ROGET'S INTERNATIONAL THESAURUS

PETER MARK ROGET

(1779–1869)

PETER MARK ROGET was born January 18, 1779, in Broad (now Broadwick) Street, a few blocks from Soho Square. His father, John Roget, hailed from Geneva and was pastor of a French Protestant church in Soho. His mother, Catherine, was a sister of Sir Samuel Romilly, the renowned law reformer. Peter was but five years old when his father died; his mother moved to Edinburgh in 1793 and in that year, at fourteen, Peter entered the university there. He was graduated from the medical school at the early age of nineteen, and soon distinguished himself by research on subjects such as pulmonary consumption and the effects of laughing gas. In 1802 he started out on a continental tour with two sons of a wealthy Manchester merchant, to whom he acted as tutor. When the Peace of Amiens was breached, Roget found himself at Geneva, a prisoner-on-parole of the French (Napoleon had annexed Geneva to France a few years earlier). He gained his freedom by pleading the Genevan—and thus French—citizenship of his family, and made his way back to England late in 1803.

In 1805 he joined the medical staff of the Public Infirmary at Manchester and made a name for himself in that city by giving a series of lectures on medical subjects. In 1808, to advance his career, he moved to London. There, in 1810, he helped establish a charity clinic, the Northern Dispensary, and contributed his services to it, gratis, for eighteen years. Combining in an unusual degree exact knowledge with a power of apt and vivid presentation, he gained eminence as a lecturer on medical and other subjects, a work he continued for nearly fifty years. He was an early member of the Medical and Chirurgical Society and edited its *Transactions* for twelve years. In 1815 he became a Fellow of the Royal Society and served as its secretary for more than twenty years. He was examiner in physiology in the University of London. He wrote numerous papers on physiology and health, among them *On Animal and Vegetable Physiology* (1834), a two-volume work on phrenology (1838), and articles for several editions of the *Encyclopædia Britannica*.

These activities would be more than enough for most men, but Roget's insatiable thirst for knowledge and his appetite for work led him into many other fields. He played an important role in the establishment of the University of London; he was a founder of the Society for the Diffusion of Knowledge and wrote for it a series of popular manuals; he devised a slide rule and spent much time trying to perfect a calculating machine; he showed remarkable ingenuity in inventing and solving chess problems and designed an inexpensive pocket chessboard. In 1828, as head of a commission to study the water supply of London, he issued a report that was the first of its kind; but, even though it graphically documented the simultaneous use of the Thames for sewage disposal and drinking water, the government took no action on its sound recommendations for pollution control.

Roget retired from professional life in 1840, and about 1848 he began preparing for publication the one work that was to perpetuate his memory. This was a catalog of words organized by their meanings, the compilation of which had been an avocation since 1805. Its first printed edition, in 1852, was called *Thesaurus of English Words and Phrases Classified and Arranged so as to Facilitate the Expression of Ideas and Assist in Literary Composition*. During his lifetime the work had twenty-eight printings; after his death it was revised and expanded by his son, John Lewis Roget, and later by John's son, Samuel Romilly Roget.

Peter Mark Roget died at West Malvern on September 12, 1869, at the age of ninety.

P. M. Roget

ROGET'S INTERNATIONAL THESAURUS™

FOURTH EDITION

REVISED BY

ROBERT L. CHAPMAN

1817

HARPER & ROW, PUBLISHERS, New York

Cambridge, Philadelphia, San Francisco, London,
Mexico City, São Paulo, Singapore, Sydney

ROGET'S INTERNATIONAL THESAURUS (Fourth Edition). Copyright 1911, 1922, 1930, 1932, 1936, 1938, 1939, 1946, 1950, ©1958, 1960, 1962, 1964, 1966, 1974, 1977 by Harper & Row, Publishers, Inc. All rights reserved. Printed in the United States of America. No part of this book may be used or reproduced in any manner whatsoever without written permission except in the case of brief quotations embodied in critical articles and reviews. For information address Harper & Row, Publishers, Inc., 10 East 53rd Street, New York, N.Y. 10022. Published simultaneously in Canada by Fitzhenry & Whiteside Limited, Toronto, and in Great Britain by William Collins Sons & Co. Ltd., P.O. Box, Glasgow G4 0NB, Great Britain.

Library of Congress Cataloging in Publication Data

Main entry under title:

Roget's international thesaurus.
   Based on: Thesaurus of English words and phrases/by Peter Mark Roget.
   Includes index.
   1. English language—Synonyms and antonyms. I. Roget, Peter Mark, 1779–1869. Thesaurus of English words and phrases. II. Chapman, Robert L.
PE1591.R73   1984   423'.1   84-47562
ISBN 0-690-00010-3 (U.S.A. and Canada)   87 88 89 90 91 27 26 25 24 23 22 21 20
ISBN 0-690-00011-1 (indexed)
ISBN 0-06-091169-7 (pbk.)   86 87 88 10 9 8 7 6 5 4
ISBN 0 00 433176-1 (cloth outside U.S.A. and Canada)
ISBN 0 00 433177-X (pbk. outside U.S.A. and Canada)

CONTENTS

HOW TO USE THIS BOOK

The *International* is a "true" thesaurus, compiled according to the plan devised originally by Peter Mark Roget. It has a text of about 250,000 words and phrases, arranged in categories by their meanings, and a comprehensive index.

The search for a word that you need is a simple, two-step process which begins in the index. Suppose that you want a word to describe something that is without a well-defined shape:

1. In the index, look up the word **shapeless** and pick the subentry closest to the meaning you want.

2. Follow its number into the text and you will find a whole paragraph of adjectives for things "shapeless" or "formless."

shaped made 167.22
   planned 654.13
shapeless
   abnormal 85.9
   formless 247.4
   inconstant 141.7
   obscure 549.15
   ugly 899.8
   unordered 62.12
   vague 514.18
shapely
   beautiful 900.17
   well-shaped 248.5
shape up
   be formed 246.8
   be in a state 7.6
   get better 691.7
   order 59.5
shard
   n. piece 55.3
   refuse 669.4
   v. pulverize 361.9
   show fragility 360.3
share
   n. allotment 816.5
   amount of stock 834.3
   part 55.1
   v. apportion 816.6
   communicate 554.7
   emotionally respond 855.12

247. FORMLESSNESS

.1 NOUNS formlessness, shapelessness; amorphousness, amorphism, amorphia; **chaos,** confusion, messiness, orderlessness; **disorder** 62; entropy; anarchy 740.2; **indeterminateness, indefiniteness,** indecisiveness, vagueness, mistiness, haziness, fuzziness, blurriness, unclearness, obscurity.

.2 unlicked cub, diamond in the rough.

.3 VERBS **deform, distort** 249.5; unform, unshape; disorder, jumble, mess up, muddle, confuse; obfuscate, obscure, fog up, blur.

.4 ADJS **formless, shapeless,** featureless, characterless, nondescript, inchoate, lumpen, blobby *or* baggy [both informal], inform; amorphous, amorphic, amorph(o)–; **chaotic, orderless,** disorderly 62.13, unordered, unorganized, confused, anarchic 740.6; kaleidoscopic; **indeterminate, indefinite,** undefined, indecisive, vague, misty, hazy, fuzzy, blurred *or* blurry, unclear, obscure.

.5 **unformed, unshaped,** unshapen, unfashioned, unlicked; uncut, unhewn.

Tracking down words in this simple fashion is the most obvious and direct use of the thesaurus. The notes that follow explain some of the broader, more subtle ways in which the unique features of the *International* will help you to solve word problems.

The thesaurus is basically a tool for transforming ideas into words. A dictionary will tell you many things about a word—spelling, pronunciation, meaning, and origins. You use a thesaurus, on the other hand, when you have an idea but do not know, or cannot remember, the word or phrase that expresses it best. You use a thesaurus also when the word that comes to mind strikes you as inadequate and you want a better one, because you know that there are always more ways than one to express an idea and that some are more effective than others. A thesaurus presents you with various possibilities and you choose the one that you think is best.

The *International*, besides being an efficient word-finder, has a structure especially designed to stimulate thought and help you to organize your ideas. The backbone of this structure is the ingenious overall arrangement of the large categories. The plan is outlined in the Synopsis of Categories, which begins on page xvii. It is not necessary to memorize this grandly methodical design; to make good use of the thesaurus all you need to remember is that it contains many sequences of closely related categories. Beginning at 448, for example, you will see HEARING, DEAFNESS, SOUND, SILENCE, FAINTNESS OF SOUND, LOUD-NESS, etc., a procession of similar, contrasting, and opposing concepts, all dealing with the perception and quality of sounds. So, when you are not quite satisfied with what you find in one place, glance at nearby categories too; it may be that your original intention was not the best. If you are having trouble framing a thought in a positive way, you may find that it can be more effectively expressed negatively. Seeing related terms, and antonyms, will often open up lines of thought that had not occurred to you.

You will have already noticed that the large categories of ideas are numbered in sequence; there are 1042 of them in this edition of Roget. Within each category the terms are presented in short paragraphs and these are numbered also. References from the index to the text are made with two-part numbers such as 247.4, the first part being the number of the category, the second the number of the paragraph within that category. This system, unique to the *International*, makes for quick and easy pinpointing of the area in which you will find the words you need.

The terms within a category are organized also by part of speech, in this order: nouns, verbs, adjectives, adverbs, prepositions, conjunctions, and interjections. An occasional mixed bag of expressions at the end is labeled simply "phrases." This grouping by parts of speech is another aspect of the *International*'s usefulness. When you are casting about for a way of saying something, rather than looking for a specific word, do not limit your search to the narrow area of the category suggested by the index reference, but examine the offerings in all parts of speech.

There is a further refinement of word arrangement. The sequence of terms within a paragraph, far from being random, is determined by close relationships. The words closest in meaning are offered in clusters that are set off with semicolons; the semicolon signals a slight change in sense or application. A close examination of the groupings will make you aware of the fine distinctions between synonyms, and you will soon recognize that few words are truly interchangeable. As a help in focusing on the *right* word, terms with special uses—foreign words, slang, informal words, and technical terms—are identified by labels in brackets.

Cross references are another convenience of the text. They suggest additional meanings of the words you are examining and sometimes they will save you the trouble of looking back again to the index. Notice also that the paragraphs of text are highlighted with terms in bold-face type. The bold words are those most commonly used for the idea at hand.

Combining forms, prefixes such as *geo-* ("earth," "of the earth") and suffixes such as *-lith* ("stone"), are inserted among the complete words that share their meanings. These are invaluable aids to vocabulary-building (and, incidentally, common fare in crossword puzzles).

The use of an apt quotation often livens up a formal speech or an essay. Here again, the *International* can help you, for it contains thousands of quotes on scores of subjects. Another bonus of the thesaurus is its dozens of word lists. These contain the names of specific things—animals, weapons, measurements, architectural ornaments—few of which have synonyms. The lists can save you many excursions to specialized reference books.

Thus, the *International* can help you in countless ways to improve your writing and speech and to enrich your vocabulary of useful words. But you should remember the caution that very few words are true synonyms and use the thesaurus in conjunction with a good dictionary whenever necessary.

PUBLISHER'S PREFACE

Like all great reference books *Roget's International Thesaurus* is the product of continuous improvement and recurring investment. This process has been going on for roughly a century and three quarters, ever since 1805, when Dr. Peter Mark Roget began compiling a list of useful words for his own convenience.

However, that catalogue of words and phrases was not like others. There have been glossaries and word lists since literature began. Roget himself knew about the thousand-year-old *Amarakosha* ("treasury of Amara"), which was a crude arrangement of words according to subjects, by the Sanskrit grammarian Amara Sinh. Roget also knew about a *Pasigraphie*, published in Paris in 1797, which tried to classify language so that it could be understood universally without translation. But Dr. Roget, this erudite physician with a flair for invention, developed a superb and revolutionary principle: *the grouping of words according to ideas*. That mechanism enables one to find just the right expression to fit one's thought without groping and without searching through the alphabet. When in 1852 he published the first book ever to carry out this concept with thoroughness and precision, he called it a "thesaurus" (from the Greek and Latin, meaning "treasury" or "storehouse"). And *thesaurus* it has remained to this day. Indeed, any attempt to produce a "thesaurus in dictionary form" is self-destructive, for it demolishes the very structure that makes the thesaurus so effective.

So successful was this *Thesaurus of English Words and Phrases, Classified and Arranged so as to Facilitate the Expression of Ideas and Assist in Literary Composition* that a second edition followed one year later in 1853. A third "cheaper edition enlarged and improved" followed in 1855 and by Dr. Roget's death in 1869 there had been no less than twenty-eight editions and printings. Peter Roget's son, Dr. John Lewis Roget, greatly expanded the book for still another edition, which appeared a decade later in 1879.

Mr. Thomas Y. Crowell acquired that property and published the first Crowell edition in 1886. Then in 1911, as one of the last acts in his distinguished career, he published a revised and reset edition which contained many additional words and phrases. Mr. Crowell had the sagacity to enlarge the size of the page and set the book in large, clear type. This has been one of its many valuable characteristics ever since.

Mr. Crowell's son, Mr. T. Irving Crowell, undertook another edition for publication in 1922. Again revised and reset, it was greatly expanded, most especially with Americanisms and with a generous increase in foreign expressions. It was now virtually a new book, and the title was changed to *Roget's International Thesaurus*—that is, *Roget's International Thesaurus* I.

This writer, Thomas Y. Crowell's grandson, carried the work forward with *Roget's International Thesaurus* II of 1946. Then much slang and substandard speech were added, together with useful quotations. The old parallel arrangement of synonyms against antonyms was converted into a more efficient tandem format. Paragraphs were numbered, and the book was equipped with a decimal finding system for the user's convenience.

Roget's International Thesaurus III appeared in 1962. In this edition some 45,000 new terms were added, together with numerous words without synonyms classified in special lists. To make the book even easier to use, all key words were set in boldface type.

Now, with a very special sense of pride, we present *Roget's International Thesaurus* IV. It has been modernized and improved throughout, to the point where there are now more than

250,000 useful words and phrases, many of them from the 1970's. Among the new features is the inclusion of combining forms such as prefixes (*cryo–*, "cold") and suffixes (*–lith*, "rock" or "stone"). The new page design with its hanging indention is a delight.

There were many and varied contributions to the excellences of the Fourth Edition; we acknowledge them here with heartfelt thanks.

Our principal debt of gratitude is to Professor Robert L. Chapman, who applied his superior lexicographic skills to every category, judiciously pruning, reorganizing, and augmenting the work of his predecessors, Lester V. Berrey and C. O. Sylvester Mawson.

The new pages owe their attractive and efficient features to Milton B. Glick; regrettably, he did not live to see his design in published form.

For the demanding work of editorial preparation we owe thanks to Tania Romero and John Alleman, who copyedited the manuscript, contributed additional textual improvements, and coded the copy for CRT composition and computer-extraction of the index.

We are especially indebted to editor Carol Cohen for her many contributions at successive stages in the translation of the manuscript to printed page. She brought to bear on the work considerable expertise in the handling of computer-processed copy, troubleshooting the sometimes arcane problems and making many editorial refinements. She also headed the very able corps of index editors, Cheryl Jimerson, Rebecca MacLean, Muriel Rosenblum, Lynn Miller, Joseph Blitman, Lorna Harbus, Sheila Brantley, James Cregan, Nancy Levering, and Susan Simon; our thanks to each of them.

Our thanks also to the many users of the *International* who have written over the years suggesting additions and calling our attention to editorial slips and typographical errors. We are dedicated to the perpetual improvement of the volume—work on *Roget's International Thesaurus* V has already begun—and we always appreciate hearing from those who want to help make a great reference book even better.

ROBERT L. CROWELL

April 11, 1977

PETER ROGET'S PREFACE

TO THE FIRST EDITION

(1852)

It is now nearly fifty years since I first projected a system of verbal classification similar to that on which the present work is founded. Conceiving that such a compilation might help to supply my own deficiencies, I had, in the year 1805, completed a classed catalog of words on a small scale, but on the same principle, and nearly in the same form, as the Thesaurus now published. I had often during that long interval found this little collection, scanty and imperfect as it was, of much use to me in literary composition, and often contemplated its extension and improvement; but a sense of the magnitude of the task, amidst a multitude of other avocations, deterred me from the attempt. Since my retirement from the duties of Secretary of the Royal Society, however, finding myself possessed of more leisure, and believing that a repertory of which I had myself experienced the advantage might, when amplified, prove useful to others, I resolved to embark in an undertaking which, for the last three or four years, has given me incessant occupation, and has, indeed, imposed upon me an amount of labor very much greater than I had anticipated. Notwithstanding all the pains I have bestowed on its execution, I am fully aware of its numerous deficiencies and imperfections, and of its falling far short of the degree of excellence that might be attained. But, in a work of this nature, where perfection is placed at so great a distance, I have thought it best to limit my ambition to that moderate share of merit which it may claim in its present form; trusting to the indulgence of those for whose benefit it is intended, and to the candor of critics who, while they find it easy to detect faults, can at the same time duly appreciate difficulties.

P. M. ROGET

April 29, 1852

FOREWORD
BY ROBERT L. CHAPMAN

This new edition of *Roget's International Thesaurus* is published in the hope and conviction that it will be more useful than its predecessors for precisely the two classes of persons Dr. Roget had in mind when he presented his original thesaurus of 1852. He expected that the book would be very welcome, first, to "those who are . . . painfully groping their way and struggling with the difficulties of composition." That is, to writers of all sorts for whom the right word has not flashed into mind. The others who might profit from his monumental effort he called "metaphysicians engaged in the more profound investigation of the Philosophy of Language." Today we would call them linguists, semanticists, or linguistic philosophers, depending on the discipline they claim.

The success of the thesaurus as a practical aid to writers has been immense. Literally millions of persons have put Roget's work to its widest proper use as a memory-jogger for words they know but cannot recall, or as a source of words new to them which, when the sense is confirmed by looking at the dictionary, can become a part of their active vocabulary. Thousands, too, have used Roget's as a browsing book, a book that stimulates thought and exploration because it uniquely collects great semantic "domains" under large conceptual headings, and shows by the manner of organization the tracks the mind may take as it ranges about in a given territory.

This edition has been prepared along lines set down by previous *International Thesaurus* editors, who have constantly improved upon the format invented by Dr. Roget. Numbered paragraphs are used to give clearly visible distinctions among sense-groups. Boldface type highlights the terms of greatest frequency within any sense-group. Everything has been done to facilitate quick consultation, while at the same time each sense-group is developed to nearly its maximum range for those whose expressive or stylistic wishes require variation, or even strangeness. Nearly every possible point-of-entry is available in the comprehensive index—one of the hallmarks of a true thesaurus.

The editor and the publisher of this fourth edition have used resources not available to previous editors. These include the newest and best general dictionaries of English and of specialized subjects, new specialized encyclopedias, and reverse-indexes of English that make the lexicon accessible in terms of sense-forming suffixes. They have used computer technology for index making, assuring a greater precision of the index than has ever been possible.

The editing policy has been exactly the same as Dr. Roget's. First, even though one cannot hope to keep up completely with our growing and shifting vocabulary, new words and phrases were carefully collected for inclusion. Second, the broadest possible range of levels and styles ("registers," as some linguists call them) has been encompassed. Noting that some of the words he entered might be condemned as vulgarisms or slang, Roget judged that "having due regard to the uses to which this Work was to be adapted, I did not feel myself justified in excluding them solely on that ground, if they possessed an acknowledged currency in general intercourse." He properly felt that choice of style was the province of the writer, and not of the reference-book maker.

For nonformal varieties of English the labels "informal" and "slang" have been used, with some trepidation. Labeling judgments are subjective and imprecise, so the designations here can hardly be taken as solidly authoritative. Nevertheless, it was felt that some sign ought to be given of the genuine semantic distinctions inherent in differences of level and style, perhaps for no better reason than that it goes against a deep semantic grain to print formal words and slang words side by side unmarked as if they were readily interchangeable.

Ready interchangeability without change of meaning is of course what makes two or more words synonymous, and a note of caution should be uttered in every thesaurus against confusing this kind of book with a synonym book. Naive users who take all the words under any heading to mean the same as the heading, and who do not read prefaces, will no doubt continue to use the thesaurus to write very strange English. Sameness or similarity of meaning is not the primary key to compiling a thesaurus. The key is membership in the cluster of linguistic signs that go to make up some very large and general concept. Most of the terms found under a major heading will in some demonstrable and logical way represent subordinate or less general parts of the larger idea. Quite inevitably, given the fact that semantic doubling or near-doubling occurs in every natural language, many of these terms will be synonymous or nearly synonymous in various parts of their range. But this is an accident of Roget's method, and not the aim of the method itself. It cannot be doubted that most users, most of the time, are in search of synonyms, and they find them, but even near-synonymity will be seen to attenuate quite rapidly as one goes along the lines of association in one direction or another.

Roget's hope that his book would "materially assist" linguistic scholars and theoreticians was largely unrealized until quite recently, but this revision has been edited in the increasing awareness that the *Thesaurus* may at last become a productive tool of linguistic research. One strain of contemporary linguistic thought, the so-called Chomskyan Revolution, has reopened speculation about the universality of language forms and elements. Roget himself worked quite consciously in the tradition of the seventeenth-century rationalist philosophers who attempted to map the totality of concepts available to the human mind, and the relations among these concepts, regardless of what language may be used to express them. The editor and the publisher believe that the new edition of the *International* constitutes the most elaborate approach yet made to the specification of possible concepts. It is the best empirical base for research in structural semantics, an area of concern generally left aside as structural linguistics worked out its theories of grammar.

To Drew University, its library, and especially to my wife, who indulged and encouraged me during the arduous years of work on this edition, I now proffer my gratitude.

SYNOPSIS OF CATEGORIES

CLASS ONE (Continued)

CLASS TWO: SPACE

CLASS TWO (Continued)

CLASS THREE: PHYSICS

CLASS FOUR: MATTER

CLASS SIX (Continued)

CLASS SEVEN: VOLITION

CLASS SEVEN (Continued)

CLASS SEVEN (Continued)

840. Debt
841. Payment
842. Nonpayment
843. Expenditure
844. Receipts

845. Accounts
846. Price, Fee
847. Discount
848. Expensiveness
849. Cheapness

850. Costlessness
851. Economy
852. Parsimony
853. Liberality
854. Prodigality

CLASS EIGHT: AFFECTIONS

I. PERSONAL AFFEC-
TIONS
A. **Emotion**
855. Feelings
856. Lack of Feelings
B. **Excitability**
857. Excitement
858. Inexcitability
859. Nervousness
860. Unnervousness
861. Patience
862. Impatience
C. **Pleasure and Pleasurableness**
863. Pleasantness
864. Unpleasantness
865. Pleasure
866. Unpleasure
867. Dislike
868. Contentment
869. Discontent
870. Cheerfulness
871. Solemnity
872. Sadness
873. Regret
874. Unregretfulness
875. Lamentation
876. Rejoicing
877. Celebration
878. Amusement
879. Dancing
880. Humorousness
881. Wit, Humor
882. Banter
883. Dullness
884. Tedium
885. Aggravation
886. Relief
887. Comfort
D. **Anticipative Emotions**
888. Hope
889. Hopelessness
E. **Concern**
890. Anxiety
891. Fear, Frightening-
ness
892. Cowardice
893. Courage
894. Rashness
895. Caution
F. **Discriminative Affections**
896. Fastidiousness
897. Taste, Tastefulness
898. Vulgarity
899. Ugliness
900. Beauty
901. Ornamentation
902. Plainness

903. Affectation
904. Ostentation
G. **Pride**
905. Pride
906. Humility
907. Servility
908. Modesty
909. Vanity
910. Boasting
911. Bluster
912. Arrogance
913. Insolence
H. **Esteem**
914. Repute
915. Disrepute
916. Honor
917. Title
918. Nobility
919. Commonalty
I. **Contemplative Emotions**
920. Wonder
921. Unastonishment

II. SYMPATHETIC
AFFECTIONS

A. **Social Relations**
922. Sociability
923. Unsociability
924. Seclusion
925. Hospitality, Wel-
come
926. Inhospitality
B. **Social Affections**
927. Friendship
928. Friend
929. Enmity
930. Hate
931. Love
932. Lovemaking, En-
dearment
933. Marriage
934. Celibacy
935. Divorce, Widow-
hood
C. **Civility**
936. Courtesy
937. Discourtesy
D. **Benevolence**
938. Kindness, Benevo-
lence
939. Unkindness, Malev-
olence
940. Misanthropy
941. Public Spirit
942. Benefactor
943. Evildoer
E. **Sympathy**
944. Pity

945. Pitilessness
946. Condolence
947. Forgiveness
948. Congratulation
F. **Gratefulness**
949. Gratitude
950. Ingratitude
G. **Ill Humor**
951. Ill Humor
952. Resentment, Anger
H. **Selfish Resentment**
953. Jealousy
954. Envy
I. **Reprisal**
955. Retaliation
956. Revenge

III. MORALITY

A. **Morals**
957. Ethics
958. Right
959. Wrong
B. **Moral Obligation**
960. Dueness
961. Undueness
962. Duty
963. Imposition
C. **Moral Sentiments**
964. Respect
965. Disrespect
966. Contempt
967. Ridicule
968. Approval
969. Disapproval
970. Flattery
971. Disparagement
972. Curse
973. Threat
D. **Moral Conditions**
974. Probity
975. Improbity
976. Justice
977. Injustice
978. Selfishness
979. Unselfishness
980. Virtue
981. Vice
982. Wrongdoing, Sin
983. Guilt
984. Innocence
985. Good Person
986. Bad Person
E. **Moral Practice**
987. Sensuality
988. Chastity
989. Unchastity
990. Indecency
991. Asceticism
992. Temperance

CLASS EIGHT (Continued)

993. Intemperance
994. Gluttony
995. Fasting
996. Intoxication
997. Sobriety
F. Moral Observance
998. Legality
999. Illegality
1000. Jurisdiction
1001. Tribunal
1002. Judge, Jury
1003. Lawyer
1004. Legal Action
1005. Accusation
1006. Justification
1007. Acquittal
1008. Condemnation
1009. Penalty
1010. Punishment
1011. Instruments of Punishment
1012. Atonement

IV. RELIGION
A. Supernatural Beings
1013. Deity
1014. Mythical and Polytheistic Gods and Spirits
1015. Angel, Saint
1016. Evil Spirits
1017. Specter
B. Supernatural Regions
1018. Heaven
1019. Hell
C. Religious Beliefs
1020. Religions, Cults, Sects
1021. Scripture
1022. Prophets, Religious Founders
1023. Theology
1024. Orthodoxy
1025. Unorthodoxy

D. Religious Quality
1026. Sanctity
1027. Unsanctity
E. Religious Sentiments
1028. Piety
1029. Sanctimony
1030. Impiety
1031. Nonreligiousness
F. Religious Practice
1032. Worship
1033. Idolatry
G. Supernaturalism
1034. Occultism
1035. Sorcery
1036. Spell, Charm
H. Churchdom
1037. The Ministry
1038. Clergy
1039. Laity
1040. Religious Rites
1041. Ecclesiastical Attire
1042. Religious Buildings

ROGET'S INTERNATIONAL THESAURUS

THESAURUS
OF ENGLISH WORDS
AND PHRASES

1. EXISTENCE

.1 NOUNS **existence, being;** subsistence, entity, essence, *ens* [L], *esse* [L], *l'être* [Fr]; **occurrence,** presence; **materiality** 376, **substantiality** 3; **life** 407; –dom, –oma *or* –ome, onto–, –ure.

.2 **reality, actuality,** factuality, empirical *or* demonstrable *or* objective existence; historicity; **truth** 516; **authenticity** 516.5; sober *or* grim reality, not a dream, more truth than poetry; accomplished fact, *fait accompli* [Fr].

.3 **fact,** the case, the truth of the matter, not opinion, not guesswork, what's what [informal]; **matter of fact,** "plain, plump fact" [R. Browning]; **bare fact,** naked fact, bald fact, **simple fact,** sober fact; **cold fact,** hard fact, **stubborn fact, brutal fact,** the nitty-gritty [informal]; **actual fact,** positive fact, absolute fact; **self-evident fact,** axiom, postulate; **accepted fact,** conceded fact, admitted fact, fact of experience, well-known fact, established fact, inescapable fact, indisputable fact, undeniable fact; **demonstrable fact,** provable fact; empirical fact; given fact, datum, **circumstance** 8; **salient fact,** significant fact.

.4 **the facts,** the information 557, the particulars, the details, the specifics, **the data;** the dope *or* the scoop *or* the score [all slang]; the picture [informal], the gen [Brit slang]; the fact *or* facts *or* truth of the matter, the facts of the case, the whole story [informal]; "irreducible and stubborn facts" [W. James]; essentials, basic *or* essential facts, brass tacks [informal].

.5 **self-existence,** uncreated being, noncontingent existence, aseity, innascibility.

.6 **mere existence,** just being, **vegetable existence,** vegetation, mere tropism; stagnation, inertia, torpor; indolence, sloth.

.7 (philosophy of being) ontology, metaphysics, existentialism.

.8 VERBS **exist, be,** be in existence, be extant, have being; breathe, **live** 407.7; subsist, stand, obtain, hold, prevail, be the case; **occur,** be present, be there, be found, be met with, have place, happen to be.

.9 **live on,** continue to exist, persist, last, endure 110.6.

.10 **vegetate,** merely exist, just be; stagnate, pass the time.

.11 **exist in, consist in,** subsist in, lie in, rest in, repose in, reside in, abide in, inhabit, dwell in, **inhere in,** be present in, be a quality of, be comprised in, be contained in, be constituted by, be coextensive with.

.12 **become,** come to be, go, get, get to be, turn out to be; be converted into, turn into 145.17; grow 148.5; be changed 139.5; –en, –ize *or* –ise.

.13 ADJS **existent, existing,** in existence; **subsistent,** subsisting; **being,** in being; –ic(al), –etic, –ar; **living** 407.11; present, **extant, prevalent, current,** in force *or* effect, on foot, under the sun, on the face of the earth.

.14 **self-existent,** self-existing, innascible; uncreated, increate.

.15 **real, actual,** factual, veritable, for real [slang], *de facto* [L]; historical; positive, undeniable, absolute; **true** 516.12; honest-to-God [slang], genuine, **authentic** 516.14; **substantial** 3.6.

.16 ADVS **really, actually; genuinely,** veritably, **truly** 516.17; **in reality,** in actuality, in effect, in fact, *de facto* [L], in point of fact, as a matter of fact; positively, absolutely; no buts about it [informal]; no ifs, ands, or buts [informal]; obviously, manifestly 555.14.

2. NONEXISTENCE

.1 NOUNS **nonexistence,** nonsubsistence; nonentity, **nonbeing,** unbeing, not-being; **nothingness,** nullity, nihility; vacancy, deprivation, emptiness, vacuity 187.2; vacuum, void 187.3; "the intense inane" [Shelley]; negativeness, negation, negativity; nonoccurrence; **unreality,** nonreality, unactuality; absence 187.

.2 **nothing,** nil, *nihil* [L], *nichts* [Ger], nix [slang], *nada* [Sp], **naught, aught;** zero, cipher, goose egg [slang]; nothing whatever, nothing at all, zilch [slang], Sweet Fanny Adams [Brit slang], nothing on earth *or* under the sun, no such thing; thing of naught 4.2.

.3 **none,** not a one, not a blessed one [informal]; never a one, ne'er a one, nary one [dial]; **not any, not a bit,** not a whit, not a hint, not a smitch *or* smidgen [dial], not a speck, not a mite, not a particle, not an iota, not a jot, not a scrap, not a trace, not a lick [informal], not a lick or smell [informal], not a suspicion, not a shadow of a suspicion, neither hide nor hair.

.4 VERBS **not exist,** not be in existence, not be met with, not occur, not be found, be absent *or* lacking.

.5 **cease to exist** *or* **be, be annihilated,** be destroyed, **be wiped out,** be extirpated, be eradicated; **go, vanish,** be no more, leave no trace, "leave not a rack behind" [Shakespeare]; **disappear** 447.2, evaporate, fade, fade away *or* out, fly, flee, dissolve, melt away, die out *or* away, pass, pass out of the picture [informal], turn to nothing *or* naught, peter out [informal]; **perish, expire,** pass away, **die** 408.19.

.6 **annihilate** 693.13, **exterminate** 693.14, eradicate, extirpate, **wipe out, stamp out** [informal], put an end to 693.12.

.7 ADJS **nonexistent,** nonsubsistent, existless, unexisting, without being, nowhere to be found; **minus, missing,** lacking, –less; **null,** nulli–, **void,** devoid; vacuous 187.13; negative.

.8 **unreal,** unactual, not real; merely nominal; **immaterial** 377.7; **unsubstantial** 4.5; **imaginary, fanciful** 535.19–22; unrealistic; illusory 519.9.

.9 **unmade,** uncreated, unborn, unbegotten, unconceived, unproduced.

.10 **no more, extinct, defunct, dead,** expired, passed away; vanished, gone glimmering; perished, annihilated; gone, all gone; all over with, had it [slang], kaput [informal], *kaputt* [Ger], done for *or* dead and done for [both informal], down the drain [slang].

.11 ADVS **none, no,** not at all, in no way, to no extent; from scratch, from the ground up.

3. SUBSTANTIALITY

.1 NOUNS substantiality, substantialness; materiality 376; **substance, body,** mass; **solidity,** density, concreteness, stere(o)–; **tangibility,** palpability, ponderability; **sturdiness, stability,** soundness, firmness, steadiness, stoutness, toughness, **strength,** durability.

.2 **substance, stuff, material, matter** 376.2; building blocks, fabric; atoms, medium; tangible.

.3 **something, thing,** –ing; an existence, **being, entity,** entelechy, unit, individual, person, persona, personality, ont(o)–; creature, critter [dial]; organism; life; body; soul, monad; **object** 376.4.

.4 **embodiment,** incarnation, materialization, substantiation, concretization; reification.

.5 VERBS **embody,** incarnate, **materialize,** body forth, lend substance to, reify, entify, hypostatize, solidify, concretize.

.6 ADJS **substantial,** substantive; **solid, concrete; tangible,** sensible, appreciable, palpable, ponderable; **material** 376.9; **real** 1.15.

.7 **sturdy,** stable, **solid,** sound, firm, steady, tough, stout, **strong,** "strong as flesh and blood" [Wordsworth], rugged; **durable,** lasting, enduring; hard, dense, unyielding; adamantine; **well-made,** well-constructed, well-built; **well-founded,** well-grounded; **massive,** bulky, heavy.

.8 ADVS **substantially,** essentially 5.10.

4. UNSUBSTANTIALITY

.1 NOUNS unsubstantiality, insubstantiality, unsubstantialness; **immateriality** 377; bodilessness, incorporeality, unsolidity, unconcreteness; **intangibility,** impalpability, imponderability; **tenuousness,** tenuity, subtlety, subtility, airiness, mistiness, vagueness, ethereality; unreality; **flimsiness** 160.2.

.2 **thing of naught,** nullity, zero; **nonentity, nobody** *or* **nebbish** [both informal]; cipher; man of straw, jackstraw, lay figure, puppet, dummy, hollow man; flash in the pan, dud [slang]; pushover [slang]; **trifle** 673.5,6; nothing 2.2.

.3 **spirit,** shadow, air, **thin air,** "airy nothing" [Shakespeare], smoke, vapor, mist, ether, **bubble,** "such stuff as dreams are made on" [Shakespeare]; "a spume that plays upon a ghostly paradigm of things" [Yeats]; illusion 519; phantom 1017.1.

.4 VERBS spiritualize, **disembody,** dematerialize; etherealize, **attenuate,** subtilize, rarefy; weaken, enervate, sap.

.5 ADJS **unsubstantial,** insubstantial, nonsubstantial, unsubstanced; intangible, impalpable, imponderable; **immaterial** 377.7; pseudo–; **bodiless,** incorporeal, unsolid, unconcrete; weightless 353.10.

.6 **tenuous, subtile, subtle; rarefied; ethereal,** airy, windy, spirituous, vaporous, gaseous; air-built, cloud-built; **chimerical,** gossamery, shadowy, phantomlike 1017.7; dreamlike, **illusory, unreal;** fatuous, fatuitous; imaginary, fanciful 535.19–22.

.7 **flimsy,** shaky, weak, unsound, infirm 160.12–16.

.8 **baseless, groundless,** ungrounded, **without foundation,** not well-founded, built on sand.

5. INTRINSICALITY

.1 NOUNS intrinsicality, internality, innerness, **inwardness; inherence,** immanence, **inbeing,** indwelling; innateness, indigenousness; essentiality, fundamentality; **subjectivity,** nonobjectivity.

.2 **essence, substance,** stuff, inner essence; quid, quiddity; **quintessence,** elixir, flower; **essential,** principle, fundamental; hypostasis, postulate, axiom; **gist,** gravamen, **nub** [informal], nucleus, center, focus, kernel, **core, pith,** meat, nuts and bolts, the nitty-gritty [both informal]; sap, marrow, **heart,** soul, spirit.

.3 **nature, character, quality,** suchness; **constitution,** crasis [archaic], composition, **characteristics,** makeup, constituents; physique 246.4, physi(o)–, physic(o)–; body-build, somatotype, system [informal], diathesis; complexion [archaic], humor or humors [both archaic]; **temperament,** temper, fiber, **disposition,** spirit, ethos, genius, dharma; tenor, way, habit, frame, cast, hue, tone, grain, vein, streak, stripe, mold, brand, stamp; **kind** 61.3, **sort, type,** ilk; **property, characteristic** 80.4; **tendency** 174; the way of it, the nature of the beast [slang].

.4 **inner nature,** inside, internal or inner or esoteric reality, true being, essential na-

ture, true inwardness, center of life, vital principle, nerve center; **spirit, soul, heart, breast, bosom, inner man;** heart of hearts, secret heart, inmost heart or soul, secret or innermost recesses of the heart, heart's core, bottom of the heart, cockles of the heart; vitals, quick, depths of one's being.

.5 VERBS **inhere,** indwell, belong to or permeate by nature; run in the blood, run in the family, be born so, be built that way [informal].

.6 ADJS **intrinsic,** internal, **inner,** inward; **inherent,** resident, implicit, immanent, indwelling; inalienable, unalienable, uninfringeable, unquestionable, unchallengeable, irreducible; **ingrained,** in the very grain; infixed, implanted, inwrought, deep-seated; **subjective,** esoteric, private, secret; self–.

.7 **innate, inborn, congenital;** native, **natural,** natural to, connatural, native to, indigenous; **constitutional,** bodily, physical, temperamental, organic; born; **inbred, genetic, hereditary,** inherited, incarnate, bred in the bone, in the blood, running in the blood or race or strain, etc.; connate, connatal, coeval 118.4; **instinctive,** instinctual, atavistic, primal.

.8 **essential,** of the essence, **fundamental; primary,** primitive, primal, elementary, elemental, original, *ab ovo* [L], radical; **basic, gut** [informal], basal, underlying; substantive, substantial, material; constitutive, constituent.

.9 ADVS **intrinsically, inherently,** innately; internally, **inwardly,** immanently; originally, primally, primitively; **naturally, congenitally,** genetically, **by birth, by nature.**

.10 **essentially, fundamentally, primarily, basically; at bottom,** *au fond* [Fr], at heart; in essence, at the core, in substance, in the main; substantially, materially; *per se* [L], of or in itself.

6. EXTRINSICALITY

.1 NOUNS **extrinsicality,** externality, outwardness, **extraneousness,** otherness, discreteness; foreignness; **objectivity,** nonsubjectivity, impersonality.

.2 **nonessential,** inessential or unessential; **accessory, extra,** collateral; other, not-self; **appendage,** appurtenance, auxiliary, **supplement,** addition, addendum, superaddition, adjunct 41; secondary, subsidiary; **contingency,** contingent, incidental, accidental, accident, happenstance, mere chance.

.3 ADJS **extrinsic, external,** outward, outside, outlying; **extraneous,** foreign; **objective,** nonsubjective, impersonal, extraorganismal.

.4 unessential, inessential *or* nonessential; **accessory, extra,** collateral, auxiliary; adventitious, appurtenant, adscititious, ascititious, **additional, supplementary,** supplemental, superadded, supervenient; **secondary,** subsidiary; **incidental,** circumstantial, contingent; accidental, fortuitous, casual, superfluous.

7. STATE

.1 NOUNS **state,** mode, modality; **status, situation,** position, posture, footing, location, bearings, spot [informal]; estate, **rank,** station, place, **standing; condition,** circumstance 8; –ance, –ancy, –cy, –ence, –ery, –hood, –ice, –ion, –ism, –ity, –ization *or* –isation, –ment, –ness, –or, –osis, –phoria, –ry, –ship, –th, –tude, –ty, –y; case, lot; **predicament,** plight, pass, pickle [slang], fix [slang], jam [slang].

.2 the state of affairs, the nature *or* shape of things, the way it shapes up [informal], the way of the world, how things stack up [slang], **how things stand,** how things are, the way of things, the way it is, like it is, where it's at, **the way things are,** the way of it, the way things go, how it goes, **how it is,** the status quo, *status in quo* [L], the size of it [informal]; how the land lies, the lay of the land [informal].

.3 good condition, bad condition; adjustment, fettle, form, order, repair, **shape** [informal], trim.

.4 mode, manner, way 657, fashion, style, form, shape, guise, complexion, tenor, tone, turn.

.5 role, capacity, character, part, quality, relation, status, position, condition.

.6 VERBS **be in** *or* **have a certain state,** be such *or* so *or* thus, **fare,** go on *or* along; **enjoy** *or* **occupy a certain position; get on** *or* **along,** come on *or* along [informal]; **manage** [informal], **contrive, make out** [informal], come through, get by; **turn out,** come out, stack up [slang], shape up [informal].

.7 ADJS conditional, modal, formal; –ate(d), –phoric; a–.

.8 in condition *or* **order** *or* repair, etc.; **out of commission** [informal], **out of kilter, out of kelter** [both informal], **out of whack** [informal], **out of order.**

8. CIRCUMSTANCE

.1 NOUNS **circumstance, occurrence, occasion, event, incident;** juncture, conjuncture, contingency, eventuality; **condition** 7.1.

.2 circumstances, total situation, existing conditions *or* situation, set of conditions, **environment** 233, context, status quo; whole picture [informal], full particulars, ins and outs.

.3 particular, instance, item, detail, point, count, case, fact, matter, article, datum, element, factor, facet, aspect, thing; respect, regard; minutia, minutiae [pl]; incidental, minor detail.

.4 circumstantiality, particularity, specificity, minuteness of detail; accuracy 516.3.

.5 circumstantiation, itemization, particularization, specification, anatomization, atomization, analysis 48.

.6 VERBS **circumstantiate, itemize, specify,** particularize, **detail,** go *or* enter into detail, descend to particulars, give full particulars, atomize, anatomize, spell out [informal]; instance, cite, adduce, document, quote chapter and verse; **substantiate** 505.12.

.7 ADJS **circumstantial,** conditional, provisional; **incidental,** occasional, contingent, adventitious, accidental, casual, unessential *or* inessential *or* nonessential, aleatory.

.8 environmental, environing, surrounding, contextual.

.9 detailed, minute, full, particular, meticulous, fussy, finicky, picayune, nice [archaic], precise, exact, specific, special.

.10 ADVS **thus, thusly** [informal], in such wise, thuswise, this way, this-a-way [dial], thus and thus, thus and so, **so,** just so, like so [informal], like this, like that, just like that; similarly 20.18, precisely 516.20.

.11 accordingly, in that case, in that event, at that rate, that being the case, such being the case, that being so, **under the circumstances,** the condition being such, as it is, as matters stand, as the matter stands, **therefore** 155.7, **consequently** 154.9; **as the case may be,** as it may be, according to circumstances; as it may happen *or* turn out, as things may fall; **by the same token,** equally.

.12 circumstantially, conditionally, provisionally; provided 507.12.

.13 fully, in full, in detail, minutely, specifically, particularly, in particular, wholly

54.13, *in toto* [L], completely 56.14–18, **at length**, *in extenso* [L].

9. RELATION

.1 NOUNS **relation, relationship, connection;** relatedness, connectedness, **association** 788, assemblage 74, **affiliation,** filiation, bond, union, alliance, tie, tie-in [informal], link, linkage, linking, liaison, **addition** 40, adjunct 41, junction 47.1, **combination** 52; deduction 42.1, disjunction 49.1, contrariety 15; **affinity, rapport,** mutual attraction, sympathy, accord 794; **closeness,** propinquity, **proximity,** approximation, contiguity, nearness 200, intimacy; **relations, dealings,** affairs, intercourse; s̄imilarity, homology.

.2 **relativity,** dependence, contingency; **interrelation, correlation** 13.

.3 **kinship,** common source *or* stock *or* descent *or* ancestry, consanguinity, agnation, cognation, enation, blood relationship 11; family relationship, affinity 12.1.

.4 **relevance, pertinence,** relatedness, materiality; **appositeness,** germaneness; application, applicability; **connection,** reference, **bearing,** concern, concernment, interest, respect, regard.

.5 VERBS **relate to,** refer to, **apply to, bear on** *or* **upon,** respect, regard, **concern, involve,** touch, affect, interest; **pertain to,** appertain to, belong to; answer to, correspond to; **have to do with,** have connection with, link with, connect, tie in with [informal], liaise with [informal], deal with, treat of, touch upon.

.6 **relate, associate, connect,** ally, link, wed, bind, tie, couple, bracket, equate, identify; bring into relation with, bring to bear upon, apply; parallel, parallelize, draw a parallel; **interrelate,** relativize, **correlate** 13.4.

.7 ADJS **relative,** relational; **connective,** linking, associative; **relating,** pertaining, appertaining, pertinent, referring, referable; **congenial,** *en rapport* [Fr], sympathetic, affinitive; **comparative,** comparable; proportional, proportionate, proportionable; **correlative** 13.10.

.8 **approximate,** approximating, approximative, proximate; **near, close** 200.14; comparable, relatable, **like,** homologous, **similar** 20.10.

.9 **related, connected; linked,** tied, coupled, knotted, twinned, wedded, wed, conjugate, bracketed, bound, yoked, spliced, joined 47.13; **associated, affiliated,** filiated, **allied,** associate, affiliate; inter-

locked, **interrelated,** interlinked, involved, implicated, **correlated** 13.10; in the same category, of that kind *or* sort *or* ilk; parallel, collateral; –al, –an, –ar, –ary, –ative, –atory, –ean, –ese, –etic, –ey, –ial, –ian, –ic(al), –ie, –ile, –ine, –ing, –istic(al), –itious, –ling, –orial, –ory, –ular, –y.

.10 **kindred, akin, related,** of common source *or* stock *or* descent *or* ancestry, agnate, cognate, enate, connate, connatural, congeneric, congenerous, consanguine(ous), genetically related, related by blood 11.6, affinal 12.4.

.11 **relevant, pertinent,** appertaining, **germane, apposite,** material, admissible, applicable, applying, pertaining, belonging, involving, appropriate, **apropos,** *à propos* [Fr], to the purpose, **to the point,** in point, *ad rem* [L].

.12 ADVS **relatively,** comparatively, proportionately, not absolutely, to a degree, to an extent; **relevantly,** pertinently, appositely, germanely.

.13 PREPS **with** *or* **in relation to,** with *or* in reference to, **with** *or* **in regard to,** with respect to, in respect to *or* of, relative to, relating to, **pertaining to,** pertinent to, referring to, in relation with, **in connection with,** apropos of, speaking of; **as to,** as for, as respects, as regards; in the matter of, on the subject of, in point of, on the score of; re, *in re* [L]; **about,** anent, of, on, upon, **concerning,** touching, respecting, **regarding.**

10. UNRELATEDNESS

.1 NOUNS **unrelatedness,** irrelation; **irrelevance,** impertinence, inappositeness, immateriality, inapplicability; inconnection *or* disconnection, inconsequence, independence; unconnectedness, separateness, discreteness, dissociation, disassociation, disjuncture, disjunction 49.1.

.2 **misconnection,** misrelation, wrong *or* invalid linking, misapplication, misapplicability, misreference; misalliance, *mésalliance* [Fr].

.3 VERBS **not concern,** not involve, not imply, not implicate, not relate to, not connect with, have nothing to do with.

.4 foist, drag in 237.6; impose on 963.7.

.5 ADJS **unrelated,** irrelative, unrelatable, **unconnected,** unallied, **unassociated,** unaffiliated *or* disaffiliated; disrelated, disconnected, dissociated, detached, discrete, disjunct, removed, separated, separate, segregate, apart, other, independent;

isolated, insular; **foreign, alien,** strange, exotic, outlandish; incommensurable, incomparable; –xene; extraneous 6.3.

.6 **irrelevant,** irrelative; **impertinent, inapposite,** inconsequent, inapplicable, immaterial, inappropriate, inadmissible; adrift, away from the point, *nihil ad rem* [L], **beside the point,** beside the mark, **beside the question,** off the subject, not to the purpose, **nothing to do with the case,** not at issue, out-of-the-way; **unessential,** nonessential, extraneous, extrinsic 6.3; incidental, parenthetical.

.7 **farfetched, remote,** distant, out-of-the-way, strained, forced, neither here nor there, brought in from nowhere, quite another thing, something else again; improbable 512.3.

.8 ADVS **irrelevantly,** irrelatively, impertinently, inappositely; without connection, without reference *or* regard.

11. RELATIONSHIP BY BLOOD

.1 NOUNS blood relationship, blood, ties of blood, consanguinity, common descent *or* ancestry, **kinship,** kindred, **relation, relationship,** sibship; propinquity; cognation; agnation, enation; filiation, affiliation; alliance, connection, **family connection** *or* **tie;** motherhood, maternity; fatherhood, paternity; patrocliny, matrocliny; patrilineage, matrilineage; patriliny, matriliny; patrisib, matrisib; brotherhood, brothership, fraternity; sisterhood, sistership; cousinhood, cousinship; **ancestry** 170.

.2 **kinsmen, kinfolk** *or* **kinsfolk, kindred,** kinnery [dial], **kin,** kith and kin, **family, relatives, relations, people,** folks [informal], connections; **blood relation** *or* **relative,** flesh, blood, flesh and blood, uterine kin, consanguinean; cognate; agnate, enate; kinsman, kinswoman, sib, sibling; german; near relation, distant relation; next of kin; collateral relative, collateral; distaff *or* spindle side, distaff *or* spindle kin; sword *or* spear side, sword *or* spear kin; **tribesman,** clansman; **ancestry** 170, **posterity** 171.

.3 **brother,** bub *or* bubba [both dial], bud *or* buddy [both informal], frater, adelpho–; brethren [pl] 1039.1; **sister,** sis [informal], sissy [informal]; sistern [pl dial]; kid brother *or* sister; blood brother *or* sister, uterine brother *or* sister, brother- *or* sister-german; half brother *or* sister, foster brother *or* sister, stepbrother *or* stepsister; **aunt,** auntie [informal]; **uncle,** unc *or*

uncs [both slang], nunks *or* nunky [both slang], nuncle [dial]; **nephew, niece; cousin,** cousin-german; first cousin, second cousin, etc.; cousin once removed, cousin twice removed, etc.; country cousin; **great-uncle, granduncle;** great-granduncle; great-aunt, grandaunt; great-grandaunt; grandnephew, grandniece; **father, mother** 170.9,10; **son, daughter** 171.3.

.4 **race, people** 418, **folk, family, house, clan, tribe, nation;** patriclan, matriclan, deme, sept, gens, phyle, phyl(o)–, phratry, totem; **lineage,** line, blood, strain, stock, stem, species, stirps, **breed,** brood, kind; plant *or* animal kingdom, class, order, etc. 61.5.

.5 **family,** brood, **house, household,** hearth, ménage, people, folks [informal], homefolks [informal]; **children,** issue, **offspring, get.**

.6 ADJS **related, kindred, akin;** consanguineous *or* consanguinean *or* consanguineal, consanguine, of the blood; cognate, uterine, agnate, enate; sib, sibling; allied, affiliated, congeneric; german, germane; collateral; foster, novercal; patrilineal, matrilineal; patroclinous, matroclinous; patrilateral, matrilateral; avuncular; intimately *or* closely related, remotely *or* distantly related.

.7 **racial, tribal, national, family,** clannish, totemic, **lineal; ethnic;** phyletic, phylogenetic, genetic; gentile, gentilic.

12. RELATIONSHIP BY MARRIAGE

.1 NOUNS **marriage relationship,** affinity, marital affinity; connection, family connection, marriage connection.

.2 **in-laws** [informal], **relatives-in-law;** brother-in-law, sister-in-law, father-in-law, mother-in-law, son-in-law, daughter-in-law.

.3 stepfather, stepmother; stepbrother, stepsister; stepchild, stepson, stepdaughter.

.4 ADJS **affinal,** affined, by marriage; step–, –in-law.

13. CORRELATION

(reciprocal or mutual relation)

.1 NOUNS **correlation,** corelation; correlativity, correlativism; **reciprocation,** reciprocity, reciprocality, relativity 9.2; mutuality, communion; community, commutuality; proportionality, direct *or* inverse relationship, direct *or* inverse ratio, direct *or* inverse proportion; **equilibrium, balance,** symmetry 248; **correspondence, equiva-lence,** equipollence, coequality.

.2 **interrelation,** interrelationship; **intercon-nection,** interlocking, interdigitation, in-tercoupling, interlinking, interlinkage, in-teralliance, interassociation, interaffilia-tion, interdependence; covariation.

.3 **interaction,** interworking, intercourse, in-tercommunication, **interplay;** alternation, seesaw; meshing, intermeshing, mesh, en-gagement; complementary distribution; **interweaving,** interlacing, intertwining 222.1; **interchange** 150, tit for tat, *quid pro quo* [L]; **concurrence** 177, coaction, **coop-eration** 786.

.4 **correlate,** correlative; **correspondent,** ana-logue, counterpart; reciprocator, recipro-catist; each other, one another.

.5 **ecology,** ecosystem; symbiosis, symbiot-ics, parasitism, commensality.

.6 VERBS **correlate,** corelate.

.7 **interrelate, interconnect,** interassociate, interlink, intercouple, interlock, interdigi-tate, interally, intertie, interjoin, interde-pend.

.8 **interact,** interwork, **interplay;** mesh, in-termesh, engage, dovetail, mortise; **inter-weave,** interlace, intertwine; **interchange;** coact, **cooperate.**

.9 **reciprocate, correspond,** correspond to, respond to, answer, answer to, comple-ment, coequal.

.10 ADJS **correlative,** corelative, correlational, corelational; **correlated,** corelated; co-.

.11 **interrelated, interconnected,** interassoci-ated, interallied, interaffiliated, inter-linked, interlocked, intercoupled, inter-tied, interdependent; inter-.

.12 **interacting,** interactive, interworking, in-terplaying; in gear, in mesh; dovetailed, mortised.

.13 **reciprocal,** reciprocative; **corresponding,** correspondent, answering, analogous, ho-mologous, equipollent, tantamount, equivalent, coequal; **complementary,** complemental; equi-.

.14 **mutual,** commutual, **common, joint,** communal, conjoint; respective, two-way.

.15 **ecological,** ecotopic; symbiotic, parasitic, commensal.

.16 ADVS **reciprocally,** back and forth, back-ward and forward, backwards and for-wards, alternately, seesaw, to and fro; vice versa, *mutatis mutandis* [L].

.17 **mutually, commonly,** communally, **jointly;** respectively, each to each; *entre nous* [Fr], *inter se* [L].

.18 ecologically; symbiotically, parasitically, commensally.

14. IDENTITY

.1 NOUNS **identity,** identicalness; **sameness,** selfsameness; indistinguishability, no dif-ference, not a bit of difference; **coinci-dence, correspondence,** agreement, con-gruence; **equivalence, equality** 30, co-equality; **synonymousness,** synonymity, synonymy; **oneness, unity,** homogeneity; selfness, selfhood, self-identity; homoou-sia, consubstantiality.

.2 **identification,** unification, coalescence, combination, union, fusion, merger, syn-thesis.

.3 **the same, selfsame,** very same, one and the same, identical same, no other, none other, very or actual thing, a distinction without a difference, the same difference [informal]; **equivalent** 20.3; **synonym;** homonym, homograph, homophone; ditto [informal], *idem* [L], *ipsissima verba* [L, the very words]; **duplicate,** dou-ble, *Doppelgänger* [Ger], twin, very im-age, dead ringer [informal], spitting im-age or spit and image [both informal] 572.3, **exact counterpart, copy** 24.1–7, rep-lica, facsimile, carbon copy.

.4 VERBS **coincide, correspond,** agree, match, tally.

.5 **identify,** make one, **unify,** unite, join, combine, coalesce, synthesize, merge, fuse 52.3.

.6 **reproduce, copy,** replicate, **duplicate,** ditto [informal].

.7 ADJS **identical,** identic; **same, selfsame, one, one and the same,** all the same, all one, of the same kidney; undifferent, in-distinguishable, without distinction, with-out difference; **alike, like** 20.10, just alike, exactly alike, alike as two peas in a pod; duplicate, twin; homoousian, consubstan-tial; aut(o)-, taut(o)-.

.8 **coinciding,** coincident, coincidental; **cor-responding,** correspondent, congruent; **synonymous, equivalent,** six of one and half a dozen of the other [informal]; **equal** 30.7, coequal, coextensive, cotermi-nous; co-, equi-, hom(o)-, is(o)-.

.9 ADVS **identically,** synonymously, **alike;** coincidentally, correspondently, corre-spondingly, congruently; **equally** 30.11, coequally, coextensively, coterminously; on the same footing, on all fours with; **likewise,** the same way, just the same, as is, ditto, same here [informal]; *ibid., ibi-dem* [both L].

15. CONTRARIETY

.1 NOUNS contrariety, **oppositeness, opposition** 790, opposure; **antithesis, contrast,** contraposition 239, counterposition, contradiction, contraindication, contradistinction; **antagonism,** perversity, repugnance, oppugnance, oppugnancy, **hostility,** inimicalness, antipathy, clashing, confrontation, showdown, collision, crosspurposes 795.2, conflict; polarity; discrepancy, inconsistency, **disagreement** 27.

.2 **opposite, the contrary,** contra, counter, **antithesis, reverse,** inverse, converse, obverse; the other side, the mirror or reverse image, the other side of the coin, the flip side [slang]; the direct or polar opposite, the other or opposite extreme; antipode, antipodes; countercheck or counterbalance or counterpoise; antipole, counterpole, counterpoint; opposite number [informal], vis-à-vis; offset, setoff, foil; **antonym,** counterterm.

.3 (contrarieties joined or coexisting) self-contradiction, **paradox** 27.2, antinomy, oxymoron, ambivalence, **irony;** equivocation, **ambiguity.**

.4 VERBS go contrary to, **run counter to,** counter, **contradict,** contravene, controvert, fly in the face of, be or play at cross-purposes; **oppose,** be opposed to, go or run in opposition to; **conflict with,** come in conflict with, oppugn, conflict, clash; contrast with, **offset,** set off, countercheck or counterbalance, countervail; **counteract,** counterwork; counterpose or contrapose, counterpoise, juxtapose in opposition.

.5 reverse, transpose 220.5.

.6 ADJS **contrary;** contrarious, perverse, **opposite,** antithetic(al), **contradictory,** counter, contrapositive, contrasted; **converse, reverse,** obverse, inverse; con–, contra–, counter–, adverse, adversative or adversive, **opposing, opposed,** oppositive, oppositional; anti [informal], dead against; **antagonistic,** repugnant, oppugnant, hostile, inimical, antipathetic(al), discordant; inconsistent, discrepant, conflicting, clashing, at cross-purposes, confronting, squared off [informal], eyeball to eyeball [slang]; contradistinct; antonymous; countervailing, counterpoised, balancing, counterbalancing, compensating; mis–, un–.

.7 **diametric(al),** diametrically opposite, ant(i)– or anth–, de(s)–, ob–, retro–; antipodal or antipodean; opposite as black and white or light and darkness or day and night or fire and water or the poles, etc., "Hyperion to a satyr" [Shakespeare].

.8 self-contradictory, **paradoxical,** antinomic, oxymoronic, ambivalent, **ironic;** equivocal, **ambiguous.**

.9 ADVS contrarily, contrariously, contra, contrariwise, conversely, inversely, **vice versa,** topsy-turvy, upside down, arsy-varsy [dial], **on the other hand,** per contra [L], **on** or **to the contrary,** tout au contraire [Fr], in flat opposition; rather, nay rather, quite the contrary, otherwise 16.11, just the other way, just the other way around, **oppositely,** just the opposite or reverse; by contraries, by way of opposition; against the grain, à rebours [Fr].

.10 PREPS **opposite,** over against, in contrast with, contrary to, vis-à-vis.

16. DIFFERENCE

.1 NOUNS **difference,** otherness, separateness, discreteness, distinctness, **distinction;** unlikeness, **dissimilarity** 21; **variation,** variance, variegation, variety, **mixture** 44, heterogeneity, diversity; **deviation,** divergence or divergency, departure; **disparity,** inequality 31; odds; **discrepancy,** inconsistency, inconsonance, incongruity, discongruity, unconformity or nonconformity, disconformity, unorthodoxy 1025, incompatibility, irreconcilability; **disagreement, dissent** 522, disaccord or disaccordance, inaccordance, discordance, dissonance, inharmoniousness, inharmony; **contrast,** opposition, **contrariety** 15; far cry, whale of a difference [slang].

.2 **margin,** wide or narrow margin, **differential;** differentia, distinction, point of difference; **nicety,** subtlety, refinement, delicacy, nice or fine or delicate or **subtle distinction,** fine point; shade or particle of difference, **nuance,** hairline, a distinction without a difference.

.3 **different thing,** different story [informal], **something else,** something else again [informal], tertium quid [L, a third something], autre chose [Fr], another kettle of fish [informal], different breed of cat [informal], horse of a different color, bird of another feather; **nothing of the kind,** no such thing, **quite another thing; other, another.**

.4 **differentiation,** differencing, **discrimination,** distinguishment, **distinction;** demarcation, **separation** 49, division, atomization, anatomization, analysis, disjunction, segregation, severance, severalization; **modification, alteration, change** 139, variation, diversification; specialization, particularization, individualization, individuation, personalization; disequalization, desynonymization.

.5 VERBS **differ, vary,** diverge, stand apart, be distinguished *or* distinct; **deviate from,** diverge from, divaricate from, depart from; **disagree with,** disaccord with, conflict with, contrast with, stand over against, clash with, jar with; bear no resemblance to 21.2, not square with, not accord with, not go on all fours with.

.6 **differentiate,** difference; **distinguish, make a distinction,** mark, mark out *or* off, **discriminate; separate,** sever, severalize, segregate, divide; set off, set apart; **modify,** vary, diversify, **change** 139.5,6; specialize, particularize, individualize, individuate, personalize; atomize, analyze, anatomize, disjoin 49.9; disequalize, desynonymize; split hairs, sharpen *or* refine a distinction, chop logic.

.7 ADJS **different,** differing; unlike, **dissimilar** 21.4; **distinct,** distinguished, differentiated, discriminated, discrete, separated, separate, disjoined 49.21, widely apart; **various,** variant, varying, varied, heterogeneous, multifarious, motley, assorted, variegated, diverse, divers, **diversified** 19.4; **several,** many; **divergent,** deviative, diverging, deviating, departing; **disparate,** unequal 31.4; **discrepant,** inconsistent, inconsonant, incongruous, incongruent, unconformable, incompatible, irreconcilable; **disagreeing,** in disagreement; at variance, at odds; inaccordant, disaccordant, discordant, dissonant, inharmonious; contrasting, contrasted, poles apart, poles asunder, worlds apart; **contrary** 15.6; all-(o)–, de–, dis–, heter(o)–, xen(o)–.

.8 **other, another,** else, otherwise, other than *or* from; not the same, not the type [informal], not that sort, of another sort, of a sort *or* of sorts [both informal]; **unique,** rare, **special,** peculiar, *sui generis* [L, of its own kind], in a class by itself.

.9 **differentiative,** differential; **distinguishing,** discriminating, discriminative, characterizing, individualizing, individuating, personalizing, differencing, separative; diagnostic, diacritical; **distinctive,** contrastive, characteristic, peculiar, idiosyncratic.

.10 ADVS **differently,** diversely, variously; in a different manner, in another way, with a difference.

.11 **otherwise,** in other ways, **in other respects;** elsewise, else, or else; than; other than; **on the other hand;** contrarily 15.9; alias.

17. UNIFORMITY

.1 NOUNS **uniformity, evenness,** equability; **steadiness,** stability 142, steadfastness, constancy, persistence, continuity, **consistency;** consonance, correspondence, accordance; unity, **homogeneity,** monolithism; equanimity, equilibrium, unruffledness, calm.

.2 **regularity, constancy,** even tenor *or* pace, smoothness, clockwork regularity; sameness, sameliness; **monotony,** monotonousness, undifferentiation, the same old thing; daily round *or* routine, treadmill; unvariation, undeviation, orderliness, invariability; monotone, drone, dingdong, singsong, monologue.

.3 VERBS **persist, prevail,** run through; run true to form *or* type, continue the same; drag on *or* along; hum, drone.

.4 **make uniform,** uniformize; **regulate,** regularize, normalize, stabilize, damp; **even, equalize,** symmetrize, harmonize, balance, equilibrize; **level,** smooth, flatten; homogenize, standardize, stereotype, assimilate to *or* with.

.5 ADJS **uniform, equable,** equal, **even; level,** flat, smooth; **regular, constant,** steadfast, persistent, continuous; **unvaried,** unruffled, unbroken, undiversified, undifferentiated, unchanged; invariable, unchangeable, immutable; **unvarying,** undeviating, unchanging, steady, stable; **ordered,** balanced, measured; **orderly,** methodic(al), systematic(al), mechanical, robotlike, automatic; **consistent,** consonant, correspondent, accordant, homogeneous, **alike,** of a piece, monolithic; equi–, hol-(o)–, hom(o)–, is(o)–, mon(o)–.

.6 **same,** samely; **monotonous, humdrum,** unrelieved, tedious 884.8, boring 884.9; repetitive, drab, gray.

.7 ADVS **uniformly,** equably, **evenly;** monotonously, in a rut *or* groove, dully, tediously, routinely, unrelievedly.

.8 **regularly; constantly, steadily,** continually; **invariably,** without exception, at every turn, never otherwise; methodically, orderly, systematically; **always** 112.11; like clockwork.

18. NONUNIFORMITY

.1 NOUNS **nonuniformity, unevenness, irregularity,** raggedness, choppiness, jerkiness, disorder 62; **difference** 16; inequality; **inconstancy, inconsistency,** variability, changeability or changeableness, mutability, capriciousness, mercuriality, wavering, **instability, unsteadiness; variation, deviation,** divergence, differentiation, divarication; versatility, **diversification,** nonstandardization; unconformity or unconformism, nonconformity or nonconformism, unorthodoxy, **pluralism;** variegation, variety, variousness, motleyness, dappleness.

.2 VERBS **diversify, vary,** variate, variegate 374.7; differentiate; divaricate, diverge; **differ** 16.5; dissent 522.4; break up, relieve, disunify.

.3 ADJS **nonuniform,** ununiform, **uneven, irregular,** ragged, choppy, jerky, jagged, rough, disorderly, unsystematic; **different** 16.7, unequal, unequable; **inconstant, inconsistent, variable,** varying, **changeable,** changing, mutable, capricious, impulsive, mercurial, erratic, spasmodic, sporadic, wavering, **unstable, unsteady;** deviating or deviative or deviatory, divergent, divaricate, erose; **diversified,** variform, diversiform, nonstandard; **nonconformist,** unorthodox; **pluralistic,** variegated, motley 374.9–15; various; diversi–, vari(o)–, heter(o)–.

.4 ADVS **nonuniformly,** ununiformly, **unequally, unevenly, irregularly,** inconstantly, **inconsistently,** unsteadily, erratically, spasmodically, capriciously, impulsively; sporadically; unsystematically, chaotically, helter-skelter, higgledy-piggledy; in all manner of ways, every which way [informal], all over the shop; here, there, and everywhere.

19. MULTIFORMITY

.1 NOUNS **multiformity,** multifariousness, **variety,** nonuniformity 18, **diversity,** diversification, variation, variegation 374, manifoldness, multiplicity, heterogeneity; omniformity, omnifariousness, everything but the kitchen sink [informal], polymorphism, heteromorphism; allotropy or allotropism [both chem]; Proteus, shapeshifting, shapeshifter; "God's plenty" [Dryden], "her infinite variety" [Shakespeare].

.2 VERBS **diversify, vary,** variate, variegate 374.7; ring changes.

.3 ADJS **multiform,** diversiform, "of every shape that was not uniform" [James Russell Lowell]; **manifold,** multifold, multiplex, multiple, multifarious, multiphase; polymorphous or polymorphic, hetero-

morphous or heteromorphic, metamorphic or metamorphotic; omniform(al), omnifarious, omnigenous; protean, proteiform; allotropic(al) [chem]; allo–, diversi–, heter(o)–, multi–, omni–, parti– or party–, poecil(o)– or poikil(o)–, poly–, vari(o)–.

.4 **diversified, varied, assorted,** heterogeneous; **various,** many and various, divers [archaic], diverse, sundry, **several, many;** of all sorts or kinds or shapes or descriptions or types.

.5 ADVS **variously, severally,** sundrily, multifariously, diversely, manifoldly.

20. SIMILARITY

.1 NOUNS **similarity, likeness,** alikeness, **sameness,** similitude; **resemblance,** semblance; **analogy, correspondence,** conformity, accordance, agreement, comparability, comparison, parallelism, parity, community, alliance, consimilarity; **approximation,** approach, closeness, nearness; assimilation, likening, **simile, metaphor; simulation, imitation,** copying, aping, mimicking; identity 14.

.2 **connaturality** or connaturalness, connature, connateness, congeneracy; congeniality, affinity; **kinship,** family likeness, family favor, generic resemblance.

.3 **likeness, like,** the like of or **the likes of** [informal]; suchlike, such; **analogue,** analogon, **parallel;** ally, associate; cognate, congener, congenator; **counterpart, complement, correspondent,** pendant, similitude, tally; coordinate, reciprocal, obverse, equivalent; correlate, correlative; **close imitation** or reproduction or copy or facsimile or replica, near duplicate, simulacrum; **close match, fellow, mate;** soul mate, kindred spirit or soul, **companion, twin,** brother, sister; mon semblable [Fr], second self, alter ego; chip off the old block; image; picture; –aria, –ee, –ella, –o, –ode, –ops(is), –type.

.4 **close** or **striking resemblance,** startling or marked or decided resemblance; close or near likeness; **faint** or **remote resemblance,** mere hint or shadow.

.5 **set, group,** matching pair or set, couple, pair, twins, look-alikes, two of a kind, birds of a feather, peas in a pod.

.6 (of words or sounds) assonance, alliteration, rhyme, slant rhyme, near rhyme, jingle, clink; pun, paronomasia.

.7 VERBS **resemble,** be like, bear resemblance; put one in mind of [informal], remind one of, bring to mind, be reminiscent of, suggest, evoke, call up, call to mind; **look like,** favor [informal], mirror; **take after,** partake of, follow, appear like, seem like, sound like; savor *or* smack of, be redolent of; **have all the earmarks of,** have every appearance of, have all the features of, have all the signs of, have every sign *or* indication of; **approximate,** approach, near, come near, come close; **compare with,** stack up with [informal]; **correspond, match, parallel;** not tell apart, not tell one from the other; **imitate** 22.5,6, **simulate,** copy, ape, mimic, counterfeit; nearly reproduce *or* duplicate *or* replicate.

.8 **similarize,** approximate, assimilate, bring near; connaturalize; –fy, –ify.

.9 **assonate,** alliterate, rhyme, chime; pun.

.10 ADJS **similar, like, alike,** something like, not unlike; **resembling,** following, favoring [informal], savoring *or* smacking of, suggestive of, **on the order of;** consimilar; **simulated, imitated,** imitation, copied, aped, mimicked, fake *or* phony [both informal], counterfeit, **mock,** synthetic, ersatz; nearly reproduced *or* duplicated *or* replicated; uniform with, homogeneous, identical 14.7; –acean, –aceous, –an, –ar, –ean, –ed, –esque, –eous, –etic, –ey, –ful, –ian, –ic(al), –ie, –ine, –ish, –like, –ly, –oid-(al), –ular, –y; hol(o)–, hom(o)– *or* home(o)–, near–, par(a)–, pseud(o)–, quasi–, semi–, syn– *or* sym–.

.11 **analogous,** comparable; **corresponding,** correspondent, equivalent; **parallel,** paralleling; **matching,** cast in the same mold, of a kind, of a size, of a piece; duplicate, twin, of the same hue *or* stripe.

.12 **such as,** suchlike, so.

.13 **connatural,** connate, cognate, agnate, enate, conspecific, correlative; congenerous, congeneric(al); congenial, affinitive; **akin, allied, connected;** brothers *or* sisters under the skin.

.14 **approximating,** approximative, approximate; **near, close;** much the same, much at one, nearly the same, same but different, "like—but oh! how different" [Wordsworth]; quasi.

.15 **very like, mighty like,** powerful like [dial], uncommonly like, remarkably like, extraordinarily like, strikingly like, **ridiculously like, for all the world like,** as like as can be; a lot alike, pretty much the same, damned little difference [informal]; as like as two peas in a pod, "as lyke as one pease is to another" [John Lyly], "as like as eggs" [Shakespeare],

comme deux gouttes d'eau [Fr, like two drops of water]; faintly *or* remotely like.

.16 **lifelike,** speaking, faithful, living, breathing, to the life, **true to life** *or* nature; realistic, natural.

.17 (of words or sounds) assonant, assonantal, alliterative, alliteral; rhyming, chiming, punning.

.18 ADVS **similarly,** correspondingly, **like, likewise,** either; in the same manner, **in like manner,** in kind; in that way, like that, like this; **thus** 8.10; so; by the same token, by the same sign; identically 14.9.

.19 **so to speak,** in a manner of speaking, **as it were,** in a manner, in a way; kind of, sort of [both informal].

21. DISSIMILARITY

.1 NOUNS **dissimilarity,** unsimilarity; **dissimilitude,** dissemblance, **unresemblance; unlikeness,** unsameness; **disparity,** diversity, divergence, **contrast, difference** 16; nonuniformity 18; incomparability, incommensurability; dissimilation, camouflage, makeup, **disguise;** poor imitation, bad likeness *or* copy, mere caricature *or* counterfeit.

.2 VERBS **not resemble, bear no resemblance,** not look like, **not compare with; differ** 16.5; have little *or* nothing in common.

.3 **dissimilate,** camouflage, **disguise;** vary 139.6.

.4 ADJS **dissimilar,** unsimilar, unresembling; **unlike, unalike,** unsame, unidentical; **disparate,** diverse, divergent, **contrasting, different** 16.7; nonuniform 18.3; scarcely like, hardly like, a bit *or* mite different; off, a bit on the off side; unmatched, odd, counter, out; offbeat; heter(o)–, near–, off–; –ish.

.5 **nothing like,** not a bit alike, not a bit of it, **nothing of the sort,** nothing of the kind, something else, something else again [informal], quite another thing, cast in a different mold, not the same thing at all; not so you could tell it, not that you would know it, **far from it,** far other [all informal]; way off, away off, a mile off, way out, no such thing, no such a thing [informal]; "no more like than an apple to an oyster" [Sir Thomas More].

.6 **not to be compared with,** not comparable to; incomparable, incommensurable, incommensurate.

.7 ADVS **dissimilarly, differently** 16.10,11, with a difference, disparately, contrastingly.

22. IMITATION

.1 NOUNS **imitation, copying, counterfeiting, repetition; emulation,** the sincerest form of flattery, **following, mirroring; simulation** 616.3; **fakery, forgery, plagiarism** or **plagiary; imposture, impersonation** 572.2, **takeoff** or hit-off [both informal], **impression; mimesis; parody, onomatopoeia.**

.2 **mimicry, mockery,** apery, parrotry; protective coloration or mimicry, aggressive mimicry, aposematic or synaposematic mimicry, cryptic mimicry, playing possum.

.3 **reproduction, duplication, imitation** 24.1, **copy** 24.1, dummy, mock-up, **replica,** facsimile, representation, paraphrase, model, version, knockoff [informal]; –een, –ette, –type; parody, burlesque, travesty 967.6.

.4 **imitator,** simulator, **impersonator, impostor** 619.6, **mimic,** mimicker, mimer, mime, –mimus, **mocker; mockingbird, cuckoo; parrot,** polly, poll-parrot or polly-parrot, ape, monkey; **echo,** echoer, echoist; **copier,** copyist, **copycat** [informal]; faker, counterfeiter, forger, plagiarist; dissimulator, dissembler, hypocrite, phony [informal], poseur; conformist, sheep.

.5 VERBS **imitate, copy, repeat,** ditto [informal]; do like [informal], do [slang], act like, go like [informal], make like [informal]; **mirror, reflect; echo,** reecho, chorus; **borrow,** steal one's stuff [slang], take a leaf out of one's book; assume, **affect; simulate** 616.21; counterfeit, fake [informal], hoke or hoke up [both slang], forge, plagiarize, crib.

.6 **mimic, impersonate,** mime, **mock;** ape, **copycat** [informal]; parrot; take off, hit off, hit off on, take off on.

.7 **emulate, follow,** follow in the steps or footsteps of, walk in the shoes of, put oneself in another's shoes, follow in the wake of, follow the example of, follow suit, follow like sheep, jump on the bandwagon; **copy after,** model after, pattern after, take after, take a leaf out of one's book, take as a model.

.8 ADJS **imitation, mock, sham** 616.26, fake or phony [both informal], counterfeit, forged, plagiarized; **pseudo,** synthetic(al), ersatz, hokey [slang], quasi; mim(o)–, ne-(o)–, near–, semi–.

.9 **imitative,** simulative; **mimic,** mimetic, **apish; emulative; echoic, onomatopoetic,** onomatopoeic; –ish, –like.

.10 imitable, copiable.

.11 ADVS imitatively, apishly; onomatopoetically; synthetically; quasi.

.12 PREPS **in imitation of,** after, in the semblance of, on the model of, à la [Fr].

23. NONIMITATION

.1 NOUNS **nonimitation, originality, novelty, newness, innovation, freshness, uniqueness; authenticity** 516.5; inventiveness, creativity or creativeness 535.3.

.2 **original, model** 25, archetype, prototype 25.1, pattern, pilot model; **innovation,** new departure.

.3 **autograph,** holograph, first edition.

.4 VERBS **originate, invent** 167.13; **innovate** 139.8; **create** 167.10; revolutionize.

.5 ADJS **original,** novel; unique; new, fresh 122.7; underived, **firsthand; authentic** 516.14, **imaginative, creative** 535.18; avant-garde; revolutionary.

.6 **unimitated,** uncopied, **unduplicated,** unreproduced, unprecedented, unexampled; prototypal 25.9, primary.

24. COPY

.1 NOUNS **copy, representation, image, likeness** 20.3, **resemblance,** semblance, similitude, picture, portrait, icon, simulacrum; ectype; pastiche, *pasticcio* [Ital]; fair copy, faithful copy; certified copy; **imitation** 22.3, **counterfeit** 616.13, forgery, fake [slang], phony [slang].

.2 **reproduction, duplication,** reduplication; reprography; transcription; tracing, rubbing; mimeography, xerography, hectography.

.3 **duplicate, duplication,** dupe [slang], ditto [informal]; **double;** clone; representation, **reproduction, replica,** replication, facsimile, model, **counterpart;** chip off the old block; triplicate, quadruplicate, etc.; repetition 103.

.4 **transcript, transcription,** apograph, tenor [law]; **transfer,** tracing, rubbing, **carbon copy,** carbon; manifold [archaic]; microcopy, microform; microfiche, fiche; recording.

.5 **print,** offprint; **impression,** impress; **reprint,** proof, second edition; photostatic copy, Photostat, stat [informal]; mimeograph copy, Ditto copy, hectograph copy, Xerox copy, Xerox [informal]; photograph, positive, negative, print, enlargement, contact print, photocopy.

.6 **cast,** casting; mold, **molding,** stamp, seal.

.7 **reflection,** reflex; **shadow,** silhouette, outline 235.2, adumbration; **echo.**

.8 VERBS **copy, reproduce,** replicate, duplicate, dupe [slang]; clone; reduplicate; transcribe; trace; double; triplicate, quadruplicate, etc.; manifold [archaic], multigraph, mimeograph, mimeo, Photostat, stat [informal], facsimile, hectograph, ditto, Xerox; microcopy, microfilm.

.9 ADVS in duplicate, in triplicate, etc.

25. MODEL

(thing copied)

.1 NOUNS model, pattern, standard, criterion, classic example, rule, mirror, paradigm; original, urtext; type, prototype, antetype, archetype, genotype, biotype, type specimen, type species, antitype; precedent, lead; representative, epitome; fugler, fugleman; imitatee.

.2 example, exemplar; representative, type, symbol, emblem; exponent; exemplification, illustration, demonstration, explanation; instance, relevant instance, case, typical example or case, case in point; object lesson.

.3 sample, specimen; piece, taste, swatch.

.4 ideal, beau ideal, ego ideal, acme, highest or perfect or best type; cynosure, apotheosis; shining example, hero, mirror, paragon, "the observed of all observers" [Shakespeare].

.5 artist's model, dressmaker's model, photographer's model, mannequin; dummy, lay figure; clay model, wood model, pilot model, mock-up.

.6 mold, form 246, cast, template, matrix, negative; die, punch, stamp, intaglio, seal, mint; last, shoe last.

.7 VERBS set an example, set the pace, lead the way; exemplify, epitomize; fit the pattern.

.8 ADJS model, exemplary, precedential, typical, paradigmatic, representative, standard, classic; ideal; type(o)–.

.9 prototypal, prototypic(al), archetypal, archetypic(al), antitypic(al).

26. AGREEMENT

.1 NOUNS agreement, accord 794, accordance; concord, concordance; harmony, cooperation 786, peace 803, rapport [Fr], concert, consort, consonance, unisonance, unison, union, chorus, oneness; correspondence, coincidence, intersection, overlap, parallelism, symmetry, tally, equivalence 14.1; congeniality, compatibility, affinity; conformity, conformance, conformation, uniformity 17; con-

gruity, congruence or congruency; consistency, self-consistency, coherence; synchronism, sync [informal], timing; assent 521.

.2 understanding, entente; mutual or cordial understanding, consortium, entente cordiale [Fr]; compact 771.

.3 (general agreement) consensus, consentaneity, consensus omnium, consensus gentium [both L], unanimity 521.5; likemindedness, meeting or intersection or confluence of minds.

.4 adjustment, adaptation, coaptation, regulation, attunement, harmonization, coordination, accommodation, squaring, integration, assimilation; reconciliation, reconcilement, synchronization, timing.

.5 fitness or fittedness, suitability, appropriateness, propriety, admissibility; aptness, aptitude, qualification; relevance 9.4, felicity, appositeness, applicability.

.6 VERBS agree, accord 794.2, harmonize, concur 521.9, cooperate 786.3,4, correspond, conform, coincide, parallel, intersect, overlap, match, tally, hit, register, lock, interlock, check [informal], square, dovetail, jibe [informal]; be consistent, cohere, stand or hold or hang together, fall in together, fit together, chime; assent 521.8, come to an agreement 521.10, be of one or the same or like mind, see eye to eye, sing in chorus; go together, go with, conform with, be uniform with, square with, sort or assort with, go on all fours with, consist with, register with, answer or respond to.

.7 (make agree) harmonize, coordinate, accord, make uniform 17.4, equalize 30.6, similarize, assimilate, homologize or homologate; adjust, set, regulate, accommodate, reconcile, synchronize, sync [informal]; adapt, fit, tailor, measure, proportion, adjust to, trim to, cut to, gear to, key to; fix, rectify, true, true up, right, set right, make plumb; tune, attune, put in tune.

.8 suit, fit, qualify, do, serve, answer, relate 9.6, be OK [informal], do the job [informal], fill the bill [informal].

.9 ADJS agreeing, in agreement; in accord, concurring, positive, affirmative, in rapport, en rapport [Fr], in harmony, in accordance, at one, on all fours, of one or the same or like mind, like-minded, consentient, consentaneous, unanimous 521.15, unisonous or unisonant; harmonious, accordant, concordant, consonant; consistent, self-consistent; uniform, coherent, conformable, of a piece, equivalent, **coinciding** 14.8, coincident, corresponding *or* correspondent; answerable, reconcilable; commensurate, proportionate; **congruous,** congruent; **agreeable,** congenial, compatible, cooperating *or* cooperative 786.5, coexisting *or* coexistent, symbiotic; synchronous, **synchronized,** in synchronization, in sync [informal]; con–, syn– *or* sym–, uni–.

.10 **apt, apposite, appropriate, suitable;** applicable, relevant, likely, sortable, seasonable, opportune; **fitting,** befitting, **suiting,** becoming; **fit,** fitted, qualified, **suited,** adapted, geared, tailored, dovetailing, meshing; **right,** just right, **pat,** happy, felicitous, just what the doctor ordered [informal]; to the point, to the purpose, *ad rem* [L], *à propos* [Fr], apropos, on the button [informal]; –ile.

.11 ADVS **in step,** in concert, **in unison,** in chorus, **in line, in keeping,** hand in glove, just right; with it [slang]; **unanimously, harmoniously,** concordantly, consonantly, **by consensus;** agreeably, congenially, compatibly; fittingly.

.12 PREPS in agreement with, together with, with, right with, in there with, right along there with; in line with, in keeping with; together on.

.13 PHRS that's it, that's the thing, that's just the thing, that's the very thing, that's the idea, that's the ticket [both informal]; right on [informal].

27. DISAGREEMENT

.1 NOUNS **disagreement, discord,** discordance *or* discordancy; **disaccord** 795, disaccordance, inaccordance; disunity, disunion; **disharmony,** unharmoniousness; dissonance, dissidence; jarring, clashing; **difference** 16, **variance,** divergence, diversity; **disparity,** discrepancy, inequality; antagonism, **opposition** 790, **conflict,** controversy, faction, oppugnancy, repugnance, dissension 795.3, argumentation 482.4; **dissent** 522, negation 524, contradiction.

.2 **inconsistency, incongruity,** asymmetry, inconsonance, incoherence; **incompatibility,** irreconcilability, incommensurability; disproportion, disproportionateness, nonconformity *or* unconformity, nonconformability *or* unconformability, heterogeneity, heterodoxy, unorthodoxy, heresy; self-contradiction, paradox, antinomy, oxymoron, **ambiguity,** ambivalence, equivocality.

.3 **unfitness, inappropriateness, unsuitability,** impropriety; **inaptness,** inaptitude, **inappositeness, irrelevance** *or* irrelevancy, infelicity, uncongeniality, inapplicability, inadmissibility; abnormality, anomaly; **maladjustment,** misjoining, misjoinder; mismatch, mismatchment; misalliance, *mésalliance* [Fr].

.4 **misfit, nonconformist,** individualist, inner-directed person, oddball [informal]; freak, sport, anomaly; naysayer, crosspatch; fish out of water, square peg in a round hole.

.5 VERBS **disagree, differ** 16.5, vary, be at cross-purposes, **disaccord** 795.8–14, **conflict,** clash, jar, jangle, jostle, collide, square off, break, break off; mismatch, mismate; **dissent** 522.4, agree to disagree, object, **negate** 524.3,4, **contradict,** counter; be *or* march out of step, "hear a different drummer" [Thoreau].

.6 ADJS **disagreeing, differing** 16.7, **discordant** 795.15,16, disaccordant; dissonant, dissident; **inharmonious,** unharmonious, disharmonious; discrepant, disproportionate; divergent, variant; at variance, **at odds,** at war, at loggerheads, at cross-purposes; hostile, antipathetic, antagonistic, repugnant; inaccordant, out of accord, out of whack [informal]; clashing, grating, jarring, jangling; **contradictory, contrary; disagreeable,** cross, cranky, negative, uncongenial, incompatible, immiscible [chem]; contra–, counter–, dis–.

.7 **inappropriate, inapt,** unapt, inapposite, **irrelevant,** malapropos, *mal à propos* [Fr]; **unsuited,** ill-suited; **unfitted,** ill-fitted; **maladjusted,** unadapted, ill-adapted; ill-sorted, ill-assorted, ill-chosen; ill-matched *or* -mated, mismatched *or* mismated, misjoined; misplaced; **unfit,** inept, unqualified; unfitting, unbefitting; **unsuitable,** improper, **unbecoming,** unseemly; infelicitous, inapplicable, inadmissible; **unseasonable,** ill-timed, untimely; **out of place,** out of line, out of keeping, out of character, out of proportion, out of joint, out of tune, out of time, out of season, out of its element; ill–, mal–, mis–.

.8 **inconsistent, incongruous, inconsonant,** inconsequent, incoherent, **incompatible,** irreconcilable; incommensurable, incommensurate; disproportionate, out of proportion, self-contradictory, paradoxical, oxymoronic, **absurd; abnormal,** anomalous.

.9 nonconformist, individualistic, inner-directed; **unorthodox,** heterodox, heretical.

.10 PREPS **in disagreement with, against,** counter to, **contrary to,** in defiance of, in contempt of, in opposition to; out of line with, not in keeping with.

28. QUANTITY

.1 NOUNS **quantity,** quantum, amount, **whole** 54; mass, **bulk,** substance, matter, magnitude, amplitude, **extent, sum; measure,** measurement; strength, force, numbers.

.2 amount, quantity, large amount 34.3,4, small amount 35.2, **sum, number,** count, **measure,** parcel, **part** 55, **portion,** group, clutch, ration, lot, deal; batch, bunch, heap [informal], pack, mess [informal], gob [slang], chunk [informal], hunk [slang], budget [archaic], dose; –ful or –full.

.3 some, somewhat, something; **aught; any,** anything.

.4 VERBS **quantify,** quantize, **count, number** 87.10, rate, fix; parcel, apportion, divide 49.18; **increase** 38.4–6, **decrease** 39.6, reduce 39.7; **measure** 490.11.

.5 ADJS **quantitative,** quantitive, quantified, quantized, measured; **some,** certain, one; a, an; **any.**

.6 ADVS **approximately,** nearly, some, about, circa; more or less, *plus ou moins* [Fr].

.7 PREPS **to the amount of,** to the tune of [informal]; as much as, all of [informal], no less than.

.8 indefinite quantities

armful	kettle(ful)
bag(ful)	lapful
barrel(ful)	mouthful
basin(ful)	mug(ful)
basket(ful)	pail(ful)
bin(ful)	pitcher(ful)
bottle(ful)	plate(ful)
bowl(ful)	pocketful
box(ful)	pot(ful)
bucket(ful)	roomful
can(ful)	sack(ful)
capful	scoop(ful)
carton(ful)	shovel(ful)
case(ful)	skepful
crate(ful)	spoon(ful)
cup(ful)	tablespoon(ful)
flask(ful)	tank(ful)
glass(ful)	teacup(ful)
handful	teaspoon(ful)
jar(ful)	thimble(ful)
keg(ful)	

29. DEGREE

.1 NOUNS **degree, grade, step,** *pas* [Fr], leap; round, rung, tread, stair; **point,** mark,

peg; **notch,** cut; plane, level, plateau; **period,** space, interval; **extent, measure,** amount, ratio, proportion, stint, standard, height, pitch, reach, remove, compass, range, scale, scope, caliber; **shade,** shadow, nuance.

.2 rank, standing, footing, **status,** station, stage, **position,** place, sphere, order, echelon, precedence, condition; rate, rating; class, caste; **hierarchy,** power structure; –ance, –ence.

.3 gradation, graduation, grading, shading.

.4 VERBS **graduate, grade,** calibrate; shade off; differentiate; **increase** 38, **decrease** 39.6,7.

.5 ADJS **gradual,** gradational, calibrated, graduated, scalar; regular, progressive; hierarchic(al); –escent.

.6 ADVS **by degrees,** degreewise; **gradually,** gradatim; **step by step,** grade by grade, *di grado in grado* [Ital], **bit by bit, little by little,** inch by inch, drop by drop; by slow degrees, by inches, by little and little, a little at a time; –meal, **inchmeal,** by inchmeal; slowly 270.13.

.7 to a degree, to some extent, in a way, in a measure, in some measure; somewhat, kind of [informal], sort of [informal], rather, pretty, quite, fairly; a little, a bit; slightly, scarcely, to a small degree 35.9,10; very, extremely, to a great degree 34.15–23.

30. EQUALITY

.1 NOUNS **equality, parity,** par, equation, **identity** 14; equivalence or equivalency, **correspondence,** parallelism, equipollence, coequality; likeness, levelness, evenness, coextension; **balance,** poise, equipoise, **equilibrium,** equiponderance; symmetry, proportion; **justice,** equity.

.2 equating or **equation; equalizing** or **equalization,** equilibration, **evening,** evening up; coordination, integration, accommodation, adjustment.

.3 the same 14.3; **tie, draw, standoff** [informal], stalemate, deadlock, dead heat, neck-and-neck race, photo finish; tied or knotted score; a distinction without a difference, six of one and half a dozen of the other, Tweedledum and Tweedledee; even break [slang], fair shake [slang].

.4 equal, match, mate, twin, fellow, **like, equivalent,** opposite number, counterpart, equipollent, coequal, parallel, ditto [informal]; **peer,** compeer, **rival.**

.5 VERBS **equal, match, rival, correspond,** reach, touch; keep pace with, keep step with, run abreast; **amount to,** come to, run to; **measure up to,** come up to, stack up with [slang], match up with; lie on a level with, **balance, parallel,** ditto [informal]; even, even off, break even [slang]; **tie, draw,** knot.

.6 **equalize; equate; even,** even up, square, level; **balance,** strike a balance, poise; compensate, counterpoise; countervail, counterbalance, cancel; coordinate, integrate, proportion; fit, accommodate, adjust.

.7 ADJS **equal, equalized,** like, **alike, even,** level, par, **on a par,** at par, au pair, commensurate, proportionate; on the same level, on the same plane, on the same footing; on terms of equality, **on even or equal terms,** on even ground; on a level, on a footing, in the same boat; **square,** quits, even stephen [informal]; half-and-half, **fifty-fifty;** nip and tuck, **drawn, tied,** deadlocked, stalemated, knotted; co–, equi– or aequi–, homal(o)–, is(o)–, pari–.

.8 **equivalent, tantamount,** equiparant, equipollent, coequal, coordinate; **identical** 14.7; corresponding or correspondent; convertible, much the same, as broad as long, neither more nor less; **all one,** all the same.

.9 **balanced, poised,** apoise, **on an even keel;** equibalanced, equiponderant or equiponderous; symmetric(al); stato–, sym–.

.10 **equisized,** equidimensional, equiproportional, equispaced; equiangular, isogonic, isometric; equilateral, equisided.

.11 ADVS **equally, correspondingly, proportionately,** equivalently, **evenly; identically** 14.9; without distinction, indifferently; to the same degree, ad eundem [L]; as, so; as well; to all intents and purposes, other things being equal, ceteris paribus [L]; as much as to say.

.12 **to a standoff** [informal], to a tie or draw.

31. INEQUALITY

.1 NOUNS **inequality, disparity, unevenness,** contrariety 15, **difference** 16, odds; **irregularity,** nonuniformity 18, heterogeneity; disproportion, asymmetry; **unbalance,** imbalance, disequilibrium, overbalance, inclination of the balance; **inadequacy,** insufficiency, shortcoming; **injustice,** inequity, unfair discrimination.

.2 VERBS unequalize, disproportion.

.3 **unbalance,** disbalance, disequilibrate, overbalance, **throw off balance,** upset, skew.

.4 ADJS **unequal,** disparate, **uneven; irregular**

18.3; disproportionate, **out of proportion,** skew, skewed, asymmetric(al); mismatched or ill-matched, ill-sorted; **inadequate,** insufficient; odd; aniso–.

.5 **unbalanced, ill-balanced,** overbalanced, off-balance, listing, heeling, leaning, canted, top-heavy; lopsided; unstable, unsteady.

.6 ADVS **unequally,** disparately, disproportionately, variously, **unevenly;** nonuniformly 18.4.

32. MEAN

.1 NOUNS **mean, median, middle** 69; **golden mean,** juste-milieu [Fr]; **medium,** happy medium; middle-of-the-road, middle course, via media [L]; middle state or ground or position or point, midpoint; **average,** balance, par, normal, norm, rule, run, generality; mediocrity; **center** 226.2.

.2 VERBS **average,** average out, **split the difference,** take the average, strike a balance, pair off; do on an average; keep to the middle, avoid extremes.

.3 ADJS **medium, mean, intermediate,** intermediary, median, medial; **average,** normal, standard; middle-of-the-road, moderate; **middling, ordinary,** usual, routine, common, mediocre, banal; **central** 226.11; medi(o)–, mes(o)–, mezzo–, semi–.

.4 ADVS **mediumly,** medianly; medially, midway 69.5, intermediately, in the mean; **centrally** 226.15.

.5 **on the average, in the long run; taking one thing with another,** taking all things together, **all in all,** on the whole, all things considered, on balance; **generally** 79.17; in round numbers.

33. COMPENSATION

.1 NOUNS **compensation, recompense,** repayment, indemnity, indemnification, measure for measure, rectification, restitution, **reparation; amends,** expiation, atonement; **redress,** satisfaction; commutation, substitution; **offsetting,** balancing, **counterbalancing,** counteraction; **retaliation** 955, revenge, lex talionis [L].

.2 **offset,** setoff; **counterbalance,** counterpoise, equipoise, counterweight, make-weight; **balance,** ballast; equivalent, consideration, something of value, quid pro quo [L, something for something], tit for tat, give-and-take 150.1.

.3 **counterclaim,** counterdemand.

.4 VERBS **compensate,** make compensation, make good, set right, rectify, **make up for,** make amends; do penance, atone, expiate; **recompense,** pay back, repay, indemnify; cover, fill up; give and take, retaliate.

.5 **offset** 15.4, set off, **counteract,** countervail, **counterbalance,** counterweigh, counterpoise; **balance,** equiponderate; square, square up.

.6 ADJS **compensating, compensatory;** recompensive, amendatory, indemnificatory, reparative, rectifying; **offsetting,** counteracting *or* counteractive, countervailing, balancing, **counterbalancing;** expiatory, penitential; retaliatory; **counter–.**

.7 ADVS **in compensation,** in return, back; in consideration, for a consideration.

.8 ADVS, CONJS **notwithstanding,** but, all the same [informal], still, yet, even; **however, nevertheless,** nonetheless; **although,** when, though; howbeit, albeit; **at all events,** in any event, **in any case,** at any rate; **be that as it may,** for all that, even so, **on the other hand,** rather, again, at the same time, just the same, **however that may be;** after all, after all is said and done.

.9 ADVS, PREPS **in spite of,** spite of [informal], **despite,** in despite of, with, even with; **regardless of,** regardless, irregardless [informal], irrespective of, without respect *or* regard to; cost what it may, regardless of cost, at any cost, at all costs.

34. GREATNESS

.1 NOUNS **greatness, magnitude,** muchness; **amplitude,** ampleness, fullness, plenitude, great scope *or* compass *or* reach; **grandeur,** grandness; **immensity,** enormousness *or* enormity, **vastness,** tremendousness, expanse, boundlessness, infinity 104; stupendousness, formidableness, prodigiousness; might, mightiness, strength, power, intensity; **largeness** 195.6, **hugeness,** gigantism, bulk.

.2 **eminence,** loftiness, prominence, distinction, consequence, notability, nobility, sublimity, **magnanimity,** majesty; fame, renown, **glory;** heroism.

.3 **quantity** 28, **quantities, much, abundance,** copiousness, superabundance, superfluity, profusion, plenty, plenitude; **volume, mass,** mountain, load; peck, bushel; bags, barrels, tons; world, worlds, acres, ocean, oceans, sea; flood, spate; **multitude** 101.3, numerousness, countlessness 104.1.

.4 **lot, lots, deal, good** *or* **great deal, considerable,** sight, **heap,** heaps, **pile,** piles, **stack,** stacks, loads, **raft,** rafts, **slew,** slews,

whole slew, spate, wad, wads, **batch,** mess, mint, peck, pack, pot, **tidy sum,** quite a little; **oodles, gobs, scads,** lashings [Brit].

.5 VERBS **loom, bulk,** loom large, bulk large, stand out; **tower,** rear, soar, outsoar; tower above, rise above, overtop; **exceed,** transcend, outstrip.

.6 ADJS **great, grand, considerable,** consequential; powerful, **mighty,** strong, irresistible, intense; main, maximum, **total, full,** plenary, comprehensive, exhaustive; grave, **serious,** heavy, deep; **–ulent.**

.7 **large** 195.16, **immense, enormous, huge** 195.20; **gigantic,** mountainous, titanic, colossal, **mammoth,** Gargantuan, monster, monstrous, outsize, sizable, overgrown, king-size, monumental; **massive,** massy, weighty, bulky, voluminous; **vast,** boundless, **infinite** 104.3, immeasurable, cosmic, astronomical, galactic; **spacious,** amplitudinous, extensive; **tremendous,** stupendous, awesome, prodigious; meg(a)–, multi–, super–.

.8 **much, many,** ample, **abundant,** copious, generous, overflowing, superabundant, multitudinous, plentiful, **numerous** 101.6, countless 104.3.

.9 **eminent, prominent,** high, elevated, towering, soaring, exalted, **lofty,** sublime; august, majestic, noble, distinguished; **magnificent,** magnanimous, heroic, godlike, superb; famous, renowned, lauded, glorious.

.10 **remarkable, outstanding,** extraordinary, superior, **marked,** of mark, signal, conspicuous, **striking; notable,** noticeable, noteworthy; **marvelous,** wonderful, formidable, exceptional, uncommon, astonishing, appalling, fabulous, fantastic, incredible, egregious.

.11 [informal terms] **terrific,** terrible, horrible, **dreadful, awful,** fearful, frightful, deadly; **whacking, thumping, rousing,** howling.

.12 **downright, outright, out-and-out;** absolute, **utter, perfect, consummate,** superlative, surpassing, the veriest, positive, definitive, classical, pronounced, decided, regular [informal], proper [Brit informal], precious, profound, stark; **thorough,** thoroughgoing, **complete,** total; **unmitigated,** unqualified, unrelieved, unspoiled, undeniable, unequivocal; **flagrant,** arrant, shocking, shattering, egregious, intolerable, unbearable, unconscionable, glaring, stark-staring, **rank,** crass, gross.

.13 **extreme, radical,** out of this world, way

or far out [informal], too much [slang]; **greatest, furthest, most, utmost,** uttermost; **ultra,** ultra-ultra; at the height *or* peak *or* limit *or* summit *or* zenith.

.14 **undiminished,** unabated, unreduced, unrestricted, unretarded, unmitigated.

.15 ADVS **greatly, largely,** to a large *or* great extent, in great measure, on a large scale; **much,** muchly [informal], pretty much, very much, so, so very much, ever so much, ever so, never so; **considerably,** considerable [dial]; abundantly, plenty [informal], no end of, no end [informal], not a little, galore [informal], **a lot,** a deal [informal], **a great deal,** *beaucoup* [Fr]; **highly,** to the skies; like *or* as all creation [informal], like *or* as all get-out [slang].

.16 **vastly, immensely, enormously, hugely, tremendously,** gigantically, colossally, titanically, prodigiously, stupendously.

.17 **by far, far and away,** far, far and wide, by a long way, by a great deal, by a long shot *or* long chalk [informal], out and away.

.18 **very, exceedingly;** awfully *or* terribly *or* terrifically [all informal], **quite,** just, so, **really,** real [informal], right [dial], **pretty,** only too, mightily, **mighty** [informal], almighty [dial], powerfully [dial], powerful [dial].

.19 (in a positive degree) **positively, decidedly, clearly,** manifestly, unambiguously, patently, **obviously,** visibly, unmistakably, observably, **noticeably,** demonstrably, sensibly, quite; **certainly,** actually, **really, truly,** verily, **undeniably,** indubitably, without doubt, assuredly, **indeed,** for a certainty, for real [slang], seriously, in all conscience.

.20 (in a marked degree) **intensely, acutely,** exquisitely, **exceptionally,** surpassingly, superlatively, eminently, preeminently; **remarkably, markedly, notably, strikingly,** signally, emphatically, pointedly, prominently, conspicuously, pronouncedly, impressively, famously, glaringly; **particularly, singularly,** peculiarly; uncommonly, extraordinarily, **unusually; wonderfully,** wondrous, amazingly, magically, surprisingly, astonishingly, marvelously, exuberantly, incredibly, awesomely; **abundantly,** richly, profusely, amply, **generously,** copiously; **magnificently,** splendidly, nobly, worthily, magnanimously.

.21 (in a distressing degree) **distressingly, sadly, sorely, bitterly,** piteously, grievously, miserably, **cruelly,** woefully, lamentably, balefully, dolorously, shockingly; **terribly, awfully, dreadfully, frightfully, horribly,** abominably, **painfully,** excruciatingly, torturously, **agonizingly,** deathly, deadly, something awful *or* fierce *or* terrible [informal], in the worst way [informal]; shatteringly, staggeringly; **excessively,** exorbitantly, extravagantly, **inordinately,** preposterously; **unduly, improperly,** intolerably, unbearably; **inexcusably,** unpardonably, unconscionably; **flagrantly,** blatantly, egregiously; **unashamedly,** baldly, nakedly, brashly, openly; **cursedly,** confoundedly, **damnably,** deucedly [informal], infernally, hellishly.

.22 (in an extreme degree) **extremely, utterly,** in the extreme, **most,** *à outrance* [Fr, to the utmost]; **immeasurably,** incalculably, indefinitely, **infinitely;** beyond compare *or* comparison, **beyond measure,** beyond all bounds, all out [informal], flat out [Brit informal]; **perfectly, absolutely,** essentially, fundamentally, radically; **purely, totally,** completely; unconditionally, unequivocally, downright, dead; with a vengeance.

.23 (in a violent degree) **violently, furiously,** hotly, fiercely, severely, **desperately,** madly, **like mad** [informal]; **wildly,** demonically, like one possessed, **frantically,** frenetically, fanatically, uncontrollably.

35. SMALLNESS

.1 NOUNS **smallness,** exiguity *or* exiguousness; **insignificance,** inconsiderableness, unimportance, pettiness, triviality, inconsequentiality; **slightness,** moderateness, scantiness, puniness, picayunishness, meanness, meagerness; daintiness, delicacy; tininess, diminutiveness, minuteness; **littleness** 196; **fewness** 102; insufficiency 662.

.2 **modicum,** minim; **minimum; little, bit,** little *or* wee *or* tiny bit [informal], **particle,** fragment, spot, **speck,** flyspeck, fleck, point, dot, jot, tittle, **iota,** ounce, **dab** [informal], mote, **mite** [informal] 196.7; whit, ace, **hair,** scruple, groat, farthing, pittance, dole, trifling amount, **smidgen** [informal], smitch [informal], pinch, gobbet, dribble, driblet, dram; grain, granule, pebble; molecule, **atom;** thimbleful, spoonful, handful, nutshell; trivia, minutiae; dwarf 196.6.

.3 **scrap,** tatter, smithereen [informal], patch, **stitch, shred,** tag; snip, **snippet,** snick, chip, nip; splinter, sliver, shiver; **morsel,** *morceau* [Fr], **crumb.**

.4 hint, *soupçon* [Fr], suspicion, suggestion, intimation; trace, touch, dash, cast, smattering, sprinkling; tinge, tincture; taste, lick, smack, sip, sup, smell; look, thought, idea; shade, shadow; gleam, spark, scintilla.

.5 hardly anything, mere nothing, next to nothing, trifle, bagatelle, a drop in the bucket *or* ocean; the shadow of a shade, the suspicion of a suspicion.

.6 ADJS small, insignificant, inconsiderable, inconsequential, negligible, trifling, petty, trivial, no great shakes, footling, picayune *or* picayunish; shallow, depthless, cursory, superficial, skin-deep; little 196.10, tiny 196.11, miniature 196.12, meager 662.10, few 102.4; short 203.8; low 208.7; mei(o)– *or* mi(o)–, sub–.

.7 dainty, delicate; subtle, subtile, tenuous, thin 205.16, rarefied 355.4.

.8 mere, sheer, stark, bare, plain, simple, unadorned, unenhanced; psil(o)–.

.9 ADVS (in a small degree) scarcely, hardly, not hardly [informal], barely, only just, by a hair, by an ace *or* whit *or* iota, slightly, lightly, exiguously, scantily, inconsequentially, insignificantly, negligibly, imperfectly, minimally, inappreciably, little; minutely, meagerly, triflingly, faintly, weakly, feebly; a little, a bit, just a bit, to a small extent, on a small scale; ever so little, *tant soit peu* [Fr], as little as may be.

.10 (in a certain or limited degree) to a degree, to a certain extent, to some degree, in some measure, to such an extent, *pro tanto* [L]; moderately, mildly, somewhat, detectably, modestly, appreciably, visibly, fairly, tolerably, partially, partly, part, in part, incompletely, not exhaustively, not comprehensively; comparatively, relatively; merely, simply, purely, only; at least, at the least, leastwise, at worst, at any rate; at most, at the most, at best, at the outside [informal]; in a manner, in a manner of speaking, in a way, after a fashion; so far, thus far.

.11 (in no degree) noway, noways, nowise, in no wise, in no case, in no respect, by no means, by no manner of means, on no account, under no circumstances, at no hand, nohow [informal], not in the least, not much, not at all, never, not by a damn sight [slang], not by a long shot [informal]; not nearly, nowhere near; not a bit, not a bit of it, not a whit, not a speck, not a jot, not an iota.

36. SUPERIORITY

.1 NOUNS superiority, preeminence, greatness 34, lead, transcendence *or* transcendency, ascendancy, prestige, favor, prepotence *or* prepotency, preponderance; predominance *or* predomination; precedence 64, priority, prerogative, privilege, right-of-way; excellence 674.1, virtuosity, inimitability, incomparability; majority, seniority, deanship; one-upmanship; success 724, accomplishment 722, skill 733.

.2 advantage, vantage, odds, inside track [informal]; upper hand, whip hand; start, head *or* flying *or* running start; edge, bulge, jump, drop [all informal]; card up one's sleeve [informal], ace in the hole [informal], something extra *or* in reserve; vantage ground *or* point, coign of vantage.

.3 supremacy, primacy, paramountcy, first place, height, acme, zenith, be-all and end-all, top spot [informal]; sovereignty, rule, control 739.5; kingship, dominion 739.6; lordship, command, imperium, sway, hegemony, directorship, management, mastery, mastership 739.7; headship, presidency, leadership; authority 739, jurisdiction, power, say [informal], authorization; influence 172; effectiveness; maximum, highest, most, *ne plus ultra* [L, no more beyond]; championship, palms, first prize, blue ribbon, new high, record.

.4 superior, chief, head, boss [informal], commander, ruler, leader, dean, *primus inter pares* [L, first among equals], master 749; higher-up [informal], senior, principal; superman, genius 733.12; prodigy, nonpareil, paragon, virtuoso, ace, star, superstar, champion, top dog [slang], laureate, fugleman, A per se, A1, A number 1, the greatest, the most [slang].

.5 the best 674.8, the best people, nobility 918; aristocracy, barons, top people [informal], elite, cream, upper crust, upper class, one's betters; the brass [informal], the VIP's [informal], lords of creation, ruling circles, establishment, power elite, power structure, ruling class, bigwigs [informal].

.6 VERBS excel, surpass, exceed, transcend, overcome, overpass, best, better, improve on, perfect, go one better [informal]; cap, trump; top, tower above *or* over, overtop; predominate, prevail, preponderate; outweigh, overbalance, overbear.

.7 **best, beat, defeat** 727.6; beat all hollow [informal], **trounce,** clobber [slang], worst, lick [informal], skin [slang], have it all over [informal]; bear the palm, take the cake [informal], bring home the bacon [informal]; **triumph** 726.3; **win** 726.4.

.8 **overshadow, eclipse, throw into the shade,** extinguish, take the shine out of [informal]; put to shame, show up [informal], put one's nose out of joint, put down [slang], fake out [slang].

.9 **outdo, outrival,** outvie, **outclass, outshine,** overmatch; **outstrip,** outgo, outrange, outreach, outpoint, **outperform;** outplay, overplay, outmaneuver, outwit; outrun, outstep, outpace, outmarch, run rings or circles around [informal]; outride, override; outjump, overjump; outleap, overleap.

.10 **outdistance, distance; pass, surpass,** overpass; **get ahead of,** shoot ahead of; leave behind, leave in the lurch; come to the front, have a healthy lead [informal], hold the field; steal a march.

.11 **take precedence, precede** 64.2; **come** or **rank first, outrank,** rank, rank out [slang]; come to the front, **lead** 292.2; play first fiddle, **star.**

.12 ADJS **superior, greater,** better, finer, major, **higher,** upper, over, super, above; ascendant, in the ascendant, in ascendancy; eminent, outstanding, rare, distinguished, marked, of choice, chosen; **surpassing, exceeding, excellent** 674.12, excelling, rivaling, eclipsing, capping, topping, **transcending,** transcendent or transcendental; **ahead,** a cut or stroke above, one up on [slang]; more than a match for; ano–, meta–, out–, pre–, preter–, super–, supra–, sur–, trans–, ultra–.

.13 **superlative, supreme, greatest, best, highest,** maximal, maximum, most, utmost; top, topmost, **uppermost,** tip-top, topnotch [informal], **first-rate** 674.15, first-class, of the first water, of the highest type, A1, A number 1; –est or –st, –most.

.14 **chief, main, principal,** paramount, **foremost,** headmost, **leading, dominant,** crowning, capital, **cardinal;** great, arch, banner, master, magisterial; central, focal, prime, **primary,** primal, first; **preeminent; predominant,** preponderant, prevailing, hegemonic(al); ruling, overruling; **sovereign** 739.17; topflight, ranking; **star,** stellar; **champion;** arch–, prot(o)–.

.15 **peerless, matchless; unmatched,** unmatchable, unrivaled, unparagoned, unparal-leled, immortal, **unequaled,** never-to-be-equaled, unpeered, unexampled, unapproached, unapproachable, **unsurpassed, unexcelled;** unsurpassable; inimitable, **incomparable,** beyond compare or comparison, **unique;** without equal or parallel, *sans pareil* [Fr], in a class by itself, *sui generis* [L], easily first, *facile princeps* [L]; second to none, *nulli secundus* [L]; **unbeatable,** invincible.

.16 ADVS superlatively, exceedingly, surpassingly; eminently, egregiously, prominently; supremely, paramountly, preeminently, **the most,** transcendently, to crown all, *par excellence* [Fr]; inimitably, incomparably, to or in the highest degree, far and away.

.17 **chiefly, mainly, in the main,** in chief; dominantly, **predominantly; mostly,** for the most part; principally, **especially,** particularly, peculiarly; **primarily, in the first place,** first of all, **above all;** indeed, even, yea, still more, more than ever, all the more, *a fortiori* [L]; ever so, never so, no end.

.18 **peerlessly, matchlessly,** unmatchably; unsurpassedly, unsurpassably; inimitably, **incomparably; uniquely,** second to none, *nulli secundus* [L]; **unbeatably,** invincibly.

.19 **advantageously,** to or with advantage, favorably; melioratively, amelioratively, improvingly.

37. INFERIORITY

.1 NOUNS **inferiority, subordinacy,** subordination, secondariness; **juniority,** minority; **subservience, subjection,** servility, lowliness, humbleness, humility; back seat [informal], second fiddle [informal], second or third string [informal].

.2 **inferior, underling,** understrapper, **subordinate,** subaltern, **junior;** secondary, second fiddle [informal], second or third stringer [informal], low man on the totem pole [informal]; lightweight, follower, pawn, cog, flunky, yes-man, creature; –ling; lower class or orders or ranks, commonalty or commonality, *hoi polloi* [Gk], masses.

.3 **inadequacy, mediocrity** 680, deficiency, imperfection, insufficiency 662; **incompetence,** maladroitness, unskillfulness 734; **failure** 725; smallness 35; littleness 196; meanness, baseness, pettiness, triviality, shabbiness, vulgarity 898; **fewness** 102; subnormality.

.4 VERBS **be inferior, not come up to,** not

measure up, fall *or* come short, fail 725.8, not make *or* hack it [slang]; want, be found wanting; **not compare,** have nothing on [slang], **not hold a candle to** [informal], not approach, not come near; serve, subserve, rank under *or* beneath, follow, play second fiddle [informal], take a back seat [informal].

.5 **bow to, hand it to** [slang], tip the hat to [informal], yield the palm; retire into the shade; give in [informal], lose face.

.6 ADJS **inferior, subordinate,** subaltern, sub, **secondary; junior, minor;** co–, par(a)–, sub–; second *or* third string, second *or* third rank, low in the pecking order; **subservient,** subject, servile, low, **lowly,** humble, modest; **lesser,** less, lower; in the shade, thrown into the shade; **common,** vulgar, **ordinary;** underprivileged, disadvantaged; **beneath one's dignity** *or* station, infra dig, demeaning.

.7 **inadequate, mediocre,** deficient, imperfect, **insufficient; incompetent,** unskillful, maladroit; small, little, mean, base, petty, trivial, shabby; **not to be compared, not comparable, not a patch on** [informal]; not in it, not in the same street with, out of it, out of the picture, **out of the running,** left a mile behind [all informal].

.8 **least, smallest,** littlest, slightest, **lowest,** shortest; minimum, minimal, minim; few 102.4.

.9 ADVS **least, less,** least of all; **under, below,** short of; under par, below the mark, at a low ebb; at the bottom of the scale, at the nadir, at the bottom of the heap [informal], in the gutter [slang]; at a disadvantage.

38. INCREASE

.1 NOUNS **increase, gain,** augmentation, greatening, **enlargement, amplification, growth,** development, widening, spread, broadening, elevation, **extension,** aggrandizement, access, accession, **increment,** accretion; **addition** 40; **expansion** 197; **inflation,** swelling, ballooning, edema, tumescence, bloating; **multiplication, proliferation,** productiveness 165; accruement, accrual, accumulation; **advance,** appreciation, ascent, mounting, crescendo, waxing, snowballing, **rise** *or* raise, boost [informal], hike [slang], **up** *or* upping [both informal], buildup; **upturn,** uptrend, upsurge, upswing; leap, jump; boom; **flood,** surge, gush.

.2 **intensification, heightening, deepening,** tightening, turn of the screw; **strengthening,** beefing-up [informal], enhancement, **magnification,** blowup, blowing up, exaggeration; aggravation, exacerbation, heating-up; **concentration,** condensation, consolidation; **reinforcement,** redoubling; pickup, step-up, **acceleration,** speedup, accelerando; explosion, population explosion, information explosion.

.3 **gains,** winnings, increase [archaic], **profits** 811.3.

.4 VERBS **increase, enlarge, aggrandize, amplify, augment, extend,** maximize, **add to; expand** 197.4, **inflate;** lengthen, broaden, fatten, fill out, thicken; **raise,** exalt, boost [informal], hike *or* hike up [both slang], jack up [informal], jump up [informal], put up, **up** [informal]; **build, build up;** pyramid, parlay.

.5 **intensify, heighten, deepen,** enhance, **strengthen,** beef up [informal], aggravate, exacerbate; exaggerate, blow up, **magnify;** whet, sharpen; **reinforce,** double, redouble, triple; **concentrate,** condense, consolidate; **complicate,** ramify, make complex; give a boost to, **step up** [informal], accelerate; key up, hop up [slang], soup up [slang], jazz up [slang]; add fuel to the flame, heat *or* hot up [informal].

.6 **increase, advance,** appreciate; **spread, widen,** broaden; **gain,** get ahead; grow, develop, wax, swell, balloon, bloat, mount, **rise,** go up, crescendo, snowball; **intensify,** gain strength, strengthen; accrue, accumulate; **multiply, proliferate,** breed; run *or* shoot up, boom.

.7 ADJS **increased, heightened,** raised, elevated; **intensified,** deepened, reinforced, strengthened, beefed-up [informal], tightened, stiffened; **enlarged, extended,** augmented, aggrandized, amplified, **enhanced,** boosted, hiked [slang]; broadened, widened, spread; **magnified, inflated, expanded,** swollen, bloated; **multiplied,** proliferated; **accelerated,** jazzed up [slang].

.8 **increasing,** crescent, **growing,** waxing, swelling, lengthening, **multiplying,** proliferating; spreading, spreading like a cancer *or* like wildfire, expanding; tightening, intensifying; incremental; **on the increase,** crescendoing, snowballing, growing like a mushroom; –er.

.9 ADVS **increasingly,** growingly, more, **more and more,** on and on, greater and greater, ever more; in a crescendo.

39. DECREASE

.1 NOUNS **decrease,** decrescence, decrement, **diminishment,** diminution, **reduction, lessening, lowering,** scaling down, miniaturization; depression, damping, dampening; **letup** [informal], abatement; alleviation, relaxation, mitigation; attenuation, extenuation, weakening, sagging, dying, dying off or away, fade-out, languishment; depreciation, **deflation; deduction** 42.1; subtraction, **abridgment** 203.3; **contraction** 198; simplicity 45.

.2 **decline,** declension, **subsidence,** slump [informal], lapse, **drop,** collapse, crash; dwindling, wane, ebb; downturn, downtrend, retreat, remission; fall, plunge, dive, decline and fall; decrescendo, diminuendo; catabasis, deceleration, slowdown.

.3 **decrement, waste, loss,** dissipation, wear and tear, erosion, ablation, depletion, corrosion, attrition, consumption, shrinkage, exhaustion; deliquescence, dissolution.

.4 **curtailment, retrenchment,** cut, cutback, rollback [informal], pullback.

.5 **minimization,** minification, **belittling,** belittlement, detraction; qualification 507.

.6 VERBS **decrease, diminish, lessen;** let up, bate, abate; **decline, subside,** shrink, wane, ebb, dwindle, languish, sink, sag, die away, tail off [informal]; **drop,** drop off, dive, plummet, plunge, fall, fall off, fall away, fall to a low ebb, run low; **waste,** wear, waste or wear away, crumble, erode, ablate, corrode, consume, consume away, be eaten away; melt away, deliquesce.

.7 **reduce, decrease, diminish, lessen,** take from; **lower, depress,** damp, dampen, **step down** [informal], tune down [informal], scale down [informal]; **downgrade;** depreciate, **deflate; curtail,** retrench; **cut,** cut down, cut back, pare, roll back [informal]; deduct 42.9; **shorten** 203.6, abridge; **compress** 198.7; **simplify** 45.4.

.8 **abate,** bate, ease; **weaken,** dilute, water down, attenuate, extenuate; alleviate, mitigate, slacken, remit.

.9 **minimize,** minify, **belittle,** detract from; dwarf, bedwarf; play down, underplay, downplay, de-emphasize.

.10 ADJS **reduced, decreased, diminished, lowered,** dropped, fallen; bated, **abated; deflated,** contracted, shrunk, shrunken; dissipated, **eroded,** consumed, ablated, **worn;** curtailed, shorn, retrenched, cut-back; weakened, attenuated, watered-down; scaled-down, miniaturized; minimized, belittled; **lower, less, lesser,** smaller, shorter.

.11 **decreasing, diminishing, lessening, subsiding, declining,** languishing, dwindling, waning, on the wane; decrescent, reductive, deliquescent, **contractive;** diminuendo, decrescendo.

.12 ADVS **decreasingly, diminishingly,** less, **less and less,** ever less; decrescendo, diminuendo; on a declining scale, at a declining rate; de–.

40. ADDITION

.1 NOUNS **addition,** accession, annexation, affixation, suffixation, prefixation, agglutination, attachment, junction, joining 47, adjunction, uniting; **increase** 38; **augmentation, supplementation,** reinforcement; superaddition, superposition, superjunction, superfetation, suppletion; juxtaposition 200.3; adjunct 41.

.2 [math terms] plus sign, plus; addend; sum, summation, total; subtotal.

.3 **adding,** computation 87.3; **adding machine,** calculator 87.19.

.4 VERBS **add,** plus [informal], put with, **join** or **unite with, affix, attach,** annex, adjoin, append, conjoin, subjoin, prefix, suffix, infix, postfix, tag, tag on, **tack on** [informal], slap on [informal], hitch on [informal]; glue on, paste on, agglutinate; superpose, superadd; burden, encumber, saddle with; **complicate,** ornament, decorate.

.5 **add to, augment, supplement; increase** 38.4; **reinforce,** strengthen, fortify; recruit, swell the ranks of.

.6 **compute,** add up 87.11,12; sum, total, total up, tot or tot up [both informal], tote or tote up [both informal], tally.

.7 **be added,** advene, supervene.

.8 ADJS **additive,** additional, additory; **cumulative,** accumulative; summative or summational.

.9 **added,** affixed, **attached,** annexed, appended, appendant; adjoined, adjunct, conjoined, subjoined; superadded, superposed, superjoined; super–, pleo– or pleio–.

.10 **additional, supplementary, supplemental; extra,** plus, further, farther, fresh, **more,** new, **other,** another, ulterior; **auxiliary,** ancillary, supernumerary, contributory, **accessory,** collateral; **surplus,** spare.

.11 ADVS **additionally, in addition, also, and** also, and all [informal], and so, **as well,** too, else, beside, **besides, to boot, into the bargain;** on top of, over, above; beyond, **plus; extra,** on the side [informal], for lagniappe; **more, moreover,** *au reste* [Fr], *en plus* [Fr], farther, further, **furthermore,** at the same time, then, again, yet; similarly, likewise, by the same token, by the same sign; item; therewith; all included, altogether; among other things, *inter alia* [L].

.12 PREPS **with, plus, including,** inclusive of, along *or* **together with,** coupled with, **in conjunction with; as well as,** to say nothing of, not to mention, let alone; over and above, **in addition to,** added to, linked to; with the addition of, attended by.

.13 CONJS **and, also,** and also.

.14 PHRS **et cetera, etc., and so forth, and so on,** *und so weiter* [Ger]; **et al.,** *et alii* [L], and all [informal], and others, and other things, *cum multis aliis* [L, with many others]; and everything else, **and more of the same, and the rest, and the like;** and suchlike *or* and all that sort of thing *or* and all that [all informal], and all like that *or* and stuff like that [both slang]; **and what not, and what have you,** and I don't know what, and God knows what, and then some [all informal]; and the following, *et sequens* [L], et seq.

41. ADJUNCT

(thing added)

.1 NOUNS **adjunct, addition,** increase, **increment,** *additum* [L], additament, additory, addendum, addenda [pl], accession, fixture; **annex,** annexation; **appendage,** appendant, pendant, appanage, tailpiece, coda; augment, augmentation, undergirding, reinforcement; appurtenance, appurtenant; **accessory,** attachment; **supplement,** complement, continuation, extrapolation, extension; offshoot, side issue, corollary, side effect, **concomitant, accompaniment** 73, **additive,** adjuvant.

.2 (written text) **postscript, appendix;** rider, allonge, codicil; **epilogue,** envoi, coda, tail; note, marginalia, scholia, commentary; **interpolation,** interlineation; affix, prefix, suffix, infix; enclitic, proclitic.

.3 (building) wing, **addition, annex,** extension, ell *or* L.

.4 **extra, bonus, premium,** something extra, extra dash, extra added attraction, lagniappe, something for good measure; **padding,** stuffing, filling; trimming, frill,

flourish, filigree, decoration, ornament; superaddition; fillip, wrinkle, twist.

42. SUBTRACTION

.1 NOUNS **subtraction, deduction,** subduction, **removal,** taking away; abstraction, ablation, sublation; erosion, abrasion; refinement, purification.

.2 **reduction, diminution,** decrease, decrement, impairment, **cut** *or* **cutting,** curtailment, shortening, truncation; dip, lessening; **shrinkage,** depletion, **attrition,** remission; **depreciation,** detraction, disparagement, derogation; retraction, retrenchment; **extraction.**

.3 **excision,** abscission, rescission, extirpation; **elimination,** exclusion, extinction, eradication, destruction, annihilation; **amputation,** mutilation.

.4 **castration,** gelding, emasculation, deballing [slang], altering, fixing [both informal]; spaying.

.5 (written text) **deletion,** erasure, cancellation, omission; editing, blue-penciling, striking *or* striking out; expurgation, bowdlerization, censoring *or* censorship; abridgment, abbreviation.

.6 [math terms] subtrahend, minuend; negative; minus sign, minus.

.7 (thing subtracted) **deduction,** decrement, minus.

.8 (result) **difference, remainder** 43, epact [astron], discrepancy, net, balance, surplus 663.5, deficit, credit.

.9 VERBS **subtract, deduct,** subduct, take away, take from, **remove,** withdraw, abstract; **reduce,** shorten, curtail, retrench, lessen, **diminish, decrease,** impair, bate, abate; **depreciate,** disparage, detract, derogate; erode, abrade, eat *or* wear *or* rub *or* shave *or* file away; **extract,** leach, drain; thin, thin out, weed; **refine,** purify.

.10 **excise,** cut out, cut, extirpate, enucleate; **eradicate,** root out, wipe *or* stamp out, **eliminate,** annihilate, extinguish; **exclude,** except, take out, rule out, bar, ban; set aside *or* apart, isolate, pick out, cull; **cut off** *or* **away,** take *or* strike *or* knock off, truncate; **amputate,** mutilate, abscind; **prune,** pare, peel, clip, crop, bob, dock, lop, nip, shear, shave, strip, strip off *or* away.

.11 **castrate,** geld, emasculate, eunuchize, spay, fix *or* alter [both informal], unsex, deball [slang].

.12 (written text) **delete,** erase, expunge, cancel, omit; **edit,** edit out, blue-pencil; strike, strike out *or* off, rub *or* blot out, cross out or off, kill, cut; void, rescind; **censor**, bowdlerize, expurgate; abridge, abbreviate.

.13 ADJS **subtractive, reductive,** deductive; ablative, erosive.

.14 PREPS **off, from; minus,** less, without, excluding, except or excepting, with the exception of, save, leaving out or aside, barring, exclusive of, not counting, exception taken of, discounting.

43. REMAINDER

.1 NOUNS **remainder, remains, remnant, residue,** residuum, **rest, balance;** holdover; **leavings, leftovers; refuse,** odds and ends, scraps, rags, **rubbish, waste,** orts, candle ends; scourings, offscourings; parings, sweepings, filings, shavings, sawdust; chaff, straw, stubble, husks; **debris,** detritus, ruins; end, fag end; stump, butt or butt end, roach [slang], rump; survival, vestige, trace, shadow, afterimage, afterglow; **fossil,** relics.

.2 **dregs, grounds, lees,** dross, slag, draff, scoria, feces; **sediment, settlings, deposits,** deposition; precipitate, precipitation, sublimate [chem]; alluvium, alluvion, diluvium; silt, loess, moraine; scum, offscum, froth; ash, ember, cinder, sinter, clinker; soot, smut.

.3 **survivor,** heir, successor; **widow,** widower, relict, **orphan.**

.4 **excess** 663, **surplus,** surplusage, overplus, overage; superfluity, redundancy.

.5 VERBS **remain, be left** or **left over, survive,** subsist, rest.

.6 **leave,** leave over, leave behind.

.7 ADJS **remaining, surviving,** over, left, **leftover,** remanent, odd; **spare,** to spare; unused, unconsumed; **surplus,** superfluous; outstanding, net.

.8 **residual,** residuary; sedimental, sedimentary.

44. MIXTURE

.1 NOUNS **mixture,** mixing, blending; **admixture,** composition, commixture, immixture, intermixture, **mingling,** minglement, commingling or comminglement, intermingling or interminglement, interlarding or interlardment; syncretism, eclecticism; **pluralism; fusion,** interfusion; amalgamation, **integration,** alloyage, coalescence; **merger, combination** 52; –mixis.

.2 **imbuement, impregnation, infusion,** suffusion, decoction, infiltration, instillment, instillation, permeation, pervasion,

interpenetration, penetration; saturation, steeping, soaking, marination.

.3 **adulteration, corruption,** contamination, denaturalization, **pollution, doctoring** [informal]; fortifying, lacing, spiking [informal]; **dilution,** cutting [informal], watering; debasement, bastardizing.

.4 **crossbreeding,** crossing, **interbreeding,** miscegenation; **hybridism,** hybridization, mongrelism, mongrelization.

.5 **compound, mixture, admixture,** intermixture, immixture, commixture, **composite, blend,** composition, confection, concoction, **combination,** combo [slang], ensemble; amalgam, alloy; paste, magma.

.6 **hodgepodge,** hotchpotch, hotchpot; **medley, miscellany,** mélange, pastiche, *pasticcio* [Ital], **conglomeration, assortment,** assemblage, mixed bag, olio, *olla podrida* [Sp], **scramble, jumble,** mingle-mangle, **mix,** mishmash, magpie, **mess,** mash, hash, patchwork, salad, gallimaufry, salmagundi, **potpourri,** stew, sauce, omnium-gatherum, Noah's ark, **odds and ends,** all sorts, everything but the kitchen sink [slang], "God's plenty" [Dryden], broad spectrum, what you will.

.7 (slight admixture) **tinge, tincture, touch, dash, smack,** taint, tinct, tint, **trace,** vestige, hint, inkling, intimation, soupçon, suspicion, suggestion, thought, shade, tempering; sprinkling, seasoning, sauce, spice, infusion.

.8 **mosaic,** chimera; pomato, potomato, topato.

.9 **hybrid, crossbreed,** cross, mixed-blood, mixblood, **half-breed,** half-bred, half blood, half-caste; **mongrel;** *ladino* [Sp]; mustee or mestee, *mestizo* [Sp], *mestiza* [Sp fem], *métis* [Fr], *métisse* [Fr fem]; Eurasian; **mulatto,** high yellow [slang], quadroon, quintroon, octoroon; sambo, zambo, *cafuso* [Brazil Pg], Cape Colored [S Africa], griqua [S Africa]; griffe; zebrule, zebrass, cattalo, mule, hinny, liger, tigon; tangelo, citrange, plumcot.

.10 **mixer, blender,** beater, agitator; cement mixer, eggbeater, churn; homogenizer, colloid mill, emulsifier; crucible, melting pot.

.11 VERBS **mix,** admix, commix, immix, **intermix, mingle,** bemingle, commingle, immingle, **intermingle,** interlace, interweave, intertwine, interlard; syncretize; **blend,** interblend; **amalgamate, integrate,** alloy, coalesce, **fuse, merge,** compound, compose, concoct; **combine** 52.3; mix up, hash, stir up, **scramble,** conglomerate, shuffle, **jumble**, mingle-mangle, throw or toss together; knead, work; homogenize, emulsify.

.12 **imbue**, imbrue, **infuse**, suffuse, transfuse, breathe, **instill**, infiltrate, **impregnate**, **permeate**, pervade, penetrate, leaven; **tinge**, **tincture**, entincture, temper, color, dye, flavor, season; saturate, steep, decoct, brew, dredge, besprinkle.

.13 **adulterate**, **corrupt**, contaminate, **debase**, denaturalize, pollute, denature, bastardize, **tamper with**, **doctor** or doctor up [both informal]; **fortify**, spike [slang], lace; **dilute**, cut [informal], water, water down [informal].

.14 **hybridize**, **crossbreed**, **cross**, **interbreed**, miscegenate, mongrelize.

.15 ADJS **mixed**, **mingled**, blended, compounded, amalgamated; **combined** 52.5; **composite**, compound, **complex**, manysided, multifaceted, intricate; **conglomerate**, pluralistic, multiracial, multinational, heterogeneous, varied, **miscellaneous**, medley, motley, dappled, patchy; promiscuous, indiscriminate, **scrambled**, **jumbled**, thrown together; half-and-half, fifty-fifty [informal]; amphibious; equivocal, **ambiguous**, ambivalent, ironic; syncretic, eclectic; mixo–.

.16 **hybrid**, **mongrel**, interbred, **crossbred**, crossed, cross; **half-breed**, half-bred, half-blooded, half-caste; demi–.

.17 miscible, mixable.

.18 PREPS **among**, amongst, 'mongst; **amid**, mid or 'mid, amidst, midst or 'midst, **in the midst of**, **in the thick of**; **with**, together with.

45. SIMPLICITY

(freedom from mixture or complexity)

.1 NOUNS **simplicity**, **purity**, simpleness, **plainness**, starkness, severity; unmixedness, monism; **unadulteration**, unsophistication, fundamentality, elementarity; **singleness**, oneness, unity, integrity, homogeneity, uniformity 17.

.2 **simplification**, streamlining, refinement, purification, distillation; **disentanglement**, disinvolvement; uncluttering, unscrambling, unsnarling; stripping, stripping down, narrowing.

.3 **oversimplification**, oversimplicity, oversimplifying; **simplism**, reductivism; intellectual childishness or immaturity, conceptual crudity.

.4 VERBS **simplify**, streamline, **reduce**, reduce to elements or essentials; purify, refine, distill; strip down; narrow; oversimplify.

.5 **disinvolve**, disintricate, unmix, disembroil, **disentangle**, untangle, **unscramble**, **unsnarl**, unknot, untwist, unbraid, unweave, untwine, unwind, uncoil, unthread, **unravel**, ravel; unclutter, clarify, clear up, sort out, get to the core or nub or essence.

.6 ADJS **simple**, **plain**, bare, mere; hapl(o)–; **single**, uniform, homogeneous, of a piece; **pure**, simon-pure, pure and simple; **essential**, elementary, indivisible, **primary**, primal, **irreducible**, **fundamental**, basic, undifferentiable or undifferentiated, undifferenced, monolithic; **austere**, chaste, unadorned, uncluttered, spare, stark, severe; homely, homespun.

.7 **unmixed**, **unmingled**, unblended, **uncombined**, uncompounded; unleavened; **unadulterated**, uncorrupted, unsophisticated, unalloyed, untinged, undiluted, unfortified; **clear**, clarified, purified, **distilled**, rectified; **neat**, **straight**, absolute, sheer, naked, bare.

.8 **uncomplicated**, **uninvolved**, incomplex, straightforward.

.9 **simplified**, streamlined, stripped down.

.10 **oversimplified**, oversimple; **simplistic**, reductive; intellectually childish or immature, conceptually crude.

.11 ADVS **simply**, **plainly**, **purely**; merely, barely; **singly**, **solely**, only, **alone**, exclusively, just, simply and solely.

46. COMPLEXITY

.1 NOUNS **complexity**, **complication**, **involvement**, involution, convolution, tanglement, **entanglement**, perplexity, **intricacy**, intricateness, ramification, complexness, crabbedness, technicality, subtlety.

.2 **complex**, perplex [informal], **tangle**, tangled skein, **mess** [informal], snafu [slang], ravel, snarl; knot, Gordian knot; **maze**, meander, Chinese puzzle, **labyrinth**; webwork, mesh; wilderness, **jungle**; Rube Goldberg contraption, wheels within wheels; rat's nest, can of worms [informal], snake pit.

.3 VERBS **complicate**, **involve**, **perplex**, ramify; **confound**, confuse, muddle, **mix up**, ball or screw or louse up [slang], foul or mess or muck up [informal], snarl up, implicate; **tangle**, entangle, embrangle, **snarl**, ravel, knot.

.4 ADJS **complex**, **complicated**, many-faceted, multifarious, ramified, perplexed, **confused**, confounded, **involved**, implicated, crabbed, **intricate**, elaborate, involuted, convoluted; **mixed up**, balled *or* screwed *or* loused up [slang], fouled *or* messed *or* mucked up [informal]; **tangled**, entangled, tangly, embrangled, **snarled**, knotted, matted, twisted, raveled; mazy, daedal, **labyrinthine**, labyrinthian, meandering; **devious**, roundabout, Byzantine, subtle.

.5 **inextricable**, irreducible, unsolvable.

47. JOINING

.1 NOUNS **joining, junction,** joinder, jointure, **connection, union,** unification, bond, bonding, conjunction, conjoining, conjugation, liaison, marriage, hookup [informal], splice, tie, tie-up *or* tie-in [both informal], knotting; merger, merging; symbiosis; **combination** 52; conglomeration, **aggregation**, agglomeration, congeries; **coupling**, copulation, accouplement, **bracketing**, yoking, pairing; **linking**, interlinking, linkage, concatenation, articulation, agglutination; **meeting**, confluence, convergence, concurrence, concourse, gathering, massing, clustering; communication, intercommunication, intercourse.

.2 **interconnection**, interjoinder, **interlinking**, interlocking, interdigitation; **interassociation**, interaffiliation.

.3 **fastening, attachment, affixation,** annexation; ligation; **binding,** bonding, gluing, sticking, tieing, lashing, trussing, girding, hooking, clasping, zipping, buckling, buttoning; knot 47.21; adhesive 50.4; splice, bond, fastener 47.20; –desis; hel(o)–, perono–.

.4 **joint, join, joining, juncture, union, connection,** link, connecting link, **coupling;** clinch, embrace; articulation [anat & bot], symphysis [anat]; **pivot, hinge; knee; elbow,** cubito–; **wrist,** carp(o)–; **ankle,** tars(o)–; **knuckle; hip,** ischi(o)–; **shoulder,** om(o)–; **neck,** cervix, trachel(o)–; ball-and-socket joint, pivot joint, hinged joint, gliding joint; toggle, toggle joint; connecting rod, tie rod; seam, suture, stitch, closure, mortise, miter, butt, scarf, dovetail, rabbet, weld; boundary, interface; arthr(o)–.

.5 VERBS (put together) **join, conjoin, unite,** unify, bond, **connect,** associate, league, band, merge, **assemble,** accumulate; **gather,** mobilize, marshal, mass, amass, **collect,** conglobulate; **combine** 52.3; **couple,** pair, accouple, copulate, conjugate, marry, **link,** yoke, knot, splice, tie, chain,

bracket; articulate, concatenate, agglutinate; glue, tape, cement, solder, weld; **put together,** fix together, lay together, piece together, clap together, tack together, stick together, lump together, roll into one; **bridge,** bridge over *or* between, span; **include,** encompass, take in, cover, embrace, comprise.

.6 **interconnect, interjoin,** intertie, interassociate, interaffiliate, **interlink,** interlock, interdigitate.

.7 **fasten, fix, attach, affix,** annex, put to, set to; graft, engraft; **secure,** anchor, moor; cement, knit, set, grapple, belay, **make fast;** clinch, clamp, cramp; tighten, trim, trice up, screw up; cinch *or* cinch up.

.8 **hook,** hitch; **clasp,** hasp, clip, snap; **button,** buckle, zipper; lock, latch; **pin,** skewer, peg, nail, tack, staple, toggle, screw, bolt, rivet; **sew,** stitch; **wedge,** jam, stick; rabbet, butt, scarf, mortise, miter, dovetail; batten, batten down; cleat; **hinge,** joint, articulate.

.9 **bind, tie,** brace, truss, **lash,** leash, rope, strap, lace, wire, chain; **splice,** bend; **gird,** girt, belt, girth, girdle, band, cinch; **tie up,** bind up, do up; **wrap,** wrap up, bundle; **bandage,** swathe, swaddle.

.10 **yoke, hitch up,** hook up; harness, harness up; halter, bridle; saddle; tether, fetter.

.11 (be joined) **join, connect, unite, meet,** merge, converge, **come together;** communicate, intercommunicate; knit, grow together; cohere, adhere, hang *or* hold together, clinch, embrace.

.12 ADJS **joint,** joined, **conjoint,** conjunct, conjugate, corporate, compact; concurrent, coincident; inclusive, comprehensive.

.13 **joined, united, connected,** copulate, **coupled,** linked, bracketed, associated, conjoined, incorporated, integrated, **merged,** gathered, assembled, **collected,** allied, leagued, banded together; hand-in-hand, hand-in-glove, intimate; unseparated, undivided; **wedded,** matched, paired, yoked, mated; **tied, bound,** knotted, spliced; ankyl(o)–, gam(o)–; –zygous, –stylic.

.14 **fast, fastened, fixed,** secure, firm, close, tight, set; **bonded,** glued, cemented, taped; **jammed,** wedged, stuck.

.15 **inseparable,** impartible, **indivisible,** undividable, indissoluble, inalienable, inseverable, bound up in *or* with.

.16 **joining, connecting,** meeting; **communicating,** intercommunicating; **connective,** connectional; conjunctive, combinative, copulative, linking, binding.

.17 jointed, articulate.

.18 ADVS **jointly**, conjointly, corporately, **together; in common**, in partnership, mutually, in concord; **all together**, as one, in unison, in agreement, in harmony; concurrently, at once.

.19 **securely, firmly, fast**, tight; **inseparably**, indissolubly.

.20 **fasteners**

anchor	hasp
band	hawser
bandage	haywire
bar	hitch
barrette	hitching post
bellyband	holdfast
belt	hook
bind	hook and eye
binding	inkle
binding stone	interlocker
binding twine	kevel [naut]
bobby pin	kingbolt
bollard	kingpin
bolt	lace
bonder	lacing
bondstone	lariat
box hook	latch
brace	latchet
braces [Brit]	leader
brad	ligament
braid	line
buckle	lock
button	loop
cable	moorings
carpet tack	nail
catch	noose
chain	nut
cinch	padlock
cincture	paper clip
clamp	pawl
clasp	peg
cleat	pin
clevis	pintle
click	*reata* [Sp, lariat]
clinch	ring
clip	rivet
clothespin	roller
corking pin [dial]	rope
cotter	safety pin
cotter pin	screw
detent	seal
dowel	sennit [naut]
drawing pin [Brit]	setscrew
fibula	skewer
fillet	snap
fishhook	snubbing post
funiculus	spike
garter	splice
girdle	staple
girth	strap
grab	string
grapnel	strop
grappler	stub tenon
grappling iron or hook	suspenders
guy	tack
guy rope	tag
hairpin	tendon
hank [naut]	terret

thole	tug
tholepin	twine
thong	vise
thumbtack	whang [Scot]
tie	wire
tie beam	withy
toggle	wrist pin
towline	zipper, slide fastener
treenail	

.21 **knots**

anchor knot	marling hitch
becket knot	Matthew Walker knot
Blackwall hitch	mesh knot
bow	midshipman's hitch
bowknot	netting knot
bowline	open hand knot
bowline knot	outside clinch
builder's knot	prolonge knot
carrick bend	reef knot
cat's-paw	reeving-line bend
clinch	rolling hitches
clove hitch	rope-yarn knot
cuckold's neck	round seizing
diamond knot	round turn and half
double hitch	hitch
Englishman's tie	running bowline
figure-of-eight knot	running knot
fisherman's bend	sheepshank
flat knot	shroud knot
Flemish knot	single knot
French shroud knot	slide knot
German knot	slipknot
granny knot	square knot
half crown	stevedore's knot
half hitch	stopper's knot
harness hitch	studding-sail halyard
hawser bend	bend
hawser fastening	stunner hitch
heaving-line bend	surgeon's knot
inside clinch	tack bend
lanyard knot	timber knot or hitch
loop knot	truckman's knot
magnus hitch	wall knot
manrope knot	weaver's knot or hitch
marlinespike hitch	Windsor knot

48. ANALYSIS

.1 NOUNS **analysis**, analyzation, **breakdown**, breaking down, breakup, breaking up; anatomy, anatomizing, dissection; separation, **division, subdivision**, segmentation, reduction to elements or parts; chemical analysis, **assay** or assaying, resolution, titration, docimasy [archaic], qualitative analysis, quantitative analysis, volumetric analysis, gravimetric analysis; ultimate analysis, proximate analysis; microanalysis, semimicroanalysis.

.2 **itemization**, enumeration, detailing; outlining, schematization, blocking, blocking out; resolution; scansion, parsing.

.3 **classification**, **categorization**, **sorting**, sorting out, sifting, sifting out, grouping, factoring, winnowing; **weighing, evaluation**, gauging, assessment, appraisal; **identification**.

.4 **outline,** structural outline, **plan,** scheme, schema, chart, graph; table, table of contents; **diagram,** block diagram, exploded view, **blueprint; catalog,** *catalogue raisonné* [Fr].

.5 **analyst, analyzer,** examiner 485.16.

.6 VERBS **analyze, break down,** break up, anatomize, dissect; **divide, subdivide,** segment; assay, titrate; separate, reduce, reduce to elements, resolve.

.7 **itemize,** enumerate, number, detail; **outline,** schematize, block out; resolve; scan, parse.

.8 **classify,** class, **categorize,** catalog, sort, sort out, sift, group, factor, winnow, thrash out; weigh, **evaluate,** gauge, assess, appraise; identify.

.9 ADJS **analytical,** analytic; segmental; classificatory, enumerative; schematic.

.10 ADVS **analytically,** by parts *or* divisions *or* sections; by categories *or* types.

49. SEPARATION

.1 NOUNS **separation, disjunction,** disjointure, disjointing, disarticulation, **disconnection,** disconnectedness, discontinuity, incoherence, disengagement, disunion, nonunion, disassociation; **parting,** alienation, **removal,** withdrawal, isolation, detachment, abstraction; **subtraction** 42; divorce, divorcement; **division,** subdivision, partition, segmentation; districting, zoning; **dislocation** 185, luxation; separability, partibility; separatism; dis–.

.2 **severance,** disseverment *or* disseverance, **sunderance,** scission, fission, cleavage, dichotomy; **cutting, slitting,** slashing, **splitting,** slicing; **rending, tearing,** ripping, laceration, hacking, chopping, butchering, mutilation; section, resection; **surgery,** amputation, excision, abscission, enucleation; –schisis, –rrhexis.

.3 **disruption, dissolution,** abruption, cataclasm; revolution 147; **disintegration** 53, breakup, **crack-up,** shattering, fragmentation; **scattering,** dispersal, diffusion; scaling, splintering, exfoliation.

.4 **break,** breakage, **breach,** burst, **rupture, fracture; crack,** cleft, **fissure, cut, split,** slit; **slash,** slice; **gap, rift,** rent, rip, tear; chip, splinter, scale.

.5 **dissection, analysis** 48, resolution, breakdown, diaeresis; anatomy.

.6 **disassembly, dismantlement,** taking down *or* apart, dismemberment, dismounting; undoing, unbuilding; stripping, divestiture, deprivation.

.7 **separator,** sieve, centrifuge, ultracentrifuge; creamer, cream separator; breaker, stripper; slicer, cutter, microtome; analyzer.

.8 VERBS **come apart,** spring apart, fly apart, come unstuck, come undone, come apart at the seams, **come** *or* **drop** *or* **fall to pieces,** go to pieces, crack up, disintegrate, unravel; come *or* fall off, peel off, carry away; get loose, give way, start.

.9 **separate, divide, disjoin, disunite,** dissociate, **disjoint,** disengage, disarticulate, **disconnect;** uncouple, unyoke; **part,** abrupt, cut the knot, **divorce,** estrange; **alienate, segregate,** sequester, isolate, shut off, set apart *or* aside, cut off *or* out *or* adrift; **withdraw, leave, depart,** split [slang]; pull out *or* away *or* back, stand apart *or* aside *or* aloof, step aside; subtract 42.9; delete 42.12; **expel,** eject, throw off *or* out, cast off *or* out.

.10 **detach, remove,** disengage, take *or* lift off, doff; **unfasten, undo,** unattach, unfix; **free, release,** liberate, loose, unloose, unleash, unfetter; **unloosen,** loosen; cast off, weigh anchor; **unhook,** unhitch, unclasp, unclinch, unbuckle, unbutton, unsnap, unscrew, unpin; unbolt, unbar; **unlock,** unlatch; **untie,** unbind, unbandage, unlace, unstrap, unchain; unstick, unglue.

.11 **sever, dissever,** cut off *or* away, ax, amputate; **cleave, split,** fissure; sunder, cut in two, dichotomize, halve, bisect; **cut,** incise, carve, **slice,** pare, prune, resect, excise 42.10; slit, snip, lance, scissor; **chop, hew,** hack, **slash;** gash, whittle, butcher; saw, jigsaw; **tear, rend,** rive, rend asunder.

.12 **break, burst,** bust [dial *or* slang], breach; **fracture, rupture; crack,** split, check, fissure; snap; chip, scale, exfoliate.

.13 **shatter, splinter,** shiver, break to *or* into pieces, break to *or* into smithereens [informal]; **smash,** crash, crush, crunch, squash, squish [informal]; **disrupt,** demolish, break up, smash up; **scatter,** disperse, diffuse; **fragment,** fission, atomize; **pulverize** 361.9, grind, cut to pieces, mince, make mincemeat of.

.14 **tear** *or* **rip apart,** take *or* pull apart, **pick** *or* **rip** *or* **tear to pieces,** tear to rags *or* tatters, **shred; dismember,** tear limb from limb, draw and quarter; **mangle,** lacerate, mutilate, maim; skin, flay, strip, peel, denude; defoliate.

.15 **disassemble,** take apart *or* down, tear down; **dismantle, demolish,** dismount, unrig [naut].

.16 **disjoint,** unjoint, **unhinge,** disarticulate,

dislocate, luxate, throw out of joint, unseat.

.17 **dissect, analyze** 48.6, anatomize, break down.

.18 **apportion, portion, section, partition,** compartmentalize, segment; **divide,** divide up, divvy or divvy up [both slang], **parcel,** parcel out, **split,** split up, cut up, subdivide; district, zone.

.19 **part company, part, separate,** split up, dispel, disband, scatter, **disperse,** break up, break it up [slang], go **separate ways,** diverge.

.20 ADJS **separate, distinct, discrete; unjoined, unconnected, unattached,** unattended, unassociated; **apart,** asunder, **in two;** discontinuous, noncontiguous, divergent; insular; noncohesive, incoherent 51.4; bipartite, dichotomous, multipartite, multisegmental; subdivided, partitioned, compartmentalized; ap(o)– or aph–, chori–, fissi–, par(a)–, schisto–, schiz(o)–, sub–.

.21 **separated,** disjoined, disjoint, disjointed, disjunct, **disconnected,** disengaged, detached, **disunited, divided,** removed, divorced, **alienated,** estranged, **segregated,** sequestered, shut off; scattered, dispersed, isolated, disarticulated, dislocated.

.22 **unfastened,** uncaught, unfixed, **undone, loose, clear, free;** unstuck, **shaky,** rickety; untied, unbound; unanchored, adrift, afloat, floating.

.23 **severed, cut,** cleft, cloven, riven, shivered, splintered, cracked, **split,** slit, reft; **rent, torn;** lacerated, lacerate, mangled, mutilated, ragged, tattered, shredded, in shreds; quartered, **dismembered,** in pieces; –clase, –fid(ate), –sect.

.24 **broken,** busted [dial or slang], **burst, ruptured;** sprung; shattered, in smithereens [informal].

.25 **separating, dividing,** parting; separative, disjunctive.

.26 **separable,** severable, **divisible,** alienable, cleavable, partible; **fissionable,** fissile, scissile; dissoluble, dissolvable.

.27 ADVS **disjointedly,** unconnectedly, sporadically, spasmodically, discontinuously, by bits and pieces, by fits and starts.

.28 **separately,** severally, piecemeal, one by one; **apart,** adrift, asunder, **in two,** in twain; apart from, away from, aside from; abstractly, in the abstract.

.29 **to pieces,** all to pieces, **to bits, to smithereens** [informal], to splinters, to shards, to tatters, to shreds.

50. COHESION

.1 NOUNS **cohesion,** cohesiveness, **coherence, adherence, adhesion,** junction 47.1, 4, sticking, cling, clinging, inseparability; cementation, conglutination, agglutination; concretion, condensation, accretion, solidification, set, congelation, congealment, clotting, coagulation; conglomeration, conglobation, compaction, agglomeration, consolidation; clustering, massing, bunching, nodality.

.2 **consistency** 26.1, connection, **connectedness;** continuity, **seriality,** sequence 65, sequentialness, **consecutiveness** 71.1, orderliness.

.3 **tenacity,** tenaciousness, **adhesiveness,** cohesiveness, retention; **tightness,** snugness; stickiness, **tackiness,** gluiness, gumminess, **viscidity,** consistency, viscosity, glutinosity; persistence or persistency, **stick-to-itiveness** [informal], toughness, **stubbornness, obstinacy,** bulldoggedness or bulldoggishness, bullheadedness.

.4 (something adhesive or tenacious) **adherent,** adherer, **adhesive** 50.13; **bulldog,** barnacle, leech, limpet, remora; burr, cocklebur, clotbur, bramble, brier, prickle, thorn; sticker, bumper sticker, decalcomania, decal; **glue, cement,** mucilage, epoxy resin, paste, stickum or gunk [both slang]; coll(o)–, gli(o)–; plaster, adhesive plaster; syrup, molasses.

.5 **conglomeration, conglomerate,** breccia [geol], **agglomerate,** agglomeration, **cluster, bunch, mass, clot;** concrete, concretion.

.6 VERBS **cohere, adhere, stick, cling,** cleave, hold, persist, stay, stay put [informal]; cling to, freeze to [informal]; hang on, hold on; take hold of, clasp, grasp, hug, embrace, clinch; **stick together, hang** or **hold together;** grow to, grow together; **solidify, set,** conglomerate, agglomerate, conglobate; **congeal,** coagulate, **clot; cluster,** mass, bunch.

.7 **be consistent** 26.6, **connect,** connect with, follow; **join** 47.11, link up.

.8 **hold fast, stick close,** stick like glue, stick like a wet shirt, stick closer than a brother, stick like a barnacle or limpet or leech, cling like ivy or a burr, hold on like a bulldog.

.9 **stick together, cement, bind, paste, glue,** agglutinate, conglutinate, gum; **weld,** fuse, **solder,** braze.

.10 ADJS **cohesive, coherent;** cohering, adhering, **sticking, clinging,** cleaving, holding together; stuck, agglutinate.

.11 **consistent** 26.9, **connected;** continuous 71.8, **serial,** uninterrupted, sequential, sequent, **consecutive** 71.9; orderly, tight; **joined** 47.13.

.12 **adhesive, adherent,** stickable, self-adhesive; **tenacious,** clingy; **sticky, tacky,** gluey, gummy, **viscid,** glutinous; **persistent,** tough, **stubborn, obstinate,** bulldoggish or bulldogged or bulldoggy, bullheaded.

.13 **adhesives**

birdlime	mucilage
cement	paste
fish glue	putty
epoxy resin	rabbitskin glue
glue	rubber cement
gluten	sealing wax
gum	size
library paste	solder
lime	viscin
lute	viscum
mastic	wafer

51. NONCOHESION

.1 NOUNS **noncohesion,** uncohesiveness, incoherence, inconsistency, discontinuity 72, nonadhesion, unadhesiveness, unadherence, untenacity; **separateness,** discreteness, aloofness; **disjunction** 49.1; **dislocation** 185; **dissolution, chaos,** anarchy, **disorder,** confusion, entropy; scattering, dispersion or dispersal; diffusion.

.2 **looseness, slackness,** bagginess, **laxness,** laxity, relaxation; sloppiness, shakiness, ricketiness.

.3 VERBS **loosen, slacken, relax;** slack, slack off; ease, ease off, let up; **loose, free,** let go, unleash; **disjoin** 49.9; unstick, unglue; scatter, disperse, diffuse.

.4 ADJS **incoherent,** uncoherent, noncoherent, **inconsistent, uncohesive, unadhesive,** nonadhesive, noncohesive, nonadherent, **untenacious, unconsolidated,** tenuous, lyo–; unjoined 49.20, disconnected, unconnected, gapped, open, **discontinuous** 72.4, broken, detached, discrete, aloof; like grains of sand.

.5 **loose, slack, lax, relaxed,** easy, sloppy; shaky, rickety; flapping, streaming; hanging, drooping, dangling; bagging, baggy.

52. COMBINATION

.1 NOUNS **combination,** combine, combo [slang], composition; hapt(o)–, zyg(o)–; **union, unification,** marriage, wedding, incorporation, embodiment, aggregation, agglomeration, conglomeration, conge-

ries; **amalgamation, consolidation,** assimilation, **integration,** solidification, **encompassment,** inclusion, ecumenism; **junction** 47.1,4; conjunction, conjugation; **alliance,** affiliation, **association** 788, merger, league, hookup [slang], tie-up [slang]; federation, confederation, confederacy, federalization, centralization, cartel; **fusion,** blend, blending, meld, melding; coalescence, coalition; synthesis, syncretism, syneresis; syndication; **conspiracy,** cabal, junta; enosis [Gk], Anschluss [Ger]; package, package deal; **agreement** 26; addition 40.

.2 **mixture** 44, **compound** 44.5.

.3 VERBS **combine, unite, unify,** incorporate, embody, **amalgamate, consolidate,** assimilate, **integrate,** solidify, coalesce, compound, put or lump together, roll into one, come together, make one; **connect, join** 47.5; **mix** 44.11; **add** 40.4; **merge, meld, blend,** shade into, fuse, flux, melt into one; interfuse, interblend; **encompass,** include, comprise; **synthesize,** syncretize; syndicate; reembody.

.4 **league, ally, affiliate, associate,** consociate; unionize, organize, cement a union; federate, confederate, federalize, centralize; **join forces,** join or unite with, join or come together [informal], join up with [informal], hook up with [slang], tie up or in with [slang], **throw in with** [slang], stand up with, go or be in cahoots [slang], **pool one's interests, join fortunes with,** stand together, make common cause with; marry, wed; **band together,** club together, bunch, bunch up [informal], gang up [informal], gang, club; team with, **team up with** [informal], couple, pair, pair off, partner; go in partnership, go in partners [informal]; **conspire,** cabal.

.5 ADJS **combined, united, amalgamated, incorporated, consolidated, integrated,** assimilated, one, **joined** 47.13, **joint** 47.12, conjoint; conjunctive, combinative or combinatory, connective, conjugate; **merged,** blended, fused; **mixed** 44.15; **synthesized,** syncretized, syncretistic, eclectic.

.6 **leagued,** enleagued, **allied, affiliated,** affiliate, **associated,** associate, corporate; federated, confederated, federate, confederate; **in league,** in cahoots [slang], in with; **conspiratorial,** cabalistic; partners with, in partnership; teamed, coupled, paired, married, wed, wedded.

.7 **combining, uniting,** incorporating; merging, blending, fusing; combinative, combinatory; associative; federative, federal; corporative, incorporative, corporational.

53. DISINTEGRATION

.1 NOUNS disintegration, decomposition, dissolution, decay, resolution, disorganization, degradation, breakup, atomization; erosion, corrosion, crumbling, dilapidation, wear, wear and tear, ablation, ravages of time; disjunction 49.1; incoherence 51.1; –diastasis, –lysis; lys(o)– or lysi–; –lyte.

.2 dissociation; catalysis, dialysis, hydrolysis, proteolysis, thermolysis, photolysis [all chem]; catalyst, hydrolyst [chem]; hydrolyte [chem]; decay, fission [phys], splitting.

.3 VERBS disintegrate, decompose, decay, dissolve, come apart 49.8, disorganize, break up, crack up, disjoin 49.9, split, fission, atomize, come or fall to pieces; erode, corrode, ablate, consume, wear or waste away, molder, crumble, crumble into dust; –lyze or –lyse.

.4 [chem terms] dissociate; catalyze, dialyze, hydrolyze, electrolyze, photolyze.

.5 ADJS disintegrative, decomposing, disintegrating, disruptive, disjunctive; erosive, corrosive, ablative; resolvent, solvent, separative; dilapidated, disintegrated, ruinous, moldering, ravaged, worn; disintegrable, decomposable, degradable, biodegradable.

.6 [chem terms] dissociative; catalytic, dialytic, hydrolytic, proteolytic, thermolytic, electrolytic, photolytic.

54. WHOLE

.1 NOUNS whole, totality, entirety, collectivity; complex; integration, embodiment; unity 89, integrity, organic unity, oneness; integer.

.2 total, sum, sum total, sum and substance, the amount, whole or gross amount, grand total.

.3 all, the whole, the entirety, everything, aggregate, assemblage, one and all, all and sundry, each and every [informal]; package, set, complement, package deal; the lot, the corpus, the ensemble; be-all, be-all and end-all, beginning and end, "alpha and omega" [Bible], A to Z, A to izzard, the whole range or spectrum, length and breadth; everything but the kitchen sink [informal].

.4 [slang terms] whole bunch, whole mess, whole caboodle, whole kit and caboodle,

whole bit or shtick, whole megillah, whole shooting match, whole hog, whole deal, whole schmear, whole shebang, whole works, the works, whole ball of wax, whole show.

.5 wholeness, totality, completeness 56, unity 89, fullness, inclusiveness, exhaustiveness, comprehensiveness; holism, holistic or total approach; universality.

.6 major part, best part, better part, most; majority, generality, plurality; bulk, mass, body, main body; lion's share; substance, gist, meat, essence, thrust, gravamen.

.7 VERBS form or make a whole, constitute a whole; integrate, unite, form a unity.

.8 total, amount to, come to, run to or into, mount up to, add up to, tot or tot up to [informal], tote or tote up to [informal], reckon up to [informal], aggregate to; aggregate, unitize; number, comprise, contain.

.9 ADJS (not partial) whole, total, entire, aggregate, gross, all; integral, integrated; one, one and indivisible; inclusive, all-inclusive, exhaustive, comprehensive, omnibus, all-embracing; holistic; universal; pan(o)– or pam– or pant(o)– or panta–, coen(o)–.

.10 intact, undamaged 677.8, unimpaired.

.11 undivided, uncut, unsevered, unclipped, uncropped, unshorn; undiminished, unreduced, complete.

.12 unabridged, uncondensed, unexpurgated.

.13 ADVS (not partially) wholly, entirely, all; totally, in toto [L], from A to Z, from A to izzard, across the board; altogether, all put together, in its entirety, tout ensemble [Fr]; in all, on all counts, in all respects, at large; as a whole, in the aggregate, in the lump, in the gross, in bulk, in the mass, en masse [Fr], en bloc [Fr]; collectively, corporately, bodily, in a body, as a body; lock, stock, and barrel; hook, line, and sinker.

.14 on the whole, in the long run, all in all, to all intents and purposes, on balance, by and large, in the main, mainly, mostly, chiefly, substantially, essentially, effectually, for the most part, almost entirely, for all practical purposes, virtually; approximately, nearly.

55. PART

.1 NOUNS part, portion, fraction; –ile, –ite, –mere, –tome; percentage; division 49.1; share, parcel, dole, quota; section, sector, segment; quarter, quadrant; item, detail, particular; installment; subdivision, subgroup, subspecies; detachment, contingent; cross section, sample, random sample, sampling; **component** 58.2; **adjunct** 41; **remainder** 43.

.2 (part of writing) section, front or back matter, text, chapter, verse, article; sentence, clause, phrase, paragraph, passage; number, book, fascicle; sheet, folio, page, signature, gathering.

.3 **piece, particle, bit, scrap** 35.3, fragment, morsel, **crumb**, shard, snatch, snack; cut, cutting, clip, clipping, paring, shaving, rasher, snip, snippet, chip, slice, collop, dollop, scoop; **tatter, shred**, stitch; **splinter**, sliver; **shiver, smithereen** [informal]; **lump**, gob [informal], gobbet, **hunk, chunk; stump**, butt, end; modicum 35.2, moiety.

.4 **member, organ**, organo–; appendage; **limb**, mel–; **branch**, imp, bough, twig, sprig, spray, switch; runner, tendril; **offshoot**, ramification, scion, spur; **arm** 287.5, **leg** 273.16, tail; hand 813.4, chir(o)–; **wing**, pinion, ali–, pter(o)–, –pterus, pteryg(o)–; lobe, lobule; joint, link.

.5 **dose, portion**; slug or shot or nip or dram [all informal].

.6 VERBS separate 49.9, apportion, divide 49.18.

.7 ADJS **partial**, part; **fractional**, sectional; segmentary, segmental; **fragmentary**; incomplete 57.4; –meric, –merous, –tomus; semi–.

.8 ADVS **partly, partially**, part, **in part**.

.9 **piece by piece, bit by bit**, part by part, **little by little**, inch by inch, foot by foot, drop by drop; –meal, **piecemeal**, inchmeal, by inchmeal; **by degrees**, by inches; **by** or **in snatches**, by or in installments, in lots, in small doses, in driblets, in dribs and drabs; in detail.

56. COMPLETENESS

.1 NOUNS **completeness, totality; wholeness** 54.5, entireness, **entirety; unity, integrity**, integrality, intactness; solidity, solidarity; **thoroughness**, exhaustiveness, inclusiveness, comprehensiveness, universality; pervasiveness, ubiquity, omnipresence.

.2 **fullness**, full; **amplitude, plenitude**; impletion, **repletion**, plethora; saturation, saturation point, satiety, congestion; overfullness 663.3, surfeit; high water, high tide, flood tide, spring tide.

.3 **full measure, fill**, full house, "good measure, pressed down, and shaken together, and running over" [Bible]; **load, capacity, complement**, lading, charge; the

whole bit [slang]; bumper, brimmer; bellyful or snootful [both slang], skinful or mouthful [both informal]; **crush**, cram [informal], jam up [informal].

.4 **completion, fulfillment, consummation**, culmination, perfection, realization, **accomplishment** 722, topping-off, closure.

.5 **limit, end** 70, **extremity**, extreme, **acme**, apogee, climax, **maximum**, ceiling, **peak**, summit, **pinnacle**, crown, top; **utmost**, uttermost, utmost extent, highest degree, nth degree or power, ne plus ultra [L]; **all, the whole** 54.3,4.

.6 VERBS (make whole) **complete**, fulfill, **accomplish** 722.4; bring to completion or fruition, mature; fill in, **fill out**, piece out, top off, eke out, round out; **make up**, make good, replenish, refill.

.7 **fill, charge, load**, lade, freight, weight; **stuff, wad**, pad, **pack**, crowd, **cram**, jam, jam-pack, ram in, chock; **fill up**, fill to the brim, brim, top off, fill to overflowing, fill the measure of; supercharge, saturate, satiate, congest; overfill 663.15, surfeit.

.8 (be thorough) **go all lengths, go all out, go the limit** [informal], go the whole way, **go the whole hog** [slang], make a federal case, **see it through** [informal], follow out or up, follow or prosecute to a conclusion; leave nothing undone, not overlook a bet [informal]; **move heaven and earth, leave no stone unturned.**

.9 ADJS **complete, whole, total, global, entire**, intact, solid; eu–, hol(o)–, integri–, pan(o)–, per–, tel(o)– or tele(o)–, teleut(o)–; **full, full-fledged**, full-dress, **full-scale**; full-grown, mature, matured, ripe, developed; **uncut**, unabbreviated, undiminished, unexpurgated.

.10 **thorough, thoroughgoing**, thoroughpaced, exhaustive, intensive, broad-based, comprehensive, all-embracing, all-encompassing, omnibus, radical, sweeping; **pervasive**, all-pervading, ubiquitous, omnipresent, **universal; unmitigated, unqualified, unconditional**, unrestricted, unreserved, **all-out**, wholesale, wholehog [slang]; out-and-out, **through-and-through**, outright, downright, straight; congenital, born, **consummate**, perfect, veritable, egregious, deep-dyed, dyed-in-the-wool; **utter, absolute, total; sheer**, clear, clean, **pure**, plumb [informal], **plain**, regular [informal].

.11 **full**, filled, **replete**, plenary, capacity, flush, round; **brimful**, brimming; **chockfull**, chuck-full, **cram-full**, topful; jam-full, jam-packed; stuffed, overstuffed, packed, crammed, *farci* [Fr]; **swollen** 197.13, bulging 256.14, bursting, ready to burst, full to bursting, fit to bust [slang]; as full as a tick, packed like sardines *or* herrings; standing room only, SRO; **saturated,** satiated, soaked; congested; overfull 663.20, surfeited; –ful.

.12 **fraught,** freighted, **laden, loaded, charged,** burdened; heavy-laden; fullladen, full-fraught, full-charged, supercharged.

.13 **completing, fulfilling,** filling; completive *or* completory, consummative *or* consummatory, culminative, perfective; **complementary,** complemental.

.14 ADVS **completely, totally, globally, entirely, wholly, fully,** integrally, roundly, **altogether,** hundred per cent, **exhaustively,** inclusively, comprehensively, largely; **unconditionally,** unrestrictedly, unreservedly; one and all; outright, *tout à fait* [Fr]; **thoroughly,** inside out [informal]; in full, in full measure; to the hilt.

.15 **absolutely, perfectly, quite,** right, stark, clean, sheer, plumb [informal], plain; irretrievably, unrelievedly, irrevocably.

.16 **utterly, to the utmost,** all the way, **all out,** flat out [Brit], *à outrance* [Fr], *à toute outrance* [Fr], **to the full, to the limit,** to the backbone, to the marrow, to the nth degree *or* power, to the sky *or* skies, to the top of one's bent, **to a farethee-well,** to a fare-you-well *or* fare-yewell, with a vengeance, all hollow [informal].

.17 **throughout, all over,** overall, **inside and out, through and through;** through thick and thin, down to the ground [informal], **from the ground up,** from the word 'go' [informal]; **to the end** *or* **bitter end,** to the death; **at full length,** *in extenso* [L], *ad infinitum* [L]; every inch, every whit, every bit; root and branch, head and shoulders, heart and soul; to the brim, to the hilt, neck deep, up to the ears, up to the eyes; **in every respect,** in all respects, you name it [informal]; **on all counts,** at all points, for good and all; lock, stock, and barrel [informal].

.18 **from beginning to end,** from end to end, **from first to last, from A to Z,** from A to izzard, from hell to breakfast [slang], from cover to cover; **from top to bottom,** *de fond en comble* [Fr]; from top to toe, **from head to foot,** *a capite ad calcem* [L], cap-a-pie; **from stem to stern,** from clew to earing, fore and aft; from soup to nuts [slang], *"ab ovo usque ad mala"* [L, from egg to apples; Horace].

57. INCOMPLETENESS

.1 NOUNS **incompleteness,** incompletion; **deficiency,** defectiveness, **inadequacy;** underdevelopment, hypoplasia, **immaturity,** callowness, arrestment; sketchiness, scrappiness, patchiness; short measure *or* weight.

.2 (part lacking) **deficiency,** want, **lack, need, deficit,** defect, **shortage;** wantage, outage, ullage; defalcation, arrearage; omission, gap, hiatus, break, lacuna, discontinuity, interval; missing link.

.3 VERBS **lack** 662.7; **fall short** 314.2.

.4 ADJS **incomplete, deficient,** defective, **inadequate;** semi–; **undeveloped,** underdeveloped, hypoplastic, **immature,** callow, infant, arrested, embryonic, **wanting, lacking,** needing, missing, **partial,** part, failing; in default, in arrear *or* arrears; **in short supply,** scanty; **short,** scant, shy [informal]; sketchy, patchy, scrappy.

.5 **mutilated,** garbled, hashed, **mangled, butchered,** docked, lopped, truncated, castrated, cut short.

.6 ADVS **incompletely, partially,** by halves, by *or* in half measures, in installments, in *or* by bits and pieces; **deficiently,** inadequately.

58. COMPOSITION

(manner of being composed)

.1 NOUNS **composition, constitution, construction, formation,** fabrication, fashioning, shaping, organization; embodiment, incorporation; make, **makeup,** getup *or* setup [both informal]; building, buildup, structure, structuring; **assembly,** assemblage, putting *or* piecing together; synthesis, syneresis; **combination** 52; **compound** 44.5; **junction** 47.1,4; **mixture** 44.

.2 **component, constituent, ingredient,** integrant, **element, factor, part** 55, part and parcel; appurtenance, adjunct 41; feature, aspect, specialty, circumstance, detail, item; contents, makings *or* fixings [both informal].

.3 VERBS **compose, constitute,** construct, fabricate; incorporate, embody; **form, organize,** structure; **enter into,** go into; make, **make up,** build, **build up, assemble,** put *or* piece together; **consist of,** be a feature of, form a part of, combine *or* unite in, merge in; **synthesize; combine** 52.3; **join** 47.5; **mix** 44.11.

.4 ADJS **composed of,** formed of, **made of,** made up of, made out of, compact of, consisting of; composing, comprising, constituting, including, inclusive of, containing, embodying, subsuming; contained in, embodied in; di(a)–; –en or –n, –ine.

.5 **component,** constituent, integrant, integral; **formative,** elementary.

59. ORDER

.1 NOUNS **order, arrangement** 60; **organization** 60.2; **disposition,** disposal, deployment, marshaling; **formation, structure,** array, lineup, setup, layout; system; routine, even tenor; **peace,** quiet, quietude, **tranquillity;** regularity, uniformity 17; symmetry, proportion, concord, **harmony,** order, the music of the spheres; "the eternal fitness of things" [Samuel Clarke], "Heav'n's first law" [Pope].

.2 **continuity,** logical order, serial order; **degree** 29; **hierarchy,** gradation, subordination, rank, place; **sequence** 65.

.3 **orderliness, trimness, tidiness, neatness,** anality; good shape [informal], good condition, fine fettle, good trim, apple-pie order [informal], a place for everything and everything in its place; **discipline,** method, methodology, methodicalness, system, systematicness.

.4 VERBS **order, arrange** 60.8, **organize, regulate;** dispose, deploy, marshal; **form,** structure, array, line up, set up, lay out; **pacify,** quiet, cool off or down [informal], **tranquilize; regularize,** harmonize; **systematize,** methodize, normalize, standardize, routinize; hierarchize, grade, rank.

.5 **form, take form,** take order, **take shape,** crystallize, **shape up;** arrange or range itself, place itself, take its place, fall in, **fall into place,** fall into line or order or series, fall into rank, take rank; come together, draw up, gather around, rally round.

.6 ADJS **orderly, ordered, regular, well-regulated, well-ordered, methodical, formal,** uniform 17.5, **systematic,** symmetrical, **harmonious;** businesslike, routine, steady, normal, habitual, usual, en règle [Fr], in hand; **arranged** 60.14.

.7 **in order, in trim,** to rights [informal], in apple-pie order [informal]; **in condition,** in good condition, in kilter or kelter [informal], **in shape,** in good shape [informal], **in good form,** in fine fettle, in good trim, in the pink [informal], in the pink of condition; **in repair,** in commission, in adjustment, in working order, fixed; up to scratch or snuff [slang].

.8 **tidy, trim, neat,** anal, spruce, sleek, slick [informal], smart, trig, dinky [Brit informal], snug, tight, **shipshape,** shipshape and Bristol fashion; **well-kept,** well-kempt, well-cared-for, well-groomed; neat as a button or pin [informal].

.9 ADVS **methodically, systematically, regularly,** uniformly, harmoniously, like clockwork.

.10 **in order, in turn, in sequence, in succession,** hierarchically, in series, seriatim [L]; step by step, by stages.

60. ARRANGEMENT

(putting in order)

.1 NOUNS **arrangement, ordering,** structuring, constitution; **disposition, disposal,** deployment, placement, marshaling; **arraying; distribution,** collation, collocation, allocation, allotment, apportionment; **formation,** formulation, form, array; regimentation; syntax; **order** 59; tax(o)– or taxi–, –taxia or –taxis.

.2 **organization, methodization,** planning, charting, codification, regulation, regularization, routinization, normalization, rationalization; **adjustment,** harmonization, **systematization,** ordination, coordination.

.3 **grouping,** categorization, taxonomy; **gradation,** subordination, **ranking,** placement; **sorting,** sorting out, assortment, sifting, screening, triage, culling, selection.

.4 **table,** code, digest, **index, inventory,** census; table of organization.

.5 **sorter,** sifter, **sieve,** riddle, **screen,** bolter, colander, grate, grating.

.6 (act of making neat) **cleanup,** red-up [dial]; tidy-up, trim-up, police-up [informal].

.7 **rearrangement, reorganization,** reconstitution, **reordering, restructuring,** shakeup; redisposition, redistribution, realignment.

.8 VERBS **arrange,** order 59.4, reduce to order, **put or set in order,** right, **put or set to rights,** put in or into shape, whip into shape [informal], unsnarl.

.9 **dispose, distribute, fix, place,** set out, collocate, allocate, **compose,** space, **marshal,** rally, array; align, line, **line up,** range; regiment; **allot, apportion,** parcel out, deal, **deal out.**

.10 **organize,** methodize, **systematize,** rationalize; **harmonize,** synchronize, **tune,** tune up; **regularize,** routinize, normalize, standardize; **regulate,** adjust, coordinate, fix, settle; **plan,** chart, codify.

.11 **classify** 61.6, **group,** categorize; **grade,** gradate, rank, subordinate; **sort,** sort out, assort; **separate,** divide; collate; **sift,** size, sieve, **screen,** bolt, riddle.

.12 tidy, **tidy up,** neaten, trim, **put in trim,** trim up, trig up, **straighten up,** fix up [informal], **clean up,** police *or* police up [both informal], groom, spruce *or* spruce up [both informal], **clear up,** clear the decks.

.13 **rearrange, reorganize,** reconstitute, **reorder, restructure,** shake up; redispose, redistribute, realign.

.14 ADJS **arranged, ordered, disposed,** composed, constituted, fixed, placed, aligned, ranged, arrayed, marshaled, grouped, ranked, **graded;** organized, methodized, **regularized,** routinized, normalized, standardized, **systematized;** regulated, harmonized, synchronized; **classified** 61.8, categorized, **sorted,** assorted; **orderly** 59.6; –tactic.

.15 **organizational,** formational.

61. CLASSIFICATION

.1 NOUNS **classification, categorization,** placement, ranging, **pigeonholing, sorting, grouping; grading,** stratification, ranking, rating; division, subdivision; **cataloging,** codification, tabulation, indexing, filing; **taxonomy,** typology; analysis 48, **arrangement** 60.

.2 **class, category, head, order, division,** branch, set, **group,** grouping, bracket, pigeonhole; **section,** heading, rubric, **label,** title; **grade,** rank, rating, status, estate, stratum, level, station, position; –age, –ate, –cy, –dom, –hood; predicament [logic]; caste, clan, race, strain, blood, kin, sept; **subdivision,** subgroup, suborder.

.3 **kind, sort, ilk, type,** lot [informal], variety, **species,** speci(o)– *or* specie–, **genus,** *genre* [Fr], gen(o)–, phylum, phyl(o)–, denomination, designation, number [informal], description, style, manner, **nature, character,** persuasion, the like *or* likes of [informal]; **stamp, brand,** feather, color, stripe, line, grain, kidney; **make,** mark, label, shape, cast, form, mold; tribe, clan, race, strain, blood, kin, breed.

.4 **hierarchy,** class structure, power structure, pyramid, establishment, pecking order; natural hierarchy, order *or* chain of

being; domain, realm, **kingdom,** animal kingdom, vegetable kingdom, mineral kingdom.

.5 (botanical and zoological classifications, in descending order) **kingdom;** subkingdom, **phylum** [zool], branch [bot]; superclass, **class,** subclass, superorder, **order,** suborder, superfamily, **family,** subfamily, tribe, subtribe, **genus,** subgenus, series, section, superspecies, **species;** subspecies, **variety;** biotype, genotype.

.6 VERBS **classify,** class; **categorize,** type, **pigeonhole,** place, **group, arrange** 60.8, range; **order** 59.4, rank, rate, **grade; sort,** assort; **divide, analyze** 48.6, subdivide, break down; **catalog,** list, file, tabulate, index, alphabetize, digest, codify.

.7 ADJS **classificational,** classificatory; **categorical, taxonomic(al),** typologic(al), ordinal; **divisional,** divisionary, subdivisional; **typical,** typal; **special,** specific, characteristic, particular, peculiar, denominative, differential, distinctive, defining.

.8 **classified, cataloged, pigeonholed,** indexed, sorted, assorted, **graded, grouped,** ranked, rated, stratified, hierarchic, pyramidal; placed; filed, on file; tabular.

.9 ADVS of any kind *or* sort, **of any description, at all,** whatever, soever, whatsoever.

62. DISORDER

.1 NOUNS **disorder,** disorderliness, **disarrangement,** derangement, disarticulation, disjunction 49.1, **disorganization;** discomposure, **dishevelment, disarray,** upset, disturbance, discomfiture, disconcertedness; **irregularity,** randomness, turbulence, perturbation, ununiformity *or* nonuniformity, unsymmetry *or* nonsymmetry, **disproportion, disharmony;** indiscriminateness, promiscuity, promiscuousness, haphazardness; entropy; **disruption** 49.3; **incoherence** 51.1; disintegration 53; "most admired disorder" [Shakespeare], "inharmonious harmony" [Horace].

.2 **confusion, chaos,** anarchy, misrule, license; **muddle,** morass, **mix-up** [informal], foul-up [informal], snafu [slang], screw-up [slang], hassle [informal]; pretty kettle of fish, pretty piece of business, nice piece of work; "Chaos and old Night" [Milton], "the seed of Chaos, and of Night" [Pope], "mere anarchy is loosed upon the world", "fabulous formless darkness" [both Yeats].

.3 **jumble, scramble, tumble, mess,** bloody *or* holy *or* unholy mess [slang], **turmoil,** welter, mishmash, hash, helter-skelter, farrago, higgledy-piggledy; **clutter, litter, hodgepodge** 44.6, rat's nest; topsy-turviness *or* topsy-turvydom, arsy-varsiness, hysteron proteron.

.4 **commotion, hubbub, tumult, turmoil, uproar, racket,** riot, **disturbance, rumpus** [informal], ruckus *or* ruction [both informal], **fracas, hassle,** shemozzle [Brit slang], shindy [slang], rampage; **ado,** to-do [informal], trouble, bother, pother, dustup [Brit informal], stir [informal], **fuss,** *brouhaha* [Fr], foofaraw [informal]; **row** [informal], **brawl,** free-for-all [informal], donnybrook *or* donnybrook fair, broil, embroilment, melee, scramble; helter-skelter, pell-mell, **roughhouse, rough-and-tumble.**

.5 **pandemonium,** "confusion worse confounded" [Milton], **hell, bedlam,** witches' Sabbath, Babel, confusion of tongues; **cacophony,** noise, static, racket.

.6 slovenliness *or* slovenry, **slipshodness,** carelessness, negligence; **untidiness,** unneatness, looseness, **messiness** [informal], **sloppiness,** dowdiness, seediness, **shabbiness,** tawdriness, chintziness [informal], shoddiness, tackiness [informal], grubbiness [informal], frowziness, blowziness; **slatternliness,** frumpishness [informal], sluttishness; **squalor,** squalidness, sordidness.

.7 **slob** [informal], **slattern, sloven,** frump [informal], sloppy Joe, schlep, schlump; drab, **slut, trollop; pig,** swine; **litterbug.**

.8 VERBS lapse into disorder, come apart 49.8, dissolve into chaos, slacken 51.3, disintegrate 53.3, degenerate, untune.

.9 **disorder, disarrange** 63.2, **disorganize,** dishevel; **confuse** 63.3, **muddle, jumble; discompose** 63.4, **upset,** unsettle, **disturb,** perturb; knock galley-west [slang].

.10 **riot,** roister, roil, carouse; **create a disturbance, make a commotion, make trouble, make an ado** *or* **to-do** [informal], raise a rumpus [informal], raise a storm [informal], raise a ruckus [informal], create a riot, **cut loose,** run wild, **run riot,** run amok, go on a rampage, go berserk.

.11 [slang or informal terms] **kick up a row,** kick up a shindy, **raise the devil,** raise the deuce *or* dickens, raise Cain, **raise hell,** raise sand, raise the roof, whoop it up, hell around, horse around; **carry on, go on,** maffick [Brit]; **cut up,** cut up rough, **roughhouse.**

.12 ADJS **unordered, orderless, disordered, unorganized, unarranged,** ungraded, unsorted, unclassified; **unmethodical,** immethodical; **unsystematic,** systemless, nonsystematic; disjunct, unjoined 49.20; disarticulated, **incoherent** 51.4; discontinuous; **formless,** amorphous, inchoate, shapeless; ununiform *or* nonuniform, unsymmetrical *or* nonsymmetrical, disproportionate, misshapen; **irregular, haphazard,** desultory, **erratic,** sporadic, spasmodic, fitful, promiscuous, indiscriminate, casual, frivolous, capricious, random, hit-or-miss, vague, dispersed, wandering, planless, undirected, **aimless,** straggling, straggly; senseless, meaningless, gratuitous; dis–.

.13 **disorderly, in disorder,** disordered, **disorganized, disarranged, discomposed,** dislocated, deranged, convulsed; **upset, disturbed,** perturbed, unsettled, discomfited, disconcerted; **turbulent,** turbid, roily; **out of order,** out of place, misplaced, shuffled; **out of kilter** *or* **kelter** [informal], **out of whack** [informal], out of gear, out of joint, out of tune, on the fritz [slang]; **cockeyed** [slang], awry, amiss, askew, haywire [informal].

.14 **disheveled, mussed up** [informal], messed up [informal], **rumpled,** tumbled, ruffled, snarled, snaggy; **tousled,** tously; uncombed, shaggy, matted.

.15 **slovenly, slipshod, careless, loose, slack,** informal, negligent; **untidy, unsightly,** unneat, **unkempt; messy** [informal], mussy [informal], **sloppy** [informal], scraggly, poky, seedy [informal], **shabby,** shoddy, lumpen, chintzy, grubby [informal], **frowzy, blowzy,** tacky [informal]; **slatternly, sluttish, frumpish,** frumpy, draggletailed, drabbletailed, draggled, bedraggled; down at the heel, out at the heels, out at the elbows, in rags, ragged, raggedy, tattered; **squalid,** sordid; dilapidated, ruinous, beat-up [slang].

.16 **confused, chaotic,** anarchic, **muddled, jumbled,** scattered, helter-skelter [informal], higgledy-piggledy, hugger-mugger, skimble-skamble, in a mess; **topsy-turvy,** arsy-varsy, upside-down, ass-backwards [slang]; **mixed up, balled** *or* **bollixed up** [slang], **screwed up** [slang], mucked up [informal], **fouled up** [informal], snafu [slang], galley-west [slang].

.17 ADVS **in disorder, in disarray, in confusion, in a jumble, in a tumble, in a muddle, in a mess; higgledy-piggledy,** helter-skelter [informal], hugger-mugger, skimble-skamble, harum-scarum [informal], willy-nilly [informal], every which way [informal]; all over, all over hell [slang],

37

all over the place, all over the shop [informal].

.18 **haphazardly, unsystematically,** unmethodically, irregularly, desultorily, **erratically,** capriciously, promiscuously, indiscriminately, **sloppily** [informal], **carelessly,** randomly, **fitfully;** by or at intervals, sporadically, spasmodically, by fits, **by fits and starts,** by or in snatches, in spots [informal]; every now and then, every once in a while [both informal]; **at random,** at haphazard, **by chance, hit or miss.**

.19 **chaotically, anarchically,** turbulently, **riotously; confusedly,** dispersedly, vaguely, wanderingly, **aimlessly,** planlessly, senselessly.

63. DISARRANGEMENT

(bringing into disorder)

.1 NOUNS **disarrangement, derangement,** misarrangement, convulsion, dislocation; **disorganization,** shuffling; **discomposure,** disturbance, perturbation; **disorder** 62; insanity 473.

.2 VERBS **disarrange, derange,** misarrange; **disorder, disorganize,** throw out of order, put out of gear, dislocate, **disarray; dishevel,** rumple, ruffle; tousle [informal], muss or muss up [both informal], mess or mess up [both informal]; **litter, clutter,** scatter.

.3 **confuse, muddle, jumble,** confound, garble, tumble, scramble, fumble, pi; **shuffle, riffle; mix up,** snarl up, **ball or bollix up** [slang], **foul up** [informal], **screw up** [slang], muck up [informal], snafu [slang]; make a hash or mess of [slang], play hob with [informal].

.4 **discompose,** throw into confusion, **upset, unsettle, disturb,** perturb, trouble, distract, throw [informal], throw into a tizzy or snit or stew [informal], agitate, convulse, embroil; **psych** or spook or bug [all slang].

.5 ADJS **disarranged** 62.13, **confused** 62.16, **disordered** 62.12.

64. PRECEDENCE

(in order)

.1 NOUNS precedence or precedency, antecedence or antecedency, anteposition, anteriority, precession; the lead, front position; **priority,** preference, urgency; top priority; prefixation, prothesis; **superiority**

36; **dominion** 739.6; **precursor** 66; prelude 66.2; preceding 292.1.

.2 VERBS **precede,** antecede, **come first,** come or go before 66.3, **go ahead of, go in advance,** stand first, stand at the head, **head,** head up [informal], front, **lead** 292.2, take precedence, have priority; lead off, kick off, usher in; head the table or board, sit on the dais; rank, outrank, rate.

.3 (place before) **prefix, preface,** premise, prelude, prologize, preamble, introduce.

.4 ADJS **preceding,** precedent, **prior,** antecedent, anterior, precessional, **leading** 292.3; **preliminary,** precursory, prevenient, prefatory, exordial, prelusive, preludial, proemial, preparatory, initiatory, propaedeutic, inaugural; **first, foremost,** headmost, **chief** 36.14.

.5 **former,** foregoing; aforesaid, aforementioned, beforementioned, above-mentioned, aforenamed, forenamed, forementioned, said, named, same.

.6 ADVS **before** 240.12; above, hereinbefore, hereinabove, *supra* [L], *ante* [L].

65. SEQUENCE

.1 NOUNS **sequence,** logical sequence, **succession,** successiveness, consecution, consecutiveness, following, coming after; descent, lineage, line; **series** 71.2; **order,** order of succession; **progression,** procession, rotation; **continuity** 71; **continuation,** prolongation, extension, posteriority; suffixation, subjunction, postposition.

.2 VERBS **succeed, follow, ensue,** come or go after, **come next,** come on, **inherit,** take the mantle of, step into the shoes or place of.

.3 (place after) suffix, append, subjoin.

.4 ADJS **succeeding, successive, following, ensuing,** sequent, sequential, sequacious, posterior, **subsequent,** consequent; eka–, rere–; proximate, **next;** appendant, suffixed, postpositive, postpositional.

66. PRECURSOR

.1 NOUNS **precursor, forerunner,** foregoer, *voorlooper* [Du], vaunt-courier, avant-courier, front or lead runner; pioneer, *voortrekker* [Du], frontiersman, bushwhacker; scout, pathfinder, explorer, point, trailblazer or trailbreaker, guide; **leader** 748.6, bellwether, fugleman; **herald,** announcer, *buccinator* [L], messenger, harbinger, stormy petrel; **predecessor,** forebear, precedent, antecedent, **ancestor; vanguard, avant-garde,** innovator, groundbreaker.

.2 prelude, preamble, preface, prologue, foreword, introduction, *avant-propos* [Fr], protasis, proem, proemium, prolegomenon or prolegomena, exordium; **prefix**, prefixture; frontispiece; **preliminary**, front matter; overture, voluntary, verse; premise, presupposition, postulate, prolepsis; **innovation** 139.3, **breakthrough** [informal], leap.

.3 VERBS **go before**, **pioneer**, blaze or break the trail, be in the van or vanguard; guide; **lead** 292.2; **precede** 64.2; herald, forerun, usher in, introduce.

.4 ADJS **preceding** 64.4; preliminary, exploratory, inaugural; **advanced**, avant-garde, original 23.5.

67. SEQUEL

.1 NOUNS **sequel**, sequela or sequelae [pl], sequelant, sequent, sequitur, **consequence** 154.1; **continuation**, continuance, **follow-up** or -through [informal]; **supplement**, addendum, appendix, back matter; postfix, suffix; postscript, PS, subscript, postface, postlude, epilogue, conclusion, peroration, codicil; refrain, chorus, coda; envoi, colophon, tag; afterthought, second thought, double take [informal], *arrière-pensée* [Fr], *esprit d'escalier* [Fr]; parting or Parthian shot; last words, swan song, dying words.

.2 afterpart, afterpiece; wake, trail, train, queue; **tail**, tailpiece; tab, tag, trailer.

.3 **aftermath**, **afterclap**, afterglow, afterimage, aftereffect, side effect, by-product, aftertaste; **aftergrowth**, aftercrop; **afterbirth**, placenta, secundines, maz(o)–; afterpain.

.4 **successor**, replacement, backup man; **descendant**, posterity, **heir**, inheritor.

68. BEGINNING

.1 NOUNS **beginning**, **commencement**, **start**, running or flying start, starting point, square one [slang], **outset**, outbreak, onset, oncoming; dawn; **creation**, **foundation**, **institution**, **origin**, origination, establishment, setting-up, setting in motion; alpha, A; **opening**, rising of the curtain; first crack out of the box [informal], kick-off or jump-off or send-off or start-off or take-off or blast-off [all informal], the word 'go' [informal]; fresh start, new departure; edge, leading edge, cutting edge, thin end of the wedge.

.2 **beginner**, **neophyte**, **tyro**; newcomer 78.4; entrant, **novice**, novitiate, probationer, catechumen; recruit, raw recruit; rookie [informal]; trainee, learner, apprentice; baby, infant; nestling, fledgling; freshman 566.6; tenderfoot, greenhorn, greeny [informal]; debutant, deb [informal].

.3 **first**, **prime**, **initial**, alpha, primitiveness or primitivity, **initiative**, first move, **first step**, *le premier pas* [Fr], first lap, first round, first inning, first stage; breaking-in, warming-up; opening move, gambit; first blush, first glance, first sight, first impression.

.4 **origin**, origination, **genesis**, **inception**, incipience or incipiency, inchoation; –geny, –escence; **birth**, parturition, pregnancy, nascency or nascence, nativity; **infancy**, babyhood, childhood, youth; freshman year; incunabula, beginnings, cradle.

.5 **inauguration**, installation or installment, induction, **introduction**, initiation; embarkation or embarkment, **launching**, floating, flotation, unveiling; debut, first appearance, coming out [informal]; opener [informal], preliminary, curtain raiser or lifter; maiden speech, inaugural address.

.6 **basics**, **rudiments**, **elements**, **principles**, principia, **outlines**, **primer**, hornbook, grammar, alphabet, ABC's; first principles, first steps; induction.

.7 VERBS **begin**, **commence**, **start**; **start in**, **start off**, **start out**, **set out**, set sail, set in, set to or about, get to, **turn to**, fall to, pitch in [informal], dive in [slang], plunge into, head into [informal], **go ahead**, fire or blast away [informal], take off or jump off or kick off or blast off or send off [all informal], get the show on the road [informal].

.8 **make a beginning**, make a move [informal], **start up**, get going [informal], get off, **get under way**, get in there [slang]; set a course, **get squared away** [informal]; make an auspicious beginning, **get off to a good start**; get in on the ground floor [informal]; **break in**, **warm up**, get one's feet wet [slang], cut one's teeth.

.9 **enter**, **enter on** or **upon**, **embark in** or on or **upon**, take up, go into; make one's debut, come out [informal].

.10 **initiate**, **originate**, **create**, invent; **precede** 64.2, **take the initiative**, **take the first step**, take the lead, pioneer 66.3; **lead**, lead off, lead the way; **head**, head up [informal], stand at the head, stand first; **break the ice**, take the plunge, break ground, cut the first turf, lay the first stone.

.11 **inaugurate**, **institute**, **found**, **establish**, set up [informal]; **install,** initiate, induct; **introduce,** broach, bring up, lift up, raise; **launch,** float; christen [informal]; **usher in,** ring in [informal]; **set on foot,** set abroach, set agoing, turn on, start up, start going, start the ball rolling [informal].

.12 **open,** open up, breach, open the door to; open fire.

.13 **originate,** take *or* have origin, be born, take birth, come into the world, **become,** come to be, get to be [informal], see the light of day, rise, **arise,** take rise, take its rise, **come forth, issue,** issue forth, come out, spring *or* crop up; burst forth, break out, erupt, irrupt.

.14 **engender, beget, procreate** 169.8; **give birth to, bear,** birth [dial], bring to birth; father, mother, sire.

.15 ADJS **beginning, initial,** initiatory *or* initiative; **incipient,** inceptive, **introductory,** inchoative, inchoate; inaugural *or* inauguratory; **prime,** primal, **primary,** primitive, primeval; acro–, arche–, eo–, ne(o)–, proto–, ur– [Ger]; primogenial; **original,** aboriginal, autochthonous; **elementary,** elemental, **fundamental,** foundational; **rudimentary,** rudimental, abecedarian; **formative, creative,** procreative, inventive; embryonic, in embryo, in the bud, budding, fetal, gestatory, parturient, pregnant, in its infancy; infant, infantile, incunabular; **natal,** nascent, prenatal, antenatal; postnatal; –escent.

.16 **preliminary, prefatory,** preludial, proemial; prepositive, prefixed.

.17 **first, foremost,** front, **head, chief, principal,** premier, **leading, main;** maiden.

.18 ADVS **first,** firstly, **at first,** first off, first thing, **in the first place,** first and foremost, before everything, *primo* [L]; **principally,** mainly, chiefly; **primarily,** initially; **originally, in the beginning,** *in limine* [L], **at the start,** at the first go-off [informal], from the ground up, from the foundations, from the beginning, from the first, **from the word 'go'** [informal], *ab origine* [L], *ab initio* [L]; *ab ovo* [L].

69. MIDDLE

.1 NOUNS **middle,** median, midmost, **midst;** thick, thick of things; **center** 226.2; **heart, core,** nucleus, kernel; **mean** 32; interior 225.2; midriff, diaphragm; waist, waistline, zone; equator; diameter.

.2 **mid-distance,** middle distance; **equidistance; half,** moiety, mediety; halfway point *or* place, midway, midcourse, halfway house; bisection.

.3 VERBS middle, bisect; average 32.2; double, fold.

.4 ADJS **middle, medial,** median, mesial, middling, mediocre, average, **medium** 32.3, mezzo [mus], **mean,** mid; **midmost,** middlemost; mid–, medi(o)–, mes(o)–, mesio–; **central** 226.11, core, nuclear; interior 225.8; **intermediate,** intermediary, intermedi(o)–; equidistant, halfway, midway, equatorial; midland, mediterranean; midships, amidships.

.5 ADVS **midway, halfway, in the middle,** betwixt and between [informal], halfway in the middle [informal]; plump *or* smack *or* slap *or* smack-dab in the middle [informal]; half-and-half, neither here nor there, *mezzo-mezzo* [Ital]; medially, mediumly; in the mean; *in medias res* [L]; **in the midst of,** in the thick of; midships, amidships.

70. END

.1 NOUNS **end,** end point, ending, **termination, terminus, terminal,** term, period, apodosis, **expiration,** cessation 144, ceasing, consummation, culmination, **conclusion, finish, finis, finale,** finality, quietus, stoppage, windup [informal], payoff [slang], curtain, curtains [slang], fall of the curtain, end of the line [informal]; decease, **death** 408; **last,** "latter end" [Bible], last gasp *or* breath, final twitch; omega, Ω, izzard, Z; **goal,** destination, stopping place, resting place; denouement, catastrophe, final solution, resolution; last *or* final words, peroration, swan song, envoi, coda, epilogue; **fate, destiny,** last things, eschatology, last trumpet, crack of doom, doom; **effect** 154.

.2 **extremity, extreme;** acr(o)–, tel(o)– *or* tele–; **limit** 56.5, **boundary,** farthest bound, jumping-off place, Thule, *Ultima Thule* [L], **pole; tip,** point, nib; tail, **tail end,** butt end, tag, tag end, fag end; bitter end; stub, stump, butt; bottom dollar [informal], bottom of the barrel [informal].

.3 **close,** closing; cessation; decline, lapse; **homestretch, last lap** *or* **round** *or* **inning** [informal], last stage; beginning of the end.

.4 **finishing stroke,** ender, **end-all,** quietus, stopper, **deathblow,** death stroke, *coup de grâce* [Fr]; **finisher,** clincher, equalizer, crusher, **settler;** knockout *or* knockout blow [both informal]; sockdolager,

KO or kayo or kayo punch [all slang]; final stroke, finishing or perfecting or crowning touch, last dab or lick [slang].

.5 VERBS **end, terminate,** determine, close, **finish, conclude,** resolve, finish or wind up [informal]; **stop, cease** 144.6; perorate; abort; scrap, scratch [both informal].

.6 **come to an end, draw to a close, expire, die** 408.19; lapse, become void or extinct or defunct, run out, run its course, have its time or have it [both informal], pass, **pass away,** die away, wear off or away, go out, blow over, be all over, be no more.

.7 **complete** 56.6, perfect, finish, finalize [informal]; **put an end to,** put a period to, put paid to [Brit], **make an end of,** bring to an end, end off [informal]; **get it over,** get over with or through with [informal]; ring down or drop the curtain; put the lid on [slang], fold up [informal]; call off [informal], call all bets off [informal]; **dispose of,** polish off [informal]; kibosh or put the kibosh on [both slang]; **kill** 409.13, extinguish, scrag [slang], zap [slang]; **give the quietus,** put the finisher or settler on [informal], knock on or in the head, knock out [informal], kayo or KO [both slang], shoot down or shoot down in flames [both slang], wipe out [slang]; **cancel, delete,** expunge.

.8 ADJS **ended, at an end, terminated, concluded, finished, complete** 56.9, perfected, settled, decided, set at rest; **over, all over,** all up [slang]; all off [informal], all bets off [slang]; **done,** done with, through or through with [both informal]; wound up [informal], washed up [slang]; all over but the shouting [informal]; **dead** 408.30, **defunct,** extinct; fini, kaput, shot, done for, SOL, zapped [all slang], wiped out [slang]; **canceled, deleted,** expunged.

.9 **ending, closing, concluding, finishing,** culminating or culminative, consummative or consummatory, perfecting or perfective, terminating, crowning, capping.

.10 **final, terminal,** terminating or terminative, determinative, definitive, **conclusive; last,** eventual, farthest, extreme, boundary, limiting, polar, **endmost, ultimate;** caudal, tail.

.11 ADVS **finally,** in fine; **ultimately, eventually; lastly,** last, **at last,** at the last or end or conclusion, at length, at long last; **in conclusion;** conclusively, once for all.

.12 **to the end, to the bitter end, all the way,** to the last gasp, the last extremity, **to a finish,** à outrance [Fr], till hell freezes over [informal], "to the edge of doom", "to the last syllable of recorded time" [both Shakespeare].

.13 PHRS **that's final, that's that,** that buttons it up [informal], that's the end of the matter, so much for that, enough said; the subject is closed, the matter is ended, the deal is off [informal]; "the rest is silence" [Shakespeare].

71. CONTINUITY

(uninterrupted sequence)

.1 NOUNS **continuity, uninterruption, uninterruptedness,** featurelessness, unrelievedness, monotony, unintermittedness, unbrokenness, **uniformity** 17, undifferentiation; fullness, plenitude; seamlessness, jointlessness, gaplessness, smoothness; **consecutiveness,** successiveness; continuousness, **endlessness, ceaselessness, incessancy; constancy** 135.2, continualness, constant flow; steadiness, steady state, equilibrium, stability 142.

.2 **series, succession, run, sequence,** consecution, progression, course, gradation; **continuum,** plenum; lineage, descent, filiation; **connection, concatenation,** catenation, catena, **chain,** chaining, articulation, reticulation, nexus; chain reaction, powder train; **train, range, rank, file, line, string,** thread, queue, row, bank, tier; windrow, swath; single file, Indian file; array; **round, cycle,** rotation, routine, recurrence, periodicity, flywheel effect, pendulum; endless belt or chain, Möbius band or strip, la ronde [Fr], endless round; gamut, spectrum, scale; drone, monotone, hum, buzz.

.3 **procession, train, column, line, string, cortege;** stream, steady stream; –cade, cavalcade, caravan, motorcade; **parade,** pomp; dress parade; promenade, review, march past, flyover [US], flypast [Brit], funeral; skimmington [Brit dial]; mule train, pack train.

.4 VERBS **continue,** be continuous, **connect, connect up, concatenate,** continuate, catenate, **join** 47.5, link, **string together,** string, thread, chain, follow in or form a series, run on, maintain continuity.

.5 **align, line, line up,** string out, rank, array, range; row, bank.

.6 **line up, get in line,** form a line, get in formation, **fall in,** fall in or into line, fall into rank, take rank, take one's place; queue, **queue up.**

.7 **file,** defile, file off; **parade,** go on parade, promenade, march past.

.8 ADJS **continuous,** continued, **continual,** continuing; **uninterrupted, unintermittent,** unintermitted, featureless, unrelieved, monotonous; **connected, joined** 47.13, linked, concatenated, catenated, articulated; **unbroken,** serried, **uniform** 17.5, undifferentiated, seamless, jointless, gapless, smooth, unstopped; unintermitting, unremitting; **incessant, constant,** steady, stable, **ceaseless,** unceasing, **endless,** unending, never-ending, **interminable,** perennial; **cyclical,** repetitive, **recurrent,** periodic; straight, running, **nonstop; round-the-clock,** twenty-four-hour; immediate, direct.

.9 **consecutive, successive,** successional, progressive; **serial,** ordinal, seriate, catenary; sequent, **sequential;** linear, lineal.

.10 ADVS **continuously, continually; uninterruptedly, unintermittently; without cease,** without stopping, without a break, unbrokenly, **connectedly, together,** cumulatively, on end; **incessantly, constantly, ceaselessly,** unceasingly, **endlessly,** *ad infinitum* [L], perennially, **interminably,** again and again, repetitively, cyclically, monotonously, unrelievedly, on and on, at or on a stretch; round the clock.

.11 **consecutively, progressively, sequentially,** successively, **in succession,** one after the other, **in turn,** turn about, turn and turn about; step by step; running, hand running [informal]; **serially,** in a series, *seriatim* [L]; **in a line,** in a row, in column, in file, in a chain, in single file, in Indian file.

72. DISCONTINUITY

(interrupted sequence)

.1 NOUNS **discontinuity,** discontinuousness, discontinuation, discontinuance, noncontinuance; **incoherence** 51.1, **disconnectedness,** disconnection, discreteness, **disjunction** 49.1; **nonuniformity** 18; irregularity, **intermittence,** fitfulness 138.1; **brokenness;** nonseriality, nonlinearity, non sequitur; incompleteness 57; episode, parenthesis; broken thread.

.2 **interruption, suspension, break,** fissure, breach, gap, hiatus, lacuna, caesura; **interval, pause,** interim 109, lull, cessation, letup [informal], **intermission.**

.3 VERBS **discontinue, interrupt** 144.6,10, **break,** break off, disjoin 49.9; **disarrange** 63.2.

.4 ADJS **discontinuous,** noncontinuous, unsuccessive, **incoherent** 51.4, nonserial, nonlinear, nonsequential, discontinued, **disconnected,** unconnected, unjoined 49.20, *décousu* [Fr], **broken;** nonuniform 18.3, irregular; broken off, **interrupted,** suspended; disjunctive, discrete, discretive; **intermittent, fitful** 138.3; scrappy, snatchy, spotty, patchy, jagged; choppy, chopped-off, herky-jerky [slang], jerky, spasmodic; episodic, parenthetic.

.5 ADVS **discontinuously, disconnectedly,** brokenly; at intervals; **haphazardly** 62.18, randomly, occasionally, infrequently, **by fits and starts,** by fits, by snatches, by catches, by jerks, by skips, skippingly, *per saltum* [L]; willy-nilly, **here and there, in spots; intermittently, fitfully** 138.4.

73. ACCOMPANIMENT

.1 NOUNS **accompaniment,** concomitance or concomitancy, withness or togetherness [both informal]; synchronism, **simultaneity** 118; coincidence, co-occurrence, **concurrence;** parallelism.

.2 **company, association,** consociation, **society, community; companionship, fellowship,** consortship, partnership.

.3 **attendant,** concomitant, corollary, **accessory,** appendage; **adjunct** 41.

.4 **accompanier, accompanist** or accompanyist; **attendant, companion, fellow, mate,** comate, consort, **partner;** companion piece.

.5 **escort, conductor, usher,** shepherd; **squire,** esquire, swain, cavalier; **chaperon,** duenna; **bodyguard,** guard, safe-conduct, **convoy;** companion, fellow traveler.

.6 **attendance, following, cortege, retinue, entourage,** suite, follower, attendant, satellite, rout, train, body of retainers; **court,** cohort; parasite 907.3–5.

.7 VERBS **accompany,** bear one company, **keep company with,** companion, companionize [informal], go or travel or run with, **go along with, attend,** wait on or upon; **associate with,** assort with, sort with, **consort with,** couple with, hang around with [informal], go hand in hand with; **combine** 52.3,4, **associate,** consociate, confederate, flock or band or herd together.

.8 **escort, conduct,** marshal, **usher,** shepherd, **guide, lead; convoy,** guard; **squire,** esquire, **attend,** wait on or upon, **take out** [informal]; **chaperon.**

.9 ADJS **accompanying, attending, attendant, concomitant,** accessory, collateral; **combined** 52.5,6, **associated, coupled,** paired; **fellow, twin, joint, joined** 47.13, conjoint, mutual; **simultaneous** 118.4, **concurrent,** coincident; correlative 13.10; parallel; co–, con– *or* col– *or* com– *or* cor–, meta–, syn– *or* sym–.

.10 ADVS hand in hand *or* glove, arm in arm, side by side, cheek by jowl, shoulder to shoulder; therewith, therewithal, herewith.

.11 **together, collectively, mutually,** jointly, unitedly, in conjunction, conjointly, *en masse* [Fr], communally, corporately, **in a body,** all at once, *ensemble* [Fr], in association, in company.

.12 PREPS **with,** in company with, along with, **together with,** in association with, coupled *or* paired *or* partnered with, in conjunction with.

74. ASSEMBLAGE

.1 NOUNS **assemblage, assembly, collection, gathering,** ingathering, **congregation,** colligation; concourse, concurrence, conflux, confluence, convergence; collocation, juxtaposition, junction 47.1,4; **combination** 52; mobilization, call-up, muster, *attroupement* [Fr]; roundup, rodeo, corralling; **comparison** 491; canvass, census, data-gathering, survey, inventory; –age, –ana *or* –iana, –ery *or* –ry, –et(te), –oma *or* –ome, –some.

.2 **assembly** (of persons), *assemblée* [Fr], **gathering, forgathering, congregation,** congress, convocation, concourse, **meeting,** meet, **get-together** [informal], turnout [informal]; convention, conventicle, synod, council, diet, **conclave,** levee; caucus; mass meeting, **rally,** sit-in; **session,** séance, sitting; panel, forum, symposium, colloquium; committee, commission; *eisteddfod* [Welsh]; plenum, quorum; **party,** festivity 878.4, fete, at home, housewarming, soiree, reception, **dance,** ball, prom, shindig *or* brawl [both slang]; rendezvous, date, assignation; –fest.

.3 **company, group,** grouping, groupment, **party, band, gang, crew,** complement, cast, outfit, pack, cohort, troop, troupe, tribe, **body,** corps, stable, bunch [informal], mob [slang], crowd [informal]; squad, platoon, battalion, regiment, brigade, division, fleet; **team,** string; covey, bevy; posse, detachment, contingent, detail, *posse comitatus* [L]; phalanx; **party, faction,** movement, wing; in-group, outgroup, peer group, age group; coterie, salon, **clique, set;** junta, cabal.

.4 **throng, multitude, horde,** host, heap [in-

formal], army, panoply, legion; flock, cluster, galaxy; **crowd,** press, crush, flood, spate, deluge, mass; **mob,** rabble, rout, ruck, jam, *cohue* [Fr], everybody and his uncle [informal].

.5 (animals) **flock, bunch, pack,** colony, host, troop, army, **herd, drove,** drive, drift, trip; pride (of lions), sloth (of bears), skulk (of foxes), gang (of elk), kennel (of dogs), clowder (of cats), pod (of seals), gam (of whales), **school** *or* shoal (of fish); (animal young) **litter** 171.2.

.6 (birds, insects) **flock, flight, swarm,** cloud; covey (of partridges), bevy (of quail), skein (of geese in flight), gaggle (of geese on water), watch (of nightingales), charm (of finches), murmuration (of starlings), spring (of teal); hive (of bees), plague (of locusts).

.7 **bunch, group,** grouping, groupment, crop, **cluster, clump,** knot; grove, copse, thicket; **batch, lot,** slew [slang], **mess** [informal]; tuft, wisp; tussock, hassock; shock, stook; botry(o)–, cym(o)– *or* kym-(o)–, staphyl(o)–.

.8 **bundle,** bindle [slang], **pack, package,** packet, deck, budget, **parcel,** fardel [dial], bale, truss, **roll,** rouleau, bolt; fagot, fascine, fasces; quiver, sheaf; bouquet, nosegay, posy.

.9 **accumulation,** cumulation, gathering, **amassment,** congeries, acervation; agglomeration, conglomeration, glomeration, conglomerate, agglomerate; aggregation, aggregate; conglobation; **mass, lump,** gob [slang], chunk *or* hunk [both informal], wad; snowball; stockpile, stockpiling.

.10 **pile, heap, stack; mound, hill;** molehill, anthill; bank, embankment, dune; haystack, hayrick, haymow, haycock, cock, mow, rick; drift, snowdrift; pyramid.

.11 **collection,** fund, treasure, holdings; corpus, **body,** data, raw data; compilation, collectanea; ana; anthology, florilegium; *Festschrift* [Ger]; chrestomathy; **museum, library,** zoo, menagerie, aquarium.

.12 **set, suit, suite, series,** outfit *or* kit [both informal]; pack, block, battery.

.13 **miscellany,** miscellanea, collectanea; **assortment, medley, variety, mixture** 44; hodgepodge, conglomerate, **conglomeration,** omnium-gatherum [informal]; **sundries,** oddments, **odds and ends.**

.14 (a putting together) **assembly,** assemblage; assembly line, production line; assembly-line production.

.15 **collector,** gatherer, accumulator; collection agent, bill collector, dunner; tax collector, farmer, exciseman [Brit], *douanier* [Fr]; pack rat, magpie, miser; connoisseur.

.16 VERBS **come together, assemble, congregate, collect,** league 52.4; **unite** 47.5; **muster, meet, gather, forgather,** gang up [informal], mass; **merge,** converge, flow together, fuse; flock together; herd together; **throng, crowd,** swarm, hive, surge, seethe, mill, stream, horde; **cluster, bunch,** bunch up, clot; gather around, gang around [slang]; rally, rally around; **huddle,** go into a huddle; rendezvous, date; **couple,** copulate, link.

.17 **convene, meet,** hold a meeting *or* session, sit; **convoke,** summon, call together.

.18 (bring *or* gather together) **assemble, gather;** muster, rally, **mobilize; collect,** raise, take up; **accumulate,** cumulate, **amass,** mass, bulk, batch; agglomerate, conglomerate, aggregate; **combine** 52.3, **join** 47.5, **bring together,** get together, **gather together,** draw *or* lump *or* batch *or* bunch together; **bunch,** bunch up; **cluster,** clump; **group,** aggroup; **gather in,** get *or* whip in; scrape together, rake *or* dredge *or* dig up; round up, corral, drive together; **put together,** make up, compile, colligate; collocate, **juxtapose,** pair, match, partner; **compare** 491.4.

.19 **pile, heap, stack,** heap *or* pile *or* stack up; mound, hill, bank, bank up; rick; pyramid; drift.

.20 **bundle,** bundle up, **package,** parcel, **pack,** truss, truss up; bale; wrap, **wrap up,** do *or* tie *or* bind up; roll up.

.21 ADJS **assembled, collected, gathered; congregate,** congregated; meeting, in session; **combined** 52.5; **joined** 47.13; joint, leagued 52.6; **accumulated,** cumulate, massed, **amassed;** heaped, stacked, piled; glomerate, agglomerate, conglomerate, aggregate; **clustered,** bunched, lumped, clumped, knotted; bundled, packaged, wrapped up; fascicled, fasciculated.

.22 **crowded, packed, crammed;** jam-packed [informal]; **compact,** firm, solid, dense, close, serried; **teeming, swarming, crawling,** bristling, populous, **full** 56.11.

.23 **cumulative,** accumulative, total, overall.

75. DISPERSION

.1 NOUNS **dispersion** *or* **dispersal, scattering,** scatterment, diffraction; **distribution, spreading,** strewing, sowing, broadcasting, **broadcast, spread,** publication 559, **dissemination,** propagation, dispensation;

radiation, divergence 299; expansion, splay; diffusion, attenuation, dilution, volatilization, evaporation, dissipation; circumfusion; fragmentation; sprinkling, spattering; peppering, buckshot *or* shotgun pattern.

.2 **decentralization,** deconcentration.

.3 **disbandment,** dispersion *or* dispersal, diaspora, separation, parting; breakup, split-up [informal]; **demobilization,** deactivation, **release,** detachment; dismissal 310.5; dissolution, disorganization, disintegration 53.

.4 VERBS **disperse, scatter,** diffract; **distribute, broadcast, sow,** disseminate, propagate, publish 559.10; diffuse, **spread,** dispread, strew, bestrew; **radiate,** diverge 299.5; splay, branch *or* fan *or* spread out; **issue, deal out,** retail, utter, dispense; sow broadcast, scatter to the winds; overscatter, overspread, oversow; circumfuse.

.5 **dissipate, dispel,** dissolve, attenuate, dilute, thin, thin out, evaporate, volatilize; drive away, clear away, cast forth, blow off.

.6 **sprinkle,** besprinkle, **spatter,** splatter; **dot,** spot, speck, speckle, stud; **pepper,** powder, dust; flour, crumb, bread; dredge.

.7 **decentralize,** deconcentrate.

.8 **disband, disperse, scatter, separate, part,** break up, split up; part company, go separate ways; **demobilize,** demob [slang], deactivate, muster out, debrief, **release,** detach, discharge, let go; dismiss 310.18; **dissolve,** disorganize, disintegrate 53.3.

.9 ADJS **dispersed, scattered, distributed,** dissipated, disseminated, strown, strewn, broadcast, **spread,** dispread; **widespread,** diffuse, discrete, sparse, **sporadic;** straggling, straggly; all over the lot *or* place [informal], from hell to breakfast [slang].

.10 **sprinkled,** spattered, splattered, **peppered,** spotted, dotted, powdered, dusted, specked, speckled, **studded.**

.11 **dispersive, scattering, spreading,** diffractive *or* diffractional, **distributive,** disseminative, diffusive, dissipative, attenuative.

.12 ADVS **scatteringly, dispersedly,** diffusely, sparsely, **sporadically,** *sparsim* [L], **here and there;** in places, **in spots** [informal]; *passim* [L], at large, everywhere, throughout, wherever you look *or* turn [informal], in all quarters.

76. INCLUSION

.1 NOUNS **inclusion, comprisal, comprehension,** envisagement, embracement, encompassment, coverage, incorporation, embodiment, assimilation, reception; **membership,** participation, admission, admissibility, eligibility; **completeness** 56, **inclusiveness, comprehensiveness,** exhaustiveness; **whole** 54; openness, toleration or tolerance.

.2 **entailment, involvement, implication;** assumption, presumption, subsumption.

.3 VERBS **include, comprise, contain, comprehend,** hold, **take in; cover,** occupy, take up, fill; fill in or out, **complete** 56.6; **embrace,** encompass, enclose, encircle, incorporate, assimilate, embody, admit, receive, envisage; **reckon in,** reckon with, reckon among, count in, **number among,** take into account or consideration.

.4 (include as a necessary circumstance or consequence) **entail, involve, implicate,** imply, assume, presume, presuppose, subsume, affect, take in, contain, comprise, **call for, require,** take, bring, lead to.

.5 ADJS **included, comprised,** comprehended, envisaged, embraced, encompassed, covered; bound up with, forming or making a part of; **involved** 176.3.

.6 **inclusive, including, containing, comprising, covering, embracing,** encompassing, enclosing, encircling, assimilating, incorporating, envisaging; counting, numbering; **super–.**

.7 **comprehensive, sweeping, complete** 56.9; **whole** 54.9; **all-comprehensive,** all-inclusive 79.14; without omission or exception, **over-all,** universal, global, **total,** blanket, omnibus, across-the-board; encyclopedic, compendious; synoptic; bird's-eye, panoramic.

77. EXCLUSION

.1 NOUNS **exclusion, barring,** debarring, debarment, preclusion, exception, omission, nonadmission; **restriction, circumscription,** narrowing, demarcation; **rejection,** repudiation; **ban,** bar, taboo, injunction; relegation; prohibition, embargo, blockade; boycott, lockout; inadmissibility.

.2 **elimination, riddance,** severance 49.2; withdrawal, **removal,** detachment, disjunction 49.1; discard, eradication, clearance, **ejection,** expulsion, suspension; **deportation, exile,** expatriation, ostracism, outlawing or outlawry; disposal, disposition; **liquidation, purge.**

.3 **exclusiveness, narrowness,** tightness; **insularity,** snobbishness, parochialism, ethnocentrism, xenophobia, know-nothingism; **segregation, separation,** division; **isolation,** insulation, seclusion; quarantine; racial segregation, apartheid, color bar, Jim Crow, race hatred; **out-group; outsider, stranger; foreigner, alien** 78.3, outcast 926.4, *persona non grata* [L].

.4 VERBS **exclude, bar,** debar, bar out, lock out, **shut out, keep out,** count out [informal], cut off, preclude; reject, turn thumbs down on [informal], ease or freeze out [informal], close the door on, send to Coventry [Brit], ostracize; repudiate, **ban,** prohibit, taboo, **leave out,** omit, pass over, ignore; relegate; blockade, embargo.

.5 **eliminate, get rid of,** rid oneself of, **get quit of,** get shut of [dial], **dispose of, remove,** abstract, eject, expel, cast off or out, chuck [slang], throw over or overboard [informal]; **deport, exile,** outlaw, expatriate; clear, clear out, clear away, clear the decks; **weed out,** pick out; **cut out,** strike off or out, elide; eradicate, root up or out; **purge, liquidate.**

.6 **segregate, separate,** divide, cordon, cordon off; **isolate,** insulate, seclude; **set apart,** keep apart; quarantine, put beyond the pale, ghettoize; **set aside,** lay aside, put aside, keep aside; **sort or pick out,** cull out, sift, screen, sieve, bolt, riddle, winnow; thresh, thrash, gin.

.7 ADJS **excluded, barred,** debarred, precluded, **shut out, left out,** left out in the cold [informal]; not included, not in it, not in the picture [informal]; **banned,** prohibited, tabooed; **expelled,** ejected, **purged,** liquidated; deported, exiled.

.8 **exclusive, excluding,** exclusory; seclusive, preclusive, exceptional, inadmissible, prohibitive, preventive, prescriptive, restrictive; separative, segregative; select, selective; narrow, insular, parochial, ethnocentric, xenophobic, snobbish.

.9 PREPS **excluding, barring,** bar, exclusive of, precluding, omitting, **leaving out; excepting,** except, **except for,** with the exception of, outside of [informal], **save,** saving, save and except, let alone; **besides,** beside, **aside from,** than; unless, without, ex.

78. EXTRANEOUSNESS

.1 NOUNS **extraneousness, foreignness;** alienism, alienage; **extrinsicality** 6; **exteriority** 224; nonassimilation, nonconformity; intrusion.

.2 **intruder,** foreign body or element, foreign intruder or intrusion; **impurity,** blemish 679; stone, speck 196.7; mote, splinter *or* sliver, **weed,** misfit 27.4; odd-ball 85.4; black sheep; monkey wrench.

.3 **alien, stranger, foreigner, outsider,** outlander, *Uitlander* [Afrikaans], tramontane, ultramontane, barbarian, foreign devil [China], *gringo* [Sp Amer]; **exile,** outlaw, wanderer, refugee, emigré, *émigré* [Fr], displaced person, D.P., *déraciné* [Fr]; the Wandering Jew.

.4 **newcomer, new arrival,** *novus homo* [L], upstart, parvenu, arriviste, Johnny-come-lately [informal], new boy [Brit]; **tenderfoot,** greenhorn; settler, emigrant, immigrant; recruit, rookie [slang]; **intruder, squatter,** gate-crasher, stowaway.

.5 ADJS **extraneous, foreign, alien,** strange, exotic; unearthly, extraterrestrial 375.26; exterior, **external** 224.6; extrinsic 6.3; ulterior, outside, outland, outlandish; barbarian, barbarous, barbaric; foreign-born; intrusive; ep(i)– *or* eph–, ex(o)– *or* ef–, xen-(o)–.

.6 ADVS **abroad,** in foreign parts; oversea, **overseas,** beyond seas; on one's travels.

79. GENERALITY

.1 NOUNS **generality, universality,** inclusiveness 76.1; worldwideness, globality *or* globalism, ecumenicity *or* ecumenicalism; catholicity; internationalism, cosmopolitanism; generalization.

.2 **prevalence, commonness,** commonality, usualness; **currency,** reign, run; **extensiveness,** widespreadness, sweepingness, rifeness, rampantness; **normality,** averageness, ordinariness, routineness, habitualness, standardness.

.3 **generality, average,** ruck, **run,** general *or* common *or* average *or* ordinary run, **run of the mill;** any Tom, Dick, or Harry, Everyman; common *or* average man, the man in the street, John Q. Public, ordinary Joe; girl next door; everyman, everywoman; *homme moyen sensuel* [Fr].

.4 **all, everyone, everybody, each and every one, one and all,** all hands [informal], every man Jack [informal], every mother's son [informal], **all the world,** *tout le monde* [Fr], the devil and all [informal], **whole, totality** 54.1.

.5 **any, anything,** any one, aught, either; **anybody, anyone.**

.6 **whatever,** whate'er, **whatsoever,** whatsoe'er, **what, whichever,** anything soever which, no matter what *or* which.

.7 **whoever, whoso, whosoever, whomever,** whomso, **whomsoever,** anyone, no matter who.

.8 (idea or expression) **generalization,** general idea, **abstraction,** generalized proposition; glittering generality, sweeping statement; **truism, platitude,** commonplace, *lieu commun* [Fr], *locus communis* [L]; **cliché,** tired cliché, bromide, trite *or* hackneyed expression.

.9 VERBS **generalize, universalize,** catholicize, ecumenicize, globalize; **broaden, widen, expand,** extend, spread; make a generalization, deal in generalities *or* abstractions.

.10 **prevail, predominate, obtain,** dominate, reign, rule; be in force *or* effect; be the rule *or* fashion, be the rage *or* thing [slang], be in [slang].

.11 ADJS **general, generalized, nonspecific,** generic, **indefinite,** indeterminate, vague, abstract, nebulous, unspecified, undifferentiated, featureless, uncharacterized, bland, neutral; **broad, wide;** collective.

.12 **prevalent, prevailing, common, popular, current,** running; regnant, reigning, **ruling, predominant,** predominating, **dominant; rife, rampant,** pandemic, epidemic, besetting; **ordinary, normal, average, usual,** routine, standard, stereotyped.

.13 **extensive, broad, wide,** liberal, diffuse, large-scale, **sweeping; widespread,** far-spread, far-stretched, **far-reaching,** far-going, far-embracing, far-extending, far-spreading, far-flying, far-ranging, **far-flung,** wide-flung, wide-reaching, wide-extending, wide-extended, wide-ranging, wide-stretching; **wholesale, indiscriminate.**

.14 **universal,** heaven-wide, galactic, planetary, world-wide, **global; total, allover;** catholic, **all-inclusive,** all-including, **all-embracing,** all-encompassing, all-comprehensive, all-comprehending, all-filling, all-pervading, all-covering; glob(o)–, omn(i)–, **pan(o)–** *or* **pam–** *or* **pant(o)–** *or* **panta–;** nonsectarian, nondenominational, ecumenic(al); cosmopolitan, international; national, country-wide, state-wide.

.15 **every, all,** any; **each,** each one; every one, each and every, each and all, **one and all, all and sundry,** all and some.

.16 **trite, commonplace,** hackneyed, platitudinous, truistic, overworked, stereotyped.

.17 ADVS **generally, in general; generally speaking,** speaking generally, **broadly,** broadly speaking, **roughly,** roughly speaking, as an approximation; **usually** 84.9, **as a rule, ordinarily, commonly, normally,** routinely, as a matter of course, in the usual course; **by and large,** at large, altogether, overall, **all things considered,** taking one thing with another, taking all things together, on balance, **all in all,** taking all in all, taking it for all in all, **on the whole,** as a whole, **in the long run,** for the most part, for better or for worse; **prevailingly, predominantly, mostly,** chiefly, mainly.

.18 **universally,** galactically, cosmically; **everywhere, all over,** the world over, internationally; in every instance, without exception, **invariably, always,** never otherwise.

80. PARTICULARITY

.1 NOUNS **particularity, individuality, singularity, differentiation,** differentness, distinctiveness, uniqueness; identity, individual **or** separate **or** concrete identity; **personality,** personship, personal identity; soul; **selfness, selfhood, egohood,** self-identity, "a single separate person" [Whitman]; oneness 89.1, wholeness, integrity; personal equation, human factor; **nonconformity** 83; **individualism,** particularism; nominalism.

.2 **speciality, specialness,** specialty, specificality, **specificness,** definiteness; special case.

.3 **the specific,** the special, **the particular,** the concrete, the individual, the unique; "all things counter, original, spare, strange" [G. M. Hopkins].

.4 **characteristic, peculiarity, singularity,** particularity, specialty, individualism, **character,** nature, **trait,** quirk, mannerism, keynote, trick, **feature,** distinctive feature, lineaments; **mark, marking, earmark,** hallmark, index; badge; token; **brand,** cast, stamp, cachet, seal, mold, cut, figure, shape, configuration; impress, impression; differential, differentia; **idiosyncrasy,** idiocrasy; **quality, property, attribute;** savor, flavor, taste, gust, aroma, odor, smack, tang, taint.

.5 **self, ego;** oneself, I, I myself, me, myself, my humble self, number one [informal], yours truly [informal]; yourself, himself, herself, itself; ourselves, yourselves; themselves; you; he, she; him, her; they, them; it; inner self, inner man; subliminal **or** subconscious self; superego, better self, ethical self; other self, alter ego, *alter, alterum* [both L].

.6 **specification, designation, stipulation,** signification, determination, denomination; allocation, attribution, fixing, selection, assignment, pinning down, precision.

.7 **particularization, specialization;** individualization, peculiarization, personalization; localization; itemization 8.5.

.8 **characterization,** distinction, **differentiation;** definition, description.

.9 VERBS **particularize, specialize; individualize,** peculiarize, personalize; **descend to particulars,** precise, get down to brass tacks [informal], get down to cases [slang], come to the point; **itemize** 8.6, detail, spell out.

.10 **characterize, distinguish, differentiate, define, describe; mark, earmark,** mark off, mark out, demarcate, **set apart,** make special **or** unique; keynote [informal], sound the keynote, set the tone **or** mood, set the pace; be characteristic, **be a feature or trait of.**

.11 **specify,** specialize, **designate, stipulate,** determine, **fix,** set, assign, pin down; **name,** denominate, state, mention, select, pick out, mark, **indicate, signify,** point out, put **or** lay one's finger on.

.12 ADJS **particular, special, especial, specific, express,** precise, **concrete; singular, individual,** individualist(ic); aut(o)–, idio–, self–; **personal,** private, intimate, inner, solipsistic, esoteric; respective, several; **fixed, definite,** defined, distinct, different, determinate, certain, absolute; **distinguished,** noteworthy, **exceptional, extraordinary;** minute, detailed.

.13 **characteristic, peculiar, singular,** single, quintessential, intrinsic, unique, **distinctive,** marked, distinguished; appropriate, proper; idiosyncratic, idiocratic, **in character,** true to form; –acean **or** –aceous, –ey **or** –y, –ious **or** –ous, –ish, –ist **or** –istic(al), –itious, –itic, –ose, –some.

.14 **this,** this and no other, this one, this single; **these; that,** that one; those.

.15 ADVS **particularly, specially, especially, specifically, expressly,** concretely, exactly, precisely, **in particular,** to be specific; **definitely, distinctly; minutely,** in detail, item by item, singly, separately.

.16 **personally,** privately, idiosyncratically, **individually; in person,** in the flesh, *in propria persona* [L]; for all me, **for my part, as far as I am concerned.**

.17 **characteristically, peculiarly,** singularly, intrinsically, **uniquely,** markedly, **distinctively,** in its own way, like no other.

.18 **namely,** nominally, **that is to say,** *videlicet* [L], viz., *scilicet* [L], scil., sc., **to wit.**

.19 **each, apiece;** severally, respectively, one by one, each to each; *per annum, per diem, per capita* [all L].

.20 PREPS per, for each.

81. SPECIALTY

(object of special attention or preference)

.1 NOUNS specialty, speciality, line, pursuit, pet subject, field, area, main interest; vocation 656.6; forte, métier, strong point, long suit; specialism, specialization; technicality; way, manner, style, type; cup of tea [informal], bag or thing [both slang], weakness [informal].

.2 special, feature, main feature; leader, lead item, leading card.

.3 specialist, specializer, expert, authority, savant, scholar, connoisseur; technical expert, technician; pundit, critic; amateur, dilettante; fan, buff, freak or nut [both slang], aficionado.

.4 VERBS specialize, feature; narrow, restrict, limit, confine; specialize in, go in for, be into [slang], have a weakness or taste for, be strong in, follow, pursue, make one's business; major in, minor in; do one's thing [slang].

.5 ADJS specialized, specialist, specialistic; technical; restricted, limited, confined; featured, feature; expert, authoritative, knowledgeable.

82. CONFORMITY

.1 NOUNS conformity; conformance, conformation other-direction; compliance, acquiescence, obedience, observance, traditionalism, orthodoxy; strictness; accordance, accord, correspondence, harmony, agreement, uniformity 17; consistency, congruity; line, keeping; accommodation, adaptation, adaption, pliancy, malleability, flexibility, adjustment; reconciliation, reconcilement; conventionality 645.1.

.2 conformist, conformer, sheep, trimmer, parrot, yes-man, organization man; conventionalist, Mrs. Grundy [Tom Morton], Babbitt [Sinclair Lewis], Philistine, middle-class type, bourgeois, burgher, Middle American, plastic person or square [both informal]; model child; teenybopper [informal]; formalist, methodologist, perfectionist, precisianist, precisian; anal character, compulsive character; pedant.

.3 VERBS conform, comply, correspond, accord, harmonize; adapt, adjust, accommodate, meet, suit, fit, shape; comply with, agree with, tally with, chime or fall in with, go by, be guided or regulated by, observe, follow, bend, yield, take the shape of; adapt to, adjust to, gear to, assimilate to, accommodate to or with; reconcile, settle, compose; rub off corners; make conform, mold, force into a mold; straighten, rectify, correct, discipline.

.4 follow the rule, do it according to Hoyle or by the book [informal], play the game [informal]; go through channels; fit in, follow the crowd, follow the fashion, swim or go with the stream or tide or current, trim one's sails to the breeze, follow the beaten path, do as others do, get or stay in line, fall into line, fall in with; keep in step, toe the mark; keep up to standard, pass muster, come up to scratch [informal].

.5 ADJS conformable, adaptable, adaptive, adjustable; compliant, pliant, complaisant, malleable, flexible, plastic, acquiescent, other-directed, submissive, tractable, obedient.

.6 conformist, conventional 645.5, square or straight [both informal]; orthodox, kosher, traditionalist(ic); bourgeois, plastic [informal]; formalistic, precisianistic, anal, compulsive; pedantic, stuffy [informal], uptight [informal]; in accord, in keeping, in line, in step; corresponding, accordant, concordant, harmonious.

.7 ADVS conformably, conformingly, obediently, pliantly, flexibly, malleably, complaisantly, yieldingly, compliantly, submissively; conventionally, traditionally; anally, compulsively; pedantically.

.8 according to rule, en règle [Fr], according to regulations; according to Hoyle, by the book, by the numbers [all informal].

.9 PREPS conformable to, in conformity with, in compliance with; according to, in accordance with, consistent with, in harmony with, in agreement with, in correspondence to; adapted to, adjusted to, accommodated to; proper to, suitable for, agreeable to, agreeably to; answerable to, in obedience to; congruent with, uniform with, in uniformity with; in line with, in step with, in lock-step with, in keeping with; after, by, per.

.10 PHRS don't rock the boat, don't make waves; when in Rome do as the Romans do.

83. NONCONFORMITY

.1 NOUNS nonconformity, unconformity, nonconformism, inconsistency, incongruity; inaccordance, disaccord, disaccordance; originality 23.1; nonconformance, disconformity; **nonobservance, noncompliance,** nonconcurrence, **dissent** 522, **protest** 522.2, disagreement, contrariety, recalcitrance, refractoriness, recusance *or* recusancy; **deviation.**

.2 **unconventionality, unorthodoxy** 1025, revisionism, heterodoxy, heresy, originality, fringiness, Bohemianism, beatnikism, hippiedom.

.3 **nonconformist,** unconformist, **original,** deviant, maverick [informal], swinger [informal], dropout, Bohemian, beatnik, hippie, freak [informal], flower child, street people, yippie; **misfit,** square peg in a round hole, ugly duckling, fish out of water; **dissenter** 522.3; **heretic** 1025.5; sectary, sectarian; nonjuror.

.4 VERBS **not conform,** nonconform, not comply; **get out of line** [informal], **rock the boat,** make waves, **leave the beaten path, go out of bounds,** break step, break bounds; drop out, opt out; **dissent** 522.4, **protest** 522.5; *"épater le bourgeois"* [Fr; Baudelaire], "hear a different drummer" [Thoreau].

.5 ADJS **nonconforming,** unconforming, nonconformable, unadaptable, unadjustable; **uncompliant,** unsubmissive; **nonobservant;** contrary, recalcitrant, refractory, recusant; **deviant; dissenting** 522.6, **dissident.**

.6 **unconventional, unorthodox,** heterodox, heretical; unfashionable, not done, not kosher, not cricket [Brit informal]; offbeat [informal], way out, far out, kinky, out in left field [informal], fringy, breakaway, **out of the way; original,** maverick, Bohemian, beat, hippie; **informal,** free and easy [informal], "at ease and lighthearted" [Whitman].

.7 **out of line, out of keeping,** out of order *or* place, misplaced, **out of step,** out of turn [informal], out of tune.

84. NORMALITY

.1 NOUNS **normality, normalcy, normalness, naturalness;** health, wholesomeness, propriety, **regularity;** naturalism, naturism, realism; **order** 59.

.2 **usualness,** ordinariness, **commonness,** commonplaceness, averageness; **generality** 79, **prevalence,** currency.

.3 **the normal, the usual, the ordinary, the common,** the commonplace, the way things are, the normal order of things; common *or* garden variety.

.4 **rule, law, principle, standard,** criterion, canon, code, maxim, prescription, guideline, regulation; **norm,** norma; **rule** *or* **law** *or* **order of nature,** natural *or* universal law; **form, formula,** formulary, formality, prescribed *or* set form; standing order; **hard and fast rule,** Procrustean law.

.5 normalization, standardization, regularization; codification, formalization.

.6 VERBS **normalize, standardize, regularize;** codify, formalize.

.7 ADJS **normal,** norm(o)-, **natural; general** 79.11; typical, unexceptional; naturalistic, naturistic, realistic; **orderly** 59.6.

.8 **usual, regular; customary,** habitual, accustomed, wonted, **normative,** prescriptive, standard, regulation, conventional; **common, commonplace, ordinary, average, everyday,** familiar, household, vernacular, stock; **prevailing, predominating,** current, popular; **universal.**

.9 ADVS **normally, naturally; normatively,** prescriptively, **regularly; usually, commonly, ordinarily, customarily, habitually, generally;** mostly, chiefly, mainly, for the most part, most often *or* frequently; **as a rule,** as a matter of course; **as usual,** as per usual [informal]; **as may be expected,** to be expected, as things go.

85. ABNORMALITY

.1 NOUNS **abnormality,** abnormity; **unnaturalness,** unnaturalism; **anomaly,** anomalousness, anomalism; **aberration,** aberrance, aberrancy; **irregularity, deviation,** divergence, **difference** 16; **eccentricity,** erraticism; teratism, monstrosity, amorphism, heteromorphism; **subnormality; inferiority** 37; **superiority** 36; **derangement** 63.1.

.2 **unusualness, uncommonness,** unordinariness, unwontedness, exceptionality; **rarity,** rareness, **uniqueness; extraordinariness, prodigiousness,** marvelousness, fabulousness, mythicalness, remarkableness, stupendousness; **incredibility** 503.3; increditability, inconceivability, **impossibility** 510.

.3 **oddity, queerness,** curiousness, quaintness, **peculiarity, absurdity** 510.1, singularity; **strangeness,** outlandishness; **bizarreness,** *bizarrerie* [Fr]; fantasticality, anticness; **freakishness, grotesqueness,** grotesquerie, weirdness, monstrousness, monstrosity, malformation, deformity, teratism.

.4 (odd person) oddity, **character** [informal], *type* [Fr], **case** [slang], natural, original, odd fellow, queer specimen; **oddball,** odd *or* queer fish, queer duck, rum one [Brit slang]; rare bird, *rara avis* [L]; eccentric 474.3; *meshuggenah* [Yid]; screwball *or* crackpot *or* kook *or* nut [all informal]; fanatic, crank, zealot; outsider, alien, pariah, loner, lone wolf, solitary, hermit; hobo, tramp; maverick; nonconformist 83.3.

.5 (odd thing) oddity, curiosity, funny *or* peculiar *or* strange thing; abnormality, anomaly; nonesuch, rarity, improbability, exception, one in a thousand *or* million; prodigy, prodigiosity; curio, conversation piece; museum piece.

.6 monstrosity, monster, miscreation, abortion, teratism, terat(o)–; freak, freak of nature, *lusus naturae* [L]; medus(i)–, –pagus.

.7 supernaturalism, supernaturalness *or* supernaturality, supranaturalism, supernormalness, preternaturalism, supersensibleness, superphysicalness, superhumanity; numinousness; unearthliness, unworldliness, otherworldliness, eeriness; transcendentalism; the supernatural, the occult, the supersensible; supernature, supranature; mystery, mysteriousness, miraculousness; faerie, witchery, elfdom.

.8 miracle, sign, prodigy, wonder, wonderwork, ferlie [Scot]; fantasy, enchantment.

.9 ADJS abnormal, unnatural; anomalous, anomalistic; irregular, eccentric, erratic, deviative, divergent, different 16.7; aberrant, stray, straying, wandering; heteroclite, heteromorphic; formless, shapeless, amorphous; subnormal; anom(o)–, anomal(o)– *or* anomali–, dys– *or* dis–, mal–, ne(o)–, par(a)–, poly–, pseud(o)–.

.10 unusual, unordinary, uncustomary, unwonted, uncommon, unfamiliar, unheard-of, *recherché* [Fr]; rare, unique, *sui generis* [L, of its own kind]; out of the ordinary, out of this world, out of the way, out of the common, out of the pale, off the beaten track, offbeat, breakaway; unexpected, not to be expected, unthought-of, undreamed-of.

.11 odd, queer, peculiar, absurd 510.7, singular, curious, oddball, kooky [informal], freaky *or* freaked out [both slang], quaint, eccentric, funny, rum [Brit slang]; strange, outlandish, off the wall [informal], passing strange, "wondrous strange" [Shakespeare]; weird, unearthly; off, out.

.12 fantastic, fantastical, fanciful, antic; unbelievable 503.10, impossible, incredible, incomprehensible, unimaginable, unexpected, unaccountable, inconceivable.

.13 freakish, freak [informal]; monstrous, deformed, malformed, misshapen, misbegotten, teratogenic, teratoid; grotesque, bizarre, baroque, rococo.

.14 extraordinary, exceptional, remarkable, noteworthy, wonderful, marvelous, fabulous, mythical, legendary; stupendous, stupefying, prodigious, portentous, phenomenal; unprecedented, unexampled, unparalleled, not within the memory of man; indescribable, unspeakable, ineffable.

.15 supernatural, supranatural, preternatural; supernormal, hypernormal, preternormal; superphysical, hyperphysical; numinous; supersensible, supersensual, pretersensual; superhuman, preterhuman, unhuman, nonhuman; supramundane, extramundane, transmundane, extraterrestrial; unearthly, unworldly, otherworldly, eerie; fey; psychic(al), spiritual, occult; transcendental; mysterious, arcane, esoteric.

.16 miraculous, wondrous, wonder-working, thaumaturgic(al), necromantic, prodigious; magical, enchanted, bewitched.

.17 ADVS unusually, uncommonly, incredibly, unnaturally, abnormally, unordinarily, uncustomarily, unexpectedly; rarely, seldom, seldom if ever, once in a thousand years, hardly, hardly ever.

.18 extraordinarily, exceptionally, remarkably, wonderfully, marvelously, prodigiously, fabulously, unspeakably, ineffably, phenomenally, stupendously.

.19 oddly, queerly, peculiarly, singularly, curiously, quaintly, strangely, outlandishly, fantastically, fancifully; grotesquely, monstrously; eerily, mysteriously, supernaturally.

.20 mythical monsters

Argus	hippocampus
basilisk	hippocentaur
Briareus	hippocerf
bucentur	hippogriff
Cacus	hircocervus
Caliban	Hydra
centaur	Kraken
Cerberus	Ladon
Ceto	Loch Ness monster
Charybdis	manticore
chimera	Medusa
cockatrice	mermaid
Cyclops	merman
dipsas	Midgard serpent
dragon	Minotaur
drake [archaic]	nixie
Echidna	ogre
Geryon	ogress
Gigantes	opinicus
Gorgon	Orthos *or* Orthros
Grendel	Pegasus
griffin	Python
Harpy	roc

Sagittary	troll
salamander	Typhoeus
satyr	Typhon
Scylla	unicorn
sea horse	vampire
sea serpent	werewolf
simurgh	windigo
siren	wivern
Sphinx	xiphopagus
Talos	zombie

86. NUMBER

.1 NOUNS **number, numeral,** *numero* [Sp], no. *or* n., **figure, digit,** binary digit *or* bit, **cipher,** character, symbol, sign, notation.

.2 (number systems) **Arabic numerals,** algorism *or* algorithm, Roman numerals; **decimal system,** binary system, octal system, duodecimal system, hexadecimal system.

.3 (numbers) finite number; infinity 104; transfinite number; **real number,** real; imaginary number *or* pure imaginary; **complex number,** complex *or* Gaussian integer; **rational number,** rational; **irrational number,** irrational; algebraic number, surd; transcendental number; **integer,** whole number; **fraction** 86.6; mixed number; round number, abbreviated number; perfect number; imperfect number, deficient *or* defective number; abundant number; prime *or* rectilinear number; Fermat number, Mersenne number; composite *or* rectangular number; figurate number, polygonal number, pyramidal number; even number, pair; odd number, impair; cardinal number, cardinal; ordinal number, ordinal, –st, –nd, –rd, –th *or* –eth; serial number.

.4 large number, astronomical number, zillion *or* jillion [both informal]; googol, googolplex; infinity, infinitude 104.1; billion, trillion, etc. 99.12,13.

.5 **sum,** summation, difference, product, **number, count,** x number, n number; account, cast, **score, reckoning, tally,** tale, the story *or* whole story [both informal], the bottom line [informal], **aggregate, amount,** quantity 28; **whole** 54, **total** 54.2; box score [informal].

.6 ratio, rate, proportion; quota, quotum; percentage, percent; fraction, proper fraction, improper fraction, compound fraction, continued fraction; geometric ratio *or* proportion, arithmetical proportion, harmonic proportion; rule of three.

.7 series, progression; arithmetical progression, geometrical progression, harmonic progression; Fibonacci numbers.

.8 ADJS numeric(al), numeral, numerary, numerative; odd, impair, even, pair; arith-

metical, algorismic *or* algorithmic; **cardinal, ordinal;** figural, **figurate,** figurative, **digital;** aliquot, submultiple, **reciprocal,** prime, fractional, decimal, exponential, **logarithmic,** logometric, differential, integral; positive, negative; rational, irrational, transcendental; surd, radical; real, imaginary; possible, impossible, finite, infinite, transfinite.

.9 **mathematical elements**

addend	index
aliquot part	integral
antilogarithm	Laplace transform
argument	least common denominator, LCD
base	
Bessel function	least common multiple, LCM
binomial	
characteristic	logarithm
coefficient	mantissa
combination	matrix
common divisor *or* measure	minuend
	mixed decimal
complement	modulus
congruence	monomial
constant	multiple
cosecant	multiplicand
cosine	multiplicator
cotangent	multiplier
cube	norm
cube root	numerator
decimal	parameter
denominator	permutation
derivative	pi (π)
determinant	polynomial
difference, remainder	power
differential	quaternion
discriminate	quotient
dividend	radical
divisor	radix
e	reciprocal
elliptical function	repeating *or* circulating decimal
equation	
exponent	root
exponential	secant
factor	sine
factorial	square root
formula	submultiple
function	subtrahend
greatest common divisor, GCD	summand
	tangent
haversine	tensor
hyperbolic function	variable
i	vector
increment	versine

87. NUMERATION

.1 NOUNS **numeration, enumeration, numbering, counting,** accounting, census, inventorying, telling, tallying; page numbering, pagination, foliation; counting on the fingers, dactylonomy; **measurement** 490; quantification, quantization.

.2 **mathematics** 87.18, math [US informal], maths [Brit informal], mathematic, **numbers, figures;** pure mathematics, abstract mathematics, applied mathematics, higher mathematics, elementary mathematics; new mathematics, new math [informal]; algorism or algorithm.

.3 **calculation, computation, estimation, reckoning,** calculus; adding, footing, casting, ciphering, totaling, toting or totting [informal].

.4 (mathematical operations) notation, **addition** 40, **subtraction** 42, **multiplication, division,** proportion, practice, equation, extraction of roots, inversion, reduction, involution, evolution, approximation, interpolation, extrapolation, transformation, differentiation, integration.

.5 **summation, summary, summing, summing up,** recount, recounting, rehearsal, capitulation, **recapitulation,** statement, **reckoning, count,** repertory, census, inventory, head count, nose count, body count; account, accounts.

.6 **account of, count of,** a reckoning of, **tab** or **tabs** of [informal], tally of, check of, track of.

.7 **figures, statistics,** indexes or indices; vital statistics.

.8 **calculator, computer,** estimator, figurer, reckoner, abacist; statistician, actuary; accountant, bookkeeper 845.7.

.9 **mathematician, arithmetician;** geometer, geometrician; algebraist, trigonometrician, statistician, geodesist, mathematical physicist.

.10 VERBS **number,** numerate, **enumerate, count, tell, tally,** give a figure to, put a figure on, call off, name or call over, run over; **count noses or heads** [informal], call the roll; census, poll; page, paginate, foliate; **measure** 490.11; quantify, quantize.

.11 **calculate, compute, estimate, reckon, figure,** cipher, cast, tally, score; **figure out,** work out, dope out [slang]; take account of, figure in [informal]; **add, subtract, multiply, divide,** algebraize, extract roots; **measure** 490.11.

.12 **sum up,** sum, summate; **figure up,** cipher up, reckon up, **count up, add up,** foot up, cast up, score up, **tally up;** total, total up, tote or tot up [informal]; **summarize, recapitulate,** recap [informal], **recount,** rehearse, recite, relate; detail, itemize, inventory.

.13 **keep account of, keep count of, keep track of, keep tab or tabs** [informal], keep tally, keep a check on or of.

.14 **check, verify** 513.12, double-check, check out; **prove,** demonstrate; balance, balance the books; **audit,** overhaul; take stock, inventory.

.15 ADJS **numerative, enumerative; calculative,** computative, estimative; **calculating,** computing, computational, estimating; statistical; quantifying, quantizing.

.16 **calculable,** computable, **reckonable,** estimable, countable, numberable, numerable; **measurable** 490.15, mensurable, quantifiable.

.17 **mathematical,** numeric(al), arithmetic(al), algebraic(al), geometric(al), trigonometric(al), analytic(al).

.18 **mathematics**

algebra	inverse geometry
algebraic geometry	Lagrangian function
analysis	Laplace's equation
analytic geometry	linear algebra
arithmetic	line geometry
associative algebra	mathematical physics
binary arithmetic	matrix algebra
Boolean algebra	metageometry
calculus	modular arithmetic
calculus of differences	multiple algebra
circle geometry	natural geometry
combinatorial mathematics	nilpotent algebra
combinatorial topology	noncommutative algebra
commutative algebra	non-Euclidean geometry
complex or double algebra	n-tuple linear algebra
denumerative geometry	number theory
descriptive geometry	plane trigonometry
differential calculus	point-set topology
division algebra	political arithmetic
elementary arithmetic	projective geometry
elementary or ordinary algebra	proper subalgebra
equivalent algebras	quadratics
Euclidean geometry	quaternian algebra
Fourier analysis	reducible algebra
game theory	Riemannian geometry
geodesic geometry	semisimple algebra
geodesy	set theory
geometry	simple algebra
Gödel's proof	solid geometry
graphic algebra	speculative geometry
group theory	spherical trigonometry
higher algebra	statistics
higher arithmetic	subalgebra
hyperalgebra	systems analysis
hyperbolic geometry	topology
infinitesimal calculus	trigonometry, trig [informal]
integral calculus	universal algebra
intuitional geometry	universal geometry
invariant subalgebra	vector algebra
	zero algebra

.19 **calculators**

abacus	electronic computer 349.16
adding machine	listing machine
analog computer	Napier's bones or rods
arithmograph	pari-mutuel machine
arithmometer	quipu
calculating machine	rule
cash register	slide rule, sliding scale
Comptometer	suan pan [Chin]
counter	tabulator
difference engine	totalizator
digital computer	

88. LIST

.1 NOUNS **list, enumeration, itemization,** items, **schedule, register,** registry; **inventory,** repertory, tally; **checklist;** tally sheet; active list, civil list [Brit], retired list, sick list; waiting list; blacklist.

.2 **table,** contents, table of contents; **chart; index,** thumb index, card index.

.3 **catalog;** classified catalog, *catalogue raisonné* [Fr]; **card catalog, bibliography,** finding list, handlist; publisher's catalog *or* list; **file,** filing system, letter file, pigeonholes.

.4 **dictionary,** word list, **lexicon, glossary, thesaurus, vocabulary,** terminology, nomenclator; promptorium, gradus; **gazetteer.**

.5 **bill,** statement, account, ledger, books; **bill of fare, menu,** carte; **bill of lading,** manifest, waybill, invoice.

.6 **roll, roster,** scroll, rota; **roll call,** muster, **census,** nose *or* head count [informal], **poll,** questionnaire, returns, census report *or* returns; property roll, tax roll, cadastre; muster roll, checkroll, checklist; jury list *or* panel; **calendar,** docket, **agenda,** order of business; **program,** dramatis personae, lineup, beadroll; honor roll, dean's list.

.7 **listing,** tabulation; **cataloging, itemization,** filing, indexing; **registration,** registry, enrollment.

.8 VERBS **list, enumerate, itemize, tabulate, catalog,** tally; **register,** post, enter, **enroll, book;** impanel; **file,** pigeonhole; **index;** inventory; calendar; score, keep score; **schedule, program.**

.9 ADJS **listed, enumerated, entered, itemized, cataloged,** tallied, inventoried; filed, **indexed, tabulated; scheduled, programmed;** inventorial, cadastral.

89. UNITY

(state of being one)

.1 NOUNS **unity, oneness, singleness,** singularity, **individuality,** identity, selfsameness; **particularity** 80; uniqueness; intactness, inviolability, purity, simplicity 45, irreducibility, **integrity,** integrality, integration, unification, fusion, combination 52; solidification, solidity, solidarity, indivisibility, undividedness, **wholeness** 54.5; univocity, organic unity; uniformity 17; "the sacredness of private integrity" [Emerson].

.2 **aloneness,** loneness, **loneliness, lonesomeness; privacy,** solitariness, **solitude;** separateness, aloofness, detachment, seclusion, sequestration, **withdrawal, alienation,** standing *or* moving *or* keeping apart, **isolation,** "splendid isolation" [Sir William Goschen]; celibacy, single blessedness.

.3 **one,** I, **unit,** ace, atom; monad; –on, –eme; one and only, none else, no other, nothing else, nought beside.

.4 **individual,** single, unit, **integer, entity,** singleton, **item,** article, point, module; person, persona, soul.

.5 VERBS **unify,** reduce to unity, make one; **integrate, unite** 52.3.

.6 **stand alone,** stand *or* move *or* keep apart, withdraw, alienate *or* seclude *or* sequester *or* isolate oneself; become an individual.

.7 ADJS **one, single, singular, individual, sole, unique,** a certain, **solitary, lone;** exclusive; **integral,** indivisible, irreducible, monadic, monistic, unanalyzable, noncompound, atomic, unitary, undivided, solid, **uniform** 17.5, **simple** 45.6, **whole** 54.9; an, any, any one, either.

.8 **alone, solitary, solo, soli–,** *solus* [L]; **isolated,** insular, apart, separate, separated, alienated, withdrawn, aloof, detached, removed; **lone, lonely, lonesome;** friendless, kithless, homeless, rootless, companionless, **unaccompanied,** unescorted, unattended; **unaided,** unassisted, unabetted, unsupported, unseconded; **single-handed;** self–.

.9 **sole, unique,** singular, absolute, unrepeated, **alone,** lone, **only,** only-begotten, **one and only,** first and last; odd, impair, unpaired, azygous, azygo–; celibate.

.10 **unitary, integrated,** integral, integrant; **unified,** united, rolled into one, composite.

.11 **unipartite, unipart, one-piece;** monadic *or* monadal; uni–, **unilateral, one-sided;** uniangulate, unibivalent, unibranchiate, unicameral, unicellular, unicuspid, unidentate, unidigitate; **unidimensional, unidirectional;** uniflorous, unifoliate, unifoliolate, unigenital, uniglobular, unilinear, uniliteral, unilobed, unilobular, unilocular, unimodular, unimolecular, uninuclear, uniocular; unipolar, **univalent, univocal.**

.12 **unifying, uniting,** unific; **combining, combinative** 52.5,7, combinatory; connective, connecting, connectional; **conjunctive** 47.16, conjunctival; coalescing, coalescent.

.13 ADVS **singly, individually,** particularly, severally, one by one, one at a time; **sin-**

gularly, in the singular; **alone,** by itself, *per se* [L]; **by oneself,** on one's own, **single-handedly;** separately, apart; **once** 136.6.

.14 **solely, exclusively, only,** merely, **purely,** simply; **entirely, wholly, totally; integrally, indivisibly,** irreducibly, unanalyzably, undividedly.

90. DUALITY

.1 NOUNS **duality, dualism, doubleness,** duplexity, **twoness;** biformity; polarity; conjugation, pairing; **doubling, duplication,** twinning, bifurcation; **dichotomy,** halving; **duplicity,** two-facedness, doublethink; **irony,** ambiguity, equivocality, **ambivalence;** Janus.

.2 **two,** twain [archaic]; **couple, pair, twosome,** set of two, **duo, duet,** brace, team, span, yoke, double harness; **match, mates; couplet,** distich, doublet; duad, dyad; the two, **both.**

.3 **deuce;** pair, doubleton; **craps** *or* **snake eyes** [both dice slang].

.4 **twins,** pair of twins [informal], identical twins, fraternal twins, exact mates; Tweedledum and Tweedledee, Siamese twins; Twin Stars, Castor and Pollux, Gemini.

.5 VERBS **pair, couple, bracket,** team, **yoke,** span, double-team, double-harness; **mate, match,** conjugate; **pair off,** couple up, team up.

.6 ADJS **two, dual, double,** duplex; **dualistic;** dyadic; duadic; biform; bipartite, bipartisan, bilateral, two-sided, double-sided; dichotomous; bifurcated; twin, identical, matched, twinned, duplicated; ambi– *or* amph(i)–, bi– *or* bin–, bis–, deut(o)– *or* deuter(o)–, di– *or* dis–, didym(o)–, duo–, dyo–, dvi–, gem–, twi–, zyg(o)–.

.7 **both,** the two, either; for two, tête-à-tête, *à deux* [Fr].

.8 **coupled, paired,** yoked, matched, mated, **bracketed;** conjugate, conjugated; biconjugate, bigeminate; bijugate.

91. DUPLICATION

.1 NOUNS **duplication, reduplication,** replication, conduplication; **reproduction, doubling;** twinning, gemination, ingemination; **repetition** 103, iteration, reiteration; **imitation** 22, parroting; **copying** 22.1; **duplicate** 24.3.

.2 **repeat,** encore, repeat performance; echo.

.3 VERBS **duplicate,** dupe [slang], ditto [informal]; **double;** multiply by two; twin, geminate, ingeminate; **reduplicate, repro-** duce, replicate, redouble; **repeat** 103.7; copy.

.4 ADJS **double, duplicate,** duple, **dual, duplex, twofold,** bifold, binary, binate; twinned, geminate, geminated; **second, secondary; twin,** biparous; biform, disomatous; bivalent; ambidextrous; two-sided, bilateral; two-faced, double-faced, bifacial, Janus-like; two-ply, two-story, two-level, conduplicate; bi–, bis–, deuter(o)–, di– *or* dis–, diphy(o)–, dipl(o)–, diss(o)–, twi–.

.5 ADVS **doubly, dually, twofold,** as much again, twice as much; twice, two times.

.6 **secondly,** second, secondarily, **in the second place** *or* instance.

.7 **again,** another time, **once more,** once again, over again, yet again, *encore, bis* [both Fr]; **anew,** afresh, new, freshly, newly; re–.

92. BISECTION

.1 NOUNS **bisection,** bipartition, bifidity, dimidiation; **dichotomy, halving, division, in half** *or* **by two,** splitting *or* cutting in two; subdivision; bifurcation, forking, ramification, branching.

.2 **half,** moiety, mediety; hemisphere, semisphere, semicircle, **fifty percent;** half-and-half *or* fifty-fifty [both informal].

.3 **bisector,** diameter, equator, halfway mark, divider, partition 237.5, line of demarcation, boundary 235.3.

.4 VERBS **bisect, halve, divide, in half** *or* **by two,** transect, subdivide; cleave, fission, **split** *or* **cut in two,** dimidiate, **dichotomize;** bifurcate, fork, ramify, branch.

.5 ADJS **half, part, partly, partial,** halfway, bi–, demi–, dich(o)–, hemi–, semi–, sam– [dial]; **one-and-a-half,** sesqui–.

.6 **halved, bisected, divided,** dimidiate; dichotomous; bifurcated, forked *or* forking, ramified, branched, branching; riven, **split,** cloven, cleft.

.7 **bipartite,** bifid, biform, bicuspid, biaxial, bicameral, binocular, binomial, binominal, biped, bipetalous, bipinnate, bisexual, bivalent, unibivalent.

.8 ADVS **in half,** in halves, **in two,** in twain, by two; half-and-half, fifty-fifty [both informal]; apart, asunder.

93. THREE

.1 NOUNS **three, trio, threesome,** trialogue, set of three, tierce [cards], leash, troika; **triad,** trilogy, trine, **trinity,** triunity, ternary, ternion; **triplet,** tercet, terzetto; trefoil, shamrock, clover; tripod, trivet; **tri-**

angle, tricorn, trihedron, trident, trisul, triennium, trimester, trinomial, trionym, triphthong, triptych, triplopy, trireme, triseme, triskelion, triumvirate; triple crown, triple threat; trey, threespot [both cards], deuce-ace [dice].

.2 **threeness**, triplicity, triality, tripleness; triunity, trinity.

.3 ADJS **three, triple,** triplex, trinal, trine, trial; triadic(al); triune, three-in-one, *tria juncta in uno* [L]; triform; **triangular,** deltoid, fan-shaped; tri–, ter–, ternati–.

94. TRIPLICATION

.1 NOUNS **triplication,** triplicity, trebleness, **threefoldness;** triplicate, second carbon.

.2 VERBS **triplicate, triple, treble, multiply by three,** threefold; cube.

.3 ADJS **triple,** triplicate, **treble, threefold,** triplex, trinal, trine, tern, ternary, ternal, ternate; three-ply; trilogic(al); cub(o)– or cubi–; ter–, tri–, tripl(o)–, tris–.

.4 **third,** tertiary, tert–, trit(o)–.

.5 ADVS **triply, trebly,** trinely; **threefold;** thrice, three times, again and yet again.

.6 **thirdly,** in the third place.

95. TRISECTION

.1 NOUNS **trisection,** tripartition, trichotomy.

.2 **third,** tierce, third part, one-third; *tertium quid* [L, a third something].

.3 VERBS **trisect, divide in thirds** or **three,** third, trichotomize; trifurcate.

.4 ADJS **tripartite,** trisected, triparted, **threeparted,** trichotomous; three-sided, trihedral, trilateral; **three-dimensional;** three-forked, three-pronged, trifurcate; trident, tridental, tridentate(d), trifid; tricuspid; three-footed, tripodic, tripedal; trifoliate, trifloral, triflorate, triflorous, tripetalous, triadelphous, triarch; trimerous, 3-merous; three-cornered, tricornered, tricorn; trigonal, trigonoid; triquetrous, triquetral; trigrammatic, triliteral; **triangular,** triangulate, deltoid; tri–.

96. FOUR

.1 NOUNS **four,** tetrad, quatern, quaternion, quaternary, quaternity, **quartet, quadruplet, foursome;** Little Joe [dice slang]; quadrennium; tetralogy; tetrapody; tetraphony, four-part diaphony; quadrille, square dance; quatrefoil or quadrifoil, four-leaf clover; tetragram, tetragrammaton; quadrangle, quad [informal], rectangle; tetrahedron; tetragon, square; bi-

quadrate; quadrinomial; quadrature, squaring; quadrilateral 251.13.

.2 **fourness,** quaternity, quadruplicity.

.3 VERBS **square, quadrate,** form or make four; form fours or squares; **cube, dice.**

.4 ADJS **four;** foursquare; quaternary, quartile, quartic, quadric, quadratic; tetrad, tetradic; quadrinomial, biquadratic; tetractinal, four-rayed, **quadruped,** four-legged; quadrivalent, tetravalent; quadrilateral 251.9; quadr(i)– or quadru–, tetr(a)–, tessar(a)–.

97. QUADRUPLICATION

.1 NOUNS **quadruplication,** quadruplicature.

.2 VERBS **quadruple, quadruplicate,** fourfold, form or make four, multiply by four; biquadrate, quadruplex.

.3 ADJS **quadruplicate, quadruple,** quadrable, **quadruplex, fourfold,** tetraploid, quadrigeminal, biquadratic; quadr(i)– or quadru–, quater–, tetr(a)–, tetrakis–.

98. QUADRISECTION

.1 NOUNS **quadrisection,** quadripartition, **quartering.**

.2 **fourth,** one-fourth, **quarter,** one-quarter, fourth part, twenty-five percent, twenty-five cents, two bits [archaic or slang]; quartern; quart; farthing; quarto or 4 to.

.3 VERBS **divide by four** or **into four; quadrisect, quarter.**

.4 ADJS quadrisected, **quartered,** quartercut; quadripartite, quadrifid, quadriform; quadrifoliate, quadrigeminal, quadripinnate, quadriplanar, quadriserial, quadrivial, quadrifurcate, quadrumanal or quadrumanous.

.5 **fourth, quarter.**

.6 ADVS **fourthly,** in the fourth place; quarterly, by quarters.

99. FIVE AND OVER

.1 NOUNS **five,** V, cinque, quint, quincunx, **quintet, fivesome, quintuplet,** pentad; five dollars; fiver or fin or five bucks [all slang]; Phoebe or Little Phoebe [both dice slang]; pentagon, pentahedron, pentagram; pentapody, pentameter, pentastich; pentarchy; Pentateuch; pentachord; pentathlon; five-pointed star, pentacle, pentalpha, mullet [her].

.2 **six,** sixer [slang], sise, Captain Hicks [dice slang], **half a dozen, sextet,** sestet, **sextuplet,** hexad; hexagon, hexahedron, hexagram, six-pointed star, estoile [her], Jewish star, star of David, *Magen David* [Heb]; hexameter, hexapody, hexastich;

hexapod; hexarchy; Hexateuch; hexastyle; hexachord.

.3 **seven,** sevener [slang], heptad; heptagon, heptahedron; heptameter, heptastich; heptarchy; Heptateuch; septet, heptachord; septuor, septennate; **week.**

.4 **eight,** eighter [slang]; eighter from Decatur [dice slang]; octagon, octahedron; octave, octavo or 8vo; octad; ogdoad, octonary; octet, octameter, octosyllable; octastyle; utas [archaic], Octateuch.

.5 **nine,** niner [slang], Nina from Carolina [dice slang], ennead; nonage, novena; nonagon, nonuplet; enneastyle.

.6 **ten,** X, tenner [slang], **decade,** Big Dick [dice slang]; decagon, decahedron; decagram, decigram, decaliter, deciliter, decare, decameter, decimeter, decastere; decapod, decastyle, decasyllable; decemvir, decemvirate, decurion; decennium, decennary, Ten Commandments or Decalogue.

.7 (eleven to ninety) **eleven; twelve, dozen,** boxcar or boxcars [both dice slang], duodecimo or twelvemo or 12mo; teens; **thirteen,** long dozen, baker's dozen; **fourteen,** two weeks, fortnight; **fifteen,** quindecima, quindene, quindecim, quindecennial; **sixteen,** sixteenmo or 16mo; **twenty, score; twenty-four,** four and twenty, two dozen, twenty-fourmo or 24mo; **twenty-five,** five and twenty, quarter of a hundred or century; **thirty-two,** thirty-twomo or 32mo; **forty,** twoscore; **fifty,** L, half a hundred; **sixty,** sexagenary; Sexagesima; sexagenarian, threescore; **sixty-four,** sixty-fourmo or 64mo or sexagesimo-quarto; **seventy,** septuagenarian, threescore and ten; **eighty,** octogenarian, fourscore; **ninety,** nonagenarian, fourscore and ten.

.8 **hundred, century,** C, one C [slang], centred, centrev or centref [both Welsh]; centennium, centennial, centenary; centenarian; cental, centigram, centiliter, centimeter, centare, centistere; hundredweight or cwt; hecatomb; centipede; centumvir, centumvirate, centurion; (120) great or long hundred; (144) gross; (150) sesquicentennial, sesquicentenary; (200) bicentenary, bicentennial; (300) tercentenary, tercentennial, etc.

.9 **five hundred,** D, five centuries; five C's [slang].

.10 **thousand,** M, chiliad; **millennium;** G or grand or thou or yard [all slang]; chiliagon, chiliahedron or chiliaëdron; chiliarchia or chiliarch; millepede; milligram,

milliliter, millimeter, kilogram or kilo, kiloliter, kilometer; kilocycle, kilohertz; **ten thousand,** myriad; **one hundred thousand,** lakh [India].

.11 **million;** ten million, crore [India].

.12 **billion,** thousand million, milliard.

.13 trillion, quadrillion, quintillion, sextillion, septillion, octillion, nonillion, decillion, undecillion, duodecillion, tredecillion, quattuordecillion, quindecillion, sexdecillion, septendecillion, octodecillion, novemdecillion, vigintillion; googol, googolplex; zillion or jillion [both informal].

.14 (division into five or more parts) quinquesection, quinquepartition, sextipartition, etc.; decimation, decimalization; fifth, sixth, etc.; **tenth, tithe,** decima.

.15 VERBS (divide by five, etc.) quinquesect; decimalize.

.16 (multiply by five, etc.) fivefold, sixfold, etc.; quintuple, quintuplicate; sextuple, sextuplicate; centuple, centuplicate.

.17 ADJS fifth, quinary; **fivefold, quintuple,** quintuplicate; quinquennial; quinquepartite, pentadic, quinquefid; quincuncial, pentastyle; pentad, pentavalent, quinquevalent; pent(a)– or pen–, quinqu(e)–, quint(i)–.

.18 **sixth,** senary; **sixfold, sextuple;** sexpartite, hexadic, sextipartite, hexapartite; hexagonal, hexahedral, hexangular; hexad, hexavalent; sextuplex, hexastyle; sexennial; hexatomic; hexamerous; hex(a)–, sex(i)–, sexti–.

.19 **seventh,** septimal; **sevenfold, septuple;** septenary; septempartite, heptadic, septemfid; heptagonal, heptahedral, heptangular; heptamerous; hept(a)–, sept(i)–.

.20 **eighth,** octonary; **eightfold, octuple;** octadic; octal, octofid, octaploid; octagonal, octahedral, octan, octangular; octosyllabic; octastyle; oct(a)– or octo–.

.21 **ninth,** novenary, nonary; **ninefold, nonuple,** enneadic; enneahedral, enneastyle; non(a)–, ennea–.

.22 **tenth,** denary, **decimal,** tithe; **tenfold, decuple;** decagonal, decahedral; decasyllabic; deca– or deka–, deci–.

.23 **eleventh,** undecennial, undecennary; undec–, hendec(a)–.

.24 **twelfth,** duodenary, duodenal; duodecimal; dodec(a)–.

.25 **thirteenth,** fourteenth, etc.; eleventeenth, umpteenth [informal]; in one's teens.

.26 **twentieth,** vicenary, vicennial, vigesimal, vicesimal; icos(a)– or icosi–, eicos(a)–.

.27 **sixtieth,** sexagesimal, sexagenary.

.28 **seventieth,** septuagesimal, septuagenary.

.29 **hundredth,** centesimal, **centennial,** centenary, centurial; **hundredfold, centuple,** centuplicate; secular; centigrado; cent(i)–, hect(o)–, hecato(n)–.

.30 **thousandth,** millenary, **millennial; thousandfold;** kilo–, milli–.

.31 millionth, meg(a)–, micro–, billionth, giga–, nano–, trillionth, pico–; quadrillionth, quintillionth, etc.

100. PLURALITY

(more than one)

.1 NOUNS **plurality,** pluralness; a greater number, a certain number; several, a few 102.2, more; plural number, the plural, –s or –es; compositeness, nonsingleness, nonuniqueness; **pluralism** 18.1, variety; numerousness 101.

.2 **majority,** plurality, more than half, the greater number, the greatest number, **most,** preponderance or preponderancy, **bulk, mass;** lion's share.

.3 pluralization, plurification.

.4 **multiplication,** multiplying, proliferation, **increase** 38; multiple, multiplier, multiplicand; tables, multiplication table.

.5 VERBS pluralize, plurify; raise to or make more than one.

.6 **multiply,** proliferate, **increase** 38.4,6.

.7 ADJS **plural,** more than one, more; some, certain; not singular, composite, nonsingle, nonunique; plurative; **pluralistic** 18.3, various; numerous 101.6.

.8 **multiple,** multiplied, multifold, multi–; –fold, **manifold; increased** 38.7; multinomial, polynomial [both math].

.9 majority, **most,** the greatest number.

.10 ADVS in majority, **in the majority;** and others, et al., et cetera 40.14.

101. NUMEROUSNESS

.1 NOUNS **numerousness, multiplicity, manyness,** multitudinousness, multifoldness, multifariousness, teemingness, swarmingness, rifeness, profuseness, profusion; **plenty, abundance** 661.2; **countlessness,** innumerability, infinitude.

.2 (indefinite number) **a number,** a certain number, one or two, two or three, **a few, several,** parcel, passel [informal]; eleventeen or umpteen [both informal].

.3 (large number) **multitude, throng** 74.4; plurality, **many; numbers, quantities,** lots 34.4, flocks, **scores;** all kinds or sorts of, quite a few, tidy sum; muchness, **large amount** 34.3,4; **host, army,** legion, rout,

ruck, mob, jam, clutter; **swarm, flock** 74.5, flight, cloud, hail, bevy, covey, shoal, hive, nest, pack, bunch 74.7; a world of, a mass of, worlds of, masses of.

.4 (immense number) **a myriad,** a thousand, **a thousand and one,** a lakh [India], a crore [India], a million, a billion, a quadrillion, a nonillion, etc. 99.10–13; a zillion or jillion [informal].

.5 VERBS **teem with,** overflow with, **abound with,** burst with, bristle with, pullulate with, **swarm with,** throng with, creep with, **crawl with, be alive with;** clutter, crowd, jam, pack; multiply 100.6; outnumber.

.6 ADJS **numerous, many,** not a few, no few; **very many,** full many, **ever so many,** considerable or quite some [both informal]; multi–, myri(o)–, pluri–, poly–, **multitudinous,** multitudinal, multifarious, multifold, multiple, **myriad,** thousand, million, billion; zillion or jillion [both informal]; heaped-up; numerous as the stars, numerous as the sands, numerous as the hairs on the head, "numerous as glittering gems of morning dew" [Edward Young].

.7 **several,** divers, **sundry,** various; fivish, sixish, etc.; some five or six, etc.; upwards of.

.8 **abundant,** copious, ample, plenteous, **plentiful** 661.7.

.9 **teeming, swarming, crowding,** thronging, overflowing, bursting, **crawling, alive with,** populous, prolific, proliferating, crowded, packed, jammed, jam-packed [informal], like sardines in a can [informal], thronged, studded, bristling, rife, lavish, prodigal, superabundant, **profuse,** in profusion, thick, **thick with,** thick-coming, thick as hail or flies; "thick as autumnal leaves that strow the brooks in Vallombrose" [Milton].

.10 **innumerable, numberless,** unnumbered, **countless,** uncounted, untold, incalculable, immeasurable, unmeasured, measureless, inexhaustible, endless, infinite, without end or limit, more than one can tell, more than you can shake a stick at [informal], no end of or to; countless as the stars or sands.

.11 **and many more,** cum multis aliis [L], and what not, and heaven knows what.

.12 ADVS **numerously,** multitudinously, **profusely,** thickly, copiously, **abundantly, prodigally; innumerably, countlessly,** infinitely, incalculably, inexhaustibly, immeasurably; in throngs, in crowds, in swarms, in heaps, *acervatim* [L]; no end [informal].

102. FEWNESS

.1 NOUNS **fewness,** infrequency, **sparsity,** sparseness, **scarcity, paucity, scantiness, meagerness,** miserliness, niggardliness, tightness, thinness, stringency, restrictedness; chintziness or chinchiness or stinginess [all informal], scrimpiness or skimpiness [both informal]; **rarity,** exiguity; smallness 35.

.2 **a few,** too few, mere or piddling few, only a few, **small number,** limited or piddling number, not enough to count or matter, **handful, scattering,** sprinkling, trickle.

.3 **minority,** least; the minority, the few; minority group; "we happy few" [Shakespeare].

.4 ADJS **few, not many,** olig(o)–; hardly or scarcely any, precious little [informal], of small number, to be counted on one's fingers.

.5 **sparse,** scant, **scanty,** exiguous, **infrequent,** scarce, scarce as hen's teeth [informal], poor, piddling, thin, slim, **meager;** miserly, niggardly, cheeseparing, tight; chintzy or chinchy or stingy [all informal], scrimpy or skimpy [both informal], skimping or scrimping [both informal]; **scattered,** sprinkled, spotty, **few and far between; rare,** seldom met with, seldom seen.

.6 **fewer, less,** smaller, not so much or many.

.7 **minority,** least.

.8 ADVS **sparsely,** *sparsim* [L], **scantily, meagerly,** exiguously, piddlingly; stingily or scrimpily or skimpily [all informal], thinly; **scarcely,** rarely, infrequently; **scatteringly,** spottily, in dribs and drabs [informal], **here and there,** in places, in spots.

103. REPETITION

.1 NOUNS **repetition, reproduction,** duplication 91, reduplication, doubling, redoubling; **recurrence,** reoccurrence, return, reincarnation, rebirth, reappearance, renewal, resumption, echo, reecho; regurgitation; **quotation; imitation** 22; plagiarism.

.2 **iteration, reiteration, recapitulation,** recap [informal], retelling, recounting, recountal, **recital, rehearsal, restatement,** rehash [informal]; reissue, reprint; review, summary, critique, résumé, summing up; going over or through, practicing; reasser-

tion, reaffirmation; elaboration, dwelling upon; **copy** 24.

.3 **redundancy, tautology,** tautologism, pleonasm, macrology, battology; tautophony, stammering, stuttering; padding, filling, expletive.

.4 **repetitiousness,** repetitiveness, stale or unnecessary repetition; harping; **monotony,** monotone, drone; **tedium** 884; **humdrum,** dingdong, singsong, chime, jingle, jingle-jangle, trot, pitter-patter; **rhyme, alliteration,** assonance, slant or near rhyme; **repeated sounds** 455.

.5 repeat, repetend, bis, ditto [informal]; **refrain,** burden, chant, undersong, chorus, bob; bob wheel, bob and wheel; ritornel, *ritornello* [Ital].

.6 **encore,** repeat performance, repeat, reprise; replay, replaying, return match.

.7 VERBS **repeat, redo,** do again, do over, do a repeat, **reproduce, duplicate** 91.3, reduplicate, double, redouble, ditto [informal], **echo,** reecho; regurgitate; renew, reincarnate, revive; come again [slang], say again, repeat oneself, **quote,** repeat word for word or verbatim, parrot, repeat like a broken record; **copy, imitate** 22.5; plagiarize.

.8 **iterate, reiterate, rehearse, recapitulate, recount,** rehash [informal], **recite, retell,** retail, **restate,** reword, review, run over, sum up, summarize, resume; reissue, reprint; do or say over again, **go over** or **through,** practice, say over, go over the same ground, give an encore, quote oneself, go the same round, fight one's battles over again; **tautologize,** battologize, pad, fill; reaffirm, reassert.

.9 **dwell on** or **upon,** insist upon, **harp on,** constantly recur or revert to, labor, belabor, hammer away at, always trot out, sing the same old song or tune, play the same old record, plug the same theme, never hear the last of; **thrash** or **thresh over,** go over again and again, go over and over.

.10 **din, ding; drum** 455.4, beat, hammer, pound; **din in the ear,** say over and over.

.11 (be repeated) **repeat, recur,** reoccur, **come again,** come up again, **return, reappear, resume;** resound, reverberate, echo; revert, turn or go back; keep coming, come again and again, happen over and over, run through like King Charles's head.

.12 ADJS **repeated,** reproduced, doubled, redoubled; duplicated, reduplicated; regurgitated; **echoed,** reechoed; **quoted,** plagia-

rized; iterated, reiterated, reiterate; retold, twice-told; warmed up or over, réchauffé [Fr].

.13 recurrent, recurring, returning, reappearing, revenant, ubiquitous, ever-recurring,
cyclical, periodic, thematic, thick-coming,
frequent, incessant, continuous 71.8,
haunting.

.14 repetitious, repetitive, repetitional or rep-
etitionary, repeating; duplicative, redupli-
cative; imitative 22.9, parrotlike; echoing,
reechoing, echoic; iterative, reiterative,
reiterant; recapitulative, recapitulatory;
battological, tautological or tautologous,
redundant; tautophon(ic)al.

.15 monotonous, monotone; tedious 884.8;
harping, labored, belabored, cliché-rid-
den; humdrum, singsong, chiming, chanting, dingdong [informal], jog-trot, jingle-
jangle; rhymed, rhyming, alliterative, al-
literating, assonant.

.16 ADVS repeatedly, often, frequently, recurrently, again and again, over and over,
over and over again, many times over,
time and again, time after time, times
without number; year after year, day after day, day by day, "tomorrow and tomorrow and tomorrow" [Shakespeare];
many times, several times, a number of
times, many a time, full many a time and
oft; every now and then, every once in a
while; re–; –s or –es.

.17 again, over, over again, once more, encore, bis [both Fr], two times, twice over,
ditto; anew, de novo [L], afresh; from the
beginning, da capo [Ital].

.18 INTERJS encore!, bis!, once more!, again!

104. INFINITY

.1 NOUNS infinity, infiniteness, infinitude;
boundlessness, limitlessness, endlessness;
illimitability, interminability, termless-
ness; immeasurability, unmeasurability,
immensity, incalculability, innumerability, incomprehensibility; measurelessness,
countlessness, numberlessness; exhaust-
lessness, inexhaustibility; universality,
"world without end" [Bible]; all-inclu-
siveness, all-comprehensiveness; eternity
112.1,2, perpetuity 112, forever; "a dark illimitable ocean, without bound" [Mil-
ton].

.2 VERBS have no limit or bounds, have or
know no end, be without end, go on and
on, go on forever, never cease or end.

.3 ADJS infinite, boundless, endless, limitless, termless, shoreless; unbounded, uncircumscribed, unlimited, illimited, infinitely continuous or extended, stretching
or extending everywhere, without bound,
without limit or end, no end of or to; illimitable, interminable, interminate; immeasurable, incalculable, innumerable,
incomprehensible, unfathomable; measureless, countless, sumless; unmeasured,
unmeasurable, immense, unplumbed, untold, unnumbered, without measure or
number or term; exhaustless, inexhaustible; all-inclusive, all-comprehensive 79.14,
universal 79.14; perpetual, eternal 112.7;
"as boundless as the sea" [Shakespeare].

.4 ADVS infinitely, illimitably, boundlessly,
limitlessly, interminably; immeasurably,
measurelessly, immensely, incalculably,
innumerably, incomprehensibly; endlessly, without end or limit; ad infinitum
[L], to infinity; forever, eternally 112.10,
in perpetuity, "to the last syllable of
recorded time" [Shakespeare].

105. TIME

.1 NOUNS time, duration, durée [Fr], lastingness, continuity 71, term, while, tide,
space; tense 586.12; period 107; cosmic
time; kairotic time; space-time 179.6;
psychological time; the past 119, the
present 120, the future 121; timebinding;
chronology 114.1.

.2 Time, Father Time, Cronus, Kronos;
"Old Time, that greatest and longest established spinner of all" [Dickens], "that
old bald cheater, Time" [Ben Jonson];
"Old Time, the clocksetter, that bald
sexton Time", "that old common arbitrator, Time", "the nurse and breeder of all
good" [all Shakespeare], "the soul of the
world" [Pythagoras], "the author of au-
thors", "the greatest innovator" [both
Francis Bacon], "the devourer of things"
[Ovid], "the illimitable, silent, never-rest-
ing thing called Time" [Carlyle], "a short
parenthesis in a long period" [Donne], "a
sandpile we run our fingers in" [Sand-
burg].

.3 tract of time, corridors of time, whirligig
of time, glass or hourglass of time, sands
of time, ravages of time, noiseless foot of
Time, scythe of Time, "the tooth of
time" [Shakespeare].

.4 passage of time, course of time, lapse of
time, progress of time, process of time,
succession of time, flow or flux of time,
sweep of time, stream or current or tide
of time, march or step of time, flight of
time, time's caravan, "Time's revolving

wheels" [Petrarch], "Time's wingèd chariot" [Andrew Marvell].

.5 VERBS **elapse**, lapse, **pass, expire**, run its course, run out, go *or* pass by; flow, run, proceed, advance, roll *or* press on, flit, fly, slip, slide, glide; continue 71.4, last, **endure**, go *or* run *or* flow on.

.6 **spend time, pass time, put in time**, employ *or* use time, fill *or* occupy time, kill time [informal], consume time, take time, take up time, while away the time; find *or* look for time; race with *or* against time, buy time, work against time, run out of time, make time stand still; weekend, winter, summer; keep time, measure time.

.7 ADJS **temporal, chronological,** chron(o)–, –chronous; durational, durative; lasting, continuous 71.8.

.8 ADVS **when, at which time,** at which moment *or* instant, what time, when as [archaic], on which occasion, **upon which, whereupon,** at which, in which time, at what time, in what period, on what occasion, whenever.

.9 **at that time,** on that occasion, at the same time as, at the same time *or* moment that, then, simultaneously, contemporaneously.

.10 in the meantime, meanwhile 109.5; during the time; for the duration; at a stretch.

.11 **then,** thereat, **at that time,** at that moment *or* instant, in that case *or* instance, on that occasion; **again,** at another time, at some other time, anon.

.12 **whenever,** whene'er, whensoever, whensoe'er, **at whatever time,** at any time, anytime, no matter when; if ever, once.

.13 in the year of our Lord, *anno Domini* [L], AD, in the Common *or* Christian Era, CE; *ante Christum* [L], AC, before Christ, BC, before the Common *or* Christian era, BCE; *anno urbis conditae* [L], AUC; *anno regni* [L], AR.

.14 PREPS **during,** pending, durante [law]; **in the course of,** in the process of, in the middle of; **in the time of,** at the time of, in the age *or* era of, intra–; over, through, **throughout,** throughout the course of, **for the period of;** until the conclusion of.

.15 **until, till,** to, unto, **up to,** up to the time of.

.16 CONJS **when, while,** whilst, the while; **during the time that,** at the time that, at the same time that, at *or* during which time; **whereas, as long as,** as far as.

.17 PHRS **time flies,** *tempus fugit* [L], time runs out, time marches on, "Time rolls

his ceaseless course" [Sir Walter Scott], "Time and tide stayeth for no man" [Richard Braithwaite].

106. TIMELESSNESS

.1 NOUNS **timelessness,** neverness, datelessness, eternity 112.1,2; no time, no time at all; time out of time, stopping *or* running out of time; everlasting moment.

.2 (a time that will never come) Greek calends, when hell freezes over, the thirtieth of February.

.3 ADJS **timeless, dateless.**

.4 ADVS **never,** ne'er, **not ever,** at no time, on no occasion, not at all; **nevermore;** never in the world, never on earth; not in donkey's years [Brit], never in all one's born days [informal], never in my life, *jamais de la vie* [Fr].

.5 without date, *sine die* [L].

107. PERIOD

(portion or point of time)

.1 NOUNS **period, point, juncture, stage; interval,** space, span, stretch; time lag; **time,** while, **moment,** minute, instant, hour, day, **season;** psychological moment; pregnant *or* fateful moment, kairos, moment of truth; **spell** 108; "this bank and shoal of time" [Shakespeare].

.2 (periods) **moment, second,** millisecond, microsecond; **minute; hour,** man-hour; **day,** sun; weekday; **week;** fortnight; **month,** moon, lunation; calendar month, lunar month; **quarter; semester,** trimester, term, session, academic year; **year,** annum, sun, twelvemonth; common year, regular year, leap year, bissextile year, defective year, perfect *or* abundant year; solar year, lunar year, sidereal year; fiscal year; calendar year; quinquennium, lustrum, luster; **decade,** decennium, decennary; **century; millennium;** –ad.

.3 **term,** time, duration, **tenure; spell** 108.

.4 **age, generation,** time, day, date, cycle; aeon; Platonic year, great year, *annus magnus* [L], indiction, cycle of indiction.

.5 **era, epoch, age;** Golden Age, Silver Age; Ice Age, glacial epoch; Stone Age, Bronze Age, Iron Age, Steel Age; Middle Ages, Dark Ages; Era of Good Feeling; Jacksonian Age; Depression Era; New Deal Era; Prohibition Era.

.6 1870's and 80's, Reconstruction Era, Gilded Age.

.7 1890's, Gay Nineties, Naughty Nineties,

Mauve Decade, Golden Age, Gilded Age.

.8 1920's, Roaring Twenties, Golden Twenties, Mad Decade, Age of the Red-Hot Mamas, Jazz Age.

.9 (modern age) Technological Age, Automobile Age, Air Age, Jet Age, Supersonic Age, Atomic Age, Electronic Age, Computer Age, Space Age, Age of Anxiety.

.10 geological time periods

Algonkian	Oligocene
Archean	Ordovician
Archeozoic	Paleocene
Cambrian	Paleozoic
Carboniferous	Pennsylvanian
Cenozoic	Permian
Comanchean	Pleistocene
Cretaceous	Pliocene
Devonian	Precambrian
Eocene	Proterozoic
Glacial	Quaternary
Holocene	Recent
Jurassic	Silurian
Lower Cretaceous	Tertiary
Lower Tertiary	Triassic
Mesozoic	Upper Cretaceous
Miocene	Upper Tertiary
Mississippian	

108. SPELL

(period of duty, etc.)

.1 NOUNS spell, fit, stretch, go [informal].

.2 turn, bout, round, inning, innings [Brit], time, time at bat, place, say, whack [slang], go [informal]; opportunity, chance; relief, spell; one's turn, one's move [informal], one's say.

.3 shift, work shift, tour, tour of duty, stint, bit, watch, trick, time, turn, relay, spell or turn of work; day shift, night shift, swing shift, graveyard shift [informal], dogwatch, anchor watch; lobster trick or tour, sunrise watch; split shift, split schedule; half time, part time, full time; overtime.

.4 term, time; tenure, continuous tenure, tenure in or of office; enlistment, hitch [informal], tour; prison term, stretch [informal].

.5 VERBS take one's turn, have a go; take turns, alternate, turn and turn about; time off, spell or spell off [both informal], relieve, cover, fill in for, take over for; put in one's time, work one's shift; stand one's watch or trick, keep a watch; have one's innings; do a stint; hold office; have tenure or tenure of appointment; enlist, sign up; reenlist, re-up [informal]; do a hitch [informal], do a tour or tour of duty; serve or do time.

109. INTERIM

(intermediate period)

.1 NOUNS interim, interval, interlude, intermission, intermittence, pause, break, recess, coffee break, half time or half-time intermission, interruption; lull, quiet spell, resting point, point of repose, plateau, letup, relief, vacation, holiday, time off, off-time, downtime, time out; respite 711.2; entr'acte; intermezzo [Ital]; interregnum.

.2 meantime, meanwhile, while, the while.

.3 VERBS intervene, interlude, interval, intermit; pause, break, recess, declare a recess; call a break or intermission; call time or time-out; take five or ten, etc., take a break [all informal].

.4 ADJS interim, temporary, tentative, provisional, provisory.

.5 ADVS meanwhile, meantime, in the meanwhile or meantime, in the interim, ad interim [L]; between acts or halves or periods, betweenwhiles, betweentimes, between now and then; till or until then; en attendant [Fr], in the intervening time, during the interval, at the same time, for the meantime, for the time being, for the nonce, for a time or season; pendente lite [L].

110. DURABILITY

(long duration)

.1 NOUNS durability, endurance, duration, durableness, lastingness, longueur [Fr], perennation, abidingness, long-lastingness, perdurability, diuturnity; continuance, maintenance, steadfastness, constancy, stability 142, persistence, permanence 140, standing, long standing; longevity, long-livedness; antiquity, age; survival, survivance, defiance or defeat of time; perpetuity 112.

.2 protraction, prolongation, continuation, extension, lengthening, drawing- or stretching- or dragging- or spinning-out, lingering; procrastination.

.3 length of time, distance of time, vista or stretch or desert of time; corridor or tunnel of time.

.4 long time, long while, long; age or ages [both informal], aeon, century, eternity, years, years on end, coon's age [informal], donkey's years [Brit informal], month of Sundays [informal], right smart spell [dial].

.5 lifetime, life, life's duration, "threescore

years and ten" [Bible], period of existence, all the days of one's life; **generation, age;** all one's born days or natural
life [informal].

.6 VERBS **endure, last** or **last out,** bide,
abide, dwell, perdure, **continue,** run, extend, **go on,** carry on, hold on, keep on,
stay on, run on; live, **live on,** continue to
be, subsist, exist, tarry, **persist;** maintain,
sustain, **remain, stay,** keep, hold, stand,
prevail, last long, hold out; **survive,** defy
or defeat time; live to fight another day;
perennate; live through, tide over; wear,
wear well.

.7 **linger on,** linger, tarry, go on, **go on and
on, wear on,** crawl, creep, drag, **drag on,**
drag along, drag its slow length along,
drag a lengthening chain.

.8 **outlast,** outwear, **outlive, survive.**

.9 **protract, prolong,** continue, **extend,
lengthen,** lengthen out, **draw out, spin
out,** drag or stretch out; linger on, dwell
on; dawdle, procrastinate, temporize,
drag one's feet.

.10 ADJS **durable,** perdurable, **lasting, enduring,** perduring, **abiding, continuing,** remaining, staying, **stable** 142.12, persisting,
persistent, perennial, meno–; inveterate,
age-long; **steadfast, constant,** intransient,
immutable, unfading, evergreen, sempervirent, **permanent** 140.7, perennial; **long-
lasting,** long-standing, of long duration or
standing, diuturnal; long-term; **long-lived,**
tough, hardy, vital, longevous or longeval;
ancient, aged, antique; macrobiotic;
chronic; **perpetual** 112.7.

.11 **protracted, prolonged,** extended, lengthened; **long,** overlong, interminable, marathon, lasting, **lingering,** languishing; long-
continued, long-continuing, long-pend-
ing; drawn- or stretched- or dragged- or
spun-out, long-drawn, **long-drawn-out;**
long-winded.

.12 daylong, nightlong, weeklong, month-
long, yearlong.

.13 lifelong, livelong, lifetime, for life.

.14 ADVS **for a long time, long, for long, interminably,** unendingly, undyingly, persistently, protractedly, enduringly; for ever
so long [informal], for many a long day,
for life or a lifetime, for an age or ages,
for a coon's or dog's age [informal], for a
month of Sundays [informal], for donkey's years [Brit informal], **forever and a
day, for years on end;** all the year round,
all the day long, the livelong day, as the
day is long; morning, noon, and night;
hour after hour, day after day, month after month, year after year; day in day
out, month in month out, year in year
out; till hell freezes over [slang], till
you're blue in the face [informal], till the
cows come home [informal], till shrimps
learn to whistle [informal], till doomsday,
from now till doomsday, from here to
eternity, till the end of time; since time
began, long ago, long since, time out of
mind, time immemorial.

111. TRANSIENCE

(short duration)

.1 NOUNS **transience** or transiency, tran-
sientness, **impermanence** or imperma-
nency, transitoriness, changeableness
141, **mutability, instability, temporari-
ness,** fleetingness, momentariness; finitude; **ephemerality,** ephemeralness; evanescence, volatility, fugacity, **short-
livedness; mortality,** death, perishability,
corruptibility, caducity.

.2 **brevity, briefness,** shortness; swiftness 269,
fleetness.

.3 **short time, little while,** little, **instant, moment** 113.3, small space, span, spurt, **short
spell;** no time, less than no time; bit or
little bit, a breath, the wink of an eye,
pair of winks [informal]; **two shakes** or
two shakes of a lamb's tail [both infor-
mal].

.4 **transient, transient guest** or **boarder,** temporary lodger; **sojourner;** passer, passerby.

.5 **ephemeron,** ephemera [pl], **ephemeral;**
ephemerid, ephemeris, ephemerides [pl];
mayfly; **bubble, smoke;** nine days' wonder, flash in the pan; snows of yesteryear,
neiges d'antan [Fr].

.6 VERBS (be transient) flit, **fly,** fleet; pass,
pass away, vanish, evaporate, evanesce,
disappear, fade, melt, sink; fade like a
shadow or dream, vanish like a dream,
burst like a bubble, **go up in smoke,** melt
like snow.

.7 ADJS **transient, transitory,** transitive; **temporary,** temporal; **impermanent,** unendur-
ing, undurable, nondurable, nonperma-
nent; frail, brittle, fragile, insubstantial;
changeable 141.6, **mutable, unstable,** inconstant 141.7; capricious, fickle, impulsive, impetuous; **short-lived, ephemeral,**
fly-by-night, evanescent, volatile, **momentary;** deciduous; **passing,** fleeting, flitting,
flying, fading, dying; fugitive, fugacious;
perishable, mortal, corruptible; "as transient as the clouds" [Robert Green Inger-
soll], here today and gone tomorrow.

.8 **brief, short,** quick, brisk, swift 269.19, fleet, speedy, "short and sweet" [Thomas Lodge]; meteoric, cometary, flashing, flickering; short-term, short-termed.

.9 ADVS **temporarily,** for the moment, for the time, *pro tempore* [L], pro tem, for the nonce, **for the time being,** for a time, awhile.

.10 **transiently,** fleetingly, flittingly, flickeringly, **briefly, shortly,** swiftly 269.21, quickly, **for a little while,** for a short time; **momentarily,** for a moment; **in an instant** 113.7.

.11 PHRS "all flesh is grass" [Bible].

112. PERPETUITY

(endless duration)

.1 NOUNS **perpetuity,** perpetualness; **eternity,** eternalness, sempiternity, infinite duration; everness, foreverness, **everlastingness, permanence** 140, ever-duringness, durability 110, perdurability, indestructibility; **constancy,** stability, immutability, continuance, continualness, perennialness *or* perenniality, **ceaselessness,** unceasingness, incessancy; timelessness 106; **endlessness,** never-endingness, **interminability; infinity** 104; coeternity.

.2 **forever, an eternity,** endless time, **time without end;** "a moment standing still for ever" [James Montgomery], "a short parenthesis in a long period" [Donne], "deserts of vast eternity" [Andrew Marvell].

.3 **immortality,** eternal life, **deathlessness,** imperishability, undyingness, incorruptibility *or* incorruption, athanasy *or* athanasia; eternal youth, fountain of youth.

.4 **perpetuation,** preservation, eternalization, immortalization; eternal re-creation, eternal return *or* recurrence, steady-state universe.

.5 VERBS **perpetuate, preserve,** preserve from oblivion, keep fresh *or* alive, perennialize, **eternalize,** eternize, **immortalize;** monumentalize; freeze, embalm.

.6 **last** *or* endure forever, **go on forever,** go on and on, live forever, **have no end,** have no limits *or* bounds *or* term, never cease *or* end *or* die *or* pass.

.7 ADJS **perpetual, everlasting,** everliving, ever-being, ever-abiding, ever-during, ever-durable, permanent 140.7, perdurable, indestructible; **eternal,** sempiternal, eterne [archaic], **infinite** 104.3, olamic, aeonian; dateless, ageless, timeless, immemorial; **endless,** unending, never-ending,

without end, **interminable,** nonterminous, nonterminating; **continual,** continuous, steady, **constant, ceaseless,** nonstop, unceasing, never-ceasing, **incessant,** unremitting, unintermitting, uninterrupted, "continuous as the stars that shine" [Wordsworth]; coeternal.

.8 **perennial,** indeciduous, **evergreen,** sempervirent, ever-new; ever-blooming, ever-bearing.

.9 **immortal,** everlasting, **deathless,** undying, never-dying, **imperishable,** incorruptible, amaranthine; fadeless, **unfading,** never-fading, ever-fresh; frozen, embalmed.

.10 ADVS **perpetually,** in perpetuity, **everlastingly, eternally, permanently** 140.9, perennially, perdurably, indestructibly, **constantly,** continually, steadily, **ceaselessly,** unceasingly, never-ceasingly, **incessantly,** never-endingly, **endlessly,** unendingly, **interminably,** without end, world without end, time without end, "from everlasting to everlasting" [Bible]; **infinitely,** *ad infinitum* [L] 104.4.

.11 **always, all along, all the time,** all the while, at all times, *semper et ubique* [L, always and everywhere]; **ever and always, invariably,** without exception, never otherwise, *semper eadem* [L, ever the same; Elizabeth I].

.12 **forever, forevermore, for ever and ever,** forever and aye; forever and a day [informal], now and forever, *ora e sempre* [Ital], "yesterday and today and forever" [Bible]; **ever, evermore,** ever and anon, ever and again; aye, for aye; **for good,** for keeps [informal], for good and all, for all time; throughout the ages, from age to age, in all ages, "for ages of ages" [Douay Bible]; **to the end of time,** till time stops *or* runs out, "to the last syllable of recorded time" [Shakespeare], to the crack of doom, to the last trumpet, till doomsday; till you're blue in the face [informal], till hell freezes over [slang], till the cows come home [informal].

.13 **for life,** for all one's natural life, for the term of one's days, while life endures, while one draws breath, in all one's born days [informal]; from the cradle to the grave, from the womb to the tomb; **till death,** till death do us part.

113. INSTANTANEOUSNESS

(imperceptible duration)

.1 NOUNS **instantaneousness** *or* instantaneity, momentariness, **momentaneousness,**

immediateness or immediacy; simultaneity 118.

.2 **suddenness, abruptness,** precipitateness or precipitatousness, precipitance or precipitancy; **unexpectedness,** unanticipation, inexpectation 540.

.3 **instant, moment, second,** sec [informal], split second, millisecond, microsecond, half a second, half a mo [Brit informal], minute, **trice,** twinkle, **twinkling, twinkling** or **twinkle of an eye,** twink, **wink,** bat of an eye [informal], flash, crack, tick, stroke, coup, breath, twitch; two shakes or shake or half a shake, **jiffy** or jiff or half a jiffy [all informal].

.4 ADJS **instantaneous,** instant, momentary, momentaneous, **immediate,** presto, quick as thought or lightning; lightning-like.

.5 **sudden, abrupt,** precipitant, **precipitate, precipitous; hasty,** headlong, impulsive, impetuous; speedy, swift, quick; **unexpected** 540.10, unanticipated, unpredicted, unforeseen, unlooked-for; **surprising** 540.11, startling, electrifying, shocking, nerve-shattering.

.6 ADVS **instantly,** instanter, momentaneously, momentarily, momently, **instantaneously, immediately; on the instant,** on the spot, on the dot [informal], on the nail, in half a mo [Brit informal]; just then, just now.

.7 **in an instant, in a trice, in a second,** in a moment, in a bit or little bit, in a jiff or jiffy or half a jiffy [informal], in a flash, in a wink [informal], in a twink, **in a twinkling, in the twinkling of an eye,** in two shakes or a shake or half a shake [informal], in two shakes of a lamb's tail [informal], before you can say 'Jack Robinson' [informal]; **in no time,** in less than no time, in nothing flat [informal], in short order; at the drop of a hat or handkerchief, like a shot, like a shot out of hell [slang]; with the speed of light.

.8 **at once,** at once and on the spot, **then and there,** now, **right now, right away, right off,** straightway, straightaway, forthwith, this minute, this very minute, **without delay,** without the least delay, in a hurry [informal], pronto [Sp], subito [Ital]; **simultaneously** 118.6, at the same instant, in the same breath; **all at once,** all together, at one time, at a stroke, at one stroke, at a blow, at one blow, at one swoop, "at one fell swoop" [Shakespeare]; at one jump, per saltum [L], uno saltu [L].

.9 **suddenly,** sudden, of a sudden, on a sud-

den, **all of a sudden, all at once:** abruptly, sharp; **precipitously** or precipitately, precipitantly, impulsively, impetuously, hastily; dash; smack, bang, slap, plop, plunk, plump, pop; **unexpectedly** 540.14, on short notice, without notice or warning, unawares, **surprisingly** 540.15, startlingly, like a thunderbolt or thunderclap, like a flash, like a bolt from the blue.

.10 PHRS no sooner said than done.

114. MEASUREMENT OF TIME

.1 NOUNS **chronology,** timekeeping, timing, clocking, horology, **chronometry,** horometry, chronoscopy; watch- or clock-making; calendar-making; dating, carbon-14 dating, dendrochronology.

.2 **time of day, time** 105, **the time; hour,** minute; stroke of the hour, time signal, bell.

.3 **standard time,** civil time, zone time, slow time [informal]; mean time, solar time, mean solar time, sidereal time, apparent time, local time; Greenwich time, Greenwich mean time or GMT, Eastern time, Central time, Mountain time, Pacific time; Atlantic time; Alaska time, Yukon time; daylight-saving time; fast time [informal], summer time [Brit]; **time zone.**

.4 **date,** point of time, time, day; postdate, antedate; datemark; date line, International Date Line.

.5 **epact,** annual epact, monthly or menstrual epact.

.6 **timepiece** 114.17, timekeeper, **timer, chronometer,** ship's watch; horologe, horologium; **clock,** Big Ben, ticker [informal], **watch,** turnip [slang]; watch or clock movement, clockworks, watchworks.

.7 **almanac,** The Old Farmer's Almanac, Ephemeris and Nautical Almanac, Information Please Almanac, Nautical Almanac, Poor Richard's Almanac, Reader's Digest Almanac, Whitaker's Almanack, World Almanac.

.8 **calendar,** calends; calendar stone, chronogram; astronomical calendar or almanac, ephemeris; perpetual calendar; Chinese calendar, church or ecclesiastical calendar, Cotsworth calendar, Gregorian calendar, Hebrew or Jewish calendar, Hindu calendar, international fixed calendar, Julian calendar, Muslim calendar, Republican or Revolutionary calendar, Roman calendar.

.9 **chronicle, chronology, register,** registry, record; **annals,** journal, diary; time sheet, time book, **log,** daybook; timecard, time ticket, clock card, check sheet; datebook; date slip; timetable; time schedule, time chart; time scale; time study, motion study, time and motion study.

.10 **chronologist,** chronologer, chronographer, horologist, horologer; watchmaker *or* clockmaker; timekeeper, timer; **chronicler,** annalist, diarist; calendar maker, calendarist.

.11 VERBS **time, fix** *or* **set the time,** mark the time; **keep time,** mark time, measure time, beat time; **clock** [informal].

.12 **punch the clock** *or* punch in *or* punch out, **time in, time out** [all informal]; ring in, ring out; clock in, clock out; check in, check out; check off.

.13 **date,** be dated, date at *or* from, bear date; fix *or* set the date, make a date; **predate,** backdate, antedate; **postdate; update,** bring up to date; datemark; date-stamp; dateline.

.14 chronologize, chronicle, calendar, intercalate.

.15 ADJS **chronologic(al),** temporal, timekeeping; **chronometric(al),** chronoscopic, chronographic(al), chronogrammatic(al), horologic(al), horometric(al), metronomic(al), calendric(al), intercalary *or* intercalated; dated; annalistic, diaristic; calendarial.

.16 ADVS **o'clock,** of the clock, by the clock; half past, half after [Brit]; a quarter of *or* to, a quarter past *or* after.

.17 **timepieces, clocks, watches**

alarm clock	metronome
alarm watch	pendule
astronomical clock	pendulum clock
atomic clock	pneumatic clock
box chronometer	pocket chronometer
calendar clock	pocket watch
calendar watch	program clock
chronograph	quartz-crystal clock
chronometer	repeater
chronopher	Riefler clock
chronoscope	sandglass
clepsydra	ship's watch
cuckoo clock	sidereal clock
dial	split-second watch
digital clock	stemwinder [informal]
digital watch	stop watch
egg glass	sundial
electric clock	telechron clock
electronic clock	telltale
gnomon	three-minute glass
grandfather clock	time ball
half-hour glass	time clock
half-minute glass	time lock
hourglass	time recorder
hunter	time switch
independent-seconds watch	traveling clock
isochronon	turret clock
journeyman	watchman's clock
marine chronometer	water clock
	wristwatch

115. ANACHRONISM

(false estimation or knowledge of time)

.1 NOUNS **anachronism,** chronological *or* historical error, **mistiming, misdating,** misdate, postdating, antedating; parachronism, metachronism, prochronism; prolepsis, anticipation; earliness, lateness, tardiness, unpunctuality.

.2 VERBS **mistime, misdate;** antedate, foredate, postdate; lag.

.3 ADJS **anachronous** *or* **anachronistic,** parachronistic, metachronistic, prochronistic; **mistimed, misdated;** antedated, foredated, postdated; ahead of time, **beforehand, early;** behind time, **behindhand, late,** unpunctual, tardy; **overdue,** past due; unseasonable, out of season; out of date, dated.

116. PRIORITY

(previous time)

.1 NOUNS **priority, previousness, earliness** 131, **antecedence** *or* **antecedency, anteriority, precedence** *or* **precedency** 64, precession; *status quo ante* [L], earlier state; preexistence; **anticipation,** predating, antedating; antedate; **past time** 119.

.2 antecedent, precedent, premise; forerunner, precursor 66, ancestor.

.3 VERBS **be prior,** be before *or* early *or* earlier, **precede, antecede,** precurse, **forerun,** come *or* go before; herald, usher in, proclaim, announce, **anticipate,** antedate, predate; preexist.

.4 ADJS **prior, previous, early** 131.7, **earlier,** *ci-devant* [Fr], **former,** fore, prime, first, **preceding** 292.3, precurrent, foregoing, anterior, **anticipatory,** antecedent; preexistent; older, elder, senior; ante– *or* anti–, fore–, pre–, pro–, prot(o)–, proter(o)–, supra–.

.5 **prewar,** ante-bellum, before the war; prerevolutionary; premundane *or* antemundane; prelapsarian, before the Fall; antediluvian, before the Flood; protohistoric, prehistoric 119.10; precultural; pre-Aryan; pre-Christian; premillenarian, premillennial; anteclassical, preclassical, pre-Roman, pre-Renaissance, preromantic, pre-Victorian.

.6 ADVS **previously, priorly, hitherto, heretofore,** theretofore; **before, early** 131.11, **earlier,** ere, erenow, ere then, or ever; already, yet; before all; **formerly** 119.13.

.7 PREPS **prior to, previous to, before,** in advance of, in anticipation of, in preparation for.

117. POSTERIORITY

(later time)

.1 NOUNS **posteriority, subsequence,** sequence, **succession, following** 293, **coming after, lateness** 132; provenience, supervenience, supervention; afterlife, next life; remainder 43, hangover [informal]; postdating; postdate; future time 121.

.2 sequel 67, **aftermath,** consequence, effect 154, conclusion 494.4; **posterity,** offspring, descendant, heir, **successor;** line, **lineage,** dynasty.

.3 VERBS **come** or **follow** or **go after, succeed,** replace, displace, overtake, supervene; **ensue,** issue, emanate, attend, result; follow up, trail, track, come close on or tread on the heels of, dog the footsteps of; step into the shoes of, take the place of.

.4 ADJS **subsequent, after, later,** posterior, **following, succeeding,** successive, sequent, lineal, consecutive, ensuing, attendant; junior, cadet, puisne, younger.

.5 **posthumous,** afterdeath; **postprandial,** postcibal, postcenal, after-dinner; **postwar,** *postbellum* [L], after the war; **postdiluvian,** postdiluvial, after the flood; postlapsarian, after the Fall; ep(i)– or eph–, infra–, meta–, post–.

.6 ADVS **subsequently, afterwards, after,** after that, after all, **later, next,** since; **thereafter,** thereon, thereupon, therewith, **then;** in the process or course of time, as things worked out, in the sequel; at a subsequent or later time, in the aftermath; *ex post facto* [L].

.7 **after which, on** or **upon which, whereupon,** whereon, whereat, whereto, whereunto, wherewith, wherefore, on, upon; hereinafter.

.8 PREPS **after, subsequent to,** later than, past, beyond, behind.

.9 PHRS *post hoc, ergo propter hoc* [L, after this, therefore on account of this].

118. SIMULTANEITY

.1 NOUNS **simultaneity** or **simultaneousness,** coincidence, concurrence, concomitance, coexistence; **contemporaneousness** or contemporaneity, coetaneousness or coetaneity, coevalness or coevalneity; unison; **synchronism,** synchronization; isochronism; accompaniment 73, agreement 26.

.2 **contemporary,** coeval, coexistent, concomitant; dead heat, draw, tie.

.3 VERBS **synchronize,** contemporize; coincide, concur, coexist, coextend; **accompany** 73.7, agree 26.6, match, go hand in hand, keep pace with, keep in step; isochronize, put or be in phase, be in time, time.

.4 ADJS **simultaneous, concurrent,** concomitant, collateral; coexistent, coexisting; **contemporaneous,** contemporary, coinstantaneous, coetaneous, coeval; coterminous, conterminous; unison, unisonous; isochronous, isochronal; coeternal; accompanying 73.9, agreeing 26.9.

.5 **synchronous,** synchronized, synchronal or synchronic, in sync [informal]; **in time,** in step, in tempo, in phase, with or on the beat.

.6 ADVS **simultaneously, concurrently,** coinstantaneously; **together,** all together, **at the same time,** at one and the same time, as one, as one man, in concert with, in chorus, with one voice, in unison, in a chorus, in the same breath; at one time, at a clip [informal]; synchronously, isochronously, in phase, in sync [informal], with or on the beat.

119. THE PAST

.1 NOUNS **the past,** past, foretime, former times, past times, times past, **days gone by, bygone times** or **days, yesterday, yesteryear,** recent past; history, past history; dead past, dead hand of the past; the years that are past, "the days that are no more" [Tennyson], "the irrevocable Past" [Longfellow], "thou unrelenting past" [William Cullen Bryant], "the eternal landscape of the past" [Tennyson].

.2 **old** or **olden times,** early times, **old days,** the olden time, times of old, **days of old, days** or **times of yore,** yore, yoretime, eld [archaic], good old times or days, lang syne or auld lang syne [both Scot], way back [informal], **long ago,** time out of mind, days beyond recall; old story, same old story.

.3 **antiquity, ancient times,** time immemorial, ancient history, remote age or time, remote or far or dim or **distant past,** distance of time, "the dark backward and abysm of time" [Shakespeare]; ancientness 123; archae(o)– or archeo–.

.4 **memory** 537, **remembrance, recollection, reminiscence, retrospection,** musing on the past, looking back; "the remembrance of things past" [Shakespeare], *"la recherche du temps perdu"* [Proust]; **reliving,** reexperiencing; revival 694.3; youth 124.

.5 [gram terms] past tense, preterit, perfect tense, past perfect tense, pluperfect, historical present tense, past progressive tense; aorist; perfective aspect; preterition.

.6 VERBS pass, be past, **be a thing of the past,** elapse, lapse, be gone, be dead and gone, be all over, have run its course, have run out, have had its day; **disappear** 447.2, die.

.7 ADJS **past, gone,** by, **gone-by, bygone,** gone glimmering, bypast, ago, **over,** departed, passed, passed away, elapsed, lapsed, vanished, dead, expired, run out, blown over, finished, forgotten, extinct, dead and buried, defunct, deceased, wound up, passé, obsolete, has-been, dated, antique, antiquated; no more, irrecoverable, never to return; archae(o)– or archeo–, ex–, pale(o)–, praeter– or preter–, retro–; –ed, y– [archaic].

.8 **reminiscent** 537.22, **retrospective, remembered** 537.23, recollected; relived, reexperienced; restored, revived.

.9 [gram terms] past, preterit or preteritive, pluperfect, past perfect; aorist, aoristic; perfective.

.10 **former,** past, fore, **previous,** late, recent, **once, onetime,** sometime, **erstwhile,** then, quondam; **prior** 116.4; **ancient, immemorial,** early, primitive, primeval, prehistoric; **old,** olden.

.11 **foregoing,** aforegoing, **preceding** 64.4; last, latter.

.12 **back,** backward, into the past; early; retrospective, retroactive, ex post facto [L], a priori [L].

.13 ADVS **formerly, previously, priorly** 116.6; **earlier, before,** before now, erenow, erst, whilom, erewhile, **hitherto, heretofore,** aforetime, beforetime, **in the past,** in times past; then; **yesterday,** only yesterday, recently; **historically,** prehistorically, in historic or prehistoric times.

.14 **once,** once upon a time, one day, one fine morning, time was.

.15 **ago, since,** gone by; back, back when; backward, to or into the past; **retrospectively,** reminiscently, retroactively.

.16 **long ago,** long since, **a long while or time ago,** some time ago or since, some time back, a way or away back [informal], ages ago, **years ago,** donkey's years ago [Brit informal]; **in times past,** in times gone by, in the old days, in the good old days; **anciently,** of old, of yore, in ancient times, in olden times, in the olden time,

in days of yore, early, in the memory of man, time out of mind.

.17 **since,** ever since, until now; **since long ago, long since,** from away back [informal], since days of yore, ages ago, **from time immemorial,** from time out of mind, aeons ago, since the world was made, since the world was young, since time began, since the year one, since Hector was a pup or since God knows when [both slang].

120. THE PRESENT

.1 NOUNS **the present,** present, presentness, the present juncture or occasion, the present hour or moment, this instant or second or moment, **the present day or time,** the present age, "the living sum-total of the whole Past" [Carlyle]; **today,** this day, **this day and age; this point,** this stage, this hour, **now,** nowadays, the now, the way things are, the nonce, **the time being; the times,** our times, these days; contemporaneousness, contemporaneity, nowness, **newness** 122, modernity; the Now Generation; historical present, present tense [both gram].

.2 ADJS **present, immediate,** instant, immanent, **latest, current,** running, extant, existent, **existing,** actual, being, that is, as is, that be; **present-day,** present-time, present-age, **modern** 122.13; topical; **contemporary,** contemporaneous; up-to-date, up-to-the-minute, fresh, new.

.3 ADVS **now, at present, at this point,** at this juncture, on the present occasion, **at this time,** at this time of day, at this moment or instant, at the present time, "upon this bank and shoal of time" [Shakespeare]; **today,** this day, in these days, **in this day and age,** in our time, **nowadays;** this night, **tonight;** here, hereat, **here and now,** hic et nunc [L], even now, but now, **just now,** as of now, as things are; on the spot; for the nonce, for the time being; for this occasion.

.4 **until now,** till now, **hereunto,** heretofore, until this time, by this time, **up to now,** up to the present, up to this time, to this day, **so far,** thus far, **as yet, to date,** yet, already, still, now or then as previously.

121. THE FUTURE

.1 NOUNS **the future,** future, futurity, imminence 152, posteriority 117, eventuality 151.1, **hereafter,** aftertime, afteryears, **time to come;** the morrow, **tomorrow,** mañana [Sp], time just ahead, **immediate** *or* **near future,** immediate prospect, offing; remote *or* deep *or* distant future; **by-and-by,** the sweet by-and-by [informal]; time ahead, course ahead, **prospect,** outlook, expectation, project, probability, prediction, forward look, foresight, prophecy, crystal ball; what is to be *or* come; determinism; future tense; futurism; the womb of time, "the past again, entered through another gate" [Pinero], "the never-ending flight of future days" [Milton].

.2 **destiny** 640.2, **fate;** what bodes *or* looms, what is fated *or* destined *or* doomed, what is in the books; **the hereafter,** the great hereafter, "the good hereafter" [Whittier], a better place, Paradise, Heaven, **afterworld,** otherworld, **next world,** world to come, life *or* world beyond the grave, **the beyond,** the great beyond, the unknown, the great unknown, **the grave,** home, abode *or* world of the dead, eternal home; "They are all gone into the world of light!" [Henry Vaughn], "the great world of light, that lies behind all human destinies" [Longfellow]; **afterlife, postexistence,** future state, **life to come,** life after death.

.3 **doomsday,** doom, day of doom, crack of doom, trumpet *or* trump of doom; **Judgment Day,** Day of Judgment, the Judgment; eschatology, last things, **last days.**

.4 **futurity,** futureness; ultimateness, eventuality, finality.

.5 **advent, coming, approach of time,** time drawing on.

.6 VERBS **come,** come on, **approach,** near, **draw on** *or* **near,** await, stare one in the face; be to be *or* come; be fated *or* destined *or* doomed, be in the books, be in the cards; loom, threaten, be imminent 152.2; lie ahead *or* in one's course; project, plot, plan, predict, expect, foresee, foretell, prophesy; hope, anticipate, look for, look forward to.

.7 **postexist,** live on, survive.

.8 ADJS **future, later,** hereafter; **coming, forthcoming, imminent** 152.3, approaching, nearing, **prospective; eventual** 151.11, ultimate, to-be, **to come; projected,** plotted, planned, looked- *or* hoped-for, desired, emergent, **predicted,** prophesied, probable, extrapolated; determined, fatal, fatidic, fated, destinal, destined; eschatological; futuristic.

.9 ADVS **in the future,** in aftertime, **afterward** *or* afterwards, **later,** at a later time, after a time *or* while, anon; **by and by,** in

the sweet by-and-by [informal]; **tomorrow,** *mañana* [Sp], the day after tomorrow; *proximo* [L], prox., **in the near** *or* **immediate future,** just around the corner, **imminently** 152.4, **soon, before long;** probably, predictably, hopefully; fatally, by destiny *or* necessity.

.10 in future, **hereafter,** hereinafter, thereafter, **henceforth, henceforward** *or* henceforwards, thence, **thenceforth,** thenceforward *or* thenceforwards, from this time forward, from this point, from this *or* that time, from then on, **from here** *or* **now on, from now on in** [informal], from here in *or* out [informal], from this moment on.

.11 **in time, in due time,** in due season *or* course, all in good time, **in the fullness of time,** in God's good time, in the course *or* process of time, **eventually** 151.12, **ultimately,** in the long run.

.12 **sometime,** somewhen, **someday, some of these days,** one of these days, some fine day *or* morning, one fine day *or* morning, some sweet day, sometime *or* other, **sooner or later,** when all is said and done.

.13 PREPS **about to,** at *or* **on the point of,** on the eve of, on the brink *or* verge of, near to, close upon, in the act of.

122. NEWNESS

.1 NOUNS **newness,** freshness, maidenhood, dewiness, pristineness, mint condition, new-mintedness, newbornness, virginity, intactness, greenness, immaturity, rawness, callowness, brand-newness; presentness, nowness; **recentness,** recency, lateness; **novelty,** novelness, gloss of novelty, newfangledness *or* newfangleness; originality; **uncommonness,** unusualness, strangeness, unfamiliarity.

.2 **novelty, innovation,** newfangled device *or* contraption [informal], **new** *or* **latest wrinkle** [informal], **the last word** *or* **the latest thing** [both informal], *dernier cri* [Fr]; what's happening, what's in, the in thing [all informal]; new look, latest fashion *or* fad; advance guard, vanguard, **avant-garde.**

.3 **modernity,** modernness; modernism; modernization, updating, *aggiornamento* [Ital].

.4 **modern,** modern man; modernist; modernizer; neologist, neoterist, neology, neologism, neoterism, neoteric; modern *or* rising *or* new generation; neonate, fledgling, stripling, *novus homo* [L], new man, upstart, arriviste, *nouveau riche* [Fr], parvenu; Young Turk, bright young man, comer [informal].

.5 VERBS innovate, invent, coin, new-mint, mint, inaugurate, neologize, neoterize; renew, renovate 694.17.

.6 modernize, streamline; update, bring up to date, move with the times.

.7 ADJS new, young, neoteric, ne(o)–, nov-(o)–; fresh, fresh as a daisy, fresh as the morning dew; unused, firsthand, original; untried, untouched, unhandled, unhandseled, untrodden, unbeaten; virgin, virginal, intact, maiden, maidenly; green, vernal; dewy, pristine, ever-new, sempervirent, evergreen; immature, undeveloped, raw, callow, fledgling, unfledged, nestling.

.8 fresh, additional, further, other, another; renewed.

.9 new-made, new-built, new-wrought, new-shaped, new-mown, new-minted, new-coined, uncirculated, in mint condition, mint, new-begotten, new-grown, new-laid; newborn, new-fledged; new-model, late-model, like new, factory-new.

.10 [informal terms] brand-new, fire-new, brand-spanking new, spanking, spanking new; just out, hot off the fire or griddle or spit, hot off the press; newfangled or newfangle.

.11 novel, original, unique, different; strange, unusual, uncommon; unfamiliar, unheard-of.

.12 recent, late, newly come, of yesterday; latter, later; cen(o)– or caen(o)–, –cene.

.13 modern, contemporary, present-day, present-time, twentieth-century; now [informal], newfashioned, fashionable, modish, mod, à la mode [Fr], up-to-date, up-to-datish, up-to-the-minute, in, abreast of the times; advanced, progressive, forward-looking, avant-garde; ultramodern, ultra-ultra, ahead of its time, far out, way out, modernistic, modernized, streamlined.

.14 newest, latest, last, most recent, newest of the new, farthest out.

•.15 ADVS newly, freshly, new, anew, once more, from the ground up, from scratch [informal], ab ovo [L], de novo [L], afresh, again; as new.

.16 now, recently, lately, latterly, of late, not long ago, a short time ago, the other day, only yesterday; just now, right now [informal].

123. OLDNESS

.1 NOUNS oldness, age, eld [archaic], hoary eld; elderliness, seniority, senility, old age 126.5; ancientness, antiquity, dust of ages, rust or cobwebs of antiquity; venerableness, eldership, primogeniture, great or hoary age, "the ancient and honourable" [Bible], inveteracy; old order, old style, ancien régime [Fr]; primitiveness, primordialism or primordiality, aboriginality; atavism.

.2 tradition, custom, common law, immemorial usage; Sunna [Muslim]; Talmud, Mishnah [both Jewish], ancient wisdom, ways of the fathers; traditionalism or traditionality; myth, mythology, legend, lore, folklore, folktale, folk motif; racial memory, archetypal myth or image or pattern, "Spiritus Mundi" [Yeats].

.3 antiquation, superannuation, staleness, disuse; old-fashionedness, unfashionableness, out-of-dateness; old-fogyishness, fogyishness, stuffiness, stodginess, fuddy-duddiness.

.4 antiquarianism; classicism, medievalism, Pre-Raphaelitism, longing or yearning or nostalgia for the past; archaeology 123.22; archaism.

.5 antiquarian, antiquary, laudator temporis acti [L], dryasdust, the Rev. Dr. Dryasdust, Jonathan Oldbuck [both Sir Walter Scott], Herr Teufelsdröckh [Carlyle]; archaeologist 123.23; classicist, medievalist, Miniver Cheevy [E. A. Robinson], Pre-Raphaelite; antique dealer, antique collector, antique-car collector; archaist.

.6 antiquity, antique, archaism; relic, relic of the past, reliquiae [pl]; remains, survival, vestige, ruin or ruins; fossil, –ite, necr(o)–, oryct(o)–; petrification, petrified wood, petrified forest; artifact, eolith, mezzolith, microlith, neolith, paleolith, plateaulith; cave painting, petroglyph; ancient manuscript 602.11.

.7 ancient, man of old, prehistoric man 123.25; preadamite, antediluvian; anthropoid, humanoid, primate, fossil man, protohuman, prehuman, missing link, apeman, hominid, Hominidae [pl]; primitive, aboriginal, aborigine, bushman, autochthon; caveman, cave dweller, troglodyte; Stone Age man, Bronze Age man, Iron Age man.

.8 (antiquated person) back number [informal]; pop or pops or dad [all informal], dodo or old dodo [both informal]; fossil or antique or relic [all informal]; mossback [informal], longhair *or* square [both informal], **mid-Victorian,** antediluvian; old liner, old believer, conservative, traditionalist, reactionary; has-been; fogy, **old fogy,** regular old fogy, old poop *or* crock [informal], **fud** *or* **fuddy-duddy** [both informal]; granny [informal], **old woman,** matriarch; **old man,** patriarch, elder, *starets* [Russ], old-timer [informal], Methuselah.

.9 VERBS **age,** grow old 126.10; **antiquate,** fossilize, date, **superannuate,** outdate; obsolesce, go out of use *or* style, molder, fust, rust, fade, perish, lose currency *or* novelty; become obsolete *or* extinct; belong to the past, be a thing of the past.

.10 ADJS **old, age-old,** auld [Scot], olden [archaic], old-time; **ancient, antique,** venerable, hoary; archae(o)– *or* archeo–, eo–, pale(o)–, proto–; of old, of yore; dateless, timeless, ageless; **immemorial,** old as Methuselah *or* Adam, old as history, old as time, old as the hills; **elderly** 126.16.

.11 primitive, prime, **primeval,** primogenial, primordial, pristine, atavistic; **aboriginal,** autochthonous; primoprimitive; ancestral, patriarchal; **prehistoric,** protohistoric, preglacial, preadamite, antepatriarchal; prehuman, protohuman, humanoid.

.12 traditional; mythological, heroic; **legendary,** unwritten, oral, handed down; trueblue, tried and true; **prescriptive, customary,** conventional, understood, admitted, recognized, acknowledged, received; **hallowed, time-honored,** immemorial; **venerable,** hoary, worshipful; **long-standing, of long standing,** long-established, established, fixed, inveterate, rooted; folk, of the folk.

.13 antiquated, grown old, **superannuated, antique,** archaic, age-encrusted, of other times, old-world; Victorian, mid-Victorian; classical, medieval, Gothic; antediluvian; fossil, fossilized, petrified.

.14 stale, fusty, musty, rusty, dusty, moldy, mildewed; **worn, timeworn,** time-scarred; **moth-eaten,** moss-grown, crumbling, moldering, gone to seed, dilapidated, ruined, ruinous.

.15 obsolete, passé, extinct, gone out, **dated, out,** out of style *or* use, gone-by, dead, disused, past, run out, **outworn.**

.16 old-fashioned, oldfangled, old-timey [informal], **out-of-date, dated,** outdated, **outmoded,** out of fashion, out of season, **unfashionable,** styleless, **behind the times,** of the old school, old hat [infor-

mal], **back-number** [informal], black-letter, has-been [informal].

.17 old-fogyish, fogyish, old-fogy; fuddy-duddy, **stuffy, stodgy;** senile, bent *or* wracked *or* ravaged with age.

.18 secondhand, used, worn, **unnew,** not new, pawed-over; hand-me-down *or* reach-me-down [both informal].

.19 older, senior, Sr., major, elder; **oldest,** eldest; first-born, firstling, primogenitary; former 119.10.

.20 archaeological, paleological; antiquarian; paleolithic, eolithic, neolithic, mezzolithic.

.21 ADVS anciently 119.16.

.22 archaeology

Assyriology	paleohistology
Egyptology	paleohydrography
epigraphy	paleolatry
fossilology	paleolimnology
human paleontology	paleolithy
micropaleontology	paleology
palaeography	paleomammology
palaeosophy	paleometeorology
palaeotypography	paleontography
palaetiology	paleontology
paleethnology	paleopathology
paleoanthropography	paleophysiography
paleoanthropology	paleophysiology
paleobiogeography	paleophytology
paleobiology	paleopotamology
paleobotany	paleopsychology
paleochorology	paleornithology
paleoclimatology	paleozoology
paleocosmology	prehistoric anthropology
paleodendrology	prehistoric archaeology
paleoecology	
paleoeremology	prehistory
paleoethnography	protohistory
paleoethnology	Sumerology
paleogeography	underwater archaeology
paleoglaciology	
paleography	
paleoherpetology	

.23 archaeologists

Assyriologist	paleographer, paleographist
Egyptologist	
epigrapher, epigraphist	paleoherpetologist
fossilologist	paleolithist
palaeotypographist	paleologist
palaetiologist	paleomammologist
paleethnographer	paleometeorologist
paleethnologist	paleontologist
paleoanthropologist	paleophysiologist
paleobiologist	paleophytologist
paleobotanist	paleornithologist
paleochorologist	paleozoologist
paleoclimatologist	prehistorian
paleodentrologist	protohistorian
paleoecologist	Sumerologist
paleoethnologist	underwater archaeologist
paleoglaciologist	

.24 Stone Age cultures

Acheulean	Azilian
Aurignacian	Chellean

Combe-Capelle	Neolithic
Cro-Magnon	Paleolithic
Eolithic	Pre-Chellean
Magdalenian	Solutrean
Mousterian	

.25 prehistoric men and manlike primates

Aurignacian man	Java man
Australanthropus	Meganthropus
Australopithecus	Neanderthal man
Brünn race	neolithic man
caveman	Oreopithecus
Cro-Magnon man	paleolithic man
Dawn man (the Pilt-	Paranthropus
down hoax)	Peking man
eolithic man	Piltdown man (hoax)
Florisbad man	Pithecanthropus
Furfooz or Grenelle	Plesianthropus
man	Rhodesian man
Galley Hill man	Sinanthropus
Gigantopithecus	Stone Age man
Grimaldi man	Swanscombe man
Heidelberg man	Zinjanthropus

.26 prehistoric animals (including types of dinosaurs)

allosaur(us)	hesperornis
ammonite	hoplophoneus
anatosaur(us)	hyaenodon
ankylosaur(us)	hyracodont
apatosaur(us)	hyracothere
archaeohippus	ichthyornis
archaeopteryx	ichthyosaur(us)
archaeornis	iguanodon(t)
archaeotherium	imperial mammoth or
archelon	elephant
arthrodiran	labyrinthodont
atlantosaur(us)	machairodont
aurochs	mammoth
bothriolepis	mastodon
brachiosaur(us)	megalosaur(us)
brontops	megathere
brontosaur(us)	merodus
brontothere	merychippus
camarasaur(us)	merycoidodon
ceratopsid	merycopotamus
ceratosaur(us)	mesohippus
cetiosaur(us)	miacis
coccostean	mosasaurus
coelodont	nummulite
compsognathus	ornithomimid
coryphodon	ornithopod
cotylosaur	ostracoderm
creodont	palaeodictyopteron
crossopterygian	palaeomastodon
cynodictis	palaeoniscid
diatryma	palaeophis
dimetrodon	palaeosaur
dinichthyid	palaeospondylus
dinothere	pelycosaur
diplodocus	phytosaur
dipnoan	plesiosaur(us)
duck-billed dinosaur	protoceratops
edaphosaurid	protohippus
elasmosaur(us)	protylopus
eohippus	pteranodon
eryopsid	pteraspid
eurypterid	pterichthys
giant sloth	pterodactyl, pterosaur
glyptodont	rhamphorhynchus
gorgosaur(us)	saber-toothed tiger or
hadrosaur(us)	cat

sauropod	titanosaur(us)
scelidosaur(us)	titanothere
smilodon	trachodon
stegocephalian	triceratops
stegodon	trilobite
stegosaur(us)	tyrannosaur(us)
struthiomimus	uintathere
teleoceras	urus
therapsid	woolly or northern
theriodont	mammoth
theropod	

124. YOUTH

.1 NOUNS **youth**, youthhood, youthhead [Scot], **youthfulness**, youthiness [Scot], **juvenility**, juvenescence, **youngness**, tenderness, tender age, early years, school age, *jeunesse* [Fr], prime of life, flower of life, salad days, springtime *or* springtide of life, seedtime of life, flowering time, bloom, florescence, budtime, "the very May-morn of his youth" [Shakespeare], "the summer of your youth" [Edward Moore], "the red sweet wine of youth" [Rupert Brooke], golden season of life, "the glad season of life" [Carlyle], heyday of youth *or* of the blood, young blood, "my burning youth" [Yeats], "my green age" [Dylan Thomas].

.2 **childhood**, "childhood's careless days" [William Cullen Bryant]; **boyhood**; **girlhood**, maidenhood *or* maidenhead; puppyhood, calfhood; subteens, pre-teens.

.3 **immaturity**, **undevelopment**, inexperience, **callowness**, **unripeness**, greenness, rawness, sappiness, freshness, juiciness, dewiness; **minority**, juniority, infancy, nonage.

.4 **childishness**, childlikeness, **puerility**; **boyishness**, boylikeness; **girlishness**, girllikeness, maidenliness.

.5 **infancy**, **babyhood**, incunabula, the cradle, the nursery, "my Angel-infancy" [Henry Vaughn].

.6 **adolescence**, maturescence, pubescence, **puberty**; nubility.

.7 **teens**, teen age, **awkward age**, age of growing pains [informal].

.8 VERBS make young, youthen; **rejuvenate**, reinvigorate.

.9 ADJS **young**, youngling, **juvenile**, juvenal, juvenescent, **youthful**, youthy [Scot], youthlike, in the flower *or* bloom of youth, florescent, flowering; "towering in confidence of twenty one" [Samuel Johnson].

.10 **immature**, unadult, impubic, inexperienced; unseasoned, unfledged, newfledged, **callow**, **unripe**, ripening, unmellowed, **raw**, **green**, vernal, primaveral, dewy, juicy, sappy, budding, tender, virginal, intact, innocent, naïve, ingenuous, **undeveloped,** growing, unformed, unlicked, not dry behind the ears; **minor,** underage.

.11 **childish,** childlike, kiddish [informal], **puerile; boyish,** boylike, beardless; **girlish,** girllike, maiden, maidenly; puppyish, puppylike, puplike, calflike, coltish, coltlike.

.12 **infant,** infantine, **infantile; babyish,** babish, baby; dollish, doll-like; kittenish, kittenlike; **newborn,** neonatal; in the cradle or crib or nursery, in swaddling clothes, in diapers, in nappies [Brit], in arms, at the breast.

.13 **adolescent,** maturescent, pubescent, hebe–; nubile.

.14 **teen-age,** teen-aged, teenish, **in one's teens;** sweet sixteen [slang].

.15 **junior,** Jr.; **younger,** puisne.

.16 PHRS "Young men are fitter to invent than to judge" [Francis Bacon]; "To be young is to be one of the Immortals" [W. C. Hazlitt], "To be young was very Heaven!" [Wordsworth].

125. YOUNGSTER

.1 NOUNS **youngster,** young person, **youth, juvenile,** youngling, young'un [dial], juvenal [archaic]; **stripling,** slip, sprig, sapling; fledgling; hopeful, young hopeful; **minor,** infant; **adolescent,** pubescent; **teenager,** teener, teenybopper [informal]; junior, younger, youngest, baby; –ling.

.2 **young people, youth,** young, **younger generation,** rising or new generation, young blood, young fry [informal], ragazze [Ital]; **children,** tots, childkind; small fry, **kids, little kids,** little guys [all informal]; boyhood, girlhood; babyhood.

.3 **child,** ped(o)– or paed(o)–, bairn [Scot]; nipper, **kid** [informal], **little one,** little fellow or guy, little bugger [slang], shaver or little shaver [both informal], little squirt [slang], **tot, little tot,** wee tot, peewee, tad or little tad, mite, chit [informal]; innocent, little innocent; darling, cherub, lamb, lambkin, kitten, **offspring** 171.3.

.4 **brat,** urchin; **minx, imp,** puck, elf, gamin, little monkey, **whippersnapper,** young whippersnapper, enfant terrible [Fr], little terror, holy terror; spoiled brat; snotnose kid [slang]; juvenile delinquent, JD [slang]; punk, punk kid [both slang].

.5 **boy, lad,** laddie, **youth,** manchild, young man, garçon [Fr], muchacho [Sp], fledg-

ling, hobbledehoy; fellow 420.5; pup, puppy, whelp, cub, colt; master; sonny, sonny boy; bud or buddy [both informal]; bub or bubba [both informal]; buck, young buck; schoolboy.

.6 **girl,** girlie [informal], **maid, maiden,** lass, girlchild, **lassie,** young thing, young creature, **damsel,** damoiselle, demoiselle, jeune fille [Fr], mademoiselle [Fr], muchacha [Sp], miss, missy, little missy, slip, wench [dial or slang], colleen; **gal,** dame, **chick,** tomato, **babe** or baby, **broad,** frail, **doll,** skirt, jill, cutie, filly, heifer [all slang]; **schoolgirl,** schoolmaid, schoolmiss, junior miss, subteen, subteener; subdebutante, subdeb [informal]; bobbysoxer [informal], teenybopper [informal], **tomboy,** hoyden, romp; piece [slang], nymphet; virgin.

.7 **infant, baby, babe,** bambino [Ital], little darling or angel or doll or cherub, bouncing baby, puling infant, mewling infant, babykins [informal], baby bunting; papoose; **toddler; suckling,** nursling, fosterling, weanling; neonate; yearling, yearold; premature baby, preemie [informal], incubator baby; preschooler.

.8 (animals) **fledgling,** birdling, nestling; **chick,** chicky, chickling; **pullet,** fryer; **duckling;** gosling; **kitten,** kit, catling; **pup,** puppy, whelp; **cub; calf,** dogie, weaner; **colt,** foal, piglet, pigling, shoat; **lamb,** lambkin; kid, yeanling; fawn; **tadpole,** polliwog; litter, nest 171.2.

.9 (plants) **sprout, seedling,** set; sucker, shoot, slip; **twig,** sprig, scion, sapling.

.10 (insects) **larva, chrysalis,** aurelia, **cocoon,** pupa; nymph, nympha; wriggler, wiggler; caterpillar, maggot, grub.

126. AGE

(time of life)

.1 NOUNS **age,** years, "the days of our years", "measure of my days" [both Bible], "slow-consuming age" [Thomas Gray], "a tyrant, which forbids the pleasures of youth on pain of death" [La Rochefoucauld].

.2 **maturity, adulthood, majority,** adultness, grown-upness, fullgrownness, mature age, legal age, voting age, driving age, drinking age, legalis homo [L]; age of consent; ripe age, riper years, full age or growth or bloom, flower of age, prime, prime of life, age of responsibility, age or years of discretion, age of matured powers; **manhood,** man's estate, virility, toga virilis

[L], manhood; **womanhood**, womanli-hood.

.3 **seniority**, eldership, deanship, primogeniture.

.4 **middle age**, middle life, meridian of life, the middle years, the wrong side of forty, the dangerous age.

.5 **old age**, oldness, eld [archaic], **elderliness**, senectitude, advanced age *or* years; geront(o)-, presby(o)-; superannuation, pensionable age, age of retirement; **ripe old age**, the golden years, senior citizenship, hoary age, gray *or* white hairs, vale of years, crabbed age, "an incurable disease" [Seneca]; **decline of life**, declining years, "the downward slope" [Seneca], the shady side [informal]; "the sere, the yellow leaf", "the silver livery of advised age" [both Shakespeare], "a crown of glory" [Bible]; sunset *or* twilight *or* evening *or* autumn *or* winter of one's days; **decrepitude**, ricketiness, infirm old age, infirmity of age, infirmity, debility, caducity, feebleness; dotage, second childhood; senility 469.10, anility; green *or* hale old age, longevity.

.6 **maturation**, maturescence, development, mellowing, ripening, seasoning, tempering; **aging**, senescence.

.7 **change of life**, menopause, climacteric, grand climacteric.

.8 **geriatrics**, gerontology.

.9 VERBS **mature**, **grow up**, grow, develop, ripen, mellow, season, temper; flower, bloom; fledge, leave the nest, **come of age**, come to maturity, attain majority, **reach one's majority**, reach twenty-one, reach voting age, reach the age of consent, reach manhood *or* womanhood, write oneself a man, come to *or* into man's estate, put on long trousers *or* pants, assume the *toga virilis*, come into years of discretion, be in the prime of life, cut one's wisdom teeth *or* eyeteeth [informal], have sown one's wild oats, settle down; put up one's hair, not be in pigtails.

.10 **age**, **grow old**, get on *or* along, **get on** *or* **along in years**, turn gray *or* white; **decline**, wane, fade, fail, sink, waste away; **dodder**, totter, shake; wither, wrinkle, shrivel, wizen; **live to a ripe old age**, cheat the undertaker [informal]; be in one's dotage *or* second childhood.

.11 **have had one's day**, have seen one's day *or* best days, **have seen better days**; **show one's age**, show marks of age, have one foot in the grave.

.12 ADJS **adult**, **mature**, **old**, **of age**, out of one's teens, big, grown, **grown-up**; old enough to know better; **marriageable**, of marriageable age, marriable, nubile; maturescent.

.13 **mature**, **ripe**, of full *or* ripe age, **developed**, fully developed, **full-grown**, full-fledged, full-blown, in full bloom, in one's prime; **mellow** *or* mellowed, seasoned, tempered, aged.

.14 **middle-aged**, mid-life, *entre deux âges* [Fr], fortyish, matronly.

.15 **past one's prime**, on the shady side [informal], overblown, overripe, of a certain age, over the hill [informal]; "fall'n into the sere, the yellow leaf" [Shakespeare].

.16 **aged**, **elderly**, **old**, grown old, in years, **along in years**, years old, advanced, advanced in life *or* years, **at an advanced age**, **ancient**, senectuous, **venerable**, old as Methuselah *or* as the hills; patriarchal; hoary, hoar, **gray**, white, gray- *or* white-headed, gray- *or* white-haired, gray- *or* white-crowned, gray- *or* white-bearded, gray *or* white with age; wrinkled, wrinkly, with crow's feet, marked with the crow's foot.

.17 **aging**, growing old, senescent, **getting on** *or* **along**, getting on *or* along in years, not as young as one used to be, long in the tooth; **declining**, sinking, waning, fading, wasting, doting.

.18 **stricken in years**, decrepit, **infirm**, weak, debilitated, feeble, gerontic *or* gerontal, timeworn, the worse for wear, rusty, moth-eaten *or* mossbacked [slang], fossilized, wracked *or* ravaged with age, run to seed; **doddering**, doddery, doddered, tottering, tottery, rickety, shaky, palsied; on one's last legs, with one foot in the grave; **wizened**, crabbed, **withered**, shriveled, like a prune, mummylike, papery-skinned; senile 469.23, anile.

127. ADULT OR OLD PERSON

.1 NOUNS **adult**, **grownup**, mature man *or* woman, grown man *or* woman, no chicken [informal]; **man**, **woman**; major, *legalis homo* [L].

.2 **old man**, **elder**, presbyter [eccl], older, oldster [informal]; golden-ager, senior citizen; old chap, old party, **old gentleman**, old gent [informal], old codger [informal], geezer *or* old geezer [both slang], gramps [slang], gaffer, old duffer [informal], old dog [informal], old-timer [informal], dotard, veteran, pantaloon; **patriarch**, graybeard, reverend *or* venerable sir;

grandfather 170.11, grandsire; Father Time, Methuselah, Nestor, Old Paar; sexagenarian, septuagenarian, octogenarian, nonagenarian, centenarian; "the quiet-voiced elders" [T. S. Eliot], "a paltry thing, a tattered coat upon a stick" [Yeats].

.3 **old woman, old lady,** dowager, granny, old granny, dame, **grandam,** grammer [Brit dial], trot or old trot [both dial]; old dame or hen or bag or girl [slang]; old battle-ax [slang], war-horse [informal]; **crone,** hag, witch, beldam, frump [informal], old wife; grandmother 170.12.

.4 (elderly couples) Darby and Joan, Baucis and Philemon.

.5 **senior,** Sr., *senex* [L], **elder,** older; dean, *doyen* [Fr], *doyenne* [Fr]; father, sire; firstling, first-born, **eldest,** oldest.

.6 VERBS mature 126.9; grow old 126.10.

.7 ADJS mature 126.12; middle-aged 126.14; aged 126.16, older 123.19.

128. SEASON

(time of year)

.1 NOUNS **season,** time of year, season of the year, "the measure of the year" [Keats], **period,** annual period; dry or rainy or cold season, dead or off season; theatrical or opera or concert season; **social season,** the season; baseball season, football season, basketball season, etc.; seasonality, periodicity 137.2; **seasonableness** 129.1.

.2 **spring,** springtide, **springtime,** seedtime or budtime, Maytime, Eastertide; *primavera* [Ital], prime, prime of the year, "the boyhood of the year" [Tennyson], "Sweet Spring, full of sweet days and roses" [George Herbert], "Daughter of heaven and earth, coy Spring" [Emerson], "the time of the singing of birds" [Bible], "when the hounds of spring are on winter's traces" [Swinburne].

.3 **summer,** summertide, **summertime,** good old summertime; growing season; midsummer; **dog days,** canicular days.

.4 **autumn, fall,** fall of the year, fall of the leaf, harvest, harvest time, harvest home; "Season of mists and mellow fruitfulness!" [Keats].

.5 **Indian summer,** St. Martin's summer, St. Luke's summer, little summer of St. Luke, St. Austin's or St. Augustine's summer, "the dead Summer's soul" [Mary Clemmer].

.6 **winter,** wintertide, **wintertime,** "ruler of th' inverted year" [William Cowper];

midwinter; Christmastime or Christmastide, Yule or Yuletide.

.7 **equinox,** vernal equinox, autumnal equinox; **solstice,** summer solstice, winter solstice.

.8 ADJS **seasonal,** in or out of season, in season and out of season; **spring,** springlike, vernal; **summer,** summery, summerly, summerlike, canicular, aestival; midsummer; **autumn,** autumnal; **winter,** wintry, wintery, hibernal, hiemal, brumal, boreal, arctic 333.14, winterlike; midwinter; equinoctial, solstitial.

129. TIMELINESS

.1 NOUNS timeliness, seasonableness, **opportuneness,** convenience; **expedience,** meetness, fittingness, fitness, appropriateness, rightness, propriety, suitability; **favorableness, propitiousness,** auspiciousness, felicitousness; **ripeness,** pregnancy, crucialness, criticality, loadedness, chargedness.

.2 opportunity, chance, time, occasion; **opening,** room, scope, place, liberty; clear stage, fair field, fair game; opportunism; a leg up, stepping-stone, rung of the ladder; time's forelock.

.3 **good opportunity, good chance,** favorable opportunity, golden opportunity, well-timed opportunity; suitable occasion, proper occasion, suitable or proper time, **good time,** high time, due season; well-chosen moment.

.4 **crisis, critical point,** crunch, crucial period, climacteric; **turning point,** hinge, turn, turn of the tide; **emergency, exigency,** juncture or conjuncture or convergence of events, critical juncture, crossroads; **pinch,** clutch [informal], rub, push, pass, strait, extremity.

.5 **crucial moment,** critical moment, loaded or charged moment, decisive moment, kairotic moment, kairos, pregnant moment, moment of truth; **psychological moment;** nick of time, eleventh hour; **zero hour,** H hour, D day, A-day, target date, deadline.

.6 VERBS **be timely,** suit or befit the time or season or occasion.

.7 **take the opportunity,** use the occasion, take the chance; take the bit in the teeth, leap into the breach, take the bull by the horns, **make one's move,** cross the Rubicon, *prendre la balle au bond* [Fr, take the ball on the rebound]; **commit oneself,** make an opening, drive an entering wedge.

.8 **improve the occasion,** "improve each

shining hour" [Isaac Watts], turn to account *or* good account, avail oneself of, **take advantage of,** put to advantage, profit by, **cash in** *or* **capitalize on;** take time by the forelock, seize the present hour, seize the day, *carpe diem* [L; Horace], make hay while the sun shines; strike while the iron is hot; not be caught flatfooted, not be behindhand.

.9 ADJS **timely, well-timed, seasonable, opportune,** convenient; **expedient,** meet, fit, fitting, befitting, suitable, sortable, appropriate; **favorable,** propitious, ripe, auspicious, lucky, providential, fortunate, happy, felicitous.

.10 **critical, crucial,** pivotal, climacteric(al), decisive; pregnant, kairotic, loaded, charged; exigent, emergent.

.11 **incidental, occasional, casual,** accidental; parenthetical, by-the-way.

.12 ADVS **opportunely, seasonably, propitiously,** auspiciously, in proper time *or* season, in due time *or* course *or* season, in the fullness of time, **in good time,** all in good time; in the nick of time, just in time, at the eleventh hour; now or never.

.13 **incidentally, by the way,** by the by; **while on the subject,** speaking of, *à propos* [Fr], apropos *or* apropos of; **in passing,** *en passant* [Fr]; parenthetically, by way of parenthesis, *par parenthèse* [Fr]; for example, *par exemple* [Fr].

130. UNTIMELINESS

.1 NOUNS **untimeliness, unseasonableness,** inopportuneness, inopportunity, unripeness, inconvenience, intempestivity; **inexpedience,** inappropriateness, irrelevance, impropriety, unfitness, unfittingness, wrongness, unsuitability; **unfavorableness,** unfortunateness, inauspiciousness, unpropitiousness, infelicity; **intrusion,** interruption; **prematurity** 131.2; **lateness** 132, thinking of it later, *esprit d'escalier* [Fr].

.2 **wrong time, bad time,** unsuitable time, unfortunate time, poor timing; evil hour, unlucky day *or* hour, off-year, contretemps.

.3 VERBS **not have time,** have other *or* better things to do, be otherwise occupied, be engaged, be preoccupied, have other fish to fry [informal].

.4 **ill-time, mistime.**

.5 **talk out of turn,** speak inopportunely, interrupt, **put one's foot in one's mouth** [informal], intrude, butt in [informal], go off half-cocked [informal], open one's big mouth *or* big fat mouth [slang], blow it [slang], speak too late *or* too soon.

.6 **miss an opportunity, miss the chance, miss the boat,** lose the opportunity, ignore opportunity's knock, lose the chance, blow the chance [slang], throw away *or* waste *or* neglect the opportunity, allow the occasion to go by, let slip through one's fingers, be left at the starting gate *or* post, oversleep, lock the barn door after the horse is stolen.

.7 ADJS **untimely, unseasonable, inopportune,** intempestive, **ill-timed,** ill-seasoned, mistimed, unripe, unready, ill-considered, too late *or* soon, out of phase *or* time; inconvenient, unhandy; **inappropriate,** irrelevant, improper, unfit, wrong, out of line, off base, unsuitable, **inexpedient,** unfitting, unbefitting, untoward, malapropos, *mal à propos* [Fr], intrusive; **unfavorable,** unfortunate, infelicitous, inauspicious, unpropitious, unhappy, unlucky; **premature** 131.8; **late** 132.16.

.8 ADVS **inopportunely, unseasonably,** inconveniently, inexpediently; **unpropitiously,** inauspiciously, unfortunately, in an evil hour, at just the wrong time.

131. EARLINESS

.1 NOUNS **earliness,** early hour, time to spare; head start, running start, ground floor, first crack, beginnings, first *or* early stage, very beginning; **anticipation, foresight,** prevision, prevenience; a stitch in time, readiness.

.2 **prematurity, prematureness; untimeliness** 130; precocity, **precociousness,** forwardness; precipitation, haste, hastiness, **overhastiness,** rush, impulse, impulsiveness.

.3 **promptness, promptitude, punctuality,** punctualness, readiness; instantaneousness 113, immediateness *or* immediacy, summariness, decisiveness, **alacrity, quickness** 269.1, speediness, swiftness, rapidity, expeditiousness, expedition, dispatch.

.4 **early bird** [informal], early riser, early comer, first arrival; **precursor** 66.

.5 VERBS **be early,** be ahead of time, take time by the forelock, be up and stirring, be beforehand *or* betimes, be ready and waiting, be off and running; gain time, draw on futurity *or* on the future.

.6 **anticipate, foresee,** foreglimpse, foretaste; **forestall,** forerun, go before, **get ahead of,** win the start, get a head start, steal a march on; **jump the gun,** go off halfcocked [informal]; take the words out of one's mouth.

.7 ADJS **early,** bright and early [informal], **beforetime,** in good time *or* season; **forehand,** forehanded; foresighted, **anticipative** *or* **anticipatory,** prevenient; **fore–.**

.8 premature, too early, too soon, oversoon; **previous** *or* a bit previous [both informal]; **untimely** 130.7; **precipitate,** hasty 113.5, **overhasty,** too soon off the mark, **unprepared,** unripe, impulsive, rushed, unmatured; unpremeditated, unmeditated, ill-considered, **half-cocked** *or* **half-baked** [both informal], unjelled, uncrystallized, not firm; **precocious, forward, advanced,** far ahead, born before one's time.

.9 prompt, punctual, immediate, instant, instantaneous 113.4, **quick** 269.19, speedy, swift, expeditious, summary, decisive, apt, alert, **ready,** Johnny on the spot [informal].

.10 earlier, previous 116.4.

.11 ADVS **early, beforehand, beforetime,** betimes, precociously, **ahead of time,** foresightedly, in advance, in anticipation, ahead, before, **with time to spare.**

.12 in time, in good time, soon enough, time enough, early enough; just in time, **in the nick of time,** with no time to spare, just under the wire, without a minute to spare.

.13 prematurely, too soon, oversoon, untimely, too early, before its *or* one's time; **precipitately,** impulsively, in a rush, hastily, **overhastily;** at half cock [informal].

.14 punctually, precisely, exactly, sharp; **on time,** on the minute *or* instant, to the minute *or* second, **on the dot** [informal], at the gun.

.15 promptly, without delay, without further delay, directly, **immediately,** immediately if not sooner [informal], **instantly** 113.6, instanter, on the instant, on the spot, **at once,** right off, **right away, straightway,** straightaway, **forthwith,** *pronto* [Sp], *subito* [Ital], PDQ *or* pretty damned quick [both slang], **quickly** 269.21–23, swiftly, speedily, with all speed, **summarily,** decisively, smartly, expeditiously, apace, in no time, in less than no time; no sooner said than done.

.16 soon, presently, directly, shortly, in a short time *or* while, **before long,** ere long, in no long time, in a while, **in a little while, after a while, by and by,** anon, betimes, *bientôt* [Fr], in due time, in due course, at the first opportunity; in a moment *or* minute, *tout à l'heure* [Fr].

132. LATENESS

.1 NOUNS **lateness, tardiness, belatedness, unpunctuality;** late hour, small hours; eleventh hour, last minute, high time; unreadiness, unpreparedness; untimeliness 130.

.2 delay, delayage, stoppage, jam *or* logjam [both informal], obstruction, tie-up [informal], bind [informal], **block,** blockage, **hang-up** [informal]; delayed reaction, double take, afterthought; **retardation** *or* retardance, slowdown *or* slow-up [both informal], slowness, lag, time lag, lagging, dragging; **detention,** suspension, holdup [informal], hindrance; **wait, halt, stay, stop,** pause, interim 109, respite; reprieve, stay of execution; moratorium; red tape, red-tapery, red-tapeism, bureaucratic delay, *paperasserie* [Fr].

.3 waiting, tarrying, **tarriance, lingering,** dawdling, dalliance, dallying, dillydallying.

.4 postponement, deferment *or* **deferral,** prorogation, putting-off, tabling; **prolongation,** protraction, continuation, extension of time; **adjournment** *or* adjournal.

.5 procrastination, hesitation 627.3; **temporization, a play for time, stall** [slang], mugwump, hold-off [informal]; Micawberism, Fabian policy; **dilatoriness,** slowness, backwardness, remissness, slackness, laxness.

.6 latecomer, late arrival; slow starter; late bloomer *or* developer; retardee; late riser.

.7 VERBS **be late, not be on time,** be overdue, be behindhand, show up late, miss the boat 130.6; keep everyone waiting; **stay late,** stay up late *or* into the small hours, burn the midnight oil, keep late hours; get up late, keep banker's hours; oversleep.

.8 delay, retard, detain, make late, slacken, lag, drag, slow down, **hold up** [informal], hold *or* keep back, check, **stay, stop,** arrest, impede, **block,** hinder, obstruct, confine; tie up with red tape.

.9 postpone, delay, defer, put off, stave off, shift off, hold off *or* up [informal], reserve, waive, **suspend,** hang up, stay, hang fire; protract, drag *or* stretch out [informal], **prolong, extend,** continue, adjourn, recess, take a recess, prorogue, prorogate; **hold over,** lay over, stand over, let the matter stand, **put aside,** lay *or* set *or* push aside, lay *or* set by, **table,** lay on the table, pigeonhole, **shelve,** put on the shelf, put on ice [informal]; consult one's pillow about, sleep on.

.10 **be left behind,** be outrun or outdistanced, make a slow start, be slow or late or last off the mark, be left at the post or starting gate; bloom or develop late.

.11 **procrastinate,** be dilatory, hesitate, hang, hang back, hang fire; **temporize,** gain or make time, **play for time,** drag one's feet [informal], hold off [informal]; **stall,** stall off, **stall for time,** stall or stooge around [slang]; talk against time, filibuster.

.12 **wait, delay, stay,** bide, abide, **bide** or **abide one's time, take one's time,** take time, mark time; **tarry, linger, loiter,** dawdle, dally, dillydally; hang around or about [informal], stick around [slang]; **hold on** [informal], sit tight [informal], hold one's breath; wait a minute or second; hold everything or hold your horses or keep your shirt on [all slang]; wait or stay up, sit up; wait and see, bide the issue, see which way the cat jumps, see how the cookie crumbles [informal]; wait for something to turn up; **await** 539.8.

.13 **wait impatiently,** sweat it out [slang], champ or chomp at the bit [informal].

.14 **be kept waiting,** be stood up [slang], be left; **kick** or **cool one's heels** [informal].

.15 **overstay, overtarry.**

.16 ADJS **late, belated, tardy,** slow, **behindhand,** never on time, backward, back, **overdue; untimely** 130.7; **unpunctual,** unready; latish; **delayed,** detained, **held up** [informal], **retarded, arrested,** blocked, **hung up** or in a bind [both informal], obstructed, stopped, jammed [informal]; in abeyance; delayed-action; moratory.

.17 **dilatory, delaying,** Micawberish; slow or late or last off the mark; **procrastinating,** procrastinative, procrastinatory; **lingering,** loitering, lagging, dallying, dillydallying, slow, sluggish, laggard, foot-dragging, shuffling, backward; easygoing, lazy, **lackadaisical; remiss,** slack, lax.

.18 later 117.4; last-minute, eleventh-hour, deathbed.

.19 ADVS **late, behind, behindhand, belatedly,** backward, slow, **behind time,** after time; far on, deep into; late in the day, at the last minute, at the eleventh hour, none too soon, in the nick of time.

.20 **tardily, slow, slowly,** deliberately, dilatorily, sluggishly, lackadaisically, leisurely, at one's leisure, lingeringly.

133. MORNING, NOON

.1 NOUNS **morning,** morn, morningtide, morning time, morntime, matins, waking time, **forenoon,** foreday; ante meridiem [L], **AM,** Ack Emma [Brit informal]; "dewy morn" [Byron], "incense-breathing morn" [Thomas Gray], "grey-eyed morn", "the morn, in russet mantle clad" [both Shakespeare], "rosy-finger'd morn" [Homer]; this morning, this AM [informal].

.2 Morning, Aurora, Eos; "daughter of the dawn" [Homer], "meek-eyed Morn, mother of dews" [James Thomson], "mild blushing goddess" [L. P. Smith].

.3 **dawn,** the dawn of day, dawning, **daybreak,** dayspring, day-peep, **sunrise, sunup** [informal], cockcrow(ing), cocklight [Brit dial], light 335, daylight, aurora; **break of day,** peep of day, **crack of dawn,** prime, prime of the morning, first blush or flush of the morning, brightening or first brightening; "the opening eyelids of the morn" [Milton], "vestibule of Day" [Bayard Taylor], "golden exhalations of the dawn" [Schiller]; chanticleer.

.4 **foredawn,** twilight, morning twilight, half-light, glow, dawnlight, first light, "the dawn's early light" [Francis Scott Key], crepuscule, aurora; **the small hours;** alpenglow.

.5 **noon, noonday,** noontide, nooning [dial], noontime, high noon, **midday,** meridian, meridiem [L], twelve o'clock, 1200 hours, eight bells, noonlight.

.6 ADJS **morning,** matin, matinal, matutinal, **antemeridian;** auroral, dawn, dawning.

.7 **noon, noonday,** noonish, **midday,** meridian, twelve-o'clock; noonlit.

.8 ADVS **in the morning,** before noon, mornings [informal]; at sunrise, at dawn, at dawn of day, at cockcrow, at first light, **at the crack of dawn;** with the sun, with the lark.

.9 at noon, at midday, at twelve-o'clock sharp.

134. EVENING, NIGHT

.1 NOUNS **afternoon,** post meridiem [L], **PM;** this afternoon, this aft [informal], this PM [informal].

.2 **evening,** eve, even, evensong, **eventide,** vesper; **close of day,** decline or fall of day, shut of day, gray of the evening, grayness 366, evening's close, when day is done; **nightfall, sunset, sundown,** setting sun, going down of the sun, cockshut

[dial]; shank of the afternoon *or* evening [informal], the cool of the evening; "the expiring day" [Dante], "evening's calm and holy hour" [S. G. Bulfinch], "the gray-hooded Ev'n" [Milton], "It is a beauteous evening, calm and free" [Wordsworth], "the pale child, Eve, leading her mother, Night" [Alexander Smith], "the evening is spread out against the sky / Like a patient etherized upon a table" [T. S. Eliot].

.3 **dusk,** duskingtide, dusk-down [dial], **twilight,** crepuscule, crepuscular light, gloam, **gloaming,** glooming; brown of dusk, brownness 367, candlelight, candlelighting, owllight *or* owl's light, cocklight [Brit dial], "the pale dusk of the impending night" [Longfellow].

.4 **night, nighttime,** nighttide, **darkness** 337, blackness 365, "sable-vested Night, eldest of things" [Milton], "sable night", "dark-eyed night" [both Shakespeare], "cowlèd night" [Francis Thompson], "empress of silence, and the queen of sleep" [Christopher Marlowe]; dark of night, "the suit of night" [Shakespeare], "the mystic wine of Night" [Louis Untermeyer]; noct(o)– *or* nocti–, nyct(o)– *or* nycti–.

.5 **eleventh hour,** curfew, bedtime.

.6 **midnight, dead of night,** hush of night, witching hour of the night; "the very witching time of night" [Shakespeare], "noonday night", "outpost of advancing day" [both Longfellow].

.7 ADJS **afternoon,** postmeridian.

.8 **evening,** evensong, vesper, vespertine; **twilight,** twilighty, crepuscular; **dusk,** dusky; sunsetty.

.9 **nocturnal,** night, **nightly,** nighttime; nightlong, all-night; night-fallen; midnight.

.10 **benighted,** night-overtaken.

.11 ADVS **nightly,** nights [informal], at *or* by night; **overnight,** through the night, all through the night, nightlong, the whole night, all night.

135. FREQUENCY

.1 NOUNS **frequency,** frequence, **oftenness; commonness,** usualness, prevalence, **common occurrence,** routineness, habitualness; incidence, relative incidence.

.2 **constancy, continualness,** steadiness, sustainment, **regularity,** noninterruption *or* uninterruption, nonintermission *or* unintermission, incessancy, ceaselessness, constant flow, continuity 71; perpetuity 112; repetition 103; **rapidity** 269.1; rapid recurrence *or* succession, rapid *or* quick fire, tattoo, **staccato,** chattering, stuttering; pulsation, vibration, **oscillation** 323.

.3 VERBS be frequent, occur often, continue 71.4, recur 137.5, vibrate 323.10.

.4 ADJS **frequent,** oftentime, many, many times, **recurrent, oft-repeated,** thick-coming; **common,** of common occurrence, not rare, **prevalent,** usual, routine, habitual, ordinary, everyday; frequentative.

.5 **constant, continual** 71.8, **perennial; steady,** sustained, **regular; incessant, ceaseless, unceasing,** unintermitting, unintermittent *or* unintermitted, unremitting, unchanging, unvarying, uninterrupted, unstopped, unbroken; **perpetual** 112.7; repeated 103.12; **rapid** 269.19, **staccato,** stuttering, chattering, machine gun; pulsating, vibrating, **oscillating** 323.15.

.6 ADVS **frequently, commonly,** usually, ordinarily, routinely, habitually; **often, oft, oftentimes,** ofttimes; **repeatedly** 103.16, **again and again; most often** *or* frequently, in many instances, **many times,** many a time, full many a time, many a time and oft, as often as can be, as often as not; **in quick** *or* **rapid succession;** often enough, not infrequently, not seldom, unseldom; as often as you wish *or* like, whenever you wish *or* like.

.7 **constantly, continually** 71.10, **steadily,** sustainedly, **regularly,** right along [informal], unvaryingly, uninterruptedly, unintermittently, **incessantly,** unceasingly, **ceaselessly,** without cease *or* ceasing, perennially, at all times, ever, ever and anon, on and on, without letup *or* break *or* intermission, without stopping; **perpetually, always** 112.10–12; **rapidly** 269.21; every day, every hour, every moment; daily, hourly, daily and hourly; **night and day,** day and night; **morning, noon, and night;** hour after hour, day after day, month after month, year after year; **day in day out,** month in month out, year in year out.

136. INFREQUENCY

.1 NOUNS **infrequency,** infrequence, unfrequentness, **seldomness; occasionalness; rarity, scarcity, scarceness,** rareness, **uncommonness,** uniqueness, unusualness; **sparsity** 102.1; **slowness** 270.

.2 ADJS **infrequent,** unfrequent, **rare, scarce, uncommon,** unique, unusual, almost unheard-of, seldom met with, seldom seen, few and far between, **sparse** 102.5; **slow** 270.10.

.3 **occasional, casual, incidental; odd,** extra,

side, off, out-of-the-way, spare, spare-time, **part-time**.

.4 ADVS **infrequently**, unfrequently, **seldom, rarely, uncommonly**, scarcely, hardly, **scarcely** *or* **hardly ever**, very seldom, not often, only now and then, at infrequent intervals, unoften; **sparsely** 102.8.

.5 **occasionally**, on occasion, **sometimes, at times**, at odd times, every so often [informal], at various times, on divers occasions, **now and then**, every now and then [informal], **once in a while**, every once in a while [informal], once and again, once or twice, betweentimes, betweenwhiles, at intervals, **from time to time**; only occasionally, only when the spirit moves, only when necessary, only now and then, at infrequent intervals, once in a blue moon *or* once in a coon's age [both informal].

.6 **once, one time**, on one occasion, just *or* only once, just this once, once and no more, once for all, once and for all *or* always.

137. REGULARITY OF RECURRENCE

.1 NOUNS **regularity**, clockwork regularity, punctuality, smoothness, **steadiness, evenness, methodicalness**, systematicalness; **repetition** 103; **uniformity** 17; **constancy** 135.2.

.2 **periodicity**, periodicalness, piston motion, pendulum motion, regular wave motion, undulation, **pulsation; rhythm** 463.22, meter, beat; **oscillation** 323; **recurrence**, reoccurrence, reappearance, return, **cyclicalness**, seasonality; **intermittence** *or* intermittency, alternation.

.3 **round, revolution, rotation, cycle**, circle, wheel, **circuit; beat**, upbeat, downbeat, thesis, arsis, **pulse**; systole, diastole; course, series, **bout, turn**, spell 108.

.4 **anniversary, commemoration**; immovable feast, annual holiday; –ennial, biennial, triennial, quadrennial, quinquennial, sextennial, septennial, octennial, decennial, tricennial, jubilee, diamond jubilee; centennial, centenary; quasquicentennial; sesquicentennial; bicentennial, bicentenary; tercentennial, tercentenary; quincentennial, quincentenary; **wedding anniversary**, silver wedding anniversary, golden wedding anniversary; **birthday**, natal day; saint's day, name day; leap year, bissextile day; holy days 1040.15.

.5 VERBS (occur periodically) **recur, reoccur, return, repeat** 103.7, reappear, **come again**, come up again, be here again,

come round *or* around, come round again, come in its turn; **rotate, revolve**, turn, circle, wheel, cycle, **roll around**, wheel around; **intermit**, alternate, **come and go**; undulate 323.11; **oscillate** 323.10, **pulse, pulsate** 323.12.

.6 ADJS **regular, systematic(al), methodical**, ordered, orderly, regular as clockwork; **uniform** 17.5; **constant** 135.5.

.7 **periodic(al), seasonal**, epochal, **cyclic(al)**, serial, isochronal, metronomic; measured, steady, even, **rhythmic(al)** 463.28; **recurrent**, recurring, reoccurring; **intermittent**, reciprocal, alternate, every other; circling, wheeling, rotary, wavelike, undulant, undulatory, oscillatory 323.15, pulsing, beating 323.18.

.8 **momentary**, momently, **hourly; daily**, diurnal, quotidian; **weekly**, tertian, hebdomadal, hebdomadary; biweekly, semiweekly; fortnightly; **monthly**, menstrual, catamenial; bimonthly, semimonthly; quarterly; biannual, semiannual, semiyearly, semestral; **yearly, annual**; biennial, triennial, decennial, etc.; centennial, centenary, secular.

.9 ADVS **regularly, systematically, methodically**, like clockwork, at regular intervals, punctually, steadily; at stated times, at fixed *or* established periods; intermittently, every so often, every now and then; **uniformly** 17.7,8; **constantly** 135.7.

.10 **periodically, recurrently, seasonally**, cyclically, epochally; rhythmically, on the beat, in time, synchronously, **hourly, daily**, etc.; every hour, every day, etc.; hour by hour, day by day, etc.; from hour to hour, from day to day, *de die in diem* [L].

.11 **alternately, by turns, in turns, in rotation**, turn about, turn and turn about, reciprocally, every other, one after the other; to and fro, up and down, from side to side; off and on, make and break, round and round.

.12 **anniversaries, holidays**

Admission Day [Ariz & Cal]	Day [Vt]
Alaska Day	Bill of Rights Day [US]
April Fools' *or* All Fools' Day	Bird Day [US]
Arbor Day [US]	Boxing Day [England]
Armed Forces Day [US]	Bunker Hill Day [Boston]
Armistice Day [US]	*Cinco de Mayo* [Mexico Sp, Fifth of May]
Army Day [US]	
Bastille Day [France]	Citizenship Day [US]
Battle of New Orleans Day [La]	Colorado Day
	Columbus Day [US]
Bennington Battle	Confederate Memo-

rial Day [US]
Constitution Day [US]
Davis' Birthday [US]
Decoration Day [US]
Defenders' Day [Md]
De Hostos' Birthday [Puerto Rico]
Dewali [India]
Discovery Day [Puerto Rico]
Dominion Day [Canada]
Double Ten [China]
Easter Monday [England]
Election Day [US]
Emancipation Day [Puerto Rico]
Empire Day [England]
Evacuation Day [Boston]
Father's Day [US]
Flag Day [US]
Forefathers' Day [New England]
Forrest's Birthday [Tenn]
Foundation Day [Canal Zone]
Fourth of July [US]
Groundhog Day [US]
Halifax Day [NC]
Halloween
Holi [India]
Ides of March
Inauguration Day [US]
Independence Day [US]
Jackson's Birthday [Tenn]
Kamehameha Day [Hawaii]
King's Birthday [England]
Kuhio Day [Hawaii]
Labor Day [US]
Lee-Jackson Day [Va]
Lee's Birthday [US]
Lenin Memorial Day [USSR]
Lincoln's Birthday [US]
Long's Birthday [La]
Loyalty Day [US]
Martin Luther King

Day [US]
Maryland Day
May Day
Mecklenburg Day [NC]
Memorial Day [US]
Midsummer Day
Mother's Day [US]
National Aviation Day [US]
Navy Day [US]
Nevada Day
New Year's Day
New Year's Eve
Orangemen's Day [N Ireland]
Pan American Day [US]
Pascua Florida Day [Fla]
Patriots' Day [Maine & Mass]
Peach Festival [Japan]
Pioneer Day [Utah]
Queen's Birthday [England]
Remembrance Day [Canada]
Rhode Island Independence Day
Roosevelt Day [Ky]
Sadie Hawkins Day [US]
Saint David's Day
Saint Patrick's Day
Saint Swithin's Day
Saint Valentine's Day
San Jacinto Day [Texas]
Seward's Day [Alaska]
Sovereign's Birthday [Canada]
State Day [US]
Tet [Vietnam]
Texas Independence Day
Thanksgiving [US]
United Nations Day
V-E Day
Veterans' Day [US]
Victoria Day [Canada]
Victory Day [RI]
V-J Day
Washington's Birthday [US]
West Virginia Day
Wyoming Day

138. IRREGULARITY OF RECURRENCE

.1 NOUNS **irregularity,** unmethodicalness, unsystematicness; **inconstancy, unevenness, unsteadiness,** uncertainty, desultoriness; **variability,** capriciousness, unpredictability, whimsicality, eccentricity, stagger, wobble, erraticness; roughness; **fitfulness, sporadicity** *or* sporadicness, spasticity, jerkiness, fits and starts, patchiness, spottiness, choppiness, brokenness, disconnectedness, discontinuity 72; **intermittence, fluctuation; nonuniformity** 18; arrhythmia, fibrillation [both med].

.2 VERBS **intermit, fluctuate,** vary, lack regularity, go by fits and starts.

.3 ADJS **irregular,** unregular, unsystematic, unmethodical *or* immethodical; **inconstant, unsteady, uneven, unrhythmical,** unmetrical, rough, unequal, uncertain, unsettled; **variable,** deviative, heteroclite; **capricious, erratic,** eccentric, wobbly, wobbling, staggering, lurching, careening; **fitful, spasmodic,** spastic, spasmatic, spasmic, **jerky,** herky-jerky [slang], halting; **sporadic,** patchy, spotty, scrappy, snatchy, catchy, choppy, **broken, disconnected, discontinuous** 72.4; **nonuniform** 18.3; **intermittent,** intermitting, **desultory, fluctuating, wavering,** wandering, rambling, veering; flickering, guttering.

.4 ADVS **irregularly,** unsystematically, unmethodically; **inconstantly, unsteadily, unevenly,** unrhythmically, roughly, uncertainly; **variably,** capriciously, unpredictably, whimsically, eccentrically, wobblingly, lurchingly, erratically; **intermittently, disconnectedly, discontinuously** 72.5; **nonuniformly** 18.4; **brokenly,** desultorily, patchily, spottily, in spots, in snatches; **by fits and starts,** by fits, by jerks, by snatches, by catches; **fitfully, sporadically, jerkily, spasmodically,** haltingly; **off and on,** at irregular intervals, sometimes and sometimes not; when the mood strikes, when the spirit moves, at random.

139. CHANGE

.1 NOUNS **change, alteration, modification; variation,** variety, difference, diversity, diversification; **deviation,** diversion, **divergence; switch, turn,** turnabout, aboutface, **reversal,** flip-flop [informal]; apostasy, defection, change of heart; **shift,** transition, **modulation,** qualification; **conversion, renewal,** revival, revivification; remaking, reshaping, re-creation, redesign, restructuring; realignment, **adaptation, adjustment,** accommodation, fitting; **reform,** reformation, **improvement,** amelioration, melioration, mitigation, constructive change, **betterment,** change for the better; gradual change, **continuity** 71; **degeneration, deterioration,** worsening, degenerative change, change for the worse; sudden change, radical *or* violent *or* total change, catastrophic change, upheaval, overthrow, **revolution, break,** break with the past, **discontinuity** 72; changeableness 141; "the ever whirling wheels of Change" [Spenser], "Nature's mighty law" [Robert Burns], "a sea-change / Into something rich and strange" [Shakespeare], "the changes and chances of this mortal life" [Book of Common Prayer].

.2 **transformation,** transmogrification [informal]; **translation; metamorphosis,** meta-morphism; **mutation,** transmutation, per-mutation, **mutant,** mutated form, sport; **transfiguration** or transfigurement; metas-tasis, metathesis, transposition, transloca-tion, **displacement,** heterotopia; **transub-stantiation,** consubstantiation; transani-mation, transmigration, reincarnation, avatar, metempsychosis; metasomatism, metasomatosis; catalysis; metabolism, anabolism, catabolism; metagenesis; transformism; –morphosis, –ody, –tropy.

.3 **innovation, introduction,** discovery, in-vention; neologism, coinage; **break-through,** leap, new phase; **novelty** 122.2.

.4 **transformer,** transmogrifier [informal]; **in-novator,** innovationist, introducer; pre-cursor 66; **alterant,** alterer, alterative, **agent,** catalytic agent, catalyst, **leaven,** yeast, ferment; **modifier,** modificator.

.5 VERBS **be changed, change, undergo a change,** go through a change, be con-verted into, turn into 145.17; **alter,** mu-tate, modulate; **vary,** checker, diversify; **deviate, diverge,** turn, **shift,** veer, jibe, tack, chop, chop and change, swerve, warp; **revive,** be renewed; **improve,** ame-liorate, meliorate, mitigate; **degenerate, deteriorate, worsen;** turn aside, take a turn, turn the corner, bottom out [infor-mal]; come about, come round or around, haul around; flop, break.

.6 (make a change) **change, work a change, alter;** mutate; **modify;** adapt; modulate, accommodate, adjust, fit, **qualify; vary, diversify; convert, renew, revamp** [infor-mal], **revive;** remake, reshape, re-create, redesign, **rebuild,** reconstruct, restructure; realign; refit; **reform, improve,** better, ameliorate, meliorate, mitigate; turn up-side down, subvert, overthrow, break up, worsen, deform, denature; ring the changes; give a turn to, give a twist to, turn the tide, turn the tables, turn the scale or balance; shift the scene; shuffle the cards; turn over a new leaf; reverse oneself; –en, –ify or –fy, –ize or –ise.

.7 **transform, transfigure, transmute,** trans-

mogrify [informal]; **translate;** transubstan-tiate, metamorphose; metabolize.

.8 **innovate,** make innovations, invent, dis-cover, **pioneer** 66.3, **revolutionize, intro-duce,** introduce new blood; neologize, coin.

.9 ADJS **changed, altered, modified,** quali-fied, **transformed,** transmuted, **metamor-phosed;** translated, metastasized; deviant, mutant; divergent; **converted, renewed,** revived, **rebuilt; reformed,** improved, **bet-ter; degenerate, worse,** unmitigated; sub-versive, **revolutionary;** changeable 141.6,7.

.10 **innovational,** innovative.

.11 **metamorphic, metabolic,** anabolic, cata-bolic; metastatic, **catalytic;** blast(o)–, meta–, re–, trans–, trop(o)–; –tropic or –trophic.

140. PERMANENCE

.1 NOUNS **permanence** or permanency, **im-mutability, changelessness,** unchanging-ness, invariableness or invariability; **fixed-ness, constancy,** steadfastness, firmness, solidity, immovableness or immovability, persistence or persistency, **lastingness, abidingness, endurance,** duration, stand-ing, long standing, inveteracy; **durable-ness, durability** 110; **perpetualness** 112.1; **stability** 142; **unchangeability** 142.4; **im-mobility,** stasis, frozenness, hardening, **ri-gidity; quiescence,** torpor.

.2 **maintenance, preservation** 701, **conserva-tion.**

.3 **conservatism, conservativeness,** opposi-tion or resistance to change, unprogres-siveness, fogyism, backwardness, old-fash-ionedness, standpattism [informal], ul-traconservatism; political conservatism, rightism 745.1; laissez-faireism 706.1; old school tie [Brit]; "adherence to the old and tried, against the new and untried" [Lincoln].

.4 **conservative,** conservatist; conservationist 701.4; ultraconservative, **diehard,** standpat or standpatter [both informal], **old fogy,** fogy, stick-in-the-mud [informal], moss-back [informal], laudator temporis acti [L], **rightist, right-winger** 745.9, "the left-over progressive of an earlier generation" [Edmund Fuller]; old school.

.5 VERBS **remain, endure** 110.6, last, stay, persist, bide, abide, stand, hold, subsist; be ever the same.

.6 **be conservative,** oppose change, stand on ancient ways; stand pat or stand still [both informal]; **let things take their course,** leave things as they are, let be, let *or* leave alone, let well enough alone, do nothing; stop *or* turn back the clock.

.7 ADJS **permanent, changeless, unchanging, immutable,** unvarying, unshifting; **unchanged,** unvaried, **unaltered,** inviolate, undestroyed, intact; **constant, persistent,** sustained, fixed, firm, solid, steadfast, like the Rock of Gibraltar; unchecked, unfailing, unfading; **lasting, enduring,** abiding, remaining, staying, continuing; **durable** 110.10; **perpetual** 112.7; **stable** 142.12; **unchangeable** 142.17; **immobile, static,** stationary, frozen, **rigid; quiescent,** torpid.

.8 **conservative, preservative,** old-line, **diehard,** standpat [informal], opposed to change; backward, old-fashioned, **unprogressive,** nonprogressive; ultraconservative, fogyish, **old-fogyish; right-wing** 745.17.

.9 ADVS **permanently,** abidingly, lastingly, steadfastly, unwaveringly, changelessly, unchangingly; enduringly, **perpetually,** invariably, **always** 112.10–12; statically, rigidly, inflexibly.

.10 *in statu quo* [L], as things are, **as is, as usual,** as per usual [informal]; at a stand *or* standstill, without a shadow of turning.

.11 PHRS *plus ça change, plus c'est la même chose* [Fr, the more it changes, the more it's the same thing].

141. CHANGEABLENESS

.1 NOUNS **changeableness,** changefulness, **changeability, alterability,** modifiability; **mutability,** permutability, impermanence, **transience,** transitoriness; mobility, movability, plasticity, malleability, rubberiness, fluidity; **resilience, adaptability,** adjustability, **flexibility,** suppleness; **nonuniformity** 18.

.2 **inconstancy, instability,** unstableness, **unsteadiness,** unsteadfastness, unfixedness, unsettledness; **uncertainty,** undependability, inconsistency, shiftiness, unreliability; **variability,** variation, variety, restlessness, deviability; unpredictability, irregularity 138.1; **desultoriness,** waywardness, wantonness; **erraticism, eccentricity;** freakishness, freakery; flightiness, impulsiveness, mercuriality, moodiness, whimsicality, **capriciousness, fickleness** 629.2,3.

.3 **fluctuation,** vicissitude, **variation, alternation,** oscillation, **vacillation,** pendulation; **wavering,** shifting, shuffling, teetering, tottering, seesawing, teeter-tottering.

.4 (comparisons) Proteus, kaleidoscope, chameleon, shifting sands, rolling stone,

April showers, cloud shapes; water; wheel of fortune; whirligig; mercury, quicksilver; the weather, weathercock, weather vane; moon, phases of the moon.

.5 VERBS **fluctuate, vary, alternate, vacillate,** oscillate, pendulate; ebb and flow, wax and wane; go through phases, **waver,** shift, shuffle, swing, sway, wobble, flounder, stagger, teeter, totter, **seesaw, teeter-totter;** back and fill, turn, blow hot and cold, ring the changes, have as many phases as the moon.

.6 ADJS **changeable, alterable,** alterative, modifiable; mutable, permutable, impermanent, transient, **transitory; variable,** checkered, ever-changing, many-sided, kaleidoscopic; mobile, movable, plastic, malleable, rubbery, fluid; **resilient, adaptable,** adjustable, **flexible,** supple, able to adapt, able to roll with the punches *or* bend without breaking; protean, proteiform; metamorphic; **nonuniform** 18.3.

.7 **inconstant, changeable,** changeful, uncertain, inconsistent, shifty, unreliable, undependable, **unstable, unfixed,** infirm, restless, **unsettled,** unstaid, **unsteady,** wishy-washy, spineless, shapeless, amorphous, indecisive, irresolute, unsteadfast, unstable as water; **variable,** deviable; unaccountable, unpredictable; vicissitudinous, vicissitudinary; whimsical, **capricious, fickle** 629.5,6; **erratic, eccentric,** freakish; volatile, giddy, dizzy, scatterbrained, mercurial, moody, flighty, impulsive, impetuous; **fluctuating,** alternating, **vacillating, wavering,** wavery, wavy, mazy, flitting, flickering, fitful, shifting, shuffling; irregular, spasmodic 138.3; **desultory,** rambling, roving, vagrant, wanton, wayward, wandering, afloat, adrift; unrestrained, undisciplined, irresponsible, uncontrolled, fast and loose.

.8 ADVS **changeably, variably, inconstantly,** uncertainly, **unsteadily,** unsteadfastly, capriciously, desultorily, erratically, waveringly; back and forth, to and fro, in and out, off and on, on and off, round and round.

142. STABILITY

.1 NOUNS **stability, firmness, soundness, substantiality, solidity;** –stasia *or* –stasis, –pexy; security, secureness, rootedness, fastness; reliability 513.4; **steadiness,** steadfastness; constancy, invariability, undeflectability; **imperturbability,** unflappability [informal], nerve, steady *or* unshakable nerves, unshakableness, **cool** [informal], *sang-froid* [Fr]; **equilibrium, balance,** stable state, stable equilibrium, homeostasis; steady state; balanced personality; aplomb; **uniformity** 17.

.2 **fixity,** fixedness, fixture, fixation; infixion, implantation, embedment; **establishment, stabilization,** confirmation, entrenchment; inveteracy, deep-rootedness, **deep-seatedness.**

.3 **immobility,** immovability, unmovability, immovableness, irremovability; inextricability; **firmness,** solidity, unyieldingness, rigidity, **inflexibility** 356.3; inertia, *vis inertiae* [L]; immobilization.

.4 **unchangeableness, unchangeability,** unalterability, unmodifiability, **immutability,** incommutability; lastingness, **permanence** 140; irrevocability, indefeasibility, **irreversibility;** irretrievability, unreturnableness, unrestorableness; intransmutability; inertness.

.5 **indestructibility, imperishability,** incorruptibility, inextinguishability, immortality, **deathlessness;** invulnerability, invincibility, inexpugnability, impregnability; ineradicability, indelibility, ineffaceability, inerasableness.

.6 (comparisons) rock, Rock of Gibraltar, bedrock, pillar, tower, foundation; leopard's spots.

.7 VERBS **stabilize,** stabilitate; firm, firm up [informal]; **steady, balance,** counterbalance, ballast; **immobilize,** freeze, keep, retain; **transfix,** stick, hold, pin *or* nail down [informal].

.8 **secure,** make sure *or* secure, tie, chain, tether, **make fast, fasten,** fasten down; **anchor,** moor; batten, batten down; belay; "build one's house upon a rock" [Bible].

.9 **fix,** define, set, **settle; establish,** found, ground, lodge, seat, **entrench,** confirm, **root; infix, ingrain,** set in, plant, implant, engraft, bed, embed; **print,** imprint, **stamp,** inscribe, **etch,** engrave; impress, impact, pack, jam, **wedge;** deep-dye, **dye in the wool;** stereotype.

.10 (become firmly fixed) **root, take root,** strike root; **stick,** stick fast, **catch, jam, lodge.**

.11 **stand fast,** stand *or* remain firm, **stand pat** [informal], stay put [informal], hold fast, not budge, not budge an inch, **stand** *or* **hold one's ground,** hold one's own, dig in one's heels, take one's stand, **stick to one's guns,** put one's foot down [informal]; **hold out,** stick it out [informal]; **hold up; weather,** weather the storm, ride it out, get home free [informal]; be im-

perturbable, be unflappable [informal], not bat an eyelash [informal], keep one's cool [informal].

.12 ADJS **stable, substantial, firm, solid, sound;** firm as Gibraltar, solid as a rock; **fast, secure; steady,** unwavering, steadfast; **balanced,** in equilibrium, in a stable state; **well-balanced;** gyr(o)-, stat(o)-; **imperturbable,** unflappable [informal], unshakable, **cool** [informal]; without nerves, without a nerve in one's body, unflinching; **reliable** 513.17, predictable; fiducial.

.13 **established,** stabilized, **entrenched,** vested, firmly established; **well-established,** well-founded, **well-grounded,** on a rock, in *or* on bedrock; old-line, long-established; **confirmed, inveterate; settled, set;** well-settled, well-set; **rooted,** well-rooted; **deep-rooted, deep-seated,** deep-set, deep-settled, deep-fixed, deep-dyed, deep-engraven, deep-grounded, deep-laid; **infixed, ingrained,** implanted, engrafted, embedded, ingrown, inwrought; impressed, indelibly impressed, imprinted; engraved, etched, graven, embossed; **dyed-in-the-wool.**

.14 **fixed,** fastened, anchored, riveted; **set, settled, stated;** staple.

.15 **immovable,** unmovable, **immobile,** immotile, immotive, unmoving, **irremovable, stationary,** frozen, not to be moved, at a standstill; **firm, unyielding,** adamant, adamantine, rigid, **inflexible** 356.12; pat, standpat [informal].

.16 **stuck, fast,** stuck fast, **fixed, transfixed, caught,** fastened, tied, chained, tethered, anchored, moored, held, inextricable; **jammed,** impacted, packed, wedged; aground, grounded, stranded, high and dry.

.17 **unchangeable,** not to be changed, changeless, unchanged, unchanging, unvarying, unvariable, **unalterable,** unaltered, unalterative, **immutable,** incommutable, inconvertible, unmodifiable; unsusceptible, insusceptible of change; **constant, invariable,** undeviating, undeflectable; lasting, unremitting, **permanent** 140.7; irrevocable, indefeasible, **irreversible,** nonreversible, reverseless; irretrievable, unrestorable, unreturnable, nonreturnable; intransmutable, inert, noble [chem].

.18 **indestructible,** undestroyable, **imperishable,** nonperishable, incorruptible; **deathless,** immortal, undying; **invulnerable, invincible,** inexpugnable, impregnable; **ineradicable,** indelible, ineffaceable, inerasable; **inextinguishable,** unquenchable, quenchless, undampable.

.19 PHRS **stet, let it stand.**

.20 **stabilizers**

balance	governor
balance piston	gyroscope
balancer	gyrostabilizer
balance rudder	hairspring
balance wheel	keel
balancing condenser	mordant
balancing flap	pendulum
ballast	pendulum wheel
centerboard damper	shock absorber
counterbalance	springs
counterweight	stabilizator
fin	stiffening
fixative	tail plane
flywheel	trim tabs

143. CONTINUANCE

(continuance in action)

.1 NOUNS **continuance, continuation,** unremittingness, **continualness** 71.1; **prolongation, extension,** protraction, **perpetuation,** lengthening; **maintenance,** sustenance, sustained action *or* activity; pursuance; run, way, straight *or* uninterrupted course; **progress,** progression; **persistence, perseverance** 625; **endurance** 110.1; **continuity** 71; **repetition** 103; staying power.

.2 **resumption, recommencement,** rebeginning, **renewal,** reopening, reentrance; **fresh start,** new beginning; another try, another shot *or* crack *or* go [informal].

.3 VERBS **continue** 71.4, **remain,** bide, **abide, stay,** tarry, linger; **go on,** go along, **keep on,** keep going, carry on, stay on, hold on, hold one's way *or* course *or* path, hold steady, run on, jog on, drag on, slog on, stagger on, put one foot in front of the other; never cease, cease not; **endure** 110.6.

.4 **sustain,** protract, prolong, **extend,** perpetuate, lengthen; **maintain,** keep, hold, retain, preserve; **keep up,** keep going, keep alive.

.5 **persist, persevere,** keep at it 625.2, stick it out, stick to it, never say die, see it through, hang in *or* hang tough [both informal]; survive, make out, manage, get along, get on, eke out an existence, keep the even tenor of one's way; go on, go on with, go on with the show [informal].

.6 **resume, recommence,** rebegin, **renew,** reenter, reopen, **return to,** go back to, begin again, take up again, make a new beginning, make a fresh start, start all over,

have another try, have another shot *or* crack *or* go [informal].

.7 ADJS **continuing, abiding** 110.10; staying, remaining, sticking; **continuous** 71.8, **unceasing,** unremitting, steady, sustained, undying, indefatigable, **persistent.**

144. CESSATION

.1 NOUNS **cessation, discontinuance,** discontinuation, breakoff [informal]; **desistance,** desinence, cease, surcease, **ceasing,** stopping, termination; **close,** closing, shutdown; relinquishment, renunciation, abandonment; –stasia *or* –stasis, stasi–.

.2 **stop,** stoppage, **halt, stay,** arrest, check, cutoff [informal]; stand, **standstill;** full stop, dead stop, grinding halt; **strike, walkout,** work stoppage, sit-down strike, lockout; **end,** ending, endgame, final whistle, gun, bell, checkmate, stalemate, deadlock, standoff [informal].

.3 **pause, rest, break,** caesura, **recess, intermission,** interim 109, intermittence, interval, interlude, *intermezzo* [Ital], **respite,** letup [informal], **interruption, suspension;** hesitation, remission, layoff [informal], abeyance, stay, drop, lull, lapse; truce, cease-fire, stand-down; vacation, holiday, day off.

.4 [gram terms] pause, juncture, boundary, caesura; (punctuation) stop *or* point *or* period, comma, colon, semicolon.

.5 (debate) **cloture,** *clôture* [Fr]; cloture by compartment, kangaroo cloture; guillotine [Brit].

.6 VERBS **cease, discontinue, end, stop, halt,** terminate, abort, cancel, scrub [informal], hold, **quit,** stay, belay [informal]; **desist,** refrain, leave off, lay off [informal], give over, **have done with;** cut it out [slang], drop it [informal], knock it off [informal], relinquish, renounce, abandon; **come to an end** 70.6.

.7 **stop, come to a stop** *or* halt, **halt,** stop in one's tracks, skid to a stop, stop dead; **bring up, pull up,** draw up, **fetch up; stop short,** come up short, bring up short, come to a screaming *or* grinding *or* shuddering halt, stop on a dime [informal], come to a full stop, come to a stand *or* standstill, fetch up all standing; stall, stick, hang fire, cease fire; run into a brick wall.

.8 (stop work) **lay off, knock off** [informal], call it a day [informal], call it quits [informal]; lay down one's tools, **shut up shop,** close shop, shut down, close down, secure [naut informal]; strike, walk out, call a strike, go or go out on strike.

.9 **pause, hesitate, rest,** let up [informal]; rest on one's oars; **recess,** take or call a recess.

.10 **interrupt, suspend,** intermit 109.3, **break, break off,** take a break [informal], cut off, break or snap the thread.

.11 **put a stop to, call a halt to,** blow the whistle on [informal], **put an end to** 70.7, put paid to [Brit informal]; **stop, stay, halt, arrest, check,** stall; block, brake, dam, stem, stem the tide or current; pull up, draw rein, put on the brakes, hit the brake pedal; **bring to a stand** or **standstill,** freeze, bring to, bring up short, **stop dead** or dead in one's tracks, stop cold, stop short, cut short, check in full career; checkmate, stalemate, deadlock.

.12 **turn off, shut off,** shut, shut down, close; kill, cut, switch off.

.13 ADVS de–, un–.

.14 INTERJS **cease!, stop!, halt!,** *halte!* [Fr], hold!, freeze!, stay!, desist!, quit it!; **let up!,** easy!, take it easy!, relax!, **leave off!,** *arrêtez!* [Fr], stop it!, forget it!, no more!, have done!, *tenez!* [Fr], **hold everything!, hold it!,** hold to!, hold on!, whoa!, that's it!, that's enough!, enough!, *basta!* [Ital].

.15 [slang or informal terms] **cut it out!,** cool it!, can it!, turn it off!, chuck it!, stow it!, drop it!, lay off!, all right already!, come off it!, **knock it off!,** break it off!, break it up!

145. CONVERSION

(change to something different)

.1 NOUNS **conversion,** reconversion, re-formation, **change-over,** turning into, becoming; **change** 139, **transformation** 139.2; **transition,** transit, switch or switch-over [both informal], passage, **shift;** lapse; **reversal,** about-face or flip-flop [both informal], *volte-face* [Fr]; growth, progress; resolution, reduction, naturalization, assimilation, assumption; alchemy.

.2 **reformation, reform, regeneration,** revival, **reclamation,** redemption, amendment, improvement 691, renewal, recrudescence, rebirth, renascence, new birth, **change of heart;** change of mind or commitment or allegiance or loyalty or conviction.

.3 apostasy, renunciation, **defection, desertion,** treason, crossing-over; degeneration 692.3.

.4 **rehabilitation,** reconditioning, readjustment, reclamation; **reeducation,** reinstruction; **repatriation.**

.5 **indoctrination,** reindoctrination, counterindoctrination; **brainwashing,** menticide; subversion, alienation, corruption.

.6 **conversion,** proselytization, proselytism, evangelization, persuasion 648.3.

.7 **convert, proselyte,** neophyte, catechumen, disciple.

.8 **apostate, defector,** turncoat, traitor, deserter, **renegade.**

.9 **converter, proselyter,** proselytizer, **missionary, apostle, evangelist** 1038.7.

.10 (instruments) melting pot, crucible, alembic, test tube, caldron, retort, mortar, potter's wheel, anvil, lathe; transformer, transducer, engine, motor, machine 348.4, 21.

.11 VERBS **convert,** reconvert; **change over,** switch or switch over [both informal], shift, make over, do over; **change, transform** 139.6,7; **change into, turn into, become,** resolve into, assimilate to, bring to, reduce to, naturalize; **make,** render; **reverse;** turn back 146.5.

.12 **re-form,** remodel, reshape, refashion; **renew,** new-model; **regenerate, reclaim,** redeem, amend, set straight; **reform,** make a new man of, restore self-respect; mend or change one's ways, **turn over a new leaf,** put on the new man.

.13 **defect,** renegade, renege, turn one's coat, desert, apostatize, change one's colors, turn against, turn traitor; degenerate 692.14.

.14 **rehabilitate,** recondition, reclaim; **reeducate,** reinstruct; **repatriate.**

.15 **indoctrinate, brainwash,** reindoctrinate, counterindoctrinate; subvert, alienate, win away, corrupt 692.14.

.16 **convince, persuade,** wean, bring over, **win over;** proselyte, **proselytize,** evangelize.

.17 be converted into, **turn into** or **to, become** 1.12, **change into,** alter into, run or fall or pass into, slide or glide into, **grow into,** ripen into, **develop** or **evolve into,** merge or blend or melt into, shift into, lapse into, open into, resolve itself or settle into, come round to.

.18 ADJS **convertible,** resolvable, transmutable, **transformable, transitional, modifiable.**

.19 **converted, changed, transformed;** naturalized, assimilated; **reformed,** regenerated, renewed, redeemed, reborn.

.20 **apostate, treasonable, traitorous,** degenerate, **renegade.**

146. REVERSION

(change to a former state)

.1 NOUNS reversion, reverting, retroversion, retrogradation, **retrogression**, retrocession, regress, **regression**, backsliding, slipping back, backing, recidivism, recidivation; reconversion; **reverse, reversal; return**, returning, revulsion; disenchantment, reclamation, return to the fold; reinstatement, rehabilitation, restitution, restoration; turn, turnabout, aboutface *or* flip-flop [both informal]; lapse, **relapse** 696.

.2 **throwback**, atavism.

.3 **returnee, repeater**; prodigal son, lost lamb; reversioner, reversionist; recidivist, habitual criminal *or* offender, two-time loser [slang]; backslider.

.4 VERBS **revert**, retrovert, **regress, retrogress**, retrograde, retrocede, **reverse, return**, return to the fold; backslide, slip back, recidivate, lapse, lapse back, relapse 696.4.

.5 **turn back, change back, go back, hark back**, cry back, **break back, turn**, turn around *or* about; do an about-face *or* flip-flop *or* do a flip-flop [all informal].

.6 **revert to, return to**, recur to, go back to; hark *or* cry back to.

.7 ADJS **reversionary**, reversional, **regressive**, recessive, **retrogressive, retrograde**; reactionary, revulsionary; recidivist *or* recidivous; retroverse, retrorse; atavistic; revertible, returnable, reversible; re–, retro–.

147. REVOLUTION

(sudden or radical change)

.1 NOUNS **revolution, radical** *or* **total change, violent change**, striking alteration, sweeping change, clean sweep, clean slate, tabula rasa; revulsion, transilience; **overthrow**, overturn, upset, *bouleversement* [Fr], convulsion, spasm, subversion, *coup d'état* [Fr]; breakup, breakdown; cataclysm, catastrophe, debacle, *débâcle* [Fr]; revolutionary war, war of national liberation; bloodless revolution, palace revolution; technological revolution, electronic *or* communications *or* computer revolution; counterrevolution; **revolt** 767.4.

.2 **revolutionism**, anarchism, syndicalism, terrorism; Bolshevism *or* Bolshevikism [both Russia], Carbonarism [Italy], Sinn Feinism [Ireland], Jacobinism [France]; sans-culottism [France], *sans-culotterie* [Fr], Castroism [Cuba], Maoism [China].

.3 **revolutionist, revolutionary**, revolutioner, revolutionizer; **rebel** 767.5; anarchist, anarch, syndicalist, criminal syndicalist, terrorist 162.9; subversive; red; Red Republican [France], *bonnet rouge* [Fr]; Jacobin [France], sans-culotte, sans-culottist; Yankee *or* Yankee Doodle *or* Continental [all US]; Puritan *or* Roundhead [both England]; Bolshevik *or* Bolshevist *or* Bolshie [all Russia], Marxist, Leninist, Communist, Commie [informal], Red, Trotskyite *or* Trotskyist, Castroist *or* Castroite, Guevarist, Maoist; Vietcong, Cong, VC, Charley [all Vietnam]; Mau-Mau [Kenya]; *Carbonaro* [Italy], Carbonarist [Italy]; Sinn Feiner, Fenian [both Ireland]; revolutionary junta.

.4 VERBS **revolutionize**, revolution, revolute [informal], **make a radical change**, make a clean sweep, break with the past; **overthrow**, overturn, upset; revolt 767.7.

.5 ADJS **revolutionary**, revolutional; revulsive, revulsionary; transilient; cataclysmic, catastrophic; **radical**, sweeping 56.10; **insurrectionary** 767.11.

.6 **revolutionist**, anarchic(al), syndical(ist), terrorist(ic), agin the government [informal]; Bolshevist(ic), Bolshevik; sans-culottic, sans-culottish; Jacobinic, Carbonarist, Fenian, Marxist, Leninist, Communist, Trotskyist *or* Trotskyite, Guevarist, Castroist *or* Castroite, Maoist, Vietcong, Mau-Mau.

148. EVOLUTION

.1 NOUNS **evolution**, evolving, evolvement; evolutionary change, gradual change, peaceful *or* nonviolent change; **development, growth**, rise; developmental change, natural growth *or* development; flowering, blossoming; ripening, maturation; accomplishment 722; **advance**, advancement, furtherance; **progress**, progression; **elaboration**, enlargement, amplification, **expansion**, explication.

.2 **unfolding**, unfoldment, unrolling, unfurling, unwinding.

.3 [biol terms] **genesis**; phylogeny, phylogenesis; ontogeny, ontogenesis; physiogeny, physiogenesis; **biological evolution**; natural selection, adaptation; horotely, bradytely, tachytely.

.4 **evolutionism**, theory of evolution; **Darwinism**, Neo-Darwinism, Haeckelism, Lamarckism *or* Lamarckianism, Neo-Lamarckism, Lysenkoism, Weismannism, Spencerianism; social Darwinism, social evolution.

.5 VERBS evolve, evolute [informal]; develop, grow, wax, progress, advance;
ripen, mellow, mature, maturate; flower,
bloom, blossom, bear fruit.

.6 elaborate, labor, work out, enlarge upon,
amplify, enlarge, expand, detail, go or enter into detail, go into, spell out [infor-
mal]; complete 722.6.

.7 unfold, unroll, unfurl, unwind, unreel,
uncoil.

.8 ADJS evolutionary, evolutional, evolution-
ist or evolutionistic; evolving, developing,
unfolding; maturing, maturational, maturative; progressing, advancing; genetic,
phylogenetic, ontogenetic, physiogenetic;
horotelic, bradytelic, tachytelic.

149. SUBSTITUTION

(change of one thing for another)

.1 NOUNS substitution, exchange, change,
switch, commutation, subrogation; vicari-
ousness, representation, deputation, delegation; deputyship, agency, power of attorney, supplanting, supplantment or
supplantation; replacement, displacement; superseding or supersedence or supersedure, supersession; tit for tat, *quid
pro quo* [L].

.2 substitute, sub [informal], substitution,
replacement, second or third string [in-
formal], utility player; change, exchange,
changeling, secondary, succedaneum; ersatz, phony or fake [both informal],
counterfeit, imitation 22, copy 24; surrogate; reserves, backup, personnel; spares;
alternate, alternative, next best thing,
supplanter, superseder; proxy, dummy;
vicar, agent, representative; deputy 781;
locum tenens, vice-president, vice-regent,
etc.; relief, fill-in, stand-in, understudy,
pinch hitter or runner [informal]; double;
equivalent, equal; ringer [slang]; ghost,
ghostwriter; substituent; analogy, comparison; metaphor, metonymy, synecdoche
[all gram]; symbol, sign, token; makeshift
670.2; allelo–, counter–, pro–, vice–.

.3 scapegoat, goat [informal], fall guy or
patsy [both slang], whipping boy.

.4 VERBS substitute, exchange, change, take
or ask or offer in exchange, switch, ring
in [informal], put in the place of, change
for, make way for, give place to; commute, redeem, compound for; rob Peter
to pay Paul; dub in; make do with, shift
with, put up with.

.5 substitute for, sub for [informal], subro-
gate; act for, double for, stand or sit in

for, understudy for, fill in for, pinch-hit for,
pinch-run [both informal]; relieve, spell
or spell off [both informal]; ghost, ghostwrite; represent 781.14; supplant, supersede, succeed, replace, displace, take the
place of, crowd out, cut out [informal],
change places with, swap places with [in-
formal], stand in the stead of, step into
the shoes of, fill one's shoes.

.6 [slang or informal terms] cover up for,
front for, go to the front for, take the rap
for, be the goat or patsy.

.7 delegate, deputize, commission 780.9, designate an agent or proxy.

.8 ADJS substitute, alternate, alternative,
equivalent, token, dummy, pinch, utility,
backup, secondary, vicarious, ersatz,
mock, quasi–, pseudo–, phony or fake
[both informal], counterfeit, imitation
22.8; proxy; makeshift, reserve, spare,
stopgap, temporary, provisional, tentative.

.9 substitutional, substitutionary, substitu-
tive; supersessive.

.10 replaceable, substitutable, supersedable,
expendable.

.11 ADVS instead, rather, *faute de mieux*
[Fr]; in its stead or place; in one's stead,
in one's behalf, in one's place, in one's
shoes; by proxy; as an alternative; *in loco
parentis* [L].

.12 PREPS instead of, in the stead of, in place
of, in the place of, in or on behalf of, in
lieu of; for, as proxy for, as a substitute
for, as representing, in preference to, as
an alternative to; replacing, as a replacement for, *vice* [L].

150. INTERCHANGE

(double or mutual change)

.1 NOUNS interchange, exchange, counterchange; transposition, transposal; mutual
transfer or replacement; mutual admiration, mutual support; cooperation 786;
commutation, permutation, intermuta-
tion; alternation; interplay, reciprocation
13.1, reciprocality, reciprocity, mutuality;
give-and-take, something for something,
quid pro quo [L], measure for measure,
tit for tat, an eye for an eye, "an eye for
an eye and a tooth for a tooth" [Bible];
retaliation, *lex talionis* [L]; cross fire; battledore and shuttlecock.

.2 trading, swapping [informal]; trade, swap
[informal], even trade, switch; barter
827.2; logrolling, back scratching, pork
barrel.

.3 interchangeability, exchangeability, changeability, standardization; commutability, permutability.

.4 VERBS interchange, exchange, change, counterchange; alternate; transpose; commute, permute; trade, swap [informal], switch; bandy, play at battledore and shuttlecock; reciprocate, respond; give and take, give a Roland for an Oliver, give as much as one takes, give as good as one gets, return the compliment, pay back, compensate, requite, return; retaliate, get back at, get even with, be quits with; logroll, scratch each other's back, cooperate 786.3.

.5 ADJS interchangeable, exchangeable, changeable, standard; equivalent; even, equal; returnable, convertible, commutable, permutable; commutative; retaliatory, equalizing; reciprocative or reciprocating, reciprocal; mutual, give-and-take; exchanged, transposed, switched, swapped [informal], traded, interchanged; allelo–, inter–.

.6 ADVS interchangeably, exchangeably; in exchange, in return; even, au pair [Fr]; reciprocally 13.16, mutually; in turn, each in its turn, every one in his turn, by turns, turn about, turn and turn about.

151. EVENT

.1 NOUNS event, eventuality, eventuation; realization, materialization, coming to be or pass, incidence; contingency, contingent; accident 156.6.

.2 event, occurrence, incident, episode, experience, adventure, hap, happening, happenstance, phenomenon, fact, matter of fact, reality, particular, circumstance, occasion, turn of events.

.3 affair, concern, matter, thing, concernment, interest, business, job [informal], transaction, proceeding, doing.

.4 affairs, concerns, matters, circumstances, relations, dealings, proceedings, doings, goings-on [informal]; course or run of things, the way of things, the way things go, what happens, current of events, march of events; the world, life, the times; order of the day; conditions, state of affairs, environing or ambient phenomena, state or condition of things.

.5 VERBS occur, happen 156.11, hap, eventuate, take place, come down [slang], transpire, be realized, come, come off, come about, come true, come to pass, pass, pass off, go off, fall, befall, betide; be found, be met with.

.6 turn up, show up [informal], come along, come one's way, cross one's path, come into being or existence, chance, crop up, spring up, pop up [informal], arise, come forth, come or draw on, appear, approach, materialize, present itself, be destined for one.

.7 turn out, result 154.5.

.8 experience, have, know, feel, taste; encounter, meet, meet with, meet up with [informal], run up against [informal]; undergo, go through, pass through, be subjected to, be exposed to, stand under, labor under, endure, suffer, sustain, pay, spend.

.9 ADJS happening, occurring, passing, taking place, on, going on, ongoing [informal], current, prevalent, prevailing, in the wind, afloat, afoot, under way, in hand, on foot, ado, doing; incidental, circumstantial, accompanying; accidental; occasional; resultant; eventuating.

.10 eventful, momentous, stirring, bustling, full of incident; phenomenal.

.11 eventual, coming, final, last, ultimate; contingent, collateral, secondary, indirect.

.12 ADVS eventually, ultimately, finally, in the long run; in the course of things, in the natural way of things, as things go, as times go, as the world goes, as the tree falls, the way the cookie crumbles [informal], as things turn out, as it may be or happen or turn out, as luck or fate or destiny wills.

.13 CONJS in the event that, if, in case, just in case, in any case, in either case, in the contingency that, in case that, if it should happen that; provided 507.12.

152. IMMINENCE

(future event)

.1 NOUNS imminence, imminency, impendence, impendency, forthcomingness; forthcoming, coming, approach, loom; immediate or near future; futurity 121.1.

.2 VERBS be imminent, impend, overhang, hang or lie over, hang over one's head, hover, threaten, menace, lower; brew, gather; come or draw on, draw near or nigh, rush up on one, forthcome, approach, near, await, face, confront, loom, stare one in the face, be in store, breathe down one's neck, be about to be borning.

.3 ADJS imminent, impending, impendent, overhanging, hanging over one's head, waiting, lurking, threatening, lowering, menacing, lying in ambush, "in danger imminent" [Spenser]; **brewing,** gathering, preparing; **coming, forthcoming, upcoming, to come,** about to be, about *or* going to happen, **approaching, nearing,** looming, looming in the distance *or* future; **near, close,** immediate, instant, **at hand,** near at hand, close at hand; **in the offing,** on the horizon, **in prospect,** already in sight, just around the corner, in view, in one's eye, in store, in reserve, **in the wind,** in the womb of time; on the knees *or* lap of the gods, in the cards [informal]; that will be, that is to be; future 121.8.

.4 ADVS **imminently,** impendingly; **any time,** any time now, any moment, any minute, any hour, any day; **to be expected,** as may be expected, as may be.

153. CAUSE

.1 NOUNS **cause, occasion,** antecedents, call, **grounds,** ground, stimulus, base, **basis,** element, principle, factor; **determinant,** determinative; causation, causality, cause and effect; etiology.

.2 **reason,** reason why, rationale, reason for *or* behind, underlying reason, rational ground, **explanation, the why,** the wherefore, the whatfor *or* whyfor [informal], **the why and wherefore,** the idea [informal], the big idea [slang]; stated cause, pretext, pretense, excuse.

.3 **immediate cause,** proximate cause; transient cause, occasional cause; formal cause; efficient cause; ultimate cause, immanent cause, remote cause, causing cause, *causa causans* [L], first cause; **final cause,** *causa finalis* [L]; provocation, **last straw,** straw that broke the camel's back, match in the powder barrel; causal sequence, chain *or* nexus of cause and effect.

.4 **author,** agent, **originator,** generator, begetter, engenderer, producer, maker, beginner, **creator,** mover; **parent, mother, father,** sire; **prime mover,** *primum mobile* [L]; causer, effector; inspirer, instigator, catalyst.

.5 **source, origin,** genesis, original, origination, **derivation, rise, beginning,** conception, inception, commencement, **head;** provenance, provenience; **root,** radix, –rhiza *or* –rrhiza, radical, taproot, grass roots; stem, stock.

.6 **fountainhead,** headwater, headstream, riverhead, springhead, headspring, **mainspring,** wellspring, wellhead, well, **spring,** fountain, fount, font, *fons et origo* [L]; mine, quarry; cren(o)–.

.7 egg, ovum 406.12, **germ,** germen [archaic], spermatozoon 406.11, nucleus 406.7, **seed; embryo** 406.14; bud 411.21; rudiment, *Anlage* [Ger]; loins.

.8 **birthplace, breeding place,** rookery, hatchery; **hotbed,** forcing bed; incubator, brooder; **nest,** nidus; **cradle,** nursery.

.9 **womb,** matrix, uterus, uter(o)–, metr(o)–, –metrium, venter.

.10 (a principle or movement) **cause, principle,** interest, issue, burning issue, commitment, faith, great cause, lifework; reason for being, *raison d'être* [Fr]; **movement,** mass movement, activity; **drive, campaign, crusade.**

.11 VERBS **cause,** be the cause of, lie at the root of; **bring about, bring to pass,** effectuate, **effect,** bring to effect, realize, occasion, **make, create, engender,** generate, **produce,** breed, work, do; –ate, –en, –ise *or* –ize; **originate,** give origin to, give occasion to, **give rise to,** give birth to, beget, bear, bring forth, labor *or* travail and bring forth, author, **father,** sire, sow the seeds of; gestate, **conceive;** set up, set afloat, **set on foot;** found, establish, inaugurate, institute.

.12 **induce,** lead, procure, get, obtain, contrive, **effect,** bring, **bring on,** draw on, **call forth, elicit, evoke,** provoke, inspire, instigate, motivate; draw down, open the door to; superinduce.

.13 **contribute to, lead to,** conduce to, redound to; **advance, forward,** influence, subserve; **determine,** decide, turn the scale, have the last word.

.14 ADJS **causal,** causative; occasional; originative, institutive, constitutive; **at the bottom of,** behind the scenes; **formative,** determinative, effectual, decisive, pivotal; etiological; etio– *or* aetio–, prot(o)–; –facient, –factive, –fic, –ic(al) *or* –etic.

.15 **original, primary,** primal, primitive, pristine, primordial, primeval, aboriginal, **elementary,** elemental, **basic,** basal, **rudimentary,** crucial, central, radical, **fundamental;** embryonic, in embryo, *in ovo* [L], germinal, seminal, pregnant; **generative,** genetic, protogenic.

154. EFFECT

.1 NOUNS **effect, result,** resultant, **consequence,** consequent, sequent, sequence, sequel, sequela; event, eventuality, eventuation, **upshot, outcome,** logical outcome, outgrowth, offshoot, offspring, issue, legacy; **product** 168, precipitate, distillate, **fruit,** harvest; development, corollary; derivative, derivation, by-product.

.2 **conclusion,** end 70, **end** *or* **final result, consummation, culmination,** denouement, catastrophe, termination, completion, finale, last act, climax, bitter end, payoff [slang].

.3 **impact,** force, **repercussion,** reaction; backwash, backlash, reflex, recoil, response; mark, print, imprint, impress, impression; clout [informal].

.4 **aftereffect, aftermath,** aftergrowth, aftercrop, **afterclap,** afterimage, afterglow, aftertaste; wake, trail, track; domino effect.

.5 VERBS **result, ensue, issue, follow,** attend; **turn out, come out,** fall out, **work out,** pan out [informal], fare; turn out to be, prove, prove to be; **become of,** come of, come about; develop, unfold; **eventuate,** terminate, end.

.6 **result from,** be the effect of, be due to, originate in *or* from, **come from,** come out of, grow from, **grow out of,** follow from *or* on, proceed from, descend from, emerge from, issue from, ensue from, emanate from, flow from, **derive from,** accrue from, rise *or* arise from, take its rise from, **spring from, stem from,** sprout from, bud from, germinate from; **depend on,** hinge *or* pivot *or* turn on, hang on, be contingent on.

.7 ADJS **resultant, resulting, following, ensuing; consequent,** consequential, sequent, sequential, sequacious; **final** 70.10; derivative, derivational.

.8 **resulting from,** coming from, arising from, deriving *or* derivable from; **owing to, due to;** attributed *or* attributable to, dependent *or* contingent on; **caused by,** occasioned by, **at the bottom of.**

.9 ADVS **consequently, as a result,** as a consequence, in consequence, naturally, *naturellement* [Fr], necessarily, of necessity, inevitably, of course, as a matter of course, and so, it follows that; **therefore; accordingly** 8.11; **finally** 70.11.

.10 PHRS one thing leads to another, *post hoc, ergo propter hoc* [L], what goes up must come down.

155. ATTRIBUTION

(assignment of cause)

.1 NOUNS **attribution, assignment,** assignation, **ascription, imputation,** arrogation, placement, application, attachment, saddling, **charge, blame; responsibility,** an-

swerability; **credit,** honor; accounting for, reference to, derivation from, connection with; etiology; palaetiology.

.2 **acknowledgment,** citation, tribute; confession; **reference;** trademark, signature; **by-line,** credit line.

.3 VERBS **attribute, assign, ascribe, impute,** give, place, put, apply, attach, refer.

.4 **attribute to, ascribe to, impute to,** assign to, **lay to,** put *or* set down to, apply to, refer to, point to; **pin on,** pinpoint [informal], fix on *or* upon, attach to, accrete to, connect with, fasten upon, hang on [slang], **saddle on** *or* **upon,** place upon, **father upon,** settle upon, saddle with; blame, **blame for,** blame on *or* upon [informal], charge on *or* upon, place *or* put the blame on, place the blame *or* responsibility for, **fix the responsibility for,** fix the burden of, **charge to,** lay to one's charge, place to one's account, set to the account of, account for, lay at the door of, bring home to; acknowledge, confess; **credit** *or* **accredit with;** put words in one's mouth.

.5 **trace to,** follow the trail to; **derive from,** trace the origin *or* derivation of; affiliate to, filiate to, father, fix the paternity of.

.6 ADJS **attributable, assignable, ascribable, imputable,** traceable, referable, accountable, explicable; owing, **due,** assigned *or* referred to, derivable from, derivative, derivational; **charged,** alleged, imputed, putative; **credited, attributed;** ap(o)− *or* aph−, de−, ep(i)−; −genous.

.7 ADVS **hence, therefore,** therefor, **wherefore,** wherefrom, whence, then, thence, *ergo* [L], for which reason; **consequently** 154.9; **accordingly** 8.11; **because of that,** for that, by reason of that, for that reason, for the reason that, from *or* for that cause, **on that account,** on that ground, thereat; **because of this, on this account,** for this cause, on account of this, *propter hoc* [L], for this reason, hereat; **thus,** thusly [informal], thuswise.

.8 **why,** whyever, whyfor *or* for why [both dial], how come [informal], how is it that, **wherefore, what for,** for which, **on what account,** on account of what *or* which, for what *or* whatever reason, from what cause, *pourquoi* [Fr].

.9 PREPS **because of,** by reason of, **as a result of,** by *or* in virtue of, **on account of,** on the score of, for the sake of, **owing to, due to,** thanks to; **considering,** in consideration of, **in view of;** after.

.10 CONJS **because,** *parce que* [Fr], **since,** as,

for, whereas, inasmuch as, forasmuch as, insofar as, insomuch as, as things go; in that, for the cause that, for the reason that, in view of the fact that, taking into account that, **seeing that,** seeing as how [dial], being as how [dial].

156. CHANCE

(absence of assignable cause)

.1 NOUNS **chance,** happenstance, hap, "heedless hap" [Spenser]; **luck;** good luck *or* fortune, serendipity, happy chance; **fortune, fate, destiny,** whatever comes, moira, **lot** 640.2; **fortuity,** fortuitousness, adventitiousness, indeterminateness *or* indeterminacy, problematicness, uncertainty 514, flukiness [informal], casualness, flip of a coin, accidentality; break [informal], the breaks [informal], run of luck, run *or* turn of the cards, fall *or* throw of the dice, the way things fall, the way the cards fall, how they fall, the way the cookie crumbles *or* the ball bounces [informal]; uncertainty principle, principle of indeterminacy, Heisenberg's principle; **probability** 511, theory of probability, law of averages, statistical probability, actuarial calculation; random sample, **risk, gamble** 515; **opportunity** 129.2.

.2 Chance, Fortune, Lady *or* Dame Fortune, wheel of fortune, Fortuna; Luck, Lady Luck; "a nickname of Providence" [de Chamfort], "blind Chance" [Lucan], "fickle Chance" [Milton], "that Power which erring men call Chance" [Milton], "the pseudonym of God when He did not want to sign" [Anatole France].

.3 **purposelessness, causelessness,** randomness, dysteleology, **unpredictability** 514.1, designlessness, **aimlessness.**

.4 **haphazard,** chance-medley, **random;** random shot; potluck.

.5 **vicissitudes,** vicissitudes of fortune, ins and outs, **ups and downs,** ups and downs of life, chapter of accidents, feast and famine, "the various turns of chance" [Dryden], fickle finger of fate; **chain of circumstances,** concatenation of events, chain reaction, vicious circle.

.6 (chance event) **happening,** hap, happenstance; **fortuity, accident,** casualty, adventure, hazard; **contingent, contingency;** fluke [informal], freak accident; chance hit, lucky shot, long shot, one in a million, long odds.

.7 **even chance,** even break [informal], fair shake [informal], even *or* square odds,

touch and go, odds; **half a chance,** fifty-fifty; toss, **toss-up,** standoff [informal].

.8 **good chance, sporting chance,** good opportunity, good possibility; odds-on, odds-on chance, **likelihood, possibility** 509, probability 511, favorable prospect, well-grounded hope; **sure bet,** sure thing [informal], a lot going for one [informal]; best bet, main chance.

.9 **small chance,** little chance, dark horse, **poor prospect** *or* prognosis, poor lookout [informal], little opportunity, poor possibility, **unlikelihood, improbability** 512, hardly a chance, not half a chance; **off chance, outside chance** [informal], **remote possibility,** bare possibility, a ghost of a chance, slim chance, gambling chance, **fighting chance** [informal]; poor bet, long odds, long shot [informal], hundred-to-one shot [informal].

.10 **no chance,** not a Chinaman's chance [slang], not a prayer, not a snowball's chance in hell [slang]; **impossibility** 510, hopelessness.

.11 VERBS **chance,** bechance, betide, come *or* happen by chance, hap, hazard, **happen** 151.5, come, come *or* happen along, **turn up,** pop up [informal], **befall;** fall to one's lot, be one's fate.

.12 **risk,** take a chance, **gamble, bet** 515.18–20; **predict** 543.9, prognosticate, make book [informal].

.13 **have a chance** *or* an opportunity, **stand a chance, run a good chance, bid** *or* **stand fair to,** admit of; be in it *or* in the running [informal]; have a chance at, have a fling *or* shot at [informal]; have a small *or* slight chance, be a dark horse, barely have a chance.

.14 **not have** *or* **stand a chance,** have no chance *or* opportunity, not have a prayer, not have a Chinaman's chance [slang], not stand a snowball's chance in hell [slang]; not be in it [informal], be out of it [informal], **be out of the running.**

.15 ADJS **chance;** chancy [informal], dicey [Brit informal], **risky** [informal]; **fortuitous, accidental,** aleatory, **casual,** adventitious, incidental, contingent, iffy [informal]; **causeless,** uncaused; indeterminate, undetermined; **unexpected** 540.10, **unpredictable** 514.14, unforeseeable, unlooked-for, **unforeseen;** fluky [informal]; fatal, fatidic, destinal.

.16 **purposeless, causeless,** designless, **aimless,** driftless, undirected, unmotivated, mindless; **haphazard, random,** dysteleological, stochastic, stray, inexplicable, unaccountable, promiscuous, indiscriminate, casual, leaving much to chance.

.17 **unintentional**, unintended, **unmeant, unplanned**, undesigned, unpurposed, unthought-of; **unpremeditated**, unmeditated, unprompted, unguided, unguarded; **unwitting, unthinking**, unconscious, involuntary.

.18 impossible 510.7; **improbable** 512.3; certain 513.13; **probable** 511.6.

.19 ADVS **by chance**, perchance, **by accident, accidentally, casually**, incidentally, **unpredictably, fortuitously;** by a piece of luck, by a fluke [informal], by good fortune; **as it chanced, as luck would have it,** by hazard, as it may happen, as it may be, as the case may be, as it may chance, as it may turn up or out; somehow, in some way, in some way or other, somehow or other, for some reason.

.20 **purposelessly, aimlessly; haphazardly**, randomly, dysteleologically, stochastically, inexplicably, unaccountably, promiscuously, indiscriminately, casually, **at haphazard, at random,** at hazard.

.21 **unintentionally, without design, unwittingly**, unthinkingly, unexpectedly, unconsciously, involuntarily.

157. POWER, POTENCY

(effective force)

.1 NOUNS **power, potency** or potence, prepotency, potentiality, **force, might**, mightiness, **vigor**, vitality, vim, push, drive, charge, puissance [archaic]; dynam(o)–, –dynamia; dint, virtue; moxie or pizzazz or poop or punch or clout or steam [all informal]; powerfulness, forcefulness; virulence, vehemence; **strength** 159; **energy** 161; **virility** 420.2; cogence or cogency, validity, effect, **effectiveness**, effectuality; productivity, productiveness; power structure; **influence** 172, pull; **authority** 739, weight; **superiority** 36; power pack, amperage, wattage; main force, *force majeure* [Fr], main strength, brute force or strength, compulsion, duress; muscle power, sinew, might and main, beef [informal], strong arm; full force, full blast; superpower; armipotence, power struggle; black power; flower power; mana; charisma.

.2 **ability**, –ability or –ibility, ableness, **capability**, capableness, **capacity**, faculty, facility, fitness, qualification, talent, flair; genius, caliber, **competence**, adequacy, sufficiency, **efficiency**, efficacy; profi-

ciency 733.1; the stuff or the goods or what it takes [all informal]; susceptibility.

.3 **omnipotence, almightiness, all-powerfulness.**

.4 **horsepower, manpower**; electric power, electropower, hydroelectric power; hydraulic power, water power; steam power, piston power; solar power; atomic power, nuclear power, thermonuclear power; rocket power, jet power; **propulsion, thrust**, impulse.

.5 force of inertia, *vis inertiae* [L]; dead force, *vis mortua* [L]; living force, *vis viva* [L]; force of life, *vis vitae* [L].

.6 centrifugal force or action, centripetal force or action, force of gravity.

.7 (science of forces) dynamics, statics.

.8 **empowerment, enablement;** investment, endowment.

.9 **work force**, hands, men; **fighting force**, troops, units, the big battalions, firepower; **personnel** 750.11; **forces.**

.10 VERBS **empower, enable;** invest, clothe, invest or clothe with power, deputize; endue, endow, **authorize** 780.9; arm.

.11 **be able**, be up to [informal], lie in one's **power**; can, may, can do; make it or make the grade [both informal]; hack it or cut it or cut the mustard [all informal]; possess authority 739.13; **take charge** 739.14.

.12 ADJS **powerful, potent**, prepotent, powerpacked, **mighty**, irresistible, **forceful**, forcible, dynamic, –dynamous; **vigorous**, vital, **energetic** 161.12, puissant, ruling, in power; **cogent**, striking, telling, effective, valid, operative, in force; **strong** 159.13; high-powered, high-tension, high-pressure, high-potency; **authoritative** 139.15; armipotent, mighty in battle.

.13 **omnipotent, almighty, all-powerful**; plenipotentiary, absolute, unlimited, **sovereign** 739.17; **supreme** 36.13.

.14 **able**, –able or –ible, –ile, **capable, equal to**, up to, **competent**, adequate, effective, effectual, efficient, efficacious; productive; **proficient** 733.20–22.

.15 ADVS **powerfully, potently, forcefully**, forcibly, mightily, with might and main, **vigorously, energetically** 161.15, dynamically; **cogently**, strikingly, tellingly; **effectively**, effectually; productively; with telling effect, to good account, to good purpose, with a vengeance.

.16 **ably, capably, competently**, adequately, effectively, effectually, **efficiently, well; to the best of one's ability**, as lies in one's power, so far as one can, as best one can; with all one's might, with everything that is in one.

.17 **by force**, by main *or* brute force, by *force majeure*, with the strong arm, with a high hand, high-handedly; **forcibly**, amain, with might and main; by force of arms, at the point of the sword, by storm.

.18 PREPS by dint of, by virtue of.

158. IMPOTENCE

.1 NOUNS impotence *or* impotency, **powerlessness**, impuissance [archaic], forcelessness; feebleness, softness, flabbiness, **weakness** 160; power vacuum.

.2 inability, incapability, incapacity, incapacitation, **incompetence** *or* incompetency, inadequacy, insufficiency, ineptitude, **inferiority** 37, inefficiency, unfitness, imbecility; disability, disablement, disqualification; legal incapacity, wardship, minority, infancy.

.3 ineffectiveness, ineffectualness, ineffectuality, inefficaciousness, **inefficacy**, counterproductiveness, counterproductivity, invalidity, **futility, uselessness**, bootlessness, failure 725, fatuity, inanity.

.4 helplessness, defenselessness, unprotection; invalidism, debilitation, effeteness.

.5 emasculation, demasculinization, effeminization; maiming, castration 42.4.

.6 impotent, weakling 160.6, invalid, incompetent; flash in the pan, blank cartridge, dud [informal]; eunuch, *castrato* [Ital], gelding.

.7 VERBS be impotent, lack force; be ineffective, avail nothing, not work *or* do, not take [informal].

.8 cannot, not be able, not have it *or* hack it *or* cut it *or* cut the mustard [informal], not make it, not make the grade [both informal].

.9 disable, disenable, unfit, **incapacitate**, drain, de-energize; enfeeble, debilitate, **weaken** 160.9,10; cripple, maim, lame, hamstring; wing, clip the wings of; **inactivate**, put out of action, put *hors de combat*; **put out of order**, put out of commission [informal], throw out of gear; bugger [slang], queer *or* queer the works [both slang], gum up *or* screw up the works [slang], throw a wrench *or* monkey wrench in the machinery [informal], sabotage, wreck; kibosh *or* put the kibosh on [both slang]; spike, spike one's guns, put a spoke in one's wheels.

.10 disqualify, invalidate, unfit, knock the bottom out of [informal].

.11 (render powerless) **paralyze**, prostrate, shoot down in flames [informal], knock out [slang], break the neck *or* back of; hamstring; handcuff, tie the hands of, hobble, enchain, manacle, hog-tie [informal], **tie hand and foot**, truss up; throttle, strangle, get a stranglehold on; muzzle, gag, silence; **disarm**, pull one's teeth, draw the teeth *or* fangs of; **take the wind out of one's sails**, deflate, knock the props out from under, cut the ground from under, not leave a leg to stand on.

.12 unman, unnerve, enervate, exhaust, etiolate, **devitalize; emasculate**, demasculinize, effeminize; desex, desexualize; sterilize; castrate 42.11.

.13 ADJS impotent, powerless, forceless; feeble, soft, flabby, **weak** 160.12; –less.

.14 unable, incapable, incompetent, inefficient, ineffective; **unqualified**, inept, unendowed, ungifted, untalented, **unfit**, unfitted; **inferior** 37.6; unable to, incapable of.

.15 ineffective, ineffectual, inefficacious, counterproductive, feckless, inadequate 37.7; **invalid, inoperative**, of no force; nugatory, nugacious; fatuous, fatuitous; **vain, futile, useless**, unavailing, bootless, fruitless; empty, inane, effete, etiolated, barren, sterile.

.16 disabled, incapacitated; crippled, hamstrung; disqualified, invalidated; disarmed; paralyzed; hog-tied [informal]; prostrate, on one's back, on one's beam-ends.

.17 out of action, out of commission [informal], out of gear; *hors de combat* [Fr], out of the battle, off the field, out of the running; laid on the shelf, obsolete.

.18 helpless, defenseless, unprotected; aidless, friendless, unfriended; fatherless, motherless; leaderless, guideless; **untenable**, pregnable, vulnerable.

.19 unmanned, unnerved, enervated, debilitated, **devitalized**; nerveless, sinewless, marrowless, pithless, lustless; **castrated**, emasculate, emasculated, gelded, eunuchized, unsexed, deballed [slang], demasculinized, effeminized.

.20 ADVS beyond one, beyond one's power *or* capacity *or* ability, beyond one's depth, out of one's league [informal], above one's head, too much for.

159. STRENGTH

(inherent power)

.1 NOUNS strength, might, mightiness, powerfulness; force, potency, power 157; energy 161; **vigor, vitality,** vigorousness, heartiness, lustiness, lustihood; **stoutness, sturdiness,** stalwartness, robustness, hardiness, ruggedness; **stamina, guts** or gutsiness [both slang], fortitude, intestinal fortitude [informal], **toughness** 359, endurance; strength of will, decisiveness, obstinacy 626; staying or sticking power.

.2 **muscularity,** brawniness; beefiness or huskiness or heftiness [all informal], thewiness, sinewiness; **brawn,** beef [informal]; **muscle,** muscul(o)–, my(o)–, –eus; thew, thews, sinew, sinews; musculature, physique; voluntary muscle 159.22, involuntary muscle; tone, elasticity 358.

.3 **firmness, soundness,** staunchness, stoutness, **sturdiness, stability,** solidity, **hardness** 356, temper.

.4 **impregnability,** impenetrability, **invulnerability,** inexpugnability, inviolability; **unassailability,** unattackableness; resistlessness, **irresistibility; invincibility,** indomitability, insuperability, unconquerableness, unbeatableness.

.5 **strengthening, invigoration,** fortification; hardening, case hardening, tempering; **restrengthening,** reinforcement; **reinvigoration,** refreshment, revivification.

.6 **strong man, stalwart, tower of strength;** powerhouse or muscle man or man mountain or big bruiser [all informal]; strong-arm man, bully, bullyboy, tough, tough guy [informal], gorilla; **giant,** Samson, Goliath; Charles Atlas; Hercules, Atlas, Antaeus, Cyclops, Briareus, colossus, Polyphemus, Titan, Brobdingnagian [Swift], Tarzan [E. R. Burroughs], Superman; the strong, the mighty.

.7 (comparisons) horse, ox, lion; oak, heart of oak; rock, Gibraltar; iron, steel, nails.

.8 VERBS **be strong,** overpower, overwhelm; have what it takes, pack a punch.

.9 **not weaken,** not flag; **bear up, hold up,** keep up, stand up; **hold out,** stay or see it out, stick or sweat it out [informal], stay the distance [informal], not give up, **never say die;** not let it get one down or take it or hang in or hang tough [all informal].

.10 **exert strength,** put beef or one's back into it [informal]; use force, muscle or strong-arm [both informal].

.11 **strengthen, invigorate, fortify,** beef up [informal], brace, buttress, prop, shore up, support, undergird, brace up; gird, gird up one's loins; steel, harden, case harden, stiffen, **toughen,** temper, nerve; confirm, sustain; **restrengthen, reinforce;**

reinvigorate, refresh, revive, recruit one's strength.

.12 **proof,** insulate, weatherproof, soundproof, fireproof, waterproof, etc.

.13 ADJS **strong, forceful,** forcible,– forcy [Scot], **mighty, powerful,** puissant [dial], **potent** 157.12; **stout, sturdy, stalwart, rugged,** hale; husky or hefty or beefy [all informal], strapping, doughty [dial], **hardy,** hard, hard as nails, iron-hard, steely; **robust,** robustious, gutty or gutsy [both slang]; strong-willed, obstinate 626.8; **vigorous, hearty,** nervy, **lusty,** bouncing, full-or red-blooded; sturdy as an ox, strong as a lion or ox or horse, strong as brandy, strong as strong; full-strength, double-strength.

.14 **able-bodied, well-built,** well-set, well-set-up [informal], well-knit, of good or powerful physique, broad-shouldered, barrel-chested, **athletic; muscular,** thickset, burly, **brawny;** thewy, sinewy, **wiry;** muscle-bound.

.15 **Herculean,** Briarean, Antaean, Cyclopean, Atlantean, gigantic, huge 195.20.

.16 **firm, sound, stout,** sturdy, **staunch, stable,** solid; sound as a dollar, solid as a rock, firm as Gibraltar, made of iron; rigid, unbreakable, infrangible.

.17 **impregnable,** impenetrable, **invulnerable,** inviolable, inexpugnable; **unassailable,** unattackable, insuperable, unsurmountable; resistless, **irresistible; invincible,** indomitable, **unconquerable,** unsubduable, unyielding 626.9, incontestable, unbeatable, more than a match for; overpowering, overwhelming.

.18 **resistant, proof, tight;** proof against, impervious to; foolproof; shatterproof; weatherproof, dampproof, watertight, leakproof; hermetic, airtight; soundproof, noiseproof; punctureproof, holeproof; bulletproof, ballproof, shellproof, bombproof, rustproof, corrosionproof; fireproof, flameproof, fire-resisting; burglarproof.

.19 **unweakened, undiminished,** unallayed, unbated, unabated, unfaded, unwithered, unshaken, unworn, unexhausted; **unweakening, unflagging;** in full force or swing, **going strong** [informal]; in the plenitude of power.

.20 (of sounds and odors) **intense, penetrating,** piercing; **loud,** deafening, thundering 456.12; **pungent,** reeking 435.10.

.21 ADVS **strongly, stoutly, sturdily,** stalwartly, **robustly,** ruggedly; **mightily, powerfully, forcefully,** forcibly; **vigorously,** heartily, lustily; **soundly, firmly,** staunchly; impregnably, invulnerably, **invincibly, irresistibly,** unyieldingly; resistantly, imperviously; **intensely; loudly,** deafeningly; **pungently.**

.22 voluntary muscles

adductor	plantaris
auricularis	platysma
biceps	pronator
brachialis	psoas
brachioradialis	pyriformis
buccinator	quadrator
coracobrachialis	quadriceps
deltoid(eus)	rectus abdominus
digastric	rectus femoris
extensor	rhomboideus
flexor	sacrospinalis
frontalis	sartorius
gastrocnemius	semimembranosus
gemellus	semitendinosus
gluteus maximus	serratus
gluteus medius	soleus
gluteus minimus	sphincter
iliacus	spinalis
infraspinatus	splenius
intercostal	sternocleidomastoid-
interosseus	(eus)
lacertus fibrosus	sternohyoid
latissimus dorsi	subclavius
levator	supraspinatus
masseter	temporalis
mentalis	tensor
mylohyoid	teres
nasalis	tibialis
oblique	trapezius
obturator	triangularis
occipitalis	triceps
omohyoid	vastus intermedius
palmaris	vastus lateralis
pectineus	vastus medialis
pectoralis	zygomaticus
peroneus	

160. WEAKNESS

.1 NOUNS **weakness,** weakliness, **feebleness, strengthlessness, flabbiness,** flaccidity, softness, **impotence** 158; gutlessness [slang], cowardice 892; **debility,** debilitation; faintness, gone or blah feeling [informal]; languor, lassitude, languishment, listlessness, weariness, fatigue 717, prostration, dullness, sluggishness; atony, anemia, bloodlessness, etiolation, asthenia, adynamia, cachexia or cachexy.

.2 **frailty,** slightness, **delicacy, daintiness,** lightness; effeminacy, womanishness; **flimsiness, unsubstantiality,** wispiness, sleaziness; **fragility,** frangibility, brittleness, breakability, destructibility, disintegration 53, collapse; human frailty, "amiable weakness" [Henry Fielding]; moral weakness, irresolution, **indecisiveness,** infirmity of will, velleity, changeableness 141; inherent vice.

.3 infirmity, unsoundness, incapacity, unfirmness, unsturdiness, **instability, unsubstantiality;** decrepitude; **unsteadiness, shakiness,** ricketiness, wobbliness, caducity, senility, invalidism; wishy-washiness, insipidity, vapidity, wateriness.

.4 **weak point, weak side,** vulnerable point, heel of Achilles; feet of clay.

.5 **weakening, enfeeblement, debilitation,** exhaustion, inanition, attrition, effemination; languishment; **devitalization,** enervation, evisceration; fatigue; attenuation, extenuation; softening, mitigation, damping, abatement, slackening, relaxation, blunting, deadening, dulling; **dilution,** reduction, thinning.

.6 **weakling,** weak or meek soul, weak sister [informal], softy [informal], softling, **jellyfish,** invertebrate, gutless wonder [slang], **baby,** big baby, crybaby, chicken [slang], Milquetoast, sop, **milksop, namby-pamby, mollycoddle,** mama's boy, mother's darling, teacher's pet; sissy or pansy or pantywaist [all slang], pushover [slang], lightweight; poor or weak or dull tool [informal], doormat, nonentity, nebbish or sad sack [both informal].

.7 (comparisons) reed, thread, hair, cobweb, gossamer, matchwood, rope of sand; house of cards, house built on sand, sand castle; water, milk and water, gruel, dishwater, cambric tea.

.8 VERBS (be weak) **shake,** tremble, quiver, cower 892.9, totter, teeter, dodder; halt, limp; be on one's last legs, have one foot in the grave.

.9 (become weak) **weaken,** grow weak or weaker, go soft [informal]; **languish, wilt,** faint, **droop,** drop, **sink, decline, flag, pine, fade, fail;** crumble, go to pieces, disintegrate 53.3; go downhill, hit the skids [slang], give way, break, collapse, cave in [informal]; give out, conk or peter or poop or peg or fizzle out [informal]; come apart, come apart at the seams, come unstuck; yield; die on the vine [informal]; wear thin or away.

.10 (make weak) **weaken, enfeeble, debilitate,** unstrengthen, unsinew, undermine, soften up [informal], unbrace, unman, unnerve, rattle, shake up [informal], **devitalize, enervate,** eviscerate; **sap,** sap the strength of, exhaust, gruel, take it out of [informal]; shake, unstring; reduce, lay low; attenuate, extenuate, mitigate, abate; blunt, deaden, dull, damp or dampen, take the edge off; cramp, cripple.

.11 **dilute, cut** [informal], **reduce, thin,** attenuate, rarefy; **water,** water down, adulterate, irrigate or baptize [both slang].

.12 ADJS **weak,** weakly, **feeble,** asthen(o)–, lept(o)–; **debilitated,** imbecile; **strengthless,** sapless, marrowless, pithless, sinewless, listless, nerveless, lustless; **impotent, powerless** 158.13; spineless, chicken or gutless [slang], cowardly 892.10; unnerved, shook-up [informal], unstrung, faint, faintish, gone; dull, slack; **soft, flabby,** flaccid, unhardened; **limp,** limber, limp or limber as a dishrag, floppy, rubbery; **languorous,** languid, **drooping,** droopy, pooped [informal]; asthenic, anemic, bloodless, effete, etiolated; not what one used to be.

.13 "weak as water" [Bible], weak as milk and water, weak as a drink of water, weak as a child or baby, weak as a chicken, weak as a kitten, weak as a mouse, "weak as a rained-on bee" [F. R. Torrence].

.14 **frail, slight, delicate, dainty,** "delicately weak" [Pope]; puny; light, lightweight, womanish, effeminate; namby-pamby, sissified, pansyish; **fragile,** frangible, **breakable,** destructible, shattery, crumbly, brittle; **unsubstantial, flimsy,** sleazy, tacky [informal], wispy, cobwebby, gossamery, papery, pasteboardy; gimcrack or gimcracky or cheap-jack [all informal]; jerry-built, jerry.

.15 **unsound, infirm,** unfirm, **unstable, unsubstantial,** unsturdy, unsolid, decrepit, crumbling, disintegrating 53.5; poor, poorish; rotten, rotten at or rotten to the core.

.16 **unsteady, shaky, rickety,** ricketish, spindly, spidery, teetering, teetery, tottery, tottering, doddering, tumbledown, ramshackle, dilapidated, rocky [informal], groggy, wobbly.

.17 **wishy-washy,** tasteless, bland, **insipid,** vapid, neutral, watery, milky, milk-and-water, mushy; halfhearted, infirm of will or purpose, **indecisive,** irresolute, changeable 141.7.

.18 **weakened, enfeebled, disabled,** incapacitated; **devitalized,** drained, exhausted, sapped, burned-out, used up, played out, spent, ausgespielt [Ger], effete; **fatigued** 717.6, **enervated,** eviscerated; **wasted, run-down,** worn, worn-out, worn to a frazzle [informal], worn to a shadow, reduced to a skeleton, "weakened and wasted to skin and bone" [Du Bartas].

.19 **diluted, cut** [informal], **reduced, thinned,** rarefied, attenuated; adulterated; watered, watered-down.

.20 **weakening, debilitating, enfeebling; devitalizing,** enervating, sapping, exhausting, fatiguing 717.11, grueling, trying, draining.

.21 **languishing, drooping, sinking, declining, flagging, pining, fading, failing.**

.22 ADVS **weakly, feebly,** strengthlessly, languorously, listlessly; faintly; delicately, effeminately, daintily; infirmly, unsoundly, unstably, unsubstantially, unsturdily, flimsily; shakily, unsteadily, teeteringly, totteringly.

161. ENERGY

.1 NOUNS **energy, vigor, force, power, vitality,** strenuousness, **intensity,** dynamism, demonic energy; **potency** 157; **strength** 159; actual or kinetic energy; dynamic energy; potential energy, ergal.

.2 **vim, verve,** fire, starch, snap [informal], bang or **punch** [both informal], **dash, drive,** push [informal], **aggressiveness, enterprise,** initiative, thrust, spunk, piss and vinegar [slang], get-up-and-go [informal]; pep or pepper or ginger or kick or zip or zing or zizz or pizzazz or poop [all informal].

.3 **animation, vivacity,** liveliness, **ardor,** glow, warmth, enthusiasm, lustiness, robustness, mettle, **zest,** zestfulness, **gusto,** élan, impetus, impetuosity, joie de vivre [Fr], brio [Ital], spiritedness, **briskness,** perkiness, pertness, **life, spirit;** activity 707.

.4 **acrimony,** acridity, acerbity, acidity, **bitterness,** tartness, **causticity,** mordancy or mordacity, **virulence; harshness,** fierceness, **rigor,** roughness, **severity, vehemence,** violence 162, stringency, astringency, stridency 458.1, **sharpness, keenness, poignancy,** trenchancy; edge, point; bite, teeth, grip, sting.

.5 **energizer, stimulus,** stimulator, arouser, restorative; **stimulant, tonic** 687.8; **activator,** motivating force, motive power; **animator,** spark plug [informal], human dynamo [informal]; life, life of the party.

.6 (units of energy) atomerg, dinamode, dyne, erg, energid, foot-pound, horsepower-hour, horsepower-year, joule, calorie 328.19, kilogram-meter, kilowatt-hour, photon, quantum.

.7 **energizing, invigoration, animation, enlivenment,** quickening, **vitalization,** revival, revitalization; **exhilaration, stimulation.**

.8 **activation,** reactivation; viability.

.9 VERBS **energize, dynamize; invigorate, animate, enliven,** liven, **vitalize, quicken,** exhilarate, stimulate, hearten, galvanize, electrify, fire, inflame, warm, kindle, rouse, arouse, act like a tonic, **pep** or snap or jazz or zip or perk up [informal], put pep or zip into it [informal].

.10 **have energy,** be energetic, be vigorous, **thrive,** burst or overflow with energy, flourish, feel one's oats, be up and doing, be full of beans or pep or ginger or zip [informal], be full of piss and vinegar [slang].

.11 **activate,** reactivate, recharge.

.12 ADJS **energetic, vigorous, strenuous, forceful, forcible, strong, dynamic,** kinetic, intense, acute, keen, incisive, trenchant, vivid, vibrant; **enterprising, aggressive,** take-over or take-charge [both informal]; **active, lively,** living, **animated, spirited,** go-go [slang], **vivacious,** brisk, lusty, **robust,** hearty, enthusiastic, mettlesome, zesty, zestful, impetuous, spanking, smacking; snappy or zippy or peppy or full of pep [all informal].

.13 **acrimonious, acrid,** acidulous, acid, **bitter,** tart, **caustic,** escharotic [med], mordant or mordacious, **virulent, violent** 162.15, **vehement,** vitriolic; **harsh,** fierce, **rigorous,** severe, rough, stringent, astringent, strident 458.12, **sharp, keen,** incisive, trenchant, **cutting,** biting, stinging, **scathing,** stabbing, **piercing, poignant,** penetrating, edged, double-edged.

.14 **energizing, vitalizing, enlivening,** quickening; tonic, bracing, rousing; **invigorating,** invigorative; **animating,** animative; **exhilarating,** exhilarative; **stimulating,** stimulative; activating; viable.

.15 ADVS **energetically, vigorously, strenuously, forcefully,** forcibly, intensely, zestfully, lustily, heartily, keenly; **actively,** briskly; **animatedly, spiritedly,** vivaciously, with pep [informal], con brio [Ital].

162. VIOLENCE

(vehement action)

.1 NOUNS **violence, vehemence, virulence, venom, furiousness, force, rigor,** roughness, harshness, ungentleness, extremity, impetuosity, inclemency, **severity, intensity,** acuteness, **sharpness; fierceness,** ferociousness, viciousness, savagery, destructiveness, vandalism; **terrorism, barbarity, brutality, atrocity,** inhumanity, bloodlust, murderousness, malignity, mercilessness, pitilessness, mindlessness, animality.

.2 **turbulence, turmoil,** chaos, upset, **fury,** furor, furore [Ital], **rage, frenzy, passion,** fanaticism, zealousness, zeal, tempestuousness, storminess, wildness, tumultuousness, **tumult, uproar,** racket, cacophony, pandemonium, hubbub, **commotion, disturbance, agitation,** bluster, broil, brawl, embroilment, brouhaha [Fr], fuss, flap [Brit informal], row, rumpus, ruckus [informal], foofaraw [informal], ferment, fume, ebullition, fomentation.

.3 **unruliness, disorderliness,** obstreperousness; **riot, rioting;** looting, pillaging, sacking; laying waste, sowing with salt; **attack** 798, **assault,** onslaught, battering; **rape, violation,** forcible seizure; **killing** 409, butchery, massacre, slaughter.

.4 **storm, tempest,** squall, line squall, **tornado, cyclone, hurricane,** typhoon, war of the elements, "Nature's elemental din" [Thomas Campbell], "tempestuous rage", "groans of roaring wind and rain" [both Shakespeare]; stormy weather, rough weather, foul weather, dirty weather; rainstorm 394.2; thunderstorm 394.3; windstorm 403.12–14; **snowstorm** 333.8.

.5 **upheaval, convulsion,** cataclysm, disaster, overthrow, breakup; **fit,** spasm, **paroxysm,** apoplexy, stroke; climax; **earthquake,** quake, temblor, diastrophism, seismo–, –seism; tidal wave, tsunami [Jap].

.6 **outburst, outbreak, eruption,** debouchment, eructation, belch, spew, flare-up; **burst,** dissiliency; **torrent,** rush, gush, spate, cascade, spurt, jet, rapids, **volcano,** volcan, burning mountain.

.7 **explosion, discharge, blowout,** blowup, detonation, fulmination, **blast, burst, report** 456.1–5; flash, flare, fulguration; bang, boom 456.4; backfire.

.8 **concussion, shock, impact,** crunch, smash; percussion, repercussion.

.9 (violent person) **violent,** berserk or berserker; **hothead, madcap,** hotspur; **devil, demon, fiend, brute,** hellhound, hellcat, hellion, hell-raiser; **beast,** wild beast, tiger, dragon, mad dog, wolf, monster, savage; rapist, mugger, killer 409.11; hardnose or tough guy or tough or hoodlum or hood [all informal], goon or gorilla [both informal], gunsel [slang], Mafioso, terror or holy terror [both informal], fire-eater [informal], spitfire, ugly customer [informal]; **fury,** virago, vixen, termagant, beldam, she-wolf, tigress, witch; firebrand, Young Turk; revolutionary 147.3, **terrorist,** incendiary, bomber.

.10 VERBS rage, storm, rant, rave, roar; rampage, ramp, tear, tear around; go or carry on [informal]; come in like a lion; destroy, wreck, ruin; sow chaos or disorder; terrorize, vandalize, barbarize, brutalize; riot, loot, burn, pillage, sack, lay waste; slaughter, butcher 409.17; rape, violate; attack, assault 798.15, batter, savage, mug, maul, hammer.

.11 seethe, boil, fume, foam, simmer, stew, ferment, stir, churn.

.12 erupt, burst forth or out, break out, blow out or open, eruct, belch, vomit, spout, spew, disgorge, discharge, eject, throw or hurl forth.

.13 explode, blow up, go off, blow out, blast, burst, bust [informal]; detonate, fulminate; touch off, set off, let off; discharge, fire, shoot; backfire.

.14 run amok, go berserk, go on a rampage, cut loose, run riot, run wild.

.15 ADJS violent, vehement, virulent, venomous, severe, rigorous, furious, fierce, intense, sharp, acute, keen, cutting, splitting, piercing; rough, tough [informal]; drastic, extreme, outrageous, excessive, exorbitant, unconscionable, intemperate, immoderate, extravagant, great.

.16 unmitigated, unsoftened, untempered, unallayed, unsubdued, unquelled; unquenched, unextinguished, unabated.

.17 turbulent, tumultuous, raging, chaotic, hellish, anarchic, storming, stormy, tempestuous, troublous, frenzied, wild, frantic, furious, infuriate, insensate, mindless, mad, angry, ravening, raving; blustering, blustery, blusterous; uproarious, rip-roaring [informal]; pandemoniac; orgastic, orgasmic.

.18 unruly, disorderly, obstreperous; unbridled 762.23; riotous, wild, rampant; terrorist(ic), revolutionary 147.5.

.19 boisterous, rampageous, rambunctious [informal], roisterous, wild, rollicking, rowdy, rough, harum-scarum [informal]; knockabout, rough-and-tumble, knock-down-and-drag-out [informal].

.20 savage, fierce, ferocious, vicious, murderous 409.24, atrocious, brutal, brutish, bestial, inhuman, pitiless, ruthless, merciless, bloody, sanguinary, kill-crazy [slang]; malign, malignant; feral, ferine; wild, untamed, tameless, ungentle; barbarous, barbaric; uncivilized, noncivilized.

.21 fiery, heated, inflamed, flaming, scorching, hot, red-hot, white-hot; fanatic, zealous, totally committed, hard-core, ardent, passionate; hotheaded, madcap.

.22 convulsive, cataclysmic, disastrous, upheaving; seismic; spasmodic, paroxysmal, spastic, jerky, herky-jerky [informal]; orgasmic.

.23 explosive, bursting, detonating, explosible, explodable, fulminating; volcanic, eruptive.

.24 ADVS violently, vehemently, virulently, venomously, rigorously, severely, fiercely; furiously, wildly, madly, like mad, like fury [informal], like blazes; all to pieces, with a vengeance.

.25 turbulently, tumultuously, riotously, uproariously, stormily, tempestuously, troublously, frenziedly, frantically, furiously, madly, insensately, mindlessly, angrily.

.26 savagely, fiercely, ferociously, atrociously, viciously, murderously, brutally or brutishly, bestially, barbarously, inhumanly, ruthlessly, pitilessly, mercilessly; tooth and nail, bec et ongles [Fr].

163. MODERATION

.1 NOUNS moderation, moderateness; restraint, constraint, control; judiciousness, prudence; steadiness, evenness, stability 142; temperateness, temperance, sobriety; self-abnegation, self-restraint, self-control, self-denial; abstinence, continence, abnegation; mildness, lenity, gentleness; calmness, serenity, tranquillity, repose, calm, cool [informal]; unexcessiveness, unextremeness, unextravagance, nothing in excess, meden agan [Gk]; happy medium, golden mean, juste-milieu [Fr], middle way or path, via media [L]; moderationism, conservatism 140.3; nonviolence, pacifism; impartiality, neutrality, dispassion.

.2 modulation, abatement, remission, mitigation, diminution, reduction, lessening, falling-off; relaxation, slackening, easing, loosening, letup or letdown [both informal]; alleviation, assuagement, allayment, palliation, leniency, lightening, tempering, softening, subduement; deadening, dulling, damping, blunting; pacification, tranquilization, mollification, demulsion, dulcification, quieting, quietening, lulling, soothing, calming, hushing.

.3 moderator, mitigator, modulator, stabilizer, temperer, assuager; calming or restraining hand, wiser head; alleviator, alleviative, palliative, lenitive; pacifier, soother, peacemaker, pacificator, mollifier; anodyne, dolorifuge, soothing syrup, tranquilizer, calmative; sedative 687.12; balm, salve; cushion, shock absorber.

.4 moderate, moderatist, moderationist,

middle-of-the-roader, centrist, neutral, compromiser; **conservative** 140.4.

.5 VERBS **be moderate, keep within bounds,** keep within compass; practice self-control or self-denial, live temperately, do nothing in excess, strike a balance, keep a happy medium or the golden mean, steer or preserve an even course, keep to the middle path or way; keep the peace, not resist, espouse or practice nonviolence, be pacifistic; not rock the boat, not make waves or static; keep one's cool [informal], keep one's head or temper; sober down, settle down; remit, relent; take in sail; go out like a lamb; be conservative 140.6.

.6 **moderate, restrain,** constrain, control, **keep within bounds; modulate, mitigate,** abate, weaken, **diminish, reduce,** slacken, lessen, slow down; **alleviate,** assuage, allay, lay, lighten, palliate, extenuate, **temper,** attemper, lenify; **soften, subdue,** tame, chasten, underplay, play down, downplay, de-emphasize, tone or tune down; deaden, dull, blunt, obtund, take the edge off, take the sting or bite out; smother, suppress, stifle; damp, dampen, bank the fire, reduce the temperature, throw cold water on, throw a wet blanket on; sober, sober down or up.

.7 **calm,** calm down, **stabilize, tranquilize, pacify,** mollify, appease, dulcify; **quiet,** hush, still, rest, compose, **lull, soothe,** gentle, rock, cradle, rock to sleep; cool, **subdue,** quell; ease, steady, smooth, smoothen, smooth over, smooth down, even out; pour oil on troubled waters, pour balm into.

.8 **cushion,** absorb the shock, **soften the blow,** break the fall, deaden, damp or dampen, soften, suppress, neutralize, offset; show pity or mercy or consideration or sensitivity, temper the wind to the shorn lamb.

.9 **relax,** unbend; ease, **ease up,** ease off, **let up,** let down; abate, bate, remit, mitigate; **slacken,** slack, slake, slack off, slack up; loose, **loosen;** unbrace, unstrain, unstring.

.10 ADJS **moderate, temperate,** sober; **mild,** soft, bland, **gentle,** tame; mild as milk or mother's milk, mild as milk and water, gentle as a lamb; nonviolent, peaceable, peaceful, pacifistic; judicious, prudent.

.11 **restrained,** constrained, limited, controlled, **stable,** in control, in hand; tempered, **softened,** hushed, **subdued,** quelled, chastened.

.12 **unexcessive,** unextreme, unextravagant, **conservative;** reasonable.

.13 **equable,** even, **cool,** even-tempered, levelheaded, dispassionate; tranquil, reposeful, serene, calm 268.12.

.14 **mitigating,** assuaging, abating, **diminishing, reducing,** lessening, allaying, **alleviating, relaxing, easing;** tempering, **softening,** chastening, **subduing;** deadening, dulling, blunting, damping, dampening, cushioning.

.15 **tranquilizing,** pacifying, mollifying, appeasing; **calming,** lulling, gentling, rocking, cradling, hushing, quietening, stilling; **soothing,** soothful, restful; dreamy, drowsy.

.16 **palliative, alleviative,** assuasive, lenitive, **calmative,** calmant, **sedative,** demulcent, anodyne; antiorgastic, anaphrodisiac.

.17 ADVS **moderately, in moderation,** restrainedly, subduedly, in or within reason, within bounds or compass, in balance; **temperately,** soberly, prudently, judiciously, dispassionately; composedly, calmly, coolly, evenly, steadily, equably, tranquilly, serenely; soothingly, conservatively.

164. OPERATION

.1 NOUNS **operation,** operance or operancy, **functioning, action, performance** or **performing,** exercise, practice, work, **working,** workings; agency; management, **conduct, running, carrying-on** or **-out,** execution; driving, steering, direction 747; **handling,** manipulation; responsibility 962.1,2; **occupation** 656.

.2 **process, procedure,** proceeding, course; act, motion; step, measure; –age, –al, –ance or –ence, –ation, –ing, –ion, –ism, –ization or –isation, –ment, –osis, –sis, –th, –ure.

.3 **workability, operability,** performability, negotiability [informal], manageability, compassability, manipulatability, maneuverability; **practicability,** viability.

.4 **operator,** operative, operant; **handler,** manipulator; **driver,** runner, steersman, pilot, engineer; conductor; functionary, agent.

.5 VERBS **operate, run, work, manage, conduct,** practice, **carry on** or **out** or **through,** make go; **handle,** manipulate, maneuver; deal with, see to, take care of; **drive, steer,** pilot, direct 147.8; perform on, play; occupy oneself with 656.10; be responsible for 962.6.

.6 operate on, **act on** or **upon,** work on, affect, influence; treat, focus *or* concentrate on; bring to bear upon.

.7 (be operative) **operate, function, work, act, perform, go, run,** be in action *or* operation *or* commission; percolate *or* perk *or* tick [all informal]; play; be effective, have effect, take effect, militate; have play, have free play.

.8 **function as,** work as, **act as,** act *or* play the part of, have the function *or* role *or* job *or* mission of.

.9 ADJS **operative, operational,** go [informal], **functional, practical; effective,** effectual, efficient, efficacious.

.10 **workable, operable, operatable, performable,** actable, doable, manageable, compassable, negotiable [informal], manipulatable, maneuverable; **practicable,** practical, viable.

.11 **operating** *or* **operational, working, functioning** *or* **functional,** acting, active, running, **going,** going on, ongoing; **in operation,** in action, **in practice, in force,** in play, in exercise, at work, on foot; **in process,** in the works, on the fire, in hand.

.12 operational, functional, agential, agentive *or* agentival; managerial; manipulational.

165. PRODUCTIVENESS

.1 NOUNS **productiveness, productivity,** productive capacity, **fruitfulness,** fructiferousness, procreativeness, **fertility,** fecundity, pregnancy; richness, **luxuriance,** lushness, exuberance, prolificacy, generousness, bountifulness, plentifulness, plenteousness, abundance 661.2, superabundance, copiousness, teemingness, swarmingness; teeming womb *or* loins.

.2 proliferation, prolification, fructification, pullulation, multiplication; **reproduction** 169, production 167.

.3 **fertilization, enrichment,** fecundation; insemination, impregnation 169.4.

.4 **fertilizer,** dressing, enrichener; organic fertilizer, manure, muck, night soil, dung, guano, compost, castor-bean meal; commercial fertilizer, inorganic fertilizer, chemical fertilizer, phosphate, superphosphate, ammonia, nitrogen, nitrate.

.5 (goddesses of fertility) Demeter, Ceres, Isis, Astarte *or* Ashtoreth; (gods) Frey, Priapus, Dionysus, Pan, Baal.

.6 (comparisons) milk cow, rabbit, Hydra, warren, seed plot, hotbed, rich soil, land flowing with milk and honey, mustard.

.7 VERBS **be productive, proliferate,** pullulate, fructify, be fruitful, **multiply,** engender, beget, teem; **reproduce** 169.7,8.

.8 **fertilize, enrich,** fatten; fructify, fecundate, fecundify, prolificate; inseminate, impregnate 169.10; dress, manure.

.9 ADJS **productive, fruitful,** fructiferous, fecund; **fertile,** pregnant, seminal, **rich,** flourishing, thriving, blooming; **prolific,** proliferous, uberous, **teeming,** swarming, bursting, bursting out, plenteous, **plentiful,** copious, generous, bountiful, **abundant** 661.7, superabundant, luxuriant, lush, exuberant; creative 167.19.

.10 **bearing, yielding, producing;** fruitbearing, fructiferous.

.11 **fertilizing, enriching,** richening, fattening, fecundative, fructificative, seminal, germinal.

166. UNPRODUCTIVENESS

.1 NOUNS **unproductiveness,** unproductivity, ineffectualness 158.3; **unfruitfulness, barrenness,** dryness, aridity, dearth, famine; sterileness, **sterility,** unfertileness, **infertility,** infecundity; wasted *or* withered loins, dry womb; **birth control, contraception,** family planning, Planned Parenthood; impotence 158.

.2 **wasteland, waste,** desolation, barren *or* **barrens,** barren land, "weary waste" [Southey], "Rock and no water and the sandy road", "An old man in a dry season" [both T. S. Eliot]; heath; **desert,** Sahara, "a barren waste, a wild of sand" [Addison], karroo [Africa], dust bowl, salt flat, Death Valley, Arabia Deserta, lunar waste *or* landscape; **wilderness,** howling wilderness, wild, wilds; bush, brush, outback [Australia].

.3 VERBS be unproductive, **come to nothing,** come to naught, hang fire, flash in the pan, fizzle *or* peter out [informal]; **lie fallow.**

.4 ADJS **unproductive,** nonproductive *or* nonproducing; **infertile,** unfertile *or* nonfertile; **unfruitful, sterile,** impotent, gelded 158.19, acarpous, infecund, unprolific *or* nonprolific, ineffectual 158.15; **barren,** desert, arid, gaunt, dry, dried-up, exhausted, drained, leached, sucked dry, wasted, **waste, desolate,** jejune; **childless,** issueless, fruitless, teemless, without issue, *sine prole* [L]; fallow, unplowed, unsown, untilled, uncultivated; celibate, virgin, menopausal.

.5 **uncreative,** noncreative, nonseminal, nongerminal, unpregnant; uninventive, unoriginal, derivative.

167. PRODUCTION, BIRTH

.1 NOUNS production; performance, execution, doing, accomplishment, achievement, realization, bringing to fruition, effectuation, operation 164; overproduction; productiveness 165.

.2 mass production, volume production, assembly-line production; production line, assembly line; modular production or assembly, standardization; division of labor, industrialization.

.3 creation, manufacture or manufacturing, making, producing, devising, fashioning, framing, forming, formation, formulation, casting, shaping, molding, machining, milling, preparation, processing, conversion, assembly, composition, elaboration; construction, building, erection, architecture; fabrication, prefabrication; workmanship, craftsmanship; handiwork, handicraft, crafting; mining, extraction, smelting, refining; growing, cultivation, raising, harvesting; –faction, –fication, –plasia or –plasy, –poiesis.

.4 establishment, foundation, constitution, institution, installation, formation, organization, inauguration, inception, setting-up, realization, materialization, effectuation.

.5 creation, origination, invention, conception, beginning, fabrication, concoction, coinage, mintage, devising, hatching, contriving, contrivance; improvisation, making do; authorship; creative effort, generation 169.6; –genesis, –geny.

.6 bearing, yielding; fruition, fruiting, fructification.

.7 birth, genesis, nativity, nascency, childbirth, childbearing, having a baby, giving birth, birthing [dial], parturition, the stork [informal], delivery, –toky, toco– or toko–; hatching; blessed event [informal]; the Nativity; multiparity; confinement, lying-in, being brought to bed, childbed, accouchement [Fr]; labor, travail, birth throes.

.8 producer, maker, craftsman, wright, smith; manufacturer, industrialist; creator, begetter, engenderer, author, mother, father, sire; ancestors 170.7; precursor 66; generator, mover; originator, initiator, inaugurator, introducer, institutor, beginner, prime mover, instigator; founder, organizer; inventor, discoverer, deviser; builder, constructor, artificer, architect, planner, conceiver, designer, shaper; executor, executrix, engineer; grower, raiser; effector, realizer; apprentice, journeyman, master, master craftsman, artist, past master; –er or –ier or –yer, –fer, –gen(e), –ist, –ment, –or.

.9 VERBS produce; perform, do, work, act, execute, accomplish, achieve, realize, engineer, effectuate, bring about, bring to fruition or into being, cause 153.11; mass-produce, volume-produce, industrialize; overproduce; be productive 165.7.

.10 create, make, manufacture, produce, form, formulate, evolve, mature, elaborate, fashion, fabricate, prefabricate, cast, shape, mold, extrude, frame; construct, build, erect, put up, set up, run up, raise, rear; make up, get up, prepare, compose, write, indite, devise, concoct, compound; put together, assemble, piece together, patch together, whomp up [slang], fudge together [informal].

.11 process, convert 145.11; mill, machine; carve, chisel; mine, extract, pump, smelt, refine; raise, rear, grow, cultivate, harvest.

.12 establish, found, constitute, institute, install, form, set up, organize, inaugurate, incept, realize, materialize, effect, effectuate.

.13 originate, invent, conceive, discover, make up, devise, contrive, concoct, fabricate, coin, mint, frame, hatch, hatch or cook up, strike out; improvise, make do with; think up, think out, dream up, design, plan, set one's wits to work, strain or crack one's invention; generate, develop, mature, evolve; breed, engender, beget, spawn, hatch; bring forth, give rise to, give being to, bring or call into being; procreate 169.8.

.14 bear, yield, produce, furnish; bring forth, usher into the world; fruit, bear fruit, fructify.

.15 give birth, bear, bear or have young, have; have a baby, bear a child; drop, cast, throw, pup, whelp, kitten, foal, calve, fawn, lamb, yean, farrow, litter; lie in, be confined, labor, travail.

.16 be born, have birth, come forth, issue forth, come into the world; hatch; be illegitimate or born out of wedlock, have the bar sinister; be born on the wrong side of the blanket, come in through a side door [informal].

.17 ADJS productional, creational, formational; executional; manufacturing, manufactural, fabricational, industrial.

.18 constructional, structural, building, housing, edificial; architectural, architectonic.

.19 creative, originative, causative, productive 165.9, **constructive,** formative, fabricative, demiurgic; inventive; generative 169.16; –facient, –factive, –ferous, –fic, –genetic, –genic, –genous, –gerous or –igerous, –ic(al) or –etic, –ive, –ory, –poietic.

.20 produced, made, caused, brought about; effectuated, executed, performed, done; grown, raised; mass-produced, volumeproduced.

.21 bearing, giving birth, –para, –parous, –tokous; **born,** given birth; **hatched;** cast, dropped, whelped, foaled, calved, etc.; "cast naked upon the naked earth" [Pliny the Elder]; née; newborn; stillborn.

.22 made, man-made; **manufactured,** created, crafted, formed, shaped, molded, cast, forged, machined, milled, fashioned, **built, constructed,** fabricated; **well-made,** well-built, well-constructed; **homemade,** homespun, **handmade,** handcrafted, selfmade; machine-made; **processed; assembled,** put together; **custom-made,** custom-built, custom, made to order; **readymade,** ready-formed, ready-prepared, ready-to-wear, ready-for-wear; prefabricated, prefab [informal]; **mined,** extracted, smelted, **refined; grown, raised,** harvested, gathered.

.23 invented, originated, **conceived,** discovered; fabricated, coined, minted, newminted; **made-up,** made out of whole cloth.

.24 manufacturable, producible, productible, causable.

.25 ADVS in production, under construction, in the works, in hand, on foot.

168. PRODUCT

.1 NOUNS product, end product; **work,** œuvre [Fr], **handiwork, artifact,** manufacture, production, **creation,** creature; offspring, child, fruit; issue, outgrowth, outcome; result, **effect** 154; **invention,** origination, coinage, mintage or new mintage, brainchild; concoction, composition; opus, opera [pl], opuscule; **extract, distillation,** essence; apprentice work, journeyman work, **masterwork, masterpiece,** *chef d'œuvre* [Fr], *Meisterstück* [Ger], work of an artist or master or past master, crowning achievement; –ade, –age, –ate, –gen(e), –ing, –ion, –ite, –ization or –isation, –ment, –plast, –state.

.2 produce, proceeds, net, **yield, output,** throughput; **crop,** harvest.

.3 by-product, outgrowth, offshoot, side issue.

.4 (amount made) make, making; batch, lot, run.

169. REPRODUCTION, PROCREATION

.1 NOUNS reproduction, remaking, re-creation, refashioning, reshaping, redoing, re-formation, **reconstruction, rebuilding,** redesign, restructuring, **revision;** reedition, reissue, reprinting; reestablishment, **reorganization,** reinstitution, reconstitution; **rebirth,** renascence, resurrection, revival; regeneration, regenesis, palingenesis; **duplication** 91, **imitation** 22, **copy** 24, **repetition** 103; **restoration** 694, renovation; producing or making or creating over or again or once more.

.2 procreation, generation, begetting, breeding, engenderment; **propagation,** multiplication, –gamy, –gony; proliferation; linebreeding; inbreeding, endogamy; outbreeding, xenogamy; dissogeny; crossbreeding 44.4.

.3 fertilization, fecundation; **impregnation,** insemination, getting with child; **pollination,** pollinization; cross-fertilization, cross-pollination; self-fertilization, heterogamy, orthogamy; isogamy, artificial insemination; conjugation, zygosis, zyg(o)–; –spermy, –myxis.

.4 conception, conceiving, coming with child; superfetation, superimpregnation.

.5 pregnancy, gestation, incubation, parturiency, gravidness or gravidity, heaviness, greatness, bigness, the family way [informal]; brooding, sitting, covering.

.6 birth 167.7, **generation, genesis; development;** procreation; abiogenesis, archigenesis, biogenesis, blastogenesis, digenesis, dysmerogenesis, epigenesis, eumerogenesis, heterogenesis, histogenesis, homogenesis, isogenesis, merogenesis, metagenesis, monogenesis, oögenesis, orthogenesis, pangenesis, parthenogenesis, phytogenesis, sporogenesis, xenogenesis; spontaneous generation.

.7 VERBS reproduce, remake, make or do over, **re-create,** regenerate, resurrect, revive, re-form, refashion, **reshape,** redo, **reconstruct, rebuild,** redesign, restructure, **revise;** reprint, reissue; reestablish, reinstitute, reconstitute, refound, **reorganize; duplicate** 91.3, **copy** 22.5, **repeat** 103.7, **restore** 694.11, renovate.

.8 procreate, generate, breed, beget, get, engender; propagate, multiply; proliferate; mother; father, sire; reproduce in kind, reproduce after one's kind, "multiply and replenish the earth" [Bible]; breed true; inbreed, breed in and in; outbreed; crossbreed 44.14; linebreed; copulate 419.23, make love 932.13.

.9 **lay** (eggs), deposit, drop, spawn.

.10 **fertilize**, fructify, fecundate, fecundify; impregnate, inseminate, spermatize; **get with child** *or* **young;** pollinate *or* pollinize, pollen; cross-fertilize, cross-pollinate *or* cross-pollinize, cross-pollen.

.11 **conceive, come with child,** (animal) catch, get in the family way [informal]; superfetate.

.12 **be pregnant,** be gravid, **be great with child, be with child** *or* **young;** be in the family way *or* have a cake in the oven *or* be expecting *or* anticipate a blessed event [all informal], be infanticipating, be knocked up [both slang], be blessedeventing [informal]; gestate, breed, carry, carry young; **incubate, hatch; brood,** sit, set, cover.

.13 **give birth** 167.15.

.14 ADJS **reproductive, re-creative, reconstructive,** re-formative; renascent, regenerative, resurgent, reappearing; reorganizational; revisional; **restorative** 694.22; Hydraheaded, Phoenixlike.

.15 **reproductive, procreative,** procreant, **propagative,** life-giving; spermatic, spermatozoic, seminal, germinal, fertilizing, fecundative; multiparous; gen(o)–, –genic; –spermic.

.16 **genetic, generative,** genial, gametic; genital, genitive; abiogenetic, biogenetic, blastogenetic, digenetic, dysmerogenetic, epigenetic, eumerogenetic, heterogenetic, histogenetic, homogenetic, isogenetic, merogenetic, metagenetic, monogenetic, oögenetic, orthogenetic, pangenetic, parthenogenetic, phytogenetic, sporogenous, xenogenetic.

.17 **bred, impregnated,** inseminated; inbred, endogamic, endogamous; outbred, exogamic, exogamous; crossbred 44.16; linebred.

.18 **pregnant,** *enceinte* [Fr], **with child** *or* **young, in the family way** [informal], gestating, breeding, teeming, parturient; heavy with child *or* young, great *or* big with child *or* young, in a delicate condition, gravid, heavy, great, big-laden; carrying, carrying a fetus *or* embryo; **expecting** [informal], anticipating *or* anticipating a blessed event [both informal], preggers [Brit informal]; knocked up [slang]; infanticipating [informal]; superfetate, superimpregnated.

170. ANCESTRY

.1 NOUNS **ancestry,** progenitorship; parentage, parenthood; grandparentage, grandfatherhood, grandmotherhood.

.2 **paternity, fatherhood,** fathership; fatherliness, paternalness.

.3 **maternity, motherhood,** mothership; motherliness, maternalness.

.4 **lineage, line, bloodline, descent,** line of descent, succession, **extraction,** derivation, birth, **blood,** breed, **family,** house, **strain,** sept, **stock,** race, stirps, seed; direct line, phylum; **branch,** stem; filiation, affiliation, apparentation; side; male line, spear *or* sword side; female line, distaff *or* spindle side; consanguinity, common ancestry 11.1.

.5 **genealogy, pedigree,** stemma, *Stammbaum* [Ger], genealogical tree, **family tree,** tree.

.6 **heredity, heritage, inheritance, birth;** patrocliny, matrocliny; endowment, inborn capacity *or* tendency *or* susceptibility *or* predisposition; diathesis; inheritability, heritability, hereditability; Mendel's law, Mendelism *or* Mendelianism; Weismann theory, Weismannism; Altmann theory, De Vries theory, Galtonian theory, Verworn theory, Wiesner theory; **genetics,** pharmacogenetics, genesiology, eugenics; **gene,** factor, inheritance factor, determiner, determinant; **character,** dominant *or* recessive character, allele *or* allelomorph; **chromosome,** chromatin, chromatid; genetic code, DNA, RNA, replication.

.7 **ancestors, antecedents, predecessors,** ascendants, **fathers, forefathers, forebears,** progenitors, primogenitors; **grandparents,** grandfathers; patriarchs, elders.

.8 **parent, progenitor, ancestor,** procreator, begetter; grandparent; ancestress, progenitress, progenitrix.

.9 **father, sire,** genitor, paternal ancestor, pater [informal], the old man [slang], governor [informal], *abba* [Heb]; **papa** *or* **pa** *or* **pap** *or* **pappy** *or* **pop** *or* **pops** *or* **dad** *or* **daddy** *or* daddums [all informal]; **patriarch, paterfamilias; stepfather;** foster father.

.10 **mother,** genetrix, dam, maternal ancestor, mater [informal], the old woman [slang]; **mama** *or* **mammy** *or* **mam** *or* **ma** *or* **mom** *or* **mommy** *or* **mummy** *or* mumsy *or* mimsy *or* motherkin *or* motherkins [all informal]; **matriarch, materfamilias; stepmother;** foster mother.

.11 **grandfather; grandpa** *or* grampa *or* gramper *or* gramp *or* gramps *or* grandpapa *or* grandpap *or* grandpappy *or* granddad *or* granddaddy *or* granddada [all informal]; grandsire *or* gramfer *or* granther [all dial]; old man 127.2; great-grandfather.

.12 **grandmother,** grandam, grannam *or* gammer [both dial]; **grandma** *or* granma *or* grandmamma *or* grandmammy *or* **granny** *or* grammy *or* gammy [all informal]; old woman 127.3; great-grandmother.

.13 ADJS **ancestral,** ancestorial, patriarchal; **parental,** parent; **paternal,** patr(o)– *or* patri–; fatherly, fatherlike; **maternal,** mother, matr(o)– *or* matri–; motherly, motherlike; grandparental; grandmotherly, grandmaternal; grandfatherly, grandpaternal.

.14 **lineal,** family, genealogical; direct, in a direct line; phyletic, phylogenetic; diphyletic.

.15 **hereditary,** patrimonial, **inherited,** hered(o)–; **innate** 5.7; genetic, genic; –clinous *or* –clinic *or* –clinal, patroclinous, matroclinous.

.16 **inheritable,** heritable, hereditable.

171. POSTERITY

.1 NOUNS **posterity, progeny, issue, offspring,** fruit, seed, brood, breed, family, descent, succession; lineage 170.4; **descendants,** heirs, inheritors, sons, **children, kids** [informal], little ones, treasures, hostages to fortune, youngsters, younglings; grandchildren, great-grandchildren; new *or* young *or* rising generation;

.2 (of animals) **young, brood,** get, nest; (fish) **spawn,** spat, fry; **litter,** drey (of squirrels), farrow (of pigs); (birds) clutch, hatch.

.3 **descendant, offspring, child, scion; son,** son and heir, chip of *or* off the old block, sonny; **daughter,** heiress; grandchild, grandson, granddaughter; stepchild, stepson, stepdaughter; foster child; ped(o)–, proli–, tecno–, toco– *or* toko–; –id, –ite.

.4 (derived or collateral descendant) **offshoot,** offset, **branch,** sprout, shoot, filiation.

.5 **bastard,** illegitimate, bantling, notho–, illegitimate *or* bastard child, whore's bird [slang], by-blow, child born out of wedlock, natural *or* love child, *nullius filius* [L]; illegitimacy, bastardy, bar sinister.

.6 **sonship,** sonhood; daughtership, daughterhood.

.7 ADJS **filial,** sonly, sonlike; **daughterly,** daughterlike.

172. INFLUENCE

.1 NOUNS **influence,** influentiality; **power** 157, force, clout [informal], potency, pressure, effect, indirect *or* incidental power, **say,** a lot to do with *or* to say about [informal], **prestige,** favor, good feeling, credit, esteem, repute, personality, leadership, charisma, magnetism, charm, enchantment; **weight,** moment, consequence, importance, eminence; **authority** 739, control, domination, hold; **sway** 741.1, reign, rule; **mastery,** ascendancy, supremacy, dominance, predominance, preponderance; upper hand, whip hand; leverage, purchase; **persuasion** 648.3, suasion, suggestion, subtle influence, insinuation.

.2 **favor,** special favor, **interest; pull** *or* drag *or* suction [all informal]; inside track [informal].

.3 **backstairs influence,** intrigues, deals, schemes, **games,** Machiavellian *or* Byzantine intrigues, ploys; connections; **wires** *or* **strings** *or* ropes [all informal]; **wirepulling** [informal]; **influence peddling;** lobbying, lobbyism.

.4 **sphere of influence,** orbit, ambit; bailiwick, vantage, stamping ground, footing, **territory,** turf, constituency.

.5 **influenceability,** swayableness, movability; **persuadability,** suasibility, openness, open-mindedness, perviousness, accessibility, receptiveness, responsiveness, amenableness; **suggestibility, susceptibility,** impressionability, malleability; **weakness** 160; putty in one's hands.

.6 (influential person or thing) **influence,** good influence; bad influence, sinister influence; man of influence; heavyweight, big wheel, very important person *or* VIP [informal]; wheeler-dealer [informal], influencer, **wire-puller** [informal]; **power behind the throne,** gray eminence, *éminence grise* [Fr], hidden hand, manipulator, friend at *or* in court, kingmaker; **influence peddler,** five-percenter, lobbyist; Svengali, Rasputin; **pressure group,** special-interest group, special interests; lobby; the Establishment, ingroup, court, powers that be 749.15, lords of creation; **key,** key to the city, access, open sesame.

.7 VERBS **influence,** make oneself felt, **affect,** weigh with, **sway,** bias, bend, incline, dispose, predispose, **move,** prompt, lead; color, tinge, tone; **induce, persuade** 648.23; work, work *or* bend to one's will; lead by the nose [informal], wear down, soften up; win friends and influence people, ingratiate oneself.

.8 (exercise influence over) **govern** 741.12, **rule, control** 741.13, order, **regulate,** direct, guide; **determine,** decide, dispose; call the shots or be in the driver's seat or wear the pants [all informal].

.9 exercise or exert influence, use one's influence, bring pressure to bear upon, act on, **work on,** bear upon, throw one's weight around or into the scale, say a few words to the right person or in the right quarter; draw, ·draw on, lead on, magnetize; **approach,** go up to with hat in hand, make advances or overtures, make up to or get cozy with [both informal]; get at or get the ear of [informal]; **pull strings** or **wires** or **ropes,** wire-pull [informal]; lobby, lobby through.

.10 **have influence, be influential, carry weight, weigh, tell, count,** cut ice, throw a lot of weight [informal], have a lot to do with or say about [informal]; be the decisive factor or the one that counts, have pull or suction or drag or leverage [informal]; have a way with one, have personality or magnetism or charisma, charm the birds out of the trees, be persuasive; have an in [informal], have the inside track [informal]; have full play.

.11 have influence or power or a hold over; **lead by the nose, twist** or **turn** or **wind around one's little finger,** keep under one's thumb, make sit up and beg or lie down and turn over; hypnotize, mesmerize, **dominate** 741.15.

.12 gain influence, **get in with** [informal], ingratiate oneself with, get cozy with [informal]; gain a footing, take hold, move in, take root, strike root in; gain a hearing, make one's voice heard, make one sit up and take notice, be listened to, be recognized; get the mastery or control of, gain a hold upon; change the preponderance, turn the scale or balance, turn the tables.

.13 ADJS **influential, powerful** 157.12, potent, strong; **effective,** effectual, efficacious, telling; **weighty,** momentous, important, consequential, substantial, **prestigious,** estimable, authoritative, reputable; **persuasive,** suasive, personable, **winning,** magnetic, charming, enchanting, charismatic.

.14 (in a position of influence) **dominant** 741.18, **predominant,** preponderant, prepotent, prepollent, regnant, ruling, swaying, prevailing, on the throne, in the driver's seat [informal]; **ascendant,** in the ascendant, in ascendancy.

.15 **influenceable, swayable, movable; persuadable,** persuasible, suasible, open, open-minded, pervious, accessible, receptive, responsive, amenable; **plastic, pliant,** pliable, malleable; **suggestible, susceptible, impressionable,** weak 160.12.

173. LACK OF INFLUENCE

.1 NOUNS lack of influence or power or force, uninfluentiality, **unauthoritativeness,** powerlessness, forcelessness, impotence 158; **ineffectiveness,** inefficaciousness, inefficacy, ineffectuality; **no say,** nothing to do with or say about [informal]; unpersuasiveness, lack of personality or charm, lack of magnetism or charisma; **weakness** 160.

.2 **uninfluenceability,** unswayableness, unmovability; **unpersuadability,** impersuadability, impersuasibility, unreceptiveness, imperviousness, unresponsiveness; unsuggestibility, **unsusceptibility,** unimpressionability; **obstinacy** 626.

.3 ADJS **uninfluential, powerless,** forceless, impotent 158.13; **weak** 160.12; unauthoritative; **ineffective,** ineffectual, inefficacious; **of no account,** no-account, without any weight, featherweight, lightweight.

.4 **uninfluenceable, unswayable, unmovable;** unpliable, unyielding, inflexible; **unpersuadable** 626.13, impersuadable, impersuasible, unreceptive, unresponsive, unamenable; impervious, closed to; **unsuggestible, unsusceptible,** unimpressionable; **obstinate** 626.8.

.5 **uninfluenced, unmoved, unaffected, unswayed.**

174. TENDENCY

.1 NOUNS **tendency, inclination, leaning,** penchant, proneness, weakness, susceptibility; **liability** 175, readiness, willingness, eagerness, aptness, aptitude, **disposition, proclivity, propensity,** predisposition, **predilection,** a thing for [informal], affinity, prejudice, liking, delight, soft spot; conduciveness; instinct or feeling for, sensitivity to; diathesis, conatus, tropism; **bent, turn, bias,** cast, warp, twist; probability 511; –ey or –y, –itis, –philia, –phoria, –trope; trop(o)–.

.2 **trend, drift, course, current,** stream, mainstream, main current, movement, glacial movement, motion, run, **tenor,** tone, **set,** set of the current, swing, bearing, line, direction, the general tendency or drift, the main course, the course of events, the way the wind blows, the way things go, trend of the times, spirit of the age or time, time spirit, *Zeitgeist* [Ger]; the way it looks.

.3 VERBS **tend,** have a tendency, **incline,** dispose, **lean, trend,** set, go, head, lead, point, verge, turn, warp, bias, bend to, work or gravitate or set toward; show a tendency or trend or set or direction, swing toward, point to, look to; **conduce,** contribute, serve, redound to.

.4 ADJS **tending,** tendent, tendentious or tendential; **leaning, inclining,** inclinatory, inclinational.

.5 **tending to, conducive to,** leading to, inclined toward, inclining toward, heading or moving or swinging or working toward.

.6 **inclined to, prone to, disposed to,** predisposed to, given to; **apt to, likely to, liable to** 175.5, calculated to, minded to, ready to, in a fair way to; –able or –ible, –atory, –ful, –tropic.

175. LIABILITY

.1 NOUNS **liability,** liableness, **likelihood** or likeliness, aptitude, aptness, **possibility** 509, **probability** 511, contingency, chance 156, eventuality 151.1; weakness, **proneness** 174.1; **obligation** 962.1,2.

.2 **susceptibility,** susceptivity, **openness,** exposure; **vulnerability** 697.4.

.3 VERBS **be liable, be subjected to,** be a pawn or plaything of, be the prey of, lie under; **expose oneself to, lay oneself open to,** open the door to; **gamble,** stand to lose or gain, stand a chance, **run the chance** or **risk, risk,** let down one's guard or defenses; **admit of,** open the possibility of, be in the way of, bid or stand fair to.

.4 **incur,** contract, invite, welcome, run, **bring on, bring down,** bring upon or down upon, bring upon or down upon oneself; **be responsible for** 962.6; fall into, fall in with; get, gain, acquire.

.5 ADJS **liable to, subject to,** standing to, in a position to, incident to, dependent on; **susceptible** or **prone to,** susceptive to, **open** or vulnerable or **exposed to,** naked to, in danger of, within range of, at the mercy of; **capable of,** ready for; **likely to, apt to** 174.6, obliged to, responsible or answerable for.

.6 CONJS **lest, that, for fear that.**

176. INVOLVEMENT

.1 NOUNS **involvement,** involution, **implication, entanglement,** enmeshment, engagement, involuntary presence or cooperation, embarrassment; relation 9; **inclusion** 76; **absorption** 530.3.

.2 VERBS **involve, implicate,** tangle, **entangle,** embarrass, enmesh, engage, **draw in,** drag or hook or suck into, catch up in, **make a party to;** interest, concern; **absorb** 530.13.

.3 ADJS **involved, implicated;** interested, concerned, a party to; **included** 76.5.

.4 **involved in, implicated in,** tangled or entangled in, enmeshed in, **caught up in,** tied up in, wrapped up in, all wound up in, dragged or hooked or sucked into; deeply involved, **up to one's neck** or **ears in,** up to one's elbows in, head over heels in, **absorbed in** 530.17, immersed or submerged in, far-gone.

177. CONCURRENCE

.1 NOUNS **concurrence, collaboration,** coaction, **co-working,** collectivity, combined effort or operation, united or concerted action, concert, synergy; **cooperation** 786; **agreement** 26; **coincidence,** simultaneity, synchronism; concomitance, accompaniment 73; **union,** junction 47.1,4, **conjunction,** combination 52, association, alliance; conspiracy, collusion, cahoots [informal]; concourse, confluence; **accordance** 794.1, concordance, correspondence, consilience; symbiosis, parasitism; saprophytism.

.2 VERBS **concur, collaborate,** coact, **co-work,** synergize; **cooperate** 786.3; conspire, collude, connive, be in cahoots [informal]; **combine** 52.3, **unite, associate** 52.4, coadunate, join, conjoin; harmonize; **coincide,** synchronize, happen together; **accord** 794.2, correspond, **agree** 26.6.

.3 **go with, go along with, go hand in hand with,** be hand in glove with, team or join up with; keep pace with, run parallel to.

.4 ADJS **concurrent,** concurring; **coacting,** coactive, **collaborative,** collective, **co-working,** cooperant, synergetic or synergic or synergistic; **cooperative** 786.5; conspiratorial, collusive; **united, joint,** conjoint, **combined, concerted,** associated, associate, coadunate; **coincident,** synchronous, coordinate; concomitant, accompanying 73.9; meeting, uniting, combining; **accordant, agreeing** 26.9, concordant, harmonious, consilient, at one with; symbiotic, parasitic, saprophytic.

.5 ADVS **concurrently,** coactively, **jointly,** conjointly, **concertedly,** in harmony or unison with, **together; with one accord,** with one voice, as one, as one man; hand in hand, hand in glove, shoulder to shoulder, cheek by jowl.

178. COUNTERACTION

.1 NOUNS **counteraction, counterworking; opposition** 790, opposure, counterposition or contraposition, confutation, **contradiction;** antagonism, repugnance, oppugnance or oppugnancy, **antipathy, conflict, friction,** interference, clashing, collision; reaction, repercussion, backlash, kick, recoil; resistance, recalcitrance, dissent 522, revolt 767.4, perverseness, nonconformity 83, crankiness, crotchetiness, renitency; going against the current, swimming upstream; **contrariety** 15.

.2 **neutralization, nullification, annulment,** cancellation, voiding, invalidation, vitiation, frustration, thwarting, undoing; **offsetting, counterbalancing.**

.3 **counteractant,** counteractive, **counteragent;** counterirritant; **antidote,** remedy, preventive or preventative, prophylactic; **neutralizer,** nullifier, offset; antacid, buffer.

.4 **counterforce,** counterinfluence, counterpressure; counterpoise, counterbalance, counterweight; countercurrent, crosscurrent, undercurrent; counterblast; head wind, foul wind.

.5 **countermeasure, counterattack,** counterstep; **counterblow** or counterstroke or countercoup or counterblast, counterfire; counterrevolution, counterinsurgency; backfire; **retort,** comeback [informal]; defense 799.

.6 VERBS **counteract,** counter, counterwork, counterattack, countervail; counterpose or contrapose, **oppose,** antagonize, **go in opposition to, go** or **run counter to, go** or **work against,** go or fly in the face of, run against, beat against, militate against, resist, **cross,** confute, **contradict,** contravene, oppugn, **conflict,** be antipathetic or hostile or inimical, interfere or conflict with, come in conflict with, **clash,** collide, meet head-on, lock horns; rub or go against the grain; swim upstream or against the current.

.7 **neutralize, nullify, annul, cancel,** cancel out, negate, negative, negativate, invalidate, vitiate, void, frustrate, stultify, thwart, come or bring to nothing, undo; **offset, counterbalance** 33.5; buffer.

.8 ADJS counteractive or counteractant, **counteracting, counterworking,** countervailing; **opposing** 790.9, oppositional; contradicting, contradictory; **antagonistic,** hostile, antipathetic, inimical, oppugnant, repugnant, **conflicting,** clashing; reactionary; resistant, recalcitrant, dissident, revolutionary, breakaway, nonconformist, perverse, cranky, crotchety, renitent; ant(i)- or anth-, contra-, counter-.

.9 **neutralizing, nullifying,** stultifying, annulling, canceling, negating, invalidating, vitiating, voiding; **offsetting,** counterbalancing; antacid, buffering.

.10 ADVS counteractively, antagonistically, opposingly, **in opposition to, counter to;** de- or des-, dis-, un-.

179. SPACE

(indefinite space)

.1 NOUNS **space, extent,** extension, spatial extension; **expanse,** expansion; spread, breadth; **measure,** volume; **dimension,** proportion; **area,** tract, surface, surface or superficial extension, field, sphere; acreage; empty space, emptiness, **void,** nothingness, infinite space, outer space, wastes of outer space, interstellar or galactic space; continuum.

.2 **range, scope, compass, reach, stretch,** radius, sweep, carry; **gamut, scale,** register, diapason; **spectrum.**

.3 **room, latitude,** swing, play, way; spare room, room to spare, room to swing a cat [informal], **elbowroom, margin, leeway;** sea room; headroom, clearance; air space.

.4 **open space,** clear space; **clearing,** clearance, glade; open country, wide-open spaces, **terrain,** prairie, steppe, plain 387; wilderness, back country, outback [Austral], desert; distant prospect or perspective, empty view, far horizon; **territory,** living space, *Lebensraum* [Ger], air space.

.5 **spaciousness, roominess,** commodiousness, capacity, capaciousness, amplitude; extensiveness, expansiveness.

.6 **fourth dimension, space-time,** time-space, space-time continuum, four-dimensional space; four-dimensional geometry; spaceworld; other continuums; **relativity,** theory of relativity, Einstein theory, principle of relativity, principle of equivalence, general theory of relativity, special or restricted theory of relativity, continuum theory; cosmic constant.

.7 VERBS **extend, reach, stretch,** sweep, spread, run, go *or* go out, cover, carry, **range,** lie; **reach** *or* stretch *or* thrust out; span, straddle, take in, hold, encompass, surround, environ.

.8 ADJS **spatial,** space, spatio–, stere(o)–; **dimensional,** proportional; two-dimensional, flat, surface *or* superficial, three-dimensional, spherical, cubic, volumetric; stereoscopic, 3-D; fourth-dimensional; space-time, spatiotemporal.

.9 **spacious, roomy, commodious, capacious,** ample; **extensive,** expansive, extended; far-reaching, extending, spreading, **vast,** broad, **wide,** deep, amplitudinous, voluminous; widespread 79.13; **infinite** 104.3.

.10 ADVS **extensively, widely,** broadly, vastly, abroad; **far and wide,** far and near; **right and left,** on all sides, on every side; infinitely.

.11 **everywhere,** everywheres [dial], **here, there, and everywhere;** in every place, in every clime *or* region, in all places, in every quarter, in all quarters; **all over,** all round, all over hell [slang], all over the map [informal], all over the world, the world over, on the face of the earth, under the sun, throughout the world, throughout the length and breadth of the land; from end to end, from pole to pole, from here to the back of beyond [Brit informal], "from Dan to Beersheba" [Bible], from hell to breakfast [slang]; **high and low,** upstairs and downstairs, inside and out, in every nook and cranny *or* hole and corner; **universally,** in all creation.

.12 **from everywhere,** everywhence, "from the four corners of the earth" [Shakespeare], "at the round earth's imagined corners" [Donne], from all points of the compass, from every quarter *or* all quarters; everywhere, everywhither, to the four winds, to the uttermost parts of the earth, "unto the ends of the earth" [Bible], to hell and back [slang].

180. REGION

.1 NOUNS **region, area, zone,** belt, **territory,** terrain; **place** 184.1; **space** 179; **country** 181, **land** 385, ground, soil; territorial waters, twelve- *or* three-mile limit, continental shelf, offshore rights; airspace; heartland; hinterland; **district, quarter, section,** department, division; salient, corridor; part, parts; **neighborhood,** vicin-

ity, vicinage, neck of the woods [informal], purlieus; premises, confines, precincts, environs, milieu, –dom, –gaea.

.2 **sphere,** hemisphere, orb, **orbit,** ambit, circle; **circuit,** judicial circuit, **beat, round,** walk; **realm,** demesne, **domain,** dominion, jurisdiction, bailiwick; border, borderland, march; **province,** precinct, department; **field,** pale, arena.

.3 **zone;** climate *or* clime [both archaic]; **longitude,** longitude in arc, longitude in time; meridian, prime meridian; **latitude,** parallel; equator, the line; tropic, Tropic of Cancer, Tropic of Capricorn; tropics, subtropics, Torrid Zone; Temperate *or* Variable Zones; Frigid Zones, Arctic Zone *or* Circle, Antarctic Zone *or* Circle; horse latitudes, roaring forties.

.4 **plot,** plot of ground *or* land, parcel of land, plat, **patch, tract, field;** lot; block, square; section (square mile), forty (sixteenth of a section); close, quadrangle, quad, enclave, pale, *clos* [Fr], croft [Brit], kraal [Africa]; real estate 810.7.

.5 (territorial divisions) **state, territory, province,** region, duchy, electorate, government, principality; **county,** shire, canton, *oblast, okrug* [both Russ], *département* [Fr], *Kreis* [Ger]; **borough, ward,** riding, *arrondissement* [Fr]; **township,** hundred, commune, wapentake; metropolis, metropolitan area, **city, town** 183; **village,** hamlet; **district,** congressional district, electoral district, precinct; magistracy, soke, bailiwick; shrievalty, sheriffalty, sheriffwick, constablewick [all England]; archdiocese, archbishopric, stake; **diocese,** bishopric, parish.

.6 (regions of the world) continent, landmass; **Old World,** the old country; **New World,** America; **Western Hemisphere, Occident,** West; **Eastern Hemisphere, Orient,** Levant, East, eastland; Far East, Middle East, Near East; Asia, Europe, Eurasia, Asia Major, Asia Minor, Africa; Antipodes, down under, Australasia, Oceania.

.7 (regions of the US) West, westland, wild West, West Coast, the Coast; Northwest, Pacific Northwest, Southwest, Middle West, North Central region; East, eastland, East Coast, Middle Atlantic; Northeast, Southeast; North, northland; South, southland; Dixie, Dixieland; Sunbelt; New England, Down East, Yankeeland [informal].

.8 ADJS **regional, territorial, geographical,** areal, sectional, zonal, topographic *or* topographical, top(o)−, zon(o)−; locational 184.18.

.9 **local, localized,** of a place, geographically limited, topical, vernacular, parochial, provincial, insular, limited, confined.

181. COUNTRY

.1 NOUNS **country,** land; **nation,** nationality, **state,** sovereign nation *or* state, polity, **body politic;** power, superpower; **republic,** people's republic, **commonwealth,** commonweal; **kingdom,** sultanate; **empire,** empery; realm, dominion, domain; **principality,** principate; duchy, dukedom; grand duchy, archduchy, archdukedom, earldom, county, palatinate, seneschalty; chieftaincy, chieftainry; toparchy, *toparchia* [L]; city-state, *polis* [Gk]; free city; province, territory, possession; colony, settlement; protectorate, mandate, mandated territory, mandant, mandatee, mandatory; buffer state; ally; satellite, puppet regime *or* government; free nation, captive nation, iron-curtain country; nonaligned *or* unaligned *or* neutralist nation.

.2 **fatherland,** *Vaterland* [Ger], *patria* [L], *la patrie* [Fr], **motherland,** mother country, the old country, **native land,** native soil, one's native heath *or* ground *or* place, **birthplace,** cradle; **home, homeland,** homeground, "home is where one starts" [T. S. Eliot], God's country.

.3 **United States,** United States of America, US, USA, **America,** Columbia, the States, Uncle Sugar [informal], Yankeeland [informal], Land of Liberty, the melting pot; stateside.

.4 **England,** Britain, Great Britain, United Kingdom, Britannia, Albion, Blighty [Brit slang], Limeyland [US slang], Tight Little Island, Land of the Rose, "This royal throne of kings, this scepter'd isle, / This earth of majesty, this seat of Mars, / This other Eden, demi-paradise" [Shakespeare], Sovereign of the Seas; British Empire, Commonwealth of Nations, British Commonwealth of Nations, the Commonwealth.

.5 (national personifications) Uncle Sam *or* Brother Jonathan (US); John Bull (England).

.6 **nationhood,** peoplehood, **nationality; statehood, sovereignty,** sovereign nationhood *or* statehood, independence, self-government, self-determination; internationality, internationalism; **nationalism.**

.7 [slang *or* derog terms] dago, Guinea, greaseball, wop (Italian); frog (Frenchman); Kraut, Krauthead, Jerry, Boche (German); Mick, Mickey, Paddy (Irishman); squarehead (Scandanavian); polack (Pole); Hunk, Hunkie, Bohunk (Eastern European); Canuck, Pepsi (French-Canadian); greaser, wetback (Mexican); spic (Latin American); Chink (Chinese); Jap (Japanese); limey (Briton); Aussie (Australian).

182. THE COUNTRY

.1 NOUNS **the country,** agricultural region, farm country, farmland, arable land, grazing region *or* country, rural district, rustic region, province *or* provinces, countryside, woodland 411.11, grassland 411.8, woods and fields, meadows and pastures, the soil, grass roots; **the sticks** *or* yokeldom *or* hickdom [all slang]; cotton belt, tobacco belt, black belt, farm belt, corn belt, fruit belt, wheat belt, citrus belt; dust bowl; highlands, moors, uplands; lowlands, veld, plains, prairies, steppes, wide-open spaces.

.2 **hinterland, back country,** outback [Austral], up-country, boondock *or* boondocks [both informal]; **the bush,** bush country, bushveld, **woods,** woodlands, **backwoods,** forests, timbers, brush; wilderness, wilds, uninhabited region, virgin land *or* territory; **wasteland** 166.2; **frontier,** borderland, outpost; wild West.

.3 **rusticity, ruralism,** inurbanity, agrarianism, bucolicism, **provincialism,** provinciality, pastorality, simplicity, unspoiledness; yokelism, hickishness, backwoodsiness; **boorishness,** churlishness, unrefinement, uncultivation.

.4 **ruralization,** countrification, rustication, pastoralization.

.5 VERBS **ruralize, countrify, rusticate,** pastoralize; farm 413.16; return to the soil.

.6 ADJS **rustic, rural, country, provincial, farm, pastoral,** bucolic, Arcadian, **agrarian,** agrestic; **agricultural** 413.20; lowland, upland.

.7 **countrified,** inurbane; country-born, country-bred, up-country, from the sticks [slang]; farmerish, hobnailed, clodhopping; **hick** *or* hicky *or* hickish *or* hickified *or* rube *or* hayseed *or* yokel *or* yokelish [all slang]; **boorish,** clownish, loutish, lumpish, lumpen, cloddish, churlish; **uncouth,** unpolished, uncultivated, uncultured, unrefined; country-style, country-fashion.

.8 **hinterland,** back, **back-country,** up-country, outback [Austral], wild, wilderness, virgin; **waste** 166.4; backwood or **backwoods,** back of beyond, backwoodsy; woodland, sylvan.

183. TOWN, CITY

.1 NOUNS **town,** township; **city, metropolis,** metropolitan area, greater city, megalopolis, conurbation, urban complex, spread city, urban sprawl, **municipality,** *urbs* [L], *polis* [Gk], *ville* [Fr], *Stadt* [Ger], –polis; **borough, burg** [informal], bourg, burgh [Scot]; **suburb,** suburbia, outskirts, *faubourg* [Fr], *banlieue* [Fr]; exurb, exurbia; market town [Brit]; boom town, ghost town.

.2 **village, hamlet;** ham or thorp or wick [all archaic]; country town, crossroads, wide place in the road; "a little one-eyed, blinking sort o' place" [Thomas Hardy], "a hive of glass, where nothing unobserved can pass" [C. H. Spurgeon].

.3 [slang terms] **one-horse town,** jerkwater town, **tank town** or station, **whistle-stop,** jumping-off place; **hick town,** rube town, hoosier town.

.4 **capital,** capital city, **seat,** seat of government; **county seat** or county site, county town [Brit], shire town.

.5 **town hall, city hall, municipal building;** courthouse; police headquarters or station, precinct house, firehouse, fire station; county building, county courthouse; community center.

.6 (city districts) East Side or End, West Side or End; downtown, uptown, midtown; city center, central city, core, inner city, suburbs, suburbia, outskirts, greenbelt, residential district, business district or section, shopping center; ghetto, Jewtown [derog]; black ghetto, niggertown [derog]; Chinatown, Little Italy, Little Hungary, etc.; barrio; the other side of the tracks, **slum** or **slums,** blighted area or neighborhood or section, urban blight, run-down neighborhood, tenement district, hell's kitchen or half-acre; tenderloin, red-light district, Bowery, **skid row** or skid road [both slang].

.7 **block,** city block, square.

.8 **square, plaza,** *place* [Fr], *piazza* [Ital], *campo* [Ital], **marketplace,** market, market cross, rialto, mart, forum, agora.

.9 **circle,** circus [Brit]; crescent.

.10 ADJS **urban, metropolitan, municipal,** burghal, **civic,** oppidan; city, town, village; citified; suburban; interurban; downtown, uptown, midtown.

184. LOCATION

.1 NOUNS **location, situation, place,** *lieu* [Fr], **placement, emplacement, position,** hole [slang], stead; **whereabouts,** whereabout; **area, district, region** 180; **locality, locale,** *locus* [L]; **abode** 191; **site,** situs; **spot, point, pinpoint,** bench mark; **bearings, latitude and longitude;** stasi–, top(o)–; –topy; –arium, –ary, –drome, –ery, –ment, –orium, –ory, –ry, –teria, –y.

.2 **station,** status, **stand, standing,** standpoint, viewpoint, angle, perspective, distance, footing, **seat, post,** base, ground, venue.

.3 **position, orientation,** lay, lie, set, **attitude,** aspect, exposure, frontage, **bearing** or **bearings,** radio bearing, azimuth; position line or line of position; **fix;** celestial navigation, dead reckoning, pilotage.

.4 **place,** stead, lieu.

.5 (act of placing) **placement, positioning, emplacement, situation, location,** localization, locating, placing, putting, pinpointing; **allocation,** collocation, **disposition,** assignment, **deployment,** posting, **stationing,** spotting; deposition, reposition, deposit; **stowage,** storage, loading, lading, packing.

.6 **establishment, foundation,** settlement, settling, colonization, population, peopling, plantation; lodgment, fixation, anchorage, mooring; **installation,** installment, inauguration, investiture, initiation.

.7 topography, geography; cartography, chorography; surveying, navigation, geodesy; geodetic satellite, orbiting geophysical observatory, OGO.

.8 VERBS **have place,** be there; have its place or slot, **belong, go, fit,** fit in.

.9 **be located** or **situated, lie, be found,** stand, rest, repose; lie in, have its seat in.

.10 **locate, situate, place, position;** emplace, spot [informal], **install,** put in place; **allocate,** collocate, **dispose, deploy,** assign; **localize,** narrow or pin down; put one's finger on, **fix,** assign or consign or relegate to a place; **pinpoint,** zero in on, home in on; find or fix or calculate one's position, triangulate, get a fix or navigational fix, navigate.

.11 **place, put, set, lay,** seat, stick [informal], **station, post;** park; pose, posit, submit.

.12 (put violently) clap, slap, **thrust, fling, hurl,** throw, cast, chuck, toss; **plump; plunk** or **plank** or **plop** [all informal].

.13 deposit, repose, reposit, rest, lay, lodge; **put down**, set down, lay down.

.14 load, lade, freight, burden; fill 56.7; **stow**, store; **pack**, pack away; ship; pile, heap, heap up, stack, mass; bag, sack, pocket; can, bottle, box, crate, barrel.

.15 establish, fix, plant, pitch, seat, set; found, base, build, ground, lay the foundation; install, invest, vest, put in, put up, set up, build in.

.16 settle, settle down, sit down, locate [informal], park [informal], ensconce; take up one's abode *or* quarters, make one's home, reside, inhabit 188.7; move, relocate, establish residence, take up residence, take residence at, put up *or* live *or* stay at, quarter *or* billet at, hang up one's hat [informal]; take *or* strike root, place oneself, plant oneself, get a footing, stand, take one's stand *or* position; anchor, drop anchor, come to anchor, moor; squat, camp, bivouac; perch, roost, nest, hive, burrow; domesticate, set up housekeeping, keep house; colonize, populate, people; set up in business, go in business for oneself, set up shop, hang up one's shingle [informal].

.17 ADJS located, placed, situated, situate, positioned, installed, emplaced, spotted [informal], set, seated; stationed, posted, deployed, assigned; established, fixed, settled, planted, ensconced, embosomed.

.18 locational, positional, situational, situal; topographic, geographic, chorographic, cartographic; navigational, geodetic; regional 180.8.

.19 ADVS in place, in position, −wise; *in situ, in loco* [both L].

.20 where, whereabouts, in what place, in which place; whither, to what *or* which place.

.21 wherever, where'er, wheresoever, wheresoe'er, whithersoever, wherever it may be; anywhere, anyplace [informal].

.22 here, hereat, in this place, just here, on the spot; hereabouts, hereabout, in this vicinity; somewhere about *or* near; aboard, on board, with *or* among us; hither, hitherward, hitherwards, hereto, hereunto, hereinto, to this place.

.23 there, thereat, in that place, in those parts; thereabout, thereabouts, in that vicinity *or* neighborhood; thither, thitherward, thitherwards, to that place; −ward(s).

.24 here and there, in places, in various places, in spots, *passim* [L].

.25 somewhere, someplace, in some place, someplace or other.

.26 PREPS at, in, on, by, a−; near, next to; with, among, in the midst of; to, toward 290.28; from 301.22.

.27 over, all over, here and there on *or* in, at about, round about; through, **all through, throughout** 56.17.

185. DISLOCATION

.1 NOUNS dislocation, displacement, −diastasis; disjointing 49.1, disarticulation, unjointing, unhinging, luxation; heterotopia; shift, removal, forcible shift *or* removal; uprooting, ripping out, deracination; disarrangement 63; incoherence 51.1; discontinuity 72; Doppler effect, red shift, violet shift [all phys].

.2 dislodgment; unplacement, unseating, upset, unsaddling, unhorsing; deposal 783.

.3 misplacement, mislaying, misputting.

.4 displaced person, DP, stateless person, Wandering Jew, man without a country, exile, deportee; displaced *or* deported population; *déraciné* [Fr].

.5 VERBS dislocate, displace, disjoint 49.9, disarticulate, unjoint, luxate, unhinge, put *or* force *or* push out of place, put *or* throw out of joint, throw out of gear, disarrange 63.2.

.6 dislodge, unplace, uproot, root up *or* out, deracinate; depose 783.4, unseat, unsaddle; unhorse, dismount; throw off, buck off.

.7 misplace, mislay, misput.

.8 ADJS dislocatory, dislocating, heterotopic.

.9 dislocated, displaced; disjointed, unjointed, unhinged; out, out of joint, out of gear; disarranged 62.13; ect(o)−.

.10 unplaced, unestablished, unsettled; unhoused, unharbored, houseless, homeless, stateless, exiled, outcast.

.11 misplaced, mislaid, misput; out of place, out of one's element, like a fish out of water, in the wrong place, in the wrong box *or* pew [informal], in the right church but the wrong pew [informal].

.12 eccentric, off-center, off-balance, unbalanced, uncentered.

186. PRESENCE

.1 NOUNS presence, being here *or* there, hereness, thereness, physical *or* actual presence, spiritual presence; immanence, indwellingness, inherence; whereness, immediacy; ubiety; availability, accessibility; occurrence 151.2, existence 1.

.2 **omnipresence,** all-presence, **ubiquity,** infinity, everywhereness.

.3 **permeation, pervasion,** penetration; **suffusion,** transfusion, diffusion, imbuement; **overrunning,** overspreading, overswarming.

.4 **attendance,** frequenting, frequence; number present; turnout *or* box office *or* draw [all informal].

.5 **attender, visitor,** –goer, **patron; fan** *or* buff [both informal], aficionado; **frequenter,** habitué, haunter; spectator 442; theatergoer 611.32; audience 448.6.

.6 VERBS **be present,** be located *or* situated 184.9, be there, be found, be met with; **occur** 151.5, exist 1.8; lie, stand, remain; fall in the way of; dwell in, indwell, inhere.

.7 **pervade, permeate,** penetrate; **suffuse,** transfuse, diffuse, leaven, imbue; **fill,** extend throughout, leave no void, occupy; **overrun,** overswarm, overspread, bespread, run through, meet one at every turn; creep with, crawl with, swarm with, teem with; honeycomb.

.8 **attend, be at,** be present at, find oneself at, **go** *or* **come to; appear,** turn up, show up [informal], show one's face, make *or* put in an appearance, give the pleasure of one's company, make a personal appearance, **visit, take in,** do [informal]; catch [informal]; sit in *or* at; be on hand, be on deck [informal]; watch, see; witness, look on, *assister* [Fr].

.9 **revisit,** return to, go back to, come again.

.10 **frequent, haunt,** resort to, hang around *or* about at *or* out at [all slang].

.11 **present oneself, report;** report for duty.

.12 ADJS **present,** attendant; **on hand,** on deck [informal], on board; **immediate,** immanent, indwelling, inherent, available, accessible, **at hand,** in view, within reach *or* sight *or* call.

.13 **omnipresent, all-present,** ubiquitous, infinite; everywhere 179.11.

.14 **pervasive,** pervading, suffusive, suffusing.

.15 **permeated,** saturated, shot through, honeycombed; crawling, creeping, swarming, teeming.

.16 ADVS **here, there.**

.17 **in person,** personally, bodily, **in the flesh** [informal], in one's own person, *in propria persona* [L].

.18 PREPS **in the presence of,** in the face of, under the eyes *or* nose of, **before.**

.19 PHRS all present and accounted for; standing room only, SRO.

187. ABSENCE

.1 NOUNS **absence,** nonpresence, awayness; nowhereness, **nonexistence** 2; want, **lack,** blank, deprivation; nonoccurrence, neverness; **subtraction** 42.

.2 **vacancy,** vacuity, voidness, **emptiness,** blankness, hollowness, inanition; **bareness,** barrenness, desolateness, bleakness, desertedness; **nonoccupance** *or* **nonoccupancy,** nonoccupation, noninhabitance, nonresidence; opening, place open, vacant post.

.3 **void, vacuum,** blank, empty space, inanity; **nothingness;** *tabula rasa* [L], clean slate; **nothing** 2.2.

.4 **absence,** nonattendance, **absenting, leaving,** taking leave, **departure** 301; running away, fleeing, abscondence, **disappearance** 447, escape 632; **absentation,** nonappearance, default, unauthorized *or* unexcused absence; **truancy, hooky** [informal], French leave, **cut** [informal]; absence without leave *or* AWOL; **absenteeism,** truantism; **leave, leave of absence,** furlough, **vacation,** holiday, day off; authorized *or* excused absence, sick leave; sabbatical leave.

.5 **absentee, truant,** no-show.

.6 **nobody, no one,** no man, not one, not a single one *or* person, **not a soul** *or* **blessed soul,** never a one, ne'er a one, nary one [dial], nobody on earth *or* under the sun, nobody present.

.7 VERBS **be absent, stay away,** keep away, keep out of the way, not come, not show up [informal], turn up missing [informal], stay away in droves [informal], fail to appear, default.

.8 **absent oneself, take leave** *or* **a leave of absence,** go on leave *or* furlough; slip off *or* away, duck *or* sneak out [informal], slip out, make oneself scarce [informal], leave the scene, bow out, exit, **depart** 301.6, **disappear** 447.2, escape 632.6.

.9 **play truant, play hooky** [informal], go AWOL, take French leave; jump ship; **cut** *or* **skip** [both informal].

.10 ADJS **absent,** not present, nonattendant, **away, gone,** departed, disappeared, vanished, absconded, out of sight; **missing,** wanting, **lacking,** not found, omitted, taken away, subtracted, deleted, nowhere to be found; a– *or* an–, dis–, e–, ectro–, lipo–, lyo–, –less; no longer present *or* with us *or* among us; **nonexistent** 2.7; conspicuous by its absence.

.11 **nonresident,** not in residence, from

home, **away from home,** on leave *or* vacation *or* holiday, on sabbatical leave; on tour, on the road; abroad, overseas.

.12 **truant,** absent without leave *or* **AWOL.**

.13 **vacant, empty,** hollow, inane, **bare, vacuous, void,** without content, with nothing inside, devoid, null, null and void, ken-(o)-, nulli–; **blank,** clear, white, bleached; featureless, unrelieved, characterless, bland, insipid; **barren** 166.4.

.14 **vacant, open, available,** free, **unoccupied,** unfilled, **uninhabited,** unpopulated, unpeopled, untaken, untenanted, tenantless, untended, unmanned, unstaffed; **deserted,** abandoned, forsaken, godforsaken [informal].

.15 ADVS **absently;** vacantly, emptily, hollowly, vacuously, blankly.

.16 **nowhere,** in no place, neither here nor there; nowhither.

.17 **away** 301.21, **elsewhere,** somewhere else, not here; elsewhither.

.18 PREPS void of, empty of, free of, **without** 662.17.

188. HABITATION

(an inhabiting)

.1 NOUNS **habitation,** inhabiting, inhabitation, habitancy, inhabitancy, **tenancy, occupancy,** occupation, **residence** *or* **residency,** residing, abiding, **living,** nesting, **dwelling,** commorancy, lodging, staying, stopping, sojourning, staying over; squatting; cohabitation; **abode** 191.

.2 **peopling,** peoplement, empeoplement, **population,** inhabiting; **colonization, settlement,** plantation.

.3 **housing,** domiciliation; lodgment, **lodging,** transient lodging, doss [Brit], **quartering,** billeting, hospitality; living quarters 191.3; **housing development,** subdivision, tract; housing problem, housing bill, lower-income housing, slum clearance, urban renewal; assembly-line housing.

.4 **camping,** tenting, **encampment,** bivouacking; camp 191.29.

.5 **sojourn,** sojournment; **stay,** stop; **stopover,** stop-off, stayover, layover.

.6 **hàbitability,** inhabitability, **livability.**

.7 VERBS **inhabit, occupy,** tenant; **reside, live, dwell, lodge, stay,** remain, abide, hang out [slang], domicile, domiciliate; **room,** bunk, berth, doss down [Brit]; **perch** *or* **roost** *or* **squat** [all informal]; nest, cohabit.

.8 **sojourn,** stop, **stay, stop over,** stay over, lay over.

.9 **people,** empeople, **populate, inhabit,** denizen; colonize, **settle,** settle in, plant.

.10 **house,** domicile, domiciliate; provide with a roof, have as a guest *or* lodger, shelter, harbor; **lodge, quarter,** put up, billet, room, bed, berth, bunk; stable.

.11 **camp, encamp,** tent; pitch, **pitch camp,** pitch one's tent, drive stakes [informal]; bivouac; go camping, camp out, sleep out, rough it.

.12 ADJS **inhabited, occupied,** tenanted; **peopled,** empeopled, **populated, colonized,** settled; populous.

.13 **resident,** residentiary, **in residence; residing, living, dwelling,** commorant, lodging, **staying,** remaining, abiding, living in; –cole, –colous, –coline.

.14 **housed,** domiciled, domiciliated, **lodged,** quartered, billeted; stabled.

.15 **habitable,** inhabitable, occupiable, lodgeable, tenantable, **livable, fit to live in;** homelike 191.33.

.16 ADVS **at home,** in the bosom of one's family, *chez soi* [Fr]; in one's element; back home *or* down home [both informal].

189. NATIVENESS

.1 NOUNS **nativeness,** nativity, native-bornness, indigenousness, aboriginality, autochthonousness, **nationality;** nativism.

.2 **citizenship,** native-born citizenship, citizenship by birth, citizenhood, subjecthood; civism.

.3 **naturalization,** naturalized citizenship, citizenship by naturalization *or* adoption, nationalization, adoption, admission, affiliation, **assimilation;** Americanization, Anglicization, etc.; acculturation, culture shock; papers, citizenship papers.

.4 VERBS **naturalize,** grant *or* confer citizenship, adopt, admit, affiliate, **assimilate;** Americanize, Anglicize, etc.; acculturate, acculturize; go native [informal].

.5 ADJS **native,** natal, **indigenous,** endemic, autochthonous, vernacular; original, aboriginal, primitive; native-born, homegrown, homebred, native to the soil *or* place *or* heath.

.6 **naturalized,** adopted, assimilated; indoctrinated, Americanized, Anglicized, etc.; acculturated, acculturized.

190. INHABITANT, NATIVE

.1 NOUNS **population, inhabitants,** habitancy, dwellers, **populace, people,** whole people, people at large, citizenry, folk; **public,** general public; community, society, **nation,** commonwealth, constituency; speech or linguistic community; ethnic or cultural community; socio–.

.2 **inhabitant,** inhabiter, habitant; **occupant,** occupier, **dweller, tenant, denizen,** inmate; **resident,** residencer, residentiary, resider; inpatient; resident physician, intern; house detective; resident or live-in maid; writer- or poet- or artist-in-residence; incumbent, *locum tenens* [L]; sojourner; addressee; –er or –ier or –yer, –cola, –ese, –ite.

.3 **native,** indigene, autochthon, earliest inhabitant, first comer, primitive settler; primitive; **aborigine,** aboriginal; local or local yokel [both informal].

.4 **citizen, national,** subject; **naturalized citizen,** nonnative citizen, citizen by adoption, immigrant, metic; hyphenated American, hyphenate; **cosmopolitan,** cosmopolite, citizen of the world.

.5 **fellow citizen,** fellow countryman, **compatriot,** congener, **countryman,** countrywoman, *landsman* [Yid], *paesano* [Ital], *paisano* [Sp]; fellow townsman, home towner [informal].

.6 **townsman;** townee or towner [both informal], **villager,** oppidan, city dweller, city man, big-city man, **city slicker** [informal]; urbanite; suburbanite; exurbanite; burgher, burgess, *bourgeois* [Fr]; townswoman, villageress; townspeople, townfolks, townfolk.

.7 **householder,** freeholder; cottager, cotter, cottier, crofter; head of household.

.8 **lodger, roomer,** paying guest; **boarder,** board-and-roomer, **transient,** transient guest or boarder; **renter, tenant,** lessee, underlessee.

.9 **settler,** *habitan(t)* [Can & Louisiana Fr]; **colonist,** colonizer, colonial, immigrant, planter; **homesteader; squatter,** nester; **pioneer;** sooner; precursor 66.

.10 **backsettler,** hinterlander, bushman [Austral]; **frontiersman,** mountain man; **backwoodsman,** woodlander, woodsman, woodman, woodhick [informal], forester; **mountaineer, hillbilly** or ridge runner [both informal], brush ape or briar-hopper [both informal]; cracker or redneck [both informal], desert rat [informal], clam digger [informal], piny [informal].

.11 (regional inhabitants) **Easterner,** eastlander; **Westerner,** westlander; **Southerner,** southlander; **Northener,** northlander, Yankee; Northman; New Englander, Down-Easter Yankee.

191. ABODE, HABITAT

(place of habitation or resort)

.1 NOUNS **abode, habitation, place, dwelling,** dwelling place, abiding place, place to live, where one lives or resides, roof over one's head, **residence,** pad or crib [both informal]; crash pad; **domicile,** *domus* [L]; **lodging,** lodgment, lodging place; seat, nest; roof, cantonment; address.

.2 **domesticity,** domesticality, homelovingness; housewifery, **housekeeping, homemaking;** householding, householdry.

.3 **quarters, living quarters; lodgings,** lodging, lodgment; diggings or digs [both Brit informal]; rooms, berth, roost, sleeping place, accommodations; **housing** 188.3, shelter, *gîte* [Fr].

.4 **home,** home sweet home, homestead, toft [Brit], home place, home roof, roof, rooftree, place where one hangs his hat; **fireside, hearth,** hearth and home, hearthstone, fireplace, *foyer* [Fr], chimney corner, ingle, ingleside or inglenook; **household,** ménage; paternal roof or domicile, family homestead, ancestral halls.

.5 **habitat,** home, **range,** locality, native environment; ec(o)– or oec(o)– or oiko–.

.6 **house,** *casa* [Sp & Ital], dwelling house; **building, structure, edifice,** fabric, erection, skyscraper; roof; lodge; manor house, hall; town house, *rus in urbe* [L]; country house, *dacha* [Russ], country seat; ranch house, farmhouse, farm; prefabricated house, Dymaxion house, living machine; sod house, adobe house; lake dwelling 398.3; houseboat; cave or cliff dwelling; penthouse; split-level; parsonage 1042.7, **rectory,** vicarage, deanery, manse; official residence, White House, 10 Downing Street, governor's mansion; presidential palace; embassy, consulate; –age.

.7 **estate,** house and grounds, house and lot, **homestead,** homecroft [Brit], place, home place, messuage [law], farmstead; **ranch,** *rancho, hacienda* [both Sp], toft or steading [both Brit], grange.

.8 **mansion,** palatial residence, **villa, château,** *hôtel* [Fr], **castle,** tower; **palace,** *palais* [Fr], *palazzo* [Ital], court.

.9 **cottage,** cot or cote, **bungalow,** box; chalet, lodge, snuggery, *pied-à-terre* [Fr]; love nest; **cabin,** cabaña; log cabin, blockhouse.

.10 **hut, hutch, shack, shanty,** crib, **shed; lean-to; booth,** bothy or boothy [both Scot], stall; tollbooth *or* tollhouse, sentry box, gatehouse, porter's lodge; **outhouse**, outbuilding; **pavilion**, kiosk; Quonset hut *or* Nissen hut.

.11 (Indian houses) wigwam, tepee, hogan, wickiup, jacal, longhouse; tupik, igloo [both Eskimo].

.12 hovel, dump [slang], hole, sty, pigsty, pigpen [both informal], tumbledown shack.

.13 summerhouse, arbor, bower, **gazebo**, pergola, kiosk, alcove, retreat; **conservatory**, **greenhouse**, glasshouse [Brit], lathhouse.

.14 apartment, flat, tenement, chambers [Brit]; suite, suite *or* set of rooms; walkup, cold-water flat; **penthouse**; garden apartment; duplex apartment; railroad flat.

.15 apartment house, flats, tenement; duplex, duplex house; cooperative apartment house, condominium; high-rise apartment building.

.16 inn, hotel, hostel, hostelry, **tavern**, ordinary [Brit], *posada* [Sp]; **roadhouse**, caravansary, guest house, **hospice**; **lodging house**, **rooming house**; **dormitory**, dorm [informal], fraternity *or* sorority house; **flophouse** *or* fleabag [both slang], doss house [Brit]; **boardinghouse**, *pension* [Fr]; public house, public *or* **pub** [both Brit informal].

.17 motel, motor court, motor inn, motor hotel, auto court; boatel.

.18 trailer, house *or* camp trailer, **mobile home**, camper, caravan [Brit]; trailer court, trailer camp, trailer park.

.19 zoo, menagerie, *Tiergarten* [Ger], zoological garden.

.20 barn, stable, stall; **cowbarn**, cowhouse, cowshed, cowbyre, byre; mews.

.21 kennel, doghouse; pound, dog pound; cattery.

.22 coop, **chicken house** *or* **coop**, henhouse, hencote, hennery; brooder.

.23 birdhouse, aviary, bird cage; dovecote, pigeon house *or* loft, columbary; roost, perch, roosting place.

.24 vivarium, terrarium, aquarium; fishpond.

.25 nest, nidus; aerie, eyrie; **beehive**, **apiary**, hive, bee tree, hornet's nest, wasp's nest, vespiary.

.26 lair, den, cave, **hole**, covert, mew, form; **burrow**, tunnel, earth, run, couch, lodge.

.27 resort, haunt, purlieu, **hangout** [slang], **stamping ground** [informal]; gathering place, rallying point, meeting place, clubhouse, club; casino, gambling house; health resort 689.29; **spa**, baths, springs, watering place.

.28 (disapproved place) **dive** [slang], **den, lair,** den of thieves; hole *or* dump *or* joint [all slang]; gyp *or* clip joint [slang]; **whorehouse**, cathouse [slang], sporting house, brothel, bordello, stews, fleshpots.

.29 camp, encampment, *Lager* [Ger]; bivouac; barrack *or* **barracks**, casern, *caserne* [Fr], cantonment, lines [Brit]; hobo jungle *or* camp; detention camp, concentration camp, *Konzentrationslager* [Ger]; campground *or* campsite.

.30 (deities of the household) lares and penates, Vesta, Hestia.

.31 VERBS **keep house**, housekeep [informal], practice domesticity, maintain a household.

.32 ADJS **residential**, residentiary; domestic, domiciliary, domal; **home, household,** mansional, manorial, palatial.

.33 homelike, homish, **homey** [informal], homely; comfortable, friendly, cheerful, peaceful, cozy, snug, intimate; simple, plain, unpretending.

.34 domesticated, **tame,** tamed, broken; housebroken.

.35 PHRS "there's no place like home" [J. H. Payne].

192. ROOM

(compartment)

.1 NOUNS **room, chamber,** *chambre* [Fr], *salle* [Fr]; ballroom, grand ballroom; rotunda.

.2 compartment, chamber, enclosed space; **cavity**, hollow, hole; **cell**, cellule; booth, stall, crib, manger; box, pew; **crypt, vault,** hold.

.3 nook, corner, cranny, **niche, recess,** cove, bay, oriel, alcove; cubicle, roomlet, carrel, hole in the wall [informal], cubby, **cubbyhole**, snuggery.

.4 hall; assembly hall, exhibition hall, convention hall; gallery; **meetinghouse; auditorium,** opera house, **theater** 611.18, music hall; stadium, **arena** 802, lecture hall, lyceum, amphitheater; concert hall, dance hall; **chapel** 1042.3.

.5 parlor, living room, sitting room, drawing room, front room, best room [informal], foreroom [dial], salon, saloon; sun parlor *or* sunroom, solarium.

.6 library, stacks; **study,** studio, atelier, workroom, office; **loft,** sail loft.

.7 bedroom, boudoir, chamber, **bedchamber,** sleeping room, cubicle, cubiculum; nursery; dormitory.

.8 (private chamber) **sanctum,** sanctum

sanctorum, holy of holies, adytum; **den,** retreat, closet, cabinet.

.9 (ships) cabin, stateroom; saloon; house, deckhouse, cuddy, shelter cabin.

.10 (trains) drawing room, stateroom, parlor car, saloon [Brit], Pullman car, roomette.

.11 **dining room,** *salle à manger* [Fr], dinette, dining hall, refectory, mess *or* messroom *or* mess hall, commons; dining car, dining saloon; **restaurant, cafeteria** 307.15.

.12 **playroom,** recreation room, rec room [informal], family room, game room, **rumpus room** [informal]; **gymnasium** 878.12.

.13 **utility room,** laundry room, sewing room.

.14 **kitchen** 330.3, **storeroom** 660.6, smoking room 434.13.

.15 **closet,** clothes closet, wardrobe, cloakroom; linen closet; dressing room, fitting room.

.16 **attic,** attic room, **garret, loft,** sky parlor; cockloft, hayloft; storeroom, junk room, lumber room [Brit].

.17 **cellar,** cellarage, **basement;** subbasement; wine cellar, potato cellar, storm cellar, cyclone cellar; coal bin *or* hole, hold, hole, bunker.

.18 **corridor, hall,** hallway; passage, **passageway; gallery,** loggia; arcade, colonnade, pergola, cloister, peristyle; areaway; breezeway.

.19 **vestibule,** portal, **portico,** entry, entryway, entrance, **entrance hall,** entranceway, **threshold; lobby, foyer;** propylaeum, stoa; narthex, galilee.

.20 **anteroom,** antechamber; side room, byroom; **waiting room,** *salle d'attente* [Fr]; **reception room,** presence chamber *or* room, audience chamber; throne room; lounge, greenroom, wardroom.

.21 **porch,** stoop, **veranda,** piazza, patio, lanai, gallery; sun porch, solarium, sleeping porch.

.22 **balcony,** gallery, terrace.

.23 **floor, story,** level, flat; first floor *or* story, ground *or* street floor, *rez-de-chaussée* [Fr]; mezzanine, mezzanine floor, *entresol* [Fr]; clerestory.

.24 **showroom,** display room, exhibition room, gallery.

.25 **hospital room; ward,** maternity ward, fever ward, charity ward, prison ward, etc.; private room, semi-private room; examining room, consultation room, treatment room; operating room *or* OR *or* surgery, labor room, delivery room, recovery room; emergency, intensive care, isolation, X ray, therapy; pharmacy, dispensary; clinic, nursery; laboratory, blood bank; nurses' station.

.26 **bathroom, lavatory, washroom** 681.10, **water closet,** WC, closet, **rest room,** comfort station, **toilet** 311.10.

.27 (for vehicles) **garage,** carport; coach *or* carriage house; carbarn; roundhouse; hangar; boathouse.

193. CONTAINER

.1 NOUNS **container, receptacle** 193.6–19, receiver 819.3, holder, vessel, utensil; –ange, –angium, –coel(e) *or* –cele, –clinium, –thecium.

.2 **bag** 193.16, **sack,** sac, poke [dial]; **pocket,** fob; **balloon, bladder,** asc(o)– *or* asci–, cyst(o)– *or* cysti–, –cyst.

.3 **belly, stomach,** gastr(o)– *or* gastri– *or* gaster(o)–, tummy *or* tum-tum [both informal], **abdomen,** abdomin(o)–, celi(o)–; **crop,** gullet 396.15, **craw,** maw, gizzard; **midriff,** diaphragm, breadbasket [informal]; swollen *or* distended *or* protruding *or* prominent belly, *embonpoint* [Fr], **paunch, gut** [slang], *kishkes* [Yid], spare tire *or* bay window [both informal]; potbelly *or* potgut *or* beerbelly [all slang], pusgut [slang], **pot** [slang], swagbelly [dial]; ventripotence; underbelly; first stomach, rumen, rumeno–; second stomach, reticulum, reticul(o)– *or* reticuli–, honeycomb stomach; third stomach, psalterium, omasum, manyplies; fourth stomach, abomasum, rennet bag.

.4 ADJS vascular, vesicular; camerated, capsular, cellular, cystic, locular, marsupial, saccular, siliquose; angi(o)–, ascidi(o)–, cotyl(o)– *or* cotyli–.

.5 **abdominal,** ventral, celiac, –coelous; stomachal *or* stomachic(al), gastric, ventricular; big-bellied 195.18.

.6 receptacles

ashcan	crock
ashtray	crucible
autoclave	dinner pail
billy *or* billycan [both	dinner plate
Austral]	dish, dishware
bucket	gallipot
caddy	garbage can
cage	GI can
can	hod
canister	holdall
cannikin	hopper
casserole	jerrican
catchall	kibble
china, chinaware	magazine
coal scuttle	messkit
coaster	milk pail
compote	mortar
creamer	mortarboard
cream pitcher	oil can

pail
palette
patera [L]
piggin
pipkin
pitcher
plate
platter
powder horn
salver
saucer
scuttle
slop pail

soup bowl *or* plate
sugar bowl
tableware
tin can, tin [Brit]
trash can
tray
trencher
vat
waiter
wastepaper basket
    669.7
watering can

stein
tankard
tasse [Fr]
tassie [Brit]
teacup

Toby-jug *or* Toby
    Fillpot jug
tumbler
tyg
wineglass

.11 ladles

bail
calabash
cyathus
dessert spoon
dipper
gourd
labis [eccl]
scoop
shovel

soupspoon
spade
spatula
spoon
sugar spoon
tablespoon
teaspoon
trowel

.7 basins

barber's basin
bathtub
bidet
bowl
catch basin *or* drain
cereal bowl
cistern
finger bowl
gravy boat
hip bath
porringer
pottinger

punch bowl
salad bowl
sauce boat
sink 682.12
sitzbath
terrine
trough
tub
tureen
vat
washbasin
washtub

.12 bottles

calabash
canteen
carafe
carboy
caster
cruet
cruse
decanter
demijohn
ewer
fifth
flacon
flagon
flask
flasket
gourd

jar
jeroboam
jug
hipflask
hot-water bottle
lota
magnum
mussuk
olla [Sp]
phial
pocket flask
stoup
thermos
vacuum bottle
vial

.8 pots

biggin
boiler
bud vase
caldron
chamber pot
coffeepot
coffee urn
cuspidor
flower bowl
flowerpot
honeypot
jardiniere
kettle

kitchen boiler
olla [Sp]
patella
paten
percolator
pipkin
potty
spittoon
teakettle
teapot
tea urn
urn
vase

.13 casks

barrel
breaker
butt
drum
firkin
harness cask *or* tub
hogshead
keg

kilderkin
pipe
puncheon
rundlet
tun
vat
water butt

.9 pans

ashpan
bakepan
boiler
brazier
bread pan
broiler
cake pan
dishpan
double boiler
dustpan
frying pan

pan broiler
piepan
posnet
roaster
saucepan
skillet
spider
stewpan
warming pan
wok

.14 cases

ammunition box
ark
attaché case
bandolier
billfold
bin
boot
box
briefcase
bunker
caisson
canister
capsule, capsula
cardcase
carton
casket
cedar chest
chest
cigarette case
cist
coffer
coffin
compact
cone
crate
crib
dispatch box

envelope
étui
file
file folder
filing box *or* case
folio
glasses *or* spectacle
    case
holster
hope chest
housewife, hussy
hutch
kit
letter file
matchbox
money box
monstrance
ostensorium
packet
packing box *or* case
pillbox
pocketcase
pod
portfolio
powder box
quiver
rack

.10 cups, drinking vessels

beaker
beer glass
blackjack
bowl
brandy snifter
cannikin
chalice
coffee cup
demitasse
drinking cup
drinking horn
eggcup
glass
goblet
highball glass
horn

jigger
jorum
liqueur glass
loving cup
mazer
mug
noggin
pannikin
pony
pottle
rummer
schooner
schooper
scyphus
shell
shot glass

reliquary
sarcophagus
scabbard
sheath
skippet
snuffbox
socket

tea chest
till
tinderbox
vanity case
vasculum
wallet

.15 baskets

bassinet
breadbasket
buck basket
bushel
clothesbasket
clothes hamper or bin
corbeil [archit]
crane
creel
dosser, dorser
flower basket
frail
fruit basket
hamper
pannier, *panier* [Fr]

picnic basket
punnet
reed basket
rush basket
sewing basket
skep
splint basket
stave basket
trug
washbasket
wastebasket
wastepaper basket
wicker basket
wire basket
wooden basket

.16 bags

bedroll or beddingroll
bindle
budget [dial]
bundle
caddie bag or cart
diplomatic pouch
evening bag
game bag
golf bag
gunny, gunny sack
handbag
mail pouch
moneybag
net
nose bag

pack sack
pocketbook
poke
pouch
purse
reticule
sack
saddlebag
schoolbag
scrip [archaic]
sleeping bag
tobacco pouch
vanity bag
wineskin

.17 luggage, baggage

attaché case
backpack
bag
bandbox
barracks bag
boodle bag
Boston bag
briefcase
carpetbag
carryall
ditty bag or box
duffel bag
flight bag
footlocker
Gladstone, Gladstone
  bag
grip
gripsack
handbag
hatbox
haversack

holdall
kit
kit bag
knapsack
locker box
musette bag
overnight bag
portmanteau
rucksack
sac de nuit [Fr]
Saratoga trunk
satchel
sea bag
shoulder bag
suitcase
tote bag or sack
traveling bag
trunk
tucker bag [Austral]
valise

.18 botany, anatomy

air bladder, phys(o)–
air sac
amnion, amnio–
bladder
bleb
blister
boll

bursa
calyx
cancelli
capsule, capsul(o)– or
  capsuli–
cell
cyst, cystis

fistula
follicle
gallbladder
legume
loculus
marsupium
musk bag
pericarp
pocket
pod
sac, sacc(o)– or sacci–
saccule
sacculus
saccus

scrotum 419.10
seedcase
silique
sinus
sound
stomach 193.3
theca
udder
utricle
vasculum
ventricle
vesica [L]
vesicle

.19 cupboards

armoire [Fr]
buffet
bunker
bureau
cabinet
Canterbury
cellaret
chest
chest of drawers
chiffonier
chifforobe
closet
clothespress
commode
credenza
davenport
desk
drawer
dresser

étagère [Fr]
escritoire
garderobe [Fr]
highboy
kitchen cabinet
locker
lowboy
press
secrétaire [Fr]
secretary
shelf
shelves
sideboard
tallboy
vargueno
vitrine
wardrobe
whatnot

194. CONTENTS

.1 NOUNS **contents, content,** what is contained or included or comprised; **insides** 225.4, innards [informal], guts; **components, constituents, ingredients,** elements, **items, parts, divisions,** subdivisions; **inventory,** index, census, list 88; part 55; whole 54; composition 58.

.2 **load, lading, cargo, freight, charge, burden; payload;** boatload, busload, carload, cartload, shipload, trailerload, trainload, truckload, vanload, wagonload.

.3 **lining, liner,** –pleura; **interlining,** interlineation; **inlayer, inlay,** inlaying; **filling,** filler; **packing,** padding, wadding, **stuffing;** facing; doubling, doublure; bushing, bush; wainscot; insole.

.4 (contents of a container) cup, cupful, etc. 28.8.

.5 (essential content) **substance, stuff, material, matter,** medium, building blocks, fabric; **sum and substance, gist, meat, nub** [informal], core, kernel, marrow, pith, sap, spirit, **essence,** quintessence, elixir, distillate, distillation, distilled essence; irreducible content; heart, soul.

.6 **enclosure,** the enclosed.

.7 VERBS **fill, pack** 56.7, **load** 184.14; **line,** interline, interlineate; inlay; face; wainscot, ceil; **pad**, wad, **stuff**; feather, fur.

195. SIZE

.1 NOUNS **size, largeness, bigness, greatness** 34, **magnitude,** order of magnitude, amplitude; mass, bulk, **volume,** body; **dimensions, proportions,** dimension, caliber, scantling, proportion; **measure,** measurement, gauge, scale; **extent, extension,** expanse, expansion, scope, reach, range, spread, coverage, area; length, height, depth, breadth, width; girth, diameter, radius; onc(o)– or onch(o)– or onci–.

.2 **capacity, volume, content,** accommodation, room, space, measure, limit, burden; poundage, tonnage, cordage; stowage, tankage; **quantity** 28.

.3 **full size,** full growth; life size.

.4 large size, economy size, family size, **king size,** giant size.

.5 **oversize,** outsize; overlargeness, overbigness; **overgrowth,** wild or uncontrolled growth, overdevelopment; **overweight,** overheaviness; overstoutness, overfatness, overplumpness; gigantism, giantism, titanism; hypertrophy.

.6 **sizableness, largeness, bigness, greatness,** grandness, grandeur, grandiosity; largishness, biggishness; voluminousness, capaciousness, generousness, copiousness, ampleness; tallness, toweringness; broadness, wideness; profundity; extensiveness, expansiveness, comprehensiveness; spaciousness 179.5.

.7 **hugeness, vastness,** enormousness, immenseness, **enormity, immensity,** tremendousness, **prodigiousness,** stupendousness, mountainousness, giantlikeness, giantship, monumentalism; monstrousness, monstrosity.

.8 **corpulence, obesity, stoutness,** *embonpoint* [Fr]; **fatness,** fattishness, adiposis or adiposity, fleshiness, beefiness, meatiness, heftiness, grossness; **plumpness,** buxomness, rotundity, fubsiness [Brit], tubbiness [informal], roly-poliness; pudginess, podginess; chubbiness, chunkiness [informal], stockiness, squattiness, dumpiness, portliness; paunchiness, bloatedness, puffiness, pursiness, blowziness; hippiness [informal]; steatopygia or steatopygy; bosominess, bustiness [informal].

.9 **bulkiness,** hulkingness or hulkiness, **massiveness,** lumpishness, clumpishness; **ponderousness,** cumbrousness, cumbersomeness; clumsiness, awkwardness, unwieldiness.

.10 **lump,** clump, **hunk** or chunk [both informal]; **mass, bulk, gob** [slang], batch, **wad,** block, loaf; pat (of butter); clod; nugget; **quantity** 28.

.11 (something large) **whopper** or thumper or lunker or whale or jumbo [all informal]; hulk.

.12 (corpulent person) lump [informal], **heavyweight,** heavy [informal], human or man mountain [informal]; **fat man, fatty** or **fatso** [both informal], roly-poly, tub, tub of lard, tun, tun of flesh, blimp [informal], hippo [informal], **potbelly,** gorbelly [archaic or dial], swagbelly.

.13 **giant** 195.26, giantess, **amazon, colossus, titan,** *nephilim* [Heb pl].

.14 **behemoth, leviathan, monster** 85.20; mammoth, mastodon; elephant, jumbo [informal]; whale; hippopotamus, hippo [informal]; **dinosaur** 123.26.

.15 VERBS **size, adjust, grade,** group, range, rank, graduate, sort, match; gauge, **measure** 490.11, proportion; **bulk** 34.5; **enlarge** 197.4–8.

.16 ADJS **large, sizable, big, great** 34.6, **grand,** tall [informal], **considerable, goodly,** healthy, tidy [informal], **substantial,** bumper, numerous 101.6; largish, biggish; large-scale; man-sized [informal]; large-size(d), good-size(d); hyper–, macr(o)–, maxi–, meg(a)–, megal(o)–, super–.

.17 **voluminous, capacious, generous, ample,** copious, broad, wide, extensive, expansive, comprehensive; spacious 179.9.

.18 **corpulent, stout, fat, overweight,** fattish, **obese,** adipose, gross, fleshy, beefy, meaty, hefty; paunchy, paunched, bloated, puffy, blowzy, distended, swollen, pursy; abdominous, big-bellied, fullbellied, potbellied, gorbellied [archaic or dial], swag-bellied, pot-gutted, pussle-gutted [both informal], **plump, buxom,** *zaftig* [Yid], full, rotund, fubsy [Brit], tubby [informal], roly-poly; **pudgy,** podgy; thickbodied, thick-girthed, **heavyset, thickset, chubby,** chunky [informal], **stocky,** squat, squatty, dumpy, pyknic, endomorphic, square; lusty, strapping [informal], stalwart, brawny, burly; **portly,** imposing; well-fed, corn-fed, grain-fed; chubbyfaced, round-faced, moonfaced; hippy [informal], full-buttocked, steatopygic or steatopygous, fat-assed or lard-assed [both slang], broad in the beam [informal]; bosomy, full-bosomed, busty [informal], top-heavy; plump as a dumpling or partridge, fat as a quail, fat as a pig or hog, "fat as a pork hog" [Malory], "fat as a porpoise" [Swift], "fat as a fool" [John Lyly], "fat as butter" [Shakespeare], fat as brawn *or* bacon.

.19 **bulky, hulky,** hulking, lumpish, lumpy, lumping [informal], clumpish, lumbering, lubberly; **massive,** massy; elephantine, hippopotamic; **ponderous,** cumbrous, cumbersome; **clumsy,** awkward, **unwieldy.**

.20 **huge, immense, vast, enormous,** astronomic(al), tremendous, prodigious, stupendous; great big, larger than life, Homeric, mighty, **titanic, colossal, monumental,** heroic(al), epic(al), towering, mountainous; profound, abysmal, deep as the ocean *or* as China; monster, monstrous; **mammoth,** mastodonic; **gigantic,** gigantean, gigant(o)–; **giant,** giantlike; Cyclopean, Brobdingnagian, Gargantuan, Herculean, Atlantean; elephantine, jumbo [informal]; dinosaurian, dinotherian; **infinite** 104.3.

.21 [slang terms] **whopping, walloping, whaling, whacking,** spanking, slapping, lolloping, thumping, thundering, bumping, banging.

.22 **full-sized,** full-size, full-scale; **full-grown, full-fledged,** full-blown; full-formed, **life-sized,** large as life.

.23 **oversize,** oversized; **outsize,** outsized, giantsize, **kingsize,** recordsize, **overlarge,** overbig, too big; **overgrown,** overdeveloped; **overweight,** overheavy; overfleshed, overstout, overfat, overplump, overfed.

.24 this big, so big, yay big [informal], this size, about this size.

.25 ADVS largely, on a large scale, in a big way; in the large; as can be.

.26 **giants**

Aegaeon	Gargantua
Aegir	Geryoneo
Alifanfaron	Gog
Amarant	Goliath
Antaeus	Grantorto
Ascapart	Gyes
Atlas	Hercules *or* Heracles
Balan	Hlér
Bellerus	Hymir
Blunderbore	Jötunn
Briareüs	Magog
Brobdingnagian	Mimir
Cormoran	Morgante
Cottus	Og
Cyclops	Orgoglio
Enceladus	Orion
Ephialtes	Pantagruel
Fafner	Paul Bunyan
Fenrir	Polyphemus
Ferragus	Titan
Fierebras	Tityus
Firbauti	Typhon
Galapas	Urdar
Galligantus	Ymir

196. LITTLENESS

.1 NOUNS **littleness, smallness** 35, smallishness, **diminutiveness,** miniatureness, slightness, exiguity; puniness, pokiness, dinkiness [slang]; tininess, **minuteness;** undersize; petiteness; dwarfishness, stuntedness, runtiness, shrimpiness; **shortness** 203; **scantiness** 102.1.

.2 **infinitesimalness,** microdimensions; inappreciability, evanescence; intangibility, impalpability, tenuousness, imponderability; imperceptibility, invisibility.

.3 (small place) **tight spot** *or* tight squeeze *or* **pinch** [all informal]; hole, pigeonhole; hole in the wall; cubby, cubbyhole; cubbyhouse, dollhouse, playhouse, doghouse.

.4 **diminutive, runt, shrimp** [informal], wart [slang], wisp, chit, slip, snip, snippet, minikin [archaic], **peewee** [informal], fingerling, small fry [informal]; lightweight, featherweight; bantam, banty [informal]; pony; minnow, mini, minny [both informal]; mouse, tit, titmouse, tomtit [informal]; nubbin, button.

.5 **miniature,** mini, minny [both informal], subminiature; –cle, –ee, –een, –el, –ella *or* –illa, –et, –ette, –idium, –idion, –ie *or* –y *or* –ey, –ium, –kin, –let, –ling, –ock, –sy, –ula, –ule, –ulum, –ulus; microcosm, microcosmos; baby; doll, puppet; microvolume; Elzevir, Elzevir edition; duodecimo, twelvemo.

.6 **dwarf,** dwarfling, **midget,** midge, **pygmy,** manikin, homunculus, atomy, micromorph, hop-o'-my-thumb; elf, gnome, brownie; dapperling, dandiprat, cocksparrow, pip-squeak; **runt, shrimp** [informal], wart [slang], peewee [informal]; Lilliputian, Pigwiggen, Tom Thumb, Thumbelina, Alberich, Alviss, Andvari, Nibelung, Regin.

.7 (minute thing) minutia, **minutiae** [pl], minim, **drop,** droplet, **mite** [informal], **point,** vanishing point, mathematical point, point of a pin, pinpoint, pinhead, **dot;** mote, fleck, **speck,** flyspeck, jot, tittle, iota; **particle,** crumb, scrap, snip, snippet; grain, grain of sand; barleycorn, millet seed, mustard seed; midge, mite, gnat; microbe, microorganism 196.18.

.8 **atom,** atomy, monad; **molecule,** ion; **electron,** proton, meson, neutrino, quark, parton, subatomic *or* nuclear particle.

.9 VERBS make small, **contract** 198.7; **shorten** 203.6; **miniaturize,** minify, scale down.

.10 ADJS **little, small** 35.6, smallish, lept(o)–, mei(o)– *or* mi(o)–, olig(o)–, parvi(o)–,

–cular, –ulous; **slight,** exiguous; **puny,** poky, pindling *or* piddling [both informal], **dinky** [informal]; cramped, limited; one-horse, two-by-four [informal]; pint-sized [informal], half-pint; knee-high, knee-high to a grasshopper; petite; short 203.8.

.11 **tiny;** teeny *or* teeny-weeny *or* eentsy-weentsy [all informal], wee *or* peewee [informal], bitty *or* bitsy *or* little-bitty *or* little-bitsy *or* itsy-bitsy *or* itsy-witsy [all informal]; **minute,** fine.

.12 **miniature, diminutive, minuscule,** mini–, minimal, miniaturized, minikin [archaic], **small-scale,** pony; bantam, banty [informal]; **baby,** baby-sized; **pocket,** pocket-sized, **vest-pocket; toy;** handy, compact; duodecimo, twelvemo; subminiature.

.13 **dwarf,** dwarfed, dwarfish, nan(o)– *or* nann(o)–; **pygmy, midget,** nanoid, elfin; Lilliputian, Tom Thumb; **undersized,** undersize, squat, dumpy; **stunted,** runty; shrunk, shrunken, wizened, shriveled; meager, scrubby, scraggy; incipient, rudimentary, rudimental.

.14 **infinitesimal, microscopic,** ultramicroscopic, micr(o)–, ultramicr(o)–; evanescent, thin, tenuous; inappreciable; impalpable, imponderable, intangible; imperceptible, indiscernible, invisible, unseeable; atomic, subatomic; molecular; granular, corpuscular, granul(o)– *or* granuli–, chondr(o)–; microcosmic(al); embryonic, germinal 406.24.

.15 **microbic,** microbial, **microorganic;** animalcular, bacterial; microzoic; protozoan, microzoan, amoebic *or* amoeboid.

.16 ADVS smally, **small,** little, **slightly** 35.9; **on a small scale,** in a small compass, in a small way, on a minuscule *or* infinitesimal scale; **in miniature,** in the small; in a nutshell.

.17 **microscopy**

electron microscopy	micromineralogy
electrophotomicrography	micropaleontology
microbiology	micropathology
microchemistry	micropetrography
microcosmography	micropetrology
microcosmology	microphotography
microcrystallography	microphysics
microgeology	microphysiography
micrography	microscopics
micrology	microspectroscopy
micromechanics	microtechnic
micrometallography	microzoology
micrometallurgy	photomicrography
micrometry	photomicroscopy

.18 **microorganisms**

amoeba	animalcule

arthrospore	nematode, nem(a)– *or*
bacillus, bacill(o)– *or*	nemo–, nemat(o)–
bacilli–	paramecium
bacteria, –bacter, bacter(o)–	phage
	pneumococcus
botulinus	protozoon, protozoa
ciliate	[pl]
coccus, cocc(o)– *or*	radiolarian
cocci–	rhizopod
colon bacillus, col(o)–	rotifer
or coli–	salmonella
diatom	saprophyte
diphtheria bacillus	schizomycete
dyad	spirillum
entozoon	spirochete
euglena	sporozoon
filterable virus	staphylococcus,
flagellate	staphyl(o)–
foraminifer	stentor
germ	streptococcus, strept(o)–
gonidium	tetrad
gregarine	triad
infusorian	trypanosome
mastigophoran	tubercle bacillus,
mastigopod	tubercul(o)–
microbe	typhoid bacillus
micrococcus	virus
microphyte	volvox
microspore	vorticellum
microzoon, microzoa	zoogloea
[pl]	zoogonidium
microzyme	zoospore
monad, monas	
moneron	

197. EXPANSION, GROWTH

(increase in size)

.1 NOUNS **expansion, extension, enlargement, increase** 38, crescendo, upping, raising, hiking, magnification, aggrandizement, amplification, ampliation [archaic], broadening, widening; **spread,** spreading, fanning out, dispersion, **flare,** splay; deployment; augmentation, **addition** 40; adjunct 41.

.2 **distension,** stretching; **inflation,** sufflation, blowing up; **dilation,** dilatation, diastole; **swelling,** swellage; swell 256.4; puffing, puff, puffiness, **bloating,** bloat, **flatulence** *or* flatulency, flatus, gassiness, windiness; turgidness *or* turgidity, turgescence; tumidness *or* tumidity, tumefaction; tumescence, intumescence; **swollenness,** bloatedness; dropsy, edema; tympanites, tympany, tympanism, meteorism.

.3 **growth, development,** maturation, growing up, upgrowth; vegetation 411.30; reproduction, procreation 169, germination, pullulation; burgeoning, sprouting; budding, gemmation; outgrowth, excrescence; overgrowth 195.5; –auxe, –megaly, –osis, –plasia *or* –plasy, –trophy; auxo–, plasto–.

.4 VERBS (make larger) **enlarge, expand, ex-**

121

tend, **widen, broaden,** build, build up, aggrandize, **amplify,** crescendo, **magnify, increase** 38.4, augment, add to 40.5, raise, up, hike *or* hike up; develop, bulk *or* bulk out; **stretch, distend, dilate, swell, inflate,** sufflate, **blow up,** puff up, huff, puff, bloat; pump, pump up; rarefy.

.5 (become larger) **enlarge, expand, extend, increase,** greaten, crescendo, **develop, widen, broaden,** bulk; **stretch, distend, dilate, swell, bloat,** tumefy, balloon, puff up, fill out; snowball.

.6 **spread,** spread out, outspread, outstretch; **expand, extend,** widen; **open, open up,** unfold; **flare,** splay; spraddle, sprangle, sprawl; **branch,** branch out, ramify; **fan,** fan out, disperse, deploy; spread like wildfire; overrun, overgrow.

.7 **grow, develop,** wax, **increase** 38.4; gather, brew; **grow up,** mature, spring up, **shoot up,** sprout up, upshoot, upspring, upsprout, upspear, overtop, tower; burgeon, **sprout** 411.31, blossom 411.32, reproduce 169.7, procreate 169.8, germinate, pullulate; vegetate 411.31; **flourish, thrive,** grow like a weed; mushroom; outgrow; overgrow, hypertrophy, overdevelop.

.8 **fatten,** fat, plump, pinguefy *or* engross [both archaic]; **gain weight,** gather flesh, take *or* put on weight, become overweight.

.9 ADJS **expansive, extensive;** expansional, extensional; expansile, extensile, elastic; expansible, inflatable; distensive, dilatant; inflationary; –plastic.

.10 **expanded, extended, enlarged, increased** 38.7, upped, raised, hiked, **amplified,** ampliate, crescendoed, widened, broadened, built-up, beefed-up [informal].

.11 **spread, spreading,** patulous; **sprawling,** sprawly; **outspread, outstretched,** spread-out, stretched-out; **open,** unfolded; widespread, wide-open; flared, spraddled, sprangled, splayed; flaring, spraddling, sprangling, splaying; splay; fanned, fanning; fanlike, fan-shaped, fan-shape, flabelliform, deltoid.

.12 **grown, full-grown, grown-up,** developed, fully developed, **mature, full-fledged; growing,** sprouting, crescent, budding, flowering 411.35, florescent, **flourishing,** blossoming, blooming, burgeoning, thriving; overgrown, hypertrophied, overdeveloped.

.13 **distended, dilated, inflated,** sufflated, **blown up, puffed up, swollen,** swelled, **bloated,** turgid, tumid, plethoric, incrassate; **puffy,** pursy; flatulent, gassy, windy,

ventose; dropsical, edematous; enchymatous; fat 194.18; phys(o)–.

198. CONTRACTION

(decrease in size)

.1 NOUNS **contraction,** contracture, systole; **compression,** compressure, compaction, compactedness, coarctation; condensation, concentration, consolidation, solidification; circumscription, narrowing; reduction, diminuendo, decrease 39; abbreviation, curtailment, shortening 203.3; **constriction,** stricture *or* striction, astriction, strangulation, stranglement; bottleneck, hourglass, hourglass figure, nipped *or* wasp waist; neck 47.4, cervix, isthmus, narrow place; astringency, constringency; puckering, pursing; knitting, wrinkling.

.2 **squeezing,** compression, clamping *or* clamping down, tightening; pressure, press, crush; **pinch, squeeze, tweak, nip.**

.3 **shrinking,** shrinkage, atrophy; **shriveling, withering;** searing, parching, drying *or* drying up; attenuation, thinning; wasting, consumption, emaciation, emaceration; preshrinking, preshrinkage, Sanforizing.

.4 **collapse,** prostration, cave-in; implosion; **deflation.**

.5 contractibility, contractility, compactability, **compressibility,** condensability; collapsibility.

.6 contractor, constrictor, clamp, compressor, vise, pincer; **astringent,** styptic; alum, astringent bitters, styptic pencil.

.7 VERBS **contract, compress,** cramp, compact, coarct, condense, concentrate, consolidate, solidify; **reduce, decrease** 39.7; abbreviate, curtail, **shorten** 203.6; **constrict,** constringe, circumscribe, **narrow,** draw, draw in *or* together; strangle, strangulate; **pucker,** pucker up, **purse; knit, wrinkle.**

.8 **squeeze,** compress, clamp, tighten; roll *or* wad up, roll up into a ball, ensphere; **press,** crush; **pinch, tweak, nip.**

.9 **shrink, shrivel, wither,** sear, parch, dry up; **wizen,** weazen; consume, waste, waste away, attenuate, thin, emaciate, macerate, emacerate; preshrink, Sanforize.

.10 **collapse, cave, cave in,** fall in; fold, fold up; implode; **deflate,** let the air out of, take the wind out of; puncture, puncture one's balloon.

.11 ADJS **contractive,** contractional, contractible, contractile, compactable; **astringent,** constringent, styptic; **compressible,** condensable; **collapsible,** foldable; deflationary; consumptive.

.12 **contracted, compressed,** cramped, compact(ed), concentrated, condensed, consolidated, solidified; **constricted,** strangled, strangulated, **squeezed,** clamped, nipped, pinched or pinched-in, waspwaisted; puckered, pursed; knitted, wrinkled.

.13 **shrunk,** shrunken; **shriveled,** shriveled up; **withered,** sear, parched, corky, dried-up; **wasted,** wasted away, consumed, emaciated, emacerated, thin, attenuated; **wizened,** wizen, weazened; wizen-faced; preshrunk, Sanforized.

.14 **deflated, flat.**

199. DISTANCE

.1 NOUNS **distance, remoteness,** farness, faroffness; **separation,** divergence, clearance, margin, leeway; **extent, length,** space 179, **reach,** stretch, range, compass, span, stride; way, ways [informal], piece [dial]; perspective, aesthetic distance; astronomical or interstellar or galactic or intergalactic distance, deep space, depths of space, **infinity** 104; **mileage,** light-years, parsecs.

.2 **long way,** good ways [informal], **great distance,** long chalk [informal], **far cry,** far piece [dial]; long step, tidy step [informal], giant step or stride; long run or haul, long road or trail; long range; apogee, aphelion.

.3 **the distance, remote distance,** offing; **horizon,** where the earth meets the sky, vanishing point, background.

.4 (remote region) **jumping-off place,** godforsaken place, God knows where, the middle of nowhere [all informal], the back of beyond, the end of the rainbow, Thule or Ultima Thule, Timbuktu, Siberia, Darkest Africa, the South Seas, Pago Pago, the Great Divide, China, Outer Mongolia, pole, antipodes, end of the earth, North Pole, South Pole, Tierra del Fuego, Greenland, Yukon, Pillars of Hercules, remotest corner of the world; outpost, outskirts; the sticks, the boondocks, the tullies [all slang]; nowhere; frontier, outback [Austral]; the moon; outer space.

.5 VERBS **reach out, stretch out,** extend out, go or go out, range out, carry out; outstretch, outlie, outdistance, outrange.

.6 **extend to,** stretch to, stretch away to, **reach to,** lead to, go to, get to, come to, run to, carry to.

.7 **keep one's distance,** remain at a distance,

maintain distance or clearance, keep at a respectful distance, **keep away,** stand off or away; keep away from, keep or stand clear of, **steer clear of** [informal], hold away from, give a wide berth to, keep a good leeway or margin or offing, keep out of the way of, keep at arm's length, keep or stay or stand aloof; maintain one's perspective, keep one's esthetic distance.

.8 ADJS **distant,** distal, **remote, removed, far, far off,** away, **faraway,** at a distance, exotic, separated, apart, asunder; long-distance, long-range; ab-, ap(o)- or aph-, dist(o)- or disti-, over-, tel(e)- or teleo-, trans-, ultra-.

.9 **out-of-the-way,** godforsaken, back of beyond; **out of reach, inaccessible,** ungetatable, unapproachable, untouchable, hyperborean, antipodean.

.10 **thither,** ulterior; **yonder,** yon; **farther, further,** remoter, more distant.

.11 **transoceanic, transmarine,** ultramarine, oversea, overseas; **transatlantic, transpacific;** tramontane, transmontane, ultramontane, transalpine; transarctic, transcontinental, transequatorial, transpolar, transpontine, ultramundane.

.12 **farthest, furthest,** farthermost, farthest off, furthermost, ultimate, extreme, remotest, most distant.

.13 ADVS **yonder,** yon; **in the distance,** in the remote distance; **in the offing,** on the horizon, in the background.

.14 **at a distance, away, off,** aloof, at arm's length; distantly, remotely.

.15 **far, far off,** far away, **afar,** afar off, a long way off, a good ways off [informal], a long cry to, "over the hills and far away" [John Gay], as far as the eye can see, out of sight; clear to hell and gone [slang].

.16 **far and wide,** far and near, distantly and broadly, wide, widely, broadly, abroad.

.17 **apart, away, aside,** wide apart, wide away, "as wide asunder as pole and pole" [J. A. Froude], "as far as the east is from the west" [Bible].

.18 **out of reach,** beyond reach, **out of range,** beyond the bounds, out of the way, out of the sphere of; out of sight, à perte de vue [Fr]; out of hearing, out of earshot or earreach.

.19 **wide, clear;** wide of the mark, abroad, all abroad, astray, afield, far afield.

.20 PREPS **as far as, to, all the way to,** the whole way to.

.21 **beyond, past, over, across,** the other or far side of.

200. NEARNESS

.1 NOUNS **nearness, closeness,** nighness, **proximity,** propinquity, immediacy; approximation, approach, convergence; **vicinity,** vicinage, **neighborhood,** environs, purlieus, confines, precinct; **foreground, immediate foreground.**

.2 **short distance, short way,** little ways, **step,** short step, brief span, short piece [dial], little; close quarters *or* range *or* grips; **stone's throw,** spitting distance [informal], bowshot, gunshot, pistol shot; earshot, earreach, whoop *or* two whoops and a holler [informal], ace, bit [informal], crack, **hair, hairbreadth** *or* hairsbreadth, hair space, finger's width, inch, span.

.3 **juxtaposition, apposition,** adjacency; **contiguity,** contiguousness, conterminousness *or* coterminousness; abuttal, abutment; adjoiningness, junction 47.1,4, connection, union; **conjunction,** conjugation; appulse, syzygy; perigee, perihelion.

.4 **meeting,** joining, **encounter;** confrontation; rencontre; near-miss, collision course, near thing, narrow squeak *or* brush.

.5 **contact, touch,** touching, *attouchement* [Fr], taction, tangency, contingence; gentle *or* tentative contact, caress, brush, glance, nudge, kiss, rub, graze; impingement, impingence; osculation.

.6 **neighbor,** neighborer, next-door *or* immediate neighbor; borderer; abutter, adjoiner; bystander, onlooker, looker-on; tangent.

.7 VERBS **near, come near,** nigh, draw near *or* nigh, **approach** 296.3; **converge.**

.8 **be near** *or* **around,** be in the vicinity *or* neighborhood of, **approximate, approach,** get warm [informal], come near, begin to.

.9 **adjoin,** join, conjoin, **connect,** butt, **abut,** abut on *or* upon, be contiguous, be in contact; **neighbor,** border, **border on** *or* **upon,** verge upon; lie by, stand by.

.10 **contact, come in contact, touch, impinge,** hit; osculate; **graze,** caress, kiss, nudge, rub, brush, glance, scrape, sideswipe, skim, skirt, shave; have a near miss, brush *or* graze *or* squeak by.

.11 **meet, encounter; come across, run across,** fall across, cross the path of; **come upon,** run upon, fall upon, light *or* alight upon; come among, fall among; **meet with,** meet up with [informal], come face to face with, **confront,** meet head-on *or* eye-

ball to eyeball; run into, **bump into** [informal], run smack into [informal], come *or* run up against [informal], run *or* fall foul of; burst *or* pitch *or* pop *or* bounce *or* plump upon [all informal]; be on a collision course.

.12 **stay near, keep close to;** stand by, lie by; go with, march with, follow close upon, breathe down one's neck, tread *or* stay on one's heels, stay on one's tail, tailgate [informal]; hang about *or* around, hang upon the skirts of, hover over; **cling to,** clasp, hug, huddle; hug the shore *or* land, keep hold of the land, stay inshore.

.13 **juxtapose** *or* juxtaposit, **appose,** join 47.5, **adjoin, abut,** neighbor; bring near, put with, place *or* set side by side.

.14 ADJS **near, close, nigh,** nearish, nighish, intimate, cheek-by-jowl, side-by-side, hand-in-hand, arm-in-arm, *bras-dessus-bras-dessous* [Fr]; **approaching,** nearing, approximate *or* approximating, proximate, proximal, propinque [archaic]; **in the vicinity** *or* **neighborhood of,** vicinal; near the mark; warm *or* hot *or* burning [all informal]; ad–, circum–, cis–, ep(i) *or* eph–, juxta–, pen(e)–, peri–, plesi(o)–, pros–, proximo–, sub–, vic–.

.15 **nearby, handy, convenient,** convenient to, propinquant *or* propinquous, at hand, ready at hand, easily reached *or* attained.

.16 **adjacent, next,** immediate, contiguous, **adjoining, abutting; neighboring,** neighbor; **juxtaposed,** juxtapositive *or* juxtapositional; **bordering,** conterminous *or* coterminous, **connecting; face to face** 239.6; end to end, endways, endwise; **joined** 47.13.

.17 **in contact,** contacting, **touching, meeting,** contingent; impinging, impingent; tangent, tangential; osculatory; grazing, glancing, brushing, rubbing, nudging.

.18 **nearer,** nigher, **closer.**

.19 **nearest,** nighest, **closest,** nearmost, next, immediate.

.20 ADVS **near, nigh, close;** hard, at close quarters; **nearby, close by,** hard by, fast by, not far *or* far off, at hand, **near** *or* **close at hand;** thereabout *or* thereabouts, hereabout *or* hereabouts; nearabout *or* nearabouts *or* nigh about [all dial]; **about, around** [informal], close about, along toward [informal]; at no great distance, only a step; as near as no matter *or* makes no difference [informal]; **within reach** *or* **range,** within call *or* hearing, within earshot *or* earreach, within a whoop *or* two whoops and a holler [informal], within a stone's throw, in spitting distance [informal], at one's elbow, at one's feet, at one's fingertips, under one's nose, at one's side, within one's grasp; just around the corner, just across the street, just next door.

.21 in juxtaposition, in conjunction, in apposition; beside 242.11,12.

.22 nearly, near, pretty near [informal], close, closely; almost, all but, not quite, as good as; well-nigh, just about; nigh, nighhand.

.23 approximately, approximatively, practically [informal], for practical purposes or all practical purposes, at a first approximation, give or take a little, more or less; roughly, roundly, in round numbers; generally, generally speaking, roughly speaking, say.

.24 PREPS near, nigh, near to, close to, near upon, close upon, hard on or upon, bordering on or upon, verging on or verging upon, on the confines of, at the threshold of, on the brink or verge of, on the edge of, at next hand, at or on the point of, on the skirts of; not far from; next door to, at one's door; nigh about or nearabout or nigh on or nigh onto [all dial].

.25 against, up against, on, upon, over against, opposite, nose to nose with, vis-à-vis, in contact with.

.26 about, around, just about, circa [L], c., somewhere about or near, near or close upon, near enough to, upwards of [informal], –ish; in the neighborhood or vicinity of.

201. INTERVAL

(space between)

.1 NOUNS interval, space 179, intervening or intermediate space, interspace, distance or space between, interstice; clearance, margin, leeway, freeboard, room 179.3; discontinuity 72, jump, leap, interruption; hiatus, caesura, lacuna; half space, single space, double space, em space, en space, hair space, time interval, interim 109.

.2 crack, cleft, cranny, chink, check, chap, crevice, fissure, scissure, incision, notch, cut, gash, slit, split, rift, rent, rime; opening, excavation, cavity, hole; gap, gape, abyss, abysm, gulf, chasm, void 187.3; breach, break, fracture, rupture; fault, flaw; slot, groove, furrow, moat, ditch, trench, dike; joint, seam; leak; ravine, gorge, dell, flume; kloof, donga; canyon or cañon, box canyon, *couloir* [Fr], cou-

lee; gully, gulch, arroyo, draw, nullah [India], wadi; clough, cleuch [both Scot]; crevasse; chimney, defile, pass, passage, col; cwm 257.8, valley 257.9.

.3 VERBS interspace, space, make a space, interval, set at intervals, space out, separate, part, dispart, set or keep apart, remove.

.4 cleave, crack, check, incise, cut, cut apart, gash, slit, split, rive, rent; open; gap, breach, break, fracture, rupture; slot, groove, furrow, ditch, trench.

.5 ADJS intervallic, interspatial, interstitial.

.6 interspaced, spaced, intervaled, spaced out, set at intervals, with intervals or an interval, separated, parted, removed.

.7 cleft, cut, cloven, cracked, sundered, rift, rent, slit, split; gaping, gappy, dehiscent; fissured, fissury; rimose, rimulose; chinky.

202. LENGTH

.1 NOUNS length, longness, lengthiness, longitude, overall length; extent, extension, measure, span, reach, stretch; distance 199; footage, yardage, mileage; infinity 104; perpetuity 112; long time 110.4; linear measures 490.17.

.2 oblongness, oblongitude.

.3 (a length) piece, portion, part; coil, strip, bolt, roll; run.

.4 line, strip, bar; stripe 568.6; string 71.2.

.5 lengthening, prolongation, elongation, production, protraction, extension, stretching, stretching or spinning or stringing out; stretch, tension, strain.

.6 VERBS be long, be lengthy, extend, be prolonged, stretch; stretch out, extend out, reach out; stretch oneself, crane, crane one's neck; stand on tiptoes; outstretch, outreach; sprawl, straggle.

.7 lengthen, prolong, prolongate, elongate, extend, produce, protract, continue; lengthen out, let out, draw out, drag out, stretch or string or spin out; stretch, draw, pull; tense, tauten, tighten, strain.

.8 ADJS long, lengthy; longish, longsome; tall 207.21; extensive, far-reaching, fargoing, far-flung; sesquipedalian, sesquipedal; as long as one's arm, a mile long; interminable, without end, no end of or to; dolich(o)–, longi–, macr(o)–, mec(o)–.

.9 lengthened, prolonged, prolongated, elongated, extended, protracted; drawn out, dragged out, stretched or spun or strung out, straggling; stretched, drawn, pulled; tense, taut, taut as a bowstring, tight, strained.

.10 oblong, oblongated, oblongitudinal, elongated; rectangular; elliptical.

.11 ADVS lengthily, extensively, at length, *in
extenso* [L], *ad infinitum* [L].

.12 lengthwise *or* lengthways, longwise *or*
longways, longitudinally, along, in length,
at length; endwise *or* endways, endlong.

203. SHORTNESS

.1 NOUNS shortness, briefness, brevity; succinctness, curtness, summariness, compendiousness, compactness; conciseness
592; littleness 196; lowness 208; transience
111, short time 111.3, instantaneousness
113.

.2 stubbiness, stumpiness [informal], stockiness, fatness 195.8, chubbiness, chunkiness
[informal], blockiness, squatness, squattiness, dumpiness; pudginess, podginess;
snubbiness *or* snubbishness.

.3 shortening, abbreviation; reduction 39.1;
abridgment, condensation, compression,
conspectus, epitome, epitomization, summary, summation, précis, abstract, recapitulation, recap [informal], synopsis; curtailment, truncation, retrenchment; tele-
scoping; elision, ellipsis, syncope, apocope; foreshortening.

.4 shortener, cutter, abridger; abstracter,
epitomizer *or* epitomist.

.5 shortcut, cut, cutoff; shortest way; beeline, air line.

.6 VERBS shorten, abbreviate, cut; reduce
39.7; abridge, condense, compress, contract, boil down, abstract, sum up, summarize, recapitulate, recap [informal],
synopsize, epitomize, capsulize; curtail,
truncate, retrench; elide, cut short, cut
down, cut off short, cut back, take in;
dock, bob, shear, shave, trim, clip, snub,
nip; mow, reap, crop; prune, poll, pollard; stunt, check the growth of; telescope; foreshorten.

.7 take a short cut, short-cut; cut across, cut
through; cut a corner, cut corners; make
a beeline, take the air line, go as the crow
flies.

.8 ADJS short, brachy– *or* brady–; brief, ab-
breviatory, "short and sweet" [Thomas
Lodge]; concise 592.6; curt, curtal, cur-
tate, decurtate; succinct, summary, syn-
optic(al), compendious, compact; little
196.10; low 208.7; transient 111.7, instantaneous 113.4,5.

.9 shortened, abbreviated; abridged, compressed, condensed, epitomized, digested,
abstracted, capsule, capsulized; curtailed,
cut short, short-cut, docked, bobbed,

sheared, shaved, trimmed, clipped, snub,
snubbed, nipped; mowed, mown, reaped,
cropped; pruned, polled, pollard; elided,
elliptic(al).

.10 stubby, stubbed, stumpy [informal],
thickset, stocky, blocky, chunky [infor-
mal], fat 195.18, chubby, tubby [infor-
mal], dumpy; squat, squatty, squattish;
pudgy, podgy; pug, pugged; snub-nosed;
turned-up, *retroussé* [Fr].

.11 short-legged, breviped; short-winged,
brevipennate.

.12 ADVS shortly, briefly, summarily, in brief
compass, economically, sparely, curtly,
succinctly; concisely 592.7,8, compendi-
ously, synoptically.

.13 short, abruptly, suddenly 113.9, all of a
sudden.

204. BREADTH, THICKNESS

.1 NOUNS breadth, width, broadness, wideness, fullness, amplitude, latitude, distance across *or* crosswise *or* crossways, extent, span, expanse, spread; beam.

.2 thickness, the third dimension, distance
through, depth; mass, bulk, body; corpulence, bodily size; coarseness, grossness
351.2; fatness 195.8.

.3 diameter, bore, caliber; radius, semidiam-
eter.

.4 VERBS broaden, widen, deepen; expand,
extend, extend to the side *or* sides;
spread 197.6, spread out *or* sidewise *or*
sideways, outspread, outstretch.

.5 thicken, grow thick, thick; incrassate, inspissate; fatten 197.8.

.6 ADJS broad, wide, deep; extensive, spread-
out 197.11, expansive; spacious, roomy
179.9; ample, full; widespread 79.13;
"broad as the world" [James Russell
Lowell], "wide as a church door" [Shake-
speare]; eury–, lati–, plat(y)–.

.7 broad of beam, broad-beamed, broad-
sterned, beamy; broad-ribbed, wide-
ribbed, laticostate; broad-toothed, wide-
toothed, latidentate.

.8 thick, three-dimensional; thickset, heavyset, thick-bodied, broad-bodied, thick-
girthed; massive, bulky 195.19, corpulent
195.18; coarse, heavy, gross, crass, fat; full-
bodied, full, viscous; dense 354.12; thick-
necked, bullnecked; hadr(o)–, pachy–.

.9 ADVS breadthwise *or* breadthways; width-
wise *or* widthways; broadwise *or* broad-
ways; broadside, broad side foremost;
sidewise *or* ways; through, depthwise *or*
ways.

.10 broad

broad-backed	wide-armed
broad-based	wide-banked
broad-billed	wide-bottomed
broad-bladed	wide-branched
broad-bosomed	wide-breasted
broad-bottomed	wide-brimmed
broad-breasted	wide-eared
broad-brimmed	wide-faced
broad-chested	wide-framed
broad-eyed	wide-hipped
broad-faced	wide-leaved
broad-gauge or	wide-lipped
-gauged	wide-nosed
broad-headed	wide-petaled
broad-leaved	wide-rimmed
broad-lipped	wide-roving
broad-mouthed	wide-set
broad-nosed	wide-spaced
broad-roomed	wide-spanned
broad-shouldered	wide-streeted
broad-tailed	wide-tracked
broad-winged	wide-wayed
wide-angle	wide-winged
wide-arched	

.11 thick

thick-ankled	thick-leaved
thick-barked	thick-legged
thick-barred	thick-lipped
thick-bottomed	thick-ribbed
thick-cheeked	thick-stalked
thick-coated	thick-stemmed
thick-eared	thick-tailed
thick-fingered	thick-toed
thick-footed	thick-toothed
thick-headed	thick-walled
thick-jawed	thick-wristed
thick-kneed	

205. NARROWNESS, THINNESS

.1 NOUNS **narrowness, slenderness; closeness,** nearness; **straitness,** restriction, restrictedness, limitation, strictness, confinement; crowdedness, incapaciousness, incommodiousness; **tightness,** tight squeeze; hair, hairbreadth or hairsbreadth; finger's breadth; narrow gauge.

.2 **narrowing, tapering,** taper; **contraction** 198; stricture, constriction, coarctation.

.3 (narrow place) narrow, **narrows, strait; bottleneck;** isthmus; channel 396, canal; pass, defile; neck, throat, der(o)–.

.4 **thinness, slenderness, slimness, frailty,** slightness, gracility, lightness, airiness, delicacy, flimsiness, wispiness, laciness, paperiness, gauziness, gossameriness, diaphanousness, insubstantiality, etherealaty, mistiness, vagueness; light or airy texture; **fineness** 351.3; **tenuity, rarity,** subtility, exility, exiguity; **attenuation;** dilution, dilutedness, wateriness 388.1; weakness.

.5 **leanness, skinniness,** fleshlessness, slightness, frailness, twigginess, spareness, meagerness, **scrawniness, gauntness,** lankness, **lankiness,** gawkiness, **boniness,** skin and bones; haggardness, poorness, paperiness, peakedness [informal], puniness, "lean and hungry look" [Shakespeare]; underweight; hatchet face, lantern jaws.

.6 **emaciation,** emaceration, attenuation, atrophy, tabes, marasmus.

.7 (comparisons) paper, wafer, lath, slat, **rail,** rake, splinter, slip, shaving, streak, vein; gruel, soup; shadow, mere shadow; **skeleton.**

.8 (thin person) **slim, lanky;** twiggy, **shadow, skeleton,** walking skeleton, corpse, barebones, bag or stack of bones; rattlebones or **spindleshanks** or spindlelegs [all informal], gangleshanks [slang], lathlegs or sticklegs [both slang], **bean pole,** beanstalk, broomstick, clothes pole, stilt.

.9 **reducing, slenderizing;** weight-watching, calorie-counting.

.10 **thinner,** solvent 391.4.

.11 VERBS **narrow,** constrict, diminish, draw in, go in; restrict, limit, straiten, confine; **taper,** snape; **contract** 198.7.

.12 **thin,** thin down, thin away or off or out; **rarefy,** subtilize, attenuate; dilute, water, water down, weaken; **emaciate,** emacerate.

.13 **slenderize, reduce,** reduce or lose or take off weight, lose flesh, weight-watch, count calories, diet; slim, **slim down,** thin down.

.14 ADJS **narrow, slender;** narrowish, narrowy; **close,** near; **tight, strait,** isthmic, isthmian; close-fitting; **restricted,** limited, circumscribed, **confined,** constricted; **cramped,** cramp; incapacious, incommodious, crowded; **meager,** scant, scanty; narrow-gauge(d); angustifoliate, angustirostrate, angustiseptal, angustisellate; angusti–, dolich(o)–, sten(o)–.

.15 **tapered,** taper, tapering, cone- or wedge-shaped.

.16 **thin, slender, slim,** gracile, "imperially slim" [E. A. Robinson]; thin-bodied, thin-set, narrow- or wasp-waisted; **svelte,** slinky, sylphlike, willowy; girlish, boyish; thinnish, slenderish, slimmish; **slight,** slight-made; **frail,** delicate, light, airy, wispy, lacy, gauzy, papery, gossamer, diaphanous, insubstantial, ethereal, misty, vague, flimsy, **fine; finespun,** thin-spun, fine-drawn, wiredrawn; threadlike, slender as a thread; **tenuous,** subtle, rare, **rarefied;** attenuated, attenuate, **watery, weak,** diluted, watered or watered-down, small; fusi– or fuso–, lept(o)–.

.17 lean, lean-looking, **skinny** [informal], fleshless, lean-fleshed, thin-fleshed, **spare,** meager, **scrawny,** scraggy, thin-bellied, **gaunt, lank, lanky; gangling** *or* gangly [both informal], gawky, **spindling,** spindly; flat-chested, flat [informal]; **bony, rawboned,** bare-boned, rattleboned [informal], skeletal, **mere skin and bones;** twiggy; **underweight,** undersized, spidery, thin *or* skinny as a lath *or* rail, "lean as a rake" [Chaucer].

.18 lean-limbed, thin-legged, lath- *or* stick-legged [slang], spindle-legged *or* -shanked [informal], gangle-shanked [slang], stilt-legged.

.19 lean- *or* horse- *or* thin-faced, thin-featured, **hatchet-faced;** wizen- *or* weazen-faced; lean- *or* thin-cheeked; lean-jawed *or* lantern-jawed.

.20 haggard, poor, puny, **peaked** *or* peaky [both informal], **pinched;** shriveled, withered; **wizened,** weazeny; **emaciated,** emaciate, emacerated, **wasted,** attenuated, corpselike, skeletal, hollow-eyed, wraithlike, cadaverous; tabetic, tabid, marantic, marasmic; **starved,** starveling, starved-looking; **undernourished,** underfed, jejune; worn to a shadow, "worn to the bones" [Shakespeare], "weakened and wasted to skin and bone" [Du Bartas].

.21 slenderizing, reducing, slimming.

.22 ADVS narrowly, closely, nearly, **barely,** hardly, only just, **by the skin of one's teeth.**

.23 thinly, thin; meagerly, sparsely, sparingly, scantily.

206. FILAMENT

.1 NOUNS filament, fili–; **fiber** 206.8, fibr(o)–, in(o)–; **thread,** mito–, nem(a)– *or* nemo– *or* nemat(o)–, –neme; **strand,** suture; **hair** 230; artificial fiber, natural fiber, animal fiber; threadlet, filamentule; fibril, fibrilla; capillament; cilium, ciliolum, cili(o)–, cilii–; **tendril,** cirrus, cirr(o)– *or* cirri– *or* cirrho– *or* cirrhi–, flagellum, blephar(o)–, mastig(o)–, –kont; gossamer, **web,** cobweb, spider *or* spider's web; skein, hank; denier.

.2 cord 206.9, chord(o)–, line, **string, twine, rope, wire, cable, yarn,** spun yarn; braid, twist, thong, brail; **ligament,** ligature, ligation, syndesm(o)–; **tendon,** teno–.

.3 cordage, cording, **ropework,** roping; tackle, tack, gear, rigging; ship's ropes 277.31.

.4 strip, strap, strop; shred, slip, list, spill; **band,** bandage, fillet, belt, girdle, fascia, taenia, taen(o)– *or* taeni–; **ribbon,** riband; **tape,** tapeline, tape measure, adhesive tape, friction tape, plastic tape, cellophane tape, Scotch tape, masking tape, cloth tape, Mystik tape, ticker tape; slat, lath, batten, spline, strake, plank; ligule, ligula.

.5 spinner, spinster; silkworm, spider; spinning wheel, spinning jenny, jenny, mule, mule-jenny; throstle; spinning frame, bobbin and fly frame; spinneret(te).

.6 VERBS (make threads) **spin;** filament, shred, gin.

.7 ADJS threadlike, thready; **stringy,** ropy, wiry; **hairlike** 230.23, hairy 230.24; filamentary, filiform; fibrous, fibered, fibroid, fibrilliform; ligamental; capillary, capilliform; cirrose, cirrous; funicular, funiculate; flagelliform; taeniate, taeniform; ligulate, ligular; gossamery, flossy, silky.

.8 fibers, threads

acetate rayon	merino
Acrilan	mohair
alpaca	near-silk
angora	nylon
Aralac	oakum
Avisco	Orlon
bast	packthread
batting	Polyfibre
cashmere	protein fibers
Celanese	raffia
Chemstrand	raw silk
coir	rayon
cotton	Rexenite
cotton batting	Sarelon
Dacron	sericin gum
darning cotton	sewing thread
Dynel	silk
Fiberfrax	sisal, sisal hemp
flax	soybean fibers
floss, floss silk	spandex
Fortisan	spun rayon
goat's hair	Terylene
harl	tussah
hemp	Velon
horsehair	Vicara
jute	vicuña
kapok	Vinyon
Lastex	wool
linen	worsted
llama hair	yarn
Manila, Manila hemp	zephyr, zephyr yarn

.9 cords

binding twine	lasso
braided rope	lead
cable	leader
catgut	marline
clothesline	mason's line
fast	monofilament
gut	pack twine
hamstring	pepper-and-salt rope
hawser	rein
lace	rope
lacing	sail twine
lariat	sennit

ship's ropes 277.31	tendon
shoelace	thew
shoestring	twine
sinew	umbilical cord
spermatic cord	whipcord
string	wire rope

207. HEIGHT

.1 NOUNS **height**, heighth [dial], vertical *or* perpendicular distance; **highness, tallness; altitude, elevation,** ceiling; **loftiness,** sublimity, exaltation; hauteur, toploftiness 912.1; eminence, prominence; **stature.**

.2 **height, elevation,** eminence, steep, acr-(o)–, hyps(o)– *or* hypsi–; **rise, raise, uprise,** lift, rising ground, vantage point *or* ground; **heights,** soaring *or* towering *or* Olympian heights, aerial heights, dizzy heights; upmost *or* uppermost *or* utmost *or* extreme height; sky, stratosphere, ether, heaven *or* heavens; zenith, apex, acme.

.3 highland, highlands, upland, uplands, moorland, moors, downs, wold, rolling country.

.4 plateau, tableland, table, mesa, table mountain, bench.

.5 **hill, down,** moor, brae [Scot], barrow, fell [Scot]; **hillock,** monticle, monticule, **knoll, hummock, mound, swell,** knob; anthill, molehill; **dune,** sand dune; butte; drumlin; foothills.

.6 ridge, arête [Fr], chine, spine, kame *or* comb [both Scot], esker; saddle, saddleback, col, horseback, hogback, hog's-back.

.7 **mountain, mount, alp,** hump, tor, ore-(o)– *or* oro–; Olympus, Everest; lofty mountains, towering alps; "the wooded mountains" [Vergil], "the hills, rock-ribbed, and ancient as the sun" [William Cullen Bryant].

.8 **peak,** pike, pic [Fr], pico [Sp], **pinnacle,** point, **crest,** spur, tor; **mountaintop; hill-top,** knoll; **summit** 211.2; precipice 213.3; lofty peak, cloud-capped *or* cloud-topped *or* snow-clad peak.

.9 **mountain range,** range, **chain,** cordillera, sierra [both Sp], massif [Fr]; Alps, Rockies, Andes, Himalayas, Caucasus; "alps on alps" [Pope], hill heaped upon hill.

.10 **watershed,** water parting, **divide;** Great Divide, Continental Divide.

.11 **tower; turret,** tour [Fr]; campanile, bell tower, belfry; lighthouse; cupola, lantern; dome; martello, martello tower; barbican; **derrick,** pole; windmill tower, observation tower, fire tower; **mast,** radio *or* television mast, antenna tower; water tower, standpipe; **spire,** pinnacle, **steeple,**

flèche [Fr]; minaret; stupa, tope, pagoda; pyramid; pylon; **shaft,** pillar, column; pilaster; obelisk; monument; colossus; skyscraper.

.12 (tall person) **longlegs** *or* longshanks *or* highpockets *or* long drink of water [all informal]; bean pole 205.8; **giant** 195.13; six-footer, seven-footer, grenadier [Brit].

.13 **high tide,** high water, flood tide, spring tide, flood.

.14 (measurement of height) altimetry, hypsometry, hypsography; altimeter, hypsometer.

.15 VERBS **tower, soar,** spire, "buss the clouds" [Shakespeare]; **rise, uprise, ascend, mount, rear;** stand on tiptoe.

.16 **rise above, tower above** *or* **over,** clear, overtop, o'ertop, outtop, **top, surmount; overlook,** look down upon *or* over; **command,** dominate, overarch, overshadow, command a view of; bestride, bestraddle.

.17 (become higher) **grow,** grow up, upgrow; uprise, **rise** *or* **shoot up,** mount.

.18 **heighten, elevate** 317.5.

.19 ADJS **high,** high-reaching, high-up, **lofty, elevated,** altitudinous, uplifted *or* upreared, eminent, exalted, prominent, steep, supernal, superlative, sublime, alti–, hyper–, super–; **towering,** towery, **soaring,** spiring, aspiring, mounting, ascending; **topping,** outtopping *or* overtopping; overarching *or* overlooking, dominating; airy, aerial, ethereal; Olympian; monumental, colossal; high as a steeple; topless; high-set, high-pitched; haughty, toplofty.

.20 skyscraping, **sky-high,** heaven-reaching *or* -aspiring, heaven-kissing, "as high as Heaven and as deep as Hell" [Beaumont and Fletcher]; cloud-touching *or* -topped *or* -capped.

.21 **giant** 195.20, gigantic, colossal, statuesque; **tall, lengthy, long** 202.8; **rangy, lanky,** lank, tall as a maypole; **gangling** *or* gangly [both informal]; **long-legged,** long-limbed, leggy.

.22 **highland,** upland; hill-dwelling, mountain-dwelling.

.23 **hilly,** knobby, rolling; **mountainous,** mountained, **alpine,** alpen, alpestrine, alpigene; subalpine; monticuline, monticulous.

.24 **higher,** superior, greater; **over, above,** supra–; upper, upmost *or* uppermost; highest 211.10.

.25 altimetric(al), hypsometrical, hypsographic(al).

.26 ADVS **on high,** high up, high; **aloft,** aloof;

up, upward, upwards, straight up, to the zenith; **above, over, o'er, overhead;** above one's head, over head and ears; skyward, airward, in the air, in the clouds; on the peak or summit or crest or pinnacle; upstairs, abovestairs; tiptoe, on tiptoe; on stilts; on the shoulders of.

208. LOWNESS

.1 NOUNS **lowness, shortness,** squatness, squattiness, stumpiness; **prostration,** supineness, proneness, recumbency, couchancy, lying, lying down, reclining; depression, debasement; subjacency.

.2 **low tide, low water,** dead low water or tide, ebb tide, neap tide, neap.

.3 **lowland, lowlands,** bottomland.

.4 **base, bottom** 212, lowest point, nadir; lowest or underlying level, lower strata, bedrock.

.5 VERBS **lie low, squat, crouch,** couch; crawl, grovel, lie prone or supine or prostrate, hug the earth; lie under, underlie.

.6 lower, debase, depress 318.4.

.7 ADJS **low, unelevated, short, squat,** squatty, stumpy, runty, chame– or chamae–; debased, depressed, prone, supine, prostrate(d), couchant, crouched, stooped, recumbent, laid low, knocked flat; **flat, low-lying,** low-set, low-hung; **low-built,** low-sized, low-statured, low-bodied; low-level, low-leveled; neap; knee-high, knee-high to a grasshopper [informal].

.8 **lower,** hyp(o)–, infra–, intra–, sub–; inferior, **under, nether,** subjacent; down; less advanced; earlier; lowest 212.7.

.9 ADVS **low,** near the ground; at a low ebb.

.10 **below,** down below, **under,** infra [L]; belowstairs, downstairs, below deck; underfoot; below par, below the mark.

.11 PREPS **below, under, underneath, beneath,** neath, at the foot of, at the base of.

209. DEPTH

.1 NOUNS **depth, deepness,** profoundness, profundity; deep-downness, extreme innerness, deep-seatedness, deep-rootedness; bottomlessness, plumblessness, fathomlessness; subterraneity, undergroundness; interiority 225.

.2 **pit, deep, depth, hole,** hollow, **cavity,** shaft, well, **gulf, chasm, abyss,** abysm, yawning abyss; crater; crevasse.

.3 **depths,** deeps, bowels, bowels of the earth; bottomless pit; infernal pit, hell, nether world, underworld; dark or unknown or yawning or gaping depths, unfathomed deeps; outer or deep space.

.4 **ocean depths, the deep sea, the deep,** trench, **the deeps, the depths,** bottomless depths, inner space, abyss; bottom waters; abyssal zone, Bassalia, bathyal zone, pelagic zone; **bottom of the sea,** ocean bottom or floor or bed, ground, benthos, Davy Jones's locker [informal].

.5 **sounding** or **soundings,** fathoming, depth sounding; **echo sounding,** echolocation; sonar; oceanography, bathometry, bathymetry; fathomage, water (depth of water).

.6 **draft,** submergence, submersion, sinkage, **displacement.**

.7 **deepening, lowering, depression;** sinking, sinkage; excavation, digging, mining, tunneling; drilling, probing.

.8 VERBS **deepen, lower, depress, sink;** countersink; **dig,** excavate, tunnel, mine, **drill;** pierce to the depths; **dive** 320.6.

.9 **sound, take soundings,** make a sounding, heave or cast or sling the lead, **fathom, plumb,** plumb-line, plumb the depths.

.10 ADJS **deep, profound,** deep-down, bath(o)– or bathy–; deepish, deepsome; **deepgoing,** deep-lying, deep-reaching; **deepset,** deep-laid; deep-sunk, deep-sunken, deep-sinking; **deep-seated, deep-rooted,** deep-fixed, deep-settled; deep-cut, deepengraven; knee-deep, ankle-deep.

.11 **abysmal,** abyssal, yawning, cavernous, gaping, plunging; **bottomless,** without bottom, soundless, unsounded, plumbless, **fathomless,** unfathomed, unfathomable; deep as a well, deep as the sea or ocean, deep as hell.

.12 **underground, subterranean,** subterraneous, buried, deep-buried.

.13 **underwater,** subaqueous; **submarine, undersea;** submerged, submersed, immersed, buried, engulfed, inundated, flooded, drowned, sunken.

.14 **deep-sea,** deep-water, blue-water; oceanographic, bathyal, bathysmal, bathybic; benthal, benthonic; abyssal, Bassalian; bathyorographic(al), bathymetric(al); benthopelagic, bathypelagic.

.15 deepest, deepmost, bedrock, rock-bottom.

.16 ADVS **deep; beyond one's depth,** out of one's depth; **over one's head,** over head and ears; at bottom, at the core, at rock bottom.

.17 depth indicators

bathometer	plumb line
bathymeter	plummet
bob	probe
depth sounder	sonic depth sounder
dipsey or deep-sea line	sound
or lead	sounding bottle
echo sounder	sounding lead
fathomer	sounding line
Fathometer	sounding machine
Kelvin machine	sounding rod
lead	sounding tube
leadline	space probe
plumb	Tanner-Blish machine
plumb bob	

210. SHALLOWNESS

.1 NOUNS **shallowness, depthlessness;** shoalness, shoaliness, no water, no depth; **superficiality,** exteriority, triviality, **cursoriness,** slightness; **surface,** superficies, skin 229, rind, epidermis; veneer, gloss; pinprick, scratch, mere scratch.

.2 **shoal, shallow,** shallows, shallow or shoal water, flat, shelf; **bank, bar,** sandbank, sandbar; **reef,** coral reef; ford; wetlands, tidal flats.

.3 VERBS **shallow,** shoal; fill in or up, silt up.

.4 **scratch the surface, touch upon,** hardly touch, skim, skim over, skim or graze the surface, hit the high spots [informal].

.5 ADJS **shallow,** shoal, **depthless,** not deep, unprofound; **surface,** on or near the surface, merely surface; **superficial, cursory,** slight, light, thin, jejune, trivial; **skin-deep,** epidermal; ankle-deep, knee-deep; shallow-rooted, shallow-rooting; shallow-draft or -bottomed or -hulled; shallow-sea.

.6 shoaly, shelfy; reefy; unnavigable.

211. TOP

.1 NOUNS **top,** top side, upper side, upside; surface 224.2; topside or topsides; upper story, top floor; clerestory; **roof,** ridgepole or roofpole; rooftop.

.2 **summit, top,** acr(o)–; **tip-top, peak,** pinnacle; **crest, brow,** loph(o)– or lophi(o)–, –loph; ridge, edge; **crown, cap, tip,** point, spire, pitch; highest pitch, no place higher, **apex,** vertex, **acme,** ne plus ultra [L], **zenith, climax,** apogee, pole; **culmination,** culmen; **extremity, maximum, limit,** upper extremity, highest point, very top, top of the world, extreme limit, utmost or upmost or uppermost, height, "the very acme and pitch" [Pope]; **sky,** heaven or heavens, seventh heaven, cloud nine [informal]; meridian, noon, high noon; mountaintop 207.8.

.3 **topping,** icing, frosting.

.4 (top part) **head,** heading, **headpiece,** cap, caput [L], capsheaf, **crown, crest;** topknot; pinhead, nailhead.

.5 **capital,** head, crown, cap; bracket capital; cornice, geisso–.

.6 **head,** headpiece, **pate, poll** [informal], crown, cephal(o)–, corono–; **sconce** or **noddle** or **noodle** or **noggin** or **bean** or dome [all informal]; brow, ridge; "the dome of Thought, the palace of the Soul" [Byron].

.7 **skull,** cranium, crani(o)–; pericranium, epicranium; brainpan, brain box or case.

.8 **phrenology,** craniology, metoposcopy, physiognomy; phrenologist, craniologist, metoposcopist, physiognomist.

.9 VERBS **top,** top off, **crown, cap,** crest, **head,** tip, peak, surmount; overtop or outtop, have the top place or spot, overarch; **culminate,** consummate, climax; ice, frost (a cake).

.10 ADJS **top,** topmost, **uppermost,** upmost, overmost, **highest;** tip-top, tip-crowning, **maximum,** maximal, ultimate; summital, apical, vertical, zenithal, climactic(al), **consummate;** acmic, acmatic; meridian, meridional; **head,** headmost, capital, chief, paramount, supreme, preeminent.

.11 **topping, crowning, capping,** heading, surmounting, overtopping or outtopping, overarching; culminating, consummating, climaxing.

.12 **topped,** headed, **crowned, capped,** crested, plumed, tipped, peaked.

.13 **topless,** headless, crownless.

.14 cephalic, encephalic, –cephalous.

.15 ADVS **on top,** at or on the top, topside [informal]; at the top of the tree or ladder, on top of the roost or heap; on the crest or crest of the wave; at the head, at the peak or pinnacle or summit.

.16 PREPS **atop, on, upon,** on top of.

.17 architectural toppings

abacus	cyma or cima
acanthus	cymatium
acroterion	dentil
annulet	drip
antefix	drop
architrave	echinus
astragal	entablature
bell	epistyle
campana	fastigium
capstone	finial
console	frieze
coping	frontispiece
coping stone	gable end
corbel	gorgerin
cornice	gutta
crown	head

headboard
header
headmold
head molding
headpiece
headpost
headsill
hoodmold
hypotrachelium
keystone
larmier
lintel
metope

modillion
mutule
neck(ing)
neckmold
neck molding
pediment
sconce
taenia
treenail
triglyph
tympanum
zoophorus

.18 **capital styles**

Byzantine
Corinthian
Doric
Gothic
Greek
Greek Corinthian
Greek Ionic

Ionic
Moorish
Roman Corinthian
Roman Doric
Romanesque
Roman Ionic
Tuscan

212. BOTTOM

.1 NOUNS **bottom,** bottom side, **underside,** nether side, lower side, downside, **underneath,** fundament; belly, underbelly; buttocks 241.4, breech; **rock bottom, bedrock,** bed, hardpan; substratum, underlayer, lowest level *or* layer *or* stratum, nethermost level *or* layer *or* stratum.

.2 **base,** basement, baso– *or* basi–, **foot,** footing, sole, toe; **nadir; foundation** 216.6; baseboard, mopboard, shoemold; wainscot, dado; chassis, frame, keel, keelson.

.3 (ground part) **ground,** earth, *terra firma* [L]; **floor,** flooring; parquet; **deck; pavement,** *pavé* [Fr], paving, surfacing; **cover,** carpet, floor covering.

.4 **bed,** bottom, floor, ground, **basin, channel,** coulee; ocean bottom 209.4.

.5 **foot,** extremity, pes, pedes [pl], *pied* [Fr], ped(o)– *or* pedi–, –pod(e), rhiz(o)–; trotter, pedal extremity, dog, tootsy [informal]; **hoof,** ungula; **paw,** pad, pug, *patte* [Fr]; forefoot, forepaw; harefoot, splayfoot, clubfoot; **toe,** digit, dactyl(o)–; **heel;** sole, pedi(o)–; instep, arch; pastern; fetlock.

.6 VERBS **base on, found on, ground on, build on,** bottom on, bed on, set on; root in; **underlie,** undergird.

.7 ADJS **bottom,** bottommost, **undermost,** nethermost, lowermost, **lowest; rock-bottom,** bedrock; ground.

.8 **basic,** basal, basilar; **underlying, fundamental,** radical, essential, elementary, elemental, primary, primal, primitive, rudimentary, original; nadiral.

.9 **pedal,** plantar; footed, hoofed, ungulate, clawed, taloned, –ped(e), –pelmous, –podous; toed, –dactylous.

213. VERTICALNESS

.1 NOUNS **verticalness,** verticality, verticalism; **erectness, uprightness,** straight up-and-downness, up-and-downness, steepness, sheerness, precipitousness, plungingness, **perpendicularity,** plumbness, aplomb; right-angledness *or* -angularity, squareness, orthogonality.

.2 **vertical, upright, perpendicular, plumb,** normal; right angle, orthodiagonal; vertical circle, azimuth circle.

.3 **precipice, cliff, steep, bluff,** wall, face, scar; crag, craig [Scot]; scarp, **escarpment; palisade,** palisades.

.4 **erection,** erecting, **elevation; rearing,** raising; **uprearing,** upraising, lofting, uplifting, heaving up *or* aloft; standing on end *or* upright *or* on its feet *or* on its base *or* on its legs.

.5 **rising, uprising;** vertical height, gradient, rise, uprise.

.6 (instruments) **square,** T square, try square, set square, carpenter's square; **plumb,** plumb line, plumb rule, plummet, bob, plumb bob, lead.

.7 VERBS **stand, stand erect, stand up, stand upright, stand up straight,** be erect, be on one's feet; hold oneself straight *or* stiff, have an upright carriage; stand at attention, stand at parade rest, stand at ease [all mil].

.8 **rise, arise, uprise, rise up, get up,** get to one's feet; **stand up, stand on end; stick up,** cock up; bristle; **rear,** ramp, uprear, rear up, rise on the hind legs; upheave; sit up, sit bolt upright; jump up, spring to one's feet.

.9 **erect, elevate, rear, raise,** pitch, **set up,** raise *or* lift *or* cast up; raise *or* heave *or* rear aloft; uprear, upraise, uplift, upheave; upright; **upend,** stand upright *or* on end; set on its feet *or* legs *or* base.

.10 **plumb,** plumb-line, set *à plomb;* **square.**

.11 ADJS **vertical, upright,** bolt upright, **erect,** upstanding, standing up, stand-up, orth(o)–, stasi–; rearing, rampant; **upended,** upraised, upreared; downright.

.12 **perpendicular, plumb,** straight-up-and-down, straight-up, **up-and-down;** sheer, steep, precipitous, plunging; **right-angled,** right-angle, right-angular, orthogonal, orthodiagonal.

.13 ADVS **vertically, erectly,** upstandingly, uprightly, **upright,** up, stark *or* bolt upright; **on end,** up on end, right on end, endwise, endways; on one's feet *or* legs, on one's hind legs [informal]; at attention.

.14 perpendicularly, sheer, sheerly; up and down, **straight up and down; plumb,** *à plomb* [Fr]; **at right angles,** square.

214. HORIZONTALNESS

.1 NOUNS **horizontalness,** horizontality, horizontalism; **levelness, flatness, planeness,** evenness, smoothness, flushness.

.2 **recumbency,** decumbency, accumbency, accubation; **prostration, proneness;** supineness, reclining, reclination; lying, lounging, **repose** 711; sprawl, loll.

.3 **horizontal, plane, level, flat,** homaloid, **dead level** *or* **flat; horizontal plane,** level plane; horizontal line, level line; horizontal projection; horizontal parallax; horizontal axis; horizontal fault; water level, sea level, mean sea level; parterre; esplanade, platform, ledge; terrace; ground, earth, floor, steppe, plain, flatland, prairie, sea of grass, bowling green, table, billiard table.

.4 **horizon, skyline,** rim of the horizon; sea line; apparent *or* local *or* visible horizon, sensible horizon, celestial *or* rational *or* geometrical *or* true horizon, artificial *or* false horizon; azimuth.

.5 VERBS **lie, lie down, lay** [informal], **recline, repose,** lounge, sprawl, loll, drape *or* spread oneself, lie limply; **lie flat** *or* **prostrate** *or* **prone** *or* **supine,** lie on one's face *or* back, lie on a level; **grovel, crawl.**

.6 **level, flatten, even, equalize,** align, **smooth** *or* **smoothen,** smooth out, flush; grade, roll, roll flat, steamroller *or* steamroll; **lay, lay down** *or* **out; raze,** rase, lay level, lay level with the ground; lay low *or* flat; **fell** 318.5.

.7 ADJS **horizontal, level, flat,** flattened, plat(y)–; **even,** smooth, smoothened, smoothed out; **tabular,** tabloid; **flush,** homaloidal, homal(o)–; **plane, plain,** plan(o)–, **plani–;** rolled, trodden, squashed, rolled *or* trodden *or* squashed flat; flat as a pancake, "flat as a cake" [Erasmus], flat as a billiard table *or* bowling green *or* tennis court, flat as a board, "flat as a flounder" [John Fletcher], level as a plain.

.8 **recumbent,** accumbent, procumbent, decumbent; **prostrate, prone,** flat; **supine,** resupine; couchant, *couché* [Fr]; **lying, reclining, reposing,** flat on one's back; sprawling, lolling, lounging; sprawled, spread, draped; groveling, crawling, flat on one's belly *or* nose.

.9 ADVS **horizontally, flat,** flatly, flatways, flatwise; **evenly, flush; level, on a level;** lengthwise, lengthways, at full length, on one's back *or* belly *or* nose.

215. PENDENCY

.1 NOUNS **pendency,** pendulousness *or* pendulosity, pensileness *or* pensility; **hanging, suspension,** dangling *or* danglement, suspense, dependence *or* dependency.

.2 **hang, droop, dangle, swing, fall; sag,** bag.

.3 **overhang, overhanging,** impendence *or* impendency, **projection,** beetling, jutting.

.4 **pendant,** hanger; **hanging,** drape; **lobe,** lobule, lobation, lappet, ear lobe, lob(o)– *or* lobi–; **uvula,** cion(o)–, staphyl(o)–.

.5 **suspender, hanger** 215.14, supporter; **suspenders,** pair of suspenders, braces [Brit], galluses [informal].

.6 VERBS **hang, hang down,** fall; **depend,** pend; **dangle, swing, flap,** flop [informal]; flow, drape, cascade; **droop,** lop; nod, weep; **sag, swag, bag; trail, drag, draggle,** drabble, daggle.

.7 **overhang,** hang over, hang out, **impend,** impend over, **project,** project over, beetle, **jut,** beetle *or* jut *or* thrust over, stick out over.

.8 **suspend, hang, hang up,** put up, fasten up; sling.

.9 ADJS **pendent, pendulous,** pendulant, pendular, penduline, pensile; **suspended, hung; hanging, pending, depending, dependent; falling; dangling,** swinging, falling loosely; weeping; flowing, cascading.

.10 **drooping,** droopy, limp, loose, nodding, floppy [informal], loppy, lop; **sagging,** saggy, swag, sagging in folds; **bagging,** baggy, ballooning; lop-eared.

.11 **overhanging,** overhung, lowering, **impending,** impendent, **pending;** incumbent, superincumbent; **projecting, jutting; beetling,** beetle; beetle-browed.

.12 **lobular,** lobar, lobate, lobated.

.13 **pendants**

apronstring	lappet
arras	lavaliere
bell rope	liripipe
bob	pendeloque
chandelier	pendicle
coattail	pendule
curtain	pendulum
drape	pigtail
drapery	plumb bob
drop	queue
eardrop	rya
earring	skirt
flap	stalactite
fringe	swing
hammock	tail
hanging	tailpiece
hangnail	tapestry
icicle	tassel

tippet	wall-hanging
trail	wattle
train	

.14 suspenders, hangers

bar	horse
belt	knob
boom	nail
button	peg
clothes hanger	pendant post
clotheshorse	pendant tackle
clothesline	pendentive
clothespin	picture hook
clothes tree	pothanger
coat hanger	pothook
crane	ring
gallows	sock suspenders
garter	spar
garter belt	stud
gibbet	suspensorium
hake	suspensory
hanger bolt	tenterhook
hanging post	yard
hat rack	yardarm
hook	

216. SUPPORT

.1 NOUNS **support, backing, aid** 785, **uphold-ing, upkeep,** carrying, carriage, mainte-nance, **sustaining,** sustainment, suste-nance, sustentation; subsidy, subvention; **moral support;** emotional *or* psychologi-cal support, security blanket [informal]; supportive relationship, supportive ther-apy; **reliance** 501.1.

.2 **supporter, support,** 216.26, **upholder,** bearer, carrier, sustainer, maintainer, –fer *or* –pher, –phor(e); staff 217.2, stave, cane, stick, walking stick, alpenstock, crook, crutch; **advocate** 787.9; **stay, prop,** ful-crum, **bracket** 216.28, **brace,** bracer, guy, guywire *or* guyline, shroud, rigging, stand-ing rigging; buttress, shoulder, arm; mast, sprit, **mainstay,** backbone, spine, neck, cervix; athletic supporter, jock *or* jock-strap [both informal], G-string; brassiere, bra [informal], bandeau, corset, girdle, foundation garment; reinforcement, rein-force *or* reinforcer, strengthener, stiff-ener; back, backing, rest, resting place.

.3 (mythology) Atlas, Hercules, Telamon, tortoise that supports the earth.

.4 **buttress,** buttressing; abutment, shoulder; **bulwark,** rampart; **embankment,** bank, re-taining wall; **breakwater,** seawall, mole, **jetty,** jutty, groin; **pier,** pier buttress, but-tress pier; flying buttress, *arc-boutant* [Fr]; hanging buttress; **beam** 217.7.

.5 **footing, foothold, toehold,** hold, perch, **purchase** 287; **standing,** stand, stance, standing place, *point d'appui* [Fr], *locus standi* [L]; footrest, footplate, footrail.

.6 **foundation,** *fond* [Fr], **base, basis, foot-**ing, basement, pavement, **ground, grounds, groundwork, seat,** sill, floor *or* flooring, fundament; bed, bedding; **sub-structure,** substruction, substratum, **un-derstructure,** understruction, underbuild-ing, undergirding, undercarriage, under-pinning, bearing wall; stereobate, stylobate; **fundamental, principle,** radi-cal, rudiment; firm *or* solid ground, *terra firma* [L]; solid rock *or* bottom, rock bot-tom, bedrock; hardpan; riprap.

.7 **foundation stone,** footstone; **cornerstone, keystone,** headstone, first stone, quoin.

.8 **base, pedestal; stand,** standard; **shaft** 217, **upright, column, pillar, post,** jack, pole, staff, stanchion, pier, pile *or* piling, king-post, queen-post, pilaster, newel-post, banister, baluster, balustrade, colonnade, caryatid; dado, die; plinth, subbase; sur-base; socle; **trunk, stem, stalk,** pedicel, pe-duncle, footstalk.

.9 **sill,** groundsel; mudsill; window sill; door-sill, threshold; doorstone.

.10 **mounting,** mount, **backing, setting;** frame, underframe, infrastructure, chas-sis, skeleton; bearing, bushing.

.11 **handle** 216.27, **hold,** grip, grasp, haft, helve.

.12 **scaffold,** scaffolding, *échafaudage* [Fr]; stage, staging.

.13 **platform; stage,** estrade, dais, floor; **ros-trum, podium, pulpit,** speaker's platform *or* stand, **soapbox** [informal]; hustings, **stump;** tribune, tribunal; emplacement; catafalque; landing stage, landing; heli-port, landing pad; launching pad; **terrace,** step terrace; **balcony, gallery.**

.14 **shelf, ledge,** shoulder, corbel, beam-end; mantel, mantelshelf, mantelpiece; reta-ble, superaltar, gradin, *gradino* [Ital], pre-della; hob.

.15 **table** 216.29, **board, stand; bench,** work-bench; **counter,** bar, buffet; **desk,** writing table, **secretary,** *secrétaire* [Fr], escritoire; **lectern,** ambo, reading desk.

.16 **trestle, horse; sawhorse,** buck *or* sawbuck; clotheshorse; trestle board *or* table, tres-tle and table; trestlework, trestling.

.17 **seat, chair** 216.30; **saddle** 216.31.

.18 (saddle parts) **pommel,** horn; **jockey;** girth, girt, surcingle, bellyband; cinch, stirrup.

.19 **sofa** 216.32, **bed** 216.33, clin(o)–, **couch, bunk;** the sack *or* the hay *or* kip *or* doss [all informal]; bedstead; **litter, stretcher,** gurney [dial].

.20 **bedding,** underbed, underbedding; **mat-tress,** paillasse, pallet; air mattress, foam-rubber mattress, innerspring mattress; sleeping bag; pad, mat, rug; litter, bedstraw; **pillow**, cushion, bolster; **springs**, bedsprings, box springs.

.21 VERBS **support, bear,** carry, **hold, sustain, maintain, bolster, reinforce,** back, shoulder, give *or* furnish *or* afford *or* supply *or* lend support; **hold up, bear up,** bolster up, keep up, buoy up, keep afloat, back up; **uphold,** upbear, upkeep; **brace, prop,** crutch, buttress; shore, **shore up;** stay, mainstay; underbrace, undergird, underprop, underpin, underset; **underlie,** be at the bottom of, form the foundation of; cra'dle; cushion, pillow; **subsidize,** subvention *or* subvenize.

.22 **rest on, stand on,** lie on, recline on, repose on, bear on, **lean on,** abut on; **sit on,** perch, ride; **straddle,** bestraddle, stride, bestride; be based on, rely on.

.23 ADJS **supporting, supportive, bearing,** carrying, burdened, –ferous *or* –phorous *or* –iferous; **holding,** upholding, maintaining, sustaining, sustentative, suspensory; bracing, propping, shoring, bolstering, buttressing; stato–.

.24 **supported, borne,** upborne, held, buoyed-up, **upheld, sustained,** maintained; **braced,** guyed, stayed, propped, shored *or* shored up, bolstered, buttressed; based *or* founded *or* grounded on.

.25 ADVS **on, across, astride, astraddle,** straddle, straddle-legged, straddleback, on the back of; horseback, on horseback; pickaback.

.26 **supports**

A-frame	raker
anvil	ratline
back rest	rib
bandage	scissors truss
block	shoe
brace	shore
crosstree	shoring
cue rest	skid
easel	sole
guy	splint
heel	stand
hob	stilts
hod	stirrup
jack	strut
lap	tripod
maulstick	trivet
music stand	truss
prop	umbrella stand

.27 **handles**

bail	handle bar
bow	handstaff
brace	helm
brake	hilt
crank	knob
crop	knocker
doorknob	loom
lug	snatch
panhandle	spindle
pull	stock
rounce	tiller
rudder	tote
sally	trigger
shaft	withe
shank	

.28 **brackets**

ancon	corbel
angle	*cul-de-lampe* [Fr]
angle bracket	gusset
angle iron	modillion
brace	shelf bracket
cantilever	shelf rest
cheek	shoulder
consol	strut

.29 **tables**

bar	gate-leg *or* gate-legged table
billiard table	head table
buffet	high table
captain's table	kitchen table
card table	laboratory table
cocktail table	lampstand
coffee table	operating table
conference table	pool table
console *or* console table	round table
counter	sideboard
deal table	side table
dinette table	taboret
dining table	tea table
dissecting table	tea wagon
dresser	trestle table
dressing table	trivet table
drop-leaf table	turntable
extension table	worktable
folding table	

.30 **seats, chairs**

armchair	dentist's chair
armless chair	dining chair
back seat	draft chair
banquette	Eames chair
barber chair	easy chair
barrel chair	elbowchair
bar stool	fan-back chair
basket chair	*fauteuil* [Fr]
batwing chair	fender stool
bed chair	folding chair
bench	foldstool
bicycle seat	form
Boston rocker	garden chair
boudoir chair	hassock
bow-back chair	high chair
Brewster chair	high seat
bucket seat	Hitchcock chair
campaign chair	horse
camp chair	ladder-back chair
campstool	lawn chair
captain's chair	long chair
channel-back chair	lounge chair
club chair	milking stool
club lounge chair	Morris chair
cocktail chair	occasional chair
comb-back chair	ottoman
contour chair	overstuffed chair
cricket	pew
cricket chair	platform rocker
deck chair	Priscilla rocker

pull-up chair
railroad chair
recliner
reclining lounge chair
rocker
rocking chair
rumble seat
saddle seat
sedan chair
settle
shooting stick
snack stool
steamer chair

step stool
stool
straight chair
swing
swing chair
swivel chair
taboret
throne
tub chair
TV chair
Windsor chair
wing chair

.31 saddles

aparejo
bicycle saddle
bridal saddle
camel saddle
cavalry saddle
cowboy saddle
English cavalry saddle
English riding saddle
English saddle
howdah
jockey saddle

motorcycle saddle
packsaddle
panel
pillion
racing saddle
riding saddle
sidesaddle
stock saddle
US cavalry saddle
Western saddle

.32 sofas

causeuse [Fr]
chaise longue [Fr]
chesterfield
couch
davenport
day bed
divan
lounge

love seat
ottoman
settee
settle
spoonholder
squab
studio couch
tête-à-tête [Fr]

.33 beds

bassinet
bed-davenport
berth
bunk
bunk bed
camp bed
Colonial bed
cot
cradle
crib
day bed
door bed
double bed
double bunk
duplex bed
feather bed
fold-away bed
folding bed
four-poster
French bed
hammock

Hollywood bed
hospital bed
king-size bed
lower berth
pallet
panel bed
pipe berth
poster bed
quarter berth
queen-size bed
roll-away bed
single bed
sofa-bed
tester bed
three-quarter bed
trestle bed
truckle bed
trundle bed
twin bed
upper berth
water bed

217. SHAFT

.1 NOUNS **shaft, pole, bar, rod, stick,** scape, scapi–; **stalk, stem;** thill; tongue, wagon tongue; pole, flagstaff; totem pole; Maypole; utility *or* telephone *or* telegraph pole; tent pole.

.2 **staff, stave; cane, stick, walking stick,** handstaff, shillelagh; Malacca cane; baton, marshal's baton, drum-major's baton, conductor's baton; swagger stick,

swanking stick; pilgrim's staff, pastoral staff, shepherd's staff, crook; crosier, cross-staff, cross, paterissa; pikestaff, alpenstock; quarterstaff; lituus, thyrsus; **crutch,** crutch-stick.

.3 **beam** 217.7, **timber,** pole, spar.

.4 **post, standard, upright;** king post, queen post, crown post; newel; banister, baluster; balustrade, balustrading; gatepost, swinging *or* hinging post, shutting post; doorpost, jamb, doorjamb; signpost, milepost; stile, mullion; stanchion; hitching post, snubbing post, Samson post.

.5 **pillar, column,** post, pier, pilaster, cion(o)–, styl(o)–, –style; colonnette, columella; caryatid; atlas, atlantes [pl]; telamon, telamones [pl]; colonnade, arcade, pilastrade, portico, peristyle.

.6 **leg** 273.16, shank; **stake,** peg; pile, spile; picket, pale, palisade.

.7 beams

angle rafter
balk
batten
boom
box girder
breastsummer
corbel
crossbeam
crosstie
footing beam
girder
hammer beam
H beam
hip rafter
I beam
joist
lattice girder
lintel
plate girder
rafter

ridgepole
ridge strut
scantling
sill
sleeper
sprit
stringpiece
strut
stud
studding
summer
summertree
tie
tie beam
transom
transverse
trave
traverse
truss
truss beam

218. PARALLELISM

(physically parallel direction or state)

.1 NOUNS **parallelism,** coextension, nonconvergence, nondivergence, collaterality, concurrence, equidistance; collineation, collimation; alignment; parallelization; parallelotropism; analogy 491.1.

.2 **parallel,** paralleler; parallel line, parallel dash, parallel bar, parallel file, parallel series, parallel column, parallel trench, parallel vector; parallelogram, parallelepiped *or* parallelepipedon.

.3 (instruments) parallel rule *or* rules *or* ruler, parallelograph, parallelometer.

.4 VERBS **parallel,** be parallel, coextend; run parallel, go alongside, go beside, run abreast; match, equal.

.5 **parallelize,** place parallel to, equidistance; line up, align, realign; collineate, collimate; match; correspond, follow, equate.

.6 ADJS **parallel,** paralleling, par(a)–; coextending, coextensive, nonconvergent, nondivergent, **equidistant,** equispaced, collateral, concurrent; lined up, aligned; equal, even; parallelogrammic(al), parallelogrammatic(al); parallelepipedal; parallelotropic; parallelodrome, parallelinervate; analogous 491.8.

.7 ADVS **in parallel,** parallelwise, parallelly; side-by-side, alongside, abreast; equidistantly, nonconvergently, nondivergently; collaterally, coextensively.

219. OBLIQUITY

.1 NOUNS **obliquity,** obliqueness; **deviation** 291, deviance, divergence, digression, divagation, vagary, excursion, skewness, aberration, squint, declination; deflection, deflexure; nonconformity 83; diagonality, crosswiseness, transverseness; indirection, indirectness, deviousness, circuitousness 321.

.2 **inclination, leaning,** lean, angularity; **slant,** slaunch [dial], rake, **slope,** –cline; **tilt, tip,** pitch, **list, cant,** swag, sway; leaning tower, tower of Pisa.

.3 **bias, bend,** bent, **crook, warp, twist, turn, skew,** slue, **veer,** sheer, **swerve,** lurch.

.4 **incline,** inclination, **slope, grade,** gradient, pitch, **ramp,** launching ramp, bank, talus, gentle or easy slope, glacis; rapid or steep slope, stiff climb, scarp, chute; helicline, inclined plane [phys]; **bevel,** bezel, fleam; hillside, side; hanging gardens; shelving beach.

.5 **declivity, descent,** dip, drop, fall, falling-off or -away, **decline;** hang, hanging; **downgrade,** downgate [Scot], **downhill.**

.6 **acclivity, ascent,** climb, **rise,** rising, uprise, uprising, rising ground; **upgrade, uphill,** upgo, upclimb, uplift, steepness, precipitousness, abruptness, verticalness 213.

.7 **diagonal,** oblique, transverse, bias, bend [her], oblique line, slash, slant, virgule, scratch comma, separatrix, solidus; oblique angle or figure, rhomboid.

.8 **zigzag,** zig, zag; zigzaggery, flexuosity, **crookedness,** crankiness; switchback, hairpin, dogleg; chevron.

.9 VERBS oblique, **deviate, diverge,** deflect, divagate, **bear off;** angle, **angle off, swerve,** sheer, shoot off at an angle, **veer,** sheer, sway, slue, **skew, twist, turn,** bend, bias; crook.

.10 **incline, lean;** slope, slant, slaunch [dial],

rake, pitch, grade, bank, shelve; **tilt, tip, list, cant,** careen, keel, sidle, swag, sway; **ascend, rise,** uprise, climb, **go uphill; descend, decline,** dip, drop, fall, fall off or away, **go downhill;** retreat.

.11 cut, cut or slant across, cut crosswise or transversely or diagonally, catercorner, diagonalize, slash, slash across.

.12 **zigzag,** zig, zag, **stagger,** crankle [archaic], wind in and out.

.13 ADJS **oblique,** lox(o)–, plagi(o)–; **devious,** deviant, deviative, divergent, digressive, divagational, deflectional, excursive; **indirect,** side, sidelong; left-handed, sinister, sinistral; backhand, backhanded; circuitous 321.7.

.14 **askew, skew,** skewed; skew-jawed, skew-gee, askewgee, agee, agee-jawed [all slang]; **awry,** wry; askance, askant, asquint, squinting, **cockeyed** [informal]; **crooked** 249.10; slaunchwise or slaunch-ways [both informal]; wamper-jawed, catawampous or catawamptious, yaw-ways [all slang], wonky [Brit slang].

.15 **inclining,** inclined, inclinatory, inclinational, –clinal, –clinic, clin(o)–; **leaning,** recumbent; **sloping,** sloped, aslope; raking, pitched; **slanting,** slanted, slant, aslant, slantways, slantwise; bias, biased; shelving, shelvy; **tilting,** tilted, atilt; tipped, **tipping,** tipsy, listing, **canting,** careening; sideling, sidelong; out of the perpendicular or square or plumb, bevel, beveled.

.16 (sloping downward) **downhill, downgrade; descending,** falling, dropping, dipping; **declining,** declined; declivous, declivitous, declivate.

.17 (sloping upward) **uphill, upgrade; rising,** uprising, **ascending,** climbing; acclivous, acclivitous, acclinate.

.18 **steep, precipitous, bluff,** plunging, abrupt, bold, **sheer,** sharp, rapid; headlong, breakneck; vertical 213.11.

.19 **transverse,** crosswise or crossways, thwart, athwart, across 221.9; **diagonal,** bendwise; catercorner or **catercornered** or cattycorner or cattycornered or kittycorner or kittycornered; slant, bias, biased, biaswise or biasways.

.20 **crooked, zigzag,** zigzagged, zigzaggy, zigzagwise or zigzagways; flexuous, twisty, hairpin, bendy, curvy; staggered, crankled [archaic]; chevrony, chevronwise or chevronways [all archit].

.21 ADVS **obliquely, deviously,** deviately, **indirectly,** circuitously 321.9; divergently, digressively, excursively, divagationally;

sideways *or* sidewise, sidelong, sideling, on *or* to one side; at an angle.

.22 **askew, awry; askance,** askant, asquint.

.23 slantingly, **slopingly,** aslant, aslope, atilt, rakingly, tipsily, slopewise, slopeways, slantwise, slantways, aslantwise, on *or* at a slant; slaunchwise *or* slaunchways [both informal]; off plumb *or* the vertical; **downhill, downgrade; uphill, upgrade.**

.24 transversely, crosswise *or* crossways, athwart, across 221.13.

.25 **diagonally,** diagonalwise; **on the bias,** bias, biaswise; **cornerwise,** cornerways; catercornerways *or* **catercorner** *or* cattycorner *or* kittycorner.

220. INVERSION

.1 NOUNS **inversion,** turning over *or* around *or* upside down; eversion, turning inside out, invagination, intussusception, ectropion; introversion, turning inward; **reversing, reversal** 146.1, turning front to back *or* side to side; reversion, turning back *or* backwards, retroversion, retroflexion, revulsion; **transposition,** transposal; topsy-turvydom *or* topsy-turviness; pronation, supination, resupination; –trope.

.2 **overturn, upset,** overset, **overthrow,** upturn, **turnover,** spill [informal]; subversion; **revolution** 147; **capsizal,** capsize; **somersault,** somerset, *culbute* [Fr]; turning head over heels.

.3 [gram terms] metastasis, metathesis; anastrophe, chiasmus, hypallage, hyperbaton, hysteron proteron, palindrome, parenthesis, synchysis, tmesis.

.4 **inverse, reverse, converse, opposite** 15.2, other side of the coin *or* picture.

.5 VERBS **invert,** inverse, turn over *or* around *or* upside down; introvert, turn in *or* inward; **turn down; turn inside out,** turn out, evert, invaginate, intussuscept; **reverse** 146.4, **transpose,** convert; put the cart before the horse; turn into the opposite, turn about, turn the tables, turn the scale *or* balance; rotate, revolve, pronate, supinate, resupinate.

.6 **overturn, turn over, turn upside down,** turn bottom side up, upturn, **upset,** overset, **overthrow,** subvert, *culbuter* [Fr]; go *or* turn ass over elbows [informal], turn a somersault, go *or* turn head over heels; **turn turtle, turn topsy-turvy,** topsy-turvy, topsy-turvify; **tip over,** keel over, topple over; **capsize;** careen, set on its beam ends.

.7 ADJS **inverted,** inversed, back-to-front, **backwards,** retroverted, **reversed,** trans-

posed; **inside out,** outside in, everted, invaginated, wrong side out; **upside-down, topsy-turvy,** ass over elbows *or* arsy-varsy [both informal]; **capsized,** head-over-heels; hyperbatic, chiastic, palindromic; resupinate; introverted.

.8 ADVS **inversely, conversely,** contrarily, contrariwise, **vice versa,** the other way around, **backwards,** turned around; **upside down,** over, topsy-turvy; **bottom up,** bottom side up; head over heels, heels over head.

221. CROSSING

.1 NOUNS **crossing, intercrossing,** intersecting, **intersection;** decussation, chiasma; traversal, transversion; cross section, transection; cruciation.

.2 **crossing, crossway, crosswalk, crossroad, crosspoint** [Brit], *carrefour* [Fr], **intersection,** intercrossing; level crossing, grade crossing; overcrossing, overpass, flyover [Brit], viaduct, undercrossing; traffic circle, rotary; cloverleaf.

.3 **network, webwork, weaving** 222, **meshwork,** tissue, crossing over and under, interlacement, intertwinement, intertexture, texture, reticulum, reticulation; crossing-out, cancellation; **net,** netting; **mesh,** meshes; **web,** webbing; weave, weft; lace, lacery, lacing, lacework; screen, screening; sieve, riddle, raddle; wicker, wickerwork; basketwork, basketry; lattice, latticework; hachure, hatching, cross-hatching; trellis, trelliswork; grate, grating; grille, grillwork; **grid,** gridiron; tracery, fretwork, fret, arabesque, filigree; plexus, plexure; reticle, reticule; wattle; dicty(o)–, reticul(o)– *or* reticuli–, –spongium.

.4 **cross, crux,** cruciform, staur(o)–; **crucifix,** rood; **crisscross,** christcross; **X,** ex, exing, chi, St. Andrew's cross, *crux decussata* [L], saltire [her]; **T,** tau, *crux commisa* [L], St. Anthony's cross; **Y,** thieves' cross, fork cross; **ankh,** key of the Nile, *crux ansata* [L]; avellan cross; cross botonée, trefled cross *or* cross of St. Lazarus; Calvary cross; Celtic *or* Iona cross; chi-rho, Christogram; crosslet, cross-crosslet; cross fitché; cross fleury, cross of Cleves; cross formée; cross fourchée; Greek cross, St. George's cross; cross grignolée; inverted cross, St. Peter's cross; Jerusalem cross, potent cross; **Latin cross,** long cross, *crux capitata* [L], *crux immissa* [L], *crux ordinaria* [L], God's mark; cross of Lorraine; **Maltese cross;** cross moline, cross ancré, cross recercelée; papal cross; patriarchal *or* archiepiscopal cross; cross patée; cross pommée, cross bourdonée; Russian cross; quadrate cross; **swastika**, gammadion, *Hakenkreuz* [Ger], *crux gammata* [L]; voided cross; pectoral cross; crossbones; dagger 586.20.

.5 **crosspiece**, traverse, transverse, transversal, transept, transom, cross bitt; **crossbar**, crossarm; swingletree, singletree, whiffletree, whippletree; doubletree.

.6 VERBS **cross**, **crisscross**, cruciate; **intersect**, intercross, decussate; **cut across**, crosscut; **traverse**, transverse, lie across; bar, crossbar.

.7 **net**, **web**, mesh; lattice, trellis; grate, grid.

.8 ADJS **cross**, **crossing**, **crossed**; **crisscross**, **crisscrossed**; **intersecting**, **intersected**, intersectional; crosscut, cut across; **decussate**, decussated; chiasmal *or* chiasmic *or* chiastic; secant.

.9 **transverse**, transversal, traverse; **across**, cross, crossway, **crosswise** *or* crossways, thwart, athwart, overthwart; oblique 219.13.

.10 **cruciform**, crosslike, cross-shaped, cruciate, X-shaped, cross, crossed; cruciferous.

.11 **netlike**, retiform, plexiform; **reticulated**, reticular, reticulate, reticulato–; cancellate, cancellated; **netted**, netty; **meshed**, meshy; laced, lacy, lacelike; filigreed; latticed, latticelike; grated, gridded; barred, crossbarred, mullioned; streaked, striped.

.12 **webbed**, webby, weblike, woven, interwoven, interlaced, intertwined; web-footed, palmiped.

.13 ADVS **crosswise** *or* crossways *or* crossway, decussatively; **cross**, **crisscross**, **across**, thwart, thwartly, thwartways, **athwart**, athwartwise, overthwart; **traverse**, traversely; **transverse**, transversely, transversally; obliquely 219.21; **sideways** *or* sidewise; contrariwise, contrawise; crossgrained, across the grain; athwartship, athwartships; di(a)–, per–, trans–.

222. WEAVING

.1 NOUNS **weaving**, weave, warpage, weftage, warp and woof *or* weft, texture, tissue; **fabric** 378.5, **web**; **interweaving**, interweavement, intertexture; **interlacing**, interlacement, interlacery; **intertwining**, intertwinement; intertieing, interknitting, interthreading, intertwisting; **lacing**, enlacement; **twining**, entwining, entwinement; wreathing, knitting, twisting; **braiding**, plaiting.

.2 **braid**, plait, **wreath**, wreathwork.

.3 **warp**; **woof**, **weft**, filling; shoot, pick.

.4 **weaver**, interlacer, webster [archaic]; weaverbird, weaver finch, whirligig beetle.

.5 **loom**, weaver; hand loom; knitting machine; shuttle.

.6 VERBS **weave**, loom, tissue; **interweave**, **interlace**, **intertwine**, interknit, interthread, intertissue, intertie, intertwist; inweave, intort; web, net; **lace**, enlace; **twine**, entwine; **braid**, plait, pleach, **wreathe**, raddle, **knit**, twist, mat, wattle; twill, loop, noose; splice.

.7 ADJS **woven**, loomed, textile; **interwoven**, **interlaced**, interthreaded, **intertwined**, interknit, intertissued, intertied, intertwisted; handwoven; **laced**, enlaced; **wreathed**, fretted, raddled, knit; **twined**, entwined; **braided**, plaited, platted, pleached.

.8 **weaving**, **twining**, entwining; **intertwining**, **interlacing**, interweaving.

223. SEWING

.1 NOUNS **sewing**, **needlework**, stitching, stitchery; suture; **fancywork**; garment making 231.31.

.2 **sewer**, needleworker; **seamstress**, sempstress, needlewoman; seamster, sempster, tailor, needleman [archaic], needler [Brit]; embroiderer, embroideress; knitter; garmentmaker 231.33–35.

.3 **sewing machine**, sewer, Singer.

.4 VERBS **sew**, **stitch**, needle; sew up; **tailor**.

.5 **sew**

appliqué	machine-stitch
backstitch	overcast
baste	overhand
bind	purl
buttonhole	quilt
chain-stitch	renter
crochet	run
cross-stitch	saddle-stitch
double-stitch	seam
embroider	single-stitch
fell	tack
finedraw	tat
gather	whip
hemstitch	whipstitch
knit	

.6 **needlework**

appliqué	crochet work
basting	cross-stitching
binding	embroidery
binding off	felling
buttonholing	finedrawing
canvas stitching	gros point
casting on	hemming
chain-stitching	hemstitching
crewelwork	knitting
crochet	knitwork
crocheting	machine stitching

macramé
needlepoint
netting
overcasting
petit point
purling

quilting
ribbing
tacking
tatting
whipstitching

.7 stitches

backstitch
bargello
buttonhole stitch
cable stitch
carpet stitch
chain stitch
continental stitch
coral stitch
cord(ing) stitch
couching stitch
cross-stitch
damask stitch
double crochet
double stitch
French knot
garter stitch
glover's stitch
half cross stitch
half stitch
hemstitch
lace stitch
lazy daisy stitch
machine stitch
needlepoint

over-and-over stitch
outline stitch
picot
rib stitch
rose stitch
running stitch
saddleback stitch
saddle stitch
saddle wire stitch
satin stitch
shell stitch
side stitch
side thread stitch
side wire stitch
single crochet
single stitch
slip stitch
stockinette
stroke stitch
suture
tent stitch
treble
twist stitch
whipstitch

.8 needles

between
blunt
crochet hook
darner
darning needle
embroidery needle
ground-down
knitting needle
knitting pin
knitting wire
long-eyed sharp

sacking needle
sailmaker's needle
sewing-machine nee-
  dle
sewing needle
sharp
straw
tacking needle
three-cornered needle
upholsterer's needle

224. EXTERIORITY

.1 NOUNS **exteriority,** externalness, externality, **outwardness,** outerness; appearance,
outward appearance, seeming, mien,
manner; openness 553.3; extrinsicality 6;
superficiality, shallowness 210; extraterri-
toriality, foreignness.

.2 **exterior,** external, **outside; surface,** superficies, covering 228, skin 229, outer skin or
layer, epidermis, integument, envelope,
crust, cortex, rind 229.2, shell 228.16; top,
superstratum; **periphery, fringe,** circumference, outline, lineaments, border; **face,**
outer face or side, façade, front, facet; ex-
trados.

.3 **outdoors,** outside, **the out-of-doors,** the
great out-of-doors, the open, **the open
air;** outland.

.4 **externalization,** exteriorization; objectification, actualization, projection, **extrapolation.**

.5 VERBS **externalize,** exteriorize; **objectify,**
actualize, project, **extrapolate.**

.6 ADJS **exterior, external;** extrinsic 6.3;
outer, outside, out, outward, outward-fac-
ing, outlying, outstanding; **outermost,**
outmost; surface, superficial 210.5, epidermic, cortical; peripheral, **fringe,** roundabout; apparent, seeming; open 555.10,
public 559.17; exomorphic; e–, ec–, ect-
(o)–, ex– or ef–, ep(i)– or eph–, extra–,
hyper–, peripher(o)–.

.7 **outdoor, out-of-door,** out-of-doors, **outside; open-air,** alfresco.

.8 extraterritorial, exterritorial; extraterrestrial, exterrestrial, extramundane; extragalactic, extralateral, extraliminal, extramural, extrapolar, extrasolar, extraprovincial,
extratribal; foreign, outlandish, alien.

.9 ADVS **externally, outwardly,** on the outside, exteriorly; **without, outside, outwards, out;** apparently, to all appearances; openly, publically, to judge by appearances; superficially, on the surface.

.10 **outdoors, out of doors, outside,** abroad;
in the open, **in the open air,** alfresco, *en
plein air* [Fr].

225. INTERIORITY

.1 NOUNS interiority, internalness, internality, **inwardness, innerness,** inness; introversion, internalization; **intrinsicality** 5;
depth 209.

.2 **interior, inside,** inner, inward, internal,
intern; inner recess, recesses, **innermost
or deepest recesses,** penetralia, secret
place or places; bosom, heart, heart of
hearts, soul, vitals, vital center; inner self,
inner life, inner landscape, inner or interior man, inner nature; intrados; core,
center 226.2.

.3 **inland,** inlands, **interior,** up-country; **midland,** midlands; heartland; hinterland
182.2.

.4 (inside parts) **insides, innards** [informal],
inwards, internals; inner mechanism,
works [informal]; **guts** [slang], **vitals, viscera,** splanchno–, *kishkes* [Yid], giblets
308.20; **heart,** –cardium, ticker or pump
[both informal], endocardium, end(o)–;
brain 466.6,7; **lung** 403.19; **liver,** hepat(o)–,
liver and lights; spleen, splen(o)–; **kidney,**
nephr(o)–, –nephros, reni– or reno–; gizzard, **stomach,** abdomen 193.3; perineum,
perineo–; pylorus, pylor(o)–; **intestine,**
enter(o)–, entrails, bowels, guts; tripes
[dial], stuffings [slang]; large intestine,
small intestine; blind gut, cecum, cec(o)–
or ceci–; foregut, hindgut; midgut, meso-

gaster; colon, col(o)– or coli–; duodenum, duoden(o)–, jejunum, jejun(o)–, ileum, ili(o)– or ile(o)–; **appendix**, vermiform appendix or process, append(o)– or appendic(o)–; rectum, rect(o)–, proct(o)– or procti–; anus 265.6, ano–.

.5 enterology, enterography, splanchnology; internal medicine.

.6 VERBS internalize, put in, keep within; enclose, embed, surround, contain, comprise, include, enfold.

.7 ADJS **interior, internal, inner, inside, inward,** intestine; **innermost,** inmost, **intimate; intrinsic** 5.6; deep 209.10; central 226.11; indoor; en– or em–, end(o)–, ent(o)–, eso–, infra–, in– or im– or il– or ir–, inter–, intra–, ob–.

.8 **inland, interior,** up-country; hinterland 182.8; **midland,** mediterranean; inshore.

.9 intramarginal, intramural, intramundane, intramontane, intraterritorial, intracoastal, intragroupal.

.10 **visceral,** splanchnic; abdominal, gastric 193.5; pyloric; **intestinal,** enteric; colonic, colic; cecal, duodenal, ileac, jejunal, mesogastric, appendical, rectal, anal; cardiac, coronary.

.11 ADVS **internally, inwardly,** interiorly, inly, **intimately,** deeply, profoundly, under the surface; **intrinsically** 5.9; centrally 226.16.

.12 **in, inside, within;** herein, therein, wherein.

.13 **inward, inwards, inwardly,** withinward, withinwards; inland, inshore.

.14 **indoors,** indoor, withindoors.

.15 PREPS **in, into; within,** at, inside, **inside** of, in the limits of; to the heart or core of.

226. CENTRALITY

.1 NOUNS **centrality,** centralness, middleness, central or middle or mid position; centricity, centricality; concentricity; centripetence, centripetalism.

.2 **center,** centr(o)– or centri–, **middle** 69, **heart, core, nucleus,** nucle(o)–, nuclei–, **kernel; pith,** metr(o)–, **marrow,** myel(o)–, medulla; **nub, hub,** nave, axis, pivot; **navel,** umbilicus, omphalos; bull's-eye; dead center; center of action or area or buoyancy or displacement or curvature or effort or figure or flotation or inversion or origin or oscillation or ossification or percussion or pressure or projection or similitude or suspension or symmetry or volume; metacenter; epicenter, centrum; storm center; center of gravity, center of

mass or inertia, centroid; "the still point of the turning world" [T. S. Eliot].

.3 [biol terms] central body, centriole, centrosome, centrosphere.

.4 **focus,** focal point, prime focus, point of convergence; **center of interest** or attention, focus of attention, center of consciousness; **center of attraction,** cynosure; polestar, lodestar; magnet.

.5 **nerve center,** ganglion, center of activity, vital center.

.6 **headquarters,** HQ, central station, central office, main office, central administration, seat, base, **base of operations,** center of authority; general headquarters, GHQ, command post, CP, company headquarters.

.7 **metropolis, capital;** urban center, art center, medical center, shopping center, shipping center, railroad center, garment center, manufacturing center, tourist center, trade center, etc.

.8 **centralization,** centering; **focalization,** focusing; convergence 298; **concentration,** concentralization, pooling; centralism.

.9 VERBS **centralize, center,** middle; center round, center on or in.

.10 **focus,** focalize, come to a point or focus, bring into focus; **concentrate,** concentralize, concenter; converge 298.2.

.11 ADJS **central,** centric, **middle** 69.4; centermost, middlemost, **midmost;** centralized, concentrated; umbilical, omphalic; axial, **pivotal,** key; centroidal; centrosymmetric; geocentric.

.12 **nuclear,** nucleal, nucleary, nucleate.

.13 **focal,** confocal; converging; centrolineal, centripetal.

.14 **concentric;** homocentric; **coaxial,** coaxal.

.15 ADVS **centrally,** in the center or middle of, at the heart of.

227. LAYER

.1 NOUNS **layer,** –cline, thickness; **level, tier,** stage, story, floor, gallery, step, ledge, deck; **stratum,** strati–, seam, couche [Fr], belt, band, **bed, course,** measures; zone; shelf; **overlayer, superstratum,** overstory, topsoil; **underlayer, substratum,** understratum, understory; floor, bedding.

.2 lamina, lamella, lamin(o)– or lamini–, lamell(i)–; **sheet,** leaf, feuille [Fr], foil, pallio–; wafer, disk; **plate,** plating; covering 228, **coat,** coating, veneer, film, patina, scum, membrane, pellicle, peel, skin; **slice,** cut, rasher, collop; **slab,** plank, deal [Brit], slat, tablet, table, plac(o)–, pinac(o)– or pinak–; panel, pane; **fold,** lap, flap, **ply**, plait; laminated glass, safety glass; laminated wood, plywood.

.3 **flake**, flock, floccule, flocculus; lepid(o)–, –lepis, phalid(o)–, squam(o)–; **scale, scurf**, dandruff; chip; shaving, paring.

.4 stratification, lamination, lamellation; foliation; delamination, exfoliation; desquamation, furfuration; flakiness, scaliness.

.5 VERBS **layer**, lay down, lay up, **stratify**, arrange in layers *or* levels *or* strata *or* tiers, **laminate;** flake, scale; delaminate, desquamate, exfoliate.

.6 ADJS **layered**, in layers; **laminated**, laminate, laminous; lamellated, lamellate, lamellar, lamelliform; two-ply, three-ply, etc.; **stratified**, stratiform; foliated, foliaceous, leaflike, leafy; spathic, spathose; filmy, scummy; membranous.

.7 **flaky**, flocculent; **scaly**, scurfy, squamous, lentiginous, furfuraceous, lepidote; scabby, scabious, scabrous, asperous.

228. COVERING

.1 NOUNS (act of covering) **covering**, coverage, obduction; **coating**, cloaking; **screening**, shielding, hiding, curtaining, **veiling**, clouding, obscuring, masking, mantling, shrouding, blanketing; blocking, blotting out, eclipse, eclipsing, occultation; **wrapping**, enwrapping, enwrapment, sheathing, envelopment; **overlaying**, overspreading, laying on *or* over, superimposition, superposition; superincumbence; upholstering, upholstery; plasterwork, stuccowork, cementwork, pargeting; incrustation.

.2 **cover** 228.38, **covering**, coverage, covert, coverture, housing, hood, cowl, cowling, **shelter; screen**, shroud, shield, veil, pall, mantle, curtain, hanging, drape, drapery; **coat**, cloak, mask, guise; vestment 231.1; **blanket.**

.3 integument, tegument, tegmen, tegmentum.

.4 **overlayer**, overlay; appliqué; **lap, overlap**, overlapping, imbrication; **flap**, fly, tent-fly.

.5 **cover, lid, top, cap;** operculum; stopper 266.4.

.6 **roof** 228.39, roofing, roofage, top, **house-top**, rooftop; roof-deck, roof garden, penthouse; roofpole, ridgepole, rooftree; shingles, slates, tiles; eaves; **ceiling**, *plafond* [Fr], overhead; skylight, lantern; widow's walk *or* captain's walk.

.7 **umbrella**, gamp *or* brolly [both Brit infor-

mal], bumbershoot [informal]; **sunshade, parasol,** beach umbrella.

.8 **tent** 228.40, canvas; top, whitetop, round top, big top; tentage.

.9 **rug, carpet** 228.41, floor cover(ing); **mat**, doormat, welcome mat; carpeting, wall-to-wall carpet(ing); drop cloth, ground cloth, ground-sheet; **flooring**, floorboards, duckboards; **tiling; pavement,** pavé.

.10 **blanket, coverlet**, coverlid [dial], cover, **spread**, robe, buffalo robe, **afghan**, rug [Brit]; lap robe; **bedspread; bedcover;** counterpane, counterpin [dial]; comfort, **comforter, quilt,** eiderdown; patchwork quilt; **bedding, bedclothes,** clothes; **linen**, bed linen; **sheet**, sheeting, bedsheet, fitted sheet, contour sheet; **pillowcase**, pillow slip, case, slip.

.11 horsecloth, **horse blanket;** caparison, housing; **saddle blanket,** saddlecloth.

.12 **coating**, coat; **veneer, facing**, revetment; pellicle, **film, scum**, skin, scale; fur; varnish, enamel, lacquer, paint 362.8.

.13 **plating**, plate; nickel plate, silver plate, gold plate, copperplate, chromium plate, anodized aluminum; electroplating, electrocoating.

.14 **crust, incrustation**, shell; piecrust, pastry shell; stalactite, stalagmite; scale, scab, eschar.

.15 **shell** 228.42, lorication, lorica, –conch; test, testa, episperm, pericarp, elytron, elytr(o)– *or* elytri–, scute, scutum; **armor**, mail, **shield**, aspid(o)–, scut(i)–; **carapace**, –stegite, –stege, steg(o)–; plate, chitin; **protective covering**, cortex, thick skin.

.16 **hull**, shell, pod, capsule, case, **husk, shuck;** cornhusk, corn shuck; **rind, peel, skin** 229, bark, jacket; chaff, bran, palea.

.17 **case**, casing, encasement; **sheath**, sheathing, cole(o)–, –theca.

.18 **wrapper**, wrapping, gift wrapping, wrap; **binder**, binding; **bandage**, bandaging; **envelope**, envelopment; **jacket**, jacketing; dust jacket.

.19 VERBS **cover**, cover up, obduce; apply to, put on, lay on; **superimpose**, superpose; **lay over**, overlay; **spread over**, overspread; **clothe, cloak**, mantle, muffle, blanket, canopy, cope, cowl, hood, **veil**, curtain, **screen, shield**, mask, cloud, obscure, block, eclipse, occult; film, scum.

.20 **wrap**, enwrap, wrap up, wrap about *or* around; **envelop, sheathe;** surround, lap, smother, enfold, embrace, invest; shroud, enshroud; swathe, swaddle; **box, case**, encase, **crate**, pack, embox, **package**, encapsulate.

.21 **top, cap,** tip, crown; put the lid on, cork, stopper; hood, hat, coif, bonnet; roof, roof in *or* over; ceil; dome, endome.

.22 **floor; carpet; pave,** causeway, cobblestone, flag, pebble; cement, concrete; blacktop, tar, asphalt, metal [archaic], macadamize.

.23 **face, veneer,** revet; **sheathe;** board, plank, weatherboard, clapboard, lath; shingle, shake; tile, stone, brick, slate; thatch; glass, glaze, fiberglass; paper, wallpaper; wall in *or* up.

.24 **coat,** spread on, **spread with;** smear, **smear on,** besmear, slap on, dab, daub, bedaub; lay on, lay it on thick, slather; undercoat, prime; enamel, gild, gloss, lacquer; butter; tar.

.25 **plaster,** parget, stucco, cement, concrete, mastic, grout, mortar; roughcast.

.26 **plate,** chromium-plate, copperplate, goldplate, nickel-plate, silver-plate; **electroplate, galvanize,** anodize.

.27 **crust, incrust,** encrust; loricate; effloresce; scab.

.28 **upholster,** overstuff.

.29 **re-cover,** reupholster, recap.

.30 **overlie,** lie over; **overlap,** lap, **lap over,** override, imbricate, jut, shingle; **extend over,** span, bridge, bestride, bestraddle, arch over, overarch, hang over, overhang.

.31 ADJS **covered,** covert, under cover; **cloaked,** mantled, blanketed, muffled, canopied, coped, cowled, hooded, **shrouded, veiled,** clouded, obscured, eclipsed, occulted, curtained, **screened,** shielded, masked; **housed;** tented, under canvas; roofed, roofed-in *or* -over; walled, walled-in; **wrapped,** enwrapped, **enveloped,** sheathed, swathed; **boxed, cased,** encased, encapsuled *or* encapsulated; **packaged; coated,** filmed, scummed; shelled, loricate, loricated; armored, hoplo–; ceiled; paved, floored.

.32 **plated,** chromium-plated, copperplated, gold-plated, nickel-plated, silver-plated; electroplated, galvanized, anodized.

.33 upholstered, overstuffed.

.34 **covering, coating;** cloaking, blanketing, shrouding, **veiling, screening,** shielding; wrapping, **enveloping,** sheathing.

.35 **overlying,** incumbent, superincumbent, superimposed; **overlapping,** lapping, shingled, equitant; imbricate, imbricated; spanning, bridging; overarched, overarching; ep(i)– *or* eph–.

.36 integumental, integumentary, tegumentary, tegumental, tegmental; vaginal, thecal.

.37 PREPS **on, upon, over,** o'er, **above, on top of.**

.38 **covers**

altar cloth *or* carpet	pall
antimacassar	pavilion
awning	persienne
baldachin	pledget
blind	purdah
canopy	pyx cloth *or* veil
centerpiece	scarf
cerecloth	screen
cerement	shade
chrismal	shamiana
ciborium	sheet
cloth	shield
cope	shroud
corporal	shutter
cozy	smoke screen
curtain	tablecloth
doily	tarpaulin, tarp [informal]
dossal	tester
fanon	tidy
fingerstall	veil
housing	veiling
jalousie	venetian blind
mantle	window shade
marquee, marquise	
mask	

.39 **roofs**

barrack roof	lean-to roof
bulkhead	mansard roof
cupola	M roof
curb roof	pantile roof
dome	penthouse roof
flat roof	pitched roof
French roof	pyramidal roof
gable roof	shed roof
gambrel roof	shingle roof
geodesic dome	slate roof
hip-and-valley roof	thatched roof
hip roof	tile roof
jerkinhead roof	

.40 **tents**

A-tent	pack tent
backpacking tent	pavilion
Baker tent	praetorium
bell tent	pup tent
bungalow tent	pyramidal tent
cabin tent	shelter tent
canoe tent	Sibley tent
circus tent	tepee
field tent	tupik
fly tent	two-man tent
highwall tent	umbrella tent
lean-to tent	wall tent
marquee, marquise	wigwam
mountain tent	

.41 **rugs, carpets**

Axminster	East Indian rug
bearskin rug	hooked rug
body Brussels	imperial Brussels
broadloom	Indian rug
Brussels carpet	indoor-outdoor carpeting
camel's hair rug	ingrain
Caucasian rug	mohair rug
chenille carpet *or* rug	moquette
Chinese rug	namda
drugget	

nammad, numdah rug	shag rug
Navaho rug	steamer rug
nylon carpeting	tapestry Brussels
Oriental rug	throw rug
Persian rug	Turkish rug
rag rug	Turkoman rug or carpet
rya	pet
Savonnerie	Wilton
scatter rug	

.42 shells

abalone shell	nautilus
armadillo shell	nutshell
chiton	oyster shell
clam shell	periwinkle
cockleshell	scallop
cocoa shell	sea shell
conch	snail shell
cowrie	tooth shell
eggshell	turtle shell
limpet	whelk
marine shell	winkle

.43 covering materials

asbestos tile	plasterboard
asphalt	plywood
asphalt tile	roofing, roofage
blacktop	roofing paper
brick	roofing tile
canvas	shake
carpeting	sheathing board
clapboard	sheeting
cobblestone	shingle
concrete	shingling
cork tile	siding
fiber glass, spun glass	slate
flag	slating
flagging	stone
flagstone	tar paper
flooring	thatch
Formica	tile
linoleum	tilestone
macadam	tiling
Masonite	veneer
pantile	wainscoting
paper	wallboard
parquet	walling
pavement	wallpaper
pavestone	weatherboard
paving	wood

.44 plaster

adobe	patching plaster
cement	plaster of Paris
chinking	Portland cement
clay	roughcast
composition, compo	scagliola
daubing	size, sizing
grout	Spackle
mastic	spackling compound
mortar	stucco
parget	

229. SKIN

.1 NOUNS **skin,** dermis, derm(a)– or dermo–, scyt(o)–; **cuticle; rind** 228.16; **flesh;** bare skin or flesh, the buff; integument, tegument; **pelt, hide** 229.8, **coat, jacket, fell, fleece, fur,** vair [her]; **leather** 229.9, rawhide; imitation leather, leather paper,

Leatheroid, Leatherette; imitation fur; peltry, skins; furring; outer skin or layer, sheath, the exterior 224.2.

.2 **peel, peeling, rind** 228.16, **skin,** epicarp; **bark;** cork, phellum, phello–; cortex, cortical tissue, cortic(o)–; periderm, phelloderm; peridium; dermatogen.

.3 **membrane,** membrana, pellicle, chorion, chori(o)–; basement membrane, membrana propria; allantoic membrane, allant(o)–; amnion, amniotic sac, amnio–; arachnoid membrane, arachn(o)–; serous membrane, serosa, membrana serosa; **eardrum,** tympanic membrane, tympanum, membrana tympana, tympan(o)–; **mucous membrane; velum,** vel–; **peritoneum,** periton(o)– or peritone(o)–; periosteum, periost(o)– or perioste(o)–; pleura, pleur(o)– or pleuri–; pericardium, pericardi(o)– or pericardo–; meninx [sing], **meninges** [pl], mening(o)– or meningi–; perineurium, neurilemma, lemmo–; conjuctiva; **hymen** or maidenhead; hymen(o)–.

.4 (skin layers) **epidermis,** epiderm(o)–, scarfskin, ecderon; hypodermis, hypoderma; dermis, derma, corium, cutis, cut(i)–, *cutis vera* [L], true skin; epithelium, pavement epithelium; endothelium, endotheli(o)–; mesoderm, mes(o)–; endoderm, entoderm; blastoderm; ectoderm, epiblast, ectoblast; enderon; connective tissue.

.5 (castoff skin) slough, cast, desquamation, exuviae [pl].

.6 ADJS **cutaneous,** cuticular; skinlike, skinny; skin-deep; **epidermal,** epidermic, ecderonic; hypodermic, hypodermal, subcutaneous; dermal, dermic, –dermatous; ectodermal, ectodermic; endermic, endermatic; cortical; epicarpal; testaceous; furry 230.24.

.7 **leather,** leathern, leathery; buff.

.8 **pelts, furs, hides**

Alaska sable	caracul
Australian seal	cat
Baltic leopard	catskin
Baltic tiger	chinchilla
bearskin	chinchillette
beaver	coast seal
beaverette	coney
beaverskin	coney leopard
black fox	coney mole
black marten	cowhide
black sable	deerskin
brook mink	doeskin
buckskin	electric beaver
calf	electric mole
calfskin	electric seal
capeskin	ermine

erminette	New Zealand seal
fleece	nutria
fox	otter
fox hair	Persian lamb
genet	pigskin
goatskin	polar seal
golden sable	rabbit
horsehide	rabbitskin
Hudson Bay seal	raccoon
jaguar	red fox
kolinsky	red sable
krimmer	Roman seal
lambskin	sable
lapin	seal
leopard	sealskin
leopardskin	shagreen
marmink	sheepskin
marmot	skunk
marten	squirrel
merino	Tartar sable
miniver	tiger
mink	water mink
mole	white fox
moleskin	wool
monkey	wool fell, woolskin
muskrat	

.9 leather

buff	Morocco
chamois, chammy	patent leather
chamois skin	sheepskin
cordovan	shoe leather
cup leather	suède
hat leather	tawed leather
kid	whitleather, white
mocha	leather

230. HAIR, FEATHERS

.1 NOUNS **hairiness, shagginess, fuzziness,** frizziness, **furriness,** downiness, fluffiness, woolliness, fleeciness, bristliness, stubbliness, burrheadedness, mopheadedness, shockheadedness, hypertrichy, hirsuteness, hirsuties, pilosity, crinosity, hispidity, villosity, pubescence; hirsutism, pilosis, pilosism; –trichia or –trichy; –thrix, –coma.

.2 **hair,** chaet(o)–, trich(o)–, pile, pil(o)– or pili–, crine, crini–; **fur,** coat; pelt 229.1,8; **fleece,** wool, lan(o)– or lani–; camel's hair, horsehair; **mane;** shag, tousled or matted hair, **mat of hair;** pubescence, pubes, pubic hair; hairlet, villus, capillament, cilium, ciliolum 206.1; seta, setula; bristle 261.3.

.3 gray hair, grizzle, silver or silvery hair, salt-and-pepper hair or beard, graying temples, "hoary hair" [Thomas Gray], "the silver livery of advised age" [Shakespeare], "a crown of glory" [Bible], "silver threads among the gold" [Eben E. Rexford].

.4 **head of hair,** head, crine; **crop,** crop of hair, mat, elflock, **thatch,** mop, shock, shag, fleece, **mane; locks, tresses,** helmet

of hair; "her native ornament of hair" [Ovid], "amber-dropping hair" [Milton].

.5 **lock, tress;** flowing locks, flowing tresses; **curl, ringlet,** "wanton ringlets wav'd" [Milton]; earlock, *payess* [Yid]; lovelock; frizz, frizzle; crimp; ponytail.

.6 **tuft, flock,** fleck; forelock, widow's peak, quiff [Brit], fetlock, cowlick; **bang, bangs,** fringe.

.7 **braid,** plait, twist; **pigtail,** rat's-tail or rat-tail, tail; **queue,** cue; coil, knot; topknot, scalplock; bun, chignon.

.8 **beard,** pogon(o)–, –pogon, **whiskers;** beaver [informal]; full beard, chin whiskers, side whiskers; **sideburns,** burnsides, **mutton chops; goatee,** tuft; imperial, **Vandyke,** spade beard; adolescent beard, pappus, down, peach fuzz, "the soft down of manhood" [Callimachus], "his phoenix down" [Shakespeare]; **stubble,** bristles.

.9 (plant beard) awn, brush, arista, pile, pappus.

.10 (animal and insect whiskers) tactile process, tactile hair, **feeler, antenna,** vibrissa; barb, barbel, barbule; cat whisker.

.11 **mustache,** mustachio, soup-strainer [informal], toothbrush, handle bars or handle-bar mustache, tash [informal].

.12 **eyelashes, lashes,** cilia; **eyebrows,** brows.

.13 false hair, switch, fall, chignon, rat [informal].

.14 **wig, peruke, toupee,** hairpiece; **periwig.**

.15 **hairdo, hairstyle, haircut, coiffure,** coif, headdress; **wave;** marcel, marcel wave; **permanent,** permanent wave; home permanent; cold wave; Afro, natural; process, conk.

.16 **feather, plume,** pinion; **quill;** pinfeather, contour feather, penna, down feather, plume feather, plumule; filoplume; hackle; scapular; **crest,** tuft, topknot, panache; penni– or penno–, pinn(i)–, pter(o)–, ptil(o)–, –ptile.

.17 (parts of feathers) quill, calamus, barrel; barb, shaft, barbule, barbicel, cilium, filament, filamentule.

.18 **plumage, feathers,** feather, feathering; contour feathers; breast feathers, mail (of a hawk); hackle; flight feathers; remiges, primaries, secondaries, tertiaries; covert, tectrices; speculum, wing bay.

.19 **down, fluff,** flue, floss, **fuzz, fur,** pile; eiderdown, eider; swansdown; thistledown; lint.

.20 VERBS grow hair; whisker, bewhisker, beard.

.21 **feather, fledge,** feather out; sprout wings.

.22 cut or dress the hair, trim, **barber,** coiffure, coif, style or shape the hair; pompadour, wave, marcel; process, conk; **bob, shingle.**

.23 ADJS **hairlike,** trichoid, capillary; filamentous, filamentary, filiform; bristlelike 261.10.

.24 **hairy, hirsute,** barbigerous, crinose, crinite, pubigerous, pubescent; pilose, pilous, pileous; **furry,** furred; villous; villose; ciliate, cirrose; hispid, hispidulous; **woolly, fleecy,** lanate, lanated, flocky, flocculent, floccose; woolly-headed, woolly-haired, ulotrichous; bushy, tufty, **shaggy,** shagged; matted, tomentose; mopheaded, burrheaded, shockheaded, unshorn; **bristly** 261.9; fuzzy; dasy–, hebe–; –chaetous, –trichous.

.25 **bearded,** whiskered, **bewhiskered,** barbate, barbigerous; mustached or mustachioed; awned, awny, pappose; goateed; unshaved, **unshaven;** stubbled, stubbly.

.26 **wigged,** periwigged, peruked, toupeed.

.27 **feathery, plumy;** hirsute; featherlike, plumelike, pinnate, pennate, pinnati–; **downy,** fluffy, nappy, velvety, peachy, fuzzy, flossy, furry.

.28 **feathered, plumaged,** flighted, **pinioned, plumed,** pennate, plumate, plumose.

.29 **tufted, crested,** topknotted.

.30 **women's hairdos**

Andalusian swirl	personality bob
bangs	pigtails
bob	pompadour
bohemian bob	ponytail
boyish bob	Psyche knot
chignon bob	roach
contour bob	Romanesque bob
coquette bob	shag
debutante bob	shingle
feathercut	short bob
Flemish bob	shortcut
French knot	straight hair shingle
Italian bob	swirl
long bob	swirl bob
long mane	ultramannish bob
mannish bob	updo
mannish wavy shingle	upswept hairdo
new moon bob	windblown bob
page-boy	

.31 **boys' haircuts**

boogie	ducktail
brushcut	flattop
butch	fuzz cut
crewcut	mohawk
d.a.	pachuco

231. CLOTHING

.1 NOUNS **clothing, clothes, apparel, wear,** wearing apparel, **dress,** dressing, **raiment,** garmenture, **garb, attire, array,** habit, habiliment, fashion, style 644, guise, costume, gear, fig or full fig [both Brit], toilette, trim, bedizenment; **vestment,** vesture, investment, investiture; **garments, raiments,** robes, robing, rags [slang], drapery, feathers; **toggery** or **togs** or **duds** or threads [all informal], sportswear; work clothes, fatigues; linen; menswear, men's clothing, womenswear, women's clothing; unisex clothing, uniwear.

.2 **wardrobe,** furnishings, things, accouterments, trappings; **outfit,** livery, harness, caparison; turnout or getup or rig [all informal]; wedding clothes, bridal outfit, trousseau.

.3 **garment, raiment,** vestment, vesture, robe, frock, gown, rag [slang], togs or duds [both informal]; –let.

.4 **ready-mades,** ready-to-wear, store or store-bought clothes [dial].

.5 **rags, tatters,** secondhand clothes, old clothes; worn clothes, **hand-me-downs** or reach-me-downs [both informal]; slops.

.6 **suit** 231.48, suit of clothes, frock, dress, rig [informal], **costume, habit,** bib and tucker [informal].

.7 **uniform** 231.49, **livery.**

.8 **mufti,** civilian dress or clothes, **civvies** or cits [both informal], plain clothes.

.9 **costume,** character dress; outfit or getup or rig [all informal]; masquerade, disguise; tights, leotards; ballet skirt, tutu; motley, cap and bells; buskin, sock.

.10 **finery, frippery, fancy dress,** fine or full feather [informal], full fig [Brit informal]; **best clothes,** best bib and tucker [informal]; **Sunday best** or Sunday clothes or Sunday-go-to-meeting clothes or Sunday-go-to-meetings [all informal], **glad rags** [slang], party dress.

.11 **formals,** formal dress, **evening dress, full dress,** white tie and tails, **soup-and-fish** [slang]; dinner clothes; dress suit, full-dress suit, tails [informal]; tuxedo, tux [informal]; **regalia,** court dress; dress uniform, full-dress uniform, special full-dress uniform, social full-dress uniform; evening gown, dinner dress or gown.

.12 **cloak,** overgarment 231.50.

.13 **coat,** jacket 231.51; overcoat 231.53, greatcoat, **topcoat,** surcoat.

.14 **waistcoat,** weskit [dial], vest.

.15 **waist, shirt** 231.54, shirtwaist, linen, sark or shift [both dial]; **blouse,** bodice, corsage; dickey.

.16 **dress** 231.55, **gown, frock; skirt,** jupe [Scot].

.17 **apron,** *tablier* [Fr]; pinafore, bib, tucker; smock.

.18 **pants, trousers** 231.56, pair of trousers, trews [Scot], **breeches,** britches [informal], breeks [Scot], **pantaloons,** jeans, **slacks.**

.19 **waistband, belt** 253.3; **loincloth,** breechcloth or breechclout, waistcloth, G-string, loinguard, dhoti, moocha; **diaper,** dydee [informal], napkins [Brit], nappies [Brit informal].

.20 **dishabille** 231.57, déshabillé [Fr], **undress,** something comfortable; **negligee,** négligé [Fr]; **wrap,** wrapper; sport clothes, **casual clothes** or **dress.**

.21 **nightwear,** night clothes; **nightdress, nightgown, nightie** [informal], bedgown; nightshirt; **pajamas,** pyjamas [Brit], PJ's [informal]; sleepers.

.22 **underclothes,** underclothing, undergarments 231.58, bodywear, **underwear, undies** [informal], Skivvies, body clothes, smallclothes, unmentionables [informal], **lingerie, linen,** underlinen; flannels, woolens.

.23 **corset,** stays, foundation garment, corselet; **girdle,** undergirdle, panty girdle; garter belt.

.24 **brassiere, bra** [informal], bandeau, underbodice, soutien-gorge [Fr], uplift brassiere; falsies [slang].

.25 **headdress,** headgear, headwear, headclothes, headtire; **millinery;** headpiece, **chapeau, cap, hat** 231.59; lid [informal]; headcloth, **kerchief,** coverchief; **handkerchief.**

.26 **veil,** veiling, veiler; yashmak [Turk]; mantilla.

.27 **footwear,** footgear, chaussure [Fr]; **shoes** 231.60, **boots;** clodhoppers or gunboats [both slang]; wooden shoes, sabots, pattens.

.28 **hosiery** 231.61, hose, stockings; **socks.**

.29 **bathing suit,** swim suit, swimming suit, tank suit, maillot [Fr]; **trunks;** bikini; wet suit.

.30 **children's wear;** rompers, jumpers; creepers; layette, baby clothes, infants' wear, baby linen; swaddling clothes, swaddle.

.31 **garment making, tailoring; dressmaking; millinery,** hatmaking, hatting; **shoemaking,** bootmaking, **cobbling;** habilimentation.

.32 **clothier, haberdasher,** draper [Brit], outfitter; costumier, costumer; glover; hosier; furrier; dry goods dealer, mercer [Brit].

.33 **garmentmaker, garmentworker;** needleworker; cutter, stitcher, finisher.

.34 **tailor,** tailoress, tailleur [Fr], sartor; fitter; busheler, bushelman; furrier; cloakmaker.

.35 **dressmaker, modiste,** couturière [Fr], couturier [Fr]; seamstress 223.2.

.36 **hatter,** hatmaker, **milliner.**

.37 **shoemaker,** bootmaker, booter, **cobbler,** souter [Scot].

.38 VERBS **clothe,** enclothe, **dress, garb, attire,** tire, array, **apparel,** raiment, garment, habilitate, **tog** [informal], dud [slang], robe, enrobe, invest, endue, **deck,** bedeck, dight, rag out or up [slang]; drape, bedrape; wrap, enwrap, lap, envelop, sheathe, shroud, enshroud; wrap or bundle or muffle up; swathe, swaddle.

.39 **cloak, mantle;** coat, jacket, gown, frock; breech; shirt; coif, bonnet, cap, hat, hood; boot, shoe; stocking, sock.

.40 **outfit,** equip, **accouter,** uniform, caparison, rig, rig out or up, fit, **fit out,** turn out, **costume,** habit, suit; disguise, masquerade, cloak oneself.

.41 **dress up, get up, doll** or **spruce up** [informal], **primp** or prink or prank [all informal], gussy up [informal], spiff or fancy or slick up [slang], pretty up [informal], deck out or up, trick out or up, tog out or up [informal], rag out or up [slang], fig out or up; titivate, dizen, bedizen; overdress; put on the dog or style [slang].

.42 **don, put on,** slip on or into, get on or into, assume, dress in; change.

.43 **wear, have on,** be dressed in, affect, sport [informal].

.44 ADJS **clothed, clad, dressed, attired, togged** [informal], tired, arrayed, **garbed,** garmented, habited, habilimented, decked, bedecked, decked out, tricked out, rigged out, dight [archaic], vested, vestmented, robed, gowned, raimented, **apparaled,** invested, endued, liveried, uniformed; **costumed,** in costume, cloaked, mantled, disguised; breeched, trousered, pantalooned; coifed, capped, bonneted, hatted, hooded; **shod,** shoed, booted, chaussé [Fr].

.45 **dressed up, dolled** or **spruced up** [informal]; spiffed or fancied or slicked up [slang], gussied up [informal]; spruce, dressed to advantage, dressed to the nines, dressed fit to kill [slang]; in Sunday best, endimanché [Fr], in one's best bib and tucker [informal], in fine or high feather; en grande tenue [Fr], en grande toilette [Fr], in full dress, in full feather, in white tie and tails, in tails; **well-dressed, chic,** soigné [Fr], stylish, modish, well turned-out.

.46 **in dishabille,** en déshabillé [Fr], **in negligee;** casual, informal, sporty.

.47 tailored, custom-made, bespoke [Brit]; ready-made, store-bought [dial], ready-to-wear; vestmental; sartorial.

.48 suits

business suit
casual suit
combination
double-breasted suit
dress suit
ensemble
foul-weather suit
jump suit
mod suit
one-piece suit
pants suit
rain suit
riding habit
sack suit
separates
shirtwaist suit
single-breasted suit
ski suit
sports suit
summer suit
sun suit
sweat suit
tailored suit
three-piece suit
town-and-country suit
track suit
tropical suit
two-piece suit
zoot suit

.49 uniforms

blues
continentals
dress blues
dress whites
fatigues
full dress
khaki
nauticals
olive-drab or OD
regimentals
sailor suit
soldier suit
stripes (prison uniform)
undress
whites

.50 cloaks, overgarments

academic gown
academic hood
academic robe
afghan
bachelor's gown
blouse
burnoose
caftan
cape
capote
cardinal
cashmere, cashmere shawl
cassock
chlamys
doctor's gown
domino
duster
frock
gaberdine
haik
houppelande
Inverness cape
judge's robe or gown
kimono
kirtle
manta
manteau
mantelet
mantelletta
mantellone
mantilla
mantle
mantua
master's gown
military cloak
monk's robe
opera cloak or cape
pallium
pelerine
pelisse
peplos
peplum
plaid
poncho
robe
roquelaure
sagum
serape
shawl
shoulderette
slop
smock
smock frock
soutane
stole
tabard
talma
tippet
toga
toga virilis
tunic
wrap-around
wrapper
wrap-up

.51 coats, jackets

blazer
blouse
body coat
bolero
bomber jacket
capuchin
car coat
chaqueta [Sp]
chesterfield
claw-hammer coat,
claw hammer
coach coat
coatee
cutaway coat, cutaway
denim jacket
dinner coat or jacket
dolman
double-breasted jacket
doublet
dress coat
dressing jacket
duffel, duffel coat
Eisenhower jacket
Eton jacket
fingertip coat
fitted coat
frock coat, frock
jerkin
jumper
jupe [Scot]
loden coat
lounging jacket
mackinaw, mackinaw coat
Mao jacket
maxicoat
mess jacket
midicoat
monkey jacket
Nehru jacket
Norfolk jacket
parka
peacoat, pea jacket
pilot jacket
Prince Albert, Prince Albert coat
redingote
reefer
sack
sack coat
san benito
shell jacket
shooting jacket
single-breasted jacket
ski jacket
sleeve waistcoat
smoking jacket
spencer
spiketail coat, spiketail
sport coat or jacket
swagger coat
swallow-tailed coat, swallowtail
tabard
tail coat, tails
tuxedo coat or jacket
watch coat
windbreaker
woolly (woolen jacket)

.52 sweaters

bolero
bulky
cardigan, cardigan jacket
cashmere sweater
crew-neck sweater
desk sweater
fisherman's sweater
hand-knit
jersey
knittie
pull-on sweater
pullover
shell
shoulderette
ski sweater
slip-on
slipover
sloppy Joe
sweat shirt
topper
turtleneck sweater
V-neck sweater
windbreaker
woolly

.53 overcoats

benjamin
Burberry
capote
chesterfield
cloth coat
dreadnought
duster
fearnought
fur coat
fur-lined coat
fur-trimmed coat
Inverness
long coat
mackintosh, mac
oilskins
paletot
raglan
raincoat
slicker
slip-on
sou'wester
surtout
tarpaulin
trench coat
ulster
waterproof
wet weathers
wrap-around
wraprascal

.54 shirts

basque
blouse
body shirt
body suit
coat shirt
dickey
doublet
dress shirt
evening shirt
gipon
habit shirt
hair shirt
halter
hickory shirt

jupe [Scot]
middy blouse
olive-drab or OD shirt
overblouse
polo shirt
pourpoint
pullover

sark
shirtwaist
short-sleeved shirt
sport shirt
tank top
top
T-shirt

robe
robe-de-chambre [Fr]

smoking jacket
wrapper

.55 dresses, skirts

ballet skirt
cheongsam
chiton
cocktail dress
crinoline
culottes
dinner dress or gown
dirndl
evening gown
farthingale
fillebeg
full skirt
grass skirt
hobble skirt
hoop skirt
jumper
kilt
kirtle
mantua
maxiskirt

microskirt
midiskirt
miniskirt
Mother Hubbard
muu-muu
overdress
overskirt
pannier
peplum
petticoat
pinafore
sack
sari
sarong
sheath
shirtdress
slit skirt
tea gown
tutu

.56 pants

bags [Brit]
bell-bottoms, bells [in-
  formal]
Bermuda shorts
bloomers
blue jeans
breeks [Scot]
buckskins
Capri pants
chivarras [Sp]
clam diggers
cords
corduroys
culottes
denims
drawers
ducks
dungarees
flannels
gabardines
galligaskins
gym pants
high-water pants
hip-huggers
hot pants
Jamaica shorts
jeans
jodhpurs
kerseys
knee breeches
knee pants
knickerbockers,

knickers
Levi's
long trousers or pants
moleskins
overalls
pajamas
pantalets
pantaloons
pedal-pushers
peg pants
pegtops
plus-fours
riding pants
rompers
sacks
shintiyan
short pants
shorts
short shorts
ski pants
slacks
smallclothes
stretch pants
sweat pants
tights
toreador pants
trews
trouserettes
trunks
tweeds
whites

.57 dishabille

bathrobe
bed jacket
boudoir dress
brunch coat
dressing gown
dressing sack or jacket

housecoat
kimono
lounging pajamas
lounging robe
morning dress
peignoir [Fr]

.58 undergarments

Balmoral
bloomers
body stocking
brassiere 231.24
briefs
bustle
BVD's
camisole
chemise
combination
corset 231.23
crinoline
drawers
foundation garment
Jockey shorts
long underwear
pannier
panties
pants

petticoat
scanties
shift
shorts
singlet [Brit]
Skivvies
slip
smock
step-ins
tournure [Fr]
T-shirt
underdrawers
underpants
undershirt
underskirt
undervest
union suit
vest [Brit]

.59 hats, caps

astrakhan
balaclava helmet
Balmoral
baseball cap
beany
bearskin
beaver
beret
billycock hat, billy-
  cock
boater
bonnet
Borsalino
boudoir cap
bowler
brass hat
busby
calash
campaign hat
capote
castor
chapeau bras [Fr]
cloche
cock-and-pinch
cocked hat
coif
coonskin cap
coxcomb
crush hat
derby
dress cap
dunce cap
Dutch cap
fantail
fedora
felt hat
fez
forage cap
fore-and-aft or -after
garrison cap
glengarry
hard hat
helmet
homburg
hood
jockey cap
kaffiyeh
kelly

kepi
leghorn
mobcap
mortarboard
nightcap
opera hat
overseas cap
Panama hat, Panama
peaked cap
picture hat
pillbox
pith hat or helmet
plug hat, plug
poke bonnet, poke
porkpie
puggree
riding hood
rumal
sailor
Salvation Army bon-
  net
scraper
shako
shovel hat
side cap
silk hat
skimmer
skullcap
slouch hat
snood
soft hat
sola topee
sombrero
sou'wester
Stetson
stocking cap
stovepipe hat, stove-
  pipe
straw hat
sunbonnet
sundown
sun hat
sun helmet
tam-o'shanter, tam
tarboosh
ten-gallon hat
three-cornered hat
tin hat

topee
top hat, topper
toque
tricorne
trilby
turban

tyrolean hat
wide-awake hat, wide-
　awake
wimple
wind-cutter
yarmulka

.60 shoes

arctics
ballet shoes or slippers
Blucher boots or
　shoes, bluchers
bootees
bootikins
boots
brogues, brogans
buskins
button shoes
campus shoes
chopines
chukka boots
clogs
combat boots
cowboy boots
creepers
desert boots
espadrilles
field shoes
flip-flops
gaiters
galoshes
getas
gumshoes, gums
gym shoes
half boots
Hessian boots, hes-
　sians
high-button shoes
high-lows
high-topped shoes
hip boots
hobnailed shoes
horseshoes

jackboots
lace shoes
Loafers
loungers
moccasins
mules
overshoes
Oxford shoes or ties,
　Oxfords
paratrooper boots
pattens
platforms
pumps
riding boots
rope shoes
rubbers
sandals
scuffs
ski boots
slippers
sneakers
snowshoes
socks
stogies
tennis shoes
thigh boots
top boots
veldschoens
Wedgies
Wellington boots,
　Wellingtons
wooden shoes
work shoes
zoris

.61 hosiery

anklets
argyles
athletic socks
bobbysocks
boothose
boot socks
crew socks
dress sheers
full-fashioned stock-
　ings
garter stockings
half hose
knee socks
lisle hose

nylons
panty-hose
rayon stockings
seamless stockings
sheer stockings, sheers
silk stockings
stocking hose
stretch stockings
sweat socks
tights
trunk hose
varsity socks
work socks

.62 leggings

antigropelos
chaps, chaparajos [Sp]
gaiters
galligaskins
gamashes
gambados

greaves
leg armor
puttees, putts
spats
spatterdashes

.63 handwear, gloves

baseball glove or mitt
boxing gloves
brass knuckles
cesta

cestus
gauntlets
hockey gloves
kid gloves, kids

mittens, mitts
mousquetaire gloves,
　mousquetaires

muff
suède gloves, suèdes

.64 neckwear

ascot, ascot tie
band
bandanna
bertha
boa
bowtie
button-down collar
celluloid collar
chemisette
choke, choker
clerical collar
collar
comforter
cravat
dog collar
fichu
four-in-hand, four-in-
　hand tie
fur
guimpe
high collar

kerchief
muffler
neckband
neckcloth
neckerchief
neckpiece
necktie
plunging neckline
rebato
Roman collar
ruff
scarf
stiff collar
stock
stole
string tie
tallith
tie
tippet
tucker
Windsor tie

.65 waistbands, belts

baldric
band
bandolier
bellyband
belt
cestus
cincture
cummerbund

fascia
girdle
girt
girth
sash
waist belt
waistcloth

.66 garment parts

arm
armhole
armlet
bosom
coattail
collar
collarband
cuff
dart
facing
fly
French cuff
gore
gusset
lap
lapel
leg

neck
neckband
pinafore
placket
pocket
pocket flap
seat
shirttail
shoulder pad
shoulder strap
sleeve
stomacher
strap
waist
wristband
yoke
zipper

232. DIVESTMENT

.1 NOUNS **divestment,** divestiture, divesture;
　removal, de–, dis–, un–; **stripping,** de-
　nudement, denudation; baring, stripping
　or laying bare, uncovering, exposure; in-
　decent exposure, exhibitionism; decorti-
　cation, excoriation; desquamation, exfoli-
　ation; exuviation, ecdysis.

.2 **disrobing,** disrobement, **undressing,** un-
　clothing, uncasing; shedding, molting,
　peeling; striptease.

.3 **nudity, nakedness,** bareness; **the nude,**
　the altogether or **the buff** [both infor-

mal], **the raw** [slang]; state of nature, **birthday suit** [informal]; not a stitch, not a stitch to one's name *or* back; décolleté, décolletage, toplessness; nudism, naturism, gymnosophy; nudist, naturist, gymnosophist; stripper, stripteaser, ecdysiast.

.4 **hairlessness, baldness,** acomia, alopecia; beardlessness, bald-headedness *or* -patedness; baldhead, baldpate, baldy [informal]; shaving, tonsure, depilation; hair remover, depilatory.

.5 VERBS **divest, strip, remove; uncover,** uncloak, unveil, **expose,** lay open, bare, lay *or* strip bare, **denude,** denudate; fleece, shear; pluck; unsheathe.

.6 **take off, remove, doff,** douse [informal], off with, put off, slip *or* step out of, cast off, throw off, drop; unwrap, undo.

.7 **undress, unclothe,** undrape, ungarment, unapparel, unarray, disarray; **disrobe,** dismantle, uncase; **strip,** strip to the buff [informal], do a strip-tease.

.8 **peel, pare, skin, strip,** flay, excoriate, decorticate, bark; scalp.

.9 **husk, hull,** pod, **shell,** shuck.

.10 **shed, cast,** throw off, **slough, molt,** exuviate.

.11 **scale, flake,** scale *or* flake off, desquamate, exfoliate.

.12 ADJS **divested, stripped, bared,** denuded, denudated, exposed, uncovered, stripped *or* laid bare, unveiled, showing.

.13 **unclad, undressed, unclothed, unattired, disrobed,** ungarmented, undraped, ungarbed, unrobed, unappareled, uncased; **clothesless,** garbless, garmentless, raimentless; half-clothed, underclothed, *en déshabillé* [Fr], in dishabille, nudish; low-necked, low-cut, décolleté, strapless, topless.

.14 **naked, nude,** gymn(o)–, nudi–; **bare,** bald, peeled, raw [slang], **in the raw** [slang], *in puris naturalibus* [L], in a state of nature, in nature's garb; in one's birthday suit, **in the buff** *or* in native buff *or* stripped to the buff, **in the altogether** [all informal], with nothing on, without a stitch, without a stitch to one's name *or* back; **stark-naked,** bare-ass [slang], bare as the back of one's hand, naked as the day one was born, naked as a jaybird [informal], starkers [Brit informal], "naked as a worm" [Chaucer], "naked as a needle" [William Langland], "naked as my nail" [John Heywood], "in naked beauty more adorned" [Milton]; nudist, naturistic, gymnosophical.

.15 **barefoot,** unshod; discalced, discalceate.

.16 bare-ankled, bare-armed, bare-backed, bare-breasted, topless, bare-chested, barefaced, bare-handed, bare-headed, bare-kneed, bare-legged, bare-necked, barethroated.

.17 **hairless,** depilous, **bald,** acomous; bald as a coot, bald as an egg; **bald-headed,** baldpated, tonsured; **beardless,** whiskerless, shaven, clean-shaven, smooth-shaven, smooth-faced; smooth, glabrous.

.18 exuvial, sloughy; desquamative, exfoliatory; denudant *or* denudatory.

.19 ADVS nakedly, barely, baldly.

233. ENVIRONMENT

.1 NOUNS **environment, surroundings, environs,** ambience, entourage, circle, circumjacencies, circumambiencies, **circumstances,** environing circumstances, *alentours* [Fr]; **precincts,** ambit, purlieus, **milieu; neighborhood, vicinity,** vicinage; **suburbs** 183.1; outskirts, outposts, borderlands; periphery, perimeter, compass, circuit; **context, situation;** habitat 191; total environment, gestalt; ec(o)– *or* oec(o)– *or* oiko–.

.2 **setting, background,** backdrop, ground, field, scene, arena, theater, locale; back, rear, hinterland, distance; stage, stage setting, stage set, *mise-en-scène* [Fr].

.3 (surrounding influence or condition) **milieu, atmosphere, climate, air,** aura, spirit, feeling, feel, quality, sense, note, tone, overtone, undertone.

.4 (natural or suitable environment) **element,** medium; ecosystem, ecodeme, ecoclimate; ecology, autecology, synecology, bioecology *or* bionomics, zoo-ecology.

.5 **surrounding, encompassment,** environment, circumambience *or* circumambiency, circumjacence *or* circumjacency; containment, **enclosure** 236; **encirclement,** cincture, encincture, circumcincture, circling, girdling, girding; **envelopment,** enfoldment, embracement; circumposition; circumflexion; inclusion 76, involvement 176.

.6 VERBS **surround, environ,** compass, **encompass,** enclose, close; go round *or* around, compass about; **envelop,** enfold, lap, wrap, enwrap, embrace, enclasp, embosom, embay, involve, invest.

.7 **encircle, circle,** ensphere, belt, belt in, zone, cincture, encincture; **girdle,** gird, begird, engird; ring, band; loop; wreathe, wreathe *or* twine around.

.8 ADJS **environing, surrounding,** encompassing, enclosing; **enveloping,** wrapping, enfolding, embracing; **encircling,** circling; circumjacent, circumferential, circumambient, ambient; circumfluent, circumfluous; peripheral; circumflex; **roundabout,** suburban, neighboring.

.9 environmental, environal; **ecological.**

.10 surrounded, environed, compassed, **encompassed,** enclosed; **enveloped,** wrapped, enfolded, lapped, wreathed.

.11 encircled, circled, ringed, cinctured, encinctured, belted, girdled, girt, begirt, zoned.

.12 ADVS **around,** round, **about,** round about, in the neighborhood *or* vicinity, close, close about.

.13 all round, all about, on every side, on all sides, on all hands, right and left; amph(i)–, circum–, peri–.

234. CIRCUMSCRIPTION

.1 NOUNS **circumscription,** circumscribing, **bounding, demarcation,** delimitation, definition, determination, specification; limit-setting, inclusion-exclusion, circling-in *or* -out, encincture, boundary-marking.

.2 limitation, restriction, confinement 236.1, prescription, proscription, restrain, discipline, moderation, continence; qualification; bounds 235, boundary, limit 235.3.

.3 patent, copyright, certificate of invention, *brevet d'invention* [Fr]; trademark, registered trademark, trade name, service mark.

.4 VERBS **circumscribe, bound; mark off** *or* mark out, stake out, lay off, rope off; **demarcate,** delimit, delimitate, draw *or* mark boundaries, circle in *or* out, set the limit, mark the periphery; **define,** determine, fix, specify; surround 233.6; enclose 236.5.

.5 limit, restrict, restrain, bound, confine; straiten, narrow; specialize; stint; scant; **condition,** qualify, hedge about; draw the line, set an end point *or* stopping place; discipline, moderate, contain, **patent, copyright,** register.

.6 ADJS **circumscribed,** circumscript; ringed *or* circled *or* hedged about; **demarcated, delimited, defined,** definite, determined, determinate, specific, stated, set, fixed; surrounded 233.10, encircled 233.11.

.7 limited, restricted, bound, **bounded, finite; confined** 236.10, prescribed, proscribed, cramped, strait, straitened, narrow; conditioned, qualified; disciplined, moderated, patented, copyrighted.

.8 restricted, out of bounds, off limits.

.9 limiting, restricting, defining, confining; limitative, limitary, restrictive, definitive, exclusive.

.10 terminal, limital; limitable, terminable.

235. BOUNDS

.1 NOUNS **bounds, limits,** boundaries, limitations, **confines, pale,** marches, bourns, verges, edges, outlines, skirts, outskirts, **fringes,** metes, metes and bounds; periphery, **perimeter;** coordinates 490.6, parameters; compass, circumference, circumscription 234.

.2 outline, contour, *tournure* [Fr], delineation, lines, lineaments, shapes, figure, figuration, **configuration,** gestalt; features, main features; **profile,** silhouette; relief; skeleton, framework.

.3 boundary, bound, limit, limitation, extremity 56.5; delimitation, hedge, break *or* breakoff point, cutoff, cutoff point, terminus, term, deadline, target date, terminal date, time allotment; finish, **end** 70; start, starting line *or* point; **limiting factor,** determinant, limit *or* boundary condition; threshold, limen; upper limit, ceiling, high-water mark; lower limit, floor, low-water mark; **confine,** march, mark, bourn, mete, compass, circumscription; **boundary line, line, border line,** frontier, division line, interface, break boundary, line of demarcation *or* circumvallation.

.4 border, bordure, limbus, board, **edge,** limb, **verge, brink,** brow, **brim, rim, margin,** marge, skirt, **fringe,** cross(o)–, thysan(o)–, **hem,** list, selvage, side; sideline; shore, bank, coast; **lip,** labium, labrum, labellum, labio–, chil(o)– *or* cheil(o)–; flange; ledge; frame, enframement; featheredge; ragged edge.

.5 frontier, border, borderland, border ground, marchland, march, marches; outskirts, outpost; frontier post; iron curtain, bamboo curtain, Berlin wall; Pillars of Hercules; three-mile *or* twelve-mile limit.

.6 curb, kerb [Brit], curbing; border stone, curbstone, kerbstone [Brit], edgestone.

.7 edging, bordering, bordure, **trimming,** binding, skirting; fringe, fimbriation, fimbria; hem, selvage, list, welt; frill, frilling; beading, flounce, furbelow, galloon, motif, ruffle, valance.

.8 VERBS **bound,** circumscribe 234.4, surround 233.6, limit 234.5, enclose 236.5, divide, separate.

.9 **outline,** contour; **delineate** 654.12; silhouette, profile, limn.

.10 **border, edge, bound, rim, skirt, hem, fringe,** befringe, lap, list, margin, marge, marginate, march, verge, line, side; **adjoin** 200.9; **frame,** enframe, set off; trim, bind; purl; purfle.

.11 ADJS **bordering, fringing,** rimming, skirting; **bounding, boundary, limiting,** limit, determining or determinant or determinative; threshold, liminal, limbic; extreme, terminal 70.10; **marginal, borderline,** frontier; coastal, littoral.

.12 **bordered,** edged; margined, marged, marginate, marginated; **fringed,** befringed, trimmed, skirted, fimbriate, fimbriated, laciniate, laciniated.

.13 lipped, labial, labiate.

.14 outlinear, delineatory; peripheral, peripher(o)–, perimetric(al), circumferential; outlined, **in outline.**

.15 ADVS **on the verge, on the brink,** on the borderline, on the point, on the edge, on the ragged edge, at the threshold, at the limit or bound; **peripherally,** marginally, at the periphery.

.16 **thus far,** so far, thus far and no farther.

236. ENCLOSURE

.1 NOUNS **enclosure; confinement,** circumscription 234, immurement, walling- or hedging- or hemming- or boxing- or fencing-in; imprisonment, incarceration; siege, beleaguerment, blockade, blockading, cordoning, quarantine, besetment; inclusion 76; **envelopment** 233.5.

.2 **packaging, packing,** package; boxing, crating, encasement; canning, tinning [Brit]; bottling.

.3 (enclosed place) **enclosure** 236.12, close, confine, enclave, pale, paling, list, cincture; **pen, coop,** fold; **yard,** park, court, courtyard, curtilage, toft; square, quadrangle, quad [informal]; **field,** delimited field, **arena,** theater, ground; **container** 193.

.4 **fence** 236.13, boundary 235.3, **barrier; wall,** stone wall; rail, railing; balustrade, balustrading.

.5 VERBS **enclose,** close in, bound, include, **contain;** compass, encompass; **surround,** encircle 233.7; **shut** or **pen in,** coop in; **fence in,** wall in, rail in; **hem** or **hedge in,** box in, pocket; shut or coop or mew up; pen, coop, corral, cage, impound, mew; **imprison,** incarcerate, jail; **besiege,** beset, beleaguer, leaguer, cordon, cordon off, quarantine, blockade; yard, yard up;

house in; chamber; stable, kennel, shrine, enshrine; **wrap** 228.20.

.6 **confine, immure;** cramp, straiten, encase; cloister, closet, cabin, crib; entomb, coffin, casket; bottle up or in, box up or in.

.7 **fence, wall,** pale, rail, bar; hem, hedge; picket, palisade; bulkhead in.

.8 parenthesize, bracket.

.9 **package, pack, parcel;** box, box up, case, encase, crate, carton; can, tin [Brit]; bottle, jar, pot; barrel, cask, tank; sack, bag; basket, hamper; capsule, encyst.

.10 ADJS **enclosed,** closed-in; **confined, bound,** immured, cloistered, "cabined, cribbed, confined" [Shakespeare]; **imprisoned,** incarcerated, jailed; caged, cramped, restrained, corralled; besieged, beleaguered, leaguered, beset, cordoned, cordoned off, quarantined, blockaded; **shut-in,** pent-up, penned, cooped, mewed, walled- or hedged- or hemmed- or boxed- or fenced-in, fenced, walled, paled, railed, barred; hemmed, hedged.

.11 enclosing, confining, claustral, parietal, parieto–; surrounding 233.8; limiting 234.9.

.12 **enclosures**

bailey	henyard
barnyard	hutch
barton	keddah [India]
basecourt	kraal
box	manger
bullpen	paddock
cage	pasture
cattlefold	pigpen, pigsty
chicken coop	pinfold, penfold
chicken yard	polygon
close	pound
compound	quadrangle, quad
corral	rink
court	run
courtyard	runway
crib	sheepcote
croft	sheepfold
dog pound	shippen
dooryard	stall
enclave	stockyard
farmyard	sty
fold	toft
hen coop	yard

.13 **fences, walls**

barbed wire	palisade
board fence	parapet
contravallation, coun-	perpend wall
tervallation	picket fence
Cyclone fence	quickset hedge
dead wall	rail fence
dike	railing
espalier	rampart
garden wall	retaining wall
hedge, hedgerow	ring fence
hoarding	scarp wall
paling	stockade

stone wall	vallum
trellis	weir
vallation	zigzag fence

237. INTERPOSITION

(a putting or lying between)

.1 NOUNS interposition, interposure, interlocation, intermediacy, interjacence; **intervention**, intervenience, intercurrence, sandwiching; **intrusion** 238.

.2 interjection, **interpolation**, introduction, throwing- or tossing-in, **injection**, insinuation, intercalation, interlineation; **insertion** 304; interlocution, remark, parenthetical or side or incidental or casual remark, *obiter dictum* [L], aside, parenthesis; episode; infix, insert.

.3 interspersion, **interfusion**, interlardment, interpenetration.

.4 **intermediary**, intermedium, mediary, medium; link, **connecting link**, tie, connection, **go-between**, liaison; middleman, broker, agent, wholesaler, jobber, distributor; **mediator** 805.3.

.5 partition, **dividing wall**, division, separation, *cloison* [Fr]; septum, interseptum, septulum, dissepiment, sept(o)- or septi-; **wall, barrier**; panel; paries; brattice; bulkhead; diaphragm, midriff, midsection; dividing line, property line, party wall; **buffer, bumper**, fender, cushion, pad, shock pad, collision mat, mat; buffer state.

.6 VERBS interpose, interject, interpolate, intercalate, interjaculate; **intervene**; put between, sandwich; **insert in**, introduce in, insinuate in, inject in, implant in; **foist in,** fudge in, work in, drag in, lug in, drag or lug in by the heels, worm in, squeeze in, smuggle in, throw in, run in, thrust in, edge in, wedge in; **intrude** 238.5.

.7 intersperse, **interfuse**, interlard, interpenetrate; intersow, intersprinkle.

.8 **partition,** set apart, separate, divide; **wall off,** fence off; panel.

.9 ADJS interjectional, interpolative, intercalary; parenthetical, episodic.

.10 **intervening**, intervenient, **interjacent**, intercurrent; **intermediate**, intermediary, medial, mean, medium, mesne, median, middle, medi(o)-, mes(o)-; inter-, intra-.

.11 partitioned, walled; mural; septal, parietal.

.12 PREPS **between, betwixt**, 'twixt, betwixt and between [informal]; **among, amongst,** 'mongst; **amid, amidst,** mid, 'mid, midst, 'midst; in the midst of, in the thick of.

238. INTRUSION

.1 NOUNS **intrusion, obtrusion, interloping;** interposition 237, interposure, imposition, insinuation, **interference,** intervention, interruption, injection, interjection 237.2; **encroachment,** entrenchment, trespass, trespassing, unlawful entry 824.4; impingement, **infringement,** invasion, incursion, inroad, influx, irruption, infiltration; entrance 302.

.2 **meddling,** intermeddling; **butting-in** or kibitzing [both informal]; **meddlesomeness, intrusiveness, forwardness,** obtrusiveness; **officiousness,** impertinence, presumption, presumptuousness; inquisitiveness 528.1.

.3 **intruder, interloper, trespasser,** buttinsky [informal]; crasher or gate-crasher [both informal], unwelcome guest; invader, encroacher, infiltrator.

.4 **meddler,** intermeddler; **busybody, pry,** Paul Pry, prier, snoop or snooper, *yenta* [Yid], **kibitzer** [informal]; backseat driver.

.5 VERBS **intrude, obtrude, interlope;** come between, **interpose** 237.6, **intervene, interfere,** insinuate, impose; **encroach, infringe,** impinge, **trespass,** trench, entrench, invade, infiltrate; **break in upon,** break in, burst in, charge in, crash in, smash in, storm in; **barge in** [informal], irrupt, **cut in,** thrust in 304.7, push in, press in, rush in, throng in, crowd in, squeeze in, elbow in; **butt in** or **horn in** or chisel in or muscle in [all informal]; appoint oneself; crash or crash the gates [both informal]; creep in, steal in, sneak in, slink in, slip in; foist in, worm or work in, edge in, put in or shove in one's oar; **foist oneself upon,** thrust oneself upon; put on or upon, impose on or upon, put one's two cents in [informal].

.6 **interrupt, put in, cut in, break in;** chime in or chip in [both informal].

.7 **meddle, intermeddle,** busybody, not mind one's business; **meddle with, tamper with,** mix oneself up with, inject oneself into, monkey with, fool with or around with [informal], mess with or around with [informal]; **pry,** Paul-Pry, snoop, nose, **stick** or poke one's nose in, stick one's long nose into; have a finger in, have a finger in the pie; kibitz [informal].

.8 ADJS **intrusive, obtrusive, interfering,** intervenient, invasive, interruptive; xen(o)-.

.9 **meddlesome,** meddling; **officious,** overofficious, self-appointed, impertinent, presumptuous; **busybody,** busy; pushing, pushy, forward; **prying,** nosy *or* snoopy [both informal]; inquisitive 528.5.

.10 PHRS **none of your business;** what's it to you?, **mind your own business,** keep your nose out of this, butt out, go soak your head, go sit on a tack, go roll your hoop, go peddle your fish, go fly a kite, go chase yourself, go jump in the lake.

239. CONTRAPOSITION

(a placing over against)

.1 NOUNS contraposition, anteposition, posing against *or* over against; **opposition,** opposing, opposure; **antithesis,** contrast, ironic *or* contrastive juxtaposition; confrontment, **confrontation;** polarity, polar opposition, **polarization; contrariety** 15; contention 796; hostility 790.2.

.2 **opposites,** antipodes, polar opposites, contraries; **poles,** opposite poles, antipoles, counterpoles, North Pole, South Pole; antipodal points, antipoints; contrapositives, contraposita; night and day, black and white.

.3 opposite side, other side, the other side of the picture *or* coin, other face; **reverse, inverse, obverse, converse;** heads, tails (of a coin).

.4 VERBS contrapose, **oppose,** contrast, match, **set over against,** pose against *or* over against, put in opposition, set *or* pit against one another; **confront,** face, front, stand *or* lie opposite, stand opposed *or* vis-à-vis, be eyeball to eyeball, bump heads, meet head-on; counteract 790.3; contend 796.14; subtend; **polarize;** contraposit.

.5 ADJS contrapositive, **opposite,** opposing, **facing,** confronting, eyeball-to-eyeball, antithetic(al); **reverse, inverse, obverse, converse; antipodal;** polar, polarized, polaric; ant(i)– *or* anth–, cat(a)– *or* cath– *or* kat(a)–, co–, contra–, counter–, enantio–, ob–.

.6 ADVS **opposite,** poles apart, at opposite extremes; contrary, contrariwise, counter; just opposite, **face to face,** vis-à-vis, *front à front* [Fr], nose to nose, eyeball to eyeball [informal], back to back.

.7 PREPS **opposite to,** in opposition to, against, over against; versus, vs.; **facing, across, fronting,** confronting, **in front of;** toward.

240. FRONT

.1 NOUNS **front, fore,** forepart, forequarter, foreside, forefront, forehand; priority, anteriority; frontier; foreland; foreground, proscenium; frontage; front page; frontispiece; preface, front matter, foreword; prefix; front view, front elevation; **head,** heading; **face,** façade, frontal; false front, window dressing, display; front man; bold *or* brave front, brave face; facet; facia; obverse (of a coin or medal), head (of a coin); lap.

.2 **vanguard,** van, point, **spearhead,** advance guard, **forefront,** avant-garde, outguard; scout, pioneer; precursor 66; front-runner; front, line, front line, battle line, front rank, first line, first line of battle; **outpost,** farthest outpost; **bridgehead,** beachhead, airhead, railhead.

.3 **prow,** prore, **bow, stem,** rostrum, figurehead, nose, beak; bowsprit, jib boom; forecastle, forepeak; foredeck.

.4 **face,** facies, **visage,** prosop(o)–; physiognomy, phiz *or* dial [both informal]; **countenance,** features, lineaments, favor; mug *or* mush *or* pan *or* kisser *or* map *or* puss [all slang].

.5 **forehead, brow.**

.6 **chin,** mentum, mento–, point of the chin, button [slang].

.7 VERBS be *or* stand in front, **lead, head,** head up; come to the front, take the lead, forge ahead; be the front-runner, pioneer.

.8 **confront, front,** affront, **face,** envisage; **meet, encounter,** breast, stem, brave, meet squarely, meet face to face *or* eyeball to eyeball, come face to face with, look in the face; **confront with, face with,** bring face to face with, tell one to one's face, cast *or* throw in one's teeth, present to, **put** *or* **bring before,** set *or* place before, lay before; bring up, bring forward; put it to, put it up to; **challenge,** dare, defy.

.9 **front on, face upon, give upon,** face *or* look toward, look out upon, look over, **overlook.**

.10 ADJS **front, frontal, anterior; fore, forward,** forehand; **foremost, headmost, leading,** first, chief, head, prime, primary; ante–, anti–, ep(i)– *or* eph–, fore–, fronto–, genio–, pre–, pro–, pros–.

.11 **fronting, facing,** opposing, eyeball-to-eyeball.

.12 ADVS **before, ahead,** out *or* up ahead, **in front,** in the front, in the lead, in the van, in advance, **in the forefront**, in the foreground; **to the fore**, to the front; foremost, headmost, first; before one's face *or* eyes, under one's nose.

.13 **frontward**, frontwards, **forward**, forwards, vanward, **headward**, headwards, **onward**, onwards; **facing** 239.7.

241. REAR

.1 NOUNS **rear, rear end, hind end**, hind part, hinder part, afterpart, rearward, **posterior, behind**, breech, stern, tail, tail end; **afterpiece**, tailpiece, heelpiece, heel; **back**, back side, reverse (of a coin *or* medal), tail (of a coin); back door, postern, postern door; back seat, rumble seat; hindhead, occiput, occipit(o)–.

.2 rear guard, rear, rear area.

.3 **back**, dorsum, dors(o)– *or* dorsi–, not(o)–, tergum, ridge; dorsal region, lumbar region; hindquarter; loin, lumb(o)–.

.4 **buttocks, rump**, hips, posterior, derrière, pyg(o)–; croup, crupper; podex; haunches; gluteal region; nates; **butt**, rear, rear end, backside, hind end, behind [all informal].

.5 [slang terms] **ass**, arse, **can**, cheeks, nether cheeks, stern, tail, rusty-dusty, bum, **fanny**, prat, keister, tuchis *or* tushy *or* tush.

.6 **tail**, cauda, caudation, caudal appendage, cerc(o)–, caud(o)– *or* caudi–, ur(o)–, –urus; tailpiece, brush (of a fox), fantail (of fowls); rattail, rat's-tail; dock, stub; **queue, cue, pigtail**.

.7 **stern**, heel; poop, counter, fantail, tail end; sternpost, rudderpost.

.8 VERBS (be behind) **bring up the rear**, come last, **follow**, come after; trail, trail behind, lag behind; fall behind, fall back, fall astern; **back up, back**, go back, go backwards, regress 295.5, retrogress; revert 146.4.

.9 ADJS **rear**, rearward, **back**, backward, retrograde, **posterior**, postern, tail; after *or* aft; **hind, hinder; hindmost**, hindermost, hindhand, posteriormost, **aftermost**, aftmost, rearmost; meta–, opisth(o)–, post–, postero–, rere–, retro–, supra–.

.10 (anatomy) posterial, dorsal, retral, tergal, lumbar, gluteal, sciatic, occipital.

.11 **tail**, caudal, caudate, caudated, tailed; taillike, caudiform, –cercal, –urous *or* –ourous.

.12 backswept, swept-back.

.13 ADVS **behind, in the rear, in back of**; in the background; behind the scenes; behind one's back; back to back; tandem.

.14 **after**; aft, abaft, baft, astern.

.15 **rearward**, rearwards, to the rear, **hindward**, hindwards, **backward**, backwards, posteriorly, retrad, tailward, tailwards.

242. SIDE

.1 NOUNS **side, flank, hand**; laterality, sidedness, handedness; unilaterality, bilaterality, etc., multilaterality, many-sidedness; border 235.4; bank, shore, coast; siding, planking; beam; broadside; quarter; hip, haunch; cheek, mel(o)–, jowl, chop; temple; profile, side-view, half-face view.

.2 **lee side, lee**, leeward; lee shore; lee tide; lee wheel, lee helm, lee anchor, lee sheet, lee tack.

.3 **windward side, windward**, windwards, weather side, weather, weatherboard; weather wheel, weather helm, weather anchor, weather sheet, weather tack, weather rail, weather bow, weather deck; weather roll; windward tide, weather-going tide, windward ebb, windward flood.

.4 VERBS **side, flank**; edge, skirt, border 235.10.

.5 **go sideways, sidle**, lateral, lateralize, **edge**, veer, skew, sidestep; go crabwise; sideslip; skid; make leeway.

.6 ADJS **side, lateral**, later(o)– *or* lateri–, pleur(o)– *or* pleuri–, ali–; flanking, skirting; next-beside; **sidelong**, sideling, **sidewise**, sideway, **sideways**, sideward, **sidewards**, glancing; leeward, lee; windward, weather; par(a)–.

.7 **sided**, flanked, –stichous; handed; lateral, –hedral; **one-sided**, unilateral; **two-sided**, bilateral, dihedral, bifacial; **three-sided**, trilateral, trihedral, triquetrous; **four-sided**, quadrilateral, tetrahedral, etc.; **many-sided**, multilateral, polyhedral.

.8 ADVS **laterally**, laterad; **sideways**, sideway, **sidewise**, sidewards, sideward, sideling, sidling, sidelong, aside, crabwise; **edgeways**, edgeway, **edgewise; askance**, askant, asquint, glancingly; broadside, **broadside on**, on the beam; on its side, on its beam-ends; on the other hand; right and left.

.9 **leeward**, to leeward, alee, downwind; **windward**, to windward, weatherward, aweather, upwind.

.10 **aside**, on one side, **to one side**, to the side, on the side, sidelong; nearby, in juxtaposition 200.20,21; away.

.11 PREPS **beside, alongside, abreast**, abeam, by, on the flank of, along by, **by the side of**, along the side of.

.12 PHRS **side by side**, cheek to cheek, cheek

by cheek, cheek by jowl, shoulder to shoulder, yardarm to yardarm.

243. RIGHT SIDE

.1 NOUNS **right side, right, right hand,** right-hand side, off side (of a horse or vehicle), starboard; Epistle side, decanal side; recto (of a book); right field; starboard tack; right wing; right-winger, conservative, reactionary.

.2 **rightness,** dextrality; dexterity, **right-handedness;** dextroversion, dextrocularity, dextroduction; dextrorotation, dextrogyration.

.3 right-hander; righty [informal].

.4 ADJS **right, right-hand,** dextral, dexter, dextr(o)–; off, **starboard;** dextrorse; dextropedal; dextrocardial; dextrocerebral; dextrocular; **clockwise,** dextrorotary, dextrogyrate, dextrogyratory; right-wing, right-wingish, conservative, reactionary.

.5 **right-handed,** dextromanual, dexterous *or* dextrous.

.6 **ambidextrous,** ambidextral, ambidexter; dextrosinistral, sinistrodextral.

.7 ADVS **rightward,** rightwards, rightwardly, **right, to the right,** dextrally, dextrad; on the right, dexter; starboard, astarboard.

244. LEFT SIDE

.1 NOUNS **left side, left, left hand,** left-hand side, wrong side [informal], near *or* nigh side (of a horse or vehicle), portside, port, larboard; Gospel side, cantorial side, verso (of a book); port tack; left wing, left-winger, radical, liberal.

.2 **leftness,** sinistrality, **left-handedness;** sinistration; levoversion, levoduction; levorotation, sinistrogyration.

.3 **left-hander, southpaw** *or* lefty [both informal].

.4 ADJS **left, left-hand,** sinister, sinistral, lev(o)– *or* laev(o)–; near, nigh; **larboard, port;** sinistrorse; sinistrocerebral; sinistrocular; **counterclockwise,** levorotatory, sinistrogyrate; left-wing, left-wingish, radical, liberal.

.5 **left-handed,** sinistromanual, sinistral, southpaw [slang].

.6 ADVS **leftward,** leftwards, leftwardly, **left, to the left,** sinistrally, sinister, sinistrad; on the left; larboard, port, aport.

245. STRUCTURE

.1 NOUNS **structure, construction,** architecture, tectonics, architectonics, frame, make, **build,** fabric, tissue, warp and woof *or* weft, web, weave, texture, con-texture, mold, shape, pattern, plan, fashion, arrangement, **organization,** organism, organic structure, **constitution, composition;** makeup, getup [informal], setup; **formation,** conformation, format; making, building, creation, production, forging, fashioning, molding, fabrication, manufacture, shaping, structuring, patterning; anatomy, physique; form 246.

.2 **structure, building, edifice, construction,** construct, erection, establishment, architecture, fabric; house 191.6; tower, pile, pyramid, skyscraper; prefabrication, prefab, packaged house; superstructure.

.3 **understructure,** understruction, underbuilding, **substructure,** substruction.

.4 **frame,** framing; **framework, skeleton,** fabric, cadre, chassis, shell; lattice, latticework; sash, casement, case, casing; window case *or* frame, doorframe; picture frame.

.5 **skeleton,** skelet(o)–, anatomy, **carcass,** frame, **bones;** endoskeleton, exoskeleton; axial skeleton, appendicular skeleton.

.6 **bone,** ossicle; osse(o)– *or* ossi– *or* oste(o)–, –ost, –osteon; cartilage, chondr(o)– *or* chondri–; tendon, ligament 206.2.

.7 (science of structure) **anatomy;** morphology, geomorphology, promorphology; tectology; histology; zootomy, anthropotomy; organology, organography; myology, myography; splanchnology, splanchnography; angiology, angiography; osteology, osteography; morphologist, anatomist, histologist.

.8 VERBS **construct** 167.10, structure.

.9 ADJS **structural,** formal, morphological, edificial, tectonic, textural; anatomic(al), organic, organismal; **architectural,** architectonic; constructional; superstructural, substructural.

.10 skeleton, skeletal.

.11 **bone,** osteal; **bony,** osseous, ossiferous; ossicular; ossified.

.12 bones

aitchbone	cranium
anklebone	cuboid
anvil	edgebone
astragalus	ethmoid bone
backbone	femur
breastbone	fibula
calcaneus	floating rib
cannon bone	frontal bone
carpal, carpus	funny bone
cheekbone	hallux
chine	hammer
clavicle	haunch bone
coccyx	heel bone
collarbone	hipbone
costa	humerus

hyoid bone	radius
ilium	rib
incus	sacrum
inferior maxillary	scaphoid
innominate bone	scapula
ischium	sesamoid bones
jawbone	shinbone
kneecap	shoulder blade
kneepan	skull
malleus	sphenoid
mandible	spinal column
mastoid	spine
maxilla	stapes
maxillary	sternum
metacarpal, metacar-	stirrup
pus	talus
metatarsal, metatarsus	tarsal, tarsus
nasal bone	temporal bone
occipital bone	thighbone
parietal bone	tibia
patella	ulna
pelvis	vertebra
phalanx, phalanges	vertebral column
[pl]	vomer
pubis	wishbone
rachidial	wristbone
rachis	zygomatic bone

246. FORM

.1 NOUNS **form, shape, figure**; figuration, **configuration**; formation, **conformation**; **structure** 245; **build**, make, frame; makeup, format, layout; cut, set, stamp, type, turn, cast, mold, impression, pattern, matrix, model, mode, modality; archetype, prototype 25.1–6, Platonic form or idea; style, fashion; aesthetic form, inner form, significant form; art form, genre; morph(o)–, –morph, –morphism or –morphy.

.2 **contour**, *tournure* [Fr], *galbe* [Fr]; broad lines, silhouette, profile, **outline** 235.2.

.3 **appearance** 446, lineaments, features.

.4 (human form) **figure, form**, shape, frame, anatomy, **physique**, build, body-build, person; body 376.3.

.5 **forming, shaping**, molding, modeling, fashioning; **formation**, efformation, formature, conformation, figuration; sculpture; morphogeny, morphogenesis; creation 167.3; –plasis.

.6 [gram terms] form, morph, allomorph, morpheme; morphology, morphemics.

.7 VERBS **form**, formalize, **shape, fashion**, tailor, frame, figure, efform, **lick into shape**; work, knead; set, fix; **forge**, dropforge; **mold**, model, sculpt or sculpture; cast, found; thermoform; stamp, mint; carve, cut, chisel, hew; roughhew, roughcast, rough out, block out, lay out, hammer or knock out; create 167.10.

.8 (be formed) **form**, shape, **shape up, take shape**; materialize.

.9 ADJS **formative**, formal, formational, plastic, morphotic; morphogen(et)ic; –form or –iform, –morphic or –morphous.

.10 [biol terms] plasmatic, plasmic, protoplasmic, plastic, metabolic.

.11 [gram terms] morphologic(al), morphemic.

247. FORMLESSNESS

.1 NOUNS **formlessness, shapelessness**; amorphousness, amorphism, amorphia; **chaos,** confusion, messiness, orderlessness; **disorder** 62; entropy; anarchy 740.2; **indeterminateness, indefiniteness**, indecisiveness, vagueness, mistiness, haziness, fuzziness, blurriness, unclearness, obscurity.

.2 unlicked cub, diamond in the rough.

.3 VERBS **deform, distort** 249.5; unform, unshape; disorder, jumble, mess up, muddle, confuse; obfuscate, obscure, fog up, blur.

.4 ADJS **formless, shapeless**, featureless, characterless, nondescript, inchoate, lumpen, blobby or baggy [both informal], inform; amorphous, amorphic, amorph(o)–; **chaotic, orderless**, disorderly 62.13, unordered, unorganized, confused, anarchic 740.6; kaleidoscopic; **indeterminate, indefinite**, undefined, indecisive, vague, misty, hazy, fuzzy, blurred or blurry, unclear, obscure.

.5 **unformed, unshaped**, unshapen, unfashioned, unlicked; uncut, unhewn.

248. SYMMETRY

.1 NOUNS **symmetry**, symmetricalness, **proportion**, proportionality, **balance**, equilibrium; **regularity**, uniformity 17, evenness; equality 30; finish; harmony, congruity, consistency, conformity 82, correspondence, keeping; eurythmy, eurythmics; dynamic symmetry; bilateral symmetry, trilateral symmetry, etc., multilateral symmetry; parallelism, polarity; shapeliness.

.2 symmetrization, regularization, balancing, harmonization; evening, equalization; coordination, integration.

.3 VERBS symmetrize, regularize, **balance**, harmonize; **proportion**, proportionate; even, even up, equalize; coordinate, integrate.

.4 ADJS **symmetric(al)**, sym–, **balanced**, proportioned, eurythmic, harmonious; **regular**, uniform 17.5, even, equal 30.7; coequal, coordinate, equilateral; **well-balanced**, well-set, well-set-up [informal]; finished.

.5 **shapely, well-shaped, well-proportioned,** well-made, **well-formed,** well-favored; comely 900.17; trim, neat, clean, clean-cut.

249. DISTORTION

.1 NOUNS **distortion,** detorsion, torsion, **contortion, crookedness,** tortuosity; **asymmetry,** unsymmetry, disproportion, lopsidedness, imbalance, irregularity, **deviation; twist,** quirk, turn, screw, wring, wrench, wrest; warp, buckle; knot, gnarl; anamorphosis, anamorphism.

.2 **perversion, corruption,** misdirection, misrepresentation, misinterpretation, misconstruction, false coloring; slanting, straining, torturing; misuse 667.

.3 **deformity,** deformation, **malformation,** malconformation, monstrosity, teratology, freakishness, misproportion, misshape; **disfigurement, defacement;** mutilation, truncation; humpback, hunchback, crookback, camelback, kyphosis [med]; swayback, lordosis [med]; wryneck, torticollis [med]; clubfoot, talipes [med], flatfoot, splayfoot; knock-knee; bowlegs; valgus [med]; harelip; cleft palate.

.4 **grimace, wry face,** wry mouth, rictus, snarl; moue, mow, pout.

.5 VERBS **distort, contort,** turn awry; **twist,** turn, screw, wring, wrench, wrest; writhe; warp, buckle, crumple; knot, gnarl; **crook,** bend, spring.

.6 **pervert, garble, put a false construction upon, give a false coloring,** color, varnish, slant, strain, torture; **bias;** misrepresent, misconstrue, misinterpret, misrender, misdirect; misuse 667.4.

.7 **deform,** misshape, disproportion; **disfigure, deface;** mutilate, truncate; blemish, mar.

.8 **grimace, make a face,** make a wry face *or* wry mouth, pull a face, **screw up one's face,** mug [slang], mouth, make a mouth, mop, mow, mop and mow; pout.

.9 ADJS distortive, contortive, contortional, torsional.

.10 **distorted, contorted, warped, twisted, crooked,** plect(o)–, strepsi–, strept(o)–, stroph(o)–; tortuous, labyrinthine, buckled, sprung, bent, bowed; cockeyed [informal], crazy; crunched, crumpled; unsymmetric(al), asymmetric(al), as– *or* asym–, nonsymmetric(al); irregular, deviative, anamorphous; one-sided, lopsided; askew 219.14.

.11 **perverted, twisted, garbled,** slanted, doctored, biased, cooked; strained, tortured; misrepresented, misquoted.

.12 **deformed, malformed, misshapen,** misbegotten, misproportioned, ill-proportioned, ill-made, ill-shaped, **out of shape;** dwarfed, stumpy; bloated; **disfigured,** defaced, blemished, marred; mutilated, truncated; grotesque, monstrous; swaybacked, round-shouldered; bowlegged, bandy-legged, bandy; knock-kneed; rickety, rachitic; club-footed, talipedic; flatfooted, splayfoot(ed), pigeon-toed; pug-nosed, snub-nosed, simous.

.13 **humpbacked, hunchbacked,** bunchbacked, crookbacked, crookedbacked, camelback, humped, gibbous, kyphotic [med].

250. STRAIGHTNESS

.1 NOUNS **straightness,** directness, unswervingness, lineality, **linearity,** rectilinearity; verticalness 213; flatness, horizontalness 214.

.2 **straight line,** straight, right line, direct line, –trix; straight course *or* stretch, straightaway; **beeline,** air line; **shortcut** 203.5; great-circle course; streamline; edge, side, diagonal, secant, transversal, chord, tangent, perpendicular, normal, segment, directrix, diameter, axis, radius, vector, radius vector [all math].

.3 **straightedge, rule,** ruler; square, T square, triangle.

.4 VERBS be straight, have no turning; arrow; go straight 289.11.

.5 **straighten, set** *or* **put straight,** rectify; **unbend,** unkink, uncurl, unsnarl, disentangle 45.5; straighten up, stand *or* sit up; straighten out, extend; flatten, smooth 214.6.

.6 ADJS **straight,** orth(o)–, rect(i)–; straightlined, dead straight, straight as an edge *or* ruler, ruler-straight, even, right, true, straight as an arrow, arrowlike; **rectilinear,** rectilineal; **linear,** lineal, in a line; **direct, undeviating, unswerving,** unbending, undeflected; **unbent, unbowed,** unturned, uncurved, undistorted; **uninterrupted, unbroken;** streamlined; straight-side, straight-front, straight-cut; upright, vertical 213.11; flat, level, smooth, horizontal 214.7.

.7 ADVS **straight,** straightly, on the straight, unswervingly, undeviatingly, **directly** 290.24; straight to the mark; down the alley *or* down the pipe *or* in the groove *or* on the beam [all informal].

159

251. ANGULARITY

.1 NOUNS **angularity**, angularness, crookedness, hookedness; orthogonality, right-angledness, right-angularity, rectangularity; flection, flexure.

.2 **angle**, –gon, goni(o)–, point, bight; vertex, apex 211.2, –ace; **corner**, quoin, coin, nook; **crook, hook,** crotchet; **bend,** swerve, veer, inflection, deflection; ell, L; cant; furcation, bifurcation, fork 299.4; zigzag, zig, zag; chevron; elbow, knee, dogleg [informal]; crank.

.3 (angular measurement) goniometry; trigonometry.

.4 (instruments) goniometer, radiogoniometer; pantometer, clinometer, graphometer, astrolabe; azimuth compass, azimuth circle; theodolite, transit theodolite, transit, transit instrument, transit circle; sextant, quadrant; bevel, bevel square; protractor, bevel protractor.

.5 VERBS **angle, crook, hook, bend,** elbow; crank; angle off or away, swerve, veer, go off on a tangent; furcate, bifurcate, branch, fork 299.7; zigzag, zig, zag.

.6 ADJS **angular,** ang–, anguli– or angulo–; cornered, **crooked, hooked, bent,** akimbo; knee-shaped, geniculate, geniculated; crotched, Y-shaped, V-shaped; furcate, furcal, forked 299.10; sharp-cornered, **sharp, pointed;** zigzag, jagged, serrate, sawtooth or saw-toothed.

.7 **right-angled, rectangular,** right-angular, right-angle; **orthogonal,** orthodiagonal, orthometric; **perpendicular,** normal.

.8 **triangular, trilateral,** trigonal, oxygonal, deltoid, trigon(o)–, hastato–; wedge-shaped, cuneiform, cuneate, cuneated, sphen(o)–.

.9 **quadrangular, quadrilateral,** quadrate, quadriform; **rectangular, square,** quadr(i)– or quadru–; foursquare, orthogonal; tetragonal, tetrahedral; **oblong;** trapezoid(al), rhombic(al), rhomboid(al), rhomb(o)–; **cubic(al),** cubiform, cuboid, cube-shaped, cubed, diced, cub(o)– or cubi–; rhombohedral, trapezohedral.

.10 pentagonal, hexagonal, heptagonal, octagonal, decagonal, dodecagonal, etc.; pentahedral, hexahedral, octahedral, dodecahedral, icosahedral, etc., –hedral.

.11 multilateral, multiangular, polygonal; polyhedral, pyramidal, pyramidic(al), pyramid(o)–; prismatic, prismoid.

.12 angles

acute angle	obtuse angle
oblique angle	reentering angle
reflex angle	solid angle
right angle	spherical angle
salient angle	straight angle

.13 angular geometric figures

acute-angled triangle	polygon
cube	polyhedron
cuboid	prism
cusp	prismoid
decagon	pyramid
dodecagon	quadrangle
dodecahedron	quadrant
equilateral triangle	quadrature
foursquare	quadrilateral
frustum of a pyramid	rectangle
gnomon	rhombohedron
heptagon	rhombus, rhomb,
hexagon	rhomboid
hexahedron	right-angled triangle,
hypercube	right triangle
icosahedron	scalene triangle
isosceles triangle	square
oblong	trapezium, trapeze
obtuse-angled triangle	trapezohedron
octagon	trapezoid
octahedron	tetragon
oxygon	tetragram
parallelepiped, parallelepipedon	tetrahedroid
	tetrahedron
parallelogram	triangle
pentagon	trigon
pentahedron	trilateral
Platonic body	truncated pyramid

252. CURVATURE

.1 NOUNS **curvature,** curving, curvity, curvation; incurvature, incurvity, incurvation; excurvature, excurvation; decurvature, decurvation; recurvature, recurvity, recurvation; rondure; **arching, vaulting,** arcuation, concameration; aduncity, aquilinity, crookedness, hookedness; sinuosity, sinuousness, tortuosity, tortuousness; circularity 253; convolution 254; rotundity 255; convexity 256; concavity 257.

.2 **curve,** curvi–, sinus; **bow, arc; crook, hook;** parabola, hyperbola; ellipse; caustic, catacaustic, diacaustic; catenary, festoon; conchoid; lituus; tracery; circle 253.2; curl 254.2.

.3 **bend,** bending; **bow,** bowing, oxbow; **turn,** turning, sweep, meander, hairpin turn or bend, S-curve, U-turn; **flexure,** flex, **flection,** conflexure, inflection, deflection; reflection; geanticline, geosyncline; trop(o)–, –tropy, –trope.

.4 **arch, span, vault,** vaulting, concameration, camber; ogive; apse; **dome,** cupola, geodesic dome, igloo, concha; cove; arched roof, ceilinged roof; **arcade, archway,** arcature; voussoir, keystone, skewback.

.5 **crescent, semicircle,** scythe, sickle, meniscus; crescent moon, half-moon; lunula, lunule; horseshoe.

.6 VERBS **curve, turn,** sweep; **crook, hook,** loop; incurve, incurvate; recurve, decurve, bend back, retroflex; sag, swag [dial]; **bend,** flex; deflect, inflect; reflect, reflex; **bow,** embow; **arch,** vault; dome; **hump,** hunch; wind, curl 254.4,5; round 255.6.

.7 ADJS **curved,** curve, curvate, curvated, **curving,** curvy, curvaceous [informal], curvesome, curviform; curvilinear, curvilineal; wavy, undulant, billowy, billowing; sinuous, tortuous, serpentine, mazy, labyrinthine, meandering; **bent;** incurved, incurving, incurvate, incurvated; recurved, recurving, recurvate, recurvated; geosynclinal, geanticlinal; –clastic, –tropic or –trophic; cyrt(o)–, sphing(o)–.

.8 **hooked, crooked, aquiline,** aduncous; **hook-shaped,** hooklike, uncinate, unciform; hamulate, hamate, hamiform; clawlike, unguiform, down-curving; **hooknosed,** beak-nosed, parrot-nosed, aquiline-nosed, Roman-nosed, crooknosed, crookbilled; **beaked,** billed; **beak-shaped,** beak-like; bill-shaped, bill-like; rostrate, rostriform, rhamphoid.

.9 turned-up, upcurving, upsweeping, retroussé.

.10 **bowed,** embowed, bandy; bowlike, bow-shaped, oxbow, Cupid's bow; **convex** 256.12, **concave** 257.16, convexoconcave; arcuate, arcuated, arcual, arciform, arc-like; **arched,** vaulted; **humped,** hunched, humpy, hunchy; gibbous, gibbose; humpbacked 249.13; tox(o)– or toxi–.

.11 **crescent-shaped,** crescentlike, crescent, crescentic, crescentiform; meniscoid(al), menisciform; S-shaped, sigmoid; **semicircular,** semilunar; horn-shaped, hornlike, horned, corniform; bicorn, two-horned; sickle-shaped, sickle-like, falcate, falciform; moon-shaped, moonlike, lunar, lunate, lunular, luniform; Cynthian; selen(o)– or seleni–.

.12 lens-shaped, lenticular, lentiform.

.13 parabolic(al), saucer-shaped; elliptic(al), ellipsoid; bell-shaped, bell-like, campanular, campanulate, campaniform.

.14 pear-shaped, pearlike, pyriform, obconic(al).

.15 heart-shaped, heartlike; cordate, cardioid, cordiform.

.16 kidney-shaped, kidneylike, reniform.

.17 turnip-shaped, turniplike, napiform.

.18 shell-shaped, shell-like; conchate, conchiform.

.19 shield-shaped, shieldlike, peltate; scutate, scutiform; clypeate, clypeiform.

.20 helmet-shaped, helmetlike, galeiform, cassideous.

.21 **arches**

fixed arch	rampant arch
flat arch	round arch
four-centered or	rowlock arch
Tudor arch	segmental arch
horseshoe arch	shouldered arch
lancet arch	three-centered or bas-
ogee arch	ket-handle arch
primitive arch	trefoil arch

253. CIRCULARITY

(simple circularity)

.1 NOUNS **circularity, roundness,** annularity, annulation.

.2 **circle,** circus, **ring,** annulus, O; **circumference,** radius; **round,** roundel, rondelle; **cycle, circuit;** orbit 375.16; cycl(o)–, gyr(o)–; closed circle or arc; vicious circle, eternal return; magic circle, fairy ring; logical circle; wheel 322.4,18; disk, discus, saucer, disc(o)– or disci–; **loop,** looplet; noose, lasso; crown, diadem, coronet, corona; garland, chaplet, wreath; halo, glory, areola, aureole, stephano–; annular muscle, sphincter.

.3 (thing encircling) **band, belt** 231.65, **cincture,** cingulum, **girdle, girth,** girt, zone, zon(o)–, fascia, fillet; collar, collarband, neckband; necklace, bracelet, armlet, wristlet, wristband, anklet; ring, earring, nose ring, finger ring, dactylio–; hoop; quoit; zodiac, ecliptic, equator, great circle.

.4 **rim,** felly; **tire,** pneumatic tire, balloon tire, tubeless tire, safety tire, nonskid tire, bias tire, belted bias tire, radial tire, belted radial tire, white sidewall tire, winter tire, snow tire, studded tire; retreaded tire, retread.

.5 circlet, **ringlet,** roundlet, annulet, eye, **eyelet,** grommet.

.6 oval, ovule, ovoid; ellipse.

.7 cycloid; epicycloid, epicycle; hypocycloid; lemniscate; cardioid; Lissajous figure.

.8 **semicircle,** half circle, hemicycle; crescent 252.5; quadrant, sextant, sector.

.9 **round,** canon; rondo, rondino, rondeau, rondelet.

.10 VERBS **circle, round;** orbit; **encircle** 233.7, surround, encompass, girdle.

.11 ADJS **circular, round,** rounded, circinate, annular, annulate or annulose, ring-shaped, ringlike; disklike, discoid; cyclic(al), cycloid(al); coronary, crownlike.

.12 **oval,** ovate, ovoid, oviform, egg-shaped, obovate [bot], ov(o)– or ovi–.

254. CONVOLUTION

(complex circularity)

.1 NOUNS **convolution,** involution, circumvolution, **winding, twisting, turning; meander, meandering;** crinkle, crinkling; circuitousness, circumlocution, circumbendibus, circumambages, ambagiousness, ambages; tortuousness, tortuosity, tortility; torsion, intorsion; sinuousness, **sinuosity,** sinuation, slinkiness; anfractuosity; snakiness; flexuousness, flexuosity; undulation, wave, waving; rivulation.

.2 **coil, whorl,** roll, **curl,** curlicue, ringlet, **spiral,** helix, volute, volution, involute, evolute, gyre, scroll; **kink, twist, twirl;** screw, corkscrew; tendril, cirrus; whirl, swirl, vortex; gyr(o)–, helic(o)–, spir(o)– or spiri–, spondyl(o)–, verticill–.

.3 curler, curling iron; curlpaper, papillote.

.4 VERBS convolve, **wind, twine,** twirl, **twist, turn, twist and turn, meander,** crinkle; serpentine, snake, slink, worm; screw, corkscrew; whirl, swirl, whorl; scallop; wring; intort; contort.

.5 **curl, coil;** crisp, kink, crimp.

.6 ADJS **convolutional, winding, twisting,** twisty, **turning; meandering,** meandrous, mazy, labyrinthine; **serpentine,** snaky, anfractuous; roundabout, circuitous, ambagious, circumlocutory; **sinuous,** sinuose, sinuate; **tortuous,** torsional, tortile; flexuous, flexuose; involutional, involute, involuted; rivose, rivulose; sigmoid(al); wreathy, wreathlike; ruffled, whorled.

.7 **snakelike, snaky,** snake-shaped, **serpentine,** serpentile, serpentoid, serpentiform; anguine [archaic], anguiform; eellike, eel-shaped, anguilliform; wormlike, vermiform, lumbriciform.

.8 **spiral,** spiroid, volute, voluted; helical, helicoid(al); anfractuous; screw-shaped, corkscrew, corkscrewy; verticillate, whorled, scrolled; cochlear, cochleate; turbinal, turbinate.

.9 **curly,** curled; **kinky,** kinked; **frizzly,** frizzy, frizzed; crispy, crisp, crisped.

.10 **wavy, undulatory,** undulative, undulant, undulating, undulate, undulated; **billowy,** billowing, surgy, rolling.

.11 ADVS **windingly, twistingly,** sinuously, tortuously, serpentinely, meanderingly, meandrously; **in and out,** round and round.

255. SPHERICITY, ROTUNDITY

.1 NOUNS **sphericity, rotundity, roundness,** rotundness, orbicularity, **sphericalness,** sphericality, globularity, globosity; spheroidity, spheroidicity; belly; cylindricality; convexity 256.

.2 **sphere,** spher(o)– or sphaer(o)–, –sphaera; **ball, orb,** orbit, **globe,** rondure; geoid; spheroid, globoid, ellipsoid, oblate spheroid, prolate spheroid; spherule, globule, globelet, orblet; glomerulus, glomerul(o)–; **pellet;** boll; bulb, bulbil, bulblet, bulb(o)–; knob, knot; gob, blob, gobbet, bolus; **balloon,** bladder, bubble.

.3 **drop,** droplet; dewdrop, raindrop, teardrop; bead, pearl.

.4 **cylinder,** cylindroid, cylindr(o)–; pillar, column; barrel, drum, cask; pipe, tube; roll, rouleau, roller, rolling pin; bole, trunk.

.5 **cone,** conoid, conelet, con(o)– or coni–; complex cone, cone of a complex; funnel; ice-cream cone, cornet [Brit]; pine cone; cop.

.6 VERBS **round,** rotund; **round out, fill out;** cone.

.7 **ball, snowball;** sphere, spherify, globe, conglobulate; bead; balloon, mushroom.

.8 ADJS **rotund, round,** rounded, rounded out, round as a ball; bellied, bellylike; convex 256.12, bulging 256.14.

.9 **spheric(al),** spheriform, spherelike, sphere-shaped; **globular, global,** globed, globous, globose, globate, globelike, globe-shaped; orbic(al), orbicular, orbiculate, orbed, orb, orby, orblike; spheroid(al), globoid, ellipsoid(al); hemispheric(al); bulbous, bulblike; ovoid, obovoid [bot].

.10 **beady,** beaded, bead-shaped, bead-like.

.11 **cylindric(al),** cylindroid(al); **columnar,** columnal, columned, columelliform; tubular, tube-shaped; barrel-shaped, drum-shaped.

.12 **conic(al),** coned, cone-shaped, conelike; conoid(al); spheroconic; funnel-shaped, funnellike, funnelled, funnelform, infundibuliform, infundibular; turbinato–.

.13 **balls**

ball bearing	eight ball
baseball	football
basketball	golf ball
billiard ball	handball
bowling ball, bowl	meatball
cannonball	medicine ball
clew	mothball
cricket ball	pinball
croquet ball	Ping-Pong ball
cue ball	polo ball

pushball
rubber ball
skittle ball
snowball
soccer ball
softball

tea ball
tennis ball
tetherball
volleyball
whiffle ball

.14 pellets

BB
bead
buckshot
bullet
grapeshot
marble 878.16

pea
pearl
pebble
pill
shot

256. CONVEXITY, PROTUBERANCE

.1 NOUNS **convexity,** convexness, convexedness; excurvature, excurvation; camber; gibbousness, gibbosity; tuberousness, tuberosity; bulging, bellying.

.2 protuberance or protuberancy, **projection, protrusion, extrusion;** prominence, eminence, salience, boldness, bulging, bellying; gibbousness, gibbosity; excrescence or excrescency; tuberousness, tuberosity; salient; relief, high relief, *altorilievo* [Ital], low relief, bas-relief, *bassorilievo* [Ital], embossment.

.3 bulge, bilge, bow, convex; **bump;** thankyou-ma'am, cahot [Can]; hill 207.5, mountain 207.7; **hump,** hunch; **lump,** clump, bunch, blob [informal]; nubbin, nubble, nub; **mole,** nevus [med]; **wart,** papilloma, verruca [med]; **knob,** boss, bulla, button, bulb; stud, jog, joggle, peg, dowel; flange, lip; tab, ear, flap, loop, ring, handle 216.27; **knot,** knur, knurl, gnarl, burl, gall; **ridge,** rib, cost(o)– or costi–, chine, spine, shoulder; welt, wale; blister, bleb, vesicle [anat], blain; bubble; condyle, condyl(o)–, style, styl(o)– or styli–, tyl(o)–; tubercle or tubercule, tubercul(o)–.

.4 swelling, swell, swollenness, edema; **rising, lump, bump,** pimple, papulo–; pock, furuncle, boil, carbuncle; corn; pustule; dilation, dilatation; turgidity, turgescence or turgescency, tumescence, intumescence; tumor, tumidity, tumefaction; wen, cyst, sebaceous cyst; bunion; distension 197.2.

.5 node, nodule, nodulus, nodulation, nodosity.

.6 breast, bosom, bust, chest, crop, brisket; thorax, thorac(o)– or thoraci–, stern(o)–, steth(o)–; pigeon breast; **breasts;** tits or titties or boobs or boobies or bubbies or jugs or headlights or knockers or knobs [all slang]; *nénés* [Fr slang]; bazoom [slang]; teat, tit or titty or mamma [all slang]; dug; **nipple,** papilla, pap [dial],

mammilla, *mamelon, teton* [both Fr]; mammillation, mamelonation; mammary gland, udder, bag.

.7 nose, nas(o)– or nasi–, rhin(o)–, olfactory organ; **snout,** rhynch(o)–, **snoot** [informal], nozzle [slang], **muzzle; proboscis,** antlia, **trunk; beak,** rostrum, rhamph(o)–, rostr(o)– or rostri–; **bill** or pecker [both slang]; nib, neb; smeller or beezer or bugle or schnozzle or schnoz or schnozzola or conk [all slang]; muffle, rhinarium; nostrils, noseholes [Brit dial], nares.

.8 (point of land) **point,** hook, spur, **cape,** tongue, bill; **promontory,** foreland, **headland,** head, mull [Scot]; naze, ness; **peninsula,** chersonese; **delta; spit,** sandspit; **reef,** coral reef; breakwater 216.4.

.9 VERBS **protrude, protuberate, project, extrude; stick out,** jut out, poke out, stand out, shoot out; **stick up,** bristle up, start up, cock up, shoot up.

.10 bulge, bilge, bouge [dial], **belly,** bag, balloon, **pouch,** pooch [dial]; pout; **goggle,** bug [dial], pop; **swell, dilate, distend,** billow; swell out, **belly out,** round out.

.11 emboss, boss, chase, raise; ridge.

.12 ADJS **convex,** convexed; excurved, excurvate, excurvated; bowed, out-bowed, arched 252.10; gibbous, gibbose; humped 252.10; rotund 255.8.

.13 protruding, protrusive, protrudent; **protuberant,** protuberating; **projecting, extruding,** jutting, outstanding; prominent, eminent, salient, bold; prognathous; excrescent, excrescential; protrusile, emissile.

.14 bulging, swelling, distended, bloated, potbellied, bellying, pouching; bagging, baggy; rounded, hillocky, hummocky, moutonnée; billowing, billowy, bosomy, ballooning, pneumatic; **bumpy,** bumped; bunchy, bunched; **bulbous,** bulbose; warty, verrucose, verrucated.

.15 bulged, bulgy; swollen 197.13, turgid, tumid, turgescent, tumescent, tumorous; bellied, ventricose; pouched, pooched [dial]; goggled, goggle; exophthalmic, bug-eyed [slang], popeyed [informal].

.16 studded, knobbed, knobby, knoblike, nubbled, nubby, nubbly, torose; **knotty, knotted; gnarled,** knurled, knurly, burled, gnarly; noded, nodal, nodiform; noduled, nodular; nodulated; tuberculous, tubercular; tuberous, tuberose.

.17 in relief, in bold or high relief, bold, raised, *repoussé* [Fr]; chased, bossed, embossed, bossy.

.18 pectoral, thoracic; pigeon-breasted; **mammary, mammillary,** mammiform; mammalian, mammate; papillary, papillose, papulous; breasted, bosomed, chested; teated, titted [slang], nippled.

.19 **peninsular**; deltaic, deltal.

257. CONCAVITY

.1 NOUNS **concavity, hollowness**; incurvature, incurvation, incurvity; depression, impression.

.2 **cavity,** concavity, concave; **hollow,** hollow shell, shell; **hole, pit, depression, dip,** sink, fold [Brit]; scoop, pocket; **basin,** trough, **bowl,** punch bowl, cup; **crater;** antrum, antr(o)–; sinus, sinu– or sino–; lacuna; alveola, alveolus, alveolation, alveol(o)–; vug [min]; follicle, crypt; armpit; socket; funnel chest or breast.

.3 **pothole, sinkhole,** pitchhole, chuckhole, **mudhole, rut** 263.1.

.4 **pit, well, shaft,** bothr(o)–; **chasm, gulf, abyss,** abysm; **excavation,** dig, diggings, workings; mine, quarry 383.6.

.5 **cave, cavern,** cove [Scot], hole, grotto, grot, antre, subterrane; lair 191.26; **tunnel, burrow,** warren; subway 272.13; bunker, foxhole, dugout, abri [Fr]; sewer.

.6 **indentation,** indent, indention, indenture, **dent,** dint; gouge, **furrow** 263; sunken part or place, **dimple; pit,** pock, pockmark; impression, impress; imprint, print; alveolus, alveolation; honeycomb; **notch** 262.

.7 **recess,** recession, **niche, nook,** inglenook, corner; cove, alcove; bay; pitchhole.

.8 (hollow in the side of a mountain) combe, cwm, cirque, corrie.

.9 **valley, vale, dale, dell,** dingle; **glen,** bottom, bottoms, bottom glade, intervale, strath [Scot], gill [Brit], wadi, grove; trench, trough, lunar rill; gap, pass, ravine 201.2.

.10 **excavator, digger;** sapper; **miner** 383.9; tunneler, sandhog or groundhog [both informal]; driller; steam shovel, navvy [Brit]; dredge, dredger.

.11 **excavation,** digging; mining; indentation, **engraving** 578.2.

.12 VERBS (be concave) **dish,** cup, bowl, hollow; retreat, retire; incurve.

.13 **hollow,** hollow out, concave, dish, cup, bowl; cave, cave in.

.14 **indent, dent,** dint, **depress,** press in, stamp, tamp, punch, punch in, impress, imprint; **pit;** pock, pockmark; dimple; **recess,** set back; set in; **notch** 262.4; engrave 578.10.

.15 **excavate, dig,** dig out, **scoop,** scoop out, **gouge,** gouge out, grub, shovel, spade,

dike, delve, scrape, scratch, scrabble; dredge; **trench,** trough, furrow, groove; **tunnel, burrow;** drive [min], sink, lower; **mine,** sap; quarry; drill, bore.

.16 ADJS **concave,** concaved, **incurved,** incurving, incurvous, –coelous; **sunk,** sunken; retreating, retiring; **hollow,** hollowed; palmshaped; dish-shaped, dished, dishing, dishlike, bowl-shaped; bowllike, cratershaped, craterlike, saucer-shaped; spoonlike; **cupped,** cup-shaped, scyphate, scyph(o)– or scyphi–; funnel-shaped, infundibular, infundibuliform; funnel-chested, funnel-breasted; boat-shaped, boatlike, navicular, naviform, cymbiform, scaphoid, scaph(o)–; **cavernous,** cavelike.

.17 **indented, dented,** depressed; **dimpled; pitted;** pocked, pockmarked; honeycombed, alveolar, alveolate, faveolate; **notched** 262.5; **engraved** 578.12.

258. SHARPNESS

.1 NOUNS **sharpness, keenness, edge;** acuteness, acuity; **pointedness,** acumination; thorniness, prickliness, spinosity, mucronation; acridity 433.1.

.2 (sharp edge) **edge,** cutting edge, knifeedge, razor-edge, featheredge; edge tool 348.2,13; weapon 801.21–25.

.3 **point** 258.18, **tip,** cusp; acumination, mucro; **nib,** neb; needle 223.8, acu–; **drill,** borer, auger, bit; **prick, prickle;** sting, aculeus.

.4 (pointed projection) **projection,** spur, jag, **snag,** snaggle; **tooth,** fang; crag, peak, arête; spire, steeple, flèche; **cog, sprocket,** ratchet; sawtooth; harrow, rake; comb, pecten, cten(o)–, pectin(i)–.

.5 **tooth,** dent(o)– or denti–, odont(o)–, **fang, tusk,** tush, scrivello; denticulation, denticle, dentil, dent, dentition; snag, snaggletooth, peg; bucktooth, gagtooth or gang tooth [both dial]; pivot tooth; cuspid, bicuspid; canine tooth, canine, dogtooth, eyetooth; molar, grinder, myl(o)–; premolar; incisor, cutter, fore tooth; wisdom tooth; milk tooth, baby tooth, deciduous tooth; permanent tooth; gold tooth; crown.

.6 **teeth,** dentition, ivories [informal]; **denture,** false teeth, set of teeth, **plate, bridgework,** dental bridge, uppers and lowers; gums, periodontal tissue, alveolar ridge, gingiv(o)–, ulo–.

.7 **thorn, bramble, brier, nettle,** burr, prickle, sticker [informal]; **spike,** spikelet, spicule, spiculum; **spine;** bristle; quill; **needle,** pine needle; **thistle,** catchweed, cleavers, goose grass, cactus; beggar's-lice, beggar's-ticks; yucca, Adam's-needle; acanth(o)–, echin(o)–.

.8 VERBS come or taper to a point, acuminate; prick, sting, stick, bite; be keen, have an edge, cut; bristle with.

.9 sharpen, edge, acuminate, aculeate, spiculate, taper; whet, hone, oilstone, file, grind; strop, strap; set, reset; point, cuspidate; barb, spur.

.10 ADJS sharp, oxy–, keen, edged, acute, acuto– or acuti–, fine, cutting, knifelike; sharp-edged, keen-edged, razor-edged, knife-edged, featheredged, sharp as broken glass; acrid 433.6; two-edged, double-edged; sharp as a razor or needle or tack, "sharp as a two-edged sword" [Bible], "sharper than a serpent's tooth" [Shakespeare]; sharpened, set.

.11 pointed, acuminate, acuate, aculeate, mucronate, acute, unbated; tapered, tapering; cusped, cuspidate; sharp-pointed; needlelike, needle-sharp, needle-pointed, needly, acicular, aculeiform; toothed, –dentate; spiked, spiky, spiculate; barbed, tined, pronged; horned, horny, cornuted, corniculate, cornified; spined, spiny, spinous, hispid, acanthoid, acanthous, "like quills upon the fretful porpentine" [Shakespeare].

.12 prickly, pricky [informal], muricate, echinate, acanaceous, aculeolate; pricking, stinging; thorny, brambly, briery, thistly; bristly.

.13 arrowlike, arrowy, arrowheaded; sagittal, sagittate, sagittiform.

.14 spearlike, hastate; lancelike, lanciform, lanceolate, lanceolar; spindle-shaped, fusiform.

.15 swordlike, gladiate, ensate, ensiform; xiph(o)– or xiphi–.

.16 toothlike, dentiform, dentoid, odontoid; dental; molar; bicuspid; toothed, toothy, fanged, tusked; snaggle-toothed, snaggled.

.17 star-shaped, starlike, star-pointed.

.18 points

antler	dibble
awl	fid
barb	fishhook
barblet	fork
barbule	gaff
barbwire, barbed wire	gaffle
bodkin	gimlet
bradawl	goad
caltrop	harpoon
carpet tack	hat pin
cheval-de-frise, chevaux-de-frise	hook
	horn
cockspur	icepick
lance	skewer
lancet	spearhead
marlinespike	spicule
nail	spiculum
oxgoad	spike
pike	spine
pin	spit
pitchfork	spur
prong	staple
punch	tack
quill	thumbtack
rowel	tine, tang [Scot]

.19 sharpeners

Carborundum	oilstone
emery	rubstone
emery wheel	steel
file	strap, strop
grindstone	whetrock
hone	whetstone
novaculite	whittle

259. BLUNTNESS

.1 NOUNS bluntness, dullness, unsharpness, obtuseness, obtundity; bluffness; abruptness; flatness; toothlessness, lack of bite or incisiveness.

.2 VERBS blunt, dull, disedge, retund, obtund, take the edge off; turn, turn the edge or point of; weaken, repress; draw the teeth or fangs; bate.

.3 ADJS blunt, dull, obtuse; bluntish, dullish; unsharp, unsharpened; unedged, edgeless; rounded, faired, smoothed; unpointed, pointless; blunted, dulled; blunt-edged, dull-edged; blunt-pointed, dull-pointed, blunt-ended; bluff, abrupt; ambly(o)–.

.4 toothless, teethless, edentate, edental, biteless.

260. SMOOTHNESS

.1 NOUNS smoothness, flatness, levelness, evenness, uniformity, regularity; sleekness, glossiness; slickness, slipperiness, lubricity, oiliness, greasiness, frictionlessness; silkiness, satininess, velvetiness; glabrousness, glabriety; downiness; suavity 936.5.

.2 polish, gloss, glaze, burnish, shine, luster, finish; patina.

.3 (smooth surface) smooth, plane, level, flat; tennis court, bowling alley or green, billiard table or ball; slide; glass, ice; marble, alabaster, ivory; silk, satin, velvet; mahogany.

.4 smoother, smooth; roller, lawn-roller; sleeker, slicker; polish, burnish; abrasive, abradant.

.5 VERBS smooth, flatten, plane, planish, level, even, equalize; dress, dub, dab; smooth down or out, lay; plaster, plaster down; harrow, drag; grade; mow, shave; lubricate, oil, grease.

.6 press, hot-press, **iron, mangle,** calender; roll.

.7 polish, shine, burnish, furbish, sleek, slick, slick down, gloss, glaze, glance, luster; **rub,** scour, **buff;** wax, varnish; finish.

.8 grind, file, sand, sandpaper, emery, pumice; sandblast.

.9 ADJS **smooth,** lio– *or* leio–, liss(o)–; smooth-textured *or* -surfaced, **even, level, plane, flat,** regular, uniform, **unbroken;** unrough, unroughened, unruffled, unwrinkled; glabrous, glabrate, glabrescent; downy; smooth as a billiard ball *or* a baby's ass; leiotrichous, lissotrichous; smooth-shaven 232.17; suave 936.18.

.10 sleek, slick, glossy, shiny, gleaming; silky, silken, satiny, velvety; **polished,** burnished, furbished; buffed, rubbed, finished; varnished, lacquered, shellacked, glazed, *glacé* [Fr]; **glassy,** smooth as glass.

.11 slippery, slippy, **slick,** slithery [informal], sliddery [dial], slippery as an eel; lubricious, lubric, oily, greasy, buttery, soaped; lubricated, oiled, greased.

.12 ADVS **smoothly, evenly,** regularly, uniformly; **like clockwork,** on wheels.

.13 smoothers

buff	mangle
buffer	plane 348.17
burnisher	planisher
calender	polisher
chamois	press
drag	presser
electric iron	roller
flatiron	rolling pin
floor polisher	sadiron
floor sander	sander
glazer	smoothing iron
goose	steamroller
grader	trouser press
harrow	trowel 348.16
hot press	waxer
iron	wringer
ironing board	

.14 polishes, abrasives

aluminum oxide	pumice
auto polish	pumice stone
colcothar	quartz sand
corundum	rasp
crocus	rottenstone
emery	rouge
emery board	sandpaper
emery paper	scouring pad
ferric oxide	shoe polish
file	silicon carbide
furniture polish	silver polish
garnet	tripoli
jeweler's rouge	wax
nail file	

261. ROUGHNESS

.1 NOUNS **roughness, unsmoothness, unevenness,** irregularity, ununiformity, nonuniformity 18, inequality, harshness, asperity; **ruggedness,** rugosity; **jaggedness,** raggedness, cragginess, scraggliness; joltiness, bumpiness; rough air, turbulence; choppiness; tooth; granulation; hispidity, bristliness, spininess; nubbiness, nubbliness.

.2 (rough surface) **rough,** broken ground; broken water, chop, lop; **corrugation,** ripple, washboard; washboard *or* corduroy road, corduroy; gooseflesh, goose bumps, goose pimples, horripilation; sandpaper.

.3 bristle, barb, barbel, striga, setule, setula, seta, seti–; **stubble.**

.4 VERBS **roughen,** rough, rough up; coarsen; granulate; gnarl, knob, stud, boss; pimple, horripilate.

.5 ruffle, wrinkle, corrugate, crinkle, crumple, **rumple; bristle; rub the wrong way,** go against the grain, set on edge.

.6 ADJS **rough, unsmooth,** trachy–; **uneven,** ununiform, unlevel, inequal, **broken,** irregular, textured; jolty, **bumpy,** rutty, rutted, pitted, pocky, potholed; horripilant, pimply; **corrugated,** ripply, wimpled; **choppy;** ruffled, unkempt; **shaggy,** shagged; **coarse,** rank, unrefined; unpolished; rough-grained, coarse-grained, cross-grained; grainy, granulated; rough-hewn, rough-cast; homespun, linsey-woolsey.

.7 rugged, ragged, harsh; rugose, rugous, wrinkled, crinkled, crumpled, corrugated; **jagged,** jaggy; **snaggy,** snagged, snaggled; scraggy, scragged, scraggly; sawtooth, sawtoothed, serrate, serrated; **craggy,** cragged; **rocky,** gravelly, stony; rockbound, ironbound.

.8 gnarled, gnarly; **knurled,** knurly; **knotted,** knotty, knobby, knobbly, nodose, nodular, studded, lumpy.

.9 bristly, bristling, bristled, hispid, hirsute, barbellate, glochidiate, setaceous, setous, setose; strigal, strigose, strigate, studded; **stubbled,** stubbly; hairy 230.24.

.10 bristlelike, setiform, aristate, setarious.

.11 ADVS **roughly,** rough, in the rough; **unsmoothly,** brokenly, **unevenly,** irregularly, raggedly, choppily, jaggedly.

.12 cross-grained, against the grain, the wrong way.

262. NOTCH

.1 NOUNS **notch, nick,** nock, **cut,** cleft, incision, **gash,** hack, blaze, scotch, **score,** kerf, crena, depression, jag; jog, joggle; **indentation** 257.6.

.2 notching, serration, serrulation; denticulation, dentil, dentil band, dogtooth; crenation, crenelation, crenulation; scallop; rickrack; picot edge, Vandyke edge; deckle edge; cockscomb, crest; saw, saw teeth, pri– *or* prion(o)–.

.3 battlement, crenel, merlon, embrasure, castellation, machicolation.

.4 VERBS **notch, nick, cut, incise, gash,** slash, chop, crimp, scotch, **score,** blaze, jag, scarify; **indent** 257.14; scallop, crenellate, crenulate, machicolate; serrate, pink, mill, knurl, tooth, picot, Vandyke.

.5 ADJS **notched, nicked,** incised, gashed, scotched, scored, chopped, blazed; **indented** 257.17; serrate, serrated, serrulated, serrato–; crenate, crenated, crenulate, crenellated, battlemented, embrasured; scalloped; dentate, dentated, toothed; **saw-toothed,** sawlike; lacerate, lacerated; **jagged,** jaggy; erose.

263. FURROW

.1 NOUNS **furrow, groove,** scratch, crack, cranny, chase, chink, score, **cut,** gash, striation, streak, stria, **gouge,** slit, incision; sulcus, sulcation; **rut,** ruck [dial], wheeltrack, well-worn groove; wrinkle 264.3; **corrugation;** flute, fluting; rifling; chamfer, bezel, rabbet, dado; microgroove; **engraving** 578.2.

.2 trench, trough, channel, ditch, dike, fosse, **canal,** cut, gutter, kennel [Brit]; moat; sunk fence, ha-ha; aqueduct 396.2; entrenchment 799.5; canalization; pleat, crimp, goffer.

.3 VERBS **furrow, groove,** score, scratch, incise, cut, carve, chisel, gash, striate, streak, gouge, slit, crack; plow; rifle; **channel, trough, flute,** chamfer, rabbet, dado; **trench,** canal, canalize, **ditch,** dike, gully, **rut; corrugate;** wrinkle 264.6; pleat, crimp, goffer; **engrave** 578.10.

.4 ADJS **furrowed, grooved,** scratched, scored, incised, cut, gashed, gouged, slit, striated; **channeled, troughed, fluted,** chamfered, rabbeted, dadoed; rifled; sulcate, sulcated; canaliculate, canaliculated; **corrugated,** corrugate; corduroy, corduroyed, **rutted,** rutty; wrinkled 264.8, pleated, crimped, goffered; **engraved** 578.12; ribbed, costate.

264. FOLD

.1 NOUNS **fold, double,** doubling, duplicature; ply; plication, plica, plicature; flec-

tion, flexure; **crease,** creasing; crimp; **tuck, gather;** ruffle, frill, ruche, ruching; flounce; lappet; lapel; dog-ear.

.2 pleat, plait, plat [dial]; accordion pleat, box pleat, knife pleat.

.3 wrinkle, corrugation, ridge, **furrow, crease,** rivel, crimp, ruck, **pucker,** cockle; **crinkle,** crankle, rimple, ripple, wimple; crumple, rumple; crow's-feet.

.4 folding, creasing, infolding, infoldment *or* enfoldment; plication, plicature; paper-folding, *origami* [Jap].

.5 VERBS **fold,** infold *or* enfold, **double,** ply, plicate; fold over, double over, lap over, turn over *or* under; **crease, crimp;** crisp; **pleat, plait, plat** [dial]; **tuck, gather;** ruffle, ruff, frill; flounce; twill, quill, flute; dog-ear; interfold.

.6 wrinkle, corrugate, shirr, ridge, **furrow, crease,** crimp, crimple, cockle, cocker, **pucker, purse; knit,** knot; ruck, ruckle; **crumple,** rumple; **crinkle,** rimple, ripple, wimple.

.7 ADJS **folded, doubled;** plicate, plicated; **pleated,** plaited; **creased,** crimped; tucked, gathered; flounced, ruffled; twilled, quilled, fluted; dog-eared; foldable, folding, flexible, pliable, plicatile.

.8 wrinkled, wrinkly; corrugated, corrugate; **creased,** rucked, **furrowed** 263.4, ridged; cockled, cockly; puckered, puckery; pursed, pursy; knitted, knotted; rugged, rugose, rugous; **crinkled,** crinkly, cranklety [dial], rimpled, rippled; crimped, crimpy; **crumpled,** rumpled.

265. OPENING

.1 NOUNS **opening, aperture, hole,** hollow, **cavity** 257.2, **orifice,** –trema, –pyle, –stome; slot, split, crack, check, leak; opening up, unstopping, uncorking, clearing, throwing open, laying open, broaching; passageway 657.4; inlet 302.5; outlet 303.9; **gap,** gape, yawn, hiatus, lacuna, gat, space, interval; **chasm, gulf;** cleft 201.2; fontanel; foramen, fenestra; stoma; pore, poro–; fistula; **disclosure** 556.

.2 gaping, yawning, oscitation, oscitancy, dehiscence, pandiculation; **gape, yawn;** the gapes.

.3 perforation, penetration, piercing, empiercement, **puncture,** goring, boring, puncturing, punching, pricking, lancing, broach, transforation, terebration; acupuncture, acupunctuation; trephining, trepanning; **impalement,** skewering, fixing, transfixion, transfixation; bore, borehole, drill hole; trypan(o)–, –tresia, –nyx-is.

.4 (holes) armhole; bullet-hole, bunghole, keyhole, knothole, loophole, manhole, mousehole, peephole, pigeonhole, pinhole, porthole, punch-hole; placket, placket hole, tap, vent, venthole, air hole, blowhole, spiracle; eye, eyelet, eye of a needle; grommet, cringle, gasket, loop, guide; deadeye.

.5 mouth, oro– or ori–, stomat(o)–, stom(o)–, –stoma, –stomum; maw, oral cavity, gob [dial], gab [Scot]; muzzle, jaw, lips, embouchure; bazoo or kisser or mug or mush or trap or yap [all slang]; jaws, mandibles, chops, chaps, jowls, maxilla, maxill(o)– or maxilli–, geny(o)–, premaxilla.

.6 anus; asshole or bumhole or bunghole [all slang]; bung.

.7 door, doorway 302.6; entrance, entry 302.5.

.8 window, casement; porthole, port, portlight; bull's-eye, œil-de-bœuf [Fr]; casement window; bay window, bow window, bay, window bay, oriel, lancet window, rose window, dormer; picture window; louver window; grille, wicket, lattice; fanlight, fan window; skylight, lantern; transom; windowpane, window glass, pane, light.

.9 porousness, porosity; sievelikeness, cribriformity, cribrosity; screen, sieve, strainer, colander, riddle, cribble, net; honeycomb; sponge.

.10 permeability, perviousness.

.11 opener; can opener, tin opener [Brit]; corkscrew, bottle screw, bottle opener, church key [informal]; latchstring; key, clavis, cleid(o)–; latchkey; passkey, passepartout [Fr], master key, skeleton key; open sesame.

.12 VERBS open, ope, open up; lay open, throw open; fly open, spring open, swing open; tap, broach; cut open, cut, cleave, split, slit, crack, chink, fissure, crevasse, incise; rift, rive; tear open, rent, tear, rip; part, dispart, separate, divide, divaricate; spread, spread out.

.13 unclose, unshut; unfold, unwrap, unroll; unstop, unclog, unblock, clear, unfoul, free, deobstruct; unplug, uncork; unlock, unlatch, undo; unseal, unclench, unclutch; uncover, uncase, unsheathe, unveil, undrape, uncurtain; disclose 556.4, expose, reveal, bare, patefy, manifest.

.14 make an opening, find an opening, make place or space, make way, make room.

.15 breach, rupture; break open, force or pry or prize open, crack or split open, rip or tear open; break into, break through; break in, burst in, bust in [informal], stave or stove in, cave in.

.16 perforate, pierce, empierce, penetrate, puncture, punch, prick, bite, hole; tap, broach; stab, stick, pink, run through; transfix, transpierce, fix, impale, spit, skewer; gore, spear, lance, spike, needle; bore, drill, auger; ream, ream out, countersink, gouge, gouge out; trepan, trephine; punch full of holes, riddle, honeycomb.

.17 gape, gap [dial], yawn, oscitate, dehisce, hang open.

.18 ADJS open, unclosed, uncovered; unobstructed, unstopped, unclogged; clear, cleared, free; wide-open, unrestricted; disclosed 555.10; bare, exposed, unhidden 555.11, naked, bald.

.19 gaping, yawning, oscitant, slack-jawed, openmouthed; dehiscent, ringent; agape, ajar.

.20 apertured, slotted, holey; pierced, perforated, perforate; honeycombed, like Swiss cheese, riddled, criblé [Fr], shot through, peppered; windowed, fenestrated.

.21 porous, porose; sievelike, cribose, cribriform; spongy, spongelike; percolating, leachy.

.22 permeable, pervious, penetrable, openable, accessible.

.23 mouthlike, oral, orificial; mandibular, maxillary.

.24 INTERJS open up!, open sesame!, gangway!, passageway!, make way!

266. CLOSURE

.1 NOUNS closure, closing, shutting, shutting up, occlusion, occlus(o)–, –clisis or –cleisis; shutdown; blockade.

.2 imperviousness, impermeability, impenetrability, impassability; imperforation.

.3 obstruction, clog, block, blockade, sealing off, blockage, strangulation, choking, choking off, stoppage, stop, bar, barrier, obstacle, impediment; congestion, jam; gorge; constipation, obstipation, costiveness; infarct, infarction; embolism, embolus; bottleneck; blind alley, blank wall, dead end, cul-de-sac, impasse; cecum, blind gut 225.4.

.4 stopper, stop, stopple, stopgap; plug, cork, bung, spike, spill, spile, tap, faucet, spigot, valve, check valve, cock, sea cock, peg, pin; lid 228.5.

.5 stopping, **wadding, stuffing,** padding, **packing,** tampon; gland; gasket.

.6 VERBS **close, shut,** occlude; close up, shut up, contract, constrict, strangle, choke, choke off, squeeze shut, fold, fold up; **fasten,** secure; **lock,** lock up, lock out, key, padlock, latch, bolt, bar, barricade; **seal,** seal up, seal off; plumb; button, button up; snap; zipper, zip up; batten, batten down; put or slap the lid on, **cover;** contain; shut the door, slam, clap, bang.

.7 **stop,** stop up; **obstruct, bar,** stay; **block,** block up; **clog,** clog up, foul; **choke,** choke up or off; **fill,** fill up; **stuff,** pack, jam; **congest,** stuff up; **plug,** plug up; stopper, stopple, **cork,** bung, spile; cover; **dam,** dam up; stanch, stench [Scot]; chink; caulk; blockade; constipate, obstipate, bind.

.8 **shut up shop,** close shop, **close up** or **down,** shut up, **shut down,** shutter, put up the shutters; cease 144.6.

.9 ADJS **closed, shut, unopen,** unopened, cleisto– or clisto–; unvented, unventilated; contracted, constricted, choked, choked off, squeezed shut, strangulated; blank; blind, cecal, dead; dead-end, blind-alley.

.10 **unpierced,** pierceless, **unperforated,** imperforate, intact; **untrodden,** pathless, wayless, trackless.

.11 **stopped, stopped up; obstructed,** infarcted, **blocked; plugged,** plugged up; **clogged,** clogged up; foul, fouled; **choked,** choked up; **full, stuffed,** packed, jammed; **congested,** stuffed up; constipated, obstipated, costive, bound.

.12 **close, tight, compact,** fast, shut fast, **snug,** staunch, firm; **sealed;** hermetic(al), hermetically sealed; airtight, dusttight or dustproof, gastight or gasproof, lighttight or lightproof, oiltight or oilproof, raintight or rainproof, smoketight or smokeproof, stormtight or stormproof, watertight or waterproof, windtight or windproof; water-repellant or -resistant.

.13 **impervious, impenetrable, impermeable; impassable,** unpassable; unpierceable, unperforable; **punctureproof,** nonpuncturable, holeproof.

267. MOTION

(motion in general)

.1 NOUNS **motion,** moto–; **movement, moving, move,** stir, unrest, restlessness; going, running, stirring; **activity** 707; kinesis, kinetics, kinematics, –kinesia, kin–, kine–

or kino–, kinesi(o)–, kinet(o)–; dynamics; kinesiatrics, kinesipathy, kinesitherapy; **actuation,** motivation; mobilization; **velocity** 269.1,2.

.2 **course, career,** set, **passage, progress,** trend, **advance,** forward motion, traject, trajet, **flow,** flux, flight, **stream, current,** run, rush, onrush, ongoing; drift, driftage; backward motion, **regression,** retrogression, sternway, backing; backflowing, reflowing, refluence, reflux, ebbing, subsiding; downward motion, **descent,** descending, sinking, plunging; upward motion, mounting, climbing, rising, **ascent,** ascending, soaring; oblique motion; sideward motion; radial motion, angular motion, axial motion; random motion, Brownian movement.

.3 **mobility, motivity,** motive power, motility, movableness; **locomotion;** motorium.

.4 **rate, gait, pace,** tread, step, stride, clip or lick [both informal]; **travel** 273, **progress,** career.

.5 VERBS **move, budge, stir;** go, run, flow, stream; **progress,** advance; **back,** back up, regress, retrogress; ebb, subside, wane; **descend,** sink, plunge; **ascend,** mount, rise, climb, soar; go sideways, go round or around, circle, rotate, gyrate, spin, whirl; travel 273.17; move over, get over; shift, change, shift or change place.

.6 **set in motion, move, actuate,** motivate, push, shove, nudge, **drive,** impel, propel; mobilize.

.7 ADJS **moving, stirring, in motion;** transitional; **mobile,** motive, motile, motor; motivational, impelling, propelling, propellant, driving; traveling 273.35; **active** 707.17; moto–, phoro–, plan(o)–, zo(o)–.

.8 **flowing,** fluent, passing, streaming, flying, **running, going, progressive,** rushing; drifting; **regressive,** retrogressive, back, **backward;** back-flowing, refluent, reflowing; descending, sinking, plunging, **downward,** down-trending; ascending, mounting, rising, soaring, **upward,** up-trending; sideward; **rotary,** rotatory, rotational; axial, gyrational, gyratory.

.9 ADVS **under way,** under sail, on one's way, on the go or move or fly or run or march, **in motion, astir;** from pillar to post.

268. QUIESCENCE

(being at rest; absence of motion)

.1 NOUNS **quiescence** or quiescency, **stillness,** silence 451, quietness, **quiet,** quietude, "lucid stillness" [T. S. Eliot]; **calmness,** restfulness, **peacefulness,** imperturbability, "wise passiveness" [Wordsworth], placidness, **placidity, tranquillity, serenity, peace, composure;** quietism, contemplation, satori, nirvana, ataraxy or ataraxia; **rest,** stato–; **repose,** silken repose, statuelike or marmoreal repose; sleep, slumber.

.2 **motionlessness, immobility; inactivity,** inaction; fixity, fixation 142.2,3.

.3 **standstill, stand,** stillstand; **stop, halt, cessation** 144; dead stop, dead stand, full stop; deadlock, lock, dead set; running or dying down, subsidence, waning, ebbing, wane, ebb.

.4 **inertness, dormancy; inertia,** vis inertiae; passiveness, passivity; suspense, abeyance, latency; torpor, apathy, indifference, indolence, lotus-eating, languor; **stagnation,** stagnancy, **vegetation,** stasis; deathliness, deadliness; catalepsy, catatonia; entropy.

.5 **calm, lull,** lull or calm before the storm; dead calm, flat calm, oily calm, windlessness, deathlike calm; doldrums, horse latitudes; anticyclone.

.6 **airlessness, closeness, oppressiveness,** oppression, **stuffiness.**

.7 VERBS **be still, keep quiet,** lie still; **rest, repose; remain, stay,** tarry; remain motionless, freeze [informal]; stand, **stand still,** be at a standstill; stand or stick fast, stick, stand firm, stay put [informal]; stand like a post; **not stir,** not stir a step; not breathe, hold one's breath; abide, abide one's time, mark time, tread water, coast; rest on one's oars, rest and be thankful.

.8 **quiet,** quieten, **lull,** soothe, quiesce, **calm,** calm down, tranquilize 163.7, pacify; **stop** 144.7, halt, bring to a standstill; **cease** 144.6, wane, subside, ebb, run or die down, dwindle, molder.

.9 **stagnate, vegetate,** fust [archaic]; sleep, slumber; smolder, hang fire; idle.

.10 **sit,** set [dial], **sit down, be seated,** remain seated; perch, roost.

.11 **becalm,** take the wind out of one's sails.

.12 ADJS **quiescent, quiet, still,** stilly [archaic], stillish, hushed; waning, subsiding, ebbing, dwindling, moldering; **at rest,** resting, reposing; restful, reposeful; cloistered, sequestered, sequestrated, isolated, secluded, sheltered; **calm, tranquil, peaceful,** peaceable, pacific, halcyon; **placid, smooth; unruffled, untroubled,** cool, undisturbed, unperturbed, unagitated, unmoved, unstirring; stolid, stoic, impassive;

even-tenored; calm as a mill pond; still as death, "quiet as a street at night" [Rupert Brooke].

.13 **motionless, unmoving,** unmoved, moveless, **immobile,** immotive, aplano–, ankyl(o)–; **still, fixed, stationary,** static, at a standstill; **stock-still,** dead-still; still as a statue, statuelike; still as a mouse; at anchor, riding at anchor; idle, unemployed, out of commission.

.14 **inert, inactive, static,** dormant, passive, sedentary; **latent,** unaroused, suspended, abeyant, in suspense or abeyance; sleeping, slumbering, smoldering; **stagnant,** standing, foul; **torpid, languorous, languid,** apathetic, phlegmatic, **sluggish,** logy, dopey [informal], groggy, heavy, leaden, **dull,** flat, slack, tame, **dead,** lifeless; catatonic, cataleptic.

.15 **untraveled, stay-at-home,** stick-in-the-mud [informal], home-keeping.

.16 **airless,** breathless, breezeless, windless; close, stuffy, oppressive, stifling, **suffocating;** not a breath of air, not a leaf stirring, "not wind enough to twirl the one red leaf" [Coleridge]; ill-ventilated, unventilated, unvented.

.17 **becalmed,** in a dead calm.

.18 ADVS quiescently, **quietly,** stilly, still; **calmly, tranquilly, peacefully; placidly,** smoothly, unperturbedly.

.19 **motionlessly,** movelessly, stationarily, fixedly.

.20 **inertly, inactively,** statically, dormantly, passively, latently; stagnantly; **torpidly, languorously, languidly; sluggishly,** heavily, dully, coldly, lifelessly, apathetically, phlegmatically; stoically, stolidly, impassively.

269. SWIFTNESS

.1 NOUNS **velocity, speed,** drom(o)–, tacho–; **rapidity,** celerity, **swiftness,** fastness, **quickness,** snappiness [informal], **speediness;** haste, hurry, flurry, rush, precipitation; dispatch, expedition, promptness, promptitude, instantaneousness; flight, flit; lightning speed; fast or swift rate, smart or rattling or spanking or lively or snappy pace, round pace; air speed, ground speed, speed over the bottom; miles per hour, knots; rpm 322.3.

.2 **speed of sound, sonic speed,** Mach, Mach number, Mach one, Mach two, etc.; subsonic speed; supersonic or ultrasonic or hypersonic or transsonic speed; sound barrier 278.40; escape velocity.

.3 **run, sprint; dash, rush,** plunge, headlong

rush or plunge, **race, scurry, scamper,** scud, scuttle, **spurt,** burst, **burst of speed;** canter, **gallop,** lope; high lope, hand gallop, full gallop; dead run; **trot,** dogtrot, jog trot; open throttle, flat-out speed [Brit], wide-open speed, heavy right foot, maximum speed; forced draft, flank speed [both naut].

.4 **acceleration, quickening; pickup,** getaway; step-up, speedup; thrust, drive, impetus.

.5 **speeder,** scorcher or hell-driver [both informal], flier, goer, stepper; hummer or hustler or sizzler [all informal]; **speed demon** or maniac or merchant [informal]; **racer, runner;** horse racer, turfman, jockey; Jehu.

.6 (comparisons) lightning, greased lightning [informal], thunderbolt, flash, streak of lightning, streak, blue streak [informal], bat out of hell [slang], light, electricity, thought, wind, shot, cannonball, rocket, arrow, dart, quicksilver, mercury, express train, jet plane, torrent, eagle, swallow, antelope, courser, gazelle, greyhound, hare, blue darter, striped snake, scared rabbit.

.7 **speedometer,** accelerometer; cyclometer; tachometer; Mach meter; log, log line, patent log, taffrail log, harpoon log, ground log; wind gauge, anemometer.

.8 VERBS **speed, go fast,** clip [informal], spank or cut along [informal], **tear along, bowl along,** thunder along, storm along, breeze or **breeze along** [both informal], tear up the track or road [informal], eat up the track or road [informal], scorch or sizzle [both informal]; **rip, zip, whiz,** whisk, sweep, brush, nip, **tear,** skim; **fly,** zing [informal], flit, fleet, wing one's way, fly low [informal], outstrip the wind; **highball** [informal], ball the jack [slang], **barrel** [informal], pour it on [informal], boom, **zoom;** make knots; foot; break the sound barrier.

.9 **rush, tear, dash, dart,** shoot, hurtle, bolt, fling, **scamper, scurry,** skedaddle [informal], **scoot,** scour, scud, scuttle, scramble, **race,** career; **hasten,** haste, make haste, **hurry,** hie, post; **step on it** [informal], step on the gas [informal], hump or hump it [both slang], stir one's stumps [slang]; march in quick or double-quick time.

.10 **run, sprint, trip,** spring, **bound,** leap; hotfoot or hightail or make tracks [all informal], **step lively** [informal], step or step along [both informal], carry the mail [informal], hop or hop along [both informal], get [slang], git [dial]; gallop, lope, canter; trot, fox-trot.

.11 **go like the wind,** go like a shot or flash, go like lightning or a streak of lightning, go like greased lightning [informal], go like a bat out of hell [slang], run like a scared rabbit [informal], run like mad [informal], go hell-bent for election [informal].

.12 **make time,** make good time, **cover ground,** get over the ground, **make strides** or **rapid strides,** make the best of one's way.

.13 **go at full blast** [informal], **go all out** [informal], run wide open, go full speed ahead, go at full tilt or steam, go flat out [Brit], let her out [informal], **open her up** [informal].

.14 **accelerate, speed up, step up** [informal], **hurry up, quicken; step on it** [slang]; **hasten** 709.4; get a move on [informal], crack on, put on, put on steam, pour on the coal, put on more speed, open the throttle; quicken one's pace; pick up speed, gain ground; give it the gas or step on its tail or give it the gun [all slang]; race (a motor), rev [informal].

.15 [naut terms] put on sail, crack or pack on sail, crowd sail, press her.

.16 **spurt,** make a spurt or dash, **dash ahead, dart ahead, shoot ahead,** rush ahead, put on or make a burst of speed.

.17 **overtake, outstrip, overhaul,** catch up, **catch up with,** come up with or to, gain on or upon, pass, lap; outpace, outrun, outsail; leave behind, leave standing or looking or flatfooted.

.18 **keep up with,** keep pace with, run neck and neck.

.19 ADJS **fast, swift, speedy, rapid,** oxy–, tachy–; **quick,** double-quick, express, **fleet, hasty, expeditious,** hustling, snappy [informal], dashing, flying, galloping, running, –dromous, spanking [informal]; **agile, nimble,** lively, nimble-footed, light-footed, light-legged, light of heel; winged, eagle-winged; mercurial; quick as lightning, quick as thought, swift as an arrow, "swifter than arrow from the Tartar's bow" [Shakespeare]; **breakneck,** reckless, headlong, precipitate; quick as a wink, quick on the trigger [informal], hair-trigger [informal]; **prompt** 131.9.

.20 **supersonic,** transsonic, ultrasonic, hypersonic, faster than sound; **high-speed,** high-velocity, high-geared.

.21 ADVS **swiftly, rapidly, quickly,** snappily

[informal], **speedily,** with speed, **fast, quick,** apace, amain, on eagle's wings, *ventre à terre* [Fr]; at a great rate, at a good clip [informal], with rapid strides, with giant strides, *à pas de geant* [Fr], in seven-league boots, **by leaps and bounds,** trippingly; **lickety-split** *or* lickety-cut [both slang]; hell-bent *or* hell-bent for election *or* hell for leather [all slang]; **posthaste,** post, **hastily,** expeditiously, promptly, with great *or* all haste, whip and spur, **hand over hand** *or* fist; double-quick, in double time, in double-quick time, on the double *or* on the double-quick [both informal]; in high gear, in high; under press of sail, under press of sail and steam, under forced draft, at flank speed [all naut].

.22 **like a shot, like a flash,** like a streak, like a blue streak [informal], like a streak of lightning, like lightning, like greased lightning [informal], **like a bat out of hell** [slang], like a scared rabbit [informal], **like a house afire** [informal]; **like sixty** [informal], **like mad** *or* crazy *or* fury [all informal], like sin [informal]; **to beat the band** *or* the Dutch *or* the deuce *or* the devil [all informal].

.23 **in short order, in no time,** instantaneously, immediately if not sooner, in less than no time, in nothing flat [informal]; in a jiff *or* jiffy [both informal], before you can say 'Jack Robinson', **in a flash,** in a twink, **in a twinkling,** "in the twinkling of an eye" [Bible], *tout de suite* [Fr], pronto [informal].

.24 **at full speed,** with all speed, at full throttle, **at the top of one's bent, for all one is worth** [informal], as fast as one's legs will carry one, as fast as one can lay feet to the ground; **at full blast,** at full drive *or* pelt; under full steam, in full sail; **all out** [slang], flat out [Brit], **wide open;** full speed ahead.

270. SLOWNESS

.1 NOUNS **slowness, leisureliness,** pokiness, slackness, creeping; sluggishness, sloth, laziness, idleness, indolence, sluggardy, languor, inertia, inertness, lentitude *or* lentor [both archaic]; deliberateness, deliberation, circumspection, tentativeness, cautiousness, reluctance, foot-dragging [informal]; drawl.

.2 **slow motion, leisurely gait,** snail's *or* tortoise's pace; **creep, crawl; walk,** footpace, dragging *or* lumbering pace, trudge, waddle, saunter, stroll; slouch, shuffle, plod, shamble; limp, claudication, hobble; dogtrot, jog trot; jog, rack; mincing steps; slow march, dead *or* funeral march, andante.

.3 **dawdling, lingering, loitering, tarrying,** dalliance, **dallying,** dillydallying, shilly-shallying, lollygagging, dilatoriness, procrastination 132.5, lag, **lagging,** goofing off [slang].

.4 **slowing, retardation,** retardment, **slackening,** flagging, slowing down; **slowdown,** slowup, **letup, letdown, slack-up, slack-off,** ease-off, ease-up; **deceleration,** negative *or* minus acceleration; **delay** 132.2, **detention, setback, holdup** [informal], check, arrest, obstruction; lag, drag.

.5 **slowpoke** [informal], **plodder,** slow goer, **slow-foot,** slowbelly, **lingerer, loiterer, dawdler,** dawdle, **laggard,** procrastinator, foot-dragger, stick-in-the-mud [informal], drone, slug, sluggard, lie-abed, sleepyhead, goof-off [slang], goldbrick [slang]; tortoise, snail.

.6 VERBS **go slow** *or* **slowly,** go at a snail's pace, get no place fast [informal]; **drag,** drag out; **creep, crawl;** laze, idle; go dead slow; inch, inch along; worm, worm along; poke, **poke along;** shuffle along, stagger along, totter along, toddle along; drag along, drag one's feet, walk, traipse *or* **mosey** [both informal]; saunter, stroll, amble, waddle, toddle [informal]; jogtrot, dogtrot; limp, hobble, claudicate.

.7 **plod,** plug [informal], peg, **trudge,** tramp, stump, lumber; plod along, plug along [informal], schlep [slang]; rub on, jog on, chug on.

.8 **dawdle, linger, loiter, tarry, delay, dally, dillydally,** shilly-shally, lollygag, waste time, **take one's time,** take one's own sweet time; goof off *or* around [slang]; lag, drag, trail; flag, falter, halt.

.9 **slow, slow down** *or* **up, let down** *or* **up, ease off** *or* **up, slack off** *or* **up, slacken,** relax, moderate, lose speed *or* momentum; **decelerate, retard, delay** 132.8, detain, impede, obstruct, arrest, stay, **check,** curb, **hold up, hold back,** keep back, set back, hold in check; draw rein, rein in; throttle down, take one's foot off the gas; brake, **put on the brakes,** put on the drag; reef, take in sail; backwater, backpedal; lose ground; clip the wings.

.10 ADJS **slow,** brady–, **leisurely,** slack, moderate, gentle, **easy,** deliberate, unhurried, relaxed, gradual, circumspect, tentative, cautious, reluctant, foot-dragging [informal]; **creeping, crawling; poking, poky,** slow-poky [informal]; tottering, staggering, toddling, trudging, **lumbering,** ambling, waddling, shuffling, **sauntering,** strolling; **sluggish,** languid, languorous, lazy, slothful, indolent, idle; **slow-going, slow-moving,** slow-creeping, slow-crawling, slow-running, slow-sailing; **slow-footed,** slow-foot, slow-legged, slow-gaited, slow-paced, slow-stepped, easy-paced, slow-winged; snail-paced, snail-like, tortoiselike, turtlelike, "creeping like snail" [Shakespeare]; limping, hobbling, hobbled, halting, claudicant; faltering, flagging; slow as slow, slow as molasses, slow as death, slower than the seven-year itch [informal].

.11 **dawdling, lingering, loitering, tarrying, dallying, dillydallying,** shilly-shallying, lollygagging, procrastinatory *or* procrastinative, dilatory, delaying 132.17, **lagging,** dragging.

.12 **retarded,** slowed down, **delayed, detained,** checked, **arrested,** impeded, set back, backward, behind; late, **tardy** 132.16.

.13 ADVS **slowly,** slow, **leisurely,** unhurriedly, relaxedly, easily, moderately, gently; creepingly, crawlingly; pokingly, pokily; **sluggishly,** languidly, languorously, lazily, indolently, idly, deliberately, with deliberation, circumspectly, tentatively, cautiously, reluctantly; **lingeringly,** loiteringly, tarryingly, dilatorily; limpingly, haltingly, falteringly; **in slow motion,** at a funeral pace, with faltering *or* halting steps; at a snail's *or* turtle's pace, "in haste like a snail" [John Heywood]; in slow tempo, in march time; with agonizing slowness; in low gear; under easy sail.

.14 **gradually,** little by little 29.6.

271. TRANSFERENCE

(removal from one place to another)

.1 NOUNS **transference, transfer; transmission,** transmittal, transmittance, –phoresis; transposition, transposal, transplacement, mutual transfer, interchange, metathesis; translocation, **transplantation,** translation; migration, transmigration; import, importation, export, exportation; deportation, extradition, expulsion, **transit,** transition, **passage; communication,** spread, spreading, dissemination, diffusion, contagion; metastasis; transmigration of souls, metempsychosis; passing over; osmosis, diapedesis; transduction, conduction, convection; transfusion, per-

fusion; transfer of property *or* right 817; delivery 818.1; travel 273.

.2 **removal, movement,** moving, relocation, shift, removement, remotion, amotion; **displacement,** delocalization.

.3 **transportation, conveyance, transport,** carrying, bearing, packing, toting [dial], lugging [informal]; **carriage,** carry, **hauling,** haulage, portage, porterage, waft, waftage; **cartage, truckage,** drayage, wagonage; ferriage, lighterage; telpherage; **freightage,** freight, expressage, railway express; airfreight, air express, airlift; **shipment,** shipping, transshipment; asportation.

.4 transferability, conveyability; transmissibility, transmittability; movability, removability; **portability,** transportability; communicability, impartability.

.5 **carrier, conveyer,** –pher, –phor(e), –phorus, –phorum; transporter, hauler, carter, wagoner, drayman, shipper, trucker, common carrier, truck driver; **bearer, porter,** redcap, skycap; coolie; litter-bearer, stretcher-bearer; caddie; shield-bearer, gun bearer; water carrier *or* bearer, water boy, bheesty [India]; the Water Bearer, Aquarius; letter carrier 561.5; busboy; cupbearer, Ganymede, Hebe; expressman, express; freighter; stevedore, cargo handler; carrier pigeon, homing pigeon.

.6 **beast of burden; pack** *or* **draft animal,** pack horse *or* mule, sumpter, sumpter horse *or* mule; **horse** 414.10–19, ass 414.20, mule; ox; camel, ship of the desert, dromedary, llama; reindeer; elephant; sledge dog, husky, malamute, Siberian husky.

.7 **freight,** freightage; **shipment, consignment,** goods [Brit]; **cargo,** payload; lading, load, pack; **baggage, luggage,** impedimenta.

.8 [geol terms] **deposit,** sediment; drift, silt, loess, moraine, scree, sinter; alluvium, alluvion, diluvium; detritus, debris.

.9 VERBS **transfer, transmit, transpose,** translocate, transplace, metathesize, switch; **transplant,** translate; **pass,** pass over, **hand over,** turn over, carry over, make over, consign, assign; **deliver** 818.13; pass on, pass the buck [informal], hand forward, hand on, relay; **import, export;** deport, extradite, expel; communicate, diffuse, disseminate, spread, impart; metastasize; transfuse, perfuse, transfer property *or* right 817.3.

.10 **remove, move, relocate, shift,** send, shunt; displace, delocalize, dislodge; **take away,** cart away, carry off *or* away; manhandle; set or lay or put aside, put or set to one side, side.

.11 **transport, convey,** freight, conduct, **take; carry, bear,** pack, tote [dial], lug [informal], manhandle; lift, waft, whisk, wing, fly.

.12 **haul, cart,** dray, truck, bus, van, wagon, coach, wheelbarrow; sled, sledge; ship, boat, barge, lighter, ferry; raft, float.

.13 (convey through a channel) **channel,** put through channels; **pipe,** tube, pipeline, flume, **siphon, funnel,** tap.

.14 **send,** send off or away, send forth; **dispatch,** transmit, remit, consign, forward; expedite; **ship,** freight, airfreight, embark, **express,** air-express; **post, mail,** airmail, drop a letter; export.

.15 **fetch, bring, go get,** go and get, go to get, **go after,** go fetch, **go for,** call for, pick up; **get, obtain,** procure, secure; **bring back, retrieve;** chase after, run after, shag, fetch and carry.

.16 **ladle, dip, scoop; bail,** bucket; **dish,** dish out or up; cup; **shovel,** spade, fork; spoon; **pour,** decant.

.17 ADJS **transferable, conveyable; transmittable,** transmissible, transmissive, consignable; **movable,** removable; **portable,** portative; transportable, transportative, transportive; conductive, conductional; transposable, interchangeable; **communicable,** contagious, impartable; transfusable; metastatic(al), metathetic(al); mailable, expressable; assignable 817.5.

.18 ADVS by transfer, from hand to hand, from door to door; by freight, by express, by rail, by trolley, by bus, by steamer, by airplane, by mail, by special delivery; trans–.

.19 **on the way,** along the way, on the road or high road, **en route, in transit,** in transitu [L], on the wing, as one goes; in passing, en passant [Fr]; in mid-progress.

272. VEHICLE

(means of conveyance)

.1 NOUNS **vehicle, conveyance,** carrier, means of carrying or transporting, medium of transportation, carriage; watercraft 277.1–9, aircraft 280; –mobile.

.2 **wagon,** waggon [Brit], wain; haywagon, milkwagon; dray, van, caravan; covered wagon, prairie schooner, Conestoga wagon.

.3 **cart,** two-wheeler; oxcart, horsecart, ponycart, dogcart; dumpcart, coup-cart [Scot]; **handcart** 272.28; jinrikisha, ricksha.

.4 **carriage,** four-wheeler, *voiture* [Fr], gharry [India]; **chaise,** shay [dial], "one hoss shay" [O. W. Holmes, Sr.].

.5 **rig, equipage,** turnout [informal], coach-and-four; team, pair, span; tandem, random; spike, spike team, unicorn; three-in-hand, four-in-hand, etc.; three-up, four-up, etc.

.6 **baby carriage,** baby buggy [informal], perambulator, pram [Brit]; gocart; **stroller,** walker.

.7 **wheel chair,** Bath chair.

.8 **cycle** 272.29, wheel [informal]; **bicycle,** bike [informal]; **tricycle,** trike [informal]; **motorcycle,** motocycle, motorbike [informal], iron [slang], road-bike [informal], pig [slang], chopper [informal], trail bike; minibike; pedicab.

.9 **automobile** 272.24, **car, auto,** motorcar, motocar, autocar, **machine,** motor, motor vehicle, motorized vehicle, *voiture* [Fr]; bus or buggy or wheels or heap or boat or crate or tub [all slang]; **jalopy** [informal], wreck [informal].

.10 **police car, patrol car; prowl car,** squad car, cruiser; **police van,** patrol wagon; wagon or paddy wagon or Black Maria [all informal]; carryall.

.11 **truck,** lorry [Brit], *camion* [Fr]; trailer truck, truck trailer, tractor trailer, semitrailer, semi [informal].

.12 (public vehicles) **bus,** omnibus, chartered bus, autobus, motorbus, motor coach, jitney [informal]; double-decker [informal]; **cab, taxicab, taxi,** hack [informal]; rental car; hired car or limousine; stage, **stagecoach,** *diligence* [Fr]; mail or post coach.

.13 **train,** railroad train; choo-choo or choo-choo train [both informal]; passenger train, Amtrak; local, way train, milk train, accommodation train; shuttle train, shuttle; express train, express; lightning express, flier, cannonball express [informal]; local express; special, limited; parliamentary train or parliamentary [Brit]; freight train, goods train [Brit], freight, freighter, rattler [slang]; baggage train, luggage train; electric train, electric [informal]; interurban; cable railroad; funicular; cog railroad or railway, rack-and-pinion railroad; subway, *métro* [Fr], tube, underground [Brit]; elevated, el [informal]; monorail; streamliner; rolling stock.

.14 **railway car,** car; passenger car, coach, carriage [Brit]; chair car, day coach; sleeping car, sleeper; Pullman, Pullman car; drawing-room car, palace car, parlor car; drawing room, roomette; dining car or compartment, diner; smoking car *or* compartment, smoker; freight car, waggon [Brit], goods waggon [Brit]; boxcar, box waggon [Brit], covered waggon [Brit]; flatcar, flat, truck [Brit]; gondola car, gondola, open waggon [Brit]; baggage car, luggage van [Brit], van [Brit]; mail car, mail van [Brit]; refrigerator car, reefer [slang]; tank car, tank; stockcar; coal car; tender; caboose; dinghy; way car, local.

.15 **streetcar, trolley** *or* trolley car, **tram** *or* tramcar [both Brit]; electric car, electric [informal]; trolley bus, trackless trolley; horsecar, horse box [Brit]; cable car, grip car.

.16 **handcar** [RR], go-devil; push car, trolley, truck car, rubble car.

.17 **tractor** 272.27, traction engine; Caterpillar tractor, Caterpillar, Cat [informal], tracked vehicle; bulldozer, dozer [informal], calfdozer.

.18 **trailer,** trail car; house trailer, mobile home; truck trailer, **semitrailer,** highway trailer; camp(ing) trailer, caravan [Brit]; **camper,** camping bus.

.19 **sled** 272.31, **sleigh,** *traîneau* [Fr]; snowmobile, Sno-Cat, weasel, Skimobile; runner, blade.

.20 **skates,** ice skates, hockey skates, figure skates; roller skates, skateboard, bob skates; **skis, snowshoes.**

.21 **hovercraft,** hovercar, air-cushion vehicle, ACV, cushioncraft, ground-effect machine, GEM, captured-air vehicle, CAV, captured-air bubble, CAB.

.22 ADJS **vehicular,** transportational; automotive, auto–, locomotive.

.23 **carriages**

araba	curricle
barouche	dearborn
berlin	desobligeant
break	dogcart
britska	*dormeuse* [Fr]
brougham	drag
buckboard	dray
buggy	droshky
bullock cart	ekka
cabriolet	fiacre
calash	fly
calèche [Fr]	four-in-hand coach
Cape cart	gig
cariole	glass coach
carryall	growler
cart	hack
charabanc	hackery
chariot	hackney, hackney
chariotee	coach
charrette [Fr]	hansom, hansom cab
clarence	jaunting *or* jaunty car
coach	jigger
Concord buggy	jinrikisha
coupé	kibitka

kittereen	sulky
landau	surrey
limber	tallyho, tallyho coach
mail phaeton	tandem
outside jaunting car	tilbury
oxcart	tonga
phaeton	trap
post chaise	troika
road cart	trolley
rockaway	tumbrel
runabout	*vettura* [Ital]
shandrydan	victoria
sidecar	vis-à-vis
sociable, sociable	voiturette
coach	wagonette
spring wagon	whiskey
stanhope	Whitechapel cart

.24 **automobiles**

air cushion car	hot rod
ambulance	hovercar
armored car	jeep
autobolide	landau
beach buggy	landaulet
beach wagon	land-rover
berlin	limousine
berlin-landaulet	locomobile
blitzbuggy	midget racer
brougham	phaeton
cabriolet	race car
camper	racer
carryall	racing car
clubmobile	rail
coach	roadster
combat car	rocket car
command car	runabout
compact car	saloon [Brit]
convertible	scout car
convertible coupe	sedan
convertible sedan	sedan limousine
coupe	shooting brake [Brit]
coupelet	sports car
crash wagon	staff car
double fueler	station wagon
dragster	steamer
dune buggy	stock car
electric brougham	swamp buggy
electromobile	torpedo
fastback	tourer [Brit]
fire engine	touring car
fueler	touring coupe
funny car	tow car
gocart	tractor
golf cart	two-seater [Brit]
hardtop	wrecker
hearse	

.25 **auto parts**

accelerator	choke
alternator	clutch
ammeter	connecting rod
automatic choke	convertible top
backup light	cowl
bearings	crank
bonnet [Brit]	crankcase
boot [Brit]	crankshaft
brake	cutout
bucket seat	cylinder
bumper	cylinder head
camshaft	dashboard, dash
carburetor	differential
chassis	directional signal

disk brakes
distributor
emergency light
exhaust, exhaust pipe
fan
fender
flywheel
gear
gearbox
gearshift
generator
headlight
headrest
hood
horn
ignition
intake, intake mani-
  fold
manifold
muffler
oil gauge
parking light
PCV valve
piston
power brakes
power steering

radiator
radius rod
rear-view mirror
rumble seat
running board
seat belt
seat cover
seat cushion
shock absorber
side mirror
spark plug
speedometer
springs
starter
steering wheel
taillight
tail pipe
top
torsion bar
transmission
universal joint, univer-
  sal
valve
windscreen [Brit]
windshield

.26 trucks

auto carrier [Brit]
autotruck
bloodmobile
bookmobile
camper
camping bus
carryall
cart
delivery truck
dolly
dray
duck, DUKW
dump truck
fork or forklift truck
freighter
garbage truck

hand truck
motor truck
moving van
panel truck
pickup
railroad truck
refrigerator truck
sedan delivery truck
six-by-six
stake truck
tongue truck
tractor, tractor truck
transfer
van
wagon truck
warehouse truck

.27 tractors

amphibian, amphibian
  tractor, amtrac [in-
  formal]
bulldozer
calfdozer
Caterpillar, Caterpil-
  lar tractor
crawler, crawler trac-
  tor
creeper, creeper trac-
  tor
duck, DUKW

farm tractor
go-devil
grader
halftrack
lawn-tractor
LVT (landing vehicle
  tracked)
Rome plow
scraper
tank
tracklayer

.28 handcarts

barrow
garden cart
handbarrow
laundry cart
lawn cart
push car

pushcart
serving cart
shopping cart
teacart
wheelbarrow

.29 cycles

bicycle
bicycle-built-for-two
folding bicycle
hydrocycle
minibike

monocycle
motorbike
motorcycle
motor scooter
push bicycle

quadricycle
safety bicycle
scooter
sidewalk bike
tandem

tandem bicycle
tricycle
unicycle
velocipede

.30 litters

brancard
cacolet [Fr]
camel litter
dandy
dolly
doolie
gocart
handbarrow
horse litter

jampan
kajawah [India]
lectica
norimon
palanquin
polki
sedan, sedan chair
stretcher
tonjon

.31 sleds

autosled
belly-bumper
bobsled, bobsleigh
cariole
coaster
cutter
dogsled
double-ripper, dou-
  ble-runner
drag

dray
jumper
kick-sled
luge
pung
scoot
skid
sledge
toboggan
troika

273. TRAVEL

.1 NOUNS **travel,** traveling, going, journeying, moving, **movement, motion, locomotion, transit, progress, passage,** course, traject, trajet, crossing, commutation; world
travel, globe-trotting [informal]; **tourism,**
touristry.

.2 **travels,** journeys, **journeyings, wanderings,**
voyagings, peregrinations, peripatetics;
odyssey.

.3 **wandering, roving, roaming, rambling,
gadding,** traipsing [dial], wayfaring, flitting, straying, drifting, gallivanting, peregrination, peregrinism, pererration, discursion, errantry, divagation; roam, rove,
ramble; **itinerancy,** itineracy; **nomadism,**
nomadization, gypsydom; vagabonding,
vagabondism, vagabondage, vagabondia;
vagrancy, hoboism, waltzing Matilda
[Austral]; bumming [slang]; the open
road; wanderyear, *Wanderjahr* [Ger];
wanderlust; "afoot and lighthearted"
[Whitman].

.4 **migration, transmigration,** passage, trek;
run (of fish), flight (of birds and insects);
swarm, swarming (of bees); **immigration,**
in-migration; **emigration,** out-migration;
expatriation; remigration; intermigration.

.5 **journey, trip,** *jornada* [Sp], peregrination,
sally, **trek;** progress, course, run; **tour,**
grand tour; round trip, circuit, turn; **expedition,** campaign; safari, hunting expedition, hunting trip, stalk, shoot; **pilgrimage,** hajj; **excursion, jaunt, junket, outing,**

pleasure trip; sight-seeing trip, rubberneck tour [slang]; package tour; **voyage** 275.6.

.6 **riding, driving; motoring,** automobiling; busing; motorcycling, bicycling, cycling, pedaling, biking [informal]; **horseback riding,** equitation; horsemanship, manège.

.7 **ride, drive;** spin or whirl [both informal]; joyride [informal]; Sunday drive; airing; lift [informal], pickup [slang].

.8 **gliding, sliding,** slipping, slithering, coasting, sweeping, flowing, sailing; **skating, skiing, tobogganing, sledding;** glide, slide, slither, sweep, skim, flow.

.9 **creeping, crawling,** going on all fours; sneaking, stealing, slinking, sidling, gumshoeing or pussyfooting [both informal], padding, prowling, nightwalking; worming, snaking; tiptoeing, tiptoe, tippytoe; creep, crawl, scramble, scrabble; all fours; herpet(o)–.

.10 **walking,** ambulation, perambulation, ambling, pedestrianism, shank's mare, going on foot or afoot, footing or hoofing, footing it; footwork, legwork [informal]; strolling, sauntering; **tramping, marching, hiking,** backpacking, footslogging, trudging, treading; lumbering, waddling; toddling, staggering, tottering; **hitchhiking** or hitching [both informal], thumbing or thumbing a ride [both informal]; jaywalking.

.11 **nightwalking,** noctambulation, noctambulism; night-wandering, noctivagation; **sleepwalking,** somnambulation, somnambulism, somnambul–; sleepwalk.

.12 **walk,** ramble, amble, **hike, march, tramp,** trudge, traipse [dial], schlep [slang], mush; **stroll,** saunter; parade; **promenade;** jaunt, airing; **constitutional** [informal], stretch; turn; peripatetic journey or exercise, peripateticism; walking tour or excursion; forced march; –grade.

.13 **step, pace, stride;** footstep, footfall, tread; hoofbeat, clop; hop, jump; skip, hippety-hop [informal].

.14 **gait, pace, walk, step, stride, tread;** saunter, stroll, strolling gait; shuffle, shamble, hobble, limp, hitch, waddle; totter, stagger, lurch; toddle, paddle; slouch, droop, drag; mince, mincing steps, scuttle; prance, flounce, stalk, strut, swagger; slink, slither, sidle; jog; swing, roll; amble, single-foot, rack, piaffer; trot, gallop 269.3; lock step; velocity 269.1,2; slowness 270.

.15 **march;** quick or quickstep march, quick-

step, quick time; double march, doublequick, double time; slow march, slow time; half step; goose step.

.16 **leg, limb, shank,** hind leg, foreleg; podite, pod(e)–; stems or trotters or hind legs or underpinnings [all informal]; pins or gams or stumps [all slang]; gamb, jamb [her]; bowlegs, baker's legs, scissor-legs; bayonet legs; shin, cnemis; ankle, tarsus, tars(o)–; hock, gambrel; calf; knee; thigh, mer(o)–; popliteal space, ham, drumstick; gigot.

.17 VERBS **travel, go,** gang [Scot], **move, pass,** fare, wayfare, fare forth, fetch, flit, hie, sashay [informal], cover ground; **progress** 294.2; move on or along, go along; wend, **wend one's way;** betake oneself, direct one's course, bend one's steps or course; course, run, flow, stream; roll, roll on; commute.

.18 (go at a given speed) go, **go at,** reach, **make, do,** hit [informal], clip off [informal].

.19 **traverse, travel over** or through, pass through, go or **pass over, cover,** measure, transit, track, range, range over or through, course, do, perambulate, pererrate, peregrinate, overpass, go over the ground; patrol, reconnoiter, scout; sweep, go or make one's rounds, scour, scour the country; ply, voyage 275.13.

.20 **journey,** make or take or go or go on a journey, **take** or **make a trip,** fare, **wayfare, trek, jaunt,** peregrinate; **tour;** hit the trail [informal], take the road, go on the road; **cruise, voyage** 275.13; go abroad, go to foreign places or shores, range the world, globe-trot [informal]; pilgrimage, pilgrim, go on or make a pilgrimage; campaign, go overseas, go on an expedition, go on safari; go on a sight-seeing trip, sight-see, rubberneck [informal].

.21 **migrate, transmigrate,** trek; flit, take wing; run (of fish), swarm (of bees); **emigrate,** out-migrate, expatriate; **immigrate,** in-migrate; remigrate; intermigrate.

.22 **wander, roam, rove,** range, nomadize, **gad,** gad about, wayfare, flit, traipse [dial], gallivant, knock around or about [informal], bat around or about [slang], mooch [slang], prowl, **drift, stray,** straggle, **meander, ramble,** stroll, saunter, jaunt, peregrinate, pererrate, divagate, go or run about, go the rounds; **tramp,** hobo, bum or go on the bum [both slang], vagabond, vagabondize, take to the road, "travel the open road" [Whitman], beat one's way; **hit the road** or trail [informal], walk the tracks or count ties [both informal].

.23 **go for an outing** or **airing, take the air,** get some air; **go for a walk** 273.28; go for a ride 273.32.

.24 **go to, repair to,** resort to, hie to, hie oneself to, arise and go to, direct one's course to, turn one's tracks to, make one's way to, bend one's steps to, betake oneself to, **visit;** make the scene [slang].

.25 **creep, crawl,** scramble, scrabble, grovel, **go on hands and knees,** go on all fours; worm, worm along, worm one's way, snake; inch, inch along; **sneak, steal,** steal along; pussyfoot or gumshoe [both informal], slink, sidle, pad, prowl, nightwalk; **tiptoe,** tippytoe, go on tiptoe.

.26 **walk,** ambulate, peripateticate, pedestrianize, traipse [dial]; **step, tread, pace, stride,** pad; foot, foot it; leg, leg it; hoof it, ankle, go on the heel and toe, ride shank's mare or pony, ride the shoeleather or hobnail express, stump it [slang]; peg or jog or shuffle on or along; perambulate; circumambulate; jaywalk.

.27 (ways of walking) **stroll,** saunter; shuffle, scuff, scuffle, straggle, shamble; stride, straddle; **trudge, plod,** peg, traipse [dial], clump, stump, slog, footslog, drag, **lumber, barge;** stamp, stomp [dial]; swing, roll, lunge; hobble, halt, limp, hitch, lurch; totter, stagger; toddle, paddle; waddle, wobble, wamble, wiggle; slouch; slink, slither, sidle; stalk; **strut, swagger;** mince, sashay [informal], scuttle, prance, tittup, flounce, trip, skip, foot; hop, jump, hippety-hop [informal]; jog, jolt; bundle, bowl along; **amble,** pace; singlefoot, rack; piaffe, piaffer.

.28 **go for a walk, take a walk, take one's constitutional** [informal], take a stretch, stretch the legs; **promenade, parade, per**ambulate.

.29 **march,** mush, footslog, **tramp, hike,** backpack; file, defile, file off; **parade,** go on parade; goose-step, do the goose step; do the lock step.

.30 **hitchhike** or **hitch** or hitch rides [all informal], beat one's way, **thumb** or **thumb one's way** [both informal], **catch a ride;** hitch or hook or bum or cadge or thumb a ride [informal].

.31 **nightwalk,** noctambulate; **sleepwalk,** somnambulate, walk in one's sleep.

.32 **ride, go for a ride** or **drive;** go for a spin [informal], take or go for a Sunday drive; **drive, chauffeur; motor,** taxi; bus; bike or cycle or wheel or pedal [all informal];

motorcycle, bicycle; go by rail, entrain; joyride or take a joyride [both informal]; catch or make a train [informal].

.33 **go on horseback;** ride bareback; mount, take horse; hack; ride hard, clap spurs to one's horse; trot, amble, pace, canter, gallop, tittup, lope; prance, frisk, curvet, piaffe, caracole.

.34 **glide, coast, skim,** sweep, flow; **sail, fly,** flit; **slide,** slip, skid, sideslip, slither, glissade; skate, ice-skate, roller-skate, skateboard; ski; toboggan, sled, sleigh; bellywhop [dial].

.35 ADJS **traveling, going, moving,** trekking, passing; **progressing** 294.5; **itinerant,** itinerary, circuit-riding; **journeying, wayfaring,** strolling; **peripatetic;** ambulant, ambulatory; ambulative; perambulating, perambulatory; peregrine, peregrinative, pilgrimlike; locomotive; **walking, pedestrian, touring,** on tour, globe-trotting [informal], globe-girdling, mundivagant [archaic]; touristic(al), touristy [informal]; expeditionary.

.36 **wandering, roving, roaming,** ranging, **rambling, meandering,** strolling, **straying,** straggling, shifting, flitting, landloping, errant, divagatory, discursive, circumforaneous; **gadding,** traipsing [dial], gallivanting; **nomad,** nomadic, floating, drifting, gypsyish or gypsy-like; **transient,** transitory, fugitive; **vagrant,** vagabond; **footloose, footloose and fancy-free; migratory,** migrational, transmigratory.

.37 **nightwalking,** noctambulant, noctambulous; night-wandering, noctivagant; **sleepwalking,** somnambulant, somnambular.

.38 **creeping, crawling, on hands and knees, on all fours;** reptant, repent, reptile, reptatorial; **on tiptoe,** on tippytoe, atiptoe, tiptoeing, tiptoe, tippytoe.

.39 **traveled,** well-traveled, cosmopolitan.

.40 **wayworn,** way-weary, road-weary, legweary, **travel-worn,** travel-weary, traveltired; travel-sated, travel-jaded; travelsoiled, travel-stained, dusty.

.41 ADVS **on the move** or **go,** en route, in transit, on the wing or fly; on the run, on the jump [informal], on the road, on the tramp or march; on the gad [informal], on the bum [informal].

.42 **on foot, afoot,** by foot, footback or on footback [both dial]; on the heel and toe, on shank's mare, on shank's pony.

.43 **on horseback,** horseback, by horse, mounted.

274. TRAVELER

.1 NOUNS traveler, goer, viator, comers and goers; wayfarer, journeyer, trekker; tourist, tourer, tripper [Brit], visiting fireman; excursionist, sightseer, rubberneck or rubbernecker [both informal]; voyager, *voyageur* [Fr], cruiser, sailor, mariner 276; globe-trotter [informal], globe-girdler, world-traveler, cosmopolite; jet set, jetsetter; pilgrim, palmer, hajji; passenger, fare; commuter, straphanger [informal]; transient; passerby; adventurer, alpinist, climber, mountaineer; explorer, fortyniner, pioneer, pathfinder, voortrekker, trailblazer, trailbreaker; camper; astronaut 282.8.

.2 wanderer, rover, roamer, rambler, stroller, straggler, mover; gad, gadabout [informal], runabout, go-about [dial]; itinerant, peripatetic, rolling stone, peregrine, peregrinator, bird of passage, visitant; drifter or floater [both informal]; Wandering Jew, Ahasuerus, Ancient Mariner [Coleridge], Argonaut, Flying Dutchman, Oisin, Ossian, Gulliver [Swift], Ulysses, Odysseus [Homer]; wandering scholar, Goliard, *vaganti* [L]; strolling player, wandering minstrel, troubadour.

.3 vagabond, vagrant, vag [slang]; bum or bummer [both slang], loafer, wastrel, losel [archaic], *lazzarone* [Ital]; tramp, turnpiker, piker, knight of the road, hobo or bo [both slang], rounder [dial], stiff or bindlestiff [both slang]; landloper, sundowner or swagman or swagsman [all Austral informal]; beggar 774.8; waif, homeless waif, dogie, stray, waifs and strays; ragamuffin, tatterdemalion; gamin, gamine, urchin, street urchin, Arab, street Arab, mudlark, guttersnipe [informal]; beachcomber, loafer, idler; ski bum, beach bum, surf bum, tennis bum; ragman, ragpicker.

.4 nomad, Bedouin, Arab; gypsy, Bohemian, Romany, *zingaro* [Ital], *Zigeuner* [Ger], *tzigane* [Fr].

.5 migrant, migrator, trekker; immigrant, inmigrant; migrant or migratory worker, wetback [informal]; emigrant, out-migrant, *émigré* [Fr]; expatriate; evacuee, *évacué* [Fr]; displaced person, DP, stateless person, exile.

.6 pedestrian, walker, walkist, –bates; foot traveler, foot passenger, hoofer [slang], footbacker [dial], ambulator, peripatetic; hiker, backpacker, trailsman, tramper; marcher, footslogger, foot soldier, infantryman, paddlefoot [slang]; hitchhiker [informal]; jaywalker.

.7 nightwalker, noctambulist, noctambule, sleepwalker, somnambulist, somnambulator, somnambule.

.8 rider, equestrian, horseman, horseback rider, horsebacker, caballero, cavalier, knight, chevalier; horse soldier, cavalryman, mounted policeman; horsewoman, equestrienne; cowboy, cowgirl, puncher or cowpuncher [both informal], *vaquero*, *gaucho* [both Sp]; broncobuster [slang], buckaroo; postilion, postboy; roughrider; jockey; steeplechaser; circus rider, trick rider.

.9 driver, reinsman, whip, Jehu, skinner [slang]; coachman, coachy [informal], *cocher* [Fr], *cochero* [Sp], *voiturier* [Fr], *vetturino* [Ital], gharry-wallah [India]; stage coachman; charioteer; harness racer; cabdriver, cabman, cabby [informal], hackman, hack, hacky [both informal], jarvey [Brit slang]; wagoner, wagonman, drayman, truckman; carter, cartman, carman; teamster; muleteer, mule skinner [slang]; bullwhacker; elephant driver, mahout; cameleer.

.10 driver, motorist, automobilist; chauffeur; taxidriver, cabdriver, cabby [informal], hackman, hack [informal], hacky [informal], hackdriver; jitney driver; truck driver, teamster, truckman, trucker; bus driver, busman; speeder 269.5, road hog [informal], Sunday driver, joyrider [informal]; hit-and-run driver; backseat driver.

.11 cyclist, cycler; bicyclist, bicycler; motorcyclist, motorcycler.

.12 engineer, engineman, engine driver [Brit]; hogger or hoghead [both slang]; Casey Jones; motorman; gripman.

.13 trainman, railroad man, railroader; conductor, guard [Brit]; brakeman, brakie [slang]; fireman, footplate man [Brit], stoker; smoke agent or bakehead [both slang]; switchman; yardman; yardmaster; trainmaster, dispatcher; stationmaster; lineman; baggage man, baggagesmasher [slang]; porter, redcap; trainboy, butcher [slang].

275. WATER TRAVEL

.1 NOUNS water travel, travel by water, marine or ocean or sea travel, navigation, navigating, seafaring, sailing, steaming, passage-making, voyaging, cruising, coasting, gunkholing [informal]; boating, yachting, motorboating, canoeing, rowing, sculling; circumnavigation, periplus; navigability.

.2 (methods) celestial navigation, astronavigation; radio navigation, radio beacon; coastal or coastwise navigation; dead reckoning; point-to-point navigation; pilotage; sonar, radar, sofar, loran, consolan, shoran, plane or traverse or spherical or parallel or middle or latitude or Mercator or great-circle or rhumbline or composite sailing; fix, line of position; sextant, chronometer, tables.

.3 **seamanship,** shipmanship; seamanliness, seamanlikeness; weather eye; sea legs.

.4 **pilotship,** pilotry, pilotage, **helmsmanship;** steerage; proper piloting.

.5 embarkation 301.3; disembarkation 300.2.

.6 **voyage,** ocean or sea trip, **cruise,** sail; course, **run, passage; crossing;** shakedown cruise; leg.

.7 **wake,** track; wash, backwash.

.8 (submarines) **surfacing,** breaking water; **submergence, dive;** stationary dive, running dive, crash dive.

.9 **way, progress; headway,** steerageway, sternway, leeway, driftway.

.10 **seaway, waterway,** fairway, road, channel, ocean or sea lane, ship route, steamer track or lane; approaches.

.11 aquatics, **swimming, bathing,** natation, balneation, nect(o)–; **swim, bathe;** crawl, Australian crawl, breaststroke, butterfly, sidestroke, dog paddle, backstroke; treading water; floating; diving 320.3; wading; fin; flipper, flapper; fishtail; waterskiing, aquaplaning, surfboarding; surfing.

.12 **swimmer, bather,** natator, merman; bathing girl, mermaid; bathing beauty; frogman; diver 320.4; –nect.

.13 VERBS **navigate, sail, cruise,** steam, run, **seafare, voyage,** ply, go on shipboard, go by ship, go on or take a voyage, "go down to the sea in ships" [Bible]; go to sea, sail the sea, sail the ocean blue; **boat, yacht,** motorboat, canoe, row, scull; steamboat; bear or carry sail; cross, traverse, make a passage or run; sail round, circumnavigate; coast.

.14 **pilot,** helm, coxswain, **steer,** guide, be at the helm or tiller, direct, manage, handle, run, operate, **conn** or cond, be at or have the conn; **navigate,** shape or chart a course.

.15 **anchor,** come to anchor, lay anchor, **cast anchor,** let go the anchor, drop the hook; carry out the anchor; kedge, kedge off; **dock, tie up; moor,** pick up the mooring;

run out a warp or rope; lash, lash and tie; foul the anchor; disembark 300.8.

.16 **ride at anchor,** ride, lie, rest; ride easy; ride hawse full; lie athwart; set an anchor watch.

.17 **lay** or **lie to,** lay or lie by; lie near or close to the wind, head to wind or windward, be under the sea; lie ahull; lie off, lie off the land; lay or lie up.

.18 **weigh anchor,** up-anchor, bring the anchor home, break out the anchor, cat the anchor, break ground, loose for sea; **unmoor,** drop the mooring, cast off or loose or away.

.19 **get under way,** put or have way upon, **put** or **push** or **shove off;** hoist the blue Peter; **put to sea,** put out to sea, go to sea, head for blue water, go off soundings; **sail,** sail away; embark 301.16.

.20 **set sail,** hoist sail, unfurl or spread sail, heave out a sail, **make sail,** trim sail; square away, square the yards; **crowd** or **clap** or **crack** or **pack on sail,** put on (more) sail; clap on, crack on, pack on; give her beans [slang].

.21 **make way,** gather way, **make headway,** make sternway; make knots, foot; **go full speed ahead,** go full speed astern; go or run or steam at flank speed.

.22 run, **run** or **sail before the wind,** run or sail with the wind, run or sail down the wind, make a spinnaker run, sail off the wind, sail free, sail with the wind aft, sail with the wind abaft the beam; tack down wind; run or sail with the wind quartering.

.23 **bring off the wind, pay off,** bear off or away, put the helm to leeward, bear or head to leeward, pay off the head.

.24 **sail against the wind,** sail on or by the wind, sail to windward, bear or head to windward; **bring in** or **into the wind,** bring by or on the wind, haul the wind or one's wind; uphelm, put the helm up; haul, haul off, haul up; **haul to, bring to, heave to;** sail in or into the wind's eye or the teeth of the wind; sail to the windward of, weather.

.25 **sail near the wind,** sail close to the wind, lie near or close to the wind, sail full and by, hold a close wind, **sail close-hauled,** close-haul; work or go or beat or eat to windward, **beat, ply;** luff, luff up, sail closer to the wind; sail too close to the wind, sail fine, touch the wind, pinch.

.26 **gain to windward of,** eat or claw to windward of, eat the wind out of, have the wind of, be to windward of.

.27 chart or plot or lay out a course; shape a course, lay or lie a course.

.28 take or follow a course, **keep or hold the course or a course**, hold on the course or a course, stand on or upon a course, stand on a straight course, maintain or keep the heading, keep her steady, keep pointed.

.29 **drift off course, yaw**, yaw off, pay off, bear off, drift, sag; sag or bear or ride or drive to leeward, make leeway, drive, fetch away; be set by the current, drift with the current, fall down.

.30 **change course**, change the heading, bear off or away, bear to starboard or port; sheer, swerve; **tack**, cast, break, yaw, slew, shift, turn; **cant**, cant round or across; **beat, ply; veer, wear, wear ship; jibe** or gybe [both Brit], jibe all standing, make a North River jibe; **put about**, come or go or bring or fetch about, beat about, cast or throw about; bring or swing or heave or haul round; **about ship**, turn or put back, turn on her heel, wind; swing the stern; box off; back and fill; stand off and on; double or round a point; miss stays.

.31 put the rudder hard left or right, put the rudder or helm hard over, put the rudder amidships, ease the rudder or helm, give her more or less rudder; starboard, port, larboard.

.32 **veer or wear short**, bring by the lee, **broach to**, lie beam on to the seas.

.33 (come to a stop) **fetch up**, haul up, fetch up all standing.

.34 **backwater**, back, reverse, go astern; **go full speed astern**; make sternway.

.35 **sail for, put away for, make for** or toward, make at, **run for**, stand for, head or steer toward, lay for, **lay a course or one's course for**, bear up for; bear up to, **bear down on** or **upon**, run or bear in with, **close with**; make, reach, fetch; heave or go alongside; lay or go aboard; lay or lie in; **put in** or into, put into port, approach anchorage.

.36 **sail away from**, head or steer away from, run from, **stand from**, lay away or off from; **stand off**, bear off, put off, shove off, haul off; stand off and on.

.37 **clear the land**, bear off the land, lay or settle the land, make or get sea room.

.38 **make land**, reach land; close with the land, stand in for the land; sight land; make a landfall.

.39 **coast**, sail coast-wise, stay in soundings, range the coast, skirt the shore, lie along the shore, **hug the shore** or **land** or **coast**.

.40 **weather the storm**, weather, ride, **ride out**, outride, ride or ride out a storm; make heavy or bad weather.

.41 **sail into**, run down, run in or into, **ram; come** or **run foul** or **afoul of, collide**, fall aboard; nose or head into, run prow or end or head on, run head and head; run broadside on.

.42 **shipwreck**, wreck, pile up [informal], cast away; **go** or **run aground**, ground, take the ground, beach, strand, run on the rocks; ground hard and fast.

.43 **careen, list, heel**, tip, cant, heave or lay down, lie along; be on her beam ends.

.44 **capsize, upset**, overset, **overturn**, turn over, turn turtle, upset the boat, keel, keel over or up; pitchpole, somersault; **sink, founder**, be lost, go down, go to the bottom, go to Davy Jones's locker; scuttle.

.45 **go overboard**, go by the board, go over the board or side.

.46 **maneuver**, execute a maneuver; heave in together, keep in formation, maintain position, **keep station**, keep pointed, steam in line, steam in line of bearing; convoy.

.47 (submarines) **surface**, break water; **submerge, dive**, go below; rig for diving; flood the tanks, flood negative.

.48 (activities aboard ship) lay, lay aloft, lay forward, etc.; traverse a yard, brace a yard fore and aft; heave, haul; kedge; warp; boom; heave round, heave short, heave apeak; log, heave or stream the log; haul down, board; spar down; ratline down, clap on ratlines; batten down the hatches; unlash, cut or cast loose; clear hawse.

.49 **trim ship**, trim, trim up; trim by the head or stern, put in proper fore-and-aft trim, give greater draft fore and aft, **put on an even keel; ballast**, shift ballast, wing out ballast; break out ballast, break bulk, shoot ballast; **clear the decks**, clear for action.

.50 **reduce sail**, shorten or take in sail, hand a sail, **reef**, reef one's sails; double-reef; lower sail, dowse sail; run under bare poles; snug down; **furl**, put on a harbor furl.

.51 **take bearings**, cast a traverse; correct distance and maintain the bearings; run down the latitude, **take a sight**, shoot the sun, bring down the sun; **box the compass; take soundings** 209.9.

.52 **signal**, make a signal, speak, hail and

speak; dress ship; unfurl *or* hoist a banner, unfurl an ensign, **break out a flag;** hoist the blue Peter; show one's colors, **exchange colors;** salute, dip the ensign.

.53 **row, paddle,** ply the oar, **pull, scull, punt;** give way, row away; catch *or* cut a crab *or* lobster [informal]; feather, feather an oar; sky an oar [informal]; row dry [Brit informal]; pace, shoot; ship oars.

.54 **float,** ride, drift; **sail, scud, run,** shoot; skim, foot; ghost, glide, slip; ride the sea, plow the deep, walk the waters.

.55 **pitch, toss, tumble,** toss and tumble, pitch and toss, **plunge,** hobbyhorse, pound, **rear, rock, roll, reel, swing, sway, lurch, yaw, heave,** scend, **flounder, welter, wallow;** make heavy weather.

.56 **swim, bathe,** go in swimming *or* bathing; tread water; **float,** float on one's back, do the deadman's float; **wade,** go in wading; skinny-dip; dive 320.6.

.57 ADJS **nautical, marine, maritime, naval, navigational; seafaring, seagoing, oceangoing,** water-borne; **seamanly, seamanlike, salty** [informal]; pelagic, oceanic 397.8.

.58 **aquatic, water-dwelling,** water-living, water-growing, water-loving; **swimming,** balneal, natant, natatory, natatorial; shore, seashore; tidal, estuarine, littoral, grallatorial; deep-sea 209.14.

.59 **navigable,** boatable.

.60 **floating, afloat,** awash; water-borne.

.61 **adrift, afloat,** unmoored, untied, loose, unanchored, aweigh; cast-off, started.

.62 ADVS **on board,** on shipboard, on board ship, **aboard,** all aboard, afloat; **on deck,** topside; aloft; in sail; before the mast; athwart the hawse, athwarthawse.

.63 **under way,** making way, with steerageway, with way on; **at sea,** on the high seas, off soundings, in blue water; **under sail** *or* **canvas,** with sails spread; under press of sail *or* canvas *or* steam; under steam *or* power; under bare poles; on *or* off the heading *or* course; in soundings, homeward bound.

.64 **before the wind,** with the wind, down the wind, running free; off the wind, with the wind aft, with the wind abaft the beam, wing and wing, under the wind, under the lee; on a reach, on a beam *or* broad reach, with wind abeam.

.65 **against the wind,** on the wind, in *or* into the wind, up the wind, by the wind, head to wind; in *or* into the wind's eye, in the teeth of the wind.

.66 **near the wind,** close to the wind, **closehauled,** on a beat, full and by.

.67 **coastward, landward,** to landward; **coastwise,** coastways.

.68 **leeward,** to leeward, alee, downwind; **windward,** to windward, weatherward, aweather, upwind.

.69 **aft,** abaft, baft, **astern;** fore and aft.

.70 **alongside,** board and board, yardarm to yardarm.

.71 **at anchor,** riding at anchor; lying to, hove to; lying ahull.

.72 **afoul,** foul, in collision; head and head, head *or* end *or* prow on; broadside on.

.73 **aground,** on the rocks; hard and fast.

.74 **overboard,** over the board *or* side, by the board; aft the fantail.

.75 INTERJS (orders, calls) ahoy!, ahoy there!, ship ahoy!; avast!, hold fast!; belay!, belay that *or* there!; aye, aye!, aye, aye, sir!; heave!, heave ho!, yo-heave-ho!, heave and awash!; lend a hand!; one hand for yourself and one for the ship!; stand by!, stand by to weigh anchor!, stand by the main sheet!, etc.; anchors aweigh!; aloft!, aloft there!; ready about!; turn out!, show a leg!, rise and shine!; man overboard!; aboard!, all aboard!, take ship!, up oars!; give way!, row away!; way enough!, ship oars!

.76 (orders to the helm) up helm!, down helm!, port!, larboard!, starboard!, helm aport!, helm astarboard!, helm alee!, helm aweather!, hard aport!, hard alee!, hard astarboard!, hard aweather!, hard over!, right!, left!, right *or* left rudder!, right *or* left standard rudder!, right *or* left five (ten etc.) degrees rudder!, right *or* left half rudder!, right *or* left full rudder!, right *or* left handsomely!, give her more rudder!, shift the rudder!, meet her!, ease the helm *or* rudder!, rudder amidships!, nothing to the right *or* left!, no nearer!, how is your rudder?, how does she head?, keep her so!, steady!, steady so!, steady as you go!, about ship!

.77 (orders to the engine room) starboard *or* port engine!, all engines!, ahead!, back!, astern!, starboard *or* port engine ahead!, full speed ahead! *or* astern!, slow ahead!, slow astern!, all engines ahead!, ahead one-third!, ahead two-thirds!, ahead standard!, ahead full!, back one-third!, back two-thirds!, back full!

.78 (submarine orders) rig for diving!, ventilate inboard!, shift the control!, stations for diving!, secure the engines!, secure the main induction!, close the conning tower hatch!, ahead both motors!, flood the tank!, blow the tank!, flood main ballast!, close main vents!, flood 2000 pounds in after trim!

276. MARINER

.1 NOUNS **mariner, seaman, sailor,** sailorman, **navigator, seafarer,** seafaring man, bluejacket, sea or water dog [informal], shipman, jack, jacky, jack afloat, jack-tar, **tar, salt** [informal], hearty, lobscouser [slang], *matelot* [Fr], windsailor, windjammer; limey or limejuicer [both slang]; lascar [India]; common or ordinary seaman, OD; able or able-bodied seaman, AB; deep-sea man, saltwater or bluewater or deepwater sailor; fresh-water sailor; fair-weather sailor; whaler, fisherman, lobsterman; viking, sea rover, buccaneer, privateer, pirate; Jason, Argonaut, Ancient Mariner, Flying Dutchman; Neptune, Poseidon, Varuna, Dylan.

.2 (novice) **lubber, landlubber;** polliwog.

.3 (veteran) **old salt** or old sea dog or shellback or barnacle-back [all informal]; **master mariner.**

.4 **navy man,** man-of-war's man, **bluejacket; gob** or swabbie or swabber [all slang]; **marine, leatherneck** [informal], gyrene, devil dog [both slang], Royal Marine, jolly [Brit informal]; horse marine; boot [informal]; **midshipman,** midshipmite, middy [informal]; cadet, naval cadet; coastguardsman, Naval Reservist, Seabee, frogman.

.5 **boatman,** boatsman, boat-handler, **boater,** waterman; **oarsman,** oar, rower, sculler, punter; galley slave; **yachtsman,** yachter; **ferryman,** ferrier; **bargeman,** barger, bargee [Brit], bargemaster; lighterman, wherryman; **gondolier,** *gondoliere* [Ital].

.6 **hand, deckhand,** deckie [Brit], roustabout [informal]; stoker, fireman, bakehead [slang]; black gang; wiper, oiler, boilerman; cabin boy; yeoman, ship's writer; purser; ship's carpenter, chips [informal]; ship's cooper, bungs or Jimmy Bungs [both informal]; ship's tailor, snip or snips [both informal]; steward, stewardess, commissary steward, mess steward, hospital steward; commissary clerk; mail orderly; navigator; radio operator, sparks [informal]; landing signalman; gunner, gun loader, torpedoman; afterguard; complement; watch.

.7 (ship's officers) **captain,** shipmaster, **master, skipper** [informal], **commander,** the Old Man [informal], *patron* [Fr]; navigator, navigating officer, sailing master; deck officer, officer of the deck, OD; watch officer, officer of the watch; **mate,** first or chief mate, second mate, third mate, boatswain's mate; **boatswain,** bos'n, pipes [informal]; quartermaster; sergeant-at-arms; chief engineer, engine-room officer; naval officer 749.20.

.8 **steersman, helmsman,** wheelman, wheelsman, boatsteerer; **coxswain,** cox [informal]; **pilot,** conner, sailing master; harbor pilot, docking pilot.

.9 **longshoreman,** wharf hand, dockhand, docker, dock-walloper [slang]; **stevedore,** loader; **roustabout** [informal], lumper.

277. SHIP, BOAT

.1 NOUNS **ship** 277.22, **boat** 277.21, **vessel, craft,** bottom, bark, argosy, hull, hulk, keel, watercraft; tub or bucket or hooker [all slang], packet; leviathan; "that packet of assorted miseries which we call a ship" [Kipling], "the ship, a fragment detached from the earth" [Joseph Conrad].

.2 **steamer, steamboat, steamship;** motor ship.

.3 **sailboat,** sailing vessel 277.23, sailing boat, sailing yacht, sailing cruiser, sailing ship, tall or taunt ship, sail, sailer, **windjammer** [informal], windship, windboat; **galley** 277.25.

.4 **motorboat, powerboat,** speedboat; **launch,** motor launch, steam launch, naphtha launch; **cruiser,** power cruiser, **cabin cruiser,** sedan cruiser, outboard cruiser.

.5 **liner, ocean liner,** ocean greyhound [informal], passenger steamer, floating hotel or palace, luxury liner.

.6 **warship,** war vessel, naval vessel 277.24, **man-of-war,** man-o'-war, ship of war, armored vessel; USS, United States Ship; HMS, His or Her Majesty's Ship; line-of-battle ship, ship of the line.

.7 **battleship,** battlewagon [informal], capital ship; **destroyer,** can or tin can [both informal].

.8 **carrier, aircraft carrier,** seaplane carrier, **flattop** [informal].

.9 **submarine, sub,** submersible, underwater craft; **U-boat,** *U-boot, Unterseeboot* [both Ger], pigboat [slang].

.10 **ships, shipping,** merchant or mercantile marine, merchant navy or fleet, bottoms, tonnage; **fleet,** flotilla, argosy; line; fishing fleet, whaling fleet, etc.; **navy** 800.26.

.11 **float, raft;** balsa, balsa raft, Kon Tiki; life raft, Carling float; boom; pontoon; buoy, life buoy; **life preserver** 701.5; surfboard; cork; bob.

.12 **rigging** 277.31, rig, **tackle,** tackling, **gear; ropework,** roping; service, serving, whipping; standing rigging, running rigging; boatswain's stores; ship chandlery.

.13 **spar** 277.29, timber; **mast,** pole, stick *or* tree [both informal]; bare pole.

.14 **sail** 277.30, **canvas,** muslin, cloth, rag [informal]; **full** *or* **plain sail,** press *or* crowd of sail; reduced sail, reefed sail; square sail; fore-and-aft sail; luff, leech, foot, earing, reef point, boltrope, clew, cringle, head.

.15 **oar,** remi–; **paddle,** scull, sweep, pole; steering oar.

.16 **anchor** 277.32, mooring, hook *or* mudhook [both informal]; **anchorage,** moorings; **berth,** slip; mooring buoy.

.17 ADJS **rigged,** decked, trimmed; square-rigged, fore-and-aft rigged, Marconi-rigged, gaff-rigged, lateen-rigged.

.18 **seaworthy,** sea-kindly, fit for sea, **snug, bold; watertight,** waterproof; **A1,** A1 at Lloyd's; stiff, tender; weatherly.

.19 **trim,** in trim; apoise, on an even keel.

.20 **shipshape,** Bristol fashion, shipshape and Bristol fashion, trim, trig, neat, tight, taut, ataunt, all ataunto, bungup and bilge-free.

.21 **boats**

airboat	dogger
almadia	dory
ark	double-ender
auxiliary, auxiliary boat	drifter
barge	dugout
bateau	eight-oar
broadhorn	*Faltboat* [Ger]
bucentaur	ferry, ferryboat
bumboat	fiber-glass boat
bunder boat	fireboat
bungo	fishing boat
buss	fishing dory
caïque	flatboat
canalboat	flyboat
canoe	foldboat
cargo boat	four-oar
catamaran	funny
catboat, cat	galley
coble	garvey
cockboat	gig
cockle	glass-bottomed boat
cockleboat	glider
cockleshell	gliding boat
cog	gondola
coracle	houseboat
cruiser 277.4	hoy
curragh	hydrocycle
cutter	hydrofoil
cutter-gig	hydroglider
dahabeah	hydroplane
dinghy	jangada
dispatch boat	johnboat
	jolly, jolly boat

kayak	rowboat, rowing boat
launch 277.4	runabout
lerret	sampan
lifeboat	scooter
lifesaving boat	scow
lighter	scull
log canoe	sea sled
longboat	shallop
mail boat, mailer	shell
motorboat	ship's boat
nuggar	showboat
outboard motorboat, outboard	skiff
outrigger canoe	small boat
pair-oar	sneakbox
pilot, pilot boat	surfboat
pinnace	towboat
piragua	trawler, trawlboat
pirogue	trimaran
pontoon	trow
post boat	tug, tugboat
pram	tuna clipper
punt	umiak
racer	wanigan
racing shell	whaleboat
radio-controlled life-boat	whale-gig
randan	wherry
	workboat
	yawl, yawl boat

.22 **ships**

argosy	packet, packet boat *or* ship
ark	
bathyscaphe	paddle boat *or* steamer
buoy-tender	
cabin boat	picket ship
cable ship	refrigeration ship
caravel	revenue cutter
cargo ship	rotor, rotor ship
coaler, collier	screw steamer
coaster	self-propelled barge
coast guard cutter	side-wheeler
container ship	slaver
derelict	spar-decker, spar-deck vessel
dredge	
excursion steamer	stage boat
fishing boat *or* vessel	steamer 277.2
floating drydock	steam schooner
freighter	steam yacht
hydrofoil	stern-wheeler
icebreaker	storeship
LASH (lighter aboard ship)	super-tanker
	tanker
lightship	tender
liner 277.5	tramp steamer
mail steamer	transport
merchant ship, merchantman	trawler
	turbine
nuclear-powered ship	turbine steamer
ocean-going tug	weather ship
oceanographic research ship	whaleback
	whaler
oiler	

.23 **sailing vessels**

baggala	bugeye
bark	bully
barkentine	buss
bastard schooner	caravel
bawley	carrack
bilander	cat
brig	catamaran
brigantine	catboat

chasse-marée [Fr]
Chesapeake canoe
class boat
clipper
corsair
corvette
cutter
dandy
dhow
dogger
dromond
felucca
fishing schooner
fishing smack
flattie
folkboat
fore-and-aft, fore-and-after
four-masted bark
four-master
Friendship sloop
frigate
full-rigged ship
gabert
galiot
galleass
galleon
hermaphrodite brig
hooker
hoy
Hudson River sloop
iceboat
ice yacht
junk
keelboat
ketch
knockabout
lateen, lateener
lorcha
lugger
motorsailer
nobby
ocean racer

outrigger
pilot boat
pinnace
piragua
pirogue
polacre, polacca
pram
proa
pungy
racing yacht
rigger
saic
sailing auxiliary
sailing barge
sailing canoe
sailing dinghy
sailing launch
sailing packet
sailing trawler
sampan
sandbagger
schooner
scooter
shallop
sharpie
shipentine
skipjack
sloop
smack
smack boat
snow
square-rigger
tartan
tea-clipper
three-master
topsail schooner
trimaran
well smack
whaler
wool-clipper
xebec
yacht
yawl

ironclad
ironclad ram
ironsides
jeep carrier
landing craft
LC (landing craft)
LCC (landing craft, control)
LCI (landing craft, infantry)
LCM (landing craft, mechanized)
LCP (landing craft, personnel)
LCT (landing craft, tank)
LCV (landing craft, vehicle)
LCVP (landing craft, vehicle-personnel)
liberty boat
light cruiser
line-of-battle ship
LSD (landing ship, dock)
LSM (landing ship, medium)
LST (landing ship, tank)
mine layer, mine ship
mine sweeper
minisub
monitor
mosquito boat
MTB (motor torpedo boat)
naval auxiliary
net-tender
nuclear or nuclear-powered submarine
patrol boat
patrol torpedo boat
PC (patrol craft)
PCE (patrol craft, escort)
PCS (patrol craft, sweeper)

picketboat
pocket battleship
Polaris submarine
privateer
protected cruiser
PT boat (patrol torpedo boat)
raider
ram
receiving ship
reconnaissance ship
repair ship
river gunboat
rocket boat
SC (scouting craft)
scout
scout cruiser
seaplane carrier
second-line battleship
second-line destroyer
ship of the line
ship of war
shipplane carrier
sloop of war
spy ship
storeship
storm boat
submarine 277.9
submarine chaser, subchaser
submarine patrol boat
submarine tender
submersible
superdreadnought
supply ship
sweeper
tanker
target boat
tender
torpedo boat
torpedo-boat destroyer or catcher
transport, transport ship or vessel
troopship
turret ship
warship

.24 naval vessels

aircraft carrier 277.8
aircraft tender
AKA boat (auxiliary cargo attack)
ammunition ship
APA boat (auxiliary personnel attack)
armored or protected cruiser
assault boat
assault transport
atomic or atomic-powered submarine
battle cruiser
battleship 277.7
blockship
bomb ketch or vessel
capital ship
caravel
carrier 277.8
coast guard cutter
communications ship
convoy
corvette
crash boat
cruiser
cutter

depot ship
destroyer 277.7
destroyer escort
destroyer leader
destroyer tender
dispatch boat
dreadnought
eagle boat
E-boat
escort carrier
escort vessel
fireboat
fire ship
first-rate
flagship
flattop [informal]
fleet submarine
floating battery
frigate
fuel ship
guard ship or boat
guided missile cruiser
gunboat
heavy cruiser
hospital ship
hunter-killer submarine

.25 galleys

bireme
foist
galiot
galleass
galley foist
half galley
hepteris
hexeris
penteconter

quadrireme
quarter galley
quinquereme
tessaraconter
triaconter
trireme
Venetian galley
war galley

.26 parts of ships

back
balance rudder
batten
beak, beakhead
beam
beam clamp
bilge keel
bilge keelson
bitt
board
bollard
bollard timber

bow
bracket plate
bridge
bulkhead
bull's-eye
bulwarks
cam cleat
capstan
carling
casemate
cathead
ceiling

centerboard
centerboard trunk
chainplate
cleat
coffee-grinder winch
companion
companion ladder
companionway
conning tower
conning tower hatch
counter
crow's nest
cutwater
daggerboard
davit
deadwood
entrance
false keel
fantail
figurehead
fin keel
forefoot
foresheets
foretop
frame
freeboard
futtock
gangplank
gangway
garboard strake
gudgeon
gunwale, gunnel
hatch
hatchway
hawse, hawsehole
hawsepiece
hawsepipe
hawse timber
head
heel
island
keel
keel and keelson
keelson
kevel
knee
knighthead
larboard
lee, lee side, leeward
leeboard
limber board
limber hole
maintop
mizzentop
monkey rail
nose
paddle wheel

pintle
planking, plank plating
Plimsoll marks
poop
port, portside
porthole
post
propeller
prow
pulpit
rail
rib
rubrail
rudder
rudderpost
rudderstock
run
scupper
scuttle
scuttlebutt
shaft tunnel
sheave hole
sheer strake
sheets
shelf, shelfpiece
sister or side keelson
sister rib
skeg
snorkel
spirketing
stanchion
starboard
steering engine
stem
stern
sternpost
stern sheets
strake
stringer
superstructure
tail end
tail shaft
tiller
transom
trimming hatch or hole
truck
waterline
waterway
weather, weather side
weatherboard
wheel
winch
windlass
windward, windward side

roundhouse
sail loft
sick bay
stateroom

.28 decks

after deck
anchor deck
boat deck
bridge deck
flight deck
forward deck
gun deck
half deck
hurricane deck
landing deck
lower deck
main deck
middle deck
orlop deck

stokehold
topside
wardroom

partial hold deck
platform, platform deck
poop, poop deck
promenade deck
protective deck
quarterdeck
runway
shelter deck
spar deck
splinter deck
superstructure deck
upper or top deck
weather deck

.29 spars, masts

boom
bowsprit
brace bumpkin
bumpkin, boomkin
club
crossjack yard
crosstree
dolphin striker
flying jib boom
fore jack
foremast
foreroyal mast
foreroyal-studding-sail boom
foreroyal yard
fore-skysail mast
fore-skysail yard
fore-topgallant mast
fore-topgallant-studding-sail boom
fore-topgallant yard
fore-topmast
fore-topmast-studding-sail boom
fore-topsail yard
fore-trysail gaff
foreyard
gaff
gooseneck
jack
jack staff
jib boom
jigger mast
king post
lazy jack
lower boom
lower mizzen-topsail yard
main-brace bumpkin
mainmast
main-royal mast
main-royal-studding-sail boom
main-royal yard

main-skysail mast
main-skysail yard
main-topgallant mast
main-topgallant-studding-sail boom
main-topgallant yard
main-topmast
main-topmast-studding-sail boom
main-topsail yard
main-trysail gaff
main yard
martingale or dolphin-striker boom
mast
masthead
mizzen, mizzenmast
mizzen-royal mast
mizzen-royal yard
mizzen-skysail mast
mizzen-skysail yard
mizzen-topgallant mast
mizzen-topgallant yard
mizzen-topmast
mizzen-topsail yard
sheer pole
skysail mast or pole
skysail yard
spanker boom
spanker gaff
spinnaker pole
spreader
sprit
tack bumpkin
topgallant mast
topgallant yard
topmast
trysail gaff
whisker boom
whisker pole
yard
yardarm

.27 compartments

below
between-decks, 'tween-decks
boiler room
brig
bunker
cabin
caboose, camboose
chain locker
chart room, chart house
conning tower
engine room, engine

space
forecastle, fo'c'sle
forepeak
galley
head
hold, hole
lazaret
officers' country
paint locker
pilothouse
quarters
radio room, radio shack

.30 sails

baby jib topsail
balance or French lug
balloon sail or jib, ballooner

batten
batten pocket
club-footed jib
club topsail

crossjack
dipping lug
fly-by-night
flying jib
flying kites
fore gaff-topsail
foreroyal
foreroyal studding sail
foresail
fore-skysail
forestaysail
fore topgallant sail
fore-topgallant studding sail
fore-topmast staysail
fore-topmast studding sail
fore-topsail
Genoa, Genoa jib
inner jib
jenny
jib
jigger
jimbo
jolly jumper
kites
lateen sail
leg-of-mutton sail
loose-footed sail
lower studding sail
lug
lugsail
main gaff-topsail
main royal
main-royal staysail
main-royal studding sail
mainsail
main skysail
main staysail
main-topgallant sail

main-topgallant studding sail
main-topmast staysail
main-topmast studding sail
main-topsail
mizzen
mizzen royal
mizzen-royal staysail
mizzen sail
mizzen skysail
mizzen staysail
mizzen-topgallant sail
mizzen-topgallant staysail
mizzen-topmast staysail
moonraker
moonsail
outer jib
parachute spinnaker
reef
reef point
royal
skysail
skyscraper [informal]
spanker
spinnaker
spitfire
spritsail
square sail
standing lug
staysail
stern staysail
storm trysail
studding sail
topgallant sail
topsail
trysail
working jib

halyard
fore-trysail vang
futtock hoop
futtock shroud
gasket
grab rope
guess-rope
guess-warp
guest rope
gunter
guy
halyard
harbor gasket
hawser
head earing
head fast
Jacob's ladder
jib guy
jib martingale
jibstay
lanyard
lee sheet
lee tack
lifeline
lift
lower-boom topping lift
main brace
main lift
main-royal brace
main-royal lift
main-royal stay
mainsheet
main-skysail brace
main-skysail lift
main-skysail stay
mainstay
main-topgallant brace
main-topgallant lift
main-topgallant stay
main-topmast stay
main-topsail lift
main-trysail peak halyard
main-trysail vang
marline

martingale
messenger
mizzen-royal brace
mizzen-royal lift
mizzen-royal stay
mizzen-skysail brace
mizzen-skysail lift
mizzen-skysail stay
mizzen stay
mizzen-topgallant brace
mizzen-topgallant lift
mizzen-topgallant stay
mizzen-topmast stay
mizzen-topsail lift
mooring pendant or pennant
outhaul
painter
pennant hoist
port tack
preventer backstay
quarter fast
ratline
reef earing
roband, ropeband
roller-reefing gear
sea gasket
sheet
shroud
span
spanker peak halyard
spanker sheet
spanker vang
spring, spring line
starboard tack
stay
stern fast
stirrup
swifter
tack
timenoguy
topping lift
vang
weather sheet
whisker jumper

.31 ropes, rigging

after shroud
anchor chain
anchor rode
backropes
backstay
becket
block
boat line
bobstay
boltrope
boom vang
bow fast
bowline
bowsprit shroud
brace
brail
breast fast
buntline
crossjack brace
crossjack lift
deadeye
downhaul
earing
fast
Flemish horse
flying jib guy
flying jib martingale
flying jib stay
footropes

forebrace
foreganger
fore lift
foreroyal backstay
foreroyal brace
foreroyal lift
foreroyal shroud
foreroyal stay
forerunner
foresheet
fore-skysail backstay
fore-skysail brace
fore-skysail lift
fore-skysail shroud
fore-skysail stay
forestay
foretack
fore-topgallant backstay
fore-topgallant brace
fore-topgallant lift
fore-topgallant shroud
fore-topgallant stay
fore-topmast backstay
fore-topmast stay
fore-topmast staysail stay
fore-topsail lift
fore-trysail peak

.32 anchors

Baldt anchor
bower
center anchor
CQR or CQR plow anchor
Danforth anchor
dinghy anchor
drag anchor
drogue
Dunn anchor
floating anchor
fluke
grapnel
kedge, kedge anchor
killick
Martin's anchor
mushroom anchor
Navy anchor

Northill anchor
parachute drogue
plow anchor
port anchor
sacred anchor
sand anchor
screw anchor
sea anchor
shank
sheet anchor
starboard anchor
stern anchor
stock
stockless anchor
stream anchor
Trotman's anchor
yachtman's anchor

.33 helms

automatic pilot
destroyer wheel
electrohydraulic steering gear

gyroscopic pilot
hand gear
lee helm
lever pilot

servo-pilot	tiller
steering gear	weather helm
telemotor	wheel

.34 equipment

anemometer	hawse bag
anemoscope	hawse hook
baggywrinkle	holystone
barograph	hygrograph
barometer	log
belaying pin	marlinespike
bilge pump	mooring swivel *or*
binnacle	shackle
boat hook	pump
caulking cotton	rigger's knife
caulking iron	sounders 209.17
compass	tackle 287.10
fid	thermograph
grapnel	toggle
grappling iron	

278. AVIATION

.1 NOUNS aviation, aeronautics, aer(o)–; airplaning, skyriding, **flying, flight,** winging; volation, volitation; aeronautism, aerodromics; powered flight, jet flight, subsonic *or* supersonic flight; cruising, cross-country flying; bush flying; **gliding,** sailplaning, soaring, sailing; volplaning; ballooning, balloonery, lighter-than-air aviation; barnstorming [informal]; high-altitude flying; blind *or* instrument flight *or* flying, instrument flight rules, IFR; contact flying, visual flight *or* flying, visual flight rules, VFR, pilotage; skywriting; cloud-seeding; in-flight training, ground school; **airline,** air service, feeder airline, scheduled airline, nonscheduled airline *or* nonsked [informal], short-hop airline; commercial aviation, general aviation, private aviation, private flying; astronautics 282.1; air show, flying circus.

.2 (allied sciences) aeroballistics, aerocartography, aerodontia, aerodynamics, aerogeography, aerogeology, aerography, aerology, aeromechanics, aerometry, aeronautical engineering, aerophotography, aeronautical meteorology, aerial photography, aerophysics, aeroscopy, aerospace research, aerostatics, aerostation, aerotechnics, aviation technology, aircraft hydraulics, avionics, climatology, acronomy, hydrostatics, jet engineering, kinematics, kinetics, meteorology, micrometry, photometry, pneumatics, rocket engineering, rocketry; supersonics, supersonic aerodynamics; aviation medicine, aeromedicine.

.3 airmanship, pilotship; **flight plan;** briefing, brief, rundown [informal], debriefing; flight *or* pilot training, flying lessons; washout [informal].

.4 air-mindedness, aerophilia; air legs.

.5 airsickness; aerophobia, aeropathy.

.6 navigation, avigation, aerial *or* air navigation; celestial navigation, astronavigation; electronic navigation, automatic electronic navigation, radio navigation, navar, radar, consolan, tacan, teleran, loran, shoran; omnidirectional range, omnirange, visual-aural range, VAR.

.7 (aeronautical organizations) Civil Aeronautics Administration, CAA, Federal Aviation Agency, FAA; Bureau of Aeronautics, BuAer; National Advisory Committee for Aeronautics, NACA; Office of Naval Research, ONR; Civil Air Patrol, CAP; Caterpillar Club; Airline Pilots Association; Aircraft Recognition Society, ARS; Air Force 800.28,29.

.8 takeoff, hopoff [informal]; taxiing, takeoff run, takeoff power, rotation; daisyclipping *or* grass-cutting [both informal]; ground loop; level-off; jet-assisted takeoff, JATO, booster rocket, takeoff rocket; catapult, electropult.

.9 flight, trip, run; hop *or* jump [both informal]; powered flight; solo flight, **solo;** inverted flight; supersonic flight; test flight, **test hop** [informal]; **airlift;** airdrop.

.10 air travel, air transport, airfreight, air cargo, airline travel; shuttle, air shuttle, shuttle service, shuttle trip, air taxi; weather *or* meteorological reconnaissance; in-flight refueling; **range,** flying range, radius of action, navigation radius.

.11 (Air Force) **mission,** flight operation; training mission; gunnery mission; combat rehearsal, **dry run** [informal]; transition mission; reconnaissance mission, reconnaissance, observation flight, search mission; **milk run** [informal]; box-top mission [informal]; combat flight; **sortie,** scramble [informal]; **air raid;** shuttle raid; bombing mission; bombing, strafing 798.7,8; **air support** (for ground troops), **air cover,** cover, umbrella, air umbrella.

.12 flight formation, formation flying, formation; close formation, loose formation, wing formation; V formation, echelon.

.13 (maneuvers) acrobatic *or* tactical evolutions *or* maneuvers, acrobatics, **aerobatics;** stunting *or* **stunt flying** [both informal], rolling, crabbing, banking, porpoising, fishtailing, diving; **dive, nose dive, power dive; zoom,** chandelle; stall, whip stall; **glide,** volplane; spiral, split 'S', lazy eight, sideslip, pushdown, pull-up, pullout.

.14 roll, barrel roll, aileron roll, outside roll, snap roll.

.15 spin, autorotation, tailspin, flat spin, inverted spin, normal spin, power spin, uncontrolled spin, falling leaf.

.16 loop, spiral loop, ground loop, normal loop, outside loop, inverted normal or outside loop, dead-stick loop, wingover, looping the loop; Immelmann turn, reverse turn, reversement; flipper turns.

.17 buzzing, flathatting or hedgehopping [both informal].

.18 landing, coming in [informal], touching down, touchdown; arrival; landing run, landing pattern; approach, downwind leg, approach leg; holding pattern, stack up [informal]; ballooning in, parachute approach; blind or instrument landing, dead-stick landing, glide landing, stall landing, fishtail landing, sideslip landing, level or two-point landing, normal or three-point landing, Chinese landing [informal], tail-high landing, tail-low landing, thumped-in landing [informal], pancake landing, belly landing, crash landing, noseover, nose-up; practice landing, bounce drill.

.19 (flying and landing guides) marker, pylon; beacon; radio beacon, radio range station, radio marker, fan marker; radar beacon, racon; beam, radio beam; beacon lights 336.10; runway lights, high-intensity runway approach lights, sequence flashers, flare path; wind indicator, wind cone or sock, air sleeve; instrument landing system, ILS, touchdown rate of descent indicator, TRODI, ground-controlled approach, GCA; talking-down system, talking down.

.20 crash, crack-up, prang [Brit informal]; crash landing; collision, midair collision; near-miss.

.21 blackout; grayout; anoxia; useful consciousness; pressure suit, antiblackout suit.

.22 airport, airfield, airdrome, aerodrome [Brit], drome, port, air harbor [Can], aviation field, landing field, landing, field, airship station; air base, air station, naval air station; airpark; heliport, helidrome; control tower, island; Air Route Traffic Control Center.

.23 runway, taxiway, strip, landing strip, airstrip, flight strip, take-off strip; fairway, launching way; stopway; clearway; transition strip; apron; flight deck, landing deck.

.24 hangar, housing, dock, airdock, shed, airship shed; mooring mast.

.25 aerocurve, aerodynamic or air volume, airplane heading, amplitude, aspect ratio, camber, décalage [Fr], equivalent monoplane, fineness ratio, flight path, margin of power, positive direction of roll, propulsive efficiency, resultant force, righting or restoring moment, skin friction, skin effect, slip, stagger, sweepback, tail force.

.26 (angle) aileron angle, blade angle, coning angle, dihedral angle, drift angle, downwash angle, elevator angle, flapping angle, flight path angle, gliding angle, helix angle, landing angle, rudder angle, trim angle, zero-lift angle, angle of attack, angle of dead rise, angle of heel, angle of incidence or wing setting, angle of pitch, angle of roll or bank, angle of sideslip, angle of stabilizer setting, angle of yaw.

.27 (center) aerodynamic center, elastic center, center of buoyancy, center of gravity, center of mass, center of pressure, center-of-pressure coefficiency.

.28 (axis) horizontal or longitudinal axis, fore-and-aft axis, X axis; lateral axis, Y axis; normal axis, Z axis; elastic axis, wing axis, drag axis, positive lift axis; yawing, yaw, positive direction of yaw.

.29 (stability) automatic stability, directional stability, dynamic stability, inherent stability, lateral stability, longitudinal stability, static stability.

.30 (load) basic load, design load, full load, normal load, ultimate load, useful load; payload, passenger capacity; offensive load; power loading, span loading, unsymmetrical loading, wing loading.

.31 (pressure) altitude or height pressure, dynamic pressure, impact pressure, manometer pressure, superpressure; center of pressure; stress, working stress, breathing stress; torsion, torsional stress, torque, propeller torque; structural fatigue.

.32 (thrust) propeller thrust, static propeller thrust, line of thrust or flight; jet thrust, pounds of thrust, augmenter or thrust augmenter, afterburner, tail-pipe burner, fan-jet; rocket assist.

.33 (propulsion) rocket propulsion, rocket power; jet propulsion, jet power; turbojet propulsion, pulse-jet propulsion, ram-jet propulsion, resojet propulsion; constant or ram pressure, air ram; reaction propulsion, reaction, action and reaction; aeromotor 280.17, aircraft engine, power plant.

.34 **pitch,** pitch ratio, aerodynamic pitch, effective pitch, geometrical pitch, zero-thrust pitch; angle of pitch, positive direction of pitch.

.35 **lift,** lift ratio, lift force or component, lift direction; aerostatic lift, dynamic lift, gross lift, useful lift, margin of lift.

.36 **drag,** resistance; drag ratio, drag force or component, induced drag, wing drag, parasite or parasitic or structural drag, profile drag, head resistance, drag direction, cross-wind force.

.37 **drift,** drift angle; lateral drift, leeway.

.38 **flow,** air flow, laminar flow; **turbulence,** turbulent flow, burble, burble point, eddies.

.39 wash, wake, stream; downwash; backwash, **slipstream,** propeller race, propwash; **exhaust,** jet exhaust, blow wash; **vapor trail,** condensation trail, contrail, vortex.

.40 (speed) **air speed,** true air speed, operating or flying speed, cruising speed, knots, minimum flying speed, hump speed, peripheral speed, pitch speed, terminal speed, sinking speed, get-away or take-off speed, landing speed, ground speed, speed over the ground; **speed of sound** 269.2; zone of no signal, Mach cone; **sound barrier,** sonic barrier or wall; sonic boom, shock wave, Mach wave.

.41 (air, atmosphere) **airspace,** navigable airspace; aerosphere; aeropause; troposphere, tropopause, substratosphere, stratosphere, stratopause, ionosphere; **aerospace;** space, empty space; **ceiling,** ballonet ceiling, service ceiling, static ceiling, absolute ceiling; cloud layer or cover, ceiling zero; visibility, visibility zero; **overcast,** undercast; fog, soup [informal]; high-pressure area, low-pressure area; trough, trough line; front; **air pocket** or air hole, air bump, pocket, hole, bump; **turbulence,** clear-air turbulence, CAT, roughness; head wind, unfavorable wind; tail wind, favorable or favoring wind; crosswind; atmospheric tides; jetstream.

.42 **airway,** air lane, air line, air route, skyway, corridor, lane, path.

.43 **course, heading,** vector; compass heading or course, compass direction, magnetic heading, true heading or course.

.44 (altitude) altitude of flight, absolute altitude, critical altitude, density altitude, pressure altitude, sextant altitude; clearance; ground elevation.

.45 VERBS **fly,** be airborne, flit, wing, take wing, wing one's way, take or make a flight, take to the air, take the air, volitate, be wafted; **jet;** aviate, airplane, aeroplane; travel by air, go or travel by airline, go by plane or by air, take to the airways, ride the skies; hop [informal]; **soar,** drift, hover; **cruise; glide,** sailplane, sail, volplane; hydroplane, seaplane; balloon; ferry; airlift; break the sound barrier; navigate, avigate.

.46 **pilot,** control, be at the controls, **fly,** manipulate, drive, fly left seat; **copilot,** fly right seat; **solo; barnstorm** [informal]; fly blind, fly by the seat of one's pants [informal]; follow the beam, ride the beam, fly on instruments; fly in formation, take position; peel off.

.47 **take off,** hop or jump off [informal], become airborne, get off or leave the ground, take to the air, go or fly aloft, clear; rotate, power off; **taxi.**

.48 **ascend,** climb, gain altitude, mount; **zoom,** hoick [informal], chandelle.

.49 (maneuver) **stunt** [informal], perform aerobatics; crab, fishtail; **spin,** go into a tail spin; **loop,** loop the loop; **roll,** wingover, spiral, undulate, porpoise, feather, yaw, sideslip, skid, bank, dip, nose down, nose up, pull up, push down, pull out, plow, mush through.

.50 **dive,** nose-dive, power-dive, go for the deck; lose altitude, settle, dump altitude [informal].

.51 **buzz,** flathat or **hedgehop** [both informal].

.52 **land,** set her down [informal], **alight, light,** touch down; **descend,** come down, fly down; come in, come in for a landing; **level off,** flatten out; upwind, downwind; overshoot, undershoot; make a dead-stick landing; pancake, thump in [informal]; bellyland, settle down, balloon in; fishtail down; **crash-land;** ditch [informal]; nose up, nose over; talk down.

.53 **crash, crack up,** prang [Brit informal], spin in, fail to pull out.

.54 **stall,** lose power, conk out [informal]; flame out.

.55 **black out,** gray out.

.56 **parachute, bail out, jump,** make a parachute jump, hit the silk, make a brollyhop [Brit informal], sky-dive.

.57 **brief,** give a briefing; debrief.

.58 ADJS **aeronautic(al),** aerial; **aviatorial,** aviational; aerodontic, aerospace, aerotechnical, aerostatic(al), aeromechanic(al), aerodynamic(al), avionic, aeronomic, aerophysical; aeromarine; aerobatic; airworthy, air-minded, air-conscious, aeromedical; air-wise; airsick.

.59 **flying,** flitting, winging; volant, volitant, volitational, hovering, fluttering; gliding; **airborne;** jet-propelled, rocket-propelled.

.60 ADVS **in flight, on the wing** or fly, while airborne.

.61 **instruments**

absolute altimeter	gyrocompass
accelerometer	Gyro Flux Gate
aerial reconnaissance	gyro horizon
camera	Gyropilot
aerograph	gyrosyn
aerometer	horn
aeroscope	hub dynamometer
air log	hygrograph
air-speed head	hygrometer
air-speed indicator	hypsometer
altigraph	inclinometer
altimeter	induction compass
altitude mixture con-	instrument board or
trol	panel
ammeter	intervalometer
anemograph	Joyce stick
anemometer	joy stick
anemoscope	macaviator
aneroid	Mach meter
automatic boost con-	magnetic compass
trol	manifold pressure
automatic or robot	gauge
pilot	meteorograph
autopilot	micrometer
autosyn	nephoscope
bank or banking indi-	octant
cator	optical altimeter
barometer	ozonometer
bearing plate	pelorus
bombing locator	photometer
bombsight	pitch or pitching indi-
Bourdon tube	cator
calorimeter	pitot-static tube
carburetor altitude	pluviometer
control	polymeter
card compass	position indicator
card magnetic com-	potentiometer
pass	pressure altimeter
ceiling-height indica-	pyrometer
tor	quadrant
chronometer	radar
climatometer	radio
compass	radio altimeter
control rod or column	radio compass
control stick	radio direction finder
directional gyro	radiogoniometer
direction finder	rate-of-climb indicator
direction indicator	recording altimeter
drift meter	recording anemome-
earth inductor or	ter
induction compass	recording hygrometer
electrical capacity	sextant
altimeter	sound-ranging altime-
engine gauge	ter
evaporimeter	Sperry antiaircraft
flight recorder	director
fuel-flow meter	spirit level
fuel quantity indica-	static tube
tor	sting
galvanometer	strike radar scanner
gosport, gosport tube	sun compass

tachometer	turn-and-bank indica-
terrain clearance indi-	tor
cator	turnmeter
thermograph	variometer
thermometer	venturi tube
thermostat	viscosimeter
throttle	yawmeter
transit instrument	yoke

279. AVIATOR

.1 NOUNS **aviator,** aeronaut, aeroplaner, airplaner, aeroplanist, airplanist, **airman, flier, pilot,** air pilot; licensed pilot, private pilot, commercial pilot, instructor; wingman; chief pilot, captain; birdman [informal]; copilot; jet pilot, jet jockey [informal]; test pilot; bush pilot; astronaut 282.8; cloud seeder, rainmaker; cropduster; barnstormer [informal]; stunt man, stunt flier.

.2 **aviatrix,** aviatress, **airwoman,** birdwoman [informal].

.3 **military pilot,** naval pilot, combat pilot; fighter pilot; bomber pilot; suicide pilot, kamikaze; observer; **aviation cadet,** air or flying cadet, pilot trainee; flyboy [slang]; ace; air force 800.28,29.

.4 crew, **aircrew,** flight crew; aircrewman; **navigator,** avigator; **bombardier;** gunner, machine gunner, belly gunner, tail gunner; crew chief; aerial photographer; meteorologist; steward, stewardess, hostess, flight attendant.

.5 **ground crew,** landing crew, plane handlers.

.6 aircraftsman, aeromechanic, aircraft mechanic, mechanic, grease monkey [slang]; rigger; aeronautical engineer, flight engineer, jet engineer, rocket engineer 281.11; ground tester, flight tester.

.7 **balloonist,** ballooner, aeronaut.

.8 **parachutist,** chutist or chuter [both informal], parachute jumper, sports parachutist; sky diver; smoke jumper; **paratrooper;** paradoctor, paramedic; jumpmaster.

.9 (mythological fliers) Daedalus, Icarus.

280. AIRCRAFT

.1 NOUNS **aircraft,** aerocraft, **airplane** 280.15, aeroplane [Brit], **plane, ship,** fixed-wing aircraft, flying machine, avion [Fr]; aerodyne, heavier-than-air craft; kite [Brit informal]; lifting body; planform.

.2 **propeller plane,** single-prop, double-prop or twin-prop, multi-prop; tractor, tractor plane; pusher, pusher plane; piston plane; turbo-propeller plane, turbo-prop, propjet.

.3 **jet plane, jet; turbojet,** ramjet, pulse-jet,

blowtorch [informal]; single-jet, twin-jet, multi-jet; Jet Liner, business jet; delta-planform jet, tailless jet, twin-tailboom jet; jumbo jet; subsonic jet; supersonic jet, supersonic transport, SST.

.4 **rocket plane**, repulsor; rocket ship, spaceship 282.2; rocket 281.2.

.5 **rotor plane**, rotary-wing aircraft, roto-craft, rotodyne; gyroplane, gyro, **autogiro**, windmill [informal]; **helicopter**, heli–; copter *or* whirlybird *or* chopper *or* egg-beater [all informal].

.6 **ornithopter**, orthopter, wind flapper, mechanical bird.

.7 **flying platform**, flying ring, Hiller-CNR machine, flying bedstead *or* bedspring; **hovercraft**, air car, ground-effect machine, air-cushion vehicle, hovercar, cushioncraft; flying crow's nest, flying motorcycle, flying bathtub.

.8 **seaplane**, waterplane, **hydroplane**, aerohydroplane, aeroboat, **floatplane**, float seaplane; **flying boat**, clipper, boat seaplane; **amphibian**, triphibian.

.9 **warplane**, battleplane, combat plane, gun boat, military aircraft; suicide plane, kamikaze; bogey, bandit, enemy aircraft; air fleet, air armada; air force 800.28,29.

.10 **trainer**; Link trainer; **flight simulator**; dual-control trainer; basic *or* primary trainer, intermediate trainer, advanced trainer; crew trainer, flying classroom; navigator-bombardier trainer, radio-navigational trainer, etc.

.11 **aerostat**, lighter-than-air craft; **airship**, ship, dirigible balloon, **blimp** [informal]; rigid airship, semirigid airship; **dirigible**, zeppelin, Graf Zeppelin; gasbag, ballonet; **balloon** 280.18, *ballon* [Fr].

.12 **glider**, gliding machine; **sailplane**, soaring plane; rocket glider; student glider; air train, glider train.

.13 **parachute**, para–; **chute** [informal], umbrella [informal], brolly [Brit informal]; pilot chute, drogue chute; rip cord, safety loop, shroud lines, harness, pack, vent; parachute jump, brolly-hop [Brit informal]; sky dive; brake *or* braking *or* deceleration parachute.

.14 **kite**, box kite, Eddy kite, Hargrave *or* cellular kite, tetrahedral kite.

.15 **airplanes**

aerobus	airliner
aerodone	air scout
air ambulance	air-sea rescue amphibian
air coach	ian
air cruiser	air-sea rescue plane
airfreighter	all-weather fighter

ambulance	interceptor
amphibian transport	intermeshing-rotor helicopter
antique plane	licopter
antisubmarine patrol	jet, jet plane 280.3
antisubmarine plane	jet bomber
arctic rescue helicopter	jet fighter
ter	jet tanker
assault transport	jet transport
assault-troop plane	killer
attack bomber	laminar-flow-control
attack plane	plane
attack transport	landplane
Autogiro	liaison plane
avion-canon [Fr]	light bomber
biplace [Fr]	light transport
biplane	liner
bomber	long-range attack aircraft
cabin plane	craft
canard	long-range bomber
cargo plane	long-range medium *or*
cargo transport	heavy bomber
carrier-based plane	long-range patrol
carrier fighter	bomber
casualty-evacuation	low-wing monoplane
plane	mailplane
club plane	maritime reconnaissance plane
commercial transport	sance plane
constant-chord-rotor	medium bomber
helicopter	meteorological reconnaissance plane
convertiplane	naissance plane
crop-duster	midwing monoplane
cruiser	military aircraft
Cub	military transport
dive bomber	mobile command post
drone	*monoplace* [Fr]
escort fighter	monoplane
evacuation ambulance	mosquito
evacuation plane	multipurpose plane
executive plane	naval aircraft
fighter	naval bomber
fighter-bomber	naval fighter
flying banana	naval interceptor
flying boxcar	night fighter
flying fortress	observation plane
flying platform 280.7	ornithopter 280.6
flying tanker	paraglider
flying wing	parasol
freighter	passenger plane
freight transport	pathfinder
general reconnaissance	patrol bomber
sance	patrol plane
glider 280.12	photo-reconnaissance
grasshopper	plane
ground-attack fighter	picket patrol plane
ground-support aircraft	pilotless aircraft
craft	*pou de ciel* [Fr]
gyrodyne	precision bomber
heavy bomber	private plane
heavy transport	propeller plane 280.2
helibus	pulse jet helicopter
helicopter 280.5	pursuit plane
helicopter gun ship	radar picket plane
high-altitude reconnaissance plane	reconnaissance plane
naissance plane	rescue helicopter
high-altitude research	rescue plane
aircraft	research plane
high-wing monoplane	robot plane
hovercraft 280.7	rocket-firing plane
hunter	rocket plane 280.4
hurricane hunter	rotor plane 280.5
in-flight refueling	scout, scout plane
tanker	seaplane 280.8

search plane
service aircraft
sesquiplane
shipboard interceptor
shipboard plane
shipplane
ski-plane
sky truck
sport plane, sports
 plane
spotter plane
spy plane
STOL (short takeoff
 and landing)
stratofreighter
stratojet
strike plane
supersonic combat
 plane
supersonic research
 plane
tactical support

bomber
tandem plane
tandem-rotor helicop-
 ter
target-tug or -tower
taxiplane
torpedo bomber
torpedo strike aircraft
trainer 280.10
trainer-bomber
trainer-fighter
transport
triplane
troop carrier
troop transport
turbojet
utility plane
VTOL (vertical take-
 off and landing)
warplane 280.9
weather reconnais-
 sance plane

instruments 278.61
intermeshing rotors
jackstay
jet pipe
jet pod
jury skid
keel
laminar-flow system
landing gear
landing lights
landing skis
launching gear
launching tube
leading edge
lift wire
longeron
monocoque [Fr]
nacelle
navigation lights
navigator's bubble
nose
nose radiator
nose turret
nosewheel
nosewheel undercar-
 riage
oleo gear
oleo leg
pants, wheel parts
parasol wing
Perspex 'chin' housing
pilot plane
pod
pontoon
projector tube
propeller, prop [infor-
 mal]
propulsive duct
radar nacelle
radar nose
radar scanner
radome
retractable landing
 gear
rocket launcher
Rogallo wing
rotors
rudder
rudder bar
rudder pedals
ruddervator
runners (for snow or
 ice)
safety wire

skid fin
skid landing gear
ski landing gear
slitwing
spinner
spoiler
spray strip
stabilizer, stabilizator
stagger or incidence
 wire
stay
stick, stick control
stressed skin
stringers
strut
stub-wing stabilizer
supersonic wings
tail
tail boom
tail fin
tail pipe
tail plane
tail rotor
tail skid
tail stinger
tail unit
tail wheel
tandem rotors
tandem seat
tractor airscrew
trailing edge
trim controls
trim tab
truss
turbine nozzle
turboprops
turret
turtleback
twin tail wheel
undercarriage
ventral airdome
ventral radome
vertical fin
V tail or vee tail
waist gun blister
walking beam
wheel cowlings
wing
wing radiator
wing rib
wing root air intake
wing roots
wing skid
wing truss

.16 airplane parts

adjustable propeller
aerothermodynamic
 duct
afterburner
aileron
air brake
air controls
airfoil
airframe
air intake
air scoop
airscrew
antidrag wire
antilift or landing wire
arresting gear
arrestor hook
astrodome
athodyd
axial-flow unit
balancing flap
ball turret
bay
beaching gear
belly tank
blister
blister canopy
body
bomb bay
bomb rack
bomb release
bonnet
booster rocket unit
bow
brace wire
bubble
bubble canopy
bubble hood
bucket seat
bumper bag
butterfly tail
cabin
canopy
cat strip
channel patch
chassis
chin
coaxial propellers
cockpit

coke-bottle fuselage
contraprops
contra-rotating air-
 screws
controls
control surface
control wires
cowl
crew compartment
dead stick
deceleron
deck
deicer
delta wing
dihedral
diving rudder
dorsal airdome
dorsal blister
double-bubble
drag strut
drag wire
drift wire
dual controls
ejection seat
ejector
elevating rudder
elevator
elevon
emergency landing
 gear
empennage
engine controls
fin
finger patch
flame trap
flap
flex wing
float
flotation gear
folding wing
fuel injector
fuselage
gas-shaft hood
gore
gull wing
gun mount
hatch
hood

.17 aircraft engines

aeromotor
arc-jet engine
athodyd
axial-flow turbojet
axial-type engine
cam engine
compound engine
compression-ignition
 engine
double-row radial
 engine
fan-jet engine
gas jet
gas turbine jet engine
impulse duct engine
intermittent duct

engine
inverted engine
jet engine
pancake engine
piston engine
propeller-drive gas tur-
 bine
propeller-jet engine
propjet
pulse jet
radial engine
ramjet
reaction engine or
 motor
reciprocating engine
resojet

resonance duct jet engine
resonance jet engine
rocket motor
rotary engine
supercharged engine
turbine
turbojet
turboprop

turbo-propeller engine
turboprop-jet
turboram-jet
twin-engines
vertical engine
V-type engine
W-type engine
X-type engine

.18 balloons

ballon-sonde [Fr]
barrage balloon
blimp 280.11
captive balloon
ceiling balloon
dirigible balloon, dirigible 280.11
fire balloon
free balloon
gasbag
gas balloon
hot-air balloon
kite balloon or sausage

montgolfier
observation balloon
pilot balloon
radiosonde balloon
rockoon (rocket-balloon)
sausage, sausage balloon
skyhook, skyhook balloon
sounding balloon
stratosphere balloon
weather balloon

.19 airship parts

ballonet
basket
car
catwalk
envelope
gas chamber or cell
gondola

landing or mooring line
mooring harness
observation car
observation platform
sandbag
side or wing car
subcloud car

281. ROCKETRY, MISSILERY

.1 NOUNS rocketry, rocket science or engineering or research or technology; missilery, missile science or engineering or research or technology; rocket or missile testing; ground test, firing test, static firing; rocket or missile project or program; instrumentation; telemetry.

.2 rocket, rocket engine or motor, reaction engine or motor, jet engine; rocket exhaust; plasma jet, plasma engine; ion engine; jetavator.

.3 rocket, missile 281.14,15, ballistic missile, guided missile; torpedo 281.16; projectile rocket, ordnance rocket, combat or military or war rocket; bird [informal]; payload; warhead, nuclear or thermonuclear warhead, atomic warhead; multiple or multiple-missile warhead.

.4 rocket bomb, flying bomb or torpedo, cruising missile; robot bomb, robomb, Vergeltungswaffe [Ger], V-weapon, P-plane; buzzbomb, bumblebomb, doodlebug.

.5 multistage rocket, step rocket; two- or three-stage rocket, two- or three-step rocket; single-stage rocket, single step rocket, one-step rocket; booster, booster

unit, booster rocket, takeoff booster or rocket; piggyback rocket.

.6 test rocket, research rocket, high-altitude research rocket, registering rocket, instrument rocket, instrument carrier, test instrument vehicle, rocket laboratory; probe.

.7 proving ground, testing ground; firing area; impact area; control center, bunker; radar tracking station, tracking station, visual tracking station; meteorological tower.

.8 rocket propulsion, reaction propulsion, jet propulsion, blast propulsion; fuel, propellant, solid fuel, liquid fuel, hydrazine, liquid oxygen or lox; charge, propelling or propulsion charge, powder charge or grain, high-explosive charge; thrust, constant thrust; exhaust, jet blast, backflash.

.9 rocket launching or firing, ignition, launch, shot, shoot; lift-off, blast-off; guided or automatic control, programming; flight, trajectory; burn; burnout, end of burning; velocity peak, Brennschluss [Ger]; altitude peak, ceiling; descent; airburst; impact.

.10 rocket launcher, projector; launching or launch pad, launching platform or rack, firing table; silo; takeoff ramp; tower projector, launching tower; launching mortar, launching tube, projector tube, firing tube; rocket gun, bazooka, antitank rocket, Panzerfaust [Ger]; superbazooka; multiple projector, calliope, Stalin organ, Katusha; antisubmarine projector, Mark 10, hedgehog [slang]; Minnie Mouse launcher, mousetrap [slang]; Meilewagon.

.11 rocket scientist or technician, rocketeer or rocketer, rocket or missile man, rocket or missile engineer.

.12 VERBS rocket, skyrocket.

.13 launch, project, shoot, fire, blast off.

.14 rockets, missiles

AAM (air-to-air missile)
AA target rocket
ABM (antiballistic missile)
airborne rocket
anchor rocket
antiaircraft rocket
antimine rocket
antimissile
antiradar rocket
antisubmarine or antisub rocket
antitank rocket
ASM (air-to-surface missile)
ATA missile (air-to-air)

ATG rocket (air-to-ground)
atom-rocket
ATS (air-to-ship)
AUM (air-to-underwater missile)
barrage rocket
bat bomb
bazooka rocket
bombardment rocket
chemical rocket
combat high-explosive rocket
Congreve rocket
countermissile
demolition rocket
fin-stabilized rocket
fireworks rocket

flare rocket
flying tank
GAPA (ground-to-air pilotless aircraft)
glide bomb
GTA rocket (ground-to-air)
GTG rocket (ground-to-ground)
guided missile
harpoon rocket
high-altitude rocket
homing rocket
HVAR (high velocity aircraft rocket)
ICBM (intercontinental ballistic missile)
incendiary antiaircraft rocket
incendiary rocket
ion rocket
IRBM (intermediate range ballistic missile)
line-throwing rocket
liquid-fuel rocket
long-range rocket
MIRV (multiple independently targetable re-entry vehicle)
MRV (multiple re-entry vehicle)
ram rocket
retro-float light
retro-rocket
rockoon
SAM (surface-to-air missile)
signal rocket

skyrocket
smokeless powder rocket
smoke rocket
snake (antimine)
solid-fuel rocket
space rocket 282.2
spinner
spin-stabilized rocket
SSM (surface-to-surface missile)
STS rocket (ship-to-shore)
submarine killer
supersonic rocket
target missile
torpedo rocket
training rocket or missile
trajectory missile
transoceanic rocket
vernier, vernier rocket
window rocket (antiradar)
winged rocket
XAAM (experimental air-to-air missile)
XASM (experimental air-to-surface missile)
XAUM (experimental air-to-underwater missile)
XSAM (experimental surface-to-air missile)
XSSM (experimental surface-to-surface missile)

.15 rocket and missile names

Aerobee	Little John
Aerojet	Lobber
Asp	Loki
Asroc	Loon
Astor	Mace
Atlas	Matador
Atlas-Agena	Mauler
Atlas-Centaur	Minnie Mouse
Bomarc	Minuteman
Bullpup	NATIV (North American test instrument vehicle)
Cajun	
Corporal	Navaho
Corvus	Nike
Crossbow	Nike Ajax
Dart	Nike Hercules
Davy Crockett	Nike Zeus
Deacon	Pershing
Delta	Petrel
Diamant	Pofo
Ding-Dong	Polaris
Dove	Poseidon
Falcon	Private A
Firebee	Private F
Genie	Quail
Hawk	Ram
Holy Moses	Rascal
Honest John	Redeye
Hound Dog	Redstone
Jupiter	Regulus I
Lacrosse	Saturn
Lark	

Scout	Tartar
Sentinel	Terrier
Sergeant	Thor
Shillelagh	Thor Able Star
Sidewinder	Thor-Agena
Skybolt	Thor-Delta
Snark	Tiny Tim
Spaerobee	Titan
Sparrow	V-1, V-2
SS-9, SS-10, SS-11	Viking
Subroc	WAC-Corporal
Super Talos	Wagtail
Talos	Zuni

.16 torpedoes

aerial torpedo
bangalore torpedo
homing torpedo
rocket torpedo

spar torpedo
submarine torpedo or fish [slang]

282. SPACE TRAVEL

.1 NOUNS **space travel, astronautics,** cosmonautics, **space flight,** navigation of empty space; interplanetary travel, space exploration; space walk; space navigation, astrogation; **space science,** space technology or engineering; **aerospace science,** aerospace technology or engineering; space or aerospace research; space or aerospace medicine, bioastronautics; astrionics; escape velocity; rocketry 281; multistage flight, step flight, shuttle flights; trip to the moon, trip to Mars, grand tour; space terminal, target planet; science fiction 608.7.

.2 **spacecraft, spaceship, space rocket,** rocket ship, manned rocket, interplanetary rocket; **rocket** 281.2; **capsule, space capsule,** ballistic capsule; module, command module, lunar excursion module, lunar module, LEM, LM; moon ship, Mars ship, etc.; deep-space ship; exploratory ship, reconnaissance rocket; ferry rocket, tender rocket, tanker ship, fuel ship; **multistage rocket** 281.5, shuttle rocket, retro rocket, attitude-control rocket, main rocket; **burn;** space docking, docking, docking maneuver; **orbit,** parking orbit; earth orbit, apogee, perigee; lunar or moon orbit, apolune, perilune, apocynthion, pericynthion; soft landing, hard landing; injection, insertion, lunar insertion, Earth insertion; **reentry, splashdown.**

.3 **flying saucer,** unidentified flying object, UFO.

.4 **rocket engine** 281.2; atomic power plant; solar battery.

.5 **space station,** astro station, **space island,** island base, cosmic stepping-stone, halfway station, advance base; manned station; inner station, outer station, transit station; space airport, **spaceport**, spaceport station, space dock, launching base; research station, space laboratory, space observatory; tracking station, radar tracking station; radar station, radio station; radio relay station, radio mirror; space mirror, solar mirror; moon station, moon base, lunar base, lunar city, observatory on the moon.

.6 **artificial satellite, satellite,** space satellite, robot satellite, unmanned satellite, sputnik; communications satellite, active communications satellite, communications relay satellite, weather satellite, orbiting observatory, geophysical satellite, navigational satellite, geodetic satellite, research satellite, interplanetary monitoring satellite, automated satellite; **probe, space probe,** geo probe, interplanetary explorer.

.7 (satellite telemetered recorders) micro-instrumentation; aurora particle counter, cosmic ray counter, gamma ray counter, heavy particle counter, impulse recorder, magnetometer, solar ultraviolet detector, solar X-ray detector, telecamera.

.8 **astronaut,** astronavigator, cosmonaut, **spaceman,** space traveler, **rocket man,** rocketeer, rocket pilot; space doctor; space crew; planetary colony, lunar colony; extraterrestrial visitor, alien, saucerman, man from Mars, Martian, little green man.

.9 **rocket society,** American Rocket Society, American Interplanetary Society, British Interplanetary Society, German Society for Space Research.

.10 (space hazards) cosmic particles, intergalactic matter, aurora particles, radiation, cosmic ray bombardment; meteors, meteorites; asteroids; meteor dust impacts, meteoric particles, space bullets; extreme temperatures; the bends, blackout, weightlessness.

.11 **space suit,** pressure suit, G suit, anti-G suit; space helmet.

.12 VERBS **travel in space,** go into outer space; orbit the earth, go into orbit, orbit the moon, etc.; navigate in space, astrogate; escape earth, break free, leave the atmosphere, shoot into space; rocket to the moon, park in space, hang or float in space, space walk.

.13 ADJS **astronautical,** cosmonautical, spacetraveling; astrogational; rocket-borne, spaceborne.

.14 **spacecraft, artificial satellites, space probes**

A-1	Mars probes
Alouette	Mercury
Anna	Midas
Apollo	Molniya
Ariel	Nimbus
ATDA	OAO (orbiting astro-
Atlas-Score	nomical observato-
ATS	ry)
Aurora 7 (Mercury)	OGO (orbiting geo-
Biosatellite	physical observato-
Comsat	ry)
Cosmos	OSO (orbiting solar
Courier	observatory)
D1-C	OV1
D2-D	OV3
Diapason	Pageos
Discoverer	Pegasus
Early Bird	Pioneer
Echo	Polyot
Elektron	Proton
ERS	Ranger
ESSA (environmental	Relay
survey satellite)	Samos
Explorer	San Marco
Faith 7 (Mercury)	Secor
FR-1	Sigma 7 (Mercury)
Freedom 7 (Mercury)	Skylab
Friendship 7 (Mercu-	Soyuz
ry)	Sputnik
GATV	Surveyor
Gemini	Syncom
Greb	Telstar
Injun	TIROS (television
Intelsat	and infrared obser-
Lageos (laser geody-	vation satellite)
namic satellite)	Transit
Lani Bird	Vanguard
Liberty Bell 7 (Mercu-	Venus probes
ry)	Viking
Lofti	Voskhod
Luna	Vostok
Lunar Orbiter	WRESAT
Lunik	Zond
Mariner	

283. IMPULSE, IMPACT

(driving and striking force)

.1 NOUNS **impulse,** impulsion, impelling force, impellent; **drive,** driving force or power; **thrust;** motive power, power 157; irresistible force; clout [informal]; **impetus; momentum;** moment, moment of force; propulsion 285.1; incitement 648.4, incentive 648.7, compulsion 756.

.2 **thrust, push, shove,** boost [informal]; press, **pressure,** piezo–, tono–; **stress,** bearing; **prod, poke, punch, jab,** dig, nudge; **bump,** jog, joggle, jolt; **jostle,** hustle; **butt,** bunt; head (of water, steam, etc.).

.3 **impact, collision, clash,** appulse, encounter, meeting, impingement, **bump, crash,** crump, whomp; **carom,** carambole, cannon; sideswipe [informal]; smash or **smashup** or **crack-up** or crunch [all informal]; **shock, brunt;** percussion, concussion; **thrusting, ramming,** bulling, **bulldozing,** shouldering; hammering, smashing, mauling, sledgehammering; onslaught 798.1.

.4 **hit, blow, stroke, knock, rap, pound,** bat [informal], slam, bang, crack, **whack, smack, thwack,** smash, dash, swipe, **belt** or **clout** [both informal], **swat** [informal], swing, **punch, poke, jab,** dig, drub, thump, pelt, yerk [dial], cut, plunk [informal], chop, **clip** or **lick** [both informal], **sock** [slang], **biff** [informal]; clump or whop or bonk [all informal], dint, slog, slug [slang], bash [informal]; drubbing, drumming, tattoo, fusillade; beating 1010.4.

.5 (boxing blows) backhander, backhand, backstroke; sidewinder; hook; short-arm blow; swing, round-arm blow, roundhouse, Long Melford; uppercut, bolo punch; haymaker; one-two, the old one-two [both slang].

.6 **tap, rap, pat,** dab, chuck, touch, tip; **snap, flick, flip,** fillip, flirt, whisk, brush; **peck,** pick.

.7 **slap, smack,** flap; **box, cuff,** buffet; **spank;** whip, lash, cut, stripe.

.8 **kick, boot;** punt, drop kick, place kick, kicking, calcitration [archaic].

.9 **stamp,** stomp [dial], drub, clump, clop.

.10 VERBS **impel,** give an impetus, **set going** or agoing, put or set in motion, give momentum; **drive, move,** animate, actuate, forward; **thrust,** power; drive or whip on; goad; **propel** 285.10; motivate, incite 648.12–21; compel 756.4.

.11 **thrust, push** 285.10, shove, boost [informal]; press, stress, **bear,** bear upon, bring pressure to bear upon; **ram,** ram down, tamp, pile drive, jam, crowd, cram; bull, bulldoze; **drive, force,** run; prod, goad, poke, punch, jab, dig, nudge; **bump,** jog, joggle, jolt, shake, rattle; **jostle,** hustle, hurtle; elbow, shoulder; **butt,** bunt, buck [informal], run or bump or butt against, knock or run one's head against; assault 798.15.

.12 **collide,** come into collision, be on a collision course, **clash,** meet, encounter, confront each other, impinge; percuss, concuss; **bump, hit, strike, knock, bang; run into, bump into,** bang into, slam into, smack into, **crash into,** smash into, dash into, carom into; **hit against,** strike against, knock against; foul, fall or run foul or afoul of; hurtle, hurt; **carom,** cannon; **sideswipe** [informal]; **crash,** smash, crump, whomp; smash up or crack up or crunch [all informal].

.13 **hit, strike, smite, knock,** knock down or out, knock for a loop [informal], knock cold [slang], **deck** [slang], coldcock [slang]; **clobber** or **belt** or **bat** or **clout** [all informal], bang, slam, dash, bash [informal], **biff** [informal], **paste** [informal], **poke, punch, jab,** thwack, smack, clap, crack, swipe, **whack;** wham or whop or clump or bonk [all informal], wallop [slang], clip [informal], cut, plunk [informal], **swat** [informal], soak or sock [both slang], slog, **slug** [slang], yerk [dial]; deal, fetch, deal or fetch a blow, hit a clip [informal], let have it; **thump,** snap; strike at 798.16.

.14 **pound, beat, hammer, maul,** sledgehammer, **knock, rap, bang,** thump, **drub,** buffet, **batter,** pulverize, paste [informal], patter, pommel, pummel, pelt, wallop [slang], larrup [informal], baste, lambaste [informal]; thresh, thrash; flail; spank, flap; whip 1010.14.

.15 **tap, rap, pat,** dab, chuck, touch, tip; **snap, flick, flip,** fillip, tickle, flirt, whisk, **graze,** brush; bunt; **peck,** pick, beak.

.16 **slap, smack,** flap; **box, cuff,** buffet; **spank;** whip 1010.14.

.17 **club,** cudgel, blackjack, sandbag, cosh [Brit].

.18 **kick,** boot, calcitrate [archaic]; punt, drop-kick, place-kick; knee.

.19 **stamp,** stomp [dial], trample, tread, drub, clump, clop.

.20 ADJS **impelling,** impellent; impulsive, pulsive, **moving,** motive, animating, actuating, **driving;** thrusting.

.21 concussive, percussive, crashing, smashing.

284. REACTION

.1 NOUNS **reaction,** retroaction; **response,** respondence, reply, answer 487.1, **rise** [slang]; **reflex,** reflection, **reflex action;** echo, bounceback, reverberation; return, revulsion; reflux, refluence; sympathetic vibration; action and reaction; predictable response, automatic or autonomic reaction; spontaneous or unthinking response, spur-of-the-moment response; conditioned reflex; –nasty, –taxia or –taxis.

.2 **recoil, rebound,** resilience, repercussion, contrecoup [Fr]; **bounce, bound, spring;** repulse, rebuff; **backlash,** backlashing, kickback, **kick,** recalcitration; **backfire, boomerang;** ricochet, carom.

.3 (a drawing back or aside) **retreat**, recoil, fallback, pullout, pullback; evasion, avoidance, sidestepping; **flinch**, wince, cringe; **side step, shy; dodge, duck** [informal].

.4 **reactionary**, reactionist, recalcitrant.

.5 VERBS **react, respond**, reply, answer, riposte, snap back, come back at [informal]; rise to the fly, take the bait.

.6 **recoil, rebound**, resile; **bounce, bound, spring; spring** or **fly back**, bounce or bound back, snap back; repercuss, have repercussions; **kick**, kick back, recalcitrate; **backfire, boomerang**; backlash, lash back; ricochet, carom, cannon, cannon off.

.7 **pull** or **draw back**, retreat, recoil, fade, **fall back**, reel back, hang back, start back, shrink back; **shrink, flinch, wince, cringe**, blink, blench, quail; **shy, start** or turn aside, evade, avoid, sidestep, weasel, weasel out; **dodge, duck** [informal]; jib, swerve, sheer off.

.8 **get a reaction**, get a response, evoke a response, ring a bell, strike a responsive chord, strike fire, strike or hit home, hit a nerve, get a rise out of [slang].

.9 ADJS **reactive**, reacting; **responsive**, respondent, responding, antiphonal; reactionary; retroactionary, retroactive; revulsive; **reflex**, reflexive; refluent; –tactic, –tropic or –trophic.

.10 recoiling, rebounding, **resilient; bouncing**, bounding, springing; repercussive; recalcitrant.

.11 ADVS **on the rebound,** on the return, on the bounce; on the spur of the moment, off the top of the head.

285. PUSHING, THROWING

.1 NOUNS **pushing, propulsion**, pulsion, **propelling**, propelment, **shoving; drive, thrust**, motive power, driving force; push, shove; butt, bunt; shunt, impulsion 283.1.

.2 steam propulsion, gas propulsion, gasoline propulsion, diesel propulsion, diesel-electric propulsion, jet propulsion, turbojet propulsion, pulse-jet propulsion, plasma-jet propulsion, ram-jet propulsion, resojet propulsion, rocket propulsion, reaction propulsion; wind propulsion.

.3 **throwing, projection**, trajection, jaculation, flinging, slinging, **pitching**, casting, hurling, lobbing, chucking, heaving; **shooting**, firing, gunnery, musketry; trapshooting, skeet or skeet shooting; archery.

.4 **throw, fling, sling, cast, hurl,** chuck, chunk, lob, **heave**, shy, **pitch, toss**, peg [informal]; **flip; put**, shot-put; (football) pass, forward pass, lateral pass, lateral; (tennis) serve, service; bowl; (baseball) fastball, curve, screwball, incurve, outcurve, upcurve, downcurve, sinker, slider, knuckleball, spitball, spitter, change-up, change of pace.

.5 **shot**, discharge; ejection 310; detonation 456.3; gunfire 798.9; **gun, cannon** 801.5,6; bullet 801.13; **salvo, volley**, fusillade, tattoo, spray; bowshot, gunshot, stoneshot, potshot.

.6 **projectile**, trajectile; ejecta, ejectamenta [both pl]; **missile** 801.12; ball 255.13; discus, quoit.

.7 **propeller**, prop [informal], airscrew; propellant, propulsor, driver; screw, wheel, screw propeller, twin screws; paddle wheel; turbine, turbo–; fan, impeller, rotor; piston.

.8 **thrower, pitcher**, hurler, chucker, heaver, tosser, flinger, slinger; bowler; shot-putter; javelin thrower; discus thrower, discobolus.

.9 **shooter**, shot; **gunner**, gun, **gunman; rifleman**, musketeer, carabineer; cannoneer, artilleryman 800.10; Nimrod, hunter 655.5; trapshooter; archer, bowman, toxophilite; **marksman**, markswoman, targetshooter, **sharpshooter**, sniper; good shot, dead shot, deadeye, **crack shot.**

.10 VERBS **push, propel**, impel, **shove**, thrust 283.11; **drive, move**, forward, advance; sweep, sweep along; butt, bunt; shunt; pole, row; pedal, treadle; **roll**, troll, bowl, trundle.

.11 **throw, fling, sling, pitch, toss, cast, hurl**, hurtle, **heave, chuck**, chunk, lob, peg [informal], shy, fire, launch, dash, let fly; catapult; **flip, snap, jerk; bowl; pass;** serve; **put**, put the shot; dart, lance, tilt; fork, pitchfork; pelt 798.27,28.

.12 **project**, traject, jaculate.

.13 **shoot, fire**, fire off, let off, let fly, **discharge**, eject 310.13; detonate 456.8; gun [informal], pistol; shoot at 798.22, gun for [informal]; strike, hit, plug [slang]; shoot down, fell, drop, stop in one's tracks; **riddle, pepper**, pelt, pump full of lead [slang]; snipe, pick off; torpedo; pot; potshoot, potshot, take a potshot; load, prime, charge; cock.

.14 **start**, start off, start up, give a start, **put** or **set in motion, set on foot**, set going or agoing, start going; **kick off** or **start the ball rolling** [both informal]; **launch**, float, set afloat; send, send off or forth; bundle, bundle off.

.15 ADJS **propulsive**, propulsory, pulsive; **propellant**, propelling; motive; **driving, pushing, shoving.**

.16 **projectile**, trajectile, jaculatory; **ballistic**, missile; ejective 310.28.

.17 jet-propelled, rocket-propelled, steam-propelled, gasoline-propelled, gas-propelled, diesel-propelled, wind-propelled, self-propelled.

286. PULLING

.1 NOUNS **pulling**, traction, drawing, draft, heaving, tugging; pulling or tractive power, **pull**; tug-of-war; towing, towage; **hauling**, haulage, drayage; attraction 288; extraction 305.

.2 **pull**, draw, draft, **heave, haul**, lug [informal], **tug**, strain, drag.

.3 **jerk**, yerk [dial], **yank** [informal], quick or sudden pull; **twitch**, tweak, pluck, hitch, wrench, snatch, start, bob; **flip**, flick, flirt, flounce; jig, **jiggle**; jog, joggle.

.4 VERBS **pull, draw, heave, haul**, hale, lug, **tug, tow**, take in tow; trail, train; **drag**, draggle, snake [informal]; troll, trawl.

.5 **jerk**, yerk [dial], **yank** [informal]; **twitch**, tweak, pluck, snatch, hitch, wrench, snake [informal]; **flip**, flick, flirt, flounce; jiggle, jig, jigget, jigger; jog, joggle.

.6 ADJS **pulling, drawing**, tractional, tractive, hauling, tugging, towing; draft.

287. LEVERAGE, PURCHASE

(mechanical advantage applied to moving or raising)

.1 NOUNS **leverage**, fulcrumage; **pry**, prize [dial].

.2 **purchase**, hold, advantage; **foothold**, toehold, footing; differential purchase; collier's purchase; traction.

.3 **fulcrum, axis, pivot**, bearing, rest, resting point, *point d'appui* [Fr]; thole, tholepin, rowlock, oarlock.

.4 **lever; pry**, prize [dial]; **bar**, pinch bar, **crowbar**, crow, iron crow, wrecking bar, ripping bar, claw bar; cant hook, peavey; **jimmy**; handspike, marlinespike; boom, spar, beam, outrigger; pedal, treadle, crank; limb.

.5 **arm**, brachi(o)–; forearm; wrist; elbow; upper arm, biceps.

.6 **tackle** 287.10, purchase.

.7 **windlass; capstan; winch**, crab; reel; Chinese windlass, Spanish windlass.

.8 VERBS **get a purchase**, get leverage, get a foothold; **pry, prize, lever**, wedge; **jimmy, crowbar**.

.9 **reel in**, wind in, draw in, pull in, crank in, trim, tighten, tauten, draw taut; windlass, winch, crank, reel; tackle.

.10 **tackle**

Bell's tackle or purchase	handy-billy
block	hatch tackle
block and fall or falls	jigger
block and tackle	luff, luff tackle
boat falls	luff upon luff
boom tackle	pulley
burton	pulley tackle
cat	runner
chain block	runner and tackle
chain fall	runner tackle
collier's purchase	single tackle
deck tackle	single-whip tackle
differential tackle	snatch block
double or twofold tackle	Spanish burton
	stay tackle
duplex purchase	tackle block
fall	threefold, fourfold, etc., tackle
fore-and-aft tackle	top burton
foretackle	yard tackle
gun tackle	

288. ATTRACTION

(a drawing toward)

.1 NOUNS **attraction**, traction 286.1, attractiveness, attractivity; attractance or attractancy; mutual attraction; pulling power, **pull**, drag, draw, tug; magnetism 342.7; gravity, gravitation, gravit(o)–; centripetal force; capillarity, capillary attraction; adduction; affinity, sympathy; **allurement** 650.

.2 attractor, attractant, attrahent; adductor; cynosure, **focus**, center, center of attraction or attention; **lure** 650.2.

.3 **magnet**, artificial magnet, field magnet, bar magnet, horseshoe magnet, electromagnet, solenoid, paramagnet, electromagnetic lifting magnet, magnetic battery; magnetic needle; lodestone, magnetite; lodestar, polestar.

.4 VERBS **attract**, pull, **draw**, drag, tug, pull or draw towards, have an attraction; **magnetize**, magnet, be magnetic; **lure** 650.4; adduct.

.5 ADJS **attracting, drawing, pulling**, dragging, tugging; **attractive, magnetic**, magnetized, attrahent; sympathetic; **alluring** 650.7; adductive, adducent.

.6 ADVS attractionally, attractively; magnetically.

289. REPULSION

(a thrusting away)

.1 NOUNS **repulsion**, repellence or repellency, **repelling**; mutual repulsion, polarization; disaffinity; centrifugal force; magnetic repulsion, diamagnetism; anti-gravity.

.2 **repulse, rebuff; dismissal,** cold shoulder, snub, spurning, brush-off, cut; refusal.

.3 VERBS **repulse, repel, rebuff, turn back,** put back, beat back, drive or push or thrust back; drive away, chase, chase off or away; send off or away, send about one's business, **send packing,** pack off, dismiss; snub, cut, brush off; spurn, refuse; **ward off,** hold off, keep off, fend off, keep at arm's length.

.4 ADJS **repulsive, repellent, repelling;** diamagnetic, of opposite polarity.

.5 ADVS repulsively, repellently.

290. DIRECTION

(compass direction or course)

.1 NOUNS **direction,** quarter, line, direction line, line of direction, point, **aim, way,** track, range, **bearing,** azimuth, compass reading, **heading, course;** current, set, tendency, inclination, bent, trend, tenor, run, drift; **orientation,** lay, lie; steering, steerage, helmsmanship, piloting; navigation 275.1,2; line of march.

.2 [naut & aero terms] vector, tack; compass direction, azimuth, compass bearing or heading, magnetic bearing or heading, relative bearing or heading, true bearing or heading or course; lee side, weather side 242.2,3.

.3 **points of the compass,** cardinal points, half points, quarter points, degrees, compass rose; compass card, lubber line; rhumb, loxodrome; **north,** northward, nor', arct(o)–; **south,** southward, austr(o)–, not(o)–; **east,** eastward, orient, sunrise; **west,** westward, occident, sunset; southeast, southwest, northeast, north-west.

.4 easting, westing, northing, southing.

.5 **orientation, bearings;** adaptation, adjustment, accommodation, alignment, collimation; disorientation.

.6 VERBS **direct, point, aim, turn, bend, train,** present, fix, set, determine; point to or at, hold on, fix on, sight on; aim at, level at, turn or train upon; directionize, give a push in the right direction.

.7 **direct to,** give directions to, lead or conduct to, point out to, show, **show** or **point the way,** steer, put on the track, put on the right track, set straight, set or put right.

.8 (have or take a direction) **bear, head,**

turn, point, aim, take or hold a heading, lead, go, steer, direct oneself, align oneself; **incline, tend,** trend, set, dispose, verge, tend to go.

.9 wester, west, western; easter, east, eastern; norther, north, northern; souther, south, southern.

.10 **head for,** bear for, **go for,** make for, hit for [informal], **steer for,** hold for, put for, **set out** or **off for,** strike out for, take off for [informal], bend one's steps for, lay for, bear up for, bear up to, make up to, set in towards; set or direct or shape one's course for, set one's compass for, sail for 275.35; align one's march; **break for,** make a break for [informal], run or dash for, make a run or dash for.

.11 **go directly, go straight,** follow one's nose, go straight on, **head straight for,** vector for, go straight to the point, steer a straight course, follow a course, keep or hold one's course, hold steady for, arrow for, cleave to the line, keep pointed; **make a beeline,** take the air line, stay on the beam.

.12 **orient,** orientate, orient or orientate oneself, orient the map or chart, **take** or **get one's bearings,** get the lay or lie of the land, see which way the land lies, see which way the wind blows; adapt, adjust, accommodate.

.13 ADJS **direct,** immediate, **straight, straight-forward,** straightaway, straightway; **undeviating,** unswerving, unveering; uninterrupted, unbroken; one-way, unidirectional, irreversible.

.14 **directable,** aimable, pointable, trainable; **steerable,** dirigible, guidable, leadable; **directed,** aimed; well-aimed or -directed or -placed, on the mark, on the nose or money [informal]; **directional,** directive.

.15 **northern,** north, northernmost, northerly, northbound, **arctic,** boreal, hyperborean; **southern,** south, southernmost, southerly, southbound, meridional, **antarctic,** austral; **eastern,** east, easternmost or easternmost, easterly, eastbound, **oriental; western,** west, westernmost, westerly, westbound, **occidental; northeastern,** northeast, northeasterly; **southeastern,** southeast, southeasterly; **southwestern,** southwest, southwesterly; **northwestern,** northwest, northwesterly.

.16 ADVS **north, N,** nor', northerly, northward, north'ard, norward, northwards, northwardly; north about.

.17 **south, S,** southerly, southward, south'ard, southwards, southwardly; south about.

.18 **east,** E, easterly, eastward, eastwards, eastwardly, where the sun rises; east-about.

.19 **west,** W, westerly, westernly, westward, westwards, westwardly; westabout.

.20 **northeast,** NE, nor'east, northeasterly, northeastward, northeastwards, northeastwardly; north-northeast, NNE; northeast by east, N by E; northeast by north, NE by N.

.21 **northwest,** NW, nor'west, northwesterly, northwestward, northwestwards, northwestwardly; north-northwest, NNW; northwest by west, NW by W; northwest by north, NW by N.

.22 **southeast,** SE, southeasterly, southeastward, southeastwards, southeastwardly; south-southeast, SSE; southeast by east, SE by E; southeast by south, SE by S.

.23 **southwest,** SW, southwesterly, southwestward, southwestwards, southwestwardly; south-southwest, SSW; southwest by south, SW by S.

.24 **directly,** direct, straight, straightly, **straightforward,** straightforwards, **undeviatingly,** unswervingly, unveeringly; **straight ahead,** dead ahead; due, dead, due north, etc.; right, forthright; –way(s), –wise, –ward(s); in a direct or straight line, in line with, in a line for, **in a beeline, as the crow flies,** straight across; straight as an arrow.

.25 **squarely,** square, right, straight, flush, full, point-blank; **plump,** plumb, plunk, kerplunk, plop, smack, smack-dab, spang; **exactly,** precisely.

.26 **clockwise,** rightward 243.7; **counterclockwise,** anticlockwise, widdershins, leftward 244.6; homeward; landward; seaward; earthward; heavenward; leeward, windward 242.9.

.27 **in every direction,** in all directions, in all manner of ways, every which way [informal], everywhither, everyway, everywhere, in all directions at once, in every quarter, on every side; around, all round, round about; forty ways or six ways from Sunday [informal]; from every quarter, everywhence; from or to the four corners of the earth, from or to the four winds.

.28 PREPS **toward,** towards, **in the direction of, to,** up, on, upon; ad– or ac– or af– or ag– or al– or ap– or as– or at–, pros–; against, over against, versus; headed for, on the way to, on the road or high road to, in transit to, en route to, on route to, in passage to.

.29 **through,** by, passing by or through, **by way of,** by the way of, **via;** over, around, round about, here and there in, all through.

291. DEVIATION

(indirect course)

.1 NOUNS **deviation,** deviance or deviancy, deviousness, **departure, digression,** diversion, **divergence,** divarication, branching off, divagation, declination, aberration, aberrancy, **variation,** indirection, exorbitation; detour, excursion, excursus, discursion; obliquity, bias, skew, slant; **circuitousness** 321; **wandering,** rambling, **straying,** errantry, pererration; drift, drifting; turning, shifting, swerving, swinging; **turn,** corner, bend, curve, dogleg, crook, hairpin, zigzag, twist, warp, swerve, **veer,** sheer, sweep; shift, double; tack, yaw; wandering or twisting or zigzag or shifting course or path; –plania.

.2 **deflection,** deflexure, flection, flexure; torsion, distortion; skewness; **refraction, diffraction, scatter,** diffusion, dispersion.

.3 VERBS **deviate, depart from, vary, diverge,** divaricate, branch off, **digress,** divagate, **turn aside,** go out of the way, detour; **swerve, veer,** sheer, curve, **shift, turn,** trend, bend, heel, bear off; tack 275.30; alter one's course, change the bearing.

.4 **stray,** go astray, lose one's way, err; take a wrong turn or turning; drift, go adrift; **wander,** ramble, rove, straggle, divagate, excurse, pererrate; meander, wind, twist, snake, twist and turn.

.5 **deflect,** deviate, **divert,** diverge, turn, bend, curve, pull, crook, dogleg, hairpin, zigzag; **warp,** bias, twist, distort, skew; refract, diffract, **scatter, diffuse, disperse.**

.6 **turn aside** or **to the side,** draw aside, side, **turn away,** jib, shy, shy off; avert; gee; haw; **sidetrack,** shove aside, shunt, switch; **head off,** turn back 289.3; **step aside,** sidestep, move aside or to the side, sidle; **steer clear of,** make way for, get out of the way of; go off, bear off, sheer off, veer off, ease off, edge off; fly off, go or fly off at a tangent; glance, glance off.

.7 ADJS **deviative,** deviatory, deviating, **deviant,** departing, aberrant, aberrational, aberrative, shifting, turning, swerving, veering; **digressive,** discursive, excursive, **circuitous; devious,** indirect, out-of-the-way; errant, erratic, zigzag, **wandering,** rambling, roving, winding, twisting, meandering, snaky, serpentine, mazy, labyrinthine, vagrant, stray, desultory, planetary, undirected.

.8 **deflective**, inflective, flectional, diffractive, refractive; refractile, refrangible; deflected, flexed, refracted, diffracted, scattered, diffuse, diffused, dispersed; distorted, skewed, skew.

292. LEADING

(going ahead)

.1 NOUNS **leading, heading,** foregoing; anteposition, the lead, *le pas* [Fr]; **preceding,** precedence 64; priority 116; front, van 240; precursor 66.

.2 VERBS **lead, head,** spearhead, stand at the head, stand first, head the line; take the lead, go in the lead, **lead the way,** be the bellwether; lead the dance; **light the way,** beacon, guide; get before, get ahead *or* in front of, come to the front, lap, outstrip, pace, set the pace; get *or* have the start, get a head start, steal a march upon; **precede** 64.2, go before 66.3.

.3 ADJS **leading, heading,** precessional, precedent, precursory, foregoing; **first, foremost,** headmost; **preceding,** antecedent 64.4; **prior** 116.4; **chief** 36.14.

.4 ADVS **before** 64.6, in front, foremost, headmost, in advance 240.12.

293. FOLLOWING

(going behind)

.1 NOUNS **following,** heeling, **trailing,** tailing [informal], shadowing; **hounding,** dogging, chasing, **pursuit,** pursual, pursuance; sequence 65; sequel 67; series 71.2.

.2 **follower,** successor, tagtail, tail [informal], shadow; **pursuer,** pursuivant; **attendant** 73.4, **satellite, hanger-on,** dangler, adherent, appendage, dependent, parasite, stooge [slang], flunky; **henchman,** ward heeler, partisan, supporter, votary, sectary; fan *or* buff [both informal]; courtier, *homme de cour* [Fr], *cavaliere servente* [Ital]; trainbearer; **public; following** 73.6; disciple 566.2.

.3 VERBS **follow,** go after *or* behind, come after *or* behind, move behind, **pursue, shadow, tail** [informal], **trail,** trail after, follow in the trail of, camp on the trail of, **heel,** follow *or* tread on the heels of, follow in the steps *or* footsteps *or* footprints of, tread close upon, follow in the wake of, hang on the skirts of, stick like the shadow of, sit on the tail of, tailgate [slang], go in the rear of, bring up the

rear, eat the dust of, take *or* swallow one's dust; tag *or* **tag after** *or* tag along [all informal]; string along [informal]; **dog,** bedog, **hound,** chase, **pursue.**

.4 **lag, lag behind,** straggle, drag, trail, **trail behind,** hang back, loiter, linger, **loiter** *or* **linger behind,** dawdle, get behind, fall behind *or* behindhand.

.5 ADJS **following,** trailing; succeeding 65.4; consecutive 71.9.

.6 ADVS **behind, after,** in the rear, in the train *or* wake of; in back of 241.13.

294 PROGRESSION

(motion forwards)

.1 NOUNS **progression, progress,** progressiveness; **passage,** course, march, career; **advance,** advancing, **advancement,** promotion, furtherance, furthering; forward motion, forwarding, forwardal; **ongoing,** ongo, go-ahead [informal], onward course, rolling, rolling on; **headway,** way; travel 273.

.2 VERBS **progress, advance, proceed, go,** go *or* move forward, step forward, go on, **go ahead,** go along, pass on *or* along; move, travel 273.17; go fast 269.8–18; **make progress,** come on, **get along,** come along [informal], **get ahead;** further oneself; **make headway, roll,** gather head, gather way; **make strides** *or* rapid strides, cover ground, get over the ground, make good time, make the best of one's way; make up for lost time, gain ground, make up leeway, make progress against, make head against, stem.

.3 **march on,** run on, rub on, **jog on, roll on,** flow on; drift along, go with the stream.

.4 **make one's way, work one's way,** weave *or* worm *or* thread one's way, inch forward, feel one's way, muddle through; go slow 270.6–9; carve one's way; push *or* force one's way, fight one's way; **forge ahead,** drive on *or* ahead, **push** *or* **press on** *or* **onward,** push *or* press forward, push, crowd.

.5 **advance, further, promote,** forward, hasten, contribute to, foster.

.6 ADJS **progressive,** progressing, advancing, proceeding, **ongoing,** oncoming, onward, forward, **forward-looking,** go-ahead [informal]; moving 273.35.

.7 ADVS **in progress,** in mid-progress; **going on.**

.8 **forward, forwards, onward, onwards, forth, on,** along, **ahead;** on the way to, on the road or high road to, en route to or for.

295. REGRESSION

(motion backwards)

.1 NOUNS **regression**, regress; recession 297; **retrogression**, retrocession, retroflexion, reflux, refluence, retrogradation, retroaction, retrusion, reaction; return, reentry; **setback**, backset, throwback, rollback, sternway; backward motion, backward step; **backsliding**, lapse, relapse, recidivism, recidivation.

.2 **retreat**, *reculade* [Fr], **withdrawal**, withdrawment, **retirement, fallback**, pullout, pullback; advance to the rear; disengagement.

.3 **reverse, reversal**, reversing, reversion; **backing**, backing up, backing off, backing out, backup; **about-face**, *volte-face* [Fr], about-turn, right-about, right-about-face, turn to the right-about, U-turn, turnaround, turnabout, swingaround; back track, back trail.

.4 **countermotion**, countermovement; countermarching, countermarch.

.5 VERBS **regress**, go backwards, **recede**, return, revert; **retrogress**, retrograde, retroflex, retrocede; pull back, jerk back, cock (the arm, fist, etc.); fall or get or go behind, fall astern, lose ground, slip back; **backslide**, lapse, relapse, recidivate.

.6 **retreat**, sound or beat a retreat, **withdraw**, retire, pull out or back, advance to the rear, disengage; **fall back**, move back, go back, stand back; run back; **draw back**, draw off; **back out or out of** [informal], back down; give ground, give place.

.7 **reverse**, go into reverse; **back, back up**, backpedal, back off or away; **backwater**, make sternway; **backtrack**, backtrail, take the back track; countermarch; reverse one's field; take the reciprocal course.

.8 **turn back**, put back; double, double back, retrace one's steps; turn one's back upon; **return**, go or come back, go or come home.

.9 **turn round** or **around** or **about**, turn, make a U-turn, turn on a dime, turn tail, **come** or **go about**, put about, fetch about; veer, veer around; **swivel, pivot**, pivot about, swing, round, swing round; wheel, wheel about, whirl, spin; heel, turn upon one's heel.

.10 **about-face**, *volte-face* [Fr], right-about-face, **do an about-face** or a right-about-face or an about-turn, perform a *volte-*

face, **face about**, turn or face to the right-about, do a turn to the right-about.

.11 ADJS **regressive**, recessive; **retrogressive**, retrocessive, retrograde; retroactive; reactionary.

.12 **reversed**, reflex, **turned around**, back, **backward**; wrong-way, wrong-way around, counter.

.13 ADVS **backwards**, backward, retrad, **hindwards**, hindward, **rearwards**, rearward, arear, astern; **back**, away, fro, *à reculons* [Fr]; **in reverse**, ass-backwards [slang]; against the grain, *à rebours* [Fr]; counterclockwise, anticlockwise, widdershins; an(a)–, re–, retro–.

296. APPROACH

(motion towards)

.1 NOUNS **approach**, approaching, coming toward, coming near, **access**, accession, nearing; approximation, proximation, appropinquation [archaic]; advance, oncoming; **advent, coming**, forthcoming; flowing toward, afflux, affluxion; appulse; nearness 200; imminence 152.

.2 **approachability, accessibility, access**, getatableness or come-at-ableness [both informal], attainability.

.3 VERBS **approach, near, draw near** or nigh, go or come near, come closer or nearer, come to close quarters; **close**, close in, close with; **accost**, encounter, confront; approximate, proximate, appropinquate [archaic]; **advance**, come, **come forward**, come on, come up, bear up, step up; ease or edge or sidle up to; bear down on or upon, be on a collision course with; gain upon, narrow the gap.

.4 ADJS **approaching, nearing**, advancing; attracted to, drawn to; **coming, oncoming, forthcoming**, upcoming, to come; approximate, proximate, approximative; near 200.14; imminent 152.3; –petal, –philic.

.5 **approachable, accessible**, getatable or come-at-able [both informal], attainable.

297. RECESSION

(motion from)

.1 NOUNS **recession**, recedence, receding, retrocedence; **retreat, retirement, withdrawal**; retraction, retractation, retractility.

.2 VERBS **recede**, retrocede; **retreat, retire, withdraw**; move off or away, stand off or away, stand out from the shore; go, **go away; die away**, fade away, drift away; diminish, decline, sink, shrink, dwindle, fade, ebb, wane; go out with the tide, fade into the distance; pull away, widen the distance.

.3 retract, withdraw, draw or pull back, pull out, draw or pull in; draw in one's claws or horns; shrink, wince, cringe, flinch, shy, duck.

.4 ADJS recessive, recessional, recessionary; recedent, retrocedent.

.5 receding, retreating, retiring; diminishing, declining, sinking, shrinking, dwindling, ebbing, waning; fading, dying.

.6 retractile, retractable, retrahent.

298. CONVERGENCE

(coming together)

.1 NOUNS convergence, converging, confluence, concourse, conflux; mutual approach, approach 296; meeting, congress, concurrence; concentration, concentralization, focalization 226.8, focus 226.4; collision course, narrowing gap; funnel, bottleneck; hub, spokes; asymptote; radius; tangent; crossing 221.

.2 VERBS converge, come together, approach 296.3, run together, meet, unite; intersect; fall in with; be on a collision course; narrow the gap, close with, close, close up, close in; funnel; taper, pinch, nip; centralize, center, come to a center; concentralize, concenter, concentrate, come or tend to a point; come to a focus 226.10.

.3 ADJS converging, convergent; meeting, uniting; concurrent, confluent, mutually approaching, approaching; connivent; focal, confocal; centrolineal, centripetal; asymptotic(al); radial, radiating; tangent, tangential.

299. DIVERGENCE

(recession from one another)

.1 NOUNS divergence or divergency, divarication; aberration, deviation 291; separation, division, decentralization; centrifugence; spread, spreading, spreading out, splaying, fanning, fanning out, deployment.

.2 radiation, ray, radius, spoke; radiance, diffusion, scattering, dispersion, emanation.

.3 forking, furcation, bifurcation, biforking, trifurcation, divarication; branching, branching off or out, ramification; arborescence, arborization, treelikeness.

.4 fork, prong, trident; Y, V; branch, ramification, stem, offshoot, –dendron; crotch, crutch; fan, delta, Δ; groin, inguen, inguin(o)–; furcula, furculum, wishbone.

.5 VERBS diverge, divaricate; aberrate; separate, divide; spread, spread out, outspread, splay, fan out, deploy; go off or away, fly or go off at a tangent.

.6 radiate, ray, diffuse, emanate, spread, disperse, scatter.

.7 fork, furcate, bifurcate, trifurcate, divaricate; branch, stem, ramify, branch off or out.

.8 ADJS diverging, divergent; divaricate, divaricating; palmate, palmated, palmi–, palmat(i)–; fanlike, fan-shaped; deltoid(al), deltalike, delta-shaped; splayed; centrifugal.

.9 radiating, radial, radiate, radiated, radio–; rayed, spoked; radiative; actin(o)–, actini–, –actinal, –actine.

.10 forked, forking, furcate, biforked, bifurcate, bifurcated, forklike, trifurcate, trifurcated, tridentlike, pronged; crotched, Y-shaped, V-shaped; branched, branching; arborescent, arboreal, arboriform, treelike, tree-shaped, dendriform, dendritic; branchlike, ramous.

300. ARRIVAL

.1 NOUNS arrival, coming, advent, approach, appearance, reaching; attainment, accomplishment, achievement.

.2 landing, landfall; docking, mooring, tying up, dropping anchor; disembarkation, disembarkment, debarkation, coming or going ashore.

.3 return, homecoming, recursion; reentrance, reentry; remigration.

.4 welcome, greetings 925.2–4.

.5 destination, goal, bourn [archaic]; port, haven, harbor, anchorage, journey's end; end of the line, terminus, terminal, terminal point; stop, stopping place, last stop.

.6 VERBS arrive, arrive at, arrive in, come, come or get to, approach, reach, hit [informal]; find, gain, attain, attain to, accomplish, achieve, make, make it [informal], fetch, fetch up at, get there, reach one's destination, come to one's journey's end; make or put in an appearance, show up [informal], turn up, pop or bob up [informal]; get in, come in, blow in [slang], pull in, roll in; check in; clock or punch or ring or time in [all informal], sign in; hit town [informal]; come to hand, be received.

.7 **arrive at**, come at, get at, **reach**, arrive upon, **come upon, hit upon**, strike upon, fall upon, light upon, pitch upon, stumble on or upon.

.8 **land**, come to land, make a landfall, set foot on dry land; reach or make land, make port; put in or into, put into port; dock, moor, tie up, drop anchor; go ashore, **disembark**, debark, unboat; **detrain**, debus, deplane, disemplane; alight 316.7, 278.52.

.9 ADJS **arriving**, approaching, entering, **coming, incoming**; inbound, inward-bound; homeward, homeward-bound.

301. DEPARTURE

.1 NOUNS departure, **leaving, going**, passing, **parting; exit**, walkout [informal]; exodus, hegira; egress 303; **withdrawal**, removal, retreat 295.2, retirement; evacuation; abandonment; decampment; escape, flight, getaway [informal].

.2 **outset**, outsetting, setout, outstart, **start**, starting, start-off, setoff, takeoff [informal].

.3 **embarkation**, embarkment, boarding; entrainment; enplanement or emplanement, **takeoff**, hopoff [informal].

.4 **leave-taking, leave, parting**, congé; **send-off, Godspeed; adieu**, one's adieus, **farewell**, aloha, **good-bye**; valedictory address, valedictory, valediction, parting words; valedictorian; viaticum; stirrup cup, one for the road, doch-an-dorrach or doch-an-dorris [both Gaelic].

.5 **point of departure, starting place** or **point**, takeoff, **start**, base, basis; line of departure; starting post or gate; stakeboat; port of embarkation.

.6 VERBS **depart**, take one's departure or leave, **leave, go**, up and go [dial], **go away, go off, get off** or **away**, get under way, come away, go one's way, go or get along, be getting along [informal], gang along [Scot], go on, get on; trot or toddle or stagger along [informal]; mosey or sashay [both informal], mosey or sashay off or along [informal]; **buzz off** or along [informal]; take wing or flight, wing it [slang]; move off or away, move out, march off or away; **pull out**; exit 303.11; take or break or tear oneself away, take oneself off.

.7 **set forth**, put forth, go forth, **sally forth**, sally, issue, issue forth, set forward, **set out** or **off**, be off, be on one's way, outset, **start, start out** or **off**, outstart, **strike out**, get off.

.8 **quit, vacate**, evacuate, abandon, turn one's back on; **withdraw, retreat, beat a retreat**, retire, remove; abscond, disappear, vanish; **bow out** [informal], make one's exit.

.9 begone, get lost or flake off [both slang], get going [informal], shove off or hit the road [both slang], **get out**, be off, take oneself off or away, get or git [both slang]; **clear out** [informal], **get the hell out** [slang], make yourself scarce [informal], vamoose [informal], beat it or scram [both slang].

.10 make off, **take off** [informal], split, dog it [both slang]; skip or skip out [both informal]; lam or take it on the lam [both slang]; powder or take a powder or take a runout powder [all slang]; skedaddle or absquatulate [both slang]; decamp.

.11 hasten off, hurry away; **scamper off, dash off**, whiz off, whip off or away, nip or nip off [both informal], tear off or out, **light out** [slang], dig or skin out [slang].

.12 **fling out** or **off**, flounce out or off.

.13 **run off** or **away**, run along, flee, take to flight, fly, take to one's heels, cut out or cut and run [both informal], hightail [slang], make tracks [informal]; run for one's life; run away from 631.10.

.14 **check out**; clock or ring or punch out [all informal], sign out.

.15 **decamp, break camp**, strike camp or tent, **pull up stakes.**

.16 **embark, go aboard**, board, go on board; go on shipboard, take ship; hoist the blue Peter; **entrain**, enplane or emplane, embus; weigh anchor, put to sea 275.19,20.

.17 say or bid good-bye or farewell, take leave, make one's adieus; bid Godspeed, give one a send-off, "speed the parting guest" [Pope]; drink a stirrup cup, have one for the road.

.18 **leave home**, go from home; leave the country, emigrate, out-migrate, expatriate.

.19 ADJS **departing, leaving; parting**, last, final, farewell; valedictory; outward-bound.

.20 **departed, left, gone**, gone off or away.

.21 ADVS **hence**, thence, whence; off, **away**, forth, out; therefrom, thereof; ab–, de–.

.22 PREPS **from, away from**; out, out of.

.23 INTERJS **farewell!, good-bye!, adieu!**, so long! [informal], cheerio! [Brit], au revoir! [Fr], ¡adios! [Sp], ¡hasta la vista! [Sp], ¡hasta luego! [Sp], ¡vaya con Dios! [Sp], auf Wiedersehen! [Ger], addio! [Ital], arrivederci!, arrivederla! [both Ital], ciao! [Ital informal], do svidanye!

[Russ], *shalom!* [Heb], *sayonara!* [Jap], *vale!, vive valeque!* [both L], aloha!, **until we meet again!**, until tomorrow!, *à demain!* [Fr], **see you later!**, see you!, I'll be seeing you!, we'll see you!, *à bientôt!* [Fr], *à toute a l'heure!* [Fr]; be good!, keep in touch!, come again!; *bon voyage!* [Fr], pleasant journey!, have a nice trip!, *tsetchem leshalom!* [Heb], *glückliche Reise!* [Ger], happy landing!; Godspeed!, peace be with you!, *pax vobiscum!* [L]; all good go with you!, God bless you!

.24 **good night!**, nighty-night! [informal], *bonne nuit!* [Fr], *gute Nacht!* [Ger], ¡*buenas noches!* [Sp], *buona notte!* [Ital].

302. INGRESS, ENTRANCE

.1 NOUNS **ingress**, ingression, introgression; **entrance**, **entry**, entree, *entrée* [Fr]; **access**; **ingoing**, **incoming**, income; **import**, importing, importation; **input**, **intake**; **penetration**, interpenetration; infiltration, percolation, seepage, leakage; insinuation; intrusion 238; introduction, **insertion** 304; admission, reception 306.

.2 **influx**, influxion, **inflow**, inflooding, indraft, indrawing, inpour, inrun, inrush; afflux, affluxion, affluence.

.3 **immigration**, in-migration, incoming population, foreign influx.

.4 **incomer**, **entrant**, comer, arrival; **visitor**, visitant; **immigrant**, in-migrant; newcomer 78.4; settler 190.9; **intruder** 238.3.

.5 **entrance**, entry, **entranceway**, entryway; **inlet**, ingress, intake, adit, approach, **access**, means of access, in [informal], way in; **opening** 265; **passageway**, corridor, companionway, hall, passage, way; gangway, gangplank; vestibule 192.19; air lock.

.6 **porch**, propylaeum; **portal**, postern, **threshold**, doorjamb, gatepost, doorpost, lintel; **door**, **doorway**, French door; **gate**, **gateway**, lych gate, barway, pylon, archway; front door, back door, side door; carriage entrance, porte cochere; cellar door, cellarway; bulkhead; hatch, hatchway, scuttle; storm door; trap door, trap; tollgate; stile, turnstile, turnpike.

.7 VERBS **enter**, go in *or* into, cross the threshold, **come in**, find one's way into, put in *or* into; be admitted, gain admittance, have an entree, have an in [informal]; **set foot in**, step in; **get in**, jump in, hop in; **drop in**, look in, visit, pop in [informal]; **breeze in**, come breezing in; break *or* burst in, bust in *or* come busting in [both slang]; **barge in** *or* come barging in [both informal]; thrust in, push *or*

press in, crowd in, jam in, wedge in, pack in, squeeze in; slip *or* creep in, wriggle *or* worm oneself into, edge in, work in, insinuate oneself; irrupt, intrude 238.5; take in, admit 306.10; insert 304.3.

.8 **penetrate** 265.16, interpenetrate, **pierce**, pass *or* go through, get through, get into, make way into, make an entrance, gain entree.

.9 **flow in**, inflow, inflood, inpour, inrush, **pour in**.

.10 **filter in**, **infiltrate**, **seep in**, percolate into, leak in, soak in.

.11 **immigrate**, in-migrate.

.12 ADJS **entering**, ingressive, **incoming**, **ingoing**; **in**, inward; **inbound**, inward-bound; inflowing, inflooding, inpouring, inrushing; invasive, intrusive, irruptive; ingrowing.

.13 ADVS **in**, inward, inwards, inwardly; en– *or* em–, in– *or* il– *or* im– *or* ir–, ob–.

.14 PREPS **into**, in, to.

303. EGRESS, EMERGENCE

.1 NOUNS **egress**, egression; **exit**, exodus; **outgoing**, outgo, going out; **outcoming**, outcome, forthcoming; departure 301; extraction 305.

.2 **emergence**, emersion; surfacing; **issue**, **issuance**; extrusion; **emission**, emanation, vent, discharge.

.3 **outburst** 162.6, ejection 310.

.4 **outflow**, outflowing; discharge; **outpour**, outpouring; effluence, effusion, exhalation; **efflux**, effluxion, defluxion; **exhaust**; **runoff**, **flowoff**; outfall; drainage, drain; gush 395.4.

.5 **leakage**, leaking, **leak**; **dripping**, drippings, **drip**, dribble, drop, trickle; distillation.

.6 **exudation**, transudation; **filtration**, exfiltration, filtering; straining; **percolation**, percolating; leaching, lixiviation; effusion, extravasation; **seepage**, seep; **oozing**, ooze; weeping, weep; **excretion** 311.

.7 **emigration**, out-migration, remigration; exile, expatriation, deportation.

.8 **export**, exporting, exportation.

.9 **outlet**, egress, **exit**, outgo, outcome, out [informal], way out; **loophole**, escape; **opening** 265; outfall, estuary; chute, flume, sluice, weir, floodgate; **vent**, ventage, venthole, port; avenue, channel; spout, tap; debouch; **exhaust**; door 302.6; outgate, sally port; vomitory; emunctory; pore; blowhole, spiracle.

.10 **outgoer**, **goer**, leaver, departer; **emigrant**, *émigré* [Fr], out-migrant.

.11 VERBS **exit,** make an exit, **make one's exit;** egress, **go out,** get out, walk out, march out, run out, pass out, bow out [informal]; depart 301.6.

.12 **emerge, come out, issue,** issue forth, extrude, **come forth,** surface, sally, sally forth; emanate, effuse, arise, come; debouch, disembogue; jump out, bail out; burst forth, break forth, erupt, break cover, **come out in the open;** protrude 256.9.

.13 **run out,** empty, find vent; **exhaust** 310.23; **drain,** drain out; **flow out,** outflow, outpour, **pour out,** sluice out, well out, gush or spout out, flow, pour, well, surge, gush, jet, spout, spurt, vomit forth, blow out, spew out.

.14 **leak, leak out, drip,** dribble, drop, trickle, trill, weep, distill.

.15 **exude,** exudate, transude, transpire, reek; **emit, discharge,** give off; **filter,** filtrate, exfiltrate; strain; **percolate;** leach, lixiviate; effuse, extravasate; **seep, ooze;** bleed; weep; excrete 311.12.

.16 **emigrate,** out-migrate, remigrate; exile, expatriate, deport.

.17 **export,** send abroad.

.18 ADJS **emerging,** emergent; **issuing,** arising, surfacing, coming, forthcoming; emanating, emanent, emanative, transeunt, transient.

.19 **outgoing, outbound,** outward-bound; **outflowing,** outpouring, effusive, effluent; effused, extravasated; extro–.

.20 exudative, transudative; percolative; porous, permeable, pervious, oozy, runny, weepy, leaky; excretory 311.19.

.21 ADVS **forth; out,** outward, outwards, outwardly.

.22 PREPS out of, ex; from; out.

304. INSERTION

(putting in)

.1 NOUNS **insertion, introduction,** insinuation, injection, infusion, perfusion, inoculation, intromission; entrance 302; penetration 265.3; interjection, interpolation 237.2; graft, grafting, transplant, transplantation; infixion, implantation, embedment, tessellation, impactment, impaction; –phoresis.

.2 **insert,** insertion; **inset, inlay;** tessera.

.3 VERBS **insert, introduce,** insinuate, inject, infuse, perfuse, inoculate, intromit; enter 302.7; penetrate 265.16; **put in, stick in,** set in, throw in, pop in, tuck in, whip in; slip in, ease in; interject 237.7.

.4 **install,** instate, inaugurate, initiate, invest, ordain; enlist, enroll, induct, sign up, sign on.

.5 **inset, inlay; embed** or bed, bed in.

.6 **graft,** engraft, **implant,** imp [archaic]; bud; inarch.

.7 **thrust in, drive in, run in, plunge in,** force in, push in, **ram in,** press in, stuff in, crowd in, squeeze in, cram in, jam in, tamp in, pound in, pack in, poke in, knock in, wedge in, impact.

.8 **implant,** infix 142.9, fit in, inlay, tessellate.

305. EXTRACTION

(taking or drawing out)

.1 NOUNS **extraction, withdrawal,** removal; **drawing, pulling,** drawing out; ripping or tearing or wresting out; eradication, **uprooting,** unrooting, deracination; squeezing out, pressing out, expression; avulsion, evulsion, cutting out, exsection, extirpation, excision, enucleation; extrication, evolvement, disentanglement, unravelment; excavation, mining, quarrying, drilling; dredging.

.2 **disinterment, exhumation,** disentombment, **unearthing.**

.3 **drawing,** drafting, sucking, **suction,** aspiration, pipetting; pumping, siphoning, tapping, broaching; milking; drainage, draining, emptying; cupping; bloodletting, bleeding, phlebotomy, venesection.

.4 **evisceration,** gutting, **disembowelment.**

.5 **elicitation,** eduction, drawing out or forth, bringing out or forth; **evocation,** calling forth; arousal.

.6 **extortion, exaction,** claim, demand; **wresting, wrenching, wringing, rending,** tearing, ripping; wrest, wrench, wring.

.7 (obtaining an extract) **squeezing, pressing,** expression; **distillation;** decoction; **rendering,** rendition; **steeping,** soaking, infusion; concentration.

.8 **extract,** extraction; **essence, quintessence, spirit, elixir;** decoction; **distillate,** distillation; **concentrate,** concentration; infusion; refinement, purification.

.9 **extractor,** separator; siphon; aspirator, pipette; pump, vacuum pump; press, wringer; corkscrew; forceps, pliers, pincers, tweezers; crowbar.

.10 VERBS **extract, take out, get out, withdraw, remove;** pull, draw; **pull out, draw out,** tear out, rip out, wrest out, pluck out, pick out, weed out, rake out; **pull up, pluck up; root up** or **out, uproot,** unroot, eradicate, deracinate, pull or pluck up by the roots; cut out, excise, exsect; gouge out, avulse, evulse; extricate, evolve, disentangle, unravel; **dig up or out**, grub up or out, excavate, **unearth**, mine, quarry; dredge, dredge up or out.

.11 **disinter, exhume**, disentomb, unbury, unsepulcher.

.12 **draw off, draft off**, draft, draw, draw from; **suck**, suck out or up, **siphon off**; pipette; pump, pump out; tap, broach; let, let out; bleed; let blood, venesect, phlebotomize; milk; **drain**, decant; exhaust, empty.

.13 **eviscerate, disembowel, gut.**

.14 **elicit**, educe, deduce, induce, derive, obtain, procure, secure; **get from**, get out of; **evoke, call up, summon up**, call or summon forth, call out; rouse, arouse, stimulate; **draw out or forth**, bring out or forth, winkle out [Brit], drag out, worm out, bring to light; wangle, wangle out of, worm out of.

.15 **extort, exact**, claim, demand; **wrest, wring from**, wrench from, rend from, wrest or tear from.

.16 (obtain an extract) **squeeze or press out**, express, wring, wring out; **distill**, elixirate [archaic]; decoct; **render**, melt down; refine; **steep**, soak, infuse; **concentrate**, essentialize.

.17 ADJS extractive, eductive; educible; eradicative, uprooting; elicitory, **evocative**, arousing; **exacting**, exactive; **extortionate**, extortionary, extortive.

.18 **essential**, quintessential, pure 45.6.

306. RECEPTION

.1 NOUNS reception, **taking in**, receipt, receiving; welcome, welcoming; refuge 700.

.2 **admission**, admittance, acceptance; immission [archaic], intromission 304.1; **installation**, instatement, inauguration, initiation; baptism, investiture, ordination; enlistment, enrollment, induction.

.3 **entree**, *entrée* [Fr], in [informal], entry, entrance 302, **access**, opening, **open door**, open arms.

.4 **ingestion**, eating, imbibition, drinking; engorgement, ingurgitation, engulfment; **swallowing**, gulping; swallow, gulp, slurp.

.5 (drawing in) **suction**, suck, sucking, myzo–; **inhalation**, inhalement, inspiration, aspiration; snuff, snuffle, sniff, sniffle.

.6 sorption, **absorption**, adsorption, chemisorption or chemosorption, engrossment; digestion, **assimilation**, infiltration;

sponging, blotting; seepage, percolation; **osmosis**, osmo–, endosmosis, exosmosis, electroosmosis; absorbency; **absorbent**, adsorbent, **sponge, blotter**, blotting paper.

.7 (bringing in) **introduction**; **import**, importing, **importation**.

.8 readmission; reabsorption, resorbence.

.9 **receptivity, receptiveness**, invitingness, openness, hospitality, recipience or recipiency; receptibility, admissibility.

.10 VERBS **receive, take in; admit, let in**, immit [archaic], intromit, give entrance or admittance to, give an entree, open the door to, give refuge or shelter or sanctuary to, throw open to.

.11 **ingest**, eat, imbibe, drink; **swallow, devour**, ingurgitate; **engulf**, engorge; **gulp**, gulp down, swill, swill down, wolf down, gobble.

.12 **draw in, suck**, suckle, suck in or up, aspirate; **inhale**, inspire, breathe in; snuff, snuffle, sniff, sniffle, snuff in or up, slurp.

.13 sorb, **absorb**, adsorb, chemisorb or chemosorb, **assimilate**, engross, digest, **drink**, imbibe, take up or in, drink up or in, slurp up, swill up; blot, **blot up, soak up**, sponge; osmose; infiltrate, filter in; **soak in, seep in**, percolate in.

.14 **bring in, introduce, import.**

.15 readmit; reabsorb, resorb.

.16 ADJS **receptive**, recipient; welcoming, open, hospitable, inviting, invitatory; introceptive; **admissive**, admissory; receivable, receptible, admissible; intromissive, intromittent; ingestive, imbibitory; end-(o)–.

.17 sorbent, **absorbent**, adsorbent, chemisorptive or chemosorptive, **assimilative**, digestive; bibulous, imbibitory, thirsty, soaking, blotting; spongy, spongeous; osmotic, endosmotic, exosmotic; resorbent.

.18 **introductory**, introductive; **initiatory**, initiative, baptismal.

307. EATING

.1 NOUNS **eating, feeding, dining**, messing; ingestion, consumption, deglutition; **tasting**, relishing, savoring; nibbling, pecking, licking, **munching; devouring**, devourment, gobbling, wolfing; **chewing**, mastication, manducation, rumination; feasting, regalement, epulation; appetite, hunger 634.7; nutrition 309; **dieting** 309.11; gluttony 994; carnivorism, carnivorousness, carnivority; herbivorism, herbivority, herbivorousness, grazing, cropping, pasturing, pasture, vegetarianism, phytophagy; omnivorism, omnivorousness, pantophagy; cannibalism, anthropophagy; omophagia *or* omophagy; phag(o)–, –phagia *or* –phagy.

.2 **bite, morsel,** swallow; mouthful, gob [slang]; cud, quid; bolus; **chew,** chaw [dial]; nip, nibble; munch; gnash; champ, chomp [dial]; snap.

.3 **drinking,** imbibing, imbibition, potation; lapping, slipping, tasting, nipping; quaffing, gulping, swigging [informal], swilling *or* guzzling [both slang], pulling [informal]; compotation, symposium; drunkenness 996.1–4.

.4 **drink,** potation, portion, libation; draft, dram, drench, **swig** [informal], swill *or* guzzle [both slang], quaff, **sip,** sup, suck, tot, bumper, snort [slang], pull [informal], lap, gulp, slurp [slang]; nip, peg; beverage 308.48,49.

.5 **meal, repast,** feed [informal], mess, spread [informal], table, board, meat, *repas* [Fr]; **refreshment,** refection, regalement, entertainment, treat.

.6 (meals) **breakfast,** *petit déjeuner* [Fr]; meat breakfast, *déjeuner à la fourchette* [Fr]; **brunch** [informal], elevenses [Brit informal]; **lunch, luncheon,** tiffin, hot luncheon; **tea,** teatime, high tea; **dinner,** *diner* [Fr]; **supper,** *souper* [Fr]; buffet supper *or* lunch; TV dinner; **picnic, cookout,** alfresco meal, fête champêtre, **barbecue,** fish fry, clambake, wiener roast *or* wienie roast; coffee break, tea break, mash [Brit informal].

.7 **light meal,** light repast, light lunch, spot of lunch [informal], collation, **snack** [informal], nosh [informal], **bite** [informal], *casse-croûte* [Fr], refreshments.

.8 **hearty meal, full meal,** healthy meal, large *or* substantial meal, heavy meal, **square meal,** man-sized meal, large order.

.9 **feast, banquet,** festal board; lavish *or* Lucullan feast; bean-feast *or* beano [both Brit informal], blow *or* blowout [both informal], groaning board.

.10 **serving,** service; **portion, helping,** help; second helping; **course;** dish, plate; antepast; entree, *entrée* [Fr]; entremets; dessert; cover, place.

.11 (manner of service) service, table service, counter service, self-service; table d'hôte, ordinary; à la carte; cover, *couvert* [Fr]; cover charge; American plan, European plan.

.12 **menu, bill of fare,** carte.

.13 **gastronomy,** gastronomics, gastrology, **epicurism,** epicureanism.

.14 **eater,** feeder, consumer, devourer; **diner,** luncher; picnicker; mouth, hungry mouth; diner-out, eater-out; boarder, board-and-roomer; **gourmet,** gastronome, epicure, connoisseur of food *or* wine, bon vivant, high liver, Lucullus, Brillat-Savarin; omnivore, pantophagist; **flesh-eater, meat-eater, carnivore,** omophagist, predacean; **man-eater, cannibal; vegetarian,** lactovegetarian, fruitarian, plant-eater, **herbivore,** phytophagan, phytophage; grasseater, graminivore; grain-eater, granivore; gourmand, trencherman, **glutton** 994.3; –phage, –vore *or* –vora.

.15 **restaurant,** eating house, dining room; eatery *or* beanery *or* hashery *or* hash house [all slang]; *trattoria* [Ital]; **lunchroom,** luncheonette; **café,** *caffè* [Ital]; tearoom, *bistro* [Fr]; **coffeehouse,** coffeeroom, **coffee shop,** tavern 191.16; chophouse; **grill,** grillroom; cookshop; buffet, smorgasbord; **lunch counter,** quick-lunch counter; hot-dog stand, hamburger stand, drive-in restaurant, drive-in; fast-food chain; **snack bar,** *buvette* [Fr], *cantina* [Sp]; pizzeria; **cafeteria,** automat; mess hall, dining hall; canteen; cookhouse, cookshack, lunch wagon, chuck wagon; **diner,** dog wagon [slang]; **kitchen** 330.3.

.16 VERBS **feed, dine,** wine and dine, mess; satisfy, gratify; regale; bread, meat; board, sustain; pasture, put out to pasture, graze, grass; forage, fodder; provision 659.9.

.17 **nourish, nurture,** nutrify, aliment, foster; **nurse, suckle,** lactate, breast-feed, wet-nurse, dry-nurse; fatten, fatten up, stuff, force-feed.

.18 **eat, feed,** fare, take, partake, partake of, break bread, break one's fast; refresh *or* entertain the inner man, put on the feed bag [slang], fall to, pitch in [informal]; **taste,** relish, savor; hunger 634.19; **diet,** go on a diet, watch one's weight, count calories.

.19 **dine,** dinner; **sup,** breakfast; lunch; picnic, cook out; **eat out, dine out;** board; mess with, break bread with.

.20 **devour, swallow,** ingest, **consume,** take in, tuck in *or* away [informal], down, take down, get down, put away [informal]; **eat up;** dispatch *or* dispose of *or* get away with [all informal]; surround *or* put oneself outside of [both slang].

.21 **gobble, gulp, bolt,** wolf, gobble *or* gulp *or* bolt *or* wolf down.

.22 **feast, banquet,** regale; eat heartily, have a good appetite, eat up, lick the platter or plate, do oneself proud [informal], do one's duty, do justice to, polish the platter, put it away [informal].

.23 **stuff, gorge** 994.4, **engorge, glut.** guttle, cram, eat one's fill, stuff *or* gorge oneself, gluttonize.

.24 **pick, peck** [informal], **nibble; snack** [informal], nosh [informal]; pick at, peck at [informal], eat like a bird, show no appetite.

.25 **chew,** chew up, chaw [dial]; **masticate,** manducate; ruminate, chew the cud; **bite,** grind, champ, chomp [dial]; **munch;** gnash; nibble, **gnaw;** mouth, mumble; gum.

.26 **feed on** *or* **upon, feast on** *or* **upon,** batten upon, fatten on *or* upon; prey on *or* upon, live on *or* upon, pasture on, browse, graze, crop.

.27 **drink,** drink in, **imbibe,** wet one's whistle [informal]; **quaff, sip, sup,** bib, swig [informal], swill *or* guzzle [both slang], pull [informal]; **suck,** suckle, suck in *or* up; drink off *or* up, toss off *or* down, drain the cup; wash down; **toast,** drink to, pledge; tipple, **booze** 996.22–24.

.28 **lap up,** sponge *or* soak up, lick, lap, slurp [slang].

.29 ADJS **eating, feeding, gastronomic(al), dining,** mensal, commensal, prandial, postprandial, preprandial; **nourishing, nutritious** 309.19; **dietetic; omnivorous,** pantophagous, **gluttonous** 994.6; **flesh-eating, meat-eating, carnivorous,** omophagous, predacious; **man-eating, cannibal,** cannibalistic; insect-eating, insectivorous; vegetable-eating, **vegetarian,** lactovegetarian, fruitarian; plant-eating, **herbivorous,** phytivorous, phytophagous; grass-eating, graminivorous; grain-eating, granivorous; –phagous, –vorous.

.30 chewing, masticatory, manducatory; ruminant, ruminating, cud-chewing.

.31 **edible, eatable,** comestible, gustable, esculent; kosher; **palatable,** succulent, **delicious,** dainty, savory.

.32 **drinkable,** potable.

.33 INTERJS chow down!, soup's on!, grub's on!, come and get it!; *bon appetit!* [Fr], eat hearty!

308. FOOD

.1 NOUNS **food,** foodstuff, food and drink, sustenance, kitchen stuff, **victuals** *or* vittles [both informal], **comestibles, edibles,** eatables, viands, **cuisine,** tucker [Austral], ingesta [pl]; fast food, junk food; **fare,** cheer, creature comfort; provision, prov-

ender; meat [archaic], bread, daily bread, bread and butter; health food 309.26; board, table, feast 307.9, spread [informal].

.2 [slang terms] **grub,** grubbery, **eats, chow,** chuck.

.3 **nutriment, nourishment,** nurture; pabulum, pap; aliment, alimentation; **refreshment,** refection; **sustenance,** support, keep.

.4 **feed, fodder, provender;** forage, pasture, eatage, pasturage; grain, sito–; corn, oats, barley, wheat; meal, bran, chop; **hay,** straw; ensilage, silage; chicken feed, scratch, scratch feed, mash; slops, swill; pet food, dog food, cat food, etc.; bird seed.

.5 **provisions, groceries,** provender, supplies, stores, larder, food supply; fresh foods, canned foods, frozen foods, dehydrated foods; commissariat, commissary, grocery.

.6 **rations,** board, meals, commons, mess, allowance, allotment, tucker [Austral]; short commons; emergency rations; K ration, C ration, garrison *or* field rations.

.7 **dish,** culinary preparation *or* concoction; cover, **course** 307.10; casserole; grill, broil, boil, roast, fry; main dish, entree, *pièce de résistance* [Fr], culinary masterpiece, dish fit for a king; side dish.

.8 **delicacy, dainty, goody** [informal], treat, kickshaw, **tidbit,** titbit; **morsel,** choice morsel, *bonne bouche* [Fr]; savory; dessert; ambrosia, nectar, cate, manna.

.9 **appetizer,** whet, *apéritif* [Fr]; foretaste, antepast, *antipasto* [Ital], *Vorspeise* [Ger]; **hors d'oeuvre;** smorgasbord; canapé.

.10 **soup,** *potage* [Fr]; consommé, gravy soup; purée; **broth,** clear soup, bouillon, stock; vegetable soup, pottage, *petite marmite* [Fr]; *potage aux herbes* [Fr]; potato soup, *vichyssoise* [Fr]; tomato soup, *potage au tomate* [Fr], *gazpacho* [Sp]; julienne, *potage à la julienne* [Fr]; chicken soup, *potage volaille à la reine* [Fr]; turtle soup, *potage à la tortue* [Fr]; oxtail soup; *pot-au-feu* [Fr]; mock turtle soup, *potage à la tête de veau* [Fr]; bisque, borscht; egg drop soup, won ton soup, bird's nest soup [all China]; miso *or* misoshiru soup [Japan]; thin soup, thick soup, gumbo, minestrone, mulligatawny, burgoo; matzo ball soup; fish soup, *bouillabaisse* [Fr], **chowder,** clam chowder.

.11 **stew,** olla, olio, *olla podrida* [Sp]; meat stew, *étuvée* [Fr]; Irish stew, mulligan stew *or* mulligan [slang]; goulash, Hungarian goulash; ragout; salmi; *bouilla-baisse* [Fr], *paella* [Catalan], oyster stew, chowder; fricassee; curry.

.12 meat, flesh, *viande* [Fr]; butcher's meat, *viande de boucherie* [Fr]; game, *menue viande* [Fr]; venison; **roast**, joint, *rôti* [Fr]; pot roast; barbecue, boiled meat, *bouilli* [Fr]; forcemeat; mincemeat, mince; hash, *hachis* [Fr]; jugged hare, *civet* [Fr]; pemmican, jerky; sausage meat, scrapple; aspic.

.13 beef, *bœuf* [Fr]; roast beef, *rosbif* [Fr]; hamburger, ground beef; corned beef; bully *or* bully beef; dried beef; chipped beef; salt beef; jerky, charqui; pastrami; beef extract, beef tea, bouillon; suet.

.14 veal, *veau* [Fr]; veal cutlet, *côtelette de veau* [Fr]; breast of veal, *poitrine de veau* [Fr]; fricandeau; calf's head, *tête de veau* [Fr]; calf's liver, *foie de veau* [Fr]; sweetbread, *ris de veau* [Fr]; calf's brains.

.15 mutton, *mouton* [Fr]; **lamb**, *agneau* [Fr]; breast of lamb, *poitrine d'agneau* [Fr]; leg of lamb, leg of mutton, *gigot* [Fr], *jambe de mouton* [Fr]; saddle of mutton; baked sheep's head.

.16 pork, *porc* [Fr], pig; sucking *or* suckling pig, *cochon de lait* [Fr]; **ham**, butt, *jambon* [Fr]; small ham, *jambonneau* [Fr]; ham steak; picnic ham; *prosciutto* [Ital]; **bacon**, *lard* [Fr]; Canadian bacon; rasher of bacon, *barde* [Fr], *tranche de lard* [Fr]; side of bacon, flitch, *flèche de lard* [Fr], gammon; salt pork, fat back, sowbelly [informal]; pork pie; spareribs; hog jowl; pigs' knuckles, pigs' feet, trotters, *pieds de cochon* [Fr]; chitterlings, haslet, cracklings; headcheese; lard.

.17 (cuts of meat) brisket, chuck, chuck roast, rolled roast, flank, flanken, knuckle, round, rump, saddle, shank, ribs, short ribs, shoulder; loin, crown roast, sirloin, tenderloin, *filet mignon* [Fr], Chateaubriand; clod, shoulder clod; plate, plate piece; roast, pot roast, rib roast, rump roast, blade roast; rack, breast; cold cuts.

.18 steak, *tranche* [Fr]; **beefsteak**, *bifteck* [Fr], *tranche de bœuf* [Fr]; club steak, fillet steak, flank steak, pinbone steak, planked steak, porterhouse steak, rib steak, round steak, rump steak, sirloin steak, shell steak, London broil, T-bone steak, tenderloin steak; cubed steak; chopped steak, ground beef, ground round, ground chuck, etc., hamburg steak, Salisbury steak, hamburger, hamburg [slang].

.19 chop, cutlet, *côtelette* [Fr]; pork chop, *côtelette de porc frais* [Fr]; mutton chop, *côtelette de mouton* [Fr], Saratoga chop; veal cutlet, veal chop, *côtelette de veau* [Fr], *Wiener Schnitzel* [Ger].

.20 (variety meats) kidneys; heart; brains; liver; gizzard; tongue; sweetbread (thymus); beef bread (pancreas); tripe (stomach); marrow; cockscomb; chitterlings *or* chitlins (intestines); prairie *or* mountain oyster (testis); haslet, giblets, *abatis* [Fr].

.21 sausage, *saucisse* [Fr], *saucisson* [Fr]; bangers [Brit]; **frankfurter**, frank, **hot dog** [informal], wienerwurst, **wiener**, wienie *or* weenie [both informal]; Vienna sausage; **bologna; salami; liverwurst**, liver sausage, braunschweiger, gooseliver, *pâté de foie gras* [Fr]; *Bratwurst* [Ger], *Knackwurst* [Ger], knockwurst; black pudding *or* blood pudding; headcheese.

.22 fowl, *volaille* [Fr]; chicken, *poulet* [Fr]; broiler, fryer, roaster, stewing chicken, capon, *chapon* [Fr]; Cornish hen, Rock Cornish hen; guinea hen; duck, *canard* [Fr]; duckling, *caneton* [Fr]; Long Island duckling; wild duck, *canard sauvage* [Fr]; goose, *oie* [Fr]; turkey, *dindon* [Fr]; pheasant, *faisan* [Fr]; partridge, *perdrix* [Fr]; grouse, *coq de bruyère* [Fr]; quail, *caille* [Fr]; pigeon; squab, *pigeonneau* [Fr].

.23 (parts of fowl) leg, drumstick, thigh, chicken foot, turkey foot, etc., wing, wishbone, breast; white meat, dark meat, giblets 308.20, pope's *or* parson's nose; oyster; neck.

.24 fish 414.65, *poisson* [Fr]; seafood; finnan haddie; kipper, kippered salmon *or* herring; smoked herring, red herring; eel, *anguille* [Fr]; fish eggs, roe, caviar.

.25 shellfish, *coquillage* [Fr]; clam, quahog, littleneck clam, soft-shell clam *or* steamer, mussel, limpet, periwinkle, scallop, whelk; oyster, *huître* [Fr]; blue point; shrimp, prawn, *crevette* [Fr]; crab, blue crab, soft-shell crab, Alaska king crab *or* Japanese crab, Dungeness crab; crayfish, crawfish, crawdad [dial], *écrevisse* [Fr]; lobster, *homard* [Fr]; rock *or* spiny lobster, *langouste* [Fr]; *écrevisse de mer* [Fr]; snail, *escargot* [Fr].

.26 eggs, *œufs* [Fr]; fried eggs, *œufs sur le plat* [Fr]; boiled eggs, *œufs à la coque* [Fr], coddled eggs; poached eggs, *œufs pochés* [Fr]; scrambled eggs, buttered eggs, *œufs brouillés* [Fr]; dropped eggs, shirred eggs, stuffed eggs, deviled eggs; omelet; soufflé.

.27 **stuffing, dressing,** forcemeat *or* farce.

.28 **bread,** *pain* [Fr], staff of life; bread stuff; white bread, French bread, Italian bread; garlic bread; dark bread, whole wheat bread, cracked-wheat bread; rye bread, *Bauernbrot* [Ger], pumpernickel, brown bread, black bread; graham bread; salt-rising bread, sourbread, sourdough bread, Irish soda bread; raisin bread, nut bread; unleavened bread, matzo, *matzoth* [Heb pl]; bread stick; **toast;** challah; pita; loaf of bread, tommy [Brit]; crust.

.29 **corn bread;** pone, ash pone, corn pone, corn tash, ash cake, hoecake, johnnycake; dodger, corn dodger, corn dab, hush puppy; cracklin' bread [dial]; *tortilla* [Sp].

.30 **biscuit,** sinker [slang]; hardtack, sea biscuit, ship biscuit, pilot biscuit *or* bread; **cracker,** soda cracker *or* saltine, graham cracker; wafer; rusk, zwieback, Melba toast, Brussels biscuit; pretzel.

.31 **bun, roll, muffin,** English muffin, crumpet, gem; popover, Yorkshire pudding; scone; cross bun, hot cross bun; Danish pastry, Danish; coffee cake; *croissant, brioche* [both Fr]; hard roll, soft roll, crescent roll, kaiser roll, Parker House roll, clover-leaf roll, pinwheel roll, onion roll, bialy *or* bialystoker; bagel.

.32 **sandwich;** double-decker sandwich, club sandwich; open-face sandwich, *canapé* [Fr], *smörgås* [Swed], *smørrebrød* [Dan]; Dagwood sandwich; –burger, **hamburger,** cheeseburger, tunaburger, etc.; **hot dog;** hot roast beef sandwich, Sloppy Joe, barbecued beef; hero sandwich, poor boy, submarine sandwich, grinder, hoagy; toasted *or* grilled cheese sandwich, tuna salad sandwich, egg salad sandwich, bacon-lettuce-tomato sandwich *or* BLT, peanut butter and jelly sandwich, pastrami sandwich, ham sandwich, corned beef sandwich, Swiss cheese sandwich, etc.

.33 **noodles,** *pasta* [Ital], Italian paste, paste; **spaghetti,** spaghettini, ziti, fedellini, fettuccine, vermicelli, **macaroni,** lasagne; ravioli, *kreplach* [Yid pl], won ton; **dumpling;** spaetzle; matzo balls, *knaydlach* [Yid pl].

.34 **cereal,** breakfast food, dry cereal, hot cereal; porridge, gruel, loblolly; **mush,** hasty pudding; oatmeal, rolled oats; farina, millet, hominy grits; grits; kasha; frumenty; cornflakes, wheatflakes, etc.; puffed wheat, puffed rice, etc.

.35 **vegetables** 308.50, produce, *légumes* [Fr];

potherbs; greens; beans, *frijoles* [Sp], *haricots* [Fr]; **potato,** spud [informal], tater [dial], *pomme de terre* [Fr], Irish potato, pratie [dial], white potato; **tomato,** love apple; eggplant, *aubergine* [Fr], mad apple; rhubarb, pieplant; cabbage, *Kraut* [Ger].

.36 **salad,** *salade* [Fr]; **green salad,** combination salad, tossed salad, potato salad, macaroni salad, Waldorf salad, fruit salad, ambrosia, salad niçoise, crab Louis, salmagundi, chef salad, Caesar salad, herring salad, tuna fish salad, chicken salad, etc.; slaw, cole slaw; aspic, molded salad, Jell-O salad.

.37 **fruit** 308.51, fructi–, produce; stone fruit, drupe; citrus fruit, citr(o)– *or* citri–; fruit compote, fruit soup, fruit cocktail.

.38 **nut** 308.52, *noix* [Fr], *noisette* [Fr]; kernel, meat; **Brazil nut** *or* nigger toe [slang]; **peanut;** goober *or* goober pea *or* ground-pea [all dial], groundnut [Brit]; salted peanuts, peanut butter; **almond,** *amande* [Fr]; burnt almond, *amande pralinée* [Fr]; bitter almond, *amande amère* [Fr]; sweet almond, *amande douce* [Fr]; blanched almonds, *amandes mondées* [Fr]; almond paste, *pâté d'amande* [Fr].

.39 **sweets,** sweet stuff, **confectionery; sweet, sweetmeat; confection; candy** 308.54; comfit, confiture; preserve, conserve; jelly, jam; marmalade; gelatin, Jell-O; compote; mousse; blancmange; tutti-frutti; maraschino cherries; honey; icing, frosting, glaze; meringue; whipped cream.

.40 **pastry,** *patisserie* [Fr]; French pastry, Danish pastry; **tart;** turnover; timbale; **pie,** *tarte* [Fr]; pasty, *pâté* [Fr], *pirog* [Russ]; blintz; *quiche* [Fr]; patty, pattycake; patty-shell, *vol-au-vent* [Fr]; rosette; dowdy, pandowdy; trifle, tipsy cake; strudel; baklava; puff, cream puff; éclair, chocolate éclair.

.41 **cake,** *gâteau* [Fr], *Torte* [Ger]; cupcake; petit four [Fr]; angel cake, angel food cake; chocolate cake, devil's food cake; white cake, yellow cake; spice cake; gingerbread; fruitcake, pound cake; marble cake; honey cake; sponge cake, génoise; shortcake; coffee cake, tea cake; cheesecake; layer cake, jumble; *baba au rhum* [Fr], savarin; Boston cream pie; upside-down cake; jelly roll, *bûche de Noël* [Fr]; baked Alaska.

.42 **cookie,** biscuit [Brit]; brownie; ginger snap; macaroon; ladyfinger; fruit bar, date bar; shortbread; sugar cookie, oatmeal cookie, chocolate chip or Toll House cookie; fortune cookie; gingerbread man; *Pfeffernüsse* [Ger pl].

.43 **doughnut,** friedcake, sinker [slang], cymbal [archaic], olykoek [dial]; French doughnut, raised doughnut; glazed doughnut; fastnacht; **cruller,** twister; jelly doughnut, bismarck; fritter, *beignet* [Fr]; apple fritter, *beignet aux pommes* [Fr].

.44 **pancake,** griddlecake, **hot cake,** battercake, flapcake, **flapjack,** flannel cake; buckwheat cake; chapatty [India]; **waffle;** blintz, cheese blintz, *crêpe, crêpe Suzette* [both Fr], *palacsinta* [Hung], *Pfannkuchen* [Ger].

.45 **pudding;** plum pudding, carrot pudding, steamed pudding, duff; vanilla pudding, chocolate pudding, tapioca pudding, etc.; trifle, Charlotte or Charlotte Russe; brown Betty; custard, flan; rennet, junket; syllabub; mousse, chocolate mousse; zabaglione; Bavarian cream.

.46 **ice,** *glace* [Fr], frozen dessert; **ice cream,** ice milk, French ice cream; **sherbet,** water ice [Brit], Italian ice; parfait; sundae, ice-cream sundae, banana split; ice-cream soda; frappé; ice-cream cone; frozen pudding; frozen custard, soft ice cream.

.47 **dairy products,** milk products; **milk,** pasteurized milk, certified milk, raw milk, homogenized milk, half-and-half, powdered milk, nonfat dry milk, evaporated milk, condensed milk, skim milk, buttermilk; **cream,** sour cream, whipping cream, heavy cream, light cream; **butter,** clarified butter, ghee; **margarine,** oleomargarine, oleo; **cheese** 308.53, tyr(o)-; curds, whey, yogurt.

.48 **beverage** 308.49, drink, thirst quencher, potation, potable, drinkable [informal], **liquor,** liquid; **soft drink,** nonalcoholic beverage, –ade; cold drink; carbonated water, soda water, **soda,** pop, soda pop, tonic; milk shake, frosted shake, thick shake, shake or frosted [both informal]; malted milk, malt [informal]; hard drink, alcoholic drink 996.38–42.

.49 **beverages, drinks**

ade	cider
alcoholic beverage 996.38–42	cocktail
ambrosia	cocoa
beef tea	coffee
birch beer	cola
bouillon	egg cream
buttermilk	eggnog
café au lait [Fr]	*espresso* [Ital]
chicory	frappé
chocolate milk	frosted shake
	fruit juice
ginger ale	mocha
ginger beer	nectar
ginger pop	orangeade
ginger punch	orange juice
grapefruit juice	phosphate
grape juice	pineapple juice
hot chocolate	punch
hydromel	root beer
ice-cream soda	root beer float
iced coffee	sarsaparilla
iced tea	seltzer
ice water	soda
juice	spring water
koumiss	sweet cider
lemonade	tea
limeade	tisane
malted milk	tomato juice
maté	Turkish coffee
milk	vichy water
milk shake	water
mineral water	

.50 **vegetables**

acorn squash	green pepper
artichoke	gumbo
asparagus	hominy
bamboo shoot	horseradish
bean	Hubbard squash
bean sprout	iceberg lettuce
beet, beetroot	kale
beet greens	kidney beans
bell pepper	kohlrabi
Bermuda onion	leaf lettuce
Bibb lettuce	leek
black-eyed pea	lentil
Boston lettuce	lettuce
broccoli	lima bean
Brussels sprouts	maize
butter bean	mushroom
butternut squash	mustard greens
cabbage	navy bean
cardoon	okra
carrot	onion
cauliflower	oyster plant
celery	parsley
celery cabbage	parsnip
celery root, celeriac	pea
celtuce	pea bean
chard, Swiss chard	pepper
chick-pea	pimento, pimiento
chicory	pinto bean
chili pepper	popcorn
Chinese cabbage	pumpkin
chive	radish
chive garlic	red cabbage
collards, collard greens	red pepper
corn	rhubarb
cos, cos lettuce	romaine, romaine lettuce
cowpea	rutabaga
cress	salsify
cucumber	scallion
dandelion greens	scarlet runners
eggplant	shallot
endive, Belgian endive	snap bean
escarole	snow pea
French bean	sorrel
garbanzos [Sp]	soy, soya
garlic	soybean, soya bean
green bean	spinach
green onion	squash
green pea	string bean

succory
sugar beet
summer squash
swede, swede turnip
sweet corn
sweet potato
taro
tomato
truffle

turnip
water chestnut
water cress
wax bean
white turnip
winter squash
yam
zucchini

watermelon

whortleberry

.52 nuts

acorn
almond
beechnut
ben nut
betel nut
black walnut
bonduc nut
Brazil nut
butternut
candlenut
cashew, cashew nut
chestnut
chinquapin
cobnut
coconut
corozo nut
cumara nut
dika nut
English walnut
filbert

groundnut
grugru nut
hazelnut
hickory nut
horse chestnut
kola, kola nut
litchi nut
Macadamia nut
palm nut
peanut
pecan
physic nut
pine nut
piñon
pistachio, pistachio
   nut
sassafras nut
souari nut
walnut

.51 fruits

akee
alligator pear
ananas
apple
apricot
avocado
banana
barberry
bearberry
berry
bilberry
blackberry
blueberry
boysenberry
breadfruit
cacao
candleberry
canistel
cantaloupe
caprifig
capulin
casaba, casaba melon
Catawba
checkerberry
cherimoya
cherry
citrange
citron
citrus, citrus fruit
civet fruit
crab apple
cranberry
currant
custard apple
damson
date
dewberry
durian
elderberry
feijoa
fig
gooseberry
granadilla
grape
grapefruit
guanabana
guava
hagberry
honeydew, honeydew
   melon
huckleberry
icaco
ilama
imbu
jaboticaba
jackfruit
Jaffa orange
jujube
kumquat
lemon
lime

lingonberry
litchi
loganberry
loquat
mammee apple
mandarin orange
mango
mangosteen
manzanilla
marang
mayapple
medlar
melon
mombin
mulberry
muscadine
muscat, muscatel
muskmelon
navel orange
nectarine
nutmeg melon
olive
orange
papaw
papaya
passion fruit
peach
pear
Persian melon
persimmon
pineapple
pippin
pitanga
plantain, *plátano* [Sp]
plum
plumcot
pomegranate
pond apple
prickly pear
prune
pulasan
quince
raisin
rambutan
raspberry
red currant
rose apple
sapodilla
sapote
Seville orange
soursop
strawberry
sugar apple
sugarplum
sweetsop
tamarind
tangelo
tangerine
ugli fruit
Valencia orange
water lemon

.53 cheeses

aettekees
Alentejo
Alise Sainte Reine
Allgäuer Bergkäse
Allgäuer Rahmkäse
American cheese
Amou
appetitost
Arrigny
Asco
Asio
Augelot
Aurore
Autun
Azeitão
Backstein
Bagnes
baker's cheese
Banon
Battelmatt
Beaufort
Beaumont
Beaupré de Roybon
Bellelay
Bel Paese
Bitto
bleu, blue cheese
Bleu d'Auvergne
Bleu de Bassilac
Bleu de Salers
Blue Dorset *or* Blue
   Vinny
Bondes
Bossons Macères
Boule de Lille
Boulette d'Avesnes *or*
   de Cambrai
Boursin
Bra
brick cheese
Brie
Brie de Coulommiers
Brie de Meaux
Brillat-Savarin
Broccio
Bruxelles
Cacciocavallo

Cachat d'Entrechaux
Caerphilly
Camembert
Canestrato
Cantal
Cardiga
Castelo Branco
Cendré Champenois
   or des Riceys
Cendré d'Aizy
Cendré de La Brie
Chabichou
Chaingy
Champenois
Chaource
Chaumont
Chavignol
Cheddar
Cheshire
Chevret
Chevrotin
Ciclo
Cierp de Luchon
clabber
Cotherstone
cottage cheese
Cottenham
Coulommiers
cream cheese
Crema Danica
Crème des Vosges
Crèmet Nantais
Cremini
croissant demi-sel
Crottin de Chavignol
Danish blue
Dansk Schweizerost
Dauphin
Decize
demi-sel
Domaci Beli Sir
Dorset Vinney
double-crème
Dunlop
Edam
Emmental *or* Emmen-
   taler

Epoisses
Ercé
Ervy
étuvé
Evarglice
Excelsior
farmer cheese
Feuille de Dreux
Fin de siécle
Fleur de Decauville
Fondue aux raisins
Fontainebleau
Fontina
Fourme d'Ambert
Fourme de Montbri-
son
Fourme de Salers
Friesche Kaas
fromage à la pie or
fromage blanc
Gammelost
Gaperon
Géromé
getmesost
getmjölkost
Gex
gjetost
Gloucester
Glux
goat cheese
Gorgonzola
Gouda
Gournay
Grana
Grana Lombardo
Grana Reggiano
gras
grated cheese
Gruyère
Guéret or Creusois
hand cheese
Harzé
Harzer-Käse
herrgårdsost
Hervé
hushållsost
Ilha
jack cheese
Kackavalj
Kasseri
Kaunas
Kefalotir
kumminost
La Bouillé
Laguiole
Lamothe Bougon or
La Mothe St. Hé-
raye
Lancashire
Langres
Leicester
Les Aydes
Les Laumes
Levroux
Leyden or Leidsche
Kaas or Kummel
Liederkranz
Limburger
Lipski
Liptauer
Livarot
Mainauer

Manicamp
Manuri
Margherita
Maroilles or Marolles
Mascherone
mesost
Metton
Mizitra
Monceau
Montasio
Mont-Cenis
Mont Dore
Morbier
mozzarella
Muenster
Murols
mysost
Nantais
Neufchâtel
New York cheese
Niolo
Nøkkelost
oka cheese
Olivet
Oloron
Óvár
Oxfordshire
Paladru
Pálpuszta
Parmesan
Paski
Pavé de Moyaux
Pecorino
Pélardon de Rioms
Persille de Savoie
Petit Gervais
Petit Gruyère
Petit-Moule
Petit Suisse
Picodon de Dieulefit
Pithiviers au Foin
Pivski
Pommel
Pont l'Évêque
Poona
Port-Salut, Port du
Salut
pot cheese
Pouligny-St. Pierre
primost
process or processed
cheese
Promessi
Provature
Provolone
Puant Macéré
pultost
Pusztadör
Rabaçal
Rahmatour
Ramadoux
Reblochon
Récollet de Gérard-
mer
Reggiano
Remoudou
ricotta
Rigotte de Condrieu
Robbiole
Rocamadur
Rokadur
Rollot

Roma
Romadur
Romano
Roquefort
Rouennais
Saint-Agathon
Saint-Florentin
Saint-Marcellin
Saint-Maure
Saint-Nectaire
Salame
sapsago
Sardo
Sassenage
Sbrinz
Schabzieger
Schmierkäse
Septmoncel
Serra da Estrella
Sjenicki
Slipcote
smaltost
smearcase
Somborski
Sorbais
Soumaintrin
Sposi
Steinbuscher-Käse
Steppe
Stilton

.54 candies

bonbon
brittle
bubble gum
butterscotch
candied apple
candy corn
caramel
chewing gum
chocolate
chocolate bar
chocolate drop
cotton candy
cough drop 687.16
cream
divinity
fondant
fudge
glacé
gum
gumdrop
hard candy
honey crisp
horehound
jelly bean, jelly egg
jujube

.55 condiments, spices

allspice
amandine
anchovies
angelica
anise
applesauce
basil
bay leaf
bell pepper
black pepper
borage
burnet
caper

store cheese
Stracchino
Suffolk
Sveciaost
Swiss cheese
Székely
Taffel
Tête de Maure
Tête de Moine
Tilsiter
Tomme
Trappe or Trappistes
Travnicki
Triple Aurore
Trôo
Troyes
Truckles
Vacherin
Valençay
Västerbottensost
Västgötaost
Velveeta
Vermont cheese
Vic-en-Bigorre
Vize
Volvet
Weisslacker Käse
Wensleydale
Wilstermarsch Käse
Wisconsin cheese

kiss
licorice
Life Saver
lollipop
lozenge
marshmallow
marzipan, marchpane
mint
nougat
peanut bar
peanut brittle
penuche or panocha
peppermint
popcorn balls
praline
rock candy
saltwater taffy
Scotch kisses
sugar candy
sugarplum
taffy
toffee
torrone [Ital]
tutti-frutti

capsicum
caraway seeds
cardamom
catsup
cayenne, cayenne pep-
per
celery salt
chervil
chili
chili pepper
chili sauce
chili vinegar
chive garlic

chives
chutney
cinnamon
cloves
coriander
cranberry sauce
cubeb
cumin
curry
dahl sauce
dill
dillseed
duck sauce
fagara
fennel, *finnochio*
  [Ital]
filé
five spice powder
garlic
garlic butter
garlic powder
garlic salt
ginger
green pepper
hedge garlic
hoisin sauce
horseradish
hyssop
juniper berries
leek
mace
marinade
marjoram
mayonnaise
mint
monosodium gluta-
  mate, MSG
mustard
nutmeg
onion

onion salt
oregano
paprika
parsley
pepper
peppercorn
peppermint
piccalilli
pickle 432.2
pimento, pimiento
pimpernel
potherb
radish
red pepper
relish
saffron
sage
salad dressing
salt
sauce-alone
savory
seasoned salt
sesame oil
sesame seeds
shallot
soy, soy sauce
spice
star anise
Tabasco, Tabasco
  sauce
tarragon
tartar sauce
thyme
tomato paste
turmeric
vanilla
vinegar
white pepper
Worcestershire sauce

.56 cold sauces

aïoli sauce
bleu cheese dressing
duck sauce
French dressing
green sauce
Italian dressing
Lorenzo dressing
mayonnaise
Mona Lisa dressing
oil and vinegar
ravigote sauce

rémoulade sauce
Ritz sauce
Russian dressing
salad dressing
sweet-and-sour sauce
tartar sauce
Thousand Island
  dressing
vinaigrette
Vincent sauce

.57 hot sauces

allemande
barbecue sauce
béarnaise
Bercy
bordelaise
bourguignonne
brown gravy
brown sauce
Colbert
cream sauce
curry sauce
demiglace
egg sauce
espagnole
gravy
hollandaise
marinara

molé
Mornay
mushroom sauce
mustard sauce
Nantua
onion sauce
pan gravy
paprika sauce
pepper sauce
poulette
roux
shallot sauce
Smitane
Soubise
velouté
white sauce

.58 dishes

arroz con pollo
atole
bacon and eggs
barbecued spareribs
beef Bourguignonne
beef Wellington
boiled dinner
Boston baked beans
bubble and squeak
cannelloni
carbonnade
cheese soufflé
chicken and dump-
  lings
chicken Cacciatore
chicken Marengo
chicken paprikás
chicken Tetrazzini
chili *or* chili con carne
chili and beans
cholent [Yid]
chop suey
chow mein
codfish balls, codfish
  cakes
compote
coquilles Saint-
  Jacques
corned beef and cab-
  bage
corned beef hash
Cornish pasty
croquettes
egg foo yong
egg roll
eggs Benedict
enchilada
felafel
fish and chips
fondue
French toast
fried rice
frittata
frog legs
galantine
gefilte fish
goulash
haggis
ham and eggs
hash
jambalaya
kabob
kidney pie
knish
lasagna
liver and onions
lobster Newburg
lobster Thermidor
macaroni and cheese

meatballs
meat loaf
meat pie
mostaccioli
moussaka
osso buco
oysters on *or* in the
  half shell
pasty
pheasant under glass
pigs in blankets
pilaf, pilau
piroshki
pizza, pizza pie
poi
porcupine balls
pork and beans
porkolt
pork pie
potpie
risotto
salmon loaf
sashimi
sauerbraten
sauerkraut
scallopini
scampi
Scotch woodcock
shepherd's pie
shish kebab
souvlaki
spaghetti and meat
  balls
Spanish rice
steak and kidney pie
Stroganoff
stuffed cabbage
stuffed derma
stuffed grape leaves
stuffed peppers
stuffed tomatoes
succotash
sukiyaki
sushi
Swedish meatballs
Swiss steak
taco
tamale
tamale pie
tempura
teriyaki
terrine
tostada
tsimmes [Yid]
veal Parmigiana
veal scallopini
Welsh rabbit, Welsh
  rarebit
Wiener schnitzel

309. NUTRITION

.1 NOUNS **nutrition, nourishment,** nutriture, –trophy; alimentation; **food** *or* **nutritive value;** food chain *or* cycle.

.2 **nutritiousness,** nutritiveness, **digestibility,** assimilability.

.3 **nutrient,** nutritive, **nutriment** 308.3; nutrilite, growth factor, growth regulator.

.4 **vitamin,** vitamin complex; provitamin; vitamer; **vitamin A:** vitamin A_1 or anti-ophthalmic factor or axerophthol, vitamin A_2, cryptoxanthin, carotene; **vitamin B,** vitamin B complex: vitamin B_1 or thiamine or aneurin or antiberi-beri factor, vitamin B_2 or vitamin G or riboflavin or lactoflavin or ovoflavin or hepatoflavin, niacin or nicotinic acid, vitamin B_6 or pyridoxine or adermin, pantothenic acid or pantothen, inositol, choline, biotin or vitamin H, folic acid or pteroylglutamic acid or vitamin M or vitamin B_c, vitamin B_{12} or cobalamin or cyanocobalamin, para-aminobenzoic acid or PABA; **vitamin C** or ascorbic acid; **vitamin D** or calciferol, ergocalciferol, cholecalciferol; **vitamin E** or tocopherol; **vitamin K** or naphthoquinone, menadione; **vitamin P** or bioflavinoid.

.5 **carbohydrate** 309.22, hydroxy aldehyde, hydroxy ketone, saccharide, sacchar(o)– or sacchari–, monosaccharide, disaccharide, trisaccharide, polysaccharide or polysaccharose; **starch,** amyl(o)–; **sugar,** glyc(o)–, sucr(o)–.

.6 **protein,** prote(o)–, proteid or protide, simple protein, conjugated protein, chromoprotein, glycoprotein, lipoprotein, nucleoprotein, phosphoprotein, scleroprotein, albuminoid; protide; **amino acid,** essential amino acid; peptide, dipeptide, polypeptide, etc.

.7 **fat,** glyceride, **lipid,** lipin, lipoid; fatty acid; steroid, sterol; cholesterol; polyunsaturated fat.

.8 **digestion,** ingestion, assimilation, absorption, –pepsia or –pepsy; primary digestion, secondary digestion; predigestion; salivary digestion, gastric or peptic digestion, pancreatic digestion, intestinal digestion; digestive system, alimentary canal, gastrointestinal tract; salivary glands, gastric glands, liver, pancreas; digestive secretions, saliva, gastric juice, pancreatic juice, intestinal juice, bile.

.9 **digestant,** digester, digestive; pepsin, pepsino–; **enzyme** 309.25, proteolytic enzyme; –ase, –in(e), –zyme, zym(o)–.

.10 **metabolism,** basal metabolism, acid-base metabolism, energy metabolism; **anabolism,** assimilation; **catabolism,** disassimilation.

.11 **diet, dieting,** dietary; dietetics; **regimen,** regime; bland diet; soft diet, pap, spoon food or meat, spoon victuals [dial]; balanced diet; diabetic diet, allergy diet, reducing diet, obesity diet; high-calorie diet, low-calorie diet; high-protein diet, low-carbohydrate diet; high-vitamin diet, vitamin-deficiency diet; acid-ash diet, alkaline-ash diet; low-salt diet, low sodium diet, salt-free diet; ulcer diet; vegetarianism, macrobiotic diet; diet book, vitamin chart, calorie chart, calorie counter.

.12 vitaminization, **fortification, enrichment,** restoration.

.13 **nutritionist, dietitian,** vitaminologist, enzymologist.

.14 (science of nutrition) **dietetics,** dietotherapeutics, dietotherapy; vitaminology; enzymology.

.15 VERBS **nourish,** nutrify [archaic]; **sustain,** strengthen.

.16 **digest,** appropriate, **assimilate,** absorb; metabolize; predigest.

.17 **diet,** go on a diet; watch one's weight, count calories.

.18 **vitaminize, fortify, enrich,** restore.

.19 ADJS **nutritious,** nutritive, nutrient, **nourishing;** alimentary, alimental; digestible, assimilable; –trophic, troph(o)–.

.20 **digestive,** assimilative; peptic.

.21 **dietary,** dietetic, dietic [archaic]; regiminal.

.22 **carbohydrates**

aldose	levulose
altrose	lyxose
arbinose	maltose
bamboo sugar	malt sugar
barley sugar	mannose
beet sugar	maple sugar
British gum	melibiose
cane sugar	milk sugar
cellobiose	molasses
cellulose	native dextran
clinical dextran	nipa sugar
corn sugar	palm sugar
date sugar	pentosan
deoxyribose	pentose sugar
dextran	raffinose
dextrin	ribose
dextro-glucose	saccharose
dextrose	sorbose
erythrose	starch
fructose, fruit sugar	sucrose
galactose	tabasheer
glucose	tagatose
glycogen	talose
grape sugar	tree molasses
gulose	tree sugar
hexose sugar	trehalose
idose	wood sugar
inulin	xylose
lactose	

.23 **proteins**

albumin	chlorophyll
albuminoid	chromoprotein
amandin	clupeine
bynin	coagulated protein
casein	collagen
caseinogen	cytoglobulin

edestin
elastin
fibroin
gliadin
globin
globulin
glutelin
glutenin
glycoprotein
helicoprotein
hemoglobin
histone
ichthulin
interferon
keratin
lactalbumin
lecithin
lecithoprotein
lipid
lipoprotein
lysozyme
metaprotein
mucin
nucleohistone

nucleoprotein
oryzenin
osseomucoid
ovalbumin
ovoglobulin
ovovitellin
peptide
peptone
phosphoaminolipide
phospholipide
phosphoprotein
prolamine
protamine
proteolipide
proteose
salmine
serum albumin
serum globulin
sturine
tendomucin
thymus histone
vegetable albumin
vitellin
zein

.24 amino acids

alanine
arginine
aspartic acid
cystine
glutamic acid
glycine
histidine
isoleucine
leucine
lysine

methionine
phenylalanine
proline
sarcosine
serine
threonine
tryptophan
tyrosine
valine

.25 enzymes

alpha-amylase
amidase
aminopeptidase
aminopolypeptidase
amylase
apoenzyme
arginase
beta-amylase
carbohydrase
carboxypeptidase
chymotrypsin
coenzyme
deoxyribonuclease
dextrinogenic enzyme
endopeptidase
esterase
glutaminase
holoenzyme
insulinase

lactase
lecithinase
lipase
lipoxidase
nuclease
nucleotidase
papain
pepsin
peptidase
phosphoglucomutase
phosphorylase
polynucleotidase
protease
proteinase
rennin
ribonuclease
saccharase
saccharifying enzyme
trypsin

.26 health foods

acidophilus milk
blackstrap molasses
brewer's yeast
buckwheat flour
caudle
cottonseed flour
fortified flour
fortified milk
fruits
liver
middlings
nonfat milk
nuts

peanut flour
powdered milk
raw vegetables
rice polish
royal jelly
soybeans
soy flour
tiger's milk
unrefined flour
wheat germ
whole wheat
whole wheat flour
yogurt

310. EJECTION

.1 NOUNS **ejection**, ejectment, throwing out, **expulsion**, **discharge**, extrusion, obtrusion, detrusion, **ousting**, **ouster**, removal, kicking or booting out [informal]; throwing or kicking downstairs; the bounce, the chuck [Brit slang]; the boot or the bum's rush or the old heave-ho [all slang]; defenestration; rejection; jettison.

.2 **eviction**, ousting, dislodgment, dispossession; ouster.

.3 **depopulation**, dispeoplement, unpeopling; devastation, desolation.

.4 **banishment**, relegation, exclusion 77; **excommunication**, disfellowship; **disbarment**, unfrocking, defrocking; **expatriation**, **exile**, exilement; outlawing or outlawry, fugitation [Scot law]; **ostracism**, ostracization, blackballing, sending to Coventry; **deportation**, transportation, **extradition**; rustication; degradation, **demotion** 783, stripping, depluming, displuming; deprivation.

.5 **dismissal**, **discharge**, forced separation, *congé* [Fr]; **firing** [informal], **cashiering**, drumming out, dishonorable discharge, rogue's march; disemployment, **layoff**, removal, surplusing, displacing, furloughing; suspension; **retirement**; the bounce, the sack [Brit informal], the chuck [Brit slang]; the boot or the gate or the ax [all slang]; walking papers or ticket [both informal], pink slip [informal]; deposal 783.

.6 **evacuation**, **voidance**, voiding; **elimination**, removal; **clearance**, **clearing**, clearage; unfouling, scouring or cleaning out; exhaustion, exhausting, venting, emptying, depletion; **unloading**, off-loading, discharging cargo or freight; draining, drainage; egress 303; **excretion**, defecation 311.2,4.

.7 **disgorgement**, disemboguement, **expulsion**, ejaculation, **discharge**, emission; **eruption**, eructation, extravasation, blowout, **outburst**; outpour, jet, spout, squirt, spurt.

.8 **vomiting**, vomition, **disgorgement**, **regurgitation**, egestion, emesis, pukes or heaves [both slang]; **retching**, heaving, gagging; nausea 686.29; **vomit**, puke or barf [both slang], spew, egesta.

.9 **belch**, **burp** [informal], wind, gas, ructation, eructation; **hiccup**.

.10 **fart** [slang], **flatulence** or flatulency, flatuosity, flatus, gas, wind.

.11 **ejector**, expeller, –fuge; **ouster**, evictor;

bouncer *or* chucker [both informal], chucker-out [Brit informal].

.12 **dischargee**, expellee; ejectee; evictee.

.13 VERBS **eject**, **expel**, **discharge**, extrude, obtrude, detrude, exclude, reject, cast, remove; **oust**, **bounce** [informal], give the hook [informal], **put out**, **turn out**, thrust out; **throw out**, cast out, chuck out, give the chuck to [Brit slang], toss out, heave out, throw *or* kick downstairs; kick *or* boot out [informal]; give the bum's rush *or* give the old heave-ho *or* throw out on one's ear [all slang]; defenestrate; jettison, throw overboard, discard, junk, throw away.

.14 **drive out**, **run out**, chase out, **rout out**; drum out; freeze out [informal], push out, force out; **hunt out**, harry out; smoke out, drive into the open; run out of town, ride on a rail.

.15 **evict**, **oust**, dislodge, dispossess, put out, turn out, turn out of doors, turn out of house and home, turn *or* put out bag and baggage; unhouse, unkennel.

.16 **depopulate**, dispeople, unpeople; devastate, desolate.

.17 **banish**, **expel**, **cast out**, thrust out, relegate, **ostracize**, disfellowship, exclude, send down, blackball, spurn, snub, cut, give the cold shoulder, send to Coventry, give the silent treatment; **excommunicate**; exile, expatriate, deport, transport, send away, **extradite**; **outlaw**, fugitate [Scot law], ban, proscribe; rusticate.

.18 **dismiss**, **send off** *or* **away**, **turn off** *or* **away**, bundle, bundle off *or* out, hustle out, pack off, **send packing**, send about one's business, send to the showers [slang]; bow out, **show the door**, show the gate; **give the gate**, give the air [both slang].

.19 **dismiss**, **discharge**, **expel**, **cashier**, drum out, disemploy, separate forcibly *or* involuntarily, **lay off**, suspend, surplus, furlough, turn off, make redundant, turn out, release, let go, let out, remove, displace, replace, strike off the rolls, give the pink slip; give one his walking papers [informal]; **fire** *or* **can** [both informal]; **sack** *or* give the sack to [both Brit informal]; **bump**, bounce, kick, boot, give the ax, give the gate [all slang]; unfrock, defrock; degrade, demote, strip, deplume, displume, deprive; depose, disbar 783.4; break, bust [slang]; **retire**, put on the retired list; pension off, superannuate; read out of; kick upstairs.

.20 **do away with**, **exterminate**, purge, liqui-

date; **shake off**, shoo, dispel; **throw off**, fling off, cast off; **eliminate**, get rid of 77.5; throw away 668.7.

.21 **evacuate**, **void**; **eliminate**, remove; **empty**, empty out, deplete, **exhaust**, vent, drain; **clear**, **purge**, clean *or* scour out, clear off *or* out *or* away, unfoul, unclog, blow, blow out, sweep out, make a clean sweep, clear the decks; defecate 311.13.

.22 **unload**, off-load, unlade, unpack, disburden, unburden, **discharge**, **dump**; unship, break bulk.

.23 **let out**, **give vent to**, give out *or* off, throw off, **emit**, **exhaust**, evacuate; **exhale**, expire, breathe out, let one's breath out, blow, puff; fume, steam, vapor, smoke, reek; open the sluices *or* floodgates, turn on the tap.

.24 **disgorge**, debouch, disembogue, **discharge**, **exhaust**, **expel**, ejaculate, throw out, **cast forth**, send out *or* forth; **erupt**, eruct, **blow out**, extravasate; **pour out** *or* **forth**, pour, outpour, decant; **spew**, **jet**, spout, squirt, **spurt**.

.25 **vomit**, spew, disgorge, regurgitate, egest, puke [slang], **throw up**, bring up, barf [slang], **be sick**, sick up [Brit informal], cast *or* heave the gorge; upchuck *or* chuck up *or* urp [all informal], shoot *or* toss one's cookies [slang]; **retch**, keck, **heave**, **gag**; reject; be seasick, feed the fish.

.26 **belch**, **burp** [informal], eruct, eructate; hiccup.

.27 **fart** [slang], let *or* lay a fart [slang], let *or* break wind.

.28 ADJS **ejective**, **expulsive**, ejaculative, emissive, extrusive, ex(o)–; eliminant; vomitive, vomitory; **eructative**; flatulent, flatuous.

.29 INTERJS **go away!**, begone!, get you gone!, go along!, get along!, **run along!**, **get along with you!**, away!, away with you!, **off with you!**, off you go!, on your way!, go about your business!, be off!, **get out of here!**, get out!, clear out!, leave!, *allez!* [Fr], *allez-vous-en!* [Fr], *va-t'-en!* [Fr], *raus mit dir!* [Ger], *heraus!* [Ger], *¡váyase!* [Sp], *via!* or *va' via!* [Ital], shoo!, scat!, git! [dial], "stand not on the order of your going, but go at once" [Shakespeare], "go and hang yourself" [Plautus].

.30 [slang terms] **beat it!**, **scram!**, buzz off!, bug off!, skiddoo!, skedaddle!, vamoose!, cheese it!, make yourself scarce!, **get lost!**, take a walk!, go chase yourself!, get the hell out!, push off!, shove off!, take a powder!, blow!

311. EXCRETION

(bodily discharge)

.1 NOUNS **excretion, egestion, extrusion, elimination, discharge; emission;** eccrisis; **exudation,** transudation; extravasation, effusion, flux, flow, –rrhea *or* –rrhoea; ejaculation, ejection 310; **secretion** 312.

.2 defecation, dejection, **evacuation,** voidance; movement, **bowel movement, BM, stool, shit** *or* **crap** [both slang]; **diarrhea,** loose bowels, flux; trots *or* runs *or* shits *or* GI's *or* GI shits [all slang]; turistas, Montezuma's revenge [both slang]; lientery; **dysentery,** bloody flux; catharsis, purgation, purge.

.3 excrement, dejection, dejecture, discharge, ejection; **waste,** waste matter; **excreta,** excretes, egesta, ejecta, ejectamenta, dejecta; exudation, exudate; transudation, transudate; extravasation, extravasate; **effluent.**

.4 feces, feculence, copr(o)–, scat(o)–; defecation, movement, bowel movement *or* BM; **stool, shit** [slang], **ordure,** night soil, jakes [Brit dial], crap [slang], ca-ca [informal]; turd [slang]; dingleberry [slang]; **manure, dung, droppings;** cow pats, cow flops [slang]; cow chips, buffalo chips; guano; coprolite, coprolith; sewage, sewerage.

.5 urine, ur(o)–, urin(o)–; water, **piss** [slang], *pish* [Yid], pee, pee-pee *or* wee-wee [both informal], piddle, stale; **urination,** micturition; urea.

.6 pus, py(o)–; **matter,** purulence, peccant humor [archaic], ichor, sanies; pussiness; **suppuration, festering,** rankling, mattering, running; gleet, leukorrhea.

.7 sweat, perspiration, water, –idrosis; exudation, exudate; diaphoresis, sudor; honest sweat, the sweat of one's brow; beads of sweat, beaded brow; cold sweat; **lather,** swelter, streams of sweat; sudoresis; body odor, **BO,** perspiration odor.

.8 hemorrhage, hemorrhea, **bleeding;** nosebleed; ecchymosis, petechia.

.9 menstruation, men(o)–, menstrual discharge *or* flow *or* flux, catamenia, catamenial discharge, flowers [archaic], **the curse,** the curse of Eve; **menses, monthlies,** courses, period *or* periods, that time.

.10 latrine, convenience, **toilet,** toilet room, water closet, WC [informal]; **john** *or* **can** *or* **crapper** [all slang]; loo [Brit slang]; **lavatory,** washroom; **bathroom,** basement; **rest room,** comfort station *or* room; ladies' *or* women's *or* girls' *or* little girls' *or* powder room [informal]; men's *or* boys' *or* little boys' room [informal]; head; privy, outhouse, backhouse, shithouse [slang], johnny house [dial], earth closet [Brit], closet *or* necessary [both dial]; urinal.

.11 toilet, stool, **water closet; john** *or* johnny *or* can *or* crapper [all slang]; latrine; commode, closestool, potty-chair [informal]; **chamber pot,** chamber, potty [informal], jerry [Brit informal], jordan [Brit dial], thunder mug [slang]; throne [slang]; chemical toilet, chemical closet; urinal; piss pot [slang]; bedpan.

.12 VERBS **excrete, egest, eliminate, discharge,** emit, give off, pass; ease *or* relieve oneself, go to the bathroom [informal]; **exude,** exudate, transude; weep; effuse, extravasate; **secrete** 312.5.

.13 defecate, shit, crap [both slang], **evacuate,** void, **stool,** dung, have a bowel movement *or* BM, take a shit *or* crap [slang], ca-ca *or* number two [both informal].

.14 urinate, pass *or* **make water, wet,** stale, **piss** [slang], piddle, pee; pee-pee *or* wee-wee *or* number one [all informal], spend a penny, pump bilge.

.15 fester, suppurate, matter, rankle, run, weep; ripen, come *or* draw to a head.

.16 sweat, perspire, exude; break out in a sweat, **get all in a lather** [informal]; sweat like a trooper *or* horse, swelter, wilt.

.17 bleed, hemorrhage, lose blood, **shed blood,** spill blood; bloody; ecchymose.

.18 menstruate, come sick, come around, have one's period.

.19 ADJS **excretory,** excretive, excretionary; **eliminative,** egestive; **exudative,** transudative; **secretory** 312.7.

.20 excremental, excrementary; **fecal,** feculent, shitty *or* crappy [both slang], scatologic *or* scatological, stercoral, stercorous, stercoraceous, dungy; **urinary,** urinative, uric, –uronic.

.21 festering, suppurative, rankling, mattering; **pussy, purulent.**

.22 sweaty, perspiry [informal]; sweating, perspiring; wet with sweat, beaded with sweat, **sticky** [informal], **clammy;** bathed in sweat, drenched with sweat, wilted; in a sweat; sudatory, sudoric, sudorific, diaphoretic.

.23 bleeding, bloody, hemorrhaging; ecchymosed.

.24 menstrual, catamenial.

312. SECRETION

.1 NOUNS **secretion**, secreta [pl], secernment, secret(o)–; **excretion** 311; external secretion, internal secretion; lactation; weeping, lacrimation.

.2 digestive secretion or juice, salivary secretion, gastric juice, pancreatic juice, intestinal juice; bile, gall, chol(e)– or cholo–; endocrine; prostatic fluid, semen, sperm; thyroxin; autacoid, hormone, chalone; mucus; tears; rheum.

.3 **saliva**, **spittle**, **sputum**, **spit**, **expectoration**, ptyal(o)–, –ptysis; salivation, ptyalism, sialorrhea, sialagogue, **slobber**, slabber, slaver, **drivel**, dribble, **drool**; froth, foam; mouth-watering.

.4 endocrinology, eccrinology, hormonology.

.5 VERBS **secrete**, secern, produce, give out; **excrete** 311.12; water; lactate; weep, tear.

.6 **salivate**, ptyalize; **slobber**, slabber, slaver, **drool**, **drivel**, dribble; **expectorate**, **spit**, spew; hawk, clear the throat.

.7 ADJS **secretory**, secretive, secretional, secretionary; **excretory** 311.19; lymphatic, serous; seminal, spermatic; watery, watering; lactational; lacteal, lacteous; lachrymal, lacrimatory, lachrymose; rheumy; salivary, salivant, salivous, sialoid, sialagogic.

.8 **glandular**, glandulous, aden(o)–; **endocrine**, humoral, exocrine, eccrine, apocrine, holocrine, merocrine; **hormonal** or hormonic; adrenal, pancreatic, gonadal; ovarian, ovar(i)– or ovaro–; luteal, luteo–; prostatic, prostat(o)–; splenetic, splen(o)–; thymic, thym(o)–; thyroidal, thyro– or thyreo–; etc.

.9 **glands**

adrenal gland, adrenal	pancreas
apocrine gland	parathyroid gland,
breast 256.6	parathyroid
corpus luteum	pineal body
ductless gland	pituitary gland, pitu-
eccrine gland	itary
endocrine gland	prostate gland, pros-
gonad	tate
holocrine gland	salivary gland
lacrimal gland	sebaceous gland
lacteal gland	spermary
liver	suprarenal gland, su-
lymph gland	prarenal
mamma	sweat gland
mammary gland	tear gland
merocrine gland	testicle, testis
ovary	thymus
ovotestis	thyroid gland, thyroid

.10 **hormones**

ACTH (adrenocorti-	adrenosterone
cotrophic hormone)	adrenotrophin
Allen-Doisy hormone	hydroxydehydrocorti-
amniotin	costerone
androgen	hydroxydesoxycorti-
androsterone	costerone
cardiac hormone	insulin
cholecystokinin	intermedin
chondrotrophic hor-	kinin
mone	lactogenic hormone
corticosterone	lipocaic
cortisone	mammin
dehydrocorticosterone	oxytocin
desoxycorticosterone	parathyrin
dexamethasone	pitocin
diiodotyrosine	pitressin
enterocrinin	progesterone
enterogastrone	progestin
epinephrine	prolactin
erythropoietin	secretin
estradiol	somatrophin
estrin	stilbestrol
estriol	testosterone
estrogen	thyroglobulin
estrone	thyrotrophin
gonadotrophin	thyroxin
growth hormone	vasopressin
hydroxycorticosterone	

313. OVERRUNNING

.1 NOUNS **overrunning**, **overgoing**, **overpassing**; overrun, overpass; **overspreading**, overgrowth; inundation, overflowing 395.6; exaggeration 617; surplus, excess 663; superiority 36.

.2 **infestation**, infestment; invasion, swarming, swarm, teeming, ravage, plague; **overrunning**, **overswarming**, overspreading; lousiness, pediculosis.

.3 **overstepping**, **transgression**, **trespass**, inroad, usurpation, incursion, intrusion, encroachment, infraction, **infringement**.

.4 VERBS **overrun**, **overgo**, **overpass**, overreach, go beyond; overstep, overstride; overleap, overjump; **overshoot**, overshoot the mark, overshoot the field; exaggerate 617.3; superabound, exceed, **overdo** 663.8–10.

.5 **overspread**, bespread, spread over; **overgrow**, grow over, run riot, cover, swarm over, teem over.

.6 **infest**, **beset**, invade, swarm, ravage, plague; **overrun**, **overswarm**, overspread; **creep with**, **crawl with**, swarm with.

.7 **run over**, overrun; **ride over**, override, **run down**, ride down; **trample**, **trample on** or **upon**, tread upon, trample underfoot, **ride roughshod over**; hit and run; inundate, overflow 395.17.

.8 **pass**, **go** or **pass by**, get or shoot ahead of; bypass; **pass over**, **cross**, go across, ford; step over, overstride, bestride, straddle.

.9 **overstep**, **transgress**, **trespass**, intrude, break bounds, overstep the bounds, go too far, know no bounds, **encroach**, in-

fringe, invade, irrupt, make an inroad *or* incursion *or* intrusion, advance upon; usurp.

.10 ADJS **overrun, overspread,** overgrown.

.11 **infested,** beset, ravaged, teeming, plagued; lousy, pediculous, pedicular; wormy, grubby; ratty.

314. SHORTCOMING

(motion short of)

.1 NOUNS **shortcoming,** falling short, not measuring up, **shortfall, shortage,** short measure, underage, deficit; **inadequacy** 57.1; insufficiency 662; delinquency; **default,** defalcation; arrear, **arrears,** arrearage; decline, slump; defectiveness, imperfection 678; **inferiority** 37; **failure** 725.

.2 VERBS **fall short, come short, run short,** stop short, not make the course, not reach, not measure up, not hack it [informal], not make it, not make out, not make the grade [informal]; want, lack, **be found wanting,** not answer, not fill the bill, not suffice; not reach to, not stretch; decline, lag, lose ground, slump, collapse, fall away; **fail** 725.8.

.3 **fall through,** fall down, **fall to the ground,** fall flat, **collapse,** break down; get bogged down, get mired, get mired down, get hung up, come to nothing, come to naught, end up *or* go up in smoke; **fizzle out** *or* peter out *or* poop out [all informal]; fall by the wayside, end "not with a bang but a whimper" [T. S. Eliot].

.4 **miss, miscarry, go amiss,** go astray, **miss the mark,** misfire; miss out, miss the boat *or* bus; miss stays, miss one's mooring.

.5 ADJS **short of,** short; **deficient, inadequate** 57.4; **insufficient** 662.9; **inferior** 37.6; **lacking,** wanting, minus; unreached.

.6 ADVS **behind, behindhand, in arrears** *or* arrear.

.7 **amiss, astray, beside the mark,** below the mark, beside the point, far from it, to no purpose, in vain, vainly, fruitlessly, bootlessly.

315. ASCENT

(motion upwards)

.1 NOUNS **ascent,** ascension, levitation, **rise, rising,** uprising, **uprise,** uprisal; **upgoing,** upgo, uphill, upslope, upping, upgang [Scot]; upcoming; **taking off,** leaving the ground, takeoff; **soaring,** zooming, gaining altitude, leaving the earth behind; spiraling *or* gyring up; shooting *or* rocketing up; jump, vault, spring, saltation, leap 319; mount, **mounting; climb, climbing,** upclimb, anabasis, clamber, escalade; surge, upsurge, upsurgence, upleap, upshoot, uprush; **gush, jet,** spurt, spout, fountain; updraft; upswing, upsweep; upgrowth; upgrade 219.6; **uplift,** elevation 317; increase 38.

.2 **upturn, uptrend,** upcast, upsweep, upbend, upcurve.

.3 **stairs, stairway, staircase,** *escalier* [Fr], **steps,** treads and risers; flight of steps, stepping-stones; spiral staircase, winding staircase; companionway, companion; stile; back stairs; perron; fire escape; landing, landing stage; ramp, incline.

.4 **ladder,** scale; stepladder, folding ladder, extension ladder; Jacob's ladder, companion ladder, accommodation ladder, side ladder, gangway ladder, quarter ladder, stern ladder.

.5 **step, stair, footstep,** rest, footrest, stepping-stone; **rung, round,** rundle, spoke, stave, scale; doorstep; tread; riser; bridgeboard, string; step stool.

.6 **climber,** ascender, upclimber; mountain climber, **mountaineer,** alpinist, rock climber, cragsman.

.7 (comparisons) rocket, skyrocket; lark, skylark, eagle.

.8 VERBS **ascend, rise, mount,** arise, up, uprise, levitate, upgo, **go up,** rise up, come up; go onwards and upwards, go up and up; upsurge, **surge,** upstream, upheave; swarm up, upswarm, sweep up; upwind, upspin, spiral, spire, curl upwards; stand up, **rear,** rear up, **tower,** loom; upgrow, grow up.

.9 **shoot up, spring up,** jump up, **leap up,** vault up, start up, fly up, pop up, bob up; float up, surface, break water; **gush, jet,** spurt, fountain; upshoot, upstart, upspring, upleap, upspear, rocket, **skyrocket.**

.10 **take off,** leave the ground, leave the earth behind, gain altitude, claw skyward; become airborne; **soar,** zoom, fly, plane, kite, fly aloft; aspire; spire, spiral *or* gyre upward; **hover,** hang, poise, float, float in the air.

.11 **climb,** climb up, upclimb, **mount,** clamber, **clamber up,** scramble *or* scrabble up, claw one's way up, struggle up, shin, shinny *or* shin up [both informal], ramp [dial], work *or* inch one's way up; **scale,** escalade, scale the heights; climb over, surmount.

.12 **mount, get on,** climb on, back; **bestride,**

bestraddle; **board**, go aboard, go on board; **get in**, jump in, hop in, pile in [informal].

.13 **upturn, turn up**, cock up; trend upwards, slope up; upcast, upsweep, upbend, upcurve.

.14 ADJS **ascending**, in the ascendant, **mounting, rising**, uprising, upgoing, upcoming; ascendant, ascensional, ascensive, anabatic; **leaping**, springing, saltatory; spiraling, skyrocketing; **upward**, upwith [Scot]; uphill, uphillward, upgrade, upsloping; uparching, rearing, rampant; climbing, scandent, scansorial.

.15 **upturned, upcast**, uplifted, **turned-up**, retroussé.

.16 ADVS **up, upward, upwards**, upwith [Scot]; skyward, heavenward; uplong, upalong; upstream, upstreamward; uphill; uphillward; upstairs; up attic or up steps [both dial]; uptown; up north; an(a)–, ano–, sur–, sursum–.

.17 INTERJS **alley-oop!, upsy-daisy!**; excelsior!, onward and upward!

316. DESCENT

(motion downward)

.1 NOUNS **descent, descending**, descension or downcome [both archaic], **comedown, down; dropping, falling**, plummeting, **drop, fall**, *chute* [Fr], **downfall**, debacle, **collapse**, crash; **swoop**, stoop, pounce, downrush, downflow, cascade, waterfall, rapids, cataract, **downpour**, defluxion; downturn, downcurve, downbend, downward trend, downtrend; declension, declination, inclination; gravitation; downgrade 219.5.

.2 sinkage, lowering, **decline, slump**, subsidence, submergence, lapse, decurrence; cadence; **droop, sag, swag**; catenary.

.3 tumble, fall, *culbute* [Fr], cropper [informal], **flop** [slang], **spill** [informal], forced landing; **header** [informal]; **sprawl; pratfall** [informal]; **stumble**, trip; dive, **plunge** 320.

.4 slide; slip, slippage; **glide**, coast, glissade; glissando; slither; **skid**, sideslip; **landslide**, landslip, subsidence; **snowslide**, snowslip [Brit]; **avalanche**.

.5 VERBS **descend**, go or **come down**, down, dip down, lose altitude; gravitate; **fall, drop**, precipitate, rain, rain or pour down, fall or drop down; **collapse**, crash; **swoop**, stoop, pounce; **pitch, plunge** 320.6, **plummet**; cascade, cataract; parachute; come down a peg [informal]; **fall**

off, drop off; trend downward, go downhill.

.6 sink, go down, sink down, submerge; **set, settle**, settle down; **decline**, lower, **subside**, give way, lapse, cave, cave in; **droop**, slouch, **sag, swag; slump**, slump down; flump, flump down; flop or flop down [both slang]; plump, plop, plump or plop down; founder 320.8.

.7 get down, alight, touch down, **light; land**, settle, perch; **dismount, get off**, unhorse; climb down.

.8 tumble, fall, fall down, come or fall or get a cropper [informal], take a fall or tumble, take a flop [slang], take a spill [informal], precipitate oneself; **sprawl**, take a pratfall [informal], spread-eagle [informal], measure one's length; fall headlong, **take a header** [informal]; fall prostrate, fall flat, fall on one's face; **fall over**, topple down or over; capsize, turn turtle; **topple**, lurch, pitch, **stumble**, stagger, totter, careen, list, tilt, trip, flounder.

.9 slide, slip, slidder [dial], slip or slide down; **glide**, skim, coast, glissade; **slither**; skid, sideslip; avalanche.

.10 light upon, alight upon, settle on; descend upon, come down on, fall on, drop on, hit or strike upon.

.11 ADJS **descending**, descendant, on the descendant; **down**, downward, decurrent, declivitous, deciduous; **downgoing**, downcoming; down-reaching; **dropping, falling**, plunging, plummeting, downfalling; **sinking**, downsinking, foundering, submerging, setting; declining, **subsiding**; collapsing, tumbledown, tottering; drooping, sagging; on the downgrade, downhill 219.16.

.12 downcast, downturned; hanging, downhanging.

.13 ADVS **down, downward, downwards**, cat(a)– or cath– or kat(a)–, cato–; downwith [Scot], adown, below; downright; downhill, downgrade; downstreet; downline; downstream; downstairs; downtown; down south.

317. ELEVATION

(act of raising)

.1 NOUNS **elevation, raising, lifting**, upping, **rearing**, escalation, erection; uprearing, uplifting; upbuoying; **uplift**, upheaval, upthrow, upcast, upthrust; **exaltation**, apotheosis, deification, beatification, canonization, enshrinement, assumption; *sursum corda* [L]; height 207; ascent 315.

.2 **lift, boost** [informal], hoist, heave; a leg up.

.3 **lifter, erector;** crane, derrick, gantry crane, crab; **jack,** jackscrew; **hoist,** lift, hydraulic lift; forklift; hydraulic tailgate; lever 287.4; windlass 287.7; tackle 287.10.

.4 **elevator,** *ascenseur* [Fr], **lift** [Brit]; escalator, moving staircase *or* stairway; dumbwaiter.

.5 VERBS **elevate, raise,** rise, **rear,** escalate, up, **erect, heighten, lift,** levitate, **boost** [informal], **hoist,** heist [dial], **heft,** heave; raise up, rear up, lift up, hold up, set up, stick up, perk up; buoy up, upbuoy; **upraise, uplift,** uphold, uprear, uphoist; upheave, upthrow, upcast; throw up, cast up; jerk up, hike, hoick; knock up, lob, loft; sky [informal].

.6 **exalt,** apotheosize, deify, beatify, canonize, enshrine; put on a pedestal.

.7 **give a lift,** give a boost, give a leg up [informal], **help up,** put on; mount, horse.

.8 **pick up,** take up, pluck up, **gather up;** draw up, fish up, haul up, drag up; dredge, dredge up.

.9 ADJS **raised, lifted, elevated;** upraised, **uplifted,** upcast; upreared, rampant; upthrown, upflung; **exalted, lofty** 207.19, sublime; stilted, on stilts; erect, upright 213.11; high 207.19.

.10 **elevating,** elevatory; lifting, **uplifting;** erective, erectile.

318. DEPRESSION

(act of lowering)

.1 NOUNS **depression, lowering, sinking;** ducking, submergence, pushing *or* thrusting under; detrusion; pushing *or* pulling *or* hauling down; reduction, de-escalation, diminution; demotion, debasement, degradation; concavity, hollowness 257.1; descent 316.

.2 **downthrow,** downcast; **overthrow,** overturn 220.2; **precipitation.**

.3 **crouch, stoop,** bend, squat; **bow,** genuflection, kneeling, kowtow, salaam, reverence, obeisance, **curtsy;** bob, duck, nod; prostration, supination.

.4 VERBS **depress, lower,** let *or* take down, debase, **sink,** bring low, reduce, couch; pull *or* haul down, take down a peg [informal]; bear down, downbear; thrust *or* press *or* push down, detrude; indent 257.14.

.5 **fell, drop, precipitate, bring down,** fetch down, **down** [informal], take down, lay low; **raze,** rase, raze to the ground; **level,**

lay level; pull down, pull about one's ears; **cut down,** chop down, hew down, whack down [informal], **mow** down; **knock down,** dash down, send headlong, **floor, deck** [slang], ground, **bowl down** *or* **over** [informal], lay out [slang]; trip, topple, tumble; **prostrate, supinate; throw,** throw *or* fling *or* cast down; bulldog; spread-eagle [informal]; blow over *or* down.

.6 **overthrow,** overturn 220.6.

.7 **drop,** let drop *or* fall.

.8 **crouch,** cringe, **cower; stoop,** bend, **squat,** get down; hunch, hunch down; scrooch *or* scrouch down [dial]; grovel, wallow, welter.

.9 **bow, bend, kneel,** genuflect, bend the knee, **curtsy,** make a low bow, make a reverence *or* obeisance, salaam, bob, duck; **kowtow,** prostrate oneself.

.10 **sit down,** seat oneself, **be seated** 268.10; squat, get down on one's hunkers [dial].

.11 **lie down,** couch, drape oneself, **recline** 214.5; prostrate, supinate, prone [dial]; flatten oneself, prostrate oneself.

.12 ADJS **depressed, lowered,** debased, reduced, **fallen;** sunk, **sunken,** submerged; downcast, downthrown; prostrate 214.8; low, at a low ebb.

319. LEAP

.1 NOUNS **leap, jump, hop, spring, skip, bound,** bounce; **pounce;** upleap, upspring, jump-off; **hurdle; vault,** pole vault; demivolt, curvet, capriole; jeté, grand jeté, tour jeté, saut de basque; jig, galliard, lavolta, Highland fling, morris; standing *or* running *or* flying jump; long jump, broad jump, standing *or* running broad jump; high jump, standing *or* running high jump; leapfrog; jump shot; handspring; buck, buckjump; ski jump, jump turn, geländesprung, gelände jump; steeplechase; hippety-hop [informal]; jump-hop; hop, skip, and jump.

.2 **caper,** dido [informal], **gambol, frisk,** curvet, cavort, capriole; **prance,** caracole; *gambade* [Fr], gambado; falcade.

.3 **leaping, jumping,** bouncing, bounding, hopping, capering, prancing, skipping, **springing,** saltation; **vaulting,** pole vaulting; **hurdling,** the hurdles, hurdle race, timber topping [slang], steeplechase; leapfrogging.

.4 **jumper,** leaper, hopper; broad jumper, high jumper; **vaulter,** pole vaulter; **hurdler,** hurdle racer, timber topper [informal]; jumping jack; bucking bronco, buckjumper, sunfisher [slang]; jumping bean; kangaroo, gazelle, stag, jackrabbit, goat, frog, grasshopper, flea; salmon.

.5 VERBS **leap, jump, vault, spring, skip, hop, bound,** bounce; upleap, upspring, updive; leap over, jump over, etc.; overleap, overjump, overskip, leapfrog; **hurdle,** clear, negotiate; curvet, capriole; buck, buckjump; ski jump; steeplechase; start, start up, start aside; **pounce,** pounce on or upon; hippety-hop [informal].

.6 **caper, cut capers,** cut a dido [informal], curvet, cavort, capriole, **gambol,** gambado, **frisk,** flounce, **trip, skip,** bob, bounce, jump about; **romp,** ramp [dial]; **prance;** caracole.

.7 ADJS **leaping, jumping,** springing, hopping, skipping, prancing, bouncing, bounding; saltant, saltatory, saltatorial.

320. PLUNGE

.1 NOUNS **plunge, dive, pitch, drop, fall;** header [informal]; **swoop, pounce,** stoop; swan dive, gainer, jackknife, cannonball; belly flop, belly buster, belly whopper [all informal]; nose dive, power dive; parachute jump, sky dive; crash dive, stationary dive, running dive.

.2 **submergence, submersion, immersion,** immergence, engulfment, **inundation,** burial; **dipping, ducking,** dousing, sousing, dunking [informal], sinking; **dip, duck, souse;** baptism.

.3 **diving,** plunging; sky diving; fancy diving, high diving, skin diving, pearl diving, deep-sea diving.

.4 **diver,** plunger; high diver; parachute jumper, jumper, sky diver; skin diver, snorkel diver, scuba diver, free diver, pearl diver, deep-sea diver, frogman; –dytes.

.5 (diving equipment) diving bell, diving chamber, bathysphere, bathyscaphe, benthoscope, aquascope; submarine 277.9; diving boat; scuba, self-contained underwater breathing apparatus, Aqua-Lung; diving goggles, diving mask, swim fins; wet suit; air cylinder; diving suit; diving helmet, diving hood; snorkel, periscope.

.6 VERBS **plunge, dive, pitch, plummet, drop, fall;** plump, plunk, plop; swoop, swoop down, stoop, **pounce,** pounce on or upon; nose-dive, make a nose dive; parachute, sky-dive; skin-dive; sound; take a header [informal].

.7 **submerge,** submerse, **immerse,** immerge, merge, **sink,** bury, engulf, **inundate,** del-

uge, drown, overwhelm, whelm; **dip, duck, dunk** [informal], douse, souse, plunge in water; baptize.

.8 **sink, scuttle,** send to the bottom, send to Davy Jones's locker; **founder, go down,** go to the bottom, sink like lead, go down like a stone; get out of one's depth.

.9 ADJS **submersible,** submergible, immersible, sinkable.

321. CIRCUITOUSNESS

.1 NOUNS **circuitousness,** circuitry, circuition [archaic], circulation; **roundaboutness,** indirection, meandering, deviance or deviancy, **deviation** 291; deviousness, **digression,** circumlocution 593.5; **excursion,** excursus; **circling, wheeling,** rounding, orbit, **orbiting; spiraling,** spiral, gyring, gyre; circumambulation, circumambience or circumambiency, circumflexion, circumnavigation, circummigration; turning, **turn** 291.1; circularity 253.

.2 **circuit, round,** revolution, circle, full circle, **cycle,** orbit, ambit; round trip, *allerretour* [Fr]; **beat, rounds, walk,** tour, turn, lap, loop.

.3 **detour, bypass, roundabout way,** roundabout, circuit, circumbendibus [informal], digression, deviation, excursion, ambages.

.4 VERBS **circuit,** make a circuit, **circle,** describe a circle, move in a circle, **circulate; go round** or **around,** go about; **wheel,** orbit, round; come full circle, close the circle, make a round trip, return to the starting point; **cycle;** spiral, gyre; go around in circles, chase one's tail; revolve 322.9; **compass,** encompass, encircle, surround; skirt, flank; go the round, make the round of, make one's rounds, circuiteer [archaic]; lap; circumvent, circumambulate, circummigrate; circumnavigate, girdle, girdle the globe, "put a girdle round about the earth" [Shakespeare].

.5 **turn, go around, round,** turn or round a corner, corner, round a bend, double or round a point.

.6 **detour,** make a detour, **go around,** go round about, go the long way around, go out of one's way, **bypass;** deviate 291.3; digress 593.9.

.7 ADJS **circuitous, roundabout, out-of-the-way, devious, oblique, indirect,** meandering, backhanded, ambagious; **deviative** 291.7, **deviating,** digressive, discursive, excursive; **circular** 253.11, **round,** wheelshaped, O-shaped; spiral, helical; orbital; rotary 322.15.

225

321.8 – 323.1

.8 circumambient, circumambulatory, circumforaneous, circumfluent, circumvolant, circumnavigatory, circumnavigable.

.9 ADVS circuitously, deviously, obliquely, indirectly, round about, about it and about, in a roundabout way, by a side door, by a side wind; circlewise, wheelwise.

322. ROTATION

.1 NOUNS rotation, revolution, volution, roll, gyration, spin, circulation, turbination; axial motion, rotational motion, angular motion, angular momentum, angular velocity; circumrotation, circumgyration, full circle; turning, whirling, swirling, spinning, wheeling, reeling, whir; centrifugation; swiveling, pivoting, swinging; rolling, volutation, trolling, trundling, bowling.

.2 whirl, wheel, reel, spin, turn, round, gyre; pirouette; swirl, twirl, eddy, gurge, surge; vortex, whirlpool, maelstrom, Charybdis; dizzy round, rat race; whirlwind 403.14.

.3 revolutions, revs [informal]; revolutions per minute, rpm.

.4 rotator, rotor; roller, rundle; whirler, whirligig, top, whirlabout; merry-go-round, carousel, roundabout; wheel, disk; Ixion's wheel; rolling stone.

.5 axle, axis, ax(o)–, axono–; pivot, gudgeon, trunnion, swivel, spindle, arbor, pole, radiant; fulcrum 216.2; pin, pintle; hub, nave; axle shaft, axle spindle, axle bar, axle-tree; distaff; mandrel; gimbal; hinge, hingle [dial]; rowlock, oarlock.

.6 axle box, journal, journal box; hotbox.

.7 bearing, ball bearing, needle bearing, roller bearing, thrust bearing, bevel bearing, bushing; jewel; headstock.

.8 (science of rotation) trochilics, gyrostatics.

.9 VERBS rotate, revolve, spin, turn, round, go round or around, turn round or around; gyrate, gyre; circumrotate, circumvolute; circle, circulate; swivel, pivot, wheel, swing; pirouette, turn a pirouette; wind, twist, screw, crank; wamble.

.10 roll, trundle, troll, bowl; roll up, furl.

.11 whirl, whirligig, twirl, wheel, reel, spin, spin like a top or teetotum, whirl like a dervish; centrifuge, centrifugate; swirl, gurge, surge, eddy, whirlpool.

.12 (move around in confusion) seethe, mill, mill around, stir, roil, moil, be turbulent.

.13 (roll about in) wallow, welter, grovel, roll, flounder, tumble.

.14 ADJS rotating, revolving, turning, gyrating; whirling, swirling, twirling, spinning, wheeling, reeling; rolling, trolling, bowling; circum–.

.15 rotary, rotational, rotatory, rotative, roto–, trocho–; trochilic, vertiginous; circumrotatory, circumvolutory, circumgyratory; gyral, gyratory, gyrational, gyroscopic, gyrostatic, gyr(o)–; whirly, swirly, gulfy; whirlabout, whirligig; vortical, cyclonic, tornadic, whirlwindy, whirlwindish.

.16 ADVS round, around, round about, in a circle; round and round, in circles, like a horse in a mill; in a whirl, in a spin; head over heels, heels over head; clockwise, counterclockwise, anticlockwise, widdershins.

.17 rotators

bobbin	rolling pin
centrifuge	rotary drill
chuck	rotor
drill 348.18	screw
extractor	spindle
fan	spin-drier
governor	spinner
gyro	spit
gyroplane	spool
gyroscope	teetotum
gyrostabilizer	top
gyrostat	treadmill
impeller	turbine
jack	turntable
propeller	ultracentrifuge
reel	whirl drill
revolving door	whirling table
revolving lever	whorl
roller	windmill

.18 wheels

balance wheel	paddle wheel
bevel gear	pinion
buffing wheel	pinwheel
cartwheel	potter's wheel
caster	prayer wheel
Catherine wheel	pulley
circular saw	ratchet wheel
cog	roulette wheel
cogwheel	spinning wheel
contrate wheel	sprocket wheel
crown wheel	spur gear
cycloidal gear	spur pinion
drive wheel	spur wheel
escape wheel	steering wheel
Ferris wheel	truck
flywheel	truckle
gear	vortex wheel
gearwheel	wagon wheel
gyrowheel	water wheel
idler wheel	wheel of fortune
mill wheel	worm wheel or gear

323. OSCILLATION

(motion to and fro)

.1 NOUNS oscillation, vibration, vibrancy, vibro–, seismo–; harmonic motion, simple harmonic motion; libration, nutation; pendulation; **fluctuation,** vacillation, wavering; libration of the moon, libration in latitude *or* longitude; vibratility; **frequency,** frequency band *or* spectrum; resonance, resonant *or* resonance frequency; periodicity 137.2.

.2 **waving,** wave motion, **undulation,** undulancy; **brandishing, flourishing,** flaunting, shaking; brandish, flaunt, flourish; wave 395.14.

.3 **pulsation, pulse, beat, throb;** beating, throbbing; rat-a-tat, staccato, rataplan, drumming 455.1; **rhythm, tempo** 463.22–24; **palpitation,** flutter, arrhythmia, pitter-patter, pitapat; **heartbeat,** heartthrob, –crotism.

.4 **wave,** wave motion, **ray;** transverse wave, longitudinal wave; electromagnetic wave, electromagnetic radiation; **light** 335; **radio wave** 344.11; mechanical wave; acoustic wave, **sound wave** 450.1; seismic wave, **shock wave;** de Broglie wave; diffracted wave, guided wave; one- *or* two- *or* three-dimensional wave; periodic wave; standing wave, node, antinode; surface wave, **tidal wave;** amplitude, crest, trough; wavelength; frequency, frequency band *or* spectrum; resonance, resonant *or* resonance frequency; period; wave number; diffraction; reinforcement, interference; in phase, out of phase; wave equation, Schrödinger equation; Huygens' principle.

.5 **alternation, reciprocation;** regular *or* rhythmic play, **coming and going,** to-and-fro, back-and-forth, ebb and flow, *va-et-vien* [Fr], flux and reflux, systole and diastole, ups and downs; sine wave, Lissajous figure *or* curve; **seesawing,** teetering, tottering, **teeter-tottering;** seesaw, teeter, teeter-totter, wigwag.

.6 **swing,** swinging, **sway,** swag; **rock, lurch, roll, reel,** careen; wag, waggle; wave, waver.

.7 **seismicity,** seismism; **seismology,** seismography, seismometry.

.8 (instruments) oscilloscope, oscillograph, oscillometer; harmonograph; vibroscope, vibrograph; kymograph; seismoscope, seismograph, seismometer.

.9 **oscillator, vibrator;** pendulum, pendulum wheel; metronome; swing; seesaw, teeter, teeter-totter, teeterboard, teetery-bender; rocker, rocking chair; rocking stone, logan stone, shuttle; shuttlecock.

.10 VERBS **oscillate, vibrate,** librate, nutate; **pendulate; fluctuate,** vacillate, waver,

wave; resonate; **swing, sway,** swag, dangle, reel, **rock, lurch, roll,** careen, toss, pitch; wag, waggle; **wobble,** coggle [Brit dial]; bob, bobble; shake, flutter 324.10–12.

.11 **wave, undulate; brandish, flourish,** flaunt, shake, swing, wield; float, fly; **flap, flutter;** wag, wigwag.

.12 **pulsate, pulse, beat, throb,** pant, **palpitate,** go pitapat; tick, ticktock; **drum** 455.4.

.13 **alternate,** reciprocate, swing, **go to and fro,** to-and-fro, **come and go,** pass and repass, ebb and flow, wax and wane, ride and tie, hitch and hike, back and fill; seesaw, teeter, **teeter-totter;** shuttle, shuttlecock, battledore and shuttlecock; **wigwag,** wibble-wabble; zigzag.

.14 (move up and down) **pump, shake.**

.15 ADJS **oscillating,** oscillatory; **vibrating,** vibratory, vibratile, harmonic; **libratory,** nutational; periodic, pendular, pendulous; **fluctuating,** fluctuational, fluctuant; wavering; vacillating, vacillatory; resonant.

.16 **waving, undulating,** undulatory, undulant.

.17 **swinging, swaying,** dangling, **reeling, rocking, lurching,** careening, **rolling,** tossing, pitching.

.18 **pulsative,** pulsatory, pulsatile; **pulsating, pulsing, beating, throbbing, palpitating,** palpitant, pitapat, staccato; **rhythmic** 463.28; –crotic.

.19 **alternate, reciprocal,** reciprocative; **sinewave; back-and-forth, to-and-fro,** up-and-down, seesaw.

.20 **seismatical,** seismological, seismographic, seismometric; **successive,** successatory, sussultatory.

.21 ADVS **to and fro, back and forth,** backward and forward, backwards and forwards, **in and out, up and down,** seesaw, shuttlewise, from side to side, from pillar to post, off and on, ride and tie, hitch and hike, round and round, like buckets in a well.

324. AGITATION

(irregular motion)

.1 NOUNS **agitation,** perturbation, **conturbation** [archaic], **trepidation,** trepidity, fidgets *or* jitters [both informal], jumpiness, nervousness, nerviness [Brit], **nervosity,** twitter, upset, **unrest,** malaise, unease, fever, feverishness, restlessness, **disquiet,** disquietude, inquietude, discomposure; **stir, churn, ferment,** fermentation, foment; seethe, seething, ebullition, boil, boiling; embroilment, roil, turbidity, fume, **disturbance, commotion,** moil, **turmoil, turbulence** 162.2, **swirl, tumult,** tumultuation, hubbub, rout, fuss, row, to-do, bluster, fluster, flurry, flutteration, flap, bustle, brouhaha, bobbery, hurly-burly; maelstrom; **excitement** 857; **disorder** 62.

.2 **shaking, quaking,** palsy, **quivering, quavering, shivering, trembling,** tremulousness, **shuddering, vibration;** succussion; jerkiness, **fits and starts,** spasms; jactation, jactitation; joltiness, bumpiness, shakes [informal], shivers *or* cold shivers [both informal], ague, chattering; chorea, St. Vitus's dance.

.3 **shake, quake, quiver, quaver,** falter, **tremor, tremble, shiver, shudder,** twitter, didder, dither; **wobble;** bob, bobble; jog, joggle; **shock, jolt,** jar, jostle; **bounce,** bump; **jerk, twitch,** tic, grimace, rictus; jig, jiggle, jigget [informal].

.4 **flutter,** flitter, flit, **flicker, waver,** dance; shake, quiver 324.3; **sputter, splutter; flap,** flop [informal]; **beat,** beating; **palpitation,** throb, pitapat, pitter-patter.

.5 **twitching, jerking,** vellication; **fidgets,** fidgetiness; itchiness, formication, pruritus.

.6 **spasm, convulsion,** cramp, **paroxysm,** throes; **orgasm,** sexual climax; epitasis, eclampsia; **seizure,** grip, attack, **fit,** access, ictus; epilepsy, falling sickness; stroke, apoplexy.

.7 **wiggle, wriggle;** wag, waggle; writhe, **squirm.**

.8 **flounder,** flounce, **stagger,** totter, **stumble,** falter; wallow, welter, volutation; **roll, rock, reel, lurch,** career, **swing, sway; toss, tumble,** pitch, plunge.

.9 (instruments) **agitator,** shaker, jiggler, vibrator; beater, paddle, whisk, eggbeater; churn.

.10 VERBS **agitate, shake, disturb, perturb,** perturbate, **disquiet, discompose, upset, trouble, stir,** swirl, flurry, fret, roughen, **ruffle,** rumple, ripple, ferment, convulse; **churn,** whip, whisk, beat, paddle; **stir up,** work up, shake up, churn up, whip up, beat up; roil, rile [dial]; **disarrange** 63.2; **excite** 857.11.

.11 **shake, quake, vibrate,** jactitate; **tremble, quiver, quaver,** falter, **shudder, shiver,** twitter, didder, chatter; shake in one's boots *or* shoes, quake *or* shake *or* tremble like an aspen leaf; have an ague; **wobble; bob,** bobble; jog, joggle; **shock, jolt,** jar, jostle, hustle, jounce, **bounce,** jump, bump.

.12 **flutter,** flitter, flit, flick, **flicker,** gutter, bicker, wave, **waver,** dance; **sputter, splutter; flap,** flop [informal], flip, beat, slat; **palpitate,** pulse, throb, pitter-patter, go pitapat.

.13 **twitch, jerk,** vellicate; itch; **jig, jiggle,** jigger *or* jigget [both informal]; **fidget,** have the fidgets.

.14 **wiggle, wriggle;** wag, waggle; **writhe, squirm,** twist and turn; have ants in one's pants [informal].

.15 **flounder,** flounce, **stagger,** totter, stumble, falter, blunder, wallop; **struggle,** labor; **wallow, welter; roll, rock, reel, lurch,** career, career, **swing, sway; toss, tumble,** thrash about, **pitch, plunge,** pitch and plunge, toss and tumble, toss and turn, be the sport of winds and waves; **seethe** 162.11.

.16 ADJS **agitated, disturbed, perturbed, disquieted, discomposed, troubled, upset, ruffled,** flurried, flustered; stirred up, shaken, shaken up; troublous, feverish, fidgety *or* jittery [both informal], **jumpy, nervous,** nervy [Brit], **restless, uneasy,** unquiet, unpeaceful; all of a twitter [informal], all of a flutter; **turbulent** 162.17; **excited** 857.18–25.

.17 **shaking, vibrating,** chattering; **quivering, quavering, quaking, shivering, shuddering, trembling, tremulous,** palsied, aspen; successive, succussatory; **shaky,** quivery, quavery, shivery, **trembly; wobbly.**

.18 **fluttering, flickering, wavering,** guttering, dancing; sputtering, spluttering, sputtery; fluttery, flickery, flicky, wavery, **unsteady,** desultory.

.19 **jerky,** twitchy *or* twitchety, jerking, **twitching, fidgety, jumpy,** jiggety [informal], vellicative; spastic, spasmodic, eclamptic, orgasmic, convulsive; fitful, saltatory.

.20 **jolting,** jolty, **joggling,** joggly, jogglety, **bouncy, bumpy,** choppy, rough; **jarring,** bone-bruising.

.21 **wriggly,** wriggling; **wiggly,** wiggling; squirmy, squirming; writhy, writhing, antsy [slang].

.22 ADVS **agitatedly, troublously, restlessly,** uneasily, unquietly, unpeacefully, nervously, feverishly.

.23 **shakily,** quiveringly, quaveringly, quakingly, **tremblingly,** shudderingly, tremulously; flutteringly, waveringly, unsteadily, desultorily; **jerkily,** spasmodically, fitfully, by jerks, by snatches, saltatorily, by fits and starts, "with many a flirt and flutter" [Pope].

325. PHYSICS

.1 NOUNS **physics**; natural *or* physical science; philosophy *or* second philosophy *or* natural philosophy *or* physic [all archaic]; acoustics, applied physics, aerophysics, astrophysics, basic conductor physics, biophysics, classical physics, chemical physics *or* chemicophysics, cryogenics, crystallography, cytophysics, geophysics, macrophysics, mathematical physics, mechanics 347, medicophysics, microphysics, molecular physics, Newtonian physics, nuclear physics 326.1, optics, physicomathematics, psychophysics, radiation physics 327.7, solar physics, solid-state physics, statics, stereophysics, theoretical physics, thermodynamics, zoophysics; physical chemistry, physicochemistry; electron physics, electrophysics, radionics, electronics 343.

.2 **physicist**, aerophysicist, astrophysicist, biophysicist, etc.

.3 ADJS **physical**, physi(o)–, physic(o)–; aerophysical, astrophysical, biophysical, etc.

326. ATOMICS

.1 NOUNS **atomics**, atomistics, atomology, atomic science; **nucleonics, nuclear physics**; atomic *or* nuclear chemistry; quantum mechanics, wave mechanics; molecular physics; thermionics; mass spectrometry, mass spectrography; radiology 327.7.

.2 (atomic theory) **quantum theory,** Bohr theory, Dirac theory, Rutherford theory, Schrödinger theory, Lewis-Langmuir *or* octet theory, Thomson's hypothesis; law of conservation of mass, law of definite proportions, law of multiple proportions, law of Dulong and Petit, law of parity, correspondence principle; atomism.

.3 **atomic scientist, nuclear physicist;** radiologist 327.8.

.4 **atom;** tracer, tracer atom, tagged atom; atomic model, nuclear atom; nuclide; **ion; shell,** subshell, planetary shell, valence shell.

.5 **isotope;** protium, deuterium *or* heavy hydrogen, tritium (isotopes of hydrogen); radioactive isotope, **radioisotope;** carbon 14, strontium 90, uranium 235, etc.; artificial isotope; isotone; isobar, isomer, nuclear isomer.

.6 **elementary particle,** atomic particle, **subatomic particle** 326.24, –on; lepton, meson, baryon, antilepton, antimeson, antibaryon; **atomic nucleus, nucleus,** nucle(o)– *or* nuclei–, *Kern* [Ger]; nuclear particle, nucleon; proton, neutron 326.25;

deuteron (deuterium nucleus), triton (tritium nucleus), alpha particle (helium nucleus); nuclear force, strong interaction; nucleosynthesis; nuclear resonance, Mössbauer effect, nuclear magnetic resonance *or* NMR; strangeness; electron, beta particle, valence electron 343.3; photon, phot(o)–.

.7 **atomic cluster, molecule;** radical, simple radical, compound radical, chain, straight chain, branched chain, side chain; ring, closed chain, cycle; homocycle, heterocycle; benzene ring *or* nucleus, Kekulé formula; lattice, space-lattice.

.8 **fission, nuclear fission,** fission reaction, fissi–; **atom-smashing,** atom-chipping, **splitting the atom;** atomic reaction; atomic disintegration *or* decay, alpha decay, beta decay, gamma decay; stimulation, dissociation, photodisintegration, ionization, nucleization, cleavage; neutron reaction, proton reaction, etc.; reversible reaction, nonreversible reaction; thermonuclear reaction; **chain reaction;** exchange reaction; breeding; disintegration series; bombardment, atomization; bullet, target; proton gun.

.9 **fusion, nuclear fusion,** fusion reaction, thermonuclear reaction, thermonuclear fusion.

.10 **fissionable material,** nuclear fuel; fertile material; **critical mass,** noncritical mass; parent element, daughter element; end product.

.11 **accelerator** 326.27, **particle accelerator,** atomic accelerator, atom smasher, atomic cannon.

.12 **mass spectrometer,** mass spectrograph.

.13 **reactor, nuclear reactor, pile,** atomic pile, reactor pile, chain-reacting pile, chain reactor, **furnace,** atomic *or* nuclear furnace, neutron factory; stellarator; power reactor, breeder reactor, power-breeder reactor; homogeneous reactor, heterogeneous reactor; plutonium reactor, uranium reactor, etc.; fast pile, intermediate pile, slow pile; lattice; bricks; rods; radioactive waste.

.14 **atomic engine, atomic** *or* **nuclear power plant,** reactor engine.

.15 **atomic energy, nuclear energy** *or* **power,** thermonuclear power; activation energy, binding energy, mass energy; energy level; atomic research, atomic project; Atomic Energy Commission, AEC.

.16 **atomic explosion, atom blast, A-blast; thermonuclear explosion,** hydrogen blast, **H-blast;** ground zero; blast wave, Mach stem; Mach front; mushroom cloud; **fallout,** airborne radioactivity, fission particles, dust cloud, radioactive dust; flash burn; A-bomb shelter, fallout shelter.

.17 VERBS **atomize,** nucleize; activate, accelerate; bombard, cross-bombard; cleave, fission, **split** or **smash the atom.**

.18 ADJS **atomic,** atomatic, atomistic; atomiferous; monatomic, diatomic, triatomic, tetratomic, pentatomic, hexatomic, heptatomic; heteratomic, heteroatomic; subatomic; dibasic, tribasic; cyclic, isocyclic, homocyclic, heterocyclic; isotopic, isobaric, isoteric.

.19 **nuclear, thermonuclear,** isonuclear, homonuclear, heteronuclear, extranuclear.

.20 **fissionable,** fissile, scissile.

.21 **atoms**

acceptor atom	isotopic isobar
asymmetric carbon atom	labeled atom
discrete atom	neutral atom
excited atom	normal atom
hot atom	nuclear isomer
impurity atom	radiation atom
isobar	recoil atom
isotere	stripped atom

.22 **theoretic atoms**

Bohr atom	Rutherford atom
cubical atom	Schrödinger atom
Dirac atom	Thomson atom
Lewis-Langmuir atom	

.23 **valent atoms and radicals**

monad	pentad
dyad	hexad
triad	heptad
tetrad	octad

.24 **subatomic particles**

antielectron	neutrino
antineutrino	neutron
antineutron	omega particle
antiparticle	phi-meson
antiproton	photon
beta particle	pion, pi-meson
electron	positron, positive electron
graviton	proton
hadron	quark
hyperon	rho particle
kaon, K-meson or K-particle	sigma particle
lambda particle	strange particle
meson, mesotron	tau-meson
muon, mu-meson	xi-particle

.25 **neutrons**

fast neutron	resonance neutron
monoenergetic neutron	slow neutron
photoneutron	thermal neutron

.26 **atomic units and constants**

atom	Avogadro number
atomic mass	Boltzmann's constant
atomic number	crystal-lattice constant
atomic weight	Dulong's constant

elementary quantum of action	Petit's constant
gram atom	Planck's constant
gram-atomic weight	quantum
magnetic quantum number	quantum number
magneton	Rydberg number or constant
mass number	valence
	valence number

.27 **accelerators**

betatron	induction accelerator
bevatron	linear accelerator
cascade transformer	microwave linear accelerator
charge-exchange accelerator	positive-ion accelerator
Cockcroft-Walton voltage multiplier	synchrocyclotron
cosmotron	synchrotron
cyclotron	Van de Graaff generator
electron accelerator	
electrostatic generator	

327. RADIATION AND RADIOACTIVITY

.1 NOUNS **radiation,** radiant energy; **radioactivity,** activity, radioactive radiation or emanation, atomic or nuclear radiation; natural radioactivity, artificial radioactivity; curiage; specific activity, high specific activity; actinic radiation, actin(o)- or actini–; radiotransparency, radiolucency; radiopacity; radiosensitivity, radiosensibility; half-life; radiocarbon dating; contamination, decontamination; saturation point; radiac or radioactivity detection identification and computation; fallout 326.16.

.2 **radioluminescence, autoluminescence;** cathode luminescence; Cerenkov radiation, synchrotron radiation.

.3 **radiorays,** nuclear rays; alpha ray, beta ray, gamma ray; alpha radiation, beta radiation, gamma radiation; X ray, Roentgen ray, X radiation; Grenz ray, infraroentgen ray; cathode ray, anode ray; Lenard ray; actinic ray; Becquerel ray; positive ray, canal ray; cosmic ray, cosmic radiation; cosmic ray bombardment, electron shower; electron emission 343.5.

.4 **radioactive particle,** radion; alpha particle, beta particle; heavy particle; high-energy particle; meson, mesotron; cosmic particle, solar particle, aurora particle, V-particle.

.5 (radioactive substance) **radiator;** alpha radiator, beta radiator, gamma radiator; fluorescent paint, radium paint; radium dial; fission products; radiocarbon, radiocopper, radioiodine, radiothorium, etc.; mesothorium; **radioelement** 327.12; radioisotope; tracer, tracer element, tracer atom, radioactive waste.

.6 **counter** 327.13, **radioscope**, radiodetector, atom-tagger; ionization chamber; ionizing event; X-ray spectrograph, X-ray spectrometer.

.7 **radiation physics**, radiology, radiological physics; radiobiology, radiochemistry, radiometallography, radiography, roentgenography, roentgenology, radiometry, spectroradiometry, radiotechnology, radiopathology; radiotherapy 689.7; radioscopy, curiescopy, roentgenoscopy, radiostereoscopy, fluoroscopy, photofluorography, orthodiography; X-ray photometry, X-ray spectrometry; tracer investigation, atom-tagging.

.8 **radiation physicist**, radiologist, atom-tagger; radiobiologist, radiochemist.

.9 VERBS **radioactivate**, activate, **irradiate**, charge; radiumize; **contaminate**, poison, infect.

.10 ADJS **radioactive**, radio–, activated, radioactivated, irradiated, charged, **hot**; **contaminated**, infected, poisoned; radiferous; radioluminescent, autoluminescent.

.11 **radiable**; radiotransparent, radioparent, radiolucent; radiopaque, radium-proof; radiosensitive.

.12 **radioactive elements**

actinium	nobelium
americium	plutonium
astatine	polonium
berkelium	promethium
californium	protactinium
curium	radium
einsteinium	radon, radium emana-
fermium	tion
francium	technetium
hahnium	thorium
mendelevium	uranium
neptunium	

.13 **radiation counters and chambers**

air-wall ionization chamber	diffusion chamber
	electronic counter
alpha pulse analyzer	expansion chamber
atom counter	externally-quenched
atom-tracing spectrometer	counter
	extrapolation ioniza-
aurora particle counter	tion chamber
	free-air ionization
beta-ray spectrograph or spectrometer	chamber
	gamma ray counter
boron counter	gas counter
Cerenkov counter	Geiger counter
cloud chamber	Geiger-counter tele-
coincidence counter	scope
compensated ioniza-	Geiger-Klemperer
tion chamber	counter
cosmic ray counter	Geiger-Müller counter
counting tube	heavy particle counter
crystal counter	integrating ionization
differential ionization	chamber
chamber	ion counter

ionization chamber	counter
kicksorter	scintillation counter
minometer	scintillator
particle counter	scintillometer
proportional counter	screen-wall counter
proportional ioniza-	self-quenched counter
tion chamber	solar gamma ray
pulse analyzer	counter
pulse ionization cham-	solar X-ray counter
ber	spark chamber
radiation pyrometer	spectroradiometer
radiometer	spinthariscope
radiomicrometer	tube counter
Rutherford-Geiger	Wilson chamber

.14 **radioactive units**

curie	millicurie
half-life	multicurie
megacurie	roentgen
microcurie	

328. HEAT

.1 NOUNS **heat, hotness,** heatedness, –thermia *or* –thermy; superheat, superheatedness; calidity *or* caloric [both archaic]; **warmth,** warmness; incalescence; radiant heat, thermal radiation, induction heat, convector *or* convected heat, coal heat, gas heat, oil heat, hot-air heat, steam heat, electric heat, solar heat, dielectric heat, ultraviolet heat, atomic heat, molecular heat; animal heat, body heat, blood heat, hypothermia; fever heat, fever 686.6; heating, burning 329.5.

.2 (metaphors) **ardor,** ardency, **fervor,** fervency, fervidness, fervidity; eagerness 635; excitement 857; **anger** 952.5–10; **sexual desire** 419.5,6; love 931.

.3 **temperature;** boiling point, cocto–; melting point, freezing point; dew point; recalescence point; zero, absolute zero.

.4 **lukewarmness,** tepidness, tepidity; tepidarium.

.5 **torridness,** torridity; extreme heat, intense heat, torrid heat, red heat, white heat, tropical heat, sweltering heat, Afric heat, Indian heat, Bengal heat, summer heat; "where the sun beats, and the dead tree gives no shelter, the cricket no relief" [T. S. Eliot]; **hot wind** 403.7.

.6 **sultriness, stuffiness, closeness,** oppressiveness; humidity, **humidness, mugginess,** stickiness [informal], swelter, temperature-humidity index, THI.

.7 **hot weather,** sunny *or* sunshiny weather; sultry weather, stuffy weather, humid weather, muggy weather, sticky weather [informal]; summer, midsummer, high summer; dog days, canicular days, canicule; **heat wave,** hot wave; broiling sun, midday sun; vertical rays; warm weather, fair weather.

.8 **hot day,** summer day; **scorcher** *or* **roaster**
or broiler *or* sizzler *or* swelterer [all informal].

.9 **hot air,** superheated air; thermal; fire
storm.

.10 **hot water,** boiling water; **steam,** vapor;
volcanic water; hot *or* warm *or* thermal
spring, thermae; geyser, Old Faithful.

.11 (hot place) **oven, furnace,** fiery furnace,
inferno, hell; steam bath; **tropics,** subtropics, Torrid Zone; equator.

.12 **glow,** incandescence, fieriness; **flush,**
blush, bloom, redness 368, rubicundity,
rosiness; whiteness 364; thermochromism;
hectic, hectic flush 686.6.

.13 **fire,** igni–, pyr(o)–; **blaze, flame,** ingle,
devouring element; **combustion, ignition,**
ignition temperature *or* point, flash *or*
flashing point; **conflagration;** flicker 335.8,
wavering *or* flickering flame, "lambent
flame" [Dryden]; smoldering fire, sleeping fire; marshfire, fen fire, ignis fatuus,
will-o'-the-wisp; fox fire; witch fire, St.
Elmo's fire, corposant; **cheerful fire,** cozy
fire, crackling fire, "bright-flaming, heatfull fire" [Du Bartas]; **roaring fire,**
blazing fire; **raging fire,** sheet of fire, sea
of flames, "whirlwinds of tempestuous
fire" [Milton]; bonfire, balefire; beacon
fire, beacon, signal beacon, watch fire;
alarm fire, two-alarm fire, three-alarm
fire, etc.; wildfire, prairie fire, forest fire;
backfire; open fire; campfire; smudge
fire; death fire, pyre, funeral pyre, crematory; burning ghat.

.14 **flare,** flare-up, **flash,** flash fire, **blaze,**
burst, outburst; deflagration.

.15 **spark,** sparkle; **scintillation,** scintilla;
ignescence.

.16 **coal,** live coal, brand, firebrand, **ember,**
burning ember; **cinder.**

.17 **fireworks** *or* firework, **pyrotechnics** *or* pyrotechnic *or* pyrotechny.

.18 (perviousness to heat) transcalency;
adiathermancy, athermancy.

.19 **thermal unit;** British thermal unit, BTU;
Board of Trade unit, BOT; centigrade
thermal unit; centigrade *or* Celsius scale,
Fahrenheit scale; **calorie,** mean calorie,
centuple *or* rational calorie, small calorie,
large *or* great calorie, kilocalorie, kilogram-calorie; therm.

.20 **thermometer,** mercury, glass; **thermostat;**
thermal detector.

.21 (science of heat) thermochemistry, thermology, thermotics, thermodynamics;
volcanology; pyrology, pyrognostics; pyro-

technics *or* pyrotechnic *or* pyrotechny,
ebulliometry; calorimetry.

.22 VERBS (be hot) **burn, scorch,** parch, scald,
swelter, roast, toast, cook, bake, fry, broil,
boil, seethe, simmer, stew; **be in heat**
419.22; shimmer with heat, give off waves
of heat, radiate heat; **blaze, combust,**
flame, flame up, **flare,** flare up; **flicker**
335.25; **glow,** incandesce, spark, flush,
bloom; smolder; steam; sweat 311.16;
gasp, pant; **suffocate, stifle,** smother,
choke.

.23 **smoke, fume,** reek; smudge.

.24 ADJS **warm,** calid [archaic], **thermal,** thermic, therm(o)–, –thermous, mild, genial;
toasty [informal], warm as toast; **sunny,**
sunshiny; summery, aestival; **temperate,**
warmish; **tropical,** equatorial, subtropical;
tepid, lukewarm, luke; room-temperature; blood-warm, blood-hot; unfrozen.

.25 **hot, heated, torrid; sweltering,** sweltry,
canicular; **burning,** parching, scorching,
searing, scalding, blistering, baking, roasting, toasting, broiling, grilling, simmering;
boiling, seething, ebullient; **piping hot,**
scalding hot, burning hot, roasting hot,
scorching hot, sizzling hot, smoking hot;
red-hot, white-hot; ardent; flushed, sweating, sweaty, sudorific; overwarm, overhot,
overheated; hot as fire, hot as hell *or*
blazes, hot as the hinges of hell, hot
enough to roast an ox, so hot you can fry
eggs on the sidewalk [informal], like a
furnace *or* oven; feverish 686.54.

.26 **fiery,** igneous, firelike, pyric; combustive,
conflagrative.

.27 **burning, ignited,** kindled, enkindled,
blazing, ablaze, ardent, flaring, flaming,
aflame, inflamed, alight, **afire, on fire,** in
flames, in a blaze, flagrant [archaic]; conflagrant, comburent; live, living; **glowing,**
aglow, in a glow, incandescent, candescent, candent; sparking, scintillating, scintillant, ignescent; **flickering,** aflicker, guttering; unquenched, unextinguished;
slow-burning; **smoldering; smoking,** fuming, reeking.

.28 **sultry, stifling, suffocating, stuffy, close,**
oppressive; **humid, sticky** [informal],
muggy.

.29 **warm-blooded, hot-blooded.**

.30 isothermal, isothermic; centigrade, Fahrenheit.

.31 diathermic, diathermal, transcalent; adiathermic, adiathermal, athermanous.

.32 pyrological, pyrognostic, pyrotechnic(al);
pyrogenic *or* pyrogenous *or* pyrogenetic;

thermochemical; thermodynamic(al).

.33 fireworks

bomb	girandole
candlebomb	ladyfinger
cannon cracker	pinwheel
cap	rocket
Catherine wheel	Roman candle
cherry bomb	serpent
cracker	skyrocket
cracker bonbon	snake
firecracker	sparkler
fizgig	squib
flare	torpedo
flowerpot	whiz-bang

.34 thermometers, thermal detectors

barretter	pyrometer
black-bulb thermometer	pyrometric cone
	pyroscope
calorimeter	pyrostat
candy thermometer	radiation pyrometer
centigrade thermometer	radiomicrometer
	register or self-registering thermometer
clinical thermometer	
cryometer	resistance pyrometer
cryoscope	resistance thermometer
cryostat	
dry-bulb thermometer	reversing thermometer
electric thermometer	telethermometer
Fahrenheit thermometer	thermel
	thermistor
galvanothermometer	thermocouple
gas thermometer	thermoelectrometer
meat thermometer	thermometrograph
metallic thermometer	thermopile
optical pyrometer	thermoregulator
oven thermometer	thermostat
platinum thermometer	wet-bulb thermometer

329. HEATING

.1 NOUNS **heating, warming,** calefaction, torrefaction, increase or raising of temperature; superheating; tepefaction; pyrogenesis; decalescence, recalescence; preheating; stove heating, furnace heating; radiant heating, panel heating; central heating; induction heating, gas heating, steam heating, oil heating, hot-water heating, hot-air heating, electric heating, electronic heating, dielectric heating; solar heating, insolation; heat exchange; cooking 330.

.2 **boiling,** seething, **stewing,** ebullition, ebullience or ebulliency, coction; decoction; **simmering;** boil; simmer; ebullioscope, ebulliometer.

.3 **melting, fusion,** running; **thawing,** thaw; liquation, fusibility; thermoplasticity.

.4 **ignition, lighting,** lighting up or off, **kindling,** firing; flammation, inflammation.

.5 **burning, combustion,** blazing, flaming; **scorching,** parching, singeing; **searing,** branding; **blistering,** vesication; **cauter**ization, cautery; **incineration,** cineration; **cremation,** concremation; suttee, self-cremation, self-immolation; the stake, burning at the stake, auto-da-fé [Pg]; scorification; carbonization; oxidation, oxidization; calcination; cupellation; deflagration; distilling, distillation; refining, smelting; pyrolysis; **c**racking, thermal cracking, destructive distillation; **spontaneous combustion,** thermogenesis.

.6 **burn,** scald, scorch, singe; sear; brand; sunburn, sunscald; windburn; mat burn; first- or second- or third-degree burn.

.7 **incendiarism, arson,** fire-raising [Brit]; **pyromania;** pyrophilia; pyrolatry, fire worship.

.8 **incendiary, arsonist; pyromaniac, firebug** [informal]; pyrophile, fire buff [informal]; pyrolater, fire worshiper.

.9 **flammability, inflammability,** combustibility.

.10 **heater, warmer; stove, furnace** 329.33; **cooker,** cookery; firebox; tuyere, tewel [archaic]; burner, jet, gas jet, pilot light or burner, element, heating element; heating pipe, steam pipe, hot-water pipe; heating duct, caliduct.

.11 **fireplace, hearth,** ingle; **fireside,** ingleside, inglenook, ingle cheek [Scot], chimney corner; hearthstone; hob, hub; fireguard, fireboard, fire screen, fender; chimney, flue; smokehole.

.12 **fire iron; andiron,** firedog; tongs, pair of tongs, fire tongs, coal tongs; poker, stove poker, salamander, fire hook; lifter, stove lifter; pothook, crook, crane, chain; trivet, tripod; spit, turnspit; grate, grating; gridiron, grid, griddle, grill, griller; damper.

.13 **incinerator,** cinerator, burner; **crematory,** cremator, crematorium, burning ghat; calcinatory.

.14 **blowtorch,** blast lamp, torch, alcohol torch, butane torch; soldering torch; blowpipe; **burner; welder** 348.24; acetylene torch or welder, cutting torch or blowpipe, oxyacetylene blowpipe or torch, welding blowpipe or torch.

.15 **cauterant,** cauterizer, cauter, cautery, thermocautery, actual cautery; hot iron, **branding iron,** brand iron, brand; moxa; electrocautery; **caustic, corrosive,** mordant, escharotic, potential cautery; acid 379.12; lunar caustic; radium.

.16 (products of combustion) scoria, sullage, slag, dross; **ashes,** ash; **cinder,** clinker, coal; coke, charcoal, brand, lava, carbon, calx; **soot**, smut, coom [Brit dial]; **smoke**, smudge, fume, reek.

.17 VERBS **heat**, raise or increase the temperature, hot or hot up [both Brit], **warm**, warm up, fire, fire up, stoke up; chafe; take the chill off; tepefy; gas-heat, oil-heat, hot-air-heat, hot-water-heat, steam-heat, electric-heat; superheat; overheat; **preheat; reheat**, recook, warm over; mull; steam; foment; cook 330.4.

.18 (metaphors) **excite, inflame** 857.11; incite, **kindle, arouse** 648.17–19; anger, **enrage** 952.21–23.

.19 insolate, sun-dry; **sun**, bask, bask in the sun, sun oneself, sunbathe.

.20 **boil, stew, simmer, seethe;** distill.

.21 **melt**, melt down, **run**, colliquate, **fuse**, flux; refine, smelt; render; **thaw**, thaw out, unfreeze; defrost, deice.

.22 **ignite, set fire to, fire, set on fire**, build a fire, **kindle**, enkindle, inflame, **light**, light up, strike a light, apply the match or torch to, torch, touch off, **burn**, conflagrate; rekindle, relight, relume; **feed**, feed the fire, **stoke**, stoke the fire, add fuel to the flame; bank; poke or stir the fire, blow up the fire, fan the flame; open the draft.

.23 **catch on fire**, catch fire, catch, take, **burn, flame**, combust, blaze, **blaze up, burst into flame.**

.24 **burn**, torrefy, **scorch, parch, sear; singe**, swinge; **blister**, vesicate; **cauterize**, brand, burn in; **char**, coal, carbonize; scorify; calcine; pyrolyze, crack; solder, weld; vulcanize; cast, found; oxidize, oxidate; deflagrate; cupel; burn off; blaze, flame 328.22.

.25 **burn up**, incendiarize, **incinerate, cremate**, consume, burn or reduce to ashes, burn to a cinder; **burn down**, burn to the ground, **go up in smoke.**

.26 ADJS **heating, warming**, chafing, calorific; calefactory, calefactive, calefacient, calorifacient, calorigenic; **burning** 328.25–27; cauterant, cauterizing; calcinatory.

.27 **inflammatory**, inflammative, **inflaming, kindling**, enkindling, lighting; **incendiary.**

.28 **flammable, inflammable, combustible**, burnable, accendible, fiery.

.29 **heated**, het or het up [both dial], hotted up [Brit], **warmed**, warmed up, centrally heated, gas-heated, oil-heated, hot-water-heated, hot-air-heated, steam-heated, electric-heated; superheated; overheated; **reheated**, recooked, **warmed-over**, *réchauffé* [Fr]; hot 328.25.

.30 **burned, burnt**, burned to the ground, incendiarized, burned-out or -down, gutted; scorched, blistered, parched, singed, seared, charred, pyrographic, adust; sunburned; **burnt-up**, incinerated, cremated, consumed, consumed by fire; ashen, ashy, carbonized, pyrolyzed, pyrolytic.

.31 **molten, melted**, fused; meltable, fusible; thermoplastic.

.32 **heaters**

Baltimore heater	induction heating machine
bedpan	
bloom heater	infrared heater
brazier	infrared lamp
brick oven	ingot heater
Bunsen burner	iron heater
calefactory	kerosene heater
car heater	kiln 576.5
defroster	orchard heater
deicer	oven
dielectric heater	plate heater
dielectric preheater	preheater
Dutch oven	radiant heater
electric blanket	radiator
electric heater	radio-frequency heater
electric pad	register
electronic heater	rivet heater
feed-water heater	sidearm heater
fireless heater	solar heater
foot warmer	space heater
forge	steam heater
gas heater	steam radiator
gas log	sun lamp
geyser [Brit]	superheater
heating pad	tire heater
heat lamp	warming house
high-frequency heater	warming pad
hot-water bag, hot-water bottle	warming pan
	water heater
hot-water heater	water oven
induction heater	

.33 **stoves, furnaces**

arc furnace	gas furnace
assay furnace	gas range
athanor	gas stove
Bessemer furnace	gasoline stove
blast furnace	induction furnace
boiler	kerosene stove
bottle-gas stove	kitchener [Brit]
box stove	kitchen range
butane stove	Norwegian stove
calefactor	oil furnace
coal furnace	oil stove
coal stove	open-hearth furnace
coke oven	potbellied stove
cook stove	Primus stove
crucible furnace	range
cupola furnace	resistance furnace
Dutch stove	reverberatory, reverbatory furnace
electric-arc furnace	
electric furnace	salamander, salamander stove
electric range	
electric stove	scorifier
foot stove	smelter
Franklin stove	

330. COOKING

.1 NOUNS **cooking, cookery, cuisine, culinary art;** home economics, domestic science, culinary science, catering, nutrition 309; baking, toasting, roasting, frying, searing, sautéing, boiling, simmering, stewing, basting, braising, poaching, shirring, barbecuing, steeping, brewing, grilling, broiling, pan-broiling; broil.

.2 **cook**, kitchener, culinarian, culinary artist; **chef**, *chef de cuisine* [Fr], chief cook; fry cook, short-order cook; **baker**, *boulanger* [Fr], pastrycook, pastry chef, *patissier* [Fr].

.3 **kitchen**, **cookroom**, cookery, **scullery**, cuisine; kitchenette; **galley**, caboose *or* camboose; cookhouse; **bakery**, bakehouse.

.4 VERBS **cook**, prepare food, prepare, do; boil, heat, stew, simmer, parboil, blanch; brew; poach, coddle; bake, fire, ovenbake; scallop; shirr; roast; toast; fry, griddle, pan; sauté, stir-fry; frizz, frizzle; sear, braise, brown; broil, grill, pan-broil; barbecue; fricassee; steam; devil; curry; baste; **do to a turn**, do to perfection.

.5 ADJS **cooking**, **culinary**, kitchen.

.6 **cooked**, heated, stewed, fried, barbecued, curried, fricasseed, deviled, sautéed, shirred, toasted; roasted, roast; broiled, grilled, pan-broiled; seared, braised, browned; boiled, simmered, parboiled; steamed; poached, coddled; baked, fired, oven-baked; scalloped.

.7 **done**, **well-done**, well-cooked, *bien cuit* [Fr], done to a turn *or* to perfection; overcooked, **overdone**; medium, medium-rare; doneness.

.8 **underdone**, undercooked, not done, **rare**, *saignant* [Fr]; sodden, fallen.

.9 **manners of cooking**

à blanc [Fr]	à la macédoine [Fr]
à la béarnaise [Fr]	à la Maintenon [Fr]
à la bonne femme [Fr]	à la maître d'hôtel [Fr]
à la bordelaise [Fr]	à la Marengo
à la bourgeoise [Fr]	à la Maryland
à la casserole	à la matelote [Fr]
à la Chateaubriand [Fr]	à l'américaine [Fr]
à la cocotte [Fr]	à la mode
à la coque [Fr]	à la mode de Caen [Fr]
à la Crécy [Fr]	à la napolitaine [Fr]
à la créole [Fr]	à la Newburg
à la Croissy [Fr]	à l'anglaise [Fr]
à la dauphine [Fr]	à la normande [Fr]
à la dauphinoise [Fr]	à la parisienne [Fr]
à la diable [Fr]	à la Périgord [Fr]
à la française [Fr]	à la polonaise [Fr]
à la godiveau [Fr]	à la printanière [Fr]
à la grecque [Fr]	à la ravigote [Fr]
à la jardinière [Fr]	à la reine [Fr]
à la julienne [Fr]	à la russe [Fr]
à la king	à la serviette [Fr]
à l'allemande [Fr]	à la Soubise [Fr]
à la lyonnaise [Fr]	à la suisse [Fr]

à la tartare [Fr]	au beurre fondu [Fr]
à l'aurore [Fr]	au beurre noire [Fr]
à la vinaigrette [Fr]	au beurre roux [Fr]
al burro [Ital]	au fromage [Fr]
al dente [Ital]	au gras [Fr]
à l'espagnole [Fr]	au gratin
à l'estragon [Fr]	au jus [Fr]
à l'etouffée [Fr]	au kirsch [Fr]
à l'italienne [Fr]	au maigre [Fr]
alla bolognese [Ital]	au naturel [Fr]
alla cacciatore [Ital]	au vert pré [Fr]
alla diavola [Ital]	au vin blanc [Fr]
alla fiorentina [Ital]	aux fines herbes [Fr]
alla marinara [Ital]	en casserole
alla milanese [Ital]	flambé
alla parmigiana [Ital]	fra diavolo [Ital]
alla pizzaiola [Ital]	in brodo [Ital]
alla romana [Ital]	maître d'hôtel
alla siciliana [Ital]	paprikás [Hung]
alla veneziana [Ital]	piccante [Ital]
al limone [Ital]	piccata [Ital]
all'italiana [Ital]	stroganoff
al Marsala [Ital]	thermidor
a piacere [Ital]	

.10 **cookers**

alcohol stove	fireless cooker
baker	fry-cooker
barbecue	galley stove
boiler	grill
broiler	hibachi
camp stove	infrared broiler
chafer	infrared cooker
chafing dish or pan	microwave oven
coffee maker	percolator
cook stove	pots, pans 193.8,9
corn popper	pressure cooker
Dutch oven	roaster
electric cooker	samovar
electric frying pan	stove 329.33
electric roaster	toaster
electric toaster	waffle iron
field range	waterless cooker

331. FUEL

.1 NOUNS **fuel**, firing, combustible *or* inflammable *or* flammable material, burnable, combustible, inflammable, flammable; coal 331.10; coke, charcoal, briquette, fireball; peat, turf; carbon, gas carbon; gasoline, kerosene 380.4; paraffin; natural gas; methane, ethane, propane, butane, pentane, hexane, heptane, octane, etc.; isooctane; benzine; alcohol, ethanol, methanol; fuel additive, dope, fuel dope; jet fuel, rocket fuel, propellant; **oil** 380; gas 401.

.2 **slack**, coal dust, coom *or* comb [both Brit dial], culm.

.3 **firewood**, stovewood, wood; **kindling**, kindlings, kindling wood; brush, brushwood; fagot, bavin [Brit]; log, backlog, yule log *or* yule clog [archaic].

.4 **lighter**, light, igniter, sparker; pocket lighter, cigar *or* cigarette lighter, butane lighter; **torch**, flambeau, taper, spill;

brand, **firebrand;** portfire; **flint,** flint and steel.

.5 **match,** lucifer; friction match, locofoco, safety match, vesuvian, vesta, fusee; Congreve, Congreve match.

.6 **tinder,** touchwood; **punk,** spunk, German tinder, amadou; tinder fungus; pyrotechnic sponge; tinderbox.

.7 **detonator,** exploder; **cap,** blasting cap, percussion cap, mercury fulminate, fulminating mercury; electric detonator *or* exploder; detonating powder; **primer,** priming; primacord; **fuse,** squib.

.8 VERBS **fuel,** fuel up, fill up, top off; refuel; coal, oil; **stoke, feed,** add fuel to the flame; detonate, explode, fulminate.

.9 ADJS **coaly,** carbonaceous, carboniferous, anthrac(o)–; anthracite, bituminous; lignitic, lign(o)– *or* ligni–.

.10 **coal**

anthracite, hard coal	grate coal
bituminous *or* soft coal	lignite, brown coal
blind coal	lump coal
broken coal	mustard-seed coal
buckwheat coal	nut coal
cannel, cannel coal	pea coal
chestnut coal	peat
egg coal	sea coal
flaxseed coal	steamboat coal
glance coal	stove coal

.11 **fuses**

base fuse	friction fuse
chemical fuse	point fuse
concussion *or* percussion fuse	proximity fuse
	time fuse
detonating fuse	variable-time *or* VT fuse
electric fuse	

332. INCOMBUSTIBILITY

.1 NOUNS **incombustibility, uninflammability,** noninflammability, **nonflammability;** unburnableness.

.2 **extinguishing,** extinguishment, extinction, **quenching,** dousing [informal], **snuffing,** putting out; **choking, damping, stifling, smothering,** smotheration; controlling; fire fighting; going out, dying, burning out, flame-out, burnout.

.3 **extinguisher, fire extinguisher;** fire apparatus, fire engine, hook-and-ladder, ladder truck; ladder pipe, snorkel, deluge set, deck gun, water cannon [Brit], pumper, super-pumper; **foam,** carbon-dioxide foam, Foamite, foam extinguisher; dry-powder extinguisher; carbon tetrachloride, carbon tet; water, soda, acid, wet blanket; sprinkler, automatic sprinkler, sprinkler system, sprinkler head; hydrant, fire hydrant, fireplug; fire hose.

.4 **fire fighter, fireman,** fire-eater [informal]; forest fire fighter, fire warden, fire-chaser, smokechaser, smokejumper; volunteer fireman, vamp [informal]; fire department, fire brigade.

.5 **fireproofing,** fire resistance; fireproof *or* fire-resistant *or* fire-resisting *or* fire-resistive *or* fire-retardant material, fire retardant; asbestos; amianthus, earth flax, mountain flax; asbestos curtain, fire wall; fire break, fire line.

.6 VERBS **fireproof,** flameproof.

.7 **extinguish, put out, quench,** out, douse [informal], **snuff,** snuff out, blow out, stamp out; **choke, damp, smother, stifle,** slack.

.8 **burn out, go out, die,** die out *or* away; fizzle *or* fizzle out [both informal]; flame out.

.9 ADJS **incombustible, uninflammable,** noninflammable, **nonflammable,** unburnable; asbestine, asbestic; amianthine.

.10 **fireproof, flameproof,** fireproofed, fire-retarded, fire-resisting *or* -resistant *or* -resistive, fire-retardant.

.11 **extinguished,** quenched, snuffed, **out.**

333. COLD

.1 NOUNS **cold, coldness; coolness,** coolth, freshness; low temperature, drop *or* decrease in temperature; **chilliness; chill, nip,** sharp air; **crispness,** briskness, nippiness; **frigidity, iciness,** frostiness, extreme *or* intense cold, gelidity, algidity; **rawness,** bleakness, keenness, sharpness, bitterness, severity, inclemency, rigor, "a hard, dull bitterness of cold" [Whittier]; cool; freezing point; cryology; cryogenics; absolute zero.

.2 (sensation of cold) **chill,** chilliness, chilling; shivering, **shivers, cold shivers,** didders [Brit dial], dithers, chattering of the teeth; creeps, **cold creeps** [informal]; **gooseflesh, goose pimples,** goose *or* duck bumps [informal], horripilation; **frostbite, chilblains,** kibe, cryopathy; ache, aching.

.3 **cold weather,** bleak weather, raw weather, bitter weather, wintry weather, **freezing weather,** zero weather, subzero weather; **cold wave,** snap, **cold snap; freeze,** frost; winter, depth of winter, hard winter; "The ways deep and the weather sharp, / The very dead of winter" [T. S. Eliot]; "When icicles hang by the wall" [Shakespeare]; wintry wind 403.8.

.4 (cold place) Siberia, Novaya Zemlya, Alaska, Iceland, the Hebrides, Greenland, "Greenland's icy mountains" [Reginald Heber], the Yukon, Tierra del Fuego, Lower Slobbovia [Al Capp]; North Pole, South Pole; Frigid Zones; the Arctic, Arctic Circle or Zone; Antarctica, the Antarctic; Antarctic Circle or Zone; tundra.

.5 **ice**, frozen water; **ice needle** or **crystal**; **icicle**, iceshockle [Brit dial]; cryosphere; ice sheet, ice field, ice barrier, ice front; **floe, ice floe**, ice island, ice raft, ice pack; ice foot, ice belt; shelf ice, pack ice; **iceberg**, berg, growler; calf; snowberg; **icecap**, jokul [Iceland]; ice pinnacle, serac, nieve penitente; **glacier**, glacieret, glaciation, glacio–, ice dike, "motionless torrents, silent cataracts" [Coleridge]; piedmont glacier; icefall; ice banner; ice cave; **sleet**, glaze, glazed frost; snow ice; névé, granular snow, firn; ground ice, anchor ice, frazil; lolly; sludge, slob; ice cubes; Dry Ice; icequake; ice storm, freezing rain.

.6 **hail**, hailstone; soft hail, graupel; **hailstorm**.

.7 **frost**, Jack Frost; **hoarfrost**, hoar, rime, rime frost, white frost; black frost; hard frost, sharp frost; killing frost; frost smoke; frost line.

.8 **snow**, chio– or chion(o)–; granular snow, corn snow, spring corn, spring snow, powder snow, wet snow; "the frolic architecture of the snow" [Emerson]; "a pure and grandfather moss" [Dylan Thomas]; **snowfall**, "feather'd rain" [William Strode], "the whitening shower" [James Thomson]; **snowstorm**, snow blast, snow squall, snow flurry, flurry, blizzard; **snowflake**, snow-crystal, flake, crystal; snow dust; **snowdrift**, snowbank, snow wreath [Brit dial], snow roller, driven snow; snowcap; snow banner; snow blanket; snow bed, snowfield, mantle of snow; snowscape; snowland; snowshed; snow line; snowball, snowman; snowslide, snowslip, avalanche; snow slush, **slush**, slosh; snowbridge; snow fence; snowhouse, igloo; mogul.

.9 VERBS **be cold**, grow cold, lose heat; **shiver, quiver**, quake, shake, tremble, shudder, didder [Brit dial], dither; **chatter; chill**, have a chill, have the cold shivers; **freeze**, freeze to death, freeze one's balls off [informal], perish with cold, horripilate, have goose pimples, have goose or duck bumps [informal]; have chilblains.

.10 (make cold) **chill**, chill to the bone or

marrow, make one shiver, make one's teeth chatter; **nip**, bite, cut, **pierce**, penetrate, go through or right through; **freeze** 334.11; frost, frostbite; numb, benumb; **refrigerate** 334.10.

.11 **hail, sleet, snow**; snow in; snow under; **frost**, ice, ice up, ice over.

.12 ADJS **cool**, coolish, temperate; **chill, chilly**, parky [Brit slang]; **fresh**, bracing, **invigorating**, stimulating; cool as a cucumber.

.13 **unheated**, unwarmed; unmelted, unthawed.

.14 **cold**, cry(o)– or kryo–, frigo–, psychro–; **crisp, brisk**, nipping, **nippy, snappy** [informal], **raw, bleak, keen, sharp**, bitter, biting, pinching, cutting, **piercing**, penetrating, inclement, severe, rigorous; snowcold; sleety; slushy; **icy**, icelike, **ice-cold**, glacial, ice-encrusted; cryospheric; supercooled; **frigid**, bitter or bitterly cold, gelid, algid; below zero, subzero; **freezing**, freezing cold, numbing; **wintry**, wintery, winterlike, winterbound, hiemal, brumal, hibernal; **arctic**, Siberian, boreal, hyperborean; stone-cold, cold as death, cold as ice, cold as marble, cold as charity, cold as a welldigger's ass, cold as a witch's tit or kiss, cold enough to freeze the tail or balls off a brass monkey, "cold as the north side of a gravestone in winter" [anon], cold as a bastard or bitch, colder than hell or the deuce or the devil.

.15 (feeling cold) **cold, cool, chilly; shivering**, shivery, shaky, dithery; algid, aguish, aguey; chattering, with chattering teeth; **frozen** 334.14, half-frozen, frozen to death, chilled to the bone, blue with cold, figé de froid [Fr], so cold one could spit ice cubes.

.16 **frosty**, frostlike; **frosted**, frost-beaded, frost-covered, frost-chequered, rimed, **hoary**, hoar-frosted, rime-frosted; frost-riven, frost-rent; frosty-faced, frosty-whiskered; frostbound, frost-fettered.

.17 **snowy**, snowlike, niveous, nival; snowblown, snow-drifted, **snow-driven; snow-covered**, snow-clad, snow-mantled, snow-robed, snow-blanketed, snow-sprinkled, snow-lined, snow-encircled, snow-laden, snow-loaded, snow-hung; **snow-capped**, snow-crested, snow-crowned, snow-tipped, snow-topped; snow-bearded; snow-feathered; snow-still.

.18 **frozen out** or **in, snowbound**, snowed-in, **icebound**.

.19 **cold-blooded**, heterothermic, poikilothermic; cryogenic; cryological.

334. REFRIGERATION

(reduction of temperature)

.1 NOUNS **refrigeration**, infrigidation, reduction of temperature; **cooling, chilling; freezing,** glacification, glaciation, congelation, congealment; refreezing, regelation; mechanical refrigeration, electric refrigeration, electronic refrigeration, gas refrigeration; food freezing, quick freezing, deep freezing, sharp freezing, blast freezing, dehydrofreezing; adiabatic expansion, adiabatic absorption, adiabatic demagnetization; cryogenics; super-cooling; **air conditioning,** air cooling.

.2 refrigeration anesthesia, crymoanesthesia, hypothermia *or* hypothermy; crymotherapy, cryo-aerotherapy; cold cautery, cryocautery; cryopathy.

.3 **cooler,** chiller; water cooler, air cooler; ventilator 402.10; fan 403.21; surface cooler; ice cube, ice pail *or* bucket, wine cooler; ice bag, ice pack, cold pack.

.4 **refrigerator,** refrigeratory, **icebox,** ice chest; Frigidaire, fridge [informal], electric refrigerator, electronic refrigerator, gas refrigerator; refrigerator car, refrigerator truck, reefer [informal]; freezer ship.

.5 **freezer, deep freeze,** deep-freezer, quick-freezer, sharp-freezer; ice-cream freezer; ice machine, ice-cube machine, freezing machine, refrigerating machine *or* engine; **ice plant,** icehouse, refrigerating plant.

.6 **cold storage;** frozen-food locker, locker, freezer locker, locker plant; frigidarium; coolhouse; coolerman.

.7 (cooling agent) **coolant; refrigerant;** cryogen; ice, Dry Ice, ice cubes; freezing mixture, liquid air, ammonia, carbon dioxide, Freon, ether; ethyl chloride; liquid air, liquid oxygen *or* lox, liquid nitrogen, liquid helium, etc.

.8 antifreeze, alcohol, ethylene glycol.

.9 refrigerating engineering, refrigerating engineer.

.10 VERBS **refrigerate,** infrigidate; **cool, chill;** refresh, freshen; ice, ice-cool; water-cool, air-cool; **air-condition;** ventilate 402.11.

.11 **freeze** 333.9,10, ice, glacify, glaciate, congeal; **deep-freeze,** quick-freeze, sharp-freeze, blast-freeze; freeze solid; **nip,** blight, blast; refreeze, regelate.

.12 ADJS **refrigerative,** refrigeratory, refrigerant, frigorific(al), algific; **cooling, chilling; freezing,** congealing; quick-freezing, deep-freezing, sharp-freezing, blast-freezing; freezable, glaciable.

.13 **cooled, chilled; air-conditioned;** iced, ice-cooled; air-cooled, water-cooled; super-cooled.

.14 **frozen,** frozen solid, glacial, gelid, congealed; **icy,** ice-cold, icy-cold, ice, icelike; deep-frozen, quick-frozen, sharp-frozen, blast-frozen; frostbitten, frostnipped.

.15 antifreeze, antifreezing.

335. LIGHT

.1 NOUNS **light,** phot(o)–, lumin(o)– *or* lumini–; radiant *or* luminous energy, visible radiation, radiation in the visible spectrum, **illumination, radiation, radiance** *or* radiancy, irradiance *or* irradiancy, irradiation, emanation; "God's first creature" [Francis Bacon], "God's eldest daughter" [Thomas Fuller, D.D.], "offspring of Heav'n firstborn" [Milton], "the first of painters" [Emerson], "the prime work of God" [Milton], "the white radiance of eternity" [Shelley]; highlight; sidelight; photosensitivity; light source 336.

.2 **shine,** shininess, **luster, sheen, gloss,** glint; **glow, gleam,** flush, sunset glow; **incandescence,** candescence; shining light; afterglow; skylight, air glow.

.3 **lightness, luminousness,** luminosity; **lucidity,** lucence *or* lucency, translucence *or* translucency.

.4 **brightness, brilliance** *or* brilliancy, **splendor,** radiant splendor, **glory, radiance** *or* radiancy, resplendence *or* resplendency, **vividness,** flamboyance; effulgence, refulgence *or* refulgency, fulgor; **glare,** blaze; bright light, brilliant light, blazing light, glaring light, dazzling light, blinding light; "the blaze of noon" [Milton]; streaming light, flood of light, burst of light.

.5 **ray,** radiation, **beam, gleam,** leam [Scot], **stream, streak, pencil, patch,** ray of light, beam of light, etc.; ribbon, ribbon of light, streamer, stream of light; violet ray, ultraviolet ray, infrared ray, X ray, gamma ray, invisible radiation; actinic ray *or* light, actinism; atomic beam, atomic ray; solar rays; radiorays 327.3; photon.

.6 **flash, blaze, flare, flame, gleam, glint, glance;** blaze *or* flash *or* gleam of light; solar flare, solar prominence, facula; Bailey's beads.

.7 **glitter, glimmer, shimmer, twinkle, blink; sparkle,** spark; **scintillation,** scintilla; coruscation; **glisten,** glister, spangle, tinsel, glittering, glimmering, shimmering, twinkling; "shining from shook foil" [G. M. Hopkins]; stroboscopic light, blinking; firefly, glowworm.

.8 **flicker, flutter, dance, quiver;** flickering, fluttering, dancing, quivering, lambency; wavering *or* flickering light, play, play of light, dancing *or* glancing light; light show; "the lambent easy light" [Dryden].

.9 **reflection,** reflectance; reflected *or* incident light, albedo; blink, iceblink, ice sky, snowblink, waterblink, water sky.

.10 **daylight,** dayshine, day glow, light of day; day, daytime, daytide; **sunlight, sunshine,** shine; noonlight, midday sun, noonday *or* noontide light; broad day *or* daylight, full sun; dusk, twilight 134.3; dawn 133.3,4; sunburst, sunbreak; **sunbeam,** sun spark, ray of sunshine; green flash.

.11 **moonlight, moonshine, moonglow; moonbeam.**

.12 **starlight,** starshine; earthshine.

.13 **luminescence,** autoluminescence, cathode luminescence, chemiluminescence *or* chemicoluminescence, crystalloluminescence, electroluminescence, photoluminescence, radioluminescence, thermoluminescence, triboluminescence; bioluminescence, noctiluscence; **fluorescence,** fluor(o)– *or* fluori–, tribofluorescence; **phosphorescence,** tribophosphorescence; luciferin, luciferase; phosphor, luminophor; ignis fatuus, will-o'-the-wisp, will-with-the-wisp, wisp, jack-o'-lantern, marshfire; friar's lantern; fata morgana; fox fire; St. Elmo's light *or* fire, witch fire, corposant; double corposant; –escence.

.14 **halo, nimbus,** aura, **aureole,** circle, ring, glory; **rainbow,** irid(o)–; solar halo, lunar halo, ring around the sun *or* moon; **corona,** solar corona, lunar corona; parhelion, parhelic circle *or* ring, mock sun, sun dog; anthelion, antisun, countersun; paraselene, mock moon, moon dog.

.15 (nebulous light) nebula 375.7; zodiacal light, Gegenschein, counterglow.

.16 polar lights, **aurora; northern lights, aurora borealis,** merry dancers; southern lights, **aurora australis;** aurora polaris; aurora glory; streamer *or* curtain *or* arch aurora; polar ray.

.17 **lightning, flash** *or* **stroke of lightning,** fulguration, fulmination, bolt, **bolt of lightning,** bolt from the blue, **thunderbolt,** thunderstroke, thunderball, fireball, firebolt, levin bolt *or* brand; "flying flame" [Tennyson], "the lightning's gleaming rod" [Joaquin Miller], "oak-cleaving thunderbolts" [Shakespeare]; fork *or* forked lightning, chain lightning, globular *or* ball lightning, summer *or* heat lightning, sheet lightning, dark lightning; Jupiter Fulgur *or* Fulminator; Thor.

.18 **iridescence,** opalescence, nacreousness, pearliness; **rainbow;** nacre, mother-of-pearl; nacreous *or* mother-of-pearl cloud.

.19 **lighting, illumination,** enlightenment; radiation, irradiation; tonality; light and shade, black and white, chiaroscuro, clairobscure, contrast, highlights; gaslighting, electric lighting, incandescent lighting, fluorescent lighting, glow lighting; arc lighting; direct lighting, indirect lighting; floodlighting, overhead lighting, stage lighting, decorative lighting, festoon lighting, strip lighting, spot lighting, diffused lighting, cove lighting.

.20 **illuminant,** luminant; electricity; gas, illuminating gas; oil, petroleum, benzine; gasoline, petrol [Brit]; kerosene, paraffin [Brit], coal oil; light source 336.

.21 (measurement of light) **candle power,** luminous intensity, luminous power, luminous flux, flux, intensity, light; quantum, **light quantum, photon;** unit of light, unit of flux; candle, international candle, British candle, Hefner candle; foot-candle, candle-foot; decimal candle, *bougie décimale* [Fr]; lux, candle-meter, lumen meter, lumeter, lumen, candle lumen; candle-hour, lamp-hour, lumen-hour; **exposure meter,** light meter, ASA scale, Scheiner scale.

.22 (science of light) photics, photology, photometry; **optics,** geometrical optics, physical optics; dioptrics, catoptrics; actinology, actinometry; heliology, heliometry, heliography.

.23 VERBS **shine,** shine forth, **burn, give light,** incandesce; **glow, beam, gleam,** glint, luster, glance; **flash, flare, blaze, flame,** fulgurate; **radiate,** shoot, shoot out rays, send out rays; spread *or* diffuse light; be bright, shine brightly, beacon; **glare;** daze, blind, dazzle, bedazzle.

.24 **glitter, glimmer, shimmer, twinkle, blink,** spangle, tinsel, coruscate; **sparkle,** spark, **scintillate; glisten,** glister, glisk [Scot].

.25 **flicker,** bicker, **flutter, waver, dance,** play, quiver.

.26 **luminesce,** phosphoresce, fluoresce; iridesce, opalesce.

.27 **grow light,** grow bright, light, **lighten,** brighten; dawn, break.

.28 **illuminate,** illumine, illume, luminate, **light, light up, lighten,** enlighten, brighten, brighten up, irradiate; bathe *or* flood with light; relumine, relume; **shed light upon,** cast *or* throw light upon, shed luster on, shine upon, overshine; spot-light, highlight; floodlight; beacon.

.29 **strike a light, light, turn** or **switch on the light,** open the light [informal], make a light, shine a light.

.30 ADJS **luminous,** luminant, luminative, lu-minificent, luminiferous, luciferous or lu-cific [both archaic], luciform, illuminant; **incandescent,** candescent; **lustrous,** ori-ent; **radiant,** irradiative, radio–; **shining,** shiny, burning, lamping, streaming; **beam-ing,** beamy; **gleaming,** gleamy, glinting; **glowing,** aglow, suffused, blushing, flush-ing; rutilant, rutilous; **sunny, sunshiny,** bright and sunny, light as day; starry, star-like, starbright.

.31 **light,** lightish, lightsome; **lucid,** lucent, lu-culent, relucent; translucent, translucid, pellucid, diaphanous, transparent; **clear,** serene; **cloudless,** unclouded, unobscured.

.32 **bright, brilliant, vivid, splendid,** splendor-ous, splendent, **resplendent,** bright and shining; fulgid [archaic], fulgent, efful-gent, refulgent; **flamboyant,** flaming; **glar-ing,** glary, garish; **dazzling,** bedazzling, blinding.

.33 **shiny,** shining, **lustrous, glossy,** glassy, *glacé* [Fr], **sheeny, polished,** burnished, shined.

.34 **flashing,** flashy, **blazing, flaming, flaring,** burning, fulgurant, fulgurating; aflame, ablaze; meteoric.

.35 **glittering, glimmering, shimmering, twin-kling, blinking, glistening,** glistering; glit-tery, glimmery, glimmerous, shimmery, twinkly, blinky, spangly, tinselly; **spar-kling, scintillating,** scintillant, scintilles-cent, coruscating, coruscant.

.36 **flickering,** bickering, **fluttering, wavering,** dancing, playing, quivering, lambent; flickery, flicky [informal], aflicker, flut-tery, wavery, quivery; blinking, flashing, stroboscopic.

.37 **iridescent,** opalescent, nacreous, pearly, pearl-like; rainbowlike.

.38 **luminescent,** photogenic; electrolumines-cent, photoluminescent, radiolumines-cent, thermoluminescent, tribolumines-cent; chemiluminescent, chemicolumines-cent; **phosphorescent,** tribophospho-rescent; **fluorescent,** tribofluorescent; autoluminescent, self-luminous, self-lumi-nescent; bioluminescent, noctilucent; lu-minal; –escent.

.39 **illuminated,** luminous, **lightened,** enlight-ened, brightened, **lighted,** lit, **lit up,** flooded or bathed with light; irradiated, irradiate; **alight,** aglow, suffused with

light, ablaze, in a blaze; lamplit, lantern-lit, candlelit, torchlit, gaslit, firelit; sunlit, moonlit, starlit; spangled, bespangled, tinseled, studded; star-spangled, star-stud-ded.

.40 **illuminating,** illumining, **lighting, lighten-ing,** enlightening, brightening.

.41 **luminary,** lumi–, photic; photologic(al), photometric(al); heliological, helio-graphic; actinic, photoactinic, actin(o)– or actini–; catoptric(al); luminal.

.42 **photosensitive;** photophobic; phototrop-ic.

336. LIGHT SOURCE

.1 NOUNS **light source,** source of light, **lumi-nary,** illuminator, luminant, illuminant, incandescent body or point, **light,** glim; **lamp,** light bulb, electric light bulb, lan-tern, candle, taper, torch, flame; match; phos–; "a lamp unto my feet, and a light unto my path" [Bible]; fire 328.13; sun, moon, stars 375.4.

.2 **candle,** taper; dip, farthing dip, tallow dip; tallow candle; wax candle, bougie; bayberry candle; rush candle, rushlight; corpse candle; votary candle.

.3 **torch,** flaming torch, flambeau, cresset, link [archaic]; **flare,** signal flare, fusee.

.4 **traffic light,** stop-and-go light; stop or red light, go or green light, caution or amber light.

.5 **firefly,** lightning bug, lampyrid, **glow-worm,** fireworm; fire beetle; lantern fly, candle fly; luciferin, luciferase; phosphor, luminophor.

.6 **chandelier,** gasolier, electrolier, hanging or ceiling fixture, luster; corona, corona lucis, crown, circlet.

.7 **wick,** taper; candlewick, lampwick.

.8 **lamps, lights**

aphlogistic lamp	Coleman lantern
arc lamp or light	cresset
Argand lamp	dark lantern
argon lamp	Davy lamp
baby spotlight or spot	daylight lamp
barn lantern	desk lamp or light
battery lamp	discharge lamp
battle lantern	electric-arc lamp
bed lamp	electric candle
bridge lamp	electric-discharge
broadside	lamp or tube
bull's-eye, bull's-eye	electric light or lamp
lantern	electric torch
calcium lamp	filament lamp
candle	Finsen light or lamp
candlelight	flame lamp
carbon light or lamp	flashbulb
Carcel lamp	flasher
carriage lamp	flashgun
Chinese lantern	flash lamp

flashlight
floodlight, flood lamp
floor lamp
fluorescent light or tube
focus lamp
fog light or lamp
footlight
gaslight, gas lamp
gasoline lantern
glow light or lamp
headlight, head lamp
Hefner lamp
high-intensity lamp
hurricane lamp
incandescent electric lamp
incandescent light or lamp
infrared lamp
instrument lamp or light
jack-o'-lantern
Japanese lantern
klieg light
lampion [archaic]
lamplet
lantern
light bulb
limelight
magic lantern
magnetite arc lamp
mercury-arc lamp, mercury lamp
mercury-vapor lamp
miner's lamp
moderator lamp
Moore light or lamp or tube
navigation light
neon light or lamp or tube
Nernst lamp
night light
oil lamp
osmium lamp

photoflash lamp
photoflood lamp
pilot light or lamp
police lantern
projector lamp
quartz lamp
railroad lantern
reading lamp
riding light
running light
rushlight
safety lamp
searchlight, search lamp
searchlight lantern
Sheringham daylight lamp
shunt lamp
side lamp
side light
sodium-vapor lamp, sodium lamp
spotlight, spot
stop light
strobe, strobe light, strobotron
stroboscope
student lamp
sun arc, sun spot
sun burner, sunlight burner
sun lamp
table lamp
taillight, tail lamp
tantalum lamp
torch, torch light
tornado lantern or lamp
tungsten lamp
ultraviolet lamp, uviol lamp
vanity lamp
vapor lamp
veilleuse [Fr]
wolfram lamp
zircon light or lamp

.9 beacons, signal lights

balefire
beacon fire
flare, flare-up, flare-up light
fusee
lighthouse
lightship
magnesium flare
occulting light
pharos

rocket
signal beacon
signal flare
signal lamp
signal lantern
signal rocket
skyrocket
Very flare
watch fire

.10 aviation beacons

airport beacon
airway beacon
anchor light
approach light
blinker light
boundary light
ceiling light or projector
course light
fixed light
flare path
flashing light

high-intensity runway approach light
identification light
landing-direction light
landing light
landmark beacon
Lindbergh light
marker, marker beacon
navigation light
obstruction light
position light

runway light

sequence flasher

.11 light holders

bracket
candelabrum, candelabra
candlestand
candlestick
chandelier
gas fixture
girandole
lamp holder

lamp socket
lampstand
light fixture
light socket
sconce
torch holder
torch staff
wall bracket

.12 burners

Argand burner
fishtail burner
gas burner
gas jet, jet

gas mantle, incandescent mantle, mantle
Welsbach mantle

337. DARKNESS, DIMNESS

.1 NOUNS **darkness, dark, lightlessness; obscurity,** obscure, tenebrosity, tenebrousness; **night** 134.4, dead of night, deep night; sunlessness, moonlessness, starlessness; **pitch-darkness,** pitch-blackness, pitchy darkness, utter or thick or total darkness, intense darkness, velvet darkness, Cimmerian or Stygian or Egyptian darkness, Erebus; "obscure darkness" [Bible], "the palpable obscure" [Milton], "darkness visible" [Milton], "a fabulous, formless darkness" [Yeats], "the suit of night" [Shakespeare], "darkness which may be felt" [Bible]; **blackness,** swarthiness 365.2.

.2 gloom, gloominess, somberness, sombrousness, somber; lowering, lower.

.3 shadow, shade, shadiness, sci(a)– or scio– or skia–; umbra, umbrage, umbrageousness; "shadows numberless" [Keats]; thick or dark shade, gloom; mere shadow, "the shadow of a shade" [Aeschylus]; penumbra; silhouette; skiagram, skiagraph.

.4 darkishness, darksomeness, **duskiness,** duskness; **murkiness, murk; dimness,** dim; **semidarkness,** semidark, partial darkness, bad light, dim light, half-light, demi-jour [Fr]; gloaming, **dusk,** twilight 133.4, 134.3.

.5 dullness, flatness, lifelessness, **drabness, deadness,** somberness, **lackluster, lusterlessness,** lack of sparkle or sheen; mat, mat finish.

.6 darkening, dimming; obscuration, obscurement, obumbration, obfuscation; eclipsing, occulting, blocking the light; **shadowing, shading,** overshadowing, overshading, overshadowment, **clouding,** overclouding, obnubilation, gathering of the clouds, overcast; blackening 365.5; extinguishment 332.2.

.7 **blackout,** dimout, brownout.

.8 **eclipse,** occultation; total eclipse, partial eclipse, central eclipse, annular eclipse; solar eclipse, lunar eclipse.

.9 VERBS **darken,** bedarken; **obscure,** obfuscate, obumbrate; **eclipse,** occult, occultate, block the light; **black out,** brown out; black, brown; blot out; **overcast,** darken over; **shadow, shade,** cast a shadow, spread a shadow or shade over, encompass with shadow, overshadow; **cloud,** becloud, encloud, cloud over, .overcloud, obnubilate; gloom, begloom, somber, cast a gloom over, murk; **dim,** bedim, dim out; blacken 365.7.

.10 **dull,** mat, deaden; **tone down.**

.11 turn or switch off the light, close the light [informal]; extinguish 332.7.

.12 **grow dark, darken,** darkle, lower; gloom [archaic], gloam [Scot]; dusk; **dim, grow dim.**

.13 ADJS **dark, black,** darksome, darkling; **lightless,** beamless, rayless, unlighted, **unilluminated,** unlit; **obscure,** caliginous, obscured, obfuscated, eclipsed, occulted, clothed or shrouded or veiled or cloaked or mantled in darkness; tenebrous, tenebrific, tenebrious, tenebrose; **pitch-dark,** pitch-black, pitchy, dark as pitch, "dark as a wolf's mouth" [Sir Walter Scott], dark as the inside of a black cat; ebon, ebony; night-dark, night-black, dark or black as night; night-clad, night-cloaked, night-enshrouded, night-mantled, night-veiled, night-hid, night-filled; sunless, moonless, starless; black 365.8.

.14 **gloomy,** gloomful [archaic], glooming, dark and gloomy, Acheronian, Acherontic, **somber,** sombrous; lowering; **funereal;** Cimmerian, Stygian; stormy, cloudy, clouded, overcast; ill-lighted, ill-lit.

.15 **darkish,** darksome, **semidark; dusky,** dusk; subfuscous, subfusc; **murky,** murksome, murk [archaic]; **dim,** dimmish, dimpsy [Brit dial]; dark-colored 365.9.

.16 **shadowy, shady,** shaded, darkling, umbral, umbrageous; overshadowed, overshaded, obumbrate, obumbrated; penumbral.

.17 **lackluster, lusterless; dull, dead,** deadened, **lifeless,** somber, drab, wan, **flat,** mat.

.18 obscuring, obscurant.

.19 ADVS **in the dark,** darkling, in darkness; in the night, in the dark of night, in the dead of night, at or by night.

338. SHADE

(a thing that shades)

.1 NOUNS **shade,** shader, **screen, light shield, curtain,** drape, drapery, blind, veil; **awning,** sunblind [Brit]; **sunshade,** parasol, **umbrella,** beach umbrella; **cover** 228.2; shadow 337.3.

.2 **eyeshade,** eyeshield, visor; goggles, colored spectacles, smoked glasses, dark glasses, **sunglasses,** shades [slang].

.3 **lamp shade;** moonshade; globe, light globe.

.4 **light filter,** filter, diffusing screen; smoked glass, frosted glass, ground glass; stained glass; butterfly; gelatin filter, Celluloid filter; frosted lens; lens hood; sunscreen.

.5 VERBS **shade, screen,** veil, curtain, shutter, draw the curtains, put up or close the shutters; cover 228.19; overshadow 337.9.

.6 ADJS **shading, screening,** veiling, curtaining; covering 228.34.

.7 **shaded, screened,** veiled, curtained; sunproof; shady 337.16.

.8 **shades**

awning	roof 228.6,39
baldacchino, baldachin	sash curtain
	screen
bamboo shade or screen	shade tree
belvedere	shutter
blind	summerhouse
brise-soleil [Fr]	sunbonnet
canopy	sun hat
curtain	sun helmet
gazebo	sunshade
hat 231.25,59	tent 228.8,40
jalousie	topee
lamp shade	umbrella 228.7
occulter, occulting screen	veil
parasol	venetian blind
persienne	visor
pith helmet	window curtain
portiere	window screen
roller blind or shade	window shade
	window shutter

339. TRANSPARENCY

.1 NOUNS **transparency,** transparence, transpicuousness, show-through, transmission or admission of light; **lucidity,** pellucidity, **clearness, clarity,** limpidity; nonopacity, uncloudedness; **crystallinity,** crystal-clearness; **glassiness,** glasslikeness, vitreousness, vitrescence; vitreosity, hyalescence; **diaphanousness,** diaphaneity, sheerness, thinness, **gossameriness,** filminess, gauziness.

.2 transparent substance, diaphane; **glass,** glassware, glasswork; vitrics; stemware;

pane, windowpane, light, windowlight, shopwindow; vitrine; showcase, display case; watch crystal or glass.

.3 VERBS be transparent, show through.

.4 ADJS **transparent**, transpicuous, light-pervious; see-through, peekaboo, revealing; **lucid**, pellucid, **clear**, limpid; nonopaque, unclouded, **crystalline**, crystal, **crystal-clear**, clear as crystal; **diaphanous**, diaphane [archaic], sheer, thin; **gossamer**, gossamery, filmy, gauzy.

.5 **glass, glassy**, glasslike, clear as glass, vitric, vitreous, vitriform, hyaline, hyalescent; hyalinocrystalline.

.6 **transparent things, translucent things**

aquamarine	gossamer
beryl	hyaline
carnelian	hyalite
cellophane	isinglass
Celluloid	Lucite
chalcedony	mica
chiffon	moonstone
chrysolite	morganite
chrysoprase	onionskin
citrine	Perspex
clear plastic	plastic wrap
Clearsite	Plexiglas
clear varnish or wax or shellac	quartz
	Saran wrap
crystal	sheers
Crystalite	tissue
diamond	tissue paper
diaphane	veil
emerald	voile
fixative varnish	water
golden beryl	window

.7 **glass**

agate glass	Lalique glass
blown glass	laminated glass, laminated safety glass
bottle glass	
bullet-resisting glass	lead glass
camphor glass	milk glass
carnival glass	opal glass
Cel-o-Glass	opaline
CM-glass	optical glass
coralene	ornamental glass
cranberry glass	Orrefors glass
CR-glass	photosensitive glass
crown glass	plastic glass
cryolite glass	plate glass
crystal, crystal glass	porcelain glass
custard glass	pressed glass
cut glass	prism glass
end-of-day glass	Pyrex
etched glass	quartz glass
fiber glass	rhinestone
flashed glass	safety glass
flat glass	Sandwich glass
flint glass	satin glass
float glass	sheet glass
Fostoria	stained glass
frosted glass	Steuben glass
fused quartz	Swedish glass
glass bead	tempered glass, tempered safety glass
glass brick	
ground glass	uranium glass
hobnail glass	Venetian glass

Vitaglass	window glass
vitreous silica	wire or wired glass
Waterford glass	

340. SEMITRANSPARENCY

.1 NOUNS **semitransparency**, semipellucidity, semidiaphaneity; semiopacity.

.2 **translucence, translucency**, lucence, lucency, translucidity, pellucidity, lucidity; transmission or admission of light.

.3 VERBS **frost**, frost over.

.4 ADJS **semitransparent**, semipellucid, semidiaphanous, semiopaque; frosty, frosted.

.5 **translucent**, lucent, translucid, lucid, pellucid; semitranslucent, semipellucid.

341. OPAQUENESS

.1 NOUNS **opaqueness**, opacity, intransparency, nontranslucency, imperviousness to light, adiaphanousness; roil, roiledness, turbidity, turbidness; cloudiness; **darkness, obscurity, dimness** 337; opaque.

.2 VERBS opaque, **darken, obscure** 337.9; **cloud**, becloud.

.3 ADJS **opaque**, intransparent, nontranslucent, adiaphanous, impervious to light; **dark, obscure** 337.13, **cloudy**, roiled, roily, grumly [Scot], turbid.

342. ELECTRICITY

.1 NOUNS **electricity**, electr(o)–, pyroelectricity, actinoelectricity, photoelectricity, ferroelectricity, piezoelectricity, thermoelectricity, faradic electricity, galvanic electricity, voltaic electricity, animal electricity, bioelectricity, neuroelectricity, organic electricity, atmospheric electricity; static electricity, friction electricity, triboelectricity, dynamic or current electricity; voltaism, galvanism; magnetic electricity, magnetoelectricity; positive electricity, negative electricity.

.2 **electric current**, electric stream or flow, rheo–, juice [informal]; direct current, DC, pulsating direct current; alternating current, AC; free alternating current, single-phase alternating current, three-phase alternating current; delta current; multiphase current, rotary current; high-frequency current, low-frequency current; galvanic current, voltaic current; magnetizing current, exciting current; induced current, induction current; active current, watt current; reactive current, wattless or idle current; absorption current, conduction current, convection current, displacement current, dielectric displacement current, ionization current, oscillating current, thermoelectric current, thermionic current, emission current; stray current, eddy current; cycle.

.3 **electric field,** static field, electrostatic field; tube of electric force, electrostatic tube of force; **magnetic field,** magnetic field of currents; **electromagnetic field;** variable field.

.4 **circuit,** path; galvanic circuit *or* circle, complete circuit, loop, closed circuit, live circuit, hot circuit; open *or* broken circuit, break, dead circuit; branch *or* lateral circuit, leg; multiple circuit *or* connection, multiple series, series multiple *or* parallel; multiplex circuit; magnetic circuit, circuital field, vector field; printed circuit, microcircuit; **short circuit, short.**

.5 **charge,** electric charge, unit quantity; live wire.

.6 **discharge,** electric discharge; aperiodic discharge, arc discharge, brush discharge, disruptive discharge, electrodeless discharge, glow discharge, oscillatory discharge, silent discharge, stratified discharge; **arc,** AC arc, Poulsen arc, arc column; **spark,** electric spark; spark gap; shock, electric shock, galvanic shock.

.7 **magnetism,** magnet(o)–, magnetic attraction; **electromagnetism;** magnetization; diamagnetism, paramagnetism, ferromagnetism; residual magnetism, magnetic remanence; magnetic memory, magnetic retentiveness; magnetic elements; magnetic dip *or* inclination, magnetic variation *or* declination; hysteresis, magnetic hysteresis, hysteresis curve, magnetic friction, magnetic lag *or* retardation, magnetic creeping; permeability, magnetic permeability, magnetic conductivity; magnetic circuit, magnetic curves, magnetic figures; magnetic flux, gilbert, weber, maxwell; magnetic moment; magnetic potential; magnetic viscosity; magnetics.

.8 **polarity,** polarization; **pole, positive pole, negative pole;** magnetic pole, magnetic axis; north pole, N pole; south pole, S pole.

.9 **magnetic force** *or* **intensity,** magnetic flux density, gauss, oersted; magnetomotive force; magnetomotivity; magnetic tube of force; line of force; **magnetic field, electromagnetic field.**

.10 **electroaffinity,** electric attraction; electric repulsion.

.11 **voltage,** volt, **electromotive force** *or* **EMF,** electromotivity, potential difference; **potential, electric potential.**

.12 **resistance,** ohm, ohmage, ohmic resis-

tance, electric resistance; surface resistance, skin effect, volume resistance; insulation resistance; **reluctance,** magnetic reluctance *or* resistance; specific reluctance, reluctivity; **reactance,** inductive reactance, capacitive reactance; **impedance.**

.13 **conduction,** electric conduction; **conductance,** conductivity, mho; superconductivity; gas conduction, ionic conduction, metallic conduction, liquid conduction, photoconduction; **conductor,** semiconductor, superconductor; **nonconductor,** dielectric, insulator.

.14 **induction;** electrostatic induction, magnetic induction, electromagnetic induction, electromagnetic induction of currents; self-induction, mutual induction; **inductance,** inductivity, henry.

.15 **capacitance,** capacity, farad; collector junction capacitance, emitter junction capacitance, resistance capacitance.

.16 **gain,** available gain, current gain, operational gain.

.17 **electric power, wattage,** watts; electric horsepower; hydroelectric power, hydroelectricity; power load.

.18 **powerhouse,** power station, power plant, central station; hydroelectric plant; nuclear *or* atomic power plant.

.19 **electrician, electrotechnician;** radio technician 344.24; wireman; **lineman,** linesman; rigger; groundman.

.20 **electrotechnologist,** electrobiologist, electrochemist, electrometallurgist, electrophysicist, electrophysiologist, **electrical engineer.**

.21 **electrification,** supplying electricity.

.22 **electrolysis;** ionization; galvanization, electrogalvanization; electrocoating, electroplating, electrogilding, electrograving, electroetching; ion, cation, anion; electrolyte, ionogen; nonelectrolyte.

.23 VERBS **electrify, galvanize,** energize, **charge;** shock; **generate,** step up, amplify, stiffen; step down; plug in, loop in; switch on *or* off, turn on *or* off, turn on *or* off the juice [informal]; short-circuit, short.

.24 **magnetize; electromagnetize;** demagnetize, degauss.

.25 **electrolyze;** ionize; galvanize, electrogalvanize; electroplate, electrogild.

.26 **insulate,** isolate; **ground.**

.27 ADJS **electric(al), electrifying;** galvanic, voltaic; dynamoelectric, hydroelectric, photoelectric, piezoelectric, etc.; electrothermal, electrochemical, electromechanical, electropneumatic, electrodynamic, static, electrostatic, stat–; electromotive; electrokinetic; electroscopic, galvanoscopic; electrometric, galvanometric, voltametric; **electrified,** electric-powered, battery-powered, cordless.

.28 **magnetic, electromagnetic;** diamagnetic, paramagnetic, ferromagnetic; **polar.**

.29 **electrolytic;** hydrolytic; ionic, anionic, cationic; ionogenic.

.30 **electrotechnical;** electroballistic, electrobiological, electrochemical, electrometallurgical, electrophysiological.

.31 **charged, electrified, live,** hot; high-tension, low-tension.

.32 **positive,** plus, electropositive; **negative,** minus, electronegative.

.33 **nonconducting,** nonconductive, insulating, dielectric.

.34 **electrical science**

electrical engineering	electrophotomicrogra-
electroballistics	phy
electrobiology	electrophysics
electrochemistry	electrophysiology
electrodynamics	electrostatics
electrokinematics	electrotechnology,
electrokinetics	electrotechnics
electromechanics	electrothermics
electrometallurgy	galvanism
electrometry	magnetics
electronics 343	magnetometry
electrooptics	thermionics

.35 **electric units**

abampere	mho
abcoulomb	microampere
abfarad	microfarad
abhenry	microhenry
abmho	micromho
abohm	micromicrofarad
abvolt	microvolt
ampere	microwatt
ampere-foot	milliampere
ampere-hour	millihenry
ampere-minute	millivolt
ampere-turn	ohm
coulomb	ohm-mile
farad	picofarad
henry	statampere
kilovolt	statcoulomb
kilovolt-ampere	statfarad
kilowatt	statvolt
kilowatt-hour	volt
megacoulomb	volt-coulomb
megampere	volt-second
megavolt	watt
megawatt	watt-hour
megohm	

.36 **electrical parts and devices**

alternator	cap, plug cap
anode	capacitor
armature	cathode
autoconverter	charger
autostarter	choking coil
autotransformer	circuit breaker
battery charger	coil
brush	commutator

compensator	oscillator
condenser	oscilloscope
controller	outlet
converter	pile
coupling	plug
cutout	pocket
distributor	points
double-pole switch	push button
double-throw switch	reactor
dynamo	receptacle
dynamotor	rectifier
electric column	relay
electric switch	resistance box
electrode	resistor
electrolytic inter-	rheostat
rupter	rotary gap
electrophorus	self-starter
electroscope	selsyn
electrostatic machine	shunt
fuse	socket
galvanoscope	spark coil
generator	spark plug
grid	starter
ground	step-down transformer
ignition	step-up transformer
induction machine	switch
inductor	synchronous converter
inductoscope	tap
insulator	terminal
interrupter	thermistor
jumper	timer
knife switch	time switch
lightning rod or ar-	toggle switch
rester	transformer
magnet 288.3	trickle charger
magneto, magneto-	voltage changer
electric machine	voltage regulator
magnetoscope	voltage transformer
mercury switch	voltaic or galvanic pile
motor-generator	Wimshurst machine

.37 **batteries**

accumulator	Leyden jar
alkaline cell	mercury cell
atomic battery	nickel-cadmium bat-
cell	tery
dry battery	primary battery
dry cell	secondary battery
electronic battery	solar battery
fuel cell	storage battery
hearing-aid battery	storage cell
lead-acid battery	voltaic battery
Leyden battery	wet cell

.38 **electric meters**

ammeter, ampereme-	milliammeter
ter	millivoltmeter
ampere-hour meter	moving-coil meter
capillary electrometer	ohm-ammeter
coulometer, coulomb	ohmmeter
meter	potentiometer
dynameter	quadrant electrometer
dynamometer, electro-	thermal ammeter
dynamometer	thermoammeter
electrometer	thermocouple, ther-
expansion ammeter	mocouple meter
faradmeter	thermoelectrometer
galvanometer	thermoelement
hysteresis meter	vacuum-tube voltme-
magnetometer	ter, VTVM
megohmmeter	variometer
mhometer	voltameter

volt-ammeter	volt-ohm meter
volt-ampere-hour	volt-ohm-milliamme-
meter	ter, VOM
voltmeter	watt-hour meter
voltmeter-milliamme-	wattmeter
ter	Wheatstone bridge

.39 electric wire

armored cable	power line
battery cable	Romex shielded wire
bell wire	or cable
BX cable	telegraph line
coaxial cable	telephone line
electric cable	three-wire cable
electric cord	transmission line
highline	triaxial cable
hookup wire	underground cable
ignition cable	way wire
lead	wire line
line	

343. ELECTRONICS

.1 NOUNS **electronics,** electro–, radionics; electron physics, electrophysics, electron dynamics; electron optics; semiconductor physics, transistor physics; photoelectronics, photoelectricity, phot(o)–; microelectronics; electronic engineering; avionics; electron microscopy; radio 344; television 345; radar 346; automation 349.

.2 (electron theory) electron theory of atoms, electron theory of electricity, electron theory of solids, free electron theory of metals, band theory of solids.

.3 **electron,** negatron, cathode particle, beta particle; photoelectron; thermion; primary electron, secondary electron; nuclear electron; recoil electron; bound electron, surface-bound electron; bonding electron; free electron, conduction electron, wandering electron; electron capture, electron transfer; spinning electrons, extranuclear electrons, planetary electrons, orbital electron; electron spin; electron state, energy level; ground state, excited state; electron pair, lone pair, shared pair, electron-positron pair, duplet, octet; electron cloud; shells, electron layers, electron shells, valence shell, valence electrons, subvalent electrons; electron affinity, relative electron affinity.

.4 **electronic effect;** Edison effect, photoelectric effect.

.5 **electron emission; thermionic emission;** photoelectric emission, photoemission; collision emission, bombardment emission, secondary emission; field emission; grid emission, thermionic grid emission; electron ray, electron beam, cathode ray, anode ray, positive ray, canal ray; glow discharge, cathode glow, cathodolumines-

cence, cathodofluorescence; electron diffraction.

.6 electron flow, electron stream; electric current; electron gas, electron cloud, space charge; photoelectric current; thermionic current, ionization current; cathode current, plate current; input current, output current; base current, base signal current; collector current, collector signal current; emitter current, emitter signal current; saturation current.

.7 **electron volt;** ionization potential; input voltage, output voltage; base signal voltage, collector signal voltage, emitter signal voltage; battery supply voltage; screen-grid voltage; inverse peak voltage; voltage saturation.

.8 electronic circuit; vacuum-tube circuit, thermionic tube circuit, transistor circuit, semiconductor circuit; equivalent circuit, coupling circuit, flip-flop circuit, trigger circuit, back-to-back switching circuit; rectifier circuit, amplifier circuit, etc.; sinusoidal circuit, nonsinusoidal circuit; astable circuit, monostable circuit, bistable circuit; small signal short circuit, small signal hybrid short circuit; small signal open circuit, small signal hybrid open circuit; printed circuit, microcircuit, wireless circuit; **circuitry.**

.9 **conductance,** input conductance, feedback conductance, transfer conductance, output conductance; grid conductance, electrode conductance, leakage conductance, plate conductance; transconductance, inversion transconductance.

.10 **resistance,** base resistance, collector resistance, emitter resistance, electrode resistance; input resistance, output resistance; image-matched input resistance, image-matched output resistance; reverse transfer resistance, forward transfer resistance; load resistance.

.11 **electron tube,** tube, valve [Brit], thermionic tube; **vacuum tube; radio tube;** discharge tube.

.12 **photoelectric tube** *or* **cell, phototube,** photocell; electron-ray tube, **electric eye.**

.13 **transistor,** semiconductor *or* solid-state device; emitter, base, collector; germanium triode, germanium crystal triode, tetrode transistor; conductivity-modulation transistor, filamentary transistor, hook-collector transistor, junction transistor, point-contact transistor, point-junction transistor, unipolar transistor; phototransistor; spacistor.

.14 **electronics engineer,** electronics physicist.

.15 ADJS **electronic;** photoelectronic, photoelectric; autoelectronic; thermionic; anodic, cathodic.

.16 electron tubes

Audion	kenotron
beam-power tube	klystron
beam tetrode	magnetron
Braun tube	mercury-vapor tube
cathode-ray tube	monoscope
cavity magnetron	multigrid tube
cold cathode tube	multiplex tube
Crookes tube	oscilloscope tube
diode	pentagrid
discharge tube	pentode
disk-seal tube	permatron
duodiode	phanotron
duodiode-triode	phasitron
duodynatron	pliotron
dynatron	reflex klystron
electron-beam tube	resnatron
electron-ray tube	secondary-emission
electron-wave tube	tube
excitron	strobotron
field-emission X-ray	tetragrid
tube	tetrode
gas-filled or gas tube	thyratron
Geissler tube	trigger tube
glow or glow discharge	triode
tube	triode-heptode
grid-glow tube	twin triode
grid-seal tube	vacuum tube
heptagrid	vapor tube
heptode	variable-mu tube
high-mu tube	X-ray diffraction tube
hot-cathode tube	X-ray tube
ignitron	

.17 photoelectric tubes and cells

electron-image tube	plier tube
gas phototube	photomultiplier tube
high-vacuum photo-	phototube
tube	photovoltaic cell
multiplier phototube	Photronic cell
photoconductor cell	soft phototube
photoelectric multi-	vacuum phototube

.18 special-purpose tubes

amplifier	mixer tube
attenuator	modulator
audio-frequency tube	multiplier
ballast regulator	multipurpose tube
ballast tube	multivibrator
beam-switching tube	oscillator
convertor	output tube
crystal detector	phase inverter
current regulator	picture tube 345.18
damper	power tube
detector	pulse generator
discriminator	radio-frequency tube
doubler	receiving tube
focus tube	rectifier tube
full-wave rectifier tube	regulator
generator	repeater
iconoscope 345.19	transducer
indicator tube	trigger tube
intermediate-fre-	tripler
quency tube	TR tube (transmit-re-
inverter	ceive)
limiter	voltage-reference tube
local-oscillator tube	voltage-regulator tube

.19 vacuum tube components

anode	loctal base
base	octal base
bayonet base	photocathode, photo-
cathode	electric cathode
control grid	plate
electrode	screen grid
electron gun	shield grid
filament	suppressor grid
grid	thermionic cathode
injection grid	trigatron

.20 electronic devices

airborne controls	Flexowriter typewriter
amplifier	fluorescent tube or
audio amplifier	lamp
automatic or robot pi-	germicidal lamp
lot	hearing aid
battery charger	high-frequency heater
calutron	image dissector
cathode-ray oscillo-	induction heater
graph	infrared cooker
cathode-ray oscillo-	isotron
scope	laser
computer	lie detector
cryotron	magnetic drum re-
cytoanalyzer	corder
depth sounder	magnetic recorder
diathermy machine	magnetic tape re-
dielectric heater	corder
dielectric preheater	magnetic wire re-
echo sounder	corder
electric eye	maser
electrocardiograph	mass spectrograph
electroencephalograph	mass spectrometer
electrograph	mass spectroscope
electron-diffraction	microprocessor
camera	microwave diathermy
electronic air condi-	machine
tioner	microwave oven
electronic air filter	neon tube or light
electronic altimeter	oscillograph
electronic battery	oscilloscope 346.21
electronic clock	pacemaker
electronic computer	photoflash bulb
349.16	polarizing microscope
electronic detector	polygraph
electronic drum	preamplifier
electronic fuel gauge	public-address system
electronic heater	radar 346
electronic nutcracker	radio 344
electronic organ	radio direction finder
electronic oscillator	radio-frequency heater
electronic pilot	radiosonde
electronic precipitator	radio telescope
electronic recorder	shortwave diathermy
electronic refrigerator	machine
electronic stenciling	sonar
machine	spectroradiometer
electronic stethoscope	stereophonic sound
electronic switch	system, stereo
electronic timer	thermal timing relay
electronic typewriter	time-delay relay
electronic watch	TR box (transmit-re-
electron-image projec-	ceive switch)
tor	trickle charger
electron lens	ultrasonic electronic
electron magnetic	machine tools
spectroscope	videotape recorder
electron microscope	X-ray microscope
Fathometer	

.21 electronic meters

count-rate meter
duodial
electronic chronome-
   ter
electronic limit gauge
electronic potentiom-
   eter
electronic potentiom-
   eter pyrometer
electronic voltmeter
events-per-unit-time
   meter

illuminometer
interferometer
ionization gauge
pH meter
radiomicrometer
sanguinometer
telemeter
tensiometer
thermionic instrument
time-interval meter
vacuum-tube elec-
   trometer

.22 photosensitive devices

electrophotometer
Geiger counter
infrared beam projec-
   tor
infrared telescope
photoelectric colorim-
   eter
photoelectric counter
photoelectric flame-
   failure detector
photoelectric image

converter
photoelectric intru-
   sion detector
photoelectric photom-
   eter
photoelectric pinhole
   detector
photoelectric recorder
photoelectric sorter
photoelectric timer
spectrophotometer

.23 electronic testing equipment

ammeter
audio-frequency oscil-
   lator
audio-IF oscillator
electric meter 342.38
field-strength meter
frequency meter
grid-dip meter
grid-dip oscillator
high-voltage probe
Lecher wires
low-capacitance probe
milliammeter
modulation monitor
ohmmeter
oscilloscope
output indicator
pulse generator
RC oscillator

regenerative wave-
   meter
resonance indicator
signal generator
standing-wave indica-
   tor
sweep generator
vacuum-tube voltme-
   ter, VTVM
variable-frequency au-
   dio-IF oscillator
vertical amplifier
voltmeter
voltmeter-milliamme-
   ter
volt-ohm-milliamme-
   ter, VOM
wavemeter

344. RADIO

.1 NOUNS radio, wireless [Brit]; radiotelephony, radiotelegraphy; communications,
telecommunication 560.1-8.

.2 radiotechnology, radio engineering, communication engineering; radio electronics, radioacoustics; radiogoniometry; conelrad (Control of Electromagnetic Radiation for Civil Defense).

.3 radio, radio receiver; radio telescope; radio set, receiver, receiving set, wireless or
wireless set [both Brit], set; cabinet, console, housing; chassis.

.4 radio transmitter, transmitter, radiator;
AM transmitter, FM transmitter, shortwave transmitter; continuous-wave transmitter, CW transmitter; radiotelephone
transmitter, RT transmitter; transmitter

receiver, transceiver [informal]; beacon,
radio beacon, radio range beacon; radio
marker, fan marker; radiosonde, radiome-
teorograph; amateur transmitter, ham
transmitter or rig [informal]; radiomicrophone, microphone 450.9.

.5 radiomobile, mobile transmitter, remote-
pickup unit.

.6 radio station, transmitting station, studio,
studio plant; AM station, FM station,
shortwave station, ultrahigh-frequency
station, clear-channel station; direction-
finder station, RDF station; relay station,
radio relay station, microwave relay station; amateur station, ham station [infor-
mal], ham shack [informal].

.7 control room, mixing room, monitor
room, monitoring booth; control desk,
console, master control desk, instrument
panel, control panel or board, jack field,
mixer [informal].

.8 network, net, radio links, hookup, communications net, circuit, network stations, network affiliations, affiliated stations; coaxial network, circuit network,
coast-to-coast hookup.

.9 radio circuit, radio-frequency circuit, audio-frequency circuit, superheterodyne
circuit, amplifying circuit; electronic circuit 343.8.

.10 radio signal, radio-frequency signal, RF
signal, direct signal, shortwave signal, AM
signal, FM signal; reflected signal,
bounce; unidirectional signal, beam; sig-
nal-noise ratio; radio-frequency amplifier,
RF amplifier, radio-frequency stage, RF
stage.

.11 radio wave, electric wave, electromagnetic wave, hertzian wave; shortwave,
long wave, microwave, high-frequency
wave, low-frequency wave; ground wave,
sky wave; carrier, carrier wave; wavelength.

.12 frequency; radio frequency, RF, intermediate frequency, IF, audio frequency, AF;
high frequency, HF; very high frequency,
VHF; ultrahigh frequency, UHF; super-
high frequency, SHF; extremely high frequency, EHF; medium frequency, MF;
low frequency, LF; very low frequency,
VLF; upper frequencies, lower frequencies; carrier frequency; spark frequency;
spectrum, frequency spectrum; cycles,
CPS, hertz, Hz, kilocycles, kilohertz,
megacycles, megahertz.

.13 band, frequency band, standard band,
broadcast band, amateur band, citizens
band, police band, shortwave band, FM

band; **channel,** radio channel, broadcast channel.

.14 **modulation;** amplitude modulation, AM; frequency modulation, FM; phase modulation, PM; sideband, side frequency, single sideband, double sideband.

.15 **amplification,** radio-frequency *or* RF amplification, audio-frequency *or* AF amplification, intermediate-frequency *or* IF amplification, high-frequency amplification.

.16 **radiobroadcasting, broadcasting,** radiocasting, standard broadcasting, AM broadcasting, FM broadcasting, shortwave broadcasting; **transmission, radio transmission;** direction *or* beam transmission, asymmetric *or* vestigial transmission; multipath transmission, multiplex transmission; mixing, volume control, sound *or* tone control, fade-in, fade-out; broadcasting regulation, Federal Communications Commission, FCC.

.17 **pickup,** outside pickup, **remote pickup,** spot pickup.

.18 **radiobroadcast, broadcast,** radiocast, **radio program;** rebroadcast, rerun; newscast, sportscast; radio fare, network show; commercial program, commercial; sustaining program, sustainer; serial, soap opera [informal]; taped program, canned show [informal], electrical transcription; sound effects.

.19 **signature, station identification,** call letters; theme song; **station break,** pause for station identification.

.20 **commercial,** commercial announcement, **spot announcement,** spot *or* plug [both informal].

.21 **reception; fading,** fade-out; **drift,** creeping, crawling; **interference,** noise interference, station interference; **static,** atmospherics, noise; blasting, blaring; blind spot.

.22 **radio listener,** listener-in *or* tuner-inner [both informal]; radio audience, listeners, listenership; hi-fi fan [informal], audiophile.

.23 **broadcaster,** radiobroadcaster, radiocaster; newscaster, sportscaster; commentator, news commentator; anchor man; announcer; disk jockey *or* DJ [both informal]; master of ceremonies, MC *or* emcee [both informal]; program director, programmer; sound-effects man, sound man; American Federation of Radio and Television Artists, AFTRA.

.24 **radioman,** radio technician, radio engineer; radiotrician, radio electrician; **radio**

operator; control engineer, volume engineer; mixer; **amateur radio operator, ham** *or* ham operator [both informal], radio amateur; Amateur Radio Relay League, ARRL; monitor; radiotelegrapher 560.16.

.25 VERBS **broadcast,** radiobroadcast, radiocast, **radio, wireless** [Brit], radiate, **transmit,** send; shortwave; beam; newscast, sportscast, put *or* go on the air, sign on; go off the air, sign off.

.26 **monitor,** check.

.27 **listen in, tune in;** tune up, tune down, tune out, tune off.

.28 ADJS **radio, wireless** [Brit]; radiosonic; neutrodyne; heterodyne; superheterodyne; shortwave; radio-frequency, audio-frequency; high-frequency, low-frequency, etc.; radiogenic.

.29 **radios, audio devices**

all-wave receiver	radiophone 560.5
AM-FM receiver	radio-phonograph
AM receiver	radio-record player
AM-FM tuner	railroad radio
AM tuner	receiver
auto radio	rechargeable-battery
aviation radio	radio
battery radio	regenerative receiver
citizens band *or* CB	relay receiver
radio, CB	ship-to-shore radio
clock radio	shortwave receiver
communications re-	superheterodyne
ceiver	table radio
crystal set	three-way *or* three-
FM receiver	power receiver
FM tuner	transceiver
mobile radio	transistor radio
multiplex receiver	transmit-receiver
pocket radio	tuner
portable radio	two-way radio
radio direction finder,	walkie-talkie
RDF	

.30 **receiver parts**

amplifier 450.10	intermediate-fre-
amplitude control	quency amplifier,
audio-frequency am-	IF amplifier
plifier, audio ampli-	intermediate-fre-
fier, AF amplifier	quency oscillator,
automatic frequency	IF oscillator
control, AFC	intermediate-fre-
baffle	quency transformer,
beat-frequency oscilla-	IF transformer
tor	knob
bypass	lead-in wire
capacitor	on-off switch
chassis	output transformer
coil	parasitic suppressor
condenser	phase control
detector	potentiometer
dial	power pack
exciter	power plug
filter	power supply
frequency control	power transformer
frequency divider	preamplifier
heater	preselector
heterodyne	program discriminator
inductor	radio-frequency ampli-

fier, RF amplifier
radio tubes 343.16–18
resistor
rheostat
selector
selsyn
speaker 450.8
tone control
transformer

transistor
trimmer
tuning condenser or
  capacitor
variable condenser or
  capacitor
vernier dial
volume control
wave trap

.31 transmitter parts

amplifier chain
broadcast loop
carrier amplifier
coaxial cable
fader
frequency changer
frequency converter
frequency doubler
frequency meter
litz wire
mixer
modulator
monitor

oscillator
power amplifier
program feed
resonance frequency
  control
signal generator
signal multiplier
transmission line
volume control
volume indicator
wave changer
wave guide

.32 aerials, antennas

antenna array
artificial antenna
auto antenna
beam antenna
bowtie antenna
colinear beam an-
  tenna
condenser antenna
dipole
directional antenna
dish
doublet
dummy antenna
eight-ball antenna
flattop antenna
FM antenna
folded dipole
frame aerial
free-space aerial
hank-type antenna
leaky wave-guide an-
  tenna
long-wire antenna
loop antenna
mast
mobile antenna
multiband antenna

nondirectional an-
  tenna
omnidirectional an-
  tenna
open aerial
parabolic antenna
pencil-beam antenna
printed antenna
rabbit ears
radar antenna 346.22
receiving antenna
reflector
resonance wave coil
rhombic antenna
rotary-beam antenna
shortwave antenna
signal squirter
telescope antenna
tower
transmitting antenna
tuned antenna
universal antenna
vertical radiator an-
  tenna
wave antenna
whip antenna
yagi

345. TELEVISION

.1 NOUNS television, tel(e)–, TV, video, telly [Brit informal]; color television, dot-sequential or field-sequential or line-sequential color television; black-and-white television; scophony; subscription television, pay TV; cable television; closed-circuit television.

.2 television broadcast, telecast, TV show; direct broadcast, live show [informal]; taped show, canned show [informal]; film pickup; colorcast; simulcast; telefilm; videotape.

.3 televising, telecasting; facsimile broad-

casting; monitoring, mixing, shading, blanking, switching; scanning, parallel-line scanning, interlaced scanning.

.4 (transmission) photoemission, audioemission; television channel, TV band; video or picture channel, audio or sound channel; picture carrier, sound carrier; beam, scanning beam, return beam; triggering pulse, voltage pulse, output pulse, timing pulse, equalizing pulse; synchronizing pulse, vertical synchronizing pulse, horizontal synchronizing pulse; video signal, audio signal; IF video signal, IF audio signal; synchronizing signal, blanking signal.

.5 (reception) **picture, image**; definition, blacker than black synchronizing; shading, black spot, hard shadow; test pattern, scanning pattern, grid; vertical interference, rain; granulation, scintillation, snow, snowstorm; flare, bloom, woomp; picture shifts, blooping, rolling; double image, multiple image, ghost; video static, noise, picture noise; signal-to-noise ratio; fringe area.

.6 television studio, TV station.

.7 **mobile unit, TVmobile**; video truck, audio truck, transmitter truck.

.8 **transmitter**, televisor; audio transmitter, video transmitter.

.9 **relay links, boosters**, booster amplifiers, relay transmitters, **booster** or **relay stations**; microwave link; aeronautical relay, stratovision; communication satellite, satellite relay; Telstar, Intelsat, Syncom; Comsat.

.10 **television camera**, telecamera, pickup camera, pickup; mobile camera.

.11 **television receiver, television** or **TV set, TV, telly** [Brit informal], televisor, boob tube or idiot box [both informal]; portable television or TV set; **screen**, telescreen.

.12 televiewer, viewer; television or viewing audience.

.13 television technician, TV man, television engineer; monitor, sound or audio monitor, picture or video monitor; pickup unit man, cameraman, sound man.

.14 VERBS televise, telecast; colorcast.

.15 teleview, watch television.

.16 ADJS televisional, televisual, televisionary, video; telegenic, videogenic; in synchronization, in sync [informal], locked in.

.17 receiver parts

audio amplifier
audio detector
audio-frequency

detector
blanking amplifier
contrast control

converter
deflection generator
electron tubes 343.16–18
FM detector
horizontal deflector
horizontal synchronizer
limiter
mixer
photocathode
photoelectric cells 343.17

picture control
picture detector
radio units 344.30
screen
shading amplifier
signal separator
sound limiter
synchronizing separator
vertical deflector
vertical synchronizer
video amplifier
video detector

.18 picture tubes

cathode-ray tube
color kinescope
direct-viewing tube
kinescope
monoscope

Oscilight
projection tube
shadow-mask kinescope

.19 camera tubes

dissector tube
iconoscope
image dissector
image iconoscope

image orthicon
orthicon
pickup tube
vidicon

.20 transmitter parts

adder
antenna filter
camera deflection generator
channel filter
encoder
exploring element
monitor screen

reproducing element
signal generator
sound units 344.31
synchronizing generator
Tel-Eye
TV-Eye

346. RADAR AND RADIOLOCATORS

.1 NOUNS **radar,** radio detection and ranging, pulse radar, microwave radar, continuous wave *or* CW radar; radar fence *or* screen; radar astronomy.

.2 airborne radar, aviation radar; **navar,** navigation and ranging; **teleran,** television radar air navigation; radar bombsight, K-1 bombsight; radar dome, radome.

.3 loran, long range aid to navigation, **shoran,** short range aid to navigation, GEE navigation, consolan.

.4 direction finder, radio direction finder, RDF, radiogoniometer, high-frequency direction finder, HFDF, huff-duff [informal]; radio compass, wireless compass [Brit].

.5 radar speed meter, electronic cop [informal]; radar highway patrol.

.6 radar station, control station; Combat Information Center, CIC; Air Route Traffic Control Center, ARTCC; beacon station, display station; fixed station, home station; portable field unit, mobile trailer unit; tracking station; direction-finder station, radio compass station; triangulation stations.

.7 radar beacon, racon; transponder; radar beacon buoy, marker buoy, radar marked beacon, ramark.

.8 (radar operations) data transmission, scanning, scan conversion, flector tuning, signal modulation, triggering signals; phase adjustment, locking signals; triangulation, three-pointing; mapping; range finding; tracking, automatic tracking, locking on; precision focusing, pinpointing; radar-telephone relay; radar navigation.

.9 (applications) detection, interception, ranging, ground control of aircraft, air-traffic control, blind flying, blind landing, storm tracking, hurricane tracking.

.10 pulse, radio-frequency *or* RF pulse, high-frequency *or* HF pulse, intermediate-frequency *or* IF pulse, trigger pulse, echo pulse.

.11 signal, radar signal; transmitter signal, output signal; return signal, echo signal, video signal, reflection, picture, target image, display, signal display, trace, reading, return, **echo, bounces, blips, pips;** spot, CRT spot; three-dimensional *or* 3-D display, double-dot display; deflection-modulated *or* DM display, intensity-modulated *or* IM display; radio-frequency *or* RF echoes, intermediate-frequency *or* IF signal; beat signal, Doppler signal, local oscillator signal; beam, beavertail beam.

.12 radar interference, deflection, refraction, superrefraction; atmospheric attenuation, signal fades, blind spots, false echoes; clutter, ground clutter, sea clutter.

.13 (radar countermeasure) **jamming;** tinfoil, aluminum foil, chaff, window [Brit].

.14 radar technician, radar engineer, radarman; air-traffic controller.

.15 VERBS **transmit, send,** radiate, beam; **jam.**

.16 reflect, return, echo, bounce back.

.17 receive, tune in, pick up, spot, home on; pinpoint; identify, trigger; lock on; sweep, scan; map.

.18 radar

AGCA radar (automatic ground control approach)
AI radar (aircraft interception)
airborne intercept radar
airport surveillance radar
antiaircraft *or* AA radar
antisubmarine radar
ASV radar (air to surface vessel)

CCA radar (close control of aircraft)
DEW Line (distant early warning line)
DME (distance measuring equipment)
Doppler radar
DVOP radar (Doppler velocity and position)
early-warning radar
FC radar (fire control)
GCA radar (ground

control approach)
GCI radar (ground control of interception)
gun-directing radar
H₂S radar (height to surface, Eng.)
H₂X (height to surface, U.S.)
IFF radar (identification, friend or foe)
interception radar
LAW radar (long-range aircraft warning)
long-range radar
MAD radar (magnetic airborne detection)
MADRE radar (magnetic drum receiving equipment)
MEW radar (microwave early warning)
MTI radar (moving target indication)

Navaglobe
Oboe (beacon bombing system)
overlap radar
panoramic radar
PAR radar (precision approach radar)
pulse-modulated radar
radar telescope
RAWIN (radio automatic wind recording)
SARAH (search rescue and homing)
SCR (Signal Corps radar)
search radar
surface or ground radar
surveillance radar
taxi radar (airport surface detection)
TRW radar (tornado radar warning)
Volscan

.19 radiolocators

automatic gun director, AGD
automatic range finder, ARF
bombing locator
compensated-loop direction finder
depth sounder
gun director
height finder

microwave height finder, MHF
position finder
radio direction finder, RDF
range finder
spaced-antenna direction finder
spaced-loop direction finder

.20 radar parts

AFC mixer
altimeter
amplifier
analyzer
ATR box (anti-transmit-receive)
ATR switch
automatic frequency control, AFC
cascade screen
cathode-ray tube, CRT
continuous wave or CW oscillator
demodulator
detector
discriminator
frequency meter
hard-tube pulser
indicator
limiter
local oscillator
magnetron
microwave mixer
mixer
modulator
network pulser
oscillator
plan position indica-

tor, PPI
position data transmitter
position tracker
potentiometer
pulse generator
pulser
pulse transformer
range-marker generator
range-sweep amplifier
range-sweep generator
receiver
reference-voltage generator
scan converter
screen
second detector
square-wave generator
synchronizer
timing unit
tracker
transmit-receive or TR unit
transmitter
TR box (transmit-receive)
TR switch
trigatron

.21 oscilloscopes, radarscopes

A-scope
B-scope
J-scope

PPI-scope
(plan position indicator scope)

.22 antennas

bedspring type
directional antenna
feed-and-reflector unit
mattress type
omnidirectional

antenna
scanner
sontenna
strike radar scanner (airborne)

.23 reflectors

beavertail reflector
corner reflector
dish reflector
horn reflector

orange peel reflector
parabolic reflector
venetian blind reflector

347. MECHANICS

.1 NOUNS **mechanics**; theoretical or analytical mechanics, pure or abstract mechanics, rational mechanics; celestial mechanics; quantum mechanics, matrix mechanics, wave mechanics; animal mechanics, zoomechanics, biomechanics; micromechanics; hydromechanics, fluid mechanics; aeromechanics; electromechanics; telemechanics, servomechanics 349.2; practical mechanics, mechanical arts; applied mechanics; statistical mechanics; leverage 287.

.2 **statics**, biostatics, electrostatics, geostatics, gyrostatics, rheostatics, stereostatics, thermostatics, hydrostatics, aerostatics.

.3 **dynamics, kinetics, kinematics,** energetics; astrodynamics, geodynamics, radiodynamics, electrodynamics, photodynamics, thermodynamics, aerodynamics, pneumodynamics, barodynamics, hydrodynamics, fluid dynamics, magnetohydrodynamics, kinesiology, biodynamics, zoodynamics, myodynamics.

.4 **hydraulics**, hydromechanics, hydrokinetics, fluidics, hydrodynamics, hydrostatics; hydrology, hydrography, hydrometry, fluviology.

.5 **pneumatics**, pneumatostatics; aeromechanics, aerophysics, aerology, aerometry, aerography, aerotechnics, aerodynamics, aerostatics.

.6 **engineering**, mechanical engineering, jet engineering, etc., see engineers 718.9.

.7 ADJS **mechanical**, mechanistic; locomotive, locomotor; zoomechanical, biomechanical, aeromechanical, hydromechanical, etc.

.8 **static**; biostatic, electrostatic, geostatic, etc.

.9 **dynamic(al), kinetic(al), kinematic(al)**; geodynamic, radiodynamic, electrodynamic, etc.

.10 **pneumatic**, pneumatological; aeromechanical, aerophysical, aerologic(al), aerotechnical, aerodynamic, aerostatic, aerographic(al).

.11 hydrologic, hydrometric(al), hydrome-chanic(al), hydrodynamic, hydrostatic, hydraulic.

348. TOOLS AND MACHINERY

.1 NOUNS **tool, instrument, implement,** utensil, –labe; **apparatus, device,** mechanical device, contrivance, contraption [informal], gadget, gizmo, gimcrack, gimmick [informal], means, mechanical means; **hand tool; power tool;** machine tool; speed tool; precision tool *or* instrument.

.2 **cutlery,** edge tools 348.13; **knife, ax,** dagger, sword, blade, cutter, whittle; **steel,** cold steel, naked steel; pigsticker *or* toad stabber *or* toad sticker [all slang]; perforator, piercer, puncturer, point 258.18; sharpener 258.19.

.3 **tableware,** dining utensils; **silverware,** silver, silver plate, stainless-steel ware; **flatware,** flat silver; **hollow ware; cutlery,** knives, forks, spoons; tablespoon, teaspoon; chopsticks.

.4 **machinery,** enginery; **machine, mechanism,** mechanical device; **engine,** motor; power plant, power source, drive, motive power; **appliance,** convenience, facility, utility, home appliance, mechanical aid; fixture; labor-saving device.

.5 **mechanism,** machinery, **movement,** movements, **action, motion, works,** workings, inner workings, innards, what makes it tick; drive train, power train; wheelwork, **wheelworks,** wheels 322.18, gear, wheels within wheels, epicyclic train; clockworks, watchworks; servomechanism 349.13,30.

.6 **gear,** gearing, gear train; gearwheel 322.18, cogwheel, rack; **gearshift;** low, intermediate, high, neutral, reverse; **differential,** differential gear *or* gearing; **transmission,** gearbox; automatic transmission; selective transmission; standard transmission, stick shift; synchromesh; fluid drive, overdrive, freewheel, Hydromatic.

.7 **clutch,** cone clutch, plate clutch, dog clutch, disk clutch, multiple-disk clutch, rim clutch, friction clutch, cone friction clutch, slip friction clutch, spline clutch, rolling-key clutch.

.8 **instrumentation, tooling,** tooling up; **retooling;** industrial instrumentation; servo instrumentation.

.9 **mechanic,** mechanician; artisan, artificer; **machinist,** machiner; auto mechanic, aeromechanic, etc.

.10 VERBS **tool,** instrument; retool; **machine,** mill; **mechanize,** motorize; sharpen 258.9.

.11 ADJS **mechanical,** machinal, machinelike, powered, power-driven, motor-driven; mechanized.

.12 **tools**

awl	nail puller
bale breaker	needlenose pliers
bar	palette knife
battering ram	peavey
belt punch	pincers
bevel, bevel square	pinch bar
bodkin	pitchfork
bradawl	planer
buffer	pliers
calipers	power sander
cant hook	puller
caulking iron *or* chisel	punch
or tool	puncheon
center punch	punch pliers
crowbar	putty knife
dibble	ram
dividers	rammer
drum sander	ramrod
edger	ripping bar
electric riveter	screwdriver
electric sander	shaper
electric soldering iron	soldering iron, solder-
emery wheel	ing gun
file	spatula
flail	square
forceps	stapler
fork	tackle 287.10
grapnel	tamp, tamper
grappling iron *or* hook	tamping bar
grease gun	tamping pick
grindstone	tamping stick
hawk	tap
hook	T bevel
jack	tire iron
jackscrew	tire tool
jointer	tongs
krenging hook	T square
lathe	tweezers
level	vise
miter box	wrecking bar
nail file	

.13 **edge tools**

adz	knife, drawshave
ax 801.25	electric razor
bistoury	gouge
bread knife	groover
broadax	grub ax
bushwhacker	grub hoe
butcher knife	hack
carving knife	hatchet
case knife	hedge trimmer
celt	hoe
chaser	hunting knife
chisel	jackknife
chopping knife	knife 801.21
clasp knife	lance
cleaver	lancet
clipper, clippers	letter-opener
cold chisel	linoleum knife
colter	machete
cutting pliers	mattock
dagger 801.22	nippers
drawing knife, draw-	panga

253

paper cutter
paper knife
paring knife
penknife
pick
pickax
plowshare
pocketknife
pruning hook
razor
razor blade
rigger's knife
ripping chisel
safety razor
saw knife
sax
scalpel
scissors
scoop

scraper
scuffle hoe
scythe
share
shears
sheath knife
sickle
sidecutters
slotter
snips
spear 801.23
spokeshave
surgical knife
sword 801.24
table knife
tin snips
wedge
wirecutters

core-box plane
dado plane
dovetail plane
edge plane
filletster plane
fore plane
grooving plane
jack plane
jointer, jointer plane
match plane
planer, planing
  machine
rabbet plane

reed plane
routing plane
sash plane
scraper plane
scrub plane
smooth or smoothing
  plane
thumb plane
tonguing plane
toothing plane
trenching plane
trying plane

.14 saws

backsaw
band saw
belt saw
bow saw
bucksaw
butcher's saw
buzz saw, circular saw
chain saw
compass saw
coping saw
cordwood saw
crosscut saw
diamond saw
double-cut saw
dovetail saw
electric saw
frame saw
fretsaw
hacksaw
handsaw
helicoidal saw
jigsaw
keyhole saw
kitchen saw

lightning or M saw
lumberman's saw
meat saw
mill saw
panel saw
pit saw
plywood saw
portable saw
power saw
pruning saw
ripsaw
rock saw
saw knife
saw machine
scribe saw
scroll saw
splitsaw
surgeon's saw
table saw
two-handed saw
vertical saw
whipsaw
wire saw
wood saw

.18 drills

accretion borer
air drill
auger
auger bit
automatic drill
bench drill
bit
bore, borer
bore bit
bow drill
brace and bit
breast auger
breast drill
broach
burr
chamfer bit
compressed-air drill
corkscrew
cross bit
diamond drill
disk drill
drill
drilling bit
drill press
electric drill
expansion bit

extension bit
flat drill
gimlet
gimlet bit
hand drill
keyway drill
portable drill
posthole auger
power drill
pump drill
push drill
ratchet drill
reamer
rotary drill
shell drill
spike bit
star drill
strap drill
tap
taper drill
tapping drill
trepan
trephine
twist bit
twist drill
wimble

.15 shovels

air shovel
air spade
backhoe
bar spade
coal shovel
ditch spade
drain spade
entrenching tool
fire shovel
garden spade
gasoline shovel
gumming spade
irrigating shovel

loy
peat spade
posthole spade
power shovel
salt shovel
scoop, scoop shovel
spade
split shovel
spud
steam shovel
stump spud
trenching spade

.19 hammers

air hammer
ball peen hammer
beetle
blacksmith's hammer
boilermaker's hammer
brick hammer, brick-
  layer's hammer
chipping hammer
claw hammer
cross peen hammer
die hammer
drop hammer
electric hammer
engineer's hammer
jackhammer

machinist's hammer
mallet
peen hammer
pile hammer
pneumatic hammer
raising hammer
riveting hammer
rubber mallet
sledge, sledgehammer
spalling hammer
steam hammer
stone hammer
tack hammer
tile setter's hammer
triphammer

.16 trowels

brick trowel
circle or cove trowel
corner trowel
curbing trowel
garden trowel

guttering trowel
plastering trowel
pointing trowel
radius trowel
slick

.20 wrenches

adjustable wrench
Allen wrench
alligator wrench
box wrench
carriage wrench
chain wrench
end wrench
lug wrench
monkey wrench
open-end wrench
pin wrench

pipe wrench
screw key
socket wrench
spanner
spark-plug wrench
Stillson wrench
S wrench
tappet wrench
tap wrench
tuning wrench
valve wrench

.17 planes

beading plane
bench plane
block plane
bullnose

capping plane
chamfer plane
circular plane
combination plane

.21 machinery

adding machine
addressing machine
automatic screw machine
automobile 272.9,24
backhoe
bulldozer
calfdozer
carryall
compressor
crab
crane
crimping machine
cutting machine
cutting press
derrick
dishwasher
dredge, dredger, dredging machine
drop hammer
dryer
dumping machine
edger
elevator dredge
folding machine
gin
grader
hoist, hoisting machine
hydraulic jack
hydraulic press
jackhammer
lawn mower, mower
machine drill
mailing machine
motorcycle 272.8,29
navvy [Brit]

packager
pile driver
planing machine
power mower
power saw
power shovel
press
printing machine
pulp machine
punching machine
pusher
roller
rose engine
ruling machine or engine
sander
saw machine
scraper
screwing machine
screw machine
sewing machine, sewer
snowblower
snowmobile
snowplow
snow-thrower
solar machine
steam hammer
steamroller
steam shovel
tractor 272.17,27
triphammer
typing machine, typewriter
washing machine
water wheel
windlass 287.7

.22 farm machinery

all-crop harvester
baler
bean harvester
beet harvester
binder
breaker
cast plow
combine
corn picker
cotton picker
cultivator
disk
disk harrow
disk plow
drag
drill
drill plow
four-bottom plow
gang plow
grain harvester
grub hook
harrow
harvester
haymaker
header
hoe drill
lister
lister cultivator
middlebreaker, middlebuster
moldboard plow
mowing machine

peg-tooth harrow
planter
plow
plow drill
prairie breaker
press drill
rake
rotary plow
scooter
seeder
seed plow
shovel plow
snap machine
sprayer
spring-tooth harrow
stag gang
subsoil plow
sulky lister
sulky plow
swather
swivel plow
tedder
three-bottom plow
thresher, thrasher, threshing machine
trench plow
turnplow
two-bottom plow
vineyard plow
walking plow
windrower

.23 mills

arrastra
ball mill
blooming mill
bone mill
cane mill
cider mill
coffee mill
cotton mill, cotton gin
drag-stone mill
feed mill
flour mill
fulling mill
grinding mill
gristmill
lapidary mill
milling machine
paper mill
pepper mill

planing mill
powder mill
rolling mill
sawmill
sheet mill
silk mill
slab mill
smoothing mill
spice mill
stamp mill
stamps
steel mill
stone mill
sugar mill
treadmill
water mill
windmill
woolen mill

.24 welders

acetylene welder
AC welder
arc welder
blowtorch 329.14
DC welder
electric welder
gas welder
oxyacetylene welder

pipe welder
spot welder
tack welder
three-phase resistance welder
welding blowpipe or torch
wire welder

.25 pumps

air lift
air pump
aspirator
beer pump
bicycle pump
bilge pump
booster pump
breast pump
bucket pump
centrifugal pump
cryo-pump
diaphragm pump
displacement pump
donkey pump, donkey
drainage pump
feed pump
float pump
force pump
forcer
hand pump

heat pump
hydraulic ram
jet pump
lift or lifting pump
piston pump
pressure pump
pulsometer
pumping engine
rotary pump
sand pump
shell pump
stirrup pump
stomach pump
suction pump
tire pump
turbine centrifugal pump
vacuum pump
water pump
wobble pump

.26 engines, motors

aeromotor 280.17
air engine or motor
alternating-current or AC motor
beam engine
blowing engine
caloric engine
cam engine
capacitor motor
commutator motor
compensated motor
compound motor
compression-ignition engine
condensing engine
Corliss engine
diagonal engine
diesel engine

direct-acting engine
direct-current or DC motor
donkey engine
double-acting or double-action engine
double-row radial engine
dynamo
dynamotor
electric motor, electromotor
external-combustion engine
fire engine
four-stroke cycle engine
gas engine

255

gas turbine engine
generator
heat engine
horizontal engine
hot-air engine
hydraulic engine
hydro-jet
impulse duct engine
inboard-outboard motor
inclined engine
induction motor
in-line engine
intermittent duct engine
internal-combustion engine
inverted engine
ion engine, ion rocket
jet, jet engine
locomotive engine
marine engine
mill-type motor
noncondensing engine
oil engine
oscillation-cylinder engine
oscillation engine
Otto engine
outboard motor
pancake engine
phase-wound rotor motor
piston engine
piston-valve engine
plasma engine
polyphase induction motor
portable engine
pulse-jet engine
pumping engine
radial engine

ramjet engine, ramjet
reaction motor or engine
reciprocating engine
refrigerating engine
resojet engine
rocket motor or engine
rotary engine
rotary-piston engine
rotor motor
series motor
servomotor
shunt motor
single-acting or single-action engine
single-phase motor
slide-valve engine
solar engine
split-phase motor
squirrel cage rotor motor
stationary engine
steam engine
supercharged engine
synchronous motor
thermal engine
three-phase motor
traction engine
triple-expansion engine
trunk engine
turbine
turbojet engine, turbojet
two-stroke cycle engine
universal motor
variable-speed motor
vernier engine
vertical engine
Wankel engine

.27 **engine parts**

bearings
boiler
cam
camshaft
connecting rod
crankcase
crankshaft
cylinder
cylinder head

differential
electrical parts 342.36
flywheel
gearbox
gears
piston
piston rod
transmission
universal joint

349. AUTOMATION

.1 NOUNS **automation,** automatic control; cybernation; **self-action,** self-activity; self-movement, self-motion, **self-propulsion;** self-direction, self-determination, self-government, automatism, self-regulation; automaticity, automatization; servo instrumentation.

.2 autonetics, automatic or automation technology, automatic electronics, automatic engineering, automatic control engineering, servo engineering, **servomechanics,** system engineering, systems analysis, feedback system engineering; cybernetics; telemechanics; radiodynamics, radio control; systems planning, systems design; circuit analysis; bionics; communication or communications theory, information theory.

.3 **automatic control,** cybernation, servo control, robot control; cybernetic control; electronic control, electronic-mechanical control; feedback control, digital feedback control, analog feedback control; cascade control, piggyback control [informal]; supervisory control; action, control action; derivative or rate action, reset action; control agent; control means.

.4 semiautomatic control; **remote control,** push-button control, remote handling, tele-action; radio control; telemechanics; telemechanism; telemetry, telemeter, telemetering; transponder; bioinstrument, bioinstrumentation.

.5 control system, **automatic control system,** servo system, robot system; closed-loop system; open-sequence system; linear system, nonlinear system; carrier-current system; integrated system, complex control system; data system, data-handling system, data-reduction system, data-input system, data-interpreting system, digital data reducing system; process-control system, annunciator system, flow-control system, motor-speed control system; automanual system; automatic telephone system; electrostatic spraying system; automated factory, automatic or robot factory, push-button plant; servo laboratory, servolab.

.6 **feedback,** closed sequence, feedback loop, closed loop; multiple-feed closed loop; process loop, quality loop; feedback circuit, current-control circuit, direct-current circuit, alternating-current circuit, calibrating circuit, switching circuit, flip-flop circuit, peaking circuit; multiplier channels; open sequence, linear operation; positive feedback, negative feedback; reversed feedback, degeneration.

.7 (functions) accounting, analysis, automatic electronic navigation, automatic guidance, braking, comparison of variables, computation, coordination, corrective action, fact distribution, forecasts, impedance matching, inspection, linear or nonlinear calibrations, manipulation, measurement of variables, missile guidance, output measurement, processing, rate determination, record keeping, statistical communication, steering, system stabilization, ultrasonic *or* supersonic flow detection.

.8 **process control,** bit-weight control, color control, density control, dimension control, diverse control, end-point control, flavor control, flow control, fragrance control, hold control, humidity control, light-intensity control, limit control, liquid-level control, load control, pressure control, precision-production control, proportional control, quality control, quantity control, revolution control, temperature control, time control, weight control.

.9 variable, process variable; simple variable, complex variable; manipulated variable; steady state, transient state.

.10 values, target values; set point; differential gap; proportional band; dead band, dead zone; neutral zone.

.11 time constants; time lead, gain; time delay, dead time; lag, process lag, hysteresis, holdup, output lag; throughput.

.12 automatic device 349.29, automatic; semiautomatic; self-actor, self-mover; **robot, automaton,** mechanical man; cyborg.

.13 **servomechanism,** servo; cybernion, automatic machine; **servomotor;** synchro, selsyn, autosyn; synchronous motor, synchronous machine.

.14 **regulator, control,** controller, **governor;** servo control, servo regulator; control element.

.15 control panel, console; coordinated panel, graphic panel; panelboard, set-up board.

.16 **computer,** electronic computer 349.31, electronic brain; information machine, thinking machine; computer unit, hardware, computer hardware 349.32.

.17 **storage,** storage system *or* unit, **memory,** high-speed memory; random access memory, RAM; memory tubes; tape *or* drum *or* disk memory.

.18 input-output *or* IO device; summing register, relay register; reader, tape reader; magnetic tape, punched tape; punched cards, punch cards; microcards, microfilm, microfiche, recorder, magnetic recorder; alphabetical printer; teletypewriter, Flexowriter typewriter; oscilloscope, oscillograph recorder; digital graph plotter, Teleplotter; **printout,** hard copy, readout.

.19 **data,** information, message, instructions, commands; **computer program,** computer software; computer routine, compiler, assembler; computer *or* machine language,

ALGOL, COBOL, FORTRAN; ruly English; computer code, alphanumeric code; single messages, multiple messages; **input data, output data,** random data, unorganized data; numeric data, alphabetic data; film data, punch-card data, oscillograph data; visible-speech data, sound-level data; angular data, rectangular data, polar data; (quantity to be controlled) input quantity, output quantity, reference quantity, controlled quantity; signals, control signals, block signals, checking signals, error signals, correcting signals, feedback signals; command pulses, feedback pulses; error, bug, play, noise; binary scale *or* system; binary digit, bit; octal system, hexadecimal system; byte.

.20 **data processing,** electronic data processing, EDP, high-speed data handling, data reduction, data retrieval, information retrieval, machine computation, telecomputing; computer typesetting; computing, scanning, analyzing, sorting, collating, integrating, classifying, reporting; computer technology.

.21 process, digital process, analog process; behavior pattern; oscillatory behavior, self-excitation; input oscillation, output oscillation; hunting, feeling; correction of error; overcorrection of error, overshoot; offset (difference between value desired and attained).

.22 **control engineer,** servo engineer, system engineer, systems analyst, automatic control system engineer, feedback system engineer, automatic technician, robot specialist; computer engineer, computer technologist, computer technician, **computer programmer;** cybernetic technologist, cyberneticist.

.23 VERBS **automate,** automatize, robotize; robot-control, servo-control; program.

.24 **self-govern,** self-control, **self-regulate,** self-direct.

.25 ADJS **automated,** cybernated, aut(o)–, automat(o)–, self–; **automatic,** automatous, **spontaneous; self-acting,** self-active; **self-operating,** self-operative, self-working; **self-regulating,** self-regulative, self-governing, self-directing; **self-regulated, self-controlled,** self-governed, self-directed, self-steered; self-adjusting, self-closing, self-cocking, self-cooking, self-dumping, self-emptying, self-lighting, self-loading, self-opening, self-priming, self-rising, self-sealing, self-starting, self-winding, automanual; semiautomatic.

.26 **self-propelled,** self-moved, horseless; **self-**

propelling, self-moving, self-propellent; self-driven, self-drive; **automotive,** automobile, automechanical; **locomotive,** locomobile.

.27 servomechanical, servo-controlled; **cybernetic;** isotronic.

.28 remote-control, remote-controlled, telemechanic; telemetered, telemetric; by remote control.

.29 automatic devices

airborne controls	automatic telephone
antiaircraft gun positioner	automatic telephone exchange
artificial feedback kidney	automaton
	autopilot
automatic block signal	chess-playing machine
automatic gun	guided missile
automatic gun director	gyroscopic pilot
	lever pilot
automatic heater	mechanical heart
automatic iron	Multiple-Stylus Electronic Printer
automatic piano	radar controls
automatic pilot	robot pilot
automatic pinspotter	robot plane
automatic pistol	robot submarine
automatic printer	self-starter
automatic rifle	speedometer
automatic sight	televox
automatic sprinkler	watcher
automatic stop	
automatic telegraph	

.30 servomechanisms

alternating-current servo	power brake
automatic feed mechanism	power servo
	selsyn
direct-current servo	servo brake
electronic servo	servomotor
Flettner control	servotab
hemostat	sine mechanism
hydraulic servo	synchro
instrument servo	synchro receiver
motor-generator servo	synchro transmitter
pneumatic servo	telemechanism

.31 electronic computers

analog computer	tor and Computer)
Audrey (Automatic Digit Recognizer)	ENIAD (Electronic Numerical Integrating and Analyzing
automatic plotter	Device)
BINAC (Binary Automatic Computer)	equation solver
data processor	ERMA (Electronic Recording
decimal digital differential analyzer	Machine—Accounting)
decoding servomechanism	high-speed digit computer
differential analyzer	IBM machine
digital computer	IDA (Integro-Differential Analyzer)
digital differential analyzer	IDP machine (Integrated Data Processing)
digital general purpose computer	Magnetronic Reservisor
digital graph plotter	
direct-reading computer	OARAC (Office of Air Research Auto-
ENIAC (Electronic Numerical Integra-	

matic Computer)	ter
printing calculator	telecomputer
Production-Control Quantometer	Teleplotter
	Telereader
RAYDAC (Raytheon Data Calculator)	tristimulus computer
selective calculator	UNIVAC (Universal Automatic Computer)
Selective Sequence Electronic Calculator	versatile digit computer
square root planime-	

.32 computer parts

adder	for Input to Computers)
analytical control unit	integrator
analyzer	memory tubes
coder	multiplier
coefficient component	phase discriminator
collator	position code converter
compiler	
decoder	position coder
detector	printer
differential	receptor
divider	relay
electrostatic storage unit	selector
	storage unit
FOSDIC (Film Optical Sensing Device	transmitter

.33 system components

actuator	modulator
amplifier	oscillator
amplifying generator	oscillator relay actuator
calibrating unit	
capacitor	phase-discriminating amplifier
clock	
control relay	pressure transducer
control resistor	reactor
converter	records-pulse generator
discriminating relay	
effector	regenerator
electropneumatic transducer	relay
	reluctance amplifier
feedback amplifier	resistor
generator	servo amplifier
inductor	thermal timing relay
load-indicating resistor	transducer
	transmitter
magnetic amplifier	uncommitted amplifier
magnetic relay	
meter relay	

.34 control mechanisms

automatic switch	flow valve
automatic trip	indicating control switch
channel selector	
check valve	internal selector
contour follower	limit switch
control transformer	line breaker
control valve	line switch
diaphragm motor valve	manostat
	manual control
electrical governor	oscillator relay control
electromechanical controller	overload breaker
	overload circuit
electronic control	overload switch
electropneumatic valve positioner	phase advancer
	positioning mechanism
emergency control	
finder switch	pressure transmitter
flowmanostat	proportioning lever

rectifier
register regulator
safety control
safety fuse
safety stop
safety switch
safety valve
selector switch

sequence switch
servo valve
speed regulator
thermoswitch
timer
voltage regulator
voltage stabilizer

.35 automatic detectors

chemical detector
electronic counter
electronic detector
error corrector
error detector
liquid-level sensor
mercury-vapor detec-
  tor
metal detector
photoelectric detector
photoelectric inspec-

tion machine
photoelectric pinhole
  detector
photoelectric sorter
sensor
temperature sensor
ultrasonic detector
ultrasonic flow detec-
  tor
ultrasonic inspector

.36 automatic analyzers

analytical spectrome-
  ter
color gauge or checker
comparator
CO_2 recorder
data analyzer
dew-point hygrometer
direct-reading spec-
  trometer
electronic comparator
gas analyzer
infrared gas and liquid

analyzer
mass spectrograph
mass spectrometer
oxygen recorder
recording analyzer
scanner
stigmatic grating spec-
  trograph
surface analyzer
vibration and stress
  analyzer

.37 automatic indicators

control indicator
count-rate meter
current indicator
density indicator
detonation indicator
differential pressure
  gauge
events-per-unit-time
  meter
fault lamp
filled-system ther-
  mometer
flowmeter
galvanometer
humidity indicator
hygrometer
integrating flowmeter
interferometer
ionization gauge
light-intensity indica-
  tor
liquid-level indicator
load indicator

logger
moisture meter
pH meter
potentiometer
pressure indicator
proximity meter
psychometer
pyrometer
radiation pyrometer
resistance thermome-
  ter
square-root flowmeter
strain gauge
tensiometer
thermistor
thermocouple
thermocouple pyrom-
  eter
time-interval meter
turn indicator
vibration meter
voltage indicator

350. FRICTION

.1 NOUNS **friction, rubbing,** rub, frottage; frication or confrication or perfrication [all archaic]; tribo–, –tribe.

.2 **abrasion, attrition, erosion, wearing away, wear,** detrition, ablation; erasure, rubbing away or off or out; **grinding, filing,** rasping, limation; fretting; galling; chafing, chafe; **scraping,** grazing, scratching, scuff-

ing; **scrape,** scratch, **scuff;** scrubbing, scouring; scrub; **polishing,** burnishing, sanding, smoothing, dressing, buffing, shining; sandblasting; abrasive 260.14.

.3 **massage,** massaging, stroking, kneading; **rubdown;** massotherapy; whirlpool bath, vibrator; facial massage, facial.

.4 massager, **masseur, masseuse;** massotherapist.

.5 (mechanics) force of friction, internal friction, starting friction, static friction, rolling friction, sliding friction, fluid friction, slip friction; force of viscosity; coefficient of friction, resistance, frictional resistance, drag; skin friction; friction loss, friction head.

.6 VERBS rub, frictionize; **massage,** knead, rub down; caress, pet, stroke 425.8.

.7 **abrade,** abrase, gnaw, gnaw away; **erode,** ablate, wear, wear away; erase, rub away or off or out; **grind, rasp, file, grate; chafe,** fret, gall; **scrape, graze,** raze [archaic], **scuff,** bark, skin; **fray, frazzle; scrub, scour.**

.8 **buff, burnish, polish,** rub up, sandpaper, **sand,** smooth, dress, shine, furbish, sandblast.

.9 ADJS **frictional,** friction; fricative; **rubbing.**

.10 **abrasive,** abradant, attritive, gnawing, erosive, ablative; **grinding, rasping;** chafing, fretting, galling.

351. TEXTURE

(surface quality)

.1 NOUNS **texture,** surface texture; **surface; finish,** feel; **grain,** granular texture, fineness or coarseness of grain; **weave,** woof 222.3, **wale; nap,** pile, shag, nub, knub, protuberance 256; **pit,** pock, indentation 257.6; structure 245.

.2 **roughness** 261; **coarseness, grossness, unrefinement,** coarse-grainedness; cross-grainedness; **graininess,** granularity, granulation, grittiness; hardness 356.

.3 **smoothness** 260, **fineness, refinement,** fine-grainedness; **delicacy, daintiness;** filminess, gossameriness 339.1; down, **downiness,** fluff, fluffiness, velvet, velvetiness, fuzz, fuzziness, peach fuzz, pubescence; satin, satininess; silk, silkiness; softness 357.

.4 VERBS **coarsen; grain,** granulate; **tooth, roughen** 261.4; smooth 260.5.

.5 ADJS **textural, textured.**

.6 **rough** 261.6, **coarse, gross, unrefined,**

coarse-grained; cross-grained; grained, grainy, granular, granulated, gritty.

.7 nappy, pily, shaggy, nubby or nubbly, studded, knobbed 256.16; pitted 257.17.

.8 smooth 260.9; fine, refined, attenuate, attenuated, fine-grained; delicate, dainty; finespun, thin-spun, fine-drawn, wiredrawn; gauzy, filmy, gossamer, gossamery 339.4, downy, fluffy, velvety, velutinous, fuzzy, pubescent; satin, satiny, silky.

352. WEIGHT

.1 NOUNS weight, heaviness, weightiness, ponderousness, ponderosity, gravity, heftiness or heft [both informal]; body weight, avoirdupois [informal], fatness 195.8, beef or beefiness [both informal]; poundage, tonnage; ponderability; deadweight, liveweight; gross weight, gr. wt.; net weight, neat weight, nt. wt., net, nett [Brit]; underweight; overweight; overbalance, overweightage.

.2 onerousness, burdensomeness, oppressiveness, cumbersomeness, cumbrousness; massiveness, massiness [archaic], bulkiness 195.9, lumpishness, unwieldiness.

.3 (sports) bantamweight, featherweight, flyweight, heavyweight, light heavyweight, lightweight, middleweight, welterweight; catchweight.

.4 counterbalance 33.2; makeweight; ballast, ballasting.

.5 [phys terms] gravity, gravitation, G; specific gravity; gravitational field, gravisphere; graviton; geotropism, positive geotropism, apogeotropism, negative geotropism; G suit, anti-G suit; mass.

.6 weight, paperweight, letterweight; sinker, lead, plumb, plummet, bob; sandbag.

.7 burden, burthen [archaic], pressure, oppression, deadweight; burdening, saddling, charging, taxing; overburdening, overtaxing, overweighting, weighing or weighting down; charge, load, loading, lading, freight, cargo, bale; cumber, cumbrance, encumbrance; incubus; incumbency or superincumbency [archaic]; handicap, drag, millstone; surcharge, overload.

.8 (systems of weight) avoirdupois weight, troy weight, apothecaries' weight; atomic weight, molecular weight.

.9 weighing, hefting [informal], balancing; weighing-in, weigh-in, weighing-out, weigh-out.

.10 VERBS weigh, weight; heft [informal], balance, weigh in the balance, strike a balance, hold the scales, put on the scales, lay in the scales; counterbalance 33.5; weigh in, weigh out; be heavy, weigh heavy, lie heavy, have weight, carry weight; tip the scales, turn or depress the scales.

.11 weigh on or upon, rest on or upon, bear on or upon, lie on, press, press down, press to the ground.

.12 weight, weigh or weight down; hang like a millstone; ballast; lead, sandbag.

.13 burden, burthen [archaic], load, lade, cumber, encumber, charge, freight, tax, handicap, hamper, saddle; oppress, weigh one down, weigh on or upon, weigh heavy on, bear or rest hard upon, lie hard or heavy upon, press hard upon, be an incubus to; overburden, overweight, overtax, overload 663.15.

.14 outweigh, overweigh, overweight, overbalance, outbalance, outpoise, overpoise.

.15 gravitate, descend 316.5,6, drop, plunge 320.6, precipitate, sink, settle, subside; tend, tend to go, incline, point, head, lead, lean.

.16 ADJS heavy, bar(o)–, gravi–, hadr(o)–; ponderous, massive, massy, weighty, hefty [informal], fat 195.18; leaden, heavy as lead; heavyweight; overweight.

.17 onerous, oppressive, burdensome, incumbent or superincumbent, cumbersome, cumbrous; massive; lumpish, unwieldy.

.18 weighted, weighed or weighted down; burdened, oppressed, laden, cumbered, encumbered, charged, loaded, fraught, freighted, taxed, saddled, hampered; overburdened, overloaded, overladen, overcharged, overfreighted, overfraught, overweighted, overtaxed.

.19 weighable, ponderable; appreciable, palpable, sensible.

.20 gravitational, mass.

.21 ADVS heavily, heavy, weightily, leadenly; burdensomely, onerously, oppressively; ponderously, cumbersomely, cumbrously.

.22 weighing instruments

alloy balance	flexure plate scale
analytical balance	lever scales
assay balance	long-arm balance
automatic indicating scale	Nicholson's hydrometer
balance	pair of scales
balance of precision	plate fulcrum scale
barrel scale	platform scale or balance
beam	
bullion balance	precision scale or balance
counter scale	
cylinder scale	Roman balance
Danish balance	scale, scales
drum scale	short-arm balance
fan scale	spiral balance

spring balance
spring scale
steelyard
torsion scale
trone [Scot]
weighbeam

weighbridge
weighing machine
weigh scales
Weightometer
weight voltameter

.23 units of weight *or* **force** *or* **mass**

assay ton
carat, c.
carat grain
centigram, cg.
decagram, dkg.
decigram, dg.
dram, dram avoirdu-
  pois, dr.
dram apothecaries',
  dr. ap.
dyne
grain, gr.
gram, g.
gram equivalent, gram
  equivalent weight
gram molecule, gram-
  molecular weight
gross ton
hectogram, hg.
hundredweight, cwt.
international carat
kilogram, kilo, kg.
kiloton
long hundredweight
long ton, l.
megaton
metric carat
metric ton, MT *or* t.

microgram, mcg.
milligram, mg.
mole, mol.
myriagram, myg.
net ton
newton
ounce, ounce avoirdu-
  pois, oz., oz. av.
ounce apothecaries',
  oz. ap.
ounce troy, oz. t.
pearl grain
pennyweight, dwt. *or*
  pwt.
pound, pound avoir-
  dupois, lb., lb. av.
poundal
pound apothecaries',
  lb. ap.
pound troy, lb. t.
quintal, q.
scruple, s. ap.
short hundredweight
short ton, s.t.
slug
sthene
stone, st.
ton, tn.

353. LIGHTNESS

.1 NOUNS **lightness, levity,** unheaviness, lack of weight; **weightlessness; buoyancy,** floatability; levitation, ascent 315; **volatility; airiness,** ethereality; foaminess, frothiness, bubbliness, yeastiness; downiness, fluffiness, gossameriness 339.1; softness, gentleness, delicacy, daintiness, tenderness.

.2 (comparisons) air, ether, feather, down, thistledown, flue, fluff, fuzz, sponge, gossamer, cobweb, fairy, straw, chaff, dust, mote, cork, chip, bubble, froth, foam, spume.

.3 lightening, easing, **easement, alleviation, relief;** disburdening, **disencumberment,** unburdening, **unloading,** unlading, unsaddling, untaxing, unfreighting; unballasting.

.4 leavening, fermentation; leaven, ferment; zym(o)–.

.5 (indeterminacy of weight) **imponderableness** *or* imponderability, unweighableness *or* unweighability; imponderables, imponderabilia.

.6 VERBS **lighten,** make light *or* lighter, reduce weight; unballast; **ease, alleviate, relieve;** disburden, disencumber, unburden,

unload, unlade, off-load; **be light,** weigh lightly, have little weight, kick the beam.

.7 **leaven, raise, ferment.**

.8 **buoy,** buoy up; float, float high, ride high, waft; **sustain, hold up,** bear up, uphold, upbear, uplift, upraise.

.9 **levitate** (opposed to gravitate), **rise,** ascend 315.8; hover, **float.**

.10 ADJS **light,** unheavy, **imponderous; weightless; airy, ethereal; volatile;** frothy, foamy, bubbly, yeasty; downy, feathery, fluffy, gossamery 339.4; *soufflé, moussé, léger* [all Fr]; "lighter than vanity" [Bible], "light as any wind that blows" [Tennyson]; light as air *or* a feather *or* gossamer, etc. 353.2.

.11 **gentle, soft, delicate,** dainty, tender, **easy.**

.12 **lightweight,** bantamweight, featherweight; underweight.

.13 **buoyant,** floaty, floatable; floating, supernatant.

.14 levitative, levitational.

.15 **lightening, easing,** alleviating, alleviative, relieving, disburdening, unburdening, disencumbering.

.16 **leavening, raising, fermenting,** fermentative, working; yeasty, barmy; enzymic, diastatic.

.17 **imponderable,** unweighable.

.18 **leavens, ferments**

bacteria
baking powder
baking soda
barm
beaten egg
brewer's yeast
buttermilk
carbon dioxide
cream of tartar
diastase
enzyme
egg whites

invertase
maltase
mother, mother of
  vinegar
pepsin
soda
sour milk
vinegar
yeast
zymase
zyme

354. DENSITY

.1 NOUNS **density, denseness, solidity, solidness,** firmness, **compactness, closeness,** dasy–, spissitude [archaic]; crowdedness, jammedness, congestedness, congestion; impenetrability, impermeability, imporosity; hardness 356; incompressibility; specific gravity, relative density; **consistency,** consistence; viscidity, viscosity, viscousness, **thickness,** gluiness.

.2 **indivisibility, inseparability,** impartibility, infrangibility, indiscerptibility; indissolubility; cohesion, coherence 50.1; unity 89; insolubility, infusibility.

.3 **densification, condensation, compression, concentration,** concretion, consolidation;

hardening, **solidification** 356.5; agglutination, clumping, clustering.

.4 **thickening,** inspissation; congelation, **congealment, coagulation,** clotting, **setting,** concretion; gelatinization, gelatination, jellification, jellying, **jelling,** gelling; curdling, clabbering.

.5 **precipitation,** deposit, sedimentation; precipitate 43.2.

.6 **solid,** solid body, body, mass; lump, clump, cluster; block, cake; node, knot; concrete, concretion; conglomerate, conglomeration.

.7 **clot,** coagulum, coagulate; blood clot, grume, thrombus, thromb(o)–, embolus, crassamentum; casein, caseinogen, paracasein, legumin; **curd,** clabber, loppered milk or bonnyclabber [both dial], clotted cream, Devonshire cream.

.8 (instruments) densimeter, densitometer; aerometer, hydrometer, lactometer, urinometer, pycnometer.

.9 VERBS **densify,** densen; **condense, compress,** compact, **consolidate, concentrate,** congest, squeeze, **press, crowd,** cram, jam, ram down; **solidify** 356.8.

.10 **thicken,** thick [archaic]; inspissate, incrassate; **congeal, coagulate, clot,** set, concrete; gelatinize, gelatinate, jelly, jellify, **jell,** gel; **curdle,** curd, clabber, lopper [dial]; cake, lump, clump, cluster, knot.

.11 **precipitate,** deposit, sediment, sedimentate.

.12 ADJS **dense, compact, close,** pycn(o)–; close-textured, close-knit, close-woven; serried, **thick, heavy,** thickset, thickpacked, thick-growing, thick-spread, thick-spreading; **condensed, compressed,** compacted, concrete, consolidated, concentrated; **crowded, jammed,** packed, jam-packed, **congested,** crammed, crammed full; **solid,** firm, substantial, massive; impenetrable, impermeable, imporous, nonporous; hard 356.10; incompressible; viscid, viscous or viscose, gluey.

.13 **indivisible,** nondivisible, undividable, **inseparable,** impartible, infrangible, indiscerptible, indissoluble; cohesive, coherent 50.10; unified 89.10; insoluble, indissolvable, infusible.

.14 **thickened,** inspissate or inspissated, incrassate; **congealed, coagulated, clotted,** grumous; **curdled,** curded, clabbered; **jellied,** jelled, gelatinized; lumpy, lumpish; caked, cakey.

.15 ADVS **densely,** compactly, **close,** closely, **thick,** thickly, heavily; solidly, firmly.

355. RARITY

.1 NOUNS **rarity,** rareness; **thinness, tenuousness,** tenuity; **subtlety,** subtility, subtilty; **fineness,** slightness, flimsiness, **unsubstantiality** or **insubstantiality** 4; **ethereality,** airiness, immateriality, incorporeality, bodilessness, insolidity; "airy nothing", "such stuff as dreams are made on" [both Shakespeare].

.2 **rarefaction,** attenuation, subtilization, etherealization; **thinning,** dilution, adulteration.

.3 VERBS **rarefy, attenuate,** thin, thin out; dilute, adulterate, water, water down, cut; subtilize, **etherealize;** expand 197.4.

.4 ADJS **rare,** rarefied; **subtle,** subtile; **thin,** thinned, dilute, attenuated, attenuate; thinned-out, diluted, adulterated, watered, watered-down, cut; **tenuous, fine,** flimsy, slight, **unsubstantial** or **insubstantial** 4.5; **airy, ethereal,** vaporous, gaseous, windy; uncompact, uncompressed.

.5 rarefactive, rarefactional.

356. HARDNESS, RIGIDITY

.1 NOUNS **hardness,** durity [archaic], induration; **callousness,** callosity; stoniness, flintiness, steeliness; **toughness** 359; solidity, impenetrability, density 354; restiveness, resistance 792; obduracy 626.1; hardness of heart 856.3.

.2 **rigidity, rigidness,** rigor [archaic]; **firmness,** renitence, renitency, **stiffness,** starchiness; **tension,** tensity, **tenseness,** tautness, tightness.

.3 **inflexibility,** unpliability, unmalleability, intractability, unbendingness, unlimberness, **stubbornness,** unyieldingness 626.2; **unalterability,** immutability; immovability 142.3; inelasticity, irresilience or irresiliency; inextensibility or unextensibility, unextendibility, inductility.

.4 **temper,** tempering; chisel temper, die temper, razor temper, saw file temper, set temper, spindle temper, tool temper; precipitation hardening, heat treating; hardness scale; indenter.

.5 **hardening, toughening,** induration, firming; **tempering,** case hardening, steeling; **solidification, setting,** concretion; crystallization, granulation; callusing; sclerosis, arteriosclerosis, atherosclerosis; lithification; lapidification [archaic]; **petrification,** petrifaction; fossilization, ossification, –ostosis; cornification, hornification; calcification; vitrification, vitrifaction; **stiffening,** rigidification.

.6 (comparisons) stone, rock 384, adamant, granite, flint, marble, diamond; steel, iron, nails; concrete, cement; brick; oak, heart of oak; bone 245.6,12.

.7 VERBS **harden**, indurate, firm, **toughen**; **callous**; **temper**, anneal, **case harden**, steel; **petrify**, lapidify [archaic], fossilize; lithify; vitrify; calcify; ossify; cornify, hornify.

.8 **solidify**, concrete, **set**, take a set, cake; condense, thicken 354.10; **crystallize**, granulate, candy.

.9 **stiffen**, rigidify, **strengthen**, back, reinforce, shore up; **tense**, **tighten**, brace, trice up, screw up.

.10 ADJS **hard**, **solid**, dure [archaic], **tough** 359.4, scler(a)– or sclero–; resistive, resistant, steely, steellike, iron-hard, ironlike; **stony**, rocky, stonelike, rocklike, lapideous, lithoid or lithoidal, lith(o)–, –lith, –lite or – lyte; diamondlike; flinty, flintlike; marble, marblelike; granitic, granitelike; concrete, cement, cemental; horny, cerat(o)– or kerat(o)–, corneous, –corn; bony, osseous; hard-boiled; hard as nails or a rock, etc. 356.6, "as firm as a stone; yea, as hard as a piece of the nether millstone" [Bible]; dense 354.12; obdurate 626.10; hardhearted 856.12.

.11 **rigid**, **stiff**, **firm**, renitent; **tense**, **taut**, **tight**, **unrelaxed**; virgate, rodlike; ramrodstiff, ramrodlike, pokerlike; stiff as a poker, stiff as buckram; starched, starchy.

.12 **inflexible**, unflexible, **unpliable**, **unpliant**, **unmalleable**, **intractable**, untractable, intractile, **unbending**, unlimber, **unyielding** 626.9, ungiving, **stubborn**, **unalterable**, immutable; **immovable** 142.15; **adamant**, adamantine; **inelastic**, nonelastic, irresilient; inextensile, inextensible, unextensible, inextensional, unextendible, nonstretchable, inductile.

.13 **hardened**, **toughened**, steeled, indurate, indurated; **case-hardened**; **callous**, calloused; **solidified**, set; crystallized, granulated; petrified, lapidified [archaic], fossilized; vitrified; sclerotic; ossified; cornified, hornified; calcified; crusted, crusty, incrusted; **stiffened**, **strengthened**, rigidified, backed, reinforced.

.14 **hardening**, **toughening**, indurative; petrifying, petrifactive.

.15 **tempered**, heat-treated, **annealed**, oil-tempered.

357. SOFTNESS, PLIANCY

.1 NOUNS **softness**, nonresistiveness, insolidity, unsolidity, nonrigidity; **gentleness**, easiness, delicacy, morbidezza, tenderness, leniency 759; **mellowness**; fluffiness, flossiness, downiness, featheriness; velvetiness, plushiness, satininess, silkiness; sponginess, pulpiness.

.2 **pliancy**, **pliability**, **plasticity**, **flexibility**, flexility, flexuousness, ductility, ductibility [archaic], tensileness, tensility, tractility, **tractability**, amenability, adaptability, facility, **elasticity**, give, bendability; **suppleness**, willowiness, springiness, **litheness**, **limberness**; **malleability**, moldability, fictility, sequacity [archaic]; **impressionability**, susceptibility, responsiveness, receptiveness, sensibility, sensitiveness; formability, formativeness; extensibility, extendibility; agreeability 622.1; submissiveness 765.3.

.3 **flaccidity**, flaccidness, **flabbiness**, **limpness**, rubberiness, floppiness; **looseness**, laxness, laxity, laxation.

.4 (comparisons) putty, clay, dough, blubber, rubber, wax, butter, pudding; velvet, plush, satin, silk; wool, fleece; pillow, cushion, kapok; puff; fluff, floss, flue; down, feathers, feather bed, eiderdown, swansdown, thistledown; breeze, zephyr, foam.

.5 **softening**, softening-up; **easing**, padding, cushioning; mollifying, mollification; **relaxation**, laxation; mellowing.

.6 VERBS **soften**, soften up; **ease**, cushion; gentle, mollify, milden; **subdue**, tone or tune down; mellow; tenderize; **relax**, laxate, loosen; **limber**, limber up, supple; massage, knead, plump, fluff, shake up; **mash**, **smash**, squash, pulp.

.7 **yield**, **give**, relent, relax, bend, unbend, give way; submit 765.6–11.

.8 ADJS **soft**, malac(o)–; nonresistive, nonrigid; mild, **gentle**, **easy**, **delicate**, **tender**; complaisant 759.8; mellow, mellowy [archaic]; **softened**, mollified; whisper-soft, soft as putty or clay or dough, etc. 357.4, soft as a kiss, soft as a sigh, "soft as sinews of the new-born babe" [Shakespeare].

.9 **pliant**, **pliable**, **flexible**, flexile, flexuous, **plastic**, **elastic**, **ductile**, sequacious or facile [both archaic], tractile, **tractable**, **yielding**, giving, bending; adaptable, **malleable**, moldable, shapable, fabricable, fictile; compliant 622.5, submissive 765.12; **impressionable**, impressible, susceptible, responsive, receptive, sensitive; **formable**, formative; **bendable**; supple, willowy, **limber**; **lithe**, lithesome, lissome, "as lissome as a hazel wand" [Tennyson], springy, whippy; extensile, extensible, extendible; like putty *or* wax *or* dough, etc. 357.4.

.10 **flaccid, flabby, limp,** rubbery, flimsy, floppy; **loose,** lax, relaxed.

.11 **spongy,** pulpy, pithy, medullary; edematous.

.12 **pasty, doughy;** loamy, clayey, argillaceous.

.13 **squashy,** squishy, squushy, squelchy.

.14 **fluffy,** flossy, **downy,** pubescent, feathery; fleecy, woolly, lanate; furry.

.15 **velvety,** velvetlike, velutinous; plushy, plush; **satiny,** satinlike; cottony; **silky,** silken, silklike, sericeous, soft as silk.

.16 **softening, easing;** subduing, mollifying, emollient; demulcent; **relaxing,** loosening.

.17 ADVS **softly, gently,** easily, delicately, tenderly; compliantly 622.9, submissively 765.17.

358. ELASTICITY

.1 NOUNS **elasticity, resilience** *or* resiliency, **give;** snap, **bounce,** bounciness; **stretch, stretchiness,** stretchability; extensibility; tone, tonus, tonicity, –tonia *or* –tony; **spring, springiness;** rebound 284.2; **flexibility** 357.2; **adaptability,** responsiveness; **buoyancy** *or* buoyance; **liveliness** 707.2.

.2 **stretching;** extension 202.5; distension 197.2; **stretch, tension, strain.**

.3 **elastic;** elastomer; **rubber,** gum elastic; stretch fabric, Lastex, spandex; gum, chewing gum 389.6; whalebone, baleen; rubber band, rubber ball, handball, tennis ball; spring; springboard; trampoline; racket, battledore; jumping jack.

.4 VERBS **stretch;** extend 202.7; distend 197.4.

.5 **give,** yield 357.7; bounce, spring, spring back 284.6.

.6 **elasticize;** rubberize, rubber; vulcanize.

.7 ADJS **elastic, resilient, springy, bouncy; stretchable, stretchy,** stretch; extensile; **flexible** 357.9; flexile; **adaptable,** adaptive, responsive; buoyant; lively 707.17.

.8 **rubber, rubbery,** rubberlike; rubberized.

.9 **rubber**

Buna	elastomer
Buna N	foam rubber
Buna S	hard rubber
Butyl rubber	India rubber
caoutchouc	Koroseal
caucho	latex
Ceará rubber	methyl rubber
cis-polyisoprene rubber	natural rubber
cold rubber	neoprene rubber
crepe, crepe rubber	nitrile rubber
crude rubber	Pará rubber
ebonite	Perbunan
	plantation rubber

polysulfide rubber	sponge rubber
polyurethane rubber	synthetic rubber
reclaimed rubber	Thiokol
rubber tissue	vulcanite
silicone rubber	vulcanized rubber

.10 **springs**

balance spring	leaf spring
bedspring	mainspring
box spring	shock absorber
coil spring	spiral spring
elliptic spring	volute spring
hairspring	

359. TOUGHNESS

.1 NOUNS **toughness, resistance; strength, hardiness, vitality, stamina** 159.1; stubbornness, **stiffness; unbreakableness** *or* **unbreakability,** infrangibility; cohesiveness, **tenacity,** viscidity 50.3; **durability,** lastingness 110.1; **hardness** 356; **leatheriness,** leatherlikeness; stringiness, ropiness.

.2 (comparisons) leather; gristle, cartilage.

.3 VERBS **toughen,** harden, stiffen, **temper,** strengthen; be tough; endure, hang tough [slang].

.4 ADJS **tough, resistant,** stubborn, stiff; **strong, hardy,** vigorous 159.13; cohesive, **tenacious,** viscid 50.12; **durable,** lasting 110.10; untiring; **hard** 356.10; chewy [informal]; leathery, leatherlike, coriaceous, tough as leather; sinewy, wiry; gristly, cartilaginous; stringy, ropy, fibrous.

.5 **unbreakable,** nonbreakable, infrangible, unshatterable, shatterproof, chip-proof, fractureproof.

.6 **toughened,** hardened, tempered, annealed.

360. BRITTLENESS, FRAGILITY

.1 NOUNS **brittleness, crispness,** crispiness; **fragility, frailty,** delicacy 160.2, flimsiness, **breakability,** breakableness, frangibility, fracturableness, crackability, crackableness, crushability, crushableness; lacerability; fissility; friability, crumbliness 361; vulnerability 697.4.

.2 (comparisons) eggshell, matchwood, old paper, piecrust, glass, china, parchment, ice, bubble, glass house, house of cards.

.3 VERBS break, shard, shatter 49.12,13, fall to pieces, disintegrate 53.3.

.4 ADJS **brittle, crisp,** crispy; **fragile, frail,** delicate 160.14, flimsy, **breakable,** frangible, crushable, crackable, fracturable; lacerable; **shatterable,** shattery, shivery, splintery; friable, crumbly 361.13; fissile; scissile; brittle as glass; vulnerable 697.16.

361. POWDERINESS, CRUMBLINESS

.1 NOUNS powderiness, pulverulence, dustiness; chalkiness; mealiness, flourines, branniness; efflorescence.

.2 granularity, graininess, granulation; sandiness, grittiness, gravelliness, sabulosity.

.3 friability, pulverableness, crispness, crumbliness; brittleness 360.

.4 pulverization, comminution, trituration, attrition, detrition; levigation; reduction to powder or dust; fragmentation, sharding; brecciation; atomization, micronization; powdering, crumbling; abrasion 350.2; grinding, grating, shredding; granulation, granulization; beating, pounding, mashing, smashing, crushing; disintegration 53.

.5 powder, dust, attritus, coni(o)– or koni-(o)–; dust ball, pussies, kittens, slut's wool, lint; efflorescence; crumb, crumble; meal, bran, flour, farina, aleuro–; grits, groats; filings, raspings, sawdust; soot, smut; airborne particles, air pollution, fallout; cosmic dust.

.6 grain, granule, granulet, granul(o)– or granuli–, chondr(o)–; grit, sand, amm(o)–, psamm(o)–; gravel, shingle; detritus, debris; breccia, collapse breccia.

.7 pulverizer, comminutor, kominuter, triturator, levigator; crusher, rock crusher; mill 348.23; grinder; granulator; grater, nutmeg grater, cheese grater; shredder; pestle, mortar and pestle; masher; millstone, quern, quernstone; roller, steamroller.

.8 koniology; konimeter.

.9 VERBS pulverize, powder, comminute, triturate, contriturate, levigate, bray, pestle, disintegrate, reduce to powder or dust, grind to powder or dust; fragment, shard; brecciate; atomize, micronize; crumble, crumb; granulate, granulize, grain; grind, grate, shred, abrade 350.7; mill, flour; beat, pound, mash, smash, crush, squash, scrunch [informal].

.10 (be reduced to powder) powder, come or fall to dust, crumble, crumble to or into dust, disintegrate 53.3, fall to pieces, break up; effloresce; granulate, grain.

.11 ADJS powdery, dusty, pulverulent, pulverous; pulverized, pulverant, powdered, disintegrated, comminute, gone to dust, reduced to powder; ground, grated, pestled, milled, comminuted, triturated, levigated; sharded, crushed; shredded; fine, impalpable; chalky, chalklike; mealy, floury, farinaceous; branny; furfuraceous, scaly, scurfy; flaky 227.7; detrited, detrital; scobiform, scobicular; efflorescent.

.12 granular, grainy, granulate, granulated; sandy, gritty, sabulous, arenarious, arenaceous; shingly, shingled, pebbled, pebbly; gravelly; breccial, brecciated.

.13 pulverable, pulverizable, pulverulent, triturable; friable, crimp [archaic], crisp, crumbly.

362. COLOR

.1 NOUNS color, hue; tint, tinct, tincture, tinge, shade, tone, cast; key; coloring, coloration; color harmony, color balance, color scheme; decorator color; complexion, skin color or coloring or tone; chromatism, chromism; achromatism 363.1; natural color; undercolor; pallor 363.2; –chroia, –chromasia, chrom(o)–, chromat(o)–, –chrome, –chromia, –chromy.

.2 warmth, warmth of color, warm color; blush, flush, glow, healthy glow or hue.

.3 softness, soft color, subtle color, pale color, pastel, pastel color.

.4 colorfulness, color, bright color, pure color, brightness, brilliance, vividness, intensity, saturation; richness, gorgeousness, gaiety; riot of color; Technicolor.

.5 garishness, loudness, luridness, gaudiness 904.3; loud or screaming color [informal]; shocking pink, jaundiced yellow, arsenic green; clashing colors, color clash.

.6 color quality; chroma, Munsell chroma, brightness, purity, saturation; hue, value, lightness; colorimetric quality, chromaticity, chromaticness; tint, tone; chromatic color, achromatic or neutral color; warm color; cool color.

.7 color system, chromaticity diagram, color triangle, Maxwell triangle; hue cycle, color circle, chromatic circle, color cycle or gamut; Munsell scale; color solid; fundamental colors; primary color, primary pigment, primary; secondary color, secondary; tertiary color, tertiary; complementary color; chromaticity coordinate; color mixture curve or function; spectral color, spectrum color, pure or full color; metamer; spectrum, solar spectrum, color spectrum, chromatic spectrum, color index; monochrome; demitint, half tint, halftone.

.8 (coloring matter) color, coloring, colorant, –phyll, tinction, tincture, pigment, pigmento–, stain; chromogen; dye, dyestuff, color filter, color gelatin; paint, distemper, tempera; coat, coating, coat of paint; undercoat, undercoating, primer, priming, prime coat, **ground, flat coat,** dead-color; interior paint, exterior paint, floor enamel; wash, wash coat, flat wash; opaque color, transparent color; medium, vehicle; drier; thinner; turpentine, turps [informal].

.9 (persons according to hair color) **brunet; blond,** goldilocks; bleached blond, peroxide blond; ash blond, platinum blond, strawberry blond, honey blond; **towhead; redhead,** carrottop.

.10 (science of colors) chromatology; chromatics, chromatography, chromatoscopy, colorimetry; spectrum analysis, spectroscopy, spectrometry.

.11 (applying color) **coloring,** coloration; **staining, dyeing; tinting,** tinging, tinction; pigmentation; illumination, emblazonry; color printing; lithography.

.12 **painting,** coating, covering; **enameling,** glossing, glazing; **varnishing,** japanning, lacquering, shellacking; staining; **calcimining, whitewashing;** gilding; stippling; frescoing, fresco; undercoating, priming.

.13 VERBS color, hue, lay on color; **tinge, tint,** tinct, **tincture,** tone, complexion; pigment; bedizen; **stain, dye,** dip; imbue; deep-dye, fast-dye, double-dye, dye in the wool; ingrain; grain; shade, shadow; illuminate, emblazon; **paint,** apply paint, **coat,** cover, face; dab, **daub,** bedaub, smear, besmear, brush on paint, slap or slop on paint; **enamel,** gloss, glaze; **varnish,** japan, **lacquer, shellac; calcimine, whitewash,** parget; wash; **gild,** begild, engild; stipple; fresco; distemper; undercoat, prime.

.14 (be inharmonious) **clash,** conflict, collide, fight.

.15 ADJS **chromatic,** colorational; **coloring,** colorific, colorative, tinctorial, tingent; pigmentary; –chroic, –chrous, monochrome, monochromic, monochromatic; dichromatic; many-colored, parti-colored, medley or motley [both archaic], rainbow, **variegated** 374.9, polychromatic; prismatic, spectral; matching, toning, harmonious; warm, glowing; cool, cold.

.16 **colored,** hued, in color, in Technicolor; **tinged, tinted,** tinctured, tinct, toned; **stained, dyed;** imbued; complexioned, complected [informal]; full-colored, full; deep, deep-colored; wash-colored.

.17 **deep-dyed, fast-dyed,** double-dyed, ·**dyed-in-the-wool;** ingrained, ingrain; colorfast, fast, fadeless, unfading, indelible, constant.

.18 **colorful,** colory; **bright, vivid,** intense,

rich, exotic, **brilliant,** burning, **gorgeous, gay,** bright-hued, bright-colored, rich-colored, gay-colored, high-colored, deep-colored.

.19 garish, lurid, loud, screaming, shrieking, glaring, flaring, flashy, flaunting, crude, blinding, overbright, raw, gaudy 904.20.

.20 **off-color,** off-tone; **inharmonious, discordant,** incongruous, **harsh,** clashing, conflicting, colliding.

.21 soft-colored, soft-hued, **soft,** softened, **subdued,** light, creamy, pastel, **pale,** subtle, mellow, delicate, quiet, tender, sweet; pearly, nacreous, mother-of-pearl, iridescent, opalescent; patinaed; somber, simple, sober, sad; flat, eggshell, semigloss, gloss.

.22 **dyes**

acid color or dye	hydroxyazobenzene
acridine dye	lake
alizarin, alizarin dye or color	madder
	madder bloom
amino azobenzene	madder extract
aniline, aniline dye	methylene
anthracene	mineral pigment
artificial or synthetic dye	mordant dye
	naphthol
azo dye	natural dye or dye-stuff
basic dye	
biological stain	phthalein
chromotrope	phthalocyanine
coal-tar dye	pincoffin
crocein	rhodamine
developing dye	trinitroaniline
direct cotton dye	trinitrophenol
disazo dye	triphenylmethane dye
eosin	vat dye
fast dye	vegetable dye
food color	woad
fuchsine	wool fast dye
garancine	xanthene dye

.23 **paints**

acrylic paint	lacquer
alkyd paint	latex paint
aluminum paint	Lucite paint
animé	luminous paint
antifouling paint	megilp
calcimine	oil-base paint
casein paint	oils, oil paints or colors
Chinese lacquer	
copal	plastic paint
copalite, copaline	polyurethane
cosmetics 900.11	poster color
deck enamel	radium paint
elemi	rubber-base paint
emulsion paint	shellac
enamel	silicate paint
engobe	stain
finger paint	synthetic lacquer
fluorescent paint	varnish
gilt, gilding	washable paint
glaze	water-base paint
gouache	watercolors
greasepaint	water glass
japan	whitewash
lac	Zanzibar copal

.24 color instruments

chromatograph	kaleidoscope
chromatometer	monochronometer
chromatoscope	prism
chromatrope	spectrograph
chromometer	spectrohelioscope
chromoscope	spectrometer
colorimeter	spectroscope 443.15

363. COLORLESSNESS

.1 NOUNS **colorlessness**, lack or absence of color, huelessness, tonelessness, achromatism, achromaticity; dullness, lackluster 337.5.

.2 **paleness, dimness,** weakness, **faintness,** fadedness; lightness, fairness; **pallor,** pallidity, pallidness, pallidi–, prison pallor, **wanness, sallowness,** pastiness, ashiness; muddiness, dullness; **anemia,** hypochromic anemia, hypochromia, chloranemia; bloodlessness, exsanguination; **ghastliness, haggardness,** lividness, sickly hue, sickliness, deadly or deathly pallor, deathly hue, cadaverousness.

.3 **decoloration,** decolorizing, decolorization, discoloration, achromatization, lightening; **fading, paling; whitening,** blanching, etiolation; **bleaching,** bleach; market bleach, madder bleach.

.4 **bleach,** bleacher, bleaching agent or substance; decolorant, decolorizer.

.5 VERBS decolor, decolorize, discolor, achromatize, etiolate; **fade, wash out; dim, dull,** tarnish, tone down; **pale, whiten,** blanch, drain, drain of color; **bleach,** peroxide, fume.

.6 lose color, **fade,** fade out; **bleach,** bleach out; **pale, turn pale,** grow pale, **change color,** turn white, **whiten, blanch,** wan.

.7 ADJS **colorless, hueless,** toneless, uncolored, achromic, achromatic, achromat(o)–, achro–, achroö–; neutral; dull, flat, mat, dead, dingy, muddy, leaden, lusterless, lackluster 337.17; **faded, washed-out,** dimmed, discolored, etiolated; **pale, dim,** weak, **faint; pallid, wan,** sallow, fallow; **white,** white as a sheet; **pasty,** mealy, waxen; **ashen,** ashy, ashenhued, gray; **anemic,** hypochromic, chloranemic; bloodless, exsanguine, exsanguinated, exsanguineous, bled white; **ghastly,** livid, lurid, **haggard,** cadaverous, sickly, deadly or deathly pale; pale as death or a ghost or a corpse, "pale as a forpined ghost" [Chaucer], "pale as his shirt" [Shakespeare]; pale-faced, tallow-faced, whey-faced.

.8 **bleached,** decolored, decolorized, whit-

ened, blanched, lightened, bleached out, bleached white; drained, drained of color.

.9 **light, fair,** light-colored, light-hued; pastel; whitish 364.8.

.10 **bleaches**

benzoyl peroxide	gray sour
bleaching clay or earth	hydrochloric acid
	hydrogen peroxide
bleaching powder	Javelle water
bleach liquor	lime
bluing	lye boil
bone charcoal	nitrogen tetroxide
calcium hypochlorite	oxalic acid
chlorine	peroxide
chlorine dioxide	sodium hypochlorite
chlorine water	sour
Clorox	sulfur dioxide
dilute acid	sulfuric acid
eau de Javelle [Fr]	white sour

364. WHITENESS

.1 NOUNS **whiteness, whitishness;** albescence; **lightness, fairness;** paleness 363.2; silveriness; snowiness, frostiness; chalkiness; pearliness; **creaminess;** blondness; hoariness, grizzliness, canescence; milkiness, lactescence; glaucousness; glaucescence; **white,** silver; albinism, albinoism, achroma, achromasia, achromatosis; albino; leukoderma, vitiligo; white race 418.2,3.

.2 (comparisons) alabaster, chalk, lily, milk, pearl, sheet, swan, fleece, foam, silver, snow, driven snow, paper, flour, ivory, maggot.

.3 **whitening,** albification, blanching; etiolation; **whitewashing; bleaching** 363.3; silvering, frosting, grizzling.

.4 **whiting,** whitening, **whitewash,** calcimine; pipe clay, Blanco [Brit].

.5 VERBS **whiten,** white [archaic], etiolate, **blanch; bleach** 363.5; silver, grizzle, frost, besnow; chalk.

.6 **whitewash,** white [archaic], calcimine; pipe-clay, Blanco [Brit]; chalk.

.7 ADJS **white,** alb(o)–, leuc(o)– or leuk(o)–; pure white, **snow-white,** snowy, niveous, white as snow, "whiter than new snow on a raven's back" [Shakespeare], frosty, frosted; **hoary,** hoar, **grizzled,** grizzly, canescent; silver, **silvery,** silvered, argent [her], argentine; platinum; chalky, cretaceous; fleece- or fleecy-white; swan-white; foam-white; **milk-white,** milky, lactescent; marble, marmoreal; lily-white, white as a lily, "white as the whitest lily on a stream" [Longfellow]; white as a sheet.

.8 **whitish,** whity, albescent; **light, fair;** pale 363.7; off-white; eggshell; glaucous, glaucescent; pearl, pearly, pearly-white, pearl-white; alabaster, alabastrine; cream, **creamy;** ivory, ivory-white; gray-white; dun-white; lint-white.

.9 **blond;** flaxen-haired, fair-haired; artificial blond, bleached-blond, peroxide-blond; ash-blond, platinum-blond, strawberry-blond, honey-blond, blond-headed, blond-haired; **towheaded,** tow-haired; golden-haired 370.5.

.10 **albino,** albinic, albinistic, albinal.

.11 **white colors and pigments**

alabaster	Kremser white
antimony white	lead carbonate
bismuth white	off white
blanc d'argent [Fr]	oyster white
blanc de fard [Fr]	Paris white
blanc d'Espagne [Fr]	pearl
blanc fixe [Fr], bar-	pearl white
ium sulfate, baryta	permanent white
white	platinum
blond	silver
bone white	snow white
Chinese white	strontium white
Dutch white	titanium white
eggshell	white lead
flake white	zinc oxide, zinc white
ivory	zinc sulfide
Kremnitz or Krems or	

365. BLACKNESS

.1 NOUNS **blackness,** nigritude, nigrescence; inkiness; **black, sable, ebony;** melanism; black race 418.2,3; darkness (absence of light) 337; –melane.

.2 **darkness, darkishness,** darksomeness, blackishness; **swarthiness,** swartness, swarth; **duskiness,** duskness; soberness, sobriety, **somberness,** graveness, sadness, funereality.

.3 **dinginess, griminess, smokiness,** sootiness, smudginess, smuttiness, blotchiness, dirtiness, **muddiness,** murkiness, fuliginousness, fuliginosity.

.4 (comparisons) ebony or ebon [archaic], jet, ink, sloe, pitch, tar, coal, charcoal, smoke, soot, smut, raven, crow, night.

.5 **blackening, darkening,** nigrification, melanization, denigration; shading; **smudging,** smutching, **smirching;** smudge, smutch, smirch, smut.

.6 **blacking,** blackening, blackwash; charcoal, burnt cork, black ink; lampblack, carbon black, stove black, gas black, soot.

.7 VERBS **blacken,** black, nigrify, melanize, denigrate; **darken,** bedarken; shade, shadow; blackwash, ink, charcoal, cork; **smudge,** smutch, **smirch,** besmirch, murk, blotch, blot, dinge; smut, soot; smoke, oversmoke; ebonize.

.8 ADJS **black,** atro–, mel(a)– or melo–, melan(o)– or melam–; **sable** [her], nigrous; **ebony,** "black as ebony" [Shakespeare]; deep black, of the deepest dye; **pitch-black, pitch-dark,** pitchy, black or dark as pitch, tar-black, tarry; night-black, night-dark, black or dark as night; midnight, black as midnight; **inky,** inky-black, atramentous, ink-black, black as ink; **jet-black,** jetty; **coal-black,** coaly, black as coal; sloe, sloe-black, sloe-colored; raven, **raven-black,** black as a crow, "cyprus black as e'er was crow" [Shakespeare]; dark 337.13–16.

.9 **dark,** dark-colored, **darkish,** darksome, blackish; nigrescent; **swarthy,** swart; **dusky,** dusk; **somber,** sombrous, **sober, grave,** sad, funereal.

.10 **dark-skinned,** black-skinned, **dark-complexioned; black, colored;** melanian, melanic, melanotic, melanistic, melanous, melano.

.11 **dingy, grimy, smoky, sooty, smudgy,** smutty, blotchy, dirty, **muddy,** murky, fuliginous, smirched, besmirched.

.12 **livid,** black and blue.

.13 **black-haired, raven-haired,** raven-tressed, black-locked; brunet.

.14 **black colors and pigments**

aniline black	ivory black
blue black	japan
bone black	lampblack
Brunswick black	naphthol blue black
carbon black	naphthylamine black
chrome black	nigrosine
corbeau	raven black
direct black	slate black
drop black, Frankfort	soot black, sooty
black	black
ink black	sulfur black

366. GRAYNESS

.1 NOUNS **grayness,** grayishness, canescence; glaucousness, glaucescence; silveriness; smokiness; mousiness; slatiness; leadenness; **gray,** neutral tint; lividness, lividity; dullness, drabness, soberness, somberness.

.2 **gray-haired** or **gray-headed person,** gray-hair, graybeard, grisard.

.3 VERBS **gray, grizzle,** silver, dapple.

.4 ADJS **gray, grayish,** gray-colored, gray-hued, gray-toned, grayed, poli(o)–; canescent; iron-gray, steely, steel-gray; Quaker-gray, Quaker-colored, acier, gray-drab; dove-gray, dove-colored; pearl-gray, pearl, pearly; silver-gray, silver, silvery, silvered; **grizzly,** grizzled, grizzle, griseous; ash-gray, ashen, ashy, cinerous, cinereous, cineritious [archaic], cinereal; dusty, dust-gray; smoky, smoke-gray; charcoal-gray; slaty, slate-colored; stone-colored; leaden, livid, lead-gray; glaucous, glaucescent; mousy, mouse-gray, mouse-colored; taupe; dapple-gray, dappled-gray, dappled, dapple; gray-spotted, gray-speckled, salt-and-pepper; gray-white, gray-black, gray-blue, gray-brown, gray-green, etc.; **dull, dingy,** dismal, **somber, sober, sad, dreary.**

.5 **gray-haired,** gray-headed, silver-headed; hoary, hoary-haired, hoaryheaded; gray-bearded, silver-bearded.

.6 gray colors and pigments

acier	mouse gray
ash	neutral tint
ash gray	olive gray
bat	opal gray
battleship gray	Oxford gray
cadet gray	oyster gray
charcoal gray	Payne's gray
cinder gray	pearl
cloud gray	pearl gray
crystal gray	pelican
dove gray	pepper-and-salt
field gray	pigeon's-neck
French gray	plumbago gray
glaucous gray	powder gray
granite gray	Quaker gray
grege	salt-and-pepper
gun metal	shell gray
iron gray	silver gray
lead gray	smoke gray
light gunmetal	steel gray
lilac gray	taupe
mole gray	zinc gray
moleskin	

367. BROWNNESS

.1 NOUNS **brownness, brownishness, brown;** browning, infuscation; brown race 418.2.

.2 VERBS **brown,** embrown, infuscate; rust; **tan, bronze,** suntan; sunburn, burn.

.3 ADJS **brown, brownish,** fusco–, pheo– or phaeo–, pyrr(o)– or pyrrh(o)–, tann(o)–; cinnamon, hazel; fuscous; **brunet,** brune; tawny, fulvous; tan, tan-colored; tan-faced, tan-skinned, tanned, sun-tanned; khaki, khaki-colored; drab, olive-drab; **dun,** dun-brown, dun-drab, dun-olive; beige, grege, ecru; **chocolate,** chocolate-colored, chocolate-brown; cocoa, cocoa-colored, cocoa-brown; coffee, coffee-colored, coffee-brown; toast, toast-brown; nut-brown; walnut, walnut-brown; seal, seal-brown; fawn, fawn-colored; grayish-brown, taupe; snuff-colored, mummy-brown; umber, umber-colored, umber-brown; olive-brown; **sepia;** sorrel; yellowish-brown, brownish-yellow; lurid [archaic]; brown as a berry, berry-brown.

.4 **reddish-brown,** brownish-red; roan; hen-na; terra-cotta; rufous, foxy; livid-brown; **mahogany,** mahogany-brown; auburn, Titian; **russet,** russety; rust, rust-colored, rusty, ferruginous, rubiginous; liver-colored, liver-brown; **bronze,** bronze-colored, bronzed, brazen; copper, coppery, copperish, cupreous, copper-colored; **chestnut,** chestnut-brown, castaneous; bay, bay-colored; bayard [archaic]; sunburned, adust [archaic].

.5 **brunet;** brown-haired; auburn-haired; xanthous.

.6 brown colors and pigments

acorn	Italian earth
alesan	Italian ocher
alizarin brown	ivory brown
anthracene brown	leather
anthragallol	Manchester brown
antique bronze	manganese brown
antique brown	maple sugar
antique drab	Mars brown
antique gold	meadow lark
Argos brown	Merida
autumn leaf	Mexican red
biscuit	mineral brown
Bismarck brown	mummy
bister	negro
bone brown	olive brown
Bordeaux	oriole
bracken	otter brown
brown madder	partridge
bunny brown	philamot
burnt almond	raw sienna
burnt umber	raw umber
cachou de Laval [Fr]	resorcin dark brown
café au lait	Roman umber
café noir	Saint Benoit
coconut	seal
Cologne brown	Sicilian umber
Cyprus earth or	suntan
umber	taupe brown
dead leaf	tawny
doeskin	tenné
drab	terra sienna
Dresden brown	terra umbra
dun	toast
feuille-morte [Fr]	topaz
foliage brown	Turkey umber
fox	umber
French nude	Vandyke brown,
Havana brown	Verona brown
hazel	

.7 reddish brown colors and pigments

Arabian red	madder brown
beef's blood	Malaga red
burgundy	oxblood
burnt ocher	oxide brown, oxide
burnt sienna	purple
Castilian brown	piccolopasso red
chestnut	red robin
Columbian red	roan
coptic	russet
cordovan	*sang de bœuf* [Fr]
henna	sienna
India red	Tanagra
Kazak	terra cotta
liver brown	Titian

368. REDNESS

.1 NOUNS **redness, reddishness,** rufosity, rubricity; **red,** *rouge* [Fr], gules; rubicundity, **ruddiness,** color, high color, floridness, floridity; rubor, erythema, erythroderma, "a fire-red cherubim's face" [Chaucer]; erythrism; reddish brown 367.7; red race 418.3; "any color, so long as it's red" [Eugene Field].

.2 **pinkness, pinkishness;** rosiness; **pink, rose.**

.3 **reddening,** rubefaction, rubification, rubescence, erubescence, rufescence; **coloring,** mantling, crimsoning, **blushing, flushing; blush,** flush, glow, bloom; hectic, hectic flush; rubefacient.

.4 VERBS (make red) **redden, rouge,** ruddle, rubify, rubric; warm, inflame; crimson, encrimson; vermilion, madder, miniate, henna, rust, carmine; incarnadine, pinkify; red-ink, lipstick.

.5 **redden,** turn *or* grow red, **color,** color up, **mantle, blush, flush, crimson;** flame, glow.

.6 ADJS **red, reddish,** gules [her], red-colored, red-hued, red-dyed, red-looking; **ruddy,** ruddied, rubicund; rubric(al), rubricate, rubricose; rufescent, rufous, rufulous; warm, hot, glowing; fiery, flaming, flame-colored, flame-red, fire-red, red as fire, lurid, red as a hot *or* live coal; reddened, inflamed; **scarlet, vermilion; crimson;** rubiate; maroon; damask; puce; stammel; cerise; iron-red; cardinal, cardinal-red; cherry, cherry-colored, cherry-red; carmine, incarmined; **ruby,** ruby-colored, ruby-red; wine, port-wine, wine-colored, wine-red, vinaceous; carnation, carnation-red; brick-red, brick-colored, bricky, tile-red, lateritious; rust, rust-red, rusty, ferruginous, rubiginous; lake-colored, laky; beet-red, red as a beet; lobster-red, red as a lobster; red as a turkey-cock; copper-red, carnelian; Titian, Titian-red; infrared; reddish-amber, reddish-gray, etc.; reddish-brown 367.4.

.7 **sanguine,** sanguineous, **blood-red,** blood-colored, bloody-red, bloody, gory, red as blood.

.8 **pink, pinkish,** pinky; **rose, rosy,** rose-colored, rose-hued, rose-red, roseate; primrose; flesh-color, flesh-colored, flesh-pink, incarnadine; coral, coral-colored, coral-red, coralline; salmon, salmon-colored, salmon-pink.

.9 **red-complexioned,** ruddy-complexioned, warm-complexioned, red-fleshed, red-faced, ruddy-faced, **ruddy,** rubicund, florid, sanguine, full-blooded; blowzy, blowzed; rosy, **rosy-cheeked;** glowing, blooming; hectic, flushed, flush; burnt, sunburned; erythematous.

.10 **redheaded,** red-haired, red-polled, red-bearded; erythristic; red-crested, red-crowned, red-tufted; carroty, chestnut, auburn, Titian, xanthous.

.11 reddening, blushing, flushing, coloring; rubescent, erubescent; rubificative, rubrific; rubefacient.

.12 **red colors and pigments**

Adrianople red	light red
alizarin	livid brown
amidonaphthol red	lobster
annatto	madder
azogrenadine	madder carmine
azolitmin	madder crimson
bright rose	madder lake
Burgundy	madder pink
burnt carmine, burnt	madder purple
crimson lake, burnt	madder red
lake	madder rose
burnt ocher	Majolica earth
cardinal	maroon
carmine	minium
carmine lake	murrey
carminette	Naples red
carnation	old red
carnelian	palladium red
casino pink	peach red
Chinese red	Persian earth
chrome red	Persian red
chrome scarlet	phenosafranine
cinnabar	Pompeian red
claret, claret red,	ponceau
claret brown	poppy
cochineal	Prussian red
Congo rubine	puce
copper red	purple lake
coquelicot	raisin
cordovan	realgar
cresol red	red lead
cramoisie	red ocher
crimson	roccellin
crimson madder	royal red
damask	rubiate
English red	rubine
faded rose	ruby
fire red	ruddle
flame red	scarlet ocher
fuchsia red	sienna
fuchsine	solferino
Goya	stammel
gridelin, gris-de-lin	strawberry
Harvard crimson	terra rosa
hellebore red	tile red
Indian red	toluidine red
infrared	Turkey red
iron red	Vandyke red
Japanese red	Venetian red
jockey	vermilionette
lake	wine

.13 **pink colors and pigments**

amaranth pink	cameo pink
annatto	carnation rose
begonia	chrome primrose
burnt rose	fiesta

flesh, flesh color
flesh red or pink
incarnadine
India pink
livid pink
madder scarlet
mallow pink
melon
moonlight
opera pink
orchid pink
orchid rose
peach
peachblossom pink

peach red
petal pink
Pompeii
primrose
red pink
rose
rose bengale
rose pink
royal pink
salmon
scarlet madder
shell pink
shocking pink
tea rose

369. ORANGENESS

.1 NOUNS **orangeness**, oranginess; **orange**.

.2 ADJS **orange**, orangeish, orangey or orangy, orange-hued, reddish-yellow; ocherous or ochery, ochrous or ochry, ochreous, ochroid, ocherish; old gold; pumpkin, pumpkin-colored; tangerine, tangerine-colored; apricot, peach; carroty, carrot-colored; orange-red, orange-yellow, red-orange, reddish-orange, yellow-orange, yellowish-orange.

.3 **orange colors and pigments**

apricot
azo-orange
burnt Italian earth
burnt ocher
burnt orange
burnt Roman ocher
burnt sienna
cadmium orange
cadmium yellow
carnelian
carotene
chrome orange
copper
copper red
Dutch orange
Florida gold
helianthin
hyacinth red
madder orange
mandarin
marigold
marigold yellow
Mars orange
methyl orange

ocher brown
ocher orange
ocher red
old gold
orange chrome yellow
orange lead
orange madder
orange mineral
orange ocher
orange vermilion
orpiment
orpiment red
pumpkin
raw sienna
realgar orange
Rubens' madder
Spanish ocher
tangerine
Tangier ocher
terra cotta
Titian
yellow carmine
zinc orange

370. YELLOWNESS

.1 NOUNS **yellowness**, yellowishness; goldenness, aureateness; yellow; gold, or; gildedness; fallowness.

.2 yellow skin, yellow complexion, sallowness; xanthochroism; **jaundice**, yellow jaundice, icterus, xanthoderma, xanthism; yellow race 418.2,3.

.3 VERBS **yellow**, turn yellow; **gild**, begild, engild; aurify; sallow; **jaundice**.

.4 ADJS **yellow**, yellowish, chrys(o)–, flav(o)–, luteo–, xanth(o)–; lutescent, luteous, luteolous; xanthic, xanthous; **gold**, **golden**, or [her], gold-colored, golden-yellow, gilt, gilded, auric, aureate; **canary**, canary-yellow; citron, citron-yellow, citreous; **lemon**, lemon-colored, lemon-yellow; sulfur-colored, sulfur-yellow; pale-yellow, **sallow**, fallow; cream, creamy, cream-colored; straw, straw-colored; flaxen, flaxen-colored, flax-colored; sandy, sand-colored; ocherous or ochery, ochrous or ochry, ochreous, ochroid, ocherish; buff, buff-colored, buff-yellow; beige, ecru; saffron, saffron-colored, saffron-yellow; primrose, primrose-colored, primrose-yellow; topaz-yellow.

.5 **yellow-haired, golden-haired**, auricomous, xanthous; blond 364.9.

.6 yellow-faced, yellow-complexioned, sallow, yellow-cheeked; **jaundiced**, xanthodermatous, icterous, icteroid.

.7 **yellow colors and pigments**

acid yellow
amber
apricot yellow
arsenic yellow
auramine
aureolin
azo flavine
azo yellow
barium chrome or chromate
barium yellow, baryta yellow
brilliant sulpho
buff
butter
cadmium yellow
California green
canarin
canary
Cassel yellow
chamois
champagne
chartreuse yellow
chrome
chrome lemon
chrome yellow
chrysophenin
Claude tint
crash
cream
crocus
curcumin
dandelion
Dutch pink
English pink
euxanthin
flax
gamboge
golden pheasant
goldenrod
golden yellow
grege
honey, honey yellow
Indian yellow
Italian pink
jonquil

king's yellow
lemon chrome
lemon yellow
madder yellow
maize
marigold yellow
massicot
metanil yellow
methyl yellow
middle stone
mikado yellow
milling yellow
naphthol yellow
oil yellow
old gold
old ivory
olivesheen
orpiment
Paris yellow
peach
pebble
permanent yellow
phosphine
primrose
primuline yellow
purree
pyrethrum yellow
quince yellow
quinoline yellow
saffron
sand
snapdragon
stil-de-grain yellow
straw
sulfur
sunflower yellow
tartrazine
yellow madder
yellow ocher
yellowstone
yolk yellow
xanthene
xanthin
xanthophyll
zinc yellow

371. GREENNESS

.1 NOUNS **greenness, greenishness; verdant-ness,** verdancy, **verdure,** virescence, viridescence, viridity; glaucousness, glaucescence; **green;** greensickness, chlorosis, chloremia, chloranemia; chlorophyll.

.2 **verdigris, patina;** patination.

.3 VERBS **green;** verdigris, patinate, patinize.

.4 ADJS **green,** chlor(o)–, verd(o)–; **verdant,** verdurous, vert [her]; grassy, leafy, leaved, foliaged; springlike, summerlike, summery, vernal, vernant, aestival; **greenish,** virescent; **grass-green,** chlorine, green as grass; citrine, citrinous; **olive,** olive-green, olivaceous; beryl-green, berylline; leek-green, porraceous [archaic]; holly, holly-green; ivy, ivy-green; emerald, emerald-green, smaragdine; chartreuse, yellow-green, yellowish-green, greenish-yellow; glaucous, glaucescent, glaucous-green; blue-green, bluish-green, green-blue, greenish-blue; greensick, chlorotic, chloremic, chloranemic.

.5 verdigrisy, verdigrised; patinous, patinaed, patinated or patinized.

.6 **green colors and pigments**

absinthe	jade
apple green	Janus green
aqua green	Kelly green
aquamarine	Kendal green
avocado green	Kildare green
beryl green	leaf green
bice	leek green
bottle green	Lincoln green
Brunswick green	malachite green
celadon	marine green
chartreuse	meadow brook
chartreuse green	methyl green
chartreuse tint	mignonette
chrome or chromium green	milori green
	Mitis green
chrome oxide green	Mittler's green
chrysolite green	Montpellier green
chrysoprase green	moss green
citron green	myrtle
civette green	Nile green
cobalt green	olive
corbeau	Paris green
cucumber green	parrot green
cypress green	patina green
duck green	pea green
Egyptian green	pistachio green
emerald	Quaker green
emeraude	reseda
fir, fir green	Rinnemann's green
gallein	sap green
glauconite	Saxony green
glaucous	Schweinfurt green
glaucous green	sea or sea-water green
grass green	serpentine green
green ocher	shamrock
Guignet's green	smalt green
Guinea green	Spanish green
holly green	terre-verte
Irish green	turquoise

verdant green	Vienna green
verdet	viridian
verd gay	viridine green
verdigris	Wedgwood green
verditer	yew green
Veronese green	zinc green

372. BLUENESS

.1 NOUNS **blueness, bluishness;** azureness; **blue, azure;** lividness, lividity; cyanosis, –cyan.

.2 VERBS **blue,** azure.

.3 ADJS **blue, bluish,** cyan(o)–, ind(i)– or indo–, cerulescent; cyanic or cyaneous or cyanean; cerulean or ceruleous; **azure** [her], azurine, azurean or azureous, azured, azure-blue, azure-colored, azure-tinted; sky-blue, sky-colored, sky-dyed; light-blue, lightish-blue, light-bluish, pale-blue; dark-blue, deep-blue; peacock-blue, pavonine, pavonian; beryl-blue, berylline; turquoise, turquoise-blue; sapphire, sapphire-blue, sapphirine; livid; cyanotic.

.4 **blue colors and pigments**

Alice blue	indigo white
aniline blue	isamine blue
aquamarine	Italian blue
azo blue	jouvence blue
azulene	lacmoid
azure	lapis lazuli blue
azurite blue	lavender blue
baby blue	Leitch's blue
benzoazurine	madder blue
beryl	marine blue
bice	methylene azure
bleu céleste [Fr]	methylene blue
blue turquoise	midnight blue
bluing	milori blue
Brunswick blue	national blue
cadet blue	navy, navy blue
calamine blue	new blue
Capri blue	old blue
cerulean	peacock blue
Chinese blue	Persian blue
ciba blue	pompadour green
cobalt	Pompeian blue
Copenhagen blue	powder blue
cornflower	Prussian blue
cyan	robin's-egg blue
cyanine blue	Saxe blue
daylight blue	sea blue
delft blue	sky blue
Dresden blue	smalt
electric blue	smoke blue
émail [Fr]	steel blue
Empire blue	trypan blue
French blue	Turnbull's blue
garter blue	turquoise
gentian blue	ultramarine
glaucous blue	water blue
Gobelin blue	Wedgwood blue
hyacinth	wisteria blue
indanthrene blue	woad
indigo	zaffer

373. PURPLENESS

.1 NOUNS **purpleness, purplishness,** purpliness; **purple;** lividness, lividity.

.2 VERBS **purple,** empurple, purpurate [archaic].

.3 ADJS **purple,** purpure [her], purpureal or purpureous or purpurean, purpurate [archaic], purpureo–, purpuri–; **purplish,** purply, purplescent; **violet,** violaceous; plum-colored, plum-purple; amethystine; **lavender,** lavender-blue; lilac; magenta; mauve; mulberry; orchid; pansy-purple, pansy-violet; raisin-colored; livid.

.4 **purple colors and pigments**

amethyst	magenta
aniline purple	mallow
Argyle purple	Mars violet
bishop's purple	mauve, mauveine
Burgundy violet	methyl violet
clematis	monsignor
dahlia	mulberry
damson	orchid
fluorite violet	pansy
fuchsia, fuchsia purple	pansy purple
fuchsia red	pansy violet
grape	Perkin's purple, Perkin's violet
grape wine	
gridelin	plum
heliotrope	pontiff purple
Hortense violet	prune purple
hyacinth	raisin black
hyacinth violet	raisin purple
imperial purple	regal purple, royal purple
king's purple	
lavender	solferino
lilac	Tyrian purple
livid purple	violet
livid violet	wine purple
madder violet	

374. VARIEGATION

(diversity of colors)

.1 NOUNS **variegation, multicolor,** particolor; medley or riot of colors; polychrome, polychromatism; dichromatism, trichromatism, etc.; dichroism, trichroism, etc.

.2 **iridescence,** iridization, irisation, **opalescence,** nacreousness, pearliness, **play of colors** or **light;** light show; moiré pattern, burelage.

.3 **spottiness,** maculation, freckliness, speckliness, mottledness, dappleness, dappledness, stippledness, spottedness, dottedness; **fleck, speck, speckle;** freckle; **spot,** dot, polka dot, macula, macule, blotch, splotch, patch, splash; **mottle, dapple; stipple,** stippling, pointillism, pointillage.

.4 **check, checker; plaid,** tartan; checkerwork, variegated pattern, harlequin, colors in patches, crazy-work, patchwork; parquet, parquetry, marquetry, mosaic, tesserae, tessellation; chessboard, checkerboard; crazy-paving [Brit].

.5 **stripe, striping, streak, streaking;** striation, striature, stria; striola, striga; crack, craze; bar, band, belt, list.

.6 (comparisons) spectrum, rainbow, iris, chameleon, leopard, jaguar, cheetah, ocelot, zebra, barber's pole, candy cane, Dalmatian, firedog, peacock, butterfly, mother-of-pearl, nacre, tortoise shell, opal, serpentine, chrysotile, antigorite, serpentine marble, marble, ophite, mackerel, mackerel sky, confetti, crazy quilt, patchwork quilt, shot silk, moiré, watered silk, marbled paper, Joseph's coat, harlequin.

.7 VERBS **variegate,** motley; polychrome, polychromize; harlequin; **mottle, dapple,** stipple, **fleck,** flake, **speck, speckle,** bespeckle, freckle, **spot,** bespot, dot, sprinkle, spangle, bespangle, pepper, stud, maculate; blotch, splotch; tattoo, stigmatize [archaic]; **check, checker;** tessellate; **stripe, streak,** striate, band, bar, vein; marble, marbleize; rainbow, iris.

.8 **iridesce,** iridize, iris; **opalesce,** opalize; moiré.

.9 ADJS **variegated, many-colored,** many-hued, divers-colored, **multicolored,** multicolor, multicolorous, **varicolored,** varicolorous, polychrome, polychromic, polychromatic, poecil(o)– or poikil(o)–, parti– or party–; parti-colored, parti-color; of all manner of colors, of all the colors of the rainbow; versicolor, versicolored, versicolorate, versicolorous; motley, medley [archaic], harlequin; colorful, colory; daedal; crazy; thunder and lightning; kaleidoscopic(al); prismatic(al), prismal, spectral; shot, shot through; bicolored, bicolor, dichromic, dichromatic; tricolored, tricolor, trichromic, trichromatic; two-color or -colored, three-color or -colored, two-tone or -toned, etc.

.10 **iridescent,** iridal, iridial, iridian, irid(o)–; irised, irisated, **rainbowy,** rainbowlike; **opalescent,** opaline, opaloid; nacreous, nacry, nacré [Fr], nacred, **pearly,** pearlish, mother-of-pearl; tortoise-shell; peacocklike, pavonine, pavonian; chatoyant; moiré, burelé.

.11 **chameleonlike,** chameleonic.

.12 **mottled, motley; pied, piebald,** skewbald, pinto; **dappled,** dapple; calico; marbled; clouded; pepper-and-salt.

.13 **spotted, dotted,** polka-dot, sprinkled, peppered, studded, pocked, pockmarked;

spotty, dotty, patchy, pocky; **speckled, specked,** speckledy, speckly, specky; **stippled,** pointillé, pointillistic; **flecked,** fleckered; spangled, bespangled; maculate, maculated, macular, macul(o)– or maculi–; punctate, punctated; freckled, frecked, freckly; blotched, blotchy, splotched, splotchy; flea-bitten.

.14 **checked,** checkered, check; **plaid,** plaided; tessellated, tessellate, mosaic.

.15 **striped,** stripy, **streaked,** streaky; **striated,** striate, striatal, striolate, strigate or strigose; barred, banded, listed; veined; **brindle,** brindled, brinded; tabby; marbled, marbleized; watered.

375. UNIVERSE

.1 NOUNS **universe, world, cosmos,** –cosm, cosm(o)–; creation, created universe, created nature, all, **all creation,** all or everything that is, all being, totality, totality of being, sum of things; omneity, allness; nature, system; wide world, whole wide world, "world without end" [Bible]; plenum; macrocosm, macrocosmos, megacosm; metagalaxy; steady-state universe, expanding universe, pulsating universe; Einsteinian universe, Newtonian universe; Ptolemaic universe, Copernican universe; sidereal universe.

.2 **heavens,** heaven, **sky, firmament,** uran(o)–; empyrean, welkin, *caelum* [L], lift or lifts [both dial]; **the blue,** blue sky, azure, cerulean, the blue serene; **ether, air,** hyaline, "the clear hyaline, the glassy sea" [Milton]; vault, cope, canopy, vault or canopy of heaven, "the arch of heaven" [Vergil], "that inverted bowl they call the sky" [Omar Khayyám], "heaven's ebon vault" [Shelley], starry heaven or heavens, "this majestical roof fretted with golden fire" [Shakespeare]; Caelus [Rom myth].

.3 **space, outer space,** cosmic space, empty space, ether space, pressureless space, celestial spaces, interplanetary or interstellar or intergalactic or intercosmic space, metagalactic space, **the void,** the void above, ocean of emptiness; chaos; outermost reaches of space; astronomical unit, light-year, parsec.

.4 **stars,** fixed stars, starry host, "living sapphires" [Milton], "all the fire-folk sitting in the air" [G. M. Hopkins], "the burning tapers of the sky" [Shakespeare], "the mystical jewels of God" [Robert Buchanan], "golden fruit upon a tree all out of reach" [George Eliot], "bright sentinels

of the sky" [William Habington], "the pale populace of Heaven" [R. Browning]; music or harmony of the spheres; orb, sphere; **heavenly body,** celestial body or sphere; **comet; morning star,** daystar, Lucifer, Phosphor, Phosphorus; **evening star,** Vesper, Hesper, Hesperus, Venus; **North Star,** polestar, polar star, lodestar, Polaris; Dog Star, Sirius, Canicula; Bull's Eye, Aldebaran.

.5 **constellation** 375.28, configuration, asterism.

.6 **galaxy, island universe,** galactic nebula, galact(o)–; spiral galaxy or nebula, spiral; barred spiral galaxy or nebula, barred spiral; elliptical or spheroidal galaxy; **Milky Way,** galactic circle, *Via Lactea* [L]; galactic cluster, supergalaxy; galactic coordinates, galactic pole, galactic latitude, galactic longitude; galactic noise, cosmic noise.

.7 **nebula,** nebulosity; gaseous nebula; dust cloud; planetary nebula; ring nebula; diffuse nebula; bright diffuse nebula; dark nebula, dark cloud, coalsack; Nebula of Lyra or Orion, Crab Nebula, the Coalsack, Black Magellanic Cloud; nebulous stars; nebular hypothesis.

.8 **star,** aster(o)–, astr(o)–, sidero–; fixed star; giant star, red giant star; main sequence star; dwarf star, white dwarf star; binary star, double star; nova, supernova; variable star, Cepheid variable; radio star, quasar, quasi-stellar radio source; pulsar; neutron star; gravity star; black hole; magnitude, stellar magnitude, relative magnitude, absolute magnitude; populations; mass-luminosity law; spectrum-luminosity diagram, Hertzsprung-Russell diagram; star catalog, star chart, sky atlas, Messier catalog, Dreyer's New General Catalog or NGC; star cloud, star cluster, globular cluster, open cluster; Pleiades or Seven Sisters, Hyades, Beehive.

.9 **planet,** wanderer, terrestrial planet, inferior planet, superior planet, secondary planet, major planet; minor planet, planetoid, asteroid; Earth; Jupiter; Mars, areo–; Mercury; Neptune; Pluto; Saturn; Uranus; Venus; solar system.

.10 **Earth, world,** *terra* [L], tellur(o)– or telluri–; **globe,** terrestrial globe, the blue planet; geosphere, biosphere; vale, vale of tears; "this pendent world", "the little O, the earth", "this goodly frame, the earth", "a stage where every man must play a part" [all Shakespeare], "a seat where gods might dwell" [Milton];

mother earth, Ge or Gaea, Tellus or Terra; whole wide world, four corners of the earth, "the round earth's imagined corners" [Donne], the length and breadth of the land; geography 385.4.

.11 **moon, satellite,** selen(o)– or seleni–; orb of night, queen of heaven, queen of night, "that orbèd maiden" [Shelley], "the wat'ry star" [Shakespeare], "the governess of floods" [Shakespeare], "a ghostly galleon tossed upon cloudy seas" [Alfred Noyes], "Maker of sweet poets" [Keats], "the wandering Moon" [Milton], "bright wanderer, fair coquette of Heaven" [Shelley], "Queen and huntress, chaste and fair" [Ben Jonson], "sovereign mistress of the true melancholy" [Shakespeare], "a ruined world, a globe burnt out, a corpse upon the road of night" [Robert Burton]; silvery moon; **new moon,** wet moon; **crescent moon,** crescent, increscent moon, increscent, waxing moon, waxing crescent moon; decrescent moon, decrescent, waning moon, waning crescent moon; gibbous moon; **half-moon,** demilune; **full moon, harvest moon,** hunter's moon; artificial satellite 282.6,14.

.12 (moon goddess, the moon personified) Diana, Phoebe, Cynthia, Artemis, Hecate or Hekate, Selene, Luna, Astarte, Ashtoreth; man in the moon.

.13 **sun,** heli(o)–; orb of day, daystar; "the glorious lamp of Heav'n, the radiant sun" [Dryden], "that orbed continent, the fire that severs day from night" [Shakespeare], "of this great world both eye and soul" [Milton], "the God of life and poesy and light" [Byron]; photosphere, chromosphere, corona; sunspot; solar flare, solar prominence; solar wind.

.14 (sun god, the sun personified) Sol, Helios, Hyperion, Titan, Phaëthon, Phoebus, Phoebus Apollo, Apollo, Ra or Amen-Ra, Shamash, Surya, Savitar.

.15 **meteor,** meteor(o)–; falling or shooting star, meteoroid, fireball, bolide; **meteorite,** meteorolite; micrometeoroid, micrometeorite; aerolite; chondrite; siderite; siderolite; tektite; meteor dust, cosmic dust; meteor trail, meteor train; meteor swarm; meteor or meteoric shower; radiant, radiant point; meteor crater.

.16 **orbit, circle, trajectory;** circle of the sphere, great circle, small circle; **ecliptic; zodiac;** zone; meridian, celestial meridian; colures, equinoctial colure, solstitial colure; equator, celestial equator, equi-

noctial, equinoctial circle or line; equinox, vernal equinox, autumnal equinox; longitude, celestial longitude, geocentric longitude, heliocentric longitude, galactic longitude, astronomical longitude, geographic or geodetic longitude; apogee, perigee; aphelion, perihelion; period.

.17 **observatory,** astronomical observatory; radio observatory, orbiting astronomical observatory or OAO, orbiting solar observatory or OSO; **planetarium;** orrery; **telescope,** astronomical telescope; reflector, refractor, Newtonian telescope, Cassegrainian telescope; **radio telescope,** radar telescope; **spectroscope,** spectrograph; spectrohelioscope, spectroheliograph; coronagraph or coronograph; heliostat, coelostat.

.18 **cosmology,** cosmography, **cosmogony;** stellar cosmogony, astrogony; cosmism, cosmic philosophy, cosmic evolution; nebular hypothesis; big bang or expanding universe theory, oscillating or pulsating universe theory, steady state or continuous creation theory.

.19 **astronomy, stargazing,** uranology, astrognosy, astrography, uranography, uranometry; astrophotography, stellar photometry; spectrography, spectroscopy, radio astronomy, radar astronomy; **astrophysics,** solar physics; celestial mechanics, gravitational astronomy; astrolithology; meteoritics; astrogeology.

.20 **astrology, stargazing,** astromancy, **horoscopy;** astrodiagnosis; natural astrology; judicial or mundane astrology; genethliacism, genethlialogy, genethliacs, genethliac astrology; **horoscope,** nativity; zodiac, **signs of the zodiac; house,** mansion; house of life, mundane house, planetary house or mansion; aspect.

.21 **cosmologist;** cosmogonist, cosmogoner; cosmographer, cosmographist; cosmic philosopher, cosmist.

.22 **astronomer,** stargazer, uranologist, uranometrist, uranographer, uranographist, astrographer, astrophotographer; radio astronomer, radar astronomer; **astrophysicist,** solar physicist; astrogeologist.

.23 **astrologer,** astrologian, astromancer, stargazer, Chaldean, astroalchemist, horoscoper, horoscopist, genethliac [archaic].

.24 ADJS **cosmic,** cosmical, **universal;** cosmologic(al), cosmogonal, cosmogonic(al); cosmographic(al).

.25 **celestial, heavenly, empyrean,** empyreal; uranic; **astral, starry, stellar,** stellary, sphery; star-spangled, star-studded; sidereal; zodiacal; equinoctial; **astronom-ic(al), astrophysical, astrologic(al)**, astrologistic, astrologous; **planetary**, planetarian, planetal, circumplanetary; planetoidal, planetesimal, asteroidal; **solar,** heliacal; terrestrial 385.6; **lunar**, lunular, lunate, lunulate, lunary, cislunar, translunar, Cynthian; semilunar; meteoric, meteoritic; extragalactic, anagalactic; galactic; nebular, nebulous, nebulose; interstellar, intersidereal; interplanetary; intercosmic.

.26 **extraterrestrial,** exterrestrial, extraterrene, extramundane, alien, space; **transmundane, otherworldly,** transcendental; extrasolar.

.27 ADVS **universally,** everywhere 179.11.

.28 **constellations**

Andromeda, the Chained Lady
Antlia or Antlia Pneumatica, the Air Pump
Apus, the Bird of Paradise
Aquarius, the Water Bearer
Aquila, the Eagle
Ara, the Altar
Argo or Argo Navis, the Ship Argo
Aries, the Ram
Auriga, the Charioteer
Big Dipper, Charles' Wain
Boötes, the Herdsman
Caelum or Caela Sculptoris, the Sculptor's Tool
Camelopardalis or Camelopardus, the Giraffe
Cancer, the Crab
Canes Venatici, the Hunting Dogs
Canis Major, the Larger Dog, Orion's Hound
Canis Minor, the Lesser Dog
Capricorn, the Horned Goat
Carina, the Keel
Cassiopeia, the Lady in the Chair
Centaurus, the Centaur
Cepheus, the Monarch
Cetus, the Whale
Chamaeleon, the Chameleon
Circinus, the Compasses
Columba or Columba Noae, Noah's Dove
Coma Berenices, Berenice's Hair

Corona Australis, the Wreath, the Southern Crown
Corona Borealis, the Northern Crown
Corvus, the Crow
Crater, the Cup
Crux, the Cross,
Cygnus, the Swan
Delphinus, the Dolphin
Dorado, the Dorado Fish
Draco, the Dragon
Equuleus, the Foal
Eridanus, the River Po
Fornax, the Furnace
Gemini, the Twins
Grus, the Crane
Hercules
Horologium, the Clock
Hydra, the Sea Serpent
Hydrus, the Water Snake
Indus, the Indian
Lacerta, the Lizard
Leo, the Lion
Leo Minor, the Lesser Lion
Lepus, the Hare
Libra, the Balance
Little Dipper
Lupus, the Wolf
Lynx, the Lynx
Lyra, the Lyre
Malus, the Mast
Mensa, the Table
Microscopium, the Microscope
Monoceros, the Unicorn
Musca, the Fly
Norma, the Rule
Northern Cross
Octans, the Octant
Ophiuchus, the Serpent Bearer

Orion, the Giant Hunter
Orion's Belt
Orion's Sword
Pavo, the Peacock
Pegasus, the Winged Horse
Perseus
Phoenix, the Phoenix
Pictor, the Painter
Pisces, the Fishes
Piscis Australis, the Southern Fish
Puppis, the Stern
Reticulum, the Net
Sagitta, the Arrow
Sagittarius, the Archer
Scorpio or Scorpius, the Scorpion
Sculptor, the Sculptor
Scutum, the Shield
Serpens, the Serpent

Sextans, the Sextant
Southern Cross
Taurus, the Bull
Telescopium, the Telescope
Triangulum, the Triangle
Triangulum Australe, the Southern Triangle
Tucana, the Toucan
Ursa Major, the Great Bear
Ursa Minor, the Lesser Bear
Vela, the Sails
Virgo, the Virgin
Volans or Piscis Volans, the Flying Fish
Vulpecula, the Little Fox

376. MATERIALITY

.1 NOUNS **materiality,** materialness; **corporeity,** corporality, corporeality, corporealness, bodiliness, embodiment, –somia; **substantiality,** concreteness 3.1; **physicalness,** physicality, physi(o)–, physic(o)–; flesh, flesh and blood, sarc(o)–, –sarc.

.2 **matter, material,** materiality, **substance** 3.2, **stuff,** hyle, hyl(o)–; brute matter; **element;** chemical element 379.1,10; the four elements; earth, air, fire, water; elementary particle, fundamental particle; elementary unit, building block, unit of being, monad; constituent, component; **atom** 326.4,21; atomic particles 326.6; **molecule;** material world, physical world, nature, natural world; hypostasis, substratum; plenum.

.3 **body,** physical body, material body, corpus [informal], anatomy [informal], person, **figure, form,** frame, **physique,** carcass [informal], bones, flesh, clay, clod, hulk; soma, somat(o)–, –some, –somus; **torso, trunk.**

.4 **object, article, thing,** material thing, affair, something; what's-its-name 584.2; something or other, *etwas* [Ger], *eppes* [Yid], *quelque chose* [Fr]; artifact; gadget 348.1; thingum, **thingumabob,** thingumadad, thingumadoodle, **thingumajig,** thingumajigger, thingumaree, thingummy, **doodad,** dofunny, **dojigger,** dojiggy, domajig, domajigger, **dohickey,** dowhacky, flumadiddle, gigamaree, **gimmick, gizmo,** dingus, hickey, jigger, hootmalalie, hootenanny, whatchy, widget [all slang or informal].

.5 **materialism,** physicism, epiphenomenalism, identity theory of mind, atomism, mechanism; physicalism, behaviorism, instrumentalism, pragmatism, pragmaticism; historical materialism, dialectical materialism, Marxism; **positivism**, logical positivism, positive philosophy, empiricism, **naturalism**; realism, natural realism, commonsense realism, commonsense philosophy, naïve realism, new realism, critical realism, representative realism, epistemological realism; substantialism; hylomorphism; hylotheism; hylozoism; worldliness, earthliness, animalism, secularism, temporality.

.6 **materialist**, physicist, atomist; historical *or* dialectical materialist, Marxist; **naturalist**; realist, natural realist, commonsense realist, commonsense philosopher, epistemological realist.

.7 **materialization**, corporealization; substantialization, substantiation; **embodiment, incorporation**, personification, **incarnation; reincarnation**, reembodiment, transmigration, metempsychosis.

.8 VERBS **materialize**, corporealize; substantialize, substantify, substantiate; **embody** 3.5, body, **incorporate**, corporify, personify, **incarnate; reincarnate**, reembody, transmigrate.

.9 ADJS **material**, materiate, hylic, **substantial** 3.6; **corporeal**, corporeous, corporal, **bodily; physical**, somatic(al), –somatous; **fleshly**; worldly, earthly, **secular**, temporal, **unspiritual**, nonspiritual.

.10 **embodied**, bodied, **incorporated, incarnate**.

.11 **materialist** *or* **materialistic**, atomistic, mechanist, mechanistic; Marxian, Marxist; **naturalist, naturalistic, positivist, positivistic**; commonsense, **realist**, realistic; hylotheistic; hylomorphous; hylozoic, hylozoistic.

377. IMMATERIALITY

.1 NOUNS **immateriality**, immaterialness; incorporeity, incorporeality, incorporealness, **bodilessness; unsubstantiality** 4, unsubstantialness; **intangibility**, impalpability, imponderability; inextension, nonextension; nonexteriority, nonexternality; **unearthliness, unworldliness; supernaturalism** 85.7; **spirituality**, spiritualness, spirituousness [archaic], otherworldliness, ghostliness, shadowiness; occultism 1034, the occult, occult phenomena; psychism, psychics, psychic *or* psychical research, psychicism; spirit world, astral plane.

.2 incorporeal, incorporeity, immateriality, unsubstantiality 4.

.3 **immaterialism, idealism,** philosophical idealism, metaphysical idealism; objective idealism; absolute idealism; epistemological idealism; monistic idealism, pluralistic idealism; critical idealism; transcendental idealism; subjectivism; solipsism; subjective idealism; **spiritualism**; personalism; panpsychism, psychism, animism, hylozoism, animatism; Platonism, Platonic realism, Berkeleianism, Cambridge Platonism, Kantianism, Hegelianism, New England Transcendentalism; Neoplatonism; Platonic idea *or* ideal *or* form, pure form, form, universal; transcendental object; transcendental.

.4 immaterialist, **idealist**; Berkeleian, Platonist, Hegelian, Kantian; Neoplatonist; **spiritualist**; psychist, panpsychist, animist.

.5 dematerialization; **disembodiment**, disincarnation; **spiritualization**.

.6 VERBS dematerialize, immaterialize, unsubstantialize, insubstantialize, desubstantialize, **disembody**, disincarnate; **spiritualize**, spiritize.

.7 ADJS **immaterial**, nonmaterial; **unsubstantial** 4.5, insubstantial, **intangible**, impalpable, imponderable; unextended, extensionless; **incorporeal**, incorporate, incorporeous; **bodiless**, unembodied, without body, asomatous; **disembodied**, disbodied, discarnate, decarnate, decarnated; **unphysical**, nonphysical; **unfleshly**; airy, ghostly, phantom, shadowy, ethereal; **spiritual**, astral, psychic(al); **unearthly, unworldly, otherworldly**, extramundane, transmundane; supernatural 85.15; occult 1034.22.

.8 **idealist, idealistic**, immaterialist, immaterialistic; solipsistic; spiritualist, spiritualistic; panpsychist, panpsychistic; animist, animistic; Platonic, Platonistic, Berkeleian, Hegelian, Kantian; Neoplatonic, Neoplatonistic.

378. MATERIALS

.1 NOUNS **materials**, substances, stuff; **raw material, staple, stock**; material resources *or* means; store, supply 660; strategic materials; matériel; –ing.

.2 (building materials) sticks and stones, lath and plaster, bricks and mortar; roofing, roofage; walling, siding; flooring, pavement 657.7, paving material, paving; masonry, flag, flagstone, ashlar, stone 384.1,12; covering materials 228.43; mortar, plasters 228.44; cement, concrete, cyclopean concrete, ferroconcrete, prestressed concrete, reinforced concrete; brick, firebrick, clinker, adobe; tile, tiling.

.3 wood 378.9, **lumber, timber,** hyl(o)–, lign(o)– or ligni–, xyl(o)–; hardwood, softwood; stick, stick of wood, stave; billet; pole, post, beam 217.3, **board,** plank; deal; two-by-four, three-by-four, etc.; slab, puncheon; slat, splat, lath; boarding, timbering, timberwork, planking; lathing, lathwork; sheeting; paneling 378.10, panelboard, panelwork; plywood, plyboard; sheathing, sheathing board; siding, sideboard; weatherboard, clapboard; shingle, shake; log; driftwood; firewood, stovewood; cordwood; cord.

.4 cane, bamboo, rattan.

.5 fabric 378.11, **cloth, rag, textile,** textile fabric, texture, tissue, stuff, weave, weft, woof, web, **material, goods,** drapery, *étoffe, tissu* [both Fr]; napery, table linen, felt, pil(o)– or pili–; silk, sereiceo–; wool 230.2; lace 378.12.

.6 paper 378.13, papyro–; sheet, leaf, page; quire, ream, stationery 602.29; cardboard.

.7 synthetic; synthetic fabric or textile or cloth; synthetic rubber; **plastic** 378.14, –plast, plasto–; thermoplastic; thermosetting plastic; resin plastic; cellulose plastic; protein plastic; cast plastic, molded plastic, extruded plastic; molding compounds; laminate; adhesive 50.13; plasticizer; polymer.

.8 VERBS gather or procure materials; **store, stock,** stock up 660.10–13; **process,** utilize.

.9 woods

acacia	hazel, hazelwood
alder	hemlock
applewood	hickory
ash	incense wood
balsa	ironwood
balsam	juniper
banyan	knotty pine
bass, basswood	lancewood
beech, beechwood	larch
birch	lemonwood
brierwood, briarwood	lignum vitae
burl	linden
buttonwood	loblolly pine
cedar, cedarwood	locust
cherry	logwood
chestnut	magnolia
cork	mahogany
cottonwood	maple
cypress	oak
dogwood	olive
ebony	orangewood
elm, elmwood	peachwood
eucalyptus	pecan
fir	Philippine mahogany
fruit wood	pine
gum, gumwood	poplar
Port Orford cedar	sycamore
redwood	teak, teakwood
rosewood	tulipwood
sandalwood	tupelo
satinwood	walnut
spruce	yew
sumac	zebrawood

.10 panelings

beaver board	Panelyte
Celotex	pegboard
Coltwood	plasterboard
Compoboard	plastic plywood
compreg	plyboard
fiberboard	plywood
firred plywood	Pregwood
Formica	pressed hardboard
hardboard	Reziwood
impreg	Sheetrock
Lamicoid	wallboard
laminated wood	Weldwood
Masonite	

.11 fabrics

acetate or acetate rayon	chintz
Acrilan	coating
alpaca	cord
Aralac	corduroy
arras	corseting
astrakhan	cotton
Avisco	cotton cambric
awning cloth	covert cloth
Axminster	crash
baize	crepe
balbriggan	crepe de chine
Banlon	cretonne
batik	crinoline
batiste	Dacron
blanketing	damask
bouclé [Fr]	denim
broadcloth	dimity
broadloom	doeskin
brocade	Donegal tweed
brocatel	double-knit
buckram	*drap d'or* [Fr]
bunting	drill
burlap	drilling
byssus	drugget
calico	duck
cambric	duffel
cambric muslin	dungaree
camel's hair	duvetyn
Canton flannel	Dynel
canvas	faille
carpeting	felt
casheen	fine linen
cashmere	flannel
cassimere	flannelette
castor	fleece
Celanese	foulard
Celanese acetate	frieze
challis	fustian
chambray	gabardine
cheesecloth	gauze
chenille	Georgette, Georgette crepe
chenille Axminster	gingham
cheviot	gossamer
chiffon	grenadine
China silk	grogram
chinchilla	grosgrain
chino	gunny

haircloth
Harris Tweed
herringbone
hessian
homespun
hop sacking
horsehair
huck
huckaback
Jacquard
jean
jersey
knitwear
lamé
Lastex
lawn
Leatherette
linen
Linene
linenette
linoleum
linsey-woolsey
lisle
list
loden
longcloth
luster
mackinaw
mackintosh
madras
malines, maline
manta
mantua
marquisette
marseilles
mat
matting
melton
messaline
mohair
moiré
moleskin
monk's cloth
mousseline [Fr]
mousseline de soie [Fr]
murrey
muslin
nainsook
nankeen
near-silk
net
netting
nylon
oilcloth
oil silk
organdy
organza
Orlon
paisley
panne, panne velvet
pepper-and-salt
percale
permanent-press fabric
piqué
plaid
plush
polyester
pongee
poplin
print

Qiana
quilting
radium
rayon
rayon casheen
rep
Revolite
rugging
russet
sackcloth
sacking
sailcloth
samite
sarcenet
Sarelon
sateen
satin
say
scrim
seersucker
serge
shalloon
shantung
sharkskin
sheers
sheeting
shirting
shoddy
shot silk
silk
spun rayon
stamin
stammel
stockinette
stuff
suède, suède cloth
swansdown
tabaret
tabby
taffeta, taffety
tapestry
tarpaulin
tartan
terry, terry cloth
Terylene
tick, ticking
toile [Fr]
toweling
tricot
tricotine
tulle
tussah
tussore
tweed
twill
Ultrasuede
veiling
Velon
velours
velure
velvet
velveteen
Vicara
vicuña
Vinyon
voile
wash-and-wear fabric
watered fabric
webbing
wool
worsted

.12 laces

Alençon lace
bobbinet
bobbin lace
bobbin net
Brussels point
Carrickmacross lace
Chantilly lace
Dieppe lace
duchesse lace
fillet, filet lace
Greek lace *or* point
guipure
Mechlin lace

mignonette lace
Milan point
needlepoint
pillow lace
point, point lace
reticella
Roman lace *or* point
Shetland lace
tambour lace
tatting
Teneriffe lace
Valenciennes
Venetian point

.13 papers

art paper
baryta paper
Bible paper
binder's board
blotting paper
blueprint paper
bond paper
butcher paper
carbon, carbon paper
cardboard
cartridge paper
cellophane
cigarette paper
cloth paper
construction paper
copy *or* copying paper
crepe, crepe paper
crown paper
curlpaper
drawing paper
endpaper
facial tissue
filter paper
flimsy
flypaper
foolscap
gift wrap
graph paper
grass paper
hand paper
hand tissue
ice paper
India paper
kraft paper
lace paper
laid paper
ledger paper
letter paper
litmus paper
manila, Manila paper

matrix paper
millboard
music paper
newspaper
newsprint
note paper
oak tag
onionskin
paperboard
paper toweling
papier-mâché
papyrus
paraffin paper
parchment
pasteboard
plate paper
proof paper
pulpboard
rag paper
rice paper
roofing paper
sepia paper
sheathing paper
shop paper
stipple paper
strawboard
sulfate paper
tar paper
tissue, tissue paper
toilet tissue *or* paper
tracing paper
transfer paper
typewriter paper
vellum
wallpaper
wastepaper
wax *or* waxed paper
wrapping paper
writing paper

.14 plastics

acetate
acetate nitrate
acrylic
alkyd
aminoplast
Bakelite
Buna
casein plastic
cellophane
Celluloid
cellulose acetate
cellulose ether

cellulose nitrate
cellulosic
coumarone-indene
epoxy
fluorocarbon plastic
Formica
furane
lignin
Lucite
melamine
multiresin
Mylar

neoprene	PVC
nitrate	polyvinyl-formalde-
nylon	hyde
Perspex	resinoid
phenolic	silicone resin
phenolic urea	Styrofoam
Plexiglas	Teflon
polyester	terpene
polyethylene	tetrafluoroethylene
polymeric amide	urea
polypropylene	urea formaldehyde
polystyrene	vinyl
polyurethane	Vinylite
polyvinyl chloride,	

379. CHEMICALS

.1 NOUNS **chemical,** chem(o)– *or* chemi–, chemic(o)–; organic chemical, biochemical, inorganic chemical; fine chemicals, heavy chemicals; **element,** chemical element; **radical; ion,** anion, cation; atom 326.4,21; **molecule,** macromolecule; **compound;** isomer, pseudoisomer, stereoisomer, diastereoisomer, enantiomer, enantiomorph, alloisomer, chromoisomer, metamer, polymer, copolymer, interpolymer, high polymer, homopolymer, monomer, dimer, trimer, etc., oligomer, –mer(e), –meride; agent, **reagent; acid,** aci–, hydracid, oxyacid, sulfacid; acidity; **base,** basi–, baso–, **alkali,** nonacid; neutralizer, antacid; alkalinity.

.2 **trace element,** microelement, micronutrient, minor element.

.3 **valence,** valency [Brit], positive valence, negative valence; monovalence, univalence, bivalence, trivalence, tervalence, quadrivalence, tetravalence, etc., multivalence, polyvalence; covalence, electrovalence.

.4 **atomic weight,** atomic mass, atomic volume, mass number; **molecular weight,** molecular mass, molecular volume; atomic number, valence number.

.5 **chemicalization;** alkalization, alkalinization; acidification, acidulation, acetification; carbonation, chlorination, hydration, hydrogenation, saturization, hydroxylation, nitration, phosphatization; oxidation, oxidization; reduction; sulfation, sulfatization, sulfonation; isomerization, metamerization, polymerization, copolymerization, homopolymerization; isomerism, geometric isomerism, optical isomerism, position isomerism, tautoisomerism, metamerism, polymerism, copolymerism; fermentation, ferment, working; catalysis 53.2; electrolysis 342.22.

.6 VERBS **chemicalize,** chemical; alkalize, alkalinize, alkalify; acidify, acidulate, ace-

tify; borate, carbonate, chlorinate, hydrate, hydrogenate, hydroxylate, nitrate, oxidize, reduce, pepsinate, peroxidize, phosphatize, sulfate, sulfatize, sulfonate; isomerize, metamerize, polymerize, copolymerize, homopolymerize; ferment, work; catalyze 53.4; electrolyze 342.25.

.7 ADJS **chemical;** biochemical, chemicobiologic; physicochemical, physiochemical, chemicophysical, chemicobiological, chemicophysiologic(al), chemicodynamic, chemicoengineering, chemicomechanical, chemicomineralogical, chemicopharmaceutical, chemurgic, electrochemical, iatrochemical, chemotherapeutic(al), chemophysiologic(al), macrochemical, microchemical, phytochemical, photochemical, radiochemical, thermochemical, zoochemical; elemental, elementary; acid 432.7; alkaline, alkali, nonacid, basic; isomeric, isomerous, metameric, metamerous, heteromerous, polymeric, polymerous, copolymeric, copolymerous, monomeric, monomerous, dimeric, dimerous, etc.

.8 valent; univalent, monovalent, monatomic, bivalent, trivalent, tervalent, quadrivalent, tetravalent, etc., multivalent, polyvalent; covalent, electrovalent.

.9 chemistry

actinochemistry	macrochemistry
alchemy	magnetochemistry
analytical chemistry	metallurgical chemis-
applied chemistry	try
astrochemistry	microchemistry
atomic chemistry	mineralogical chemis-
biochemistry	try
biogeochemistry	neurochemistry
business chemistry	nuclear chemistry
chemiatry	organic chemistry
chemical dynamics	pathological chemis-
chemical engineering	try, pathochemistry
chemicobiology	petrochemistry
chemicoengineering	pharmacochemistry
chemicophysics	photochemistry
chemophysiology	physical chemistry,
chemurgy	physicochemistry
colloid chemistry	physiological chemis-
colorimetry, color-	try, physiochemistry
imetric analysis	phytochemistry
crystallochemistry	piezochemistry
cytochemistry	polymer chemistry
electrochemistry	psychobiochemistry,
engineering chemistry	psychochemistry
galactochemistry	pure chemistry
geological chemistry,	radiochemistry
geochemistry	soil chemistry
hydrochemistry	spectrochemistry
iatrochemistry	stereochemistry
immunochemistry	structural chemistry
industrial chemistry	synthetic chemistry
inorganic chemistry	theoretical chemistry
lithochemistry	thermochemistry

topochemistry
ultramicrochemistry
zoochemistry, zoo-

chemy
zymochemistry,
    zymurgy

,10 chemical elements

actinium, Ac
aluminum, Al
americium, Am
antimony, Sb
argon, Ar or A
arsenic, As
astatine, At
barium, Ba
berkelium, Bk
beryllium, Be
bismuth, Bi
boron, B
bromine, Br
cadmium, Cd
calcium, Ca
californium, Cf
carbon, C
cerium, Ce
cesium, Cs
chlorine, Cl
chromium, Cr
cobalt, Co
columbium, Cb
copper, Cu
curium, Cm
dysprosium, Dy
einsteinium, Es or E
erbium, Er
europium, Eu
fermium, Fm
fluorine, F
francium, Fr
gadolinium, Gd
gallium, Ga
germanium, Ge
gold, Au
hafnium, Hf
hahnium, Ha
helium, He
holmium, Ho
hydrogen, H
indium, In
iodine, I
iridium, Ir
iron, Fe
krypton, Kr
lanthanum, La
lawrencium, Lw
lead, Pb
lithium, Li
lutetium, Lu
magnesium, Mg
manganese, Mn
mendelevium, Md or

Mv
mercury, Hg
molybdenum, Mo
neodymium, Nd
neon, Ne
neptunium, Np
nickel, Ni
niobium, Nb
nitrogen, N
nobelium, No
osmium, Os
oxygen, O
palladium, Pd
phosphorus, P
platinum, Pt
plutonium, Pu
polonium, Po
potassium, K
praseodymium, Pr
promethium, Pm
protactinium, Pa
radium, Ra
radon, Rn
rhenium, Re
rhodium, Rh
rubidium, Rb
ruthenium, Ru
rutherfordium, Rf
samarium, Sm
scandium, Sc
selenium, Se
silicon, Si
silver, Ag
sodium, Na
strontium, Sr
sulfur, S
tantalum, Ta
technetium, Tc
tellurium, Te
terbium, Tb
thallium, Tl
thorium, Th
thulium, Tm
tin, Sn
titanium, Ti
tungsten or wolfram,
    W
uranium, U
vanadium, V
xenon, Xe
ytterbium, Yb
yttrium, Y
zinc, Zn
zirconium, Zr

.11 chemicals

absolute alcohol
acetate
acetone
alcohol
aldehyde
amine
ammonia
amyl alcohol
anhydride
arsenate
arsenite

basic anhydride
benzoate
bicarbonate
bicarbonate of soda
bichloride of mercury
bisulfate
borate
borax
bromide
calcium carbonate
calcium hydroxide

carbide
carbohydrate 309.22
carbonate
carbon dioxide
carbon monoxide
Chile saltpeter
chlorate
chloride
chlorite
chromate
citrate
copperas
cyanide
dehydrated alcohol
dichromate
dioxide
disulfide
ester
ether
ethyl, ethyl alcohol,
    ethanol
fluoride
formaldehyde
fulminate
halide
halogen
hydrate
hydride
hydrocarbon
hydroxide
hypochlorite
iodide
isopropyl alcohol, iso-
    propanol

ketone
lactate
lye
methane
methyl
methyl alcohol, meth-
    anol
monoxide
niter
nitrate
nitride
nitrite
oxalate
oxide
permanganate
peroxide
petrochemical
phosphate
phosphide
potash, potassium hy-
    droxide
potassium nitrate
sal ammoniac
salt
saltpeter
silicate
sodium bicarbonate
sodium chloride
sulfate
sulfide
sulfite
tartrate
thiosulfate
trioxide

.12 acids

acetic acid
acetylsalicylic acid, as-
    pirin
acrylic acid
amino acid 309.24
ammono acid
aqua fortis
aqua regia
arsenic acid
ascorbic acid
battery acid
benzoic acid
boric acid
butyric acid
carbolic acid
carbonic acid
chloric acid
chlorous acid
chromic acid
citric acid
cyanic acid
fluoric acid
folic acid
formic acid
fumaric acid
gallic acid
hydrobromic acid
hydrochloric acid
hydrocyanic acid
hydrofluoric acid
hydroiodic acid

hypochlorous acid
iodic acid
lactic acid
lauric acid
lignosulphonic acid
linoleic acid
maleic acid
malic acid
muriatic acid
niacin, nicotinic acid
nitric acid
nucleic acid
oil of vitriol
oleic acid
oxalic acid
palmitic acid
pectic acid
perboric acid
perchloric acid
phenol
phosphoric acid
picric acid
prussic acid
salicylic acid
stearic acid
sulfanilic acid
sulfuric acid
tartaric acid
undecylenic acid
uric acid
vitriol

.13 chemical apparatus

alembic
aspirator
beaker

blowpipe
Büchner funnel
Bunsen burner

burette	Kipp's apparatus,
capillary tube	Kipp generator
centrifuge	matrass
condenser	pestle and mortar
crucible	pipette
deflagrating spoon	precision balance
desiccator	reagent bottle
distiller	receiver
Erlenmeyer flask	reflex condenser
etna	retort
evaporating dish	separatory funnel
funnel	still
graduated cylinder,	test tube
graduate	volumetric flask

380. OILS, LUBRICANTS

.1 NOUNS **oil,** ole(o)– *or* oli–, *oleum* [L]; **fat,** lipid, lip(o)–, lipar(o)–, **grease;** ester; cerate; sebum, sebo–, sebi–; tallow, steat(o)–; mineral oil, vegetable oil, animal oil; fixed oil, fatty oil, nonvolatile oil, volatile oil, essential oil; saturated fat, hydrogenated fat, unsaturated fat, polyunsaturated fat; drying oil, semidrying oil, nondrying oil.

.2 **lubricant,** lubricator, lubricating oil, lubricating agent, antifriction; graphite, plumbago, black lead; silicone; glycerin; wax 380.15, cer(o)–; mucilage, mucus, synovia.

.3 **ointment, balm, salve, lotion, cream, unguent,** unguentum, inunction, inunctum, unction, chrism; soothing syrup, lenitive, embrocation, demulcent, emollient; spikenard, nard; balsam; **pomade,** pomatum, brilliantine; cold cream, hand lotion, face cream, lanolin; eye-lotion, eyewash, collyrium.

.4 **petroleum,** petr(o)– *or* petri–, rock oil, fossil oil; crude oil, crude; **gasoline,** gas [informal], **petrol** [Brit]; aviation gasoline, avgas; ethyl, ethyl gas, premium gas, high-test, high-octane gas; regular, regular gas; low-lead gas, lead-free gas, white gas; **kerosene,** paraffin 331.1; diesel oil, diesel fuel; motor oil.

.5 **oiliness, greasiness, unctuousness,** unctiousness, unctuosity; **fattiness,** fatness, pinguidity; richness; sebaceousness; adiposis, adiposity; **soapiness,** saponacity *or* saponaceousness; smoothness, slickness, sleekness, **slipperiness,** lubricity.

.6 **lubrication,** lubricating, **oiling, greasing,** lubrification [archaic]; grease job *or* lube [both informal]; **anointment,** unction, inunction; chrismatory, chrismation.

.7 lubritorium, lubritory; grease rack, grease pit.

.8 VERBS **oil, grease; lubricate,** lubrify [archaic]; **anoint,** salve, unguent, embrocate, dress, pour oil *or* balm upon; smear, daub; slick, slick on [informal]; pomade; lard; glycerolate, glycerinate, glycerinize; wax, beeswax; smooth the way, soap the ways, grease the wheels.

.9 ADJS **oily, greasy; unctuous,** unctional; unguinous; **oleaginous,** oleic; unguentary, **unguent,** unguentous; chrismal, chrismatory; **fat, fatty,** adipose, adip(o)–; pinguid, pinguedinous, pinguescent; rich; sebaceous; blubbery, tallowy, suety; lardy, lardaceous; buttery, butyraceous; soapy, saponaceous; paraffinic; mucoid; smooth, slick, sleek, **slippery.**

.10 **lubricant,** lubricating, **lubricative,** lubricatory, lubricational; lenitive, emollient, soothing.

.11 **mineral and fuel oils**

absorber oil	mineral oil
anthracene oil	mineral seal oil
asphalt-base oil	mineral sperm oil
Barbados tar	mineral spirits
benzine	naphtha
carbolic oil	naphthalene
coal oil	naphthene-base oil
creosote	paraffin *or* paraffine
creosote oil	[Brit]
derv [Brit]	paraffin-base oil
fuel oil	petrolatum
furnace oil	petroleum
gas oil	petroleum benzine
green oil	petroleum jelly
hidyne [Brit]	petroleum spirit
jet fuel	road oil
kerosene	saturating oil
lamp oil	shale naphtha *or* spirit
light oil	shale oil
liquid petrolatum	signal oil
lube oil	stove oil
medicinal oil	technical oil
middle oil	white oil

.12 **vegetable oils**

absinthe	flaxseed oil
almond oil	fusel oil
anise *or* aniseed oil	grain oil
avocado oil	gum spirit
bay *or* bayberry oil	hempseed oil
beechnut oil	kekuna oil
camphor	kokum butter
candlenut oil	laurel butter *or* oil
carapa oil	lemon oil
castor *or* ricinus oil	linseed oil
cedarwood oil	Macassar oil
China wood oil	mace butter
citronella	maize oil
clove oil	nut oil
cocoa butter	oil of almonds
coconut oil *or* butter	oil *or* spirits of turpen-
colza *or* rape oil	tine
copaiba	oleoresin
copra oil	olive oil
corn oil	palm-kernel oil, palm
cotton *or* cottonseed	butter
oil	palm oil
croton oil	peanut oil
eucalyptus oil	peppermint oil

perilla oil
pine-needle oil
pine oil
pine tar
pine-tar oil
poppyseed oil
rapeseed oil
resin oil
rosin grease
rosin oil
safflower oil
sesame oil

soybean oil
spearmint oil
spikenard
sunflower oil
sweet or edible oil
tung oil
turpentine
walnut oil
wintergreen oil
wood oil
wood turpentine

.13 animal oils, fats

adipose tissue
beef tallow
blubber
bone oil
bottlenose oil
butter
butterfat
cod-liver oil
cod oil
doegling oil
dripping, drippings
fat
fish oil
ghee
goose grease
halibut-liver oil
Haliver Oil
hog lard
lanolin
lard
lard oil
lipid

lipoma
margarine
menhaden oil
mutton tallow
neat's-foot oil
oleo
oleomargarine
oleo oil
porpoise oil
salmon oil
sardine oil
seal oil
shark or shark-liver oil
shortening
sperm oil
suet
tallow
tallow oil
tuna oil
whale oil
wool fat or grease
wool oil

.14 glyceryl esters

glycerin
glycerin jelly
glycerite, glycerole
glycerogel
glycerogelatin
glycerol
margarin

olein
palmitin
stearin
trimargarin
triolein
tripalmitin
tristearin

.15 waxes

ader wax
ambergris
beeswax
candelilla wax
carnauba wax
casting wax
cerate
ceresin
fig wax
floor wax
fossil wax
Ghedda wax

gondang wax
lac wax
mineral wax
ozokerite
paraffin scale
paraffin wax
pisang wax
scale wax
sealing wax
ski wax
vegetable wax

381. RESINS, GUMS

.1 NOUNS **resin,** resina, resino–, retin(a)– or retini–; **gums,** gum resins; oleoresins; hard or varnish resins; acaroid resins, gum acaroides, coumarone resins, fossil resins, amber, succin(o)–, lac resins, pine resins, vegetable resins; resinoid, synthetic resin, plastic; resene; resinate, rosin, gum rosin, colophony, colophonium.

.2 VERBS resin, resinize, resinate; rosin.

.3 ADJS **resinous,** resinic, resiny; resinoid; rosiny; **gummy,** gummous, gumlike; pitchy.

.4 resins, gums

acacia
agar
algin
amber
ambergris
ammoniac
amyrin
animé
asa dulcis
asafetida
balsam
bassorin
Bengal kino
benjamin
benzoin
British Indian gum
butea gum, butea kino
cachibou
camphor
Canada balsam
carob gum
carrageenin
cherry-tree gum
chewing gum
chicle
colophony, colophonium
Congo copal
conima
copaiba
copal
copaline
dammar
dragon's blood
elemi
euphorbium
fossil copal
frankincense
galbanum
garnet lac
ghatti
guacin
guaiac, guaiacum
guar gum
gum ammoniac
gum animé
gum arabic
gum archipin
gum benjamin or benzoin
gum butea
gum copal
gum dammar
gum elemi

gum euphorbium
gum galbanum
gum guaiac or guaiacum
gum juniper
gum kauri
gum kino
gum labdanum
gum-lac
gum myrrh
gum olibanum
gum opoponax
gum resin
gum rosin
gum sagapenum
gum sandarac
gum shellac
gum storax
gutta-percha
hard resin
herabol myrrh
incense resin
karaya
kauri, kauri resin or gum
kino
Kordofan gum
labdanum
lac
lacquer
liquidambar
locust-kernel gum
mastic
megilp
mesquite gum
myrrh
oleoresin
olibanum
opoponax
pitch
quince-seed gum
rosin
sagapenum
sandarac
seed-lac
Senegal gum
shellac
Sonora lac
sterculia gum
stick lac
storax
tragacanth
wood rosin
Zanzibar copal

382. INORGANIC MATTER

.1 NOUNS **inorganic matter,** nonorganic matter; inanimate or lifeless or nonliving matter, inorganized or unorganized matter, **brute matter;** mineral kingdom or world.

.2 **inanimateness,** inanimation, **lifelessness,** inertness; **insensibility,** insentience, insensateness, senselessness, unconsciousness, unfeelingness.

.3 inorganic chemistry; chemicals 379.

.4 ADJS **inorganic,** unorganic, nonorganic; **mineral,** nonbiological; unorganized, inorganized.

.5 **inanimate,** inanimated, unanimated, exanimate, azoic, abio–, abiotic, nonliving, **lifeless,** soulless; inert; insentient, unconscious, nonconscious, **insensible,** insensate, senseless, unfeeling; dumb, mute.

383. MINERALS AND METALS

.1 NOUNS **mineral;** –ine, –ite, –lite or –lyte, –lyth; inorganic substance, lifeless matter found in nature, oryct(o)–; extracted matter or material; **mineral world** or **kingdom;** mineral resources; mineraloid, gel mineral, metamict substance; mineralization.

.2 **ore,** mineral; mineral-bearing material; unrefined or untreated mineral; natural or native mineral.

.3 **metal;** metallics; native metals, alkali metals, earth metals, alkaline-earth metals, noble metals, precious metals, base metals, rare metals, rare-earth metals or elements; metalloid, semimetal, nonmetal; bullion (gold or silver); gold dust; metal leaf, metal foil; metalwork, metalware; metallicity, metalleity.

.4 **alloy,** alloyage, fusion, compound; **amalgam.**

.5 **cast, casting; ingot, bullion;** pig, sow; sheet metal; button, gate, regulus.

.6 **mine,** pit; **quarry; diggings, workings;** open cut, opencast; bank; shaft; coal mine, colliery; strip mine; gold mine, silver mine, etc.

.7 **deposit,** mineral deposit, pay dirt; **vein, lode,** dike, ore bed; shoot or chute, ore shoot or ore chute; chimney; stock; placer, placer deposit, placer gravel; country rock; lodestuff, gangue, matrix, veinstone.

.8 **mining;** coal mining, gold mining, etc.; strip mining; placer mining; hydraulic mining; prospecting; mining claim, lode claim, placer claim; gold fever; gold rush.

.9 **miner,** mineworker, pitman; coal miner, collier [Brit]; gold miner, gold digger; gold panner; placer miner; quarry .miner; **prospector,** desert rat, sourdough; **fortyniner;** hand miner, rockman, powderman, driller, draw man; butty.

.10 **mineralogy;** mineralogical chemistry; crystallography; **petrology,** petrography, microetrography; **geology** 385.4; mining geology, mining engineering.

.11 **metallurgy;** metallography, metallurgical chemistry, metallurgical engineering, physical metallurgy, powder metallurgy, electrometallurgy, hydrometallurgy, pyrometallurgy.

.12 **mineralogist; metallurgist,** electrometallurgist, metallurgical engineer; **petrologist,** petrographer; **geologist** 385.5; mining engineer.

.13 VERBS mineralize; petrify 356.7.

.14 **mine;** quarry; pan, pan for gold; prospect; hit pay dirt.

.15 ADJS **mineral,** –litic; inorganic 382.4; mineralized, petrified; asbestine, carbonous, graphitic, micaceous, alabastrine, quartzose, silicic; sulfurous, sulfuric; ore-bearing, ore-forming.

.16 **metal, metallic,** metallike, metall(o)– or metal(o)–, metalline, metalloid or metalloidal, metalliform; semimetallic; nonmetallic; metallo-organic or metallorganic, organometallic; bimetallic, trimetallic; metalliferous, metalbearing.

.17 brass, brassy, brazen; bronze, bronzy; copper, coppery, cuprous, cupreous; gold, golden, gilt, aureate; nickel, nickelic, nickelous, nickeline; silver, silvery; iron, ironlike, ferric, ferrous, ferruginous; steel, steely; tin, tinny; lead, leaden; pewter, pewtery; mercurial, mercurous, quicksilver; gold-filled, gold-plated, silver-plated, etc.

.18 **mineralogical, metallurgical,** petrological, crystallographic.

.19 **minerals**

alabaster	clay
amphibole	coal 331.10
antimony, stib(o)– or	coke
stibi(o)–	corundum
apatite	cryolite
aplite	diatomite
argillite	elaterite
arsenic, ars–	emery
asbestos	epidote
asphalt	epsomite
azurite	feldspar
barite	fluorite
bauxite	fluorspar
bitumen	fool's gold
boron, bor(o)–	garnet
brimstone	glauconite
bromine, brom(o)–	graphite
brookite	gypsum
brucite	hatchettine
calcite	holosiderite
carbon, carb(o)–	hornblende
celestite	ilmenite
chalcedony	iolite
chlorite	iron pyrites
chromite	jet

kaolinite
kyanite
lazurite
lignite
lime
magnesite
malachite
maltha
marcasite
marl
meerschaum
mica
mineral charcoal
mineral coal
mineral oil 380.11
mineral salt
mineral tallow
mineral tar
mineral wax
molybdenite
monazite
obsidian
olivine
orthoclase
ozokerite
peat
perlite
phosphate rock
phosphorus, phosph-
   (o)–, phosphor(o)–
pitchblende
pumice

pumicite
pyrite
pyrites
pyroxene
quartz
realgar
red clay
rhodonite
rock crystal
rocks 384
rutile
salt, hal(o)–
selenite
selenium, selen(o)– or
   seleni–
siderite
silica
silicate
silicon, sil–, silic(o)–
spar
spinel
spodumene
sulfur, sulf(o)–
talc, talcum, talc(o)–
tellurium, tellur(o)–,
   telluri–
tourmaline
tripoli
vermiculite
wollastonite
wulfenite
zeolite

polonium
potassium
praseodymium
promethium
protactinium
radium, radio–
rhenium
rubidium
ruthenium, ruthen(o)–
   or ruthenio–
samarium
scandium
silver, argent(o)– or
   argenti–, argyr(o)–
sodium, natr(o)–
strontium
tantalum, tantal(o)–
   or tantali–

technetium
terbium
thallium
thorium
thulium
tin, stann(o)– or stan-
   ni–
titanium, titan(o)–
tungsten, tungst(o)–,
   wolfram, wol-
   fram(o)–
uranium, uran(o)–
vanadium, vanad(o)–
ytterbium
yttrium
zinc, zinco–
zirconium

.22 alloys

admiralty metal
air-hardened steel
alloy iron
alloy steel
alnico
aluminum bronze
babbitt or babbitt
   metal
basic iron
bearing steel
bell metal
beryllium bronze
brass, chalc(o)– or
   chalk(o)–
britannia metal
bronze, chalc(o)– or
   chalk(o)–
bush metal
Carboloy
carbon steel
cartridge brass
case-hardened steel
cast iron
cheoplastic metal
chisel steel
chrome or chromium
   steel
chrome-nickel steel
cinder pig
coin nickel
coin silver
constantan
cupronickel
damask or Damascus
   steel
decarbonized iron
dental gold
die steel
drill steel
Duralumin
Duriron
electrum
elinvar
fuse metal
galvanized iron
German silver
gilding metal
graphite steel
green gold
grid metal
gun metal
hard lead

high brass
high-speed steel
hot-work steel
hypernik
inconel
ingot iron
invar
leaded bronze
low brass
manganese bronze
mine pig
misch metal
Monel Metal
Muntz metal
naval brass
nichrome
nickel bronze
nickel silver
ni-hard iron
ni-resist iron
oil-hardened steel
Permalloy
perminvar
pewter
phosphor bronze
pig, pig iron
pig lead
pinchbeck
red brass
rose metal
shot metal
silicon bronze
silicon steel
solder
spiegeleisen
stainless steel
steel
Stellite
sterling silver
structural iron
structural steel
Swedish steel
tin bronze
tombac
tool steel
tula metal
type metal
white gold
white metal
Wood's metal
wrought iron
yellow brass

.20 ores

argentite
arsenopyrite
bauxite
cassiterite
chalcocite
chalcopyrite
cinnabar
galena
göthite
hematite
iron ore

ironstone
limonite
lodestone
magnetite
mispickel
pyrite
siderite
stibnite
tinstone
turgite
zincite

.21 elementary metals

aluminum, aluminium
   [Brit], alumin(o)–
americium
barium
beryllium
bismuth, bismut(o)–
cadmium
calcium, calcio–
cerium
cesium
chromium or chrome,
   chrom(o)–
cobalt, cobalti– or
   cobalto–
copper, cupr(o)– or
   cupri–, chalc(o)– or
   chalk(o)–
dysprosium
erbium
europium
gadolinium
gallium
germanium, germano–
gold, auro–
hafnium

holmium
indium
iridium, irid(o)–
iron, ferro– or ferri–,
   sider(o)–
lanthanum
lead, plumb(o)–,
   molybd(o)–
lithium, lithi(o)–
lutetium
magnesium or magne-
   sia, magnesio–
manganese,
   mangan(o)– or man-
   gani–
mercury, mercur(o)–
molybdenum,
   molybd(o)–
neodymium
nickel
niobium
osmium, osm(o)–
palladium
phosphorus
platinum, platin(o)–

yellow gold   yellow metal

.23 leaf metals

aluminum foil	lead foil
Dutch foil *or* leaf *or*	silver foil
gold	silver leaf
gold foil	tin foil
gold leaf	

384. ROCK

.1 NOUNS **rock, stone,** petr(o)– *or* petri–, saxi–, lith(o)–, –lith; living rock; **igneous rock,** plutonic *or* abyssal rock, hypabyssal rock; volcanic rock, extrusive *or* effusive rock, scoria; magma, intrusive rock; granite, grano–, basalt, porphyry, –phyre; **lava,** aa, pahoehoe, ropy lava, corded pahoehoe, elephant-hide pahoehoe, entrail pahoehoe, festooned pahoehoe, sharkskin pahoehoe, shelly pahoehoe, slab pahoehoe, block lava, pillow lava, ellipsoidal lava *or* basalt; **sedimentary rock;** limestone, sandstone; **metamorphic rock,** blast(o)–, –blast, orth(o)–, par(a)–; schist, gneiss; conglomerate, pudding stone, breccia, –clast; rubble, rubblestone, scree, talus, tuff, tufa, brash; sarsen, sarsen stone, druid stone; monolith; crag, craig [Scot]; bedrock; mantlerock, regolith; saprolite, geest, laterite.

.2 sand, amm(o)–, psamm(o)–; grain of sand; sands of the sea; sand pile, sand dune, sand hill; sand reef, sandbar.

.3 gravel, shingle, chesil [Brit].

.4 pebble, pebblestone, gravelstone, chuckie [Scot]; jackstone *or* checkstone [both dial]; fingerstone; slingstone; drakestone; spall.

.5 boulder, river boulder, shore boulder, glacial boulder.

.6 precious stone, gem, gem stone, crystal, stone; semiprecious stone; gem of the first water; birthstone.

.7 petrification, petrifaction, lithification, crystallization.

.8 geology, petrology, crystallography; petrochemistry.

.9 VERBS **petrify,** lithify, crystallize, turn to stone; harden 356.7.

.10 ADJS **stone, rock;** lithic, –litic; petrified; petrogenic, petrescent; adamant, adamantine; flinty, flintlike; marbly, marblelike; granitic, granitelike; slaty, slatelike.

.11 stony, rocky, lapideous; stonelike, rocklike, lithoid *or* lithoidal; sandy, gritty 361.12; gravelly, shingly, shingled; pebbly, pebbled, –clastic; porphyritic, –phyric; trachytic, trachy–; crystal, crystalline, crystall(o)–; bouldery, rock- *or* boulder-strewn, rock-studded, rock-ribbed; craggy; monolithic.

.12 stones

anthraconite	lava
aplite	limestone
aventurine	lodestone
basalt	Lydian stone
basanite	marble
beetlestone	milkstone
brimstone	mudstone
brownstone	obsidian
buhr, buhrstone	phonolite
cairngorm	pitchstone
chalk	porphyry
clinkstone	pumice
corundophilite	quarrystone
dendrite	quartz
diabase	quartzite
diorite	rance
dolerite	rottenstone
dolomite	sandstone
dripstone	serpentine
eaglestone	shale
emery rock	slabstone
fieldstone	slate
flag, flagstone	smokestone
flint	snakestone
floatstone	soapstone
freestone	stalactite
geode	stalagmite
gneiss	starstone
goldstone	steatite
granite	stinkstone
granulite	tinstone
greenstone	touchstone
grit	trap, traprock
gritrock, gritstone	tufa
hairstone	wacke
ironstone	whitestone

.13 gem stones

adamant [archaic]	heliotrope
adder stone	hyacinth
agate	jacinth
alexandrite	jade, jadestone
amethyst	jargoon
aquamarine	jasper
beryl	kunzite
black opal	lapis lazuli
bloodstone	moonstone
brilliant	morganite
carbuncle	onyx
carnelian	opal
cat's-eye	peridot
chalcedony	plasma
chrysoberyl	rose quartz
chrysolite	ruby
chrysoprase	sapphire
citrine	sard
coral	sardonyx
demantoid	spinel, spinel ruby
diamond	star sapphire
emerald	sunstone
fire opal	topaz
garnet	tourmaline
girasol	turquoise
harlequin opal	zircon

.14 specialized stones

bakestone	capstone
bondstone	cobble, cobblestone

copestone, coping	keystone
stone	kneestone
cornerstone	knockstone
crowstone	lapstone
curbstone	milestone
dogstone	millstone
doorstone	oilstone
edgestone	pavestone
footstone	rubstone
gravestone	stepstone, stepping-
grindstone	stone
hagstone	tilestone
hammerstone	tombstone
headstone	topstone
kerbstone [Brit]	whetstone

385. LAND

.1 NOUNS **land, ground,** earth, ge(o)–, **soil,** agro–, ped(o)–, glebe [archaic], **sod, clod, dirt, dust, clay,** marl, **mold** [Brit dial]; terra [L], **terra firma;** terrain; **dry land;** arable land; marginal land; grassland 411.8, woodland 411.11; **crust,** earth's crust, lithosphere; regolith; topsoil, subsoil; alluvium, alluvion; eolian or subaerial deposit; **real estate, real property,** landholdings, acres, territory, freehold; region 180; the country 182.

.2 **shore, coast,** côte [Fr]; **strand,** playa [Sp], **beach,** shingle, plage, lido, riviera, sands, berm; **waterside, waterfront;** shoreline, coastline; foreshore; bank, embankment; riverside; **seashore, seacoast, seaside, seaboard,** seabeach, seacliff, seabank, sea margin, tidewater, coastland, littoral; drowned or submerged coast; rockbound coast, ironbound coast; loom of the land.

.3 **landsman,** landman, **landlubber.**

.4 (science of land or the earth) **geography,** geographics; physiography, physical geography; geoscopy; geomorphology; geodesy, geodetics 490.9; geophysics; geodynamics; **geology,** geognosy, dynamic geology, hydrogeology, physical geology, physiographic geology, stratigraphic geology, stratigraphy, paleontological geology, cosmical geology, geomorphogeny, historical geology, structural or geotectonic geology, mining geology, geological chemistry, geological engineering; mineralogy 383.10; geodesy, geodetics 490.9; soil science, pedology, soil mechanics.

.5 (scientists) **geographer,** physiographer, geodesist 490.10, **geologist,** geognost, geomorphogenist, geophysicist, geological engineer; mineralogist 383.12; soil scientist, pedologist.

.6 ADJS **terrestrial,** terrene [archaic], **earth, earthly,** telluric, tellurian; earthbound; sublunar, subastral; geophilous; terraqueous; fluvioterrestrial.

.7 **earthy,** soily, loamy, marly, gumbo; clayey, clayish; adobe.

.8 **alluvial,** estuarine, fluviomarine.

.9 **coastal, littoral, seaside, shore,** shoreside; shoreward; riparian or riparial or riparious; riverain, riverine; riverside.

.10 **geographic(al), physiographic(al),** geodesic, geodetic; geophysical, geologic(al), geognostic(al).

.11 ADVS **on land,** on dry land, on terra firma; onshore, ashore; alongshore; shoreward; by land, overland.

.12 **on earth,** on the face of the earth or globe, in the world, in the wide world, in the whole wide world; **under the sun,** under the stars, beneath the sky, under heaven, below, **here below.**

.13 **soils**

adobe	latosolic soil
alluvial soil	leaf mold
argil	lithosol
bog soil	loam
bole	loess
boulder clay	marl
chernozemic soil	mold
china clay	podsolic soil
clay	porcelain clay
clunch	potter's clay
desertic soil	red clay
dust	regosol
fuller's earth	regur soil
gilgai soil	residual clay
gumbo, gumbo soil	sand
humus	sedimentary clay
indurated clay	silt
kaolin	till
kaolinite	tundra soil
laterite	wiesenboden

386. BODY OF LAND

.1 NOUNS **continent, mainland,** main [archaic], landmass; North America, South America, Africa, Europe, Asia, Eurasia, Eurasian landmass, Australia, Antarctica; subcontinent, peninsula 256.8.

.2 **island, isle,** neso–; **islet,** holm, ait [Brit dial]; continental island; oceanic island; **key, cay;** sandbank, sandbar, bar; **reef,** coral reef, coral head; coral island, atoll; archipelago, island group or chain; insularity; islandology.

.3 **continental,** mainlander; continentalist.

.4 **islander,** islandman, island-dweller, islesman, insular; islandologist.

.5 VERBS insulate, isolate, island, enisle; island-hop.

.6 ADJS **continental,** mainland.

.7 **insular,** insulated, isolated; island, islandy or islandish, islandlike; islanded, isleted, island-dotted; seagirt; archipelagic or archipelagian.

387. PLAIN

(open country)

.1 NOUNS **plain, plains;** peneplain; flat, flat country, flatland, **flats,** level, pedi(o)–; champaign country, champaign, open country, **wide-open spaces; prairie,** grassland 411.8, **steppe, pampas,** *pampa* [Sp], savanna, tundra, vega, campo, llano, sebkha; **veld,** grass veld, bushveld, tree veld; wold, weald; **moor,** moorland, down, **downs,** lande, **heath,** fell [Brit]; lowland, lowlands, bottomland; basin, playa; salt marsh; salt pan; salt flat, alkali flat; **desert** 166.2; **plateau,** upland, tableland, table, **mesa,** mesilla; coastal plain, alluvial plain, delta; mare, lunar mare.

.2 **plainsman,** plainswoman; moorman, moorlander; veldman; plainsfolk, flatlanders, lowlanders.

.3 ADJS champaign, **plain, flat,** open; campestral *or* campestrian.

388. LIQUIDITY

.1 NOUNS **liquidity, fluidity,** fluidness, liquidness, liquefaction 391; **fluency,** flow, flux, fluxion, fluxility [archaic]; wateriness; rheuminess; **juiciness,** sappiness, succulence; milkiness, lactescence; lactation; chylifaction, chylification; serosity; suppuration; moisture 392.

.2 **fluid, liquid;** liquor, drink, beverage; liquid extract, fluid extract; **juice, sap,** opo–; **blood;** latex, milk, whey 308.47; water 392.3; semiliquid 389.5; fluid mechanics, hydraulics, etc. 347.1–4; hydrogeology.

.3 (body fluids) humor, **lymph,** lymph(o)–; chyle, chyl(o)– *or* chyli–, –chylia; rheum; serous fluid, serum, sero–; **pus, matter,** purulence, peccant humor [archaic]; suppuration; ichor, sanies; discharge; gleet, leukorrhea, the whites; **mucus,** mucor, muc(o)– *or* muci–, mucoso–, myx(o)–; **phlegm,** snot [slang]; **saliva** 312.3; **urine** 311.5; **sweat** 311.7; **tear,** teardrop, lachryma; **milk,** lact(o)– *or* lacti–, galact(o)–, mother's milk, colostrum, lactation.

.4 **blood,** hem(o)– *or* hema– *or* hemi–, hemat(o)–, sangui(ni)–, sanguin(o)–; lifeblood, venous blood, arterial blood, **gore,** ichor, humor; grume; **serum,** blood serum; blood substitute; **plasma,** plasm(o)–, plasmato–; synthetic plasma, plasma substitute, dextran, clinical dextran; **blood cell** *or* **corpuscle,** hemocyte; **red corpuscle** *or* **blood cell,** erythrocyte, erythr(o)–; **white corpuscle** *or* **blood cell,** leukocyte, leuk(o)–, leukocyt(o)–, lymphocyte, lym-

ph(o)–, lymphat(o)–, neutrophil, neutro–, phagocyte, phag(o)–; blood platelet; **hemoglobin;** blood pressure; circulation; **blood group** *or* **type,** type O *or* A *or* B *or* AB; Rh-type, Rh-positive, Rh-negative; **Rh factor,** Rhesus factor; antigen, antibody, isoantibody, globulin; opsonin, opson(o)–; blood grouping; blood count, blood picture; hematoscope, hematoscopy, hemometer; bloodstream; hematics, hematology, hematologist; bloodmobile; blood bank, blood donor center; blood donor.

.5 flowmeter, fluidmeter, hydrometer.

.6 ADJS **fluid,** fluidal, fluidic, **fluent, flowing,** flexible *or* fluxile [both archaic], fluxional, fluxionary [archaic], runny; **liquid,** liquidy; watery 392.16; **juicy,** sappy, succulent.

.7 (physiology) **lymphatic,** rheumy, humoral, phlegmy, ichorous, serous, sanious; chylific, chylifactive, chylifactory; **pussy,** purulent, suppurated *or* suppurating, suppurative; tearlike, **lachrymal,** lacrimatory; bloody 368.7.

.8 **milky,** lacteal, lacteous, **lactic;** lactescent, lactiferous; milk, milch.

389. SEMILIQUIDITY

.1 NOUNS semiliquidity, semifluidity; butteriness, creaminess; pulpiness 390.

.2 **viscosity,** viscidity, viscousness, slabbiness, lentor [archaic]; thickness, spissitude, heaviness, stodginess; **stickiness, tackiness,** glutinousness, glutinosity, toughness, tenaciousness, tenacity, adhesiveness, **gumminess,** gauminess [dial], gumlikeness; **ropiness, stringiness;** clamminess, sliminess, mucilaginousness; gooeyness [informal]; **gluiness,** gluelikeness; syrupiness, treacliness [Brit]; gelatinousness, jellylikeness, gelatinity; colloidality; doughiness, pastiness; **thickening,** curdling, clotting, coagulation, incrassation, inspissation, clabbering *or* loppering [dial], jellification.

.3 **mucosity,** mucidness, mucousness, pituitousness [archaic], snottiness [slang].

.4 **muddiness,** muckiness, **slushiness,** sloshiness, sludginess, **sloppiness,** slobbiness, slabbiness [archaic], squashiness, squelchiness, **ooziness,** miriness, **turbidity,** turbidness, dirtiness.

.5 **semiliquid,** semifluid; **goo** *or* **goop** *or* gook *or* gunk *or* glop [all informal], sticky mess, gaum [dial]; **paste,** pap, pudding, putty, **butter,** cream; **pulp** 390.2; **jelly,** gelatin, jell, gel, jam; **glue;** size; **gluten;** mucilage; mucus; **dough**, batter; **syrup**, molasses, treacle [Brit], rob; egg white, albumen, glair; starch, cornstarch; **curd**, clabber, bonnyclabber; gruel, porridge, loblolly [dial]; soup, gumbo, purée.

.6 **gum** 381, chewing gum, bubble gum; chicle, chicle gum.

.7 **emulsion**, emulsoid; emulsification; emulsifier; **colloid**, colloider.

.8 **mud, muck, slush, slosh,** sludge, slob [Ir], squash, **slime,** swill, **slop, ooze, mire;** clay, slip; gumbo; pel(o)–.

.9 **mud puddle,** puddle, loblolly [dial], slop; **mudhole,** slough, muckhole, chuckhole, chughole [dial]; hog wallow.

.10 VERBS **emulsify,** emulsionize; colloid, colloidize; cream; churn, whip, beat up; **thicken,** inspissate, incrassate, curdle, clot, coagulate, clabber or lopper [both dial]; jell, jelly, jellify.

.11 ADJS **semiliquid,** semifluid, semifluidic; buttery; creamy; emulsive, colloidal; **pulpy** 390.6; half-frozen, half-melted.

.12 **viscous, viscid,** viscose, visc(o)–, slabby; **thick,** heavy, stodgy, thickened, inspissated, incrassated; curdled, clotted, grumous, coagulated, clabbered or loppered [both dial]; **sticky, tacky,** tenacious, adhesive, tough; gluey, gluelike, glutinous, glutenous, glutinose, gli(o)–, gloe(o)– or gloio–; gumbo, gumbolike; **gummy,** gaumy [dial], gummous, gumlike, **syrupy;** ropy, stringy; mucilaginous, clammy, slimy, slithery; gooey [informal]; **gelatinous,** jellylike, jellied, jelled, tremelloid or tremellose; glairy; **doughy, pasty;** starchy, amylaceous.

.13 **mucous,** muculent, mucoid, mucinous, pituitous [archaic], snotty [slang]; mucific, muciferous.

.14 **muddy,** mucky, **slushy, sloshy,** sludgy, **sloppy,** slobby, slabby [archaic], splashy, **squashy,** squishy, **squelchy, oozy,** soft, miry, sloughy, plashy, sposhy [dial]; **turbid, dirty.**

390. PULPINESS

.1 NOUNS **pulpiness,** pulpousness; **softness** 357; flabbiness; **mushiness,** mashiness, squashiness; **pastiness,** doughiness; **sponginess,** pithiness; fleshiness, succulence.

.2 **pulp, paste, mash, mush,** smash, squash, crush; pudding, porridge, sponge; sauce, butter; poultice, cataplasm, plaster; pith; paper pulp, wood pulp, sulfate pulp, sulfite pulp, rag pulp; pulpwood; pulp lead, white lead; dental pulp.

.3 **pulping,** pulpification, pulpefaction;

blending; digestion; **maceration,** mastication.

.4 **pulper,** pulpifier, macerator, pulp machine or engine, digester; **masher,** smasher, potato masher, beetle.

.5 VERBS **pulp,** pulpify; **macerate,** masticate, chew; **mash,** smash, squash, crush.

.6 ADJS **pulpy,** pulpous, pulpal, pulpar, pulplike, pulped; **pasty,** doughy; pultaceous; **mushy;** macerated, masticated, chewed; **squashy,** squelchy, squishy; soft, flabby; fleshy, succulent; **spongy,** pithy, baccate.

391. LIQUEFACTION

.1 NOUNS liquefaction, liquidization, fluidification, fluidization; liquescence or liquescency, deliquescence, deliquium [archaic]; dissolution, solution, dissolving, decoagulation, unclotting, melting, thawing, running, fusing, fusion; solubilization; colliquation; lixiviation, percolation, leaching.

.2 **solubility,** solubleness, dissolvability, dissolvableness, dissolubility, dissolubleness; meltability, fusibility.

.3 **solution,** decoction, infusion, mixture; chemical solution; lixivium, leach, leachate.

.4 **solvent** 391.10, dissolvent, dissolver, dissolving agent, resolvent, resolutive, **thinner,** dilutant or diluent; anticoagulant; liquefier, liquefacient; menstruum; universal solvent, alkahest; flux.

.5 VERBS **liquefy,** liquidize, liquesce, fluidify, fluidize; **melt, run,** thaw, colliquate; melt down; fuse, flux; deliquesce; **dissolve,** solve; thin, cut; solubilize; hold in solution; unclot, decoagulate; leach, lixiviate, percolate; decoct, infuse.

.6 ADJS **liquefied, melted, molten,** thawed; unclotted, decoagulated; in solution, in suspension, liquescent, deliquescent.

.7 **liquefying,** liquefactive; colliquative, **melting,** fusing, thawing; **dissolving,** dissolutive, dissolutional.

.8 **solvent,** dissolvent, resolvent, resolutive, thinning, cutting, diluent; alkahestic.

.9 **liquefiable; meltable,** fusible, thawable; **soluble, dissolvable,** dissoluble.

.10 **solvents**

acetone	chloroform
alcohol	ether
aqua regia	ethyl acetate
benzene	furfural
benzine, benzol	gasoline
carbolic acid	kerosene
carbon disulfide	naphtha
carbon tetrachloride,	phenol
carbon tet	toluene

turpentine xylene, xylol
water

392. MOISTURE

.1 NOUNS **moisture, hygr(o)–, damp, wet; dampness, moistness,** moistiness, **wetness,** wettishness, **wateriness,** humor *or* humectation [both archaic]; soddenness, soppiness, sogginess; swampiness, bogginess, marshiness; dewiness; mistiness, fogginess 404.3; raininess, pluviosity, showeriness; rainfall; exudation 303.6.

.2 **humidity,** humidness, **dankness,** dankishness, **mugginess,** stickiness; absolute humidity, relative humidity; dew point; humidification.

.3 **water,** *aqua* [L], *agua* [Sp], *eau* [Fr], hydr-(o)–, hydrat(o)–, aqui– *or* aqua–; Adam's ale *or* wine, H_2O; hydrol; hard water, soft water; heavy water; drinking water; rain water, rain 394; ground water, spring water, well water; sea water, salt water; limewater; mineral water *or* waters; steam, water vapor; hydrosphere; hydrometeor; head, hydrostatic head; hydrothermal water; wetting agent, wetting-out agent.

.4 **dew, dewdrops,** dawn dew, night dew, evening damp; fog drip, false dew.

.5 **sprinkle, spray,** sparge, shower; spindrift, spume, froth, foam; **splash,** plash, swash, slosh; **splatter,** spatter.

.6 **wetting, moistening, dampening,** damping; humidification; dewing, bedewing; **watering, irrigation;** hosing, wetting *or* hosing down; **sprinkling, spraying,** sparging, aspersion, aspergation; **splashing,** swashing, splattering, spattering; affusion, baptism; bath, bathing, rinsing, laving; **flooding,** drowning, inundation, deluge; **immersion, submersion** 320.2.

.7 **soaking,** soakage, soaking through, sopping, **drenching,** imbruement, sousing; ducking, dunking [informal]; soak, drench, souse; **saturation,** permeation; **steeping,** maceration, seething, infusion, brewing, imbuement; injection, impregnation; infiltration, percolation, leaching, lixiviation; pulping 390.3.

.8 **sprinkler,** sparger, sparge, sprayer, speed sprayer, concentrate sprayer, mist concentrate sprayer, spray, spray can, atomizer, aerosol; nozzle; aspergil, aspergillum; **shower,** shower bath, shower head, needle bath; syringe, fountain syringe, douche, enema, clyster; sprinkling *or* watering can, watering pot, watercart; sprinkling system, sprinkler head.

.9 (science of humidity) hygrology, hygrometry, psychrometry.

.10 (instruments) hygrometer, hair hygrometer, hygrograph, hygrodeik, hygroscope, hygrothermograph; psychrometer, sling psychrometer; humidor; hygrostat.

.11 VERBS be damp, not have a dry thread; **drip,** weep; **seep, ooze,** percolate; exude 303.15; sweat 311.16.

.12 **moisten, dampen,** damp, **wet,** wet down; humidify, humect *or* humectate [both archaic]; **water, irrigate;** dew, bedew; **sprinkle,** besprinkle, **spray,** sparge, asperge; **splash,** dash, **swash, slosh, splatter, spatter,** bespatter; dabble, paddle; slop, slobber; hose, hose down; syringe, douche; sponge.

.13 **soak, drench,** drouk [Scot], imbrue, **souse, sop,** sodden; **saturate,** permeate; **bathe,** lave, wash, rinse, douche, flush; watersoak, waterlog; **steep,** seethe, macerate; infuse, imbue, brew, impregnate, inject; infiltrate, percolate, leach, lixiviate.

.14 **flood,** float, **inundate, deluge,** turn to a lake *or* sea, swamp, whelm, drown; duck, dip, dunk [informal]; **submerge** 320.7; sluice, pour on, flow on; rain 394.9.

.15 ADJS **moist,** moisty; **damp,** dampish; **wet,** wettish; undried, tacky; **humid, dank, muggy, sticky;** dewy, roric; roriferous; rainy 394.10; marshy, swampy, fenny, boggy.

.16 **watery,** waterish, **aqueous, aquatic;** liquid 388.6; **splashy,** plashy, sloppy, swashy [Brit]; hydrous, hydrated; hydraulic.

.17 **soaked, drenched,** soused, bathed, steeped, macerated; **saturated,** permeated; **watersoaked, waterlogged; soaking, sopping; wringing wet,** soaking wet, sopping wet, wet to the skin, like a drowned rat; **sodden,** soppy, **soggy,** soaky; dripping, **dripping wet;** dribbling, seeping, weeping, oozing; flooded, overflowed, whelmed, swamped, engulfed, inundated, deluged, drowned, submerged, submersed, immersed, dipped, dunked [informal]; awash, weltering.

.18 **wetting,** dampening, moistening, watering, humectant; **drenching, soaking,** sopping; **irrigational,** irriguous [archaic].

.19 **hygric,** hygrometric, hygroscopic, hygrophilous, hygrothermal.

393. DRYNESS

.1 NOUNS **dryness, aridness,** aridity, waterlessness; **drought;** juicelessness, saplessness; **thirst,** thirstiness; corkiness; watertightness, watertight integrity.

.2 (comparisons) dust, bone, parchment, stick, mummy, biscuit, cracker.

.3 **drying, desiccation,** drying up; **dehydration,** anhydration; evaporation; air-drying; insolation; drainage; withering, mummification; dehumidification.

.4 **drier,** desiccator, desiccative, siccative, exsiccative, exsiccator, **dehydrator,** dehydrant; dehumidifier; evaporator; hairdrier, clothes-drier.

.5 VERBS thirst; drink up, soak up, sponge up.

.6 **dry, desiccate,** exsiccate, dry up, **dehydrate,** anhydrate; evaporate; dehumidify; air-dry; insolate, sun, sun-dry; smoke, smoke-dry; cure; torrefy, burn, fire, kiln, **bake, parch,** scorch, sear; **wither, shrivel;** wizen, weazen; mummify; sponge, blot, soak up; **wipe,** rub, swab, brush; towel; drain 305.12.

.7 ADJS **dry, arid,** xer(o)–, scler(a)– or sclero–; **waterless,** unwatered, undamped, anhydrous, anhydr(o)–, dehydr(o)–; **bonedry,** dry as dust, dry as a bone; like parchment; droughty; juiceless, sapless; **thirsty,** thirsting, athirst; high and dry; sandy, dusty; desert, Saharan.

.8 rainless, fine, fair, bright and fair, pleasant.

.9 **dried, dehydrated, desiccated,** dried-up, exsiccated; evaporated; **parched, baked,** sunbaked, burnt, scorched, **seared,** sear or sere, sun-dried, adust; wind-dried, airdried; **withered, shriveled,** wizened, weazened; corky; mummified.

.10 **drying, dehydrating, desiccative,** desiccant, exsiccative, exsiccant, siccative, siccant; evaporative.

.11 **watertight, waterproof,** moistureproof, dampproof, leakproof, seepproof, dripproof, stormproof, stormtight, rainproof, raintight, floodproof.

394. RAIN

.1 NOUNS rain, ombro–, hyet(o)–; **rainfall,** fall, **precipitation,** moisture, wet; **shower,** sprinkle, flurry, patter, pitter-patter, splatter; streams of rain, sheet of rain, splash or spurt or gout of rain; **drizzle,** mizzle; **mist,** misty rain, Scotch mist; evening mist; rainwater; blood rain; raindrop, unfrozen hydrometeor.

.2 **rainstorm,** brash or scud [both Scot]; **cloudburst,** rainburst, burst of rain, torrent of rain, waterspout, spout, rainspout, **downpour,** downflow, downfall, pour, pouring or pelting or teeming or drowning rain, spate [Scot], plash [dial], **deluge,**

flood, heavy rain, driving or gushing rain, drenching or soaking rain, drencher, soaker.

.3 **thunderstorm,** thundersquall, thundergust, thundershower, thunder [dial]; ceraun(o)– or keraun(o)–.

.4 **wet weather, raininess,** rainy weather, stormy or dirty weather, cat-and-dog weather [informal], spell of rain, wet; rainy day; **rains,** rainy or wet season, spring rains, **monsoon;** predominance of Aquarius, reign of St. Swithin.

.5 **rainmaking,** seeding, cloud-seeding, nucleation, artificial nucleation; **rainmaker,** rain doctor, cloud seeder; Dry Ice, silver iodide.

.6 Jupiter Pluvius, Zeus; Thor.

.7 **rain gauge,** pluviometer, pluvioscope, pluviograph; ombrometer, ombrograph; udometer, udomograph; hyetometer, hyetometrograph, hyetograph.

.8 (science of precipitation) hydrometeorology, hyetology, hyetography; pluviography, pluviometry, ombrology.

.9 VERBS **rain, precipitate,** fall; weep; **shower,** shower down; **sprinkle,** spit [informal], spatter, patter, pitter-patter; **drizzle,** mizzle; **pour,** stream, pour with rain, **pelt,** drum, tattoo, come down in torrents or sheets or buckets, **rain cats and dogs** [informal], "rain dogs and polecats" [Richard Brome], rain tadpoles or bullfrogs or pitchforks [informal], "rain daggers with their points downward" [Robert Burton].

.10 ADJS **rainy, showery;** pluvious or pluviose or pluvial; **drizzly,** drizzling, mizzly, drippy; **misty,** misty-moisty; pouring, streaming, pelting, drumming, driving, blinding, cat-and-doggish [informal].

.11 pluviometric or pluvioscopic or pluviographic, ombrometric or ombrographic, udometric or udographic, hyetometric, hyetographic, hyetometrographic; hydrometeorologic(al), hyetologic(al).

395. STREAM

(running water)

.1 NOUNS **stream, waterway, watercourse** 396.2, channel 396; meandering stream, flowing stream, lazy stream, racing stream, braided stream; spill stream; adolescent stream; **river,** fluvi(o)–; navigable river, underground or subterranean river, "moving road" [Pascal], "a strong brown god" [T. S. Eliot]; wadi, arroyo [Sp]; **brook,** branch; kill, bourn, run [Brit dial], creek, crick [dial]; rivulet, rill, streamlet, brooklet, runlet, runnel, rundle [dial], rindle [Brit dial], beck [Brit], gill [Brit], burn [Scot], sike [Brit dial]; freshet, fresh; millstream, race; midstream, midchannel; stream action, fluviation.

.2 headwaters, headstream, headwater, head, riverhead; source, fountainhead 153.5,6.

.3 tributary, feeder, branch, fork, prong [dial], confluent, confluent stream, affluent; effluent, anabranch; bayou; billabong [Austral]; dendritic drainage pattern.

.4 flow, flowing, flux, fluency, profluence, fluid motion or movement, rheo–, –rrhea or –rrhoea; stream, current, set, trend, tide, water flow; drift, driftage; course, onward course, surge, gush, rush, onrush, spate, run, race; millrace, mill run; undercurrent, undertow; crosscurrent, crossflow; affluence, afflux, affluxion, confluence, concourse, conflux; downflow, downpour, defluxion; inflow 302.2; outflow 303.4.

.5 torrent, river, flood, waterflood, deluge; spate, pour, freshet, fresh; cataract, Niagara.

.6 overflow, spillage, spill, spill-over, overflowing, overrunning, alluvion, alluvium, inundation, flood, deluge, whelming, engulfment, submersion 320.2, cataclysm; the Flood, the Deluge; washout.

.7 trickle, tricklet, dribble, drip, dripping, stillicide [archaic], drop, spurtle; percolation, leaching, lixiviation; distillation, condensation, sweating; seeping, seepage.

.8 lap, swash, wash, slosh, plash, splash; lapping, washing, etc.

.9 jet, spout, spurt, spurtle, squirt, spit, spew, spray, spritz [dial]; rush, gush, flush; fountain, fount, font, jet d'eau [Fr]; geyser, spouter [informal].

.10 rapids, rapid; ripple, riffle, riff [dial]; chute, shoot, sault.

.11 waterfall, cataract, fall, falls, Niagara, cascade, force [Brit], linn [Scot], sault; nappe; watershoot.

.12 eddy, back stream, gurge, swirl, twirl, whirl; whirlpool, vortex, gulf, maelstrom; Maelstrom, Charybdis; countercurrent, counterflow, counterflux, backflow, reflux, refluence, regurgitation, backwash, backwater.

.13 tide, tidal current or stream, tidal flow or flood, tide race; tidewater; tideway, tide gate; tide rip, riptide, rip; direct tide, opposite tide; spring tide; high tide, high water, full tide; low tide, low water; neap tide, neap; lunar tide, solar tide; flood tide, ebb tide; rise of the tide, flux, flow, flood; ebb, reflux, refluence; ebb and flow, flux and reflux; tidal amplitude, tidal range; tide chart or table, tidal current chart; tide gauge, thalassometer.

.14 wave, cym(o)– or kym(o)–, billow, surge, swell, heave, undulation, lift, rise, send, scend; trough, peak; sea, heavy swell, ground swell; roller, roll; comber, comb; surf, breakers; wavelet, ripple, riffle; tidal wave, tsunami; gravity wave, water wave; tide wave; bore, tidal bore, eagre; whitecaps, white horses; rough or heavy sea, rough water, dirty water or sea, choppy or chopping sea, popple, lop, chop, choppiness.

.15 water gauge, fluviograph, fluviometer; marigraph; Nilometer.

.16 VERBS flow, stream, issue, pour, surge, run, course, rush, gush, flush, flood; set, make, trend; flow in 302.9; flow out 303.13; flow back, surge back, ebb, regurgitate.

.17 overflow, flow over, run over, well over, brim over, overbrim, overrun, pour out or over, spill, slop, slosh, spill out or over; cataract, cascade; inundate, engulf, swamp, sweep, whelm, overwhelm, flood, deluge, submerge 320.7.

.18 trickle, dribble, dripple, drip, drop, spurtle; filter, percolate, leach, lixiviate; distill, condense, sweat; seep, weep; gurgle 452.11.

.19 lap, plash, splash, wash, swash, slosh.

.20 jet, spout, spurt, spurtle, squirt, spit, spew, spray, spritz [dial], play, gush, well, surge; vomit, vomit out or forth.

.21 eddy, gurge, swirl, whirl, purl, reel, spin.

.22 billow, surge, swell, heave, lift, rise, send, scend, toss, popple, roll, wave, undulate; peak, draw to a peak, be poised; comb, break, dash, crash, smash; rise and fall, ebb and flow.

.23 ADJS streamy, rivery, brooky, creeky; streamlike, riverine; fluvial, fluviatile or fluviatic.

.24 flowing, streaming, running, pouring, fluxive, fluxional, coursing, racing, gushing, rushing, surging, surgy, fluent, profluent, affluent, defluent, decurrent, confluent, diffluent; tidal; gulfy, vortical; meandering, mazy, sluggish, serpentine.

.25 flooded, deluged, inundated, engulfed, swamped, swept, whelmed, drowned, overwhelmed, afloat, awash; washed, water-washed; in flood, at flood, in spate.

396. CHANNEL

.1 NOUNS channel, conduit, duct, course; way, passage, passageway; trough, troughway, troughing; tunnel; ditch, trench 263.2; adit; ingress, entrance 302; egress, exit 303.1.

.2 watercourse, waterway, aqueduct, water channel, water gate, water carrier, culvert; streamway, riverway; bed, stream bed, river bed, creek bed, runnel; dry bed; water gap; arroyo [Sp], wadi, donga [Africa], nullah [India], gully, gullyhole, gulch, canal; swash, swash channel; race, headrace, tailrace; flume; sluice; spillway; spillbox; irrigation ditch, water furrow; waterworks.

.3 gutter, trough, eave or eaves trough; chute, shoot; pentrough, penstock; guide.

.4 (metal founding) gate, ingate, runner, sprue, tedge.

.5 drain, sough [Brit], sluice, scupper; sink, sump, piscina; gutter, kennel; sewer, cloaca, headchute; cloaca maxima.

.6 tube, tubi–, solen(o)–; pipe, aul(o)–; tubing, piping, tubulation; tubulure; nipple, pipette, tubulet, tubule, tubuli–; reed, stem, straw; hose, hosepipe, garden hose, fire hose; pipeline; standpipe; water pipe, gas pipe, steam pipe; organ pipe, reed pipe, flue pipe; drainpipe, waste pipe, soil pipe; catheter; siphon, siphon(o)– or siphoni–; tap; efflux tube, adjutage; funnel; snorkel; siamese, siamese connection or joint.

.7 main, water main, gas main, fire main.

.8 spout, beak, waterspout, downspout; gargoyle.

.9 nozzle, bib nozzle, pressure nozzle, spray nozzle, nose, snout; rose, rosehead; shower head, sprinkler head.

.10 valve, gate; faucet, spigot, tap; cock, petcock, draw cock, stopcock, sea cock, drain cock, ball cock; ball valve; bunghole; needle valve; valvule, valvula.

.11 floodgate, flood-hatch, gate, head gate, penstock, water gate, sluice, sluice gate; tide gate, aboideau [Can]; weir; lock, lock gate, dock gate; air lock.

.12 hydrant, fire hydrant, plug, water plug, fireplug.

.13 (anatomy) duct, vessel, canal, angi(o)–, vasi– or vaso–; vas, meatus, meat(o)–; thoracic duct, lymphatic, lymphangio–; emunctory [archaic]; pore; intestines 225.4; urethra, ureter, urethr(o)–, uretero–; vagina, vagin(i)–, elytr(o)– or elytri–; oviduct, Fallopian tube, fall(o)–; salpinx, salping(o)–; Eustachian tube; ostium; fistula.

.14 blood vessel; artery, arteri(o)–, aorta, aort(o)–, pulmonary artery, carotid; vein, ven(o)– or veni–, phleb(o)–, jugular vein, vena cava, pulmonary vein; portal vein, pyl(o)– or pyle–; varicose vein; venation; capillary, arteriole, veinlet, venule.

.15 gullet, throat, esophagus, esophag(o)–, gorge, hals [dial], weasand [archaic], wizen [Brit dial], goozle or guzzle [both dial]; fauces, isthmus of the fauces; pharynx, pharyng(o)–.

.16 windpipe, trachea, trache(o)–, weasand [archaic], wizen [Brit dial]; bronchus, bronchi [pl], bronchial tube, bronchi(o)–; epiglottis.

.17 air passage, air duct, airway, air shaft, shaft, air hole, air tube; blowhole, breathing hole, spiracle; nostril, naris 256.7; touchhole; spilehole, vent, venthole, ventage, ventiduct; ventilator, ventilating shaft; transom, louver, louverwork; wind tunnel.

.18 chimney, flue, flue pipe, funnel, stovepipe, stack, smokestack, smokeshaft; Charley Noble; fumarole.

.19 VERBS channel, channelize, canalize, conduct, convey, put through; pipe, funnel, siphon; trench 263.3.

.20 ADJS tubular, tubate, tubiform, tubelike, tubulo–, pipelike; tubed, piped; cannular; fistular; bronchial, tracheal.

.21 vascular, vesicular, vascul(o)–; arterial; venous or venose, veinous; capillary.

.22 throated, throatlike, jugular.

.23 valvular, valval, valvelike.

397. OCEAN

.1 NOUNS ocean, sea, ocean sea, mari–, thalass(o)–; great or main sea, thalassa [Gk], main or ocean main, the bounding main, tide, salt sea, salt water, blue water, the brine, the briny [informal], the briny deep, "the vasty deep" [Shakespeare], the deep, the deep sea, the deep blue sea, drink or big drink [both slang], high sea, high seas; the seven seas; hydrosphere; ocean depths 209.4.

.2 "great Neptune's ocean", "unpath'd waters", "the always wind-obeying deep" [all Shakespeare], "thou deep and dark blue ocean" [Byron], "Uterine Sea of our dreams and Sea haunted by the true dream", "Sea of a thousand creases, like the infinitely pleated tunic of the god in the hands of women of the sanctuary" [both S.-J. Perse], "the great naked sea shouldering a load of salt" [Sandburg], "the wine-dark sea" [Homer], "the wavy waste" [Thomas Hood], "old ocean's gray and melancholy waste" [William Cullen Bryant], "the world of waters wild" [James Thomson], "the rising world of waters dark and deep" [Milton], "the glad, indomitable sea" [Bliss Carman], "the clear hyaline, the glassy sea" [Milton].

.3 (oceans) Atlantic, Pacific, Arctic, Antarctic, Indian.

.4 spirit of the sea, "the old man of the sea" [Homer], sea devil, Davy, **Davy Jones**; sea god, **Neptune**, Poseidon, Oceanus, Triton, Nereus, Oceanid, Nereid, Thetis; Varuna, Dylan; **mermaid**, siren; merman, seaman.

.5 (ocean zones) pelagic zone, benthic zone, estuarine area, sublittoral, littoral, intertidal zone, splash zone, supralittoral.

.6 oceanography, thalassography, hydrography, bathymetry; marine biology; aquiculture.

.7 oceanographer, thalassographer, hydrographer.

.8 ADJS **oceanic, marine, maritime**, pelagic, thalassic, –alian; nautical 275.57; oceanographic(al), hydrographic(al), bathymetric(al), bathyorographical, thalassographic(al); terriginous; deep-sea 209.14.

.9 ADVS **at sea**, on the high seas; afloat 275.62,63; by water, by sea.

.10 **oversea, overseas**, beyond seas, over the water, transmarine, across the sea.

.11 **oceanward**, oceanwards, **seaward**, seawards, off; offshore, off soundings, out of soundings, in blue water.

398. LAKE, POOL

.1 NOUNS **lake**, landlocked water, loch [Scot], lough [Ir], nyanza [Africa], mere, freshwater lake; oxbow lake, bayou lake, glacial lake; volcanic lake; tarn; inland sea; **pool**, lakelet, **pond**, pondlet, limn-(o)– or limni–, –limnion, linn [Scot], dike [Brit dial], *étang* [Fr]; standing water, still water, stagnant water, dead water; **water hole**, water pocket; farm pond; fishpond; millpond, millpool; salt pond, salina, tidal pond or pool; **puddle**, plash, sump [dial]; **lagoon**, *laguna* [Sp]; **reservoir**, artificial lake; dam; **well, cistern**, tank.

.2 **lake dweller**, lacustrian, lacustrine dweller or inhabitant, **pile dweller** or builder; laker.

.3 **lake dwelling**, lacustrine dwelling, **pile house** or **dwelling**, palafitte; crannog.

.4 limnology, limnologist; limnimeter, limnograph.

.5 ADJS **lakish**, laky, lakelike; lacustrine, lacustral, lacustrian; pondy, pondlike, lacuscular; limnologic(al).

399. INLET, GULF

.1 NOUNS **inlet, cove**, creek [Brit], arm of the sea, arm, armlet, reach, loch [Scot], **bay, fjord**, bight; **gulf; estuary**, firth or frith, bayou, mouth, *boca* [Sp]; **harbor**, natural harbor; road or roads, roadstead; **strait** or straits, kyle [Scot], **narrow** or narrows, euripus, belt, gut, narrow seas; **sound**.

.2 ADJS **gulfy**, gulflike; gulfed, bayed, embayed; estuarine, fluviomarine, tidewater.

400. MARSH

.1 NOUNS **marsh**, marshland, **swamp**, swampland, fen, fenland, **morass**, mere or marish [both archaic], *marais* [Fr], **bog, mire, quagmire**, sump [dial], wash, baygall; glade, everglade; slough, swale, wallow, hog wallow, buffalo wallow, sough [Brit]; bottom, **bottoms**, bottomland, slob land, holm [Brit], meadow; **moor**, moorland, moss [Scot], peat bog; **salt marsh**; quicksand; taiga; mud flat, **mud** 389.8,9; helo–, paludi–.

.2 VERBS **mire**, bemire, sink in, **bog**, mire or bog down, stick in the mud; stodge.

.3 ADJS **marshy, swampy**, swampish, **moory**, moorish, fenny, marish [archaic], paludal or paludous; **boggy**, boggish, **miry**, mirish, quaggy, quagmiry, spouty, poachy; **muddy** 389.14; swamp-growing, uliginous.

401. VAPOR, GAS

.1 NOUNS **vapor**, volatile, vapo–, vapori–, atm(o)–; **fume, reek**, exhalation, breath, effluvium; **fluid**; **miasma**, mephitis, malaria [archaic], fetid air; **smoke**, smudge; wisp or plume or puff of smoke; **damp**, chokedamp, blackdamp, firedamp, afterdamp; flatus; **steam**, water vapor; cloud 404.

.2 **gas**, aer(o)–, mano–, pneum(o)–, pneumat(o)–; rare or noble or inert gas, –on, halogen gas; fluid; **atmosphere, air** 402; pneumatics, aerodynamics 347.5.

.3 **vaporousness**, vaporiness; vapor pressure or tension; **aeriness; ethereality**, etherialism; **gaseousness**, gaseous state, gassiness, gaseity; **flatulence**, windiness, flatuosity [archaic]; **fluidity**.

.4 **volatility**, vaporability, vaporizability, evaporability.

.5 **vaporization, evaporation**, volatilization, gasification; sublimation; distillation, fractionation; etherification; aeration, aerification; fluidization; atomization; exhalation; fumigation; smoking; steaming; etherealization.

.6 **vaporizer, evaporator**; atomizer, aerosol, spray; still, retort.

.7 **vaporimeter**, manometer, pressure gauge; gas meter, gasometer; pneumatometer, spirometer; aerometer, airometer; eudiometer.

.8 VERBS **vaporize, evaporate**, volatilize, **gasify**; sublimate, sublime; distill, fractionate; etherify; **aerate**, aerify; carbonate, oxygenate, hydrogenate, chlorinate, halogenate, etc.; atomize, spray; fluidize; **reek, fume**; exhale, give off, emit, send out; **smoke; steam**; fumigate, perfume; **etherize**.

.9 ADJS **vaporous**, vaporish, vapory, vaporlike; **airy, aery, aerial, ethereal; gaseous**, in the gaseous state, gasified, gassy, gaslike, gasiform; vaporing; **reeking**, reeky; miasmic or miasmal or miasmatic, mephitic; **fuming**, fumy; smoky, smoking; steamy, steaming; ozonic; oxygenous; oxyacetylene; pneumatic, aerostatic, aerodynamic.

.10 **volatile**, volatilizable; **vaporable**, vaporizable, vaporescent; **evaporative**, evaporable.

.11 **gases**

acetylene	marsh gas
air gas	methane
ammonia	mustard gas
argon	natural gas
asphyxiating gas	neon
butane	nerve gas
carbon dioxide	nitrogen, nitr(o)–
carbon monoxide	oil gas
chlorine, chlor(o)–	oxygen, oxy–
coal gas	ozone, ozon(o)–
ethane	phosgene
ether	poison gas
ethylene	propane
fluorine, fluor(o)–	radon
formaldehyde	sewer gas
helium	sneeze gas
hydrogen, hydr(o)–	tear gas
illuminating gas	vesicatory gas
krypton	war gas
laughing gas	water gas
lewisite	xenon

402. AIR

.1 NOUNS **air**, aero–; ether; ozone [informal]; thin air.

.2 **atmosphere**, atm(o)–; aerosphere, gaseous envelope or environment or medium, welkin, lift [dial]; biosphere, ecosphere, noosphere.

.3 (atmospheric layers) stratum, layer, belt; lower atmosphere, upper atmosphere, outer atmosphere; troposphere; substratosphere, tropopause; stratosphere, strato–, isothermal region; ionosphere, Heaviside or Heaviside-Kennelly layer or region; Appleton layer, F layer; Van Allen belt or radiation belt; photosphere, chemosphere.

.4 **weather, climate**, clime; **the elements**, forces of nature; microclimate, macroclimate; fair weather, calm weather, halcyon days, good weather; stormy weather 162.4; rainy weather 394.4; windiness 403.15; hot weather 328.7; cold weather 333.3; meteor(o)–.

.5 **weather map**; isobar, isobaric or isopiestic line; isotherm, isothermal line; isometric, isometric line; high, high-pressure area; low, low-pressure area; front, front(o)–, wind-shift line, squall line; cold front, polar front, cold sector; warm front; occluded front, stationary front; air mass; cyclone, anticyclone.

.6 **meteorology**, weather science, aerology, aerography, weatherology, climatology, climatography, microclimatology, forecasting, long-range forecasting; barometry; pneumatics 347.5; anemology 403.16; nephology 404.4.

.7 **meteorologist**, weather scientist, aerologist, aerographer, weatherologist; climatologist, microclimatologist; **weatherman, weather forecaster**, weather prophet; **weather report**, weather forecast; weather bureau; weather ship; weather station; weather-reporting network.

.8 **weather instrument**, meteorological or aerological instrument; **barometer**, aneroid barometer, glass, weatherglass; barograph, barometrograph, recording barometer; aneroidograph; vacuometer; hygrometer; weather balloon, radiosonde; weather satellite; hurricane-hunter aircraft; weather vane 403.17.

.9 **ventilation**, cross-ventilation, **airing**, aerage, perflation, refreshment; **aeration; air conditioning**, air cooling; oxygenation, oxygenization.

.10 **ventilator; aerator; air conditioner**, air filter, air cooler, ventilating or cooling system; blower; air passage 396.17; fan 403.21.

.11 VERBS **air**, air out, **ventilate**, cross-ventilate, wind, refresh, freshen; **air-condition**, air-cool; **fan**, winnow; **aerate**, airify; oxygenate, oxygenize.

.12 ADJS **airy**, aery, **aerial**, aeriform, airlike, **pneumatic**, ethereal; exposed, roomy, light; airish, breezy 403.25; open-air, alfresco; **atmospheric**, tropospheric, stratospheric.

.13 **climatal**, climatic(al), climatographic(al), **elemental**; meteorologic(al), aerologic(al), aerographic(al), climatologic(al); macroclimatic, microclimatic, microclimatologic(al); barometric(al), baric, barographic; isobaric, isopiestic, isometric; high-pressure, low-pressure; cyclonic, anticyclonic.

403. WIND

(air flow)

.1 NOUNS **wind**, venti– or vento–, current, **air current**, current of air, movement of air, stream, stream of air, flow of air; updraft, downdraft; crosscurrent, undercurrent; monsoon; fall wind, gravity wind, katabatic wind, head wind, tail wind, following wind; jetstream; **draft**; **inspiration, inhalation, indraft**, inflow, inrush.

.2 "scolding winds" [Shakespeare], "the felon winds" [Milton], "the wings of the wind" [Bible], "O wild West Wind, thou breath of Autumn's being" [Shelley], "the wind that sang of trees uptorn and vessels tost" [Wordsworth].

.3 (wind god; the wind personified) Aeolus, Vayu; Boreas (north wind); Eurus (east wind); Zephyr or Zephyrus, Favonius (west wind); Notus (south wind); Caurus (northwest wind); Afer (southwest wind).

.4 **puff**, puff of air or wind, breath, breath of air, flatus, waft, capful of wind, whiff, whiffet, stir of air.

.5 **breeze**, light or gentle wind or breeze, softblowing wind, **zephyr**, gale [archaic], air, light air, moderate breeze; fresh or stiff breeze; cool or cooling breeze; sea breeze, onshore breeze, ocean breeze, cat's-paw.

.6 **gust**, wind gust, **blast**, blow, flaw, **flurry**, scud [Scot].

.7 **hot wind**; snow eater, thawer; chinook, **chinook wind**; simoom, samiel; foehn; khamsin; harmattan; sirocco; solano; Santa Ana; volcanic wind.

.8 **wintry wind**, winter wind, raw wind, chilling or freezing wind, bone-chilling wind, sharp or piercing wind, cold or icy wind, biting wind, the hawk [slang], nipping or nippy wind, "a nipping and an eager air" [Shakespeare], icy blasts; Arctic or boreal or hyperboreal or hyperborean blast.

.9 **north wind, norther**, mistral, bise, tramontane; northeaster, **nor'easter**, Euroclydon, gregale, Tehuantepec wind, Tehuantepecer; northwester, **nor'wester**; southeaster, **sou'easter**; southwester, **sou'-wester**, kite-wind; **east wind**, easter, easterly, levanter; **west wind**, wester, westerly; **south wind**, souther, southerly buster [Austral].

.10 prevailing wind; polar easterlies; prevailing westerlies, antitrades; trade wind, trades; doldrums, wind-equator; horse latitudes; roaring forties.

.11 [naut terms] **head wind, beam wind, tail wind**, following wind, fair or favorable wind, apparent or relative wind, backing wind, veering wind, slant of wind.

.12 **windstorm**, big or great or fresh or strong or stiff or high or howling or spanking wind, ill or dirty or ugly wind; storm, storm wind, stormy winds, **tempest**, tempestuous wind; williwaw; **blow**, violent or heavy blow; **squall**, thick squall, black squall, white squall; squall line, wind-shift line, line squall; line storm; equinoctial; **gale**, half a gale, whole gale; tropical cyclone, **hurricane**, typhoon, tropical storm, **blizzard** 333.8; **thundersquall**, thundergust.

.13 **dust storm, sandstorm**, shaitan, peesash, devil, khamsin, sirocco, simoom, samiel, harmattan.

.14 **whirlwind**, whirlblast, wind eddy; **cyclone, tornado, twister**, rotary storm, typhoon, *baguio* [Sp]; sandspout, sand column, dust devil; waterspout, rainspout.

.15 **windiness**, gustiness; airiness, **breeziness**; draftiness.

.16 **anemology**, anemometry; **wind direction; wind force, Beaufort scale**, half-Beaufort scale, International scale; wind rose, barometric wind rose, humidity wind rose, hyetal or rain wind rose, temperature wind rose, dynamic wind rose; wind arrow, wind marker.

.17 **weather vane, weathercock**, vane, cock, wind vane, wind indicator, wind cone or sleeve or sock, anemoscope; anemometer, wind-speed indicator, anemograph, anemometrograph.

.18 **breathing, respiration**, aspiration, spiro–, pneumat(o)–, –pnea or –pnoea; **inspiration, inhalation; expiration, exhalation**; insufflation, exsufflation; **breath**, wind, breath of air; pant, puff; wheeze, asthmatic wheeze; broken wind; gasp, gulp; snoring, snore, stertor; sniff, sniffle, snuff, snuffle; sigh, suspiration; sneeze, sternutation; cough, hack; hiccup; **artificial respiration,** mouth-to-mouth resuscitation; inhalator; iron lung; scuba, self-contained underwater breathing apparatus, Aqua-Lung; oxygen mask, oxygen tent.

.19 **lungs,** pneumon(o)–, bellows, lights; **gills,** branchiae, branchi(o)–; ctenidia.

.20 **blower,** bellows; blowpipe, blowtube, blowgun.

.21 **fan,** flabellum, flabelli–, rhipi– *or* rhipid(o)–; punkah, thermantidote, electric fan, blower, exhaust fan; ventilator 402.10; windsail, windscoop, windcatcher.

.22 VERBS **blow, waft; puff,** huff, whiff; whiffle; **breeze;** breeze up, freshen; **gather, brew,** set in, blow up, pipe up, come up, **blow up a storm;** bluster, squall; **storm,** rage, "blow, winds, and crack your cheeks, rage, blow" [Shakespeare], blast, blow great guns, blow a hurricane; blow over.

.23 **sigh,** sough, whisper, mutter, murmur, **sob, moan,** groan, growl, snarl; **wail, howl,** scream, screech, shriek, **roar,** whistle, pipe, sing, sing in the shrouds.

.24 **breathe, respire; inhale, inspire,** breathe in; **exhale, expire,** breathe out, exhaust, expel; **puff,** huff, **pant,** suck one's breath *or* wind, breathe hard *or* heavily, blow; **gasp,** gulp; snore; wheeze; **sniff,** sniffle, snuff, snuffle, snort; **sigh,** suspire; sneeze; cough, hack; hiccup.

.25 ADJS **windy, blowy; breezy, drafty,** airy, airish; brisk, fresh; **gusty,** blasty, puffy, flawy; **squally;** blustery, blustering, blusterous; aeolian, favonian, boreal.

.26 **stormy, tempestuous,** raging, storming, angry; turbulent 162.17; dirty, foul; cyclonic, tornadic, typhonic, typhoonish; rainy 394.10; cloudy 404.7.

.27 **windblown,** blown; **windswept,** bleak, raw, exposed.

.28 anemological, anemographic, anemometric(al).

.29 **respiratory,** breathing; inspiratory, expiratory; nasal, rhinal; pulmonary, pulmonic, pneumonic; puffing, huffing, snorting, wheezing, wheezy, asthmatic, stertorous, snoring, panting, heaving; sniffy, sniffly, sniffling, snuffy, snuffly, snuffling; sneezy, sternutative, sternutatory, errhine.

404. CLOUD

.1 NOUNS **cloud,** high fog, nepho–, "the clouds—the only birds that never sleep" [Victor Hugo], "the argosies of cloudland" [J. T. Trowbridge], "islands on a dark-blue sea" [Shelley], "fair, frail, palaces" [T. B. Aldrich], "the low'ring element" [Milton]; fleecy cloud, cottony cloud, billowy cloud; cloud bank, cloud mass, cloud drift; cloudling, cloudlet; **nimbus,** nimbus cloud, rain cloud, water carrier; storm cloud, squall cloud; thundercloud, thunderhead; **cumulus,** cumulus cloud, woolpack, cloud street, fractocumulus; cumulo-nimbus, anvil cloud; **stratus,** stratus cloud, strato–, cirro-stratus, cumulo-cirro-stratus, cirro-velum; strato-cumulus, cumulo-stratus, snail cloud; mammatocumulus, festoon cloud; cloud funnel; alto-cumulus, alto-stratus; **cirrus,** cirrus cloud, curl cloud, cirr(o)– *or* cirri–; cirro-cumulus, cumulo-cirrus, cirromacula; mackerel sky; cirro-nebula, cirrus haze; cirro-fillum, cirrus stripe; mare's-tail, colt's-tail, cat's-tail, cocktail; goat's hair; banner cloud, cap cloud, cloudcap; scud; mushroom cloud, cloudscape, cloud band; cloudland, Cloudcuckooland *or* Nephelococcygia [Aristophanes].

.2 **fog,** pea soup [informal], peasouper *or* pea-soup fog [both informal]; London fog, London special [Brit informal]; **smog** (smoke-fog), smaze (smoke-haze); frost smoke; mist, drizzling mist, drisk [dial]; haze, gauze, film; vapor 401.

.3 **cloudiness, haziness, mistiness, fogginess,** nebulosity, nubilation, nimbosity, **overcast,** heavy sky, dirty sky.

.4 **nephology,** nephelognosy; nephologist.

.5 **nephelometer,** nepheloscope.

.6 VERBS **cloud,** becloud, encloud, cloud over, overcloud, cloud up, clabber up [dial], **overcast,** overshadow, shadow, shade, **darken** 337.9, darken over, nubilate, obnubilate, obscure; **smoke,** oversmoke; **fog,** befog; smog; **mist,** bemist, enmist; **haze.**

.7 ADJS **cloudy,** nebulous, nubilous, nimbose; **clouded,** overclouded, **overcast;** dirty, heavy; dark 337.13; **gloomy** 337.14; cloud-flecked; cirrous, cirrose; cumulous, cumuliform, stratous, stratiform; lenticularis, mammatus, castellatus; thunderheaded, stormy, squally.

.8 **cloud-covered,** cloud-laden, cloud-curtained, cloud-crammed, cloud-crossed, cloud-hidden, cloud-wrapped, cloud-enveloped, cloud-surrounded, cloud-girt, cloud-flecked, cloud-eclipsed, **cloud-capped,** cloud-topped.

.9 **foggy,** soupy *or* pea-soupy [both informal]; smoggy; hazy, misty.

.10 nephological.

405. BUBBLE

.1 NOUNS **bubble**, bleb, **globule**; vesicle, bulla, **blister**, blood blister, fever blister; balloon, bladder 193.2; air bubble, soap bubble.

.2 **foam, froth,** aphr(o)–; **spume**, sea foam, scud; **spray, surf**, breakers, white water, spoondrift *or* **spindrift**, "stinging, ringing spindrift" [Kipling]; **suds, lather**, soapsuds; **scum**, offscum; head, collar; puff, mousse, soufflé, meringue.

.3 **bubbling**, bubbliness, **effervescence** *or* effervescency, **sparkle**, spumescence, frothiness, frothing, foaming; **fizz**, fizzle, carbonation; **ebullience** *or* ebulliency; **ebullition**, boiling; **fermentation**, ferment.

.4 VERBS **bubble**, bubble up, burble; **effervesce, fizz, fizzle**; hiss, **sparkle**; **ferment**, work; **boil**, seethe, simmer; plop, blubber; guggle, gurgle; bubble over, boil over.

.5 **foam, froth**, spume, cream; **lather**, suds, sud; scum, mantle; **aerate**, whip, beat, whisk.

.6 ADJS **bubbly**, burbly, **bubbling**, burbling; **effervescent**, spumescent, **fizzy, sparkling**, *mousseux* [Fr]; carbonated; ebullient; puffed, soufflé *or* soufléed, beaten, whipped, chiffon; **blistered**, blistery, blebby, vesicated, vesicular; blistering, vesicant, vesicatory.

.7 **foamy**, foam-flecked, **frothy**, spumy, spumous *or* spumose; yeasty, barmy; **sudsy**, suddy, **lathery**, soapy, soapsudsy, soapsuddy; heady, with a head *or* collar on.

406. ORGANIC MATTER

.1 NOUNS **organic matter**, animate *or* living matter, all that lives, living nature, organic nature, organized matter; flesh, tissue, fiber, brawn, plasm, cre(o)– *or* kre(o)–, creat(o)–, hist(o)–, in(o)–, –plasm-(a); **flora and fauna**, plant and animal life, animal and vegetable kingdom, biosphere, biota, ecosphere, noosphere.

.2 **organism**, organization, organic being, **living being** *or* **thing**, being, creature, created being, **individual**, genetic individual, physiological individual, morphological individual; zoon, zooid; virus; aerobic organism, anaerobic organism; heterotrophic organism, autotrophic organism; microbe, microorganism 196.18; –ont, –id.

.3 biological classification *or* taxonomy, kingdom, phylum, etc. 61.5.

.4 **cell**, bioplast, cellule, cellul(o)– *or* cellul(i)–, cyt(o)– *or* cyti–, –cyte, –plast; procaryotic cell, eucaryotic cell; plant cell, animal cell; germ cell, somatic cell; corpuscle; unicellularity, multicellularity; **protoplasm**, energid; trophoplasm; chromatoplasm; cytoplasm, cyt(o)–, plasm-(o)–, plasmato–, plasto–; ectoplasm, endoplasm; cellular tissue, –enchyma; reticulum; plasmodium, coenocyte, syncytium, plasmod(o)– *or* plasmodi(o)–.

.5 organelle; plastid; chromoplast, plastosome, chloroplast; mitochondrion; Golgi apparatus; ribosome; spherosome, microbody; vacuole; central apparatus, cytocentrum; centroplasm; central body, microcentrum; centrosome; centrosphere; centriole, basal body; pili, cilia, flagella, spindle fibers; aster, astr(o)–; kinoplasm; plasmodesmata; cell membrane.

.6 metaplasm; cell wall, cell plate; structural polysaccharide; bast, phloem, xylem, xyl-(o)–, cellulose, chitin.

.7 **nucleus**, nucle(o)– *or* nuclei–, kary(o)– *or* cary(o)–; macronucleus, meganucleus; micronucleus; nucleolus, nucleol(o)–, pyren(o)–; plasmosome; karyosome, chromatin strands; nuclear envelope; chromatin, karyotin, chromat(o)–; basichromatin, heterochromatin, oxychromatin.

.8 **chromosome**, –some; allosome; heterochromosome, sex chromosome, idiochromosome; W chromosome; X chromosome, accessory chromosome, monosome; Y chromosome; Z chromosome; euchromosome, autosome; homologous chromosomes; univalent chromosome, chromatid; centromere; gene-string, chromonema; genome; chromosome complement; chromosome number, diploid number, haploid number; polyploidy.

.9 **gene**, gen(o)–; allele; operon; structural gene, regulator gene, operator gene; deoxyribonucleic acid, **DNA**; DNA double helix; nucleotide, codon; ribonucleic acid, **RNA**; messenger RNA, mRNA; transfer RNA, tRNA; ribosomal RNA; anticodon; gene pool, gene complex, gene flow, genetic drift; genotype, biotype; **hereditary character**, heredity 170.6.

.10 **gamete, germ cell**, reproductive cell; macrogamete, megagamete; microgamete; planogamete; genetoid; gamone; gametangium, gametophore; gametophyte; germ plasm, idioplasm.

.11 **sperm, spermatozoa, seed, semen**, scum *or* protein [both slang], sperm(o)– *or* sperm(a)– *or* sperm(i)–, spermat(o)–; seminal *or* spermatic fluid, milt; **sperm cell**, male gamete; spermatozoon, spermatozoid, antherozoid; antheridium; spermatium, spermatiophore or spermatophore, spermagonium; pollen, pollin(i)–; spermatogonium; androcyte, spermatid, spermatocyte.

.12 **ovum, egg, egg cell,** female gamete, oösphere; oöcyte; oögonium; ovicell, ooecium; ovule; stirp.

.13 **spore,** sporule, spor(o)– or spori–, coni-(o)–, conidi(o)–; microspore; macrospore; megaspore; swarm spore, zoospore, planospore; spore mother cell, sporocyte; zygospore; sporocarp, cystocarp; basidium, basidi(o)–; sporangium, megasporangium, microsporangium; sporocyst; gonidangium; sporogonium, sporophyte; sporophore; sorus.

.14 **embryo,** embry(o)–, zygote, oösperm, oöspore, blast(o)–, –blast; blastula; *Anlage* [Ger]; **fetus,** fet(o)– or feti– or foet-(o)– or foeti–; germ, germen [archaic], rudiment; **larva,** larvi–, nymph.

.15 **egg,** ov(o)– or ovi–, o– or oö–; ovule; bird's egg; **roe,** fish eggs, caviar, spawn; **yolk,** yellow, vitellus, vitell(o)–, lecith(o)–; white, **egg white,** albumen, albumin(o)– or albumini–; glair, eggshell.

.16 **cell division; mitosis,** mit(o)–; amitosis; metamitosis; eumitosis; endomitosis; promitosis; haplomitosis, mesomitosis; karyomitosis; karyokinesis; interphase, prophase, metaphase, anaphase, telophase, diaster, cytokinesis; **meiosis.**

.17 (science of organisms) **biology,** biological science, life science; aerobiology, agrobiology, astrobiology or exobiology or xenobiology, **bacteriology, biochemistry** or biochemy or biochemics, bioecology or ecology or bionomics 233.4, biometry or biometrics, bionics, biophysics, cell physiology, cybernetics, cryobiology, cytology, electrobiology, **embryology,** enzymology, ethnobiology, gnotobiotics, microbiology, molecular biology, paleontology, pharmacology, **physiology,** radiobiology, taxonomy, virology; **anatomy** 245.7; **zoology** 415; **botany** 412; **genetics** 170.6.

.18 **biologist,** bacteriologist, biochemist, biophysicist, biometrist, cytologist, ecologist, embryologist, geneticist, physiologist; naturalist, natural scientist; botanist 412.2; zoologist 415.2; anatomist 245.7.

.19 ADJS **organic,** organ(o)–; organized; **animate, living,** vital, zoetic; **biological,** biotic; physiological, physi(o)–.

.20 **protoplasmic,** plasmic, plasmatic, –plastic; **genetic,** genic, hereditary.

.21 **cellular,** cellulous; unicellular, multicellular; corpuscular.

.22 gametic, gamic, sexual; **spermatic,** spermic, **seminal,** spermatozoal, spermatozoan, spermatozoic; sporal, sporous, sporoid, –sporic; sporogenous.

.23 **nuclear,** nucleal, nucleary, nucleate; multinucleate; nucleolar, nucleolate, nucleolated; **chromosomal;** chromatinic; –zygous; –ploid, haploid, hapl(o)– or apl(o)–, diploid, dipl(o)–, polyploid; –somic.

.24 **embryonic, germinal,** germinant, germinative, germinational; larval; fetal; in the bud; –blastic; germiparous.

.25 **egglike,** ovicular, eggy; ovular; albuminous, albuminoid; yolked, yolky; oviparous.

407. LIFE

.1 NOUNS **life, living, vitality,** being alive, having life, animation, animate existence; liveliness, animal spirits, vivacity, spriteliness; long life, longevity; viability; lifetime 110.5; immortality 112.3; birth 167; existence 1; bi(o)–, organ(o)–; –biosis.

.2 "one dem'd horrid grind" [Dickens], "a beauty chased by tragic laughter" [John Masefield], "a little gleam of Time between two eternities" [Carlyle], "a tale told by an idiot, full of sound and fury, signifying nothing" [Shakespeare], "a perpetual instruction in cause and effect" [Emerson], "a flame that is always burning itself out" [G. B. Shaw], "a dome of many-colored glass" [Shelley], "a long lesson in humility" [J. M. Barrie], "a fiction made up of contradiction" [William Blake], "a fatal complaint, and an eminently contagious one" [O. W. Holmes, Sr.], "a play of passion" [Sir W. Raleigh], "a comedy to those who think, a tragedy to those who feel" [H. Walpole].

.3 **life force, soul,** spirit, force of life, living force, *vis vitae, vis vitalis* [both L], **vital force** or vital energy, animating force or power or principle, inspiriting force or power or principle, *élan vital* [Fr], impulse of life, vital principle, **vital spark** or **flame,** spark of life, divine spark, life principle, vital spirit, vital fluid, anima; **breath,** life breath, **breath of life,** breath of one's nostrils, divine breath, life essence, essence of life, pneuma; prana, atman, jivatma, jiva; blood, **lifeblood,** heartblood, heart's blood; **heart,** heartbeat, beating heart; seat of life; growth force, bathmism; **life process;** biorhythm, biological clock, life cycle.

.4 **the living,** the living and breathing, all

animate nature, the quick; the quick and the dead.

.5 vivification, vitalization, animation, quickening.

.6 biosphere, ecosphere, noosphere; biochore, biotope, biocycle.

.7 VERBS **live,** be alive *or* animate *or* vital, have life, exist 1.8, breathe, respire, live and breathe, fetch *or* draw breath, draw the breath of life, walk the earth, subsist.

.8 **come to life,** come into existence *or* being, come into the world, see the light, be incarnated, **be born** *or* begotten *or* conceived; quicken; **revive, come to,** come alive, show signs of life; **awake, awaken;** rise again, live again, rise from the grave, resurge, resuscitate, reanimate, return to life.

.9 **vivify, vitalize, energize, animate, quicken,** inspirit, imbue *or* endow with life, give life to, put life *or* new life into, breathe life into, bring to life, bring *or* call into existence *or* being; conceive 167.13; give birth 167.15.

.10 **keep alive,** keep body and soul together, endure, survive, persist, last, hang on, be spared, have nine lives like a cat; support life; cheat death.

.11 ADJS **living, alive,** having life, live, very much alive, alive and kicking [informal], conscious, breathing, quick [archaic], **animate,** animated, **vital,** zoetic, instinct with life, imbued *or* endowed with life, vivified, enlivened, inspirited; in the flesh, among the living, in the land of the living, on this side of the grave, aboveground; existent 1.13; long-lived, tenacious of life; capable of life *or* survival, viable; –biotic, –coline *or* –colous.

.12 **life-giving,** animating, animative, quickening, vivifying, energizing.

408. DEATH

.1 NOUNS **death, dying,** somatic death, clinical death, biological death, **decease, demise,** thanat(o)–, necr(o)–; perishing, release, **passing away,** passing, passing over, "crossing the bar" [Tennyson], leaving life, making an end, departure, parting, going, going off *or* away, exit, ending, end 70, end of life, cessation of life, **loss of life,** ebb of life, expiration, **dissolution, extinction,** bane, annihilation, extinguishment, quietus; doom, summons of death, final summons, sentence of death, death knell, knell; **sleep, rest,** eternal rest *or* sleep, last sleep, last rest; **grave** 410.16; reward, debt of nature, last debt;

last muster, last roundup, curtains [slang]; jaws of death, hand *or* finger of death, shadow *or* shades of death.

.2 "the journey's end", "the undiscovered country from whose bourn no traveler returns", "dusty death" [all Shakespeare], "that dreamless sleep" [Byron], "a debt we all must pay" [Euripides], "the tribute due unto nature" [Laurence Sterne], "the sleeping partner of life" [Horace Smith], "a knell that summons thee to heaven or to hell", "that fell arrest without all bail" [both Shakespeare], "kind Nature's signal of retreat" [Samuel Johnson], "the latter end", "a little sleep, a little slumber, a little folding of the hands to sleep" [both Bible], "the seamouth of mortality" [Robinson Jeffers], "that good night" [Dylan Thomas], "the downward path" [Horace], "the gate of life" [St. Bernard], "the crown of life" [Edward Young], "an awfully big adventure" [J. M. Barrie].

.3 (personifications and symbols) **Death,** "Black Death" [Ovid], "Pale Death" [Horace], "the pale priest of the mute people" [R. Browning], "that grim ferryman", "that fell sergeant" [both Shakespeare], "Hell's grim Tyrant" [Pope], "the king of terrors" [Bible], **Grim Reaper,** Reaper; pale horse; pale horse, pale rider; angel of death, death's bright angel, Azrael; scythe *or* sickle of Death; **skull,** death's-head, grinning skull, crossbones, skull and crossbones; *memento mori* [L]; white cross.

.4 river of death, Styx, Stygian shore, Acheron; Jordan, Jordan's bank; "valley of the shadow of death" [Bible]; Heaven 1018; Hell 1019.

.5 early death, early grave, **untimely end;** sudden death; stroke of death, death stroke; deathblow 409.10.

.6 **violent death;** killing 409; suffocation, smothering, smotheration [informal]; asphyxiation; choking, choke, strangulation, strangling; drowning, watery grave; starvation; liver death, serum death; megadeath.

.7 **natural death;** easy *or* quiet *or* peaceful death *or* end, euthanasia, blessed *or* welcome release.

.8 dying day, deathday, "the supreme day and the inevitable hour" [Vergil]; final *or* fatal hour, dying hour, running-out of the sands, deathtime.

.9 moribundity, extremity, last *or* final extremity; **deathbed;** deathwatch; death struggle, agony, last agony, death agonies, death throes, throes of death; last breath or gasp, dying breath; **death rattle, death groan.**

.10 **swan song,** *chant du cygne* [Fr], death song.

.11 **bereavement** 812.1.

.12 **deathliness,** deathlikeness, deadliness; **weirdness, eeriness, uncanniness,** unearthliness; ghostliness, ghostlikeness; **ghastliness, grisliness, gruesomeness,** macabreness; paleness, haggardness, wanness, luridness, pallor; cadaverousness, corpselikeness; *facies Hippocratica* [L], Hippocratic face or countenance, mask of death.

.13 **death rate,** death toll; **mortality,** mortalness; transience 111; mutability 141.1.

.14 **obituary,** obit, necrology, necrologue; register of deaths, roll of the dead, death roll, mortuary roll, bill of mortality; casualty list; martyrology; body count.

.15 **terminal case; dying.**

.16 **corpse,** dead body, necr(o)–, dead man or woman, dead person, **cadaver, carcass, body;** *corpus delicti* [L]; **stiff** [slang]; **the dead, the defunct, the deceased,** the departed, the loved one; **decedent,** late lamented; **remains,** mortal or organic remains, bones, skeleton, dry bones, relics, reliquiae; dust, ashes, earth, clay, tenement of clay; **carrion,** crowbait, food for worms; **mummy,** mummification; embalmed corpse.

.17 **dead,** the majority, the great majority; one's fathers, one's ancestors; the choir invisible.

.18 **autopsy, postmortem, inquest,** postmortem examination, ex post facto examination, necropsy, necroscopy, medical examiner, coroner, mortality committee.

.19 VERBS **die, decease, succumb, expire, perish,** be taken by death, up and die [dial], cease to be or live, part, depart, quit this world, make one's exit, go, go the way of all flesh, go out, pass, pass on or over, **pass away, meet one's death or end or fate,** end one's life or days, depart this life, "shuffle off this mortal coil" [Shakespeare], put off mortality, **lose one's life,** fall, be lost, relinquish or surrender one's life, resign one's life or being, **give up the ghost,** yield the ghost or spirit, yield one's breath, take one's last breath, breathe one's last, stop breathing, fall asleep, close one's eyes, take one's last sleep, pay the debt of or to nature, go out with the

ebb, "go the way of all earth" [Bible], return to dust or the earth.

.20 [slang terms] **croak, go west, kick the bucket, kick in, pop off, drop off, step off,** go to the wall, **knock off, pipe off, kick off, shove off, pass out, peg out,** go for a burton [Brit], take the last count; **check out, check in, cash in, hand or pass or cash in one's checks or chips;** turn up one's toes, slip one's cable; have one's time or have it or buy it [all Brit].

.21 **meet one's Maker,** go to glory, go to kingdom come [informal], go to the happy hunting grounds, go to or reach a better place or land or life or world, go to one's rest or reward, go home, go home feet first [informal], go to one's last home, go to one's long account, go over to or join the majority or great majority, **be gathered to one's fathers,** join one's ancestors, join the angels, join the choir invisible, die in the Lord, go to Abraham's bosom, pass over Jordan, "walk through the valley of the shadow of death" [Bible], cross the Stygian ferry, give an obolus to Charon; awake to life immortal, "put on immortality" [Bible].

.22 **drop dead, fall dead,** fall down dead, bite the dust [informal]; come to an untimely end.

.23 die in harness, die with one's boots on, make a good end, die fighting, die in the last ditch, die like a man.

.24 die a natural death; die a violent death, be killed 409.21; OD [slang]; **starve,** famish; **smother, suffocate; asphyxiate; choke, strangle; drown,** go to a watery grave, go to Davy Jones's locker [informal]; catch one's death, catch one's death of cold.

.25 **lay down** or **give one's life for one's country,** die for one's country, *"pro patria mori"* [Horace], make the supreme sacrifice, do one's bit.

.26 **die out** 2.5, become extinct.

.27 **be dead, be no more,** sleep or be asleep with the Lord, sleep with one's fathers or ancestors; lie in the grave, lie in Abraham's bosom; push up daisies [informal].

.28 **bereave;** leave, leave behind; orphan, widow.

.29 ADJS **deathly, deathlike, deadly; weird, eerie, uncanny,** unearthly; ghostly, ghostlike; **ghastly, grisly, gruesome, macabre;** pale, deathly pale, wan, lurid, blue, livid, haggard; **cadaverous,** corpselike; mortuary.

.30 **dead, lifeless,** breathless, without life, inanimate 382.5, exanimate, without vital functions, sapro–; **deceased, demised, defunct,** croaked [slang], departed, departed this life, destitute of life, **gone, passed on,** gone the way of all flesh, gone west [informal], dead and gone, done for [informal], dead and done for [informal], no more, finished [informal], taken off or away, released, fallen, bereft of life, gone for a burton [Brit informal]; **at rest,** resting easy [informal], still, out of one's misery; **asleep,** sleeping, reposing; asleep in Jesus, with the Lord, asleep or dead in the Lord; **called home,** out of the world, gone to a better world or place or land, launched into eternity, gone to glory, gone to kingdom come [informal], "gathered to his fathers" [Bible], with the saints, sainted, numbered with the dead; in the grave six feet under, pushing up daisies [both informal]; carrion, food for worms; martyred; death-struck, death-stricken, smitten with death; stillborn; late, late lamented.

.31 **stone-dead;** dead as a doornail, dead as a herring, dead as mutton [all informal]; cold, stone-cold, "as cold as any stone" [Shakespeare], stiff [slang].

.32 **drowned,** in a watery grave or bier, in Davy Jones's locker.

.33 **dying,** expiring, going, slipping, slipping away, sinking, low, despaired of, given up, given up for dead, hopeless, bad, **moribund,** near death, near one's end, at the end of one's rope [informal], done for [informal], at the point of death, **at death's door,** at the portals of death, in articulo mortis [L], in extremis [L], in the jaws of death, facing or in the face of death; **on one's last legs** [informal], with one foot in the grave, tottering on the brink of the grave; on one's deathbed; at the last gasp; terminal; nonviable, incapable of life.

.34 **mortal, perishable,** subject to death, ephemeral, transient 111.7, mutable 141.6.

.35 **bereaved,** bereft, deprived; widowed; orphan, **orphaned,** parentless, fatherless, motherless.

.36 **postmortem,** postmortal, postmortuary, postmundane, post-obit, postobituary, **posthumous.**

.37 ADVS **deathly, deadly;** to the death, à la mort [Fr].

.38 PHRS one's hour is come, one's days are numbered, one's race is run, one's doom is sealed, life hangs by a thread, one's number is up, Death knocks at the door,

Death stares one in the face, the sands of life are running out.

409. KILLING

.1 NOUNS **killing, slaying, slaughter, dispatch, extermination, destruction,** destruction of life, taking of life, dealing death, bane; **kill; bloodshed,** bloodletting, blood, gore, flow of blood; mercy killing, euthanasia; ritual murder or killing, immolation, sacrifice; auto-da-fé [Pg], martyrdom, martyrization; lynching; stoning, lapidation; braining; shooting; poisoning; execution 1010.7.

.2 **homicide, manslaughter; murder,** bloody murder [informal]; bumping-off [slang]; foul play; **assassination;** removal, elimination, liquidation, purge, purging; thuggery, thuggism, thuggee.

.3 (killer or killing of) genocide (race), homicide (person), parenticide (parent), patricide (father), matricide (mother), fratricide (brother), sororicide (sister), parricide (kinsman), suicide (self), uxoricide (wife), mariticide (spouse, especially husband), regicide (king), tyrannicide (tyrant), vaticide (prophet), giganticide (giant), infanticide (infant), aborticide or feticide (fetus), pesticide (pest), rodenticide (rodent), vermicide or filaricide (worms), insecticide (insects), microbicide or germicide (germs), fungicide (fungi), herbicide (plants).

.4 **butchery,** butchering, **slaughter,** shambles, occision, slaughtering, hecatomb.

.5 **carnage, massacre, bloodbath, decimation,** saturnalia of blood; **mass murder, mass destruction,** wholesale murder, pogrom, race-murder, genocide, race extermination, **holocaust,** final solution.

.6 **suicide,** self-murder, self-destruction, death by one's own hand, felo-de-se [L], self-immolation, self-sacrifice; **disembowelment,** ritual suicide, hara-kiri, seppuku [both Jap], suttee, sutteeism; car of Jagannath or Juggernaut; mass suicide, race suicide.

.7 **suffocation,** smothering, smotheration, **asphyxiation,** asphyxia; **strangulation,** strangling, burking, throttling, stifling, garrote, garroting; **choking,** choke; **drowning.**

.8 **fatality,** fatal accident, violent death, **casualty,** disaster, calamity.

.9 **deadliness, lethality,** mortality, fatality; **malignance** or malignancy, malignity, **virulence, perniciousness,** banefulness.

.10 **deathblow,** death stroke, final stroke, fatal or mortal or lethal blow, *coup de grâce* [Fr].

.11 **killer, slayer, slaughterer, butcher,** bloodshedder; massacrer; **manslayer, homicide, murderer,** man-killer, bloodletter, Cain; **assassin,** assassinator; **cutthroat,** thug, desperado, bravo, gorilla [slang], apache, gunman; hit man or button man or gun or trigger man or torpedo or gunsel [all slang]; **hatchet man;** poisoner; strangler, garroter, burker; cannibal, maneater, anthropophagus; head-hunter; mercy killer; thrill killer, homicidal maniac; executioner 1010.8; matador; exterminator, eradicator; –cide 409.3, –ctonus; poison, pesticide 676.3.

.12 (place of slaughter) aceldama, field of blood or bloodshed; **slaughterhouse,** butchery [Brit], shambles, abattoir; stockyard; gas chamber, concentration camp; Auschwitz, Belsen, etc.

.13 VERBS **kill, slay, put to death,** deprive of life, bereave of life, **take life,** take the life of, take one's life away, **do away with,** make away with, **put out of the way,** put to sleep, end, **put an end to,** end the life of, **dispatch, do to death,** do for, finish, finish off, take off, **dispose of, exterminate, destroy,** annihilate; liquidate, purge; carry off or away, remove from life; put down, put away, put one out of one's misery; launch into eternity, send to glory, send to kingdom come [informal], send to one's last account; martyr, martyrize; immolate, sacrifice; lynch; cut off, cut down, nip in the bud; poison; chloroform; starve; execute 1010.19.

.14 [slang terms] rub out, croak, bump off, polish off, blot out, erase, wipe out, zap, blast, do in, off, hit, ice, waste, gun down, lay out, take care of, take for a ride, give the business or works, get, fix, settle.

.15 **shed blood,** spill blood, let blood, bloody one's hands with, dye one's hands in blood, pour out blood like water, wade knee-deep in blood.

.16 **murder,** commit murder; **assassinate;** remove, **purge, liquidate,** eliminate, get rid of.

.17 **slaughter, butcher, massacre, decimate,** commit carnage, depopulate, murder or kill or slay en masse; commit mass murder or destruction, murder wholesale, commit genocide.

.18 **strike dead,** fell, bring down, lay low; drop, drop or stop in one's tracks; **shoot,** shoot down, pistol, shotgun, machine-gun, gun down, riddle, shoot to death; cut down, cut to pieces or ribbons, **put to the sword,** stab to death, jugulate, cut or slash the throat; **deal a deathblow,** give the quietus or *coup de grâce,* silence; knock in or on the head; **brain,** blow or knock or dash one's brains out, poleax; **stone,** lapidate, stone to death; blow up, blow to bits or pieces or kingdom come, frag; disintegrate, vaporize; burn to death, incinerate, burn at the stake.

.19 **strangle, garrote, throttle, choke,** burke; **suffocate, stifle, smother, asphyxiate,** stop the breath; **drown.**

.20 **condemn to death,** sign one's death warrant, strike the death knell of, finger [slang], give the kiss of death to.

.21 **be killed,** get killed, die a violent death, **come to a violent end,** meet with foul play, welter in one's own blood.

.22 **commit suicide, take one's own life, kill oneself,** die by one's own hand, do away with oneself, put an end to oneself; blow one's brains out, take an overdose (of a drug), OD [informal]; commit hara-kiri.

.23 ADJS **deadly, deathly,** deathful, **killing, destructive,** death-dealing, death-bringing, feral [archaic]; savage, brutal; internecine; **fatal, mortal, lethal,** –cidal; **malignant,** malign, **virulent, pernicious,** baneful.

.24 **murderous,** slaughterous; cutthroat; redhanded; **homicidal,** man-killing; genocidal; suicidal, self-destructive; cruel 939.24; **bloodthirsty,** bloody-minded; **bloody,** gory, sanguinary.

410. INTERMENT

.1 NOUNS **interment, burial,** burying, inhumation, sepulture, **entombment;** encoffinment, inurning, inurnment, urn burial; primary burial; secondary burial, reburial; disposal of the dead; burial or funeral or funerary customs.

.2 **cremation, incineration,** burning, reduction to ashes; pyre, funeral pile.

.3 **embalmment,** embalming; mummification.

.4 **last offices,** last honors, **last rites,** funeral rites, last duty or service, funeral service, burial service, exequies, **obsequies;** Office of the Dead, Memento of the Dead, requiem, requiem mass, dirge [archaic]; **extreme unction;** viaticum; funeral oration or sermon, eulogy; **wake,** deathwatch.

.5 **funeral, burial,** burying; funeral procession, cortege; dead march, muffled drum, last post [Brit], taps; dirge 875.5; burial at sea, deep six [slang].

.6 **knell**, passing bell, death bell, funeral ring, tolling, tolling of the knell.

.7 **mourner**, griever, lamenter, keener; mute, professional mourner; **pallbearer**, bearer.

.8 **undertaker, mortician**, funeral director; embalmer; gravedigger; sexton.

.9 **mortuary, morgue**, deadhouse [archaic], charnel house, lichhouse [Brit dial] **funeral home** or **parlor**, undertaker's establishment; **crematorium**, crematory, cinerarium, burning ghat.

.10 **hearse**, funeral car or coach; catafalque.

.11 **coffin, casket**, burial case, box, kist [Scot]; wooden kimono or overcoat [slang]; **sarcophagus**; mummy case.

.12 **urn**, cinerary urn, funerary or funeral urn or vessel, bone pot, ossuary.

.13 **bier**, litter.

.14 **graveclothes, shroud**, winding sheet, cerecloth, cerements; pall.

.15 **graveyard, cemetery, burial ground** or **place**, burying place or ground, *campo santo* [Ital], boneyard [slang], burial yard, necropolis, polyandrium, **memorial park**, city or village of the dead; **churchyard**, God's acre; **potter's field**; Golgotha, Calvary; lych-gate.

.16 **tomb, sepulcher**; grave, burial, pit, deep six [slang]; resting place, "the lone couch of his everlasting sleep" [Shelley]; last home, long home, narrow house, house of death, low house, low green tent; **crypt, vault**, burial chamber; ossuary, ossuarium; charnel house, bone house; **mausoleum; catacombs;** mastaba; cist grave, box grave, passage grave, shaft grave, beehive tomb; **shrine**, reliquary, monstrance, tope, stupa; cenotaph; dokhma, tower of silence; pyramid, mummy chamber; burial mound, tumulus, barrow, cist, cromlech, dolmen.

.17 **monument**, gravestone 570.12.

.18 **epitaph**, inscription, *hic jacet* [L], tombstone marking.

.19 VERBS **inter**, inhume, **bury**, sepulture, inearth [archaic], **lay to rest, consign to the grave**, lay in the grave or earth, lay under the sod, put six feet under [slang]; tomb, **entomb**, ensepulcher, hearse; enshrine; inurn; encoffin, coffin; hold or conduct a funeral.

.20 **cremate, incinerate, burn**, reduce to ashes.

.21 **lay out; embalm;** mummify; lie in state.

.22 ADJS **funereal**, funeral, funerary, funebrial, funebrous or funebrious, *funèbre*

[Fr], mortuary, exequial, obsequial, feral; sepulchral, tomblike; cinerary; necrological, obituary, epitaphic; **dismal** 872.24; **mournful** 872.26; dirgelike 875.18.

.23 ADVS beneath the sod, underground, six feet under [slang], "in the dark union of insensate dust" [Byron]; at rest, resting in peace.

.24 PHRS RIP, *requiescat in pace* [L sing], *requiescant in pace* [L pl], rest in peace; *hic jacet* [L], *ci-gît* [Fr], here lies; ashes to ashes and dust to dust [Book of Common Prayer].

411. PLANTS

.1 NOUNS **plants, vegetation; flora, plant life**, vegetable life; **vegetable kingdom,** plant kingdom; herbage, flowerage, verdure, greenery, greens; botany 412; vegetation spirit 413.4.

.2 **growth**, stand, crop; plantation, planting; **clump**, tuft, tussock, hassock.

.3 **plant**, phyt(o)–, –phyte; **vegetable; weed;** seedling; cutting; vascular plant; seed plant, spermatophyte; gymnosperm; angiosperm, flowering plant; monocotyledon or monocot or monocotyl; dicotyledon or dicot or dicotyl; polycotyledon or polycot or polycotyl; thallophyte, fungus; gametophyte, sporophyte; exotic, hothouse plant; ephemeral, annual, biennial, triennial, perennial; evergreen, deciduous plant; cosmopolite; aquatic plant, hydrophyte, amphibian.

.4 (varieties) **legume**, pulse, vetch, bean, pea, lentil, phac(o)– or phak(o)–; **herb;** succulent; **vine**, viti–, grapevine, ampel(o)–, creeper, ivy, climber, liana; **fern**, –pteris, bracken; **moss**, bry(o)–, musc(o)– or musci–; **wort**, liverwort; **algae**, phyc(o)–; brown algae, fucus; green algae, conferva, confervoid; red algae, blue-green algae; planktonic algae, phytoplankton, diatom; **seaweed**, kelp, sea moss, rockweed, gulfweed, sargasso or sargassum, sea lentil, wrack, sea wrack; **fungus**, fungi–, myc(o)–, –mycete, mold, rust, smut, puffball, mushroom, toadstool; lichen; parasitic plant, parasite, saprophyte, perthophyte, heterophyte, autophyte; plant families 412.3–6; fruits and vegetables 308.50,51.

.5 **grass**, gramin(i)–, gramineous or graminaceous plant, pasture or forage grass, lawn grass, ornamental grass; aftergrass, fog [dial]; **cereal**, cereal plant, farinaceous plant, **grain**, grani–, corn [Brit]; sedge, caric(o)–; rush, reed, cane, bamboo.

.6 turf, sod, **sward**, greensward; divot.

.7 **green, lawn**; artificial turf, Astroturf; grassplot, greenyard; grounds; **common, park, village green**; golf course or links, fairway; bowling green, putting green.

.8 **grassland**, grass; **meadow**, meadow land, mead [archaic], swale, lea, haugh or haughland [Scot], vega; **pasture**, pasturage, pasture land, park [Brit dial]; **range**, grazing; **prairie, savanna, steppe**, steppeland, **pampas**, pampa, campo, llano, **veld**, grass veld.

.9 **shrubbery; shrub, bush**, thamn(o)–; scrub, bramble, brier, brier bush.

.10 **tree**, timber, dry(o)–, dendr(o)–, –dendron; shade tree, fruit tree, timber tree; softwood tree, hardwood tree; sapling, seedling; pollard; conifer, evergreen.

.11 **woodland, wood, woods, timberland**, hyl(o)–; **timber**, stand of timber, **forest**, forest land, forest preserve, state or national forest; forestry, dendrology, silviculture; afforestation, reforestation; rain forest, cloud forest; climax forest; sprout forest; selection forest; protection forest; index forest; fringing forest, gallery forest; primeval forest; virgin forest; greenwood; **jungle**, jungles; boondocks [informal]; wildwood, **bush**, scrub; bushveld, tree veld; shrubland, scrubland; pine barrens, palmetto barrens; hanger; **park**, chase [Brit]; park forest; arboretum.

.12 **grove, woodlet**; holt [dial], hurst, spinney [Brit], tope [India], shaw [dial], bosk [archaic]; **orchard**; wood lot; coppice, copse; bocage [Fr].

.13 **thicket**, thickset, **copse, coppice**, copsewood, frith [Brit dial]; bosket [archaic], boscage; covert; motte; **brake**, canebrake; chaparral; chamisal; ceja.

.14 **brush, scrub**, bush, **brushwood**, shrubwood, scrubwood.

.15 **undergrowth, underwood, underbrush**, copsewood, undershrubs, boscage, frith [Brit dial].

.16 **foliage, leafage**, leafiness, umbrage, foliation; frondage, frondescence; vernation.

.17 **leaf, frond**, phyll(o)–, –phyllum; leaflet, foliole; ligule, ligul(i)–; lamina, **blade**, spear, spire, pile, flag; **needle**, pine needle; floral leaf, **petal**, sepal; bract, bractlet, bracteole, spathe, involucre, involucrum, glume, lemma; cotyledon, seed leaf, –cotyl; stipule, stipula.

.18 **branch, fork, limb, bough**; deadwood; **twig, sprig**, switch; spray; **shoot**, offshoot, spear, frond; scion; **sprout**, sprit, slip, burgeon, thallus, thall(o)– or thalli–, clad(o)–; sucker; **runner**, stolon, flagellum, sarmentum, sarment; bine; **tendril**; ramage; branchiness, branchedness, ramification.

.19 **stem, stalk, stock**, axis, caulis [L], caul(o)– or cauli–, –dendron; **trunk**, bole, corm(o)–; spear, spire; straw; reed; cane; culm, haulm [Brit]; caudex; footstalk; pedicel, peduncle, pod(o)–; leafstalk, petiole, petiolus, petiolule; seedstalk; caulicle; tigella; funicule, funiculus; stipe, anthrophore, carpophore, gynophore.

.20 **root**, radix, radicle, –rhiza or –rrhiza; rootlet; **taproot**, tap; **rhizome**, rootstock; **tuber**, tubercle; **bulb**, bulbil, bulb(o)–; corm, earthnut.

.21 **bud**, burgeon, gemma; gemmule, gemmula; plumule, acrospire; leaf bud, flower bud.

.22 **flower, posy, blossom, bloom**, flori–, anth(o)–, **blow** [archaic]; floweret, floret, floscule; **wildflower; gardening**, horticulture, floriculture; hortorium.

.23 **bouquet, nosegay, posy**, boughpot, flower arrangement; **boutonniere**, buttonhole [Brit]; **corsage; spray; wreath**; festoon; **garland**, chaplet, lei.

.24 **flowering**, florescence, efflorescence, flowerage, **blossoming, blooming**; inflorescence; **blossom, bloom**, blowing, blow; unfolding, unfoldment; anthesis, full bloom.

.25 (types of inflorescence) raceme, corymb, umbel, umbell(i)–, panicle, cyme, thyrse, spadix, verticillaster; head, capitulum; spike, spikelet; ament, catkin; strobile, cone, pine cone.

.26 (flower parts) petal, perianth; calyx, calyc(o)–, epicalyx; corolla, corolla tube, corona; androecium, anther, stamen, stamin(i)–, microsporophyll; pistil, pistill–, gynoecium; style, styl(o)– or styli–; stigma, carpel, megasporophyll; receptacle, torus, –clinium.

.27 **ear**, spike; auricle; ear of corn, mealie; **cob**, corncob.

.28 **seed vessel, seedcase**, seedbox, pericarp, angi(o)–; hull, husk; **capsule, pod**, cod [dial], seed pod; pease cod, legume, legumen, boll, burr, follicle, silique.

.29 **seed**, sperm(o)– or sperma– or spermi–, spermat(o)–; **stone, pit, nut**, pyren(o)–; acorn, balan(o)–; pip; fruit, carp(o)–, –carp, –carpium; **grain, kernel, berry**, cocc(o)– or cocci–; flaxseed, linseed, hayseed; bird seed.

.30 **vegetation, growth**; germination, pullulation; burgeoning, sprouting; budding, luxuriation.

.31 VERBS **vegetate, grow**; germinate, pullulate; root, take root, strike root; sprout up, shoot up, upsprout, upspear; **burgeon**, put forth, burst forth; **sprout**, shoot; **bud**, gemmate, put forth *or* put out buds; **leaf**, leave, leaf out, put out *or* put forth leaves; flourish, luxuriate, riot, grow rank *or* lush; overgrow, overrun.

.32 flower, be in flower, **blossom, bloom**, be in bloom, blow, effloresce, floreate, burst into bloom.

.33 ADJS **vegetable**, vegetal, vegetative, vegetational, vegetarian; **plantlike**, –phytic; **herbaceous**, herbal, herbous, herbose, herby; leguminous, leguminose, leguminiform; cereal, farinaceous; weedy; fruity, fruitlike, –carpic, –carpous; tuberous, bulbous; rootlike, rhizoid, radicular, radicated, radiciform; botanic(al) 412.8.

.34 algal, fucoid, confervoid; phytoplanktonic, diatomaceous; fungous, fungoid, fungiform.

.35 floral; **flowery**, florid [archaic]; **flowered**, floreate, floriate, floriated, –florate, –florous, –anthous; **flowering, blossoming, blooming**, bloomy, florescent, inflorescent, efflorescent, in flower, in bloom, in blossom; uniflorous, multiflorous; radiciflorous, rhizanthous; **garden**, horticultural, hortulan, floricultural.

.36 arboreal, arborical, arboresque, arboreous, arborary; **treelike**, arboriform, arborescent, dendroid, dendriform, dendritic; deciduous, nondeciduous; evergreen; softwood, hardwood; piny; coniferous; citrous; bushy, shrubby, scrubby, scrubbly; bushlike, shrublike, scrublike.

.37 sylvan, woodland, forest, forestal; dendrologic(al), silvicultural, afforestational, reforestational; **wooded**, timbered, forested, arboreous; **woody**, woodsy, bushy, shrubby, scrubby; bosky, copsy, braky.

.38 leafy, leavy [archaic], bowery; foliated, foliate, foliose, foliaged, leaved, –phyllous, –folious; **branched**, branchy, branching, ramified, ramate, ramous *or* ramose; twiggy.

.39 verdant, verdurous, verdured; **mossy**, moss-covered, moss-grown; **grassy**, grasslike, gramineous, graminaceous; turfy, swardy, turflike, caespitose, tufted; meadowy.

.40 luxuriant, flourishing, **rank, lush**, riotous, exuberant; dense, impenetrable, thick, heavy, gross; jungly, jungled; overgrown,

overrun; **weedy**, unweeded, weed-choked, weed-ridden; gone to seed.

.41 perennial, ephemeral; hardy, half-hardy; **deciduous**, evergreen.

.42 algae

brown algae	pond scum
conferva	red algae
dulse	reindeer moss
fucoid	rockweed
fucus, fuc(o)– *or* fuci–	sargasso, sargassum
green algae	scum
gulfweed	sea lettuce
Iceland moss	sea moss
Irish moss	seaweed
kelp	sea wrack
lichen	stonewort
phytoplankton, plankton	wrack

.43 ferns

adder's fern	lip fern
basket fern	maidenhair
beech fern	marsh fern
bladder fern	moonwort
boulder fern	oak fern
bracken	osmunda
chain fern	ostrich fern
cliff brake	rattlesnake fern
climbing fern	rock brake
curly grass	shield fern
grape fern	snuffbox fern
hart's tongue	walking fern
holly fern	wall fern
lady fern	wood fern

.44 flowers

acacia	Christmas rose
African violet	chrysanthemum
amaryllis	cineraria
anemone	clematis
arbutus	clethra
arrowhead	cockscomb
asphodel	columbine
aster	cornel
azalea	cornflower
baby-blue-eyes	cosmos
baby's breath	cowslip
bachelor button	crocus
begonia	cyclamen
bitterroot	daffodil
black-eyed Susan	dahlia
bleeding heart	daisy
bloodroot	dandelion
bluebell	delphinium
bluet	dogwood
bridal wreath	duckweed
broom	Dutchman's-breeches
buttercup	edelweiss
cactus	eglantine
calendula	fireweed
camas	flax
camellia	*fleur-de-lis* [Fr]
camomile	forget-me-not
campanula	forsythia
candytuft	foxglove
carnation	foxtail
cat's-paw	fuchsia
cattail	gardenia
century plant	gentian
Chinese lantern	geranium

gladiolus
goldenrod
groundsel
harebell
hawthorn
heather
hepatica
hibiscus
hollyhock
honeysuckle
horehound
hyacinth
hydrangea
impatience
Indian paintbrush
indigo
iris, irid(o)–
jack-in-the-pulpit
japonica
jasmine
jonquil
knotweed
lady's-slipper
larkspur
lavender
lilac
lily
lily of the valley
lobelia
lotus
love-lies-bleeding
lupine
magnolia
mallow
marguerite
marigold
marshmallow
marsh marigold
mayflower
mignonette
mimosa
moccasin flower
mock orange
monkshood
morning-glory
moss rose
motherwort
myrtle
narcissus
nasturtium
oleander

opium poppy,
  mecon(o)–
orchid
oxalis
pansy, viol–
passion flower
peony
periwinkle
petunia
phlox
pink
poinsettia
poppy
portulaca
primrose
Queen Anne's lace
ranunculus
resurrection plant
rhododendron
rose, rhod(o)–
shooting star
smilax
snapdragon
snowball
snowberry
snowdrop
spiraea
stock
strawflower
sunflower
sweet alyssum
sweet pea
sweet William
trillium
trumpet vine
tulip
umbrella plant
Venus's flytrap
verbena
vetch
viburnum
viola
violet
wallflower
water lily, nymph(o)–
  or nymphi–
wisteria
wolfbane
yarrow
yucca
zinnia

.45 fungi

blight
blue mold
bread mold
ergot, ergo–
green mold
mildew
mold
mushroom
penicillium
puffball
rot

rust
slime mold
smut
tinea
toadstool
truffle
tuckahoe
verticillium, verticilli–
water mold
yeast

.46 grasses, grains

alfilaria
bamboo
barley
  ..ach grass
  ..d grass
  ..al grass

bent, bent grass
Bermuda grass
black bent
bluegrass
bluejoint
bog grass

bristly foxtail grass
broomcorn
buckwheat
buffalo grass
bulrush
bunch grass
canary grass
cane
China grass
cocksfoot grass
corn
cotton grass
crab grass
durra
eelgrass
English rye grass
feather grass
finger-comb grass
finger grass
flyaway grass
four-leaved grass
gama or sesame grass
grama or mesquite
  grass
guinea grass
hairgrass
hassock grass
herd's grass
horsetail
Indian corn
Italian rye grass
Japanese lawn grass
Kentucky bluegrass
little quaking grass
lovegrass
lyme grass
maize
meadow fescue
meadow foxtail
meadow grass
millet
myrtle grass

oats
orchard grass
paddy
palm-leaved grass
pampas grass
papyrus
peppergrass
pin grass
plume grass
pony grass
redtop
reed
ribbon grass
rice, oryz(o)– or oryzi–
rush
rye
scutch
sedge
sesame
sheep's fescue
silk grass
sorghum
spear grass
squirrel tail grass
star grass
striped grass
sugar cane
switch grass
sword grass
tear grass
timothy
tufted hair grass
viper's grass
wheat
wild oats
wire grass
wood meadow grass
woolly beard grass
worm grass
yellow-eyed grass
zebra grass
zoysia

.47 herbs

angelica
anise, anis(o)–
balm
basil
belladonna
boneset
borage
burning bush
calendula
camomile
caraway
cardamom
castor-oil plant
catnip, catmint
chervil
chicory
clover
coriander
Cretan dittany
deadly nightshade
death camas
dill
dittany
fennel
feverroot
figwort
fraxinella, gas plant
ginseng

hemp
henbane
horehound
hyssop
licorice
liverwort
mandrake
marijuana
marjoram
mayapple
mint
monkshood
mullein
mustard
oregano, origanum
parsley
peppermint
rosemary
rue
sage
savory
sorrel
spearmint
sweet cicely
sweet woodruff
tansy
tarragon
thyme

tobacco
wild marjoram

wintergreen

.48 mosses

club moss
Florida moss
flowering moss
ground pine
hair cap moss
lycopodium
peat moss

red tipped moss
scale moss
sphagnum moss
staghorn moss
tree moss
white moss

.49 shrubs

alder
azalea
barberry
bayberry
blackberry
blackthorn
blueberry
box
broom
caper
chokeberry
cinchona, quin(o)–
coca
coffee
cranberry
currant
daphne
elder
forsythia
frangipani
fuchsia
furze
gardenia
genista
gooseberry
gorse
greasewood
guava
guayule
haw
heather
hemp tree
henna
hibiscus
holly
huckleberry
hydrangea
indigo
Juneberry
juniper
jute
kalmia
laurel, laur(o)–

leatherleaf
lilac
magnolia
manzanita
mesquite
milkwort
mock orange
mountain lilac
myrica
myrtle
nandin, nandina
ninebark
oleander
Persian berry
photinia
poison sumac
privet
pussy willow
queen of the meadow
rabbit berry
red brush
rhododendron
rosebay
rosemary
rose of Sharon
sage, sagebrush
sand myrtle
sisal
snowberry
snow wreath
spiraea
sumac
symplocos
syringa
tamarisk
turkey berry
veronica
whin
wintercreeper
witch hazel
yellowroot
zenobia

.50 trees

acacia
ailanthus
alder
allspice
almond
apple
apricot
ash
aspen
avocado, alligator
   pear
bald cypress
balsa
balsam

banyan
basswood
bay
bayberry
beech
betel palm
birch
boxwood
Brazil-nut
breadfruit
buckeye
butternut
buttonwood
cacao

camphor tree
candleberry
cashew
cassia
catalpa
cedar
cherry
chestnut
chinaberry tree, China
   tree
chinquapin
cinnamon
citron
clove
coconut, coco
cork oak
cottonwood
cypress
date palm
dogwood
ebony
elder
elm
eucalyptus
fig
fir
frankincense
ginkgo
grapefruit
guava
gum
hawthorn
hazel, hazelnut
hemlock
henna
hickory
holly
hop tree
hornbeam
horse chestnut
ironwood
juniper
kumquat
laburnum
lancewood
larch
laurel
lemon
lignum vitae
lime
linden
litchi, litchi nut
locust
logwood

madroña
magnolia
mahogany
mango
mangrove
maple
medlar
mimosa
mountain ash
mulberry
nutmeg
nux vomica
oak
olive
orange
palm, palmi–
papaw
papaya
peach
pear
pecan
persimmon
pine
pistachio
plane
plum
pomegranate
poplar
quince
raffia palm
rain tree
redwood
rosewood
sandalwood
sassafras
satinwood
senna
sequoia
serviceberry
silk oak
spruce
sycamore
tamarack
tamarind
tangerine
teak
thorn tree
tulip oak
tulip tree
upas
walnut
willow
witch hazel
yew

.51 vines

bittersweet
clematis
dewberry
English ivy
grape
greenbrier
honeysuckle
hop

ivy
jasmine
liana
morning glory
poison ivy
trumpet creeper
Virginia creeper
wisteria

.52 weeds

beggar's-ticks
bindweed
brake
burdock
burr
Canada thistle

cat's ear
chickweed
chicory
crab grass
crazyweed
creeping buttercup

dandelion	prickly lettuce
dock	purslane
fireweed	quack grass
horsetail	ragweed
jimsonweed	sandburr
knawel	scarlet pimpernel
knotweed	sheep's sorrel, sheep
lady's thumb	sorrel
locoweed	shepherd's purse
mallow	skunk cabbage
mayweed	smartweed
milkweed	speedwell
mustard	spotted spurge
nettle	spurry
pigweed	stinkweed
plantain	tarweed
poison ivy	thistle
poke, pokeweed	tumbleweed

412. BOTANY

.1 NOUNS **botany**, phytology; phytography, phytonomy; algology, phycology, bryology, dendrology, fungology, hydroponics, aquiculture, mycology, paleobotany, physiological botany, phytobiology, phytochemistry, phytoecology, phytogeography, phytomorphology, phytopaleontology, phytopathology, phytotaxonomy, phytoteratology, phytotomy, phytotopography, pomology, structural botany, systematic botany, vegetable *or* plant anatomy, vegetable *or* plant pathology, vegetable *or* plant physiology.

.2 **botanist**, phytologist, herbalist [archaic]; phytographer, phytonomist; algologist, phycologist, bryologist, dendrologist, ecologist, fungologist, herbalist, mycologist, phytobiologist, phytoecologist, phytogeographer, phytopaleontologist, phytopathologist, phytoteratologist, pomologist.

.3 **Thallophyta** (thallus plants), thallogens, thallophytes: algae; Cyanophyceae (blue-green algae); Chlorophyceae (green algae); Phaeophyceae, Ectocarpales, Fucales (brown algae); Rhodophyceae (red algae); fungi, molds; Schizomycetes (fission fungi, bacteria); Myxomycetes (slime molds); Phycomycetes (algal fungi, water molds); Ascomycetes (sac fungi, lichen, lichen fungi); Penicillium (blue and green molds); Basidiomycetes (basidium fungi, rusts, smuts, puffballs, mushrooms, toadstools).

.4 **Bryophyta** (moss plants), bryophytes: Hepaticae (liverworts); Musci (mosses).

.5 **Pteridophyta** (fern plants), pteridophytes: Lycopodiales (ground pines, club mosses, ball worts); Lycopodiaceae (club moss-Selaginellaceae; Sigillaria, Stigmaria; etaceae, Equisetales (horsetails),

equisetum; Calamites, calamite; Filicales, Filices (ferns), filicoids; Cycadofilicales, Cycadofilices (cycad ferns), cycadofilicales; Lepidodendraceae (fossil trees): Lepidodendron, lepidodendroids, lepidodendrids.

.6 **Spermatophyta** (seed plants), spermatophytes: Gymnospermae (naked-seeded plants), gymnosperms; Cycadales, cycads; Gnetales, gnetums; Ginkgoales, ginkgoes; Pinales *or* Coniferae (cone-bearing evergreens), conifers; Angiospermae (covered-seeded plants), angiosperms; Monocotyledones, Endogenae (cereals, palms, lilies, orchids, bananas, pineapples, etc.); monocotyledons, endogens; Dicotyledones (oaks, apples, sunflowers, peas, etc.), dicotyledons.

.7 VERBS botanize, herbalize.

.8 ADJS **botanic(al)**, phytologic(al); phytobiological, phytochemical, pomological, etc. 412.1.

413. AGRICULTURE

.1 NOUNS **agriculture, farming, husbandry;** cultivation, culture, geoponics, tillage, tilth; agrology, agronomy, agronomics; thremmatology; agrogeology, agricultural geology; dry farming, dryland farming, dirt farming [informal], truck farming, contour farming, mixed farming, intensive farming, subsistence farming, tank farming, hydroponics, grain farming, strip farming, fruit farming, sharecropping; rural economy *or* economics, farm economy *or* economics, agrarian economy *or* economics, agrarianism.

.2 **horticulture, gardening;** landscape gardening, landscape architecture, groundskeeping; truck gardening, market gardening, olericulture; flower gardening, flower-growing, floriculture; viniculture, viticulture; orcharding, fruit-growing, pomiculture, citriculture.

.3 **forestry**, arboriculture, tree farming, silviculture, forest management; Christmas tree farming; forestation, afforestation, reforestation; lumbering, logging; woodcraft.

.4 (agricultural deities) vegetation spirit *or* daemon, fertility god *or* spirit, year-daemon, forest god *or* spirit, corn god, Ceres, Demeter, Gaea *or* Gaia; Triptolemus *or* Triptolemos; Dionysus *or* Dionysos; Persephone, Proserpina *or* Proserpine *or* Persephassa, Kore *or* Cora; Flora; Aristaeus; Pomona; Frey.

.5 **agriculturist**, agriculturalist; agrologist,

agronomist; **farmer**, granger, husbandman, **yeoman**, cultivator, tiller, **tiller of the soil**; peasant, *Bauer* [Ger], rustic 919.8,9; **rancher**, ranchman; **grower**, raiser; **planter**, tea-planter, coffee-planter, etc.; gentleman farmer; dirt farmer [informal]; dry farmer; truck farmer; tree farmer; peasant holder or propietor, *kulak, muzhik* [both Russ]; tenant farmer, crofter [Brit]; sharecropper, cropper, collective farm worker, *kolkhoznik* [Russ], *kibbutznik* [Yid]; farmhand, farm laborer, migrant or migratory worker or laborer, picker; plowman, plowboy; planter, sower; reaper, harvester, harvestman; haymaker.

.6 **horticulturist, nurseryman, gardener;** landscape gardener, landscapist, landscape architect; truck gardener, market gardener, olericulturist; **florist**, floriculturist; vinegrower, viniculturist, viticulturist, vintager, *vigneron* [Fr]; orchardist, orchardman, fruit-grower.

.7 **forester;** arboriculturist, silviculturist, tree farmer; conservationist; **ranger**, forest ranger; woodsman, woodman [Brit], woodcraftsman; **logger, lumberman,** timberman, lumberjack; woodcutter, wood chopper.

.8 **farm**, farmplace, farmstead, farmhold [archaic], farmery [Brit], **grange**, location [Austral], pen [Jamaica]; **plantation**, cotton plantation, etc., *hacienda* [Sp]; **ranch**, rancho, rancheria, station [Austral]; dude ranch; croft, homecroft [Brit]; **homestead**, steading; toft [Brit]; mains [Brit dial]; demesne, homefarm, demesne farm, manor farm; **barnyard**, farmyard, barton [Brit dial]; collective farm, *kolkhoz* [Russ], *kibbutz* [Heb]; dry farm, truck farm, stock farm, grain farm, fur farm, fruit farm, orchard, dairy farm, chicken farm or ranch, poultry farm, sheep farm or ranch, cattle ranch; factory farm; tree farm; farmland, arable land, plowland, fallow; grassland, pasture 411.8.

.9 **field, tract, plat, plot, patch,** piece or parcel of land; cultivated land; clearing; hayfield, corn field, wheat field, etc.; paddy, rice paddy.

.10 **garden**, *jardin* [Fr]; paradise; garden spot; kitchen garden, vegetable garden, victory garden, market or truck garden, flower garden, rock garden, alpine garden, bog garden, tea garden, roof garden, Japanese garden, ornamental garden, sunken garden; botanical garden, *jardin des plantes* [Fr], arboretum; pinetum; shrubbery;

vineyard, vinery, grapery, grape ranch; bed, **flower bed**, border; **herbarium**, dry garden, hortus siccus; –arium, –etum, –ery.

.11 **nursery; conservatory, greenhouse**, forcing house, summerhouse, glasshouse, lathhouse, **hothouse,** coolhouse; force or forcing bed, forcing pit, **hotbed**, cold frame; seedbed; cloche; pinery, orangery.

.12 **growing, raising**, rearing; **green thumb.**

.13 **cultivation**, cultivating, culture, **tilling,** dressing, working; harrowing, plowing, contour plowing, furrowing, listing, fallowing, weeding, hoeing, pruning, thinning.

.14 **planting**, setting; **sowing, seeding**, semination, insemination; **dissemination**, broadcast, broadcasting; transplantation, resetting; retimbering, reforestation.

.15 **harvest**, harvesting, **reaping, gleaning,** gathering, cutting; nutting; crop 811.5.

.16 VERBS **farm, ranch; grow, raise,** rear; **crop;** dryfarm; sharecrop; **garden.**

.17 **cultivate**, culture, **dress, work, till,** till the soil, dig, delve, spade; mulch; **plow, list,** fallow, backset [W US]; **harrow, rake; weed,** weed out, hoe, cut, prune, thin, thin out; force; fertilize 165.8.

.18 **plant**, implant [archaic], **set,** put in; **sow, seed,** seed down, seminate, inseminate; **disseminate,** broadcast, sow broadcast, scatter seed; drill; bed; dibble; **transplant,** reset, pot; forest; **retimber, reforest.**

.19 **harvest, reap, crop, glean, gather,** gather in, bring in, get in the harvest, reap and carry; **pick,** pluck; dig, grabble [S US]; mow, cut; hay; nut; crop herbs.

.20 ADJS **agricultural, agrarian,** agro–, geoponic(al), agronomic(al); **farm, farming;** arable; **rural** 182.6.

.21 **horticultural;** olericultural; **vinicultural,** viticultural; arboricultural, silvicultural.

414. ANIMALS, INSECTS

.1 NOUNS **animal life, animal kingdom,** brute creation, **fauna,** Animalia [zool], animality, zo(o)–; birds, beasts, and fish; the beasts of the field, the fowl of the air, and the fish of the sea; domestic animals, **livestock,** stock [informal], cattle; wild animals or beasts, beasts of field, **wildlife,** denizens of the forest or jungle or wild, furry creatures; beasts of prey; game, big game, small game.

.2 **animal, creature,** –zoon, critter [dial], living being or thing, creeping thing; **brute, beast,** varmint [dial], dumb animal or creature, dumb friend.

.3 (varieties) vertebrate 415.7-8, invertebrate 415.3-6; biped, quadruped; mammal, mammalian 414.58; primate 414.59, –anthropus; marsupial, marsupialian; canine; feline; rodent, gnawer; ungulate; ruminant; insectivore, herbivore, carnivore, omnivore; cannibal; scavenger; reptile 414.30,31,60,61; amphibian 414.32,62; aquatic; cosmopolite; vermin, varmint [dial].

.4 pachyderm; elephant, Jumbo, hathi [India]; mammoth, woolly mammoth; mastodon; rhinoceros, rhino; hippopotamus, hippo, river horse.

.5 (hoofed animals) deer, buck, doe, fawn; red deer, stag, hart, hind; roe deer, roe, roebuck; musk deer; fallow deer; hog-deer; white-tailed or Virginia deer; mule deer; elk, wapiti; moose; reindeer, caribou; deerlet; antelope; gazelle, kaama, gnu, wildebeest, hartebeest, springbok, dik-dik, eland or Cape elk, koodoo; camel, dromedary, ship of the desert; giraffe, camelopard, okapi.

.6 cattle 414.69, kine [archaic pl], neat; beef cattle, beef, beeves [pl]; dairy cattle or cows; bovine animal, bovine, critter [dial]; cow, bossy [informal]; milk or milch cow, milker, milcher, dairy cow; bull, bullock, tauro– or tauri(o)–, top cow [dial]; steer, stot [Brit dial], ox, oxen [pl]; calf, heifer, yearling, fatling, stirk [Brit]; dogie, leppy [both W US]; maverick [W US]; hornless cow, butthead, muley head [both dial], muley cow; zebu, Brahman; yak; musk-ox; buffalo, water buffalo, Indian buffalo, carabao; bison, aurochs, wisent.

.7 sheep 414.70, jumbuck [Austral]; lamb, lambkin, yeanling; teg [Brit]; ewe, ewe lamb; ram, tup [Brit], wether; bellwether; mutton.

.8 goat; he-goat, buck, billy goat or billy [both informal]; she-goat, doe, nanny goat or nanny [both informal]; kid, doeling; mountain goat.

.9 swine 414.71, pig, hog, porker, hyo–, –choerus; shoat, piggy, piglet, pigling; sucking or suckling pig; gilt; boar, sow; barrow; wild boar, tusker, razorback; babirusa.

.10 horse 414.68, hipp(o)–, –hippus; horse-flesh, hoss [dial], critter [dial]; equine, mount, nag [informal]; steed, prancer, dobbin; charger, courser, war-horse, destrier [archaic]; Houyhnhnm [Swift]; colt, foal, filly; mare, brood mare; stallion, studhorse, stud, top horse [dial], entire

horse, entire; gelding, purebred horse, blood horse; wild horse, Przewalsky's horse, tarpan.

.11 pony, Shetland pony, Shetland, shelty, Iceland pony, Galloway.

.12 bronco, bronc, range horse, Indian pony, cayuse, mustang; bucking bronco, buckjumper, sunfisher, broomtail; cow-cutting horse, stock horse, roping horse, cow pony.

.13 (colored horses) bay, bayard, chestnut, gray, dapple-gray, grizzle, roan, sorrel, dun, buckskin [W US], pinto, paint, piebald, skewbald, calico pony, painted pony.

.14 (inferior horse) nag, plug, hack, jade, crock, garron [Scot & Ir], crowbait [slang], scalawag, rosinante; goat or stiff or dog [all slang]; roarer, whistler; balky horse, balker, jughead; rogue.

.15 (scrawny horse) rackabones, scrag, stack of bones.

.16 hunter; stalking-horse; saddle horse, saddler, rouncy [archaic], riding horse, rider, palfrey, mount; remount; polo pony; post-horse; cavalry horse; driving horse, road horse, roadster, carriage horse, coach horse, gigster; hack, hackney; draft horse, dray horse, cart horse, workhorse, plow horse; shaft horse, pole horse, thill horse, thiller, fill horse or filler [both dial]; wheelhorse, wheeler, lead, leader; pack horse, jument [archaic], sumpter, sumpter horse, bidet.

.17 race horse, racer, bangtail, pony [both slang]; steeplechaser; entry, starter, nomination in the race; stake horse, staker; plate horse, plater; mudder; pole horse; favorite; stable, string.

.18 gaited horse; galloper, trotter, pacer, sidewheeler [slang]; stepper, high-stepper, cob, prancer; ambler, padnag, pad; racker; single-footer.

.19 (famous horses) Al Borak (Mohammed's winged horse of ascension), Baiardo (Rinaldo's bay horse), Black Beauty, Black Bess (Dick Turpin's horse), Black Saladin (Warwick's horse), Bucephalus (Alexander the Great's horse), Buttermilk (Dale Evans' horse), Champion (Gene Autrey's horse), Copenhagen (Wellington's horse at Waterloo), Grani (Sigurd's magic horse), Incitatus (the horse of Caligula, the Roman Emperor), Marengo (Napoleon's white horse), Pegasus (winged horse of the Muses), Roan Barbary (favorite horse of Richard II), Rosinante (Don Quixote's bony horse), Silver (the

Lone Ranger's horse), Sleipnir (Odin's eight-legged horse), Trigger (Roy Rogers' horse), Topper (Hopalong Cassidy's horse), Traveller (Robert E. Lee's horse), Vegliantino or Veillantif (Orlando's horse), White Surrey (favorite horse of Richard III); (race horses) Assault, Citation, Kelso, Man O'War, Nashua, Native Dancer, Seabiscuit, Secretariat, Swaps, Whirlaway.

.20 ass, donkey, burro, neddy or cuddy [both Brit dial], moke [Brit slang], Rocky Mountain canary [W US]; jackass, jack, dickey [Brit dial]; jenny, jenny ass, jennet.

.21 mule, sumpter mule, sumpter; hinny, jennet.

.22 dog 414.72, canine, cyn(o)–, pooch [informal], bowwow [slang]; pup, puppy, puppy-dog [informal], whelp; bitch, gyp [S US], slut; toy dog, lap dog; working dog; watchdog, bandog; sheep dog, shepherd or shepherd's dog; Seeing Eye dog, guide dog; sled dog; show dog, fancy dog; kennel, pack of dogs.

.23 sporting dog, hunting dog, hunter, field dog, bird dog, gun dog, water dog.

.24 cur, mongrel, lurcher [Brit], mutt [informal]; pariah dog.

.25 fox, reynard; wolf, lyc(o)–, timber wolf, lobo [W US], coyote, brush wolf, prairie wolf, medicine wolf [W US]; dingo, jackal, hyena; Cape hunting dog, African hunting dog.

.26 cat 414.73, feline, ailur(o)– or aelur(o)–; pussy or puss or pussycat [all informal], tabby, grimalkin; house cat; kitten, kitty or kitty-cat [both informal]; kit, kitling [Brit dial]; tomcat, tom; gib or gib-cat [both Brit dial]; mouser; Cheshire cat, Chessycat [informal]; silver cat, Chinchilla cat; blue cat, Maltese cat; tiger cat, tabby cat; tortoise-shell cat, calico cat; alley cat.

.27 (wild cats) lion, Leo [informal], simba [Swah]; tiger, Siberian tiger; leopard, panther, jaguar, cheetah; cougar, painter [S US], puma, mountain lion, catamount or cat-a-mountain; lynx, ocelot; wildcat, bobcat.

.28 (wild animals) bear, bar [dial], arct(o)–; guinea pig, cavy; hedgehog, porcupine, quill pig [slang]; woodchuck, groundhog, whistle-pig [dial]; prairie dog, prairie squirrel; raccoon, coon; opossum, possum; weasel, mousehound [Brit]; wolverine, glutton; ferret, monk [informal]; skunk, polecat [dial]; zoril, stink cat [S

Africa], Cape polecat; foumart; ape, pithec(o)–, –pithecus; monkey, monk [informal], chimpanzee, chimp.

.29 hare, lag(o)–, leveret, jackrabbit; rabbit, bunny [informal], lapin; cottontail; Belgian hare, leporide; buck, doe.

.30 reptile 414.60, reptilian; lizard, saur(o)–, –saur(us); saurian, dinosaur; crocodile, crocodilian, alligator, gator [informal]; tortoise, turtle, terrapin.

.31 serpent, snake 414.61, ophidian, herpet(o)–, ophi(o)–, –ophis; viper, pit viper; sea snake.

.32 amphibian 414.62, batrachian, croaker, batrach(o)–, –batrachus, paddock [dial]; frog, rani–, tree toad or frog, bullfrog; toad, hoptoad or hoppytoad; newt, salamander; tadpole, polliwog.

.33 bird 414.66, fowl, –ornis; birdy or birdie [both informal]; fowls of the air, birdlife, avifauna; baby bird, chick, nestling, fledgling; wildfowl, game bird; waterfowl, water bird, wading bird, diving bird; sea bird; shore bird; migratory bird, migrant, bird of passage; songbird, oscine bird, warbler, passerine bird, perching bird; cage bird; flightless bird, ratite; seed-eating bird, insect-eating bird, fruit-eating bird, fish-eating bird, bird of prey; eagle, aeto–, –aetus, bird of Jove, eaglet; owl, bird of Minerva, bird of night; peafowl, peahen, peacock, bird of Juno; swan, cygnet; pigeon, dove, squab; stormy or storm petrel, Mother Carey's chicken; fulmar, Mother Carey's goose.

.34 poultry, fowl, domestic fowl, barnyard fowl, barn-door fowl, dunghill fowl; chicken 414.67, chick, chicky or chickabiddy [both informal]; cock, rooster, chanticleer; hen, biddy [informal], partlet; cockerel, pullet; setting hen, brooder, broody hen; capon, poulard; broiler, fryer, spring chicken, roaster, stewing chicken; Bantam, banty [informal]; game fowl; guinea fowl, guinea cock, guinea hen; goose, gander, gosling; duck, drake, duckling; turkey, gobbler, turkey gobbler; turkey-cock, tom, tom turkey; hen turkey; poult.

.35 marine animal 414.63, denizen of the deep; whale, cetacean 414.64, cet(o)–; porpoise, dolphin, –delphis, sea pig; sea serpent, sea snake, Loch Ness monster, sea monster, Leviathan [Bible]; fish 414.65, ichthy(o)–, –ichthys, pisci–, game fish, tropical fish, panfish; shark, man-eating shark, man-eater; salmon, kipper, grilse, smolt, parr, alevin; minnow or minny

[dial], fry, fingerling; **sponge,** spongi(o)–
or spong(o)–, –spongia; **plankton,** zoo-
plankton, nekton, benthon, benthos, zoo-
benthos.

.36 **bug; beetle;** arthropod; hexapod, myria-
pod; centipede, chilopod; millipede or
millepede, diplopod; **mite,** acar(o)– or ac-
ari–; arachnid, **spider,** arachn(o)–; taran-
tula, black widow spider, daddy longlegs
or harvestman; **scorpion; tick;** larva, maggot, nymph, **caterpillar,** eruci–, –campa;
insect 414.74; **fly,** musci–, myi(o)–, –myia.

.37 **ant,** myrmec(o)–, emmet [dial], pismire,
pissant [dial], antymire [dial]; red ant,
black ant, fire ant, house ant, agricultural
ant, carpenter ant, army ant; slave ant,
slave-making ant; **termite,** termito–,
white ant; queen, worker, soldier.

.38 **bee,** api–; honeybee, bumblebee; queen,
queen bee, worker, drone; **wasp; hornet,**
yellow jacket.

.39 **locust,** acridian; **grasshopper,** hopper,
hoppergrass [dial]; **cricket;** cicada, cicala,
dog-day cicada, seventeen-year locust.

.40 **vermin;** parasite; **louse,** head louse, body
louse, grayback, cootie [slang]; crab, crab
louse; weevil; nit; **flea,** sand flea, dog flea,
cat flea, chigoe, chigger, jigger, red bug,
mite, harvest mite; **roach, cockroach,** cu-
caracha [Sp].

.41 bloodsucker, parasite; **leech,** bdell(o)–,
–bdella; tick, wood tick; **mosquito,**
skeeter [dial], culex, culic(i)–; bedbug,
housebug [Brit].

.42 **worm** 414.75, vermi–, –scolex; earthworm,
angleworm, fishworm, night crawler,
nightwalker [N US]; measuring worm,
inchworm; tapeworm, helminth, hel-
minth(o)–, ligul(i)–, taen(o)– or
taeni(o)–.

.43 ADJS **animal,** animalian, animalic, animalistic, zoic, zooidal; zoologic(al); **brutish,
brutal,** brute, brutelike; **bestial, beastly,**
beastlike; subhuman; dumb, "that wants
discourse of reason" [Shakespeare]; instinctual or instinctive, mindless, nonrational.

.44 **vertebrate,** chordate, mammalian; marsupial, cetacean.

.45 **canine,** doggish, doggy, doglike; vulpine,
foxy, foxlike; lupine, wolfish, wolflike.

.46 **feline,** felid, cattish, catty, catlike; kittenish; leonine, lionlike; tigerish, tigerlike.

.47 **ursine,** bearish, bearlike.

.48 **rodent,** rodential; verminous; mousy,
mouselike; ratty, ratlike.

.49 **ungulate,** hoofed, hooved; **equine,** hippic,
horsy, horselike; **equestrian;** asinine, mul-

ish; bovid, ruminant; **bovine,** cowlike,
cowish; bull-like, bullish, taurine; cervine,
deerlike; caprine, caprid, hircine, goatish,
goatlike; ovine, sheepish, sheeplike; por-
cine, swinish, piggish, hoggish.

.50 elephantlike, elephantine, pachydermous.

.51 **reptile,** reptilian, **reptilelike,** reptiloid,
reptiliform; reptant, repent, creeping,
crawling, slithering; **lizardlike,** saurian;
crocodilian; **serpentine,** serpentile, serpentoid, serpentiform, **serpentlike;** snak-
ish, **snaky, snakelike,** ophidian, anguine
[archaic]; viperish, viperous, vipery, viper-
ine, viperoid, viperiform, viperlike; colu-
brine, colubriform; amphibian, batrachian, froggy, toadish, salamandrian.

.52 **birdlike,** birdy; avian, avicular; gallina-
ceous, rasorial; oscine, passerine, perching; columbine, columbaceous, dovelike;
psittacine; aquiline, hawklike; anserine,
anserous, goosy; nidificant, nesting, nest-
building; nidicolous, altricial; nidifugous,
precocial.

.53 **fishlike,** fishy; piscine, pisciform; piscatorial, piscatory; eellike; selachian, shark-
like, sharkish.

.54 **invertebrate,** invertebral; protozoan, pro-
tozoal, protozoic; crustaceous, crustacean; molluscan, molluscoid.

.55 **insectile, insectlike,** buggy; verminous;
lepidopterous, lepidopteran; weevily.

.56 **wormlike,** vermicular, vermiform; wormy.

.57 planktonic, nektonic, benthonic, zoo-
planktonic, zoobenthoic.

.58 **mammals**

aardvark	bassarisk
aardwolf	bat, –nycteris
addax	bear
agouti	beaver
alpaca	Belgian hare
American lion	bettong
Angora goat	bezoar goat
anoa	bighorn sheep
ant bear	binturong
anteater	bison
antelope	black bear
antelope chipmunk or	black buck
squirrel	black cat
aoudad	black fox
apar	black sheep
Arctic fox	blue fox
Arctic hare	boar
argali	bobcat
armadillo	brown bear
ass	brush deer
aurochs	brush wolf
babirusa	buffalo
Bactrian camel	buffalo wolf
badger	burro
bandicoot	burro deer
banteng	bush baby
baronduki	cachalot

Caffre cat
camel
camelopard
Cape buffalo
capybara, carpincho
carabao
caracal
carcajou
caribou
Cashmere goat
cat
catamount or cat-a-
  mountain
cat squirrel
cattalo
cavy
chamois
cheetah
chevrotain
chickaree
chigetai
chinchilla
chipmunk
cinnamon bear
civet cat
coati
coon
coon cat
cotton mouse
cotton rat
cottontail rabbit
cougar
cow
coyote
coypu
deer
deer mouse
deer tiger
dingo
dog
donkey
dormouse
dromedary
duckbill, duckbill
  platypus
echidna
eland
elephant
elk
ermine
eyra
fallow deer
ferret
field mouse
fisher
fitch
flickertail
flying fox
flying lemur
flying marmot
flying phalanger
flying squirrel
foumart
fox
fox squirrel
gaur
gazelle
gemsbok
genet
gerbil
giant ground sloth
giraffe

glutton
gnu
gnu goat
goat
goat antelope
gopher
grasshopper mouse
gray fox
gray wolf
grison
grizzly bear
groundhog
ground squirrel
guanaco
guib
guinea pig
hackee
hamster
hare
harnessed antelope
hartebeest
harvest mouse
hedgehog
herring hog
hippopotamus
hog
horse
hyena
hyrax
ibex
ice bear
imperial mammoth
Indian buffalo
jabalina
jackal
jackass
jackrabbit
jaguar
jaguarundi
jerboa
jerboa kangaroo
jumping mouse
kaama [Africa]
kangaroo
kangaroo mouse
kangaroo rat
karakul
kiang
kinkajou
kit fox
koala
Kodiak bear
koodoo
lapin
lemming
leopard
leopard cat
lion
llama
loris
lynx
mammoth
manul
mara
Marco Polo's sheep
margay
markhor
marmot
marten
mastodon
mazama
meadow mouse

meerkat
mink
mole, talpi–
mongoose
moose
mouflon
mountain goat
mountain lion
mountain sheep
mouse, my(o)–, –mys
mouse deer
mule
mule deer
muntjac
musk deer
musk hog
musk-ox
muskrat, musquash
nilgai
nutria
ocelot
okapi
onager
oont [India]
opossum
oryx
otter
ounce
ox
pack rat
painter [S US]
Pallas's cat
panda
pangolin
panther
pasang
peba
peccary
peludo
phalanger
pig
pika
pine mouse
platypus
pocket gopher
pocket mouse
pocket rat
polar bear
polar fox
polecat
porcupine
possum
potto
pouched rat
poyou
prairie dog
prairie fox
prairie wolf
pronghorn, pronghorn
  antelope
puma
rabbit
rabbit bandicoot
raccoon
rat
red deer
red fox
red squirrel
reindeer
rhinoceros
ring-tailed cat
rock squirrel

Rocky Mountain goat
roe, roe deer, roebuck
saber-toothed tiger or
  cat
sable
sable antelope
saiga
sambar
sand cat
serval
sheep
shrew
shrew mole
sika
silver fox
skunk
skunk bear
sloth
snowshoe rabbit
springbok
squirrel
steenbok
stoat
suslik
swamp rabbit
swine
Syrian bear
takin
tamandua
tamarin
tapir
tarpan
tatou
tatouay
tatou peba
tayra
Thian Shan sheep
tiger
tiger cat
timber wolf
tree shrew
tree squirrel
tsine
urial
urus
Virginia deer
vole
wallaby
wapiti
warthog
waterbuck
water buffalo or ox
weasel
wharf rat
whistler
white fox
whitetail, whitetailed
  deer
white wolf
wild ass
wild boar
wildcat
wildebeest
wild goat
wild ox
wild pig
wild sheep
wolf
wolverine
wombat
woodchuck
wood mouse

wood rat
woolly mammoth
yak

zebra
zebu
zoril

.59 primates

angwantibo
anthropoid ape
ape
aye-aye
baboon
Barbary ape
bonnet monkey *or*
  macaque
capuchin
chacma
chimpanzee
colobus
drill
entellus
gibbon
gorilla
grivet
guenon

guereza
hanuman
langur
lemur
lion-tailed monkey *or*
  macaque
macaque
man 417
mandrill
marmoset
mountain gorilla
orangutan, orang
proboscis monkey
rhesus
saki
siamang
spider monkey

.60 reptiles

agama
alligator
alligator lizard
alligator snapper *or*
  turtle *or* terrapin
anole
basilisk
beaded lizard
bearded lizard
blindworm
box turtle
butterfly agama
cayman
chameleon
crocodile
diamondback, dia-
  mondback terrapin
dinosaurs 123.26
dragon, flying dragon
false map turtle
gavial
gecko
Gila monster
girdle-tailed lizard
glass snake
green turtle

hawksbill turtle,
  hawksbill
horned toad *or* lizard,
  horny-toad [dial]
iguana
leatherback
lizard
loggerhead, logger-
  head turtle
matamata
monitor
mugger
sand lizard
sea turtle *or* tortoise
skink
slow-worm
snapping turtle
soft-shelled turtle
stump-tailed lizard,
  stump tail
teju
terrapin
tortoise
tuatara
turtle

.61 snakes

adder
anaconda
asp
black snake
blind snake
boa
boa constrictor
bull snake
bushmaster
cobra
cobra de capello
constrictor
copperhead
coral snake
cottonmouth
daboia
diamondback, dia-
  mondback rattle-
  snake

fer-de-lance
garter snake
gopher snake
hamadryad
harlequin snake
hog-nose snake
horned rattlesnake
horned viper
king cobra
king snake
krait
mamba
milk snake
moccasin
pine snake
puff adder
python
racer
rat snake

rattlesnake, rattler
Russell's viper
shovel-nose
sidewinder
spectacled cobra
thunder snake

tic-polonga
urutu
viper
water moccasin
water snake
worm snake

.62 amphibians

bullfrog
caecilian
congo snake *or* eel
eft
frog
grass frog
green frog
hellbender
leopard frog
midwife toad
mud puppy

newt
pickerel frog
salamander
siren
spring frog
Surinam toad
toad
tree frog
water dog
wood frog

.63 marine animals

crustacean 415.5
dugong
elephant seal
fur seal
harbor seal
manatee
mollusk 415.5
octopus, octopod
sea calf

sea cow
sea dog
sea elephant
seal
sea lion
sea urchin, echin(o)–
shellfish 308.25
squid
walrus

.64 cetaceans

baleen whale
beluga
blackfish
blue whale
cachalot
dolphin
finback
grampus
humpback

killer, killer whale
narwhal
porpoise
right whale
rorqual
sperm whale
sulfur-bottom whale
whalebone whale
zeuglodon

.65 fish

albacore
alewife
alligator gar
amber jack
anchovy
angel fish
archerfish
argusfish
balloonfish
barbel
barn door skate
barracuda
basking shark
bass
black bass
blackfish
black sea bass
bleak
blind fish
blowfish
blue fish
bluegill
blue shark
bonefish
bonito
bowfin
bream
brook trout
brown trout

buffalo fish
bullhead
burbot
butterfish
candlefish
capelin
carp
catfish
channel bass
char
chimaera
Chinook salmon
chub
cichlid
cisco
cobia
cod, codfish
coelacanth
conger, conger eel
crappie
croaker
cutlass fish
cutthroat trout
dace
darter
devilfish
doctor fish
dogfish
Dolly Varden trout

dorado
dragon fish
drum, drumfish
eel
eelpout
electric eel
electric fish
electric ray, narc(o)–
filefish
flame tetra
flatfish
flounder
fluke
flying fish
flying gurnard
gar, garfish, gar pike
giant bass
globefish
goatfish
goby
golden trout
goldfish
gourami
grayling
grouper
grunion
grunt
gudgeon
guitarfish
gunnel
guppy
haddock
hake
halibut
hammerhead shark
herring
hogfish
horse mackerel
jewfish
kingfish
lake trout
lamprey
lantern fish
ling
loach
lung fish
mackerel
mako shark
manta
marlin
menhaden
miller's-thumb
minnow
moray eel
mudfish
muskellunge
oquassa
paddlefish
papagallo
perch
permit
pickerel
pike
pike perch
pilchard
pilot fish
piranha
plaice

pollack
pompano
porbeagle, porbeagle
  shark
porgy
puffer
rabbitfish
rainbow trout
ray
redfin
redfish
roach
roosterfish
sailfish
salmon
salmon trout
sardine
sawfish
scup
sea bass
sea bream
sea horse, hippocam-
  pus
sea perch
sea trout
sergeant fish
shark
shiner
shovelhead catfish
shovelhead shark
silver salmon
skate
smelt
snapper
snook
sole
speckled trout
sprat
steelhead, steelhead
  trout
stickleback
sting ray
striped bass
sturgeon
sucker
Sunapee trout
sunfish
swordfish
tarpon
tautog
tench
thornback ray
thresher, thresher
  shark
toadfish
tope
torpedo fish
triggerfish
trout
tuna, tunny
turbot
veiltail
wahoo
walleye, walleyed pike
weakfish
whitefish
whiting
yellowtail

.66 birds

aberdevine
adjutant bird

albatross
argala

Audubon's warbler,
  Audubon warbler
auk
auklet
avocet
bald eagle, American
  eagle
baldpate
bank swallow
barbet
barnacle goose
barn owl
barn swallow
bird of paradise
bittern
blackbird
Blackburnian warbler
blackcap
black game
black grouse
bluebill
bluebird
blue jay
bobolink
bobwhite, bobwhite
  quail
booby
brant
brown thrasher
brush turkey
budgerigar
bullfinch
bunting
bushtit
bush wren
bustard
butcher bird
buzzard
Canada goose
canary
canvasback, canvas-
  back duck
capercaillie
caracara
carancho
cardinal, cardinal bird
cassowary
catbird
cattle egret
cedarbird
cedar waxwing
chaffinch
chat
chewink
chickadee
chicken hawk
chimney swift
chipping sparrow
cliff swallow
cockatiel
cockatoo
condor
coot
cormorant
cowbird
crake
crane
creeper
crossbill
crow
cuckoo
curlew

cushat [Scot]
dabchick
darter
dipper
dodo
dove
duck
dunlin
eagle
egret
eider, eider duck
emu
English sparrow
erne
falcon
finch
fish hawk
flamingo
flicker
flycatcher
fly-catching warbler
fool duck
frigate bird
fulmar
gallinule
gannet
garganey
gnatcatcher
goatsucker
godwit
golden eagle
goldeneye
goldfinch
goose
goshawk
grackle
grebe
greylag goose
grosbeak
grouse
guillemot
guinea fowl
gull
gyrfalcon
hangbird
harpy eagle
harrier
hawk
hawk owl
hermit thrush
heron
hobby
honker
hoopoe
hoot owl
horned owl
horned screamer
house finch
house martin
hummingbird
ibis
indigo bunting
jackdaw
jay
junco
jungle fowl
kea
kestrel
killdeer, killdee [dial]
kingbird
kingfisher
kinglet

kite
kittiwake
kiwi
kookaburra
lammergeier
lapwing
lark
laughing jackass
linnet
loon
lovebird
lyrebird
macaw
magpie
mallard
man-o'-war bird
marabou, marabou
   stork
martin
mavis
meadow lark
merganser
merl
mew
mistle or missel thrush
moa
mockingbird
moor hen
mourning dove
mud hen
murre
mute swan
myna, myna bird
nighthawk
night-heron
nightingale
nightjar
nutcracker
nuthatch
oriole
ortolan
osprey
ostrich
ouzel
owl
oyster catcher
parakeet
parrot
partridge
passenger pigeon
peafowl
peewee
pelican
penguin
peregrine falcon
petrel
pewit
phalarope
pheasant
phoebe, phoebe bird
pigeon
pigeon hawk
pintail
pipit
plover
pochard
poorwill
ptarmigan
puffin
purple martin
quetzal, quetzal bird
rail

raven
razorbill
redbird
red grouse
redhead
red-headed wood-
   pecker
redpoll
redshank
redstart
redwing
reedbird
rhea
ricebird
ringdove
ring-necked pheasant
ring ouzel
ringtail
roadrunner
robin
rock dove
rook
ruddy duck
ruffed grouse
sage grouse, sage hen
sand martin
sandpiper
sapsucker
scarlet tanager
scaup duck
screech owl
sea duck
sea eagle
sea gull
sea mew
sea swallow
secretary bird
sheldrake
shoebill, shoebird
shoveler
shrike
siskin
snipe
snowbird
snow bunting
snow goose
solan goose
songbird
song sparrow
song thrush
sparrow
sparrow hawk
spoonbill
sprig
starling
stilt, stilt plover
stone curlew
stork
stormy or storm petrel
swallow
swan
swan goose
swift
tanager
teal, teal duck
tern
thrasher
thrush
tit
titlark
titmouse
toucan

towhee
tragopan
tree swallow
trumpeter
turkey
turkey buzzard, turkey
   vulture
turnstone
turtledove
veery
vesper sparrow
vireo
vulture
warbler
waxwing
weaverbird, weaver
wheatear
whippoorwill

whistler
whooper swan
widgeon
wild duck
willet
woodcock
wood duck
wood owl
woodpecker
wood pigeon
wren
wren-tit
wryneck
yellowbird
yellowhammer
yellowlegs
yellowthroat
zebra finch

.67 breeds of chickens

Ancona
Andalusian
Australorp
Bantam
Barred Plymouth
   Rock
black Minorca
black Orpington
black Spanish
black Sumatra
blue Andalusian
blue Orpington
Brahma
buff Orpington
Campine
Cochin
Cornish
dark Cornish
Dorking
Faverolle
Hamburg

Houdan
Jersey white giant
Langshan
Leghorn
Minorca
New Hampshire
New Hampshire red
Orpington
Plymouth Rock
Rhode Island red
Rhode Island white
Rock Cornish
speckled Sussex
Sumatra
Sussex
white Leghorn
white Orpington
white Plymouth Rock
white Wyandotte
Wyandotte

.68 breeds of horses

American quarter
   horse
American saddle horse
American trotter
Appaloosa
Arabian
Barbary horse, Barb
Belgian
Cleveland Bay
Clydesdale
French coach horse
Galloway
German coach horse
hackney pony
Hambletonian
jennet or genet
Lippizaner
Morgan

Narragansett pacer
palomino
Percheron
Plantation walking
   horse
quarter horse
saddle horse
Shetland, Shetland
   pony
Shire, Shire horse
standardbred
Suffolk, Suffolk punch
Tennessee walking
   horse
thoroughbred
Turk
Waler
Welsh pony

.69 breeds of cattle

Aberdeen Angus,
   Angus, black Angus
Africander
Alderney
Ayrshire
Belted Galloway
Brahman, Brahmany
Brown Swiss
Charbray

Charolais
Devon
Dexter
Durham
Dutch Belted
French Canadian
Galloway
Guernsey
Hereford

Holstein, Holstein-
Friesian
Jersey
Lincoln Red, Lincoln
Red Shorthorn
Longhorn
Polled Durham *or*
Shorthorn

Polled Hereford
Red Poll, Red Polled
Santa Gertrudis
Shorthorn
Sussex
Welsh, Welsh Black
West Highland

.70 breeds of sheep

black face Highland
blackhead Persian
broadtail
Cheviot
Columbia
Corriedale
Cotswold
Dorset Down
Hampshire, Hamp-
shire Down
Karakul
Kerry Hill
Leicester
Lincoln
Merino
Oxford *or* Oxfordshire

Down
Panama
Rambouillet
Romanov
Romeldale
Romney, Romney
Marsh
Ryeland
Scottish blackface
Shropshire
Southdown
Suffolk
Targhee
Welsh Mountain
Wensleydale

.71 breeds of swine

Berkshire
Cheshire
Chester White
Duroc, Duroc-Jersey
Hampshire
Hereford
Landrace
large black

large white
Mangalitza
middle white
Poland China
Spotted Poland China
Tamworth
Wessex saddleback
Yorkshire

.72 breeds of dogs

affenpinscher
Afghan hound
Airedale, Airedale ter-
rier
Alaskan malamute
Alsatian
American foxhound
American water span-
iel
Australian terrier
badger dog
barbet
Basenji
basset, basset hound
beagle
Bedlington terrier
Belgian sheep dog *or*
shepherd
Bernese mountain dog
Blenheim spaniel
bloodhound, sleuth,
sleuthhound
boarhound
Border terrier
borzoi
Boston bull *or* terrier
Bouvier des Flandres
boxer
Briard
Brittany spaniel
Brussels griffon
bulldog, bull
bull mastiff
bull terrier

Cairn terrier
Chesapeake Bay
retriever
Chihuahua
chow, chow chow
clumber spaniel
Clydesdale terrier
cocker spaniel
collie
coonhound
dachshund
Dalmatian, coach dog
Dandie Dinmont ter-
rier
deerhound
Doberman pinscher
elkhound
English bulldog
English cocker spaniel
English foxhound
English setter
English springer span-
iel
English toy spaniel
Eskimo dog
field spaniel
flat-coated retriever
foxhound
fox terrier
French bulldog
gazelle hound
German shepherd,
police dog
German short-haired

pointer
German wire-haired
pointer
giant schnauzer
golden retriever
Gordon setter
Great Dane
Great Pyrenees
greyhound
griffon
Groenendael
harrier
hound, hound-dog [S
US]
husky
Irish setter
Irish terrier
Irish water spaniel
Irish wolfhound
Italian greyhound
Japanese spaniel
keeshond
Kerry blue terrier
King Charles spaniel
komondor
kuvasz
Labrador retriever
lakeland terrier
Lhasa apso
malamute
Malinois
Maltese
Manchester terrier
mastiff
Mexican hairless
miniature poodle
miniature pinscher
miniature schnauzer
Newfoundland
Norfolk spaniel
Norwegian elkhound
Norwich terrier
Old English sheep
dog
otterhound
papillon
Pekingese
pointer
Pomeranian

poodle
pug
puli
rat terrier
retriever
Rhodesian ridgeback
Rottweiler
Russian owtchar
Russian wolfhound
Saluki
St. Bernard
Samoyed
schipperke
schnauzer
Scottish deerhound
Scottish terrier
Sealyham terrier
setter
shepherd dog
Shetland sheep dog
Shih Tzu
Siberian husky
silky terrier
Skye terrier
spaniel
spitz
springer spaniel
staghound
Sussex spaniel
terrier
toy poodle
toy spaniel
toy terrier
turnspit
Vizsla
water spaniel
Weimaraner
Welsh collie
Welsh corgi
Welsh springer span-
iel
Welsh terrier
West Highland white
terrier
whippet
wire-haired terrier
wolfhound
Yorkshire terrier

.73 breeds of cats

Abyssinian cat
Angora cat
Archangel cat
Burmese cat
coon cat [dial]
domestic shorthair cat
Egyptian cat
Havana brown cat

Himalayan cat
Manx cat
Persian cat
Rex cat
Russian blue cat
Siamese cat
Turkish cat

.74 insects

ant
ant lion
aphid, aphis
assassin bug
bedbug
bee
bee fly
beetle
billbug, billbeetle
blowfly
bluebottle

boll weevil
borer, peachtree
borer, appletree
borer, etc.
botfly
bristletail
buffalo bug
buffalo carpet beetle
buprestid beetle
butterfly
caddis fly

Cecropia moth
chafer
chigoe, chigger
chinch, chinch bug
cicada
cicala
cockchafer
cockroach
codling moth
Colorado beetle,
   Colorado potato
   beetle
cone-nose
crane fly
cricket
Croton bug
cucumber flea beetle
curculio
damselfly
deer fly
dobson fly
dragonfly
drosophila
dung beetle
earwig
elm leaf beetle
ephemerid
firebrat
firefly
flea
flea beetle
flour moth
fly
fruit fly
fruit-tree bark beetle
gadfly
gallfly
glowworm
gnat
grain beetle
grasshopper
greenbottle fly
harlequin cabbage
   bug
hawkmoth
hornet
horn fly
horntail
horsefly
housefly
Japanese beetle
jigger, jigger flea
June bug or beetle
katydid
kissing bug

lacewing
ladybug, ladybird,
   lady beetle
lantern fly
leafhopper
Lepisma
locust
louse
mantis, praying man-
   tis
mayfly
mealworm
mealybug
midge
miller
mole cricket
mosquito
mosquito hawk
moth
pill bug
podura
potato bug or beetle
punkie
roach
robber fly
rose beetle
rove beetle
St. Mark's fly
sawfly
scarab, scarab beetle
scorpion fly
shad fly
silverfish
snout beetle
sow bug
springtail
squash bug
stag beetle
stinkbug
stone fly
syrphus fly
termite
thrips
tiger moth
tsetse fly
tumblebug
walkingstick
wasp
water bug
weevil, grain weevil,
   rice weevil, etc.
wood tick
wood wasp
yellow jacket

.75 worms

angleworm
armyworm
bollworm
bookworm
cankerworm
cotton worm
cutworm
earthworm
earworm
fireworm
hellgrammite
inchworm, measuring
   worm, looper
leech
nematode

pinworm
planarian
roundworm
shipworm, spileworm
silkworm
tapeworm
teredo
tobacco worm
tomato worm
trematode
tussah
webworm
wireworm
woodworm

415. ZOOLOGY

.1 NOUNS zoology, anthropology 417.7, biology 406.17, anatomy 245.7, comparative anatomy or zootomy, animal physiology or zoonomy, conchology, ecology, zooecology, entomology, ethology, helminthology, herpetology, ichthyology, malacology, mammalogy, ophiology, ornithology, protozoology, taxonomy or zootaxy, zoogeography or zoography, zoopathology, zoophysics; taxidermy.

.2 zoologist, anthropologist 417.7, biologist 406.18, animal physiologist or zoonomist, conchologist, ecologist, zoo-ecologist, entomologist or bugologist [informal], ethologist, helminthologist, herpetologist, ichthyologist, malacologist, mammalogist, ophiologist, ornithologist, protozoologist, zoographer, zoopathologist, zoophysicist, zootaxonomist; taxidermist.

.3 Subkingdom Protozoa (one-celled animals): Protozoa: Mastigophora, Sarcodina, Sporozoa, Ciliata, Suctoria.

.4 Subkingdom Parazoa (many-celled animals without a true digestive cavity): Porifera (sponges).

.5 Subkingdom Metazoa (many-celled animals with true digestive cavities): Mesozoa; Coelenterata: Scyphozoa (jellyfishes), Anthozoa (sea anemones, corals); Ctenophora (comb jellies); Platyhelminthes (flatworms): Turbellaria (free-living flatworms), Trematoda (flukes), Cestoda (tapeworms); Nemertinea or Nemertea (ribbon worms); Entoprocta; Ectoprocta or Bryozoa (moss animals); Aschelminthes: Rotifera (wheel animalcules or wheel worms), Nematoda (roundworms), Nematomorpha (hair snakes); Acanthocephala (spiny-headed worms); Phoronidea; Pogonophora (beard worms); Brachiopoda (lamp shells); Echinodermata: Crinoidea (sea lilies), Asteroidea (starfishes), Ophiuroidea (brittle stars), Echinoidea (sea urchins), Holothurioidea (sea cucumbers); Chaetognatha (arrowworms); Mollusca: Gastropoda (univalve mollusks such as limpets, slugs, snails), Pelecyopoda (bivalve mollusks such as clams), Cephalopoda (octopuses, squids), Scaphopoda (tooth shells), Amphineura (chitons), Monoplacophora; Annelida (segmented worms): Polychaeta (sandworms), Oligochaeta (earthworms), Hirudinea (leeches); Sipunculoidea (peanut worms); Priapuloidea; Echiuroidea; Arthropoda: Arachnida (spiders), Crustacea (lobsters, shrimp, etc.), Insecta (insects), Chilopoda (centipedes), Diplopoda (millipedes); Chordata.

.6 Phylum Chordata: Hemichordata (tongue worms), Cephalochordata (lancelets), Tunicata (sea squirts), Vertebrata.

.7 Subphylum Vertebrata: Cyclostomata (lampreys, hagfishes), Chondrichtyes (cartilaginous fishes such as sharks, rays, skates), Osteichthyes (bony fishes), Amphibia (amphibians), Reptilia (reptiles), Mammalia (mammals).

.8 Class Mammalia: Monotremata (platypuses, echidnas), Marsupialia (kangaroos, opossums), Insectivora (shrews, moles), Dermoptera (flying lemurs), Chiroptera (bats), Primates (man, apes, monkeys), Edentata (anteaters, armadillos, sloths), Pholidota (pangolin), Lagomorpha (hares, rabbits), Rodentia (rodents), Cetacea (whales, dolphins), Carnivora (carnivores), Tubulidentata (aardvarks), Proboscidea (elephants), Hyracoidea (coneys), Sirenia (manatees or sea cows), Perissodactyla (horses, tapirs, rhinoceroses), Artiodactyla (antelopes, cattle, pigs).

.9 ADJS zoologic(al), entomologic(al); taxidermic, taxidermal.

416. ANIMAL HUSBANDRY

.1 NOUNS animal husbandry, animal rearing or raising or culture, stock raising; zooculture, zootechnics, zootechny; thremmatology; gnotobiotics; herding, grazing, keeping flocks and herds, running livestock; breeding, stockbreeding, stirpiculture; horse training, dressage, manège; horsemanship; pisciculture, fish culture; apiculture, bee culture, beekeeping; cattle raising; sheepherding; pig-keeping; dairy-farming, chicken-farming, pig-farming, etc.; cattle-ranching, mink-ranching, etc.

.2 stockman, stock raiser, stockkeeper [Austral]; breeder, stockbreeder; sheepman; cattleman, cow keeper, cowman, grazier [Brit]; rancher, ranchman, ranchero; dairyman, dairy farmer; stableman, stableboy, groom, hostler, equerry; trainer, breaker, tamer; broncobuster or buckaroo [both slang]; horseshoer, farrier.

.3 herder, drover, herdsman, herdboy; shepherd, shepherdess, sheepherder, sheepman; goatherd; swineherd, pigman, pigherd, hogherd; gooseherd, gooseboy, goosegirl; swanherd; cowherd, neatherd

[Brit], cowboy, cowgirl, cowhand, puncher or cowpuncher [both informal], waddy [W US], cowman, cattleman, vaquero [Sp], gaucho; horseherd, wrangler, horse wrangler.

.4 apiarist, apiculturist, beekeeper, beeherd.

.5 animal enclosure 191.19–26, 236.12.

.6 VERBS raise, breed, rear, grow, hatch, feed, nurture, fatten; keep, run; ranch, farm; culture.

.7 tend; groom, rub down, brush, curry, currycomb; water, drench, feed, fodder; bed, bed down, litter; milk; harness, saddle, hitch, bridle, yoke; gentle, handle, manage; tame, train, break.

.8 drive, herd, drove [Brit], punch cattle, shepherd, ride herd on; spur, goad, prick, lash, whip; wrangle, round up; corral, cage.

417. MANKIND

.1 NOUNS mankind, humankind, man, human species, human race, race of man, human family, humanity, mortals, mortality, flesh, mortal flesh, clay; generation of man [archaic], le genre humain [Fr], "the plumeless genus of bipeds" [Plato], homo, genus Homo, Homo sapiens, Hominidae, hominid; human nature, frail or fallen humanity, Adam, Adam's seed or offspring.

.2 people 418, persons, folk, folks, gentry, men, people in general; public, populace, population, citizenry, general public; John Q. Public, Everyman, man in the street, common man, you and me, John Doe, everyman, everywoman, everyone, everybody; community, commonwealth, nation, nationality, state; estate [archaic], polity, body politic; society, world, world or community at large.

.3 person, human, human being, man, homo, anthrop(o)–, homin(i)–, prosop(o)–; member of the human race, Adamite; mortal, life, soul, living soul; being, creature, individual, "single, separate person" [Whitman], personage, personality, body; somebody, one, someone; fellow or chap or customer or party or character [all informal]; guy or cat or duck or joker [all slang]; bloke or cove or johnny [all Brit slang]; earthling, groundling, terran, worldling, tellurian; head, hand, nose.

.4 God's image, lord of creation; homo faber, symbol-using animal; "a god in ruins" [Emerson], "the aristocrat amongst the animals" [Heine], "the measure of all things" [Protagoras], "a reasoning animal" [Seneca], "the most intelligent of animals—and the most silly" [Diogenes], "a thinking reed" [Pascal], "a tool-using animal" [Carlyle], "a tool-making animal" [Benjamin Franklin], "the only animal that blushes. Or needs to" [Mark Twain], "an intelligence served by organs" [Emerson], rational animal, animal capable of reason, "an ingenious assembly of portable plumbing" [Christopher Morley], "Nature's sole mistake" [W. S. Gilbert], "that unfeather'd two-legged thing" [Dryden], "but breath and shadow, nothing more" [Sophocles], "this quintessence of dust" [Shakespeare], "political animal" [Aristotle]; "the naked ape" [Desmond Morris].

.5 humanness, humanity, mortality; human nature, the way you are; frailty, human frailty, weakness, human weakness, weakness of the flesh, "thy nature's weakness" [Whittier], "one touch of nature" [Shakespeare], the weaknesses human flesh is heir to; human equation.

.6 humanization; anthropomorphism, pathetic fallacy, anthropopathism, anthropomorphology.

.7 anthropology, science of man; anthropogeny, anthropography, anthropogeography, human geography, demography, human ecology, anthropometry, craniometry, craniology, ethnology, ethnography; behavioral science, sociology, socio-, psychology 690; anatomy 245.7; anthropologist, ethnologist, sociologist.

.8 humanism; naturalistic humanism, scientific humanism; Religious Humanism; Christian humanism, integral humanism; new humanism; anthroposophy.

.9 VERBS humanize, anthropomorphize, make human, civilize.

.10 ADJS human; hominal; creaturely, creatural; Adamite or Adamitic; frail, weak, fleshly, finite, mortal; only human; earthborn, of the earth, earthy, tellurian, unangelic; humanistic; man-centered, homocentric, anthropocentric; anthropological.

.11 manlike, anthropoid, humanoid, hominid; anthropomorphic, anthropopathic.

.12 personal, individual, private, peculiar, idiosyncratic.

.13 public, general, common; communal, societal, social; civic, civil; national, state; international, cosmopolitan, supernational, supranational.

.14 ADVS humanly, mortally, after the manner of men.

418. PEOPLES

.1 NOUNS people; race, strain, stock, ethno-, gen(o)-; culture 642.3, society, speech community, ethnic group; community, nationality, nation.

.2 (races) Caucasoid or Caucasian or white race; Nordic race, Alpine race, Mediterranean race; xanthochroi, melanochroi; Archaic Caucasoid or archaic white or Australoid race; Polynesian race; Negroid or black race; Nilotic race, Melanesian race, Papuan race; Pygmoid race; Bushman race; Mongoloid or Mongolian or yellow race; Malayan or Malaysian or brown race; prehistoric races 123.25.

.3 Caucasian, white man, white; WASP [informal]; paleface, ofay, the Man, Mister Charley [all slang]; whitey or honky [both derog]; Australian aborigine, blackfellow [Austral]; Negro, black man, black, colored person; darky [slang]; spade, nigger, niggra, coon, burrhead, jigaboo, jungle bunny, boy [all derog]; pygmy, Negrito, Negrillo; Bushman; Indian, American Indian, Amerind, Red Indian [Brit], red man; injun or redskin [both slang]; Mongolian, yellow man, Oriental; gook or slant-eye [both derog]; Malayan, brown man.

.4 crossbreed, mulatto 44.9.

419. SEX

.1 NOUNS sex, gender, gen(o)-; maleness, masculinity 420, femaleness, femininity 421.

.2 sexuality, sexualism, gam(o)-; love 931, lovemaking 932, marriage 933; carnality, sensuality 987; sexiness, voluptuousness, flesh, fleshliness; libido, sex drive, sexual instinct or urge; potency 420.2; impotence; frigidity, coldness.

.3 sex appeal, sexual attraction or attractiveness or magnetism.

.4 sex object; piece, meat, piece of meat, ass, piece of ass, hot number [all slang]; sex queen, sex goddess; stud [slang].

.5 sexual desire, sensuous or carnal desire, bodily appetite, biological urge, venereal appetite or desire, sexual longing, lust, desire, lusts or desires of the flesh, itch, passion, carnal or sexual passion, fleshly lust, prurience or pruriency, concupiscence, hot blood, aphrodisia, hot pants [slang]; lustfulness, goatishness, horniness, libidinousness; lasciviousness 989.5; eroticism, erotism, eroto-; indecency 990; erotomania, eromania, eroticomaniac, *hysteria libidinosa* [L]; nymphomania, andromania, *furor uterinus* [L]; satyrism, satyriasis, gynecomania; infantile sexuality, polymorphous perversity.

.6 **heat, rut;** frenzy *or* fury of lust; estrus, estrum, estral cycle, estruation.

.7 **aphrodisiac, love potion,** philter; cantharis, blister beetle, Spanish fly.

.8 **copulation, sex act,** *le sport* [Fr], coupling, mating, coition, **coitus,** pareunia, venery, copula [law], **sex, intercourse, sexual intercourse,** cohabitation, commerce, sexual commerce, congress, sexual congress, sexual union, sexual relations, relations, marital relations, marriage act, act of love, sleeping together *or* sleeping with; screwing, balling, diddling, making it with [all slang]; meat, ass [both slang], intimacy, connection, carnal knowledge, aphrodisia; orgasm, climax, sexual climax; adultery, fornication 989.7; coitus interruptus, onanism; **lovemaking** 932; **procreation** 169; germ cell, sperm, ovum 406.10–12.

.9 **masturbation,** autoeroticism, self-abuse, onanism, manipulation, playing with oneself, hand job [slang]; oral-genital stimulation, fellatio *or* fellation, irrumation, cunnilingus; anal intercourse, buggery, sodomy, pederasty; bestiality.

.10 **genitals,** genitalia, sex organs, reproductive organs, pudenda, private parts, privy parts, privates, ede(o)–, meat [slang]; **male organs; penis, phallus,** phallo–, *lingam* [Skt]; gonads; **testes, testicles,** didym(o)–; balls *or* nuts *or* rocks [all slang], cods [dial], cullions [archaic], ballocks, family jewels [both slang]; spermary; scrotum, bag *or* basket [both slang], cod [archaic], scrot(o)– *or* scroti–; **female organs,** –gyne; **vulva,** vulv(o)–, episio–, *yoni* [Skt]; **vagina;** clitoris; labia, labia majora, labia minora, lips, nymphae, nymph(o)– *or* nymphi–; cervix; ovary, ovar(o)– *or* ovari–; uterus, womb 153.9; secondary sex characteristic, pubic hair, beard 230.8, breasts 256.6.

.11 **sexlessness,** asexuality, neuterness.

.12 **sexual preference;** sexual normality; **heterosexuality; homosexuality,** homosexualism, homoeroticism, sexual inversion; autoeroticism, **bisexuality,** bisexualism, amphierotism, swinging both ways [slang]; **lesbianism,** sapphism, tribadism *or* tribady; paraphilia; zoophilia, zooerastia; pedophilia; algolagnia, algolagny, sadomasochism; active algolagnia, **sadism;** passive algolagnia, **masochism;** fetishism;

narcissism; exhibitionism; necrophilia; coprophilia; scotophilia, voyeurism; transvestitism; **incest,** incestuousness.

.13 **perversion,** sexual deviation, sexual deviance, sexual perversion, sexual abnormality; sexual pathology; psychosexual disorder; sexual psychopathy, *psychopathia sexualis* [L]; **sex crime.**

.14 **intersexuality,** intersexualism, epicenism, epicenity; hermaphroditism, pseudohermaphroditism; androgynism, androgyny, gynandry, gynandrism; transsexuality, transsexualism.

.15 **heterosexual, straight** [slang].

.16 **homosexual,** homosexualist, homophile, invert; homo, queer, faggot, fag, fruit [all derog]; flit, fairy, pansy, nance, auntie [all derog], queen [slang]; catamite, pathic; chicken, punk, gunsel [all derog]; **bisexual,** bi-guy [slang]; **lesbian,** sapphist, tribade, fricatrice [archaic]; dyke *or* bull dyke [both derog], butch, femme [both slang].

.17 **sodomist, sodomite,** bugger; pederast; paraphiliac; zoophiliac; pedophiliac; sadist; masochist; fetishist; transvestite; narcissist; exhibitionist; necrophiliac; coprophiliac; scotophiliac, voyeur; erotomaniac, nymphomaniac, satyr; rapist 989.12.

.18 **pervert, deviant,** deviate, sex *or* sexual pervert, sex *or* sexual deviant, sex *or* sexual deviate; sex fiend, sex criminal, sexual psychopath.

.19 **intersex,** sex-intergrade, epicene; hermaphrodite, pseudohermaphrodite; androgyne, gynandroid; transsexual.

.20 **sexology,** sexologist; sexual customs *or* mores *or* practices; sexual morality; new morality, sexual revolution; sexual freedom, free love; trial marriage.

.21 VERBS **sex,** sexualize.

.22 **lust, lust after,** itch for, have a lech *or* hot pants for [slang], **desire; be in heat** *or* **rut,** rut, come in, estruate.

.23 **copulate, couple, mate,** unite in sexual intercourse, **have sexual relations, have sex,** make out [slang], perform the act of love *or* marriage act, come together, cohabit, be intimate; sleep with, lie with, go to bed with; **screw, lay, ball, frig, diddle, make it with** [all slang]; cover, mount, serve *or* service (of animals); commit adultery, fornicate 989.19; **make love** 932.13.

.24 **masturbate,** play with *or* abuse oneself; fellate; sodomize, bugger, ream [slang].

.25 **climax, come,** achieve satisfaction,

achieve *or* reach orgasm; **ejaculate, get off** [slang].

.26 ADJS **sexual, sex,** sexlike, gamic, libidinal; **erotic,** amorous 931.24; nuptial 933.19; venereal; **carnal, sensual** 987.5,6, voluptuous, fleshly; **sexy; heterosexual, straight** [informal]; erogenous, erogenic, erotogenic; sexed, oversexed, undersexed; procreative 169.15; potent 420.12.

.27 **genital,** genito–; **phallic,** penile, penial; testicular; scrotal; spermatic, seminal, gon(o)–; vulvar, vulval; vaginal; clitoral; cervical; ovarian; uterine.

.28 **aphrodisiac,** aphroditous, **arousing,** stimulating, eroticizing, venereal.

.29 **lustful, prurient, hot,** steamy, sexy, concupiscent, lickerish, libidinous, **salacious** 990.9, **passionate,** hot-blooded, itching, **horny** [slang], randy, goatish; sex-starved, unsatisfied; lascivious 989.29; **orgasmic,** orgastic, **ejaculatory.**

.30 **in heat, burning, hot; in rut,** rutting, rutty, ruttish; **in must, must,** musty; estrous, estral, estrual.

.31 **unsexual,** unsexed; **sexless, asexual, neuter,** neutral; castrated, emasculated, eunuchized; **cold, frigid; impotent;** frustrated.

.32 **homosexual,** homoerotic, **gay** [informal], **queer** [derog]; **bisexual,** bisexed, amphierotic, **AC-DC** [informal], autoerotic; lesbian, sapphic, tribadistic; mannish 420.13, butch; effeminate 421.14; transvestite; **perverted,** deviant.

.33 **hermaphrodite,** hermaphroditic, pseudohermaphrodite, pseudohermaphroditic, epicene, monoclinous; androgynous, androgynal, gynandrous, gynandrian.

420. MASCULINITY

.1 NOUNS **masculinity,** masculineness, maleness; **manliness,** manlihood, **manhood,** manfulness, manlikeness; mannishness; gentlemanliness, gentlemanlikeness.

.2 **virility,** virileness, potence *or* **potency,** sexual power, manly vigor, *machismo* [Sp]; ultramasculinity.

.3 **mankind, man, men, manhood,** menfolk *or* menfolks [both dial], sword side; **male sex.**

.4 **male,** male being, masculine; he, him, his; **man,** male person, *homme* [Fr], *hombre* [Sp]; **gentleman;** andr(o)–.

.5 **fellow,** feller, lad, chap, **guy** [all informal]; cat, bird, duck, stud, **joker,** character, jasper, bugger, bastard [all slang]; bloke *or* cove *or* johnny [all Brit slang].

.6 **he-man** *or* two-fisted man [both infor-

mal], jockstrap, jock [both slang], man with hair on his chest; caveman, bucko [both slang].

.7 (forms of address) **Mister, Mr.,** Messrs. [pl], Master; **sir;** *monsieur, M.* [both Fr], *messieurs, MM.* [both Fr pl]; *signor, signore* [both Ital], *signorino* [Ital], *señor, Sr.* [both Sp], *don* [Sp], *senhor* [Pg]; *Herr* [Ger]; *mein Herr* [Ger]; *mijnheer* [Du], *sahib* [Hind], *bwana* [Swahili].

.8 (male animals) cock, rooster, chanticleer; cockerel; drake; gander; peacock; tom turkey, tom, turkey-cock, bubbly-jock [Scot], gobbler, turkey gobbler; dog; boar; stag, hart, buck; stallion, studhorse, stud, top horse [dial], entire horse, entire; tomcat, tom; he-goat, billy goat, billy; ram, tup [Brit]; wether; bull, bullock, top cow [dial]; steer, stot [Brit dial].

.9 (mannish female) **amazon,** virago, androgyne; lesbian 419.16, butch, dyke [both slang]; **tomboy,** hoyden, romp.

.10 VERBS masculinize, virilize.

.11 ADJS **masculine, male,** bull, he–; **manly, manlike, mannish,** manful, andric; uneffeminate; **gentlemanly,** gentlemanlike.

.12 **virile, potent,** viripotent; ultramasculine, **macho** [Sp], **he-mannish** [informal], two-fisted [informal], broad-shouldered, hairychested.

.13 **mannish,** mannified; **unwomanly, unfeminine,** uneffeminate, viraginous; **tomboyish,** hoyden, rompish.

421. FEMININITY

.1 NOUNS **femininity,** femineity, feminality, feminacy, feminineness, femaleness; **womanliness,** womanlikeness, womanishness, **womanhood,** womanity, muliebrity; girlishness, little-girlishness; maidenhood, maidenliness; **ladylikeness,** gentlewomanliness; **matronliness,** matronage, matronhood, matronship; the eternal feminine, *"das Ewig-Weibliche"* [Ger; Goethe].

.2 **effeminacy, unmanliness,** effeminateness, epicenity, epicenism, **womanishness,** muliebrity, **sissiness** [informal], prissiness [informal]; androgyny, feminism.

.3 **womankind, woman, women,** femininity, **womanhood,** womenfolk *or* womenfolks [both dial], distaff side; **female sex;** second sex, **fair sex,** softer sex, **weaker sex,** weaker vessel.

.4 **female,** female being; she, her; –ess, –ette, –ine, –trix; gyne–, gyn(o)–, gyneo–, gyneco–, –gyne.

.5 **woman,** Eve, daughter of Eve, Adam's Rib, *femme* [Fr], distaff [archaic], weaker vessel; frow, *Frau* [Ger], *vrouw* [Du], *donna* [Ital], wahine [Hawaii]; **lady,** milady, gentlewoman, *domina* [L]; **matron,** dame, **dowager;** squaw; lass, girl 125.6.

.6 [slang terms] **dame,** hen, biddy, skirt; Jane, **broad, doll, chick,** wench, bird [Brit], tomato, bitch, minx.

.7 "a rag and a bone and a hank of hair" [Kipling], "God's second mistake" [Nietzche], "the last thing civilized by man" [George Meredith], "sphinxes without secrets" [Oscar Wilde], "the female of the human species, and not a different kind of animal" [G. B. Shaw], "O fairest of creation! last and best of all God's works" [Milton], "frailty, thy name is woman!" [Shakespeare], "a necessary evil" [Latin proverb], "a temple sacred by birth, and built by hands divine" [Dryden].

.8 (forms of address) Mistress [archaic], **Mrs.;** madam *or* ma'am; *madame, Mme* [both Fr]; *mesdames, Mmes* [both Fr pl]; *Frau* [Ger], *vrouw* [Du], *signora* [Ital], *señora* [Sp], *senhora* [Pg], *mem-sahib* [Hind]; dame [archaic], *donna* [Ital], *doña* [Sp], *dona* [Pg], lady; **Ms.; Miss;** *mademoiselle, Mlle* [both Fr]; *Fräulein* [Ger]; *signorina* [Ital], *señorita* [Sp], *senhorita* [Pg].

.9 (female animals) hen, Partlet, biddy; guinea hen; peahen; bitch, slut, gyp; sow; ewe, ewe lamb; she-goat, nanny goat *or* nanny; doe, hind, roe; jenny; mare, brood mare; filly; cow, bossy; heifer; vixen; tigress; lioness; she-bear, she-lion, etc.

.10 (effeminate male) **mollycoddle,** effeminate; **mother's darling, mama's boy,** Lord Fauntleroy, sissy, Percy, goody-goody; **pantywaist,** nancy *or* nance, chicken, lily; cream puff, weak sister, milksop; old woman.

.11 feminization, womanization, effemination, effeminization, sissification [informal].

.12 VERBS feminize; womanize, demasculinize, effeminize, effeminatize, effeminate, soften, sissify [informal]; emasculate, castrate, geld.

.13 ADJS **feminine, female,** she–; gynic, gynecic, gynecoid, –gynous; muliebral, distaff, **womanly, womanish, womanlike,** petticoat; **ladylike,** gentlewomanlike, gentlewomanly; **matronly,** matronal, matronlike; **girlish,** little-girlish, kittenish; maidenly 124.11.

.14 **effeminate, womanish,** old-womanish, **unmanly,** muliebrous, soft, chicken, prissy, **sissified,** sissy, **sissyish.**

422. SENSATION

(physical sensibility)

.1 NOUNS **sensation, sense, feeling;** sense impression, sense-datum *or* -data, percept, perception, sense perception; experience, sensory experience; **consciousness,** awareness; response, response to stimuli.

.2 **sensibility,** sensibleness, physical sensibility, sentience *or* sentiency; openness to sensation, readiness of feeling, receptiveness, receptivity; sensation level, threshold of sensation, limen; impressionability, impressibility, affectibility; **susceptibility,** susceptivity; perceptibility.

.3 **sensitivity, sensitiveness;** perceptivity, perceptiveness; responsiveness; tact, tactfulness, considerateness, sympathy; empathy, identification; passibility; delicacy, exquisiteness, tenderness, fineness; **oversensitiveness,** oversensibility, hypersensitivity, **thin skin,** hyperesthesia, hyperpathia, supersensitivity, overtenderness; **irritability,** prickliness, soreness, **touchiness,** tetchiness; ticklishness, nervousness 859; allergy, anaphylaxis; sensitization; photophobia.

.4 **sore spot,** sore point, soft spot, raw, exposed nerve, raw nerve, nerve ending, tender spot, the quick, where the shoe pinches.

.5 **senses, five senses,** sensorium; touch, taste, smell, sight, hearing; sixth sense; sense *or* sensory organ, sensillum, receptor; synesthesia, chromesthesia, color hearing; phonism, photism.

.6 **nerve,** nerv(o)– *or* nervi–, neur(o)–; **neuron;** sensory *or* afferent neuron, sensory cell; motor *or* efferent neuron; association *or* internuncial neuron; axon, dendrite, myelin *or* medullary sheath; **synapse;** effector organ; nerve trunk; **ganglion,** gangli(o)–; plexus, solar plexus; **spinal cord,** spin(o)– *or* spini–, myel(o)–; **brain** 466.6,7; cerebral cortex, sensory area, sensorium; gray matter, white matter; **nervous system;** central nervous system, peripheral nervous system; autonomic nervous system; sympathetic *or* thoracolumbar nervous system, parasympathetic *or* craniosacral nervous system.

.7 neurology; neurologist, neurosurgeon.

.8 VERBS **sense, feel,** experience, **perceive,** apprehend, be sensible of, be conscious *or* aware of; taste 427.7, smell 435.8, see 439.12, hear 448.11,12, touch 425.6; respond, respond to stimuli.

.9 **sensitize,** make sensitive; sensibilize, sensify; sharpen, whet, quicken, stimulate, excite, stir, cultivate, refine.

.10 **touch a sore spot**, touch a soft spot, touch on the raw, touch to the quick, touch a nerve *or* nerve ending, touch where it hurts, hit one where he lives [slang].

.11 ADJS **sensory**, sensatory, sensorial, senso-(ri)–; **sensitive, receptive**; sensuous; sensorimotor, sensimotor.

.12 **neural, nervous,** nerval; neurological.

.13 sensible, sentient, sensile; **susceptible,** susceptive; **receptive,** impressionable, impressive [archaic], impressible; **perceptive; conscious,** cognizant, **aware,** sensitive to, alive to.

.14 **sensitive,** responsive, sympathetic; empathic, empathetic; passible; delicate, tactful, tender, refined; **oversensitive, thin-skinned;** oversensible, hyperesthetic, hyperpathic, hypersensitive, supersensitive, overtender, overrefined; **irritable, touchy,** tetchy [dial], itchy, ticklish, prickly; goosy, skittish; nervous 859.10; allergic, anaphylactic.

.15 (keenly sensitive) **exquisite,** poignant, **acute,** sharp, **keen,** vivid, intense, extreme, excruciating.

423. INSENSIBILITY

(physical unfeeling)

.1 NOUNS **insensibility,** insensibleness, **insensitivity,** insensitiveness, insentience, impassibility; **unperceptiveness,** imperceptiveness, imperception, imperceptivity, imperceptiveness, imperceptivity, imperceptiveness, obtuseness; inconsiderateness, **unfeeling,** unfeelingness; thick skin *or* hide, callousness 856.3; **numbness,** dullness, **deadness,** ambly(o)–, brady–, narc-(o)–; pins and needles; anesthesia, analgesia; narcosis, electronarcosis; narcotization.

.2 **unconsciousness, senselessness;** nothingness, oblivion, obliviousness, nirvana; nirvana principle; **faint, swoon, blackout,** syncope, lipothymy *or* lipothymia; **coma; stupor;** catalepsy, catatony *or* catatonia, sleep 712; knockout, KO *or* kayo [both slang]; semiconsciousness, grayout.

.3 **anesthetic,** analgesic, **pain-killer,** tranquilizer, **sedative,** sleeping pill, knockout drop *or* Mickey Finn [both slang], dope [slang], drug, narcotic, opiate 687.12.

.4 VERBS (render insensible) **deaden, numb,** benumb, blunt, dull, obtund, **desensitize;** paralyze, palsy; **anesthetize, put to sleep,** slip one a Mickey *or* Mickey Finn

[slang], chloroform, etherize; narcotize, drug, dope [slang]; freeze, **stupefy, stun,** bedaze, besot; knock unconscious, knock senseless, **knock out, KO** *or* kayo [both slang], lay out, coldcock [both slang], knock stiff.

.5 **faint, swoon,** drop, succumb, keel over [informal], fall in a faint, fall senseless, **pass out** [informal], **black out,** go out like a light; gray out.

.6 ADJS **insensible, unfeeling, insensitive,** insentient, insensate, impassible; **unperceptive,** imperceptive, impercipient, thick-skinned, thick-witted, **dull,** obtuse, obdurate; **numb,** numbed, benumbed, dead, **deadened,** asleep, unfelt; callous 856.12.

.7 **stupefied, stunned,** dazed, bedazed.

.8 **unconscious, senseless, oblivious,** comatose, asleep, dead, **dead to the world,** cold, out, **out cold;** nirvanic; half-conscious, semiconscious; drugged, narcotized; doped, stoned, spaced out, strung out, zonked, zonked out, out of it [all slang]; catatonic, cataleptic.

.9 **deadening,** numbing, dulling; **anesthetic,** analgesic, narcotic; stupefying, stunning.

424. PAIN

(physical suffering)

.1 NOUNS **pain,** alg(o)–, –algy *or* –algia, noci–, –odynia, –pathy, –agra; **suffering, hurt,** hurting, misery [dial], **distress,** *Schmerz* [Ger], dolor [archaic]; **discomfort,** malaise; aches and pains.

.2 **pang,** throes; seizure, spasm, paroxysm; **twinge,** twitch, wrench, jumping pain; crick, kink, hitch, cramp *or* cramps; **nip,** thrill, pinch, tweak, bite, prick, **stab,** stitch, sharp *or* piercing *or* stabbing pain, acute pain, **shooting pain,** darting pain, fulgurant pain, lancinating pain, shooting, shoot; gnawing, gnawing *or* grinding *or* boring pain; griping, tormen [archaic]; girdle pain; stitch in the side; charley horse [informal].

.3 **smart,** smarting, **sting,** stinging, urtication, **tingle,** tingling; **burn,** burning, burning pain, fire.

.4 **soreness, irritation,** inflammation, tenderness, sensitiveness; algesia; rankling [archaic], festering; sore 686.35; sore spot 422.4.

.5 **ache,** aching, throbbing pain; **headache,** cephalalgia, misery in the head [dial]; splitting headache, **sick headache, migraine,** megrim, hemicrania; **backache, earache,** otalgia; **toothache,** odontalgia;

stomachache, tummyache [informal], bellyache *or* gut-ache [slang]; **colic,** collywobbles, gripes, gripe, gnawing, gnawing of the bowels, fret [dial]; **heartburn,** pyrosis; **angina.**

.6 **agony, anguish, torment, torture,** rack, excruciation, crucifixion, martyrdom, martyrization, excruciating *or* agonizing *or* atrocious pain.

.7 VERBS **pain,** give *or* inflict pain, **hurt, wound, afflict, distress,** ail; **burn;** sting; nip, bite, tweak, pinch; pierce, prick, stab, cut, lacerate; **irritate, inflame;** chafe, gall, fret, rasp, rub, grate; gnaw, grind; gripe; fester, rankle [archaic]; **torture, torment,** rack, put to torture, put *or* lay on the rack, **agonize, harrow,** crucify, martyr, martyrize, excruciate, wring, twist, convulse; prolong the agony, kill by inches.

.8 **suffer, feel pain,** feel the pangs, anguish 866.19; **hurt, ache,** have a misery [dial], ail; **smart, tingle;** throb, pound; shoot; twinge, thrill, twitch; **wince,** blench *or* blanch, shrink, make a wry face, grimace; **agonize,** writhe.

.9 ADJS **pained,** in pain, **hurt,** hurting, **suffering,** afflicted, wounded, distressed, in distress; **tortured, tormented, racked, agonized, harrowed,** lacerated, crucified, martyred, martyrized, wrung, twisted, convulsed; on the rack, under the harrow.

.10 **painful,** –pathic; hurtful, **hurting,** distressing, afflictive; **acute, sharp,** piercing, stabbing, shooting, stinging, biting, gnawing; **poignant,** pungent, **severe,** cruel, harsh, grave, hard; griping, cramping, spasmic, spasmatic, spasmodic, paroxysmal; **agonizing, excruciating,** atrocious, torturous, tormenting, racking, **harrowing.**

.11 **sore, raw;** smarting, tingling, **burning; irritated, inflamed, tender,** sensitive, fiery, angry, red; algetic; chafed, galled; **festering,** rankling [archaic].

.12 **aching,** achy, **throbbing;** headachy, migrainous, backachy, toothachy, stomachachy, colicky, griping.

.13 **irritating,** irritative, irritant; **chafing, galling,** fretting, rasping, grating, grinding, stinging, scratchy.

425. TOUCH

.1 NOUNS **touch,** thigmo–; sense of touch, tactile sense, cutaneous sense; taction, **contact** 200.5; **feel,** feeling; hand-mindedness; light touch, lambency, whisper, breath, **kiss, caress;** lick, lap; **brush,** graze,

glance; stroke, rub; tap, flick 283.6; fingertip caress, tentative poke.

.2 **touching, feeling, fingering,** palpation; **handling,** manipulation; petting, caressing, stroking, rubbing, frottage, friction 350; pressure 283.2.

.3 **touchableness, tangibility, palpability,** tactility.

.4 **feeler,** tactile organ, tactor; tactile cell; tactile process, tactile corpuscle, **antenna;** tactile hair, vibrissa; cat whisker; barbel, barbule; palp, palpus.

.5 **finger, digit,** digiti–, dactyl(o)–; forefinger, index finger, index; ring finger, annulary; middle finger, medius, dactylion; little finger, pinkie [informal], minimus; thumb, pollex.

.6 VERBS **touch, feel,** feel of, palpate; **finger,** pass *or* run the fingers over, feel with the fingertips, thumb; **handle, palm, paw; manipulate,** wield, ply; twiddle; poke at, prod 283.11; tap, flick 283.15; come in contact 200.10.

.7 **touch lightly,** touch upon; kiss, **brush,** sweep, graze, brush by, glance, scrape, skim.

.8 **stroke, pet, caress,** fondle; **nuzzle,** nose, rub noses; feel up [slang]; rub, rub against, massage, knead 350.6.

.9 **lick, lap,** tongue, mouth.

.10 ADJS **tactile,** tactual; hand-minded.

.11 **touchable, palpable, tangible,** tactile.

.12 **lightly touching,** lambent, playing lightly over, barely touching.

426. SENSATIONS OF TOUCH

.1 NOUNS **tingle,** tingling, thrill, buzz; **prickle,** prickles, prickling, pins and needles; **sting,** stinging, urtication; paresthesia.

.2 **tickle,** tickling, **titillation,** pleasant stimulation, **ticklishness,** tickliness.

.3 **itch, itching,** itchiness, psor(o)–, yeuk [Scot]; pruritus.

.4 **creeps** *or* **cold creeps** *or* shivers *or* **cold shivers** [all informal], creeping of the flesh; **gooseflesh, goose bumps,** goose pimples; formication.

.5 VERBS **tingle,** thrill; **itch;** scratch; **prickle,** prick, sting.

.6 **tickle, titillate.**

.7 **feel creepy,** feel funny, creep, crawl, **have the creeps** *or* **cold creeps** [informal]; have gooseflesh *or* goose bumps.

.8 ADJS **tingly,** tingling, atingle; **prickly,** prickling.

.9 **ticklish,** tickling, tickly, **titillative.**

.10 **itchy,** itching.

.11 creepy, crawly, formicative.

427. TASTE

(sense of taste)

.1 NOUNS **taste**, gust [archaic], *goût* [Fr]; **flavor**, sapor; **smack, tang; savor, relish,** sapidity; palate, tongue, tooth, stomach; taste in the mouth; sweet, sour, bitter, salt; aftertaste; savoriness 428.

.2 **sip, sup, lick, bite.**

.3 tinge, hint 35.4.

.4 **sample, specimen, taste,** taster, little bite, little smack; example 25.2.

.5 taste bud *or* bulb *or* goblet, taste *or* gustatory cell, taste hair; **tongue,** lingua, lingu(o)– *or* lingui–, gloss(o)–; **palate,** palat(o)–, staphyl(o)–, uran(o)–.

.6 **tasting, savoring,** gustation.

.7 VERBS **taste, sample; savor;** sip, sup [dial], roll on the tongue; smack, taste of.

.8 ADJS **gustatory,** gustative; tastable, gustable [archaic].

.9 **flavored,** flavorous, flavory, sapid, saporous, saporific; savory, flavorful 428.8,9.

.10 **lingual,** glossal; tonguelike, linguiform, lingulate.

428. SAVORINESS

.1 NOUNS **savoriness, palatableness,** palatability, **tastiness,** toothsomeness, goodness, good taste, right taste, **deliciousness,** gustatory delightfulness, scrumptiousness *or* yumminess [both informal], lusciousness, delectability, **flavorfulness,** flavorsomeness, flavorousness, flavoriness, good flavor, fine flavor, sapidity; full flavor, full-bodied flavor; gourmet quality.

.2 **savor, relish, zest, gusto,** *goût* [Fr].

.3 **flavoring, flavor,** flavorer; **seasoning,** seasoner, **relish, condiment, spice,** condiments 308.55.

.4 VERBS **taste good,** tickle *or* flatter *or* delight the palate, tempt *or* whet the appetite, make the mouth water.

.5 **savor, relish,** like, love, be fond of, be partial to, enjoy, delight in, appreciate; smack the lips; taste 427.7.

.6 **savor of, taste of, smack of,** have a relish of, have the flavor of, taste like.

.7 **flavor, savor; season,** salt, pepper, **spice,** sauce.

.8 ADJS **tasty,** good-tasting, **savory,** savorous, **palatable, toothsome,** gusty [Scot], gustable [archaic], sapid, **good,** good to eat, nice, agreeable, likable, pleasing, to one's taste, **delicious,** delightful, delectable, exquisite; delicate, dainty; juicy, succulent,

luscious, lush; ambrosial, nectarous, nectareous; fit for a king, fit for a gourmet, of gourmet quality; scrumptious *or* yummy [both informal].

.9 **flavorful, flavorsome,** flavorous, flavory, well-flavored; full-flavored, full-bodied; nutty, fruity; **rich,** rich-flavored.

.10 **appetizing, mouth-watering, tempting,** tantalizing, provocative, piquant.

429. UNSAVORINESS

.1 NOUNS **unsavoriness, unpalatableness,** unpalatability, **distastefulness.**

.2 **acridness,** acridity, tartness, sharpness, causticity, astringence *or* astringency, acerbity, **sourness** 432; pungency 433; **bitterness,** –picrin; gall, gall and wormwood, wormwood, bitter pill.

.3 **nastiness, foulness, vileness, loathsomeness, repulsiveness, obnoxiousness,** odiousness, offensiveness, disgustingness, nauseousness; **rankness,** rancidity, rancidness, overripeness, rottenness, fetidness; repugnance 867.2; nauseant, emetic, sickener.

.4 VERBS **disgust, repel,** turn one's stomach, nauseate.

.5 ADJS **unsavory, unpalatable, unappetizing,** untasty, ill-flavored, foul-tasting, **distasteful,** dislikable, unlikable, uninviting, unpleasant, unpleasing, displeasing, disagreeable.

.6 **bitter,** picr(o)–, bitter as gall, amaroidal; **acrid,** sharp, caustic, tart, astringent; hard, harsh, rough, coarse; acerb, acerbic, sour 432.6; pungent 433.7.

.7 **nasty, offensive** 864.18, fulsome, noisome, noxious, rebarbative, mawkish, cloying, brackish, **foul, vile,** bad; icky [informal], yucky [slang], **sickening, nauseating,** nauseous, nauseant, vomity *or* barfy [both slang]; poisonous 864.7, rank, rancid, maggoty, weevily, spoiled, overripe, high, rotten, stinking, fetid.

.8 **inedible, uneatable,** not fit to eat *or* drink, undrinkable, impotable; unfit for human consumption.

430. INSIPIDNESS

.1 NOUNS **insipidness,** insipidity, **tastelessness, flavorlessness,** savorlessness, saplessness, unsavoriness; **weakness, thinness,** mildness, **wishy-washiness;** flatness, staleness, lifelessness, deadness; vapidity, inanity, jejunity, jejuneness.

.2 ADJS **insipid, tasteless, flavorless,** spiceless, **savorless,** sapless, unsavory, unflavored; pulpy, pappy, gruelly; **weak, thin, mild,**

wishy-washy, washy, watery, watered, watered-down, diluted, dilute, milk-and-water; **flat, stale,** dead, *fade* [Fr]; vapid, inane, jejune; indifferent, neither one thing nor the other.

431. SWEETNESS

.1 NOUNS **sweetness,** sweet, sweetishness, saccharinity, dulcitude [archaic]; **sugariness,** syrupiness; oversweetness, mawkishness, cloyingness, sickly-sweetness.

.2 **sweetening,** edulcoration [archaic]; sweetener; sugar 309.5,22; artificial sweetener, saccharin, cyclamates, sodium cyclamate, calcium cyclamate; molasses, blackstrap, treacle [Brit]; syrup, maple syrup, cane syrup, corn syrup, sorghum; **honey,** meli- *or* melli-, honeycomb, honeypot, comb honey, clover honey; honeydew; **nectar, ambrosia;** sugarcoating; sweets 308.39; sugar-making; sugaring off; saccharification.

.3 VERBS **sweeten,** dulcify, edulcorate *or* dulcorate [both archaic]; **sugar,** honey; sugarcoat, glaze, candy; mull; saccharify; sugar off.

.4 ADJS **sweet,** sweetish, sweetened; sacchar(o)- *or* sacchari-, sacchariferous; **sugary,** sugared, candied, **honeyed,** syrupy; mellifluous, mellifluent [archaic]; melliferous, nectarous, nectareous, ambrosial; sugarsweet, honeysweet, sweet as sugar *or* honey, sweet as a nut; sugarcoated; bittersweet; sour-sweet, sweetsour, sweet and sour, sweet and pungent.

.5 **oversweet,** saccharine, rich, **cloying,** mawkish, luscious [archaic], sickly-sweet.

432. SOURNESS

.1 NOUNS **sourness,** sour, sourishness, **tartness,** tartishness, acerbity, verjuice; acescency; acidity, acidulousness; hyperacidity, subacidity; vinegarishness, vinegariness; unsweetness, **dryness; pungency** 433; greenness, unripeness.

.2 **sour; vinegar,** acidulant; **pickle,** sour pickle, dill pickle, bread-and-butter pickle; verjuice; lemon, lime, crab apple, green apple, chokecherry; sour grapes; sour balls; sourdough; sour cream, yogurt; **acid** 379.1,12.

.3 **souring,** acidification, acidulation, acetification, acescence; fermentation.

.4 VERBS **sour,** turn sour *or* acid, **acidify,** acidulate, acetify; ferment; set the teeth on edge.

.5 ADJS **sour,** soured, sourish; **tart,** tartish; crab, **crabbed;** acerb, acerbic, acerbate;

acescent; **vinegarish,** vinegary, sour as vinegar; pickled; **pungent** 433.6; unsweet, unsweetened, **dry,** sec; green, unripe.

.6 **acid,** acidulous, acidulent, acidulated; acetic, acetous, acetose; hyperacid; subacid, subacidulous.

433. PUNGENCY

.1 NOUNS **pungency,** piquancy, poignancy; **sharpness, keenness,** edge, **causticity,** astringency, mordancy, severity, asperity, trenchancy, cuttingness, bitingness, harshness, roughness, **acridity; bitterness** 429.2; acerbity, acidulousness, acidity, **sourness** 432.

.2 **zest,** zestfulness, zestiness, **briskness,** liveliness, raciness; **nippiness, tanginess,** snappiness; **spiciness,** pepperiness, hotness, fieriness; **tang, spice,** relish; **nip, bite;** punch, snap, zip, ginger; **kick,** guts [slang].

.3 **strength,** strongness; high flavor, highness, rankness, gaminess.

.4 **saltiness, salinity,** brininess; brackishness; **salt,** sali-, salin(o)- *or* salini-; **brine.**

.5 VERBS **bite, nip,** bite the tongue, sting, make the eyes water, go up the nose.

.6 ADJS **pungent, piquant, poignant; sharp, keen,** piercing, penetrating, nose-tickling, stinging, **biting, acrid,** astringent, irritating, harsh, rough, severe, asperous, cutting, trenchant; **caustic,** vitriolic, mordant, escharotic; **bitter** 429.6; acerbic, acid, **sour** 432.6.

.7 **zestful,** zesty, **brisk,** lively, racy, zippy, **nippy,** snappy, **tangy,** with a kick; spiced, seasoned, high-seasoned; **spicy,** curried, **peppery,** hot, burning, hot as pepper.

.8 **strong,** strong-flavored, strong-tasting; **high,** high-flavored, high-tasted; **rank,** gamy.

.9 **salty,** salt, salted, saltish, **saline, briny;** brackish; pickled.

434. TOBACCO

.1 NOUNS **tobacco,** *tabac* [Fr], nicotia *or* nicotian [both archaic], nicotin(o)-; **the weed** [informal], fragrant weed, Indian weed *or* drug, filthy weed, sot-weed [archaic], "pernicious weed" [Cowper], "thou weed, who art so lovely fair and smell'st so sweet" [Shakespeare], "sublime tobacco" [Byron], "divine tobacco" [Spenser]; carcinogenic substance.

.2 (tobaccos) flue-cured *or* bright, firecured, air-cured; Broadleaf, Burley, Cuban, Havana, Havana seed, Latakia, Turkish, Russian, Maryland, Virginia;

plug tobacco, bird's-eye, canaster, leaf, lugs, seconds, shag.

.3 **smoking tobacco,** smokings [dial], smoke *or* smokes [both informal].

.4 **cigar,** seegar [dial]; rope *or* stinker [both slang]; **cheroot, stogie,** corona, belvedere, Havana, colorado, trichinopoly; cigarillo; box of cigars, cigar box, cigar case, humidor; cigar cutter.

.5 **cigarette;** butt *or* cig *or* fag *or* coffin nail *or* cancer stick [all slang]; cigarette butt, **butt,** stub; snipe [slang]; pack *or* deck of cigarettes, box *or* carton of cigarettes, cigarette case.

.6 **pipe,** tobacco pipe; corncob, corncob pipe, Missouri meerschaum; briar pipe, briar; clay pipe, clay, churchwarden [Brit]; meerschaum; water pipe, hookah, nargileh, calean, hubble-bubble; peace pipe, calumet; pipe rack, pipe cleaner, tobacco pouch.

.7 **chewing tobacco,** eating tobacco [dial]; navy *or* navy plug, cavendish, twist, pigtail, cut plug; **quid,** cud, fid [Brit dial], chew, chaw [dial]; tobacco juice.

.8 **snuff,** snoose [slang]; rappee; pinch of snuff; snuff bottle, snuffbox, snuff mill [Scot].

.9 **nicotine,** nicotia [archaic].

.10 **smoking,** smoking habit, habitual smoking; chain-smoke; smoke, puff, drag [slang]; **chewing;** tobacco *or* nicotine addiction, tobaccoism, tabacosis, tabacism, tabagism, nicotinism.

.11 **tobacco user, smoker,** cigarette *or* pipe *or* cigar smoker, chewer, snuffer, snuff dipper.

.12 **tobacconist;** snuffman; tobacco store *or* shop, cigar store.

.13 **smoking room,** smoking car, **smoker.**

.14 VERBS (use tobacco) **smoke;** inhale, puff, draw, drag [informal], pull; smoke like a furnace *or* chimney; chain-smoke; **chew,** chaw [dial]; **take snuff,** dip *or* inhale snuff.

.15 ADJS **tobacco,** tobaccoy, tobaccolike; **nicotinic;** smoking, chewing; snuffy.

435. ODOR

.1 NOUNS **odor, smell, scent,** aroma, flavor [archaic], savor, osm(o)–; **essence,** definite odor, redolence, effluvium, emanation, exhalation, fume, breath, subtle odor, whiff, trace, detectable odor; trail, spoor; fragrance 436; stench 437.

.2 **odorousness, smelliness,** headiness, pungency 433.

.3 **smelling,** olfaction, nosing, scenting;

sniffing, snuffing, snuffling, whiffing, odorizing, odorization.

.4 **sense of smell,** smell, smelling, scent, olfaction, olfactory sense, –osphresia *or* –osphrasia.

.5 **olfactory organ;** olfactory pit, olfactory cell, olfactory area, **nose** 256.7; **nostrils,** noseholes [dial], nares; olfactory nerves; **olfactories.**

.6 VERBS (have an odor) **smell,** be aromatic, smell of, be redolent of; emit *or* emanate *or* give out a smell, reach one's nostrils, yield an odor *or* aroma, breathe, exhale; reek, **stink** 437.4.

.7 **odorize;** scent, perfume 436.8.

.8 **smell, scent, nose; sniff,** snuff, snuffle, inhale, breathe, breathe in; get a noseful of, smell of, catch a smell of, get *or* take a whiff of, whiff.

.9 ADJS **odorous,** odoriferous, odored, odorant, **smelling,** smellful [Austral], smellsome, **smelly,** redolent, aromatic; effluvious; **fragrant** 436.9; **malodorous** 437.5.

.10 **strong,** strong-smelling, strong-scented; **pungent,** penetrating, nose-piercing, sharp; reeking, suffocating.

.11 **smellable,** sniffable, whiffable.

.12 **olfactory,** olfactive.

.13 **keen-scented,** quick-scented, sharp- *or* keen-nosed, **with a nose for.**

436. FRAGRANCE

.1 NOUNS **fragrance,** fragrancy [archaic], **perfume, aroma,** scent, redolence, balminess, **incense, bouquet,** nosegay [archaic], sweet smell, sweet savor; **odor** 435; spice, spiciness; muskiness; fruitiness.

.2 **perfumery,** *parfumerie* [Fr]; **perfume,** *parfum* [Fr], **scent, essence,** extract; aromatic, ambrosia; attar, essential *or* volatile oil; aromatic water; balsam, **balm,** aromatic gum; balm of Gilead, balsam of Mecca; myrrh; bay oil, myrcia oil; champaca oil; rose oil, attar of roses, "the perfumed tincture of the roses" [Shakespeare]; lavender oil, heliotrope, jasmine oil, bergamot oil; fixative, musk, civet, ambergris.

.3 **toilet water,** Florida water; rose water, *eau de rose* [Fr]; lavender water, *eau de lavande* [Fr]; *eau de jasmin* [Fr]; cologne, cologne water, eau de Cologne; bay rum; **lotion,** after-shave lotion.

.4 **incense;** joss stick; pastille; frankincense *or* olibanum; agalloch *or* aloeswood, calambac, lignaloes *or* linaloa, sandalwood.

.5 **perfumer,** *parfumeur* [Fr]; thurifer, censer bearer; **perfuming,** censing, thurification, odorizing.

.6 (articles) perfumer, *parfumoir* [Fr], fumigator, scenter, odorator, odorizer; atomizer, purse atomizer, spray; censer, thurible, incensory, incense burner; vinaigrette, scent bottle, smelling bottle, scent box, scent ball; scent bag, sachet; pomander, pouncet-box [archaic]; potpourri.

.7 VERBS **be fragrant,** smell sweet, **smell good,** please the nostrils.

.8 **perfume, scent,** cense, incense, thurify, aromatize, odorize, fumigate, embalm.

.9 ADJS **fragrant, aromatic,** odoriferous, redolent, perfumy, **perfumed, scented,** odorate *or* essenced [both archaic], **sweet, sweet-smelling,** sweet-scented, savory, balmy, ambrosial, incense-breathing; thuriferous; **odorous** 435.9; sweet as a rose, fragrant as new-mown hay; flowery; fruity; musky; spicy.

437. STENCH

.1 NOUNS **stench, stink,** malodor, fetidness, fetidity, fetor, foul odor, offensive odor, offense to the nostrils, bad smell, rotten smell, noxious stench, "the rankest compound of villainous smell that ever offended nostril" [Shakespeare], frowst [Brit], smell *or* stench of decay, **reek,** reeking, nidor; mephitis, miasma, graveolence [archaic]; body odor, BO; halitosis, **bad breath,** foul breath.

.2 **fetidness,** fetidity, malodorousness, **smelliness,** stinkingness, **odorousness,** noisomeness, **rankness, foulness,** putridness, offensiveness; repulsiveness; **mustiness,** funkiness, must, frowst [Brit], moldiness, mildew, fustiness, frowiness [dial], frowziness, frowstiness [Brit], stuffiness; **rancidness,** rancidity, reastiness [Brit dial]; rottenness 692.7.

.3 **stinker,** stinkard; skunk *or* polecat *or* rotten egg; stink ball, stinkpot, stink bomb.

.4 VERBS **stink,** smell, **smell bad,** assail *or* offend the nostrils, stink in the nostrils, smell to heaven *or* high heaven, **reek;** smell up, stink up; stink out.

.5 ADJS **malodorous, fetid,** olid, **odorous, stinking, reeking,** reeky, nidorous, smelling, bad-smelling, ill-smelling, heavy-smelling, **smelly,** smellful [Austral], stenchy; **foul,** vile, putrid, bad, fulsome, noisome, fecal, offensive, repulsive, noxious, sulfurous, graveolent [archaic]; rotten 692.41; **rank,** strong, high, gamy; **rancid, reasty** *or* **reasy** [both Brit dial], reechy [archaic]; **musty,** funky, fusty,

frowy [dial], frowzy, frowsty [Brit], stuffy, moldy, mildewed, mildewy; mephitic, miasmic, miasmal.

438. ODORLESSNESS

.1 NOUNS **odorlessness, inodorousness,** scentlessness, smell-lessness.

.2 **deodorizing,** deodorization, fumigation, ventilation 402.9.

.3 **deodorant,** deodorizer; fumigant, fumigator.

.4 VERBS **deodorize,** fumigate; ventilate 402.11, freshen the air.

.5 ADJS **odorless,** inodorous, nonodorous, smell-less, **scentless,** unscented.

.6 **deodorant,** deodorizing.

439. VISION

.1 NOUNS **vision,** seeing, opto–, –opsia *or* –opsy, –opsis; **sight, eyesight,** sightedness, –opy *or* –opia; eye, power of sight, sense of sight, visual sense; **perception,** discernment; perspicacity, perspicuity, sharp *or* acute *or* keen sight, visual acuity, quick sight; farsight, farsightedness; clear sight, unobstructed vision; rod vision, scotopia; cone vision, photopia; color vision, twilight vision, daylight vision, day vision, night vision; eye-mindedness; **field of vision,** visual field, scope, ken, purview, horizon, sweep, range; peripheral vision, peripheral field; field of view 444.3.

.2 **observation,** observance; **looking, watching, viewing,** –scopy; witnessing, espial; **notice,** note, respect, **regard;** watch, lookout; spying, espionage.

.3 **look, sight,** looksee [informal], dekko [Brit informal], eye, view, regard, eyeful [informal]; sidelong look; leer, leering look, lustful leer; sly look; look-in; preview; scene, prospect 446.6.

.4 **glance,** glance of the eye, squiz [Austral], slant [informal], rapid glance, cast, sideglance; **glimpse,** flash, quick sight; **peek, peep;** wink, blink, flicker *or* twinkle of an eye; causal glance, **half an eye;** *coup d'œil* [Fr].

.5 **gaze, stare,** gape, goggle; sharp *or* piercing *or* penetrating look; **ogle,** glad eye, come-hither look [informal], bedroom eyes [slang]; **glare, glower,** glaring *or* glowering look; evil eye, *malocchio* [Ital], whammy [slang].

.6 **scrutiny,** overview, **survey,** contemplation, the eye [slang]; examination, visual examination, vetting [Brit informal], ocular inspection, eyeball inspection [informal], **inspection** 485.3.

.7 **viewpoint, standpoint, point of view,** vantage, vantage point, point or coign of vantage; where one stands; **outlook,** angle, angle of vision; mental outlook 525.2.

.8 observation post or point; **observatory; lookout,** outlook, overlook; **watchtower,** tower; Texas tower; beacon, lighthouse, pharos; gazebo, belvedere; bridge, conning tower, crow's nest; peephole, sighthole, loophole; **ringside,** ringside seat; **grandstand,** bleachers; **gallery,** top gallery; paradise or peanut gallery [informal].

.9 **eye,** visual organ, organ of vision, oculus, optic, **orb,** ocul(o)–, ophthalm(o)–, **peeper** [informal], baby blues [informal]; clear eyes, bright eyes, starry orbs; saucer eyes, banjo eyes [slang], popeyes, goggle eyes; **naked eye,** unassisted or unaided eye; corner of the eye; eyeball; retina, retin(o)–; lens, phak(o)–; cornea, corne(o)–; sclera, scler(o)–; optic nerve, iris, irid(o)–; pupil; eyelid, lid, blephar(o)–, nictitating membrane.

.10 **sharp eye,** keen eye, piercing or penetrating eye, gimlet eye, X-ray eye; **eagle eye;** peeled eye [informal], watchful eye; **weather eye.**

.11 (comparisons) eagle, hawk, cat, lynx, ferret, weasel; Argus.

.12 VERBS **see, behold, observe, view, witness, perceive, discern, spy,** espy, **sight,** have in sight, make out, pick out, descry, spot [informal], twig [Brit informal], discover, notice, distinguish, recognize, ken [dial], **catch sight of,** get a load of [slang], take in, get an eyeful of [informal], look on or upon, cast the eyes on or upon, **set** or **lay eyes on, clap eyes on** [informal]; **glimpse,** get or catch a glimpse of; see at a glance, see with half an eye; see with one's own eyes.

.13 **look, peer,** direct the eyes, turn or bend the eyes, cast one's eye, lift up the eyes; **peek, peep,** pry, take a peep or peek; play peekaboo.

.14 **look at,** take a look at, eye, eyeball [informal], have a looksee [informal], look on or upon, gaze at or upon; **watch, observe, view, regard;** keep one's eyes peeled or skinned, be watchful or observant or vigilant, keep one's eyes open; keep in sight or view, hold in view; look after, keep under observation, spy upon, keep an eye on, follow; **reconnoiter,** scout, get the lay of the land.

.15 **scrutinize, survey, eye,** contemplate, look over, give the eye [slang], give the once-over [slang]; **ogle,** ogle at, **leer,** leer at,

give one the glad eye; examine, vet [Brit informal], **inspect** 485.23; **pore,** pore over, peruse; take a close or careful look; take a long, hard look; size up [informal]; take stock of.

.16 **gaze,** gloat [archaic], fix one's gaze, fix or fasten or rivet the eyes upon, keep the eyes upon; **eye, ogle; stare,** stare at, stare hard, look, goggle, **gape, gawk** [informal], gaup [dial], gaze open-mouthed; crane, crane the neck, stand on tiptoe; strain one's eyes; look straight in the eye, look full in the face, hold one's eye or gaze, stare down.

.17 **glare, glower,** look daggers, look black; give one the evil eye, give one a whammy [slang].

.18 **glance, glimpse,** glint, cast a glance, glance at or upon, give a coup d'œil, take a glance at, take a squint at [informal].

.19 **look askance** or askant, give a sidelong look; squint, look asquint; cock the eye; **look down one's nose** [informal].

.20 **look away,** look aside, **avert the eyes,** look another way, break one's eyes away, stop looking, turn away from, turn the back upon; drop one's eyes or gaze, cast one's eyes down; avoid one's gaze.

.21 ADJS **visual, seeing, ocular, eyeball** [informal], **optic(al);** ophthalmic; visible 444.6.

.22 **clear-sighted,** clear-eyed; **farsighted,** far-seeing, telescopic; **sharp-sighted,** keen-sighted, sharp-eyed, **eagle-eyed,** hawk-eyed, ferret-eyed, lynx-eyed, cat-eyed, Argus-eyed; **eye-minded.**

.23 ADVS **at sight,** as seen, visibly, at a glance; by sight, by eyeball [informal], visually; at first sight, **at the first blush,** prima facie [L].

440. DEFECTIVE VISION

.1 NOUNS faulty eyesight, bad eyesight, defect of vision or sight, imperfect vision, blurred vision, reduced sight, partial blindness; **astigmatism,** astigmia; nystagmus; albinism; double vision, double sight; tunnel vision; blindness 441.

.2 **dim-sightedness,** dull-sightedness, near-blindness, amblyopia, gravel-blindness, sand-blindness, **purblindness,** dim eyes, ambly(o)–; blurredness, blearedness, bleariness, redness, lippitude [archaic].

.3 **nearsightedness, myopia,** shortsightedness, short sight.

.4 **farsightedness,** hyperopia, longsightedness, long sight; presbyopia.

.5 **strabismus,** heterotropia, –tropia; cast, cast in the eye; **squint,** squinch [dial];

cross-eye, cross-eyedness; convergent strabismus, esotropia; upward strabismus, anoöpsia; walleye, exotropia.

.6 (defective eyes) cross-eyes, cockeyes, squint eyes, swivel eyes [slang], goggle eyes, walleyes, bug-eyes or popeyes [both slang], saucer eyes [slang].

.7 winking, blinking, fluttering the eyelids, nictitation; winker, blinkard [archaic].

.8 VERBS see badly or poorly, barely see, be half-blind; have a mote in the eye; see double.

.9 squint, squinch ˙[dial], squint the eye, look asquint, screw up the eyes, skew, goggle [archaic].

.10 wink, blink, nictitate, bat the eyes [informal].

.11 ADJS poor-sighted; astigmatic(al); nystagmic; nearsighted, shortsighted, myopic, mope-eyed [archaic]; farsighted, longsighted, presbyopic; squinting, squinty, asquint, squint-eyed, squinch-eyed [dial], strabismal, strabismic; winking, blinking, blinky, blink-eyed.

.12 cross-eyed, cockeyed, swivel-eyed [slang], goggle-eyed, bug-eyed or popeyed [both slang], walleyed, saucer-eyed, glare-eyed; one-eyed, monocular; moon-eyed.

.13 dim-sighted, dim, dull-sighted, dim-eyed, weak-eyed, feeble-eyed, mole-eyed; purblind, half-blind, gravel-blind, sand-blind; bleary-eyed, blear-eyed; filmy-eyed, film-eyed.

441. BLINDNESS

.1 NOUNS blindness, sightlessness, cecity, ablepsia, unseeingness, sightless eyes, lack of vision, eyelessness; stone-blindness, total blindness; darkness, "ever-during dark", "total eclipse without all hope of day" [both Milton], "the precious treasure of his eyesight lost" [Shakespeare]; economic blindness; partial blindness, reduced sight, blind side; blind spot; dim-sightedness 440.2; snow blindness, niphablepsia; amaurosis, gutta serena [L], drop serene; cataract; glaucoma; trachoma; mental or psychic blindness, mind-blindness, soul-blindness, benightedness, unenlightenment, spiritual blindness; blinding, making blind, depriving of sight, putting out the eyes, excecation [archaic]; blurring the eyes, blindfolding, hoodwinking.

.2 day blindness, hemeralopia; night blindness, nyctalopia; moon blindness, moon-blind.

.3 color blindness; dichromatism; monochromatism, achromatopsia; red blind-

ness, protanopia, green blindness, deuteranopia, red-green blindness, Daltonism; yellow blindness, xanthocyanopia; blue-yellow blindness, tritanopia; violet-blindness.

.4 the blind, the sightless, the unseeing; blind man; bat, mole; "blind leaders of the blind" [Bible].

.5 blindfold; eye patch; blinkers, blinds, blinders, rogue's badge.

.6 (aids for the blind) sensory aid, Braille, New York point, Gall's serrated type, Boston type, Howe's American type, Moon or Moon's type, Alston's Glasgow type, Lucas's type, sight-saver type, Frere's type; line letter, string alphabet, writing stamps; noctograph, writing frame, embosser, high-speed embosser; visagraph; talking book; optophone, Visotoner, Optacon; personal sonar, Pathsounder; ultrasonic spectacles; cane; Seeing Eye dog, guide dog.

.7 VERBS blind, blind the eyes, deprive of sight, strike blind, render or make blind, excecate [archaic]; darken, dim, obscure, eclipse; put one's eyes out, gouge; blindfold, hoodwink, bandage; throw dust in one's eyes, benight; dazzle, bedazzle, daze; glare; snow-blind.

.8 be blind, not see, walk in darkness, grope in the dark, feel one's way; go blind, lose one's sight or vision; be blind to, close or shut one's eyes to, wink or blink at, look the other way, blind oneself to, wear blinkers; have a blind spot or side.

.9 ADJS blind, sightless, ableptical, eyeless, visionless, unseeing, undiscerning, unobserving, unperceiving; in darkness, rayless, bereft of light, dark [dial], "dark, dark, dark, amid the blaze of noon" [Milton]; stone-blind, stark blind, blind as a bat, blind as a mole, blind as an owl; amaurotic; dim-sighted 440.13; hemeralopic; nyctalopic; color-blind; mind-blind, soul-blind, mentally or psychically or spiritually blind, benighted, unenlightened.

.10 blinded, excecate [archaic], darkened, obscured; blindfolded, blindfold, hoodwinked; dazzled, bedazzled, dazed; snow-blind, snow-blinded.

.11 blinding, obscuring; dazzling, bedazzling.

442. SPECTATOR

.1 NOUNS spectator, observer, –scopus; looker, onlooker, looker-on, watcher, gazer, gazer-on, gaper, goggler, viewer, seer, beholder, perceiver, percipient; spectatress, spectatrix; witness, eyewitness; bystander, passerby; sidewalk superintendent; kibitzer; girl-watcher, ogler, drugstore cowboy [informal]; bird-watcher; television-viewer, televiewer, video-gazer, TV-viewer.

.2 **attender** 186.5; theatergoer 611.32; audience 448.6.

.3 **sightseer**, excursionist, tourist, rubberneck *or* **rubbernecker** [both slang]; slummer.

.4 **sight-seeing**, rubbernecking [slang], lionism [Brit informal]; excursion, **rubberneck tour** [slang].

.5 VERBS spectate [informal], look on, eye, ogle, gape 439.16; take in, **look at, watch** 439.14; attend 186.8.

.6 **sight-see**, see the sights, take in the sights, lionize *or* see the lions [both Brit informal]; **rubberneck** [slang]; go slumming.

.7 ADJS spectating, spectatorial, –scopic; onlooking; sight-seeing, rubberneck [slang].

443. OPTICAL INSTRUMENTS

.1 NOUNS lens, glass, phak(o)– *or* phac(o)–; achromatic lens, astigmatic lens, coated lens; meniscus, concavo-convex lens, concave lens, convex lens, toric lens; telephoto lens; zoom lens, varifocal lens; eyepiece, eyeglass, ocular; objective, object glass; prism, objective prism; hand lens, magnifying glass, magnifier; reading glass, reader; condenser, bull's-eye, burning glass; camera 577.11,20.

.2 **spectacles, specs** [informal], **glasses, eyeglasses**, pair of glasses *or* spectacles, barnacles [Brit slang], cheaters *or* peepers [both slang]; reading glasses, readers; bifocals, divided spectacles, trifocals, pince-nez, nippers [informal]; lorgnette, *lorgnon* [Fr]; horn-rimmed glasses; harlequin glasses; granny glasses; mini-specs [informal]; colored glasses, sunglasses, sun-specs [informal], dark glasses, Polaroid glasses, shades [slang]; goggles, blinkers; eyeglass, monocle, quizzing glass; contact lens.

.3 **telescope**, scope, **spy glass**, terrestrial telescope, glass, **field glass; binoculars**, zoom binoculars, opera glasses.

.4 **sight**; sighthole; finder, viewfinder; panoramic sight; bombsight; peep sight, open sight, leaf sight.

.5 **mirror**, glass, **looking glass**, seeing glass [Brit dial], reflector, speculum; hand mirror, window mirror, rear-view mirror, cheval glass, pier glass, shaving mirror; steel mirror; convex mirror, concave mirror, distorting mirror.

.6 **optics**, optical physics; **optometry**; microscopy, microscopics, micro–; telescopy; stereoscopy; spectroscopy, spectrometry, spectro–; infrared spectroscopy; spectrophotometry; electron optics; **photography** 577.

.7 **oculist**, ophthalmologist, **optometrist**; microscopist, telescopist; optician.

.8 ADJS **optic(al)**, ophthalmic, ophthalmologic(al), optometrical, optico–, opto–.

.9 –**scopic**, microscopic, telescopic, etc.; stereoscopic, stereo–, three-dimensional, 3-D.

.10 **spectacled, bespectacled**, four-eyed [informal]; goggled; monocled.

.11 **optical instruments**

diffractometer	photometer
eriometer	photomultiplier
goniometer	prism
image orthicon	rangefinder
laser	stereopticon
microfilm viewer *or* reader	thaumatrope viewer
optometer	

.12 **scopes**

abdominoscope	pharyngoscope
amblyoscope	photoscope
bronchoscope	polariscope
chromatoscope	polemoscope
chromoscope	pseudoscope
cystoscope	radarscope
diaphanoscope	radioscope
epidiascope	retinoscope
gastroscope	sniperscope
kaleidoscope	snooperscope
ophthalmoscope	spectroscope
oscilloscope	stereoscope
periscope	stroboscope

.13 **microscopes**

binocular microscope	phase contrast microscope, phase microscope
blink microscope	
compound microscope	pinion focusing microscope
dark-field microscope	
dissecting microscope	polarizing microscope
electron microscope	power microscope
field ion microscope	projecting microscope
fluorescence microscope	simple *or* single microscope
gravure microscope	stereomicroscope, stereoscopic microscope
laboratory microscope	
metallurgical microscope	
	surface microscope
optical microscope	ultramicroscope
oxyhydrogen microscope	ultraviolet microscope
	X-ray microscope

.14 **telescopes**

astronomical telescope	guiding telescope
	inverting telescope
Cassegrainian telescope	mercurial telescope
	Newtonian telescope
double-image telescope	optical telescope
	panoramic telescope
elbow telescope	prism telescope
finder telescope	radio telescope

reflecting telescope
refracting telescope
Schmidt telescope
spotting scope
terrestrial telescope
tower telescope

twin telescope
vernier telescope
water telescope
zenith telescope,
zenith tube

.15 spectroscopes, spectrometers

analytical spectrometer
diffraction spectroscope
direct-reading spectrometer
direct-reading spectroscope
microspectrophotometer

microspectroscope
monochromator
ocular spectroscope
prism spectroscope
reversion spectroscope
spectrograph
spectrophotometer
spectroradiometer
star spectroscope

444. VISIBILITY

.1 NOUNS **visibility,** visibleness, perceptibility, discernibleness, observability, visuality, seeableness; exposure; manifestation; outcrop, outcropping; the visible, the seen, what is revealed, what can be seen; revelation, epiphany.

.2 **distinctness, plainness,** evidence [archaic], evidentness, obviousness, patentness, manifestness; **clearness, clarity,** crystal-clearness; **definiteness,** definition; percipi; prominence, conspicuousness, conspicuity; high or low visibility; atmospheric visibility, seeing, ceiling, ceiling unlimited, visibility unlimited, visibility zero.

.3 **field of view,** field of vision, range or scope of vision, **sight,** limit of vision, eyereach, **eyesight,** eyeshot, ken; **vista, view, horizon, prospect, perspective, outlook,** survey, –scape; range, scan, scope; line of sight, sightliness; naked eye; command, domination, outlook over.

.4 VERBS **show,** show up, show through, shine out or through, **appear** 446.8, **be visible,** be seen, be revealed, be evident, be noticeable, meet the gaze, impinge on the eye, present to the eye, meet or catch or hit or strike the eye; **stand out,** stand forth, loom large, glare, **stare one in the face,** hit one in the eye, **stick out like a sore thumb.**

.5 **be exposed,** be conspicuous, have high visibility, stick out, hang out [slang], crop out; live in a glass house.

.6 ADJS **visible,** visual, **perceptible,** perceivable, **discernible, seeable,** viewable, witnessable, beholdable, observable, detectable, noticeable, recognizable, to be seen, phaner(o)–; **in sight,** in view, in plain sight, in full view, present to the eyes, before one's eyes, under one's eyes, open, naked, outcropping, hanging out [slang],

exposed, showing, open or exposed to view; **evident,** in evidence, **manifest, apparent;** revealed, disclosed, unhidden, unconcealed, unclouded, undisguised.

.7 **distinct, plain, clear, obvious, evident, patent,** unmistakable, not to be mistaken, plain to be seen, for all to see, showing for all to see; **definite, defined, well-defined,** well-marked, well-resolved, in focus; **clear-cut,** clean-cut; crystal-clear, clear as crystal; as clear as day, as plain as a pikestaff [informal], as plain as the nose on one's face, under one's nose, as plain as plain can be; **conspicuous,** glaring, staring, **prominent,** pronounced, well-pronounced, in bold or strong or high relief.

.8 ADVS **visibly, perceptibly,** perceivably, discernibly, seeably, recognizably, observably, markedly, noticeably; **manifestly, apparently,** evidently; **distinctly, clearly,** with clarity or crystal clarity, **plainly,** obviously, patently, definitely, unmistakably; conspicuously, undisguisedly, unconcealedly, prominently, pronouncedly, glaringly, starkly, staringly.

445. INVISIBILITY

.1 NOUNS **invisibility,** imperceptibility, unperceivability, indiscernibility, unseeableness, viewlessness; nonappearance; disappearance 447; the invisible, the unseen; unsubstantiality 4, immateriality 377, secrecy 614, concealment 615.

.2 **inconspicuousness,** half-visibility, semivisibility, low profile; **indistinctness, unclearness,** unplainness, **faintness,** paleness, feebleness, weakness, **dimness,** bleariness, darkness, shadowiness, **vagueness,** vague appearance, indefiniteness, obscurity, uncertainty, indistinguishability; **blurriness,** blur, soft focus, defocus, **fuzziness, haziness,** mistiness, filminess, fogginess.

.3 VERBS be invisible or unseen, escape notice; lie hid 615.8, **blush unseen;** disappear 447.2.

.4 **blur, dim, pale,** soften, film, mist, fog; defocus, lose resolution or sharpness or distinctness, go soft at the edges.

.5 ADJS **invisible,** aphan(o)–; **imperceptible,** unperceivable, **indiscernible,** undiscernible, **unseeable,** viewless, unbeholdable, unapparent, insensible; **out of sight,** *à perte de vue* [Fr]; secret 614.11–16; **unseen,** sightless, unbeheld, unviewed, unwitnessed, unobserved, unnoticed, unperceived; behind the curtain or scenes; disguised, camouflaged, hidden, **concealed** 615.11–14; latent, unrealized, submerged.

.6 **inconspicuous**, half-visible, semivisible, low-profile; **indistinct, unclear**, unplain, **indefinite**, undefined, ill-defined, ill-marked, **faint**, pale, feeble, weak, **dim**, dark, **shadowy**, **vague**, obscure, indistinguishable, unrecognizable; half-seen, merely glimpsed; uncertain, confused, out of focus, **blurred, blurry**, bleared, bleary, blear, **fuzzy, hazy**, misty, filmy, foggy.

446. APPEARANCE

.1 NOUNS **appearance, appearing**, apparition, coming, forthcoming, coming-forth, coming into being, rising, rise, arising, **emergence**, issuance; **materialization** 376.7, **materializing**, occurrence, **manifestation**, realization, incarnation, revelation, epiphany, theophany, avatar; presentation, disclosure, exposure, opening, unfolding, unfoldment, showing, showing forth, rising of the curtain.

.2 **appearances**, exteriors, externals; **mere externals, façade**, ostent, show, **outward show**, display, front [informal], outward *or* external appearance, surface appearance, surface show, vain show, apparent character, public image; gaudiness, speciousness, meretriciousness, **superficiality**.

.3 **aspect**, look, view; feature, lineaments; **seeming, semblance, image**, imago, eidolon, likeness, simulacrum; effect, impression, total effect *or* impression; **form, shape**, figure, configuration, gestalt; **manner**, fashion, wise, guise, style; **respect, regard**, reference, light; **phase**, phasis, phaso–; **facet**, side, angle, viewpoint 439.7, slant [informal], twist [informal].

.4 **looks, features, lineaments**, traits, lines; **countenance**, face, visage, feature, favor, brow, physiognomy; cast of countenance, **cut of one's jib** [informal], facial appearance *or* expression, cast, turn; **air, mien**, demeanor, carriage, bearing, port, posture, stance, presence; guise, garb, complexion, color.

.5 (thing appearing) **apparition, appearance**, phenomenon; **vision, image, shape, form**, figure, presence; false image, mirage, phasm [archaic], **phantom** 1017.1; –phane.

.6 **view, scene, sight**; prospect, **outlook, lookout, vista, perspective; scenery**, scenic view; panorama, sweep; scape, **landscape**, seascape, riverscape, waterscape, airscape, skyscape, cloudscape, cityscape, townscape; bird's-eye view.

.7 **spectacle, sight**; exhibit, **exhibition**, exposition, **show, stage show** 611.4, **display, presentation**, representation; tableau, tableau vivant; panorama, diorama, cosmorama, myriorama, cyclorama, georama; **phantasmagoria**, shifting scene, light show; psychedelic show; **pageant**, pageantry; parade, pomp.

.8 VERBS **appear**, become visible, **make one's appearance**, make *or* put in an appearance, appear on the scene, appear to one's eyes, meet *or* catch *or* strike the eye, **come in sight** *or* view, show, show oneself, show one's face, **show up** [informal], **turn up**, come, **materialize** 376.8, present oneself, present oneself to view, **manifest oneself**, become manifest, **reveal oneself**, discover oneself, uncover oneself, declare oneself, expose *or* betray oneself; **come to light**, see the light, see the light of day; **emerge**, issue, issue forth, stream forth, come forth, come out, come forward, come to hand; enter 302.7, come upon the stage; **rise, arise**, rear its head; look forth, peer *or* peep out; crop out, outcrop; loom, heave in sight, appear on the horizon; fade in.

.9 **burst forth**, break forth, debouch, erupt, irrupt; **pop up, bob up** [informal], start up, spring up, burst upon the view; flare up, flash, gleam.

.10 **appear to be**, seem to be, **appear, seem**, look, feel, sound, look to be, appear to one's eyes, have *or* present the appearance of, give the feeling of, strike one as; **appear like, seem like, look like**, have *or* wear the look of, **sound like; have every appearance of**, have all the earmarks of, have all the features of, have every sign *or* indication of; assume the guise of, take the shape of, exhibit the form of.

.11 ADJS **apparent**, appearing, **seeming**, ostensible; outward, surface, superficial; **visible** 444.6.

.12 ADVS **apparently, seemingly, ostensibly, to all appearances**, to all seeming, as it seems, to the eye; on the face of it, *prima facie* [L]; on the surface, outwardly, superficially; at first sight *or* view, at the first blush.

447. DISAPPEARANCE

.1 NOUNS **disappearance**, disappearing, **vanishing**, vanishment; going, passing, departure; dissipation, dispersion; dissolution, dissolving, melting, evaporation, evanescence, dematerialization 377.5; fadeout, fading, fadeaway, blackout; wipe, wipe-off, erasure; eclipse, occultation, blocking; vanishing point; elimination 77.2; extinction 693.6.

.2 VERBS **disappear, vanish,** vanish from sight, do a vanishing act [slang], depart, fly, **flee** 631.10, go, be gone, **go away,** pass, pass out or away, pass out of sight, exit, leave the scene or stage, pass out of the picture, retire from sight, become lost to sight, be seen no more; **perish, die,** die out or away, fade, **fade out** or **away,** do a fade-out [slang]; sink, sink away, dissolve, melt, melt away, "melt, thaw, and dissolve itself" [Shakespeare], dematerialize 377.6, evaporate, evanesce, **vanish into thin air,** go up in smoke; disperse, dispel, dissipate; cease, cease to exist 2.5, **cease to be;** leave no trace, "leave not a rack behind" [Shakespeare]; waste, waste away, erode, be consumed, wear away, dwindle; undergo or suffer an eclipse; **hide** 615.8.

.3 ADJS **vanishing, disappearing,** passing, fleeting, fugitive, transient, flying, fading, dissolving, melting, evaporating, evanescent.

.4 **gone,** away, gone away, past and gone, extinct, missing, no more, lost, lost to sight or view, **out of sight;** nonexistent 2.7.

448. HEARING

.1 NOUNS **hearing,** audition, audio–, audit(o)–, –acousia or –acusia; sense of hearing, auditory or aural sense, ear; listening, heeding, attention, hushed attention, rapt attention, eager attention; auscultation, aural examination, examination by ear; audibility.

.2 **audition,** hearing, tryout [informal], **audience, interview,** conference; attention, favorable attention, ear; **listening,** listening in; **eavesdropping,** wiretapping, electronic surveillance, bugging [informal].

.3 **good hearing,** refined or acute sense of hearing, sensitive ear, nice or quick or sharp or correct ear; **an ear for;** musical ear, ear for music; ear-mindedness; bad ear, no ear, tin ear.

.4 **earshot,** earreach, **hearing,** range, auditory range, reach, carrying distance, **sound.**

.5 **listener,** hearer, auditor, audient, hearkener; **eavesdropper,** overhearer, little pitcher with big ears, snoop, listener-in [informal].

.6 **audience,** auditory [archaic], **house,** congregation; theater, gallery; orchestra, pit; groundling, spectator 442.

.7 **ear,** aur(i)–, oto–, lug [Scot], auditory apparatus; external ear, **outer ear;** auricle, pinna, auriculo–; cauliflower ear; concha, conch, shell; ear lobe, lobe, lobule; auditory canal, acoustic or auditory meatus; **middle ear,** tympanic cavity, tympanum; eardrum, drumhead, tympanic membrane; auditory ossicles; malleus, hammer, incus, anvil; stapes, stirrup; mastoid process; Eustachian or auditory tube; **inner ear;** round window, secondary eardrum; oval window; bony labyrinth, membraneous labyrinth; perilymph, endolymph; vestibule; semicircular canals; cochlea; basilar membrane, organ of Corti; auditory nerve.

.8 **hearing aid,** hard-of-hearing aid; electronic hearing aid, transistor hearing aid; vacuum-tube hearing aid; ear trumpet; amplifier, speaking trumpet, megaphone; stethoscope.

.9 (science of hearing) otology; otoscopy, auriscopy; otoneurology, otopathy, otography, otoplasty, otolaryngology, otorhinolaryngology; acoustic phonetics, phonetics 594.14; auriscope, otoscope; audiometer.

.10 otologist, ear specialist, otolaryngologist, otorhinolaryngologist, ear, nose, and throat specialist.

.11 VERBS **listen, hark, hearken, heed, hear, attend,** give attention, **give ear,** give or lend an ear, bend an ear; **listen to,** listen at [dial], attend to, give a hearing to, give audience to, sit in on; **listen in; eavesdrop,** wiretap, tap, intercept, bug [informal]; **keep one's ears open,** be all ears [informal], listen with both ears, strain one's ears; prick up the ears, cock the ears; hang on the lips of; hear out; auscultate, examine by ear.

.12 **hear,** catch, get [informal], take in; **overhear; hear of,** hear tell of [dial]; get an earful [slang]; have an ear for.

.13 be heard, **fall on the ear,** sound in the ear, catch or reach the ear, come to one's ear, register, make an impression, get across [informal]; **have one's ear,** reach, contact, get to; make oneself heard, get through to, gain a hearing, reach the ear of; ring in the ear; caress the ear; assault or split or assail the ear.

.14 ADJS **auditory,** audio, audile, **hearing, aural,** auricular, otic; audio-visual; audible 449.15; otological, otoscopic, otopathic, etc.; acoustic(al), phonic.

.15 **listening, attentive,** open-eared, **all ears** [informal].

.16 **eared,** auriculate; big-eared, cauliflower-eared, crop-eared, dog-eared, droop-eared, flap-eared, flop-eared, lop-eared, long-eared, mouse-eared, prick-eared; **sharp-eared;** tin-eared; ear-minded.

.17 INTERJS **hark!,** hark ye!, hear ye!, hearken!, hear!, oyez!, hear ye, hear ye!, list!, **listen!,** attend!, attention!, hist!, whisht!, psst!

.18 **phones**

autophone	Interphone
Dictaphone	kinetophone
earphone	magnetophone
electrophone	microphone
Geophone	optophone
headphone	radiophone
hydrophone	radiotelephone
idiophone	telephone 560.4–6,21

449. DEAFNESS

.1 NOUNS **deafness, hardness of hearing,** dull hearing, deaf ears, "ears more deaf than adders" [Shakespeare]; **stone-deafness;** nerve-deafness; mind deafness, word deafness; **tone deafness;** impaired hearing, hearing or auditory impairment; loss of hearing, hearing loss; **deaf-muteness,** deaf-mutism, surdimutism [archaic].

.2 **the deaf,** the hard-of-hearing; **deaf-mute,** surdo-mute [archaic], deaf-and-dumb person; lip reader.

.3 deaf-and-dumb alphabet, manual alphabet, finger alphabet; dactylology, sign language; lip reading, oral method.

.4 VERBS **be deaf;** have no ears, be earless; lose one's hearing, suffer hearing loss or impairment, go deaf; shut or stop or close one's ears, **turn a deaf ear;** fall on deaf ears.

.5 **deafen, stun,** split the ears or eardrums.

.6 ADJS **deaf, hard of hearing,** dull or thick of hearing, deaf-eared, dull-eared; surd [archaic]; deafened, stunned; **stone-deaf,** deaf as a stone, deaf as a door or a doorknob or doornail, **deaf as a post,** deaf as an adder, "like the deaf adder that stoppeth her ear" [Bible]; **unhearing;** earless; word-deaf; tone-deaf; half-deaf, quasi-deaf; **deaf and dumb,** deaf-mute.

450. SOUND

.1 NOUNS **sound, sonance,** acoustic(al) phenomenon; audio–, audito–, phon(o)–, –phone, –phonia or –phony, son(o)– or soni–; auditory phenomenon or stimulus, auditory effect; noise; ultrasound; sound wave, sound propagation; sound intensity, sound intensity level, amplitude, loudness 453; phone, speech sound 594.13.

.2 **tone, pitch, frequency,** audio frequency, AF; monotone, monotony, tonelessness; overtone, harmonic, partial, partial tone; fundamental tone, fundamental; intonation 594.7; ton(o)–.

.3 **timbre, tonality, tone quality,** tone color, color, coloring, clang color or tint, *Klangfarbe* [Ger].

.4 **sounding,** sonation, sonification.

.5 **acoustics, phonics,** radioacoustics; acoustical engineer, acoustician.

.6 **sonics;** subsonics; **supersonics,** ultrasonics; speed of sound 269.2; sound barrier, sonic barrier or wall; sonic boom.

.7 (sound unit) **decibel,** bel, phon.

.8 **loudspeaker, speaker;** dynamic speaker, electrodynamic speaker, excited-field speaker, moving-coil speaker, permanent magnet speaker, coaxial speaker, triaxial speaker, electromagnetic speaker, electrostatic speaker, capacitor speaker; high-fidelity speaker, full-fidelity speaker; **tweeter,** high-frequency speaker; **woofer,** low-frequency speaker; midrange speaker; monorange speaker; speaker unit, speaker system; crossover network; voice coil; cone, diaphragm; acoustical network; horn; **headphone, earphone,** headset.

.9 **microphone, mike** [informal]; radiomicrophone; **bug** [slang].

.10 **audio amplifier, amplifier; preamplifier,** preamp [informal].

.11 sound reproduction system, audio sound system; **high-fidelity** system, hi-fi [informal]; **record player, phonograph,** Gramophone, Victrola; **jukebox,** nickelodeon; radio-phonograph combination; monophonic or monaural system, **mono** [informal], stereophonic or binaural system, stereo [informal]; four-channel stereo system, discrete four-channel system, derived four-channel system, quadraphonic sound system; pickup or cartridge, magnetic pickup or cartridge, ceramic pickup or cartridge, crystal pickup, photoelectric pickup; stylus, needle; tone arm; turntable, transcription turntable, record changer, changer; **public-address system,** PA or PA system; sound truck; loudhailer, bullhorn; intercommunication system, **intercom** [informal], squawk box or bitch box [both informal]; **tape recorder,** tape deck; hi-fi fan [informal], audiophile.

.12 **record, phonograph record,** disc, wax; transcription, electrical transcription; recording, wire recording, tape recording; tape, tape cassette, cassette; tape cartridge, cartridge.

.13 **audio distortion, distortion;** scratching, shredding, hum, 60-cycle hum, rumble, hissing, howling, blurping, blooping, woomping, fluttering, flutter, wow, wowwows, squeals, whistles, birdies, motorboating; feedback; static 344.21.

.14 VERBS **sound,** make a sound *or* noise, give forth *or* emit a sound; noise; speak 594.20; resound.

.15 ADJS **sounding,** sonorous, soniferous; **sounded;** tonal; monotone, monotonic, toneless, droning.

.16 **audible,** hearable; **distinct, clear,** plain, definite, articulate; distinctive, contrastive; high-fidelity, hi-fi [informal].

.17 **acoustic**(al), phonic, **sonic;** subsonic, supersonic, ultrasonic, hypersonic; transonic *or* transsonic, faster than sound.

.18 ADVS **audibly, aloud,** out, **out loud;** distinctly, clearly, plainly.

.19 **microphones**

antinoise microphone	phone
capacitor microphone	moving-conductor
carbon microphone	microphone
cardioid microphone	noise-canceling micro-
ceramic microphone	phone
close-talking micro-	nondirectional micro-
phone	phone
combination micro-	omnidirectional
phone	microphone
condenser micro-	parabolic-reflector
phone	microphone
contact microphone	phase-shift micro-
crystal microphone	phone
double-button carbon	piezoelectric micro-
microphone	phone
dynamic microphone	pressure microphone
flame microphone	push-pull microphone
glow-discharge micro-	ribbon microphone
phone	shotgun microphone
gradient microphone	single-button carbon
hot-wire microphone	microphone
lapel microphone	standard microphone
lavaliere microphone	stereo microphone
line microphone	throat microphone
lip microphone	unidirectional micro-
magnetostriction	phone
microphone	variable-reluctance
mask microphone	microphone
moving-coil micro-	velocity microphone

451. SILENCE

.1 NOUNS silence, silentness, **soundlessness,** noiselessness, **stillness,** "lucid stillness" [T. S. Eliot], **quietness,** quietude, quiescence 268, **quiet, still,** peace, whisht [Scot & Ir], **hush,** mum; lull, rest; golden silence; deathlike silence, tomblike silence, solemn *or* awful silence, silence of the grave *or* tomb; hush *or* dead of night,

dead; tacitness, taciturnity; inaudibility; tranquillity.

.2 **muteness,** mutism, **dumbness,** voicelessness, tonguelessness; speechlessness, wordlessness; inarticulateness; anaudia, aphasia, aphonia; hysterical mutism; deafmuteness 449.1.

.3 **mute,** dummy; deaf-mute 449.2.

.4 **silencer, muffler,** muffle, **mute,** baffler, quietener, cushion; **damper,** damp; dampener; **soft pedal,** sordine, sourdine, *sordino* [Ital]; hushcloth, silence cloth; **gag, muzzle;** antiknock; **soundproofing,** acoustic tile, sound-absorbing material, soundproofing insulation.

.5 VERBS **be silent,** keep silent *or* silence, **keep still** *or* **quiet; keep one's mouth shut, shut up** [informal], **hold one's tongue,** keep one's tongue between one's teeth, put a bridle on one's tongue, seal one's lips, shut *or* close one's mouth, muzzle oneself, save one's breath [informal], **not breathe a word,** not let out a peep [informal], say nothing, not say 'boo' [informal], forswear speech *or* speaking, **keep mum, hold one's peace,** not let a word escape one, not utter a word; make no sign, keep to oneself, play dumb; not have a word to say, be mute, stand mute.

.6 [slang terms] keep one's trap *or* yap shut, button up, button one's lip, shut one's bazoo, dummy up, clam up, close up like a clam.

.7 **fall silent, hush,** quiet, quieten, quiesce, **quiet down,** pipe down [informal], check one's speech.

.8 **silence, put to silence, hush,** hush-hush, **shush, quiet,** quieten, **still; soft-pedal,** put on the soft pedal; squash, squelch [informal], stifle, choke, choke off, throttle, put the kibosh on [slang], put the lid on *or* shut down on [both informal], put the damper on [informal], **gag, muzzle,** muffle, stop one's mouth, cut one short; strike dumb *or* mute, dumbfound.

.9 **muffle, mute, dull, soften, deaden,** cushion, baffle, damp, **dampen,** deafen; subdue, stop, tone down, **soft-pedal,** put on the soft pedal.

.10 ADJS **silent, still,** stilly, **quiet,** quiescent 268.12, **hushed,** whist [Brit dial], **soundless,** noiseless; echoless; **inaudible,** subaudible, below the limen *or* threshold of hearing, unhearable; quiet as a mouse, mousy; silent as a post *or* stone, "noiseless as fear in a wide wilderness" [Keats], "silent as the shadows" [Coleridge], so quiet that one might hear a feather *or* pin drop; silent as the grave *or* tomb, still as death, "hush as death" [Shakespeare]; **unsounded, unvoiced,** unvocalized, unpronounced, unuttered, unarticulated.

.11 **tacit, wordless, unspoken,** unuttered, unexpressed, unsaid; **implicit** 546.7–9.

.12 **mute, mum, dumb,** voiceless, tongueless, **speechless,** wordless, breathless; inarticulate; **tongue-tied,** stricken dumb, dumbstruck, dumbstricken, dumbfounded; anaudic, aphasic, aphonic.

.13 ADVS **silently, in silence, quietly,** soundlessly, noiselessly; inaudibly.

.14 INTERJS **silence!, hush!, shush!, sh!,** sh-sh!, whist! *or* whish! [both Brit dial], whisht! [Scot & Ir], peace!, pax!, *tais toi!* [Fr], **be quiet!, be silent!,** be still!, **keep still!,** keep quiet!, quiet!, quiet please!, soft!, belay that! *or* there!, stow it!; **hold your tongue!,** hold your jaw! *or* lip!, **shut up!** [informal], **shut your mouth!** [informal], save your breath!, not another word!, not another peep out of you!, mum!, mum's the word!; hush your mouth!, shut your trap!, shut your face!, button your lip!, pipe down!, clam up!, dry up!, can it! [all slang].

452. FAINTNESS OF SOUND

.1 NOUNS **faintness, lowness, softness,** gentleness, subduedness, dimness, feebleness, weakness; indistinctness, unclearness, flatness; subaudibility; decrescendo.

.2 muffled tone, veiled voice, *voce velata* [Ital]; **mutedness; dullness, deadness,** flatness.

.3 **thud,** dull thud; **thump,** flump, crump [Brit informal], clop, clump, clunk, plunk, tunk, plump, bump; pad, pat; **patter,** pitter-patter, pitapat; **tap,** rap, **click,** tick, flick, pop; tinkle, clink, chink.

.4 **murmur,** murmuring, murmuration; **mutter,** muttering; **mumble,** mumbling; soft voice, low voice, small *or* little voice, "still small voice" [Bible]; **undertone,** underbreath, bated breath; susurration, susurrus; **whisper,** whispering, stage whisper, breathy voice; breath, sigh, exhalation, aspiration.

.5 **ripple, splash,** ripple of laughter, ripple of applause.

.6 **rustle,** rustling, froufrou, "a little noiseless noise among the leaves" [Keats].

.7 **hum, humming,** thrumming, low rumbling, booming, bombilation, bombination, **droning, buzzing,** whizzing, whirring, purring.

.8 **sigh, sighing, moaning,** sobbing, whining, soughing.

.9 VERBS **steal** *or* **waft on the ear,** melt in the air, float in the air.

.10 **murmur, mutter, mumble,** mussitate [archaic], maffle [Brit dial]; coo; susurrate; **whisper,** whisper in the ear; breathe, sigh, aspirate.

.11 **ripple, babble, burble, bubble, gurgle,** guggle, **purl, trill;** lap, plash, **splash,** swish, swash, slosh, wash.

.12 **rustle,** crinkle; **swish,** whish.

.13 **hum,** thrum, bum [Brit dial], boom, bombilate, bombinate, **drone, buzz,** whiz, whir, burr, birr [Scot], purr.

.14 **sigh, moan, sob, whine,** keen, wail, sough.

.15 **thud, thump, patter,** clop, clump, clunk, plunk; pad, pat; **tap,** rap, **click,** tick, pop; tinkle, clink, chink.

.16 ADJS **faint, low, soft, gentle, subdued, dim, feeble, weak,** faint-sounding, low-sounding, soft-sounding; soft-voiced, low-voiced, faint-voiced, weak-voiced; murmured, whispered; half-heard, scarcely heard; distant; indistinct, unclear; barely audible, subaudible, near the limit *or* threshold of hearing; piano, pianissimo; decrescendo.

.17 **muffled, muted, softened, dampened,** damped, **smothered,** stifled, bated, dulled, deadened, subdued; **dull, dead, flat,** *sordo* [Ital].

.18 **murmuring,** murmurous, murmurish, **muttering, mumbling;** susurrous, susurrant; **whispering,** whisper, whispery; **rustling.**

.19 **rippling, babbling, burbling, bubbling, gurgling,** guggling, **purling, trilling;** lapping, splashing, plashing, sloshing, swishing.

.20 **humming,** thrumming, **droning,** booming, bombinating, **buzzing,** whizzing, whirring, purring, burring, birring [Scot].

.21 ADVS **faintly, softly,** gently, subduedly, hushedly, dimly, feebly, weakly, low; piano, pianissimo; *sordo* [Ital], *sordamente* [Ital], *à la sourdine* [Fr].

.22 **in an undertone,** *sotto voce* [Ital], **under one's breath,** with bated breath, in a whisper, between the teeth; aside, in an aside; out of earshot.

453. LOUDNESS

.1 NOUNS **loudness,** loudishness, intensity, volume; fullness, sonorousness, sonority; surge of sound, surge, crescendo, swell, swelling.

.2 **noisiness,** noisefulness, **uproariousness,**

racketiness, tumultuousness, thunderousness, clamorousness, clangorousness, boisterousness, obstreperousness; vociferousness 459.5.

.3 **noise,** loud noise, **blast** 456.3, tintamarre, **racket, din,** chirm [dial], **clamor;** outcry, **uproar,** hue and cry, noise and shouting; howl; clangor, clatter, clap, jangle, rattle; roar, thunder, thunderclap 456.5, brouhaha, **tumult, hubbub,** flap, hullabaloo; row, bobbery [India], fracas, brawl, commotion, drunken brawl, shindy, donnybrook, free-for-all, shemozzle [Brit slang], rumble *or* rhubarb [both slang], dustup [Brit informal], rumpus [informal], ruckus [informal], ruction [dial], rowdydow [informal]; **pandemonium,** bedlam, hell *or* bedlam let loose, hell broke loose [slang]; charivari, shivaree [dial]; discord 461.

.4 **blare, blast,** shriek 458.4, peal; **toot,** tootle, **honk,** beep, blat, trumpet; bay, bray; **whistle,** tweedle, squeal; trumpet call, trumpet blast *or* blare, sound *or* flourish of trumpets, **fanfare,** tarantara, tantara, tantarara; tattoo; taps.

.5 **noisemaker;** ticktack, bull-roarer, catcall, whizzer, whizgig, snapper, cricket, clapper, clack, clacker, cracker; firecracker, cherry bomb; rattle, rattlebox; horn, Klaxon; whistle, steam whistle, siren; boiler room, boiler factory.

.6 VERBS **din;** boom, thunder 456.9; **resound,** ring, peal, ring *or* resound in the ears, din in the ear, **blast the ear,** pierce *or* split *or* rend the ears, rend *or* split the eardrums, split one's head; **deafen,** stun; blast 456.8, crash 456.6; **rend the air** *or* skies *or* firmament, rock the sky, fill the air, make the welkin ring; shake *or* rattle the windows; awake *or* startle the echoes, set the echoes ringing, awake the dead; surge, swell, rise, crescendo.

.7 drown out, outshout, outroar, shout down, overpower, overwhelm; jam.

.8 **be noisy, make a noise** *or* **racket,** raise a clamor *or* din *or* hue and cry, noise, racket, chirm [dial], **clamor,** roar, clangor; brawl, row, rumpus; **make an uproar,** kick up a dust *or* racket, kick up *or* raise a hullabaloo, raise the roof, raise Cain *or* Ned, howl like all the devils of hell, raise the devil, raise hell, whoop it up, maffick [Brit]; not be able to hear oneself think.

.9 **blare,** blast; shriek 458.8; **toot,** tootle, sound, peal, wind, blow, blat; pipe, trumpet, bugle, clarion; bay, bell, bray; **whistle,** tweedle, squeal; **honk,** honk *or* sound *or* blow the horn, beep; sound taps, sound a tattoo.

.10 ADJS **loud,** loudish, loud-sounding, stentorian, stentorious, stentoraphonic, forte, fortissimo; **resounding,** ringing, plangent, pealing; full, sonorous; **deafening,** ear-deafening, **ear-splitting,** head-splitting, ear-rending, ear-piercing, piercing; thunderous, tonitruous, tonitruant; booming 456.12; window-rattling, earthshaking, enough to wake the dead *or* the seven sleepers.

.11 **loud-voiced, loudmouthed,** fullmouthed, full-throated, big-voiced, clarion-voiced, trumpet-voiced, trumpet-tongued, brazen-mouthed, stentorian, boanergean.

.12 **noisy,** noiseful, rackety, clattery, clangorous, clanging, **clamorous,** clamoursome [Brit dial], clamant, blatant, blaring, brassy, brazen, blatting; uproarious, **tumultuous,** turbulent, blustering, brawling, **boisterous,** rip-roaring, rowdy, mafficking [Brit], strepitous, strepitant, obstreperous; vociferous 459.10.

.13 ADVS **loudly, aloud,** loud, lustily; **noisily,** uproariously; ringingly, resoundingly; with a loud voice, at the top of one's voice, at the pitch of one's breath, in full cry, with one wild yell, with a whoop and a hurrah; forte, *fortemente* [Ital], fortissimo.

454. RESONANCE

.1 NOUNS **resonance, sonorousness,** sonority, plangency, **vibrancy;** mellowness, richness, fullness; deepness, lowness, bassness; hollowness.

.2 **reverberation, resounding; rumble,** rumbling, thunder, thundering, boom, booming, growl, growling, grumble, grumbling, reboation; rebound, resound, **echo,** re-echo.

.3 **ringing,** tintinnabulation, **pealing, chiming, tinkling,** tingling, **jingling,** dinging, donging; **tolling,** knelling; clangor, clanking, clanging; **ring, peal, chime; toll,** knell; **tinkle,** tingle, **jingle,** dingle, ding, dingdong, ding-a-ling, ting-a-ling; clink, tink, ting, chink; clank, clang; jangle, jingle-jangle; change ringing, peal ringing; tinnitus.

.4 **bell,** tintinnabulum; **gong,** triangle, **chimes;** dinner bell *or* gong *or* chimes, doorbell, jingle bell, hand bell, telephone bell, fire bell, sacring bell, passing bell, gong bell, church bell, sleigh bell, cowbell, sheepbell; clapper, tongue.

.5 **resonator,** resounder, reverberator; **sound-**

ing board, sound box; resonant chamber *or* cavity; echo chamber; loud pedal, damper pedal, sustaining pedal.

.6 VERBS resonate, vibrate, pulse, throb.

.7 reverberate, resound, sound, rumble, roll, boom, echo, reecho, rebound, bounce back, be reflected, be sent back, echo back, send back, return.

.8 ring, tintinnabulate, peal, sound; toll, knell, sound a knell; chime; gong; tinkle, tingle, jingle, ding, dingdong, dong; clink, tink, ting, chink; clank, clang, clangor; jangle, jinglejangle; ring on the air; ring changes *or* peals; ring in the ear.

.9 ADJS resonant, vibrant, sonorous, plangent, rolling; mellow, rich, full; resonating, vibrating, pulsing, throbbing.

.10 deep, deep-toned, deep-pitched, deepsounding, deepmouthed, deep-echoing; hollow, sepulchral; low, low-pitched, lowtoned, grave, heavy; bass; baritone; contralto.

.11 reverberating, reverberant, reverberatory, reboant, resounding, rebounding, repercussive, sounding; rumbling, thundering, booming, growling; echoing, reechoing, echoic; undamped; persistent, lingering.

.12 ringing, pealing, tolling, sounding, chiming; tinkling, tingling, jingling, dinging; tintinnabular *or* tintinnabulary *or* tintinnabulous.

455. REPEATED SOUNDS

.1 NOUNS staccato; drum, thrum, beat, pound, roll; drumming, tom-tom, beating, pounding, thumping; throb, throbbing, pulsation 323.3; palpitation, flutter; sputter, spatter, splutter; patter, pitterpatter, pitapat; rub-a-dub, rattattoo, rataplan, rat-a-tat, rat-tat, rat-tat-tat, tat-tat, tat-tat-tat; tattoo, devil's tattoo, ruff, ruffle, paradiddle; drumbeat, drum music; drumfire, barrage.

.2 clicking, ticking, tick, ticktock, ticktack, ticktick.

.3 rattle, rattling, brattle [Scot], ruckle [Brit dial], rattletybang; clatter, clitter, clunter [Brit dial], clitterclatter, chatter, clack, clacket [dial]; racket 453.3.

.4 VERBS drum, thrum, beat, pound, thump, roll; palpitate, flutter; sputter, splatter, splutter; patter, pitter-patter, go pitapat *or* pitter-patter; throb, pulsate 323.12; beat *or* sound a tattoo, beat a devil's tattoo, ruffle, beat a ruffle.

.5 tick, ticktock, ticktack.

.6 rattle, ruckle [Brit dial], brattle [Scot];

clatter, clitter, chatter, clack; rattle around, clatter about.

.7 ADJS staccato; drumming, thrumming, beating, pounding, thumping; throbbing; palpitant, fluttering; sputtering, spattering, spluttering; clicking, ticking.

.8 rattly, rattling, chattering, clattery, clattering.

456. EXPLOSIVE NOISE

.1 NOUNS report, crash, crack, clap, bang, wham, slam, clash, burst, bust [dial]; knock, rap, tap, smack, whack, thwack, whop, whap, swap [dial], whomp, splat, crump [Brit informal], bump, slap, slat [Brit dial], flap, flop.

.2 snap, crack; click, clack; crackle, snapping, cracking, crackling, crepitation, decrepitation, sizzling, spitting.

.3 detonation, blast, explosion, fulmination, discharge, burst, bang, pop, crack, bark; shot, gunshot; volley, salvo, fusillade.

.4 boom, booming, cannonade, peal, rumble, grumble, growl, roll, roar.

.5 thunder, thundering, bront(o)–, ceraun(o)– *or* keraun(o)–; clap *or* crash *or* peal of thunder, thunderclap, thunderpeal, thundercrack, thunderstroke; "heaven's artillery", "the thunder, that deep and dreadful organ-pipe", "dread rattling thunder", "deep, dread-bolted thunder" [all Shakespeare], "the crashing of the chariot of God" [William Cullen Bryant], "dry sterile thunder without rain" [T. S. Eliot]; thunderstorm 394.3; Thor *or* Donar, Jupiter Tonans, Indra.

.6 VERBS crack, clap, crash, wham, slam, bang, clash; knock, rap, tap, smack, whack, thwack, whop, whap, swap [dial], whomp, splat, crump [Brit informal], bump, slat [Brit dial], slap, flap.

.7 snap, crack; click, clack; crackle, crepitate, decrepitate; spit.

.8 blast, detonate, explode, discharge, burst, go off, bang, pop, crack, bark, fulminate; burst on the ear.

.9 boom, thunder, peal, rumble, grumble, growl, roll, roar.

.10 ADJS snapping, cracking, crackling, crepitant.

.11 banging, crashing, bursting, exploding, explosive, blasting, cracking, popping; knocking, rapping, tapping; slapping, flapping, slatting [Brit dial].

.12 thundering, thunderous, thundery, fulminating, tonitruous, tonitruant, thunderlike; booming, pealing, rumbling, rolling, roaring; cannonading, volleying.

457. SIBILATION

(hissing sounds)

.1 NOUNS sibilation, sibilance *or* sibilancy; **hiss, hissing,** siss, sissing, white noise; hush, hushing, shush, shushing; sizz, sizzle, sizzling; fizz, fizzle, fizzling, effervescing, effervescence; swish, whish, whoosh; whiz, buzz, zip; siffle; wheeze, *râle* [Fr], rhonchus; whistle, whistling; sneeze, sneezing, sternutation; snort; snore, stertor; sniff, sniffle, snuff, snuffle; spit, sputter, splutter; squash, squish, squelch; sigmatism, lisp; assibilation; frication, frictional rustling.

.2 VERBS sibilate; **hiss,** siss; hush, shush; sizzle, sizz; fizzle, fizz, effervesce; whiz, buzz, zip; swish, whish, whoosh; whistle; wheeze; sneeze; snort; snore; sniff, sniffle, snuff, snuffle; spit, sputter, splutter; squash, squish, squelch; lisp; assibilate.

.3 ADJS **sibilant; hissing,** hushing, sissing; sizzling, fizzling, effervescent; sniffing, sniffling, snuffling; snoring; wheezing, wheezy.

458. STRIDOR

(harsh and shrill sounds)

.1 NOUNS stridence *or* stridency, **stridor,** stridulousness; **shrillness,** highness, sharpness, acuteness, arguteness; **screechiness, squeakiness,** creakiness, reediness, pipingness.

.2 **raucousness, harshness,** raucity; discord, cacophony 461.1; coarseness, rudeness, ugliness, roughness, gruffness; **raspiness,** scratchiness, scrapiness, **hoarseness,** huskiness, dryness; stertorousness; roupiness [Scot]; gutturalness, gutturalism, gutturality, thickness, throatiness; cracked voice.

.3 **rasp, scratch, scrape,** grind; crunch, craunch, scranch [archaic], scrunch, crump; burr, chirr, buzz; snore; **jangle, clash, jar;** clank, clang, clangor, twang, twanging; blare, blat, bray; croak, caw, cackle; belch; growl, snarl; grumble, groan.

.4 **screech, shriek, scream, squeal,** shrill, keen, squeak, squawk, skirl, screak, skreak [dial], skriech *or* skreigh [both Scot], creak; whistle, pipe; whine, wail, howl, ululation, yammer; caterwaul.

.5 (insect sounds) **stridulation,** cricking, creaking, chirking [Scot]; crick, creak, chirk, chirp, chirrup.

.6 (high voices) soprano, mezzo-soprano, treble; tenor, alto; male alto, counter-

tenor; head register, head voice, head tone, falsetto.

.7 VERBS **stridulate,** crick, creak, chirk, chirp, chirrup.

.8 **screech, shriek,** screak, skreak [dial], skriech *or* skreigh [both Scot], creak, squeak, squawk, **scream, squeal,** shrill, keen; whistle, pipe, skirl; whine, wail, howl, wrawl [Brit dial], yammer, ululate; caterwaul.

.9 (sound harshly) **jangle, clash, jar;** blare, blat, bray; croak, caw, cackle; belch; burr, chirr, buzz; snore; growl, snarl; grumble, groan; clank, clang, clangor; twang.

.10 **grate, rasp, scratch, scrape,** grind; crunch, craunch, scranch [archaic], scrunch, crump.

.11 **grate on,** jar on, grate upon the ear, jar upon the ear, offend the ear, pierce *or* split *or* rend the ears, harrow *or* lacerate the ear, **set the teeth on edge, get on one's nerves,** jangle *or* wrack the nerves, make one's skin crawl.

.12 ADJS **strident,** stridulant, stridulous; strident-voiced.

.13 **high,** high-pitched, high-toned, high-sounding; treble, soprano, mezzo-soprano, tenor, alto, falsetto, countertenor.

.14 **shrill, thin, sharp,** acute, argute, keen, keening, **piercing,** penetrating, ear-piercing; **screechy,** screeching, shrieky, shrieking, **squeaky,** squeaking, screaky, creaky, creaking; whistling, piping, skirling, reedy; whining, wailing, howling, ululating, ululant.

.15 **raucous,** raucid, **harsh,** harsh-sounding; coarse, rude, rough, gruff, ragged; **hoarse, husky,** roupy [Scot], cracked, dry; **guttural,** thick, throaty, croaky, croaking; choked, strangled; squawky, **squawking;** brassy, brazen, tinny, metallic; stertorous.

.16 **grating, jarring,** grinding; **jangling,** jangly; **rasping,** raspy; scratching, scratchy; scraping, scrapy.

459. CRY, CALL

.1 NOUNS **cry, call, shout, yell,** hoot; halloo, hollo, yo-ho; **whoop, holler** [informal]; **cheer, hurrah** 867.2; **howl,** yowl, yawl [Brit dial]; bawl, bellow, roar; **scream, shriek,** screech, squeal, squall, caterwaul; yelp, yap, yammer, yawp, bark; war cry, battle cry, war whoop, rallying cry.

.2 **exclamation,** ejaculation, outburst, blurt, ecphonesis; expletive.

.3 hunting cry; tallyho, yoicks [archaic], view halloo.

.4 outcry, vociferation, clamor, gaff; hulla-baloo, hubbub, **uproar** 453.3; **hue and cry.**

.5 vociferousness, vociferance, clamorous-ness, clamoursomeness [Brit dial], bla-tancy; noisiness 453.2.

.6 VERBS **cry, call, shout, yell, holler** [infor-mal], hoot; hail, halloo, hollo; **whoop; cheer** 876.6; **howl,** yowl, yammer, yawl [Brit dial]; squawk, yawp; **bawl, bellow,** roar, roar or bellow like a bull; **scream, shriek,** screech, squeal, squall, caterwaul; yelp, yap, bark.

.7 **exclaim,** give an exclamation, ejaculate, burst out, blurt, blurt out.

.8 **vociferate,** outcry, **cry out,** call out, bel-low out, yell out, holler out [informal], shout out, sing out, pipe up, **clamor** 453.7, make or raise a clamor; make an outcry, **raise a hue and cry,** make an uproar.

.9 cry aloud, raise or lift up the voice, give voice or tongue, shout or cry or thunder at the top of one's voice, split the throat or lungs, strain the voice or throat, rend the air 453.6.

.10 ADJS **vociferous,** vociferant, vociferating; **clamorous,** clamoursome [Brit dial]; **bla-tant;** obstreperous, brawling; **noisy** 453.12; crying, shouting, **yelling, hollering** [infor-mal], **bawling,** screaming; yelping, yap-ping, yammering; loudmouthed, open-mouthed, boanergean.

.11 **exclamatory,** ejaculatory, blurting.

460. ANIMAL SOUNDS

.1 NOUNS animal noise; **call, cry;** mating call or cry; grunt, howl, bark, howling, ulula-tion, barking, etc.; birdcall, note, wood-note, clang; stridulation 458.5.

.2 VERBS cry, call; **howl,** yowl, yawp, yawl [dial], ululate; wail, whine, pule; **squeal,** squall, scream, screech, screak, squeak; troat; **roar;** bellow, blare, **bawl;** moo, low; **bleat,** blate, blat; **bray;** whinny, neigh, whicker, nicker; **bay,** bay at the moon, bell; **bark,** latrate [archaic], give voice or tongue; **yelp,** yap, yip; mew, mewl, meow, miaow, caterwaul.

.3 **grunt,** gruntle [Brit dial], oink; **snort.**

.4 **growl,** snarl, grumble, gnarl, snap; hiss, spit.

.5 (birds) **warble, sing,** carol, call; pipe, whis-tle; **trill,** chirr, roll; **twitter,** tweet, twit, chatter, chitter; **chirp,** chirrup, chirk, **cheep,** peep, pip; **quack,** honk, cronk; **croak, caw; squawk,** scold; **crow,** cock-a-doodle-doo; **cackle,** gaggle, gabble, gug-gle, **cluck,** clack, chuck; **gobble; hoot,** hoo; **coo; cuckoo;** drum.

.6 ADJS **howling,** yowling, crying, wailing, whining, puling, bawling, ululant, bla-tant, etc.; lowing, mugient.

461. DISCORD

(dissonant sounds)

.1 NOUNS **discord,** discordance or discor-dancy, **dissonance** or dissonancy, di-aphony, **cacophony;** stridor 458; **inharmo-niousness,** unharmoniousness, dishar-mony, inharmony; **unmelodiousness,** unmusicalness, unmusicality, untuneful-ness, tunelessness [archaic]; atonality, atonalism; flatness, sharpness, sourness [informal]; dissonant chord, wolf; sour note or clinker [informal], off note.

.2 **clash, jangle, jar; noise,** mere noise, con-fusion or conflict or jarring or jostling of sounds; Babel, witches' or devils' chorus; harshness 458.2; clamor 453.3.

.3 VERBS sound or hit a sour note [infor-mal], hit a clinker [informal]; **clash, jar, jangle,** conflict, jostle; grate 458.10,11; un-tune, unstring.

.4 ADJS **dissonant, discordant, cacophonous,** absonant [archaic], disconsonant, dia-phonic; strident, shrill, harsh, raucous, grating 458.12–16; **inharmonious,** unhar-monious, disharmonious, disharmonic, in-harmonic; **unmelodious,** immelodious, nonmelodious; **unmusical,** musicless, un-tuneful, tuneless [archaic]; untunable, un-tuned, atonal; cracked, **out of tune,** out of tone, out of pitch; **off-key, off-tone, off-pitch,** off; flat, sharp, **sour** [informal]; "above the pitch, out of tune, and off the hinges" [Rabelais], "like sweet bells jangled, out of tune and harsh" [Shake-speare].

.5 **clashing, jarring, jangling,** jangly, con-fused, conflicting, jostling, warring, ajar; **harsh, grating** 458.15,16.

462. MUSIC

.1 NOUNS **music,** "the speech of angels" [Carlyle], "the mosaic of the Air" [An-drew Marvell], "the harmonious voice of creation; an echo of the invisible world" [Giuseppe Mazzini], "the only universal tongue" [Samuel Rogers], "the universal language of mankind" [Longfellow], "the poor man's Parnassus" [Emerson], "the brandy of the damned" [G. B. Shaw], "nothing else but wild sounds civilized into time and tune" [Thomas Fuller, D.D.].

.2 **melody,** melodiousness, **tunefulness,** musicalness, musicality; **tune, tone,** musical sound, musical quality, tonality; sweetness, dulcetness, mellifluence, mellifluousness.

.3 harmony, concord, concordance, concert, consonance or consonancy, consort, accordance, **accord,** monochord, concentus, symphony, diapason; synchronism, synchronization; **attunement,** tune, attune; chime, chiming; unison, unisonance, homophony, monody; **euphony;** light or heavy harmony; two-part or three-part harmony, etc.; harmony or music of the spheres; harmonics 462.

.4 air, aria, **tune, melody,** melodia, line, melodic line, refrain, note, **song,** solo, solo part, soprano part, treble, lay, descant, **strain,** measure; canto, cantus; melo–.

.5 piece, opus, **composition,** production, work; **score; arrangement,** adaptation, orchestration, harmonization; instrumental music; electronic music; aleatory, aleatory music; **incidental music;** chamber music, string quartet, trio, chamber orchestra, string orchestra; sonata, sonatina; ricercar; absolute music, program music; nocturne, *Nachtmusik* [Ger]; étude, study, exercise; invention; variation, descant, *air varié* [Fr], theme and variations.

.6 medley, potpourri; *divertissement* [Fr]; fantasia, *Fantasiestück* [Ger]; caprice, capriccio, humoresque; romance, romanza.

.7 classical music, classic; concert music, serious music, longhair music [informal], symphonic music; **symphony,** symphonia, *sinfonietta* [Ital], symphonic ode or poem, tone poem or poetry; **concerto,** concertino, concertstück, concerto grosso; rhapsody; semiclassic, semiclassical music.

.8 popular music, pop music or pop, light music, popular song or air or tune, ballad; hit, song hit, hit tune.

.9 dance music, ballroom music, **suite,** musical suite, suite of dances; **dances** 879.7; syncopated music, **syncopation; ragtime** or rag; **jazz;** hot jazz, **swing,** jive [slang]; bebop, bop [slang]; mainstream jazz; avant-garde jazz, the new music [informal]; boogie-woogie; rock-and-roll, rock, hard rock, acid rock, folk rock, country rock; rhythm-and-blues.

.10 folk music, folk songs, ethnic music, ethnomusicology; folk ballads, balladry; border ballads; country music, hillbilly music; country-and-western music, western swing; old-time country music or old-

timey music; bluegrass; field holler; the blues, country blues, city blues.

.11 march, martial or military music; military march, quick or quickstep march; processional march, recessional march; funeral or dead march; wedding march.

.12 vocal music, song; singing, caroling, warbling, lyricism, vocalism, **vocalization;** operatic singing, bel canto, coloratura, bravura; choral singing; folk singing; croon, crooning; yodel, yodeling; scat, scat singing; intonation; hum, humming; solmization, tonic sol-fa, solfeggio, solfège, sol-fa, sol-fa exercise.

.13 song, lay, lied, *chanson* [Fr], carol, **ditty,** canticle, lilt; **ballad,** ballade, *ballata* [Ital]; *canzone* [Ital]; canzonet, *canzonetta* [Ital], cavatina; chant; folk song, *Volkslied* [Ger]; calypso; **art song,** *Kunstlied* [Ger]; drinking song, *brindisi* [Ital]; war song; **love song,** *Liebeslied* [Ger], love-lilt, torch song [informal]; serenade, serenata, *serena* [Provençal]; *matin* [Fr], *aubade* [Fr], *alba* [Provençal], *canso* [Provençal]; blues, blues song; croon, croon song; **carol,** Christmas carol, noël; **anthem,** national anthem; wedding song, bridal hymn, hymeneal, *Brautlied* [Ger], epithalamium, prothalamium; barcarole, boat song, chantey; minstrel song, minstrelsy; theme song; **dirge** 875.5.

.14 solo; aria; arietta, arioso; *aria buffa, aria da capo, aria d'agilità, aria da chiesa, aria d'imitazione, aria fugata, aria parlante* [all Ital]; bravura, *aria di bravura* [Ital]; coloratura, *aria di coloratura* [Ital]; cantabile, *aria cantabile* [Ital]; recitative, *recitativo* [Ital].

.15 lullaby, cradlesong, *berceuse* [Fr], *Schlummerlied, Wiegenlied* [both Ger].

.16 sacred music, church music, liturgical music; **hymn,** hymn-tune, **psalm,** chorale, choral fantasy, anthem; motet; **oratorio;** passion; **mass;** requiem mass, requiem; offertory, offertory sentence or hymn; **cantata;** doxology, introit, canticle, paean; prosodion; recessional; **spiritual,** Negro spiritual; white spiritual, gospel music, gospel; psalmody, hymnody, hymnology.

.17 part music, polyphonic music, part song, part singing, ensemble music, ensemble singing; **duet,** duo, **duettino** [Ital]; **trio,** terzet, terzetto; **quartet; quintet; sextet,** sestet; **septet,** septuor; **octet.**

.18 chorus, choral singing, unison; glee; cantata, lyric cantata; madrigal, madrigaletto; oratorio.

.19 round, rondo, rondeau, **roundelay,** catch,

troll; rondino, rondoletto; **fugue,** canon, fugato.

.20 **polyphony,** polyphonism; **counterpoint,** contrapunto; Gregorian chant, Ambrosian chant; *faux-bourdon* [Fr]; musica ficta, false music.

.21 monody, monophony, homophony.

.22 **part,** melody *or* voice part, **voice** 463.5, **line;** descant, canto, cantus, cantus planus *or* firmus, plain song, plain chant; prick song, cantus figuratus; soprano, tenor, treble, alto, contralto, baritone, bass, bassus; undersong; drone; **accompaniment;** continuo, basso continuo, figured bass, thorough bass; ground bass, basso ostinato.

.23 **response,** responsory report, answer; echo; antiphon, antiphony, antiphonal chanting *or* singing.

.24 **passage, phrase,** musical phrase, strain, part, **movement;** introductory phrase, anacrusis; statement, exposition, development, variation; division; period, musical sentence; section; **measure;** figure; **verse, stanza;** burden, bourdon; **chorus, refrain,** response; folderol, **ornament** 463.18, cadence 463.23, harmonic close, resolution; **coda,** tailpiece; ritornello; intermezzo, interlude; bass passage; tutti, tutti passage; bridge, bridge passage.

.25 (fast, slow, etc. passages) presto, prestissimo; allegro, allegretto; scherzo, scherzando; adagio, adagietto; andante, andantino; largo, larghetto, larghissimo; crescendo; diminuendo, decrescendo; rallentando, ritardando; ritenuto; piano, pianissimo; forte, fortissimo; staccato, marcato, marcando; pizzicato; spiccato; legato; stretto.

.26 **overture, prelude,** *Vorspiel* [Ger], **introduction,** operatic overture, dramatic overture, concert overture, voluntary, descant, vamp; curtain raiser.

.27 **impromptu, extempore, improvisation, interpolation;** cadenza, flourish; vamp; lick, hot lick, riff.

.28 **score,** musical score *or* copy, **music,** notation, musical notation, written music, copy, draft, transcript, transcription, version, edition, text, arrangement; part; full *or* orchestral score, compressed *or* short score, piano score, vocal score, instrumental score; tablature, lute tablature; opera score, opera; **libretto;** sheet music; **songbook,** songster; hymnbook, hymnal; music paper; music roll.

.29 **staff,** stave [Brit]; line, ledger line; bar, bar line; space, degree; brace.

.30 **theme,** motive, **motif,** subject, phrase 462.24, figure; leitmotiv.

.31 **execution, performance; rendering,** rendition, music-making, **touch, expression;** fingering; pianism; intonation; repercussion; pizzicato, staccato, spiccato, parlando, legato, cantando, rubato, demilegato, mezzo staccato, slur; glissando.

.32 **musicianship;** musical talent *or* flair, musicality; virtuosity; musical ear, ear for music; musical sense, sense of rhythm; absolute *or* perfect pitch; relative pitch.

.33 **musicale;** choral service, service of song, sing [informal], singing, community singing *or* sing, singfest, sing-in; folk-sing *or* hootenanny [both informal]; music festival; opera festival; folk-music festival, jazz festival, rock festival; *Sängerfest* [Ger], *eisteddfod* [Welsh]; jam session [informal]; swan song, farewell performance.

.34 **performance,** musical performance, **program,** musical program, program of music; **concert,** symphony concert, chamber concert; Philharmonic concert, philharmonic; popular concert, pops, pop concert [both informal]; promenade concert, prom [informal]; band concert; recital; service of music; concert performance (of an opera); –log(ue).

.35 musical theater, lyric theater, musical stage, lyric stage; **music drama,** lyric drama; song-play, *Singspiel* [Ger]; **opera,** grand opera, light opera, ballad opera; comic opera, *opéra bouffe* [Fr], *opera buffa* [Ital]; **operetta; musical comedy; musical;** Broadway musical; **ballet,** *opéra ballet* [Fr], comedy ballet, *ballet d'action* [Fr], *ballet divertissement* [Fr]; dance drama; chorus show; **song-and-dance act;** minstrel, minstrel show.

.36 VERBS **harmonize,** be harmonious, be in tune *or* concert, chord, **accord,** symphonize, synchronize, **chime, blend,** tune, attune, atone, sound together, sound in tune; assonate; melodize, musicalize.

.37 **tune, tune up,** attune, atone, chord, **put in tune;** voice, string; tone up, tone down.

.38 **strike up,** strike up a tune, **strike up the band,** break into music, pipe up, pipe up a song, yerk out [dial], **burst into song.**

.39 **sing, vocalize,** carol, descant, lilt, troll; **warble,** trill, tremolo, quaver, shake; **chirp,** chirrup, twit [Brit dial], **twitter;** pipe, whistle, tweedle, tweedledee; **chant; intone,** intonate; **croon; hum; yodel;** roulade; chorus, choir, sing in chorus; **hymn,** anthem, psalm, "make a joyful noise unto the Lord" [Bible]; sing the praises of; minstrel; ballad; **serenade;** sol-fa, do-re-mi, solmizate.

.40 **play, perform, execute, render,** do; interpret; make music; concertize; symphonize; chord; accompany; play by ear.

.41 **strum, thrum, pluck,** plunk, **pick,** twang, sweep the strings.

.42 **fiddle** [informal], play violin or the violin; scrape or saw [both informal], bow.

.43 **blow a horn,** sound or wind the horn, sound, blow, wind, **toot,** tootle, pipe, tweedle; bugle, carillon, clarion, fife, flute, trumpet, whistle; bagpipe, doodle [Brit dial]; lip, tongue, double-tongue, triple-tongue.

.44 **syncopate,** play jazz, swing, jive [slang], rag [informal].

.45 **beat time,** keep time, tap, tap out the rhythm; count, count the beats; beat the drum, **drum** 455.4, play drum or the drums, thrum, beat, thump, pound; tom-tom; ruffle; beat or sound a tattoo.

.46 **conduct, direct,** lead, wield the baton.

.47 **compose, write, arrange, score, set, set to music,** put to music; musicalize, melodize, **harmonize; orchestrate;** instrument, instrumentate; **adapt,** make an adaptation; transcribe, transpose.

.48 ADJS **musical, musically inclined,** musicianly, with an ear for music; virtuoso, virtuose, virtuosic; **music-loving,** music-mad, musicophile, philharmonic.

.49 **melodious,** melodic; **musical,** music-like; **tuneful,** tunable; fine-toned, **pleasant-sounding,** agreeable-sounding, pleasant, appealing, agreeable, catchy, singable; **euphonious** or euphonous or euphonic, **lyric(al),** melic; songful, songlike; **sweet, dulcet,** sweet-sounding, achingly sweet, sweet-flowing; honeyed, mellifluent, mellifluous, mellisonant, music-flowing; rich, mellow; sonorous, canorous; golden, golden-toned; silvery, silver-toned; sweet-voiced, golden-voiced, silver-voiced, silver-tongued, golden-tongued, music-tongued; ariose, arioso, cantabile.

.50 **harmonious,** harmonic(al), symphonious; harmonizing, **chiming,** blending, well-blended, blended; **concordant,** consonant, accordant, according, **in accord,** in concord, in concert; synchronous, synchronized, in sync [informal], **in tune,** tuned, attuned; in unison, in chorus; unisonous, unisonant; homophonic, monophonic, monodic; assonant, assonantal.

.51 **vocal,** singing; **choral,** choric; operatic; hymnal; psalmic, psalmodic, psalmodial;

sacred, liturgical; treble, soprano, tenor, alto, falsetto; coloratura, lyric, bravura, dramatic, heroic; baritone; bass.

.52 **instrumental,** orchestral, symphonic, concert; dramatico-musical; jazz, syncopated, jazzy, rock, swing.

.53 **polyphonic, contrapuntal.**

.54 ADJS, ADVS (directions, style) legato; staccato; spiccato; pizzicato; forte, fortissimo; piano, pianissimo; sordo; crescendo, accrescendo; decrescendo, diminuendo, morendo; dolce; amabile; affettuoso, con affetto; amoroso, con amore; lamentabile; agitato, con agitazione; leggiero; agilmente, con agilità; capriccioso, a capriccio; scherzando, scherzoso; appassionato, appassionatamente; abbandono; brillante; parlando; a cappella; trillando, tremolando, tremoloso; sotto voce; stretto.

.55 (slowly) largo, larghetto, allargando; adagio, adagietto; andante, andantino, andante moderato; calando; a poco; lento; ritardando, rallentando.

.56 (fast) presto, prestissimo; veloce; accelerando; vivace, vivacissimo; desto, con anima, con brio; allegro, allegretto; affrettando, moderato.

463. HARMONICS, MUSICAL ELEMENTS

.1 NOUNS **harmonics, harmony;** melodics; rhythmics; musicality; **music, music theory,** theory; musicology; musicography.

.2 **harmonization; orchestration, instrumentation;** arrangement, setting, adaptation, transcription; phrasing, modulation, intonation, preparation, suspension, solution, resolution; tone painting.

.3 **tone, tonality** 450.2,3.

.4 **pitch, tune, tone, key, note,** register, tonality; height, depth; classical pitch, high pitch, diapason or normal or French pitch, international or concert or new philharmonic pitch, standard pitch, low pitch, Stuttgart or Scheibler's pitch, philharmonic pitch, philosophical pitch.

.5 **voice,** voce [Ital]; voce di petto [Ital], chest voice; voce di testa [Ital], head voice; bass, drone, drone bass, bourdon, burden; coloratura, treble, falsetto.

.6 **scale, gamut, register,** compass, range, diapason; tuning, temperament; diatonic scale, chromatic scale, enharmonic scale, major scale, minor scale, natural or harmonic or melodic minor, whole-tone scale; great scale; octave scale, dodecuple scale, pentatonic scale.

.7 **sol-fa,** tonic sol-fa, do-re-mi; Guidonian

syllables, sol-fa syllables, do, re, mi, fa, sol, la, ti, do; fixed-do system, movable-do system; solmization; bobization.

.8 (diatonic series) tetrachord, chromatic tetrachord, enharmonic tetrachord, Dorian tetrachord; hexachord, pentachord; –chord.

.9 octave, *ottava* [Ital], eighth; *ottava alta* [Ital], *ottava bassa* [Ital]; small octave, great octave; contraoctave, subcontraoctave, double contraoctave; one-line octave, two-line octave, four-line octave, two-foot octave, four-foot octave; twelve-tone row, tone row.

.10 mode, octave species; major mode, minor mode; Greek modes, Ionian mode, Dorian mode, Phrygian mode, Lydian mode, mixolydian mode, Aeolian mode, Locrian mode; hypoionian mode, hypodorian mode, hypophrygian mode, hypolydian mode, hypoaeolian mode, hypomixolydian mode, hypolocrian mode; Gregorian *or* ecclesiastical *or* church *or* medieval mode; plagal mode, authentic mode; Indian *or* Hindu mode, raga.

.11 form, arrangement, pattern, model, design; song *or* lied form, primary form; sonata form, sonata allegro, symphonic form, canon form, toccata form, fugue form, rondo form.

.12 notation, character, mark, symbol, signature, sign, *segno* [Ital]; dot; custos, direct; cancel; bar, measure; measure *or* time signature, key signature; tempo mark, metronome *or* metronomic mark; fermata, hold, pause; *presa* [Ital], lead; slur, tie, ligature, vinculum, enharmonic tie; swell; accent, accent mark, expression mark.

.13 clef; C clef, soprano clef, alto clef, tenor clef; F clef *or* bass clef, G clef *or* treble clef.

.14 note, musical note, notes of a scale; tone 450.2; sharp, flat, natural; accidental; double whole note, breve; whole note, semibreve; half note, minim; quarter note, crotchet; eighth note, quaver; sixteenth note, semiquaver; thirty-second note, demisemiquaver; sixty-fourth note, hemidemisemiquaver; tercet, triplet; sustained note, dominant, dominant note; enharmonic, enharmonic note; staccato, spiccato; responding note, report; shaped note, patent note.

.15 key, key signature, tonality; keynote, tonic; tonic key; major, minor, major *or* minor key, tonic major *or* minor; supertonic, mediant, submediant, dominant,

subdominant, subtonic; pedal point, organ point.

.16 harmonic, harmonic tone, overtone, upper partial tone; flageolet tone.

.17 chord, major *or* minor chord, tonic chord, dominant chord; seventh chord, diminished seventh chord, sixth chord; consonant chord, concord; enharmonic chord, enharmonic; broken chord, arpeggio; unbroken chord, *concento* [Ital]; key chord, tonic triad, major triad, minor triad, common chord; triad, augmented triad.

.18 ornament, grace, arabesque, embellishment, *fioritura* [Ital]; flourish, roulade, flight, run; passage, division 462.24; florid phrase *or* passage; coloratura; incidental, incidental note; grace note, appoggiatura; acciaccatura; mordent, single mordent, double *or* long mordent; inverted mordent, pralltriller; turn, back *or* inverted turn; cadence, cadenza.

.19 trill, trillo; trillet, *trilleto* [Ital]; tremolo, tremolant, tremolando; quaver, quiver, tremble, tremor, flutter, falter, shake; vibrato, *Bebung* [Ger].

.20 interval, degree, step, note, tone; second, third, fourth, fifth, sixth, seventh, octave; prime *or* unison interval, major *or* minor interval, harmonic *or* melodic interval, enharmonic interval, diatonic interval; parallel *or* consecutive intervals, parallel fifths, parallel octaves; whole step, major second; half step, halftone, semitone, minor second; diatonic semitone, chromatic semitone, less semitone, quarter semitone, tempered *or* mean semitone; quarter step, enharmonic diesis; augmented interval; diatessaron, diapason; –chord.

.21 rest, pause; whole rest, breve rest, semibreve rest, half rest, minim, quarter rest, eighth rest, sixteenth rest, thirty-second rest, sixty-fourth rest.

.22 rhythm, beat, meter, measure, number *or* numbers, movement, lilt, swing; prosody, metrics; rhythmic pattern *or* phrase.

.23 cadence *or* cadency, authentic cadence, plagal cadence, mixed cadence, perfect *or* imperfect cadence, half cadence, deceptive *or* false cadence, interrupted *or* suspended cadence.

.24 tempo, time, beat, time pattern, timing; simple time *or* measure, compound time *or* measure; two-part *or* duple time, three-part *or* triple time, triplet, four-part *or* quadruple time, five-part *or* quintuple time, six-part *or* sextuple time, seven-part *or* septuple time, nine-part *or* nonuple

347

time; two-four time, six-eight time, etc.; tempo rubato, rubato; mixed times; **syncopation,** syncope; **ragtime,** rag [informal]; waltz time, three-four *or* three-quarter time, andante tempo, march tempo, etc.; largo, etc. 462.55, presto, etc. 462.56.

.25 **accent,** accentuation, rhythmical accent *or* accentuation, ictus, emphasis, stress arsis, thesis; grammatical accent, rhetorical accent; musical *or* pitch *or* tone accent, stress accent; intonation, intonation pattern *or* contour.

.26 **beat,** throb, pulse, pulsation; downbeat, upbeat, offbeat; bar beat.

.27 ADJS **tonal,** tonic; chromatic, enharmonic; semitonic.

.28 **rhythmic(al),** cadent, cadenced, **measured, metric(al);** in rhythm, in numbers; beating, throbbing, pulsing, pulsating, pulsative, pulsatory.

.29 **syncopated; ragtime,** ragtimey [informal]; **jazz;** jazzy *or* jazzed *or* jazzed up [all informal], hot, swingy [informal].

.30 ADVS **in time,** in tempo 463.24, *a tempo* [Ital].

464. MUSICIAN

.1 NOUNS **musician,** musico, **music maker,** professional musician, minstrel, minstrelsy, **player,** performer, executant, interpreter, tunester, artiste, artist, concert artist, **virtuoso,** virtuosa; maestro; recitalist; **soloist,** duettist; –ist.

.2 **syncopator;** ragtimer [informal]; **jazz musician, jazzman;** swing musician, swingster [informal]; Tin Pan Alley.

.3 **instrumentalist,** instrumentist; bandman, bandsman; orchestral musician; symphonist; concertist; accompanist, accompanyist; ripieno.

.4 **wind musician,** wind-instrumentalist, horn player, hornist, horner, piper, tooter; bassoonist, bugler, clarinetist, cornettist, fifer, oboist, piccoloist, saxophonist, trombonist; trumpeter, trumpet major; flutist, flautist.

.5 **string musician,** strummer, picker [informal], thrummer, twanger; banjoist, banjo-picker [informal], citharist, guitarist, guitar-picker [informal], classical guitarist, folk guitarist, lute player, lutenist, lutanist, lutist, lyrist, mandolinist, theorbist; violinist, fiddler [informal]; bass violinist, bassist, bass player, contrabassist; violoncellist, cellist *or* 'cellist, celloist; violist; harpist, harper; zitherist, psalterer.

.6 **xylophonist,** marimbaist.

.7 **pianist,** pianiste, pianofortist, piano

player, ivory tickler *or* thumper [slang]; harpsichordist, clavichordist, monochordist; accordionist, concertinist.

.8 **organist,** organ player.

.9 **organ-grinder,** hurdy-gurdist, hurdy-gurdyist, hurdy-gurdy man.

.10 **drummer, percussionist,** timpanist, kettledrummer; taborer.

.11 **cymbalist,** cymbaler; bell-ringer, **carilloneur,** campanologist, campanist.

.12 **orchestra, band, ensemble,** combo [informal], group; string orchestra, chamber orchestra; **symphony orchestra,** symphony, Philharmonic; gamelan orchestra; **brass band,** military band, German band, concert band, ragtime band, string band, dixieland band, steel band *or* orchestra, **jazz band,** big band, swing band; street band, callithumpian band, jug band, skiffle band; rock-and-roll group; waits; strings, woodwind *or* woodwinds, brass *or* brasses, string *or* woodwind *or* brass section, string *or* woodwind *or* brass choir; desks; trio, **quartet,** quintet, sextet; **string quartet,** string trio; woodwind quartet, etc.; brass quintet, etc.

.13 **vocalist,** vocalizer, voice, **singer, songster,** songbird, warbler, canary [slang], lead singer, caroler, melodist, cantor; songstress, singstress, cantatrice; chanter, chantress; aria singer, lieder singer, opera singer, diva, prima donna; improvisator; blues singer, torch singer [informal]; crooner, rock *or* rock-and-roll singer; yodeler; psalm singer, hymner; Meistersinger; **bass,** basso, basso profundo, deep bass, *basso cantante* [Ital], lyric bass; *basso buffo* [Ital], comic bass; **baritone,** baritenor; **tenor,** countertenor, lyric tenor, heroic tenor, *Heldentenor* [Ger]; **soprano,** lyric soprano, coloratura soprano, dramatic soprano, mezzo-soprano; **alto,** contralto.

.14 **minstrel, ballad singer,** balladeer, **bard,** rhapsode, rhapsodist; wandering *or* strolling minstrel, **troubadour,** trovatore, trouvère, minnesinger, scop, gleeman, fili, jongleur; street singer, wait; serenader; **folk singer,** folk-rock singer; country-and-western singer;

.15 **choral singer,** choir member, chorister, chorus singer, choralist; choirman, **choirboy; chorus girl,** chorine [slang].

.16 **choir, chorus,** choral group, choral society, oratorio society, chamber chorus, *Kammerchor* [Ger], chorale, men's *or* women's chorus, mixed chorus, ensemble, voices; **glee club,** *Liedertafel, Lieder-*

kranz [both Ger], singing club *or* society; *a cappella* choir; choral symphony.

.17 **conductor,** leader, symphonic conductor, **music director,** director, *Kapellmeister* [Ger]; **orchestra leader, band leader, bandmaster,** band major, drum major.

.18 **choirmaster,** choral director *or* conductor, song leader, *maestro di cappella* [Ital]; choir chaplain, minister of music, precentor, cantor, chorister.

.19 **concertmaster,** concertmeister, *Konzertmeister* [Ger], first violinist.

.20 **composer, scorer, arranger,** musicographer; melodist, melodizer; harmonist, harmonizer; **orchestrator;** symphonist; tone poet; ballad maker *or* writer, balladeer, balladist, balladmonger; madrigalist; lyrist; hymnist, hymnographer, hymnologist; contrapuntist; song writer, songsmith, tunesmith; lyricist, librettist; musicologist, ethnomusicologist.

.21 **music lover,** philharmonic, **music fan, music buff** [both informal], musicophile; musicmonger; concertgoer, operagoer; tonalist.

.22 (patrons) the Muses, the Nine, sacred Nine, tuneful Nine, Pierides; Apollo, Apollo Musagetes; Orpheus; Erato, Euterpe, Polymnia *or* Polyhymnia, Terpsichore.

.23 **songbird,** singing bird, **songster,** feathered songster, warbler; nightingale, Philomel; bulbul, canary, cuckoo, lark, mavis, mockingbird, oriole, ringdove, song sparrow, thrush.

465. MUSICAL INSTRUMENTS

.1 **musical** instrument, –ina, –phone, –chord.

.2 **string** *or* **stringed instrument,** chordophone; strings, string choir.

.3 **harp; lyre,** aeolian harp *or* lyre; bell harp; claviharp; Irish harp, clarsach; Autoharp; **cither,** cithara, **zither,** cittern, gittern; psaltery; dulcimer, symphonia; langspiel; polychord, heptachord, hexachord.

.4 **lute,** archlute; theorbo, oud; bandore, *bandurria* [Sp], pandora, pandura; **banjo,** banjer [dial]; banjo-zither; banjorine; **ukulele,** uke [informal]; banjo-ukulele, banjo-uke [informal], banjuke, banjulele; **guitar,** Spanish guitar, Hawaiian guitar, classical guitar, concert guitar, centerhole guitar, F-hole guitar, electric guitar, Dobro guitar, steel guitar, bass guitar; **mandolin,** mandola, mandore, mandolute, mando-bass, mando-cello, balalaika,

tamboura, samisen, troubadour fiddle, vina, sitar.

.5 **viol,** vielle; viol family; violette, viola pomposa; treble viol, descant viol; alto *or* tenor viol, viol *or* viola da braccio; bass viol, viol *or* viola da gamba, viola bastarda, baritone; viol *or* viola d'amore, viol *or* viola da spalla, viol *or* viola di bordone, viol *or* viola di fagotto; rebec; trumpet marine, tromba marina.

.6 **violin, fiddle** [informal], crowd [Brit dial]; violinette, violino piccolo; kit, kit violin, pocket *or* kit fiddle; **viola,** tenor violin, violotta; **violoncello, cello** *or* 'cello; violoncello piccolo; **bass viol,** contrabass, **bass, double bass,** violone, **bull fiddle** [informal], *basso da camera* [Ital]; viola alta; Stradivarius, Stradivari, Strad [informal]; Amati, Cremona, Guarnerius; bow, fiddlestick, fiddlebow; bridge, sound hole, soundboard, fingerboard, tuning peg, scroll; string 465.23, G string, D string, A string, E string.

.7 **wind instrument,** wind; aerophone; **horn,** pipe, tooter; mouthpiece, embouchure, lip; valve, bell, reed, double reed, key, slide.

.8 **brass wind,** brass *or* brass-wind instrument; brasses, brass choir; **bugle,** bugle horn; **trumpet,** valve trumpet, key trumpet, pocket trumpet, tromba; **clarion;** post horn; lituus; lur; **cornet,** cornet-à-pistons, cornopean; **trombone;** slide trombone, sliphorn [slang], sackbut, valve trombone; **saxhorn,** saxtuba, saxcornet, flugelhorn; **althorn** *or* alto horn, ballad horn; baritone, tenor tuba, euphonium, double-bell euphonium; **tuba,** helicon, bombardon, bass horn, sousaphone; ophicleide, serpent; **French horn,** horn, orchestral horn, *corno di caccia* [Ital]; hunting horn; mellophone; alphorn, alpenhorn.

.9 **woodwind,** wood *or* woodwind instrument; woods, woodwind choir; **flute;** aul(o)–; recorder, fipple flute *or* pipe, flageolet; **fife;** pipe, tabor pipe; **piccolo;** ocarina, sweet potato [informal]; hornpipe, pibgorn; whistle, tin-whistle, penny-whistle; aulos; reed instrument, **reed;** double-reed instrument, **double reed; oboe,** hautboy, *oboe d'amore* [Ital]; bass *or* basset oboe, heckelphone; tenoroon, *oboe da caccia* [Ital]; musette; shawm, bombard, bombardon, pommer; **bassoon;** double bassoon, contrabassoon, contrafagotto; sonorophone; single-reed instrument, **single reed; clarinet,** licorice stick [slang];

basset horn; **English horn**, *cor anglais* [Fr]; krummhorn, cromorne; **saxophone, sax** [informal]; panpipe, Pandean pipe, oaten reed, syrinx, shepherd's pipe.

.10 **bagpipe** *or* bagpipes, pipes, union pipes, doodlesack, *Dudelsack* [Ger]; cornemuse, musette; sordellina; chanter, drone.

.11 **mouth organ**, mouth harp, harp, French harp [dial], **harmonica**, harmonicon; Jew's harp, mouth bow; kazoo.

.12 **accordion**, piano accordion; **concertina**; squeeze box [informal]; mellophone; bandonion.

.13 **piano**, pianoforte; pianette, pianino; **grand piano**, grand, Steinway; baby grand, parlor grand, concert grand; square piano, upright piano, upright; spinet; cottage piano; clavier, *Klavier* [Ger]; **harpsichord**, clavicymbal, clavicembalo, cembalo, hammer dulcimer, dulcimer harpsichord; **clavichord**, clarichord, monochord, manichord *or* manichordon; clavicittern, clavicytherium; virginal, pair of virginals, couched harp; lyrichord; violin piano, piano-violin, melodion, harmonichord, sostinente pianoforte, melopiano.

.14 **player piano**, mechanical piano, Pianola; street piano; music roll, piano player roll.

.15 **organ**, pipe organ, reed organ, church organ; baroque organ; **electric organ**, Hammond organ, electro-pneumatic organ, tubular-pneumatic organ, tracker-action organ, hydraulic organ; choralcelo, harmonium, melodeon, melodica, organophone, seraphine, symphonion, vocalion; steam organ, calliope, calliophone; orchestrelle.

.16 **hurdy-gurdy**, vielle, **barrel organ**, hand organ, grind organ, street organ.

.17 **music box**, musical box; orchestrion, orchestrina.

.18 **percussion instrument**, percussion, percussive, idiophone; percussions, battery; **cymbals**, potlids [slang], highhat [informal], crash cymbal; sizzler; **triangle; gong**, tam-tam, tonitruone; **bells**, tubular bells, handbells, tintinnabula; chime, **chimes; orchestral bells**, glockenspiel, lyra; **vibraphone**, vibraharp, vibes [informal]; **xylophone, marimba**, metallophone; celesta; gamelan; **clappers**, snappers, **castanets**, finger cymbals, bones, rattle, rattlebones, maraca.

.19 **drum**, membranophone, tympan, tympanum, tympanon, timpani; **kettledrum**, kettle, timbal, naker, nagara [India]; **snare drum**, side drum; tenor drum, **bass drum, tom-tom**, tam-tam; **bongo drum; conga; timbrel**, tabor, **tambourine**, tambourin; taboret, tabret; troll-drum; war drum, drumhead, drumskin; snare; drumstick, jazz stick, tymp stick.

.20 **keyboard**, fingerboard; console, **keys**, manual, claviature; piano keys, ivories [slang], eighty-eight [slang], organ manual, great, swell, choir, solo, echo; pedals.

.21 **carillon**, chimes 465.18, chime of bells; electronic carillon.

.22 **stop**, organ stop, rank, register; **foundation stop**; principal, diapason, violin *or* string diapason; **flute stop**; melodia, claribel, octave, piccolo, twelfth; concert flute, harmonic flute, stopped flute, bourdon, gedeckt, stopped diapason, quintaten, rohr flute, koppel flute, block flute; **string stop**; cello, viola, gamba, dulciana, viol d'orchestre; **reed stop**, trumpet, trombone, posaune, cornopean, clarion, cromorna, shawm, bombard, ranket, bassoon, English horn, clarinet, oboe; **mutation stop**; nazard, tierce, quint, larigot, septième; **mixture**; cornet, sesquialtera, fourniture, plein jeu, cymbel; **hybrid stop**; spitz flute, gemshorn; **voix céleste**, vox angelica, unda maris; **tremolo**, vibrato, vox humana.

.23 **string**, chord, steel string, wound string, nylon string; fiddlestring, catgut; horsehair; music wire, piano wire.

.24 **plectrum**, plectron, pick.

.25 (aids) metronome, rhythmometer; tone measurer, monochord, sonometer; tuning fork, tuning bar, diapason; pitch pipe, tuning pipe; mute; music stand, music lyre; baton, conductor's baton, stick [informal].

466. INTELLECT

(mental faculty)

.1 NOUNS **intellect, mind**, *mens* [L], menti–, noo–, psych(o)–; mental *or* intellectual faculty, nous, **reason, rationality**, rational *or* reasoning faculty, power of reason, *Vernunft* [Ger], *esprit* [Fr], *raison* [Fr], ratio, discursive reason, "discourse of reason" [Shakespeare], **intelligence**, mentality, mental capacity, **understanding**, reasoning, intellection, conception; **psyche**; brain, **brains**, smarts [slang], gray matter [informal]; head, headpiece.

.2 **wits, senses, faculties**, parts, capacities, intellectual gifts *or* talents; intellectuals [archaic]; consciousness 475.2.

.3 **inmost mind**, inner recesses of the mind,

mind's core, deepest mind, center of the mind; inner man 5.4; subconscious, subconscious mind 690.35; inmost heart 855.2.

.4 **psyche, spirit,** spiritus, **soul,** âme [Fr], **heart, mind,** anima, *anima humana* [L]; shade, shadow, manes; breath, pneuma, breath of life, divine breath; *atman, purusha, buddhi, jiva, jivatma* [all Skt]; ba, khu [both Egypt myth]; *ruach, nephesh* [both Heb]; spiritual being, inner man, "the Divinity that stirs within us" [Addison]; ego, the self, the I.

.5 **life principle,** vital principle, vital spirit *or* soul, **vital force,** prana [Hinduism]; essence *or* substance of life, individual essence, *ousia* [Gk]; divine spark, vital spark *or* flame.

.6 **brain,** cerebr(o)–, encephal(o)–; seat *or* organ of thought, sensory, sensorium; encephalon; gray matter, head, pate *or* sconce *or* noddle [all informal]; noodle *or* noggin *or* bean *or* upper story [all slang]; sensation 422.

.7 (parts of the brain) prosencephalon, forebrain; telencephalon, endbrain; cerebrum; cerebral hemispheres, corpus callosum, cerebral cortex, mantle, pallium, archipallium, neopallium; lobe, frontal lobe, temporal lobe, parietal lobe, occipital lobe, limbic lobe; diencephalon, between brain; hypothalamus, hypothalam(o)–, subthalamus, thalamus, thalam(o)–; midbrain, mesencephalon; pons; optic chiasm; hindbrain, rhombencephalon; metencephalon, myelencephalon; cerebellum, little brain; hippocampus; fornix; corpus striatum, lenticular nucleus, globus pallidus, pallido–; folia, arbor vitae, cerebellar hemispheres, vermis; medulla oblongata; reticular system; brain stem; meninges, dura mater, pia mater, arachnoid; ventricle; convolution, fissure, gyrus; cerebrospinal fluid; pituitary body; pineal body; gray matter, poli(o)–, white matter; glial cells.

.8 ADJS **mental, intellectual, rational, reasoning, thinking,** noetic, conceptive, conceptual, phrenic; intelligent 467.12; noological; endopsychic, psychic(al), psychologic(al), spiritual; cerebral; subjective, internal.

467. INTELLIGENCE, WISDOM

(mental capacity)

.1 NOUNS **intelligence, understanding,** *Verstand* [Ger], **comprehension,** apprehen-

sion, **mental** *or* **intellectual grasp,** intellectual power, thinking power, power of mind *or* thought; ideation, conception; integrative power, esemplastic power; rationality, reasoning *or* deductive power; **sense, wit,** mother wit, natural *or* native wit; intellect 466; **intellectuality,** intellectualism; capacity, mental capacity, **mentality,** caliber, reach *or* compass *or* scope of mind; **IQ,** intelligence quotient, mental ratio, mental age; sanity 472; knowledge 475.

.2 **smartness, braininess,** smarts *or* savvy [both slang], **brightness, brilliance, cleverness,** aptness, aptitude, native cleverness, mental alertness, nous, **sharpness, keenness,** acuity, acuteness, gifts, giftedness, talent, flair, genius; quickness, nimbleness, adroitness, dexterity; sharp-wittedness, keen-wittedness, quick-wittedness, nimble-wittedness; nimble mind, mercurial mind, quick parts, clear *or* quick thinking; ready wit, quick wit, sprightly wit, *esprit* [Fr].

.3 **shrewdness, artfulness, cunning,** cunningness, canniness, **craft, craftiness,** wiliness, guilefulness, slickness, **slyness,** pawkiness [Brit], foxiness [informal], peasant *or* animal cunning, low cunning; subtility, subtilty, **subtlety;** insidiousness, deviousness.

.4 **sagacity,** sagaciousness, **astuteness, acumen,** longheadedness; **foresight,** foresightedness, providence; **farsightedness,** farseeingness, longsightedness; **discernment, insight,** penetration, acuteness, acuity; perspicacity, perspicaciousness, perspicuity, perspicuousness; incisiveness, trenchancy, cogency; **perception,** perceptiveness, percipience, apperception; sensibility 422.2.

.5 **wisdom,** ripe wisdom, seasoned understanding, mellow wisdom, wiseness, sageness, sapience, good *or* sound understanding; Sophia; erudition 475.4,5; **profundity,** profoundness, depth; broadmindedness 526.

.6 **sensibleness, reasonableness,** reason, rationality, sanity, saneness, **soundness; practicality,** practical wisdom, practical mind; **sense,** good *or* common *or* plain sense, **horse sense** [informal]; due sense of; level head, cool head, **levelheadedness,** balance, coolheadedness, coolness; soberness, sobriety, **sober-mindedness.**

.7 **judiciousness, judgment,** good *or* sound judgment, cool judgment, soundness of judgment; **prudence,** prudentialism, providence, policy, polity; weighing, consideration, circumspection, circumspectness, reflection, reflectiveness, **thoughtfulness; discretion,** discreetness; **discrimination.**

.8 **genius,** *Geist* [Ger], spirit, soul; daimonion, demon, daemon; **inspiration,** afflatus, divine afflatus; Muse; fire of genius; **creativity;** talent 733.4; creative thought 535.2.

.9 (intelligent being) **intelligence, intellect,** head, brain, mentality, consciousness; wise man 468.

.10 VERBS **have all one's wits about one,** have all one's marbles [slang], have smarts *or* savvy [slang], have a head on one's shoulders [informal], have one's head screwed on right; use one's head *or* wits; know what's what 733.18, be wise as a serpent *or* owl; be reasonable, listen to reason.

.11 be brilliant, **scintillate,** sparkle, coruscate.

.12 ADJS **intelligent,** intellectual [archaic]; ideational, conceptual, conceptive, discursive; sophic, noetic; **knowing, understanding, reasonable, rational, sensible, bright;** sane 472.4; not so dumb [informal], strong-minded.

.13 **clear-witted,** clearheaded, clear-sighted; awake, **wide-awake,** alive, **alert,** on the ball [slang].

.14 **smart, brainy** [informal], **bright, brilliant,** scintillating; **clever,** apt, **gifted,** talented; **sharp,** keen; **quick,** nimble, adroit, dexterous; **sharp-witted,** keen-witted, needle-witted, **quick-witted,** quick-thinking, steel-trap, nimble-witted, quick on the trigger *or* uptake [informal]; smart as a whip, sharp as a tack [slang]; nobody's fool *or* no dumbbell *or* not born yesterday [all informal].

.15 **shrewd, artful, cunning, knowing, crafty, wily,** guileful, canny, slick, sly, pawky [Brit], foxy [informal], crazy like a fox [slang]; **subtle,** subtile; insidious, devious, Byzantine, calculating.

.16 **sagacious, astute,** longheaded, argute; **understanding, discerning,** penetrating, incisive, acute, trenchant, cogent, piercing; **foresighted,** foreseeing; forethoughted, forethoughtful, provident; **farsighted,** farseeing, longsighted; **perspicacious,** perspicuous; **perceptive** 422.13, percipient, apperceptive, appercipient.

.17 **wise, sage,** sapient, **knowing; learned** 475.21; **profound,** deep; wise as an owl *or* serpent, wise as Solomon; wise beyond one's years, in advance of one's age, wise in one's generation; broad-minded 526.8.

.18 **sensible, reasonable, rational, logical; practical,** pragmatic; philosophical; com-

monsense, commonsensical [informal]; **levelheaded,** balanced, coolheaded, cool, **sound, sane,** sober, **sober-minded,** well-balanced.

.19 **judicious,** judicial, judgmatic(al), **prudent,** prudential, politic, careful, provident, **considerate,** circumspect, **thoughtful,** reflective, reflecting; **discreet;** discriminative, discriminating; **well-advised,** well-judged, enlightened.

.20 ADVS **intelligently, understandingly,** knowingly, discerningly; **reasonably,** rationally, sensibly; **smartly, cleverly; shrewdly,** artfully, cunningly; **wisely,** sagaciously, astutely; **judiciously, prudently,** discreetly, providently, considerately, circumspectly, thoughtfully.

468. WISE MAN

.1 NOUNS **wise man, sage,** sapient, man of wisdom; **master,** authority, **mastermind,** master spirit of the age, oracle; **philosopher,** thinker, lover of wisdom; rabbi; doctor; great soul, mahatma, guru, rishi; *starets* [Russ], elder, wise old man, elder statesman; illuminate; seer; mentor; **intellect,** man of intellect; mandarin, **intellectual** 476; savant, **scholar** 476.3.

.2 Solomon, Socrates, Plato, Mentor, Nestor, Confucius, Buddha, Gandhi.

.3 **the wise,** the intelligent, the sensible, the prudent, the knowing, the understanding.

.4 Seven Wise Men of Greece, Seven Sages, Seven Wise Masters; Solon, Chilon, Pittacus, Bias, Periander, Epimenides, Cleobulus, Thales.

.5 Magi, Three Wise Men, Wise Men of the East, Three Kings; Three Kings of Cologne; Gaspar *or* Caspar, Melchior, Balthasar.

.6 **wiseacre,** wisehead, wiseling, **witling,** wisenheimer [slang], wise guy, smart ass [slang]; wise fool; Gothamite, wise man of Gotham, wise man of Chelm.

469. UNINTELLIGENCE

.1 NOUNS **unintelligence,** unintellectuality [archaic], unwisdom, unwiseness, intellectual *or* mental weakness; **senselessness, witlessness, mindlessness,** brainlessness, primal stupidity, *Urdummheit* [Ger], reasonlessness, lackwittedness, lackbrainedness, slackwittedness, slackmindedness; **irrationality; ignorance** 477; **foolishness** 470; incapacity, ineptitude; low IQ.

.2 **unperceptiveness,** imperceptiveness, insensibility, impercipience, undiscerningness, unapprehendingness, **incomprehen-**

sion, nonunderstanding; **blindness**, mind-blindness, purblindness; **shortsightedness**, nearsightedness, dim-sightedness.

.3 **stupidity**, stupidness, *bêtise* [Fr], **dumbness** [informal], **doltishness**, boobishness, duncery [archaic], dullardism, blockishness, cloddishness, lumpishness, sottishness, **asininity**, ninnyism, simpletonianism; oafishness, oafdom, yokelism, loutishness; **density**, denseness, opacity; grossness, crassness, crudeness, boorishness; **dullness**, dopiness [slang], **obtuseness**, sluggishness, bovinity, cowishness, slowness, lethargy, stolidity, hebetude; **dim-wittedness**, dimness, **dull-wittedness**, slow-wittedness, beef-wittedness, dull-headedness, **thick-wittedness**, thick-headedness, unteachability, ineducability; wrongheadedness.

.4 [informal terms] **blockheadedness**, woodenheadedness, klutziness, dunderheadedness, jolterheadedness *or* joltheadedness [both Brit], chowderheadedness, chuckleheadedness, beetleheadedness, chumpiness, numskulledness *or* numskullery, cabbageheadedness, sapheadedness, muttonheadedness, fatheadedness, boneheadedness, knuckleheadedness, blunderheadedness.

.5 **muddleheadedness**, addleheadedness, addlepatedness, puzzleheadedness; dizziness [informal].

.6 **empty-headedness**, empty-mindedness, absence of mind; **vacuity**, vacuousness, vacancy, vacuum, emptiness, mental void, blankness, hollowness, inanity, vapidity, jejunity.

.7 **superficiality**, **shallowness**, **unprofundity**, lack of depth, unprofoundness, thinness; shallow-wittedness, shallow-mindedness; **frivolousness**, flightiness, lightness, fluffiness, frothiness, volatility.

.8 **feeblemindedness**, weak-mindedness; infirmity, weakness, feebleness, softness.

.9 **mental deficiency**, mental retardation, amentia, mental handicap, subnormality, mental defectiveness; **arrested development**, infantilism, retardation, retardment, backwardness; **simplemindedness**, simple-wittedness, simpleness, simplicity; **idiocy**, idiotism [archaic], profound idiocy, **imbecility**, **half-wittedness**, blithering idiocy; moronity, moronism, **cretinism**; mongolism, mongolianism, mongoloid idiocy, Down's syndrome; insanity 473.

.10 **senility**, senilism, senile weakness, senile debility, caducity, decrepitude, senecti-

tude, decline; **childishness**, **second childhood**, **dotage**, **dotardism**; anility; senile dementia, senile psychosis.

.11 **puerility**, puerilism, immaturity, **childishness**; **infantilism**, babyishness.

.12 VERBS **be stupid**, etc.; drool, slobber, drivel, dither, blither, blather, maunder, dote, burble; not see an inch beyond one's nose, not have enough sense to come in out of the rain, not find one's way to first base.

.13 ADJS **unintelligent**, unintellectual [archaic], **unthinking**, **unreasoning**, **irrational**, unwise, inept, **not bright**; ungifted, untalented; **senseless**, insensate; **mindless**, **witless**, **reasonless**, **brainless**, pin-brained, pea-brained, of little brain, headless; **lackwitted**, lackbrained, slackwitted, slackminded, lean-minded, lean-witted, shortwitted; **foolish** 470.8; **ignorant** 477.12.

.14 **undiscerning**, **unperceptive**, imperceptive, impercipient, insensible, unapprehending, uncomprehending, nonunderstanding; **shortsighted**, myopic, nearsighted, dim-sighted; **blind**, purblind, mind-blind, blind as a bat; blinded, blindfold, blindfolded.

.15 **stupid**, **dumb**, dullard, **doltish**, blockish, klutzy *or* klutzish [both slang], duncish, duncical, cloddish, clottish [Brit], chumpish [informal], lumpish, **oafish**, boobish, sottish, **asinine**, lamebrained, Boeotian; **dense**, thick [informal], opaque, gross, crass, fat; bovine, cowish, beef-witted, beef-brained, beefheaded; unteachable, ineducable; wrongheaded; dead from the neck up, dead above *or* between the ears, muscle-bound between the ears.

.16 **dull**, dull of mind, **dopey** [slang], **obtuse**, blunt, dim, wooden, heavy, sluggish, slow, **slow-witted**, hebetudinous, **dim-witted**, **dull-witted**, blunt-witted, dull-brained, dull-headed, dull-pated, **thick-witted**, thick-headed, thick-pated, thick-skulled, thick-brained, fat-witted, gross-witted, gross-headed.

.17 [informal terms] **blockheaded**, woodenheaded, stupidheaded, dumbheaded, dunderheaded, blunderheaded, jolterheaded *or* joltheaded [both Brit], chowderheaded, chuckleheaded, beetleheaded, nitwitted, numskulled, cabbageheaded, pumpkin-headed, sapheaded, lunkheaded, muttonheaded, fatheaded, boneheaded, knuckleheaded, clodpated, shitheaded [slang].

.18 **muddleheaded**, **fuddlebrained** [informal], scramblebrained [informal], muddled, addled, addleheaded, **addlepated,** addle-brained, muddybrained, puzzleheaded, blear-witted; dizzy [informal], muzzy, foggy.

.19 **empty-headed,** empty-minded, empty-noddled, empty-pated, empty-skulled; **vacuous,** vacant, empty, hollow, inane, vapid, jejune, blank; **rattlebrained,** rattleheaded; scatterbrained 532.16.

.20 **superficial, shallow, unprofound;** shallow-witted, shallow-minded, shallow-brained, shallow-headed, shallow-pated; **frivolous,** flighty, light, volatile, frothy, fluffy, **featherbrained, birdwitted, birdbrained.**

.21 **feebleminded, weak-minded,** weak, feeble, infirm, soft, soft in the head, weak in the upper story [informal].

.22 **mentally deficient,** mentally defective, mentally handicapped, retarded, **mentally retarded,** backward, arrested, subnormal, not right in the head, **not all there** [informal]; **simpleminded,** simplewitted, simple, simpletonian; **half-witted,** half-baked [informal]; **idiotic, moronic, imbecile,** imbecilic, cretinous, cretinistic, mongoloid; **crackbrained,** cracked, crazy 473.25; babbling, driveling, slobbering, drooling, blithering, dithering, maundering, burbling.

.23 **senile,** decrepit, doddering, doddery; **childish,** childlike, in one's second childhood, **doting,** doited [Scot].

.24 **puerile,** immature, childish; childlike; **infantile,** infantine; **babyish,** babish.

.25 ADVS **unintelligently, stupidly;** foolishly 470.12.

470. FOOLISHNESS

.1 NOUNS **foolishness, folly, foolery, fool-headedness, stupidity, asininity,** niaiserie [Fr], **bêtise** [Fr]; **inanity, fatuity,** fatuousness; ineptitude; **silliness; frivolousness,** frivolity, giddiness; triviality, triflingness, nugacity, desipience; **senselessness, witlessness, thoughtlessness,** brainlessness, mindlessness; **idiocy, imbecility; craziness, madness,** lunacy, **insanity; eccentricity, queerness,** crankiness, crackpottedness; weirdness; screwiness or nuttiness or wackiness or goofiness or daffiness or battiness or sappiness [all slang]; zaniness, zanyism, **clownishness, buffoonery.**

.2 **unwiseness,** unwisdom, **injudiciousness, imprudence;** indiscreetness, **indiscretion,** inconsideration, thoughtlessness, witlessness, inattention, unthoughtfulness; un-

reasonableness, **unsoundness, unsensibleness,** senselessness, reasonlessness, **irrationality, unreason,** inadvisability; recklessness; childishness, immaturity, puerility, callowness; inexpedience 671; unintelligence 469; pompousness, stuffiness.

.3 **absurdity,** absurdness, **ridiculousness;** ludicrousness 880.1; **nonsense,** nonsensicality, stuff and nonsense; **preposterousness,** fantasticalness, monstrousness, wildness, **outrageousness.**

.4 (foolish act) **folly, stupidity,** act of folly, absurdity, sottise [Fr], foolish or stupid thing, dumb thing to do [slang]; fool or fool's trick, dumb trick [informal]; **imprudence, indiscretion,** imprudent or unwise step; blunder 518.5.

.5 **stultification;** infatuation.

.6 VERBS **be foolish;** be stupid 469.12; **act or play the fool;** get funny, do the crazy act or bit or shtick [slang]; **fool, tomfool** [informal], **trifle, frivol; fool around** [informal], horse around [informal], **clown, clown around; make a fool of oneself,** make a monkey of oneself [slang], stultify oneself, invite ridicule, put oneself out of court, play the buffoon; **lose one's head, take leave of one's senses,** go haywire; pass from the sublime to the ridiculous; strain at a gnat and swallow a camel.

.7 **stultify,** infatuate, turn one's head, befool; gull, dupe; **make a fool of,** make a monkey of [slang], play for a sucker [slang], put on [slang].

.8 ADJS **foolish,** fool [informal], **foolheaded** [informal], **stupid, dumb** [slang], **asinine,** wet [Brit]; buffoonish; **silly,** apish, dizzy [informal]; **fatuous,** fatuitous, **inept, inane;** futile; **senseless, witless, thoughtless,** brainless; **idiotic,** moronic, imbecile, **crazy, mad,** daft, **insane;** cockeyed or screwy or nutty or wacky or goofy or daffy or loony or batty or sappy or kooky or flaky [all slang]; infatuated, besotted, credulous, gulled, befooled, beguiled, fond, doting, gaga; sentimental, maudlin; dazed, fuddled.

.9 **unwise, injudicious, imprudent, impolitic; indiscreet;** inconsiderate, thoughtless, mindless, witless, unthoughtful, unthinking, unreflecting, unreflective; **unreasonable, unsound, unsensible,** senseless, insensate, reasonless, **irrational,** reckless, inadvisable; inexpedient 671.5; **ill-advised, ill-considered,** ill-gauged, ill-judged, ill-imagined, ill-contrived, ill-devised, unconsidered; unadvised, misadvised, misguided; undiscerning; unforeseeing, unseeing, shortsighted, myopic.

.10 **absurd, nonsensical,** ridiculous, poppycockish, laughable, ludicrous 880.4; **foolish, crazy;** preposterous, cockamamie [informal], fantastic(al), grotesque, monstrous, wild, weird, **outrageous,** incredible, beyond belief, *outré* [Fr], extravagant, bizarre; high-flown.

.11 foolable, befoolable, gullible; naïve, artless, inexperienced, green.

.12 ADVS **foolishly, stupidly,** sillily, idiotically; **unwisely,** injudiciously, imprudently, indiscreetly, inconsiderately; senselessly, unreasonably, thoughtlessly, witlessly, unthinkingly; absurdly, ridiculously.

471. FOOL

.1 NOUNS **fool, tomfool,** perfect fool, born fool; *schmuck* [Yid]; ass, jackass, stupid ass, egregious ass; zany, **clown, buffoon,** doodle; sop, milksop; mooncalf, softhead; figure of fun; **lunatic** 473.15; **ignoramus** 477.8.

.2 [slang terms] **chump, booby, boob, sap,** prize sap, klutz, **dingbat,** dingdong, **ding-a-ling, saphead, mutt, jerk,** jerk-off, asshole, **goof,** schlemiel, sawney [Brit], galoot.

.3 **dolt, dunce,** clod, Boeotian, **dullard,** *niais* [Fr], donkey, stupid, **ninny,** ninnyhammer, **nincompoop,** looby, noddy, jobbernowl [Brit informal], thickwit, **dope, nitwit,** dimwit, lackwit, lamebrain, put, lightweight, witling, gaby [Brit dial]; **dummy** or **dumb cluck** or **dumbbell** or **dumb bunny** [all slang], block [slang], loon [slang], gowk [Brit dial].

.4 **blockhead,** dolthead, dumbhead, stupidhead, dullhead, bufflehead [dial], bonehead, jughead, thickhead, thickskull, **numskull, lunkhead,** chucklehead, **knucklehead,** chowderhead, jolterhead [Brit informal], muttonhead, beefhead, **meathead,** noodlehead, pinhead, pinbrain, peabrain, cabbagehead, pumpkin head, **fathead,** blubberhead, muddlehead, puzzlehead, addlebrain, addlehead, **addlepate,** tottyhead [archaic], puddinghead, mushhead, blunderhead, dunderhead, dunderpate, clodpate, clodhead, clodpoll.

.5 **oaf, lout,** boor, lubber, **gawk,** gawky, **lummox,** yokel, rube, hick, hayseed, bumpkin, clod, clodhopper.

.6 **silly,** silly Billy, **silly ass, goose.**

.7 **scatterbrain,** scatterbrains, shatterbrain, shatterpate [both archaic], **rattlebrain,** rattlehead, rattlepate, **harebrain,** featherbrain, shallowbrain, shallowpate [archaic], featherhead, giddybrain, giddyhead, giddypate, **flibbertigibbet.**

.8 **simpleton,** simp [slang], juggins or jiggins [both slang], clot [Brit], golem, **idiot,** driveling or blithering or congenital idiot; **imbecile, moron, half-wit,** natural, natural idiot, born fool, natural-born fool, ament, defective; cretin, mongolian or mongoloid idiot.

.9 **dotard,** senile; fogy, **old fogy,** fuddy-duddy, old fart or fud.

472. SANITY

.1 NOUNS **sanity, saneness,** sanemindedness, soundness, **soundness of mind,** soundmindedness, sound mind, healthy mind, right mind [informal], senses, reason, **rationality,** reasonableness, lucidity, balance, wholesomeness; normalness, normality, normalcy; **mental health;** mental hygiene; mental balance or poise or equilibrium; sobriety, sober senses; a sound mind in a sound body, *"mens sana in corpore sano"* [L; Juvenal]; contact with reality; lucid interval.

.2 VERBS **come to one's senses,** sober down or up, recover one's sanity or balance or equilibrium, get things into proportion; see in perspective; have all one's marbles [slang].

.3 **bring to one's senses,** bring to reason.

.4 ADJS **sane,** sane-minded, **rational,** reasonable, sensible, **lucid,** normal, wholesome, clearheaded, clearminded, balanced, **sound,** mentally sound, of sound mind, *compos mentis* [L], sound-minded, healthy-minded, right, right in the head, **in one's right mind,** in possession of one's faculties or senses, together, all there [both slang].

473. INSANITY, MANIA

.1 NOUNS **insanity,** insaneness, unsaneness, **lunacy, madness,** *folie* [Fr], **craziness, daftness,** oddness, strangeness, queerness, abnormality; loss of touch or contact with reality, loss of mind or reason; dementedness, dementia, brainsickness, mindsickness, mental sickness, sickness, **mental illness, mental disease,** –phrenia; brain damage; rabidness, **mania,** furor; alienation, aberration, mental disturbance, **derangement,** distraction, disorientation, mental derangement or disorder, unbalance, mental instability, unsoundness, **unsoundness of mind,** unbalanced mind, diseased or unsound mind, sick mind, disturbed or troubled or clouded mind, shattered mind, mind overthrown or unhinged, darkened mind, disordered mind or reason; senselessness, witlessness, reasonlessness, irrationality; possession, pixilation; mental deficiency 469.1.

.2 [informal terms] daffiness, nuttiness, battiness, screwiness, goofiness, kookiness, wackiness, dottiness, looniness, balminess; bats in the belfry, a screw loose; lame brains.

.3 psychosis, psychopathy, psychopathia, psychopathic condition; organic psychosis, metabolic psychosis, toxic psychosis, functional psychosis; reactive or situational psychosis; certifiability; neurosis 690.19; senile dementia, senile psychosis, senility, Pick's disease; presenile dementia, Alzheimer's disease; syphilitic paresis, dementia paralytica, paralytic dementia, general paresis, general paralysis; arteriosclerotic psychosis; Korsakoff's psychosis or syndrome; prison psychosis; psychopathia sexualis, sexual pathology 419.12–14; pathological drunkenness or intoxication, dipsomania 993.3; pharmacopsychosis, drug addiction 642.9; moral insanity, psychopathic personality 690.16, folie du doute [Fr], abulia 627.4.

.4 schizophrenia, dementia praecox, schiz-(o)–; mental dissociation, dissociation of personality; split personality, alternating personality, dual or double personality, multiple personality; catatonic schizophrenia, catatonia, hebephrenia, hebephrenic schizophrenia; schizothymia; schizophasia; paranoia, paraphrenia, paranoiac or paranoid psychosis; paranoid schizophrenia.

.5 melancholia, "moping, melancholy and moonstruck madness" [Milton]; melancholia hypochondriaca; involutional melancholia or involutional psychosis; stuporous melancholia, melancholia attonita; flatuous melancholia; melancholia religiosa; manic-depressive psychosis; cyclothymia.

.6 rabies, hydrophobia, lyssa, canine madness; dumb or sullen rabies, paralytic rabies; furious rabies.

.7 frenzy, furor, fury, maniacal excitement, fever, rage; seizure, attack, fit, paroxysm, spasm, convulsion; amok, murderous insanity or frenzy; psychokinesis; furor epilepticus.

.8 delirium, deliriousness, brainstorm; calen-ture of the brain, afebrile delirium, lingual delirium, delirium mussitans; incoherence, wandering, raving, ranting.

.9 delirium tremens, mania or dementia a potu, delirium alcoholicum or ebriositatis.

.10 [slang or informal terms] the DT's, the horrors, the shakes, the heebie-jeebies, the jimjams, the beezie-weezies, the screaming meemies, blue Johnnies, blue devils, pink elephants, pink spiders, snakes, snakes in the boots.

.11 fanaticism, fanaticalness, rabidness, overzealousness, overenthusiasm, ultrazealousness, zealotry, zealotism, bigotry, perfervidness; extremism, extremeness, extravagance, excessiveness, overreaction; overreligiousness 1028.3.

.12 mania 473.36, craze, infatuation, enthusiasm, passion, fascination, crazy fancy, bug [slang], rage, furore, furor; manic-depressive psychosis.

.13 obsession, prepossession, preoccupation, hang-up [slang], fixation, tic, complex, fascination; hypercathexis; compulsion, morbid drive, obsessive compulsion, irresistible impulse; monomania, ruling passion, fixed idea, idée fixe [Fr], one-track mind; possession.

.14 insane asylum, asylum, lunatic asylum, madhouse, mental institution, mental home, bedlam; bughouse or nuthouse or laughing academy or loonybin or booby hatch [all slang]; mental hospital, psychopathic hospital or ward, psychiatric ward; padded cell.

.15 lunatic, madman, dement, phrenetic, fanatic [both archaic], fou, aliéné [both Fr], noncompos; bedlamite, Tom o' Bedlam; demoniac, energumen; loon or loony or nut or crackpot or screwball or weirdie or weirdo or kook or flake or crackbrain [all slang]; meshuggenah [Yid]; maniac, raving lunatic; borderline case; idiot 471.8.

.16 psychotic, psycho [informal], mental, mental case, certifiable case, psychopath, psychopathic case; psychopathic personality; paranoiac, paranoid; schizophrenic, schizophrene, schizoid; schiz or schizy or schizo [all slang]; catatoniac; hebephreniac; manic-depressive.

.17 fanatic, infatuate, bug [slang], nut [slang], buff or fan [both informal], freak [slang], fanatico, aficionado [both Sp], devotee, zealot, enthusiast, energumen; monomaniac, crank [informal]; lunatic fringe.

.18 psychiatry, alienism; psychiatrist, alienist 690.12.

.19 VERBS **be insane, be out of one's mind,** not be in one's right mind, not be right in the head, **not be all there** [informal], have a demon or devil; have bats in the belfry or have a screw loose, not have all one's buttons or marbles [slang]; **wander, ramble; rave, rage, rant;** dote, babble; drivel, drool, slobber, slaver; froth or foam at the mouth, run mad, run amok.

.20 **go mad, go crazy, take leave of one's senses,** lose one's senses or reason or wits, **crack up, go off one's head** [informal].

.21 [slang terms] go off one's nut or rocker, go off the track or trolley, go out of one's skull, blow one's top or stack, flip one's lid or wig, go ape, go bananas, go crackers [Brit], blow one's mind, freak out.

.22 addle the wits, **affect one's mind, go to one's head.**

.23 **madden,** dement, **craze,** mad [archaic], make mad, send mad, **unbalance, unhinge,** undermine one's reason, **derange,** distract, frenzy, shatter, **drive insane** or mad or **crazy,** put or send out of one's mind, overthrow one's mind or reason.

.24 **obsess, possess,** beset, infatuate, **preoccupy, be uppermost in one's thoughts,** have a thing about [informal]; grip, hold, get a hold on, not let go; **drive, compel, impel.**

.25 ADJS **insane, unsane, mad, stark-mad, stark-staring mad,** maddened, **crazy, sick,** crazed, loco [informal], mental, psycho [informal], **lunatic, moon-struck, daft, non compos mentis,** non compos, **unsound,** of unsound mind, **demented, deranged,** deluded, disoriented, unhinged, **unbalanced,** unsettled, distraught, wandering, mazed, **cracked** [informal], **crackbrained, brainsick, sick in the head,** not right, not right in the head [informal], not in one's right mind, **touched,** tetched [dial], touched in the head, off one's head [informal], **out of one's mind,** out of one's head [informal], out of one's senses or wits, bereft of reason, reasonless, irrational, deprived of reason, senseless, witless, **not all there** [informal], *meshuggah* [Yid]; hallucinated; manic; queer, odd, strange, off, flighty [archaic]; abnormal 85.9, mentally deficient 469.22.

.26 [slang terms] **daffy, dotty,** dippy, **loony, goofy, wacky, balmy** or barmy, flaky, **kooky, potty, batty,** bats, nuts, **nutty,** fruity, fruitcakey, **screwy,** screwball, screwballs, crackers [Brit], **bananas,** bonk-ers, loopy, beany, **buggy, bughouse,** bugs, **cuckoo,** slaphappy, flipped, freaked-out, off the wall, gaga, haywire, out of one's skull, off in the upper story, off one's nut or rocker, off the track or trolley, off the hinges, round the bend [Brit], minus some buttons, nobody home, with bats in the belfry, just plain nuts.

.27 **psychotic, psychopathic, mentally ill,** mentally sick, certifiable; disturbed, neurotic 690.45; schizophrenic, schizoid, schiz [slang], schizy; manic-depressive; paranoiac, paranoid; catatonic; brain-damaged, brain-injured.

.28 **possessed,** possessed with a demon or devil, **pixilated, bedeviled,** demonized, devil-ridden.

.29 **mad as a hatter,** mad as a March hare, crazier than a bedbug or coot or loon, nutty as a fruitcake [slang].

.30 **rabid, maniac** or **maniacal,** raving mad, stark-raving mad, **frenzied, frantic,** frenetic; **mad, madding, wild, furious, violent;** desperate; **beside oneself,** like one possessed, uncontrollable; **raving, raging,** ranting; frothing or foaming at the mouth; **amok, berserk,** running wild; maenadic, corybantic, bacchic, Dionysiac.

.31 **delirious, out of one's head** [informal], **off one's head** [informal], off; **giddy,** dizzy, lightheaded; **wandering, rambling, raving, ranting,** babbling, incoherent.

.32 **fanatic(al), rabid;** overzealous, ultrazealous, overenthusiastic, zealotic, bigoted, perfervid; **extreme,** extremist, extravagant, inordinate, ultra–, hyper–; **unreasonable, irrational; wild-eyed,** wild-looking, haggard; overreligious 1028.4.

.33 **obsessed, possessed,** prepossessed, **infatuated,** preoccupied, fixated, **hung-up** [slang], besotted, gripped, held; monomaniac or monomaniacal.

.34 **obsessive,** obsessional; **obsessing, possessing, preoccupying,** gripping, holding; driving, impelling, **compulsive, compelling.**

.35 ADVS madly, insanely, crazily; deliriously; fanatically, rabidly, etc.

.36 **manias**

abluto– (bathing)	delusions)
acro– (incurable insanity)	America– (United States)
agora– (open spaces)	andro– (men)
agyio– (streets)	Anglo– (England)
ailuro– (cats)	antho– (flowers)
alcoholo– (alcohol)	aphrodisio– (sexual pleasure)
amaxo– (being in vehicles)	api– (bees)
ameno– (pleasing	arithmo– (counting)

auto– (solitude)
autophono– (suicide)
ballisto– (bullets)
biblio– (books)
biblioklepto– (book theft)
bruxo– (gritting one's teeth)
cacodemono– (demonic possession)
chero– (gaiety)
China– (China)
chiono– (snow)
choreo– (dancing)
chremato– (money)
clino– (bed rest)
coprolalo– (foul speech)
cremno– (cliffs)
creso– (great wealth)
cyno– (dogs)
Danto– (Dante)
demo– (crowds)
dipso– (liquor)
dora– (fur)
drapeto– (running away)
dromo– (traveling)
ecdemio– (wandering)
edeo– (genitals)
ego– (one's self)
eleuthro– (freedom)
empleo– (public employment)
eno– (wine)
entheo– (religion)
entomo– (insects)
eremio– (stillness)
ergasio– (activity)
ergo– (work)
erotico– (erotica)
eroto– (sexual desire)
erotographo– (erotic literature)
erythro– (blushing)
ethero– (ether)
flori– (plants)
Franco– (France)
Gallo– (France)
gamo– (marriage)
gephyro– (crossing bridges)
Germano– (Germany)
grapho– (writing)
Greco– (Greece)
gymno– (nakedness)
gyneco– (satyriasis)
hamarto– (sin)
hedono– (pleasure)
helio– (sun)
hiero– (priests)
hippo– (horses)
hodo– (travel)
homicido– (murder)
hydro– (water)
hydrodipso– (drinking water)
hylo– (woods)
hyper– (acute mania)
hypno– (sleep)
hypo– (mild mania)
hystero– (nymphoma-

nia)
ichthyo– (fish)
icono– (icons)
idolo– (idols)
Italo– (Italy)
kaino– (novelty)
kathiso– (sitting)
kineso– (movement)
klepto– (stealing)
lalo– (speech)
letheo– (narcotics)
logo– (talking)
lyco– (lycanthropy)
lype– (deep melancholy)
macro– (becoming larger)
megalo– (own importance)
melo– (music)
mentulo– (the penis)
mesmero– (hypnosis)
metro– (writing verse)
micro– (becoming smaller)
mono– (one subject)
musico– (music)
muso– (mice)
mytho– (lies; exaggerations)
necro– (death; the dead)
nocti– (night)
noso– (imagined disease)
nosto– (return home)
nudo– (nudity)
nympho– (female lust)
ochlo– (crowds)
oestro– (nymphomania)
oiko– (home)
oino– (wine)
oligo– (a few subjects)
onio– (buying)
ophidio– (reptiles)
opio– (opium)
opso– (a special food)
orchido– (testicles)
ornitho– (birds)
para– (joy in complaints)
parousia– (second coming of Christ)
patho– (moral insanity)
phago– (food; eating)
phanero– (picking at growths)
pharmaco– (medicines)
philopatrido– (homesickness)
phono– (noise)
photo– (light)
phronemo– (thinking)
phthisio– (tuberculosis)
pluto– (great wealth)
politico– (politics)
porio– (wanderlust)

pornographo– (pornography)
poto– (drinking; delirium tremens)
pseudo– (falsities)
pyro– (fires)
Russo– (Russia)
satyro– (male lust)
scribble– (writing)
scribo– (writing)
siderodromo– (railroad travel)
sito– (food)
sopho– (one's own wisdom)
squander– (spending)
sub– (mild mania)
symmetro– (symmetry)
Teutono– (Germany)
thalasso– (the sea)
thanato– (death)

theatro– (theater)
theo– (that one is God)
timbro– (postage stamps)
tomo– (surgery)
tricho– (hair)
trichorrhexo– (pinching off one's hair)
trichotillo– (plucking one's hair)
tristi– (melancholia)
tromo– (delirium tremens)
Turko– (Turkey)
typo– (writing for publication)
utero– (nymphomania)
verbo– (words)
xeno– (foreigners)
zoo– (animals)

474. ECCENTRICITY

.1 NOUNS eccentricity, idiosyncrasy, idiocrasy, erraticism, erraticness, queerness, oddity, peculiarity, strangeness, singularity, freakishness, freakiness, quirkiness, crotchetiness, dottiness, crankiness, crankism, crackpotism; whimsy, whimsicality; abnormality, anomaly, unnaturalness, irregularity, deviation, deviancy, differentness, divergence, aberration; nonconformity, unconventionality 83.2.

.2 quirk, twist, kink, crank, quip, trick, mannerism, crotchet, conceit, whim, maggot, maggot in the brain, bee in one's bonnet or head [informal].

.3 eccentric, erratic; freak or character or crank [all informal]; crackpot or nut or screwball or weirdie or weirdo or kook or queer potato or oddball or flake [all slang] 85.4; strange duck [informal]; nonconformist 83.3, recluse 924.5.

.4 ADJS eccentric, erratic, idiocratic(al), idiosyncratic(al), queer, queer in the head [informal], odd, peculiar, strange, fey, singular, anomalous, freakish, funny; unnatural, abnormal, irregular, divergent, deviative, deviant, different, exceptional; unconventional 83.6; crotchety, quirky, dotty, maggoty [Brit], cranky, crank, crankish, whimsical, kinky, twisted; screwy or screwball or nutty or wacky or kooky or flaky or oddball [all slang].

475. KNOWLEDGE

.1 NOUNS knowledge, knowing, ken, –gnosia or –gnosis or –gnosy, –sophy; acquaintance, familiarity, intimacy; private knowledge, privity; information, data, datum, facts, factual base, corpus; intelligence;

practical knowledge, **experience, know-how,** expertise, technic, technics, technique; self-knowledge; ratio cognoscendi.

.2 **cognizance;** cognition, noesis; **recognition, realization; perception,** insight, apperception; **consciousness, awareness,** mindfulness, note, notice, sensibility; appreciation, appreciativeness.

.3 **understanding, comprehension, apprehension,** intellection, prehension; conception, conceptualization, ideation; savvy [informal]; grasp, mental grasp, grip, command, mastery; precognition, foreknowledge 542.3, clairvoyance 1034.8; intelligence, wisdom 467.

.4 **learning, enlightenment, education, instruction,** edification, illumination; acquirements, acquisitions, attainments, accomplishments; sophistication; store of knowledge; liberal education; acquisition of knowledge 564.

.5 **scholarship, erudition,** eruditeness, **learnedness,** reading, letters; **intellectuality,** intellectualism; **literacy; culture;** book learning, booklore; **bookishness, bookiness, pedantry,** pedantism, donnishness [Brit]; bluestockingism; bibliomania, book madness, bibliolatry, bibliophilism; classicism, classical scholarship, humanism, humanistic scholarship.

.6 **profound knowledge,** deep knowledge; specialized or special knowledge; expertise, proficiency 733.1; wide or vast or extensive knowledge, general knowledge, interdisciplinary or cross-disciplinary knowledge, encyclopedic knowledge, polymathy, polyhistory, pansophy; **omniscience,** all-knowingness.

.7 slight knowledge 477.6.

.8 tree of knowledge, tree of knowledge of good and evil; forbidden fruit.

.9 **lore, body of knowledge,** body of learning, store of knowledge, system of knowledge, treasury of information; literature, literature of the field, publications, materials; bibliography; encyclopedia, cyclopedia.

.10 **science,** ology, **art, study, discipline,** –gnomy, –logy, –nomy, –urgy; **field,** field of inquiry, concern, province, domain, area, arena, sphere, branch or field of study, branch or department of knowledge, specialty, academic specialty, academic discipline; **technology, technics,** technicology, –techny; social science, natural science; applied science, pure science, experimental science.

.11 **scientist,** man of science; **technologist;** practical scientist, experimental scientist; savant, **scholar** 476.3; authority, expert; intellectual 476.

.12 VERBS **know, perceive, apprehend,** prehend, cognize, recognize, discern, see, make out; conceive, conceptualize; **realize, appreciate, understand, comprehend,** fathom; savvy [informal]; wot or wot of [both Brit dial], ken [Scot]; have, possess, **grasp,** seize; have knowledge of, be informed, be apprised of, have information about, be acquainted with, be conversant with, be cognizant of, be conscious or aware of.

.13 **know well, know full well,** know damn well or darn well [informal], have a good or thorough knowledge of, be well-informed, be learned in, **be up on** [informal], be master of, command, be thoroughly grounded in, **have down pat** or **cold** [both informal], have it taped [Brit informal], have at one's fingers' ends or tips, have in one's head, **know by heart** or rote, **know like a book,** know like the back of one's hand, **know backwards,** know backwards and forwards, **know inside out,** know down to the ground [informal], **know one's stuff** or know one's onions [both informal], be expert in; **know the ropes,** know all the ins and outs, know the score [informal], know all the answers [informal]; know what's what 733.18.

.14 learn (acquire knowledge) 564.6–15; come to one's knowledge 557.14.

.15 ADJS **knowing, knowledgeable,** –gnostic; **cognizant, conscious, aware, mindful, sensible;** intelligent 467.12; **understanding, comprehending,** apprehensive, apprehending; **perceptive,** insightful, apperceptive, percipient, perspicacious, appercipient, prehensile; shrewd, sagacious, wise 467.15–17; omniscient, all-knowing.

.16 **cognizant of, aware of, conscious of, mindful of, sensible to** or **of, appreciative of,** no stranger to, seized of [Brit]; privy to, in the secret, let into, in the know [slang], behind the scenes or curtain; alive to, awake to; **wise to** [informal], hep to or on to [both slang]; streetwise; apprised of, informed of; undeceived, undeluded.

.17 [slang or informal terms] **hep, hip,** on the beam, go-go, **with it,** into, really into, groovy.

.18 **informed, enlightened, instructed,** versed, well-versed, educated, schooled, **taught;** posted, briefed, primed, trained;

up on, up-to-date, abreast of, *au courant* [Fr].

.19 versed in, informed in, read or well-read in, up on, strong in, at home in, master of, expert or authoritative in, proficient in, **familiar with**, at home with, **conversant with, acquainted with**, intimate with.

.20 well-informed, well-posted, well-educated, **well-grounded, well-versed, well-read**, widely read.

.21 learned, erudite, educated, cultured, cultivated, lettered, literate, civilized, **scholarly, scholastic**, studious; wise 467.17; **profound**, deep, abstruse; encyclopedic, pansophic, polymath or polymathic, polyhistoric.

.22 book-learned, book-read, literary, book-taught, book-fed, book-wise, **bookish**, booky, book-minded; book-loving, bibliophilic, bibliophagic; **pedantic**, donnish [Brit], scholastic, inkhorn; **bluestocking**.

.23 intellectual 466.8, intellectualistic; **highbrow** or highbrowed or highbrowish [all informal]; elitist.

.24 self-educated, self-taught, autodidactic.

.25 knowable, cognizable, recognizable, **understandable, comprehensible**, apprehendable, apprehensible, prehensible, graspable, seizable, discernible, conceivable, appreciable, perceptible, distinguishable, ascertainable, discoverable.

.26 known, recognized, ascertained, conceived, grasped, apprehended, prehended, seized, perceived, discerned, appreciated, **understood, comprehended**, realized; pat or **down pat** [both informal].

.27 well-known, well-kenned [Scot], well-understood, well-recognized, **widely known**, commonly known, universally recognized, generally or universally admitted; **familiar**, familiar as household words, household, **common, current; proverbial**; public, notorious; known by every schoolboy; talked-of, talked-about, in everyone's mouth, **on everyone's tongue; commonplace**, trite 883.9, hackneyed, platitudinous, truistic.

.28 scientific, scientifico–; **technical, technological**, technicological, techno–; **scholarly**; disciplinary.

.29 ADVS knowingly, consciously, wittingly, with forethought, understandingly, intelligently, studiously, learnedly, eruditely, as every schoolboy knows.

.30 to one's knowledge, **to the best of one's knowledge**, as far as one can see or tell, as far as one knows, as well as can be said.

476. INTELLECTUAL

.1 NOUNS intellectual, intellect, intellectualist, literate, member of the intelligentsia, white-collar intellectual; brainworker, thinker; Brahmin, mandarin, egghead [slang]; **highbrow** [informal]; wise man 468.

.2 intelligentsia, literati, illuminati; intellectual elite.

.3 scholar, scholastic [archaic], clerk or learned clerk [both archaic]; a gentleman and a scholar; student 566; **learned man**, man of learning, giant of learning, colossus of knowledge, mastermind, **savant**, pundit; genius 733.12; polymath, polyhistor, **mine of information**, walking encyclopedia; literary man, *littérateur* [Fr] or litterateur, **man of letters**; philologist, philologue; philomath, lover of learning; philosopher, philosophe; bookman; **academician**, schoolman; classicist, classicist, Latinist, humanist.

.4 bookworm, bibliophage; **grind** or greasy grind [both slang]; **booklover, bibliophile**, bibliophilist, philobiblist, bibliolater, bibliolatrist; bibliomaniac, bibliomane.

.5 pedant; **formalist, precisionist**, precisian, purist, *précieux* [Fr], **bluestocking**, *bas bleu* [Fr], *précieuse* [Fr fem]; Dr. Pangloss [Voltaire].

.6 dilettante, **half scholar**, sciolist, **dabbler**, dabster, amateur, trifler, smatterer; grammaticaster, philologaster, criticaster, philosophaster, Latinitaster.

477. IGNORANCE

.1 NOUNS ignorance, ignorantness, **unknowingness**, unknowing, nescience; lack of information, knowledge-gap, hiatus of learning; empty-headedness, blankmindedness, vacuousness, vacuity, inanity; tabula rasa; **unintelligence** 469; **unacquaintance, unfamiliarity; greenness**, greenhornism, rawness, callowness, unripeness, green in the eye, **inexperience** 734.2; innocence, simpleness, simplicity; crass or gross or primal or pristine ignorance; ignorantism, know-nothingism, obscurantism; agnosticism.

.2 "blind and naked Ignorance" [Tennyson], "the mother of devotion" [Robert Burton], "the mother of prejudice" [John Bright], "the dominion of absurdity" [J. A. Froude].

.3 **incognizance, unawareness, unconsciousness, insensibility,** unwittingness, nonrecognition; nonrealization, incomprehension; **unmindfulness;** mindlessness; blindness 441, deafness 449.

.4 **unenlightenment, benightedness,** benightment, dark, darkness; savagery, barbarism, paganism, heathenism, Gothicism; age of ignorance, dark age; rural idiocy.

.5 **unlearnedness, inerudition,** ineducation, unschooledness, unletteredness; **unscholarliness,** unstudiousness; **illiteracy,** illiterateness, functional illiteracy; **unintellectuality,** unintellectualism, Philistinism, bold ignorance.

.6 **slight knowledge,** vague notion, imperfect knowledge, a little learning, glimmering, glimpse [archaic], smattering, **smattering of knowledge,** smattering of ignorance, **half-learning,** semi-learning, semi-ignorance, sciolism; **superficiality,** shallowness, surface-scratching; **dilettantism,** dilettantship, amateurism.

.7 **the unknown,** the unknowable, the strange, the unfamiliar, the incalculable; **matter of ignorance,** sealed book, riddle, enigma, mystery, puzzle 514.3, 549.8,9; *terra incognita* [L], unexplored ground or territory; frontier, frontiers of knowledge, **unknown quantity,** x, y, z, n; dark horse.

.8 **ignoramus, know-nothing;** no scholar, puddinghead, dunce, fool 471; **illiterate; lowbrow** [informal]; unintelligentsia, illiterati; **greenhorn,** greeny [informal], tenderfoot; **dilettante,** dabbler 476.6; **middlebrow** [informal].

.9 VERBS **be ignorant,** be green, have everything to learn, **know nothing,** know from nothing [slang]; wallow in ignorance; not know any better; **not know what's what,** not know what it is all about, not know the score [informal], not be with it [informal], not know any of the answers; not know the time of day or what o'clock it is, not know beans, not know the first thing about, not know one's ass from one's elbow [slang], not know the way home, not know enough to come in out of the rain, not know chalk from cheese, **not know up from down,** not know which way is up.

.10 **be in the dark,** be blind, labor in darkness, walk in darkness, be benighted, grope in the dark, "see through a glass, darkly" [Bible].

.11 **not know,** not rightly know [dial], know not, know not what, know nothing of, wot not of [Brit dial], be innocent of, have no idea or notion or conception, **not have the first idea, not have the least** or **remotest idea,** not have idea one, not have the foggiest [slang], **not pretend to say,** not take upon oneself to say; not know the half of it; not know from Adam, not know from the man in the moon; wonder, wonder whether; half-know, have a little learning, scratch the surface, know a little, smatter, dabble, toy with, coquet with; pass, give up.

.12 ADJS **ignorant,** nescient, **unknowing,** uncomprehending, **know-nothing;** simple, **dumb** [informal], empty, empty-headed, blankminded, vacuous, inane, **unintelligent** 469.13; **uninformed, unenlightened,** unilluminated, unapprized, unposted [informal]; **unacquainted, unconversant,** unversed, uninitiated, **unfamiliar,** strange to; **inexperienced** 734.17; **green,** callow, innocent, gauche, awkward, naïve, unripe, raw; groping, tentative, unsure.

.13 **unaware, unconscious, insensible, unknowing,** incognizant; mindless, witless; unprehensive, unrealizing, nonconceiving, **unmindful,** unwitting, unsuspecting; unperceiving, impercipient, unhearing, unseeing, uninsightful; unaware of, in ignorance of, unconscious of, unmindful of, insensible to, out of it [informal], not with it [informal]; **blind to, deaf to,** dead to, a stranger to; asleep, napping, **off one's guard,** caught napping, caught tripping.

.14 **unlearned, inerudite,** unerudite, **uneducated,** unschooled, uninstructed, untutored, unbriefed, untaught, unedified, unguided; ill-educated, misinstructed, misinformed, mistaught, led astray; hoodwinked, deceived; **illiterate,** functionally illiterate, unlettered, grammarless; **unscholarly,** unscholastic, unstudious; **unliterary, unread,** unbookish, unbooklearned, bookless [archaic], unbooked; **uncultured,** uncultivated, unrefined, rude, Philistine; barbarous, pagan, heathen; Gothic; nonintellectual, **unintellectual; lowbrow** or lowbrowed or lowbrowish [all informal].

.15 **half-learned,** half-baked [informal], half-cocked or half-assed [both slang], sciolistic; **shallow, superficial;** immature, sophomoric(al); **dilettante,** dilettantish, smattering, dabbling, amateur, amateurish; **wise in one's own conceit.**

.16 **benighted, dark,** in darkness, in the dark.

.17 **unknown,** unbeknown [informal], un-

heard [archaic], **unheard-of**, unappre-
hended, unapparent, unperceived, unsuspected; unexplained, unascertained; unin-
vestigated, unexplored; unidentified, unclassified, uncharted, unfathomed,
unplumbed, virgin, untouched; undisclosed, unrevealed, undivulged, undiscovered, unexposed, sealed; **unfamiliar,**
strange; incalculable, **unknowable,** incognizable, undiscoverable; able; enigmatic
549.17, mysterious, puzzling 514.25.

.18 ADVS **ignorantly, unknowingly,** unmindfully, unwittingly, witlessly, unsuspectingly, **unawares;** unconsciously, insensi-
bly; for anything or aught one knows, not
that one knows.

.19 INTERJS **God knows!,** God only knows!,
Lord knows!, Heaven knows!, nobody
knows!, damned if I know!, **it beats me!,**
it has me guessing!, it's Greek to me!;
search me!, you've got me!, I give up!, I
pass!, **who knows?,** how should I know?, I
don't know what!

478. THOUGHT

(exercise of the intellect)

.1 NOUNS **thought, thinking, cogitation,** log-
(o)–; cerebration, ideation, noesis, menta-
tion, intellection, intellectualization, ratiocination; workings of the mind; **reasoning** 482; **brainwork, headwork,** mental
labor or effort, mental act or process, act
of thought, mental or intellectual exercise; heavy thinking; straight thinking;
conception, conceit [archaic], conceptualization; abstract thought, imageless
thought; excogitation, thinking out or
through; thinking aloud; **idea** 479; creative thought 535.2.

.2 **consideration, contemplation, reflection,
speculation, meditation, musing, rumination, deliberation,** lucubration, brooding,
study, **pondering,** weighing, revolving,
turning over in the mind; advisement,
counsel.

.3 **thoughtfulness,** contemplativeness, speculativeness, reflectiveness; **pensiveness,**
wistfulness, reverie, musing, melancholy;
preoccupation, absorption, engrossment,
abstraction, brown study, deep or profound thought; **concentration,** study,
close study.

.4 **thoughts,** inmost thoughts, secret
thoughts, mind's core; **train of thought,**
current or flow of thought or ideas, succession or sequence or chain of thought

or ideas; **stream of consciousness; association,** association of ideas.

.5 **mature thought,** developed thought, ripe
idea; **afterthought,** *arrière-pensée* [Fr], *esprit d'escalier* [Fr], second thought or
thoughts; **reconsideration,** reappraisal, revaluation, rethinking, re-examination, review, thinking over.

.6 **introspection,** self-communion, self-coun-
sel, self-consultation, subjective inspection or speculation.

.7 subject for thought, food for thought,
something to chew on, something to get
one's teeth into.

.8 VERBS **think, cogitate,** cerebrate, intellectualize, ideate, conceive, conceptualize,
form ideas, entertain ideas; **reason** 482.15;
use one's head, use or exercise the mind,
set the brain or wits to work, bethink
oneself, put on one's thinking or considering cap [informal].

.9 **think hard,** think one's head off, **rack** or
ransack one's brains, crack one's brains
[informal], **beat** or **cudgel one's brains,**
work one's head to the bone, do some
heavy thinking, bend or apply the mind;
sweat or stew over [informal], hammer or
hammer away at; puzzle, **puzzle over.**

.10 **concentrate,** concentrate the mind or
thoughts, concentrate on or upon, attend
closely to, **focus on** or **upon,** give or devote the mind to, glue the mind to,
cleave to the thought of, fix the mind or
thoughts upon, bend the mind upon,
bring the mind to bear upon; gather or
collect one's thoughts, pull one's wits together, focus or fix one's thoughts, marshal or arrange one's thoughts or ideas.

.11 **think about,** cogitate, **give** or **apply the
mind to,** put one's mind to, apply oneself
to, bend or turn the mind or thoughts to,
direct the mind upon, **give thought to,
trouble one's head about,** occupy the
mind or thoughts with; think through or
out, puzzle out, sort out, reason out, excogitate.

.12 **consider, contemplate, speculate, reflect,
study, ponder,** perpend, **weigh, deliberate, debate, meditate, muse, brood, ruminate,** chew the cud [informal], digest; introspect, be abstracted; fall into a brown
study, retreat into one's mind or
thoughts; **toy with, play with,** play
around with, flirt or coquet with the
idea.

.13 **think over, ponder over, brood over,
muse over, mull over, reflect over,** con
over, **deliberate over,** run over, **meditate**

over, ruminate over, chew over, digest, turn over, **revolve**, revolve in the mind, turn over in the mind, deliberate upon, meditate upon, muse on or upon, bestow thought or consideration upon.

.14 **take under consideration,** entertain, take under advisement, take under active consideration, inquire into, **think it over,** see about [informal]; **sleep upon,** consult or advise with or take counsel of one's pillow.

.15 **reconsider, re-examine,** review; revise one's thoughts, reappraise, revaluate, rethink; view in a new light, have second thoughts, think better of.

.16 **think of,** bethink oneself of, **entertain the idea of,** entertain thoughts of; have an idea of, have thoughts about; **have in mind, contemplate, consider;** take it into one's head; **bear in mind, keep in mind,** hold the thought; harbor an idea, keep or hold an idea, cherish or foster or nurse or nurture an idea.

.17 (look upon mentally) **contemplate, look upon, view, regard,** see, view with the mind's eye, **envisage,** envision, **visualize** 535.15, imagine, image.

.18 **occur to,** occur to one's mind, occur, **come to mind,** rise to mind, rise in the mind, come into one's head, impinge on one's consciousness, claim one's mind or thoughts, pass through one's head or mind, dawn upon one, **enter one's mind,** pass in the mind or the thoughts, **cross one's mind,** race or tumble through the mind, flash on or across the mind; **strike,** strike one, strike the mind, grab one [slang], **suggest itself,** present itself, offer itself, present itself to the mind or thoughts.

.19 **impress, make an impression, strike,** grab [slang], hit; catch the thoughts, arrest the thoughts, seize one's mind, sink or penetrate into the mind, embed itself in the mind, lodge in the mind, **sink in** [informal].

.20 **occupy the mind** or **thoughts,** engage the thoughts, monopolize the thoughts, fasten itself on the mind, seize the mind, fill the mind, take up one's thoughts; **preoccupy,** occupy, **absorb, engross,** absorb or enwrap or engross the thoughts, obsess the mind, run in the head; foster in the mind; come uppermost, be uppermost in the mind; have in or on one's mind, **have on the brain** [informal], have constantly in one's thoughts.

.21 ADJS **cognitive,** prehensive, **thought,** conceptive, conceptual, conceptualized, ideative, noetic, mental; **thoughtful,** cogitative, **contemplative, reflective, speculative, deliberative, meditative, ruminative,** ruminant, museful [archaic]; **pensive,** wistful; introspective; thinking, reflecting, contemplating, pondering, deliberating, excogitating, excogitative, meditating, ruminating, musing; sober, serious, deep-thinking; concentrating, concentrative.

.22 absorbed or engrossed in thought, **absorbed, engrossed,** introspective, rapt, **wrapped in thought, lost in thought,** abstracted, immersed in thought, buried in thought, engaged in thought, occupied, preoccupied.

.23 ADVS **thoughtfully,** contemplatively, reflectively, meditatively, ruminatively, musefully [archaic]; **pensively,** wistfully; on reconsideration, on second thought.

.24 **on one's mind, on the brain** or on one's chest [both informal], in the thoughts; in the heart, in petto [Ital], in one's inmost thoughts.

479. IDEA

.1 NOUNS **idea,** ideo–; **thought,** mental or intellectual object, **notion, fancy, concept, conception,** conceit; **perception, impression,** mental impression, image, **mental image,** representation, recept; imago; memory-trace; **sentiment,** apprehension; reflection, observation; **opinion** 501.6; supposition, **theory** 499.

.2 (philosophy) ideatum, ideate; noumenon; universal, universal concept or conception; idée-force; Platonic idea or form, archetype, prototype, subsistent form, eternal object, transcendent universal, eternal universal, pattern, model, exemplar, ideal, transcendent idea or essence, universal essence, innate idea; Aristotelian form, form-giving cause, formal cause; complex idea, simple idea; percept; construct of memory and association; Kantian idea, supreme principle of pure reason, regulative first principle, highest unitary principle of thought, transcendent nonempirical concept; Hegelian idea, highest category, the Absolute, the Absolute Idea, the Self-determined, the realized ideal; noosphere [Teilhard de Chardin]; history of ideas, Geistesgeschichte [Ger]; **idealism** 377.3.

.3 **abstract idea, abstraction,** abstract.

.4 **main idea,** leading or principal idea, fundamental idea, idée-maitresse [Fr], guiding principle, **big idea** [informal].

.5 **novel idea,** new or **latest wrinkle** [informal], new slant or twist [informal].

.6 **good idea,** not a bad idea; **bright thought,** bright or brilliant idea, **brainchild** or **brainstorm** [both informal], **inspiration.**

.7 **absurd idea,** crazy idea, fool notion, brainstorm [both informal].

.8 **ideology,** system of ideas, body of ideas, system of theories; world view, *Weltanschauung* [Ger]; philosophy; **ethos.**

.9 ADJS ideational, ideal, **conceptual, notional,** fanciful; **theoretical** 499.13; **ideological.**

.10 **ideaed, notioned, thoughted.**

480. ABSENCE OF THOUGHT

.1 NOUNS **thoughtlessness,** thoughtfreeness; **vacuity,** vacancy, **emptiness of mind, empty-headedness,** blankness, mental blankness, blankmindedness; fatuity, inanity, foolishness 470; tranquillity, calm of mind; **nirvana;** oblivion; quietism, passivity; blank mind, fallow mind, tabula rasa; unintelligence 469.

.2 VERBS **not think, make the mind a blank,** let the mind lie fallow; **not think of,** not consider, be unmindful of; **not enter one's mind** or **head,** be far from one's thoughts.

.3 **get it off one's mind, get it off one's chest** [informal], clear the mind, relieve one's mind; **put it out of one's thoughts,** dismiss from the mind or thoughts, push from one's thoughts, put away thought.

.4 ADJS **thoughtless, thoughtfree,** incogitant, **unthinking,** unreasoning; unideaed; unintellectual; **vacuous,** vacant, blank, blankminded, relaxed, empty, **empty-headed,** fatuous, inane 469.19; unoccupied; calm, tranquil; nirvanic; oblivious; quietistic, passive.

.5 **unthought-of, undreamed-of,** unconsidered, unconceived, unconceptualized; unimagined, unimaged; imageless.

481. INTUITION

.1 NOUNS **intuition, intuitiveness, sixth sense;** intuitive reason or knowledge, direct apprehension, unmediated perception, subconscious perception, unconscious or subconscious knowledge, immediate cognition, knowledge without thought or reason; **insight,** inspiration, aperçu; anticipation, a priori knowledge; *satori* [Jap], *buddhi* [Skt]; woman's intuition; second sight, second-sightedness,

precognition 542.3, clairvoyance 1034.8; intuitionism, intuitivism.

.2 **instinct,** natural instinct, unlearned capacity, innate or inborn proclivity, native or natural tendency, **impulse,** blind or unreasoning impulse, vital impulse; **libido, id,** primitive self; archetype, archetypal pattern or idea; unconscious or subconscious urge or drive; collective unconscious; "the *not ourselves,* which is in us and all around us" [Matthew Arnold], "an unfathomable Somewhat, which is *Not we*" [Carlyle], "that which is imprinted upon the spirit of man by an inward instinct" [Francis Bacon].

.3 **hunch** [informal], **presentiment, premonition,** preapprehension, intimation, foreboding 544; suspicion, **impression,** intuition, intuitive impression, **feeling,** forefeeling, vague feeling or idea, funny feeling [informal], feeling in one's bones.

.4 VERBS **intuit, sense, feel,** feel intuitively, **feel in one's bones** [informal], **have a feeling,** have a funny feeling [informal], **get** or **have the impression, have a hunch** [informal], just know, know instinctively.

.5 ADJS **intuitive,** intuitional, sensing, feeling; **second-sighted, precognitive** 542.7, clairvoyant 1034.23.

.6 **instinctive,** natural, **inherent, innate,** unlearned; unconscious, subliminal; **involuntary, automatic,** spontaneous, impulsive; libidinal.

.7 ADVS **intuitively,** by intuition; **instinctively,** automatically, spontaneously, on or by instinct.

482. REASONING

.1 NOUNS **reasoning, reason,** logical thought, discursive reason, rationalizing, rationalization, ratiocination; induction, inductive reasoning, deduction, deductive reasoning; rationalism, **rationality,** discourse or discourse of reason [both archaic]; sweet reason, reasonableness; demonstration, proof 505; specious reasoning, sophistry 483; philosophy 500.

.2 **logic,** logics, logico–; **dialectics,** dialectic, dialecticism; art of reason, science of discursive thought; formal logic, material logic; doctrine of terms, doctrine of the judgment, doctrine of inference, traditional or Aristotelian logic, Ramist or Ramistic logic, modern or epistemological logic, pragmatic or instrumental or experimental logic; psychological logic, psychologism; symbolic or mathematical logic, logistic; propositional calculus, calculus of individuals, functional calculus, combinatory logic, algebra of relations, algebra of classes, set theory, Boolean algebra.

.3 (methods) a priori reasoning, a fortiori reasoning, a posteriori reasoning; discursive reasoning; **deduction, deductive reasoning,** syllogism, syllogistic reasoning; **induction, inductive reasoning,** epagoge; philosophical induction, inductive *or* Baconian method; **inference; generalization,** particularization; synthesis, analysis; hypothesis and verification.

.4 **argumentation, argument, controversy, dispute, disputation, polemic,** disceptation [archaic], eristic; **contention, wrangling, bickering,** hubbub 453.3, bicker, setto [informal], rhubarb *or* hassle [both slang], passage of arms; war of words, verbal engagement *or* contest, logomachy, flyting; paper war, *guerre de plume* [Fr]; academic disputation, defense of a thesis; defense, apology, apologia, apologetics; pilpul, casuistry; polemics; litigation.

.5 **argument,** *argumentum* [L]; **case, plea,** pleading, *plaidoyer* [Fr]; special pleading; **reason, consideration; refutation,** elenchus, ignoratio elenchi; pros, cons, **pros and cons;** talking point.

.6 **syllogism;** prosyllogism; mode; figure; mood; pseudosyllogism, paralogism; sorites, progressive *or* Aristotelian sorites, regressive *or* Goclenian sorites; categorical syllogism; enthymeme; dilemma; **rule,** rule of deduction, transformation rule; modus ponens, modus tollens.

.7 **premise, proposition, position,** assumed position, sumption, **assumption,** supposal, presupposition, **hypothesis, thesis, theorem,** lemma, **statement,** affirmation, categorical proposition, assertion, basis, ground, foundation; **postulate, axiom, postulation,** postulatum; data; major premise, minor premise; first principles; a priori principle, apriorism; philosophical proposition, philosopheme; hypothesis ad hoc; sentential *or* propositional function, truth-function, truth table, truth-value.

.8 **conclusion** 494.4.

.9 **reasonableness,** reasonability, **logicalness,** logicality, **rationality, sensibleness, soundness,** justness, justifiability, admissibility; **sense,** common sense, sound sense, sweet reason, **logic, reason;** plausibility 511.3.

.10 **good reasoning, right thinking,** sound reasoning, ironclad reasoning, irrefutable logic; **cogent argument, cogency;** strong argument, knockdown argument; good

case, good reason, sound evidence, strong point.

.11 **reasoner,** ratiocinator, **thinker; rationalist;** rationalizer; **logician,** logistician; logicaster; dialectician; syllogist, syllogizer; sophist 483.6; philosopher 500.6,12,13.

.12 **arguer, controversialist, disputant, debater,** argufier [informal], wrangler, mooter, Philadelphia lawyer [informal], guardhouse lawyer [informal], disceptator [archaic], pilpulist, casuist; polemic, polemist, polemicist; logomacher, logomachist; apologist.

.13 **contentiousness,** litigiousness, **quarrelsomeness,** argumentativeness, disputatiousness, combativeness 797.15; ill humor 951.

.14 **side,** interest; **the affirmative,** pro, aye; **the negative,** con, no, nay.

.15 VERBS **reason;** logicalize, logicize; rationalize, provide a rationale; intellectualize; bring reason to bear, apply *or* use reason, put two and two together; **deduce, infer, generalize; synthesize, analyze; theorize,** hypothesize; philosophize; syllogize.

.16 **argue,** argufy [informal], **dispute,** discept [archaic], logomachize, polemize, polemicize, moot, **bandy words, chop logic, plead,** pettifog [informal], join issue, give and take, cut and thrust, try conclusions, cross swords, lock horns, **contend, contest,** spar, **bicker, wrangle,** hassle [slang], have it out; thrash out; take one's stand upon, **put up an argument** [informal]; take sides, take up a side; argue to no purpose; **quibble, cavil** 483.9.

.17 **be reasonable, be logical, make sense,** figure [informal], **stand to reason,** be demonstrable, be irrefutable; hold good, hold water [informal]; have a leg to stand on.

.18 ADJS **reasoning, rational,** ratiocinative *or* ratiocinatory; analytic(al).

.19 **argumentative, argumental, dialectic(al), controversial, disputatious, contentious, quarrelsome,** litigious, combative 797.25, ill-humored 951.18–26, eristic(al), polemic(al), logomachic(al), pilpulistic, pro and con.

.20 **logical, reasonable, rational, cogent, sensible, sane, sound,** wholesome, legitimate, just, justifiable, admissible; credible 501.24; plausible 511.7; as it should be, as it ought to be; **well-argued, well-founded, well-grounded.**

.21 **reasoned, advised, considered, calculated,**

meditated, contemplated, deliberated, studied, weighed, thought-out.

.22 dialectic(al), maieutic; syllogistic(al), enthymematic(al), soritical, epagogic, inductive, deductive, inferential, synthetic(al), analytic(al), discursive; a priori, a fortiori, a posteriori; categorical, hypothetical, conditional.

.23 **deducible, derivable, infenible;** sequential, following.

.24 ADVS **reasonably, logically, rationally,** by the rules of logic, **sensibly,** sanely, soundly; syllogistically, analytically; **in reason,** in all reason, within reason, within the bounds or limits of reason, within reasonable limitations, **within bounds,** within the bounds of possibility, as far as possible, in all conscience.

483. SOPHISTRY

(specious reasoning)

.1 NOUNS **sophistry,** sophistication, sophism, philosophism, **casuistry,** jesuitry, jesuitism, subtlety, oversubtlety; **false** or **specious reasoning, rationalization,** evasive reasoning, vicious reasoning, sophistical reasoning, special pleading; **fallacy,** fallaciousness; **speciousness,** speciosity, superficial or apparent soundness, plausibleness, plausibility; **insincerity, disingenuousness; equivocation,** equivocalness; perversion, distortion, misapplication; vicious circle, circularity; mystification, obfuscation, obscurantism.

.2 **illogicalness,** illogic, illogicality, **unreasonableness, irrationality, reasonlessness, senselessness, unsoundness,** unscientificness, invalidity, untenableness, inconclusiveness; **inconsistency,** incongruity, antilogy.

.3 (specious argument) **sophism,** sophistry, insincere argument, mere rhetoric, philosophism, solecism; paralogism, pseudosyllogism; claptrap, moonshine, empty words, "sound and fury, signifying nothing" [Shakespeare]; bad case, weak point, flaw in an argument, "lame and impotent conclusion" [Shakespeare]; **fallacy,** logical fallacy, formal fallacy, material fallacy, verbal fallacy; *argumentum ad hominem, argumentum ad baculum, argumentum ad captandum, argumentum ad captandum vulgus* [all L], crowd-pleasing argument, argument by analogy, *tu quoque* argument, *petitio principii* [L], begging the question, **circular argument,** undis-

tributed middle, *non sequitur* [L], *hysteron proteron* [Gk].

.4 **quibble,** quiddity, quodlibet, quillet [archaic], jesuitism, **cavil,** quip, quirk, shuffle, dodge.

.5 **quibbling, caviling,** boggling, captiousness, nit-picking, **bickering; logic-chopping, hairsplitting,** trichoschistism; subterfuge, chicane, chicanery, pettifoggery; **equivocation,** tergiversation, prevarication, **evasion, hedging, pussyfooting** [informal], **sidestepping,** dodging, shifting, shuffling, fencing, parrying, boggling, paltering.

.6 **sophist,** sophister, philosophist [archaic], **casuist,** Jesuit; choplogic [archaic], logic-chopper; paralogist.

.7 **quibbler, caviler,** pettifogger, hairsplitter, captious or picayune critic, nitpicker; **equivocator,** mystifier, mystificator, obscurantist, prevaricator, palterer, tergiversator, shuffler, **hedger;** pussyfoot or **pussyfooter** [both informal].

.8 VERBS reason speciously, reason ill, paralogize, reason in a circle, argue insincerely, pervert, distort, misapply; rationalize; prove that black is white and white black; not have a leg to stand on.

.9 **quibble, cavil, bicker,** boggle, chop logic, **split hairs,** nitpick; **equivocate,** mystify, obscure, prevaricate, tergiversate, palter, fence, parry, shift, **shuffle, dodge,** shy, **evade, sidestep, hedge, pussyfoot** [informal], evade the issue; **beat about** or **around the bush,** not come to the point, **beg the question;** blow hot and cold; strain at a gnat and swallow a camel, pick nits.

.10 ADJS **sophistical,** sophistic, philosophistic(al) [archaic], casuistic(al), jesuitic(al), **fallacious, specious,** colorable, plausible, hollow, superficially or apparently sound; deceptive, illusive, empty; overrefined, oversubtle, **insincere, disingenuous.**

.11 **illogical, unreasonable, irrational, reasonless,** contrary to reason, **senseless,** without reason, **without rhyme or reason; unscientific,** nonscientific, unphilosophical; **invalid,** inauthentic, unauthentic, faulty, flawed, paralogical, fallacious; inconclusive, inconsequent, inconsequential, not following; **inconsistent,** incongruous, absonant [archaic], loose, unconnected; contradictory, **self-contradictory,** self-annulling, self-refuting.

.12 **unsound, unsubstantial,** insubstantial, weak, feeble, poor, flimsy, unrigorous, inconclusive, unproved, unsustained, poorly argued.

.13 **baseless, groundless,** ungrounded, **unfounded,** ill-founded, unbased, **unsupported,** unsustained, **without foundation,** without basis or sound basis; **untenable, unsupportable,** unsustainable; **unwarranted,** idle, empty, vain.

.14 **quibbling, caviling, equivocatory,** captious, nit-picking [slang], **bickering;** picayune, petty, trivial, trifling; paltering, shuffling, hedging, pussyfooting [informal], **evasive; hairsplitting,** trichoschistic, logic-chopping, choplogic(al) [archaic].

.15 ADVS **illogically, unreasonably, irrationally, reasonlessly, senselessly;** baselessly, groundlessly; untenably, unsupportably, unsustainably; out of all reason, out of all bounds.

.16 PHRS *post hoc, ergo propter hoc* [L, after this, therefore because of this].

484. TOPIC

.1 NOUNS **topic, subject,** subject of thought, **matter, subject matter,** what it is about, **concern,** focus of interest or attention, **theme,** burden, **text,** motif, motive, business at hand, **case,** matter in hand, **question, problem, issue; point,** point at issue, point in question, main point, gist 672.6; item on the agenda; head, heading, chapter, rubric; substance, meat, essence, material part, basis; living issue, topic of the day.

.2 **caption, title, heading, head,** superscription, rubric; **headline;** overline; banner, banner head or line, streamer; **scarehead,** screamer; spread, spreadhead; drop head, dropline, hanger; running head or title, jump head; **subhead, subheading,** subtitle; legend, motto, epigraph; title page.

.3 VERBS **caption, title, head,** head up [informal]; **headline;** subtitle, subhead.

.4 ADJS **topical, thematic.**

485. INQUIRY

.1 NOUNS **inquiry,** inquiring, inquirendo, **inquest** 408.18, inquisition; inquiring mind; analysis 48.

.2 **examination,** examen, **exam** [informal], **test, trial, quiz;** oral examination, oral, doctor's oral, master's oral, viva voce examination, viva [informal]; **audition, hearing;** written examination, written [informal], blue book [informal]; midterm, midyear, midsemester; qualifying examination, preliminary examination, prelim [informal]; take-home examination; final

examination, **final** [informal], comprehensive examination, comps [informal], great go [archaic] or greats (Oxford); honors [Brit], tripos (Cambridge).

.3 **examination, inspection, scrutiny,** –opsy; **survey, review, perusal,** perlustration, **study,** look-through, scan, run-through; visitation; overhaul, overhauling; quality control.

.4 **investigation,** indagation [archaic], **research,** legwork [informal], inquiry into; sifting, gathering or amassing evidence; perscrutation, probe, searching investigation, close inquiry, exhaustive study; police inquiry or investigation, criminal investigation, detective work, detection, sleuthing; investigative bureau or agency, bureau or department of investigation; legislative investigation, congressional investigation, hearing; witch-hunt; fishing expedition.

.5 preliminary or tentative examination; quick or cursory inspection, quick look; grope, prod, feel.

.6 **checkup, check;** spot check; physical examination, **physical,** physical checkup, health examination; exploratory examination.

.7 **re-examination,** reinquiry, recheck, **review,** reappraisal, revaluation, rethinking, revision, rebeholding, second or further look.

.8 **reconnaissance;** recce or recco or recon [all slang]; **reconnoitering,** reconnoiter, exploration, **scouting.**

.9 **surveillance,** shadowing, following, trailing, tailing [informal], 24-hour surveillance, observation, stakeout [informal]; **spying, espionage,** espial, **intelligence,** military intelligence, intelligence work, cloak-and-dagger work [informal]; intelligence agency, secret service, secret police; counterespionage, counterintelligence; wiretap, wiretapping, bugging, electronic surveillance.

.10 **question, query, inquiry,** demand [archaic], **interrogation,** interrogatory; interrogative; **problem, issue, topic** 484, case or point in question, bone of contention, controversial point, question before the house, debating point, question or point at issue, **moot point** or case, question mark, *quodlibet* [L]; vexed or knotty question, burning question; leader, leading question; feeler, trial balloon, fishing question; cross-question, rhetorical question; cross-interrogatory; catechism.

.11 **questioning, interrogation, querying,** asking, seeking, pumping, probing, inquiring; **quiz**, quizzing, **examination;** challenge, dispute; interpellation, bringing into question; catechizing, catechization; catechetical method, Socratic method *or* induction.

.12 **grilling,** the grill [slang], inquisition; police interrogation; **third-degree** [informal]; direct examination, redirect examination, **cross-examination,** cross-interrogation, **cross-questioning.**

.13 **canvass, survey, inquiry, questionnaire,** questionary; **poll, public-opinion poll,** opinion poll *or* survey, statistical survey, opinion sampling, voter-preference survey, consumer-preference survey; consumer research.

.14 **search,** searching, **quest, hunt,** hunting, stalk, stalking, still hunt, dragnet, frisk [slang]; posse, search party; search warrant; search-and-destroy operation *or* mission; **rummage, ransacking,** turning over *or* upside down; **forage;** house-search, perquisition, domiciliary visit; exploration, probe.

.15 **inquirer, asker, prober,** querier, querist, **questioner,** questionist, interrogator; interrogatrix; interpellator; **quizzer,** examiner, catechist; inquisitor, inquisitionist; cross-questioner, cross-interrogator, **cross-examiner;** interlocutor; **pollster,** poller, sampler, opinion-sampler; **interviewer; detective** 781.10; **secret agent** 781.9.

.16 **examiner,** examinant, **tester; inspector,** scrutinizer, scrutator; scrutineer, quality-control inspector, check-out pilot; observer; visitor, visitator; **investigator,** indagator [archaic].

.17 seeker, hunter, searcher, perquisitor; rummager, ransacker; digger, delver; zetetic; **researcher,** researchist, research worker.

.18 **examinee,** examinant, examinate, questionee, quizzee; informant, subject, interviewee; witness.

.19 VERBS **inquire, ask, question, query; make inquiry,** take up *or* institute *or* pursue *or* follow up *or* conduct *or* carry on an inquiry, ask about, ask questions, put queries; inquire of, require an answer, ask a question, put a question to, pose *or* set *or* propose *or* propound a question; bring into question, interpellate; **demand** [archaic], **want to know.**

.20 **interrogate, question, query, quiz, test, examine;** catechize; **pump,** pump for information, shoot questions at, pick the brains of, worm out of; interview.

.21 **grill,** put on the grill [informal], inquisi-

tion, make inquisition; roast [informal], put the pressure on [informal], put the screws to, go over [both slang]; **cross-examine, cross-question,** cross-interrogate; third-degree [slang], put through the third degree [informal]; put to the question; extract information, pry *or* prize out.

.22 **investigate,** indagate [archaic], sift, **explore, look into,** peer into, **search into, go into, delve into,** dig into, poke into, pry into; **probe, sound, plumb, fathom.**

.23 **examine, inspect, scrutinize, survey,** canvass, **look at,** peer at, **observe, scan, peruse, study; look over,** run the eye over, cast *or* pass the eyes over, go over, run over, pass over, pore over; overlook, overhaul; **monitor, review,** pass under review; set an examination, give an examination; **take stock of,** size *or* **size up,** take the measure [informal]; **check, check out, check over** *or* **through; check up on;** autopsy, postmortem 408.18.

.24 **make a close study of,** scrutinize, examine thoroughly, vet [Brit], **go deep into,** look closely at; examine point by point, go over step by step, subject to close scrutiny, view *or* try in all its phases, get down to nuts and bolts [informal]; perscrutate, perlustrate.

.25 **examine cursorily,** take a cursory view of, give a quick *or* cursory look, give a dekko [Brit slang], **scan, skim, skim over** *or* **through,** slur, slur over, slip *or* skip over *or* through, **glance at,** give the once-over [slang], pass over lightly, zip through, **dip into, touch upon,** touch upon lightly *or* in passing, **hit the high spots; thumb through,** flip through the pages, turn over the leaves, leaf *or* page through.

.26 **re-examine, recheck, reinquire, reconsider,** reappraise, revaluate, rethink, **review,** revise, rebehold, take another *or* a second *or* a further look; retrace, retrace one's steps, go back over.

.27 **reconnoiter,** make a reconnaissance, case [informal], scout, **scout out,** spy, **spy out,** play the spy, peep; **watch,** put under surveillance, stake out [informal]; bug.

.28 **canvass, survey,** make a survey; **poll,** conduct a poll, sample, **questionnaire** [informal].

.29 **seek, hunt,** look [archaic], **quest, pursue,** go in pursuit of, follow, go in search of, prowl after, see to, try to find; **look up, hunt up; look for,** look around *or* about for, **search for,** seek for, **hunt for,** cast *or* beat about for, **fish for, angle for,** bob for, dig for, delve for; **ask for,** inquire for; **gun for,** go gunning for; still-hunt [informal].

.30 **search, hunt, explore;** research; **hunt through, search through, look through, go through;** dig, delve, burrow, root, poke, pry; look round or around, poke around, nose around, smell around; beat the bushes; forage; frisk [slang].

.31 **grope,** grope for, **feel for,** fumble, grabble, scrabble, feel around, poke around, pry around, beat about, grope in the dark; **feel or pick one's way.**

.32 **ransack, rummage, rake, scour, comb;** rifle; **look everywhere,** look into every hole and corner, **look high and low,** look upstairs and downstairs, **look all over,** look all over hell [slang], search high heaven, turn upside down, turn inside out, **leave no stone unturned;** shake down or shake or toss [all slang].

.33 **search out, hunt out, spy out,** scout out, **ferret out,** fish out, pry out, dig out, root out, grub up.

.34 **trace, stalk, track, trail; follow,** follow up, shadow, tail [informal], dog the footsteps of; nose, nose out, **smell or sniff out,** follow the trail or scent or spoor of; follow a clue; **trace down, hunt down, track down, run down,** run to earth.

.35 ADJS **inquiring, questioning, querying,** quizzing; **quizzical, curious;** interrogatory, interrogative, interrogational; **inquisitorial,** inquisitional; catechistic(al), catechetic(al).

.36 **examining,** examinational; examinatorial; **testing,** trying, **tentative;** groping, feeling; **inspectional;** inspectorial; **investigative,** indagative [archaic]; zetetic; heuristic, investigatory, investigational; **exploratory,** explorative, explorational; fact-finding; analytic(al).

.37 **searching, probing, prying, nosy** [informal]; poking, digging, fishing, delving; in search or quest of, looking for, **out for,** on the lookout for, **in the market for,** loaded or out for bear [informal]; all-searching.

.38 ADVS **in question, at issue,** in debate or dispute, **under consideration,** under active consideration, **under advisement,** sub judice [L], under examination, under investigation, under surveillance, up or open for discussion; **before the house, on the docket, on the agenda, on the table, on the floor.**

486. ANSWER

.1 NOUNS **answer, reply, response,** responsory, responsion, replication; answering, respondence; riposte or repost, **retort, rejoinder,** reaction 284, return, **comeback** [slang], back answer, short answer, back talk; **repartee,** backchat, clever or ready or witty reply or retort, snappy comeback [slang]; yes-and-no answer, evasive reply; **acknowledgment,** receipt; rescript, rescription; antiphon; **echo,** reverberation 454.2.

.2 **rebuttal, counterstatement,** counterreply, counterclaim, counterblast, counteraccusation, countercharge, tu quoque [L, you too], contraremonstrance; **rejoinder,** replication, defense, rebutter, surrebutter or surrebuttal, surrejoinder; confutation, refutation.

.3 **answerer, replier,** responder, **respondent,** responser.

.4 VERBS **answer,** make or give answer, return answer, return for answer, **reply, respond,** say, say in reply; **retort,** riposte, **rejoin,** return, flash back; come back or come back at or come right back at [all slang], answer back or talk back [informal], shoot back [informal]; **react; acknowledge,** make or give acknowledgment; echo, reecho, reverberate 454.7.

.5 **rebut,** make a rebuttal; **rejoin,** surrebut, surrejoin; counterclaim, countercharge; confute, refute.

.6 ADJS **answering, replying, responsive,** respondent, responding; rejoining, returning; antiphonal; echoing, echoic, reechoing 454.11; confutative, refutative.

.7 ADVS in answer, in reply, in response, in return, in rebuttal.

487. SOLUTION

(answer to a problem)

.1 NOUNS **solution, resolution, answer, reason, explanation** 552.4; **finding,** determination, ascertainment; **outcome, upshot,** denouement, **result,** issue, end 70, end result, accomplishment 722; **solving,** working, **working-out,** finding-out, resolving, **clearing up,** cracking; **unriddling,** riddling, unscrambling, unraveling, sorting out, untwisting, unspinning, unweaving, untangling, disentanglement; **decipherment,** decoding; interpretation 552.

.2 VERBS **solve, resolve,** find the solution or answer, **clear up,** get, get right, do, work, **work out, find out, figure out,** dope or dope out [both slang]; sort out, puzzle out; debug; psych or psych out [both slang]; **unriddle,** riddle, unscramble, undo, untangle, disentangle, untwist, unspin, unweave, unravel, ravel, ravel out; **decipher, decode, crack; make out,** interpret 552.9; answer, explain 552.10; unlock, pick or open the lock; find the key of, find a clue to; **get to the bottom of, fathom,** plumb, bottom; have it, hit it, hit upon a solution, hit the nail on the head, hit it on the nose [informal]; guess, divine, guess right.

.3 ADJS **solvable,** soluble, **resolvable,** open to solution, capable of solution, workable, doable, answerable; explainable, explicable, determinable, ascertainable; **decipherable,** decodable.

488. DISCOVERY

.1 NOUNS discovery, finding, finding out, determining; **detection,** spotting, catching, espial; recognition, determination, distinguishment; **locating, location; disclosure, exposure,** revelation, **uncovering,** unearthing, exhumation, excavation, bringing to light; **find,** trove, treasure trove, trouvaille [Fr], strike, lucky strike; accidental or chance discovery, casual discovery; serendipity; rediscovery; invention 167.5.

.2 VERBS **discover, find, find out, determine,** get; strike, hit; put or lay one's hands on, lay one's fingers on, **locate** 184.10; **hunt down,** trace down, track down, **run down, run to earth;** trace; rediscover; invent 167.13.

.3 **come across, run across, meet with,** meet up with [informal], fall in with, **encounter, run into,** bump into [informal], come or run up against [informal], **come on** or **upon, hit upon,** light upon, alight upon, tumble on; **chance upon, happen upon, stumble on** or **upon,** stub one's toe upon, blunder upon, discover serendipitously.

.4 **uncover, unearth,** disinter, exhume, excavate; **disclose, expose,** reveal, **bring to light; turn up,** dig up, root up, fish up; worm out, ferret out.

.5 **detect, spot** [informal], **spy,** espy, descry, sense, pick up, notice, discern, see, **perceive, make out, recognize,** distinguish, identify.

.6 **scent,** catch the scent of, sniff, smell, **get wind of;** sniff or scent or smell out, nose out; be on the right scent, be near the truth, be warm [informal], burn [informal].

.7 **catch,** catch out; catch off side, catch off base; catch tripping, **catch napping, catch off-guard** or off one's guard, catch asleep at the switch; **catch at,** catch in the act, **catch red-handed,** catch in flagrante delicto, **catch with one's pants down** [slang], catch flat-footed, have the goods on [slang].

.8 (detect the hidden nature of) **see through, penetrate,** see as it really is, see in its true colors, see the inside of, see the cloven hoof; open the eyes to, tumble to, catch on to, wise up to [informal]; **be on to, be wise to, be hep to** [slang], have one's measure, **have one's number,** have dead to rights [slang].

.9 **turn up, show up,** be found; discover itself, expose or betray itself; hang out [slang]; materialize, **come to light,** come out; come along, come to hand.

.10 ADJS on the right scent, **on the right track,** on the trail of; **hot** or **warm** [both informal]; **discoverable,** determinable, findable, **detectable,** spottable, disclosable, exposable, locatable, **discernible.**

.11 INTERJS eureka!, I have it!, at last!, at long last!, finally!, thalassa!, thalatta! [both Gk].

489. EXPERIMENT

.1 NOUNS **experiment, experimentation,** empirio– or empirico–; experimental method; testing, trying, **trial;** research and development, R and D; **trial and error,** hit and miss, cut and try [informal]; empiricism, experimentalism, pragmatism, instrumentalism; **rule of thumb;** tentativeness, tentative method; control experiment, controlled experiment, **control;** experimental design; experimental proof or verification; noble experiment.

.2 **test, trial, try;** essay; docimasy [archaic], assay; determination, blank determination; **proof,** verification; touchstone, standard, criterion 490.2; crucial test; acid test; ordeal, crucible; probation; **feeling out, sounding out,** kiteflying; test case; first or rough draft, brouillon [Fr]; rough sketch.

.3 **tryout** or **workout** [both informal]; **rehearsal,** practice; pilot plan or program; **dry run;** Gedankenexperiment [Ger]; road test; **trial run,** practical test; shakedown, shakedown cruise, bench test; flight test, test flight or run; audition, hearing.

.4 **feeler, probe,** sound, sounder; **trial balloon,** ballon d'essai [Fr], pilot balloon, barometer; weather vane, weathercock;

straw to show the wind, straw vote; sample, random sample, experimental sample.

.5 **laboratory, lab** [informal], research laboratory, research establishment *or* facility, experiment station, field station, research and development *or* R and D establishment; think tank [informal], **proving ground.**

.6 **experimenter,** experimentist, experimentalist, **researcher,** research worker, R and D worker; experimental engineer; **tester,** tryer-out, test driver, test pilot; essayer; assayer; analyst, analyzer.

.7 **experimentee,** testee, patient, **subject,** laboratory animal, experimental *or* test animal, **guinea pig.**

.8 VERBS **experiment,** experimentalize, **research,** make an experiment, **run an experiment,** run a sample *or* specimen; **test, try,** essay, cut and try [informal], **test** *or* **try out,** have a dry run *or* rehearsal *or* test run; put to the test, **put to the proof, prove, verify,** validate, substantiate, confirm, put to trial, bring to test, make a trial of, give a trial to; **give a try,** have a go, give it a go [informal]; sample, taste; assay; play around with [informal], fool around with [slang]; try out under controlled conditions; give a tryout *or* workout [informal], **road-test,** shake down; try one out, put one through his paces; experiment *or* practice upon; try it on; try on, try it for size [informal]; try one's strength, see what one can do.

.9 **sound out, feel out, sound,** get a sounding *or* reading *or* sense, probe, **feel the pulse,** read; **put** *or* **throw out a feeler,** send up a trial balloon, fly a kite; **see which way the wind blows,** see how the land lies; take a straw vote, take a random sample, use an experimental sample.

.10 **stand the test, stand up, hold up, hold up in the wash,** pass, **pass muster,** get by [informal], hack it [slang], meet *or* satisfy requirements.

.11 ADJS **experimental, test, trial;** pilot; testing, proving, trying; probative, probatory, verificatory; probationary; **tentative,** provisional; empirical; trial-and-error, hit-or-miss, cut-and-try; heuristic.

.12 **tried, tested, proved,** verified, confirmed, tried and true.

.13 ADVS **experimentally,** by rule of thumb, by trial and error, by hit and miss, hit or miss, by guess and by God.

.14 **on trial,** under examination, **on** *or* **under probation,** under suspicion, **on approval.**

490. MEASUREMENT

.1 NOUNS **measurement, measure,** –metry; mensuration, measuring, gauging; admeasurement; metage; **estimation,** estimate, rough measure, approximation; **quantification,** quantitation, quantization; **appraisal,** appraisement, **assessment,** determination, rating, valuation, evaluation; assizement, assize; **survey,** surveying; triangulation; **instrumentation;** telemetry, telemetering; metric system; English system of measurement; calibration, correction; computation, calculation 87.3.

.2 **measure, gauge,** barometer, **rule, yardstick,** measuring rod *or* stick, **standard,** norm, canon, **criterion,** test, touchstone, check; **pattern,** model, type; **scale,** graduated *or* calibrated scale; meter-reading, reading, readout, value, degree, quantity; parameter.

.3 **extent** (quantity) 28, (degree) 29, (size) 195, (distance) 199, (length) 202, (breadth) 204; **weight** 352.

.4 (measuring device) **measure,** measurer, **gauge,** gauger; **meter;** instrument.

.5 (measures) US liquid measure, British imperial liquid measure, US dry measure, British imperial dry measure, apothecaries' measure, linear measure, square measure, circular measure, cubic measure, volume measure, surface measure, surveyor's measure, land measure, board measure.

.6 **coordinates,** Cartesian coordinates, rectangular coordinates, polar coordinates, cylindrical coordinates, spherical coordinates, equator coordinates; latitude, longitude; altitude, azimuth; declination, right ascension; ordinate, abscissa.

.7 **waterline;** watermark, tidemark, floodmark, **high-water mark;** load waterline, load line mark, Plimsoll mark *or* line.

.8 **measurability,** mensurability, computability, determinability, quantifiability.

.9 (science of measurement) **mensuration;** metrology; **geodesy,** geodetics, geodetic engineering; **surveying;** oceanography, bathymetry; topography, cartography, chorography; cadastration; planimetry; stereometry; goniometry; hypsometry, hypsography, altimetry; craniometry; biometry, biometrics; psychometry; psychometrics.

.10 **measurer,** meter, gauger; **geodesist,** geodetic engineer; **surveyor,** land surveyor, quantity surveyor; topographer, cartographer, oceanographer, chorographer; appraiser, assessor; assayer; valuer, valuator, evaluator; estimator.

.11 VERBS **measure, gauge, quantify,** mete [archaic], take the measure of, mensurate, triangulate, apply the yardstick to; quantize; **estimate,** make an approximation; **assess, rate, appraise, valuate, value,** evaluate, appreciate, prize; **assay;** size *or* size up [both informal], take the dimensions of; **weigh** 352.10; survey; plumb, probe, sound, fathom; span, pace, step; calibrate, graduate; divide; caliper, dial; meter; read the meter, take a reading, check a parameter; compute, calculate 87.11.

.12 **measure off, mark off, lay off,** set off, rule off; **step off,** pace off; **measure out,** mark out, lay out.

.13 ADJS **measuring, metric(al),** mensural, mensurative, mensurational; valuative, valuational; **quantitative,** numerative; approximative, estimative; geodetic(al), geodesic(al), hypsographic(al), hypsometric(al); topographic(al), chorographic(al), cartographic(al), oceanographic(al).

.14 **measured, gauged,** metered, **quantified;** quantized; **appraised, assessed, valuated,** valued; **assayed; surveyed,** plotted, mapped, admeasured, triangulated; known by measurement.

.15 **measurable,** mensurable, **quantifiable,** numerable, meterable, gaugeable, fathomable, **determinable,** computable, calculable; quantizable; estimable; assessable, appraisable; appreciable, perceptible, noticeable.

.16 ADVS **measurably, appreciably, perceptibly,** noticeably.

.17 linear measures

absolute angstrom	footstep
Admiralty mile	furlong, fur.
angstrom, angstrom	hand
unit, a. *or* å. *or* A.	handbreadth, hands-
or Å.	breadth
arpent	hectometer, hm.
astronomical unit	inch, in.
block	international ang-
board foot, bd. ft.	strom
cable length	kilometer, km.
centimeter, cm.	land mile
chain, Gunter's chain,	league
chn.	light-year
cubit	line
decameter, dekame-	link, li.
ter, dkm.	meter, m.
decimeter, dm.	micron, μ
ell	mil
em	mile, mi.
en	millimeter, mm.
fathom, fthm.	millimicron, micromil-
fingerbreadth, finger	limeter
foot, ft.	myriameter, mym.

nail	point, pt.
nautical mile, naut.	pole, p.
mi.	rod, r.
pace	statute mile, stat. mi.
palm	step
parsec	stride
perch	wavelength
pica	yard, yd.

.18 area measures

acre, a. *or* ac.	rood
are, a.	section, sec.
arpent	square inch, foot,
centare, ca.	mile, etc.
hectare, ha.	square meter, kilome-
perch	ter, etc.
pole, p.	township

.19 volume measures

barrel	gill, gi.
bushel, bu.	hectoliter, hl.
centiliter, cl.	hogshead, hhd.
cord, cd.	jeroboam
cubic foot, yard, etc.	jigger
cubic meter	kiloliter, kl.
cup	liquid pint, quart, etc.
decaliter, dekaliter,	liter, l.
dkl.	magnum
decastere, dks.	milliliter, ml.
deciliter, dl.	minim, min.
drop	peck, pk.
dry pint, quart, etc.	pint, pt.
fifth	pony
finger	quart, qt.
fluidounce, fl. oz.	stere, s.
fluidram, fl. dr.	tablespoon, tbs.
gallon, gal.	teaspoon, ts.

.20 gauges

alidade	micrometer caliper
calipers	octant
chain	plumb 209.17
compass	plumb rule
dial	precision block
dipstick	protractor
dividers	quadrant
engineer's chain	rod
feeler gauge	rule
foot rule	ruler
gauge block	scale
goniometer	sector
gradiometer	set square
graduated scale	sextant
graduated tape	size stick
Gunter's *or* surveyor's	spirit level
chain	square
Gunter's scale	tape, tapeline, tape
Johansson block, Jo	measure
block	theodolite
level	transit
line	transit theodolite
log	try square
log line	T square
measuring machine	vernier
meterstick	vernier caliper
micrometer	yardstick

491. COMPARISON

.1 NOUNS **comparison,** compare, examining side by side, matching, proportion [archaic], comparative judgment *or* estimate;

likening, comparing, analogy; parallelism; comparative relation; weighing, balancing; opposing, opposition, contrast; contrastiveness, distinctiveness, distinction 492.3; confrontment, confrontation; relation 9; correlation 13; simile, similitude, metaphor, allegory, figure *or* trope of comparison; comparative degree; comparative method; comparative linguistics, comparative grammar, comparative literature, comparative anatomy, etc.

.2 collation, comparative scrutiny, point-by-point comparison; verification, confirmation, checking; check, cross-check.

.3 comparability, comparableness, comparativeness; analogousness, equivalence, commensurability; proportionateness *or* proportionability [both archaic]; ratio, proportion, balance; similarity 20.

.4 VERBS compare, liken, assimilate, similize, liken to, compare with; make *or* draw a comparison, run a comparison, do a comparative study, bring into comparison; analogize, bring into analogy; relate 9.6; metaphorize; draw a parallel, parallel; match; examine side by side, view together; weigh *or* measure against; confront, contrast, oppose, set in opposition, set off against, set in contrast, put *or* set over against, place against, counterpose, set over against one another, set against one another; compare and contrast, note similarities and differences; weigh, balance.

.5 collate, scrutinize comparatively, compare point by point, painstakingly match; verify, confirm, check, cross-check.

.6 compare notes, exchange views *or* observations, match data *or* findings.

.7 be comparable, compare, compare to *or* with, not compare with 21.2, admit of comparison, be commensurable, be of the same order, be worthy of comparison, be fit to be compared; measure up to, come up to, match up with, stack up with [informal], hold a candle to [informal]; match, parallel; vie, vie with, rival; resemble 20.7.

.8 ADJS comparative, relative 9.7, comparable, commensurate, commensurable, parallel, matchable, analogous; analogical; collatable; correlative 13.10; much at one, much of a muchness [informal]; similar 20.10.

.9 incomparable, incommensurable, not to be compared, of different orders; unlike, dissimilar 21.4.

.10 ADVS comparatively, relatively; comparably.

.11 PREPS compared to, compared with, as compared with, by comparison with, in comparison with, beside, over against, taken with; than.

492. DISCRIMINATION

.1 NOUNS discrimination, discriminateness, discriminatingness, discriminativeness; seeing *or* making distinctions, appreciation of differences; analytic power *or* faculty; criticalness; finesse, refinement, delicacy; niceness of distinction, nicety, subtlety, refined discrimination, critical niceness; tact, tactfulness, feel, feeling, sense, sensitivity 422.3, sensibility 422.2; appreciation, appreciativeness; judiciousness 467.7; taste, discriminating taste, aesthetic *or* artistic judgment; palate, fine *or* refined palate, connoisseurship, selectiveness, fastidiousness 896.

.2 discernment, critical discernment, penetration, perception, perceptiveness, insight, perspicacity; flair; judgment, acumen 467.4.

.3 distinction, contradistinction, distinctiveness [archaic]; distinguishment, differentiation 16.4, separation, division, segregation, demarcation; nice *or* subtle distinction, nuance, shade of difference, microscopic distinction; hairsplitting, trichoschistism.

.4 VERBS be discriminating, exercise discrimination; be tactful, show *or* exercise tact; be tasteful, use one's palate, pick and choose; use advisedly.

.5 discriminate, distinguish, contradistinguish, separate, divide, analyze, subdivide, segregate, sever, severalize, differentiate, demark, demarcate, mark the interface, set off, set apart, sift, sift out, sieve, sieve out, winnow, screen, screen out, sort, sort out; pick out, select 637.14; separate the sheep from the goats, separate the men from the boys, separate the wheat from the tares *or* chaff, winnow the chaff from the wheat; draw the line, fix *or* set a limit; split hairs, make a fine *or* nice *or* subtle distinction, subtilize.

.6 make a distinction, draw distinctions, distinguish between, appreciate differences, see nuances *or* shades of difference, see the difference, tell apart, tell one thing from another, know which is which, know what's what [informal], "know a hawk from a handsaw" [Shakespeare], know one's ass from one's elbow [slang].

.7 ADJS **discriminating, discriminate,** discriminative, selective; **tactful, sensitive** 422.14; appreciative; **critical;** distinctive [archaic], **distinguishing;** differential; precise, accurate, exact; nice, fine, delicate, subtle, refined; fastidious 896.9.

.8 **discerning, perceptive** 422.13, perspicacious, insightful; **astute, judicious** 467.16, 19.

.9 ADVS **discriminatingly,** discriminatively, discriminately; with finesse; **tactfully; tastefully.**

493. INDISCRIMINATION

.1 NOUNS **indiscrimination,** indiscriminateness, undiscriminatingness, undiscriminativeness, unselectiveness, **uncriticalness, unparticularness;** syncretism; unfastidiousness; lack of refinement, coarseness *or* crudeness *or* crudity of intellect; **casualness,** promiscuousness, **promiscuity; indiscretion,** indiscreetness, **imprudence** 470.2; **untactfulness,** tactlessness, lack of feeling, **insensitivity,** insensibility 423, unmeticulousness, unpreciseness 534.4.

.2 **indistinction,** indistinctness, vagueness 445.2; uniformity 17; **indistinguishableness,** undistinguishableness, indiscernibility; a distinction without a difference.

.3 VERBS **confound, confuse,** mix, muddle, tumble, jumble, jumble together, **blur,** blur distinctions, overlook distinctions.

.4 **use loosely,** use unadvisedly.

.5 ADJS **undiscriminating, indiscriminate,** indiscriminative, undiscriminative, undifferentiating, unselective; wholesale, general, blanket; **uncritical,** uncriticizing, undemanding, nonjudgmental; **unparticular,** unfastidious; unsubtle; **casual, promiscuous;** unexacting, unmeticulous 534.13; **indiscreet,** undiscreet, **imprudent** 470.9; **untactful,** tactless, insensitive.

.6 **indistinguishable,** undistinguishable, undistinguished, indiscernible, **indistinct,** indistinctive, **without distinction,** not to be distinguished, undiscriminated, undifferentiated, **alike,** six of one and half a dozen of the other [informal]; standard, interchangeable, stereotyped, uniform 17.5.

494. JUDGMENT

.1 NOUNS **judgment,** judging, adjudgment, adjudication, judicature, deeming [archaic]; **arbitrament,** arbitration 805.2; good judgment 467.7; **choice** 637; **discrimination** 492.

.2 **criticism, censure** 969.3; approval 968; cri-

tique, review, notice, critical notice, report, comment; book review, literary criticism, critical journal, critical bibliography.

.3 **estimate, estimation; view, opinion** 501.6; **assessment,** assessing, **appraisal,** appraisement, appraising, appreciation, reckoning, valuation, valuing, **evaluation,** evaluating, evaluative criticism, analyzing, weighing, gauging, ranking, **rating;** measurement 490.

.4 **conclusion, deduction, inference,** consequence, consequent, corollary; derivation, illation; induction.

.5 **verdict, decision,** resolution [archaic], **determination, finding;** diagnosis, prognosis; **decree, ruling,** consideration, order, **pronouncement,** deliverance; **award,** action, **sentence; condemnation,** doom; dictum; precedent.

.6 **judge,** judger, adjudicator, justice; arbiter 1002.1; referee, umpire.

.7 **critic,** criticizer; connoisseur, *cognoscente* [Ital]; literary critic, man of letters; textual critic; editor; social critic, muckraker; captious critic, smellfungus, caviler, carper, faultfinder; criticaster, criticule, critickin; **censor,** censurer; **reviewer, commentator,** commenter; scholiast, annotator.

.8 VERBS **judge,** exercise judgment *or* the judgment; adjudge, adjudicate; be judicious *or* judgmental; **consider, regard,** hold, **deem, esteem, count, account,** think of; allow [dial], **suppose,** presume 499.9,10, opine, form an opinion, give *or* pass *or* express an opinion.

.9 **estimate,** form an estimate, make an estimation; **reckon,** call, guess, figure [informal]; **assess, appraise,** give an appreciation, **gauge, rate, rank,** class, mark, **value, evaluate,** valuate, place *or* set a value on, prize, appreciate; size up *or* take one's measure [informal], **measure** 490.11.

.10 **conclude,** draw a conclusion, **come to** *or* **arrive at a conclusion; find; deduce, derive,** take as proved *or* demonstrated, extract, **gather,** collect, glean, fetch; **infer,** draw an inference; induce; **reason,** reason that; put two and two together.

.11 **decide, determine; find,** ascertain; resolve; **settle,** fix; make a decision, come to a decision, **make up one's mind,** settle one's mind.

.12 **sit in judgment,** hold the scales, hold court; **hear,** give a hearing to; **try** 1004.17; **referee, umpire,** officiate; arbitrate 805.6.

.13 **pass judgment,** utter a judgment, deliver

or pronounce judgment; agree on a verdict, return a verdict, **bring in a verdict, find,** find for *or* against; pronounce on, act on, **pronounce,** report, **rule,** decree, order; **sentence,** pass sentence, doom, condemn.

.14 **criticize,** critique; **censure** 969.13,14; **review;** comment upon, annotate; moralize upon.

.15 **rank, rate,** count, be regarded, be thought of, be in one's estimation.

.16 ADJS **judicial, judiciary,** judicative, judgmental; juridic(al), juristic(al); **judicious** 467.19; **critical** 969.24.

.17 ADVS **all things considered, on the whole, taking one thing with another,** on balance, taking everything into consideration *or* account; everything being equal, other things being equal, *ceteris paribus* [L], taking into account, considering, after all, this being so; therefore, wherefore; *sub judice* [L], in court, before the bench *or* bar *or* court.

495. PREJUDGMENT

.1 NOUNS **prejudgment,** prejudication, forejudgment; **preconception, presumption, presupposition,** presupposal, presurmise, preapprehension, prenotion, **prepossession; predilection,** predisposition; preconsideration, **predetermination,** predecision, preconclusion, premature judgment; *parti pris* [Fr], **prejudice** 527.3.

.2 VERBS **prejudge,** forejudge; **preconceive, presuppose, presume,** presurmise; **be predisposed;** predecide, predetermine, preconclude, judge beforehand *or* prematurely, judge before the evidence is in, **jump to a conclusion,** go off half-cocked *or* at half cock [informal], jump the gun [slang].

.3 ADJS **prejudged,** forejudged, **preconceived,** preconceptual, **presumed, presupposed,** presurmised; predetermined, predecided, preconcluded, judged beforehand *or* prematurely; **predisposed,** predispositional; prejudicial, prejudging, prejudicative.

496. MISJUDGMENT

.1 NOUNS **misjudgment,** poor judgment, error in judgment, warped *or* skewed judgment; **miscalculation,** miscomputation, **misreckoning, misestimation,** misappreciation, misevaluation, misvaluation, misconjecture, wrong impression; **misreading,** wrong construction, misconstruction,

misinterpretation 553; error 518; injudiciousness 470.2.

.2 VERBS **misjudge,** judge amiss, **miscalculate, misestimate, misreckon,** misappreciate, misevaluate, misvalue, miscompute, misdeem, misesteem, misthink, misconjecture; misconstrue, **misinterpret** 553.2; err 518.9; fly in the face of facts; put the wrong construction on things, get a wrong impression, misread the situation *or* case.

497. OVERESTIMATION

.1 NOUNS **overestimation,** overestimate, **overreckoning,** overcalculation, **overrating,** overassessment, overvaluation, overappraisal; **overreaction; overstatement, exaggeration** 617.

.2 VERBS **overestimate, overreckon,** overcalculate, overcount, overmeasure, **overrate,** overassess, overappraise, overesteem, **overvalue,** overprize, think *or* make too much of, idealize, see only the good points of; overreact to; **overstate, exaggerate** 617.3.

.3 ADJS **overestimated, overrated,** puffed up, overvalued, on the high side; **exaggerated** 617.4.

498. UNDERESTIMATION

.1 NOUNS **underestimation,** misestimation, underestimate, **underrating, underreckoning,** undervaluation, misprizing, misprizal, misprision; **belittlement, depreciation,** deprecation, **minimization,** disparagement 971.

.2 VERBS **underestimate,** misestimate, **underrate,** underreckon, **undervalue,** underprize, **misprize; make little of,** attach little importance to, not do justice to, sell short, think little of, make *or* think nothing of, set little by, miss on the low side, set no store by, set at naught, make light of, shrug off; depreciate, minimize, belittle, deprecate, disparage 971.8.

.3 ADJS **underestimated, underrated,** undervalued, on the low side; unvalued, unprized.

499. THEORY, SUPPOSITION

.1 NOUNS **theory,** theorization, *theoria* [Gk]; theoretics, theoretic, theoric [archaic]; **speculation,** mere theory; doctrinairism, doctrinality, doctrinarity; analysis, **explanation,** abstraction; theoretical basis *or* justification.

.2 **theory, explanation,** proposed *or* tentative explanation, statement covering the facts or evidence; body of theory, theoretical structure *or* construct; unified theory.

.3 **supposition, supposal,** supposing; **presupposition,** presupposal; **assumption, presumption, conjecture, inference, surmise, guesswork; hypothesis,** working hypothesis; **postulate,** postulation, *postulatum* [L], set of postulates; **proposition, thesis, premise** 482.7; **axiom** 517.2.

.4 **guess, conjecture,** unverified supposition, perhaps, speculation, surmise; hunch [informal]; shot *or* stab [both informal]; rough guess, wild guess, blind guess, bold conjecture, shot in the dark [informal].

.5 (vague supposition) **suggestion,** bare suggestion, **suspicion, inkling, hint, intimation, impression, notion,** mere notion, sneaking suspicion [informal], trace of an idea, half an idea, vague idea, hazy idea, **idea** 479.

.6 **supposititiousness, presumptiveness,** presumableness, theoreticalness, hypotheticalness, conjecturableness, speculativeness.

.7 **theorist, theorizer,** theoretic, **theoretician,** notionalist [archaic]; **speculator;** hypothesist, hypothesizer; **doctrinaire,** doctrinarian; armchair authority *or* philosopher.

.8 **supposer,** assumer, surmiser, **conjecturer, guesser,** guessworker.

.9 VERBS **theorize, hypothesize, speculate,** have *or* entertain a theory, espouse a theory.

.10 **suppose, assume, presume, surmise,** expect, **suspect, infer, understand, gather, conclude, deduce, consider,** reckon, divine, **imagine, fancy,** dream, conceive, **believe, deem,** repute, feel, **think,** be inclined to think, opine, say, daresay, be afraid [informal]; take, take it, take it into one's head, take for, take to be, take for granted, take as a precondition, **presuppose, presurmise,** prefigure; provisionally accept *or* admit, grant, take it as given, let, let be.

.11 **conjecture, guess,** give a guess, talk off the top of one's head [informal], hazard a conjecture, venture a guess, risk assuming *or* stating, tentatively suggest, go out on a limb [informal].

.12 **postulate, predicate, posit,** set forth, lay down, assert; pose, advance, **propose, propound** 773.5.

.13 ADJS **theoretical,** theoretico–; **hypothetic(al),** postulatory, notional; **speculative,**

conjectural; abstract, ideal; academic, moot; impractical, armchair.

.14 **supposed,** suppositive, **assumed, presumed, conjectured, inferred,** understood, deemed, **reputed,** putative, alleged, accounted as; suppositional, supposititious; assumptive, **presumptive;** given, granted, taken as *or* for granted; **postulated,** postulational, premised.

.15 **supposable, presumable,** assumable, conjecturable, surmisable, imaginable, premissable.

.16 ADVS **theoretically, hypothetically,** *ex hypothesi* [L], ideally; **in theory,** in idea, in the abstract, on paper.

.17 **supposedly,** supposably, **presumably,** presumedly, assumably, assumedly, presumptively, assumptively, reputedly; suppositionally, supposititiously; **seemingly,** in seeming, quasi; as it were.

.18 conjecturably, **conjecturally;** to guess, to make a guess, **as a guess,** as a rough guess.

.19 CONJS **supposing,** supposing that, **assuming that,** allowing that, on the assumption *or* supposition that, if, as if, as though, by way of hypothesis.

500. PHILOSOPHY

.1 NOUNS **philosophy,** "life's guide" [Cicero], "a handmaid to religion" [Francis Bacon]; philosophical inquiry *or* investigation, philosophical speculation; inquiry *or* investigation into first causes; school of philosophy, philosophic system, school of thought; philosophic doctrine, philosophic theory; theory of knowledge, **epistemology,** gnosiology; mental philosophy, moral philosophy; **metaphysics,** ontology, first philosophy, theory *or* science of being, phenomenology, cosmology, casuistry, **ethics** 957; **aesthetics,** theory of beauty; axiology, value theory; **logic;** philosophastry, philosophastering; sophistry 483.

.2 Platonic philosophy, Platonism, philosophy of the Academy; Aristotelian philosophy, Aristotelianism, philosophy of the Lyceum, Peripateticism, Peripatetic school; Stoic philosophy, Stoicism, philosophy of the Porch *or* Stoa; Epicureanism, philosophy of the Garden.

.3 **materialism** 376.5; **idealism** 377.3.

.4 monism, philosophical unitarianism, mind-stuff theory; pantheism, cosmotheism; hylozoism.

.5 pluralism; dualism, mind-matter theory.

.6 **philosopher,** philosophizer, philosophe; philosophaster; **thinker,** speculator; casuist; metaphysician, cosmologist; sophist 483.6.

.7 VERBS **philosophize**, reason 482.15.

.8 ADJS **philosophic(al)**, sophistical 483.10; philosophicohistorical, philosophicolegal, philosophicojuristic, philosophicopsychological, philosophicoreligious, philosophicotheological.

.9 acosmistic, animatistic, animist or animistic, atomistic, cosmotheistic, Cyrenaic, eclectic(al), Eleatic, empirical, Epicurean, eudaemonistic(al), existential, hedonist or hedonistic, hedonic(al), humanist, humanistic(al), idealistic(al); materialistic 376.11, mechanistic, Megarian, metaphysical, monistic, naturalistic, nominalist or nominalistical, panlogical, panlogistical, pantheistic, positivist, positivistic, pragmatic, pragmatist, instrumentalist, rationalistic, realist or realistic, scholastic, neo-scholastic, sensationalistic, Stoic, syncretistic, theistic, transcendentalist or transcendentalistic, utilitarian, vitalistic, voluntarist or voluntaristic.

.10 Aristotelian, Peripatetic; Augustinian, Averroist or Averroistic, Bergsonian, Berkeleian, Cartesian, Comtian or Comptean, Hegelian, Neo-Hegelian, Heideggerian, Heraclitean, Humean, Husserlian, Kantian, Leibnizian, Parmenidean, Platonic, Neoplatonic, pre-Socratic, Pyrrhonic, Pyrrhonian, Pythagorean, Neo-Pythagorean, Sartrian, Schellingian, Schopenhauerian, Scotist, Socratic, Spencerian, Thomist or Thomistic, Viconian, Wittgensteinian.

.11 philosophies

acosmism	dialectical materialism
aestheticism	dualism
African school	eclecticism
agnosticism	egoism
Alexandrian school	egoistic hedonism
analytic philosophy	Eleaticism, Elean
animalism	school
animatism	empiricism
animism	Epicureanism
Aristotelianism	Eretrian school
atomism	eristic school
Augustinianism	essentialism
Averroism	ethicism
Bergsonism	ethics 957
Berkeleianism	eudaemonism
Bonaventurism	existentialism, existen-
Bradleianism	tial philosophy
Cartesianism	Fichteanism
Comtism	hedonism
cosmotheism	Hegelianism
criticism, critical phi-	Heideggerianism
losophy	Heracliteanism
Cynicism	Herbartianism
Cyrenaic hedonism,	humanism
Cyrenaicism	Humism
deism	hylomorphism

hylotheism	nism
hylozoism	philosophy of signs
idealism	philosophy of the
immaterialism	ante-Nicene Fathers
individualism	philosophy of the
instrumentalism	post-Nicene Fathers
intuitionism	physicalism
Ionian school	physicism
Kantianism	Platonism
Leibnizianism	pluralism
logical empiricism,	positivism
logical positivism	pragmaticism, pragma-
Marxism	tism
materialism	psychism
mechanism	psychological hedo-
Megarianism	nism
mentalism	Purva Mimamsa
Mimamsa	Pyrrhonism
monism	Pythagoreanism
mysticism	rationalism
naturalism	realism
neocriticism	Sankhya
Neo-Hegelianism	Sartrianism
Neoplatonism	Schellingism
Neo-Pythagoreanism	Scholasticism
neo-scholasticism	Schopenhauerism
new ethical move-	Scotism
ment	secular humanism
nominalism	semiotic, semiotics
noumenalism	sensationalism
Nyaya	sensism
ontologism	skepticism
ontology	Socratism
optimism	Sophism, Sophistry
ordinary language phi-	Spencerianism
losophy	Spinozism
organicism	Stoicism
organic mechanism	substantialism
panlogism	syncretism
panpneumatism	theism
panpsychism	Thomism
pantheism	transcendentalism
panthelism	universalistic hedo-
Parmenidean school	nism
patristicism	utilitarianism
patristic philosophy	Uttara Mimamsa
Peripateticism	vitalism
pessimism	voluntarism
phenomenalism	zetetic philosophy
philosophy of orga-	

.12 adherents

acosmist	egoist
agnostic	Eleatic
analytic philosopher	empiricist
animalist	Epicurean
animatist	Eretrian
animist	eristic
Aristotelian	essentialist
atomist	eudaemonist
Averroist	existentialist, existen-
Bergsonian	tial philosopher
Berkeleian	Fichtean
Cartesian	hedonist
Comtist	Hegelian
cosmotheist	Heideggerian
Cynic	Heraclitean
Cyrenaic	Herbartian
deist	humanist
dialectical materialist	Humist
dualist	Husserlian
eclectic	hylomorphist

hylotheist
hylozoist
idealist
immaterialist
individualist
intuitionist
Kantian
Kierkegaardian
Leibnizian
logical empiricist, logi-
  cal positivist
Marxist
materialist 376.6
mechanist
Megarian
mentalist
monist
mystic
naturalist
Neo-Hegelian
Neoplatonist
Neo-Pythagorean
nominalist
ontologist
organicist
organic mechanist
panpsychist
pantheist
Parmenidean
Peripatetic
phenomenalist
physicalist

physicist
Platonist
pluralist
positivist
pragmatist
psychist
Pyrrhonist
Pythagorean
rationalist
realist
Sartrian
Scholastic
Scotist
secular humanist
sensationalist
sensist
skeptic
Socratist
Sophist
Spencerian
Spinozist
Stoic
substantialist
syncretist
theist
Thomist
transcendentalist
utilitarian
vitalist
voluntarist
Wittgensteinian
zetetic

.13 philosophers

Abelard
Albertus Magnus
Albinus
Alexander, Hartley
  Burr
Alexander, Samuel
Ammonius Saccas
Anaxagoras
Anaximander
Anaximenes
Anselm
Apollonius
Apuleius
Aristippus
Aristotle
Augustine
Averroes
Ayer
Bacon, Francis
Bacon, Roger
Bautain
Bayle
Bentham
Bergson
Berkeley
Boethius
Bonaventure
Boodin
Bosanquet
Bowne
Bradley
Brightman
Broad
Bruno
Cabanis
Caird, Edward
Caird, John
Carnap

Cassirer
Chubb
Cicero
Clifford
Cohen, Hermann
Comte
Condillac
Condorcet
Confucius
Cousin
Croce
Democritus
Descartes
Dewey
d'Holbach
Diderot
Dilthey
Drake
Dreisch
Duns Scotus
Empedocles
Engels
Epictetus
Epicurus
Erigena
Eucken
Euhemerus
Fechner
Feigl
Fichte
Flewelling
Franke
Frege
Fullerton
Gentile
Geulincx
Gilson
Green

Grotius
Haeckel
Hahn
Haldane
Hamann
Harris
Hartmann
Hegel
Heidegger
Heraclitus
Herbart
Herder
Hobbes
Holt
Howison
Hume
Husserl
Hutcheson
Jacobi
James
Jaspers
Kant
Kierkegaard
La Mettrie
Langer
Leibniz
Leucippus
Locke
Lotze
Lovejoy
Lucretius
Mach
Maimonides
Maine de Biran
Malebranche
Marcus Aurelius
Maritain
Marvin
Marx
Maximus
McGilvary
M'Taggart
Mead
Meinong
Mencius
Mendelssohn, Moses
Mill, James
Mill, John Stuart
Moderatus
Montague
Moore
Morgan
Natorp
Neurath
Nietzsche
Numenius
Ockham

Ortega y Gasset
Paley
Parmenides
Pascal
Peirce
Perry
Philo
Plato
Plotinus
Porphyry
Pratt
Pritchard
Protagoras
Pyrrho
Pythagoras
Reid
Reynaud
Rogers
Ross
Rousseau
Royce
Russell
Santayana
Sartre
Scheler
Schelling
Schiller, Ferdinand
Schleiermacher
Schlick
Schopenhauer
Sellars
Seneca
Shaftesbury
Sidgwick
Socrates
Spaulding
Spencer
Spinoza
Stern
Stevenson
Stirling
Strong
Thales
Theophrastus
Thomas Aquinas
Tindal
Toland
Vico
Waismann
Whitehead
Windelband
Wittgenstein
Wolff
Woodbridge
Xenophanes
Zeno of Citium
Zeno of Elea

501. BELIEF

.1 NOUNS **belief, credence, credit, faith, trust;** hope; **confidence,** assuredness, **assurance;** sureness, surety, **certainty 513; reliance, dependence,** reliance on or in, dependence on, stock or store [both informal]; acceptation, acception, reception, acquiescence; suspension of disbelief; fideism; **credulity 502.**

.2 a **belief, tenet, dogma,** precept, **principle, principle** or **article** of **faith,** canon, maxim, axiom; **doctrine**, teaching; –ism, –logy or –logia.

.3 **system of belief; religion, faith** 1020.1; school, cult, ism, ideology, *Weltanschauung* [Ger], world view; political faith or belief or philosophy; **creed, credo,** credenda; articles of religion, creedal or doctrinal statement, formulated belief; gospel; catechism;

.4 **statement of belief** or **principles, manifesto,** position paper; solemn declaration; deposition, affidavit.

.5 **conviction, persuasion,** convincement; **firm belief,** implicit or **staunch belief,** settled judgment, mature judgment or belief, fixed opinion, unshaken confidence, steadfast faith, rooted or deeprooted belief.

.6 **opinion, sentiment, feeling, impression,** reaction, **notion, idea, thought,** mind, thinking, **way of thinking, attitude,** stance, posture, position, **view,** eye, sight, lights, observation, **conception, concept,** conceit, **estimation,** estimate, consideration, **theory** 499, assumption, presumption, **conclusion, judgment** 494, personal judgment; **point of view** 525.2; public opinion, public belief, general belief, prevailing belief or sentiment, *consensus gentium* [L], common belief, community sentiment, popular belief, *vox populi* [L], climate of opinion; ethos; mystique.

.7 **profession, confession, declaration, profession** or **confession** or **declaration of faith.**

.8 **believability,** believableness, **credibility, credit,** trustworthiness, **plausibility,** tenability, acceptability, conceivability; **reliability** 513.4.

.9 **believer, truster;** religious believer 1028.4; true believer; the assured, the faithful, the believing; fideist.

.10 VERBS **believe, credit, trust, accept,** receive, buy [slang]; give credit or credence to, give faith to, put faith in, take stock in or set store by [informal], attach some weight to; be led to believe; accept implicitly, believe without reservation, take for granted, take or accept for gospel, take as gospel truth [informal], take on faith, take on trust or credit; take at face value; **take one's word for,** trust one's word, take at one's word; swallow 502.6; be certain 513.9.

.11 **think, opine,** be of the opinion, be afraid [informal], **have the idea,** have an idea, **suppose, assume, presume, judge** 494.8, **guess, surmise,** have a hunch [informal],

have an inkling, suspect, expect [informal], have an impression, be under the impression, conceive, ween, trow [both archaic], **imagine, fancy,** daresay; **deem, esteem, hold, regard, consider, maintain,** reckon, estimate; hold as, account as, set down as or for, view as, look upon as, take for, take, take it.

.12 **state, assert,** declare, **affirm,** vow, avow, avouch, warrant, asseverate, **confess,** swear, profess, express the belief, swear to a belief.

.13 **hold the belief, have the opinion,** entertain a belief or opinion, adopt or embrace a belief; foster or nurture or cherish a belief, be wedded to or espouse a belief; get hold of an idea, get it into one's head, form a conviction.

.14 **be confident,** have confidence, **be satisfied, be convinced, be certain,** be easy in one's mind about, be secure in the belief, **feel sure, rest assured,** rest in confidence; doubt not, **have no doubt,** have no misgivings or diffidence or qualms, have no reservations, have no second thoughts.

.15 **believe in, have faith in,** pin one's faith to, confide in, **have confidence in,** place or repose confidence in, place reliance in, put oneself in the hands of, **trust in,** put trust in, have simple or childlike faith in, rest in, repose in or hope in [both archaic].

.16 **rely on** or **upon, depend on** or **upon,** place reliance on, rest on or upon, repose on, lean on, **count on,** calculate on, reckon on, **bank on** or **upon** [informal]; **trust to** or **unto, swear by,** take one's oath upon; **bet on** or gamble on or lay money on or bet one's bottom dollar on [all informal]; take one's word for.

.17 **trust, confide in, rely on, depend on,** repose, place trust or confidence in, **trust in** 501.15, trust implicitly, deem trustworthy, think reliable or dependable, take one's word.

.18 **convince,** convict, **convert, win over,** bring over, bring round, talk over, talk one around, bring to reason, bring to one's senses, **persuade, lead to believe; satisfy, assure;** put one's mind at rest on; sell or sell one on [both informal]; carry one's point, bring or drive home to; cram down one's throat; be convincing, carry conviction; inspire belief or confidence.

.19 **convince oneself, persuade oneself,** sell oneself [informal], make oneself easy about, make oneself easy on that score, satisfy oneself on that point, make sure of, make up one's mind.

.20 **find credence, be believed,** be accepted, be received; be swallowed *or* **go down** *or* pass current [all informal]; produce *or* carry conviction; have the ear of, gain the confidence of.

.21 ADJS **believing, undoubting, undoubtful,** doubtless [archaic]; faithful [archaic], pistic, pious, pietistic, **devout;** under the impression, impressed with; **convinced, confident,** positive, dogmatic, secure, **persuaded,** sold on, **satisfied, assured; sure, certain** 513.13–21; fideistic.

.22 **trusting, trustful,** trusty [archaic], **confiding, unsuspecting, unsuspicious,** without suspicion; childlike, innocent, guileless, naïve 736.5; **credulous** 502.8; relying, depending, reliant, dependent.

.23 **believed, credited, trusted, accepted;** received; **undoubted,** unsuspected, **unquestioned,** undisputed, uncontested.

.24 **believable, credible; tenable,** conceivable, **plausible,** colorable; worthy of faith, trustworthy, trusty; fiduciary; reliable 513.17; unimpeachable, unexceptionable, **unquestionable** 513.15.

.25 fiducial, fiduciary, pistic; convictional.

.26 **convincing,** convictional, **persuasive,** assuring, impressive, satisfying, satisfactory; decisive, absolute, conclusive, determinative; authoritative.

.27 **doctrinal, creedal,** canonical, dogmatic, confessional.

.28 ADVS **believingly, undoubtingly,** undoubtfully, without doubt, unquestioningly; **trustingly,** trustfully, unsuspectingly, unsuspiciously; piously, devoutly; with faith; **with confidence,** on *or* upon trust, on faith.

.29 **in one's opinion, to one's mind,** in one's thinking, **to one's way of thinking,** the way one thinks, **in one's estimation,** according to one's lights, as one sees it, to the best of one's belief; in the opinion of, in the eyes of.

502. CREDULITY

.1 NOUNS **credulity, credulousness,** inclination *or* disposition to believe, ease of belief, will *or* willingness to believe, wishful belief *or* thinking; **blind faith,** unquestioning belief; uncritical acceptance, premature *or* unripe acceptation, hasty *or* rash conviction; **trustfulness, unsuspiciousness,** unsuspectingness; uncriticalness, unskepticalness; overcredulity, overcredulousness, overtrustfulness, overopen-

ness to conviction *or* persuasion, gross credulity; infatuation, fondness, dotage; one's blind side.

.2 **gullibility, dupability,** cullibility, **deceivability,** seduceability, persuadability, hoaxability; easiness [informal], softness, weakness; **simpleness,** simplicity, **ingenuousness, unsophistication; greenness,** naïveness, **naïveté,** naivety 736.1.

.3 **superstition,** superstitiousness; popular belief, **old wives' tale;** tradition, lore, folklore; charm, spell 1036.

.4 **trusting soul; dupe** 620; sucker *or* patsy [both slang].

.5 VERBS **be credulous,** accept unquestioningly; not boggle at anything, **believe anything,** be easy of belief *or* persuasion, be uncritical, believe at the drop of a hat, be a dupe, think the moon is made of green cheese.

.6 [slang *or* informal terms] kid oneself; **swallow,** swallow anything, swallow whole, not choke *or* gag on, swallow hook, line, and sinker; **eat up,** lap up, devour, gulp down, gobble up *or* down; bite, nibble, rise to the fly, take the bait; swing at; go for, **fall for,** tumble for; **be taken in,** be a sucker *or* patsy *or* easy mark.

.7 **be superstitious;** knock on wood, keep one's fingers crossed.

.8 ADJS **credulous,** easy of belief, ready *or* inclined to believe, easily taken in; **undoubting** 501.21; **trustful, trusting; unsuspicious, unsuspecting;** uncritical, unskeptical; overcredulous, overtrustful, overtrusting, overconfiding; fond, infatuated, doting; **superstitious.**

.9 **gullible, dupable,** cullible, **deceivable, foolable, deludable, exploitable,** victimizable, seduceable, persuadable, hoaxable, humbugable, hoodwinkable; soft, easy [informal], **simple; ingenuous, unsophisticated, green, naïve** 736.5.

503. UNBELIEF

.1 NOUNS **unbelief, disbelief,** nonbelief, unbelievingness; refusal *or* inability to believe; discredit; **incredulity** 504; **denial** 524.2, **rejection** 638; misbelief, heresy 1025.2; infidelity, atheism, **agnosticism** 1031.6; minimifidianism, nullifidianism.

.2 **doubt, doubtfulness, dubiousness,** dubiety; half-belief; **question,** question in one's mind; **skepticism,** skepticalness; total skepticism, Pyrrhonism; **suspicion,** suspiciousness, wariness, leeriness, **distrust, mistrust, misdoubt,** distrustfulness, mistrustfulness; **misgiving,** self-doubt, diffidence; scruple, scrupulousness [both archaic]; apprehension 891.4; **uncertainty** 514; shadow of doubt.

.3 **unbelievability,** unbelievableness, **incredibility, implausibility,** inconceivability, untenableness; **doubtfulness, questionableness;** credibility gap; unreliability 514.6.

.4 doubter, doubting Thomas; unbeliever 1031.11,12.

.5 VERBS **disbelieve,** unbelieve, misbelieve, **not believe,** find hard to believe, not admit, refuse to admit, not buy [slang], take no stock in or set no store by [both informal]; **discredit,** refuse to credit, refuse credit or credence to, give no credit or credence to; gag on, **not swallow** 504.3; negate, **deny** 524.3,4; **reject** 638.2.

.6 **doubt, be doubtful, be dubious, be skeptical,** doubt the truth of, beg leave to doubt, **have one's doubts,** have or harbor or entertain doubts or suspicions, half believe, have reservations, **take with a grain of salt,** scruple [archaic], **distrust, mistrust,** misgive; **be uncertain** 514.9,10; **suspect,** smell a rat [informal]; **question,** query, **challenge, contest, dispute,** greet with skepticism, treat with reserve, bring or call in question, raise a question, throw doubt upon, awake a doubt or suspicion; **doubt one's word,** give one the lie; doubt oneself, be diffident.

.7 **be unbelievable,** be incredible, pass belief, be hard to believe, strain one's credulity, **stagger belief;** shake one's faith, undermine one's faith; perplex, stagger, fill with doubt.

.8 ADJS **unbelieving, disbelieving,** nonbelieving; faithless, without faith; unconfident, unconvinced, unconverted; nullifidian, minimifidian, creedless; **incredulous** 504.4; repudiative; **heretical** 1025.9; **irreligious** 1031.17.

.9 **doubting, doubtful, in doubt, dubious; questioning; skeptical,** Pyrrhonic, from Missouri [informal]; **distrustful, mistrustful, untrustful,** mistrusting, untrusting; **suspicious,** suspecting, scrupulous [archaic], shy, wary, leery; **agnostic; uncertain** 514.14.

.10 **unbelievable, incredible,** unthinkable, **implausible,** unimaginable, inconceivable, not to be believed, **hard to believe,** hard of belief, beyond belief, unworthy of belief, not meriting or not deserving belief, tall [informal]; **staggering belief,** passing belief; preposterous, absurd, ridic-

ulous, unearthly, ungodly; **doubtful, dubious,** doubtable, dubitable, **questionable,** problematic(al), **unconvincing,** open to doubt or suspicion; **suspicious,** suspect; thin or a bit thin [both informal]; thick or a bit thick or a little too thick [all informal].

.11 unreliable 514.19.

.12 **doubted, questioned, disputed,** contested, moot; **distrusted, mistrusted; suspect,** suspected, **under suspicion,** under a cloud; **discredited,** exploded, **disbelieved.**

.13 ADVS **unbelievingly,** doubtingly, **doubtfully, dubiously,** questioningly, **skeptically,** suspiciously; **with a grain of salt,** with reservations, with some allowance, with caution.

504. INCREDULITY

.1 NOUNS **incredulity, incredulousness,** uncredulousness, refusal or disinclination to believe, resistance or resistiveness to belief, tough-mindedness, **inconvincibility,** unconvincibility, unpersuadability, unpersuasibility; **suspiciousness,** suspicion, wariness, leeriness, guardedness, cautiousness, caution; **skepticism** 503.2.

.2 **ungullibility,** uncullibility, **undupability,** undeceivability, unhoaxability, unseduceability; **sophistication.**

.3 VERBS **refuse to believe,** resist believing, **not allow oneself to believe,** be slow to believe or accept; not kid oneself [slang]; **disbelieve** 503.5; **be skeptical** 503.6; **not swallow,** not be able to swallow or down [informal], not go for or **not fall for** [both slang], not be taken in by; **not accept, reject** 638.2.

.4 ADJS **incredulous,** uncredulous, **hard of belief,** shy of belief, disposed to doubt, indisposed or disinclined to believe, unwilling to accept; impervious to persuasion, **inconvincible,** unconvincible, unpersuadable, unpersuasible; **suspicious, suspecting,** wary, leery, cautious, guarded; **skeptical** 503.9.

.5 **ungullible,** uncullible, **undupable,** undeceivable, **unfoolable, undeludable,** unhoaxable, unseduceable, hoaxproof; **sophisticated, wise, hardheaded,** practical, realistic, **tough-minded;** nobody's fool, not born yesterday, nobody's sucker or patsy [slang].

505. EVIDENCE, PROOF

.1 NOUNS **evidence, proof; reason to believe,** grounds for belief; **grounds,** material grounds, **facts, data,** premises, basis for belief; piece or item of evidence, **fact, datum,** relevant fact; **indication, manifestation,** sign, symptom, mark, token, mute witness; body of evidence, documentation; **muniments,** title deeds and papers; chain of evidence; **clue** 568.8; exhibit.

.2 evidence in chief, primary or secondary evidence, prima facie evidence, external or extrinsic evidence, internal or intrinsic evidence, direct evidence, indirect evidence, circumstantial or presumptive evidence, documentary evidence, oral evidence, word-of-mouth evidence, ex parte evidence, collateral evidence, cumulative evidence, incriminating evidence, hearsay evidence, hearsay, state's evidence; *corpus delicti* [L], body of the crime.

.3 **testimony, attestation,** attest [archaic], **witness;** testimonial, testimonium [archaic]; **statement, declaration, assertion,** asseveration, affirmation 523, avouchment, avowal, averment, allegation, admission, **disclosure** 556, profession, word; **deposition,** legal evidence, sworn evidence or testimony; *procès-verbal* [Fr]; compurgation; affidavit, sworn statement; instrument in proof, *pièce justificative* [Fr].

.4 **proof, demonstration,** ironclad proof; **determination, establishment, settlement; conclusive evidence,** indisputable evidence, incontrovertible evidence, damning evidence, unmistakable sign, sure sign, absolute indication; burden of proof, onus, *onus probandi* [L]; the proof of the pudding.

.5 **confirmation, substantiation,** proof, proving, proving out, bearing out, affirmation, attestation, **authentication, validation, certification,** ratification, **verification; corroboration, support,** supporting evidence, corroboratory evidence, fortification, buttressing, bolstering, backing, backing up, reinforcement, undergirding, strengthening, circumstantiation; **documentation.**

.6 **citation, reference,** quotation; **exemplification,** instance, example, case, case in point, particular, item, illustration, demonstration; cross reference.

.7 **witness, eyewitness,** spectator, earwitness; **bystander,** passerby; **deponent, testifier,** attestant, attester, attestator, voucher, swearer; **informant,** informer; character witness; cojuror, compurgator.

.8 **provability, demonstrability,** determinability; confirmability, supportability, verifiability.

.9 VERBS **evidence, evince,** furnish evidence, **show, go to show,** tend to show; **demonstrate, illustrate,** exhibit, manifest, display, express, set forth; approve; **attest; indicate, signify,** signalize, symptomatize, mark, **denote, betoken, point to,** give indication of, show signs of; **connote, imply, suggest,** involve; argue, breathe, tell, bespeak; **speak for itself,** speak volumes.

.10 **testify, attest, give evidence,** witness, **give or bear witness; disclose** 556.4–7; **vouch,** state one's case, **depose,** depone, **warrant, swear,** take one's oath, acknowledge, avow, **affirm,** avouch, aver, allege, asseverate, **certify, give one's word.**

.11 **prove, demonstrate, show,** afford proof of, prove to be, prove true; **establish, fix, determine, ascertain,** make out, remove all doubt; **settle,** settle the matter; **set at rest;** clinch or cinch or nail down [all informal]; **prove one's point,** make one's case, bring home to, make good, have or make out a case; hold good, hold water; follow, follow from, follow as a matter of course.

.12 **confirm,** affirm, **attest,** warrant, uphold [Brit dial], **substantiate, authenticate, validate, certify,** ratify, **verify;** circumstantiate, **corroborate, bear out,** support, buttress, **sustain,** fortify, bolster, back, back up, reinforce, undergird, strengthen; **document;** probate, prove.

.13 **adduce,** produce, **advance, present,** bring to bear, **offer,** allege [archaic], plead, **bring forward,** bring on; rally, marshal, deploy, array.

.14 **cite, name,** call to mind; **instance,** cite a particular or particulars, cite cases or a case in point, itemize, particularize, produce an instance, give a for-instance [informal]; **exemplify,** example [archaic], **illustrate,** demonstrate; **document; quote,** quote chapter and verse.

.15 **refer to,** direct attention to, **appeal to,** invoke; make reference to; cross-refer, make a cross-reference; reference, cross-reference.

.16 **have evidence** or **proof,** have a case, possess incriminating evidence, **have something on** [informal]; **have the goods on** or **have dead to rights** [both slang].

.17 ADJS **evidential,** evidentiary, **factual,** symptomatic, **significant, indicative,** attestative, attestive, probative; founded on, grounded on, based on; implicit, suggestive; **material,** telling, convincing, weighty; overwhelming, damning; **conclusive,** determinative, **decisive,** final, incontrovertible, irresistible, indisputable, irrefutable, sure, certain, absolute; documented, documentary; **valid, admissible;** adducible; firsthand, authentic, reliable 513.17, eye-witness; hearsay, circumstantial, presumptive, nuncupative, cumulative, ex parte.

.18 **demonstrative,** demonstrating, demonstrational; evincive, apodictic.

.19 **confirming,** confirmatory, confirmative; substantiating, **verifying,** verificative; **corroborating,** corroboratory, **corroborative,** supportive, **supporting.**

.20 **provable, demonstrable,** demonstratable, apodictic, evincible, attestable, **confirmable,** checkable, **substantiatable, establishable,** supportable, sustainable, **verifiable,** validatable, authenticatable.

.21 **proved, proven, demonstrated,** shown; **established,** fixed, **settled, determined,** ascertained; **confirmed, substantiated,** attested, **authenticated, certified, validated, verified;** circumstantiated, **corroborated,** borne out.

.22 **unrefuted,** unconfuted, unanswered, uncontroverted, uncontradicted, **undenied; unrefutable** 513.15.

.23 ADVS **evidentially,** according to the evidence, on the evidence, as attested by; **in confirmation, in corroboration of, in support of;** at first hand, at second hand.

.24 **to illustrate,** to prove the point, as an example, as a case in point, to name an instance, by way of example, **for example, for instance,** to cite an instance, as an instance, e.g., *exempli gratia* [L]; as, thus.

.25 **which see, q.v.,** *quod vide* [L]; *loco citato* [L], loc. cit.; *opere citato* [L], op. cit.

.26 PHRS **it is proven,** *probatum est* [L], there is nothing more to be said, it must follow; QED, *quod erat demonstrandum* [L].

506. DISPROOF

.1 NOUNS **disproof,** disproving, disproval, **invalidation,** disconfirmation, explosion, negation, redargution [archaic]; exposure, exposé; *reductio ad absurdum* [L].

.2 **refutation, confutation,** confounding, refutal, **rebuttal, answer,** complete answer, crushing *or* effective rejoinder, squelch; discrediting; **overthrow,** overthrowal, upset, upsetting, subversion, undermining, demolition; **contradiction,** controversion, denial 524.2.

.3 **conclusive argument, knockdown argument, floorer,** sockdolager [slang]; **clincher** *or* crusher *or* settler *or* finisher *or* squelcher [all informal].

.4 VERBS **disprove, invalidate,** disconfirm, discredit, prove the contrary, belie, give the lie to, redargue [archaic]; **negate,** negative; **expose, show up; explode,** blow up, blow sky-high, **puncture, deflate, shoot** *or* **poke full of holes; knock the bottom out of** [informal], knock the props *or* chocks out from under, take the ground from under, undercut, cut the ground from under one's feet, not leave a leg to stand on, have the last word, leave nothing to say.

.5 **refute, confute, confound, rebut,** parry, answer, **answer conclusively,** dismiss, dispose of; **overthrow,** overturn, overwhelm, upset, subvert, defeat, demolish, undermine; argue down; floor *or* finish *or* settle *or* squash *or* squelch [all informal], crush, smash all opposition; silence, put *or* reduce to silence, shut up, stop the mouth of; nonplus, take the wind out of one's sails; **contradict,** controvert, **deny** 524.4.

.6 ADJS **refuting, confuting, confounding,** confutative, refutative, refutatory; contradictory, contrary 524.5.

.7 **disproved,** disconfirmed, **invalidated,** negated, negatived, discredited, belied; **exposed,** shown up; **punctured,** deflated, **exploded; refuted,** confuted, confounded; **upset, overthrown,** overturned; **contradicted,** disputed, denied, impugned; dismissed, discarded, rejected 638.3.

.8 **unproved,** not proved, unproven, **undemonstrated,** unshown; **untried,** untested; **unestablished,** unfixed, **unsettled, undetermined,** unascertained; **unconfirmed, unsubstantiated,** unattested, **unauthenticated,** unvalidated, uncertified, **unverified; uncorroborated,** unsustained, **unsupported,** unsupported by evidence, **groundless,** without grounds *or* basis, **unfounded** 483.13; **inconclusive,** indecisive; not following.

.9 **unprovable,** controvertible, **undemonstrable,** undemonstratable, unattestable, unsubstantiatable, **unsupportable,** unconfirmable, unsustainable, unverifiable.

.10 **refutable,** confutable, **disprovable,** defeasible.

507. QUALIFICATION

.1 NOUNS **qualification, limitation, restriction,** circumscription, **modification,** hedge, hedging; specification; **allowance, concession,** cession, grant; grain of salt; **reservation, exception,** waiver, exemption; specialness, special circumstance, special case, special treatment; **mental** reservation, salvo, *arrière-pensée* [Fr]; extenuating circumstances.

.2 **condition, provision, proviso, stipulation,** whereas; **specification,** parameter, given, *donnée* [Fr], limiting condition, boundary condition; **catch** or joker or kicker [all informal], string, a string to it [informal]; **requisite, prerequisite,** obligation; *sine qua non* [L], *conditio sine qua non* [L]; clause; escape clause, escape hatch, saving clause; escalator clause; **terms,** provisions; grounds; small or fine print [informal], fine print at the bottom [informal]; ultimatum.

.3 VERBS **qualify, limit,** condition [archaic], hedge, hedge about, **modify, restrict,** restrain, circumscribe, set limits or conditions, box in [informal], narrow; adjust to, regulate by; alter 139.6; **temper, season,** leaven, soften, modulate, moderate, assuage, **mitigate,** palliate, abate, reduce, diminish.

.4 **make conditional,** make contingent, **condition;** make it a condition, attach a condition or proviso, **stipulate;** insist upon, make a point of; **have a catch** [informal], have a joker or kicker [informal], have a joker in the deck [informal], have a string attached [informal].

.5 **allow for, make allowance for,** provide for, take account of, **take into account** or **consideration, consider,** consider the circumstances; allow, **grant, concede,** admit, admit exceptions, see the special circumstances; relax, relax the condition, waive, set aside, lift temporarily; disregard, **discount,** leave out of account; consider the source, **take with a grain of salt.**

.6 **depend,** hang, rest, hinge; **depend on** or **upon, hang on** or **upon, rest on** or **upon,** rest with, repose upon, lie on, lie with, stand on or upon, be based on, be bounded or limited by, be dependent on, be predicated on, **be contingent** or **conditional on; hinge on** or **upon, turn on** or **upon,** revolve on or upon, have as a fulcrum.

.7 ADJS **qualifying,** qualificative, qualificatory, **modifying,** modificatory, altering; **limiting, restricting,** limitative, restrictive, bounding; **extenuating,** extenuatory, **mitigating,** mitigative, mitigatory, modulatory, palliative, assuasive, lenitive, softening.

.8 **conditional, provisional,** provisory, stipulatory; specificative; **specified, stipulated,** fixed, stated, given.

.9 **contingent, dependent, depending;** contingent on, **dependent on, depending on,** predicated on, based on, hanging or hinging on, turning on, revolving on; depending on circumstances; circumscribed by, hedged or hedged about by; boxed in [informal]; **subject to,** incidental to, incident to.

.10 **qualified, modified, conditioned, limited, restricted,** hedged, hedged about; **tempered, seasoned,** leavened, softened, **mitigated,** modulated.

.11 ADVS **conditionally, provisionally, with qualifications,** with a string or catch or joker or kicker to it [informal]; with a reservation or exception, with a grain of salt.

.12 CONJS **provided,** provided that, provided always, **providing,** with this proviso, it being provided; **on condition,** on condition that, **with the stipulation,** with the understanding, according as, subject to.

.13 **granting, admitting, allowing,** admitting that, allowing that; exempting, waiving.

.14 **if,** an or an' [both archaic], if and when, only if, if only, if and only if, if it be so, if it be true that, if it so happens or turns out.

.15 **so,** just so, so that [archaic], so as, **so long as, as long as.**

.16 **unless,** unless that, **if not, were it not,** were it not that; **except, excepting,** except that, with the exception that, save, **but.**

508. NO QUALIFICATIONS

.1 NOUNS **unqualifiedness,** unlimitedness, **unconditionality,** unrestrictedness, **unreservedness,** uncircumscribedness; categoricalness; **absoluteness,** definiteness, **explicitness;** decisiveness.

.2 ADJS **unqualified, unconditional,** unconditioned, **unrestricted,** unhampered, **unlimited,** uncircumscribed, unmitigated, **categorical,** straight, **unreserved,** without reserve; **implicit,** unquestioning, undoubting, unhesitating; **explicit, express, unequivocal,** clear, unmistakable; **peremptory,** indisputable, inappealable; **without exception,** admitting no exception, unwaivable; **positive, absolute,** definite, definitive, determinate, decided, decisive, fixed, final, conclusive; round, flat, **complete, entire, whole, total,** global, omn(i)–; **utter,** perfect, downright, outright, out-and-out, **straight-out** [informal], all-out, flat-out [dial].

.3 ADVS [informal terms] **no strings attached,** no holds barred, **no catch** or joker or kicker, no joker in the deck, no small print or fine print, no fine print at the bottom; no ifs, ands, or buts; downright.

509. POSSIBILITY

.1 NOUNS possibility, possibleness, the realm of possibility, the domain of the possible, conceivableness, conceivability, thinkability, thinkableness, imaginability; probability, likelihood 511; what may be, what might be, what is possible, what one can do, what can be done, the possible, the attainable, the feasible; potential, potentiality, virtuality; contingency, eventuality; chance, prospect; outside chance [informal], off chance, remote possibility; hope, outside hope, small hope; good possibility, good chance, even chance 156.7,8; bare possibility 156.9.

.2 practicability, practicality, feasibility; workability, operability, actability, performability, realizability, negotiability; viability, viableness; achievability, doability, compassability, attainability; surmountability, superability.

.3 accessibility, access, approachability, openness, reachableness, come-at-ableness, getatableness [both informal]; penetrability, perviousness; obtainability, obtainableness, availability, procurability, procurableness, securableness, gettableness, acquirability.

.4 VERBS be possible, could be, might be, have or stand a chance or good chance, bid fair to.

.5 make possible, enable, permit, clear the road or path for, smooth the way for, open the way for, open up the possibility of.

.6 ADJS possible, within the bounds or realm or range or domain of possibility, in one's power, in one's hands, humanly possible; probable, likely 511.6; conceivable, conceivably possible, imaginable, thinkable, cogitable; plausible 511.7; potential; contingent.

.7 practicable, practical, feasible; workable, actable, performable, effectible [archaic], realizable, compassable, operable, negotiable, doable; viable; achievable, attainable; surmountable, superable, overcomable.

.8 accessible, approachable, come-at-able or getatable [both informal], reachable, within reach; open, open to; penetrable, getinable [informal], pervious; obtainable, attainable, available, procurable, securable, findable, gettable, to be had.

.9 ADVS possibly, conceivably, imaginably, feasibly; perhaps, perchance, haply; maybe, it may be, for all or aught one knows.

.10 by any possibility, by any chance, by any means, by any manner of means; in any way, in any possible way, at any cost, at all, if at all, ever; on the bare possibility, on the off chance, by merest chance.

.11 if possible, if humanly possible, God willing, wind and weather permitting.

510. IMPOSSIBILITY

.1 NOUNS impossibility, impossibleness, the realm or domain of the impossible, inconceivability, unthinkability, unimaginability, what cannot be, what can never be, what cannot happen, hopelessness, no chance 156.10; self-contradiction, absurdity, paradox, oxymoron, logical impossibility; impossible, the impossible, impossibilism.

.2 impracticability, unpracticability, impracticality, unfeasibility; unworkability, inoperability, unperformability; unachievability, unattainability; unrealizability, uncompassability; insurmountability, insuperability.

.3 inaccessibility, unaccessibility; unapproachability, un-come-at-ableness [informal], unreachableness; impenetrability, imperviousness; unobtainability, unobtainableness, unattainability, unavailability, unprocurableness, unsecurableness, ungettableness [informal], unacquirability; undiscoverability, unascertainableness.

.4 VERBS be impossible, be an impossibility, not have a chance, be a waste of time; contradict itself, be a logical impossibility, be a paradox; fly in the face of reason.

.5 attempt the impossible, try for a miracle, look for a needle in a haystack or in a bottle of hay, try to be in two places at once, try to fetch water in a sieve or catch the wind in a net or weave a rope of sand or get figs from thistles or gather grapes from thorns or make bricks from straw or make cheese of chalk or make a silk purse out of a sow's ear or change the leopard's spots or get blood from a turnip; ask the impossible, cry for the moon.

.6 make impossible, rule out, disenable, disqualify, close out, **bar**, prohibit, put out of reach, leave no chance.

.7 ADJS **impossible, not possible**, beyond the bounds of possibility *or* reason, contrary to reason, at variance with the facts; **inconceivable, unimaginable, unthinkable, not to be thought of, out of the question**; hopeless; **absurd**, ridiculous, preposterous; **self-contradictory**, paradoxical, oxymoronic, logically impossible; **ruled-out**, excluded, closed-out, **barred**, prohibited.

.8 **impracticable, impractical, unfeasible; unworkable**, unperformable, inoperable, undoable, unnegotiable; **unachievable, unattainable**, uneffectible [archaic]; unrealizable, uncompassable; insurmountable, unsurmountable, **insuperable**, unovercomable; **beyond one**, beyond one's power, beyond one's control, out of one's depth, too much for.

.9 **inaccessible**, unaccessible; **unapproachable**, un-come-at-able [informal]; **unreachable**, beyond reach, out of reach; **impenetrable**, impervious; closed to, denied to, lost to, closed forever to; **unobtainable, unattainable, unavailable**, unprocurable, unsecurable, ungettable [informal], unacquirable; not to be had, **not to be had for love or money**; undiscoverable, unascertainable.

.10 ADVS **impossibly, inconceivably**, unimaginably, unthinkably.

511. PROBABILITY

.1 NOUNS **probability, likelihood**, likeliness, liability, aptitude, verisimilitude; **chance, odds; expectation, outlook**, prospect; favorable prospect, well-grounded hope, some *or* reasonable hope, fair expectation; **good chance** 156.8; presumption, presumptive evidence; tendency; probable cause, reasonable ground *or* presumption; probabilism.

.2 **mathematical probability**, statistical probability, statistics, **predictability**; probability theory, game theory, theory of games; operations research; probable error, standard deviation; probability curve, frequency curve, frequency polygon, frequency distribution, probability function, probability density function, probability distribution, cumulative distribution function; **statistical mechanics**, quantum mechanics, uncertainty *or* indeterminacy principle, Maxwell-Boltzmann distribution law, Bose-Einstein statistics, Fermi-Dirac statistics; **mortality table**, actuarial table, life table, com-

bined experience table, Commissioners Standard Ordinary table.

.3 **plausibility**; reasonability 482.9; credibility 501.8.

.4 VERBS **be probable, seem likely**, offer a good prospect, offer the expectation, have *or* run a good chance; **promise**, be promising, make fair promise, **bid fair to**, stand fair to, show a tendency, be in the cards, have the makings of, have favorable odds, lead one to expect; **make probable**, probabilize, make more likely, smooth the way for; increase the chances.

.5 **think likely, daresay**, venture to say; **presume**, suppose 499.10.

.6 ADJS **probable, likely, liable, apt**, verisimilar, in the cards, odds-on; **promising, hopeful**, fair, in a fair way; foreseeable, **predictable; presumable**, presumptive; mathematically *or* statistically probable, predictable within limits.

.7 **plausible, apparent** [archaic]; **reasonable** 482.20; **credible** 501.24; conceivable 509.6.

.8 ADVS **probably, in all probability** *or* likelihood, **likely, most likely, very likely**; very like *or* like enough *or* like as not [all informal]; **doubtlessly**, doubtless, **no doubt**, indubitably; **presumably**, presumptively; by all odds, ten to one, a hundred to one, dollars to doughnuts.

.9 PHRS **there is reason to believe**, I am led to believe, it can be supposed, it would appear, it stands to reason, it might be thought, one can assume, appearances are in favor of, the chances *or* odds are, you can bank on it, you can make book on it, you can bet on it, you can bet your bottom dollar, you can just bet, you can't go wrong; I daresay, I venture to say.

512. IMPROBABILITY

.1 NOUNS **improbability, unlikelihood**, unlikeliness; **doubtfulness**, dubiousness, **questionableness; implausibility**, incredibility 503.3; little expectation, low order of probability, poor possibility, bare possibility, faint likelihood, poor prospect, poor outlook; **small chance** 156.9.

.2 VERBS **be improbable, not be likely**, be a stretch of the imagination, strain one's credulity, go beyond reason, go far afield, go beyond the bounds of reason *or* probability.

.3 ADJS **improbable, unlikely**, unpromising, hardly possible, scarcely to be expected *or* anticipated; **doubtful, dubious, questionable**, doubtable, dubitable, more than doubtful; **implausible**, incredible 503.10.

.4 PHRS **not likely!**, no fear!, never fear!, I ask you!, you should live so long! [slang], don't hold your breath!

513. CERTAINTY

.1 NOUNS **certainty, certitude,** certainness, **sureness, surety, assurance, assuredness,** certain knowledge; **positiveness, absoluteness, definiteness,** dead or moral or absolute certainty; unequivocalness, unmistakableness, unambiguity, nonambiguity, univocity, univocality; **infallibility,** infallibilism, inerrability, inerrancy; **necessity,** determinacy, determinateness, noncontingency, Hobson's choice, ineluctability, predetermination, predestination, **inevitability** 639.7; **truth** 516; **proved fact, probatum.**

.2 [slang terms] **sure thing,** dead-sure thing, sure bet, sure card, **cinch,** lead-pipe cinch, **open-and-shut case.**

.3 **unquestionability, undeniability,** indubitability, indubitableness, **indisputability,** incontestability, incontrovertibility, **irrefutability,** unrefutability, unconfutability, irrefragability, unimpeachability; **doubtlessness, questionlessness; demonstrability,** demonstratability, provability, verifiability, confirmability; factuality, **reality,** actuality 1.2.

.4 **reliability, dependability, validity, trustworthiness,** faithworthiness; unerringness; predictability, calculability; stability, substantiality, firmness, **soundness,** solidity, staunchness, steadiness, **steadfastness;** secureness, **security;** invincibility 159.4; **authoritativeness, authenticity.**

.5 **confidence,** confidentness, conviction, belief, fixed or settled belief, **sureness, assurance, assuredness,** surety, security, certitude; **faith,** subjective certainty; trust 501.1; **positiveness, cocksureness; self-confidence, self-assurance, self-reliance;** poise 858.3; courage 893; **overconfidence, oversureness,** overweening [archaic], overweeningness, hubris; pride 905, arrogance 912, pomposity 904.7, self-importance 909.1.

.6 **dogmatism,** dogmaticalness, **positiveness,** positivism, peremptoriness, **opinionatedness,** self-opinionatedness; bigotry; infallibilism.

.7 **dogmatist,** dogmatizer, opinionist, doctrinaire, bigot; positivist; infallibilist.

.8 **ensuring, assurance;** reassurance, reassurement; **certification;** ascertainment, determination, establishment; **verification,** substantiation, validation, collation, check, checking; **confirmation** 505.5.

.9 VERBS **be certain, be confident, feel sure, rest assured, have no doubt,** doubt not; know, just know, know for certain; **bet on** or **gamble on** or **bet one's bottom dollar on** [all informal]; admit of no doubt; **go without saying,** aller sans dire [Fr], be axiomatic or apodictic.

.10 **dogmatize,** lay down the law, pontificate, oracle, oraculate, proclaim.

.11 **make sure, make certain,** make sure of, make no doubt, make no mistake; remove or dismiss or expunge or erase all doubt; **assure, ensure,** insure, **certify, ascertain; find out,** get at, see to it, see that; **determine,** decide, **establish,** settle, fix, nail down [informal], clinch or cinch [both informal], clear up, sort out, set at rest; assure or satisfy oneself, make oneself easy about or on that score; **reassure.**

.12 **verify, confirm** 505.12, test, prove, audit, **collate,** validate, **check,** check up or on or out [informal], check over or through, **double-check,** triple-check, cross-check, recheck, check and doublecheck, check up and down, check over and through, check in and out, "make assurance double sure" [Shakespeare].

.13 ADJS **certain, sure,** sure-enough [informal]; **bound; positive, absolute, definite,** perfectly sure, apodictic; decisive, conclusive; clear, clear as day, clear and distinct, unequivocal, **unmistakable,** unambiguous, nonambiguous, univocal; **necessary,** determinate, ineluctable, predetermined, predestined, **inevitable** 639.15; **true** 516.12.

.14 [informal or slang terms] **dead sure,** sure as death, sure as death and taxes, sure as fate, sure as can be, sure as shooting, sure as God made little green apples, sure as hell or the devil, as sure as I live and breathe.

.15 **unquestionable, undeniable, indubitable, indisputable, incontestable, irrefutable,** unrefutable, unconfutable, **incontrovertible,** irrefragable, unanswerable, inappealable, **unimpeachable, absolute;** admitting no question or dispute or doubt or denial; **demonstrable,** demonstratable, **provable,** verifiable, testable, confirmable; self-evident, axiomatic; factual, **real,** historical, actual 1.15.

.16 **undoubted,** indubious, **unquestioned, undisputed, uncontested,** uncontradicted, unchallenged, uncontroverted, uncontroversial; **doubtless, questionless,** beyond a shade *or* shadow of doubt, past dispute, beyond question.

.17 **reliable, dependable, sure,** surefire [informal], **trustworthy, trusty,** faithworthy, **to be depended** *or* **relied upon,** to be counted *or* reckoned on; predictable, calculable; **secure, solid, sound, firm, fast, stable, substantial,** staunch, steady, **steadfast, faithful, unfailing;** invincible 159.17; well-founded, well-grounded.

.18 **authoritative, authentic,** magisterial, **official;** cathedral, ex cathedra; standard, approved, accepted, received.

.19 **infallible, inerrable,** inerrant, unerring.

.20 **assured,** made sure; **determined, decided, ascertained; settled, established,** fixed, cinched [informal], set [informal], stated, determinate, secure; **certified, attested,** guaranteed, warranted, tested, tried, proved; **open-and-shut** [informal], **nailed down** [informal], **in the bag** *or* on ice [both slang].

.21 **confident, sure,** secure, assured, reassured, decided, determined; **convinced,** persuaded, positive, **cocksure; unhesitating,** unfaltering, unwavering; **undoubting** 501.21; **self-confident, self-assured, self-reliant,** sure of oneself; poised 858.13; unafraid 893.19; **overconfident, oversure,** overweening, hubristic; proud 905.8, arrogant 912.9, pompous 904.22, self-important 909.8.

.22 **dogmatic(al),** dogmatizing, pronunciative, **positive,** positivistic, peremptory, pontifical, oracular; **opinionated,** opinioned, opinionative, conceited 909.11; **self-opinionated,** self-opinioned; doctrinarian, doctrinaire; bigoted.

.23 ADVS **certainly, surely, assuredly, positively, absolutely, definitely,** decidedly; decisively, distinctly, clearly, unequivocally, unmistakably; **for certain,** for sure *or* for a fact [both informal], in truth, certes *or* forsooth [both archaic], and no mistake [informal]; **for a certainty,** to a certainty, à coup sûr [Fr]; **most certainly,** most assuredly; **indeed,** indeedy [informal]; truly 516.17; **of course,** as a matter of course; **by all means,** by all manner of means; at any rate, at all events; nothing else but [informal], no two ways about it, no buts about it [informal]; no ifs, ands, or buts.

.24 **surely, sure, to be sure,** sure enough; sure thing *or* surest thing you know [both informal].

.25 **unquestionably, undoubtedly, indubitably, admittedly, undeniably,** indisputably, incontestably, incontrovertibly, irrefutably, irrefragably; **doubtlessly,** doubtless, **no doubt, without doubt,** beyond doubt *or* question, out of question.

.26 **without fail,** whatever may happen, **come what may,** come hell or high water [slang]; cost what it may, *coûte que coûte* [Fr]; rain or shine, live or die, sink or swim.

.27 PHRS **it is certain,** there is no question, there is not a shadow of doubt, that's for sure [slang]; that goes without saying, *cela va sans dire* [Fr]; that is evident, that leaps to the eye, *cela saute aux yeux* [Fr].

514. UNCERTAINTY

.1 NOUNS **uncertainty, incertitude, unsureness,** uncertainness; indemonstrability, unverifiability, unprovability, unconfirmability; **unpredictability,** unforeseeableness, incalculability, unaccountability; **indetermination,** indeterminacy, indeterminism; **randomness, chance,** chanciness, hit-or-missness, **luck; indecision,** indecisiveness, undecidedness, undeterminedness; **hesitation, hesitancy; suspense,** suspensefulness, agony *or* state of suspense; **fickleness, capriciousness,** whimsicality, **erraticness,** erraticism, **changeableness** 141; **vacillation, irresolution** 627; indeterminacy *or* uncertainty principle.

.2 **doubtfulness, dubiousness, doubt,** dubiety, dubitancy, dubitation [archaic]; **questionableness, disputability,** contestability, controvertibility, refutability, confutability, deniability; disbelief 503.1.

.3 **bewilderment,** disconcertion, disconcertedness, disconcert, disconcertment, **embarrassment, confoundment,** discomposure, unassuredness, **confusion** 532.3; **perplexity,** puzzlement, baffle, **bafflement,** predicament, plight, **quandary, dilemma,** horns of a dilemma, nonplus; **puzzle,** problem, riddle, mystery, enigma; fix *or* jam *or* pickle *or* scrape *or* stew [all informal]; perturbation, disturbance, upset, bother, pother.

.4 **vagueness, indefiniteness, indecisiveness,** indeterminateness, indeterminableness, indefinableness, **unclearness, indistinctness,** haziness, fogginess, mistiness, blurriness, fuzziness; **obscurity,** obscuration; **looseness, laxity, inexactness,** inaccuracy, imprecision; **broadness, generality,** sweepingness; ill-definedness, amorphousness, shapelessness, blobbiness, inchoateness, disorder, incoherence.

.5 equivocalness, equivocality, polysemousness, ambiguity 550.

.6 unreliability, undependability, untrustworthiness, unfaithworthiness, treacherousness, treachery; unsureness, insecurity, unsoundness, infirmity, insolidity, unsolidity, instability, insubstantiality, unsubstantiality, unsteadfastness, unsteadiness, desultoriness, shakiness; precariousness, hazard, danger, risk, riskiness, peril, perilousness, ticklishness, slipperiness, shiftiness, shiftingness; speculativeness; unauthoritativeness, unauthenticity.

.7 fallibility, errability, errancy, liability to error.

.8 (an uncertainty) gamble, guess, piece of guesswork, chance, wager, toss-up, touch and go; contingency, double contingency, possibility upon a possibility; question, open question; undecided issue; borderline case; blind bargain, pig in a poke, sight-unseen transaction; leap in the dark.

.9 VERBS be uncertain, feel unsure; doubt, have one's doubts, question, puzzle over, agonize over; wonder, wonder whether; not know what to make of, not be able to make head or tail of; be at sea, float in a sea of doubt; be at one's wit's end, not know which way to turn, be of two minds, not know where one stands, not know whether one stands on one's head or one's heels, be in a dilemma or quandary, flounder, grope, beat about, thrash about, go around in circles; go off in all directions at once.

.10 hang in doubt, stop to consider, think twice; falter, dither, hesitate, vacillate 627.8.

.11 depend, pend [dial], all depend, be contingent or conditional on, hang on or upon; hang, hang in the balance, be touch and go, tremble in the balance, hang in suspense; hang by a thread, hang by the eyelids.

.12 bewilder, disconcert, discompose, upset, perturb, disturb, dismay, abash, embarrass, put out, pother, bother, moider [Brit dial], flummox [informal].

.13 perplex, baffle, confound, boggle [Brit dial], daze, amaze [archaic], maze, addle, fuddle, muddle, buffalo [slang], bamboozle [informal], mystify, puzzle, nonplus, stick [informal], stump [informal], floor [informal], throw [slang], get [informal], beat [informal], lick [slang], put to one's wit's end; keep one guessing, keep in suspense.

.14 make uncertain, obscure, muddle, muddy, fuzz, fog, confuse 532.7.

.15 ADJS uncertain, unsure; doubting, agnostic, skeptical, unconvinced, unpersuaded; chancy, dicey [Brit], touch-and-go; unpredictable, unforeseeable, incalculable, unaccountable, undivinable; indemonstrable, unverifiable, unprovable, unconfirmable; equivocal, polysemous, ambiguous 550.3; fickle, capricious, whimsical, erratic, variable, wavering, changeable 141.6; hesitant, hesitating; indecisive, irresolute 627.9.

.16 doubtful, iffy [informal]; in doubt, in dubio [L]; dubitable, doubtable, dubious, questionable, problematic(al), speculative, conjectural, suppositional; debatable, moot, arguable, disputable, contestable, controvertible, controversial, refutable, confutable, deniable; mistakable; suspicious, suspect; open to question or doubt; in question, in dispute, at issue.

.17 undecided, undetermined, unsettled, unfixed, unestablished; untold, uncounted; pendent, dependent, pending, depending, contingent, conditional, conditioned; open, in question, at issue, in the balance, up in the air, up for grabs [slang], in suspense, in a state of suspense, suspenseful.

.18 vague, indefinite, indecisive, indeterminate, indeterminable, undetermined, unpredetermined, undestined; random, stochastic, chance, chancy [informal], aleatory or aleatoric, hit-or-miss; indefinable, undefined, ill-defined, unclear, unplain, indistinct, fuzzy, obscure, confused, hazy, shadowy, shadowed forth, foggy, blurred, blurry, veiled; loose, lax, inexact, inaccurate, imprecise; nonspecific, unspecified; broad, general, sweeping; amorphous, shapeless, blobby; inchoate, disordered, orderless, chaotic, incoherent.

.19 unreliable, undependable, untrustworthy, unfaithworthy, treacherous, unsure, not to be depended or relied on; insecure, unsound, infirm, unsolid, unstable, unsubstantial, insubstantial, unsteadfast, unsteady, desultory, shaky; precarious, hazardous, dangerous, perilous, risky, ticklish; shifty, shifting, slippery; provisional, tentative, temporary.

.20 unauthoritative, unauthentic, unofficial, nonofficial, apocryphal; uncertified, unverified, unchecked, unconfirmed, uncorroborated, unauthenticated, unvalidated, unattested, unwarranted; **un-demonstrated, unproved.**

.21 **fallible, errable,** errant, liable *or* open to error, error-prone.

.22 **unconfident, unsure, unassured, insecure,** unsure of oneself; **unselfconfident,** unselfassured, unselfreliant.

.23 **bewildered, dismayed,** distracted, distraught, abashed, **disconcerted, embarrassed,** discomposed, **put-out, disturbed, upset,** perturbed, **bothered,** all hot and bothered [informal]; **confused** 532.12; clueless, without a clue, guessing, mazed, in a maze; turned around, going around in circles, like a chicken with its head cut off [informal]; in a fix *or* stew *or* pickle *or* jam *or* scrape [informal]; **lost, astray,** abroad, adrift, **at sea,** off the track, out of one's reckoning, out of one's bearings, disoriented.

.24 **in a dilemma,** on the horns of a dilemma; **perplexed, confounded, mystified, puzzled, nonplussed, baffled,** bamboozled [informal], **buffaloed** [slang]; **at a loss, at one's wit's end,** fuddled, addled, muddled, **dazed, beat** [informal], licked [slang]; **stuck** *or* floored *or* **stumped** *or* thrown [all informal]; **on tenterhooks,** in suspense.

.25 **bewildering, confusing, distracting, disconcerting,** discomposing, **dismaying, embarrassing,** disturbing, **upsetting,** perturbing, bothering; **perplexing, baffling, mystifying, mysterious, puzzling,** confounding; **problematic(al);** intricate 46.4; **enigmatic** 549.17.

.26 ADVS **uncertainly,** in an uncertain state, **unsurely; doubtfully, dubiously;** in suspense, on the horns of a dilemma; perplexedly, disconcertedly, confusedly, dazedly, mazedly, in a daze, in a maze.

.27 **vaguely, indefinitely,** indeterminably, indefinably, **indistinctly,** indecisively, **obscurely; broadly, generally,** in broad *or* general terms.

515. GAMBLE

.1 NOUNS **gamble, chance, risk, hazard; speculation, venture,** play; flier *or* plunge [both slang]; calculated risk; uncertainty 514; fortune, luck 156.1,2.

.2 matter of chance, sporting chance, gambling chance, luck of the draw, chance at odds; hazard of the die, cast *or* throw of the dice, turn *or* roll of the wheel, turn of the table, turn of the cards, fall of the cards, flip of the coin; toss-up, toss; heads or tails, touch and go; blind bargain, pig

in a poke; leap in the dark, shot in the dark; potshot, random shot; potluck.

.3 **wager, bet, stake, hazard;** play *or* chunk *or* shot [all slang]; **ante;** parlay; **book,** handbook.

.4 betting system; **sweepstakes, sweepstake, sweeps;** pari-mutuel; **daily double, exacta, perfecta; quinella; superfecta; martingale; double-or-nothing.**

.5 **pot, jackpot, pool, stakes, kitty; bank,** tiger.

.6 **odds,** price; equivalent odds; **even** *or* **square odds,** even break; **short odds,** ten-to-one shot; **long odds,** long shot, hundred-to-one shot; even chance, good chance, small chance, no chance 156.10.

.7 **gambling,** gaming, sporting [archaic], **speculation,** play, playing; **betting, wagering,** hazarding, risking, staking; drawing *or* casting lots, sortition; cardsharping.

.8 (games of chance) chuck-a-luck, chuck farthing, **crack-loo** [slang], **craps,** crap shooting, crap game, **fan-tan,** hazard, horse racing, keno, lotto, bingo, pinball, policy *or* the numbers game, the numbers [informal]; pitch and toss *or* chuck and toss, roulette, *trente-et-quarante, rouge et noir* [both Fr], shell game; **sweepstake** *or* **sweepstakes;** card games 878.35.

.9 die [sing]; **dice, bones** [informal]; **ivories** *or* **cubes** *or* devil's bones *or* teeth [all slang]; **craps,** crap shooting, crap game; poker dice; loaded dice, false *or* crooked dice; bird cage.

.10 (throw of dice) **throw, cast, roll, shot, hazard of the die;** dice throws (snake eyes, etc.) 90.3, 93.1, 96.1, 99.1–7; crap, craps; **natural, nick.**

.11 **lottery,** drawing, **sweepstakes** *or* **sweepstake** *or* **sweep;** draft lottery; **raffle;** lotto, bingo, keno, tombola [Brit], Genoese *or* number lottery; interest lottery, Dutch *or* class lottery; numbers pool; tontine; grab bag *or* barrel *or* box.

.12 (gambling device) gambling wheel, wheel of fortune, Fortune's wheel; roulette wheel; raffle wheel; pinball machine; slot machine, one-armed bandit [informal]; gambling table, crap table.

.13 pari-mutuel, pari-mutuel machine; totalizator, totalizer, tote [informal].

.14 **counter, check, chip.**

.15 **gambling house, gaming house,** betting house, betting parlor, gambling hall, sporting house [archaic], **gambling den, gambling hell;** hell *or* joint *or* flat *or* crib [all slang]; casino; poolroom.

.16 **bookmaker, bookie** [informal]; **numbers runner**; **bagman**.

.17 **gambler, gamester, player,** sportsman or sporting man [both archaic], sport, hazarder [archaic]; venturer, adventurer; **bettor, wagerer, punter; speculator,** speculatist; plunger [slang]; petty gambler, piker [slang]; tinhorn or tinhorn gambler [both slang]; **sharper** or sharpie or sharp [all slang]; **cardsharp** or cardshark, cardsharper; crap shooter [informal], boneshaker [slang]; betting ring; compulsive gambler; tipster, tout [Brit].

.18 VERBS **gamble,** game, sport [archaic], play, **try one's luck** or fortune; **speculate; draw lots,** draw straws, lot, cut lots, **cast lots;** cut the cards or deck; match coins, toss, flip a coin, call, call heads or tails; shoot craps, play at dice; play the ponies [informal]; raffle off.

.19 **chance, risk, hazard,** set at hazard, venture, wager, take a flier [informal]; **gamble on,** take a gamble on; **take a chance,** take one's chance, take the chances of, try the chance, **chance it,** "stand the hazard of the die" [Shakespeare]; **take** or **run the risk,** run a chance; **take chances,** tempt fortune; **leave** or **trust to chance** or **luck,** rely on fortune, take a leap in the dark; buy a pig in a poke; take potluck.

.20 **bet, wager, gamble, hazard, stake,** punt, lay, lay down, **make a bet, lay a wager; plunge** [slang]; **bet on** or **upon, back; bet** or **play against; parlay; ante, ante up; meet a bet, see, call, cover, fade; pass; stand pat.**

.21 ADJS speculative, **uncertain** 514.15; **hazardous, risky** 697.10.

516. TRUTH

(conformity to fact or reality)

.1 NOUNS **truth, trueness,** verity, **very truth,** sooth or good sooth [both archaic]; **unerroneousness, unfalseness,** unfallaciousness; historical truth, **objective truth, actuality,** historicity, **fact, reality** 1.2–3; the true, ultimate truth; eternal verities; truthfulness, veracity 974.3.

.2 **the truth,** the truth of the matter, the case; what's what or how it is or how things are or like it is or where it's at [all informal], the unvarnished truth, the simple truth, **the naked truth,** the plain truth, the unqualified truth, the honest truth, dinkum oil [Austral slang], the sober truth, the exact truth, the straight truth; the straight of it or the honest-to-

God truth or God's truth [all informal], the absolute truth, the intrinsic truth, the unalloyed truth, **the hard truth,** the stern truth, **gospel, gospel truth, Bible truth,** revealed truth; the truth, the whole truth and nothing but the truth.

.3 **accuracy, correctness,** care for truth, attention to fact, right, **rightness, rigor, rigorousness, exactness, exactitude; preciseness, precision;** mathematical precision, pinpoint precision, scientific exactness; **faultlessness,** perfection, absoluteness, flawlessness; **faithfulness, fidelity;** literalness, literality, literalism, textualism, the letter; strictness, severity, rigidity; niceness, nicety, delicacy, subtlety, fineness, refinement; **meticulousness** 533.3.

.4 **validity, soundness,** solidity, substantiality, **justness;** authority, **authoritativeness; cogency,** weight, force.

.5 **genuineness, authenticity,** bona fideness, **legitimacy; realness, realism,** photographic realism, absolute realism, realistic representation, **naturalism,** naturalness, truth to nature, **lifelikeness,** truth to life, true-to-lifeness, verisimilitude, absolute likeness, **literalness,** literality, literalism, truth to the letter; **inartificiality,** unsyntheticness; **unspuriousness, unspeciousness,** unfictitiousness, artlessness, unaffectedness; **honesty, sincerity;** unadulteration 45.1.

.6 **the real thing,** the very model, **the genuine article,** the very thing, it [informal]; the article or the goods or the McCoy or **the real McCoy** [all slang], the real Simon Pure, not an illusion.

.7 VERBS **be true,** be the case; conform to fact, square with the facts or evidence; **prove true,** prove to be, prove out, be so in fact; **hold true, hold good, hold water** [informal], hold or stick together [informal], **hold up, hold up in the wash** [slang], **wash** [informal], **stand up,** stand the test, be consistent or self-consistent, hold, remain valid; **be truthful.**

.8 **seem true, ring true, sound true, carry conviction,** hold the ring of truth.

.9 **be right, be correct,** be just right; be OK [informal], add up; **hit the nail on the head,** hit it on the nose [informal], score a bull's eye.

.10 **be accurate, dot the i's and cross the t's,** draw or cut it fine [informal], be precise; **make precise, precise,** particularize.

.11 **come true, come about,** attain fulfillment, **turn out, come to pass,** happen as expected.

.12 ADJS **true, truthful,** eu–; **unerroneous,** not in error, in conformity with the facts *or* evidence; **unfalse, unfallacious, unmistaken; real, veritable,** sure-enough [slang], true to the facts, **factual, actual,** effectual, **historical,** documentary; objectively true; **certain,** undoubted, unquestionable 513.13–16; unrefuted, unconfuted, undenied; **ascertained, proved, verified,** validated, **certified,** demonstrated, confirmed, determined, established, attested, substantiated, **authenticated,** corroborated; true as gospel; substantially true, categorically true; **veracious** 974.16.

.13 **valid, sound, well-grounded, well-founded,** solid, substantial; consistent, self-consistent, logical; **good, just,** sufficient; **cogent, weighty, authoritative; legal, lawful,** legitimate, **binding.**

.14 **genuine, authentic,** veridical, **real, natural, realistic, naturalistic,** true to reality, **true to nature, lifelike,** true to life, verisimilar; **literal,** following the letter, true to the letter; verbatim, verbal, **word-for-word;** true to the spirit; **legitimate,** rightful, lawful; **bona fide,** card-carrying [informal], **good,** sure-enough [slang], **sincere, honest;** candid, honest-to-God [slang], dinkum [Austral slang]; **inartificial, unsynthetic; unspurious, unspecious, unsimulated, unfaked, unfeigned, undisguised,** uncounterfeited, **unpretended, unaffected, unassumed; unassuming, simple,** unpretending, unfeigning, undisguising; **unfictitious,** unfanciful, unfabricated, unconcocted, uninvented, unimagined; unromantic; **original,** unimitated, uncopied; unexaggerated, undistorted; unflattering, unvarnished, uncolored, unqualified; **unadulterated** 45.7; **pure,** simon-pure; **sterling,** twenty-four carat, all wool and a yard wide [informal].

.15 **accurate, correct, right,** proper, just; all right *or* OK *or* okay [all informal], just right, dead right, bang on [Brit informal], straight, straight-up-and-down; **faultless,** flawless, absolute, **perfect;** letter-perfect; **meticulous** 533.12.

.16 **exact, precise,** express; even, square; absolutely *or* definitely *or* positively right; **faithful;** direct; **unerring,** undeviating, constant; **infallible,** inerrant, inerrable; strict, close, severe, **rigorous,** rigid; mathematically exact, mathematical; mechanically *or* micrometrically precise; scientifically exact, scientific; religiously exact, religious; **nice,** delicate, subtle, **fine,** refined; pinpoint, microscopic.

.17 ADVS **truly, really,** really-truly [informal], **verily,** veritably, forsooth *or* in very sooth [both archaic], **in truth,** in good *or* very truth, **actually,** historically, **in reality, in fact,** factually, in point of fact, as a matter of fact, to tell the truth, to state the fact *or* truth, of a truth, with truth; **indeed,** indeedy [informal]; **certainly,** undoubtedly 513.25; no buts about it [informal], nothing else but.

.18 **genuinely, authentically, really,** naturally, **legitimately, honestly,** veridically; warts and all; unaffectedly, unassumedly.

.19 **accurately, correctly,** rightly, properly, straight; **perfectly, faultlessly,** flawlessly; **just right,** just so; so, sic.

.20 **exactly, precisely,** expressly; **just, dead,** right, straight, even, square, **plumb,** directly, squarely, point-blank; unerringly, undeviatingly; verbatim, **literally,** *literatim* [L], verbally, word for word, word by word, word for word and letter for letter, *verbatim et litteratim* [L], in the same words, *ipsissimis verbis* [L], to the letter, according to the letter, *au pied de la lettre* [Fr]; **faithfully, strictly, rigorously,** rigidly; **definitely, positively, absolutely; in every respect,** in all respects, for all the world, neither more nor less.

.21 **to be exact, to be precise,** strictly speaking, not to mince the matter, by the book.

.22 **to a nicety, to a T** *or* tittle, to a turn, to a hair, to *or* within an inch.

.23 PHRS **that's right, that is so,** right on!, amen!, that's it, that's just it, it is that, *c'est ça* [Fr]; **you are right,** right you are, right as rain, you've got it, you better believe it, you've got something there, I'll say, it is for a fact, you speak truly, as you say, right, righto [informal], quite, rather! [informal]; **you said it,** you said a mouthful, now you're talking, you can say that again, you're not kidding, that's for sure, ain't it the truth?, you're darn tootin' [both dial]; don't I know it?, you're telling me?

517. MAXIM

.1 NOUNS **maxim, aphorism, apothegm, epigram, dictum, adage,** axiom, dictate [archaic], **proverb,** gnome, words of wisdom, **saw, saying,** witticism, sentence, expression, phrase, catchword, word, byword, mot, motto, moral; **precept,** prescript, teaching, text, verse, sutra, distich, sloka; golden saying, proverbial saying; common *or* current saying, stock saying, pithy saying, wise saying *or* expression, oracle, sententious expression *or* saying; ana, analects, proverbs, wisdom, wisdom literature, collected sayings.

.2 **axiom, truth,** a priori truth, postulate, **truism,** self-evident truth, general *or* universal truth; theorem; **proposition;** brocard, **principle,** *principium* [L], settled principle; **formula; rule, law,** dictate, **dictum;** golden rule.

.3 **platitude, cliché, commonplace, banality,** bromide, **chestnut** [informal], corn [slang], triticism [archaic], trite saying, hackneyed *or* stereotyped saying, commonplace expression, *lieu commun* [Fr], *locus communis* [L], **familiar tune,** old song *or* story, old saw; twice-told tale, retold story; reiteration 103.2; prosaicism, prosaism; prose; old joke 881.9.

.4 **motto, slogan,** watchword, catchword, tag line; **device;** epithet; inscription, epigraph.

.5 VERBS aphorize, apothegmatize, epigrammatize, coin a phrase; proverb.

.6 ADJS **aphoristic, proverbial,** epigrammatic(al), **axiomatic(al);** sententious, pithy, gnomic, pungent, succinct, terse, crisp, pointed; formulistic, formulaic; **platitudinous** 883.9.

.7 ADVS **proverbially, as the saying is** *or* **goes,** as they say, as the fellow says [informal], as it has been said, as it was said of old.

518. ERROR

.1 NOUNS **error, erroneousness; untrueness,** untruthfulness, **untruth; wrongness, wrong; falseness, falsity; fallacy,** fallaciousness, self-contradiction; **fault, faultiness,** defectiveness; sin, sinfulness, peccancy, flaw, flawedness, *hamartia* [Gk]; misdoing, misfeasance; errancy, aberrancy, aberration, **deviancy; heresy,** unorthodoxy, heterodoxy; perversion, **distortion;** misconstruction, misapplication; **delusion, illusion** 519; misjudgment 496; misinterpretation 553.

.2 **inaccuracy,** inaccurateness, **incorrectness, uncorrectness, inexactness,** unfactualness, inexactitude, **unpreciseness, imprecision,** looseness, laxity, unrigorousness; tolerance, allowance; negligence; approximation; **deviation,** standard deviation, probable error, predictable error.

.3 **mistake, error,** *erratum* [L], *corrigendum* [L]; **fault,** *faute* [Fr]; human error; **misconception, misapprehension, misunderstanding;** misstatement, misquotation;

misreport; **misprint, typographical error,** typo [informal], printer's error, typist's error; clerical error; misidentification; **misjudgment, miscalculation** 496.1; misplay; misdeal; miscount; misuse; failure, miss, miscarriage.

.4 **slip,** slipup *or* miscue [both informal]; **lapse,** *lapsus* [L], **oversight,** omission, bevue, balk [archaic], inadvertence *or* inadvertency, loose thread; **misstep,** trip, stumble, false *or* wrong step, wrong *or* bad *or* false move; **slip of the tongue,** *lapsus linguae* [L]; **slip of the pen,** *lapsus calami* [L].

.5 **blunder, faux pas, gaffe,** solecism; stupidity, indiscretion 470.4; **botch, bungle** 734.5.

.6 [slang *or* informal terms] **goof, boo-boo,** foozle, bloomer, **blooper,** boot, **bobble, boner,** bonehead play *or* trick, dumb trick, boob stunt, fool mistake; howler, screamer; **screw-up,** foul-up, muck-up, louse-up; pratfall.

.7 **grammatical error, solecism,** anacoluthon, misusage, missaying, mispronunciation; **bull, Irish bull,** fluff, **malapropism,** malaprop, Mrs. Malaprop [R. B. Sheridan]; Pickwickian sense; spoonerism, marrowsky; hypercorrection, hyperform; folk etymology; catachresis.

.8 VERBS **not hold water** *or* not hold together [both informal], not stand up, not square, not figure [informal], not add up, **not hold up, not hold up in the wash** *or* not wash [both informal].

.9 **err, fall into error, go wrong, go amiss,** go astray, go out of line, go awry, stray, **deviate,** wander; **lapse, slip, slip up, trip, stumble; miscalculate** 496.2.

.10 **be wrong, be mistaken, be in error, be at fault,** be out of line, be off the track, be in the wrong, miss the truth, miss by a mile [informal], have another think coming [informal]; receive a false impression, take the shadow for the substance, be misled, be misguided; deceive oneself, be deceived, delude oneself; labor under a false impression.

.11 **bark up the wrong tree, back the wrong horse,** count one's chickens before they are hatched.

.12 **misdo,** do amiss; **misuse, misemploy,** misapply; **misconduct, mismanage;** miscall, miscount, misdeal, misplay, misfield; misprint, miscite, misquote, misread, misreport, misspell.

.13 **mistake, make a mistake;** miscue, make a miscue [both informal]; **misidentify;** misunderstand, misapprehend, misconceive, misinterpret 553.2.

.14 blunder, make a blunder, make a faux pas, make a false or wrong step, make a misstep; misspeak, misspeak oneself, trip over one's tongue; blunder into; botch, bungle 734.11.

.15 [slang or informal terms] make or pull a boner or boo-boo or blooper; drop a brick [Brit], goof, fluff, duff [Brit], foozle, boot, bobble, blow; screw up, foul up, muck up, louse up; put one's foot in it or in one's mouth; muff one's cue, fluff one's lines, fall flat on one's face or ass, drop the ball.

.16 ADJS erroneous, untrue, not true, not right; unfactual, wrong, all wrong; peccant, perverse, corrupt; false, fallacious, self-contradictory; illogical 483.11; unproved 506.8; faulty, faultful, flawed, defective, at fault; out, off, all off, off the track or rails; wide [archaic], wide of the mark, beside the mark; amiss, awry, askew, deviant, deviative, deviational; erring, errant, aberrant; straying, astray, adrift; heretical, unorthodox, heterodox; abroad, all abroad; perverted, distorted; delusive, deceptive, illusory 519.9.

.17 inaccurate, incorrect, inexact, unfactual, unprecise, imprecise, loose, lax, unrigorous; negligent; approximate, approximative; out of line, out of plumb, out of true, out of square.

.18 mistaken, in error, erring, under an error, wrong, all wet [slang]; off or out in one's reckoning; in the wrong box, in the right church but the wrong pew.

.19 unauthentic or inauthentic, unauthoritative, unreliable 514.19,20; misstated, misreported, miscited, misquoted, garbled; unfounded 483.13; spurious 616.26.

.20 ADVS erroneously, falsely, fallaciously; faultily, faultfully; untrue [archaic], untruly; wrong, wrongly; mistakenly; amiss, astray.

.21 inaccurately, incorrectly, inexactly, unprecisely.

.22 PHRS you are wrong, you are mistaken, you're all wet [slang], you're way off [informal], you have another guess coming [informal], don't kid yourself [slang].

519. ILLUSION

.1 NOUNS illusion, delusion, deluded belief; deception 618, trick; self-deception, self-deceit, self-delusion; dereism, autism; misconception, misbelief, false belief, wrong impression, warped or distorted conception; bubble, chimera, vapor, "airy nothing" [Shakespeare]; ignis fatuus [L], will-o'-the-wisp; dream, dream vision; dreamworld, dreamland; daydream; pipe dream [informal]; trip [informal]; fool's paradise, castle in the air.

.2 illusoriness, illusiveness, delusiveness; falseness, fallaciousness; unreality, unactuality; unsubstantiality, airiness, immateriality; idealization 535.7; seeming, semblance, simulacrum, appearance, false or specious appearance, show, false show, false light; magic, sorcery 1035, illusionism, sleight of hand, prestidigitation, magic show, magic act; magician, sorcerer 1035.5, illusionist, Prospero [Shakespeare].

.3 fancy, imagination 535.

.4 phantom, phantasm, phantasma, wraith, specter; shadow, shade; phantasmagoria; fantasy, wildest dream; figment of the imagination 535.5, phantom of the mind; apparition, appearance; vision, waking dream, image [archaic]; shape, form, figure, presence; eidolon, idolum; "such stuff as dreams are made on" [Shakespeare].

.5 optical illusion, trick of eyesight; afterimage, spectrum, ocular spectrum.

.6 mirage, fata morgana, looming.

.7 hallucination; hallucinosis; tripping [informal], mind-expansion; consciousness-expansion; delirium tremens 473.9,10; dream 535.9.

.8 VERBS go on a trip or blow one's mind [both informal], freak out [slang]; hallucinate; expand one's consciousness.

.9 ADJS illusory, illusive; illusional, illusionary; Barmecide or Barmecidal; delusory, delusive; delusional, delusionary, deluding, pseud(o)–; dereistic, autistic; dreamy, dreamlike; visionary; imaginary 535.19; erroneous 518.16; deceptive 618.19; self-deceptive, self-deluding; chimeric(al), fantastic; unreal, unactual, unsubstantial 4.5,6; airy; unfounded 483.13; false, fallacious, misleading; specious, seeming, apparent, ostensible, supposititious, all in the mind; spectral, apparitional, phantom, phantasmal; phantasmagoric.

.10 hallucinatory, hallucinative, hallucinational; hallucinogenic, psychedelic, consciousness-expanding, mind-expanding, mind-blowing [informal].

520. DISILLUSIONMENT

.1 NOUNS disillusionment, disillusion, disenchantment, undeception, unspelling, return to reality, loss of one's illusions, loss of innocence, cold light of reality, enlightenment, bursting of the bubble; awakening, rude awakening, bringing back to earth; disappointment 541; debunking [slang].

.2 VERBS disillusion, disillude, disillusionize; disenchant, unspell, uncharm, break the spell or charm; disabuse, undeceive; correct, set right or straight, put straight, tell the truth, enlighten, let in on; clear the mind of; open one's eyes, awaken, wake up, unblindfold; disappoint 541.2; dispel or dissipate one's illusions, rob or strip one of one's illusions; bring one back to earth, let down easy [informal]; burst or prick the bubble, puncture one's balloon [informal]; let the air out of, take the wind out of; knock the props out from under, take the ground from under; debunk [slang]; expose, show up 556.4.

.3 be disillusioned, be disenchanted, get back to earth, get one's feet on the ground, return to or embrace reality; charge to experience.

.4 ADJS disillusioning, disillusive, disillusionary, disenchanting, disabusing, undeceiving, enlightening.

.5 disillusioned, disenchanted, unspelled, uncharmed, disabused, undeceived, stripped or robbed of illusion, enlightened, set right, put straight; with one's eyes open, sophisticated, blasé; disappointed 541.5.

521. ASSENT

.1 NOUNS assent, acquiescence, concurrence, compliance, agreement, acceptance, accession; eager or hearty or warm assent, welcome; assentation; agreement in principle, general agreement; support; consent 775.

.2 affirmative; yes, yea, aye, amen; nod, nod of assent; thumbs-up; affirmativeness, affirmative attitude, yea-saying.

.3 acknowledgment, recognition, acceptance; appreciation; admission, confession, concession, allowance; avowal, profession, declaration.

.4 ratification, endorsement, acceptance, approval, approbation 968.1, sanction, OK or okay [both informal], imprimatur, green light or go-ahead [both informal], permission, nod, the nod, certification, confirmation, validation, authentication, authorization, warrant; affirmation, affirmance; stamp, rubber stamp, stamp of approval; seal, signet, sigil; subscription, signature, John Hancock [informal];

countersignature; visa, visé [Fr]; notarization.

.5 unanimity, unanimousness; like-mindedness, meeting of minds, one or same mind; total agreement; understanding, mutual understanding; concurrence, consent, general consent, common assent or consent, consentaneity, accord, accordance, concord, concordance, agreement, general agreement; consensus, consensus of opinion [informal]; consensus omnium [L], universal agreement or accord, consensus gentium [L], agreement of all, sense of the meeting; acclamation, general acclamation; unison, harmony, chorus, concert, one or single voice, one accord; general voice, vox populi [L].

.6 assenter, consenter, accepter, covenanter, covenantor; assentator, yea-sayer, yesman.

.7 endorser, subscriber, ratifier, approver, upholder, certifier, confirmer; signer, signatory; cosigner, cosignatory, party; underwriter, guarantor, insurer; notary, notary public.

.8 VERBS assent, give or yield assent, acquiesce, consent 775.2, comply, accede, agree, agree to or with; take kindly to or hold with [both informal]; accept, receive, buy [slang], take one up on [informal]; subscribe to, acquiesce in, abide by; yes, say 'yes' to; nod, nod assent, give the nod, give a nod of assent; vote for, cast one's vote for, give one's voice for; welcome, hail, cheer, acclaim, applaud, accept in toto.

.9 concur, accord, coincide, agree, agree with, agree in opinion; enter into one's view, enter into the ideas or feelings of, see eye to eye, be at one with, be of one mind with, go with, go along with, fall or chime or strike in with, close with, meet, conform to, side with, identify oneself with; echo, ditto [informal], say 'ditto' to, say 'amen' to; join in the chorus, go along with the crowd [informal], run with the pack, go or float or swim with the stream or current; get on the bandwagon [informal].

.10 come to an agreement, agree, agree with, agree on or upon, arrive at an agreement, come to an understanding, come to terms, strike a bargain, covenant, get together [informal]; shake hands on, shake on it [informal]; come around to.

.11 acknowledge, admit, own, confess, allow, avow, grant, warrant, concede, yield [archaic]; accept, recognize; agree in principle, express general agreement, go along with, not oppose or deny, agree provisionally or for the sake of argument; assent grudgingly or under protest.

.12 ratify, endorse, second, support, **certify, confirm, validate, authenticate, accept, OK** [informal], **give the green light** or go-ahead [informal], give the imprimatur, permit, give permission, **approve** 968.9; sanction, **authorize,** warrant, accredit; **pass,** pass on or upon, give thumbs up [informal]; amen, say amen to; visa, *visé* [Fr]; underwrite, subscribe to; **sign,** undersign, sign on the dotted line, put one's John Hancock on [informal], initial, put one's mark or cross on; autograph; cosign, countersign; seal, sign and seal, set one's seal, **set one's hand and seal;** affirm, swear and affirm, take one's oath, swear to; rubber stamp [informal]; notarize.

.13 ADJS **assenting, agreeing,** acquiescing, **acquiescent, compliant,** consenting, submissive, conceding, concessive, assentatious, agreed, content.

.14 accepted, approved, received; acknowledged, admitted, allowed, granted, conceded, recognized, professed, confessed, avowed, warranted; ratified, endorsed, certified, confirmed, validated, authenticated; **signed,** sealed, signed and sealed, countersigned, underwritten; stamped; sworn to, notarized, affirmed, sworn and affirmed.

.15 unanimous, solid, consentaneous, **with one consent** or voice; uncontradicted, unchallenged, uncontroverted, uncontested, unopposed; **concurrent,** concordant, **of one accord; agreeing, in agreement,** likeminded, **of one mind,** of the same mind; of a piece, **at one,** at one with, agreed on all hands, carried by acclamation.

.16 ADVS **affirmatively,** assentingly, in the affirmative.

.17 **unanimously,** concurrently, consentaneously, **by common** or **general consent,** with one consent, **with one accord,** with one voice, without contradiction, *nemine contradicente* [L], nem con, without a dissenting voice, *nemine dissentiente* [L], in chorus, in unison, to a man, **together,** all together, all agreeing, **as one,** as one man, one and all, on all hands; by acclamation.

.18 INTERJS **yes, yea,** aye, *oui* [Fr], *sí* [Sp], *da* [Russ], *ja* [Ger]; **yeah** or yep or uh-huh [all informal]; yes sir, yes ma'am; yes sirree [informal], why yes, *mais oui* [Fr]; in-

deed, indeedy [informal], yes indeed, yes indeedy [informal]; **surely, certainly,** assuredly, most assuredly, **exactly, precisely,** just so, absolutely, positively, really, truly, rather [Brit], quite, to be sure; sure or sure thing or surest thing you know [all slang]; **all right,** alright [informal], **right,** righto [informal], alrighty [informal]; **OK** or **okay** [both informal], Roger [informal]; fine [informal], **good,** well and good, good enough, **very well,** *très bien* [Fr]; naturally, *naturellement* [Fr]; **of course,** as you say, **by all means,** by all manner of means; **amen;** hear, hear [Brit].

.19 PHRS **so be it,** be it so, so mote it be [archaic], so shall it be, *amen* [Heb]; so it is, so is it; agreed; done; *c'est bien* [Fr]; that's right 516.23; **you bet,** you bet your life, you bet your boots [all slang].

522. DISSENT

.1 NOUNS **dissent, dissidence,** dissentience; nonassent, nonconsent, nonconcurrence, nonagreement, agreement to disagree; minority opinion or position; **disagreement, difference, variance,** diversity, disparity; **dissatisfaction, disapproval,** disapprobation; repudiation; **rejection; opposition** 790; dissension, disaccord 795; **alienation,** withdrawal, dropping out, secession; recusance or recusancy, nonconformity 83; apostasy 628.2; counter-culture, underground.

.2 objection, protest; **kick** or **beef** [both informal]; bitch or squawk or howl [all slang], protestation; **remonstrance, remonstration,** expostulation; **challenge; demur,** demurrer, **scruple,** compunction, qualm; **complaint,** grievance; **exception;** peaceful or nonviolent protest; **demonstration,** protest demonstration, rally, march, sit-in, teach-in, boycott, strike, picketing, indignation meeting; grievance committee.

.3 **dissenter, dissentient, dissident,** recusant; **objector,** demurrer; minority or opposition voice; **protester,** protestant; **separatist,** schismatic; sectary, sectarian, opinionist; nonconformist 83.3; apostate 628.5.

.4 VERBS **dissent,** dissent from, be in dissent, **disagree,** discord with, **differ,** not agree, disagree with, agree to disagree or differ; divide on, be at variance; **take exception,** withhold assent, **take issue, beg to differ,** rise to a point of order; be in opposition to, oppose 790.2; withdraw, drop out, secede, separate *or* disjoin oneself.

.5 object, protest, kick *or* beef [both informal], put up a struggle *or* fight; bitch *or* squawk *or* howl *or* holler *or* put up a squawk *or* raise a howl [all slang]; cry out against, yell bloody murder; remonstrate, expostulate; raise *or* press objections, raise one's voice against, enter a protest; complain, state a grievance; dispute, challenge, call in question; demur, scruple, boggle; demonstrate, demonstrate against, rally, march, sit in, teach in, boycott, strike, picket.

.6 ADJS dissenting, dissident, dissentient, recusant; disagreeing, differing; opposing 790.8, in opposition; alienated; counterculture, antiestablishment, underground; breakaway [Brit]; at variance with, at odds with; schismatic(al), sectarian, sectary; nonconforming 83.5.

.7 protesting, protestant; objecting, expostulative, expostulatory, remonstrative, remonstrant; under protest.

523. AFFIRMATION

.1 NOUNS affirmation, affirmance, assertion, asseveration, averment, declaration, vouch [archaic], allegation; avouchment, avowal; position, stand, stance; profession, statement, word, say, saying, say-so [informal], positive declaration *or* statement; manifesto, position paper; creed 501.3; pronouncement, proclamation, announcement, annunciation, enunciation; proposition, conclusion; predication, predicate; protest, protestation; utterance, dictum, *ipse dixit* [L].

.2 deposition, sworn statement, statement under oath, notarized statement, sworn testimony, affirmation; vouching, swearing; attestation; certification; testimony 505.3; affidavit.

.3 oath, vow, avow [archaic], word, assurance, guarantee, warrant, solemn oath *or* affirmation *or* word *or* declaration; pledge 770.1; Bible oath, ironclad oath; judicial oath, extrajudicial oath; oath of office, official oath; oath of allegiance, loyalty oath, test oath.

.4 VERBS affirm, assert, assever [archaic], asseverate, aver, protest, lay down, avouch, avow, declare, say, have one's say, speak, speak up *or* out, state, set down, express, put, put it; allege, profess; stand on *or* for; predicate; issue a manifesto *or* position paper, manifesto; announce, pronounce, annunciate, enunciate, proclaim;

maintain, have, contend, argue, insist, hold, submit, maintain with one's last breath.

.5 depose, depone; testify 505.10; warrant, attest, certify, guarantee, assure; vouch, swear, swear to, swear the truth, assert under oath; make *or* take one's oath, vow; swear by bell, book, and candle; call heaven to witness, declare *or* swear to God, swear on the Bible, kiss the book, swear to goodness, hope to die, cross one's heart and hope to die [informal]; swear till one is black *or* blue in the face [informal].

.6 administer an oath, place *or* put under oath, put to one's oath, put upon oath; swear, swear in, adjure [archaic].

.7 ADJS affirmative, affirming, affirmatory; assertive, assertative, assertional; declarative, declaratory; predicative, predicational; positive, absolute, emphatic, decided.

.8 affirmed, asserted, asseverated, avouched, avowed, averred, declared; alleged, professed; stated, pronounced, announced, enunciated; predicated; manifestoed; deposed, warranted, attested, certified, vouched, vouched for, vowed, pledged, sworn, sworn to.

.9 ADVS affirmatively, assertively, declaratively, predicatively; positively, absolutely, decidedly; emphatically, with emphasis; without fear of contradiction; under oath.

524. NEGATION, DENIAL

.1 NOUNS negation, abnegation; negativeness, negativity, negativism, negative attitude, naysaying; negative, no, nay, nix [slang].

.2 denial, disavowal, disaffirmation, disownment, disallowance; disclamation, disclaimer; renunciation, retraction, retractation, repudiation, recantation; revocation, nullification, annulment, abrogation; abjuration, abjurement, forswearing; contradiction, flat *or* absolute contradiction, contravention, contrary assertion, controversion, countering, crossing, gainsaying, impugnment; refutation, disproof 506.

.3 VERBS negate, abnegate, negative; say 'no'; shake the head.

.4 deny, not admit, not accept, refuse to admit *or* accept; disclaim, disown, disaffirm, disavow, disallow, abjure, forswear, renounce, retract, take back, recant; revoke, nullify, repudiate; contradict, cross,

assert the contrary, contravene, controvert, impugn, **dispute,** gainsay, **oppose,
counter,** contest, take issue with, join issue upon; belie, give the lie to, give one
the lie direct *or* in his throat; **refute** 506.5,
disprove 506.4.

.5 ADJS **negative,** negatory, abnegative; **denying, disclaiming,** disowning, disaffirm-
ing, disallowing, disavowing, renunciative,
renunciatory, repudiative, recanting, abjuratory, revocative *or* revocatory; **contradictory,** contradicting, **opposing, contrary,** adversative, repugnant; a– *or* an–,
dis–, e– *or* ef– *or* ex–, in– *or* il– *or* im– *or*
ir–, mis–, non–, nulli–, un–.

.6 ADVS **negatively, in the negative;** in denial, in contradiction.

.7 CONJS **neither,** not either, **nor,** nor yet, or
not, and not, also not.

.8 INTERJS **no, nay,** negative, *non* [Fr], *nein*
[Ger], *nyet* [Russ]; certainly not, absolutely no; no sir, no ma'am; **not,** not a bit
or whit *or* jot, I think not, not really; to
the contrary, *au contraire* [Fr], quite the
contrary, far from it; no such thing, nothing of the kind *or* sort, not so.

.9 **by no means, by no manner of means;** on
no account, in no respect, **in no case,
under no circumstances,** on no condition,
no matter what; **not at all,** not in the
least, **never;** in no wise, noways, noway,
nohow [dial]; out of the question; **not for
the world,** not if one can help it, not if I
know it, not at any price, not for love or
money, not for the life of me; to the contrary, *au contraire* [Fr], quite the contrary, far from it; God forbid 969.27.

.10 [slang *or* informal terms] **nope,** nix, **unh-
unh,** no sirree; **no way, not on your life,**
not by a long chalk, not by a long shot *or*
sight, not by a darn *or* damn sight, not a
bit of it, not much, not a chance, fat
chance, **nothing doing, forget it.**

525. MENTAL ATTITUDE

.1 NOUNS **attitude,** mental attitude; psychology; **position, posture,** stance; **way of
thinking,** way of looking at things; **feeling, sentiment,** the way one feels; feeling
tone, affect, affectivity, emotion, emotiv-
ity; opinion 501.6.

.2 **outlook,** mental outlook; *Anschauung*
[Ger], **point of view, viewpoint, standpoint;** position, stand, place, situation;
side; footing, basis; where one is *or* sits *or*
stands; **view,** sight, light, eye; respect, regard; angle, angle of vision, slant; **frame
of reference,** framework, universe of dis-

course, universe, system, reference system.

.3 **disposition, character, nature, temper,
temperament,** mettle, constitution [ar-
chaic], makeup, stamp, type, stripe, kidney, make, mold; **turn of mind, inclination,** mind, **tendency,** grain, set, mental
set, mind-set, **leaning,** animus, propensity, proclivity, predilection, preference,
predisposition; **bent, turn, bias,** slant,
cast, warp, twist; idiosyncrasy, eccentricity, individualism; diathesis, aptitude;
strain, streak.

.4 **mood, humor, temper, frame of mind,**
state of mind, morale, cue *or* frame [both
archaic], tone, note, **vein; mind, heart,**
spirit *or* **spirits.**

.5 (pervading attitudes) **climate,** mental *or*
intellectual climate, spiritual climate,
moral climate, mores, norms, climate of
opinion, **ethos,** ideology, *Weltanschauung* [Ger], world view.

.6 VERBS **take the attitude,** feel about it,
look at it, **view,** look at in the light of; **be
disposed to,** tend *or* incline toward, prefer, lean toward.

.7 ADJS **temperamental, dispositional,** constitutional; emotional, affective; mental,
intellectual; spiritual; characteristic 80.13;
innate 5.7.

.8 **disposed,** dispositioned, **predisposed,
prone, inclined, given,** bent, apt, likely,
–tempered, **minded, in the mood** *or* **humor.**

.9 ADVS **temperamentally, dispositionally,**
constitutionally; emotionally; mentally,
intellectually; morally, spiritually; **by temperament** *or* **disposition,** by virtue of
mind-set, by the logic of character *or*
temperament; from one's standpoint *or*
viewpoint *or* angle; within the frame of
reference *or* framework *or* reference system *or* universe of discourse.

526. BROAD-MINDEDNESS

.1 NOUNS **broad-mindedness,** wide-minded-
ness, large-mindedness, "the result of flattening high-mindedness out" [George
Saintsbury]; **breadth,** broadness, broad
gauge, latitude; **unbigotedness,** unhide-
boundness, unprovincialism, noninsular-
ity, unparochialism, cosmopolitanism; ecumenicity, ecumenicism, ecumenicalism,
ecumenism; broad mind, spacious mind.

.2 **liberalness, liberality,** catholicity, **liberal-
mindedness;** liberalism, libertarianism,
latitudinarianism; freethinking, free
thought.

.3 **open-mindedness, openness,** receptiveness, receptivity; persuadableness, persuadability, persuasibility; open mind.

.4 **tolerance,** toleration; **indulgence,** lenience *or* leniency, condonation, lenity; **forbearance, patience,** long-suffering; easiness, permissiveness; **charitableness,** charity, **generousness, magnanimity** 979.2.

.5 **unprejudicedness, unbiasedness; impartiality,** evenhandedness, equitability, **fairness,** justness, objectivity, **detachment, dispassionateness, disinterestedness;** indifference, neutrality; unopinionatedness.

.6 **liberal,** liberalist; **libertarian; freethinker,** latitudinarian, ecumenist, ecumenicist; big person, broad-gauge person.

.7 VERBS **keep an open mind,** be big [informal], judge not, not write off, suspend judgment, listen to reason, open one's mind to, see both sides; **live and let live;** lean over backwards, **tolerate** 861.5; **accept,** be easy with, **view with indulgence, condone,** brook, abide with, be content with; **live with** [informal]; shut one's eyes to, look the other way, wink at, blink at, **overlook, disregard, ignore;** "swear allegiance to the words of no master" [Horace].

.8 ADJS **broad-minded,** wide-minded, large-minded, **broad, wide,** broad-gauged, catholic, spacious of mind; **unbigoted,** unfanatical, **unhidebound,** unprovincial, cosmopolitan, noninsular, unparochial; ecumenistic, ecumenical.

.9 **liberal, liberal-minded,** liberalistic; **libertarian;** freethinking, latitudinarian.

.10 **open-minded, open, receptive,** admissive; **persuadable,** persuasible.

.11 **tolerant,** tolerating; **indulgent, lenient, condoning;** forbearing, forbearant [archaic], **patient,** long-suffering; **charitable, generous, magnanimous** 979.6.

.12 **unprejudiced, unbiased, unprepossessed, unjaundiced; impartial,** evenhanded, **fair,** just, equitable, objective, **dispassionate, impersonal, detached, disinterested;** indifferent, neutral; **unswayed, uninfluenced,** undazzled.

.13 **unopinionated,** unopinioned, unwedded to an opinion; **unpositive, undogmatic;** uninfatuated, unbesotted, unfanatical.

.14 **broadening,** enlightening.

527. NARROW-MINDEDNESS

.1 NOUNS **narrow-mindedness, narrowness,** illiberality, uncatholicity; **little-mindedness, small-mindedness, smallness, littleness, meanness, pettiness; bigotry,** bigotedness, fanaticism, *odium theologicum* [L]; insularity, insularism, provincialism, parochialism; **hideboundness,** straitlacedness, stuffiness [informal]; authoritarianism; **shortsightedness,** nearsightedness, purblindness; blind side, blind spot, blinders; closed mind, mean mind, petty mind, shut mind; narrow views *or* sympathies, cramped ideas.

.2 **intolerance,** intoleration; **uncharitableness,** ungenerousness; unforbearance.

.3 **prejudice,** prejudgment, forejudgment, **predilection, prepossession,** preconception; **bias,** bent, leaning, inclination, twist; **jaundice,** jaundiced eye; **partiality,** partialism, partisanship, favoritism, onesidedness, undispassionateness, undetachment.

.4 **discrimination,** social discrimination, minority prejudice; xenophobia, know-nothingism; **chauvinism,** ultranationalism, superpatriotism; fascism; **class consciousness,** class prejudice, class distinction, class hatred, class war; anti-Semitism; redbaiting [informal]; **racism,** racialism, race hatred, **race prejudice,** race snobbery, racial discrimination; white *or* black supremacy, white *or* black power; **color line,** color bar; **social barrier,** Jim Crow, Jim Crow law; **segregation,** apartheid, sex discrimination, sexism, male chauvinism.

.5 **bigot,** intolerant, illiberal, little person; **racist; pig** [slang]; **chauvinist,** ultranationalist, jingo, superpatriot; male chauvinist, sexist; **dogmatist, doctrinaire** 513.7; **fanatic** 473.17.

.6 VERBS **close one's mind,** shut the eyes of one's mind, take narrow views, put on blinders, blind oneself, have a blind side *or* spot, constrict one's views; not see beyond one's nose *or* an inch beyond one's nose; **view with a jaundiced eye,** see but one side of the question, look only at one side of the shield.

.7 **prejudge,** forejudge, judge beforehand, precondemn, prejudicate [archaic], take one's opinions ready-made, accede to prejudice.

.8 **discriminate against, draw the line,** draw the color line, red-bait.

.9 **prejudice,** prejudice against, prejudice the issue, prepossess, **jaundice, influence, sway, bias,** bias one's judgment; warp, twist, bend, distort.

.10 ADJS **narrow-minded,** narrow, narrow-gauged, closed, closed-minded, cramped, constricted, *borné* [Fr], little-minded, small-minded, mean-minded, petty-minded, narrow-hearted, narrow-souled, narrow-spirited, mean-spirited, small-souled; **small, little, mean, petty;** uncharitable, ungenerous; bigot, **bigoted,** fanatical; **illiberal,** unliberal, uncatholic; provincial, insular, parochial; **hidebound,** creedbound, **straitlaced,** stuffy [informal]; authoritarian; **shortsighted,** nearsighted, purblind; deaf, deaf-minded, deaf to reason.

.11 **intolerant,** untolerating; **unindulgent,** uncondoning, unforbearing.

.12 **prejudiced,** prepossessed, **biased, jaundiced,** colored; **partial,** one-sided, partisan; influenced, swayed, warped, twisted; interested, nonobjective, **undetached,** undispassionate; xenophobic, know-nothing; **chauvinistic,** ultranationalist, superpatriotic; **racist,** anti-Negro, antiblack; anti-Semitic; sexist; dogmatic, doctrinaire, **opinionated** 513.22.

528. CURIOSITY

.1 NOUNS **curiosity,** curiousness, **inquisitiveness; interest,** interestedness, lively interest; thirst or desire or lust or itch for knowledge, mental acquisitiveness, inquiring or curious mind; nosiness or snoopiness [both informal], prying; officiousness, meddlesomeness 238.2; morbid curiosity, ghoulishness, voyeurism, scopophilia, prurience, prurient interest.

.2 **inquisitive,** quidnunc; **inquirer,** questioner, querier, querist, inquisitor, inquisitress; **busybody,** gossip, yenta [Yid], **pry,** Paul Pry, **snoop,** snooper, nosy Parker [informal]; sightseer; rubbernecker or rubberneck [slang]; eavesdropper; Peeping Tom, voyeur, scopophiliac; Lot's wife.

.3 VERBS **be curious, want to know, take an interest in,** take a lively interest, burn with curiosity; prick up the ears; interrogate, quiz, question, inquire, query; stare, gape, peer, gawk, rubber or rubberneck [both slang]; seek, dig up, dig around for, nose out, nose around for.

.4 **pry, snoop,** peep, peek, spy, nose, have a long or big nose, poke or stick one's nose in; meddle 238.7.

.5 ADJS **curious, inquisitive,** inquiring, interested, quizzical; burning with curiosity, eaten up or consumed with curiosity, curious as a cat; agape, agog, all agog, openmouthed, open-eyed; gossipy; overcurious, supercurious; morbidly curious, morbid, ghoulish; prurient, itchy, voyeuristic, scopophiliac.

.6 **prying,** snooping, **nosy** or **snoopy** [both informal]; meddlesome 238.9.

529. INCURIOSITY

.1 NOUNS **incuriosity,** incuriousness, **uninquisitiveness; boredom; uninterestedness,** disinterest, disinterestedness, **unconcern,** uninvolvement, **indifference** 636, indifferentness, indifferentism, **apathy,** impassivity, impassiveness, listlessness, stolidity, **lack of interest;** carelessness, heedlessness, regardlessness, insouciance, unmindfulness; aloofness, detachment, withdrawal; intellectual inertia.

.2 VERBS **take no interest in, not care;** mind one's own business, pursue the even tenor of one's way, glance neither to the right nor to the left.

.3 ADJS **incurious, uninquisitive,** uninquiring; **bored; uninterested,** unconcerned, disinterested, uninvolved, **indifferent, apathetic,** impassive, stolid, phlegmatic, listless; careless, heedless, regardless, insouciant, mindless, unmindful; aloof, detached, distant, withdrawn.

530. ATTENTION

.1 NOUNS **attention, attentiveness,** mindfulness, regardfulness, heedfulness; **attention span; heed,** ear; consideration, thought; awareness, consciousness, alertness 533.5; **observation,** observance, advertence, advertency, **note, notice,** remark, **regard,** respect; **intentness,** intentiveness, concentration; diligence, assiduity, assiduousness, earnestness; **care** 533.1.

.2 **interest, concern,** concernment; **curiosity** 528; **enthusiasm,** passion; cathexis; matter of interest, special interest.

.3 **engrossment, absorption, intentness,** single-mindedness, **concentration, application,** study, studiousness, **preoccupation,** engagement, **involvement, immersion,** submersion; obsession, monomania; rapt attention, absorbed attention or interest; deep study, deep or profound thought, contemplation, meditation.

.4 **close attention,** close study, scrutiny, fixed regard, rapt or fascinated attention, whole or total or undivided attention; minute or meticulous attention, attention to detail, finicalness, finickiness; constant or unrelenting attention, harping, strict attention; special consideration.

.5 VERBS **attend to,** look to, **see to,** advert to, be aware of; **pay attention to,** pay regard to, give mind to, pay mind to [informal], not forget, spare a thought for, **give heed to;** have a look at; **turn to,** give thought to, trouble one's head about; give one's mind to, direct one's attention to, turn or bend or set the mind or attention to; **devote oneself to,** devote the mind or thoughts to, fix or rivet or focus the mind or thoughts on, set one's thoughts on, apply the mind or attention to, apply oneself to, **occupy oneself with, concern oneself with,** give oneself up to, be absorbed or engrossed in, **lose oneself in;** hang on one's words, hang on the lips; **drink in,** drink in with rapt attention.

.6 **heed, attend,** tend, **mind, watch, observe, regard,** look, see, view, mark, remark, animadvert [archaic], **note, notice,** take note or notice.

.7 **hearken to, hark, listen, hear,** give ear to, lend an ear to, incline or bend an ear to, prick up the ears, strain one's ears, **keep one's ears open,** unstopper one's ears, have or keep an ear to the ground, listen with both ears, **be all ears.**

.8 **pay attention** or heed, **take heed,** give heed, **look out, watch out** [informal], **take care** 533.7; look lively or alive, **look sharp,** stay or be alert, sit up and take notice; be on the ball or keep one's eye on the ball or not miss a trick or not overlook a bet [all informal]; miss nothing; keep one's eyes open 533.8; attend to business, mind one's business; pay close or strict attention, strain one's attention, not relax one's concern, give one's undivided attention, give special attention to; keep in the center of one's attention, keep uppermost in one's thought; **concentrate on,** focus or fix on; **study,** scrutinize; be obsessed with.

.9 **take cognizance of, take note** or **notice of, take heed of, take account of, take into consideration** or **account, bear in mind,** keep or hold in mind, reckon with, keep in sight or view, not lose sight of, have in one's eye, have an eye to, have regard for.

.10 **call attention to,** direct attention to, **bring under** or **to one's notice,** bring to attention, pick out, focus on, call or bring to notice, direct to the attention; **direct to,** address to; **mention, specify,** mention in passing, touch on, cite, **refer to,** allude to; **point out, point to,** point at, put or lay one's finger on.

.11 **meet with attention,** fall under one's notice; **catch the attention,** draw or hold or focus the attention, catch or meet or strike the eye, attract notice or attention, arrest or engage attention, fix or rivet one's attention, arrest the thoughts, awaken the mind or thoughts, **excite notice,** arouse notice, arrest one's notice, invite or solicit attention, claim or demand attention.

.12 **interest, concern,** involve in or with, affect the interest; **pique, titillate,** tantalize, tickle, **attract,** invite, **fascinate, provoke, stimulate, excite,** pique one's interest, excite interest, excite or whet one's interest, arouse one's passion or enthusiasm, turn one on [slang].

.13 **engross, absorb,** immerse, **occupy, preoccupy, engage,** involve, monopolize, exercise, take up; **obsess; grip, hold, arrest, hold the interest, fascinate, enthrall,** spellbind, **hold spellbound,** grab [slang], charm, enchant, mesmerize, hypnotize, catch; absorb the attention, claim one's thoughts, engross the mind or thoughts, engage the attention, involve the interest, occupy the attention, monopolize one's attention, engage the mind or thoughts.

.14 **come to attention,** stand at attention.

.15 ADJS **attentive, heedful, mindful, regardful,** advertent; **intent,** intentive, diligent, assiduous, intense, earnest, concentrated; **careful** 533.10; **observing,** observant; watchful, aware, conscious, alert 533.13,14; agog, openmouthed; open-eared, open-eyed, **all eyes, all ears,** all eyes and ears; on the job [informal], on the ball, Johnny on the spot [both slang]; meticulous, nice, finical, finicky, finicking, niggling.

.16 **interested,** concerned; **curious** 528.5; tantalized, piqued, titillated, tickled, **attracted,** fascinated, excited, turned-on [slang]; keen on or about, enthusiastic, passionate; cathectic.

.17 **engrossed, absorbed,** totally absorbed, single-minded, **occupied, preoccupied, engaged,** devoted, devoted to, intent, intent on, monopolized, obsessed, monomaniacal, swept up, taken up with, **involved, caught up in,** wrapped in, **wrapped up in,** engrossed in, **absorbed in** or with or by, **lost in, immersed in,** submerged in, buried in; over head and ears in, head over heels in [informal], up to one's elbows in, up to one's ears in; contemplating, contemplative, studying, studious, meditative, meditating.

.18 **gripped, held, fascinated, enthralled, rapt, spellbound,** charmed, enchanted, mesmerized, **hypnotized,** fixed, caught, arrested.

.19 **interesting, stimulating, provocative,** provoking, thought-provoking, thought-challenging, thought-inspiring; **titillating,** tickling, **tantalizing, inviting, exciting; piquant,** lively, racy, juicy, succulent, spicy, rich; readable.

.20 **engrossing, absorbing,** consuming, **gripping,** holding, **arresting,** engaging, attractive, **fascinating, enthralling, spellbinding,** enchanting, magnetic, hypnotic, mesmerizing, mesmeric; obsessive, obsessing.

.21 ADVS **attentively,** with attention; **heedfully,** mindfully, regardfully, advertently; observingly, observantly; **interestedly,** with interest; **raptly,** with rapt attention; engrossedly, absorbedly, preoccupiedly; devotedly, **intently,** without distraction, **with undivided attention.**

.22 INTERJS **attention!,** look!, see!, look you!, look here!, looky! [informal], witness!; lo!, behold!, lo and behold!; **hark!,** listen!, hark ye!, hear ye!, oyez!; *nota bene* [L, note well], NB.

.23 **hey!,** hail!, ahoy!, hello!, hollo!, hallo!, halloo!, halloa!, ho!, heigh!, hi!, hist!; hello there!, ahoy there!, etc.

531. INATTENTION

.1 NOUNS **inattention,** inattentiveness, **heedlessness, unheedfulness, unmindfulness, thoughtlessness,** inconsideration; **incuriosity** 529, **indifference** 636; inadvertence *or* inadvertency; unintentness, unintentiveness; disregard, disregardfulness, regardlessness; **flightiness** 532.5, giddiness 532.4, lightmindedness; levity, frivolousness, flippancy; shallowness, superficiality; **inobservance,** unobservance, nonobservance; **unalertness,** unwariness, unwatchfulness; **obliviousness,** unconsciousness, unawareness; **carelessness,** negligence 534.1–4; distraction, **absentmindedness** 532.2.

.2 VERBS **be inattentive, pay no attention,** pay no mind [dial], not attend, not notice, **take no note** *or* **notice of,** take no thought *or* account of, miss, not heed, give no heed, pay no regard to, not listen, hear nothing, not hear a word; **disregard, overlook, ignore,** pass over *or* by, have no time for, let pass *or* get by *or* get past; think little of, **slight,** make light of; **close** *or* **shut one's eyes to,** see nothing, be blind to, turn a blind eye, **look the other way, blink at, wink at,** connive at; stick one's head in the sand; **turn a deaf**

ear to, stop one's ears, let come in one ear and go out the other; let well enough alone; not trouble oneself with, not trouble one's head with *or* about; **be unwary,** be off one's guard, be caught out.

.3 **wander, stray,** divagate, wander from the subject; have no attention span, have a short attention span, let one's attention wander, get off the track [informal].

.4 **dismiss,** dismiss *or* drive from one's thoughts; **put out of mind,** put out of one's head *or* thoughts, wean one's thoughts from, think nothing of, force one's thoughts from, **think no more of, forget, forget it,** forget about it, **let it go** [informal], let slip, not give it another *or* a second thought, **drop the subject,** give it no more thought; turn one's back upon, turn away from, turn one's attention from, abandon, leave out in the cold [informal]; put *or* set *or* lay aside, push *or* thrust aside *or* to one side, put on the back burner [informal]; **turn up one's nose at,** sneeze at; shrug off, brush off *or* aside; laugh off *or* away, dismiss with a laugh.

.5 **escape notice** *or* **attention,** escape one, get by, be missed, pass one by, not enter one's head, fall on deaf ears, not register.

.6 ADJS **inattentive, unmindful,** inadvertent, thoughtless, **incurious** 529.3, **indifferent** 636.6,7; **heedless,** unheeding, unheedful, regardless, *distrait* [Fr], disregardful, disregardant; **unobserving,** inobservant, unobservant, unnoticing, unnoting, unremarking, unmarking; **distracted** 532.10; careless, negligent 534.10.

.7 **oblivious, unconscious,** insensible, dead to the world; blind, deaf; **preoccupied** 532.11.

.8 **unalert, unwary, unwatchful, unvigilant,** uncautious, incautious; **unprepared,** unready; unguarded, **off one's guard,** off-guard; **asleep,** sleeping, nodding, napping, **asleep at the switch** [informal], asleep on the job *or* **not on the job** [both informal], goofing off *or* looking out the window [both slang].

532. DISTRACTION, CONFUSION

.1 NOUNS **distraction,** distractedness, **diversion,** separation *or* withdrawal of attention, divided attention; **inattention** 531.

.2 **abstractedness, abstraction,** preoccupation, absorption, engrossment, depth of thought, fit of abstraction; **absentmindedness,** absence of mind; bemusement, musing, musefulness [archaic]; **woolgath-**

ering, mooning [informal], moonraking [archaic], stargazing, **dreaming, daydreaming,** fantasying, pipe-dreaming [informal], castle-building; **brown study,** study, reverie, muse, dreamy abstraction, quiet *or* muted ecstasy, trance; dream, **daydream,** fantasy, pipe dream [informal]; daydreamer, Walter Mitty.

.3 **confusion, fluster, flummox** [informal], **flutter,** flurry, ruffle; disorientation, **muddle, muddlement,** fuddle *or* fuddlement [both informal], befuddlement, daze, maze [dial]; unsettlement, disorganization, **disorder,** chaos, **mess** [informal], shuffle, jumble, discomfiture, discomposure, disconcertion, discombobulation [informal], **bewilderment, embarrassment,** disturbance, perturbation, **upset,** frenzy, pother, bother, botheration *or* stew [both informal], pucker [archaic]; tizzy *or* swivet *or* sweat [all informal]; haze, fog, mist, cloud; maze; **perplexity** 514.3.

.4 **dizziness, vertigo,** vertiginousness, spinning head, swimming, swimming of the head, **giddiness,** wooziness [informal], **lightheadedness;** tiddliness [Brit informal], **drunkenness** 996.1–4.

.5 **flightiness, giddiness,** volatility, mercuriality; **thoughtlessness,** witlessness, brainlessness, empty-headedness, foolishness 470.

.6 VERBS **distract, divert,** detract, distract the attention, divert *or* detract attention, divert the mind *or* thoughts, draw off the attention, call away, take the mind off of, relieve the mind of, cause the mind to stray *or* wander, put off the track, throw off the scent, lead the mind astray, beguile; throw off one's guard.

.7 **confuse,** throw into confusion, **fluster;** flummox, fuss *or* fuss up [all informal], **flutter,** put into a flutter, **flurry, rattle,** ruffle, moider [Brit dial], **mix up,** ball up [slang], entangle, **muddle,** fuddle [informal], **befuddle, addle,** addle the wits, **daze, maze, dazzle,** bedazzle; **upset, unsettle,** raise hell, disorganize; throw into a tizzy *or* swivet, etc.; **disconcert, discomfit, discompose,** discombobulate [informal], disorient, **bewilder, embarrass, put out, disturb, perturb, bother,** pother, bug [slang]; fog, mist, cloud, becloud; **perplex** 514.13.

.8 **dizzy, make one's head swim,** cause vertigo, send one spinning, whirl the mind, swirl the senses, make one's head reel *or* whirl *or* spin *or* revolve, go to one's head; **intoxicate** 996.21,22.

.9 **muse, moon** [informal], **dream, daydream,** pipe-dream [informal], fantasy; abstract oneself, be lost in thought, let one's attention wander, let one's mind run on other things, dream of *or* muse on other things; **wander, stray,** divagate, let one's thoughts *or* mind wander, give oneself up to reverie, go woolgathering, let one's wits go bird's nesting, be in a brown study, be absent, be somewhere else, stargaze.

.10 ADJS **distracted, distraught,** *distrait* [Fr]; **wandering, rambling; wild, frantic, beside oneself.**

.11 **abstracted, bemused,** museful [archaic], **musing, preoccupied, absorbed, engrossed,** taken up; **absentminded, absent,** faraway, elsewhere, somewhere else, not there; pensive, meditative; lost, **lost in thought,** wrapped in thought; rapt, transported, ecstatic; dead to the world, **unconscious, oblivious; dreaming, dreamy,** drowsing, nodding, half-awake, betwixt sleep and waking, napping; **daydreaming,** daydreamy, pipe-dreaming [informal]; **woolgathering,** mooning *or* moony [both informal], moonraking [archaic], castle-building, in the clouds, off in the clouds, stargazing, in a reverie.

.12 **confused, mixed-up,** balled-up [slang]; **fluttered,** fluttered, **ruffled, rattled,** fussed [informal]; **upset, unsettled,** disorganized, **disordered,** chaotic, jumbled, in a jumble, shuffled; shaken, shook [slang], **disconcerted, discomposed,** discombobulated [informal], **embarrassed, put-out, disturbed, perturbed,** bothered, all hot and bothered [informal]; in a stew *or* botheration [informal], in a pucker [archaic]; in a tizzy *or* swivet *or* sweat [informal], in a pother; **perplexed** 514.24.

.13 **muddled,** in a muddle; fuddled [informal], **befuddled;** muddleheaded, fuddlebrained [informal]; puzzleheaded, puzzlepated; **addled,** addleheaded, addlepated, addlebrained; foggy, fogged, in a fog, hazy, muzzy [informal], misted, misty, cloudy, beclouded.

.14 **dazed,** mazed, **dazzled,** bedazzled, in a daze; **silly,** knocked silly; **groggy** [informal], **dopey** [slang], woozy [informal], **punch-drunk** [informal], punchy, **slaphappy** [both slang].

.15 **dizzy, giddy,** vertiginous, swimming, turned around, going around in circles; lightheaded, **tiddly** [Brit informal], **drunken** 996.30–33.

.16 **scatterbrained,** shatterbrained *or* shatterpated [both archaic], rattlebrained, rattleheaded, rattlepated, scramblebrained, harebrain, harebrained, **giddy, dizzy,** gaga [informal], **giddy-brained,** giddy-headed, giddy-pated, giddy-witted, giddy as a goose, fluttery, frivolous, featherbrained, featherheaded; **thoughtless, witless, brainless, empty-headed** 469.19.

.17 **flighty,** volatile, mercurial.

533. CAREFULNESS

(close or watchful attention)

.1 NOUNS **carefulness, care, heed, concern, regard; attention** 530; **heedfulness,** regardfulness, mindfulness, **thoughtfulness;** consideration, solicitude, loving care, tender loving care, TLC [informal]; circumspectness, circumspection; forethought, anticipation, preparedness; **caution** 895.

.2 **painstakingness,** painstaking, **pains; diligence,** assiduousness, assiduity, sedulousness, industriousness, industry; **thoroughness,** thoroughgoingness.

.3 **meticulousness,** exactingness, **scrupulousness,** scrupulosity, **conscientiousness,** punctiliousness, attention to detail, **particularness,** particularity, circumstantiality; **fussiness, criticalness,** criticality; **finicalness,** finickingness, finickiness, finicality; **exactness, exactitude, accuracy, preciseness, precision,** precisionism, precisianism, punctuality, correctness; **strictness,** rigidness, **rigor,** rigorousness; nicety, niceness, delicacy, detail, subtlety, refinement, minuteness, exquisiteness.

.4 **vigilance, wariness,** prudence, **watchfulness,** watching, observance, **surveillance; watch, vigil, lookout;** *qui vive* [Fr]; invigilation, proctoring, monitoring; watch and ward; custody, custodianship, guardianship, stewardship; **guard,** guardedness; watchful eye, weather *or* peeled eye [informal], sharp eye, eagle eye, lidless *or* sleepless *or* unblinking *or* unwinking eye.

.5 **alertness, attentiveness; attention** 530; **wakefulness,** sleeplessness; **readiness,** promptness, promptitude, punctuality; **quickness,** agility, nimbleness; **smartness,** brightness, keenness, sharpness, acuteness, acuity.

.6 VERBS **care, mind, heed,** reck, think, consider, regard, take heed *or* thought of; **take an interest,** be concerned; **pay attention** 530.8.

.7 **be careful, take care** *or* good care, take heed, have a care, exercise care; **be cautious** 895.5; **take pains,** take trouble, be

painstaking, go to great pains, go to great lengths, bend over backwards [informal]; mind what one is doing *or* about, mind one's business, **mind one's P's and Q's** [informal]; **watch one's step** [informal], pick one's steps, tread on eggs, place one's feet carefully, feel one's way; treat gently, **handle with gloves** *or* **kid gloves.**

.8 **be vigilant,** be watchful, never nod *or* sleep, **be on the watch** *or* **lookout,** be on the *qui vive,* keep a good *or* sharp lookout, keep in sight *or* view; **keep watch,** keep watch and ward, keep vigil; **watch, look sharp,** look about one, look with one's own eyes, **be on one's guard,** sleep with one eye open, have all one's eyes *or* wits about one, keep one's eyes open, keep a weather eye open [informal], **keep one's eyes peeled** [informal], keep the ears on *or* to the ground, keep a nose to the wind; keep alert, **be on the alert; look out, watch out** [informal]; look lively *or* alive; stop, look, and listen.

.9 **look after, tend, take care of** 699.19.

.10 ADJS **careful, heedful, regardful, mindful, thoughtful, considerate,** solicitous, loving, tender, curious [archaic]; circumspect; **attentive** 530.15; **cautious** 895.8.

.11 **painstaking, diligent, assiduous,** sedulous, **thorough, thoroughgoing,** operose, industrious, elaborate.

.12 **meticulous, exacting, scrupulous, conscientious,** religious, **punctilious, punctual, particular, fussy, critical, attentive,** scrutinizing; **finical,** finicking, finicky; **exact, precise,** precisionistic, precisianistic, **accurate, correct;** close, narrow; **strict,** rigid, **rigorous,** exigent, demanding; nice, delicate, subtle, fine, refined, minute, detailed, exquisite.

.13 **vigilant, wary, prudent, watchful,** lidless, sleepless, observant; **on the watch, on the lookout,** *aux aguets* [Fr]; **on guard,** on one's guard, guarded; with open eyes, with one's eyes open, with one's eyes peeled *or* with a weather eye open [both informal]; open-eyed, sharp-eyed, keeneyed, Argus-eyed, eagle-eyed, hawk-eyed; **all eyes, all ears, all eyes and ears;** custodial.

.14 **alert, on the alert,** on the *qui vive,* **on one's toes,** on the job *or* on the ball [both informal], **attentive; awake,** wakeful, **wide-awake,** sleepless, unsleeping, unblinking, unwinking, unnodding, alive, ready, prompt, quick, agile, nimble, quick on the trigger *or* draw [informal]; **smart, bright, keen, sharp.**

.15 ADVS **carefully, heedfully,** regardfully, **mindfully,** thoughtfully, **considerately,** solicitously, tenderly, lovingly; circumspectly; **cautiously** 895.12; **with care,** with great care; **painstakingly, diligently,** assiduously, industriously, sedulously, thoroughly, thoroughgoingly.

.16 **meticulously, exactingly, scrupulously, conscientiously,** religiously, punctiliously, punctually, fussily; strictly, rigorously; exactly, **accurately, precisely, with exactitude, with precision;** nicely, with great nicety, refinedly, minutely, in detail, exquisitely.

.17 **vigilantly, warily,** prudently, **watchfully,** observantly; **alertly,** attentively; sleeplessly, unsleepingly, unwinkingly, unblinkingly, lidlessly, unnoddingly.

534. NEGLECT

.1 NOUNS **neglect,** neglectfulness, **negligence,** inadvertence *or* inadvertency, dereliction, *culpa* [L], culpable negligence; **remissness,** laxity, laxness, slackness, looseness, laches; unrigorousness, permissiveness; noninterference, *laissez-faire* [Fr], nonrestriction; **disregard,** slight; **inattention** 531; **oversight,** overlooking; omission, nonfeasance, nonperformance, lapse, failure, default; poor stewardship *or* guardianship *or* custody; procrastination 132.5.

.2 **carelessness, heedlessness, unheedfulness,** disregardfulness, regardlessness; unsolicitude, unsolicitousness, **thoughtlessness,** tactlessness, inconsiderateness, **inconsideration;** unthinkingness, unmindfulness, oblivion, forgetfulness; **unpreparedness,** unreadiness, lack of foresight *or* forethought; **recklessness** 894.2; **indifference** 636; **laziness** 708.5; perfunctoriness; cursoriness, hastiness, offhandedness, casualness; easiness; nonconcern, insouciance; abandon, careless abandon, *sprezzatura* [Ital].

.3 **slipshodness,** slipshoddiness, **slovenliness,** slovenry, sluttishness, untidiness, **sloppiness** *or* **messiness** [both informal]; haphazardness; slapdash, slapdashness, a lick and a promise [all informal], loose ends; bad job, sad work, botch, slovenly performance; bungling 734.4.

.4 **unmeticulousness,** unexactingness, **unscrupulousness,** unrigorousness, **unconscientiousness,** unpunctiliousness, unpunctuality, unparticularness, unfussiness, unfinicalness, **uncriticalness;** inexactness, inexactitude, inaccuracy, imprecision, unpreciseness.

.5 **neglecter,** negligent [archaic], ignorer, disregarder; **procrastinator,** waiter on Providence, Micawber [Dickens]; slacker, shirker, malingerer, dodger, goof-off *or* goldbrick [both slang], idler; skimper [informal]; trifler 673.9; sloven, slut; bungler 734.8.

.6 VERBS **neglect, overlook, disregard,** not heed, take for granted, **ignore;** not care for, not take care of; **pass over,** gloss over; **let slip, let slide** [informal], **let go,** let ride [slang], let take its course; let the grass grow under one's feet; not think *or* consider, not give a thought to, take no thought *or* account of, blind oneself to, turn a blind eye to, leave out of one's calculation; lose sight of, lose track of; **be neglectful** *or* **negligent,** fail in one's duty, **fail, lapse, default,** let go by default; not get involved; nod, sleep [archaic], be caught napping, be asleep at the switch [informal].

.7 **leave undone,** leave, **let go,** leave half-done, pretermit, **skip,** jump, **miss, omit,** cut [informal], let be *or* alone, pass over, pass up [informal], abandon; leave a loose thread, leave loose ends, let dangle; slack, shirk, malinger, goof off *or* goldbrick [both slang]; trifle 673.13; **procrastinate** 132.11.

.8 **slight;** turn one's back on, turn a cold shoulder to, cold-shoulder [informal], leave out in the cold; scamp, skimp [informal]; slur, **slur over,** pass over, slubber over, slip *or* **skip over,** dodge, fudge, blink, carefully ignore; skim, **skim over,** skim the surface, **touch upon,** touch upon lightly *or* in passing, pass over lightly, go once over lightly, **hit the high spots** *or* **give a lick and a promise** [both informal]; **cut corners,** cut a corner.

.9 **do carelessly,** do by halves, do in a slipshod fashion, do anyhow, do in any old way [informal]; botch, **bungle** 734.11; **trifle with,** play *or* play at fast and loose with, mess around *or* about with [informal]; **do offhand,** dash off, knock off *or* throw off [both informal], **toss off** *or* **out** [informal]; **roughhew,** roughcast, rough out; **knock out** [informal], hammer *or* pound out, bat out [slang]; toss *or* **throw together,** knock together, patch together, patch, patch up, fudge up, fake up, whomp up [informal], lash up [Brit informal], slap up [informal]; jury-rig.

.10 ADJS **negligent, neglectful,** neglecting,

derelict, culpably negligent; inadvertent, uncircumspect; **inattentive** 531.6; unwary, unwatchful, off-guard, unguarded; **remiss**, slack, lax, relaxed, loose, unrigorous, permissive, overly permissive; noninterfering, *laissez-faire* [Fr], nonrestrictive; slighting; slurring, scamping, skimping [informal]; procrastinating 132.17.

.11 **careless, heedless, unheeding, unheedful, disregardful,** disregardant, regardless, **unsolicitous,** tactless, respectless, **thoughtless, unthinking, inconsiderate,** untactful, undiplomatic, mindless of, **unmindful,** forgetful, oblivious; **unprepared,** unready; **reckless** 894.8; **indifferent** 636.6,7; lazy 708.18; perfunctory, cursory, casual, offhand; easygoing, *dégagé* [Fr], airy, flippant, insouciant, free and easy.

.12 **slipshod,** slipshoddy, **slovenly,** sloppy *or* **messy** [both informal], sluttish, untidy; **clumsy, bungling** 734.20; **haphazard, promiscuous, hit-or-miss,** hit-and-miss; deficient, half-assed [slang], botched.

.13 unmeticulous, unexacting, unpainstaking, **unscrupulous,** unrigorous, **unconscientious,** unpunctilious, unpunctual, **unparticular, unfussy, unfinical, uncritical;** inexact, inaccurate, unprecise.

.14 **neglected,** unattended to, untended, unwatched, unchaperoned, uncared-for; **disregarded,** unconsidered, unregarded, **overlooked, missed,** omitted, passed by, passed over, passed up [informal], **ignored, slighted;** unasked, unsolicited; half-done, undone, left undone; deserted, abandoned; in the cold *or* out in the cold [both informal]; shelved, pigeonholed, **put** *or* **laid aside,** sidetracked *or* sidelined [both informal], shunted.

.15 **unheeded, unobserved, unnoticed, unnoted, unperceived, unseen,** undiscerned, undescried, unmarked, unremarked, unregarded, unminded, unconsidered, unthought-of, unmissed.

.16 **unexamined, unstudied,** unconsidered, unsearched, unscanned, unweighed, unsifted, unexplored, unconned.

.17 ADVS **negligently, neglectfully,** inadvertently; **remissly,** laxly, slackly, loosely; **unrigorously,** permissively; nonrestrictively; **slightingly,** lightly, slurringly; scampingly, skimpingly [informal].

.18 **carelessly, heedlessly,** unheedingly, **unheedfully,** disregardfully, regardlessly, **thoughtlessly, unthinkingly, unsolicitously,** tactlessly, **inconsiderately,** unmindfully, forgetfully; **inattentively, unwarily,** unvigilantly, unguardedly, un-

watchfully; **recklessly** 894.11; perfunctorily; once over lightly, cursorily; casually, offhand, offhandedly, airily; clumsily, bunglingly 734.24; **sloppily** *or* **messily** [both informal]; haphazardly, promiscuously, hit or miss, hit and miss, helter-skelter, slapdash [both informal], anyhow, any old way, any which way [both informal].

.19 unmeticulously, **unscrupulously, unconscientiously,** unfussily, **uncritically;** inexactly, inaccurately, unprecisely, imprecisely, unpunctually.

535. IMAGINATION

.1 NOUNS **imagination,** imagining, imaginativeness, **fancy, fantasy,** conceit [archaic]; mind's eye, "that inward eye which is the bliss of solitude" [Wordsworth]; flight of fancy, fumes of fancy; fantasticism.

.2 **creative thought,** conception; productive *or* constructive *or* creative imagination, creative power *or* ability, esemplastic imagination *or* power, shaping imagination, poetic imagination, artistic imagination; mythopoeia, *mythopoesis* [Gk]; mythification, mythicization; inspiration, muse; Muses: Calliope (epic poetry), Clio (history), Erato (lyric and love poetry), Euterpe (music), Melpomene (tragedy), Polyhymnia (sacred song), Terpsichore (dancing and choral song), Thalia (comedy), Urania (astronomy); genius 467.8.

.3 **invention, inventiveness, originality, creativity,** creativeness, **ingenuity;** productivity, prolificacy, **fertility,** fecundity; rich *or* teeming imagination, fertile *or* pregnant imagination, seminal *or* germinal imagination, fertile mind.

.4 **lively imagination,** active fancy, **vivid imagination,** colorful *or* highly colored *or* lurid imagination, warm *or* ardent imagination, fiery *or* heated imagination, excited imagination, bold *or* daring *or* wild *or* fervent imagination; verve, vivacity of imagination.

.5 **figment of the imagination,** creature of the imagination, creation *or* coinage of the brain, fiction of the mind, maggot, whim, whimsy, figment, imagination, invention; brainchild; **imagining,** fancy, idle fancy, vapor, fantasque, "thick-coming fancies" [Shakespeare], imagery; **fantasy, make-believe;** phantom, vision, apparition, insubstantial image, eidolon, **phantasm** 519.4; **fiction,** myth, romance; wildest dreams, stretch of the imagination; **chimera, bubble, illusion** 519; hallucination, delirium, sick fancy; trip *or* drug trip [both slang].

.6 **visualization, envisioning,** envisaging, picturing, objectification, imaging, calling to *or* before the mind's eye, figuring *or* portraying *or* representing in the mind; depicting *or* delineating in the imagination; conceptualization; **picture, vision, image,** mental image, mental picture, visual image, vivid *or* lifelike image, eidetic image, concept, **conception,** mental representation *or* presentation, *Vorstellung* [Ger]; **imagery,** word-painting; poetic image, poetic imagery; imagery study; imagism, imagistic poetry.

.7 **idealism, idealization; ideal,** ideality; visionariness, **utopianism;** flight of fancy, play of fancy, imaginative exercise; **romanticism,** romance; **quixotism,** quixotry; dreamery; **impracticality,** unpracticalness, **unrealism,** unreality; **wishful thinking,** wish fulfillment, wish-fulfillment fantasy, autistic thinking, dereistic thinking, autism, dereism, autistic distortion.

.8 **dreaminess,** dreamfulness, musefulness, pensiveness; dreamlikeness; **dreaming, musing; daydreaming,** pipe-dreaming [informal], dreamery, fantasying, castle-building.

.9 **dream,** oneir(o)– *or* onir(o)–; **reverie, daydream,** pipe dream [informal]; **brown study** 532.2; **vision; nightmare,** incubus, bad dream.

.10 **air castle, castle in the air,** castle in the sky *or* skies, castle in Spain; Xanadu, pleasure dome of Kubla Khan [both Coleridge].

.11 **utopia** *or* **Utopia** [Sir Thomas More], **paradise, heaven** 1018, **heaven on earth;** millennium, kingdom come; **dreamland,** lotus land, land of dreams, land of enchantment, land of heart's desire, wonderland, cloudland, fairyland, land of faerie, faerie; Eden, Garden of Eden; promised land, land of promise, land of plenty, land of milk and honey, Canaan, Goshen; Shangri-la, New Atlantis [Francis Bacon], Arcadia, Agapemone, Happy Valley [Samuel Johnson], land of Prester John, Eldorado, Seven Cities of Cibola, Quivira; Laputa [Swift]; Cockaigne, Big Rock-Candy Mountain, Fiddler's Green, Never-Never-land [J. M. Barrie], Neverland, Cloudcuckooland *or* Nephelococcygia [Aristophanes], Erewhon [Samuel Butler], Land of Youth; dystopia *or* kakotopia; Pandemonium.

.12 **imaginer, fancier, fantast; fantasist;** myth-maker, mythopoet; mythifier, mythicizer; **inventor; creative artist,** poet.

.13 **visionary, idealist; prophet, seer; dreamer, daydreamer,** dreamer of dreams, castle-builder, lotus-eater, **wishful thinker; romantic,** romanticist, romancer; **Quixote,** Don Quixote; utopian, utopianist, utopianizer; **escapist;** enthusiast, rhapsodist.

.14 VERBS **imagine, fancy, conceive,** conceit [archaic], conceptualize, ideate, figure to oneself; **invent, create, originate,** think up, dream up, shape, mold, coin, hatch, concoct, fabricate, produce; **suppose** 499.10; **fantasize; fictionalize; give free rein to the imagination,** let one's imagination riot *or* run riot *or* run wild, allow one's imagination to run away with one; experience imaginatively *or* vicariously.

.15 **visualize, vision, envision, envisage, picture, image,** objectify; picture in one's mind, picture to oneself, **view with the mind's eye,** contemplate in the imagination, form a mental picture of, represent, see, just see, have a picture of; **call up,** summon up, conjure up, **call to mind,** realize.

.16 **idealize,** utopianize, quixotize, rhapsodize; **romanticize,** romance; paint pretty pictures of, paint in bright colors; see through rose-colored glasses; **build castles in the air.**

.17 **dream; dream of,** dream on; **daydream,** pipe-dream [informal], indulge in wish-fulfillment; fantasy, conjure up a vision, "see visions and dream dreams" [Bible]; blow one's mind *or* go on a trip *or* trip *or* freak out [all slang].

.18 ADJS **imaginative,** conceptual, conceptive, ideational, ideative, notional; **inventive, original,** originative, esemplastic, shaping, **creative, ingenious; productive, fertile,** fecund, prolific, seminal, germinal, teeming, pregnant; **inspired,** visioned.

.19 **imaginary,** imaginational, notional; **imagined, fancied; unreal,** unactual, nonexistent; fictive, visional, supposititious, **all in the mind; illusory** 519.9.

.20 **fanciful, notional,** notiony [dial], whimsical, maggoty [Brit]; brain-born; fancy-bred, fancy-born, fancy-built, fancy-framed, fancy-woven, fancy-wrought; dream-born, dream-built, dream-created; **fantastic(al),** fantasque, extravagant, preposterous, outlandish, wild, baroque, rococo, florid; bizarre, grotesque, Gothic.

.21 **fictitious, make-believe, figmental,** fictional, fictive, pseud(o)–; nonhistorical, nonfactual, nonactual, nonrealistic; **fabu-**

lous, **mythic**(al), mythological, legendary; mythified, mythicized.

.22 **chimeric**(al), **aerial**, **ethereal**, phantasmal; vaporous, vapory; air-built, cloud-built, cloud-born, cloud-woven.

.23 **ideal**, **idealized**; utopian, Arcadian, Edenic, paradisal; pie in the sky [informal]; heavenly, celestial; millennial.

.24 **visionary**, **idealistic**, **quixotic**(al); **romantic**, **romanticized**, romancing, romantico–; poetic(al); storybook; **impractical**, **unpractical**, **unrealistic**; wish-fulfilling, autistic, dereistic; starry-eyed, dewy-eyed; in the clouds, with one's head in the clouds; airy, **otherworldly**, transmundane, transcendental.

.25 **dreamy**, **dreamful**; **dreamy-eyed**, dreamy-minded, dreamy-souled; dreamlike; daydreamy, **dreaming**, **daydreaming**, pipedreaming [informal], castle-building; **entranced**, tranced, in a trance, dream-stricken, enchanted, spellbound, spelled, charmed.

.26 **imaginable**, **fanciable**, **conceivable**, **thinkable**, cogitable; **supposable** 499.15.

536. UNIMAGINATIVENESS

.1 NOUNS **unimaginativeness**, unfancifulness; **prosaicness**, prosiness, prosaism, prosaicism, unpoeticalness; **staidness**, **stuffiness** [informal]; stolidity; **dullness**, **dryness**; aridness, aridity, **barrenness**, infertility, infecundity; **unoriginality**, uncreativeness, uninventiveness, dearth of ideas.

.2 (practical attitude) **realism**, realisticness, **practicalness**, **practicality**, **practical-mindedness**, sober-mindedness, **hardheadedness**, **matter-of-factness**; down-to-earthness, earthiness, worldliness, secularism; pragmatism, pragmaticism, positivism, scientism; unidealism, unromanticalness, unsentimentality; sensibleness, saneness, reasonableness, rationality; freedom from illusion, lack of sentimentality; lack of feelings 856.

.3 **realist**, pragmatist, positivist, practical person.

.4 VERBS **keep both feet on the ground**, stick to the facts, call a spade a spade; **come down to earth**, come down out of the clouds.

.5 ADJS **unimaginative**, **unfanciful**; unideal, unidealized, unromantic, unromanticized; **prosaic**, prosy, prosing, unpoetic(al); **literal**, literal-minded; earthbound, mundane; **staid**, **stuffy** [informal]; stolid;

dull, dry; arid, barren, infertile, infecund; **unoriginal**, uninspired; uninventive 166.5.

.6 **realistic**, realist, **practical**; pragmatic(al), scientific, scientistic, positivistic; **unidealistic**, unideal, **unromantic**, **unsentimental**, **practical-minded**, sober-minded, **hardheaded**, straight-thinking, **matter-of-fact**, **down-to-earth**, **with both feet on the ground**; worldly, earthy, secular; sensible, sane, reasonable, rational, sound, sound-thinking.

537. MEMORY

.1 NOUNS **memory**,–mnesia; **remembrance**, **recollection**, mind, *souvenir* [Fr]; memory trace, engram; mind's eye, eye of the mind, mirror of the mind, tablets of the memory; corner or recess of the memory, inmost recesses of the memory; Mnemosyne, mother of the Muses; computer memory, information storage, disk memory, tape memory, drum memory, memory bank, memory circuit; collective memory, mneme, race memory; atavism; cover or screen memory, affect memory; anterograde memory; eye or visual memory, kinesthetic memory; skill, verbal response, emotional response.

.2 "that inward eye" [Wordsworth], "the warder of the brain" [Shakespeare], "the treasury and guardian of all things" [Cicero], "storehouse of the mind, garner of facts and fancies" [M. F. Tupper], "the hearing of deaf actions, and the seeing of blind" [Plutarch], "the diary that we all carry around with us" [Oscar Wilde].

.3 **retention**, **retentiveness**, retentivity, memory span; good memory, retentive memory or mind; total memory, eidetic memory or imagery, photographic memory, total recall; camera-eye.

.4 **remembering**, **remembrance**, **recollection**, recollecting, exercise of memory, **recall**, recalling; reflection, reconsideration; **retrospect**, retrospection, hindsight, looking back; flashback, **reminiscence**, review, contemplation of the past, review of things past; **memoir**; **memorization**, memorizing, **rote**, rote memory, rote learning, study, learning by heart, commitment to memory.

.5 **recognition**, **identification**, **reidentification**, distinguishment; realization 475.2.

.6 **reminder**, **remembrance**, remembrancer; **prompt**, prompter, tickler; prompting, cue, hint; jogger [informal], flapper; *aide-mémoire* [Fr], memorandum 570.4.

.7 **memento**, **remembrance**, **token**, **trophy**,

souvenir, keepsake, relic, remembrancer, favor, token of remembrance; commemoration, memorial 570.12; *memento mori* [L]; **memories, memorabilia, memorials.**

.8 memorability, rememberability.

.9 mnemonics, memory training, mnemotechny, mnemotechnics, mnemonization; mnemonic, mnemonic device, *aide-mémoire* [Fr].

.10 VERBS **remember, recall, recollect,** mind [dial]; reflect; **think of,** bethink oneself [archaic]; **call** *or* **bring to mind,** recall to mind, call up, summon up, conjure up, evoke, reevoke, revive, recapture, call back, bring back, "call back yesterday, bid time return" [Shakespeare]; **think back,** go back, **look back,** cast the eyes back, carry one's thoughts back, look back upon things past, use hindsight, retrospect, **see in retrospect,** go back over, hark back, retrace; review, review in retrospect.

.11 reminisce, rake *or* dig up the past.

.12 recognize, know, tell, distinguish, make out; identify, place, have; spot *or* nail *or* peg [all informal], reidentify, know again, recover *or* recall knowledge of; realize 475.12.

.13 keep in memory, bear in mind, keep *or* hold in mind, hold *or* retain the memory of, keep in view, have in mind, hold in the thoughts, carry in one's thoughts, retain in the thoughts, store in the mind, retain, keep; tax *or* burden the memory, treasure, cherish, treasure up in the memory, enshrine *or* embalm in the memory, cherish the memory of; keep up the memory of, keep the memory alive, keep alive in one's thoughts, brood over, dwell on *or* upon, fan the embers.

.14 be remembered, sink in the mind, sink in, penetrate, make an impression; live *or* dwell in one's memory, be easy to recall, remain in one's memory, be green *or* fresh in one's memory, remain indelibly impressed on the memory, be stamped on one's memory, never be forgotten; haunt one's thoughts, obsess, run in the head, be in one's thoughts, be on one's mind; be burnt into one's memory, plague one; rankle, rankle in the breast.

.15 recur, recur to the mind, return to mind, come back.

.16 come to mind, pop into one's head, come to one, come into one's head, flash on the mind, pass in review.

.17 memorize, commit to memory, con; study; learn by heart, get by heart, learn

or get by rote, get letter-perfect, learn word for word, learn verbatim, swot up [Brit informal]; know by heart, have by heart *or* rote, have at one's fingers' ends *or* tips; repeat by heart *or* rote, give word for word, recite, repeat, parrot, repeat like a parrot, say one's lesson.

.18 fix in the mind *or* memory, instill, infix, inculcate, impress, imprint, stamp, inscribe, etch, grave, engrave; impress on the mind, get into one's head, drive *or* hammer into one's head; burden the mind with, task the mind with, load *or* stuff *or* cram the mind with; inscribe *or* stamp *or* rivet in the memory, set in the tablets of memory, etch indelibly in the mind.

.19 refresh the memory, review, restudy, brush up, rub up, polish up [informal], get up on.

.20 remind, put in mind, remember, put in remembrance, bring back to the memory, bring to recollection, refresh the memory of; remind one of, recall, suggest, put one in mind of; take one back, carry back, carry back in recollection; jog the memory, awaken *or* arouse the memory, flap the memory, give a hint *or* suggestion; prompt, prompt the mind, give the cue, hold the promptbook; nudge, pull by the sleeve, nag.

.21 try to recall, think hard, rack *or* ransack one's brains, cudgel one's brains, crack one's brains [informal]; have on the tip of one's tongue, have on the edge of one's memory *or* consciousness.

.22 ADJS **recollective, memoried;** mnemonic; retentive; **retrospective,** in retrospect; **reminiscent, mindful, remindful, suggestive,** redolent, evocative.

.23 remembered, recollected, recalled; retained, pent-up in the memory, kept in remembrance, enduring, lasting, unforgotten; present to the mind, lodged in one's mind, stamped on the memory; vivid, eidetic, fresh, green, alive.

.24 remembering, mindful, keeping *or* bearing in mind, holding in remembrance; unable to forget, haunted, plagued, obsessed, nagged, rankled.

.25 memorable, rememberable, recollectable; notable 672.18.

.26 unforgettable, never to be forgotten, never to be erased from the mind, indelible, indelibly impressed on the mind, fixed in the mind; haunting, persistent, recurrent, nagging; obsessive.

.27 memorial, commemorative.

.28 ADVS **by heart,** *par cœur* [Fr], **by rote, by**
or **from memory,** without book; **memora-**
bly; rememberingly.

.29 **in memory of,** to the memory of, in remembrance *or* commemoration, *in me-*
moriam [L]; *memoria in aeterna* [L], in
perpetual remembrance.

538. FORGETFULNESS

.1 NOUNS **forgetfulness,** unmindfulness, absentmindedness, **memorylessness;** short
memory, short memory span, little retentivity *or* recall, mind *or* memory like a
sieve; loose memory, vague *or* fuzzy
memory, dim *or* hazy recollection; **lapse**
of memory, decay of memory; **oblivious-**
ness, oblivion, nirvana; obliteration;
Lethe, Lethe water, waters of Lethe *or*
oblivion, river of oblivion; nepenthe; **for-**
getting; heedlessness 534.2; forgiveness
947.

.2 **amnesia,** failure *or* loss of memory, **mem-**
ory gap, blackout [informal]; fugue; anterograde amnesia, retrograde amnesia,
retroanterograde amnesia; infantile amnesia; lacunar amnesia, partial amnesia;
agnosia, unrecognition; paramnesia, false
memory, misremembrance; auditory *or*
verbal amnesia, word deafness *or* blindness, amnesic *or* amnestic aphasia; tactile
amnesia, astereognosis; systematic amnesia; amnesiac.

.3 **block,** blocking, **mental block,** memory
obstruction; repression, suppression, defense mechanism, conversion, sublimation, symbolization.

.4 VERBS **be forgetful,** be absentminded,
have a short memory, have a mind *or*
memory like a sieve, have a short memory span, be unable to retain, have little
recall, forget one's own name.

.5 **forget,** clean forget [informal]; **not re-**
member, disremember *or* disrecollect
[both informal], fail to remember, forget
to remember, **have no remembrance** *or*
recollection of, be unable to recollect *or*
recall, draw a blank [informal]; lose, lose
sight of; have on the tip of the tongue;
blow *or* fluff one's lines; misremember,
misrecollect.

.6 **efface** *or* **erase from the memory,** consign
to oblivion, unlearn, obliterate, **dismiss**
from one's thoughts 531.4; **forgive** 947.3–5.

.7 **be forgotten,** escape one, slip one's mind,
fade *or* die away from the memory, slip
or escape the memory, drop from one's
thoughts; fall *or* sink into oblivion, go in
one ear and out the other.

.8 ADJS **forgotten,** clean forgotten [infor-
mal], **unremembered,** disremembered *or*
disrecollected [both informal], **unrecol-**
lected, unretained, unrecalled, past recollection *or* recall, out of the mind, lost,
erased, effaced, obliterated, gone out of
one's head *or* recollection, consigned to
oblivion, buried *or* sunk in oblivion; out
of sight out of mind; misremembered,
misrecollected.

.9 **forgetful, forgetting,** inclined to forget,
memoryless, unremembering, unmindful,
absentminded, **oblivious,** insensible to
the past, with a mind *or* memory like a
sieve; suffering from *or* stricken with amnesia, amnesic, amnestic; blocked, repressed, suppressed, sublimated, converted; heedless 534.11; Lethean.

.10 **forgettable, unrememberable, unrecol-**
lectable.

.11 ADVS **forgetfully,** forgettingly, unmindfully, absentmindedly, **obliviously.**

539. EXPECTATION

.1 NOUNS **expectation,** expectance *or* **expec-**
tancy, state of expectancy; **anticipation,**
prospect, thought; contemplation; probability 511; confidence, reliance 501.1; certainty 513; imminence 152; unastonishment 921.

.2 **sanguine** *or* **cheerful expectation,** optimism, **hope** 888.

.3 **suspense,** state of suspense, cliff-hanging
[informal]; **waiting,** expectant waiting;
uncertainty 514; anxiety, dread, pessimism, apprehension 890.1.

.4 **expectations,** prospects, outlook, hopes,
apparent destiny *or* fate, future prospects; likelihoods, probabilities.

.5 VERBS **expect,** be expectant, **anticipate,**
have in prospect, face, think, **contem-**
plate, have in contemplation *or* mind, envisage; **hope** 888.7; presume 499.10; dread
891.18; **take for granted;** not be surprised
or a bit surprised; foresee 542.5.

.6 **look forward to,** reckon *or* calculate *or*
count on; look to, **look for, watch for,**
look out for, watch out for, be on the
watch *or* lookout for, keep a good *or*
sharp lookout for; be ready for; forestall.

.7 **be expected,** be one's probable fate *or*
destiny, be one's outlook *or* prospect, be
in store.

.8 **await,** wait, wait for, wait on *or* upon,
stay *or* tarry for; lie in wait for; watch,
watch and wait; **bide one's time,** bide,
abide, **mark time;** cool one's heels [infor-
mal]; be in suspense, hold one's breath,

bite one's nails; sweat *or* sweat out *or* sweat it *or* sweat it out [all slang]; **wait up for,** stay up for, sit up for.

.9 **expect to, plan on** 653.4–7.

.10 **be as expected,** be as one thought *or* looked for, turn out that way, come as no surprise; **be just like one,** be one all over [slang]; **expect it of,** think that way about, **not put it past** [informal]; **impend,** be imminent 152.2; lead one to expect 544.13.

.11 ADJS **expectant,** expecting, in expectation *or* anticipation; **anticipative,** anticipant, anticipating, anticipatory; **waiting,** awaiting, waiting for; forewarned, forearmed, forestalling, ready, prepared; **looking forward to,** looking for, watching for, on the watch *or* lookout for; gaping, agape, agog, all agog, eager 635.9; sanguine, optimistic, hopeful 888.11; sure, confident 501.21, 513.21; certain 513.13; unsurprised, not surprised.

.12 **in suspense, on tenterhooks, on tiptoe, on edge, with bated breath,** tense, taut, with muscles tense, quivering, keyed-up, biting one's nails; anxious, **apprehensive** 890.6.

.13 **expected,** anticipated, awaited, foreseen; presumed 499.14; probable 511.6; **looked-for,** hoped-for; **due,** promised; long-expected, overdue; **in prospect, prospective; in view,** in one's eye, on the horizon; imminent 152.3.

.14 **to be expected,** as expected, up to *or* according to expectation, just as one thought, just as predicted, on schedule, **as one may have suspected,** as one might think *or* suppose; **expected of,** counted on, **taken for granted;** just like one, one all over [slang], in character.

.15 ADVS **expectantly,** expectingly; anticipatively, **anticipatingly,** anticipatorily; hopefully 888.14; **with bated breath,** with breathless expectation; with ears pricked up, with eyes *or* ears strained.

540. INEXPECTATION

.1 NOUNS **inexpectation,** nonexpectation, inexpectance *or* inexpectancy, no expectation, **unanticipation; unexpectedness;** unforeseeableness, unpredictableness, unpredictability; unreadiness, unpreparedness; the unforeseen, the unlooked-for, the last thing one expects; **improbability** 512.

.2 **surprise,** surprisal; astonishment 920.1–2; surpriser, startler, shocker, **blow,** staggerer [informal], **eye-opener,** revelation; **bolt out of** *or* **from the blue,** thunderbolt, thunderclap; **bombshell,** bomb; blockbuster, earthshaker; sudden turn *or* development, *peripeteia* [Gk], switch; surprise ending, kicker *or* joker *or* catch [all informal]; surprise package; surprise party.

.3 **start, shock, jar, jolt, turn.**

.4 VERBS **not expect,** hardly expect, **not anticipate, not look for,** not bargain for, **not foresee,** not think of, have no thought of, have no expectation, think unlikely *or* improbable.

.5 **be startled, be taken by surprise,** be given a start, be given a turn *or* jar *or* jolt; **start, startle, jump,** jump a mile [informal], jump out of one's skin; **shy,** start aside, flinch.

.6 **be unexpected, come unawares,** come as a surprise *or* shock, appear unexpectedly, turn up, pop up *or* bob up [both informal], drop from the clouds, appear like a bolt out of the blue, come *or* burst like a thunderclap *or* thunderbolt, burst *or* flash upon one, come *or* fall *or* pounce upon, steal *or* creep up on.

.7 **surprise, take by surprise,** do the unexpected, spring a surprise [informal], **open one's eyes,** give one a revelation; **catch** *or* **take unawares,** catch *or* take short, pull up short, **catch off-guard** 488.7; come from behind, come from an unexpected quarter, come upon unexpectedly *or* without warning, spring *or* pounce upon; spring a mine under, ambush, bushwhack; drop in on [informal]; give a surprise party; **astonish** 920.6,7.

.8 **startle, shock, electrify, jar, jolt, shake, stun, stagger, give one a turn** [informal], make one jump out of his skin, take aback, take one's breath away, throw on one's beam ends, bowl down *or* over [informal], strike all of a heap [informal]; **frighten** 891.23.

.9 ADJS **inexpectant,** nonexpectant, unexpecting; **unanticipative,** unanticipating; **unsuspecting, unaware,** unguessing; uninformed, unwarned, unforewarned, unadvised, unadmonished; unready, unprepared; off one's guard 531.8.

.10 **unexpected, unanticipated, unlooked for,** unhoped for, unprepared for, undivined, unguessed, unpredicted, **unforeseen;** unforeseeable, unpredictable; **improbable** 512.3; contrary to expectation, beyond *or* past expectation, out of one's reckoning, more than expected, more than one bargained for; **out of the blue,** dropped from the clouds, from out in left field [slang]; without warning, unheralded, unannounced; sudden 113.5; out-of-the-way, **extraordinary.**

.11 **surprising, astonishing** 920.12; **startling, shocking,** electrifying, staggering, stunning, jarring, jolting.

.12 **surprised,** struck with surprise; **astonished** 920.9; **taken by surprise,** taken unawares, caught short.

.13 **startled, shocked, electrified,** jarred, jolted, shaken, shook [slang], staggered, **given a turn** or **jar** or **jolt,** taken aback, bowled down or over [informal], struck all of a heap [informal], able to be knocked down with a feather.

.14 ADVS **unexpectedly,** unanticipatedly, improbably, implausibly, unpredictably, unforeseeably, *à l'improviste* [Fr], **by surprise, unawares,** against or contrary to all expectation, as no one would have predicted, without notice or warning, in an unguarded moment, like a thief in the night; **out of a clear sky, out of the blue, like a bolt from the blue;** suddenly 113.9.

.15 **surprisingly, startlingly, to one's surprise,** to one's great surprise; shockingly, staggeringly, stunningly, **astonishingly** 920.16.

541. DISAPPOINTMENT

.1 NOUNS **disappointment,** sad or sore disappointment, bitter or cruel disappointment, failed or blasted expectation; **dashed hope, blighted hope,** betrayed hope, hope deferred, forlorn hope; **dash** [archaic], dash to one's hopes; blow, buffet; **frustration,** discomfiture, bafflement, defeat, balk, foiling; **comedown,** setback, **letdown** [informal]; failure, fizzle [informal], fiasco; **disillusionment** 520; tantalization, mirage, tease; **dissatisfaction** 869.1; fallen countenance.

.2 VERBS **disappoint,** defeat expectation or hope; **dash,** dash or blight or blast or crush one's hope; **balk, bilk, thwart, frustrate, baffle, defeat,** foil, cross; **put one's nose out of joint; let down,** cast down; **disillusion** 520.2; tantalize, tease; dissatisfy 869.4.

.3 **be disappointing,** not come up to expectation, not live or measure up to expectation, go wrong, turn sour, disappoint one's expectations, come or fall short; **peter out** or **fizzle** or **fizzle out** [all informal], not make it or not hack it [both slang].

.4 **be disappointed,** not realize one's expectations, fail of one's hopes or ambitions, be let down; look blue, laugh on the

wrong side of one's mouth [informal]; be crestfallen or chapfallen.

.5 ADJS **disappointed,** bitterly or sorely disappointed; **let down,** betrayed, ill-served, ill done-by; **dashed,** blighted, blasted, crushed; **balked,** bilked, **thwarted, frustrated,** baffled, crossed, dished [Brit], defeated, foiled; hoist by one's own petard, caught in one's own trap; disillusioned 520.5; crestfallen, chapfallen, out of countenance; soured; dissatisfied 869.5; regretful 873.8.

.6 **disappointing,** not up to expectation, falling short, out of the running, not up to one's hopes, second- or third-best; tantalizing, teasing; **unsatisfactory** 869.6.

542. FORESIGHT

.1 NOUNS **foresight,** foreseeing, looking ahead, **prevision,** forecast [archaic]; **prediction** 543; **foreglimpse,** foreglance, foregleam; preview, prepublication; **prospect,** prospection; **anticipation,** contemplation, envisionment, envisagement; **foresightedness; farsightedness,** longsightedness, farseeingness; sagacity, providence, discretion, preparation, provision, forehandedness, readiness, prudence 467.4–7.

.2 **forethought, premeditation,** predeliberation, preconsideration 653.3; caution 895.

.3 **foreknowledge,** foreknowing, forewisdom, **precognition,** prescience, presage, presentiment, **foreboding** 544; clairvoyance 1034.8; foreseeability 543.8.

.4 **foretaste,** antepast [archaic], prelibation.

.5 VERBS **foresee,** see beforehand or ahead, foreglimpse, foretaste, **anticipate,** contemplate, envision, envisage, **look forward to,** look ahead, look beyond, look or pry or peep into the future; **predict** 543.9.

.6 **foreknow,** know beforehand, precognize; smell in the wind, scent from afar; **have a presentiment, have a premonition** 544.11; feel in one's bones [informal], just know, intuit 481.4.

.7 ADJS **foreseeing, foresighted; foreknowing, precognizant,** precognitive, prescient; divinatory 543.11; **forethoughted,** forethoughtful; anticipant, anticipatory; **farseeing, farsighted,** longsighted; sagacious, provident, providential, forehanded, prepared, ready, prudent 467.16–19; intuitive 481.5; clairvoyant 1034.23.

.8 foreseeable 543.13; foreseen 543.14.

.9 ADVS **foreseeingly, foreknowingly,** with foresight; against the time when, for a rainy day.

543. PREDICTION

.1 NOUNS prediction, foretelling, foreshowing, forecasting, prognosis, prognostication, presage [archaic], presaging; prophecy, prophesying, vaticination; soothsaying, soothsay; prefiguration, prefigurement, prefiguring; preshowing, presignifying, presigning [archaic]; forecast, promise; apocalypse; prospectus; foresight 542; presentiment, foreboding 544; omen 544.3,6; guesswork, speculation, hariolation; probability 511, statistical prediction, actuarial prediction; improbability 512.

.2 divination, divining, –mancy; augury, haruspication, haruspicy, pythonism, mantic, mantology [archaic]; fortunetelling, crystal gazing, palm-reading, palmistry; crystal ball; horoscopy, astrology 375.20; sorcery 1035; clairvoyance 1034.8.

.3 dowsing, witching, water witching; divining rod or stick, wand, witch or witching stick, dowsing rod, doodlebug; dowser, water witch or witcher.

.4 predictor, foreteller, prognosticator, seer, foreseer, foreshower, foreknower, presager [archaic], prefigurer; forecaster; prophet, prophesier, soothsayer, vates [L]; diviner, divinator, augur; psychic 1034.13; prophetess, seeress, divineress, pythoness; Druid; fortuneteller; crystal gazer; palmist; geomancer; haruspex, astrologer 375.23; weather prophet 402.7; prophet of doom, calamity howler, Cassandra; religious prophets 1022.

.5 [slang terms] dopester, tipster, tout or touter.

.6 sibyl; Pythia, Pythian, Delphic sibyl; Babylonian or Persian sibyl, Cimmerian sibyl, Cumaean sibyl, Erythraean sibyl, Hellespontine or Trojan sibyl, Libyan sibyl, Phrygian sibyl, Samian sibyl, Tiburtine sibyl.

.7 oracle; Delphic or Delphian oracle, Python, Pythian oracle; Delphic tripod, tripod of the Pythia; Dodona, oracle or oak of Dodona.

.8 predictability, divinability, foretellableness, calculability, foreseeability, foreknowableness.

.9 VERBS predict, make a prediction, foretell, soothsay, prefigure, forecast, prophesy, prognosticate, make a prophecy or prognosis, vaticinate, forebode, presage, see or tell the future, read the future, see in the crystal ball; foresee 542.5; dope or dope out [both slang]; call the turn or call one's shot [both informal]; divine; witch or dowse for water; tell fortunes, fortune-tell, cast one's fortune; read one's hand, read palms, read tea leaves, cast a horoscope or nativity; guess, speculate, hariolate.

.10 portend, foretoken 544.10–12.

.11 ADJS predictive, predictory, predictional; foretelling, forewarning, forecasting; prefiguring, prefigurative, presignifying, presignificative; prophetic(al), fatidic(al), apocalyptic(al); vaticinatory, vaticinal, mantic, sibyllic, sibylline; divinatory, oracular, auguring, augural; haruspical; foreseeing 542.7; presageful, presaging; prognostic, prognosticative, prognosticatory; fortunetelling; weather-wise.

.12 ominous, premonitory, foreboding 544.16–17.

.13 predictable, divinable, foretellable, calculable, anticipatable; foreseeable, foreknowable, precognizable; probable 511.6; improbable 512.3.

.14 predicted, prophesied, presaged, foretold, forecast, foreshown; foreseen, foreglimpsed, foreknown.

.15 forms of divination

aeromancy	halomancy
alectryomancy	haruspicy
aleuromancy	hieromancy
alphitomancy	hieroscopy
anthracomancy	hippomancy
anthropomancy	horoscopy
arithmomancy	hydromancy
aspidomancy	I Ching
astrodiagnosis	ichthyomancy
astrology 375.20	idolomancy
astromancy	lithomancy
augury	logomancy
austromancy	margaritomancy
axinomancy	meteoromancy
belomancy	molybdomancy
bibliomancy	myomancy
botanomancy	necromancy
capnomancy	nomancy
cephalomancy	numerology
ceromancy	oenomancy
chalcomancy	omoplatoscopy
chirognomy	oneiromancy
chiromancy	onomancy
chronomancy	onychomancy
cleidomancy	ophiomancy
cleromancy	ornithomancy
coscinomancy	osteomancy
crithomancy	palmistry
crystallomancy	podomancy
cubomancy	psephomancy
dactyliomancy	psychomancy
extispicy	pyromancy
gastromancy	rhabdomancy
geloscopy	scapulimancy
genethlialogy,	scatomancy
genethliacs	sciomancy
geomancy	scyphomancy
gyromancy	sideromancy

sortes Biblicae [L]
sortes Homericae [L]
sortes Praenestinae [L]
sortes Vergilianae [L]
sortilege
spatulamancy

spodomancy
stichomancy
sycomancy
theomancy
xylomancy
zoomancy

544. PRESENTIMENT

.1 NOUNS presentiment, premonition, preapprehension, forefeeling, presage, presagement; hunch 481.3; prediction 543.

.2 foreboding, boding; apprehension, misgiving; chill or quiver along the spine, shudder of the flesh.

.3 omen, portent; augury, auspice, soothsay, prognostic, prognostication; premonitory sign or symptom, premonitory shiver or chill, foretoken, foretokening, tokening, betokening, betokenment, foreshowing, prefiguration, presigning [archaic], presignifying, presignification, preindication, indicant, indication, sign, token, type, promise, sign of the times; foreshadow, foreshadowing, shadow, adumbration.

.4 warning, forewarning, "warnings, and portents and evils imminent" [Shakespeare], handwriting on the wall, "mene, mene, tekel, upharsin" [Aramaic; Bible].

.5 harbinger, forerunner, precursor, messenger [archaic], herald, announcer, buccinator novi témporis [L]; presager, premonitor, foreshadower.

.6 (omens) bird of ill omen, owl, raven, stormy petrel, Mother Carey's chicken; gathering clouds, clouds on the horizon, dark or black clouds, angry clouds, storm clouds, thundercloud, thunderhead; black cat; broken mirror; rainbow; ring around the moon; shooting star; halcyon bird.

.7 ominousness, portentousness, portent, bodefulness, presagefulness, suggestiveness, significance, meaning 545; fatefulness, fatality, doomfulness, sinisterness, banefulness, balefulness, direness.

.8 inauspiciousness, unpropitiousness, unfavorableness, unfortunateness, unluckiness, ill-fatedness, ill-omenedness; fatality.

.9 auspiciousness, propitiousness, favorableness; luckiness, fortunateness, prosperousness, beneficence, benignity, benignancy, benevolence; brightness, cheerfulness, cheeriness; good omen, good auspices, auspicium melioris aevi [L].

.10 VERBS foreshow, presage; omen, be the omen of, auspicate [archaic]; foreshadow, shadow, adumbrate, shadow forth, cast

their shadows before; predict 543.9; have an intimation, have a hunch [informal].

.11 forebode, bode, portend, croak; threaten, menace, lower, look black; warn, forewarn; have a premonition or presentiment, apprehend, preapprehend.

.12 augur, hint, divine [archaic]; foretoken, preindicate, presignify, presign, presignal, pretypify, prefigure, betoken, token, typify, signify, mean 545.8, spell, indicate, point to, be a sign of.

.13 promise, suggest, hint, imply, give prospect of, make likely, give ground for expecting, raise expectation, lead one to expect, hold out hope, make fair promise, bid fair, stand fair to.

.14 herald, harbinger, forerun, run before; announce, proclaim, preannounce; give notice, notify.

.15 ADJS augured, foreshadowed, foreshown; indicated, signified; preindicated, prognosticated, foretokened, prefigured, pretypified, presignified, presigned [archaic]; presignaled; presaged; promised, threatened; predicted 543.14.

.16 premonitory, forewarning, augural, monitory, warning, presageful, presaging, foretokening, preindicative, indicative, prognostic, prognosticative, presignificant, prefigurative; significant, meaningful 545.10; foreshowing, foreshadowing; big or pregnant or heavy with meaning; forerunning, precursory, precursive; intuitive 481.5; predictive 543.11.

.17 ominous, portentous, portending; foreboding, boding, bodeful; inauspicious, ill-omened, ill-boding, of ill or fatal omen, of evil portent, loaded or laden or freighted or fraught with doom; fateful, doomful; apocalyptic; unpropitious, unpromising, unfavorable, unfortunate, unlucky; sinister, dark, black, gloomy, somber, dreary; threatening, menacing, lowering; bad, evil, ill, untoward; dire, baleful, baneful, ill-fated, ill-starred, evil-starred.

.18 auspicious, of good omen, of happy portent; propitious, favorable, favoring, fair, good; promising, of promise, full of promise; fortunate, lucky, prosperous; benign, benignant, bright, happy, golden.

.19 ADVS ominously, portentously, bodefully, forebodingly; significantly, sinisterly; threateningly, menacingly, loweringly.

.20 inauspiciously, unpropitiously, unpromisingly, unfavorably, unfortunately, unluckily.

.21 auspiciously, propitiously, promisingly, favorably; fortunately, luckily; brightly.

545. MEANING

.1 NOUNS **meaning, significance, signification**, *significatum* [L], *signifié* [Fr], **point, sense,** idea, **purport, import; implication, connotation,** reference, referent; intension, extension; **denotation;** dictionary meaning, lexical meaning; emotive *or* affective meaning, undertone, overtone, coloring; relevance, bearing, **relation,** pertinence; **substance, gist,** pith, spirit, essence; **drift,** tenor; sum, sum and substance; **literal meaning, true** *or* **real meaning, unadorned meaning; effect,** force, impact, consequence, practical consequence; totality of associations *or* references *or* relations, value; syntactic *or* structural meaning, grammatical meaning; symbolic meaning; metaphorical *or* transferred meaning; semantic field, semantic cluster; range *or* span of meaning, scope.

.2 **intent, intention, purpose, aim, object, design,** plan.

.3 **explanation, definition,** construction, **interpretation** 552.

.4 **acceptation,** acception, accepted *or* received meaning; **usage,** acceptance.

.5 **meaningfulness,** suggestiveness, expressiveness, pregnancy; **significance,** significancy, significantness; intelligibility, interpretability, readability; pithiness, meatiness, sententiousness.

.6 (units) **sign, symbol, signifiant, significant, type, token, icon, lexeme, sememe, morpheme, glosseme, word,** term, **phrase,** lexical form *or* item, semantic *or* semiotic *or* semasiological unit.

.7 **semantics,** semiotic, semiotics, **significs,** semasiology; lexicology.

.8 VERBS **mean, signify, denote, connote,** import, spell, have the sense of, be construed as, have the force of; **stand for, symbolize; imply,** suggest, argue, breathe, bespeak, betoken, **indicate; refer to.**

.9 **intend,** have in mind 653.7.

.10 ADJS **meaningful,** meaning, **significant,** significative; **denotative, connotative,** denotational, connotational, intensional, extensional, associational; **referential; symbolic, metaphorical,** figurative, allegorical; transferred, extended; intelligible, interpretable, definable, readable; **suggestive,** indicative, **expressive; pregnant,** full of meaning, loaded *or* laden *or* fraught *or* freighted *or* heavy with significance; **pithy, meaty,** sententious, **substantial,** full of substance; pointed, full of point.

.11 **meant,** implied 546.7, **intended** 653.9.

.12 **semantic,** semantological, semiotic, semasiological; lexologic(al); **symbolic, signific,** iconic, lexemic, sememic, glossematic, morphemic, **verbal,** phrasal, lexical.

.13 ADVS **meaningfully,** meaningly, **significantly;** suggestively, indicatively; **expressively.**

546. LATENT MEANINGFULNESS

.1 NOUNS latent meaningfulness, **latency,** latentness, delitescence, latent content; **potentiality,** virtuality, possibility; dormancy 268.4.

.2 **implication, connotation, import,** latent *or* underlying *or* implied meaning, ironic suggestion *or* implication; meaning 545; **suggestion,** allusion; coloration, tinge, undertone, overtone, undercurrent, more than meets the eye *or* ear, something between the lines, intimation, touch, nuance, innuendo, **hint** 557.4; **inference, supposition,** presupposition, assumption, presumption; secondary *or* transferred *or* metaphorical sense, undermeaning; subsidiary sense, subsense; hidden *or* esoteric *or* arcane meaning, occult meaning; **symbolism, allegory.**

.3 VERBS **be latent, underlie, lie under the surface, lurk,** lie hid *or* low, lie beneath, hibernate, lie dormant, smolder; make no sign, escape notice.

.4 **imply, implicate, involve,** import, connote, entail 76.4; mean 545.8; **suggest,** bring to mind; **hint, insinuate, infer, intimate** 557.10; **allude to,** point indirectly to; write between the lines; allegorize; **suppose, presuppose,** assume, presume, take for granted; mean to say *or* imply *or* suggest.

.5 ADJS **latent, lurking,** lying low, delitescent, **hidden** 615.11, obscured, obfuscated, veiled, muffled, covert, occult, mystic [archaic], cryptic; esoteric; **underlying, under the surface,** submerged; **between the lines;** hibernating, sleeping, dormant 268.14; **potential,** unmanifested, virtual, possible.

.6 **suggestive, allusive,** allusory, **indicative, inferential; insinuating,** insinuative, insinuatory; ironic; **implicative,** implicatory, implicational; referential.

.7 **implied,** implicated, involved; **meant,** indicated; **suggested, intimated, insinuated, hinted; inferred, supposed,** assumed, presumed, presupposed.

.8 **tacit, implicit, implied, understood,** taken for granted.

.9 unexpressed, unpronounced, **unsaid, unspoken, unuttered,** undeclared, unbreathed, unvoiced, wordless, silent; **unmentioned,** untalked-of, **untold,** unsung, unproclaimed, unpublished; unwritten, unrecorded.

.10 symbolic(al), allegoric(al), figurative, **metaphoric(al);** anagogic(al).

.11 ADVS **latently,** underlyingly; **potentially,** virtually.

.12 suggestively, allusively, **inferentially,** insinuatingly; impliedly.

.13 tacitly, **implicitly,** unspokenly, wordlessly, silently.

547. MEANINGLESSNESS

.1 NOUNS **meaninglessness,** unmeaningness, **senselessness,** nonsensicality; **insignificance,** unsignificancy; **noise,** mere noise, empty sound, talking to hear oneself talk, phatic communion; inanity, emptiness, nullity; "sounding brass and a tinkling cymbal" [Bible], "a tale told by an idiot, full of sound and fury, signifying nothing" [Shakespeare]; purposelessness, aimlessness, futility; dead letter.

.2 **nonsense, stuff and nonsense,** pack of nonsense, **folderol, balderdash,** *niaiserie* [Fr], flummery, trumpery, **rubbish,** trash, *narrishkeit* [Yid], vaporing, fudge; **humbug,** gammon, hocus-pocus; rant, claptrap, fustian, rodomontade, bombast, absurdity 470.3; stultiloquence, **twaddle,** twattle [Brit dial], twiddle-twaddle, fiddle-faddle, fiddledeedee, waffling [Brit], **blather, babble,** babblement, bibble-babble, **gabble,** gibble-gabble, **blabber, gibber, jabber,** prate, **prattle,** palaver, rigmarole *or* rigamarole, galimatias, skimble-skamble, drivel, drool; **gibberish,** jargon, mumbo jumbo, **double-talk,** amphigory, gobbledygook [informal].

.3 [slang terms] **bullshit, shit, crap, bull,** poppycock, bosh, bunkum, **bunk, guff,** gup [Brit], scat, bop, bilge, piffle, moonshine, flapdoodle, tommyrot, **rot, hogwash,** malarkey, hokum, hooey, bushwa, **blah** *or* blah-blah, baloney, tripe, **hot air,** gas, wind.

.4 VERBS **be meaningless, mean nothing,** signify nothing, not mean a thing, not convey anything; not register, not ring any bells.

.5 **talk nonsense, twaddle,** twattle [Brit dial], **piffle,** waffle [Brit], **blather, blabber, babble, gabble,** gibble-gabble, **jabber, gibber,** prate, **prattle,** rattle; talk through one's hat; gas, bull, **bullshit, throw the bull** [all slang]; **drivel,** vapor, drool, run off at the mouth.

.6 ADJS **meaningless, unmeaning, senseless,** purportless, importless, nondenotative, nonconnotative; **insignificant,** unsignificant; empty, inane, null; phatic, garbled, scrambled; **purposeless, aimless,** designless, **without rhyme or reason.**

.7 **nonsensical,** silly, poppycockish [informal]; **foolish, absurd** 470.8,10; twaddling, twaddly; rubbishy, trashy; skimble-skamble; Pickwickian.

.8 ADVS **meaninglessly,** unmeaningly, nondenotatively, nonconnotatively, **senselessly, nonsensically;** insignificantly, unsignificantly; **purposelessly,** aimlessly.

548. INTELLIGIBILITY

.1 NOUNS **intelligibility, comprehensibility, apprehensibility,** prehensibility, **understandability,** knowability, cognizability, scrutability, penetrability, fathomableness; recognizability, readability; articulateness.

.2 **clearness, clarity; plainness, distinctness,** explicitness, clear-cutness, definition; **lucidity,** limpidity, pellucidity, crystallinity, perspicuity, transpicuity, transparency; **simplicity,** straightforwardness, directness; unmistakableness, unequivocalness, unambiguousness; **coherence,** connectedness, consistency, structure; plain style, plain English, plain speech, unadorned style.

.3 legibility, decipherability, **readability.**

.4 VERBS **be understandable, make sense;** be plain *or* clear; **speak for itself,** tell its own tale, speak volumes, have no secrets, put up no barriers; read easily [informal].

.5 (be understood) **get over** *or* **across** [informal], come through, **register** [informal], **penetrate, sink in,** soak in; dawn on, be glimpsed.

.6 **make clear,** make it clear, **let it be understood,** make oneself understood, get *or* put over *or* across [informal]; **simplify,** put in plain words *or* plain English, put in words of one syllable, spell out [informal]; elucidate, **explain,** explicate, **clarify** 552.10; put one in the picture [Brit]; make available to all, popularize, vulgarize.

.7 **understand, comprehend, apprehend,** have, **know, conceive, realize,** appreciate, ken [Scot], savvy [slang], sense, **read,** dig [slang], **fathom, follow,** get the idea, be with one *or* with it [informal], get the picture [informal], get into *or* through one's head or thick head [informal]; grasp, seize, get hold of, grasp or seize the meaning, get [slang], take, take in, catch, catch on [informal], get the meaning of, get the hang of, catch or get the drift [informal]; master, learn, have it taped [Brit informal], assimilate, absorb, digest.

.8 perceive, see, discern, make out, descry; see the light, see daylight [informal], come alive; see through, see to the bottom of, penetrate, see into, pierce, plumb; see at a glance, see with half an eye.

.9 ADJS intelligible, comprehensible, apprehensible, prehensible, knowable, cognizable, scrutable, fathomable, plumbable, penetrable; understandable, easily understood, easy to understand, exoteric; readable; articulate.

.10 clear, crystal-clear, clear as crystal, clear as day, clear as the nose on one's face; plain, distinct; definite, defined, well-defined, clear-cut, clean-cut, crisp; direct, simple, straightforward; explicit, express; unmistakable, unequivocal, univocal, unambiguous, unconfused; loud and clear; lucid, pellucid, limpid, crystalline, perspicuous, transpicuous, transparent, translucent, luminous; coherent, connected, consistent.

.11 legible, decipherable, readable, fair; uncoded, unenciphered, in the clear.

.12 ADVS intelligibly, understandably, comprehensibly, apprehensibly; articulately; clearly, lucidly, limpidly, pellucidly, perspicuously, simply, plainly, distinctly, definitely; coherently; explicitly, expressly; unmistakably, unequivocally, unambiguously; in plain terms or words, in plain English, in no uncertain terms.

.13 legibly, decipherably, readably, fairly.

549. UNINTELLIGIBILITY

.1 NOUNS unintelligibility, incomprehensibility, inapprehensibility, ununderstandability, unknowability, incognizability, inscrutability, impenetrability, unfathomableness, unsearchableness, numinousness; incoherence, unconnectedness, ramblingness; inarticulateness; ambiguity 550.

.2 abstruseness, reconditeness; crabbedness, crampedness, knottiness; complexity, intricacy, complication 46.1; hardness, difficulty; profundity, profoundness, deepness; esoterica.

.3 obscurity, obscuration, obscurantism, obfuscation, mumbo jumbo [informal], mystification; perplexity; unclearness,

unclarity, unplainness, opacity; vagueness, indistinctness, indeterminateness, fuzziness, shapelessness, amorphousness; murkiness, murk, mistiness, mist, fogginess, fog, darkness, dark.

.4 illegibility, unreadability; undecipherability, indecipherability; scribble, scrawl.

.5 unexpressiveness, inexpressiveness, expressionlessness, impassivity; straight face, dead pan [slang], poker face [informal].

.6 inexplicability, unexplainableness, uninterpretability, indefinability, undefinability, unaccountableness; insolvability, inextricability; enigmaticalness, mysteriousness, mystery.

.7 (something unintelligible) Greek, Choctaw, double Dutch; gibberish, babble, jargon, gobbledygook, noise, Babel; scramble, jumble, garble; argot, cant, slang, secret language, Aesopian language, code, cipher, cryptogram; glossolalia, gift of tongues.

.8 enigma, mystery, puzzle, puzzlement; Chinese puzzle, crossword puzzle, jigsaw puzzle; problem, puzzling or baffling problem, why; question, question mark, vexed or perplexed question, enigmatic question, sixty-four dollar question [informal]; perplexity; knot, knotty point, crux, point to be solved; puzzler, poser, brain twister or teaser [informal], sticker [slang]; mind-boggler, floorer or stumper [all informal]; nut to crack, hard or tough nut to crack; tough proposition [informal], "a perfect nonplus and baffle to all human understanding" [Southey].

.9 riddle, conundrum, charade, rebus; logogriph, anagram; riddle of the Sphinx.

.10 VERBS be incomprehensible, not make sense, be too deep, go over one's head, be beyond one, beat one [informal], elude or escape one, lose one, need explanation or clarification or translation, be Greek to, pass comprehension or understanding, not penetrate; baffle, perplex 514.13, riddle, be sphinxlike, speak in riddles; speak in tongues; talk double Dutch, babble, gibber.

.11 not understand, be unable to comprehend, not have the first idea, be unable to get into or through one's head or thick skull; be out of one's depth, be at sea, be lost; not know what to make of, make nothing of, not be able to account for, not be able to make head or tail of; be unable to see, not see the wood for the trees; give up, pass [informal].

.12 make unintelligible, scramble, jumble,

garble; **obscure,** obfuscate, mystify, shadow; **complicate** 46.3.

.13 ADJS **unintelligible, incomprehensible,** in-apprehensible, **ununderstandable,** un-knowable, incognizable; **unfathomable, inscrutable,** impenetrable, unsearchable, numinous; **ambiguous** 550.3; **incoherent,** unconnected, rambling; **inarticulate; past comprehension,** beyond one's comprehension, beyond understanding; Greek to one.

.14 **hard to understand, difficult, hard,** tough [informal], beyond one, **over one's head,** beyond or out of one's depth; knotty, cramp, crabbed; intricate, **complex,** over-technical, perplexed, **complicated** 46.4; **scrambled,** jumbled, **garbled; obscure,** obscured, obfuscated.

.15 **obscure, vague, indistinct,** indeterminate, fuzzy, shapeless, amorphous; unclear, unplain, opaque, muddy, **clear as mud** or clear as ditch water [both informal]; **dark,** dim, blind [archaic], shadowy; **murky,** cloudy, foggy, hazy, misty, nebulous; transcendent.

.16 **recondite, abstruse,** abstract, transcendental; **profound, deep; hidden** 615.11; arcane, **esoteric,** occult; **secret** 614.11.

.17 **enigmatic(al),** cryptic(al); sphinxlike; **perplexing, puzzling** 514.25; riddling, logogriphic.

.18 **inexplicable, unexplainable,** uninterpretable, undefinable, indefinable, **unaccountable; insolvable,** unsolvable, insoluble, inextricable; mysterious, **mystic(al),** shrouded or wrapped or enwrapped in mystery.

.19 **illegible, unreadable, unclear; undecipherable,** indecipherable.

.20 **inexpressive,** unexpressive, impassive; **expressionless; vacant, empty, blank;** glassy, fishy, wooden; deadpan, poker-faced [informal].

.21 ADVS **unintelligibly, incomprehensibly,** inapprehensibly, ununderstandably.

.22 **obscurely, vaguely, indistinctly,** indeterminately; **unclearly,** unplainly; illegibly.

.23 **reconditely, abstrusely;** esoterically, occultly.

.24 **inexplicably, unexplainably,** undefinably, **unaccountably, enigmatically; mysteriously,** mystically.

.25 **expressionlessly, vacantly, blankly, emptily,** woodenly, glassily, fishily.

.26 PREPS **beyond,** past, above; **too deep for.**

.27 PHRS **I don't understand, I can't see, I** don't see how or why, **it beats me** [informal], **you've got me** [informal], **it's be-**yond me, it's too deep for me, it has me guessing, I don't have the first idea, it's Greek to me; **I give up, I pass** [informal].

550. AMBIGUITY

.1 NOUNS **ambiguity,** ambiguousness; **equivocalness,** equivocacy, equivocality; **double meaning,** amphibology, multivocality, polysemy, polysemousness; punning, paronomasia; **double reference,** double entendre; **uncertainty** 514; irony; **levels of meaning,** richness of meaning, complexity of meaning.

.2 (ambiguous word or expression) **ambiguity,** equivoque, equivocal, equivocality; equivocation, amphibology, **double entendre;** counterword, portmanteau word; polysemant; **weasel word;** squinting construction; **pun** 881.8.

.3 ADJS **ambiguous, equivocal,** equivocatory; multivocal, polysemous, polysemantic, amphibolous, amphibological; **uncertain** 514.15; ironic; **obscure,** mysterious, enigmatic 549.14–18.

551. FIGURE OF SPEECH

.1 NOUNS **figure of speech, figure, image,** trope, turn of expression, manner or way of speaking, ornament, device, flourish, flower; purple passage; imagery, nonliterality, nonliteralness, figurativeness, figurative language; figured or florid or flowery style, asiaticism, floridity, euphuism.

.2 VERBS **metaphorize,** figure [archaic]; similize; personify, personalize; **symbolize** 572.6.

.3 ADJS **figurative,** tropological; **metaphorical,** trolatitious; allusive, referential; mannered, figured, ornamented, **flowery** 601.11.

.4 ADVS **figuratively,** tropologically; **metaphorically;** symbolically; **figuratively speaking,** so to say or speak, in a manner of speaking, **as it were.**

.5 figures of speech

agnomination	catachresis
alliteration	chiasmus
allusion	circumlocution
anacoluthon	climax
anadiplosis	conversion
analogy	ecphonesis
anaphora	emphasis
anastrophe	enallage
antiphrasis	epanaphora
antithesis	epanodos
antonomasia	epanorthosis
apophasis	epidiplosis
aporia	epiphora
aposiopesis	eroteme
apostrophe	exclamation

gemination
hendiadys
hypallage
hyperbaton
hyperbole
hypozeugma
hypozeuxis
hysteron-proteron
inversion
irony
kenning
litotes
malapropism
meiosis
metalepsis
metaphor
metonymy
onomatopoeia, ono-
　matopy
oxymoron
paradiastole
paralepsis

paregmenon
parenthesis
periphrasis
personification
pleonasm
ploce
polyptoton
polysyndeton
preterition
prolepsis
prosopopoeia
regression
repetition
rhetorical question
sarcasm
simile, similitude
spoonerism
syllepsis
symploce
synecdoche
Wellerism
zeugma

552. INTERPRETATION

.1 NOUNS interpretation, construction, reading, way of seeing or understanding or putting; diagnosis; definition, description; meaning 545.

.2 rendering, rendition; text, edited text, diplomatic text, normalized text; version; reading, lection, variant, variant reading; edition, critical or scholarly edition; conflation, composite reading or text.

.3 translation, transcription, transliteration; paraphrase, loose or free translation; decipherment, decoding; amplification, restatement, rewording; metaphrase, literal or verbal or faithful or word-for-word translation; pony or trot or crib [all informal]; interlinear, interlinear translation, bilingual text or edition; gloss, glossary; key, clavis [L].

.4 explanation, explication, elucidation, illumination, enlightenment, light, clarification, éclaircissement [Fr], simplification; exposition, expounding, exegesis; illustration, demonstration, exemplification; reason, rationale; euhemerism, demythologization, allegorization; decipherment, decoding, cracking, unlocking, solution 487; editing, emendation.

.5 (explanatory remark) comment, word of explanation; annotation, notation, note, note of explanation, footnote, gloss, scholium; exegesis; apparatus criticus [L]; commentary, commentation [archaic].

.6 interpretability, construability; definability, describability; translatability; explicability, explainableness, accountableness.

.7 interpreter, exegete, exegetist, exegesist, hermeneut; commentator, annotator, scholiast; critic, textual critic, editor, dia-

skeuast, emender, emendator; cryptographer, cryptologist, decoder, decipherer, cryptanalyst; explainer, lexicographer, definer, explicator, exponent, expositor, expounder, clarifier; demonstrator, euhemerist, demythologizer, allegorist; go-between 781.4; translator, metaphrast, paraphrast; oneirocritic; guide, cicerone [Ital], dragoman.

.8 (science of interpretation) exegetics, hermeneutics; tropology; criticism, literary criticism, textual criticism; paleography, epigraphy; cryptology, cryptography, cryptanalysis; lexicography; diagnostics, symptomatology, semeiology, semeiotics; pathognomy; physiognomics, physiognomy; metoposcopy; oneirology, oneirocriticism.

.9 VERBS interpret, diagnose; construe, put a construction on, take; understand, understand by, take to mean, take it that; read; read into, read between the lines; see in a special light, read in view of, take an approach to, define, describe.

.10 explain, explicate, expound, exposit; give the meaning, tell the meaning of; spell out, unfold; account for, give reason for; clarify, elucidate, clear up, make clear, make plain; simplify, popularize; illuminate, enlighten, shed or throw light upon; rationalize, euhemerize, demythologize, allegorize; tell or show how, show the way; demonstrate, show, illustrate, exemplify; decipher, crack, unlock, find the key to, unravel, solve 487.2; explain oneself; explain away.

.11 comment upon, commentate, remark upon; annotate, gloss; edit, make an edition.

.12 translate, render, transcribe, transliterate, put or turn into, transfuse the sense of; construe; English.

.13 paraphrase, rephrase, reword, restate, rehash; give a free or loose translation.

.14 ADJS interpretative, interpretive, interpretational, exegetic(al), hermeneutic(al); constructive, constructional; diagnostic; symptomatological, semeiological; tropological; definitional, descriptive.

.15 explanatory, explaining, exegetic(al), explicative, explicatory; expository, expositive; clarifying, elucidative; illuminating, illuminative, enlightening; demonstrative, illustrative, exemplificative; glossarial, annotative, critical, editorial, scholiastic; rationalizing, rationalistic, euhemeristic, demythologizing, allegorizing.

.16 **translational,** translative; paraphrastic, metaphrastic.

.17 **interpretable, construable; definable,** describable; translatable, renderable; Englishable [archaic]; explainable, explicable, accountable.

.18 ADVS **by interpretation,** as here interpreted, as here defined, according to this reading; **in explanation, to explain; that is,** that is to say, *id est* [L], i.e.; **to wit, namely,** *videlicet* [L], viz., *scilicet* [L], sc.; **in other words,** in words to that effect.

553. MISINTERPRETATION

.1 NOUNS **misinterpretation, misunderstanding,** *malentendu* [Fr], misintelligence, **misapprehension, misreading, misconstruction,** malobservation, **misconception; misrendering,** mistranslation, eisegesis; misexplanation, misexplication, misexposition; misapplication; gloss; **perversion, distortion,** wrenching, twisting, contorting, torturing, squeezing, garbling; abuse of terms, misuse of words, catachresis; misquotation, miscitation; "blunders round about a meaning" [Pope]; misjudgment 496; **error** 518.

.2 VERBS **misinterpret, misunderstand,** misconceive, **mistake, misapprehend; misread, misconstrue,** put a false construction on, **take wrong, get wrong,** get one wrong; misapply; **misexplain,** misexplicate, misexpound; **misrender,** mistranslate; quote out of context; **misquote,** miscite, give a false coloring, give a false impression *or* idea, gloss; **garble, pervert, distort,** wrench, contort, torture, squeeze, twist the words *or* meaning, stretch *or* strain the sense *or* meaning, misdeem, **misjudge** 496.2.

.3 ADJS **misinterpreted, misunderstood, mistaken, misapprehended, misread,** eisegetical, **misconceived, misconstrued;** garbled, perverted, distorted, catachrestic(al).

.4 **misinterpretable, misunderstandable,** mistakable.

554. COMMUNICATION

.1 NOUNS **communication,** communion, congress, **commerce, intercourse; speaking, speech, talking,** linguistic intercourse, speech situation, speech circuit, converse, **conversation** 597; **contact, touch, connection; intercommunication,** intercommunion, **interplay,** interaction; **exchange,** interchange; answer, response, reply; one-way communication, two-way communication; **dealings,** dealing, **traffic, truck**

[informal]; **information** 557; **message** 558.4; ESP, telepathy 1034.8,9; **correspondence** 604; social intercourse 922.4.

.2 **impartation,** impartment, imparting, **conveyance, telling, transmission,** transmittal, transfer, transference, sharing, giving; notification, **announcement** 559.2, publication 559, **disclosure** 556.

.3 **communicativeness, talkativeness** 596, **sociability** 922; **unreserve,** unreservedness, **unreticence, unrestraint, unconstraint,** unrestriction; **unrepression,** unsuppression; **unsecretiveness,** untaciturnity; **candor, frankness** 974.4; **openness,** plainness, freeness, **outspokenness,** plainspokenness; **accessibility,** approachability, **conversableness; extroversion,** outgoingness.

.4 **communicability, impartability, conveyability, transmittability,** transmissibility, transferability; **contagiousness** 686.3.

.5 **communications,** electronic communications, communications industry, media, communications medium *or* media, communications network; **telecommunication** 560.1–3; radiocommunication, wire communication; communication *or* information theory 557.7.

.6 VERBS **communicate, be in touch** *or* **contact, be in connection** *or* intercourse, have intercourse, hold communication; **intercommunicate,** interchange, commune with; commerce with, **deal with, traffic with, have dealings with, have truck with** [informal]; **speak, talk,** be in a speech situation, **converse** 597.9.

.7 **communicate, impart,** render, **convey, transmit,** transfer, send, **disseminate,** broadcast, pass, **pass on** *or* **along, hand on; report, make known, get** across *or* over; give *or* send *or* leave word; **signal;** share, share with; **give** 818.12; **tell** 557.8.

.8 **communicate with, get in touch** *or* **contact with, contact** [informal], **make contact with,** raise, reach, get to, make *or* establish connection, get in connection with; **make advances,** make overtures, **approach,** make up to [informal]; relate to; keep in touch *or* contact with, maintain connection; **answer,** respond *or* reply to; **question, interrogate; correspond** 604.11.

.9 ADJS **communicational, communicating, communional; transmissional; speech, verbal,** linguistic, oral; **conversational** 597.13; **intercommunicational,** intercommunicative, intercommunional, interactional, interactive, interacting, interresponsive, responsive, answering; questioning, interrogative, interrogatory; tele-pathic 1034.23.

.10 communicative, talkative 596.9, gossipy, newsy; sociable 922.18; unreserved, unreticent, unshrinking, unrestrained, unconstrained, unhampered, unrestricted; demonstrative, expansive, effusive; unrepressed, unsuppressed; unsecretive, unsilent, untaciturn; candid, frank 974.17; self-revealing, self-revelatory; open, free, outspoken, free-speaking, free-spoken, free-tongued; accessible, approachable, conversable, easy to speak to; extroverted, outgoing.

.11 communicable, impartable, conveyable, transmittable, transmissible, transferable; contagious 686.58.

555. MANIFESTATION

.1 NOUNS manifestation, appearance, –phany; expression, evincement; indication, evidence, proof 505; embodiment, incarnation, materialization 376.7; epiphany, theophany, angelophany, Satanophany, Christophany, pneumatophany, avatar; revelation, disclosure 556; dissemination, publication 559.

.2 display, demonstration, show, showing, phen(o)– or phaeno–; presentation, presentment, ostentation [archaic], exhibition, exhibit, exposition, retrospective; production, performance, representation, enactment, projection; opening, unfolding, unfoldment; unveiling, exposure, varnishing day, vernissage [Fr].

.3 manifestness, apparentness, obviousness, plainness, clearness, crystal-clearness, perspicuity, distinctness, patentness, palpability, tangibility; evidentness, evidence [archaic], self-evidence; openness, openness to sight, overtness; visibility 444; unmistakableness, unquestionability 513.3.

.4 conspicuousness, prominence, salience or saliency, bold or high or strong relief, boldness, noticeability, pronouncedness, strikingness, outstandingness; obtrusiveness; flagrance or flagrancy, arrantness, blatancy, notoriousness, notoriety; ostentation 904.

.5 VERBS manifest, show, exhibit, demonstrate, display, breathe, unfold, develop, present, represent [archaic], evince, evidence; indicate, give sign or token, token, betoken, mean 545.8; express, show forth, set forth; make plain, make clear; produce, bring out, roll out, trot out [informal], bring forth, bring forward or to the front, bring to notice, expose to view,

bring to or into view; reveal, divulge, disclose 556.4; illuminate, highlight, spotlight, bring to the fore, place in the foreground, bring out in bold or strong or high relief; flaunt, dangle, wave, flourish, brandish, parade; affect, make a show of; perform, enact, dramatize; embody, incarnate, materialize 376.8.

.6 (manifest oneself) come out into the open, come forth; show one's colors or true colors, wear one's heart upon one's sleeve; speak up, speak out, raise one's voice, assert oneself, let one's voice be heard, stand up and be counted, take a stand; open up, show one's mind, have no secrets; appear, materialize.

.7 be manifest, be there for all to see, be no secret or revelation, lie on the surface, be seen with half an eye; need no explanation, speak for itself, tell its own story or tale; go without saying, aller sans dire [Fr]; leap to the eye, sauter aux yeux [Fr], stare one in the face, hit one in the eye, strike the eye, glare, shout; come across, project; stand out, stick out, stick out a mile, stick out like a sore thumb, hang out [slang].

.8 ADJS manifest, apparent, evident, self-evident, axiomatic, indisputable, obvious, plain, clear, perspicuous, distinct, palpable, patent, tangible; visible, perceptible, perceivable, discernible, seeable, observable, noticeable; to be seen, easy to be seen, plain to be seen; plain as day, plain as the nose on one's face, plain as a pikestaff; crystal-clear, clear as crystal; express, explicit, unmistakable, not to be mistaken, open-and-shut [informal]; self-explanatory, self-explaining; indubitable 513.15.

.9 manifesting, manifestative, showing, displaying, demonstrating, demonstrative, presentational, expository, expositional, exhibitive, exhibitional, expressive; evincive, evidential; indicative, indicatory; appearing, incarnating, incarnational, materializing; epiphanic, theophanic, angelophanic; Satanophanic, Christophanic, pneumatophanic; revelational, revelatory, disclosive 556.10; promulgatory 559.18.

.10 open, overt, open to all, open as day; unclassified; revealed, disclosed, exposed; bare, bald, naked.

.11 unhidden, unconcealed, unscreened, uncurtained, unshaded, veilless; unobscure, unobscured, undarkened, unclouded; undisguised, uncamouflaged.

.12 conspicuous, noticeable, notable, ostensible, **prominent**, **bold**, **pronounced**, **salient**, in relief, in bold or high or strong relief, **striking**, **outstanding**, in the foreground, sticking or hanging out [slang]; obtrusive; **flagrant**, arrant, blatant, notorious; **glaring**, staring, stark-staring.

.13 **manifested**, demonstrated, exhibited, shown, displayed; **manifestable**, demonstrable, exhibitable, displayable.

.14 ADVS **manifestly**, **apparently**, **evidently**, **obviously**, **patently**, **plainly**, **clearly**, distinctly, **unmistakably**, expressly, explicitly, palpably, tangibly; **visibly**, **perceptibly**, perceivably, discernibly, observably, **noticeably**.

.15 **openly**, **overtly**, before one, **before one's eyes** or very eyes, under one's nose [informal]; to one's face, face to face; **publicly**, in public; **in the open**, out in the open, in open court, **in plain sight**, in broad daylight, in the face of day or heaven, for all to see, in public view, in plain view, in the marketplace; aboveboard, on the table.

.16 **conspicuously**, **prominently**, **noticeably**, ostensibly, **notably**, **markedly**, **pronouncedly**, **saliently**, **strikingly**, **boldly**, **outstandingly**; obtrusively; arrantly, flagrantly, blatantly, notoriously; glaringly, staringly.

556. DISCLOSURE

.1 NOUNS **disclosure**, disclosing; **revelation**, revealment, revealing, patefaction [archaic]; apocalypse; discovery, discovering; manifestation 555; unfolding, unfoldment, **uncovering**, unwrapping, uncloaking, taking the wraps off, taking from under wraps, removing the veil, unveiling, **unmasking**; **exposure**, exposition, **exposé**; **baring**, stripping, stripping or laying bare; **showing up**, showup.

.2 **divulgence**, **divulging**, divulgement, divulgation, evulgation, letting out [Brit]; **betrayal**, unwitting disclosure, indiscretion; leak, communication leak; **giveaway** or dead giveaway [both informal]; telltale, telltale sign, obvious clue; **blabbing** or blabbering [both informal], babbling; **tattling**.

.3 **confession**, shrift, **acknowledgment**, **admission**, concession, avowal, owning, owning up [informal], unbosoming, unburdening oneself, making a clean breast; rite of confession 1040.4.

.4 VERBS **disclose**, **reveal**, **let out**, **show**, impart, discover, develop [both archaic]; manifest 555.5; unfold, unroll; **open**, open up, lay open, break the seal, bring into the open; **expose**, **show up**; **bare**, strip or lay bare; take the lid off, **bring to light**, hold up to view; hold up the mirror to; **unmask**, dismask, tear off the mask, **uncover**, unveil, take out from under wraps, take the wraps off, lift or draw the veil, raise the curtain, let daylight in, unscreen, uncloak, undrape, unshroud, unfurl, unsheathe, unwrap, unpack, unkennel; show one's hand or cards, put or lay one's cards on the table.

.5 **divulge**, divulgate, evulgate; **reveal**, **make known**, **tell**, breathe, utter, vent, ventilate, air, give vent to, **give out**, **let out** [Brit], let get around, out with [informal], come out with; break it to, **break the news**; let in on or to, **confide**, confide to, let into the secret; **publish** 559.10,11.

.6 **betray**, inform, **inform on** 557.12, talk or peach [both informal], rat or stool or sing or squeal [all slang], turn state's evidence; leak [informal], spill [slang], **spill the beans** [informal]; **let the cat out of the bag** [informal], speak before one thinks, be unguarded or indiscreet, **give away** or give the show away [both informal], betray a confidence, tell secrets, reveal a secret; have a big mouth or bazoo [slang], **blab** or blabber [both informal]; babble, **tattle**, tell or tattle on, tell tales, **tell tales out of school**; talk out of turn, let slip, let fall or drop; **blurt**, **blurt out**.

.7 **confess**, break down and confess, **admit**, **acknowledge**, allow, avow, concede, grant, **own**, **own up** [informal], let on, implicate or incriminate oneself, come clean [slang]; spill or spill it or spill one's guts [all slang]; **tell the truth**, tell all, admit everything, let it all hang out [informal], throw off all disguise; **plead guilty**, own oneself in the wrong, cop a plea [slang]; **unbosom oneself**, **make a clean breast**, **get it off one's chest** [informal], **get it out of one's system** [informal], disburden or unburden one's mind or conscience or heart, **take the load off one's mind**; out with it or spit it out or open up [all informal].

.8 **be revealed**, **become known**, **come to light**, appear, manifest itself, come to one's ears, transpire, **leak out**, **get out**, **come out**, out, break forth, show its face; show its colors, be seen in its true colors, stand revealed, blow one's cover [slang].

.9 ADJS **revealed**, **disclosed** 555.10.

.10 **disclosive**, **revealing**, revelatory, revelational, apocalyptic(al); **disclosing**, showing, exposing, betraying; eye-opening; talkative 554.10, 596.9.

.11 confessional, admissive.

557. INFORMATION

.1 NOUNS **information**, info [informal], **facts, datum** [sing], **data, knowledge** 475; general information, gen [Brit informal]; factual information, hard information; **evidence, proof** 505; **enlightenment,** light; incidental information, sidelight; **acquaintance,** familiarization, briefing; **instruction** 562.1; **intelligence;** the know or the dope or the goods or the scoop [all slang]; transmission, **communication** 554; **report, word,** message, presentation, account, **statement,** mention; white paper, white book, blue book, command paper [Brit]; dispatch, bulletin, communiqué, handout [informal], release; publicity, promotional material; **notice,** notification; announcement, publication 559; directory, guidebook 748.10.

.2 **inside information,** private or confidential information; the lowdown or inside dope or inside wire or hot tip [all slang]; insider; pipeline [informal].

.3 **tip** or **tip-off** or **pointer** [all informal], clue, cue; steer or office [both slang]; **advice;** whisper, passing word, **word to the wise,** word in the ear, bug in the ear [informal]; warning, caution, monition, alerting.

.4 **hint,** gentle hint, **intimation, indication, suggestion, suspicion,** inkling, whisper, **glimmer, glimmering; cue, clue,** index, symptom, sign, spoor, track, scent, telltale; **implication, insinuation, innuendo;** broad hint, gesture, signal, nod, wink, look, nudge, kick, prompt.

.5 **informant, informer, source,** teller, interviewee, enlightener; **adviser,** monitor; **reporter,** notifier, **announcer,** annunciator; spokesman, mouthpiece; communicator, communicant, publisher; **authority,** witness, expert witness; **tipster** [informal], **tout** [slang]; newsmonger, gossipmonger; **information medium** or **media,** press, radio, television; channel, grapevine; information center; public relations officer.

.6 **informer, betrayer,** delator; **snitch** or snitcher [both slang]; whistle-blower [informal]; **tattler, tattletale, telltale, talebearer; blab** or blabber or blabberer or blabbermouth [all informal]; **squealer** or peacher or **stool pigeon** or stoolie or **fink** or narc [all slang]; **spy** 781.9.

.7 information or communication theory; data storage or retrieval, EDP, electronic data processing; signal, noise; encoding, decoding; bit; redundancy, entropy; channel; information or communication explosion.

.8 VERBS **inform, tell, speak, apprize, advise, advertise,** advertise of, **give word,** mention to, **acquaint, enlighten,** familiarize, brief, verse, wise up [slang], give the facts, give an account of, give by way of information; **instruct** 562.11; possess or seize one of the facts; **let know, have one to know, give one to understand;** tell once and for all; notify, give notice or notification, serve notice; **communicate** 554.6,7; bring or send or leave word; **report** 558.11; **disclose** 556.4–7; put in a new light, shed new or fresh light upon.

.9 **post** or **keep one posted** [both informal]; fill one in, bring up to date, put one in the picture [Brit].

.10 **hint, intimate, suggest, insinuate, imply, indicate,** adumbrate, lead or leave one to gather, justify one in supposing, give or drop or throw out a hint, give an inkling of, **hint at; allude to,** make an allusion to, glance at [archaic]; **prompt,** give the cue; put in or into one's head.

.11 **tip** or **tip off** or **give one a tip** [all informal], alert; **give a pointer to** [informal]; put hep or hip [slang], **let in on,** let in on the know [slang]; let next to or put next to or **put on to** or put on to something hot [all slang]; **confide,** confide to, entrust with information, give confidential information, mention privately or confidentially, whisper, buzz, breathe, whisper in the ear, **put a bug in one's ear** [informal].

.12 **inform on** or **against, tell on** [informal], **betray;** tattle, blab [informal]; **snitch** or squeal or peach or sell out or rat or stool or fink or narc or put the finger on or snitch on or squeal on [all slang]; turn informer; blow the whistle [informal]; testify against, **bear witness against;** turn state's evidence, turn king's or queen's evidence [Brit].

.13 come to know, have it reported, get the facts, **get wise to** [informal], **get hep to** or **next to** or **on to** [all slang]; learn; become conscious or aware of, become alive or awake to, awaken to, open one's eyes to.

.14 be informed or apprised, have the facts; **come to one's knowledge,** come to or reach one's ears; be told, hear, overhear, hear tell of or hear say [both informal];

get scent *or* wind of; **know** 475.12; **know well** 475.13.

.15 **keep informed,** keep posted [informal], stay briefed, **keep up on,** keep up to date *or* au courant, keep abreast of the times; **keep track of,** keep count *or* account of, keep tab *or* tabs on [informal], keep a check on, keep an eye on.

.16 ADJS informed 475.18–20; informed of, in the know 475.16.

.17 informative, informing, informational; **instructive, enlightening;** educative, educational 562.19; advisory, monitory; **communicative** 554.11.

.18 telltale, tattletale.

.19 ADVS from information received, according to reports *or* rumor, from notice given, as a matter of general information, by common report, from what one can gather.

558. NEWS

.1 NOUNS news, tidings, intelligence, information, word, advice; newsiness [informal]; newsworthiness; a nose for news; journalism, reportage; the press, the fourth estate, broadcast journalism; news medium *or* media, newspaper, newsletter, newsmagazine, radio, television, press association, news service, news agency, wire service, telegraph agency.

.2 good news, good word, glad tidings; gospel, evangel; bad news.

.3 news item, piece *or* budget of news; article, story, piece; copy; scoop *or* beat [both slang], exclusive; spot news.

.4 message, dispatch, word, communication, communiqué, advice, release; express [Brit]; embassy, embassage [archaic]; letter 604.2; telegram 560.14; pneumatogram, *petit bleu* [Fr].

.5 bulletin, news report, flash.

.6 report, rumor, flying rumor, unverified *or* unconfirmed report, hearsay, *on-dit* [Fr], scuttlebutt *or* latrine rumor [both informal]; talk, whisper, buzz, rumble, bruit, cry; idea afloat, news stirring; common talk, town talk, talk of the town, topic of the day, *cause célèbre* [Fr]; grapevine; canard, roorback.

.7 gossip, gossiping, gossipry, gossipmongering, back-fence gossip [informal], newsmongering; talebearing, taletelling; tattle, tittle-tattle, chitchat, talk, idle talk; "putting two and two together, and making it five" [Pascal]; piece of gossip, groundless rumor, tale, story.

.8 scandal, dirt [informal], malicious gossip, "gossip made tedious by morality" [Oscar Wilde]; juicy morsel, tidbit, choice bit of dirt [informal]; scandalmongering; gossip column; character assassination, slander 971.3; whispering campaign.

.9 newsmonger, rumormonger, scandalmonger, gossip, gossipmonger, gossiper, *yenta* [Yid], quidnunc, busybody, tabby [informal]; talebearer, taleteller, telltale, tattletale [informal], tattler, tittle-tattler, "a tale-bearing animal" [J. Harrington]; gossip columnist; reporter, newspaperman 605.22.

.10 (secret news channel) grapevine, grapevine telegraph, bush telegraph [Austral]; pipeline.

.11 VERBS report, give a report, give an account of, tell, relate, rehearse [archaic]; write up, make out *or* write up a report; bring word, tell the news, break the news, give tidings of; bring glad tidings, give the good word; announce 559.12; rumor 559.10; inform 557.8.

.12 gossip, talk over the back fence [informal]; tattle, tittle-tattle; clatter [Scot], talk; retail gossip, dish the dirt [informal], tell idle tales.

.13 ADJS newsworthy, front-page, with news value, newsy.

.14 gossipy, gossiping, newsy; talebearing, taletelling.

.15 reported, rumored, whispered; rumored about, talked about, whispered about, bruited about, bandied about; in the news, in circulation, in the air, going around, going about, current, rife, afloat, in every one's mouth, on all tongues, all over the town; made public 559.17.

.16 ADVS as they say, as it is said, as the story goes *or* runs, as the fellow says [informal], it is said.

559. PUBLICATION

.1 NOUNS publication, publishing, promulgation, evulgation, propagation, dissemination, diffusion, broadcast, broadcasting, spread, spreading, spreading abroad, circulation, ventilation, airing, noising, bandying, bruiting, bruiting about; display; issue, issuance; telecasting, videocasting; printing 603; book, periodical 605.

.2 announcement, annunciation, enunciation; proclamation, pronouncement, pronunciamento; report, communiqué, declaration, statement; program, programma, notice, notification, public notice; circular, encyclical, encyclical letter; manifesto, position paper; white paper, white book; ukase, edict 752.4; bulletin board.

.3 **press release,** release, handout, bulletin, notice.

.4 **publicity, publicness,** notoriety, **fame,** famousness, **celebrity,** *réclame, éclat* [both Fr]; **limelight** or **spotlight** [both informal], daylight, bright light, glare, **public eye** or consciousness, **exposure, currency,** common or public knowledge, widest or maximum dissemination; **ballyhoo** or hoopla [both slang]; report, public report; cry, hue and cry; **public relations, PR; publicity story,** press notice; **write-up, puff** [informal], **plug** [slang], **blurb** [informal].

.5 **promotion, buildup** [informal], flack [informal], publicization, publicizing, promoting, advocating, advocacy, bruiting, drumbeating, tub-thumping, press-agentry; **advertising,** salesmanship 829.2, advertising campaign; advertising agency; advertising medium or media.

.6 **advertisement, ad** [informal], notice; **commercial,** message, important message, message from the sponsor; spot commercial or spot, network commercial; reader, reading notice; display ad; want ad [informal], classified ad; spread, two-page spread; testimonial.

.7 **poster, bill, placard, sign,** show card, banner, *affiche* [Fr]; **signboard, billboard,** highway sign, hoarding [Brit]; sandwich board; marquee.

.8 **advertising matter,** promotional material, public relations handout or release, **literature** [informal]; **leaflet,** leaf, **folder, handbill, bill, flier,** throwaway, handout, **circular,** broadside, broadsheet.

.9 **publicist,** publicizer, public relations man, public relations officer, PR man, public relations specialist, **publicity man** or agent, **press agent,** flack [slang]; **advertiser; adman,** huckster, pitchman [all informal]; ad writer [informal], copywriter; **promoter, booster** [informal], plugger [slang]; **ballyhooer** or **ballyhoo man** [both slang]; **barker,** spieler [slang], skywriter; billposter; sandwich boy or man.

.10 VERBS **publish, promulgate, propagate, circulate,** circularize, **diffuse, disseminate,** distribute, **broadcast,** televise, telecast, videocast, air, **spread,** spread around or about, spread far and wide, publish abroad, **pass the word around,** bruit, **bruit about, advertise,** repeat, retail, put about, **bandy about, noise about,** cry about or abroad, noise or sound abroad,

set news afloat, **spread a report; rumor,** launch a rumor, voice [archaic], whisper, buzz, **rumor about,** whisper or buzz about.

.11 **make public,** bring or lay or drag before the public, **display,** take one's case to the public, **give** or **put out,** give to the world, **make known; divulge** 556.5; **ventilate,** air, give air to, bring into the open, open up, broach.

.12 **announce,** annunciate, enunciate; **declare, state,** declare roundly, affirm, pronounce, give notice; **report,** make an announcement or report, make or issue a statement, publish or issue a manifesto, present a position paper, issue a white paper, hold a press conference.

.13 **proclaim,** cry, cry out, **promulgate,** celebrate, **herald,** herald abroad; **blazon,** blaze, blaze or blazon about or abroad, blare, blare forth or abroad, thunder, declaim, shout, trumpet, trumpet or thunder forth, announce with flourish of trumpets or beat of drum; shout from the housetops, proclaim at the crossroads or market cross, proclaim at Charing Cross [Brit].

.14 **issue, bring out, put out, get out,** get off, emit, put or give or send forth, offer to the public.

.15 **publicize,** give publicity; bring or drag into the limelight, throw the spotlight on [informal]; **advertise, promote,** build up, cry up, sell, puff [informal], **boost** [informal], **plug** [slang], **ballyhoo** [slang]; put on the map, make a household word of, establish; bark, spiel [both slang]; make a pitch for or beat the drum for or thump the tub for [all informal]; **write up,** give a write-up, press-agent [informal]; circularize; bulletin; bill; **post bills,** post, post up, placard; skywrite.

.16 (be published) **come out,** break, **issue,** fo or come forth, find vent, **see the light,** become public; **circulate, spread,** spread about, have currency, **get around** or about, get abroad, get afloat, get exposure, go or fly or buzz or blow about, **go the rounds,** pass from mouth to mouth, be on everyone's lips, go through the length and breadth of the land; spread like wildfire.

.17 ADJS **published, public,** made public, **circulated,** in circulation, promulgated, propagated, **disseminated,** spread, diffused, distributed; in print; **broadcast,** telecast, televised; **announced,** proclaimed, declared, **stated,** affirmed; reported, brought to notice; common knowledge, common property, current; **open,** accessible, open to the public.

.18 publicational, promulgatory, propagatory; proclamatory, annunciatory, enunciative; declarative, declaratory; heraldic.

.19 ADVS **publicly, in public; openly** 555.15; in the public eye, in the glare of publicity, in the limelight or spotlight [informal].

560. COMMUNICATIONS

.1 NOUNS **communications,** signaling, telecommunication, tel(e)– or telo–; electronic communication, electrical communication; wire communication, wireless communication; communication engineering, communication technology; communications engineer; media, communications medium or media; communication or information theory 557.7; communication or information explosion.

.2 **telegraphy,** telegraphics; railroad telegraphy, submarine telegraphy; simplex telegraphy, multiplex telegraphy, duplex telegraphy, quadruplex telegraphy; single-current telegraphy, closed-circuit telegraphy; teleprinter, teletypewriter, Teletype, typotelegraph, teleprinter exchange or telex; TelAutograph, facsimile telegraph; wire service, Teletype network, Teletyping, teletypewriting, typotelegraphy, TelAutography; **ticker,** stock ticker, news ticker; code 614.6; electricity 342; **key,** interrupter, transmitter, sender; receiver, **sounder.**

.3 **radio** 344, radiotelephony, **radiotelegraphy,** wireless [Brit], wireless telephony, wireless telegraphy; line radio, wire or wired radio, wired wireless [Brit], wire wave communication; radiophotography; **television** 345; electronics 343.

.4 **telephone, phone** [informal], telephone set; telephony, telephonics, telephone mechanics, telephone engineering; high-frequency telephony; receiver, telephone receiver; mouthpiece, transmitter, telephone extension, extension; wall telephone, desk telephone; dial telephone, push-button telephone; telephone booth, call box [Brit], public telephone, coin telephone, pay station.

.5 **radiophone, radiotelephone,** wireless telephone, wireless; headset, headphone 450.8.

.6 **intercom** [informal], Interphone, intercommunication system.

.7 **telephone exchange,** telephone office, central office, **central;** automatic exchange, machine-switching office; step-by-step switching, panel switching, crossbar switching, electronic switching.

.8 **switchboard; PBX,** private branch or business exchange; in or A board, out or B board.

.9 **telephone operator, operator,** switchboard operator, telephonist, **central;** long distance; PBX operator.

.10 **telephone man;** telephone mechanic; telephonic engineer; lineman 342.19.

.11 **telephoner,** phoner [informal], caller, **party,** calling party.

.12 **telephone number, phone number** [informal]; telephone directory, phone book [informal]; telephone exchange, exchange; telephone area, area code.

.13 **telephone call, phone call** [informal], **call, ring** or buzz [both informal]; local call, toll call, long-distance call; long distance, direct distance dialing, DDD; station-to-station call, person-to-person call; collect call; mobile call; dial tone, busy signal.

.14 **telegram, telegraph, wire** [informal], **telex; cablegram, cable; radiogram,** radiotelegram; **day letter, night letter;** fast telegram.

.15 **Telephoto,** Wirephoto, facsimile, telephotograph, radiophotograph, Photoradiogram.

.16 **telegrapher,** telegraphist, telegraph operator; **sparks** or brass pounder or dit-da artist [all informal]; radiotelegrapher; wireman, wire chief.

.17 **line,** wire line, telegraph line, telephone line; private line, party line; trunk, trunk line; WATS or wide area telecommunications service, WATS line; cable, telegraph cable; concentric cable, coaxial cable, co-ax [informal].

.18 VERBS **telephone, phone** [informal], **call,** call on the phone [informal], put in or make a call, **call up, ring,** ring up, give a ring or buzz [informal], buzz [informal]; dial; listen in; hold the phone or wire; hang up, ring off [Brit].

.19 **telegraph, telegram,** flash, **wire** or send a wire [both informal], telex; **cable;** Teletype; radio; sign on, sign off.

.20 ADJS **communicational,** telecommunicational, **communications,** communication, signal; **telephonic,** magnetotelephonic, microtelephonic, monotelephonic, thermotelephonic; **telegraphic; Teletype;** Wirephoto, facsimile; phototelegraphic, telephotographic; **radio**, wireless [Brit]; radiotelegraphic.

.21 telephones

carbon telephone	Picturephone
dial telephone	push-button tele-
extension phone	phone
field telephone	radiotelephone
French telephone,	sound-powered tele-
hand set	phone
light-beam telephone	string telephone
magnetotelephone	thermophone, ther-
mechanical telephone	motelephone
microtelephone	wall telephone
monotelephone	wireless telephone
pantelephone	

.22 telegraphs

autotelegraph	multiplex
dial telegraph	needle telegraph
disk telegraph	pantelegraph
electric telegraph	phototelegraph
engine-room telegraph	quadruplex
facsimile telegraph	radiotelegraph
field telegraph	semaphore telegraph
heliograph	solar telegraph
indicator telegraph	TelAutograph
magnetotelegraph	telectrograph
marconigraph	telegraphoscope
Morse telegraph	typewriting telegraph
multiple telegraph	writing telegraph

.23 teleprinters

news ticker	Teletypesetter
printer	teletypewriter
printing telegraph	TFX
stock ticker	ticker
telecon	typewriting telegraph
teleprinter	typotelegraph
Teletype	

.24 telegraph recorders

phototransceiver	telegraphonograph
siphon recorder	telegraphophone
telegraphone	

561. MESSENGER

.1 NOUNS **messenger**, message-bearer, **dispatch-bearer**, commissionaire [Brit], nuncio [archaic], **courier**, diplomatic courier, carrier, **runner**, express [Brit], dispatchrider, post [archaic], postboy, postrider, *estafette* [Fr]; go-between 781.4; **emissary** 781.6; Mercury, Hermes, Iris, Pheippides, Paul Revere.

.2 **herald**, **harbinger**, forerunner; evangel, evangelist, bearer of glad tidings; herald angel, Gabriel.

.3 **announcer**, annunciator, enunciator; nunciate [archaic]; **proclaimer**; **crier**, **town crier**, bellman.

.4 errand boy, office boy, copyboy; bellhop [slang], bellboy, bellman, callboy, caller.

.5 **postman**, **mailman**, mail carrier, letter carrier; postmaster, postmistress; postal clerk.

.6 (mail carriers) carrier pigeon, carrier,

homing pigeon, homer [informal]; pigeon post; post-horse, poster; post coach, mail coach; post boat, packet boat *or* ship, mail boat, mail packet, mailer [archaic]; mail train, mail car, post car, post-office car, railway mail car; mail truck; mailplane.

562. TEACHING

.1 NOUNS **teaching, instruction, education, schooling, tuition**; edification, **enlightenment**, illumination; tutelage, tutorage, tutorship; tutoring, coaching, private teaching; spoon-feeding; direction, guidance; **pedagogy**, pedagogics, didactics; catechization; programmed instruction; self-teaching, self-instruction; information 557; reeducation 145.4.

.2 **inculcation, indoctrination**, catechization, inoculation, **implantation**, infixation, infixion, **impression, instillment**, instillation, impregnation, **infusion**, imbuement; absorption and regurgitation; dictation; conditioning, brainwashing; reindoctrination 145.5.

.3 **training, preparation**, readying [informal], **conditioning, grooming**, cultivation, development, improvement; **discipline**; breaking, housebreaking; **upbringing, bringing-up**, fetching-up [dial], **rearing, raising, breeding, nurture**, nurturing, fostering; **practice**, rehearsal, **exercise, drill**, drilling; **apprenticeship**, in-service training, on-the-job training; military training, basic training; manual training, sloyd; vocational training *or* education.

.4 preinstruction, pre-education; **priming**, cramming [informal].

.5 elementary education; initiation, introduction, propaedeutic; **rudiments**, first steps, elements, **ABC's**; reading, writing, and arithmetic, **three R's**; primer, hornbook, abecedarium, abecedary.

.6 **instructions, directions, orders**; briefing, final instructions.

.7 **lesson, teaching, instruction, lecture**, lecture-demonstration, harangue, **discourse**, disquisition, exposition, **talk**; homily, **sermon**, preachment; chalk talk [informal]; skull session [informal]; **recitation**, recital; **assignment, exercise**, task, set task, homework; **moral**, morality, moralization, moral lesson; object lesson.

.8 **study**, branch of learning; **discipline**, subdiscipline; **field, specialty**, academic specialty, area; **course**, course of study, **curriculum**; **subject**; **major, minor**; elective; refresher course; **seminar**, proseminar;

classical education; scientific education, technical education; religious education; liberal arts, humanities, trivium, quadrivium; general education, general studies, core curriculum.

.9 physical education, physical culture, gymnastics, calisthenics, eurythmics.

.10 primary education, elementary education; secondary education, higher education; vocational education; liberal education; graduate education, professional education, graduate-professional education; postgraduate education; continuing education, adult education.

.11 VERBS **teach, instruct,** give instruction, give lessons in, **educate, school; edify, enlighten,** civilize, illumine; **direct, guide;** inform 557.8; **show,** show how, demonstrate; give an idea of; put in the right, set right; improve one's mind, enlarge *or* broaden the mind; sharpen the wits, open the eyes *or* mind; teach a lesson, give a lesson to; **ground,** teach the rudiments *or* elements; catechize; teach an old dog new tricks; reeducate 145.14.

.12 **tutor, coach; prime, cram** [informal], cram with facts, stuff with knowledge.

.13 **inculcate, indoctrinate,** catechize, inoculate, **instill, infuse,** imbue, impregnate, **implant,** infix, impress; **impress upon the mind** *or* **memory,** urge on the mind, beat into, beat *or* knock into one's head; condition, brainwash, program.

.14 **train; drill, exercise; practice,** rehearse; keep in practice, keep one's hand in; **prepare,** ready, **condition, groom,** fit, put in tune, form, **lick into shape** [informal]; **rear, raise, bring up,** fetch up [dial], bring up by hand, **breed; cultivate,** develop, improve; **nurture, foster,** nurse; **discipline,** take in hand; put through the mill *or* grind [informal]; break, break in, housebreak, house-train [Brit]; put to school, send to school, apprentice.

.15 **preinstruct,** pre-educate; **initiate,** introduce.

.16 **give instructions,** give directions; **brief,** give a briefing.

.17 **expound,** exposit; explain 552.10; **lecture, discourse,** harangue, hold forth, give *or* read a lesson; **preach,** sermonize; **moralize,** point a moral.

.18 **assign,** give *or* make an assignment, give homework, set a task, set hurdles; lay out a course, make a syllabus.

.19 ADJS **educational,** educative, educating, teaching, **instructive,** instructional, **tuitional,** tuitionary; **cultural, edifying, en**-

lightening, illuminating; informative 557.17; didactic, preceptive; self-instructional, self-teaching, autodidactic; lecturing, preaching, hortatory, exhortatory, homiletic(al); initiatory, introductory, propaedeutic; **disciplinary;** coeducational.

.20 **scholastic, academic, schoolish; scholarly; pedagogical** 565.12; graduate, professional, graduate-professional, postgraduate; interdisciplinary, cross-disciplinary; curricular.

.21 extracurricular, extraclassroom; nonscholastic, noncollegiate.

563. MISTEACHING

.1 NOUNS **misteaching,** misinstruction; **misguidance,** misdirection, misleading; sophistry 483; perversion, corruption; mystification, obscuration, obfuscation, obscurantism; **misinformation,** misknowledge; the blind leading the blind; college of Laputa.

.2 **propaganda;** propagandism, indoctrination; **propagandist,** agitprop.

.3 VERBS **misteach,** misinstruct, miseducate; **misinform;** misadvise, **misguide,** misdirect, **mislead;** pervert, corrupt; mystify, obscure, obfuscate.

.4 **propagandize,** carry on a propaganda; indoctrinate.

.5 ADJS **mistaught,** misinstructed; **misinformed;** misadvised, **misguided,** misdirected, **misled.**

.6 misteaching, misinstructive, miseducative, **misinforming; misleading,** misguiding, misdirecting.

564. LEARNING

.1 NOUNS **learning,** intellectual acquirement *or* acquisition *or* attainment, stocking *or* storing the mind, mental cultivation, mental culture, improving *or* broadening the mind; mastery of skills; **self-education,** self-instruction; **knowledge, erudition** 475.5,6; education 562.1; memorization 537.4.

.2 **absorption,** ingestion, imbibing, assimilation, taking-in, soaking-up, digestion.

.3 **study, studying,** application, conning; **reading,** perusal, –lexia; restudy, restudying, review; **contemplation** 478.2; **inspection** 485.3; **engrossment** 330.3; **brainwork, headwork,** lucubration, mental labor; exercise, **practice, drill;** grind *or* grinding *or* boning [all informal], **cramming** *or* cram [both informal], swotting [Brit informal]; extensive study, wide reading; subject 562.8.

.4 studiousness, scholarliness, scholarship; bookishness 475.4, diligence 707.6.

.5 teachableness, teachability, educability, trainableness; aptness, aptitude, quickness, readiness; receptivity, mind like a blotter; willingness, motivation; docility, malleability, moldability, pliability, facility, plasticity, impressionability, susceptibility, formability; brightness, cleverness, intelligence 467.

.6 VERBS learn, get, get hold of [informal], get into one's head; gain knowledge, pick up information, gather or collect or glean knowledge or learning; stock or store the mind, improve or broaden the mind; stuff or cram the mind; burden or load the mind; find out, ascertain, discover, find, determine; become informed, gain knowledge or understanding of, acquire information or intelligence about, learn about, find out about; acquaint oneself with, make oneself acquainted with, become acquainted with; be informed 557.14.

.7 absorb, get by osmosis, take in, ingest, imbibe, assimilate, digest, soak up, drink in; soak in, seep in, percolate in.

.8 memorize 537.17; fix in the mind 537.18.

.9 master, attain mastery of, make oneself master of, gain command of, become adept in, become familiar or conversant with, become versed or well-versed in, get up in or on, gain a good or thorough knowledge of, learn all about, get down pat [informal], get down cold [slang], get taped [Brit informal]; get the hang or knack of; learn the ropes, learn the ins and outs; know well 475.13.

.10 learn by experience, learn by doing, live and learn, go through the school of hard knocks; learn a lesson, be taught a lesson.

.11 receive instruction, undergo schooling, pursue one's education, attend classes, go to or attend school, take lessons; train, prepare oneself, ready oneself, go into training; serve an apprenticeship; apprentice oneself to; study with, read with, sit at the feet of, learn from, have as one's master.

.12 study, regard studiously, apply oneself to, con; read, peruse, go over; restudy, review; contemplate 478.12; examine 485.23; give the mind to 530.5; pore over, vet [Brit informal]; bury oneself in, wade through, plunge into; dig or grind or bone [all informal], swot [Brit informal]; lucubrate, elucubrate, burn the midnight oil; make a study of; practice, drill.

.13 browse, scan, skim, dip into, thumb over or through, run over or through, glance or run the eye over or through, turn over the leaves, have a look at, hit the high spots.

.14 study up, brush up, polish up [informal], rub up, get up; study up on, read up on, get up on; cram or cram up [both informal], bone up [slang].

.15 study to be, study for, read for, read law, etc.; specialize in, go in for, make one's field; major in, minor in.

.16 ADJS educated, learned 475.18–23; self-taught, self-instructed, autodidactic.

.17 studious, devoted to studies, scholarly, scholastic, academic, professorial, donnish; owlish; rabbinic, mandarin; pedantic, dryasdust; bookish 475.22; diligent 707.22.

.18 teachable, instructable, educable, schoolable, trainable; apt, quick, ready, ripe for instruction; receptive, willing, motivated; thirsty for knowledge; docile, malleable, moldable, pliable, facile, plastic, impressionable, susceptible, formable; bright, clever, intelligent 467.12.

565. TEACHER

.1 NOUNS teacher, instructor, educator, educationist, preceptor, mentor; rabbi, melamed [Heb], pandit, pundit, guru, mullah [Per], starets [Russ]; master, maestro; pedagogue, pedagogist; schoolteacher, schoolmaster, schoolkeeper; dominie [Scot], abecedarian [archaic], certified teacher; professor, docent, don [Brit], doctor, fellow; guide 748.7.

.2 instructress, educatress, preceptress, mistress; schoolmistress; schoolma'am or schoolmarm, dame, schooldame; tutoress; governess, duenna.

.3 schoolman, academician.

.4 (academic ranks) professor, associate professor, assistant professor, instructor, tutor, associate, assistant, lecturer, reader [Brit]; visiting professor; emeritus, professor emeritus, retired professor.

.5 teaching fellow, teaching assistant; teaching intern, intern; practice teacher, apprentice teacher, student or pupil teacher; teacher's aide, paraprofessional; monitor, proctor, prefect, praepostor [Brit]; student assistant, graduate assistant.

.6 tutor, tutorer; coach, coacher; private instructor, Privatdocent, Privatdozent [both Ger]; crammer [Brit informal].

.7 **trainer, handler, groomer;** driller, drill-master; **coach,** athletic coach.

.8 **lecturer,** lector, **reader** [Brit], praelector, **preacher,** homilist.

.9 **principal, headmaster,** headmistress; president, chancellor, vice-chancellor, rector, provost, master; **dean,** academic dean, dean of the faculty, dean of women, dean of men; administrator, educational administrator; administration.

.10 **faculty,** faculty members, professorate, professoriate, professors, professordom, teaching staff.

.11 **instructorship, teachership,** preceptorship, schoolmastery; **tutorship,** tutorhood, tutorage, tutelage; **professorship,** professorhood, professorate, professoriate; **chair,** chair of English, etc.; lectureship, readership [Brit]; fellowship.

.12 ADJS **pedagogic(al),** preceptorial, tutorial; **teacherish,** teachery, teacherlike, teachy, **schoolteacherish,** schoolteachery, **schoolmasterish,** schoolmasterly, schoolmastering, schoolmasterlike; schoolmistressy, schoolmarmish [dial]; **professorial,** professorlike, academic, donnish; pedantic 475.22.

566. STUDENT

.1 NOUNS **student, pupil, scholar,** learner, studier, educatee, **trainee,** élève [Fr]; inquirer; self-taught person, autodidact; auditor; monitor, prefect, praepostor [Brit]; –log or –logue.

.2 **disciple, follower,** apostle; convert, proselyte 145.7.

.3 self-taught man, autodidact.

.4 **school child,** school kid [informal]; **schoolboy,** school lad; **schoolgirl;** preschool child, preschooler, nursery school child, infant [Brit]; kindergartner, grade schooler, primary schooler, intermediate schooler; secondary schooler, prep schooler, preppie [informal], high schooler; schoolmate, schoolfellow, fellow student, classmate.

.5 **college student, collegian,** collegiate, **varsity student** [Brit informal], college boy or girl; co-ed [informal]; seminarian, seminarist; bahur [Heb], yeshiva bocher [Yid].

.6 **undergraduate,** undergrad [informal], cadet, midshipman; underclassman, **freshman,** freshie [informal], plebe, **sophomore,** soph [informal]; **upperclassman, junior, senior.**

.7 [Brit terms] commoner, pensioner, sizar, servitor [archaic], exhibitioner, fellow commoner; sophister, questionist [both archaic]; wrangler, optime; passman.

.8 **graduate,** grad [informal]; **alumnus,** alumni [pl], alumna [fem], alumnae [fem pl]; **graduate student,** master's degree candidate, doctoral candidate; **postgraduate,** postgrad [informal]; degrees 917.6,9; college graduate, college man, educated man, educated class; meritocracy.

.9 **novice,** novitiate, **tyro,** abecedarian, alphabetarian, **beginner** 68.2, entrant, **neophyte, tenderfoot** or greenhorn [both informal], freshman, **fledgling;** catechumen, initiate, debutant; new boy, newcomer 78.4; ignoramus 477.8; **recruit, raw recruit,** inductee, rookie [informal], boot; **probationer,** probationist, postulant; **apprentice,** articled clerk.

.10 **grind** or greasy grind [both informal], swotter or mugger [both Brit informal]; bookworm 476.4; overachiever; failing student, flunkee [informal], underachiever.

.11 **class, form** [Brit], **grade;** track.

.12 ADJS **studentlike,** schoolboyish, schoolgirlish; undergraduate, graduate, postgraduate; **collegiate,** college-bred; sophomoric(al); autodidactic; **studious** 564.17; **learned, bookish** 475.21,22.

.13 **probationary,** probational, on probation.

567. SCHOOL

.1 NOUNS **school, educational institution,** teaching institution, academic or scholastic institution, teaching and research institution, **institute, academy,** seminary, Schule [Ger], école [Fr], escuela [Sp].

.2 **public school,** common school, district school; union school, regional school, **central school, consolidated school; private school;** day school, country day school; **boarding school,** pensionat [Fr]; **finishing school;** dame school, blab school; **special school,** school for the handicapped; **night school,** evening school; **summer school,** vacation school; correspondence school, extension, university extension; school of continuing education, continuation school; platoon school; progressive school; free school, nongraded school, informal school, open classroom school; alternate or alternative school, street academy, storefront school, school without walls.

.3 [Brit terms] provided school, council school, board school; voluntary school, nonprovided school, national school, charity school.

.4 **preschool,** infant school [Brit], nursery,

nursery school; day nursery, day-care center, crèche; kindergarten.

.5 **elementary school, grade school** *or* graded school, the grades; **primary school;** junior school [Brit]; **grammar school;** folk school, *Volksschule* [Ger].

.6 **secondary school,** middle school, **academy,** *Gymnasium* [Ger]; *lycée* [Fr], lyceum; **high school,** high [informal]; **junior high school,** junior high [informal], intermediate school; **senior high school,** senior high [informal]; **preparatory school,** prep school [informal], public school [Brit], seminary; **grammar school** [Brit], Latin school, *Progymnasium* [Ger]; *Realschule* [Ger]; *Realgymnasium* [Ger].

.7 **college,** four-year college, degree-granting institution, institution of higher learning; alma mater; college of general studies, university college, college of liberal arts, liberal-arts college; **university,** varsity [Brit informal], *université* [Fr]; multiversity; **junior college,** two-year college; community college; **graduate school,** postgraduate school; teachers' college, college *or* school of education; normal school, normal; law school, medical school, library school, journalism school, school of communications, school *or* college of business administration; engineering school, college of engineering, institute of technology; coeducational school; academe, academia, the groves of Academe, **the campus,** the halls of learning, ivied halls.

.8 **vocational school, trade school,** occupational school; business college *or* school, commercial school, secretarial school; industrial school; technical school, technical training institute, technological school *or* institute; polytechnic school, polytechnic; manual arts school; school of arts and crafts.

.9 **conservatory,** *conservatoire* [Fr]; school of fine arts; **art school,** school of art, school of graphic arts, school of design; school *or* college of architecture; school of the performing arts; **music school,** college *or* academy of music; singing school, choir school, schola cantorum; **dancing school,** *salle de danse* [Fr]; acting school, school *or* college of dramatic arts, school of drama.

.10 **religious school,** denominational school, **church school, parochial school,** parish school; convent school; Hebrew school, *heder* [Yid], Talmud Torah; yeshiva, mesivta; **seminary, divinity school,** theological seminary, theological school; **Bible school,** Bible institute; **Sunday school,** Sabbath school; vacation church school.

.11 **gymnasium,** palaestra; wrestling school; fencing school, *salle d'armes* [Fr].

.12 **riding school** *or* academy, manège.

.13 **military school** *or* **academy;** US Military Academy, West Point; Royal Military Academy (at Woolwich); Royal Military College, Sandhurst; *Ecole Speciale Militaire Interarmes*, St. Cyr; naval school *or* academy; US Naval Academy, Annapolis; US Coast Guard Academy (at New London); US Merchant Marine Academy, Kings Point; Royal Naval College, Dartmouth; *École Navale* (at Brest); US Air Force Academy (at Colorado Springs); Royal Air Force College, Cranwell; *École de l'Air* (at Salon-de-Provence); war college, naval college, staff college, command and general staff school, air university.

.14 **reform school, reformatory,** industrial school, training school; borstal *or* borstal school *or* remand school [all Brit].

.15 **schoolhouse,** school building; little red schoolhouse; classroom building; hall; campus.

.16 **schoolroom, classroom;** recitation room; lecture room *or* hall; auditorium; theater, amphitheater.

.17 **governing board, board;** board of education, school board; college board, board of regents, board of trustees, board of visitors.

.18 ADJS **scholastic, academic,** institutional, **school,** classroom; **collegiate; university;** preschool; interscholastic, intercollegiate, extramural; intramural.

568. INDICATION

.1 NOUNS **indication,** signification, identification, differentiation, denotation, **designation,** denomination; characterization, highlighting; specification, naming, pointing, pointing out *or* to, fingering [informal], picking out, selection; symptomaticness, indicativeness; **meaning** 545; hint, suggestion 557.4; **expression, manifestation** 555; show, showing, disclosure 556.

.2 **sign,** telltale sign, sure sign, **index,** indicant, **indicator,** signal [archaic], measure; **symptom;** note, keynote, **mark, earmark,** hallmark, **badge,** device, banner, stamp, signature, sigil, seal, trait, **characteristic,** character, peculiarity, idiosyncrasy, **property,** differentia; image, picture, **representation,** representative; insignia 569.

.3 symbol, emblem, token, cipher [archaic], type; allegory; symbolism, symbology, iconology, charactery; conventional symbol; symbolic system; symbolization; ideogram, logogram, pictogram; logotype; totem, totem pole; love knot.

.4 pointer, index, lead; direction, guide; fist, index finger or mark; arrow; hand, hour hand, minute hand, needle, compass needle, lubber'line; signpost, guidepost, finger post, direction post; milepost; blaze; guideboard, signboard 559.7.

.5 mark, marking; watermark; scratch, scratching, engraving, graving, score, scotch, cut, hack, gash, blaze; nick, notch 262; scar, cicatrix, scarification, cicatrization; brand, earmark; stigma; stain, discoloration 679.2,3; blemish, macula, spot, blotch, splotch, flick, patch, splash; mottle, dapple; dot, point; polka dot; tittle, jot; speck, speckle, fleck; tick, freckle, lentigo, mole; birthmark, strawberry mark, nevus; caste mark; check, checkmark; prick, puncture; tattoo, tattoo mark.

.6 line, score, stroke, slash, virgule, diagonal, dash, stripe, strip, streak, striation, striping, streaking, bar, band; hairline; dotted line; lineation, delineation; sublineation, underline, underlining, underscore, underscoring; hatching, cross-hatching, hachure.

.7 print, imprint, impress, impression; dint, dent, indent, indentation, indention, concavity; sitzmark; stamp, seal, sigil, signet; colophon; fingerprint, thumbprint, thumbmark, dactylogram, dactylograph; footprint, footmark, footstep, step, vestige; pad, paw print, pawmark, pug, pugmark; fossil print or footprint, ichnite, ichnolite; bump, boss, stud, pimple, lump, excrescence, convexity, embossment.

.8 track, trail, path, course, piste [Fr], line, wake; vapor trail, contrail, condensation trail; spoor, signs, traces, scent.

.9 clue, cue, key, tip-off [informal], telltale, straw in the wind; trace, vestige, spoor, scent, whiff; lead [informal], hot lead [informal]; catchword, cue word, key word; evidence 505; hint, intimation, suggestion 557.4.

.10 marker, mark; bookmark; landmark, seamark; bench mark; milestone, milepost; cairn, menhir, catstone; lighthouse, lightship, tower, platform, watchtower, pharos; monument 570.12.

.11 identification, identification mark; badge, identification badge, identification tag, dog tag [mil], ID card, tessera, card, calling card, visiting card, carte de visite [Fr], press card; letter of introduction; signature, initials, monogram, calligram; credentials; serial number; countersign, countermark.

.12 password, watchword, countersign, tessera; token; open sesame; secret grip; shibboleth.

.13 label, tag; ticket, docket [Brit], tally; stamp, sticker; seal, sigil, signet; cachet; stub, counterfoil; token, check; brand, trade name, trademark name; trademark, registered trademark; government mark, government stamp, broad arrow [Brit]; hallmark, countermark; price tag; plate, bookplate, book stamp, colophon, ex libris [L], logotype or logo; masthead, imprint, title page; letterhead, billhead; running head or title.

.14 gesture, gesticulation; motion, movement; carriage, bearing, posture, poise, pose, stance, way of holding oneself; body language, kinesics; beck, beckon; shrug; charade, dumb show, pantomime; sign language, gesture language; dactylology, deaf-and-dumb alphabet; hand signal; chironomy.

.15 signal, sign; high sign or the wink or the nod [all informal]; wink, flick of the eyelash, glance, leer; look in one's eyes, tone of one's voice; nod; nudge, elbow in the ribs, poke, kick, touch; alarm 704; beacon, signal beacon, marker beacon, radio beacon; signal light, signal lamp or lantern; blinker; signal fire, beacon fire, watch fire, balefire; flare, parachute flare; rocket, signal rocket, Roman candle; signal gun, signal shot; signal siren or whistle, signal bell, bell, signal gong, police whistle, watchman's rattle; aid to navigation, sailing aid; fog signal or alarm, fog bell, foghorn, fog whistle; buoy, spar buoy, bell buoy, gong buoy; traffic signal, traffic light, red or stop light, amber or caution light, green or go light; heliograph; signal flag; semaphore, semaphore telegraph, semaphore flag; wigwag, wigwag flag; international alphabet flag, international numeral pennant; red flag; white flag; yellow flag, quarantine flag; blue peter; pilot flag or jack; signal post, signal mast, signal tower; telecommunications 560.1–3.

.16 call, summons; whistle; moose call, birdcall, duck call, hog call, goose call, crow call, hawk call, dog whistle; bugle call, trumpet call; **reveille, taps,** last post [Brit]; alarm, alarum; **battle cry,** war cry, rebel yell, rallying cry; Angelus, Angelus bell.

.17 VERBS **indicate,** be indicative of, be an indication of, be significant of, connote, denominate, argue, bespeak, be symptomatic *or* diagnostic of, symptomize, symptomatize, **characterize, mark,** highlight, be the mark *or* sign of, give token, **betoken, signify,** stand for, identify, differentiate, note [archaic], **denote, mean** 545.8; testify, give evidence 505.10; **show, express, display, manifest** 555.5, **hint,** suggest 557.10, reveal, **disclose** 556.4; entail, involve 76.4.

.18 **designate, specify;** denominate, name, denote; stigmatize; **symbolize, stand for,** typify, be taken as, symbol, emblematize, figure [archaic]; **point to,** refer to, advert to, allude to, make an allusion to; pick out, select; **point out,** point at, put *or* lay one's finger on, finger [slang].

.19 **mark,** make a mark, put a mark on; pencil, chalk; mark out, demarcate, delimit, define; **mark off, check, check off,** tick, tick off, chalk up; punctuate, point; **dot, spot,** blotch, splotch, dash, **speck, speckle,** fleck, freckle; mottle, dapple; blemish; **brand,** stigmatize; **stain, discolor** 679.6; stamp, seal, punch, impress, imprint, **print, engrave** 578.12; **score, scratch,** gash, scotch, scar, scarify, cicatrize; nick, notch 262.4; **blaze,** blaze a trail; **line, seam,** trace, **stripe, streak, striate;** hatch; **underline, underscore;** prick, puncture, tattoo, riddle, pepper.

.20 **label, tag,** tab, ticket; stamp, seal; **brand, earmark;** hallmark.

.21 **gesture, gesticulate; motion,** motion to; beckon, wiggle the finger at; wave the arms, saw the air; shrug, shrug the shoulders; pantomime, mime.

.22 **signal,** signalize, sign, give a signal, make a sign; speak; flash; **give the high sign** *or* **the nod** [informal]; nod; nudge, poke, kick, dig one in the ribs, touch; wink, glance, raise one's eyebrows, leer; hold up the hand; **wave,** wave the hand, wave a flag, **flag,** flag down; **unfurl a flag,** hoist a banner, break out a flag; **show one's colors,** exchange colors; **salute,** dip; dip a flag, hail, hail and speak; half-mast; give *or* sound an alarm, raise a cry; beat the drum, sound the trumpet.

.23 ADJS **indicative,** indicatory; connotative, indicating, signifying, signalizing; **significant,** significative, meaningful; symptomatic, symptomatologic(al), diagnostic, pathognomonic(al); evidential, **designative,** denotative, denominative, naming; **suggestive,** implicative; **expressive,** demonstrative, exhibitive; representative 572.10, 11; identifying, identificational; individual, peculiar, idiosyncratic; **emblematic(al); symbolic(al),** symbolistic, symbological, typical; figurative, figural, metaphorical; ideographic; semiotic, semantic.

.24 **gestural,** gesticulative, gesticulatory; kinesic; pantomimic, **in pantomime,** in dumb show.

569. INSIGNIA

.1 NOUNS **insignia, regalia,** ensigns, **emblems, badges, symbols,** markings; badge, badge of office, mark of office, chain, chain of office, collar; wand, verge, *fasces* [L], mace, staff, baton; livery, uniform, mantle, dress; tartan, tie, old school tie, regimental tie; ring, school ring, class ring; pin, button, lapel pin *or* button; cap and gown, mortarboard; cockade; brassard; figurehead, eagle; cross 221.4, skull and crossbones, swastika, hammer and sickle, rose, thistle, shamrock, fleur-de-lis; medal, **decoration** 916.5,6; **heraldry,** armory, blazonry, sigillography, sphragistics.

.2 [her terms] heraldic device, achievement, bearings, coat of arms, arms, armorial bearings, armory, blazonry, blazon; hatchment; shield, escutcheon, scutcheon, lozenge; charge, field; crest, torse, wreath, garland, bandeau, chaplet, mantling, helmet; crown, coronet; device, motto; pheon, broad arrow; animal charge, lion, unicorn, griffin, yale, cockatrice, falcon, alerion, eagle, spread eagle; marshaling, quartering, impaling, impalement, dimidiating, differencing, difference; ordinary, bar, bend, bar sinister, bend sinister, baton, chevron, chief, cross, fess, pale, paly, saltire; subordinary, billet, bordure, canton, flanch, fret, fusil, gyron, inescutcheon, mascle, orle, quarter, rustre, tressure; fess point, nombril point, honor point; cadency mark, file, label, crescent, mullet, martlet, annulet, fleur-de-lis, rose, cross moline, octofoil; tincture, gules, azure, vert, sable, purpure, tenne; metal, or, argent; fur, ermine, ermines, erminites, erminois, pean, vair; heraldic officials 749.21.

.3 (royal insignia) regalia; scepter, rod, rod of empire; orb; armilla; purple, ermine, robe of state *or* royalty; purple pall;

crown, royal crown, coronet, tiara, diadem; cap of maintenance or dignity or estate, triple plume, Prince of Wales's feathers; uraeus; seal, signet, great seal, privy seal.

.4 (ecclesiastical insignia) tiara, triple crown; ring, keys; miter, crosier, crook, pastoral staff; pallium; cardinal's hat, red hat.

.5 (military insignia) insignia of rank, grade insignia, chevron, stripe; star, bar, eagle, spread eagle, chicken [slang], pip [Brit], oak leaf; branch of service insignia, insignia of branch or arm; unit insignia, organization insignia, shoulder patch, patch; shoulder sleeve insignia, badge, aviation badge or wings; parachute badge, submarine badge; service stripe, hash mark [informal], overseas bar, Hershey bar [slang]; epaulet.

.6 flag, banner, oriflamme, standard, gonfalon or gonfanon, guidon, vexillum [L], labarum [L]; pennant, pennon, pennoncel, banneret, banderole, swallowtail, burgee, streamer; bunting; coachwhip, long pennant; national flag, colors; royal standard; ensign, merchant flag, jack, Jolly Roger, black flag; house flag; (US) Old Glory, Stars and Stripes, Star-Spangled Banner, red, white, and blue; (Confederacy) Stars and Bars; (France) tricolor, le drapeau tricolore [Fr]; (Britain) Union Jack, Union Flag, white or red or blue ensign; (Denmark) Dannebrog; signal flag 568.15.

570. RECORD

.1 NOUNS record, recording, documentation, –gram; chronicle, annals, history; roll, rolls, pipe roll [Brit]; account; register, registry, rota, roster, scroll, catalog, inventory, table, list 88; letters, correspondence; vestige, trace, memorial, token, relic, remains.

.2 archives, public records, government archives, government papers, presidential papers, historical documents, historical records, memorabilia; cartulary; biographical records, life records, biographical material, papers, ana; parish rolls or register or records.

.3 registry, register office; archives, files; chancery.

.4 memorandum, memo [informal], memoir, aide-mémoire [Fr], memorial; reminder 537.6; note, notation, annotation, jotting, docket, marginal note, marginalia, scholium, scholia, adversaria, foot-

note; entry, register, registry, item; minutes.

.5 document, official document, legal document, legal paper, legal instrument, instrument, writ, paper, parchment, scroll, roll, writing, script, scrip; holograph, chirograph; papers, ship's papers; docket, file, personal file, dossier; blank, form.

.6 certificate, certification, ticket; authority, authorization; credential, voucher, warrant, warranty, testimonial; note; affidavit, sworn statement, notarized statement, deposition, witness, attestation, procès-verbal [Fr]; visa, visé [Fr]; bill of health, clean bill of health; navicert [Brit]; diploma, sheepskin [informal]; certificate of proficiency, testamur [Brit].

.7 report, bulletin, brief, statement, account, accounting; account rendered, compte rendu [Fr]; minutes, the record, proceedings, transactions, acta; yearbook, annual; returns, census report or returns, election returns, tally.

.8 (official documents) state paper, white paper; blue book, green book, Red Book [Brit], white book, yellow book, livre jaune [Fr]; gazette, official journal, Congressional Record, Hansard.

.9 (registers) genealogy, pedigree, studbook; Social Register, blue book; directory; Who's Who; Almanach de Gotha, Burke's Peerage; Red Book, Royal Kalendar; Lloyd's Register.

.10 (recording media) bulletin board; scoresheet, scorecard, scoreboard; tape, magnetic tape, videotape, ticker tape; phonograph record, disc, platter [informal]; film, motion-picture film; slip, card, index card, filing card; library catalog, catalog card; microcard, microfiche, microdot, microfilm; file 88.3.

.11 (record books) notebook, pocketbook, pocket notebook, blankbook; loose-leaf notebook, spiral notebook; memorandum book, memo book [informal], commonplace book, adversaria; address book; workbook; blotter, police blotter; docket, court calendar; calendar, desk calendar, appointment calendar, appointment schedule, engagement book; tablet, table [archaic], writing tablet; diptych, triptych; pad, scratch pad; scrapbook, memory book, album; diary, journal; log, ship's log, logbook; account book, ledger, daybook; cashbook, petty cashbook; Domesday Book; catalog, classified catalog; yearbook, annual.

.12 monument, monumental or memorial

record, **memorial**; necrology, obituary, **memento**, remembrance, testimonial; cup, trophy, prize, ribbon, plaque; **marker**; inscription; **tablet**, stone, hoarstone [Brit], boundary stone, memorial stone; **pillar**, stela, shaft, column, memorial column, rostral column; cross; arch, memorial arch; memorial statue, bust; monolith, obelisk, **pyramid; tomb**, grave 410.16; **gravestone, tombstone**; memorial tablet, brass; headstone, footstone; mausoleum; cenotaph; cairn, mound, barrow, cromlech, dolmen, megalith, menhir, cyclolith; **shrine**, reliquary, tope, stupa.

.13 recorder, registrar 571.1.

.14 register, recording instruments 571.3.

.15 **registration, register, registry; recording,** record keeping, recordation; minuting, **enrollment**, matriculation, enlistment; impanelment; **listing, tabulation, cataloging**, inventorying, indexing; chronicling; **entry**, insertion, entering, posting; docketing, inscribing, **inscription; booking**, logging.

.16 VERBS **record**, put or place upon record; **inscribe**, enscroll; **register, enroll**, matriculate, check in; impanel; poll; **file**, index, catalog, calendar, **tabulate, list**, docket; **chronicle**; minute, put in the minutes or on the record, spread on the record; **write**, commit or reduce to writing, put in writing, put in black and white, put on paper; **write out; make out**, fill out; **write up**, chalk, chalk up; **write down, mark down, jot down, put down, set down, take down**; note, **note down**, make a note, make a memorandum; **post**, post up; **enter**, make an entry, insert, write in; **book, log**; cut, carve, grave, engrave, incise; put on tape, tape, tape-record; record, cut; videotape.

.17 ADJS **recording**, recordative [archaic], registrational; self-recording.

.18 **recorded**, registered; inscribed, written down, down; **filed**, indexed, enrolled, **entered**, logged, booked, posted; documented; minuted; **on record**, on file, on the books; official, legal, of record.

.19 **documentary**, documentational, documental, archival; epigraphic, inscriptional; necrological, obituary; testimonial.

571. RECORDER

.1 NOUNS **recorder**, recordist; **registrar**, register, prothonotary; archivist, documentalist; master of the rolls [Brit], *custos rotulorum* [L]; librarian; **clerk**, record clerk, filing clerk; bookkeeper, accountant; **scribe**, scrivener; **secretary**, amanuensis; **stenographer** 602.17; notary, notary public; marker; scorekeeper, scorer, official scorer, timekeeper; engraver, stonecutter.

.2 **annalist**, genealogist, chronicler, historian 608.11.

.3 **recording instruments**

anemograph	recording meter
autograph, auto-	register
graphic recorder	seismochronograph
barograph camera	seismograph
cash register	seismoscope
chronograph	self-registering barom-
Dictaphone	eter, thermometer,
differential recorder	etc.
dynagraph	siphon recorder
electrograph	sound recorder
facsimile telegraph	spectrograph
frequency recorder	sphygmograph
Gramophone	stethograph
Graphophone	tape recorder
hydrograph	TelAutograph
hygrograph	telegraphone
kymograph	Teletype, teletype-
odometer	writer
oscillograph	telltale
pari-mutuel, pari-mu-	thermograph, ther-
tuel machine	mometrograph
pedometer, passome-	ticker
ter	time clock
pluviograph	totalizator
pneumatograph, pneu-	turnstile
mograph	videotape recorder
recording barometer,	voting machine
potentiometer,	votograph
pyrometer, etc.	wire recorder

572. REPRESENTATION

.1 NOUNS **representation, delineation**, presentment, drawing, **portrayal, portraiture, depiction**, depictment, rendering, rendition, characterization, charactering [archaic], picturization, figuration, limning, imaging; prefigurement; **illustration**, exemplification, demonstration; projection, **realization**; imagery, iconography; **art** 574; **drama** 611.1,4–6; conventional representation, plan, diagram, schema, blueprint, chart, map; **notation**, mathematical notation, musical notation, score, tablature, dance notation, choreography; writing, script, alphabet, syllabary; letter, ideogram, pictogram, logogram, logograph, hieroglyphic; printing 603; **symbol** 568.3.

.2 **impersonation**, personation; mimicry, mimicking, miming, pantomime, pantomiming, aping, dumb show; mimesis, **imitation** 22; personification, embodiment, incarnation; **characterization**, portrayal; **acting**, playing, enacting, enactment, performing, performance; **posing**, masquerade.

.3 **image, likeness,** eid(o)–; **resemblance,** semblance, similitude, simulacrum; **effigy, icon, idol; copy** 24; **picture** 574.12; **portrait** 574.16; **photograph** 577.3–7; **perfect** or **exact likeness, duplicate, double;** match, fellow, mate, companion, **twin;** living image, very image, very picture, living picture, dead ringer [informal], spitting image or spit and image [both slang]; miniature, model; **reflection,** shadow, mirroring; trace, tracing; rubbing.

.4 **figure, figurine; doll,** dolly [informal]; **puppet, marionette,** fantoccini [pl]; **mannequin** or manikin, model, dummy, lay figure; wax figure, waxwork; scarecrow, man of straw, snowman, gingerbread man; **sculpture, bust, statue, statuette,** statuary, monument [archaic]; portrait bust or statue; carving, wood carving; figurehead.

.5 **representative,** representation, **type, specimen,** typification, embodiment; **cross section;** exponent; **example** 25.2.

.6 VERBS **represent, delineate, depict,** render, characterize, hit off, character [archaic], **portray, picture,** picturize, limn, draw, **paint** 574.20; register, convey an impression of; take or catch a likeness; notate, write, print, map, chart, diagram, schematize; trace, trace out, trace over; rub, take a rubbing; **symbolize** 568.18.

.7 **go for, pass for,** count for, answer for, stand in the place of, be taken as, be regarded as, be the equivalent of; **pass as, serve as,** go as, be accepted for.

.8 **image, mirror,** hold the mirror up to nature, reflect, figure; **embody,** body forth, incarnate, **personify,** personate, impersonate; **illustrate,** demonstrate, exemplify; project, realize; shadow, shadow forth; **prefigure, pretypify,** foreshadow, adumbrate.

.9 **impersonate,** personate; **mimic,** mime, pantomime, take off, do or give an impression of; ape, copy; **pose as, masquerade as,** affect the manner or guise of, pass for, pretend to be, represent oneself to be; **act,** enact, perform, do; **play, act as,** act or play a part, act the part of, act out.

.10 ADJS **representational, representative, depictive, delineatory; illustrative,** illustrational; pictorial, graphic, vivid; ideographic, pictographic, figurative; **representing, portraying,** limning, illustrating; **typifying, symbolizing,** personifying, incarnating, embodying; imitative, mimetic, simulative, apish, mimish; echoic, onomatopoeic.

.11 **typical,** typic, typal; exemplary, sample; **characteristic,** distinctive, distinguishing, quintessential; **realistic, naturalistic; natural, normal,** usual, regular; **true to type, true to form,** the nature of the beast [informal].

573. MISREPRESENTATION

.1 NOUNS **misrepresentation, perversion, distortion,** deformation, garbling, twisting, slanting; inaccuracy; **coloring,** miscoloring, **false coloring; falsification** 616.9; misteaching 563; injustice, unjust representation; misdrawing, mispainting; misstatement, misreport, misquotation; nonrepresentationalism, nonrealism, abstractionism, expressionism, calculated distortion; overstatement, exaggeration, hyperbole, overdrawing; understatement, litotes.

.2 bad likeness, **daub,** botch; scribble, scratch; distortion, distorted image, anamorphosis; travesty, parody, caricature, burlesque.

.3 VERBS **misrepresent, belie,** give a wrong idea; put in a false light, **pervert, distort, garble, twist,** warp, wrench, slant, twist the meaning of; **color,** miscolor, **give a false coloring,** put a false construction or appearance upon, falsify 616.16–23; misteach 563.3; **disguise,** camouflage; misstate, misreport, misquote; overstate, exaggerate, overdraw; understate; travesty, parody, caricature, burlesque.

.4 **misdraw, mispaint;** daub, botch, scribble, scratch.

574. ART

.1 NOUNS **art,** the arts; **fine arts,** beaux arts [Fr]; arts of design, **design,** designing; art form; abstract art, representative art; **graphic arts;** plastic art; **arts and crafts;** primitive art, cave art; folk art; calligraphy; sculpture 575; ceramics 576; photography 577; etching, engraving 578.2; decoration 901.1; artist 579.

.2 "a treating of the commonplace with the feeling of the sublime" [J. F. Millet], "the conveyance of spirit by means of matter" [Salvador de Madariaga], "the expression of one soul talking to another" [Ruskin], "an instant arrested in eternity" [James Huneker], "a handicraft in flower" [George Iles], "science in the flesh" [Jean Cocteau], "life upon the larger scale" [E. B. Browning], "the perfection of nature" [Sir Thomas Browne], "the conscious utterance of thought, by speech or action, to any end" [Emerson], "the wine of life" [Jean Paul Richter], "a shadow of the divine perfection" [Michelangelo], "life seen through a temperament" [Zola], "a form of catharsis" [Dorothy Parker].

.3 **craft, manual art,** industrial art, **handicraft,** artisan work, craftwork, artisanship; industrial design; woodcraft, metalcraft, stonecraft; techno–.

.4 **architecture,** "frozen music", "music in space" [both Schelling], "the art of significant forms in space" [Claude Bragdon], "the printing press of all ages" [Lady Morgan]; landscape architecture, landscape gardening; civil architecture; functionalism.

.5 (act or art of painting) **painting,** coloring, –chromy, "a noble and expressive language" [Ruskin]; the brush; **portraiture** 572.1; **illustration,** picturization; watercoloring, *gouache* [Fr], oil painting, acrylic painting, tempera painting, encaustic painting, encaustic cerography, wash, wash drawing; grisaille, impasto; finger painting; monochrome; portrait painting, historical painting, still-life painting, nude painting, landscape painting, marine painting, genre painting; mural painting, fresco painting, poster painting, decorative painting, flower painting, miniature painting; illumination; sand painting.

.6 (art of drawing) **drawing, sketching, delineation; black and white,** charcoal; mechanical drawing, drafting; freehand drawing.

.7 scenography, ichnography, orthographic *or* orthogonal projection.

.8 **artistry, art, talent,** artistic skill, flair, artistic flair, artistic invention; artiness *or* arty-craftiness *or* artsy-craftsiness [all informal]; artistic temperament; virtu, artistic quality.

.9 **style,** pencil; lines; genre; **school,** movement; the grand style.

.10 **treatment; technique,** draftsmanship, brushwork, painterliness; **composition, design,** arrangement; grouping, balance; **color,** values; atmosphere, tone; shadow, shading; **line;** perspective.

.11 **work of art, object of art,** *objet d'art* [Fr], art object, art work, artistic production, piece, **work, study, design, composition;** creation, brainchild; virtu, article *or* piece of virtu; **masterpiece,** *chef d'œuvre*

[Fr], masterwork, master [archaic], old master, classic; museum piece; grotesque; statue 572.4; mobile, stabile; nude, still life; pastiche, *pasticcio* [Ital]; artware, artwork; bric-a-brac; kitsch.

.12 **picture,** picto–; **image, likeness, representation,** tableau; "a poem without words" [Horace]; photograph 577.3; **illustration,** illumination; miniature; copy, reproduction; print, color print; engraving 578.2, stencil 578.5, block print; daub; abstraction, abstract; mural, fresco, wall painting; cyclorama, panorama, montage, collage; still life, study in still life; tapestry, mosaic, stained glass window, **icon,** altarpiece, diptych, triptych.

.13 **scene, view, scape; landscape;** waterscape, riverscape, seascape, seapiece; airscape, skyscape, cloudscape; snowscape; cityscape, townscape; farmscape; pastoral; treescape; diorama; exterior, interior.

.14 **drawing,** –gram; **delineation;** line drawing; **sketch, draft; black and white,** chiaroscuro; **charcoal, crayon, pen-and-ink,** pencil drawing, charcoal drawing, pastel, pastel painting; silhouette; vignette; doodle; rough draft *or* copy, rough outline, cartoon, sinopia, **study,** design; *brouillon, ébauche, esquisse* [all Fr]; diagram, graph; silver-print drawing, tracing.

.15 **painting, canvas,** easel-picture, "a pretty mocking of the life" [Shakespeare], "silent poetry" [Simonides], "the intermediate somewhat between a thought and a thing" [Coleridge]; **oil painting,** oil; **watercolor,** water, aquarelle, wash, wash drawing; finger painting; tempera, egg tempera; *gouache* [Fr].

.16 **portrait, portraiture, portrayal;** head; profile; silhouette, shadow figure; miniature.

.17 **cartoon, caricature; comic strip;** comic section, comics [both informal], funny paper *or* funnies [both slang]; comic book; animated cartoon.

.18 **studio,** *atelier* [Fr]; **gallery** 660.9.

.19 (art equipment) palette; easel; paintbox; art paper, drawing paper; sketchbook, sketchpad; canvas, artists' canvas; canvas board; scratchboard; lay figure; camera obscura, camera lucida; maulstick; palette knife, spatula; brush, paintbrush; air brush, spray gun; pencil, drawing pencil; crayon, charcoal, chalk, pastel; stump; painter's cream; ground; pigments, medium; siccative, drier; fixative, varnish; **paint** 362.8,23.

.20 VERBS **portray, picture,** picturize, **depict, limn,** draw *or* paint a picture; **paint**

362.13; color, tint; spread *or* lay on a color; **daub** [informal]; scumble; **draw, sketch, delineate; draft;** pencil, chalk, crayon, charcoal; dash off, scratch [informal]; doodle; design; diagram; cartoon; copy, trace; stencil; hatch, crosshatch, shade.

.21 ADJS **artistic**, painterly; **arty** *or* arty-crafty *or* artsy-craftsy [all informal]; **art-minded,** art-conscious; **aesthetic; tasteful; beautiful** 900.16; **ornamental** 901.10; **well-composed,** well-grouped, well-arranged, well-varied; of consummate art; in the grand style.·

.22 **pictorial,** pictural, **graphic, picturesque;** picturable; photographic 577.17; scenographic; painty, pastose; scumbled; monochrome, polychrome; freehand.

.23 **art schools, groups, movements**

American	Mannerist
Art Nouveau	Milanese
Ashcan school, the	Modenese
Eight	Momentum
Barbizon	'N'
Bauhaus	Neapolitan
Bolognese	New Objectivity
British	New York
classical abstraction	Origine
Cobra	Paduan
Der Blaue Reiter	Parisian
De Stijl	Phases
Die Brücke	plein-air
Dutch	Pre-Raphaelite
eclectic	Raphaelite
Flemish	Reflex
Florentine	Restany
Fontainebleau	Roman
French	Scottish
Honfleur	Sienese
Hudson River	Spur
Italian	Suprematism
L'Age d'or	The Ten
letrist	Tuscan
Lombard	Umbrian
Madinensor	Venetian
Madrid	Washington

.24 **art styles**

abstract classicism	cubism
abstract expressionism	Dadaism
abstractionism	display art
action painting	divisionism
activist art	earth art
analytical cubism	elementarism
art autre [Fr]	existentialism
art brut [Fr]	expressionism
art deco	expressionistic abstraction
art nouveau	tion
attitude art	Fauvism
baroque	free abstraction
baroque formalism	free expressionism
classicism, classicalism	futurism
cloisonnism	geometricism
conceptual art	gesture calligraphy
concrete art	gesture painting
constructivism	Gothicism
conventionalism	hallucinatory painting

idealism	photomontage
impressionism	poetic kinetics
informalism	poetic realism
intimism	poetic tachism
intuitionism	pointillism
invisible painting	pop art
kinetic art	poptical art
linear chromatism	postconcretism
luminodynamism	postexpressionism
lyrical abstraction	postimpressionism
magic realism	postpainterly abstrac-
matter informalism	tion
matter painting	pre-Columbian art
minimal art	preimpressionism
modernism	primitivism
mysticism	purism
naturalism	quietistic painting
neoclassicism	realism
neoconcrete art	representationism,
neoconstructivism	representationalism
neocubism	romanticism
neodadaism	social realism
neoexpressionism	spatialism
neofigural postsurreal-	suprarational automa-
ism	tism
neoimpressionism	suprematism
neoplasticism	surrealism
neotraditionalism	surrealist tachism
nonaction calligraphy	symbolism
nonobjectivism	synchromism
nonrepresentational-	synthesism
ism	tachism
nuagism	traditionalism
objectivism	unism
op art	vorticism
ornamentalism	

.25 **architecture styles**

academic	high Renaissance
baroque	international
Bauhaus	Italian
Beaux Arts	medieval
Byzantine	Mesopotamian
early Renaissance	modern
Egyptian	Neo-Gothic
English	new brutalism
French	Persian
German	Renaissance
Gothic	Roman
Greco-Roman	Romanesque
Greek	Spanish
Greek Revival	

575. SCULPTURE

.1 NOUNS **sculpture, sculpturing;** plastic art, **modeling; statuary;** monumental sculpture, architectural sculpture, decorative sculpture, garden sculpture, portrait sculpture; stone sculpture, clay sculpture, glass sculpture, metal sculpture, wire sculpture, paper sculpture, CYSP sculpture, earth art; **stonecutting;** gem-cutting; **wood carving,** xyloglyphy; whittling; bone-carving, shell-carving, ivory-carving, scrimshaw; wax modeling, ceroplastics; relief-carving, relief, relievo, glyptic, anaglyphy, anaglyptics, anaglyptography; embossing, **engraving** 578.2, **chasing,** toreutics, founding, casting, molding, plaster casting, lost-wax process, *cire perdue* [Fr]; sculptor 579.6,14.

.2 (sculptured piece) **sculpture; statue** 572.4; marble, bronze, terra cotta; mobile, stabile; cast 24.6.

.3 **relief,** relievo; **embossment,** boss; half relief, *mezzo-rilievo* [Ital]; high relief, *alto-rilievo* [Ital]; low relief, bas-relief, *basso-rilievo* [Ital], *rilievo stiacciato* [Ital]; sunk relief, *cavo-rilievo* [Ital], coelanaglyphic sculpture, **intaglio,** *intaglio rilievo, intaglio rilevato* [both Ital]; *repoussé* [Fr]; glyph, anaglyph; glyptograph; **mask;** plaquette; **medallion; medal; cameo,** cameo glass, sculptured glass; cut glass.

.4 (tools, materials) chisel, point, mallet, modeling tool, spatula; cutting torch, welding torch, soldering iron; solder; modeling clay, Plasticine, sculptor's wax.

.5 VERBS **sculpture,** sculp *or* sculpt [both informal], insculpture [archaic]; **carve,** chisel, cut, grave, engrave, chase; weld, solder; assemble; **model, mold;** cast, found.

.6 ADJS **sculptural,** sculpturesque, sculptitory; statuary; **statuesque,** statuelike; **monumental,** marmoreal.

.7 **sculptured,** sculpted; sculptile; **molded, modeled,** ceroplastic; **carved,** chisled; **graven,** engraven; in relief, in high *or* low relief; glyphic, glyptic, anaglyphic, anaglyptic; anastatic; embossed, chased, hammered, toreutic; *repoussé* [Fr].

576. CERAMICS

.1 NOUNS **ceramics, pottery.**

.2 **ceramic ware,** ceramics; **pottery,** crockery; **china, porcelain;** enamelware; refractory, cement; bisque, biscuit; pot, crock, vase, urn, jug, bowl; tile, tiling; brick, firebrick, refractory brick, adobe; glass 339.2.

.3 (materials) clay, argill(o)– *or* argilli–; potter's clay *or* earth, fireclay, refractory clay; porcelain clay, kaolin, china clay; china stone, petuntse; flux; slip; glaze.

.4 **potter's wheel,** wheel; kick wheel, pedal wheel, power wheel.

.5 **kiln, oven, stove, furnace;** acid kiln, brickkiln, cement kiln, enamel kiln, muffle kiln, limekiln, reverberatory, reverberatory kiln; pyrometer, pyrometric cone, Seger cone.

.6 VERBS pot, shape, **throw,** throw *or* turn a pot; mold; **fire,** bake; glaze.

.7 ADJS **ceramic,** clay, enamel, china, porcelain; refractory.

.8 **ceramics**

Albion ware	jasper, jasper ware
Allervale pottery	Kinkozan ware
basalt, basaltes	Leeds pottery
Belleek ware	Limoges, Limoges
Berlin ware	ware
biscuit ware	Lowestoft ware
blackware	lusterware, luster pottery
bone china	tery
Castleford ware	majolica
Castor ware	Meissen ware
champlevé, champlevé	Nabeshima ware
enamel	Old Worcester ware
china, chinaware	Palissy ware
clayware	Parian ware
cloisonné, cloisonné	porcelain
enamel	queensware
cottage china	refractory ware
crackle, crackleware	Rockingham ware
crouch ware	salt-glazed ware
Crown Derby ware	Satsuma ware
delft, delftware	Seto ware
Dresden china	Sèvres, Sèvres ware
earthenware	soft-paste porcelain
eggshell porcelain	Spode
enamel, enamelware	spongeware
faience	Staffordshire ware
glassware 339.2,7	stoneware
glazed ware	terra cotta
gombroon	ting ware
hard-paste porcelain	Toft ware
Hirado ware	Wedgwood ware
Hizen porcelain	whiteware, white pottery
Imari ware	tery
ironstone, ironstone	Worcester ware
china	yi tsing ware
Jackfield ware	

577. PHOTOGRAPHY

.1 NOUNS **photography,** picture-taking; **cinematography,** motion-picture photography; color photography; photochromy, heliochromy; **3-D,** three-dimensional photography; photofinishing; photogravure; radiography, X-ray photography; photogrammetry, phototopography.

.2 photographer 579.5.

.3 **photograph, photo** [informal], heliograph, **picture,** shot [informal]; **snapshot,** snap [informal]; black-and-white photograph; color photograph, color print, heliochrome; slide, diapositive, transparency; candid photograph; still, still photograph; photomural; montage, photomontage; aerial photograph, photomap; telephotograph, Telephoto, Wirephoto; photomicrograph, microphotograph; metallograph; microradiograph; electron micrograph; photochronograph, chronophotograph; **portrait;** pinup [informal]; cheesecake *or* beefcake [both slang]; **mug** *or* mug shot [both slang]; rogues' gallery; photobiography.

.4 **tintype** *or* ferrotype, ambrotype, daguerreotype, calotype *or* talbotype, collotype, photocollotype, autotype, vitrotype.

.5 **print**, photoprint, positive; glossy, matte, semi-matte; **enlargement, blowup;** photocopy, Photostat, photostatic copy, Xerox, Xerox copy; microprint, microcopy; blueprint, cyanotype; **slide**, transparency, lantern slide; contact printing, projection printing; photogravure; hologram.

.6 shadowgraph, shadowgram, skiagraph, skiagram; radiograph, radiogram, scotograph; **X ray**, X-ray photograph, roentgenograph, roentgenogram; photofluorogram; photogram.

.7 spectrograph, spectrogram; spectroheliogram.

.8 (motion pictures) **shot; take, retake;** close-up, long shot, medium shot, full shot, group shot, deuce shot, matte shot, process shot, boom shot, travel shot, trucking shot, follow-focus shot, pan shot *or* panoramic shot, rap shot, reverse *or* reverse-angle shot, wild shot, zoom shot; motion picture 611.16; kinescope.

.9 **exposure**, time exposure; shutter speed; f-stop, lens opening; film rating, **film speed**, film gauge, ASA exposure index, DIN number; exposure meter, light meter.

.10 **film; negative;** printing paper, photographic paper; **plate;** dry plate; vehicle; motion-picture film, panchromatic film, monochromatic film, orthochromatic film, black-and-white film, color film, color negative film, color reversal film; microfilm, bibliofilm; sound-on-film, sound film; sound track, soundstripe; roll, cartridge; pack, bipack, tripack; frame; emulsion, dope, backing.

.11 **camera**, Kodak; motion-picture camera, cinematograph *or* kinematograph [both Brit].

.12 **projector;** motion-picture projector, cinematograph *or* kinematograph [both Brit], vitascope; **slide projector**, magic lantern, stereopticon; slide viewer.

.13 **processing solution;** developer, soup [informal]; fixer, fixing bath, sodium thiosulfate *or* sodium hyposulfite *or* hypo; stop bath, short-stop, short-stop bath.

.14 VERBS **photograph, shoot** [informal], take a photograph, **take a picture**, take one's picture; **snap**, snapshot, snapshoot; **film**, get *or* capture on film; **mug** [slang]; daguerreotype, talbotype, calotype; Photostat; Xerox; microfilm; photomap; pan; **X-ray**, radiograph, roentgenograph.

.15 **process; develop; print;** blueprint; **blow up, enlarge.**

.16 **project, show, screen.**

.17 ADJS **photographic,** photo; **photogenic;** photosensitive, photoactive; panchromatic; telephotographic, telephoto; tintype; three-dimensional, 3-D.

.18 **types of photography**

aerophotography, aerial photography, air photography	miniature photography
animation photography	phonophotography
astrophotography	photoheliography
candid photography	photomacrography
chronophotography	photomicrography
cinematography	pyrophotography
cinephotomicrography	radiography
color photography	schlieren photography
electrophotography	skiagraphy
heliophotography	spectroheliography
holography	spectrophotography
infrared photography	stereophotography
integral photography	stroboscopic photography
laser photography	telephotography
macrophotography	uranophotography
microphotography	xerography
	X-ray photography

.19 **photographic equipment**

burning-in tool	lens hood
changing bag	light meter
closeup lens	periscopic lens
darkroom	photoelectric cell meter
darkroom timer	photoflash, photoflash lamp
developing tank	
diaphragm	photoflood, photoflood lamp
dodging tool	
dryer	photographometer
drying blotter	photometer
easel	polarizing filter
electronic-flash unit	portrait lens
enlarger	range finder
exposure meter	reflected light meter
filter	reflector
finder	safelight
fisheye lens	self-timer
flashbulb	shutter
flashcube	stroboscopic *or* strobe light
flashgun	
flashlight	telephoto lens
flash powder	timer
flash synchronizer	tripod
flash tube	varifocal lens
gadget bag	viewfinder
incident light meter	wide-angle lens
iris diaphragm	zoom lens
lens	
lens cover	

.20 **cameras**

aerial reconnaissance camera	flash camera
astrograph	folding camera
box camera	hand camera
camera obscura	Iconoscope
candid camera	image orthicon
cinematograph [Brit]	laboratory camera
color camera	magazine camera
electron-diffraction camera	microcamera
	miniature camera, minicam

motion-picture camera, movie camera	press camera
photochronograph	reflex camera
photocopier	single-lens reflex, SLR
photographic telescope	spectroscopic camera
photomicrographic camera	stereo camera
photomicroscope	still camera
photopitometer	telescopic camera
photospectroscope	television camera
Photostat	tripod camera
pinhole camera	twin-lens reflex
Polaroid Land camera	vest-pocket camera
portrait camera	Xerox machine
precision camera	X-ray diffraction camera
	X-ray machine

578. GRAPHIC ARTS

.1 NOUNS graphic arts, graphics; printmaking; painting 574.5; drawing 574.6; relief-carving 575.1; photography 577; printing 603; graphic artist 579.8.

.2 engraving, engravement, graving, enchasing, tooling, chiseling, incising, incision, lining, scratching, slashing, scoring; inscription, inscript; gem-engraving, glyptic, glyptography; glass-cutting; type-cutting; marking, line, scratch, slash, score; hatching, cross-hatching; etch, etching; stipple, stippling; tint, demitint, half tint; burr.

.3 (engraving processes) steel engraving, zincography, plate engraving, copperplate engraving, chalcography; relief method; woodcut, wood engraving, xylography; linocut; metal cut, *manière criblée* [Fr], cribbling; relief etching, zinc etching; intaglio; drypoint, etching, soft-ground etching, aquatint, mezzotint, stipple engraving, crayon engraving; cerography; pyrography, pyrogravure, woodburning, xylopyrography; photoengraving 603.1.

.4 lithography, planography, autolithography, artist lithography; chromolithography; photolithography, offset lithography 603.1.

.5 stencil printing, stencil; silk-screen printing, serigraphy; monotype; glass printing, decal, decalcomania; cameography.

.6 print, imprint, impression, impress; negative; color print; engraving, engravement; etching; aquatint, mezzotint; lithograph; autolithograph; chromolithograph; lithotype; copperplate, copperplate print *or* engraving; crayon engraving, graphotype; block, block print, linoleum-block print, rubber-block print, wood engraving, woodprint, xylograph, cut, woodcut, woodblock; vignette.

.7 plate, steel plate, copperplate, chalcograph; zincograph; stone, lithographic stone; printing plate 603.8.

.8 proof, artist's proof, proof before letter, open-letter proof, remarque proof.

.9 engraving tool, graver, burin, style, point, etching point, needle, etching needle; etching ball; etching ground *or* varnish; scorper; rocker; die, punch, stamp, intaglio, seal.

.10 VERBS engrave, grave, tool, enchase, incise, sculpture, inscribe, character, mark, line, crease, score, scratch, scrape, cut, carve, chisel; groove, furrow 263.3; stipple, cribble; hatch, crosshatch; lithograph, autolithograph; be a printmaker *or* graphic artist; make prints *or* graphics; print 603.14.

.11 etch, eat, eat out, corrode, bite, bite in.

.12 ADJS engraved, graven, graved, glypt(o)–; tooled, enchased, inscribed, incised, marked, lined, creased, cut, carved, glyphic, sculptured, insculptured, "insculp'd upon" [Shakespeare]; grooved, furrowed 263.4; printed, imprinted, impressed, stamped.

.13 glyptic(al), glyptographic, lapidary, lapidarian; xylographic, wood-block; lithographic, autolithographic, chromolithographic; aquatint, aquatinta, mezzotint.

579. ARTIST

.1 NOUNS artist, *artiste* [Fr], "a dreamer consenting to dream of the actual world" [Santayana], creator, maker; master, old master; dauber, daubster; copyist; craftsman, artisan 718.6.

.2 limner, delineator, depicter, picturer, portrayer, imager; illustrator; illuminator; calligrapher; commercial artist.

.3 drawer, sketcher, delineator; draftsman, architectural draftsman; crayonist, charcoalist, pastelist; cartoonist, caricaturist.

.4 painter, *artiste-peintre* [Fr]; colorist; luminist, luminarist; oil painter, oil-colorist; watercolorist; aquarellist; finger painter; monochromist, polychromist; genre painter, historical painter, landscapist, miniaturist, portrait painter, portraitist, marine painter, still-life painter; pavement artist; scene painter, scenewright, scenographer.

.5 photographer, photographist, cameraman; cinematographer; snapshotter, snap shooter, shutterbug [informal]; daguerreotypist, calotypist, talbotypist; skiagrapher, shadowgraphist, radiographer, X-ray photographer.

.6 sculptor, sculptress, sculpturer; earth artist; statuary; figurer, *figuriste* [Fr], modeler, molder, wax modeler, clay modeler;

graver, chaser, carver; stonecutter, mason, monumental mason, wood carver, xyloglyphic artist, whittler; ivory carver, bone carver, shell carver; gem carver, glyptic *or* glyptographic artist.

.7 ceramist, ceramicist, potter; china decorator *or* painter, tile painter, majolica painter; glassblower, glazer, glass decorator, pyroglazer, glass cutter; enamelist, enameler.

.8 printmaker, graphic artist; **engraver,** graver, burinist; inscriber, carver; **etcher;** line engraver; **lithographer,** autolithographer, chromolithographer; serigrapher, silk-screen artist; cerographer, cerographist; chalcographer; gem engraver, glyptographer, lapidary; wood engraver, xylographer; pyrographer, xylopyrographer; zincographer.

.9 designer, stylist, styler; costume designer, dress designer, *couturier* [Fr], *couturière* [Fr fem]; furniture designer, rug designer, textile designer.

.10 architect, civil architect; landscape architect, landscape gardener; city *or* urban planner, urbanist; functionalist.

.11 decorator, expert in decor, ornamentist, ornamentalist; **interior decorator,** house decorator, room decorator, floral decorator, table decorator; window decorator *or* dresser; confectionery decorator.

.12 stylists

abstract classicist
abstract expressionist
abstractionist
actionist
action painter
activist
analytical cubist
attitudist
baroque formalist
classicist
conceptual artist
concretist
constructivist
conventionalist
cubist
Dadaist
divisionist
earth artist
eclectic
elementarist
existentialist
expressionist
expressionistic abstractionist
Fauvist
free abstractionist
free expressionist
futurist
geometricist
gesture calligraphist
gesturist
idealist
impressionist
informalist
intimist
kineticist
linear chromatist
luminist
luminodynamist
lyrical abstractionist
magic realist
mannerist
matter informalist
modernist
mystic
naturalist
neoclassicist
neoconcretist
neoconstructivist
neocubist
neodadaist
neoexpressionist
neofigural postsurrealist
neoimpressionist
neoplasticist
neotraditionalist
nonaction calligraphist
nonobjectivist
nonrepresentationist
nuagist
objectivist
op artist
plein-airist
poetic kineticist
poetic realist
poetic tachist
pointillist
pop artist
poptical artist
postconcretist
postexpressionist
postimpressionist
postpainterly abstractionist
preimpressionist
primitive, primitivist
purist
realist
representationist, representationalist
romanticist
social realist
spatialist
suprarational automatist
suprematist
surrealist
surrealist tachist
symbolist
synchromist
synthesist
tachist
traditionalist
unist
vorticist

.13 painters

Albright
Bacon
Baziotes
Bellini
Bellows
Benton
Blake
Boccioni
Bonnard
Botticelli
Boucher
Braque
Brueghel
Buffet
Carrà
Cassatt
Cézanne
Chagall
Chardin
Chirico
Constable
Copley
Corot
Correggio
Courbet
Dali
Daumier
David
da Vinci
Degas
de Kooning
Delacroix
Dubuffet
Duchamp
Dufy
Dürer
Eakins
El Greco
Ensor
Ernst
Feininger
Fra Angelico
Fragonard
Friesz
Gainsborough
Gauguin
Giotto
Gleizes
Goya
Graves
Greuze
Gris
Grosz
Guardi
Hals
Hobbema
Hodler
Hogarth
Hokusai
Holbein
Homer
Hopper
Ingres
Jongkind
Kandinsky
Kent
Kirchner
Klee
Kline
Kokoschka
Kollwitz
LeBrun
Léger
Leonardo
Limburg
Lippi
Lorenzetti
Manet
Mantegna
Marc
Marin
Marquet
Masaccio
Masolino
Masson
Matisse
Michelangelo
Millet
Miró
Modigliani
Mondrian
Monet
Moses
Motherwell
Munch
Murillo
Nolde
Orozco
Ozenfant
Picabia
Picasso
Pissarro
Pollock
Poussin

Raphael	Stella
Redon	Stuart
Rembrandt	Tintoretto
Remington	Titian
Renoir	Tobey
Reynolds	Toulouse-Lautrec
Riley	Turner
Rivera	Utrillo
Rockwell	van der Weyden
Romney	Vandyke
Rosa	van Eyck
Rossetti	van Gogh
Rothko	van Ruisdael
Rouault	Velázquez
Rousseau	Vermeer
Rubens	Veronese
Ryder	Vlaminck
Sargent	Vuillard
Schmidt-Rottluff	Warhol
Seurat	Watteau
Severini	Whistler
Signac	Wood
Siqueiros	Wyeth
Sisley	Zadkine
Soutine	

.14 sculptors

Arp	Maillol
Borglum	Michelangelo
Brancusi	Milles
Calder	Moore
Cellini	Oldenburg
della Robbia	Phidias
Donatello	Picasso
Epstein	Pisano
French	Praxiteles
Ghiberti	Rodin
Giacometti	Saint-Gaudens
Lipchitz	

580. LANGUAGE

.1 NOUNS **language, speech, tongue,** *lingua* [L], lingu(o)– *or* lingui–, gloss(o)–, glott-(o)–; **talk, parlance, locution,** phraseology, **idiom, lingo** [informal]; dialect; idiolect, personal usage, individual speech habits *or* performance, parole; code *or* system of oral communication, individual speech competence, langue; **usage.**

.2 **dead language,** ancient language, lost language; parent language; classical language; living language, vernacular.

.3 **mother tongue,** native language *or* tongue, native speech, vernacular.

.4 **standard language,** standard *or* prestige dialect; national language, official language; educated speech *or* language; literary language, written language, formal written language; classical language; correct *or* good English, **Standard English, the King's** *or* **Queen's English,** Received Standard, Received Pronunciation.

.5 **informal language** *or* **speech,** informal standard speech, **spoken language, colloquial language** *or* **speech,** vernacular language *or* speech, vernacular; colloquialism, colloquial usage, conversationalism, vernacularism; informal English, conversational English, colloquial English, English as it is spoken.

.6 **substandard language** *or* **speech,** nonstandard language *or* speech; vernacular language *or* speech, **vernacular,** vulgate, vulgar tongue, common speech; uneducated speech, illiterate speech; substandard usage; **slang.**

.7 **dialect,** idiom; class dialect; regional *or* local dialect; subdialect; folk speech *or* dialect, patois; **provincialism, localism, regionalism,** regional accent 594.9; Canadian French, French Canadian; Pennsylvania Dutch, Pennsylvania German; Yankee, New England dialect; Brooklynese; Cockney; Yorkshire; Midland, Midland dialect; Anglo-Indian; Australian English; Gullah; Acadian, Cajun; dialect atlas, linguistic atlas; isogloss, bundle of isoglosses; speech community; linguistic community, linguistic ambience; speech *or* linguistic island, relic area; dialect dictionary, Dictionary of American Regional English.

.8 (idioms) Anglicism, Briticism, Englishism; Americanism, Yankeeism; Gallicism, Frenchism; Irishism, Hibernicism; Canadianism, Scotticism, Germanism, Russianism, Latinism, etc.

.9 **jargon, lingo** [informal], **cant, argot, patois, patter, vernacular;** vocabulary, **phraseology;** gobbledygook, mumbo jumbo, gibberish; **slang;** taboo language, vulgar language; obscene language, scatology.

.10 (jargons) Academese, cinemese, collegese, economese, sociologese, legalese, pedagese, societyese, stagese, telegraphese, Varietyese, Wall Streetese, journalese, newspaperese, officialese, federalese, Pentagonese, Washingtonese, medical Greek, medicalese, businessese, computerese, commercialism, business English; shoptalk.

.11 **lingua franca,** jargon, **pidgin,** trade language; auxiliary language, interlanguage; creolized language, creole language, creole; koine; pidgin English, talkeetalkee, Bêche-de-Mer, Beach-la-mar; Kitchen Kaffir; Chinook *or* Oregon Jargon; Sabir; artificial international languages 580.24.

.12 **linguistics,** linguistic science, science of language; glottology, glossology [archaic]; linguistic analysis; historical linguistics, comparative linguistics, general linguistics, descriptive linguistics, structural linguistics, structuralism, theoretical linguistics, areal linguistics, dialectology, geolinguistics, dialect or linguistic geography, glottochronology or lexicostatistics, computational or mathematical linguistics, psycholinguistics, sociolinguistics, metalinguistics; transformational linguistics, glossematics; etymology, derivation; **philology;** bowwow theory, dingdong theory, pooh-pooh theory; lexicology 582.15; semantics 545.7; syntactics, linguistic structure; **grammar** 586; phonology, phonemics, phonetics 594.14; morphophonemics, morphology 582.3; graphemics, paleography; language study, foreign-language study.

.13 linguist, linguistic scientist, linguistician, linguistic scholar; philologist, philologer, philologian; philologaster; **grammarian,** grammatist; grammaticaster; **etymologist,** etymologer; **lexicologist; lexicographer,** glossographer, glossarist; phoneticist, phonetician, phonemicist, phonologist, orthoepist; dialectician, dialectologist; semanticist, semasiologist; paleographer.

.14 polyglot, linguist, **bilingual** or diglot, trilingual, multilingual, –glot.

.15 colloquializer; jargonist, jargoneer, jargonizer; slangster.

.16 VERBS **speak, talk,** use language, communicate orally or verbally; use informal speech or style, colloquialize, vernacularize; jargon, jargonize, cant; patter.

.17 ADJS **linguistic,** lingual, glottological; descriptive, structural, glottochronological, lexicostatistical, psycholinguistic, sociolinguistic, metalinguistic; **philological;** lexicological, lexicographic(al); syntactic(al), **grammatic(al);** semantic 545.12; phonetic 594.31, phonemic, phonological; morphological 582.22; morphophonemic, graphemic, paleographic(al).

.18 vernacular, colloquial, conversational, unliterary, informal, spoken; unstudied, familiar, common, everyday; **substandard,** nonstandard, uneducated.

.19 jargonish, jargonal; **slang,** slangy; taboo; scatological.

.20 idiomatic; dialect, dialectal, dialectological; provincial, regional, local.

.21 types of languages

affixing	inflectional
agglutinative	isolating
analytic	monosyllabic
fusional	polysyllabic
incorporative	polysynthetic
polytonic	synthetic
symbolic	

.22 groups of languages

Adamawa-Eastern	Latinian
Afro-Asiatic	Luorawetlan
Algonquian	Malayo-Polynesian,
Anatolic, Anatolian	Malayo-Indonesian
Annam-Muong	Manchu
Araucanian	Mande
Arawakan	Mayan
Aryan	Melanesian
Athapaskan	Micronesian
Austric	Mongolic
Austroasiatic	Mon-Khmer
Austronesian	Munda
Aymara	Muran
Baltic	Muskogean
Balto-Slavic	Na-dene
Bantu	Nahuatlan
Berber	Niger-Congo
Brythonic	Nilotic
Bushman	Osco-Umbrian
Caddoan	Otomanguean
Cariban	Paleo-Asiatic, Paleo-
Caspian	Siberian
Caucasian	Papuan
Celtic	Penutian
Chad	Permian
Chari-Nile	Piman
Chibchan	Polynesian
Chinookan	Quechuan
Cushitic	Ritwan
Dard	Romance, Romanic
Dravidian	Sabellian
Eskimo-Aleut	Salish
Finnic	Samoyed, Samoyedic
Finno-Ugric, Finno-	Sanskritic
Ugrian	Scandinavian
Germanic	Semitic
Goidelic	Shahaptian
Gur	Shoshonean
Haida	Sino-Tibetan
Hamitic	Siouan
Hamito-Semitic	Skittagetan
Hellenic	Slavic, Slavonic
Hokan	Sudanic
Hokan-Coahuiltecan,	Tagala
Hokaltecan	Takilman
Hokan-Siouan	Tanoan
Indic, Indo-Aryan	Taracahitian
Indo-Chinese	Tarascan
Indo-European, Indo-	Teutonic
Germanic	Thraco-Illyrian
Indo-Hittite	Thraco-Phrygian
Indo-Iranian	Tibeto-Burman,
Indonesian	Tibeto-Burmese
Iranian	Tsimshian
Iroquoian	Tungusic
Italic	Tupi-Guaranian
Jicaquean	Turanian
Karankawa	Turkic, Turko-Tartar
Kartvelian	Ugric
Kechumaran	Ural-Altaic
Keresan	Uralian
Khoin	Uto-Aztecan
Khoisan	Xincan
Kitunahan	Yeniseian
Koluschan	Yukaghir
Kuki-Chin	Yukian
Kunama	Zuñian
Kwa	

.23 languages

Abnaki	Dalmatian	Kabyle	Makassar
Afghan, Afghani	Danish	Kachin	Malagasy
Afrikaans	Dinka	Kafiri	Malay
Ainu	Dutch	Kalmuck	Malayalam
Akan	Dyak	Kamasin	Maltese
Akkadian	Edo	Kamchadal, Kamchat-	Malto
Albanian	Efatese	kan	Manchu
Aleut	Egyptian	Kanarese	Mandarin
Algonquin	Elamitic	Kara-Kalpak	Mandingo
Amharic	English	Karamojong	Mangarevan
Andaman	Eskimo	Karankawa	Manobo
Anglo-French, Anglo-	Estonian	Karelian	Manx
Norman	Ethiopic	Karen	Maori
Anglo-Saxon	Euskarian	Kashmiri	Marathi
Annamese	Ewe	Kashubian	Marquesan
Anzanite	Faeroese	Kazan Tatar	Marshall, Marshallese
Apache	Faliscan	Keres	Maya
Arabic	Fijian	Ket	Meithei
Aramaic	Finnish	Khamti	Mende
Araucanian	Flemish	Kharia	Messapian
Arawak	Fox	Khasi	Middle English
Armenian	French	Khmer	Middle Greek
Assamese	Frisian	Khondi	Middle High German
Austral	Fulani, Fula	Khosa	Middle Persian
Avestan	Gadaba	Khotanese	Mishmi
Aymara	Gaelic	Khowar	Mishongnovi
Aztec	Galcha	Kickapoo	Misima
Balinese	Galla	Kiowa	Miskito
Baluchi	Garo	Kiowa Apache	Mon
Bashkir	Gaulish	Kiranti	Mongolian
Basque	Geez	Kirghiz	Mordvin, Mordvinian
Batak	Georgian	Kiriwina	Moro
Bellacoola	German	Kodagu	Mru
Bengali	Gilbertese	Kohistani	Mundari
Berber	Gold, Goldi	Koiari	Muong
Bhili	Gondi	Kolami	Mura
Bihari	Gothic	Komi	Murmi
Bikol	Greek	Kongo	Muskogee
Bini	Guanche	Konkani	Naga
Blackfoot	Guarani	Korean	Nepali
Brahui	Gujarati	Korwa	Newari
Breton	Gypsy	Koryak	Ngala
Buginese	Haida	Kui	Ngbaka
Bulgarian	Haitian Creole	Kuki	Niasese
Burmese	Hausa	Kumyk	Nicobarese
Burushaski	Hawaiian	Kunama	Niuean
Buryat	Hebrew	Kurdish	Nogai
Byelorussian	High German	Kurukh	Nootka
Cantonese	Hindustani	Kutchin	Norwegian
Carib	Hittite	Kutenai	Old English
Carolinian	Ho	Ladino	Oraon
Castilian	Hopi	Lahnda	Oriya
Catalan	Hottentot	Lampong	Oscan
Cham	Iban	Lamut	Osmanli
Chamorro	Ibanag	Lao	Ossetic
Cheremis	Ibo	Lapp	Ostyak
Cherokee	Icelandic	Latin	Pahari
Chibcha	Igorot	Latvian, Lettish	Pahlavi
Chin	Illyrian	Libyan	Palaic
Chinese	Ilocano	Ligurian	Palau
Choctaw	Irish, Irish Gaelic	Limbu	Palaung
Chukchi	Italian	Lithuanian	Pali
Chuvash	Ivatan	Livonian	Pampango
Coptic	Jagatai	Loucheux	Pangasinan
Cornish	Jakun	Low German	Panjabi, Punjabi
Cuman	Japanese	Lusatian	Pashto
Czech	Javanese	Luwian	Paya
Dafla	Juang	Lycian	Persian
Dagomba	Judeo-German	Lydian	Phrygian
Dakota	Judeo-Spanish	Macedonian	Plattdeutsch
		Madurese	Polabian
		Magyar	Polish

Portuguese
Prakrit
Provençal, *langue
d'oc* [Fr]
Punic
Punjabi
Puyi
Quechua
Quiché
Rajasthani
Riffian
Romaic
Romansh, Rhaeto-Ro-
manic, Rhaetian
Romany
Ronga
Ruanda
Rumanian
Rundi
Russian
Ruthenian
Sabellian
Saharan
Saho
Sakai
Salar
Samoan
Sanskrit
Santali
Sardinian
Sasak
Savara
Scottish Gaelic
Selung
Semang
Serbo-Croatian
Shan
Shina
Shluh, Shilha
Siamese
Sindhi
Sinhalese
Slovak
Slovene, Slovenian
Sogdian
Somali
Sorbian
Soyot
Spanish
Sumerian
Susian
Swahili
Swedish
Syriac
Syryenian
Taal
Tagalog

Tagula
Tahitian
Tajiki
Takelma
Talamanca
Talishi
Tamashek
Tamaulipec
Tamil
Tatar
Tavgi
Taw-Sug
Teleut
Telugu
Thracian
Tibetan
Tigre
Tigrinya
Tino
Tipura
Tocharian
Toda
Tonga
Tuamotu
Tuareg
Tulu
Tungus
Tupi
Turkish
Turkoman
Ugaritic
Uighur
Ukrainian
Umbrian
Urdu
Uzbek
Venetic
Veps
Vietnamese
Visayan
Vogul
Vote
Votyak
Wa
Welsh
Wendish
White Russian
Xhosa
Yakut
Yenisei
Yiddish
Yoruba
Yurak
Zenaga
Zulu
Zuñi

.24 artificial languages

Antido
Arulo
Blaia Zimondal
Esperantido
Esperanto
Europan
Idiom Neutral
Ido
Interlingua
Latinesce
Latino, Latino sine
flexione
Lingualumina

Lingvo Kosmopolita
Monario
Nov-Esperanto
Novial
Nov-Latin
Occidental
Optez
Pasigraphy
Ro
Romanal
Solresol
Volapük

581. LETTER

.1 NOUNS **letter, written character, character, sign, symbol,** graph, grapheme, allo-
graph, alphabetic character *or* symbol,
phonetic character *or* symbol; logographic *or* lexigraphic character *or* symbol; ideographic *or* ideogrammic *or* ideo-
grammatic character *or* symbol; syllabic
character *or* symbol, syllabic, syllabo-
gram; pictographic character *or* symbol;
cipher, device; monogram; graphy, *mater
lectionis* [L]; **writing** 602.

.2 (phonetic and ideographic symbols) **pho-
nogram;** phonetic symbol; **logogram,**
logograph, grammalogue; word letter;
ideogram, ideograph, phonetic, radical,
determinative; **pictograph,** pictogram; **hieroglyphic,** hieroglyph, hieratic symbol,
demotic character; **rune,** runic character
or symbol; **cuneiform, character;** wedge,
arrowhead, ogham; kana, hiragana, kata-
kana; **shorthand** 602.8; hieroglyphics.

.3 writing system, script, letters; alphabet,
letters of the alphabet, **ABC's;** christ-
cross-row; **phonetic alphabet,** International Phonetic Alphabet, IPA; Initial
Teaching Alphabet, ITA; phonemic alphabet; runic alphabet, futhark; alpha-
betism; **syllabary;** alphabetics, alphabetol-
ogy, graphemics; paleography; speech
sound 594.13.

.4 spelling, orthography; phonetic spelling,
phonetics, phonography; spelling reform;
spelling match *or* bee, spelldown; bad
spelling, cacography; spelling pronunciation.

.5 lettering, initialing; **inscription,** epigraph,
graffito; alphabetization; transliteration,
transcription.

.6 VERBS **letter, initial, inscribe,** character,
sign, mark; **capitalize; alphabetize,** alphabet; transliterate, transcribe.

.7 spell, orthographize; spell out, write out,
trace out; spell backward; outspell, spell
down; syllabify, syllabize, syllable, syllabi-
cate.

.8 ADJS **literal, lettered; alphabetic(al);** abecedarian; graphemic, allographic; large-
lettered, majuscule, majuscular, uncial;
capital, capitalized, upper-case; small-let-
tered, minuscule, minuscular, lower-case;
logographic, logogrammatic, lexigraphic,
ideographic, ideogrammic, ideogram-
matic, pictographic; transliterated, transcribed.

.9 writing systems

Arabic	kanji
Armenian	katakana
Assyrian	Kharoshthi
Avestan	Korean
Babylonian	Latin
Berber	Lemnian
Brahmi	Libyan
Chalcidian	Linear A
Cherokee	Linear B
Coptic	Lycian
Cretan	Lydian
Cypriot	Manchu
Cypro-Minoan	Mayan
Cyrillic	Minoan
Devanagari	Mitannic
Egyptian demotic	Mongolian
Egyptian hieratic	Nagari
Egyptian hieroglyphic	Nubian
Elamitic	ogham
Ethiopian	Oscan
Etruscan	Pahlavi
Georgian	Permian
Glagolitic	Persian
Gothic	Phoenician
Grantha	Phrygian
Greek	runic
Hebrew	Sanskrit
hiragana	Scandinavian
Hittite hieroglyphic	Semitic
Iberian	Sinaitic
Indus Valley	Sogdian
Initial Teaching	Sumerian
Alphabet	Szeklian
International Pho-	Tuareg
netic Alphabet	Turkish runic
Ionian	Uighur
Irish	Umbrian
Kalmuck	Vietnamese
kana	

582. WORD

.1 NOUNS **word,** log(o)-, onomato-, -onym, -onymy; **term,** expression, locution, linguistic form, lexeme, free form, minimum free form, *logos* [Gk], *verbum* [L]; verbalism, vocable, utterance, articulation; **usage;** syllable, polysyllable; homonym, homophone, homograph; monosyllable; synonym; metonym; antonym.

.2 **root,** etymon, primitive; eponym; derivative, derivation; cognate; doublet.

.3 **morphology,** morphemics; morphophonemics; **morpheme;** morph, allomorph; bound morpheme *or* form, free morpheme *or* form; difference of form, formal contrast; accidence; **inflection,** conjugation, declension; paradigm; derivation, word-formation; formative; root, radical; theme, stem; **affix, suffix, prefix,** infix; proclitic, enclitic; affixation, infixation, suffixation, prefixation; morphemic analysis, immediate constituent *or* IC analysis, cutting; morphophonemic analysis.

.4 **word form,** formation, construction; back formation; clipped word; spoonerism; **compound;** *tatpurusha, dvandva, karmadharaya, dvigu, avyayibhava, bahuvrihi* [all Skt]; endocentric compound, exocentric compound; acronym, acrostic; paronym, conjugate.

.5 **technical term,** technicality; jargon word.

.6 **barbarism, corruption, vulgarism, impropriety,** taboo word; **colloquialism, slang, localism** 582.6.

.7 **loan word,** borrowing, borrowed word, paronym; loan translation, calque; foreignism.

.8 **neologism,** neology, neoterism, new word *or* term, newfangled expression; **coinage;** new sense *or* meaning; nonce word; ghost word *or* name.

.9 **catchword,** catch phrase, shibboleth, slogan, cry; **pet expression,** byword; vogue word, fad word, cliché.

.10 long word, hard word, jawbreaker [informal], polysyllable; sesquipedalian, sesquipedalia [pl]; lexiphanicism, grandiloquence 601.

.11 hybrid word, **hybrid;** macaronicism, macaronic; hybridism, contamination; blendword, blend, portmanteau word, portmanteau, portmantologism, telescope word.

.12 **portmanteau word,** portmanteau, **counterword.**

.13 **archaism,** archaicism, antiquated word *or* expression; obsoletism, obsolete.

.14 **vocabulary, lexis, words, wordage, verbiage,** wordhoard, stock of words; phraseology; thesaurus; lexicon 605.7.

.15 **lexicology; lexicography,** lexigraphy, glossography; onomastics, onomatology; onomasiology; semantics, semasiology.

.16 **etymology, derivation, origin,** word history, semantic history; historical linguistics, comparative linguistics; eponymy, folk etymology.

.17 echoic word, onomatopoeic word, onomatope; onomatopoeia; bowwow theory.

.18 **neologist, word-coiner,** neoterist; phraser, phrasemaker, phrasemonger.

.19 ADJS **verbal,** vocabular, vocabulary.

.20 lexical, lexicologic(al); lexigraphic(al), **lexicographic(al),** glossographic(al); etymologic(al), derivative; onomastic, onomatologic; onomasiologic(al); echoic, onomatopoeic; conjugate, paronymous, paronymic.

.21 neological, neoteric(al).

.22 **morphological,** morphemic; morphophonemic; inflective, inflectional, paradigmatic, derivational; affixal, prefixal, infixal, suffixal.

583. NOMENCLATURE

.1 NOUNS **nomenclature, terminology,** orismology, glossology [archaic]; onomatology, onomastics; toponymy, place-names, place-naming; antonomasia; polyonymy; **taxonomy,** classification, systematics, biosystematy, biosystematics, cytotaxonomy, binomial nomenclature, binomialism, Linnaean method, trinomialism; kingdom, phylum, class, order, family, genus, species.

.2 **naming, calling, denomination,** appellation, designation, styling, terming, definition, identification; **christening,** baptism; dubbing; nicknaming.

.3 **name,** onomato–, –onym, –onymy; **appellation,** appellative, **denomination, designation, style,** *nomen* [L], **cognomen,** cognomination; proper name *or* noun; moniker *or* handle [both slang]; **title,** honorific; empty title *or* name; **label, tag; epithet,** byword; **scientific name,** trinomen, trinomial name, binomen, binomial name; nomen nudum, hyponym; tautonym; typonym; middle name; eponym; namesake; secret name, cryptonym, euonym.

.4 **first name, forename, Christian name, given name,** baptismal name.

.5 **surname, last name, family name, cognomen,** byname; **maiden name;** married name; patronymic, matronymic.

.6 (Latin terms) *praenomen, nomen, agnomen, cognomen.*

.7 **nickname, sobriquet,** byname, cognomen; **pet name,** diminutive, hypocoristic, affectionate name.

.8 **alias, pseudonym,** anonym, **assumed name,** false *or* fictitious name, *nom de guerre* [Fr]; **pen name, nom de plume;** stage name, *nom de theatre* [Fr], professional name; John Doe, Jane Doe, Richard Roe.

.9 **misnomer,** wrong name.

.10 **signature,** sign manual, **autograph, hand, John Hancock** [informal]; mark, mark of signature, cross, christcross, X; initials; subscription; countersignature, countersign, countermark, counterstamp; endorsement; visa, *visé* [Fr]; monogram, cipher, device; seal, sigil, signet.

.11 VERBS **name, denominate,** nominate, **designate, call, term, style, dub;** specify; define, identify; **title, entitle; label, tag; nickname; christen,** baptize.

.12 **misname,** misnomer, **miscall,** misterm, misdesignate.

.13 **be called, be known by** *or* **as, go by, go as, go by the name of,** go *or* pass under the name of, bear the name of, rejoice in the name of; go under an assumed *or* false name, have an alias.

.14 ADJS **named, called,** yclept [archaic], **styled, titled,** denominated, denominate [archaic], **known as,** known by the name of, designated, termed, dubbed, identified as; christened, baptized; what one may well *or* fairly *or* properly *or* fitly call.

.15 **nominal,** cognominal; **titular, in name only,** nominative, formal; **so-called,** quasi; would-be, *soi-disant* [Fr]; **self-called, self-styled,** self-christened; honorific; epithetic(al); hypocoristic, diminutive; by name, by whatever name, under any other name.

.16 denominative, nominative, appellative; eponymous, eponymic.

.17 **terminological,** nomenclatural, orismological; onomastic; toponymic, toponymous; taxonomic, classificatory, binomial, Linnaean, trinomial.

584. ANONYMITY

.1 NOUNS **anonymity, anonymousness, namelessness; incognito;** anonym.

.2 **what's-its-name** *or* **what's-his-name** *or* **what's-his-face** *or* what's-her-name *or* **what-you-may-call-it** *or* what-you-may-call-'em *or* what-d'ye-call-'em *or* what-d'ye-call-it *or* whatzit [all informal]; *je ne sais quoi* [Fr], I don't know what; such-and-such; **so-and-so,** certain person, Mr. X; you-know-who.

.3 ADJS **anonymous, anon.; nameless, unnamed,** unidentified, undesignated, unspecified, innominate, without a name, **unknown;** undefined; unacknowledged; **incognito;** cryptonymous, cryptonymic.

585. PHRASE

.1 NOUNS **phrase, expression, locution, utterance,** usage, term, verbalism, –logy *or* –logia; **word-group,** construction, endocentric construction, headed group, syntagm; syntactic structure; noun phrase, verb phrase, verb complex, adverbial phrase, adjectival phrase, prepositional phrase; **clause; sentence,** period, periodic sentence; **paragraph; idiom,** idiotism, phrasal idiom; turn of phrase *or* expression, peculiar expression, manner *or* way of speaking; set phrase *or* term; conventional *or* common *or* standard phrase; phraseogram, phraseograph.

.2 **diction, phrasing** 588.1.

.3 **phraser, phrasemaker,** phrasemonger, phraseman.

.4 ADJS **phrasal,** phrase; phrasey.

.5 ADVS in set phrases *or* terms, in good set terms, in round terms.

586. GRAMMAR

.1 NOUNS **grammar,** rules of language; "the rule and pattern of speech" [Horace]; grammaticalness, grammaticality, grammatical theory; traditional grammar, school grammar; descriptive grammar, structural grammar, phrase-structure grammar; generative grammar, transformational grammar, transformational generative grammar; tagmemic analysis; glossematics; stratificational grammar; **parsing,** grammatical analysis; **morphology** 582.3; **phonology** 594.14.

.2 **syntax, structure, syntactic structure,** word order, word arrangement; syntactics, syntactic analysis; immediate constituent analysis, IC analysis, cutting; phrase structure; surface structure, shallow structure, deep structure, underlying structure; levels, ranks, strata; tagmeme, form-function unit, slot, filler, slot and filler; **function, subject, predicate, complement, object,** direct object, indirect object, **modifier,** qualifier, sentence *or* construction modifier, appositive, attribute, attributive.

.3 **part of speech,** form class, major form class, function class; function *or* empty *or* form word; **adjective,** adjectival, attributive; **adverb,** adverbial; **preposition;** verbal adjective, gerundive; **participle,** present participle, past participle, perfect participle; **conjunction,** subordinating conjunction, coordinating conjunction, conjunctive adverb, adversative conjunction, copulative, copulative conjunction, correlative conjunction, disjunctive, disjunctive conjunction; **interjection,** exclamatory noun *or* adjective; **particle.**

.4 **verb,** transitive, transitive verb, intransitive, intransitive verb, impersonal verb, neuter verb, deponent verb, defective verb, finite verb, linking verb, copula; verbal; **infinitive; auxiliary verb,** auxiliary, modal auxiliary; verb phrase.

.5 **noun, pronoun,** substantive, common noun, proper noun, abstract noun, collective noun, quotation noun, hypostasis, adherent noun, adverbial noun; verbal noun, gerund; nominal; noun phrase.

.6 **article,** definite article, indefinite article; determiner, noun determiner, determinative.

.7 **person;** first person; second person, proximate; third person; fourth person, obviative.

.8 **number;** singular, dual, trial, plural.

.9 **case;** common case, subject case, nominative; object *or* objective case, accusative, dative, possessive case, genitive; local case, locative, essive, superessive, inessive, adessive, abessive, lative, allative, illative, sublative, elative, ablative, delative, terminative, approximative, prolative, perlative, translative; comitative, instrumental, prepositional, vocative; oblique case.

.10 **gender,** masculine, feminine, neuter, common gender; grammatical gender, natural gender; animate, inanimate.

.11 **mood,** mode; indicative, subjunctive, imperative, conditional, potential, obligative, permissive, optative, jussive.

.12 **tense; present;** historical present; **past,** preterit; aorist; imperfect; future; **perfect,** present perfect, future perfect; past perfect, **pluperfect;** progressive tense, durative; point tense.

.13 **aspect;** perfective, imperfective, inchoative, iterative, frequentative, desiderative.

.14 **voice;** active voice, active, passive voice, passive; middle voice, middle; medio-passive; reflexive.

.15 **punctuation,** punctuation marks; diacritical mark *or* sign; reference mark, reference; point, tittle; stop, end stop.

.16 VERBS grammaticize; **parse,** analyze; inflect, **conjugate, decline; punctuate,** mark, point; parenthesize, hyphenate, bracket.

.17 ADJS **grammatic(al), correct, syntactic(al),** formal, structural; tagmemic, glossematic; **functional;** substantive, nominal, pronominal; verbal, transitive, intransitive; linking, copulative; attributive, adjectival, adverbial, participial; prepositional, postpositional; conjunctive.

.18 **punctuation marks**

ampersand (&)	periods (. . . *or* * * *)
angle brackets (⟨ ⟩)	
apostrophe (')	exclamation mark *or*
braces ({ })	point (!)
brackets ([ ])	hyphen (-)
colon (:)	parentheses, parens
comma (,)	[informal] ( )
dash (—, -)	period, full stop
ellipsis, suspension	[Brit], point, deci-

mal point, dot (.)
question mark, interrogation mark *or* point (?)
quotation marks, quotes (" ")

semicolon (;)
single quotation marks, single quotes (' ')
virgule, diagonal, solidus, slash mark (/)

.19 diacritical marks

acute accent (´)
breve (˘)
cedilla (¸)
circumflex accent (ˆ, ˆ, *or* ˜)

diaeresis, umlaut (¨)
grave accent (`)
haček [Cz], wedge (ˇ)
macron (¯)
tilde (˜)

.20 reference marks

asterisk, star (*)
asterism (*∗*)
bullet, centered dot (●)
caret (∧)
dagger, obelisk (†)
ditto mark (")
double dagger,

diesis (‡)
double prime (")
index, fist (☞)
leaders (. . . .)
paragraph (¶)
parallels (‖)
prime (´)
section (§)

587. UNGRAMMATICALNESS

.1 NOUNS **ungrammaticalness,** bad *or* faulty grammar, faulty syntax; lack of concord *or* agreement, faulty reference, misplaced *or* dangling modifier, shift of tense, shift of structure, anacoluthon, faulty subordination, faulty comparison, faulty coordination, faulty punctuation, lack of parallelism, sentence fragment, comma fault, comma splice; abuse of terms, corruption of speech, broken speech, talkee-talkee.

.2 solecism, ungrammaticism, **misusage, missaying, misconstruction,** barbarism, infelicity; corruption; antiphrasis, malapropism 518.7.

.3 VERBS **solecize,** commit a solecism, use faulty *or* inadmissible *or* inappropriate grammar, ignore *or* disdain *or* violate grammar, murder the King's *or* Queen's English, break Priscian's head [archaic].

.4 ADJS **ungrammatic(al),** solecistic(al), **incorrect,** barbarous; faulty, erroneous 518.16; infelicitous, improper 27.7; careless, slovenly, slipshod 62.15; loose, imprecise 518.17.

588. DICTION

.1 NOUNS **diction,** use *or* choice of words, **phraseology,** phrase, **phrasing, wording, wordage, verbiage,** rhetoric, speech, talk [informal], **language,** dialect, parlance, locution, expression, formulation; **grammar;** usage, *usus loquendi* [L]; **idiom;** composition.

.2 style; mode, manner, strain, vein; fashion, way 657; **rhetoric; manner of speaking,** mode of expression, literary style, style of writing, command of language *or* idiom,

form of speech, expression of ideas; feeling for words *or* language, sense of language, *Sprachgefühl* [Ger]; power *or* grace of expression; linguistic tact *or* finesse; personal style; mannerism, trick, peculiarity; affectation; "the dress of thoughts" [Dickens], "a certain absolute and unique manner of expressing a thing, in all its intensity and color" [Walter Pater]; inflation, exaggeration, grandiloquence 601; the grand style, the sublime style, the sublime; the plain style; **stylistics,** stylistic analysis.

.3 stylist, master of style; rhetorician, rhetor, rhetorizer [archaic]; mannerist.

.4 VERBS **phrase, express,** find a phrase for, give expression *or* words to, **word,** state, **frame,** conceive, style, couch, **put in words,** clothe *or* embody in words, couch in terms, express by *or* in words, find words to express; put, present, set out; **formulate,** formularize; paragraph; rhetorize [archaic].

.5 ADJS **phrased,** expressed, worded, formulated, styled, put, presented, couched.

589. ELEGANCE

(*of language*)

.1 NOUNS **elegance,** elegancy; **grace,** gracefulness, gracility; **taste,** tastefulness, good taste; **correctness,** seemliness, comeliness, **propriety; refinement,** discrimination, **restraint; polish, finish,** terseness, neatness; smoothness, flow, **fluency; felicity,** felicitousness, **ease;** clarity, clearness, lucidity, limpidity, pellucidity, perspicuity; distinction, dignity; **purity,** chastity, chasteness; **plainness,** straightforwardness, directness, **simplicity,** naturalness, unaffectedness, Atticism, Attic quality; classicism, classicalism; well-rounded *or* well-turned periods, flowing periods; the right word in the right place, fittingness, appropriateness.

.2 harmony, proportion, symmetry, **balance,** equilibrium, order, orderedness, measure, measuredness, concinnity; rhythm; **euphony,** sweetness, beauty.

.3 (affected elegance) **affectation,** affectedness, studiedness, **pretentiousness, mannerism,** manneredness, artifice, artfulness, **artificiality,** unnaturalness; **euphuism,** Gongorism, Marinism; **preciousness,** preciosity; euphemism; purism; overelegance, overelaboration, overniceness, overrefinement, hyperelegance, etc.

.4 purist, classicist, Atticist, plain stylist.

.5 euphuist, Gongorist, Marinist, *précieux* [Fr], *précieuse* [Fr fem]; phrasemaker, phrasemonger.

.6 ADJS **elegant, tasteful, graceful,** gracile, **polished,** finished, round, terse; neat, trim, **refined, restrained; clear,** lucid, limpid, pellucid, perspicuous; **simple, unaffected, natural,** unlabored, **easy; pure,** chaste; **plain,** straightforward, direct; classic(al); Attic, Ciceronian.

.7 **appropriate, fit, fitting,** just [archaic], **proper, correct, seemly,** comely; **felicitous,** happy, **apt,** well-chosen, **well-put,** well-expressed, inspired.

.8 **harmonious, balanced,** symmetrical, orderly, ordered, measured, concinnate, concinnous; **euphonious,** euphonic, euphonical [archaic], sweet; **smooth,** tripping, smooth-sounding, fluent, flowing.

.9 (affectedly elegant) **affected,** euphuistic(al); elaborate, elaborated; **pretentious, mannered, artificial, unnatural,** studied; precious, *précieux, précieuse* [both Fr], overnice, overrefined, overelegant, overelaborate, hyperelegant, etc.; Gongoristic, Gongoresque, Marinistic.

590. INELEGANCE

(of language)

.1 NOUNS **inelegance,** inelegancy; inconcinnity, infelicity; **clumsiness,** cumbrousness, leadenness, heaviness, stiltedness, **ponderousness,** unwieldiness; sesquipedalianism, sesquipedality; turgidity, bombasticness, pompousness 601.1; **gracelessness,** ungracefulness; **tastelessness,** bad taste, **impropriety,** indecorousness, unseemliness; incorrectness, impurity; **vulgarity,** vulgarism, Gothicism [archaic], barbarism, barbarousness, **coarseness, unrefinement,** roughness, grossness, rudeness, crudeness, uncouthness; dysphemism; cacology, poor diction; cacophony, uneuphoniousness, harshness; loose *or* slipshod construction, ill-balanced sentences; lack of finish *or* polish.

.2 ADJS **inelegant, clumsy, graceless,** ungraceful, inconcinnate, inconcinnous, infelicitous, unfelicitous; **tasteless,** in bad taste, offensive to ears polite; **incorrect, improper; indecorous, unseemly,** uncourtly, undignified; **unpolished, unrefined;** impure, unclassical; **vulgar,** barbarous, barbaric, rude, **crude, uncouth,** Doric, outlandish; low, gross, **coarse,** dysphemistic, doggerel; cacologic(al), ca-

cophonous, uneuphonious, harsh, ill-sounding.

.3 **stiff, stilted, formal,** Latinate, *guinde* [Fr], **labored,** ponderous, elephantine, lumbering, cumbrous, leaden, heavy, unwieldy, sesquipedalian, inkhorn, turgid, bombastic, pompous 601.8; **forced,** awkward, cramped, halting.

591. PLAIN SPEECH

.1 NOUNS **plain speech,** plain speaking, plain style, unadorned style, **plain English,** plain words, common speech, vernacular, household words; **plainness,** simpleness, simplicity; soberness, restrainedness; severity, austerity; spareness, leanness, baldness, bareness, starkness, unadornedness; naturalness, unaffectedness; directness, straightforwardness, calling a spade a spade, making no bones about it [informal]; unimaginativeness, prosaicness, matter-of-factness, prosiness, unpoeticalness; homespun, rustic style; candor, frankness, openness.

.2 VERBS **speak plainly,** waste no words, **call a spade a spade,** come to the point, not beat about the bush, make no bones about it *or* talk turkey [both informal].

.3 ADJS **plain-speaking,** simple-speaking; **plain,** common; **simple,** unadorned, unvarnished, pure, neat; sober, severe, austere, ascetic, spare, lean, bald, bare, stark, Spartan; **natural, unaffected;** direct, straightforward; commonplace, homely, homespun, rustic; candid, plain-spoken, frank, open; **prosaic,** prosing, prosy; unpoetical, unimaginative, dull, dry, **matter-of-fact.**

.4 ADVS **plainly, simply,** naturally, unaffectedly, matter-of-factly; in plain words, **in plain English,** in words of one syllable; point-blank, to the point.

592. CONCISENESS

.1 NOUNS **conciseness,** concision, briefness, brachylogy, **brevity,** "the soul of wit" [Shakespeare]; shortness, compactness; **curtness,** brusqueness, **crispness, terseness,** summariness; taciturnity 613.2, reserve 613.3; **pithiness,** succinctness, pointedness, sententiousness; compendiousness.

.2 laconicness, laconism, laconicism, economy of language; laconics.

.3 aphorism, epigram 517.1; **abridgment** 607.

.4 **abbreviation,** shortening, clipping, cutting, pruning, truncation; ellipsis, aposiopesis, contraction, syncope, apocope, elision, crasis, syneresis [all gram].

.5 VERBS **be brief, come to the point, make a long story short,** cut the matter short, **be telegraphic,** waste no words, put it in few words, give more matter and less art; shorten, condense, **abbreviate** 203.6.

.6 ADJS **concise, brief, short,** "short and sweet" [Thomas Lodge]; **condensed, compressed,** tight, close, compact; **compendious** 203.8; **curt,** brusque, **crisp, terse,** summary; taciturn 613.9; reserved 613.10; **pithy, succinct; laconic,** Spartan; **abridged, abbreviated,** synopsized, shortened, clipped, cut, pruned, contracted, truncated, docked; elliptic, aposiopestic; sententious, epigrammatic(al), gnomic, aphoristic(al) 517.6, **pointed,** to the point.

.7 ADVS **concisely, briefly,** shortly; laconically; **curtly,** brusquely, **crisply, tersely,** summarily; **pithily, succinctly,** pointedly; sententiously, aphoristically, epigrammatically.

.8 **in brief, in short,** in substance, in epitome, in outline, **in a nutshell,** in a capsule; **in a word,** in two words, in a few words, without wasting words; **to be brief,** to come to the point, to cut the matter short, **to make a long story short.**

593. DIFFUSENESS

.1 NOUNS **diffuseness,** diffusiveness, diffusion; **formlessness** 247; **profuseness,** profusiveness, profusion; **effusiveness,** effusion, gush, gushing; outpour, tirade; logorrhea, talkativeness 596, cloud of words; **copiousness, exuberance,** rampancy, amplitude, extravagance, prodigality, fertility, fecundity, rankness, teemingness, prolificity, prolificacy, productivity, abundance, overflow, fluency [archaic]; superfluity, superflux, superabundance; redundancy, pleonasm, repetitiveness, reiterativeness, reiteration, tautology, macrology; repetition for effect or emphasis, palilogy.

.2 **wordiness, verbosity,** verbiage, verbalism, verbality; **prolixity, long-windedness,** longiloquence; flow or flux of words, cloud of words; logorrhea, talkativeness 596.

.3 discursiveness, desultoriness, digressiveness, aimlessness; rambling, maundering, meandering, wandering, roving.

.4 **digression, departure,** deviation, **discursion,** excursion, excursus, sidetrack, side path, side road, byway, bypath; episode.

.5 **circumlocution, roundaboutness,** circuitousness, ambages [archaic]; deviousness, obliqueness, **indirection;** periphrase, periphrasis.

.6 **expatiation, amplification, enlargement,** expansion, dilation; elaboration; **development,** explication, unfolding, working-out.

.7 VERBS **expatiate, amplify, dilate, expand,** enlarge, **enlarge upon,** elaborate; relate or rehearse in extenso; detail, particularize; **develop,** evolve, unfold; work out, explicate; descant, relate at large.

.8 **protract, extend, spin out,** string out, draw out, stretch out, **drag out,** run out; pad, fill out; perorate, **speak at length,** spin a long yarn, never finish; chatter, talk one to death 596.5,6.

.9 **digress,** wander, **get off the subject, wander from the subject,** get sidetracked, excurse, ramble, maunder, stray, go astray; depart, deviate, turn aside; **go off on a tangent,** go up blind alleys.

.10 circumlocute [informal], **go round about,** go around and around, **beat around** or **about the bush,** go round Robin Hood's barn; periphrase.

.11 ADJS **diffuse,** diffusive; **formless** 247.4; **profuse,** profusive; **effusive,** gushing, gushy; copious, exuberant, extravagant, prodigal, fecund, teeming, prolific, productive, abundant, superabundant, overflowing; redundant, pleonastic, repetitive, reiterative, tautologous.

.12 **wordy, verbose; talkative** 596.9; **prolix,** windy [informal], **long-winded,** longiloquent; **protracted,** extended, de longue haleine [Fr], lengthy, long, **long-drawn-out,** long-spun, spun-out, endless, unrelenting; padded, filled out.

.13 **discursive, aimless,** loose; **rambling, maundering, wandering,** roving; excursive, **digressive,** deviative, **desultory,** episodic; by the way.

.14 **circumlocutory,** circumlocutional, **roundabout, circuitous,** ambagious [archaic], oblique, indirect; periphrastic.

.15 **expatiating,** dilative, dilatative, enlarging, amplifying, expanding; **developmental.**

.16 ADVS **at length,** at large, in full, in extenso [L], in detail.

594. SPEECH

(utterance)

.1 NOUNS **speech,** log(o)–, lalo–, phon(o)–; **language** 580, **talk,** talking, speaking, **discourse,** oral communication, comment, parole, **palaver, prattle, gab** [informal]; rapping or yakking or yakkety-yak [all slang]; **words, accents;** chatter 596.3; conversation 597; elocution 599.1.

.2 "the mirror of the soul" [Publilius Syrus],

"the image of life" [Democritus], "a faculty given to man to conceal his thoughts" [Talleyrand], "but broken light upon the depth of the unspoken" [George Eliot].

.3 **utterance, speaking**, locution [archaic], phonation; parole, speech act, linguistic act *or* behavior; string, utterance string, sequence of phonemes; **voice, tongue;** word of mouth, parol, the spoken word; vocable, **word** 582.

.4 **remark, statement, comment,** crack [slang], one's two cents' worth [informal], **word,** say, **saying, utterance,** observation, reflection, expression; note, thought, **mention;** assertion, averment, allegation, affirmation, pronouncement, position, dictum; **declaration;** interjection, exclamation; question 485.10; answer 486; address, greeting, apostrophe; sentence, phrase; subjoinder, Parthian shot.

.5 **articulateness,** articulacy, readiness *or* facility of speech; eloquence 600.

.6 **articulation,** phonation, voicing, **vocalization; pronunciation, enunciation,** utterance; **delivery, attack.**

.7 **intonation, inflection, modulation;** intonation pattern *or* contour, intonation *or* inflection of voice, speech tune *or* melody; suprasegmental, suprasegmental phoneme; **tone, pitch;** pitch accent.

.8 manner of speaking, way of saying, mode of expression; **tone of voice, voice,** *voce* [Ital], **tone;** voice quality, **timbre;** voice qualifier; paralinguistic communication.

.9 regional accent, foreign accent, **accent;** brogue, twang, burr, drawl, broad accent.

.10 juncture, open juncture, close juncture; terminal, clause terminal, rising terminal, falling terminal; sandhi; word boundary, clause boundary; pause.

.11 **accent,** accentuation, stress accent; **emphasis, stress;** ictus, beat, rhythmical stress; rhythm, rhythmic pattern, **cadence;** prosody, prosodics, metrics 609.8; stress pattern; level of stress; primary stress, secondary stress, tertiary stress, weak stress.

.12 vowel quantity, **quantity,** mora; long vowel, short vowel, full vowel, reduced vowel.

.13 **speech sound,** phone, vocable; articulation, manner of articulation; **stop, plosive,** explosive, mute, check, occlusive, **affricate,** continuant, **liquid,** lateral, **nasal;** point *or* place of articulation; labial, bilabial, labiodental, labiovelar, dental, apico-dental, alveolar, apico-alveolar, pala-

tal, cerebral, cacuminal, retroflex, velar, guttural, pharyngeal, glottal, laryngeal; lingual; **voice,** voicing; sonority; aspiration, palatalization, labialization, pharyngealization, glottalization; surd, voiceless sound; sonant, voiced sound; **consonant; semivowel,** glide, transition sound; vocalic, syllabic nucleus, syllabic peak, peak; vocoid; **vowel;** monophthong, **diphthong,** triphthong; **phoneme,** segmental phoneme, morphophoneme; modification, assimilation, dissimilation; **allophone;** parasitic vowel, epenthetic vowel, svarabhakti vowel, prothetic vowel; **syllable.**

.14 **phonetics,** articulatory phonetics, acoustic phonetics; phonology; morphophonemics; orthoepy; sound *or* phonetic law; sound shift, *Lautverschiebung* [Ger]; umlaut, mutation, ablaut, gradation; rhotacism, betacism; Grimm's law, Verner's law, Grassmann's law.

.15 **phonetician,** phonetist, phoneticist; orthoepist.

.16 **ventriloquism,** ventriloquy; **ventriloquist.**

.17 talking machine, sonovox, voder, vocoder.

.18 **talker, speaker,** sayer, utterer, patterer; chatterbox 596.4; conversationalist 597.8.

.19 **vocal** *or* **speech organ,** articulator; tongue, apex, tip, blade, dorsum, back; vocal cords *or* bands, vocal processes, vocal folds; voice box, larynx, Adam's apple, laryng(o)–; syrinx; arytenoid cartilages; glottis, vocal chink; lips, teeth, palate, hard palate, soft palate, velum, alveolus, teeth ridge, alveolar ridge; nasal cavity, oral cavity; pharynx, throat *or* pharyngeal cavity.

.20 VERBS **speak, talk; patter** *or* **gab** *or* wag the tongue [all informal]; mouth; chatter 596.5; converse 597.9; declaim 599.10.

.21 [slang terms] **yap,** yak, yakkety-yak, spiel, **chin,** jaw, shoot off one's face, shoot *or* bat the breeze, beat the gums.

.22 **speak up, speak out, pipe up, open one's mouth,** open one's lips, say out, lift *or* raise one's voice, break silence; take the floor; put in a word, get in a word edgewise.

.23 **say, utter, breathe,** sound, **voice,** vocalize, phonate, **articulate, enunciate, pronounce,** lip, give voice, give tongue, give utterance; whisper; **express,** give expression, verbalize, put in words, find words to express; **word,** formulate, phrase 588.4; **present,** deliver; **emit,** give, raise, **let out,** out with, come *or* give out with, put *or* set forth, pour forth; throw off, fling off;

chorus, chime; **tell, communicate** 554.6,7; **convey, impart, disclose** 556.4,5; have or say one's say, speak one's mind.

.24 **state, declare, assert,** aver, affirm, asseverate, allege; **relate, recite;** quote; proclaim, nuncupate.

.25 **remark, comment, observe, note; mention,** speak [archaic], let drop or fall, say by the way, make mention of; refer to, allude to, make reference to, call attention to; muse, reflect; opine [dial]; interject; blurt, blurt out, exclaim.

.26 (utter in a certain way) murmur, mutter, mumble, whisper, breathe, buzz, sigh; gasp, pant; exclaim, yell 459.6–9; sing, lilt, warble, chant, coo, chirp; pipe, flute; cackle, crow; bark, yelp, yap; growl, snap, snarl; hiss, sibilate; grunt, snort; roar, bellow, blare, trumpet, bray, blat, bawl, thunder, rumble, boom; scream, shriek, screech, squeal, squawk, yawp, squall; whine, wail, keen, blubber, sob; drawl, twang.

.27 **address, speak to, talk to,** bespeak, beg the ear of; **appeal to,** invoke; apostrophize; **approach; buttonhole,** take by the button or lapel; take aside, talk to in private, closet oneself with; **accost, call to, hail,** halloo, greet, salute, speak, speak fair.

.28 **pass one's lips, escape one's lips,** fall from the lips or mouth.

.29 inflect, modulate, intonate.

.30 ADJS **speech, linguistic,** lingual; **spoken, uttered, said,** vocalized, **voiced, pronounced, sounded, articulated, enunciated;** vocal, voiceful; **oral, verbal, unwritten,** viva voce [L], nuncupative, parol; acroamatic(al).

.31 **phonetic,** phonic; intonated; pitched, pitch, **tonal,** tonic, oxytone, oxytonic, paroxytonic, barytone; **accented, stressed,** strong, heavy; unaccented, unstressed, weak, light, pretonic, atonic, posttonic; articulated; stopped, muted, checked, occlusive, nasal, nasalized, twangy, continuant, liquid, lateral, affricated; labial, bilabial, labiodental, labiovelar, dental, apico-dental, alveolar, apico-alveolar, palatal, cerebral, cacuminal, retroflex, velar, guttural, throaty, thick, pharyngeal, glottal; lingual, glossal; apical, laminal, dorsal; low, high, mid, open, broad, close; front, back, central; wide, lax, tense, narrow; voiced, sonant, voiceless, surd; rounded, unrounded, flat; aspirated; labialized; palatalized, soft, mouillé [Fr]; unpalatalized, hard; pharyngealized, glottal-

ized; **consonant,** consonantal, semivowel, glide, **vowel;** vowellike, vocoid, vocalic, syllabic; monophthongal, diphthongal, triphthongal; **phonemic;** assimilated, dissimilated.

.32 **speaking, talking;** articulate, talkative 596.9; eloquent 600.8, well-spoken; truespeaking, clean-speaking, plain-speaking, plain-spoken, **outspoken,** free-speaking, free-spoken, loud-speaking, loud-spoken, soft-speaking, soft-spoken; English-speaking, etc.

.33 ventriloquial, ventriloquistic.

.34 ADVS **orally, vocally, verbally, by word of mouth,** viva voce [L]; from the lips of, from his own mouth.

595. IMPERFECT SPEECH

.1 NOUNS **speech defect,** speech impediment, impairment of speech, –lalia or –laly, –phasia or –phasy, –phemia, –phonia, –phrasia; dysarthria, dysphasia, dysphrasia; dyslalia, dyslogia; idioglossia, idiolalia; **broken speech,** cracked or broken voice, broken tones or accents; indistinct or blurred or muzzy speech; loss of voice, aphonia; **nasalization,** nasal tone or accent, **twang,** nasal twang, talking through one's nose; **falsetto,** childish treble, artificial voice; **shake, quaver,** tremor; **lisp,** lisping; hiss, sibilation; **croak,** choked voice, hawking voice; crow; harshness, dysphonia, hoarseness 458.2.

.2 **inarticulateness,** inarticulacy; thickness of speech.

.3 **stammering, stuttering,** hesitation, faltering, traulism, dysphemia, balbuties [L]; palilalia; stammer, stutter.

.4 **mumbling, muttering,** maundering; droning, drone; mumble, mutter; jabber, jibber, gibber, gibbering, gabble; whispering, whisper, susurration; mouthing; murmuring.

.5 **mispronunciation,** misspeaking, cacology, cacoepy; lallation, lambdacism, paralambdacism; rhotacism, pararhotacism; gammacism; mytacism; **corruption.**

.6 **aphasia,** motor aphasia, paraphasia, jargon aphasia, paranomia; aphrasia; loss of speech, mutism, muteness 451.2.

.7 VERBS **speak poorly,** talk incoherently, be unable to put two words together; have an impediment in one's speech, have a bone in one's neck or throat; speak thickly; **croak; lisp; shake, quaver; drawl;** mince, clip one's words.

.8 **stammer, stutter,** hesitate, falter, halt,

mammer [Brit dial], stumble; hem, haw, hum, **hum and haw, hem and haw.**

.9 **mumble, mutter,** maunder; drone; swallow one's words, speak drunkenly or incoherently; jabber, gibber, gabble; splutter, sputter; blubber, sob; whisper, susurrate; murmur; mouth.

.10 nasalize, **speak through one's nose,** twang, snuffle.

.11 **mispronounce,** misspeak, missay, **murder the King's** or Queen's **English.**

.12 ADJS (imperfectly spoken) inarticulate, indistinct, blurred, muzzy; **mispronounced; shaky,** shaking, **quavering,** tremulous, titubant; **drawling,** drawly; **lisping; throaty, guttural,** thick, velar; stifled, choked, choking, strangled; **nasal, twangy,** breathy, adenoidal, snuffling; croaking, hawking; harsh, dysphonic, hoarse 458.12–16.

.13 **stammering, stuttering,** halting, hesitating, faltering, stumbling, balbutient.

596. TALKATIVENESS

.1 NOUNS **talkativeness, loquacity,** loquaciousness; **overtalkativeness,** loose tongue, big mouth [informal]; **gabbiness** or windiness or gassiness [all informal]; **garrulousness, garrulity; long-windedness,** prolixity, verbosity 593.2; multiloquence, multiloquy; **volubility, fluency, glibness;** fluent tongue, flowing tongue, **gift of gab** [informal]; openness, candor, frankness 974.4; effusion, gush, slush; gushiness, **effusiveness** 593.1; flow or flux or spate of words; flux de bouche, flux de mots, flux de paroles [all Fr]; **communicativeness** 554.3; gregariousness, sociability, conversableness 922.

.2 logomania, logorrhea, diarrhea of the mouth, verbal diarrhea, cacoëthes loquendi, furor loquendi [both L].

.3 **chatter, jabber,** gibber, **babble,** babblement, prate, **prating, prattle, palaver,** chat, natter [Brit], **gabble, gab** [informal], blab, **blabber, blather,** blether, blethers [Scot], clatter, clack, cackle, talkee-talkee; caquet, caqueterie, bavardage [all Fr], twaddle, twattle, **gibble-gabble, bibble-babble, chitter-chatter, prittle-prattle, tittle-tattle,** mere talk, idle talk or chatter, "the hare-brained chatter of irresponsible frivolity" [Disraeli]; **guff** or gas or hot air or blah-blah or yak or yakkety-yak [all slang]; **gossip;** nonsense talk 547.2.

.4 **chatterer, chatterbox, babbler, jabberer, prater, prattler, gabbler,** gibble-gabbler, **gabber** [informal], **blabberer,** blatherer,

patterer, word-slinger, moulin à paroles [Fr], blab, rattle, "agreeable rattle" [Goldsmith]; magpie, jay; **windbag** or gasbag or windjammer or hot-air artist [all slang]; idle chatterer, talkative person, **big** or great **talker** [informal], spendthrift of one's tongue.

.5 VERBS **chatter, chat, prate, prattle, patter, palaver, babble, gab** [informal], natter [Brit], **gabble, gibble-gabble,** tittle-tattle, **jabber,** gibber, **blab, blabber, blather,** blether, clatter, twaddle, twattle, rattle, clack, waffle [Brit], haver [Brit], dither, spout or **spout off** [both informal], pour forth, **gush,** talk to hear one's head rattle [informal]; **jaw** or gas or yak or yakkety-yak or run off at the mouth or beat one's gums [all slang], **shoot off one's mouth** or face [slang]; reel off; **talk on,** talk away, **go on** [informal], run on, rattle on, run on like a mill race; ramble on; talk oneself hoarse, talk till one is blue in the face, talk oneself out of breath; "varnish nonsense with the charms of sound" [Charles Churchill]; **talk too much;** gossip; talk nonsense 549.5.

.6 **talk one to death, talk one's head** or ear **off,** talk one deaf and dumb, talk one into a fever, talk the hind leg off a mule.

.7 **outtalk, outspeak, talk down,** outlast; filibuster.

.8 be loquacious or garrulous, be a windbag or gasbag [slang]; have a big mouth or bazoo [slang].

.9 ADJS **talkative, loquacious, talky, big-mouthed** [informal], **overtalkative, garrulous, chatty;** gossipy, newsy; gabby or windy or gassy [all slang], all jaw [slang]; **multiloquent,** multiloquious; **long-winded, prolix, verbose** 593.12; **voluble, fluent; glib,** flip [informal], smooth; candid, frank 974.17; **effusive,** gushy; expansive, **communicative** 554.11; conversational; gregarious, sociable 922.18.

.10 **chattering, prattling, prating,** gabbling, jabbering, gibbering, blabbing, blabbering, blathering.

.11 ADVS **talkatively, loquaciously,** garrulously; **volubly, fluently,** glibly; effusively, gushingly.

597. CONVERSATION

.1 NOUNS **conversation, converse,** conversing, rapping [slang]; interlocution, colloquy; **exchange;** verbal intercourse, interchange of speech, give-and-take; **discourse,** colloquial discourse; **communion, intercourse, communication** 554.

.2 **the art of conversation,** "a game of circles", "our account of ourselves" [both Emerson]; "the sweeter banquet of the mind", "the feast of reason and the flow of soul" [both Pope].

.3 **talk, palaver, speech, words;** confabulation, **confab** [informal]; **chinfest** *or* **talkfest** *or* **bull session** [all informal]; **dialogue,** duologue, trialogue; question-and-answer session.

.4 **chat,** cozy chat, friendly chat *or* talk, **little talk,** coze, causerie, **visit** [informal], gam, *tête-à-tête* [Fr], **heart-to-heart talk.**

.5 **chitchat,** chitter-chatter, tittle-tattle, **small talk,** cocktail-party chitchat, beauty-parlor chitchat, tea-table talk, table talk, idle chat *or* gossip, backchat.

.6 **conference, congress, convention, parley, palaver, confab** [informal], confabulation, **conclave, powwow, huddle** [informal], **consultation,** *pourparler* [Fr], **meeting;** session, sitting, séance; exchange *or* interchange of views; **council,** council of war; **discussion; interview, audience; news conference,** press conference; high-level talk, conference at the summit, summit, summit conference; summitry; negotiations, bargaining, bargaining session; confrontation, eyeball-to-eyeball encounter [informal]; council fire.

.7 **discussion, debate,** debating, **deliberation, dialogue,** exchange of views, canvassing, ventilation, airing, review, **treatment, consideration,** investigation, **examination, study, analysis,** logical analysis; logical discussion, dialectic; buzz session [informal], rap *or* rap session [both slang]; panel discussion, open discussion, joint discussion, symposium, colloquium, conference, seminar; forum, open forum, town meeting.

.8 **conversationalist,** converser, conversationist; talker, discourser, confabulator; colloquist, colloquialist, collocutor; conversational partner; interlocutor, interlocutress *or* interlocutrice *or* interlocutrix; parleyer, palaverer; dialogist; Dr. Johnson.

.9 VERBS **converse, talk together, talk** *or* **speak with,** converse with, visit with [informal], discourse with, **commune with,** communicate with, take counsel with, commerce with, **have a talk with,** have a word with, **chin** [slang], **chew the rag** *or* **fat** [slang], **shoot the breeze** [slang], hold *or* carry on *or* join in *or* engage in a conversation; confabulate, confab [informal]; colloque, colloquize; "inject a few raisins of conversation into the tasteless dough

of existence" [O. Henry]; **bandy words; communicate** 554.6,7.

.10 **chat, visit** [informal], gam, coze, have a friendly *or* cozy chat; **have a little talk,** have a heart-to-heart talk, let one's hair down; talk with one in private, talk with one *tête-à-tête*, be closeted with, make conversation *or* talk; **prattle,** prittle-prattle, tittle-tattle; **gossip.**

.11 **confer,** hold conference, parley, palaver, powwow, sit down together, meet around the conference table, **go into a huddle** [informal], deliberate, take counsel, counsel, **lay** *or* **put heads together;** collogue; **confer with,** sit down with, **consult with, advise with, discuss with, take up with,** reason with; **discuss,** talk over; **consult,** refer to, call in; **compare notes,** exchange observations *or* views; have conversations; negotiate, bargain.

.12 **discuss, debate, reason, deliberate,** deliberate upon, exchange views *or* opinions, talk, **talk over,** talk of *or* about, rap [slang], comment upon, reason about, discourse about, **consider, treat,** handle, deal with, take up, **go into, examine,** investigate, **analyze,** sift, **study,** canvass, review, pass under review, controvert, ventilate, air, thresh out, reason the point, consider pro and con; **kick** *or* **knock around** [slang].

.13 ADJS conversational, colloquial, confabulatory, interlocutory; communicative 554.11; chatty, chitchatty, cozy.

.14 ADVS conversationally, colloquially; *tête-à-tête* [Fr].

598. SOLILOQUY

.1 NOUNS **soliloquy,** monology; **monologue;** aside; solo; monodrama.

.2 **soliloquist,** soliloquizer, Hamlet; **monologist.**

.3 VERBS **soliloquize,** monologize; **talk to oneself,** say to oneself, tell oneself, think out loud *or* aloud; address the four walls; say aside; do all the talking, monopolize the conversation, hold forth without interruption.

.4 ADJS soliloquizing, monologic(al), apostrophic; soloistic; monodramatic.

599. PUBLIC SPEAKING

.1 NOUNS **public speaking, declamation, speechmaking, speaking,** speechification [informal], lecturing, speeching; **oratory,** platform oratory *or* speaking; campaign oratory, stump speaking; **elocution; rhet-**

oric, art of public speaking; eloquence 600; forensics, **debating**; speechcraft, wordcraft; homiletics; demagogism, demagoguery, rabble-rousing; **pyrotechnics**.

.2 **speech**, speeching, speechification [informal], **talk, oration, address**, declamation, harangue; public speech or address, formal speech, set speech, prepared speech or text; say; **tirade**, screed, **diatribe**, jeremiad, philippic, invective; after-dinner speech; funeral oration, eulogy; allocution, exhortation, hortatory address, forensic, forensic address; **recitation**, recital, reading; salutatory, salutatory address; valediction, valedictory, valedictory address; inaugural address, inaugural; chalk talk [informal]; pep talk [informal]; pitch, sales talk 829.5; talkathon, filibuster; peroration; debate.

.3 **lecture**, prelection, **discourse**, log(o)–, –log(ue), –logia, –logy; **sermon**, sermonette, homily, religious discourse; preachment, preaching, preachification [informal]; travelogue.

.4 **speaker, talker, public speaker, speechmaker**, speecher, speechifier [informal], spieler or jawsmith [both slang]; after-dinner speaker; **spokesman**, spokeswoman; **demagogue**, rabble-rouser; declaimer, ranter, tub-thumper [informal], haranguer, spouter [informal]; panelist, debater.

.5 **lecturer**, praelector, discourser, reader; **preacher**; sermonizer, sermonist, sermoner, homilist [archaic], pulpitarian, pulpiteer, Boanerges; **expositor**, expounder; chalk talker [informal].

.6 **orator, public speaker**, platform orator or speaker; rhetorician, rhetor; silver-tongued orator, **spellbinder**; Demosthenes, Cicero, Franklin D. Roosevelt, Winston Churchill, William Jennings Bryan; **soapbox orator**, soapboxer, stump orator.

.7 **elocutionist**, elocutioner; recitationist, reciter, diseur, diseuse; reader; improvisator, *improvvisatore* [Ital].

.8 **rhetorician**, teacher of rhetoric, rhetor, elocutionist.

.9 VERBS **make a speech, give a talk, deliver an address**, speechify [informal], **speak, talk, discourse**; address; stump [informal], go on or take the stump; platform, soapbox; take the floor.

.10 **declaim**, hold forth, **orate**, elocute [informal], spout [informal], spiel [informal], mouth; **harangue, rant**, "out-herod Herod" [Shakespeare], tub-thump, perorate,

rodomontade; **recite**, read; debate; demagogue, rabble-rouse.

.11 **lecture**, prelect, read or deliver a lecture; **preach**, preachify [informal], **sermonize**, read a sermon.

.12 ADJS **declamatory, elocutionary, oratorical, rhetorical**, forensic; eloquent 600.8; demagogic(al).

600. ELOQUENCE

.1 NOUNS **eloquence, rhetoric, silver tongue**, eloquent tongue, facundity; **articulateness; gift of gab** [informal], **glibness**, smoothness, slickness; **felicitousness**, felicity; **oratory** 599.1; expression, **expressiveness**, command of words or language, gift of expression, vividness, graphicness; pleasing or effective style; **meaningfulness** 545.5.

.2 **fluency**, flow; **smoothness, facility, ease; grace**, gracefulness, poetry; **elegance** 589.

.3 **vigor, force**, power, strength, vitality, drive, sinew, sinewiness, nervousness, nervosity, vigorousness, forcefulness, effectiveness, impressiveness, punch or guts [both informal]; incisiveness, trenchancy, cuttingness, poignancy, bitingness, bite, mordancy; strong language, "thoughts that breathe and words that burn" [Thomas Gray].

.4 **spirit**, pep [informal], liveliness, raciness, sparkle, vivacity, dash, verve, vividness; piquancy, poignancy, pungency.

.5 **vehemence, passion**, impassionedness, enthusiasm, **ardor**, ardency, **fervor**, fervency, fire, fieriness, glow, warmth.

.6 **loftiness**, elevation, sublimity; grandeur, **nobility**, stateliness, majesty, gravity, solemnity, dignity.

.7 VERBS **have the gift of gab** [informal], have a tongue in one's head; spellbind; shine, "pour the full tide of eloquence along" [Pope].

.8 ADJS **eloquent, silver-tongued, silver**; well-speaking, well-spoken, **articulate**, facund; **glib, smooth**, smooth-spoken, smooth-tongued, **slick; felicitous**; spellbinding; Demosthenic, Demosthenian; Ciceronian, Tullian.

.9 **fluent, flowing**, tripping; **smooth**, pleasing, facile, **easy, graceful, elegant** 589.6.

.10 **expressive, graphic, vivid**, suggestive, imaginative; **meaningful** 545.10.

.11 **vigorous, strong, powerful**, imperative, **forceful**, forcible, vital, driving, sinewy, sinewed, nervous, punchy or gutsy [both informal], **striking, telling, effective**, impressive; incisive, trenchant, cutting, biting, piercing, poignant, penetrating, slashing, mordant, acid, corrosive; sensational.

.12 **spirited, lively,** peppy [informal], **racy,** sparkling, vivacious; piquant, poignant, pungent.

.13 **vehement,** emphatic, **passionate, impassioned,** enthusiastic, **ardent,** fiery, **fervent,** burning, glowing, warm; urgent, stirring, exciting, stimulating, provoking.

.14 **lofty, elevated, sublime, grand, majestic,** noble, stately, grave, solemn, dignified; serious, weighty; moving, inspiring.

.15 ADVS **eloquently; fluently,** smoothly, glibly, trippingly on the tongue; **expressively,** vividly, graphically; **meaningfully** 545.13; **vigorously,** powerfully, forcefully, spiritedly; tellingly, strikingly, effectively, impressively; **vehemently, passionately,** ardently, fervently, warmly, glowingly, in glowing terms.

601. GRANDILOQUENCE

.1 NOUNS **grandiloquence,** magniloquence, lexiphanicism, **pompousness,** pomposity, orotundity; **rhetoric,** mere rhetoric, rhetoricalness; high-flown diction, big or tall talk [informal]; grandioseness, grandiosity; loftiness, stiltedness; fulsomeness; **pretentiousness,** pretension, **affectation** 589.3; ostentation; showiness, flashiness, gaudiness, meretriciousness, bedizenment, garishness; sensationalism, luridness, Barnumism; **inflation, inflatedness,** swollenness, turgidity, turgescence, flatulence or flatulency, tumidness, tumidity; sententiousness, pontification; swollen phrase or diction, swelling utterance; platitudinous ponderosity, polysyllabic profundity, pompous prolixity; Johnsonese; prose run mad; convolution, tortuosity, tortuousness, ostentatious complexity or profundity.

.2 **bombast,** bombastry, **fustian,** highfalutin [informal], **rant,** rodomontade; **hot air** [slang]; balderdash, gobbledygook [slang].

.3 high-sounding words, lexiphanicism, hard words; **sesquipedalian word,** big or long word, two-dollar word [slang], **jawbreaker,** jawtwister, mouthful; antidisestablishmentarianism, honorificabilitudinitatibus [Shakespeare], pneumonoultramicroscopicsilicovolcanoconiosis; polysyllabism, sesquipedalianism, sesquipedality; Latinate diction; academic choctaw, technical jargon.

.4 **ornateness, floweriness,** floridness, floridity, lushness, luxuriance; flourish, flourish of rhetoric, flowers of speech or rhetoric,

purple patches or passages, beauties, fine writing; **ornament,** ornamentation, **adornment, embellishment,** elegant variation, **embroidery, frill,** colors or colors of rhetoric [both archaic], figure, **figure of speech** 551.

.5 **phrasemonger,** rhetorician; phraseman, phrasemaker, fine writer, wordspinner; euphuist, Gongorist, Marinist; pedant.

.6 VERBS **talk big** [informal], talk highfalutin [informal], **pontificate, blow** [slang], **vapor,** Barnumize; inflate, bombast, lay or pile it on [informal], lay it on thick or lay it on with a trowel [both informal]; smell of the lamp.

.7 **ornament, decorate, adorn, embellish, embroider,** enrich; overcharge, overlay, overload, load with ornament, festoon, weight down with ornament, flourish [archaic]; **gild,** trick out, varnish; paint in glowing colors, tell in glowing terms; "to gild refined gold, to paint the lily, to throw a perfume on the violet" [Shakespeare]; elaborate, convolute, involve.

.8 ADJS **grandiloquent,** magniloquent, **pompous, orotund; grandiose; fulsome;** lofty, elevated, tall [informal], **stilted; pretentious, affected** 589.9; overdone, overwrought; **showy, flashy, ostentatious,** gaudy, meretricious, flamboyant, flaming, bedizened, flaunting, garish; lurid, sensational, sensationalistic; **high-flown, highfalutin** [informal], high-flying; high-flowing, **high-sounding, big-sounding,** greatsounding, grandisonant [archaic], sonorous; **rhetorical,** declamatory; **pedantic,** inkhorn, lexiphanic [archaic]; sententious, Johnsonian; convoluted, tortuous, labyrinthine, overelaborate, overinvolved; euphuistic, Gongoresque.

.9 **bombastic,** fustian, mouthy, **inflated, swollen,** swelling, turgid, turgescent, tumid, tumescent, flatulent, windy or gassy [both informal].

.10 **sesquipedalian,** sesquipedal, polysyllabic, jawbreaking [informal].

.11 **ornate, purple** [informal], colored, **fancy;** adorned, **embellished, embroidered,** decorated, festooned, overcharged, overloaded, befrilled; **flowery, florid,** lush, luxuriant; figured, **figurative** 551.3.

.12 ADVS **grandiloquently,** magniloquently, **pompously,** grandiosely, loftily, stiltedly; pretentiously; **ostentatiously,** showily; **bombastically,** turgidly, tumidly, flatulently, windily [informal].

.13 **ornately,** fancily; **flowerily,** floridly.

602. WRITING

.1 NOUNS **writing**, scrivening *or* scrivenery [both archaic], inscription, lettering, grapho–, –graphy, –graphia; engrossment; pen, **pen-and-ink**; inkslinging *or* ink spilling [both slang], pen *or* pencil driving *or* pushing [slang]; **typing, typewriting**; macrography, micrography; stroke *or* dash of the pen, *coup de plume* [Fr]; secret writing, cryptography 614.6.

.2 **authorship, writing**, authorcraft, pencraft, **composition**, inditement; pen; **creative writing**, literary composition, literary production, verse-writing, short-story writing, novel-writing, playwriting, drama-writing; essay-writing; **expository writing**; technical writing; journalism, editorial-writing, feature-writing, rewriting; songwriting, lyric-writing, libretto-writing; artistry, literary power, literary artistry, literary talent *or* flair, skill with words *or* language, facility in writing, ready pen; **writer's itch**, graphomania, scribblemania, graphorrhea, *cacoethes scribendi* [L]; automatic writing; writer's cramp, graphospasm.

.3 **handwriting, hand, script**, scription, fist [informal], chirography, **calligraphy**, autography; **manuscript**, scrive [Scot]; **penmanship**, penscript, pencraft; stylography; graphology, graphanalysis, graphometry; paleography.

.4 (style of handwriting) **longhand**, cursive; bold hand, round hand, slanting hand, perpendicular hand, letter hand, book hand, Spencerian writing, Italian hand, law hand, court hand, charter hand, chancery hand, text hand, copperplate hand; cursive hand, minuscule script; uncial, majuscule script; **printing**, handprinting, block letter, **lettering**.

.5 (good writing) **calligraphy**, fine writing, elegant penmanship, **good hand**, fine hand, good fist [informal], fair hand, copybook hand.

.6 (bad writing) **cacography, bad hand**, poor fist [informal], cramped *or* crabbed hand, botched writing, childish scrawl, illegible handwriting, *griffonage* [Fr].

.7 **scribbling**, scribblement; **scribble**, scrabble, **scrawl, scratch**, *barbouillage* [Fr]; *pattes de mouche* [Fr], hen tracks, hen scratches, pothookery, pothooks, pothooks and hangers.

.8 **stenography, shorthand**, brachygraphy, tachygraphy; Speedwriting, phonography, stenotypy; contraction.

.9 **letter, written character** 581.1; **alphabet, writing system** 581.3,9; punctuation 586.15, 18–20.

.10 (written matter) **writing, piece**, –graph, –gram; piece of writing, screed; **copy, matter**; printed matter, literature, reading matter; the written word, *literae scriptae* [L]; nonfiction; fiction 608.7,8; **composition, work**, opus, production, literary production, literary artefact *or* artifact, brainchild; essay, article 606.1; poem 609.6; play 611.4–6; letter 604.2; **document** 570.5-8; **paper**, parchment, scroll; **script**, scrip, scrive [Scot]; **penscript, typescript; manuscript**, MS., Ms., ms., holograph, autograph; **draft**, first draft, second draft, etc., recension, **version**; edited version, finished version, final draft; transcription, transcript, fair copy, engrossment; flimsy; original, author's copy; printout, computer printout.

.11 (ancient manuscript) **codex**; scroll; palimpsest, *codex rescriptus* [L]; papyrus, parchment.

.12 **literature, letters, belles lettres**, polite literature, humane letters, *litterae humaniores* [L], republic of letters; serious literature; **classics**, ancient literature; medieval literature, Renaissance literature, etc.; national literature, English literature, French literature, etc.; contemporary literature; underground literature; pseudonymous literature; folk literature; travel literature; wisdom literature; erotic literature, erotica, pornographic literature, pornography, porn [slang], obscene literature, scatological literature; popular literature, pop literature [slang]; kitsch.

.13 **writer, scribbler** [slang], **penman**, pen, penner, –grapher; pen *or* pencil driver *or* pusher [slang], word-slinger, **inkslinger** *or* ink spiller [both slang], knight of the plume *or* pen *or* quill [informal]; **scribe, scrivener, amanuensis, secretary**, recording secretary, **clerk**; letterer; **copyist**, copier, transcriber; chirographer, calligrapher.

.14 **writing expert**, graphologist, handwriting expert, graphometrist; paleographer.

.15 **author, writer**, scribe [informal], composer, inditer; authoress, penwoman; **creative writer**, *littérateur* [Fr], literary artist, literary craftsman *or* artisan *or* journeyman, belletrist, man of letters, literary man; wordsmith, word painter; free lance, free-lance writer; ghostwriter, ghost [informal]; collaborator, coauthor; prose writer, logographer; story writer, **short-**

story writer; storyteller 608.10; **novelist**, novelettist; diarist; **newspaperman** 605.22; **annalist** 608.11; **poet** 609.13; **dramatist** 611.27, humorist 881.12; scriptwriter, scenario writer, scenarist; nonfiction writer; article writer, magazine writer; **essayist;** monographer; reviewer, critic, literary critic, music critic, art critic, drama critic, dance critic; columnist; pamphleteer; technical writer; copywriter, advertising writer; compiler, encyclopedist, bibliographer.

.16 **hack writer**, hack, literary hack, Grub Street writer [Brit], **penny-a-liner, scribbler** [slang], **potboiler** [informal].

.17 **stenographer**, brachygrapher, tachygrapher; phonographer, stenotypist.

.18 **typist;** printer.

.19 VERBS **write, pen, pencil,** drive or push the pen or pencil [slang]; stain or spoil paper [informal], shed or spill ink [informal], **scribe**, scrive [Scot]; inscribe, scroll; superscribe; enface; take pen in hand; **put in writing,** put in black and white; **draw up, draft, write out,** make out; **write down, record** 570.16; take down in shorthand; **type; transcribe,** copy out, engross, make a fair copy, copy; trace; **rewrite, revise, edit,** recense, make a recension, make a critical revision.

.20 **scribble, scrabble, scratch, scrawl;** doodle.

.21 **write,** author, **compose, indite,** formulate, produce, prepare; dash off, knock off or out [informal], throw on paper; free-lance; collaborate, coauthor; ghostwrite, ghost [informal]; novelize; scenarize; pamphleteer; editorialize.

.22 ADJS **written,** penned, penciled; **inscribed;** engrossed; **in writing, in black and white,** on paper; scriptural, scriptorial, graphic; calligraphic, chirographic(al); stylographic(al); manuscript, autograph, autographic(al), holograph, holographic(al), in one's own hand, under one's hand; **longhand,** in longhand; **shorthand,** in shorthand; italic, italicized; cursive, running, flowing; graphologic(al), graphometric(al); graphoanalytic(al); typewritten; printed.

.23 **scribbled,** scrabbled, **scratched, scrawled;** scribbly, scratchy, scrawly.

.24 **literary,** belletristic; classical.

.25 auctorial, authorial; polygraphic; graphomaniac(al), scribblemaniac(al), scripturient [archaic].

.26 **alphabetic,** ideographic, etc. 581.8.

.27 stenographic(al), tachygraphic(al), **shorthand,** in shorthand; phonographic(al).

.28 clerical, secretarial.

.29 stationery

biblus	paper
bond paper	papyrus
carbon paper	parchment
copy or copying paper	rice paper
demy	scratch pad
flimsy	scroll
foolscap	stencil
lambskin (parchment)	tracing paper
legal-size paper	typing paper
letter paper	vellum
note paper	writing paper
pad	

.30 writing materials

ballpoint pen	lettering pen
blackboard	nib
cartridge pen	pen
chalk	penpoint
China or Chinese ink	plume
copying ink	printer's ink
crayon	quill
drawing ink	reed
eraser	secret or invisible or
felt-tip pen	sympathetic ink
fountain pen	slate
India or Indian ink	snorkel pen
ink	stencil
ink cartridge	style
ink eradicator	stylograph, stylograph
ink eraser	pen
inkhorn	stylus
inkpot	table
inkstand	tablet
inkwell	typewriter ribbon
lead pencil	writing brush

.31 writing machines

addressing machine	stenotype
Addressograph	teleprinter
Composaline	Teletype, teletype-
electric typewriter	writer
Flexowriter	ticker, stock ticker
Selectric	typewriter
stenograph	VariTyper

603. PRINTING

.1 NOUNS **printing,** publishing, publication, –typy; photographic reproduction, photochemical process, phototypography, phototypy; **photoengraving; letterpress,** relief printing, **typography,** letterpress photoengraving; zincography, photozincography; line engraving, halftone engraving; stereotypy; wood-block printing, xylotypography, chromoxylography; intaglio printing, **gravure;** rotogravure, rotary photogravure; planographic printing, planography, **lithography,** typolithography, photolithography, lithogravure, lithophotogravure; offset lithography, offset, dry offset, photo-offset; photogelatin process, albertype, collotype; electronography, electrostatic printing, onset, xerography, xeroprinting; stencil, mimeograph, silk-screen printing; color printing, chromotypography, chromotypy, two-color printing, three-color printing; book printing, job printing, sheetwork; history of printing, palaeotypography; photography 577; **graphic arts, printmaking 578.1.**

.2 composing, composition, typesetting, setting; hand composition, machine composition; hot-metal typesetting, cold-type typesetting, photosetting, photocomposition; imposition; justification; composing stick, galley chase, furniture, quoin; typesetting machine, Linotype, Intertype, Monotype, phototypesetter, phototypesetting machine; computerized typesetting; line of type, slug; layout, dummy.

.3 print, imprint, stamp, impression, impress, letterpress; reprint, reissue; offprint; offcut; offset, setoff, mackle.

.4 copy, printer's copy, manuscript, typescript; **matter;** composed matter, live matter, dead matter, standing matter.

.5 proof, proof sheet, pull [Brit], trial impression; galley, **galley proof,** slip; page proof, foundry proof, plate proof, stone proof, press proof, cold-type proof, color proof, computer proof, engraver's proof, reproduction or repro proof, blueprint, blue [informal], vandyke, progressive proof; author's proof; revise.

.6 **type, print, stamp, letter;** type body or shank or stem, body, shank, stem, shoulder, belly, back, bevel, beard, feet, groove, nick, face, counter; ascender, descender, serif; lower case, minuscule; upper case, majuscule; capital, cap [informal], small capital, small cap [informal]; ligature, logotype; bastard type, bottleassed type, fat-faced type; pi; type lice; **font; face,** typeface; type class, roman, sans serif, script, italic, black letter; case, typecase; point, pica; en, em; typefounders, typefoundry.

.7 **space,** patent space, justifying space, justification space; spaceband, slug; quadrat, quad; em quad, en quad; em, en; three-em space, thick space; four-em space, five-em space, thin space; hair space.

.8 **printing surface, plate,** printing plate; typeform, locked-up page; duplicate plate, electrotype, stereotype, plastic plate, rubber plate; zincograph, zincotype; stone.

.9 presswork, makeready; **press, printing press,** printing machine [Brit]; platen press, flatbed cylinder press, cylinder press, rotary press, web press, rotogravure press; bed, platen, web.

.10 **printed matter; reading matter, text,** letterpress [Brit]; advertising matter; advance sheets.

.11 press, printing office, printshop, printery, printers; publishers, **publishing house; pressroom,** composing room, proofroom.

.12 **printer, pressman; compositor, typesetter,** typographer, Linotyper; keyboarder; stoneman, makeup man; proofer; stereotyper, stereotypist, electrotyper; apprentice printer, devil, **printer's devil.**

.13 proofreader, reader, printer's reader [Brit]; **copyreader,** copy editor, copyholder.

.14 VERBS **print; imprint, impress, stamp,** enstamp [archaic]; engrave 578.10; run, run off, strike; **publish, issue, bring out, put out, get out;** put to press, put to bed, see through the press; prove, proof, prove up, make or pull a proof, pull; overprint; reprint, reissue; mimeograph, hectograph; multigraph.

.15 autotype, electrotype, linotype, monotype, palaeotype, stereotype; keyboard.

.16 compose, set, set in print; **make up,** impose; justify, overrun; pi, pi a form.

.17 copy-edit; **proofread,** read, read or correct copy.

.18 (be printed) go to press, come out, appear in print.

.19 ADJS **printed, in print;** typeset.

.20 **typographic(al);** phototypic, phototypographic; chromotypic, chromotypographic; stereotypic, palaeotypographic(al); **boldface,** bold-faced, blackface, black-faced, full-faced; **lightface,** light-faced; **upper-case, lower-case.**

.21 typesetting machines

Alphatype	Ludlow
Composaline	Monophoto
Diatype	Monotype
Elrod	Monotype caster
Fotomatic	Monotype keyboard
Fotosetter	Photon
Fototronic	phototypesetter
Intertype	Tapetron
Linasec	VideoComp
Linofilm	V-I-P
Linotron	Zip
Linotype	

.22 type sizes

3-point, excelsior	10-point, elite or long
3½-point, brilliant	primer
4-point, gem	11-point, small pica
4½-point, diamond	12-point, pica
5-point, pearl	14-point, English
5½-point, agate, ruby	16-point, Columbian
6-point, nonpareil	18-point, great primer
7-point, minion	20-point, paragon
8-point, brevier	48-point, canon
9-point, bourgeois	

.23 type styles, typefaces

antique	bold
Baskerville	extracondensed
blackface	Futura
black letter	Garamond
block-serifed	German text
Bodoni	Gothic
boldface, bold	Goudy
Bulmer	Granjon
Caledonia	grotesque
Caslon	Ionic
Caslon Old Style	italic
Century	Janson
Clarendon	lightface
condensed	modern
cursive	Old English
display	old style
Doric	roman
Egyptian	sans serif
Electra	script
Elzevir	Times Roman
expanded	Transitional
extended	Typewriter
extraboldface, extra-	

.24 presses

copying press	Multigraph
cylinder press	offset lithography
electrotype press	press
flatbed press, flat	perfecting press
press	platen press
foundry press	proof press
four-color press	rotary press
galley press	sheet-fed press
gravure press	two-color press
hand press	web press, web-fed
letterpress	press

.25 copying machines

Ditto	Multigraph
duplicator	pantograph
hectograph	spirit duplicator
mimeograph	Xerox machine

.26 printing equipment

bearer	galley
bed	gripper
bevel	guide
blanket	gutter, gutter stick
boss	ink bell, inking bell
box	inking roller
brayer	line gauge
burr	matrix
case	overlay
chase	page gauge
composing frame	platen
composing rule	quoin
composing stick	ratchet
drawsheet	reglet
footstick	rounce
form	turtle
frame	tympan, tympan sheet
frisket	type mold
furniture	underlay

604. CORRESPONDENCE

.1 NOUNS correspondence, letter writing, written communication, epistolary inter-course or communication; personal corre-spondence, business correspondence.

.2 letter, epistle, message, communication, dispatch, missive, favor [archaic]; personal letter, business letter; note, line, chit, billet [archaic]; **reply, answer, acknowledgment,** rescript.

.3 air letter, aerogram; airgraph [Brit], V-mail; drop letter; fan letter; love letter, *billet-doux* [Fr]; poison-pen letter; open letter; chain letter; form letter; circular letter, newsletter, encyclical, encyclical letter; round robin; bull, apostolic or papal brief; monitory, monitory letter; pastoral letter, Pastoral Epistle; paschal letter; dimissory letter, dimissorial; letter of credence, letters credential, letters overt, letters patent, letters rogatory, letters testamentary; letters of marque; letter of delegation, letters of request, letter of credit; letter of introduction; dead letter, nixie; letter book.

.4 card, postcard, postal card, lettercard; picture postcard.

.5 mail, post [Brit], **letters, correspondence;** airmail, surface mail, seapost, sea mail; **parcel post, PP;** letter post, printed paper, halfpenny post, newspaper post, book post [all Brit]; first-class or second-class or third-class or fourth-class mail; junk mail [informal]; rural free delivery, RFD, rural delivery, RD; **special delivery,** special handling, express or express delivery [both Brit]; registered mail, certified mail; frank; letter bag; post day [Brit]; mailing list; direct mail, direct-mail advertising or selling, mail-order selling; fan mail.

.6 postage; stamp, postage stamp; frank; postmark, cancellation.

.7 mailbox, postbox, letter box, pillar box [Brit]; drop, letter drop; mailing machine; mailbag, postbag [Brit].

.8 postal service, postal system; post office, PO, general post office, GPO, sub post office, sea post office.

.9 correspondent, letter writer, writer, communicator; pen pal [informal]; addressee.

.10 address, name and address, direction [archaic], **destination,** superscription; zone, postal zone, zip code; letterhead, billhead.

.11 VERBS correspond, correspond with, communicate with, write, write to, write a letter, send a letter to, send a note, **drop a line** [informal]; use the mails; keep up a correspondence, exchange letters.

.12 reply, answer, acknowledge; reply by return mail.

.13 mail, post, dispatch, send; airmail.

.14 address, direct, superscribe.

.15 ADJS epistolary, epistolatory; **postal**, post.

.16 PHRS please reply, RSVP, *répondez s'il vous plaît* [Fr].

605. BOOK, PERIODICAL

.1 NOUNS book, volume, tome, biblio–; publication, writing, work, opus, production; title; opusculum, opuscule; magnum opus, great work, classic; standard work, definitive work; nonbook; folio; serial; paperback, pocket book, soft-cover, soft-bound book, limp-cover book; cloth-bound book, hardback, hard-cover book, hard book, bound book, cased book; playbook 611.26; songbook 462.28; notebook 570.11; storybook, **novel** 608.8; best seller; trade book; children's book, juvenile book, juvenile; picture book; coloring book, sketchbook; prayer book, psalter, psalmbook.

.2 edition, issue; volume, number; printing, impression; copy; series, set, collection, library; library edition; back number; **trade edition, trade book**; subscription edition, subscription book; school edition, text edition.

.3 rare book, early edition; first edition; Elzevir, Elzevir book *or* edition; Aldine, Aldine book *or* edition; manuscript, scroll, codex; incunabulum, cradle book.

.4 compilation, omnibus; symposium; collection, collectanea, miscellany; collected works, selected works, complete works, *œuvres* [Fr], canon; miscellanea, analects; ana; chrestomathy, delectus; **anthology**, garland, florilegium; flowers, beauties; garden; *Festschrift* [Ger]; quotation book; album, photograph album; scrapbook.

.5 handbook, manual, enchiridion, vade mecum, gradus, how-to book [informal]; cookbook, cookery book [Brit]; nature book, field guide; travel book, **guidebook** 748.10.

.6 reference book, work of reference; **encyclopedia**, cyclopedia; **concordance; catalog**; calendar; index; classified catalog, *catalogue raisonné* [Fr], dictionary catalog; **directory**, city directory; telephone directory, telephone book, phone book [informal]; **atlas, gazetteer**; studbook; polyglot, diatesseron, harmony; source book, casebook; record book 570.11.

.7 dictionary, lexicon, wordbook, Webster's; glossary, gloss, **vocabulary**, onomasticon, nomenclator; **thesaurus**, Roget's, storehouse *or* treasury of words, thesaurus dictionary, synonym dictionary, synonymy; phrase book; gradus; general dictionary, unabridged dictionary, semi-unabridged dictionary, desk dictionary, college dictionary; specialized dictionary; bilingual dictionary, foreign-language dictionary, polyglot dictionary; dialect dictionary; idiom dictionary, slang dictionary; rhyming dictionary; etymological dictionary; etymologicon; children's dictionary, juvenile dictionary, school dictionary, elementary dictionary; biographical dictionary; geographical dictionary, gazetteer; dictionary of quotations; science dictionary, electronics dictionary, geological dictionary, chemical dictionary, psychological dictionary, etc.

.8 textbook, text, schoolbook, **manual**, manual of instruction; **primer**, alphabet book, abecedary, abecedarium; hornbook, battledore; gradus, exercise book, workbook; **grammar, reader**; spelling book, speller, casebook.

.9 booklet, pamphlet, brochure, chapbook, leaflet, folder, tract; circular 559.8; comic book.

.10 periodical, serial, journal, gazette; ephemeris; **magazine**, pulp magazine, slick magazine, newsmagazine, women's magazine, men's magazine, children's magazine, trade magazine; pictorial; review; organ, house organ; daily, weekly, biweekly, bimonthly, fortnightly, monthly, quarterly; annual, yearbook; daybook, diary 570.11.

.11 newspaper, news, **paper**, sheet *or* rag [both slang], **gazette**, daily newspaper, daily, weekly newspaper, weekly, neighborhood newspaper, national newspaper; newspaper of record; **tabloid**, extra, special, extra edition, special edition.

.12 makeup; front matter, preliminaries, text, back matter; head, fore edge, back, tail; page, leaf, folio; type page; trim size; flyleaf, endpaper, endleaf, endsheet, signature; recto, verso *or* reverso; title page, half-title page; title, bastard title, binder's title, subtitle, running title; copyright page, imprint, printer's imprint, colophon; catchword, catch line; dedication, inscription; acknowledgments, preface, foreword, introduction; contents, contents page, table of contents; errata; bibliography; index.

.13 part, section, book, volume; article; serial, installment, *livraison* [Fr]; fascicle; **passage**, phrase, clause, verse, paragraph, chapter, column.

.14 (sizes) –mo; folio; quarto, 4to; octavo,

8vo; duodecimo, twelvemo, 12mo; sexto-decimo, sixteenmo, 16mo; octodecimo, eighteenmo, 18mo; imperial, super, royal, medium, crown.

.15 **bookbinding**, bibliopegy; **binding, cover, book cover**, case, bookcase, hard binding, soft binding, mechanical binding, spiral binding, plastic binding; library binding; headband, footband, tailband; jacket, book jacket, dust jacket, dust cover, wrapper; slipcase, slipcover; book cloth, binder's cloth, binder's board, binder board; folding, tipping, gathering, collating, sewing; **signature**; collating mark, niggerhead; Smyth sewing, side sewing, saddle stitching, wire stitching, stapling, perfect binding; smashing, gluing-off, trimming, rounding, backing, lining, lining-up; casemaking, stamping, casing-in.

.16 (bookbinding styles) Aldine, Arabesque, Byzantine, Canevari, cottage, dentelle, Etruscan, fanfare, Grolier, Harleian, Jansenist, Maioli, pointillé, Roxburgh.

.17 **library**, bookroom, bookery [archaic], *bibliothèque* [Fr], *bibliotheca* [L], athenaeum; **public library, circulating library, lending library** [Brit]; **rental library; book wagon, bookmobile**; Bibliothèque Nationale, Bodleian Library, British Museum, Deutsche Bücherei, Library of Congress, Vatican Library; American Library Association, ALA.

.18 **bookstore, bookshop**, *librairie* [Fr], bookseller's; **bookstall, bookstand; book club**.

.19 **bibliography**, bibliography of bibliographies, annual bibliography, annotated bibliography, critical bibliography; index, Art Index, Education Index, etc.; periodical index, Reader's Guide to Periodical Literature; Bibliography Index; Books in Print, Paperbound Books in Print; Cumulative Book Index; National Union Catalog, Library of Congress Catalog, General Catalogue of Printed Books [Brit], Union List of Serials; **publisher's catalog**, publisher's list, backlist.

.20 **bookholder, bookrest, book support, book end; bookcase**, revolving bookcase *or* bookstand, bookrack, bookstand, **bookshelf**; stack, bookstack; book table, book tray, book truck; folder, folio; **portfolio**.

.21 **bookman**, bibliographer, bibliognost; **bookmaker; publisher, book publisher; editor**, trade editor, reference editor, juvenile editor, textbook editor, dictionary editor, college editor, acquisitions editor, executive editor, managing editor,

editor-in-chief, copy editor, production editor, permissions editor; **printer**, book printer; **bookbinder**, bibliopegist; **bookdealer, bookseller**, book agent, book salesman; bibliopole, bibliopolist; **librarian**, bibliothec, bibliothecary, *bibliothécaire* [Fr], reference librarian, cataloger, children's librarian; chief librarian, library director, curator; **booklover**, philobiblist, bibliophile, bibliolater, book collector, bibliomane, bibliomaniac, bibliotaph; **bookworm**, bibliophage; book-stealer, biblioklept.

.22 **journalist, newspaperman, newsman**, pressman [Brit], newswriter, gazetteer [archaic], gentleman *or* representative of the press; **reporter, leg man** [informal], interviewer; **cub reporter**; newspaperwoman, sob sister [slang]; **correspondent, foreign correspondent**, war correspondent, special correspondent, own correspondent; publicist; rewriter, **rewrite man**; reviser, diaskeuast; **editor**, subeditor, managing editor, city editor, news editor, sports editor, woman's editor, feature editor, **copy editor**, copyman, copy chief, slotman; reader, **copyreader**; editorial writer, leader writer [Brit]; **columnist**, paragrapher, paragraphist.

.23 **the press**, public press, **fourth estate**; print medium *or* media, public print; Fleet Street; **journalism**; Associated Press, AP; United Press International, UPI; Reuters; **publishing**, book publishing, magazine publishing; publishing industry, communications, communications industry.

.24 **bibliology**, bibliography; bookcraft, bookmaking, book production, book manufacturing, bibliogenesis, bibliogony; bookselling, bibliopolism.

.25 ADJS **bibliological**, bibliographic(al); bibliothecal, bibliothecary; bibliopolic; bibliopegic.

.26 **journalistic**, journalese [informal]; **periodical**, serial; magazinish, magaziny; newspaperish, newspapery; **editorial**; reportorial.

606. TREATISE

.1 NOUNS **treatise**, piece, treatment, tractate, tract, –logy *or* –logia; examination, survey, **discourse, discussion**, disquisition, descant, exposition, screed; homily; memoir; dissertation, **thesis; essay**, theme; pandect; excursus; **study**, lucubration, étude; **paper**, research paper, term paper; **sketch**, outline, aperçu; causerie; **monograph**, research monograph; *morceau* [Fr], paragraph, **note;** preliminary study, introductory study, first approach, prolegomenon; **article,** feature, special article.

.2 **commentary,** commentation [archaic]; **comment, remark; criticism,** critique, *compte-rendu critique* [Fr], analysis; **review,** critical review, **report,** notice, **write-up** [informal]; **editorial,** leading article *or* leader [both Brit]; gloss, running commentary.

.3 **discourser,** disquisitor, expositor; descanter; **essayist;** monographer, monographist; tractation, tractator [archaic]; **writer, author** 602.15.

.4 **commentator,** commenter; expositor, expounder; annotator, scholiast; glossarist, glossographer; **critic; reviewer,** book reviewer; **editor;** editorial writer, editorialist, leader writer [Brit]; news analyst; publicist.

.5 VERBS **write upon,** touch upon, **discuss, treat, treat of, deal with,** take up, handle, go into, inquire into, survey; discourse, dissert, dissertate, descant; **comment upon,** remark upon; **criticize, review, write up.**

.6 ADJS dissertational, disquisitional, discoursive; expository, expositorial, expositive; essayistic; monographic(al); commentative, commentatorial; critical.

607. ABRIDGMENT

.1 NOUNS **abridgment,** compendium, compend, *abrégé* [Fr], **condensation,** short *or* shortened version, condensed version, abbreviation, abbreviature, brief, digest, **abstract,** epitome, **précis, capsule, sketch,** thumbnail sketch, **synopsis,** conspectus, syllabus, apercu, **survey, review,** overview, pandect, bird's-eye view; **outline,** skeleton, draft; topical outline; head, rubric.

.2 **summary, résumé,** recapitulation, recap [informal], rundown, run-through; **summation;** sum, substance, sum and substance; pith, meat, gist, core, essence, main point 672.6.

.3 **excerpt, extract, selection,** extraction, excerption; passage, selected passage.

.4 **excerpts,** *excerpta* [L], **extracts, gleanings,** cuttings, clippings, flowers, florilegium, **anthology** 605.4; fragments; analects; **miscellany,** miscellanea; **collection,** collectanea; ana.

.5 VERBS **abridge, condense; summarize, brief, outline, sketch,** sketch out, hit the high spots; **capsule, capsulize; nutshell,**

put in a nutshell; synopsize; shorten 203.6.

.6 ADJS **abridged,** condensed; compendious, **brief** 203.8.

.7 ADVS in brief, in summary, in sum, in a nutshell 592.8.

608. DESCRIPTION

.1 NOUNS **description, portrayal,** portraiture, **depiction,** rendering, rendition, **delineation,** limning, **representation** 572; imagery; **word painting** *or* **picture, picture, portrait, image,** photograph; evocation, impression; **sketch,** vignette, cameo; **characterization,** character, character sketch, profile; vivid description, exact description, realistic *or* naturalistic description, slice of life, *tranche de vie* [Fr], graphic account; specification, particularization, details, itemization, catalog, cataloging.

.2 **narration, narrative, relation, recital,** rehearsal, telling, retelling, recounting, recountal, review; **storytelling,** tale-telling, yarn spinning *or* yarning [both informal].

.3 **account, statement, report, word.**

.4 **chronicle, record** 570; **history, annals,** chronicles, memorabilia, chronology; **biography, memoir,** memorial, **life, story, life story,** adventures, fortunes, experiences; life and letters; legend, saint's legend, hagiology, hagiography; **autobiography, memoirs,** memorials; **journal, diary,** confessions; **profile, biographical sketch,** résumé, curriculum vitae; obituary, necrology, martyrology; photobiography; case history; historiography, theory of history; Clio, Muse of history.

.5 (history) "a set of lies agreed upon" [Napoleon], "the unrolled scroll of prophecy" [Garfield], "the chart and compass for national endeavor" [Sir Arthur Helps], "a voice forever sounding across the centuries the laws of right and wrong" [J. A. Froude], "a cyclic poem written by Time upon the memories of man" [Shelley], "the crystallisation of popular belief" [Donn Piatt], "philosophy learned from examples" [Dionysius of Halicarnassus], "history is bunk" [Henry Ford], "history is merely gossip" [Oscar Wilde].

.6 **story, tale, yarn, account, narrative,** narration, chronicle; **anecdote,** anecdotage; **epic, epos, saga.**

.7 **fiction,** work of fiction; **fairy tale,** *Märchen* [Ger]; **legend, myth,** mythos, mythology, folktale, folk story, **fable,** *fabliau* [Fr], **parable, allegory,** apologue; **fantasy;**

romance, gest; love story; bedtime story; nursery tale; adventure story; suspense story, thriller *or* shocker [both informal]; detective story *or* yarn, whodunit [informal]; mystery story, mystery; ghost story; Western story, Western, Westerner, horse opera [informal]; **science fiction,** sci-fi; space fiction, space opera [informal], scientifiction [archaic].

.8 (fictional forms) **short story,** storiette; short-short; vignette; **novel,** *roman* [Fr]; novelette; novella, *nouvelle* [Fr]; **dime novel,** dreadful, penny dreadful, shilling shocker [Brit informal]; epistolary novel, historical novel, psychological novel, novel of ideas, comic novel, picaresque novel, *roman à clef* [Fr], *roman-fleuve* [Fr], river novel, thesis novel, novel of manners, detective novel, sociological novel, sentimental novel, propaganda novel, proletarian novel, novel of character, novel of incident, novel of the soil, regional novel, Gothic novel, problem novel, satirical novel, novel of sensibility, science-fiction novel, *Bildungsroman* [Ger], stream-of-consciousness novel; erotic novel, pornographic novel.

.9 (story elements) **plot,** fable, argument, story, line, subplot, secondary plot, mythos; plan, **structure,** architecture, architectonics, scheme, design; subject, topic, theme, motif; thematic development, development, continuity; **action,** movement; incident, episode; **complication;** rising action, falling action, *peripeteia* [Gk], switch [informal]; *anagnorisis* [Gk], recognition; denouement, catastrophe; *deus ex machina* [L]; device, contrivance, **gimmick** [informal]; angle *or* slant *or* twist [all informal]; **characterization; tone,** atmosphere, mood; background, color, **local color.**

.10 **narrator,** relator, reciter, recounter, *raconteur* [Fr]; **anecdotist;** storyteller, storier, taleteller, teller of tales, spinner of yarns *or* yarn spinner [both informal]; word painter; short-story writer; **novelist,** novelettist, fictionist; fabulist, fableist, fabler, mythmaker, mythopoet; romancer, romancist; sagaman.

.11 **chronicler,** annalist; **historian,** historiographer; **biographer,** memorialist, Boswell; autobiographer, autobiographist; diarist.

.12 VERBS **describe,** portray, **picture,** render, **depict, represent,** delineate, limn, **paint,** draw; evoke, bring to life, make one see; outline, sketch; **characterize,** character;

express, set forth, give words to; **write** 602.21.

.13 **narrate, tell, relate, recount,** report, **recite,** rehearse, give an account of; tell a story, unfold a tale, fable, fabulize; storify, fictionalize; romance; novelize; mythicize, mythify, mythologize, allegorize; retell.

.14 **chronicle,** historify; biograph, biography, biographize; **record** 570.16.

.15 ADJS **descriptive, depictive,** expositive, **representative, delineative; expressive, vivid, graphic,** well-drawn; realistic, naturalistic, true to life, lifelike, faithful.

.16 **narrative, narrational;** storied, storified; **anecdotal,** anecdotic; epic(al).

.17 **fictional;** fictionalized; mythic(al), mythological, **legendary, fabulous;** mythopoeic, mythopoetic(al); parabolic(al), allegoric(al); **romantic,** romanticized.

.18 historic(al), historiographic(al), historied, historico–; chronologic(al); **traditional, legendary;** biographical, autobiographical; hagiographic(al), martyrologic(al); necrologic(al).

.19 ADVS **descriptively,** representatively; **expressively, vividly, graphically;** faithfully, realistically, naturalistically.

609. POETRY

.1 NOUNS **poetry,** poesy, verse, song, rhyme; "musical thought", "the harmonious unison of man with nature" [both Carlyle], "the supreme fiction" [Wallace Stevens], "the spontaneous overflow of powerful feelings recollected in tranquility" [Wordsworth], "the rhythmical creation of beauty" [Poe], "painting with the gift of speech" [Simonides], "the poet's innermost feeling issuing in rhythmic language" [John Keble], "the record of the best and happiest moments of the happiest and best minds" [Shelley], "the journal of a sea animal living on land, wanting to fly in the air", "the achievement of the synthesis of hyacinths and biscuits" [both Sandburg], "the best words in the best order" [Coleridge], "the rhythmic, inevitably narrative, movement from an overclothed blindness to a naked vision" [Dylan Thomas], "not the thing said but a way of saying it" [A. E. Housman], "the art of uniting pleasure with truth, by calling imagination to the help of reason" [Samuel Johnson], "the emotion of life rhythmically remembering beauty" [Fiona MacLeod], "the music of the soul, and above all of great and of feeling souls" [Voltaire].

.2 **poetics,** poetcraft, versecraft, versification, versemaking, *ars poetica* [L]; "my craft and sullen art" [Dylan Thomas]; poetic language, poeticism; poetic license, poetic justice.

.3 **bad poetry,** versemongering, poetastering, poetastery; poesy.

.4 **lyric poetry,** melic poetry, elegiac poetry *or* verse; **narrative poetry,** epic poetry *or* verse, epos, *épopée* [Fr], runic verse, heroic poetry, –ad; mock-heroic poetry, Hudibrastic verse; dramatic poetry, amoebean verse, stichomythia; pastoral poetry, didactic poetry, metaphysical poetry, erotic poetry, satirical poetry, satire, Goliardic verse, light verse, society verse, *vers de société* [Fr], occasional verse; modernist verse, imagist verse, symbolist verse, cubist poetry, concrete poetry; oral poetry; polyphonic prose, prose poetry.

.5 **doggerel,** crambo, crambo clink *or* jingle [Scot], Hudibrastic verse; nonsense verse, amphigory; macaronics, macaronic verse; lame verses, limping meters, halting meters.

.6 **poem, verse, rhyme,** "imaginary gardens with real toads in them" [Marianne Moore]; verselet, versicle; **jingle;** anacreontic, ballad, ballade, cento, clerihew, dithyramb, epode, elegy, epigram, ghazel, limerick, lyric, madrigal, nursery rhyme, ode, Pindaric ode, Sapphic ode, Horatian ode, narrative poem, palinode, satire, sestina, sonnet, English sonnet, Shakespearean sonnet, Italian sonnet, Petrarchan sonnet, sonnet sequence, sloka, song, villanelle; troubadour poem, Provençal poem, canso, chanson, balada, tenso, tenzone, pastourelle, pastorela, alba; epic, epos, *épopée* [Fr], epopoeia; pastoral, eclogue, idyll, pastoral elegy, bucolic, georgic; rondeau, rondel, roundel, roundelay, triolet, virelay; haiku, tanka; epithalamium, prothalamium; dirge, threnody, monody.

.7 **book of verse,** garland, **anthology** 605.4; poetic works, poesy.

.8 **metrics, prosody, versification;** scansion, scanning; metrical pattern *or* form, prosodic pattern *or* form, meter, numbers, measure; quantitative meter, syllabic meter, accentual meter; free verse, *vers libre* [Fr]; alliterative meter, *Stabreim* [Ger].

.9 **meter, measure,** numbers; **rhythm, cadence,** movement, lilt, jingle, swing; sprung rhythm; **accent,** accentuation, metrical accent, stress, emphasis, ictus, **beat;** arsis, thesis; quantity, mora; metrical unit; foot, metrical foot; triseme, tetraseme; metrical group, metron, colon, period; dipody, syzygy, tripody, tetrapody, pentapody, hexapody, heptapody; iamb *or* iambus *or* iambic, anapest, trochee, dactyl, spondee, pyrrhic; amphibrach, antispast, bacchius, chloriambus *or* chloriamb, cretic *or* amphimacer, dochmiac, epitrite, ionic, molossus, paeon, proceleusmatic, tribrach; dimeter, trimeter, tetrameter, pentameter, hexameter, heptameter; **iambic pentameter, dactylic hexameter;** Alexandrine; Saturnian meter; elegiac, elegiac couplet *or* distich, elegiac pentameter; heroic couplet; counterpoint; caesura, diaeresis, masculine caesura, feminine caesura; catalexis; anacrusis; –stich.

.10 **rhyme;** clink, crambo; **consonance, assonance; alliteration;** eye rhyme; male *or* masculine *or* single rhyme, female *or* feminine *or* double rhyme; initial rhyme, end rhyme; tail rhyme, rhyme royal; near rhyme, slant rhyme; rhyme scheme; rhyming dictionary; unrhymed poetry, blank verse.

.11 (poetic divisions) **measure, strain; syllable; line; verse; stanza,** stave; strophe, antistrophe, epode; **canto,** book; **refrain, chorus,** burden; envoi; monostich, distich, tristich, tetrastich, pentastich, hexastich, heptastich, octastich; **couplet;** triplet, tercet, *terza rima* [Ital]; **quatrain;** sextet, sestet; septet; octave, octet, *ottava rima* [Ital]; rhyme royal; Spenserian stanza.

.12 **Muse;** the Muses, Pierides, *Camenae* [L]; Apollo, Apollo Musagetes; Calliope, Polyhymnia, Erato, Euterpe; Helicon, Parnassus; Castilian Spring, Pierian Spring, Hippocrene; Bragi; **poetic genius,** poesy, afflatus, fire of genius, **creative imagination** 535.2, **inspiration** 467.8.

.13 **poet,** poetess, poetress [archaic], maker [archaic]; "the painter of the soul" [Disraeli], "a nightingale who sits in darkness and sings to cheer its own solitude with sweet sounds", "the unacknowledged legislators of the world" [both Shelley], "all who love, who feel great truths, and tell them" [Philip James Bailey], "literalists of the imagination" [Marianne Moore]; ballad maker, balladmonger; **bard, minstrel,** scop, fili, skald, **jongleur, troubadour,** *trovatore* [Ital], trouveur, *trouvère* [Fr], *Meistersinger* [Ger], minnesinger;

minor poet, major poet, arch-poet; laureate, **poet laureate**; occasional poet; **lyric poet**; epic poet; pastoral poet, pastoralist, idyllist, bucoliast [archaic]; rhapsodist, rhapsode; vers-librist, *vers libriste* [Fr]; elegist, librettist; lyricist, lyrist; odist; satirist; sonneteer; modernist, imagist, symbolist; Parnassian; beat poet.

.14 **bad poet;** rhymester, rhymer; metrist; versemaker, versesmith, versifier, verseman, versemonger; poetling, **poetaster,** poeticule; balladmonger.

.15 VERBS **poetize, versify,** verse, write *or* compose poetry, build the stately rime, sing deathless songs, make immortal verse; tune one's lyre, climb Parnassus, mount Pegasus, **sing,** "lisp in numbers" [Pope]; elegize; poeticize.

.16 **rhyme,** assonate, alliterate; **scan;** jingle; cap verses *or* rhymes.

.17 ADJS **poetic(al),** poetlike; **lyric(al), narrative,** dramatic, lyrico-dramatic; bardic; runic, skaldic; epic, heroic; mock-heroic, Hudibrastic; pastoral, bucolic, eclogic, idyllic, Theocritean; didactic; elegiac(al); dithyrambic, rhapsodic(al), Alcaic, Anacreontic, Homeric, Pindaric, sapphic; Castalian, Pierian; poetico-mythological; poetico-mystical, poetico-philosophic.

.18 **metric(al), prosodic(al); rhythmic(al), measured,** cadenced, –semic; scanning; iambic, dactylic, spondaic, pyrrhic, trochaic, anapestic, antispastic; –stichous.

.19 **rhyming; assonant,** assonantal; **alliterative;** jingling.

.20 ADVS **poetically, lyrically; metrically, rhythmically,** in measure.

610. PROSE

.1 NOUNS **prose,** "words in their best order" [Coleridge]; prose fiction, nonfiction prose, expository prose; prose rhythm; prose style; poetic prose, polyphonic prose, prose poetry.

.2 **prosaism, prosaicism, prosaicness,** prosiness, **unpoeticalness; matter-of-factness,** unromanticism, unidealism; **unimaginativeness** 536; **plainness,** commonness, commonplaceness, unembellishedness; insipidness, flatness, vapidity; **dullness** 883.

.3 VERBS **prose,** write prose *or* in prose.

.4 ADJS **prose,** in prose; unversified, nonpoetic, nonmetrical.

.5 **prosaic, prosy, prosing;** unpoetic(al), poetryless; **plain, common, commonplace, ordinary,** unembellished, mundane; **matter-of-fact, unromantic, unidealistic,** unimpassioned; pedestrian, **unimaginative**

536.5; insipid, vapid, flat; humdrum, tiresome, **dull** 883.6.

611. SHOW BUSINESS

.1 NOUNS **show business,** show biz [informal], entertainment industry; **the theater, the footlights, the stage, the boards,** the scenes [archaic], traffic of the stage; stagedom, theater world, stage world, stageland, playland; **drama,** legitimate stage *or* theater, legit [slang], Broadway, off Broadway, off-off-Broadway; repertory drama *or* theater, stock; summer stock, strawhat *or* strawhat circuit [both informal]; **vaudeville,** variety; **burlesque; circus,** carnival; theatromania, theatrophobia.

.2 **dramatics;** dramaticism, dramatism; **theatrics,** theatricism, **theatricalism,** theatricality, staginess; theatricals, amateur theatricals; **histrionics,** histrionism; dramatic *or* histrionic *or* Thespian art; dramatic stroke, *coup de théâtre* [Fr]; **melodramatics,** sensationalism; **dramaturgy,** dramatic structure, play construction, dramatic form; dramatic irony.

.3 **theatercraft, stagecraft,** stagery, scenecraft; **showmanship.**

.4 **stage show, show; play,** stage play, piece, vehicle, work; **drama,** dramatic play; comedy drama; playlet, skit, sketch; well-made play, *pièce bien faite* [Fr]; closet drama; straight drama, legitimate drama; **melodrama,** sensational play; Grand Guignol; suspense drama, cliff hanger [slang]; Tom show; sociodrama, psychodrama; problem play; **pageant,** spectacle, extravaganza; mystery play, mystery, miracle play, miracle, morality play, morality; Passion play; pastoral, pastoral drama; masque, antimasque; charade; pantomime 568.14; improvisational drama, happening; experimental theater, total theater; epic theater; documentary drama; theater of the absurd; theater of cruelty; tableau, *tableau vivant* [Fr]; dramalogue; monologue, monodrama; duologue, duodrama, dialogue; **vaudeville show,** vaudeville; **variety show; revue** *or* review, musical revue; minstrel show; burlesque show; music drama, opera, ballet 462.35; television drama *or* play *or* show, teleplay; radio drama *or* play *or* show; broadcast drama; dramatic series, serial, daytime serial, soap opera *or* soap [both informal]; quiz show, giveaway, giveaway show, panel show, talk show [informal]; situation comedy, sitcom [informal]; telethon; **hit** or hit show [both informal], gasser [slang], success, critical success, audience success, word-of-mouth success; failure, **flop** or bomb [both slang].

.5 **tragedy,** tragic drama; classical tragedy, Greek tragedy, Aeschylean tragedy, Sophoclean tragedy, Euripidean tragedy, Senecan tragedy; Renaissance tragedy; revenge tragedy, romantic tragedy, domestic tragedy; tragic flaw; buskin, cothurnus; tragic muse, Melpomene.

.6 **comedy;** tragicomedy; sentimental comedy, *comédie larmoyante* [Fr]; light comedy, comedietta; comedy of ideas, comedy of manners, realistic comedy, romantic comedy, comedy of humors, comedy of intrigue, domestic comedy, comedy of situation, **situation comedy,** black comedy, dark comedy, high comedy; comedy of character; genteel comedy; low comedy, broad or raw comedy, *comédie rosse* [Fr]; **burlesque;** mime, satyr play; **slapstick,** slapstick comedy; **farce,** farce comedy, exode; camp, high camp, low camp [all slang]; commedia dell'arte; harlequinade, *arlequinade* [Fr]; musical comedy, **musical** [informal]; comedy ballet; comic opera, burletta, *opera buffa* [Ital], *comédie bouffe* [Fr]; comic relief, comedy relief; comic muse, Thalia.

.7 (comedy symbols) sock, coxcomb, cap and bells, motley, bladder, slapstick.

.8 **act, scene, number, turn,** bit or shtick [both slang], routine [informal]; curtain raiser or lifter; introduction; expository scene; **prologue,** epilogue; **entr'acte,** intermezzo, intermission, interlude, *divertissement* [Fr], *divertimento* [Ital]; **finale,** afterpiece; exodus, exode; chaser [slang]; curtain call, curtain; hokum or hoke act [slang]; song and dance; burlesque act, striptease; stand-up comedy act; sketch, skit.

.9 **acting, playing,** playacting, performing, **performance,** taking a role or part; **representation, portrayal, characterization,** projection; **impersonation,** personation, miming, mimicking, mimicry, mimesis; pantomiming, mummery; ham or hammy acting or hamming or hamming up [all slang], overacting; stage presence; stage directions, **business,** stage business, *jeu de théâtre* [Fr], acting device; stunt or gag [both informal]; hokum or hoke [both slang]; buffoonery, slapstick; patter; stand-up comedy [informal].

.10 **repertoire, repertory;** stock.

.11 **role, part,** piece [slang]; cue, **lines,** side;

cast; **character,** person, personage; lead, starring or lead role, fat part, leading man, leading woman or lady, hero, heroine; antihero; title role, protagonist, principal character; supporting role, supporting character; ingenue, *jeune première* [Fr]; soubrette; villain, heavy [informal], antagonist; bit, bit part, minor role; feeder, straight part; walking part, walk-on; **actor** 612.2.

.12 **engagement,** playing engagement, booking; **run; stand,** one-night stand; **circuit,** vaudeville circuit, borscht circuit; **tour;** date.

.13 theatrical performance, **performance,** show, **presentation,** presentment, **production,** entertainment, stage presentation or performance; bill; **exhibit, exhibition;** benefit performance, benefit; personal appearance, flesh show [slang]; tryout; premiere, premier performance, debut; farewell performance, swan song [slang].

.14 **production,** mounting, staging, putting on; stage management; **direction,** *mise-en-scène* [Fr]; **rehearsal,** dress rehearsal, walk-through, run-through.

.15 (shows) repertory show, rep show [slang]; **floor show;** variety show, vaudeville show; leg or girl or girly show [slang], burlesque show, hootchy-kootchy show, cooch or coochie show [slang]; magic show; **rodeo; circus,** the big top, **carnival, sideshow;** puppet show, fantoccini [pl], Punch-and-Judy show; peep show, raree-show; galanty show, shadow show, *ombres chinoises* [Fr]; light show.

.16 **motion picture, moving picture, movie** [informal], **picture,** picture show, motion-picture show, moving-picture show, **film,** flicker or flick [both informal], cinema [Brit], photoplay, photodrama, cine–; silent film, silent; talkie [informal], talking picture; **feature;** preview, sneak preview, trailer; selected short subject, **short;** documentary film, **documentary;** educational film; newsreel; Grade B movie; Western, horse opera or shoot-'em-up [both slang], spaghetti Western [informal]; horror picture; thriller or chiller or creepie [all slang]; pornographic film, nudie [informal], porno or skin flick [both slang]; animated cartoon, cartoon; 3-D; Cinemascope, Cinerama; black-and-white film, color film; Technicolor, underground film or movie; experimental film.

.17 **the cinema, the movies** or the pictures [both informal], the screen, the silver screen; art film, *cinéma vérité, nouvelle vague* [both Fr].

.18 **theater,** theatr(o)–; **playhouse,** house, theatron, odeum; **auditorium; opera house,** opera; **hall,** music hall, concert hall; **amphitheater;** circle theater, arena theater, theater-in-the-round; vaudeville theater; burlesque theater; **little theater,** community theater; open-air theater, outdoor theater; Greek theater; Elizabethan theater, Globe Theatre; showboat; cabaret, nightclub, club, night spot, *boîte de nuit* [Fr].

.19 **motion-picture theater,** moving-picture theater, movie theater [informal], movie house, picture palace *or* picture house [both Brit], cinema *or* cinema theater [both Brit], cinematograph *or* kinematograph [both Brit]; drive-in, drive-in theater; nickelodeon.

.20 **auditorium;** parquet, orchestra, pit [Brit]; **orchestra circle,** parquet circle, parterre; **dress circle;** fauteuil *or* theatre stall *or* stall [all Brit]; box, box seat, loge, *baignoire* [Fr]; stage box; proscenium boxes, parterre boxes; balcony, gallery; **peanut gallery** *or* paradise *or* nigger heaven [all slang]; standing room.

.21 **stage,** the boards; acting area, playing *or* performing area; apron, apron stage, forestage; proscenium stage, proscenium arch, proscenium; bridge; revolving stage; orchestra, pit, orchestra pit; **bandstand,** shell, band shell; stage right, R; stage left, L; backstage; **wings,** coulisse; dressing room, greenroom; flies, fly gallery, fly floor; gridiron, grid [informal]; board, lightboard, switchboard; dock; prompter's box.

.22 (stage requisites) **property, prop;** practical piece *or* prop [informal]; costume 231.9; theatrical makeup, makeup, greasepaint, blackface, clown white; spirit gum.

.23 **lights; footlights,** foots [informal], floats; floodlight, flood; bunch light; **limelight,** spotlight, spot [informal], arc light, arc, klieg light; color filter, medium, gelatin; dimmer; marquee; light plot.

.24 **setting, stage setting,** stage set, **set,** *mise-en-scène* [Fr].

.25 **scenery,** decor; **scene;** screen, **flat;** cyclorama; stage screw; side scene, **wing,** coulisse; border; tormentor, **teaser;** wingcut, woodcut; transformation, transformation scene; flipper; batten; counterweight; **curtain,** rag [slang], hanging; **drop,** drop scene, drop curtain, scrim, cloth; **backdrop,** back cloth [Brit]; act drop *or* curtain; tab, tableau; fire curtain, curtain board, asbestos, asbestos board.

.26 **playbook, script,** text, **libretto;** promptbook; book; **score; scenario,** continuity, shooting script; scene plot; lines, actor's lines, cue, side.

.27 **dramatist; playwright,** playwriter, dramaturge; play doctor *or* play fixer [both informal]; dramatizer; **scriptwriter, scenario writer,** scenarist, scenarioist, screenwriter; gagman, joke writer, jokesmith; **librettist;** tragedian, comedian; farcist, *farceur, farceuse* [both Fr], farcer; melodramatist; monodramatist; mimographer; **choreographer.**

.28 **theater man,** theatrician; **showman,** exhibitor, **producer, impresario; director,** auteur; stage director, **stage manager;** set designer, scenewright; costume designer, costumer, *costumier, costumière* [both Fr]; wigmaker; makeup man *or* artist; prompter; callboy; playreader; master of ceremonies, MC *or* emcee [both informal]; ticket collector; usher, usherer, usherette; ringmaster, equestrian director; barker, ballyhoo man *or* spieler [both informal].

.29 **stage technician, stagehand,** machinist [archaic], sceneman, **sceneshifter;** flyman; carpenter; **electrician;** scene painter, scenic artist, scenewright.

.30 **agent, actor's agent,** playbroker, ten-percenter [slang]; **booking agent;** advance agent, advance man; publicity man *or* agent.

.31 **patron,** patroness; **backer, angel** [informal]; Dionysus.

.32 **playgoer, theatergoer;** attender 186.5, spectator 442, audience 448.6; moviegoer [informal], **motion-picture fan** [informal]; first-nighter; standee, groundling [archaic]; *claqueur* [Fr], hired applauder; pass holder, deadhead [informal].

.33 VERBS **dramatize,** theatricalize; melodramatize; scenarize; **present, stage, produce,** mount, **put on,** put on the stage; **put on a show;** try out, preview; give a performance; premiere; **open,** open a show, open a show cold [informal]; set the stage; ring up the curtain, ring down the curtain; **star, feature** [informal], bill, **headline,** give top billing to; succeed, make *or* be a hit [informal], be a gas *or* gasser [slang]; fail, flop *or* bomb [both slang].

.34 **act, perform, play,** playact, tread the boards, strut one's stuff [slang]; appear, **appear on the stage;** act like a trouper;

register; emotionalize, emote [informal]; pantomime, mime; patter; sketch; troupe, barnstorm [informal]; steal the show, upstage; make one's debut or bow, come out; act as foil or feeder, stooge [slang], be straight man for; star, play the lead, get top billing, have one's name in lights.

.35 enact, act out; represent, depict, portray; act or play or perform a part or role, take a part, sustain a part, act or play the part of; create a role or character; impersonate, personate; play opposite, support.

.36 overact, overdramatize, chew up the scenery [informal], act all over the stage; ham or ham it up [both informal]; mug [slang], grimace; spout, rant, roar, declaim, "out-herod Herod" [Shakespeare]; milk a scene; underact, throw away [informal].

.37 rehearse, practice, go through, run through, go over; go through one's part, read one's lines; con or study one's part; be a fast or slow study.

.38 ADJS dramatic, dramatical [archaic], dramaturgic(al); theatrical, histrionic, thespian; scenic; stagy; theaterlike, stagelike; spectacular; melodramatic; ham or hammy [both slang]; overacted, overplayed, milked [informal]; underacted, underplayed, thrown away; film, filmic, movie [informal], cinematic, cinematographic; monodramatic; vaudevillian; operatic; ballet, balletic; legitimate; stellar, all-star; stagestruck, starstruck; stageworthy, actor-proof.

.39 tragic, heavy; buskined, cothurned.

.40 comic, light; tragicomic(al), farcical, slapstick; camp or campy [both slang].

.41 ADVS on the stage or boards, before an audience, before the footlights; in the limelight or spotlight; onstage; downstage, upstage; backstage, off stage, behind the scenes; down left, DL; down right, DR; up left, UL; up right, UR.

612. ENTERTAINER

.1 NOUNS entertainer, public entertainer, performer; artist, artiste; impersonator, female impersonator; vaudevillian, vaudevillist; dancer 879.3, hoofer [slang]; song and dance man; chorus girl, show girl, chorine [informal]; coryphée; chorus boy or man; burlesque queen [informal], stripteaser, exotic dancer, ecdysiast; stripper or peeler or stripteuse [all slang]; dancing girl, nautch girl, belly dancer; go-go dancer; geisha, geisha girl; mountebank; magician, conjurer, prestidigitator,

sleight-of-hand artist; mummer, guiser or guisard [both Scot]; singer, musician 464.

.2 actor, player, stage player or performer, playactor, histrion, histrio, thespian, Roscius, theatrical [informal], trouper; actress; child actor; mummer, pantomime, pantomimist; monologist, diseur, diseuse; reciter; dramatizer; mime, mimer, mimic; strolling player, stroller; barnstormer [informal]; character actor, character man or woman, character; villain, antagonist, bad guy or heavy [both informal]; juvenile, ingenue; soubrette; foil, feeder or stooge [both slang], straight man; utility man; protean actor; matinee idol [informal].

.3 circus artist or performer; trapeze artist, aerialist, flier [informal]; high-wire artist, tightrope walker, slack-rope artist, equilibrist; acrobat, tumbler; bareback rider; juggler; lion tamer, sword swallower; snake charmer; clown; ringmaster, equestrian director.

.4 motion-picture actor, movie actor [informal]; movie star [informal], film star; starlet.

.5 ham or ham actor [both informal]; grimacer.

.6 lead, leading man or lady, principal, star, superstar, headliner, headline or feature attraction; hero, heroine, protagonist; juvenile lead, jeune premier, jeune première [both Fr]; first tragedian, heavy lead [informal]; prima donna, diva, singer 464.13; première danseuse, prima ballerina, danseur noble [Fr].

.7 supporting actor; support, supporting cast; supernumerary, super or supe [both informal], spear-carrier [informal], extra; bit player; walking gentleman or lady [slang], walk-on, mute; figurant, figurante; understudy, stand-in, standby, substitute.

.8 tragedian, tragedienne.

.9 comedian, comedienne, comic, funnyman; farcist, farcer, farceur, farceuse [both Fr]; stand-up comic or comedian [informal]; light comedian, genteel comedian, low comedian, slapstick comedian, hokum or hoke comic [slang].

.10 buffoon, buffo [Ital], clown, fool, jester, zany, merry-andrew, jack-pudding, pickle-herring, motley fool, motley, wearer of the cap and bells; harlequin; Pantaloon, Pantalone; Punch, Punchinello, Pulcinella, Polichinelle; Punch and Judy; Hanswurst; Columbine; Harlequin; Scaramouch.

.11 **cast,** cast of characters, characters, persons of the drama, *dramatis personae* [L]; supporting cast; **company,** acting company, **troupe;** repertory company, stock company; ensemble, chorus, *corps de ballet* [Fr]; circus troupe.

613. UNCOMMUNICATIVENESS

.1 NOUNS **uncommunicativeness,** closeness, indisposition to speak, disinclination to communicate; unconversableness, **unsociability** 923; secretiveness 614.1; lack of message *or* meaning, meaninglessness 547.

.2 **taciturnity, untalkativeness,** unloquaciousness; **silence** 451; **speechlessness,** wordlessness, dumbness, **muteness** 451.2; obmutescence; quietness, quietude; laconicalness, laconism, curtness, shortness, terseness; brusqueness, briefness, brevity, conciseness, economy *or* sparingness of words, pauciloquy [archaic].

.3 **reticence** *or* reticency; **reserve,** reservedness, restraint, **constraint;** guardedness, discreetness, discretion; suppression, repression; subduedness; backwardness, retirement; **aloofness, standoffishness,** distance, remoteness, **detachment,** withdrawal, withdrawnness; impersonality; **coolness,** coldness, frigidity, iciness, frostiness, chilliness; **inaccessibility, unapproachability; undemonstrativeness,** unexpansiveness, unaffability, uncongeniality; **introversion;** modesty, bashfulness 908.1–4; expressionlessness, blankness, impassiveness, impassivity.

.4 **prevarication, equivocation,** tergiversation, evasion, shuffle, fencing, dodging, parrying; *suppressio veri* [L]; weasel words.

.5 **man of few words,** clam [informal], laconic [archaic]; Spartan, Laconian.

.6 VERBS **keep to oneself,** keep one's own counsel; not open one's mouth, not say a word, stand mute, **hold one's tongue** 451.5; have little to say, refuse comment, say neither yes nor no, waste no words, save one's breath; retire; **keep one's distance,** keep at a distance, keep oneself to oneself, **stand aloof,** hold oneself aloof; keep secret 614.7.

.7 **prevaricate, equivocate,** waffle [informal], tergiversate, evade, dodge, sidestep, parry, duck, weasel [informal], palter; hum and haw, **hem and haw,** back and fill; **mince words,** mince the truth, euphemize.

.8 ADJS **uncommunicative,** indisposed *or* disinclined to communicate; unconversa-

tional, unconversable [archaic]; **unsociable** 923.5; **secretive** 614.15; meaningless 547.6.

.9 **taciturn, untalkative,** unloquacious, indisposed to talk; **silent, speechless,** wordless, mum; **mute** 451.12, dumb, quiet; close, closemouthed, close-tongued, snug [dial], **tight-lipped;** tongue-tied, word-bound; **laconic,** curt, brief, terse, brusque, short, concise, **sparing of words,** economical of words.

.10 **reticent, reserved,** restrained, constrained; **suppressed,** repressed; subdued; guarded, discreet; backward, **retiring,** shrinking; **aloof, standoffish,** offish [informal], standoff, **distant,** remote, removed, **detached,** Olympian, withdrawn; impersonal; **cool,** cold, frigid, icy, frosty, chilled, chilly; **inaccessible, unapproachable,** forbidding; **undemonstrative,** unexpansive, unaffable, uncongenial, ungenial; **introverted;** modest, bashful 908.9–12; expressionless, blank, impassive.

.11 **prevaricating, equivocal,** tergiversating, tergiversant, **evasive,** weasel-worded.

614. SECRECY

.1 NOUNS **secrecy,** secretness, airtight secrecy, close secrecy; crypticness; the dark; hiddenness, **concealment** 615; **secretiveness,** closeness; discreetness, discretion; **uncommunicativeness** 613; **evasiveness,** evasion, subterfuge; hugger-mugger, hugger-muggery.

.2 **privacy,** retirement, isolation, sequestration, seclusion; incognito, anonymity; **confidentialness,** confidentiality; closed meeting, executive session, private conference.

.3 **veil of secrecy, veil,** curtain, pall, wraps; iron curtain, "curtains of fog and iron" [Churchill], bamboo curtain; wall *or* barrier of secrecy; **suppression,** repression, stifling, smothering; **censorship,** blackout [informal], **hush-up; seal of secrecy,** official secrecy; security, ironbound security; pledge *or* oath of secrecy.

.4 **stealth,** stealthiness, furtiveness, **clandestineness,** clandestinity, clandestine behavior, **surreptitiousness, covertness,** slyness, shiftiness, sneakiness, slinkiness, underhand dealing, undercover *or* underground activity; prowl, prowling; stalking.

.5 **secret, confidence;** private *or* personal matter, privity [archaic]; confidential *or* **privileged communication;** deep, dark secret; solemn secret; guarded secret, classified information, restricted information;

mystery, enigma, arcanum; esoterica, cabala, the occult, hermetism, hermeticism, hermetics; deep or profound secret, sealed book, mystery of mysteries; skeleton in the closet or cupboard.

.6 cryptography, cryptoanalysis, cryptoanalytics; code, cipher; secret language; secret writing, coded message, cryptogram, cryptograph; secret or invisible or sympathetic ink; cryptographer.

.7 VERBS keep secret, keep mum, veil, keep dark; keep it a deep, dark secret; secrete, conceal 615.7; keep to oneself 613.6, keep in petto, bosom, keep close, keep snug [dial], keep back, keep from, withhold, hold out on [slang]; not let it go further, keep within these walls, keep within the bosom of the lodge, keep between us; not tell, hold one's tongue 451.5, never let on [informal], make no sign, not breathe a word, be the soul of discretion; not give away [informal], "tell it not in Gath" [Bible], keep it under one's hat [informal], keep under wraps [informal], keep buttoned up [informal], keep one's own counsel; play dumb; not let the right hand know what the left is doing; keep in ignorance, keep or leave in the dark; classify; file and forget.

.8 hush up, hush, hush-hush, huggermugger; suppress, repress, stifle, muffle, smother, squash, quash, squelch, kill, sit on or upon, put the lid on [slang]; censor, black out [informal].

.9 tell confidentially, tell for one's ears only, mention privately, whisper, breathe, whisper in the ear; tell one a secret; take aside, see one alone, talk to in private, speak in privacy.

.10 code, encode, encipher, cipher.

.11 ADJS secret, close, closed, cryptic, dark; unuttered, unrevealed, undivulged, undisclosed, unspoken, untold; hush-hush [informal], top secret, classified, restricted, under wraps [informal], under security or security restrictions; censored, suppressed, stifled, smothered, hushed-up, under the seal or ban of secrecy; unrevealable, undivulgable, undisclosable, untellable, unwhisperable, unbreatheable, unutterable; latent, ulterior, concealed, hidden 615.11; arcane, esoteric, occult, cabalistic, hermetic; enigmatic, mysterious 549.18.

.12 covert, clandestine, quiet, unobtrusive, hugger-mugger, hidlings [Scot], surreptitious, undercover, underground, under-the-counter, under-the-table, back-door, hole-and-corner [informal], underhand, underhanded; furtive, stealthy, privy, backstairs, sly, shifty, sneaky, sneaking, skulking, slinking, slinky, feline.

.13 private, privy; intimate, inmost, innermost, interior, inward, personal; closet; secluded, sequestered, isolated, withdrawn, retired; incognito, anonymous.

.14 confidential, auricular, inside [slang], esoteric; in petto [Ital], close to one's chest [informal], under one's hat [informal]; off the record, not for the record, not to be minuted, within these four walls, in the bosom of the lodge, for no other ears, eyes-only, between us; not to be quoted, not for publication or release; not for attribution; unquotable, unpublishable, sealed; sensitive, privileged, under privilege.

.15 secretive, secret, close, dark; discreet; evasive, shifty; uncommunicative, closemouthed 613.8,9.

.16 coded, encoded; ciphered, enciphered; cryptographic(al).

.17 ADVS secretly, in secret, in or up one's sleeve; nobody the wiser; covertly, in hidlings [Scot], undercover, à couvert [Fr], under the cloak of; behind the scenes, in the background, in a corner, in the dark, in darkness, behind the veil or curtain, behind the veil of secrecy; sub rosa [L], under the rose; underground; sotto voce [Ital], under the breath, with bated breath, in a whisper.

.18 surreptitiously, clandestinely, secretively, furtively, stealthily, slyly, shiftily, sneakily, sneakingly, skulkingly, slinkingly, slinkily; by stealth, on the sly, on the quiet, on the q.t. [both slang], à la dérobée [Fr], en tapinois [Fr], behind one's back, by a side door, like a thief in the night, underhand, underhandedly, under the table, in holes and corners or in a hole-and-corner way [both informal].

.19 privately, privily, in private, in privacy, in privy; apart, aside; behind closed doors, januis clausis [L], à huis clos [Fr], in camera [L], in chambers, in secret or closed meeting, in executive session, in private conference.

.20 confidentially, in confidence, in strict confidence, under the seal of secrecy, off the record; between ourselves, strictly between us, entre nous [Fr], inter nos [L], for your ears only, between you and me, from me to you, between you and me and the bedpost or lamppost [informal].

615. CONCEALMENT

.1 NOUNS **concealment, hiding, secretion;** burial, burying, interment, putting away; **covering,** covering up, masking, screening 228.1; mystification, obscuration; darkening, obscurement, clouding 337.6; **hiddenness,** concealedness, covertness, occultation; **secrecy** 614; uncommunicativeness 613; invisibility 445; **subterfuge, deception** 618.

.2 veil, curtain, **cover, screen** 228.2; wraps; disguise 618.10.

.3 ambush,· ambushment, **ambuscade,** *guetapens* [Fr]; surveillance, shadowing 485.9; lurking hole or place; blind, stalkinghorse; booby trap, trap 618.11.

.4 hiding place, hideaway, hideout, hidey hole [slang], hiding, concealment, **cover,** secret place; recess, corner, dark corner, nook, cranny, niche; **hole,** bolt-hole, foxhole, funk hole, dugout, lair, den; **asylum, sanctuary, retreat, refuge** 700; covert, coverture, undercovert; **cache,** stash [informal]; cubbyhole, cubby.

.5 secret passage, covert way, secret exit; **back way,** back door, side door; **bolt-hole,** escape route, escape hatch; secret staircase, *escalier dérobé* [Fr], **back stairs; underground,** underground route, underground railroad.

.6 VERBS **conceal, hide,** ensconce; **cover, cover up,** blind, **screen, cloak, veil,** curtain, blanket, shroud, enshroud, envelop; **disguise, camouflage, mask,** dissemble; whitewash [informal]; gloss over, varnish, slur over; distract attention from; **obscure,** obfuscate, cloud, becloud, befog, throw out a smoke screen, shade, throw into the shade; **eclipse,** occult; put out of sight, sweep under the rug, keep under cover; cover up one's tracks, lay a false scent, hide one's trail; hide one's light under a bushel.

.7 secrete, hide away, keep hidden, put away, store away, stow away, file and forget, bottle up, lock up, seal up, put out of sight; **keep secret** 614.7; **cache,** stash [informal], deposit, plant [slang]; **bury;** bosom, embosom [archaic].

.8 (hide oneself) **hide, conceal oneself, take cover, hide out** [informal], hide away, **go into hiding,** go to ground; stay in hiding, **lie hid** or **hidden, lie low** [informal], lie *perdue,* lie snug or close [dial], lie doggo or sit tight [both slang], burrow [archaic], **hole up** [slang], **go underground;** play peekaboo or bopeep or hide and seek;

keep out of sight, retire from sight, drop from sight, disappear 447.2, crawl or retreat into one's shell, keep in the background, stay in the shade; **disguise oneself,** masquerade, take an assumed name, change one's identity, go under an alias, remain anonymous, be incognito, go under false colors, wear a mask.

.9 lurk, couch; **lie in wait,** lay wait; **sneak, skulk, slink, prowl,** nightwalk, **steal, creep,** pussyfoot [slang], gumshoe [slang], tiptoe; stalk, shadow 485.34.

.10 ambush, ambuscade, **waylay; lie in ambush,** lay wait for, **lie in wait for,** lay for [informal]; set a trap for 618.18.

.11 ADJS **concealed, hidden, hid,** occult, recondite [archaic], blind, adel(o)–, crypt(o)– or krypt(o)–; **covered** 228.31; **covert, under cover,** under wraps [informal]; **obscured,** obfuscated, clouded, clouded over, wrapped in clouds, in a cloud or fog or mist or haze, beclouded, befogged; eclipsed, in eclipse, under an eclipse; in the wings; buried; underground; close, secluded, secluse, sequestered; in purdah, under house arrest, incommunicado; **obscure,** abstruse, mysterious 549.15–18; **secret** 614.11,12; unknown 477.17, latent 546.5.

.12 unrevealed, undisclosed, undivulged, unexposed; unapparent, **invisible, unseen,** unperceived, unspied, undetected; undiscovered, unexplored, untraced, untracked; unexplained, unsolved.

.13 disguised, camouflaged, in disguise; masked, masquerading; **incognito,** incog [informal].

.14 in hiding, hidden out, under cover, in a dark corner, lying hid, doggo [slang]; in ambush or ambuscade; waiting concealed, lying in wait; in the wings; lurking, skulking, prowling, sneaking, stealing; pussyfooted, pussyfoot, on tiptoe; stealthy, furtive, surreptitious 614.12.

.15 concealing, hiding, obscuring; covering 228.34; unrevealing, nonrevealing, undisclosing.

616. FALSENESS

.1 NOUNS **falseness, falsehood,** falsity, inveracity, untruth, **truthlessness, untrueness; fallaciousness,** fallacy, **erroneousness** 518.1.

.2 spuriousness, phoniness [slang], bogusness [informal], **ungenuineness, unauthenticity,** unrealness, artificiality, factitiousness, syntheticness.

.3 sham, fakery, faking, falsity, feigning, pretending; feint, pretext, **pretense,** hollow pretense, **pretension, false pretense** or **pretension;** humbug, humbuggery; **bluff,** bluffing, four-flushing [informal]; speciousness, meretriciousness; cheating, fraud; imposture 618.6; deception, delusion 618.1; acting, playacting; representation, **simulation,** simulacrum; dissembling, **dissemblance, dissimulation;** seeming, semblance, appearance, face, ostentation, **show, false show,** outward show, **false air;** window dressing, front, **false front, façade,** gloss, varnish; gilt; color, coloring, false color; masquerade, disguise 618.10; posture, pose, posing, attitudinizing; affectation 903.

.4 **falseheartedness, falseness,** doubleheartedness, doubleness of heart, doubleness of heart, **duplicity, two-facedness,** double-facedness, **double-dealing,** ambidexterity; **dishonesty,** improbity, lack of integrity, Machiavellianism, bad faith; low cunning, cunning, artifice, wile 735.1–3; **deceitfulness** 618.3; faithlessness, treachery 975.5,6.

.5 **insincerity, uncandidness,** uncandor, **unfrankness,** disingenuousness; emptiness, hollowness; mockery, hollow mockery; crossed fingers, tongue in cheek, unseriousness; sophistry, jesuitry, casuistry 483.1.

.6 **hypocrisy,** hypocriticalness; Tartuffery, Tartuffism, Pecksniffery, pharisaism, **sanctimony** 1029, sanctimoniousness, religiosity, false piety, ostentatious devotion; **mealymouthedness, unctuousness,** oiliness; **cant,** mummery, snuffling [archaic]; **mouthing; lip service;** tokenism; token gesture, empty gesture; sweet talk or soft soap [both informal]; crocodile tears.

.7 **quackery,** quackishness, quackism, **mountebankery, charlatanry,** charlatanism; imposture; humbug, humbuggery.

.8 **untruthfulness, dishonesty,** falsehood, **unveracity,** unveraciousness, truthlessness, **mendaciousness, mendacity;** credibility gap; **lying, fibbing,** fibbery, pseudology; pathological lying, mythomania, *pseudologia phantastica* [L].

.9 **falsification,** falsifying; confabulation; perversion, distortion, straining; **misrepresentation,** misconstruction, misstatement, coloring, false coloring, miscoloring; **exaggeration** 617; **prevarication,** equivocation 613.4; **perjury,** false swearing, oath breaking.

.10 **fabrication, invention, concoction;** canard; **forgery; fiction,** figment, **myth,** fable, romance, extravaganza.

.11 **lie, falsehood,** falsity, **untruth,** untruism, mendacity, **prevarication, fib,** taradiddle [informal], flimflam or flam, *blague* [Fr]; **fiction,** pious fiction, legal fiction; **story** [informal], **trumped-up story,** farrago; **yarn** [informal], **tale,** fairy tale [informal], ghost story; farfetched story, tall tale or **tall story** [both informal], **cock-and-bull story,** fish story [informal]; exaggeration 617; half-truth, stretching of the truth, slight stretching, white lie, little white lie; *suggestio falsi* [L]; a pack of lies.

.12 monstrous lie, consummate lie, deep-dyed falsehood, out-and-out lie, **whopper** [informal], gross or flagrant or shameless falsehood, **barefaced lie, dirty lie** [slang]; **slander, libel** 971.3; the big lie.

.13 **fake, fakement** [informal], **phony** [slang], **rip-off** [slang], **sham, mock, imitation,** simulacrum, dummy; paste, tinsel, *clinquant* [Fr], pinchbeck, shoddy, junk; **counterfeit, forgery;** put-up job or frame-up [both informal], put-on [informal]; **hoax, cheat, fraud, swindle** 618.7–9; whited sepulcher, whitewash job [informal]; impostor 619.6.

.14 **humbug,** humbuggery; **bunk** [slang], **bunkum;** hooey or hoke or hokum [all slang], **bosh** [informal], bull or **bullshit** or balls or crap [all slang], baloney [slang], flimflam, flam, claptrap, moonshine, eyewash, hogwash, gammon [informal], *blague* [Fr], jiggery-pokery [Brit].

.15 VERBS ring false, **not ring true.**

.16 **falsify, belie, misrepresent,** miscolor; misstate, misquote, misreport, miscite; overstate, understate; **pervert, distort,** strain, warp, **slant, twist;** garble; put a false appearance upon, give a false coloring, give a color to, **color, gild,** gloss, gloss over, whitewash, varnish; fudge [informal], dress up, titivate, embellish, embroider, trick or prink out; deodorize, make smell like roses; **disguise, camouflage, mask.**

.17 **tamper with, manipulate, fake, juggle,** sophisticate, **doctor** or **cook** [both informal], rig; pack, stack; **adulterate** 44.13; retouch; **load; salt,** plant [slang], salt a mine.

.18 **fabricate, invent, manufacture, trump up, make up, hatch, concoct, cook up** [informal], fudge [informal], fake, hoke up [slang]; **counterfeit, forge;** fantasize, fantasize about.

.19 **lie, tell a lie,** falsify, speak falsely, speak with forked tongue [informal], be untruthful, trifle with the truth, deviate from the truth, **fib, story** [informal]; **stretch the truth,** strain or bend the truth; draw the longbow; **exaggerate** 617.3; lie flatly, lie in one's throat, lie through one's teeth, lie like a trooper, **prevaricate,** equivocate 613.7; deceive, mislead 618.13,15.

.20 swear falsely, forswear oneself [archaic], **perjure oneself, bear false witness.**

.21 **sham, fake** [informal], **feign, counterfeit, simulate,** gammon [informal]; **pretend,** make a pretense, **make believe, make a show of,** make like [informal], make as if *or* as though; go through the motions [informal]; let on, let on like [informal]; **affect,** profess, **assume,** put on; **dissimulate, dissemble,** cover up; **act, play,** playact, **put on an act** [informal], act *or* play a part; **put up a front** [informal], put on a front *or* false front [informal]; four-flush [slang], **bluff,** pull *or* put up a bluff [informal]; **play possum** [informal], roll over and play dead.

.22 **pose as, masquerade as,** impersonate, pass for, assume the guise *or* identity of, set up for, act the part of, represent oneself to be, claim *or* pretend to be, **make false pretenses,** go under false pretenses, **sail under false colors.**

.23 **be hypocritical, act** *or* **play the hypocrite;** cant, be holier than the Pope, reek of piety; snuffle [archaic], snivel, mouth; give mouth honor, render *or* give lip service; sweet-talk, soft-soap, blandish 970.5.

.24 **play a double game** *or* **role, play both ends against the middle,** work both sides of the street, have it both ways at once, have one's cake and eat it too, run with the hare and hunt with the hounds [Brit]; two-time [informal].

.25 ADJS **false, untrue, truthless, not true,** void *or* devoid of truth, contrary to fact, in error, **fallacious, erroneous** 518.16; unfounded 483.13.

.26 **spurious, ungenuine, unauthentic,** supposititious, bastard, **pseudo, quasi,** apocryphal, **fake** [informal], **phony** [slang], **sham, mock, counterfeit,** colorable, **bogus,** queer [slang], **dummy, make-believe,** so-called, **imitation** 22.8, noth(o)–; not what it is cracked up to be [slang]; **falsified;** dressed up, titivated, embellished, embroidered; garbled; twisted, distorted, warped, perverted; **simulated, faked, feigned,** colored, fictitious, fictive, **counterfeited, pretended, affected, assumed, put-on; artificial, synthetic,** ersatz; **unreal;** factitious, unnatural, man-made; illegitimate; *soi-disant* [Fr], self-styled;

pinchbeck, brummagem [Brit], tinsel, shoddy, tin, junky.

.27 **specious, meretricious,** gilded, tinsel, **seeming,** apparent, colored, colorable, plausible, **ostensible.**

.28 **quack, quackish; charlatan, charlatanish,** charlatanic.

.29 **fabricated,** invented, manufactured, **concocted, hatched, trumped-up, made-up,** put-up, cooked-up [informal]; **forged;** fictitious, fictional, figmental, **mythical,** fabulous, legendary; fantastic, fantasied, fancied.

.30 **tampered** with, **manipulated, cooked** *or* **doctored** [both informal], juggled, **rigged,** engineered; packed.

.31 **falsehearted, false,** false-principled, false-dealing; double, duplicitous, ambidextrous, **double-dealing,** doublehearted, double-minded, double-tongued, double-faced, **two-faced,** Janus-faced; Machiavellian, dishonest; **crooked, deceitful** 618.20; artful, cunning, crafty 735.12; faithless, perfidious, treacherous 975.20,21.

.32 **insincere, uncandid, unfrank, mealy-mouthed,** disingenuous; dishonest; **empty, hollow;** tongue in cheek, unserious; sophistic(al), jesuitic(al), casuistic 483.10.

.33 **hypocritic(al),** canting, Pecksniffian, pharisaic(al), pharisean, **sanctimonious, goody-goody** [informal], holier than the Pope, holier-than-thou, simon-pure; **mealymouthed,** unctuous, oily.

.34 **untruthful, dishonest, unveracious,** unveridical, truthless, **lying, mendacious;** perjured, forsworn; prevaricating, equivocal 613.11.

.35 ADVS **falsely, untruly,** truthlessly; **erroneously** 518.20; **untruthfully,** unveraciously; **spuriously, ungenuinely;** artificially, synthetically; unnaturally, factitiously; speciously, seemingly, apparently, plausibly, ostensibly; nominally, in name only.

.36 **insincerely,** uncandidly; emptily, hollowly; unseriously; **hypocritically,** mealymouthedly, unctuously.

617. EXAGGERATION

.1 NOUNS **exaggeration, exaggerating; overstatement, big** *or* **tall talk** [informal], **hyperbole, hyperbolism; superlative; extravagance,** profuseness, prodigality 854; **magnification, enlargement,** amplification [archaic], dilation, dilatation, **inflation,** expansion, blowing up, puffing up, aggrandizement; **heightening,** enhancement; **stretching,** overemphasis; overestimation 497; exaggerated lengths, **extreme,** overkill, exorbitance, inordinacy, **excess** 663; burlesque, travesty, caricature; sensationalism, puffery *or* ballyhoo [both informal], touting, huckstering; grandiloquence 601.

.2 **overreaction, much ado about nothing,** storm *or* tempest in a teapot, making a mountain out of a molehill.

.3 VERBS **exaggerate,** hyperbolize; **overstate,** overspeak [archaic], **overreach, overdraw,** overcharge; **overstress; overdo, carry too far, go to extremes;** overestimate 497.2; overpraise, oversell, tout, puff *or* ballyhoo [both informal]; **stretch,** stretch the truth, draw the longbow; **magnify,** amplify [archaic]; aggrandize, build up; pile *or* lay it on [informal], **lay it on thick** [informal], lay it on with a trowel [slang]; pile Pelion on Ossa; talk big [informal], talk in superlatives, deal in the marvelous, make much of; **overreact,** make a mountain out of a molehill; caricature, travesty, burlesque.

.4 ADJS **exaggerated,** hyperbolic(al), **magnified,** amplified [archaic], **inflated,** aggrandized; **stretched,** disproportionate, **blown up out of all proportion;** overpraised, oversold, touted, puffed *or* ballyhooed [both informal]; overemphasized, overemphatic, overstressed; **overstated, overdrawn; overdone,** overwrought; overestimated 497.3; overlarge, overgreat; **extreme,** exorbitant, inordinate, **excessive** 663.16; **superlative, extravagant,** profuse, **prodigal** 854.8; high-flown, grandiloquent 601.8.

.5 **exaggerating, exaggerative,** hyperbolic(al).

618. DECEPTION

.1 NOUNS **deception,** calculated deception, **deceptiveness, subterfuge,** snow job [slang], song and dance [informal], **trickiness; falseness** 616; fallaciousness, fallacy; self-deception, fond illusion, wishful thinking, willful misconception; vision, hallucination, phantasm, mirage, will-o'-the-wisp, **delusion,** delusiveness, illusion 519; deceiving, **victimization, dupery;** bamboozlement [informal], hoodwinking; swindling, defrauding, conning, flimflam *or* flimflammery [both informal]; **fooling,** befooling, tricking, **kidding** *or* putting on [both informal]; spoofing *or* spoofery [both informal]; bluffing; circumvention, overreaching, outwitting; ensnarement, entrapment, enmeshment, entanglement.

.2 **misleading, misguidance, misdirection;** bum steer [slang]; misinformation 563.1.

.3 **deceit, deceitfulness, guile, falseness,** insidiousness, **underhandedness; shiftiness, furtiveness,** surreptitiousness, indirection; hypocrisy 616.6; **falseheartedness, duplicity** 616.4; **treacherousness** 975.6; artfulness, craft, **cunning** 735; sneakiness 614.4; sneak attack.

.4 **chicanery,** chicane, **skulduggery** [informal], **trickery,** dodgery, pettifogging, pettifoggery, *supercherie* [Fr], **artifice,** sleight, machination; **sharp practice, underhand dealing, foul play;** connivery, connivance, collusion, conspiracy, covin.

.5 **juggling,** jugglery, **trickery,** *escamotage* [Fr], prestidigitation, conjuration, **legerdemain, sleight of hand;** mumbo jumbo, **hocus-pocus,** hanky-panky [informal], monkey business, hokey-pokey [informal], jiggery-pokery [Brit].

.6 **trick, artifice, device,** ploy, gambit, stratagem, **scheme,** design, *ficelle* [Fr], **subterfuge,** blind, **ruse, wile,** chouse [informal], shift, **dodge,** artful dodge, sleight, pass, feint, fetch, chicanery; **bluff;** gimmick, joker, catch; curve, curve-ball; googly *or* bosey *or* wrong'un [all Brit informal]; **dirty trick,** dirty deal, fast deal, scurvy trick; sleight of hand, sleight-of-hand trick, hocus-pocus [archaic]; juggle, juggler's trick; **bag of tricks,** tricks of the trade.

.7 **hoax, deception,** spoof [informal], **humbug, flam, fake** *or* fakement [both informal], **rip-off** [slang], **sham;** mare's nest.

.8 **fraud, fraudulence** *or* fraudulency, **dishonesty; imposture; imposition, cheat, cheating,** cozenage, diddle *or* diddling [both slang], **swindle,** scam [slang], flimflam *or* flam, dodge [slang], **gyp** [slang], ramp [Brit slang], fishy transaction, piece of sharp practice; **gyp joint** [slang]; **racket** [informal], illicit business 826; **graft** [informal], grift [slang]; bunco; cardsharping; ballot-box stuffing, gerrymandering.

.9 **confidence game, con game** [slang], **skin game** [slang], **bunco game; shell game,** thimblerig, thimblerigging; bucket shop, boiler room [slang]; goldbrick.

.10 **disguise, camouflage,** protective coloration; **false colors, false front** 616.3; **incognito;** smoke screen; **masquerade,** masque, mummery; **mask,** visor, vizard, vizard mask [archaic], false face, domino, domino mask.

.11 **trap, gin; pitfall,** trapfall, deadfall; flytrap, mousetrap, mole trap, rattrap, bear trap; deathtrap, firetrap; Venus's flytrap, Dionaea; spring gun, set gun; baited trap; **booby trap, mine; decoy** 619.5, 650.2.

.12 **snare,** springe; **noose,** lasso, lariat; bola; **net, trawl, dragnet,** seine, purse seine, pound net, gill net; cobweb; **meshes, toils; fishhook, hook,** sniggle; **bait,** ground bait; **lure,** fly, jig, squid, plug, wobbler, spinner; lime, birdlime.

.13 VERBS **deceive, beguile, trick, hoax, dupe, gammon, gull,** pigeon, **bamboozle** [informal], **snow** [slang], **hornswaggle** [slang], **diddle** [slang], **humbug, take in,** hocus-pocus [informal], string along, **put something over** or **across,** slip one over on [informal], pull a fast one on; **delude,** mock; **betray,** let down, leave in the lurch, leave holding the bag, play one false, **double-cross** [informal], cheat on; two-time [informal]; juggle, conjure; **bluff;** cajole, **circumvent,** get around, forestall; **overreach,** outreach, outwit, outmaneuver, outsmart.

.14 **fool, befool,** make a fool of, practice on one's credulity, **pull one's leg,** make an ass of; **trick; spoof** or **kid** [both informal], put one on [informal]; **play a trick on,** play a practical joke upon, send on a fool's errand; fake out [slang].

.15 **mislead, misguide, misdirect,** lead astray, lead up the garden path, **give a bum steer** [slang]; throw off the scent, put on a false scent, drag or draw a red herring across the trail; throw a curve or curve ball, bowl a googly or bosey or wrong 'un [Brit informal]; misinform 563.3.

.16 **hoodwink,** blindfold, blind, blind one's eyes, blear the eyes of [archaic], throw dust in one's eyes, **pull the wool over one's eyes.**

.17 **cheat, victimize, gull,** pigeon, fudge, **swindle, defraud,** practice fraud upon, scam [slang], euchre, **con,** finagle, **fleece,** shave [dial], mulct, beat [informal], **rook** [informal], **gyp,** fob [archaic], **bilk, flam** or **flimflam** [both informal], **diddle** [slang], **screw, have** [informal], ramp [Brit slang], **stick** [informal], **sting** [slang], burn [informal], **gouge** [informal], **chisel** [slang], cozen, cog [archaic]; chouse or hocus or hocus-pocus [all informal]; **do out of,** chouse out of [informal], beguile of or out of; **play** or **take for a sucker** [slang], make a patsy of [slang], **sell one a bill of goods** [informal], do in [slang], obtain under false pretenses; live by one's wits; bunco, play a bunco game; sell gold bricks [informal]; shortchange, shortweight; stack the cards or deck, pack the

deal [slang], deal off the bottom of the deck, play with marked cards; cog the dice, load the dice; thimblerig; crib [slang]; throw a fight or game [informal], take a dive [slang].

.18 **trap, entrap, gin, catch, catch out,** catch in a trap; **ensnare, snare, hook, hook in,** sniggle, noose; inveigle 650.4; net, mesh, enmesh, snarl [archaic], ensnarl, wind, tangle, entangle, entoil, enweb; trip, trip up; **set** or **lay a trap for,** bait the hook, spread the toils; lime, birdlime; **lure,** allure, **decoy** 650.4.

.19 ADJS **deceptive, deceiving, misleading,** beguiling, **false, fallacious,** delusive, delusory; hallucinatory, illusive, **illusory** 519.9; tricky, trickish, tricksy [archaic], catchy; **fishy** [informal], questionable, dubious.

.20 **deceitful, false; fraudulent, sharp, guileful, insidious,** slippery, **shifty, tricky,** trickish, finagling, chiseling [slang]; underhand, **underhanded, furtive, surreptitious,** indirect; collusive, covinous; **false-hearted, two-faced** 616.31; **treacherous** 975.21; **sneaky** 614.12; **cunning,** artful, **wily, crafty** 735.12; calculating, scheming 654.14.

.21 ADVS **deceptively,** beguilingly, **falsely,** fallaciously, delusively, **trickily, misleadingly,** with intent to deceive; under false colors, under cover of, under the garb of, in disguise.

.22 **deceitfully, fraudulently, guilefully,** insidiously, **shiftily, trickily; underhandedly,** furtively, surreptitiously, indirectly, like a thief in the night; **treacherously** 975.25.

619. DECEIVER

.1 NOUNS **deceiver, deluder, duper,** misleader, **beguiler, bamboozler** [informal]; actor, playactor [informal], role-player; **dissembler,** dissimulator; **double-dealer,** Machiavelli, Machiavel, Machiavellian; dodger, Artful Dodger [Dickens], **counterfeiter, forger, faker;** plagiarizer, plagiarist; entrancer, **enchanter,** charmer, befuddler, hypnotizer, mesmerizer; **seducer,** Don Juan, Casanova; tease, teaser; jilt, jilter; gay deceiver; **fooler, joker,** jokester, **hoaxer,** practical joker; spoofer, **kidder,** ragger, leg-puller [all informal].

.2 **trickster, tricker; juggler;** sleight-of-hand performer, magician, illusionist, conjurer, **prestidigitator,** escamoteur [Fr].

.3 **cheat, cheater; swindler, defrauder,** cozener, **gypper** or gyp artist [both slang], flimflammer or flimflam man [both informal], **blackleg** [informal], magsman

[Brit slang], **chiseler** [slang], bilker [informal], diddler [informal], **crook** [slang], juggler; two-timer [informal].

.4 **sharper, sharp**, sharpie [informal], **shark**, jackleg [informal], slicker [informal]; spieler, pitchman; **confidence man, con man** *or* **con artist** [both informal], **bunco artist, bunco steerer** [slang], carpetbagger; **horse trader**, horse coper [Brit]; **cardsharp**, cardsharper; thimblerigger; shortchanger; **shyster** *or* pettifogger [both informal]; land shark, land pirate, landgrabber, mortgage shark; crimp.

.5 **shill**, decoy, **come-on man** [slang], plant, capper, stool pigeon, stoolie [informal]; *agent provocateur* [Fr].

.6 **impostor, ringer; impersonator; pretender**; sham, shammer, **humbug**, *blagueur* [Fr], **fraud** [informal], **fake** *or* **faker** [both informal], **phony** [slang], **fourflusher** [slang], bluff, bluffer; **charlatan, quack,** quacksalver, quackster, **mountebank**, saltimbanco; **wolf in sheep's clothing**, ass in lion's skin, jackdaw in peacock's feathers; poser, poseur; malingerer.

.7 **masquerader**, masker; **impersonator**, personator; mummer, guiser *or* guisard [both Scot]; incognito, incognita.

.8 **hypocrite, phony** [slang], sanctimonious fraud, pharisee, whited sepulcher, **canter**, snuffler, mealymouth, "a saint abroad and a devil at home" [Bunyan]; Tartuffe, Pecksniff, Uriah Heep, Joseph Surface; **false friend, fair-weather friend**; summer soldier.

.9 **liar, fibber**, fibster, fabricator, fabulist, pseudologist; falsifier; **prevaricator**, equivocator, palterer; **storyteller**; yarner, yarn spinner, spinner of yarns [all informal]; Ananias; Satan, Father of Lies; Baron Munchausen; Sir John Mandeville; consummate liar, "liar of the first magnitude" [Congreve], *menteur à triple étage* [Fr], dirty liar; pathological liar, mythomaniac, pseudologue, confirmed *or* habitual liar; **perjurer, false witness**.

.10 **traitor**, treasonist, **betrayer, quisling, rat** [slang], serpent, snake, cockatrice, **snake in the grass, double-crosser** [slang], double-dealer; double agent; trimmer, timeserver 628.4; **turncoat** 628.5; informer 557.6; archtraitor; Judas, Judas Iscariot, Benedict Arnold, Quisling, Brutus; **schemer, plotter**, intriguer, *intrigant* [Fr], conspirer, **conspirator**, conniver, machinator.

.11 **subversive**; saboteur, **fifth columnist**; fellow traveler, crypto; security risk; collaborationist, collaborator, fraternizer; **fifth column, underground**; Trojan horse.

620. DUPE

.1 NOUNS **dupe, gull**, cull [Brit dial]; pigeon, patsy, fall guy [all slang]; mug [Brit slang], sucker *or* fish [both informal], gudgeon, *gobe-mouches* [Fr]; victim; gullible *or* dupable *or* credulous person, **easy mark** [informal], **sitting duck**, trusting soul, innocent, *naïf* [Fr], babe, babe in the woods; pushover *or* cinch *or* lead-pipe cinch [all informal], easy pickings, greenhorn, greeny *or* greener [both informal]; toy, plaything; monkey, chump [informal], boob [slang], schlemiel [slang], sap *or* saphead *or* prize sap [all slang], fool 471; stooge, **cat's-paw** 658.3.

621. WILL

.1 NOUNS **will, volition**, –boulia *or* –bulia; **choice**, determination, **decision** 637.1; **wish**, velleity, **mind, fancy, discretion, pleasure, inclination, disposition**, liking, appetence, appetency, desire 634; appetite, passion, lust, sexual desire 419.5; animus, **objective, intention** 653; **command** 752; free choice, one's own will *or* choice *or* discretion *or* initiative, free will 762.6; conation, conatus; will power, **resolution** 624.

.2 VERBS **will**, see *or* think fit, think good, think proper, **choose to, have a mind to; choose**, determine, **decide** 637.13–16; resolve 624.7; command, decree 752.9; wish, desire 634.14–20.

.3 have one's will, **have one's way, write one's own ticket**, have it all one's way, do *or* go as one pleases, please oneself; take the bit in one's teeth, take charge of one's destiny; stand on one's rights; take the law into one's own hands; have the last word, impose one's will.

.4 ADJS **volitional; willing, voluntary**; conative; –willed, –boulic *or* –bulic.

.5 ADVS **at will**, at choice, at pleasure, *al piacere* [Ital], **at one's pleasure,** *a beneplacito* [Ital], at one's will and pleasure, at one's own sweet will, **at one's discretion**, *à discrétion* [Fr], *ad arbitrium* [L]; *ad libitum* [L], ad lib; as one wishes, as it pleases *or* suits oneself, **in one's own way**, in one's own sweet way [informal], **as one thinks best**, as it seems good *or* best, as far as one desires; of one's own free will, of one's own accord, on one's own; without coercion, unforced.

622. WILLINGNESS

.1 NOUNS willingness, gameness [informal], readiness; unreluctance, unloathness, ungrudgingness; agreeableness, agreeability, favorableness; acquiescence, consent 775; compliance, cooperativeness; receptivity, receptiveness, responsiveness; amenability, tractableness, tractability, docility, pliancy, pliability; eagerness, promptness, forwardness, alacrity, zeal, zealousness, ardor, enthusiasm; goodwill, cheerful consent; willing heart or mind or humor, favorable disposition, right or receptive mood, willing ear.

.2 voluntariness, volunteering; gratuitousness; spontaneity, spontaneousness, unforcedness; self-determination, self-activity, self-action, autonomy, autonomousness, independence, free will 762.5–7; voluntaryism, voluntarism; volunteer.

.3 VERBS be willing, be game [informal], be ready; be of favorable disposition, find one's heart [archaic], have a willing heart; incline, lean 173.3; look kindly upon; be open to, agree, be agreeable to; acquiesce, consent 775.2,3; not hesitate to, would as lief, would as leave [dial], would as. lief as not, not care or mind if one does [informal]; go along with [informal]; be eager, be dying to, be spoiling for, be champing at the bit; enter with a will, go into heart and soul, plunge into; cooperate, collaborate 786.3; lend or give or turn a willing ear.

.4 volunteer, do voluntarily, do of one's own accord, do of one's own volition, do of one's own free will or choice; do independently.

.5 ADJS willing, willinghearted, ready, game [informal]; disposed, inclined, minded, willed, fain, prone [archaic]; well-disposed, well-inclined, favorably inclined or disposed; predisposed; favorable, agreeable, cooperative; compliant, content [archaic], acquiescent, consenting 775.4; eager; prompt, quick, alacritous, forward, ready and willing, zealous, ardent, enthusiastic; in the mood or vein or humor or mind, in a good mood; receptive, responsive; amenable, tractable, docile, pliant.

.6 ungrudging, ungrumbling, unreluctant, unloath, nothing loath, unaverse, unshrinking.

.7 voluntary, volunteer; gratuitous; spontaneous, free, freewill, willful [archaic]; offered, proffered; discretionary, discretional, nonmandatory, optional, elective; arbitrary; self-determined, self-determining, autonomous, independent, self-active, self-acting; unsought, unbesought, unasked, unrequested, unsolicited, uninvited, unbidden, uncalled-for; unforced, uncoerced, unpressured, unrequired, uncompelled; unprompted, uninfluenced.

.8 ADVS willingly, with a will, with good will, with right good will, de bonne volonté [Fr]; eagerly, with zest, with relish, with open arms, zealously, ardently, enthusiastically; readily, promptly, at the drop of a hat [informal].

.9 agreeably, favorably, compliantly; lief, lieve [dial], fain, as lief, as lief as not; ungrudgingly, ungrumblingly, unreluctantly, nothing loath, without reluctance or demur or hesitation.

.10 voluntarily, freely, gratuitously, spontaneously, willfully [archaic]; optionally, electively, by choice; of one's own accord, of one's own free will, of one's own volition, of one's own choice, at one's own discretion; without coercion or pressure or compulsion or intimidation; independently 762.32.

623. UNWILLINGNESS

.1 NOUNS unwillingness, disinclination, nolition, indisposition, indisposedness, reluctance, renitency, renitence, grudgingness, grudging consent; unenthusiasm, lack of enthusiasm or zeal or eagerness, slowness, backwardness, dragging of the feet or foot-dragging [both informal]; sullenness, sulk, sulks, sulkiness; cursoriness, perfunctoriness; recalcitrance or recalcitrancy, disobedience, refractoriness, fractiousness, intractableness, indocility, mutinousness; averseness, aversion, repugnance, antipathy, distaste, disrelish; obstinacy, stubbornness 626.1; refusal 776; opposition 790; resistance 792; disagreement, dissent 795.2,3.

.2 demur, demurral, scruple, qualm, qualm of conscience, compunction; hesitation, hesitancy or hesitance, pause, boggle, falter; qualmishness, scrupulousness, scrupulosity; stickling, boggling; faltering; shrinking; shyness, diffidence, modesty, bashfulness; recoil; protest, objection 522.2.

.3 VERBS be unwilling, would rather not, not care to, not feel like [informal], not find it in one's heart to, not have the heart or stomach to; mind, object to, draw the line at, balk at; grudge, begrudge.

.4 demur, scruple, have qualms *or* scruples; stickle, stick at, boggle, strain; falter, waver; hesitate, pause, hang back, hang off, hold off; fight shy of, shy at, shy, shrink, recoil, blench, flinch, wince, quail, pull back; make bones about *or* of.

.5 ADJS unwilling, disinclined, indisposed, not in the mood, averse; unconsenting 776.6; opposed 790.8; resistant 792.5; disagreeing, differing, at odds 795.15,16; disobedient, recalcitrant, refractory, fractious, sullen, sulky, indocile, mutinous; cursory, perfunctory; involuntary, forced.

.6 reluctant, renitent, grudging, loath; backward, laggard, dilatory, slow, slow to; unenthusiastic, unzealous, indifferent, apathetic, perfunctory; balky, balking, restive.

.7 demurring, qualmish, boggling, stickling, squeamish, scrupulous; diffident, shy, modest, bashful; hesitant, hesitating, faltering; shrinking.

.8 ADVS unwillingly, involuntarily, against one's will, *à contre cœur* [Fr]; under compulsion *or* coercion *or* pressure; in spite of oneself, *malgré soi* [Fr].

.9 reluctantly, grudgingly, sullenly, sulkily; unenthusiastically, perfunctorily; with dragging feet, with a bad *or* an ill grace, under protest; with a heavy heart, with no heart *or* stomach.

624. RESOLUTION

.1 NOUNS resolution, resolvedness, determination, decision, resolve, fixed *or* firm resolve, will, purpose; resoluteness, determinedness, determinateness, decisiveness, decidedness, purposefulness; definiteness; earnestness, seriousness, sincerity, devotion, dedication, commitment, total commitment; "the dauntless spirit of resolution", "the native hue of resolution" [both Shakespeare]; single-mindedness, relentlessness, persistence, tenacity, perseverance 625; self-will, obstinacy 626.

.2 firmness, firmness of mind *or* spirit, staunchness, settledness, steadiness, constancy, steadfastness, fixedness; concentration; flintiness, steeliness; inflexibility, rigidity, unyieldingness 626.2; trueness, loyalty 974.7.

.3 pluck, spunk [informal], mettle, backbone [informal], grit, true grit, spirit, stamina, guts *or* moxie [both slang], pith [archaic], bottom, toughness [informal]; pluckiness, spunkiness [informal], gameness, mettlesomeness; courage 893.

.4 will power, will, power, strong-mindedness, strength of mind, strength *or* fixity of purpose, strength, fortitude, moral fiber; iron will, will of iron; a will *or* mind of one's own; the courage of one's convictions, moral courage.

.5 self-control, self-command, self-possession, self-mastery, self-government, self-domination, self-restraint, self-conquest, self-discipline, self-denial; control, restraint, constraint, discipline; composure, possession, aplomb; independence 762.5.

.6 self-assertion, self-assertiveness, forwardness, nerve *or* pushiness [both informal], importunateness, importunacy; self-expression, self-expressiveness.

.7 VERBS resolve, determine, decide, will, purpose, make up one's mind, make *or* take a resolution, make a point of; settle, fix, seal; conclude, come to a determination *or* conclusion, determine once for all.

.8 be determined, be resolved; have a mind *or* will of one's own, know one's own mind; be in earnest, mean business [informal], mean what one says; have blood in one's eyes *or* be out for blood [both informal], set one's mind *or* heart upon; put one's heart into, devote *or* commit *or* dedicate oneself to, give oneself up to; buckle oneself, buckle down, buckle to; steel oneself, brace oneself, grit one's teeth, set one's teeth *or* jaw; put *or* lay *or* set one's shoulder to the wheel; take the bull by the horns, take the plunge, cross the Rubicon; nail one's colors to the mast, burn one's bridges *or* boats, go for broke [slang], kick down the ladder, throw away the scabbard; never say die, die hard, die fighting, die with one's boots on.

.9 remain firm, stand fast *or* firm, hold out, hold fast, take one's stand, set one's back against the wall, stand *or* hold one's ground, keep one's footing, hold one's own, hang in *or* hang in there *or* hang tough [all slang], dig in, dig one's heels in; stick to one's guns, stick, stick fast, stick to one's colors, adhere to one's principles; not listen to the voice of the siren; take what comes, stand the gaff; put one's foot down [informal], stand no nonsense.

.10 not hesitate, think nothing of, think little of, make no bones about [informal], have *or* make no scruple of [archaic], stick at nothing, stop at nothing; not look back; go the whole hog [informal], carry through, face out.

.11 ADJS **resolute, resolved, determined, bound** or **bound and determined** [both informal], **decided,** decisive, **purposeful;** definite; **earnest, serious,** sincere; devoted, dedicated, committed, wholehearted; single-minded, relentless, persistent, tenacious, persevering 625.7; **obstinate** 626.8.

.12 **firm, staunch,** fixed, settled, steady, steadfast, constant, set or sot [both dial], flinty, steely; unshaken, not to be shaken, **unflappable** [informal]; undeflectable, **unswerving,** not to be deflected; immovable, unbending, inflexible, **unyielding** 626.9; true, loyal 974.20.

.13 **unhesitating,** unhesitant, **unfaltering,** unflinching, unshrinking; stick-at-nothing [informal].

.14 **plucky, spunky** [informal], gritty [informal], gutty or gutsy [both slang], **mettlesome,** dauntless, **game,** game to the backbone, game to the last or end; **courageous** 893.17–21.

.15 **strong-willed, strong-minded,** firm-minded; **self-controlled,** controlled, self-disciplined, self-restrained; **self-possessed; self-assertive,** self-asserting, forward, pushy [informal], importunate; self-expressive; **independent** 762.21.

.16 **determined upon,** resolved upon, decided upon, intent upon, fixed upon, settled upon, **set on,** dead set on [informal], sot on [dial], **bent on,** hell-bent on [slang].

.17 ADVS **resolutely, determinedly, decidedly,** decisively, resolvedly, **purposefully, with a will;** firmly, steadfastly, steadily, fixedly, with constancy, staunchly; **seriously,** in all seriousness, **earnestly,** in earnest, in good earnest, sincerely; devotedly, with total dedication, committedly; hammer and tongs, tooth and nail, bec et ongles [Fr]; heart and soul, with all one's heart, wholeheartedly; **unswervingly;** single-mindedly, relentlessly, persistently, tenaciously, like a bulldog, like a leech, perseveringly 625.8; **obstinately, unyieldingly,** inflexibly 626.14,15.

.18 **pluckily, spunkily** [informal], **mettlesomely, gamely,** dauntlessly, manfully, like a man; on one's mettle; **courageously, heroically** 893.22.

.19 **unhesitatingly,** unhesitantly, **unfalteringly,** unflinchingly, unshrinkingly.

.20 **come what may,** venga lo que venga [Sp], vogue la galère [Fr], **cost what it may,** coûte que coûte [Fr], whatever the cost, at any price or cost or sacrifice, at all risks or hazards, **whatever may happen,** ruat caelum [L], though the heavens may fall, at all events, live or die, survive or perish, sink or swim, rain or shine, come hell or high water; in some way or other.

625. PERSEVERANCE

.1 NOUNS **perseverance, persistence** or persistency, **insistence** or insistency, singleness of purpose; resolution 624; **steadfastness, steadiness,** stability 142; **constancy, permanence** 140.1; loyalty, fidelity 974.7; single-mindedness, concentration, unswerving attention, engrossment, preoccupation 530.3; **endurance, stick-to-itiveness** [informal], staying power, **pertinacity,** pertinaciousness, **tenacity,** tenaciousness, **doggedness,** unremittingness, relentlessness, dogged perseverance, bulldog tenacity; plodding, plugging, slogging; **obstinacy, stubbornness** 626.1; **diligence,** application, sedulousness, sedulity, industry, industriousness, assiduousness, assiduity; **tirelessness, indefatigability, stamina; patience,** patience of Job 861.1.

.2 VERBS **persevere, persist, carry on,** go on, **keep on,** keep up, keep at, **keep at it,** keep going, keep driving, keep trying, try and try again, **keep the ball rolling,** keep the pot boiling, keep up the good work; not take 'no' for an answer; not accept compromise or defeat; **endure, last, continue** 110.6.

.3 keep doggedly at, **plod,** drudge, slog or slog away, put one foot in front of the other, peg away or at or on; **plug,** plug at, plug away or along; pound or hammer away; **keep one's nose to the grindstone.**

.4 **stay with it, hold on,** hold fast, **hang on,** hang on for dear life [informal], hang on like a bulldog or leech, hang in or hang in there or hang tough [all slang]; **stick to it** or stick with it [both informal], **stick** [slang], **stick to one's guns;** not give up, **never say die,** not give up the ship [informal], not strike one's colors; come up fighting, come up for more; **stay it out, stick it** or stick it out [both informal], tough it out [slang], stick out, **hold out;** hold up, **bear up,** stand up; **live with it,** live through it; stay the distance [informal]; "wear this world out to the ending doom", "bears it out even to the edge of doom" [both Shakespeare]; brazen it out.

.5 prosecute to a conclusion, **go through with it, carry through, follow through, see it through** [informal], see out, follow out or up; go to the bitter end, go all the way, go to any length, go the whole length; go the limit, **go the whole hog**, go all out, go for broke [all slang]; **leave no stone unturned**, leave no avenue unexplored, overlook nothing, exhaust every move; move heaven and earth, go through fire and water, go through hell and high water [informal].

.6 **die trying**, die in the last ditch, die in harness, **die with one's boots on** or die in one's boots, die at one's post, die in the attempt, die game, die hard, **go down with flying colors**.

.7 ADJS **persevering**, perseverant, **persistent**, persisting, insistent; **enduring**, permanent, **constant**, lasting; continuing 140.7; **stable, steady, steadfast** 142.12; immutable, inalterable 142.17; **resolute** 624.11; **diligent, assiduous, sedulous**, industrious; dogged, plodding, slogging, plugging; **pertinacious, tenacious, stick-to-itive** [informal]; loyal, faithful 974.20; **unswerving**, unremitting, unabating, unintermitting, uninterrupted; single-minded, utterly attentive; rapt, preoccupied 530.17,18; **unfaltering, unwavering, unflinching**; relentless, **unrelenting**; **obstinate, stubborn** 626.8; **unrelaxing**, unfailing, **untiring**, unwearying, unflagging, never-tiring, **tireless**, weariless, **indefatigable**, unwearied, unsleeping, undrooping, unnodding, unwinking, sleepless; undiscouraged, undaunted, indomitable, unconquerable, invincible, game to the end; **patient**, patient as Job 861.9.

.8 ADVS **perseveringly, persistently**, persistingly, insistently; **resolutely** 624.17; loyally, faithfully, **devotedly** 974.25; **diligently**, industriously, assiduously, sedulously; **doggedly**, sloggingly, ploddingly; pertinaciously, tenaciously; unremittingly, unabatingly, unintermittingly, uninterruptedly; unswervingly, unwaveringly, unfalteringly, unflinchingly; relentlessly, unrelentingly; **indefatigably, tirelessly**, weariessly, untiringly, unwearyingly, unflaggingly, unrestingly, unsleepingly; **patiently** 861.12.

.9 **through thick and thin**, through fire and water, come hell or high water, through evil report and good report, rain or shine, fair or foul, in sickness and in health; **come what may** 624.20.

626. OBSTINACY

.1 NOUNS **obstinacy**, obstinateness, pertinacity, restiveness, **stubbornness, willfulness**, self-will, hardheadedness, **headstrongness**,

strongheadness; mind or will of one's own, set or fixed mind, inflexible will; **doggedness, determination**, tenaciousness, tenacity, "tough tenacity of purpose" [J. A. Symonds], perseverance 625; **bullheadedness, pigheadedness, mulishness**; obduracy, unregenerateness; stiff neck, stiff-neckedness; sullenness, sulkiness; balkiness; uncooperativeness; bitterendism [informal]; dogmatism, opinionatedness 513.6; overzealousness, fanaticism 473.11; intolerance, bigotry 527.1,2.

.2 **unyieldingness**, unbendingness, stiff temper, **inflexibility**, inelasticity, impliability, ungivingness, **obduracy**, toughness, **firmness**, stiffness, adamantness, rigorism, **rigidity**; hard-bittenness, hard-nosedness [informal]; unalterability, unchangeability, immutability, immovability; irreconcilability, uncompromisingness, **intransigence** or intransigency, *intransigeance* [Fr], intransigentism; **implacability**, inexorability, **relentlessness**, unrelentingness; sternness, grimness, dourness, flintiness, steeliness.

.3 **perversity**, *perversité* [Fr], perverseness, **contrariness, wrongheadedness, waywardness**, frowardness, difficultness, crossgrainedness, cantankerousness, orneriness [informal], **cussedness** or pure cussedness [both informal]; sullenness, sulkiness, dourness, stuffiness [informal]; irascibility 951.2.

.4 **ungovernability, unmanageability**, uncontrollability; indomitability, untamableness, **intractability**, refractoriness, shrewishness; incorrigibility; **unsubmissiveness**, unbiddability [Brit], **indocility**; irrepressibility, insuppressibility; unmalleability, unmoldableness; **recalcitrance** or recalcitrancy, contumacy, contumaciousness; **unruliness**, obstreperousness, restiveness, fractiousness, wildness, breachiness [dial]; defiance 793; resistance 792.

.5 **unpersuadableness**, deafness, blindness; positiveness, dogmatism 513.6.

.6 (obstinate person) **mule**, donkey, ass, perverse fool; bullethead or pighead [both slang]; hardnose [informal]; standpat or **standpatter** [both informal], **stickler**; **intransigent**, *intransigeant* [Fr], maverick; dogmatist, positivist, bigot, fanatic, purist; **diehard, bitter-ender** [informal], last-ditcher.

.7 VERBS **balk, stickle**; hold one's ground, not budge, **stand pat** [informal], **not yield an inch**, stick to one's guns; hold out, stand out; take no denial, not take 'no' for an answer; take the bit in one's teeth; die hard; **persevere** 625.2.

.8 ADJS **obstinate, stubborn, pertinacious, restive; willful, self-willed,** strong-willed, hardheaded, **headstrong,** strongheaded, *entêté* [Fr]; **dogged,** bulldogged, **tenacious,** persevering 625.7; **bullheaded,** bulletheaded [informal], **pigheaded, mulish,** stubborn as a mule; **set, set in one's ways,** case-hardened, stiff-necked; **sullen, sulky;** balky, balking; unregenerate, uncooperative; bigoted, intolerant 527.11, overzealous, fanatic(al) 473.32; dogmatic, opinionated 513.22.

.9 **unyielding, unbending, inflexible, hard,** inelastic, impliable, ungiving, **firm, stiff, rigid,** rigorous; rock-ribbed; **adamant,** adamantine; unmoved, unaffected; **immovable,** not to be moved; **unalterable,** unchangeable, immutable; **uncompromising,** intransigent, irreconcilable, hardshell, hard-core [both informal]; implacable, inexorable, **relentless,** unrelenting; stern, grim, dour; iron, cast-iron, flinty, steely.

.10 **obdurate,** tough, **hard,** hard-set, hardmouthed, hard-bitten, hard-nosed [informal].

.11 **perverse, contrary, wrongheaded, wayward, froward, difficult,** cross-grained, cantankerous, ornery [informal]; sullen, sulky, stuffy [informal]; irascible 951.19.

.12 **ungovernable, unmanageable, uncontrollable, indomitable, untamable, intractable, refractory;** shrewish; **incorrigible; unsubmissive,** unbiddable [Brit], **indocile;** irrepressible, insuppressible; unmalleable, unmoldable; **recalcitrant,** contumacious; obstreperous, **unruly, restive,** wild, fractious, breachy [dial]; beyond control, out of hand; resistant, resisting 792.5; defiant 793.7.

.13 **unpersuadable,** deaf, blind; positive; dogmatic 513.22.

.14 ADVS **obstinately, stubbornly,** pertinaciously; willfully, headstrongly; **doggedly,** tenaciously; **bullheadedly,** pigheadedly, mulishly; unregenerately; uncooperatively; with set jaw, with sullen mouth, with a stiff neck.

.15 **unyieldingly, unbendingly, inflexibly, adamantly,** obdurately, **firmly,** stiffly, rigidly, rigorously; unalterably, unchangeably, immutably, immovably, unregenerately; uncompromisingly, intransigently, irreconcilably; implacably, inexorably, relentlessly, unrelentingly; sternly, grimly, dourly.

.16 **perversely, contrarily,** contrariwise, waywardly, wrongheadedly, frowardly, cross-grainedly, cantankerously, sullenly, sulkily.

.17 **ungovernably, unmanageably, uncontrollably,** indomitably, untamably, intractably; shrewishly; incorrigibly; unsubmissively; irrepressibly, insuppressibly; contumaciously; unrulily, obstreperously, restively, fractiously.

627. IRRESOLUTION

.1 NOUNS irresolution, indecision, unsettlement, unsettledness, irresoluteness, undeterminedness, **indecisiveness,** undecidedness, infirmity of purpose; mugwumpery, mugwumpism, fence-sitting, fence-straddling; double-mindedness, **ambivalence,** ambitendency; dubiety, dubiousness, **uncertainty** 514; **instability, inconstancy,** changeableness 141; capriciousness, mercuriality, fickleness 629.2,3; change of mind, second thoughts, tergiversation 628.1.

.2 **vacillation, fluctuation,** oscillation, pendulation, **wavering,** wobbling, shilly-shally, **shilly-shallying,** blowing hot and cold; equivocation 613.4.

.3 **hesitation,** hesitance, **hesitancy,** hesitating; falter, faltering, shilly-shally, shilly-shallying; diffidence, tentativeness, caution, cautiousness.

.4 **weak will, weak-mindedness;** feeblemindedness [archaic], **weakness,** feebleness, faintness, faintheartedness, **frailty, infirmity; spinelessness,** invertebracy; abulia; fear 891; cowardice 892; **pliability** 357.2.

.5 **vacillator, shillyshallyer,** shilly-shally, **waverer,** wobbler; mugwump, fence-sitter, fence-straddler; ass between two bundles of hay; weakling, jellyfish, Milquetoast.

.6 VERBS **not know one's own mind,** not know where one stands, **be of two minds,** have two minds; stagger, stumble, boggle.

.7 **hesitate, pause, falter, hang back,** hover; shilly-shally, hum and haw, **hem and haw;** wait to see how the cat jumps or the wind blows, scruple, jib, demur [archaic], stick at, stickle, strain at; think twice about, stop to consider, ponder, debate, deliberate, see both sides of the question, balance, weigh one thing against another, consider both sides of the question; come down squarely in the middle, sit on or straddle the fence, fall between two stools; yield, back down 765.7; retreat, withdraw 295.6; pull back, shy 284.7; fear

891.9; not face up to, hide one's head in the sand 633.13.

.8 **vacillate, waver, fluctuate,** pendulate, oscillate, wobble, teeter, totter [archaic], dither, swing from one thing to another, **shilly-shally,** back and fill, keep off and on, will and will not; blow hot and cold 629.4; **equivocate** 613.7; change one's mind, tergiversate 628.6; vary, **alternate** 141.5; shift, **change** 139.5.

.9 ADJS **irresolute,** irresolved, **unresolved; undecided, indecisive, undetermined,** unsettled, infirm of purpose; dubious, **uncertain** 514.15; at loose ends, at a loose end; **of two minds,** double-minded, ambivalent, ambitendent; changeable, mutable 141.6; capricious, mercurial, fickle 629.5,6; mugwumpian, mugwumpish, fence-sitting, fence-straddling.

.10 **vacillating,** vacillatory, oscillatory, wobbly, **wavering, fluctuating,** pendulating, oscillating, **shilly-shallying,** shilly-shally, "at war 'twixt will and will not" [Shakespeare].

.11 **hesitant,** hesitating; faltering; shilly-shallying; diffident, tentative, timid, cautious; scrupling, jibbing, demurring [archaic], sticking, straining, stickling.

.12 **weak-willed, weak-minded,** feebleminded [archaic], **weak-kneed, weak,** feeble, faint, fainthearted, **frail, infirm;** spineless, invertebrate; without a will of one's own, unable to say 'no'; abulic; afraid 891.30–34, cowardly 892.10–13; **pliable** 357.9.

.13 ADVS **irresolutely,** irresolvedly, **undecidedly, indecisively, undeterminedly; uncertainly** 514.26; hesitantly, hesitatingly, falteringly; waveringly, vacillatingly, shilly-shally, shilly-shallyingly.

628. CHANGE OF ALLEGIANCE

.1 NOUNS **tergiversation,** tergiversating; **reverse, reversal,** flip or flip-flop [both slang], turnabout, turnaround, **about-face,** volte-face [Fr], right-about-face, right-about, a turn to the right-about; **change of mind;** second thoughts, better thoughts, afterthoughts, mature judgment.

.2 **apostasy,** recreancy; treason, misprision of treason, betrayal, turning traitor, ratting [slang], going over, **defection;** bolt, secession, breakaway; **desertion** 633.2; recidivism, recidivation, backsliding 696.2; faithlessness, disloyalty 975.5.

.3 **recantation, withdrawal, disavowal, denial,** reneging, **unsaying, repudiation,** palinode, palinody, **retraction,** retractation;

disclaimer, disclamation, **disownment,** disowning, abjurement, abjuration, revokement or revocation [both archaic]; **renunciation,** renouncement, forswearing; expatriation.

.4 **timeserver,** timepleaser [archaic], temporizer, formalist, trimmer, weathercock; chameleon, Vicar of Bray.

.5 **apostate, turncoat,** turnabout, **recreant, renegade,** renegado, renegate [archaic], runagate, **defector,** tergiversator, tergiversant; **deserter, turntail,** quisling, fifth columnist, collaborationist, collaborator, traitor 619.10; strikebreaker 789.6; **bolter,** mugwump, **seceder,** secessionist, **separatist,** schismatic; **backslider,** recidivist; reversionist; convert, proselyte.

.6 VERBS **change one's mind, tergiversate, change one's song** or **tune** or **note,** sing a different tune; come round, wheel, do an about-face, reverse oneself, do a flip-flop [slang]; swing from one thing to another; think better of it, have second thoughts, be of another mind.

.7 **be a timeserver,** trim, temporize, change with the times.

.8 **apostatize** or apostacize, go over, change sides, switch, switch over, change one's allegiance, **defect; turn one's coat,** turn cloak; secede, break away, bolt, fall off or away; desert 633.6.

.9 **recant, retract, repudiate, withdraw, take back,** renege, **abjure, disavow, disown, deny, disclaim, unsay,** revoke [archaic]; **renounce, forswear, eat one's words,** swallow, eat crow, eat humble pie; **back down** or **out,** climb down, crawfish out [informal], backwater.

.10 ADJS **timeserving, trimming, temporizing;** supple, neither fish nor fowl.

.11 **apostate, recreant, renegade,** tergiversating, tergiversant; treasonous, treasonable, traitorous, collaborative; faithless, disloyal 975.20.

.12 **repudiative,** repudiatory; abjuratory, revocatory [archaic]; renunciative, renunciatory; schismatic; **separatist,** secessionist, breakaway [informal], mugwumpian, mugwumpish.

629. CAPRICE

.1 NOUNS **caprice, whim,** capriccio [Ital], boutade [Fr], humor, **whimsy,** freak, whim-wham; **fancy,** fantasy, **conceit, notion,** flimflam, toy, freakish inspiration, crazy idea, fantastic notion, fool notion [informal], harebrained idea, brainstorm, **vagary,** megrim; **fad, craze, passing fancy;**

quirk, crotchet, crank, kink; maggot, maggot in the brain, bee in one's bonnet [informal], flea in one's nose [informal].

.2 capriciousness, caprice, whimsicalness, whimsy, whimsicality; humorsomeness, fancifulness, fantasticality, freakishness; crankiness, crotchetiness, quirkiness; moodiness, temperamentalness; petulance 951.5; arbitrariness, motivelessness.

.3 fickleness, flightiness, skittishness, inconstancy, lightness, levity, légèreté [Fr]; volatility, mercurialness, mercuriality; faddishness, faddism; changeableness 141; unpredictability 514.1; unreliability, undependability 975.4; coquettishness 932.8; frivolousness 469.7.

.4 VERBS blow hot and cold, keep off and on, have as many phases as the moon, chop and change, fluctuate 141.5, vacillate 627.8.

.5 ADJS capricious, whimsical, freakish, humorsome, vagarious; fanciful, notional, fantasied [archaic], fantastic(al), maggoty, crotchety, kinky, harebrained, cranky, flaky [slang], quirky; wanton, wayward, vagrant; arbitrary, unreasonable, motiveless; moody, temperamental; petulant 951.21; unrestrained 762.23.

.6 fickle, flighty, skittish, light; coquettish, flirtatious, toying; versatile, inconstant, changeable 141.7; vacillating 627.10; volatile, mercurial, quicksilver; faddish; unpredictable 514.15; unreliable, undependable 975.19.

.7 ADVS capriciously, whimsically, fancifully, at one's own sweet will [informal]; flightily, lightly; arbitrarily, unreasonably, without rhyme or reason.

630. IMPULSE

.1 NOUNS impulse; natural impulse, blind impulse, instinct, urge, drive; vagrant or fleeting impulse; involuntary impulse, reflex, automatic response; gut response [slang]; notion, fancy; sudden thought, flash, inspiration, brainstorm, brain wave, quick hunch.

.2 impulsiveness, impetuousness, impetuosity; hastiness, overhastiness, haste, quickness, suddenness; precipitateness, precipitance, precipitancy, precipitation; recklessness, rashness 894; impatience 862.

.3 thoughtlessness, unthoughtfulness, heedlessness, carelessness, inconsideration, inconsiderateness; caprice 629.

.4 unpremeditation, indeliberation, undeliberateness, uncalculatedness, undesignedness, spontaneity, spontaneousness,

unstudiedness; involuntariness 639.5; snap judgment or decision; snap shot, offhand shot.

.5 improvisation, extemporization, improvision, extempore [archaic], impromptu, ad lib, ad-libbing or playing by ear [both informal]; extemporaneousness, extemporariness; temporary measure or arrangement, pro tempore measure or arrangement, stopgap, makeshift, jury-rig [naut].

.6 improviser, improvisator, improvvisatore, improvvisatrice [both Ital], extemporizer, ad-libber [informal].

.7 VERBS act on the spur of the moment, obey one's impulse, let oneself go; blurt out, come out with, say what comes uppermost, say the first thing that comes into one's head.

.8 improvise, extemporize, improvisate, talk off the top of one's head [informal], throw away or depart from the prepared text, throw away the speech, scrap the plan, ad-lib [informal], do offhand, wing it [slang], vamp, fake [informal], play by ear [informal]; dash off, strike off, knock off, throw off, toss off or out; make up, whip up, cook up, whomp up [informal], lash up [Brit], throw together; jury-rig.

.9 ADJS impulsive, impetuous, hasty, overhasty, quick, sudden, precipitate, headlong; reckless, rash 894.7–9; impatient 862.6.

.10 unthinking, unreasoning, unreflecting, uncalculating, unthoughtful, thoughtless, inadvertent, reasonless, heedless, careless, inconsiderate; unguarded; arbitrary, capricious 629.5.

.11 unpremeditated, unmeditated, uncalculated, undeliberated, spontaneous, undesigned, unstudied; unintentional, unintended, inadvertent, unwilled, indeliberate, undeliberate; involuntary, reflex, reflexive, automatic, gut [slang], unconscious; unconsidered, unadvised, snap, casual; ill-considered, ill-advised, ill-devised.

.12 extemporaneous, extemporary, extempore, impromptu, unrehearsed, improvised, improvisatory, improvisatorial, improviso, improvisé [Fr]; ad-lib, ad libitum [L]; stopgap, makeshift, jury-rigged; offhand, off-the-cuff [informal].

.13 ADVS impulsively, impetuously, hastily, suddenly, quickly, precipitately, headlong; recklessly, rashly 894.10,11.

.14 on impulse, on a sudden impulse, on the spur of the moment; without premeditation, unpremeditatedly, uncalculatedly, undesignedly; unthinkingly, unreflectingly, unreasoningly, unthoughtfully, thoughtlessly, heedlessly, carelessly, inconsiderately, unadvisedly; unintentionally, inadvertently, without willing, indeliberately, involuntarily.

.15 extemporaneously, extemporarily, extempore, à l'improviste [Fr], impromptu, ad lib, offhand, out of hand; at or on sight; by ear, off the hip [slang], off the cuff [informal]; at short notice.

631. AVOIDANCE

.1 NOUNS avoidance, shunning; forbearance, refraining; hands-off policy, nonintervention, noninvolvement, neutrality; evasion, elusion; getting around [informal], circumvention; prevention, forestalling, forestallment 730.2; escape 632; evasive action, the runaround [slang]; zigzag, jink, slip, dodge, duck, side step, shy; shunting off, sidetracking; evasiveness, elusiveness; equivocation 613.4; avoiding reaction, defense mechanism or reaction.

.2 shirking, slacking, goldbricking [informal], soldiering, goofing or goofing off [both slang]; clock-watching; malingering, skulking [Brit]; dodging, ducking; welshing [slang]; truancy; tax evasion, tax dodging.

.3 shirker, shirk, slacker, eye-servant or eye-server [both archaic], soldier or old soldier, goldbricker, goldbrick [informal]; clock watcher; welsher [slang]; malingerer, skulker or skulk [both Brit]; truant; tax dodger.

.4 flight, fugitation, exit, quick exit, making oneself scarce or getting the hell out [both informal], bolt, disappearing act [slang], hasty retreat; running away, decampment; skedaddle, skedaddling, scramming, absquatulation [all slang]; elopement; disappearance 447; French leave, absence without leave, AWOL; desertion 633.2; hegira.

.5 fugitive, fleer, runaway, runagate, bolter, skedaddler [informal]; absconder, eloper; refugee, evacuee, émigré [Fr]; displaced person, DP, stateless person; escapee 632.5.

.6 VERBS avoid, shun, fight shy of, keep from, keep away from, keep clear of, steer clear of [informal], give a miss to [informal], keep or get out of the way of, give a wide berth, keep remote from, stay detached from; make way for, give place to; keep one's distance, keep at a respectful distance, keep or stand or hold aloof; give the cold shoulder to [informal], have

nothing to do with, have no association with, have no truck with [informal]; not meddle with, let alone, let well enough alone, keep hands off, not touch, not touch with a ten-foot pole; turn away from, turn one's back upon, slam the door in one's face.

.7 evade, elude, beg, get out of, shuffle out of, circumvent, skirt, double, get around [informal]; give one the run-around; ditch or shake or shake off [all slang], get away from; throw off the scent; play at hide and seek; lead one a chase or merry chase, lead one a dance or pretty dance; escape 632.6–9.

.8 dodge, duck; shy, shy off or away; swerve, sheer off; pull away or clear; pull back, shrink, recoil 284.6,7; sidestep, step aside; parry, fence, ward off; shift, shift or put off; hedge, pussyfoot [informal], be or sit on the fence, beat around or about the bush, hem and haw, beg the question, equivocate 613.7.

.9 shirk, slack, lie or rest upon one's oars, not pull fair; lie down on the job [informal]; soldier, duck duty, goof off or dog it [both slang], goldbrick [informal]; malinger, skulk [Brit]; get out of, sneak or slip out of, slide out of, dodge, duck; welsh [slang].

.10 flee, fly, take flight, take to flight, take wing, fugitate, run, cut and run [informal], make a precipitate departure, run off or away, run away from, decamp, absquatulate or skedaddle [both informal], take to one's heels, make off, clear out [informal], depart 301.6, do the disappearing act, make a quick exit, make oneself scarce [informal], get the hell out [informal], beat a retreat, turn tail, show the heels, show a clean or light pair of heels; run for it, "show it a fair pair of heels and run for it" [Shakespeare], bolt, make a break for it [informal], run for one's life; advance to the rear, make a strategic withdrawal; take French leave, go AWOL, slip the cable; desert 633.6; skip or skip out [both informal], jump [informal]; abscond, levant [Brit], elope, run away with; skip or jump bail.

.11 [slang terms] beat it, blow, scram, lam, take it on the lam, take a powder or run-out powder, split, skin out, duck out, duck and run, dog it; vamoose.

.12 slip away, steal away, sneak off, slink off, slide off, slither off, skulk away, mooch off [slang], duck out [slang], slip out of.

.13 not face up to, hide one's head in the

sand, not come to grips with, put off, procrastinate, temporize.

.14 ADJS **avoidable, escapable,** eludible; evadable; preventable.

.15 evasive, elusive, elusory; **shifty,** slippery, cagey [slang]; shirking, malingering.

.16 **fugitive, runaway,** in flight, on the lam [slang], hot [slang]; disappearing 447.3; –fugal.

632. ESCAPE

.1 NOUNS escape; **getaway** or break or breakout [all informal]; **deliverance; delivery,** riddance, **release,** setting-free, freeing, **liberation, extrication,** rescue; emergence, issuance, issue, outlet, vent; **leakage,** leak; jailbreak, prisonbreak; evasion 631.1; flight 631.4; escapism.

.2 **narrow escape,** hairbreadth escape, **close call** [informal], **close shave** [informal], **near miss,** near go or near thing [both Brit informal], near or narrow squeak [Brit informal], close squeak or tight squeeze [both informal].

.3 (means of escape) bolt-hole, escape hatch, fire escape, life net, lifeboat, life raft, life buoy, lifeline, sally port, slide, inflatable slide, ejection seat, emergency exit.

.4 **loophole, way out,** way of escape, hole to creep out of, escape hatch, escape clause, saving clause; pretext 649; **alternative,** choice 637.

.5 escapee, escaper; escape artist; escapist; **fugitive** 631.5.

.6 VERBS escape, make or effect one's escape, make good one's escape; **get away, make a getaway** [informal]; **free oneself,** deliver oneself, gain one's liberty, **get free, get clear of,** bail out, **get out, get out of,** get well out of; **break loose,** cut loose, break away, break one's bonds or chains, slip the collar, shake off the yoke; **jump** or **skip** [both informal]; **break jail** or **prison,** escape prison, fly the coop [slang]; leap over the wall; evade 631.7; flee 631.10.

.7 **get off, go free,** win freedom, go at liberty, **go scot free,** escape with a whole skin, escape without penalty; **get away with** [slang], get by, get away with murder, **get off cheap;** cop a plea or cop out [both slang].

.8 scrape or squeak through, escape with or by the skin of one's teeth.

.9 **slip away, give one the slip,** slip through one's hands or fingers; slip or sneak through; **slip out of,** slide out of, crawl or creep out of, sneak out of, wiggle or wriggle or squirm or shuffle or worm out of, find a loophole.

.10 **find vent,** issue forth, come forth, exit, **emerge, issue,** debouch, erupt, break out, break through, come out, run out, **leak out,** ooze out.

.11 ADJS **escaped, loose,** on the loose, disengaged, out of, well out of; fled, flown; fugitive, runaway; scot-free; at large, **free** 762.19.

633. ABANDONMENT

.1 NOUNS abandonment, forsaking, leaving, lipo–; jettison, jettisoning, throwing overboard or away, casting away; **withdrawal,** evacuation, pulling out, absentation; cessation 144; disuse, desuetude.

.2 **desertion, defection,** ratting [slang]; dereliction; **secession,** bolt, breakaway, walkout; betrayal 975.8; schism, apostasy 628.2; deserter 628.5.

.3 (giving up) relinquishment, surrender, resignation, renouncement, renunciation, abdication, waiver, abjurement, abjuration, cession, handing over, **yielding, forswearing; withdrawing, dropping out** [informal].

.4 derelict, castoff; jetsam, flotsam, lagan, **flotsam and jetsam;** waifs and strays; rubbish, junk, trash, refuse; waif, orphan, dogie [dial]; **castaway;** foundling; wastrel, reject, discard 668.3.

.5 VERBS **abandon, forsake;** quit, **leave,** leave behind, take leave of, depart from, absent oneself from, turn one's back upon, turn one's tail upon, say goodbye to, bid a long farewell to; **withdraw, back out, drop out** [informal], pull out, stand down [informal]; **go back on, go back on one's word;** cry off [Brit], beg off, renege; **vacate,** evacuate; quit cold or leave flat [both informal]; jilt, throw over [informal]; maroon; **jettison,** discard 668.7; let fall into disuse or desuetude.

.6 desert, **leave in the lurch,** rat [slang], let down, **walk** or **run out on** [informal], turn one's back upon; apostatize 628.8; **defect, secede, bolt,** break away, pull out [informal], withdraw one's support; sell out [slang], betray 975.14.

.7 **give up, relinquish, surrender,** yield, waive, **forgo, resign,** renounce, throw up, abdicate, **abjure, forswear, have done with,** cede, hand over, lay down, wash one's hands of, drop, drop all idea of, drop like a hot potato; **cease** 144.6, **desist from,** leave off, give over; hold or stay one's hand, cry quits, acknowledge defeat, throw up the cards, throw in the sponge, throw in the towel 765.8.

.8 ADJS **abandoned, forsaken, deserted,** left; disused; **derelict,** castaway, jettisoned; marooned; discarded 668.11.

634. DESIRE

.1 NOUNS **desire, wish,** wanting, **want, need,** desideration; **hope; fancy; will, mind, pleasure,** will and pleasure; heart's desire; **urge,** drive, libido, pleasure principle; concupiscence; horme; wish fulfillment, fantasy; passion, ardor, sexual desire 419.5; **curiosity,** intellectual curiosity, thirst for knowledge, lust for learning; **eagerness** 635; –philia, –orexia.

.2 **liking, likes** [pl], **love, fondness;** infatuation, crush; **affection;** relish, taste, gusto, gust [Scot]; **passion, weakness** [informal].

.3 **inclination, penchant, partiality, fancy, favor, predilection, preference,** propensity, proclivity, leaning, bent, turn, bias, **affinity;** mutual affinity or attraction; **sympathy,** fascination.

.4 **wistfulness,** wishfulness, yearnfulness, **nostalgia;** wishful thinking; sheep's eyes, longing or wistful eye; daydream, daydreaming.

.5 **yearning, yen** [informal]; **longing,** desiderium, **hankering** [informal], **pining,** honing [dial], aching; languishment, languishing; **nostalgia, homesickness,** *Heimweh* [Ger], *mal du pays, maladie du pays* [both Fr]; nostomania.

.6 **craving, coveting; hunger, thirst, appetite,** "an universal wolf" [Shakespeare], appetition, appetency or appetence; aching void; **itch, itching,** prurience or pruriency; **sexual desire** 419.5; cacoëthes, mania 473.12.

.7 **appetite,** stomach, relish, taste; **hunger,** hungriness, –phagia; tapeworm [slang], eyes bigger than the stomach, wolf in the stomach, canine appetite; empty stomach, emptiness [informal], hollow hunger; **thirst,** thirstiness, drought [dial], dryness; polydipsia; torment of Tantalus; sweet tooth [informal].

.8 **greed,** greediness, graspingness, **avarice, cupidity, avidity, voracity, rapacity, lust,** avariciousness, –lagnia or –lagny; avidness, esurience, wolfishness; voraciousness, ravenousness, rapaciousness, sordidness, **covetousness,** acquisitiveness; itching palm; grasping; **piggishness, hoggishness,** swinishness; **gluttony** 994; inordinate

desire, fury or frenzy of desire, overgreediness; insatiable desire, insatiability; incontinence, intemperateness 993.1.

.9 **aspiration,** hitching one's wagon to a star, reaching high, upward looking; "the desire of the moth for the star" [Shelley]; high goal or aim or purpose, dream, ideals; **idealism** 535.7.

.10 **ambition,** ambitiousness, vaulting ambition; climbing, status-seeking, social climbing, careerism; power-hunger; "the mind's immodesty" [D'Avenant], "the way in which a vulgar man aspires" [Henry Ward Beecher], "the evil shadow of aspiration" [George Macdonald], "the avarice of power" [G. G. Coulton], "avarice on stilts and masked" [W. S. Landor]; noble or lofty ambition, magnanimity [archaic]; "the spur that makes man struggle with destiny" [Donald G. Mitchell].

.11 (object of desire) **desire,** heart's desire, desideration, *desideratum* [L]; **wish; hope;** catch, plum, prize, trophy; forbidden fruit, temptation; lodestone, magnet; golden vision, glimmering goal; land of heart's desire 535.11; something to be desired, "a consummation devoutly to be wish'd" [Shakespeare]; dearest wish, ambition, the height of one's ambition.

.12 **desirer,** wisher, wanter, hankerer [informal], yearner, coveter; fancier, collector; addict, freak [slang], devotee, votary 635.6; **aspirant,** aspirer, solicitant, hopeful [informal], candidate; lover, suitor 931.11.

.13 **desirability; agreeability,** acceptability, unobjectionableness; **attractiveness,** attraction, magnetism, **appeal,** seductiveness, provocativeness; likability, lovability 931.7.

.14 VERBS **desire,** desiderate, be desirous of, **wish,** lust after, **want,** have a mind to, choose [dial]; would fain do or have, would be glad of; **like,** fancy, take to, **take a fancy to,** have a fancy for; have an eye to, have one's eye on, aim at; set one's cap for, have designs on; wish very much, wish to goodness; **love** 931.18; lust 419.22; prefer, favor 637.17.

.15 **want to, wish to, like to,** love to, dearly love to, choose to; **itch to,** burn to; ache to [informal], long to, **be dying to.**

.16 **wish for, hope for, yearn for,** yen for or have a yen for [both informal], **itch for,** lust for, pant for, **long for, pine for,** hone for [dial], ache for, be hurting for [dial], weary for, languish for, **be dying for,** thirst for, sigh for, gape for [archaic]; cry for, clamor for; spoil for [informal].

.17 **want with all one's heart, want in the worst way; set one's heart on, have one's heart set on,** give one's kingdom in hell for or one's eyeteeth for [slang].

.18 **crave, covet, hunger after,** thirst after, crave after, **lust after,** pant after, run mad after, **hanker after** [informal]; crawl after; aspire after, be consumed with desire.

.19 **hunger,** hunger for, feel hungry, starve [informal]; be ravenous, raven; **have a good appetite,** be a good trencherman, have a tapeworm [slang], have a wolf in one's stomach; eye hungrily, lick one's chops [informal]; **thirst,** thirst for.

.20 **aspire, be ambitious;** aspire to, try to reach; aim high, keep one's eyes on the stars, "hitch one's wagon to a star" [Emerson].

.21 ADJS **desirous,** desiring, desireful [archaic], lickerish, **wanting, wishing,** needing, hoping; tempted; appetitive, desiderative, optative, libidinous, libidinal; hormic; **eager** 635.9; lascivious, **lustful** 419.29.

.22 **desirous of** or **to,** keen on, set on [dial], bent on; fond of, with a liking for, partial to [informal]; fain of or to; inclined toward, leaning toward; **itching for** or **to,** aching for or to, **dying for** or **to;** spoiling for [informal]; mad on or for, wild to or for [informal]; crazy to or for [informal].

.23 **wistful,** wishful; **longing, yearning,** yearnful, **hankering** [informal], **languishing, pining,** honing [dial]; **nostalgic, homesick.**

.24 **craving,** coveting; **hungering,** hungry, thirsting, thirsty, athirst; **itching,** prurient; fervid; **devoured by desire,** in a frenzy or fury of desire, mad with lust, consumed with desire.

.25 **hungry,** hungering, peckish [dial]; empty [informal], unfilled; ravening, **ravenous,** voracious, sharp-set, wolfish, dog-hungry [slang], hungry as a bear; **starved, famished,** starving, famishing, perishing or pinched with hunger; fasting; half-starved, half-famished.

.26 **thirsty,** thirsting, athirst; **dry, parched,** droughty [dial].

.27 **greedy,** avaricious, avid, voracious, rapacious, esurient, **ravening, grasping, grabby** [slang], acquisitive, mercenary, sordid, overgreedy; ravenous, gobbling, devouring; miserly, money-hungry, money-mad, venal; **covetous,** coveting; **piggish, hoggish,** swinish, a hog for, greedy as a hog; **gluttonous** 994.6; omnivorous, all-devour-

ing; insatiable, insatiate, unsatisfied, unsated, unappeased, unappeasable, limitless, bottomless, unquenchable, quenchless, unslaked, unslakeable, slakeless.

.28 **aspiring, ambitious,** sky-aspiring, upward-looking, high-reaching; high-flying, social-climbing, careerist, careeristic, on the make [informal]; power-hungry.

.29 **desired, wanted,** coveted; **wished-for,** hoped-for, longed-for; in demand, popular.

.30 **desirable,** to be desired, **much to be desired; enviable,** worth having; **likable, pleasing,** after one's own heart; **agreeable,** acceptable, unobjectionable; **attractive,** taking, winning, **seductive, provocative,** tantalizing, exciting 650.7; appetizing, tempting, toothsome, mouth-watering; **lovable,** adorable 931.23.

.31 ADVS **desirously, wistfully,** wishfully, longingly, **yearningly,** piningly, languishingly; cravingly, itchingly; hungrily, thirstily; aspiringly, ambitiously.

.32 **greedily, avariciously,** avidly, ravenously, raveningly, voraciously, rapaciously, **covetously,** graspingly, devouringly; wolfishly, **piggishly, hoggishly,** swinishly.

635. EAGERNESS

.1 NOUNS **eagerness, anxiousness,** anxiety; **avidity,** avidness, keenness, forwardness, **readiness,** promptness, quickness, **alacrity,** cheerful readiness, *empressement* [Fr]; keen desire, **appetite** 634.7; zest, zestfulness, gusto, gust [Scot], verve, **liveliness,** life, **vitality,** vivacity, élan, spirit, animation; **impatience,** breathless impatience 862.1.

.2 **zeal, ardor, ardency, fervor, fervency, fervidness, spirit, warmth, fire, heat,** heatedness, **passion,** passionateness, impassionedness, heartiness, intensity, **abandon,** vehemence; intentness, resolution 624; **devotion,** devoutness, devotedness, dedication, commitment, committedness; **earnestness, seriousness,** sincerity; loyalty, faithfulness, faith, **fidelity** 974.7.

.3 **enthusiasm,** enthusiasticalness; keen interest, fascination; **craze** 473.12.

.4 **overzealousness, overeagerness,** overanxiousness, overanxiety; **overenthusiasm, infatuation; overambitiousness; frenzy, fury; zealotry,** zealotism; mania, **fanaticism** 473.11.

.5 **enthusiast, zealot, infatuate,** energumen, **eager beaver** [informal], rhapsodist, great one for [informal]; addict; hound, fiend, demon, freak, nut, bug [all slang]; faddist; pursuer; sucker for [slang]; hobbyist, collector; **fanatic** 473.17; visionary 535.13.

.6 **devotee, votary, fan** or **buff** [both informal], **fancier,** admirer, **follower; groupie;** worshiper, idolizer, idolater; amateur, dilettante; collector; **rooter** or **booster** [both informal].

.7 VERBS **jump at,** catch, grab, grab at, snatch, snatch at, fall all over oneself, get excited about; desire 634.14–20.

.8 **be enthusiastic, rave, enthuse** [informal]; **rhapsodize, carry on over** [informal], make much of, **make a fuss over,** make an ado or much ado about, make a to-do over [informal], take on over [informal], go on over or about [informal], rave about [informal], whoop it up about [slang]; gush, gush over; effervesce, bubble over.

.9 ADJS **eager, anxious, agog,** all agog; **avid, keen,** forward, prompt, quick, ready, ready and willing, alacritous, bursting to, raring to; **zestful, lively, full of life, vital,** vivacious, vivid, spirited, **animated; impatient** 862.6; breathless, panting, champing at the bit; **desirous** 634.21.

.10 **zealous, ardent, fervent, fervid,** perfervid, **spirited, intense,** hearty, vehement, abandoned, **passionate,** impassioned, **warm,** heated, hot, hot-blooded, red-hot, fiery, white-hot, flaming, burning, afire, on fire; **devout, devoted;** dedicated, committed; **earnest, sincere, serious,** in earnest; loyal, faithful 974.20; intent, intent on, resolute 624.11.

.11 **enthusiastic,** enthused [informal], glowing, full of enthusiasm, gung-ho [slang]; enthusiastic about, infatuated with, **keen** on or about.

.12 [slang terms] **wild about, crazy about, mad about,** ape about or over, gone on, all in a dither over, gaga over, starry-eyed over, all hopped up about, hepped up over, hot about or for or on, steamed up about, **turned-on;** hipped on, **cracked on,** bugs on, freaked-out, **nuts on** or **over** or **about.**

.13 **overzealous,** ultrazealous, **overeager,** overanxious; **overambitious;** overdesirous; **overenthusiastic, infatuated;** feverish, perfervid, febrile, at fever pitch; hectic, frenetic, furious, **frenzied,** frantic, **wild,** hysteric(al), delirious; **insane** 473.25–34; **fanatical** 473.32.

.14 ADVS **eagerly, anxiously; impatiently,** breathlessly; **avidly,** promptly, quickly, keenly, readily; zestfully, vivaciously, animatedly; **enthusiastically,** with enthusi-

asm; **with alacrity,** with zest, with gusto, with relish, with open arms.

.15 **zealously, ardently, fervently, fervidly,** perfervidly, heatedly, heartily, vehemently, **passionately,** impassionedly; intently, intensely; **devoutly, devotedly;** earnestly, sincerely, seriously.

636. INDIFFERENCE

.1 NOUNS **indifference,** indifferentness; indifferentism; halfheartedness, **zeallessness,** perfunctoriness, fervorlessness; **coolness,** coldness, chilliness, chill, iciness, frostiness; tepidness, **lukewarmness,** Laodiceanism; **neutrality,** neutralness, neuterness; insipidity, vapidity.

.2 **unconcern, disinterest, detachment; disregard, dispassion,** insouciance, **carelessness,** regardlessness; easygoingness; **heedlessness,** mindlessness, inattention 531; **unmindfulness, incuriosity** 529; disregardfulness, recklessness, negligence 534.1,2; unsolicitousness, unanxiousness; pococurantism; **nonchalance,** inexcitability 858, ataraxy or ataraxia; indiscrimination, casualness 493.1; **listlessness,** lackadaisicalness, lack of feeling or affect, sloth, accidia, acedia, **apathy** 856.4.

.3 **undesirousness,** desirelessness; nirvana; lovelessness, passionlessness; uneagerness, **unambitiousness;** lack of appetite, inappetence, anorexia, anorexia nervosa.

.4 VERBS **not care, not mind, not give** or **care a damn,** not give a hoot or shit [slang], care nothing for or about, not care a straw about; shrug off; **take no interest in,** have no desire for, have no taste or relish for; hold no brief for.

.5 **not matter to,** be all one to, take it or leave it.

.6 ADJS **indifferent, halfhearted,** zealless, perfunctory, fervorless; **cool, cold** 929.9; tepid, **lukewarm,** Laodicean; neither hot nor cold, neither one thing nor the other, "neither fish, nor flesh, nor good red herring" [John Heywood]; **neuter, neutral.**

.7 **unconcerned, uninterested, disinterested,** turned-off, **dispassionate,** insouciant, **careless,** regardless, easygoing; incurious 529.3; mindless, **unmindful, heedless,** inattentive 531.6, perfunctory, disregardful; **devil-may-care,** reckless, negligent 534.10, 11; unsolicitous, unanxious; pococurante, **nonchalant,** inexcitable 858.10; ataractic; **blasé;** undiscriminating, casual 493.5; **listless,** lackadaisical; **apathetic** 856.13.

.8 **undesirous,** unattracted, desireless; loveless, passionless; inappetent; nirvanic; **un-**

enthusiastic, uneager; **unambitious**, unaspiring.

.9 ADVS **indifferently, with indifference,** with utter indifference; coolly, coldly; lukewarmly, halfheartedly; perfunctorily; for aught one cares.

.10 **unconcernedly, uninterestedly, disinterestedly,** dispassionately, insouciantly, carelessly, regardlessly; mindlessly; **unmindfully, heedlessly,** recklessly, negligently 534.17,18; **nonchalantly**; listlessly, lackadaisically; **apathetically** 856.14,15.

.11 PHRS **who cares?,** I don't care, I couldn't care less; it's a matter of sublime indifference; never mind!, **what does it matter?,** what's the difference?, what's the diff? [slang], what are the odds?, what of it?, what boots it?, **so what?,** what the hell [slang], it's all one to me, it's all the same to me [slang].

.12 **I should worry?,** I should fret?, that's your lookout, I feel for you but I can't reach you; that's your pigeon [slang], that's your tough luck, tough titty *or* tough shit [both slang].

637. CHOICE

.1 NOUNS **choice, selection, election,** preference, decision, **pick, choosing,** free choice; alternativity; co-option, co-optation; **will,** volition, free will 762.6,7; preoption, first choice; the pick 674.8.

.2 **option, discretion, pleasure,** will and pleasure; optionality; possible choice, alternative, alternate choice.

.3 **dilemma,** Scylla and Charybdis, the devil and the deep blue sea; *embarras de choix* [Fr]; choice of Hercules; Hobson's choice, no choice, only choice.

.4 **adoption, embracement,** acceptance, espousal; affiliation.

.5 **preference, predilection,** proclivity, bent, affinity, prepossession, predisposition, partiality, inclination, leaning, bias, tendency, taste; favor, fancy; prejudice; personal choice, particular choice [archaic], chosen kind *or* sort, style, cup of tea [informal], type, bag *or* thing [both slang]; druthers [dial].

.6 **vote, voting, suffrage,** franchise, enfranchisement, voting right, right to vote; **voice, say;** representation; **poll, polling,** canvass, canvassing, division, counting heads *or* noses; **ballot,** secret ballot, Australian ballot; **plebiscite,** plebiscitum, **referendum**; yeas and nays, yea, aye, yes, nay, no; voice vote, *viva voce* vote; rising vote; hand vote, show of hands; absentee

vote, proxy; casting vote, deciding vote; write-in vote, write-in; fagot vote [Brit]; graveyard vote; single vote, plural vote; transferable vote, nontransferable vote; Hare system, list system, cumulative voting, preferential voting, proportional representation; straw vote, record vote, snap vote, plumper [Brit].

.7 **selector, chooser, optant,** elector, **voter; electorate.**

.8 **nomination, designation,** naming, proposal.

.9 **election, appointment;** political election 744.15.

.10 **selectivity,** selectiveness, picking and choosing; **choosiness** 896.1; eclecticism; **discrimination** 492.

.11 **eligibility, qualification, fitness,** fittedness, **suitability,** acceptability, worthiness, desirability; eligible.

.12 **elect,** elite, chosen; chosen people.

.13 VERBS **choose, elect,** opt, opt for, co-opt, make *or* take one's choice, make choice of, use *or* take up *or* exercise one's option; pick and choose.

.14 **select,** make a selection; **pick,** handpick, **pick out, single out,** choose out; extract, excerpt; **decide between; cull,** glean, winnow, sift; separate the wheat from the chaff *or* tares, separate the sheep from the goats.

.15 **adopt;** approve, ratify, pass, carry; **take up,** go in for [informal]; accept, **embrace,** espouse; affiliate.

.16 **decide upon, determine upon,** settle upon, fix upon; make *or* take a decision, **make up one's mind.**

.17 **prefer,** have preference, **favor,** like better *or* best, prefer to, set before *or* above, regard *or* honor before; rather [dial], **had** *or* **have rather,** choose rather; think proper, see *or* think fit, think best, please; incline *or* lean *or* tend toward, have a bias *or* partiality.

.18 **vote,** cast one's vote, ballot, cast a ballot; hold up one's hand, stand up and be counted; plump [Brit]; divide; poll, canvass.

.19 **nominate, name, designate;** put up, propose, submit, name for office; run, run for office.

.20 **elect, vote in,** place in office; **appoint.**

.21 **put to choice,** offer, present, set before; put to vote, have a show of hands.

.22 ADJS **elective;** volitional, voluntary; **optional,** discretional; **alternative,** disjunctive.

.23 **selective,** selecting, choosing; eclectic(al);

elective, electoral; appointing, appointive, constituent; adoptive; discriminating 492.7; choosy [informal], particular 896.9.

.24 eligible, qualified, fit, fitted, suitable, acceptable, admissible, worthy, desirable; with voice, with vote, with voice and vote, enfranchised.

.25 preferable, of choice or preference, better, preferred, to be preferred, more desirable, favored; preferential, preferring, favoring.

.26 chosen, selected, picked; select, elect; handpicked; adopted, accepted, embraced, espoused, approved, ratified, passed, carried; elected, unanimously elected, elected by acclamation; appointed; nominated, designated, named.

.27 ADVS at choice, at one's will, at one's will and pleasure, at one's pleasure, electively, at one's discretion, at the option of, if one wishes; on approval; optionally; alternatively.

.28 preferably, by choice or preference, in preference; by vote, by election or suffrage; rather than, sooner than, first, sooner, rather, before.

.29 CONJS or, either . . . or; and/or.

638. REJECTION

.1 NOUNS rejection, repudiation; abjurement, abjuration, renouncement 633.3; disownment, disclamation, recantation 628.3; exclusion, exception 77.1; disapproval, nonacceptance, nonapproval, declining, declination, refusal 776; contradiction, denial 524.2; passing by or up [informal], ignoring, nonconsideration, discounting, dismissal, disregard 531.1; throwing out or away, putting out or away, chucking or chucking out [both informal]; discard 668.3; turning out or away, repulse, rebuff 289.2; spurning, scouting, despising, despisal, contempt 966.

.2 VERBS reject, repudiate, abjure, forswear, renounce 633.7, disown, disclaim, recant 628.9, except, exclude 77.4; disapprove, decline, refuse 776.3; contradict, deny 524.4; pass by or up [informal], waive, ignore, refuse to consider, discount, dismiss; disregard 531.2; throw out or away, chuck or chuck out [both informal], discard 668.7; turn out or away, shove away, brush aside, push aside, repulse, repel, rebuff 289.2; spurn, scout, disdain, contemn, despise 966.3.

.3 ADJS rejected, repudiated; renounced, forsworn, disowned; denied, refused; ex-

cluded, excepted; disapproved, declined; ignored, discounted, not considered, dismissed, dismissed out of hand; discarded; repulsed, rebuffed; spurned, scouted, disdained, scorned, contemned, despised; out of the question, not to be thought of, declined with thanks.

.4 rejective; renunciative, abjuratory; declinatory; dismissive; contemptuous, despising, scornful, disdainful.

639. NECESSITY

.1 NOUNS necessity, necessariness, necessitude [archaic], necessitation; mandatoriness, mandatedness, obligatoriness, obligation, obligement; compulsoriness, compulsion, duress 756.3.

.2 requirement, requisite, requisition; necessity, need, want, occasion; need for, call for, demand, demand for; desideratum, desideration; prerequisite, prerequirement; must, must item; essential, indispensable; the necessary, the needful; necessities, necessaries, essentials, bare necessities.

.3 needfulness, requisiteness; essentiality, essentialness, vitalness; indispensability, indispensableness; irreplaceability; irreducibleness, irreducibility.

.4 urgent need, dire necessity; exigency or exigence, urgency, imperative, imperativeness, immediacy, pressingness, pressure; "necessity's sharp pinch" [Shakespeare]; matter of necessity, case of need, matter of life and death; predicament 731.4.

.5 involuntariness, unwilledness, instinctiveness; compulsiveness; reflex action, conditioning, automatism; echolalia, echopraxia; automatic writing; instinct, impulse 630; blind impulse or instinct, sheer chemistry.

.6 choicelessness, no choice, no alternative, Hobson's choice, only choice; that or nothing; not a pin to choose, six of one and half a dozen of the other, distinction without a difference; indiscrimination 493.

.7 inevitability, inevitableness, unavoidableness, necessity, inescapableness, inevasibleness, unpreventability, undeflectability, ineluctability; irrevocability, indefeasibility; uncontrollability; relentlessness, inexorability, unyieldingness, inflexibility; fatefulness, certainty, sureness; force majeure, vis major, act of God, inevitable accident, unavoidable casualty; predetermination, fate 640.2,3.

.8 VERBS **necessitate, oblige,** dictate, **constrain;** insist upon, **compel** 756.4.

.9 **require, need, want,** feel the want of, have occasion for, be in need of, be hurting for [dial], stand in need of, not be able to dispense with, not be able to do without; **call for,** cry for, cry out for, clamor for; **demand,** ask, claim, exact; prerequire [archaic]; need *or* want doing, take doing [informal], be indicated.

.10 **be necessary,** lie under a necessity, be one's fate; can't be avoided, can't be helped; be under the necessity of, be in for; be obliged, **must,** need *or* needs must [archaic], **have to,** have got to [informal], should, need, **need to,** have need to; can't keep from, can't help, **cannot help but,** cannot do otherwise; be forced *or* driven.

.11 **have no choice** *or* **alternative,** have one's options reduced *or* eliminated, have no option but, cannot choose but, be robbed *or* relieved of choice; be pushed to the wall, be driven into a corner; take it or leave it [informal], have that or nothing.

.12 ADJS **necessary, obligatory, compulsory,** mandatory; **exigent, urgent,** necessitous, importunate, **imperative;** choiceless, without choice, out of one's hands *or* control.

.13 **requisite, needful, required, needed,** necessary, **wanted, called for,** indicated; **essential, vital, indispensable,** unforgoable, irreplaceable; irreducible, irreductible; prerequisite.

.14 **involuntary, instinctive, automatic, mechanical,** reflex, reflexive, conditioned; **unconscious,** unthinking, blind; **unwitting,** unintentional, independent of one's will, unwilling, unwilled, against one's will; **compulsive;** forced; **impulsive** 630.9–12.

.15 **inevitable, unavoidable,** necessary, **inescapable,** inevasible, unpreventable, undeflectable, ineluctable, irrevocable, indefeasible; uncontrollable, unstoppable; relentless, inexorable, unyielding, inflexible; irresistible, resistless; **certain,** fateful, **sure,** sure as fate, sure as death, sure as death and taxes; **fated** 640.9.

.16 ADVS **necessarily,** needfully, requisitely; **of necessity,** from necessity, need *or* needs [both archaic], perforce; without choice; **willy-nilly,** *nolens volens* [L], willing or unwilling, *bon gré mal gré* [Fr], whether one will or not; come what may; compulsorily 756.12.

.17 **if necessary, if need be,** if worst comes to worst; for lack of something better, *faute de mieux* [Fr].

.18 **involuntarily, instinctively, automatically, mechanically,** by reflex, reflexively; blindly, **unconsciously,** unthinkingly; **unwittingly,** unintentionally; **compulsively; unwillingly** 623.8.

.19 **inevitably, unavoidably,** necessarily, **inescapably,** inevasibly, unpreventably, ineluctably; irrevocably, indefeasibly; uncontrollably; relentlessly, inexorably, unyieldingly, inflexibly; fatefully, **certainly, surely.**

.20 PHRS **it is necessary, it must be,** it needs must be *or* it must needs be [both archaic], it will be, there's no two ways about it, it must have its way; it cannot be helped, there is no helping it *or* help for it, that's the way the cookie crumbles *or* the ball bounces [informal], what will be will be, it's God's will; the die is cast; it is fated 640.11.

640. PREDETERMINATION

.1 NOUNS **predetermination, predestination,** foredestiny, **preordination,** foreordination, foreordainment; decree; foregone conclusion; **necessity** 639; foreknowledge, prescience 542.3.

.2 **fate,** fatality, **fortune, lot,** cup, portion, appointed lot, kismet, weird, *moira* [Gk], future 121; **destiny,** destination, **end,** final lot; **doom,** foredoom [archaic], God's will, will of Heaven; **inevitability** 639.7; handwriting on the wall; book of fate; Fortune's wheel, wheel of fortune *or* chance; astral influences, stars, planets, constellation, astrology 375.20; unlucky day, ides of March, Friday, Friday the thirteenth, *dies funestis* [L].

.3 **Fates,** *Fata* [L], **Parcae,** *Moirai* [Gk], Clotho, Lachesis, Atropos; Nona, Decuma, Morta; Weird Sisters, Weirds; Norns; Urdur, Verthandi, Skuld; Fortuna, Lady *or* Dame Fortune, *Tyche* [Gk]; Providence, Heaven, "a divinity that shapes our ends, rough-hew them how we will" [Shakespeare].

.4 **determinism, fatalism,** necessitarianism, necessarianism, predeterminism; predestinarianism, Calvinism, election.

.5 **determinist, fatalist,** necessitarian, necessarian; predestinationist, predestinarian, Calvinist.

.6 VERBS **predetermine, predecide,** preestablish; **predestine,** predestinate, **preordain,** foreordain.

.7 **destine,** destinate [archaic], **ordain,** fate,

mark, appoint [archaic]; have in store for; **doom**, foredoom, devote.

.8 ADJS **predetermined**, **predecided**, **preestablished**, **predestined**, predestinate, **preordained**, foreordained; forgone.

.9 **destined**, **fated**, fateful, fatal [archaic], ordained, written, in the cards, marked, appointed [archaic], in store; **doomed**, foredoomed, devoted; inevitable 639.15.

.10 **deterministic**, **fatalistic**, necessitarian, necessarian.

.11 PHRS **it is fated**, **it is written**, it's in the cards; what will be will be, *che sarà sarà* [Ital], *que será será* [Sp].

641. PREARRANGEMENT

.1 NOUNS **prearrangement**, preordering, preconcertedness; premeditation, plotting, planning, scheming; **put-up job** [informal], **frame-up** [slang], packed *or* rigged jury [slang], setup [slang], packed deal *or* stacked deck [both slang]; directed verdict.

.2 **schedule**, **program**, programma, bill, card, **calendar**, docket, slate; playbill; batting order, **lineup** [informal], **roster**; blueprint, budget; **prospectus**; schedule *or* program of operation, **order of the day**, things to be done, **agenda**, list of agenda; protocol; bill of fare, menu, *carte du jour* [Fr].

.3 VERBS **prearrange**, precontrive, predesign [archaic], preorder, preconcert; premeditate, plot, plan, scheme; **fix** *or* **rig** [both informal]; pack [slang], set up *or* cook up [both slang]; **stack the cards** *or* pack the deal [both slang]; put in the bag *or* sew up [both slang]; frame *or* frame up [both slang].

.4 **schedule**, **line up** [informal], **slate**, **book**, bill, program, calendar, docket, budget; put on the agenda.

.5 ADJS **prearranged**, precontrived, predesigned [archaic], preordered, preconcerted, cut out; premeditated, plotted, planned, schemed; **fixed** *or* rigged [both informal], packed *or* stacked [both slang], **put-up** [informal], set-up *or* cooked-up [both slang]; in the bag *or* on ice *or* cinched *or* sewed up [all slang]; cut-and-dried, cut-and-dry.

.6 **scheduled**, **slated**, booked, billed, to come.

642. CUSTOM, HABIT

.1 NOUNS **custom**, **convention**, use, **usage**, standard usage, standard behavior, **wont**, wonting, **way**, established way, time-honored practice, **tradition**, standing custom, **folkway**, manner, **practice**, praxis, prescription, **observance**, ritual, consuetude, **mores** [pl]; proper thing, what is done, **social convention** 645; *bon ton* [Fr], **fashion** 644; manners, etiquette 646.3; conformity 82.

.2 "a sort of second nature" [Cicero], "the universal sovereign" [Pindar], "that unwritten law, by which the people keep even kings in awe" [D'Avenant], "often only the antiquity of error" [Cyprian].

.3 **culture**, **society**, **civilization**; trait, culture trait; key trait; complex, culture complex, trait-complex; culture area; culture center; **folkways**, **mores**, system of values, **ethos**, **culture pattern**; cultural change; cultural lag; culture conflict; acculturation, culture contact [Brit], cultural drift.

.4 **habit**, habitude, **custom**, **second nature**; use, **usage**, trick, **wont**, **way**, practice, praxis; bad habit; stereotype; "the petrifaction of feelings" [L. E. Landon]; pattern, **habit pattern**; stereotyped behavior; force of habit; creature of habit; automatism 639.5; peculiarity, characteristic 80.4.

.5 **rule**, procedure, **common practice**, form, prescribed *or* set form; common *or* ordinary run of things, matter of course; standard operating procedure, SOP, drill [Brit]; standing orders [pl].

.6 **routine**, run, **round**, beat, track, beaten path; jog trot, **rut**, **groove**, well-worn groove; **treadmill**, squirrel cage; grind *or* daily grind [both informal]; **red tape**, redtapeism, **bureaucracy**, bureaucratism, *chinoiserie* [Fr].

.7 **customariness**, accustomedness, wontedness, **habitualness**; **inveteracy**, inveterateness, confirmedness, settledness, fixedness; commonness, prevalence 79.2.

.8 **habituation**, **accustoming**; **conditioning**, seasoning, training; **familiarization**, naturalization [archaic], breaking-in [informal], orientation; **domestication**, **taming**, breaking, housebreaking; acclimation, acclimatization; **inurement**, hardening, case hardening; adaption, adjustment, accommodation 82.1.

.9 **addiction**, addictedness; dependence, psychological dependence, drug dependence; craving 634.6; habituation; cocainism; physical dependence; **drug addiction**, a habit [informal]; tolerance, acquired tolerance; withdrawal sickness, withdrawal symptoms; amphetamine withdrawal symptoms, crash [slang]; opiate addiction, morphinism; barbiturism, barbiturate addiction; **alcoholism** 996.3, chronic alcoholism, acute alcoholism, dipsomania; nicotine addiction 434.10, chain smoking; drug culture.

.10 **addict**, fiend [informal], habitual; **drug user**, user [informal], tripper [slang], drug abuser; doper *or* freak *or* **head** [all slang]; marijuana smoker, **pothead** [slang]; cocaine sniffer, cokie *or* snowbird [both slang]; pillhead [slang]; methhead *or* **speed freak** [both slang]; LSD user; **acid freak** *or* acidhead *or* cubehead [all slang]; **drug addict**; narcotics addict; opium eater; **dope fiend** [informal]; **junkie** *or* hype *or* hophead [all slang]; alcoholic, dipsomaniac, **drunkard** 996.10,11; heavy smoker, **chain smoker**, nicotine addict [informal]; glue sniffer.

.11 VERBS accustom, habituate, wont; **condition**, season, train; familiarize, naturalize [archaic], break in [informal], orient, orientate; **domesticate**, domesticize, **tame**, break, gentle, housebreak; acclimatize, acclimate, inure, harden, case harden; adapt, adjust, accommodate 26.7; confirm, fix, establish 142.9.

.12 **become a habit**, take root, **grow on one**, take hold of one, take one over.

.13 **be used to**, be wont, wont, **make a practice of**; get used to, get into the way of, **take to**, accustom oneself to; contract *or* fall into a habit, addict oneself to.

.14 **get in a rut**, be in a rut, move *or* travel in a groove *or* rut, run on in a groove, follow the beaten path, go round like a horse in a mill, go on in the old jog-trot way.

.15 ADJS **customary, wonted**, consuetudinary; traditional, time-honored; familiar, everyday, ordinary, **usual** 84.8; **established**, received, accepted; set, prescribed, prescriptive; normal 84.7; **standard**, regular, stock, regulation; prevalent, widespread, obtaining, generally accepted, popular, **current** 79.12; **conventional** 645.5; conformable 82.5.

.16 **habitual, regular**, frequent, constant, persistent; repetitive, recurring, recurrent; stereotyped; automatic 639.14; **routine**, well-trodden, well-worn, beaten; trite, hackneyed 883.9.

.17 **accustomed, wont, wonted**, used to; **conditioned**, trained, seasoned; experienced, **familiarized**, naturalized [archaic], broken-in, run-in [informal], oriented, orientated; acclimated, acclimatized; inured,

hardened, case-hardened; adapted, adjusted, accommodated.

.18 **used to, familiar with**, conversant with, **at home in** *or* **with**, no stranger to, an old hand at.

.19 **habituated**, *habitué* [Fr]; **in the habit of**, used to; **addicted to, hooked on** [slang], dependent on; never free from; **in a rut; addicted, hooked** *or* strung out *or* spaced out *or* hyped [all slang], dependent.

.20 **addictive, habit-forming**, habituating, conditioning; hard [informal], physiologically addictive, psychologically addictive.

.21 **confirmed, inveterate, chronic**, established, long-established, **fixed, settled, rooted**, thorough; incorrigible, irreversible; **deep-rooted**, deep-set, deep-settled, **deep-seated**, deep-fixed, deep-dyed; **infixed, ingrained**, fast, dyed-in-the-wool; implanted, inculcated, instilled; set, **set in one's ways**, settled in habit.

.22 ADVS **customarily**, conventionally, accustomedly, wontedly; normally, **usually** 84.9; **as is the custom**; as is usual, *comme d'habitude* [Fr]; as things go, as the world goes.

.23 **habitually, regularly**, routinely, frequently, persistently, repetitively, recurringly; **inveterately, chronically**; from habit, **by** *or* **from force of habit**, as is one's wont.

643. UNACCUSTOMEDNESS

.1 NOUNS **unaccustomedness**, unwontedness, disaccustomedness, unusedness, unhabituatedness; **unfamiliarity**, unacquaintance, unconversance, unpracticedness, newness to; inexperience 734.2; ignorance 477.

.2 VERBS **disaccustom, cure, break of**, stop, **wean**.

.3 **break the habit, cure oneself of**, disaccustom oneself, wean oneself from, break the pattern, break one's chains *or* fetters; **give up**, leave off, **abandon**, drop, stop, discontinue, kick *or* shake [both slang], throw off, rid oneself of; get on the wagon, swear off 992.8.

.4 ADJS **unaccustomed**, disaccustomed, **unused, unwonted**; uninured, unseasoned, untrained, unhardened; unhabituated, **not in the habit of**; out of the habit of, rusty; weaned; **unused to, unfamiliar with**, unacquainted with, unconversant with, unpracticed, new to, a stranger to; inexperienced 734.17; ignorant 477.12.

644. FASHION

.1 NOUNS **fashion, style, mode, vogue,** trend, prevailing taste; proper thing, *bon ton* [Fr], custom 642; convention 645.1,2; swim [informal], current *or* stream of fashion; height of fashion; the new look, the season's look; high fashion, *haute couture* [Fr].

.2 **fashionableness,** *bon ton* [Fr], **fashionability, stylishness, modishness,** voguishness; **popularity,** prevalence, currency 79.2.

.3 **smartness, chic,** elegance; style-consciousness, clothes-consciousness; **spruceness, nattiness,** neatness, trimness, sleekness, **dapperness,** jauntiness; sharpness *or* spiffiness *or* classiness *or* niftiness [all slang]; swankness *or* **swankiness** [both informal]; foppery, foppishness, coxcombry, dandyism.

.4 **the rage,** the thing, **the last word** [informal], *le dernier cri* [Fr], **the latest thing,** the latest wrinkle [informal].

.5 **fad, craze, rage;** wrinkle [informal]; novelty 122.2; **faddishness,** faddiness [informal], **faddism; faddist.**

.6 **society,** *société* [Fr], fashionable society, **polite society, high society,** high life, *beau monde, haut monde* [both Fr], good society; best people, people of fashion, right people; *monde* [Fr], world of fashion, Vanity Fair; **smart set** [informal]; the Four Hundred, **upper crust** *or* upper cut [both informal]; cream of society, elite, carriage trade; café society, jet set, beautiful people, in-crowd; *jeunesse dorée* [Fr]; drawing room, salon; social register.

.7 person of fashion, fashionable, man-about-town, man *or* woman of the world, *mondain, mondaine* [both Fr], leader *or* arbiter of fashion, taste-maker, trend-setter, tone-setter, *arbiter elegantiae* [L]; ten best-dressed, fashion plate, clothes-horse, "the glass of fashion and the mold of form" [Shakespeare], Beau Brummel; fop, dandy 903.9; **socialite** [informal]; **clubwoman,** clubman; jet setter; swinger [informal]; **debutante,** subdebutante, deb *or* subdeb [both informal].

.8 VERBS **catch on,** become popular, **become the rage.**

.9 **be fashionable, be the style, be the rage,** be the thing; have a run; cut a figure in society [informal], give a tone to society, set the fashion *or* style *or* tone; dress to kill.

.10 **follow the fashion, get in the swim** [informal], get *or* jump on the bandwagon [slang], join the parade, follow the crowd, go with the stream *or* tide *or* current; keep in step, do as others do; keep up, **keep up appearances,** keep up with the Joneses.

.11 ADJS **fashionable, in fashion, smart, in style, in vogue; all the rage,** all the thing; **popular,** prevalent, current 79.12; **up-to-date,** up-to-datish, up-to-the-minute, hip *or* mod [both slang], trendy [informal], newfashioned, modern, new 122.9–14; **in the swim.**

.12 **stylish, modish,** voguish, vogue; *soigné or soignée* [both Fr]; *à la mode* [Fr], in the mode.

.13 **chic, smart,** elegant; style-conscious, clothes-conscious; **well-dressed,** well-groomed, *soigné or soignée* [both Fr], dressed to advantage, dressed to kill, dressed to the teeth, dressed to the nines, well-turned-out; **spruce, natty,** neat, trim, sleek, smug, trig, tricksy [archaic]; **dapper,** dashing, jaunty, braw [Scot]; sharp *or* spiffy *or* classy *or* nifty *or* snazzy [all slang]; **swank** *or* **swanky** [both informal], posh [informal], ritzy [informal], swell *or* nobby [both slang]; genteel; exquisite, *recherché* [Fr]; cosmopolitan, sophisticated 733.26.

.14 **ultrafashionable,** ultrastylish, ultrasmart; chichi; foppish, dandified, dandyish, dandiacal.

.15 **faddish,** faddy [informal].

.16 **socially prominent,** in society, high-society, elite; café-society, jet-set; lace-curtain, silk-stocking.

.17 ADVS **fashionably, stylishly, modishly,** *à la mode* [Fr], in the latest style *or* mode.

.18 **smartly,** chicly, elegantly, exquisitely; **sprucely, nattily,** neatly, trimly, sleekly; **dapperly,** jauntily, dashingly, swankly *or* swankily [both informal]; foppishly, dandyishly.

645. SOCIAL CONVENTION

.1 NOUNS **social convention, convention,** conventional usage, **social usage, form, formality; custom** 642; conformity 82; **propriety, decorum,** decorousness, correctness, *convenance, bienséance* [both Fr], decency, seemliness, civility [archaic], good form, etiquette 646.3; **conventionalism, conventionality, Grundyism; Mrs. Grundy.**

.2 **the conventions, the proprieties, the mores,** the right things, accepted *or* sanctioned conduct, what is done, civilized behavior; **dictates of society**, dictates of Mrs. Grundy.

.3 conventionalist, Grundy, Mrs. Grundy; conformist 82.2.

.4 VERBS **conform**, observe the proprieties, play the game, follow the rules 82.3,4.

.5 ADJS **conventional, decorous,** orthodox, **correct,** right, **proper,** decent, seemly, meet; **accepted, recognized,** acknowledged, received, admitted, approved, being done; *comme il faut, de rigueur* [both Fr]; **traditional, customary** 642.15; formal 646.7; conformable 82.5.

.6 ADVS **conventionally,** decorously, orthodoxly; **customarily, traditionally;** correctly, properly, as is proper, as it should be, *comme il faut* [Fr]; according to use *or* custom, according to the dictates of society *or* Mrs. Grundy.

646. FORMALITY

.1 NOUNS **formality,** form, formalness; **ceremony,** ceremonial, **ceremoniousness; ritual,** rituality; extrinsicality, impersonality 6.1; formalization, stylization, conventionalization; **stiffness, stiltedness,** primness, rigidness, starchiness, buckram [archaic], **dignity,** gravity, weight, **solemnity** 871; **pomp** 904.6; pomposity 904.7.

.2 **formalism, ceremonialism, ritualism;** legalism; pedantry, pedantism, pedanticism; precisianism, preciseness, preciousness, preciosity, purism; punctiliousness, punctilio, scrupulousness.

.3 **etiquette,** social code, rules of conduct; **formalities,** social procedures, social conduct; **manners,** good manners, exquisite manners, quiet good manners, **politeness,** *politesse* [Fr], natural politeness, comity, civility 936.1; **amenities,** decencies, civilities, elegancies, **social graces, mores, proprieties;** decorum, good form; **courtliness,** elegance 589; **protocol,** diplomatic code; punctilio, point of etiquette; convention, social usage.

.4 (ceremonial function) **ceremony,** ceremonial; **rite, ritual, formality; solemnity, service, function,** office, **observance,** performance; **exercise,** exercises; **celebration,** solemnization; **liturgy,** religious ceremony 1040.3; **rite of passage,** *rite de passage* [Fr]; convocation; commencement, commencement exercises; graduation, graduation exercises; baccalaureate service; inaugural, inauguration; initiation; formal; empty formality *or* ceremony, mummery.

.5 VERBS **formalize,** ritualize, solemnize, celebrate, dignify; **observe;** conventionalize, stylize.

.6 **stand on ceremony,** observe the formalities, follow protocol.

.7 ADJS **formal,** formulary; formalist, formalistic; legalistic; pedantic(al); stylized, conventionalized; extrinsic, outward, impersonal 6.3; surface, **superficial** 224.6, nominal 583.15.

.8 **ceremonious, ceremonial; ritualistic, ritual;** hieratic(al), sacerdotal, liturgic 1040.22; **solemn** 871.3; **pompous** 904.22; **stately** 904.21; well-mannered 936.16; **conventional,** decorous 645.5.

.9 **stiff, stilted,** prim, rigid, starch, starched, buckram, in buckram.

.10 **punctilious, scrupulous, precise,** precisian, precisionist, precious, puristic; exact, meticulous 533.12; **orderly, methodical** 59.6.

.11 ADVS **formally,** in due form, in set form; **ceremoniously, ritually,** ritualistically; solemnly 871.4; for form's sake, *pro forma* [L], **as a matter of form.**

.12 **stiffly, stiltedly,** starchly, primly, rigidly.

647. INFORMALITY

.1 NOUNS **informality, informalness, unceremoniousness; casualness,** offhandedness, **ease, easiness,** easygoingness; **relaxedness;** affability, graciousness, cordiality, sociability 922; Bohemianism, unconventionality 83.2; **familiarity; naturalness,** simplicity, plainness, homeliness, homeyness, folksiness [informal], common touch, **unaffectedness,** unpretentiousness 902.2; unconstraint, unconstrainedness, looseness; irregularity.

.2 VERBS **not stand on ceremony,** let one's hair down [slang], be oneself, come as you are.

.3 ADJS **informal, unceremonious; casual, offhand,** offhanded, unstudied, easy, easygoing, free and easy; *dégagé* [Fr]; **relaxed;** affable, gracious, cordial, sociable 922.18; Bohemian, unconventional 83.6; **familiar; natural,** simple, plain, homely, homey, folksy [informal], *haymish* [Yid]; **unaffected, unassuming** 902.7; unconstrained, loose; irregular; unofficial.

.4 ADVS **informally, unceremoniously,** without ceremony, *sans cérémonie, sans façon* [both Fr]; **casually,** offhand, offhandedly; relaxedly; familiarly; **naturally,** simply, plainly; **unaffectedly, unassumingly** 902.11; unconstrainedly, unofficially; *en famille* [Fr].

648. MOTIVATION, INDUCEMENT

.1 NOUNS motive, reason, cause, source, spring, mainspring; matter, score, consideration; ground, basis 153.1; sake; goal 653.2; ideal, principle, ambition, aspiration, inspiration, guiding light or star, lodestar; calling, vocation; intention 653; ulterior motive.

.2 motivation, moving, actuation, prompting, stimulation, animation; direction, inner-direction, other-direction; influence 172.

.3 inducement, enlistment, engagement, solicitation, persuasion, suasion; exhortation, hortation, preaching, preachment; selling, sales talk, salesmanship; jawboning [informal]; lobbying; coaxing, wheedling, working on [informal], cajolery, cajolement, conning, snow job [slang], blandishment, sweet talk or soft soap [both informal]; allurement 650.

.4 incitement, incitation, instigation, stimulation, arousal, excitement, excitation, fomentation, agitation, inflammation, firing, stirring, stirring-up, impassioning, whipping-up, rabble-rousing; provocation, irritation, exasperation; pep talk, pep rally.

.5 urging, pressure, pressing; encouragement, abetment; insistence, instance; goading, prodding, spurring, pricking, needling.

.6 urge, urgency; impulse, impulsion, compulsion; press, pressure, drive, push; sudden or rash impulse; constraint, exigency, stress, pinch.

.7 incentive, inducement, encouragement, persuasive, invitation, provocation, incitement; stimulus, stimulation, stimulative, fillip, whet; carrot; reward, payment 841; profit 811.3; bait, lure 650.2; bribe 651.2; sweetening or sweetener [both informal], interest, percentage, what's in it for one [informal].

.8 goad, spur, prod, prick [archaic], sting, gadfly; oxgoad; rowel; whip, lash, whiplash, gad [dial].

.9 inspiration, infusion, infection; fire, firing; animation, exhilaration, enlivenment; afflatus, divine afflatus; genius, animus, moving or animating spirit.

.10 prompter, mover, prime mover, impeller, energizer, galvanizer, inducer, actuator, animator, moving spirit; encourager, abettor, inspirer, firer, spark, sparker, spark plug [informal]; persuader; stimula-

tor, gadfly; tempter 650.3; coaxer, coax [informal], wheedler, cajoler, pleader.

.11 instigator, inciter, exciter, urger; provoker, provocateur [Fr], agent provocateur [Fr], catalyst; agitator, fomenter, inflamer; agitprop; rabble-rouser, rouser, demagogue; firebrand, incendiary; seditionist, seditionary; troublemaker, mischief-maker, ringleader.

.12 VERBS motivate, move, set in motion, actuate, move to action, impel, propel; ego-involve; stimulate, energize, galvanize, animate, spark; promote, foster; force, compel 756.4.

.13 prompt, provoke, evoke, elicit, call up, summon up, muster up, call forth, inspire; bring about, cause 153.11.

.14 urge, press, push, work on [informal], twist one's arm [slang]; importune, nag, pressure, high-pressure, bring pressure to bear upon, throw one's weight around, throw one's weight into the scale, jawbone [informal]; lobby; coax, wheedle, cajole, blandish, plead with, sweet-talk or soft-soap [both informal], exhort, call on or upon, advocate, recommend; insist, insist upon 753.7.

.15 goad, prod, poke [archaic], nudge, spur, prick, sting, needle; whip, lash, flog [Brit].

.16 urge on or along, egg on [informal], hound on, hie on, hasten on, hurry on, speed on; goad on, spur on, drive on, whip on; cheer on, root on [informal].

.17 incite, instigate, put up to [slang]; set on, sic on; foment, ferment, agitate, arouse, excite, stir up, work up, whip up; rally; inflame, incense [archaic], fire, heat, heat up, impassion; provoke, pique, whet, tickle; nettle; lash into a fury or frenzy; pour oil on the fire, feed the fire, add fuel to the flame, fan, fan the flame, blow the coals, stir the embers.

.18 kindle, enkindle, fire, spark, trigger, touch off, set off, light the fuse.

.19 rouse, arouse, raise, raise up, waken, awaken, wake up, turn on [slang], stir, stir up, set astir, pique.

.20 inspire, inspirit, spirit, spirit up; fire, fire one's imagination; animate, exhilarate, enliven; infuse, infect, inject, inoculate, imbue or embue, inform.

.21 encourage, give encouragement, pat or clap on the back; invite, ask for; abet, aid and abet, countenance, keep in countenance; foster, nurture, nourish, feed.

.22 induce, prompt, move one to, influence, sway, incline, dispose, carry, bring, lead,

lead one to; lure 650.4; **tempt** 650.5; determine, decide; enlist, procure, engage [archaic], interest in, get to do.

.23 **persuade, prevail on** or **upon,** prevail with, **sway,** convince, **bring round,** bring to reason, bring to one's senses; **win, win over,** bring over, draw over, gain, gain over; **talk over, talk into,** argue into, outtalk [informal]; wangle, wangle into; hook or hook in [both slang], con, sell or sell one on [both informal], **charm, captivate** 650.6; wear down, overcome one's resistance, twist one's arm [slang].

.24 **persuade oneself, make oneself easy about,** make sure of, make up one's mind; be persuaded, rest easy.

.25 ADJS **motivating, motivational, motive, moving, animating, actuating, impelling,** impulsive, inducive [archaic], directive; **urgent, pressing, driving;** compelling 756.9; causal, causative 153.14.

.26 **inspiring, inspirational,** inspiriting; infusive; animating, exhilarating, enlivening.

.27 **provocative, provoking,** piquant, **exciting,** challenging, prompting, **rousing, stirring, stimulating,** stimulant, stimulative, energizing, galvanizing, galvanic; **encouraging,** inviting, **alluring** 650.7; auxo–.

.28 **incitive,** inciting, incentive; **instigative,** instigating; **agitative,** agitational; **inflammatory, incendiary,** fomenting, rabble-rousing.

.29 **persuasive,** suasive, persuading; wheedling, cajoling; hortative, hortatory; exhortative, exhortatory.

.30 **moved, motivated, prompted, impelled, actuated;** stimulated, animated; minded, inclined, of a mind to, with half a mind to; inner-directed, other-directed.

.31 **inspired, fired,** afire, on fire.

649. PRETEXT

.1 NOUNS **pretext, pretense, pretension,** lying pretension, **show,** ostensible or announced or public motive; **front,** façade, **sham** 616.3; **excuse,** apology, protestation, poor excuse, lame excuse; **put-off;** handle, peg to hang on, leg to stand on, locus standi [L]; **subterfuge,** refuge, device, stratagem, feint, **trick** 618.6; dust thrown in the eye, smoke screen, **screen, cover,** stalking-horse, **blind;** guise, semblance; mask, cloak, veil; gloss, varnish, color; cover-up, cover story, alibi.

.2 **claim,** profession, allegation.

.3 VERBS **pretext, make a pretext of,** take as an excuse or reason or occasion, urge as a motive, **pretend,** make a pretense of; put up a front or false front; allege, claim, profess, purport, avow; protest too much.

.4 **hide under,** cover oneself with, shelter under, take cover under, wrap oneself in, cloak or mantle oneself with, take refuge in; conceal one's motive with.

.5 ADJS pretexted, **pretended, alleged, claimed, professed, purported,** avowed; **ostensible,** hypocritical, **specious;** so-called, in name only.

.6 ADVS **ostensibly, allegedly,** purportedly, professedly, avowedly; for the record, for public consumption; under the pretext of, **as a pretext,** as an excuse, as a cover or cover-up or alibi.

650. ALLUREMENT

.1 NOUNS **allurement, allure, enticement, inveiglement,** invitation, agacerie [Fr], blandishment, cajolery; **inducement** 648.7; **temptation,** tantalization; **seduction,** seducement; beguilement, beguiling, come-hither [dial]; **fascination, captivation,** enthrallment, entrapment, snaring; **enchantment,** witchery, bewitchery, bewitchment; **attraction, interest, charm, glamour, appeal,** magnetism; charisma; sex appeal, SA [slang]; **attractiveness,** charmingness, **seductiveness,** winsomeness, winning ways; song of the Sirens, voice of the tempter; forbidden fruit; wooing 932.6; flirtation 932.8.

.2 **lure,** charm, **come-on** [slang], drawing card, drawcard; **decoy,** decoy duck; **bait,** ground bait, baited trap; **snare,** trap, hook; **endearment** 932.

.3 **tempter, seducer, enticer,** inveigler, **charmer,** enchanter, fascinator, tantalizer, teaser; coquette, flirt; Don Juan; Pied Piper of Hamelin; **temptress,** enchantress, seductress, **siren;** Siren, Circe, Lorelei, Parthenope; **vampire,** vamp [slang], femme fatale [Fr].

.4 VERBS **lure, allure, entice, seduce, inveigle, decoy,** draw, **draw on, lead on;** give the come-on or bat the eyes at [both slang], flirt with, flirt 932.18; **woo** 932.19; coax, cajole, blandish; **ensnare** 618.18; draw in, suck in or rope in [both slang]; bait, offer bait to, bait the hook, angle with a silver hook.

.5 **attract, interest, appeal, engage,** fetch [informal], attract one's interest, be attractive, take or tickle one's fancy; **invite,** summon, beckon; **tempt, tantalize, titillate,** tickle, **tease,** whet the appetite, make one's mouth water, dangle before one.

.6 fascinate, **captivate**, **charm**, becharm, spell, spellbind, cast a spell, put under a spell, **beguile**, **intrigue**, **enthrall**, infatuate, **enrapture**, **transport**, **enravish**, **entrance**, **enchant**, witch, **bewitch**, vamp [slang], carry away, turn one's head; hypnotize, mesmerize.

.7 ADJS **alluring**, **fascinating**, **captivating**, **charming**, **glamorous**, exotic, **enchanting**, spellful, spellbinding, **entrancing**, ravishing, **enravishing**, **intriguing**, **enthralling**, witching, **bewitching**; attractive, **interesting**, **appealing**, engaging, taking, fetching [informal], catching, winning, winsome, prepossessing; exciting; charismatic; **seductive**, seducing, **beguiling**, **enticing**, **inviting**, come-hither [informal]; flirtatious, coquettish; coaxing, cajoling, blandishing; **tempting**, **tantalizing**, teasing, titillating, titillative, tickling; **provocative**, *provoquant* [Fr]; appetizing, mouth-watering, piquant; **irresistible**; siren, sirenic; hypnotic, mesmeric.

.8 ADVS **alluringly**, **fascinatingly**, captivatingly, charmingly, enchantingly, entrancingly, enravishingly, intriguingly, beguilingly, glamorously, bewitchingly; attractively, appealingly, engagingly, winsomely; **enticingly**, **seductively**, with bedroom eyes [slang]; **temptingly**, provocatively; **tantalizingly**, teasingly; piquantly, appetizingly; irresistibly; hypnotically, mesmerically.

651. BRIBERY

.1 NOUNS **bribery**, bribing, subornation, **corruption**, **graft**, bribery and corruption.

.2 **bribe**, bribe money, sop, sop to Cerberus, gratuity, gratification [archaic], payoff [informal], boodle [slang]; hush money [slang]; payola [slang]; protection.

.3 VERBS **bribe**, throw a sop to; grease [informal], **grease the palm** or hand, tickle the palm or tickle in the palm; **purchase**; buy or **buy off** or pay off [all informal]; suborn, corrupt, tamper with; reach or get at or get to [all informal]; approach, try to bribe; **fix**, **take care of**.

.4 ADJS **bribable**, corruptible, purchasable, buyable; approachable; fixable; on the take [slang], on the pad [slang]; **venal**, corrupt.

652. DISSUASION

.1 NOUNS **dissuasion**, talking out of [informal], remonstrance, expostulation, admonition, monition, **warning**, caveat, **caution**, cautioning; intimidation, determent, deterrence, scaring or frightening off.

.2 **deterrent**, determent; **discouragement**, disincentive; damp, damper, **wet blanket**, cold water, chill.

.3 VERBS **dissuade**, convince to the contrary, **talk out of** [informal], kid out of [slang]; unconvince, unpersuade; remonstrate, expostulate, admonish, cry out against; **warn**, **caution**; intimidate, scare or frighten off, daunt 891.26.

.4 **disincline**, **indispose**, disaffect, disinterest; **deter**, repel, turn from, turn away or aside; divert, deflect; distract, put off or turn off [both slang]; wean from; **discourage**; **throw cold water on**, throw or lay a wet blanket on, damp, dampen, cool, chill, quench, blunt.

.5 ADJS **dissuasive**, dissuading, disinclining, **discouraging**; **deterrent**; expostulatory, admonitory, monitory, cautionary; intimidating.

653. INTENTION

.1 NOUNS **intention**, **intent**, intendment, **aim**, effect, counsel [archaic], meaning, view, study, animus, **point**, **purpose**, function, set or settled or fixed purpose; sake; **design**, **plan**, project, idea; **proposal**, prospectus; **resolve**, resolution, mind, will; **motive** 648.1; determination 624.1; desideratum, desideration, **ambition**, aspiration, **desire** 634; striving, nisus.

.2 **objective**, **object**, **aim**, **end**, **goal**, destination, mark, pursuit, object in mind, **end in view**; **target**, butt, bull's-eye, quintain; quarry, prey, game; reason for being, *raison d'être* [Fr]; by-purpose, by-end; final cause, ultimate aim, "the be-all and the end-all" [Shakespeare], teleology.

.3 **intentionality**, **deliberation**, **deliberateness**, express intention, expressness, **premeditation**, **predeliberation**, preconsideration, **calculation**, **calculatedness**, predetermination, preresolution, forethought, aforethought.

.4 VERBS **intend**, **purpose**, **plan**, purport, **mean**, have every intention, think, **propose**; **resolve**, determine 624.7; project, **design**, destine; **aim**, aim at, drive at, aspire to or after, set one's sights on, go for, be after, set before oneself, purpose to oneself; harbor a design; **desire** 634.14–20.

.5 **intend to**, **mean to**, **aim to**, **propose to**, resolve to.

.6 **plan on**, **figure on**, count on, calculate

on, reckon on, bank on *or* upon; bargain for.

.7 contemplate, meditate; envisage, envision, have in mind, have in view; have an eye to, have a mind to, have half a mind to, have a good *or* great mind to.

.8 premeditate, calculate, preresolve, predetermine, predeliberate, preconsider, forethink, work out beforehand; plan 654.9; plot, scheme 654.10.

.9 ADJS intentional, intended, proposed, purposed, projected, designed, of design, aimed, aimed at, meant, purposeful, purposive, willful, voluntary, deliberate; deliberated; considered, studied, advised, calculated, contemplated, envisaged, envisioned, meditated, conscious, knowing, witting; planned 654.13; teleological.

.10 premeditated, predeliberated, preconsidered, predetermined, preresolved, prepense, aforethought.

.11 ADVS intentionally, purposely, purposefully, purposively, on purpose, with purpose, deliberately, designedly, willfully, voluntarily; pointedly; wittingly, consciously, knowingly; advisedly, calculatedly, contemplatedly, meditatedly, premeditatedly, with premeditation, with intent, with full intent, by design, with one's eyes open; with malice aforethought, in cold blood.

.12 PREPS, CONJS for, to; in order to *or* that, so, so that, so as to; for the purpose of, to the end that, with the intent that, with the view of, with a view to, with an eye to; in contemplation of, in consideration of; for the sake of.

654. PLAN

.1 NOUNS plan, scheme, design, method, program, device, contrivance, game, envisagement, conception, enterprise, idea; organization, rationalization, systematization, schematization; charting, mapping, graphing, blueprinting; planning, calculation, figuring; planning function; long-range planning, long-range plan; master plan, the picture *or* the big picture [both informal]; approach, attack; way, procedure 657.1; arrangement, prearrangement, system, disposition, layout, setup, lineup; schedule; schema, schematism, scheme of arrangement; blueprint, guidelines, program of action; methodology; working plan, ground plan, tactical plan, strategic plan; tactics, strategy; operations research; intention 653; forethought, foresight 542.

.2 project, projection; proposal, prospectus, proposition; scenario, game plan [informal].

.3 diagram, plot, chart, blueprint, graph, table; design, pattern, copy [archaic], cartoon; sketch, draft, drawing, working drawing, rough; *brouillon, ébauche, esquisse* [all Fr]; outline, delineation, skeleton, figure, profile; house plan, ground plan, ichnography; elevation, projection.

.4 map, chart; general reference map, special map, thematic map; political map; road map, transportation map; physical map, terrain map, relief map, contour map, topographic chart; photomap; globe, terrestrial globe, celestial globe; atlas; mariner's chart, hydrographic chart; aeronautical chart; weather map, weather chart, climatic chart; celestial chart, astronomical chart, heliographic chart; hachure, contour line, isoline, layer tint; scale, graphic scale, representative fraction; legend; grid line, meridian, parallel, latitude, longitude; index; projection, map projection; azimuthal projection, azimuthal equidistant projection, gnomonic projection; cylindrical projection, Mercator projection, Miller projection; conic projection, Lambert conformal conic projection *or* Lambert conformal projection, polyconic projection; sinusoidal projection; cartography, chorography, topography, photogrammetry, phototopography; cartographer, map maker, mapper, chorographer, topographer, photogrammetrist.

.5 policy, polity, principles, guiding principles; procedure, course, line, plan of action; creed 501.3; platform; position paper.

.6 intrigue, web of intrigue, plot, scheme, deep-laid plot *or* scheme, underplot, game *or* little game [both informal], trick, stratagem, finesse; counterplot; conspiracy, confederacy, covin, complot [archaic], cabal; complicity, collusion, connivance; artifice 735.3; contrivance, contriving; scheming, schemery, plotting; finagling [informal], machination, manipulation, maneuvering, engineering, rigging; frame-up [informal]; wire-pulling [informal].

.7 planner, designer, deviser, contriver, framer, projector; enterpriser, entrepreneur; organizer, promoter, developer; architect, tactician, strategist, strategian.

.8 schemer, plotter, counterplotter, finagler [informal], Machiavellian; intriguer, *intri-*

gant, intrigante [both Fr]; **conspirer, conspirator,** coconspirator, **conniver;** maneuverer, machinator, operator [informal], opportunist, exploiter; wire-puller [informal].

.9 VERBS **plan, devise, contrive, design,** frame, shape, cast, concert, lay plans; organize, rationalize, systematize, schematize, methodize; **arrange,** prearrange, make arrangements, set up, work up, work out; **schedule;** lay down a plan, shape *or* mark out a course; program; **calculate,** figure; **project,** cut out, make a projection, forecast [archaic], plan ahead; intend 653.4.

.10 **plot, scheme, intrigue,** be up to something; **conspire, connive,** collude, complot [archaic], cabal; **hatch, hatch up,** cook up [informal], brew, concoct, hatch *or* lay a plot; **maneuver,** machinate, finesse, operate [informal], engineer, rig, wangle [informal], angle, finagle [informal]; frame *or* frame up [both informal]; counterplot, countermine.

.11 **plot, map, chart, blueprint; diagram,** graph; **sketch;** draw up a plan; map out, plot out, **lay out,** sketch out, set out, mark out; lay off, mark off.

.12 **outline,** line, **delineate,** chalk out, brief; **sketch, draft,** trace; block in *or* out; rough in, rough out.

.13 ADJS **planned, devised, designed,** shaped, set, **blueprinted,** charted, **contrived; plotted;** arranged; organized, rationalized, systematized, schematized, methodized; worked out, calculated, figured; **projected; scheduled,** on the agenda, in the works, on the calendar, on the docket, on the anvil, on the carpet, on the tapis [archaic], *sur le tapis* [Fr]; tactical, **strategic,** strategetic.

.14 **scheming, calculating, designing, contriving,** plotting, intriguing; Machiavellian, Byzantine; **conniving,** connivent [archaic], conspiring, collusive; stratagemical; up to.

.15 schematic, diagrammatic.

655. PURSUIT

.1 NOUNS **pursuit,** pursuing, pursuance, prosecution [archaic]; **quest,** seeking, hunting, searching 485.14; **following,** follow, follow-up; tracking, trailing, tracking down, dogging, shadowing, stalking; **chase,** hot pursuit; hue and cry.

.2 **hunting,** gunning, shooting, venery, cynegetics, sport, sporting; **hunt, chase,** chevy *or* chivy [both Brit], shikar [India], cours-

ing; fox hunting; hawking, falconry; stalking, still hunt.

.3 **fishing,** fishery, **angling,** piscation, halieutics; rod and reel; harpooning; whaling; casting, fly fishing; still-fishing; trolling; trawling; jigging; guddling.

.4 **pursuer,** pursuant, **chaser,** follower; hunter, quester, **seeker.**

.5 **hunter, huntsman,** sportsman, **Nimrod;** huntress, sportswoman; stalker; courser; trapper; big game hunter, shikari [India], white hunter; jacklighter, jacker, beater.

.6 **fisher, fisherman, angler,** *piscator* [L], piscatorian, piscatorialist; Waltonian, "the compleat angler" [Izaak Walton]; dibber, dibbler, troller, trawler, jacker, jigger, guddler, drifter, drift netter, whaler.

.7 **quarry, game, prey,** venery, beasts of venery, victim, the hunted; kill; big game.

.8 VERBS **pursue,** prosecute [archaic], **follow,** follow up, **go after,** take out after [informal], run after, run in pursuit of, make after, go in pursuit of; raise the hunt, raise the hue and cry, hollo after; **chase, give chase,** chivy; hound, dog; **quest,** quest after, **seek,** seek out, hunt, search 485.29,30.

.9 **hunt,** go hunting, hunt down, chase, run, shikar [India], sport; shoot, gun; course; ride to hounds, follow the hounds; **track,** trail; **stalk,** prowl after, still-hunt; hound, dog; hawk, falcon; fowl; flush, start; drive, beat; jack, jacklight.

.10 **fish,** go fishing, **angle;** cast one's hook *or* net; bait the hook; shrimp, whale, clam, grig; still-fish, fly-fish, troll, bob, dap, dib *or* dibble, gig, jig, spin; torch, jack, jacklight; guddle; net, trawl, seine; drive.

.11 ADJS **pursuing,** pursuant, following; **questing, seeking, searching** 485.37; **in pursuit,** in hot pursuit, in full cry; hunting, cynegetic, fishing, piscatory, piscatorial, halieutic(al).

.12 PREPS **after, in pursuit** *or* **pursuance of,** in search of, on the lookout for, in the market for, out for; on the track *or* trail of, on the scent of.

.13 INTERJS (hunting cries) view halloo!, yoicks! [archaic]; so-ho!, tallyho!, tallyho over!, tallyho back!

656. BUSINESS, OCCUPATION

.1 NOUNS **business, occupation, employment, service,** employ, **activities,** activity, function, enterprise, undertaking, **work, affairs,** labor; thing *or* bag [both slang]; **affair, matter, concern,** concernment, interest, lookout [informal]; what one is doing or about; **commerce** 827.

.2 **task, work, stint, job,** labor, job of work, piece of work, **chore,** chare, odd job; **assignment, charge,** project, errand, **mission,** commission, **duty,** service, exercise; things to do, matters in hand, irons in the fire, fish to fry; homework; busywork, make-work.

.3 **function, office, duty, job,** province, place, role, *rôle* [Fr], part; **capacity,** character, **position.**

.4 (sphere of work or activity) **field, sphere,** province, department, area, discipline, subdiscipline, orb, orbit, realm, domain, demesne, walk; beat, round.

.5 **position, situation, job,** employment, service, **office,** post, –ate, –cy, –dom, –ship, –ure, –y; **place,** station, berth, billet, **appointment,** engagement, gig [slang]; incumbency, tenure; opening, vacancy; second job, moonlighting [informal].

.6 vocation, occupation, business, **work, line, line of work,** line of business or endeavor, number [informal], walk, **walk of life, calling,** mission, **profession, practice, pursuit, specialty,** specialization, *métier* [Fr], mystery [archaic], **trade,** racket or game [both slang]; **career,** lifework, life's work; **craft,** art, handicraft; careerism, career building.

.7 **avocation, hobby,** hobbyhorse [archaic], sideline, by-line, side interest, pastime, spare-time activity.

.8 **professionalism,** professional standing or status.

.9 **nonprofessionalism, amateurism,** amateur standing or status.

.10 VERBS **occupy, engage, busy,** devote, spend, **employ,** occupy oneself, busy oneself, go about one's business, devote oneself; pass or employ or spend the time; occupy one's time, take up one's time; attend to business, attend to one's work; mind one's business, mind the store [informal], stick to one's last or knitting.

.11 **busy oneself with, do,** occupy or engage oneself with, employ oneself in or upon, pass or employ or spend one's time in; **engage in, take up,** devote oneself to, apply oneself to, address oneself to, have one's hands in, turn one's hand to; concern oneself with, make it one's business; **be about, be doing,** be occupied with, be engaged or employed in, be at work on; practice, follow as an occupation 705.7.

.12 **work,** work at, work for, have a job, be employed, **ply one's trade,** labor in one's

vocation, do one's number [informal], follow a trade, practice a profession, carry on a business or trade, keep up; **do** or **transact business,** carry on business 827.14; set up shop, set up in business, hang out one's shingle [informal]; stay employed, hold down a job [informal]; moonlight [informal]; labor, toil 716.13, 14.

.13 officiate, function, serve; **perform as, act as,** act or play one's part, **do duty,** discharge or perform or exercise the office or duties or functions of, serve in the office or capacity of.

.14 **hold office,** fill an office, occupy a post.

.15 ADJS **businesslike,** working; practical, realistic 536.6; banausic, moneymaking, breadwinning, utilitarian 665.18; materialistic 1031.16; workaday, workday, prosaic 883.8; **commercial** 827.21.

.16 occupational, vocational, functional; **professional, pro** [informal]; official; technical, industrial; all in the day's work.

.17 avocational, amateur, nonprofessional.

.18 ADVS **professionally,** vocationally; as a profession or vocation; in the course of business.

657. WAY

.1 NOUNS **way, wise, manner, means, mode,** form [archaic], **fashion, style,** tone, guise [archaic]; **method,** methodology, **system;** algorithm [math]; **approach,** attack, tack; **technique, procedure, process,** proceeding, course, practice; order; lines, line, line of action; *modus operandi* [L], mode of operation, MO, manner of working, mode of procedure; **routine;** the way of, the how, the drill [Brit].

.2 **route, itinerary, course,** path, track, run, line, road; trajectory, traject, *trajet* [Fr]; circuit, tour, orbit; walk, beat, round; trade route, **sea lane, air lane,** flight path; path of least resistance, primrose path; shortcut 202.5.

.3 **path, track, trail,** –ode; **pathway,** footpath, footway; walkway, catwalk; **sidewalk, walk,** fastwalk, *trottoir* [Fr], foot pavement [Brit]; boardwalk; hiking trail; public walk, promenade, esplanade, alameda, parade, *prado* [Sp], mall; towpath or towing path; bridle path or road or trail or way; bicycle path; berm; run, runway; beaten track or path, rut, groove; garden path.

.4 passageway, pass, passage, defile; avenue, artery; corridor, aisle, alley, lane; channel, conduit 396.1; ford, ferry, traject, *trajet*

[Fr]; opening, aperture; access, inlet 302.5; exit, outlet 303.9; connection, communication; covered way, gallery, arcade, portico, colonnade, cloister, ambulatory; underpass, overpass; tunnel, railroad tunnel, vehicular tunnel; junction, interchange, **intersection** 221.2.

.5 byway, bypath, byroad, by-lane, bystreet, side road, side street; **bypass, detour,** roundabout way; bypaths and crooked ways; back way, back stairs, back door, side door; back road, back street.

.6 road, roadway, carriageway [Brit], right-of-way; **main road,** main drag [slang], **thoroughfare, arterial,** artery; **highway,** highroad [Brit], arterial highway, primary highway, **freeway, superhighway, expressway, turnpike,** pike, **thruway,** speedway, **parkway,** motorway [Brit], *Autobahn* [Ger], *autostrada* [Ital], *autoroute* [Fr]; state highway, US highway, interstate highway, *route nationale* [Fr], King's or Queen's highway, royal road, *camino real* [Sp]; secondary road, local road, county road, township road; private road, byway, driveway; highways and byways; dirt road, gravel road, paved road, *pavé* [Fr], plank road, corduroy road; **street,** through street, arterial street, **avenue, boulevard, drive;** place, row, court, lane, terrace, crescent, vennel [Scot]; **alley, alleyway,** mews, wynd [Scot], close [Brit], dead-end street, blind alley, cul-de-sac; toll road or highway; controlled access highway; post road; bypass, circumferential, belt highway, ring road; causeway, causey, *chaussée* [Fr], dike; roadbed.

.7 **pavement,** paving; macadam, blacktop, bitumen, asphalt, tarmacadam, Tarmac, Tarvia, bituminous macadam; cement, concrete; tile, brick, paving brick; stone, paving stone, pavestone, flag, flagstone, flagging; cobblestone, cobble; road metal; gravel; washboard; curbstone, kerbstone [Brit], edgestone; curb, kerb [Brit], curbing.

.8 **railway, railroad,** rail, line, track, railway or railroad or rail line; tram or tramline or tramway or tramroad [all Brit], trolley line, streetcar line, street railway; elevated railway; elevated or el or L [all informal]; subway, underground [Brit], *métro* [Fr], tube [Brit informal]; electric railway, cable railway, horse railway; cog railway, rack railway, rack-and-pinion railway; gravity-operated railway; monorail; light railroad; main line, trunk, trunk line; branch, feeder, feeder line; siding,

sidetrack, turnout; switchback; junction; terminus, terminal, the end of the line; roadway, roadbed, embankment, trestle.

.9 **cableway,** ropeway, wireway, wire ropeway, cable or rope railway, funicular or funicular railway; telpher, telpherway, telpher ropeway, telpher line or railway; ski lift.

.10 **bridge, span, viaduct;** overpass, overcrossing, overbridge or flyover [both Brit]; drawbridge, bascule bridge, lift bridge, swing bridge; floating bridge, bateau bridge, pontoon bridge; **suspension bridge;** cantilever bridge; arch bridge; footbridge; gangplank, gangboard, gangway, catwalk; rope bridge; toll bridge; stepping-stone, stepstone; Bifrost.

.11 ADVS **how, in what way** or **manner,** by what mode or means; to what extent; in what condition; by what name; at what price; after this fashion, in this way, in such wise, along these lines; **thus, so,** thus and so; as, like, on the lines of; a–, –ally, –ling, –ly, –wise, –way or –ways.

.12 **anyhow, anyway,** anywise, in any way, by any means, by any manner of means; in any event, at any rate, in any case; **nevertheless, nonetheless, however, regardless,** irregardless [informal]; at all, nohow [dial].

.13 **somehow, in some way,** in some way or other, someway [informal], by some means, **somehow or other,** somehow or another, in one way or another, in some such way, after a fashion; no matter how, **by hook or by crook,** by fair means or foul.

658. MEANS

.1 NOUNS **means,** ways, **ways and means,** means to an end; **wherewithal,** wherewith; funds 835.14; **resources,** disposable resources, capital 835.15; stock, supply 660; power, capacity, ability 157.1,2; recourses, resorts, devices; method 657.1, –ment.

.2 **instrumentality, agency;** machinery, **mechanism;** mediation, going between, intermediation, service; **expedient,** recourse, resort, device 670.2.

.3 **instrument, tool, implement, appliance,** device; contrivance, lever, mechanism; **vehicle, organ; agent** 781; medium, mediator, intermedium, intermediary, intermediate, interagent, go-between 781.4; midwife, servant, slave, handmaid, handmaiden, *ancilla* [L]; **cat's-paw, puppet, dummy, pawn,** creature, minion, stooge [slang], Charlie McCarthy [informal]; toy, plaything; dupe 620.

.4 VERBS **find means, find a way,** provide the wherewithal; get by hook or by crook, obtain by fair means or foul; beg, borrow, or steal.

.5 be instrumental, **serve, subserve,** minister to, act for, act in the interests of, promote, advance, forward, assist, facilitate; mediate, go between.

.6 ADJS **instrumental, implemental;** agential, agentive, agentival; **useful,** handy, employable, **serviceable; helpful,** conducive, forwarding, favoring, promoting, assisting, facilitating; subservient, ministering, ministerial; mediating, mediatorial, intermediary.

.7 ADVS, PREPS **by means of, by** or **through the agency of,** by or through the good offices of, through the instrumentality of, by the aid of, thanks to, by use of, **by way of,** by dint of, by the act of, through the medium of, by or in virtue of, at the hand of, at the hands of; **with;** herewith, therewith, wherewith, wherewithal; whereby, thereby, hereby; **through, by,** per; on, upon [archaic].

659. PROVISION, EQUIPMENT

.1 NOUNS **provision,** providing; **equipment, accouterment,** fitting out, outfitting; **supply,** supplying, finding; **furnishing,** furnishment; chandlery, **retailing, selling** 829.2; logistics; procurement 811.1; investment, endowment, subvention, subsidy, subsidization; provisioning, victualing, purveyance, catering; armament; resupply, replenishment, reinforcement; **preparation** 720.

.2 **provisions, supplies** 660.1; provender 308.5; **merchandise** 831.

.3 accommodations, accommodation, facilities; **lodgings** 188.3; bed, board; **board and room,** bed and board; **subsistence,** keep.

.4 **equipment,** matériel, equipage, munitions; **furniture, furnishings,** furnishments [archaic]; **fixtures, fittings, appointments, accouterments, appurtenances,** installations, plumbing; **appliances,** utensils, **conveniences; outfit, apparatus, rig,** machinery; stock-in-trade; **plant,** facility, facilities; paraphernalia, things, **gear,** impedimenta [pl], **tackle;** rigging; armament, munition; **kit,** duffel.

.5 **harness,** caparison, trappings, tack, tackle; headgear, bridle, halter, headstall, cavesson, hackamore, jaquima; bit, snaffle,

curb, noseband, chinband, cheekpiece, blinds, blinders, winker braces, browband, crownband, gag swivel, side check, breeching, britchen [dial], bellyband, girth, cinch, surcingle; collar; reins, lines, ribbons; yoke, tug, hames, hametugs, shaft tug; jerk line, checkrein, bearing rein, martingale or pole strap; saddle or back band; backstrap, crupper, hip straps.

.6 **provider, supplier,** furnisher; **donor** 818.11; patron; **purveyor,** provisioner, **caterer,** victualer, sutler; *vivandier, vivandière* [both Fr]; chandler, retailer, merchant 830.2,3; commissary, commissariat, quartermaster, storekeeper, stock clerk, steward, manciple.

.7 VERBS **provide, supply,** find, **furnish;** accommodate; invest, clothe, endow, fund, subsidize; donate, give, afford, contribute, yield, present 818.12,14; make available; stock, store; provide for, make provision or due provision for; prepare 720.6; support, maintain, keep; fill, fill up; replenish, recruit.

.8 **equip, furnish, outfit,** gear, **prepare, fit,** fit up or out, **rig,** rig up or out, **turn out,** appoint, accouter, dress; arm, heel [slang], munition; man, staff; –ate, –ize.

.9 **provision,** provender, cater, victual; feed; forage; fuel, gas, gas up, fill up, top off, coal, oil, bunker; **purvey,** sell 829.8,9.

.10 **accommodate,** furnish accommodations; lodge 188.10; **put up,** board.

.11 **make a living,** earn a living or livelihood, **make** or **earn one's keep.**

.12 **support oneself,** make one's way; **make ends meet, keep body and soul together, keep the wolf from the door,** keep or hold one's head above water, keep afloat; **survive, subsist, cope, eke out,** make out, scrape along, manage, get by.

.13 ADJS **provided, supplied, furnished,** provisioned, purveyed, catered; invested, endowed; **equipped, fitted,** fitted out, outfitted, **rigged,** accoutered; armed, heeled [slang]; **prepared** 720.16.

.14 **well-provided, well-supplied, well-furnished,** well-stocked, well-found; **well-equipped, well-fitted,** well-appointed; well-armed.

660. STORE, SUPPLY

.1 NOUNS **store, hoard, treasure,** treasury; plenty, plenitude, abundance, cornucopia; heap, mass, stack, pile, dump, rick; **collection, accumulation,** cumulation, **amassment,** budget, **stockpile; backlog;** repertory, repertoire; stock-in-trade; **in-**

ventory, stock, supply on hand; **stores, supplies, provisions,** provisionment, rations; larder, commissariat, commissary; munitions; matériel; material, materials 378.

.2 **supply, fund, resource, resources; means, assets,** liquid assets, balance, **capital,** capital goods, capitalization, available means *or* resources; grist, grist to the mill; holdings, property 810.

.3 **reserve, reserves,** reservoir, resource, **stockpile, cache,** reserve supply, something in reserve *or* in hand, something to fall back on, reserve fund, **nest egg, savings,** sinking fund; backlog, unexpended balance, ace in the hole [slang], a card up one's sleeve.

.4 **source of supply,** source, staple, resource; well, fountain, fount, font [archaic]; spring, wellspring; mine, **gold mine, bonanza;** quarry, lode, vein; cornucopia.

.5 **storage, stowage;** preservation, conservation, safekeeping, warehousing; cold storage, dry storage, dead storage; storage space, shelf-room; custody, guardianship 699.2.

.6 **storehouse, storeroom,** stock room, lumber room, store, storage, **depository, repository,** conservatory [archaic], reservoir, repertory, depot, supply depot, supply base, magazine, *magasin* [Fr], warehouse, godown; bonded warehouse, *entrepôt* [Fr]; dock; hold, cargo dock; attic, cellar, basement; closet, cupboard; wine cellar, buttery; **treasury,** treasure house, treasure room, exchequer; bank, vault 836.12,13; archives, library, stack room; armory, arsenal, dump; lumberyard; drawer, shelf; bin, bunker, bay, crib; rack, rick; vat, tank; crate, box; chest, locker, hutch; bookcase, stack, glory hole.

.7 **garner, granary,** grain bin, elevator, grain elevator, **silo;** mow, haymow, hayloft, hayrick; crib, corncrib.

.8 **larder, pantry,** buttery [dial]; spence [Brit dial], stillroom [Brit]; root cellar; dairy, dairy house *or* room.

.9 **museum; gallery,** art gallery, picture gallery, pinacotheca; salon; Metropolitan Museum, National Gallery, Museum of Modern Art, Guggenheim Museum, Tate Gallery, British Museum, Louvre, Hermitage, Prado, Uffizi, Rijksmuseum; museology, curatorship.

.10 VERBS **store, stow,** lay in store; **lay in,** lay in a supply *or* stock *or* store, store away, stow away, **put away, lay away,** pack away, bundle away, lay down, stow down,

salt down *or* away [informal]; **deposit,** reposit, lodge; **cache,** stash [slang]; **bank,** coffer, hutch [archaic]; warehouse, reservoir; file, file away.

.11 **store up, stock up, lay up,** put up, **save up,** hoard up, treasure up, garner up, **heap up,** pile up, build up a stock *or* inventory; **accumulate,** cumulate, **collect, amass, stockpile;** backlog; garner, gather into barns; **hoard,** treasure, save, keep, hold, squirrel, squirrel away; hide, secrete 615.7.

.12 **reserve, save, conserve, keep,** retain, husband, husband one's resources, keep *or* hold back, withhold; **keep in reserve,** keep in store, keep on hand, keep by one; **preserve** 701.7; **set** *or* **put aside,** set *or* put apart, put *or* lay *or* set by; save up, save to fall back upon, keep as a nest egg, **save for a rainy day,** provide for *or* against a rainy day.

.13 **have in store** *or* **reserve,** have to fall back upon, have something to draw on, have something laid by, have something laid by for a rainy day.

.14 ADJS **stored, accumulated,** amassed, laid up; gathered, garnered, collected; **stockpiled;** backlogged; **hoarded,** treasured.

.15 **reserved, preserved, saved,** conserved, put by, kept, retained, held, withheld, held back, kept *or* held in reserve; spare.

.16 ADVS **in store,** in stock, in supply, **on hand.**

.17 **in reserve,** back, aside, by.

661. SUFFICIENCY

.1 NOUNS sufficiency, sufficientness, **adequacy,** adequateness, **enough,** competence *or* competency, satisfactoriness, satisfaction, satisfactory amount; good *or* adequate supply; exact measure, right amount, no more and no less; bare sufficiency, minimum, bare minimum, just enough, enough to get by on.

.2 **plenty, plenitude, plentifulness,** plenteousness; myriad, myriads, numerousness 101; **amplitude,** ampleness; substantiality, substantialness; **abundance, copiousness;** exuberance, riotousness; **bountifulness,** bountiousness, liberalness, **liberality,** generousness, **generosity; lavishness, extravagance, prodigality;** luxuriance, fertility, teemingness, productiveness 165; **wealth, opulence** *or* opulency, richness, affluence; more than enough; maximum; **fullness,** full measure, repletion, repleteness; overflow, outpouring, flood, flow, shower, spate, stream, gush, avalanche; landslide;

prevalence, profuseness, profusion, riot; **superabundance** 663.2; great abundance, great plenty, "God's plenty" [Dryden], quantities, much, lots, scads 34.4; bumper crop, rich harvest, foison [archaic]; rich vein, bonanza; ample sufficiency, enough and to spare, enough and then some; fat of the land.

.3 cornucopia, horn of plenty, horn of Amalthea, endless supply.

.4 VERBS **suffice, do,** just do, serve, **answer;** work, be equal to, **avail;** answer *or* serve the purpose; qualify, meet, fulfill, **satisfy,** meet requirements; **pass muster,** make the grade [informal], hack it [slang], **fill the bill** [informal]; get by [slang], do it, do'er [dial], do in a pinch, **pass,** pass in the dark [informal]; hold, stand, stand up, take it, bear; stretch [informal], reach, go around.

.5 **abound,** exuberate [archaic], teem, **teem with,** creep with, crawl with, swarm with, bristle with; proliferate 165.7; **overflow,** run over; flow, stream, rain, pour, shower, gush.

.6 ADJS **sufficient,** sufficing; **enough, ample,** substantial, **plenty, satisfactory, adequate,** decent, due; competent, up to the mark; commensurate, proportionate, corresponding 26.9; suitable, fit 26.10; good, **good enough,** plenty good enough [informal]; sufficient for *or* to *or* unto, up to, equal to; barely sufficient, minimal, minimum.

.7 **plentiful,** plenty, **plenteous,** plenitudinous, "plenty as blackberries" [Shakespeare]; **galore** [informal], in plenty, in quantity *or* quantities, aplenty [informal]; numerous 101.6; much, many 34.8; **ample,** all-sufficing; wholesale; well-stocked, well-provided, well-furnished, well-found; abundant, abounding, **copious,** exuberant, riotous; flush; **bountiful, bounteous, lavish, generous, liberal,** extravagant, prodigal; luxuriant, fertile, productive 165.9, **rich,** fat, **wealthy, opulent, affluent;** maximal; **full,** replete, well-filled, running over, overflowing; inexhaustible, exhaustless, bottomless; **profuse,** profusive, effuse, diffuse; **prevalent,** prevailing, rife, rampant, epidemic; teeming 101.9; **superabundant** 663.19; a dime a dozen.

.8 ADVS **sufficiently, amply,** substantially, **satisfactorily, enough;** competently, **adequately;** minimally.

.9 **plentifully,** plenteously, **aplenty** [informal], **in plenty,** in quantity *or* quantities, in good supply; **abundantly,** in abundance, copiously, no end [informal]; **superabundantly** 663.24; **bountifully,** bounteously, **lavishly, generously, liberally,** extravagantly, prodigally; maximally; **fully,** in full measure, to the full, overflowingly; inexhaustibly, exhaustlessly, bottomlessly; exuberantly, luxuriantly, riotously; richly, opulently, affluently; **profusely,** diffusely, effusely.

662. INSUFFICIENCY

.1 NOUNS **insufficiency, inadequacy,** insufficientness, inadequateness, –penia; short supply, seller's market, none to spare; nonsatisfaction, nonfulfillment, coming *or* falling short *or* shy; too little, too late; incompetence, unqualification, unsuitability 27.3.

.2 **meagerness,** exiguousness, exiguity, scrimpiness, skimpiness, scantiness, scantness, spareness; meanness, miserliness, niggardliness, narrowness [dial], stinginess, parsimony; smallness, slightness, puniness, paltriness; thinness, leanness, slimness, slim pickings [informal], slenderness, scrawniness; jejuneness, jejunity; austerity; Lenten fare.

.3 **scarcity,** scarceness; **sparsity,** sparseness; **scantiness,** scant sufficiency; **dearth, paucity,** poverty; **rarity,** rareness, uncommonness.

.4 **want, lack, need, deficiency, deficit, shortage,** shortfall, wantage, **incompleteness,** defectiveness, shortcoming 314, imperfection; **absence,** omission; **destitution,** impoverishment, beggary, deprivation; starvation, famine, drought.

.5 **pittance,** dole, scrimption [dial]; drop in the bucket; **mite,** bit 35.2; short allowance, short commons, half rations, cheeseparings and candle ends; mere subsistence, starvation wages.

.6 **dietary deficiency,** vitamin deficiency, **malnutrition** 686.10.

.7 VERBS **want, lack, need, require;** miss, feel the want of; run short of.

.8 **be insufficient,** not qualify, be found wanting, not make it [informal], kick the beam, not hack it [slang], **fall short,** fall shy, come short, not come up to; run short; want, lack, fail, fail of *or* in.

.9 ADJS **insufficient,** unsufficing, **inadequate,** hyp(o)–, mal–, olig(o)–, sub–, –privic; found wanting, defective, incomplete, imperfect, deficient, lacking, failing, wanting; too little, not enough; unsatisfactory, unsatisfying; unequal to, incompetent, unqualified, not up to snuff.

.10 **meager, slight,** scrimpy, scrimp, skimp, skimpy, exiguous; scant, **scanty,** spare; miserly, niggardly, stingy, narrow [dial], parsimonious, mean; austere, Lenten, Spartan, abstemious, ascetic; stinted, frugal, sparing; poor, impoverished; small, puny, paltry; thin, lean, slim, slender, scrawny; dwarfish, dwarfed, stunted; straitened, limited; jejune, watered, watery, unnourishing, unnutritious; subsistence, starvation.

.11 **scarce, sparse, scanty; in short supply,** at a premium; **rare,** uncommon; scarcer than hen's teeth [informal]; not to be had, not to be had for love or money, not to be had at any price; out of print, out of stock *or* season.

.12 **ill-provided,** ill-furnished, ill-equipped, ill-found, ill off; **unprovided,** unsupplied, unreplenished; bare-handed; unfed, underfed, undernourished; shorthanded, undermanned; **empty-handed, poor,** pauperized, impoverished, beggarly; starved, half-starved, on short commons, starving, starveling, famished.

.13 **wanting, lacking, needing, missing, in want of;** for want of, in default of, in the absence of; short, **short of,** scant of; shy, **shy of** *or* **on; out of,** destitute of, bare of, void of, empty of, devoid of, forlorn of, bereft of, deprived of, denuded of, unpossessed of, unblessed with, bankrupt in; out of pocket; at the end of one's rope *or* tether.

.14 ADVS **insufficiently; inadequately,** unsubstantially, incompletely.

.15 **meagerly, slightly,** sparely, punily, scantily, poorly, frugally, sparingly.

.16 **scarcely, sparsely, scantily,** skimpily, scrimpily; **rarely,** uncommonly.

.17 PREPS **without,** minus, less, sans.

663. EXCESS

.1 NOUNS **excess, excessiveness, inordinance,** inordinacy [archaic], inordinateness, nimiety, **immoderateness,** immoderacy, immoderation, **extravagance** *or* extravagancy, intemperateness, incontinence, overindulgence, **intemperance** 993; unrestrainedness, abandon; gluttony 994; **extreme,** extremity, **extremes; boundlessness** 104.1; overlargeness, overgreatness, monstrousness, enormousness 34.1; overgrowth, overdevelopment, hypertrophy, gigantism, giantism; **overmuch,** overmuchness, too much, too-muchness; exor-

bitance *or* exorbitancy, undueness, **outrageousness,** unconscionableness, **unreasonableness;** radicalism, extremism 745.4; egregiousness; fabulousness, hyperbole, **exaggeration** 617.

.2 **superabundance,** overabundance, **superflux, plethora,** redundancy, overprofusion, **overplentifulness,** overplenteousness, overplenty, **oversupply,** overaccumulation, **oversufficiency,** overmuchness, overcopiousness, overlavishness, overluxuriance, overbounteousness, overnumerousness; lavishness, **extravagance** *or* extravagancy, **prodigality; plenty** 661.2; **more than enough, enough and to spare,** enough in all conscience; **overdose,** overmeasure, "enough, with over-measure" [Shakespeare]; too much of a good thing, egg in one's beer [slang]; drug on the market; spate, avalanche, landslide, deluge, flood, inundation; *embarras de richesses* [Fr], money to burn [informal]; overpopulation.

.3 **overfullness,** plethora, **surfeit, glut;** satiety 664; engorgement, repletion, congestion; hyperemia, **saturation,** supersaturation; **overload,** overburden, overcharge, surcharge, overfreight, overweight; **overflow,** overbrimming, overspill.

.4 **superfluity,** superfluousness, fat; **redundancy,** redundance; unnecessariness, needlessness; featherbedding, payroll padding; duplication, duplication of effort, overlap; **luxury,** extravagance, frill *or* frills [both informal]; frippery, overadornment, bedizenment, gingerbread; **ornamentation, embellishment** 901.1; expletive, padding, filling; pleonasm, tautology; verbosity, prolixity 593.2; more than one really wants to know.

.5 **surplus,** surplusage, plus, **overplus,** overstock, **overage,** overset, overrun, **overmeasure, oversupply;** margin; **remainder, balance, leftover, extra, spare,** something extra *or* to spare; bonus, dividend, lagniappe [dial], gratuity, tip, *pourboire* [Fr].

.6 **overdoing,** overcarrying, **overreaching,** supererogation; overimportance, overemphasis; overuse; overreaction; **overwork, overexertion,** overexercise, overexpenditure, overtaxing, overstrain, tax, strain; too many irons in the fire, too much at once.

.7 **overextension, overdrawing,** drawing *or* spreading too thin, **overstretching,** overstrain, overstraining, stretching, straining, stretch, strain, tension, extreme tension, snapping or breaking point; **overexpansion;** inflation, distension, overdistension, 'swelling, bloat, bloating 197.2.

.8 VERBS **superabound,** overabound, **know no bounds, swarm,** pullulate, run riot, luxuriate, **teem;** overflow, flood, overbrim, overspill, spill over, overrun, overspread, overswarm, overgrow, fill; meet one at every turn; hang heavy on one's hands, remain on one's hands.

.9 **exceed, surpass, pass, transcend, go beyond;** overpass, overstep, overrun, **overreach,** overshoot, overshoot the mark.

.10 **overdo, go too far,** pass all bounds, know no bounds, overact, **carry too far,** overcarry, go to an extreme, **go to extremes, go overboard;** run into the ground; overemphasize, overstress; overplay, overplay one's hand [informal]; overreact, protest too much; overreach oneself; **overtax, overtask, overexert, overexercise, overstrain,** overdrive, overspend, exhaust, overexpend, overuse; overtrain; **overwork,** overlabor; overelaborate, overdevelop, tell more than one wants to know; overstudy; burn the candle at both ends; have too many irons in the fire, do too many things at once; **exaggerate** 617.3; **overindulge** 993.5.

.11 **pile it on,** lay it on, **lay it on thick,** lay it on with a trowel [slang].

.12 **carry coals to Newcastle,** teach fishes to swim, teach one's grandmother to suck eggs, kill the slain, beat or flog a dead horse, labor the obvious, butter one's bread on both sides, paint or gild the lily, "to gild refined gold, to paint the lily, to throw a perfume on the violet" [Shakespeare].

.13 **overextend, overdraw, overstretch, overstrain,** stretch, strain; reach the breaking or snapping point; **overexpand,** overdistend, overdevelop, inflate, swell 197.4.

.14 **oversupply, overprovide,** overlavish, overfurnish, overequip; **overstock;** overprovision, overprovender; overdose; flood the market, oversell; **flood, deluge, inundate,** engulf, swamp, whelm, overwhelm; lavish with, be prodigal with.

.15 **overload,** overlade, **overburden,** overweight, **overcharge,** surcharge; **overfill,** stuff, crowd, cram, jam, pack, jam-pack, **congest,** choke; **overstuff,** overfeed; gluttonize 994.4; **surfeit, glut, gorge,** satiate 664.4; **saturate,** soak, drench, supersaturate, supercharge.

.16 ADJS **excessive, inordinate,** arch–, hyper–, super–, sur–, ultra–; **immoderate,** over-

weening, **intemperate, extravagant,** incontinent; **unrestrained, unbridled,** abandoned; gluttonous 994.6; **extreme; overlarge, overgreat,** overbig, **monstrous,** enormous, gigantic 34.7; overgrown, overdeveloped, hypertrophied; **overmuch,** too much, a bit much; **exorbitant, undue, outrageous,** unconscionable, **unreasonable;** fancy or high or stiff or steep [all informal]; **out of bounds** or all bounds, out of sight or out of this world [both informal], **boundless** 104.3; egregious; fabulous, hyperbolic, **exaggerated** 617.4.

.17 **superfluous, redundant; excess, in excess;** unnecessary, unessential, nonessential, expendable, dispensable, **needless,** unneeded, gratuitous, uncalled-for; expletive; pleonastic, tautologous, tautologic(al); verbose, prolix 593.12; de trop [Fr], supererogatory, supererogative; spare, to spare; on one's hands.

.18 **surplus,** overplus; **remaining,** unused, **leftover; over,** over and above; **extra, spare,** supernumerary, for lagniappe [dial], as a bonus.

.19 **superabundant,** overabundant, plethoric, **overplentiful,** overplenteous, overplenty, **oversufficient, overmuch; lavish, prodigal,** overlavish, overbounteous, overgenerous, overliberal; overcopious, overluxuriant, riotous, overexuberant; overprolific, overnumerous; **swarming,** pullulating, **teeming,** overpopulated, overpopulous; plentiful 661.7.

.20 **overfull, overloaded, overladen, overburdened,** overfreighted, overfraught, overweighted, **overcharged,** surcharged, **saturated,** drenched, soaked, supersaturated, supercharged; **surfeited, glutted,** gorged, overfed, satiated 664.6, **stuffed,** overstuffed, **crowded, crammed,** jammed, packed, jam-packed; choked, **congested,** stuffed up; **overstocked, oversupplied; overflowing,** in spate, running over, filled to overflowing; plethoric, hyperemic; **bursting,** ready to burst, bursting at the seams, at the bursting point, overblown, distended, **swollen, bloated** 197.13.

.21 **overdone, overwrought;** overdrawn, overstretched, overstrained.

.22 ADVS **excessively, inordinately, immoderately, intemperately,** overweeningly, **overly, over, overmuch,** too much; **too,** too-too [informal]; **exorbitantly, unduly, unreasonably,** unconscionably, **outrageously.**

.23 **in** or **to excess, to extremes,** to the extreme, all out [informal], flat out [Brit informal], to a fault, too far, out of all proportion.

.24 **superabundantly**, overabundantly, **lavishly, prodigally, extravagantly**; more than enough, plentifully 661.9; without measure, out of measure, beyond measure.

.25 **superfluously, redundantly**, supererogatorily; tautologously; unnecessarily, needlessly, beyond need, beyond reason, overplus [archaic].

.26 PREPS **in excess of**, over, beyond, past, above, **over and above**, above and beyond.

664. SATIETY

.1 NOUNS **satiety, satiation, satisfaction, fullness, surfeit, glut**, repletion, engorgement; **fill, bellyful** or skinful [both informal], snootful [slang]; **saturation**, saturatedness, supersaturation; saturation point; more than enough, enough in all conscience, all one can stand or take; too much of a good thing, much of a muchness [informal].

.2 **satedness**, surfeitedness, cloyedness, jadedness; overfullness, fed-upness [informal].

.3 cloyer, surfeiter, sickener; **overdose**; a diet of cake; warmed-over cabbage, "cabbage repeatedly" [Juvenal].

.4 VERBS **satiate, sate, satisfy, slake, allay; surfeit, glut, gorge, engorge**; cloy, jade, pall; **fill**, fill up; saturate, oversaturate, supersaturate; **stuff, overstuff, cram; overfill**, overgorge, overdose, overfeed.

.5 **have enough**, have about enough of, have quite enough, **have one's fill**; have too much, have too much of a good thing, **have a bellyful** or skinful [informal], have a snootful [slang], have an overdose of, be fed up [informal], have all one can take or stand, have it up to here [informal], have had it.

.6 ADJS **satiated, sated, satisfied**, slaked, allayed; **surfeited, gorged**, replete, engorged, **glutted; cloyed**, jaded; **full, full of**, with one's fill of, **overfull**, saturated, oversaturated, supersaturated; **stuffed**, overstuffed, crammed, overgorged, overfed; **fed-up** or fed to the gills or fed to the teeth [all informal], stuffed to the gills [informal]; **with a bellyful** or skinful [informal], with a snootful [slang], with enough of; disgusted, **sick of**, tired of, sick and tired of.

.7 **satiating**, sating, satisfying, filling; surfeiting, overfilling; jading, **cloying**, cloysome.

665. USE

.1 NOUNS **use, employment**, employ [archaic], **usage; exercise, exertion**, active use; good use; ill use, wrong use, misuse 667; hard use, hard or rough usage; **application**, appliance; using up, **consumption** 666.

.2 **usage, treatment, handling**, management; way or means of dealing; stewardship, custodianship, guardianship, care.

.3 **utility, usefulness, usability, use**, utilizability, **serviceability**, helpfulness, functionality, profitability, applicability, availability, **practicability**, practicality, practical utility, operability, **effectiveness**, efficacy, efficiency.

.4 **benefit, use, service, avail, profit, advantage**, point, percentage [informal], what's in it for one [slang], convenience; interest, behalf, behoof; **value, worth**.

.5 **function, use, purpose**, role, end use, immediate purpose, ultimate purpose, operational purpose, operation; work, duty, office.

.6 **functionalism, utilitarianism**; pragmatism, pragmaticism; functional design, functional furniture or housing, etc.

.7 [law terms] usufruct, imperfect usufruct, perfect usufruct, right of use, user, enjoyment of property; *jus primae noctis* [L], *droit du seigneur* [Fr].

.8 **utilization**, using; **employment**, management, manipulation, handling, working, operation, **exploitation**.

.9 **user**, employer; **consumer**, enjoyer.

.10 VERBS **use, utilize, make use of**, do with; **employ**, practice, ply, work, manage, handle, manipulate, operate, **wield**, play; **have or enjoy the use of**; exercise, **exert**.

.11 **apply, put to use**, carry out, put into execution, **put in practice** or operation, put in force, enforce; bring to bear upon.

.12 **treat, handle**, manage, use, **deal with**, cope with, contend with, do with; steward, care for.

.13 **spend**, consume, expend, **pass, employ, put in**; devote, bestow, give to or give over to, devote or consecrate or dedicate to; while, while away, wile; use up 666.2.

.14 **avail oneself of**, resort to, have recourse to, turn to, look to, recur to, refer to, take to [informal], betake oneself to; revert to, fall back upon; convert or turn to use, put in or into requisition, press or enlist into service, impress, call or bring into play.

.15 **take advantage of, make the most of**, use

to the full, make good use of, improve, **turn to use** or **profit** or **account** or **good account,** turn to one's advantage, use to advantage, put to advantage, find one's account or advantage in; improve the occasion 129.8; **profit by, benefit from,** reap the benefit of; **exploit, capitalize on, make capital of,** make a good thing of [informal], make hay [informal], **trade on,** cash in on [informal]; make the best of, make a virtue of necessity.

.16 (take unfair advantage of) **exploit, take advantage of, use,** make use of, **use for one's own ends;** make a pawn or cat's-paw of, play for a sucker [slang]; **manipulate,** work on, work upon, stroke, play on or upon; **impose upon,** presume upon; use ill, ill-use, abuse, misuse 667.4,5; milk, bleed, bleed white [informal]; drain, suck the blood of or from, suck dry; exploit one's position, feather one's nest [informal].

.17 **avail,** be of use, serve, **suffice,** do, answer, answer or serve the purpose, serve one's need, fill the bill or do the trick [both informal]; bestead [archaic], **stand one in stead** or **good stead,** be handy, stand one in hand [dial]; advantage, be of advantage or service to; **profit, benefit,** pay or pay off [both informal], give good returns, yield a profit.

.18 ADJS **useful,** employable, of use, of service, **serviceable,** commodious [archaic]; good for; **helpful,** of help 785.21; **advantageous,** beneficial 674.12; **practical,** banausic, pragmatical, **functional, utilitarian,** of general utility or application; **fitting,** proper, appropriate, expedient 670.5.

.19 **handy, convenient; available,** accessible, **ready, at hand,** to hand, **on hand,** on tap, **on deck** [informal], on call, at one's call or beck and call, at one's elbow, at one's fingertips, just around the corner, at one's disposal; versatile, adaptable, all-around [informal], of all work.

.20 **effectual, effective,** active, efficient, efficacious, operative.

.21 **valuable,** of value, **profitable,** yielding a return, well-spent, **worthwhile,** rewarding; gainful, remunerative 811.15.

.22 **usable, utilizable; applicable,** appliable; practical, operable; **reusable; exploitable;** manipulable, pliable, compliant 765.12–14.

.23 **used, employed,** exercised, exerted, **applied,** techno–; secondhand 123.18.

.24 **in use, in practice,** in force, in effect, in service, in operation, in commission.

.25 ADVS **usefully,** to good use; **profitably, advantageously, to advantage,** to profit, to good effect; **effectually, effectively,** efficiently; **serviceably, functionally, practically;** handily, conveniently.

666. CONSUMPTION

.1 NOUNS **consumption, using** or **eating up;** burning up; absorption, assimilation, digestion, ingestion, **expenditure,** expending, spending; squandering, wastefulness 854.1; finishing; **depletion,** drain, **exhaustion,** impoverishment, waste, wastage, wasting away, erosion, ablation, wearing down, wearing away, attrition.

.2 VERBS **consume, spend, expend, use up;** absorb, assimilate, digest, ingest, eat, **eat up,** swallow, swallow up, gobble, gobble up; burn up; **finish,** finish off; **exhaust, deplete,** impoverish, drain, drain of resources; suck dry, bleed white [informal], suck one's blood; wear away, erode, ablate; waste away; squander 854.3,4.

.3 **be consumed,** be used up, waste; **run out, give out,** peter out [informal]; run dry, dry up.

.4 ADJS **used up, consumed,** eaten up, burnt up; finished, gone; **spent,** exhausted, effete, dissipated, depleted, impoverished, drained, worn-out; worn away, eroded, ablated; **wasted** 854.9.

.5 **consumable, expendable,** spendable; replaceable; disposable, throwaway, no-deposit, no-deposit-no-return.

667. MISUSE

.1 NOUNS **misuse, misusage, abuse; misemployment, misapplication; mishandling,** mismanagement, poor stewardship; corrupt administration, malversation, breach of public trust, maladministration; diversion, defalcation, misappropriation, conversion, **embezzlement,** peculation, pilfering; perversion, prostitution; profanation, violation, pollution, fouling, befoulment, desecration, defilement, debasement; malpractice, abuse of office, misconduct, malfeasance, misfeasance.

.2 **mistreatment, ill-treatment, maltreatment, ill-use,** ill-usage, **abuse;** molestation, violation, outrage, violence, injury, atrocity; cruel and unusual punishment.

.3 **persecution,** oppression, harrying, hounding, tormenting, harassment, victimization; **witch-hunting,** witch-hunt, red-baiting [informal], McCarthyism.

.4 VERBS **misuse, misemploy, abuse, misapply; mishandle,** mismanage, maladminister; divert, misappropriate, convert, defalcate [archaic], embezzle, pilfer, peculate, feather one's nest [informal]; pervert, prostitute; profane, violate, pollute, foul, foul one's own nest, befoul, desecrate, defile, debase.

.5 **mistreat, maltreat, ill-treat, ill-use, abuse,** injure, molest; do wrong to, do wrong by; outrage, do violence to, do one's worst to; mishandle, manhandle; buffet, batter, bruise, savage, maul, knock about, rough, rough up.

.6 **persecute,** oppress, **torment,** victimize, **harass,** molest, harry, hound, beset; pursue, hunt 654.8,9.

668. DISUSE

.1 NOUNS **disuse, disusage, desuetude; nonuse,** nonemployment, abstinence, abstention; nonprevalence, unprevalence; **obsolescence,** obsoleteness, obsoletism, obsoletion; superannuation, retirement, pensioning off.

.2 **discontinuance,** cessation, desistance; relinquishment, forbearance, resignation, renunciation, renouncement, abjurement, abjuration; waiver, nonexercise; abeyance, suspension, cold storage [informal]; **abandonment** 633.

.3 **discard, discarding,** jettison, deep six [slang], disposal, dumping; **scrapping, junking** [informal]; removal, elimination 77.2; **rejection** 638; **reject,** throwaway, castaway, castoff, rejectamenta [pl]; refuse 669.4,5.

.4 VERBS **cease to use,** relinquish, **discontinue, disuse,** quit, stop, drop [informal], give up, give over, put behind one, let go, leave off, come off [slang], cut out, desist, have done with; waive [archaic], resign, renounce, abjure; nol-pros, not pursue with or proceed with.

.5 **not use, do without,** dispense with, **let alone,** not touch, hold off; **abstain, refrain,** forgo, forbear, spare, waive; keep or hold back, reserve, save, keep in hand, have up one's sleeve.

.6 **put away,** lay away, **put aside,** lay or set or push aside, sideline [informal], lay or set by; stow, store 660.10; **pigeonhole, shelve,** put on the shelf, put in mothballs; **table,** lay on the table; table the motion, pass to the order of the day; postpone, delay 132.8.

.7 **discard, reject, throw away, throw out,** chuck [informal], eighty-six [slang], cast, cast off or away or aside; **get rid of,** get quit of, get shut or shet of [dial], rid oneself of, **dispose of,** slough, **dump, ditch** [informal], **jettison, throw** or **heave** or **toss overboard,** deep-six [slang], throw out the window, throw or cast to the dogs, cast to the winds; throw over, jilt; part with, give away; **abandon** 633.5; remove, eliminate 77.5.

.8 **scrap, junk** [informal], consign to the scrap heap, throw on the junk heap [informal]; superannuate, retire, pension off, put out to pasture or grass.

.9 **obsolesce,** fall into disuse, go out, pass away; be superseded; superannuate.

.10 ADJS **disused, abandoned,** deserted, **discontinued,** done with; out, **out of use;** old; relinquished, resigned, renounced, abjured; **outworn,** worn-out, past use, not worth saving; **obsolete,** obsolescent, superannuated, superannuate; superseded, outdated, out-of-date, outmoded; retired, pensioned off; on the shelf; antique, antiquated, old-fashioned, archaic.

.11 **discarded,** rejected, **cast-off,** castaway.

.12 **unused,** unutilized, **unemployed,** unapplied, unexercised; in abeyance, suspended; waived; **unspent,** unexpended, unconsumed; held back, held out, put by, put aside, saved, held in reserve, in hand, spare, to spare, extra, reserve; stored 660.14; untouched, unhandled; untapped; untrodden, unbeaten; **new,** original, pristine, fresh, mint.

669. USELESSNESS

.1 NOUNS **uselessness,** inutility; **needlessness,** unnecessity; unserviceability, **unusability,** unemployability, inoperativeness, inoperability, disrepair; unhelpfulness; inapplicability, unsuitability, unfitness; functionlessness; otiosity; **superfluousness** 663.4.

.2 **futility,** vanity, emptiness, hollowness; **fruitlessness,** bootlessness, unprofitableness, profitlessness, unprofitability, otiosity, worthlessness, valuelessness; triviality, nugacity; unproductiveness 166; **ineffectuality,** ineffectiveness, inefficacy 158.3; impotence 158.1; **pointlessness,** meaninglessness, purposelessness, aimlessness, fecklessness; the absurd, absurdity; inanity, fatuity; vicious circle; **rat race** [informal].

.3 **labor in vain,** labor lost, labor of Sisyphus; work of Penelope, Penelope's web; **wild-goose chase,** snipe hunt, bootless errand; waste of labor, waste of breath, waste of time.

.4 **refuse, waste,** wastage, waste matter, offal; **leavings,** sweepings, dust [Brit], scraps, orts; garbage, gash [slang], swill, slop, slops, hogwash [informal]; draff, lees, **dregs** 43.2; **offscourings**, scourings, rinsings, dishwater; parings, raspings, filings, shavings; **scum;** chaff, stubble, husks; weeds, tares; deadwood; rags, bones, wastepaper, shards, potsherds; scrap iron; slag, culm, slack.

.5 **rubbish, rubble, trash, junk** [informal], shoddy, riffraff, raff [Brit dial], **scrap,** dust [Brit], **debris, litter,** lumber, clamjamfry [Scot], truck [informal].

.6 **trash pile,** rubbish heap, dustheap, midden, kitchen midden; wasteyard, **junkyard** [informal], **dump.**

.7 wastepaper basket, wastebasket; wastebin, garbage can, dustbin [Brit], trash can.

.8 VERBS **labor in vain,** go on a **wild-goose chase,** beat the air, lash the waves, tilt at windmills, sow the sand, bay at the moon, waste one's breath, preach *or* speak to the winds, beat *or* flog a dead horse, roll the stone of Sisyphus, milk the ram, milk a he-goat into a sieve, pour water into a sieve, hold a farthing candle to the sun, look for a needle in a haystack, lock the barn door after the horse is stolen.

.9 ADJS **useless,** of no use, no go [informal]; **aimless,** meaningless, **purposeless,** of no purpose, **pointless,** feckless; **unavailing,** of no avail; ineffective, **ineffectual** 158.15; impotent 158.13–19; **superfluous** 663.17.

.10 **needless, unnecessary, unessential,** nonessential, **unneeded, uncalled-for,** unrequired.

.11 **worthless, valueless, good-for-nothing,** good-for-naught, no-good *or* NG [both informal], no-account [dial], dear at any price, worthless as tits on a boar [dial], not worthwhile, not worth having, not worth mentioning *or* speaking of, not worth a thought, not worth a rap *or* a continental *or* a damn, not worth the powder to blow it to hell, not worth the powder and shot, not worth the pains, of no earthly use, fit for the junk yard [informal]; trivial, nugatory, nugacious; **junk** *or* **junky** [both informal]; **cheap,** shoddy, trashy, **shabby** 673.18.

.12 **fruitless,** gainless, profitless, bootless, otiose, **unprofitable,** unremunerative, nonremunerative, **unrewarding,** rewardless; abortive; barren, sterile, **unproductive** 166.4.

.13 **vain, futile,** hollow, empty, "weary, stale, flat, and unprofitable" [Shakespeare], idle; absurd; inane, fatuous, fatuitous.

.14 **unserviceable, unusable,** unemployable, inoperative, inoperable, unworkable; out of order, out of whack [informal], in disrepair; **unhelpful,** unconducive; inapplicable; unsuitable, unfit; functionless, nonfunctional, otiose, nonutilitarian.

.15 ADVS **uselessly; needlessly,** unnecessarily; bootlessly, fruitlessly; **futilely, vainly;** purposelessly, to little purpose, to no purpose, **aimlessly, pointlessly,** fecklessly.

670. EXPEDIENCE

.1 NOUNS **expedience** *or* **expediency,** advisability, politicness, **desirability,** recommendability; **fitness, fittingness, appropriateness,** propriety, decency [archaic], seemliness, **suitability,** rightness, feasibility, **convenience;** seasonableness, timeliness, **opportuneness; usefulness** 665.3; **advantage, advantageousness,** beneficialness, **profit,** profitability, percentage [informal], worthwhileness, fruitfulness; wisdom, **prudence** 467.5–7.

.2 **expedient, means,** means to an end, **measure, step, action,** effort, **stroke,** stroke of policy, coup, **move, countermove,** maneuver, demarche, course of action; tactic, **device, contrivance,** artifice, **stratagem, shift; gimmick** *or* dodge *or* trick [all informal]; **resort,** resource; answer, solution; working proposition, working hypothesis; **temporary expedient, improvisation,** ad hoc measure, jury-rigged expedient, **makeshift,** stopgap, shake-up, jury-rig; **last expedient, last resort** *or* resource, *pis aller* [Fr], last shift, trump.

.3 VERBS **expedite one's affair,** work to one's advantage, not come amiss, be just the thing, be just what the doctor ordered [informal]; forward, advance, promote, profit, advantage, benefit; **work,** serve, answer, fill the bill *or* do the trick [both informal]; suit the occasion, **be fitting,** fit, befit, be right.

.4 **make shift, make do,** make out [dial], cope, **manage,** manage with, get along on, get by on, do with; do as well as one can.

.5 ADJS **expedient, desirable,** to be desired, much to be desired, **advisable, politic,** recommendable; **appropriate, meet, fit,** fitten [dial], **fitting,** befitting, **right, proper,** good, decent [archaic], **becoming,** seemly, likely, congruous, **suitable,** sortable, feasible, **convenient,** happy, felicitous; timely, seasonable, opportune, welltimed; **useful** 665.18; **advantageous,** favorable; **profitable,** fructuous, worthwhile, worth one's while; **wise** 467.17–19.

.6 **practical,** practicable, pragmatic(al), banausic; feasible, workable, operable, realizable; **efficient,** effective, **effectual** 665.20.

.7 **makeshift,** makeshifty, **stopgap,** band-aid [informal], improvised, improvisational, **jury-rigged; ad hoc;** temporary, provisional, tentative.

.8 ADVS **expediently, fittingly, fitly, appropriately, suitably,** sortably, congruously, rightly, properly, decently [archaic], feasibly, conveniently; practically; seasonably, opportunely; desirably, advisably; advantageously, to advantage, all to the good.

671. INEXPEDIENCE

.1 NOUNS inexpedience or inexpediency, **undesirability, inadvisability,** impoliticness or impoliticalness; unwiseness 470.2; **unfitness, unfittingness, inappropriateness, unsuitability,** incongruity, **unmeetness,** wrongness, unseemliness, inconvenience or inconveniency [both archaic], ineptitude, inaptitude; unseasonableness, untimeliness, inopportuneness; unfortunateness, infelicity; disadvantageousness, unprofitableness, unprofitability, worthlessness, futility, uselessness 669.

.2 **disadvantage, drawback, liability; detriment,** impairment, prejudice, loss, damage, hurt, harm, mischief, injury; step backward, loss of ground; **handicap** 730.6.

.3 **inconvenience,** discommodity, incommodity, disaccommodation [archaic], **trouble, bother;** inconvenientness, inconveniency, **unhandiness,** awkwardness, clumsiness, unwieldiness, troublesomeness.

.4 VERBS **inconvenience,** put to inconvenience, **put out, discommode,** incommode, disaccommodate [archaic], disoblige, **trouble, bother,** put to trouble, **impose upon;** harm, disadvantage 675.6.

.5 ADJS **inexpedient, undesirable, inadvisable,** impolitic(al), not to be recommended; **ill-advised, ill-considered, unwise** 470.9; **unfit, unfitting,** unbefitting, **inappropriate, unsuitable,** unmeet, inapt, inept, unseemly, improper, wrong, bad, out of place, incongruous, ill-suited; malapropos, mal à propos [Fr], inopportune, untimely, ill-timed, unseasonable; infelicitous, unfortunate, unhappy; unprofitable 669.12; futile 669.13.

.6 **disadvantageous,** unadvantageous, **unfavorable;** unprofitable, unrewarding, worthless, useless 669.9–11; **detrimental,** deleterious, injurious, harmful, prejudicial, disserviceable.

.7 **inconvenient, incommodious,** discommodious; **unhandy, awkward,** clumsy, unwieldy, troublesome.

.8 ADVS **inexpediently, inadvisably,** impoliticly or impolitically, **undesirably; unfittingly, inappropriately, unsuitably,** ineptly, inaptly, incongruously; inopportunely, unseasonably; infelicitously, unfortunately, unhappily.

.9 **disadvantageously,** unadvantageously, unprofitably, unrewardingly; uselessly 669.15; **inconveniently,** unhandily, with difficulty, ill.

672. IMPORTANCE

.1 NOUNS **importance, significance, consequence,** consideration, **import,** note, mark, **moment, weight;** materiality; concern, concernment, interest; **first order,** high order, high rank; **priority,** primacy, precedence, preeminence, paramountcy, superiority, **supremacy;** value, worth, merit, excellence 674.1; emphasis, stress, accent; consequentiality, self-importance 909.1.

.2 **notability, noteworthiness,** remarkableness, salience, memorability; **prominence, eminence, greatness,** distinction; prestige, esteem, repute, reputation, honor, glory, renown, dignity, fame 914.1.

.3 **gravity, seriousness,** solemnity, weightiness; no joke, no laughing matter.

.4 **urgency,** imperativeness, exigency; **press,** pressure, high pressure, **stress,** tension, **pinch;** clutch or crunch [both informal]; **crisis, emergency.**

.5 **matter of importance,** thing of interest, point of interest, matter of concern, object of note, one for the book or something to write home about [both informal], something special; vital concern or interest, matter of life or death; notabilia, memorabilia, great doings.

.6 **salient point,** cardinal point, high point, great point; important thing, chief thing, **the point, main point,** main thing, essential matter, **essence,** the bottom line [informal], substance, gravamen, *sine qua non* [L], issue, real issue, prime issue, name of the game [informal]; **essential,** fundamental, substantive point, material point; **gist, nub** [informal], **heart,** meat, pith, kernel, **core; crux,** crucial or pivitol or critical point, pivot; turning point, climax, crisis; keystone, cornerstone; landmark, milestone, bench mark.

.7 **feature, highlight,** high spot, outstanding feature.

.8 **personage, important person,** person of importance *or* consequence, **great man,** big man [informal], man of mark *or* note, **somebody,** something [informal], **notable,** notability, figure; **celebrity,** famous person, person of renown, lion [informal], personality; name, big name, big gun [informal]; nabob, **mogul,** panjandrum, person to be reckoned with, very important person, **VIP** [informal], **bigwig** [informal]; sachem; brass hat [informal]; **worthy,** pillar of society, elder, father; **dignitary,** dignity; **magnate;** tycoon [informal], baron; **power;** power elite, Establishment; interests; brass, top brass; top people, the great; ruling circle, lords of creation, "the choice and master spirits of the age" [Shakespeare]; the top, the summit.

.9 [slang terms] **big shot,** wheel, **big wheel,** big cheese, big noise, big-timer, big-time operator, **high-muck-a-muck** *or* high-muckety-muck, his nibs; big man on campus, BMOC.

.10 **chief, principal,** paramount, biggest frog in the pond [slang]; honcho [slang], top dog *or* Mr. Big [both slang]; **king,** electronics king, etc.; leading light, luminary, master spirit, **star,** superstar, prima donna, lead 612.6.

.11 VERBS **matter,** import [archaic], signify, **count, tell, weigh, carry weight,** cut ice *or* cut some ice [both informal], be prominent, stand out, mean much; be something, be somebody, amount to something; have a key to the executive washroom; be featured, star, get top billing.

.12 **value, esteem, treasure, prize,** appreciate, **rate highly,** think highly of, think well of, **think much of,** set store by; give *or* attach *or* ascribe importance to; make much of, make a fuss *or* stir about, make an ado *or* much ado about.

.13 **emphasize, stress,** lay emphasis *or* stress upon, place emphasis on, give emphasis to, **accent, accentuate, punctuate, point up,** bring to the fore, put in the foreground; **highlight,** spotlight; **star, underline, underscore,** italicize; overemphasize, overstress, overaccentuate, rub in; harp on; dwell on, belabor; attach too much importance to, make a federal case of, make a mountain out of a molehill.

.14 **feature,** headline [informal]; **star,** give top billing to.

.15 **dramatize, play up** [informal], splash, make a production of.

.16 ADJS **important, major, consequential, momentous, significant, considerable, substantial, material, great,** grand, big; **superior,** world-shaking, earthshaking; bigtime *or* big-league *or* major-league *or* heavyweight [all informal]; high-powered [informal], double-barreled [slang]; bigwig *or* bigwigged [both informal]; name *or* big-name [both informal], self-important 909.8.

.17 **of importance, of significance, of consequence,** of note, of moment, of weight; of concern, of concernment, of interest, not to be overlooked *or* despised, not to be sneezed at [informal]; viable.

.18 **notable, noteworthy, celebrated, remarkable, marked,** of mark, signal; **memorable,** rememberable, unforgettable, never to be forgotten; **striking,** telling, salient; **eminent, prominent,** conspicuous, noble, **outstanding, distinguished;** prestigious, esteemed, estimable, reputable 914.15–19; **extraordinary, out of the ordinary,** exceptional, special, rare.

.19 **weighty, heavy, grave,** sober, **solemn, serious,** earnest; portentous, fateful, fatal; formidable, awe-inspiring, imposing.

.20 **emphatic, decided, positive, forceful,** forcible; **emphasized, stressed,** accented, accentuated, punctuated, pointed; underlined, underscored, starred, italicized; in red letters, in letters of fire.

.21 **urgent, imperative,** imperious, **compelling, pressing,** high-priority, high-pressure, crying, clamorous, insistent, instant, exigent; crucial, critical, pivotal, acute.

.22 **vital,** of vital importance, life-and-death *or* life-or-death; **essential, fundamental,** indispensable, basic, substantive, bedrock, material; **central, focal.**

.23 **paramount, principal, leading, foremost, main, chief,** premier, **prime, primary,** preeminent, **supreme,** capital [archaic], cardinal; **highest, uppermost, topmost,** toprank, ranking, of the first rank, **dominant, predominant,** master, controlling, **overruling,** overriding, all-absorbing.

.24 ADVS **importantly, significantly,** consequentially, materially, momentously, greatly, grandly; eminently, prominently, conspicuously, outstandingly, saliently, signally, notably, markedly, remarkably.

673. UNIMPORTANCE

.1 NOUNS **unimportance, insignificance,** inconsequence, inconsequentiality, indifference, **immateriality**; inessentiality; ineffectuality; unnoteworthiness, unimpressiveness; inferiority, secondariness, low order of importance, low priority; marginality; **smallness**, littleness, slightness, inconsiderableness, negligibility; **pettiness**, puniness, pokiness, picayune, picayunishness; irrelevance 10.1.

.2 **paltriness**, poorness, **meanness**, sorriness, sadness, pitifulness, contemptibleness, pitiableness, despicableness, miserableness, wretchedness, vileness, crumminess [slang], shabbiness, shoddiness, cheapness, beggarliness, worthlessness, unworthiness, meritlessness; meretriciousness, gaudiness 904.3.

.3 **triviality**, trivialness, triflingness, nugacity; **superficiality**, shallowness; slightness, slenderness, flimsiness; **frivolity**, frivolousness, lightness, levity; **foolishness**, silliness; inanity, emptiness, vacuity; triteness, vapidity; vanity, idleness, futility; **much ado about nothing**, tempest or storm in a teacup or teapot, much cry and little wool, big deal [slang].

.4 **trivia**, **trifles**; **trumpery**, gimcrackery, knickknackery, bric-a-brac; **rubbish**, trash, chaff; peanuts, chicken feed or chickenshit [both slang], small change; small beer; froth, "trifles light as air" [Shakespeare]; minutiae, details, minor details.

.5 **trifle**, **triviality**, bagatelle, fribble, **gimcrack**, gewgaw, frippery, **trinket**, bibelot, curio, **bauble**, gaud, toy, **knickknack**, knickknackery, kickshaw, minikin [archaic], whim-wham, folderol; pin, button, hair, straw, rush, feather, fig, bean, hill of beans [informal], molehill, row of pins or buttons [informal], sneeshing [Brit dial], pinch of snuff; bit, snap; a curse, a continental, a hoot [informal], a damn, a darn, shit [slang], a tinker's damn; picayune, rap, sou, halfpenny, farthing, brass farthing, cent, red cent, two cents, twopence or tuppence [both Brit]; peppercorn; drop in the ocean, drop in the bucket; fleabite, pinprick; joke, jest, farce, mockery, child's play.

.6 **insignificancy**, inessential, marginal matter or affair, trivial or paltry affair, small or trifling or minor matter, **no great matter**; a little thing, peu de chose [Fr], hardly or scarcely anything, matter of no importance or consequence, matter of indifference; **nothing**, **naught**, mere nothing, nothing in particular, nothing to signify, nothing to speak or worth speaking of, nothing to think twice about, nothing

to boast of, nothing to write home about, thing of naught, rien du tout [Fr], nullity, nihility; **technicality**.

.7 **a nobody**, **insignificancy**, jackstraw [archaic], **little fellow**, little guy [informal], **man in the street**; common man 79.3; **nonentity**, nebbish [informal], obscurity, a nothing, cipher, "an O without a figure" [Shakespeare], nobody one knows; lightweight, mediocrity; whippersnapper, whiffet, pip-squeak, squirt, shrimp, scrub, runt [all informal]; squit [Brit informal], punk [slang]; small potato, small potatoes; man of straw, dummy, figurehead 749.4; **small fry**, Mr. and Mrs. Nobody, John Doe and Richard Roe or Mary Roe; Tom, Dick, and Harry; Brown, Jones, and Robinson.

.8 **trifling**, dallying, **dalliance**, flirtation, coquetry; toying, fiddling, playing, fooling, monkeying or monkeying around [both informal], horsing or fooling or kidding or messing or playing or screwing or mucking or farting around [informal]; jerking off [slang]; **puttering**, tinkering, pottering, piddling; dabbling, smattering; loitering, idling 708.4.

.9 **trifler**, **dallier**, fribble; **putterer**, potterer, piddler, smatterer, dabbler; amateur, dilettante, Sunday painter; **flirt, coquet**.

.10 VERBS **be unimportant**, be of no importance, not signify, **not matter**, not count, cut no ice [informal], signify nothing, matter little, **not make any difference**; **not amount to anything**, not amount to a hill of beans [informal], not amount to a damn [slang].

.11 **attach little importance to**, give little weight to; make little of, underplay, de-emphasize, downplay, play down, minimize, **make light of**, think little of, **make** or **think nothing of**, take no account of, set little by, set no store by, set at naught; snap one's fingers at; not care a straw about; not give a shit or a hoot or two hoots for [slang], not give a damn about, not give a dime a dozen for; deprecate, depreciate 971.8.

.12 **make much ado about nothing**, make mountains out of molehills, have a storm or tempest in a teacup or teapot.

.13 **trifle**, **dally**; **flirt, coquet**; toy, fiddle, fiddle-faddle [informal], fribble, frivol [informal], **play, fool**, monkey or **monkey around** [both informal], horse or fool or play or mess or kid or screw or muck or fart around [informal]; jerk off [slang], **putter, potter**, tinker, piddle; dabble, smatter; toy with, fiddle with, fool with, play with, finger with, fidget with, twiddle; idle, loiter 708.11–13.

.14 ADJS **unimportant, of no importance,** of little or small importance, of no great importance, **of no account,** of no significance, of no concern, of no matter, of little or no consequence, no great shakes [informal]; no skin off one's nose or elbow [informal]; inferior, secondary, of a low order of importance, low-priority; marginal.

.15 **insignificant, inconsequential, immaterial;** nonessential, unessential, inessential, **not vital,** back-burner [informal], dispensable; unnoteworthy, unimpressive; **inconsiderable,** inappreciable, negligible; **small, little,** minute, dinky [slang], petit [archaic], minor, inferior; technical; irrelevant 10.6.

.16 **trivial, trifling;** fribble, fribbling, nugacious, nugatory; catchpenny; **slight,** slender, flimsy; **superficial, shallow; frivolous, light,** windy, airy, frothy; idle, futile, vain, otiose; **foolish,** fatuous, asinine, **silly; inane,** empty, vacuous; trite, vapid; unworthy of serious consideration.

.17 **petty, puny,** measly [slang], **poky, piddling,** piffling, niggling, pettifogging, picayune, picayunish; **small-time** or two-bit or tinhorn or punk [all slang]; **one-horse** or **two-by-four** or jerkwater [all informal]; small-beer.

.18 **paltry, poor,** common, **mean, sorry, sad, pitiful,** pitiable, pathetic, **despicable, contemptible,** beneath contempt, **miserable, wretched,** beggarly, vile, **shabby,** scrubby, scruffy, shoddy, scurvy, scuzzy [slang], scummy, **crummy** or cheesy [both slang], **trashy,** rubbishy, garbagey [informal], trumpery, gimcracky [informal]; tinpot [slang]; **cheap,** worthless, valueless, twopenny or twopenny-halfpenny [both Brit], two-for-a-cent or -penny, dime-a-dozen; meretricious, gaudy 904.20.

.19 **unworthy, worthless,** meritless, unworthy of regard or consideration, beneath notice.

.20 ADVS **unimportantly, insignificantly, inconsequentially,** immaterially, unessentially; **pettily,** paltrily; **trivially,** triflingly; superficially, shallowly; frivolously, lightly, idly.

.21 PHRS **it does not matter,** it matters not, it does not signify, **it is of no consequence** or **importance, it makes no difference,** it cannot be helped, it is all the same; n'importe, de rien, ça ne fait rien [all Fr]; it will all come out in the wash [informal], it will be all the same a hundred years from now.

.22 **no matter, never mind,** think no more of it, do not give it another or a second thought, don't lose any sleep over it, let it pass, let it go [informal], ignore it, forget it [informal], skip it or drop it [both slang].

.23 **what does it matter?, what matter?, what's the difference?,** what's the diff? [slang], what do I care?, what of it?, what boots it?, what's the odds?, so what?, what else is new?; for aught one cares, big deal [informal].

674. GOODNESS

(good quality or effect)

.1 NOUNS **goodness, excellence, quality, class** [informal]; **virtue,** grace; **merit,** desert; **value, worth; fineness,** goodliness, fairness, niceness; **superiority,** first-rateness, **skillfulness** 733.1; wholeness, **soundness,** healthiness 683.1; **virtuousness** 980.1; **kindness, benevolence,** benignity 938.1; beneficialness, helpfulness 785.10; favorableness, auspiciousness 544.9; expedience, advantageousness 670.1; **usefulness** 665.3; pleasantness, agreeableness 863.1; cogency, validity 516.4; profitableness, rewardingness 811.4.

.2 **superexcellence,** supereminence, preeminence, supremacy, primacy, paramountcy, peerlessness, unsurpassedness, matchlessness, superfineness; **superbness,** exquisiteness, **magnificence,** splendidness, splendiferousness, marvelousness.

.3 **tolerableness,** tolerability, goodishness, passableness, fairishness, **adequateness, satisfactoriness,** acceptability, admissibility; sufficiency 661.

.4 **good, welfare,** well-being, **benefit; interest, advantage; behalf,** behoof; blessing, benison, boon; **profit,** avail [archaic], gain; world of good.

.5 **good thing,** a thing to be desired, "a consummation devoutly to be wish'd" [Shakespeare]; **treasure, gem, jewel,** diamond, pearl; **boast, pride, pride and joy; prize, trophy,** plum; **winner** [informal]; **catch, find** [informal], trouvaille [Fr]; **godsend, windfall.**

.6 **first-rater** or **topnotcher** [both informal]; **wonder, prodigy, genius, star, superstar; luminary, leading light,** one in a thousand.

.7 [slang or informal terms] **dandy, jim-**

dandy, dilly, humdinger, **pip**, **pippin**, **peach**, ace, beaut, **lulu**, **daisy**, darb, honey, sweetheart, dream, lollapaloosa, corker, whiz, **crackerjack**, knockout, killer-diller, the nuts, the cat's pajamas or meow.

.8 **the best**, the very best, the best ever, the tops [informal]; **quintessence**, prime, optimum, superlative; **choice**, **pick**, **select**, elect, elite, *corps d'élite* [Fr], chosen; **cream**, **flower**, fat; cream of the crop, *crème de la crème* [Fr], salt of the earth; *pièce de résistance* [Fr]; prize, champion, queen; nonesuch, paragon, nonpareil; gem of the first water.

.9 **harmlessness**, hurtlessness, uninjuriousness, **innocuousness**, benignity, benignancy; unobnoxiousness, inoffensiveness; innocence.

.10 VERBS **do good**, profit, avail; do a world of good; **benefit**, **help**, serve, advance, advantage, favor 785.11–19; be the making of, make a man of; do no harm, break no bones.

.11 **be as good as**, equal, emulate, rival, vie, vie with, challenge comparison.

.12 ADJS **good**, **excellent**, eu–, *bueno* [Sp], *bon* [Fr], bonny [Brit], **fine**, **nice**, goodly, fair; **splendid**, **capital**, **grand**, elegant [informal], braw [Scot], famous [informal], noble; royal, regal, fit for a king; very good, *très bon* [Fr]; commendable, laudable, **estimable** 968.20; skillful 733.20–26; **sound**, healthy 683.5; virtuous 980.7; kind, benevolent 938.13–17; beneficial, helpful 785.21; profitable 811.15; favorable, auspicious 544.18; expedient, advantageous 670.5; useful 665.18; pleasant 863.6; cogent, valid 516.13.

.13 [slang terms] **great**, swell, dandy, jim-dandy, neat, cool, bully, tough, mean, heavy, bad, groovy, out of sight, fab, marvy, gear, something else, ducky, keen, hot, nifty, spiffy, spiffing, ripping, nobby, peachy, peachy-keen, delicious, scrumptious, out of this world, hunky-dory, crackerjack, boss, stunning, corking, smashing, solid, all wool and a yard wide; rum or wizard [both Brit], bonzer [Austral]; bang-up, jam-up, slap-up, ace-high, fine and dandy, just dandy, but good, OK, okay, A-OK.

.14 **superior**, above par, **crack** [informal]; **high-grade**, **high-class**, high-quality, high-caliber, high-test.

.15 **first-rate**, **first-class**, in a class by itself, first-chop [informal]; **tip-top**, **top-notch**, topflight, top-drawer, tops [all informal];

topping or top-hole [both Brit informal]; A1 or A number 1 [both informal].

.16 **up to par**, up to standard, **up to snuff** [informal]; **up to the mark**, up to the notch or up to scratch [both informal].

.17 **superb**, super [slang], **superexcellent**, **supereminent**, superfine, **exquisite**; **magnificent**, **splendid**, splendiferous, tremendous, **immense**, **marvelous**, **wonderful**, glorious, divine, heavenly, terrific, sensational; **sterling**, golden; gilt-edged or gilt-edge [both informal]; of the highest type, of the best sort, of the first water, as good as good can be, as good as they come, as good as they make 'em [informal], out of this world [slang].

.18 **best**, very best, greatest [informal], **prime**, optimum, optimal, aristo–; **choice**, **select**, elect, elite, **picked**, handpicked; **prize**, **champion**; **supreme**, paramount, **unsurpassed**, surpassing, unparalleled, unmatched, unmatchable, matchless, **peerless**; quintessential; for the best, all for the best.

.19 **tolerable**, goodish, fair, fairish, moderate, tidy [informal], **decent**, respectable, presentable, good enough, **pretty good**, not bad, not amiss, not half bad, not so bad, **adequate**, **satisfactory**, **all right**, OK or okay [both slang]; better than nothing; **acceptable**, admissible, **passable**, unobjectionable, unexceptionable; workmanlike; sufficient 661.6.

.20 **harmless**, hurtless, unhurtful, **uninjurious**, undamaging, **innocuous**, innoxious, innocent; unobnoxious, inoffensive; nonmalignant, **benign**; nonpoisonous, nontoxic, nonvirulent, nonvenomous.

.21 ADVS **excellently**, **nicely**, **finely**, **capitally**, **splendidly**, **famously**, royally; **well**, very well, **fine** [informal], right, aright.

.22 **superbly**, exquisitely, **magnificently**, tremendously, immensely, terrifically, **marvelously**, **wonderfully**, gloriously, divinely; out–.

.23 **tolerably**, **fairly**, fairishly, moderately, respectably, **adequately**, **satisfactorily**, passably, **acceptably**, unexceptionably, presentably, decently; fairly well, well enough, pretty well; **rather**, **pretty**.

675. BADNESS

(bad quality or effect)

.1 NOUNS **badness**, **evilness**, viciousness, damnability, reprehensibility; moral badness, peccancy, wickedness 981.4; unhealthiness 684.1; inferiority 680.3; unskillfulness 734.1; unkindness, malevolence 939; inauspiciousness, unfavorableness 544.8; inexpedience 671; unpleasantness 864; invalidity 158.3; inaccuracy 518.2; improperness 959.1.

.2 **terribleness, dreadfulness,** direness, **awfulness** [informal], horribleness; **atrociousness, outrageousness,** heinousness, nefariousness; **notoriousness, egregiousness,** scandalousness, shamefulness, **infamousness; abominableness,** odiousness, **loathsomeness, detestableness,** despicableness, contemptibleness, hatefulness; **offensiveness,** grossness, obnoxiousness; squalor, squalidness, sordidness, **wretchedness,** filth, **vileness,** fulsomeness, **nastiness,** rankness, **foulness,** noisomeness; disgustingness, repulsiveness; uncleanness 682; beastliness, bestiality, brutality; **rottenness** or lousiness [both informal], the pits [slang]; shoddiness, shabbiness; scurviness, **baseness** 915.3; **worthlessness** 673.2.

.3 **evil, bad, wrong, ill; harm, hurt, injury, damage, detriment; destruction** 693; despoliation 824.5; mischief, havoc; outrage, atrocity; abomination, grievance, vexation, woe, crying evil; poison 676.3; blight, venom, toxin, **bane** 676; **corruption,** pollution, infection, befoulment, defilement; fly in the ointment, worm in the apple or rose; skeleton in the closet; snake in the grass; "something rotten in the state of Denmark" [Shakespeare]; ills the flesh is heir to, "all ills that men endure" [Abraham Cowley]; the worst.

.4 **bad influence,** malevolent influence, evil star, **ill wind;** evil genius, **hoodoo** or **jinx** [both informal], Jonah; curse, enchantment, whammy [slang], spell, hex, voodoo; evil eye, *malocchio* [Ital].

.5 **harmfulness, hurtfulness,** injuriousness, banefulness, balefulness, detrimentalness, deleteriousness, perniciousness, mischievousness, noxiousness, venomousness, poisonousness, toxicity, virulence, noisomeness, **malignance** or **malignancy, malignity, viciousness;** unhealthiness 684.1; deadliness, lethality 409.8; ominousness 544.7.

.6 **VERBS work evil, do ill; harm, hurt; injure,** scathe, wound, **damage; destroy** 693.10–21; despoil 824.16, prejudice, disadvantage, impair, disserve, distress; **wrong,** do wrong, do wrong by, aggrieve, do evil, do a mischief, do an ill office to; **molest,** afflict; lay a hand on; get into trouble; abuse, outrage, violate, maltreat, mistreat 667.5; torment, harass, persecute, savage,

crucify, torture 866.18; play mischief or havoc with, wreak havoc on, play hob with [informal]; **corrupt,** deprave, taint, pollute, infect, befoul, defile 682.19; poison, envenom, blight; curse, hex, jinx, bewitch; threaten, menace 973.2; doom; condemn 1008.3.

.7 **ADJS bad, evil, ill,** untoward, cac(o)– or kako–, dis– or dys–, mal–; black, sinister; **wicked, wrong,** peccant, **vicious, sinful** 981.16; criminal 982.6; unhealthy 684.5; **inferior** 680.9,10; unskillful 734.15–20; unkind, malevolent 939.14–24; inauspicious, unfavorable 544.17; inexpedient 671.5; unpleasant 864.17; invalid 158.15; inaccurate 518.17; improper 959.3.

.8 [slang terms] **dirty,** punk, bum, shitty, crappy, cheesy, **crummy,** grim, putrid, icky, yecchy, vomity, barfy, stinking, stinky, creepy, hairy, godawful, goshawful.

.9 **terrible, dreadful, awful** [informal], dire, horrible, horrid; atrocious, outrageous, heinous, villainous, nefarious; enormous, monstrous; **deplorable,** lamentable, regrettable, pitiful, pitiable, woeful, grievous, sad 864.20; flagrant, **scandalous,** shameful, **shocking,** infamous, **notorious,** arrant, **egregious;** unclean 682.20–25; shoddy, schlock [slang], shabby, scurvy, **base** 915.12; **odious, obnoxious,** offensive, gross, **disgusting,** repulsive, loathsome, **abominable, detestable, despicable, contemptible,** beneath contempt, hateful; blameworthy, **reprehensible** 969.26; rank, fetid, foul, filthy, vile, **rotten** or **lousy** [both informal], fulsome, noisome, **nasty,** squalid, sordid, **wretched;** beastly, brutal; as bad as they come, as bad as they make 'em [informal], as bad as bad can be; worst; too bad; worthless 673.19

.10 **execrable, damnable;** cursed 972.9,10; infernal, hellish, devilish, fiendish, satanic, ghoulish, demoniac, demonic(al), diabolic(al), ungodly.

.11 **evil-fashioned, ill-fashioned, evil-shaped, ill-shaped, evil-qualitied, evil-looking, ill-looking, evil-favored, ill-favored, evil-hued, evil-faced, evil-minded, evil-eyed, ill-affected** [archaic], **evil-gotten, ill-gotten, ill-conceived.**

.12 **harmful, hurtful,** scatheful, **baneful,** baleful, distressing, **injurious, damaging, detrimental,** deleterious, counterproductive, **pernicious,** mischievous; noxious, venomous, venenate, poisonous, venenous, veneniferous, toxic, virulent, noisome; **malignant,** malign, malevolent, malefic, vicious; prejudicial, disadvantageous, disserviceable; corruptive, corrupting, corrosive, corroding 692.45; deadly, lethal 409.23; ominous 544.17.

.13 ADVS **badly**, bad [informal], **ill**, evil, evilly, wrong, wrongly, amiss; to one's cost.

.14 **terribly, dreadfully**, dreadful [dial], **horribly**, horridly, **awfully** [informal], **atrociously, outrageously;** flagrantly, scandalously, shamefully, shockingly, infamously, notoriously, egregiously, grossly, offensively, nauseatingly, fulsomely, odiously, **vilely**, obnoxiously, **disgustingly,** loathsomely; wretchedly, sordidly, shabbily, basely, abominably, detestably, despicably, contemptibly, foully, nastily; brutally, bestially, savagely, viciously; something fierce or terrible [informal].

.15 **harmfully, hurtfully, banefully,** balefully, **injuriously, damagingly, detrimentally,** deleteriously, counterproductively, **perniciously,** mischievously; noxiously, venomously, poisonously, toxically, virulently, noisomely; **malignantly,** malignly, malevolently, malefically, **viciously;** prejudicially, disadvantageously, disserviceably; corrosively, corrodingly.

676. BANE

.1 NOUNS **bane, curse, affliction,** infliction, visitation, **plague, pestilence,** pest, calamity, **scourge, torment,** open wound, running sore, grievance, woe, burden, crushing burden; disease 686; death 408; evil, harm 675.3; destruction 693; vexation 866.2; thorn, thorn in the flesh or side, pea in the shoe; bugbear, bête noire [Fr], nemesis.

.2 **blight,** blast; canker, cancer; mold, fungus, mildew, smut, must, rust; rot, dry rot; **pest;** worm, worm in the apple or rose; moth [archaic], "moth and rust" [Bible].

.3 **poison, venom,** venin, virus [archaic], toxic, toxin, toxicant, tox(o)– or toxi–; eradicant, **pesticide; insecticide;** insect powder, bug bomb [informal]; roach powder, roach paste; stomach poison, contact poison, systemic insecticide or systemic, fumigant, chemosterilant; chlorinated hydrocarbon insecticide, organic chlorine; organic phosphate insecticide; carbamate insecticide; miticide, acaricide, vermicide, anthelmintic; rodenticide, rat poison; **herbicide,** defoliant, **weed killer;** fungicide; microbicide, germicide, antiseptic, disinfectant, antibiotic; **toxicology.**

.4 **miasma, mephitis,** malaria [archaic]; effluvium, exhaust, exhaust gas; coal gas, chokedamp, blackdamp, firedamp.

.5 sting, stinger, dart; **fang,** tang [dial]; beesting, snakebite.

.6 **poisons**

aconite	hydrocyanide
aldrin	hydrogen cyanide
alkaloid	hyoscyamine
antimony	lead
arsenic	lead arsenate
arsenic trioxide, arsenious oxide	lindane
	Malathion
arsenious acid	mercuric chloride
beryllium	mercury
bichloride of mercury	methoxychlor,
cadmium	methoxy DDT
calcium arsenate	mustard gas
carbolic acid	nerve gas
carbon monoxide	nicotine
carbon tetrachloride	parathion
chlordane	Paris green
chlorine	phenol
corrosive sublimate	poison gas
curare	potassium cyanide
cyanide	prussic acid
cyanide gas	pyrethrum
DDD	red squill
(dichlorodiphenyl-dichloroethane)	rotenone
	selenium
DDT	strychnine
(dichlorodiphenyl-trichloroethane)	tartar emetic
	2,4-D
dieldrin	2,4,5-T
endrin	warfarin
hydrocyanic acid	white arsenic

.7 **poisonous plants**

aconite	locoweed
amanita	mayapple
banewort	mescal bean
bearded darnel	monkshood
belladonna	nightshade
black henbane	nux vomica
black nightshade	ordeal tree
castor-oil plant	poison bean
corn cackle	poisonberry
datura	poison bush
deadly nightshade	poison hemlock, poison parsley
death camas	
death cup, death angel	poison ivy
	poison oak
ergot	poison rye grass
foxglove	poison sumac
Gastrolobium	poison tobacco
hellebore	poisonweed
hemlock	pokeweed
henbane	sheep laurel
horsetail	upas
jequirity, jequirity bean	water hemlock
	white snakeroot
jimsonweed	wolfsbane
larkspur	

677. PERFECTION

.1 NOUNS **perfection,** finish; **faultlessness, flawlessness,** defectlessness, indefectibility, impeccability, absoluteness; infallibility; spotlessness, stainlessness, taintlessness, purity, immaculateness; sinlessness 980.4; chastity 988.

.2 **soundness, integrity, intactness, wholeness,** entireness, completeness; **fullness,** plenitude.

.3 **acme of perfection, pink, pink of perfection,** culmination, perfection, height, top, acme, ultimate, summit, pinnacle, peak, highest pitch, climax, consummation, *ne plus ultra* [L], last word.

.4 pattern *or* standard *or* mold *or* norm of perfection, very model, quintessence; archetype, prototype, exemplar, mirror; **classic,** masterwork, masterpiece, *chef d'œuvre* [Fr]; **ideal** 25.4; **paragon** 985.4.

.5 VERBS **perfect,** develop, ripen, mature; improve 691.7; crown, culminate, complete 722.6; do to perfection 722.7.

.6 ADJS **perfect, ideal, faultless, flawless,** unflawed, defectless, not to be improved, **impeccable,** absolute; **just right;** spotless, stainless, taintless, unblemished, untainted, unspotted, immaculate, **pure,** uncontaminated, unadulterated, unmixed; sinless 980.9; chaste 988.4; indefective [archaic], indefectible; infallible; beyond all praise, irreproachable, unfaultable, *sans peur et sans reproche* [Fr], peerless 36.15.

.7 **sound, intact, whole, entire, complete,** integral; **full;** total, utter, unqualified 508.2.

.8 **undamaged, unharmed, unhurt, uninjured,** unscathed, **unspoiled,** virgin, inviolate, **unimpaired;** harmless, scatheless; **unmarred,** unmarked, unscarred, unscratched, undefaced, unbruised; **unbroken,** unshattered, untorn; undemolished, undestroyed; undeformed, unmutilated, unmangled, unmaimed; unfaded, unworn, unwithered, bright, fresh, untouched, pristine, mint.

.9 **perfected, finished,** polished, refined; **classic(al),** masterly, masterful, expert, proficient; ripened, ripe, matured, mature, developed, fully developed; **consummate,** quintessential, archetypical, exemplary, model.

.10 ADVS **perfectly,** ideally; **faultlessly, flawlessly, impeccably; just right;** spotlessly; immaculately, purely; infallibly; **wholly, entirely, completely, fully,** thoroughly, totally, absolutely 56.14,15.

.11 **to perfection, to a turn, to a T** [informal], to a finish, to a nicety; to a fare-thee-well *or* fare-you-well *or* fare-ye-well [informal].

678. IMPERFECTION

.1 NOUNS **imperfection,** imperfectness; **unperfectedness; faultiness, defectiveness,** defectibility; **shortcoming, deficiency,** lack, want, shortage, **inadequacy,** inadequateness; erroneousness, **fallibility;** inaccuracy, inexactness, inexactitude 518.2; **unsoundness,** incompleteness, patchiness, sketchiness, unevenness; **impairment** 692; mediocrity 680; immaturity, undevelopment 721.4; impurity, adulteration 44.3.

.2 **fault,** *faute* [Fr], **defect, deficiency, inadequacy,** imperfection, kink, defection [archaic]; **flaw,** hole, bug [slang]; something missing; catch [informal], fly in the ointment, problem, little problem, snag, drawback; **crack, rift; weakness,** frailty, infirmity, failure, **failing, foible, shortcoming;** weak point, Achilles' heel, vulnerable place, chink in one's armor, weak link; **blemish,** taint 679.

.3 VERBS **fall short,** come short, miss, miss out, not qualify, fall down [slang], **not measure up,** not come up to par, not come up to the mark, not come up to scratch [informal], not pass muster, not bear inspection, miss the mark, not hack it [slang], not make it [informal], not make the grade.

.4 ADJS **imperfect,** not perfect, atel(o)–; **unperfected; defective, faulty, inadequate, deficient,** short, lacking, wanting, found wanting, "weighed in the balance and found wanting" [Bible]; off; erroneous, **fallible;** inaccurate, inexact, imprecise 518.17; **unsound, incomplete,** unfinished, partial, patchy, sketchy, uneven, unthorough; makeshift 670.7; **damaged, impaired** 692.29–44; mediocre 680.7,8; **blemished** 679.8; immature, undeveloped 721.11,12; impure, adulterated, mixed 44.15.

.5 ADVS **imperfectly, inadequately,** deficiently; **incompletely,** partially; **faultily, defectively.**

679. BLEMISH

.1 NOUNS **blemish, disfigurement,** disfiguration, **defacement;** scar, keloid, cicatrix; needle scar, track *or* crater [both slang]; scratch; scab; blister, vesicle, bulla, bleb; weal, wale, welt, wen, sebaceous cyst; port-wine stain *or* port-wine mark, hemangioma, strawberry mark; pock, pustule; pockmark, pit; nevus, birthmark, mole; freckle, lentigo; milium, whitehead, blackhead, comedo, pimple, hickey, sty; wart, verruca; **crack,** craze, check, rift, split; **deformity**, deformation, warp, twist, kink, **distortion**; flaw, defect, fault 678.2.

.2 **discoloration**, discolorment, discolor [archaic]; bruise 692.9.

.3 **stain, taint, tarnish**; mark, brand, **stigma**; maculation, macule, macula; **spot, blot**, blur, **blotch**, patch, speck, speckle, fleck, flick, flyspeck; daub, dab; **smirch, smudge**, smutch *or* smouch, smut, **smear**; splotch, splash, splatter, spatter; bloodstain; eyesore; macul(o)– *or* maculi–.

.4 VERBS **blemish, disfigure**, deface, **flaw, mar**; scab; scar, cicatrize, scarify; **crack**, craze, check, split; **deform**, warp, twist, kink, **distort**.

.5 **spot**, bespot, blot, blotch, speck, speckle, bespeckle, maculate [archaic]; freckle; flyspeck; **spatter, splatter**, splash, splotch.

.6 **stain**, bestain, **discolor**, smirch, besmirch, taint, attaint, **tarnish**; mark, stigmatize, brand; smear, besmear, daub, bedaub, slubber [Brit dial]; blur, slur [dial]; **darken, blacken**; smoke, besmoke; scorch, singe, sear; dirty, soil 682.16.

.7 **bloodstain, bloody**, ensanguine.

.8 ADJS **blemished, disfigured**, defaced, **marred**, scarred, keloidal, cicatrized, scarified, scabbed, scabby; pimpled, pimply; cracked, crazed, checked, split; deformed, warped, twisted, kinked, distorted; faulty, flawed, defective 678.4.

.9 **spotted, spotty**, maculate, maculated, macular, blotched, **blotchy**, splotched, splotchy; **speckled**, speckly, bespeckled; freckled, freckly, freckle-faced; spattered, splattered, splashed.

.10 **stained, discolored**, foxed, foxy, **tainted, tarnished**, smirched, besmirched; stigmatized, stigmatic, stigmatiferous; darkened, blackened, murky, smoky, inky; **soiled** 682.21.

.11 **bloodstained**, blood-spattered, **bloody**, sanguinary, **gory**, ensanguined.

680. MEDIOCRITY

.1 NOUNS **mediocrity**, mediocreness, fairishness, modestness, modesty, moderateness, middlingness, **indifference**; respectability, passableness, **tolerableness** 674.3; **dullness**, lackluster, tediousness 883.1.

.2 **ordinariness**, averageness, normality, **commonness, commonplaceness**; common *or* garden variety [informal]; unexceptionality, unremarkableness, unnoteworthiness, conventionality.

.3 **inferiority**, inferiorness, **poorness**, lowliness, humbleness, **baseness, meanness**,

commonness, coarseness; **second-rateness**, third-rateness, fourth-rateness.

.4 **low grade**, low class, low quality; second best.

.5 **mediocrity, second-rater**, third-rater, fourth-rater, nothing *or* nobody special, no prize, not much of a bargain, small potatoes *or* small beer [both slang]; tinhorn [slang]; nonentity 673.7; middle class, middle order *or* orders, bourgeoisie, burgherdom; suburbia; Middle America, silent majority.

.6 **irregular**, second, third; *schlock, schmatte* [both Yid].

.7 ADJS **mediocre, middling, indifferent, fair, fairish, fair to middling** [informal], moderate, modest, medium, betwixt and between; respectable, passable, **tolerable** 674.19; **so-so**, *comme ci comme ça* [Fr]; of a kind, of a sort, of sorts [informal]; nothing to brag about, not much to boast of, nothing to write home about; "not below mediocrity nor above it" [Johnson]; dull, lackluster, tedious 883.6; insipid, vapid, wishy-washy, namby-pamby.

.8 **ordinary, average**, normal, **common, commonplace**, garden *or* garden-variety [both informal], run-of-mine *or* -mill, run-of-the-mine *or* -mill; **unexceptional, unremarkable, unnoteworthy**, unspectacular, no great shakes [informal]; conventional; middle-class, bourgeois, plastic [slang]; suburban; usual, regular 84.8.

.9 **inferior, poor**, punk [slang], **base, mean, common**, coarse, cheesy *or* tacky [both informal], tinny; shabby, seedy 692.34; cheap, Mickey Mouse [informal], paltry 673.18; irregular; second-best; **second-rate**, third-rate, fourth-rate; **second-class**, third-class, fourth-class; **low-grade, low-class**, low-quality, low-test.

.10 **below par**, below standard, **below the mark** [informal], substandard, **not up to scratch** [informal], not up to snuff [informal], not up to sample *or* standard *or* specification, off.

.11 ADVS **mediocrely, middlingly**, fairly, fairishly, middling well, fair to middling [informal], moderately, modestly, **indifferently, so-so**; passably, **tolerably** 674.23.

.12 **inferiorly, poorly**, basely, meanly, commonly.

681. CLEANNESS

.1 NOUNS **cleanness, cleanliness**; **purity**, pureness; **immaculateness**, immaculacy; **spotlessness**, unspottedness, stainlessness, whiteness; freshness; fastidiousness, daintiness, cleanly habits; asepsis, sterility, hospital cleanliness; tidiness 59.3.

.2 **cleansing, cleaning, detersion; purge,** purging, purgation, abstersion [archaic]; **purification,** lustration, catharsis; expurgation, bowdlerization; dry cleaning, steam cleaning.

.3 **sanitation, hygiene,** hygenics; **disinfection, decontamination, sterilization,** antisepsis; pasteurization, flash pasteurization; fumigation, disinfestation, delousing.

.4 **refinement, clarification, purification,** depuration; **straining,** colature; elution, elutriation; extraction 305.8; **filtering,** filtration; **percolation,** leaching, edulcoration [archaic], lixiviation; **sifting,** separation, **screening,** sieving, bolting, riddling, winnowing; essentialization; sublimation; **distillation,** destructive distillation, spiritualization [archaic].

.5 **washing, ablution;** lavation, laving, lavage; lavabo; **wash, washup;** soaping, lathering; rinse, rinsing; sponge, sponging; shampoo; washout, elution, elutriation; irrigation, flush, flushing, flushing out; douche, douching; enema; **scrub,** scrubbing, swabbing, mopping, scouring; **cleaning up** or **out,** washing up, scrubbing up or out, mopping up, wiping up.

.6 **laundering, laundry,** tubbing; **wash, washing;** washday.

.7 **bathing,** balneation, balne(o)–.

.8 **bath,** bathe [Brit], tub [informal]; **shower,** shower bath, needle bath, hot or cold shower; douche; sponge bath, sponge; hip bath, sitz bath; sweat bath, Turkish bath, hummum, Russian bath, Swedish bath, Finnish bath, sauna or sauna bath, Japanese bath, whirlpool bath, plunge bath.

.9 **dip, bath;** acid bath, mercury bath, fixing bath; sheep dip.

.10 **bathing place, bath, baths,** public baths, **bathhouse,** bagnio [archaic], sauna; *balneum, balneae, thermae* [all L]; mikvah; watering place, spa; lavatory, washroom, bathroom; steam room, sweat room, sudatorium, sudarium, caldarium, tepidarium; rest room.

.11 **washery, laundry;** washhouse, washshed; **Laundromat, launderette,** coin laundry, coin-operated laundry; automatic laundry; hand laundry; car wash.

.12 **washbasin, washbowl,** washdish, basin; **lavatory, washstand; bathtub,** tub, bath; bidet; **shower,** showers, shower room,

shower bath, shower stall, shower head, shower curtain; **sink,** kitchen sink; dishwasher, automatic dishwasher; washing machine; washer; piscina, lavabo, ewer, aquamanile; washtub, washpot, washing pot, wash boiler, dishpan; finger bowl; wash barrel.

.13 **refinery; refiner,** purifier, clarifier; **filter;** strainer, colander; **percolator,** lixiviator; **sifter, sieve, screen,** riddle, cribble; winnow, winnower, winnowing machine, winnowing basket or winnowing fan; cradle, rocker.

.14 **cleaner,** cleaner-up, cleaner-off, cleaner-out; **janitor,** janitress, custodian; cleaning woman or lady or man, charwoman or char [both Brit].

.15 **washer,** launderer; **laundress,** laundrywoman, **washerwoman,** washwoman, washerwife [Scot]; **laundryman,** washerman, washman; dry cleaner; **dishwasher,** pot-walloper [slang], scullion, scullery maid; dishwiper.

.16 **sweeper; street sweeper,** crossing sweeper, whitewing, cleanser or scavenger [both Brit]; **chimney sweep** or sweeper, sweep, flue cleaner.

.17 **cleanser, cleaner;** cleaning agent; lotion, cream; cold cream, cleansing cream, **soap, detergent,** synthetic detergent, abstergent; shampoo; rinse; **solvent** 391.10, cleaning solvent; purifier, depurant; mouthwash, wash; dentifrice, **toothpaste, tooth powder;** pumice stone, holystone; purge, purgative, cathartic, enema, diuretic, emetic, nauseant.

.18 VERBS **clean, cleanse, purge,** deterge, depurate; **purify,** lustrate; sweeten, **freshen;** whiten, bleach; clean up or out, clear out, sweep out; reform, clean house, delouse; spruce, **tidy** 60.12; scavenge; **wipe,** wipe up or out, wipe off; dust, dust off; steam-clean, **dry-clean;** expurgate, bowdlerize.

.19 **wash, bathe,** bath [Brit], shower, lave; **launder,** tub; wash up or out; **rinse,** rinse out, flush, flush out, irrigate, sluice, sluice out; ritually immerse, baptize, *toivel* [Yid]; sponge; **scrub,** scrub up or out, **swab, mop,** mop up; **scour,** holystone; soap, lather; shampoo; syringe, douche; gargle.

.20 **groom,** dress, fettle [Brit dial], **brush up;** preen, plume; manicure.

.21 **comb,** curry, card, hackle or hatchel, heckle [dial], rake.

.22 **refine, clarify,** clear, purify, rectify, depurate, decrassify; try; **strain;** elute, elutriate; **extract** 305.10; **filter,** filtrate; **percolate,** leach, lixiviate, edulcorate [archaic]; **sift,** separate, sieve, **screen,** bolt, winnow; sublimate, sublime; **distill,** spiritualize [archaic], essentialize.

.23 **sweep,** sweep up *or* out, **brush,** brush off, whisk, broom; vacuum [informal], vacuum-clean.

.24 **sanitize,** sanitate, hygienize; **disinfect, decontaminate, sterilize,** antisepticize; autoclave, boil; pasteurize, flash-pasteurize; disinfest, fumigate, delouse; chlorinate.

.25 ADJS **clean, pure; immaculate, spotless,** stainless, white, fair, dirt-free, soil-free; **unsoiled, unsullied,** unmuddied, unsmirched, unbesmirched, unblotted, unsmudged, unstained, untarnished, **unspotted,** unblemished; smutless, smut-free; bleached, whitened; bright, shiny 335.32, 33; **unpolluted,** nonpolluted, untainted, unadulterated, **undefiled;** kosher, *tahar* [Heb], ritually pure *or* clean; clean as a whistle *or* a new penny *or* a hound's tooth; sweet, **fresh; cleanly,** fastidious, dainty, of cleanly habits; well-washed, well-scrubbed, tubbed [informal].

.26 **cleaned, cleansed,** cleaned up; purged, purified; expurgated, bowdlerized; reformed; refined; spruce, spick and span, **tidy** 59.8.

.27 **sanitary, hygienic, prophylactic; sterile,** aseptic, antiseptic, **uninfected;** disinfected, decontaminated, sterilized; autoclaved, boiled; pasteurized.

.28 **cleansing, cleaning;** detergent, abstergent, depurative; **purifying,** purificatory, lustral; expurgatory; purgative, purging, cathartic, diuretic, emetic.

.29 ADVS **cleanly,** clean; **purely, immaculately,** spotlessly.

.30 **cleansers**

anion detergent	cation detergent
benzine, benzol	cleaning fluid
bleach 363.10	detergent
borax	lye
Carbona	sodium carbonate, sal
carbon tetrachloride,	soda, soda
carbon tet [informal]	washing powder
	washing soda

.31 **soaps**

amole	kosher soap
bar soap	laundry soap
bath soap	lead soap
brown soap	lime soap
castile soap, castile	liquid soap
deodorant soap	marine soap
floating soap	metallic soap
glycerin soap	milled soap
granulated soap	neat soap
green soap	olive-oil castile soap

powdered soap, soap	soda soap
powder	soft soap
pumice soap	tar soap
saddle soap	toilet soap
shaving soap	wash ball
soap flakes	

.32 **cleaning devices**

autoclave	nail brush
automatic washer	napkin
automatic washer-	paper towel
dryer	pumice stone
bath brush	purificator
bath towel	push broom
broom, besom	rag mop
brush	rake
carpet cleaner *or*	scouring pad
sweeper	scraper
chamois cloth	scrubber
cleansing tissue	scrub *or* scrubbing
comb	brush
currycomb	serviette [Brit]
dishcloth	soap pad
dishmop	sponge
dishrag	sponge mop
dish towel	steam cleaner
dishwasher	sterilizer
doormat	sudarium, sudary [ar-
dustcloth	chaic]
duster	swab
dust mop, dry mop	toilet paper
dustpan	toothbrush
eyeglass cloth	toothpick
facecloth	towel
face towel	Turkish towel
feather duster	vacuum cleaner
hackle	washboard
hairbrush	washcloth
hand brush	washer
handkerchief	washing engine
hand towel	washing machine
holystone	washrag
hose	whisk broom, whisk
mop	wisp [Brit]
mop bucket *or* pail	wringer
mundatory	wringer washer

682. UNCLEANNESS

.1 NOUNS **uncleanness,** immundity; **impurity,** unpureness; **dirtiness,** grubbiness, dinginess, griminess, messiness [informal], scruffiness, slovenliness, untidiness 62.6; miriness, muddiness 389.4; uncleanliness.

.2 **filthiness, foulness,** vileness, scumminess [informal], feculence, shittiness [slang], muckiness, ordurousness, nastiness, ickiness [informal]; scurfiness, scabbiness; rottenness, putridness 692.7; rankness, fetidness 437.2; odiousness, repulsiveness 864.2; nauseousness, disgustingness 429.3; hoggishness, piggishness, swinishness, beastliness.

.3 **squalor,** squalidness, squalidity, **sordidness;** slumminess [informal].

.4 **defilement, befoulment,** dirtying, soiling, besmirchment; **pollution, contamination,** infection; abomination; ritual uncleanness or impurity or contamination.

.5 **soil**, soilure, soilage, smut; **smirch, smudge,** smutch, smear, **spot,** blot, blotch, **stain** 679.3.

.6 **dirt, grime;** dust; soot, smut; **mud** 389.8.

.7 **filth, muck,** slime, mess, sordes, foul matter; ordure, **excrement** 311.3,4; mucus, snot [slang]; scurf, furfur, dandruff; scuz [slang]; putrid matter, pus, corruption [dial], gangrene, decay, carrion, **rot** 692.7; **obscenity,** smut [informal] 990.4.

.8 **slime, slop,** scum, sludge, slush, splosh [dial], slosh, slab [dial], slob [dial], glop or gunk [both informal], **muck, mire,** ooze.

.9 **offal,** slough, **offscourings,** scurf, scum, riffraff, scum of the earth; **carrion; garbage, swill,** slop, slops; dishwater, ditchwater, bilgewater, bilge; **sewage,** sewerage; **refuse** 669.4.

.10 **dunghill, manure pile,** midden, mixen [Brit dial], colluvies; compost heap; dump, garbage dump, kitchen midden, refuse heap.

.11 **sty, pigsty,** pigpen; **stable,** Augean stables; dump or hole [both slang], tenement; warren, **slum,** rookery; the slums; plague spot, pesthole; hovel 191.12.

.12 (receptacle of filth) **sink;** sump, **cesspool,** septic tank; **sewer,** drain, cloaca, cloaca maxima [both L]; **dump,** garbage dump; **swamp,** bog, mire, quagmire, marsh.

.13 **pig, swine, hog,** slut, sloven, slattern 62.7; Struwwelpeter.

.14 VERBS wallow in the mire, live like a pig.

.15 **dirty,** dirty up, dirt [archaic], grime, **begrime;** muck, muck up [informal]; **muddy,** bemud [archaic]; mire, bemire; slime; dust; soot, smoke, besmoke.

.16 **soil,** besoil; black, **blacken; smirch,** besmirch, sully, slubber [Brit dial], smutch or smouch, besmutch, smut, **smudge,** smear, besmear, daub, bedaub; **spot, stain** 679.5,6.

.17 **defile, foul, befoul; sully;** nasty or benasty [both dial], mess or mess up [both informal]; **pollute, corrupt, contaminate, infect; taint,** tarnish.

.18 **spatter, splatter, splash, bespatter,** dabble, bedabble, spot, splotch.

.19 **draggle,** bedraggle, **drabble, bedrabble,** daggle [archaic], drabble in the mud.

.20 ADJS **unclean, unwashed,** unbathed, unscrubbed, unscoured, unswept, unwiped; **impure,** unpure; **polluted, contaminated, infected, corrupted;** ritually unclean or impure or contaminated, tref [Yid], tere-

fah [Heb], nonkosher; not to be handled without gloves; **uncleanly.**

.21 **soiled, sullied, dirtied, smirched,** besmirched, smudged, spotted, **tarnished, tainted, stained; defiled,** fouled, **befouled;** draggled, drabbled, bedraggled.

.22 **dirty, grimy, grubby,** grungy [slang], smirchy, dingy, messy [informal]; scruffy, slovenly, untidy 62.15; miry, **muddy** 389.14; **dusty;** smutty, smutchy, smudgy; sooty, smoky; snuffy.

.23 **filthy, foul,** vile, mucky, **nasty,** icky or yecchy [both informal]; malodorous, mephitic, rank, fetid 437.5; **putrid, rotten** 692.41; nauseating, disgusting; **odious, repulsive** 864.18; **slimy,** scummy [informal]; barfy or vomity or puky [all slang]; sloppy, sludgy, slushy, sloshy, sposhy [dial], slabby [archaic], gloppy or gunky [both informal], scurfy, scabby; wormy, maggoty, flyblown; feculent, ordurous, crappy or shitty [both slang], fecal 311.20.

.24 **hoggish, piggish, swinish,** beastly.

.25 **squalid, sordid,** wretched, shabby; slumlike, slummy.

.26 ADVS **uncleanly, impurely,** unpurely; dirtily, grimily; filthily, foully, nastily, vilely.

683. HEALTHFULNESS

.1 NOUNS **healthfulness, healthiness,** salubrity, salubriousness, salutariness, wholesomeness, beneficialness, goodness.

.2 **hygiene,** hygienics; sanitation 681.3; public health, epidemiology; health physics; preventive medicine, prophylaxis, preventive dentistry, prophylactodontia; prophylactic psychology, mental hygiene.

.3 **hygienist,** hygeist, **sanitarian;** public health doctor or physician, epidemiologist; health physicist; preventive dentist, prophylactodontist; dental hygienist.

.4 VERBS **make for health,** conduce to health, **be good for,** agree with.

.5 ADJS **healthful, healthy, salubrious, salutary, wholesome,** health-preserving, health-enhancing, **beneficial,** benign, good, **good for; hygienic(al),** hygeian, sanitary; **constitutional,** for one's health; bracing, refreshing, invigorating, tonic.

684. UNHEALTHFULNESS

.1 NOUNS **unhealthfulness, unhealthiness, insalubrity,** insalubriousness, unsalutariness, **unwholesomeness,** badness; noxiousness, noisomeness, injuriousness, harmfulness 675.5; pathenogenicity; health hazard, threat or danger or menace to health; contamination, pollution, environmental pollution, air *or* water *or* noise pollution.

.2 innutritiousness, indigestibility.

.3 poisonousness, toxicity, venomousness; virulence *or* virulency, malignancy, noxiousness, destructiveness, deadliness; infectiousness, infectivity, contagiousness, communicability; poison, venom 676.3.

.4 VERBS disagree with, not be good for.

.5 ADJS unhealthful, unhealthy, insalubrious, unsalutary, unwholesome, peccant, bad, bad for; noxious, noisome, injurious, harmful 675.12; polluted, contaminated, tainted, foul, septic; unhygienic, unsanitary, insanitary; morbific, pathogenic, pestiferous.

.6 innutritious, indigestible, unassimilable.

.7 poisonous, toxic(al), toxicant; venomous, envenomed, venenate, venenous; veneniferous, toxiferous; virulent, noxious, malignant, malign, destructive, deadly; pestiferous, pestilential; mephitic, miasmal, miasmic, miasmatic; infectious, infective, contagious, communicable, catching.

685. HEALTH

.1 NOUNS health, well-being; fitness, physical fitness; bloom, flush, glow, rosiness; mental health, emotional health; physical condition; Hygeia.

.2 healthiness, healthfulness, soundness, wholesomeness; healthy body, good *or* healthy constitution; good health, good state of health, "good estate of body" [Bible], *"mens sana in corpore sano"* [L; Juvenal], a sound mind in a sound body; robust health, rugged health, rude health, glowing health, picture of health, "health that snuffs the morning air" [Grainger]; fine fettle, fine whack [informal], fine *or* high feather [informal], good shape, good trim, fine shape, top shape [informal], good condition, mint condition; eupepsia, good digestion; clean bill of health.

.3 haleness, heartiness, robustness, vigorousness, ruggedness, vitality, lustiness, hardiness, strength, vigor; longevity.

.4 immunity, resistance, nonproneness *or* nonsusceptibility to disease; acquired immunity, artificial immunity, congenital immunity, familial immunity, inherent immunity, inherited immunity, innate *or* racial immunity, natural immunity, nonspecific immunity, specific immunity, opsonic immunity, phagocytic immunity, toxin-antitoxin immunity, active immunity, passive immunity; immunization 689.17; antibody, antigen 687.27.

.5 VERBS enjoy good health, have a clean bill of health, be in the pink; be in the best of health; feel good, feel fine, feel like a million [informal], never feel better; feel one's oats, be full of pep; burst with health, bloom, glow, flourish; keep fit, stay in shape; wear well, stay young.

.6 get well, mend, recuperate 694.19; recover 694.20.

.7 ADJS healthy, healthful, enjoying health, fine, in health, in shape, in condition, fit, fit and fine; in good health, in the pink [informal], in the pink of condition, in mint condition, in good case, in good *or* fine shape, in fine fettle, in fine whack [informal], in fine *or* high feather [informal], chipper [informal], fit as a fiddle [informal]; alive and kicking [informal], bursting with health, full of life and vigor, bright-eyed and bushy-tailed; full of beans *or* of piss and vinegar [slang], feeling one's oats; eupeptic.

.8 well, unailing, unsick, unsickly, unfrail; all right, doing nicely, up and about, sitting up and taking nourishment.

.9 sound, whole, wholesome; unimpaired 677.8; sound of mind and body, sound in wind and limb, sound as a dollar [informal].

.10 hale, hearty, hale and hearty, robust, robustious, robustuous, vital, vigorous, strong, strong as a horse, stalwart, stout, sturdy, rugged, rude, hardy, lusty, bouncing, flush [archaic].

.11 fresh, green, youthful, blooming; flush, flushed, rosy, rosy-cheeked, ruddy, pink, pink-cheeked; fresh as a daisy *or* rose, fresh as April.

.12 immune, resistant, nonprone *or* nonsusceptible to disease.

686. DISEASE

.1 NOUNS disease, illness, sickness, malady, ailment, indisposition, disorder, complaint, morbidity, *morbus* [L], affliction, affection, distemper [archaic], infirmity, –ia, –iasis, –pathy, –sis, nos(o)–; disability, defect, handicap; deformity 249.3; birth defect, congenital defect; abnormality, condition, pathological condition; signs, symptoms, pathology, symptomatology, symptomology, syndrome; sickishness, malaise, seediness *or* rockiness [both informal], the pip [informal]; complication, secondary disease *or* condition; contageous *or* infectious disease; bacterial disease, protozoan disease; worm disease; fungus disease, –osis *or* –ose; virus disease; allergy, allergic disease; nutritional disease, deficiency disease; geriatric disease; congenital disease, genetic disease, hereditary disease; iatrogenic disease; occupational disease; degenerative disease, wasting disease, atrophy, necr-(o)–; organic disease, functional disease; psychogenic or psychosomatic disease; circulatory disease, cardiovascular disease, respiratory disease, endocrine disease, gastrointestinal disease, urinogenital or urogenital disease, muscular disease, neurological disease; epidemic disease, pandemic disease, endemic disease, endemic; acute disease or condition, chronic disease or condition; plant disease, blight 676.2.

.2 unhealthiness, healthlessness; **ill health,** poor health, delicate or shaky or frail or fragile health; **sickliness,** peakedness [informal], **feebleness,** delicacy, weakliness, fragility, **frailty** 160.2; **infirmity, unsoundness,** debility, debilitation, enervation, exhaustion, decrepitude; wasting, languishing, languishment [archaic], cachexia or cachexy; chronic ill health, invalidity, invalidism; unwholesomeness, morbidity, morbidness; hypochondria, hypochondriasis, valetudinarianism.

.3 infection, contagion, contamination, taint, virus; aerial infection, airborne infection, contact infection, direct infection, cryptogenic infection, droplet infection, dust infection, hand infection, indirect infection, phytogenic infection, primary infection, pyogenic infection, secondary infection, subclinical infection, waterborne infection, zoogenic infection; **contagiousness, infectiousness, communicability;** epidemicity, inoculability; carrier, vector; epidemiology.

.4 epidemic, plague, pestilence, pest, pandemic, pandemia, scourge; epizootic, epiphytotic, murrain; bubonic plague, black plague, hemorrhagic plague, ambulatory plague, larval plague, glandular plague, cellulocutaneous plague, defervescing plague, pneumonic plague, premonitory plague, septicemic plague, siderating plague, black death; white plague, tuberculosis 686.15; pesthole, plague spot.

.5 seizure, attack, access, visitation; arrest; blockage, stoppage, occlusion, thrombosis, thromboembolism; **stroke,** ictus, apoplexy; **spasm, throes, fit, paroxysm, convulsion,** eclampsia, frenzy; **epilepsy,** epilept(o)– or epilepti–, falling sickness; grand mal, haute mal, epilepsia major,

epilepsia gravior; petit mal, epilepsia minor, epilepsia mitior; abdominal epilepsy, acquired epilepsy, activated epilepsy, affect epilepsy, akinetic epilepsy, autonomic epilepsy, cardiac epilepsy, cortical epilepsy, cursive epilepsy, diurnal epilepsy, focal epilepsy, hysterical epilepsy, Jacksonian epilepsy or Rolandic epilepsy, larval epilepsy or latent epilepsy, laryngeal epilepsy, matutinal epilepsy, menstrual epilepsy, musicogenic epilepsy, myoclonous epilepsy or Unterricht's disease, nocturnal epilepsy, epilepsia nutans, physiologic epilepsy, psychic epilepsy, psychomotor epilepsy, reflex epilepsy, epilepsia, rotatoria or torsion spasm, sensory epilepsy, serial epilepsy, epilepsia tarda or tardy epilepsy, tonic epilepsy, traumatic epilepsy, ucinate epilepsy; cryptogenic or essential or idiopathic epilepsy; tonic spasm, tetany, lockjaw, trismus, tetanus; laryngospasm, laryngismus; clonic spasm, clonus; cramp.

.6 fever, feverishness, febrility, febricity, pyrexia, febri–, pyr(o)–, pyret(o)–; hyperpyrexia, hyperthermia; **heat, fire, fever heat;** flush, hectic flush; calenture; hectic fever or hectic; intermittent fever, remittent fever or remittent, continued fever, eruptive fever, recurrent or relapsing fever; irritation fever, water fever, protein fever, vaccinal fever, urethral fever, urinal fever; traumatic fever, wound fever; childbed fever, puerperal fever; delirium 473.8.

.7 collapse, breakdown, crackup [informal], **prostration,** exhaustion; nervous prostration or breakdown or exhaustion, neurasthenia; circulatory collapse.

.8 (disease symptoms) anemia; ankylosis; asphyxiation, anoxia, cyanosis; ataxia; bleeding, hemorrhage; colic; dizziness, vertigo; ague, chill, chills; dropsy, hydrops, edema; fainting; fatigue 717; fever 686.6; constipation; diarrhea, flux, dysentery; indigestion, upset stomach, dyspepsia 686.28; inflammation 686.9; necrosis 686.37; insomnia; itching, pruritus; jaundice 686.21, icterus, ictero–; backache, lumbago; vomiting, nausea 686.29; paralysis 686.25; skin eruption, rash 686.33,34; sore, abscess 686.35; hypertension, high blood pressure; hypotension, low blood pressure; tumor, growth 686.36; shock 686.24; convulsion, seizure, spasm 686.5; pain 424; fibrillation, tachycardia; labored breathing, apnea, dyspnea, asthma; blennorhea; nasal discharge, rheum, coughing, sneezing; wasting, cachexia *or* cachexy, tabes, tabo–, marasmus, emaciation, atrophy, necr(o)–; sclerosis.

.9 **inflammation**, –itis; acute inflammation, adhesive inflammation, chronic inflammation, catarrhal inflammation, diffuse inflammation, exudative inflammation, focal inflammation, hyperplastic inflammation, hypertrophic inflammation, metastatic inflammation, necrotic inflammation, obliterative inflammation, reactive inflammation, seroplastic inflammation, serous inflammation, simple inflammation, specific inflammation, suppurative inflammation, toxic inflammation, traumatic inflammation; atrophic inflammation, cirrhotic inflammation, fibroid inflammation, sclerosing inflammation; **appendicitis; arthritis;** rheumatoid arthritis, atrophic arthritis, arthritis deformans, chronic infectious arthritis, proliferative arthritis, arthritis pauperum, poor man's gout, osseous rheumatism; **gout,** podagra, gouty arthritis, uratic arthritis; gonococcal arthritis, gonorrheal arthritis, blennorrhagic arthritis, urethral arthritis, syphilitic arthritis; tuberculous arthritis, arthritis fungosa; menopausal arthritis, climactic arthritis; hypertrophic arthritis, degenerative arthritis; acute arthritis, dysenteric arthritis, hemophilic arthritis, infectional arthritis, suppurative arthritis, vertebral arthritis; osteoarthritis; **rheumatism,** rheumatiz *or* rheumatics [both dial]; gonorrheal rheumatism, rheumatism of the heart, Heberden's rheumatism, subacute rheumatism, tuberculous rheumatism *or* Poncet's rheumatism, visceral rheumatism; **bursitis,** bunion, housemaid's knee, tennis elbow; **colitis,** ulcerative colitis, mucous colitis, irritable bowel syndrome, spastic colon; nephritis, pyonephritis; **hepatitis,** infectious hepatitis, serum hepatitis; gastritis, enteritis; catarrh; bronchitis; **laryngitis;** pharyngitis; carditis, pericarditis, endocarditis; arteritis; phlebitis, thrombophlebitis, milk leg; capillaritis; mastoiditis; meningitis, cerebral meningitis, cerebrospinal meningitis, spinal meningitis, alcoholic meningitis, mumps meningitis, brain fever, cerebritis, cerebellitis, encephalitis, equine encephalomyelitis, myelitis; neuritis; osteitis, osteomyelitis; peritonitis; adrenitis; penitis *or* priapitis, orchitis *or* testitis, prostatitis; vaginitis, vulvitis, clitoritis, metritis *or* uteritis, ovaritis; ureteritis, cystitis, urethritis; lymphangitis; otitis; glossitis; tonsilitis, adenoiditis; ophthalmia, ophthalitis, conjunctivitis; rhinitis; sinusitis; pyorrhea, pyorrhea alveolaris, paradental pyorrhea, gingivitis, periodontitis, Rigg's disease; wryneck *or* torticollis, lumbago *or* lumbar rheumatism, collagen disease.

.10 (deficiency diseases) anemia, deficiency anemia, pernicious anemia, chlorosis, greensickness; goiter, struma; protein deficiency, kwashiorkor; malnutrition, cachexia; vitamin deficiency; night blindness, keratomalacia, xerophthalmia; pellagra, Italian *or* Lombardy leprosy, maidism; ariboflavinosis, beriberi; scurvy; rickets *or* rachitis, osteomalacia, osteoporosis; dermatitis.

.11 (genetic diseases) sickle-cell anemia *or* disease, thalassemia; hemophilia; dichromatic vision, achromatic vision, color blindness; mongolism *or* mongolianism, Down's syndrome; Turner's syndrome; Christmas disease; Hartnup disease; maple syrup urine disease; Milroy's disease; Niemann-Pick disease, lipid histiocytosis; Tay-Sachs disease; Werdnig-Hoffmann disease; cystic fibrosis, pancreatic fibrosis, mucoviscidosis; albinism; Huntington's chorea; muscular dystrophy; ichthyosis; dysautonomia.

.12 (infectious diseases) **dysentery,** amebic dysentery, amebiasis, bacillary dysentery, viral dysentery; anthrax, splenic fever, woolsorter's disease, ragsorter's disease, milzbrand, anthrac(o)–; bubonic plague, black death 686.4; **cholera,** Asiatic cholera; **chicken pox,** varicella; cowpox, vaccinia; **smallpox,** variola; diphtheria; elephantiasis; erysipelas, St. Anthony's fire; dengue *or* dengue fever, dandy fever, breakbone fever; histoplasmosis; leprosy, lepra, hansenosis, Hansen's disease; influenza, **flu** [informal], grippe 686.14; herpes, herpes simplex, herpet(o)–; herpes zoster, zoster, zona, shingles; jungle rot; kala azar, black fever, dumdum fever, cachectic fever, ponos; **hepatitis** 686.21; loaiasis, loa loa; hookworm; **malaria,** malarial fever, malari(o)–, ague, blackwater fever, Chagres fever, marsh fever; yellow fever, yellow jack; meningitis 686.9; **mononucleosis,** infectious mononucleosis, glandular fever, kissing disease [slang]; **measles,** rubeola; **German measles,** bastard measles, rubella; mumps, parotitis; leptospirosis, swamp fever; osteomyelitis; paratyphoid fever; pneumonia 686.14; infantile paralysis, poliomyelitis, polio [informal]; strep throat, septic sore throat, streptococcus tonsilitis; scarlet fever, scarlatina; rheumatic fever, acute articular rheumatism, inflammatory rheumatism, cerebral rheumatism, polyarthritis rheumatism; ringworm, tinea; rabies, hydrophobia, lyssa, madness; rat-bite fever, Haverhill fever; Rocky Mountain spotted fever; rickettsialpox, Kew Gardens spotted fever; schistosomiasis, snail fever; sleeping sickness, sleepy sickness [Brit], African lethargy, encephalitis lethargica; **tetanus, lockjaw,** tetan(o)–; trench fever, five-day fever; trench mouth, Vincent's infection; tularemia, deer fly fever, rabbit fever, alkali disease; psittacosis, parrot fever, ornithosis; tuberculosis 686.15; typhoid fever *or* typhoid, enteric fever, typh(o)–; typhus *or* typhus fever, jail fever, spotted fever; famine fever, relapsing fever; brucellosis, undulant fever; whooping cough, pertussis; thrush; yaws, frambesia; venereal disease 686.16.

.13 (eye diseases) **conjunctivitis,** pink eye; trachoma, blepharitis, iritis, sty, keratitis, choroiditis, uveitis, optic neuritis; detached retina; glaucoma; cataract; esotropia, cross-eye, walleye; retinoblastoma; amaurosis, gutta serena; eye defect, defective vision 440.

.14 (respiratory diseases) **bronchitis,** acute bronchitis, chronic bronchitis; catarrh, rheum, **cold,** common cold, coryza, the sniffles, the snuffles; influenza, flu [informal], grippe, *la grippe* [Fr]; Asian *or* Asiatic flu, Hong Kong flu; swine flu; bronchiectasis; pleurisy, pleuritis, dry pleurisy, wet pleurisy; **pneumonia,** pneum(o)–; lobar pneumonia, pneumococcal pneumonia, croupous pneumonia, fibrinous pneumonia, lung fever, pneumonic fever; atypical pneumonia, virus pneumonia; bronchopneumonia, bronchial pneumonia, bronchiolitis; double pneumonia; empyema; **emphysema;** epidemic pleurodynia, devil's grip; pneumothorax, collapsed lung; pneumoconiosis, coniosis, silicosis, silic(o)–, aluminosis, asbestosis, berylliosis, byssinosis, chalicosis, siderosis, siderosilicosis, mason's lung, farmer's lung; bituminosis, anthracosis, anthracosilicosis, coal-miner's lung, miner's lung, miner's asthma, miner's consumption, miner's phthisis, black lung [informal]; lipoid pneumonia; lung cancer; whooping cough; hay fever, asthma 686.32; tonsilitis, amygdalitis, quinsy; adenoiditis; croup; pharyngitis, sore throat; laryngitis.

.15 **tuberculosis,** TB, tubercul(o)–, white plague, phthisis, **consumption;** pulmonary tuberculosis *or* phthisis; inhalation *or* aerogenic tuberculosis; scrofula, tuberculosis of the lymphatic glands; scrofuloderma, colliquation, tuberculosis cutis, lupus vulgaris, tuberculosis luposa; cerebral tuberculosis, tuberculous meningitis; tuberculosis of the bones and joints, tuberculosis of the intestines, tuberculosis of the kidney and bladder, tuberculosis of the larynx, tuberculosis of the serous membranes; miliary *or* disseminated tuberculosis.

.16 **venereal disease, VD,** social disease, Cupid's itch *or* Venus's curse, dose [slang]; **syphilis,** syph [informal], syphil(o)–, pox, great pox, French disease *or* pox *or* plague [archaic], Italian *or* Spanish pox [archaic], *morbus Gallicus* [L]; acquired syphilis, congenital syphilis; primary *or* secondary *or* tertiary syphilis, latent syphilis, constitutional syphilis; paresis, general paresis, paralytic dementia, cerebral tabes, syphilitic meningoencephalitis; tabes, tabes dorsales, syphilitic posterior spinal sclerosis, locomotor ataxia; **gonorrhea,** clap *or* claps [both slang], dose of clap *or* claps [slang]; chancre, hard chancre, chancroid, simple chancre, soft chancre; granuloma inguinale, granuloma venereum, pudendal ulcer; lymphogranuloma venereum, Frei's disease, Nicolas-Favre disease, fifth venereal disease, climatic bubo, tropical bubo; balanitis gangrenosa.

.17 (cardiovascular diseases) heart disease, heart condition; angina, angina pectoris; congenital heart disease, rheumatic heart disease, coronary *or* ischemic heart disease, hypertensive heart disease; carditis, endocarditis, myocarditis, pericarditis, pyopericarditis; palpitation of the heart, palpitation, tachycardia, arrhythmia, extrasystole, premature beat, paroxysmal tachycardia, atrial fibrillation, auricular fibrillation, ventricular fibrillation; cardiac insufficiency, coronary insufficiency, myocardial insufficiency, myovascular insufficiency, pseudoaortic insufficiency; insufficiency of the valves, aortic insufficiency, mitral insufficiency, pulmonary insufficiency, tricuspid insufficiency; cardiac stenosis, aortic stenosis, mitral stenosis, pulmonary stenosis, tricuspid stenosis; **heart attack, heart failure,** heart *or* cardiac shock, cardiac arrest; cardiac *or* myocardial infarction, heart block; thrombosis, cardiac thrombosis, coronary thrombosis, coronary; sclerosis, atherosclerosis, arteriosclerosis, hardening of the arteries; armored heart, beriberi heart, chaotic heart, encased heart, fat *or* fatty heart, cor adiposum, hairy heart *or* cor villosum, fibroid heart, flask-shaped heart, frosted heart, round heart, stony heart, tabby-cat *or* thrush-breast *or* tiger *or* tiger-lily heart, turtle heart, ox heart *or* cor bovinum, cor juvenum; cor biloculare, cor pseudotriloculare biatriatum, cor triloculare biatriatum, cor triloculare biventriculare, cor triatriatum; hypertension, high blood pressure, systolic hypertension, diastolic hypertension; apoplexy, stroke, apoplectic stroke, paralytic stroke; arterial aneurism; varicose veins, varix, hemorrhoid, pile, lingual hemorrhoid.

.18 (blood diseases) **anemia;** hypochromic anemia, iron deficiency anemia, pernicious anemia, macrocytic anemia, microcytic anemia, aplastic anemia, hypoplastic anemia, Fanconi's syndrome, hemolytic anemia, primary anemia; hemoglobinopathy, sickle-cell anemia *or* disease, thalassemia *or* Mediterranean anemia; polycythemia *or* erythrocytosis; purpura, idiopathic thrombocytopenic purpura, purpura hemorrhagica; hemophilia, bleeder's disease, hemophilia A; Christmas disease, hemophilia B; hemophilia C; angiohemophilia, pseudohemophilia, vascular hemophilia; afibrinogenemia; neutropenia, cyclic neutropenia, Banti's syndrome, Felty's syndrome; panhematopenia; leukemia, acute leukemia, chronic leukemia, lymphoid *or* lymphogenous *or* lymphatic leukemia, myeloid *or* myelogenous leukemia, monocytic leukemia, lymphosarcoma; lymphoma; Hodgkin's disease, infectious granuloma, malignant granuloma, malignant lymphoma, anemia lymphatica, pseudoleukemia; reticulum cell sarcoma, lymphoblastoma, leukemic reticuloendotheliosis, Gaucher's disease, Letterer-Siwe syndrome, xanthomatosis, Hand-Schuller-Christian disease; multiple myeloma, plasma cell leukemia, plasmacytoma.

.19 (gland diseases) acromegaly, giantism, dwarfism, sexual precocity, sexual infantilism, panhypopituitarism, persistent lactation, diabetes insipidus; hyperthyroidism, thyrotoxicosis, toxic goiter, Graves' disease, hypothyroidism, cretinism, myxedema; hyperparathyroidism, hypoparathyroidism; Addison's disease, hypercorticoidism, Cushing's disease, androgenital

syndrome, pheochromocytoma; eunuchoidism, choriocarcinoma, Kleinfelter's syndrome; hypo-ovarianism, hyperovarianism; diabetes, diabetes mellitus, hypoglycemia; hyperglycemia.

.20 (metabolic diseases) acidosis, alkalosis, ketosis; gout, podagra; galactosemia, lactose intolerance, fructose intolerance; phenylketonuria *or* PKU, maple syrup urine disease, congenital hypophosphatasia.

.21 (liver diseases) **jaundice** *or* icterus, **cirrhosis, hepatitis,** infectious hepatitis, serum hepatitis, hepatoma; cholecystitis, gallstone *or* biliary calculus, cholangitis.

.22 (kidney diseases) nephritis, Bright's disease, glomerulonephritis; nephrosis, nephrosclerosis, nephrolithosis, uremia, hematuria, renal hematuria; kidney stone, nephrolith, renal calculus.

.23 nervous disorder, neuropathy, brain disease; neuritis, shingles *or* herpes zoster, sciatica *or* sciatic neuritis, writer's cramp, polyneuritis, pressure neuropathy, Bell's palsy, radiculitis; neuralgia, ischialgia, glossopharyngeal neuralgia, trigeminal neuralgia, *tic douloureux* [Fr]; **headache,** cephalalgia, **migraine; epilepsy,** falling sickness 686.5; palsy, shaking palsy, paralysis agitans, Parkinson's disease, Parkinsonism; cerebral palsy, spastic paralysis; chorea, the jerks [informal], St. Vitus's dance, Huntington's chorea; multiple sclerosis *or* MS, amyotrophic lateral sclerosis *or* Lou Gehrig's disease; brain tumor; priapism; organic psychosis, toxic psychosis 473.3; emotional disorder 690.17.

.24 **shock,** traumatism; secondary shock; allergic shock, anaphylactic shock, histamine shock, serum shock, cardiogenic shock, cerebral shock, hematogenic shock, neurogenic shock; protein shock; insulin shock, hypoglycemic shock; postoperative shock, surgical shock, traumatic shock, wound shock; mental shock, **trauma;** thanatosis; shell shock, combat *or* battle fatigue 690.19.

.25 paralysis, paralyzation, palsy, impairment of motor function, –plegia *or* –plegy, –lysis; stroke, apoplexy; paresis; motor paralysis, sensory paralysis; hemiplegia, paraplegia, diplegia; cataplexy, catalepsy; infantile paralysis, poliomyelitis, polio [informal].

.26 **heatstroke;** heat prostration *or* exhaustion; sunstroke, *coup de soleil* [Fr], siriasis, insolation; calenture, thermic fever.

.27 (diseases of the digestive tract) stomach

condition; gastritis; **ulcer**, peptic ulcer, stomach ulcer, duodenal ulcer, esophagal ulcer; esophagitis, duodenitis; hiatal hernia, abdominal hernia, diverticulosis; diverticulitis, peritonitis; megacolon; polyp; colitis 686.9.

.28 **indigestion**, dyspepsia; heartburn, cardialgia, pyrosis; colic, gripe, gripes; cholera morbus; **constipation, irregularity**, obstipation, costiveness; **diarrhea**, dysentery, flux, trots [slang], lientery, looseness of the bowels.

.29 **nausea**, nauseation, queasiness, squeamishness, qualmishness; qualm, pukes [slang]; motion sickness, seasickness, *mal de mer* [Fr], airsickness, car sickness; vomiting 310.8.

.30 **poisoning**, intoxication, venenation; septic poisoning, blood poisoning, sepsis, septicemia, toxemia, pyemia, septicopyemia; autointoxication; food poisoning, ptomaine poisoning, milk sickness, ergotism, St. Anthony's fire.

.31 (environmental and occupational diseases) motion sickness 686.29; jet lag; altitude sickness, anoxia, anoxemia, anoxic anoxia; frostbite, chilblain, immersion foot, trench foot; radiation sickness, radionecrosis; lead poisoning; Minamata disease, mercury poisoning; *itai* [Jap], cadmium poisoning; sunstroke 686.26; aeroembolism, caisson disease, decompression sickness, diver's palsy, the bends [informal]; red-out; pneumoconiosis, black lung [informal] 686.14; writer's cramp *or* palsy *or* spasm; housemaid's knee; anthrax, woolsorter's disease.

.32 **allergy**, allergic disorder; allergic rhinitis, **hay fever**, rose cold, pollinosis; **asthma**, bronchial asthma; **hives**, urticaria; eczema; conjunctivitis; cold sores; allergic gastritis; cosmetic dermatitis; allergen.

.33 (skin diseases) dermatosis, dermatitis, –derma; **eczema**, tetter; **acne**, acne vulgaris; dermamycosis, **athlete's foot**, jungle rot; itch, scabies, pruigo, pruritus; psora, psoriasis; erysipelas, St. Anthony's fire; erythema; elephantiasis; herpes, herpes simplex; herpes zoster, shingles; ringworm; hives; impetigo; lichen, lichen primus; miliaria, prickly heat, heat rash; pemphigus; lupus, lupus vulgaris; leprosy; skin cancer, epithelioma; exanthem.

.34 **skin eruption**, eruption, **rash**, efflorescence, breaking out, –anthema, –id(e); diaper rash; drug rash, vaccine rash; prickly heat, heat rash; hives, urticaria, nettle rash; papular rash; rupia.

.35 **sore, lesion;** pustule, papule, papula, papulo–, fester, pimple; pock; ulcer, ulceration; bed sore; tubercle; blister, bleb, bulla, blain; whelk, wheal, welt, wale; boil, furuncle, furunculus; carbuncle; canker; canker sore; cold sore, fever blister; sty; abscess, gathering, aposteme [archaic]; gumboil, parulis; whitlow, felon, paronychia; bubo; chancre; soft chancre, chancroid; hemorrhoids, piles; bunion; chilblain, kibe; polyp; stigma, petechia; scab, eschar; fistula; suppuration, festering; wound 692.8; swelling, rising 256.4.

.36 **growth**, neoplasm, –phyte; **tumor**, intumescence, –cele, –oma, onch(o)– *or* onchi– *or* onci–; benign tumor, nonmalignant tumor, innocent tumor; malignant tumor, malignant growth, metastatic tumor, **cancer**, carcin(o)–, sarcoma, carcinoma; morbid growth; excrescence, outgrowth; proud flesh; exostosis; cyst, wen; fungus, fungosity; callus, callosity, **corn**, clavus; **wart**, verruca; **mole**, nevus.

.37 **gangrene**, mortification, necrosis, sphacelus, sphacelation; noma; moist gangrene, dry gangrene, gas gangrene; caries, cariosity; slough; necrotic tissue.

.38 (animal diseases) anthrax, splenic fever, charbon, milzbrand, malignant pustule; malignant catarrh *or* malignant catarrhal fever; bighead; blackleg, black quarter, quarter evil *or* ill; cattle plague, rinderpest; glanders; foot-and-mouth disease, hoof-and-mouth disease, aphthous fever; distemper; gapes; heaves, broken wind; hog cholera; loco, loco disease, locoism; mange, scabies; pip; rot, liver rot, sheep rot; staggers, megrims, blind staggers, mad staggers; swine dysentery, bloody flux; stringhalt; Texas fever, blackwater; John's disease, paratuberculosis, pseudotuberculosis; rabies, hydrophobia.

.39 **germ**, pathogen, bug [informal], disease-causing agent, disease-producing microorganism; **microbe**, microorganism; **virus**, filterable virus, nonfilterable virus, adenovirus, echovirus, reovirus, rhinovirus, enterovirus, picornavirus; rickettsia; bacterium, **bacteria** [pl], coccus, streptococcus, staphylococcus, bacillus, spirillum, vibrio, spirochete, gram-positive bacteria, gram-negative bacteria, aerobe, aerobic bacteria, anaerobe, anaerobic bacteria; protozoon, protozoa [pl], amoeba, trypanosome; fungus, mold, spore.

.40 **sick person**, sufferer, –path; valetudinarian, **invalid, shut-in**; incurable, terminal case; **patient, case**; inpatient, outpatient;

apoplectic, consumptive, dyspeptic, epileptic, rheumatic, arthritic, spastic; **the sick, the infirm.**

.41 **carrier,** vector, biological vector, mechanical vector; Typhoid Mary.

.42 **cripple,** defective, **handicapped person,** incapable; amputee; paraplegic, quadriplegic, paralytic; deformity 249.3; the crippled, the handicapped, "the halt, the lame, and the blind" [Bible]; idiot, imbecile 471.8.

.43 VERBS **ail, suffer,** labor under, be affected with, complain of; **feel ill,** feel under the weather, feel awful [informal], feel something terrible, not feel like anything [informal], feel like the walking dead; look green about the gills [informal].

.44 **take sick** or **ill, sicken; catch, contract, get,** take, sicken for [Brit], **come down with** [informal], be stricken or seized by, fall a victim to; catch cold; take one's death [dial]; **break out,** break out with, break out in a rash, erupt; run a temperature, fever; be laid by the heels, be struck down, be brought down, be felled; drop in one's tracks, **collapse;** overdose, OD [slang]; go into shock, be traumatized.

.45 **fail, weaken, sink, decline,** run down, lose strength, lose one's grip, dwindle, droop, flag, wilt, wither, wither away, fade, **languish,** waste, waste away, pine, peak, "dwindle, peak, and pine" [Shakespeare].

.46 **go lame,** founder.

.47 **afflict, disorder, derange; sicken, indispose; weaken, enfeeble,** enervate, reduce, debilitate, devitalize; **invalid,** incapacitate, **disable;** lay up, hospitalize.

.48 **infect, disease, contaminate,** taint.

.49 **poison,** empoison [archaic], envenom.

.50 ADJS **unhealthy,** healthless, in poor health; **infirm, unsound,** invalid, valetudinary, valetudinarian, debilitated, cachectic, enervated, exhausted, drained; **sickly,** peaky or peaked [both informal]; **weakly, feeble, frail** 160.12–18,21; weakened, with low resistance, **run-down,** reduced, reduced in health; moribund, languishing, failing 160.21; pale 363.7.

.51 **unwholesome, unhealthy,** unsound, morbid, diseased, pathological, path(o)–.

.52 **ill, ailing, sick, unwell, indisposed,** taken ill, down, bad, on the sick list; **sickish, seedy** or **rocky** [both informal], **under the weather, out of sorts** [informal], below par [informal], off-color, off one's feed [informal]; not quite right, not oneself; faint, faintish, feeling faint; feeling awful,

feeling something terrible [both informal]; sick as a dog, laid low; in a bad way, critically ill, in danger, on the critical list; mortally ill, sick unto death.

.53 **nauseated,** nauseous, **queasy, squeamish, qualmish,** qualmy; **sick to one's stomach,** sick to or sick at the stomach; pukish or puky or barfy [all slang]; seasick, carsick, airsick.

.54 **feverish,** fevered, feverous, in a fever, febrile, pyretic; **flushed,** inflamed, **hot, burning,** fiery, hectic; hyperpyretic, hyperthermic; delirious 473.31.

.55 **laid up, invalided,** hospitalized, in hospital [Brit]; **bedridden, bedfast, sick abed; down,** prostrate, flat on one's back; in childbed, confined.

.56 **diseased, morbid, pathological,** bad, **infected, contaminated,** tainted, peccant, –pathic, kako– or caco–; **poisoned,** septic; cankerous, cankered, ulcerous, ulcerated, gangrenous, gangrened, mortified, sphacelated.

.57 anemic, chlorotic; bilious; dyspeptic, colicky; dropsical, edematous, hydropic; gouty, podagric; neuritic, neuralgic; palsied, paralytic; pneumonic, pleuritic, tubercular, tuberculous, phthisic, consumptive; rheumatic, arthritic; rickety, rachitic; syphilitic, pocky, luetic; tabetic, tabid [archaic]; allergic; apoplectic; hypertensive; diabetic; encephalitic; epileptic; laryngitic; leprous; malarial; measly; nephritic; scabietic, scorbutic, scrofulous; variolous, variolar; tumorous; cancerous, malignant; carcinogenic, tumorigenic.

.58 **contagious, infectious,** infective, **catching,** taking, spreading, **communicable,** zymotic, inoculable; pestiferous, pestilential, **epidemic,** epidemial, pandemic; epizootic, epiphytotic; endemic; sporadic.

687. REMEDY

.1 NOUNS **remedy, cure, corrective,** alterative, remedial measure, sovereign remedy; **relief, help, aid, assistance,** succor; balm, balsam; healing agent; restorative, analeptic; healing quality or virtue; specific, specific remedy; **prescription,** recipe, receipt.

.2 **nostrum,** patent medicine, quack remedy; snake oil.

.3 **panacea, cure-all,** universal remedy, theriac, catholicon; polychrest, broad-spectrum drug or antibiotic; elixir, elixir of life, *elixir vitae* [L].

.4 **medicine, medicament, medication,** medicinal, theraputant, **drug, physic,** preparation, mixture, pharmacon, pharmac(o)–; herbs, medicinal herbs, simples, vegetable remedies, "the physic of the field" [Pope]; balsam, balm; tisane, ptisan; drops; powder; inhalant; electuary, elixir, syrup, lincture, linctus; officinal; prescription drug, ethical drug; over-the-counter drug, nonprescription drug, proprietary medicine *or* drug, proprietary, patent medicine; proprietary name, generic name; materia medica.

.5 **dangerous drug, drug**; dope, junk, candy, stuff [all informal]; hard drug, hard stuff [informal]; addictive drug.

.6 **dose, draft, potion**, portion, **shot**, injection; broken dose; booster, booster dose, recall dose, booster shot; narcotic shot; overdose; **fix** *or* hit *or* bang [all slang], mainlining [slang]; popping *or* skin-popping [both slang]; dropping; drug packet, bag *or* deck [both slang].

.7 **pill**, bolus, **tablet, capsule**, lozenge, troche.

.8 **tonic, bracer**, cordial, restorative, analeptic, roborant, **pick-me-up** [informal]; **shot in the arm** [slang]; vitamin shot.

.9 **stimulant** 687.52, upper [slang]; cocaine, coke *or* snow [both slang], C [slang]; amphetamine, pep pill [informal], jolly bean [slang]; amphetamine sulfate, Benzedrine, Benzedrine pill, bennie *or* benzie [both slang]; dextroamphetamine sulfate, Dexedrine, Dexedrine pill; dexie *or* heart *or* football [all slang]; Dexamyl, Dexamyl pill, purple heart [slang]; methamphetamine hydrochloride, Methedrine, Methedrine pill; meth *or* speed *or* crystal *or* businessman's trip [all slang].

.10 **palliative, alleviative, lenitive, assuasive**, assuager.

.11 **balm** 687.51, lotion, salve, ointment, unguent, *unguentum* [L], cerate, unction, balsam, oil, emollient, demulcent; liniment, embrocation; vulnerary; collyrium, eyesalve, eyewater [archaic], eyewash.

.12 **sedative, depressant** 687.54, depressor, downer [slang]; **calmative, tranquilizer** 687.55, soother, soothing syrup, quietener, pacifier; **analgesic** 687.56, **anodyne**, paregoric [archaic], **pain killer** *or* pain pill [both informal]; hypnotic, soporific, somnifacient, sleep-inducer, sleeping draught, **sleeping pill**, goofball *or* sleeper [both slang]; barbiturate, barbiturate pill, barb [slang]; phenobarbital sodium, Nembutal, Nembutal pill; yellow jacket *or* yellow *or* nemmie [all slang]; secobarbital sodium, Seconal, Seconal pill, red *or* red

devil [both slang]; amobarbital sodium, Amytal, Amytal pill; blue, blue angel, blue heaven, blue bird, blue devil [all slang]; Tuinal, Tuinal pill, rainbow *or* tooie [both slang]; sodium thiopental, phenobarbital, Luminal, Luminal pill, purple heart [slang]; chloral hydrate, knockout drops *or* Mickey Finn [both slang]; **narcotic**, narc(o)–; **opiate; opium**, mecon(o)–; pen yan, hop, tar, black stuff [all slang]; codeine, codeine cough syrup, turps [slang]; tincture of opium, laudanum; paregoric, blue velvet [slang]; morphine, morphia, M *or* Miss Emma [both slang]; diacetyl morphine, heroin; **H, hard stuff, horse, junk, scag, shit, smack**, white stuff [all slang]; meperidine, Demerol; methadone, Dolophine, dolly [slang]; lotus; alcohol, liquor 996.12–14.

.13 **psychoactive drug**, psychochemical, mind-altering drug; **tranquilizer** 687.55, ataractic; psychic energizer, antidepressant; **hallucinogen, psychedelic**, psychedelic drug, mind-expanding drug, mind-blowing drug, psychotomimetic; lysergic acid diethylamide, LSD-25, **LSD**, acid *or* 25 [both slang]; STP; dimethyltryptamine, DMT; diethyltryptamine, DET; psilocybin, psilocin; mescal, mescal button, peyote, mescaline, mesc [slang]; mescal bean; morning glory seeds; kava; **marijuana; gage, grass**, hay, **pot**, tea, hemp, weed, Mary Jane [all slang]; marijuana cigarette; **joint** *or* **stick** *or* **reefer** [all slang], roach [slang]; hashish, hash [slang]; ganja [India]; tetrahydrol cannabinol, THC.

.14 **antipyretic** 687.64, febrifuge, fever-reducer, fever pill [informal].

.15 **anesthetic** 687.57; local *or* topical *or* general anesthetic; differential anesthetic.

.16 **cough medicine**, cough syrup, cough drops; horehound.

.17 **laxative** 687.62, **cathartic, physic, purge, purgative**, aperient, carminative, diuretic, –agogue.

.18 **emetic**, vomitive *or* vomit [both archaic], nauseant.

.19 **enema**, clyster, clysma, lavage, lavement [archaic].

.20 **prophylactic, preventive**, preventative, protective.

.21 **antiseptic** 687.58, **disinfectant** 687.59, fumigant, fumigator, **germicide**, bactericide, microbicide.

.22 **dentifrice, toothpaste**, tooth powder; mouthwash, gargle.

.23 **contraceptive**, birth control device, prophylactic; condom; **rubber** *or* skin *or* bag [all slang]; oral contraceptive, **birth control pill, the pill** [informal]; diaphragm, pessary; spermicide, spermicidal jelly, contraceptive foam; intrauterine device, IUD.

.24 **vermifuge,** vermicide, worm medicine, anthelmintic.

.25 **antacid** 687.63, gastric antacid, alkalizer.

.26 **antidote,** counterpoison, alexipharmic, theriaca or theriac.

.27 **antitoxin,** antitoxic serum; **antivenin; serum,** antiserum; interferon; **antibody,** antigen-antibody product, anaphylactic antibody, incomplete antibody, inhibiting antibody, sensitizing antibody; gamma globulin, serum gamma globulin, immune globulin, antitoxic globulin; lysin, precipitin, agglutinin, anaphylactin, bactericidin; antiantibody; antigen, Rh antigen, Rh factor; allergen; **immunosuppressive drug.**

.28 **vaccine,** stock vaccine, bovine vaccine, humanized vaccine; univalent vaccine, homologous or autogenous vaccine, heterogenous vaccine, multivalent or polyvalent vaccine; live-virus vaccine, killed-virus vaccine; T.A.B. vaccine, typhoid-paratyphoid A and B vaccine, triple vaccine; measles vaccine; rubella vaccine; BCG vaccine (bacillus Calmette-Guérin), Calmette's vaccine; polio vaccine, Salk vaccine, Sabin vaccine; toxoid, tetanus toxoid, diphtheria toxoid.

.29 **miracle drugs, wonder drugs,** magic bullets; **antibiotic** 687.60; bacteriostat; **sulfa drug** 687.61, sulfa, sulfanilamide, sulfonamide.

.30 **diaphoretic,** sudorific.

.31 **vesicant,** vesicatory, epispastic.

.32 (other drugs) antihistamine; antiperiodic; antiphlogistic; antispasmodic; counterirritant; decongestant; carminative; adjuvant; expectorant; emmenagogue; maturative; vasodilator, vasoconstrictor; **hormone** 312.10; **vitamin** 309.4.

.33 **dressing, application,** epithem [archaic]; plaster, court plaster, mustard plaster, sinapism; **poultice,** cataplasm; formentation; **compress,** pledget; stupe; tent; tampon; **bandage, bandaging,** band [archaic], binder, cravat, triangular bandage, roller or roller bandage, four-tailed bandage; bandage compress, adhesive compress, Band-Aid; elastic bandage, Ace elastic bandage, Ace bandage; rubber bandage; plastic bandage; **tourniquet;** sling; splint, brace; cast, plaster cast; tape, **adhesive tape;** lint, cotton, gauze, sponge.

.34 **pharmacology, pharmacy, pharmaceutics;** posology; materia medica.

.35 **pharmacist,** pharmaceutist, pharmacopolist, **druggist, chemist** [Brit], **apothecary,** dispenser, gallipot; pharmacologist, pharmaceutical chemist, posologist.

.36 **drugstore, pharmacy,** chemist or chemist's shop [both Brit], apothecary's shop, dispensary, dispensatory.

.37 **pharmacopoeia,** pharmacopedia, dispensatory.

.38 VERBS remedy, cure 694.13–15; prescribe; treat 689.30.

.39 ADJS **remedial, curative, therapeutic, healing, corrective,** alterative, restorative, analeptic, sanative, sanatory; adjuvant; **medicinal,** medicative, theriac(al), iatric.

.40 **palliative, lenitive, alleviative, assuasive,** soothing, balmy, balsamic, demulcent, emollient.

.41 **antidotal,** alexipharmic; **antitoxic; antibiotic,** bacteriostatic, antimicrobial; antiluetic, antisyphilitic; antiscorbutic; antiperiodic; antipyretic, febrifugal; vermifugal, anthelmintic; **antacid.**

.42 **prophylactic, preventive,** protective.

.43 **antiseptic, disinfectant, germicidal,** bactericidal.

.44 **tonic, stimulating, bracing, invigorating,** reviving, refreshing, restorative, analeptic, strengthening, roborant, corroborant.

.45 **sedative, calmative,** calmant, depressant, **soothing, tranquilizing, quietening;** narcotic, opiatic; **analgesic,** anodyne, paregoric [archaic]; hypnotic, soporific, somniferous, somnifacient, sleep-inducing.

.46 **psychochemical,** psychoactive; ataractic; antidepressant; hallucinogenic, **psychedelic,** mind-expanding, psychotomimetic.

.47 **anesthetic,** deadening, numbing.

.48 **cathartic,** laxative, purgative, aperient; carminative; diuretic.

.49 **emetic,** vomitive, vomitory [archaic].

.50 **pharmaceutic(al),** pharmacological.

.51 **balms**

arnica	menthol
balm of Gilead	Mentholatum
balsam	mercurial ointment
blue ointment	olive oil
glycerin	petrolatum, petroleum jelly
glycerite, glycerole	
glycerogel, glycerogelatin	Vaseline
	Vicks Vaporub
glycerol	witch hazel
lanolin	zinc ointment
melissa	

.52 **stimulants**

Adrenalin, adrenaline	ammonium carbonate
aloes	amphetamine

amphetamine sul-
  phate
arnica
aromatic spirits of
  ammonia
Benzedrine
benzoin
caffeine
chocolate
cocaine
cocoa
coffee
colocynth
desoxyephedrine
Dexamyl
Dexedrine, dex-
  troamphetamine

sulfate
digitalin, digitalis
epinephrine
kola nut, kola
Methedrine, meth-
  amphetamine
  hydrochloride
nikethamide
nux vomica
picrotoxin
quassia
quinine
smelling salts, salts
sodium phosphate
strychnine
tea

.53 hallucinogens, psychoactive drugs

belladonna
cannabis, bhang
DET, diethyltrypt-
  amine
DMT, dimethyl-
  tryptamine
hashish
hemp, ganja
hyoscyamus, henbane
Indian hemp
jimsonweed
LSD, lysergic acid

diethylamide
marijuana
mescal
mescaline
morning glory seeds
peyote
psilocin
psilocybin
stramonium
THC, tetrahydrol can-
  nabinol

.54 depressants

aconite
alcohol
Amytal, amobarbital
  sodium
atropine
barbital, barbitone
  [Brit]
barbituric acid
belladonna
bromide
chloral hydrate, chlo-
  ral
codeine
Demerol
Dial, diallylbarbituric
  acid
heroin
hyoscyamine
laudanum
Luminal

meperidine
methadone
morphine
Nembutal
opium
paraldehyde
pentobarbital
phenobarbital
Quaalude
reserpine
scopolamine
Seconal, secobarbital
  sodium
sodium bromide
Sulfonal, sulfonmeth-
  ane
thalidomide
Trional, sulfonethyl-
  methane
Tuinal

.55 tranquilizers

chlorpromazine
Equanil
Librium
meprobamate
Miltown
phenoglycodol
phenothiazine
rauwolfia

reserpine
Serpasil
thalidomide
thioridazine
Thorazine
Triavil
Valium

.56 analgesics

acetanilide
acetophenetidin
aminopyrine
Anacin
aspirin, acetylsalicylic
  acid
Bufferin, buffered
  aspirin

Darvon
Empirin
Excedrin
headache powder
phenacetin
Pyramidon
sodium salicylate

.57 anesthetics

A.C.E. mixture (alco-
  hol, chloroform and
  ether)
anesthyl
Avertin
benzocaine
butacaine sulfate,
  butacaine
C.E. mixture (chloro-
  form and ether)
chloroform
cocaine
cyclopropane
dibucaine
ether
ethyl chloride
ethylene
gas

halocaine
laughing gas
menthol
Metycaine
nitrous oxide
novocaine, Novocain
Nupercaine
Pantocain
piperocaine
procaine
protoxide of nitrogen
tetracaine
thiopental sodium,
  Pentothal, truth
  serum
tribromoethanol
trichloromethane
urethane

.58 antiseptics

A.B.C. powder (boric
  acid, bismuth subni-
  trate and calomel)
alcohol
Argyrol
boric acid
calomel
camphor
carbolic acid
chloramine, chlora-
  mine-T
cresol
gentian violet
gramicidin
hexachloraphene
hydrogen peroxide

iodine
iodoform
Mercurochrome, mer-
  bromin
mercurous chloride
Merthiolate
peroxide
phenol
phenyl salicylate
resorcinol
Salol
silver vitellin
spirits of camphor
thimerosal
thymol
tincture of iodine

.59 disinfectants

bichloride of mercury
bleaching powder
carbolic acid
chlorine
chloride of lime
cresol
formaldehyde
hypochlorous acid
lye

Lysol
mercuric chloride,
  mercury chloride
phenol
potassium permanga-
  nate
sodium hydroxide
sodium hypochlorite

.60 antibiotics

actinomycin
amphotericin
ampicillin
antimycin A
Aureomycin
azaserine
bacitracin
carbomycin
cephaloridine
Chloromycetin, chlor-
  amphenicol
chlortetracycline
cloxacillin
cycloserine
dihydrostreptomycin
erythromycin
fradicin
gramicidin
griseofulvin
kanamycin
methicillin
mitomycin

mycomycin
neomycin
novobiocin
nystatin
oxacillin
oxytetracycline
penicillin
phenethicillin
polymyxin
pyocyanase
pyocyanin
spectinomycin
Staphcillin
streptomycin
streptothricin
subtilin
Terramycin
tetracycline
tylocin
tyrothricin
vancomycin
viomycin

.61 sulfa drugs

Gantrisin	sulfamethazine
Neoprontosil	sulfanilamide
phthalylsulfathiazole	sulfapyrazine
Prontosil	sulfapyridine
succinylsulfathiazole	Sulfasuxidine
sulfadiazine	Sulfathalidine
sulfadimethoxine	sulfathiazole
sulfaguanidine	sulfisoxazole
sulfamerazine	

.62 laxatives

agar	magnesia, magnesium
aloes	oxide
bran	mercurous chloride
calomel	milk of magnesia,
cascara, cascara	magnesium hydrox-
sagrada	ide
castor oil	mineral oil
citrate of magnesia,	mineral water
magnesium citrate	phenolphthalein
colocynth	podophyllin
Culver's root	prunes
epsom salts, epsom	psyllium seed
salt	Rochelle powders
figs	salts
Glauber's salt	Seidlitz powders
jalop	senna
leptandra	sodium phosphate

.63 antacids

Alka-Seltzer	magnesium hydrox-
bicarbonate of soda	ide
Brioschi	Pepto-Bismol
Bromo Seltzer	Rolaids
calcium carbonate	seltzer, seltzer water
Maalox	sodium bicarbonate
magnesia, magnesium	sodium phosphate
oxide	Tums
milk of magnesia,	

.64 antipyretics

acetanilide	phenazone
antipyrine	quinacrine
aspirin, acetylsalicylic	quinidine
acid	quinine
Atabrine	sodium salicylate
mepacrine [Brit]	

.65 miscellaneous drugs

ammonium chloride	ergot
Antabus	ipecac, ipecacuanha
atropine, belladonna	milk of bismuth
bismuth	podophyllin
curare	quassia
Dilantin, diphenylhy-	sal ammoniac
dantoin	sassafras
ephedrine	syrup of ipecac

688. HEALING ARTS

.1 NOUNS **medicine,** leechcraft, physic or leechdom [both archaic]; therapy 689; anatomic medicine, biomedicine, comparative medicine, clinical medicine, constitutional medicine, dosimetric medicine, experimental medicine, folk medicine, general medicine, group medicine, holistic medicine, industrial medicine, internal medicine, materia medica, neo-Hippocratic medicine, physical medicine, preclinical medicine, preventive medicine, public health medicine, tropical medicine, veterinary medicine; psychosomatic medicine 690.4; socialized medicine, state medicine, federal medicine; Medicare, Medicaid; forensic or legal medicine, medical jurisprudence; military medicine, naval medicine, air medicine, aviation medicine, aerospace medicine, space medicine.

.2 (systems) osteopathy; chiropractic, chiropraxis; Galenic medicine; naturopathy; eclectic medicine, eclecticism; allopathy; homeopathy; ayurveda, ayurvedic medicine.

.3 **surgery,** –chirurgia; operative surgery, clinical surgery, general surgery; major surgery, minor surgery; veterinary surgery; aseptic surgery, antiseptic surgery; dental surgery or oral surgery, neurosurgery, brain surgery, urological surgery, orthopedic surgery, thoracic surgery, heart surgery, open-heart surgery, plastic surgery or reconstructive surgery, chiroplasty, reparative surgery, prosthetics, cryosurgery; microsurgery; electrosurgery; radiosurgery; operation 689.21–25; organ transplantation.

.4 **dentistry,** general dentistry; operative dentistry, oral surgery, surgical dentistry; prosthetic dentistry, prosthodontics, prosthodontia; orthodontics, orthodontia; periodontics, periodontia; exodontics, exodontia; endodontics, endodontia; radiodontics, radiodontia.

.5 **healer, therapist,** therapeutist, **medic,** –path, –iatrist, iatro–; bonesetter; oculist; **optometrist; midwife;** homeopath, homeopathist; **osteopath; chiropractor.**

.6 **doctor,** doc [informal], **physician,** Doctor of Medicine, **MD, medical practitioner, medical man, medico** [informal], leech [archaic], croaker or sawbones [both slang]; allopath, allopathist; general practitioner, GP; family doctor; country doctor; **intern; resident,** house physician, resident physician; physician in ordinary; medical attendant, attending physician; **medical examiner,** coroner.

.7 **quack,** quacksalver, **charlatan, medicaster,** medicine man, medicine monger, horse doctor.

.8 **specialist; orthopedist; pediatrician,** pediatrist; **chiropodist, podiatrist,** foot doctor; **dermatologist,** skin man [slang]; **internist;** cardiologist; **neurologist; psychia-**

trist 690.12,13; gynecologist; obstetrician; gerontologist, geriatrician; otolaryngologist, eye-ear-nose-throat specialist; **oculist,** ophthalmologist, eye doctor; otologist; **pathologist;** immunologist, serologist; anesthesiologist; radiologist.

.9 **surgeon,** sawbones [slang]; operator, operative surgeon.

.10 **dentist,** tooth doctor, toothdrawer; **dental surgeon,** operative dentist; DDS, Doctor of Dental Surgery; DDSc, Doctor of Dental Science; DMD, Doctor of Dental Medicine; **orthodontist,** periodontist, prosthodontist, exodontist, endodontist; radiodontist.

.11 **veterinary, veterinarian, vet** [informal], veterinary surgeon [Brit], horse doctor.

.12 **nonmedical therapist;** theotherapist; Christian *or* spiritual *or* divine healer; **Christian Science practitioner,** healer; **faith healer.**

.13 **nurse,** sister *or* nursing sister [both Brit]; trained nurse, graduate nurse; registered nurse, RN; practical nurse, licensed practical nurse, LPN; charge nurse, general-duty nurse, private-duty nurse, surgical nurse, scrub nurse; community nurse, district nurse, visiting nurse, public health nurse, school nurse; student nurse; probe [informal], **probationer,** probationist.

.14 (hospital staff) paramedic; orderly, attendant, nurse's aide; dresser; anesthetist; radiographer, X-ray technician; laboratory technician; radiotherapist; physical therapist, physiotherapist; dietitian; hospital administrator.

.15 **Hippocrates,** Galen; Aesculapius, Asclepius.

.16 **practice of medicine,** medical practice; general practice, restricted practice; internship; residency; Hippocratic oath.

.17 VERBS **practice medicine,** doctor [informal]; treat 689.30; intern.

.18 ADJS **medical,** medico–, iatric, surgical; chiropodic, pediatric, orthopedic, obstetric(al), neurological; dental, dent(o)– *or* denti–; orthodontic, periodontic, prosthodontic, exodontic; osteopathic, chiropractic, naturopathic, hydropathic, allopathic, homeopathic; clinical, clinico–.

.19 **branches of medicine**

anatomy	dentistry
anesthesiology	dermatology
audiology	diagnostics
bacteriology	embryology
cardiography	endocrinology
cardiology	epidemiology
chiropody	etiology
dental surgery	exodontics

fluoroscopy	otolaryngology
general medicine	otology
geriatrics, gerontology	parasitology
gynecology	pathology
hematology	pediatrics
hygiene	periodontics
immunochemistry	physical medicine
immunology	physiopathology
internal medicine	podiatry
materia medica	psychiatry
mental hygiene	psychoanalysis
midwifery	psychology 690
mycology	radiology
neurology	serology
neurosurgery	surgery
nosology	surgical anatomy
nutrition	symptomatology,
obstetrics	semeiology
ophthalmology	teratology
optometry	therapeutics 689.1
orthodontics	tocology
orthopedics	toxicology

689. THERAPY

.1 NOUNS **therapy, therapeutics,** therapeusis, **treatment, medical care** *or* **treatment,** medication, –iatric(s) *or* –iatry, –pathic(s) *or* –pathy, –praxis; healing arts 688; psychotherapy 690; medicines 687.

.2 actinotherapy, aerosol therapy, aerotherapy *or* aerotherapeutics, arsenotherapy, autoserum therapy, bacterial therapy, bacteriotherapy, bibliotherapy, biotherapy, buffer therapy, cardiotherapy, chemotherapy, chrysotherapy, climatotherapy, cold therapy, collapse therapy, constitutional therapy, contact therapy, crymotherapy, dermatotherapy, dietotherapy 309.14, dye therapy, endocrinotherapy, fever therapy, frigotherapy, galactotherapy, glandular therapy, gold therapy, hemotherapy, heterovaccine therapy, hyperbaric therapy, immunization therapy, infrared therapy, intravenous therapy, iodotherapy, maggot therapy, malariotherapy, mechanotherapy, Metrazol therapy, nonspecific therapy, occupational therapy, opsonic therapy, organotherapy, oxygen therapy, pharmacotherapy, physical therapy *or* physiotherapy, phototherapy, protein therapy, pyretotherapy, radium therapy, ray therapy, replacement therapy, serotherapy, shock therapy 690.7, specific therapy, substitution therapy, suggestion therapy 690.6, surgicotherapy, ultrasonic therapy, ultraviolet therapy, vaccine therapy, X-ray therapy.

.3 **nonmedical therapy;** theotherapy; **healing;** Christian *or* spiritual *or* divine healing; **faith healing.**

.4 **hydrotherapy,** hydrotherapeutics; hydropathy, water cure; cold-water cure; contrast bath, whirlpool bath.

.5 **heat therapy,** thermotherapy; heliotherapy, solar therapy; fangotherapy; hot bath, sweat bath, sunbath.

.6 **diathermy,** medical diathermy; electrotherapy, electrotherapeutics; **radiothermy,** high-frequency treatment; shortwave diathermy, ultrashortwave diathermy, microwave diathermy; ultrasonic diathermy; surgical diathermy, radiosurgery, electrosurgery, electroresection, electrocautery, electrocoagulation.

.7 **radiotherapy,** radiotherapeutics, radio–; curietherapy, ray therapy, radiation therapy, irradiation therapy, irradiation; interstitial irradiation therapy, intercavitary irradiation therapy; X-ray therapy, roentgenotherapy or roentgentherapy, roentgen ray therapy, roentgenization; X-ray dosimetry, roentgenometry; isotope therapy; radium therapy, radiumization; cobalt therapy.

.8 **radiology,** radiography, radioscopy, fluoroscopy, etc. 327.7.

.9 (radiotherapeutic substances) radium; cobalt; radioisotope, tracer, labeled or tagged element, radioelement; radiocarbon, carbon 14, radiocalcium, radiopotassium, radiosodium, radioiodine; atomic cocktail.

.10 (diagnostic pictures and graphs) **X ray,** radiograph, radiogram, roentgenogram or roentgenograph; photofluorograph; X-ray movie; chest X-ray; pyelogram; orthodiagram; encephalograph, encephalogram; electroencephalograph, electroencephalogram, EEG; electrocorticogram; electrocardiogram, ECG, EKG; electromyogram.

.11 case history, medical history, anamnesis; associative anamnesis; catamnesis, follow-up.

.12 **diagnostics,** prognostics; symptomatology, semeiology, semeiotics.

.13 **diagnosis,** differential diagnosis, postmortem diagnosis; biological diagnosis, clinical diagnosis, laboratory diagnosis; cytodiagnosis, serum diagnosis or serodiagnosis; physical diagnosis, anatomic diagnosis; examination, physical examination, digital examination, oral examination, etc.; study, test, work-up [informal]; urinalysis, uroscopy; biopsy; Pap test or smear; electrocardiography, electroencephalography, electromyography; mammography.

.14 **prognosis,** prognostication; prognostic, **symptom,** sign.

.15 **treatment,** medical treatment or attention; **cure,** curative measures; **medication,** medicamentation; regimen, regime; first aid; hospitalization.

.16 (methods) prophylaxis or prophylaxy, preventive treatment; active treatment, adjuvant treatment, causal treatment, conservative treatment, empiric treatment, expectant treatment, palliative treatment, perennial treatment, preseasonal treatment, rational treatment, specific treatment, supporting treatment, symptomatic treatment; antigen treatment, crossfire treatment, cross-firing, diathermic treatment, dietetic treatment, drip treatment, drug treatment, electrotherapeutic treatment, fever treatment, heat treatment, hot-air treatment, light treatment, radiotherapeutic treatment, shock treatment, starvation treatment, surgical treatment, tonic treatment, vibration treatment.

.17 **immunization;** immunization therapy, immunotherapy; vaccine therapy, vaccinotherapy; toxin-antitoxin immunization; serum therapy, serotherapy, serotherapeutics; tuberculin test, scratch test, patch test; **immunology,** immunochemistry; immunity theory, side-chain theory; immunity.

.18 **inoculation, vaccination; injection,** hypodermic, hypodermic injection, shot [informal], hypospray or jet injection; booster, booster shot [informal]; antitoxin, vaccine 687.27,28; narcotic injection; bang or fix or hit [all slang]; mainlining or shooting up or skin-popping [all slang].

.19 (methods of injection) cutaneous, percutaneous, subcutaneous, intradermal, intramuscular, intravenous, intramedullary, intracardiac, intrathecal, intraspinal.

.20 **transfusion,** blood transfusion; arterial transfusion, direct transfusion, drip transfusion, exchange transfusion, exsanguination transfusion, exsanguino transfusion, plasma transfusion, reciprocal transfusion, replacement transfusion, serum transfusion, venous transfusion; serum 388.4; blood bank, blood donor center, bloodmobile; blood donor; perfusion.

.21 **surgery,** surgical treatment; cautery, cauterization; bloodless surgery; electrolysis, electrolyzation; electrocautery, electrosurgery, surgical diathermy, electroresection; laser surgery; radiosurgery.

.22 operation, surgical operation, surgical intervention, surgical technique *or* measure, the knife [informal]; major operation, minor operation; capital operation, serious operation; ablative operation, anastomotic operation, bloodless operation, compensating operation, crescent operation, elective operation, emergency operation, exploratory operation, fenestration operation, interval operation, palliative operation, radical operation; **section, resection; excision,** removal; **amputation; transplant,** organ transplant *or* transplantation, heart transplant, kidney transplant, corneal transplant.

.23 (surgical removal) –ectomy, adenoidectomy, appendectomy, arteriectomy, cervicectomy, cholecystectomy, craniectomy, cricoidectomy, cystectomy, enterectomy, gastrectomy, hemorrhoidectomy, hysterectomy, mammectomy *or* mastectomy, mastoidectomy, nephrectomy, omphalectomy, oophorectomy *or* ovariectomy, oophorocystectomy, orchidectomy, pancreatectomy, penectomy, pericardiectomy, phrenicectomy, pneumonectomy, prostatectomy, salpingectomy, stapedectomy, tonsillectomy, ureterectomy, urethrectomy, vasectomy, venectomy; castration.

.24 (surgical incision) –tomy, amygdalotomy, ankylotomy, arteriotomy, blepharotomy, cardiotomy, cecotomy, celiotomy, cholecystotomy, cirsotomy, coccygotomy, colpotomy, craniotomy, cystotomy, duodenotomy, elytrotomy, embryotomy, enterotomy, gastroenterotomy, gastrotomy, glossotomy, hebotomy, herniotomy, hysterotomy, laparotomy, lithotomy, lobotomy, mastotomy, nephrotomy, neurotomy, ovariotomy, pancreatotomy, phrenicotomy, pneumonotomy, prostatotomy, salpingotomy, sclerotomy, thoracotomy, thyrotomy, tonsillotomy, ureterotomy, urethrotomy; prefrontal lobotomy, psychosurgery; caesarean, caesarean section *or* operation.

.25 plastic surgery, –plastic *or* –plasty; reparative surgery, plastic operation, reconstructive operation, cosmetic operation; **facelifting;** balanoplasty, blepharoplasty, batrachoplasty, bronchoplasty, canthoplasty, colpoplasty, cystoplasty, dermoplasty, genyoplasty, heteroplasty, labioplasty, mammilloplasty, otoplasty, rhinoplasty.

.26 bloodletting, bleeding, venesection, phlebotomy; leeching; cupping.

.27 hospital, *hôpital* [Fr], **infirmary;** sick bay *or* berth; **clinic,** polyclinic, inpatient clinic, outpatient clinic, policlinic, wellbaby clinic; general hospital, teaching hospital, special hospital; community hospital, government hospital, public hospital, voluntary hospital, private hospital, proprietary hospital; veterans hospital, VA hospital; surgical hospital, osteopathic hospital, convalescent hospital, children's hospital, maternity *or* lying-in hospital, mental hospital 473.14; base hospital, field hospital, station hospital, evacuation hospital; **sanatorium;** asylum, home; **nursing home,** convalescent home, *maison de santé* [Fr]; rest home, ward, sickroom; sickbed.

.28 pesthouse, lazar house, lazaretto *or* lazaret, lock hospital [Brit]; isolation ward.

.29 health resort, spa, watering place, baths; mineral spring, warm *or* hot spring; pump room, pump house.

.30 VERBS **treat, doctor,** minister to, care for, give care to; **diagnose;** nurse; **cure, remedy, heal;** dress the wounds, bandage, poultice, plaster, strap, splint; lick one's wounds; bathe; massage, rub; operate on; physic, purge, flux [archaic].

.31 medicate, medicine, drug, dope [slang], dose; salve, oil, anoint, embrocate.

.32 irradiate, radiumize, **X-ray,** roentgenize.

.33 bleed, let blood, leech, phlebotomize; cup; **transfuse,** give a transfusion; perfuse.

.34 immunize, inoculate, vaccinate, shoot [informal].

.35 undergo treatment, take the cure, doctor [dial], take medicine; go under the knife [informal].

.36 medical and surgical instruments

artificial heart	heat lamp
artificial kidney	hemostat
aspirator	hypodermic, hypo
bedpan	[slang], hypodermic
bistoury	needle, hypodermic
bronchoscope	syringe
cardiograph	kidney basin
cardioscope	lancet, lance
catheter	laparotomy pack, lap
clinical thermometer	pack [informal]
cystoscope	manometer
dialysis machine	mechanical heart
diaphanoscope	microscope
diathermy machine	microwave diathermy
drain	machine
drain tube	nebulizer
electrocardiograph	needle
electroencephalograph	ophthalmoscope
electromyograph	orthodiagraph
fluoroscope	orthoscope
forceps	otoscope
gastroscope	percussion hammer
germicidal lamp	pneumatometer
heart-lung machine	pneumograph,

pneumatograph	splint
probe	stethograph
pus basin	stethometer
radio knife	stethoscope
resectoscope	stomach pump
respirometer	stomach tube
roentgenoscope	stylet
rubber gloves	surgical or suture nee-
scalpel	dle
shortwave diathermy	suture
machine	swab
sound	syringe
specimen bottle	tongue depressor or
speculum	blade
sphygmograph	trephine, trepan
sphygmomanometer	trocar
sphygmometer	urinalysis kit
spirograph	X-ray machine
spirometer	

.37 respirators

heart-lung machine	oxygen tank
inhalator	oxygen tent
inspirator	Pulmotor
iron lung	resuscitator
oxygen mask	

690. PSYCHOLOGY AND PSYCHOTHERAPY

.1 NOUNS **psychology,** psych(o)–; science of the mind, science of human behavior; mental philosophy; psychonomics, psychonomy; reactology, reflexology; abnormal psychology, academic psychology, analytical psychology, applied psychology, animal psychology, association psychology, child psychology, clinical psychology, cognitive psychology, comparative psychology, constitutional psychology, criminal psychology, depth psychology, developmental psychology, differential psychology, dynamic psychology, ecological psychology, educational psychology, experimental psychology, existential psychology, faculty psychology, folk psychology, functional psychology, genetic psychology, group psychology, hormic psychology, individual psychology, industrial psychology, morbid psychology, neuropsychology, phenomenological psychology, popular psychology, physiological psychology, race psychology, rational psychology, self psychology, social psychology, structural psychology; parapsychology 1034.4; psychobiochemistry, psychobiology, psychodiagnostics, psychodynamics, psychogenetics, psychogeriatrics, psycholinguistics, psychometrics, psychopathology, psychopharmacology, psychophysics, psychophysiology, psychosociology; psychosomatics, psychotechnics, psychotechnology, psychothera-

peutics; psychological medicine, psychological warfare.

.2 (systems) Freudian psychology, Freudianism, psychoanalysis, psychoanalytic theory, metapsychology; Jungian psychology, analytical psychology; Adlerian psychology; Reichian psychology, orgone theory; Horneyan psychology; Gestalt psychology, configurationism; behavior or behavioristic psychology, **behaviorism,** stimulus-response psychology, Watsonian psychology, Skinnerian psychology, Pavlovian psychology; structuralism; association psychology, associationism, mental chemistry; apperceptionism; dianetics.

.3 psychiatry, psychological medicine; neuropsychiatry; social psychiatry; prophylactic psychiatry.

.4 psychosomatic medicine, psychological medicine, medicopsychology; psychosocial medicine.

.5 psychotherapy, psychotherapeutics, mind cure; group therapy, group psychotherapy, conjoint therapy; humanistic therapy; gestalt therapy, psychodrama, bioenergetics, encounter therapy, rational-emotive therapy, marriage encounter, confrontation therapy; training group or T-group, sensitivity training, sensory awareness training or SAT, consciousness raising, group sensitivity training, group relations training; marathon, est or Erhard Seminars Training; New Consciousness, behavior modification, behavior therapy; biofeedback; transpersonal therapy, Arica movement, psychosynthesis, transcendental meditation or TM; transactional analysis or TA, assertiveness training; regression therapy, primal therapy, scream therapy; family training, radical therapy, feminist therapy; occupational therapy, vocational therapy; recreational therapy, play therapy; reality therapy; release therapy; supportive therapy; directive therapy, nondirective therapy; narcotherapy, narcoanalysis, narcosynthesis, Pentothal interview; sleep treatment, prolonged narcosis; hypnotherapy, hypnoanalysis; hypnotism, hypnosis, narcohypnosis; psychosurgery; **counseling,** psychological counseling; pastoral counseling.

.6 suggestion therapy, suggestionism; hypnotherapy, hypnotism, hypnosis, hypnotic suggestion, posthypnotic suggestion; **autosuggestion,** self-suggestion, self-hypnosis; suggestibility, power of suggestion.

.7 shock therapy, shock treatment; convulsive therapy; electroshock therapy, electroshock, electronarcosis, Metrazol shock therapy; hypoglycemic shock therapy, insulin shock therapy.

.8 **psychoanalysis, analysis,** psychanalysis, the couch [informal]; psychoanalytic therapy, psychoanalytic method; **depth psychology,** psychology of depths; group analysis; psychognosis, psychognosy; dream analysis, interpretation of dreams, dream symbolism; depth interview.

.9 **psychodiagnostics,** psychodiagnosis, psychological or psychiatric evaluation; Rorschach method.

.10 **psychometrics,** psychometry; **intelligence testing;** psychological screening; psychography; psychogram, psychograph, psychological profile; psychometer, IQ meter [informal]; lie detector, polygraph, psychogalvanometer.

.11 **psychological test,** mental test; standardized test; achievement test; **aptitude test,** Oseretsky test, Stanford scientific aptitude test; **personality test,** Bernreuter personality inventory, Brown personality inventory, Minnesota multiphasic personality inventory; interest inventory; **association test,** word association test, controlled association test, free association test; **apperception test,** thematic apperception test, TAT; **Rorschach test,** inkblot test; Szondi test; **intelligence test,** IQ test; alpha test, beta test, Babcock-Levy test, Binet or Binet-Simon test, Stanford-Binet test, Stanford revision, Goldstein-Sheerer test, Kent mental test; Wechsler-Bellevue intelligence scale, Gesell's development schedule, Minnesota preschool scale, Cattell's infant intelligence scale; intelligence quotient, IQ.

.12 **psychologist,** psychologue; clinical psychologist; **psychiatrist, alienist;** neuropsychiatrist; psychopathist, psychopathologist; psychotechnologist, industrial psychologist; psychobiologist, psychochemist, psychophysiologist, psychophysicist; psychographer; somatist; Freud, Adler, Jung, Reich, Horney, Watson, Skinner, Pavlov.

.13 **psychotherapist,** psychotherapeutist; **clinical psychologist; psychiatrist;** narcotherapist; hypnotherapist; behavior therapist; **psychoanalyst,** psychoanalyzer, **analyst;** headshrinker or shrinker or shrink [all slang].

.14 **personality tendency,** complexion [archaic], humor; somatotype; **introversion,** introvertedness, ingoingness; inner-directed-

ness; **extroversion,** extrovertedness, outgoingness; other-directedness; syntony, ambiversion; schizothymia, schizothymic or schizoid personality; cyclothymia, cyclothymic or cycloid personality; mesomorphism, mesomorphy; endomorphism, endomorphy; ectomorphism, ectomorphy.

.15 (personality type) **introvert, extrovert,** syntone, ambivert; schizothyme, schizoid; cyclothymic, cyclothyme, cycloid; choleric, melancholic, sanguine, phlegmatic; endomorph, mesomorph, ectomorph.

.16 (pathological personality types) neurotic personality, **neurotic, psychoneurotic,** neuropath; weak personality, maladjusted personality, inadequate personality, inferior personality, immature personality, disordered personality, disturbed personality, emotionally unstable personality, perverse personality, hostile personality; paranoid personality; schizoid personality, schizoid; dual personality, double personality, multiple personality, split personality, alternating personality; seclusive personality, shut-in personality; escapist; antisocial personality, sociopath, psychopathic personality, moral insanity, **psychopath;** psychotic personality, **psychotic** 473.16; mentally defective personality, idiot 471.8; hypochondriac, hypochondriast, valetudinarian, valetudinary, imaginary invalid, *malade imaginaire* [Fr]; **alcoholic** 996.10,11; drug user 642.10; sexual psychopath 419.16–19.

.17 **mental disorder, emotional disorder,** functional nervous disorder; reaction; emotional instability; **maladjustment,** social maladjustment; nervous breakdown, crack-up [slang]; problems in living; **insanity, mental illness** 473.1; psychosis 473.3; **schizophrenia,** schiz(o)–; paranoia 473.4; **manic-depressive psychosis,** melancholia 473.5; **neurosis;** personality disorder; brain disease, nervous disorder 686.23.

.18 **personality disorder, character disorder,** moral insanity, sociopathy, **psychopathy; psychopathic personality;** sexual pathology, sexual psychopathy 419.12–14.

.19 **neurosis, psychoneurosis,** neuroticism, neurotic or psychoneurotic disorder; psychasthenia; accident neurosis, anxiety neurosis, association neurosis, blast neurosis, compensation neurosis, conversion neurosis, expectation neurosis, fixation neurosis, fright neurosis, homosexual neurosis, hypochondria or hypochondriasis, occupational neurosis, pathoneurosis, regression neurosis, traumatic neurosis, transference neurosis, compulsion neurosis, obsessional neurosis, obsessive-compulsive neurosis; hysteria; anxiety hysteria, conversion hysteria; phobia 891.1; reactive neurosis, situational neurosis; combat *or* war neurosis, combat *or* battle fatigue, shell shock, psychopathia martialis.

.20 (neurotic reactions) anxiety reaction, avoidance reaction, compensatory reaction, conversion reaction, depressive reaction, dissociation reaction, emotional instability reaction, flight reaction, immaturity reaction, neurotic-depressive reaction, obsessive-compulsive reaction, passive-aggressive reaction, passive-dependence reaction, phobic reaction, psychasthenic reaction, somatization reaction, shock reaction, stress reaction.

.21 **psychological stress, stress; frustration,** external frustration, internal frustration; conflict, ambivalence, ambivalence of impulse; trauma, traumatism, mental *or* emotional shock, decompensation.

.22 (psychosomatic symptoms) analgesia, anesthesia, bulimia, depraved appetite, neurasthenia, paresthesia, parorexia, pica; anxiety equivalent; speech abnormality.

.23 (symptoms of emotional disorder) mental distress, psychalgia; emotionalism; anxiety, anxiety state, anxiety equivalent, free-floating anxiety; hysteria, hysterics, hyster(o)–; melancholia, hypochondria, psycholepsy, **depression,** dejection; detachment, alienation, withdrawal, abstraction, preoccupation; **apathy,** lethargy, indifference, unresponsiveness, insensibility; stupor, catatonic stupor; psychomotor disturbance, tic, twitching; amimia, paramimia; euphoria, elation; *folie du doute* [Fr], pathological indecisiveness, abulia; mania 473.12,36; obsession, compulsion 473.13.

.24 (thought disturbances) blocking, **block,** psychological block, mental block; paralogia; mental confusion, disorientation; agnosia; flight of ideas; **delusion,** delusion of persecution, delusion of grandeur, paranoid delusion, delusion of reference; nihilism, nihilistic delusion; hallucination, hallucinosis 519.7; delirium 473.8.

.25 (speech abnormalities) dysarthria, dysphasia; aphonia, hysterical aphonia, psychophonasthenia; incoherence; echolalia, verbigeration; schizophasia; mutism; imper-

fect speech, speech defect 595.1; aphasia 595.6.

.26 (trance states) **trance,** daze, stupor; catatonic stupor, catalepsy; cataplexy; dream state, reverie, daydreaming 532.2; somnambulism, sleepwalking; hypnotic trance; fugue, fugue state; **amnesia** 538.2.

.27 **dissociation,** mental *or* emotional dissociation, disconnection; dissociation of personality, personality disorganization *or* disintegration; **schizoid personality;** double *or* dual personality; multiple personality, split personality, alternating personality; schizoidism, schizothymia, **schizophrenia** 473.4; depersonalization; **paranoid personality; paranoia** 473.4.

.28 **fixation,** libido fixation *or* arrest, **arrested development;** infantile fixation, pregenital fixation, father fixation, Freudian fixation, mother fixation, parent fixation; **regression,** retreat to immaturity.

.29 **complex,** inferiority complex, superiority complex, parent complex, Oedipus complex, mother complex, Electra complex, father complex, Diana complex, persecution complex; castration complex.

.30 **defense mechanism,** defense reaction; ego defense, psychotaxis; biological *or* psychological *or* sociological adjustive reactions; resistance; dissociation 690.27; **negativism, alienation; escapism,** escape mechanism, avoidance mechanism; escape, flight, **withdrawal; isolation,** emotional insulation; **fantasy,** fantasizing, escape into fantasy, dreamlike thinking, autistic *or* dereistic thinking, wishful thinking, autism, dereism; wish-fulfillment, wish-fulfillment fantasy; **compensation,** overcompensation, decompensation; substitution; **sublimation; projection,** blame-shifting; displacement; **rationalization.**

.31 **suppression, repression, inhibition,** resistance, restraint, censorship; block, psychological block, blockage, blocking; reaction formation; rigid control; **suppressed desire.**

.32 **catharsis,** purgation, abreaction, motor abreaction, psychocatharsis, **emotional release,** outlet; release therapy, acting-out, psychodrama.

.33 **conditioning,** classical *or* Pavlovian conditioning; instrumental conditioning, operant conditioning; psychagogy, reeducation, reorientation; conditioned reflex, conditioned stimulus, conditioned response; reinforcement, positive reinforcement, negative reinforcement; simple reflex, unconditioned reflex, **reflex** 284.1; **behavior** 737.

.34 **adjustment,** adjustive reaction; **readjustment, rehabilitation;** psychosynthesis, integration of personality; fulfillment, self-fulfillment; integrated personality, syntonic personality.

.35 **psyche,** psychic apparatus, **personality, self; mind** 466.1–5; preconscious, foreconscious, coconscious; **subconscious, unconscious,** subconscious *or* unconscious mind, submerged mind, subliminal, subliminal self; **libido,** psychic *or* libidinal energy, motive force, vital impulse, ego-libido, object libido; **id,** primitive self, pleasure principle, life instinct, death instinct; **ego,** conscious self; **superego,** ethical self, conscience; ego ideal; ego-id conflict; anima, persona; collective unconscious, racial unconscious.

.36 **engram,** memory trace, traumatic trace *or* memory; unconscious memory; archetype, archetypal pattern *or* image *or* symbol; imago, image, father image, etc.; memory 537.

.37 **symbol,** universal symbol, father symbol, mother symbol, phallic symbol, fertility symbol, etc.; symbolism, symbolization.

.38 **surrogate,** substitute; father surrogate, father figure, father image; mother surrogate, mother figure.

.39 **gestalt,** pattern, figure, configuration, sensory pattern; figure-ground.

.40 **association, association of ideas,** mental linking; controlled association, free association, association by contiguity, association by similarity; association by sound, clang association; stream of consciousness; transference, identification, positive transference, negative transference; synesthesia 422.5.

.41 **cathexis,** desire concentration; charge, energy charge, cathectic energy; anticathexis, countercathexis, counterinvestment; hypercathexis, overcharge.

.42 VERBS **psychologize, psychoanalyze.**

.43 ADJS **psychological; psychiatric,** neuropsychiatric; psychometric; **psychopathic,** psychopathological; **psychosomatic,** psychophysical, psychophysiological, psychobiological; psychogenic, psychogenetic, functional; psychodynamic, psychoneurological, psychosexual, psychosocial, psychotechnical; **psychotic** 473.27.

.44 **psychotherapeutic;** psychiatric, psychoanalytic(al).

.45 **neurotic, psychoneurotic,** disturbed, disordered; neurasthenic, psychasthenic; hysteric(al), hypochondriac, phobic.

.46 **introverted,** introvert, introversive, **subjective, ingoing,** inner-directed.

.47 **extroverted,** extrovert, extroversive, **outgoing,** extrospective; other-directed.

.48 **subconscious, unconscious;** subliminal, extramarginal; preconscious, foreconscious, coconscious.

691. IMPROVEMENT

.1 NOUNS **improvement, betterment,** bettering, change for the better; meliration, **amelioration; mend,** mending, **amendment; progress,** progression, headway; **advance,** advancement; upward mobility; **promotion, furtherance,** preferment; **rise,** ascent, **lift, uplift,** upswing, uptrend, upbeat; upping *or* boost *or* pickup [all informal]); Great Leap Forward; **enhancement, enrichment;** euthenics, eugenics; **restoration,** revival, recovery 692.2,8.

.2 **development, refinement,** elaboration, **perfection;** beautification, embellishment; maturation, ripening, evolution, seasoning.

.3 **cultivation, culture, refinement, polish,** civility; cultivation of the mind; **civilization;** acculturation; enculturation, socialization; enlightenment, education 475.4, 562.1–3.

.4 **revision,** revise, revisal; revised edition; **emendation, amendment, correction, rectification;** editing, redaction, recension, revampment; **rewrite,** rewriting, rescript, rescription [archaic].

.5 **reform, reformation;** regeneration 145.2; **transformation** 139.2; **conversion** 145; reformism, meliorism; gradualism, Fabianism, revisionism; utopianism; progressivism, progressism; radical reform, extremism, radicalism 745.4; revolution 147.

.6 **reformer,** reformist, meliorist; gradualist, Fabian, revisionist; utopian, utopist; progressive, progressivist, progressionist, progressist; radical, extremist 745.12; revolutionary 147.3.

.7 VERBS (get better) **improve, grow better,** show improvement, **mend,** amend [archaic], meliorate, ameliorate; **look up** *or* **pick up** *or* **perk up** [all informal]; **develop,** shape up; **advance, progress, make progress, make headway, gain,** gain ground, go forward, get *or* go ahead, come on, come along [informal], get along; make strides *or* rapid strides, take off *or* skyrocket [both informal], make up for lost time; graduate.

.8 **rally,** come about or round, **take a favorable turn,** take a turn for the better, gain strength; **recuperate, recover** 694.19,20.

.9 (make better) **improve, better,** change for the better, make an improvement; transform, transfigure 139.7; improve upon, refine upon, **mend, amend,** emend [archaic]; meliorate, **ameliorate; advance, promote,** foster, favor, nurture, forward, bring forward; **lift,** elevate, **uplift,** raise, boost [informal]; upgrade; **enhance, enrich,** fatten, lard [archaic]; make one's way, better oneself; be the making of; **reform;** reform oneself, turn over a new leaf, mend one's ways, straighten out, straighten oneself out, go straight [informal]; **civilize,** acculturate, socialize; enlighten, edify; **educate** 562.11.

.10 **develop,** elaborate; beautify, embellish; **cultivate, refine,** polish, finish, **perfect;** mature, ripen, evolve, season.

.11 **touch up,** tone up, **brush up, furbish,** furbish up, spruce, **spruce up,** freshen, vamp, vamp up, rub up, brighten up, polish, polish up, shine [informal]; retouch; **revive, renovate** 694.16,17; **repair, fix** 694.14.

.12 **revise,** redact, recense, **revamp, rewrite,** redraft, **rework,** work over; **emend, amend,** emendate, **rectify,** correct; **edit,** blue-pencil.

.13 ADJS **improved, bettered,** eu–; changed for the better, advanced, ameliorated, enhanced, enriched; developed, perfected; beautified, embellished; **reformed; transformed,** transfigured, converted; **cultivated,** cultured, **refined,** polished, civilized; **educated** 475.18.

.14 **better,** better off, better for, all the better for.

.15 **improving, bettering;** meliorative, ameliorative; progressive, progressing, advancing, ongoing; mending, **on the mend;** on the lift or rise or upswing or upbeat or upgrade [informal], looking up [informal].

.16 **emendatory, corrective;** revisory, revisional; reformatory, reformative, reformational; **reformist,** reformistic, melioristic; gradualistic, Fabian, revisionist; utopian, radical 745.20; revolutionary 147.5.

.17 **improvable,** ameliorable, corrigible, perfectible; **emendable** 694.25.

692. IMPAIRMENT

.1 NOUNS **impairment, damage, injury, harm,** mischief, scathe, **hurt, detriment,** loss, weakening, sickening; disablement, incapacitation; encroachment, inroad, in-fringement 238.1; **disrepair, dilapidation,** ruinousness; breakage; **breakdown, collapse,** crack-up [informal]; bankruptcy; hurting, spoiling, ruination; sabotage; mayhem, mutilation, crippling, hobbling, laming, maiming; destruction 693.

.2 **corruption, pollution, contamination,** vitiation, **defilement,** fouling, befouling; **poisoning,** envenoming; infection, festering, suppuration; **perversion,** prostitution, misuse 667; denaturing, adulteration.

.3 **deterioration, decadence** or decadency, **degradation, debasement,** derogation, deformation; **degeneration,** degeneracy, degenerateness, effeteness; loss of tone, failure of nerve; depravation, depravedness; **retrogression,** retrogradation, retrocession, **regression;** devolution, involution; demotion 783; downward mobility; **decline,** declination, declension, comedown, **descent,** downtrend, downward trend, downturn, depreciation, **drop, fall,** falling-off, slippage, slump, lapse, fading, dying, failing, failure, wane, ebb.

.4 **waste,** wastage, **consumption;** withering, atrophy, wilting, marcescence; emaciation 205.6.

.5 **wear,** use; **wear and tear;** erosion, weathering, ablation, ravages of time.

.6 **decay, decomposition, disintegration, dissolution,** resolution, degradation, biodegradation, breakup, disorganization, **corruption, spoilage, dilapidation;** corrosion, oxidation, oxidization, rust; mildew, mold 676.2; degradability, biodegradability.

.7 **rot, rottenness, foulness, putridness,** putridity, rancidness, rancidity, rankness, **putrefaction,** putrescence, spoilage, decay, decomposition; **mortification,** necrosis, gangrene, sphacelation, sphacelus, slough; caries, tooth decay, carrion; dry rot.

.8 (an impairment) **injury, hurt, lesion; wound, trauma;** sore 686.35; cut, incision, scratch, gash; puncture, stab, stab wound; laceration, mutilation; abrasion, scuff, scrape, chafe, gall; frazzle, fray; run, **rip,** rent, slash, **tear;** burn, scald, scorch, first- or second- or third-degree burn; flash burn; break, fracture, rupture; crack, chip, craze, check, crackle; wrench; concussion; mortal wound, "wounds immedicable" [Milton]; blemish 679.

.9 **bruise, contusion,** ecchymosis, **black-and-blue mark; black eye,** shiner or mouse [both slang].

.10 **wreck, ruins, ruin,** hulk, carcass, skeleton;

mere wreck, wreck of one's former self; nervous wreck; rattletrap.

.11 VERBS **impair, damage,** endamage, **injure, harm, hurt,** irritate; **worsen,** make worse, deteriorate, put back, aggravate, exacerbate, embitter; **weaken; dilapidate;** add insult to injury, rub salt in the wound.

.12 spoil, mar, botch, ruin, wreck, blight, play havoc with; destroy 693.10–21.

.13 [slang or informal terms] queer, screw up, foul up, louse up, snafu, snarl up, bugger, bugger up, gum up, ball up, bollix, bollix up, mess up, hash up, muck up; play hob with, play hell with, play merry hell with, play the devil with; cook, sink, shoot down in flames.

.14 corrupt, debase, degrade, degenerate, deprave, debauch, defile, violate, desecrate, deflower, ravish, ravage, despoil; contaminate, confound, pollute, vitiate, poison, infect, taint; canker, ulcerate; pervert, warp, twist, distort; prostitute, misuse 667.4; denature; cheapen, devalue; coarsen, vulgarize, drag in the mud; adulterate, alloy.

.15 (inflict an injury) injure, hurt; wound, scotch [archaic]; traumatize; stab, stick, pierce, puncture; cut, incise, slit, slash, gash, scratch; abrade, scuff, scrape, chafe, fret, gall, bark, skin; break, fracture, rupture; crack, chip, craze, check; lacerate, claw, tear, rip, rend; run; frazzle, fray; burn, scorch, scald; mutilate, maim, make mincemeat of, maul, savage; sprain, strain, wrench; bloody; blemish 679.4–7.

.16 bruise, contuse, bung or bung up [both slang]; buffet, batter, bash [informal], maul, pound, beat, beat black and blue; give a black eye.

.17 cripple, lame, maim; hamstring, hobble; wing; emasculate, castrate; incapacitate, disable 158.9.

.18 undermine, sap, mine, sap the foundations of, honeycomb; sabotage.

.19 deteriorate, sicken, worsen, get or grow worse, get no better fast [informal], disimprove, degenerate; slip back, retrogress, retrograde, regress, relapse, fall back; go to the bad 693.24; let oneself go, let down, slacken; be the worse for, be the worse for wear, have seen better days.

.20 decline, sink, fail, fall, slip, fade, die, wane, ebb, subside, lapse, run down, go down, go downhill, fall away, fall off, go off [informal], slide, slump, hit a slump; hit the skids [slang]; reach the depths, hit or touch bottom, hit rock bottom, have no lower to go.

.21 languish, pine, droop, flag, wilt; fade, fade away; wither, shrivel, shrink, diminish, dry up, desiccate, wizen, sear; "fall'n into the sere, the yellow leaf" [Shakespeare].

.22 waste, waste away, wither away, atrophy, consume, consume away, emaciate, pine away; trickle or dribble away; run to waste, run to seed.

.23 wear, wear away, wear down, wear off; abrade, fret, rub off; fray, frazzle, tatter, wear ragged; wear out; weather, erode, ablate.

.24 corrode, erode, eat, gnaw, eat into, eat away, nibble away, gnaw at the root of; canker; oxidize, rust.

.25 decay, decompose, disintegrate; go or fall into decay, go or fall to pieces, break up, crumble, crumble into dust; spoil, corrupt, canker, go bad; rot, putrefy, putresce; fester, suppurate, rankle [informal]; mortify, necrose, gangrene, sphacelate; mold, molder, mildew.

.26 break, break up, fracture, come apart, come unstuck, come or fall to pieces, disintegrate; burst, rupture; crack, split, fissure; snap; break open, give way or away, start, spring a leak, come apart at the seams.

.27 break down, founder, collapse; cave or fall in, come crashing or tumbling down, topple, topple down or over, tremble or nod or totter to one's fall; totter, sway.

.28 get out of order, get out of whack [informal], get out of kilter [informal], get out of commission [informal], get out of gear; get out of joint; go wrong, go kaput [slang], go on the blink or fritz [slang], go haywire [slang], give out, break down, pack up [Brit informal], conk out [slang].

.29 ADJS impaired, damaged, hurt, injured, harmed; deteriorated, worsened, aggravated, exacerbated, irritated, embittered; weakened; worse, worse off, the worse for, all the worse for; imperfect 676.4; lacerated, mangled, cut, split, rent, torn, slit, slashed, mutilated; broken 49.24, shattered, smashed, in bits, in pieces, in shards, burst, busted [dial], ruptured, sprung; cracked, chipped, crazed, checked; burned, scorched, scalded.

.30 spoiled or spoilt, marred, botched, blighted, ruined, wrecked; destroyed 693.28.

.31 [slang or informal terms] queered, screwed up, fouled up, loused up, snafued, buggered, buggered up, gummed up, snarled up, balled up, bollixed up, messed up, hashed up, mucked up; cooked, sunk, shot.

.32 crippled, game [informal], bad, handicapped, maimed; lame, halt, halting, hobbling, limping; hamstrung; spavined; disabled, incapacitated; emasculated, castrated.

.33 worn, well-worn, deep-worn, worn-down, the worse for wear, dog-eared; timeworn; shopworn, shelfworn; worn to the stump, worn to the bone; worn ragged, worn to rags, worn to threads; threadbare, bare, sere [archaic].

.34 shabby, shoddy, seedy, scruffy, tacky [informal], dowdy, tatty, ratty; holey, full of holes; raggedy, ragged, tattered, torn; patchy; frayed, frazzled; in rags, in tatters, in shreds; out at the elbows, out at the heels, down-at-heel or -heels, down-at-the-heel or -heels.

.35 dilapidated, ramshackle, decrepit, tottery, slummy [informal], tumbledown, broken-down, run-down, in ruins, ruinous, ruined, derelict, gone to wrack and ruin, the worse for wear; battered, beaten up, beat-up [informal].

.36 weatherworn, weather-beaten, weathered, weather-battered, weather-wasted, weather-eaten, weather-bitten, weather-scarred; eroded; faded, washed-out, bleached, blanched.

.37 wasted, atrophied, shrunken; withered, sere, shriveled, wilted, wizened, dried-up, desiccated; wrinkled, wrinkled like a prune; brittle, papery, parchmenty; emaciated 205.20; worn to a shadow, reduced to a skeleton, "worn to the bones" [Shakespeare].

.38 worn-out, used up [informal], worn to a frazzle, frazzled, fit for the dust hole or wastepaper basket; exhausted, tired, fatigued, pooped [slang], spent, effete, played out, ausgespielt [Ger], shotten [dial], jaded, emptied, done or done up [both informal]; run-down, laid low, at a low ebb, in a bad way, far-gone, on one's last legs.

.39 in disrepair, out of order, out of working order, out of condition, out of repair, inoperative, out of whack or kilter or kelter [informal], out of commission [informal], out of tune, out of gear; out of joint; on the fritz or on the blink [both slang], haywire [slang], packed-up [Brit informal]; broken 49.24.

.40 putrefactive, putrefacient, rotting, septic; saprogenic, saprogenous; saprophilous, saprophytic, saprobic, sapro–.

.41 decayed, decomposed; spoiled, corrupt, peccant, bad, gone bad; rotten, rotting, putrid, putrefied, foul; putrescent, mortified, necrosed, necrotic, sphacelated, gangrened, gangrenous; carious; cankered, ulcerated, festering, suppurating, suppurative; rotten at or to the core.

.42 tainted, off, blown, frowy [dial]; stale; sour, soured, turned; rank, reechy [archaic], rancid, strong [informal], high, gamy.

.43 blighted, blasted, ravaged, despoiled; blown, flyblown, wormy, weevily, maggoty; moth-eaten, worm-eaten; moldy, moldering, mildewed, smutty, smutted; musty, fusty, frowzy or frowsy, frowsty [Brit].

.44 corroded, eroded, eaten; rusty, rust-eaten, rust-worn, rust-cankered.

.45 corrupting, corruptive; corrosive, corroding; erosive, eroding, damaging, injurious 675.12.

.46 deteriorating, worsening, disintegrating, coming apart or unstuck, crumbling, cracking, fragmenting, going to pieces; decadent, degenerate, effete; retrogressive, retrograde, regressive, from better to worse; declining, sinking, failing, falling, waning, subsiding, slipping, sliding, slumping; languishing, pining, drooping, flagging, wilting; ebbing, draining, dwindling; wasting, fading, withering, shriveling; tabetic, marcescent.

.47 on the wane, on the decline, on the downgrade, on the downward track, on the skids [slang]; tottering, nodding to its fall.

.48 degradable, biodegradable, decomposable, putrefiable, putrescible.

693. DESTRUCTION

.1 NOUNS destruction, ruin, ruination, blue ruin [slang]; perdition, damnation, eternal damnation; universal ruin; wreck, wrack [dial], wrack and ruin; devastation, ravage, havoc, holocaust, hecatomb, carnage, shambles, slaughter, bloodbath, desolation; waste, consumption; decimation; dissolution, disintegration, breakup, disruption, disorganization, undoing, lysis; vandalism, depredation, spoliation, despoliation, despoilment; the road to ruin.

.2 end, fate, doom, death, death knell, bane, deathblow, coup de grâce [Fr], quietus.

.3 fall, downfall, prostration; overthrow, overturn, upset, upheaval, bouleverse-

ment [Fr]; convulsion, subversion, sabotage.

.4 debacle, disaster, cataclysm, catastrophe; breakup, breaking up; breakdown, collapse; crash, smash, smashup, crack-up [informal]; wreck, wrack, shipwreck; cave-in, cave; washout; total loss.

.5 demolition, demolishment; wrecking, wreckage, leveling, razing, flattening, smashing, tearing down, bringing to the ground; dismantlement, disassembly, unmaking.

.6 extinction, extermination, elimination, eradication, extirpation; rooting out, deracination, uprooting, tearing up root and branch; annihilation, extinguishment, snuffing out; abolition, abolishment; annulment, nullification, voiding, negation; liquidation, purge; suppression; choking, choking off, suffocation, stifling, strangulation; silencing.

.7 obliteration, erasure, effacement, expunction, blot [archaic], blotting, blotting out, wiping out; washing out, scrubbing [informal], cancellation, cancel; deletion.

.8 destroyer, ruiner, wrecker, demolisher, –clast; vandal, hun; exterminator, annihilator; iconoclast, idoloclast, idol breaker; biblioclast; nihilist; terrorist, syndicalist; bomber, dynamiter, dynamitard; burner, arsonist.

.9 eradicator, expunger; eraser, rubber, India rubber, sponge.

.10 VERBS destroy, deal or unleash destruction, unleash the hurricane; ruin, ruinate [dial], bring to ruin, lay in ruins; throw into disorder, upheave; wreck, wrack, shipwreck; damn, seal the doom of, condemn, confound; devastate, desolate, waste, lay waste, ravage, havoc, wreak havoc, despoil, depredate; vandalize; decimate; devour, consume, engorge, gobble, gobble up, swallow up; gut, gut with fire, incinerate, vaporize, ravage with fire and sword; dissolve, lyse.

.11 do for, fix [informal], settle, sink, cook [informal], cook one's goose, dish, scuttle, put the kibosh on [slang], do in, undo, knock in or on the head, torpedo, knock out, KO [slang], deal a knockout blow to, shoot down or shoot down in flames [both informal]; break the back of; make short work of; defeat 727.6.

.12 put an end to, make an end of, end, finish, finish off [informal], put paid to [Brit], give the *coup de grâce* to, give the quietus to, deal a deathblow to, dispose of, get rid of, do away with; cut off, take off, be the death of, sound the death knell of; put out of the way, put out of existence, slaughter, make away with, kill 409.13; nip, nip in the bud or head; cut short.

.13 abolish, nullify, void, abrogate, annihilate, annul, repeal, revoke, negate, negative, invalidate, undo, cancel, bring to naught.

.14 exterminate, eliminate, eradicate, deracinate, extirpate, annihilate; wipe out [informal]; cut out, root up or out, uproot, pull or pluck up by the roots, cut up root and branch, strike at the root of, lay the ax to the root of; liquidate, purge; remove, sweep away.

.15 extinguish, quench, snuff out, put out, stamp or trample out, trample underfoot; smother, choke, stifle, strangle, suffocate; silence; suppress, quash, squash or squelch [both informal], quell, put down.

.16 obliterate, expunge, efface, erase, raze [archaic], blot, sponge, wipe out, wipe off the map, rub out, blot out, sponge out; cancel, strike out, cross out, scratch, scratch out, rule out; delete, dele.

.17 demolish, wreck, total or wrack up [both slang], undo, unbuild, unmake, dismantle, disassemble; take apart, tear apart, rend, take or pull or pick or tear to pieces, pull in pieces, tear to shreds or rags or tatters; sunder, cleave, split; disintegrate, fragment, break to pieces, make mincemeat of, reduce to rubble, atomize, pulverize, smash, shatter 49.13.

.18 blow up, blast, spring, blow to pieces or bits, bomb, bombard, blitz; mine.

.19 raze, rase, fell, level, flatten, smash, prostrate, raze to the ground or dust; steamroller, bulldoze; pull down, tear down, take down, bring down, bring down about one's ears, bring tumbling or crashing down, break down, throw down, cast down, beat down, knock down or over; cut down, chop down, mow down; blow down; burn down.

.20 overthrow, overturn; upset, overset, upend, subvert, throw down or over; undermine, honeycomb, sap, sap the foundations, weaken.

.21 overwhelm, whelm, swamp, engulf; inundate.

.22 (be destroyed) fall, fall to the ground, tumble, come tumbling or crashing down, topple, tremble or nod to its fall, bite the dust [informal]; break up, crumble, crumble to dust, disintegrate, go or fall to pieces; go by the board, go out the window, go up the spout [informal].

.23 **perish, expire, succumb, die, cease, end,** come to an end, go, pass, **pass away, vanish, disappear,** fade away, run out, peg *or* conk out [slang], come to nothing *or* naught, be no more, be done for; be all over with, be all up with [informal].

.24 **go to ruin, go to wrack and ruin,** go to rack and manger [archaic], **go to the bad,** go wrong, **go to the dogs** *or* **go to pot** [both informal], go to the deuce *or* devil [informal], go to hell [slang], go to the wall, go to perdition *or* glory [informal]; go up [informal], go under; **go to smash,** go to shivers, go to smithereens [informal].

.25 **drive to ruin,** drive to the bad, **force to the wall,** drive to the dogs [informal], hound *or* harry to destruction.

.26 ADJS **destructive,** destroying, –clastic, ant-(i)– *or* anth–; **ruinous,** ruining; demolishing, demolitionary; **disastrous, calamitous, cataclysmic,** cataclysmal, **catastrophic;** fatal, fateful, doomful, baneful; **deadly** 409.23; consumptive, consuming, withering; **devastating, desolating,** ravaging, wasting, wasteful, spoliative, depredatory; vandalic, vandalish, vandalistic; subversive, subversionary; nihilist, nihilistic; suicidal, self-destructive; fratricidal, internecine, internecive.

.27 **exterminative,** exterminatory, **annihilative, eradicative,** extirpative, extirpatory; all-destroying, all-devouring, all-consuming.

.28 **ruined, destroyed, wrecked, blasted, undone, done for** [informal], done in [informal], finished, *ausgespielt* [Ger], kaput [slang]; down-and-out, broken, bankrupt; spoiled 692.30; irremediable 889.15; fallen, overthrown; **devastated, desolated, ravaged,** blighted, wasted; ruinous, in ruins; gone to wrack and ruin, gone to pot *or* gone to the dogs [both informal].

694. RESTORATION

.1 NOUNS **restoration, restitution, reestablishment, reinstatement,** reinstation, reformation [archaic], reinvestment, reinvestiture, instauration, reversion, reinstitution, reconstitution, replacement, **rehabilitation,** redintegration [archaic], reconversion, reactivation, reenactment; improvement 691.

.2 **reclamation, recovery, retrieval,** redemption, salvation, salvage.

.3 **revival,** revivification, revivescence *or* re-

vivescency, **renewal,** resurrection, resuscitation, reanimation, resurgence, recrudescence; **refreshment** 695; second wind; *renaissance* [Fr], renascence, **rebirth,** new birth; **rejuvenation,** rejuvenescence, second youth, new lease on life; **regeneration,** regeneracy, regenerateness; regenesis, palingenesis, palingenesy.

.4 **renovation, renewal;** refreshment, **reconditioning,** furbishment, refurbishment; retread *or* retreading [both informal]; facelifting *or* face-lift; slum clearance, urban renewal.

.5 **reconstruction, re-creation, remaking,** remodeling, **rebuilding,** refabrication, refashioning; reassembling, reassembly; reformation.

.6 **reparation, repair,** repairing, **fixing, mending;** overhaul, overhauling; troubleshooting [informal]; **rectification, correction, remedy; redress,** making right, amends, satisfaction, compensation, recompense.

.7 **cure,** curing, **healing, remedy** 687; **therapy** 689.

.8 **recovery, rally, comeback** [informal], return; **recuperation, convalescence.**

.9 **restorability, reparability,** curability, recoverability, reversibility, remediability, retrievability, redeemability, corrigibility.

.10 **mender, fixer,** doctor [informal], restorer, renovator, repairer, **repairman,** maintenance man, **serviceman;** trouble man *or* **troubleshooter** [both informal]; Mr. Fixit *or* little Miss Fixit [both informal]; **mechanic** *or* mechanician; tinker; cobbler.

.11 VERBS **restore, put back, replace, return,** place in *statu quo ante;* **reestablish,** reform [archaic], **reinstate,** reenact, **reinstall,** reinvest, revest, reinstitute, reconstitute, recruit, **rehabilitate,** reintegrate, reconvert, reactivate; refill, replenish; give back 823.4.

.12 **redeem, reclaim, recover, retrieve;** ransom; rescue; salvage, recycle; win back, **recoup.**

.13 **remedy, rectify, correct, right,** emend, amend, **redress,** make good *or* right, **put right,** set right, put *or* set to rights, put *or* set straight, set up, make all square; pay reparations, give satisfaction, requite, recompense, compensate, remunerate.

.14 **repair, mend, fix,** fix up [informal], do up, doctor [informal], put in repair, put in shape, set to rights, put in order *or* condition; **condition, recondition,** commission, put in commission, ready; **service, overhaul;** patch, **patch up;** tinker,

tinker up; cobble; sew up, darn; recap, re-tread.

.15 **cure, work a cure, recure** [archaic], **remedy, heal, restore to health,** bring round *or* around, pull round *or* around, give a new *or* fresh lease on life, make better, make well, fix up, pull through, set on one's feet *or* legs; snatch from the jaws of death.

.16 **revive, revivify, renew,** recruit; **reanimate,** reinspire, **regenerate, rejuvenate, revitalize,** put *or* breathe new life into; **refresh** 695.2; **resuscitate,** bring to; recharge; **resurrect,** bring back, call back, recall to life, raise from the dead; rewarm, warm up *or* over; **rekindle,** relight, reheat the ashes, stir the embers.

.17 **renovate, renew; recondition,** refit, revamp, furbish, refurbish; refresh, face-lift.

.18 **remake,** reconstruct, remodel, re-create, **rebuild,** refabricate, re-form, refashion, reassemble.

.19 **recuperate,** recruit, **gain strength,** recruit *or* renew one's strength, **get better;** improve 691.7; **rally, pick up,** perk up *or* brace up [both informal], take a new *or* fresh lease on life; **take a favorable turn,** turn the corner, be out of the woods, take a turn for the better; **convalesce;** sleep it off.

.20 **recover, rally, revive, get well, get over, pull through,** pull round *or* around, come round *or* around [informal], come back [informal], make a comeback [informal]; get about, get back in shape [informal], be oneself again; **survive,** weather the storm; **come to,** come to oneself, show signs of life; come up smiling, bounce back [both informal]; come *or* pull *or* snap out of it [informal].

.21 **heal, heal over,** close up, scab over, cicatrize, granulate; heal *or* right itself; **knit, set.**

.22 ADJS **restorative, restitutive,** restitutory, analeptic; **reparative, reparatory;** remedial, **curative** 687.39.

.23 **recuperative,** recuperatory; **reviviscent; convalescent;** buoyant, resilient, elastic.

.24 **renascent,** *redivivus* [L], resurrected, renewed, revived, reborn, resurgent, recrudescent, reappearing.

.25 **remediable, curable,** medicable; **emendable,** amendable, **correctable,** rectifiable, corrigible; **improvable,** ameliorable; **reparable,** repairable, **mendable, fixable;** restorable, recoverable, retrievable, reversible, reclaimable, recyclable, redeemable.

695. REFRESHMENT

.1 NOUNS **refreshment,** refection, refreshing, **bracing, exhilaration, stimulation,** enlivenment, vivification, **invigoration,** reinvigoration, reanimation, revival, revivification, revivescence *or* revivescency, renewal, recreation; regalement, regale; tonic, bracer, pick-me-up [informal], cordial.

.2 VERBS **refresh, freshen,** refreshen, freshen up, fresh up [informal]; **revive, revivify, reinvigorate,** reanimate; **exhilarate, stimulate, invigorate,** fortify, enliven, animate, vivify, quicken, **brisk, brisken; brace, brace up,** buck up *or* pick up [both informal], perk up *or* chirk up [both informal], set up, set on one's legs *or* feet [informal]; renew one's strength, put *or* breathe new life into; renew, recreate; **regale, cheer,** refresh the inner man.

.3 ADJS **refreshing,** refreshful, **fresh,** brisk, crisp, crispy, zesty, zestful, **bracing, tonic,** cordial, **exhilarating, stimulating, invigorating,** rousing, energizing; regaling, cheering.

.4 **refreshed, invigorated, exhilarated,** stimulated, energized, recharged, animated, reanimated, **revived,** renewed, recreated.

.5 **unwearied, untired, unfatigued,** unexhausted.

696. RELAPSE

.1 NOUNS **relapse, lapse,** falling back; **reversion, regression** 146.1; **reverse, reversal,** backward deviation, **setback,** backset; **return,** recurrence, renewal, recrudescence; throwback, atavism.

.2 **backsliding,** backslide; **fall, fall from grace;** recidivism, recidivation; apostasy 628.2.

.3 **backslider,** recidivist, reversionist; apostate 628.5.

.4 VERBS **relapse, lapse, backslide,** slide back, lapse back, **slip back,** sink back, **fall back,** have a relapse, **return to, revert to,** recur to, yield again to, fall again into, recidivate; revert, **regress** 146.4; **fall, fall from grace.**

.5 ADJS **relapsing, lapsing, backsliding,** recidivous; **recrudescent; regressive** 146.7; apostate 628.11.

697. DANGER

.1 NOUNS **danger, peril, jeopardy, hazard, risk; endangerment, imperilment;** cause for alarm, **menace, threat** 973; **crisis, emergency,** pass, pinch, strait, plight, predicament 731.4; rocks or breakers ahead, gathering clouds, storm clouds; dangerous ground, yawning or gaping chasm, quicksand, thin ice; house of cards, cardhouse.

.2 **dangerousness, hazardousness, riskiness,** chanciness [informal], diceyness [Brit informal], **perilousness; unsafeness,** unhealthiness [informal]; criticalness; **precariousness, ticklishness,** slipperiness, touchiness, delicacy, ticklish business [informal]; **insecurity,** unsoundness, instability, unsteadiness, shakiness, totteriness; sword of Damocles; **unreliability,** undependability, untrustworthiness 514.6; **unsureness,** unpredictability, **uncertainty,** doubtfulness, dubiousness 514.1,2.

.3 **exposure, openness,** liability, nonimmunity, susceptibility; **unprotectedness, defenselessness,** nakedness, helplessness.

.4 **vulnerability, pregnability,** penetrability, assailability, vincibility; weakness 160; **vulnerable point, weak link, weak point, soft spot,** heel of Achilles, chink, chink in one's armor, "the soft underbelly of Europe" [Sir Winston Churchill].

.5 (hidden danger) snags, rocks, reefs, ledges; coral heads; shallows, shoals; sandbank, sandbar, sands; quicksands; rockbound or ironbound coast, lee shore; undertow, undercurrent; **pitfall** 618.11; snake in the grass.

.6 VERBS **endanger, imperil,** peril, periclitate; **risk, hazard, gamble, gamble with; jeopardize,** jeopard, jeopardy, compromise, put in danger, **put in jeopardy,** put on the spot or lay on the line [both slang]; **expose,** lay open; incur danger, run into or encounter danger.

.7 **take chances, take a chance, chance, risk, gamble,** hazard, **run the chance or risk or hazard;** go out on a limb [informal], **expose oneself,** lower one's guard, **lay oneself open to,** open the door to; **tempt Providence,** forget the odds, **defy danger,** skate on thin ice, court destruction, dance on the razor's edge, go in harm's way, stand or sleep on a volcano, sit on a barrel of gunpowder, build a house of cards, put one's head in the lion's mouth, "beard the lion in his den" [Sir Walter Scott], march up to the cannon's mouth, play with fire, go through fire and water, go out of one's depth, go to sea in a sieve, carry too much sail, sail too near the wind; risk one's life, **take one's life in one's hand,** dare, face up to, brave 893.10, 11.

.8 **be in danger,** be in peril, be in extremis, be in desperate case, have one's name on the danger list, have the chances or odds against one; be despaired of; hang by a thread; tremble on the verge, totter on the brink; feel the ground sliding from under one; have to run for it; be threatened, be on the spot [informal].

.9 ADJS **dangerous,** dangersome [dial], **perilous,** periculous, parlous, jeopardous, bad, ugly, serious, critical, explosive, attended or beset or fraught with danger; alarming, **menacing, threatening** 973.3.

.10 **hazardous, risky, chancy** [informal], dicey [Brit informal], aleatory, riskful, full of risk; **adventurous,** venturous, venturesome; **speculative,** wildcat.

.11 **unsafe,** unhealthy [informal]; **unreliable, undependable, untrustworthy,** treacherous, **insecure, unsound,** unstable, unsteady, shaky, tottery, rocky; **unsure, uncertain,** unpredictable, doubtful, dubious 514.15,16.

.12 **precarious, ticklish, touchy,** touch-and-go, **critical, delicate;** slippery, slippy; on thin ice, on slippery ground; hanging by a thread, trembling in the balance.

.13 **in danger, in jeopardy, in peril,** in a bad way; **endangered, imperiled, jeopardized;** at the last extremity, in extremis [L], in desperate case; threatened, on the spot [informal]; between the hammer and the anvil, between Scylla and Charybdis, between two fires, between the devil and the deep blue sea; in a predicament 731.20; cornered 731.23.

.14 **unprotected, unshielded, unsheltered,** uncovered, unscreened, **unguarded, undefended,** unattended, unwatched, unfortified; unarmored, **unarmed,** bare-handed, weaponless, anopl(o)–; guardless, ungarrisoned, **defenseless, helpless;** unwarned, unsuspecting.

.15 **exposed, open,** out in the open, naked; out on a limb [informal]; liable, susceptible, nonimmune.

.16 **vulnerable, pregnable,** penetrable, expugnable; assailable, attackable, surmountable; conquerable, beatable [informal], vincible; weak 160.12–17.

.17 ADVS **dangerously, perilously, hazardously, riskily,** critically, unsafely; **precariously,** ticklishly.

698. SAFETY

.1 NOUNS **safety,** safeness, **security,** surety [archaic], assurance; risklessness, immunity, clear sailing; **protection,** safeguard

699.3; harmlessness 674.9; invulnerability 159.4.

.2 VERBS **be safe, be on the safe side; keep safe, come through;** weather, ride out, weather the storm; keep one's head above water, tide over; land on one's feet; save one's bacon [informal], save one's neck; lead a charmed life, possess nine lives.

.3 **play safe** [informal], **keep on the safe side,** give danger a wide berth, take precautions 895.6; assure oneself, make sure, look before one leaps; **save** 701.7, **protect** 699.18.

.4 ADJS **safe, secure, safe and sound;** immune, immunized; insured; **protected** 699.21; on the safe side; unthreatened, unmolested; unhurt, unharmed, unscathed, intact, untouched, with a whole skin, undamaged.

.5 **unhazardous, undangerous, unperilous, unrisky,** riskless, **unprecarious;** fail-safe; guaranteed, warranteed; dependable, reliable, trustworthy, sound, stable, steady, firm 513.17; "founded upon a rock" [Bible]; as safe as houses; harmless 674.20; invulnerable 159.17.

.6 **in safety, out of danger,** past danger, out of the meshes *or* toils, home free [informal], **in the clear, out of harm's reach** *or* **way;** under cover, under lock and key; in shelter, in harbor *or* port, at anchor *or* haven, in the shadow of a rock; on sure *or* solid ground, on *terra firma,* high and dry, above water.

.7 **snug, cozy;** airworthy, seaworthy, seakindly.

.8 ADVS **safely, securely,** reliably, dependably; with safety, **with impunity.**

.9 INTERJS **all's well!,** all clear!, all serene!; ally-ally out'n free!

.10 PHRS the danger is past, the storm has blown over, the coast is clear.

699. PROTECTION

.1 NOUNS **protection, guard, safekeeping; eye,** watchful eye; protective custody; safety 698; **shelter, cover,** shade, shadow [archaic], lee; **refuge** 700; preservation 701; **defense** 799.

.2 **protectorship, guardianship,** stewardship, custodianship; **care, charge, keeping, custody; hands,** safe hands, wing; **auspices, patronage, tutelage, guidance; ward,** wardship, wardenship, watch and ward; cure, pastorship, pastorage, pastorate; **oversight,** jurisdiction, management, min-

istry, administration, government, governance.

.3 **safeguard,** palladium, **guard; shield,** scut(i)–, aspid(o)–, –aspis; **screen,** aegis; umbrella, protective umbrella; patent, copyright; **bulwark** 799.4; backstop; **fender,** mudguard, **bumper, buffer, cushion,** pad, padding; seat belt; protective clothing; shin guard, knuckle guard, knee guard, nose guard, hand guard, arm guard, ear guard, finger guard, foot guard; goggles, mask, face mask, welder's mask, fencer's mask; safety shoes; helmet, hard hat [informal], crash helmet, sun helmet; cowcatcher, pilot; dashboard; windshield, windscreen [Brit], dodger; life preserver 701.5; lifeline, safety rail, guardrail, handrail; governor; safety, safety switch, interlock; safety valve, safety plug; fuse, circuit breaker; insulation; safety glass, laminated glass; lightning rod, lightning conductor; prophylactic, preventive 687.20; contraceptive 687.23.

.4 **insurance,** assurance [Brit]; group insurance, fraternal insurance; reciprocal insurance, interinsurance; term insurance; reinsurance; straight *or* ordinary life insurance, limited payment insurance, endowment insurance, family income policy, family maintenance policy, retirement income insurance, joint life insurance, industrial life insurance, group life insurance, business life insurance, savings bank life insurance, credit life insurance; **casualty insurance; health insurance,** hospitalization insurance, hospital service contract, major medical insurance, disability insurance, accident insurance, workmen's compensation insurance; **automobile insurance,** collision insurance; no-fault insurance; aviation insurance; fire insurance, flood insurance; burglary insurance, theft insurance, robbery insurance, fidelity insurance, fidelity bond, forgery bond; credit insurance; bond, surety bond, license bond, permit bond, customs bond, bail bond, court bond; business interruption insurance; title insurance; liability insurance, public liability insurance, automobile liabilitity insurance, malpractice insurance; marine insurance, ocean marine insurance, inland marine insurance; **annuity,** variable annuity; government insurance, **social security** 745.7; **insurance company,** stock company, mutual company; **insurance policy,** policy, certificate of insurance; deductible; insurance man, underwriter, insurance broker, insurance agent, insurance adjuster, actuary.

.5 **protector**, protectress, safekeeper; patron, patroness; tower, pillar, tower of strength, rock; champion, **defender** 799.7.

.6 **guardian, warden,** governor; **custodian,** steward, **keeper, caretaker,** warder [Brit], attendant; next friend, prochein ami, guardian *ad litem*; **curator,** conservator; janitor; castellan; **shepherd;** game warden, gamekeeper; ranger, forest ranger; lifeguard, lifesaver [Brit]; air warden; guardian angel 1014.22.

.7 **chaperon,** duenna; **governess.**

.8 **nurse, nursemaid,** nurserymaid, nanny [informal], amah, ayah [India], mammy [dial]; dry nurse, wet nurse; **baby-sitter,** sitter [informal].

.9 **guard,** guarder, guardsman [archaic], warder; **outguard, outpost; picket,** outlying picket, inlying picket; advance guard, **vanguard, van; rear guard;** coast guard; armed guard, security guard; jailer 761.10; bank guard; railway *or* train guard; goalkeeper, goaltender, goalie [informal]; **garrison;** cordon, *cordon sanitaire* [Fr].

.10 **watchman, watch,** watcher, watchkeeper; **lookout,** lookout man; **sentinel, picket, sentry; scout,** vedette; forward observer, spotter; **patrol, patrolman,** patroller, roundsman; night watchman, Charley [slang]; fireguard, fire patrolman, fire warden; airplane spotter; Argus.

.11 **watchdog,** bandog, guard dog; Cerberus.

.12 **doorkeeper, doorman, gatekeeper,** cerberus, warden, **porter, janitor,** concierge [Fr], ostiary, usher; receptionist.

.13 **picket,** picketer, demonstrator, picket line.

.14 **bodyguard,** safeguard; **convoy, escort;** guards, praetorian guard; guardsman; yeoman *or* yeoman of the guard *or* beefeater, gentleman-at-arms, Life Guardsman [all England].

.15 **policeman, constable, officer, police officer,** *flic* [Fr slang], *gendarme* [Fr], *carabiniere* [Ital]; peace officer, law enforcement agent, arm of the law; military policeman, MP; detective 781.10; policewoman, police matron; patrolman, police constable [England]; trooper, mounted policeman; reeve, portreeve; **sheriff, marshal;** deputy sheriff, deputy, bound bailiff, catchpole, beagle [slang], bombailiff [Brit slang]; sergeant, police sergeant; roundsman; lieutenant, police lieutenant; captain, police captain; inspector, police inspector; superintendent,

chief of police; commissioner, police commissioner; government man, federal, fed *or* G-man [both informal]; narc [slang]; **bailiff,** tipstaff, tipstaves [pl]; mace-bearer, lictor, sergeant at arms; beadle.

.16 [slang *or* informal terms] cop, copper, John Law, bluecoat, bull, flatfoot, gumshoe, gendarme, shamus, dick, flattie, bobby *or* peeler [both Brit], pig, Dogberry; the cops, the law, the fuzz; New York's finest.

.17 **police, police force,** law enforcement agency; **constabulary;** state police, troopers, highway patrol, county police, provincial police; security force; special police; tactical police, riot police; **posse,** *posse comitatus* [L]; **vigilantes,** vigilance committee; secret police, political police; FBI, Federal Bureau of Investigation; military police, MP; shore patrol, SP; Scotland Yard [England]; Sûreté [France]; Cheka, NKVD, MVD, OGPU [all USSR]; Gestapo [Germany]; Royal Canadian Mounted Police, RCMP, Mounties [all Canada]; Interpol, International Criminal Police Commission.

.18 VERBS **protect, guard, safeguard, secure, keep,** bless, make safe, police; keep from harm; **insure,** underwrite; ensure, guarantee 772.9; patent, copyright, register; **cushion;** champion, go to bat for [slang], ride shotgun for [informal], fend, defend 799.8; **shelter, shield, screen, cover,** cloak, shroud [archaic]; **harbor, haven;** nestle; compass about, fence; arm, armor.

.19 **care for, take care of;** preserve, conserve; provide for, support; take charge of, **take under one's wing,** make one a *protégé*; **look after,** see after, **attend to, minister to,** look *or* see to, look *or* watch out for [informal], keep an eye on *or* upon, keep a sharp eye on *or* upon, **watch over,** keep watch over, **watch, mind, tend;** keep tab *or* tabs on [informal]; **shepherd,** ride herd on [slang]; **chaperon,** matronize; baby-sit [informal]; **foster, nurture, cherish, nurse; mother,** be a mother *or* father to.

.20 **watch, keep watch, keep guard,** keep vigil, keep watch and ward; stand guard, stand sentinel; be on the lookout 533.8; mount guard; **police, patrol,** go on one's beat.

.21 ADJS **protected, guarded,** safeguarded, defended; safe 698.4–7; patented, copyrighted; **sheltered, shielded,** screened, covered, cloaked; policed; armed 799.14; invulnerable 159.17,18.

.22 **under the protection of,** under the shield of, under the aegis of, **under one's wing,** under the wing of, under the shadow of one's wing.

.23 **protective, custodial,** guardian, tutelary; vigilant, watchful; prophylactic, preventive; immunizing; protecting, guarding, safeguarding, sheltering, **shielding,** screening, covering; fostering, parental; defensive 799.11.

700. REFUGE

.1 NOUNS **refuge, sanctuary,** safehold, **asylum, haven, port,** harborage, **harbor;** harbor of refuge, port in a storm, snug harbor, safe haven; game sanctuary, bird sanctuary, preserve, forest preserve, game preserve; stronghold 799.6.

.2 **recourse, resource, resort;** last resort or resource, *dernier ressort, pis aller* [both Fr]; **hope; expedient** 670.2.

.3 **shelter, cover, covert,** coverture; concealment 615; *abri* [Fr], dugout, cave, earth, funk hole [informal], foxhole; bunker; trench; storm cellar, storm cave, cyclone cellar; air-raid shelter, bomb shelter, bombproof, fallout shelter, safety zone or isle or island.

.4 **asylum, home,** retreat; **poorhouse,** almshouse, workhouse [Brit], poor farm; **orphanage; hospice,** hospitium; old folks' home, rest home, nursing home, old soldiers' home, sailors' snug harbor; foster home; halfway house.

.5 **retreat,** recess, hiding place, **hideaway,** hideout; **sanctum, sanctum sanctorum,** holy of holies, adytum; privacy [archaic], secret place; **den,** lair, mew; **cloister,** hermitage, ashram, cell; **ivory tower.**

.6 **harbor, haven, port,** seaport; harborage, **anchorage,** anchorage ground, protected anchorage, moorings; **roadstead, road,** roads; berth, slip; **dock,** dockage, marina, basin; dry dock; shipyard, dockyard; **wharf, pier,** quay; landing, landing place or stage, jetty, jutty [archaic]; breakwater, mole, groin; seawall, embankment, bulkhead.

.7 VERBS **take refuge, take shelter,** seek refuge, **claim sanctuary,** run into port; fly to, throw oneself into the arms of; bar the gate, lock or bolt the door, raise the drawbridge, let the portcullis down; take cover 615.8.

.8 **find refuge** or sanctuary, make port, reach safety.

701. PRESERVATION

.1 NOUNS **preservation,** preserval, **conservation,** conservancy, **saving, salvation,** salvage, **keeping, safekeeping,** maintenance, upkeep, support; protection 699; conservationism, environmental conservation; soil conservation, forest conservation, forest management, wildlife conservation, stream conservation, water conservation, wetlands conservation.

.2 (means of preservation) **curing,** seasoning, salting, brining, pickling, marination, corning; **drying,** dry-curing, jerking; dehydration, anhydration, evaporation, desiccation; **smoking,** fuming, smoke-curing, kippering; **refrigeration,** freezing, quick-freezing, blast-freezing; freeze-drying, lyophilization; irradiation; **embalming,** mummification; taxidermy, stuffing; **canning,** tinning [Brit]; bottling, potting.

.3 **preservative,** preservative medium; salt, brine, vinegar, formaldehyde, Formalin, embalming fluid.

.4 **preserver,** saver, conservator, keeper, safe-keeper; taxidermist; lifesaver, rescuer, deliverer, savior; **conservationist,** preservationist; National Wildlife Service, Audubon Society, Sierra Club; ranger, forest ranger, game warden.

.5 **life preserver,** life jacket, life vest, life belt, cork jacket, Mae West [informal]; life buoy, life ring, buoy; water wings; breeches buoy; lifeboat, life raft, rubber dinghy [Brit]; life net; lifeline; safety belt; **parachute,** ejection seat or ejector seat, ejection capsule.

.6 (place set apart for conservation) **preserve, reserve, reservation; park,** paradise; national park; forest preserve or reserve; national or state forest; wilderness preserve; Indian reservation; game reserve, bird sanctuary, wildlife preserve, **sanctuary** 700.1; museum, library, archives, bank, store 660.

.7 VERBS **preserve, conserve, save,** spare; **keep,** keep safe, keep inviolate or intact; patent, copyright, register; not endanger, not destroy; not use up, not waste, not expend; **guard, protect** 699.18; **maintain, sustain,** uphold, support, **keep up,** keep alive.

.8 (preserve from decay) preservatize; **cure,** season, salt, brine, marinate or marinade, pickle, corn, **dry, dry-cure,** jerk, dry-salt; dehydrate, anhydrate, evaporate, desiccate; **smoke,** fume, **smoke-cure,** smoke-dry, kipper; **refrigerate,** freeze, quick-freeze, blast-freeze; freeze-dry, lyophilize; irradiate; **embalm**, mummify; stuff.

.9 **put up**, do up; **can**, tin [Brit]; bottle, jar, pot.

.10 ADJS **preservative**, preservatory, conservative, conservatory; **conservational**, conservationist; preserving, conserving, saving, keeping; **protective** 699.23.

.11 **preserved**, conserved, **kept**, saved, spared; protected 699.21; **untainted, unspoiled;** intact, undamaged 677.7,8; **well-preserved,** well-conserved, **well-kept**, in a good state of preservation.

702. RESCUE

.1 NOUNS **rescue, deliverance,** delivery, saving; lifesaving; **extrication, release, freeing, liberation** 763; **salvation, salvage, redemption,** ransom; **recovery, retrieval.**

.2 **rescuer,** lifesaver, lifeguard; coast guard, lifesaving service, air-sea rescue; savior 942.2; lifeboat.

.3 VERBS **rescue,** come to the rescue, **deliver, save,** be the saving of, **redeem,** ransom, **salvage; recover, retrieve** 823.6; **free,** set free, **release, extricate,** extract, **liberate** 763.4–6; snatch from the jaws of death; save one's bacon or save one's neck or bail one out [all informal].

.4 ADJS **rescuable, savable;** redeemable; deliverable, extricable.

703. WARNING

.1 NOUNS **warning, caution,** caveat, **admonition,** monition, admonishment; **notice,** notification; **word to the wise,** *verbum sapienti* [L], verb. sap.; flea in one's ear [informal]; hint, tip-off [informal]; **lesson,** object lesson, **example,** deterrent example, warning piece; moral, moral of the story; **alarm** 704; final warning or notice, ultimatum; **threat** 973.

.2 **forewarning,** prewarning, **premonition,** precautioning; advance notice, plenty of notice, prenotification, prenotice; presentiment, **foreboding** 544; **portent,** "warnings, and portents and evils imminent" [Shakespeare].

.3 **warning sign,** premonitory sign, **danger sign;** preliminary sign or signal; **symptom,** early symptom, premonitory symptom, prodrome, prodroma, prodromata [pl]; **precursor** 66; **omen** 544.3,6; **handwriting on the wall,** "mene, mene, tekel, upharsin" [Aramaic; Bible]; straw in the wind; gathering clouds, clouds on the horizon; thundercloud, thunderhead; falling barometer or glass; storm or stormy petrel,

Mother Carey's chicken; **red light,** red flag; quarantine flag, yellow flag, yellow jack; death's-head, skull and crossbones; **high sign** [slang], **warning signal.**

.4 **warner,** cautioner, admonisher, monitor; prophet of doom, Cassandra, Jeremiah; **lookout,** lookout man; **sentinel, sentry; signalman,** signaler, flagman; lighthouse keeper.

.5 VERBS **warn, caution, advise, admonish; give warning,** give fair warning, utter a caveat, address a warning to, put a flea in one's ear [informal], say a word to the wise; tip or tip off [both informal]; notify, give notice, tell once and for all; issue an ultimatum; **threaten** 973.2; **alert,** warn against, put on one's guard; **give the high sign** [slang]; cry havoc, sound the alarm 704.3.

.6 **forewarn,** prewarn, precaution, premonish; prenotify, tell in advance, give advance notice; **portend, forebode** 544.10.

.7 ADJS **warning,** cautioning, **cautionary; monitory,** monitorial, admonitory, admonishing; notifying, notificational; exemplary, deterrent.

.8 **forewarning, premonitory; portentous,** foreboding 544.17; **precautionary,** precautional; precursive, precursory, forerunning, prodromal, prodromic.

704. ALARM

.1 NOUNS **alarm,** alarum, alarm signal, **alert;** hue and cry; note of alarm; air-raid alarm; all clear; tocsin, alarm bell; signal of distress, SOS, Mayday, upside-down flag; fiery cross, crostarie; storm warning, storm flag or pennant or cone, hurricane warning, gale warning, small-craft warning; fog signal or alarm, foghorn, fog bell; burglar alarm; fire alarm, fire bell, fire flag, still alarm; siren, whistle, horn, Klaxon; hooter [Brit], buzzer; police whistle, watchman's rattle; alarm clock; five-minute gun, two-minute gun; lighthouse, beacon; blinking light, flashing light, occulting light.

.2 **false alarm,** cry of wolf; bugbear, bugaboo; bogy; flash in the pan, dud [informal].

.3 VERBS **alarm, alert, arouse,** put on the alert; **warn** 703.5; fly storm warnings; **sound the alarm,** give or raise or beat or turn in an alarm, ring or sound the tocsin, cry havoc, raise a hue and cry; give a false alarm, **cry wolf; frighten** 891.23, startle 540.8.

.4 ADJS **alarmed, aroused;** alerted; **fright-ened** 891.33; startled 540.13.

705. ACTION

(voluntary action)

.1 NOUNS **action, act, acting, doing,** –ade, –esis, –ice, –y; not words but action; **practice, praxis,** –praxia; **exercise; operation,** working, function, functioning; **operations;** workings, **movements;** employment, work, occupation; swing, play; **activism; activity** 707; **behavior** 737.

.2 **performance, execution,** enactment; transaction; **discharge, dispatch;** conduct, **handling,** management, administration [archaic]; **achievement, accomplishment, effectuation, implementation; commission, perpetration;** completion 722.2.

.3 **act, action, deed, doing,** thing, thing done; **turn; feat, stunt** [informal], *tour de force* [Fr], **exploit,** adventure, gest, **enterprise,** achievement, accomplishment, **performance,** production; effort, endeavor, job, undertaking; **transaction,** passage; operation, proceeding, step, measure, **maneuver, move;** coup, stroke; blow, go [informal]; accomplished fact, *fait accompli* [Fr]; overt act [law]; *acta, res gestae* [both L], **doings, dealings; works;** work, handiwork, hand.

.4 VERBS **act, serve, function; operate, work,** practice, do one's stuff [slang]; do one's thing [slang]; **move,** proceed; make, play, **behave** 737.4.

.5 **take action, take steps** or **measures; proceed,** proceed with; **do something, do something about, act on** or **upon,** get with it [slang]; go; **lift a finger, take** or **bear a hand;** play a role or part in; stretch forth one's hand, strike a blow; **maneuver.**

.6 **do, effect,** effectuate, **make; bring about,** bring to pass, **bring off, produce, achieve, accomplish,** realize 722.4,5; **render, pay; inflict, wreak,** do to; **commit, perpetrate;** pull off [informal]; go and do, up and do or take and do [both dial].

.7 **practice, exercise, employ,** use; **carry on,** conduct, prosecute, **wage; follow, pursue; engage in,** work at, devote oneself to, do, apply oneself to, employ oneself in; **take up,** take to, **undertake, tackle,** take on, address oneself to, have a go at, turn one's hand to, **go in** or **out for** [informal], make it one's business, follow as an occupation; specialize in 81.4.

.8 **perform, execute, enact; transact;** dis-charge, dispatch; conduct, **manage, handle;** dispose of, take care of, **deal with,** cope with; **make, accomplish,** complete 722.4–6.

.9 **carry out,** carry through, go through, fulfill, work out; **bring off,** carry off; **put through,** get through; **implement; put into effect, put in** or **into practice,** carry into effect, carry into execution, **translate into action;** suit the action to the word; rise to the occasion, come through [informal].

.10 ADJS **acting,** performing, practicing, serving, functioning, **functional, operating, operational,** working; **in action** 164.11; **behavioral** 737.7.

706. INACTION

(voluntary inaction)

.1 NOUNS **inaction,** passiveness, "a wise passiveness" [Wordsworth], **passivity,** passivism; **passive resistance, nonviolent resistance;** nonresistance, **nonviolence;** pacifism; neutrality, neutralness, neutralism, **nonparticipation, noninvolvement;** standpattism [informal]; **do-nothingism,** do-nothingness, do-nothing policy, *laissez-faire* policy, **laissez-faireism;** *laissez-faire, laissez-aller* [both Fr]; watching and waiting, watchful waiting, waiting game; **inertia,** inertness, **immobility,** dormancy, stagnation, stagnancy, vegetation, stasis, paralysis; **procrastination; idleness,** indolence, **inactivity** 708; **quiescence** 268; **quietism,** contemplation, meditation, passive self-annihilation; contemplative life, *vita contemplativa* [L].

.2 VERBS **do nothing,** not stir, not budge, **not lift a finger** or **hand,** not move a foot, **sit back, sit on one's hands** [informal], sit on one's ass or butt or duff [slang], sit on the sidelines, be a sideliner, sit it out, fold one's arms, twiddle one's thumbs; **cool one's heels** [informal]; **bide one's time, delay,** watch and wait, wait and see, play a waiting game, hang fire; lie or rest upon one's oars, rest, be still 268.7; repose on one's laurels; drift, coast; **stagnate, vegetate,** lie dormant, hibernate; idle 708.11.

.3 **refrain, abstain,** hold, **spare, forbear, forgo,** keep from; hold or stay one's hand.

.4 **let alone,** leave alone, **leave** or **let well enough alone;** not make waves, not rock the boat; **let be,** leave be [slang], let things take their course, let it have its way; leave things as they are, let sleeping dogs lie; *laisser faire, laisser passer, laisser aller* [all Fr], live and let live; **take no part in,** not get involved in, **have nothing to do with,** have no hand in, stand *or* hold aloof.

.5 **let go, let pass, let slip, let slide** *or* let ride [both informal]; **procrastinate.**

.6 ADJS **passive; neutral,** neuter; **standpat** [informal], **do-nothing;** *laissez-faire, laissez-aller* [both Fr]; **inert,** immobile, dormant, stagnant, stagnating, vegetative, vegetable, static, stationary, motionless, paralyzed, paralytic; procrastinating; **inactive, idle** 708.16,17; quiescent 268.12; quietist, quietistic, contemplative, meditative.

.7 ADVS **at a stand** *or* **standstill,** at a halt.

707. ACTIVITY

.1 NOUNS **activity, action,** activeness; **movement,** motion, **stir;** proceedings, doings, goings-on, –fest, –ics; **activism,** political activism, **militancy;** business 656.

.2 **liveliness, animation, vivacity,** vivaciousness, **sprightliness, spiritedness,** bubbliness, **ebullience, effervescence, briskness,** breeziness, **peppiness** [informal]; **life, spirit, verve,** energy; moxie *or* pizzazz *or* piss and vinegar [all slang], pep [informal], vim 161.2.

.3 **quickness, swiftness, speediness,** alacrity, **readiness,** smartness, sharpness, briskness; **promptness, promptitude;** dispatch, expeditiousness, expedition; **agility, nimbleness,** spryness.

.4 **bustle, fuss, flurry, flutter,** fluster, **scramble,** ferment, stew, sweat, whirl, swirl, vortex, maelstrom, **stir,** hubbub, hullabaloo, **flap** [informal], feery-fary [Scot], ado, todo, bother, botheration, pother; fussiness, flutteriness; tumult, commotion, **agitation** 857.3; **restlessness,** unquiet, fidgetiness 857.4; **spurt, burst,** fit, spasm.

.5 **busyness, press of business;** plenty to do, many irons in the fire; **the battle of life,** the rat race [informal].

.6 **industry,** industriousness, assiduousness, **assiduity, diligence, application,** concentration, laboriousness, sedulity, **sedulousness,** unsparingness, relentlessness, zealousness, ardor, fervor, vehemence; **energy,** energeticalness, strenuousness, tirelessness, indefatigability.

.7 **enterprise,** enterprisingness, dynamism, **initiative,** aggression, **aggressiveness,** force, forcefulness, pushfulness, pushingness, **pushiness, push, drive, hustle, go,** getup, get-up-and-get *or* **get-up-and-go,**

go-ahead, go-getting, go-to-itiveness [informal], **up-and-comingness;** adventurousness, venturousness, venturesomeness, adventuresomeness; **spirit,** gumption *or* spunk [both informal]; **ambitiousness** 634.10.

.8 **man of action, doer,** man of deeds; **hustler** [informal], bustler; go-getter *or* ball of fire *or* live wire *or* powerhouse *or* human dynamo [all informal]; beaver, busy bee, **eager beaver** [informal]; operator *or* big-time operator *or* wheeler-dealer [all slang]; winner [informal]; **activist,** political activist, **militant;** enthusiast 635.5; new broom, take-charge guy [slang].

.9 **overactivity,** hyperactivity; **hyperkinesia** *or* hyperkinesis; franticness, frenziedness; overexertion, overextension; officiousness 238.2.

.10 VERBS **be busy, have one's hands full,** have many irons in the fire; not have a moment to spare, not have a moment that one can call one's own; have other things to do, have other fish to fry; **work, labor, drudge** 716.12–14; busy oneself 656.10,11.

.11 **stir, stir about, bestir oneself,** stir one's stumps [informal], be up and doing.

.12 **bustle, fuss,** make a fuss, **flutter,** rush around *or* about, tear around, hurry about, buzz *or* whiz about, dart to and fro, go around like a chicken with its head cut off.

.13 **hustle** [informal], **drive,** drive oneself, **push, scramble,** go all out [informal], **make things hum,** step lively [informal], make the sparks *or* chips fly; make up for lost time; press on, drive on; go ahead, forge ahead, shoot ahead, go full steam ahead.

.14 [slang terms] **hump,** get cutting, break one's neck, bear down on it, **hit the ball,** pour it on, lean on it, shake a leg, go to town on.

.15 **keep going, keep on,** keep on the go, **carry on,** peg *or* plug away [informal], **keep at it,** keep moving, keep driving, **keep the pot boiling,** keep the ball rolling; keep busy, **keep one's nose to the grindstone,** stay on the treadmill.

.16 make the most of one's time, improve the shining hour, make hay while the sun shines, not let the grass grow under one's feet; get up early.

.17 ADJS **active, lively, animated, spirited,** bubbly, **ebullient, effervescent, vivacious, sprightly,** chipper *or* perky [both informal], pert; **spry, breezy, brisk, energetic,** smacking, spanking; alive, live, full of life, full of pep or full of go [both informal]; **peppy** or snappy or zingy [all informal]; frisky, bouncing, bouncy; mercurial, quicksilver; **activist,** activistic, **militant.**

.18 **quick, swift, speedy, expeditious,** alacritous, dispatchful [archaic], **prompt,** ready, smart, sharp, quick on the trigger [informal]; **agile, nimble, spry.**

.19 **astir, stirring,** afoot, **on foot;** in full swing.

.20 **bustling,** fussing, fluttering, **fluttery,** fussy; **fidgety,** restless, fretful, jumpy, unquiet, unsettled 857.25; **agitated, turbulent** 857.21,22.

.21 **busy,** full of business; **occupied, engaged, employed, working;** at it; **at work,** on duty, on the job, in harness; **hard at work, hard at it; on the move, on the go,** on the run, **on the hop** or **jump** [informal]; busy as a bee or beaver, busier than a one-armed paper hanger [informal]; up to one's ears or elbows in; tied up.

.22 **industrious, assiduous, diligent, sedulous,** laborious, **hardworking;** hard, unremitting, unsparing, relentless, zealous, ardent, fervent, vehement; **energetic,** strenuous; never idle; sleepless, unsleeping; tireless, unwearied, unflagging, indefatigable 625.7.

.23 **enterprising, aggressive, dynamic,** driving, forceful, **pushing,** pushful, **pushy, up-and-coming, go-ahead** or **hustling** [both informal]; adventurous, venturous, venturesome, adventuresome; **ambitious** 634.28.

.24 **overactive,** hyperactive; hectic, frenzied, frantic, frenetic; hyperkinetic; intrusive, officious 238.8,9.

.25 ADVS **actively, busily; lively,** sprightly, **briskly, breezily, energetically, animatedly, vivaciously, spiritedly,** with life and spirit; allegro, allegretto; full tilt, in full swing, all out [informal].

.26 **quickly, swiftly, expeditiously,** with dispatch, readily, **promptly; agilely, nimbly, spryly.**

.27 **industriously, assiduously, diligently, sedulously,** laboriously; unsparingly, relentlessly, zealously, ardently, fervently, vehemently; **energetically,** strenuously, tirelessly, indefatigably.

708. INACTIVITY

.1 NOUNS **inactivity, inaction,** inactiveness; lull, suspension; suspended animation; dormancy, hibernation; immobility, motionlessness, quiescence 268; **inertia** 706.1; underactivity.

.2 **idleness,** unemployment, otiosity, inoccupation; idle hands, idle hours, time hanging on one's hands; "a life of dignified otiosity" [Thackeray].

.3 **unemployment,** inoccupation; layoff, furlough; normal unemployment, seasonal unemployment, technological unemployment, cyclical unemployment; unemployment insurance.

.4 **idling, loafing,** lazing, *flânerie* [Fr], goofing off [slang], goldbricking [informal]; *dolce far niente* [Ital]; trifling; dallying, dillydallying, mopery, dawdling; loitering, tarrying, lingering; lounging, lolling.

.5 **indolence, laziness, sloth,** slothfulness, lotus-eating; laggardness, slowness, dilatoriness, remissness, do-nothingness, faineancy, *fainéantise* [Fr]; inexertion, inertia; **shiftlessness,** dolessness [dial], hoboism, vagrancy; spring fever; ergophobia.

.6 **languor,** languidness, languorousness, languishment [archaic], lackadaisicalness, **listlessness,** lifelessness, inanimation, enervation, slowness, lenitude or lentor [both archaic], **dullness, sluggishness,** heaviness, dopiness [informal], hebetude, supineness, **lassitude, lethargy,** oscitancy, kef; phlegm, apathy, indifference, passivity; torpidness, **torpor,** torpitude, torpidity; stupor, stupefaction; **sloth,** slothfulness, acedia; **sleepiness, somnolence, drowsiness** 712.1; **weariness, fatigue** 717; jadedness, satedness 664.2; world-weariness, ennui, boredom 884.3.

.7 **lazybones,** lazyboots, lazylegs, indolent, lie-abed, slugabed.

.8 **idler, loafer, lounger,** loller, lotus-eater, *flâneur, flâneuse* [both Fr], **do-nothing,** dolittle, *fainéant* [Fr], goof-off [slang], goldbrick or goldbricker [both informal]; **sluggard,** slug, slouch, sloucher, lubber, stick-in-the-mud [informal], gentleman of leisure; **time waster,** time killer; **dallier, dillydallier,** mope, moper, doodler, diddler [informal], **dawdler,** dawdle, laggard, **loiterer,** lingerer; waiter on Providence; trifler, **putterer,** potterer; clock watcher.

.9 **bum,** stiff [slang], derelict, skid-row bum, Bowery bum, *lazzarone* [Ital]; beachcomber; **good-for-nothing,** good-fornaught, **ne'er-do-well,** wastrel; vagrant, hobo, tramp 274.3; beggar 774.8.

.10 **nonworker, drone;** cadger, bummer or moocher [both slang], **sponger,** freeloader, lounge lizard [informal], social parasite, parasite, spiv [Brit]; beggar, mendicant, panhandler [slang]; **the unemployed;** the unemployable; lumpen proletariat; leisure class, rentiers, coupon clippers, idle rich.

.11 VERBS idle, do nothing, laze, lazy [informal], take one's ease, take one's time, loaf, lounge; lie around, lounge around, loll around, lollop around [Brit informal], moon, moon around, sit around, sit on one's ass or butt or duff [slang], stand around, hang around, loiter about or around, slouch, slouch around, bum around or mooch around [both slang]; goof off or lie down on the job [both slang]; sleep at one's post; let the grass grow under one's feet; twiddle one's thumbs, fold one's arms.

.12 waste time, consume time, kill time, idle or trifle or fritter or fool away time, loiter away or loiter out the time, beguile the time, while away the time, pass the time, lose time, waste the precious hours, burn daylight [archaic]; trifle, dabble, fribble, footle, putter, potter, piddle, diddle, doodle.

.13 dally, dillydally, piddle, diddle, diddle-daddle, doodle, dawdle, loiter, lollygag [dial], linger, lag, poke, take one's time.

.14 take it easy, take things as they come, drift, drift with the current, swim with the stream, coast, lead an easy life, live a life of ease, eat the bread of idleness, lie or rest upon one's oars; rest or repose on one's laurels, lie back on one's record.

.15 lie idle, lie fallow; aestivate, hibernate, lie dormant; lie or lay off, recharge one's batteries [informal]; lie up, lie on the shelf; ride at anchor, lay or lie by, lay or lie to; have nothing to do, have nothing on [slang].

.16 ADJS inactive, unactive; stationary, static, at a standstill; sedentary; quiescent, motionless 268.12–14.

.17 idle, fallow, otiose; unemployed, unoccupied, disengaged, désœuvré [Fr], jobless, out of work, out of employ, out of a job, out of harness; free, available, at liberty, at leisure; at loose ends; unemployable, lumpen; leisure, leisured; off duty, off work, off.

.18 indolent, lazy, bone-lazy, slothful, work-shy, ergophobic; do-nothing, fainéant [Fr], laggard, slow, dilatory, procrastinative, remiss, slack, lax; easy; shiftless, doless [dial]; unenterprising, nonaggressive; good-for-nothing, ne'er-do-well; drony, dronish, spivvish [Brit], parasitic, cadging, sponging, scrounging.

.19 languid, languorous, listless, lifeless, inanimate, enervated, debilitated, pepless [in-

formal], lackadaisical, slow, wan, lethargic, hebetudinous, supine, lymphatic, apathetic, sluggish, dopey [slang], drugged, droopy, dull, heavy, leaden, lumpish, torpid, stultified, inert, stagnant, stagnating, vegetative, vegetable, dormant; phlegmatic, numb, benumbed; moribund, dead, exanimate; sleepy, somnolent 712.21; pooped [slang], weary 717.6; jaded, sated 664.6; blasé, world-weary, bored 884.10,11.

709. HASTE

.1 NOUNS haste, hurry, scurry, rush, race, dash, drive, scuttle, scamper, scramble, hustle [informal], bustle, flutter, flurry, hurry-scurry, helter-skelter; no time to be lost.

.2 hastiness, hurriedness, quickness, swiftness, expeditiousness, alacrity, promptness 707.3; speed 269.1,2; furiousness, feverishness; precipitousness, precipitance or precipitancy, precipitation; suddenness, abruptness; impetuousness, impetuosity, impulsiveness, rashness.

.3 hastening, hurrying, festination, speeding, forwarding, quickening, acceleration; forced march, double time, double-quick time, double-quick.

.4 VERBS hasten, haste, hurry, accelerate, speed, speed up, hurry up, hustle up [informal], rush, quicken, hustle [informal], bustle, bundle, precipitate, forward; dispatch, expedite; whip, whip along, spur, urge 648.14–16; push, press; crowd, stampede; hurry on, hasten on, drive on, hie on, push on; hurry along, rush along, speed along, speed on its way; push through, railroad through [informal].

.5 make haste, hasten, festinate, hurry, get moving or going [informal], get a move on [informal], hurry up, race, run, post, rush, chase, tear, dash, spurt, leap, plunge, scurry, hurry-scurry, scamper, scramble, scuttle, hustle [informal], bundle, bustle; bestir oneself, move quickly 269.8–13; hurry on, dash on, press or push on, crowd; double-time, go at the double; break one's neck or fall all over oneself [both informal]; lose no time, not lose a moment; rush through, hurry through; dash off; make short work of, make the best of one's time or way, make up for lost time.

.6 [slang terms] step on it, snap to it, hop to it, hotfoot, bear down on it, shake it up, get cracking, get the lead out, get the lead out of one's ass, get one's ass in gear, hump, hump it, hump oneself, shag ass, tear ass, **get a hustle** or **move** or **wiggle on**, stir one's stumps, not spare the horses.

.7 **rush into, plunge into,** dive into, plunge, plunge headlong; **not stop to think,** go off half-cocked or at half cock [informal], leap before one looks.

.8 **be in a hurry,** have no time to lose or spare, not have a moment to spare, work against time, work under pressure.

.9 ADJS **hasty, hurried,** festinate, **quick,** flying, **expeditious,** prompt 707.18; **immediate,** instant, on the spot; **swift, speedy** 269.19; **urgent** 672.21; furious, feverish; slap-bang, slapdash, **cursory,** passing, snap [informal], superficial; last-minute.

.10 **precipitate,** precipitant, precipitous; **sudden,** abrupt; **impetuous, impulsive, rash;** headlong, breakneck; breathless, panting.

.11 **hurried, rushed,** pushed, pressed, crowded, **pressed for time,** hard-pushed or -pressed, hard-run; double-time, double-quick, on or at the double.

.12 ADVS **hastily, hurriedly, quickly; expeditiously,** promptly, with dispatch; apace, amain, hand over fist, **immediately,** instantly, at once; **swiftly, speedily** 269.21; with haste, with great or all haste, with a rush; furiously, feverishly, in a sweat or lather of haste, hotfoot; by forced marches; **helter-skelter, hurry-scurry,** pellmell; slapdash, cursorily, superficially, on the run or fly, in passing.

.13 **posthaste,** in posthaste; post, express; by express, by airmail, by return mail; by cable, by telegraph.

.14 **in a hurry, in haste,** in hot haste, in all haste; in short order 269.23; against time, against the clock.

.15 **precipitately,** precipitantly, precipitously, slap-bang; **suddenly,** abruptly; **impetuously, impulsively, rashly; headlong,** headfirst, headforemost, head over heels, heels over head [archaic], à corps perdu [Fr].

.16 INTERJS **make haste!,** make it quick!, **hurry up!;** now!; at once!, rush!, immediate!, **urgent!,** instanter!, step lively!, look alive!, on the double!

.17 [slang terms] **step on it!,** snap to it!, **make it snappy!,** get a move on!, get a wiggle on!, chop-chop!, shake a leg!, stir your stumps!, get the lead out!, **get moving!, get going!,** get cracking!, get with it!, hop to it!, move your tail!, move your fanny!, get on the ball!, don't spare the horses!

710. LEISURE

.1 NOUNS **leisure, ease, convenience,** freedom; retirement, semiretirement; rest, repose 711; **free time, spare time,** goof-off time [slang], odd moments, idle hours; time to spare or burn or kill, time on one's hands, time at one's disposal or command; time, one's own sweet time [informal].

.2 **leisureliness, unhurriedness,** unhastiness, hastelessness, relaxedness; dolce far niente [Ital]; **inactivity** 708; **slowness** 270; deliberateness, deliberation.

.3 VERBS **have time,** have time enough, have time to spare, have plenty of time, have nothing but time, be in no hurry.

.4 **take one's leisure,** take one's ease, **take one's time, take one's own sweet time** [informal], do at one's leisure or convenience or pleasure; go slow 270.6–9.

.5 ADJS **leisure, leisured;** idle, unoccupied, free, open, spare; retired, semiretired.

.6 **leisurely, unhurried,** unhasty, hasteless, easy, relaxed; deliberate; inactive 708.16, 17; slow 270.10.

.7 ADVS **at leisure, at one's leisure,** at one's **convenience,** at one's own sweet time [informal], when one gets around to it, when it is handy, when one has the time, when one has a minute to spare, when one has a moment to call one's own.

711. REST, REPOSE

.1 NOUNS **rest, repose, ease, relaxation;** slippered or unbuttoned ease; **comfort** 887; restfulness, quiet, tranquillity 268.1; inactivity 708; sleep 712.

.2 **respite, recess,** rest, pause, halt, stay, lull, **break,** surcease, suspension, interlude, **intermission,** spell [Austral], letup [informal], **time out** [informal], time to catch one's breath; **breathing spell,** breathing time, breathing place, breathing space, breath, **breather;** coffee break, tea break, cigarette break; cocktail hour, happy hour [informal]; enforced respite, downtime.

.3 **vacation,** holiday [Brit]; **time off;** paid vacation, paid holiday [Brit]; **leave, leave of absence, furlough; liberty,** shore leave; **sabbatical,** sabbatical leave or year; **weekend;** busman's holiday.

.4 **holiday** 137.12, **day off; red-letter day,** gala day, fete day, festival day, day of festivities; **legal holiday,** bank holiday [Brit]; High Holiday, High Holy Day; holy day 1040.14,15; feast, feast day, high day, church feast, fixed feast, movable feast; half-holiday.

.5 **day of rest,** *dies non* [L]; **Sabbath,** Sunday, Lord's day, First day.

.6 VERBS **rest, repose,** take rest, take one's ease, **take it easy** [informal], rest from one's labors, take life easy; go to rest, settle to rest; lie down, go to bed, snug down, curl up, bed, bed down, couch, recline, lounge, drape oneself, sprawl, loll; take off one's shoes, unbuckle one's belt.

.7 **relax, unlax** [slang], **unbend, unwind,** slack, slacken, ease; **ease up, let up,** slack up, slack off, **ease off, let down, slow down,** let up on.

.8 **take a rest, take a break, break, take time out** [informal], pause, lay off, **knock off** [informal], recess, **take a recess,** take ten *or* take five [both slang]; stop for breath, catch one's breath, breathe; stop work, suspend operations, call it a day.

.9 **vacation,** holiday, take a holiday, make holiday; **take a leave of absence,** take leave, go on leave, go on furlough, take one's sabbatical; weekend; Sunday, Christmas, etc.

.10 ADJS **vacational, holiday,** ferial [archaic], festal; sabbatical; **comfortable** 887.11,12; **restful,** quiet 268.12.

.11 ADVS **at rest, at ease,** at one's ease; abed, in bed.

.12 **on vacation,** on leave, on furlough; off duty, on one's own time.

712. SLEEP

.1 NOUNS **sleepiness, drowsiness,** doziness, heaviness, lethargy, oscitation, somnolence *or* somnolency, yawning, stretching, oscitancy, pandiculation; languor 708.6; sand in the eyes, heavy eyelids; REM sleep.

.2 **sleep, slumber,** narc(o)–, somni–; **repose,** silken repose, *somnus* [L], the arms of Morpheus; bye-bye *or* beddy-bye [both informal]; doss [Brit slang], blanket drill *or* shut-eye [both slang]; light sleep, fitful sleep, **doze, drowse,** snoozle [dial]; beauty sleep [informal]; sleepwalking, somnambulism; somniloquy; **land of Nod,** slumberland, sleepland, dreamland; hibernation, winter sleep, aestivation; bedtime, sack time [slang]; unconsciousness 423.2.

.3 **nap, snooze** [informal], **cat nap,** wink, **forty winks** [informal], wink of sleep, spot of sleep; **siesta,** blanket drill [slang].

.4 **sweet sleep, balmy sleep,** downy sleep, soft sleep, gentle sleep, smiling sleep, golden slumbers; "folded sleep" [Tennyson], "dewy-feathered sleep" [Milton], "care-charmer Sleep, son of the sable night" [Samuel Daniel], "the honey-heavy dew of slumber" [Shakespeare]; peaceful sleep, sleep of the just; restful sleep, good night's sleep, "sleep that knits up the ravell'd sleave of care" [Shakespeare], "Brother of Death" [Sir Thomas Browne].

.5 **deep sleep,** profound sleep, heavy sleep, **sound sleep,** unbroken sleep, wakeless sleep, drugged sleep, dreamless sleep, the sleep of the dead, "sleep such as makes the darkness brief" [Martial].

.6 **stupor,** sopor, **coma,** swoon, lethargy [archaic]; **trance;** narcosis, narcohypnosis, narcoma, narcotization, narcotic stupor *or* trance; sedation; high [slang]; nod [informal]; narcolepsy; catalepsy; thanatosis; shock 686.24; sleeping sickness, encephalitis lethargica.

.7 **hypnosis,** mesmeric *or* **hypnotic sleep, trance,** somnipathy, hypnotic somnolence; lethargic hypnosis, somnambulistic hypnosis, cataleptic hypnosis, animal hypnosis; narcohypnosis; autohypnosis, self-hypnosis; hypnotherapy 690.5.

.8 **hypnotism, mesmerism;** hypnology; hypnotization, mesmerization; **animal magnetism,** od, odyl, odylic force; hypnotic suggestion, posthypnotic suggestion, autosuggestion.

.9 **hypnotist, mesmerist,** hypnotizer, mesmerizer; Svengali, Mesmer.

.10 **sleep-inducer,** sleep-producer, sleep-provoker, sleep-bringer, hypnotic, soporific, somnifacient; poppy, mandrake, mandragora, opium, opiate, morphine, morphia; nightcap; sedative 687.12; anesthetic 687.57; lullaby 462.15.

.11 **Morpheus,** Somnus, Hypnos; "sweet father of soft rest" [Wm. Drummond]; sandman, dustman [Brit].

.12 **sleeper, slumberer;** sleeping beauty; **sleepyhead,** lie-abed, slugabed, sleepwalker, somnambulist; somniloquist.

.13 VERBS **sleep, slumber,** rest in the arms of Morpheus; **doze, drowse; nap,** take a nap, catch a wink; sleep soundly, **sleep like a top** *or* **log,** sleep like the dead; snore, saw wood *or* saw logs [both slang]; oversleep.

.14 [slang *or* informal terms] **snooze,** get some shut-eye, get some sack time, take forty winks; pound the ear, kip *or* doss [both Brit].

.15 **hibernate,** aestivate, lie dormant.

.16 **go to sleep,** settle to sleep, go off to sleep, **fall asleep,** drop asleep, **drop off,** "drift gently down the tides of sleep" [Longfellow]; **doze off, drowse off,** nod off, dope off [slang]; close one's eyes, "let fall the shadow of mine eyes" [Shakespeare].

.17 **go to bed, retire;** lay me down to sleep; bed, bed down; go night-night or go bye-bye or go beddy-bye [all informal].

.18 [slang or informal terms] **hit the hay, hit the sack,** crash, turn in, crawl in, flop, sack out, sack up, kip down or doss down [both Brit].

.19 **put to bed,** bed; nestle, cradle; **tuck in.**

.20 **put to sleep;** lull to sleep, rock to sleep; **hypnotize, mesmerize,** magnetize; **entrance,** trance, put in a trance; narcotize, drug, dope [slang]; anesthetize, put under; sedate.

.21 ADJS **sleepy, drowsy, dozy,** snoozy [informal], **slumberous,** slumbery, dreamy; **half asleep,** asleep on one's feet; sleepful, sleep-filled; yawny, stretchy [informal], oscitant, yawning, napping, **nodding,** ready for bed; heavy, **heavy-eyed, heavy with sleep,** sleep-swollen, sleep-drowned, sleep-drunk, drugged with sleep; **somnolent,** soporific; **lethargic,** comatose, narcose or narcous, stuporose or **stuporous, in a stupor,** out of it [informal]; narcoleptic; cataleptic; narcotized, drugged, doped [slang]; sedated; anesthetized; **languid** 708.19.

.22 **asleep, sleeping, slumbering,** in the arms or lap of Morpheus, in the land of Nod; **sound asleep, fast asleep,** dead asleep, deep asleep, in a sound sleep, flaked-out [slang]; **unconscious, oblivious, out;** comatose; dormant; dead, **dead to the world;** unwakened, unawakened.

.23 **sleep-inducing,** sleep-producing, sleep-bringing, sleep-causing, sleep-compelling, sleep-inviting, sleep-provoking, sleep-tempting; **narcotic, hypnotic, soporific, somniferous,** somnifacient; sedative 687.45.

.24 **hypnotic,** hypnoid(al), **mesmeric;** odylic; narcohypnotic.

713. WAKEFULNESS

.1 NOUNS **wakefulness,** wake; **sleeplessness,** restlessness, tossing and turning; **insomnia,** insomnolence or insomnolency, "the wakey nights" [Sir Thomas Wyatt]; vigil, all-night vigil, lidless vigil, *pervigilium* [L]; insomniac; consciousness, sentience; alertness 533.5.

.2 **awakening, wakening,** rousing, **arousal;** rude awakening; reveille [mil].

.3 VERBS **keep awake,** keep one's eyes open; keep alert, be vigilant 533.8; stay awake, **toss and turn,** not sleep a wink, not shut one's eyes, count sheep.

.4 **awake, awaken, wake, wake up, get up,** rouse, come alive [informal]; open one's eyes, stir [informal].

.5 (wake someone up) **awaken, waken, rouse, arouse,** awake, wake, **wake up,** shake up, knock up [Brit].

.6 **get up,** get out of bed, **arise,** rise, **rise and shine** [informal], greet the day, **turn out** [informal]; roll out or pile out or show a leg or hit the deck [all slang].

.7 ADJS **wakeful, sleepless, slumberless, unsleeping,** insomniac, insomnious; restless.

.8 **awake,** conscious, **up; wide-awake,** broad awake; alert 533.14.

.9 ADVS **sleeplessly, unsleepingly; wakefully,** with one's eyes open; alertly 533.17.

714. ENDEAVOR

.1 NOUNS **endeavor,** effort, striving, struggle, strain; **exertion** 716; determination, resolution 624.

.2 **attempt, trial, effort, essay,** assay [archaic], **endeavor, undertaking;** approach, move; stroke, step; **try** or **go** or **fling** or shot [all informal]; **crack** or **whack** or **stab** or **lick** [all slang]; gambit, offer, **bid,** strong bid; experiment, tentative; tentation, trial and error.

.3 **one's best,** one's level best [informal], **one's utmost,** one's damndest or darndest [slang], one's best effort or endeavor, the best one can, the best one knows how, all one can do, all one's got or one's all [both informal], the top of one's bent, as much as in one lies.

.4 VERBS **endeavor, strive, struggle,** strain, sweat, sweat blood, labor, **exert oneself,** apply oneself; spend oneself; seek, study, aim; resolve, be determined 624.7–9.

.5 **attempt, try, essay,** assay, offer; **undertake** 715.3, **approach,** come to grips with, engage, take the bull by the horns; venture, venture on or upon, chance; **make an attempt** or **effort,** lift a finger or hand.

.6 [slang or informal terms] **tackle, take on, make a try, give a try,** try on for size, **have a fling at,** give a fling, take a fling at, have a go at, give a go, give a whirl, **take a crack** or **whack at, make a stab at, have a shot at.**

.7 **try to, try and** [informal], **attempt to, endeavor to,** strive to, seek to, study to, aim to, venture to, dare to, pretend to.

.8 **try for, strive for,** strain for, struggle for,

contend for, pull for [informal], bid for, make a bid or strong bid for, make a play for [informal].

.9 **see what one can do,** see what can be done, see if one can do, do what one can, use one's endeavor; try anything once; **try one's hand,** try one's luck; make a cautious or tentative move, experiment, feel one's way.

.10 **make a special effort,** go out of the way, go out of one's way, **put oneself out,** put oneself out of the way, lay oneself out or bend over backwards [both informal], trouble oneself, **go to the trouble,** take trouble, **take pains,** redouble one's efforts.

.11 **try hard, push** [informal], make a bold push, **put one's back to or into,** put one's heart into, try until one is blue in the face, knock oneself out [slang], break one's neck [informal], bust one's ass [slang], rupture oneself, do it or break a leg, do it or bust a gut [slang]; die trying, **try and try;** try, try again; exert oneself 716.9.

.12 **do one's best,** do one's level best [informal], **do one's utmost,** try one's best or utmost, do or try one's damndest or darndest [slang], **do all or everything one can,** do the best one can, **do the best one knows how,** do all in one's power, do as much as in one lies, do what lies in one's power; put all one's strength into, put one's whole soul in, **strain every nerve; go all out** or go the limit [both informal], go for broke or shoot the works [both slang], give it one's all or give it all one's got [both informal]; be on one's mettle.

.13 **make every effort, spare no effort or pains, go all lengths, go to great lengths,** go the whole length, go through fire and water, not rest, not relax, not slacken, move heaven and earth, leave no stone unturned, leave no avenue unexplored.

.14 ADJS trial, tentative, experimental; venturesome, willing; determined, resolute 624.11,12.

.15 ADVS **out for,** out to, trying for, **on the make** [informal].

.16 **at the top of one's bent,** to one's utmost, as far as possible.

715. UNDERTAKING

.1 NOUNS undertaking, enterprise, operation, work, venture, project, proposition or deal [both informal]; **program, plan** 654; **affair, business, task** 656.2; effort, at-

tempt 714.2; engagement, contract, obligation, commitment 770.2.

.2 **adventure,** emprise, **mission;** quest, pilgrimage; expedition, exploration.

.3 VERBS **undertake, assume,** accept, **take on, take upon oneself,** take upon one's shoulders, **tackle,** attack; engage or contract or obligate or commit oneself; **put** or set or **turn one's hand to,** engage in, **devote oneself to, apply oneself to,** betake oneself to [archaic], address oneself to, give oneself up to; busy oneself with 656.11; **take up,** move into, go into, **go in or out for** [informal], **enter on or upon,** proceed to, embark in or upon, **venture upon,** go upon, launch forth, set forward, set going, get under way; set about, go about, lay about, go to do; **set to, turn to, buckle to, fall to; pitch into** [informal], plunge into, fall into, **launch into** or upon; go at, set at, have at [informal], knuckle or buckle down to; put one's hand to the plow, put or lay one's shoulder to the wheel; take the bull by the horns; **endeavor, attempt** 714.4,5.

.4 **have in hand, have one's hands in,** have on one's hands or shoulders.

.5 **be in progress or process,** be on the anvil, be in the fire, be in the works or hopper or pipeline [informal], **be under way.**

.6 **bite off more than one can chew** [informal], overextend or overreach oneself, have too many irons in the fire.

.7 ADJS **undertaken, assumed,** accepted, **taken on** [informal]; **ventured,** attempted, chanced; **in hand,** on the anvil, in the fire, **in progress or process,** in the works or hopper or pipeline [informal], **under way.**

.8 **enterprising,** venturesome, adventurous.

716. EXERTION

.1 NOUNS exertion, effort, energy, elbow grease; **endeavor** 714; **trouble, pains;** great or mighty effort, might and main, muscle, nerve and sinew, hard or strong or long pull, "a long pull, a strong pull, and a pull all together" [Dickens].

.2 **strain,** straining, stress, stressfulness, **stress and strain,** taxing, **tension,** stretch, rack; tug, pull, haul, heave; overexertion, overstrain, overtaxing, overextension, overstress.

.3 **struggle, fight, battle, tussle, scuffle, wrestle,** hassle [informal].

.4 **work,** erg(o)–; **labor, employment, industry, toil,** moil, travail, toil and trouble, sweat of one's brow; **drudgery, sweat,** slavery, spadework, donkeywork; rat race [informal]; treadmill; unskilled labor, hewing of wood and drawing of water; dirty work, scut work; tedious or stupid or idiot or tiresome work, grind [informal], fag; **manual labor,** handwork, handiwork; hand's turn, stroke of work, stroke; lick or lick of work or stitch of work [all informal]; task 656.2; fatigue 717.

.5 **hard work** or **labor, backbreaking work,** warm work, uphill work, hard or tough grind [informal]; **hard job** 731.2; **laboriousness, toilsomeness,** effortfulness, **strenuousness, arduousness,** operosity, operoseness; onerousness, oppressiveness, burdensomeness; troublesomeness.

.6 **exercise, exercising; practice, drill, workout;** athletics, gymnastics, calisthenics, gymnastic exercises, physical jerks [Brit], setting-up exercises, daily dozen, isometric exercises, isometrics; yoga; constitutional [informal], stretch; violent exercise, breather [informal]; physical education.

.7 exerciser; horizontal bar, parallel bars, horse, side horse, long horse, rings; trapeze; trampoline; Indian club; medicine ball; punching bag; rowing machine; weight, dumbbell, barbell.

.8 VERBS **exert, exercise, ply, employ, use, put forth,** put out [informal].

.9 **exert oneself,** put forth one's strength, bend one's effort, bend might and main, spare no effort, tax one's energies; put oneself out or lay oneself out or go all out [all informal]; endeavor 714.4; **do one's best** 714.12; **apply oneself;** hump or hump it or hump oneself [all slang], **buckle down** or **knuckle down** [both informal], bear down on it [slang], lay to; lay to the oars, ply the oar.

.10 **strain, tense, stress, stretch, tax,** press, rack; **pull, tug,** haul, **heave;** strain the muscles, strain every nerve or every nerve and sinew; put one's back into it [informal]; sweat blood; overexert, overstrain, overtax, overextend; drive or whip or flog oneself.

.11 **struggle, strive, contend, fight, battle,** buffet, scuffle, tussle, wrestle, hassle [informal], work or fight one's way, agonize, huff and puff, grunt and sweat, sweat it [slang], make heavy weather of it.

.12 **work, labor;** busy oneself 656.10,11; turn a hand, do a hand's turn, do a lick of work; chore, do the chores, char or do chars, chare [Brit].

.13 **work hard;** scratch or hustle or sweat [all informal], **slave, sweat and slave** [informal]; **hit the ball** or bear down on it or pour it on [all slang]; work one's head off [informal], work one's fingers to the bone; work like a horse or cart horse or dog, work like a slave or galley slave, work like a coal heaver, work like a Trojan; work overtime, do double duty, work double hours or tides, **work day and night, burn the midnight oil;** lucubrate, elucubrate; overwork 663.10.

.14 **drudge, grind** or **dig** [both informal], **fag, grub, toil, moil,** toil and moil, travail, **plod, slog, peg, plug** [informal], hammer, peg away or along, plug away or along [informal], hammer away, pound away, work away; **keep one's nose to the grindstone;** wade through.

.15 **set to work, get busy,** roll up one's sleeves, spit on one's hands; fall to work, **fall to, buckle** or **knuckle down to** [informal], **turn to, set to** or **about,** put or set one's hand to, start in, enter on or upon, **get on the job** or get going [both informal]; go to it or get with it or get cracking or have at it [all slang]; hop or jump to it [slang]; **attack,** set at, **tackle** [informal]; **plunge into,** dive into; **pitch in** or **into** [informal]; light into or wade into or tear into or sail into [all informal], put or lay one's shoulder to the wheel, put one's hand to the plow; take on, undertake 715.3.

.16 **task, work, busy,** keep busy, fag, sweat [informal], **drive, tax;** overtask, overtax, **overwork,** overdrive; burden, oppress 352.13.

.17 ADJS **laboring, working; struggling, striving, straining; drudging, toiling,** slaving, sweating or grinding [both informal], grubbing, **plodding,** slogging, pegging, plugging [informal]; hardworking 707.21.

.18 **laborious, toilsome, arduous, strenuous,** painful, effortful, operose, troublesome, onerous, oppressive, burdensome; wearisome 717.11; **heavy,** hefty [informal], tough [informal], uphill, **backbreaking,** grueling, punishing, crushing, killing, Herculean; **labored,** forced, strained; hard-fought, hard-earned.

.19 ADVS **laboriously, arduously, toilsomely, strenuously,** operosely; effortfully, with effort, **hard,** by the sweat of one's brow; the hard way; with all one's might, for all one is worth, with a will, **with might and main,** with a strong hand, manfully; **hammer and tongs, tooth and nail,** *bec et* *ongles* [Fr], heart and soul; **industriously** 707.27.

717. FATIGUE

.1 NOUNS **fatigue, tiredness, weariness,** wearifulness; overtiredness, overstrain; faintness, goneness, weakness, enfeeblement, enervation, debility, debilitation 160.1; jadedness; lassitude, languor 707.6; tension fatigue, stance fatigue; mental fatigue, brain fag [informal]; strain, mental strain, heart strain, eyestrain; sleepiness 712.1.

.2 **exhaustion,** exhaustedness, draining; **collapse, prostration,** breakdown, crack-up [informal], nervous exhaustion *or* prostration.

.3 **breathlessness, shortness of breath,** windedness, short-windedness; panting, gasping; dyspnea, labored breathing.

.4 VERBS **fatigue, tire, weary, exhaust,** fag *or* tucker [both informal], wilt, flag, jade, harass, frazzle, beat, poop [slang]; **wear, wear on** *or* **upon, wear down; tire out, wear out, fag out** *or* **tucker out** [both informal], knock out *or* poop out [both slang], burn out; **use up,** do up *or* knock up [both informal]; take the tuck out of, **do in; wind,** put out of breath; overtire, overweary, overfatigue, overstrain; weaken, enervate, debilitate 160.10; weary *or* tire to death; prostrate.

.5 **get tired, grow weary, tire, weary, fatigue,** jade; **flag, droop, faint,** sink, wilt; **play out, poop out** [slang], peter out [informal], run out, run down, burn out; gasp, wheeze, pant, puff, blow, puff and blow, puff like a grampus; collapse, break down, crack up [informal], give out, drop, drop in one's tracks, succumb.

.6 ADJS **fatigued, fagged** [informal], **tired, weary,** wearied, weariful, jaded, **frazzled,** run ragged, run-down, good and tired; unrefreshed, unrestored, in need of rest, ready to drop; **faint, fainting,** feeling faint, **weak,** enfeebled, enervated, debilitated, seedy [informal], weakened 160.12, 13,18; drooping, droopy, wilting, flagging, sagging; languid 708.19; worn, worn-down, **worn to a frazzle** *or* shadow, toilworn, weary-worn; wayworn, way-weary; footweary, weary-footed, footsore; tiredarmed; tired-winged, weary-winged; weary-laden, "tired and weary-laden" [Bible].

.7 tired-looking, weary-looking, tired-eyed, tired-faced, haggard, hollow-eyed, ravaged, drawn, worn, wan.

.8 **exhausted,** drained, **spent,** gone; **tired out, worn-out, fagged out** [informal], **tuckered out** [informal], **played out; pooped out** *or* knocked out *or* wiped out [all slang]; used up *or* done up *or* beat up [all informal], washed-up [informal]; **all in** *or* **bushed** *or* **pooped** *or* **beat** [all slang], whacked [Brit informal], beaten; done *or* **done in** [both informal]; bonetired, bone-weary; **dog-tired,** dog-weary; **dead** [informal], **dead-tired,** dead beat, **tired to death,** weary unto death, deadalive *or* dead-and-alive, more dead than alive, dead on one's feet, ready to drop, on one's last legs; prostrate.

.9 **overtired, overweary,** overwearied, overstrained, overdriven, overfatigued, overspent.

.10 **breathless, winded;** wheezing, puffing, panting, **out of breath,** short of breath *or* wind; short-winded, short-breathed, broken-winded, touched in the wind, dyspneic.

.11 **fatiguing, wearying,** wearing, **tiring,** straining, stressful, trying, **exhausting,** draining, **grueling,** punishing, killing; **tiresome,** fatiguesome, **wearisome,** weariful; toilsome 716.18.

.12 ADVS **out,** to the point of exhaustion.

718. WORKER, DOER

.1 NOUNS **doer,** actor, **performer, worker, practitioner,** perpetrator; **producer, maker,** creator, fabricator, **author,** mover, prime mover; architect; **agent,** medium; **executor,** executant, executrix; **operator,** operative, operant; subject; –ant *or* –ent, –arian, –ator, –ee, –eer, –er *or* –ier *or* –yer, –ist, –ster.

.2 (working person) **worker, laborer, toiler,** moiler; proletarian, blue-collar worker, laboring man, stiff *or* working stiff [both slang]; **workman, workingman; workwoman, workingwoman,** working girl, workgirl; industrial worker, factory worker; white-collar worker, office worker; **jobholder,** wageworker, **wage earner,** salaried worker; **breadwinner;** wage slave; employee, servant 750; **hand, workhand;** common laborer, unskilled laborer, navvy [Brit], day laborer, roustabout; **casual,** casual laborer; **migrant** worker, migrant; menial, flunky; pieceworker, jobber; full-time worker, parttime worker; temporary employee, temporary, office temporary; free-lance worker, free lance, free-lancer; self-employed person.

.3 drudge, grub, hack, fag, plodder, **slave,** galley slave, **workhorse,** beast of burden, slogger; "hewers of wood and drawers of water" [Bible]; grind or greasy grind [both slang], swot [Brit informal].

.4 **professional,** professionist, pro or old pro [both informal], seasoned professional; gownsman; the profession.

.5 **amateur, nonprofessional;** layman.

.6 **craftsman, handicraftsman;** craftswoman; **artisan,** artificer, artist [archaic], mechanic; wright; **technician;** apprentice, prentice [informal]; **journeyman,** skilled laborer; **master,** master craftsman, master workman, master carpenter, etc.

.7 **smith,** farrier [Brit], forger, forgeman, metalworker; Vulcan, Hephaestus, Wayland or Völund.

.8 craftsmen, workers

architect	manicurist
armorer	mason
barber	mechanic
beautician	miller
brazier	paperhanger
bricklayer	plumber
builder	potter
cabinetmaker	puddler
carpenter	puttier
carver	rigger
chandler	roofer
contractor	saddler
cooper	spinner
electrician	steam fitter
farmhand	steeplejack
fitter	stonecutter
forger	stonemason
founder	tanner
fuller	tinker
gas fitter	tinner
glassblower	turner
glazer	upholsterer
glazier	weaver
hairdresser	welder
lather	woodcutter
machinist	wrecker

.9 engineers

aeronautical engineer	hydraulic engineer
aerospace engineer	illuminating engineer
agricultural engineer	industrial engineer
architectural engineer	irrigation engineer
army engineer	marine engineer
automotive engineer	mechanical engineer
ceramic engineer	metallurgical engineer, metallurgist
chemical engineer	
civil engineer	military engineer
communications engineer	mining engineer
	municipal engineer
construction engineer	naval engineer
electrical engineer	nuclear engineer
electronics engineer	ordnance engineer
fire-protection engineer	petroleum engineer
	power engineer
fuel engineer	power-supply engineer
furnace engineer	product engineer
geological engineer	radar engineer
highway engineer	radio engineer
railroad engineer	textile engineer
refrigerating engineer	tool engineer
research engineer	transportation engineer
rocket engineer	
sanitary engineer	ventilation engineer
steam engineer	water-supply engineer
structural engineer	welding engineer
telephone engineer	

.10 smiths

anglesmith	keysmith
arrowsmith	knifesmith
blacksmith	locksmith
bladesmith	runesmith
brightsmith	shoeingsmith
bronzesmith	silversmith
chainsmith	stonesmith
clocksmith	tinsmith
coppersmith	toolsmith
goldsmith	versesmith 609.14
gunsmith	wagonsmith
hammersmith	weaponsmith
housesmith	whitesmith
ironsmith	wiresmith
jawsmith 599.4	wordsmith 602.15
jokesmith 881.12	

.11 wrights

cartwright	scenewright
housewright	shipwright
millwright	wagonwright, wainwright
pitwright	
playwright 611.27	wheelwright
plowwright	woodwright

.12 makers

anvil maker	cake maker
arrow maker	candlemaker
ax maker	candymaker
bag maker	canvas maker
balance maker	cap maker
barrel maker	carpet maker
basket maker	cart maker
bed maker	casemaker
beer maker	cement maker
bell maker	chain maker
bellows maker	chairmaker
belt maker	cheese maker
blanket maker	chest maker
block maker	chisel maker
board maker	cider maker
bobbin maker	cigarette maker
bodice maker	cigar maker
body maker	cloak maker
boilermaker	clockmaker
bolt maker	clog maker
bookmaker	cloth maker
boot maker	coach maker
bottle maker	coffin maker
bow maker	collar maker
box maker	combmaker
brake maker	cord maker
bread maker	coremaker
brickmaker	couch maker
bridge maker	cradle maker
broom maker	crate maker
brush maker	cup maker
bucket maker	diemaker
bullet maker	dish maker
butter maker	doll maker
button maker	door maker
cabinetmaker	dressmaker

dye maker
fan maker
felt maker
fiddle maker
file maker
garment maker
glassmaker
glove maker
glue maker
gunmaker
harness maker
hat maker
hook maker
hub maker
ice maker
ink maker
iron maker
kettle maker
lace maker
lamp maker
leather maker
lens maker
lockmaker
lute maker
map maker
matchmaker 933.13
model maker
nail maker
needle maker
netmaker
papermaker
patternmaker
pen maker
pie maker
pinmaker
plate maker
porcelain maker

pot maker
powder maker
ribbon maker
road maker
rope maker
rug maker
sack maker
saddle maker
safe maker
sailmaker
salt maker
sausage maker
saw maker
scale maker
scarf maker
screw maker
scythe maker
shirtmaker
shoemaker
soapmaker
steelmaker
sugar maker
sword maker
tentmaker
thread maker
tile maker
tool-and-die maker
toolmaker
tubemaker
tub maker
wagonmaker
watchmaker
web maker
wheel maker
whip maker
wigmaker
wine maker

.13 workers

brainworker
brassworker
clothworker
fieldworker
flintworker
garmentworker
glassworker
goldworker
ironworker
laceworker
leatherworker
metalworker
millworker
mineworker

needleworker
plateworker
saltworker
sawworker
shellworker
silverworker
steelworker
stoneworker
tinworker
waxworker
wireworker
woodworker
woolworker

719. WORKPLACE

.1 NOUNS **workplace,** work site, **workshop, shop,** –ery, –y; work space, working space, loft; **bench,** workbench, worktable; **desk;** establishment, facility, installation; **company,** institution, house, firm, concern, agency, organization, **corporation;** workhouse; sweatshop; workroom; studio, atelier; parlor, beauty parlor, funeral parlor, etc.; barbershop, beauty shop, butcher shop, etc.

.2 hive, hive of industry, beehive; factory or mill or manufacturing town; hub of industry, center of manufacture.

.3 **plant; factory,** manufactory, manufacturing plant, *usine* [Fr]; main plant, assembly plant, subassembly plant, feeder plant; push-button plant, automated or cybernated or automatic or robot factory; assembly or production line; defense plant, munitions plant, armory, arsenal; **power plant** 342.18; atomic energy plant; **machine shop; mill,** sawmill, flour mill, etc. 348.23; **yard,** yards, brickyard, shipyard, dockyard, boatyard; mint; refinery, oil refinery, sugar refinery, etc.; distillery, brewery, winery; boilery; bindery, bookbindery; packing house; cannery; dairy, creamery; pottery; tannery; **factory district,** industrial zone, industrial park, factory belt, manufacturing quarter.

.4 **works,** bleachworks, bottling works, brassworks, copperworks, dye works, gasworks, glassworks, ironworks, metalworks, paper works, printworks, saltworks, scrapworks, soapworks, starchworks, steelworks, tileworks, tubeworks, tryworks, waterworks, wireworks.

.5 **foundry,** metalworks; steelworks, steel mill; forge, furnace, bloomery; smelter; smithy, smithery, stithy, blacksmith shop or blacksmith's shop.

.6 **repair shop,** fix-it shop [informal]; **garage;** roundhouse; hangar.

.7 **laboratory, lab** [informal]; research laboratory, research installation or facility or center.

.8 **office,** shop [informal]; home or head or main office, headquarters, executive office, corporate headquarters; chambers; closet, cabinet [archaic], **study,** den; embassy, consulate, legation, chancery, chancellery; box office, booking office, ticket office; branch, branch office, local office.

720. PREPARATION

.1 NOUNS **preparation,** preparing, prep or prepping [both informal], fixing [informal], **readying,** making ready, makeready; warm-up; mobilization; **prearrangement** 641; **planning** 654.1; trial, **tryout** 489.2,3; **provision, arrangement;** preparatory or preliminary act or measure or step; **preliminary, preliminaries,** clearing the decks [informal]; propaedeutic, preparatory study or instruction; basic training, familiarization, briefing; prerequisite; processing, treatment, pretreatment; equipment 659; training 562.3; manufacture 167.3; **spadework,** groundwork, foundation 216.6.

.2 **fitting, fit** [informal]; **conditioning; adaptation, adjustment,** tuning; **qualification,** capacitation, enablement; **equipment, furnishing** 659.1.

.3 (a preparation) **concoction,** decoction, *decoctum* [L], brew, **confection; composition, mixture** 44.5, **combination** 52.

.4 **preparedness, readiness; fitness,** fittedness, suitedness, suitableness, **suitability;** condition, trim; **qualification,** qualifiedness, **competence** *or* competency, **ability, capability, proficiency,** mastery; ripeness, maturity, seasoning, tempering.

.5 **preparer,** preparator, preparationist; trainer, coach, instructor, mentor, teacher; **trailblazer, pathfinder; forerunner** 66.1; **paver of the way.**

.6 VERBS **prepare, make** *or* **get ready, prep** [informal], trim [archaic], **ready, fix** [informal]; provide [archaic], **arrange; make preparations** *or* **arrangements,** sound the note of preparation, clear the decks [informal], clear for action, settle preliminaries; mobilize, marshal, deploy; **prearrange** 641.3; **plan** 654.9; **try out** 489.8; fix up *or* ready up [both informal], put in *or* into shape; dress; treat, pretreat, process; cure, tan.

.7 **make up, get up, fix up** [informal]; **concoct,** decoct, brew; **compound, compose, put together, mix** 44.11; **make** 167.10.

.8 **fit, condition, adapt, adjust,** suit, tune, attune, put in tune *or* trim *or* working order; **qualify, enable,** capacitate; **equip, furnish** 659.7–9.

.9 **prime, load,** charge, cock, set; wind, wind up; steam up, get up steam, warm up.

.10 **prepare to, get ready to,** get set for [informal], fix to [dial]; be about to, be on the point of; ready oneself to, hold oneself in readiness.

.11 **prepare for, provide for,** arrange for, make arrangements *or* dispositions for, look out for, **make provision** *or* **due provision for;** provide against, make sure against, forearm, **provide for** *or* **against a rainy day,** prepare for the evil day; lay in provisions, lay up a store, keep as a nest egg, save to fall back upon, lay by, husband one's resources, salt *or* squirrel something away; set one's house in order.

.12 **prepare the way, pave the way,** smooth the path *or* road, **clear the way,** open the way, open the door to; **break the ice;** go in advance, **blaze the trail; prepare the ground,** cultivate the soil, sow the seed; do the spadework, lay the groundwork *or* foundation, lay the first stone; lead up to.

.13 **prepare oneself,** brace oneself, **get ready, get set** [informal], strip for action, roll up one's sleeves, spit on one's hands, limber up, warm up, flex one's muscles, gird up one's loins, buckle on one's armor, get into harness, shoulder arms; sharpen one's tools, whet the knife *or* sword.

.14 **be prepared, be ready,** stand by, stand ready, hold oneself in readiness, keep one's powder dry, "put your trust in God, my boys, and keep your powder dry" [Cromwell].

.15 (be fitted) **qualify, measure up,** check out [informal], have the qualifications *or* prerequisites.

.16 ADJS **prepared, ready,** prepped [informal], in readiness *or* ready state, all ready, good and ready, prepared and ready, psyched up [informal]; **vigilant** 533.13; **ripe, mature; set** *or* all set, on the mark [informal]; **prearranged** 641.5; **planned** 654.13; primed, loaded, cocked, loaded for bear [slang]; familiarized, briefed, informed, put into the picture [Brit informal]; groomed, coached; ready for anything, "prepared for either course" [Vergil]; in the saddle, booted and spurred; armed and ready, in arms, up in arms, **armed** 799.14; in battle array, mobilized; **provided, equipped** 659.13; **well-prepared.**

.17 **fitted, adapted, adjusted, suited; qualified, fit, competent, able, capable,** proficient; checked out [informal]; well-qualified, well-fitted, well-suited.

.18 **prepared for, ready for,** alert for, set *or* all set for [informal]; loaded for, primed for; up for [slang]; equal to, up to.

.19 **ready-made,** ready-formed, ready-mixed, ready-furnished, ready-dressed, ready-cooked; ready-built, prefabricated, prefab [informal]; ready-to-wear, ready-for-wear; ready-cut, cut-and-dried *or* cut-and-dry.

.20 **preparatory, preparative;** propaedeutic; prerequisite; provident, provisional.

.21 ADJS, ADVS **in readiness, in store, in reserve;** in anticipation.

.22 **in preparation,** in course of preparation, **in progress** *or* **process,** under way, **going on,** in embryo, **in production,** on stream, under construction, **in the works** *or* hopper *or* pipeline [informal], on the way, **in the making, in hand,** on the anvil, on the fire, in the oven; under revision; brewing, forthcoming.

.23 **afoot, on foot, afloat, astir.**

.24 PREPS in preparation for, against, for; in order to.

721. UNPREPAREDNESS

.1 NOUNS unpreparedness, unreadiness, unprovidedness, nonpreparedness, nonpreparation, lack of preparation; vulnerability 697.4; extemporaneousness, improvisation, ad lib [informal], planlessness; unfitness, unfittedness, unsuitedness, unsuitableness, unsuitability, unqualifiedness, unqualification, disqualification, incompetence, incapability.

.2 improvidence, thriftlessness, unthriftiness, poor husbandry, lax stewardship; shiftlessness, fecklessness, thoughtlessness, heedlessness; happy-go-luckiness; hastiness 709.2; negligence 534.1.

.3 (raw or original condition) naturalness, inartificiality; natural state, nature, state of nature, nature in the raw; pristineness, intactness, virginity; natural man, "unaccommodated man" [Shakespeare]; artlessness 736.

.4 undevelopment, nondevelopment; immaturity, immatureness, callowness, unfledgedness, rawness, unripeness, greenness; unfinish, unfinishedness, unpolishedness, unrefinement, uncultivation; crudity, crudeness, rudeness, coarseness, roughness, the rough; oversimplification, oversimplicity, simplism, reductionism.

.5 raw material; crude, crude stuff [informal]; ore, rich ore, rich vein; unsorted or unanalyzed mass; rough diamond, diamond in the rough; unlicked cub; virgin soil.

.6 VERBS be unprepared or unready, not be ready; go off half-cocked or at half cock [informal]; be taken unawares or aback, be caught napping, be caught with one's pants down [slang], be surprised; extemporize, improvise, ad-lib or play by ear [both informal]; have no plan, be innocent of forethought.

.7 make no provision, take no thought of tomorrow or the morrow, seize the day, carpe diem [L; Horace], let tomorrow take care of itself, live for the day, live like the grasshopper, live from hand to mouth; eat, drink, and be merry.

.8 ADJS unprepared, unready, unprimed; surprised, caught short, caught napping, caught with one's pants down [slang], taken by surprise, taken aback, taken unawares, caught off balance, caught off base [informal], tripped up; unarranged, unorganized, haphazard; makeshift,

rough-and-ready, extemporaneous, extemporized, improvised, ad-lib or off the top of one's head [both informal]; impromptu, snap [informal]; unmade, unmanufactured, unconcocted, unhatched, uncontrived, undevised, unplanned, unpremeditated, undeliberated, unstudied; hasty, precipitate 709.9–11; unbegun.

.9 unfitted, unfit, ill-fitted, unsuited, unadapted, unqualified, disqualified, incompetent, incapable; unequipped, unfurnished, unarmed, ill-equipped, ill-furnished, unprovided, ill-provided 662.12.

.10 raw, crude; uncooked, unbaked, unboiled; underdone, undercooked, rare, red.

.11 immature, unripe, underripe, unripened, impubic, raw, green, callow, unfledged, fledgling, unseasoned, unmellowed; ungrown, half-grown, adolescent, juvenile; undigested, ill-digested; half-baked [informal]; half-cocked or at half cock [both informal].

.12 undeveloped, unfinished, unlicked, unformed; unfashioned, unwrought, unlabored, unworked, unprocessed, untreated; unblown; uncut, unhewn; underdeveloped; backward, arrested, stunted; crude, rude, coarse, unpolished, unrefined; uncultivated, uncultured; rough, roughcast, roughhewn, in the rough; rudimentary, rudimental, lyo–, pro–; embryonic, in embryo, in ovo [L]; oversimple, simplistic, reductive, reductionistic.

.13 (in the raw or original state) natural, native, in a state of nature, in the raw; inartificial, artless 736.5; virgin, virginal, pristine, untouched, unsullied.

.14 fallow, untilled, uncultivated, unsown.

.15 improvident, unproviding; thriftless, unthrifty, uneconomical; grasshopper; hand-to-mouth; shiftless, feckless, thoughtless, heedless; happy-go-lucky; negligent 534.10, 11.

722. ACCOMPLISHMENT

(act of accomplishing; entire performance)

.1 NOUNS accomplishment, achievement, fulfillment, performance, execution, effectuation, implementation, carrying out or through, discharge, dispatch, consummation, realization, attainment, production, fruition; success 724; fait accompli [Fr], accomplished fact; mission accomplished.

.2 completion, completing, finish, finishing,

conclusion, end, ending, **termination,** terminus, **close, windup** [informal], rounding off or out, topping off; **perfection,** culmination 677.1,3; ripeness, maturity, maturation, full development.

.3 **finishing touch,** final touch, last touch, last stroke, final or finishing stroke, finisher [informal], copestone, capstone, crown, crowning of the edifice; climax 211.2.

.4 VERBS **accomplish, achieve, effect, effectuate, compass, consummate, do, execute, produce, make,** enact, **perform, discharge, fulfill,** realize, **attain,** fetch [dial]; **work,** work out; **dispatch, dispose of,** knock off [informal], polish off [slang], take care of [informal], **deal with,** put away, make short work of; **succeed,** manage 724.6–12; do the job [informal], **do** or **turn the trick** [slang].

.5 **bring about, bring to pass,** bring to effect, bring to a happy issue; **implement, carry out, carry through,** carry into execution; **bring off, carry off, pull off** [informal]; **put through,** get through, **put over** or **across** [informal]; come through with [informal].

.6 **complete, perfect, finish, finish off, conclude, terminate, end,** carry to completion, prosecute to a conclusion; **get through, get done;** get through with, get it over, get it over with, **finish up;** clean up or wind up or button up or wrap up or mop up [all informal], close up or out; put the lid on it [slang], call it a day [informal]; **round off** or out, **top off;** top out, **crown,** cap 211.9; climax, culminate; **give the finishing touches** or **strokes,** put the finishing touches or strokes on, finalize.

.7 **do to perfection, do up brown** [slang], **do to a turn,** do to a T [informal], do to a frazzle [slang], do down to the ground [informal], not do by halves, do oneself proud [informal], leave no loose ends, leave nothing hanging; go all lengths, go to all lengths, go the whole length or way; go the limit or go whole hog or go all out or shoot the works or go for broke [all slang].

.8 **ripen,** ripe [dial], **mature,** maturate; bloom, blow, blossom, flourish; come to fruition, bear fruit; **mellow;** grow up, reach maturity, reach its season; come or draw to a head; bring to maturity, bring to a head.

.9 ADJS **completing,** completive, completory, **finishing,** consummative, culminat-

ing, terminative, conclusive, **concluding,** fulfilling, finalizing, crowning; ultimate, **last, final,** terminal.

.10 **accomplished, achieved, effected,** effectuated, implemented, **consummated, executed, discharged, fulfilled, realized,** compassed, **attained; dispatched, disposed of,** set at rest; wrought, wrought out.

.11 **completed, done, finished, concluded, terminated, ended,** finished up; cleaned up or wound up or wrapped up or mopped up [all informal]; washed up [informal], **through,** done with; all said and done, all over but the shouting; perfective.

.12 **complete, perfect, consummate,** polished; exhaustive, thorough 56.10; fully realized.

.13 **ripe, mature,** matured, maturated, seasoned, **mellow,** full-grown, fully developed; tel(o)– or tele–.

.14 ADVS to completion, to the end, to the full, to the limit; to a turn, to a T [informal], to a finish, to a frazzle [slang].

723. NONACCOMPLISHMENT

.1 NOUNS **nonaccomplishment, nonachievement, nonperformance,** inexecution, nonexecution, nondischarging, **noncompletion,** nonconsummation, nonfulfillment, unfulfillment; nonfeasance, omission; neglect 534; loose ends, rough edges; endless task, work of Penelope, Sisyphean labor or toil or task; failure 725.

.2 VERBS neglect, leave undone 534.7, fail 725.8–16.

.3 ADJS **unaccomplished, unachieved, unperformed,** unexecuted, undischarged, unfulfilled, unconsummated, unrealized, unattained; **unfinished, uncompleted, undone;** neglected 534.14.

724. SUCCESS

.1 NOUNS **success, successfulness;** go [informal]; fortunate outcome, prosperous issue; **prosperity** 728; accomplishment 722; victory 726.

.2 sure success, **winner** or **natural** [both informal]; shoo-in or **sure thing** or sure bet or **cinch** or lead-pipe cinch [all slang].

.3 **great success,** howling or roaring success [informal], **triumph,** resounding triumph, brilliant success, striking success, meteoric success; **killing** [informal]; **hit** or big hit [both informal]; **smash** or **smash hit** or gas or gasser or riot or wow or sensation or overnight sensation [all slang]; brief or momentary success, nine days' wonder, flash in the pan, fad; best seller.

.4 **score, hit, bull's-eye;** goal, touchdown; slam, grand slam; strike; hole, hole in one; home run, homer [informal].

.5 (successful person) **winner, star,** star in the firmament, success; comer [slang]; victor 726.2.

.6 VERBS **succeed, prevail,** be successful, be crowned with success, meet with success; **go, come off,** go off; prosper 728.7; fare well, work well, do or work wonders, go to town or go great guns [both informal]; **make a hit** [informal], **click** or **connect** [both slang], **catch on** or **take** [both informal]; **go over** [informal], go over big [slang]; pass, graduate, qualify, win one's spurs, get one's credentials, be blooded; come through or pass with flying colors.

.7 **achieve one's purpose, gain one's end** or **ends,** secure one's object, attain one's objective, do what one set out to do, reach one's goal; make one's point; play it or handle it just right [informal], not put a foot wrong, play it like a master.

.8 **score a success,** score, hit it, hit the mark, ring the bell [informal], turn up trumps, break the bank or make a killing [both informal], hit the jackpot [slang].

.9 **make good, come through, achieve success,** make a success, **make it** [informal], **make one's mark, give a good account of oneself,** bear oneself with credit, do all right by oneself or do oneself proud [both informal]; **advance, progress,** make one's way, make headway, **get on,** come on [informal], **get ahead** [informal]; go places, **go far;** rise, **rise in the world,** work one's way up, claw or scrabble one's way up, mount the ladder of success; **arrive,** get there [slang], make the scene [informal]; come out on top, come out on top of the heap [slang]; **be a success,** have it made [informal], have the world at one's feet; **make a noise in the world** [informal], cut a swath, set the world or river or Thames on fire; break through, score or make a breakthrough.

.10 **succeed with,** crown with success; **make a go of it;** accomplish, compass, achieve 722.4; **bring off, carry off, pull off** [informal], turn or do the trick [informal], **put through,** bring through; **put over** or **across** [informal]; get away with it or get by [both slang].

.11 **manage, contrive, succeed in; make out, get on** or **along** [informal], come on or along [informal], go on; **scrape along,** worry along, **muddle through** [Brit], get by, **manage somehow; make it** [informal], **make the grade,** cut the mustard or hack it [both slang]; **clear,** clear the hurdle; **negotiate** [informal], **engineer; swing** [informal], put over [slang], put through, swing the deal.

.12 **win through, win out** [informal], come through [slang], rise to the occasion, beat the game or beat the system [both informal]; **triumph** 726.3; weather out, **weather the storm,** live through, keep one's head above water; come up fighting or smiling, not know when one is beaten, persevere 625.2–6.

.13 ADJS **successful,** succeeding, crowned with success; **prosperous,** fortunate 728.12–14; **triumphant** 726.8; ahead of the game, out in front, on top, on top of the heap [slang]; assured of success, surefire, made; coming or on the up-and-up [both informal].

.14 ADVS **successfully,** swimmingly [informal], well, to some purpose, to good purpose; beyond all expectation, beyond one's fondest dreams.

725. FAILURE

.1 NOUNS **failure, unsuccessfulness,** unsuccess, successlessness, nonsuccess; no go [informal]; ill success; futility, uselessness 669; **defeat** 727; losing game; "lame and impotent conclusion" [Shakespeare]; nonaccomplishment 723; **bankruptcy** 842.4.

.2 [slang or informal terms] **flop, floperoo,** bust, frost, **fizzle, lemon, washout,** turkey, bomb, flat failure, dull thud, total loss.

.3 **collapse, crash,** smash, comedown, breakdown, **fall,** pratfall [slang], stumble, tumble, **downfall,** cropper [informal]; nose dive or tailspin [both slang]; deflation, bursting of the bubble.

.4 **miss,** near-miss; **slip, slipup** [informal], slip 'twixt cup and lip; **error, mistake** 518.3.

.5 **abortion, miscarriage,** miscarrying, abortive attempt, vain attempt; wild-goose chase, merry chase; **misfire, flash in the pan,** wet squib, dud [slang].

.6 **fiasco, botch,** bungle, hash, mess, muddle, foozle or bollix [both informal]; **flunk** [informal], washout [slang].

.7 (unsuccessful person) **failure, loser** [informal]; flop or washout or false alarm [all slang], flash in the pan, **dud** [slang], also-ran; bankrupt 842.4.

571

.8 VERBS **fail,** be unsuccessful, fail of success, not work *or* not come off [both informal], come to grief, **lose;** not make the grade, be found wanting, not come up to the mark; not pass, **flunk** *or* **flunk out** [both informal]; go to the wall, **go on the rocks;** labor in vain 669.8; go bankrupt 842.7.

.9 [slang *or* informal terms] **lose out,** get left, **not make it,** not hack it, not get to first base, drop the ball, **flop,** flummox, lay an egg, go over like a lead balloon, draw a blank, bomb, drop a bomb; **fold,** fold up; take it on the chin, take the count; crap out; strike out, fan, whiff.

.10 **sink, founder,** go down, go under [informal]; **slip,** go downhill, be on the skids [slang].

.11 **fall, fall down** [slang], fall down on the job [informal]; **fall short, fall through,** fall to the ground; fall between two stools; **fall dead,** fall stillborn; **fall flat,** fall on one's face *or* fall flat on one's face [both informal], fall on one's ass [slang]; **collapse,** fall in; **crash,** go to smash [informal].

.12 **come to nothing,** hang up *or* get nowhere [both informal]; **poop out** *or* go phut [both slang]; be all over *or* up with; fail miserably *or* ignominiously; fizz out *or* **fizzle** *or* fizzle out [all informal]; **misfire,** flash in the pan; **blow up, explode, end** *or* **go up in smoke,** go up like a rocket and come down like a stick.

.13 **miss,** miss the mark, miss one's aim; slip, slip up [informal], goof [slang], bungle, blunder, foozle [informal]; err 518.9.

.14 **miscarry, abort;** go amiss, go astray, **go wrong,** go on a wrong tack, take a wrong turn.

.15 **stall,** stick, die, go dead, **conk out** [slang], sputter and stop, run out of steam, come to a shuddering halt, come to a dead stop.

.16 **flunk** *or* **flunk out** [both informal]; **fail,** pluck *or* plough [both Brit slang], bust *or* wash out [both slang].

.17 ADJS **unsuccessful,** successless, failing; failed, *manqué* [Fr], stickit [Scot]; **unfortunate** 729.14; **abortive,** par(a)–; miscarrying, miscarried, stillborn; fruitless, bootless, futile, useless 669.9–14; lame, **ineffectual,** ineffective, inefficacious, of no effect.

.18 ADVS **unsuccessfully,** successlessly, **without success;** fruitlessly, bootlessly, ineffectually, ineffectively, inefficaciously; to little *or* no purpose, **in vain.**

726. VICTORY

.1 NOUNS **victory, triumph, conquest,** subduing, subdual; a feather in one's cap [informal]; total victory, grand slam; championship; **winning,** win [informal]; knockout, KO [slang]; easy victory, walkover *or* walkaway [both informal], pushover *or* picnic [both slang]; runaway victory, landslide victory, landslide; Pyrrhic victory, Cadmean victory; moral victory; winning streak [informal]; **success** 724; ascendancy 739.6,7; mastery 741.2.

.2 **victor, winner,** triumpher; **conqueror,** defeater, **vanquisher,** subduer, subjugator, *conquistador* [Sp]; top dog [informal]; master, master of the situation; hero, conquering hero; **champion,** champ [slang]; easy winner, sure winner, shoo-in [slang]; pancratiast; runner-up.

.3 VERBS **triumph, prevail, be victorious, come out on top** [informal], chain victory to one's car; **succeed** 724.6; break the record, set a new mark [informal].

.4 **win, gain, capture, carry;** win out [informal], win through, carry it, carry off *or* away; **win** *or* **carry** *or* **gain the day,** win the battle, come out first, finish in front, make a killing [informal], remain in possession of the field; **win the prize,** win the palm *or* bays *or* laurels, bear the palm, **bring home the bacon** [informal], take the cake [slang], win one's spurs; fluke *or* win by a fluke [both slang].

.5 **win hands down** *or* win going away [both informal], win in a canter *or* walk *or* waltz [all informal], romp home *or* breeze [both informal], **walk off** *or* **away with,** waltz off with [informal], walk off with the game, **walk over** [informal]; have the game in one's own hands, have it all one's way; **take** *or* **carry by storm,** sweep aside all obstacles, carry all before one, make short work of.

.6 **triumph over, prevail over, best, beat** [informal], **get the better** *or* **best of; surmount, overcome,** rise above, **defeat** 727.6.

.7 **gain the ascendancy,** get on top [slang], **get the advantage, gain the upper** *or* **whip hand,** dominate the field, get the edge on *or* jump on *or* drop on [slang], get a leg up on [slang], get a stranglehold on.

.8 ADJS **victorious, triumphant,** triumphal, **winning, prevailing;** conquering, vanquishing, defeating, overcoming; ascendant, in the ascendant, in ascendancy, dominant 741.18; successful 724.13; flushed with success or victory.

.9 **undefeated, unbeaten, unvanquished, unconquered,** unsubdued, unquelled, unbowed.

.10 ADVS **triumphantly, victoriously, in triumph.**

727. DEFEAT

.1 NOUNS **defeat; beating,** drubbing, thrashing, hiding, lathering, whipping, lambasting, trimming, licking [all informal], trouncing; **vanquishment, conquest, conquering,** mastery, subjugation, subduing, subdual; **overthrow, overturn,** overcoming; **fall, downfall,** collapse, smash, crash, undoing, **ruin,** debacle, **destruction** 693; deathblow, quietus; Waterloo; failure 725.

.2 **discomfiture, rout, repulse,** rebuff; **frustration,** bafflement, confusion; **checkmate, check,** balk, foil [archaic]; **reverse,** reversal, **setback.**

.3 **utter defeat,** total defeat, overwhelming defeat, crushing defeat, smashing defeat, decisive defeat; no contest; smearing or pasting or creaming or clobbering or shellacking or whopping or whomping [all slang]; whitewash or whitewashing [both informal], **shutout.**

.4 **ignominious defeat,** abject defeat, inglorious defeat, disastrous defeat, utter rout, bitter defeat, stinging defeat.

.5 **loser, defeatee** [informal]; the vanquished; good loser, game loser, sport or **good sport** [both informal]; **underdog, also-ran;** booby or duck [both slang]; stooge or fall guy [both slang]; victim 866.11.

.6 VERBS **defeat, worst, best, get the better** or **best of,** be too good for, be too much for, be more than a match for; **outdo,** outgeneral, outmaneuver, outclass, outshine, outpoint, outsail, outrun, outfight, etc.; **triumph over** 726.6; **beat,** drub, **lick,** whip, thrash, trim, hide, lather, trounce, lambaste [all informal]; **skin** or skin alive [both slang]; **fix** or **settle** or settle one's hash or make one say 'uncle' or put one's nose out of joint [all informal]; do in [slang], **knock on the head,** deal a deathblow to, put hors de combat; **undo, ruin, destroy** 693.10–21; lick to a frazzle [informal], beat hollow or all hollow [informal]; beat by a nose [informal].

.7 **overcome, surmount; overpower, overmaster,** overmatch; **overthrow, overturn,** overset; put the skids to [informal]; **up-**set, trip, trip up, lay by the heels, send flying or sprawling; silence, floor, deck, make bite the dust; overcome oneself, master oneself; kick one's habit [slang].

.8 **overwhelm,** whelm, snow under [informal], overbear, defeat utterly, deal a crushing or smashing defeat; bulldoze or steamroller [both informal]; **smear** or paste or cream or **clobber** or shellac or whop or skunk or whomp [all slang]; schmear [Yid], blank or whitewash [both informal], **shut out.**

.9 **discomfit, rout, put to rout, put to flight,** scatter, stampede, panic; confound; put out of court.

.10 **conquer, vanquish, quell, suppress, put down, subdue, subjugate,** put under the yoke, master; **reduce,** prostrate, fell, **flatten, break, smash, crush, humble,** bend, **bring one to his knees;** roll or trample in the dust, tread or trample underfoot, trample down, ride down, ride or run roughshod over, override.

.11 **thwart, frustrate, dash, check,** deal a check to, **checkmate** 730.15,16.

.12 **lose,** lose out [informal], lose the day, come off second best, **get** or **have the worst of it, meet one's Waterloo; fall,** succumb, tumble, bow, go down, go under, **bite** or **lick the dust,** take the count [slang]; snatch defeat from the jaws of victory; throw in the towel, say uncle; have enough.

.13 ADJS **lost,** unwon.

.14 **defeated, worsted, bested, outdone; beaten,** beat, **licked,** whipped, trimmed, lathered, trounced, lambasted, settled, fixed [all informal]; skinned or skinned alive [both slang], thrown for a loss [slang]; **discomfited,** put to rout, **routed,** scattered, stampeded, panicked; confounded; **overcome, overthrown,** upset, overturned, overmatched, **overpowered, overwhelmed,** whelmed, **overmastered,** overborne, overridden; **fallen,** down; floored, silenced; done in [slang], **undone, done for** [informal], **ruined, on the skids** [informal], hors de combat [Fr]; all up with [informal].

.15 **shut out,** blanked or whitewashed [both informal], unscoring.

.16 **conquered, vanquished,** quelled, suppressed, put down, **subdued, subjugated,** mastered; **reduced,** prostrate(d), felled, **flattened,** smashed, **crushed,** broken; **humbled,** brought to one's knees.

.17 **overpowering, overcoming, overwhelming, overmastering,** overmatching.

728. PROSPERITY

.1 NOUNS **prosperity,** prosperousness, thriving *or* flourishing condition; **success** 724; **welfare, well-being,** weal, happiness, felicity; comfortable *or* easy circumstances, **comfort, ease,** security; **life of ease,** the life of Riley [informal], **the good life; clover** *or* **velvet** [both informal], **bed of roses, luxury,** lap of luxury, Easy Street [informal]; the affluent life, gracious life, gracious living; fat of the land; fleshpots, fleshpots of Egypt; milk and honey, loaves and fishes; a chicken in every pot, a car in every garage; purple and fine linen; high standard of living; upward mobility; **affluence, wealth** 837.

.2 **good fortune** *or* **luck,** happy fortune, **fortune, luck,** the breaks [slang]; **fortunateness, luckiness,** felicity [archaic]; blessing, smiles of fortune, fortune's favor.

.3 **stroke of luck,** piece of good luck; blessing; **fluke** *or* **lucky strike** *or* **scratch hit** *or* **break** [all slang], good *or* lucky break [slang]; **run** *or* **streak of luck** [informal].

.4 **good times,** piping times, bright *or* palmy *or* halcyon days, rosy era; heyday; prosperity, era of prosperity; fair weather, sunshine; golden era, **golden age,** golden time, Saturnian age, reign of Saturn, *Saturnia regna* [L]; age of Aquarius, millennium; utopia 535.11; heaven 1018.

.5 **roaring trade, land-office business** [informal], bull market, seller's market; booming economy, boom [informal], expanding economy.

.6 **fortunate, lucky dog** [informal], fortune's favorite, favorite of the gods, fortune's child, destiny's darling; man of substance 837.6.

.7 VERBS **prosper,** enjoy prosperity, **fare well,** get on well, do well, have everything going one's way, get on swimmingly; **turn out well, go well,** take a favorable turn; **succeed** 724.6; come on *or* along [informal], get on [informal]; **advance,** progress, make progress, make headway, get ahead [informal].

.8 **thrive, flourish,** boom; blossom, bloom, flower; batten, fatten, grow fat; be fat, dumb, and happy [informal].

.9 **be prosperous, make good, make one's mark,** rise *or* get on in the world, make a noise in the world [informal], do all right by oneself [informal], **make one's fortune;** grow rich 837.9; drive a roaring trade, do a land-office business [informal], rejoice in a seller's market.

.10 **live well, live in clover** *or* on velvet [informal], **live a life of ease,** live the life of Riley, **live high, live high on the hog** [informal], live on *or* off the fat of the land, roll in the lap of luxury; bask in the sunshine, have one's place in the sun; have a good *or* fine time of it.

.11 **be fortunate, be lucky,** be in luck, have all the luck, have one's moments [informal], **lead** *or* **have a charmed life;** fall into the shithouse and come up with a five-dollar gold piece [slang]; **get a break** *or* get the breaks [both slang]; hold aces *or* turn up trumps [both informal]; have a run of luck *or* hit a streak of luck [both informal]; have it break good for one [slang], have a stroke of luck; strike it lucky *or* make a lucky strike *or* strike oil [all slang], **strike it rich** [informal], hit it big [slang], strike a rich vein, come into money, drop into a good thing.

.12 ADJS **prosperous,** in good case; **successful** 724.13; **affluent, wealthy** 837.13; **comfortable,** comfortably situated, easy; on Easy Street [informal], **in clover** *or* on velvet [both informal], on a bed of roses, in luxury, high on the hog [informal]; up in the world, on top of the heap [slang].

.13 **thriving, flourishing, prospering, booming** [informal]; vigorous, exuberant; in full swing, going strong [informal]; halcyon, palmy, balmy, rosy, piping, clear, fair; blooming, blossoming, flowering, fruiting; fat, sleek, in good case; fat, dumb, and happy [informal].

.14 **fortunate, lucky, providential; in luck; blessed,** blessed with luck, favored; born under a lucky star, born with a silver spoon in one's mouth, born on the sunny side of the hedge; **auspicious** 544.16.

.15 ADVS **prosperously, thrivingly, flourishingly,** boomingly, swimmingly [informal].

.16 **fortunately, luckily,** providentially.

729. ADVERSITY

.1 NOUNS **adversity,** adverse circumstances, difficulties, hard knocks [informal], **hardship, trouble,** troubles, "sea of troubles" [Shakespeare]; rigor, vicissitude, care, stress, pressure, stress of life; hardcase, **hard life,** a dog's life, vale of tears; wretched *or* miserable *or* hard *or* unhappy lot, hard row to hoe [informal], ups and downs of life, things going against one; bummer *or* downer [both slang]; annoyance, irritation, aggravation; **difficulty** 731; **trial,** tribulation, cross, curse, blight, **affliction** 866.8; plight, predicament 731.4.

.2 **misfortune, mishap,** ill hap, **misadventure, mischance,** *contretemps* [Fr], grief; **disaster, calamity, catastrophe, cataclysm, tragedy; shock, blow,** hard *or* nasty *or* staggering blow; **accident,** casualty; collision, crash; **wreck,** shipwreck; smash *or* smashup *or* crack-up *or* pileup [all informal], "the slings and arrows of outrageous fortune" [Shakespeare].

.3 **reverse, reversal,** reverse of fortune, **setback,** check, severe check, backset, throwback [informal]; **comedown,** descent, down.

.4 **unfortunateness, unluckiness,** lucklessness, ill success; unprosperousness; starcrossed *or* ill-fated life; inauspiciousness 544.8.

.5 **bad luck,** ill luck, **hard luck,** hard lines [Brit], **tough** *or* **rotten luck** [informal], raw deal [slang], bad *or* tough *or* rotten break [informal], devil's own luck; **ill fortune,** bad fortune, evil fortune, evil star, ill wind, evil dispensation; frowns of fortune.

.6 **hard times,** bad times, sad times; evil day, rainy day; hard *or* stormy *or* heavy weather; **depression, recession, slump,** economic stagnation, bust [informal].

.7 **unfortunate,** poor unfortunate, the plaything *or* toy *or* sport of fortune, fortune's fool; **loser** *or* sure loser [both informal]; hardcase *or* sad sack *or* hard-luck guy [all slang]; *schlemiel, schlimazel* [both Yid]; the wretched of the earth; victim 866.11.

.8 VERBS **go hard with,** go ill with; run one hard; **oppress, weigh on** *or* **upon,** weigh heavy on, weigh down, **burden,** overburden, load, overload, bear hard upon, lie on, lie hard *or* heavy upon; try one, put one out.

.9 **have trouble;** be born to trouble, be born under an evil star, be "born unto trouble, as the sparks fly upward" [Bible]; **have a hard time of it,** be up against it [informal], make heavy weather of it, meet adversity, have a bad time; bear the brunt, bear more than one's share; be put to one's wit's end, not know which way to turn.

.10 **come to grief,** have a mishap, suffer a misfortune, be stricken *or* staggered, be poleaxed, be felled, be clobbered [slang]; run aground, go on the rocks *or* shoals, split upon a rock; sink, drown, founder.

.11 **fall on evil days, go down in the world,** go downhill, slip, be on the skids [slang],

come down, have a comedown, fall from one's high estate; **deteriorate,** degenerate, sink, decline; **go to pot** [informal], go to the dogs; reach the depths, touch bottom, hit rock bottom; have seen better days.

.12 bring bad luck; hoodoo *or* hex *or* jinx *or* Jonah *or* put the jinx on [all informal]; put the evil eye on, whammy [slang].

.13 ADJS **adverse, untoward, detrimental, unfavorable,** mis–; **sinister; hostile,** antagonistic, inimical; **contrary, counter,** counteractive, conflicting, opposing, opposed, opposite, in opposition; **difficult, troublesome, troublous, hard,** trying, rigorous, stressful; wretched, miserable 866.26; not easy 731.16; harmful 675.12.

.14 **unfortunate, unlucky, unprovidential,** unblessed, **unprosperous,** sad, unhappy, hapless, fortuneless, luckless, donsie [Brit dial]; **out of luck,** short of luck; **down on one's luck** [informal], badly *or* ill off, down in the world, in adverse circumstances; underprivileged, depressed; ill-starred, evil-starred, born under a bad sign, born under an evil star, planet-stricken, planet-struck, star-crossed; fatal, dire, doomful, funest, **ominous, inauspicious** 544.17.

.15 **disastrous, calamitous, catastrophic, cataclysmic,** cataclysmal, **tragic,** ruinous, wreckful [archaic], **fatal, dire, black,** grievous; destructive 693.26.

.16 ADVS **adversely, untowardly,** detrimentally, **unfavorably;** contrarily, conflictingly, opposingly, oppositely.

.17 **unfortunately, unluckily,** unprovidentially, sadly, unhappily, **as ill luck would have it;** by ill luck, by ill hap; in adverse circumstances, if worst comes to worst.

.18 **disastrously,** calamitously, catastrophically, cataclysmically, grievously, tragically, crushingly, shatteringly.

730. HINDRANCE

.1 NOUNS **hindrance,** hindering, **hampering, let, let** *or* **hindrance; check, arrest,** arrestment, arrestation; fixation; **impediment,** holdback; **resistance, opposition** 790; **suppression, repression, restriction, restraint** 760; **obstruction,** blocking, blockage, clogging, occlusion; **interruption,** interference; **retardation,** retardment, **detention,** detainment, **delay,** holdup, setback; **inhibition;** constriction, squeeze, stricture, cramp, stranglehold; **closure,** closing up *or* off; obstructionism, negativism, footdragging [informal]; nuisance value.

.2 **prevention, stop, stoppage, stopping,** arrestation, estoppel; **stay, halt; prohibition,** forbiddance; debarment; **determent,** deterrence, **discouragement; forestalling,** preclusion, obviation, foreclosure.

.3 **frustration, thwarting, balking, foiling;** discomfiture, disconcertion, bafflement, confounding; **defeat,** upset; **check, checkmate, balk, foil** [archaic].

.4 **obstacle, obstruction,** obstructive; **hangup** [informal]; **block, blockade, cordon,** curtain; **difficulty,** hurdle, hazard; **deterrent,** determent; **drawback,** objection; **stumbling block,** stumbling stone, stone in one's path; fly in the ointment, one small difficulty [informal], **hitch, catch,** joker [informal], rub, **snag;** bottleneck.

.5 **barrier, bar;** gate, portcullis; **fence; wall,** stone wall, brick wall; seawall, jetty, groin, mole, breakwater; **bulwark, rampart,** defense, buffer, bulkhead, parapet, breastwork, work, earthwork, mound; bank, embankment, levee, dike; ditch, moat; dam, weir, leaping weir, barrage, milldam, beaver dam, cofferdam, wicket dam, shutter dam, bear-trap dam, hydraulic-fill dam, rock-fill dam, arch dam, arch-gravity dam, gravity dam; boom, jam, logjam; roadblock; backstop; iron curtain, bamboo curtain.

.6 **impediment,** embarrassment, hamper; encumbrance, cumbrance; **trouble,** difficulty 731; **handicap,** disadvantage, inconvenience, penalty; white elephant; **burden** or burthen [archaic], imposition, onus, cross, weight, deadweight, millstone around one's neck; **load, pack,** cargo, freight, charge; impedimenta, lumber.

.7 **curb, check,** countercheck, arrest, **stay, stop,** damper, holdback; **brake,** clog, drag, drogue, remora; chock, scotch, spoke, spoke in one's wheel; doorstop; checkrein, bearing rein, martingale; bit, snaffle, pelham, curb bit; shackle, chain, fetter, trammel 760.4; sea anchor, drift anchor, drift sail, drag sail or sheet.

.8 **hinderer,** impeder, **marplot,** obstructer; frustrater, thwarter; obstructionist, negativist; filibuster, filibusterer.

.9 **spoilsport,** wet blanket, **killjoy,** grouch, sourpuss [informal], malcontent, **dog in the manger** [informal].

.10 VERBS **hinder, impede, inhibit, arrest, check,** countercheck, scotch, **curb,** snub; **resist, oppose** 790.3; suppress, **repress** 760.8; **interrupt,** intercept [archaic]; intervene, interfere, intermeddle, **meddle**

238.7; damp, dampen, throw cold water on; **retard,** slacken, **delay,** detain, **hold back, keep back,** set back, hold up [informal]; **restrain** 760.7; keep or hold in check, bottle up, dam up.

.11 **hamper, impede, cramp,** embarrass; trammel, entrammel, enmesh, entangle, ensnarl, entrap, entwine, involve, entoil, toil, net, lime, tangle, snarl; fetter, shackle, tie one's hands; **encumber,** cumber, **burden,** lumber, **saddle with,** weigh down, press down; hang like a millstone round one's neck; **handicap,** put at a disadvantage; lame, cripple, hobble, hamstring.

.12 **obstruct, stand in the way;** dog, **block, blockade,** block up, occlude; **jam, crowd, pack; bar,** barricade, bolt, lock; **debar,** shut out; shut off, **close,** close off or up, close tight, shut tight; constrict, squeeze, squeeze shut, strangle, strangulate, stifle, suffocate, **choke,** choke off, chock; stop up 266.7.

.13 **stop, stay, halt,** bring to a stop, put a stop or end to; **brake,** slow down, put on the brakes; **block, stall, stymie,** deadlock; nip in the bud.

.14 **prevent, prohibit, forbid; bar,** estop; **save,** help, **keep from; deter, discourage,** dishearten; **avert, keep off, ward off, stave off, fend off,** fend, repel, deflect, turn aside; **forestall, foreclose, preclude,** exclude, debar, **obviate,** anticipate; rule out.

.15 **thwart, frustrate, foil, cross, balk, stonewall** [slang]; spike, scotch, checkmate; **counter,** contravene, counteract, countermand, counterwork; stand in the way of, confront, brave, defy, challenge; **defeat** 727.6–11; **discomfit,** upset, **disrupt, confound,** flummox [slang], discountenance, put out of countenance, **disconcert, baffle,** nonplus, perplex, stump [informal], throw on one's beam ends; **circumvent,** elude; sabotage, **spoil, ruin,** dish [informal], dash, blast; **destroy** 693.10; throw a wrench in the machinery, **throw a monkey wrench into the works** [informal]; put a spoke in one's wheel, scotch one's wheel, spike one's guns, put one's nose out of joint [informal], upset one's applecart; take the wind out of one's sails, steal one's thunder, cut the ground from under one, knock the chocks or props from under one, knock the bottom out of [informal]; tie one's hands, clip the wings of.

.16 [slang terms] **queer, crab, foul up, louse**

up, snafu, bollix, gum, **gum up**, gum up the works; crimp, cramp, **put a crimp in,** cramp one's style.

.17 ADJS **hindering,** hindersome [dial], troublesome; **inhibitive,** inhibiting, suppressive, repressive; constrictive, strangling, stifling, choking; restrictive 760.12; **obstructive,** obstructing, occlusive, obstruent [archaic]; contrary, crosswise; counterproductive; interruptive, interrupting; in the way.

.18 hampering, **impeding, impedimental,** impeditive; onerous, oppressive, burdensome, cumbersome, cumbrous, encumbering.

.19 **preventive,** preventative, prophylactic, ant(i)– or anth–; **prohibitive, forbidding;** deterrent, deterring, **discouraging;** preclusive, forestalling.

.20 **frustrating,** confounding, disconcerting, baffling, defeating.

.21 ADVS under handicap, at a disadvantage, on the hip [archaic], with everything against one.

731. DIFFICULTY

.1 NOUNS **difficulty,** difficultness; **hardness, toughness,** rigor, rigorousness, ruggedness; **arduousness,** laboriousness, strenuousness, toilsomeness; **troublesomeness,** bothersomeness; onerousness, oppressiveness, burdensomeness; formidability, hairiness [slang]; complication, intricacy, complexity 46; abstruseness 549.2.

.2 **tough proposition** [informal], large or tall order [informal]; **hard job, tough job** [informal], backbreaker, ballbuster [slang], **chore,** man-sized job; brutal task, Herculean task, Augean task; **uphill work** or going, rough go [informal], **heavy sledding,** hard pull [informal], dead lift [archaic]; tough lineup to buck [slang], hard road to travel; tough nut to crack or hard row to hoe or hard row of stumps [all informal]; bitch [slang]; **handful** [informal], all one can manage.

.3 **trouble, matter;** headache [slang], problem, besetment, **inconvenience, disadvantage;** ado, great ado; peck of troubles, "sea of troubles" [Shakespeare]; hornet's nest, Pandora's box, can of worms [informal]; **evil** 675.3; **bother, annoyance** 864.7; **anxiety, worry** 890.1,2.

.4 **predicament, plight, pickle** or hobble [both informal], **strait,** straits, parlous straits, **pinch, bind,** pass, clutch, crunch [informal]; pretty pass, pretty pickle [informal], nice or pretty predicament, **sorry**

plight, fine kettle of fish [informal], how-do-you-do or fine how-do-you-do [both informal]; **spot** or **tight spot** or **squeeze** or tight squeeze [all informal], tightrope, ticklish or tricky spot [informal], sticky wicket [Brit informal]; **scrape** or **jam** or **hot water** [all informal]; tail in a gate or tit in the wringer [both slang]; slough, quagmire, morass, swamp, quicksand; **embarrassment,** embarrassing position or situation; **complication,** imbroglio, **mess,** holy or unholy mess [informal], mix or stew [both informal]; the devil to pay, hell to pay [slang].

.5 **impasse, corner** or box or hole [all informal]; **cul-de-sac, blind alley, dead end,** dead-end street; **extremity, end of one's rope** or **tether,** wit's end, nowhere to turn; **stalemate,** deadlock; stand, standstill, halt, stop.

.6 **dilemma,** horns of a dilemma, **quandary,** nonplus; **vexed question,** thorny problem, knotty point, knot, crux, node, nodus, Gordian knot, poser, teaser, perplexity, puzzle, enigma 549.8; paradox, oxymoron; asses' bridge, *pons asinorum* [L].

.7 **crux,** hitch, pinch, rub, snag, catch, joker [informal], where the shoe pinches.

.8 **unwieldiness, unmanageability; unhandiness,** inconvenience, impracticality; **awkwardness, clumsiness; cumbersomeness,** ponderousness, bulkiness, hulkiness.

.9 VERBS be difficult, present difficulties, **take some doing** [informal].

.10 **have difficulty, have trouble, have a hard time of it,** have one's hands full, be hard put, have much ado with; labor under difficulties, labor under a disadvantage; struggle, **flounder,** beat about, make heavy weather of it; swim against the current; walk on eggshells or hot coals, dance on a hot griddle.

.11 **get into trouble,** plunge into difficulties; **let oneself in for, put one's foot in it** [informal]; **get in a jam** or **hot water** or **the soup** [informal], **get into a scrape** [informal], **get in a mess** or hole or box or bind [informal]; paint oneself into a corner [informal], get one's ass in a bind or put oneself in a spot [both slang], put one's foot in one's mouth; have a tiger by the tail; burn one's fingers; get all tangled or snarled or wound up, get all balled up or bollixed up [slang].

.12 **trouble,** beset; **bother,** pother, **disturb, perturb,** irk, plague, **torment,** harass, **vex, distress** 866.13–16; inconvenience, **put out,** put out of the way, discommode 671.4;

concern, worry 890.3,4; puzzle, perplex 514.13; put to it, give one trouble, complicate matters; give one a hard time or give one a bad time or make it tough for [all informal]; be too much for; ail, be the matter.

.13 cause trouble, bring trouble, "sow the wind and reap the whirlwind" [Bible]; bring down upon one, bring down upon one's head, bring down around one's ears; stir up a hornet's nest, bring a hornet's nest about one's ears, open Pandora's box, open a can of worms [informal]; raise hob or hell [informal]; raise merry hell or play hob or play hell [all informal], play the deuce or devil [informal].

.14 put in a hole [informal], put in a spot [slang]; embarrass; involve, enmesh, entangle.

.15 corner, run or drive into a corner [both informal], tree [informal], chase up a tree or stump [informal], drive or force to the wall, put one's back to the wall, have one on the ropes [informal].

.16 ADJS difficult, difficile, dys– or dis–; not easy, no picnic; hard, tough, rough, rugged, rigorous, brutal, severe; wicked or mean or hairy [all slang], formidable; arduous, strenuous, toilsome, laborious, operose, Herculean; steep, uphill; hard-fought; hard-earned; jawbreaking; knotty, knotted; thorny, spiny, set with thorns; delicate, ticklish, tricky, critical, easier said than done; exacting, demanding; intricate, complex 46.4; abstruse 549.16.

.17 troublesome, besetting; bothersome, irksome, vexatious, painful, plaguey [informal], annoying 864.22; burdensome, oppressive, onerous, heavy or hefty [both informal], crushing, backbreaking; trying, grueling.

.18 unwieldy, unmanageable, unhandy; inconvenient, impractical; awkward, clumsy, cumbersome, unmaneuverable; contrary, perverse, crosswise; ponderous, bulky, hulky, hulking.

.19 troubled, beset, sore beset; bothered, vexed, irked, annoyed 866.21; plagued, harassed 866.24; distressed, perturbed 866.22; inconvenienced, embarrassed; put to it or hard put to it [both informal]; worried, anxious 890.6,7; puzzled 514.24.

.20 in a predicament, in a sorry plight, in a pretty pass; in a mess or in a scrape or in a jam or in hot water or in the soup [all informal]; in a spot or in a fix or in a tight spot or in a hole or in a bind or in a box [all informal], in a pickle [informal],

in a nice or pretty pickle [informal]; in trouble, in Dutch [slang], on the spot or behind the eight ball [both informal]; on Queer Street [informal]; out on a limb [informal]; in deep water, out of one's depth.

.21 in a dilemma, on the horns of a dilemma, in a quandary; between two stools; between Scylla and Charybdis, between the devil and the deep blue sea.

.22 at an impasse, at one's wit's end, at a loss, at a stand or standstill; nonplussed, at a nonplus; baffled, perplexed, bewildered, mystified, stuck or stumped [both informal].

.23 cornered, in a corner, with one's back to the wall; treed or up a tree or up a stump [all informal]; at bay, aux abois [Fr].

.24 straitened, reduced to dire straits, in desperate straits, pinched, sore or sorely pressed, hard pressed, hard up [slang], up against it [slang]; driven from pillar to post; desperate, in extremities, in extremis [L], at the end of one's rope or tether.

.25 stranded, grounded, aground, on the rocks, high and dry; stuck, stuck or set fast; foundered, swamped; castaway, marooned, wrecked, shipwrecked.

.26 ADVS with difficulty, difficultly, with much ado, mogi–; hardly, painfully; the hard way, arduously, strenuously, laboriously, toilsomely.

.27 unwieldily, unmanageably, unhandily, inconveniently; awkwardly, clumsily, cumbersomely; ponderously.

732. FACILITY

.1 NOUNS facility, ease, easiness, facileness, effortlessness; lack of hindrance, smoothness, freedom; clear coast, clear road or course; smooth road, royal road, highroad; easy going, plain sailing, smooth or straight sailing; clarity, intelligibility 548; uncomplexity, uncomplicatedness, simplicity 45.

.2 wieldiness, wieldableness, manageability, manageableness, maneuverability, handiness; convenience, practicality, untroublesomeness; flexibility, pliancy, pliability, ductility, malleability; adaptability, feasibility.

.3 easy thing, mere child's play, simple twist of the wrist; cinch or snap or pushover or setup or breeze or duck soup or velvet or picnic or pie [all slang], piece of cake [Brit slang]; easy target, sitting duck [informal]; sinecure.

.4 **facilitation, easing,** smoothing; **speeding,** expediting, expedition, quickening, hastening; streamlining; simplifying, **simplification, clarification.**

.5 **disembarrassment, disentanglement, disencumbrance,** disinvolvement, uncluttering, unscrambling, unsnarling, disburdening, unhampering; **extrication,** disengagement, **freeing,** clearing.

.6 VERBS **facilitate, ease; grease the wheels** [informal]; **smooth, smooth** or **pave the way,** grease the ways, soap the ways [both informal], prepare the way, **clear the way,** make all clear for, make way for; run interference for [informal], open the way, open the door to; **open up, unclog, unblock,** unjam, unbar, loose 763.6; **lubricate,** remove friction, grease, oil; **speed, expedite,** quicken, hasten; **help along,** help on its way; **aid** 785.11; **explain** 552.11, make clear 548.6; **simplify** 45.4.5.

.7 **do easily,** make short work of, do with one's hands tied behind one's back, do with both eyes shut.

.8 **disembarrass, disencumber,** disburden, unhamper; **disentangle,** disembroil, disinvolve, unclutter, unscramble, unsnarl; **extricate,** disengage, **free, free up,** clear; **liberate** 763.4.

.9 **go easily, run smoothly,** work well, work like a machine, go like clockwork; present no difficulties, give no trouble, be painless, be effortless; **flow, roll, glide, slide,** coast, sweep, sail.

.10 **have it easy, have it soft** [informal], have it all one's own way, have the game in one's hands; **win easily;** breeze in or walk over the course or win in a walk or win in a canter or win hands down [all informal].

.11 **take it easy** or **go easy** [both informal], swim with the stream, drift with the current, go with the tide; cool it or not sweat it [both slang]; take it in one's stride, make little or light of, think nothing of.

.12 ADJS **easy, facile, effortless,** smooth, casual, painless; **soft** [informal], cushy [slang]; **plain,** uncomplicated, straightforward, **simple** 45.6–9, Mickey Mouse [informal], simple as ABC [informal], easy as pie or easy as falling off a log [both informal], like shooting fish in a barrel, like taking candy from a baby; **clear** 548.10; **glib; light,** unburdensome; nothing to it.

.13 **smooth-running,** frictionless, easy-running, easy-flowing; well-oiled, well-greased.

.14 **wieldy, wieldable;** tractable; flexible, pliant, yielding, malleable, ductile, pliable, **manageable,** maneuverable; handy, **convenient,** foolproof, practical, untroublesome; adaptable, feasible.

.15 ADVS **easily, facilely, effortlessly, readily, simply,** lightly, swimmingly [informal], without difficulty; no sweat or like nothing or slick as a whistle [all slang]; hands down [informal], with one hand tied behind one's back, with both eyes closed; **smoothly,** like clockwork; on easy terms.

733. SKILL

.1 NOUNS **skill, skillfulness, expertness, proficiency,** craft, expertise, **cleverness; dexterity,** dexterousness or dextrousness; **adroitness,** address, **adeptness, deftness,** handiness, practical ability; coordination, timing; quickness, readiness; **competence,** capability, capacity, ability; efficiency; **facility, prowess;** grace, style, finesse; **tact, tactfulness, diplomacy;** savoir-faire [Fr]; **artistry;** artfulness; **craftsmanship,** workmanship, artisanship; **know-how** [informal], savvy [slang]; technical skill, **technique;** technical brilliance, technical mastery, **virtuosity,** bravura, wizardry; brilliance 467.2; **cunning** 735; **ingenuity,** ingeniousness, resource, resourcefulness, wit; **mastery,** mastership, **command,** control, grip; marksmanship, seamanship, airmanship, horsemanship, etc.; –ery or –ry, –ics, –ship, –manship, –urgy.

.2 **agility, nimbleness, spryness,** lightness, featliness.

.3 **versatility, ambidexterity,** many-sidedness, all-roundedness [informal], Renaissance versatility; **adaptability,** adjustability, flexibility; Renaissance man.

.4 **talent,** flair, strong flair, **gift, endowment,** dowry, dower, natural gift or endowment, **genius,** instinct, **faculty,** bump [informal]; **power, ability, capability, capacity,** potential; caliber; **forte,** speciality, métier, long suit, strong point; **equipment, qualification;** talents, powers, naturals [archaic], parts; the goods or the stuff or what it takes [all slang], makings.

.5 **aptitude,** inborn or innate aptitude, aptness, felicity, flair; **bent, turn,** propensity, leaning, inclination, tendency; turn for, capacity for, gift for, genius for; an eye for, an ear for, a hand for.

.6 **knack, art, hang, trick,** way; **touch, feel.**

.7 **art, science, craft; skill; technique,** technic, **technics,** technology, technical knowledge or skill, technical know-how [informal]; **mechanics,** mechanism; method 657.1.

.8 **accomplishment, acquirement, attainment;** finish.

.9 **experience, practice,** practical knowledge or skill; background, past experience, seasoning, tempering; **worldly wisdom,** knowledge of the world, blaséness, sophistication; sagacity 467.4.

.10 **masterpiece, masterwork,** *chef d'œuvre* [Fr]; **master stroke,** *coup de maître* [Fr]; **feat,** *tour de force* [Fr].

.11 **expert, adept,** proficient, –an or –ean or –ian, –ician, –ist; **artist, craftsman,** artisan, skilled workman, journeyman; technician; seasoned or experienced hand; shark or sharp [both informal], no slouch [slang]; graduate; **professional, pro** [informal]; **jack-of-all-trades,** handy man, Admirable Crichton [J. M. Barrie]; **authority,** professor, **consultant,** expert consultant, attaché, technical adviser, savant 476.3; diplomatist, diplomat; politician, statesman, elder statesman; connoisseur, *connaisseur* [Fr]; *cordon bleu* [Fr]; marksman, crack shot, dead shot.

.12 **talented person, talent,** man of parts, gifted person, prodigy, **genius;** mental genius, intellectual genius, intellectual prodigy, mental giant; gifted child, **child prodigy,** boy wonder [informal]; natural [informal].

.13 **master, past master;** master hand, **good hand,** skilled or practiced hand; ace or star or superstar or crackerjack or great or all-time great or topnotcher or first-rater [all informal]; **prodigy, wizard** or whiz [both informal], magician; **virtuoso; genius,** man of genius; **mastermind;** mahatma, sage 468.1.

.14 **champion, champ** [slang], world champion; **record holder,** world-record holder; laureate; medal winner, Olympic medal winner, medalist, award winner, prizeman, prizetaker, **prizewinner;** hall-of-famer.

.15 **veteran, vet** [informal], seasoned veteran, **old pro** [informal]; **old hand, old-timer** [informal]; old campaigner, war-horse [informal]; salt or old salt or old sea dog [all informal], shellback [slang].

.16 **sophisticate,** man of experience, **man of the world;** slicker or city slicker [both informal]; man-about-town; **cosmopolitan,** cosmopolite, citizen of the world.

.17 VERBS **excel in** or **at, shine in** or **at** [informal], **be master of; be at home in; have a gift** or **flair** or **talent** or **bent** or **faculty** or

turn for, have a bump for [informal], **have a good head for,** have an ear for, have an eye for, be born for, show aptitude or talent for; have the knack or touch, have the hang of it; have something on the ball or plenty on the ball [slang].

.18 **know backwards and forwards, know one's stuff** or **know one's onions** [both slang], **know the ropes** or **know all the ins and outs** [both informal], know from A to Z or from alpha to omega, know from the ground up, know all the tricks, know all the tricks of the trade, know all the moves of the game; **know what's what, know a thing or two,** know what it's all about, know the score or know all the answers [both slang], "know a hawk from a handsaw" [Shakespeare]; have savvy [slang]; **know one's way about,** know the ways of the world, have been around [slang], have been through the mill [informal], have cut one's wisdom teeth or eyeteeth [informal], be long in the tooth, **not be born yesterday;** get around [informal].

.19 **exercise skill,** handle oneself well, demonstrate one's ability, **strut one's stuff** [slang], show expertise; cut one's coat according to one's cloth, play one's cards well.

.20 ADJS **skillful, good,** goodish, excellent, **expert, proficient; dexterous** or dextrous, **adroit, deft, adept, coordinated,** well-coordinated, **apt,** no mean, **handy;** quick, ready; **clever,** cute or slick [both informal], neat, clean; fancy, graceful, stylish; some or quite some or quite a or every bit a [all informal]; **masterly, masterful;** magisterial; authoritative, professional; the compleat or the complete; crack or crackerjack [both informal]; **virtuoso,** bravura, technically superb; **brilliant** 467.14; cunning 735.12; tactful, diplomatic, politic, statesmanlike; **ingenious,** resourceful, daedal, Daedalian; **artistic; workmanlike, well-done.**

.21 **agile, nimble, spry,** sprightly, fleet, featly, peart [dial], light, graceful, nimble-footed, light-footed, sure-footed; nimble-fingered, neat-fingered, neat-handed.

.22 **competent, capable, able, efficient, qualified, fit, fitted, suited, worthy;** journeyman; fit or fitted for; **equal to, up to;** up to snuff [slang], up to the mark [informal], *au fait* [Fr]; well-qualified, well-fitted, well-suited.

.23 **versatile, ambidextrous,** two-handed, all-around [informal], **many-sided**, generally capable; **adaptable**, adjustable, flexible, resourceful, supple; amphibious.

.24 **skilled, accomplished; practiced; professional**, career; trained, coached, prepared, primed, finished; at one's best, at concert pitch; initiated, initiate; technical; conversant 475.20.

.25 **skilled in**, proficient in, adept in, versed in, **good at**, expert at, **handy at, a hand** *or* **good hand at**, master of, strong in, at home in; **up on**, well up on, well-versed 475.19,20.

.26 **experienced, practiced**, mature, matured, ripe, ripened, **seasoned**, tried, tried and true, **veteran**, old, an old dog at [informal]; sagacious 467.16–19; **worldly, worldly-wise**, world-wise, wise in the ways of the world, knowing, **sophisticated**, cosmopolitan, cosmopolite, blasé, dry behind the ears, not born yesterday, long in the tooth.

.27 **talented, gifted, endowed**, with a flair; born for, made for, cut out for [informal], with an eye for, with an ear for, with a bump for [informal].

.28 **well-laid, well-devised**, well-contrived, well-designed, well-planned, well-worked-out; well-invented, *ben trovato* [Ital]; **well-weighed, well-reasoned**, well-considered, well-thought-out; **cunning, clever**.

.29 ADVS **skillfully, expertly, proficiently**, excellently, well; **cleverly**, neatly, ingeniously, resourcefully; cunningly 735.13; **dexterously** *or* dextrously, **adroitly, deftly, adeptly**, aptly, handily; agilely, nimbly, featly, spryly; **competently, capably, ably**, efficiently; **masterfully**; brilliantly, superbly, with genius, with a touch of genius; **artistically**, artfully; with skill, with consummate skill, with finesse.

734. UNSKILLFULNESS

.1 NOUNS **unskillfulness**, skill-lessness, **inexpertness, unproficiency, uncleverness**; unintelligence 469; inadeptness, **undexterousness** *or* undextrousness, indexterity, **undeftness**; inefficiency; **incompetence** *or* **incompetency, inability, incapability, incapacity**, inadequacy; **ineffectiveness, ineffectuality; mediocrity**, pedestrianism; **inaptitude**, inaptness, unaptness, **ineptness**, maladroitness; unfitness, unfittedness; untrainedness, unschooledness; thoughtlessness, inattentiveness; maladjustment; rustiness [informal].

.2 **inexperience**, unexperience, unexperiencedness, unpracticedness; **rawness**, greenness, unripeness, callowness, unfledgedness, immaturity; ignorance 477; **unfamiliarity**, unacquaintance, unacquaintedness, unaccustomedness; **amateurishness**, amateurism, unprofessionalness, unprofessionalism.

.3 **clumsiness, awkwardness**, bumblingness, **maladroitness, unhandiness**, left-handedness, heavy-handedness, ham-handedness [informal]; handful of thumbs; **ungainliness**, uncouthness, **ungracefulness**, gracelessness, inelegance; **gawkiness**, gawkishness; **lubberliness, oafishness**, loutishness, boorishness, clownishness, lumpishness; **cumbersomeness**, hulkiness, **ponderousness; unwieldiness, unmanageability** 731.8.

.4 **bungling, blundering**, boggling, **fumbling**, muffing, **botching**, botchery, blunderheadedness; **sloppiness, carelessness** 534.2; too many cooks.

.5 **bungle, blunder, botch**, flub, boner *or* bonehead play [both slang], boggle, bobble *or* boo-boo [both slang], foozle [informal], bevue; **fumble, muff**, fluff, miscue [slang]; **slip**, trip, stumble; *gaucherie, étourderie, balourdise* [all Fr]; hash *or* mess [both informal]; bad job, sad work, clumsy performance; off day; **error, mistake** 518.3.

.6 **mismanagement, mishandling**, misdirection, misguidance, misconduct, **misgovernment**, misrule; misadministration, maladministration; malfeasance, malpractice, misfeasance, wrongdoing 982; nonfeasance, omission, **negligence**, neglect 534.6; bad policy, impolicy, inexpedience *or* inexpediency 671.

.7 **incompetent**, incapable; dull tool, mediocrity, **no conjuror**; one who will not set the Thames on fire [Brit]; greenhorn 477.8.

.8 **bungler, blunderer**, blunderhead, boggler, slubberer, bumbler, **fumbler, botcher**; bull in a china shop, ox; lubber, looby, **lout, oaf**, gawk, gowk [Brit dial], *klutz* [Yid], boor, **clown**, slouch; clodhopper, clodknocker, yokel; **clod**, clot [Brit], **dolt**, blockhead 471.3,4; awkward squad.

.9 [slang *or* informal terms] **goof**, goofer, goofball, foul-up, foozler, clumsy, fumble-fist, **butterfingers**, muff, muffer, stumblebum, stumblebunny, duffer, lummox, **slob**, lump, dub; rube, hick.

.10 VERBS **not know how**, not have the knack, not have it in one [informal]; not be up to [informal]; not be versed.

.11 **bungle, blunder**, bumble, boggle, **muff**, muff one's cue, **fumble**, be all thumbs, have a handful of thumbs; **flounder, muddle, lumber;** stumble, **slip,** trip, trip over one's own feet, get in one's own way, miss one's footing, miscue; commit a *faux pas*, commit a gaffe; blunder on *or* upon *or* into; blunder away, be not one's day; **botch,** mar, **spoil, butcher, murder,** make sad work of; play havoc with, play the mischief with.

.12 [slang *or* informal terms] bobble, **goof,** put one's foot in it, stub one's toe, drop a brick, bonehead into it; bitch, bitch up, hash up, **mess up,** flub, **make a mess** *or* **hash of,** foul up, goof up, **screw up,** louse up, gum up, gum up the works, bugger, bugger up, play the deuce *or* devil *or* hell *or* merry hell with; go at it ass-backwards.

.13 **mismanage, mishandle, misconduct,** misdirect, misguide, **misgovern, misrule;** misadminister, maladminister; be negligent 534.6.

.14 not know what one is about, not know one's interest, make an ass of oneself, make a fool of oneself, stultify oneself, put oneself out of court, stand in one's own light, not know on which side one's bread is buttered, kill the goose that lays the golden egg, cut one's own throat, dig one's own grave, behave self-destructively, play with fire, burn one's fingers, jump out of the frying pan into the fire, "sow the wind and reap the whirlwind" [Bible], lock the barn door after the horse is stolen, count one's chickens before they are hatched, buy a pig in a poke, aim at a pigeon and kill a crow, put the cart before the horse, put a square peg into a round hole, run before one can walk.

.15 ADJS **unskillful,** skill-less, artless, **inexpert, unproficient, unclever;** inefficient; **undexterous** *or* undextrous, **undeft, inadept, unfacile;** unapt, inapt, inept, half-assed [slang], **poor;** mediocre, pedestrian; thoughtless, inattentive; unintelligent 469.13.

.16 **unskilled, unaccomplished, untrained,** untaught, unschooled, untutored, uncoached, uninitiated, **unprepared,** unprimed, unfinished, unpolished; **untalented, ungifted, unendowed;** amateurish, unprofessional, unbusinesslike, semiskilled.

.17 **inexperienced,** unexperienced, unversed, unconversant, **unpracticed;** undeveloped, unseasoned; **raw, green,** green as grass, unripe, callow, unfledged, immature, unmatured, fresh, not dry behind the ears,

untried; unskilled in, unpracticed in, unversed in, unconversant with, unaccustomed to, unused to, unfamiliar *or* unacquainted with, new to, uninitiated in, a stranger to, a novice *or* tyro at; ignorant 477.12.

.18 out **of practice,** out of training *or* form, soft [informal], out of shape *or* condition, stiff, **rusty;** gone *or* run to seed [informal], not what one used to be [informal], losing one's touch, slipping, on the downgrade.

.19 **incompetent, incapable, unable, inadequate, unequipped, unqualified,** ill-qualified, **unfit, unfitted,** unadapted, not equal *or* up to, not cut out for [informal]; ineffective, **ineffectual;** unadjusted, maladjusted.

.20 **clumsy, awkward, bungling, blundering,** blunderheaded, bumbling, fumbling; **maladroit, unhandy,** left-hand, left-handed, heavy-handed, ham-handed *or* ham-fisted [both informal], clumsy-fisted, butterfingered [informal], **all thumbs,** fingers all thumbs, with a handful of thumbs; stiff; **ungainly, uncouth, ungraceful,** graceless, inelegant, *gauche* [Fr]; **gawky, gawkish; lubberly, loutish, oafish,** boorish, clownish, lumpish, slobbish [slang]; **sloppy, careless** 534.11; **ponderous, cumbersome,** lumbering, hulking, hulky; **unwieldy** 731.18.

.21 **botched, bungled,** fumbled, muffed, spoiled, **butchered,** murdered; **ill-managed,** ill-done, ill-conducted, ill-devised, ill-contrived, ill-executed; mismanaged, misconducted, **misdirected, misguided;** impolitic, ill-considered, ill-advised 470.9; negligent 534.10–13.

.22 [slang *or* informal terms] bobbled, bitched, bitched up, hashed up, **messed up,** fouled up, **screwed up, loused up,** gummed up, buggered, buggered up; assbackwards.

.23 ADVS **unskillfully, inexpertly, unproficiently, uncleverly;** inefficiently; **incompetently, incapably,** inadequately, unfitly; **undexterously, undeftly, inadeptly,** unfacilely; unaptly, inaptly, ineptly, poorly.

.24 **clumsily, awkwardly; bunglingly, blunderingly; maladroitly,** unhandily; **ungracefully,** gracelessly, inelegantly, uncouthly; **ponderously, cumbersomely,** lumberingly, hulkingly, hulkily; ass-backwards [slang].

735. CUNNING

.1 NOUNS **cunning,** cunningness, **craft, craftiness, callidity, artfulness, art, artifice,** wiliness, wiles, guile, **slyness**, insidiousness, suppleness [Scot], **foxiness**, slipperiness, shiftiness, trickiness; gamesmanship *or* one-upmanship [both informal]; **canniness, shrewdness, sharpness**, acuteness, astuteness, **cleverness** 733.1; resourcefulness, ingeniousness, wit, inventiveness, readiness; subtlety, subtilty, subtleness, Italian hand, fine Italian hand, finesse; sophistry 483; "the dark sanctuary of incapacity" [Chesterfield], "the ape of wisdom" [Locke]; satanic cunning, the cunning of the serpent; sneakiness, **stealthiness, stealth** 614.4; cageyness [informal], wariness 895.2.

.2 **Machiavellianism, Machiavellism; politics, diplomacy,** diplomatics; jobbery, jobbing.

.3 **stratagem, artifice,** art [archaic], **craft, wile,** strategy, **device,** wily device, **contrivance, expedient, design, scheme, trick,** cute trick, fetch, fakement [informal], gimmick [slang], **ruse, red herring, shift,** tactic, **maneuver,** move, coup, gambit, **ploy, dodge,** artful dodge; **game,** little game, racket *or* grift [both slang]; **plot,** conspiracy, **intrigue** 654.6; sleight, feint, jugglery; **subterfuge,** blind, dust in the eyes; chicanery, knavery, deceit, trickery 618.3,4.

.4 **machination, manipulation, wire-pulling** [informal]; influence, political influence, behind-the-scenes influence *or* pressure; **maneuvering,** maneuvers, tactical maneuvers; **tactics,** devices, expedients.

.5 **circumvention,** getting round *or* around; **evasion,** elusion, the slip [informal]; the runaround *or* buck-passing *or* passing the buck [all informal]; **frustration, foiling, thwarting** 730.3; **outwitting,** outsmarting, outguessing, **outmaneuvering.**

.6 **slyboots,** sly dog [informal], **fox,** reynard, dodger, Artful Dodger [Dickens], crafty rascal, smooth *or* slick citizen [informal], glib tongue, smooth *or* sweet talker, charmer; **trickster,** shyster [slang], Philadelphia lawyer [informal]; horse trader, Yankee horse trader; **swindler** 619.3.

.7 **strategist, tactician;** maneuverer, **machinator, manipulator,** wire-puller [informal]; calculator, schemer; **intriguer** 654.8.

.8 **Machiavellian,** Machiavel, Machiavellianist; **diplomat,** diplomatist, **politician** 746; political realist; influence peddler *or* power broker [both informal].

.9 VERBS **live by one's wits,** play a deep game; use one's fine Italian hand, finesse; shift, dodge, twist and turn, zig and zag;

hide one's hand, cover one's path; **trick, deceive** 618.13–18.

.10 **maneuver, manipulate,** pull strings *or* wires; **machinate, contrive,** angle [informal], **jockey, engineer;** play games [informal]; **plot, scheme, intrigue** 654.10; **finagle, wangle;** gerrymander.

.11 **outwit, outsmart,** outguess, outfigure, **outmaneuver,** outgeneral, outflank, outplay; get the better *or* best of, go one better, know a trick worth two of that; **overreach, outreach; circumvent,** get round *or* around, **evade,** stonewall [slang], **elude, frustrate, foil,** give the slip *or* runaround [informal]; pass the buck [informal]; pull a fast one [slang], steal a march on; make a fool of, make a sucker *or* patsy of [slang]; be too much for, be too deep for; **deceive, victimize** 618.13–18.

.12 ADJS **cunning, crafty, artful, wily,** guileful, **sly,** insidious, supple [Scot], **shifty,** pawky [Brit], **arch, smooth, slick** [informal], **slippery,** snaky, serpentine, **foxy,** vulpine, feline; **canny, shrewd,** knowing, sharp, cute, acute, astute, **clever** 733.20; resourceful, ingenious, inventive, ready; subtle, subtile; sophistical 483.10; **tricky,** trickish, tricksy [archaic]; **Machiavellian,** Machiavellic, politic, diplomatic; strategic, tactical; deep, deep-laid; cunning as a fox *or* serpent, crazy like a fox [slang], slippery as an eel, too clever by half; sneaky, **stealthy** 614.12; cagey [informal], wary 895.9; **scheming, designing** 654.14; **deceitful** 618.20.

.13 ADVS **cunningly, craftily, artfully,** wilily, guilefully, insidiously, shiftily, foxily, trickily, smoothly, slick [slang]; **slyly,** on the sly; **cannily, shrewdly,** knowingly, astutely, **cleverly** 733.29; subtlely, subtilely; cagily [informal], warily 895.13.

736. ARTLESSNESS

.1 NOUNS **artlessness, ingenuousness, guilelessness; simplicity,** simpleness, plainness; **simpleheartedness, simplemindedness; unsophistication,** unsophisticatedness; *naïveté* [Fr], naïvety, naïveness, childlikeness; **innocence;** trustfulness, trustingness, unguardedness, unwariness, unsuspiciousness; **openness,** openheartedness, sincerity, candor 974.4; single-heartedness, single-mindedness, singleness of heart; directness, bluffness, bluntness, 'outspokenness.

.2 **naturalness,** naturalism, nature; state of nature; **unspoiledness; unaffectedness,** unaffectation, **unassumingness,** unpretendingness, unpretentiousness, undisguise; **inartificiality**, unartificialness, genuineness.

.3 **unsophisticate**, simple soul, naïf, **ingenue, innocent, child**, mere child, infant, **babe**, babe in the woods, lamb, dove; child of nature, noble savage; yokel, rube *or* hick [both slang]; oaf, lout 471.5; dupe 620.

.4 VERBS wear one's heart on one's sleeve, look one in the face.

.5 ADJS **artless, simple**, plain, **guileless**; simplehearted, simpleminded; **ingenuous**, *ingénu* [Fr]; **unsophisticated, naïve**; childlike, born yesterday; **innocent**; trustful, trusting, unguarded, unwary, unreserved, confiding, unsuspicious; **open**, openhearted, sincere, candid, **frank** 974.17; single-hearted, single-minded; direct, bluff, blunt, outspoken.

.6 **natural**, naturelike, native; in the state of nature; unspoiled; **unaffected, unassuming, unpretending**, unpretentious, unfeigning, undisguising, undissimulating, undissembling, undesigning; **genuine, inartificial**, unartificial, unadorned, unvarnished, unembellished; homespun; pastoral, rural, arcadian, bucolic.

.7 ADVS **artlessly, ingenuously, guilelessly**; simply, plainly; **naturally, genuinely**; naïvely; openly, openheartedly.

737. BEHAVIOR

.1 NOUNS **behavior, conduct, deportment, comportment, manner, manners, demeanor, mien**, *maintien* [Fr], **carriage, bearing**, port, poise, posture, guise, **air**, address, presence; –phoria; tone, style, lifestyle; way of life, modus vivendi; way, ways; methods, method, methodology; practice, praxis; procedure, proceeding; **actions**, acts, goings-on, doings, movements, moves, tactics; action, doing 705.1; activity 707; objective *or* observable behavior; motions, gestures; pose, affectation 903; pattern, behavior pattern; culture pattern, behavioral norm, folkway, custom 642; behavioral science, social science.

.2 **good behavior**, sanctioned behavior; good citizenship; good manners, correct deportment, etiquette 646.3; courtesy 936; sociability 922; bad *or* poor behavior, misbehavior 738; discourtesy 937.

.3 **behaviorism**, behavior *or* behavioristic psychology; behavior therapy.

.4 VERBS **behave, act, do**, go on; **behave oneself, conduct oneself**, manage oneself, **handle oneself**, guide oneself, **comport oneself, deport oneself, demean oneself, bear oneself, carry oneself**; acquit oneself, quit oneself [archaic]; proceed, move; misbehave 738.4.

.5 **behave oneself, behave**, act well, **be good**, be nice, **do right**, do what is right, do the right *or* proper thing, keep out of mischief, play the game *or* mind one's P's and Q's [both informal], be on one's good *or* best behavior.

.6 **treat, use, do by**, deal by, **act** *or* **behave toward**, conduct oneself toward, act with regard to, conduct oneself vis-à-vis *or* in the face of; **deal with**, cope with, **handle**; respond to.

.7 ADJS **behavioral**; behaviorist, behavioristic; **behaved**, behaviored, **mannered**, demeanored, –phoric.

738. MISBEHAVIOR

.1 NOUNS **misbehavior, misconduct**, misdemeanor [archaic]; unsanctioned *or* nonsanctioned behavior; frowned-upon behavior; **naughtiness**, badness; impropriety; venial sin; **disorderly conduct**, disorder, disorderliness, disruptiveness, disruption, **rowdiness**, rowdyism, ruffianism, hooliganism; vandalism; roughhouse, horseplay; discourtesy 937; vice 981; misdoing, wrongdoing 982.

.2 **mischief, mischievousness**; **devilment, deviltry**, devilry; **roguishness**, roguery, scampishness; **waggery**, waggishness; **impishness**, devilishness, puckishness, elfishness; **prankishness**, pranksomeness; sportiveness, playfulness, *espièglerie* [Fr]; high spirits, youthful spirits; foolishness 470.

.3 **mischief-maker**, mischief, **rogue, devil**, knave, **rascal**, rapscallion, scapegrace, **scamp**; **wag** 881.12; buffoon 612.10; funmaker, joker, jokester, practical joker, prankster, life of the party, **cutup** [slang]; **rowdy**, ruffian, hoodlum, hood [informal], hooligan; **imp, elf, puck**, pixie, **minx**, bad boy, bugger *or* booger [both informal], little devil, little rascal, little monkey, *enfant terrible* [Fr].

.4 VERBS **misbehave**, misdemean [archaic], **misbehave oneself, misconduct oneself**, misdemean oneself [archaic], behave ill; get into mischief; act up *or* carry on *or* carry on something scandalous [all informal], sow one's wild oats; cut up [slang], horse around [informal], roughhouse *or* cut up rough [both slang]; play the fool 470.6.

.5 ADJS **misbehaving**, unbehaving; **naughty, bad**; improper, not respectable; out-of-order *or* off-base *or* out-of-line [all informal]; disorderly, disruptive, **rowdy**, rowdyish, **ruffianly**.

.6 **mischievous**, mischief-loving, full of mischief; **roguish**, scampish, scapegrace, arch, knavish; **devilish; impish, puckish, elfish,** elvish; **waggish, prankish, pranky,** pranksome, trickish, tricksy; **playful,** sportive, high-spirited, *espiègle* [Fr]; foolish 470.8–10.

.7 ADVS **mischievously, roguishly,** knavishly, scampishly, devilishly; impishly, puckishly, elfishly; waggishly; prankishly, playfully, sportively, in fun.

739. AUTHORITY

.1 NOUNS **authority, prerogative, right, power,** faculty, competence *or* competency; regality, royal prerogative; constituted authority, vested authority; inherent authority; legal *or* lawful *or* rightful authority, legitimacy; derived *or* delegated authority, vicarious authority, indirect authority; **the say** *or* **the say-so** [both informal]; divine right, *jus divinum* [L]; absolute power, absolutism 741.9,10.

.2 **authoritativeness, authority, power,** powerfulness, magisterialness, **potency** *or* potence, puissance, **strength,** might, mightiness, clout [slang].

.3 **authoritativeness, masterfulness, lordliness,** magistrality, magisterialness; **arbitrariness,** peremptoriness, imperativeness, **imperiousness,** autocraticalness, highhandedness, dictatorialness, overbearingness, overbearance, overbearing, domineering, domineeringness, tyrannicalness, authoritarianism, bossism [informal].

.4 **prestige, authority, influence,** influentialness; pressure, **weight,** weightiness, moment, **consequence;** eminence, **stature,** rank, seniority, priority, precedence; **greatness** 34; **importance, prominence** 672.1,2.

.5 **governance, authority, jurisdiction, control, command, power, rule, reign,** regnancy, **dominion,** sovereignty, empire, empery, raj [India], **sway; government** 741; administration, disposition 747.3; grip, claws, **clutches,** hand, hands, iron hand, talons.

.6 **dominance** *or* dominancy, **dominion, domination;** preeminence, supremacy, superiority 36; **sovereignty,** suzerainty, suzerainship, **overlordship;** primacy, principality, **predominance** *or* predominancy, predomination, prepotence *or* prepotency; preponderance, **ascendance** *or* ascendancy; **upper** *or* **whip hand,** balance of power; eminent domain.

.7 **mastership,** masterhood, masterdom, **mastery; leadership, headship, lordship;** hegemony; supervisorship, directorship 747.4; hierarchy, nobility, aristocracy, **ruling class** 749.15; chairmanship; chieftainship, chieftaincy, chieftainry, chiefery *or* chiefry; presidentship, presidency; premiership, prime-ministership, prime-ministry; governorship; princeship, princedom, principality; rectorship, rectorate; suzerainty, suzerainship; regency, regentship; prefectship, prefecture; proconsulship, proconsulate; provostship, provostry; protectorship, protectorate; seneschalship, seneschalsy; pashadom, pashalic; sheikhdom; emirate, viziership, vizierate; magistrateship, magistrature, magistracy; mayorship, mayoralty; sheriffdom, sheriffcy, sheriffalty, shrievalty; consulship, consulate; chancellorship, chancellery, chancellorate; seigniory; tribunate, aedileship; deanery; patriarchate, patriarchy [archaic]; bishopric, episcopacy; archbishopric, archiepiscopacy, archiepiscopate; metropolitanship, metropolitanate; popedom, popeship, popehood, papacy, pontificate, pontificality; dictatorship, dictature.

.8 **sovereignty, royalty,** regnancy, **majesty,** empire, empery, imperialism, **emperorship; kingship,** kinghood; queenship, queenhood; kaisership, kaiserdom; czardom; rajaship; sultanship, sultanate; caliphate; the throne, the crown, the purple; royal insignia 569.3.

.9 **scepter, rod, staff,** staff *or* rod of office, wand, wand of office, baton, mace, truncheon, fasces; crosier, crook, cross-staff; caduceus; gavel; mantle; chain of office; portfolio.

.10 (seat of authority) **saddle** [informal], **helm, driver's seat** [informal]; seat, chair, bench; woolsack [England]; seat of state, seat of power; curule chair; dais.

.11 **throne,** royal seat; musnud *or* gaddi [both India]; Peacock throne.

.12 (acquisition of authority) **accession; succession,** rightful *or* legitimate succession; **usurpation,** arrogation, assumption, taking over, seizure; anointment, anointing, consecration, coronation; **delegation,** deputation, assignment, **appointment; election; authorization,** empowerment.

.13 VERBS **possess** *or* **wield authority, have power,** have the power, have the right, have the say *or* say-so· [informal], hold the prerogative; carry authority, have clout [slang], have what one says go, have one's own way; show one's authority, crack the whip, throw one's weight around [informal]; rule 741.14, dominate 741.15, govern 741.12, control 741.13; supervise 747.10.

.14 take command, take charge, take over, take the helm, take the reins of government, take the reins into one's hand, get the power into one's hands, gain or get the upper hand, take the lead; ascend or mount or succeed to or accede to the throne; assume command, assume, usurp, arrogate, seize; usurp or seize the throne or crown or mantle, usurp the prerogatives of the crown; seize power, execute a *coup d'état.*

.15 ADJS authoritative, clothed with authority, commanding, imperative; governing, controlling, ruling 741.18; preeminent, supreme, leading, superior 36.12–14; powerful, potent, puissant, mighty; dominant, ascendant, hegemonic, hegemonistic; influential, prestigious, weighty, momentous, consequential, eminent, substantial, considerable; great 34.6; important, prominent 672.18; ranking, senior; authorized, empowered, duly constituted, competent; official, *ex officio* [L]; authoritarian; absolute, autocratic, monocratic; totalitarian.

.16 imperious, imperial, masterful, authoritative, feudal, aristocratic, lordly, magistral, magisterial; arrogant 912.9; arbitrary, peremptory, imperative; absolute, absolutist, absolutistic; dictatorial, authoritarian; bossy [informal], domineering, highhanded, overbearing, overruling; autocratic, monocratic, despotic, tyrannical; tyrannous, grinding, oppressive 864.24; repressive, suppressive 760.11; strict, severe 757.6.

.17 sovereign; regal, royal, majestic, purple; kinglike, kingly, "every inch a king" [Shakespeare]; imperial, imperious or imperatorious [both archaic]; imperatorial; monarchic(al), monarchal, monarchial; tetrarchic; princely, princelike; queenly, queenlike; dynastic.

.18 ADVS authoritatively, with authority; commandingly, imperatively; powerfully, potently, puissantly, mightily; influentially, weightily, momentously, consequentially; officially, *ex cathedra* [L].

.19 imperiously, masterfully, magisterially; arbitrarily, peremptorily; autocratically, dictatorially, high-handedly, domineer-

ingly, overbearingly, despotically, tyrannically.

.20 by authority of, in the name of, in or by virtue of.

.21 in authority, in power, in charge, in control, in command, at the reins, at the head, at the helm, at the wheel, in the saddle or driver's seat [informal], on the throne; "drest in a little brief authority" [Shakespeare].

740. LAWLESSNESS

(absence of authority)

.1 NOUNS lawlessness; licentiousness, license, uncontrol, unrestraint 762.3; indiscipline, insubordination, mutiny, disobedience 767; irresponsibility, unaccountability; willfulness, unchecked or rampant will; interregnum, power vacuum.

.2 anarchy, anarchism; disorderliness, unruliness, misrule, disorder, disruption, disorganization, confusion, turmoil, chaos, primal chaos, tohubohu; antinomianism; nihilism; syndicalism, anarcho-syndicalism, criminal syndicalism, lynch law, mob rule or law, mobocracy, ochlocracy; law of the jungle; revolution 147; rebellion 767.4.

.3 anarchist, anarch; antinomian; nihilist, syndicalist, anarcho-syndicalist; revolutionist 147.3; mutineer, rebel 767.5.

.4 VERBS reject or defy authority, enthrone one's own will; take the law in one's own hands, act on one's own responsibility; do or go as one pleases, indulge oneself; be a law unto oneself, answer to no man, "swear allegiance to the words of no master" [Horace].

.5 ADJS lawless; licentious, ungoverned, undisciplined, unrestrained 762.33; insubordinate, mutinous, disobedient 767.8–11; uncontrolled, uncurbed, unbridled, unchecked, rampant, unreined, reinless; irresponsible, wildcat, unaccountable; self-willed, willful, headstrong, heady.

.6 anarchic(al), anarchial, anarchistic; unruly, disorderly, disorganized, chaotic; antinomian; nihilistic, syndicalistic.

.7 ADVS lawlessly, licentiously; anarchically, chaotically.

741. GOVERNMENT

.1 NOUNS government, governance, discipline, regulation; direction, management, administration, dispensation, disposition, oversight, supervision 747.2; regime, regimen; rule, sway, sovereignty, reign, regnancy; empire, empery; civil government, political government; form or system of government, political organization, polity; –archy, –cracy or –ocracy.

.2 **control, mastery, mastership, command, power, jurisdiction, dominion, domination; hold, grasp,** grip, gripe; **hand, hands, iron hand,** clutches; talons, claws; helm, reins of government.

.3 **the government, the authorities; the powers that be,** the Establishment; Uncle Sam, Washington; John Bull, the Crown, His or Her Majesty's Government, Whitehall.

.4 (governments) federal government, federation; unitary government; republic, commonwealth, democracy, representative government, representative democracy, direct or pure democracy; constitutional or parliamentary government; "government of the people, by the people, for the people" [Lincoln]; social democracy, welfare state; mob rule, tyranny of the majority, mobocracy [informal], ochlocracy; pantisocracy; aristocracy, hierarchy, oligarchy; feudal system; monarchy, absolute monarchy, constitutional monarchy, limited monarchy; dictatorship, tyranny, autocracy, autarchy; dyarchy, duarchy, duumvirate; triarchy, triumvirate; totalitarian government or regime, police state; stratocracy, military government, militarism, garrison state; martial law, rule of the sword; regency; hierocracy, theocracy, thearchy; patriarchy, patriarchate; gerontocracy; technocracy, meritocracy; autonomy, self-government, home rule, self-determination; heteronomy, dominion rule, colonial government, colonialism, neocolonialism; provisional government; coalition government.

.5 matriarchy, matriarchate, gynarchy, gynocracy, gynecocracy; petticoat government.

.6 [slang or informal terms] foolocracy, gunocracy, mediocracy, moneyocracy, landocracy, cottonocracy, beerocracy, oiligarchy, parsonarchy, pedantocracy, pornocracy, snobocracy, squirearchy.

.7 **supranational government,** supergovernment, **world government,** World Federalism; League of Nations, United Nations 743.

.8 (principles of government) democratism, republicanism; constitutionalism, parliamentarism, parliamentarianism; monarchism, royalism; feudalism, feudality; imperialism; fascism, neofascism, Nazism, national socialism; statism, governmental-ism; collectivism, communism 745.5, socialism 745.6; federalism; centralism; pluralism; political principles 745.

.9 absolutism, dictatorship, despotism, tyranny, autocracy, autarchy, monarchy, absolute monarchy; **authoritarianism;** totalitarianism; one-man rule, one-party rule; Caesarism, Stalinism, kaiserism, czarism; benevolent despotism, paternalism.

.10 **despotism, tyranny, fascism,** domineering, domination, oppression; heavy hand, high hand, iron hand, iron heel or boot; big stick, *argumentum baculinum* [L]; **terrorism,** reign of terror; thought control.

.11 **officialism, bureaucracy;** beadledom, bumbledom; **red-tapeism,** red-tapery, **red tape** [all informal]; official jargon 744.37.

.12 VERBS **govern, regulate; wield authority** 739.13; **command,** officer, captain, **head, lead,** be master, be at the head of, **preside over,** chair; **direct, manage, supervise, administer,** administrate 747.8–11; discipline; stand over.

.13 **control, hold in hand,** have in one's power, gain a hold upon; hold the reins, hold the helm, be in the driver's seat or the saddle [informal]; have control of, **have under control, have in hand** or **well in hand;** be master of the situation, have it all one's own way, have the game in one's own hands; pull the strings or wires.

.14 **rule, sway, reign,** bear reign, have the sway, wield the scepter, wear the crown, sit on the throne; rule over, overrule.

.15 **dominate, predominate,** preponderate, prevail; **have the ascendancy, have the upper** or **whip hand,** have at a disadvantage, have on the hip [archaic]; **master,** have the mastery of; bestride; dictate, lay down the law; **rule the roost** or wear the pants [both informal]; take the lead, play first fiddle; **lead by the nose, twist** or **turn around one's little finger; keep under one's thumb,** bend to one's will.

.16 **domineer,** domineer over, **lord it over;** browbeat, henpeck [informal], intimidate, bully, cow, bulldoze [informal], walk over, walk all over; castrate, unman; daunt, terrorize 891.26–28; **tyrannize,** tyrannize over, despotize; **grind,** grind down, break, **oppress,** suppress, repress, weigh or press heavy on; keep under, keep down, beat down, clamp down on [informal]; overbear, overmaster, overawe; override, ride over, trample or stamp or tread upon, trample or tread down, **trample** or **tread underfoot,** crush under an iron heel, **ride roughshod over;** hold *or* keep a tight hand upon, rule with a rod of iron, rule with an iron hand *or* fist; enslave, subjugate 764.8; compel, coerce 756.4–7.

.17 ADJS **governmental,** gubernatorial; **political, civil,** civic; **official,** bureaucratic; democratic, republican, fascist, fascistic, oligarchal, oligarchic(al), aristocratic(al), theocratic, **federal,** federalist, federalistic, **constitutional,** parliamentary, parliamentarian; monarchic(al), monarchial, monarchal [archaic]; autocratic, monocratic, absolute, **authoritarian;** despotic, **dictatorial; totalitarian;** pluralistic; patriarchal, patriarchic(al); matriarchal, matriarchic(al); heteronomous; autonomous, self-governing.

.18 **governing, controlling, regulating,** regulative, regulatory, **commanding; ruling, reigning, sovereign,** regnant; **master, chief,** general, **boss** [informal], **head; dominant, predominant,** predominate, preponderant, preponderate, prepotent, prepollent, prevalent, **leading, paramount, supreme,** hegemonic, hegemonistic; ascendant, in the ascendant, in ascendancy; at the head, in chief; in charge 739.21.

.19 **executive, administrative,** ministerial; official, bureaucratic; **supervisory, directing, managing** 747.12–14.

.20 ADVS **under control, in hand,** well in hand; **in one's power,** under one's control.

742. LEGISLATURE, GOVERNMENT ORGANIZATION

.1 NOUNS **legislature,** legislative body; **parliament, congress, assembly,** general assembly, house of assembly, legislative assembly, **national assembly, chamber of deputies,** federal assembly, diet, soviet, court; unicameral legislature, bicameral legislature; legislative chamber, upper chamber *or* house, lower chamber *or* house; state legislature, state assembly; provincial legislature, provincial parliament; city council, city board, board of aldermen, common council, commission; representative town meeting, town meeting.

.2 **Parliament** (Afghanistan, Austria, Barbados, Belgium, Canada, Ethiopia, Fiji, France, West Germany, India, Iran, Italy, Jamaica, Laos, Liechtenstein, Malagasy Republic, Malaysia, Rhodesia, Singapore, South Africa, Swaziland, Trinidad and Tobago, United Kingdom), Federal Parliament (Australia), National Assembly (Bhutan, Botswana, Bulgaria, Republic of China, El Salvador, Gabon, Guinea, Equatorial Guinea, Guyana, Hungary, Ivory Coast, Jordan, Kenya, South Korea, Kuwait, Malawi, Mauritania, Pakistan, Rwanda, Senegal, Tanzania, Thailand, Tunisia, Uganda, Upper Volta, North Vietnam, Zaïre, Zambia), Legislative Assembly (Costa Rica, Mauritius, Nauru, Western Samoa, Tonga), Federal Assembly (Czechoslovakia, Switzerland, Yugoslavia), Federal National Assembly (Cameroon), Grand National Assembly (Rumania, Turkey), People's Assembly (Albania, Egypt), Supreme People's Assembly (North Korea), Congress (Chile, Colombia, Honduras, Liberia, Mexico, US, Venezuela), National Congress (Brazil, Dominican Republic, Ecuador, Guatemala), National People's Congress (People's Republic of China), People's Consultative Congress (Indonesia), House of Representatives (Cyprus, Gambia, Malta, New Zealand, Sierra Leone), People's Council (Maldive Islands, Syria), Great and General Council (San Marino), Council of the Valleys (Andorra), National Council (Monaco), Chamber of Deputies (Lebanon, Luxembourg), Legislative Chamber (Haiti), Chamber of Representatives (Morocco), Diet (Japan), Cortes (Spain), Eduskunta (Finland), Folketing (Denmark), Riksdag (Sweden), Althing (Iceland), Great People's Khural (Mongolia), Storting (Norway), States General (Netherlands), Supreme Soviet (USSR), Knesset (Israel), Volkskammer (East Germany), Oireachtas (Ireland), Sejm (Poland).

.3 **upper house, upper chamber; Senate** (Australia, Barbados, Belgium, Brazil, Canada, Chile, Colombia, Dominican Republic, Ecuador, Ethiopia, Fiji, France, Iran, Ireland, Italy, Jamaica, Liberia, Malagasy Republic, Malaysia, Mexico, Nicaragua, Paraguay, Philippines, Rhodesia, South Africa, Swaziland, Trinidad and Tobago, US, Venezuela), House of Elders (Afghanistan), Chamber of Nations (Czechoslovakia), Bundesrat (Austria, West Germany), Rajya Sabha (India), House of Councillors (Japan), Chamber of Notables (Jordan), King's Council (Laos), First Chamber (Netherlands), Lagting (Norway), Corporative Chamber (Portugal), Council of Nationalities (USSR), Council of States (Switzerland), Republican Senate (Turkey), **House of Lords** (United Kingdom).

.4 lower house, lower chamber; **House of Representatives,** House [informal] (Australia, Fiji, Jamaica, Japan, Liberia, Malaysia, Philippines, US), House of the People (Afghanistan), House of Assembly (Barbados, Rhodesia, South Africa, Swaziland), Chamber of Representatives (Belgium, Colombia), **Chamber of Deputies** (Brazil, Chile, Dominican Republic, Ecuador, Ethiopia, Italy, Jordan, Mexico, Nicaragua, Paraguay, Venezuela), National Assembly (France, Laos, Malagasy Republic, Portugal, Turkey), **House of Commons** (Canada, United Kingdom), Chamber of the People (Czechoslovakia), Bundestag (West Germany), Lok Sabha (India), Majlis (Iran), Dáil (Ireland), Second Chamber (Netherlands), Odelsting (Norway), Council of the Union (USSR), National Council (Switzerland).

.5 (US Senate committees) Aeronautical and Space Sciences; Agriculture and Forestry; Appropriations; Armed Services; Banking, Housing and Urban Affairs; Budget; Commerce; District of Columbia; Finance; Foreign Relations; Government Operations; Interior and Insular Affairs; Judiciary; Labor and Public Welfare; Post Office and Civil Service; Public Works; Rules and Administration; Veterans' Affairs.

.6 (US House of Representatives committees) Agriculture; Appropriations; Armed Services; Banking, Currency and Housing; Budget; District of Columbia; Education and Labor; Government Operations; House Administration; Interior and Insular Affairs; Internal Security; International Relations; Interstate and Foreign Commerce; Judiciary; Merchant Marine and Fisheries; Post Office and Civil Service; Public Works and Transportation; Rules; Science and Technology; Small Business; Standards of Official Conduct; Veterans' Affairs; Ways and Means.

.7 (US executive departments) Department of State; Department of the Treasury; Department of Justice; Department of Defense; Department of the Interior; Department of Agriculture; Department of Commerce; Department of Labor; Department of Health, Education, and Welfare; Department of Housing and Urban Development; Department of Transportation.

.8 cabinet, ministry, **council,** advisory council, council of state, privy council, divan; shadow cabinet; kitchen cabinet, camarilla.

.9 (US Cabinet) Secretary of State; Secretary of the Treasury; Secretary of Defense; Secretary of the Interior; Secretary of Agriculture; Secretary of Commerce; Secretary of Labor; Secretary of Health, Education, and Welfare; Attorney General; Secretary of Housing and Urban Development; Secretary of Transportation.

.10 (British Cabinet) Prime Minister; First Lord of the Treasury; Chief Secretary, Treasury; Lord Chancellor; Lord President of the Council; Lord Privy Seal; Chancellor of the Exchequer; First Secretary of State; Secretary of State for Foreign and Commonwealth Affairs; Secretary of State for the Home Department; Secretary of State for Employment and Productivity; Secretary of State for Defence; Secretary of State for Economic Affairs; Secretary of State for Scotland; Secretary of State for Education and Science; Secretary of State for Wales; First Lord of the Admiralty; President of the Board of Trade; Paymaster-General; Minister of Housing and Local Government; Minister of Technology; Minister of Transport; Minister of Power; President of the Board of Education; Minister of Agriculture, Fisheries and Food.

.11 (US Agencies) ACTION; Administrative Conference of the United States; Agency for International Development; American Battle Monuments Commission; American National Red Cross; Appalachian Regional Commission; Architect of the Capitol; Atomic Energy Commission, AEC; Central Intelligence Agency, CIA; Civil Aeronautics Board, CAB; Commission of Fine Arts; Commission on Civil Rights; Council of Economic Advisors; Council on Environmental Quality; Council on International Economic Policy; District of Columbia; Domestic Council; Economic Development Administration, EDA; Energy Research Development Administration; Environmental Protection Agency, EPA; Equal Employment Opportunity Commission, EEOC; Export-Import Bank of the United States, EIB; Farm Credit Administration, FCA; Federal Aviation Agency,

FAA; Federal Bureau of Investigation, FBI; Federal Communications Commission, FCC; Federal Deposit Insurance Corporation, FDIC; Federal Energy Administration; Federal Home Loan Bank Board; Federal Maritime Commission; Federal Mediation and Conciliation Service; Federal Power Commission, FPC; Federal Reserve System; Federal Trade Commission, FTC; Food and Drug Administration, FDA; Foreign Claims Settlement Commission of the United States; General Accounting Office, GAO; General Services Administration, GSA; Government Printing Office; Indian Claims Commission; Interstate Commerce Commission, ICC; Library of Congress; National Academy of Sciences; National Academy of Engineering; National Aeronautics and Space Administration, NASA; National Aeronautics and Space Council; National Credit Union Administration; National Foundation on the Arts and the Humanities; National Labor Relations Board, NLRB; National Mediation Board; National Science Foundation, NSF; National Security Council; Occupational Safety and Health Review Commission; Office of Consumer Affairs; Office of Economic Opportunity, OEO; Office of Intergovernmental Relations; Office of Management and Budget; Office of Science and Technology; Office of the Special Representative for Trade Negotiations; Panama Canal Company; Railroad Retirement Board; Renegotiation Board; St. Lawrence Seaway Development Corporation; Securities and Exchange Commission, SEC; Selective Service System; Small Business Administration; Smithsonian Institution; Tennessee Valley Authority, TVA; United States Arms Control and Disarmament Agency; United States Civil Service Commission; United States Information Agency, USIA; United States Postal Service; United States Tariff Commission; United States Tax Court; Veterans Administration, VA.

.12 **capitol, statehouse; courthouse;** city hall.

.13 **legislation, lawmaking,** legislature [archaic]; **enactment,** enaction, constitution, passage, passing; **resolution,** concurrent resolution, joint resolution; act 998.3.

.14 (legislative procedure) introduction, first reading, committee consideration, tabling, filing, second reading, deliberation, **debate,** third reading, **vote,** division, roll call; **filibustering,** filibuster, talkathon [slang]; cloture 144.5; **logrolling;** steamroller methods.

.15 **veto,** executive veto, absolute veto, qualified or limited veto, suspensive or suspensory veto, item veto, pocket veto; veto power; veto message; senatorial courtesy.

.16 **referendum,** constitutional referendum, statutory referendum, optional or facultative referendum, compulsory or mandatory referendum; **mandate; plebiscite,** plebiscitum; initiative, direct initiative, indirect initiative; recall.

.17 **bill,** omnibus bill, hold-up bill, companion bills amendment; **clause, proviso;** enacting clause, dragnet clause, escalator clause, saving clause; **rider;** joker [informal]; **calendar, motion;** question, previous question, privileged question.

.18 VERBS **legislate,** make or enact laws, **enact, pass,** constitute, ordain, put in force; **put through, jam** or **steamroller** or **railroad through** [informal], lobby through; table, pigeonhole; take the floor, get the floor, have the floor; yield the floor; **filibuster; logroll,** roll logs; **veto, pocket, kill; decree** 752.9.

.19 ADJS **legislative,** legislatorial, lawmaking; deliberative; **parliamentary, congressional;** senatorial; bicameral, unicameral.

743. UNITED NATIONS, INTERNATIONAL ORGANIZATIONS

.1 NOUNS **United Nations, UN;** League of Nations.

.2 (organs) Secretariat; General Assembly; Security Council; Trusteeship Council; International Court of Justice; Economic and Social Council, ECOSOC.

.3 (agencies) Food and Agricultural Organization, FAO; General Agreement on Tariffs and Trade, GATT; Intergovernmental Maritime Consultative Organization, IMCO; International Atomic Energy Agency, IAEA; International Bank for Reconstruction and Development, World Bank; International Civil Aviation Organization, ICAO; International Development Association, IDA; International Finance Corporation, IFO; International Labor Organization, ILO; International Monetary Fund, the Fund; International Telecommunication Union, ITU; United Nations Children's Fund, UNICEF; United Nations Educational, Scientific, and Cultural Organization, UNESCO; Universal Postal Union, UPU; World Health Organization,

WHO; World Meteorological Organization, WMO.

.4 (ECOSOC commissions) Statistical Commission; Commission on Human Rights, Subcommission on Prevention of Discrimination and the Protection of Minorities; Social Development Commission; Commission on the Status of Women; Commission on Narcotic Drugs; Population Commission; Economic Commission for Europe, ECE; Economic Commission for Asia and the Far East, ECAFE; Economic Commission for Latin America, ECLA; Economic Commission for Africa.

.5 (non-UN international organizations) World Council of Churches, WCC; Organization for Economic Cooperation and Development, OECD; North Atlantic Treaty Organization, NATO; Council of Europe; European Economic Community, Common Market, EEC; European Coal and Steel Community, ECSC; European Atomic Energy Community, Euratom; European Free Trade Association, EFTA; Colombo Plan for Cooperative Development in South and Southeast Asia, Colombo Plan; Central Treaty Organization, CENTO; Organization of American States, OAS; Latin American Free Trade Association, LAFTA; Central American Common Market, CACM; Arab League, AL; Organization of Petroleum Exporting Countries, OPEC; Organization of African Unity, OAU; Southeast Asia Treaty Organization, SEATO; ANZUS Council; African-Malagasy-Mauritius Common Organization, OCAM; Asian and Pacific Council, ASPAC; Bank for International Settlements, BIS; Council for Mutual Economic Assistance, COMECON; Eastern European Mutual Assistance Treaty, Warsaw Pact; French Community; International Bureau of Weights and Measures; International Committee of the Red Cross, ICRC; International Criminal Police Organization, Interpol; Nordic Council; Commonwealth of Nations, British Commonwealth [informal].

744. POLITICS

.1 NOUNS politics, polity, the art of the possible, "economics in action" [Robert La Follette]; practical politics, *Realpolitik* [Ger]; empirical politics; party *or* partisan politics, partisanism, –partism; reform politics; power politics, *Machtpolitik* [Ger]; machine politics, bossism [informal], Tammany Hall, Tammanism [informal]; pressure-group politics; confrontation politics; consensus politics; career politics; petty politics, peanut politics [slang]; pork-barrel politics; kid-glove politics [slang]; silk-stocking politics [slang]; ward politics.

.2 **political science**, poli-sci [slang], **politics, government, civics**; political philosophy, political theory; political behavior; political economy, comparative government, international relations, public administration; political geography, geopolitics, *Geopolitik* [Ger].

.3 **statesmanship, statecraft**, political *or* governmental leadership, national leadership; transpartisan *or* suprapartisan leadership; "the wise employment of individual meanness for the public good" [Lincoln]; kingcraft, queencraft; senatorship.

.4 **policy, polity**, public policy; line, **party line**, party principle *or* doctrine *or* philosophy, **position**, bipartisan policy; noninterference, nonintervention, *laissez-faire* [Fr], laissez-faireism; free enterprise; go-slow policy; government control, governmentalism; planned economy, managed currency, price supports, pump-priming [informal]; autarky, economic self-sufficiency; free trade; protection, protectionism; bimetallism; strict constructionism; localism, sectionalism, states' rights, nullification.

.5 **foreign policy, foreign affairs**; world politics; **diplomacy**, diplomatic *or* diplomatics [both archaic]; shirt-sleeve diplomacy; shuttle diplomacy; dollar diplomacy, dollar imperialism; brinkmanship; **nationalism, internationalism**; expansionism, imperialism, manifest destiny, colonialism, neocolonialism; spheres of influence; balance of power; containment; deterrence; militarism, preparedness; tough policy, the big stick [informal], twisting the lion's tail; nonresistance, isolationism, neutralism, coexistence, peaceful coexistence; détente; compromise, appeasement; peace offensive; good-neighbor policy; open-door policy, open door; Monroe Doctrine; Truman Doctrine; Eisenhower Doctrine; Nixon Doctrine.

.6 **program**; Square Deal [Theodore Roosevelt], New Deal [F. D. Roosevelt], Fair Deal [Truman], New Frontier [J. F. Kennedy], Great Society [L. B. Johnson]; austerity program; Beveridge Plan [Brit];

five-year plan; Cultural Revolution [China]; Point Four; Marshall Plan.

.7 **platform,** party platform, **program,** declaration of policy; **plank; issue;** keynote address, keynote speech.

.8 **political convention, convention;** conclave, powwow [informal]; national convention, quadrennial circus [informal]; state convention, county convention, preliminary convention, nominating convention; constitutional convention.

.9 **caucus,** legislative or congressional caucus, packed caucus; secret caucus.

.10 **candidacy,** candidature [Brit], **running, running for office,** throwing one's hat in the ring [informal], standing or standing for office [both Brit].

.11 **nomination,** caucus nomination, direct nomination, petition nomination; acceptance speech.

.12 **electioneering,** campaigning, politicking [informal], **stumping** or **whistle-stopping** [both informal]; **rally,** clambake [informal]; campaign dinner, $100-a-plate dinner, fund-raising dinner.

.13 **campaign,** all-out campaign, hard-hitting campaign, hoopla or hurrah campaign [informal]; **canvass, solicitation;** front-porch campaign; grass-roots campaign; stump excursion or stumping tour or whistle-stop campaign [all informal]; TV or media campaign; campaign commitments or promises; campaign fund, campaign contribution; campaign button.

.14 **smear campaign,** mudslinging campaign; **whispering campaign;** muckraking, **mudslinging** or **dirty politics** [both informal], character assassination; political canard, roorback; last-minute lie.

.15 **election,** general election, by-election; congressional election, presidential election; partisan election, nonpartisan election; **primary,** primary election; direct primary, open primary, closed primary, nonpartisan primary, mandatory primary, optional primary, preference primary, presidential primary, presidential preference primary, runoff primary; caucus 744.9; runoff, runoff election; disputed or contested election; referendum.

.16 **election district, precinct, ward, borough;** congressional district; safe district; swing district [informal]; close borough, pocket borough, rotten borough [all Brit]; gerrymander, gerrymandered district, shoestring district; silk-stocking district or ward; single-member district or constituency.

.17 **suffrage, franchise, the vote,** right to vote; universal suffrage, manhood suffrage, woman or female suffrage; suffragism, suffragettism; suffragist, woman-suffragist, suffragette; household franchise; one man, one vote.

.18 **voting,** going to the polls, casting one's ballot; preferential voting, preferential system, alternative vote; proportional representation, PR, cumulative system or voting, Hare system, list system; single system or voting, single transferrable vote; plural system or voting; single-member district 744.16; absentee voting; proxy voting, card voting; voting machine; election fraud, colonization, floating, repeating, ballot-box stuffing; vote 637.6.

.19 **ballot, slate, ticket,** proxy [dial]; straight ticket, split ticket; Australian ballot; Massachusetts ballot, office-block ballot; Indiana ballot, party-column ballot; absentee ballot; long ballot, blanket ballot, jungle ballot [informal]; short ballot; nonpartisan ballot; sample ballot; party emblem.

.20 **polls,** poll, polling place, polling station [Brit], balloting place; voting booth, polling booth; ballot box; voting machine; pollbook.

.21 **returns,** election returns, **poll,** count, official count; **recount;** landslide, tidal wave.

.22 **electorate,** electors; **constituency,** constituents; electoral college.

.23 **voter, elector, balloter;** registered voter; fraudulent voter, floater, repeater, ballot-box stuffer; proxy.

.24 **political party, party,** major party, minor party, third party, splinter party; "the madness of many for the gain of a few" [Pope]; Republican Party, GOP (Grand Old Party); Democratic Party; Conservative Party, Liberal Party, Socialist Party, Socialist Labor Party, Socialist Workers Party, Communist Party, Prohibition Party; Anti-Masonic Party, Anti-Monopoly Party, Constitutional Union Party, Democratic-Republican Party, States' Rights Democratic Party or Dixiecrats [informal], Farmer-Labor Party, Federalist Party, Free Soil Party, Greenback Party, American Party or Know-Nothing Party, Liberal Republican Party, Liberty Party, National Republican Party, People's Party or Populist Party, Progressive Party, Bull Moose Party, Whig Party; Conservative Party or Tory Party, Liberal Party, Labour Party [all England]; party in power, opposition party, loyal opposition; faction, camp; machine, political *or* party machine, Tammany Hall; city hall; one-party system, two-party system, multiple party system.

.25 partisanism, partisanship, partisanry; Republicanism; Conservatism, Toryism; Liberalism; Whiggism, Whiggery.

.26 nonpartisanism, independence, neutralism; mugwumpery, mugwumpism.

.27 partisan, party member, party man; regular, stalwart, loyalist; wheelhorse, party wheelhorse; heeler, ward heeler, party hack; party faithful; Republican, Democrat, etc.; registered Republican, registered Democrat; Labourite, Conservative, Tory, Liberal, Whig [all England].

.28 nonpartisan, independent, neutral, mugwump, undecided *or* uncommitted voter; swing vote.

.29 political influence, wire-pulling [informal]; social pressure, public opinion, special-interest pressure, group pressure; influence peddling; lobbying, lobbyism; logrolling, back scratching.

.30 wire-puller [informal]; influence peddler, four-percenter, power broker, fixer [informal], five-percenter [slang]; logroller.

.31 pressure group, interest group, special-interest group, special interests; vested interests; financial interests, farm interests, labor interests, etc.; minority interests, ethnic vote, black vote, Jewish vote, Italian vote, etc.; Black Power, White Power, Polish Power, etc.

.32 lobby, legislative lobby, special-interest lobby; lobbyist, registered lobbyist, lobbyer, parliamentary agent [England].

.33 front, movement, coalition, political front; popular front, people's front, communist front, etc.; grass-roots movement, ground swell.

.34 (political corruption) graft, boodling [slang], jobbery; pork-barrel legislation *or* pork-barreling; political intrigue.

.35 spoils of office; graft, boodle [slang]; slush fund [slang]; campaign fund, campaign contribution; public tit *or* public trough [both slang]; spoils system; cronyism, nepotism.

.36 political patronage, patronage, favors of office, pork *or* pork barrel [both informal], plum, melon [informal].

.37 political *or* official jargon; officialese, federalese, Washingtonese, gobbledygook [all informal]; bafflegab [slang]; political doubletalk, bunkum [informal]; pussyfooting; pointing with pride and viewing with alarm.

.38 VERBS politick [informal], politicize; look after one's fences *or* mend one's fences [both informal]; caucus; gerrymander.

.39 run for office, run; throw *or* toss one's hat in the ring [informal], enter the lists *or* arena, stand *or* stand for office [both Brit]; contest a seat [Brit].

.40 electioneer, campaign; stump, take the stump, take to the stump, stump the country, take to the hustings, hit the campaign trail, whistle-stop [all informal]; canvass, go to the voters *or* electorate, solicit votes, ring doorbells; shake hands and kiss babies.

.41 support, back *or* back up [both informal], endorse; go with the party, follow the party line; get on the bandwagon [informal]; nominate, elect, vote 637.18–20.

.42 hold office, hold *or* occupy a post, fill an office, be the incumbent, be in office.

.43 ADJS political, politic, politico–; governmental, civic; geopolitical; statesmanlike; diplomatic; suffragist; politico-commercial, politico-diplomatic, politico-ecclesiastical, politico-economic(al), politico-ethical, politico-geographical, politico-judicial, politico-military, politico-moral, politico-religious, politico-scientific, politico-social, politico-theological.

.44 partisan, party; bipartisan, biparty, two-party.

.45 nonpartisan, independent, neutral, mugwumpian *or* mugwumpish [both informal], on the fence.

745. POLITICO-ECONOMIC PRINCIPLES

.1 NOUNS conservatism, conservativeness, rightism; "an unhappy crossbreed, the mule of politics that engenders nothing" [Disraeli]; old school tie [Brit]; standpattism, unprogressiveness, backwardness; ultraconservatism, reaction, reactionism, reactionarism, reactionaryism, reactionariness, die-hardism [informal], Toryism, Bourbonism; extreme rightism, radical rightism, know-nothingism; extreme right, extreme right wing; social Darwinism; laissez-faireism 706.1; royalism, monarchism.

.2 moderatism, moderateness, moderantism; middle of the road, moderate position, fence [informal], center, third force.

.3 liberalism, progressivism, leftism; left, left wing.

.4 radicalism, extremism, ultraism; radicalization; revolutionism; ultraconservatism 745.1; extreme left, extreme left wing, left-wing extremism; New Left, Old Left; Jacobinism, sans-culottism, *sans-culotterie* [Fr]; **anarchism, nihilism,** syndicalism, anarcho-syndicalism, criminal syndicalism.

.5 **communism, Bolshevism, Marxism,** Marxism-Leninism, Leninism, Trotskyism, Stalinism, Maoism, Titoism, Castroism, revisionism; Marxian socialism; dialectical materialism; democratic centralism; dictatorship of the proletariat; **Communist Party;** Communist International, Comintern; Communist Information Bureau, Cominform; iron curtain 730.5.

.6 **socialism,** collective ownership, public ownership; **collectivism;** creeping socialism; state socialism, *Staatssozialismus* [Ger]; guild socialism; Fabian socialism, Fabianism; utopian socialism; Marxian socialism, Marxism 745.5; phalansterism; Owenism; Saint-Simonianism, Saint-Simonism; **nationalization.**

.7 **welfarism,** welfare statism; womb-to-tomb security, cradle-to-grave security; social welfare; social security, social insurance; old-age and survivors insurance; unemployment compensation, unemployment insurance; workmen's compensation, workmen's compensation insurance; health insurance, Medicare, Medicaid, state medicine, **socialized medicine;** sickness insurance; public assistance, **welfare, relief,** welfare payments, aid to dependent children, ADC, old-age assistance, aid to the blind, aid to the permanently and totally disabled; guaranteed income, guaranteed annual income; welfare state; welfare capitalism.

.8 **capitalism,** capitalistic system, **free enterprise,** private enterprise, free-enterprise economy, free-enterprise system, free economy; finance capitalism; *laissez-faire* [Fr], laissez-faireism; private sector; private ownership; state capitalism; **individualism,** rugged individualism.

.9 **conservative,** conservatist, **rightist, right-winger;** Bircher; "a person who has something to conserve" [Edward Young], "the leftover progressive of an earlier generation" [Edmund Fuller]; standpat *or* standpatter [both informal]; hard hat; social Darwinist; ultraconservative, extreme right-winger, **reactionary,** reactionarist, reactionist, diehard, Bourbon, Tory; **royalist, monarchist,** imperialist; **right, right wing; radical right.**

.10 **moderate,** moderatist, moderationist,

moderantist, centrist, middle-of-the-roader [informal]; center.

.11 **liberal,** liberalist, **progressive,** progressivist, **leftist, left-winger;** welfare stater; Lib-Lab [Brit informal]; **left.**

.12 **radical, extremist,** ultra, ultraist; **revolutionary,** revolutionist; subversive; extreme left-winger, left-wing extremism, **red** [informal], Bolshevik; yippie; Jacobin, sansculotte; **anarchist,** nihilist, syndicalist, anarcho-syndicalist; Wobbly [slang]; mild radical, parlor Bolshevik [informal], pink *or* parlor pink [both slang], pinko [derog]; lunatic fringe.

.13 **Communist,** Bolshevist; Bolshevik, **Red** [informal], bolshie [slang], commie [derog]; Marxist, Leninist, Marxist-Leninist, Trotskyite *or* Trotskyist, Stalinist, Maoist, Titoist, Castroite, revisionist; card-carrying Communist, avowed Communist; fellow traveler, Communist sympathizer, comsymp [slang].

.14 **socialist,** collectivist; state socialist; Fabian, Fabian socialist; Marxist 745.13; utopian socialist; Fourierist, phalansterian; Saint-Simonian; Owenite.

.15 **capitalist,** individualist, rugged individualist; rich man 837.6,7.

.16 VERBS **politicize;** democratize, republicanize, socialize, communize; nationalize 815.7.

.17 ADJS **conservative, right-wing,** right of center; old-line, die-hard, standpat [informal], unprogressive, nonprogressive; ultraconservative, **reactionary,** reactionist.

.18 **moderate,** centrist, middle-of-the-road [informal].

.19 **liberal,** liberalistic, liberalist, **progressive,** progressivistic; **leftist, left-wing,** on the left, left of center.

.20 **radical, extreme, extremist,** extremistic, ultraist, ultraistic; revolutionary, revolutionist; subversive; ultraconservative 745.17; extreme left-wing, **red** [informal]; anarchistic, nihilistic, syndicalist, anarcho-syndicalist; mildly radical, pink [slang].

.21 **Communist, communistic,** Bolshevik, Bolshevist, bolshie [slang], Red [informal], commie [derog]; **Marxist,** Leninist, Marxist-Leninist, Trotskyite *or* Trotskyist, Stalinist, Maoist, Titoist, Castroite, revisionist.

.22 **socialist, socialistic,** collectivistic; Fabian; Fourieristic, phalansterian; Saint-Simonian.

.23 **capitalist, capitalistic,** bourgeois, individualistic, nonsocialistic, free-enterprise, private-enterprise.

746. POLITICIAN

.1 NOUNS **politician,** politico, political leader, professional politician, –crat or –ocrat; party leader, party boss or party chieftain [both informal]; machine politician, political hack, Tammany man; pol [informal]; old campaigner, war-horse; wheelhorse; reform politician, reformer.

.2 **statesman,** stateswoman, solon, public man, national leader; "a politician who is held upright by equal pressure from all directions" [Eric Johnston], "a successful politician who is dead" [Thomas B. Reed]; elder statesman.

.3 **legislator, lawmaker,** solon, lawgiver; **congressman,** congresswoman, Member of Congress; **senator; representative;** Speaker of the House; majority leader, minority leader; floor leader; whip, party whip; Member of Parliament, MP; state senator, assemblyman, chosen freeholder, councilman, alderman, city father.

.4 (petty politician) **two-bit** or **peanut politician** [slang], politicaster, statemonger [archaic], political dabbler; hack, party hack.

.5 (corrupt politician) **dirty** or **crooked politician** [informal], jackleg politician [slang]; **grafter,** boodler [informal]; spoilsman, spoilsmonger; influence peddler 744.30.

.6 (political intriguer) strategist, machinator, gamesman, wheeler-dealer [slang]; operator or finagler or **wire-puller** [all informal]; **logroller,** pork-barrel politician; Machiavellian 654.8; behind-the-scenes operator, gray eminence, *éminence grise* [Fr], power behind the throne, kingmaker [informal].

.7 (political leader) **boss** [slang], cacique, sachem, man higher up [informal]; keynoter [informal], policy maker; standardbearer; ringleader 648.11.

.8 **henchman,** hanger-on; heeler or **ward heeler** [both informal]; hatchet man.

.9 **candidate, aspirant,** hopeful or political hopeful [both informal], office seeker or hunter, baby kisser [slang]; running mate; **dark horse;** stalking-horse; favorite son; presidential timber; defeated candidate, also-ran or dud [both slang]; lame duck.

.10 **campaigner,** electioneer, **stumper** [informal], whistle-stopper [slang], stump speaker or orator [informal].

.11 **officeholder,** office-bearer [Brit], jack-in-office, public servant, public official, incumbent, holdover, lame duck; new broom [slang]; president-elect; ins, the powers that be.

.12 **political worker, committeeman, committeewoman,** precinct captain, precinct leader, district leader; party chairman, state chairman, national chairman, chairman of the national committee.

.13 ADJS **statesmanlike,** statesmanly.

747. DIRECTION, MANAGEMENT

.1 NOUNS **direction, management, managing,** managery [archaic], handling, **running** [informal], **conduct;** governance, **command, control, government** 741; **authority** 739; **regulation,** ordering, husbandry; manipulation; **guidance, lead, leading;** steering, steerage, pilotage, the conn, the helm, the wheel.

.2 **supervision, superintendence,** intendance, **bossing** [informal]; **surveillance,** oversight, eye; **charge, care, auspices, jurisdiction; responsibility,** accountability 962.2.

.3 **administration,** executive function or role, command function; **decision-making; disposition,** disposal, **dispensation;** officiation.

.4 **directorship, directorate, managership,** leadership, headship, governorship, chairmanship, convenership [Brit], presidency, generalship, captainship; mastership 739.7; **dictatorship, sovereignty** 739.8; superintendence or **superintendency,** intendancy, foremanship, overseership, supervisorship; stewardship, custody, guardianship, proctorship.

.5 **helm,** rudder, tiller, wheel, **reins,** reins of government.

.6 **domestic management, housekeeping,** homemaking, housewifery, ménage, husbandry [archaic]; domestic economy, home economics.

.7 **efficiency engineering,** scientific management, industrial engineering, management engineering, management consulting; management theory; efficiency expert, management consultant; time and motion study, time-motion study, time study.

.8 VERBS **direct, manage, regulate, conduct, carry on, handle, run** [informal]; **control, command, govern** 741.12; pull the strings or **mastermind** [both informal]; quarterback, call the signals; **order, prescribe;** lay down the law, make the rules; **head, head up,** officer, captain, skipper [informal];

lead, take the lead, lead on; manipulate, maneuver, engineer; take command 739.14; be responsible for.

.9 guide, steer, drive, run [informal]; herd, shepherd; pilot, take the helm, be at the helm *or* wheel *or* tiller *or* rudder, hold the reins, be in the driver's seat.

.10 supervise, superintend, boss [informal], oversee, overlook, ride herd on [informal], stand over, keep an eye on *or* upon, keep in order; cut work out for; strawboss [informal]; take care of 699.19.

.11 administer, administrate; officiate; preside, preside over, preside at the board; chair, chairman, occupy the chair.

.12 ADJS directing, directive, directory, directorial; managing, managerial; commanding, controlling, governing 741.18; regulating, regulative, regulatory; head, chief; leading, guiding.

.13 supervising, supervisory, overseeing, superintendent, boss [informal]; in charge 739.21.

.14 administrative, administrating; ministerial, executive; officiating, presiding.

.15 ADVS in the charge of, in the hands of, in the care of; under the auspices of, under the aegis of; in one's charge, on one's hands, under one's care, under one's jurisdiction.

748. DIRECTOR

.1 NOUNS director, *directeur* [Fr], governor, rector, manager, administrator, intendant, conductor; person in charge, responsible person; ship's husband, supercargo; impresario, producer; deputy, agent 781.

.2 superintendent, super [informal]; supervisor, foreman, monitor, head, headman, overman, Big Brother [Orwell], boss [informal], chief, gaffer, ganger [both Brit], taskmaster; sirdar [India], overseer, overlooker; inspector, surveyor, visitor; proctor; subforeman, straw boss [informal]; slave driver; boatswain; floorman, floorwalker, floor manager; noncommissioned officer 749.19; controller, comptroller, auditor.

.3 executive, executive officer, executive director, executive secretary; officer, official; president, prexy [slang], chief executive officer, chief executive, managing director, provost, prefect, warden, archon; magistrate; chairman of the board; chancellor, vice-chancellor; vice-president, VP, veep [informal]; secretary; treasurer;

dean; management, the administration 748.11.

.4 steward, bailiff [Brit], factor [Scot], seneschal; majordomo, butler, housekeeper, *maître d'hôtel* [Fr]; master of ceremonies, MC *or* emcee [both informal], master of the revels; proctor, procurator, attorney; guardian, custodian 699.6–12; curator, librarian; landreeve; croupier.

.5 chairman, chairwoman, chair, convener [Brit], speaker, presiding officer.

.6 leader, conductor [archaic]; file leader, fugleman; pacemaker, pacesetter; bellwether, bell mare, bell cow, Judas goat; standard-bearer, torchbearer; leader of men, born leader, charismatic leader *or* figure, inspired leader; messiah, Mahdi; führer, duce; forerunner 66.1; ringleader 648.11; precentor, coryphaeus, choragus, symphonic conductor, choirmaster 464.17, 18.

.7 guide, guider; shepherd, herd, herdsman, drover, cowherd, goatherd, etc.; tour guide, tour director *or* conductor, cicerone, mercury [archaic], courier, dragoman; pilot, river pilot, navigator, helmsman, timoneer, steersman, steerer, coxswain, boatsteerer, boatheader; automatic pilot, Gyropilot; pointer, guidepost 568.4.

.8 guiding star, cynosure [archaic], polestar, polar star, lodestar, Polaris, North Star.

.9 compass, magnetic compass, gyrocompass, gyroscopic compass, gyrostatic compass, Gyrosin compass, surveyor's compass, mariner's compass; needle, magnetic needle; direction finder, radio compass, radio direction finder, RDF; inertial guidance *or* inertial navigation system; loran, shoran.

.10 directory, guidebook, handbook, Baedeker; city directory, business directory; telephone directory, telephone book, phone book [informal], classified directory, Yellow Pages; bibliography; catalog, index, handlist, checklist, finding list; itinerary, road map, roadbook; reference book 605.6.

.11 directorate, directory, management, the administration, the brass *or* top brass [both informal], the people upstairs *or* the people in the front office [both informal], executive hierarchy; the executive, executive arm *or* branch; cabinet; board, governing board *or* body, board of directors, board of trustees, board of regents; steering committee, executive committee, interlocking directorate; cadre, executive council; infrastructure; council 755.

749. MASTER

.1 NOUNS master, lord, lord and master, overlord, seigneur or seignior, paramount, lord paramount, liege, liege lord, *padrone* [Ital], *patron, chef* [both Fr], patroon; **chief** or **boss** [both informal], sahib [India], *bwana* [Swahili]; employer; husband, man of the house, master of the house, goodman [archaic or dial], paterfamilias; patriarch, elder; teacher, rabbi, guru, starets; church dignitary, ecclesiarch 1038.9.

.2 **mistress**, governess, dame, madam; **matron, housewife**, homemaker, goodwife [Scot], lady of the house, chatelaine; housemistress, housemother; rectoress, abbess, mother superior; great lady, first lady; matriarch, dowager.

.3 **chief**, principal; top dog or kingpin or kingfish [all informal]; master, dean, doyen, doyenne [fem], high priest [informal], superior, senior; **leader** 748.6; important person, personage 672.8–10.

.4 **figurehead**, nominal head, dummy, lay figure, front man or front [both informal], stooge or Charlie McCarthy [both slang], puppet, creature.

.5 **governor, ruler**, –arch, –crat or –ocrat; **captain**, master, **commander**, commandant, intendant, castellan, chatelain, chatelaine; **director, manager**, executive 748.3.

.6 **head of state, chief of state**; premier, **prime minister, chancellor**, grand vizier, dewan [India]; doge; **president**, chief executive, the man in the White House.

.7 **potentate, sovereign, monarch, ruler, prince**, dynast, **crowned head, emperor**, *imperator* [L], king-emperor, **king**, anointed king, majesty, royalty, royal, royal personage; petty king, tetrarch, kinglet; grand duke; paramount, lord paramount, suzerain, overlord, overking, high king; **chief, chieftain**, high chief; prince consort 918.7.

.8 (rulers) **caesar**, *Kaiser* [Ger], **czar;** Holy Roman Emperor; Dalai Lama; **pharaoh;** pendragon, rig, ardri; **mikado**, tenno; shogun, tycoon; khan or cham; shah, padishah; negus; bey; **sheikh;** sachem, sagamore; Inca; cacique; kaid.

.9 (princes of India) **raja, maharaja**, rana, nizam, jam; Great Mogul, Mogul.

.10 (Muslim rulers) **sultan**, Grand Turk, grand seignior; caliph; imam; hakim; khan or cham; nizam, nawab; emir; Great Mogul, Mogul.

.11 **sovereign queen, sovereign princess, princess, queen**, queen regent, queen regnant, **empress, czarina**, *Kaiserin* [Ger]; rani, maharani [both India]; grand duchess; queen consort.

.12 **regent**, protector, prince regent, queen regent.

.13 (regional governors) **governor**, governor-general, lieutenant governor; **viceroy**, vice-king, exarch, proconsul, khedive, stadtholder; nabob, nawab, subahdar [all India]; gauleiter; eparch; palatine; tetrarch; burgrave; collector; hospodar, vaivode; dey, bey or beg, beglerbeg, wali or vali, satrap; provincial.

.14 **tyrant, despot**, warlord; **autocrat**, autarch; oligarch; absolute ruler or master or monarch, omnipotent or all-powerful ruler; **dictator**, duce, führer, commissar, pharaoh, caesar, czar; usurper, arrogator; **oppressor, hard master**, driver, **slave driver**, Simon Legree [Harriet B. Stowe]; **martinet, disciplinarian**, stickler.

.15 **the authorities, the powers that be**, ruling class or classes, **the Establishment**, the interests, the power elite, the power structure; **they**, them; the inner circle; the ins or the ingroup [both informal]; **management, the administration**; higher echelons, **top brass** [informal]; higher-ups, the people upstairs or the people in the front office [all informal]; **the top** [informal], the corridors of power; prelacy, hierarchy; ministry; **bureaucracy, officialdom**; directorate 748.11.

.16 **official, officer**, officiary, functionary or functionnaire, *fonctionnaire* [Fr]; **public official**, public servant; officeholder, office-bearer or placeman [both Brit]; civil servant; bureaucrat, mandarin, red-tapist; petty tyrant, jack-in-office.

.17 (public officials) **minister**, secretary, secretary of state [Brit], undersecretary, cabinet minister, cabinet member, minister of state [Brit]; **chancellor**; warden; archon; magistrate; syndic; commissioner; commissar; county commissioner; **city manager, mayor**, *maire* [Fr], lord mayor, burgomaster or burghermaster; headman, induna [Africa]; **councilman**, councilwoman, councillor, city councilman, elder, city father, alderman, bailie [Scot], selectman; supervisor, county supervisor; reeve, portreeve; legislator 746.3.

.18 **commissioned officer, officer;** top brass, the brass [both informal]; **commander in chief**, generalissimo, captain general; hetman, sirdar; general of the army, general of the air force, five-star general [informal], **marshal,** *maréchal* [Fr], field marshal; general officer, **general,** four-star general [informal]; lieutenant general, three-star general [informal]; major general, two-star general [informal], brigadier general, one-star general [informal], brigadier [Brit]; field officer; **colonel,** chicken colonel [slang]; lieutenant colonel; **major;** company officer; **captain,** subahdar, risaldar [both India]; subaltern [Brit], **lieutenant,** jemadar [India]; first lieutenant; second lieutenant, shavetail [slang], sublieutenant [Brit]; **commander,** commandant, the Old Man [slang]; **commanding officer,** CO, executive officer, exec [slang]; chief of staff; aide, aide-de-camp, ADC; officer of the day, OD, orderly officer [Brit]; staff officer; senior officer, junior officer.

.19 **noncommissioned officer,** noncom [informal], NCO; warrant officer, chief warrant officer; centurion; sergeant, sarge [slang], havildar [India]; first sergeant, top sergeant [informal], topkick [slang]; sergeant major, master sergeant, sergeant first class, technical sergeant, platoon sergeant, staff sergeant, mess sergeant, color sergeant, acting sergeant, lance sergeant [Brit]; **corporal,** naik [India]; acting corporal, lance corporal [Brit], lance-jack [Brit slang].

.20 **naval officer;** fleet admiral, navarch, **admiral,** vice admiral, rear admiral, **commodore, captain, commander,** lieutenant commander, **lieutenant,** lieutenant junior grade, ensign; warrant officer; petty officer, master chief petty officer, senior chief petty officer, chief petty officer, petty officer first class, petty officer second class, petty officer third class; skipper.

.21 (heraldic officials) herald, king of arms, king at arms, earl marshal; Garter, Garter King of Arms, Clarenceux, Clarenceux King of Arms, Norroy and Ulster, Norroy and Ulster King of Arms, Norroy, Norroy King of Arms, Lyon, Lyon King of Arms; College of Arms.

750. SERVANT, EMPLOYEE

.1 NOUNS **retainer,** dependent, follower; myrmidon, yeoman; vassal, liege, liege man, feudatory, homager; inferior, **underling, subordinate,** understrapper; **minion,** creature, hanger-on, lackey, flunky, stooge [informal]; peon, serf, slave 764.7.

.2 **servant,** servitor, help; domestic, domes-

tic servant, house servant; **menial,** drudge, slavey [informal]; scullion, turnspit.

.3 **employee;** pensioner, **hireling, mercenary,** myrmidon; hired man, hired hand, man *or* girl Friday, right-hand man, assistant 787.6; worker 718.

.4 **man,** manservant, serving man, gillie [Scot], **boy,** *garçon* [Fr], houseboy, houseman; butler; valet, *valet de chambre* [Fr], gentleman, gentleman's gentleman; driver, chauffeur, coachman; gardener; lord-in-waiting, lord of the bedchamber, equerry.

.5 **attendant,** tender, usher, squire, yeoman; errand boy, errand girl, gofer [slang], office boy, office girl, copyboy; page, footboy; bellboy, bellman, bellhop; cabin boy; printer's devil; chore boy; caddie; bootblack, boots [Brit]; trainbearer; cupbearer, Ganymede, Hebe; orderly, batman [Brit]; steward, **stewardess, hostess,** airline stewardess, airline hostess.

.6 **lackey, flunky,** livery *or* liveried servant; **footman,** *valet de pied* [Fr].

.7 **waiter, waitress;** carhop; counterman, soda jerk [informal]; busboy; headwaiter, *maître d'hôtel* [Fr], maitre d' [informal]; hostess; wine steward, sommelier; bartender, barkeeper *or* barkeep, barman, barmaid [Brit].

.8 **maid, maidservant,** servitress, **girl,** servant girl, *bonne* [Fr], serving girl, wench, biddy [informal], hired girl; lady-help [Brit], au pair girl, ayah [India], amah [China]; live-in maid, live-out maid; **handmaid,** handmaiden; **lady's maid,** waiting maid *or* woman, gentlewoman, abigail, soubrette; lady-in-waiting, maid-in-waiting, lady of the bedchamber; companion; chaperon; betweenmaid, tweeny [both Brit]; duenna; parlormaid; kitchenmaid, scullery maid; cook; housemaid, chambermaid, *femme de chambre, fille de chambre* [both Fr], upstairs maid; nursemaid 699.8.

.9 **factotum, do-all** [archaic], general servant [Brit], man of all work; maid of all work, domestic drudge, slavey [informal].

.10 **majordomo, steward,** house steward, **butler,** chamberlain, *maître d'hôtel* [Fr], seneschal; **housekeeper.**

.11 **staff, personnel, employees,** help, hired help, the help, **crew, gang,** men, force, servantry, retinue 73.6.

.12 **service,** servitude [archaic], servitorship, *servitium* [L]; **employment, employ;** ministry, ministration, attendance, tendance; serfdom, peonage, slavery 764.1.

.13 VERBS serve, work for, be in service with; minister or administer to, pander to, do service to; help 785.11; care for, do for [informal], look after, take care of; wait, wait on or upon, attend, tend, attend on or upon, dance attendance upon, wait on hand and foot; lackey, valet, maid, chore; drudge 716.14.

.14 ADJS serving, servitorial, servitial, ministering, waiting, attending, attendant; in the train of, in one's pay or employ; helping 785.20; menial, servile 907.12.

751. PRECEPT

.1 NOUNS precept, prescript, prescription, teaching; instruction, direction, charge, commission, injunction, dictate; order, command 752.

.2 rule, law, canon, rubric, maxim, dictum, moral; norm, convention; formula, form; rule of action or conduct, moral precept; commandment, mitzvah [Heb]; ordinance, imperative, regulation, règlement [Fr]; principle, principium, settled principle, general principle or truth, tenet; standard; guideline, working rule, working principle; guiding principle, golden rule; code.

.3 formula, form [archaic], recipe, receipt; prescription; formulary.

.4 ADJS preceptive, didactic, instructive, prescriptive; prescript, prescribed, mandatory, hard and fast, binding, dictated; formulary, standard, regulation, official, authoritative, canonical, statutory, rubric(al).

752. COMMAND

.1 NOUNS command, commandment, order, direct order, bidding, behest, hest [archaic], imperative, dictate, dictation, will, pleasure, say-so [informal], word, word of command, mot d'ordre [Fr]; special order.

.2 injunction, charge, commission, mandate.

.3 direction, directive, instruction, rule, regulation; prescript, prescription, precept 751; general orders.

.4 decree, decreement [archaic], decretum, decretal, rescript, fiat, edict, edictum [L]; law 998.3; rule, ruling, dictum, ipse dixit; ordinance, ordonnance [Fr], appointment [archaic]; proclamation, pronouncement, pronunciamento, declaration, ukase; bull, brevet [archaic]; decree-law,

décret loi [Fr]; senatus consultum [L], senatus consult; diktat.

.5 summons, bidding, beck, call, calling, nod, beck and call, preconization; convocation, evocation, calling forth, invocation; requisition, indent [Brit].

.6 (legal order) injunction, interdict, mandatory injunction, prohibitory injunction; mandate; writ, process, precept; notice, notification; warrant, bench warrant, justice's warrant, search warrant, death warrant, warrant of arrest, warrant of attorney; mittimus, mandamus, caveat, capias, nisi prius [Brit], fieri facias, levari facias, elegit, habere facias possessionem, habere facias seisinam.

.7 summons, writ of summons, subpoena, citation, monition; certiorari; venire or venire facias, venire facias de novo or venire de novo; habeas corpus, writ of habeas corpus, habeas corpus ad faciendum et recipiendum or habeas corpus cum causa, habeas corpus ad prosequendum, habeas corpus ad subjiciendum, habeas corpus ad testificandum; garnishment.

.8 process server, summoner.

.9 VERBS command, order, dictate, direct, instruct, mandate, bid, enjoin, charge, commission, call on or upon; issue a writ or injunction; decree, rule, ordain, promulgate; give an order or direct order, issue a command, say the word, give the word or word of command; call the tune [informal], call the signals or play [slang]; order about or around; proclaim, declare, pronounce 559.12,13.

.10 prescribe, require, demand, dictate, impose, lay down, set, appoint, make obligatory or mandatory; authorize 777.11.

.11 lay down the law, put one's foot down [informal], read the riot act.

.12 summon, call, demand, preconize; call for, send for or after, bid come; cite, summons [informal], subpoena, serve; page; convoke, convene, call together; call away; muster, invoke, conjure; order up, summon up, muster up, call up, conjure up; evoke, call forth, summon forth, call out; recall, call back, call in; requisition, indent [Brit].

.13 ADJS mandatory, mandated, imperative, compulsory, prescript, prescriptive, obligatory, must [informal]; dictated, imposed, required, entailed, decretory; decisive, final, peremptory, absolute, hard-and-fast, ultimate, conclusive, binding, irrevocable, without appeal.

.14 commanding, imperative, jussive, peremptory; **directive, instructive; mandating,** dictating, compelling, obligating, **prescriptive,** preceptive; decretory, decretive, decretal.

.15 ADVS **commandingly, imperatively,** peremptorily.

.16 **by order** *or* **command,** at the word of command, as ordered *or* required, to order; mandatorily, compulsorily, obligatorily.

753. DEMAND

.1 NOUNS **demand, claim, call; requisition,** requirement, order, rush order, indent [Brit]; call for, demand for; heavy demand, draft, drain, levy, tax, taxing; imposition, impost, tribute, duty, contribution; insistent demand, rush; exorbitant *or* extortionate demand, exaction, extortion, blackmail; **ultimatum,** nonnegotiable demand; notice, warning 703.

.2 **stipulation, provision,** proviso, condition, term, string [informal], exception, reservation; qualification 507.

.3 **insistence, importunity,** importunateness, importunacy, **demandingness,** pertinaciousness, pertinacity; pressure, pressingness, urgency, exigency 672.4; persistence 625.1.

.4 VERBS **demand, ask, ask for,** make a demand; **call for,** call on *or* upon one for, appeal to one for; cry for, clamor for; **claim, challenge, require;** levy, **impose,** impose on one for; **exact, extort,** screw; blackmail; **requisition,** make *or* put in requisition, indent [Brit]; **order,** put in *or* place an order, order up; deliver *or* issue an ultimatum; warn 703.5.

.5 **claim, pretend to, lay claim to, challenge;** assert *or* vindicate a claim *or* right *or* title to.

.6 **stipulate,** stipulate for, specifically provide, set conditions *or* terms, make reservations; qualify 507.3,4.

.7 **insist, insist on** *or* **upon,** stick to [slang], set one's heart *or* mind upon; **take one's stand upon,** stand on *or* upon; stand upon one's rights, **put one's foot down** [informal]; brook *or* take no denial, not take 'no' for an answer; **maintain, contend,** assert 523.4; urge, press 648.14; **persist** 625.2–6.

.8 ADJS **demanding, exacting,** exigent; draining, taxing, exorbitant, extortionate, grasping; **insistent,** instant, **importunate,** urgent, pertinacious, pressing, loud, clamant, crying, clamorous; persistent 625.7.

.9 **requisitorial,** requisitory.

.10 ADVS **demandingly, exactingly,** exigently; exorbitantly, extortionately; **insistently, importunately, urgently,** pressingly, clamorously, loudly, clamantly.

.11 **on demand,** at demand, **on call,** upon presentation.

754. ADVICE

.1 NOUNS **advice, counsel, recommendation, suggestion;** proposal; advising, advocacy; **direction, instruction,** guidance, briefing; **exhortation,** hortation, expostulation, remonstrance; **admonition,** monition, caution, caveat, **warning** 703; **idea,** thought, opinion 501.6; **consultation,** parley 597.6; council 755.

.2 **piece of advice, word of advice, word to the wise,** *verbum sapienti* [L], verb. sap. *or* verbum sap., word in the ear, **flea in the ear** [informal], **tip** [informal], a few words of wisdom, one's two cents' worth [informal].

.3 **adviser, counsel, counselor, consultant,** professional consultant, expert; instructor, guide, **mentor,** nestor, orienter; confidant, personal adviser; admonisher, monitor, Dutch uncle; Polonius [Shakespeare], preceptist; **teacher** 565; meddler, buttinsky [slang], kibitzer *or* backseat driver [both informal].

.4 **advisee,** counselee.

.5 VERBS **advise, counsel, recommend, suggest, advocate,** propose, submit; **instruct,** coach, guide, direct, brief; prescribe; give a piece of advice, put a flea in one's ear [informal], speak words of wisdom; meddle, kibitz [informal]; confer, consult with 597.11.

.6 **admonish, exhort,** expostulate, remonstrate, preach; **enjoin, charge,** call upon one to; caution, issue a caveat; warn 703.5,6; move, prompt, **urge, incite, encourage, induce,** persuade 648.12–23.

.7 **take** *or* **accept advice, follow advice,** follow, follow implicitly; solicit advice, desire guidance, implore counsel; **be advised by;** have at one's elbow, take one's cue from.

.8 ADJS **advisory,** recommendatory; consultative, consultatory; directive, instructive; **admonitory,** monitory, monitorial, cautionary, **warning** 703.7; **expostulative,** expostulatory, **remonstrative,** remonstratory, remonstrant; **exhortative,** exhortatory, hortative, hortatory, preachy [informal], **didactic,** moralistic, sententious.

755. COUNCIL

.1 NOUNS **council,** *concilium* [L], deliberative *or* advisory body, deliberative assembly, consultative assembly; chamber, **board,** court, bench; **congress,** diet, synod, soviet; legislature 742; **cabinet,** divan, council of ministers, council of state, US Cabinet 742.9, British Cabinet 742.10; kitchen cabinet, camarilla; staff; junta, directory; Sanhedrin; privy council, common council, county council, parish council, borough council, city council; brain trust [informal], group *or* corps *or* body of advisers; council of war; council fire; syndicate, **association** 788; **conference** 597.6; **assembly** 74.2; tribunal 1001.

.2 **committee,** subcommittee, standing committee, special committee, ad hoc committee; committee of one.

.3 **forum,** discussion group, **round table, panel;** open forum.

.4 ecclesiastical council, chapter, classis, conclave, conference, congregation, consistory, convention, convocation, presbytery, session, synod, vestry; parochial council, parochial church council; diocesan conference, diocesan court; provincial court, plenary council; ecumenical council; Council of Nicaea, Council of Trent, Lateran Council, Vatican Council; conciliarism.

.5 ADJS **conciliar,** council; consultative, deliberative, advisory; synodal, synodic(al).

.6 ADVS **in council, in conference, in consultation, in a huddle** [slang], in conclave; **in session,** sitting.

756. COMPULSION

.1 NOUNS **compulsion,** obligation, obligement; necessity 639; inevitability 639.7; **irresistibility,** compulsiveness; forcing, enforcement; **constraint,** coaction; **restraint** 760.

.2 **force,** *ultima ratio* [L]; **brute force,** naked force, rule of might, big battalions, **main force,** physical force; the right of the strong, the law of the jungle; **tyranny** 741.10; steamroller [informal].

.3 **coercion,** intimidation, **duress; the strong arm** *or* strong-arm tactics [both informal], the sword, the mailed fist, the bludgeon, the boot in the face, the jackboot, the big stick, the club, *argumentum baculinum* [L]; **pressure, high pressure,** high-pressure methods; **violence** 162.

.4 VERBS **compel, force, make;** have, cause, cause to; **constrain, bind,** tie, tie one's

hands; **restrain** 760.7; enforce, **drive,** impel; use force upon, force one's hand.

.5 **oblige, necessitate, require,** exact, demand, **dictate,** impose, call for; take *or* brook no denial; leave no option *or* escape, admit of no option.

.6 **press; pressure** *or* **high-pressure** *or* lean on *or* squeeze [all informal], twist one's arm [slang]; ram *or* cram down one's throat; **bring pressure to bear upon, put pressure on,** bear down on, bear down upon, bear against, bear hard upon; put the screw *or* screws on [informal], put the screw *or* screws to [informal].

.7 **coerce,** use violence, intimidate, **strong-arm** [slang], bully, steamroller *or* bulldoze [both informal], bludgeon, blackjack; hijack, shanghai, dragoon.

.8 **be compelled, be coerced,** have to 639.10.

.9 ADJS **compulsory, compulsive,** compulsatory, **compelling; pressing, driving,** imperative, imperious; constraining, coactive; **restraining** 760.11; **irresistible.**

.10 **obligatory, compulsory,** imperative, mandatory, required, dictated, **binding;** involuntary; **necessary** 639.12; **inevitable** 639.15.

.11 **coercive, forcible;** steamroller *or* bulldozer *or* sledgehammer *or* strong-arm [all informal]; violent 162.15.

.12 ADVS **compulsively,** compulsorily, **compellingly,** imperatively, imperiously.

.13 **forcibly, by force,** by main force, by *force majeure,* by a strong arm; by force of arms, *vi et armis* [L].

.14 **obligatorily,** compulsorily, mandatorily, by stress of, under press of; at the point of a gun, at the point of the sword *or* bayonet, at bayonet point; under the lash; of necessity.

757. STRICTNESS

.1 NOUNS **strictness, severity, harshness, stringency,** astringency; **discipline,** strict *or* tight *or* rigid discipline, regimentation; **austerity, sternness,** grimness, ruggedness, **toughness** [informal]; Spartanism; authoritarianism; demandingness, exactingness; **meticulousness** 533.3.

.2 **firmness, rigor, rigorousness,** rigidness, rigidity, stiffness, **hardness,** obduracy, obdurateness, **inflexibility,** inexorability, unyieldingness, unbendingness, impliability, unrelentingness, **relentlessness; uncompromisingness;** stubbornness, obstinacy 626; purism; precisianism, puritanism, fundamentalism, orthodoxy.

.3 **firm hand, iron hand,** heavy hand, strong hand, tight hand, tight rein; tight ship.

.4 VERBS **hold** or **keep a tight hand upon,** keep a firm hand on, keep a tight rein on, rule with an iron hand, rule with a rod of iron; regiment, discipline; run a tight ship, keep in line; maintain the highest standards, not spare oneself nor anyone else.

.5 **deal hardly** or **harshly with,** deal hard measure to, lay a heavy hand on, bear hard upon, not pull one's punches [slang]; throw one's back at [informal].

.6 ADJS **strict, exacting,** exigent, demanding, not to be trifled with, **stringent,** astringent; **severe, harsh,** dour, unsparing; **stern, grim, austere,** rugged, **tough** [informal]; Spartan, Spartanic; authoritarian; **meticulous** 533.12.

.7 **firm, rigid, rigorous,** rigorist, rigoristic, stiff, **hard,** iron, obdurate, **inflexible,** ironhanded, inexorable, dour, **unyielding,** unbending, impliable, **relentless,** unrelenting, procrustean, muscle-bound; **uncompromising;** stubborn, obstinate 626.8; purist, puristic; puritan, puritanic(al), fundamentalist, orthodox; ironbound, rockbound, ironclad [informal]; straitlaced or straightlaced, hidebound.

.8 ADVS **strictly, severely, stringently, harshly;** sternly, grimly, **austerely,** ruggedly, toughly [informal].

.9 **firmly, rigidly, rigorously,** stiffly, hardly, obdurately, **inflexibly,** impliably, inexorably, unyieldingly, unbendingly; **uncompromisingly, relentlessly,** unrelentingly; ironhandedly, with a firm or strong or heavy or tight or iron hand.

758. LAXNESS

.1 NOUNS **laxness, laxity, slackness, looseness,** relaxedness; loosening, relaxation; imprecision, sloppiness [informal], carelessness, remissness, negligence 534.1–4; indifference 636; leniency 759; permissiveness; overpermissiveness, overindulgence, softness; easygoingness, easiness; weakness 160; impotence 158; unrestraint 762.3.

.2 **unstrictness,** nonstrictness, undemandingness, unsevereness, unharshness; unsternness, unaustereness; flexibility, pliancy.

.3 VERBS **hold a loose rein, give free rein to,** give the reins to, **give one his head,** give a free course to, give rope enough to; permit all or anything.

.4 ADJS **lax, slack, loose,** relaxed; imprecise, sloppy [informal], careless, slipshod; remiss, negligent 534.10–13; indifferent 636.6–8; lenient 759.7; permissive; overpermissive, overindulgent, soft; easy, easygo-

ing; weak 160.12; impotent 158.13–15; unrestrained 762.23.

.5 **unstrict,** undemanding, **unexacting; unsevere, unharsh; unstern,** unaustere; **flexible, pliant,** yielding.

759. LENIENCY

.1 NOUNS **leniency** or **lenience,** lenientness, lenity; **clemency,** clementness, **mercifulness,** mercy, **humaneness,** humanity, pity, **compassion** 944.1; **mildness, gentleness,** tenderness, softness, moderateness; **easiness,** easygoingness; laxness 758; **forbearance,** forbearing, patience 861; acceptance, **tolerance** 526.4.

.2 **compliance, complaisance,** obligingness, accommodatingness, **agreeableness;** affability, graciosity, graciousness, generousness, decency, amiability; kindness, kindliness, benignity, **benevolence** 938.

.3 **indulgence, humoring,** obliging; favoring, gratification, pleasing; **pampering,** cosseting, **coddling,** mollycoddling, **spoiling;** permissiveness, overpermissiveness, overindulgence.

.4 **spoiled child,** *enfant gâté* [Fr], pampered darling, mama's boy, mollycoddle; *enfant terrible* [Fr], naughty child.

.5 VERBS **be easy on,** handle with kid gloves or velvet gloves, use a light hand or light rein, spare the rod; **tolerate,** bear with 861.5.

.6 **indulge, humor, oblige;** favor, please, gratify, satisfy, **cater to; give way to,** yield to, let one have his own way; **pamper,** cosset, **coddle,** mollycoddle, **spoil;** spare the rod and spoil the child.

.7 ADJS **lenient, mild, gentle,** tender, humane, compassionate, **clement,** merciful 944.7; soft, moderate, **easy,** easygoing; lax 758.4,5; forgiving 947.6; **forbearing, forbearant,** patient 861.9; accepting, **tolerant** 526.11.

.8 **indulgent, compliant,** complaisant, **obliging, accommodating, agreeable,** amiable, gracious, generous, benignant, affable, decent, kind, kindly, benign, benevolent 938.13–15; permissive, overpermissive, overindulgent.

.9 **indulged, pampered, coddled, spoiled,** spoiled rotten [informal].

760. RESTRAINT

.1 NOUNS **restraint, constraint; inhibition;** legal restraint, injunction, interdict; **control, curb, check,** rein, arrest, arrestation; **retardation,** deceleration, slowing down; cooling or cooling off or cooling down [all informal]; retrenchment, curtailment; self-control 624.5; **hindrance** 730; rationing; thought control; restraint of trade, monopoly, protection, protectionism, protective tariff, tariff wall; **prohibition** 778.

.2 suppression, repression; subdual, quelling, putting down, smashing, crushing; quashing, squashing or squelching [both informal]; smothering, stifling, suffocating, strangling, throttling; extinguishment, quenching; crackdown [informal]; censorship.

.3 **restriction, limitation, confinement;** circumscription 234; stint, cramping, cramp; qualification 507.

.4 **shackle,** restraint, **restraints, fetter, hamper,** trammel, trammels, **manacle,** gyves, bond, **bonds,** irons, chains, Oregon boat; stranglehold; **handcuffs,** cuffs; stocks, bilbo, pillory; hobbles, hopples; straitjacket or straightjacket, strait-waistcoat [Brit], camisole; yoke, collar; bridle, halter; **muzzle, gag;** tether; leash, leading strings; reins.

.5 **lock,** bolt, bar, padlock; barrier 730.5.

.6 restrictionist, protectionist, monopolist; censor.

.7 VERBS **restrain, constrain, control, govern,** guard, contain, keep under control, put or lay under restraint; **inhibit,** straiten [archaic]; enjoin, prohibit 778.3; **curb, check, arrest, bridle,** rein, snub; **retard,** slow down, decelerate; **cool** or **cool off** or **cool down** [all informal]; retrench, curtail; hold, keep, withhold, hold up [informal], **keep from;** hinder 730.10; **hold back, keep back,** pull, set back; **hold in, keep in,** pull in, rein in; **hold** or **keep in check, hold at bay,** dompt, hold in leash; hold fast, keep a tight hand on; restrain oneself, not go too far, not go off the deep end [informal].

.8 **suppress, repress,** stultify; **keep down,** hold down, keep under; **subdue, quell, put down,** smash, **crush; quash, squash** or **squelch** [both informal]; **extinguish,** quench, stanch, damp down, pour water on, drown, kill; **smother, stifle,** suffocate, asphyxiate, strangle, throttle, choke off, **muzzle, gag;** censor, silence; sit on or sit down on [both slang]; jump on or crack down on or clamp down on or shut down on [all informal], put or keep the lid on [slang]; bottle up, cork, cork up.

.9 **restrict, limit, narrow, confine,** tighten; circumscribe 234.4; keep in or within bounds, keep from spreading, localize,

hem, hem in, box, box in or up; **cramp,** stint; qualify 507.3.

.10 **bind, restrain, tie,** tie up, **strap,** lash, leash, pinion, fasten, secure, make fast; **hamper, trammel,** entrammel; rope; **chain,** enchain; **shackle, fetter, manacle,** gyve, **put in irons; handcuff, tie one's hands; tie hand and foot,** hog-tie [informal]; straitjacket; hobble, hopple; tether, picket, moor, anchor; tie down, pin down, peg down; get a stranglehold on, put a half nelson on [informal]; **bridle.**

.11 ADJS **restraining, constraining; inhibiting,** inhibitive; **suppressive, repressive,** stultifying.

.12 **restrictive,** limitative, restricting, **narrowing, limiting, confining,** cramping.

.13 **restrained, constrained, inhibited,** pent-up; guarded; controlled, curbed, bridled; **under restraint,** under control, in check, under discipline; slowed down, retarded, arrested, in remission; in or on leash, in leading strings.

.14 **suppressed, repressed; subdued,** quelled, put down, smashed, crushed; quashed, squashed or squelched [both informal]; smothered, stifled, suffocated.

.15 **restricted, limited, confined;** circumscribed 234.6, hemmed in, hedged in or about, boxed in; landlocked; weatherbound, windbound, icebound, snowbound; cramped, stinted; qualified 507.10.

.16 **bound, tied,** tied up, tied down, strapped, hampered, trammeled, shackled, handcuffed, fettered, manacled, tethered; **in bonds,** in irons or chains, ironbound.

761. CONFINEMENT

.1 NOUNS **confinement,** locking up, lockup, caging, penning, impoundment, **restraint,** restriction; check, constraint 760.1.

.2 **quarantine, isolation,** cordoning off, segregation, separation, seclusion; sanitary cordon, cordon sanitaire [Fr], cordon; quarantine flag, yellow flag, yellow jack.

.3 **imprisonment, jailing,** incarceration, **internment,** immurement, immuration; **detention, captivity,** duress, durance, durance vile; close arrest, house arrest; term of imprisonment.

.4 **commitment,** committal, consignment; recommitment, remand; mittimus [law].

.5 **custody,** custodianship, keep [archaic], **keeping, care, charge, ward,** guarding, hold, protective or preventive custody; protection, safekeeping 699.1.

.6 **arrest,** arrestment, arrestation, pinch or

bust [both slang]; **capture, apprehension, seizure,** netting [informal].

.7 **place of confinement;** limbo, hell, purgatory; pound, pinfold or penfold; **cage; enclosure,** pen, coop 236.3.

.8 **prison,** prisonhouse, **penitentiary,** pen [slang], keep, penal institution, bastille, state prison, federal prison; house of detention, detention home; **jail, gaol** [Brit], jailhouse, lockup, tollbooth [Scot], bridewell [Brit]; maximum-security prison, minimum-security prison; **guardhouse, stockade; brig; dungeon,** oubliette, black hole; **reformatory,** house of correction, reform school, training school, industrial school, borstal or borstal institution [both Brit], debtor's prison, sponging house; **prison camp,** internment camp, detention camp, labor camp, forced-labor camp, **concentration camp;** prisoner-of-war camp or stockade, POW camp; cell; bullpen; solitary confinement, the hole [slang]; condemned cell, death cell, death house or death row; penal settlement or colony, Devil's Island.

.9 [slang or informal terms] **jug, can, coop, cooler,** hoosegow, slammer, stir, clink, pokey, quod or chokey [both Brit].

.10 **jailer, gaoler** [Brit], **keeper, warder,** prison guard, **turnkey,** bull or screw [both slang]; **warden,** governor [Brit], commandant, principal keeper; custodian, guardian 699.6; **guard** 699.9.

.11 **prisoner, captive,** *détenu* [Fr], cageling; **convict,** con [slang]; **jailbird** [informal], gaolbird [Brit informal], stir bird [slang]; **internee; prisoner of war,** POW; political prisoner; lifer [informal]; trusty; parolee, ticket-of-leave man or ticket-of-leaver [both Brit]; ex-convict; chain gang.

.12 VERBS **confine, shut in,** coop in, hem in, fence in, wall in, rail in; **shut up, coop up, pen up,** box up, mew up, bottle up, cork up, seal up, **impound;** pen, coop, pound [archaic], crib, mew, cloister, immure, cage, encage; **enclose** 236.5; **hold, keep in,** hold or keep in custody, **detain,** keep in detention, constrain, **restrain,** hold in restraint; check, inhibit 760.7; restrict 760.9; shackle 760.10.

.13 **quarantine, isolate,** segregate, separate, seclude; **cordon, cordon off,** seal off, rope off.

.14 **imprison, incarcerate, intern,** immure; **jail, gaol** [Brit], jug [slang], throw into jail, throw under the jailhouse [dial]; throw or cast in prison, clap up, clap in jail or prison; **lock up,** lock in, bolt in,

put or keep under lock and key; hold captive, hold prisoner, hold in captivity; hold under close or house arrest.

.15 **arrest,** make an arrest, put under arrest, pick up, **take captive, take prisoner, apprehend, capture,** seize, net [informal], lay by the heels, **take into custody.**

.16 [slang or informal terms] **bust, pinch,** make a pinch, nab, pull in, **run in,** collar.

.17 **commit,** consign, commit to prison, send to jail, send up or send up the river [both slang]; commit to an institution, institutionalize; recommit, remit, remand.

.18 **be imprisoned, do** or **serve time** [informal].

.19 ADJS **confined,** in confinement, **shut-in,** pent, **pent-up,** kept in, under restraint; "cabined, cribbed, confined" [Shakespeare]; impounded; **detained;** restricted 760.15; cloistered, enclosed 236.10.

.20 **quarantined,** isolated, segregated, separated; cordoned, cordoned or sealed or roped off.

.21 **jailed,** jugged [slang], **imprisoned, incarcerated, interned,** immured; **in prison,** in stir [slang], in captivity, **behind bars,** locked up, under lock and key, in durance vile.

.22 **under arrest, in custody,** in hold, in charge [Brit], under or in detention; under close arrest, under house arrest.

762. FREEDOM

.1 NOUNS **freedom, liberty; license,** loose [archaic]; run or the run of [both informal], "the right to live as we wish" [Epictetus], "the will to be responsible to ourselves" [Nietzsche], "political power divided into small fragments" [Thomas Hobbes], "the choice of working or starving" [Samuel Johnson]; the Four Freedoms [F. D. Roosevelt], freedom of speech and expression, freedom of worship, freedom from want, freedom from fear; constitutional freedom; academic freedom, *Lehrfreiheit, Lernfreiheit* [both Ger].

.2 **right, rights, civil rights,** civil liberties, constitutional rights, legal rights; Bill of Rights, Petition of Right, Declaration of Right, Declaration of the Rights of Man, Magna Charta or Magna Carta; **unalienable rights, human rights,** natural rights, "life, liberty, and the pursuit of happiness" [Thomas Jefferson].

.3 **unrestraint, unconstraint,** noncoercion, nonintimidation; **unreserve,** irrepressibility, uninhibitedness; immoderacy, intemperance, incontinence, uncontrol, unruliness, indiscipline; **abandon**, abandonment, **licentiousness**, wantonness, riotousness, wildness; permissiveness, unstrictness, laxness 758.

.4 **latitude, scope, room**, range, way, field, maneuvering space or room; **margin**, clearance, **space**, open space, elbowroom, **leeway** [informal], sea room, wide berth; **tolerance; free scope**, full or ample scope, **free hand**, free play, free course; **carte blanche**, blank check; no holds barred; swing, play, full swing; rope, long rope or tether, rope enough to hang oneself.

.5 **independence, self-determination, self-government**, self-direction, **autonomy**, home rule; autarky, autarchy, self-containment, self-sufficiency; **individualism**, rugged individualism, **self-reliance**, self-dependence; inner-direction; Declaration of Independence.

.6 **free will**, free choice, **discretion**, option, choice, say, say-so [informal], free decision; **full consent**; absolute or unconditioned or noncontingent free will.

.7 **own free will, own account, own accord, own hook** or own say-so [both informal], own discretion, own choice, **own initiative**, personal initiative, own responsibility, personal or individual responsibility, own volition, own authority, own power; own way, own sweet way [informal].

.8 **exemption**, exception, **immunity; release**, discharge; **franchise**, license, charter, patent, liberty; diplomatic immunity; congressional or legislative immunity; privilege 958.4; permission 777.

.9 **noninterference, nonintervention**; isolationism; laissez-faireism, let-alone principle or doctrine or policy; *laissez-faire, laissez-aller* [both Fr]; liberalism, free enterprise, free competition, self-regulating market; capitalism 745.8; free trade.

.10 **liberalism**, libertarianism, latitudinarianism; broad-mindedness, open-mindedness, toleration, tolerance; unbigotedness 526.1; libertinism, **freethinking**, free thought; **liberation** 763.

.11 **freeman**, freewoman; citizen, free citizen, burgess; franklin; freedman, freedwoman, deditician.

.12 **independent, free lance; individualist**, rugged individualist; free spirit; **liberal**, libertarian, latitudinarian; libertine, freethinker; free trader; **nonpartisan**, neutral, mugwump; isolationist; nonaligned nation; third world, third force.

.13 VERBS **liberalize**, ease; **free, liberate** 763.4.

.14 **exempt, free, release**, discharge, **let go** or **let off** [both informal], **excuse**, spare, except, grant immunity, dispense from; give dispensation from; dispense with, save the necessity; remit, remise; absolve 1007.4.

.15 **give a free hand**, let one have his head, **give one his head; give the run of** [informal], give the freedom of; give one leeway [informal], give full play; give one scope or space or room; **give rein** or **free rein to**, give the reins to, give bridle to, give one line, give one rope; **give one carte blanche, give one a blank check;** let go one's own way, let one go at will.

.16 **not interfere, leave** or **let alone, let be**, leave be [informal], **leave** or **let well enough alone**, let sleeping dogs lie; **keep hands off**, not tamper, not meddle, not involve oneself, not get involved, butt out or not butt in [both slang], let it take its course, live and let live, leave to oneself; mind one's own business.

.17 **be free**, feel free, feel at liberty; **go at large**, breathe the air of freedom; **have free scope**, have a free hand, have the run of [informal]; be at home, feel at home.

.18 **let oneself go**, let go, let loose or cut loose [both informal], **give way to**, open up, let it all hang out [informal]; go all out, go flat out [Brit], pull out all the stops; go unrestrained, run wild, have one's fling, sow one's wild oats.

.19 (be independent or self-sufficient) **shift for oneself, fend for oneself**, strike out for oneself, look out for number one [slang]; **go it alone, be one's own man**, pull a lone oar, play a lone hand [informal], **paddle one's own canoe** [informal]; stand on one's own legs or own two feet, stand on one's own [informal], suffice to oneself, do for oneself, make one's own way; ask no favors, ask no quarter; **be one's own boss** [informal], ask leave of no man; **go one's own way**, take one's own course; do on one's own, do on one's own initiative, do on one's own hook or say-so [informal], do in one's own sweet way [informal]; **have a will of one's own**, have one's own way, do what one likes or wishes or chooses, **do as one pleases**, go as one pleases, please oneself [informal], **suit oneself**; have a free mind, free-lance.

.20 ADJS **free**, eleuther(o)–; **at liberty, at large**, on the loose, **loose**, unengaged, disengaged, detached, unattached, uncommitted, uninvolved, clear, in the clear, go-as-you-please, easygoing, footloose,

footloose and fancy-free, "afoot and lighthearted" [Whitman], free and easy; free as air, free as a bird, free as the wind; scot-free; **freeborn; freed, liberated, emancipated,** released.

.21 **independent,** self-dependent, self–; free-spirited, freewheeling, **self-determined,** self-directing, one's own man; inner-directed, **individualistic;** self-governed, **self-governing, autonomous,** sovereign; self-reliant, self-sufficient, self-subsistent, self-supporting, self-contained, autarkic, autarchic; nonpartisan, neutral, **nonaligned;** third-world, third-force.

.22 **free-acting,** free-going, free-moving, free-working; freehand, freehanded; **free-spoken,** outspoken, **plain-spoken, open,** direct, candid, blunt 974.17.

.23 **unrestrained, unconstrained, unforced,** uncompelled, uncoerced; unmeasured, **uninhibited, unsuppressed, unrepressed,** unreserved, go-go; uncurbed, unchecked, **unbridled,** unmuzzled; **unreined,** reinless; **uncontrolled,** unmastered, unsubdued, ungoverned, **unruly;** out of control, out of hand, out of one's power; **abandoned,** intemperate, immoderate, **incontinent, licentious,** loose, wanton, rampant, riotous, wild; irrepressible; lax 758.4,5.

.24 **nonrestrictive,** unrestrictive; **permissive;** indulgent 759.8; lax 758.4,5; **liberal,** libertarian, latitudinarian; broad-minded, open-minded, tolerant; unbigoted 526.8; libertine; freethinking.

.25 **unhampered, untrammeled, unhandicapped, unimpeded,** unhindered, unprevented, unclogged, unobstructed; clear, unencumbered, unburdened, unladen, unembarrassed, disembarrassed.

.26 **unrestricted, unconfined, uncircumscribed,** unbound [archaic], unbounded, unmeasured; **unlimited,** limitless, illimitable; unqualified, unconditioned, **unconditional,** without strings, no strings; **absolute,** perfect, unequivocal, full, plenary, open, **wide-open** [informal].

.27 **unbound,** untied, **unfettered,** unshackled, unchained; unmuzzled, ungagged; uncensored.

.28 **unsubject,** ungoverned, unenslaved, **unenthralled;** unvanquished, unconquered, unsubdued, unquelled, untamed, unbroken.

.29 **exempt, immune;** exempted, **released,** excused, excepted, let off [informal], spared; **privileged, licensed,** favored, chartered; permitted; **unliable,** unsubject, ir-

responsible, unaccountable, unanswerable.

.30 **quit, clear, free, rid; free of, clear of, quit of, rid of, shut of** [informal], **shed of** [dial].

.31 ADVS **freely, free; without restraint,** without stint, **unreservedly,** with abandon; outright.

.32 **independently, alone, by oneself,** all by one's lonesome [informal], under one's own power, **on one's own** or **on one's own hook** [both informal], on one's own initiative; **on one's own account** or **responsibility,** on one's own say-so [informal]; **of one's own free will, of one's own accord,** of one's own volition, at one's own discretion.

763. LIBERATION

.1 NOUNS **liberation, freeing,** setting free, setting at liberty; **deliverance, delivery;** rescue 702; **emancipation,** disenthrallment, manumission; enfranchisement, affranchisement; Emancipation Proclamation; women's liberation 958.6; gay liberation.

.2 **release,** unhanding, **loosing,** unloosing; unbinding, untying, unbuckling, unshackling, unfettering, unlashing, unstrapping, untrussing or unpinioning [both archaic], unmanacling, unleashing, unchaining, untethering, unhobbling, unharnessing, unyoking, unbridling; unmuzzling, ungagging; unlocking, unlatching, unbolting, unbarring; unpenning, uncaging; **discharge, dismissal;** parole; demobilization, separation from the service.

.3 **extrication,** freeing, releasing, clearing; **disengagement, disentanglement,** untangling, unsnarling, unraveling, disentwining, disinvolvement, unknotting, disembarrassment, disembroilment; dislodgment, breaking out or loose.

.4 VERBS **liberate, free, deliver, set free,** set at liberty, set at large; **emancipate,** manumit, disenthrall; enfranchise, affranchise; rescue 702.3.

.5 **release, unhand,** let go, **let loose, turn loose,** cast loose, let out, let off, let go free; **discharge, dismiss;** let out on bail, grant bail to, go bail for [informal]; parole, put on parole; demobilize, separate from the service.

.6 **loose,** loosen, unloose, unloosen; **unbind, untie,** unstrap, unbuckle, unlash, untruss or unpinion [both archaic]; **unfetter, unshackle,** unmanacle, unchain, unhandcuff, untie one's hands; unleash, untether, unhobble; unharness, unyoke, unbridle; unmuzzle, ungag; unlock, unlatch, unbolt, unbar; unpen, uncage.

.7 **extricate, free, release, clear,** get out; **disengage,** disentangle, untangle, unsnarl, unravel, disentwine, disinvolve, unknot, disembarrass, disembroil; dislodge, break out or loose, cut loose, tear loose.

.8 **free oneself from,** deliver oneself from, **get free of,** get quit of, **get rid of,** get clear of, **get out of,** get well out of; **throw off, shake off; escape** 632.6.

.9 **go free,** go scot free, go at liberty, **get off,** get off scot-free, get out of.

.10 ADJS **liberated, freed, emancipated, released;** delivered, rescued, ransomed, redeemed; extricated, unbound, untied, unshackled, etc.; **free** 762.20; on parole.

764. SUBJECTION

.1 NOUNS **subjection, subjugation; domination** 741.2; **restraint, control** 760.1; **bondage, captivity; thrall, thralldom,** enthrallment; **slavery,** enslavement; **servitude,** compulsory or involuntary servitude, servility, bond service, indentureship; **serfdom,** serfhood, villenage, **vassalage;** helotry, helotism; debt slavery, **peonage;** feudalism, feudality; absolutism, tyranny 741.9,10; deprivation of freedom, disenfranchisement, disfranchisement.

.2 **subservience** or subserviency, subjecthood, subordinacy, **subordination,** juniority, **inferiority;** lower status, subordinate role, satellite status; **service,** servitorship 750.12.

.3 **dependence** or dependency, tutelage, chargeship, wardship; clientship, clientage.

.4 **subdual, quelling,** crushing, trampling or treading down, reduction, humbling, humiliation; **breaking, taming,** domestication, gentling; **conquering** 727.1; **suppression** 760.2.

.5 **subordinate,** junior, secondary, **inferior; underling,** understrapper, low man on the totem pole [informal]; assistant, **helper** 787.6; right-hand man 787.7; servant, employee 750.

.6 **dependent, charge, ward,** client, protégé, encumbrance; pensioner, pensionary; public charge, ward of the state.

.7 **subject, vassal,** liege, liege man, liege subject, homager; **captive; slave,** servant, chattel, chattel slave, **bondsman,** bondman, **bondslave,** theow, thrall; indentured servant; bondwoman, bondswoman, bondmaid; odalisque, concubine;

galley slave; **serf,** helot, villein; churl; debt slave, **peon.**

.8 VERBS **subjugate, subject, subordinate; dominate** 741.15; disfranchise, disenfranchise, divest or deprive of freedom; **enslave,** enthrall, make a chattel of; take captive, lead captive or into captivity; **hold in subjection,** hold in bondage, **hold captive,** hold in captivity; **hold down,** keep down, keep under; **keep under one's thumb,** have tied to one's apron strings, hold in leash, hold in leading strings, hold in swaddling clothes, hold or keep at one's beck and call; vassalize, make dependent or tributary; peonize.

.9 **subdue, master,** overmaster, **quell, crush, reduce,** beat down, **break,** break down, overwhelm; tread underfoot, trample underfoot, roll in the dust, trample in the dust, drag at one's chariot wheel; **suppress** 760.8; **conquer** 727.10; tyrannize 741.16; unman 158.12; bring low, **bring to terms, humble,** humiliate, bend, **bring one to his knees, bend to one's will.**

.10 **have subject,** twist or turn or wind around one's little finger, make lie down and roll over, have eating out of one's hand, **lead by the nose,** make a puppet of, make putty of, make a sport or plaything of; use as a doormat, treat like dirt under one's feet.

.11 **domesticate, tame, break, bust** [slang]; **gentle** [informal], break in, break to harness; housebreak.

.12 **depend on,** be at the mercy of, be the sport or plaything or puppet of, be putty in the hands of; not dare to say one's soul is one's own.

.13 ADJS **subject, dependent,** tributary, client; **subservient, subordinate, inferior;** servile; liege, **vassal,** feudal, feudatory.

.14 **subjugated,** subjected, **enslaved, enthralled, captive,** bond, unfree; disenfranchised, disfranchised, **oppressed, suppressed** 760.14; **in subjection, in bondage, in captivity,** in slavery, in bonds, in chains; under the lash, under the heel; **in one's power,** in one's control, in one's hands or clutches, in one's pocket, **under one's thumb,** at one's mercy, under one's command or orders, at one's beck and call, at one's feet.

.15 **subdued, quelled,** crushed, broken, reduced, humbled, humiliated, brought to one's knees, brought low, made to grovel; **tamed, domesticated,** broken to harness, housebroken or housebroke.

.16 **downtrodden,** downtrod [archaic], kept

down or under, ground down, overborne, trampled, **oppressed; abused,** misused; **henpecked, browbeaten,** led by the nose, in leading strings, tied to one's apron strings, ordered around [informal], regimented, tyrannized; slavish, servile, submissive 765.12–16; unmanned 158.19; treated like dirt under one's feet.

.17 PREPS **under, below, beneath,** underneath, subordinate to; at the feet of; under the heel of; at the beck and call of.

.765. SUBMISSION

.1 NOUNS **submission,** submittal, **yielding; compliance,** complaisance, **acquiescence, acceptance;** going along with [informal], assent 521; consent 775; **obedience** 766; subjection 764; **resignation,** resignedness; **deference,** homage, kneeling, obeisance; **passivity,** passiveness, supineness, nonresistance, nonopposition, nonopposal, nondissent.

.2 **surrender, capitulation;** renunciation, giving over, abandonment, relinquishment, **cession;** giving up or in, backdown [informal]; retreat, recession, recedence.

.3 **submissiveness, docility, tractability,** biddability, yieldingness, compliableness [archaic], pliancy, pliability, flexibility, malleability, moldability, ductility, plasticity, facility; agreeableness, agreeability; subservience, **servility** 907.

.4 **manageability, governability, controllability,** manipulability, manipulatability, corrigibility, untroublesomeness; **tameness,** housebrokenness; tamableness, domesticability.

.5 **meekness, gentleness, tameness, mildness,** peaceableness, quietness, lamblikeness, dovelikeness; humility 906.

.6 VERBS **submit, comply, take, accept,** go along with [informal], **acquiesce,** be agreeable, accede, **assent** 521.8; **consent** 775.2; relent, **succumb,** resign, resign oneself, not resist; take one's medicine, swallow the pill, face the music; **knuckle down** or **under,** knock under [archaic], take it, swallow it; take it lying down; put up with it, grin and bear it, make the best of it, **live with it;** obey 766.2.

.7 **yield, give way, give ground, back down, give up, give in,** cave in [informal], withdraw from or quit the field, break off combat, cease resistance, have no fight left.

.8 **surrender, capitulate,** acknowledge defeat, **cry quits,** cry pax [Brit], **say uncle** [informal], beg a truce, pray for quarter,

implore mercy, **throw in the towel, throw in the sponge** [both informal], show or wave the white flag, lower or haul down or strike one's flag or colors, throw down or lay down or deliver up one's arms, hand over one's sword, yield the palm, pull in one's horns [informal], come to terms; renounce, abandon, relinquish, **cede,** give over.

.9 **submit to, yield to, defer to,** bow to, give way to, knuckle under to, succumb to.

.10 **bow down,** bow, bend, stoop, crouch, **bow one's head,** bend the neck, bow submission; genuflect, curtsy; **bow to,** bend to, knuckle to [informal], bend or bow to one's will, bend to one's yoke; kneel to, **bend the knee to, fall on one's knees before,** crouch before, **fall at one's feet,** throw oneself at the feet of, prostrate oneself before, **truckle to,** cringe to; **kowtow,** bow and scrape, grovel, do obeisance or homage.

.11 **eat dirt, eat crow, eat humble pie,** lick the dust, kiss the rod.

.12 ADJS **submissive, compliant,** compliable [archaic], complaisant, complying, **acquiescent,** consenting 775.4; **assenting,** accepting, agreeable; subservient, abject, **obedient** 766.3; servile; **resigned,** uncomplaining; unassertive; **passive, supine, unresisting,** nonresisting, unresistant, nonresistant, nonresistive, nonopposing, nondissenting.

.13 **docile, tractable,** biddable, **yielding,** pliant, pliable, flexible, malleable, moldable, ductile, plastic, facile [archaic], like putty in one's hands.

.14 **manageable, governable, controllable,** manipulable, manipulatable, handleable, corrigible, restrainable, untroublesome; domitable, tamable, domesticable.

.15 **meek, gentle, mild,** peaceable, pacific, quiet; **subdued, chastened, tame,** tamed, broken, housebroken, domesticated; lamblike, gentle as a lamb, dovelike; humble 906.9.

.16 **deferential, obeisant; subservient, obsequious,** servile 907.12,13; crouching, prostrate, prone, on one's belly, on one's knees, on one's marrowbones [informal], on bended knee.

.17 ADVS **submissively, compliantly,** complaisantly, acquiescently, agreeably; **obediently** 766.6; **resignedly,** uncomplainingly, with resignation; **passively,** supinely, unresistingly, unresistantly, nonresistively.

.18 **docilely, tractably,** biddably, **yieldingly,**

pliantly, pliably, malleably, flexibly, plastically, facilely [archaic].

.19 meekly, gently, tamely, mildly, peaceably, pacifically, quietly, like a lamb.

766. OBEDIENCE

.1 NOUNS obedience or obediency, compliance; acquiescence, submission, submissiveness 765.1–5; servility 907; willingness, dutifulness, duteousness; service, servitium, homage, fealty, allegiance, loyalty, faith, suit and service or suit service, observance [archaic]; conformity 82; law-abidingness.

.2 VERBS obey, mind, heed, keep, observe, listen or hearken to; comply, conform 82.3; stay in line or not get out of line or not get off base [all informal], toe the line or mark, obey the rules, follow the book, do what one is told; do as one says, do the will of, defer to, do one's bidding, come at one's call, lie down and roll over for [slang]; take orders, attend to orders, do suit and service, follow the lead of; submit 765.6–11.

.3 ADJS obedient, compliant, complying; acquiescent, submissive 765.12–15; willing, dutiful, duteous; loyal, faithful, devoted; conforming; law-abiding.

.4 at one's command, at one's pleasure, at one's disposal, at one's nod, at one's call, at one's beck and call.

.5 henpecked, tied to one's apron strings, on a string, on a leash, in leading strings.

.6 ADVS obediently, compliantly; acquiescently, submissively 765.17; willingly, dutifully, duteously; loyally, faithfully, devotedly; in obedience to, in compliance or conformity with.

.7 at your service or command or orders, as you please, as you will, as thou wilt [archaic].

767. DISOBEDIENCE

.1 NOUNS disobedience, nonobedience, noncompliance; undutifulness, unduteousness; willful disobedience; insubordination, indiscipline; unsubmissiveness, intractability, indocility 626.4, recusancy; nonconformity 83; lawlessness, waywardness, frowardness, naughtiness; violation, transgression, infraction, infringement, lawbreaking; civil disobedience, passive resistance; uncooperativeness, noncooperation.

.2 refractoriness, recalcitrance or recalcitrancy, recalcitration, contumacy, contumaciousness, obstreperousness, defiance,

defiance of authority, unruliness, restiveness, fractiousness, orneriness [informal]; wildness, breachiness [dial]; obstinacy, stubbornness 626.1.

.3 rebelliousness, mutinousness; riotousness; insurrectionism, insurgentism; factiousness, sedition, seditiousness; treasonableness, traitorousness, subversiveness; extremism 745.4.

.4 revolt, rebellion, revolution, mutiny, insurrection, insurgence or insurgency, émeute [Fr], uprising, rising, outbreak, general uprising, levée en masse [Fr], riot, civil disorder; peasant revolt, jacquerie [Fr]; putsch, coup d'état [Fr].

.5 rebel, revolter; insurgent, insurrectionary, insurrecto, insurrectionist; malcontent, frondeur [Fr]; mutineer, rioter, brawler; maverick [informal], insubordinate, nonconformist 83.3; agitator 648.11; extremist 745.12; revolutionary, revolutionist 147.3; traitor, subversive 619.10,11.

.6 VERBS disobey, not mind, not heed, not keep or observe, not listen or hearken, pay no attention to, ignore, disregard, defy, set at defiance, fly in the face of, snap one's fingers at, scoff at, flout, go counter to, set at naught, set naught by, care naught for; be a law unto oneself, refuse to cooperate; not conform 83.4; violate, transgress 769.4; break the law 999.5.

.7 revolt, rebel, kick over the traces, reluct, reluctate; rise up, rise, arise, rise up in arms, mount the barricades; mutiny, mutineer [archaic]; insurge, insurrect, riot, run riot; revolutionize, revolution, revolute, subvert, overthrow 147.4; strike 789.8.

.8 ADJS disobedient, transgressive, uncomplying, violative, lawless, wayward, froward, naughty; recusant, nonconforming 83.5; undutiful, unduteous; self-willed, willful, obstinate 626.8; undisciplined, ill-disciplined, indisciplined.

.9 insubordinate, unsubmissive, indocile, uncompliant, uncooperative, noncooperative, noncooperating, intractable 626.12.

.10 refractory, recalcitrant, contumacious, obstreperous, defiant, unruly, restive, impatient of control or discipline, fractious, ornery [informal]; wild, breachy [dial].

.11 rebellious, rebel, breakaway; mutinous, mutineering; insurgent, insurrectionary, riotous, turbulent; factious, seditious, seditionary; revolutionary, revolutional; traitorous, treasonable, subversive; extreme, extremistic 745.20.

.12 ADVS disobediently, uncompliantly, against or contrary to order and discipline; **insubordinately, unsubmissively,** in-docilely, **uncooperatively;** unresignedly; disregardfully, floutingly, **defiantly;** intractably 626.17; obstreperously, contumaciously, restively, fractiously; **rebelliously,** mutinously; riotously.

768. OBSERVANCE

.1 NOUNS **observance,** observation; **keeping,** adherence, heeding; compliance, conformance, conformity, accordance; **performance, practice,** execution, discharge, carrying out or through; acquittal, acquittance [both archaic], fulfillment, satisfaction; respect, heed, care 533.1.

.2 VERBS **observe, keep, heed, follow;** regard, **respect,** attend to, **comply with,** conform to; hold by, **abide by,** adhere to; **live up to,** act up to, **be faithful to,** keep faith with, do justice to, do the right thing by; **fulfill,** fill, meet, satisfy; **make good,** keep or make good one's word or promise, be as good as one's word, redeem one's pledge, stand to one's engagement.

.3 **perform, practice,** do, execute, discharge, carry out or through, carry into execution, do one's office, fulfill one's role, discharge one's function.

.4 ADJS **observant,** regardful, mindful; **faithful,** devout, devoted, true, loyal, constant; dutiful, duteous, as good as one's word; practicing, active; compliant, conforming; punctual, punctilious, scrupulous, meticulous, conscientious 533.12.

769. NONOBSERVANCE

.1 NOUNS **nonobservance,** inobservance, unobservance, nonadherence; nonconformity, disconformity, **nonconformance, noncompliance;** inattention, **disregard** 531.1; laxity 758.1; **nonfulfillment, nonperformance,** nonfeasance, failure, dereliction, delinquency, omission, default, slight, oversight; negligence; neglect 534.

.2 **violation, infraction, breach,** breaking; **infringement, transgression, trespass,** contravention; offense 999.4; breach of promise, breach of contract, breach of trust or faith, bad faith, breach of privilege; breach of the peace.

.3 VERBS **disregard,** pay no regard to 531.3; neglect 534.6.

.4 **violate, break;** infringe, transgress, **trespass,** contravene, trample on or upon, trample underfoot, do violence to, make a mockery of; **defy,** set at defiance, flout, set at naught, set naught by; take the law

into one's own hands; break one's promise, break one's word, etc.

.5 ADJS **nonobservant,** inobservant, unobservant, nonadherent; nonconforming, unconforming, noncompliant, uncompliant; inattentive, **disregardful** 531.6; **negligent** 534.10; unfaithful, untrue, unloyal, inconstant.

770. PROMISE

.1 NOUNS **promise, pledge,** troth, plight, faith, parole, **word, word of honor,** solemn declaration or word; **oath, vow** 523.3; avouch, avouchment; **assurance, guarantee,** warranty.

.2 **engagement, undertaking, commitment, agreement,** obligation, recognizance; **understanding,** gentlemen's agreement; verbal agreement, informal agreement, pactum [law]; contract 771.1,3; preengagement.

.3 **betrothal,** betrothment, espousal, **engagement,** handfasting or affiance [both archaic], troth, marriage contract or vow, plighted troth or faith or love; banns, banns of matrimony.

.4 VERBS **promise,** give or make a promise, hold out an expectation; **pledge, plight,** troth, **vow; give one's word,** pledge or pass one's word, give one's parole, **give one's word of honor,** plight one's troth or faith, pledge or plight one's honor; **swear** 523.5; **vouch,** avouch, **warrant, guarantee, assure;** underwrite, countersign.

.5 **engage, undertake, commit,** obligate, bind, **agree to,** answer for, be answerable for, take on oneself, be responsible for, be security for, go bail for, accept obligation or responsibility, bind oneself to; have an understanding; enter into a gentlemen's agreement; take the vows or marriage vows; shake hands on; contract 771.6.

.6 **affiance, betroth,** troth, **plight, engage,** contract, contract an engagement, pledge or promise in marriage; **plight one's troth, become engaged;** publish the banns.

.7 ADJS **promissory,** votive; under or upon oath, on one's word, on one's word of honor, on the Book, under hand and seal.

.8 **promised, pledged, bound, committed,** compromised, **obligated; sworn,** warranted, **guaranteed,** assured, underwritten; contracted 771.12; **engaged, plighted, affianced, betrothed,** intended.

771. COMPACT

.1 NOUNS compact, pact, contract, legal contract, valid contract, covenant, convention, transaction, paction [Scot], accord, agreement, mutual agreement, formal agreement, legal agreement, stipulation, understanding, arrangement, bargain, dicker or deal [both informal]; union contract, wage contract, employment contract, collective agreement; cartel, consortium; protocol; bond, binding agreement, ironclad agreement, covenant of salt; gentleman's agreement or gentlemen's agreement; promise 770.

.2 treaty, international agreement, entente, entente cordiale [both Fr], concord, concordat, cartel, convention, paction, capitulation; alliance, league; nonaggression pact, mutual-defense treaty; NATO, North Atlantic Treaty Organization; SEATO, Southeast Asia Treaty Organization.

.3 (contracts) indenture, indent; deed, deed poll, title deed, contract by deed; deed of arrangement, arrangement; specialty contract, specialty, formal contract, special contract; parol contract, simple contract; quasi contract, contract quasi, implied contract; deed or covenant of indemnity, recognizance; contract of record; insurance policy, policy, group policy; bond, promissory note, debenture, debenture bond; mortgage deed, deed of trust.

.4 arrangement, settlement; signing, signature, sealing, closing, conclusion; adjustment, accommodation; solemnization.

.5 execution, completion; transaction; carrying out, discharge, fulfillment, prosecution, effectuation; enforcement; observance 768.

.6 VERBS contract, compact, covenant, bargain, agree, engage, undertake, make a deal [informal], do a deal [Brit informal], stipulate, agree to, bargain for; promise 770.4.

.7 treat with, negotiate, bargain, make terms, sit down with, sit down at the bargaining table.

.8 sign, shake hands, seal, formalize, make legal and binding; agree on terms, come to an agreement 521.10; strike a bargain 827.18.

.9 arrange, settle; adjust, accommodate, compose, fix, make up, straighten out, work out; conclude, close, close with, settle with.

.10 execute, complete, transact, promulgate, make; make out, fill out; discharge, fulfill, render, administer; carry out, carry through, put through, prosecute; effect, effectuate, implement; enforce, put in force; abide by, honor, adhere to, observe 768.2.

.11 ADJS contractual, covenantal, conventional.

.12 contracted, compacted, covenanted, agreed, bargained for, stipulated; engaged, undertaken; promised 770.8; arranged, settled; under hand and seal, signed, sealed; signed, sealed, and delivered.

.13 ADVS as agreed upon, as promised, as contracted for, according to the contract or bargain or agreement.

772. SECURITY

(thing given as a pledge)

.1 NOUNS security, surety, indemnity, guaranty, guarantee, warranty, warrant, insurance, assurance; bond, tie; stocks and bonds 834.1–4.

.2 pledge, gage, pignus, vadium [both L]; undertaking; earnest, earnest money, god's penny, handsel; escrow; token payment; pawn, hock [slang]; bail, bond, vadimonium, replevin, replevy, recognizance; mainprise; hostage, surety.

.3 deposit, stake, forfeit; caution money, caution; collateral, collateral security or warranty; margin.

.4 mortgage, mortgage deed, deed of trust, lien, security agreement; vadium mortuum or mortuum vadium; dead pledge; vadium vivum, living pledge, antichresis; hypothec, hypothecation, bottomry, bottomry bond; adjustment mortgage, blanket mortgage, chattel mortgage, closed mortgage, participating mortgage, installment mortgage, leasehold mortgage, trust mortgage; first mortgage, second mortgage, third mortgage.

.5 lien, general lien, particular lien; pignus legale, common-law lien, statutory lien, judgment lien, pignus judiciale, tax lien, mechanic's lien; mortgage bond.

.6 guarantor, warrantor, guaranty, guarantee; mortgagor; insurer, underwriter; sponsor, surety; godparent, godfather, godmother; bondsman, bailsman, mainpernor.

.7 warrantee, mortgagee; insuree, policyholder; godchild, godson, goddaughter.

.8 guarantorship, sponsorship, sponsion.

.9 VERBS **secure, guarantee, guaranty, warrant, assure, insure,** ensure, bond, **certify;** countersecure; **sponsor,** be sponsor for, sign for, sign one's note, **back,** stand behind, stand up for; **endorse;** sign, **underwrite,** undersign, subscribe to; confirm, attest 505.12.

.10 pledge, impignorate, handsel [Brit], **deposit, stake,** post, **put up,** put up as collateral; **pawn,** put in pawn, spout or put up the spout [both archaic], **hock** or **put in hock** [both informal]; mortgage, hypothecate, bottomry, bond; go bail.

.11 ADJS **secured,** covered, **guaranteed, warranted,** certified, **insured,** ensured, **assured;** certain, sure 513.13.

.12 pledged, staked, posted, deposited, **put up,** put up as collateral; on deposit, at stake; as earnest; **pawned, in pawn, in hock** [informal], up the spout [archaic].

.13 in trust, held in trust, held in pledge, fiduciary; in escrow.

773. OFFER

.1 NOUNS **offer, offering,** proffer, presentation, **bid,** submission; **advance, overture,** approach, invitation; hesitant or tentative or preliminary approach, **feeler** [informal]; asking price.

.2 proposal, proposition, suggestion, instance; **motion,** resolution; sexual advance or approach or invitation or overture, indecent proposal, pass [slang], improper suggestion; request 774.

.3 ultimatum, last word, final offer, firm price.

.4 VERBS **offer, proffer, present,** tender, **put up, submit, extend,** prefer [archaic], **hold out,** hold forth, place in one's way, lay at one's feet, put or place at one's disposal.

.5 propose, submit, prefer; **suggest,** recommend, **advance,** proposition [informal], commend to attention, **propound, pose, put forward,** bring forward, put or set forth, put it to, put or set or lay or bring before; **bring up, broach, moot,** introduce, open up, launch, start; **move, make a motion,** offer a resolution; postulate 499.12.

.6 bid, bid for, make a bid.

.7 make advances, approach, overture, **make an overture;** make a pass or throw a pass [both slang], proposition [informal], solicit, importune.

.8 urge upon, press upon, ply upon, push upon, force upon, thrust upon; **press, ply;** insist 753.7.

.9 volunteer, come or step forward, offer or proffer or present oneself, be at one's service, not wait to be asked, not wait for an invitation, need no prodding.

774. REQUEST

.1 NOUNS **request,** asking; the touch [slang]; desire, wish, expressed desire; **petition,** petitioning, impetration, address; **application; requisition,** indent [Brit]; demand 753.

.2 entreaty, appeal, plea, bid, suit, call, cry, clamor, cri du cœur [Fr]; **supplication, prayer,** rogation, **beseechment,** imploring, imploration, obsecration, obtestation, adjuration, imprecation; **invocation,** invocatory plea or prayer.

.3 importunity, importunateness, urgency, pressure, **urging, pressing, plying;** buttonholing; dunning; **teasing,** pestering, plaguing, nagging; **coaxing,** wheedling, cajolery, cajolement, blandishment.

.4 invitation, invite or **bid** [both informal], engraved invitation, bidding, biddance, **call,** calling, **summons.**

.5 solicitation, canvass; suit, addresses; **courting, wooing.**

.6 beggary, mendicancy, mendicity; **begging,** cadging, scrounging; mooching or bumming or panhandling [all slang].

.7 petitioner, supplicant, suppliant, suitor; **solicitor** 830.7; **applicant,** solicitant, claimant; **aspirant,** seeker; **candidate,** postulant; bidder.

.8 beggar, mendicant, scrounger, **cadger; bum** or bummer or **moocher** or **panhandler** [all informal]; schnorrer [Yid]; hobo, tramp 274.3; loafer 708.8; mendicant friar; mendicant order.

.9 VERBS **request, ask,** make a request, **beg leave,** make bold to ask; **desire,** wish, express a wish for, crave; **ask for,** order, put in an order for, bespeak, call for, trouble one for; whistle for [informal]; **requisition,** make a requisition, indent [Brit]; make application, **apply for,** file for, **put in for;** demand 753.4.

.10 petition, present or prefer a petition, sign a petition, circulate a petition; **pray,** sue; apply to, **call on** or **upon;** memorialize.

.11 entreat, implore, beseech, beg, crave, **plead, appeal, pray, supplicate,** impetrate, obtest; adjure, conjure; invoke, imprecate [archaic], **call on** or **upon,** cry on or upon, **appeal to,** cry to, run to; go cap in hand to; kneel to, go down on one's knees to, fall on one's knees to, go on bended knee to, throw oneself at the feet of, get or come down on one's marrowbones [informal]; plead for, clamor for, cry for; call for help.

.12 importune, urge, press, pressure [informal], apply or exert pressure, push, ply; dun; beset, buttonhole, besiege; work on [informal], tease, pester, plague, nag, nag at, bug [slang]; coax, wheedle, cajole, blandish.

.13 invite, ask, call, summon, call in, bid come, extend or issue an invitation, request the presence of, request the pleasure of one's company.

.14 solicit, canvass; court, woo, address, sue, sue for, pop the question [informal]; seek, bid for, look for; fish for, angle for.

.15 beg, scrounge, cadge; mooch or bum or panhandle [all informal]; hit or hit up or touch or put the touch on or make a touch [all slang]; pass the hat [informal].

.16 ADJS supplicatory, suppliant, supplicant, supplicating, prayerful, precative; petitionary; begging, mendicant, cadging, scrounging, mooching [slang]; on one's knees or bended knees, on one's marrowbones [informal]; with joined or folded hands.

.17 imploring, entreating, beseeching, begging, pleading, appealing, precatory, precative, adjuratory.

.18 importunate; teasing, pestering, plaguing, nagging, dunning; coaxing, wheedling, cajoling; insistent, demanding, urgent 753.8.

.19 invitational, inviting, invitatory.

.20 INTERJS please, prithee [archaic], pray, pray do; be so good as to, be good enough, have the goodness; will you, may it please you; if you please, s'il vous plaît [Fr]; I beg you, je vous en prie [Fr]; for God's or goodness or heaven's or mercy's sake.

775. CONSENT

.1 NOUNS consent, assent, agreement, accord [archaic], acceptance, approval, blessing, approbation, sanction, endorsement, ratification; affirmation, affirmative, affirmative voice or vote, aye, okay or OK [both informal]; permission 777; willingness, readiness, promptness, promptitude, eagerness, unreluctance, unloathness, ungrudgingness, tacit or unspoken or silent or implicit consent, connivance; acquiescence, compliance; submission 765.

.2 VERBS consent, assent, give consent, yield assent, accede to, accord to or grant [both archaic], say yes, say aye, vote affirmatively, vote aye, nod, nod assent; accept, agree to, go along with [informal]; be in accord with, be in favor of, take kindly to, approve of, hold with; approve, give one's blessing to, okay or OK [both informal]; sanction, endorse, ratify; consent to silently or by implication, wink at, connive at; be willing, turn a willing ear; deign, condescend 906.7; have no objection, not refuse; permit 777.9.

.3 acquiesce, comply, comply with, fall in with, be persuaded, come round or around, come over, come to [dial]; submit 765.6–11.

.4 ADJS consenting, assenting, affirmative, approving, agreeing, favorable, accordant, consentient; sanctioning, endorsing, ratifying; acquiescent, compliant, compliable [archaic]; submissive 765.12–16; willing, agreeable, content; ready, prompt, eager, unreluctant, unloath, nothing loath, ungrudging, unrefusing; permissive 777.14.

.5 ADVS consentingly, assentingly, affirmatively, approvingly, favorably, agreeably, accordantly; acquiescently, compliantly; willingly 622.8; yes 521.18.

776. REFUSAL

.1 NOUNS refusal, rejection, turndown or turning down [both informal]; thumbsdown [informal]; nonconsent, nonacceptance; declining, declination, declension, declinature; denial, disclamation, disclaimer, disallowance; repudiation 638.1; disagreement, dissent 522; recantation 628.3; contradiction 524.2; negation, abnegation, negative, negative answer, nay, no, nix [slang]; unwillingness 623; disobedience 767; noncompliance, nonobservance 769; withholding, holding back, retention, deprivation.

.2 repulse, rebuff, peremptory or flat or point-blank refusal, summary negative; slap in the face [informal], kick in the teeth [slang]; short shrift.

.3 VERBS refuse, decline, not consent, refuse consent, reject, turn down [informal], decline to accept, not buy [slang]; not think of, not hear of [both informal]; say no, say nay, vote nay, vote in the negative, disagree, dissent 522.4; vote negatively, shake one's head, negative, negate; turn thumbs down on [informal]; be unwilling 623.3; turn one's back upon, turn a deaf ear to, set oneself against, set one's face against, be unmoved, harden one's heart, resist entreaty or persuasion; stand aloof, have nothing to do with, wash one's hands of; hold out against; put or set one's foot down [informal], refuse point-blank or summarily; decline politely or with thanks, beg off; repudiate, disallow, disclaim 638.2.

.4 deny, withhold, hold back; grudge, begrudge; close the hand or purse; deprive one of.

.5 repulse, rebuff, repel, slap one in the face [informal], kick one in the teeth [slang], give one short shrift, shut or slam the door in one's face, turn one away, send to the right-about [informal]; deny oneself to, refuse to receive, not be at home to, cut, snub 966.5–7.

.6 ADJS unconsenting, nonconsenting, negative; unwilling 623.5; uncompliant, uncomplying, uncomplaisant, inacquiescent, uncooperative; disobedient 769.8–11; rejective, declinatory; deaf to, not willing to hear of.

.7 PHRS I refuse, I won't, I will not, I will no such thing; over my dead body, far be it from me, not if I can help it, not likely, not on your life, count me out, include me out, I'm not taking any, I won't buy it, it's no go, like hell I will, I'll be hanged if I will, try and make me, you have another guess coming, you should live so long, I'll see you in hell first, nothing doing [all informal]; out of the question, not to be thought of, impossible; no, by no means.

777. PERMISSION

.1 NOUNS permission, leave, allowance, vouchsafement; consent 775; permission to enter, admission, ticket, ticket of admission; license, liberty 762.1; okay or OK or the go-ahead or the green light [all informal]; special permission, charter, patent, dispensation, release, waiver.

.2 sufferance, tolerance, toleration, indulgence; winking, overlooking, connivance; permissiveness.

.3 authorization, authority, sanction, countenance, warrant, warranty, fiat; empowerment, enabling, entitlement, enfranchisement, certification; clearance, security clearance; ratification 521.4.

.4 carte blanche, blank check [informal], full authority, full power, free hand, open mandate.

.5 grant, concession; charter, franchise, liberty, diploma, patent, letters patent, brevet; royal grant.

.6 permit, license, warrant; building permit, learner's permit; driver's license, marriage license, hunting license, fishing license, etc.; nihil obstat, imprimatur.

.7 pass, passport, safe-conduct, safeguard, protection; visa; clearance, clearance papers; bill of health, clean bill of health, pratique, full pratique.

.8 permissibility, permissibleness, allowableness; admissibility, admissibleness; justifiableness, warrantableness, sanctionableness; validity, legitimacy, lawfulness, licitness, legality.

.9 VERBS permit, allow, admit, let, leave [dial], give permission, give leave, make possible; consent 775.2; grant, accord, vouchsafe; okay or OK or give the go-ahead or give the green light [all informal], say the word or give the word [both informal]; dispense, release.

.10 suffer, countenance, have, tolerate, brook, condone, endure, stomach, bear, bear with, put up with, stand for, hear of [informal]; indulge 759.6; shut one's eyes to, wink at, blink at, overlook, connive at; leave the door or way open.

.11 authorize, sanction, warrant; give official sanction or warrant, legitimize, validate, legalize; empower, give power, enable, entitle; license, privilege; charter, patent, enfranchise, franchise; certificate, certify; ratify 521.12.

.12 give carte blanche, issue or accord or give a blank check [informal], give full power or authority, give an open mandate, give a free hand, leave alone, leave it to one; permit all or anything, open the floodgates, remove all restrictions.

.13 may, can, have permission, be permitted or allowed.

.14 ADJS permissive, admissive, permitting, allowing; consenting 775.4; unprohibitive, nonprohibitive; tolerating, suffering, tolerant; indulgent, lenient 759.7; lax 758.4,5.

.15 permissible, allowable, admissible; justifiable, warrantable, sanctionable; licit, lawful, legitimate, legal, legitimized, legalized.

.16 permitted, allowed, admitted; tolerated, on sufferance; unprohibited, unforbidden.

.17 authorized, empowered, entitled; warranted, sanctioned; licensed, privileged; chartered, patented; franchised, enfranchised.

.18 ADVS permissively, admissively; tolerantly, indulgently.

.19 permissibly, allowably, admissibly; with permission, by one's leave; licitly, lawfully, legitimately, legally.

.20 PHRS **by your leave,** with your permission, if you please, may I?

778. PROHIBITION

.1 NOUNS **prohibition, forbidding,** forbiddance; **ruling out, disallowance,** denial, rejection 633; **refusal** 776; **repression, suppression** 760.2; **ban, embargo, injunction,** prohibitory injunction, **proscription,** inhibition, **interdict,** *interdictum* [L], interdiction; index, index expurgatorius, index librorum prohibitorum; **taboo;** thou-shalt-not *or* don't *or* no-no [all informal]; **law,** statute 998.3; **preclusion, exclusion, prevention** 730.2; **forbidden fruit,** contraband; Eighteenth Amendment, Volstead Act, Prohibition Party; sumptuary laws *or* ordinances; **zoning,** zoning laws, restrictive covenants.

.2 veto, negative [archaic]; absolute veto, qualified *or* limited negative *or* veto, suspensive *or* suspensory veto, item veto, pocket veto.

.3 VERBS **prohibit, forbid; disallow, rule out;** deny, reject 638.2; **say no to, refuse** 776.3; **bar,** debar, **preclude, exclude,** exclude from, shut out, shut the door to, **prevent** 730.14; **ban,** put under the ban, **outlaw; repress, suppress** 760.8; **enjoin,** put under an injunction, issue an injunction against, issue a prohibitory injunction; **proscribe,** inhibit, **interdict,** put *or* lay under an interdict *or* interdiction; put on the Index; **embargo, lay** *or* **put an embargo on; taboo.**

.4 not permit *or* **allow, not have, not suffer** *or* **tolerate,** not endure, not stomach, not bear, not bear with, not countenance, not brook, brook no, not condone, not accept, **not put up with,** not go along with [informal]; not stand for *or* not hear of [both informal], **put** *or* **set one's foot down on** [informal].

.5 veto, put one's veto upon, decide *or* **rule against, negative, kill.**

.6 ADJS **prohibitive, prohibitory, prohibiting, forbidding;** inhibitive, inhibitory, **repressive, suppressive** 760.11,12; **proscriptive, interdictive, interdictory; preclusive, exclusive, preventive** 730.19.

.7 prohibited, forbidden, forbade, forbid, *verboten* [Ger], **barred; vetoed; unpermissible,** nonpermissible, not permitted *or* allowed, **unallowed;** disallowed, ruled out; off limits, out of bounds; unauthorized, **unsanctioned,** unlicensed; banned, under the ban, **outlawed,** contraband; **taboo,** tabooed, untouchable; **illegal,** unlawful, illicit.

779. REPEAL

.1 NOUNS **repeal, revocation,** revoke, revokement, renege, **rescinding,** rescindment, rescission, **abrogation,** cassation, reversal; suspension; waiving, **waiver, setting aside; countermand,** counterorder; **annulment,** nullification, withdrawal, **invalidation,** voiding, voidance, vacation, vacatur, defeasance; **cancellation,** canceling, cancel, write-off; **abolition,** abolishment; **recall,** retraction, recantation 628.3.

.2 VERBS **repeal, revoke, rescind,** reverse, **abrogate,** renege, renig [informal]; suspend; **waive, set aside; countermand,** counterorder; **abolish,** do away with; **cancel,** write off; **annul,** nullify, disannul, withdraw, **invalidate,** void, vacate, make void, declare null and void; **overrule,** override; **recall,** retract, recant 628.9.

.3 ADJS **repealed, revoked, rescinded,** etc.; **invalid, void, null and void.**

780. COMMISSION

.1 NOUNS **commission,** commissioning, **delegation,** devolution, devolvement, **deputation;** commitment, entrusting, entrustment, **assignment,** consignment; **errand, task, office; care,** cure, **responsibility,** purview, jurisdiction; **mission,** legation, embassy; **authority,** authorization, power to act, full power, plenipotentiary power, empowerment, vicarious *or* delegated authority; **warrant,** license, **mandate, charge, trust,** brevet, exequatur; **agency,** agentship, factorship; regency, regentship; lieutenancy; trusteeship, executorship; **proxy,** procuration, power of attorney.

.2 appointment, assignment, designation, **nomination,** naming, selection, tabbing [informal]; **ordainment,** ordination; posting, transferral.

.3 installation, installment, **instatement,** induction, placement, **inauguration,** investiture, taking office; **accession,** accedence; coronation, enthronement.

.4 engagement, employment, hiring, appointment, taking on [informal]; retainment, briefing [Brit]; preengagement, bespeaking; reservation, booking.

.5 rental, rent; lease, let [Brit]; hire, hiring; sublease, subrent; **charter,** bareboat charter; lend-lease.

.6 enlistment, enrollment; conscription, draft, drafting, induction, impressment, press; call, draft call, call-up, summons, call to the colors, letter from Uncle Sam [informal]; **recruitment**, recruiting; **muster**, levy; mobilization; selective service, compulsory military service.

.7 indenture, binding over; **apprenticeship.**

.8 **assignee, appointee,** selectee, nominee, candidate; licensee, licentiate; **deputy, agent** 781.

.9 VERBS **commission, authorize,** empower, accredit; **delegate,** devolute, devolve, devolve upon, depute; **deputize; assign,** consign, **commit, charge, entrust,** give in charge; license, charter, warrant; detail, detach, post, transfer, send out, mission, send on a mission.

.10 **appoint, assign,** designate, **nominate,** name, select, tab [informal]; **ordain,** ordinate [archaic].

.11 **install,** instate, induct, **inaugurate,** invest, put in, place, **place in office;** chair; crown, throne, enthrone, anoint.

.12 **be instated, take office,** accede; take *or* mount the throne; attain to.

.13 **employ, hire,** give a job to, take into employment, take into one's service, take on [informal], recruit, **engage,** sign up *or* on [informal]; retain, brief [Brit]; bespeak, preengage; sign up for [informal], **reserve,** book.

.14 **rent, lease,** let [Brit], hire, job, **charter;** sublease, sublet, underlet.

.15 **rent out,** rent; **lease,** lease out; let *or* let off *or* let out [all Brit]; **hire out,** hire; charter; **sublease, sublet,** underlet; lendlease, lease-lend; lease-back; farm, farm out; job.

.16 **enlist,** list [archaic], **enroll, sign up** *or* on [informal]; **conscript, draft, induct,** press, impress, commandeer; detach, detach for service; summon, call up, call to the colors; **mobilize,** call to active duty; **recruit, muster,** levy, raise, muster in; join 788.14.

.17 indenture, article, bind, bind over; **apprentice.**

.18 ADJS **commissioned, authorized, accredited;** delegated, deputized, appointed.

.19 **employed, hired, hireling, paid,** mercenary; rented, leased, let [Brit]; sublet, subleased; chartered.

.20 **indentured,** articled, bound over; **apprenticed, apprentice,** prentice *or* 'prentice.

.21 ADVS for hire, for rent, to let, to lease.

781. DEPUTY, AGENT

.1 NOUNS **deputy, proxy, representative, substitute,** vice, vicegerent, **alternate,** backup *or* backup man [both informal], alter ego, **surrogate,** procurator, secondary, stand-in, understudy, pinch hitter [informal], utility man; second in command, executive officer; exponent, advocate, pleader, paranymph, attorney, champion; lieutenant, vicar, vicar general; locum tenens, locum [informal]; amicus curiae; co–; dummy, figurehead 749.4.

.2 **delegate, legate; commissioner,** commissary, *commissionaire* [Fr], commissar; **messenger, herald, emissary, envoy; minister,** secretary.

.3 **agent, instrument,** implement, **tool; steward** 748.4; **functionary; official** 749.16; clerk, **secretary;** amanuensis; factor, consignee; general agent, special agent; actor's agent, baggage agent, business agent *or* walking delegate, claim agent, commercial agent, commission agent, customer agent, federal agent, Federal [informal], fed [slang], freight agent, insurance agent, land agent, law agent, literary agent, loan agent, news agent, passenger agent, press agent, parliamentary agent, purchasing agent, real estate agent, sales agent, station agent, theatrical agent, ticket agent, travel agent; puppet, cat's-paw 658.3; dupe 620.

.4 **go-between, middleman, intermediary, medium,** intermedium, intermediate, interagent, **internuncio,** broker; connection [slang], **contact; negotiator,** negotiant; interpleader; arbitrator, mediator 805.3.

.5 **spokesman,** spokeswoman, official spokesman, speaker, **voice,** mouthpiece [informal]; herald; prolocutor, prolocutress *or* prolocutrix; reporter, rapporteur.

.6 **diplomat,** diplomatist, diplomatic agent, diplomatic [archaic]; **emissary, envoy, legate, minister,** foreign service officer; **ambassador,** ambassadress, ambassador-at-large; envoy extraordinary, plenipotentiary, **minister plenipotentiary;** nuncio, internuncio, apostolic delegate; vice-legate; resident, minister resident; *chargé d'affaires* [Fr], chargé; secretary of legation, chancellor [Brit]; **attaché,** commercial attaché, military attaché; **consul,** consul general, vice-consul, consular agent; career diplomat.

.7 **foreign office, foreign service,** diplomatic service; diplomatic mission, diplomatic staff *or* corps, *corps diplomatique* [Fr]; **embassy, legation;** consular service.

.8 vice-president, vice-chairman, vice-governor, vice-director, vice-master, vice-chancellor, vice-premier, vice-warden, vice-consul, vice-legate; vice-regent, viceroy, vicegerent, vice-king, vice-queen, vice-reine.

.9 secret agent, operative, cloak-and-dagger operative, undercover man, inside man [slang]; spy, espionage agent; counterspy, double agent; spotter; scout, reconnoiterer; intelligence agent or officer; CIA man, military-intelligence man, naval-intelligence man; spy-catcher [informal], counterintelligence agent.

.10 detective, operative, investigator, sleuth, Sherlock Holmes [A. Conan Doyle]; police detective, Bow Street runner or officer [England], plainclothesman; private detective, private investigator, inquiry agent [Brit]; hotel detective, house detective, house dick [slang], store detective; arson investigator; narcotics agent, narc [slang]; FBI agent, G-man [informal], treasury agent, T-man [informal], revenuer [slang], Federal [informal], fed [slang]; Federal Bureau of Investigation, FBI; Secret Service.

.11 [slang or informal terms] dick, gumshoe, gumshoe man, hawkshaw, sleuthhound, beagle, flatfoot, tec; eye, private eye; skip tracer, spotter.

.12 secret service, intelligence service, intelligence bureau or department; intelligence, military intelligence, naval intelligence; counterintelligence.

.13 (group of delegates) delegation, deputation, commission, mission; committee, subcommittee.

.14 VERBS represent, act for, act on behalf of, substitute for, appear for, answer for, speak for, hold the proxy of, hold a brief for, act in the place of, stand in for, stand in the stead of, serve in one's stead, pinch-hit for [informal]; understudy, back up [informal]; front for [slang]; deputize, commission 780.9.

.15 ADJS deputy, deputative; acting, representative; vice–.

.16 diplomatic, ambassadorial, consular, ministerial, plenipotentiary.

.17 ADVS by proxy, indirectly; in behalf of 149.12.

782. PROMOTION

.1 NOUNS promotion, preferment, advancement, advance, upping [informal], rise, elevation, upgrading, step up, step up the ladder; raise, pay raise, boost [informal]; exaltation, aggrandizement; ennoblement, knighting; graduation, passing.

.2 VERBS promote, advance, prefer [archaic], up [informal], elevate, upgrade; kick upstairs [informal]; raise, raise one's pay, up one's pay or boost one's pay [both informal]; exalt, aggrandize; ennoble, knight; pass, graduate.

783. DEMOTION, DEPOSAL

.1 NOUNS demotion, degrading, degradation, disgrading, downgrading, debasement, abasement, humbling, casting down, reduction, bump or bust [both slang]; stripping of rank, depluming, displuming.

.2 deposal, deposition, removal, displacement, deprivation, ousting, unseating; cashiering, firing [informal], dismissal 310.5; forced resignation; kicking upstairs [informal]; superannuation, pensioning off, retirement; suspension; impeachment; purge, liquidation; overthrow, overthrowal; dethronement, disenthronement, discrownment; disbarment, disbarring; unfrocking, defrocking, unchurching; deconsecration, expulsion, excommunication 310.1,4.

.3 VERBS demote, degrade, disgrade, downgrade, debase, abase, humble, lower, reduce, bump or bust [both slang]; strip of rank, cut off one's spurs, deplume, displume.

.4 depose, remove from office, give the gate [slang], divest or deprive or strip of office, remove, displace, oust; suspend; cashier, drum out, strip of rank, break, bust [slang]; dismiss 310.19; purge, liquidate; overthrow; retire, superannuate, pension, pension off, put out to pasture [informal]; kick upstairs [informal]; unseat, unsaddle; dethrone, disenthrone, unthrone, uncrown, discrown; disbar; unfrock, defrock, unchurch; strike off the roll, read out of; expel, excommunicate 310.13,17; deconsecrate.

784. RESIGNATION

(retirement from office)

.1 NOUNS resignation, demission, withdrawal, retirement, retiral [Brit], superannuation, emeritus status; abdication; voluntary resignation; forced resignation, deposal 783; relinquishment 633.3.

.2 VERBS resign, demit, quit, leave, vacate, withdraw from; retire, superannuate, be superannuated, be pensioned or pensioned off, be put out to pasture [informal]; relinquish, give up 633.7; retire from office, stand down, stand or step aside, give up one's post, hang up one's spurs [informal]; **tender** or **hand in one's resig-nation**, send in one's papers, turn in one's badge or uniform; **abdicate**, re-nounce the throne, give up the crown; pension off 783.4.

.3 ADJS **retired**, in retirement, superannu-ated, on pension, pensioned, pensioned off, emeritus, emerita [fem].

785. AID

.1 NOUNS **aid, help, assistance, support, suc-cor, relief, comfort**, ease, remedy; **service, benefit** 665.4; ministry, ministration, of-fice, offices, good offices; yeoman's ser-vice; therapy 689; protection 699; rescue 702.

.2 **assist**, helping hand, hand, **lift; boost** or **leg** or **leg up** [all informal]; help in time of need.

.3 **support, maintenance, sustainment,** sus-tentation, **sustenance, subsistence,** provi-sion; **keep, upkeep; livelihood, living,** meat, bread, daily bread; **nurture, nour-ishment;** mothering, care, tender loving care, TLC [informal]; manna, manna in the wilderness; economic support, price support, subsidy, subsidization, subven-tion, endowment.

.4 **patronage, fosterage, tutelage, sponsor-ship, auspices,** aegis, care, guidance, **championship;** seconding; interest, advo-cacy, encouragement, **backing, abetment;** countenance, **favor, goodwill,** charity, sympathy.

.5 **furtherance, helping along, advancement,** advance, **promotion, forwarding,** facilita-tion, speeding, easing or smoothing of the way, clearing of the track, greasing of the wheels, expedition, expediting, rush-ing; special or preferential treatment.

.6 **self-help,** self-helpfulness, **self-support,** self-sustainment, self-improvement; inde-pendence 762.5.

.7 **helper, assistant** 787.6; **benefactor** 942.

.8 **reinforcements, support, relief,** auxilia-ries, reserves, reserve forces.

.9 **facility, accommodation, appliance, con-venience,** amenity, appurtenance; advan-tage.

.10 **helpfulness,** aidfulness [archaic]; service-ability, utility, **usefulness** 665.3; **advanta-geousness,** profitability, favorableness, beneficialness 674.1.

.11 VERBS **aid, help, assist,** comfort, abet [ar-chaic], **succor,** relieve, ease, doctor, rem-edy; be of some help; do good, do a world of good, **benefit, avail** 674.10; **favor, befriend; give help,** render assistance,

proffer aid, come to the aid of, rush or fly to the assistance of, lend one aid, **give** or **lend** or **bear a hand** or **helping hand,** stretch forth or hold out a helping hand; take by the hand, take in tow; **give an as-sist, give a leg up** [informal], give a lift or give a boost [both informal], help a lame dog over a stile; **save,** redeem, bail out [informal], **rescue** 702.3; protect 699.18–20; set up, put on one's feet; give new life to, resuscitate, rally, reclaim, revive, **restore** 694.11–21; be the making of; see one through.

.12 **support, lend support,** give or furnish or afford support; **maintain, sustain, keep,** upkeep [Brit]; **uphold,** hold up, bear, up-bear, **bear up,** bear out; reinforce, under-gird, bolster, **bolster up,** buttress, shore, shore up, prop, prop up, crutch; **finance,** fund, subsidize, subvention, subvention-ize; pick up the tab or check [informal].

.13 **back, back up, stand behind, stand back of,** get behind, get in behind, get in back of; **stand by,** stick by or **stick up for** [both informal], **champion; second, take the part of,** take up or adopt or espouse the cause of, **go to bat for** [informal], take up the cudgels for, run interference for [informal]; **side with,** take sides with, associate oneself with, join oneself to, align oneself with, come down or range oneself on the side of.

.14 **abet, aid and abet, encourage,** hearten, embolden, comfort [archaic]; advocate, hold a brief for [informal], countenance, keep in countenance, **endorse, lend one-self to,** lend one's countenance to, lend one's favor or support to, lend one's of-fices, put one's weight in the scale, plump for or thump the tub for [both in-formal], lend one's name to, give one's support or countenance to, give moral support to, hold one's hand, make one's cause one's own; subscribe [Brit], **favor, go for** [informal], smile upon, shine upon.

.15 **patronize, sponsor,** take up.

.16 **foster, nurture, nourish,** mother, care for, lavish care on, feed, sustain, cultivate, **cherish;** pamper, coddle, cosset, fondle [archaic]; **nurse,** suckle, cradle; dry-nurse, wet-nurse; spoon-feed.

.17 **further, forward, advance, promote,** en-courage, **boost** [informal], favor, advan-tage, **facilitate,** set or put or push for-ward, give an impulse to; speed, expedite, quicken, hasten, lend wings to; conduce to, make for, contribute to.

.18 serve, render service to, do service for, **work for, labor in behalf of; minister to,** pander to, cater to; attend 750.13.

.19 **oblige, accommodate, favor,** do a favor, do a service.

.20 ADJS **helping,** assisting, serving; **assistant, auxiliary,** adjuvant, subservient, subsidiary, ancillary, accessory; ministerial, ministering, ministrant; fostering, nurtural, nutricial; instrumental 658.6.

.21 **helpful,** aidful [archaic]; **profitable, salutary,** good for, **beneficial** 674.12; remedial, therapeutic; **serviceable, useful** 665.18–22; contributory, conducive, constructive, positive, furthersome [archaic]; at one's service, at one's command, at one's beck and call.

.22 **favorable, propitious;** kind, kindly, kindly-disposed, **well-disposed,** well-affected, well-intentioned, well-meant, **well-meaning;** benevolent, beneficent, benign, benignant; friendly, amicable, neighborly; cooperative.

.23 self-helpful, self-helping, self-improving; **self-supporting, self-sustaining;** self-supported, self-sustained; independent 762.21.

.24 ADVS **helpfully,** helpingly; **beneficially,** favorably, profitably, advantageously, to advantage, to the good; serviceably, **usefully** 665.25.

.25 PREPS helped by, with the help or assistance of, by the aid of; **by means of** 658.7.

.26 **for, on** or **in behalf of,** in aid of, in the name of, on account of, **for the sake of,** in the service of, in furtherance of, in favor of; remedial of.

.27 **behind, back of** [informal], supporting, **in support of.**

786. COOPERATION

.1 NOUNS **cooperation, collaboration, coaction,** concurrence, synergy, synergism; community, harmony, concordance, concord, fellowship, fellow feeling, solidarity, concert, **teamwork;** pulling together, joining of forces, pooling, pooling of resources; bipartisanship, mutualism, mutuality, mutual assistance, coadjuvancy; reciprocity; joint effort, common effort, combined or joint operation, common enterprise or endeavor, collective or united action, mass action; coagency; coadministration, cochairmanship, codirectorship, duet, duumvirate; trio, triumvirate, troika; quartet, quintet, sextet, septet, octet; symbiosis, commensalism; **cooperativeness,** collaborativeness, team

spirit, morale, esprit, *esprit de corps* [Fr]; communism, communalism, communitarianism, collectivism; ecumenism, ecumenicism, ecumenicalism; **collusion,** complicity 654.6.

.2 **affiliation, alliance, alignment, association,** combination, **union,** unification, **coalition,** fusion, merger, coalescence, coadunation, amalgamation, **league, federation, confederation,** confederacy, consolidation, incorporation, inclusion, integration; hookup or tie-up or tie-in [all informal]; **partnership,** copartnership, copartnery, cahoots [slang]; colleagueship, collegialism, collegiality; **fraternity,** confraternity, fraternization, fraternalism; sorority; **fellowship,** sodality, comradeship, freemasonry.

.3 VERBS **cooperate, collaborate,** do business with or **play ball** [both slang], coact, concur; concert, harmonize, concord; **join,** band, league, **associate, affiliate, ally, combine, unite,** fuse, merge, coalesce, amalgamate, federate, confederate, consolidate; hook up or tie up or tie in [all informal]; partner, be in league, **go into partnership with,** go partners [informal], go or be in cahoots with; **join together,** club together, league together, band together, etc.; **work together,** get together or team up [both informal], work as a team, act together, act in concert, **pull together; hold together, hang together,** keep together, **stand together,** stand shoulder to shoulder; lay or put or get heads together; make common cause, throw in together [slang], unite efforts, join in; reciprocate; **conspire,** collude 654.10.

.4 **side with,** take sides with, **unite with; join, join with;** join up with or get together with or team up with [all informal], strike in with [archaic]; **throw in with** or string along with or swing in with [all informal], **go along with; line up with** [informal], align with, align oneself with, range with, range oneself with, stand in with [slang]; **join hands with,** be hand in glove with, go hand in hand with; act with, take part with, **go in with;** cast in one's lot with, join one's fortunes with, stand shoulder to shoulder with, be cheek by jowl with, sink or swim with, stand or fall with; make common cause with, pool one's interests with; enlist under the banner of, rally round, flock to.

.5 ADJS **cooperative, cooperating,** cooperant;

collaborative, coactive, coacting, coefficient, synergetic, synergic(al), synergistic(al); **fellow**, co–; concurrent, concurring, concerted; harmonious, harmonized, concordant, **common, communal,** collective; **mutual,** reciprocal; **joint, combined** 52.5; coadjuvant, coadjutant; symbiotic, commensal; uncompetitive, noncompetitive, communalist, communalistic, communist, communistic, communitarian, collectivist, collectivistic, ecumenic(al); **conniving, collusive** 654.14.

.6 ADVS **cooperatively,** cooperatingly, coactively, coefficiently, concurrently, **jointly,** combinedly, **conjointly,** concertedly, in concert with; harmoniously, concordantly; communally, collectively, **together;** as one, with one voice, unanimously, in chorus, in unison, as one man; **side by side, hand in hand, hand in glove, shoulder to shoulder, back to back,** "all for one, one for all" [Dumas père].

.7 **in cooperation,** in collaboration, in partnership, in cahoots [slang], in collusion, in league.

.8 PREPS **with, in cooperation with,** etc.

787. ASSOCIATE

.1 NOUNS **associate, confederate,** consociate, **colleague,** fellow member, **companion, fellow,** bedfellow, **crony,** consort, cohort, compeer, compatriot, confrere, **brother, brother-in-arms, ally,** adjunct, coadjutor; **comrade** 928.3; –ster; co–.

.2 **partner,** pardner or pard [both dial], **mate, teammate,** comate, copemate or copesmate [both archaic], copartner, side partner, **buddy** [informal], **sidekick** or sidekicker [both slang]; playmate, messmate, tentmate, roommate, classmate, pewmate, waymate, cupmate, shopmate, shipmate, jailmate, schoolmate, tablemate, cradlemate, bedmate, housemate, lovemate, shelfmate, couchmate, birthmate, watchmate, clubmate; nominal or holding-out or ostensible or quasi-partner, general partner, special partner, silent partner, secret partner, dormant or sleeping partner.

.3 **accomplice,** cohort, confederate, fellow conspirator, coconspirator, partner or accomplice in crime; particeps criminis, socius criminis [both L]; **accessory,** accessory before the fact, accessory after the fact; **abettor.**

.4 **collaborator,** cooperator; coauthor; **collaborationist.**

.5 **co-worker,** workfellow, fellow worker, **buddy** [informal], butty [Brit informal]; **teammate, yokefellow,** yokemate; benchfellow, shopmate.

.6 **assistant, helper,** auxiliary, aider, **aid,** aide, paraprofessional; **help, helpmate, helpmeet;** deputy, agent 781; **attendant, second,** acolyte, acolythist [archaic]; best man, paranymph; servant 750; adjutant, aide-de-camp; lieutenant, executive officer; coadjutant, coadjutor; coadjutress, coadjutrix; supporting actor or player, supporting instrumentalist, sideman.

.7 **right-hand man,** right hand, strong right hand, **man Friday,** fidus Achates, second self, alter ego, confidant.

.8 **man, henchman,** gillie; hanger-on, satellite, **follower,** disciple, adherent, votary; creature, lackey, flunky, stooge [slang], jackal, minion, myrmidon; sycophant 907.3; goon [slang], thug 943.3–4; puppet, cat's-paw 658.3; dummy, figurehead 749.4.

.9 **supporter, upholder,** maintainer, sustainer; support, **mainstay, standby** [informal], stalwart, reliance, dependence; **abettor, seconder,** second; endorser, sponsor; **backer, promoter,** angel [slang], **patron,** Maecenas; friend at or in court; **champion,** defender, apologist, **advocate,** –arian, –ist, –ite, paranymph, exponent, protagonist; **well-wisher,** favorer, encourager, sympathizer; **partisan,** sider [archaic], sectary, votary; **fan** or buff [both informal], aficionado, **admirer,** lover.

788. ASSOCIATION

.1 NOUNS **association, society, body; alliance, coalition, league, union;** council; bloc, axis; **partnership; federation, confederation,** confederacy; grouping, assemblage 74; **combination,** combine; Bund, Verein [both Ger]; **gang** or **ring** or mob [all informal]; machine, political machine; economic community, common market, free trade area, customs union; credit union; cooperative, cooperative society, consumer cooperative, Rochdale cooperative; college, **group,** corps, band 74.3.

.2 **community, society, commonwealth;** body; kinship group, **clan,** moiety, totem, phyle, phratry or phratria, gens, caste, subcaste, endogamous group; **family,** extended family, nuclear family; **order, class,** social class, economic class; colony, settlement; **commune,** ashram; socio–.

.3 **fellowship,** sodality; **society,** guild, order; **brotherhood, fraternity,** confraternity, confrerie, fraternal order; **sisterhood, sorority; club,** country club; secret society.

.4 **party, interest, camp, side;** interest group, pressure group, ethnic group; minority group, vocal minority; silent majority; **faction,** division, sect, wing, **caucus,** splinter, splinter group, breakaway group, offshoot; political party 744.24.

.5 **school, sect,** class, order; **denomination, communion,** confession, faith, church; **persuasion,** ism; disciples, followers, adherents.

.6 **clique, coterie, set, circle,** ring, junto, junta, cabal, camarilla, **clan,** group; **crew** or mob or **crowd** or **bunch** or outfit [all informal]; cell; cadre, inner circle; closed or charmed circle; ingroup, we-group; elite, elite group.

.7 **team,** squad, string; eleven, nine, eight, five; **crew,** rowing crew; varsity, first team, first string; reserves, second team, second string, third string; platoon; complement; **cast, company.**

.8 **organization,** establishment, foundation, **institution, institute.**

.9 **company, firm, concern, house,** *compagnie* [Fr], *compañía* [Sp]; **business, industry, enterprise,** business establishment, commercial enterprise; **partnership,** copartnership; joint-stock association, joint-stock company, *Aktiengesellschaft* [Ger], *aktiebolag* [Swed]; **corporation,** corporate body, body corporate, conglomerate corporation, conglomerate, diversified corporation; holding company, consolidating company; **trust, syndicate, cartel,** combine, pool, consortium, plunderbund [slang]; combination in restraint of trade; stock company 833.15; operating company; utility, public utility; chamber of commerce, junior chamber of commerce; trade association.

.10 **branch, organ, division,** wing, arm, offshoot, **affiliate; chapter,** lodge, post; **local;** branch office.

.11 **member,** affiliate, belonger, insider, initiate, one of us, cardholder, card-carrier, card-carrying member; **enrollee,** enlistee; **associate,** socius, **fellow;** brother, sister; comrade; honorary member; life member; member in good standing, dues-paying member; charter member; clubman, clubwoman, clubber [informal]; fraternity man, Greek [slang], sorority woman, sorority girl; guildsman; committeeman; conventionist, conventioner, conventioneer; joiner [informal]; pledge.

.12 **membership,** members, associates, affiliates, body of affiliates, constituency.

.13 **partisanism,** partisanship, **partiality; factionalism, sectionalism,** faction; sectarianism, denominationalism; **cliquism,** cliquishness, cliqueyness; **clannishness,** clanship; exclusiveness; ethnocentricity; party spirit, *esprit de corps* [Fr]; the old college spirit.

.14 VERBS **join,** join up [informal], **enter, go into,** come into, get into, make oneself part of, swell the ranks of; **enlist, enroll, affiliate, sign up** or on [informal], take up membership, take out membership; inscribe oneself, put oneself down; associate oneself with, affiliate with, league with, team or team up with; sneak in, creep in, insinuate oneself into; **combine, associate** 52.3,4.

.15 **belong,** hold membership, be a member, be on the rolls, be inscribed, subscribe, hold or carry a card.

.16 ADJS **associated, corporate,** incorporated; **combined** 52.5.

.17 **associational, social, society, communal; organizational;** coalitional; sociable 922.18.

.18 **cliquish,** cliquey, **clannish;** ethnocentric.

.19 **partisan,** party; **partial,** interested; **factional, sectional,** sectarian, sectary, denominational.

.20 ADVS **in association, conjointly** 786.6,7.

789. LABOR UNION

.1 NOUNS **labor union,** trade union, trade guild [Brit]; organized labor; collective bargaining; craft union, horizontal union; industrial union, vertical union; **local,** union local, local union; company union.

.2 **union shop,** preferential shop, **closed shop;** open shop; nonunion shop; **labor contract, union contract;** maintenance of membership.

.3 **labor unionist, trade unionist, union member,** unionist, cardholder; shop steward, bargainer, negotiator; business agent; union officer; union or labor organizer, organizer.

.4 **striker;** sitdown striker; holdout [informal].

.5 (strike enforcer) **picket; goon** [slang], strong-arm man; flying squadron or squad, **goon squad** [slang].

.6 **strikebreaker, scab** or **rat** or **fink** or scissorbill [all slang], **blackleg** [Brit].

.7 **strike, walkout** or tie-up [both informal], turnout [Brit informal], job action; slowdown, rulebook slowdown, sick-in or sickout [both informal]; work stoppage, sit-down strike, sit-down, wildcat strike, outlaw strike; sympathy strike; **boycott,** boycottage; buyer's *or* consumer's strike; **lockout;** revolt 767.4.

.8 VERBS **organize, unionize.**

.9 **strike, go on strike, go out, walk out;** shut it down; slow down; sit down; **boycott;** picket; hold out [informal]; **lock out;** revolt 767.7.

.10 **break a strike; scab** *or* **rat** *or* **fink** [all slang], **blackleg** [Brit].

790. OPPOSITION

.1 NOUNS **opposition,** opposing, opposure, crossing, traversal, oppugnation, **bucking** [informal], standing against; contraposition 15.1; **resistance** 792; **contention** 796; negation 524; **rejection** 638; **counteraction,** counterworking 178.1; refusal 776; **contradiction,** challenge, contravention, contraversion, rebutment, rebuttal, denial, impugnation, impugnment; crosscurrent, undercurrent, head wind.

.2 **hostility, antagonism, repugnance,** oppugnancy, **antipathy,** enmity, bad blood, inimicalness; contrariness, contrariety, perverseness, **obstinacy** 626; fractiousness, refractoriness, recalcitrance 767.2; uncooperativeness, noncooperation, negativeness; **friction, conflict,** clashing, **collision,** cross-purposes, dissension, disaccord 795; rivalry, vying, competition 796.2.

.3 VERBS **oppose, counter, cross,** traverse, **go** *or* **act in opposition to, go against,** run against, **run counter to,** fly in the face of, fly in the teeth of; **protest** 522.5; set oneself against, set one's face against, be *or* play at cross-purposes; **take issue with, take one's stand against,** declare oneself against, stand and be counted against, vote against; make a stand against, make a dead set against; join the opposition; not put up with, not abide, not be content with; counteract, counterwork, countervail 178.6; **resist,** withstand 792.3.

.4 **contend against,** militate against, **contest, combat, battle,** reluct, reluctate, **fight against, strive against,** struggle against, labor against, **take on** [informal], grapple with, join battle with, close with, antagonize [archaic], **fight, buck** [informal], buffet, beat against, beat up against, breast, stem, breast *or* stem the tide *or* current *or* flood, breast the wave, buffet the waves; rival, compete with *or* against, vie with *or* against; offer resistance 792.3.

.5 **confront, affront, front, meet, face;** encounter 796.16.

.6 **contradict,** cross, traverse, contravene, controvert, rebut, deny, **gainsay;** challenge, contest; oppugn, call into question; **belie,** be contrary to, come in conflict with, negate 524.3,4; **reject** 638.2.

.7 **be against,** be agin [dial]; discountenance 969.10,11; not hold with, not have anything to do with; have a crow to pluck *or* pick, have a bone to pick.

.8 ADJS **oppositional, opponent, opposing, opposed; anti** [informal], enantio–; **adverse, adversary,** adversative, oppugnant, antithetic(al), repugnant, **con** [informal], **contrary, counter; negative; opposite,** oppositive; overthwart [archaic], cross; **contradictory;** unfavorable, unpropitious 544.17; **hostile, antagonistic,** unfriendly, enemy, inimical, alien, antipathetic(al); fractious, refractory, recalcitrant 767.10; uncooperative, noncooperative; perverse, obstinate 626.8–11; **conflicting, clashing,** dissentient, disaccordant 795.15; rival, competitive 796.26.

.9 ADVS **in opposition, in confrontation,** eyeball-to-eyeball [slang], **at variance, at cross-purposes, at odds,** at issue, at war with, up in arms, with crossed bayonets, at daggers drawn, at daggers, in hostile array, poised against one another; **contra,** contrariwise, counter, cross, athwart; against the tide *or* wind *or* grain.

.10 PREPS **opposed to, adverse to,** counter to, **in opposition to,** in conflict with, at cross-purposes with; **against,** agin [dial], dead against, athwart; **versus, vs.; con,** contra, face to face with, *vis-à-vis* [Fr].

791. OPPONENT

.1 NOUNS **opponent, adversary, antagonist, assailant, foe,** foeman, **enemy;** adverse *or* opposing party, opposite camp, **the opposition,** the loyal opposition; **combatant** 800.

.2 **competitor, contestant,** contender, vier, player, entrant; **rival,** corrival, emulator; the field.

.3 **oppositionist,** opposer; obstructionist, obstructive, negativist, naysayer; **objector, protester,** dissident, dissentient; **resister;** noncooperator; **disputant,** litigant, plaintiff, defendant; quarreler, irritable man, scrapper [slang], wrangler, brawler; diehard, bitter-ender, last-ditcher, intransigent, irreconcilable.

792. RESISTANCE

.1 NOUNS **resistance**, withstanding, renitence or renitency, repellence or repellency; **defiance** 793; **opposition** 790; **stand;** **repulsion,** repulse, rebuff; **objection, protest,** remonstrance, **dispute,** challenge, demur, **complaint;** dissentience, **dissent** 522; reaction, hostile or combative reaction, counteraction 178; revolt 767.4; recalcitrance or recalcitrancy, recalcitration, fractiousness, refractoriness 767.2; **reluctance** 623.1; **obstinacy** 626; passive resistance, noncooperation; uncooperativeness, negativism.

.2 VERBS **resist, withstand; stand; endure** 861.5; **stand up, bear up, hold up, hold out; defy** 793.3–6; be proof against, bear up against; **repel, repulse, rebuff.**

.3 **offer resistance,** not turn the other cheek, show fight, **withstand,** stand, **take one's stand,** make a stand, make a stand against, take one's stand against, **stand up to,** stand up against, stand at bay; front, **confront,** meet head-on, **face up to,** face down, face out; **object, protest,** remonstrate, **dispute,** challenge, **complain,** complain loudly, **dissent** 522.4,5; reluct, make a determined resistance; kick against, recalcitrate, "kick against the pricks" [Bible]; put up a fight or struggle [informal], not take lying down; **revolt** 767.7; **oppose** 790.3; **contend with** 796.18; **strive against** 790.4.

.4 **stand fast, stand** or **hold one's ground,** make a resolute stand, **hold one's own,** remain firm, stick or stick fast [both informal], **stick to one's guns, stay it out, stick it out** [informal], **hold out,** not back down, not give up, not submit, **never say die; fight to the last ditch,** die hard, sell one's life dearly, go down with flying colors.

.5 ADJS **resistant, resistive,** resisting, renitent, **withstanding,** repellent; obstructive, retardant, retardative; **unyielding,** unsubmissive 626.9–12; rebellious 767.11; **proof against** 159.18; objecting, protesting, disputing, disputatious, complaining, dissentient, dissenting 522.6,7; recalcitrant, fractious, refractory 767.10; **reluctant** 623.5–7; noncooperative, uncooperative; up in arms, on the barricades, not lying down.

793. DEFIANCE

.1 NOUNS **defiance,** defying, defial [archaic]; **daring,** daringness, **audacity,** boldness, bold front, brash bearing, brashness, brassiness [informal], brazenness, bravado, insolence; arrogance 912; sauciness, cheekiness [informal], pertness, impudence, impertinence; bumptiousness, cockiness; **contempt,** contemptuousness, derision, **disdain,** disregard, despite.

.2 **challenge, dare,** double dare; **defy** or defi; gage, gage of battle, gauntlet, glove, chip on the shoulder, slap of the glove, invitation or bid to combat; war cry, war whoop, battle cry, rebel yell.

.3 VERBS **defy,** bid defiance, hurl defiance, snarl or shout or scream defiance; **dare,** double-dare, outdare; **challenge,** call out, throw or fling down the gauntlet or glove or gage, knock the chip off one's shoulder; beard, face, face out, stare down, **confront, affront,** front; pluck by the beard, slap one's face, double or shake one's fist at; show fight, show one's teeth, bare one's fangs; dance the war dance; **brave** 893.11.

.4 **flout,** disregard, **slight,** slight over, treat with contempt, set at defiance, fly in the teeth or face of, **snap one's fingers at; thumb one's nose at,** cock a snook at, bite the thumb at; **disdain, despise, scorn** 966.3; laugh at, laugh to scorn, laugh out of court, laugh in one's face; hold in derision, scout, scoff at, **deride** 967.8,9.

.5 **show** or **put up a bold front,** bluster, throw out one's chest, crow, look big, stand with arms akimbo.

.6 **take a dare,** accept a challenge, **take one up on** or **call one's bluff** [both informal]; take up the gauntlet.

.7 ADJS **defiant,** defying, challenging; **daring, bold,** brash, brassy [informal], brazen, **audacious,** insolent; arrogant 912.9–14; saucy, cheeky [informal], pert, impudent, impertinent; bumptious, cocky; **contemptuous,** disdainful, derisive, disregardful, greatly daring, regardless of consequences.

.8 ADVS **in defiance of,** in the teeth of, in the face of, under one's very nose.

794. ACCORD

(harmonious relationship)

.1 NOUNS **accord,** accordance, **concord,** concordance, **harmony,** symphony; **rapport;** good vibrations [informal], good vibes [slang]; amity 927.1; frictionlessness; rapprochement [Fr]; **sympathy,** empathy, identity, feeling of identity, fellow feeling, **fellowship,** kinship, **affinity; agreement, understanding, like-mindedness;**

congeniality, **compatibility; oneness,** uni-ty, unison, union; **community,** com-munion, community of interests; solidar-ity, team spirit, esprit, *esprit de corps* [Fr]; mutuality, sharing, reciprocity, mu-tual supportiveness; bonds of harmony, ties of affection, cement of friendship; happy family; peace 803; **love,** *agape* [Gk], charity, *caritas* [L], brotherly love; correspondence 26.1.

.2 VERBS **get along, harmonize, agree with, agree, get along with,** get on with, cotton to *or* hit it off with [both informal], har-monize with, **be in harmony with,** be in tune with, fall *or* chime in with, blend in with, go hand in hand with, **be at one with;** sing in chorus, be on the same wavelength [informal]; **sympathize,** em-pathize, identify with, respond to, under-stand one another, enter into one's views, enter into the ideas *or* feelings of; **accord,** correspond 26.6; reciprocate, interchange 150.4.

.3 ADJS **in accord,** accordant [archaic], **har-monious, in harmony,** in tune, attuned, agreeing, in concert, **in rapport, en rap-port** [Fr], amicable 927.14–20; frictionless; **sympathetic,** empathic, empathetic, **un-derstanding,** sympathetico– *or* sympa-tho–; **like-minded,** akin, of the same mind, of one mind, at one, united, to-gether; concordant, corresponding 26.9; agreeable, congenial, **compatible; peace-ful** 803.9,10.

795. DISACCORD

(unharmonious relationship)

.1 NOUNS **disaccord, discord,** discordance *or* discordancy, **unharmoniousness,** inharmo-niousness, disharmony, inharmony, disaf-finity, incompatibility, incompatibleness; noncooperation; **conflict,** open conflict, **friction,** rub; jar, jangle, clash, clashing; strained relations, **tension; unpleasant-ness;** mischief; **contention** 796; **enmity** 929; Eris, Discordia.

.2 **disagreement, difficulty, misunderstand-ing, difference,** difference of opinion, agreement to disagree, **variance,** division, dividedness; **odds,** cross-purposes; polarity of opinion, polarization; disparity 27.1.

.3 **dissension, dissent,** dissidence, flak [infor-mal]; bickering, infighting, faction, fac-tiousness, partisanship, partisan spirit; **di-visiveness; quarrelsomeness;** litigiousness; pugnacity, bellicosity, combativeness, **ag-gressiveness,** contentiousness, belligerence

797.15; irritability, shrewishness, iras-cibility 951.2.

.4 **falling-out, breach of friendship,** parting of the ways; **alienation, estrangement, disaffection,** disfavor; **breach, break, rup-ture, schism, split, rift,** cleft, **disunity, dis-union, disruption,** separation, cleavage, divergence, division, dividedness; division in the camp, house divided against itself; open rupture, breaking off of negotia-tions, recall of ambassadors.

.5 **quarrel,** open quarrel, **dispute, argument,** polemic, slanging match [Brit], fliting [ar-chaic or dial], **controversy,** altercation, **fight, squabble, contention,** strife, **tussle,** bicker, wrangle, snarl, **tiff, spat,** fuss; **fracas,** donnybrook *or* donnybrook fair; broil, embroilment, imbroglio; words, sharp words, logomachy; **feud,** blood feud, vendetta; brawl 796.5.

.6 [slang or informal terms] row, rumpus, ruckus, ruction, shindy, barney [Brit], set-to, run-in, **scrap, hassle,** rhubarb, dustup; knock-down-and-drag-out, knock-down-and-drag-out quarrel *or* fight.

.7 **bone of contention,** apple of discord, sore point, tender spot, delicate *or* tick-lish issue, rub; **bone to pick,** crow to pluck *or* pick *or* pull; *casus belli* [L], grounds for war.

.8 VERBS **disaccord, disagree, differ,** differ in opinion, hold opposite views, **be at variance,** not get along, pull different ways, be at cross-purposes, have no mea-sures with, misunderstand one another; **conflict, clash,** collide, jostle, jangle, jar; live like cat and dog, live a cat-and-dog life.

.9 **have a bone to pick with,** have a crow to pluck with *or* pick with *or* pull with.

.10 **fall out,** have a falling-out, **break with, split,** separate, **diverge,** divide, agree to disagree, **part company,** come to *or* reach a parting of the ways.

.11 **quarrel, dispute,** differ [archaic], flite [ar-chaic or dial], altercate, **fight, squabble,** tiff, spat, **bicker, wrangle,** spar, broil, have words, set to, join issue, make the fur fly; **feud;** brawl 796.14.

.12 [slang or informal terms] **row, scrap, has-sle,** make *or* kick up a row; lock horns, bump heads.

.13 **pick a quarrel,** fasten a quarrel on, look for trouble, pick a bone with, pluck a crow with; have a chip on one's shoulder.

.14 **sow dissension,** stir up trouble, make trouble; **alienate, estrange,** separate, **di-vide, disunite,** disaffect, **come between;**

irritate, provoke, aggravate; **set at odds,** set at variance; **set against,** pit against, **sic on** *or* **at, set on,** set by the ears, set at one's throat; fan the flame, pour oil on the blaze, light the fuse.

.15 ADJS **disaccordant, unharmonious,** inharmonious, disharmonious, **discordant,** out of accord, dissident, dissentient, **disagreeing, differing; conflicting,** clashing, colliding; like cats and dogs.

.16 **at odds, at variance, at loggerheads,** at square [archaic], at cross-purposes; at war, at strife, at feud, at daggers *or* at daggers drawn, up in arms.

.17 **partisan,** polarizing, **divisive, factional,** factious; **quarrelsome,** bickering, disputatious, wrangling, eristic(al), polemic(al); litigious, pugnacious, combative, **aggressive,** bellicose, belligerent 797.25; irritable, shrewish, irascible 951.19.

796. CONTENTION

.1 NOUNS **contention, contest,** contestation, combat, **conflict, strife, war, struggle,** cut and thrust; **warfare** 797; **hostility,** enmity 929; **quarrel,** altercation, controversy, polemic, debate, argument, dispute, **disputation,** litigation; words, war of words, paper war, logomachy; **fighting,** scrapping [slang]; **quarreling, bickering, wrangling, squabbling;** contentiousness, **quarrelsomeness** 795.3; cat-and-dog life; Kilkenny cats.

.2 **competition, rivalry,** vying, emulation, jockeying [informal]; cutthroat competition; run for one's money; gamesmanship, lifemanship, one-upmanship.

.3 **contest, engagement, encounter, match,** matching, meet, meeting, derby, **trial, test,** *concours, rencontre* [both Fr]; fight, bout, go [informal]; joust, tilt; tournament, tourney; rally; **game** 878.9,34,35; **games,** Olympic games, Olympics, gymkhana.

.4 **fight, battle, fray,** affray, combat, action, conflict, embroilment, **clash; brush, skirmish,** scrimmage; tussle, **scuffle, struggle,** scramble, shoving match; exchange of blows, *passage d'arms* [Fr], passage at *or* of arms, clash of arms; **quarrel** 795.5; pitched battle, battle royal, hand-to-hand fight, stand-up fight [informal], running fight *or* engagement; tug-of-war; bullfight, tauromachy; dogfight, cockfight; street fight, rumble [informal]; air *or* aerial combat, sea *or* naval combat, ground combat, armored combat, infantry combat, fire fight, hand-to-hand combat, house-to-house combat.

.5 **free-for-all,** knock-down-and-drag-out [informal], **brawl,** broil, melee, scrimmage, **fracas,** donnybrook *or* donnybrook fair; riot; rumpus, ruckus, ruction, row [all informal].

.6 **death struggle, life-and-death** *or* **life-or-death struggle, fight to the death,** *guerre à mort, guerre à outrance* [both Fr], all-out war, total war, last-ditch fight, fight to the last ditch.

.7 **duel,** single combat, monomachy, satisfaction, **affair of honor.**

.8 **fencing, swordplay.**

.9 **boxing, fighting,** noble *or* manly art of self-defense, **fisticuffs, pugilism, prizefighting,** the fights [informal], the ring; **boxing match, prizefight,** spar, bout; shadowboxing; close fighting, infighting, the clinches [informal]; Chinese boxing; savate.

.10 **wrestling,** rassling [dial], grappling, *sumo* [Jap]; **martial arts;** jujitsu, judo, karate, *aikido* [all Jap], *t'ai chi chu'an, kung-fu, wu-su* [all Chin], *tae-kwan-do* [Korean]; catch-as-catch-can; wrestling match, wrestling meet; Greco-Roman wrestling, Cornish wrestling, Westmorland wrestling, Cumberland wrestling.

.11 **racing, track,** track sports; **horse racing,** the turf, the sport of kings; dog racing, automobile racing.

.12 **race,** contest of speed *or* fleetness; derby; **heat, lap;** footrace, **run,** dash, hundred-yard dash, etc.; sprint, sprint race; marathon, marathon race; relay, relay race; torch race, match race, obstacle race, hurdle race, cross-country race, point-to-point race, three-legged race, sack race, potato race; walk; automobile race, road race, endurance race, track race *or* speedway race, stock-car race, drag race; Grand Prix, Le Mans, Indianapolis 500; motorcycle race, bicycle race; boat race, yacht race, regatta; air race; dog race.

.13 **horse race,** flat race, harness race, trotting race, quarter-horse race, steeplechase *or* chase, hurdle race; invitational race, claiming race, plate race [informal], purse race, stake race *or* stake, sweepstakes *or* sweepstake, sweep [informal], handicap race *or* handicap; Kentucky Derby, Preakness Stakes, Belmont Stakes; Grand National, Derby.

.14 VERBS **contend, contest,** jostle; **fight, battle, combat, war,** put up a fight [informal]; wage war 797.18; **strive, struggle,** scramble, **tussle, scuffle; quarrel** 795.11,12; clash, collide; **wrestle,** rassle [dial], grapple, grapple with, go to the mat with; **come to blows,** close, **mix it up** [slang], exchange blows *or* fisticuffs, **box,** spar, give and take; cut and thrust, **fence,** thrust and parry; **joust, tilt, tourney,** run a tilt *or* a tilt at, break a lance with; **duel,** fight a duel, give satisfaction; feud; skirmish; fight one's way; fight the good fight; **brawl, broil; riot.**

.15 **lift** *or* **raise one's hand against;** make war on 797.19; draw the sword against, take up the cudgels, couch one's lance; square up *or* off [informal], come to the scratch; have at, jump; lay on, lay about one; **pitch into** *or* **sail into** [both informal], light into *or* lay into [both slang], strike the first blow, draw first blood; **attack** 798.15.

.16 **encounter, come up against,** fall *or* run foul *or* afoul of; close with, come to close quarters, bring to bay, meet *or* fight hand-to-hand.

.17 **engage, take on** [informal], enter the ring *or* arena with, put on the gloves with, match oneself against; **join issue,** try conclusions, **join battle, do** *or* **give battle,** engage in battle.

.18 **contend with, engage with,** cope with, **fight with, strive˙ with, struggle with,** wrestle with, grapple with, bandy with [archaic], try conclusions with, measure swords with, tilt with, **cross swords with;** exchange shots, shoot it out with [informal]; **lock horns** *or* **bump heads** [both informal], fall *or* go to loggerheads [archaic]; **tangle with** *or* **mix it up with** [both slang], have a brush with; have it out, fight *or* battle it out, settle it; fight tooth and nail, fight like devils, ask and give no quarter, make blood flow freely, battle *à outrance,* fight to the death.

.19 **compete, compete with, challenge,** jockey [informal], **vie, vie with,** cope [archaic], enter into competition with, **meet;** try *or* test one another; **rival,** emulate, outvie.

.20 **race,** race with, run a race; horse-race, boat-race.

.21 **contend for, strive for, struggle for, fight for,** vie for; stickle for, stipulate for, make a point of.

.22 **dispute, contest,** take issue with; **fight over,** quarrel over, wrangle over, squabble over, bicker over, strive *or* contend about.

.23 ADJS **contending, contesting; contestant,** disputant; striving, struggling; fighting, battling, warring; **warlike** 797.25; **quarrelsome** 795.17.

.24 **competitive,** competing, **vying,** rivaling, **rival,** emulous, in competition, in rivalry; **cutthroat.**

797. WARFARE

.1 NOUNS **warfare, war,** warring, warmaking, **combat, fighting,** *la guerre* [Fr], –machy; armed conflict, armed combat, military operations, the sword, arbitrament of the sword, appeal to arms *or* the sword, resort to arms, force *or* might of arms, bloodshed; **state of war, hostilities,** belligerence *or* belligerency, open war *or* warfare *or* hostilities; **hot war, shooting war;** total war, all-out war; **wartime; battle** 796.4; **attack** 798.

.2 "an epidemic insanity" [Emerson], "a brain-spattering, windpipe-slitting art", "the feast of vultures, and the waste of life" [both Byron], "the business of barbarians" [Napoleon], "the trade of kings" [Dryden], "a by-product of the arts of peace" [Ambrose Bierce], "a conflict which does not determine who is right— but who is left" [anon], "the continuation of politics by other means" [von Clausewitz], "an emblem, a hieroglyphic, of all misery" [Donne], "politics with bloodshed" [Mao Tse-tung].

.3 civil war, revolutionary war, religious war *or* holy war *or* jihad, war of independence, people's war, war of national liberation; limited war, brushfire war, police action; undeclared war; preventive war, war to end war; world war, general war, global war; Armageddon.

.4 air *or* aerial warfare, sea *or* naval warfare, amphibious warfare, land warfare, three-dimensional war; submarine warfare; trench warfare, siege warfare, underground warfare; offensive warfare, defensive warfare; war of movement, mobile warfare; motorized warfare, mechanized warfare; position warfare, war of position; irregular warfare, guerrilla warfare, bushfighting; jungle warfare; chemical warfare, gas warfare; biological warfare, bacteriological warfare, virus warfare, germ warfare; psychological warfare; conventional war *or* warfare; atomic war *or* warfare, atom war, A-war, H-war; push-button warfare, technological warfare, slide-rule warfare, missile warfare; war of attrition.

.5 **cold war,** inactive war, phony war, twilight war, armed neutrality; **psychological warfare, war of nerves;** economic warfare.

.6 **battle array,** order of battle, **disposition, deployment;** open order; close formation; echelon.

.7 **campaign,** war, **drive, expedition,** hostile expedition; **crusade,** holy war, jihad.

.8 **operation,** action; **movement; mission; operations,** military operations, naval operations; combined operations, joint operations, coordinated operations; active operations, amphibious operations, airborne operations, fluid operations, major operations, minor operations, night operations, overseas operations; war plans, staff work; logistics; war game, dry run, kriegspiel, maneuver, maneuvers.

.9 **strategy, tactics;** applied tactics; offensive strategy, defensive strategy; aerial tactics, infantry tactics, airborne tactics, paratroop tactics, cavalry tactics, guerrilla tactics, mobile tactics, armored tactics, columnar tactics, mob tactics, fire tactics, barrier tactics, shock tactics, blitzkrieg tactics, scorched-earth tactics, linear tactics, grand tactics, maneuver tactics; diversion, feint, diversionary movement; encirclement, investment, encircling movement, pincers movement; infiltration.

.10 **warcraft,** war, arms, **military science,** art or rules or science of war; siegecraft; **generalship,** soldiership; chivalry, knighthood, knightly skill.

.11 **declaration of war,** challenge; defiance 793.

.12 **call to arms, call-up,** call to the colors, **rally; mobilization; muster,** levy; conscription, recruitment 780.6; **rallying cry,** slogan, watchword, catchword, exhortation; **battle cry,** war cry, war whoop, rebel yell; banzai, gung ho, St. George, Montjoie, Geronimo, go for broke; **bugle call,** trumpet call, clarion, clarion call.

.13 **service,** duty; active service or duty; military obligation; selective service, national service [Brit].

.14 **militarization, activation, mobilization;** war or wartime footing, national emergency; martial law, suspension of civil rights; garrison state, military dictatorship; remilitarization, reactivation; arms race; war clouds, war scare.

.15 **warlikeness,** unpeacefulness, war or warlike spirit, ferocity, fierceness; **combativeness, contentiousness; hostility, antagonism;** unfriendliness 929.1; aggression, **aggressiveness; belligerence** or belligerency,

pugnacity, pugnaciousness, bellicosity, **truculence,** fight [informal]; chip on one's shoulder [informal]; militancy, **militarism,** martialism, militaryism; saber rattling; **chauvinism, jingoism,** hawkishness [informal], bellicism, **warmongering,** waving of the bloody shirt; warpath; quarrelsomeness 795.3.

.16 (rallying devices and themes) battle flag, banner, colors, gonfalon, bloody shirt, fiery cross or crostarie, atrocity story, enemy atrocities; martial music, war song, battle hymn, national anthem; national honor, face; foreign threat, totalitarian threat, Communist threat, colonialist or neocolonialist or imperialist threat, Western imperialism, yellow peril; expansionism, manifest destiny; independence, self-determination.

.17 war-god, Mars, Ares, Odin or Woden or Wotan, Tyr or Tiu or Tiw; war-goddess, Athena, Minerva, Bellona, Enyo, Valkyrie.

.18 VERBS **war, wage war, make war, carry on war** or **hostilities,** engage in hostilities, wield the sword; battle, **fight** 796.14; spill or shed blood.

.19 **make war on,** levy war on, "let slip the dogs of war" [Shakespeare]; **attack** 798.15–28; **declare war, challenge,** throw or fling down the gauntlet; defy 793.3–6; open hostilities, plunge the world into war; launch a holy war on, go on a crusade against.

.20 **go to war,** break the peace, take up the gauntlet, **go on the warpath, rise up in arms, take** or **resort to arms,** take arms, take up arms, take up the cudgels or sword, fly or appeal to the sword, unsheathe one's weapon, come to cold steel; take the field.

.21 **campaign,** undertake operations, pursue a strategy, make an expedition, go on a crusade.

.22 **serve,** do duty; fulfill one's military obligation, wear the uniform; **soldier,** see or do active duty; **bear arms,** carry arms, shoulder arms, shoulder a gun; see action or combat, hear shots fired in anger.

.23 **call to arms, call up,** call to the colors, **rally; mobilize; muster,** levy; conscript, recruit 780.16; give the battle cry, wave the bloody shirt, beat the drums, blow the bugle or clarion.

.24 **militarize, activate, mobilize,** go on a wartime footing, gird or gird up one's loins, muster one's resources; reactivate, remilitarize, take out of mothballs [informal].

.25 ADJS **warlike, militant,** fighting, warring, battling; **martial, military,** soldierly, soldierlike; **combative, contentious,** gladiatorial; trigger-happy [informal]; **belligerent, pugnacious, truculent, bellicose,** scrappy [slang], full of fight; **aggressive,** offensive; fierce, ferocious, savage, bloody, bloody-minded, bloodthirsty, sanguinary, sanguineous; **unpeaceful,** unpeaceable, unpacific; **hostile, antagonistic, enemy,** inimical; unfriendly 929.9; quarrelsome 795.17.

.26 militaristic, warmongering, saber-rattling; **chauvinistic,** chauvinist, **jingoistic,** jingoist, jingoish, jingo; hawkish [informal], of the war party.

.27 embattled, battled, engaged, at grips, in combat; arrayed, deployed, ranged, in battle array, in the field; armed 799.14.

.28 ADVS at war, up in arms; in the midst of battle, in the thick of the fray or combat; in the cannon's mouth, at the point of the gun; at swords' points, at the point of the bayonet or sword.

.29 wars

Algerian War	Peloponnesian Wars
American Revolution	Persian Wars
Arab-Israeli War	Punic Wars
Balkan Wars	Russian Revolution
Boer War	Russo-Japanese War
Civil War (American)	Samnite Wars
Civil War (English)	Seven Weeks' War
Civil War (Spanish)	Seven Years' War
Civil Wars (Chinese)	Sino-Japanese War
Civil Wars (Roman)	Six Day War
Crimean War	Southeast Asian War
Crusades	Spanish-American
Franco-Prussian War	War
French and Indian	Thirty Years' War
War	Vietnam War
French Revolution	War Between the
Gallic Wars	States
Greco-Persian Wars	War of 1812
Hundred Years' War	War of the Austrian
Indian Wars	Succession
Indochina War	War of the Polish
Italian Wars of Inde-	Succession
pendence	War of the Spanish
Korean War	Succession
Macedonian-Persian	Wars of the French
War	Revolution
Manchurian War	Wars of the Roses
Mexican War	World War I
Napoleonic Wars	World War II

.30 battles

Actium	Arbela-Gaugamela	Marne River
Adrianople	Ardennes	Marston Moor
Aegates Isles	Austerlitz	Metaurus River
Aegospotami	Ayacucho	Meuse River-Argonne
Agincourt	Balaclava	Forest
Antietam	Bannockburn	Midway
Anzio	Bataan-Corregidor	Minden
Battle of Britain		Monmouth
Battle of the Bulge		Mukden
Belleau Wood		Naseby
Bennington		Nashville
Bismarck Sea		Navarino
Blenheim		New Orleans
Borodino		Nile River
Bosworth Field		Normandy
Bouvines		Novgorod
Boyne		Okinawa
Brunanburh		Omdurman
Buena Vista		Orleans
Bull Run		Panipat
Bunker Hill		Passero Cape
Cannae		Pearl Harbor
Caporetto		Petersburg
Caudine Forks		Pharsalus
Chaeronea		Philippi
Châlons-sur-Marne		Philippine Sea
Chancellorsville		Plassey
Château-Thierry		Plataea
Chattanooga		Plevna
Chickamauga		Poitiers
Constantinople		Port Arthur
Coral Sea		Pydna
Crécy		Quebec
Cunaxa		Ravenna
Cynoscephalae		Rocroi
Dardanelles		Rossbach
Dienbienphu		Saint-Mihiel
Drogheda		Saipan
Dunkirk		Salamis
El Alamein		Salerno
Flodden		Santiago de Cuba
Fontenoy		Saratoga
Fredericksburg		Sedan
Gaza		Sempach
Gettysburg		Sevastopol
Granicus River		Shiloh
Guadalcanal		Singapore
Hampton Roads		Soissons
Hastings		Solferino
Hohenlinden		Somme River
Inchon		Spanish Armada
Ipsus		Spotsylvania
Issus		Stalingrad
Ivry-la-Bataille		Syracuse
Iwo Jima		Tannenberg
Jena-Auerstedt		Tarawa-Makin
Jutland		Tertry
Khartoum		Teutoburger Wald
Kwajalein-Eniwetok		Thermopylae
Lake Erie		Tours
Lake Trasimenus		Trafalgar
Langside		Valmy
Leipzig		Verdun
Leningrad		Vicksburg
Lepanto		Vienna
Leuctra		Wagram
Lexington and Con-		Wake Island
cord		Waterloo
Leyte		Yalu River
Long Island		Yorktown
Lucknow		Ypres
Lüleburgaz		Zama
Lützen		
Maldon		
Manila Bay		
Mantinea		
Marathon		
Marengo		
Mariana Islands		

798. ATTACK

.1 NOUNS **attack, assault,** assailing, assailment; **offense, offensive; aggression; onset, onslaught; strike;** descent on or upon; **charge, rush,** dead set at, run at or against; **drive, push** [informal]; **sally, sortie;** infiltration; coup de main [Fr]; frontal attack or assault, head-on attack, flank attack; mass attack; banzai attack or charge; hit-and-run attack; breakthrough; **counterattack, counteroffensive;** amphibious attack; gas attack; diversionary attack, diversion; assault and battery, simple assault, mugging [informal], aggravated assault, armed assault, unprovoked assault; **blitzkrieg, blitz,** lightning attack, lightning war, panzer warfare, sudden or devastating or crippling attack, shock tactics; atomic or thermonuclear attack, first-strike capacity, megadeath, overkill.

.2 **surprise attack,** surprise, surprisal, unforeseen attack, **sneak attack** [informal]; Pearl Harbor.

.3 **thrust,** pass, lunge, swing, cut, stab, jab; feint; home thrust.

.4 **raid,** foray, razzia; **invasion, incursion,** inroad, irruption; **air raid, air strike,** air attack, shuttle raid, fire raid, saturation raid; escalade, scaling, boarding.

.5 **siege, besiegement, beleaguerment;** encompassment, investment, encirclement, envelopment; blockading, blockade; cutting of supply lines; vertical envelopment; pincer movement.

.6 **storm,** storming, taking by storm.

.7 **bombardment, cannonade;** strafe, strafing; **air raid, blitzkrieg, blitz,** lightning attack, lightning war.

.8 **bombing, blitz,** dive-bombing, glide-bombing, skip-bombing, shuttle bombing, area bombing, interdiction bombing, pattern bombing, carpet bombing, precision bombing, pinpoint bombing, saturation bombing, tactical bombing, strategic bombing, high-altitude bombing, low-altitude bombing.

.9 **gunfire, fire, firing,** musketry, **shooting,** fireworks or gunplay [both informal]; gunfight, shoot-out; shellfire; rocket fire; antiaircraft fire, flak or flack; automatic-weapons fire, cross fire, curtain fire, direct fire, dry fire, file fire, ground fire, horizontal fire, interdiction fire, machine-gun fire, mortar fire, vertical fire, percussion fire, pistol fire, platoon fire, plunging fire, high-angle fire, raking fire, rapid fire, ricochet fire, rifle fire, rolling fire, time fire, zone fire, fire of demolition; firepower.

.10 **volley, salvo,** burst, spray, **fusillade,** drumfire, **cannonade,** cannonry, **broadside,** enfilade; **barrage,** antiaircraft barrage, box barrage, emergency barrage, mortar barrage, normal barrage, standing barrage, rolling or creeping barrage.

.11 **stabbing,** piercing; **knifing,** bayonetting; the sword; **impalement, transfixion.**

.12 **stoning,** lapidation.

.13 **assailant,** assailer, **attacker;** assaulter, mugger [informal]; **aggressor;** invader, raider.

.14 **zero hour, H hour; D day,** target day.

.15 VERBS **attack, assault, assail,** harry, assume or take the offensive; commit an assault upon, mug [informal]; **strike, hit, pound** 283.13,14; **go at, come at,** have at, lay at [dial], go for [informal], **launch out against,** make a set or dead set at; **pitch into** or **light into** or **sail into** or wade into or lay into [all informal]; **fall on** or **upon, set on** or **upon, descend on** or **upon,** come down on, swoop down on; pounce upon, land on, land on like a ton of bricks, crack down on [informal]; **lift** or **raise a hand against,** draw the sword against, take up the cudgels against; **lay hands on,** lay a hand on, bloody one's hands with; gang up on, attack in force; jump or bushwhack [both informal], surprise, **ambush; blitz,** attack or hit like lightning.

.16 **lash out at,** let drive at, let fly at, strike out at; **strike at,** hit at, poke at, thrust at, **swing at,** swing on, **take a swing** or **crack** or **swipe** or **poke** or **shot at** [informal], make a thrust or pass at, lunge at, aim or deal a blow at, flail at, flail away at, take a fling or shy at; **cut and thrust; feint.**

.17 **launch an attack,** kick off an attack, mount an attack, **push, thrust,** mount or open an offensive, **drive; advance against** or **upon, march upon** or **against,** bear down upon; **infiltrate; strike; flank;** press the attack, follow up the attack; **counterattack; gas.**

.18 **charge,** rush, **rush at, fly at,** run at, dash at, make a dash or rush at; tilt at, go full tilt at, make or run a tilt at, ride full tilt against; **jump off,** go over the top [informal].

.19 **besiege, lay siege to,** encompass, surround, **encircle,** envelop, invest, set upon on all sides, get in a pincers, close the jaws of the pincers or trap; **blockade;** beset, beleaguer, harry, harass, drive or press one hard; soften up.

.20 raid, foray, make a raid; invade, inroad, make an inroad, make an irruption into; escalade, scale, scale the walls, board; storm, take by storm, overwhelm, inundate.

.21 pull a gun on, draw a gun on; get the drop on or beat to the draw [both slang].

.22 fire upon, fire at, shoot at, pop at or take a pop at [both slang], take or fire or let off a shot at; open fire, commence firing, open up on [slang]; aim at, take aim at, zero in on, take dead aim at, draw a bead on; snipe, snipe at; bombard, blast, strafe, shell, cannonade, mortar, barrage, blitz; pepper, fusillade, fire a volley; rake, enfilade; pour a broadside into; cannon; torpedo; shoot 285.13.

.23 bomb, drop a bomb, lay an egg [slang]; dive-bomb, glide-bomb, skip-bomb, pattern-bomb, etc.; atom-bomb, hydrogen-bomb.

.24 mine, plant a mine, trigger a mine.

.25 stab, stick [informal], pierce, plunge in; run through, impale, spit, transfix, transpierce; spear, lance, poniard, bayonet, saber, sword, put to the sword; knife, dirk, dagger, stiletto; spike.

.26 gore, horn, tusk.

.27 pelt, stone, lapidate [archaic], pellet; brickbat or egg [both informal].

.28 hurl at, throw at, cast at, heave at, chuck at [informal], fling at, sling at, toss at, shy at, fire at, let fly at; hurl against, hurl at the head of.

.29 ADJS attacking, assailing, assaulting, charging, driving, thrusting, advancing; invading, invasive, invasionary, incursive, incursionary, irruptive.

.30 offensive, combative, on the offensive or attack; aggressive 797.25.

.31 ADVS under attack, under fire; under siege.

.32 INTERJS attack!, advance!, charge!, over the top!, up and at 'em!, give 'em hell!, let 'em have it!, fire!, open fire!; banzai!

799. DEFENSE

.1 NOUNS defense, defence [Brit], guard, ward; protection 699; resistance 792; self-defense, self-protection, self-preservation; deterrent capacity; defense in depth; the defensive; defenses, psychological defenses, ego defenses, defense mechanism, escape mechanism, avoidance reaction, negative taxis or tropism.

.2 civil defense; Office of Emergency Planning, OEP, Office of Civil Defense, OCD, Air Defense Command; conelrad (control of electromagnetic radiation for civil defense), Emergency Broadcast System, EBS, Civil Defense Warning System; radar defenses, distant early warning or DEW Line; antimissile missile, antiballistic-missile system, ABM.

.3 armor, armature; armor plate; body armor, suit of armor, plate armor, panoply, harness; mail, chain mail, chain armor, coat of mail, hauberk, habergeon; bulletproof vest; shield, buckler; protective covering, cortex, thick skin, shell 228.15; spines, needles.

.4 fortification; bulwark, rampart, parapet, battlement, merlon; vallation [archaic], vallum, contravallation, circumvallation; earthwork, work, bank [archaic], dike, mound, parados; stockade, palisade; barricade; abatis; entanglement, barbed-wire entanglement; fieldwork; casemate; breastwork; mantelet; ravelin; redan; lunette; bastion, demibastion, banquette, curtain, tenaille; advanced work, outwork, barbican, redoubt, sconce, fortalice [archaic]; glacis; scarp, escarp, escarpment, counterscarp; machicolation, loophole, balistraria; bartizan; drawbridge, portcullis, cheval-de-frise or chevaux-de-frise; postern gate, sally port; fence, barrier 730.5; enclosure 236.3.

.5 entrenchment, trench, ditch, fosse; moat; dugout, abri; bunker; foxhole, slit trench; approach trench, communication trench, fire trench, gallery, parallel, coupure; tunnel, fortified tunnel; sap, single or double sap, flying sap; mine, countermine.

.6 stronghold, hold, safehold, fasthold, fastness, keep, ward, bastion, donjon, citadel, castle, tower, tower of strength, strong point; mote or motte; fort, fortress, post; bunker, pillbox, blockhouse, garrison, garrison house; acropolis; peel, peel tower; rath; martello tower, martello; bridgehead, beachhead.

.7 defender, champion, advocate; upholder; supporter 787.9; vindicator, apologist; protector 699.5; guard 699.9; paladin.

.8 VERBS defend, guard, shield, screen, secure, guard against; defend tooth and nail; safeguard, protect 699.18–20; stand by the side of, flank; advocate, champion 1006.10.

.9 fortify, embattle, battle [archaic]; arm; armor, armor-plate; man; garrison, man the garrison; barricade, blockade; bulwark, wall, palisade, fence; castellate, crenellate; bank; entrench, **dig in**; mine.

.10 **fend off, ward off, stave off, hold off,** keep off, beat off, parry, fend, counter, turn aside; **hold** or **keep at bay,** keep at arm's length; stop, check, block, hinder, obstruct; **repel, repulse, rebuff, drive back,** put back, push back; go on the defensive, fight a holding or delaying action, fall back to prepared positions.

.11 ADJS **defensive,** defending, **guarding,** shielding, screening; **protective** 699.23; self-defensive, self-protective, self-preservative.

.12 **fortified,** battlemented, embattled, battled [archaic]; castellated, crenellated, casemated, machicolated.

.13 **armored,** armor-plated; in armor, panoplied, armed cap-a-pie, armed at all points, in harness, "in complete steel" [Shakespeare]; mailed, mailclad, ironclad; loricate, loricated.

.14 **armed,** hoplo–; heeled or carrying [both slang]; accoutered, **in arms,** bearing or wearing or carrying arms, under arms, sword in hand; **well-armed,** heavy-armed, full-armed, bristling with arms, **armed to the teeth;** light-armed.

.15 **defensible,** defendable, tenable.

.16 ADVS **defensively, in defense,** in self-defense; **on the defensive,** on guard; **at bay,** *aux abois* [Fr], with one's back to the wall.

.17 **armor**

aegis	habergeon
armet	hauberk
backplate	headpiece
bard	heaume
basinet	helm
beaver	helmet
brassard	jamb
breastplate	jambeau
brigandine	knee plate
buckler	lorica
bulletproof vest	mail
burganet	morion
byrnie	nasal
cabasset	nosepiece
camail	pallette
casque	pavise
casquetel	*Pickelhaube* [Ger]
chamfron	plate
coif	rerebrace
corselet	rondel
cubitiere	sallet
cuirass	shield
cuisse	skirt of tasses
épaulière	solleret
face guard	tasse
gas mask	tuille
gauntlet	vambrace
gorget	visor
greaves	

800. COMBATANT

.1 NOUNS **combatant, fighter, battler,** scrapper [slang]; **contestant, contender, competitor, rival;** disputant, wrangler, squabbler, bickerer, quarreler; struggler, tussler, scuffler; brawler, rioter; feuder; **belligerent,** militant; gladiator; jouster, tilter; **knight,** belted knight; swordsman, blade, sword, *sabreur, beau sabreur* [both Fr]; fencer, foilsman, swordplayer [archaic]; duelist; gamecock, fighting cock; **tough,** rough, rowdy, **ruffian, thug, hoodlum, hood** [informal], hooligan, streetfighter, bully, bullyboy, bravo; gorilla or goon or plug-ugly [all slang], hatchet man or enforcer [both informal], strong-arm man, strong arm, strong-armer; swashbuckler.

.2 **pugilist,** pug or palooka [both slang], **boxer, fighter, prizefighter,** fisticuffer, bruiser, sparrer; flyweight, bantamweight, featherweight, lightweight, welterweight, middleweight, light heavyweight, heavyweight; judo or jujitsu or karate expert, brown belt, black belt; Chinese boxer; savate expert.

.3 **wrestler,** rassler [dial], grappler, scuffler, matman.

.4 **bullfighter,** toreador, *torero* [Sp]; banderillero, picador, matador.

.5 **militarist, warmonger,** war dog or hound, war hawk, **hawk** [informal]; **chauvinist, jingo,** jingoist.

.6 **serviceman,** military man; navy man 276.4; air serviceman 279.3,4; **soldier, warrior,** brave, fighting man, legionary, hoplite, **man-at-arms,** rifleman, rifle; **cannon fodder,** food for powder; warrioress, Amazon; spearman, pikeman, halberdier.

.7 (common soldiers) GI, GI Joe, **doughboy, Yank;** Tommy Atkins or Tommy or Johnny or swaddy [all Brit]; redcoat; *poilu* [Fr]; Aussie, Anzac, digger [all Austral]; jock [Scot]; Fritz, Jerry, Heinie, Hun [derog], Boche [derog], Kraut [derog] (German soldier); Janissary (Turkish soldier); sepoy [India]; askari [Africa].

.8 **enlisted man,** noncommissioned officer 749.19; **common soldier, private,** buck private [slang]; private first class, pfc.

.9 **infantryman, foot soldier;** footslogger or paddlefoot or doughfoot or **dogface** or grunt [all slang]; light infantryman, chasseur, *Jäger* [Ger], Zouave; **rifleman,** rifle, musketeer; fusileer, carabineer; **sharpshooter,** marksman, expert rifleman, *bersagliere* [Ital]; **sniper;** grenadier.

.10 **artilleryman,** artillerist, **gunner,** guns

[slang], cannoneer, machine gunner; **bomber,** bomb thrower, bombardier.

.11 **cavalryman,** mounted infantryman, **trooper;** dragoon, light *or* heavy dragoon; lancer, lance, uhlan, hussar; cuirassier; spahi; cossack.

.12 **tank corpsman, tanker,** tank crewman.

.13 **engineer,** combat engineer, pioneer, Seabee; sapper, sapper and miner.

.14 **elite troops,** special troops, **shock troops,** storm troops, elite corps; commandos, rangers, Special Forces, Green Berets, marines, paratroops, guardsmen, Schutzstaffel, SS, Waffen-SS, Gurkhas.

.15 **irregular,** casual; **guerrilla,** partisan, franctireur; **bushfighter,** bushwhacker [slang]; underground, resistance, maquis; Vietcong, VC, Charley [slang]; *maquisard* [Fr], underground *or* resistance fighter.

.16 **mercenary, hireling,** *condottiere* [Ital], free lance, free companion, **soldier of fortune,** adventurer; gunman, gun, hired gun, hired killer, professional killer.

.17 **recruit,** rookie [slang], conscript, drafted man, **draftee, inductee,** selectee, enlistee, enrollee, trainee, boot [slang]; **raw recruit,** tenderfoot; awkward squad [slang]; draft, levy.

.18 **veteran, vet** [informal], campaigner, old campaigner, old soldier, war-horse [informal].

.19 (military units) **unit, organization,** tactical unit, **outfit** [informal]; **army,** field army, army group, corps, **division,** wing, regiment, battle group, battalion, garrison, **company,** troop, brigade, legion, phalanx, cohort, **platoon,** section, **battery,** maniple, combat team, combat command; task force; **squad,** squadron; detachment, detail, posse; kitchen police, KP; column, flying column; rank; file; train, field train; cadre.

.20 **corps;** army corps, *corps d'armée* [Fr]; corps troops; air corps, armored corps, tank corps, engineer corps, corps of engineers, army service corps, drum corps, bugle corps, quartermaster corps, signal corps, corps of signals, medical corps, rifle corps, marine corps, staff corps, motor corps, adjutant general corps, judge advocate general corps, ordnance corps, chemical corps, transportation corps, dental corps, veterinary corps, army nurse corps, military police corps; corps of cadets.

.21 **arm, branch, service,** arm *or* branch of the service.

.22 **army,** this man's army [slang], **armed force, armed service,** fighting machine;

the **military,** military establishment; **soldiery, forces, troops, host,** array, legions; ranks, rank and file; **standing army, regular army,** regulars, professional *or* career soldiers; the line, troops of the line; line of defense, first *or* second line of defense; ground forces, ground troops; storm troops; paratroops, ski troops; occupation force.

.23 **militia,** organized militia, national militia, mobile militia, territorial militia, reserve militia; home reserve; **National Guard,** Air National Guard, state guard; home guard; minutemen, trainband, yeomanry.

.24 **reserves, auxiliaries, second line of defense,** landwehr, army reserves, home reserves, territorial reserves, territorial *or* home defense army, supplementary reserves, organized reserves; US Army Reserve, US Naval Reserve, US Marine Corps Reserve, US Air Force Reserve, US Coast Guard Reserve.

.25 **volunteers,** volunteer army, volunteer militia, volunteer navy.

.26 **navy,** naval forces, **first line of defense; fleet,** flotilla, argosy, armada, squadron, escadrille, division, task force, task group; mosquito fleet; United States Navy, USN; Royal Navy, RN; marine, mercantile *or* merchant marine, merchant navy, merchant fleet; naval militia; naval reserve; coast guard; Seabees, Naval Construction Battalion.

.27 **marines,** sea soldiers, Marine Corps, Royal Marines; **leathernecks** *or* devil dogs *or* gyrenes [all slang], jollies [Brit informal].

.28 **air force,** air corps, air service, air arm; strategic air force, tactical air force; squadron, escadrille, flight, wing.

.29 **air force;** US Air Force, USAF; US Army Air Force, USAAF; Royal Air Force, RAF; Royal Canadian Air Force, RCAF; Royal Australian Air Force, RAAF; US National Air Service, USNAS; Naval Air Division, NAD, Navy Air, Fleet Air Arm; Army-Navy Air Corps, ANAC; Far East Air Force, FEAF; Air Command, Bomber Command, Coastal Command; Strategic Air Command, SAC, Air Transport Command, ATC; Air Transport Service, ATS; Military Air Transport Service, MATS; Naval Air Transport Service, NATS; Carrier Aircraft Service Unit, CASU; Airborne Reconnaissance Force, ARF.

.30 (women's services) Women Accepted for

Volunteer Emergency Service, WAVE, Waves; Women's Army Corps, WAC, Wacs; Women's Royal Army Corps, WRAC, Wracs; Women's Army Auxiliary Corps, WAAC, Waacs; Women's Royal Naval Corps, WREN, Wrens; Women's Air Force, WAF, Wafs; Women's Royal Air Force, WRAF, Wrafs; Women's Auxiliary Air Force, WAAF, Waafs; Women's Air Force Service Pilots, WASP, Wasps; Women's Reserve of the Marine Corps, WAM, Wams; Women's Auxiliary of the US Coast Guard, Spars; Army Nurse Corps, Navy Nurse Corps.

.31 **guards,** household troops; **yeomen of the guard,** beefeaters, Life Guards, Horse Guards, Foot Guards, Grenadier Guards, Coldstream Guards, Scots Guards, Irish Guards; Swiss Guards.

.32 **war-horse, charger,** courser, trooper.

801. ARMS

.1 NOUNS **arms, weapons,** deadly weapons, instruments of destruction; **weaponry, armament, munitions, ordnance,** munitions of war, *apparatus belli* [L]; musketry; missilery; small arms; side arms; stand of arms; conventional weapons, nonnuclear weapons; **nuclear weapons,** atomic weapons, thermonuclear weapons, A-weapons; biological weapons; weapons of mass destruction.

.2 **armory, arsenal,** magazine, dump; ammunition depot, ammo dump [informal]; park, gun park, artillery park, park of artillery; atomic arsenal, thermonuclear arsenal.

.3 **ballistics, gunnery,** musketry, artillery; rocketry, missilery; archery.

.4 **sword, blade,** good or trusty sword; steel, **cold steel;** Excalibur.

.5 **gun, firearm;** shooting iron or gat or rod or heater or piece [all slang]; shoulder weapon or gun or arm; **rifle,** musket, recoilless rifle; shotgun, smoothbore gun or weapon, sawed-off shotgun; **pistol,** handgun, automatic, repeater, **revolver,** six-shooter or six-gun [both informal], Saturday night special [informal]; flamethrower, flame projector; **blowgun,** blowpipe, sumpit or sumpitan; peashooter.

.6 **artillery, cannon,** cannonry, **ordnance,** engines of war; field artillery; heavy artillery, heavy field artillery; siege artillery, bombardment weapons, breakthrough weapons; siege engine; mountain artil-

lery, coast artillery, trench artillery, antiaircraft artillery, flak [slang]; battery.

.7 **antiaircraft gun,** AA gun, ack-ack [slang], pom-pom [informal], *Fliegerabwehrkanone* [Ger], skysweeper, Bofors, Oerlikon.

.8 **ammunition,** ammo [informal], **powder and shot,** iron rations [informal].

.9 **explosive,** high explosive; **powder,** nitro powder, smokeless powder; **gunpowder,** "villanous saltpetre" [Shakespeare]; **guncotton,** nitrocotton; cellulose nitrate, pyroxylin, **nitroglycerin,** melinite, cordite, gelignite, lyddite, Ballistite; **TNT,** trinitrotoluene, trinitrotoluol; **dynamite,** giant powder; plastic explosive.

.10 **charge, load;** blast; warhead, payload.

.11 **cartridge,** cartouche, **shell;** ball cartridge; blank cartridge, dry ammunition.

.12 **missile, projectile,** bolt; brickbat, stone, rock, Irish confetti [slang]; boomerang; bola; throwing-stick, throw stick, waddy [Austral]; countermissile; **rocket** 281.2–6, 14,15; **torpedo** 281.16.

.13 **shot,** bar shot, bird shot, buckshot, canister shot, cannon shot, case shot, chain shot, crossbar shot, duck shot, langrage or langrel shot, round shot, split shot, swan shot; grapeshot, grape; **ball,** cannonball, rifle ball, minié ball; **bullet,** slug, pellet; dumdum bullet, expanding bullet, explosive bullet, manstopping bullet, manstopper; tracer bullet, tracer; **shell,** high-explosive shell, **shrapnel.**

.14 **bomb,** bombshell; time bomb, infernal machine; **grenade,** hand grenade, rifle grenade, concussion grenade, smoke grenade, incendiary grenade, wall grenade, gas grenade, tear-gas grenade; petard, carcass; depth charge, depth bomb, ash can [slang]; aerial bomb, fire bomb, incendiary bomb, antipersonnel bomb.

.15 **atomic bomb, atom bomb, A-bomb,** fission bomb, nuclear explosive, atomic warhead, nuclear warhead, thermonuclear warhead; **hydrogen bomb, H-bomb,** fusion bomb, thermonuclear bomb, super-bomb, hell bomb; cobalt bomb; **plutonium bomb;** clean bomb, dirty bomb; nuclear artillery, tactical nuclear weapons, low-yield or limited nuclear weapons, nukes [slang].

.16 **arrow, shaft, dart,** reed, **bolt,** tox(o)– or toxi–; quarrel; chested arrow, footed arrow, bobtailed arrow, cloth yard shaft; arrowhead, barb; flight, volley.

.17 **bow,** crossbow, longbow, carriage bow; **bow and arrow.**

.18 **sling, slingshot;** throwing-stick, throw stick, spear-thrower, atlatl, wommera; **catapult,** arbalest, ballista, trebuchet.

.19 **launcher,** projector, bazooka; rocket launcher 281.10.

.20 **brass knuckles;** knucks *or* brass knucks [both informal], knuckles, knuckle-dusters.

.21 **knives**

barong	shiv [slang]
bolo	switchblade knife,
bowie knife, bowie	switchblade
edge tool 348.2,13	throwing knife *or* iron
gravity knife	trench knife
machete	yataghan
parang	

.22 **daggers**

bayonet	misericord
dirk	poniard, poignard
dudgeon [archaic]	skean, skean dhu
kris	stiletto
kuttar	

.23 **spears**

assegai	lance
bill	partisan
gisarme	pike
halberd	spontoon
javelin	

.24 **swords**

backsword	glaive [archaic]
bilbo	rapier
broadsword	saber
claymore	scimitar
cutlass	smallsword
épée	Toledo
falchion	tuck [archaic]
foil	

.25 **axes**

battle-ax	Lochaber ax
broadax	poleax
halberd	tomahawk
hatchet	

.26 **clubs**

bastinado	mace
bat	morning star
billy, billy club	nightstick
blackjack	paddle
bludgeon	quarterstaff
cane	ram, battering ram
clavi–	sandbag
cosh [Brit slang]	shillelagh
cudgel	spontoon
ferule	staff
knobkerrie	stave
knobstick	stick
life preserver	truncheon
loaded cane	war club

.27 **guns and launchers**

air gun	antitank gun
air pistol	antitank rifle
air rifle	arquebus
antiaircraft gun, AA gun	atomic cannon
antisubmarine mortar	atomic gun, atom gun
	automatic

automatic pistol	M-14
automatic rifle, auto-rifle	mine thrower, *Minenwerfer* [Ger]
ball-turret gun	*mitrailleuse* [Fr]
bazooka	M-1
BB gun	mortar
belly-gun	mountain gun
Big Bertha	M-16
blunderbuss	musket
bolt-action rifle	musketoon
bombard	muzzle-loader
breechloader	needle gun
Bren gun, Bren	pedrero
brown Bess	petronel
Browning automatic rifle, BAR	pistol
bulldog	pom-pom
burp gun [informal]	popgun
caliver	pump gun
cane gun	recoilless rifle
cannon	repeater
carbine	revolver
carronade	rifle
chassepot	riot gun
culverin	rocket launcher
dart gun	semiautomatic rifle, semiautomatic
derringer	shotgun
escopeta	shoulder arm *or* gun *or* weapon
falconet	siege gun
field gun, fieldpiece	six-gun, six-shooter [informal]
firelock	
flintlock	skysweeper
forty-five, .45	smoothbore
forty-four, .44	Sten gun, Sten
fowling piece	submachine gun
fusil	swivel, swivel gun
Garand rifle, Garand	tear-gas gun
Gatling gun	thirty-eight, .38
hackbut	thirty-thirty, .30-30
handgun	thirty-two, .32
harpoon gun	Thompson submachine gun, tommy gun [informal]
harquebus	
hedgehog	
horse pistol	trench mortar
howitzer	turret gun
lever-action rifle	twenty-two, .22
Lewis gun	wind-gun [archaic]
Long Tom	Y-gun
machine gun	zip gun
machine pistol	
matchlock	

.28 **gun makes**

Armstrong	Marlin
Benet-Mercie	Martini-Henry
Beretta	Mauser
Bofors	Maxim
Browning	Minié
Colt	Mossberg
Enfield	Oerlikon
Flobert	Paixhans
Garand	Parrott
Garling	Remington
Gatling	Savage
Hotchkiss	Smith and Wesson
Krupp	Snider
Lancaster	Spandau
Lee-Enfield	Springfield
Lee-Metford	Stevens
Lewis	Vickers
Luger	Vickers-Maxim
Mannlicher	Webley-Scott

Westley Richards   Winchester
Whitworth

.29 gun parts

barrel	hair trigger
bolt	hammer
breech	lock
butt	magazine
chamber	muzzle
cock	receiver
cylinder	sear
flintlock	sear pin
gun carriage	sight
gunflint	stock
gunlock	trigger
gunstock	

.30 bombs

aerial bomb	hydrobomb
antipersonnel bomb	hydrogen bomb,
antisubmarine bomb	H-bomb
atomic bomb,	incendiary, incendiary
A-bomb	bomb
azon bomb, azon	petard
blockbuster	pipe bomb
citybuster	plutonium bomb
concussion bomb	razon bomb
delayed-action bomb	robot bomb
demolition bomb	roc
depth bomb, depth	rocket bomb 281.4
charge	satchel charge
dynamite bomb	smoke bomb
fireball	stench bomb, stink
fire bomb	bomb
fission bomb	tear-gas bomb
fragmentation bomb	thermonuclear bomb
fusion bomb	time bomb
gas bomb	

.31 mines

aerial mine	land mine
antenna mine	Leon mine
antipersonnel mine	limpet mine
antitank mine	magnetic mine
booby trap	oyster mine
buoyant mine	pressure mine
castrator mine	set gun
Claymore mine	sonic mine, acoustic
floating mine	mine
fougasse	spring gun
ground mine	submarine mine

802. ARENA

.1 NOUNS **arena, scene of action, site,** scene, setting, background, **field, ground,** terrain, sphere, place, locale, milieu, precinct, purlieu; course, range, walk [archaic]; campus; **theater,** stage, stage set *or* setting, scenery; **platform; forum,** agora, marketplace, open forum, public square; **amphitheater,** circus, hippodrome, **coliseum,** colosseum, **stadium, bowl; hall, auditorium;** gymnasium, gym [informal], palaestra; **lists,** tiltyard, tilting ground; floor, **pit,** cockpit; bear garden; **ring,** prize ring, boxing ring, canvas, squared circle [informal], wrestling ring, mat, bull ring; parade ground; athletic field 878.12.

.2 **battlefield, battleground,** battle site, **field,** combat area, **field of battle;** field of slaughter, field of blood *or* bloodshed, aceldama, killing ground, shambles; **the front,** front line, **line,** enemy line *or* lines, firing line, battle line, line of battle; combat zone; **theater, theater of operations,** theater *or* seat of war; communications zone, zone of communications; no-man's-land; demilitarized zone, DMZ; jump area, landing beach.

.3 campground, camp, encampment, bivouac, tented field.

803. PEACE

.1 NOUNS **peace,** *pax* [L]; **peacetime,** piping time of peace, the storm blown over; freedom from war, cessation of combat, exemption from hostilities, public tranquillity, "liberty in tranquillity" [Cicero]; **harmony,** accord 794.

.2 **peacefulness, tranquillity, serenity, calmness, quiet,** peace and quiet, quietude, quietness, quiet life, restfulness; order, orderliness, law and order.

.3 **peace of mind,** peace of heart, peace of soul *or* spirit, peace of God, "peace which passeth all understanding" [Bible].

.4 **peaceableness, unpugnaciousness,** uncontentiousness, nonaggression; irenicism, dovishness [informal], **pacifism,** pacificism; peaceful coexistence; **nonviolence.**

.5 **noncombatant,** nonbelligerent, nonresistant, nonresister; **civilian,** citizen.

.6 **pacifist,** pacificist, peacenik [informal], **peace lover, dove,** dove of peace [both informal]; pacificator, peacemaker, peacemonger; **conscientious objector,** conchie [slang].

.7 VERBS **keep the peace,** remain at peace, wage peace; refuse to shed blood, keep one's sword in its sheath; forswear violence, beat one's swords into plowshares; pursue the arts of peace.

.8 [Bible] "be at peace among yourselves", "follow after the things which make for peace", "follow peace with all men", "as much as lieth in you, live peaceably with all men", "seek peace, and pursue it", "have peace one with another", "be of one mind, live in peace".

.9 ADJS **pacific, peaceful, peaceable;** tranquil, serene; idyllic, pastoral; halcyon, soft, piping, calm, quiet, restful, untroubled, orderly, at peace; concordant 794.3; bloodless; peacetime.

.10 **unbelligerent, unhostile,** unbellicose, **unpugnacious, uncontentious,** unmilitant, unmilitary, **nonaggressive**, noncombative, nonmilitant; noncombatant, civilian; **pacific, peaceable**, peace-loving, dovish [informal]; **pacifistic**, pacifist, irenic; **nonviolent**; conciliatory 804.12.

.11 INTERJS **peace!, peace be with you!,** peace be to you!, *pax vobiscum!, pax tecum!* [both L]; *shalom!, shalom aleichem!* [both Heb], *salaam aleikum!* [Arab]; "peace be to this house!", "peace be within thy walls, and prosperity within thy palaces", "let the peace of God rule in your hearts" [all Bible]; go in peace!, *vade in pace!* [L].

804. PACIFICATION

.1 NOUNS pacification, peacemaking, peacemongering, **conciliation, propitiation, placation, appeasement, mollification,** dulcification; **calming, soothing,** tranquilization 162.2; détente, relaxation of tension, easing of relations; mediation 805; placability; peace-keeping force, United Nations troops.

.2 **peace offer,** offer of parley, parley; **peace feelers; peace offering,** propitiatory gift; **olive branch; white flag,** truce flag, flag of truce; calumet, peace pipe, **pipe of peace;** downing of arms, hand of friendship, empty hands, outstretched hand.

.3 **reconciliation,** reconcilement, *rapprochement* [Fr], **reunion,** shaking of hands, making up *or* kissing and making up [both informal].

.4 **adjustment,** accommodation, resolution, composition of differences, compromise, arrangement, settlement, terms.

.5 **truce, armistice,** peace; pacification, treaty of peace, suspension of hostilities, **cease-fire,** stand-down, breathing spell, cooling-off period; Truce *or* Peace of God, Pax Dei, Pax Romana; temporary arrangement, *modus vivendi* [L]; hollow truce, *pax in bello* [L]; demilitarized zone, buffer zone, neutral territory.

.6 **disarmament,** reduction of armaments; **demilitarization,** deactivation, disbanding, disbandment, **demobilization,** mustering out, reconversion, decommissioning.

.7 VERBS **pacify, conciliate, placate, propitiate, appease, mollify,** dulcify; **calm, soothe,** tranquilize 163.7; smooth, smooth over, smooth down, smooth one's feathers; allay, lay, lay the dust; pour oil on troubled waters, pour balm on, take the edge off of, take the sting out of; cool [slang], defuse.

.8 **reconcile, bring to terms, bring together,** reunite, heal the breach; bring about a détente; **harmonize,** restore harmony, put in tune; adjust, settle, compose, accommodate, arrange matters, settle differences, resolve, compromise; **patch things up,** fix up [informal], patch up a friendship *or* quarrel, weave peace between, smooth it over; mediate 805.6.

.9 **make peace,** cease hostilities, raise a siege; **bury the hatchet, smoke the pipe of peace;** negotiate a peace, dictate peace; make a peace offering, hold out the olive branch, hoist *or* show *or* wave the white flag.

.10 **make up** *or* **kiss and make up** *or* make it up *or* make matters up [all informal], **shake hands,** come round, come together, come to an understanding, **come to terms,** let the wound heal, let bygones be bygones, forgive and forget, put it all behind one, settle *or* compose one's differences.

.11 **disarm, lay down one's arms,** down *or* ground one's arms, sheathe the sword, turn swords into plowshares; **demilitarize,** deactivate, **demobilize, disband,** reconvert, decommission.

.12 ADJS pacificatory, **pacific,** irenic, **conciliatory,** reconciliatory, **propitiatory,** propitiative, **placative,** placatory, **mollifying, appeasing; pacifying,** soothing 163.15.

.13 **pacifiable, placable, appeasable.**

805. MEDIATION

.1 NOUNS **mediation,** intermediation, **intercession; intervention,** interposition, putting oneself between, stepping in, declaring oneself in, involvement, interagency.

.2 **arbitration,** arbitrament, compulsory arbitration, binding arbitration; umpirage, refereeship, mediatorship.

.3 **mediator,** intermediator, intermediate agent, intermediate, intermedium, **intermediary,** interagent, internuncio; **medium; intercessor,** interceder; ombudsman; **intervener,** interventor, interventionist; **go-between,** middleman 781.4; connection [slang]; front *or* front man [both slang]; deputy, agent 781; **spokesman,** spokeswoman, **mouthpiece; negotiator,** negotiant, negotiatress *or* negotiatrix.

.4 **arbitrator,** arbiter, impartial arbitrator, third party, unbiased observer; **moderator; umpire, referee, judge;** magistrate 1002.1.

.5 **peacemaker,** make-peace, reconciler,

smoother-over; **pacifier**, pacificator; **conciliator**, propitiator, **appeaser**; marriage counselor, family counselor.

.6 VERBS **mediate**, intermediate, **intercede**, go between; **intervene**, interpose, step in, declare oneself a party, involve oneself, put oneself between disputants, use one's good offices, act between; represent 781.14; **negotiate**, bargain, treat with, make terms, meet halfway; **arbitrate**, moderate; **umpire**, referee, judge.

.7 **settle**, **arrange**, adjust, straighten out, bring to terms or an understanding; make peace 804.9.

.8 ADJS **mediatory**, mediatorial, mediative, mediating, going or coming between; intermediatory, intermediary, intermedial, intermediate, **middle**, intervening, mesne, interlocutory; interventional, arbitrational, arbitrative; **intercessory**, intercessional; pacificatory 804.12.

806. NEUTRALITY

.1 NOUNS **neutrality**, **neutralism**, strict neutrality; noncommitment, noninvolvement; **independence**, **nonpartisanism**, **nonalignment**; anythingarianism or nothingarianism [both informal]; mugwumpery, mugwumpism, fence-sitting; **evasion**, **cop-out** [slang], abstention; **impartiality** 976.4.

.2 **indifference**, indifferentness, Laodiceanism; passiveness 706.1; apathy 856.4.

.3 **middle course** or **way**, *via media* [L]; **middle ground**, neutral ground, center, **middle of the road**, fence [informal]; medium, **happy medium**; mean, **golden mean**; moderation, moderateness 163.1; compromise 807; halfway measures, half measures, half-and-half measures.

.4 **neutral**, neuter; **independent, nonpartisan**; mugwump, fence-sitter; anythingarian or nothingarian [both informal]; third force, third world.

.5 VERBS **remain neutral**, stand neuter, sit it out [informal], **keep in the middle of the road, sit on the fence** or straddle [both informal], trim; **evade**, evade the issue, duck the issue [informal], **cop out** [slang], abstain.

.6 **steer a middle course**, hold or keep or preserve a middle course, walk a middle path, follow the *via media*, strike or preserve a balance, **keep a happy medium**, keep the golden mean, avoid both Scylla and Charybdis; be moderate 163.5.

.7 ADJS **neutral**, neuter; noncommitted, uncommitted, noninvolved, uninvolved; **in-**different, Laodicean; passive 706.6; apathetic 856.13; neither one thing nor the other, neither hot nor cold; even, half-and-half, fifty-fifty [informal]; **on the fence** [informal], **in the middle of the road**, centrist, moderate, midway; **independent, nonpartisan; nonaligned**, third-force, third-world; **impartial** 976.10.

807. COMPROMISE

(mutual concession)

.1 NOUNS **compromise**, composition, adjustment, accommodation, settlement, mutual concession, give-and-take; abatement of differences; bargain, deal [informal], arrangement, understanding; **concession**, giving way, yielding; surrender, desertion of principle, evasion of responsibility, cop-out [slang].

.2 VERBS **compromise**, make or reach a compromise, compound, compose, accommodate, adjust, settle, make an adjustment or arrangement, **make a deal** [informal], come to an understanding, strike a bargain; strike a balance, take the mean, **meet halfway**, split the difference, go fifty-fifty [informal], give and take; play politics; steer a middle course 806.6; **make concessions**, give way, yield; surrender, desert one's principles, evade responsibility, duck responsibility [informal], cop out [slang].

808. POSSESSION

.1 NOUNS **possession**, possessing, **owning**, having title to; seisin, nine points of the law, *de facto* possession, *de jure* possession, lawful or legal possession; property rights, proprietary rights; **title,** derivative title, original title; adverse possession, squatting, squatterism, squatter's right; claim, legal claim; usucapion, prescription; **occupancy**, occupation; **hold, holding, tenure;** tenancy, tenantry, **lease,** leasehold, sublease, underlease, undertenancy; gavelkind; villenage, villein socage, villeinhold; socage, free socage; burgage; frankalmoign, lay fee; tenure in chivalry, knight service; fee fief, fiefdom, feud, feodum; freehold, alodium; fee simple, fee tail, fee simple absolute, fee simple conditional, fee simple defeasible or fee simple determinable; fee position; dependency, colony, mandate; prepossession [archaic], preoccupation, preoccupancy; chose in possession, bird in hand; property 810.

.2 **ownership,** possessorship, *dominium* [L], **proprietorship,** proprietary; lordship, overlordship, seigniory; dominion, sovereignty 739.5; landownership, landowning, landholding, land tenure.

.3 **monopoly,** monopolization; **corner,** cornering, a corner on [all informal]; exclusive possession; engrossment, forestallment.

.4 VERBS **possess, have, hold,** have and hold, **occupy, fill, enjoy,** boast; be possessed of, have tenure of, have in hand, be seized of, have in one's grip *or* grasp, have in one's possession, be enfeoffed of; **command,** have at one's command *or* pleasure *or* disposition *or* disposal; claim, usucapt; squat, squat on, claim squatter's right.

.5 **own,** have for one's own *or* very own, have to one's name, call one's own, have title to, have the deed for, hold in fee simple.

.6 **monopolize,** hog [slang], take it all, have all to oneself, have exclusive possession of *or* exclusive rights to; engross, forestall, tie up; **corner** *or* get a corner on *or* corner the market [all informal].

.7 **belong to,** pertain to, appertain to; vest in.

.8 ADJS **possessed, owned,** held; –an *or* –ean *or* –ian; in seisin, in fee, in fee simple, free and clear; **own,** of one's own; **in one's possession, in hand,** in one's grip *or* grasp, at one's command *or* disposal; on hand, by one, in stock, in store.

.9 **possessing, having, holding,** having and holding, **occupying, owning; in possession of, possessed of,** seized of, master of; tenured; enfeoffed; endowed with, blessed with; worth; propertied, property-owning, landed, landowning, landholding; –ed *or* –'d.

.10 **possessive,** possessory, **proprietary.**

.11 **monopolistic,** monopoloid, monopolizing, hogging *or* hoggish [both slang].

809. POSSESSOR

.1 NOUNS **possessor, holder,** keeper, haver, enjoyer, –er; have [informal].

.2 **proprietor,** proprietary, **owner;** *rentier* [Fr]; titleholder, deedholder; proprietress, proprietrix; **master, mistress, lord,** laird [Scot]; **landlord, landlady;** lord of the manor, mesne lord, mesne, feudatory, feoffee; squire, country gentleman; householder; beneficiary, cestui, cestui que trust, cestui que use.

.3 **landowner,** landholder, property owner,

propertied *or* landed person, man of property, freeholder; landed interests, landed gentry, slumlord, rent gouger; absentee landlord.

.4 **tenant, occupant,** occupier, incumbent, **resident; lodger,** roomer, paying guest; **renter,** hirer [Brit], **lessee,** leaseholder; subtenant, sublessee, underlessee, undertenant; tenant at sufferance, tenant at will; tenant from year to year, tenant for years, tenant for life; squatter; homesteader.

.5 **trustee,** fiduciary, holder of the legal estate; depository, depositary.

810. PROPERTY

.1 NOUNS **property, properties, possessions, holdings,** havings, goods, chattels, goods and chattels, **effects,** estate and effects, what one can call one's own, what one has to one's name; hereditament, corporeal hereditament, incorporeal hereditament; acquest.

.2 **belongings, appurtenances,** trappings, paraphernalia, appointments, accessories, perquisites, appendages, appanages, choses local; **things,** material things, mere things; choses, choses in possession, choses in action; personal effects, chattels personal, movables, choses transitory; one's all.

.3 **impedimenta,** luggage, dunnage, baggage, bag and baggage, traps, tackle, apparatus, gear, outfit, duffel.

.4 **estate, interest, equity, stake,** part, percentage; **right, title, claim,** holding; use, trust, benefit; absolute interest, vested interest, contingent interest, beneficial interest, equitable interest; easement, right of common, common, right of entry; limitation; settlement, strict settlement.

.5 (estates) particular estate, legal estate, equitable estate, paramount estate, vested estate, estate at sufferance, estate at will, estate in possession, estate for years, estate for life, estate pour autre vie; feudal estate, fee, feud, feod [archaic], feodum, fief, estate in fee; fee simple; fee tail, estate tail *or* in tail; copyhold; lease, leasehold; remainder; reversion; estate in expectancy.

.6 **freehold,** estate of freehold; alodium, alod; frankalmoign, lay fee, tenure in *or* by free alms; mortmain, dead hand.

.7 **real estate, realty,** real property, chattels real, tenements; *praedium* [L], landed property *or* estate, **land, lands,** property, grounds, acres; lot, lots, parcel, plot, plat, quadrat; demesne, domain [archaic]; messuage, manor, honor, toft [Brit].

.8 **assets, means, resources;** stock, stock-in-trade; one's worth, what one is worth; circumstances, funds 835.14; **wealth** 837; **material assets,** tangible assets, tangibles; intangible assets, intangibles; current assets, deferred assets, fixed assets, frozen assets, liquid assets, quick assets, assets and liabilities, net assets, net worth; assessed valuation.

.9 ADJS **propertied,** proprietary; **landed.**

.10 real, praedial; manorial, seignioral, seigneurial; feudal, feudatory, feodal.

.11 freehold, leasehold, copyhold; alodial.

811. ACQUISITION

.1 NOUNS **acquisition,** gaining, getting, getting hold of [informal], coming by, **acquirement, obtainment,** obtention, **attainment,** securement, winning; trover; accession; addition 40; **procurement,** procural, procurance, procuration; **earnings,** making, pulling or dragging down [slang], moneymaking, moneygetting, moneygrubbing.

.2 **collection, gathering,** gleaning, bringing together, assembling, **accumulation,** cumulation, **amassment.**

.3 **gain, profit,** percentage [informal], get [Brit dial], **take,** take-in [informal], rake-off [slang]; **gains, profits, earnings, winnings, return, returns, proceeds,** gettings, makings; **income** 841.4; **receipts** 844; pickings, gleanings; pelf, lucre, filthy lucre; perquisite, perk or perks [both Brit]; cleanup or killing [both slang]; net or neat profit, clean or clear profit, net; gross profit, gross; paper profits; capital gains; interest, dividends; hoard, store 660; wealth 837.

.4 **profitableness, profitability,** gainfulness, remunerativeness, rewardingness.

.5 **yield, output,** make, production; **proceeds,** produce, product; **crop, harvest,** fruit, vintage, bearing; second crop, aftermath; bumper crop.

.6 **find,** finding, **discovery;** trove, *trouvaille* [Fr]; treasure trove, buried treasure; foundling; waifs, waifs and strays; **windfall,** windfall money, windfall profit, **bonus, gravy** [slang], bunce [Brit slang].

.7 **godsend, boon, blessing;** manna, manna from heaven, loaves and fishes.

.8 VERBS **acquire, get, gain, obtain, secure, procure; win;** score; **earn, make,** pull down or drag down [both slang]; **reap, harvest;** contract; take, catch, capture,

corral [informal]; **net,** bag, sack; come or enter into possession, **come into, come by,** come in for, be seized of; draw, derive.

.9 **take possession, take up,** take over, get hold of [informal], get at, **lay hands on,** get one's fingers or hands on, make one's own; grab, glom on to [both slang], annex.

.10 **collect, gather, glean, pick, pluck,** cull, **take up,** pick up, get or gather in, gather to oneself, bring or get together, scrape together; amass, assemble, accumulate 660.11; **scrape up,** rake up, **dig up,** grub, grub up, round up, scare up [informal].

.11 **profit, make** or **draw** or **realize** or **reap profit, make money;** coin money, make a killing, clean up; gain by, **capitalize on,** commercialize, make capital out of, **cash in on** or make a good thing of [both informal], turn to profit or account, **realize on,** make money by, obtain a return, turn a penny or an honest penny; **gross, net; realize, clear.**

.12 **be profitable,** pay, repay, pay off [informal], yield a profit, be gainful, be worthwhile or worth one's while, be a good investment.

.13 ADJS **obtainable, attainable, available,** accessible, to be had.

.14 **acquisitive,** acquiring; grasping, grabby [slang]; greedy 634.27.

.15 **gainful,** productive, **profitable, remunerative, lucrative,** fat, **paying,** well-paying; advantageous, worthwhile; banausic, moneymaking, breadwinning.

.16 ADVS **profitably, gainfully,** remuneratively, lucratively, **at a profit,** in the black; for money; advantageously, to advantage, to profit, to the good.

812. LOSS

.1 NOUNS **loss, losing,** privation, **deprivation, bereavement,** taking away; stripping, dispossession, despoilment, spoliation, robbery; divestment, denudation; **sacrifice,** forfeit, **forfeiture,** denial, nonrestoration; expense, cost, debit; detriment, injury, damage; destruction, ruin, perdition, total loss, dead loss; losing streak [informal]; **loser** 727.5.

.2 **waste,** wastage, **exhaustion, depletion,** depreciation, dissipation, wearing, wearing away, erosion, ablation, using, using up, consumption, expenditure, impoverishment, drain, shrinkage, leakage, evaporation; decrement, decrease 39.

.3 **losses, losings.**

.4 VERBS **lose**, incur loss, **suffer loss**, undergo privation, be bereaved of or bereft of, have no more, meet with a loss; drop, kiss good-bye [both slang]; let slip, let slip through one's fingers; **forfeit**, default; **sacrifice**; miss, wander from, go astray from; **mislay**, misplace; lose out.

.5 **waste**, **deplete**, **depreciate**, dissipate, wear, wear away, erode, ablate, consume, drain, **shrink**, dribble away; decrease 39.6; squander 854.3,4.

.6 **go to waste**, come to nothing, come to naught, go up in smoke or go down the drain [both informal]; run to waste, go to pot [informal], run or go to seed; dissipate, leak, leak away, scatter to the winds, "waste its sweetness on the desert air" [Thomas Gray].

.7 ADJS **lost**, gone; forfeited, forfeit; by the board, out the window; long-lost; lost to; wasted, consumed, depleted, dissipated, expended, worn away, eroded, ablated, used, used up, shrunken; squandered 854.9; irretrievable 889.15.

.8 **bereft**, bereaved, divested, denuded, **deprived of**, shorn of, parted from, bereaved of, stripped of, dispossessed of, despoiled of, robbed of; **out of**, minus [informal], wanting, lacking; cut off, cut off without a cent.

.9 ADVS **at a loss**, unprofitably, to the bad [informal]; in the red [slang]; out, out of pocket.

813. RETENTION

.1 NOUNS **retention**, retainment, **keeping**, **holding**, **maintenance**, **preservation**; prehension; keeping or holding in, **bottling up** or corking up [both informal], locking in, suppression, repression, inhibition, retentiveness, retentivity; **tenacity** 50.3.

.2 **hold**, **purchase**, **grasp**, **grip**, gripe, **clutch**, **clamp**, **clinch**, **clench**; seizure 822.2; bite, nip; **cling**, clinging; toehold, foothold, footing; **clasp**, **hug**, **embrace**, bear hug; grapple; firm hold, tight grip, iron grip, grip of steel, death grip.

.3 (wrestling holds) half nelson, full nelson, quarter nelson, three-quarter nelson, stranglehold, toehold, lock, hammerlock, headlock, scissors, bear hug.

.4 (prehensile organs) **clutches**, **claws**, **talons**, pounces, unguals, ungues, ungulae [both L], chel(i)-, onych(o)-, ungui-; **nails**, fingernails; **pincers**, nippers, chelae; **tentacles**; **fingers**, digits, hooks [slang]; **hands**, paws, meathooks, mitts [both slang]; palm, palmi-; prehensile tail; **jaws**, mandibles, maxillae; **teeth**, fangs.

.5 VERBS **retain**, **keep**, **save**, save up, **maintain**, **preserve**; keep or hold in, **bottle up** or cork up [both informal], lock in, suppress, repress, inhibit, keep to oneself; persist in; hold one's own, hold one's ground.

.6 **hold**, **grip**, gripe, **grasp**, **clutch**, clip, **clinch**, **clench**; bite, nip; grapple; **clasp**, **hug**, **embrace**; **cling**, **cling to**, cleave to, stick to, adhere to, freeze to; **hold on to**, hold fast or tight, hang on to, keep a firm hold upon; **hold on, hang on** [informal], hold on like a bulldog, stick like a leech, cling like a winkle, hang on for dear life; keep hold of, never let go.

.7 **hold**, **keep**, **harbor**, bear, have, have and hold, hold on to; **cherish**, fondle, entertain, treasure, treasure up; **foster**, **nurture**, **nurse**; embrace, hug, clip [Brit dial], cling to; bosom or embosom [both archaic], take to the bosom.

.8 ADJS **retentive**, keeping, holding, gripping, grasping; **tenacious**, clinging; viselike.

.9 **prehensile**, raptorial; fingered, digitate or digitated, digital; clawed, taloned, jawed, toothed, dentate, fanged.

.10 **incommunicable**, noncommunicable, **unimpartable**; inalienable, indefeasible; noninfectious, noncontagious, not catching.

.11 ADVS **for keeps** [informal], to keep, **for good**, for good and all, for always; forever 112.12.

.12 **gripping instruments**

chuck	grip
clamp	holdfast
clasp	jaws
clinch	nippers
clip	paper clip
cramp	pincers
dog	pincette
forceps	pliers
grab	tie clip
grabhook	tongs
grapnel, grapple, grappler	tweezers
grappling iron or hook	vise
	wrench 348.20

814. RELINQUISHMENT

.1 NOUNS **relinquishment**, **release**, giving up, letting go, dispensation; **disposal**, disposition, riddance, getting rid of, dumping 668.3; **renunciation**, forgoing, forswearing, swearing off, resignation, abjuration, **abandonment** 633; recantation, retraction 628.3; **surrender**, cession, **yielding**; sacrifice.

.2 **waiver, quitclaim**, deed of release.

.3 VERBS **relinquish, give up**, render up, **surrender, yield**, cede; spare; resign, vacate; drop, **waive**, dispense with; **forgo**, do without, get along without, forswear, abjure, **renounce**, swear off, **abandon** 633.5–7; recant, retract 628.9; disgorge, throw up; have done with, wash one's hands of; **part with**, give away, dispose of, rid oneself of, get rid of, dump 668.7; kiss goodbye [slang]; **sacrifice**, make a sacrifice; quitclaim.

.4 **release, let go**, leave go [dial], **let loose of**, unhand, unclutch, unclasp, relax one's grip or hold.

.5 ADJS **relinquished**, released, disposed of; waived, dispensed with; forgone, forsworn, renounced, abjured, **abandoned** 633.8; recanted, retracted; **surrendered**, ceded, yielded; sacrificed.

815. PARTICIPATION

.1 NOUNS **participation, partaking, sharing**, having a part or share or voice, contribution, association; involvement, engagement; complicity; **voting** 744.18, **suffrage** 744.17; partnership, copartnership, copartnery, joint control, cochairmanship, joint chairmanship; joint tenancy, cotenancy; joint ownership, condominium.

.2 **communion**, community, communal effort or enterprise, **cooperation**, cooperative society; **collectivity**, collectivism, collective enterprise, collective farm, kibbutz, kolkhoz; **democracy**, participatory democracy, town meeting; collegiality; common ownership, public ownership, state ownership, communism, socialism 745.5,6; profit sharing; sharecropping.

.3 **communization**, communalization, **socialization, nationalization, collectivization**.

.4 **participator, participant, partaker, sharer**; party, **a party to**, accomplice, accessory; partner, copartner; cotenant; shareholder.

.5 VERBS **participate, partake, contribute**, chip in, involve or engage oneself; **have a hand in**, have a finger in, have a finger in the pie, have to do with, have a part in, be an accessory to, be implicated in, be a party to; **participate in**, partake of or in, **take part in**, take an active part in, **join, join in**, make oneself part of, join oneself to, associate oneself with, play or perform a part in, get in the act [slang]; **have a voice in**, help decide, be in on the decisions, vote, have suffrage, be enfranchised; **enter into**, go into; make the

scene [slang]; sit in, sit in on; bear a hand, pull an oar.

.6 **share, share in**, come in for a share, **go shares**, be partners in, have a stake in, have a percentage or piece of [informal], **divide with, divvy up with** [slang], halve, go halves; go halvers or go **fifty-fifty** or go even stephen [all informal], split the difference, **share and share alike**; do one's share or part, pull one's weight; cooperate 786.3; apportion 816.6.

.7 **communize, communalize, socialize, collectivize, nationalize**.

.8 ADJS **participating, participative**, participant, participatory; involved, engaged; implicated, accessory; **partaking, sharing**.

.9 **communal, common**, general, public, collective, popular, social, societal; **mutual**, commutual [archaic], reciprocal, associated, **joint**, conjoint, **in common**, share and share alike; **cooperative** 786.5; profit-sharing; collectivistic, **communistic**, socialistic 745.21,22.

816. APPORTIONMENT

.1 NOUNS **apportionment, portioning**, division, divvy [slang], **partition**, repartition, partitionment, partitioning, parceling, budgeting, rationing, **dividing, sharing**, sharing out, splitting, cutting, slicing, cutting the pie [informal], divvying up [slang].

.2 **distribution**, dispersion, **disposal**, disposition; dole, doling, doling out, giving out, passing around; **dispensation**, administration, issuance; disbursal, disbursement, paying out.

.3 **allotment, assignment, appointment**, setting aside, **earmarking**, tagging; appropriation; **allocation**.

.4 **dedication, commitment, devotion**, consecration, hallowing, ordainment, ordination.

.5 **portion, share, interest, part**, stake, stock, **piece**, bit, segment, –ile; **bite** or **cut** or **slice** or **chunk** [all informal], a piece of the action [informal], **lot, allotment, end** [informal], **proportion, percentage**, measure, quantum, **quota**, deal or dole [both archaic], meed, moiety, mess, helping; contingent; dividend; **commission**, rakeoff [slang]; equal share, half, halver [informal]; **lion's share**, bigger half, big end [slang]; small share, modicum; **allowance, ration, budget**; fate, destiny 640.2.

.6 VERBS **apportion, portion, parcel, partition, part, divide**, share; share with, share and share alike, divide with, go halvers or fifty-fifty *or* even stephen with [informal]; divide into shares, **share out** *or* **around**, divide up, divvy up [slang], **split**, split up, carve, cut, slice, carve up, slice up, cut up, cut *or* slice the pie *or* melon [informal].

.7 **proportion**, proportionate, prorate, divide *pro rata*.

.8 **parcel out**, **portion out**, measure out, spoon out, **deal out**, **dole out**, **mete out**, ration out, give out, pass around; mete, dole, deal; **distribute**, disperse; **dispense**, dispose [archaic], issue, administer; disburse, pay out.

.9 **allot**, **lot**, **assign**, **appoint**, **set**, detail; **allocate**, make assignments *or* allocations, schedule; **set apart** *or* **aside**, **earmark**, **tag**, mark out for; set off, mark off, portion off; assign to, appropriate to *or* for; reserve, restrict to, restrict 234.5; **ordain**, **destine**, **fate**.

.10 **budget**, **ration**; allowance, put on an allowance.

.11 **dedicate**, **commit**, **devote**, **consecrate**, set apart.

.12 ADJS **apportioned**, portioned out, parceled, allocated, etc.; **apportionable**, divisible, distributable, dispensable, severable.

.13 **proportionate**, proportional; prorated, *pro rata* [L]; half; halvers *or* fifty-fifty *or* even stephen [all informal], half-and-half, equal; **distributive**, distributional; **respective**, particular, per head, per capita, several.

.14 ADVS **proportionately**, in proportion, *pro rata* [L]; **distributively**; **respectively**, severally, each to each; share and share alike, in equal shares, half-and-half; fifty-fifty *or* even stephen [both informal].

817. TRANSFER OF PROPERTY OR RIGHT

.1 NOUNS **transfer**, transference; **conveyance**, conveyancing; **giving** 818; **delivery**, deliverance; **assignment**, assignation; **consignment**, consignation; conferment, conferral, settling, settlement; vesting; bequeathal 818.10; **sale** 829; surrender, cession; transmission, transmittal; disposal, disposition; demise; alienation, abalienation; amortization, amortizement; enfeoffment; deeding; bargain and sale; lease and release; **exchange**, barter, trading.

.2 **devolution**, succession, reversion; shifting use, shifting trust.

.3 VERBS **transfer**, **convey**, **deliver**, hand, pass, negotiate; give 818.12–21; **hand over**, **turn over**, **pass over**; assign, consign, confer, settle, settle on; cede, surrender; bequeath 818.18; **sell** 829.8–12; **make over**, **sign over**, sign away; transmit, **hand down**, **hand on**, **pass on**, devolve upon; demise; alienate, alien, abalienate, amortize; enfeoff; **deed**, deed over, give title to; **exchange**, barter, trade.

.4 **change hands**, change ownership; devolve, pass on, descend, succeed [archaic].

.5 ADJS **transferable**, **conveyable**, negotiable, alienable; **assignable**, consignable; devisable, bequeathable; heritable, inheritable.

818. GIVING

.1 NOUNS **giving**, **donation**, **bestowal**, bestowment; **endowment**, gifting [informal], **presentation**, presentment; **award**, awarding; grant, granting; accordance, vouchsafement [archaic]; conferment, conferral; investiture; delivery, deliverance, surrender; **concession**, communication, impartation, impartment; **contribution**, subscription; accommodation, supplying, furnishment, provision 659; **offer** 773; **liberality** 853.

.2 **commitment**, **consignment**, assignment, **delegation**, relegation, commendation, remanding, **entrustment**; enfeoffment, infeudation *or* infeodation.

.3 **charity**, almsgiving; **philanthropy** 938.4.

.4 **gift**, **present**, presentation, *cadeau* [Fr], **offering**, fairing [Brit]; tribute, **award**; oblation 1032.7; handsel; box [Brit]; Christmas present *or* gift, birthday present *or* gift; peace offering; white elephant [informal].

.5 **gratuity**, **largess**, **bounty**, liberality, donative, sportula; perquisite, perks [Brit informal]; consideration, fee [archaic], **tip**, *pourboire* [Fr], *Trinkgeld* [Ger], sweetener, inducement; grease *or* salve *or* palm oil [all slang]; **premium**, **bonus**, something extra, gravy [slang], bunce [Brit slang], lagniappe; honorarium; incentive pay, time and a half, double time; bribe 651.2.

.6 **donation**, donative; **contribution**, subscription; alms, pittance, **charity**, **dole**, **handout** [slang], alms fee, widow's mite; Peter's pence; **offering**, offertory, votive offering, collection; tithe.

.7 **benefit**, benefaction, benevolence, **blessing**, **favor**, **boon**, grace; manna.

.8 **subsidy**, subvention, subsidization, support, price support, depletion allowance, tax benefit *or* write-off; **grant,** grant-in-aid, bounty; **allowance, stipend,** allotment; **aid,** assistance, financial assistance; **help,** pecuniary aid; scholarship, fellowship; **welfare,** public welfare, public assistance, relief, relief *or* welfare payments, welfare aid, dole, aid to dependent children; guaranteed annual income; alimony; annuity; pension, old-age insurance, retirement benefits.

.9 **endowment,** investment, **settlement,** foundation; **dowry,** *dot* [Fr], portion, marriage portion; **dower,** widow's dower; jointure, legal jointure, thirds; appanage.

.10 **bequest,** bequeathal, **legacy,** devise; inheritance 819.2; **will, testament,** last will and testament; probate, attested copy; codicil.

.11 **giver, donor,** donator, gifter [informal], presenter, bestower, conferrer, grantor, awarder, imparter, vouchsafer; fairy godmother, lady bountiful, Santa Claus, sugar daddy [informal]; cheerful giver; **contributor, subscriber,** supporter, backer, financer, funder, angel [informal]; patron, patroness, Maecenas; almsgiver, almoner; **philanthropist** 938.8; assignor, consignor; settler; testate, testator, testatrix; feoffor.

.12 VERBS **give, present, donate,** slip [slang], let have; **bestow, confer, award, allot, render,** bestow on; impart, communicate; **grant,** accord, **allow,** vouchsafe, yield, afford; **tender,** proffer, offer, extend, issue, dispense, administer; serve, help to; deal, dole, mete; **give out, deal out, dole out, mete out, hand out** or dish out [both informal], fork out *or* shell out [both slang]; make a present of, gift *or* gift with [both informal], give as a gift; be generous *or* liberal with, give freely; pour, shower, rain, snow, heap, lavish 854.3.

.13 **deliver, hand, pass,** reach, forward, render, put into the hands of; transfer 271.9; **hand over,** give over, deliver over, fork over [slang], **pass over, turn over,** come across with [informal]; hand out, give out, pass out, distribute, circulate; hand in, give in; **surrender,** resign.

.14 **contribute, subscribe,** chip in [informal], kick in [slang], give one's share *or* fair share; put oneself down for, pledge; contribute to, give to, **donate to,** gift *or* gift with [both informal]; put something in the pot, sweeten the kitty.

.15 **furnish, supply, provide, afford,** provide for; **accommodate with,** favor with, indulge with; **heap upon,** pour on, shower down upon, **lavish upon.**

.16 **commit, consign, assign, delegate,** relegate, confide, commend, remit, remand, give in charge; **entrust,** trust, give in trust; enfeoff, infeudate.

.17 **endow,** invest, vest; endow with, favor with, bless with, grace with, vest with; **settle on** *or* **upon; dower.**

.18 **bequeath, will,** will and bequeath, **leave, devise, will to,** hand down, hand on, pass on, transmit; **make a will,** draw up a will, execute a will, make a bequest, write one's last will and testament, write into one's will; add a codicil; entail.

.19 **subsidize, finance,** fund; **aid, assist, support, help,** pay the bills, pick up the check *or* tab [informal]; pension, pension off.

.20 **thrust upon, force upon, press upon,** push upon, obtrude on, ram *or* cram down one's throat.

.21 **give away,** dispose of, part with, sacrifice, spare.

.22 ADJS philanthropic, eleemosynary, **charitable** 938.15; **generous** 853.4.

.23 **giveable,** presentable, bestowable; impartable, communicable; bequeathable, devisable; allowable.

.24 **given,** allowed, accorded, granted, vouchsafed, bestowed, etc.; gratuitous 850.5; God-given, providential.

.25 **donative,** contributory; concessive; testate, testamentary; intestate.

.26 **endowed,** dowered, invested; dower, dowry, dotal; subsidiary, stipendiary, pensionary.

.27 ADVS as a gift, gratis, on one, on the house, free; to his heirs, to the heirs of his body, to his heirs and assigns, to his executors *or* administrators and assigns.

819. RECEIVING

.1 NOUNS **receiving, receival, receipt, getting, taking;** acquisition 811; derivation; **assumption, acceptance;** admission, admittance; **reception** 306.

.2 **inheritance,** heritance [archaic], **heritage, patrimony, birthright, legacy, bequest,** bequeathal; reversion; entail; heirship; **succession,** line of succession, mode of succession, law of succession; primogeniture, ultimogeniture, postremogeniture, borough-English, coheirship, coparcenary, gavelkind; hereditament, corporeal *or* incorporeal hereditament; **heritable; heirloom.**

.3 **recipient, receiver,** accepter, getter, taker,

acquirer, obtainer, procurer; payee, endorsee; addressee, consignee; holder, trustee; **hearer**, viewer, beholder, audience, auditor, listener, looker, spectator; –ee.

.4 **beneficiary**, allottee, **donee, grantee**, patentee; **assignee, assign;** devisee, **legatee**, legatary [archaic]; feoffee; almsman, almswoman; stipendiary; pensioner, pensionary; annuitant; –ee.

.5 **heir**, heritor, inheritor, *heres* [L]; **heiress**, inheritress, inheritrix; coheir, joint heir, fellow heir, coparcener; heir portioner [Scot]; heir expectant; **heir apparent**, apparent heir; **heir presumptive**, presumptive heir; statutory next of kin; legal heir, heir at law, heir general, heir of line *or* heir whatsoever [both Scot]; heir of inventory *or* beneficiary heir [both Scot]; heir of provision [Scot], heir by destination; heir of the body; heir in tail, heir of entail; fideicommissary heir, fiduciary heir; reversioner; remainderman; **successor**, next in line.

.6 VERBS **receive, get, gain, secure,** have, come by, be in receipt of; **obtain, acquire** 811.8–10; **admit, accept, take,** take off one's hands, **take in** 306.10; assume, take on, take over; **derive, draw,** draw *or* derive from; have an income of, drag down *or* pull down [both slang]; have coming in, have in prospect, come in for.

.7 **inherit,** heir [dial], **come into,** come in for, come by, step into a fortune; step into the shoes of, succeed to.

.8 **be received, come in,** come to hand, pass *or* fall into one's hands, go into one's pocket, come *or* fall to one, fall to one's share *or* lot; **accrue,** accrue to.

.9 ADJS **receiving,** on the receiving end; **receptive,** recipient 306.16.

.10 **received, accepted, admitted, recognized, approved.**

820. LENDING

.1 NOUNS **lending, loaning;** moneylending, lending at interest; **advance, advancing,** advancement; **usury,** loan-sharking *or* shylocking [both slang]; lend-lease.

.2 **loan,** lend [dial], **advance,** accommodation; secured loan, collateral loan; unsecured loan; call loan, call money, demand loan; time loan, time money; term loan, long-term loan, short-term loan; installment loan; clearance loan, day loan, morning loan; selfliquidating loan; bank loan, Wall Street loan; policy loan; foreign loan, external loan.

.3 **lender, loaner;** loan officer; **moneylender,** moneymonger; money broker; banker 836.10; **usurer,** Shylock, loan shark [informal]; **pawnbroker;** mortgagee, mortgage holder.

.4 **lending institution,** savings and loan association, finance company *or* corporation, loan office, mortgage company; **bank** 836.13; **credit union;** pawnshop, **pawnbroker,** pawnbrokery, **hock shop** [informal], *mont-de-piété* [Fr], sign of the three balls.

.5 VERBS **lend, loan, advance,** accommodate with; loan-shark [slang]; float *or* negotiate a loan; lend-lease, lease-lend.

.6 ADJS **loaned, lent.**

.7 ADVS **on loan,** on security; in advance.

821. BORROWING

.1 NOUNS **borrowing,** money-raising; touching *or* hitting *or* hitting-up [all slang]; **pawning,** pledging, hocking [slang]; financing, mortgaging; installment buying, installment plan, hire purchase [Brit]; debt, debtor 840.4.

.2 **adoption, appropriation, taking,** deriving, **derivation, assumption; imitation,** simulation, copying, mocking; borrowed plumes; plagiarism, plagiary, pastiche, pasticcio; infringement, pirating.

.3 VERBS **borrow,** borrow the loan of, get on credit *or* trust, get on tick *or* get on the cuff [both informal]; get a loan, float *or* negotiate a loan, go into the money market, **raise money;** touch *or* hit up *or* hit one for [all slang]; run into debt 840.6; pawn 772.10.

.4 **adopt, appropriate,** take, take on, take over, assume, make use of, derive from; **imitate, simulate,** copy, mock, steal one's stuff [slang]; plagiarize, steal; pirate, infringe.

822. TAKING

.1 NOUNS **taking,** possession, taking possession, taking away; **claiming,** staking one's claim; **acquisition** 811; **reception** 819.1; **theft** 824.

.2 **seizure, grab,** grabbing, snatching, snatch, –lepsy; **kidnapping, abduction,** forcible seizure; power grab, coup, *coup d'état* [Fr], seizure of power; hold 813.2; **catch,** catching; **capture,** collaring [informal], nabbing [slang]; **apprehension,** prehension; **arrest,** arrestation, taking into custody; picking up *or* taking in *or* running in [all informal]; dragnet.

.3 **sexual possession,** taking; sexual assault,

ravishment, **rape**, violation; defloration, deflowerment, devirgination.

.4 **appropriation, taking over, takeover** [informal], **adoption, assumption, usurpation**, arrogation; requisition, indent [Brit]; preoccupation, prepossession, preemption; **conquest**, occupation, subjugation, enslavement, colonization.

.5 (seizure and appropriation) **attachment, annexation**, annexure [Brit]; **confiscation**, sequestration; impoundment; **commandeering, impressment**; expropriation, nationalization, socialization, communalization, communization, collectivization; levy; distraint, distress; garnishment; execution; eminent domain, angary, right of eminent domain, right of angary.

.6 **deprivation**, deprivement, **privation, divestment, bereavement**; relieving, disburdening, disburdenment; curtailment, abridgment [archaic]; disentitlement.

.7 **dispossession**, disseisin, expropriation; reclaiming, repossessing, **repossession**, foreclosure; **eviction** 310.2; disendowment; **disinheritance**, disherison, disownment.

.8 **extortion, shakedown** [informal], **blackmail**, bloodsucking, vampirism; protection racket; badger game.

.9 **rapacity**, rapaciousness, ravenousness, sharkishness, wolfishness, **predaciousness**, predacity; pillaging, looting 824.5.

.10 **take, catch, bag**, capture, seizure, **haul**; booty 824.11.

.11 **taker**; partaker; **catcher, captor, capturer**.

.12 **extortionist**, extortioner, **blackmailer**, racketeer, shakedown artist [informal], **bloodsucker**, leech, **vampire**; raptor, predator, harpy, **vulture**, shark; profiteer; rackrenter.

.13 VERBS **take**, possess, take possession; **get**, get into one's hold or possession; pocket, palm; draw off, drain off; **claim, stake one's claim**, enforce one's claim; partake; **acquire** 811.8–11; **receive** 819.6; **steal** 824.13–19.

.14 **seize**, take or get hold of, **lay hold of**, catch or grab hold of, glom on to [slang], **lay hands on**, lay one's hands on, clap hands on [informal], get into one's grasp or clutches; get one's fingers or hands on, get between one's finger and thumb; **grab, grasp, grip**, gripe [archaic], **grapple, snatch**, nip, nail [slang], **clutch, claw**, clinch, clench; **clasp, hug, embrace**; snap up, nip up, whip up, catch up; pillage, loot 824.16; take by assault or storm; **kidnap, abduct**, carry off; shanghai; take by the throat, throttle.

.15 **possess sexually, take; rape**, ravish, violate, assault sexually, lay violent hands on; deflower, deflorate, devirginate.

.16 **seize on** or **upon**, fasten upon; spring or pounce upon, jump [informal], swoop down upon; **catch at, snatch at**, snap at, jump at, make a grab for, scramble for.

.17 **catch, take**, land or nail [both informal], hook, **snag, snare**, sniggle, spear, harpoon; ensnare, enmesh, entangle, tangle, foul, tangle up with; **net**, mesh; **bag**, sack; **trap**, entrap; lasso, rope, noose.

.18 **capture, apprehend, collar** [informal], **nab** [slang], grab [informal], lay by the heels, take prisoner; **arrest**, place or put under arrest, take into custody; pick up or take in or run in [all informal].

.19 **appropriate, adopt, assume, usurp**, arrogate, accroach; requisition, indent [Brit]; **take possession of**, possess oneself of, take for oneself, arrogate to oneself, take up, **take over, help oneself to**, make use of, make one's own, make free with, dip one's hands into; take it all, take all of, hog, monopolize, sit on; preoccupy, prepossess, preempt; jump a claim; **conquer**, overrun, occupy, subjugate, enslave, colonize; squat on.

.20 (seize and appropriate) **attach, annex; confiscate**, sequester, sequestrate, impound; **commandeer**, press, **impress**; expropriate, nationalize, socialize, communalize, communize, collectivize; exercise the right of eminent domain, exercise the right of angary; levy, distrain, replevy, replevin; garnishee, garnish.

.21 **take from**, take away from, **deprive of**, relieve one of, disburden one of, lighten one of, ease one of; **deprive, bereave, divest**; tap, milk, mine, drain, bleed, curtail, abridge [archaic]; cut off; disentitle.

.22 **wrest**, wring, wrench, **rend**, rip; **extort, exact**, squeeze, screw, **shake down** [informal], **blackmail**, levy blackmail, badger or play the badger game [both slang]; **force from, wrest from, wrench from, wring from, tear from**, rip from, **rend from**, snatch from, pry loose from.

.23 **dispossess**, disseise, expropriate, foreclose; **evict** 310.15; disendow; **disinherit**, disherison, **disown**, cut out of one's will, **cut off**, cut off with a shilling, cut off without a cent.

.24 **strip**, strip bare or clean, fleece [informal], **shear**, denude, skin or pluck [both slang], flay, **despoil, divest**, pick clean, pick the bones of; deplume, displume; **milk**; bleed, **bleed white**; exhaust, drain, dry, suck dry; **impoverish**, eat out of house and home.

.25 ADJS **taking, catching;** privative, deprivative; confiscatory, annexational, expropriatory; **thievish** 824.20,21.

.26 **rapacious, ravenous,** ravening, vulturous, vulturine, sharkish, **wolfish,** lupine, predacious, **predatory,** raptorial; vampirish, **bloodsucking,** parasitic; **extortionate; grasping,** grabby [slang]; all-devouring, all-engulfing.

823. RESTITUTION

.1 NOUNS **restitution, restoration,** restoring, giving back, sending back, **return;** reddition [archaic]; extradition, rendition; repatriation; recommitment, remandment, remand; remitter.

.2 **reparation, recompense,** paying back, squaring [informal], repayment, reimbursement, refund, **compensation, indemnification,** retribution, atonement, redress, satisfaction, **amends,** making good, **requital.**

.3 **recovery,** regainment; **retrieval,** retrieve; **recuperation,** recoup, recoupment; **retake,** retaking, recapture; **repossession,** resumption, reoccupation; **reclamation,** reclaiming, revindication; **redemption,** ransom, salvage, trover; replevin, replevy; revival, restoration 694.

.4 VERBS **restore, return, give back,** take back, bring back, put back; remit, send back; repatriate; extradite; recommit, remand.

.5 **make restitution,** make reparation, **make amends,** make good, make up for, atone, give satisfaction, redress, **recompense,** pay back, square [informal], repay, reimburse, refund, **compensate, requite,** indemnify, make it up to; pay damages, pay reparations; pay conscience money.

.6 **recover, regain, retrieve,** recuperate, **recoup, get back,** come by one's own; **redeem,** ransom; **reclaim,** revindicate; **repossess,** resume, reoccupy; **retake,** recapture, take back; replevin, replevy; revive, renovate, restore 694.11–18.

.7 ADJS **restitutive,** restitutory, **restorative;** compensatory, indemnificatory, retributive, reparative; reversionary, reversional, revertible; redeeming, redemptive, redemptional.

.8 ADVS **in restitution,** in reparation, in recompense, in compensation, in retribution, in requital, in amends, in atonement, to atone for.

824. THEFT

.1 NOUNS **theft, thievery,** stealage, **stealing,** thieving, **purloining,** klept(o)–; swiping *or* lifting *or* snatching *or* snitching *or* pinching [all slang]; conveyance [archaic], **appropriation,** conversion, liberation [slang], annexation [informal]; **pilfering,** pilferage, **filching,** scrounging [informal], moonlight requisition [informal]; abstraction; sneak thievery; shoplifting, boosting [slang]; poaching; **graft; embezzlement** 667.1; **fraud, swindle** 618.8.

.2 **larceny,** petit *or* petty larceny, petty theft, grand larceny, grand theft, simple larceny, mixed *or* aggravated larceny.

.3 **robbery,** robbing; bank robbery; banditry, **highway robbery;** armed robbery, **holdup,** heist *or* stickup [both slang], holdup *or* stickup job [slang]; assault and robbery, **mugging** [slang]; purse snatching; **pocket picking; hijacking** [informal]; asportation; cattle stealing, **cattle rustling** *or* cattle lifting [both informal]; extortion 822.8.

.4 **burglary,** burglarizing, housebreaking, **breaking and entering,** break and entry, break-in, unlawful entry; second-story **work** [slang]; safebreaking, **safecracking** *or* safeblowing [both informal].

.5 **plundering, pillaging, looting, sacking,** freebooting, ransacking, rifling, spoiling, **despoliation,** despoilment, despoiling; rapine, spoliation, depredation, direption [archaic], **raiding,** reiving [Scot], ravage, ravaging, ravagement, rape, ravishment; **pillage, plunder,** sack; brigandage, brigandism, banditry; **marauding,** foraging; raid, foray, razzia.

.6 **piracy, buccaneering, privateering, freebooting;** letters of marque, letters of marque and reprisal; air piracy, airplane hijacking, skyjacking.

.7 **plagiarism,** plagiarizing, plagiary, **piracy,** literary piracy, appropriation, borrowing, cribbing; infringement of copyright; autoplagiarism.

.8 **abduction, kidnapping;** shanghaiing, impressment, crimping.

.9 **grave-robbing,** body-snatching [informal], resurrectionism.

.10 **theft, steal, grab, filch, pinch** *or* **lift** [both slang]; **rip-off** [slang]; **heist** *or* **job** *or* caper [all slang]; robbery, burglary, etc.

.11 **booty, spoil, spoils, loot, swag** [slang]; illgotten gains, **plunder,** prize, haul, take, pickings, stealings, stolen goods, hot goods *or* items [slang]; **boodle** *or* squeeze *or* **graft** [all informal]; perquisite, perks

[Brit informal], pork barrel, spoils of office, public trough; till, public till; blackmail.

.12 **thievishness**, larcenousness, taking ways [slang], light fingers, sticky fingers; kleptomania, bibliokleptomania.

.13 VERBS **steal, thieve, purloin, appropriate**, annex or borrow [both informal], **take**, snatch, palm, bag [informal], **make off with**, walk off with, run off or away with, abstract, disregard the distinction between *meum* and *tuum*; **lift** or hook or crib or cop or **pinch** or nip or snitch or snare [all slang], have one's hand in the till; **pilfer, swipe** [slang], **filch**, scrounge [informal]; shoplift, boost [slang]; poach; rustle; **embezzle** 667.4; defraud, swindle 618.17; **extort** 822.22.

.14 **rob**, commit robbery; pick one's pockets; hold up, stick up [informal]; mug [slang]; hijack [informal]; heist or knock over [both slang], rip off [slang].

.15 **burglarize**, burgle [informal], commit burglary, crack a crib [slang]; crack or blow a safe [informal].

.16 **plunder, pillage, loot, sack**, ransack, rifle, freeboot, spoil, spoliate, despoil, depredate, prey on or upon, **raid**, reive [Scot], ravage, ravish, raven, sweep, gut; **fleece** 822.24; maraud, foray, forage.

.17 **pirate**, buccaneer, privateer, freeboot.

.18 **plagiarize, pirate**, borrow or crib [both informal], appropriate; **pick one's brains**; infringe a copyright.

.19 **abduct**, abduce, spirit away, **carry off** or **away**, run off or away with; **kidnap**, snatch [slang], hold for ransom; skyjack; **shanghai**, crimp, impress.

.20 ADJS **thievish, thieving, larcenous, light-fingered, sticky-fingered**; kleptomaniac(al), burglarious; brigandish, piratic(al), piratelike; fraudulent 618.20.

.21 **plunderous, plundering, looting, pillaging**, ravaging, marauding, spoliatory; predatory, predacious.

.22 **stolen**, pilfered, purloined; pirated, plagiarized; hot [informal].

825. THIEF

.1 NOUNS **thief, robber**, stealer, purloiner, lifter [slang], *ganef* [Yid], **crook** [informal]; larcenist, larcener; **pilferer, filcher**, petty thief, chicken thief, scrounger [slang]; sneak thief, prowler; shoplifter, booster [slang]; poacher; **grafter**, petty grafter; jewel thief, **swindler**, con man 619.3,4; land pirate, land shark, land-grabber; grave robber, body snatcher, resur-

rectionist, ghoul; embezzler, peculator, white-collar thief; den of thieves.

.2 **pickpocket**, cutpurse, fingersmith or dip [both slang]; mobsman or swell-mobsman [both Brit]; **purse snatcher**; light-fingered gentry.

.3 **burglar**, yegg or cracksman [both slang]; housebreaker, cat burglar, cat man, second-story thief or worker; **safecracker**, safebreaker, safeblower; pete blower or pete man or peterman [all slang].

.4 **bandit, brigand**, dacoit; **gangster** [informal], mobsman, mobster, racketeer; **thug, hoodlum** 943.4.

.5 **robber, holdup man** or stickup man [both informal]; highwayman, highway robber, footpad, road agent, bushranger [Austral]; mugger [slang], sandbagger; train robber; bank robber, **hijacker** [informal].

.6 **plunderer, pillager, looter, marauder**, rifler, sacker, spoiler, despoiler, spoliator, depredator, **raider**, moss-trooper, freebooter, rapparee, reiver [Scot], forayer, forager, ravisher, ravager; wrecker.

.7 **pirate, corsair, buccaneer, privateer**, sea rover, rover, picaroon; viking, sea king; Blackbeard (Edward Teach), Captain Kidd, Jean Lafitte, Henry Morgan; Captain Hook [J. M. Barrie], Long John Silver [Stevenson]; air pirate, airplane hijacker, skyjacker.

.8 **cattle thief**, abactor, rustler or **cattle rustler** [both informal].

.9 **plagiarist**, plagiarizer, cribber [informal], **pirate**, literary pirate, copyright infringer.

.10 **abductor, kidnapper; shanghaier**, crimp, crimper.

.11 (famous thieves) Barabbas, Robin Hood, Jesse James, Clyde Barrow, John Dillinger, Claude Duval, Jack Sheppard, Willie Sutton, Dick Turpin, Jonathan Wild; Autolycus, Macheath [John Gay], Thief of Baghdad, Jean Valjean [Hugo], Jimmy Valentine [O. Henry], Raffles [E. W. Hornung], Bill Sikes [Dickens].

826. ILLICIT BUSINESS

.1 NOUNS **illicit business**, illegitimate business, illegal operations, illegal commerce or traffic, shady dealings, **racket** [informal]; **the rackets** [informal], the syndicate, **organized crime, Mafia**, Cosa Nostra; **black market**, gray market; narcotics traffic; prostitution, traffic in women, white slavery; usury, loan-sharking [slang]; protection racket; bootlegging, moonshining [informal]; gambling 515.7.

.2 smuggling, contrabandage, contraband; narcotics smuggling, dope smuggling [slang], jewel smuggling, cigarette smuggling; gunrunning, rumrunning.

.3 contraband, smuggled goods; narcotics, drugs, dope [slang], jewels, cigarettes; bootleg liquor 996.17; stolen goods or property, hot goods or items [slang].

.4 racketeer; Mafioso; **black marketeer,** gray marketeer; bootlegger, moonshiner [informal]; pusher or dealer [both informal], narcotics or dope or drug pusher [informal].

.5 smuggler, contrabandist, runner; gunrunner, rumrunner.

.6 fence, receiver, **receiver of stolen goods,** swagman or swagsman [both slang].

.7 VERBS (deal in illicit goods) push or shove [both slang]; **sell under the counter; black-market,** black-marketeer; bootleg, moonshine [informal]; fence [informal].

.8 smuggle, run, sneak.

827. COMMERCE, ECONOMICS

.1 NOUNS commerce, trade, traffic, truck, intercourse, **dealing, dealings; business, business dealings** or affairs or relations, commercial affairs or relations; the business world, the world of trade or commerce, the marketplace; merchantry, mercantile business; **market,** marketing, state of the market, buyers' market, sellers' market; **industry** 716.4; big business, small business; fair trade, free trade, reciprocal trade, unilateral trade, multilateral trade; balance of trade; restraint of trade.

.2 trade, trading, doing business, trafficking; barter, bartering, **exchange,** interchange, swapping [informal]; give-and-take, horse trading [informal], **dealing,** wheeling and dealing [informal]; **buying and selling; wholesaling,** jobbing; brokerage, agency; **retailing,** merchandising 829.2.

.3 negotiation, bargaining, haggling, higgling, **dickering, chaffering,** chaffer, haggle; hacking out or working out or hammering out a deal, coming to terms; collective bargaining, package bargaining, pattern bargaining.

.4 transaction, business or commercial transaction, **deal,** business deal, negotiation [archaic], operation, turn; package deal.

.5 bargain, deal [informal], dicker; **trade, swap** [informal]; horse trade [informal]; trade-in; blind bargain, pig in a poke; hard bargain.

.6 custom, patronage, trade; **goodwill,** repute, good name.

.7 economy, economic system, national economy, world economy, local economy, town economy, urban economy, village economy, farm economy, rural economy, handicraft economy, industrial economy, mercantile economy, barter economy, diversified economy, consumer economy, war economy, planned economy, collectivized economy, capitalist or capitalistic economy, free-enterprise or private-enterprise economy, laissez-faire economy, socialist or socialistic economy; hot or overheated economy; healthy or sound economy; **gross national product,** GNP.

.8 standard of living, standard of life, standard of comfort; real wages, take-home pay or take-home; cost of living; cost-of-living index, consumer price index.

.9 business cycle, economic cycle, business fluctuations; peak, peaking; low, bottoming out [informal]; prosperity, boom [informal]; crisis, recession, **depression,** slowdown, cooling off, slump or bust [both informal], downturn; upturn, expanding economy, recovery; **growth,** economic growth, high growth rate, expansion, market expansion, economic expansion.

.10 economics, eco or econ [both informal], economic science, the dismal science; political economy; dynamic economics; theoretical economics, plutology; classical economics; Keynesian economics, Keynesianism; econometrics; economism, economic determinism; economic man.

.11 economist, economic expert or authority; political economist.

.12 commercialism, mercantilism; industrialism; Mercury, Hermes.

.13 commercialization; industrialization.

.14 VERBS trade, deal, traffic, truck, buy and sell, do business; barter; exchange, change, interchange, give in exchange, take in exchange, **swap** [informal], switch; swap horses or horse-trade [both informal]; trade off; trade in; trade sight unseen, make a blind bargain, sell a pig in a poke; **ply one's trade** 656.12.

.15 deal in, trade in, traffic in, handle, carry, be in; market, merchandise, **sell,** retail, wholesale, job.

.16 trade with, deal with, traffic with, do business with, have dealings with, have truck with, transact business with; frequent as a customer, shop at, trade at, **patronize,** take one's business or trade to;

open an account with, have an account with.

.17 **bargain, drive a bargain, negotiate, haggle,** higgle, chaffer, huckster, **dicker,** hack out *or* work out *or* hammer out a deal; **bid,** bid for, cheapen, beat down, jew down [derog]; underbid, outbid; drive a hard bargain.

.18 **strike a bargain,** make a bargain, make a dicker, **make a deal,** get oneself a deal, put through a deal, shake hands, shake on it [informal]; bargain for, agree to; **come to terms** 521.10; be a bargain, be a go *or* be a deal [both informal], be on [slang].

.19 put on a business basis *or* footing, make businesslike; commercialize; industrialize.

.20 (adjust the economy) cool *or* cool off the economy; heat *or* heat up the economy.

.21 ADJS **commercial, business, trade,** trading, **mercantile,** merchant; commercialistic, mercantilistic; industrial; wholesale, retail.

.22 **economic;** socio-economic, politico-economic(al); ec(o)– *or* oec(o)– *or* oik(o)–.

828. PURCHASE

.1 NOUNS **purchase, buy,** emption; **buying, purchasing; shopping, marketing;** window-shopping; impulse buying; shopping spree; repurchase, rebuying; mail-order buying, catalog buying; installment buying, hire purchase [Brit]; buying up, cornering, coemption [archaic]; buying power, purchasing power; consumer sovereignty, consumer power, consumerism; money illusion.

.2 **emption,** right of emption, right of sole emption; **option,** first option, **first refusal,** refusal, preemption, right of preemption, prior right of purchase.

.3 **clientele,** clientage, **patronage, custom,** trade, carriage trade; **market,** public, purchasing public; urban market, rural market, youth market, suburban market, etc.

.4 **customer, client; patron,** patronizer [informal], regular customer *or* buyer, regular; **prospect;** mark *or* sucker [both slang].

.5 **buyer,** purchaser, emptor, **consumer,** vendee; **shopper,** marketer; window-shopper, browser; purchasing agent, customer agent.

.6 **by-bidder,** decoy, come-on man *or* shill [both slang].

.7 VERBS **purchase, buy,** procure, make *or* complete a purchase, make a buy, make a deal for, blow oneself to [slang]; **buy up,** regrate, **corner,** monopolize, engross; buy

out; buy off; buy in, buy into, buy a piece of; repurchase, rebuy, buy back; buy on credit, buy on the installment plan.

.8 **shop, market, go shopping,** go marketing; window-shop, browse.

.9 **bid,** make a bid, offer, offer to buy, make an offer; give the asking price; by-bid, shill [slang]; bid up; bid in.

.10 ADJS **purchasing, buying,** in the market; cliental.

.11 **bought,** store-bought, boughten *or* store-boughten [both dial], purchased.

829. SALE

.1 NOUNS **sale; wholesale, retail; market, demand,** outlet; buyers' market, sellers' market; mass market; conditional sale; tie-in sale, tie-in; turnover; bill of sale.

.2 **selling, merchandising, marketing; wholesaling,** jobbing; **retailing;** mail-order selling, direct-mail selling, catalog selling; **vending, peddling, hawking, huckstering;** market *or* marketing research, consumer research, consumer preference study, consumer survey; sales campaign, promotion, sales promotion; **salesmanship,** high-pressure salesmanship, hard sell [informal], low-pressure salesmanship, soft sell [informal]; sellout.

.3 **sale,** closing-out sale, going-out-of-business sale, inventory-clearance sale, distress sale, fire sale; bazaar; rummage sale, white elephant sale, garage sale, flea market; tax sale.

.4 **auction,** auction sale, vendue, outcry, sale at *or* by auction, sale to the highest bidder; Dutch auction; **auction block, block.**

.5 **sales talk, sales pitch,** patter; **pitch** *or* spiel *or* ballyhoo [all slang].

.6 **sales resistance,** consumer *or* buyer resistance.

.7 **salability,** salableness, merchandisability, **marketability,** vendibility.

.8 VERBS **sell, merchandise, market,** move, turn over, sell off, make *or* effect a sale; convert into cash, turn into money; **sell out,** close out; sell up [Brit]; **retail,** sell retail, sell over the counter; **wholesale,** sell wholesale, job, be jobber *or* wholesaler for; dump, unload, flood the market with; sacrifice, sell at a sacrifice *or* loss; resell, sell over; undersell, undercut, cut under; sell short; sell on consignment.

.9 **vend,** dispense, **peddle, hawk, huckster.**

.10 **put up for sale,** put up, ask bids *or* offers for, offer for sale, offer at a bargain.

.11 **auction, auction off, auctioneer,** sell at

auction, sell by auction, put up for auction, **put on the block**, bring under the hammer; knock down, sell to the highest bidder.

.12 **be sold, sell**, bring, realize, sell for.

.13 ADJS **sales**, selling, market, **marketing, merchandising, retail,** retailing, wholesale, wholesaling.

.14 **saiable, marketable,** retailable, merchandisable, merchantable, vendible; in demand.

.15 **unsalable,** nonsalable, **unmarketable;** on one's hands, on the shelves, not moving, not turning over, unbought, unsold.

.16 ADVS **for sale,** to sell, up for sale, in *or* on the market, in the marts of trade; at a bargain, marked down.

.17 **at auction,** at outcry, at public auction *or* outcry, by auction, **on the block,** under the hammer.

830. BUSINESSMAN, MERCHANT

.1 NOUNS **businessman,** businesswoman; enterpriser, entrepreneur, man of commerce; small *or* little businessman; big businessman, magnate, tycoon [informal], baron, king, top executive, business leader; director, manager 748.1; big boss; **industrialist,** captain of industry; banker, financier 836.9,10.

.2 **merchant,** merchandiser, marketer, **trader,** trafficker, **dealer,** monger, chandler; **tradesman,** tradeswoman; **storekeeper, shopkeeper;** regrater; **wholesaler,** jobber, middleman; importer, exporter; **distributor; retailer,** retail merchant, retail dealer *or* seller.

.3 (merchants) grocer, groceryman; greengrocer; fruiterer; butcher; baker; poulterer; fishmonger, fishwife; ironmonger [Brit], hardwareman; drysalter [Brit]; perfumer; haberdasher, furnisher, clothing merchant; draper; shoe *or* footwear merchant; bookseller, bookdealer; chandler; confectioner; florist; furrier; jeweler; newsdealer; saddler; stationer; tobacconist; wine merchant, vintner, liquor merchant.

.4 **salesman,** seller, salesperson, salesclerk; **saleswoman,** saleslady, salesgirl; **clerk,** shop clerk, store clerk, shop assistant; floorwalker; **agent, sales agent,** selling agent; scalper *or* ticket scalper [both informal]; sales engineer; sales manager; salespeople, sales force, sales personnel.

.5 **traveling salesman, traveler, commercial traveler,** traveling agent, traveling man *or* woman, knight of the road, bagman

[Brit], drummer; detail man; door-to-door salesman, canvasser.

.6 **vendor, peddler, huckster, hawker,** higgler, cadger [Scot], colporteur, chapman [Brit]; cheap-jack *or* cheap-john [both informal]; coster *or* costermonger [both Brit]; sidewalk salesman.

.7 **solicitor,** canvasser; tout, touter, **pitchman, barker, spieler,** ballyhooer, **ballyhoo man** [all informal].

.8 **auctioneer,** auction agent.

.9 **broker,** note broker, bill broker [Brit], discount broker, cotton broker, hotel broker, insurance broker, mortgage broker, diamond broker, furniture broker, ship broker, grain broker; stockbroker 833.10; pawnbroker 820.3; money broker, money changer, cambist; land broker, real estate broker, Realtor, real estate agent, estate agent [Brit].

.10 **ragman,** old-clothesman, rag-and-bone man [Brit]; junkman, junk dealer.

.11 **tradesmen, tradespeople,** tradesfolk, merchantry.

831. MERCHANDISE

.1 NOUNS **merchandise, commodities, wares, goods,** effects, vendibles, **consumer goods,** consumer items, goods for sale; stock, staples, stock-in-trade; inventory; line, line of goods; sideline; job lot; mail-order goods, catalog goods.

.2 **commodity, ware,** vendible, **product, article, item,** article of commerce *or* merchandise; staple, staple item, standard article; special, feature, leader, lead item, loss leader; seconds; drug, drug on the market.

.3 **dry goods, soft goods;** textiles 378.5,11; yard goods, white goods, linens, napery; men's wear, ladies' wear, children's wear, infants' wear; sportswear, sporting goods; leatherware, leather goods.

.4 **hard goods, durables,** durable goods; fixtures, white goods, **appliances** 659.4; tools and machinery 348; **hardware,** ironmongery [Brit]; sporting goods, **housewares,** housefurnishings, kitchenware; tableware, dinnerware; flatware, hollow ware; metalware, brassware, copperware, silverware, ironware, tinware; woodenware; glassware; chinaware, earthenware, clayware, stoneware, graniteware; enamelware; ovenware.

.5 **furniture,** furnishings, home furnishings.

.6 **notions, sundries,** novelties, knickknacks, odds and ends; toilet goods, toiletries; cosmetics; giftware.

.7 **groceries**, grocery [Brit], food items, baked goods, packaged goods, canned goods, tinned goods [Brit]; green goods, **produce, truck.**

832. MARKET

(place of trade)

.1 NOUNS **market, mart, store, shop,** salon, boutique, wareroom, emporium, house, establishment, *magasin* [Fr]; **retail store; wholesale house, discount store, discount house,** warehouse, mail-order house; general store, country store; **department store; co-op** [informal], cooperative; **variety store,** variety shop, **dime store; ten-cent store** or five-and-ten or five-and-dime [all informal]; chain store; concession; **trading post,** post; **supermarket;** countinghouse.

.2 **marketplace, mart, market, open market,** market overt; **shopping center,** shopping plaza, plaza, shopping mall, shopping or shop or commercial complex; emporium, rialto; staple; **bazaar, fair,** trade fair, show, auto show, boat show, etc., exposition; flea market, flea fair, street market, *marché aux puces* [Fr].

.3 **booth, stall, stand;** newsstand, kiosk, news kiosk.

.4 (stores) hardware store, ironmongery [Brit]; stationery store, stationers; toy shop; hobby shop; novelty shop; confectionery, candy store, sweet shop; drugstore, pharmacy, apothecary, chemist or chemist's shop [both Brit]; tobacco store, cigar store, tobacconists, smoke shop; secondhand store, secondhand shop, thrift shop; antique store; gift shop; bookstore 605.18; trimming store, dry goods store; clothing store, clothiers, sweater shop, dress shop, specialty shop, haberdashery, men's-wear shop, ladies'-wear shop, children's shop; florists; fur salon; furniture store; jewelry store, jewelers; leather goods store, luggage shop; saddlery; shoe store, bootery; hat shop, milliners; sporting goods store; liquor store, package store; automobile showroom, used-car lot; schlock shop or schlock house [both slang].

.5 **grocery,** grocery store, food store, food shop; **supermarket;** *bodega* [Sp], superette, groceteria; delicatessen, deli [informal], appetizing store; health food store; vegetable store or market, greengrocery, fruit stand; butcher shop, meat market,

pork store, *charcuterie* [Fr]; bakery, bakeshop; dairy, creamery.

.6 **commissary, canteen, post exchange, PX.**

.7 **gas station, filling station, service station.**

.8 **vending machine,** vendor, coin machine, coin-operated machine, slot machine, **automat.**

.9 **salesroom,** wareroom; showroom; auction room.

.10 **counter,** shopboard [archaic]; notions counter; showcase; peddler's cart, pushcart.

833. STOCK MARKET

.1 NOUNS **stock market, the market, Wall Street;** ticker market; open market, competitive market; steady market, strong market, hard or stiff market; unsteady market, spotty market; weak market; long market; top-heavy market; market index, stock price index, Dow-Jones Industrial Average.

.2 **active market,** brisk market, lively market.

.3 **inactive market,** slow market, stagnant market, flat market, tired market, sick market; investors on the sidelines.

.4 **rising market,** booming market, buoyant market; **bull market,** bullish market.

.5 **declining market,** sagging market, retreating market, off market, soft market; **bear market,** bearish market; **slump,** sag; break, break in the market; **crash,** smash.

.6 **rigged market,** manipulated market, pegged market, put-up market.

.7 **stock exchange, exchange,** Wall Street, 'change [Brit], **stock market,** bourse, **board;** the Exchange, New York Stock Exchange, the Big Board; American Stock Exchange, Amex, curb, curb market, curb exchange; over-the-counter market, telephone market, outside market; third market; exchange floor; commodity exchange, pit, corn pit, wheat pit, etc.; quotation board; **ticker,** stock ticker; ticker tape.

.8 **financial district,** Wall Street, the Street; Lombard Street.

.9 **stockbrokerage,** brokerage, brokerage house, brokerage office; wire house; bucket shop, boiler room [both slang].

.10 **stockbroker,** sharebroker [Brit], **broker,** jobber, stockjobber, dealer, stock dealer; Wall Streeter; stock-exchange broker, *agent de bourse* [Fr]; floor broker, floor trader, floorman, specialist; pit man; curb broker; odd-lot dealer; two-dollar broker; broker's agent, customer's broker or customer's man, registered representative; bond crowd.

.11 speculator, adventurer, operator; big operator, smart operator; **plunger,** gunslinger; scalper; stag [Brit]; lame duck; margin purchaser.

.12 bear, short, short seller; shorts, short interest, short side; short account, bear account.

.13 bull, long, longs, long interest, long side; long account, bull account.

.14 stockholder, stockowner, **shareholder;** bondholder, coupon clipper [slang]; stockholder of record.

.15 stock company, joint-stock company; issuing company; stock insurance company.

.16 trust, investment company; investment trust, holding company; closed-end investment company, closed-end fund; open-end fund, mutual fund; load fund, no-load fund; growth fund, income fund, dual purpose fund.

.17 pool, bear pool, bull pool, blind pool.

.18 stockbroking, brokerage, stockbrokerage, jobbing, stockjobbing, stockjobbery, stock dealing; bucketing, legal bucketing.

.19 speculation, agiotage; stockjobbing, stockjobbery; **venture,** flutter; flier, plunge; scalping; liquidation, profit taking; arbitrage; buying in, covering shorts; short sale; spot sale; round trade or transaction, turn; risk or venture capital, equity capital.

.20 manipulation, rigging; raid, bear raid, bull raid; **corner,** corner in, corner on the market, monopoly; washing, washed or wash sale.

.21 option, stock option, right, **put, call,** put and call, right of put and call; straddle, spread; strip; strap.

.22 panic, bear panic, rich man's panic.

.23 VERBS speculate, venture, operate, **play the market,** buy or sell or deal in futures; **plunge,** take a flier; scalp; bucket, bucketshop; stag or stag the market [both Brit]; trade on margin; pyramid; be long, go long, be long of the market, be on the long side of the market; be short, be short of the market, be on the short side of the market; margin up, apply or deposit margin; wait out the market, hold on; be caught short, miss the market, overstay the market; scoop the market, make a scoop or killing.

.24 sell, convert, liquidate; throw on the market, dump, unload; **sell short,** go short, make a short sale; cover one's short, fill a short sale; make delivery, clear the trade; close out, sell out, terminate the account.

.25 manipulate the market, rig the market; bear, **bear the market;** bull, **bull the market;** raid the market; hold or peg the market; whipsaw; wash sales.

.26 corner, get a corner on, **corner the market;** monopolize, engross; buy up, absorb.

834. SECURITIES

.1 NOUNS securities, stocks and bonds, investment securities; active securities, marketable securities; obsolete securities; digested securities, undigested securities; gilt-edged securities; speculative securities, cats and dogs [slang]; international securities, foreign securities, American Depository Receipts; government securities, governments, treasury bill, treasury note, treasury certificate, treasury bond, short-term note; municipal securities; corporation securities; outstanding securities; registered securities, unregistered securities; senior securities, junior securities; listed securities; unlisted securities, outside securities, over-the-counter securities; negotiable securities, negotiables; callable securities, subject to call; noncallable securities, not subject to call; convertible securities, convertibles; stamped securities; margined securities; legal securities; certificate of deposit; banker's acceptance; note; warrant; futures contract; portfolio.

.2 stock, stocks, shares [Brit], equity, equities, equity security, corporate stock, capital stock; authorized capital stock, issued capital stock, unissued capital stock; floating stock; treasury stock; active stock, inactive stock; **preferred stock,** preference stock [Brit], cumulative preferred stock, convertible preferred stock, cumulative convertible preferred stock, participating preferred stock; **common stock,** ordinary shares [Brit]; voting stock; nonvoting stock, voting-right certificate; assessable stock; nonassessable stock; no-par stock; letter stock; guaranteed stock; deferred stock; ten-share unit stock; quarter stock, eighth stock; high-grade stock, quality stock, seasoned stock, standard stock, blue chip stock, blue chip, pale blue chip; fancies [slang]; penny stock; speculative stock; growth stock; income stock; cyclical stock; defensive stock, protective stock; specialty stock; hot issue, glamour issue, high-flier [informal]; new issue; special situation stock; long stock, short stock; borrowed stock, loaned stock; hypothecated stock; watered stock; industrials, rails, utilities, steels, coppers, etc.; stock split, split; reverse split; stock list; stock ledger, share ledger [Brit].

.3 **share, lot;** preference share; dummy share; holding, holdings, stockholding, stockholdings; block; round lot, full lot, even lot, board lot; odd lot, fractional lot.

.4 **bond, debenture;** negotiable bond, non-negotiable bond; long-term bond, short-term bond; government bond; savings bond, Series E bond, appreciation bond, Series H bond, current income bond; war bond, defense bond, Liberty bond; treasury bond; Federal Agency bond, Fannie Mae, Ginnie Mae; municipal bond, tax-exempt bond, corporation stock [Brit], state bond, revenue bond, general obligation bond, turnpike bond, bond anticipation note, tax anticipation note; corporate bond; bearer bond, bearer certificate, coupon bond; registered bond, registered certificate; interchangeable bond; callable bond, redeemable bond; noncallable bond; optional bond; convertible bond, convertible debenture; participating bond; installment bond; serial bond; perpetual bond, annuity bond; consolidated annuities, consolidated stock, consols; tax-free bond; definitive bond; guaranteed bond; interim bond; deferred bond, extended bond; refunding bond; assented bond; assumed bond; adjustment bond; joint bond; voting bond; income bond; small bond, baby bond; secured bond, unsecured bond; sinking-fund bond; mortgage bond, general mortgage bond, trustee mortgage bond, purchase money bond, first mortgage bond, firsts [pl], second mortgage bond, seconds [pl]; collateral trust bond; equipment bond, equipment note, equipment trust bond, equipment trust certificate, equipment trust; high-grade bond; premium bond; par bond; discount bond, deep-discount bond; indenture, trust indenture; nominal rate, coupon rate, current yield, yield to maturity.

.5 **stock certificate,** certificate of stock; street certificate; interim certificate; **coupon.**

.6 **issue,** issuance; **flotation;** stock issue, secondary issue; bond issue.

.7 **dividend;** regular dividend; extra dividend, special dividend, plum or melon [both slang]; cumulative dividend, accumulated dividends, accrued dividends; interim dividend; cash dividend; stock dividend; optional dividend; scrip dividend; liquidating dividend; phony dividend; **interest** 840.3.

.8 **assessment,** Irish dividend.

.9 **price, quotation;** bid-and-asked prices, bid price, asked or asking or offering price; actual or delivery or settling price, put price, call price; opening price, closing price; high, low; market price, quoted price, flash price; issue price; fixed price; parity; **par,** issue par; par value, nominal value, face value; stated value; book value; market value; bearish prices, bullish prices; swings, fluctuations; flurry, flutter; rally, decline.

.10 **margin;** thin margin, shoestring margin; exhaust price.

.11 (commodities) spots, spot grain, etc.; futures, future grain, etc.

.12 VERBS **issue, float, put on the market;** issue stock, go public [informal]; float a bond issue.

.13 **declare a dividend,** cut a melon [slang].

.14 ADVS dividend off, ex dividend; dividend on, cum dividend; coupon off, ex coupon; coupon on, cum coupon; warrants off, ex warrants; warrants on, cum warrants; when issued.

835. MONEY

.1 NOUNS **money, currency, legal tender, medium of exchange,** circulating medium, sterling [Brit], **cash,** hard cash, cold cash; specie, coinage, mintage, coin of the realm, gold; **silver;** dollars; pounds, shillings, and pence; **the wherewithal,** the wherewith; lucre, **filthy lucre** [informal], the almighty dollar, pelf, root of all evil, mammon; "the sinews of war" [Libanius], "the sinews of affairs" [Laertius], "the ruling spirit of all things" [Publilius Syrus], "coined liberty" [Dostoyevsky]; **hard currency,** soft currency; fractional currency, postage currency, postal currency; managed currency; necessity money, scrip, emergency money.

.2 [slang or informal terms] **dough, bread, jack, kale,** mazuma, mopus, gelt, gilt, rhino, spondulics, oof, ooftish, wampum, possibles, moolah, boodle, blunt, dinero, **sugar,** brass, tin, rocks, simoleons, shekels, berries, chips, **bucks,** green, green stuff, the needful, grease, ointment, oil of palms, cabbage.

.3 **wampum,** wampumpeag, peag, sewan, roanoke; cowrie.

.4 **specie,** hard money; coin, piece, piece of money, piece of silver or gold; roll of coins, rouleau; **gold piece;** ten-dollar gold piece, eagle; five-dollar gold piece, half eagle; twenty-dollar gold piece, double eagle; guinea, sovereign, pound sovereign, crown, half crown; doubloon; ducat; napoleon, louis d'or; moidore.

.5 **paper money; bill,** dollar bill, etc.; **note,** negotiable note, legal-tender note; **bank note,** Federal Reserve note; national bank note; government note, treasury note; silver certificate; gold certificate; scrip; fractional note, shinplaster [slang]; fiat money, assignat.

.6 [slang or informal terms] **folding money,** the long green, mint leaves, lettuce, greenbacks, frogskins, skins.

.7 (US denominations) mill; cent, penny, copper, red cent [informal]; five cents, nickel; ten cents, dime; twenty-five cents, quarter, two bits [informal]; fifty cents, half dollar, four bits [informal]; dollar, dollar bill; buck or smacker or frogskin or fish or skin [all slang]; silver dollar, cartwheel or iron man [both slang]; two-dollar bill, two-spot [slang]; five-dollar bill; fiver or five-spot or fin [all slang]; ten-dollar bill; tenner or ten-spot or sawbuck [all slang]; twenty-dollar bill, double sawbuck [slang]; fifty-dollar bill, half a C [slang]; hundred-dollar bill; C or C-note or century [all slang]; five hundred dollars, half grand [slang], five-hundred-dollar bill, half G [slang]; thousand dollars, G of grand [both slang], thousand-dollar bill, G-note or yard [both slang].

.8 (British denominations) mite; farthing; halfpenny or ha'penny, bawbee [Brit informal], mag or meg [both Brit dial]; penny; pence, p; new pence, np; twopence or tuppence; threepence or thrippence, threepenny bit or piece; fourpence, fourpenny, groat; sixpence, tanner [Brit slang], teston; shilling, bob [Brit slang]; florin; half crown, half dollar [Brit informal]; crown, dollar [Brit informal]; pound, quid [slang]; guinea; fiver (£5), tenner (£10), pony (£25), monkey (£500), plum (£100,000), marigold (£1,000,000) [all Brit slang].

.9 (foreign denominations) afghani (Afghanistan), anna, pie or pai (India), azteca (Mexico), baht or tical (Thailand), balboa (Panama), bolivar (Venezuela), cent (Australia, Netherlands, etc.), centavo (Portugal, Argentina, Mexico, etc.), centesimo (Italy, Uruguay); centime (Belgium, France, Switzerland), centimo (Spain, Venezuela, etc.), colón (Costa Rica, El Salvador), conto, cruzeiro (Brazil), cordoba (Nicaragua), dinar (Algeria, Kuwait, Iraq, Iran, Yugoslavia); dirham (Morocco); dollar (Australia, Liberia, Malaysia, etc.), dong (North Vietnam), drachma (Greece), ekpwele (Equatorial Guinea), escudo (Chile, Portugal), florin, guilder, gulden, stiver (Netherlands), forint (Hungary), franc (France, Belgium, Switzerland, Burundi, Cameroon, Central African Republic, Chad, Congo, Dahomey, Gabon, Guinea, Ivory Coast, Luxembourg, Malagasy Republic, Mali, Niger, Rwanda, Senegal, Togo, Upper Volta), gourde (Haiti), groschen (Austria), guaraní (Paraguay), kip (Laos), kopeck, ruble (Russia), koruna (Czechoslovakia), krona (Sweden); krone (Denmark, Norway, Austria), kwacha (Malawi, Zambia), kyat (Burma), lek (Albania), lempira (Honduras), leone (Sierra Leone), leu (Romania), lev (Bulgaria), lilangeni (Swaziland), lira (Italy, Turkey); Mark, Deutschmark, Reichsmark, Pfennig (Germany), markka (Finland), piaster (South Vietnam), milreis, reis (Brazil), ouguiya (Mauritania), peseta (Spain), peso (Argentina, Mexico, etc.), pistareen, piece of eight (Spain), pound (United Kingdom, Cyprus, United Arab Republic, Gambia, Ghana, Ireland, Israel, Lebanon, Malta, New Zealand, Nigeria, Sudan, Syria, Turkey), quetzal (Guatemala), rand (South Africa), rial (Iran), riel (Cambodia), riyal (Saudi Arabia), rupee (India, Pakistan, etc.), rupiah (Indonesia), schilling (Austria), shekel (ancient Near East), shilling (Kenya, Tanzania, Uganda), sol (Peru), sucre (Ecuador), soldo (Italy), sou (France), taka (Bangladesh), tugrik (Mongolia), won (South Korea), yen (Japan), yuan (China), zaïre (Zaïre), zloty (Poland).

.10 **counterfeit,** counterfeit money, phony or bogus money [informal], false or bad money, queer [slang], base coin, green goods [slang]; **forgery,** bad check, rubber check or kite [both slang].

.11 **negotiable instrument** or **paper,** commercial paper, paper, bill; **bill of exchange,** bill of draft; certificate, certificate of deposit, CD; **check,** cheque [Brit]; blank check; bank check, teller's check; treasury check; cashier's check, certified check;

traveler's check or banker's check; letter of credit, commercial letter of credit; **money order, MO**; postal order or post-office order [both Brit]; draft, warrant, voucher, debenture; **promissory note, note, IOU**; note of hand; acceptance, acceptance bill, bank acceptance, trade acceptance; due bill; demand bill, sight bill, demand draft, sight draft; time bill, time draft; exchequer bill or treasury bill [both Brit]; checkbook.

.12 **token, counter**, slug; **scrip, coupon; check, ticket**, tag; hat check, baggage check.

.13 **sum**, amount of money; round sum, lump sum.

.14 **funds, finances, moneys**, exchequer, purse, budget, pocket; treasure, substance, **assets**, resources, **pecuniary resources, means**, wherewithal, command of money; balance; pool, **fund, kitty** [informal]; checking account, bank account; Swiss bank account, unnumbered or unregistered bank account; reserves, cash reserves; savings, savings account, nest egg [informal]; life savings; bottom dollar [informal].

.15 **capital, fund**; moneyed capital; principal, corpus; circulating capital, floating capital; fixed capital, working capital, equity capital, risk or venture capital; capital structure; capital gains distribution; capitalization.

.16 **money market**, supply of short-term funds; tight money, cheap money; **borrowing** 821; **lending** 820; discounting, note discounting, note shaving, dealing in commercial paper.

.17 **bankroll**; roll or wad [both slang]; shoestring [informal].

.18 **ready money**, the ready [informal], available funds, **cash, money in hand, cash in hand**, balance in hand, immediate resources, liquid assets, cash supply; treasury.

.19 **petty cash, pocket money, pin money**, spending money, **change**, small change.

.20 precious metals; **gold**, yellow stuff [slang]; nugget, gold nugget; **silver, copper, nickel**, coin gold or silver; bullion, ingot, bar.

.21 standard of value, gold standard, silver standard; monometallism, bimetallism; money of account.

.22 (science of coins) **numismatics**, numismatology; numismatist, numismatologist.

.23 monetization; issuance, circulation; remonetization; demonetization; revaluation, devaluation.

.24 **coining**, coinage, mintage, striking, stamping; **counterfeiting, forgery**; coin-clipping.

.25 **coiner**, minter, mintmaster, moneyer; **counterfeiter, forger**; coin-clipper.

.26 VERBS monetize; **issue, utter, circulate**; remonetize, reissue; demonetize; revalue, devalue, devaluate.

.27 discount, discount notes, deal in commercial paper, shave; borrow 820.3, lend 820.5.

.28 **coin, mint; counterfeit, forge**; utter, pass or shove the queer [slang].

.29 **cash**, cash in [informal], liquidate, convert into cash.

.30 ADJS **monetary, pecuniary**, nummary, **financial**; capital; fiscal; sumptuary; numismatic; sterling.

.31 convertible, liquid, negotiable.

836. FINANCE, INVESTMENT

.1 NOUNS finance, finances, money matters; world of finance, **high finance**, investment banking, international banking, Wall Street banking, Lombard Street; economics 851.

.2 **financing, funding, backing**, financial backing, **sponsorship, patronization**, support, financial support; **stake** or **grubstake** [both informal]; subsidy 818.8; provision of capital, capitalization; deficit financing.

.3 **investment, venture, risk**, plunge [informal], speculation; prime investment.

.4 **banking**, money dealing, money changing; investment banking.

.5 **financial condition**, state of the exchequer; **credit rating**, Dun and Bradstreet rating.

.6 **solvency**, soundness, solidity; credit standing; unindebtedness.

.7 **crisis**, financial crisis; dollar crisis, dollar gap.

.8 **financier**, moneyman, **capitalist**, finance capitalist; Wall Streeter; investor; financial expert, economist, authority on money and banking.

.9 **financer, backer**, funder, **sponsor, patron, supporter**, angel [slang]; staker or grubstaker [both informal], meal ticket [slang].

.10 **banker, money dealer**, moneymonger; money broker; discounter, note broker, bill broker [Brit]; moneylender 820.3; money changer, cambist; investment banker; bank president, bank manager, bank officer, loan officer, trust officer, banking executive; bank clerk, cashier, teller.

.11 **treasurer,** financial officer, bursar, purser, purse bearer, **cashier,** cashkeeper; accountant, auditor, controller *or* comptroller, bookkeeper; chamberlain, curator, steward, trustee; depositary, depository; receiver, liquidator, **paymaster;** Secretary of the Treasury, Chancellor of the Exchequer.

.12 **treasury, treasure-house;** subtreasury; **depository,** repository; storehouse 660.6; gold depository, Fort Knox; **strongbox, safe,** money chest, **coffer, locker, chest;** piggy bank, penny bank, bank; **vault,** strong room; safe-deposit *or* safety-deposit box *or* vault; cashbox, coin box, cash register, **till;** bursary; exchequer, fisc; public treasury, pork barrel, public crib *or* trough *or* till [informal].

.13 **bank;** commercial bank, trust company; national bank, state bank; **savings bank,** mutual savings bank; savings and loan association; central bank, branch bank; Federal Reserve bank, reserve bank, member bank, nonmember bank; land bank, federal land bank, federal intermediate credit bank, federal home loan bank, farm loan bank *or* association; moneyed corporation; investment banking house, investment bank, Wall Street bank, Lombard Street bank; international bank; Bank of England, Old Lady of Threadneedle Street; Bank of France; Swiss bank; World Bank, International Monetary Fund; clearing house.

.14 **purse, wallet, pocketbook, bag, handbag,** porte-monnaie, **billfold,** money belt, money clip, poke [slang], pocket; moneybag; purse strings.

.15 VERBS **finance, back, fund, sponsor, patronize, support,** provide for, capitalize, provide capital *or* money for, pay for, bankroll [informal], angel [slang], put up the money; **stake** *or* **grubstake** [both informal]; subsidize 818.19; set up, set up in business; refinance.

.16 **invest,** place, put, sink; **risk, venture;** make an investment, lay out money, place out *or* put out at interest; reinvest, plow back into [informal]; **invest in, put money in,** sink money in, pour money into, tie up one's money in; buy in *or* into, buy a piece *or* share of; financier; plunge [informal], speculate 833.23.

.17 ADJS **solvent, sound,** substantial, solid, good, sound as a dollar; **able to pay,** good for, unindebted 841.23.

.18 **insolvent,** unsound, indebted 840.8.

837. WEALTH

.1 NOUNS **wealth, riches, opulence** *or* **opulency** 661.2, **luxuriousness** 904.5; richness, wealthiness; **prosperity,** prosperousness, **affluence,** comfortable *or* easy circumstances, independence; **money,** lucre, pelf, gold, mammon; **substance, property, possessions,** material wealth; **assets** 835.14; **fortune, treasure,** handsome fortune; full *or* heavy *or* well-lined *or* bottomless *or* fat *or* bulging purse, moneybags [informal]; *embarras de richesses* [Fr], money to burn [informal]; high income, six-figure income; high tax bracket, upper bracket.

.2 **large sum,** good sum, tidy sum *or* **pretty penny** [both informal], **king's ransom,** mint, pot *or* potful [both informal]; power *or* mint *or* barrel *or* raft *or* load of money [informal]; heaps of gold, pile *or* wad [both slang]; thousands, millions, cool million.

.3 (rich source) **mine,** mine of wealth, **gold mine,** bonanza, lode, rich lode, mother lode, Eldorado, Golconda, Seven Cities of Cibola; gravy train [informal]; rich uncle.

.4 **the golden touch,** Midas touch; philosophers' stone; Pactolus.

.5 **the rich, the wealthy,** the well to do, the haves [informal]; **plutocracy,** timocracy.

.6 **rich man,** wealthy man, warm man [Brit informal], **moneyed man,** man of wealth, **man of means** *or* **substance,** fat cat [slang], richling, moneybags [informal], Daddy Warbucks [Harold Gray], **nabob; capitalist, plutocrat,** bloated plutocrat; **millionaire,** multimillionaire, billionaire; parvenu 919.10.

.7 Croesus, Midas, Plutus, Dives, Timon of Athens, Danaë; Rockefeller, Vanderbilt, Whitney, DuPont, Ford, Getty, Rothschild, Onassis, Hughes, Hunt.

.8 VERBS **enrich, richen.**

.9 **grow rich, get rich,** fill *or* line one's pockets, feather one's nest, **make** *or* **coin money,** have a gold mine, have the golden touch, **make a fortune,** make one's pile [slang]; **strike it rich;** come into money; make good, get on in the world, do all right by oneself [informal].

.10 **have money,** command money, **be loaded** [informal], have the wherewithal, have means, have independent means; **afford,** well afford.

.11 **live well,** live high, live high on the hog [informal], **live in clover,** roll or wallow in wealth, roll in the lap of luxury; have all the money in the world, have a mint, have money to burn [informal].

.12 worship mammon, worship the golden calf.

.13 ADJS **wealthy, rich, loaded** [informal], warm [Brit informal], **affluent, moneyed,** in the money [informal], in funds or cash, **well-to-do,** well-to-do in the world, **well-off, well-situated, well-fixed** [informal], **prosperous,** comfortable, provided for, well provided for, fat, **flush,** flush with or of money, abounding in riches, made of money, **rolling in money,** rolling or wallowing in wealth, worth a great deal, frightfully rich, disgustingly rich, big-rich [dial], rich as Croesus; **well-heeled** or oofy or lousy rich or filthy rich [all slang]; independent, independently rich, independently wealthy; **luxurious** 904.21; **opulent** 661.7.

838. POVERTY

.1 NOUNS **poverty, poorness,** impecuniousness, impecuniosity; **straits,** difficulties, **hardship** 729.1; distress, embarrassment, **embarrassed** or **reduced** or **straitened circumstances,** tight squeeze, hard pinch, slender or narrow means, insolvency, light purse; unprosperousness; broken fortune; genteel poverty; vows of poverty, voluntary poverty.

.2 **indigence, penury, pennilessness,** moneylessness; **pauperism,** pauperization, **impoverishment,** grinding poverty, chronic pauperism; **beggary,** beggarliness, mendicancy; homelessness; **destitution, privation, deprivation; neediness, want,** need, lack, pinch, gripe, necessity, disadvantagedness, necessitousness; **hand-to-mouth existence,** bare subsistence, wolf at the door, bare cupboard, empty purse or pocket.

.3 **the poor, the needy,** the have-nots [informal], the **down-and-out,** the disadvantaged, the underprivileged, the distressed; the urban poor, ghetto-dwellers, barrio-dwellers; welfare rolls, welfare clients, welfare families; "wretched of the earth" [E. Pottier]; the other America; the forgotten man, "the forgotten man at the bottom of the economic pyramid" [F. D. Roosevelt]; depressed population, depressed area, chronic poverty area; underdeveloped nation.

.4 **poor man,** poorling, poor devil, **down-and-out, down-and-outer, pauper,** indigent, penniless man, hardcase, starveling; **beggar** 774.8; welfare client; almsman, almswoman, charity case, casual; **bankrupt** 842.4.

.5 VERBS **be poor,** be hard up [informal], find it hard going, have seen better days, be on one's uppers, be pinched or strapped, **be in want,** want, need, lack; **starve,** not know where one's next meal is coming from, **live from hand to mouth,** eke out or squeeze out a living; **not have a penny** or sou, not have a penny to bless oneself with, not have one dollar to rub against another; go on welfare.

.6 **impoverish,** reduce, **pauperize, beggar;** eat out of house and home; **bankrupt** 842.8.

.7 ADJS **poor, ill off,** badly or poorly off, hard up [informal], **impecunious, unmoneyed; unprosperous;** reduced, in reduced circumstances; **straitened,** in straitened circumstances, narrow, in narrow circumstances, feeling the pinch, strapped, **embarrassed,** distressed, **pinched,** squeezed, put to one's shifts or last shifts, at the end of one's rope, on the edge or ragged edge [informal], down to bedrock, in Queer Street; short, **short of money** or funds or cash, out of pocket; unable to make ends meet, unable to keep the wolf from the door; poor as a church mouse, "poor as Job" [John Gower]; land-poor.

.8 **indigent, poverty-stricken; needy,** necessitous, **in need, in want,** disadvantaged, deprived, underprivileged; **beggared,** beggarly, mendicant; **impoverished, pauperized,** starveling; ghettoized; bereft, bereaved; stripped, fleeced; **down at heels,** down at the heel, on or down on one's uppers, out at the heels, out at elbows, in rags; on welfare, on relief, on the dole [Brit].

.9 **destitute, down-and-out,** in the gutter; **penniless,** moneyless, fortuneless, out of funds, **without a sou,** without a penny to bless oneself with, without one dollar to rub against another; insolvent, in the red, **bankrupt** 842.11; homeless; propertyless, landless.

.10 [slang terms] **broke, busted, flat, flat broke, stone-broke,** stony, **strapped,** skint [Brit], beat, oofless; down to one's last penny or cent.

839. FINANCIAL CREDIT

.1 NOUNS **credit, trust, tick** [informal]; borrowing power *or* capacity; commercial credit, cash credit, bank credit, book credit, tax credit, investment credit; line of credit; installment plan, installment credit, consumer credit, hire purchase plan *or* never-never [both Brit]; rating, credit rating, Dun and Bradstreet rating; credit insurance; credit union.

.2 **account,** credit account, charge account; bank account, savings account, checking account; bank balance; expense account.

.3 **credit instrument;** paper credit; **letter of credit,** *lettre de créance* [Fr], circular note; credit slip, deposit slip, certificate of deposit; negotiable instruments 835.11; **credit card,** charge card, charge plate.

.4 **creditor,** creditress; debtee; mortgagee, mortgage-holder; note-holder; credit man; bill collector, collection agent; dunner, dun.

.5 VERBS **credit,** accredit; **credit to one's account,** place to one's credit *or* account.

.6 **give** *or* **extend credit,** sell on credit, trust, entrust; give tick [informal]; carry, carry on one's books.

.7 **receive credit,** take credit, **charge,** charge to one's account, keep an account with, go on tick [informal], buy on credit, buy on the cuff [informal], buy on the installment plan; go in hock for [slang]; have one's credit good for.

.8 ADJS **accredited,** credited, of good credit, **well-rated.**

.9 ADVS **to one's credit** *or* **account,** to the credit *or* account of, to the good.

.10 **on credit, on account, on trust,** on tick *or* **on the cuff** [both informal]; on terms, on good terms, on easy terms, on budget terms, in installments.

840. DEBT

.1 NOUNS **debt, indebtedness,** indebtment, **obligation, liability,** financial commitment, due, **dues,** score, pledge, unfulfilled pledge, amount due, outstanding debt; **bill, bills,** chits, **charges;** floating debt; funded debt; accounts receivable; accounts payable; borrowing 821; maturity; bad debts, uncollectibles; national debt, public debt.

.2 **arrears,** arrear, arrearage, back debts, back payments; **deficit,** default, deferred payments; overdraft, bounced *or* bouncing check; dollar gap, unfavorable balance of payments; deficit financing.

.3 **interest, premium, price, rate;** interest rate, rate of interest, prime interest rate, bank rate, price of money; discount rate; **usury,** excessive *or* exorbitant interest; mortgage points; simple interest, compound interest; net interest, gross interest; compensatory interest; lucrative interest; penal interest.

.4 **debtor,** borrower; mortgagor.

.5 VERBS **owe, be indebted,** be obliged *or* obligated for, be financially committed, lie under an obligation, be bound to pay.

.6 **go in debt,** get into debt, run into debt, plunge into debt, incur *or* contract a debt, go in hock [slang], **run up a bill** *or* a score *or* an account; run *or* show a deficit, operate at a loss; borrow 820.3.

.7 **mature, accrue, fall due.**

.8 ADJS **indebted, in debt,** plunged in debt, in difficulties, embarrassed, in embarrassed circumstances, in the hole [informal], in the red, in hock [slang], encumbered, mortgaged, mortgaged to the hilt, tied up, involved; deep in debt, involved *or* deeply involved in debt, burdened with debt, head over heels in debt, up to one's ears in debt.

.9 **chargeable, obligated, liable,** pledged, responsible, answerable for.

.10 **due, owed, owing, payable,** receivable, redeemable, mature, **outstanding, unpaid,** in arrear *or* arrears, back.

841. PAYMENT

.1 NOUNS **payment, paying,** paying off, paying up [informal], payoff; **defrayment,** defrayal; paying out, doling out, **disbursal** 843.1; **discharge, settlement, clearance, liquidation, amortization,** amortizement, retirement, satisfaction; quittance; acquittance *or* acquitment *or* acquittal [all archaic]; debt service, interest payment, sinking-fund payment; remittance; installment, installment plan; hire purchase *or* hire purchase plan *or* never-never [all Brit]; regular payments, monthly payments, weekly payments, quarterly payments, etc.; down payment, deposit, earnest, earnest money, binder; god's penny; cash, spot cash, cash payment, cash on the nail *or* cash on the barrelhead [both informal]; prepayment; payment in kind.

.2 **reimbursement,** recoupment, return, restitution; **refund,** refundment, kickback [informal]; **repayment** 823.2.

.3 **recompense, remuneration, compensation;** requital, requitement, quittance, **retribution, reparation, redress,** satisfaction, atonement, amends, return, restitution 823; blood money, wergild; **indemnity, indemnification**; price, consideration; **reward**, meed, guerdon; honorarium; workmen's compensation, solatium, damages, smart money; salvage.

.4 **pay, payment, remuneration, compensation**, total compensation, wages plus fringe benefits, pay and allowances, financial remuneration; **salary, wage, wages, income, earnings**, hire; real wages, purchasing power; take-home pay, take-home [informal], pay *or* income *or* wages after taxes, pay *or* income *or* wages after deductions, net income *or* wages *or* pay *or* earnings, taxable income; gross income; living wage; minimum wage, base pay; portal-to-portal pay; severance pay, discontinuance *or* dismissal wage; wage scale; escalator plan, escalator clause, sliding scale; payroll; wage freeze, wage rollback, wage reduction, wage control; guaranteed annual wage, guaranteed income plan.

.5 **fee, stipend, allowance**, emolument, tribute; **reckoning**, account, bill; assessment, scot; initiation fee, footing [archaic]; retainer, retaining fee; hush money, blackmail; blood money; mileage.

.6 (extra pay or allowance) **bonus, premium, fringe benefit** *or* **benefits**, bounty, perquisite, perquisites, perks [Brit informal], gravy [slang], lagniappe, solatium; **tip** 818.5; overtime pay; bonus system.

.7 **dividend; royalty; commission**, rake-off *or* cut [both slang].

.8 (the bearing of another's expense) **treat**, standing treat, picking up the check *or* tab [informal]; paying the bills, maintenance, support 785.3; subsidy 818.8.

.9 **payer**, remunerator, compensator, recompenser; paymaster, purser, bursar, cashier, treasurer 836.11; defrayer; liquidator; taxpayer, ratepayer [Brit].

.10 VERBS **pay**, render, tender; **recompense, remunerate, compensate, reward**, guerdon, indemnify, satisfy; salary, fee; remit; prepay; pay by installments, pay on, pay in.

.11 **repay**, pay back, **reimburse**, recoup; **requite**, quit, **atone**, redress [archaic], **make amends**, make good, make up for, make up to, make restitution, make reparation 823.4,5; pay in kind, pay one in his own coin, give tit for tat; **refund**, kick back [informal].

.12 **settle with**, reckon with, account with [archaic], pay out, **settle** *or* **square ac-**

counts with, square oneself with, get square with, **get even** *or* **quits with**; even the score [slang], wipe *or* clear off old scores, pay old debts, clear the board.

.13 **pay in full, pay off, pay up** [informal], **discharge, settle, square, clear, liquidate, amortize**, retire, take up, lift, take up and pay off, honor, acquit oneself of [archaic]; satisfy; meet one's obligations *or* commitments, redeem, redeem one's pledge *or* pledges, tear up *or* burn one's mortgage, have a mortgage-burning party, settle *or* square accounts, make accounts square, strike a balance; pay the bill, pay the shot.

.14 **pay out, fork out** *or* **shell out** [both slang]; **expend** 843.5.

.15 **pay over**, hand over; **ante, ante up**, put up; put down, lay down, lay one's money down.

.16 [slang or informal terms] **kick in, fork over**, pony up, cough up, stump up [Brit], come across, come through with, come across with, come down with, come down with the needful, plank down, plunk down, post, tickle *or* grease the palm, cross one's palm with, lay on one; pay to the tune of.

.17 **pay cash**, make a cash payment, cash, **pay spot cash, pay cash down**, pay cash on the barrelhead [informal], plunk down the money *or* put one's money on the line [both slang], pay at sight; pay in advance; pay as you go; pay cash on delivery, pay COD.

.18 **pay for**, pay *or* stand the costs, **bear the expense** *or* **cost**, pay the piper [informal]; **finance, fund** 836.15; **defray**, defray expenses; pay the bill, **foot the bill** [informal], pick up the check *or* tab [informal]; honor a bill, acknowledge, redeem; pay one's way; pay one's share, chip in [informal], go Dutch [informal].

.19 **treat**, treat to, **stand treat**, go treat, stand to [informal], pick up the check *or* tab [informal], pay the bill, set up, blow to [slang]; stand drinks; maintain, support 785.12; subsidize 818.19.

.20 **be paid, draw wages**, be salaried, work for wages, be remunerated, collect for one's services, **earn**, get an income, pull down *or* drag down [both slang].

.21 ADJS **paying, remunerative; compensating**, compensative, compensatory; retributive, retributory; **rewarding**, rewardful; lucrative, moneymaking, profitable 811.15; repaying, satisfying, reparative.

.22 **paid**, discharged, settled, liquidated, acquitted [archaic], paid in full, receipted, remitted; **spent, expended;** salaried, waged, hired; prepaid, postpaid.

.23 **unindebted,** unowing, **out of debt,** above water, **clear,** all clear, free and clear, all straight; solvent 836.17.

.24 ADVS **in compensation,** as compensation, in recompense, for services rendered, for professional services, **in reward,** in requital, in reparation, in retribution, in restitution, **in amends,** in atonement, to atone for.

.25 **cash,** cash on the barrelhead [informal], strictly cash; **cash down, money down,** down; cash on delivery, **COD;** on demand, on call; pay-as-you-go.

842. NONPAYMENT

.1 NOUNS **nonpayment, default, delinquency,** delinquence [archaic], nondischarge of debts, nonremittal, failure to pay; defection; protest, repudiation; dishonor, dishonoring; bad debt, uncollectible, dishonored or protested bill.

.2 **moratorium,** grace period; **write-off,** cancellation, obliteration 693.7.

.3 **insolvency, bankruptcy,** receivership, **failure; crash,** collapse, bust [slang]; run upon a bank; insufficient funds, overdraft, overdrawn account, bounced or bouncing check, kited check.

.4 **insolvent,** insolvent debtor, lame duck [informal]; **bankrupt,** failure.

.5 **defaulter,** delinquent, nonpayer; **welsher** [slang], levanter; tax evader, tax dodger [informal].

.6 VERBS **not pay;** dishonor, repudiate, disallow, protest, stop payment, refuse to pay; **default, welsh** [slang], levant; button up one's pockets, draw the purse strings.

.7 **go bankrupt, go broke** [informal], go into receivership, become insolvent or bankrupt, **fail,** break, bust [slang], crash, collapse, **fold, fold up,** go up or **go under** [both informal], shut down, shut one's doors, go out of business, **be ruined,** go to ruin, go on the rocks, go to the wall, go to pot [informal], go to the dogs.

.8 **bankrupt, ruin, break,** bust [slang]; put out of business, drive to the wall, scuttle, sink; impoverish 838.6.

.9 declare a moratorium; write off, absolve, cancel, nullify, wipe the slate clean; wipe out, obliterate 693.16.

.10 ADJS **defaulting,** nonpaying, **delinquent;** behindhand, in arrear or arrears.

.11 **insolvent, bankrupt,** in receivership, broken, **broke** [informal], busted [slang],

ruined, failed, unable to pay one's creditors, unable to meet one's obligations, on the rocks; destitute 838.9.

.12 **unpaid, unremunerated,** uncompensated, unrecompensed, **unrewarded,** unrequited.

.13 **unpayable,** irredeemable, inconvertible.

843. EXPENDITURE

.1 NOUNS **expenditure, spending,** disbursal, **disbursement;** debit, debiting; budgeting, scheduling; costing, costing-out; **payment** 841; deficit spending.

.2 **spendings,** outgoings, outgo, outflow, **outlay,** money going out.

.3 **expenses, costs,** charges, budget, budget items, disbursals, liabilities; **expense, cost,** burden of expenditure; **overhead,** operating expense or expenses or costs or budget, general expenses; expense account, swindle sheet [slang]; direct costs, indirect costs; distributed costs, undistributed costs; material costs; labor costs; carrying charge; unit cost; replacement cost; prime cost; cost of living, cost-of-living index, cost-of-living allowance.

.4 **spender,** expender, expenditor, disburser.

.5 VERBS **spend, expend, disburse, pay out,** fork or shell out [slang], **lay out,** outlay; **pay** 841.10; put one's hands in one's pockets, open the purse, loosen or untie the purse strings; throw money around [informal], go on a spending spree, splurge, spend money as if it were going out of style, go or run through, **squander** 854.3; **invest,** sink money in [informal], put out; **incur costs** or **expenses;** budget, schedule, cost, cost out.

.6 **be spent,** burn in one's pocket, burn a hole in one's pocket.

.7 **afford,** well afford, spare, **spare the price,** bear, stand, support, endure, undergo, meet the expense of.

844. RECEIPTS

.1 NOUNS **receipts,** receipt, **income, revenue, profits, earnings, returns, proceeds,** avails [archaic], **take,** takings, intake, take-in [informal], get [Brit dial]; credit, credits; gains 811.3; gate receipts, gate, box office; net receipts, net; gross receipts, gross; net income, gross income; earned income, unearned income; dividend, dividends; royalties, commissions; receivables; disposable income; make, produce, **yield, output** 168.2.

.2 (written acknowledgment) **receipt, acknowledgment, voucher,** warrant [Brit]; canceled check; **receipt in full,** receipt in full of all demands, release, acquittance, quittance, discharge.

.3 VERBS receive 819.6; acquire 811.8–12; acknowledge receipt of, receipt, mark paid.

.4 yield, bring in, afford, pay, pay off [informal], return; gross, net.

845. ACCOUNTS

.1 NOUNS accounts; outstanding accounts, uncollected or unpaid accounts; accounts receivable, receipts, assets; accounts payable, expenditures, liabilities; budget, budgeting, costing-out.

.2 account, reckoning, tally, score; profit and loss account, debtor and creditor account, open or running account, cash account, suspense account, income account, revenue account, selling account, stock account, control account, provision account, valuation account, sales account; account current; account rendered, *compte rendu* [Fr], account stated; balance.

.3 statement, bill, itemized bill, bill of account, account, reckoning, check, *l'addition* [Fr], score or tab [both slang]; dun; invoice, manifest, bill of lading.

.4 account book, ledger, journal, daybook; register, registry, record book, books; log, logbook; cashbook; purchase ledger, accounts payable ledger, sales ledger, sales journal, accounts receivable ledger, card ledger, suspense ledger, stock ledger, bank ledger, stores ledger, inventory, cost ledger, factory ledger; bankbook, passbook; balance sheet; cost sheet, cost card.

.5 entry, item, minute, note, notation; single entry, double entry; credit, debit.

.6 accounting, accountancy, bookkeeping, double-entry bookkeeping or accounting, single-entry bookkeeping or accounting; business or commercial or monetary arithmetic; cost accounting, cost system, cost-accounting system; audit, auditing.

.7 accountant, bookkeeper; clerk, actuary [archaic], registrar, recorder, journalizer; calculator, reckoner; cost accountant, cost keeper; certified public accountant, CPA; chartered accountant or CA [both Brit]; auditor, bank examiner; bank accountant; accountant general; comptroller or controller.

.8 VERBS keep accounts, keep books, make up or cast up accounts; make an entry, enter, post, post up, journalize, book, docket, log, note, minute; credit, debit; charge off; capitalize; carry, carry on one's books; carry over; balance, balance accounts, balance the books, strike a balance; close the books, close out.

.9 take account of, take stock, overhaul; inventory; audit, examine or inspect the books.

.10 falsify accounts, garble accounts, cook or doctor accounts [informal], salt; surcharge.

.11 bill, send a statement; invoice; call, call in, demand payment, dun.

.12 ADJS accounting, bookkeeping.

846. PRICE, FEE

.1 NOUNS price, cost, expense, expenditure, charge, –age; rate, figure, amount, price tag [informal]; damage or score or tab [all slang].

.2 quotation, quoted price; cash price; bargain price, cut price; asking price, offered price, bid, bid price; selling price; current price, going price, market price, price current, current quotation; wholesale price, trade price; list price, recommended price; net or neat price, net; fixed price; controlled price, managed price, fair-trade price; flat rate; *prix fixe* [Fr]; package price; unit price; piece price; price list, prices current; stock market quotations 834.9.

.3 worth, value, account, rate; face value, face; par value; market value; net worth; conversion factor or value; money's worth, pennyworth, value received.

.4 valuation, evaluation, pricing, price determination, assessment, appraisal, appraisement, apprizal, estimation, rating; unit pricing, dual pricing.

.5 price index, business index; consumer price index; cost-of-living index; price level; price ceiling, ceiling price, ceiling, top price; floor price, floor, bottom price; demand curve; rising prices, inflation, inflationary spiral.

.6 price controls, price-fixing, valorization; managed prices, fair-trading, fair trade, fair-trade agreement; price supports, rigid supports, flexible supports; price freeze; rent control.

.7 fee, dues, toll, charge, charges, demand, exaction, exactment, scot, shot, scot and lot; hire; fare, carfare; license fee; entrance or admission fee, admission; cover charge; portage, towage; wharfage, anchorage, dockage; pilotage; storage, cellarage; brokerage; salvage.

.8 freightage, freight, haulage, carriage, cartage, drayage, expressage, lighterage; poundage, tonnage.

.9 **rent, rental;** rent-roll; rent charge; rack rent, quitrent.

.10 **tax, taxation, duty, tribute,** contribution, **assessment,** cess [Brit], **levy, toll, impost,** imposition; **tithe;** surtax, supertax; direct tax, indirect tax; progressive tax *or* taxation, graduated taxation; proportional tax, ad valorem tax; regressive tax *or* taxation; single tax; withholding tax, tax withholding; tax return, separate returns, joint return; tax dodging, tax evasion; conscience money; tax exemption, tax-exempt status; tax structure, tax base; taxable income *or* goods *or* land *or* property, ratables [Brit].

.11 (kinds of tax) excise, excise tax, internal revenue tax; **duty,** customs, customs duty, **tariff,** tariff duty, specific duty, ad valorem duty, revenue tariff, protective tariff; import tax, export tax; poll tax, poll, head tax, capitation tax, capitation; salt tax, gabelle; federal tax, state tax, provincial tax, local tax, rates [Brit]; property tax, land tax, property-increment tax, personal property tax; school tax; death tax, estate tax, death duty *or* estate duty [both Brit], inheritance tax; liquor tax, alcohol tax; capital gains tax, corporation tax, excess profits tax, value added tax, VAT; gift tax; income tax; license tax, franchise tax; automobile registration tax, gasoline tax; telephone tax, luxury tax, window tax, nuisance tax; amusement tax; doomage, assessment on default; sales tax, use tax; severance tax.

.12 taxer, taxman; **tax collector,** publican, collector of internal revenue, internal revenue agent; tax farmer, farmer; assessor, **tax assessor;** exciseman [Brit], revenuer; Internal Revenue Service, IRS; customs, US Customs Service, Bureau of Customs and Excise [Eng]; customhouse.

.13 VERBS **price,** set a price on, fix the price of; place a value on, **value, evaluate,** valuate, **appraise, assess, rate,** prize; quote a price; set an arbitrary price on, control *or* manage the price of, valorize; fair-trade.

.14 **charge, demand, ask,** require; **exact, assess, levy, impose; tax,** assess a tax upon, slap a tax on [slang], lay *or* put a duty on, make dutiable, subject to a tax *or* fee *or* duty, collect a tax *or* duty on; tithe; prorate, assess *pro rata*; charge for, stick for [informal].

.15 **cost, sell for, fetch, bring,** bring in, afford [archaic], set one back [slang]; **come to,** run to *or* into, **amount to,** mount up to, come up to, total up to.

.16 ADJS **priced, valued,** evaluated, assessed, appraised, rated, prized; **worth,** valued at; good for; ad valorem, pro rata.

.17 **chargeable, taxable,** ratable [Brit], assessable, dutiable, leviable; tithable.

.18 tax-free, nontaxable, nondutiable, tax-exempt; deductible, tax-deductible.

.19 ADVS **at a price,** for a consideration; to the amount of, to the tune of [informal].

847. DISCOUNT

.1 NOUNS **discount, cut, deduction,** abatement, reduction, price reduction, price-cutting, price-cut, rollback [informal]; underselling; rebate, rebatement; bank discount, cash discount, chain discount, time discount, trade discount; write-off, charge-off; **depreciation; allowance,** concession; setoff; drawback, **refund,** kickback [slang]; **premium,** percentage, agio, contango, backwardation [both Brit]; breakage, salvage; tare, tret; penalty, penalty clause.

.2 VERBS **discount, cut, deduct,** bate, abate; **take off,** write off, charge off; **depreciate,** reduce; **allow,** make allowance; rebate, **refund,** kick back [slang]; take a premium *or* percentage.

.3 ADVS **at a discount,** at a reduction, below par.

848. EXPENSIVENESS

.1 NOUNS **expensiveness, dearness,** high *or* great cost, **costliness,** highness, stiffness *or* steepness [both informal], priceyness [Austral]; richness, sumptuousness, luxuriousness.

.2 **preciousness, dearness, value,** high *or* great value, **worth,** extraordinary worth, price *or* great price [both archaic], **valuableness; pricelessness, invaluableness.**

.3 **high price,** high *or* big price tag [informal], **fancy price,** good price, steep *or* stiff price [informal], luxury price, pretty penny *or* an arm and a leg [both informal], exorbitant *or* unconscionable *or* extortionate price; famine price, scarcity price; rack rent; inflationary prices, rising *or* soaring *or* spiraling prices, soaring costs; sellers' market; **inflation,** inflationary trend *or* pressure, hot economy, inflationary spiral, inflationary gap.

.4 **exorbitance,** exorbitancy [archaic], **extravagance,** excess, **excessiveness,** inordinateness, immoderateness, immoderation, undueness, unreasonableness, outrageousness, preposterousness; unconscionableness, extortionateness.

.5 **overcharge,** surcharge, overassessment; usury, shylocking or loan-sharking [both slang]; **extortion,** exploitation, **holdup** or highway robbery [both slang]; profiteering.

.6 VERBS **cost much,** cost money or cost you [both informal], cost a pretty penny or an arm and a leg [informal], cost a packet, **run into money;** be overpriced, price out of the market.

.7 **overprice,** set the price tag too high; **overcharge,** surcharge, overtax; **hold up** or soak or stick or sting or clip [all slang], **make pay through the nose, gouge;** victimize, swindle 618.13–18; exploit, skin [slang], fleece, screw, bleed, bleed white; profiteer; rack or rack up the rents, rackrent.

.8 **overpay,** overspend, pay too much, pay more than it's worth, **pay dearly,** pay exorbitantly, pay, **pay through the nose,** be had [informal].

.9 **inflate,** heat or heat up the economy.

.10 ADJS precious, dear, valuable, worthy, rich, golden, of great price [archaic], worth a pretty penny [informal], worth a king's ransom, worth its weight in gold, good as gold, precious as the apple of one's eye; **priceless, invaluable,** inestimable, **beyond price,** not to be had for love or money, too precious for words.

.11 **expensive, dear, costly,** of great cost, dear-bought, **high, high-priced,** premium, top; **fancy** or stiff or steep [all informal], pricey [Austral]; beyond one's means, not affordable, more than one can afford; unpayable; rich, sumptuous, **luxurious** 904.21.

.12 **overpriced,** grossly overpriced, **exorbitant, excessive, extravagant, inordinate, immoderate,** undue, unwarranted, unreasonable, fancy, unconscionable, outrageous, preposterous, out of bounds, out of sight [informal], **prohibitive; extortionate,** cutthroat, **gouging, usurious,** exacting; **inflationary,** spiraling, skyrocketing.

.13 ADVS dear, dearly; at a high price, at great cost, at a premium, at a great rate, at heavy cost, at great expense.

.14 **preciously, valuably,** worthily; **pricelessly,** invaluably, inestimably.

.15 **expensively,** richly, sumptuously, luxuriously.

.16 **exorbitantly, excessively,** grossly, **extravagantly, inordinately,** immoderately, unduly, unreasonably, unconscionably, outrageously, preposterously; **extortionately,** usuriously, gougingly.

849. CHEAPNESS

.1 NOUNS **cheapness, inexpensiveness,** reasonableness, modestness, moderateness, nominalness; drug or glut on the market; shabbiness, shoddiness 673.2.

.2 **low price, nominal price,** reasonable price, modest or manageable price, sensible price, moderate price; low or nominal or reasonable charge; bargain prices, budget prices, economy prices, easy prices, popular prices, rock-bottom prices; buyers' market; low or small price tag [informal], low tariff [informal]; **reduced price,** cut price, sale price; cheap or reduced rates.

.3 **bargain,** advantageous purchase, **buy** [informal], **good buy, steal** [slang]; money's worth, pennyworth, good pennyworth.

.4 **cheapening, depreciation, devaluation,** reduction, lowering; deflation, cooling or cooling off of the economy; decline, plummet, plummeting, plunge, dive, nose dive or slump or sag; price fall, break; **price cut** or reduction, cut, slash, **markdown.**

.5 VERBS **be cheap,** cost little, not cost anything or cost nothing [both informal], cost next to nothing; **buy dirt cheap,** buy for a song, buy for nickels and dimes, buy at a bargain, buy for a mere nothing; get one's money's worth, get a good pennyworth; buy at wholesale prices or at cost.

.6 **cheapen, depreciate, devaluate,** lower, reduce, **mark down, cut prices, cut,** slash, shave, trim, pare, knock the bottom out of [informal]; deflate, cool or cool off the economy; beat down, jew down [derog]; come down or fall in price; **fall,** decline, plummet, dive, nose-dive [informal], head for the bottom, plunge, sag; slump; break, give way; reach a new low.

.7 ADJS **cheap, inexpensive,** unexpensive, **low, low-priced,** frugal, reasonable, sensible, manageable, modest, moderate, to fit the pocketbook, budget, easy, economy, economic(al); within means; nominal, token; worth the money, well worth the money; cheap or good at the price, cheap at half the price; shabby, shoddy 673.18.

.8 **dirt cheap,** cheap as dirt, dog-cheap [informal], **a dime a dozen,** two-for-a-penny, twopenny-halfpenny, sixpenny, bargain-basement, five-and-ten, dime-store.

.9 **reduced,** cut, slashed, **marked down;** cut-rate; half-price; **giveaway** [informal], sacrificial; **lowest,** rock-bottom, bottom, best.

.10 ADVS **cheaply, cheap,** on the cheap [Brit informal]; **inexpensively,** reasonably, moderately, nominally; **at a bargain,** *à bon marché* [Fr], for a song *or* mere song, for pennies, for nickels and dimes, at small cost, at a low price, at budget prices, at piggy-bank prices, at a sacrifice; at cost *or* cost price, at prime cost, wholesale, at wholesale; at reduced rates.

850. COSTLESSNESS

(absence of charge)

.1 NOUNS **costlessness,** gratuitousness, gratuity, **freeness,** expenselessness, complimentariness, no charge; free ride [informal]; freebie [slang]; labor of love; **gift** 818.4–6.
.2 **complimentary ticket, pass,** free pass *or* ticket, paper [slang], free admission, guest pass *or* ticket, Annie Oakley [slang]; discount ticket, twofer [informal].
.3 **freeloader,** free rider, pass holder, deadhead [informal], paper [slang]; paper house [informal].
.4 VERBS **give, present** 818.12; freeload, sponge 907.11.
.5 ADJS **gratuitous, gratis, free, free of charge,** for free, **for nothing,** free for nothing, free for the asking, free gratis *or* free gratis for nothing [both informal], for love, free as air; freebie *or* freebee *or* freeby [all slang]; costless, expenseless, untaxed, without charge, free of cost *or* expense; unbought, unpaid-for; **complimentary, on the house;** given 818.24; giftlike; eleemosynary, charitable 938.15.
.6 ADVS **gratuitously, gratis, free, free of charge,** for nothing, for the asking, without charge, with the compliments of the management, as our guest.

851. ECONOMY

.1 NOUNS **economy, thrift, thriftiness,** economicalness, savingness, sparingness, unwastefulness, **frugality,** frugalness; tight purse strings; parsimony, parsimoniousness 852.1; false economy; carefulness, care, chariness, canniness; **prudence,** providence, forehandedness; **husbandry,** management, good management *or* stewardship, prudent *or* prudential administration; austerity, austerity program; economic planning; economy of means 852.1.
.2 **economizing,** economization, reduction of spending *or* government spending; **saving,** scrimping, skimping [informal], scraping, sparing, cheeseparing; **retrench-**ment, **curtailment,** reduction of expenses, cutback, slowdown, cooling, cooling off *or* down, low growth rate.
.3 **economizer,** economist, **saver.**
.4 VERBS **economize, save,** make *or* enforce economies; **scrimp, skimp** [informal], **scrape,** scrape and save; **manage, husband,** husband one's resources; keep within compass [archaic], keep within one's means *or* budget, balance income with outgo, live within one's income, make ends meet, cut one's coat according to one's cloth; put something aside, save for a rainy day, have a nest egg.
.5 **retrench, cut down,** cut *or* pare down expenses, **curtail expenses;** cut corners, tighten one's belt, cut back, roll back [informal], take a reef, slow down.
.6 ADJS **economic(al), thrifty, frugal,** unwasteful, conserving, **saving,** economizing, spare, **sparing;** Scotch; **prudent,** prudential, provident, forehanded; careful, chary, canny; scrimping, skimping [informal], cheeseparing; penny-wise; parsimonious 852.7; labor-saving, time-saving, money-saving.
.7 ADVS **economically, thriftily, frugally,** husbandly [archaic]; prudently, providently; carefully, charily, cannily; sparingly, with a sparing hand.

852. PARSIMONY

.1 NOUNS **parsimony,** parsimoniousness; frugality 851.1; **stinting, pinching, scrimping,** skimping, cheeseparing; economy, economy of means, economy of assumption, law of parsimony, Ockham's razor, elegance.
.2 **niggardliness,** penuriousness, **meanness,** minginess, shabbiness, sordidness.
.3 **stinginess, ungenerosity, illiberality, cheapness** *or* tightness [both informal], tight purse strings, nearness, closeness, closefistedness, closehandedness [archaic], tightfistedness, hardfistedness, **miserliness,** penny-pinching, hoarding; **avarice** 634.8.
.4 **niggard, tightwad** [slang], **miser,** hard man with a buck [slang], **skinflint,** scrooge, penny pincher, pinchfist, pinchgut [archaic], churl, curmudgeon [archaic], muckworm, save-all [dial], Harpagon [Molière], Silas Marner [George Eliot].
.5 VERBS **stint, scrimp, skimp, scamp,** scant, screw, **pinch,** starve, famish; **pinch pennies,** rub the print off a dollar bill, rub the picture off a nickel; live upon nothing; grudge, begrudge.

.6 **withhold**, hold back, hold out on [slang].

.7 ADJS **parsimonious, sparing,** cheeseparing, **stinting, scamping, scrimping,** skimping; frugal 851.6; too frugal, overfrugal, frugal to excess; penny-wise, penny-wise and pound-foolish.

.8 **niggardly, niggard, pinchpenny,** penurious, **grudging, mean,** mingy, shabby, sordid.

.9 **stingy, illiberal, ungenerous, miserly,** save-all, **cheap** or **tight** [both informal], **near, close, closefisted,** closehanded [archaic], **tightfisted, pinchfisted, hardfisted;** near as the bark on a tree, "as close as a vise" [Hawthorne]; pinching, **penny-pinching; avaricious** 634.27.

.10 ADVS **parsimoniously, stintingly,** scrimpingly, skimpingly.

.11 **niggardly, stingily, illiberally,** ungenerously, **closefistedly, tightfistedly;** meanly, shabbily, sordidly.

853. LIBERALITY

.1 NOUNS **liberality, liberalness, freeness, freedom; generosity, generousness,** largeness, **unselfishness, munificence,** largess; **bountifulness, bounteousness, bounty;** hospitality, welcome, graciousness; **openhandedness,** freehandedness, open or free hand, easy purse strings; **givingness;** openheartedness, bigheartedness, largeheartedness, greatheartedness, freeheartedness; open heart, big or large or great heart; **magnanimity** 979.2.

.2 **cheerful giver,** free giver.

.3 VERBS **give freely,** give cheerfully, give with an open hand, give with both hands, put one's hands in one's pockets, open the purse, loosen or untie the purse strings; **spare no expense,** spare nothing, not count the cost, let money be no object; **heap upon,** lavish upon, shower down upon; give the coat or shirt off one's back, give more than one's share, **give until it hurts;** give of oneself, give of one's substance, not hold back, offer oneself; keep the change!

.4 ADJS **liberal, free,** free with one's money, free-spending; **generous, munificent,** large, princely, handsome; **unselfish, ungrudging; unsparing, unstinting,** stintless, unstinted; **bountiful, bounteous, lavish,** profuse; hospitable, gracious; **openhanded,** freehanded, open; **giving;** openhearted, **bighearted, largehearted,** greathearted, freehearted; **magnanimous** 979.6.

.5 ADVS **liberally, freely; generously, munificently,** handsomely; **unselfishly,** ungrudgingly; **unsparingly, unstintingly; bountifully,** bounteously, **lavishly,** profusely; hospitably, graciously; **openhandedly,** freehandedly; openheartedly, bigheartedly, largeheartedly, greatheartedly, freeheartedly; with open hands, with both hands, with an unsparing hand, without stint.

854. PRODIGALITY

.1 NOUNS **prodigality, overliberality,** overgenerousness, overgenerosity; **profligacy, extravagance,** pound-foolishness, reckless spending or expenditure; incontinence, intemperance 993; lavishness, profuseness, profusion; **wastefulness, waste; dissipation, squandering,** squandermania; carpe diem; slack or loose purse strings, leaking purse; conspicuous consumption or waste.

.2 **prodigal, wastrel,** waster, **squanderer; spendthrift,** wastethrift, spender, spend-all, big-time spender [informal]; Diamond Jim Brady; prodigal son.

.3 VERBS **squander, lavish, slather,** blow [slang], play ducks and drakes with; **dissipate,** scatter [archaic], sow broadcast, scatter to the winds; **run through,** go through; **throw away,** throw one's money away, **spend money like water,** hang the expense, let slip or flow through one's fingers, spend as if money grew on trees, spend money as if it were going out of style, throw money around, spend like a drunken sailor; gamble away; burn the candle at both ends; seize the day, live for the day, let tomorrow take care of itself.

.4 **waste, consume, spend, expend, use up, exhaust;** lose; spill, pour down the drain or rathole; pour water into a sieve, cast pearls before swine, kill the goose that lays the golden egg, *manger son blé en herbe* [Fr], throw out the baby with the bath water.

.5 **fritter away,** fool away, fribble away, dribble away, drivel away, **trifle away,** dally away, potter away, piss away [slang], muddle away, diddle away [informal], squander in dribs and drabs; idle away, while away.

.6 **misspend, throw good money after bad,** throw the helve after the hatchet.

.7 **overspend,** spend more than one has, spend what one hasn't got; overdraw, overdraw one's account, live beyond one's means, have champagne tastes on a beer budget.

.8 ADJS **prodigal, extravagant, lavish,** profuse, **overliberal,** overgenerous, overlavish, **spendthrift, wasteful,** profligate, dissipative; incontinent, intemperate 993.7;
pound-foolish, penny-wise and pound-
foolish; easy come, easy go.
.9 **wasted, squandered, dissipated,** consumed, spent, used, lost; **gone to waste,**
run to seed; down the drain or spout or
rathole [informal]; misspent.

855. FEELINGS

.1 NOUNS **feelings, emotions, affections,
sentiments, passions, sensibilities, susceptibilities, sympathies,** tender susceptibilities, finer feelings; the logic of the heart;
emotional life; affectivity, affective faculty; feeling tone.
.2 (seat of affections; hence, affections,
deepest feelings) **heart, soul, spirit,** *esprit*
[Fr], **breast, bosom,** inmost heart or soul,
heart of hearts, secret or inner recesses of
the heart, secret places, heart's core,
heartstrings, cockles of the heart, bottom
of the heart, being, innermost being, core
of one's being; viscera, pit of one's stomach, guts [slang]; bones.
.3 **feeling, emotion, affection,** emotional
charge, path(o)–, thym(o)–; **sentiment,
passion,** heartthrob; sense, deep or profound sense, **sensation** 422; impression,
undercurrent; presentiment 481.3; foreboding 544; experience; affect; reaction,
response, gut reaction [informal]; feeling
tone, emotional shade or nuance.
.4 (capacity of emotion) **sensibility, sensitivity, sensitiveness,** delicacy, affectivity, susceptibility, impressionability 422.2.
.5 **sympathetic response, sympathy, fellow
feeling,** responsiveness, relating, caring,
concern; response, echo, chord, sympathetic chord, vibrations, vibes [slang]; **empathy,** identification; involvement, sharing; pathos.
.6 **tender feeling, tenderness,** softness, gentleness, delicacy; **tenderheartedness,** softheartedness, warmheartedness, tender or
sensitive or warm heart, soft place or spot
in one's heart; fondness, weakness 634.2.
.7 **bad feeling, hard feelings;** immediate dislike, disaffinity, personality conflict, **hostility,** animosity 929.3,4; **hardheartedness**
856.3.
.8 **sentimentality, sentiment, sentimental-
ism,** oversentimentality, oversentimental-
ism, bathos; nostalgia, nostomania; romanticism; sweetness and light, hearts-
and-flowers; bleeding heart; mawkishness, cloyingness, maudlinness, namby-
pamby, namby-pambyness, namby-pam-
byism; mushiness or sloppiness [both
informal]; **mush** or slush or slop or goo or
schmaltz [all slang]; sob story or tear-
jerker [both slang], soap opera.
.9 **emotionalism,** emotionality, emotionaliz-
ing, emotionalization; emotiveness, emo-
tivity, visceralness; nonrationalness, un-
reasoningness; demonstrativeness; theatricality, theatrics, histrionics, making
scenes; **sensationalism, melodrama,** melodramatics, blood and thunder, yellow
journalism; emotional appeal, human interest, love interest.
.10 **fervor, fervency,** fervidness, **passion,** passionateness, impassionedness, **ardor, ardency,** *empressement* [Fr], warmth of
feeling, **warmth, heat, fire,** verve, furor,
fury, vehemence; heartiness, gusto, relish,
savor; spirit, heart, soul; **liveliness** 707.2;
zeal 635.2; **excitement** 857; ecstasy 857.7.
.11 VERBS **feel,** entertain or harbor or cherish
or nurture a feeling; **feel deeply,** feel in
one's viscera or bones, feel in one's guts
[slang]; experience 151.8; have a sensation, get or receive an impression, **sense,
perceive** 422.8.
.12 **respond, react,** be moved, be affected or
touched, be inspired, echo, catch the
flame or infection, be in tune, be turned
on to [slang], enter into the spirit of, be
imbued with the spirit of; care about,
sympathize with, empathize with, identify with, relate to emotionally, dig
[slang], be turned on by [slang], be involved, share; color with emotion, change
color.
.13 **take to heart,** lay to heart, nourish in
one's bosom, feel in one's breast, cherish
at the heart's core, treasure up in the
heart; lie at the heart.
.14 **have deep feelings, be all heart, have a
tender heart,** be a man of heart or sentiment; have a soft place or spot in one's
heart; be a prey to one's feelings; love
931.18–20; hate 930.5.
.15 **emotionalize, emote** [informal], give free
play to the emotions, make a scene; be
theatrical, theatricalize, ham it up [infor-
mal]; **sentimentalize,** gush [informal],
slobber over [slang], slop over [informal].
.16 **affect, touch, move, stir; melt, soften,**
melt the heart; **penetrate,** pierce, go
through one, go deep; touch a chord,
**touch a sympathetic chord, touch one's
heart,** tug at the heart or heartstrings, go
to one's heart; come home to; **touch to**

the quick, touch on the raw, flick one on the raw, smart, sting.

.17 impress, affect, strike, hit, smite, rock; make an impression, make a dent in, make an impact upon, sink in [informal], strike home, come home to, hit the mark [informal]; tell, have a strong effect, traumatize, strike hard, impress forcibly.

.18 impress upon, bring home to, make it felt; stamp, stamp on, etch, engrave, engrave on.

.19 ADJS emotional, emotive, affectional, affective, feeling; soulful, of soul, of heart, of feeling, of sentiment; visceral, gut [slang]; glandular; emotiometabolic, emotiomotor, emotiomuscular, emotiovascular; demonstrative, overdemonstrative.

.20 emotionalistic, emotive, overemotional, hysteric(al), sensational, sensationalistic, melodramatic, theatrical, histrionic, hammy [informal], nonrational, unreasoning.

.21 sensitive, sensible, emotionable, passible, delicate; responsive, sympathetic, receptive; susceptible, impressionable 422.13; tender, soft, tenderhearted, softhearted, warmhearted.

.22 sentimental, sentimentalized, soft, mawkish, maudlin, cloying; sticky or gooey or schmaltzy or sappy [all slang], oversentimental, oversentimentalized, bathetic; mushy or sloppy or gushing or teary or beery [all informal]; tear-jerking [slang]; namby-pamby, romantic; nostalgic, nostomanic.

.23 fervent, fervid, passionate, impassioned, intense, ardent; hearty, cordial, enthusiastic, exuberant, unrestrained, vigorous; keen, breathless, excited 857.18–25; lively 707.17; zealous 635.10; warm, burning, heated, hot, red-hot, fiery, flaming, glowing, ablaze, afire, on fire, boiling over, steaming, steamy; delirious, fevered, feverish, febrile, flushed; intoxicated, drunk.

.24 affecting, touching, moving, emotive, pathetic.

.25 affected, moved, touched, impressed; impressed with or by, penetrated with, seized with, imbued with, devoured by, obsessed, obsessed by; wrought up by; stricken, wracked, racked, torn, agonized, tortured.

.26 deep-felt, deepgoing, heartfelt, homefelt [archaic]; deep, profound, indelible; pervading, absorbing; penetrating, piercing; poignant, keen, sharp, acute.

.27 ADVS feelingly, emotionally, affectingly,

touchingly, movingly, with feeling, poignantly.

.28 fervently, fervidly, passionately, impassionedly, intensely, ardently, zealously; keenly, breathlessly, excitedly; warmly, heatedly, glowingly; heartily, cordially; enthusiastically, exuberantly, vigorously; kindly, heart and soul, with all one's heart, from the bottom of one's heart.

.29 sentimentally, mawkishly, maudlinly, cloyingly; mushily or sloppily or gushingly [all informal].

856. LACK OF FEELINGS

.1 NOUNS unfeeling, unfeelingness, lack of affect, lack of feeling or feeling tone, emotional deadness or numbness or paralysis, anesthesia, emotionlessness, unemotionalism, unexcitability; dispassion, dispassionateness, unpassionateness, objectivity; passionlessness, spiritlessness, heartlessness, soullessness; coldness, coolness, frigidity, chill, chilliness, frostiness, iciness; coldheartedness, cold-bloodedness; cold heart, cold blood; unresponsiveness, unsympatheticness; lack of touch or contact, autism, self-absorption, withdrawal, catatonia; unimpressionableness, unimpressibility; insusceptibility, unsusceptibility; impassiveness, impassibility, impassivity; straight face or poker face [both informal], dead pan [slang]; immovability, untouchability; dullness, obtuseness; inexcitability 858.

.2 insensibility, insensibleness, unconsciousness, unawareness, obliviousness, oblivion.

.3 callousness, callosity, callus; insensitivity, insensitiveness, Philistinism; hardness, hardenedness, hardheartedness, hardness of heart, hard heart, heart of stone, stoniness, flintiness; obduracy, obdurateness, induration, inuredness; imperviousness, thick skin, rhinoceros hide, thick or hard shell, armor, formidable defenses.

.4 apathy, indifference, unconcern, disinterest; withdrawnness, aloofness, detachment, ataraxy or ataraxia, dispassion; passiveness, passivity, supineness, insouciance, nonchalance; inappetence, lack of appetite; listlessness, spiritlessness, blah or blahs [both slang], heartlessness, plucklessness, spunklessness; lethargy, phlegm, lethargicalness, phlegmaticalness, phlegmaticness, hebetude, dullness, sluggishness, languidness; soporifousness, sopor, comatoseness, torpidness, torpor, torpidity, stupor, stupefaction; acedia, sloth;

resignation, resignedness; **numbness**, benumbedness; hopelessness 889.

.5 VERBS not be affected by, remain unmoved, not turn a hair; have a thick skin, have a heart of stone; be cold as ice, be a cold fish, be an icicle.

.6 **callous, harden**, case harden, **harden one's heart**, ossify, steel, indurate, inure; brutalize.

.7 **dull, blunt**, desensitize, obtund, hebetate.

.8 **numb, benumb**, paralyze, **deaden**, anesthetize, freeze, **stun, stupefy**, drug.

.9 ADJS **unfeeling, unemotional**, nonemotional, emotionless, affectless, emotionally dead or numb or paralyzed, anesthetized, drugged; **unpassionate, dispassionate**, unimpassioned, **objective**; passionless, **spiritless, heartless**, soulless; **cold, cool, frigid**, frozen, chill, chilly, arctic, frosty, frosted, icy, **coldhearted, coldblooded**, cold as charity; **unaffectionate**, unloving; **unresponsive**, unresponding, **unsympathetic**; out of touch or contact; in one's shell or armor, behind one's defenses; autistic, self-absorbed, catatonic; unimpressionable, unimpressible, insusceptible, unsusceptible; **impassive**, impassible; immovable, untouchable; dull, obtuse, blunt; **inexcitable** 858.10.

.10 **insensible, unconscious**, unaware, **oblivious**, blind to, deaf to, dead to, lost to.

.11 **unaffected, unmoved, untouched**, unimpressed, unstruck, **unstirred**, unruffled, unanimated, uninspired.

.12 **callous, calloused, insensitive**, Philistine; **thick-skinned**, pachydermatous; **hard, hardhearted, hardened**, case-hardened, indurated, stony, flinty, steely, impervious, inured, steeled against, proof against, as hard as nails.

.13 **apathetic, indifferent, unconcerned**, uncaring, Laodicean, **disinterested, uninterested; withdrawn, aloof, detached**, Olympian; **passive**, supine; stoic; insouciant, nonchalant, blasé; **listless, spiritless**, blah [slang], heartless, pluckless, spunkless; **lethargic, phlegmatic**, hebetudinous, **dull**, desensitized, sluggish, torpid, languid, slack, soporific, comatose, **stupefied**, in a stupor, **numb**, numbed, benumbed; resigned; hopeless 889.12.

.14 ADVS **unfeelingly, unemotionally**, emotionlessly; with a straight or poker face [informal], deadpan [slang]; **dispassionately**, unpassionately; **spiritlessly, heartlessly**, coldly, coldheartedly, cold-bloodedly, **in cold blood**; with dry eyes.

.15 **apathetically, indifferently, unconcernedly**, disinterestedly, uninterestedly, impassively; **listlessly, spiritlessly**, heartlessly, plucklessly, spunklessly; **lethargically, phlegmatically**, dully, numbly.

857. EXCITEMENT

.1 NOUNS **excitement**, emotion, excitedness, **arousal, stimulation, exhilaration**; a high [slang], manic state or condition.

.2 **thrill, sensation**, titillation; **tingle**, tingling; quiver, shiver, shudder, tremor, **tremor of excitement**, rush [slang]; flush, rush of emotion, surge of emotion; **kick** or charge or boot or bang or lift [all slang], jollies [slang].

.3 **agitation, perturbation**, ferment, **turbulence, turmoil**, tumult, embroilment, uproar, **commotion**, disturbance, ado, brouhaha [Fr], feery-fary [Scot], to-do [informal]; pell-mell, **flurry**, ruffle, bustle, stir, swirl, swirling, whirl, vortex, eddy, hurry, hurry-scurry, hurly-burly; fermentation, yeastiness, effervescence, ebullience, ebullition; fume.

.4 **trepidation**, trepidity; **disquiet**, disquietude, inquietude, **unrest, restlessness**, fidgetiness; **fidgets** or **shakes** or shivers or dithers [all informal]; **quivering, quavering, quaking, shaking**, trembling; **quiver**, quaver, shiver, shudder, didder [Brit dial], twitter, **tremor**, tremble, flutter; palpitation, pitapatation [informal], pitapat, pitter-patter; **throb**, throbbing; panting, heaving.

.5 **dither, tizzy** [informal], swivet, foofaraw, **pucker** [informal], **twitter**, twitteration [informal], **flutter, fluster**, flusteration or flustration [both informal], **fret, fuss**, pother, bother, lather or stew [both informal], flap.

.6 **fever of excitement**, fever, heat, fever heat, fire; sexual excitement, rut 419.6.

.7 **fury, furor**, furore [Brit], fire and fury; **ecstasy**, transport, **rapture**, ravishment; intoxication, abandon; **passion, rage**, raging or tearing passion, towering rage or passion; **frenzy**, orgy, orgasm; madness, craze, **delirium**, hysteria.

.8 **outburst**, outbreak, **burst, flare-up**, blaze, **explosion**, eruption, irruption, upheaval, convulsion, spasm, seizure, fit, paroxysm; storm, tornado, whirlwind, cyclone, hurricane, gale, tempest, gust.

.9 **excitability**, excitableness, perturbability, agitatibility; emotional instability, explosiveness, eruptiveness, inflammability, combustibility, tempestuousness, violence, latent violence; **irascibility** 951.2; irritability, edginess, touchiness, prickliness, **sensitivity** 422.3; skittishness, startlishness, **nervousness** 859; emotionalism 855.9.

.10 **excitation, excitement, arousal,** arousing, **stirring,** stirring up, working up, working into a lather [informal], lathering up, whipping up, steaming up, **agitation, perturbation; stimulation, stimulus, exhilaration,** animation; electrification, galvanization; **provocation, irritation,** aggravation, exasperation, exacerbation, fomentation, inflammation, infuriation, **incitement** 648.4.

.11 VERBS **excite, impassion, arouse, rouse,** blow up [archaic], **stir, stir up,** set astir, stir the feelings, stir the blood, play on the feelings; **work up,** work into, work up into a lather [informal], lather up, whip up, **key up,** steam up; **move** 648.12; **foment, incite** 648.17; turn on [slang]; awaken, awake, wake, waken, wake up; call up, summon up, call forth; **kindle,** enkindle, light up, light the fuse, **fire, inflame,** heat, warm, set fire to, set on fire, fire or warm the blood; fan, fan the fire or flame, blow the coals, stir the embers, feed the fire, add fuel to the fire or flame, pour oil on the fire; raise to a fever heat or pitch, bring to the boiling point; overexcite; **annoy, incense** 952.22; **enrage, infuriate** 952.23; frenzy, madden 473.23.

.12 **stimulate, whet, sharpen,** pique, provoke, quicken, enliven, pick up, jazz up [slang], animate, **exhilarate,** invigorate, galvanize, fillip, give a fillip to; infuse life into, give new life to, revive, renew, resuscitate.

.13 **agitate, perturb, disturb, trouble, disquiet, discompose,** discombobulate [informal], unsettle, stir, **ruffle, shake, shake up, shock, upset,** jolt, jar, rock, stagger, electrify, bring or pull one up short, give one a turn [informal]; fuss [slang], flutter, flurry, rattle, disconcert, **fluster.**

.14 **thrill, tickle,** titillate, flush, give a thrill, **give one a kick** or boot or charge or bang or lift [informal]; intoxicate, fascinate, take one's breath away.

.15 **be excitable,** have a short fuse [informal], excite easily; **get excited,** get into a dither or tizzy or swivet or pucker, get into a stew [informal]; catch the infection, **work oneself up,** work oneself into a sweat or lather [informal], get hot under the collar [informal], run a temperature or race one's motor [both slang]; turn a hair; ex-

plode, **blow up** [informal], blow one's top or stack [informal], blow one's cool [slang], flip or flip one's lid [both slang], blow a gasket [slang]; **flare up,** flash up, flame up, fire up, catch fire, take fire; **fly into a passion, fly off the handle** or **hit the ceiling** [both informal]; go into hysterics, have a tantrum or temper tantrum, come apart; **rage, rave, rant,** rant and rave, bellow, **storm,** ramp; be angry, smolder, **seethe** 952.15.

.16 (be excited) **thrill, tingle, tingle with excitement,** glow; swell, swell with emotion, be full of emotion; thrill to; flip out [slang]; turn on to or get high on or freak out on [all slang]; heave, pant; **throb,** palpitate, go pitapat; **tremble, shiver, quiver, quaver, quake,** flutter, twitter, **shake,** shake like an aspen leaf, have the shakes [informal]; shit in one's pants [slang]; **fidget,** have the fidgets [informal]; toss and turn, toss, tumble, twist and turn, wriggle, wiggle, writhe, squirm; twitch, jerk.

.17 **change color,** turn color, go all colors; **pale,** whiten, blanch, turn pale; darken, look black; turn blue in the face; **flush, blush,** crimson, glow, mantle, color, redden, turn red.

.18 ADJS **excited,** impassioned; **thrilled,** agog, tingling, tingly, atingle, aquiver, atwitter; **stimulated, exhilarated, high** [slang]; manic; **moved, stirred,** stirred up, **aroused, roused,** on one's mettle, fired, inflamed, **wrought up, worked up,** worked up into a lather [informal], lathered up, whipped up, steamed up, keyed up, hopped up [slang]; turned-on [slang]; carried away; bursting, ready to burst; effervescent, yeasty, ebullient.

.19 **in a dither, in a tizzy** [informal], in a swivet, in a foofaraw, **in a pucker** [informal], in a quiver, **in a twitter,** in a flutter, all of a twitter or flutter, in a fluster, in a flurry, in a pother, in a bother, in a ferment, in a turmoil, in an uproar, in a stew or in a sweat [both informal], in a lather [slang].

.20 **heated, passionate, warm, hot,** red-hot, flaming, **burning, fiery, glowing, fervent, fervid; feverish,** febrile, hectic, flushed; sexually excited, in rut 419.30; burning with excitement, het up [dial], hot under the collar [informal]; seething, boiling, boiling over, steamy, steaming.

.21 **agitated, perturbed, disturbed, troubled, disquieted, upset,** unsettled, **discomposed, flustered,** ruffled, **shaken.**

.22 **turbulent,** tumultuous, tempestuous, boisterous, clamorous, uproarious.

.23 **frenzied, frantic; ecstatic,** transported, enraptured, ravished, in a transport or ecstasy; intoxicated, abandoned; orgiastic, orgasmic; raging, raving, roaring, bellowing, ramping, storming, howling, ranting, fulminating, frothing or foaming at the mouth; **wild,** hog-wild [slang]; **violent,** fierce, ferocious, feral, **furious; mad,** madding, **rabid,** maniac(al), demoniac(al), possessed; carried away, **distracted, delirious, beside oneself,** out of one's wits; uncontrollable, running mad, amok, berserk; **hysterical,** in hysterics; wild-eyed, wild-looking, haggard; blue in the face.

.24 **overwrought,** overexcited; **overcome,** overwhelmed, overpowered, overmastered; **upset,** bouleversé [Fr].

.25 **restless,** restive, **uneasy,** unquiet, unsettled, unrestful, tense; **fidgety, fussy,** fluttery.

.26 **excitable, emotional,** highly emotional, perturbable, agitable; emotionally unstable; explosive, volcanic, eruptive, inflammable; irascible 951.19; irritable, edgy, touchy, prickly, **sensitive** 422.13; **skittish,** startlish; **high-strung,** high-spirited, mettlesome, high-mettled; **nervous** 859.10.

.27 **passionate, fiery, vehement,** hotheaded, **impetuous,** violent, furious, fierce, **wild;** tempestuous, stormy, tornadic; simmering, volcanic, ready to burst forth.

.28 **exciting, thrilling,** thrilly [informal], **stirring, moving, breathtaking,** excito–; agitating, perturbing, disturbing, upsetting, troubling, disquieting, unsettling, distracting, jolting, jarring; heart-stirring, heart-thrilling, heart-swelling, heart-expanding, soul-stirring, spirit-stirring, deep-thrilling, mind-blowing [slang]; impressive, striking, telling; **provocative** 648.27, provoking, piquant, tantalizing 650.7; **inflammatory** 648.28; **stimulating,** stimulative; exhilarating, heady, intoxicating, maddening, ravishing; **electric,** galvanic, charged; **overwhelming,** overpowering, overcoming, overmastering, more than flesh and blood can bear; suspensive, **suspenseful,** cliff-hanging [informal].

.29 **penetrating, piercing,** stabbing, cutting, stinging, biting, keen, brisk, sharp, caustic, astringent.

.30 **sensational, lurid,** yellow, **melodramatic,** Barnumesque; spine-chilling; blood-and-thunder, cloak-and-dagger.

.31 ADVS **excitedly, agitatedly,** perturbedly; with beating or leaping heart, with heart beating high, with heart going pitapat or pitter-patter, thrilling all over, with heart in mouth; with glistening eyes, all agog, all aquiver or atwitter or atingle; in a sweat or stew or dither or tizzy.

.32 **heatedly, passionately,** warmly, hotly, glowingly, fervently, fervidly, **feverishly.**

.33 **frenziedly, frantically,** wildly, furiously, violently, fiercely, madly, rabidly, distractedly, deliriously, till one is blue in the face.

.34 **excitingly, thrillingly,** stirringly, movingly; **provocatively,** provokingly; stimulatingly, exhilaratingly.

858. INEXCITABILITY

.1 NOUNS **inexcitability,** inexcitableness, unexcitableness, **imperturbability,** imperturbableness, unflappability [informal]; inirritability, unirritableness; **dispassion,** dispassionateness, unpassionateness, ataraxy or ataraxia; steadiness; stoicism; **even temper,** steady or smooth temper, good or easy temper; unnervousness 860; **patience** 861; **impassiveness,** impassivity, stolidity; bovinity, dullness.

.2 **composure,** countenance; **calmness,** calm disposition, **placidity, serenity,** tranquillity, soothingness, peacefulness; mental composure, peace or calm of mind; calm or quiet mind, easy mind; philosophicalness, philosophy, philosophic composure; quiet, quietude; imperturbation, indisturbance, unruffledness; **coolness,** coolheadedness, cool [slang], sangfroid; icy calm; Oriental calm, Buddha-like composure.

.3 **equanimity,** equilibrium, equability, balance; **levelheadedness,** level head, well-balanced or well-regulated mind; poise, aplomb, **self-possession,** self-control, self-command, self-restraint, restraint, possession, **presence of mind;** confidence, assurance, **self-confidence, self-assurance.**

.4 **sedateness, staidness,** soberness, sobriety, sober-mindedness, seriousness, gravity, solemnity, sobersidedness; temperance, moderation; sobersides.

.5 **nonchalance,** casualness, offhandedness; easygoingness, lackadaisicalness; **indifference,** unconcern 636.2.

.6 VERBS **compose, calm** 163.7; **set one's mind at ease or rest,** make one easy.

.7 **compose oneself, control oneself,** restrain oneself, collect oneself, **get hold of oneself, get** organized [informal], master one's feelings; **calm down, cool off,** sober down, simmer down [informal], cool it [slang]; **relax,** unwind, take it easy [informal].

.8 (control one's feelings) **suppress, repress,** keep under, smother, stifle, inhibit; sublimate.

.9 **keep cool,** keep one's cool [slang], **keep calm,** keep one's head, keep one's shirt on [slang], not turn a hair; take things as they come, roll with the punches [informal]; keep a stiff upper lip.

.10 ADJS **inexcitable, imperturbable,** undisturbable, **unflappable** [informal]; **unirritable,** inirritable; **dispassionate,** unpassionate; **steady;** stoic(al); **even-tempered; impassive,** stolid; bovine, dull; unnervous 860.2; **patient** 861.10.

.11 **unexcited, unperturbed,** undisturbed, untroubled, unagitated, **unruffled,** unflustered, unstirred, unimpassioned.

.12 **calm, placid,** quiet, **tranquil, serene,** peaceful; **cool, coolheaded,** cool as a cucumber [informal]; philosophical.

.13 **composed, collected,** recollected, **levelheaded; poised,** together [slang], in equipoise, equanimous, equilibrious, **balanced,** well-balanced; **self-possessed,** self-controlled, self-restrained; confident, assured, **self-confident, self-assured.**

.14 **sedate, staid,** sober, sober-minded, serious, grave, solemn, sobersided; temperate, moderate.

.15 **nonchalant, blasé; indifferent,** unconcerned 636.6,7; **casual, offhand; easygoing,** easy, free and easy, devil-may-care, lackadaisical, *dégagé* [Fr].

.16 ADVS inexcitably, **imperturbably,** inirritably, **dispassionately;** steadily; stoically; **calmly, placidly,** quietly, **tranquilly, serenely; coolly, composedly,** levelheadedly; impassively, stolidly, stodgily, stuffily.

.17 **sedately, staidly, soberly,** sobersidedly.

.18 **nonchalantly, casually,** offhandedly, easygoingly, lackadaisically.

859. NERVOUSNESS

.1 NOUNS **nervousness, nerves,** nervosity, **uneasiness, apprehensiveness;** undue or morbid excitability, excessive irritability, state of nerves, case of nerves, spell of nerves, attack of nerves; **agitation, trepidation** 857.3,4; fear 891; panic, panickiness; **fidgets,** fidgetiness; twitching, tic, vellication; stage fright, buck fever [informal]; nervous stomach.

.2 [slang or informal terms] **jitters, willies, heebie-jeebies,** jimjams, **jumps, shakes,** quivers, trembles, dithers, all-overs, butterflies, shivers, cold shivers, sweat, cold sweat.

.3 **tension,** tenseness, tautness, **strain, stress,** stress and strain, mental strain, nervous tension or strain, pressure.

.4 frayed nerves, frazzled nerves, jangled nerves, shattered nerves, raw nerves, twanging nerves; neurosis 690.19; neurasthenia, nervous prostration, nervous breakdown 686.7.

.5 **nervous wreck,** wreck, a bundle of nerves.

.6 VERBS **fidget,** have the fidgets; **jitter,** have the jitters, etc.; **tremble** 857.16.

.7 lose self-control, go into hysterics; lose courage 892.8; **crack** or **crack up** [informal], go haywire [slang]; **flip** or flip one's lid or wig [slang], **go to pieces,** have a nervous breakdown, come unstuck or come apart [both informal], go up the wall [informal].

.8 **get on one's nerves,** jangle the nerves, **grate on, jar on, put on edge, set the teeth on edge, go against the grain;** irritate 866.14.

.9 **unnerve, unman, undo, unstring,** unbrace, **demoralize, shake, upset,** psych out [informal], dash, knock down, **crush,** overcome, prostrate.

.10 ADJS **nervous,** nervy [Brit informal]; **highstrung,** overstrung, all nerves; **uneasy, apprehensive;** nervous as a cat; **excitable** 857.26; **irritable, edgy, on edge,** nerves on edge, on the ragged edge [informal], panicky, fearful, frightened 891.31–33.

.11 **jittery** [informal], **jumpy,** skittery [dial], twittery, all-overish [informal]; **shaky,** shivery, quivery, in a quiver; tremulous, tremulant, trembly; jumpy as a cat on a hot tin roof; **fidgety,** fidgeting; fluttery, all of a flutter or twitter; twitchy; **agitated** 857.21; shaking, trembling, quivering, shivering; shook up or all shook up [both slang].

.12 **tense,** uptight [informal], **strained,** stretched tight, taut, unrelaxed, **under a strain.**

.13 **unnerved, unmanned, unstrung, undone,** reduced to jelly, unglued [informal], **demoralized, shaken, upset,** dashed, stricken, **crushed; shot,** shot to pieces; neurasthenic, prostrate, prostrated, overcome.

.14 **nerve-racking,** nerve-rending, nerve-shaking, nerve-jangling, nerve-trying, nerve-stretching; jarring, grating.

.15 ADVS **nervously, shakily,** shakingly, tremulously, tremblingly, quiveringly.

860. UNNERVOUSNESS

.1 NOUNS unnervousness, nervelessness; calmness, inexcitability 858; unshakiness, untremulousness; steadiness, steady-handedness, steady nerves; no nerves, strong nerves, iron nerves, nerves of steel, icy nerves; cool head.

.2 ADJS unnervous, nerveless, without a nerve in one's body; strong-nerved, iron-nerved, steel-nerved; coolheaded, calm, inexcitable 858.10–12; cool, calm, and collected; steady, rock-steady, steady-nerved, steady-handed; unshaky, unshaken, unquivering, untremulous, without a tremor; unflinching, unfaltering, unwavering, unshrinking, unblenching, unblinking; relaxed, unstrained.

861. PATIENCE

.1 NOUNS patience, patientness; tolerance, toleration, acceptance; indulgence, lenience, leniency 759; sweet reasonableness; forbearance, forbearing, forbearingness; sufferance, endurance; long-suffering, long-sufferance, longanimity; stoicism, fortitude, self-control; patience of Job; "the art of hoping" [Vauvenargues], "a minor form of despair, disguised as a virtue" [Ambrose Bierce]; waiting game, waiting it out; perseverance 625.

.2 resignation, meekness, humility, humbleness; obedience; amenability; submission, submissiveness 765.3; acquiescence, compliance, uncomplainingness; nonresistance, quietism, passivity, passiveness 706.1; passive resistance, nonviolent resistance; Quakerism.

.3 stoic, Spartan, man of iron.

.4 VERBS be patient, forbear, bear with composure, wait, wait it out, play a waiting game, watch for one's moment, keep one's shirt on [slang], not hold one's breath [informal]; contain oneself, possess oneself, possess one's soul in patience; carry on, carry through; "have patience and endure" [Ovid].

.5 endure, bear, stand, support, sustain, suffer, tolerate, abide, bide; persevere, stick [informal]; hang in or hang in there or hang tough [all slang]; bear with, put up with, take up with, abide with, stand for [informal], brook, brave; lump or lump it [both informal].

.6 accept, condone, countenance; overlook, not make an issue of, let go by, let pass; reconcile oneself to, resign oneself to,

yield or submit to, obey; accustom oneself to, accommodate oneself to, adjust oneself to; accept one's fate, lay in the lap of the gods, take things as they come, roll with the punches [informal]; make the best of it, make the most of it, make the best of a bad bargain, make a virtue of necessity; submit with a good grace, grin and bear it, grin and abide, shrug, shrug it off; take in good part, take in one's stride; rise above.

.7 take, pocket, swallow, down, stomach, eat, digest, disregard, turn a blind eye, ignore; swallow an insult, pocket the affront, turn the other cheek, take it lying down, turn aside provocation.

.8 bear up under, bear the brunt, stand the gaff [slang], take it [informal], take it on the chin [slang], take it like a man, not let it get one down [informal].

.9 ADJS patient, armed with patience, with a soul possessed in patience, patient as Job; tolerant, tolerative, tolerating, accepting; understanding, indulgent, lenient 759.8; forbearing; philosophical; long-suffering, longanimous; enduring, endurant; stoic(al), Spartan; disciplined, self-controlled; persevering 625.7.

.10 resigned, reconciled; meek, humble; obedient, amenable, submissive 765.12; acquiescent, compliant; accommodating, adjusting, adapting, adaptive; unresisting, passive 706.6; uncomplaining.

.11 ADVS patiently, enduringly, stoically; tolerantly, indulgently, leniently, forbearantly, forbearingly, philosophically, more in sorrow than in anger; "like patience on a monument smiling at grief" [Shakespeare]; perseveringly 625.8.

.12 resignedly, meekly, submissively, passively, acquiescently, compliantly, uncomplainingly.

862. IMPATIENCE

.1 NOUNS impatience, impatientness, unpatientness, breathless impatience; anxiety, eagerness 635; tense readiness, restlessness, restiveness, ants in one's pants [slang]; disquietude, unquietness, uneasiness; sweat or lather or stew [all informal], fretfulness, fretting, chafing; impetuousness 630.2; haste 709; excitement 857.

.2 intolerance, intoleration, unforbearance, nonendurance.

.3 the last straw, the straw that breaks the camel's back, the limit, the limit of one's patience, all one can bear or stand.

.4 VERBS be impatient, hardly wait; hasten

709.4–8; itch to, burn to; **champ at the bit, pull at the leash,** not be able to sit down *or* stand still; **chafe, fret, fuss,** squirm; **stew,** sweat, sweat and stew, get into a dither, get into a stew [informal], work oneself into a lather *or* sweat [informal], get excited 857.15; wait impatiently, sweat it out [slang]; jump the gun [informal].

.5 **have no patience with,** be out of all patience; **lose patience,** run out of patience, call a halt, have had it [informal], blow the whistle [slang].

.6 ADJS **impatient,** unpatient; breathless; champing at the bit, rarin' to go [slang]; **anxious, eager** 635.9; hopped-up [slang], in a lather [informal], in a sweat *or* stew [informal], excited 857.18,19; edgy, **on edge; restless,** restive, unquiet, uneasy; **fretful,** fretting, chafing, antsy-pantsy *or* antsy [both slang], squirming, squirmy, about to piss one's pants [slang]; **impetuous** 630.9; **hasty** 709.9–11.

.7 **intolerant,** unforbearing, unindulgent.

.8 ADVS **impatiently,** breathlessly; **anxiously** 635.14; fretfully; restlessly, restively, uneasily; intolerantly.

863. PLEASANTNESS

.1 NOUNS **pleasantness,** pleasingness, pleasance, pleasure, pleasurefulness, **pleasurableness,** pleasurability, pleasantry [archaic], felicitousness, **enjoyableness; bliss,** blissfulness; sweetness, mellifluousness, *douceur* [Fr]; mellowness; **agreeableness,** agreeability, complaisance, rapport, harmoniousness; compatibility; welcomeness; geniality, congeniality, cordiality, affability, amicability, amiability; amenity, graciousness; goodness, goodliness, niceness.

.2 **delightfulness,** exquisiteness, loveliness; **charm,** winsomeness, grace, **attractiveness, appeal,** appealingness, winningness; **glamour;** captivation, enchantment, entrancement, bewitchment, witchery, enravishment, **fascination** 650.1; invitingness, temptingness, tantalizingness; voluptuousness, sensuousness; luxury.

.3 **delectability,** delectableness, deliciousness, lusciousness; tastiness, flavorsomeness, savoriness; juiciness, succulence.

.4 **cheerfulness;** brightness, sunniness; sunny side, bright side; fair weather.

.5 VERBS make pleasant, brighten, sweeten, gild, gild the lily *or* pill.

.6 ADJS **pleasant, pleasing, pleasureful, pleasurable,** hedy–; fair, fair and pleasant, enjoyable, pleasure-giving; felicitous, felicific; **likable, desirable,** to one's liking, to one's taste, to *or* after one's fancy, after one's own heart; **agreeable,** complaisant, harmonious, *en rapport* [Fr], compatible; **blissful;** sweet, mellifluous, honeyed, dulcet; mellow; **gratifying,** satisfying, rewarding, heart-warming, grateful; **welcome,** welcome as the roses in May; genial, congenial, cordial, affable, amiable, amicable, gracious; good, goodly, nice, fine; cheerful 870.11.

.7 **delightful, exquisite, lovely; thrilling,** titillative; **charming, attractive, engaging, appealing,** prepossessing, **enchanting,** bewitching, witching, entrancing, enthralling, intriguing, fascinating 650.7; captivating, irresistible, ravishing, enravishing; **winning,** winsome, taking, fetching, heart-robbing; inviting, tempting, tantalizing; voluptuous, sensuous; luxurious.

.8 **blissful,** beatific, saintly, divine; sublime; **heavenly,** paradisiac(al), paradisial, paradisian, paradisic(al), empyreal *or* empyrean, Elysian; out of this world [slang].

.9 **delectable, delicious,** luscious; tasty, flavorsome, savory; juicy, succulent.

.10 **bright, sunny,** fair, mild, balmy; halcyon, Saturnian.

.11 ADVS **pleasantly, pleasingly, pleasurably, fair, enjoyably;** blissfully; gratifyingly, satisfyingly, agreeably, genially, affably, cordially, amiably, amicably, graciously, kindly; cheerfully 870.17.

.12 **delightfully, exquisitely; charmingly, engagingly, appealingly, enchantingly,** bewitchingly, entrancingly, intriguingly, fascinatingly 650.8; ravishingly, enravishingly; **winningly,** winsomely; invitingly, temptingly, tantalizingly, voluptuously, sensuously; luxuriously.

.13 **delectably,** deliciously, lusciously, tastily, succulently.

864. UNPLEASANTNESS

.1 NOUNS **unpleasantness,** unpleasingness, displeasingness, displeasure; **disagreeableness,** disagreeability, *désagrément* [Fr]; **undesirability,** unappealingness, unattractiveness, unengagingness, uninvitingness; **distastefulness,** unsavoriness, unpalatability, **undelectability; ugliness** 899.

.2 **offensiveness,** objectionability, objectionableness; repugnance, contrariety, **odiousness, repulsiveness,** repellence *or* repellency, rebarbativeness, disgustingness, nauseousness; **loathsomeness,** hatefulness, beastliness [informal]; **vileness, foulness,** putridness, putridity, rottenness, noxiousness; nastiness, fulsomeness, noisomeness, **obnoxiousness**, abominability, heinousness; contemptibility, despicability, despicableness, baseness, ignobility; harshness; unspeakableness; grossness, crudeness, obscenity.

.3 **dreadfulness, horribleness,** horridness, atrociousness, atrocity, hideousness, terribleness, awfulness [informal]; grimness, direness, banefulness.

.4 **agony,** agonizingness, excruciation, excruciatingness, **torture,** torturesomeness, torturousness, **torment,** tormentingness; desolation, desolateness, heartbreak, heartsickness.

.5 **distressfulness, distress, grievousness, grief; painfulness,** pain 424; bitterness, sharpness; lamentability, lamentableness, deplorability, deplorableness, pitiableness, pitifulness, pitiability, regrettableness; **sadness, sorrowfulness, mournfulness,** lamentation, woefulness, woebegoneness, pathos, poignancy; comfortlessness, discomfort; dreariness, cheerlessness, joylessness, dismalness, **depression,** bleakness.

.6 **mortification,** humiliation, embarrassment; disconcertedness, awkwardness.

.7 **vexatiousness, irksomeness, annoyance,** annoyingness, aggravation, exasperation, provocation, provokingness, tiresomeness, wearisomeness; **troublesomeness, bothersomeness,** harassment; worrisomeness, plaguesomeness, peskiness or pestiferousness [both informal].

.8 **oppressiveness, burdensomeness,** onerousness, weightiness, heaviness.

.9 **intolerability,** intolerableness, unbearableness, insupportableness, insufferableness, **unendurability.**

.10 VERBS **be unpleasant; displease;** be disagreeable or undesirable or distasteful, etc.

.11 **offend,** give offense, **repel,** put off, re**volt, disgust,** nauseate, sicken, make one sick, make one sick to or in the stomach, make one vomit or puke or retch, turn the stomach, gross out [slang]; stink in the nostrils; stick in one's throat, stick in one's crop or craw or gizzard [informal]; **horrify, appall,** shock; make the flesh creep or crawl, make one shudder.

.12 **agonize,** excruciate, **torture, torment,** desolate.

.13 **mortify,** humiliate, embarrass, disconcert, disturb.

.14 **distress, dismay,** grieve, mourn, lament, sorrow; pain, discomfort.

.15 **vex, irk, annoy, aggravate,** exasperate, provoke; **trouble, worry,** plague, harass, bother.

.16 **oppress, burden,** weigh upon, weight down, wear one down, be heavy on one, crush one; **tire, exhaust,** weary, wear out, wear upon one; prey on the mind, prey on or upon; **haunt,** haunt the memory, obsess.

.17 ADJS **unpleasant, unpleasing, unenjoyable;** displeasing, **disagreeable; unlikable,** dislikable; **undesirable,** unattractive, unappealing, unengaging, uninviting, unalluring; unwelcome, thankless; **distasteful,** untasteful, **unpalatable,** unsavory, unappetizing, undelicious, **undelectable; ugly** 899.6–11; sour, **bitter.**

.18 **offensive, objectionable, odious, repulsive,** repellent, rebarbative, **repugnant,** revolting, forbidding; disgusting, sickening, loathsome, beastly [informal], **vile, foul, nasty, nauseating** 429.7; fulsome, mephitic, miasmal, miasmic, malodorous, stinking, fetid, noisome, noxious; gross, crude, obscene; **obnoxious, abhorrent, hateful, abominable,** heinous, **contemptible, despicable,** detestable, execrable, beneath or below contempt, **base,** ignoble.

.19 **horrid, horrible,** horrific, **horrifying,** horrendous, unspeakable; **dreadful, atrocious, terrible, rotten,** awful or beastly [both informal], hideous; **tragic;** dire, grim, baneful; appalling, shocking.

.20 **distressing,** distressful, dismaying; afflicting, afflictive; **painful, sore, bitter,** sharp; **grievous,** dolorous, dolorific, dolorogenic; **lamentable, deplorable,** regrettable, pitiable, piteous, rueful, woeful, woebegone, **sad,** sorrowful, wretched, mournful, **depressing,** depressive; **pathetic,** affecting, touching, moving, saddening, poignant; comfortless, discomforting, uncomfortable; dreary, cheerless, joyless, dismal, bleak.

.21 **mortifying,** humiliating, **embarrassing,** crushing, disconcerting, awkward, disturbing.

.22 **annoying, irritating,** galling, **provoking, aggravating** [informal], **exasperating; vexatious,** vexing, irking, **irksome,** tiresome, wearisome; **troublesome, bothersome, worrisome,** bothering, troubling, disturbing, plaguing, plaguesome, plaguey [informal], pestilent, pestilential, **pesky** or pestiferous [both informal]; tormenting, harassing, worrying; pestering, teasing; importunate, importune.

.23 **agonizing, excruciating, harrowing,** racking, rending, **desolating,** consuming; **tormenting,** torturous; **heartbreaking,** heart-rending, **heartsickening,** heartwounding.

.24 **oppressive, burdensome,** onerous, heavy, weighty; harsh, wearing, wearying, exhausting; overburdensome, tyrannous, grinding.

.25 **insufferable, intolerable, insupportable, unendurable, unbearable,** past bearing, not to be borne *or* endured, **too much** *or* a bit much [informal], more than flesh and blood can bear, enough to drive one mad, enough to provoke a saint, enough to make a preacher swear [informal], enough to try the patience of Job.

.26 ADVS **unpleasantly,** unpleasingly; **displeasingly, offensively, objectionably,** odiously, **repulsively,** repellently, rebarbatively, repugnantly, **revoltingly, disgustingly, sickeningly, loathsomely, vilely,** foully, nastily, fulsomely, mephitically, malodorously, fetidly, noisomely, noxiously, obnoxiously, **abhorrently, hatefully, abominably,** contemptibly, **despicably, detestably,** execrably, nauseatingly.

.27 **horridly, horribly, dreadfully, terribly,** hideously; **tragically;** grimly, direly, banefully; appallingly, shockingly.

.28 **distressingly,** distressfully; **painfully,** sorely, **grievously,** lamentably, deplorably, pitiably, ruefully, woefully, sadly, pathetically; **agonizingly, excruciatingly,** harrowingly, heartbreakingly.

.29 **annoyingly, irritatingly, aggravatingly** [informal], **provokingly, exasperatingly;** vexatiously, **irksomely,** tiresomely, wearisomely; **troublesomely, bothersomely,** worrisomely.

.30 **insufferably, intolerably, unbearably, unendurably, insupportably.**

.31 INTERJS eeyuck! *or* yeeuck! *or* yeeuch!, phew! *or* pugh!, ugh!; *feh!* [Yid].

865. PLEASURE

.1 NOUNS **pleasure, enjoyment;** quiet pleasure, euphoria, well-being, **contentment,** content, ease, comfort 887; coziness; **gratification, satisfaction,** great satisfaction, hearty enjoyment, keen pleasure *or* satisfaction; self-gratification, self-indulgence; luxury; **relish, zest, gusto,** *joie de vivre* [Fr]; sweetness of life, *douceur de vivre* [Fr]; kicks [informal], fun, entertainment, amusement 878; intellectual pleasure, pleasures of the mind; physical pleasure, creature comforts, bodily pleasure, sense *or* sensuous pleasure; sexual pleasure, voluptuousness, sensual pleasure, *volupté* [Fr], animal pleasure, animal comfort, bodily comfort, fleshly *or* carnal delight; forepleasure, titillation, endpleasure, fruition.

.2 **happiness, gladness, delight,** delectation; **joy, joyfulness,** joyance; **cheer,** cheerfulness, exhilaration, exuberance, high spirits, **glee,** sunshine; gaiety 870.4, overjoyfulness, overhappiness; intoxication; **rapture,** ravishment, bewitchment, **enchantment,** unalloyed happiness; elation, exaltation; **ecstasy,** ecstatics, transport; **bliss,** blissfulness; beatitude, beatification, blessedness, felicity; paradise, heaven, seventh heaven, cloud nine.

.3 **treat, regalement,** regale, revelment, feast, round of pleasures, mad round, banquet, feast *or* banquet of the soul; festivity, celebration, merrymaking, revel, revelry, jubilation, joyance.

.4 pleasure-loving, pleasure principle, hedonism, hedonics; epicureanism, Cyrenaicism, eudaemonism.

.5 VERBS **please, give pleasure,** afford one pleasure, be to one's liking, sit well with one, meet one's wishes, take *or* strike one's fancy, strike one right, hit the spot [slang], be just the ticket *or* be just what the doctor ordered [both informal], make a hit [informal], go over big [slang].

.6 **gratify, satisfy,** sate, satiate; slake, appease, allay, assuage, quench; regale, feed, feast; do one's heart good, warm the cockles of the heart.

.7 **gladden,** make happy, happify; bless, beatify; cheer 870.7.

.8 **delight,** delectate, **tickle, titillate, thrill,** tickle to death *or* tickle pink [both informal]; wow *or* slay *or* knock out *or* knock dead [all slang]; **enrapture, enthrall, enchant,** entrance, fascinate, captivate, bewitch, **charm,** becharm; enravish, ravish, imparadise; transport, carry away, send *or* freak out [both slang].

.9 **be pleased, feel happy,** sing, purr, smile, laugh, be wreathed in smiles, beam; **delight,** joy, take great satisfaction; look like the cat that swallowed the canary, walk *or* tread on air, be in heaven *or* seventh heaven *or* paradise, be on cloud nine; fall *or* go into raptures; die with delight *or* pleasure.

.10 **enjoy,** be pleased with, receive *or* derive pleasure from, take delight *or* pleasure in, get a kick *or* boot *or* bang *or* charge *or* lift out of [slang]; like, love, adore [informal]; **delight in, rejoice in,** indulge in, luxuriate in, revel in, riot in, bask in, wallow in, swim in; groove on *or* get high on *or* freak out on [all slang]; feast on, gloat over *or* on; **relish, appreciate,** roll under the tongue, savor, smack the lips; devour, eat up.

.11 **enjoy oneself,** have a good time.

.12 ADJS **pleased, delighted; glad,** gladsome; **charmed,** intrigued [informal]; **thrilled; tickled,** tickled to death *or* tickled pink [both informal], exhilarated; **gratified, satisfied;** pleased with, taken with, favorably impressed with, sold on [slang]; pleased as Punch, pleased as a child with a new toy; euphoric, eupeptic; **content, contented,** easy, **comfortable** 887.11,12, cozy, in clover.

.13 **happy, glad, joyful, joyous,** flushed with joy, radiant, beaming, glowing, starry-eyed, sparkling, laughing, smiling, smirking, chirping, purring, singing, dancing, leaping, capering, **cheerful, gay** 870.11–16; **blissful,** "throned on highest bliss" [Milton]; blessed; beatified, beatific; thrice happy, "thrice and four times blessed" [Vergil]; happy as a lark, happy as a king, happy as the day is long, happy as a baby boy, happy as a clam at high water.

.14 **overjoyed,** overjoyful, overhappy, bursting with happiness; **rapturous,** raptured, **enraptured, enchanted,** entranced, enravished, ravished, rapt, possessed; sent *or* high *or* freaked out [all slang], **in raptures,** transported, in a transport of delight, **carried away,** rapt *or* ravished away, beside oneself, beside oneself with joy, all over oneself [slang]; **ecstatic,** in ecstasies, rhapsodic(al); imparadised, **in paradise,** in heaven, in seventh heaven, on cloud nine; **elated,** elate, exalted, jubilant, exultant, flushed.

.15 **pleasure-loving,** pleasure-seeking, fun-loving, hedonic, hedonistic; epicurean, Cyrenaic, eudaemonic.

.16 ADVS **happily, gladly, joyfully, joyously, delightedly,** with pleasure, to one's delight; **blissfully,** blessedly; **ecstatically,** rhapsodically, **rapturously; elatedly,** jubilantly, exultantly.

.17 INTERJS **goody!,** goody, goody!, goody gumdrops!, good-o!; whee!, **wow!,** u-mm!, mmmm!, oooo!, oo-la-la!; oh boy!, boy oh boy!, boy!, man!, hot dog!, hot ziggety!, hot diggety!, wowie zowie!, out of sight! *or* outa sight!, groovy!, keen-o!, keen-o-peachy!

866. UNPLEASURE

.1 NOUNS unpleasure, lack of pleasure, joylessness, cheerlessness; unsatisfaction, nonsatisfaction, ungratification, nongratification; grimness; discontent 869; displeasure, dissatisfaction, **discomfort,** uncomfortableness, malaise, **painfulness; disquiet,** inquietude, **uneasiness,** unease, discomposure, vexation of spirit, **anxiety;** angst, anguish, dread, nausea, existential woe, existential vacuum; the blahs [slang]; **dullness,** flatness, staleness, tastelessness, savorlessness; ashes in the mouth; **boredom,** ennui, tedium, tediousness, spleen; emptiness, spiritual void, death of the heart *or* soul; unhappiness 872.2; dislike 867.

.2 **annoyance, vexation,** bothersomeness, exasperation, **aggravation** [informal]; **nuisance, pest, bother,** botheration [informal], **trouble, problem,** difficulty, trial; **bore,** crashing bore [informal]; **drag,** downer [both slang]; **worry,** worriment [informal]; bad news [informal]; **headache** [informal], **pain in the neck** *or* **pain in the ass** [both slang]; **harassment,** molestation, persecution, dogging, hounding, harrying; devilment, bedevilment; vexatiousness 864.7.

.3 **irritation,** exacerbation, salt in the wound, embitterment, **provocation;** fret, gall, chafe; irritant; pea in the shoe.

.4 **mortification, chagrin, distress;** embarrassment, abashment, discomfiture, disconcertion, disconcertment, discountenance, discomposure, disturbance, confusion; skeleton in the closet.

.5 **pain, distress, grief,** stress, stress of life, suffering, passion, dolor; ache, aching; pang, wrench, throes, cramp, spasm; wound, injury, hurt; **sore,** sore spot, tender spot, lesion; cut, stroke; shock, blow, hard *or* nasty blow.

.6 **wretchedness, despair,** bitterness, infelicity, **misery, anguish, agony, woe,** bale; **melancholy,** melancholia, **depression, sadness, grief** 872.10; **heartache,** aching heart, heavy heart, bleeding heart, broken heart, agony of mind *or* spirit; suicidal despair; **desolation,** prostration, crushing; extremity, depth of misery.

.7 **torment, torture,** cruciation, crucifixion, passion, rack, laceration, clawing, lancination; persecution; martyrdom; purgatory, "frigid purgatorial fires" [T. S. Eliot], hell, hell upon earth; holocaust; nightmare, horror.

.8 **affliction,** infliction; **curse, woe,** distress, grievance, **sorrow,** *tsures* [Yid]; **trouble,** peck *or* pack of troubles, "sea of troubles" [Shakespeare]; care, burden of care, cankerworm of care; **burden, oppression, cross, load,** encumbrance, weight, albatross around one's neck, millstone around one's neck; thorn, thorn in the side, crown of thorns; bitter pill, bitter draft, bitter cup, cup *or* waters of bitterness; gall, gall and wormwood; "the thousand natural shocks that flesh is heir to" [Shakespeare], "all the ills that men endure" [Abraham Cowley].

.9 **trial, tribulation,** trials and tribulations; ordeal, fiery ordeal, the iron entering the soul.

.10 **tormentor,** torment; **pest,** pesterer, nag, nudzh [slang], *nudnik* [Yid]; **tease,** teaser; annoyer, harasser, harrier, badgerer, heckler, plaguer, persecutor; sadist; **bully.**

.11 **sufferer,** victim, prey; **wretch,** poor devil, object of compassion; martyr.

.12 VERBS **give no pleasure** *or* joy *or* cheer *or* comfort, **disquiet,** discompose, leave unsatisfied; discontent 869.4; taste like ashes in the mouth; **bore,** be tedious.

.13 **annoy, irk, vex, nettle, provoke, pique,** miff *or* peeve [both informal], distemper, **ruffle, disturb,** discompose, **roil, rile** [informal], aggravate [informal], **exasperate,** exercise, try the patience; **put one's back up,** bristle; **gripe;** give one a pain [informal]; **get, get one's goat;** get under one's skin, get in one's hair; burn up *or* brown off [both slang]; **torment, molest, bother,** pother; **harass, harry,** drive up the wall [informal], **hound, dog, nag,** nudzh [slang], **persecute; heckle, badger, hector,** bait, bullyrag, worry, nip at the heels of, chivy, fash [Scot]; bug [slang], be on the back of *or* be at *or* ride [all slang], **pester, tease, needle, devil, bedevil, pick on** [informal], tweak the nose, pluck the beard, give a bad time to [slang]; **plague, beset.**

.14 **irritate,** exacerbate, rub salt in the wound, provoke, **gall, chafe, fret, grate,** grit *or* gravel [both informal], rasp; **get on one's nerves, grate on, set on edge, set the teeth on edge, go against the grain; rub the wrong way.**

.15 **chagrin, embarrass, abash, discomfit, disconcert,** discompose, **confuse,** throw into confusion, **upset, confound,** cast down, mortify, put out, put out of face *or* countenance, put to the blush.

.16 **distress, afflict, trouble, burden, load** with care, bother, disturb, perturb, disquiet, discomfort, agitate, upset, put to it.

.17 **pain, grieve,** aggrieve, anguish; **hurt, wound,** bruise, **hurt the feelings;** pierce, prick, stab, cut, sting; **cut up** [informal], **cut to the heart,** wound *or* sting *or* cut to the quick; touch a soft spot *or* tender spot, touch a raw nerve, touch where it hurts, hit one where he lives [slang]; step on one's corns; barb the dart, twist the knife.

.18 **torture, torment, agonize, harrow,** savage, **rack,** scarify, crucify, impale, excruciate, lacerate, claw, rip, bloody, lancinate, macerate, convulse, wring; prolong the agony, kill by inches; martyr, martyrize; punish 1010.10.

.19 **suffer, hurt, ache, bleed;** anguish, **suffer anguish; agonize,** writhe; go hard with, have a bad time of it; quaff the bitter cup, drain the cup of misery to the dregs, be nailed to the cross.

.20 ADJS **pleasureless,** joyless, cheerless, depressed 872.22, grim; **sad, unhappy** 872.20–28; unsatisfied, unfulfilled, ungratified; **bored;** anguished, anxious, suffering angst *or* dread *or* nausea, uneasy, unquiet, prey to malaise; **repelled, revolted, disgusted,** sickened, nauseated, nauseous.

.21 **annoyed, irritated,** bugged [slang]; galled, chafed; **bothered, troubled, disturbed, ruffled, roiled,** riled [informal]; **irked, vexed, piqued, nettled, provoked,** peeved *or* miffed [both informal], griped, aggravated [informal], **exasperated;** burnt-up *or* browned-off [both slang], resentful, angry 952.24–29.

.22 **distressed, afflicted, put-upon,** beset; **troubled, bothered, disturbed, perturbed, disquieted,** discomforted, discomposed, agitated; hung up [informal]; **uncomfortable,** uneasy, ill at ease; **chagrined, embarrassed,** abashed, discomfited, **disconcerted, upset, confused,** mortified, **put-out,** out of countenance, cast down, chapfallen.

.23 **pained, grieved,** aggrieved; **wounded, hurt, injured, bruised,** mauled; **cut, cut to the quick; stung;** anguished, aching, bleeding.

.24 **tormented, plagued, harassed, harried, dogged, hounded, persecuted,** beset; nipped at, worried, chivied, **heckled,** badgered, hectored, baited, bullyragged, ragged, **pestered, teased, needled, deviled, bedeviled, picked on** [informal], **bugged** [slang].

.25 **tortured, harrowed,** savagèd, **agonized,**

convulsed, wrung, racked, crucified, impaled, lacerated, clawed, ripped, bloodied, lancinated; on the rack, under the harrow.

.26 **wretched, miserable; woeful,** woebegone; crushed, stricken, **cut up** [informal], heartsick, heart-stricken, heart-struck; deep-troubled; desolate, disconsolate, suicidal.

.27 ADVS to one's displeasure, to one's disgust.

867. DISLIKE

.1 NOUNS **dislike, distaste, disrelish; disaffection, disfavor,** disinclination; disaffinity; **displeasure, disapproval,** disapprobation.

.2 **hostility,** antagonism, **enmity** 929; **hatred, hate** 930; **aversion, repugnance,** repulsion, **antipathy,** allergy [informal], abomination, **abhorrence, horror,** mortal horror; **disgust, loathing;** nausea; shuddering, cold sweat, creeping flesh.

.3 VERBS **dislike,** mislike, disfavor, not like, have no liking for, **have no use for** [informal], **not care for,** have a disaffinity for, entertain *or* conceive *or* take a dislike to, not be able to bear *or* endure *or* abide, **disapprove of; disrelish,** have no taste for, not have the stomach for; be hostile to; **hate, abhor, loathe** 930.5.

.4 **feel disgust,** be nauseated, **sicken at,** choke on, have a bellyful of [slang]; **gag, retch,** keck, heave, vomit, puke, upchuck *or* barf [both slang].

.5 **shudder at,** have one's flesh creep *or* crawl at the thought of; shrink from, **recoil, revolt at; grimace,** make a wry face *or* wry mouth; turn up one's nose at, look down one's nose at, look askance at, take a dim view of, show distaste for, disapprove of.

.6 **repel, disgust** 864.11.

.7 ADJS **unlikable, distasteful,** mislikable, dislikable, **uncongenial, displeasing, unpleasant** 864.17; **not to one's taste,** not one's sort, not one's cup of tea, against one's grain, counter to one's preferences, offering no delight, uninviting; **unlovable; abhorrent, odious** 864.18; **intolerable** 864.25.

.8 **averse, allergic** [informal], undelighted, out of sympathy, disaffected, disenchanted, **disinclined, displeased,** put off [informal], **not charmed; unfriendly, hostile** 929.9–13; –phobic.

.9 **disliked, uncared-for, unvalued, unprized; despised,** lowly; **unpopular, out of favor,** gone begging; **unappreciated,** misunderstood, misprized; unsung, thankless; unwept, unlamented, unmourned, undeplored, unmissed, unregretted.

.10 **unloved,** unbeloved, uncherished, loveless; **lovelorn,** forsaken, **rejected,** jilted, thrown over [informal], spurned, crossed in love.

.11 **unwanted,** unwished, undesired; **unwelcome,** unasked, unbidden, uninvited, uncalled-for, unasked-for.

868. CONTENTMENT

.1 NOUNS **contentment, content,** contentedness, satisfiedness; **satisfaction,** entire satisfaction, fulfillment; ease, peace of mind, composure 858.2; comfort 887; wellbeing, euphoria; **happiness** 865.2; **acceptance,** resignation, reconcilement, reconciliation.

.2 **complacence** *or* complacency, bovinity; smugness, **self-complacence** *or* self-complacency, **self-satisfaction, self-content,** self-contentedness.

.3 **satisfactoriness, adequacy, sufficiency** 661; **acceptability,** admissibility, **tolerability,** agreeability, unobjectionability, unexceptionability, tenability, viability.

.4 VERBS **content, satisfy;** gratify 865.6; put *or* set at ease, set one's mind at ease *or* rest, achieve inner harmony.

.5 **be content, rest satisfied, rest easy,** rest and be thankful, be reconciled to, take the good the gods provide, accept one's lot, let well enough alone; come to terms with oneself, learn to live in one's own skin; have no kick coming [slang], can't complain; content oneself with, settle for; **be pleased** 865.9.

.6 **be satisfactory, suffice** 661.4.

.7 ADJS **content, contented, satisfied; pleased** 865.12; **happy** 865.13; **easy, at ease,** at one's ease, easygoing; **composed** 858.13; **comfortable** 887.11,12, of good comfort; euphoric, eupeptic; without care, *sans souci* [Fr]; accepting, resigned, reconciled; uncomplaining, unrepining.

.8 **untroubled, unbothered, undisturbed, unperturbed** 858.11, unworried, unvexed, unplagued, untormented.

.9 **well-content, well-pleased,** well-contented, **well-satisfied,** highly satisfied.

.10 **complacent,** bovine; **smug, self-complacent, self-satisfied,** self-content, **self-contented.**

.11 **satisfactory, satisfying; sufficient** 661.6, sufficing, **adequate,** commensurate, proportionate, proportionable, ample, equal to.

.12 acceptable, admissible, **agreeable**, unobjectionable, unexceptionable, tenable, viable; **OK** or okay or all right or alright [all informal]; **passable**, good enough.

.13 tolerable, bearable, endurable, **supportable, sufferable**.

.14 ADVS contentedly, to one's heart's content; satisfiedly, with satisfaction; complacently, smugly, self-complacently, self-satisfiedly, self-contentedly.

.15 satisfactorily, satisfyingly; **acceptably, agreeably**, admissibly; sufficiently, adequately, commensurately, amply, enough; **tolerably, passably**.

.16 to one's satisfaction, to one's delight, to one's great glee; to one's taste, to the king's or queen's taste.

869. DISCONTENT

.1 NOUNS discontent, discontentment, discontentedness; **dissatisfaction, unsatisfaction**, dissatisfiedness, unfulfillment; resentment, envy 954; restlessness, restiveness, uneasiness; rebelliousness 767.3; disappointment 541; unpleasure 866; unhappiness 872.2; ill humor 951; **disgruntlement**, sulkiness, sourness, petulance, peevishness, querulousness; vexation of spirit; cold comfort; divine discontent; Faustianism.

.2 unsatisfactoriness, dissatisfactoriness; **inadequacy, insufficiency** 662; **unacceptability**, inadmissibility, unsuitability, undesirability, objectionability, untenability, indefensibility; intolerability 864.9.

.3 malcontent, *frondeur* [Fr]; **complainer**, complainant, **faultfinder, grumbler**, growler, **murmurer**, mutterer, griper, croaker, peevish or petulant or querulous person, whiner, *kvetch* [Yid]; kicker or grouch or crank or crab or grouser or beefer [all informal]; **bellyacher** or bitcher or sorehead [all slang]; reactionary, reactionist; rebel 767.5.

.4 VERBS **dissatisfy, discontent, disgruntle, displease**, disappoint, dishearten, put out [informal].

.5 ADJS discontented, dissatisfied, disgruntled, unaccepting, unaccommodating, **displeased**, disappointed; **unsatisfied, ungratified**, unfulfilled; resentful, dog-in-the-manger; envious 954.4; restless, restive, uneasy; rebellious 767.11; malcontent, malcontented, **complaining**, complaintful, **faultfinding**, grumbling, growling, murmuring, muttering, griping, croaking,

peevish, **petulant**, sulky, **querulous**, querulant, whiny; grouchy or cranky or beefing or crabby or crabbing or grousing [all informal]; bellyaching or bitching [both slang]; unhappy 872.21; out of humor 951.17.

.6 unsatisfactory, dissatisfactory; **unsatisfying, ungratifying**, unfulfilling; **displeasing** 864.17, disappointing, disheartening, not up to expectation, not good enough; **inadequate**, incommensurate, **insufficient** 662.9.

.7 unacceptable, inadmissible, unsuitable, undesirable, **objectionable**, exceptionable, impossible, untenable, indefensible; intolerable 864.25.

.8 ADVS discontentedly, dissatisfiedly.

.9 unsatisfactorily, dissatisfactorily; **unsatisfyingly, ungratifyingly; inadequately, insufficiently; unacceptably**, inadmissibly, unsuitably, undesirably, objectionably; intolerably 864.30.

870. CHEERFULNESS

.1 NOUNS cheerfulness, cheeriness, **good cheer, cheer**, cheery vein or mood; blitheness, blithesomeness; **gladness**, gladsomeness; **happiness** 865.2; **pleasantness**, winsomeness, geniality; brightness, radiance, sunniness; sanguineness, sanguinity, sanguine humor, euphoric or eupeptic mien; optimism, rosy expectation, hopefulness.

.2 good humor, good spirits; **high spirits, exhilaration**, rare good humor.

.3 lightheartedness, lightsomeness, lightness, levity; **buoyancy**, resilience, bounce [informal]; **jauntiness**, perkiness, debonairness, carefreeness; **breeziness**, airiness, pertness, chirpiness, light heart.

.4 gaiety, gayness, *allégresse* [Fr]; **liveliness, vivacity, vitality**, life, **animation, spiritedness, spirit**, esprit, élan, sprightliness, zestfulness, zest, vim, zip [informal], vigor, verve, gusto, **exuberance**, heartiness; **spirits**, animal spirits; piss and vinegar [slang]; **friskiness**, skittishness, coltishness, rompishness, rollicksomeness, capersomeness; **sportiveness, playfulness, frolicsomeness**, gamesomeness.

.5 merriment, merriness; **hilarity**, hilariousness; **joy, joyfulness**, joyousness; **glee**, gleefulness, high glee; **jollity**, jolliness, **joviality**, jocularity, jocundity; frivolity, levity; **mirth**, mirthfulness, **amusement** 878; **fun; laughter** 876.4.

.6 VERBS exude cheerfulness, radiate cheer, **beam**, glow, sparkle, sing, lilt, whistle, **chirp**, chirrup, chirp like a cricket, dance, skip, caper, frolic, gambol, romp, caracole; smile, laugh 876.7,8.

.7 **cheer, gladden, brighten,** put in good humor; **encourage, hearten, pick up** [informal]; **inspire,** inspirit, warm the spirits, **raise the spirits,** elevate one's mood, buoy up, boost, give a lift [slang], put one on top of the world *or* on cloud nine [both informal]; **exhilarate,** animate, invigorate, liven, enliven, vitalize; **rejoice,** rejoice the heart, do the heart good.

.8 **elate, exalt,** elevate, lift, uplift, flush.

.9 **cheer up, take heart,** drive dull care away; **brighten up,** light up, **perk up; buck up** *or* brace up *or* chirk up [all informal]; come out of it, snap out of it [slang], revive.

.10 be of good cheer, bear up, keep one's spirits up, keep one's chin up [informal], keep one's pecker up [Brit informal], keep a stiff upper lip [slang], grin and bear it.

.11 ADJS cheerful, cheery, of good cheer, in good spirits; in high spirits, exalted, elated, exhilarated, high [slang]; irrepressible; **blithe,** blithesome; **glad, gladsome; happy** 865.13; **pleasant, genial,** winsome; **bright,** sunny, bright and sunny, **radiant,** riant, sparkling, beaming, glowing, flushed, rosy, smiling, laughing; sanguine, sanguineous, euphoric, eupeptic; optimistic, hopeful.

.12 **lighthearted,** light, lightsome; **buoyant,** corky [informal], resilient; **jaunty,** perky, **debonair, carefree,** free and easy; **breezy,** airy.

.13 **pert,** peart [dial], chirk [dial], chirrupy, **chirpy, chipper** [informal].

.14 **gay,** gay as a lark; **spirited,** sprightly, lively, **animated, vivacious,** vital, zestful, zippy [informal], **exuberant,** hearty; frisky, antic, skittish, coltish, rompish, capersome; **full of beans** *or* **feeling one's oats** [both informal], full of piss and vinegar [slang]; **sportive, playful,** playful as a kitten, frolicsome, gamesome; rollicking, rollicky, rollicksome.

.15 **merry, mirthful, hilarious; joyful, joyous,** rejoicing 876.9; **gleeful,** gleesome; **jolly,** buxom; **jovial,** jocund, jocular; **frivolous;** laughter-loving, mirth-loving, risible; merry as a cricket *or* grig, "as merry as the day is long" [Shakespeare].

.16 **cheering, gladdening; encouraging, heartening,** heart-warming; **inspiring,** inspiriting; **exhilarating,** animating, enlivening, invigorating; cheerful, cheery, glad, joyful.

.17 ADVS **cheerfully,** cheerily, with good cheer, with a cheerful heart; irrepressibly; **lightheartedly,** lightly; jauntily, perkily, airily; **pleasantly,** genially, blithely; **gladly, happily, joyfully,** smilingly; optimistically, hopefully.

.18 **gaily, exuberantly, heartily, spiritedly, animatedly, vivaciously,** zestfully, with zest, with vim, with élan, with zip [informal], with verve, with gusto.

.19 **merrily, gleefully, hilariously; jovially,** jocundly, jocularly; frivolously; **mirthfully,** laughingly.

871. SOLEMNITY

.1 NOUNS **solemnity, solemnness, soberness, sobriety, gravity,** weightiness, **somberness, grimness; sedateness, staidness;** demureness, decorousness; **seriousness, earnestness, thoughtfulness, sober-mindedness,** sobersidedness; sobersides; long face, straight face; **formality** 646.

.2 VERBS **keep a straight face,** look serious, compose one's features, wear an earnest frown, repress a smile, not crack a smile [slang], wipe the smile off one's face, keep from laughing.

.3 ADJS **solemn, sober, grave,** unsmiling, weighty, **somber,** frowning, **grim; sedate, staid;** demure, decorous; **serious, earnest, thoughtful,** serio–; **sober-minded,** sobersided; straight-faced, long-faced, grim-faced, grim-visaged, stone-faced; sober as a judge, grave as an undertaker; **formal** 646.7–10.

.4 ADVS **solemnly, soberly,** gravely, somberly, grimly; **sedately, staidly,** demurely, decorously; **seriously, earnestly,** thoughtfully, sober-mindedly, sobersidedly; with a straight face; formally 646.11,12.

872. SADNESS

.1 NOUNS **sadness, sadheartedness;** heaviness, **heavyheartedness,** heavy heart, **heaviness of heart;** pathos, bathos.

.2 **unhappiness,** infelicity; displeasure 866.1; discontent 869; **uncheerfulness,** cheerlessness; **joylessness,** unjoyfulness; mirthlessness, unmirthfulness, humorlessness, infestivity; **grimness; wretchedness, misery.**

.3 **dejection, depression, oppression,** dejectedness, **downheartedness,** downcastness; **discouragement, disheartenment,** dispiritedness; *Schmerz, Weltschmerz* [both Ger]; malaise 866.1; lowness, lowness *or* depression *or* oppression of spirit, downer, down trip [both slang]; **low spirits,** drooping spirits, sinking heart; despondence or **despondency**, despondentness, spiritlessness, heartlessness; black or blank despondency, Slough of Despond; hopelessness 889, **despair** 889.2, pessimism 889.6, suicidal despair, death wish, self-destructive urge, weariness of life, *taedium vitae* [L].

.4 **hypochondria**, hypochondriasis, morbid anxiety.

.5 **melancholy**, **melancholia**, melancholiness; gentle melancholy, romantic melancholy; **pensiveness**, **wistfulness**, tristfulness.

.6 **blues** or blue devils [both informal], mulligrubs [slang], mumps, **dumps** [informal], **doldrums**, dismals, dolefuls [informal], blahs [informal], mopes, megrims, sulks.

.7 **gloom**, gloominess, darkness, **dismalness**, **bleakness**, grimness, **somberness**, **gravity**, **solemnity**; **dreariness**, drearisomeness; wearifulness, wearisomeness.

.8 **glumness**, grumness, **moroseness**, **sullenness**, sulkiness, **moodiness**, mumpishness, dumpishness; mopishness, mopiness [informal].

.9 **heartache**, aching **heart**, bleeding heart; heartsickness, heartsoreness; **heartbreak**, **broken heart**, brokenheartedness, heartbrokenness.

.10 **sorrow**, sorrowing, **grief**, **care**, carking care, **woe**; heartgrief, heartfelt grief; languishment, pining; **anguish**, **misery**, **agony**; prostration; lamentation 875.

.11 **sorrowfulness**, **mournfulness**, ruefulness, **woefulness**, **dolefulness**, dolorousness, **plaintiveness**, plangency, grievousness, aggrievedness, lugubriousness, funerealness; tearfulness 875.2.

.12 **disconsolateness**, disconsolation, **inconsolability**, comfortlessness; **desolation**, desolateness; forlornness.

.13 **sourpuss** or gloomy Gus [both slang]; mope, brooder; melancholic, melancholiac; depressive.

.14 **killjoy**, spoilsport, crepehanger [informal]; damp, damper, **wet blanket**; skeleton at the feast; pessimist 889.7.

.15 VERBS **hang one's head**, pull or make a long face, look blue, sing the blues [informal]; hang crepe [informal].

.16 **despond**, **lose heart**, give way, give oneself up or over to; **despair** 889.10, be or become suicidal, lose the will to live; **droop**, sink, languish; reach or plumb the depths, touch bottom, hit rock bottom.

.17 **grieve**, **sorrow**; mourn 875.8–14; be dumb with grief; **pine**, pine away; **brood over**, mope, fret, take on [informal]; **eat one's heart out**, break one's heart over; **agonize**, ache, bleed.

.18 **sadden**, darken, cast a pall or gloom upon, weigh or weigh heavy upon; **deject**, **depress**, **oppress**, press down, **cast down**, lower, lower the spirits, get one down [informal], **discourage**, **dishearten**, take the heart out of, **dispirit**; damp, dampen, damp or dampen the spirits; dash, knock down, beat down; sink, sink one's soul, plunge one into despair.

.19 **aggrieve**, **oppress**, **grieve**, **sorrow**, plunge one into sorrow, embitter; draw tears, bring to tears; **anguish**, **cut up** [informal], wring or pierce or lacerate or rend the heart, pull at the heartstrings; afflict 866.16, torment 866.18; **break one's heart**, **make one's heart bleed**; desolate, leave an aching void; prostrate, break down, crush, inundate, overwhelm.

.20 ADJS **sad**, saddened; sadhearted, **sad of heart**; **heavyhearted**, heavy; oppressed, weighed upon, weighed or weighted down, burdened or laden with sorrow; sad-faced, long-faced; sad-eyed; sad-voiced.

.21 **unhappy**, **uncheerful**, uncheery, **cheerless**, **joyless**, **unjoyful**, unsmiling; mirthless, unmirthful, humorless, infestive; **grim**; **out of humor**, out of sorts, in bad humor or spirits; **sorry**, sorryish; discontented 869.5; **wretched**, **miserable**; pleasureless 866.20–26.

.22 **dejected**, **depressed**, **downhearted**, **down**, **downcast**, cast down, bowed-down, subdued; **discouraged**, **disheartened**, **dispirited**, dashed; **low**, feeling low, low-spirited, **in low spirits**; **down in the mouth** [informal], **in the doldrums**, **in the dumps** or in the doleful dumps [both informal], **in the depths**; **despondent**, desponding; **despairing** 889.12, weary of life, suicidal, world-weary; pessimistic 889.16; spiritless, heartless, **woebegone**; **drooping**, droopy, languishing, pining; hypochondriac or hypochondriacal.

.23 **melancholy**, melancholic, **blue** [informal], funky; atrabilious, atrabiliar; **pensive**, **wistful**, tristful.

.24 **gloomy**, **dismal**, **bleak**, **grim**, **somber**, sombrous, **solemn**, **grave**, *triste* [Fr], **funereal**, funebrial, crepehanging [informal], saturnine; **dark**, black, gray; **dreary**, drear, drearisome; weary, weariful, wearisome.

.25 **glum**, grum, **morose**, **sullen**, sulky, mumpish, dumpish, long-faced, crestfallen, chapfallen; **moody**, moodish, **brooding**,

broody; mopish, mopey [informal], moping.

.26 sorrowful, sorrowing, sorrowed, mournful,
rueful, woeful, doleful, plaintive, plangent; anguished; dolorous, grievous, lamentable, lugubrious; tearful 875.17; careworn; grieved, grief-stricken, grieffull, aggrieved, in grief, plunged in grief, dumb
with grief.

.27 sorrow-stricken, sorrow-wounded, sorrow-
struck, sorrow-torn, sorrow-worn, sorrow-
wasted, sorrow-beaten, sorrow-blinded,
sorrow-clouded, sorrow-shot, sorrow-
burdened, sorrow-laden, sorrow-sighing,
sorrow-sobbing, sorrow-sick.

.28 disconsolate, inconsolable, unconsolable,
comfortless, forlorn; desolate, désolé [Fr];
sick, sick at heart, heartsick, soul-sick,
heartsore.

.29 overcome, crushed, overwhelmed, inundated, stricken, cut up [informal], desolated, prostrate(d), broken-down, undone; heart-stricken, heart-struck; heartbroken, brokenhearted.

.30 depressing, down [slang], depressive, depressant, oppressive; discouraging, disheartening, dispiriting.

.31 ADVS sadly, gloomily, dismally, drearily,
heavily, bleakly, grimly, somberly, som-
brously, solemnly, funereally, gravely,
with a long face.

.32 unhappily, uncheerfully, cheerlessly, joylessly, unjoyfully.

.33 dejectedly, downheartedly; discouragedly,
disheartenedly, dispiritedly; despon-
dently, despairingly, spiritlessly, heartlessly; disconsolately, inconsolably, un-
consolably, forlornly.

.34 melancholily, pensively, wistfully, trist-
fully.

.35 glumly, grumly, morosely, sullenly; moodily, moodishly, broodingly, broodily;
mopishly, mopily [informal], mopingly.

.36 sorrowfully, mournfully, ruefully, woefully, dolefully, dolorously, plaintively,
grievously, grieffully, lugubriously; heart-
brokenly, brokenheartedly; tearfully, with
tears in eyes.

873. REGRET

.1 NOUNS regret, regretting, regretfulness;
remorse, remorsefulness, remorse of conscience, ayenbite of inwit [archaic];
shame, shamefulness, shamefacedness,
shamefastness; sorrow, grief, sorriness, repining; contrition, contriteness, attrition;
bitterness; regrets, apologies; wistfulness
634.4.

.2 compunction, qualms, scruples, pangs,
pangs of conscience, throes, sting or
pricking or twinge or twitch of conscience, touch of conscience, voice of
conscience, pricking of heart, better self.

.3 self-reproach, self-reproachfulness, self-ac-
cusation, self-condemnation, self-convic-
tion, self-punishment, self-humiliation,
self-debasement, self-hatred, self-flagella-
tion; self-analysis, soul-searching, examination of conscience.

.4 penitence, repentance, change of heart;
apology, humble or heartfelt apology, abject apology; reformation 145.2; deathbed
repentance; mea culpa [L]; saeta [Sp];
penance 1012.3; wearing a hairshirt or
sackcloth or sackcloth and ashes, mortification of the flesh.

.5 penitent, confessor, "a sadder and a wiser
man" [Coleridge]; prodigal son, prodigal
returned; Magdalen.

.6 VERBS regret, deplore, repine, be sorry
for; rue, rue the day; bemoan, bewail;
curse one's folly, reproach oneself, kick
oneself [slang], bite one's tongue, accuse
or condemn or blame or convict or punish oneself, flagellate oneself, humiliate
or debase oneself, hate oneself for one's
actions; examine one's conscience, search
one's soul, analyze or search one's motives; cry over spilled milk, waste time in
regret.

.7 repent, think better of, change one's
mind; plead guilty, own oneself in the
wrong, humble oneself, apologize 1012.5,
beg pardon or forgiveness, throw oneself
on the mercy of the court; do penance
1012.6; reform.

.8 ADJS regretful, remorseful, full of remorse, ashamed, shameful, shamefaced,
shamefast, sorry, rueful, repining, unhappy about; conscience-stricken, con-
science-smitten; self-reproachful, self-re-
proaching, self-accusing, self-condemning,
self-convicting, self-punishing, self-flagel-
lating, self-humiliating, self-debasing, self-
hating; wistful 634.23.

.9 penitent, repentant; penitential, penitentiary; contrite, abject, humble, humbled,
sheepish, apologetic, touched, softened,
melted.

.10 regrettable, much to be regretted; deplorable 675.9.

.11 ADVS regretfully, remorsefully, sorrily,
ruefully, unhappily.

.12 penitently, repentantly, penitentially;
contritely, abjectly, humbly 906.15, sheepishly, apologetically.

874. UNREGRETFULNESS

.1 NOUNS **unregretfulness, unremorsefulness, unsorriness,** unruefulness; **remorselessness,** regretlessness, sorrowlessness; **shamelessness,** unashamedness.

.2 **impenitence,** impenitentness; nonrepentance, irrepentance; **uncontriteness,** unabjectness; seared conscience, heart of stone, callousness 856.3; **hardness of heart,** hardness, induration, obduracy; insolence 913.

.3 VERBS **harden one's heart,** steel oneself; **have no regrets,** not look backward, not cry over spilled milk; have no shame.

.4 ADJS **unregretful,** unregretting, **unremorseful, unsorry, unsorrowful,** unrueful; **remorseless,** regretless, sorrowless, griefless; unsorrowing, ungrieving, unrepining; **shameless,** unashamed.

.5 **impenitent, unrepentant,** unrepenting; **uncontrite,** unabject; untouched, unsoftened, unmelted, callous 856.12; **hard,** hardened, obdurate; insolent 913.8–10.

.6 **unregretted,** unrepented.

.7 ADVS **unregretfully, unremorsefully,** unruefully; **remorselessly,** sorrowlessly, impenitently, shamelessly, unashamedly; **without regret,** without looking back, **without remorse,** without compunction, without any qualms or scruples.

875. LAMENTATION

.1 NOUNS **lamentation, lamenting, mourning, moaning, grieving, sorrowing, wailing, bewailing, bemoaning,** keening, howling, ululation, "weeping and gnashing of teeth" [Bible]; **sorrow** 872.10.

.2 **weeping, sobbing, crying, bawling,** greet [Scot]; blubbering, whimpering, sniveling; **tears,** flood of tears, fit of crying; cry or good cry [both informal]; **tearfulness,** weepiness [informal], lachrymosity, melting mood; tearful eyes, swimming or brimming or overflowing eyes; **tear,** teardrop, lachryma, dacry(o)–; lacrimatory, tear bottle.

.3 **lament,** plaint, planctus [L]; **murmur,** mutter; **moan, groan; whine,** whimper; **wail,** wail of woe; **sob,** cri du cœur [Fr], cry, outcry, scream, howl, yowl, bawl, yawp, keen, ululation; jeremiad, tirade, dolorous tirade.

.4 **complaint, grievance,** peeve, pet peeve, groan; dissent, protest 522; beef or kick or gripe or grouse [all informal]; **bellyache** or howl or holler or squawk or bitch [all slang]; **complaining,** scolding, groaning, faultfinding 969.4, sniping, destructive criticism, **grumbling, murmuring;** beefing or grousing or kicking or griping [all informal]; **bellyaching** or squawking or bitching or yapping [all slang]; whining, petulance, peevishness, querulousness.

.5 **dirge, funeral** or **death song,** coronach, keen, elegy, epicedium, requiem, monody, threnody, threnode, knell, death knell, passing bell, funeral or dead march, muffled drums; eulogy, funeral or graveside oration.

.6 (mourning garments) **mourning, weeds,** widow's weeds, crape, black; deep mourning; sackcloth, sackcloth and ashes; cypress, cypress lawn, yew; mourning band; mourning ring.

.7 **lamenter, griever, mourner** 410.7; **complainer,** malcontent 869.3.

.8 VERBS **lament, mourn, moan, grieve, sorrow,** keen, weep over, **bewail, bemoan, deplore, repine, sigh,** give sorrow words; sing the blues [informal], elegize, dirge, knell.

.9 **wring one's hands,** tear one's hair, gnash one's teeth, beat one's breast, roll on the ground.

.10 **weep, sob, cry,** greet [Scot], **bawl,** boohoo; blubber, whimper, snivel; **shed tears,** drop a tear; **burst into tears,** give way to tears, melt or dissolve in tears, break down, break down and cry; cry one's eyes out, cry oneself blind.

.11 **wail,** ululate; **moan, groan; howl,** yowl, yawl [Brit dial]; **cry,** squall, bawl, yawp, **yell, scream,** shriek; cry out, make an outcry; bay at the moon; tirade.

.12 **whine, whimper,** yammer [dial], pule.

.13 **complain, groan;** kick or gripe or beef [all informal], **grumble, murmur, mutter,** grouch [informal], growl, clamor, croak, grunt, yelp, howl or raise a howl [both informal], put up a squawk or howl [slang]; **squawk** or holler or crab or grouse [all informal]; **bitch** or bellyache or yap [all slang]; **take on** [informal], fret, fuss, make a fuss about, fret and fume; air a grievance, lodge or register a complaint.

.14 **go into mourning;** put on mourning, wear mourning.

.15 ADJS **lamenting, grieving, mourning, moaning, sorrowing;** wailing, bewailing, bemoaning; **in mourning,** in sackcloth and ashes.

.16 **plaintive,** plangent, **mournful,** moanful, wailful, lamentive, ululant; **sorrowful** 872.26,27; **complaining, faultfinding** 969.24, **querulous, fretful,** petulant, peevish; **howling,** Jeremianic; whining, whiny, whimpering, puling.

.17 **tearful,** teary, **weepy** [informal]; lachrymal, lachrymose, lacrimatory; in the melting mood, on the edge of tears, ready to cry; **weeping, sobbing, crying;** blubbering, whimpering, sniveling; **in tears,** with tears in one's eyes, with tearful or watery eyes, with swimming or brimming or overflowing eyes, with eyes suffused, bathed or dissolved in tears, "like Niobe, all tears" [Shakespeare].

.18 dirgelike, knell-like, elegiac(al), epicedial, threnodic.

.19 ADVS **lamentingly, plaintively, mournfully,** moanfully, wailfully; **sorrowfully** 872.36; complainingly, groaningly, querulously, fretfully, petulantly, peevishly.

876. REJOICING

.1 NOUNS **rejoicing, jubilation,** jubilance, jubilant display, jubilee, show of joy, raucous happiness; **exultation,** elation, triumph; whoopee or hoopla [both informal], festivity 878.3,4, merriment 870.5; celebration 877.

.2 **cheer, hurrah, huzzah,** hurray, hooray, yippee, rah; **cry, shout, yell;** hosanna, hallelujah, alleluia, paean, paean or chorus of cheers; **applause** 968.2.

.3 **smile,** smiling; bright smile, gleaming or glowing smile, beam; silly smile or grin; **grin,** grinning; broad grin, ear-to-ear grin, toothful grin; stupid grin, idiotic grin; sardonic grin, **smirk, simper.**

.4 **laughter,** laughing, **hilarity** 870.5, risibility; **laugh;** boff or boffola or yuck [all slang]; **titter; giggle; chuckle, chortle;** cackle, crow; **snicker,** snigger, snort; ha-ha, hee-haw, hee-hee, ho-ho, tee-hee, yuk-yuk; guffaw, **horselaugh; hearty laugh, belly laugh** [slang], Homeric laughter, cachinnation; **shout, shriek,** shout of laughter, burst or outburst of laughter, peal or roar of laughter, gales of laughter; fit of laughter, convulsion, "laughter holding both his sides" [Milton].

.5 VERBS **rejoice, jubilate, exult, glory, joy, delight,** bless or thank one's stars, congratulate oneself, hug oneself, rub one's hands, clap hands; dance or skip for joy, dance, skip, frisk, rollick, revel, frolic, caper, gambol, caracole, romp; sing, carol, chirp, chirrup, chirp like a cricket, whistle, lilt.

.6 **cheer,** give a cheer, **cry, shout, yell,** cry for joy, yell oneself hoarse; huzzah, hurrah, hurray, hooray; shout hosanna or hallelujah, "make a joyful noise unto the Lord" [Bible]; **applaud** 968.10.

.7 **smile,** crack a smile [slang], break into a smile; **beam,** smile brightly; **grin,** grin like a Cheshire cat or chessy-cat [informal]; **smirk, simper.**

.8 **laugh,** burst out laughing, burst into laughter, burst out, laugh outright; laugh it up [slang]; **titter; giggle; chuckle, chortle;** cackle, crow; **snicker,** snigger, snort; ha-ha, hee-haw, hee-hee, ho-ho, tee-hee, yuk-yuk; **guffaw,** horselaugh; **shout, shriek,** give a shout or shriek of laughter; **roar,** cachinnate, roar with laughter; shake with laughter, shake like jelly; be convulsed with laughter, go into convulsions; burst or split with laughter, break up [slang], split [informal], **split one's sides,** laugh fit to burst or bust [slang], bust a gut or pee one's pants laughing [both slang], **be in stitches** [informal], hold one's sides; laugh oneself sick or silly or limp, die or nearly die laughing; laugh in one's sleeve, laugh up one's sleeve, laugh in one's beard.

.9 ADJS **rejoicing,** delighting, exulting; **jubilant, exultant, elated,** elate, flushed.

.10 ADVS **rejoicingly,** delightingly, exultingly; **jubilantly, exultantly, elatedly.**

877. CELEBRATION

.1 NOUNS **celebration,** celebrating; **observance,** formal or solemn or ritual observance, **solemnization;** marking the occasion; **commemoration,** memorialization, remembrance, memory; jubilee; holiday 711.4; anniversaries 137.12; **festivity** 878.3,4; **revel** 878.6; rejoicing 876; **ceremony,** rite 646.4; religious rites 1040; ovation, triumph; **tribute;** testimonial, testimonial banquet or dinner; toast; **salute;** salvo; flourish of trumpets, fanfare, fanfaronade; dressing ship.

.2 VERBS **celebrate, observe, keep, mark,** solemnly mark, honor; **commemorate,** memorialize; **solemnize,** signalize, hallow, mark with a red letter; hold jubilee, jubilize, jubilate, maffick [Brit informal]; **make merry** 878.26; kill the fatted calf; sound a fanfare, blow the trumpet, beat the drum, fire a salute; dress ship.

.3 ADJS **celebrative,** celebrating; **commemorative,** commemorating; memorial; solemn.

.4 ADVS **in honor of, in commemoration of,** in memory or remembrance of, to the memory of.

878. AMUSEMENT

.1 NOUNS amusement, entertainment, diversion, solace, divertisement, *divertissement* [Fr], recreation, relaxation, regalement; pastime, *passe-temps* [Fr]; mirth 870.5; pleasure, enjoyment 865.

.2 fun, action [informal]; funmaking, fun and games, play, sport, game; good time, lovely time, pleasant time; big time or high time or high old time [all informal], picnic or laughs or lots of laughs or ball [all slang], great fun, time of one's life; a short life and a merry one.

.3 festivity, merrymaking, merriment, gaiety, jollity, jollification [informal], joviality, conviviality, whoopee or hoopla [both informal]; larking [informal], skylarking, racketing, mafficking [Brit informal], holiday-making; revelry, revelment, reveling, revels.

.4 festival, festivity, festive occasion, *fiesta* [Sp], fete, –fest, gala, gala affair, blowout [slang], jamboree [slang]; high jinks, do, great doings [all informal]; *fête champêtre* [Fr]; feast, banquet 307.9; picnic 307.6; party 922.11; waygoose [Brit dial], wayzgoose; fair, carnival; kermis; *Oktoberfest* [Ger]; Mardi Gras; Saturnalia; field day, gala day, feria.

.5 frolic, play, romp, rollick, frisk, gambol, caper, dido [informal].

.6 revel, lark, escapade, ploy; celebration 877; spree, bout, fling, wingding, randy [Scot], randan [dial]; bust or tear or bender or binge or toot or bat [all slang]; carouse, carousal; orgy, debauch; drinking bout 996.5.

.7 round of pleasure, mad round, whirl, merry-go-round, the rounds, the dizzy rounds.

.8 sports; athletics, agonistics; gymnastics, palaestra; acrobatics, tumbling; track, track and field; soccer, association football; Rugby, rugger [informal]; swimming, bathing, natation.

.9 game, sport 878.34; play; contest 796.3; race 796.12; event, meet; bout, match, go [informal]; singles, doubles; twosome, threesome, foursome; double-header; pentathlon, decathlon; play-off, runoff; games of chance 515.8.

.10 tournament, tourney, gymkhana, field day; rally; regatta; carousel; meet, track meet; games, Olympic games, the Olympics; Olympiad, Highland games.

.11 entertainment industry; show business, show biz [informal]; theater 611.18–20;

cabaret, tavern, roadhouse; café dansant, café chantant; nightclub, night spot or nitery [both informal], *boîte, boîte de nuit* [both Fr]; juke joint [slang], discothèque; dance hall, dancing pavilion, ballroom, dance floor; casino; amusement park, fun-fair [Brit]; resort 191.27.

.12 playground; field, athletic field, playing field; football field, gridiron; baseball field, diamond; infield, outfield; soccer field; archery ground, cricket ground, polo ground, croquet ground or lawn, bowling green; bowling alley; links, golf links, golf course; fairway, putting green; gymnasium, gym [informal]; court, badminton court, basketball court, tennis court, racket court, squash court; billiard parlor, poolroom, pool hall; racecourse, track, course, turf, oval; stretch; rink, glaciarium, ice rink, skating rink; playroom 192.12.

.13 swimming pool, pool, swimming bath [Brit], plunge, plunge bath, natatorium; swimming hole; wading pool.

.14 park, public park, pleasure garden or ground, pleasance, paradise, common, commons.

.15 merry-go-round, carousel, roundabout, whirligig, whip, flying horses; Ferris wheel; seesaw, teeter-totter; swing; roller coaster; chutes, chute-the-chutes; –drome.

.16 toy, plaything, sport; bauble, knickknack, gimcrack, gewgaw, kickshaw, whim-wham, trinket; doll, paper doll, rag doll, puppet, marionette, toy soldier; dollhouse, doll carriage; hobbyhorse, cockhorse, rocking horse; top, teetotum; pinwheel; jack-in-the-box; jacks, jackstones; jackstraws, pick-up sticks; blocks; checkerboard, chessboard; marble, mig, agate, steelie, taw; athletic equipment; ball 255.13; racket, battledore; bat, baseball bat, cricket bat; cue; club, golf club.

.17 playing cards, cards; picture cards, face cards, court cards: king, queen, jack or knave; bower, right or left bower, best bower; spot cards: ace, deuce, trey; joker; diamonds, hearts, clubs, spades; hand; dummy; royal flush, flush, full house, straight, three of a kind, pair; singleton; trump, ruff; trick; rubber, round; pack, deck.

.18 chessman, man, piece; bishop, knight, king, queen, pawn, rook or castle.

.19 player, frolicker, frisker, funmaker, gamboler; pleasure-seeker, pleasurer, pleasurist, playboy [slang]; reveler, merrymaker, rollicker, skylarker, **carouser,** cutup [slang]; contestant 791.2.

.20 athlete, jock [slang], **player,** amateur athlete, professional athlete, competitor, sportsman, sport, gamester, games-player; ballplayer, baseballer, cricketer; batter, catcher, baseman, infielder, outfielder, shortstop, outfield, battery; footballer, lineman, offensive lineman, defensive lineman, halfback, blocking back, wingback, tailback, quarterback, fullback, end, tackle; center; guard, linebacker; golfer; poloist; pugilist, wrestler 800.2,3; racer 269.5; jumper 319.4; skater; archer, bowman, toxophilite; coach, games master or mistress [Brit].

.21 gymnast, palaestrian; pancratiast; **acrobat,** tumbler, contortionist; funambulist, high wire artist, ropewalker, tightrope walker, ropedancer; aerialist, man on the flying trapeze; weightlifter.

.22 master of ceremonies, MC or **emcee** [both informal], marshal; **toastmaster;** master of the revels, revel master; Lord of Misrule, Abbot of Unreason [Scot]; social director.

.23 VERBS **amuse, entertain, divert,** regale, beguile, solace, recreate, refresh, enliven, exhilarate, put in good humor; **relax,** loosen up; **delight, tickle, titillate,** tickle the fancy; raise a smile or laugh, convulse, set the table on a roar, be the death of one; wow or slay or knock dead or kill or break one up or fracture one [all slang].

.24 amuse oneself, take one's pleasure, give oneself over to pleasure, be on pleasure bent; **relax,** let oneself go, loosen up; **have fun, have a good time,** have a ball or have lots of laughs [both slang], live it up or laugh it up [both slang]; drown care, drive dull care away; beguile the time, kill time, while away the time.

.25 play, sport, disport; **frolic, rollick, gambol, frisk, romp, caper,** cut capers [informal], antic, curvet, cavort, caracole, flounce, trip, skip, dance; cut up [slang], cut a dido [informal], horse around [slang], fool around, carry on [informal].

.26 make merry, revel, roister, jolly, lark [informal], skylark, **make whoopee** [slang], let oneself go, **blow or let off steam;** cut loose, let loose, let go, whoop it up, **kick up one's heels;** hell around or raise hell or blow off the lid [all slang]; step out [informal], go places and do things, go on the town, see life, **paint the town red** [slang]; go the dizzy rounds, go on the

merry-go-round [slang]; **celebrate** 877.2; spree, **go on a spree,** go on a bust or toot or bender or binge or rip or tear [all slang]; **carouse,** jollify [informal], wanton, debauch, **sow one's wild oats, have one's fling.**

.27 "eat, drink, and be merry" [Bible], feast, banquet.

.28 ADJS **amused, entertained; diverted, delighted, tickled, titillated;** "pleased with a rattle, tickled with a straw" [Pope].

.29 amusing, entertaining, diverting, beguiling; **fun** [informal], more fun than a barrel of monkeys [informal]; recreative, recreational; **delightful,** titillative, titillating; humorous 880.4.

.30 festive, festal; merry, gay, jolly, jovial, joyous, joyful, gladsome, convivial, gala, hilarious; **merrymaking,** on the loose [informal].

.31 playful, sportive, sportful; **frolicsome,** gamesome, rompish, larkish, capersome; waggish 738.6.

.32 sporting, sports; **athletic,** agonistic; **gymnastic,** palaestral; **acrobatic.**

.33 ADVS **in fun,** for amusement, **for fun,** for the fun of it; for kicks or for laughs [both slang], for the heck or hell of it [slang], for the devil of it [slang]; just to be doing.

.34 sports, games

acey-deucy	cricket
acrostics	croquet
anagrams	curling
archery	deck tennis
association football	discus
backgammon	dominoes
badminton	draughts
bagatelle	fencing
ball	fishing
balloon ball	fives
bandy	football
baseball	fox and geese
basketball	French and English
battledore and shut-	Frisbee
tlecock	ghost
billiards	gliding
bingo, beano	go
blindman's buff	gobang
bobsledding	golf
boccie	go maku
boloball	Halma
bowling, bowls	hammer throwing
boxing 796.9	handball
captain ball	hide-and-seek
cat	hiking
catch	hockey
charades	hopscotch
checkers	horseshoes
chess	hunting
Chinese checkers	hurdling
climbing	ice hockey
court tennis	ice skating
crambo	jacks, jackstones

jackstraws	shinny	put-and-take	snipsnapsnorum
jai alai	shogi	quadrille	solitaire
keno	shooting	quinze	speculation
lacrosse	shot-put	reverse	squeezers
lawn tennis	shuffleboard, shovel-	rouge et noir	straight poker
leapfrog	board	rum	stud poker
lotto	skating	rummy	thirty-one
luging	skeet, skeet shooting	Russian bank	twenty-one
Mah-Jongg	skiing	seven-up	vingt-et-un
marbles	ski-jumping	skat	whist
merels	skin-diving		
Monopoly	skittles		
motorcycling	sky-diving		
mountaineering	sledding		
mumble-the-peg,	snowmobiling		
mumblety-peg	snooker		
ninepins	snorkel diving		
paddle tennis	soccer		
pall-mall	softball		
pallone	squash, squash rac-		
parachuting	quets		
Parcheesi	stickball		
pelota	surfing		
Ping-Pong	table tennis		
polo	tennis		
pool	tenpins		
post office	tent pegging		
pushball	tetherball		
pyramids	three-dimensional		
quintain	chess		
quoits	ticktacktoe		
racquets	tiddlywinks		
riding	tilting		
roller skating	tipcat		
rounders	tivoli		
rowing	tobogganing		
Rugby	trap bat and ball		
sailing	trapshooting		
sailplaning	tug of war		
Scrabble	volleyball		
scuba diving	water polo		
sculling	waterskiing		
sharpshooting	wrestling 796.10		

.35 card games

all fours	flinch
auction bridge	fright
authors	frog
baccarat	gin
banker	gin rummy
beggar-my-neighbor	goat
bezique	go fish
blackjack	hearts
blind poker	keno
bluff	lansquenet
Boston	loo
brag	lottery
bridge	lotto
canasta	matrimony
casino	Milles Bornes
commerce	monte
commit	napoleon
connections	old maid
contract bridge, con-	ombre
tract	pairs
cribbage	patience
draw poker	penny ante
Earl of Coventry	picquet
écarté	pinochle
euchre	Pit
faro	poker
five hundred	Polish bank

879. DANCING

.1 NOUNS **dancing,** terpsichore, dance, chore(o)–, chorio–; **the light fantastic;** **choreography; ballet,** classical ballet, modern ballet, comedy ballet; **modern dance;** dance drama, choreodrama; hoofing [slang]; tap dancing, soft-shoe dancing, clog dancing; solo dancing, choral dancing, ballroom dancing, social dancing, folk dancing, country dancing, square dancing, round dancing, couple dancing.

.2 **dance, hop** [informal], **shindig** or shindy [both slang]; **ball,** *bal* [Fr]; masked ball, masque, mask, masquerade ball, masquerade, *bal masqué* [Fr], *bal costumé* [Fr], fancy-dress ball; promenade, **prom** [informal]; country dance, square dance, barn dance; mixer, stag dance; record hop; tea dance, *thé dansant* [Fr]; gay dance [informal].

.3 **dancer,** *danseur* [Fr], terpsichorean, **hoofer** [slang], step dancer, tap dancer, clog dancer, heel-and-toe dancer; solo dancer, choral dancer, ballroom dancer, social dancer, folk-dancer, country dancer, square-dancer, round-dancer; figure dancer, figurant, figurante; skirt dancer; ballet dancer, ballet girl, **ballerina,** danseuse, coryphée; *première danseuse* [Fr], *danseur noble* [Fr]; **modern dancer; chorus girl,** chorus boy or man; geisha or geisha girl; nautch girl, bayadere; hula girl; taxi dancer.

.4 **ballroom, dance hall,** dancery; dance palace; casino.

.5 VERBS **dance, trip the light fantastic,** trip, skip, hop, foot, prance [informal], **hoof** [slang], clog, tap-dance; shake, shimmy, shuffle; waltz, one-step, two-step, foxtrot, etc.

.6 ADJS **dancing, dance,** terpsichorean; balletic; choreographic.

.7 dances

allemande	*ventre* [Fr]
apache dance	bolero
barn dance	boogaloo
beguine	bourrée
belly dance, *danse du*	boutade

branle	mambo
breakdown	mazurka
bubble dance	merengue
bunny hop	Mexican hat dance
cakewalk	minuet
can-can	monkey
cantico	morris dance
Castle walk	one-step
cha-cha	ox dance
Charleston	pachanga
chonchina	pas de deux
clog	paso doble
conga	passamezzo
cotillion	pas seul
country dance	peabody
courante	polka
eagle rock	polonaise
fan dance	Portland fancy
fandango	quadrille
flamenco	rain dance
fling	reel
folk dance	rigadoon
fox trot	Road to the Isles
frug	round dance
funky chicken	rumba
furlana	salsa
galliard	saltarello
gallopade	samba
galop	saraband
gavotte	schottische
german, german cotil-	Scotch reel
lion	shimmy
habañera	Sir Roger de Coverley
Highland fling	skirt dance
hokey-pokey	snake dance
hootchy-kootchy	square dance
hopak	strathspey
hora	swim
hornpipe	sword dance
hula, hula-hula	tango
hustle	tap dance
interpretative dance	tarantella
jig	trepak
jota	turkey trot
juba	twist
kola	two-step
Lambeth Walk	Virginia reel
lancers	waltz, valse
limbo	war dance
lindy, lindy hop	Watusi
longways dance	ziganka
malagueña	

.8 dance steps

arabesque	grapevine
buck-and-wing	heel-and-toe
chassé	pas
coupé	pigeonwing
double shuffle	quickstep
gambado, gambade	shuffle

880. HUMOROUSNESS

.1 NOUNS humorousness, funniness, amus-
ingness, laughableness, laughability, hilarity; wittiness 881.2; drollness, drollery;
whimsicalness, quizzicalness; ludicrousness, ridiculousness, absurdity, absurdness, quaintness, eccentricity, incongruity, bizarreness, bizarrerie; richness, pricelessness [informal]; the funny side.

.2 comicalness, comicality; farcicalness, far-
cicality, slapstick quality, broadness.

.3 bathos; anticlimax, comedown.

.4 ADJS humorous, funny, amusing; witty
881.15; droll, whimsical, quizzical; laughable, risible, good for a laugh; ludicrous,
ridiculous, hilarious, absurd, quaint, eccentric, incongruous, bizarre; rich, priceless [informal], screaming, too funny or
too killing for words [informal].

.5 comic or comical; farcical, slapstick,
broad; burlesque 967.14; tragicomic, serio-
comic, mock-heroic.

.6 ADVS humorously, amusingly, funnily,
laughably; wittily 881.18; drolly, whimsically, quizzically; comically, farcically,
broadly; ludicrously, ridiculously, absurdly, quaintly, eccentrically, incongruously, bizarrely.

881. WIT, HUMOR

.1 NOUNS wit, humor, pleasantry, esprit
[Fr], salt, spice or savor of wit; Attic wit
or salt, Atticism; ready wit, quick wit,
nimble wit, agile wit, pretty wit; dry wit,
subtle wit; comedy 611.6; black humor,
sick humor, gallows humor; satire, sarcasm, irony; parody, lampoon, travesty,
caricature, burlesque, squib; farce, mere
farce; slapstick, slapstick humor, broad
humor; visual humor.

.2 wittiness, humorousness, funniness; face-
tiousness, pleasantry, jocularity, jocose-
ness, jocosity; joking, joshing [informal];
smartness, cleverness, brilliance; pungency, saltiness; keenness, sharpness;
keen-wittedness, quick-wittedness, nimble-wittedness.

.3 drollery, drollness; whimsicality, whimsicalness, humorsomeness, antic wit.

.4 waggishness, waggery; roguishness 738.2;
playfulness, sportiveness, levity, frivolity,
flippancy, merriment 870.5; prankishness,
pranksomeness; trickery, trickiness, tricks-
iness, trickishness.

.5 buffoonery, buffoonism, clownery, harlequinade; clownishness, buffoonishness;
foolery, fooling, tomfoolery; horseplay;
shenanigans or monkeyshines [both infor-
mal]; banter 882.

.6 joke, jest, gag [informal], wheeze, jape,
fun, sport, play; story, yarn, funny story,
good story; dirty story or joke, blue story
or joke, double entendre [Fr]; shaggy-dog
story; sick joke [informal]; ethnic joke;
capital joke, good one, laugh, belly laugh,
rib tickler, sidesplitter, howler, wow,
scream, riot, panic; visual joke, sight gag

[informal]; **point**, cream of the jest; **jest-book**.

.7 **witticism, pleasantry,** *plaisanterie, boutade* [both Fr]; **play of wit,** *jeu d'esprit* [Fr]; **crack** *or* smart crack *or* **wisecrack** [all informal]; **quip,** conceit, bright *or* happy thought, bright *or* brilliant idea; **mot, bon mot,** smart saying, stroke of wit; epigram, turn of thought, aphorism, apothegm; flash of wit, scintillation; **sally,** flight of wit; **repartee,** retort, riposte, snappy comeback [slang]; facetiae [pl], quips and cranks; **gibe, dirty** *or* **nasty crack** [informal]; persiflage 882.1.

.8 **wordplay, play on words,** *jeu de mots* [Fr], missaying, corruption, paronomasia, *calembour* [Fr], abuse of terms; **pun,** punning; equivoque, equivocality; anagram, logogram, logogriph, metagram; acrostic, double acrostic; amphiboly, amphibologism; palindrome; spoonerism; malapropism.

.9 **old joke,** old wheeze, old turkey, **trite joke,** hoary-headed joke, joke with whiskers; **chestnut** *or* **corn** *or* **corny joke** *or* **oldie** [all slang]; Joe Miller, Joe Millerism; twice-told tale, retold story, warmed-over cabbage [informal].

.10 **prank, trick, practical joke,** waggish trick, *espièglerie* [Fr], antic, caper, frolic; **monkeyshines** *or* **shenanigans** [both slang].

.11 **sense of humor, risibility,** funny bone.

.12 **humorist, wit, funnyman, comic,** *bel-esprit* [Fr], life of the party; **joker,** jokester, gagman [informal]; **jester, quipster, wisecracker** *or* **gagster** [both informal]; **wag,** wagwit; zany, madcap, cutup [slang]; **prankster; comedian,** banana [slang]; **clown** 612.10; punster, punner; epigrammatist; satirist, ironist; burlesquer, caricaturist, parodist, lampooner; reparteeist; witling; gag writer [slang], jokesmith.

.13 VERBS **joke, jest, wisecrack** *or* crack wise [both informal], utter a mot, **quip,** jape, josh [informal], fun [informal], make fun, **kid** *or* **kid around** [both informal]; **make a funny** [informal]; **crack a joke,** get off a joke, tell a good story; pun, play on words; scintillate, sparkle; **make fun of,** gibe at, fleer at, mock, scoff at, poke fun at, make the butt of one's humor, be merry with; ridicule 967.8–11.

.14 **trick, play a practical joke,** play tricks *or* pranks, **play a joke** *or* **trick on,** make merry with; pull one's leg, put one on [slang].

.15 ADJS **witty,** *spirituel* [Fr]; **humorous, funny;** jocular, joky [informal], **joking,**

jesting, jocose; **facetious,** joshing [informal], **whimsical, droll,** humorsome; smart, clever, brilliant, scintillating, sparkling, sprightly; keen, sharp, rapier-like, pungent, pointed, biting, mordant; salty, salt, Attic; keen-witted, quick-witted, nimble-witted.

.16 **clownish,** buffoonish.

.17 **waggish;** roguish 738.6; **playful, sportive; prankish,** pranky, pranksome; tricky, trickish, tricksy.

.18 ADVS **wittily, humorously;** jocularly, jocosely; **facetiously; whimsically, drolly.**

.19 **in fun, in sport, in play, in jest,** in joke, as a joke, jokingly, jestingly, with tongue in cheek; for fun, for sport.

882. BANTER

.1 NOUNS **banter, badinage, persiflage, pleasantry, fooling, fooling around, kidding** *or* **kidding around** [both informal], **raillery, rallying, sport,** good-natured banter, harmless teasing; ridicule 967; **chaff, twit,** jest, joke, jape, josh [informal]; jive [slang]; exchange, give-and-take.

.2 **bantering, twitting, chaffing, joking, jesting,** japing, **fooling, teasing,** hazing, joshing [informal]; **jollying** *or* **kidding** [both informal]; **ribbing** *or* **ragging** *or* **razzing** *or* roasting [all slang].

.3 **banterer,** *persifleur* [Fr], **chaffer, twitter; jollyer** *or* **kidder** *or* **josher** [all informal]; ribber *or* roaster *or* razzer *or* ragger [all slang].

.4 VERBS **banter, twit, chaff,** rally, **joke, jest, jape, tease,** haze; **jolly** *or* **kid** *or* **josh** *or* **put on** [all informal], ride *or* needle [both informal]; rib *or* rag *or* razz *or* roast *or* jive [all slang].

.5 ADJS **bantering, chaffing, twitting; jollying** *or* **kidding** *or* **joshing** [all informal], **fooling, teasing,** quizzical.

883. DULLNESS

(being uninteresting)

.1 NOUNS **dullness, dryness,** dustiness, uninterestingness; **stuffiness, stodginess,** woodenness, stiffness; barrenness, sterility, aridity, jejunity; **insipidness,** insipidity, vapidness, vapidity, inanity, hollowness, emptiness, superficiality, **flatness,** tastelessness; characterlessness, colorlessness, pointlessness; **deadness,** lifelessness, spiritlessness, bloodlessness, paleness, pallor, etiolation, effeteness; **slowness,** pokiness, dragginess [informal], unliveliness; **tediousness** 884.2; **dreariness,** drearisomeness, dismalness; **heaviness**, leadenness, ponderousness; inexcitability 858; solemnity 871; lowness of spirit 872.3.

.2 **prosaicness,** prosiness; prosaism, prosaicism, prose, plainness; **matter-of-factness,** unimaginativeness; matter of fact.

.3 **triteness,** corniness *or* squareness [both slang], **banality,** banalness, unoriginality, **hackneyedness, commonplaceness,** commonness, familiarness, platitudinousness; **staleness,** mustiness, fustiness; cliché 517.3.

.4 VERBS **fall flat,** fall flat as a pancake; leave one cold, go over like a lead balloon [slang], lay an egg, bomb [slang]; **wear thin.**

.5 prose, platitudinize, sing a familiar tune.

.6 ADJS **dull, dry,** dusty, dryasdust; **stuffy, stodgy,** wooden, stiff; arid, barren, blank, sterile, jejune; **insipid,** vapid, inane, hollow, empty, superficial; fade, blah [informal], **flat,** tasteless; characterless, colorless, pointless; **dead,** lifeless, spiritless, bloodless, pale, pallid, etiolated, effete; cold; **slow,** poky, draggy [informal], pedestrian, plodding, unlively; **tedious** 884.8; **dreary,** drearisome, dismal; **heavy,** leaden, ponderous, elephantine; ho-hum [informal]; dull as dish water, "weary, stale, flat and unprofitable" [Shakespeare]; inexcitable 858.10; solemn 871.3; low-spirited 872.22.

.7 **uninteresting,** uneventful, **unexciting; unentertaining,** unenjoyable, **unamusing,** unfunny, unwitty.

.8 **prosaic,** prose, prosy, prosing, plain; **matter-of-fact,** unimaginative, unimpassioned.

.9 **trite;** corny *or* square *or* square-John *or* Clyde [all slang], fade, **banal,** unoriginal, platitudinous, **stereotyped,** stock, set, **commonplace, common,** truistic, **familiar,** bromidic [slang], old hat [informal], back-number, bewhiskered, warmed-over, **cut-and-dried; hackneyed,** hackney; well-known 475.27; **stale,** musty, fusty; **worn,** timeworn, well-worn, moth-eaten, threadbare, **worn thin.**

.10 ADVS **dully, dryly,** dustily, **uninterestingly;** stuffily, stodgily; aridly, barrenly, jejunely, **insipidly, vapidly,** inanely, hollowly, emptily, superficially, tastelessly, **colorlessly,** pointlessly; lifelessly, spiritlessly, bloodlessly, pallidly, effetely; slowly, draggily [informal], ploddingly; **tediously** 884.12; drearily, drearisomely, dismally; heavily, ponderously.

.11 **tritely,** cornily [slang], **banally,** common-

placely, commonly, familiarly, hackneyedly, unoriginally, truistically, stalely.

884. TEDIUM

.1 NOUNS **tedium, monotony, humdrum,** irksomeness, irk; **sameness,** sameliness, samesomeness [dial], wearisome sameness, the same old thing, the same damn thing [slang]; broken record; undeviation, unvariation, invariability; the round, the daily round, the weary round, the treadmill, the squirrel cage, the beaten track *or* path; time on one's hands, time hanging heavily on one's hands.

.2 **tediousness, monotonousness; humdrumness,** humdrumminess; **dullness** 883; **wearisomeness,** wearifulness; **tiresomeness, irksomeness,** drearisomeness; **boresomeness,** boringness; prolixity, long-windedness.

.3 **weariness, tiredness,** wearifulness; jadedness, fed-upness, satiation, satiety; **boredom,** boredness; **ennui,** spleen, melancholy, life-weariness, *taedium vitae* [L], world-weariness, dispiritedness 872.3.

.4 **bore,** crashing bore [informal], frightful bore; **pest, nuisance; headache** *or* **pain in the neck** *or* pain in the ass [all slang]; dryasdust, dusty, humdrum; drag [slang], proser, twaddler; **drip** *or* **pill** *or* **flat tire** [all slang]; **wet blanket;** buttonholer.

.5 VERBS **be tedious, drag on,** go on forever; have a certain sameness, be infinitely repetitive; **weary, tire, irk,** wear, wear on *or* upon, **make one tired,** fatigue, weary *or* tire to death, jade; give one a swift pain in the ass *or* give one a bellyful *or* make one fed-up [all slang], pall, satiate, glut.

.6 **bore,** leave one cold, set *or* send to sleep; **bore stiff** [informal], bore to tears, bore to death *or* extinction, bore to distraction, bore out of one's life, bore out of all patience; buttonhole.

.7 **harp on** *or* **upon, dwell on** *or* **upon,** harp upon one *or* the same string, play *or* sing the same old song *or* tune, play the same broken record.

.8 ADJS **tedious, monotonous, humdrum,** singsong, jog-trot, treadmill, unvarying, invariable, uneventful, broken-record, harping, everlasting, too much with us [informal]; blah [informal], **dreary,** drearisome, dry, dryasdust, dusty, **dull** 883.6; prolix, long-winded.

.9 **wearying,** wearing, **tiring; wearisome,** weariful, fatiguing, **tiresome, irksome; boring, boresome,** stupefyingly boring, stuporific, yawny [informal].

.10 **weary,** weariful; **tired,** wearied, irked; good and tired, tired to death, weary unto death; sick, **sick of, tired of, sick and tired of;** jaded, satiated, fed-up [slang]; blasé; splenetic, melancholy, melancholic, life-weary, world-weary, tired of living, dispirited 872.22.

.11 **bored,** uninterested; bored stiff [slang], bored to death or extinction, bored to tears, stupefied or stuporous with boredom.

.12 ADVS tediously, monotonously, harpingly, everlastingly, unvaryingly, endlessly; long-windedly; **boringly,** boresomely; **wearisomely,** fatiguingly, wearyingly, tiresomely, irksomely, drearisomely; dully 883.10.

.13 on a treadmill, in a squirrel cage, on the beaten track, on the same old round; without a change of menu or scenery or pace.

.14 PHRS ho, hum!, heigh ho!, what a life!; *plus ça change, plus c'est la même chose* [Fr, the more it changes, the more it's the same thing]; so what else is new?

885. AGGRAVATION

.1 NOUNS **aggravation, worsening; exacerbation,** embittering, embitterment, souring; deterioration; **intensification, heightening,** sharpening, deepening, increase, enhancement, amplification, enlargement, magnification, augmentation; **exasperation,** annoyance, irritation 866.2,3; deliberate aggravation, provocation; contentiousness 797.15.

.2 VERBS **aggravate, worsen,** make worse; **exacerbate,** embitter, sour; deteriorate; **intensify, heighten,** sharpen, make acute or more acute, bring to a head, deepen, increase, enhance, amplify, enlarge, magnify, build up; augment; rub salt in the wound, add insult to injury, pour oil on the fire, heat up [informal], hot up [slang]; **exasperate, annoy, irritate** 866.13, 14; provoke, be an *agent provocateur.*

.3 **worsen,** get or grow worse, go from push to shove; **go from bad to worse, jump out of the frying pan into the fire,** avoid Scylla and fall into Charybdis, "sow the wind and reap the whirlwind" [Bible].

.4 ADJS **aggravated, worsened, worse,** exacerbated, embittered, soured; **intensified, heightened,** increased, enhanced, amplified, magnified, enlarged, augmented, heated up [informal], hotted up [slang]; **exasperated, irritated, annoyed** 866.21; provoked, deliberately provoked.

.5 **aggravating,** aggravative; **exasperating,** exasperative; **annoying, irritating** 864.22; provocative; contentious.

.6 ADVS **aggravatingly, exasperatingly; annoyingly** 864.29.

.7 **from bad to worse,** worse and worse, out of the frying pan into the fire.

886. RELIEF

.1 NOUNS **relief, easement, easing, ease; reduction,** diminishment, diminution, lessening, abatement; **remedy** 687; **alleviation, mitigation, palliation,** softening, assuagement, allayment, appeasement, mollification, subduement; soothing, salving; lulling; dulling, deadening, numbing, anesthesia, anesthetizing, analgesia.

.2 **release, deliverance, freeing,** removal; suspension, intermission, respite, surcease, reprieve; discharge; catharsis, purging, purgation, purge, cleansing, cleansing away, emotional release.

.3 **lightening, disburdening,** unburdening, unweighting, unloading, disencumbrance, disembarrassment, easing of the load, a load off one's mind, something out of one's system.

.4 sense or feeling of relief, sigh of relief.

.5 VERBS **relieve,** give relief; **ease,** ease matters; **reduce,** diminish, lessen, abate; **alleviate, mitigate, palliate,** soften, pad, cushion, assuage, allay, lay, appease, mollify, subdue, soothe; salve; pour balm into, pour oil on; poultice, foment, stupe; slake, slacken; lull; **dull, deaden,** dull or deaden the pain, numb, benumb, anesthetize; temper the wind to the shorn lamb, lay the flattering unction to one's soul.

.6 **release, free, deliver,** reprieve, remove, free from; suspend, intermit, give respite or surcease; discharge; act as a cathartic, purge, purge away, cleanse, cleanse away; give release.

.7 **lighten, disburden,** unburden, unweight, unload, unfreight, disencumber, disembarrass, ease one's load; **set one's mind at ease or rest,** set at ease, **take the load off one's mind,** smooth the ruffled brow of care.

.8 **be relieved, feel relief,** feel better about it, get something out of one's system, feel or be oneself again; **breathe easy or easier,** breathe more freely, breathe again; **heave a sigh of relief,** draw a long or deep breath.

.9 ADJS **relieving, easing, alleviative,** alleviating, **mitigative,** mitigating, **palliative,** lenitive, assuasive, softening, subduing, soothing, demulcent, emollient, balmy, balsamic; **remedial** 687.39; dulling, deadening, numbing, benumbing, anesthetic, analgesic, anodyne, pain-killing; cathartic, purgative, cleansing.

887. COMFORT

.1 NOUNS **comfort, ease, well-being;** contentment 868; clover, velvet [slang], bed of roses; life of ease 728.1; solid comfort.

.2 **comfortableness, easiness; restfulness,** reposefulness, peace, peacefulness; softness, cushiness [informal], cushioniness; **coziness, snugness;** friendliness, warmness; **homelikeness,** homeyness [informal], homeliness; **commodiousness,** roominess, convenience; luxuriousness 904.5; hospitality 925.

.3 **creature comforts, comforts, conveniences,** excellent accommodations, amenities, good things of life, cakes and ale, egg in one's beer [slang], all the comforts of home, all the heart can desire.

.4 **consolation, solace,** solacement, easement, heart's-ease, **encouragement,** aid and comfort, **assurance, reassurance,** support, **comfort,** crumb or shred of comfort, "kind words and comfortable" [William Cowper]; condolence 946, sympathy; **relief** 886.

.5 **comforter,** consoler, solacer, encourager, paraclete.

.6 VERBS **comfort, console, solace,** give comfort, bear up; condole with, sympathize with; ease, **put** or **set at ease;** relieve 886.5; **assure, reassure; encourage, hearten,** pat on the back; **cheer** 870.7; wipe away the tears, "rejoice with them that do rejoice, and weep with them that weep" [Bible].

.7 **be comforted, take comfort, take heart,** pull oneself together, pluck up one's spirits.

.8 **be at ease,** be or feel easy, stand easy [Brit]; **make oneself comfortable,** make oneself at home, feel at home; **relax,** be relaxed; live a life of ease 728.10.

.9 **snug,** snug down or up; tuck in.

.10 **snuggle, nestle, cuddle,** croodle [Brit dial], cuddle up, curl up; bundle; snuggle up to, snug up or together [archaic].

.11 ADJS **comfortable,** comfy [informal]; contented 868.7–10; **easy,** easeful; **restful,** reposeful, peaceful, **relaxing;** soft, cushioned, cushy [informal], cushiony; **cozy, snug,** snug as a bug in a rug; friendly, warm; **homelike,** homey [informal],

homely, lived-in; **commodious,** roomy, convenient; luxurious 904.21.

.12 **at ease, at one's ease,** easy, relaxed, at rest; **at home,** in one's element.

.13 **comforting, consoling,** consolatory, of good comfort; condoling, condolent, condolatory, sympathetic; **assuring, reassuring,** supportive; **encouraging, heartening; cheering** 870.16; relieving 886.9; hospitable 925.11.

.14 ADVS **comfortably, easily,** with ease; **restfully,** reposefully, peacefully; **cozily, snugly; commodiously,** roomily, conveniently; luxuriously, voluptuously.

.15 **in comfort,** in ease, **in clover, on** or **in velvet** [slang], on a bed of roses.

.16 **comfortingly, consolingly,** assuringly, reassuringly, supportively, encouragingly, hearteningly; hospitably.

888. HOPE

.1 NOUNS **hope, hopefulness,** hoping, **hopes,** fond or fervent hope, good hope, good cheer; aspiration, **desire** 634; **expectation** 539; sanguine expectation, happy or cheerful expectation; **trust, confidence, faith,** assured faith, **reliance,** dependence; conviction, assurance, security, well-grounded hope; assumption, presumption; **promise,** prospect, prospects, good or bright or fair prospect, good or hopeful prognosis; great expectations, high hopes; hoping against hope, prayerful hope; doomed hope or hopes.

.2 "the second soul of the unhappy" [Goethe], "the dream of those that wake" [Matthew Prior], "the thing with feathers that perches in the soul" [Emily Dickinson], "the worst of all evils, because it prolongs the torments of man" [Nietzsche].

.3 **optimism,** optimisticalness, Pollyannaism, cheerful or bright or rosy outlook; **cheerfulness** 870; bright side, silver lining; "the noble temptation to see too much in everything" [Chesterton], "the mania of maintaining that everything is well when we are wretched" [Voltaire]; philosophical optimism, Leibnizian optimism, utopianism, perfectionism, perfectibilism; millenarianism, chiliasm, millennialism.

.4 **ray of hope,** gleam or glimmer of hope; faint hope.

.5 **airy hope,** unreal hope, dream, golden dream, pipe dream [informal], bubble, chimera, fool's paradise, quixotic ideal, utopia 535.11.

.6 **optimist,** hoper, Pollyanna [Eleanor Porter], ray of sunshine [slang], irrepressible optimist; "a proponent of the doctrine that black is white" [Ambrose Bierce], "one who makes the best of it when he gets the worst of it" [anon], "one who makes the most of all that comes and the least of all that goes" [Sara Teasdale], Leibnizian optimist, philosophical optimist, utopian, perfectionist, perfectibilist, perfectibilitarian; millenarian, chiliast, millennialist, millennian; aspirer, aspirant, hopeful [informal].

.7 VERBS **hope**, be or live in hopes, entertain or harbor the hope, cling to the hope, cherish or foster or nurture the hope; **expect** 539.5; **trust**, confide, presume, feel confident, rest assured; pin one's hope upon, put one's trust in, hope in, rely on, count on, lean upon, bank on; hope for, **aspire to, desire** 634.14–16; **hope against hope**, hope and pray, hope to God [informal].

.8 **be hopeful, get one's hopes up,** keep one's spirits up, never say die, take heart, be of good hope, be of good cheer, keep hoping, keep hope alive; **hope for the best**, knock on wood, keep one's fingers crossed, allow oneself to hope; catch at straws.

.9 **be optimistic, look on the bright side, look through rose-colored glasses,** voir en couleur de rose [Fr], think positively or affirmatively, be upbeat [informal], think the best of, **make the best of it,** say that all is for the best, put a good or bold face upon, put the best face upon; count one's chickens before they are hatched, count one's bridges before they are crossed.

.10 **give hope, raise hope,** yield or afford hope, hold out hope, justify hope, inspire hope, **raise one's hopes,** raise expectations, **lead one to expect; cheer** 870.7; inspire, inspirit; **assure, reassure,** support; **promise,** hold out promise, augur well, bid fair or well, make fair promise, have good prospects.

.11 ADJS **hopeful, hoping, in hopes,** full of hope, in good heart, of good hope, of good cheer; **aspiring** 634.28; **expectant** 539.11; **sanguine,** fond; **confident,** assured; undespairing.

.12 **optimistic,** upbeat [informal], bright, sunny; **cheerful** 870.11–15; **rosy,** roseate, rose-colored, couleur de rose [Fr]; Leibnizian, utopian 535.23, perfectionist, perfectibilitarian, millenarian, chiliastic, millennialistic.

.13 **promising,** of promise, full of promise, bright with promise, pregnant of good, **favorable,** looking up; **auspicious, propitious** 544.18; inspiring, inspiriting, **encouraging,** cheering, reassuring, supportive.

.14 ADVS **hopefully,** hopingly; **expectantly** 539.15; **optimistically; cheerfully** 870.17; sanguinely, fondly; confidently.

889. HOPELESSNESS

.1 NOUNS **hopelessness,** unhopefulness, no hope, not a prayer [informal], small hope, bleak outlook or prospect or prognosis, blank future; inexpectation 540; futility 669.2; impossibility 510.

.2 **despair, desperation,** desperateness; no way [informal], no way out, no exit, despondency 872.3; disconsolateness 872.12; forlornness; cave of despair, cave of Trophonius; acedia, sloth; apathy 856.4.

.3 **irreclaimability, irretrievability,** irredeemability, irrecoverableness, unsalvageability, unsalvability; incorrigibility, irreformability; irrevocability, **irreversibility; irreparability, incurability,** irremediableness, curelessness, remedilessness, immedicableness; unrelievability, unmitigability.

.4 **forlorn hope,** vain expectation, doomed or foredoomed hope, counsel of perfection.

.5 **dashed hopes,** blighted hope, hope deferred; disappointment 541.

.6 **pessimism, cynicism,** malism, nihilism; uncheerfulness 872.2; **gloominess,** dismalness, gloomy outlook; negativism; defeatism; retreatism; "the name that men of weak nerve give to wisdom" [Bernard De Voto].

.7 **pessimist, cynic,** malist, nihilist; killjoy 872.14, calamity howler [informal], worrywart [slang], seek-sorrow, Job's comforter, prophet of doom, Cassandra, Eeyore; negativist; defeatist; retreatist; "one who is not happy except when he is miserable" [anon], "a man who feels bad when he feels good for fear he'll feel worse when he feels better" [George Burns], "one who is always building dungeons in the air" [John Galsworthy], "a man who thinks everybody as nasty as himself, and hates them for it" [G. B. Shaw].

.8 **hopeless case; goner** or gone goose or gosling or dead duck [all slang]; terminal case.

.9 VERBS **be hopeless,** have not a hope or prayer, look bleak or dark; **be pessimistic, look on the dark side,** be or think downbeat [informal], think negatively, think or make the worst of, put the worst face upon; "fancy clouds where no clouds be" [Thomas Hood].

.10 **despair,** despair of, **despond** 872.16, falter, lose hope, **lose heart, abandon hope,** give up hope, **give up,** give up all hope *or* expectation, give way, fall *or* sink into despair, give oneself up *or* yield to despair, turn one's face to the wall.

.11 **shatter one's hopes,** dash *or* crush *or* blight one's hope, dash the cup from one's lips, disappoint 541.2, drive to despair *or* desperation.

.12 ADJS **hopeless,** unhopeful, without hope, affording no hope, bleak, grim, dismal, cheerless, comfortless; **desperate, despairing, in despair;** despondent 872.22; disconsolate 872.28; forlorn; apathetic 856.13.

.13 futile, vain 669.13; **doomed, foredoomed.**

.14 **impossible,** out of the question, not to be thought of, no go [informal].

.15 **past hope, beyond recall,** past praying for; **irretrievable, irrecoverable, irreclaimable,** irredeemable, unsalvageable, unsalvable; incorrigible, irreformable; **irrevocable, irreversible; irremediable, irreparable,** inoperable, **incurable,** cureless, remediless, immedicable, beyond remedy, terminal; unrelievable, unmitigable; **ruined,** undone; lost, gone.

.16 **pessimistic,** pessimist, downbeat [informal], **cynical,** nihilistic; uncheerful 872.21; **gloomy,** dismal; negative, negativistic; defeatist; Cassandran *or* Cassandrian, Cassandra-like.

.17 ADVS **hopelessly, desperately,** forlornly; impossibly.

.18 **irreclaimably, irretrievably, irrecoverably,** irredeemably, unsalvageably, unsalvably; irrevocably, **irreversibly; irremediably, incurably, irreparably.**

890. ANXIETY

(troubled thought)

.1 NOUNS **anxiety, anxiousness; apprehension, apprehensiveness,** misgiving, **foreboding, forebodingness,** suspense, strain, tension, nervous strain *or* tension; **dread, fear** 891; **concern, concernment, anxious concern, solicitude,** zeal 635.2; **care,** cankerworm of care; **distress,** trouble, vexation; **uneasiness, perturbation, disturbance,** upset, **agitation, disquiet,** disquietude, inquietude, unquietness; **nervousness** 859; malaise, angst 866.1; pucker *or* stew *or* all-overs [all informal], pins and needles; overanxiety; anxious seat *or*

bench; anxiety neurosis 690.19, anxiety hysteria 690.19.

.2 **worry, worriment** [informal], **worriedness; worries,** worries and cares; **worrying, fretting;** harassment, torment.

.3 VERBS **concern,** give concern, **trouble, bother, distress, disturb, upset,** frazzle, **disquiet, agitate;** rob one of ease *or* sleep *or* rest, keep one on edge *or* on tenterhooks *or* on pins and needles.

.4 (make anxious) **worry, vex,** fret, **harass,** harry, **torment,** dog, hound, plague, persecute, haunt, beset.

.5 (feel anxious) **worry,** worry oneself, worry one's head about, worry oneself sick, be a prey to anxiety; **fret, fuss, chafe,** stew *or* take on [both informal], fret and fume; bite one's nails.

.6 ADJS **anxious, concerned, apprehensive,** foreboding, misgiving, suspenseful, strained, tense; **fearful** 891.31,32; **solicitous,** zealous 635.9,10; **troubled, bothered; uneasy, perturbed, disturbed, disquieted, agitated; nervous** 859.10–12; **on pins and needles,** on tenterhooks, on the anxious seat *or* bench; anxioused up [dial], all hot and bothered [slang]; all-overish *or* in a pucker *or* in a stew [all informal]; **overanxious, overapprehensive.**

.7 **worried, vexed,** fretted; **harassed,** harried, tormented, dogged, hounded, persecuted, haunted, beset, plagued; worried sick, worried to a frazzle, worried stiff [slang].

.8 **careworn,** heavy-laden.

.9 **troublesome, bothersome, distressing,** distressful, **disturbing, upsetting, disquieting; worrisome,** worrying; fretting, chafing; **harassing,** tormenting, plaguing; **annoying** 864.22.

.10 ADVS **anxiously, concernedly, apprehensively,** misgivingly, **uneasily;** worriedly; solicitously, zealously 635.14,15.

891. FEAR, FRIGHTENINGNESS

.1 NOUNS **fear, fright,** affright, phob(o)–; **scare, alarm, consternation, dismay; dread,** unholy dread, **awe; terror, horror,** horrification, mortal *or* abject fear; **phobia;** funk *or* blue funk [both informal]; **panic,** panic fear *or* terror; stampede; **cowardice** 892.

.2 **frighteningness, frightfulness, awfulness, scariness,** fearfulness, fearsomeness, alarmingness, dismayingness, disquietingness, startlingness, disconcertingness, terribleness, **dreadfulness,** horribleness, hideousness, appallingness, direness, **ghastliness,** grimness, grisliness, **gruesomeness,** ghoulishness; **creepiness, spookiness,** eeriness, weirdness, uncanniness.

.3 **fearfulness,** afraidness; **timidity, timorousness, shyness;** shrinkingness, bashfulness, diffidence, stage fright, mike fright [informal]; skittishness, startlishness, jumpiness.

.4 **apprehension,** apprehensiveness, **misgiving, qualm,** qualmishness, all-overs [informal]; **anxiety** 890; doubt 503.2; foreboding 544.

.5 **trepidation,** trepidity, perturbation, **fear and trembling; quaking, agitation** 857.3,4; **uneasiness, disquiet,** disquietude, inquietude; nervousness 859; palpitation, heartquake; shivers or cold shivers [both informal], creeps or cold creeps [both informal], chills of fear or terror, icy fingers or icy clutch of dread, jimjams [slang]; horripilation, gooseflesh, goose bumps [informal]; sweat, cold sweat; thrill of fear, spasm or quiver of terror; sinking stomach.

.6 **frightening, intimidation,** bullying, browbeating, cowing, bulldozing [informal], hectoring; **demoralization,** psychological warfare, war of nerves.

.7 **terrorization,** horrification, scaremongering; **terrorism,** terror or terroristic tactics, *Schrecklichkeit* [Ger], rule by terror, reign of terror.

.8 **alarmist,** scaremonger; **terrorist,** bomber, assassin.

.9 **frightener, scarer;** scarebabe, **bogey,** bogey man, **bugaboo,** bugbear; hobgoblin; **scarecrow; horror, terror,** holy terror; **ogre,** ogress, **monster,** vampire, werewolf, ghoul, bête noire, fee-faw-fum; incubus, succubus, nightmare; **ghost,** specter, phantom, revenant; Frankenstein, Dracula, Wolf-man; mythical monsters 85.20.

.10 (fear of people, etc.) androphobia (men), gynephobia (women), parthenophobia (young girls), pedophobia (children); tyrannophobia (tyrants), hagiophobia (saints), hierophobia (priests), papaphobia (the Pope), anthropophobia (people), agoraphobia or demophobia (crowds), ochlophobia (mobs), harpaxophobia (robbers); xenophobia (foreigners), Anglophobia (English), Francophobia or Gallophobia (French), Germanophobia or Teutonophobia (Germans), gringophobia (gringos), Japanophobia (Japanese), Judeophobia (Jews), Negrophobia (Negroes), Russophobia (Russians), Sinophobia (Chinese); theophobia (God), Satanophobia (Satan), demonophobia

(demons), phasmophobia (ghosts), pneumatophobia (spirits).

.11 (fear of animals) ailurophobia (cats), cynophobia (dogs), hippophobia (horses), musophobia (mice), taurophobia (bulls), zoophobia (animals); batrachophobia or herpetophobia (reptiles), ophiciophobia or ophiophobia or snakephobia (snakes); ornithophobia (birds); ichthyophobia (fish); vermiphobia or helminthophobia (worms); acarophobia (mites), apiphobia (bees), arachnephobia (spiders), entomophobia (insects), pediculophobia (lice); bacillophobia or microbiophobia (microbes), bacteriophobia (bacteria), spermophobia or spermatophobia (germs); teratophobia (monsters).

.12 (fear of things) anthophobia (flowers), aulophobia (flutes), ballistophobia (bullets), belonephobia (needles), crystallophobia (crystals), eisoptrophobia (mirrors), enetophobia (pins); koniophobia or amathophobia (dust), linonophobia (string), mysophobia (dirt), necrophobia (corpses); hydrophobia (water); metallophobia (metal), aurophobia (gold), chrometophobia (money); mechanophobia (machinery), ochophobia (vehicles), telephonophobia (telephone); chaetophobia or trichophobia (hair), dermatosiophobia (skin), doraphobia (fur), odontophobia (teeth), ommetaphobia (eyes), pogonophobia (beards), pteronophobia (feathers), rectophobia (rectum); blennophobia or myxophobia (slime), coprophobia (feces), hemaphobia or hematophobia or hemophobia (blood), proteinphobia (protein), urophobia (urine); cibophobia or sitophobia or sitiophobia (food), potophobia (drink), pharmacophobia (drugs), toxiphobia or toxophobia or toxicophobia (poison); microphobia (small things), neophobia (new things), monophobia (one thing), panphobia or pantophobia (everything).

.13 (fear of natural phenomena) cometophobia (comets), heliophobia (sun), siderophobia (stars); barophobia (gravity); astraphobia or astrapophobia (lightning), brontophobia or tonitrophobia or keraunophobia (thunder), ancraophobia (wind), aerophobia (draft), homichlophobia (fog); nephophobia (clouds); chionophobia (snow); antlophobia (floods), cymophobia (waves); cheimaphobia or cheimatophobia (cold), thermophobia (heat), pyrophobia (fire); photophobia (light), selaphobia (light flashes), electrophobia (electricity); eosophobia (dawn), achluophobia or scotophobia (darkness), sciophobia (shadows), nyctophobia (night); acousticophobia (sound); bromidrosiphobia (body odor); cryophobia (ice, frost).

.14 (fear of diseases) acarophobia (the itch), albuminurophobia (albumin in the urine), anemophobia (anemia), cancerphobia or canceriophobia or carcinophobia (cancer), cardiophobia (heart disease), cholerophobia (cholera), cnidophobia (insect stings), coprostasophobia (constipation), dermatopathophobia (skin disease), diabetophobia (diabetes), diplopiaphobia (double vision), emetophobia (vomiting), febriphobia (fever), helminthophobia (worms), hormephobia (shock), hydrophobophobia (rabies), lyssophobia or maniaphobia (insanity), meningitophobia (meningitis), nephophobia or pathophobia (disease), parasitophobia (parasites), pellagraphobia (pellagra), scabiophobia (scabies), syphilophobia (syphilis), traumatophobia (wound, injury), trichinophobia (trichinosis), trichopathophobia (hair disease), tuberculophobia or phthisiophobia (tuberculosis), venereophobia (venereal disease).

.15 (fear of situations) acerophobia or acerbophobia (sourness), acrophobia (sharpness), anginophobia (narrowness), asthenophobia (weakness), bathophobia (depth), hygrophobia (dampness); algophobia (pain), dikephobia (justice), eleutherophobia (freedom), hedonophobia (pleasure), kopophobia (fatigue), peniaphobia (poverty), phobophobia (fear), poinephobia (punishment), zelophobia (jealousy); chromophobia (color), chronophobia (duration), dromophobia or kinetophobia (motion), symmetrophobia (symmetry), tachophobia (speed), tredecaphobia or triskaidekaphobia (13); autophobia or monophobia or ermitophobia (being alone), atephobia (ruin), atelophobia (imperfection), hypegiaphobia (responsibility), kakorraphiaphobia (failure); erotophobia or genophobia (sex), gametophobia (marriage), patroiophobia (heredity), gymnophobia or nudophobia (nudity); ideophobia (ideas), logophobia (words), onomatophobia (names), philosophobia (philosophy), politicophobia (politics), rhabdophobia (magic); apeirophobia (infinity), kenophobia (void).

.16 (fear of places) agoraphobia (open places), claustrophobia (enclosed places), acrophobia or altophobia or batophobia or hypsophobia (high places); cremnophobia (precipices), limnophobia (lakes), potamophobia (rivers), thalassophobia (sea); ecclesiophobia (church), ecophobia or oecophobia or oikophobia (home); uranophobia or ouranophobia (heaven), hadephobia or stygiophobia (hell); topophobia (certain places).

.17 (fear of activities) agyrophobia (crossing a street), gephyrophobia (crossing a bridge), batophobia (passing high buildings), hodophobia (travel); clinophobia (going to bed), coitophobia (coitus), ergophobia (work), graphophobia (writing), hypnophobia (sleep), kleptophobia (stealing), lalophobia or laliophobia or glossophobia or phonophobia (speech), phagophobia (swallowing), rypophobia (soiling), stasophobia (standing), thaasophobia (being idle); erythrophobia (blushing), geumatophobia (taste), haptophobia or haphophobia or thixophobia (touch), olfactophobia or osmophobia or ophresiophobia (smell), phronemophobia (thinking), tremophobia (trembling); katagelophobia (ridicule), mastigophobia (beating), pnigophobia or pnigerophobia (smothering), trypanophobia or vaccinophobia (inocculation); tocophobia (childbirth), thanatophobia (death); musicophobia (music); hamartophobia or peccatiphobia (sin).

.18 VERBS fear, be afraid; apprehend, have qualms, misgive, eye askance; dread, stand in dread or awe of, be in mortal dread of, stand aghast; be on pins and needles, sit upon thorns; have one's heart in one's mouth.

.19 take fright, take alarm, push the panic button [informal]; funk or go into a funk [both informal], get wind up [Brit slang]; lose courage 892.8; pale, grow or turn pale, change or turn color; look as if one had seen a ghost; freeze, be paralyzed with fear; shit in one's pants [slang].

.20 start, startle, jump, jump out of one's skin, jump a mile, leap like a startled gazelle; shy, fight shy, start aside, boggle, jib; panic, stampede, skedaddle [informal].

.21 flinch, shrink, draw back, recoil, funk [informal], quail, cringe, wince, blench, blink.

.22 tremble, shake, quake, shiver, quiver, quaver; tremble or quake in one's boots or shoes, tremble like an aspen leaf, quiver like a rabbit, shake all over.

.23 **frighten,** fright, affright; **funk** [informal]; **scare,** spook [slang]; give one a fright *or* scare *or* turn; **alarm,** disquiet, raise apprehensions; shake, stagger; **startle** 540.8; **unnerve, unman,** unstring; give one gooseflesh, horripilate, make one's flesh creep, chill one's spine, make one's nerves tingle, make one's hair stand on end, make one's blood run cold, freeze *or* curdle the blood, make one's teeth chatter, make one tremble, take one's breath away, make one shit one's pants [slang].

.24 **put in fear,** put the fear of God into, **throw a scare into** [slang], scare the life out of, scare the pants off of, scare hell out of *or* scare the shit out of [both slang]; **panic,** stampede, send scuttling, throw blind fear into.

.25 **terrify, awe,** strike terror into; **horrify, appall, shock,** make one's flesh creep; **frighten out of one's wits** *or* **senses,** frighten from one's propriety, **scare stiff** *or* **shitless** [slang], scare to death; strike dumb, **stun, stupefy, paralyze, petrify,** freeze.

.26 **daunt, deter,** shake, stop; **discourage, dishearten;** faze [informal]; **awe, overawe.**

.27 **dismay, disconcert, appall, astound, confound, abash, discomfit, put out, take aback** [informal].

.28 **intimidate, cow, browbeat, bulldoze** [informal], bludgeon, dragoon; **bully, hector, harass,** huff; bluster, bluster out of *or* into; **terrorize,** put in bodily fear, use terror *or* terroristic tactics, pursue a policy of *Schrecklichkeit,* systematically terrorize; **threaten** 973.2; **demoralize.**

.29 **frighten off, scare away,** bluff off, put to flight.

.30 ADJS **afraid, scared,** spooked [slang]; feared *or* afeared [both dial]; **fearstricken, fear-struck;** haunted with fear; –phobic.

.31 **fearful,** fearing, fearsome, **in fear; cowardly** 892.10; **timorous, timid, shy,** rabbity *or* mousy [both informal]; **shrinking, bashful, diffident;** scary; **skittish, skittery** [dial], startlish, jumpy, goosy [slang], trigger-happy [informal]; **tremulous,** trembling, trepidant, shaky, shivery; **nervous** 859.10.

.32 **apprehensive, misgiving,** all-overish [informal], **qualmish, qualmy;** anxious 890.6.

.33 **frightened,** affrighted, in a fright, in a funk *or* blue funk [informal]; **alarmed, disquieted;** consternated, **dismayed,** daunted; **startled** 540.13; more frightened than hurt.

.34 **terrified, terror-stricken, terror-struck,** terror-smitten, terror-shaken, terror-troubled, terror-riven, terror-ridden, terror-driven, terror-crazed, terror-haunted; **awestricken, awestruck; horrified,** horror-stricken, horror-struck; **appalled, astounded, aghast;** frightened out of one's wits, **scared to death, scared stiff** *or* **shitless** [slang]; unnerved, unstrung, unmanned, undone, **cowed,** awed, **intimidated; stunned, petrified, stupefied,** paralyzed, frozen; white as a sheet, pale as death *or* a ghost, deadly pale, ashen, blanched, pallid, gray with fear.

.35 **panicky,** panic-prone, panicked, in a panic, panic-stricken, panic-struck, out of one's mind with fear, prey to blind fear.

.36 **frightening, frightful; fearful,** fearsome, fear-inspiring; **scary** [informal], scaring, chilling; **alarming, startling,** disquieting, dismaying, disconcerting; **daunting,** deterring, **deterrent,** discouraging, disheartening, fazing, awing, overawing.

.37 **terrifying,** terrorful, terror-striking, terror-inspiring, terror-bringing, terror-giving, terror-breeding, terror-breathing, terror-bearing, terror-fraught; **bloodcurdling, hair-raising** [informal]; petrifying, paralyzing, stunning, stupefying; **terror, terroristic.**

.38 **terrible,** terrific, tremendous, din(o)– *or* dein(o)–; **horrid, horrible, horrifying,** horrific, horrendous, *schrecklich* [Ger]; **dreadful, dread,** dreaded; **awful;** awesome, awe-inspiring; **shocking, appalling,** astounding; **dire,** direful, fell; formidable, redoubtable; **hideous, ghastly,** morbid, grim, grisly, gruesome, ghoulish, macabre.

.39 **creepy, spooky, eerie, weird, uncanny,** unco *or* uncolike [both Scot].

.40 ADVS **fearfully, apprehensively, diffidently,** for fear of; **timorously, timidly, shyly,** mousily [informal], bashfully, shrinkingly; **tremulously, tremblingly,** quakingly, **with** *or* **in fear and trembling;** with heart in mouth, with bated breath.

.41 **in fear, in terror,** in awe, in alarm, in consternation; in mortal fear, in fear of one's life.

.42 **frightfully, fearfully; alarmingly, startlingly,** disquietingly, dismayingly, disconcertingly; **shockingly, appallingly,** astoundingly; **terribly,** terrifically, tremendously; **dreadfully, awfully; horridly, horribly,** horrifyingly, horrifically, horrendously.

892. COWARDICE

.1 NOUNS cowardice, cowardliness; fear 891; **faintheartedness**, faintheart, weakheartedness, chickenheartedness, henheartedness, pigeonheartedness; **yellowness**, white-liveredness or lily-liveredness or chicken-liveredness [all informal], weakkneedness; weakness, softness; unmanliness, unmanfulness; timidness, **timidity**, timorousness, milksoppiness, milksoppishness, milksopism.

.2 uncourageousness, unvaliantness, unvalorousness, unheroicness, ungallantness, unintrepidness; **plucklessness, spunklessness** or gritlessness [both informal], gutlessness [slang], spiritlessness, heartlessness.

.3 **dastardliness**, pusillanimousness, **pusillanimity**, poltroonery, poltroonishness, poltroonism, baseness, **cravenness**; desertion under fire, skedaddling [informal].

.4 **cold feet** [slang], weak knees, **faint heart**, chicken heart, **yellow streak** [slang], white feather.

.5 **coward**, jellyfish, invertebrate, **weakling**, weak sister [informal], milksop, Milquetoast, mouse, **sissy**, baby, **big baby**, **chicken** [slang]; white liver or lily liver or chicken liver [all informal], white feather; fraid-cat or fraidy-cat or scaredy-cat [all slang]; funk or funker [both informal]; "one who in a perilous emergency thinks with his legs" [Ambrose Bierce]; –phobe.

.6 **dastard, craven, poltroon**, recreant, caitiff, arrant coward; **sneak**.

.7 VERBS **dare not; have a yellow streak** [slang], **have cold feet** [slang], be unable to say 'boo' to a goose.

.8 **lose one's nerve**, lose courage, **get cold feet** [slang], **show the white feather**; falter, boggle, funk [informal], **chicken** [slang]; back out, funk out [informal], **chicken out** [slang]; desert under fire, skedaddle [informal], **run scared** [slang], scuttle.

.9 **cower, quail, cringe, crouch, skulk, sneak**, slink.

.10 ADJS **cowardly**, coward; afraid, fearful 891.30–35; timid, timorous, overtimorous, overtimid, rabbity or mousy [both informal]; **fainthearted**, weakhearted, chickenhearted, henhearted, pigeonhearted; white-livered or lily-livered or chicken-livered or milk-livered [all informal]; **yellow** or with a yellow streak [both informal]; **weak-kneed, chicken** [slang], afraid of one's shadow; weak, soft; unmanly, un-

manful, sissy, sissified; milksoppy, milksoppish; panicky, panic-prone, funking or funky [both informal]; daunted, dismayed, unmanned, cowed, intimidated.

.11 **uncourageous, unvaliant, unvalorous, unheroic**, ungallant, **unintrepid, undaring**, unable to say 'boo' to a goose; unsoldierlike, unsoldierly; **pluckless, spunkless** or gritless [both informal], **gutless** [slang], spiritless, heartless.

.12 **dastardly**, dastard; **poltroonish**, poltroon; **pusillanimous**, base, craven, recreant, caitiff; dunghill, dunghilly.

.13 **cowering, quailing, cringing; skulking, sneaking, slinking**, sneaky, slinky.

.14 ADVS **cravenly**, poltroonishly, like a coward, **uncourageously, unvaliantly, unvalorously, unheroically**, ungallantly, unintrepidly, undaringly; plucklessly, spunklessly or gritlessly [both informal], spiritlessly, heartlessly; faintheartedly, weakheartedly, chickenheartedly.

893. COURAGE

.1 NOUNS **courage, courageousness; bravery**, braveness, **boldness, valor**, valorousness, valiance, valiancy, **gallantry**, conspicuous gallantry, gallantry under fire, gallantness, **intrepidity**, intrepidness, **prowess**, virtue; doughtiness, stalwartness, stoutness, stoutheartedness, lionheartedness, greatheartedness; **heroism**, heroicalness; chivalry, chivalrousness, knightliness; military or martial spirit, soldierly quality or virtues; **manliness**, manfulness, **manhood**; Dutch courage [informal], pot-valor.

.2 "fear that has said its prayers" [Dorothy Bernard], "fear holding on a minute longer" [George Patton], "taking hard knocks like a man when occasion calls" [Plautus], "doing without witnesses that which we would be capable of doing before everyone" [La Rochefoucauld].

.3 **fearlessness**, dauntlessness, **undauntedness, unfearfulness**, unfearingness, unafraidness, **unapprehensiveness; confidence** 513.5; untimidness, untimorousness, unshrinkingness, unshyness, unbashfulness.

.4 **fortitude, hardihood**, hardiness; **pluckiness; spunkiness** or grittiness or nerviness [all informal], mettlesomeness; **gameness**, gaminess; **resolution** 624, resoluteness, tenaciousness, tenacity, pertinaciousness, pertinacity, bulldog courage.

.5 **nerve**, *chutzpah* [Yid], **spunk** [informal], **pluck, grit, stamina**, toughness, **backbone** [informal], pith, **mettle**, bottom; **guts** or gutsiness or guttiness [all slang], **intestinal fortitude** [informal]; heart, spirit; stout heart, heart of oak.

.6 **daring,** derring-do; **bravado, bravura; audacity,** audaciousness, overboldness, balls [slang]; **adventurousness,** venturousness, **venturesomeness,** adventuresomeness, enterprise; foolhardiness 894.3.

.7 **exploit, feat, deed, enterprise, achievement, adventure,** gest, **bold stroke,** heroic act or deed; aristeia.

.8 (brave person) **hero, heroine;** brave, stalwart, gallant, valiant, man of courage or mettle, a man, valiant knight, good soldier; demigod, paladin; demigoddess; the brave; decorated hero; Hector, Achilles, Roland, David, Samson; lion, tiger, bulldog, fighting cock, gamecock; *chutzpanik* [Yid].

.9 **encouragement, heartening, inspiration,** inspiriting, inspiritment, emboldening, assurance, reassurance, pat or clap on the back.

.10 VERBS **dare, venture, make bold to,** make so bold as to, **have the nerve, have the guts** [slang], have the courage of one's convictions, be a man, "dare do all that may become a man" [Shakespeare], "be strong, and quit yourselves like men" [Bible]; defy 793.3.

.11 **brave, face, confront,** affront, front, look straight in the eyes, meet eyeball to eyeball [informal], meet, meet boldly; set at defiance 793.4; speak up, speak out, stand up and be counted; **face up to, stand up to,** not flinch or shrink from, bite the bullet [informal], look full in the face, put a bold face upon, show or present a bold front, **meet head-on,** face up, face the music [informal]; **brazen,** brazen out or through; beard, "beard the lion in his den" [Sir Walter Scott]; put one's head in the lion's mouth, fly into the face of danger, take the bull by the horns, march up to the cannon's mouth, bell the cat, go through fire and water, go in harm's way, run the gauntlet, take one's life in one's hands, put one's life on the line [informal].

.12 **outbrave, outdare; outface,** face down, face out; **outbrazen,** brazen out; **outlook, outstare,** stare down, stare out of countenance.

.13 **steel oneself, get up nerve,** nerve oneself, muster or summon up or gather courage, pluck up heart, screw up one's nerve or courage, "screw your courage to the stick-

ing place" [Shakespeare], stiffen one's backbone [informal].

.14 **take courage, take heart,** take heart of grace; **brace up or buck up** [informal].

.15 **keep up one's courage,** bear up, **keep one's chin up** [informal], **keep a stiff upper lip** [informal], hold up one's head, take what comes; hang in or hang in there or hang tough or stick it out [all slang], stick to one's guns.

.16 **encourage, hearten, embolden, nerve,** pat or clap on the back, **assure, reassure,** bolster, support; **inspire,** inspirit; buck up or brace up [both informal]; put upon one's mettle, make a man of; cheer 870.7.

.17 ADJS **courageous, brave, bold, valiant, valorous, gallant, intrepid,** doughty, **hardy,** stalwart, stout, stouthearted, ironhearted, lionhearted, greathearted, bold-spirited, bold as a lion; **heroic,** herolike; **chivalrous,** chivalric, knightly, knightlike, soldierly, soldierlike; **manly,** manful.

.18 **plucky; spunky or gritty or nervy** [all informal], **gutsy or gutty** [both slang], tough, **resolute, game,** gamy; **spirited,** spiritful, red-blooded, mettlesome; bulldoggish, tenacious, pertinacious.

.19 **unafraid, unfearing, unfearful; unapprehensive,** undiffident; **confident** 513.21; **fearless, dauntless,** aweless, dreadless; **unfrightened,** unscared, unalarmed, unterrified; **untimid,** untimorous, unshy, unbashful.

.20 **undaunted, undismayed,** uncowed, unintimidated, unappalled, unabashed, unawed; **unflinching, unshrinking,** unquailing, uncringing, unwincing, unblenching, unblinking.

.21 **daring, audacious,** overbold; **adventurous, venturous, venturesome,** adventuresome, enterprising; foolhardy 894.9.

.22 ADVS **courageously, bravely, boldly, heroically, valiantly,** valorously, **gallantly, intrepidly,** doughtily, stoutly, hardily, stalwartly; **pluckily, spunkily** [informal], gutsily [slang], **resolutely, gamely,** tenaciously, pertinaciously, bulldoggishly, **fearlessly,** unfearingly, unfearfully; **daringly,** audaciously; chivalrously, knightly, yeomanly; like a man, like a soldier.

894. RASHNESS

.1 NOUNS **rashness, brashness,** brazen boldness, **incautiousness, overboldness, imprudence, indiscretion,** injudiciousness, **improvidence; unwariness,** unchariness; overcarelessness; **overconfidence,** oversureness, overweeningness; **impudence,** insolence 913; gall *or* brass *or* cheek [all informal], *chutzpah* [Yid]; hubris; temerity, temerariousness; heroics.

.2 **recklessness,** devil-may-careness; heedlessness, **carelessness** 534.2; **impetuousness** 630.2, impetuosity, hotheadedness; **haste** 709, **hastiness,** hurriedness, overeagerness, overzealousness, overenthusiasm; **furiousness,** desperateness, wantonness, wildness; **precipitateness,** precipitousness, precipitance, precipitancy, precipitation.

.3 **foolhardiness,** harebrainedness; **audacity,** audaciousness; *courage fou* [Fr]; forwardness, boldness, **presumption,** presumptuousness; **daring,** daredeviltry, daredevilry, fire-eating; playing with fire, flirting with death, courting disaster, stretching one's luck, going for broke [slang], brinkmanship; adventurousness 893.6.

.4 **daredevil,** devil, **madcap,** madbrain, wild man, hotspur, hellcat, rantipole, harumscarum *or* fire-eater [both informal]; **adventurer,** adventuress; brazenface.

.5 VERBS be rash, be reckless, carry too much sail, sail too near the wind, go out of one's depth, go too far, go to sea in a sieve, take a leap in the dark, buy a pig in a poke, count one's chickens before they are hatched, catch at straws, lean on a broken reed, put all one's eggs in one basket, live in a glass house; go out on a limb [informal], leave oneself wide open [slang], drop one's guard, stick one's neck out *or* ask for it [both slang].

.6 **court danger,** mock *or* defy danger, thumb one's nose at the consequences, **tempt Providence,** tweak the devil's nose, bell the cat, play a desperate game, ride for a fall; play with fire, flirt with death, stretch one's luck, go for broke [slang], march up to the cannon's mouth, put one's head in a lion's mouth, beard the lion in his den, sit on a barrel of gunpowder, sleep on a volcano, play Russian roulette.

.7 ADJS **rash, brash,** incautious, overbold, **imprudent, indiscreet,** injudicious, improvident; **unwary, unchary;** overcareless; overconfident, oversure, overweening, **impudent,** insolent, brazenfaced, brazen 913.8–10; hubristic; temerarious.

.8 **reckless,** devil-may-care; careless 534.11; **impetuous,** hotheaded; **hasty** 709.9–11, hurried, overeager, overzealous, overenthusiastic; **furious,** desperate, mad, wild, wanton, harum-scarum [informal]; precipitate, **precipitous, precipitant;**

headlong, breakneck; slapdash, slap-bang; accident-prone.

.9 **foolhardy, harebrained,** madcap, **wild,** wild-ass [slang], madbrain, madbrained; **audacious;** forward, bold, **presumptuous; daring,** daredevil, fire-eating, death-defying; adventurous 893.21.

.10 ADVS **rashly, brashly, incautiously, imprudently, indiscreetly,** injudiciously, improvidently; **unwarily,** uncharily; overconfidently, overweeningly, **impudently,** insolently, **brazenly,** hubristically, temerariously.

.11 **recklessly,** happen what may; heedlessly, **carelessly** 534.18; **impetuously,** hotheadedly; **hastily,** hurriedly, overeagerly, overzealously, overenthusiastically; **furiously,** desperately, wildly, wantonly, **madly,** like mad [informal], like crazy [slang]; **precipitately,** precipitously, precipitantly; **headlong,** headfirst, headforemost, **head over heels,** heels over head, *à corps perdu* [Fr]; slapdash, slap-bang *or* slam-bang [both informal]; helter-skelter, ramble-scramble [informal], hurry-scurry, holus-bolus.

.12 **foolhardily, daringly, audaciously,** presumptuously, harebrainedly.

895. CAUTION

(provident care)

.1 NOUNS **caution, cautiousness;** slowness to act *or* commit oneself *or* make one's move; **care, heed, solicitude; carefulness, heedfulness,** mindfulness, regardfulness, thoroughness; **gingerliness,** guardedness; uncommunicativeness 613; **tentativeness,** hesitation, unprecipitateness, slow and careful steps, deliberate stages, wait and see policy; **prudence,** prudentialness, **circumspection, discretion,** canniness [Scot], pawkiness [Brit], judiciousness; calculation, **deliberateness,** deliberation, careful consideration, prior consultation; **safeness,** safety first, no room for error; **hedge, hedging,** hedging one's bets, cutting one's losses.

.2 **wariness, chariness, cageyness** *or* **leeriness** [both slang]; **suspicion,** suspiciousness; **distrust,** distrustfulness, mistrust, mistrustfulness.

.3 **precaution,** precautiousness; **forethought, foresight,** foresightedness, forehandedness, forethoughtfulness; **providence,** provision, forearming; precautions, steps, measures, steps and measures; **safeguard,** protection 699, preventive measure; insurance.

.4 overcaution, overcautiousness, overcarefulness, overwariness.

.5 VERBS be cautious, be careful; think twice, give it a second thought; make haste slowly, take it easy [informal]; put the right foot forward, take one step at a time, pick one's steps, go step by step, feel one's ground or way; pussyfoot, tiptoe, go on tiptoe, walk on eggshells; draw in one's horns.

.6 take precautions, take steps or measures, take steps and measures; prepare or provide for or against, forearm; guard against, make sure against, make sure, "make assurance double sure" [Shakespeare]; play safe [informal], keep on the safe side; leave no stone unturned, forget or leave out nothing, overlook no possibility, leave no room for error, leave nothing to chance, consider every angle; look before one leaps; see how the land lies or the wind blows, see how the cat jumps [informal]; clear the decks, batten down the hatches, shorten sail, reef down, tie in or tuck in or take in a reef, get out a sheet-anchor, have an anchor to windward; hedge, provide a hedge, hedge one's bets, cut one's losses; take out insurance; keep something for a rainy day.

.7 beware, take care, have a care, take heed, take heed at one's peril; keep at a respectful distance, keep out of harm's way; mind, mind one's business; be on one's guard, be on the watch or lookout, be on the qui vive; look out, watch out [informal]; look sharp, keep one's eyes open, keep a weather eye open [informal], keep one's eye peeled [slang], watch one's step [slang], look about one; stop, look, and listen; not stick one's neck out [slang], not go out on a limb [informal], not expose oneself, not be too visible, lie low, stay in the background; hold one's tongue 451.5-7.

.8 ADJS cautious, careful, heedful, mindful, regardful, thorough; prudent, circumspect, slow to act or commit oneself or make one's move, canny [Scot], pawky [Brit], discreet, politic, judicious, noncommittal; unadventurous, unenterprising, undaring; gingerly; guarded, on guard, on one's guard; uncommunicative 613.8-10; tentative, hesitant, unprecipitate; deliberate; safe, on the safe side, leaving no stone unturned, forgetting or leaving out nothing, overlooking no possibility, leaving no room for error.

.9 wary, chary, cagey [slang], leery [slang], suspicious, suspecting, distrustful, mistrustful, shy.

.10 precautious, precautionary, precautional; forethoughtful, forethoughted, foresighted, foreseeing, forehanded; provident, provisional.

.11 overcautious, overcareful, overwary.

.12 ADVS cautiously, carefully, heedfully, mindfully, regardfully; prudently, circumspectly, cannily [Scot], pawkily [Brit], discreetly, judiciously; gingerly, guardedly, easy [informal], with caution, with care.

.13 warily, charily, cagily [slang]; askance, askant, suspiciously, leerily [slang], distrustfully.

.14 INTERJS careful!, be careful!, take care!, have a care!, look out!, watch out!, watch your step!, watch it!, steady!, look sharp!, easy!, take it easy!, easy does it!, go easy!

896. FASTIDIOUSNESS

.1 NOUNS fastidiousness, particularity, particularness; scrupulousness, scrupulosity; punctiliousness, punctilio; preciseness, precision; meticulousness, conscientiousness, criticalness; taste 897; sensitivity, discrimination 492, discriminatingness, discriminativeness; selectiveness, selectivity, pickiness [slang], choosiness; strictness 533.3, perfectionism, precisianism, purism; puritanism, priggishness, prudishness, censoriousness.

.2 finicalness, finickiness, finickingness, finicality; fussiness, pernicketiness or persnicketiness [both informal]; squeamishness, queasiness, pawkiness [Brit].

.3 nicety, niceness, delicacy, delicateness, daintiness, exquisiteness, fineness, refinement.

.4 overfastidiousness, overscrupulousness, overparticularity, overconscientiousness, overmeticulousness, overniceness, overnicety; overcriticalness, hypercriticism, hairsplitting; overrefinement; oversqueamishness, oversensitivity, hypersensitivity, morbid sensibility.

.5 exclusiveness, selectness, selectiveness, selectivity; cliquishness, clannishness; snobbishness, snobbery, snobbism.

.6 perfectionist, precisian, precisianist, stickler, nitpicker [slang], captious critic 494.7.

.7 fuss-budget or fusspot [both informal], fuss, fusser, fuddy-duddy [slang], granny, old woman, old maid.

.8 VERBS be hard to please, fuss, pick and choose; turn up one's nose at, look down one's nose at, disdain, scorn, spurn.

.9 ADJS fastidious, particular, scrupulous,

meticulous, conscientious, exacting, precise, punctilious; **sensitive, discriminating** 492.7, discriminative; **selective,** picky [slang], choosy, choicy [slang]; critical 969.24, "nothing if not critical" [Shakespeare]; **strict** 533.12, perfectionistic, precisianistic, puristic; puritanic(al), priggish, prudish, censorious.

.10 **finical, finicky,** finicking, finikin; **fussy,** fuss-budgety [informal]; **squeamish,** queasy, pawky [Brit], pernickety or persnickety [both informal], difficult, hard to please.

.11 **nice, dainty, delicate,** *délicat* [Fr], fine, refined, exquisite.

.12 **overfastidious, overparticular, overscrupulous, overconscientious,** overmeticulous, **overnice,** overprecise; **overcritical,** hypercritical, ultracritical, hairsplitting; overrefined; oversqueamish, oversensitive, hypersensitive, morbidly sensitive.

.13 **exclusive, selective, select,** elect; **cliquish,** clannish; **snobbish,** snobby.

.14 ADVS **fastidiously, particularly,** scrupulously, **meticulously, conscientiously,** critically, punctiliously; discriminatingly, discriminatively, selectively; **finically,** finickily, finickingly; **fussily; squeamishly,** queasily.

897. TASTE, TASTEFULNESS

.1 NOUNS **taste, good taste,** sound critical judgment, discernment or appreciation of excellence, preference for the best, *goût raffiné* [Fr]; **tastefulness,** quality, excellence, choiceness, **elegance,** grace, gracefulness, gracility, graciousness, graciosity; **refinement,** finesse, **polish, culture, cultivation,** civilizedness, refined or cultivated or civilized taste; niceness, nicety, delicacy, daintiness, subtlety, sophistication, **discrimination** 492, fastidiousness 896; acquired taste, "caviare to the general" [Shakespeare].

.2 "good sense delicately put in force" [Chévier], "the microscope of the judgment" [Rousseau], "a fine judgment in discerning art" [Horace], "the literary conscience of the soul" [Joseph Joubert], "the enemy of creativeness" [Picasso].

.3 **decorousness, decorum,** decency, properness, propriety, rightness, **seemliness,** becomingness, fittingness, fitness, appropriateness, suitability, meetness, happiness, felicity; gentility, genteelness; civility, urbanity 936.1.

.4 **restraint,** restrainedness, understatement,

unobtrusiveness, quietness, subduedness, quiet taste; simplicity 902.1.

.5 **aesthetic** or **artistic taste,** virtuosity, virtu, **expertise,** expertism, connoisseurship; dilettantism; fine art of living; epicurism, epicureanism; gastronomy, *friandise* [Fr]; aesthetics.

.6 **aesthete,** man of taste, lover of beauty.

.7 **connoisseur,** *connaisseur* [Fr], *cognoscente* [Ital]; **judge,** good judge, **critic, expert,** authority, maven [slang], arbiter, arbiter of taste, *arbiter elegantiarum* [L]; **epicure,** epicurean; **gourmet, gourmand,** *bon vivant* [Fr], good or refined palate; virtuoso; dilettante, amateur; collector.

.8 ADJS **tasteful, in good taste,** in the best taste; **excellent,** of quality, of the best; **aesthetic,** artistic, pleasing, well-chosen, choice, of choice; pure, chaste; classic(al), Attic, restrained, understated, unobtrusive, quiet, subdued, simple, unaffected 902.6,7.

.9 **elegant,** graceful, gracile, gracious; **refined, polished, cultivated,** civilized, **cultured;** nice, fine, delicate, dainty, subtle, sophisticated, **discriminating** 492.7,8, fastidious 896.9.

.10 **decorous,** decent, proper, right, **seemly, becoming,** fitting, appropriate, suitable, meet, happy, felicitous; genteel; civil, urbane 936.14.

.11 ADVS **tastefully, with taste,** in good taste, in the best taste; aesthetically, artistically; elegantly, gracefully; decorously, genteelly, decently, properly, seemly, becomingly; quietly, unobtrusively; simply 902.10.

898. VULGARITY

.1 NOUNS **vulgarity,** vulgarness, vulgarism; **inelegance** or inelegancy, **indelicacy, impropriety, indecency, indecorum,** indecorousness, unseemliness, unbecomingness, unfittingness, inappropriateness, unsuitableness, unsuitability; ungentility; **untastefulness,** tastelessness, unaestheticness, unaestheticism; low or bad or poor taste, *mauvais goût* [Fr]; vulgar taste, bourgeois taste, Babbittry, philistinism; popular taste, pop culture or pop [both slang]; campiness, camp, high or low camp; kitsch.

.2 **coarseness, grossness,** *grossièreté* [Fr], **rudeness, crudeness,** crudity, **crassness,** rawness, roughness, **earthiness;** ribaldness, ribaldry; **obscenity** 990.4; meretriciousness, **loudness** [informal], **gaudiness** 904.3.

.3 **unrefinement, uncouthness,** uncultivation, uncultivatedness, unculturedness; uncivilizedness, wildness; impoliteness, incivility, ill breeding 937.1; **barbarism,** barbarousness, barbarity, philistinism, Gothicism; **savagery,** savagism; **brutality,** brutishness, bestiality, animality; Neanderthalism, troglodytism.

.4 **boorishness, churlishness,** carlishness, **loutishness,** lubberliness, lumpishness, cloddishness, clownishness, yokelism; ruffianism, rowdyism, hooliganism; parvenuism, arrivism, upstartness.

.5 **commonness, commonplaceness,** ordinariness, homeliness; **lowness, baseness, meanness;** ignobility, plebeianism.

.6 **vulgarian,** low *or* vulgar *or* ill-bred fellow, mucker [slang], guttersnipe [informal], *épicier* [Fr]; Babbitt, Philistine, bourgeois; *parvenu, arriviste, nouveau riche* [all Fr], upstart; bounder [informal], cad, **boor,** churl, clown, **lout,** looby, peasant, groundling, yokel; rough, **ruffian,** roughneck [slang], **rowdy,** hooligan; vulgarist, ribald.

.7 **barbarian, savage,** Goth, animal, brute; Neanderthal, troglodyte.

.8 vulgarization, coarsening; popularization; *haute vulgarisation* [Fr].

.9 VERBS vulgarize, coarsen; popularize.

.10 ADJS **vulgar, inelegant, indelicate, indecorous, indecent, improper, unseemly,** unbeseeming, unbecoming, unfitting, inappropriate, unsuitable, **ungenteel,** undignified; **untasteful,** tasteless, in bad *or* poor taste, chintzy; **offensive,** offensive to gentle ears.

.11 **coarse, gross, rude, crude, crass,** raw, rough, **earthy;** ribald; **obscene** 990.5–9; meretricious, **loud** [informal], **gaudy** 904.20.

.12 **unrefined, unpolished, uncouth,** unkempt, uncombed, unlicked; **uncultivated, uncultured; uncivilized,** noncivilized; impolite, uncivil, ill-bred 937.4–6; **wild,** untamed, agrio–; **barbarous,** barbaric, barbarian; outlandish, Gothic; primitive; **savage, brutal,** brutish, bestial, animal; Neanderthal, troglodytic; wild-and-woolly, rough-and-ready.

.13 **boorish, churlish,** carlish, **loutish,** lubberly, lumpish, cloddish, clownish, loobyish, yokelish 182.7; rowdy, **rowdyish, ruffianly,** roughneck [slang], hooliganish, raffish, raised in a barn.

.14 **common, commonplace, ordinary;** plebeian 919.11; homely, homespun; **general, public, popular,** pop [slang]; vernacular;

Babbittish, Philistine, bourgeois; campy, high-camp, low-camp, kitschy.

.15 **low, base, mean, ignoble,** vile, scurvy, sorry, scrubby, beggarly; low-minded, base-minded.

.16 ADVS **vulgarly, uncouthly, inelegantly,** indelicately, indecorously, indecently, improperly, unseemly, untastefully, offensively; **coarsely, grossly, rudely, crudely,** crassly, roughly; ribaldly.

899. UGLINESS

.1 NOUNS **ugliness, unsightliness, unattractiveness,** uncomeliness, unhandsomeness, unbeautifulness, unprettiness, unloveliness, unaestheticness, unpleasingness 864.1; unprepossessingness, ill-favoredness, inelegance; **homeliness,** plainness; unshapeliness, shapelessness; ungracefulness, gracelessness, clumsiness, ungainliness 734.3; **uglification, uglifying, disfigurement,** defacement; dysphemism; cacophony.

.2 **hideousness,** horridness, horribleness, frightfulness, dreadfulness, terribleness, awfulness [informal]; **repulsiveness** 864.2, repugnantness, offensiveness, forbiddingness, loathsomeness; ghastliness, gruesomeness, grisliness; **deformity,** misshapenness.

.3 forbidding countenance, vinegar aspect, wry face, face that would stop a clock.

.4 **eyesore,** blot, blemish, **sight** [informal], **fright,** mess, no beauty, ugly duckling; baboon; scarecrow, gargoyle, monster, **monstrosity,** teratism; witch, bag *or* dog [both slang], **hag,** harridan.

.5 VERBS **offend** 864.9, offend the eye, offend one's aesthetic sensibilities, **look bad;** look something terrible *or* look like hell *or* look like the devil *or* look a sight *or* look a fright *or* look a mess *or* look like something the cat dragged in [all informal]; **uglify, disfigure,** deface, blot, blemish, mar, spoil; dysphemize.

.6 ADJS **ugly, unsightly, unattractive, unhandsome, unpretty, unlovely,** uncomely, **inelegant; unbeautiful,** unbeauteous, beautiless, unaesthetic, unpleasing 864.17; **homely, plain;** not much to look at, not much for looks, short on looks [informal], hard on the eyes [slang]; ugly as sin, ugly as the wrath of God, ugly as hell, homely as a mud fence, homely enough to sour milk, homely enough to stop a clock, not fit to be seen; **uglified, disfigured,** defaced, blotted, blemished, marred, spoiled; dysphemized, dysphemistic; cacophonous, cacophonic.

.7 **unprepossessing, ill-favored,** hard-favored, evil-favored, ill-featured; ill-looking, evil-looking; hard-featured, hard-visaged; grim, grim-faced, grim-visaged.

.8 **unshapely,** shapeless, **ill-shaped,** ill-made, ill-proportioned; **deformed,** misshapen, misproportioned, malformed, misbegotten; grotesque, scarecrowish, gargoylish; monstrous, teratic, cacogenic.

.9 **ungraceful,** ungraced, graceless; clumsy, **ungainly** 734.20.

.10 **inartistic,** unartistic, **unaesthetic;** unornamental, undecorative.

.11 **hideous, horrid, horrible, frightful, dreadful, terrible,** awful [informal]; **repulsive** 864.18, repelling, **repugnant,** offensive, foul, forbidding, loathsome, revolting; **ghastly,** gruesome, grisly.

.12 ADVS **uglily,** homelily, uncomelily, **unattractively, unhandsomely, unbeautifully,** unprettily.

.13 **hideously, horridly, horribly, frightfully, dreadfully, terribly,** awfully [informal]; **repulsively, repugnantly,** offensively, forbiddingly, loathsomely, revoltingly; gruesomely, ghastly.

900. BEAUTY

.1 NOUNS **beauty, beautifulness,** beauteousness, **prettiness, handsomeness, attractiveness** 863.2, **loveliness, pulchritude, charm,** grace, elegance, exquisiteness; bloom, glow; the beautiful; source of aesthetic pleasure or delight; beauty unadorned.

.2 "truth's smile when she beholds her own face in a perfect mirror" [Tagore], "the sensible image of the Infinite" [Bancroft], "God's handwriting" [Emerson], "a form of genius" [Oscar Wilde], "the power by which a woman charms a lover and terrifies a husband" [Ambrose Bierce].

.3 **comeliness, fairness,** sightliness, personableness, becomingness, pleasingness 863.1, goodliness, bonniness, agreeability, agreeableness.

.4 **good looks,** good appearance, good effect; good proportions, aesthetic proportions; **shapeliness,** good figure, good shape, *belle tournure* [Fr], nice body, lovely build, physical or bodily charm, curvaceousness, curves [informal], pneumaticness, sexy body; bodily grace, **gracefulness,** gracility; good points, **beauties, charms, delights,** perfections, good features.

.5 **daintiness, delicacy,** delicateness; **cuteness** or cunningness [both informal].

.6 **gorgeousness,** ravishingness; **gloriousness,** heavenliness, sublimity; **splendor,** splendidness, splendorousness, splendrousness, resplendence; **brilliance,** brightness, radiance, luster; **glamour** 650.1.

.7 **thing of beauty,** vision, picture [informal], poem, eyeful [informal], **sight** or **treat for sore eyes** [slang].

.8 **beauty, charmer,** *charmeuse* [Fr]; **beaut** or **dream** or **looker** or **good looker** or **stunner** or **dazzler** or **fetcher** or **peach** or **knockout** or **raving beauty** [all slang]; beauty queen, beauty contest winner, Miss America, bathing beauty, cover girl, model, pinup girl, pinup, bunny, cute or slick chick [slang], pussycat or sex kitten [both slang]; **belle,** reigning beauty, great beauty, lady fair; beau ideal, paragon; enchantress 650.3; "the face that launch'd a thousand ships" [Marlowe].

.9 (famous beauties) Venus, Venus de Milo; Aphrodite, Hebe; Adonis, Apollo, Apollo Belvedere, Hyperion, Antinoüs, Narcissus; Astarte; Balder, Freya; Helen of Troy, Cleopatra; the Graces, houri, peri.

.10 **beautification,** prettification, **adornment;** decoration 901.1; beauty treatment; facial [informal]; manicure; hairdressing.

.11 **makeup, cosmetics;** war paint or drugstore complexion [both informal]; powder, talcum, talcum powder; rouge, paint, lip rouge; nail polish; greasepaint, clown white; mascara, eye shadow; cold cream, hand cream or lotion, vanishing cream, foundation cream; foundation, base; mudpack; lipstick; eyebrow pencil; puff, powder puff; compact, vanity case.

.12 **beautician,** beautifier; hairdresser, *coiffeur, coiffeuse* [both Fr]; barber; manicurist.

.13 **beauty parlor** or **salon** or **shop,** *salon de beauté* [Fr]; barbershop.

.14 VERBS **beautify, prettify;** pretty up or gussy up or doll up [all informal], grace, **adorn; decorate** 901.8; set off, set off to advantage or good advantage, become one; glamorize.

.15 **look good;** look like a million or look fit to kill or knock dead or knock one's eyes out [all slang]; take the breath away, beggar description; shine, beam, bloom, glow.

.16 ADJS **beautiful, beauteous,** endowed with beauty, cal(o)– or call(o)– or cali– or calli–; heavy [slang]; **pretty, handsome, at-**

tractive 863.7, pulchritudinous, **lovely**, **graceful**, gracile, habro–; **elegant**, fine, exquisite, flowerlike; aesthetic, aesthetically appealing; eye-filling or easy on the eyes or not hard to look at or long on looks or looking fit to kill [all slang]; pretty as a picture, "lovely as the day" [Longfellow], "fair as is the rose in May" [Chaucer]; tall, dark, and handsome.

.17 **comely**, **fair**, **good-looking**, well-favored, **personable**, presentable, agreeable, becoming, pleasing 863.6, goodly, bonny, likely [dial], **sightly**, braw [Scot]; pleasing to the eye, lovely to behold; **shapely**, well-built, built, well-shaped, well-proportioned, well-made, well-formed, stacked, well-stacked, curvaceous, curvy [slang], pneumatic, amply endowed, built for comfort or built like a brick shithouse [both slang], buxom, callipygian, callipygous; Junoesque, statuesque, goddess-like; slender 205.16.

.18 **dainty**, **delicate**; *mignon* [Fr], **cute**, cunning [informal], cute as a bug's ear.

.19 **gorgeous**, **ravishing**; raving or **devastating** or **stunning** or killing [all slang]; **glorious**, heavenly, divine, sublime; **resplendent**, splendorous, splendrous, splendid, resplendently beautiful; **brilliant**, bright, radiant, shining, beaming, glowing, blooming, sparkling, **dazzling**; **glamorous** 650.7.

.20 **beautifying**, cosmetic; decorative 901.10.

.21 ADVS **beautifully**, beauteously, **prettily**, **handsomely**, **attractively**, **becomingly**, comelily; elegantly, exquisitely.

.22 **daintily**, **delicately**; **cutely**, cunningly [informal].

.23 **gorgeously**, **ravishingly**; ravingly or devastatingly or stunningly [all slang]; **gloriously**, divinely, sublimely; **resplendently**, splendidly, splendorously, splendrously; **brilliantly**, brightly, radiantly, glowingly, **dazzlingly**.

901. ORNAMENTATION

.1 NOUNS **ornamentation**, **ornament**; **decoration**, decor; **adornment**, **embellishment**, embroidery, elaboration; nonfunctional addition or adjunct; garnish, garnishment, garniture; trimming, trim; flourish; emblazonment, emblazonry; illumination; **color**, color patterns, color compatibility, color design, color arrangement; **arrangement**, flower arrangement, floral decoration, furniture arrangement; table setting or decoration; window dressing; **interior decoration** or decorating, room decoration.

.2 **ornateness**, **elegance**, **fanciness**, fineness, **elaborateness**; **ostentation** 904; richness, luxuriousness, luxuriance; **floweriness**, floridness, floridity; flamboyance; **overelegance**, overelaborateness, overornamentation; baroqueness, baroque, rococo, arabesque, moresque, chinoiserie.

.3 **finery**, **frippery**, gaudery, gaiety, bravery, trumpery, flashery [slang], folderol, trickery, chiffon, trappings, festoons, superfluity; **frills**, frills and furbelows, **frillery**, frilling, frilliness; foofaraw [dial], fuss [informal], froufrou; gingerbread; **tinsel**, clinquant, pinchbeck, paste; gilt, gilding.

.4 **trinket**, gewgaw, **knickknack**, knack, **gimcrack**, kickshaw, whim-wham, **bauble**, fribble, bibelot, toy, gaud; bric-a-brac.

.5 **jewelry**, bijouterie, ice [slang]; costume jewelry, glass, paste, junk jewelry [informal], scatter pins.

.6 **jewel**, bijou, **gem**, stone, precious stone, dactylio–; rhinestone; pin, brooch, stickpin, breastpin, chatelaine; ring, circle, earring, nose ring; bracelet, wristlet, wristband, armlet, anklet; chain, necklace, torque; locket; beads, chaplet, wampum; bangle; charm; fob; crown, coronet, diadem, tiara.

.7 **motif**, ornamental motif, **figure**, **detail**, form, touch, repeated figure; **pattern**, **theme**, design, ornamental theme, ornamental or decorative composition; foreground detail, background detail; **background**, setting, foil, **style**, ornamental or decorative style, national style, **period style**.

.8 VERBS **ornament**, **decorate**, **adorn**, **dress**, **trim**, **garnish**, array, **deck**, bedeck, dizen, bedizen; prettify, **beautify** 900.14; **redecorate**, refurbish, redo 694.17; **embellish**, **furbish**, embroider, enrich, grace, set off or out, paint, color, blazon, emblazon, paint in glowing colors; **dress up**; **spruce up** or gussy up or doll up or fix up [all informal], **primp up**, prink up, prank up, trick up or out, deck out, fig out; primp, prink, prank, preen; smarten, smarten up, dandify, titivate.

.9 **figure**, filigree; **spangle**, **bespangle**; bead; tinsel; jewel, bejewel, gem, diamond; ribbon, beribbon; flounce; flower, garland, wreathe; feather, plume; flag; illuminate; paint 362.13; engrave 578.10.

.10 ADJS **ornamental**, **decorative**, adorning, embellishing.

.11 **ornamented**, **adorned**, **decorated**, **embellished**, **bedecked**, decked out, tricked out, garnished, trimmed, bedizened; figured; flowered; festooned, befrilled, wreathed; spangled, bespangled, spangly; jeweled, bejeweled; beaded; studded; plumed, feathered; beribboned.

.12 **ornate, elegant, fancy,** fine, chichi, pretty-pretty; picturesque; **elaborate,** labored, high-wrought; **ostentatious** 904.18–22; **rich, luxurious,** luxuriant; **flowery, florid; flamboyant; fussy, frilly; overelegant,** overelaborate, overlabored, overworked, overwrought, busy; **baroque,** rococo, arabesque, moresque.

.13 **ornamentations**

aglet	frostwork
aigrette	garland
appliqué	graffito
arabesque	guilloche
arras	hanging
batik	helix
beading	imbrication
beaten work	inlay
bouquet	lacework
boutonniere	metalwork
bow	motif
bugle	niello
chaplet	nosegay
coronal	openwork
corsage	panache
crown	panelwork
cul-de-lampe [Fr]	parquetry
cuspidation	passementerie
cutwork	plume
damascene, damask	pom-pom
decoupage	posy
diaper, diapering	quilting
drapery	reeding
drawnwork	rosette
egret	ruffle
embroidery	scroll
epaulet	sequin
fancywork	snood
feather	spangle
festoon	spiral
figure work	stenciling
filigree	strapwork
fillet	striping
finial	tapestry
fleuron [Fr]	tassel
foliage	tooling
foliation	tracery
fretwork	vermiculation
fringe	vignette
frog	wreath

.14 **architectural ornamentations**

acanthus	cyma
apophyge	fascia
astragal	fillet
beading	finial
beak	foil
billet	fret
boss	frieze
cartouche	listel
cavetto	molding
cinquefoil	ogee
congé [Fr]	ovolo
cornice	patera
cusp	pendant

quatrefoil	terminal
reed	torus
scotia	trefoil
scrollhead	volute
splay	

902. PLAINNESS

(unaffectedness)

.1 NOUNS **plainness, simplicity, simpleness, ordinariness, commonness, commonplaceness,** homeliness, prosaicness, prosiness, matter-of-factness; **purity,** chasteness, classic *or* classical purity, Attic simplicity.

.2 **naturalness,** inartificiality; **unaffectedness, unassumingness, unpretentiousness;** directness, straightforwardness.

.3 **unadornment, unembellishment,** unornamentation; **uncomplexity,** uncomplication, uncomplicatedness, **unsophistication,** unadulteration; bareness, baldness, nakedness, nudity, undress, beauty unadorned.

.4 **inornateness, unelaborateness,** unfanciness, unfussiness; austerity, severity, starkness, Spartan simplicity.

.5 VERBS simplify, chasten, restrain, purify.

.6 ADJS **simple, plain, ordinary, nondescript, common, commonplace, prosaic,** prosy, **matter-of-fact, homely, homespun,** everyday, workday, workaday, household, garden, common- *or* garden-variety; pure, **pure and simple,** chaste, classic *or* classical, Attic.

.7 **natural,** native; **inartificial,** unartificial; **unaffected, unpretentious,** unpretending, unassuming, unfeigning, direct, straightforward, honest, candid.

.8 **unadorned, undecorated, unornamented, unembellished,** ungarnished, unfurbished, unvarnished, untrimmed; **uncomplex,** uncomplicated, **unsophisticated,** unadulterated; **undressed,** undecked, unarrayed; bare, bald, blank, naked, nude.

.9 **inornate,** unornate, **unelaborate,** unfancy, unfussy; austere, severe, stark, Spartan.

.10 ADVS **plainly, simply,** ordinarily, commonly, commonplacely, prosaically, matter-of-factly.

.11 **unaffectedly, naturally,** unpretentiously, unassumingly, directly, straightforwardly.

903. AFFECTATION

.1 NOUNS **affectation, affectedness;** pretension, **pretense, airs,** putting on airs, put-on [informal]; **show, false show,** mere show; front, false front [informal], **façade,** mere façade, **image,** public image; feigned belief, **hypocrisy** 616.6; sham

616.3; artificiality, unnaturalness, insincerity; prunes and prisms, airs and graces; stylishness, mannerism.

.2 **mannerism**, *minauderie* [Fr], **trick of behavior**, trick, **quirk**, habit, peculiarity, peculiar trait, idiosyncrasy, trademark; –ism.

.3 **posing, pose, posturing**, attitudinizing, attitudinarianism; peacockery, peacockishness.

.4 **foppery, foppishness, dandyism**, coxcombry, puppyism, conceit.

.5 **overniceness**, overpreciseness, **overrefinement, elegance**, exquisiteness, preciousness, preciosity; goody-goodyism *or* goody-goodness [both informal]; purism, formalism, formality, pedantry, precisionism, precisianism; euphuism; euphemism.

.6 **prudery, prudishness, priggishness, primness, smugness, stuffiness** [informal], oldmaidishness, **straitlacedness**, stiff-neckedness, hideboundness, narrowness, censoriousness, sanctimony, sanctimoniousness, **puritanicalness**, Quakerishness; **false modesty**, overmodesty, demureness, demurity, *mauvaise honte* [Fr].

.7 **affecter**; mannerist; **phony** [slang], **fake** *or* **fraud** [informal], **pretender**, actor, playactor [informal], performer; **paper tiger**, hollow man, straw man, man of straw; deceiver 619.

.8 **poser**, poseur, striker of poses, **posturer**, posturist, posture maker, attitudinarian, attitudinizer.

.9 **dandy, fop, coxcomb**, macaroni, gallant, dude *or* swell [both informal], sport [slang], exquisite, blood, fine gentleman, puppy, jackanapes, jack-a-dandy, fribble, clotheshorse, fashion plate; beau, Beau Brummel, spark, blade, ladies' man, ladykiller [slang], masher; man-about-town, boulevardier.

.10 **fine lady**, *grande dame, précieuse* [both Fr]; belle, toast.

.11 **prude, prig, puritan, bluenose**, goodygoody [informal], old maid; Victorian, mid-Victorian.

.12 VERBS **affect, assume, put on**, assume *or* put on airs, wear, **pretend, simulate, counterfeit, sham, fake** [informal], **feign**, make out like [informal], make a show of, play, playact [informal], act *or* play a part, play a scene, do a bit [informal], put up a front [slang], dramatize, histrionize, lay it on thick [informal], overact, tug the heartstrings.

.13 **pose, posture, attitudinize**, peacock, strike a pose, strike an attitude, pose for effect.

.14 **mince**, mince it, prink [Brit dial]; **simper**, smirk, bridle.

.15 ADJS **affected, pretentious**, la-di-da; **mannered**, *maniéré* [Fr]; **artificial, unnatural, insincere**; theatrical, stagy, histrionic; overdone, overacted.

.16 **assumed, put-on, pretended**, simulated, **phony** [slang], **fake** *or* **faked** [informal], feigned, counterfeited; spurious, sham 616.26; hypocritical 616.33.

.17 **foppish, dandified**, dandy, coxcombical, conceited.

.18 (affectedly nice) **overnice, overprecise, precious**, *précieuse* [Fr], exquisite, **overrefined, elegant**, mincing, simpering, namby-pamby; **goody-goody** *or* goody good-good [both informal]; puristic, formalistic, pedantic, precisionistic, precisian, precisianistic, euphuistic, euphemistic.

.19 **prudish, priggish, prim, smug, stuffy** [informal], old-maidish, **overmodest**, demure, **straitlaced**, stiff-necked, hidebound, narrow, censorious, sanctimonious, **puritanical**, Quakerish, Victorian, mid-Victorian.

.20 ADVS **affectedly, pretentiously**; elegantly, mincingly; for effect, for show.

.21 **prudishly, priggishly**, primly, smugly, stuffily [informal], straitlacedly, stiffneckedly, puritanically.

904. OSTENTATION

.1 NOUNS **ostentation, ostentatiousness, ostent; pretentiousness, pretension, pretense**; loftiness, lofty affectations.

.2 **pretensions**, vain pretensions; **airs**, lofty airs, vaporing, highfalutin *or* highfaluting ways [informal], side, swank [informal].

.3 **showiness, flashiness**, flamboyance, panache, dash, jazziness [slang], jauntiness, sportiness [informal], gaiety, glitter, glare, dazzle, dazzlingness; extravaganza; **gaudiness**, gaudery, **tawdriness**, meretriciousness; gorgeousness, colorfulness; **garishness**, loudness [informal], **blatancy**, flagrancy, shamelessness, brazenness, luridness, extravagance, sensationalism, obtrusiveness, vulgarness, crudeness, extravagation.

.4 **display, show, demonstration**, manifestation, **exhibition, parade**, *étalage* [Fr]; **pageantry, pageant, spectacle**; vaunt, fanfaronade, blazon, flourish, flaunt, flaunting; daring, brilliancy, éclat, bravura, flair; dash *or* splash *or* splurge [all informal]; figure; **exhibitionism**, showing-off;

theatrics, histrionics, dramatics, staginess; false front, sham 616.3.

.5 **grandeur**, grandness, grandiosity, **magnificence**, gorgeousness, **splendor**, splendidness, splendiferousness, resplendence, brilliance, glory; nobility, proudness, **state, stateliness, majesty;** impressiveness, imposingness; **sumptuousness, elegance, elaborateness, lavishness, luxuriousness;** ritziness or poshness or plushness or swankness or swankiness [all informal]; **luxury,** barbaric or Babylonian splendor.

.6 **pomp,** circumstance, pride, **state,** solemnity 871, formality 646; **pomp and circumstance,** "pride, pomp, and circumstance" [Shakespeare]; heraldry, "trump and solemn heraldry" [Coleridge].

.7 **pompousness, pomposity,** pontification, pontificality, **stuffiness** [informal], **self-importance,** inflation; grandiloquence 601, turgidity, orotundity.

.8 **swagger, strut,** swank [informal], bounce, brave show; swaggering, strutting; swash, **swashbucklery,** swashbuckling, swashbuckling; peacockishness, peacockery.

.9 **stuffed shirt** [slang], blimp [slang], Colonel Blimp; bloated aristocrat.

.10 **strutter, swaggerer,** swanker [Brit], swash, swasher, **swashbuckler,** peacock, miles gloriosus.

.11 **show-off** [informal], **exhibitionist,** flaunter; **grandstander** or grandstand player or hot dog or **hotshot** or showboat [all slang].

.12 VERBS **put** or **thrust oneself forward,** come forward, step to the front or fore, step into the limelight, take center stage, attract attention, make oneself conspicuous.

.13 **cut a dash,** make a show, put on a show, make one's mark, cut a swath, **cut** or **make a figure;** make a splash or a splurge [informal]; **splurge** or splash [both informal]; shine, glitter, glare, dazzle.

.14 **give oneself airs, put on airs,** put on, put on side, put on the dog [informal], put up a front [slang], ritz it [slang], look big, **swank** [slang], swell, swell it, act the grand seigneur; pontificate, play the pontiff.

.15 **strut, swagger,** swank [Brit], prance, stalk, peacock, swash, swashbuckle.

.16 **show off** [informal], **grandstand** or hot dog [both slang], play to the gallery or galleries [informal], please the crowd; exhibit or parade one's wares [informal], strut one's stuff [slang], go through one's paces, show what one has.

.17 **flaunt,** vaunt, **parade, display, demonstrate,** manifest, **exhibit,** air, put forward, put forth, hold up, flash or sport [both informal]; advertise; **flourish,** brandish, wave; dangle, dangle before the eyes; emblazon, blazon forth; trumpet, trumpet forth.

.18 ADJS **ostentatious, pretentious,** ambitious, vaunting, **lofty, highfalutin** or highfaluting [both informal], **high-flown,** high-flying; **high-toned,** tony [both informal], **fancy,** classy [slang], flossy [informal].

.19 **showy, flaunting, flashy,** snazzy, flashing, glittering, **jazzy** [slang], splashy or splurgy [both informal]; exhibitionistic, show-offy [informal], bravura; **gay,** jaunty, rakish, **dashing;** gallant, brave, braw [Scot], daring; **sporty** or dressy [both informal]; frilly [informal], frothy, chichi.

.20 **gaudy, tawdry;** gorgeous, colorful; **garish,** loud [informal], **blatant, flagrant,** shameless, **brazen,** brazenfaced, lurid, extravagant, sensational, **spectacular,** glaring, flaring, flaunting, screaming [informal], obtrusive, vulgar, crude; meretricious.

.21 **grandiose, grand, magnificent, splendid,** splendiferous [informal], splendacious [slang], **glorious,** superb, fine, superfine, fancy, superfancy, swell [slang]; **imposing, impressive,** awful, awe-inspiring; **noble, proud, stately, majestic,** princely; **sumptuous, elegant, elaborate, luxurious,** extravagant, deluxe; plush or posh or ritzy or swank or swanky [all informal], Corinthian; palatial, Babylonian; barbaric.

.22 **pompous, stuffy** [informal], **self-important,** impressed with oneself, pontifical; **inflated, swollen,** bloated, tumid, turgid, flatulent, gassy [informal], stilted; **grandiloquent, bombastic** 601.8,9; solemn 871.3, formal 646.7–10.

.23 **strutting, swaggering;** swashing, **swashbuckling,** swashbuckling; peacockish, peacocky.

.24 **theatrical, stagy, dramatic, histrionic;** spectacular.

.25 ADVS **ostentatiously, pretentiously,** loftily; with flourish of trumpet, with beat of drum, with flying colors.

.26 **showily, flauntingly,** flashily, with a flair, glitteringly; gaily, jauntily, **dashingly;** gallantly, bravely, daringly.

.27 **gaudily, tawdrily;** gorgeously, colorfully; **garishly, blatantly, flagrantly,** shamelessly, **brazenly,** brazenfacedly, luridly, sensationally, **spectacularly,** glaringly, flaringly, obtrusively.

.28 **grandiosely, grandly, magnificently,**

splendidly, splendiferously, splenda-ciously, gloriously, superbly; nobly, proudly, majestically; imposingly, impres-sively; **sumptuously, elegantly,** elabo-rately, luxuriously, **extravagantly;** palatial-ly.

.29 **pompously,** stuffily [informal], **self-impor-tantly;** stiltedly; **bombastically** 601.12.

905. PRIDE

.1 NOUNS **pride,** proudness, pridefulness; **self-esteem, self-respect,** self-confidence, self-reliance, self-consequence, face, inde-pendence, self-sufficiency; pardonable pride; obstinate or stiff-necked pride, stiff-neckedness; **vanity, conceit** 909.4; haughtiness, **arrogance** 912; boastfulness 910.1; purse-pride.

.2 **proud bearing,** pride of bearing, **dignity,** dignifiedness, **stateliness,** courtliness, grandeur, **loftiness;** pride of place; **nobil-ity,** lordliness, princeliness; **majesty,** regal-ity, kingliness, queenliness; worthiness, augustness, venerability; **sedateness, so-lemnity** 871, gravity, sobriety.

.3 proudling, highflier; stiff neck; egoist 909.5; boaster 910.5; the proud.

.4 VERBS **be proud,** hold up one's head, hold one's head high, stand up straight, hold oneself erect, never stoop; look one in the face or eye.

.5 **pride oneself, preen oneself,** plume one-self on, pique oneself, **congratulate one-self,** hug oneself; **be proud of, take pride in,** glory in, exult in.

.6 **make proud,** do proud [informal], **gratify, elate,** flush, turn one's head.

.7 **save face,** save one's face, preserve one's dignity, guard or preserve one's honor, be jealous of one's repute or good name.

.8 ADJS **proud, prideful,** proudful [dial]; **self-esteeming, self-respecting;** self-confident, self-reliant, independent, self-sufficient; proudhearted, proud-minded, proud-spir-ited, proud-blooded; proud-looking; as proud as Punch, proud as Lucifer, proud as a peacock; erect, stiff-backed, stiff-necked; purse-proud, house-proud.

.9 **vain, conceited** 909.8–12; haughty, **arro-gant** 912.9; boastful 910.10.

.10 **puffed up,** swollen, bloated, swollen or bloated with pride; elated, flushed, flushed with pride.

.11 **lofty, elevated,** high, high-flown, highfalu-tin or highfaluting [both informal], high-toned [informal]; high-minded, lofty-minded; high-headed, high-nosed [infor-mal].

.12 **dignified, stately, imposing, grand, courtly,** magisterial, aristocratic; **noble,** lordly, princely; **majestic,** regal, royal, kingly, queenly; worthy, **august, venera-ble;** statuesque; **sedate, solemn** 871.3, so-ber, grave.

.13 ADVS **proudly,** pridefully, **with pride;** self-esteemingly, self-respectingly, self-confi-dently, self-reliantly, independently, self-sufficiently; erectly, with head erect, with head held high, with nose in air; stiff-neckedly; like a lord, en grand seigneur [Fr].

.14 **dignifiedly, with dignity;** nobly, stately, imposingly, loftily, grandly, magisterially; majestically, regally, royally; worthily, au-gustly, venerably; sedately, solemnly, so-berly, gravely.

906. HUMILITY

.1 NOUNS **humility, humbleness, meekness; lowliness,** lowlihood, poorness, mean-ness, smallness, ingloriousness, undistin-guishedness; unimportance 673; innocu-ousness 674.9; teachableness 564.5; submis-siveness 765.3; **modesty,** unpretentiousness 908.1; plainness, simpleness, homeliness.

.2 **humiliation, mortification;** embarrass-ment 866.4; **abasement,** debasement, **let-down,** setdown, put-down, dump [infor-mal], **comedown,** descent, deflation, wounded or humbled pride; self-dimin-ishment, **self-abasement, self-abnegation** 979.1; **shame, disgrace;** shamefacedness, shamefastness, hangdog look.

.3 **condescension,** condescendence, deign-ing, lowering oneself, stooping from one's high place.

.4 VERBS **humiliate, humble;** mortify, **em-barrass** 866.15; put out, put out of face or countenance; **shame, disgrace,** put to shame, put to the blush; **deflate,** prick one's balloon, let down; take it out of, take the shine out of [informal], take the wind out of one's sails, take the starch out of [slang]; put one's nose out of joint [informal], put a tuck in one's tail or make one sing small [both informal].

.5 **abase, debase, crush,** abash, **degrade, re-duce,** diminish, **demean,** lower, **bring low,** bring down, trip up, take down, set down, put down, dump or dump on [both informal], knock one off his perch; take down a peg or a peg or two [infor-mal].

.6 **humble oneself, demean oneself,** abase oneself, climb down [informal], get down from one's high horse [informal]; put one's pride in one's pocket; **eat humble pie**, eat crow, eat dirt, swallow one's pride, lick the dust; come on bended knee, come hat in hand; go down on one's knees; draw in one's horns *or* sing small [both informal], lower one's note *or* tone, tuck one's tail; come down a peg *or* a peg or two; **deprecate** *or* **depreciate oneself**, diminish oneself, discount oneself, belittle oneself.

.7 **condescend, deign, vouchsafe; stoop, descend,** lower oneself, set one's dignity aside *or* to one side; be so good as to, so forget oneself.

.8 **be humiliated,** be put out of countenance; **be crushed, feel small, feel cheap,** look foolish *or* silly, could sink through the floor; **take shame, be ashamed, feel ashamed of oneself,** be put to the blush, have a very red face; hang one's head, hide one's face, not dare to show one's face, not have a word to say for oneself; drink the cup of humiliation to the dregs.

.9 ADJS **humble, lowly, low, poor, mean,** small, inglorious, undistinguished; unimportant 673.14–19; innocuous 674.20; teachable 564.18; **modest, unpretentious** 908.9; **plain, simple,** homely; humble-looking, humble-visaged; humblest, lowliest, lowest, least.

.10 humblehearted, humble-minded, humble-spirited, poor in spirit; **meek,** meekhearted, meek-minded, meek-spirited; **abject,** submissive 765.12–16.

.11 **self-abasing, self-abnegating, self-deprecating,** self-depreciating, self-doubting.

.12 **humbled,** reduced, diminished, lowered, brought down, brought low, set down, bowed down, in the dust; on one's knees, on one's marrowbones [informal].

.13 **humiliated, humbled,** mortified, **embarrassed, chagrined, abashed, crushed,** out of countenance; blushing, red-faced, **ashamed, shamed,** ashamed of oneself, shamefaced, shamefast; crestfallen, chapfallen, hangdog.

.14 **humiliating,** humiliative, humbling, chastening, mortifying, **embarrassing,** crushing.

.15 ADVS **humbly, meekly;** modestly 908.14; with due deference, with bated breath, "with bated breath and whispering humbleness" [Shakespeare]; submissively 765.17–19; **abjectly,** on bended knee, **on one's knees,** on one's marrowbones [informal], on all fours, with one's tail between one's legs, hat in hand.

907. SERVILITY

.1 NOUNS **servility, slavishness,** subservience *or* subserviency, menialness, abjectness, **baseness, meanness; submissiveness** 765.3; slavery, helotry, helotism, serfdom, peonage.

.2 **obsequiousness, sycophancy,** fawnery, toadyism, flunkyism, parasitism, sponging; ingratiation, insinuation; **truckling, fawning, toadying,** toadeating, groveling, cringing, footlicking, **bootlicking** [slang], backscratching, tufthunting; **apple-polishing** *or* **handshaking** [both informal]; asslicking *or* ass-kissing *or* brown-nosing [all slang]; timeserving; obeisance, prostration; mealymouthedness.

.3 **sycophant, flatterer, toady,** toad, toadeater, footlicker, bootlick *or* **bootlicker** [both slang], lickspit, lickspittle, **truckler, fawner,** courtier, led captain, tufthunter, kowtower, groveler, cringer, spaniel; **backslapper,** backscratcher, clawback [dial]; **handshaker** *or* **apple-polisher** *or* **yes-man** [all informal]; suck *or* ass-licker *or* asskisser *or* brown-nose *or* brown-noser *or* brownie [all slang]; flunky, lackey, stooge [slang], jackal; timeserver; creature, **puppet,** minion, **tool,** cat's-paw, dupe, instrument, faithful servant, slave, helot, serf, peon; mealymouth.

.4 **parasite,** barnacle, leech, parasit(o)– *or* parasiti–; **sponger,** sponge [informal], freeloader [slang], smell-feast; beat *or* deadbeat [both slang].

.5 **hanger-on, adherent,** dangler, appendage, **dependent, satellite, follower,** retainer, servant, man, shadow, tagtail, **henchman,** heeler *or* ward heeler [both informal].

.6 VERBS **fawn, truckle; flatter; toady,** toadeat; **bootlick** [slang], lickspittle, lick one's shoes, lick the feet of; **grovel,** crawl, creep, cower, cringe, crouch, stoop, kneel, bend the knee, fall on one's knees, prostrate oneself, throw oneself at the feet of, fall at one's feet, kiss one's feet, kiss the hem of one's garment, lick the dust, make a doormat of oneself; **kowtow, bow, bow and scrape.**

.7 **toady to, truckle to, pander to, cater to; wait on** *or* **upon,** wait on hand and foot, do service, fetch and carry, do the dirty work of, do *or* jump at the bidding of.

.8 **curry favor, court, pay court to,** make court to, run after [informal], dance attendance on; **shine up to,** make up to [informal]; **suck up to** *or* **play up to** *or* **act up to** [all slang]; be a yes man [informal], agree to anything; fawn upon, fall over *or* all over [slang]; **handshake** *or* **polish the apple** [both informal]; lick one's ass *or* kiss one's ass *or* brown-nose [all slang].

.9 **ingratiate oneself,** insinuate oneself, worm oneself in, creep into the good graces of, get next to [informal], **get on the good** *or* **right side of,** rub the right way [informal].

.10 **attach oneself to,** pin *or* fasten oneself upon, hang about *or* around, dangle, hang on the skirts of, hang on the sleeve of, become an appendage of, **follow,** follow at heel; follow the crowd, get on the bandwagon, go with the stream, hold with the hare and run with the hounds.

.11 **sponge** *or* **sponge on** [both informal]; feed on, fatten on, batten on, live off of, use as a meal ticket.

.12 ADJS **servile, slavish,** subservient, **menial, base,** mean; **submissive** 765.12.

.13 **obsequious, flattering, sycophantic(al), toadyish, fawning, truckling, ingratiating, toadying,** toadeating, **bootlicking** [slang], footlicking, backscratching; **groveling,** sniveling, cringing, cowering, crouching, crawling; **parasitic,** leechlike, sponging [informal], par(a)–; timeserving; **abject,** beggarly, hangdog; obeisant, prostrate, on one's knees, on one's marrowbones [slang], on bended knee; mealymouthed.

.14 ADVS **servilely, slavishly,** subserviently, menially, "in a bondman's key" [Shakespeare]; **submissively** 765.17.

.15 **obsequiously, sycophantically, ingratiatingly, fawningly, trucklingly;** hat-in-hand, cap-in-hand; **abjectly,** obeisantly, grovelingly, on one's knees; parasitically.

908. MODESTY

.1 NOUNS **modesty, meekness; humility** 906; **unpretentiousness,** unassumingness, **unpresumptuousness, unostentatiousness,** unambitiousness, unobtrusiveness, unboastfulness.

.2 **self-effacement, self-depreciation,** self-deprecation, self-detraction, undervaluing of self, **self-doubt, diffidence;** weak ego, lack of self-confidence *or* self-reliance, self-distrust.

.3 **reserve, restraint, constraint,** backwardness, retiring disposition.

.4 **shyness, timidity,** timidness, timorousness, **bashfulness,** shamefacedness, shamefastness, **coyness, demureness,** demurity, skittishness, mousiness; self-consciousness, embarrassment; stammering, confusion; stagefright, mikefright [informal].

.5 **blushing, flushing,** coloring, mantling, reddening, crimsoning; **blush, flush,** suffusion; pudicity, pudency.

.6 shrinking violet, modest violet, mouse.

.7 VERBS **efface oneself,** depreciate *or* deprecate *or* doubt *or* distrust oneself; reserve oneself, retire, shrink, **retire into one's shell, keep in the background,** keep oneself to oneself, keep one's distance, remain in the shade, take a back seat [informal], hide one's face, hide one's light under a bushel, avoid the limelight; pursue the noiseless tenor of one's way, blush unseen, "do good by stealth and blush to find it fame" [Pope].

.8 **blush, flush, mantle, color,** change color, color up, redden, crimson, turn red, get red in the face, blush up to the eyes; stammer; squirm with self-consciousness *or* embarrassment.

.9 ADJS **modest, meek; humble** 906.9; **unpretentious,** unpretending, **unassuming,** unpresuming, unpresumptuous, **unostentatious, unobtrusive, unimposing,** unboastful; unambitious, unaspiring.

.10 **self-effacing, self-depreciative, self-depreciating, self-deprecating; diffident,** deprecatory, deprecative, self-doubting, unselfconfident, unselfreliant, self-distrustful.

.11 **reserved, restrained, constrained;** quiet; **backward, retiring, shrinking.**

.12 **shy, timid,** timorous, **bashful,** shamefaced, shamefast, **coy, demure,** skittish, mousy; **self-conscious,** conscious, confused; stammering, inarticulate.

.13 **blushing,** blushful; **flushed, red, ruddy,** red in the face; **sheepish; embarrassed.**

.14 ADVS **modestly, meekly; humbly** 906.15; **unpretentiously,** unpretendingly, **unassumingly,** unpresumptuously, **unostentatiously, unobtrusively;** quietly, without ceremony, *sans façon* [Fr].

.15 **shyly, timidly,** timorously, **bashfully, coyly, demurely,** diffidently; **shamefacedly,** shamefastly, **sheepishly,** blushingly, with downcast eyes.

909. VANITY

.1 NOUNS **vanity, vainness;** overproudness, overweening pride; **self-importance,** consequentiality, **self-esteem,** self-respect, self-assumption; **self-admiration, self-delight,** self-worship, self-endearment, **self-love,** *amour-propre* [Fr], self-infatuation, **narcissism,** narcism; autoeroticism, autoerotism; **self-satisfaction, self-content,** ego trip [informal], self-approbation, self-congratulation, self-gratulation, self-complacency, **smugness**, complacency, self-sufficiency; vainglory, vaingloriousness; "an itch for the praise of fools" [R. Browning].

.2 **pride** 905; arrogance 912; **boastfulness** 910.1.

.3 **egotism, egoism**, egoisticalness, egotisticalness, **ego** [informal], self-interest, individualism, "the tongue of vanity" [Chamfort]; **egocentricity**, egocentrism, self-centeredness, self-centerment; selfishness 978.

.4 **conceit, conceitedness, self-conceit, self-conceitedness, immodesty,** side, self-assertiveness; **stuck-upness** [informal], chestiness [slang], swelled-headedness, swelled head; **cockiness** [informal], pertness, perkiness; aggressive self-confidence, obtrusiveness, bumptiousness.

.5 **egotist, egoist, egocentric,** individualist; **swellhead** [slang], narcissist, narcist, Narcissus; **braggart** 910.5, know-it-all, smart aleck 913.5, no modest violet, "a person of low taste, more interested in himself than in me" [Ambrose Bierce].

.6 VERBS **be stuck on oneself** [slang], be impressed or overly impressed with oneself; ego-trip, be or go on an ego trip [all informal]; think well of oneself, think one is it or one's shit doesn't stink [slang], get too big for one's breeches, have a swelled head, know it all, have no false modesty, have no self-doubt, love the sound of one's own voice, be blinded by one's own glory, lay the flattering unction to one's soul; fish for compliments; toot one's own horn, **boast** 910.6–8; be vain as a peacock, give oneself airs 904.14.

.7 **puff up, inflate,** swell; go to one's head, turn one's head.

.8 ADJS **vain, vainglorious,** overproud, overweening; **self-important, self-esteeming,** self-respecting, self-assuming, consequential; **self-admiring,** self-delighting, self-worshiping, self-loving, self-endeared, self-infatuated, narcissistic, narcistic, narcissan, narcissine; **self-satisfied, self-content,** self-contented, self-approving, self-gratulating, self-gratulatory, self-congratulating, self-congratulatory, self-complacent, **smug,** complacent, self-sufficient.

.9 **proud** 905.8; arrogant 912.9; boastful 910.10.

.10 **egotistic(al),** egoistic(al), self-interested; **egocentric,** egocentristic, self-centered, narcissistic, narcistic, narcissan, narcissine; selfish 978.5.

.11 **conceited, self-conceited, immodest,** self-opinionated; **stuck-up** [informal], **puffed up, chesty** [slang], **swelled-headed,** too big for one's shoes or britches; biggety [dial]; **cocky** [informal], pert, perk, perky; peacockish, peacocky; know-it-all, smart-alecky 913.9, overwise, wise in one's own conceit; aggressively self-confident, obtrusive, bumptious.

.12 **stuck on oneself** [informal], impressed with oneself, pleased with oneself, full of oneself, all wrapped up in oneself.

.13 ADVS **vainly,** self-importantly; **egotistically,** egoistically; **conceitedly,** self-conceitedly, immodestly; cockily [informal], pertly, perkily.

910. BOASTING

.1 NOUNS **boasting, bragging,** vaunting; **boastfulness, braggadocio, braggartism; boast, brag,** vaunt; side, bombast, bravado, vauntery, fanfaronade, gasconade, gasconism, rodomontade; bluster, swagger 911.1; vanity, conceit 909.4; jactation, jactitation; heroics.

.2 [slang or informal terms] **big talk,** fine talk, fancy talk, tall talk, highfalutin or highfaluting, **hot air,** gas, bunk, bunkum, **bullshit;** tall story, fish story.

.3 **self-approbation,** self-praise, self-laudation, self-gratulation, self-applause, self-puffery, self-vaunting, self-advertising, self-advertisement, self-glorification; vainglory, vaingloriousness.

.4 **crowing,** exultation, elation, triumph, jubilation; **gloating.**

.5 **braggart, boaster,** brag, braggadocio, hector, fanfaron, Gascon, gasconader, miles gloriosus; **blowhard** or blower or big mouth or bullshit artist or hot-air artist or gasbag or windbag or big bag of wind or windjammer or windy [all slang]; blusterer 911.2; Texan, Fourth-of-July orator; Braggadocchio [Spenser], Captain Bobadil [Ben Jonson], Thraso [Terence], Parolles [Shakespeare].

.6 VERBS **boast, brag,** make a boast of, vaunt, flourish, gasconade, vapor, puff, draw the longbow, advertise oneself, **blow one's own trumpet, toot one's own horn,** sing one's own praises, exaggerate one's own merits; bluster, swagger 911.3; speak for Buncombe.

.7 [slang or informal terms] **blow,** blow off, **blow hard, talk big,** shoot the shit, spread oneself, lay it on thick, brag oneself up.

.8 **flatter oneself,** conceit oneself, **congratulate oneself,** hug oneself, shake hands with oneself, **pat oneself on the back,** take merit to oneself.

.9 **exult,** triumph, glory, delight, joy, jubilate; **crow** or crow over, crow like a rooster or cock; **gloat,** gloat over.

.10 ADJS **boastful, boasting, braggart, bragging,** thrasonical, thrasonic, big-mouthed [slang], vaunting, vaporing, gasconading, Gascon, fanfaronading, fanfaron; vain, conceited 909.8–12; **vainglorious,** self-glorious, self-lauding, self-applauding, self-praising, self-flattering, self-vaunting, self-advertising.

.11 **inflated, swollen, windy** or gassy [both informal], **bombastic,** high-swelling, **high-flown, highfalutin** or highfaluting [both informal], **pretentious,** extravagant, big, tall [informal].

.12 **crowing,** exultant, exulting, elated, elate, jubilant, **triumphant, flushed,** cock-a-hoop, in high feather; **gloating.**

.13 ADVS **boastfully,** boastingly, braggingly, vauntingly, vaingloriously.

.14 **exultantly,** exultingly, elatedly, jubilantly, triumphantly, in triumph; **gloatingly.**

911. BLUSTER

.1 NOUNS **bluster,** blustering, hectoring, bullying, **swagger,** swashbucklery, side; **bravado,** rant, rodomontade, fanfaronade; sputter, splutter; fuss, bustle, fluster, flurry; bluff, bluster and bluff; intimidation 891.6; **boastfulness** 910.1.

.2 **blusterer, swaggerer,** swasher, swashbuckler, fanfaron, bravo, **bully,** bullyboy, bucko, roisterer, cock of the walk, vaporer, blatherskite [informal]; ranter, raver, hectorer, hector, Herod; slanger [Brit]; bluff, bluffer; **braggart** 910.5.

.3 VERBS **bluster,** hector; **swagger,** swashbuckle; bully; bounce, vapor, roister, rollick, gasconade, kick up a dust [informal]; sputter, splutter; rant, rage, rave, storm, "out-herod Herod" [Shakespeare]; slang [Brit]; bluff, bluster and bluff, put up a bluff [informal]; intimidate 891.28; **brag** 910.6.

.4 ADJS **blustering,** blustery, blusterous, hectoring, **bullying, swaggering,** swashing, swashbuckling, boisterous, roisterous, roistering, rollicking; ranting, raging, raving, storming; tumultuous 162.17; noisy, "full of sound and fury" [Shakespeare].

912. ARROGANCE

.1 NOUNS **arrogance,** arrogantness; overbearingness, overbearing pride, overweening pride, stiff-necked pride, assumption of superiority, domineering, domineeringness; **pride,** proudness; superbia, sin of pride, chief of the deadly sins; **haughtiness, hauteur; loftiness,** Olympian loftiness or detachment; **toploftiness** or stuckupness or uppishness or uppityness [all informal], side, hoity-toitiness, hoity-toity; haughty airs, airs of de haut en bas, cornstarchy airs [informal]; high horse [informal]; **condescension,** condescendence, patronizing, patronization, patronizing attitude; purse-pride.

.2 **presumptuousness,** presumption, overweening, overweeningness, assumption, total self-assurance; hubris; **insolence** 913.

.3 **lordliness, imperiousness,** masterfulness, magisterialness, **high-and-mightiness,** aristocratic presumption; elitism.

.4 **aloofness, standoffishness,** offishness [informal], chilliness, coolness, distantness, remoteness.

.5 **disdainfulness, disdain,** aristocratic disdain, **contemptuousness, superciliousness,** contumeliousness, cavalierness, you-be-damnedness [slang].

.6 **snobbery, snobbishness,** snobbiness, snobbism; **priggishness, priggery,** priggism; snootiness or snottiness or sniffiness or high-hattedness or high-hattiness [all slang]; tufthunting.

.7 **snob, prig;** elitist; **highbrow** or egghead [both slang], Brahmin, mandarin; namedropper, tufthunter; "he who meanly admires a mean thing" [Thackeray].

.8 VERBS **give oneself airs** 904.14; **hold one's nose in the air,** look down one's nose, toss the head, bridle; mount or get on one's high horse or ride the high horse [informal]; **condescend, patronize,** deal with or treat de haut en bas.

.9 ADJS **arrogant, overbearing, superior, domineering, proud, haughty; lofty, toplofty** [informal] 207.19; **high-flown,** highfalutin or high-faluting [both informal]; **high-headed; high-nosed** or **stuck-up** or **uppish** or uppity or **upstage** [all informal]; **hoity-toity,** big, big as you please, six feet above contradiction; on one's high horse; **condescending, patronizing,** de haut en bas [Fr]; purse-proud.

.10 **presumptuous,** presuming, assuming, overweening, would-be, self-elect, self-elected, self-appointed; **insolent** 913.8.

.11 **lordly, imperious,** aristocratic, totally self-assured; hubristic; **masterful,** magisterial, **high and mighty;** elitist; U [Brit informal]; dictatorial 739.16.

.12 **aloof, standoffish,** standoff, offish [informal], chilly, cool, distant, remote, above all that; Olympian.

.13 **disdainful,** dismissive, **contemptuous,** supercilious, contumelious, cavalier, you-be-damned [slang].

.14 **snobbish,** snobby, **priggish,** snippy [informal]; **snooty** or **snotty** or **sniffy** [all slang]; **high-hat** or high-hatted or high-hatty [all slang]; patronizing, condescending.

.15 ADVS **arrogantly, haughtily, proudly,** aloofly; **condescendingly, patronizingly,** *de haut en bas* [Fr]; loftily, toploftily [informal]; imperiously, magisterially; Olympianly; **disdainfully, contemptuously,** superciliously, contumeliously; with nose in air, with nose turned up, with head held high, with arms akimbo.

.16 **presumptuously,** overweeningly, aristocratically; hubristically; **insolently** 913.11.

.17 **snobbishly,** snobbily, **priggishly;** snootily or snottily [both slang].

913. INSOLENCE

.1 NOUNS **insolence,** procacity, bumptiousness, contumely; **audacity, effrontery,** boldness, assurance, hardihood; hubris; **presumption,** presumptuousness, overweening, overweeningness; **arrogance** 912, uppishness or uppityness [both informal], obtrusiveness, pushiness [informal].

.2 **impudence, impertinence,** flippancy, **cockiness** or **cheekiness** [both informal], freshness [slang], **brazenness,** brazenfacedness, brassiness [informal], face of brass, **rudeness** 937.1, brashness, disrespectfulness, contempt 966, derision, ridicule 967.

.3 **cheek** or face or brass [all informal]; **nerve** or **gall** or crust [all slang]; *chutzpah* [Yid].

.4 **sauciness,** sassiness [informal], **sauce** [informal], sass [dial], lip [slang], **back talk** or backchat [both informal].

.5 (impudent person) malapert, saucebox [informal]; minx, hussy; whippersnapper, puppy, pup, upstart; smarty or smart-ass or wise-ass [all slang], **smart aleck** or smarty-pants [both informal], wise guy [slang]; boldface, brazenface; *chutzpanik* [Yid]; swaggerer 911.2.

.6 VERBS **have the audacity, have the cheek; have the gall** or have a nerve or have one's nerve [all informal]; **get fresh** [slang], get smart [informal], forget one's place, **dare, presume,** take liberties, make bold; hold in contempt 966.3–6, ridicule, taunt, deride 967.8–10.

.7 **sauce** [informal], sass [dial], **talk back,** answer back [informal], lip or give one the lip [both slang], provoke.

.8 ADJS **insolent,** insulting, **audacious,** procacious, bumptious, contumelious; **arrogant** 912.9, uppish or uppity [both informal]; hubristic; **presumptuous,** presuming, over-presumptuous, overweening; **forward,** pushy [informal], obtrusive, familiar; cool, cold, **disdainful** 912.13.

.9 **impudent, impertinent, pert,** malapert, flip [informal], flippant, **cocky** or cheeky [both informal], **fresh** [slang], facy [dial]; crusty or gally or nervy [all slang], *chutzpadik* [Yid]; uncalled-for, gratuitous, biggety [dial]; **rude** 937.4–7, **disrespectful,** contemptuous 966.8, derisive 967.12, brash, bluff; **saucy,** sassy [dial]; smart or smart-alecky [both informal], smart-ass or wise-ass [both slang].

.10 **brazen,** brazenfaced, boldfaced, barefaced, **brassy** [informal], **bold,** bold as brass [informal], unblushing, unabashed, aweless, **shameless,** dead or lost to shame; swaggering 911.4.

.11 ADVS **insolently, audaciously,** procaciously, bumptiously, contumeliously; **arrogantly** 912.15; **presumptuously,** obtrusively, pushily [informal].

.12 **impudently, impertinently,** pertly, flippantly, **cockily** or cheekily [both informal], saucily; **rudely** 937.8, brashly, disrespectfully, contemptuously 966.9, derisively 967.15, in a smart-alecky way [informal], in a smart-ass fashion [slang].

.13 **brazenly,** brazenfacedly, **boldly,** boldfacedly, **shamelessly,** unblushingly.

914. REPUTE

.1 NOUNS **repute, reputation,** "the bubble reputation" [Shakespeare]; **name,** character, figure; **fame, famousness, renown,** "that last infirmity of noble mind" [Milton], **kudos,** report, glory; éclat, **celebrity, popularity,** recognition, a place in the sun; **acclaim, public acclaim,** réclame, publicity, vogue, **notoriety,** notoriousness, talk of the town.

.2 **reputability,** reputableness; good reputation, good name, **good** or **high repute,** good report, good odor, fair name, name to conjure with; jealousy of one's repute, maintenance of one's good name; facesaving.

.3 **esteem,** estimation, **honor, regard, respect,** approval, approbation, account, favor, consideration, credit, worth.

.4 **prestige,** kudos, **dignity;** face; **rank, standing,** stature, high place, position, station, **status.**

.5 **distinction, mark, note; importance,** consequence, significance; **notability, prominence, eminence, greatness,** conspicuousness, outstandingness; elevation, exaltation, loftiness, high mightiness; nobility, grandeur, sublimity; excellence 674.1, supereminence 674.2.

.6 **illustriousness,** luster, brilliance *or* brilliancy, radiance, splendor, resplendence *or* resplendency, glory, blaze of glory, nimbus, halo, aura, envelope; charisma, mystique, glamour, numinousness, magic.

.7 (posthumous fame) **memory, remembrance,** legend, heroic legend *or* myth; **immortality,** lasting *or* undying fame, niche in the hall of fame, secure place in history; immortal name, "ghost of a great name" [Lucan].

.8 **glorification, ennoblement,** dignification, **exaltation,** elevation, magnification, aggrandizement; enthronement; immortalization, enshrinement; beatification, canonization, sainting, sanctification; deification, apotheosis; lionization.

.9 **celebrity,** man of mark *or* note, person of note *or* consequence, **notable, notability, luminary, great man,** master spirit, worthy, name, **big name,** figure, public figure, **somebody; important person, personage** 672.8; cynosure, "the observed of all observers" [Shakespeare], idol, popular idol, lion, social lion; hero, heroine, popular hero, pop hero [slang], folk hero; star, superstar; immortal; luminaries, galaxy, pleiad, constellation.

.10 VERBS **be somebody,** be something; figure, make *or* cut a figure, cut a dash *or* make a splash [both informal], **make a noise in the world,** make *or* leave one's mark; live, flourish; shine, glitter, gleam, glow.

.11 **gain recognition,** be recognized, come into one's own, come to the front *or* fore, come into vogue.

.12 **honor,** confer *or* bestow honor upon; **dignify,** adorn, grace; **distinguish,** signalize, confer distinction on.

.13 **glorify,** glamorize; **exalt,** elevate, raise, uplift, set up, **ennoble,** aggrandize, magnify, exalt to the skies; crown; throne, enthrone; immortalize, enshrine, hand one's name down to posterity, make legendary; beatify, canonize, saint, sanctify; deify, apotheosize, apotheose; **lionize.**

.14 **reflect honor on,** shed a luster on, redound to one's honor.

.15 ADJS **reputable,** highly reputed, **estimable, esteemed,** much *or* highly esteemed, **honorable,** honored; meritorious, noble,

worthy, creditable; respected, respectable, highly respectable; revered, reverend, venerable, venerated, worshipful; **well-thought-of,** highly regarded, held in esteem, in good odor, in favor, in high favor; in one's good books; prestigious.

.16 **distinguished,** distingué; **noted, notable,** marked, of note, of mark; **famous, famed,** honored, **renowned, celebrated, popular,** acclaimed, much acclaimed, **notorious, well-known,** in everyone's mouth, on everyone's tongue *or* lips, talked-of, talked-about; far-famed, far-heard; fabled, legendary, mythical.

.17 **prominent, conspicuous, outstanding,** to the front, in the limelight [informal]; **important,** consequential, significant.

.18 **eminent, high, exalted,** elevated, lofty, sublime, held in awe, awesome; immortal; **great,** big [informal], **grand;** excellent 674.12-15, supereminent 674.17,18, mighty, high and mighty; glorified, ennobled, magnified, aggrandized; enthroned, throned; immortalized, shrined, enshrined; beatified, canonized, sainted, sanctified; deified, apotheosized.

.19 **illustrious,** lustrous, glorious, brilliant, radiant, splendid, splendorous, splendrous, splendent, resplendent, bright, shining; charismatic, glamorous, numinous, magic(al).

.20 ADVS **reputably, estimably, honorably,** nobly, respectably, worthily, creditably.

.21 **famously, notably, notedly, notoriously,** popularly, celebratedly; **prominently, eminently,** conspicuously, outstandingly; illustriously, gloriously.

915. DISREPUTE

.1 NOUNS **disrepute, ill repute,** bad repute, bad *or* poor reputation, evil repute *or* reputation, ill fame, shady *or* unsavory reputation, **bad name,** bad odor, bad report, bad character; **disesteem, dishonor,** public dishonor, **discredit; disfavor,** ill-favor; disapprobation 969.1.

.2 **disreputability,** disreputableness, **notoriety;** discreditableness, dishonorableness, unsavoriness, **unrespectability;** disgracefulness, **shamefulness.**

.3 **baseness, lowness, meanness, crumminess** [slang], poorness, pettiness, paltriness, smallness, littleness, pokiness, beggarliness, shabbiness, shoddiness, squalor, scrubbiness, scumminess, scabbiness, scurviness, scruffiness, abjectness, wretchedness, miserableness, despicableness, contemptibleness, contemptibility, abominableness, execrableness, obnoxiousness, **odiousness, vileness** 864.2, foulness, rankness, fulsomeness, grossness, nefariousness, heinousness, **atrociousness,** monstrousness, enormity; degradation, debasement, depravity.

.4 **infamy,** infamousness; **ignominy,** ignominiousness; ingloriousness, **ignobility,** odium, obloquy, opprobrium, "a long farewell to all my greatness" [Shakespeare]; depluming, displuming, loss of honor *or* name *or* repute, degradation, demotion 783.

.5 **disgrace, scandal, humiliation; shame,** dirty shame *or* low-down dirty shame [both slang], crying *or* burning shame; **reproach,** byword, byword of reproach, a disgrace to one's name.

.6 **stigma,** stigmatism, onus; **brand,** badge of infamy; **slur,** reproach, censure, reprimand, imputation, aspersion, reflection, stigmatization; pillorying; **black eye** [informal], black mark; **disparagement** 971; **stain, taint,** attaint, **tarnish,** blur, **smirch,** smutch, smudge, smear, spot, blot, blot on *or* in one's escutcheon *or* scutcheon; bend *or* bar sinister [her]; baton, champain, point champain [all her]; mark of Cain; broad arrow [Brit].

.7 VERBS **incur disgrace,** incur disesteem *or* dishonor *or* discredit, be shamed, earn a bad name, forfeit one's good opinion, fall into disrepute, seal one's infamy; lose one's good name, **lose face,** lose countenance, lose credit, **lose caste; disgrace oneself,** lower oneself, demean oneself, degrade *or* debase oneself, act beneath oneself, derogate, stoop, descend, ride to a fall, fall from one's high estate, foul one's own nest; put one's good name in jeopardy; compromise oneself.

.8 **disgrace, dishonor, discredit,** reflect discredit upon, bring into discredit, reproach, cast reproach upon, be a reproach to; **shame, put to shame,** impute shame to, hold up to shame; hold up to public shame *or* public scorn *or* public ridicule, pillory, bring shame upon; **humiliate** 906.4; **degrade, debase** 783.3, deplume, displume, defrock, unfrock, bring low.

.9 **stigmatize, brand; stain,** tarnish, taint, attaint, blot, **blacken, smear,** bespatter, **sully,** soil, defile, vilify, **slur,** cast a slur upon, blow upon; disapprove 969.10–15; **disparage, defame** 971.8,9; censure, reprimand, **give a black eye** [informal], give a black mark, put in one's bad *or* black

books; give a bad name, give a dog a bad name; expose, expose to infamy; pillory, gibbet; burn *or* hang in effigy.

.10 ADJS **disreputable, discreditable, dishonorable,** unsavory, shady, seamy, sordid, **unrespectable, ignoble, ignominious, infamous,** inglorious; notorious; unpraiseworthy 969.25,26; derogatory 971.13.

.11 **disgraceful, shameful,** pitiful, deplorable, opprobrious, sad, sorry, too bad; degrading, debasing, demeaning, beneath one, beneath one's dignity, *infra indignitatem* [L], infra dig [informal], unbecoming, unworthy of one; cheap, gutter; **humiliating,** humiliative; **scandalous,** shocking, outrageous.

.12 **base, low,** low-down [informal], **mean,** crummy [slang], poor, petty, paltry, small, little, **shabby, shoddy,** squalid, lumpen, scrubby, scummy, scabby, **scurvy,** scruffy, mangy [informal], measly *or* cheesy [both slang], poky, beggarly, **wretched, miserable,** abject, **despicable, contemptible,** abominable, execrable, obnoxious, **disgusting, odious** 864.18, vile, foul, dirty, rank, fulsome, gross, flagrant, grave, arrant, nefarious, heinous, reptilian, **atrocious,** monstrous, unmentionable; degraded, debased, depraved.

.13 **in disrepute,** in bad repute, in bad odor; **in disfavor,** in discredit, **in bad** [informal], in one's bad *or* black books, out of favor, out of countenance, at a discount; **in disgrace,** in Dutch [informal], **in the doghouse** [slang], under a cloud; stripped of reputation, disgraced, discredited, dishonored, shamed, loaded with shame, unable to show one's face.

.14 **unrenowned,** renownless, nameless, inglorious, **unnotable, unnoted,** unnoticed, unremarked, **undistinguished, unfamed,** uncelebrated, unsung, unhonored, unglorified, unpopular; no credit to; **unknown,** little known, obscure, unheard-of, *ignotus* [L].

.15 ADVS **disreputably, discreditably, dishonorably, unrespectably, ignobly, ignominiously, infamously,** ingloriously.

.16 **disgracefully, scandalously,** shockingly, deplorably, outrageously; **shamefully,** to one's shame, to one's shame be it spoken.

.17 **basely, meanly,** poorly, pettily, **shabbily, shoddily,** scurvily, **wretchedly, miserably,** abjectly, **despicably, contemptibly,** abominably, execrably, obnoxiously, **odiously** 864.26, **vilely,** foully, grossly, flagrantly, arrantly, nefariously, heinously, **atrociously,** monstrously.

916. HONOR

(token of esteem)

.1 NOUNS **honor**, great honor, distinction, glory, credit, ornament; "blushing honors" [Shakespeare].

.2 **award, reward, prize**; first prize, second prize; consolation prize; booby prize; Nobel Prize, Pulitzer Prize; sweepstakes; jackpot; Oscar, Academy Award.

.3 **trophy**, laurel, **laurels**, bays, palm, palms, crown, chaplet, wreath, garland, **feather in one's cap** [informal]; civic crown *or* garland *or* wreath; cup, loving cup, pot [slang]; America's Cup, Old Mug.

.4 **citation**, eulogy, mention, honorable mention, kudos, **accolade, tribute**, praise 970.1.

.5 **decoration**, decoration of honor, order, ornament; ribbon, riband; blue ribbon, *cordon bleu* [Fr]; red ribbon, red ribbon of the Legion of Honor; cordon, grand cordon; garter; star, gold star.

.6 **medal**, order, medallion; military medal, service medal, war medal, soldier's medal; Congressional Medal of Honor, Medal of Honor, Distinguished Service Medal, Distinguished Service Cross, Navy Cross, Distinguished Flying Cross, Air Medal, Silver Star Medal, Bronze Star Medal, Order of the Purple Heart, Unit Citation, Distinguished Unit Citation; Distinguished Conduct Medal, Military Cross, Victoria Cross, Distinguished Service Order; Croix de Guerre, Médaille Militaire; Carnegie hero's medal.

.7 scholarship, fellowship.

.8 VERBS **honor, do honor**, pay regard to; give *or* pay *or* render honor to; **cite; decorate**, pin a medal on; **crown**, crown with laurel; pay tribute, praise 970.5.

.9 ADJS **honored, distinguished**; laureate, crowned with laurel.

.10 **honorary, honorific, honorable**.

.11 ADVS **with honor**, with distinction; *cum laude, magna cum laude, summa cum laude, insigne cum laude, honoris causa* [all L].

917. TITLE

(appellation of dignity or distinction)

.1 NOUNS **title, honorific, honor**, title of honor; **handle** *or* handle to one's name [both slang].

.2 (honorifics) Excellency, Eminence, Reverence, Grace, Honor, Worship, Your *or* His *or* Her Excellency; Lord, My Lord, milord, Lordship, Your *or* His Lordship; Lady, My Lady, milady, Ladyship, Your *or* Her Ladyship; Highness, Royal Highness, Imperial Highness, Serene Highness, Your *or* His *or* Her Highness; Majesty, Royal Majesty, Imperial Majesty, Serene Majesty, Your *or* His *or* Her Majesty.

.3 Sir, sire, sirrah; Esquire; Master, Mister 420.7; mirza, effendi, sirdar, emir, khan, sahib.

.4 Mistress, madame 421.8.

.5 (ecclesiastical titles) Reverend, His Reverence, His Grace; Monsignor; Holiness, His Holiness; Dom, Brother, Sister, Father, Mother; Rabbi.

.6 **degree**, academic degree; **bachelor**, baccalaureate, *baccalaureus* [L], bachelor's degree; **master**, master's degree; **doctor**, doctorate, doctor's degree.

.7 ADJS **titular**, titulary; honorific.

.8 the Noble, the Most Noble, the Most Excellent, the Most Worthy, the Most Worshipful; the Honorable, the Most Honorable, the Right Honorable; the Reverend, the Very Reverend, the Right Reverend, the Most Reverend.

.9 **academic degrees**

AA, Associate of Arts	MBA, Master in Business Administration
AB, Bachelor of Arts (Artium Baccalaureus)	MD, Doctor of Medicine
AdjA, Adjunct in Arts	MDiv, Master of Divinity
AM, Master of Arts (Artium Magister)	MFA, Master of Fine Arts
BA, Bachelor of Arts	MLS, Master of Library Science
BD, Bachelor of Divinity	MRE, Master of Religious Education
BS, Bachelor of Science	MS, Master of Science
DD, Doctor of Divinity	
DDS, Doctor of Dental Surgery	MusD, Doctor of Music
DEd, Doctor of Education	PhD, Doctor of Philosophy
DPhil, Doctor of Philosophy	SB, Bachelor of Science
EdD, Doctor of Education	ScD, Doctor of Science
JD, Doctor of Jurisprudence	SM, Master of Science
LittD, Doctor of Letters	STD, Doctor of Sacred Theology
LLD, Doctor of Laws	ThD, Doctor of Theology
MA, Master of Arts	

918. NOBILITY

(noble rank or birth)

.1 NOUNS **nobility**, nobleness; **aristocracy**, aristocraticalness; **gentility**, genteelness; quality, rank, distinction; birth, high *or* noble birth, ancestry, high or honorable descent; blood, **blue blood**; royalty 739.8.

.2 **nobility**, noblesse, **aristocracy**, aristo–; elite, elect, the classes, **upper classes** or circles, upper cut or **upper crust** [both informal], upper ten [Brit informal], **upper ten thousand**, the Four Hundred, high society, high life, haut monde [Fr]; old nobility, ancienne noblesse [Fr], noblesse de robe, noblesse d'épée [both Fr]; First Families of Virginia, FFVs; **peerage**, baronage, lords temporal and spiritual; baronetage; knightage, chivalry; royalty.

.3 **gentry**, gentlefolk, gentlefolks, gentlepeople, better sort; lesser nobility, petite noblesse [Fr]; samurai [Jap]; landed gentry, squirearchy.

.4 **nobleman**, noble, gentleman; peer; **aristocrat**, patrician, Brahman, blue blood, thoroughbred, silk-stocking, lace-curtain, swell or upper-cruster [both slang]; **grandee**, magnifico, magnate, optimate; **lord**, laird [Scot], lordling; seignior, seigneur, hidalgo [Sp]; **duke**, grand duke, archduke, marquis, **earl**, **count**, viscount, **baron**, daimio, baronet; squire; esquire; armiger; palsgrave, waldgrave, margrave, landgrave.

.5 **knight, cavalier**, chevalier, caballero [Sp], Ritter [Ger], "a verray parfit gentil knight" [Chaucer]; **knight-errant**, knight-adventurer; companion; bachelor, knight bachelor; baronet, knight baronet; banneret, knight banneret; Bayard, Gawain, Lancelot, Sidney, Sir Galahad, Don Quixote.

.6 **noblewoman**, peeress, gentlewoman; **lady**, dame, doña [Sp], khanum; **duchess**, grand duchess, archduchess, marchioness, viscountess, **countess**, baroness, margravine.

.7 **prince**, Prinz, Fürst [both Ger], knez, atheling, sheikh, sherif, mirza, khan, emir, shahzada [India]; princeling, princelet; crown prince, heir apparent; heir presumptive; prince consort; prince regent; **king** 749.7; princes of India 749.9; Muslim rulers 749.10.

.8 **princess**, princesse [Fr], infanta [Sp], rani, maharani, begum, shahzadi, kumari or kunwari, raj-kumari, malikzadi; crown princess; **queen** 749.11.

.9 (rank or office) lordship, ladyship; dukedom, marquisate, earldom, barony, baronetcy; viscountship, viscountcy, viscounty; knighthood, knight-errantship; seigniory, seigneury, seignioralty; pasha-ship, pashadom; princeship, princedom; kingship, queenship 739.8.

.10 ADJS **noble**, of rank, high, exalted; **aristocratic**, patrician; **gentle**, genteel, of gentle blood; gentlemanly, gentlemanlike; ladylike, quite the lady; knightly, chivalrous; ducal, archducal; princely, princelike; kingly, kinglike, "every inch a king" [Shakespeare]; queenly, queenlike; titled.

.11 **wellborn**, well-bred, blue-blooded, of good breed; **thoroughbred**, purebred, pure-blooded, pur sang [Fr], full-blooded; **highborn**, highbred; born to the purple.

919. COMMONALTY

.1 NOUNS **commonalty**, commonality, commonage, commoners, commons; **common people**, vulgus [L], ordinary people, common sort, plain people, plain folks, common run [informal], rank and file, neither nobility nor clergy, the third estate, the salt of the earth; **proletariat**, working class, working people, toiling class, toilers, laborers, lumpen proletariat; **bourgeoisie**, middle class, middle orders, upper middle class, lower middle class, linendrapers, shopkeepers, small tradesmen; **lower classes**, lower orders, the lower cut [informal], the other half; peasantry.

.2 **the people**, **the populace**, hoi polloi [Gk], the population, the citizenry, **the public**, the general public, John Q. Public; demos [Gk]; Tom, Dick, and Harry; Brown, Jones, and Robinson.

.3 **the masses**, **the hoi polloi**, the many, **the multitude**, the crowd, **the mob**, the horde, the million, **the majority**, the mass of the people, the herd, the great unnumbered, the great unwashed, **the vulgar** or **common herd**; profanum vulgus, ignobile vulgus, mobile vulgus [all L]; "the multitude of the gross people" [Erasmus], "many-headed multitude" [Sir Philip Sidney], "the beast with many heads" [Shakespeare], "the blunt monster with uncounted heads, the still-discordant wavering multitude" [Shakespeare].

.4 **rabble**, rabblement, rout, ruck, common ruck, canaille, ragtag [informal], "the tag-rag people" [Shakespeare], **ragtag and bobtail**; rag, tag, and bobtail.

.5 **riffraff**, raff, chaff, trash, **rubbish**, dregs, sordes, offscourings, offscum, scum, **scum of the earth**, dregs or scum or offscum or **offscourings of society**, swinish multitude, vermin, cattle.

.6 **the underprivileged,** the disadvantaged, the poor, ghetto-dwellers, slum-dwellers, welfare cases, chronic poor, depressed class, poverty subculture, the wretched of the earth, outcasts, the dispossessed, the powerless.

.7 **common man, commoner,** little man, little fellow, **average man,** ordinary man, typical man, **man in the street,** one of the people, man of the people, Everyman; **plebeian,** pleb [slang]; **proletarian,** bourgeois, *roturier* [Fr]; Cockney; Joe Doakes, John Smith, Mr. *or* Mrs. Brown *or* Smith.

.8 **peasant, countryman,** countrywoman, **provincial,** son of the soil, tiller of the soil; **peon,** hind, fellah, muzhik; sons of Martha, "hewers of wood and drawers of water" [Bible].

.9 **rustic,** bucolic [informal]; **yokel, hick, rube, hayseed** [all slang], **bumpkin,** country bumpkin, **clod, clodhopper** [informal], **hillbilly** *or* **woodhick** [both slang], **boor,** clown, lout, looby, farmer 413.5.

.10 **upstart, parvenu,** adventurer, sprout [slang], "an upstart crow beautified in our feathers" [Robert Greene]; *bourgeois gentilhomme* [Fr], would-be gentleman; *nouveau riche, nouveau roturier* [both Fr], **newly-rich,** pig in clover [slang]; social climber, name-dropper, tufthunter; status seeker.

.11 ADJS **common,** commonplace, **plain,** ordinary, **lowly,** low, mean, **humble,** homely; **lowborn,** lowbred, baseborn, earthborn, plebeian; non-noble, nonclerical; third-estate; ungenteel, shabby-genteel; vulgar, rude 898.10–15; below the salt; cockney, born within sound of Bow bells.

.12 **middle-class,** bourgeois; **proletarian,** working-class.

.13 **parvenu, upstart,** mushroom, risen from the ranks; **newly-rich,** *nouveau-riche* [Fr].

920. WONDER

.1 NOUNS **wonder, wonderment,** sense of wonder, marveling, marvel, **astonishment, amazement,** amaze, **astoundment;** dumbfoundment, stupefaction; **surprise, awe,** breathless wonder *or* awe, sense of mystery, admiration; beguilement, fascination 650.1; bewilderment, puzzlement 514.3.

.2 **marvel, wonder, prodigy, miracle, phenomenon,** astonishment, amazement, marvelment, wonderment, wonderful thing, nine days' wonder, amazing *or* astonishing thing, quite a thing, really something, **sensation,** stunner [slang]; one for the book *or* something to brag about *or* something to shout about *or* something to write home about *or* something else [all informal]; **rarity,** nonesuch, exception, one in a thousand, one in a way; curiosity, gazingstock, sight, spectacle; wonders of the world.

.3 **wonderfulness,** wondrousness, **marvelousness,** miraculousness, phenomenalness, prodigiousness, stupendousness, remarkableness, extraordinariness; beguilingness, fascination, enchantingness, enticingness, seductiveness, glamorousness; awesomeness, mysteriousness, mystery, numinousness.

.4 **inexpressibility, ineffability,** inenarrability, noncommunicability, noncommunicableness, incommunicability, incommunicableness, indescribability, indefinableness, **unutterability, unspeakability,** unnameableness, innominability, unmentionability.

.5 VERBS **wonder, marvel, be astonished** *or* amazed *or* astounded, be seized with wonder; **gaze, gape,** look *or* stand aghast *or* agog, gawk, **stare,** stare openmouthed, open one's eyes, rub one's eyes, hold one's breath; not be able to account for, not know what to make of, not believe one's eyes *or* ears *or* senses.

.6 **astonish, amaze, astound, surprise,** startle, **stagger, bewilder, perplex** 514.12,13, flabbergast [informal], confound, overwhelm, boggle; **awe,** awestrike, strike with wonder *or* awe; **dumbfound, dumbfounder,** strike dumb, strike dead; strike all of a heap *or* throw on one's beam ends [both informal], bowl down *or* over [informal], dazzle, bedazzle, daze, bedaze; stun, stupefy, petrify, paralyze.

.7 take one's breath away, turn one's head, make one's head swim, make one's hair stand on end, make one's tongue cleave to the roof of one's mouth, make one stare, make one sit up and take notice, carry one off his feet.

.8 beggar *or* baffle description, stagger belief.

.9 ADJS **wondering,** wrapped *or* rapt in wonder, marveling, **astonished, amazed, surprised, astounded,** flabbergasted [informal], **bewildered,** puzzled 514.23,24, confounded, **dumbfounded,** dumbstruck, staggered, overwhelmed, unable to believe one's senses *or* eyes; **aghast,** agape, agog, all agog, gazing, gaping, at gaze, staring, gauping, wide-eyed, popeyed, open-eyed, openmouthed, **breathless; thunderstruck,** wonder-struck, wonder-stricken, awestruck, struck all of a heap [informal]; awed, in awe, in awe of; spellbound, fascinated, captivated, under a charm, beguiled, enthralled, enraptured, enravished, enchanted, entranced, bewitched, hypnotized, mesmerized, stupefied, lost in wonder or amazement.

.10 **wonderful, wondrous, marvelous, miraculous,** fantastic, fabulous, phenomenal, prodigious, stupendous, unheard-of, unprecedented, extraordinary, exceptional, rare, unique, **remarkable,** striking, **sensational; strange,** passing strange, "wondrous strange" [Shakespeare]; **beguiling, fascinating** 650.7; incredible, inconceivable, outlandish, unimaginable, incomprehensible; **bewildering, puzzling** 514.25, enigmatic.

.11 **awesome,** awful, awing, awe-inspiring; **mysterious,** numinous; weird, eerie, uncanny, bizarre.

.12 **astonishing, amazing, surprising,** startling, **astounding,** confounding, staggering, stunning [slang], eye-opening, breathtaking, overwhelming, mind-boggling; **spectacular.**

.13 **indescribable, ineffable,** inenarrable, inexpressible, unutterable, unspeakable, noncommunicable, incommunicable, indefinable, undefinable, unnameable, innominable, unwhisperable, unmentionable.

.14 ADVS **wonderfully,** wondrously, **marvelously, miraculously,** fantastically, fabulously, phenomenally, prodigiously, stupendously, extraordinarily, exceptionally, remarkably, strikingly, **sensationally;** strangely, outlandishly, incredibly, inconceivably, unimaginably, incomprehensibly, **bewilderingly, puzzlingly,** enigmatically; **beguilingly,** fascinatingly 650.8.

.15 **awesomely,** awfully, awingly, awe-inspiringly; **mysteriously,** numinously, weirdly, eerily, uncannily, bizarrely.

.16 **astonishingly, amazingly, astoundingly,** staggeringly, confoundingly; **surprisingly,** startlingly, to one's surprise or great surprise, to one's astonishment or amazement; for a wonder, strange to say.

.17 **indescribably, ineffably,** inexpressibly, unutterably, unspeakably, inenarrably, indefinably, unnameably, unmentionably.

.18 in wonder, in astonishment, in amazement, in bewilderment, in awe, in admiration, with gaping mouth.

.19 INTERJS (astonishment or surprise) my word!, I declare!, well I never!, of all things!, as I live and breathe!, what!, indeed!, really!, surely!, how now!, what on earth!, what in the world!, I'll be jiggered!, holy Christ!, holy Christmas!, holy cow!, holy mackerel!, holy Moses!, holy smoke!, holy shit! [slang], hush or shut my mouth!, blow me down!, strike me dead!, shiver my timbers!

.20 oh!, O!, ah!, la!, lo!, lo and behold!, hello!, halloo!, hey!, whew!, phew!, wow!, yipes!, yike!

.21 my!, oh, my!, dear!, dear me!, goodness!, gracious!, goodness gracious!, gee!, my goodness!, my stars!, good gracious!, good heavens!, good lack!, lackadaisy!, welladay!, hoity-toity!, zounds!, 'sdeath!, gadzooks!, gad so!, bless my heart!, God bless me!, heavens and earth!, for crying out loud! [slang].

.22 imagine!, fancy!, fancy that!, just imagine!, only think!, well!, I never!, can you feature that!, can you beat that!, it beats the Dutch!, do tell!, you don't say!, the devil or deuce you say!, I'll be!, what do you know!, what do you know about that!, how about that!, who would have thought it!, did you ever!, can it be!, can such things be?, will wonders never cease!

921. UNASTONISHMENT

.1 NOUNS **unastonishment, unamazement,** unamazedness, nonastonishment, nonamazement, nonamazedness, nonwonder, nonwondering, nonmarveling, unsurprise, unsurprisedness, awelessness, wonderlessness, calmness, coolness, **cool** [slang], cool or calm or nodding acceptance, composure, inexcitability 858, expectation 539, unimpressibleness, refusal to be impressed or awed or amazed.

.2 VERBS **accept, take for granted,** take as a matter of course, treat as routine, show no amazement, refuse to be impressed, not blink an eye, not turn a hair, keep one's cool [slang].

.3 ADJS **unastonished, unsurprised, unamazed,** unmarveling, unwondering, unastounded, undumbfounded, unbewildered; undazzled, undazed; unawed, aweless, wonderless; **unimpressed,** unmoved; calm, **cool,** composed, inexcitable 858.10–15; expecting, expected 539.11–14.

922. SOCIABILITY

.1 NOUNS **sociability,** sociality, sociableness, fitness or fondness for society, social-mindedness, **gregariousness, affability,** companionability, compatibility, geniality, **congeniality**; hospitality 925; clubbability [informal], clubbishness, clubbism; intimacy, familiarity; amiability, **friendliness** 927.1; **communicativeness** 554.3; social grace, civility, urbanity, courtesy 936.

.2 **camaraderie**, comradery, comradeship, **fellowship**, good-fellowship; consorting, hobnobbing.

.3 **conviviality**, joviality, jollity, gaiety, heartiness, cheer, good cheer, festivity, merrymaking, merriment, revelry.

.4 **social intercourse**, social activity, **intercourse, communication, communion,** intercommunion, **fellowship,** intercommunication, **community,** collegiality, commerce, congress, converse, conversation, social relations.

.5 (social grouping) **social circle** or **set,** social class, one's crowd or set; **association** 788.

.6 **association,** consociation, affiliation, **fellowship, companionship, company, society;** fraternity, fraternization; membership, participation, partaking, sharing, cooperation 786.

.7 **visit, social call,** call; formal visit, duty visit, required visit; visiting, visitation; round of visits; social round, social whirl, mad round.

.8 **appointment, engagement, date** [informal], double date, blind date [both informal]; arrangement, interview; engagement book.

.9 **rendezvous, tryst, assignation, meeting;** trysting place, meeting place, place of assignation; assignation house; love nest [informal].

.10 **social gathering, social,** sociable, social affair, affair, gathering, get-together [informal]; **reception,** at home, salon, levee; soiree; matinee; reunion, family reunion; wake.

.11 **party, entertainment,** blowout [slang]; **festivity** 878.3,4; shindig or shindy; **ball** 879.2; stag or stag party [both informal]; hen party [slang]; house party; housewarming, house-raising; shower, donation party; surprise party; garden party, lawn party, fête champêtre [Fr]; costume party, masquerade party, masquerade, masque, mask; coffee party, coffee klatch, Kaffeeklatsch [Ger]; cocktail party; dinner party, dinner; smoker [informal].

.12 **tea,** afternoon tea, five-o'clock tea, high tea; **tea party.**

.13 **bee,** quilting bee, raising bee, husking bee, cornhusking, corn shucking, husking.

.14 **debut, coming out** [informal], presentation, coming-out party [informal].

.15 (sociable person) joiner, mixer or **good mixer** [both informal], good or pleasant company, excellent companion, life of the party, bon vivant; man-about-town, playboy, social lion, nightclub habitué; clubman, clubwoman.

.16 VERBS **associate with,** assort with, sort with, consort with, hobnob with, **mingle with, mix with, touch elbows** or **shoulders with,** eat off the same trencher; **fraternize,** fellowship, join in fellowship; **keep company with,** bear one company, walk hand in hand with; join, take up with [informal], tie up with [slang]; **flock together,** herd together, club together, clique or clique with [both informal], gang up with [slang], hang around with [informal], hunt or run in couples; chum, **chum with** or chum together [both informal]; pal or pal with [both informal], pal up with or around with [slang], run around with, run with, hang out with.

.17 **visit,** make or pay a visit, **call on** or **upon, drop in,** run in, look in, look one up, see, stop off or over [informal], drop or run or stop by; leave one's card.

.18 ADJS **sociable, social,** social-minded, fit for society, fond of society, **gregarious, affable; companionable,** companionate, compatible, genial, **congenial;** hospitable 925.11; clubby, clubbable [both informal], clubbish; **communicative** 554.10; amiable, **friendly** 927.14; civil, urbane, courteous 936.14–17.

.19 **convivial,** boon, free and easy, hail-fellow-well-met; **jovial, jolly,** hearty, festive, gay.

.20 **intimate, familiar,** cozy, chatty, tête-à-tête.

.21 ADVS **sociably,** socially, gregariously, affably; companionably, arm in arm, hand in hand.

923. UNSOCIABILITY

.1 NOUNS **unsociability,** insociability, unsociableness, dissociability; **ungregariousness,** uncompanionability; unclubbableness or unclubbability [both informal], ungeniality, **uncongeniality;** incompatibility, social incompatibility; **unfriendliness** 929.1; **uncommunicativeness** 613; sullenness, mopishness, moroseness; self-sufficiency, self-containment; autism; bashfulness 908.4.

.2 **aloofness, standoffishness,** offishness,

withdrawnness, **remoteness,** distance, detachment; **coolness,** coldness, frigidity, chill, chilliness, iciness, frostiness; inaccessibility, unapproachability.

.3 seclusiveness, exclusiveness; **seclusion** 924.

.4 VERBS **keep to oneself,** keep oneself to oneself, enjoy or prefer one's own company, stay at home, shun companionship, **stand aloof,** hold oneself aloof or apart, keep one's distance, keep at a distance, keep in the background, retire, retire into the shade, creep into a corner.

.5 ADJS **unsociable,** insociable, dissociable, unsocial; **ungregarious,** nongregarious; **uncompanionable,** ungenial, uncongenial; incompatible, socially incompatible; unclubbable [informal]; **unfriendly** 929.9; **uncommunicative** 613.8; sullen, mopish, mopey, morose; close, snug; self-sufficient, self-contained; autistic; bashful 908.12.

.6 **aloof, standoffish,** offish, standoff, **distant,** remote, withdrawn, removed, detached, Olympian; **cool,** cold, frigid, chilly, icy, frosty; seclusive, exclusive; inaccessible, unapproachable.

924. SECLUSION

.1 NOUNS **seclusion,** reclusion, **retirement, withdrawal, retreat,** recess; renunciation or forsaking of the world; **sequestration,** quarantine, separation, detachment, apartness; segregation, apartheid, Jim Crow; **isolation,** "splendid isolation" [Sir William Goschen]; **privacy,** privatism, **secrecy;** rustication; privatization; isolationism.

.2 **hermitism,** hermitry, eremitism, anchoritism, cloistered monasticism.

.3 **solitude,** solitariness, **aloneness,** loneness, singleness; **loneliness, lonesomeness.**

.4 **forlornness, desolation;** friendlessness, kithlessness, fatherlessness, motherlessness, homelessness; helplessness, defenselessness; abandonment, desertion.

.5 **recluse, loner,** solitaire, solitary, solitudinarian; **shut-in,** invalid, bedridden invalid; cloistered monk or nun; **hermit,** eremite, anchorite; marabout; hermitess, anchoress; **ascetic;** closet cynic; stylite, pillarist, pillar saint; Hieronymite, Hieronymian; Diogenes, Timon of Athens, St. Simeon Stylites, St. Anthony, desert saints, desert fathers; outcast, pariah 926.4; **stay-at-home,** homebody; isolationist, seclusionist.

.6 VERBS **seclude oneself,** go into seclusion, retire, go into retirement, retire from the world, abandon or forsake the world, live in retirement, lead a retired life, lead a cloistered life, be or remain incommunicado, shut oneself up, live alone, live apart; stay at home; rusticate; take the veil; cop out [slang], opt out or drop out of society.

.7 ADJS **secluded, retired, withdrawn; isolated,** shut off, insular, **separate,** separated, **apart,** detached, removed; segregated, quarantined; **remote, out-of-the-way,** in a backwater, out-of-the-world; **unfrequented,** unvisited.

.8 **private,** privy, **secret, hidden.**

.9 **recluse, sequestered, cloistered,** shut up or in; **hermitic(al),** eremitic(al), hermitish; anchoritic(al); stay-at-home, domestic.

.10 **solitary, alone; in solitude,** by oneself, all alone; **lonely, lonesome, lone.**

.11 **forlorn,** lorn; **abandoned, forsaken, deserted, desolate,** godforsaken [informal], friendless, unfriended, kithless, fatherless, motherless, homeless; helpless, defenseless; outcast 926.10.

.12 ADVS **in seclusion, in retirement,** in retreat, in solitude; in privacy, in secrecy; "far from the madding crowd's ignoble strife" [Thomas Gray], "the world forgetting by the world forgot" [Pope].

925. HOSPITALITY, WELCOME

.1 NOUNS **hospitality,** hospitableness, receptiveness; **cordiality,** amiability, graciousness, **friendliness,** neighborliness, geniality, heartiness, bonhomie, **generosity,** liberality, openheartedness, warmth, warmness, warmheartedness; open door.

.2 **welcome,** welcoming, **reception,** accueil [Fr]; cordial or warm or hearty welcome, pleasant or smiling reception, the glad hand [slang], open arms; embrace, hug; welcome mat.

.3 **greetings, salutations,** salaams; **regards,** best wishes 936.8.

.4 **greeting, salutation,** salute; **hail, hello,** how-do-you-do; accost, address; nod, bow, bob; curtsy 964.2; wave; handshake, hand-clasp; embrace, hug, kiss; smile, smile of recognition.

.5 **host,** mine host; hostess, receptionist; landlord 809.2.

.6 **guest, visitor,** visitant, xen(o)–; **caller,** company; frequenter, habitué; uninvited guest, gate-crasher [informal]; moocher or freeloader [both slang].

.7 VERBS **receive, admit,** accept, take in, let in, open the door to; **be at home to,** have the latchstring out, keep a light in the window, put out the welcome mat, keep the door open, keep an open house.

.8 **entertain,** entertain guests, guest; host, preside, do the honors [informal]; give a party, throw a party [slang]; spread oneself [informal].

.9 **welcome,** make welcome, bid one welcome, make one feel welcome *or* at home, hold out the hand, extend the right hand of friendship; glad hand, give the glad hand *or* glad eye [all informal]; **embrace, hug, receive with open arms;** give a warm reception to, "kill the fatted calf" [Bible].

.10 **greet, hail, accost,** address; **salute,** make one's salutations; **bid** *or* **say hello,** bid good day *or* good morning, etc.; exchange greetings, **pass the time of day; give one's regards** 936.13; shake hands, shake [slang], press *or* squeeze one's hand; nod to, bow to; curtsy 964.6; tip the hat to, lift the hat, touch the hat *or* cap; take one's hat off to, uncover; pull the forelock; kiss, greet with a kiss, kiss hands *or* cheeks.

.11 ADJS **hospitable, receptive,** welcoming; **cordial,** amiable, gracious, **friendly,** neighborly, genial, hearty, open, openhearted, warm, warmhearted; **generous,** liberal; –xenous.

.12 **welcome,** welcome as the roses in May; **agreeable,** desirable, acceptable; **grateful,** gratifying, pleasing.

.13 ADVS **hospitably, with open arms.**

.14 INTERJS **welcome!,** *soyez le bienvenu!* [Fr], *¡bien venido!* [Sp], *benvenuto!* [Ital], *Willkommen!* [Ger]; glad to see you!

.15 **greetings!,** salutations!, **hello!,** hullo!, hail!, hey! *or* heigh!, **hi!,** aloha!, *¡hola!* [Sp]; **how do you do?, how are you?,** *comment allez-vous?, comment ça va?* [both Fr], *¿cómo está Usted?* [Sp], *come sta?* [Ital], *wie geht's?* [Ger]; **good morning!,** *guten Morgen!* [Ger]; good day!, *bon jour!* [Fr], *¡buenos días!* [Sp], *buon giorno!* [Ital], *guten Tag!* [Ger]; **good afternoon!,** *¡buenas tardes!* [Sp]; **good evening!,** *bon soir!* [Fr], *buona sera!* [Ital], *guten Abend!* [Ger].

.16 [informal terms] **howdy!,** howdy-do!, how-de-do!, how-do-ye-do!, how-d'ye-do!, how you doin'?, hi ya!; how's things?, how's tricks?, how goes it?, how's every little thing?, how's the world treating you?

926. INHOSPITALITY

.1 NOUNS **inhospitality,** inhospitableness, unhospitableness, unreceptiveness; **uncordialness,** ungraciousness, **unfriendliness,** unneighborliness; nonwelcome, nonwelcoming.

.2 unhabitability, uninhabitability, unlivability.

.3 **ostracism,** ostracization; **banishment** 310.4; **proscription, ban; boycott,** boycottage; **blackball,** blacklist.

.4 **outcast,** social outcast, outcast of society, **castaway, derelict,** Ishmael; **pariah, untouchable,** leper; outcaste; *déclassé* [Fr]; **outlaw; expellee, evictee; displaced person, DP; exile, expatriate,** man without a country; undesirable; *persona non grata* [L], unacceptable person.

.5 VERBS **have nothing to do with,** have no truck with [informal], refuse to associate with, steer clear of [informal], **spurn, turn one's back upon;** deny oneself to, refuse to receive, not be at home to; shut the door upon.

.6 **ostracize,** disfellowship; **banish** 310.17; **proscribe, ban, outlaw,** put under the ban; **boycott, blackball,** blacklist.

.7 ADJS **inhospitable, unhospitable; unreceptive,** closed; **uncordial,** ungracious, **unfriendly,** unneighborly.

.8 **unhabitable, uninhabitable,** nonhabitable, unoccupiable, untenantable, **unlivable, unfit to live in,** not fit for man or beast.

.9 **unwelcome, unwanted; unagreeable,** undesirable, unacceptable; **uninvited,** unasked, unbidden.

.10 **outcast, cast-off, castaway, derelict;** outside the pale, outside the gates; **rejected, disowned; abandoned, forsaken** 924.11.

927. FRIENDSHIP

.1 NOUNS **friendship, friendliness; amicability,** amicableness, amity, peaceableness, unhostility; **amiability,** amiableness, **congeniality,** well-affectedness; neighborliness, neighborlikeness; sociability 922; love 931; kindness 938.

.2 **fellowship, companionship, comradeship,** colleagueship, chumship [informal], palship [slang], freemasonry, consortship, boon companionship; **brotherhood, fraternity,** fraternalism, sodality, confraternity; **sisterhood, sorority;** brotherliness, sisterliness; community of interest, *esprit de corps* [Fr].

.3 **good terms, good understanding,** good

footing, friendly relations; **harmony,** sympathy, fellow feeling, **rapport** 794.1; **favor, goodwill, good graces, regard,** respect, mutual regard, favorable regard, the good *or* right side of [informal]; an in [informal].

.4 **acquaintance,** acquaintedness, close acquaintance; **introduction,** presentation, knockdown [slang].

.5 **familiarity, intimacy,** intimate acquaintance, closeness, nearness, inseparableness; affinity, special affinity; chumminess [informal], palliness [slang], mateyness [Brit informal].

.6 **cordiality, geniality,** heartiness, bonhomie, ardency, warmth, warmness, warm-heartedness; hospitality 925.

.7 **devotion, devotedness;** dedication, commitment; fastness, steadfastness, firmness, constancy, staunchness; triedness, trueness, tried-and-trueness.

.8 cordial friendship, warm *or* ardent friendship, devoted friendship, bosom friendship, intimate *or* familiar friendship, sincere friendship, beautiful friendship, fast *or* firm friendship, staunch friendship, loyal friendship, lasting friendship, undying friendship.

.9 VERBS **be friends,** have the friendship of, have the ear of; **know, be acquainted with;** associate with 922.16; cotton to *or* hit it off [both informal], get on well with, hobnob with, fraternize with; be close friends with, be inseparable; **be on good terms,** enjoy good *or* friendly relations with; keep on good terms, have an in with [informal].

.10 **befriend, make friends with,** gain the friendship of, **strike up a friendship,** get to know one another, take up with [informal], shake hands with, **get acquainted,** make *or* scrape acquaintance with, pick up an acquaintance with; get chummy with [informal], buddy up [slang]; play footsie with [slang]; win friends, win friends and influence people.

.11 **cultivate,** cultivate the friendship of, **court,** pay court to, pay addresses to, seek the company of, **run after** [informal], **shine up to,** make up to [informal], play up to *or* suck up to [both slang], hold out *or* extend the right of friendship *or* fellowship; **make advances,** approach, break the ice.

.12 **get on good terms with, get into favor,** win the regard of, **get in the good graces of, get in good with,** get in with [informal], get on the in with *or* get next to

[both informal], **get on the good** *or* **right side of** [informal].

.13 **introduce, present, acquaint,** make acquainted, give an introduction, give a knockdown [slang], do the honors [informal].

.14 ADJS **friendly,** friendlike; **amicable, peaceable,** unhostile; **harmonious** 794.3; **amiable, congenial,** *simpático* [Sp], *simpatico* [Ital], *sympathique* [Fr], pleasant, agreeable, favorable, well-affected, well-disposed, well-intentioned, well-meaning, well-meant; brotherly, fraternal; sisterly; neighborly, neighborlike; sociable 922.18; kind 938.13–17.

.15 **cordial, genial,** hearty, ardent, warm, warmhearted; hospitable 925.11.

.16 **friends with,** friendly with, at home with; **acquainted.**

.17 **on good terms,** on a good footing, on friendly *or* amicable terms, **on speaking terms,** on a first-name basis, on visiting terms; **in good with,** in with [informal], on the in with, in [both slang], **in favor, in one's good graces,** in one's good books, on the good *or* right side of [informal].

.18 **familiar, intimate, close,** near, inseparable, on familiar *or* intimate terms; handin-hand, hand and glove; **thick, thick as thieves** [informal].

.19 **chummy** [informal], matey [Brit informal]; pally *or* palsy *or* palsy-walsy *or* buddy-buddy [all slang].

.20 **devoted,** dedicated, committed, **fast,** steadfast, constant, faithful, staunch; tried, true, **tried and true,** tested.

.21 ADVS **amicably,** friendly, friendliwise; **amiably, congenially,** pleasantly, agreeably, favorably; **cordially, genially,** heartily, ardently, warmly, with open arms; familiarly, intimately; arm in arm, hand in hand.

928. FRIEND

.1 NOUNS **friend, acquaintance,** close acquaintance; confidant, confidante, repository; **intimate,** familiar, **close friend,** intimate *or* familiar friend; **bosom friend,** friend of one's bosom, inseparable friend, **best friend;** alter ego, other self; brother, fellow, fellowman, fellow creature, neighbor; **sympathizer,** well-wisher, partisan, advocate, favorer, backer, **supporter** 787.9; casual acquaintance; pickup [informal]; lover 931.11,12.

.2 **good friend,** great friend, **devoted friend,** warm *or* ardent friend, **faithful friend,** trusted *or* trusty friend, *fidus Achates*

[L], constant friend, staunch friend, fast friend, "a friend that sticketh closer than a brother" [Bible]; **friend in need**, friend indeed.

.3 **companion, fellow,** fellow companion, **comrade,** *camarade* [Fr], amigo [informal], mate [Brit], comate, company, **associate** 787, consociate, compeer, confrere, consort, **colleague, partner,** pardner *or* pard [both slang], copartner, side partner, **sidekick** [slang], crony, old crony, gossip; **chum** *or* **buddy** *or* buddy-boy *or* bosom buddy [all informal], **pal** [informal], ace [slang], butty [Brit informal]; girl friend [informal]; **roommate,** chamberfellow; bunkmate, bunkie [informal]; bedfellow, bedmate; **schoolmate,** schoolfellow, classmate, classfellow, school companion, school chum, fellow student *or* pupil; **playmate,** playfellow; **teammate,** yokefellow, yokemate; workfellow 787.5; shipmate; messmate.

.4 **boon companion,** boonfellow; **good fellow,** jolly fellow, hearty, *bon vivant* [Fr]; pot companion.

.5 (famous friendships) Achilles and Patroclus, Castor and Pollux, Damon and Pythias, David and Jonathan, Diomedes and Sthenelus, Epaminondas and Pelopidas, Hercules and Iolaus, Nisus and Euryalus, Pylades and Orestes, Theseus and Pirithoüs, Christ and the beloved disciple; The Three Musketeers.

929. ENMITY

.1 NOUNS **enmity, unfriendliness,** inimicality; **uncordiality,** unamiability, ungeniality, disaffinity, incompatibility, incompatibleness; personal conflict, strain, **tension;** coolness, coldness, chilliness, chill, frost, iciness; inhospitality 926, unsociability 923.

.2 **disaccord** 795; ruffled feelings, strained relations, alienation, estrangement 795.4.

.3 **hostility, antagonism, repugnance, antipathy,** spitefulness, spite, despitefulness, malice, malevolence, malignity, **hatred, hate** 930; **conflict, contention** 796, collision, clash, clashing, **friction;** quarrelsomeness 795.3; belligerence 797.15.

.4 **animosity,** animus; **ill will,** ill feeling, bitter feeling, **hard feelings,** no love lost; **bad blood,** ill blood, feud, vendetta; **bitterness,** sourness, soreness, **rancor,** acrimony, virulence, venom, vitriol.

.5 **grudge, spite,** crow to pick *or* pluck *or* pull, bone to pick; peeve *or* pet peeve [both informal].

.6 **enemy, foe,** foeman, **adversary, antagonist;** bitter enemy; sworn enemy; open enemy; public enemy; archenemy, devil; "my nearest and dearest enemy" [Thomas Middleton].

.7 VERBS **antagonize,** set against, set at odds, set at each other's throat, sick on each other [informal]; aggravate, exacerbate, heat up, **provoke,** envenom, **embitter,** infuriate, madden; **alienate,** estrange 795.14.

.8 **bear ill will,** bear malice, have it in for [informal], hold it against, be down on [informal]; **bear a grudge,** owe a grudge, have a bone to pick with; have a crow to pick *or* pluck *or* pull with; **hate** 930.5.

.9 ADJS **unfriendly, inimical, unamicable; uncordial,** unamiable, ungenial, incompatible; strained, tense; disaccordant, unharmonious 795.16; cool, cold, chill, chilly, frosty, icy; inhospitable 926.7; unsociable 923.5.

.10 **hostile, antagonistic,** repugnant, antipathetic, set against, spiteful, despiteful, malicious, malevolent, malignant, hateful, full of hate *or* hatred; virulent, **bitter,** sore, rancorous, acrid, caustic, venomous, vitriolic; conflicting, clashing, colliding; quarrelsome 795.17; belligerent 797.25.

.11 **alienated, estranged,** disaffected, separated, divided, disunited, torn; irreconcilable.

.12 **at outs, on the outs** [informal], at enmity, at variance, **at odds,** at loggerheads, at cross-purposes, at sixes and sevens, at each other's throat, at daggers drawn.

.13 **on bad terms,** not on speaking terms; in bad with [informal], in bad odor with, in one's bad *or* black books, on one's shitlist [slang].

.14 ADVS **unamicably,** inimically; **uncordially,** unamiably, ungenially; coolly, coldly, chillily, frostily; **hostilely, antagonistically.**

930. HATE

.1 NOUNS **hate, hatred,** mis(o)–; **dislike** 867; **detestation, abhorrence, aversion, antipathy,** repugnance, **loathing,** execration, **abomination,** odium; **spite,** spitefulness, despitefulness, malice, malevolence, malignity; vials of hate *or* wrath; misanthropy, misandry, misogyny; anti-Semitism; race hatred, racism; bigotry; Anglophobia, Russophobia, xenophobia, etc. 891.10–17.

.2 **enmity** 929; bitterness, **animosity** 929.4.

.3 (hated thing) **anathema, abomination,**

detestation, aversion, abhorrence, antipathy, execration, hate; peeve, pet peeve;
phobia.

.4 hater, man-hater, woman-hater, misanthropist, misanthrope, misogynist, anti-
Semite, racist, bigot; Anglophobe, Russo-
phobe, xenophobe, etc.

.5 VERBS hate, detest, loathe, abhor, execrate, abominate, hold in abomination,
take an aversion to, shudder at, utterly
detest.

.6 dislike, disrelish 867.3.

.7 ADJS hating, abhorrent, loathing; averse
to 867.8; disgusted 866.20.

.8 hateful, detestable 864.18; despiteful; unlikable 867.7.

931. LOVE

.1 NOUNS love, affection, attachment, devotion, phil(o)–, –phily; fondness, sentiment, weakness [informal], like, liking,
fancy, shine [slang]; passion, tender feeling or passion, ardor, ardency, fervor,
heart, flame; physical love, Amor, Eros,
bodily love, libido, sexual love, sex 419;
desire, yearning 634.1–5; lasciviousness
989.5; charity, caritas [L], brotherly love,
Christian love, agape [Gk]; spiritual love,
Platonic love; adoration, worship, hero
worship; regard, admiration; idolization,
idolism, idolatry; popular regard, popularity; faithful love, truelove; married
love, conjugal love, uxoriousness; free
love, free-lovism; lovemaking 932.

.2 "an insatiate thirst of enjoying a greedily
desired object" [Montaigne], "the heart's
immortal thirst to be completely known
and all forgiven" [Henry Van Dyke],
"Nature's second sun" [George Chap-
man], "tyrant sparing none" [Corneille],
"the blood of life, the power of reunion
of the separated" [Tillich], "the reflection of a man's own worthiness from
other men" [Emerson], "a spiritual coupling of two souls" [Ben Jonson].

.3 amorousness, amativeness, lovingness,
meltingness, affection, affectionateness,
demonstrativeness; sexiness; goatishness,
horniness [slang]; romanticism, sentimentality, susceptibility; lovesickness, love-
lornness; ecstasy, rapture 857.7; enchantment 865.2.

.4 infatuation, infatuatedness, passing fancy; crush or mash or pash or case [all
slang]; puppy love or calf love [both in-
formal].

.5 parental love, natural affection, mother

or maternal love, father or paternal love;
filial love.

.6 love affair, affair, affair of the heart,
amour, romance, romantic tie or bond,
something between, liaison, entanglement, intrigue; flirtation, hanky-panky;
triangle, eternal triangle; illicit love, forbidden love, adulterous affair, adultery,
unfaithfulness, infidelity, cuckoldry.

.7 lovability, likability, adorability, sweetness, loveliness, lovesomeness, amiability,
attractiveness 863.2, desirability, agreeability; charm, appeal, allurement 650; winsomeness, winning ways.

.8 (gods) Love, Cupid, Amor, Eros, Kama;
(goddesses) Venus, Aphrodite, Astarte,
Freya.

.9 (symbols) cupid, cupidon, amor, amou-
rette, amoretto, amorino [Ital].

.10 sweetheart, sweetie [informal], sweet pa-
tootie [slang]; honey 932.5; date [infor-
mal]; steady [slang]; flirt, coquette; vampire, vamp; conquest, catch, captive.

.11 lover, admirer, adorer, amorist, –phile; infatuate, paramour, suitor, wooer, pursuer,
follower.

.12 beau, inamorato, swain, man, gallant,
cavalier, squire, esquire, caballero [Sp];
amoroso, cavaliere servente [both Ital];
sugar daddy [slang]; gigolo; boyfriend or
fellow or young man or flame [all infor-
mal]; old man [informal]; love-maker;
petter or necker [both slang]; seducer,
lady-killer, ladies' man, sheik, philanderer; Lothario, Casanova, Romeo, Don
Juan.

.13 loved one, love, beloved, darling, dear,
dear one, dearly beloved, well-beloved,
truelove, beloved object, object of one's
affections, light of one's eye or life, light
of love; crush.

.14 lady love, inamorata, amorosa [Ital],
lady, mistress; old lady [informal]; girl or
girl friend or best girl or dream girl [all
informal], lass, lassie, jo [Scot], gill, jill,
Dulcinea.

.15 favorite, preference; darling, idol, jewel,
apple of one's eye, man after one's own
heart; pet, fondling, cosset, minion;
spoiled child or darling, enfant gâté [Fr];
teacher's pet; matinee idol.

.16 fiancé, fiancée, bride-to-be, affianced, betrothed, future, intended [informal].

.17 loving couple, soul mates, lovebirds, turtledoves, bill-and-cooers; Romeo and Juliet, Antony and Cleopatra, Tristan and
Isolde, Pelléas and Mélisande, Abélard

and Héloïse, Daphnis and Chloë, Aucassin and Nicolette.

.18 VERBS **love, be fond of,** be in love with, **care for, like, fancy,** have a fancy for, have eyes for [informal], go for [slang], take an interest in, **dote on** or **upon,** be sweet on [informal]; have a crush or mash or case on [slang]; be desperately in love, have it bad [slang], burn with love; be partial to, have a soft spot in one's heart for, have a weakness or fondness for.

.19 **cherish, hold dear,** prize, treasure; **admire, regard,** esteem, revere; **adore, idolize,** worship, dearly love, think worlds or the world of, love to distraction.

.20 **fall in love,** lose one's heart, **become enamored,** be smitten [informal]; take to, **take a liking** or fancy to, take a shine to or fall for [both slang], cotton to [informal], become attached to, bestow one's affections on; fall head and ears or head over heels in love, be swept off one's feet.

.21 **enamor, endear;** win one's heart, win the love or affections of, take the fancy of, make a hit with [slang]; **charm, becharm, infatuate,** hold in thrall, **fascinate,** attract, allure, **captivate,** bewitch, enrapture, carry away, sweep off one's feet, turn one's head, inflame with love; **seduce,** vamp [slang], draw on, tempt, tantalize.

.22 ADJS **beloved, loved, dear, darling, precious;** pet, favorite; **adored, admired,** esteemed, revered; **cherished,** prized, treasured, held dear; **well-liked,** popular; **well-beloved,** dearly beloved, dear to one's heart, after one's heart or own heart, dear as the apple of one's eye.

.23 **lovable, likable, adorable,** admirable, **lovely,** lovesome, sweet, winning, winsome; **charming** 650.7; angelic, seraphic; caressable, kissable; cuddlesome, cuddly.

.24 **amorous,** amatory, amative, erotic; **sexual** 419.26–30; loverly, loverlike; **passionate, ardent,** impassioned; desirous 634.21–28; lascivious 989.29.

.25 **loving,** lovesome, **fond, adoring, devoted, affectionate,** –philic, –philous; demonstrative, **romantic, sentimental, tender,** soft [informal], melting; lovelorn, lovesick, languishing; wifely, husbandly, conjugal, uxorious, faithful; parental, paternal, maternal, filial.

.26 **enamored, charmed, becharmed, fascinated, captivated,** bewitched, enraptured 857.23, enchanted 865.14; **infatuated,** infatuate; **smitten** [informal], heartsmitten.

.27 **in love,** head over heels in love, over head and ears in love.

.28 **fond of, enamored of,** partial to, **sweet on** or **upon** [informal], **stuck on** [slang], **in love with,** attached to, wedded to, devoted to, wrapped up in; **taken with,** smitten with [informal], struck with; gone on or far gone on or hipped on or keen about or **wild about** or **mad about** or crazy about [all informal]; nuts about [slang], have a thing about [informal].

.29 ADVS **lovingly, fondly, affectionately, tenderly, dearly, adoringly,** devotedly; amorously, ardently, passionately; with love, with affection, with all one's love.

932. LOVEMAKING, ENDEARMENT

.1 NOUNS **lovemaking,** dalliance, amorous dalliance, billing and cooing; **petting** or **necking** or spooning [all informal], smooching [slang], lollygagging [dial]; **fondling, caressing,** hugging, kissing; cuddling, snuggling, nestling, nuzzling; bundling; sexual intercourse 419.8.

.2 **embrace, hug,** squeeze, clasp, enfoldment, bear hug [informal].

.3 **kiss,** buss, smack, smooch [slang], **osculation.**

.4 **endearment; caress,** pat; sweet talk, soft words, honeyed words, sweet nothings; blandishments, artful endearments.

.5 **darling, dear,** deary, **sweetheart, sweetie, sweet,** sweets, sweetkins, **honey,** hon, **honey bunch,** honey child, sugar, love, lover, precious, precious heart, pet, petkins, babe, **baby, doll,** baby-doll, cherub, angel, chick, chickabiddy, buttercup, duck, duckling, lamb, lambkin, snookums.

.6 **courtship, courting, wooing;** court, suit, suing, amorous pursuit, addresses; gallantry; serenade.

.7 **proposal,** marriage proposal, offer of marriage; engagement 770.3.

.8 **flirtation, coquetry,** dalliance; flirtatiousness, coquettishness, coyness; sheep's eyes, goo-goo eyes [slang], amorous looks, coquettish glances, come-hither look; ogle, side-glance.

.9 **philandering,** philander, lady-killing [slang]; lechery, licentiousness, unchastity 989.

.10 **flirt, coquette,** gold digger or vamp [both slang]; strumpet, whore 989.14–16.

.11 **philanderer,** philander, woman chaser, **ladies' man,** heartbreaker; masher, ladykiller, wolf, skirt chaser, man on the make or make-out artist [both slang]; libertine, lecher, seducer 989.10–12.

.12 love letter, billet-doux, mash note [slang]; valentine.

.13 VERBS make love, bill and coo; pet or neck or spoon [all informal], make out [slang], smooch [slang], lollygag [dial]; dally, toy, trifle, wanton; sweet-talk [dial], whisper sweet nothings; copulate 419.23.

.14 caress, pet, pat; fondle, dandle, coddle, cocker, cosset; pat on the head or cheek, chuck under the chin.

.15 cuddle, snuggle, nestle, nuzzle; lap; bundle.

.16 embrace, hug, clasp, press, squeeze [informal], fold, enfold, bosom, embosom, put or throw one's arms around, take to one's arms, fold to the heart, press to the bosom.

.17 kiss, osculate, buss, smack, smooch [slang]; blow a kiss.

.18 flirt, coquet; gold-dig; philander, gallivant, run around, play around; make eyes at, ogle, eye, cast coquettish glances, cast sheep's eyes at, make goo-goo eyes at [slang], faire les yeux doux [Fr], look sweet upon [informal].

.19 court, woo, sue, press one's suit, pay court or suit to, make suit to, pay one's court to, address, pay one's addresses to, pay attention to, lay siege to, throw oneself at the head of; pursue, follow; chase [slang]; set one's cap at or for [informal]; serenade; spark [informal], squire, esquire, beau, sweetheart [informal], swain.

.20 propose, pop the question [informal], ask for one's hand; become engaged 770.6.

.21 ADJS amatory, amative 931.24; sexual 419.26–30; caressive; flirtatious, flirty; coquettish, coy.

933. MARRIAGE

.1 NOUNS marriage, matrimony, wedlock, –gamy; holy matrimony, holy wedlock, match, union, matrimonial union, alliance, "a world-without-end bargain" [Shakespeare], "a dignified and commodious sacrament" [T. S. Eliot], marriage sacrament, sacrament of matrimony, bond of matrimony, wedding knot, conjugal bond or tie or knot, nuptial bond or tie or knot; married state or status, wedded state or status, wedded bliss, weddedness, wifehood, husbandhood, spousehood; coverture, cohabitation; bed, marriage bed, bridebed; intermarriage, mixed marriage, interfaith marriage, interracial marriage; miscegenation; misalliance, mésalliance [Fr], ill-assorted marriage.

.2 (kinds of marriage) monogamy, monogyny, monandry; serial polygamy; digamy, deuterogamy; bigamy; trigamy, polygamy, polygyny, polyandry; morganatic marriage, left-handed marriage; marriage of convenience, mariage de convenance [Fr]; love match; levirate, leviration; beena marriage; companionate marriage, trial marriage; common-law marriage; picture marriage; concubinage; homosexual marriage.

.3 marriageability, nubility, ripeness.

.4 wedding, marriage, marriage ceremony, nuptial mass; church wedding, civil wedding, civil ceremony; espousement, bridal; banns; nuptials, spousals, espousals, hymeneal rites; chuppah [Heb], wedding canopy; wedding song, marriage song, nuptial song, prothalamium, epithalamium, epithalamy, hymen, hymeneal; wedding veil, saffron veil or robe; bridechamber, bridal suite, nuptial apartment; honeymoon; forced marriage, shotgun wedding; Gretna Green wedding, elopement.

.5 wedding party; wedding attendant, usher; best man, bridesman, groomsman; paranymph; bridesmaid, bridemaiden, maid or matron of honor.

.6 newlywed; bridegroom, groom; bride, plighted bride, blushing bride; war bride, GI bride [slang]; honeymooner.

.7 spouse, mate, yokemate, partner, consort, better half [informal], "bone of my bones, and flesh of my flesh" [Bible].

.8 husband, married man, man, benedict, goodman [archaic], old man [slang].

.9 wife, married woman, wedded wife, goodwife or goody [both archaic], squaw, woman, lady, matron, old lady or old woman [both slang], feme, feme covert, better half [informal], helpmate, helpmeet, rib, wife of one's bosom; wife in name only; wife in all but name, concubine, common-law wife.

.10 married couple, wedded pair, man and wife, husband and wife, man and woman, vir et uxor [L], one flesh; newlyweds, bride and groom.

.11 harem, seraglio, serai, gynaeceum; zenana, purdah.

.12 monogamist, monogynist; bigamist; digamist, deuterogamist; trigamist; polygamist, polygynist, polyandrist; Mormon; Bluebeard.

.13 **matchmaker, marriage broker,** matrimonial agent, *shadchen* [Yid]; matrimonial agency *or* bureau.

.14 (god) Hymen; (goddesses) Hera, Teleia; Juno, Pronuba; Frigg.

.15 VERBS (join in marriage) **marry,** wed, nuptial, **join, unite, hitch** [slang], **splice** [informal], couple, match, make *or* arrange a match, join together, **unite in marriage,** join *or* unite in holy wedlock, tie the nuptial *or* wedding knot, make one; give away, give in marriage; marry off, find a mate for, find a husband *or* wife for.

.16 (get married) **marry, wed,** contract matrimony, mate, couple, espouse, wive, **take to wife,** take to oneself a wife, **get hitched** [slang], **be spliced** [informal], become one, be made one, pair off, give one's hand to, bestow one's hand upon, lead to the altar, take for better or for worse; remarry, rewed; intermarry, interwed, miscegenate.

.17 **honeymoon,** go on a honeymoon.

.18 **cohabit,** live together, live as man and wife, share one's bed and board.

.19 ADJS **matrimonial, marital, conjugal, connubial, nuptial,** wedded, married, hymeneal; epithalamic; spousal, husbandly, wifely; bridal; –gamous.

.20 **monogamous,** monogynous, monandrous; **bigamous,** digamous; **polygamous,** polygynous, polyandrous; morganatic; miscegenetic.

.21 **marriageable,** nubile, ripe, of age, of marriageable age.

.22 **married, wedded,** one, one bone and one flesh, mated, matched, coupled, partnered, paired.

934. CELIBACY

.1 NOUNS **celibacy, singleness,** single blessedness, single state *or* condition; unwed state *or* condition; **bachelorhood,** bachelordom, bachelorism, bachelorship; **spinsterhood,** maidenhood, maidenhead, **virginity,** maiden *or* virgin state; **monasticism,** monachism; misogamy, misogyny; continence 988.3.

.2 **celibate,** *célibataire* [Fr]; monk, monastic, priest, nun; misogamist, misogynist; unmarried, single [informal].

.3 **bachelor,** bach *or* old bach [both slang], confirmed bachelor, **single man.**

.4 **spinster,** spinstress, **old maid,** maid, maiden, bachelor girl, single girl, single woman, lone woman, maiden lady, feme sole; **virgin,** vestal, vestal virgin; parthen(o)–.

.5 VERBS **be unmarried, be single,** live alone, enjoy single blessedness, **bach** *or* **bach it** [both slang], keep bachelor quarters, keep one's freedom.

.6 ADJS **celibate; monastic,** monachal, **monkish;** misogamic, misogynous.

.7 **unmarried, unwedded, unwed, single,** sole, spouseless, wifeless, husbandless; **bachelorly,** bachelorlike; **spinsterly,** spinsterish, spinsterlike; **old-maidish,** old-maidenish; maiden, maidenly; virgin, virginal.

935. DIVORCE, WIDOWHOOD

.1 NOUNS **divorce,** divorcement, grasswidowhood, **separation,** legal *or* judicial separation, separate maintenance; interlocutory decree; dissolution of marriage; annulment, decree of nullity; broken marriage, broken home.

.2 **divorcée,** divorced person, divorced man, *divorcé* [Fr], divorced woman, *divorcée* [Fr]; divorcer; grass widow, grass widower.

.3 **widowhood,** viduity [archaic]; **widowerhood,** widowership; weeds, widow's weeds.

.4 **widow,** widow woman [dial], relict; dowager, queen dowager, etc.; **widower,** widowman [dial].

.5 VERBS **divorce, separate,** part, split up [informal], unmarry, put away, obtain a divorce, come to a parting of the ways, untie the knot, sue for divorce, file suit for divorce; grant a divorce, grant a final decree; grant an annulment, grant a decree of nullity, annul a marriage, put asunder.

.6 **widow,** bereave.

.7 ADJS widowly, widowish, widowlike; **widowed,** widowered; **divorced;** separated, legally separated.

936. COURTESY

.1 NOUNS **courtesy, courteousness, politeness, civility,** amenity, agreeableness, urbanity, comity, affability; **graciousness,** gracefulness; complaisance; **thoughtfulness, considerateness,** tactfulness, tact, solicitousness, solicitude; **respect,** respectfulness, deference.

.2 **gallantry,** gallantness, **chivalry,** chivalrousness, knightliness; courtliness, courtly politeness, *noblesse oblige* [Fr].

.3 **mannerliness, manners, good manners,** excellent *or* exquisite manners, good *or* polite deportment, good *or* polite behavior, *bienséance* [Fr]; *savoir-faire, savoir-vivre* [both Fr]; correctness, correctitude.

.4 **good breeding, breeding; refinement, polish, culture, cultivation; gentility,** gentleness, genteelness, elegance; **gentlemanliness,** gentlemanlikeness, ladylikeness.

.5 **suavity, suaveness, smoothness, smugness,** blandness, **unctuousness,** oiliness, **glibness,** fulsomeness; sweet talk, fair words, soft words *or* tongue, sweet *or* honeyed words *or* tongue, incense; soft soap *or* butter [both informal].

.6 **courtesy, civility,** amenity, urbanity, attention, polite act, act of courtesy *or* politeness, graceful gesture; favor 938.7.

.7 **amenities, civilities,** gentilities, graces, elegancies; dignities; formalities, ceremonies, rites, rituals.

.8 **regards, compliments, respects,** *égards, devoirs* [both Fr]; **best wishes,** one's best, good wishes, best regards, kind *or* kindest regards, love, best love; greetings 925.3; remembrances, kind remembrances; compliments of the season.

.9 **gallant, cavalier,** chevalier, **knight,** "a verray parfit gentil knight" [Chaucer].

.10 "the very pink of courtesy" [Shakespeare], "the very pineapple of politeness" [R. B. Sheridan], "the mirror of all courtesy" [Shakespeare].

.11 VERBS **mind one's manners,** mind one's P's and Q's [informal]; keep a civil tongue in one's head; mend one's manners; observe etiquette, observe *or* follow protocol.

.12 **pay one's respects to, make one's compliments to,** present oneself, pay attentions to, do service, wait on *or* upon.

.13 **give one's regards, give one's compliments,** give one's love, give one's best regards, give one's best, send one's regards *or* compliments, etc.; wish one joy, wish one luck, bid Godspeed.

.14 ADJS **courteous, polite, civil, urbane, gracious,** graceful, agreeable, affable, fair; complaisant; obliging, accommodating; **thoughtful, considerate,** tactful, solicitous; respectful, deferential, attentive.

.15 **gallant, chivalrous,** chivalric, knightly; **courtly; formal,** ceremonious; old-fashioned, old-world.

.16 **mannerly, well-mannered,** good-mannered, **well-behaved,** well-spoken; **correct,** correct in one's manners *or* behavior.

.17 **well-bred,** highbred, **well-brought-up; cultivated, cultured, polished, refined,** gen-

teel, gentle; gentlemanly, gentlemanlike, ladylike.

.18 **suave, smooth, smug,** bland, glib, **unctuous,** oily, soapy *or* buttery [both informal], fulsome, ingratiating, disarming; suave-spoken, fine-spoken, fair-spoken, soft-spoken, smooth-spoken, smooth-tongued, oily-tongued, honey-tongued, honey-mouthed.

.19 ADVS **courteously, politely, civilly,** urbanely, mannerly; **gallantly, chivalrously,** courtly, knightly; **graciously,** gracefully, with a good grace; complaisantly, complacently; obligingly, accommodatingly; respectfully, attentively, deferentially.

937. DISCOURTESY

.1 NOUNS **discourtesy,** discourteousness; **impoliteness,** unpoliteness; **rudeness, incivility,** inurbanity, **ungraciousness, ungallantness,** uncourtliness, ungentlemanliness, **unmannerliness,** mannerlessness, bad *or* ill manners, **ill breeding,** conduct unbecoming a gentleman, caddishness; inconsiderateness, unsolicitousness, tactlessness, insensitivity; grossness, gross behavior, vulgarity, offensiveness, coarseness, crudeness, loutishness.

.2 disrespectfulness 965.1; **insolence** 913.

.3 **gruffness, brusqueness,** *brusquerie* [Fr], **curtness,** shortness, sharpness, abruptness, bluntness, brashness; **harshness,** roughness, severity; truculence, aggressiveness 797.15; **surliness,** crustiness, bearishness, beastliness, churlishness, **boorishness,** nastiness.

.4 ADJS **discourteous, uncourteous; impolite,** unpolite; **rude, uncivil, ungracious, ungallant,** uncourtly, inaffable, uncomplaisant, unaccommodating; **disrespectful** 965.5; **insolent** 913.8.

.5 **unmannerly,** unmannered, mannerless, **ill-mannered, ill-behaved,** ill-conditioned.

.6 **ill-bred, ungenteel,** ungentle, caddish; inconsiderate, unsolicitous, tactless, insensitive; **ungentlemanly,** ungentlemanlike; **unladylike,** unfeminine; **vulgar, boorish, unrefined** 898.10–13, offensive, coarse, crude, loutish, louty, nasty.

.7 **gruff, brusque, curt,** short, sharp, snippy [informal], abrupt, blunt, bluff, brash; **cavalier; harsh,** rough, severe; truculent, aggressive 797.25; **surly,** crusty, bearish, beastly, churlish.

.8 ADVS **discourteously, impolitely, rudely,** uncivilly, ungraciously, ungallantly, ungenteelly, caddishly; inconsiderately, unsolicitously, tactlessly, insensitively.

.9 gruffly, brusquely, curtly, shortly, sharply, snippily [informal], abruptly, bluntly, bluffly, brashly, cavalierly; harshly, crustily, bearishly, churlishly, **boorishly,** nastily.

938. KINDNESS, BENEVOLENCE

.1 NOUNS kindness, kindliness, kindly disposition; **benignity,** benignancy; **goodness,** niceness; **graciousness; kindheartedness,** warmheartedness, softheartedness, tenderheartedness, affectionateness, warmth, goodness *or* warmth of heart, **loving kindness,** "milk of human kindness" [Shakespeare]; soul of kindness, heart of gold; **brotherhood,** fellow feeling, **sympathy,** compassion, fraternal feeling, feeling of kinship; **humaneness,** humanity.

.2 good nature, good humor, good disposition, good temper, sweetness, sweet temper *or* nature, goodnaturedness, goodhumoredness, goodtemperedness, bonhomie; **amiability,** affability, geniality, cordiality; **gentleness,** mildness, lenity.

.3 considerateness, consideration, **thoughtfulness,** mindfulness, heedfulness, regardfulness, attentiveness, **solicitousness,** solicitude, thought, regard, concern, delicacy, tact, tactfulness; indulgence, toleration, leniency 759; complaisance, accommodatingness, **helpfulness,** obligingness, agreeableness.

.4 benevolence, benevolentness, benevolent disposition, well-disposedness, **beneficence, charity,** charitableness, **philanthropy;** altruism, philanthropism, **humanitarianism,** welfarism, do-goodism; utilitarianism, Benthamism, greatest good of the greatest number; **goodwill,** grace, brotherly love, Christian charity *or* love, *caritas* [L], love of mankind, good will to *or* toward man, love, *agape* [Gk], flower power; BOMFOG (brotherhood of man and fatherhood of God); **bigheartedness,** largeheartedness, greatheartedness; **generosity** 853; giving 818.

.5 welfare; welfare work, social service, social welfare, social work; child welfare, etc.; commonweal, public welfare; welfare state, welfare statism, welfarism.

.6 benevolences, philanthropies, charities; works, **good works.**

.7 kindness, favor, mercy, **benefit,** benefaction, benevolence, benignity, blessing, **service,** turn, **good turn, good** *or* **kind deed,** *mitzvah* [Heb], office, good *or* kind offices, obligation, grace, act of

grace, courtesy, act of kindness, kindly act, labor of love.

.8 philanthropist, altruist, benevolist, **humanitarian,** man of good will, **do-gooder,** well-doer, power for good; welfare worker, social worker; welfare statist; almsgiver, almoner; Robin Hood.

.9 VERBS be kind, be good *or* nice to, show kindness to; treat well, do right by; favor, oblige, accommodate.

.10 be considerate, consider, respect, regard, think of, **be thoughtful of,** have consideration *or* regard for.

.11 be benevolent, bear good will, wish well, have one's heart in the right place; practice the golden rule, do as you would be done by, do unto others as you would have others do unto you; make love, not war.

.12 do a favor, do good, do a kindness, do a good turn, do a good *or* kind deed, use one's good offices, render a service, confer a benefit; benefit, help 785.11.

.13 ADJS kind, kindly, kindly-disposed; **benign,** benignant; **good, nice,** decent; **gracious; kindhearted, warm, warmhearted,** softhearted, tenderhearted, tender, loving, affectionate; **sympathetic,** sympathizing, compassionate; **brotherly,** fraternal; humane, human; Christian, Christly, Christlike.

.14 good-natured, well-natured, **good-humored, good-tempered,** bonhomous, **sweet, sweet-tempered; amiable, affable, genial, cordial; gentle,** mild; easy, easy-natured, easy to get along with, **agreeable.**

.15 benevolent, charitable, beneficent, philanthropic, altruistic, humanitarian; **bighearted,** largehearted, greathearted, freehearted; **generous** 853.4; almsgiving, eleemosynary; **welfare,** welfarist(ic), welfare statist.

.16 considerate, thoughtful, mindful, heedful, regardful, solicitous, attentive, delicate, tactful, mindful of others; complaisant, **accommodating,** accommodative, **helpful,** agreeable, **obliging,** indulgent, tolerant, lenient 759.7,8.

.17 well-meaning, well-meant, well-affected, well-disposed, **well-intentioned.**

.18 ADVS kindly, benignly, benignantly; **good,** nicely, well, favorably; **kindheartedly, warmly,** warmheartedly, softheartedly, tenderheartedly; humanely, humanly.

.19 good-naturedly, good-humoredly, bonhomously; **sweetly; amiably,** affably, genially, cordially; graciously, in good part.

.20 benevolently, beneficently, charitably,

philanthropically, altruistically, bigheartedly, with good will.

.21 **considerately, thoughtfully,** mindfully, heedfully, regardfully, tactfully, solicitously, attentively; well-meaningly, well-disposedly.

939. UNKINDNESS, MALEVOLENCE

.1 NOUNS **unkindness, unkindliness;** unbenignity, unbenignness; **unamiability,** uncordiality, ungraciousness, inhospitality, inhospitableness, ungeniality, unaffectionateness; unsympatheticness, uncompassionateness; disagreeableness.

.2 **unbenevolentness, uncharitableness,** ungenerousness.

.3 **inconsiderateness, inconsideration, unthoughtfulness,** unmindfulness, unheedfulness, **thoughtlessness,** heedlessness, respectlessness, disregardfulness, forgetfulness; **unhelpfulness,** unobligingness, unaccommodatingness.

.4 **malevolence, ill will,** bad will, bad blood, bad temper, ill nature, ill-disposedness, ill *or* evil disposition; evil eye, *malocchio* [Ital], whammy [slang], blighting glance.

.5 **malice, maliciousness,** maleficence; malignance *or* **malignancy,** malignity; **meanness** *or* orneriness *or* cussedness *or* bitchiness [all informal], hatefulness, nastiness, invidiousness; **wickedness,** iniquitousness 981.4; deviltry, devilry, devilment; malice prepense *or* aforethought, evil intent; **harmfulness, noxiousness** 675.5.

.6 **spite,** despite; **spitefulness, cattiness;** gloating pleasure, unwholesome *or* unholy joy, *Schadenfreude* [Ger].

.7 **rancor, virulence,** venomousness, **venom,** vitriol, gall.

.8 **causticity,** causticness, corrosiveness, mordancy, mordacity, bitingness; **acrimony, asperity,** acidity, acidness, acidulousness, acridity, acerbity, **bitterness,** tartness; sharpness, keenness, incisiveness, piercingness, stabbingness, trenchancy; "sharptoothed unkindness" [Shakespeare].

.9 **harshness, roughness,** ungentleness; **severity,** austerity, hardness, sternness, grimness, inclemency; stringency, astringency.

.10 **heartlessness, unfeeling,** unnaturalness, unresponsiveness, insensitivity, coldness, **coldheartedness,** coldbloodedness; **hardheartedness,** hardness, hardness of heart, heart of stone; **callousness,** callosity; obduracy; **pitilessness, unmercifulness** 945.1.

.11 **cruelty,** cruelness, sadistic cruelty, sadism, wanton cruelty; **ruthlessness** 945.1; inhumaneness, **inhumanity,** atrociousness;

brutality, brutalness, brutishness, bestiality, beastliness, animality; **barbarity,** barbarousness, vandalism; **savagery, viciousness,** violence, fiendishness, truculence; fierceness, ferociousness, ferocity; bloodthirst, bloodthirstiness, bloodlust, bloodiness, bloody-mindedness, sanguineousness; cannibalism.

.12 (brutal act) **atrocity,** cruelty, brutality, barbarity, inhumanity.

.13 **bad deed, disservice,** ill service, **ill turn,** bad turn.

.14 ADJS **unkind, unkindly,** ill; **unbenign,** unbenignant; **unamiable,** disagreeable, **uncordial, ungracious,** inhospitable, **ungenial,** unaffectionate, unloving; **unsympathetic,** unsympathizing, **uncompassionate,** uncompassioned.

.15 **unbenevolent,** unbeneficent, **uncharitable,** unphilanthropic, unaltruistic, ungenerous.

.16 **inconsiderate, unthoughtful,** unmindful, unheedful, disregardful, **thoughtless,** heedless, respectless, mindless, unthinking, forgetful; uncomplaisant; **unhelpful, unaccommodating, unobliging,** disobliging, uncooperative.

.17 **malevolent, ill-disposed,** evil-disposed, **ill-natured,** ill-affected, ill-conditioned, ill-intentioned.

.18 **malicious,** maleficent, malefic; **malignant,** malign; **mean** *or* **ornery** *or* cussed *or* bitchy [all informal], hateful, nasty, baleful, invidious; **wicked,** iniquitous 981.16; **harmful, noxious** 675.12.

.19 **spiteful,** despiteful; **catty,** cattish.

.20 **rancorous, virulent,** vitriolic; **venomous,** venenate, envenomed.

.21 **caustic,** mordant, mordacious, corrosive, corroding; **acrimonious,** acrid, acid, acidic, acidulous, acidulent, acerb, acerbate, acerbic, **bitter,** tart; **sharp,** keen, incisive, trenchant, **cutting,** penetrating, piercing, biting, **stinging,** stabbing, **scathing, scorching,** withering.

.22 **harsh, rough,** rugged, ungentle; **severe,** austere, **stringent,** astringent, hard, stern, dour, grim, inclement, unsparing.

.23 **heartless, unfeeling,** unnatural, unresponsive, insensitive, **cold,** cold of heart, **coldhearted, coldblooded; hard, hardened,** hard of heart, **hardhearted,** stonyhearted, marblehearted, flinthearted; **callous,** calloused; obdurate; **unmerciful** 945.3.

.24 **cruel,** cruel-hearted, sadistic; **ruthless** 945.3; **brutal,** brutish, brute, bestial, beastly, animal; subhuman, dehumanized, brutalized; sharkish, wolfish, slavering; **barbarous,** barbaric, uncivilized, unchristian; savage, **ferocious,** feral, **vicious,** fierce, **atrocious,** truculent, fell; **inhumane,** inhuman, unhuman; fiendish, fiendlike; demoniac *or* demoniacal, diabolic(al), devilish, satanic, hellish, infernal; **bloodthirsty,** bloody-minded, bloody, sanguineous, sanguinary; cannibalistic, anthropophagous; murderous 409.24; Draconian, Tartarean.

.25 ADVS **unkindly,** ill; **unbenignly,** unbenignantly; **unamiably,** disagreeably, uncordially, ungraciously, inhospitably, ungenially, unaffectionately, unlovingly; unsympathetically, uncompassionately.

.26 **unbenevolently,** unbeneficently, **uncharitably,** unphilanthropically, unaltruistically, ungenerously.

.27 **inconsiderately,** unthoughtfully, thoughtlessly, heedlessly, unthinkingly; unhelpfully, uncooperatively.

.28 **malevolently, maliciously,** maleficently, **malignantly; meanly** *or* ornerily *or* cussedly *or* bitchily [all informal], hatefully, nastily, invidiously, balefully; **wickedly,** iniquitously 981.19; **harmfully,** noxiously 675.15, **spitefully,** in spite; with bad intent, with malice prepense *or* aforethought.

.29 **rancorously, virulently,** vitriolically; venomously, venenately.

.30 **caustically,** mordantly, mordaciously, corrosively, corrodingly; **acrimoniously,** acridly, acidly, acerbly, acerbically, **bitterly,** tartly; **sharply,** keenly, incisively, trenchantly, **cuttingly,** penetratingly, piercingly, bitingly, **stingingly,** stabbingly, **scathingly,** scorchingly, witheringly.

.31 **harshly, roughly; severely,** austerely, stringently, sternly, grimly, inclemently, unsparingly.

.32 **heartlessly, unfeelingly, callously,** coldheartedly; cold-bloodedly, **in cold blood.**

.33 **cruelly, brutally,** brutishly, bestially, subhumanly, sharkishly, wolfishly, slaveringly; **barbarously, savagely, ferociously,** ferally, **viciously,** fiercely, **atrociously,** truculently; **ruthlessly** 945.4; **inhumanely,** inhumanly, unhumanly; fiendishly, diabolically, devilishly.

940. MISANTHROPY

.1 NOUNS **misanthropy,** misanthropism, Timonism, cynicism, antisociality, antisocial sentiments *or* attitudes; unsociability 923.

.2 **misanthrope,** misanthropist; man-hater,

cynic; misogynist, **woman-hater;** sexist; Alceste, Timon.

.3 ADJS **misanthropic,** Timonistic, **antisocial;** unsociable 923.5,6; man-hating, cynical; misogynous, woman-hating; sexist.

941. PUBLIC SPIRIT

.1 NOUNS **public spirit,** social consciousness; **civism,** citizenship, citizenism.

.2 **patriotism,** love of country; "the last refuge of a scoundrel" [Samuel Johnson]; **nationalism,** nationality, ultranationalism; Americanism, Anglicism, Briticism, etc.; **chauvinism, jingoism,** overpatriotism; patriotics, flag waving.

.3 **patriot;** nationalist; ultranationalist; **chauvinist,** chauvin, **jingo,** jingoist; patrioteer [informal], flag waver, superpatriot, hard hat [informal], hundred-percenter, hundred-percent American.

.4 ADJS **public-spirited, civic; patriotic; nationalistic;** ultranationalist, ultranationalistic; overpatriotic, superpatriotic, flag-waving, **chauvinist(ic),** jingoist(ic).

942. BENEFACTOR

.1 NOUNS **benefactor,** benefactress, **benefiter,** succorer, befriender; ministrant, ministering angel; Samaritan, **good Samaritan; helper,** aider, assister, help, aid, helping hand, "a very present help in time of trouble" [Bible]; jack-at-a-pinch; **patron, backer** 787.9; **good person** 985.

.2 **savior, redeemer,** deliverer, **liberator,** rescuer, freer, **emancipator,** manumitter.

943. EVILDOER

.1 NOUNS **evildoer, wrongdoer,** worker of ill *or* evil, **malefactor,** malfeasant, malfeasor, misfeasor, malevolent, public enemy, **sinner, villain,** transgressor, delinquent; **criminal,** outlaw, felon, **crook** [informal], lawbreaker, gangster *or* mobster [both informal], racketeer, thief; **bad person** 986; deceiver 619.

.2 **troublemaker, mischief-maker;** agitator 648.11.

.3 **ruffian,** rough, bravo, **rowdy, thug,** desperado, cutthroat, kill-crazy animal, mad dog; gunman; bully, bullyboy, bucko; devil, hellcat, hell-raiser; killer 409.11.

.4 [slang *or* informal terms] **roughneck, tough,** bruiser, mug, mugger, ugly customer, **hoodlum, hood, hooligan,** gorilla, plug-ugly, strong-arm man, muscle man, **goon;** gun, gunsel, trigger man, rodman, torpedo, hatchet man; hellion, terror, holy terror.

.5 **savage, barbarian, brute, beast, animal,** tiger, shark, hyena; wild man; cannibal, man-eater, anthropophagite; **wrecker, vandal,** nihilist, destroyer.

.6 **monster, fiend,** fiend from hell, **demon, devil,** devil incarnate, hellhound, hellkite; **vampire,** lamia, **harpy, ghoul;** werewolf, ape-man; ogre, ogress; Frankenstein's monster.

.7 **witch, hag, vixen,** hellhag, hellcat, she-devil, virago, termagant, grimalkin, Jezebel, beldam, she-wolf, tigress, wildcat, bitch-kitty [slang], siren, fury.

944. PITY

.1 NOUNS **pity, sympathy,** feeling, fellow feeling in suffering, **commiseration,** condolence; **compassion, mercy,** ruth, humanity; **clemency,** quarter, reprieve, mitigation, relief 886, favor, grace; **leniency,** forbearance 759.1; **kindness, benevolence** 938; pardon, **forgiveness** 1007.1; self-pity; **pathos.**

.2 **compassionateness, mercifulness,** ruthfulness, softheartedness, tenderness, lenity, gentleness; bowels of compassion *or* mercy; bleeding heart.

.3 VERBS **pity,** be *or* **feel sorry for,** feel sorrow for; **commiserate,** compassionate; sympathize, **sympathize with,** feel for, weep for, lament for, bleed, bleed for, have one's heart bleed for, condole with 946.2.

.4 **have pity, have mercy upon, take pity on** *or* **upon;** melt, thaw; relent, forbear, relax, give quarter, spare, temper the wind to the shorn lamb, go easy on *or* let up on [both informal], reprieve, pardon, forgive 1007.4; put out of one's misery; be cruel to be kind.

.5 (excite pity) **move, touch,** affect, reach, **soften,** melt, melt the heart, appeal to one's better feelings; sadden, grieve 872.17,18.

.6 **beg for mercy,** ask for pity, cry for quarter, beg for one's life; fall on one's knees, throw oneself at the feet of.

.7 ADJS **pitying, sympathetic,** sympathizing, commiserative, condolent, understanding; **compassionate, merciful,** ruthful, **clement,** gentle, soft, melting, bleeding, tender, **tenderhearted,** softhearted, warmhearted; **humane,** human; lenient, forbearant 759.7,8; charitable 938.15.

.8 **pitiful, pitiable, pathetic, piteous,** touching, moving, affecting, heartrending, grievous, doleful 872.26.

.9 self-pitying, self-pitiful, sorry for oneself.

.10 ADVS **pitifully,** sympathetically; **compassionately, mercifully,** ruthfully, clemently, humanely.

945. PITILESSNESS

.1 NOUNS **pitilessness, unmercifulness, uncompassionateness,** unsympatheticness, mercilessness, **ruthlessness,** unfeelingness, inclemency, relentlessness, inexorableness, unyieldingness 626.2, unforgivingness; **heartlessness,** hardness, flintiness, harshness, **cruelty** 939.10,11; remorselessness, unremorsefulness; short shrift, tender mercies.

.2 VERBS **show no mercy,** give no quarter, turn a deaf ear to, claim one's pound of flesh, harden one's heart.

.3 ADJS **pitiless,** unpitying, unpitiful; **unsympathetic,** unsympathizing; **uncompassionate,** uncompassioned; **merciless, unmerciful,** without mercy, **ruthless,** dog-eat-dog; unfeeling, bowelless, inclement, relentless, inexorable, unyielding 626.9, unforgiving; **heartless,** hard, flinty, harsh, **cruel** 939.23,24; remorseless, unremorseful.

.4 ADVS **pitilessly,** unsympathetically; mercilessly, **unmercifully, ruthlessly,** uncompassionately, inclemently, relentlessly, inexorably, unyieldingly, unforgivingly; heartlessly, harshly, cruelly 939.33; remorselessly, unremorsefully.

946. CONDOLENCE

.1 NOUNS **condolence,** condolement, **consolation,** comfort, balm, soothing words, **commiseration, sympathy,** sharing of grief *or* sorrow.

.2 VERBS **condole with, commiserate, sympathize with,** feel with, express sympathy for, send one's condolences; **console,** wipe away one's tears, comfort, speak soothing words, bring balm to one's sorrow; sorrow with, share *or* help bear one's grief, grieve *or* weep with, grieve *or* weep for, share one's sorrow, "weep with them that weep" [Bible].

.3 ADJS condolent, consolatory, comforting, commiserative, **sympathetic.**

947. FORGIVENESS

.1 NOUNS **forgiveness,** forgivingness; unresentfulness, unrevengefulness; **condonation,** overlooking, disregard; **patience** 861; **indulgence, forbearance,** longanimity, long-suffering; **kindness, benevolence** 938; **magnanimity** 979.2; **tolerance** 526.4.

.2 **pardon,** excuse, sparing, **amnesty,** indemnity, exemption, immunity, reprieve, grace; **absolution**, shrift, remission, remission of sin; **redemption**; **exoneration**, **exculpation** 1007.1.

.3 VERBS **forgive, pardon, excuse,** give *or* grant forgiveness, spare; amnesty, grant amnesty to, grant immunity *or* exemption; **absolve,** remit, give absolution, shrive, grant remission; **exonerate, exculpate** 1007.4; blot out one's sins, wipe the slate clean.

.4 **condone, overlook, disregard, ignore,** take [informal], pass over, let it go [informal], give one another chance, let one off this time *or* let one off easy [both informal], close *or* shut one's eyes to, **blink** or **wink** at, connive at; allow for, make allowances for; bear with, endure, regard with indulgence; pocket the affront, leave unavenged, turn the other cheek.

.5 **forget, forgive and forget,** dismiss from one's thoughts, think no more of, not give it another *or* a second thought, let it go [informal], let it pass, **let bygones be bygones;** write off, charge off, charge to experience; bury the hatchet.

.6 ADJS **forgiving,** sparing, placable, conciliatory; **kind, benevolent** 938.13–17; **magnanimous, generous** 979.6; **patient** 861.9,10; **forbearing,** longanimous, long-suffering; unresentful, unrevengeful; **tolerant** 526.11, more in sorrow than in anger.

.7 **forgiven, pardoned, excused,** spared, amnestied, reprieved, remitted; overlooked, disregarded, forgotten, not held against one, wiped away, removed from the record, blotted, canceled, **condoned,** indulged; absolved, shriven; redeemed; exonerated, exculpated, acquitted; unresented; unavenged, unrevenged; uncondemned.

948. CONGRATULATION

.1 NOUNS **congratulation,** gratulation, **felicitation,** blessing, **compliment,** pat on the back; good wishes, best wishes.

.2 VERBS **congratulate,** gratulate, **felicitate,** bless, **compliment,** tender *or* offer one's congratulations *or* felicitations *or* compliments; shake one's hand, pat on the back; **rejoice with,** wish one joy.

.3 ADJS **congratulatory,** congratulant, congratulational; gratulatory, gratulant; **complimentary.**

.4 INTERJS **congratulations!,** take a bow!; nice going!, bravo!, well done!, right on! [slang], good show! [Brit].

949. GRATITUDE

.1 NOUNS **gratitude, gratefulness, thankfulness, appreciation, appreciativeness;** obligation, sense of obligation *or* indebtedness.

.2 **thanks, thanksgiving,** praise, hymn, paean, benediction; grace, prayer of thanks; **thank-you; acknowledgment,** cognizance, **credit,** crediting, recognition; thank offering.

.3 VERBS **be grateful, be obliged,** feel *or* be *or* lie under an obligation, be obligated *or* indebted, be in the debt of; **be thankful,** thank God, thank *or* bless one's stars; **appreciate,** be appreciative of; never forget; overflow with gratitude.

.4 **thank,** bless; give one's thanks, **express one's appreciation; offer thanks, give thanks,** tender *or* render thanks, return thanks; acknowledge, make acknowledgments of, credit, recognize, give *or* render credit *or* recognition; fall on one's knees.

.5 ADJS **grateful, thankful; appreciative,** sensible; **obliged, much obliged,** beholden, indebted to, crediting, under obligation, acknowledging, cognizant of.

.6 INTERJS **thanks!, thank you!,** I thank you!, *merci!* [Fr], *¡gracias!* [Sp], *grazie!* [Ital], *danke!, danke schön!* [both Ger], gramercy!, **much obliged!,** many thanks!, thank you kindly!; I thank you very much!, *merci beaucoup!, je vous remercie beaucoup!* [both Fr].

950. INGRATITUDE

.1 NOUNS **ingratitude, ungratefulness, unthankfulness,** thanklessness, unappreciation, **unappreciativeness;** nonacknowledgment, nonrecognition, denial of due *or* proper credit; "benefits forgot" [Shakespeare]; grudging *or* halfhearted thanks.

.2 **ingrate,** ungrateful wretch.

.3 VERBS **be ungrateful,** feel no obligation, **not appreciate,** owe one no thanks; look a gift horse in the mouth; bite the hand that feeds one.

.4 ADJS **ungrateful, unthankful,** thankless, unappreciative, unmindful.

.5 **unthanked, unacknowledged,** unrecognized, uncredited, denied due *or* proper credit, unrequited, unrewarded, forgotten, neglected, unduly *or* unfairly neglected, ignored; ill-requited, ill-rewarded.

951. ILL HUMOR

.1 NOUNS **ill humor,** bad humor, **bad temper,** ill temper, **ill nature,** filthy *or* rotten *or* evil humor; sourness, biliousness; choler, bile, gall, spleen; causticity, corrosiveness, asperity 939.8; **anger** 952.5; discontent 869.

.2 irascibility, irritability, excitability, **crossness,** crabbedness, **crankiness, testiness,** crustiness, huffiness, huffishness, **cantankerousness** [informal], churlishness, bearishness, snappishness, waspishness; **meanness** *or* **orneriness** *or* **bitchiness** *or* cussedness [all informal], disagreeability, ugliness [informal]; **perversity,** crossgrainedness, fractiousness.

.3 hot temper, temper, quick *or* short temper, irritable temper, warm temper, fiery temper, fierce temper, short fuse [slang], pepperiness, spunkiness [informal], **hot-headedness,** hot blood.

.4 touchiness, tetchiness, ticklishness, prickliness, quickness to take offense, **sensitiveness,** oversensitiveness, hypersensitiveness, sensitivity, oversensitivity, hypersensitivity, thin skin; temperamentalness.

.5 petulance *or* petulancy, peevishness, pettishness, **querulousness, fretfulness,** resentfulness; shrewishness, vixenishness.

.6 grouchiness, **crabbiness, grumpiness,** grumpishness, gruffness.

.7 contentiousness, quarrelsomeness 795.3; **disputatiousness, argumentativeness,** litigiousness; **belligerence** 797.15.

.8 sullenness, sulkiness, surliness, **moroseness, glumness,** grumness, grimness, mumpishness, dumpishness, *bouderie* [Fr]; **moodiness,** moodishness; mopishness, mopiness [informal]; dejection, melancholy 872.3–5.

.9 scowl, frown, lower, glower, pout, moue, mow, grimace, wry face; sullen looks, black looks, long face.

.10 sulks, sullens, **mopes,** mumps, dumps, grumps [informal], frumps [Brit dial], **blues,** blue devils, mulligrubs, dorts *or* dods [both Scot], **pouts.**

.11 (ill-humored person) **sorehead, grouch, crank, crosspatch,** feist [dial], **bear,** grizzly bear; fury, Tartar, dragon, ugly customer [slang]; **hothead,** hotspur; fire-eater.

.12 bitch [slang], **shrew, vixen,** virago, termagant, fury, witch, beldam, cat, tigress, she-wolf, she-devil, spitfire; fishwife; **scold,** common scold; battle-ax [slang].

.13 VERBS have a temper, have a short fuse [slang], have a devil in one, be possessed of the devil.

.14 sulk, mope; grump *or* grouch *or* bitch [all informal], fret; get oneself in a sulk.

.15 look sullen, look black, look black as

thunder, gloom, pull *or* make a long face; **frown, scowl,** knit the brow, lower, **glower, pout,** make a moue *or* mow, grimace, make a wry face, make a lip, hang one's lip.

.16 sour, acerbate, exacerbate; **embitter,** bitter, envenom.

.17 ADJS out of humor, out of temper, out of sorts, **in a bad humor,** in a shocking humor, feeling evil [slang]; caustic, corrosive, acid 939.21; angry 952.26; discontented 869.5.

.18 ill-humored, bad-tempered, ill-tempered, evil-humored, evil-tempered, **ill-natured,** ill-affected, ill-disposed.

.19 irascible, irritable, excitable, **cross, cranky, testy,** feisty, crusty, huffy, huffish, shirty [Brit slang], **cantankerous** [informal], cankered, crabbed, spiteful, spleeny, splenetic, churlish, bearish, snappish, waspish; **mean** *or* **ornery** *or* cussed *or* **bitchy** [all informal], disagreeable, ugly [informal]; **perverse,** fractious, crossgrained.

.20 touchy, tetchy, miffy, ticklish, prickly, quick to take offense, **thin-skinned,** sensitive, oversensitive, hypersensitive, highstrung, temperamental.

.21 peevish, petulant, pettish, **querulous, fretful,** resentful; catty; shrewish, vixenish, vixenly; nagging, naggy.

.22 grouchy, crabby, grumpy, grumpish, gruff, grumbly, grumbling, growling.

.23 sour, soured, **sour-tempered,** vinegarish; choleric, dyspeptic, bilious, jaundiced; **bitter,** embittered.

.24 sullen, sulky, surly, morose, dour, mumpish, dumpish, **glum,** grum, grim; **moody,** moodish; **mopish,** mopey [informal], moping; **glowering,** lowering, **scowling, frowning;** dark, black; black-browed, beetle-browed; dejected, melancholy 872.22, 23.

.25 hot-tempered, hotheaded, passionate, hot, fiery, peppery, spunky [informal], **quick-tempered, short-tempered;** hasty, quick, "sudden and quick in quarrel" [Shakespeare], explosive, volcanic, combustible.

.26 contentious, quarrelsome 795.17; **disputatious,** controversial, litigious, polemic(al); **argumentative,** argumental; scrappy [slang], fighty [dial]; cat-and-doggish, cat-and-dog; **belligerent** 797.25.

.27 ADVS ill-humoredly, ill-naturedly; **irascibly, irritably, crossly, crankily, testily,** huffily, cantankerously [informal], crabbedly, sourly, churlishly, crustily, bearishly, snappily; perversely, fractiously, cross-grainedly.

.28 peevishly, petulantly, pettishly, querulously, fretfully.

.29 grouchily [informal], crabbily, grumpily, grumblingly.

.30 sullenly, sulkily, surlily, morosely, mumpishly, glumly, grumly, grimly; moodily, mopingly; gloweringly, loweringly, scowlingly, frowningly.

952. RESENTMENT, ANGER

.1 NOUNS resentment, resentfulness; displeasure, disapproval, disapprobation, dissatisfaction, discontent; vexation, irritation, annoyance, aggravation [informal], exasperation.

.2 offense, umbrage, pique; glower, scowl, angry look, dirty look [slang], glare, frown.

.3 bitterness, bitter resentment, bitterness of spirit, heartburning; rancor, virulence, acrimony, acerbity, asperity; causticity 939.8; choler, gall, bile, spleen, acid, acidity, acidulousness; hard feelings, animosity 929.4; soreness, rankling, slow burn [informal]; gnashing of teeth.

.4 indignation, indignant displeasure, righteous indignation.

.5 anger, wrath, ire, saeva indignatio [L], mad [informal]; angriness, irateness, wrathfulness, soreness [informal], "a transient madness" [Horace]; infuriation, enragement; vials of wrath, grapes of wrath; heat, more heat than light [informal].

.6 temper, dander or Irish [both informal], monkey [Brit slang]; bad temper 951.1.

.7 dudgeon, high dudgeon; huff, pique, pet, tiff, miff or stew [both informal], fret, fume, ferment.

.8 fit, fit of anger, fit of temper, rage, wax [Brit slang], tantrum, temper tantrum; duck fit or cat fit or conniption or conniption fit [all informal], paroxysm, convulsion.

.9 outburst, outburst of anger, burst, explosion, eruption, blowup or flare-up [both informal], access, blaze of temper; storm, scene, high words.

.10 rage, passion; fury, furor; towering rage or passion, blind or burning rage, raging or tearing passion, furious rage; vehemence, violence; the Furies, the Eumenides, the Erinyes; Nemesis; Alecto, Tisiphone, Megaera.

.11 provocation, affront, offense, "head and front of one's offending" [Shakespeare]; casus belli [L], red rag, red rag to a bull,

sore point, sore spot, tender spot, raw nerve, slap in the face.

.12 VERBS resent, be resentful, feel or harbor or nurse resentment, feel hurt, smart, feel sore or have one's nose out of joint [both informal].

.13 take amiss, take ill, take in bad part, take to heart, not take it as a joke, mind; take offense, take umbrage, get miffed or huffy [informal].

.14 (show resentment) redden, color, flush, mantle; growl, snarl, gnarl, snap, show one's teeth, spit; gnash or grind one's teeth; glower, lower, scowl, glare, frown, give a dirty look [slang], look daggers.

.15 (be angry) burn, seethe, simmer, sizzle, smoke, smolder; be pissed or pissed off or browned off [all slang], be livid, be beside oneself, fume, stew [informal], boil, fret, chafe; foam at the mouth; breathe fire and fury; rage, storm, rave, rant, bluster; take on or go on or carry on [all informal], rant and rave, kick up a row or dust or shindy [slang]; raise Cain or raise hell or raise the devil or raise the roof [all slang], tear up the earth; throw a fit, have a conniption or conniption fit or duck fit or cat fit [informal], go into a tantrum; stamp one's foot.

.16 vent one's anger, vent one's rancor or choler or spleen, pour out the vials of one's wrath; snap at, bite or snap one's nose off, bite or take one's head off, jump down one's throat; expend one's anger on, take it out on [informal].

.17 (become angry) anger, lose one's temper, forget oneself, let one's angry passions rise; get mad or get sore [both informal]; get one's gorge up, get one's blood up, get one's dander or Irish up [informal], get one's monkey up [Brit slang]; bridle, bridle up, bristle, bristle up, raise one's hackles, get one's back up; see red [informal]; get hot under the collar [slang], flip out [slang], work oneself into a lather or sweat or stew [informal], do a slow burn [informal], reach boiling point, boil over.

.18 flare up, blaze up, fire up, flame up, spunk up, ignite, kindle, take fire.

.19 fly into a rage or passion or temper, fly out, fly off at a tangent; fly off the handle or hit the ceiling or go into a tailspin or have a hemorrhage [all slang]; explode, blow up [informal]; blow one's top or stack [slang], blow a fuse or gasket [slang], flip one's lid or wig [slang].

.20 offend, give offense, give umbrage, affront, outrage; grieve, aggrieve; wound, hurt, **sting**, hurt the feelings; step *or* tread on one's toes.

.21 **anger, make angry, make mad** *or* **sore** [informal], **tick off** [slang], **raise one's gorge** *or* **choler, raise one's dander** [informal], **put** *or* **get one's dander** *or* **Irish up** [informal], **put** *or* **get one's monkey up** [Brit slang], **get one's mad up** [informal]; **make hot under the collar** *or* **burn one up** [both slang]; **piss one off** [slang].

.22 **provoke, incense**, arouse, inflame, **embitter; vex, irritate, annoy, aggravate** [informal], **exasperate, nettle,** fret, **chafe; pique, peeve** *or* **miff** [both informal], **huff; ruffle, roil, rile** [informal], **ruffle one's feathers, rankle**; bristle, **put** *or* **get one's back up, set up, put one's hair** *or* **fur** *or* **bristles up**; **stick in one's craw** [informal]; **stir up, work up, stir one's bile, stir the blood.**

.23 **enrage, infuriate, madden,** drive one mad, frenzy, lash into fury, work up into a passion, make one's blood boil.

.24 ADJS **resentful,** resenting; **bitter,** embittered, **rancorous,** virulent, **acrimonious,** acerb, acerbic, acerbate; **caustic** 939.21; **choleric,** splenetic, acid, acidic, acidulous, acidulent; **sore** [informal], rankled, burning *or* stewing [both informal].

.25 **provoked, vexed, piqued; peeved** *or* **miffed** *or* **huffy** [all informal], **nettled, irritated, annoyed,** aggravated [informal], exasperated, put-out.

.26 **angry,** angered, **incensed, indignant, irate,** ireful; **pissed** *or* **pissed-off** *or* **PO'd** *or* **teed off** *or* **TO'd** *or* **ticked off** *or* **browned-off** [all slang], **livid,** livid with rage, **beside oneself, wroth, wrathful,** wrathy, **mad** *or* **sore** [both informal], **cross,** waxy [Brit slang]; **wrought-up,** worked up, riled up [informal].

.27 **hot** [slang], **het up** [dial], **hot under the collar** [slang]; **burning, seething,** simmering, smoldering, sizzling, boiling; flushed with anger.

.28 **in a temper, in a huff, in a pet,** in a stew [informal], in a wax [Brit slang], **in high dudgeon.**

.29 **infuriated,** infuriate, in a rage *or* passion *or* fury; **furious,** fierce, wild, savage; **raving mad** [informal], **rabid,** foaming *or* frothing at the mouth; **fuming,** in a fume; **enraged, raging, raving, ranting, storming;** mad as a hornet, mad as a wet hen; fighting mad *or* roaring mad *or* good and mad *or* hopping mad [all informal], fit to be tied [slang].

.30 ADVS **angrily, indignantly, irately,** wrath-

fully, **infuriatedly,** infuriately, furiously, heatedly; **in anger,** in hot blood, in the heat of passion.

953. JEALOUSY

.1 NOUNS **jealousy,** *jalousie* [Fr], **jealousness, heartburning,** heartburn, **jaundice,** jaundiced eye, **green in the eye** [informal], "the jaundice of the soul" [Dryden]; "green-eyed jealousy", "green-eyed monster", "a monster begot upon itself, born on itself" [all Shakespeare], Othello's flaw, horn-madness; **envy** 954.

.2 **suspiciousness,** suspicion, doubt, misdoubt, mistrust, distrust, distrustfulness.

.3 VERBS suffer pangs of jealousy, **have green in the eye** [informal], **be possessive** *or* overpossessive, view with a jaundiced eye; **suspect,** distrust, mistrust, doubt, misdoubt.

.4 ADJS **jealous, jaundiced,** jaundice-eyed, yellow-eyed, green-eyed, yellow, green, green with jealousy; horn-mad; **invidious, envious** 954.4; **suspicious,** distrustful.

954. ENVY

.1 NOUNS **envy, enviousness, covetousness;** invidia, deadly sin of envy, invidiousness; **grudging,** grudgingness; **jealousy** 953; rivalry.

.2 "the tax which all distinction must pay" [Emerson], "emulation adapted to the meanest capacity" [Ambrose Bierce], "a kind of praise" [John Gay].

.3 VERBS **envy, be envious** *or* **covetous of, covet,** cast envious eyes, desire for oneself; **grudge, begrudge.**

.4 ADJS **envious,** envying, invidious, green with envy; **jealous** 953.4; **covetous,** desirous of; **grudging, begrudging.**

955. RETALIATION

.1 NOUNS **retaliation, reciprocation,** exchange, interchange, give-and-take; **retort, reply,** return, **comeback** [informal]; counter, counterblow, counterstroke, counterblast, recoil, boomerang.

.2 **reprisal, requital, retribution; recompense, compensation** 33, **reward,** comeuppance [informal], desert, **deserts, just deserts, what is merited, what is due** *or* **condign, what one has coming** [informal]; **quittance, return of evil for evil; revenge** 956; **punishment** 1010.

.3 **tit for tat, measure for measure,** like for like, **quid pro quo,** something in return, blow for blow, a Roland for an Oliver, a game two can play, **an eye for an eye,** a tooth for a tooth, "eye for eye, tooth for tooth, hand for hand, foot for foot" [Bible], law of retaliation *or* equivalent retaliation, *lex talionis* [L], talion.

.4 VERBS **retaliate, retort,** counter, **strike back,** hit back at [informal], give in return; **reciprocate,** give in exchange, give and take; **get back at** [slang], come back at [informal], turn the tables upon.

.5 **requite,** quit, make requital *or* reprisal *or* retribution, get satisfaction, recompense, compensate, make restitution, indemnify, reward, redress, make amends, **repay, pay, pay back,** pay off; **give one his comeuppance** [informal], give one his deserts, serve one right, give one what is coming to him [informal].

.6 **give in kind,** cap, match, give as good as was sent; repay in kind, **pay one in his own coin** *or* currency, give one a dose of his own medicine [informal]; return the like, return the compliment; return like for like, **return evil for evil;** return blow for blow, **give one tit for tat,** give a quid pro quo, give as good as one gets, give measure for measure, give *or* get an eye for an eye and a tooth for a tooth, follow *or* observe the *lex talionis*.

.7 **get even with** [informal], even the score, **settle with, settle** *or* **square accounts** [informal], settle the score [informal], fix [informal], pay off old scores, pay back in full measure, be *or* make quits; **take revenge** 956.4; **punish** 1010.10–12.

.8 ADJS **retaliatory,** retaliative; **retributive,** retributory; **reparative,** compensatory, restitutive, recompensing, recompensive, reciprocal; **punitive** 1010.25.

.9 ADVS **in retaliation,** in exchange, in reciprocation; **in return,** in reply; **in requital, in reprisal,** in retribution, in reparation, in amends; **in revenge,** *en revanche* [Fr].

956. REVENGE

.1 NOUNS **revenge, vengeance, avengement,** sweet revenge, getting even, evening of the score; revanche, revanchism; **retaliation, reprisal** 955.2; vendetta, feud, blood feud.

.2 **revengefulness, vengefulness, vindictiveness,** rancor, grudgefulness, irreconcilableness, unappeasableness, implacableness, implacability.

.3 **avenger, vindicator;** revanchist; Nemesis, the Furies, the Erinyes, the Eumenides.

.4 VERBS **revenge, avenge, take revenge,** have one's revenge, wreak one's ven-

geance; **retaliate, even the score, get even with** 955.4–7; launch a vendetta.

.5 **harbor revenge,** breathe vengeance; have accounts to settle, have a crow to pick *or* pluck *or* pull with; nurse one's revenge, brood over, dwell on *or* upon, keep the wound open.

.6 ADJS **revengeful, vengeful,** avenging; **vindictive,** vindicatory; revanchist; **punitive,** punitory; rancorous, grudgeful, irreconcilable, unappeasable, implacable, unwilling to forgive and forget, unwilling to let bygones be bygones; **retaliatory** 955.8.

957. ETHICS

.1 NOUNS **ethics, principles,** standards, **morals,** moral principles; **code,** ethical *or* moral code, **ethic,** code of morals *or* ethics, ethical system, value system, axiology; **norm,** behavioral norm, normative system; moral climate, ethos, *Zeitgeist* [Ger]; Ten Commandments, decalogue; new morality; social ethics, professional ethics, medical ethics, legal ethics, business ethics, etc.

.2 **ethical** *or* **moral philosophy,** ethology, ethonomics, aretaics, eudaemonics, casuistry, deontology, empiricism, evolutionism, hedonism, ethical formalism, intuitionism, perfectionism, Stoicism, utilitarianism, categorical imperative, golden rule; egoistic ethics, altruistic ethics, Christian ethics, situation ethics; comparative ethics.

.3 **morality, morals,** morale; virtue 980; ethicality, ethicalness.

.4 **amorality,** unmorality; amoralism.

.5 **conscience,** grace, **sense of right and wrong;** inward monitor, inner arbiter, moral censor, censor, ethical self, superego; **voice of conscience,** still small voice within; tender conscience; social conscience; conscientiousness 974.2; twinge of conscience 873.2.

.6 ADJS **ethical, moral,** moralistic; ethological; axiological.

.7 **amoral,** unmoral, nonmoral.

958. RIGHT

.1 NOUNS **right,** rightfulness, rightness; what is right *or* proper, what should be, what ought to be, the seemly, the thing, the proper thing, the right *or* proper thing to do, what is done.

.2 **propriety, decorum, decency;** correctness, correctitude, rightness, properness, decorousness, goodness, niceness, seemliness; fitness, fittingness, appropriateness, suit-

739

ability 670.1; normativeness, normality; proprieties, decencies; righteousness 980.1.

.3 (a right or privilege) **right, due,** droit; **prerogative,** power, authority; faculty, appurtenance; **claim,** proper claim, demand, **interest, title,** pretension, pretense, prescription; birthright; natural right, presumptive right, inalienable right; divine right; vested right or interest; property right; conjugal right.

.4 **privilege, license, liberty, freedom, immunity;** franchise, patent, copyright, grant, warrant, blank check, carte blanche; favor, indulgence, **special favor,** dispensation.

.5 **human rights,** rights of man; constitutional rights, **civil rights** 762.2.

.6 **women's rights,** rights of women; **feminism, women's liberation,** women's lib [informal], women's liberation movement, sisterhood.

.7 **women's rightist, feminist, women's liberationist,** women's liberation advocate or adherent or activist, women's libber, libber [both informal]; **suffragette,** suffragist.

.8 ADJS **right,** rightful; fit, suitable 670.5; **proper, correct, decorous,** good, nice, decent, seemly, **due, appropriate,** fitting, condign, **right and proper,** as it should be, as it ought to be; kosher, according to Hoyle [both informal]; in the right; normative, normal; righteous 980.7–9; orth(o)–.

.9 ADVS **rightly, rightfully,** right; **by rights,** by right, with good right, **as is right** or **only right; properly,** correctly, as is proper or fitting, **duly, appropriately,** fittingly, condignly, **in justice,** in equity; in reason, in all conscience.

959. WRONG

.1 NOUNS **wrong, wrongfulness, wrongness; impropriety, indecorum;** incorrectness, improperness, indecorousness, unseemliness; unfitness, unfittingness, inappropriateness, unsuitability 671.1; infraction, violation, delinquency, criminality, illegality, unlawfulness; abnormality, deviance or deviancy, aberrance or aberrancy; sinfulness, wickedness, unrighteousness 981.3–5.

.2 **abomination,** terrible thing; **scandal, disgrace, shame, pity,** atrocity, profanation, desecration, violation, sacrilege, infamy, ignominy.

.3 ADJS **wrong, wrongful; improper, incorrect, indecorous,** undue, unseemly; unfit, unfitting, inappropriate, unsuitable 671.5; delinquent, criminal, illegal, unlawful; abnormal, deviant, aberrant; evil, sinful, wicked, unrighteous 981.16; not the thing, hardly the thing, not done; **off-base** or **out-of-line** or **off-color** [all informal]; abominable, terrible, scandalous, disgraceful, shameful, shameless, atrocious, sacrilegious, infamous, ignominious; mis–.

.4 ADVS **wrongly, wrongfully,** wrong; **improperly,** incorrectly, indecorously.

960. DUENESS

.1 NOUNS **dueness, entitlement,** entitledness, deservingness, deservedness, meritedness, expectation, just or justifiable expectation; **justice** 976.

.2 **due,** one's due, what one merits, what one has earned, what is owing, what one has coming, what is coming to one, acknowledgment, cognizance, credit, crediting, recognition; **right** 958.3.

.3 **deserts,** just deserts, deservings, merits, dues, due reward or punishment, **comeuppance** [informal], all that is coming to one.

.4 VERBS **be due,** be one's due, **be entitled to,** have a right or title to, have a rightful claim to or upon, claim as one's right, **have coming.**

.5 **deserve, merit,** earn, rate or be in line for [both informal], **be worthy of,** be deserving, richly deserve.

.6 **get one's deserts,** get one's dues, **get one's comeuppance** [informal], get his or get hers [both slang], get what is coming to one; get justice; serve one right, be rightly served; get for one's pains, reap the fruits or benefit of, reap where one has sown.

.7 ADJS **due, owed, owing,** payable, redeemable, coming, **coming to.**

.8 **rightful,** condign, appropriate, proper 958.8; fit, becoming 670.5; **fair, just** 976.8–10.

.9 **warranted, justified, entitled,** qualified, worthy; **deserved, merited,** richly deserved, earned, well-earned.

.10 **due, entitled to,** with a right to; **deserving, meriting, meritorious, worthy of;** attributable, ascribable.

.11 ADVS **duly,** rightfully, condignly, as is one's due or right.

961. UNDUENESS

.1 NOUNS **undueness, undeservedness,** undeservingness, unentitledness, unentitlement, unmeritedness; disentitlement; lack of claim *or* title, false claim *or* title, invalid claim *or* title, no claim *or* title, empty claim *or* title; **inappropriateness** 671.1; **impropriety** 959.1; **excess** 663.

.2 **presumption, assumption, imposition; license,** licentiousness, **undue liberty,** liberties, familiarity, **presumptuousness,** freedom *or* liberty abused, hubris; **lawlessness** 740.

.3 (taking to oneself unduly) **usurpation, arrogation,** seizure, **appropriation,** assumption, adoption, infringement, encroachment, invasion, trespass, trespassing; playing God.

.4 **usurper,** arrogator, pretender.

.5 VERBS **not be entitled to,** have no right *or* title to, have no claim upon, not have a leg to stand on.

.6 **presume, assume, venture, hazard, dare,** pretend, attempt, **make bold,** make free, **take the liberty,** take upon oneself.

.7 **presume on** *or* **upon, impose on** *or* **upon,** encroach upon, obtrude upon; **take liberties,** take a liberty, overstep, overstep one's rights *or* bounds *or* prerogatives, make free with *or* of, abuse one's rights, abuse a privilege, give an inch and take an ell; **inconvenience,** bother, trouble, cause to go out of one's way.

.8 (take to oneself unduly) **usurp, arrogate,** seize, **appropriate,** assume, adopt, take over, arrogate *or* accroach to oneself, pretend to, infringe, encroach, invade, trespass; play God.

.9 ADJS **undue, unowed, unowing,** not coming, not outstanding; **undeserved, unmerited,** unearned; **unwarranted, unjustified;** unentitled, undeserving, unmeriting, nonmeritorious, unworthy; preposterous, outrageous.

.10 **inappropriate** 671.5; **improper** 959.3; **excessive** 663.16–21.

.11 **presumptuous, presuming,** licentious; hubristic.

962. DUTY

(moral obligation)

.1 NOUNS **duty, obligation,** charge, onus, burden, mission, devoir, must, ought, imperative, **bounden duty,** proper *or* assigned task, what ought to be done, what one is responsible for, "stern daughter of the voice of God" [Wordsworth], deference, **respect** 964, fealty, allegiance, loyalty, homage, devotion, dedication, commitment, self-imposed duty; **business,**

place 656.3; **ethics** 957; line of duty; call of duty; duties and responsibilities.

.2 **responsibility,** incumbency; **liability,** accountability, accountableness, answerability, answerableness, amenability; **responsibleness, dutifulness,** duteousness, devotion *or* dedication to duty, sense of duty *or* obligation.

.3 VERBS **should, ought to,** had best, had better, be expedient.

.4 **behoove, become,** befit, beseem, be bound, be obliged *or* obligated, be under an obligation; **owe it to,** owe it to oneself.

.5 **be the duty of, be incumbent on** *or* **upon,** stand on *or* upon, be a must *or* an imperative for, duty calls one to.

.6 **be responsible for,** stand responsible for, **be liable for,** be answerable *or* accountable for, have to answer for.

.7 **be one's responsibility,** be one's office, be one's charge *or* mission, **rest with,** lie upon, devolve on, rest on the shoulders of, lie on one's head, lie at one's door, fall to one, fall to one's lot.

.8 **incur a responsibility,** become bound to, become sponsor for.

.9 **take** *or* **accept the responsibility, take upon oneself,** take upon one's shoulders, commit oneself, **answer for,** respect *or* defer to one's duty; sponsor, be *or* stand sponsor for; do at one's own risk *or* peril; **take the blame,** take the rap for [slang].

.10 **do one's duty,** perform *or* fulfill *or* discharge one's duty, do what one has to do, pay one's dues [informal], **do what is expected,** do the needful, do justice to, **do** *or* **act one's part,** play one's proper role; answer the call of duty, do one's bit.

.11 **meet an obligation,** satisfy one's obligations, stand to one's engagement, stand up to, **acquit oneself, make good,** redeem one's pledge.

.12 **obligate, oblige, require,** make incumbent *or* imperative, tie, **bind,** pledge, commit, saddle with, put under an obligation.

.13 ADJS **dutiful, duteous;** moral, ethical, conscientious, scrupulous, observant; **obedient** 766.3; deferential, **respectful** 964.8.

.14 **incumbent on** *or* **upon,** chargeable to, behooving.

.15 **obligatory, binding, imperative,** imperious, peremptory, mandatory, must, *de rigueur* [Fr]; **necessary, required** 639.12,13.

.16 **obliged, obligated, obligate, under obligation; bound, duty-bound,** in duty bound, tied, pledged, committed, saddled, beholden, bounden; **obliged to,** beholden to, bound *or* bounden to, **indebted to.**

.17 **responsible, answerable; liable, accountable,** amenable, unexempt from, chargeable; responsible for, at the bottom of; to blame.

.18 ADVS **dutifully, duteously, in the line of duty,** as in duty bound; beyond the call of duty.

963. IMPOSITION

(a putting or inflicting upon)

.1 NOUNS imposition, infliction, laying on, charging, taxing, tasking; burdening, weighting, freighting, loading, loading down, imposing an onus; **exaction, demand** 753; unwarranted demand, obtrusiveness, presumptuousness 913.1; inconvenience, trouble, bother; inconsiderateness 939.3.

.2 administration, giving, bestowal; applying, application, dosing, dosage, meting out, prescribing; forcing, forcing on, enforcing.

.3 **charge, duty, tax,** task; **burden,** weight, freight, cargo, load, onus.

.4 VERBS **impose, impose on** *or* **upon, inflict on** *or* **upon, put on** *or* **upon, lay on** *or* **upon,** enjoin; **put, place, set, lay,** put down; **levy, exact, demand** 753.4; **tax,** task, **charge,** burden with, weight *or* freight with, weight down with, yoke with, **fasten upon,** saddle with; subject to.

.5 **inflict, wreak, do to,** bring, bring upon, bring down upon, visit upon.

.6 **administer, give, bestow; apply, put on** *or* **upon,** lay on *or* upon, **dose, dose with,** mete out, to prescribe for; **force, force upon,** enforce upon.

.7 **impose on** *or* **upon,** take advantage of 665.16; **presume upon** 961.7; **deceive** 618.13, play *or* work on, put on *or* upon, put over *or* across [slang]; palm *or* pass off on, fob *or* foist on; shift the blame *or* responsibility, **pass the buck** [informal].

964. RESPECT

.1 NOUNS **respect, regard,** consideration, appreciation, favor, approbation, approval; **esteem,** estimation, prestige; **reverence, veneration,** awe; **deference,** deferential *or* reverential regard; **honor, homage,** duty; great respect, high regard, admiration, adoration, breathless adoration, exaggerated respect, worship, hero worship, **idol-**

ization 1033.8; idolatry, deification, apotheosis; courtesy 936.

.2 **obeisance,** reverence, homage; **bow, nod, bob,** bend, inclination, inclination of the head, **curtsy, salaam, kowtow,** scrape, bowing and scraping, making a leg; **genuflection,** kneeling, bending the knee; prostration; salute, salutation, presenting arms, dipping the colors *or* ensign, standing at attention; **submissiveness, submission** 765; obsequiousness, **servility** 907.

.3 **respects, regards,** *égards* [Fr], duties, *devoirs* [Fr], attentions.

.4 VERBS **respect,** entertain respect for, accord respect to, **regard, esteem,** hold in esteem *or* consideration, favor, **admire,** think much of, think well of, think highly of, have *or* hold a high opinion of; **appreciate, value,** prize; **revere, reverence,** hold in reverence, **venerate, honor, look up to, defer to,** exalt, put on a pedestal, **worship,** hero-worship, **deify, apotheosize, idolize, adore,** worship the ground one walks on, stand in awe of.

.5 **do** *or* **pay homage to,** show *or* demonstrate respect for, pay respect to, pay tribute to, **do** *or* **render honor to; doff one's cap to,** take off one's hat to; salute, present arms, dip the colors *or* ensign, stand at *or* to attention.

.6 **bow, make obeisance, salaam, kowtow,** make one's bow, bow down, **nod,** incline *or* bend *or* bow the head, bend the neck, **bob, bob down, curtsy,** bob a curtsy, bend, make a leg, scrape, **bow and scrape; genuflect, kneel,** bend the knee, get down on one's knees, throw oneself on one's knees, fall on one's knees, fall down before, fall at the feet of, prostrate oneself, kiss the hem of one's garment.

.7 **command respect,** inspire respect, stand high, have prestige, rank high, be widely reputed; awe 920.6.

.8 ADJS **respectful, regardful,** attentive; **deferential,** conscious of one's place, dutiful, honorific, ceremonious, cap in hand; **courteous** 936.14.

.9 **reverent, reverential;** admiring, **adoring, worshiping,** worshipful, hero-worshiping, **idolizing,** idolatrous, deifying, apotheosizing; **venerative, venerational;** awestruck, awestricken, awed, in awe; solemn 871.3.

.10 **obeisant,** prostrate, on one's knees, on bended knee; **submissive** 765.12–16; **obsequious** 907.13.

.11 **respected, esteemed, revered,** reverenced, adored, worshiped, **venerated, honored,** well-thought-of, admired, much-admired, appreciated, valued, prized, in high esteem or estimation, highly considered, well-considered, held in respect or regard or favor or consideration, prestigious.

.12 **venerable, reverend, estimable, honorable,** worshipful, august, awe-inspiring, awesome, awful, dreadful; time-honored.

.13 ADVS, PREPS **in deference to,** with due respect, with all respect, **with all due respect to** or for, saving, excusing the liberty, saving your reverence, sir-reverence.

965. DISRESPECT

.1 NOUNS **disrespect, disrespectfulness,** lack of respect, **disesteem, dishonor, irreverence;** ridicule 967; disparagement 971; **discourtesy** 937; **impudence,** insolence 913.

.2 **indignity, affront, offense, injury,** humiliation; scurrility, contempt 966, contumely, despite, flout, flouting, mockery, jeering, jeer, mock, scoff, gibe, taunt, brickbat [informal]; **insult, aspersion,** uncomplimentary remark, left-handed or backhanded compliment, slap in the face, damning with faint praise; cut, "most unkindest cut of all" [Shakespeare]; dump or **put-down** [both slang]; **outrage, atrocity,** enormity.

.3 VERBS **disrespect,** not respect, **disesteem,** hold a low opinion of, rate or rank low, hold in low esteem, not care much for; **show disrespect for,** show a lack of respect for, **be disrespectful,** treat with disrespect, be overfamiliar with; trifle with, make bold or free with, take a liberty, take liberties with, play fast and loose with; ridicule 967.8–11; **disparage** 971.8–12.

.4 **offend, affront,** give offense to, disoblige, outrage; dishonor, humiliate, treat with indignity; flout, mock, jeer at, scoff at, fleer at, gibe at, taunt; insult, call names, hurl a brickbat [informal], slap in the face, damn with faint praise, take or pluck by the beard; dump on or put down [both slang]; **add insult to injury.**

.5 ADJS **disrespectful, irreverent,** aweless; **discourteous** 937.4; **insolent, impudent** 913.8,9; ridiculing, **derisive** 967.12–14; **disparaging** 971.13.

.6 **insulting, insolent, abusive,** offensive, humiliating, degrading, contumelious, calumnious; scurrilous, scurrile; backhand, backhanded, left-handed; outrageous, atrocious, unspeakable.

.7 **unrespected, unregarded, unrevered,** unvenerated, unhonored, unenvied.

966. CONTEMPT

.1 NOUNS **contempt, disdain, scorn,** contemptuousness, disdainfulness, superciliousness, snootiness, snottiness, sniffiness, toploftiness, scornfulness, despite, contumely, sovereign contempt; snobbishness; clannishness, cliquishness, exclusiveness; hauteur, airs, arrogance 912; ridicule 967; insult 965.2; disparagement 971.

.2 **snub, rebuff, repulse; slight,** humiliation, spurning, spurn, disregard, the go-by [slang]; cut, cut direct, **the cold shoulder** [informal]; sneer, snort, sniff.

.3 VERBS **disdain, scorn, despise, contemn,** disprize, misprize, rate or rank low, be contemptuous of, feel contempt for, **hold in contempt,** hold cheap, look down upon, feel superior to, be above, hold beneath one or beneath contempt, look with scorn upon, view with a scornful eye; **put down** or dump on [both slang]; deride, **ridicule** 967.8–11; insult 965.4; **disparage** 971.8–12; thumb one's nose at, sniff at, sneeze at, snap one's fingers at, sneer at, snort at, curl one's lip at, shrug one's shoulders at; care nothing for, couldn't care less about, think nothing of, set at naught.

.4 **spurn, scout, turn up one's nose at,** scorn to receive or accept, not want any part of; spit upon.

.5 **snub, rebuff,** repulse; **high-hat** or upstage [both slang]; **look down one's nose at,** look cool or coldly upon; cold-shoulder or turn a cold shoulder upon or **give the cold shoulder** or give or turn the shoulder [informal]; turn one's back upon, turn away from, turn on one's heel, set one's face against, slam the door in one's face, show one his place, put one in his place; not be at home to, not receive.

.6 **slight, ignore,** pooh-pooh [informal], make little of, dismiss, pretend not to see, disregard, overlook, neglect, pass by, pass up or give the go-by [both slang], leave out in the cold [informal], take no note or notice of, look right through [informal], pay no attention or regard to, refuse to acknowledge or recognize; cut or cut dead [both informal].

.7 **avoid** 631.6, shun, dodge, steer clear of or have no truck with [both informal]; **keep one's distance,** keep at a respectful distance, **keep** or **stand** or **hold aloof;** keep at a distance, keep at arm's length; **be stuck-up** [informal], act holier than thou, give oneself airs.

.8 ADJS **contemptuous, disdainful,** supercilious, snooty, snotty, sniffy, toplofty, top-
loftical, **scornful,** sneering, withering,
contumelious; snobbish, snobby; clannish, cliquish, exclusive; haughty, arrogant 912.9.

.9 ADVS **contemptuously, scornfully, disdainfully;** in or with contempt, in disdain, in scorn; sneeringly, with a sneer,
with curling lip.

.10 INTERJS **bah!, pah!,** phooey!, boo!, phoo!,
pish!, ecch!, yeech!, eeyuck! or eeyuch!,
yeeuck!, *feh!* [Yid].

967. RIDICULE

.1 NOUNS **ridicule, derision, mockery, raillery,** rallying, chaffing; panning or razzing
or roasting or ragging [all slang], **scoffing,
jeering, sneering,** snickering, sniggering,
smirking, grinning, leering, fleering, snorting, levity, flippancy, smartness, smart-al-
eckiness or joshing [both informal], fooling, twitting, taunting, booing, hooting,
catcalling, hissing; **banter** 882.

.2 **gibe, scoff, jeer,** fleer, flout, mock, bar-
racking [Brit], **taunt, twit,** quip, jest,
jape, put-on or leg-pull [both informal],
foolery; scurrility, caustic remark; **cut,**
cutting remark, verbal thrust; dump or
put-down or rank-out or dirty dig [all
slang], crack [slang], **slap, slam** or **swipe**
[both informal], jab [slang], dig [infor-
mal], gibing retort, rude reproach, short
answer, back answer, comeback [slang],
parting shot, Parthian shot.

.3 **boo, booing, hoot, catcall;** Bronx cheer or
raspberry or razz [all slang]; **hiss, hissing,**
the bird [slang].

.4 scornful laugh or smile, snicker, snigger,
smirk, sardonic grin, leer, fleer, **sneer,**
snort.

.5 **sarcasm, irony, cynicism, satire,** satiric wit
or humor, invective, innuendo; causticity
939.8.

.6 **burlesque, lampoon,** squib, **parody, satire,
farce,** mockery, imitation, wicked imitation or pastiche, takeoff [informal], **travesty, caricature.**

.7 **laughingstock,** jestingstock, gazingstock,
derision, mockery, **figure of fun,** byword,
byword of reproach, jest, joke, **butt,** target, stock, **goat** [informal], toy, game, **fair
game,** victim, dupe, fool, everybody's
fool, monkey, mug [Brit slang].

.8 VERBS **ridicule, deride,** ride [informal],
make a laughingstock or mockery of; **pan**
or razz or roast or rag [all slang]; **make
fun** or **game of,** poke fun at, make merry

with, put one on or pull one's leg [both
informal]; **laugh at,** laugh in one's face,
grin at, smile at, snicker or snigger at;
laugh to scorn, hold in derision, laugh
out of court; point at, point the finger of
scorn; pillory.

.9 **scoff, jeer,** gibe, barrack [Brit], **mock,** re-
vile, rail at, rally, chaff, **twit, taunt,** jape,
flout, scout, have a fling at, cast in one's
teeth; cut at; dump on or put down or
rank out [all slang], slap at, slam or swipe
[both informal], jab, jab at, dig at; pooh,
pooh-pooh; sneer, **sneer at,** fleer, curl
one's lip.

.10 **boo, hiss, hoot,** catcall, give the raspberry
or Bronx cheer [slang], give the bird
[slang], whistle at.

.11 **burlesque, lampoon, satirize, parody,** car-
icature, travesty, hit or take off on.

.12 ADJS **ridiculing, derisive,** derisory; **mocking, railing, rallying,** chaffing; panning or
razzing or roasting or ragging [all slang],
scoffing, jeering, sneering, snickering,
sniggering, smirking, grinning, leering,
fleering, snorting, flippant, smart, smart-
alecky [informal], smart-ass [slang], joshing [informal], fooling, twitting, taunting,
booing, hooting, catcalling, hissing, bantering, kidding, teasing, quizzical.

.13 **sarcastic, ironic(al), sardonic, cynical, sa-
tiric(al),** Rabelaisian, dry; caustic 939.21.

.14 **burlesque, satiric(al), farcical,** parodic,
caricatural, macaronic, doggerel.

.15 ADVS **derisively, mockingly,** scoffingly,
jeeringly, sneeringly, "with scoffs and
scorns and contumelious taunts" [Shake-
speare].

968. APPROVAL

.1 NOUNS **approval, approbation;** sanction,
acceptance, countenance, **favor;** admira-
tion, esteem, respect 964; endorsement,
vote, favorable vote, yea vote, yea, voice,
adherence, blessing, seal of approval,
nod, stamp of approval, OK 521.4.

.2 **applause,** plaudit, éclat, **acclaim, acclamation; popularity;** clap, handclap, **clapping,** handclapping, clapping of hands;
cheer 876.2; burst of applause, peal or
thunder of applause; round of applause,
hand, big hand; ovation, standing ovation; encore.

.3 **commendation,** good word, acknowledgment, recognition, appreciation; boost or
buildup [both slang]; **puff,** promotion;
blurb or **plug** or promo or hype [all
slang]; honorable mention.

.4 **recommendation,** recommend [Brit informal]; **advocacy**, advocating, advocation, patronage; **reference, credential,** voucher, **testimonial;** character reference, character, certificate of character; letter of introduction.

.5 **praise,** bepraisement; **laudation,** laud; **glorification,** glory, exaltation, magnification, **honor**; eulogy, *eloge, hommage* [both Fr], eulogium; **encomium,** accolade, kudos, panegyric; paean; **tribute,** homage, meed of praise; congratulation 948.1; flattery 970; overpraise, excessive praise, idolizing, idolatry, deification, apotheosis, adulation, lionizing, hero worship.

.6 **compliment,** polite commendation, complimentary *or* flattering remark; **bouquet** *or* posy [both informal], trade-last *or* TL [both informal].

.7 **praiseworthiness, laudability,** laudableness, commendableness, estimableness, meritoriousness, exemplariness, admirability.

.8 **commender,** eulogist, eulogizer; **praiser,** lauder, extoller, encomiast, panegyrist, **booster** [informal], puffer, promoter; plugger *or* tout *or* touter [all slang]; **applauder,** claqueur; claque; rooter *or* fan *or* buff [all informal], adherent; appreciator.

.9 VERBS **approve, approve of,** think well of; **sanction, accept; admire, esteem, respect** 964.4; **endorse, bless,** OK 521.12; **countenance,** keep in countenance; **hold with,** uphold; **favor,** be in favor of, view with favor, take kindly to.

.10 **applaud, acclaim, hail; clap,** clap the hands, give a hand *or* big hand, hear it for [slang]; **cheer** 876.6; root for [informal], cheer on; encore; cheer *or* applaud to the very echo.

.11 **commend, speak well** *or* **highly of,** speak in high terms of, speak warmly of, have *or* say a good word for; boost *or* give a boost to [both informal], puff, promote, cry up; plug *or* tout *or* hype [all slang]; **recommend, advocate,** put in a word *or* good word for, support, back, lend one's name *or* support *or* backing to.

.12 **praise,** bepraise; **laud, belaud; eulogize,** panegyrize, pay tribute, salute; **extol, glorify,** magnify, exalt, bless; cry up, blow up, puff, puff up; boast of, brag about [informal], make much of; celebrate, emblazon, sound *or* resound the praises of, ring one's praises, sing the praise of, trumpet; praise to the skies, *porter aux nues* [Fr]; flatter 970.5; overpraise, praise

to excess, idolize, deify, apotheosize, adulate, lionize, hero-worship.

.13 **espouse,** take up, take for one's own; **campaign for, crusade for,** put on a drive for; carry the banner of, march under the banner of; beat the drum for, thump the tub for; lavish oneself on, fight the good fight for; devote *or* dedicate oneself to, spend *or* give *or* sacrifice oneself for.

.14 **compliment, pay a compliment,** make one a compliment, give a bouquet *or* posy [informal], say something nice about; hand it to *or* have to hand it to [both slang], pat on the back, take off one's hat to, doff one's cap to, congratulate 948.2.

.15 **meet with approval,** find favor with, pass muster, recommend itself, do credit to; redound to the honor of; ring with the praises of.

.16 ADJS **approbatory, commendatory, complimentary, laudatory,** acclamatory, eulogistic, panegyric, encomiastic, **appreciative; admiring, regardful, respectful** 964.8; flattering 970.8.

.17 **approving, favorable,** favoring, in favor of, **pro,** well-disposed, well-inclined, supporting, backing, **advocating.**

.18 **uncritical,** uncriticizing, **uncensorious,** unreproachful; overpraising, overappreciative, unmeasured *or* excessive in one's praise, idolatrous, adulatory, lionizing, hero-worshiping, fulsome.

.19 **approved,** favored, backed, advocated, supported; favorite; **accepted,** received, admitted; recommended, highly touted [informal], **admired** 964.11, **applauded,** well-thought-of, in good odor, **acclaimed,** cried up; **popular.**

.20 **praiseworthy,** worthy, **commendable,** estimable, **laudable,** admirable, meritorious, creditable; exemplary, model, unexceptionable; deserving, well-deserving; beyond all praise, *sans peur et sans reproche* [Fr].

.21 PREPS **in favor of, for, pro,** all for.

.22 INTERJS **bravo!,** bravissimo!, **well done!,** ¡ole! [Sp], bene! [Ital], hear, hear!, aha!; hurrah!; **good!,** fine!, excellent!, great!, beautiful!, swell!, good for you!, good enough!, not bad!, now you're talking!; attaboy!, attababy!, attagirl!, attagal!, good boy!, good girl!; that's the idea!, that's the ticket!; encore!, bis! [Fr], take a bow!, one cheer more!

.23 **hail!,** all hail!, ave! [L], vive! [Fr], viva!, evviva! [both Ital], long life to!, glory be to!, honor be to!

969. DISAPPROVAL

.1 NOUNS disapproval, disapprobation, disfavor, disesteem, disrespect 965; dim view, poor or low opinion, low estimation; displeasure, distaste, dissatisfaction, discontent, discontentment, discontentedness, disgruntlement, indignation, unhappiness; disillusion, disillusionment, disenchantment, disappointment; disagreement, opposition 790, opposure; rejection, thumbs-down, exclusion, ostracism, blackballing, blackball, ban; complaint, protest, objection, dissent 522.

.2 deprecation, discommendation, dispraise, denigration, disvaluation; ridicule 967; depreciation, disparagement 971; contempt 966.

.3 censure, reprehension, stricture, reprobation, blame, denunciation, denouncement, decrial, impeachment, arraignment, indictment, condemnation, damnation, fulmination, anathema; castigation, flaying, skinning alive [informal], fustigation, excoriation; pillorying.

.4 criticism, adverse criticism, hostile criticism, flak [informal], bad notices, bad press, animadversion, imputation, reflection, aspersion, stricture, obloquy; knock or swipe or slam or rap or hit [all informal], home thrust; minor or petty criticism, niggle, cavil, quibble, exception, nit [informal]; censoriousness, reproachfulness, priggishness; faultfinding, taking exception, carping, caviling, pettifogging, quibbling, captiousness, niggling, nit-picking, pestering, nagging; hypercriticism, hypercriticalness, overcriticalness, hairsplitting, trichoschistism.

.5 reproof, reproval, reprobation; rebuke, reprimand, reproach, reprehension, scolding, chiding, rating, upbraiding, objurgation; admonishment, admonition; correction, castigation, chastisement, spanking, rap on the knuckles; lecture, lesson, sermon.

.6 [slang or informal terms] piece or bit of one's mind, talking-to, speaking-to, roasting, raking-down, raking-over, raking over the coals, dressing, dressing-down, set-down; bawling-out, cussing-out, calling-down, jacking-up, going-over, chewing-out, chewing, reaming-out, reaming, ass-chewing, ass-reaming, what-for.

.7 berating, rating, jawing [slang], tongue-lashing; revilement, vilification, blackening, execration, abuse, vituperation, invective, contumely, hard or cutting or bitter words; tirade, diatribe, jeremiad, screed, philippic; attack, assault, onslaught, assailing.

.8 reproving look, dirty or nasty look [slang], black look, frown, scowl.

.9 faultfinder, frondeur [Fr], momus; critic 494.7, captious critic, criticizer, nitpicker [informal], smellfungus, belittler, censor, censurer, carper, caviler, quibbler, pettifogger; scold, common scold.

.10 VERBS disapprove, disapprove of, not approve; disfavor, view with disfavor, frown at or upon, look black upon, look askance at, make a wry face at, grimace at, turn up one's nose at, shrug one's shoulders at; take a dim view of [informal], not think much of, think ill of, think little of, not take kindly to, not hold with, hold no brief for [informal]; not go for or not get all choked up over or be turned off by [all slang]; not want or have any part of, wash one's hands of, dissociate oneself from; object to, take exception to; oppose 790.3–7, set oneself against, set one's face against; reject, categorically reject, disallow, not hear of; turn thumbs down on or thumb down [both informal], frown down, exclude, ostracize, blackball, ban; say no to, shake one's head at; dissent from, protest, object 522.4,5.

.11 discountenance, not countenance, not tolerate, not brook, not condone, not suffer, not abide, not endure, not bear with, not put up with, not stand for [informal].

.12 deprecate, discommend, dispraise, disvalue, not be able to say much for, denigrate, put down [slang]; ridicule 967.8–11; depreciate, disparage 971.8; hold in contempt, disdain, despise 966.3.

.13 censure, reprehend; blame, lay or cast blame upon; reproach, impugn; condemn, damn, damn with faint praise; fulminate against, anathematize, anathemize, put on the Index; denounce, denunciate, accuse 1005.7–11, decry, cry down, impeach, arraign, indict, call to account, exclaim or declaim or inveigh against, cry out against, cry out on or upon, cry shame upon, raise one's voice against, raise a hue and cry against, shake up [archaic]; reprobate, hold up to reprobation; animadvert on or upon, reflect upon, cast reflection upon, cast a reproach or slur upon, complain against; throw a stone at, cast or throw the first stone.

.14 criticize; pan or knock or slam or hit or rap or take a rap or swipe at [all informal], snipe at.

.15 find fault, take exception, fault-find, pick holes, cut up, pick or pull or tear apart, pick or pull or tear to pieces; carp, cavil, quibble, nitpick, pettifog, catch at straws.

.16 nag, niggle, carp at, fuss at, fret at, yap at or pick at [both informal], peck at, nibble at, pester, henpeck, pick on [informal], bug or hassle [both slang].

.17 reprove, rebuke, reprimand, reprehend, scold, chide, rate, admonish, upbraid, objurgate, have words with; lecture, read a lesson or lecture to; correct, rap on the knuckles, chastise, spank, turn over one's knees; take to task, call to account, bring to book, call on the carpet, read the riot act; take down, set down, set straight, straighten out.

.18 [informal terms] call down, dress down, speak or talk to, tell off, tell a thing or two, give a piece or bit of one's mind, rake or haul over the coals, rake up one side and down the other, give it to, trim, come down on or upon, jump on, jump all over, jump down one's throat.

.19 [slang terms] bawl out, give a bawling out, chew, chew out, chew ass, ream, ream out, ream ass, cuss out, jack up, sit on or upon, lambaste, give a going-over, tell where to get off; give what-for, give the deuce or devil, give hell, give hail Columbia.

.20 berate, rate, betongue, jaw [slang], clapper-claw [dial], tongue-lash, rail at, rag, thunder or fulminate against, rave against, yell at, bark or yelp at; revile, vilify, blacken, execrate, abuse, vituperate, load with reproaches.

.21 (criticize or reprove severely) attack, assail 798.15; castigate, flay, skin alive [informal], lash, slash, excoriate, fustigate, scarify, scathe, roast [informal], scorch, blister, trounce.

.22 ADJS disapproving, disapprobatory, unapproving, turned-off, displeased, dissatisfied, discontented, disgruntled, indignant, unhappy; disillusioned, disenchanted, disappointed; unfavorable, low, poor, opposed 790.8, opposing, con, against, agin [informal], dissenting 522.6, 7; uncomplimentary; unappreciative.

.23 condemnatory, censorious, damnatory, denunciatory, reproachful, blameful, reprobative, objurgatory, priggish, judgmental; deprecative, deprecatory; derisive, ridiculing, scoffing 967.12–14; deprecia-

tive, disparaging 971.13; contemptuous 966.8; invective, inveighing; reviling, vilifying, blackening, execrating, execratory, ecratory, abusive, vituperative.

.24 critical, faultfinding, carping, caviling, quibbling, pettifogging, captious, cynical; nagging, niggling; hypercritical, ultracritical, overcritical, hairsplitting, trichoschistic.

.25 unpraiseworthy, illaudable; uncommendable, discommendable; objectionable, exceptionable, unacceptable, not to be thought of.

.26 blameworthy, blamable, to blame; reprehensible, censurable, reproachable, reprovable, open to criticism or reproach; culpable, chargeable, impeachable, accusable, indictable, arraignable, imputable.

.27 ADVS disapprovingly, askance, askant, unfavorably; censoriously, critically, reproachfully; captiously.

.28 INTERJS God forbid!, Heaven forbid!, Heaven forfend!, forbid it Heaven!; by no means!, not for the world!, not on your life!, over my dead body!, not if I know it!, nothing doing!, no way!, perish the thought!, I'll be hanged or damned if . . . !

970. FLATTERY

.1 NOUNS flattery, adulation; praise 968.5; blandishment, palaver, cajolery, cajolement, wheedling; blarney or bunkum or soft soap or soap or butter salve [all informal], oil, grease, eyewash [slang]; sweet talk, fair or sweet or honeyed words, soft or honeyed phrases, incense, pretty lies, sweet nothings; compliment 968.6; fawning, sycophancy 907.2.

.2 unction, "that flattering unction" [Shakespeare]; unctuousness, oiliness; slobber, gush, smarm; flattering tongue; insincerity 616.5.

.3 overpraise, overprizing, excessive praise, overcommendation, overlaudation, overestimation; idolatry 968.5.

.4 flatterer, flatteur [Fr], adulator, courtier; cajoler, wheedler; backslapper, backscratcher; blarneyer or soft-soaper [both informal]; sycophant 907.3.

.5 VERBS flatter, adulate, conceit; cajole, wheedle, blandish, palaver; slaver or slobber over, beslobber, beslubber; oil the tongue, lay the flattering unction to one's soul, make fair weather; praise, compliment 968.12,14; fawn upon 907.6–9.

.6 [slang or informal terms] soft-soap, butter, honey, butter up, soften up; stroke;

blarney, jolly, pull one's leg; lay it on, lay it on thick, overdo it, soap, oil; string along, kid along; play up to, get around; lay it on with a trowel.

.7 **overpraise,** overprize, overcommend, overlaud; overesteem, overestimate; idolize 968.12.

.8 ADJS **flattering, adulatory; complimentary** 968.16; **blandishing, cajoling, wheedling,** blarneying or soft-soaping [both informal]; fair-spoken, fine-spoken, smooth-spoken, smooth-tongued, **mealymouthed,** honey-mouthed, honey-tongued, honeyed, oily-tongued; fulsome, slimy, slobbery, gushing, smarmy, insinuating, oily, buttery [informal], soapy [slang]; **unctuous,** smooth, bland; insincere 616.32; courtly, courtierly; **fawning, sycophantic, obsequious** 907.13.

971. DISPARAGEMENT

.1 NOUNS **disparagement, depreciation, detraction,** derogation, running down or knocking [both informal], putting down [slang], **belittling;** sour grapes; slighting, minimizing, faint praise, lukewarm support, discrediting, decrial; disapproval 969; contempt 966; indignity, disgrace, comedown [informal].

.2 **defamation,** malicious defamation, defamation of character, injury of or to one's reputation; **vilification,** revilement, defilement, blackening, denigration; **smear,** character assassination, ad hominem attack, name-calling, smear word, smear campaign; **muckraking, mudslinging.**

.3 **slander, scandal, libel,** traducement; calumny, calumniation; backbiting, cattiness or bitchiness [both informal].

.4 **aspersion, slur, reflection,** imputation, insinuation, suggestion, sly suggestion, innuendo, whispering campaign; disparaging or uncomplimentary remark; personality, personal remark.

.5 **lampoon,** pasquinade, pasquin, pasquil, squib, **satire,** malicious parody, **burlesque** 967.6; poison pen, hatchet job.

.6 **disparager, depreciator,** decrier, detractor, belittler, debunker, deflater, slighter, derogator, **knocker** [informal], caustic critic, hatchet man; **slanderer,** libeler, defamer, backbiter; calumniator, traducer; **muckraker, mudslinger,** social critic; cynic, railer, Thersites.

.7 **lampooner,** lampoonist, **satirist,** pasquinader; poison-pen writer.

.8 VERBS **disparage, depreciate, belittle,** slight, minimize, make little of, degrade, debase, **run down** or **knock** [informal], **put down** [slang]; **discredit,** bring into discredit, reflect discredit upon, disgrace; detract from, derogate from, cut down to size [slang]; **decry,** cry down; speak ill of, speak slightingly of, not speak well of; disapprove of 969.10; hold in contempt 966.3; submit to indignity or disgrace, bring down, bring low.

.9 **defame, malign, bad-mouth** [informal]; **asperse, cast aspersions on,** cast reflections on, injure one's reputation, damage one's good name; **slur,** cast a slur on, do a number on [informal]; give a bad name, give a dog a bad name.

.10 **vilify, revile, defile, sully, soil, smear,** smirch, besmirch, bespatter, tarnish, **blacken,** denigrate, blacken one's good name, give a black eye [informal]; stigmatize 915.9; **muckrake, throw mud at,** heap dirt upon, drag through the mud; call names, engage in personalities.

.11 **slander, libel;** calumniate, traduce; stab in the back, backbite, speak ill of behind one's back.

.12 **lampoon, satirize,** pasquinade, dip the pen in gall, **burlesque** 967.11.

.13 ADJS **disparaging, derogatory,** derogative, **depreciatory,** depreciative, deprecatory, slighting, belittling, minimizing, detractory, pejorative, back-biting, catty or bitchy [both informal], contumelious, contemptuous, derisive, derisory, ridiculing 967.12; censorious 969.23; **defamatory,** vilifying, **slanderous, scandalous, libelous;** calumnious, calumniatory; **abusive,** scurrilous, scurrile.

972. CURSE

.1 NOUNS **curse, malediction,** malison, damnation, denunciation, commination, imprecation, execration; blasphemy; anathema, fulmination, thundering, excommunication; ban, proscription; hex, evil eye, malocchio [Ital], whammy [slang].

.2 **vilification, abuse,** revilement, **vituperation, invective,** opprobrium, obloquy, contumely, calumny, scurrility, blackguardism.

.3 **cursing, cussing** [informal], **swearing, profanity,** profane swearing, foul or profane or obscene or blue or bad or strong or unparliamentary or indelicate language, vulgar language, vile language, colorful language, unrepeatable expressions, dysphemism, billingsgate, ribaldry, evil speaking, **dirty language** or **talk** [informal], obscenity, scatology, **filthy language, filth.**

.4 **oath,** profane oath, curse; cuss *or* cuss word *or* dirty word *or* four-letter word *or* **swearword** [all informal], naughty word, no-no [informal], foul invective, **expletive, epithet,** dirty name [slang], dysphemism, obscenity.

.5 VERBS curse, accurse, **damn,** darn, **confound,** blast, anathematize, fulminate *or* thunder against, execrate, imprecate; excommunicate; call down evil upon, call down curses on the head of; put a curse on; curse up hill and down dale; curse with bell, book, and candle; blaspheme; hex, give the evil eye, throw a whammy [slang].

.6 **curse, swear, cuss** [informal], curse and swear, execrate, rap out *or* rip out an oath, take the Lord's name in vain; swear like a trooper, cuss like a sailor, make the air blue, swear till one is blue in the face; **talk dirty** [informal], scatologize, dysphemize.

.7 **vilify, abuse, revile,** vituperate, blackguard, call names, epithet, epithetize; **swear at,** damn, cuss out [informal].

.8 ADJS cursing, maledictory, imprecatory, **damnatory,** denunciatory, epithetic(al); **abusive,** vituperative, contumelious; calumnious, calumniatory; execratory, comminatory, fulminatory, excommunicative, excommunicatory; scurrilous, scurrile; blasphemous, profane, foul, vile, **dirty** [informal], **obscene,** dysphemistic, scatologic(al); ribald, Rabelaisian, raw, risqué.

.9 **cursed,** accursed, bloody [Brit slang], **damned, damn, damnable,** goddamned, goddamn, **execrable.**

.10 (euphemisms) **darned,** danged, **confounded,** deuced, blessed, **blasted,** dashed, blamed, goshdarn, doggone *or* doggoned, goldarned, goldanged, dadburned; blankety-blank; ruddy [Brit].

.11 INTERJS damn!, damn it!, God damn it! *or* goddam it!, confound it!, hang it!, devil take!, a plague upon!, a pox upon!, *parbleu!* [Fr].

.12 (euphemistic oaths) darn!, dern!, dang!, dash!, drat!, blast!, doggone!, goldarn!, goldang!, golding!, gosh-darn!

973. THREAT

.1 NOUNS **threat, menace,** threateningness, threatfulness, promise of harm, knife poised at one's throat, arrow aimed at one's heart, sword of Damocles; denunciation, commination; imminence 152;

foreboding 544; **warning** 703; saber rattling, bulldozing, **intimidation** 891.6; veiled *or* implied threat, idle *or* hollow *or* empty threat.

.2 VERBS **threaten, menace,** bludgeon, bulldoze, **intimidate** 891.28; utter threats against, shake *or* double *or* clench one's fist at; hold over one's head; denounce, comminate; **lower,** look threatening; **be imminent** 152.2; **forebode** 544.11; **warn** 703.5.

.3 ADJS **threatening, menacing,** threatful, minatory, minacious; **lowering; imminent** 152.3; **ominous,** foreboding 544.17; denunciatory, comminatory, abusive; fear-inspiring, **intimidating,** bludgeoning, bulldozing, browbeating, bullying, hectoring, blustering, terrorizing, terroristic.

974. PROBITY

.1 NOUNS **probity,** assured probity, **honesty, integrity, rectitude, uprightness,** upstandingness, erectness, **virtue,** virtuousness, **righteousness, goodness;** cleanness, **decency; honor,** honorableness, worthiness, estimableness, reputability, nobility; unimpeachableness, unimpeachability, irreproachableness, irreproachability, blamelessness; immaculacy, unspottedness, stainlessness, pureness, purity; respectability; principles, high principles, high ideals, high-mindedness; **character,** good character, moral strength, moral excellence; **fairness,** justness, justice 976.

.2 **conscientiousness, scrupulousness,** scrupulosity, **scruples,** punctiliousness, meticulousness; scruple, point of honor, punctilio; qualm 623.2; twinge of conscience 873.2; overconscientiousness, overscrupulousness; fastidiousness 896.

.3 **veracity,** veraciousness, verity, **truthfulness,** truth, veridicality, truth-telling, truth-speaking; truth-loving; credibility, absolute credibility.

.4 **candor, candidness, frankness,** sincerity, genuineness, plain dealing; ingenuousness; artlessness 736; **openness,** openheartedness; freedom, freeness; **unreserve,** unrestraint, unconstraint; **forthrightness, directness, straightforwardness; outspokenness,** plainness, plainspokenness, plain speaking, roundness, broadness; **bluntness,** bluffness, brusqueness.

.5 **undeceptiveness, undeceitfulness, guilelessness.**

.6 **trustworthiness,** faithworthiness, trustiness, trustability, **reliability, dependability,** responsibility, sureness; unfalseness, unperfidiousness, untreacherousness; incorruptibility, inviolability.

.7 **fidelity, faithfulness, loyalty,** faith; **constancy, steadfastness,** staunchness, firmness, trueness, troth, true blue; good faith, *bona fides* [L], *bonne foi* [Fr]; **allegiance, fealty,** homage; bond, tie; attachment, adherence, adhesion; devotion, devotedness.

.8 **man of honor,** man of his word, gentleman, *gentilhomme* [Fr], *galantuomo* [Ital]; **honest man,** good man; woman of honor, woman of her word, lady, real lady; honest woman, good woman; salt of the earth; square *or* straight shooter [informal]; true blue, truepenny; trusty, faithful.

.9 VERBS **keep faith,** not fail, **keep one's word** *or* **promise,** keep troth, be as good as one's word, redeem one's pledge, play by the rules, acquit oneself, make good.

.10 shoot straight [informal], draw a straight furrow, **put one's cards on the table,** level with [slang].

.11 **speak** *or* **tell the truth,** speak *or* tell true, paint in its true colors, tell the truth and shame the devil; tell the truth, the whole truth, and nothing but the truth.

.12 **be frank,** speak plainly, speak out, speak one's mind, say what one thinks, **call a spade a spade,** tell it like it is.

.13 ADJS **honest, upright,** uprighteous, **upstanding,** erect, right, **righteous, virtuous, good,** clean, **decent; honorable,** full of integrity, **reputable,** estimable, creditable, worthy, noble, sterling, manly, yeomanly, Christian [informal]; unimpeachable, irreproachable, blameless, immaculate, spotless, stainless, unstained, unspotted, unblemished, untarnished, unsullied, undefiled, pure; **respectable,** highly respectable; **ethical, moral; principled, high-principled,** high-minded, right-minded; uncorrupt, uncorrupted, inviolate; truehearted, true-souled, true-spirited; true-dealing, true-disposing, true-devoted; **law-abiding,** law-loving, law-revering; fair, just 976.8–10.

.14 **straight, square,** foursquare, **fair and square; square-dealing,** square-shooting, straight-shooting, up-and-up, **on the up-and-up, on the level,** on the square; open, aboveboard, open and aboveboard; bona fide, good-faith; authentic, veritable, genuine 516.14; single-hearted; honest as the day is long.

.15 **conscientious,** tender-conscienced; **scrupulous,** careful 533.10–14; punctilious,

punctual, meticulous, religious, strict, nice; fastidious 896.9; overconscientious, overscrupulous.

.16 **veracious, truthful,** true, veridical; truth-telling, truth-speaking, truth-declaring, truth-passing, truth-bearing, truth-loving, truth-seeking, truth-desiring, truth-guarding, truth-filled; true-speaking, true-meaning, true-tongued.

.17 **candid, frank, sincere,** genuine, ingenuous, frankhearted; **open,** openhearted, transparent; artless 736.5; **straightforward, direct,** straight [informal], **forthright,** downright, straight-out [informal]; plain, broad, round; **unreserved,** unrestrained, unconstrained, unchecked; unguarded; free; **outspoken, plain-spoken,** free-spoken, free-speaking, free-tongued; explicit, unequivocal; **blunt,** bluff, brusque; heart-to-heart.

.18 **undeceptive, undeceitful, undissembling,** undissimulating, undeceiving, undesigning, uncalculating; **guileless, unbeguiling,** unbeguileful; unassuming, unpretending, unfeigning, undisguising, unflattering; undissimulated, undissembled; unassumed, unaffected, unpretended, unfeigned, undisguised, unvarnished, untrimmed.

.19 **trustworthy, trusty,** trustable, faithworthy, **reliable, dependable, responsible,** straight [slang], sure, to be trusted, **to be depended** *or* **relied upon,** to be counted *or* reckoned on, as good as one's word; tried, true, **tried and true,** tested, proven; unfalse, unperfidious, untreacherous; incorruptible, inviolable.

.20 **faithful, loyal,** devoted; **true, true-blue,** true to one's colors; **constant, steadfast,** steady, consistent, stable, unfailing, staunch, firm, "marble-constant" [Shakespeare].

.21 ADVS **honestly, uprightly, honorably,** upstandingly, erectly, **virtuously, righteously, decently,** worthily, reputably, nobly; unimpeachably, irreproachably, blamelessly, immaculately, unspottedly, stainlessly, purely; high-mindedly, morally; **conscientiously, scrupulously,** punctiliously, meticulously, fastidiously 896.14.

.22 **truthfully, truly,** veraciously; to tell the truth, to speak truthfully; in truth, in sooth [archaic], of a truth, with truth, in good *or* very truth.

.23 **candidly, frankly, sincerely,** genuinely, in all seriousness *or* soberness, in all conscience; in plain words *or* English, straight from the shoulder, not to mince the matter, not to mince words, without equivocation, with no nonsense, all joking aside or apart; openly, openheartedly, unreservedly, unrestrainedly, unconstrainedly, forthrightly, directly, straightforwardly, outspokenly, plainly, plain-spokenly, broadly, roundly, bluntly, bluffly, brusquely.

.24 trustworthily, trustily, reliably, dependably, responsibly; undeceptively, undeceitfully, guilelessly; incorruptibly, inviolably.

.25 faithfully, loyally, devotedly; constantly, steadfastly, steadily, responsibly, consistently, staunchly, firmly; in or with good faith, bona fide [L].

975. IMPROBITY

.1 NOUNS improbity, dishonesty, dishonor; unscrupulousness, unconscientiousness; corruption, corruptness, corruptedness; crookedness, criminality, feloniousness, fraudulence or fraudulency, underhandedness, unsavoriness, fishiness or shadiness [both informal], indirection, shiftiness, slipperiness, deviousness, evasiveness, unstraightforwardness, trickiness.

.2 knavery, roguery, rascality, rascalry, villainy, reprobacy, scoundrelism; chicanery 618.4; knavishness, roguishness, scampishness, villainousness; baseness, vileness, degradation, turpitude, moral turpitude.

.3 deceitfulness 618.4; falseheartedness 616.4; perjury, forswearing, untruthfulness 616.8, credibility gap; insincerity, unsincereness, uncandidness, uncandor, unfrankness, disingenuousness; sharp practice 618.4; fraud 618.8; artfulness, craftiness 735.1; intrigue 654.6.

.4 untrustworthiness, unfaithworthiness, untrustiness, unreliability, undependability, irresponsibility.

.5 infidelity, unfaithfulness, unfaith, faithlessness, trothlessness; inconstancy, unsteadfastness, fickleness; disloyalty, unloyalty; falsity, falseness, untrueness; disaffection, recreancy, dereliction; bad faith, mala fides [L], Punic faith; breach of promise, breach of trust or faith, barratry.

.6 treachery, treacherousness; perfidy, perfidiousness, falseheartedness; duplicity, double-dealing, foul play; dirty work or dirty pool or dirty trick [all slang].

.7 treason, petty treason, misprision of treason, high treason; lese majesty, sedition; quislingism, fifth-column activity; collaboration, fraternization.

.8 betrayal, betrayment, letting down [informal], double cross [slang], sellout [slang], Judas kiss, stab in the back.

.9 corruptibility, venality, bribability, purchasability.

.10 criminal 986.10, scoundrel 986.3, traitor 619.10, deceiver 619.

.11 VERBS (be dishonest) live by one's wits; shift, shift about, evade; deceive 618.13; cheat 618.17; falsify 616.16; lie 616.19.

.12 be unfaithful, not keep faith with, go back on [informal], fail, break one's word or promise, go back on one's word [informal], break faith, perjure or forswear oneself; forsake, desert 633.5,6; pass the buck [informal]; shift the responsibility or blame.

.13 play one false, prove false; stab in the back, knife [slang]; bite the hand that feeds one; play dirty pool [slang].

.14 betray, double-cross or two-time [both slang], sell out or sell down the river [both slang], turn in; let down or let down one's side [both informal]; inform on 557.12.

.15 act the traitor, quisle, turn against, go over to the enemy, turn one's coat, sell oneself; collaborate, fraternize.

.16 ADJS dishonest, dishonorable; unconscientious, unconscienced, conscienceless, unconscionable, shameless, without shame or remorse, unscrupulous, unprincipled, unethical, immoral, amoral; corrupt, corrupted, rotten; crooked, criminal, felonious, fraudulent; underhand, underhanded; shady [informal], not kosher, unsavory, dark, sinister, insidious, indirect, slippery, devious, tricky, shifty, evasive, unstraightforward; fishy [informal], questionable, suspicious, doubtful, dubious; ill-gotten, ill-got.

.17 knavish, roguish, scampish, rascally, scoundrelly, blackguardly, villainous, reprobate, recreant, base, vile, degraded; infamous, notorious.

.18 deceitful 618.20; falsehearted 616.31; perjured, forsworn, untruthful 616.34; insincere, unsincere, uncandid, unfrank, disingenuous; artful, crafty 735.12; calculating, scheming 654.14.

.19 untrustworthy, unfaithworthy, untrusty, trustless, unreliable, undependable, fly-by-night, irresponsible, unsure, not to be trusted, not to be depended or relied upon.

.20 unfaithful, faithless, of bad faith, trothless; inconstant, unsteadfast, fickle; disloyal, unloyal; false, untrue, not true to; disaffected, recreant, derelict, barratrous.

.21 **treacherous,** **perfidious,** falsehearted; **shifty,** slippery, tricky; **double-dealing,** double, ambidextrous; **two-faced** 616.31.

.22 **traitorous,** turncoat, double-crossing *or* two-timing [both slang], betraying; Judas-like, Iscariotic; **treasonable,** treasonous; quisling, quislingistic, fifth-column, Trojan-horse.

.23 **corruptible, venal,** bribable, purchasable, mercenary, hireling.

.24 ADVS **dishonestly, dishonorably; unscrupulously,** unconscientiously; **crookedly,** criminally, feloniously, **fraudulently,** underhandedly, like a thief in the night, insidiously, deviously, shiftily, evasively, fishily [informal], suspiciously, dubiously, by fair means or foul; **deceitfully** 618.22; knavishly, roguishly, villainously; basely, vilely; infamously, notoriously.

.25 **perfidiously,** falseheartedly; **unfaithfully,** faithlessly; **treacherously;** traitorously, treasonably.

976. JUSTICE

.1 NOUNS **justice, justness; equity,** equitableness, evenhandedness, measure for measure, give-and-take; **right, rightness,** rightfulness, meetness, properness, propriety, what is right; dueness 960; justification, **justifiableness,** justifiability, warrantedness, warrantability, defensibility; poetic justice; retributive justice, nemesis; summary justice, drumhead justice, rude justice; scales of justice; lawfulness, legality 998.

.2 "truth in action" [Disraeli], "right reason applied to command and prohibition" [Cicero], "the firm and continuous desire to render to everyone that which is his due" [Justinian].

.3 **fairness,** fair-mindedness, candor; the fair thing, the right *or* proper thing, the handsome thing [informal]; **square deal** [informal], **fair shake** [slang]; **fair play,** cricket [informal]; sportsmanship, good sportsmanship, sportsmanliness, sportsmanlikeness.

.4 **impartiality,** detachment, **dispassion,** loftiness, Olympian detachment, **dispassionateness, disinterestedness,** disinterest, unbias, unbiasedness, a fair field and no favor; **neutrality** 806; selflessness, unselfishness 979.

.5 (personifications) Justice, Justitia, blind *or* blindfolded Justice; Rhadamanthus, Minos; (deities) Jupiter Fidius, Deus Fidius; Fides, Fides publica Romani, Fides

populi Romani; Nemesis, Dike, Themis; Astraea.

.6 VERBS **be just, be fair,** do the fair thing, do the handsome thing [informal], do the right thing by; **do justice to,** see justice done, see one righted *or* redressed, redress a wrong *or* injustice, remedy an injustice, serve one right, shoot straight with *or* **give a square deal** [both informal], give a fair shake [slang]; give the Devil his due; give and take; bend over backwards, lean over backwards.

.7 **play fair, play the game** [informal], be a good sport, show a proper spirit.

.8 ADJS **just, fair,** square, **fair and square; equitable,** balanced, level [informal], **even,** evenhanded; **right, rightful;** justifiable, justified, warranted, warrantable, defensible; **due** 960.7–10, deserved, merited; meet, meet and right, right and proper, fit, **proper, good,** as it should *or* ought to be; lawful, legal 998.10.

.9 **fair-minded; sporting, sportsmanly,** sportsmanlike; square-dealing *or* square-shooting [both informal].

.10 **impartial, impersonal,** candid, **dispassionate, disinterested,** detached, lofty, Olympian; **unbiased,** uninfluenced, unswayed; **neutral** 806.7; selfless, unselfish 979.5,6.

.11 ADVS **justly, fairly,** fair, in a fair manner; rightfully, rightly, duly, deservedly, meetly, properly; **equitably, equally, evenly,** upon even terms; justifiedly, justifiably, warrantably, warrantedly; **impartially, impersonally, dispassionately, disinterestedly,** without distinction, without regard *or* respect to persons, without fear or favor.

.12 **in justice,** in equity, in reason, in all conscience, in all fairness, **to be fair,** as is only fair *or* right, as is right *or* just *or* fitting *or* proper.

977. INJUSTICE

.1 NOUNS **injustice, unjustness; inequity,** iniquity, inequitableness, iniquitousness; **wrong, wrongness,** wrongfulness, unmeetness, improperness, **impropriety;** undueness; what should not be, what ought not *or* must not be; unlawfulness, illegality 999.

.2 **unfairness;** unsportsmanliness, **unsportsmanlikeness;** foul play, foul, a hit below the belt.

.3 **partiality, one-sidedness; bias,** leaning, inclination; undispassionateness, undetachment, interest, involvement, **partisanism,** partisanship, parti pris; unneutrality; **fa-**

voritism, preference, nepotism; unequal or preferential treatment, discrimination, unjust legal disability, inequality.

.4 **injustice, wrong, injury**, grievance, disservice, raw deal [slang]; imposition; mockery or miscarriage of justice; great wrong, grave or gross injustice; atrocity, outrage.

.5 **unjustifiability, unwarrantability**, indefensibility; **inexcusability**, unconscionableness, **unpardonability**, unforgivableness, inexpiableness, irremissibility.

.6 VERBS not play fair, hit below the belt, give a raw deal [slang].

.7 **do one an injustice, wrong**, do wrong, do wrong by, **do one a wrong**, do a disservice; do a great wrong, do a grave or gross injustice, commit an atrocity or outrage.

.8 **favor**, prefer, show preference, **play favorites**, treat unequally, discriminate.

.9 ADJS **unjust, inequitable**, unequitable, iniquitous, **unbalanced, uneven, unequal; wrong, wrongful,** unrightful; **undue,** unmeet, undeserved, unmerited; unlawful, illegal 999.6,7.

.10 **unfair**, not fair; **unsporting**, unsportsmanly, **unsportsmanlike**, not cricket [informal]; foul, below the belt.

.11 **partial, interested,** involved, **partisan,** unneutral, **one-sided,** all on one side, undetached, **undispassionate, biased,** warped, influenced, swayed.

.12 **unjustifiable, unwarrantable,** unallowable, unreasonable, indefensible; **inexcusable,** unconscionable, **unpardonable, unforgivable,** inexpiable, irremissible.

.13 ADVS **unjustly, unfairly;** wrongfully, wrongly, undeservedly; inequitably, iniquitously, unequally, unevenly; partially, interestedly, one-sidedly, undispassionately; **unjustifiably, unwarrantably,** unallowably, unreasonably, indefensibly; inexcusably, unconscionably, unpardonably, unforgivably, inexpiably, irremissibly.

978. SELFISHNESS

.1 NOUNS **selfishness**, selfism, **self-seeking,** self-serving, self-pleasing, **self-indulgence,** self-advancement, careerism, personal ambition, self-devotion, self-jealousy, self-sufficiency, **self-consideration,** self-solicitude, self-absorption, ego trip, self-occupation; self-containment, autism, remoteness 923.1,2; **self-interest,** self-interestedness, interest; self-esteem, self-admiration 909.1; **self-centeredness, narcissism, egotism** 909.3; possessiveness, greed, graspingness, acquisitiveness; **individualism** 762.5,

personalism, privatism, private or personal desires, private or personal aims.

.2 **ungenerousness, unmagnanimousness, illiberality,** meanness, smallness, littleness, paltriness, minginess, pettiness; **niggardliness, stinginess** 852.2,3.

.3 **self-seeker,** self-pleaser, self-advancer; **narcissist, egotist** 909.5; timepleaser, timeserver, temporizer; fortune hunter, tufthunter; self-server, careerist; monopolist, hog, road hog; dog in the manger; **individualist,** loner or lone wolf [both informal].

.4 VERBS **please oneself,** gratify oneself; egotrip, be or go on an ego trip [all informal]; indulge or pamper or coddle oneself, consult one's own wishes, look after one's own interests, take care of or look out for number one [both informal].

.5 ADJS **selfish, self-seeking, self-serving,** self-pleasing, **self-advancing,** careerist, ambitious for self, **self-indulgent,** self-jealous, self-sufficient, **self-interested,** self-considerative, self-besot, self-devoted, self-occupied, self-absorbed, wrapped up in oneself, self-contained, autistic, remote 923.5, 6; self-esteeming, self-admiring 909.8; **self-centered, narcissistic, egotistical** 909.10; possessive, greedy, grasping, acquisitive; **individualistic** 762.21, personalistic, privatistic.

.6 **ungenerous, illiberal,** unchivalrous, mean, small, little, paltry, mingy, petty; **niggardly, stingy** 852.8,9.

.7 ADVS **selfishly, for oneself,** in one's own interest, from selfish or interested motives, to gain some private ends.

979. UNSELFISHNESS

.1 NOUNS **unselfishness, selflessness;** altruism; self-subjection, self-subordination, self-abasement, self-effacement; **humility** 906; modesty 908; self-neglect, self-neglectfulness, self-forgetfulness; **self-renunciation,** self-renouncement; **self-denial,** self-abnegation; **self-sacrifice,** sacrifice, self-immolation, self-devotion, devotion, dedication, commitment, consecration; disinterest, disinterestedness; unpossessiveness, unacquisitiveness.

.2 **magnanimity,** magnanimousness, **generosity,** generousness, openhandedness, **liberality,** liberalness; **bigness, bigheartedness,** greatheartedness, largeheartedness, big or large or great heart, greatness of heart or soul; noble-mindedness, high-mindedness, idealism; **nobleness,** nobility, princeliness, greatness, **loftiness,** elevation, exaltation, sublimity; chivalry, chivalrousness, knight-liness, errantry, knight-errantry; heroism.

.3 VERBS not have a selfish bone in one's body, think only of others; put oneself out, go out of the way, lean over backwards; sacrifice, make a sacrifice; subject oneself, subordinate oneself, abase oneself.

.4 observe the golden rule, do as one would be done by, do unto others as you would have others do unto you.

.5 ADJS **unselfish, selfless**; altruistic; self-unconscious, self-forgetful, self-abasing, self-effacing; **humble** 906.9; **unpretentious, modest** 908.9–13; self-neglectful, self-neglecting; **self-denying**, self-renouncing, self-abnegating, self-abnegatory; **self-sacrificing**, self-immolating, sacrificing, self-devotional, self-devoted, devoted, dedicated, committed, consecrated, unsparing of self, disinterested; unpossessive, unacquisitive.

.6 magnanimous, generous, openhanded, liberal; big, bighearted, greathearted, largehearted, great of heart or soul; noble-minded, high-minded, idealistic; **noble**, princely, handsome, great, high, elevated, **lofty**, exalted, sublime; chivalrous, knightly; heroic.

.7 ADVS **unselfishly, altruistically**, forgetful of self; for others.

.8 magnanimously, generously, openhandedly, **liberally**; bigheartedly, greatheartedly, largeheartedly; **nobly**, handsomely; chivalrously, knightly.

980. VIRTUE

(moral goodness)

.1 NOUNS virtue, virtuousness, goodness, **righteousness**, rectitude, right conduct, the straight and narrow; probity 974; **morality**, moral rectitude or virtue, morale; **saintliness**, saintlikeness, angelicalness; **godliness** 1028.2.

.2 "the health of the soul" [Joseph Joubert], "the fount whence honour springs" [Marlowe], "the adherence in action to the nature of things" [Emerson], "victorious resistance to one's vital desire to do this, that or the other" [James Branch Cabell], "to do unwitnessed what we should be capable of doing before all the world" [La Rochefoucauld].

.3 purity, immaculacy, **chastity** 988; guiltlessness, innocence 984.

.4 uncorruptness, uncorruptedness, incorruptness; **unsinfulness**, sinlessness; un-

wickedness, uniniquitousness; undegenerateness, undepravedness, undissoluteness, undebauchedness.

.5 cardinal virtues, natural virtues; prudence, justice, temperance, fortitude; theological virtues or supernatural virtues; faith, hope, charity or love.

.6 VERBS **be good**, do no evil; keep in the right path, walk the straight path, follow the straight and narrow, keep on the straight and narrow way or path; fight the good fight.

.7 ADJS **virtuous, good, moral; upright, honest** 974.13–20; **righteous**, just, straight, right-minded; **angelic**, seraphic; **saintly**, saintlike; **godly** 1028.9.

.8 chaste, immaculate, pure 988.4; guiltless, innocent 984.6.

.9 uncorrupt, uncorrupted, incorrupt, incorrupted; **unsinful**, sinless; **unwicked**, uniniquitous, unerring, unfallen; undegenerate, undepraved, undemoralized, undissolute, undebauched.

981. VICE

(moral badness)

.1 NOUNS **vice**, viciousness; criminality, **wrongdoing** 982; **immorality**, unmorality, **evil**; **amorality** 957.4; **unvirtuousness**, ungoodness; **unrighteousness, ungodliness**, unsaintliness, unangelicalness; **uncleanness**, impurity, **unchastity** 989; waywardness, wantonness, prodigality; delinquency, moral delinquency; peccability; backsliding, recidivism; **evil nature, carnality** 987.2.

.2 vice, weakness, weakness of the flesh, flaw, moral flaw, **frailty, infirmity; failing**, failure; weak point, weak side, foible; bad habit, besetting sin; **fault, imperfection** 678.

.3 iniquity, evil, bad, wrong, error, obliquity, villainy, knavery, reprobacy, peccancy, **abomination, atrocity**, shame, disgrace, scandal, **infamy; sin** 982.2.

.4 wickedness, badness, naughtiness, **evilness, viciousness, sinfulness, iniquitousness; baseness**, rankness, **vileness**, foulness, arrantness, nefariousness, heinousness, villainousness, flagitiousness; fiendishness, hellishness; devilishness, devilry, deviltry.

.5 turpitude, moral turpitude; corruption, corruptedness, corruptness, rottenness, moral pollution or pollutedness; **decadence** or decadency, debasement, degradation, demoralization, abjection; degeneracy, degenerateness, degeneration, reprobacy, **depravity**, depravedness, depravation; **dissoluteness, profligacy;** abandonment, abandon.

.6 **obduracy, hardheartedness, hardness, callousness,** heartlessness, hardness of heart, heart of stone.

.7 **sink, sink of corruption; den of iniquity,** den, **fleshpots, hellhole;** hole *or* joint [both slang]; Sodom, Gomorrah, Babylon; **brothel** 989.9.

.8 VERBS **do wrong, sin** 982.5.

.9 **go wrong, go astray, err,** deviate from the path of virtue, leave the straight and narrow; **fall,** lapse, slip, trip; **degenerate** 692.19; **go to the bad** 693.24; backslide 696.4.

.10 **demoralize,** vitiate, drive to the dogs; **corrupt** 692.14; **sully, soil, defile.**

.11 ADJS **vice-laden,** vice-prone, **vicious,** steeped in vice; **immoral,** unmoral; **amoral,** nonmoral.

.12 **unvirtuous,** virtueless, ungood; **unrighteous, ungodly,** unsaintly, unangelic; **unclean,** impure, **unchaste** 989.23; fleshly, carnal 987.6, wayward, wanton, prodigal; erring, fallen, lapsed, postlapsarian; frail, weak, infirm; Adamic; peccable; backsliding, recidivist, recidivistic; of easy virtue 989.26.

.13 **diabolic(al), devilish,** demoniac *or* demoniacal, satanic, Mephistophelian; **fiendish,** fiendlike; **hellish,** hellborn, **infernal.**

.14 **corrupt,** corrupted, vice-corrupted, polluted, morally polluted, rotten, tainted, contaminated, vitiated; warped, perverted; **decadent,** debased, degraded, reprobate, **depraved, debauched, dissolute, degenerate,** profligate, abandoned, gone to the bad *or* dogs, sunk *or* steeped in iniquity, rotten at *or* to the core.

.15 **evil-minded,** evilhearted, **blackhearted; base-minded,** low-minded; low-thoughted, dirty *or* dirty-minded [all slang].

.16 **wicked, evil, vicious, bad, naughty, wrong, sinful, iniquitous,** peccant, reprobate; dark, black; base, low, vile, foul, rank, flagrant, arrant, nefarious, heinous, villainous, criminal, knavish, flagitious; abominable, atrocious, monstrous, unspeakable, execrable, damnable; shameful, disgraceful, scandalous, **infamous, unpardonable,** unforgivable; **improper,** reprehensible, blamable, blameworthy, unworthy.

.17 **hardened, hard, case-hardened, obdurate,** inured, indurated; **callous,** calloused,

seared; **hardhearted,** heartless; **shameless,** lost to shame, lost to all sense of honor, conscienceless, unblushing, **brazen.**

.18 **irreclaimable,** irredeemable, unredeemable, unregenerate, **irreformable,** incorrigible, past praying for; shriftless, graceless; **lost.**

.19 ADVS **wickedly, evilly, sinfully, iniquitously,** peccantly, **viciously;** basely, vilely, foully, rankly, arrantly, flagrantly, flagitiously.

982. WRONGDOING, SIN

.1 NOUNS **wrongdoing, evildoing, misdoing, wrong conduct, misconduct, misdemeanor,** misfeasance, malfeasance, malversation, **malpractice,** evil courses, machinations of the devil; **sin,** "thou scarlet sin" [Shakespeare], "the transgression of the law" [Bible]; **crime, criminality,** lawbreaking, feloniousness, criminal tendency, criminosis; viciousness, **vice** 981; misprision, negative *or* positive misprision, misprision of treason *or* felony.

.2 **misdeed, misdemeanor,** misfeasance, malfeasance, malefaction, criminal *or* guilty *or* sinful act, **offense,** injustice, injury, **wrong, iniquity, evil,** peccancy, *malum* [L]; **tort; error, fault,** breach; **impropriety,** slight *or* minor wrong, venial sin, **indiscretion,** peccadillo, trip, slip, lapse; **transgression,** trespass; **sin,** "deed without a name" [Shakespeare]; deadly *or* mortal sin, grave *or* heavy sin, unutterable sin, unpardonable *or* unforgivable *or* inexpiable sin; sin against the Holy Ghost; sin of commission; sin of omission, nonfeasance, omission, failure, dereliction, delinquency; **crime, felony;** capital crime; war crime, crime against humanity, genocide; **outrage, atrocity,** enormity.

.3 **deadly sin, seven deadly sins: pride,** superbia; **envy,** invidia; **avarice,** greed, avaritia; **sloth,** acedia; **wrath,** anger, ira; **gluttony,** gula; **lust,** luxuria.

.4 **original sin,** fall from grace, fall, fall of man, fall of Adam *or* Adam's fall, sin of Adam.

.5 VERBS **do wrong,** do amiss, misdemean oneself, **err,** offend; **sin,** commit sin; **transgress,** trespass.

.6 ADJS wrongdoing, evildoing, malefactory, malfeasant; **wrong,** iniquitous, **sinful, wicked** 981.16; **criminal,** felonious.

983. GUILT

.1 NOUNS **guilt, guiltiness; criminality,** peccancy; **culpability,** reprehensibility, blamability, blameworthiness; chargeability, censurability, censurableness, reproachability, reproachableness, reprovability, reprovableness, inculpation, implication, involvement, complicity, impeachability, impeachableness, indictability, indictableness, arraignability, arraignableness; red-handedness, dirty hands, red or bloody hands, "hangman's hands" [Shakespeare]; guilty conscience, guilt-feelings; onus, burden.

.2 VERBS be guilty, look guilty, look like the cat that swallowed the canary, blush, stammer.

.3 ADJS **guilty,** peccant, **criminal, to blame, at fault,** faulty, on one's head; **culpable,** reprehensible, censurable, reproachable, reprovable, inculpated, implicated, involved, impeachable, indictable, arraignable.

.4 ADVS **red-handed,** red-hand, **in the act,** in the very act, *in flagrante delicto* [L].

.5 **guiltily,** shamefacedly, sheepishly, with a guilty conscience.

984. INNOCENCE

.1 NOUNS **innocence,** innocency, innocentness; unfallen or unlapsed or prelapsarian state; unguiltiness, **guiltlessness,** faultlessness, blamelessness, reproachlessness, **sinlessness,** offenselessness; **spotlessness,** stainlessness, taintlessness, unblemishedness; **purity,** cleanness, cleanliness, whiteness, immaculacy, impeccability; clean hands, clean slate, clear conscience, nothing to hide.

.2 childlikeness 736.1; lamblikeness, dovelikeness, angelicness; unacquaintance with evil, uncorruptedness, incorruptness, pristineness, undefiledness.

.3 **inculpability,** unblamability, unblamableness, **unblameworthiness,** irreproachability, irreproachableness, impeccability, impeccableness, unexceptionability, unexceptionableness, **irreprehensibility,** irreprehensibleness, uncensurability, uncensurableness, unimpeachability, unimpeachableness, unindictableness, unarraignableness.

.4 **innocent,** babe, newborn babe, infant, babe in the woods, child, mere child, lamb, dove, angel.

.5 VERBS know no wrong, have clean hands, have a clear conscience, look as if butter would not melt in one's mouth.

.6 ADJS **innocent;** unfallen, unlapsed, prelapsarian; **unguilty,** not guilty, **guiltless, faultless, blameless,** reproachless, **sinless,** offenseless, with clean hands, "blameless in life and pure of crime" [Horace]; clear, in the clear; without reproach, *sans reproche* [Fr]; innocent as a lamb, lamblike, dovelike, angelic, childlike 736.5; unacquainted with or untouched by evil, uncorrupted, incorrupt, pristine, undefiled.

.7 **spotless,** stainless, taintless, unblemished, unspotted, **untainted, unsoiled, unsullied, undefiled; pure, clean, immaculate,** impeccable, white, "without unspotted, innocent within" [Dryden].

.8 **inculpable,** unblamable, unblameworthy, **irreproachable,** irreprovable, **irreprehensible,** uncensurable, unimpeachable, unindictable, unarraignable, unobjectionable, unexceptionable, above suspicion.

.9 ADVS **innocently, guiltlessly, unguiltily,** with a clear conscience; **unknowingly,** unconsciously, unawares.

985. GOOD PERSON

.1 NOUNS good person, good man or woman or child, worthy, prince, nature's nobleman, man after one's own heart; *persona grata* [L], acceptable person; **good fellow,** capital fellow, **good sort,** right sort, a decent sort of fellow, good lot [Brit informal], no end of a fellow; real man or woman, **mensch** [Yid]; **gentleman,** perfect gentleman, a gentleman and a scholar; **lady,** perfect lady; **gem,** jewel, pearl, diamond; rough diamond, diamond in the rough; honest man 974.8.

.2 [slang or informal terms] **good guy,** crackerjack, brick, trump, good egg, stout fellow, nice guy, good Joe, likely lad, no slouch, doll, pussycat.

.3 **good** or **respectable citizen,** excellent or exemplary citizen, good neighbor, burgher, **pillar of society,** pillar of the church, salt of the earth; Christian or true Christian [both informal].

.4 **paragon, ideal,** beau ideal, nonpareil, *chevalier sans peur et sans reproche* [Fr], **good example,** shining example; exemplar, **model, pattern, standard,** mirror, "the observed of all observers" [Shakespeare]; *Übermensch* [Ger; Nietzsche]; one in a thousand or ten thousand, man of men, a man among men.

.5 **hero, god, demigod,** phoenix; **heroine, goddess,** demigoddess; **idol.**

.6 holy man; great soul, mahatma; guru, *rishi* [Skt]; *starets* [Russ]; saint, angel 1017.

986. BAD PERSON

.1 NOUNS **bad person, bad man** or **woman**
or **child**, **unworthy** or **disreputable per-**
son, unworthy, disreputable, **undesirable**,
persona non grata [L], unacceptable or
unwanted or objectionable person, bad
news [informal]; bad example; –eer.

.2 **wretch**, mean wretch, **beggarly fellow**,
beggar, **blighter** [Brit slang]; **bum** or bummer or lowlifer or lowlife or **mucker** [all
slang], caitiff, budmash [India], pilgarlic;
devil, **poor devil**, *pauvre diable* [Fr], poor
creature, *mauvais sujet* [Fr]; **sad case**, sad
sack or sad sack of shit [both slang];
good-for-nothing, **good-for-naught**, **no-**
good [informal], **ne'er-do-well**, wastrel,
vaurien [Fr], worthless fellow; **derelict**,
skid-row bum, Bowery bum, tramp, hobo,
beachcomber, **drifter**, drunkard, vagrant,
vag [informal], vagabond, truant, stiff or
bindlestiff [both slang], swagman or sundowner [both Austral]; human wreck.

.3 **rascal**, precious rascal, rogue, knave,
scoundrel, villain, blackguard, **scamp**,
scalawag [informal], spalpeen [Ir], rapscallion, **devil**; shyster; sneak.

.4 "a rascally yeaforsooth knave", "a foul-
mouthed and calumnious knave", "poor
cuckoldy knave", "a poor, decayed, ingenious, foolish, rascally knave", "an arrant,
rascally, beggarly, lousy knave", "a slipper
and subtle knave, a finder of occasions",
"a whoreson, beetle-headed, flap-ear'd
knave", "filthy, worsted-stocking knave; a
lily-livered, action-taking knave", "a
knave; a rascal; an eater of broken meats;
a base, proud, shallow, beggarly, three-
suited, hundred-pound, filthy, worsted-
stocking knave" [all Shakespeare].

.5 **reprobate**, recreant, **miscreant**, bad or
sorry lot [both Brit informal], bad egg
[informal], bad'un or wrong'un [both
slang]; scapegrace, black sheep; lost soul,
lost sheep, *âme damnée* [Fr], backslider,
recidivist, fallen angel; degenerate, pervert; profligate, **lecher** 989.10,11; trollop,
whore 989.14–16; **pimp** 989.18.

.6 [slang or informal terms] **bastard**, **son of**
a bitch, SOB, **jerk**, creep, mother, **shit**,
turd, shithead, fart, **louse**, **meanie**, **heel**,
shitheel, **rat**, **stinker**, stinkard, pill, bugger; **hood**, hooligan 943.3,4.

.7 beast, **animal**; cur, dog, hound, whelp,
mongrel; **reptile**, viper, serpent, snake;
vermin, varmint [dial], hyena; **swine**, pig;
skunk, polecat; insect, worm.

.8 cad, bounder or rotter [both informal].

.9 **wrongdoer, malefactor, sinner**, transgressor, delinquent; malfeasor, misfeasor,
nonfeasor; misdemeanant, misdemeanist;
culprit, offender; evil person, evil man or
woman or child, evildoer 943.

.10 **criminal, felon, crook** [informal], public
enemy, **lawbreaker, scofflaw**; **gangster** or
mobster [both informal], **racketeer**; swindler 619.3,4; thief 825; thug 943.3,4; **desper-**
ado, desperate criminal; **outlaw**, fugitive,
convict, jailbird, gaolbird [Brit]; gallows
bird [informal]; **traitor**, betrayer, quisling,
Judas, double-dealer, two-timer [slang],
deceiver 619.

.11 **the underworld**, gangland, gangdom, organized crime, the rackets, the mob, the
syndicate, the Mafia, Cosa Nostra, Black
Hand.

.12 **the wicked**, the bad, the evil, the unrighteous, the reprobate; sons of men, sons of
Belial, sons or children of the devil, limbs
of Satan, children of darkness; **scum of**
the earth, dregs of society.

987. SENSUALITY

.1 NOUNS **sensuality**, sensualness, sensual-
ism; appetitiveness, appetite; **voluptuous-**
ness, luxuriousness, luxury; **unchastity**
989; **pleasure-seeking**; sybaritism; **hedo-**
nism, Cyrenaic hedonism, Cyrenaicism,
ethical hedonism, psychological hedonism, hedonics, hedonic calculus; epicurism, epicureanism; pleasure principle,
Lustprinzip [Ger].

.2 **carnality**, carnal-mindedness; **fleshliness**,
flesh; animal or carnal nature, the flesh,
the beast, Adam, the Old Adam, the offending Adam, fallen state or nature,
lapsed state or nature, postlapsarian state
or nature; **animality, animalism**, bestiality, beastliness, brutishness, **brutality**;
coarseness, grossness; swinishness; **earthi-**
ness, unspirituality, nonspirituality, materialism.

.3 **sensualist**, sensuist; **voluptuary, pleasure-**
seeker, sybarite, Cyrenaic, Sardanapalus,
Heliogabalus, **hedonist**, *bon vivant* [Fr],
carpet knight; epicure, epicurean; gourmet, gourmand; swine.

.4 VERBS **sensualize**, carnalize, coarsen, bru-
tify.

.5 ADJS **sensual**; **appetitive**; **voluptuous**, luxurious; **unchaste** 989.23, **hedonistic**, **plea-**
sure-seeking, pleasure-bent, bent on pleasure, luxury-loving, epicurean, sybaritic;
Cyrenaic.

.6 **carnal**, carnal-minded, **fleshly**, bodily,
physical; Adamic, fallen, lapsed, postlap-

sarian; animal, animalistic; **brutish, brutal,** brute; **bestial,** beastly, beastlike; Circean; coarse, gross; swinish; orgiastic; **earthy,** unspiritual, nonspiritual, material, materialistic.

988. CHASTITY

.1 NOUNS **chastity, virtue,** virtuousness, honor; **purity,** cleanness, cleanliness; whiteness, snowiness; **immaculacy,** immaculateness, spotlessness, stainlessness, taintlessness, blotlessness, unspottedness, unstainedness, unblottedness, untaintedness, unblemishedness, unsoiledness, unsulliedness, undefiledness, untarnishedness; uncorruptness 980.4; sexual innocence, innocence 984.

.2 **decency,** seemliness, propriety, decorum, decorousness, elegance, delicacy; **modesty,** shame, pudicity, pudency.

.3 **continence** or continency; abstinence 992.2; celibacy; **virginity,** intactness, maidenhood, maidenhead; Platonic love; marital fidelity or faithfulness.

.4 ADJS **chaste, virtuous; pure,** purehearted, pure in heart; **clean,** cleanly; **immaculate, spotless,** blotless, stainless, taintless, white, snowy; **unsoiled, unsullied, undefiled,** untarnished, unstained, unspotted, untainted, unblemished, unblotted, uncorrupt 980.9; "as chaste as Diana", "as chaste as unsunn'd snow" [both Shakespeare], "chaste as morning dew" [Edward Young]; sexually innocent, innocent 984.6–8.

.5 **decent, modest, decorous,** delicate, elegant, proper, becoming, seemly.

.6 **continent;** abstinent 992.10; celibate; **virginal, virgin,** maidenly, vestal, intact; Platonic.

.7 **undebauched, undissipated, undissolute,** unwanton, unlicentious.

989. UNCHASTITY

.1 NOUNS **unchastity,** unchasteness; unvirtuousness; **impurity,** uncleanness, uncleanliness, taintedness, soiledness, sulliedness, maculacy; **indecency** 990.

.2 **incontinence,** uncontinence; intemperance 993; unrestraint 762.3.

.3 **profligacy,** dissoluteness, licentiousness, license, unbridledness, wildness, fastness, rakishness, gallantry, **libertinism,** libertinage; **dissipation, debauchery,** debauchment; venery, wenching, whoring, womanizing.

.4 **wantonness, waywardness; looseness,** laxity, lightness, loose morals, easy virtue, whorishness, chambering, **promiscuity,** sleeping around [informal]; swinging [informal].

.5 **lasciviousness, lechery, lecherousness, lewdness,** bawdiness, **dirtiness,** salacity, salaciousness, **carnality,** animality, fleshliness, **sexuality, sexiness, lust, lustfulness,** prurience or pruriency; **obscenity** 990.4; concupiscence, lickerishness, libidinousness, randiness, horniness [slang], lubricity, lubriciousness, **sensuality,** eroticism, goatishness; satyrism, satyriasis, gynecomania; nymphomania, furor uterinus, hysteromania, uteromania, clitoromania; erotomania, eroticomania, aphrodisiomania.

.6 **seduction,** seducement, **betrayal; violation,** abuse; **debauchment, defilement,** ravishment, ravage, despoilment, fate worse than death; priapism; defloration, deflowering; **rape,** sexual or criminal assault.

.7 (illicit sexual intercourse) **adultery,** criminal conversation or congress or cohabitation, extramarital or premarital sex, extramarital or premarital relations, extracurricular sex or relations [informal], **fornication;** free love, free-lovism; **incest;** concubinage; cuckoldry.

.8 **prostitution,** harlotry, whoredom, **streetwalking;** soliciting, solicitation; Mrs. Warren's profession; whoremonging, whoremastery, pimping, pandering.

.9 **brothel, house of prostitution,** house of assignation, house of joy or ill repute or ill fame, **whorehouse,** bawdyhouse, sporting house, disorderly house, **cathouse, bordello,** bagnio, stew, dive, den of vice, den or sink of iniquity, crib, joint; panel house or panel den; red-light district, tenderloin, stews, street of fallen women.

.10 **libertine, swinger** [informal], **profligate, rake,** rakehell, rip [informal], roué, wanton, womanizer, walking phallus, debauchee, rounder [archaic], **wolf** [slang], woman chaser, skirt chaser [slang], gay dog, gay deceiver, gallant, philanderer, lover-boy [informal], lady-killer, Lothario, Don Juan, Casanova.

.11 **lecher, satyr, goat,** old goat, **dirty old man;** whorer or whoremonger [both archaic], whoremaster, whorehound [slang]; Priapus; gynecomaniac; erotomaniac, eroticomaniac, aphrodisiomaniac.

.12 **seducer, betrayer,** deceiver; **debaucher, ravisher,** ravager, violator, despoiler, defiler; **raper, rapist.**

.13 adulterer, fornicator; adulteress, fornicatress, fornicatrix.

.14 strumpet, trollop, **wench, hussy, slut,** jade, baggage, *cocotte* [Fr], grisette; **tart** or **chippy** or **floozy** or broad [all slang], bitch, drab, trull, quean, harridan, Jezebel, wanton, whore [informal], bad woman, **loose woman,** easy woman [informal], easy lay [slang], woman of easy virtue, frail sister; pickup; nymphomaniac, nympho [slang], hysteromaniac, uteromaniac, clitoromaniac; nymphet.

.15 demimonde, demimondaine, demirep; **courtesan,** adventuress, **seductress,** femme fatale, vampire, vamp, temptress; hetaera, houri, harem girl, odalisque; Jezebel, Messalina, Delilah, Thais, Phryne, Aspasia, Lais.

.16 **prostitute, harlot, whore,** *fille de joie* [Fr], daughter of joy, call girl or B-girl [both informal], **scarlet woman,** unfortunate woman, painted woman, fallen woman, erring sister; **streetwalker,** hustler or **hooker** [both slang], woman of the town, *poule* [Fr], stew, meretrix, Cyprian, Paphian; white slave.

.17 **mistress,** woman, **kept woman,** kept mistress, **paramour,** concubine, doxy, playmate, spiritual or unofficial wife.

.18 **procurer, pimp,** pander or panderer, *maquereau* [Fr], **bawd; gigolo,** fancy man; procuress, **madam** [informal]; white slaver.

.19 VERBS **be promiscuous,** sleep around, swing [informal]; **debauch, wanton,** rake, chase women, womanize, whore, sow one's wild oats; **philander** 932.18; **dissipate** 993.6; fornicate, commit adultery; grovel, wallow, wallow in the mire.

.20 **seduce, betray, deceive,** mislead, lead astray; **debauch, ravish,** ravage, despoil, ruin; **deflower,** pop one's cherry [slang]; **defile,** soil, sully; **violate,** abuse; **rape,** force.

.21 **prostitute;** pimp, procure, pander.

.22 **cuckold,** father upon; wear horns, wear the horn.

.23 ADJS **unchaste, unvirtuous,** unvirginal; **impure, unclean; indecent** 990.5; soiled, sullied, smirched, besmirched, defiled, tainted, maculate.

.24 **incontinent,** uncontinent; **orgiastic; intemperate** 993.7; unrestrained 762.23.

.25 **profligate, licentious,** unbridled, free; **dissolute, dissipated, debauched,** abandoned; **wild, fast,** gallant, gay, rakish; rakehell, rakehellish, rakehelly.

.26 **wanton, wayward,** Paphian; **loose,** lax, slack, loose-moraled, of loose morals, of easy virtue, easy [informal], **light,** no better than she should be, whorish, chambering, **promiscuous.**

.27 **freeloving; adulterous,** illicit, extramarital, premarital; incestuous.

.28 **prostitute, prostituted, whorish, harlot,** scarlet, fallen, meretricious, streetwalking, hustling [slang], on the town or streets, on the *pavé.*

.29 **lascivious, lecherous, sexy, salacious, carnal,** animal, **sexual, lustful,** ithyphallic, **hot,** prurient, concupiscent, lickerish, libidinous, randy, horny [slang], lubricious; **lewd, bawdy,** dirty, obscene 990.9; erotic, **sensual,** fleshly; goatish, satyric, priapic; gynecomaniacal; nymphomaniacal, hysteromaniacal, uteromaniacal, clitoromaniacal; erotomaniacal, eroticomaniacal, aphrodisiomaniacal.

990. INDECENCY

.1 NOUNS **indecency, indelicacy, inelegance** or **inelegancy, indecorousness,** indecorum, **impropriety,** inappropriateness, unseemliness, indiscretion, indiscreetness; **unchastity** 989.

.2 **immodesty,** unmodestness, impudicity; exhibitionism; **shamelessness,** unembarrassedness; **brazenness,** forwardness, boldness, flagrancy, notoriousness.

.3 **vulgarity, uncouthness, coarseness, grossness,** rankness, rawness; **earthiness,** frankness; raciness, saltiness, spiciness.

.4 **obscenity, dirtiness,** bawdry, **ribaldry, pornography,** porno or porn [both informal], hard-core or soft-core pornography, salacity, **smut, dirt, filth; lewdness, bawdiness,** salaciousness, **smuttiness, foulness, filthiness,** nastiness, vileness, offensiveness; scurrility, fescenninity; Rabelaisianism; erotic art or literature, pornographic art or literature; sexploitation; blue movie or dirty movie or porno film or skin flick [all slang], stag film [informal], X-rated movie; pornographomania, erotographomania, iconolagny.

.5 ADJS **indecent, indelicate, inelegant, indecorous, improper,** inappropriate, **unseemly, unbecoming,** indiscreet.

.6 **immodest,** unmodest; exhibitionistic; **shameless,** unashamed, unembarrassed, unabashed, unblushing, **brazen,** brazenfaced; **forward,** bold, flagrant, notorious.

.7 **risqué,** risky, **racy,** salty, spicy, **off-color,** suggestive, scabrous.

.8 **vulgar, uncouth, coarse, gross,** rank, raw, broad, low; gutter; **earthy,** frank.

.9 **obscene, lewd, bawdy,** ithyphallic, **ribald, pornographic, salacious,** sultry [informal], lurid, **dirty, smutty,** raunchy [slang], blue, smoking-room, impure, unchaste, unclean, **foul, filthy, nasty,** vile, fulsome, offensive, unprintable, unrepeatable, not fit for mixed company; scurrilous, scurrile, Fescennine; foul-mouthed, foul-tongued, foul-spoken; Rabelaisian.

991. ASCETICISM

.1 NOUNS **asceticism, austerity, self-denial,** rigor; **puritanism,** eremitism, anchoritism, anchorite *or* anchoritic monasticism, monasticism, monachism; Sabbatarianism; Albigensianism, Waldensianism, Catharism; Yoga; mortification, self-mortification, maceration, flagellation; **abstinence** 992.2; fasting 995; voluntary poverty, mendicantism, Franciscanism; Trappism.

.2 **ascetic, puritan,** Sabbatarian; Albigensian, Waldensian, Catharist; **abstainer** 992.4; anchorite, **hermit** 924.5; yogi, yogin; sannyasi, bhikshu, dervish, fakir, flagellant; mendicant, Franciscan; Trappist.

.3 ADJS **ascetic, austere,** self-denying, rigoristic, **puritanical,** eremitic, anchoritic 924.9, Sabbatarian; Albigensian, Waldensian, Catharist; **abstinent** 992.10; mendicant, wedded to poverty, Franciscan; Trappist; flagellant.

992. TEMPERANCE

.1 NOUNS **temperance,** temperateness, **moderation,** moderateness, sophrosyne; golden mean; nothing in excess, sobriety, soberness, frugality, forbearance, abnegation; renunciation, renouncement; denial, **self-denial;** restraint, constraint, **self-restraint; self-control,** self-mastery, self-discipline.

.2 **abstinence,** abstention, abstainment, **abstemiousness,** refraining, refrainment, avoidance, eschewal, passing up [informal]; **total abstinence, teetotalism,** nephalism, Rechabitism; the pledge; Encratism, Shakerism; Pythagorism, Pythagoreanism; sexual abstinence, celibacy 934; chastity 988; gymnosophy; Stoicism; vegetarianism, fruitarianism; plain living, spare diet, simple diet; Spartan fare, Lenten fare; fish day, Friday, banyan day; fast 995.2,3; **continence** 988.3; asceticism 991.

.3 **prohibition,** prohibitionism; Eighteenth Amendment, Volstead Act.

.4 **abstainer,** abstinent; **teetotaler,** teetotalist; nephalist, Rechabite, hydropot, water-drinker; vegetarian, fruitarian; banian, banya; gymnosophist; Pythagorean, Pythagorist; Encratite, Apostolici, Shaker; ascetic 991.2.

.5 **prohibitionist, dry** [slang]; Anti-Saloon League; Women's Christian Temperance Union, WCTU.

.6 VERBS **restrain oneself,** constrain oneself, curb oneself, hold back, **avoid excess;** limit oneself, restrict oneself; **control oneself,** control one's appetites, repress *or* inhibit one's desires, contain oneself, discipline oneself, master oneself, exercise self-control *or* self-restraint, keep oneself under control, keep in *or* within bounds, keep within compass *or* limits, know when one has had enough; live plainly *or* simply *or* frugally; mortify oneself, mortify the flesh, control the fleshly lusts, control the carnal man *or* the old Adam, "let the passions be amenable to reason" [Cicero]; eat to live, not live to eat; eat sparingly.

.7 **abstain,** abstain from, refrain, **refrain from, forbear, forgo,** spare, withhold, hold back, **avoid, shun,** eschew, **pass up** [informal], **keep from,** keep *or* stand *or* hold aloof from, have nothing to do with, take no part in, have no hand in, **let alone,** let well enough alone, let go by, **deny oneself,** do without, not *or* never touch.

.8 **swear off, renounce,** forswear, **give up,** abandon, stop, discontinue; take the pledge, get on the wagon *or* water wagon [slang].

.9 ADJS **temperate, moderate,** sober, frugal, restrained, **sparing,** stinting, measured.

.10 **abstinent,** abstentious, **abstemious;** teetotal, sworn off, on the wagon *or* water wagon [slang]; nephalistic, Rechabite; Encratic, Apostolic, Shaker; Pythagorean; sexually abstinent, celibate, chaste; Stoic; vegetarian, fruitarian; Spartan, Lenten; **continent** 988.6; **ascetic** 991.3.

.11 prohibitionist, antisaloon, dry [informal].

.12 ADVS **temperately, moderately, sparingly,** stintingly, frugally, in moderation, within compass *or* bounds.

993. INTEMPERANCE

.1 NOUNS **intemperance,** intemperateness, **indulgence, self-indulgence; overindulgence,** overdoing; **unrestraint,** unconstraint, indiscipline, uncontrol; **immoderation,** immoderacy, immoderateness; inordinacy, inordinateness; **excess, excessiveness,** too much, too-muchness [informal]; prodigality, extravagance; crapulence or crapulency, crapulousness; **incontinence** 989.2; **swinishness, gluttony** 994; **drunkenness** 996.1.

.2 **dissipation, licentiousness; riotous living,** free living, high living [informal], fast or killing pace; **debauchery,** debauchment; **carousal,** carouse; **debauch, orgy,** saturnalia.

.3 **dissipater,** rounder [archaic], free liver, high liver [informal]; nighthawk or night owl [both informal].

.4 VERBS **indulge,** indulge oneself, indulge one's appetites, "indulge in easy vices" [Samuel Johnson], deny oneself nothing or not at all; **give oneself up to,** give free course to, give free rein to; live well or high, live high on the hog [slang], live off the fat of the land; indulge in, luxuriate in, wallow in; roll in.

.5 **overindulge, overdo, carry to excess,** carry too far, go the limit, go whole hog [slang], not know when to stop; dine not wisely but too well.

.6 **dissipate,** plunge into dissipation, **debauch, wanton, carouse,** run riot, live hard or fast, squander one's money in riotous living, burn the candle at both ends, keep up a fast or killing pace, sow one's wild oats, have one's fling, "eat, drink, and be merry" [Bible].

.7 ADJS **intemperate, indulgent, self-indulgent; overindulgent,** overindulging, unthrifty, unfrugal, **immoderate,** inordinate, **excessive,** too much, prodigal, extravagant, extreme, unmeasured, unlimited; crapulous, crapulent; undisciplined, uncontrolled, unbridled, unconstrained, **unrestrained** 762.23; **incontinent** 989.24; swinish, gluttonous 994.6; bibulous 996.34.

.8 **licentious, dissipated, riotous, dissolute, debauched;** free-living, high-living [informal].

.9 **orgiastic,** saturnalian, corybantic.

.10 ADVS **intemperately,** prodigally, **immoderately,** inordinately, excessively, **in** or **to excess,** to extremes, beyond all bounds or limits, without restraint; high, high on the hog [slang].

994. GLUTTONY

.1 NOUNS **gluttony, gluttonousness, greed, greediness,** voraciousness, voracity, ravenousness, edacity, crapulence or crapulency, gulosity, rapacity, insatiability; omnivorousness; **piggishness, hoggishness,**
swinishness, "swinish gluttony" [Milton]; overindulgence, overeating, polyphagia, hyperphagia; intemperance 993.

.2 **epicurism, epicureanism, gourmandise,** gastronomy.

.3 **glutton,** greedy eater, hefty or husky eater [informal], trencherman, trencherwoman, belly-god, greedygut or greedyguts [both slang], gorger, **gourmand,** gourmandizer, gormand, gormandizer, guttler, cormorant; **hog** or **pig** [both informal].

.4 VERBS **gluttonize,** gormandize, **indulge one's appetite,** live to eat; **gorge,** engorge, glut, cram, **stuff,** batten, guttle, guzzle, **devour,** raven, bolt, gobble, gulp, **wolf,** gobble or gulp or bolt or wolf down, eat like a horse, eat one's head off [informal], eat out of house and home.

.5 **overeat,** overgorge, **overindulge, make a pig** or **hog of oneself.**

.6 ADJS **gluttonous, greedy,** voracious, ravenous, edacious, rapacious, insatiable, polyphagic, hyperphagic, Apician; **piggish, hoggish,** swinish; crapulous, crapulent; intemperate 993.7; omnivorous, all-devouring; **gorging,** cramming, glutting, guttling, stuffing, guzzling, wolfing, bolting, **gobbling, gulping,** gluttonizing.

.7 **overfed,** overgorged, overindulged.

.8 ADVS **gluttonously, greedily,** voraciously, ravenously, edaciously; **piggishly, hoggishly,** swinishly.

995. FASTING

.1 NOUNS **fasting,** abstinence from food; starvation; restriction of intake; punishment of Tantalus.

.2 **fast,** lack of food; spare or meager diet, Lenten diet, Lenten fare, "Lenten entertainment" [Shakespeare]; short commons or rations, starvation diet, bread and water, bare subsistence; xerophagy, xerophagia; Barmecide or Barmecidal feast.

.3 **fast day,** jour maigre [Fr]; **Lent,** Quadragesima; Yom Kippur, Tishah B'Av or Ninth of Av; Ramadan.

.4 VERBS **fast,** not eat, go hungry, dine with Duke Humphrey; eat sparingly.

.5 ADJS **fasting,** uneating, unfed; **Lenten,** quadragesimal.

996. INTOXICATION

.1 NOUNS **intoxication, inebriation, inebriety,** insobriety, besottedness, sottedness, **drunkenness, tipsiness,** befuddlement, fuddle, fuddlement, fuddledness, tipsification or tiddliness [both informal]; a high; Dutch courage, pot-valiance *or* pot-valiancy, pot-valor; hangover, katzenjammer, morning after [informal].

.2 **bibulousness,** bibacity, bibaciousness, bibulosity, sottishness; serious drinking; crapulence, crapulousness; **intemperance** 993; bacchanalianism; Bacchus, Dionysus.

.3 **alcoholism, dipsomania,** oenomania *or* oinomania, alcoholic psychosis *or* addiction, pathological drunkenness, problem drinking, heavy drinking, habitual drunkenness, ebriosity; delirium tremens 473.9, 10; grog blossom *or* bottle nose [both informal]; gin drinker's liver, cirrhosis of the liver.

.4 **drinking, imbibing; social drinking; tippling,** guzzling, gargling, bibbing; winebibbing, winebibbery; toping, **boozing** *or* **swilling** [both informal], **hitting the booze** *or* **bottle** *or* **sauce** [slang].

.5 **spree, drinking bout,** bout, **celebration,** potation, compotation, symposium, wassail, guzzle, **carouse, carousal,** drunken carousal *or* revelry; **binge, drunk,** bust, tear; **bender** *or* **toot** *or* **bat** *or* **jag** [all slang], pub-crawl [Brit informal]; bacchanal, bacchanalia, bacchanalian; **debauch, orgy.**

.6 **drink, dram,** potation, potion, libation, **nip, draft, drop, spot,** finger or two, **sip, sup, suck,** drench, guzzle, gargle, jigger; peg, swig, swill, pull; **snort, jolt, shot,** snifter, wet; **round; round of drinks.**

.7 **bracer, refresher,** reviver, pickup *or* **pick-me-up** [both informal], hair of the dog *or* hair of the dog that bit one [both informal].

.8 **drink, cocktail, highball,** mixed drink 996.42; **punch; eye-opener** [informal], **nightcap** [informal], sundowner [Brit informal]; **chaser** [informal], *pousse-café* [Fr], *apéritif* [Fr]; parting cup, stirrup cup, doch-an-dorrach *or* wee doch-an-dorrach [both Scot]; Mickey Finn *or* Mickey *or* knockout drops [all slang].

.9 **toast, pledge.**

.10 **drinker, imbiber, social drinker,** tippler, bibber; winebibber, oenophilist; **drunkard, drunk, inebriate,** *shikker* [Yid], sot, toper, guzzler, swiller, soaker, lovepot, tosspot, barfly, thirsty soul, **serious drinker,** devotee of Bacchus; **boozer** [informal], swigger; hard drinker, heavy drinker, big drunk [slang]; **alcoholic, dipsomaniac, problem drinker,** chronic alcoholic, chronic drunk, pathological drinker, alcoholic addict; carouser, reveler, wassailer; bacchanal, bacchanalian; pot companion.

.11 [slang terms] **lush,** lusher, **soak, sponge,** hooch hound, **boozehound,** ginhound, elbow bender *or* crooker, bottle sucker, swillbelly, swillpot, swillbowl; **souse, stew,** bum, rummy, rum hound; wino.

.12 **liquor,** intoxicating liquor, "the luscious liquor" [Milton], **hard liquor, schnapps, spirits, ardent spirits,** strong waters, **intoxicant,** toxicant, inebriant, **potable,** potation, **beverage, drink, strong drink,** alcoholic drink *or* beverage, **alcohol,** aqua vitae, water of life, brew, **grog,** social lubricant, nectar of the gods; **booze** [informal]; **rum,** the Demon Rum, John Barleycorn; the bottle, the cup, the cup that cheers, "the ruddy cup" [Sir Walter Scott], little brown jug; punch bowl, the flowing bowl.

.13 [slang terms] **likker, hooch, sauce,** firewater, tiger milk; **medicine,** snake medicine, corpse reviver.

.14 (bad liquor) **rotgut, poison,** rat poison, formaldehyde, embalming fluid, shellac, panther piss [all slang].

.15 **beer** 996.38, "barmy beer" [Dryden]; swipes [Brit informal], suds [informal]; small beer.

.16 **wine** 996.39, *vin* [Fr], *vino* [Sp & Ital], oen(o)– *or* en(o)–; vintage wine, nonvintage wine; red wine, white wine, rosé wine, pink wine; dry *or* sweet wine, heavy *or* light wine, full *or* thin wine, rough *or* smooth wine, still wine, sparkling wine; extra sec *or* demi-sec *or* sec *or* brut champagne; new wine, must; imported wine, domestic wine.

.17 **bootleg liquor, moonshine** [informal]; hooch *or* shine *or* mountain dew [all slang], white lightning *or* white mule [both slang]; bathtub gin; home brew.

.18 **liquor dealer,** liquor store owner; **vintner,** wine merchant; **bartender,** mixologist, barkeeper, barkeep, barman [Brit], tapster, publican [Brit]; barmaid, tapstress; **brewer,** brewmaster; **distiller; bootlegger, moonshiner** [informal].

.19 **bar, barroom,** bistro, cocktail lounge; taproom; **tavern, pub,** pothouse, alehouse, rumshop, grogshop, dramshop, groggery, gin mill [slang], **saloon,** drinking saloon, saloon bar [Brit]; public house [Brit]; public *or* local [both Brit informal]; beer parlor, beer garden, rathskeller; **nightclub, cabaret;** café, wine shop; barrel house *or* honky-tonk *or* dive [all slang]; **speakeasy** *or* blind tiger *or* blind pig *or* after-hours joint [all slang].

.20 distillery, still, distiller; **brewery**, brewhouse; **winery**, wine press; bottling works.

.21 VERBS **intoxicate, inebriate, addle, befuddle**, bemuse, besot, go to one's head, make one see double, make one tiddly.

.22 [slang or informal terms] **plaster**, pickle, swack, crock, stew, souse, stone, pollute, tipsify, booze up, boozify, fuddle, overtake.

.23 **tipple, drink**, dram [Brit], nip; grog, **guzzle**, gargle; **imbibe**, have a drink *or* nip *or* dram *or* guzzle *or* gargle, soak, bib, quaff, sip, sup, lap, lap up, take a drop, slake one's thirst, cheer *or* refresh the inner man, drown one's sorrows, commune with the spirits; toss off *or* down, toss one's drink, knock back, drink off *or* up, drain the cup, drink bottoms-up, drink deep; **drink hard**, drink like a fish, drink seriously, **tope**; take to drink *or* drinking, "follow strong drink" [Bible].

.24 [slang or informal terms] **booze**, swig, swill, moisten *or* wet one's whistle; **liquor, liquor up**, lush, souse, tank up, **hit the booze** *or* **bottle** *or* **sauce**, exercise *or* bend *or* crook *or* raise the elbow, dip the beak, splice the main brace; chug-a-lug, chug.

.25 **get drunk**, be stricken drunk, get high, put on a high, take a drop too much; **get plastered** *or* **pickled**, etc. [slang], tie one on *or* get a bun on [both slang].

.26 **be drunk**, be intoxicated, have a drop too much, have more than one can hold, have a jag on [slang], see double, be feeling no pain; **stagger, reel; pass out** [slang].

.27 **go on a spree**, go on a binge *or* drunk *or* toot *or* bat *or* bender [slang], **carouse, spree, revel**, wassail, debauch, "eat, drink, and be merry" [Bible], paint the town red [slang], pub-crawl [Brit informal].

.28 **drink to, toast, pledge**, drink a toast to, drink *or* pledge the health of, give you.

.29 **distill; brew**; bootleg, moonshine [informal], moonlight [slang].

.30 ADJS **intoxicated, inebriated**, inebriate, inebrious, **drunk, drunken**, *shikker* [Yid], **tipsy**, in liquor, **in one's cups, under the influence**, the worse for liquor; nappy, beery; **tiddly, giddy, dizzy**, muddled, addled, flustered, bemused, reeling, seeing double; **mellow, merry**, jolly, happy, gay, glorious; **full**, fou [Scot]; **besotted**, sotted, sodden, drenched, far-gone; drunk as a lord, drunk as a fiddler *or* piper, drunk as an owl; staggering drunk, blind drunk; crapulent, crapulous; **maudlin**.

.31 [slang or informal terms] **fuddled, muzzy**, boozy, overtaken; **swacked, plastered**, stewed, **pickled**, pissed, **soused**, soaked, boiled, fried, canned, tanked, potted, corned, bombed, smashed; bent, **crocked**, crocko, shellacked, tight, lushy, squiffy, afflicted, jug-bitten, oiled, lubricated, polluted, raddled, organized, **high**, elevated, high as a kite, lit, **lit up**, lit to the gills, illuminated, **loaded, stinko**, stinking drunk, pie-eyed, pissy-eyed, cockeyed, cockeyed drunk, roaring *or* rip-roaring drunk, skunk-drunk; half-seas over, three sheets to the wind.

.32 **full of Dutch courage, pot-valiant**, pot-valorous.

.33 **dead-drunk**, blind drunk, blind [informal], overcome, out [informal], **out cold** *or* passed out [both slang], **blotto** *or* **stiff** [both slang], helpless, under the table; paralyzed [informal], **stoned** [slang].

.34 **bibulous**, bibacious, drunken, sottish, liquorish, given *or* addicted to drink, **liquor-loving**, liquor-drinking, drinking, swilling [informal], toping, tippling, winebibbing.

.35 **intoxicating**, intoxicative, **inebriating**, inebriative, inebriant, heady.

.36 **alcoholic, spirituous, ardent, strong, hard**, with a kick [slang]; winy, vinous.

.37 INTERJS (toasts) skoal!, *skôl!* [Norw], prosit! *or* prost!, *à votre santé!* [Fr], *¡salud!* [Sp], *l'chaim!* [Heb], *sláinte!* [Ir], *salute!* [Ital], *na zdorov'e!* [Russ], *nazdrowie!* [Pol], to your health!, cheerio!, cheers!, down the hatch!, bottoms up!, here's how!, here's to you!, here's looking at you!, here's mud in your eye!, here's good luck!, here's to absent friends!

.38 **brews**

ale	metheglin
beer	Munich beer
bitters [Brit]	near beer
bock beer	Pilsner
dark beer	porter
half-and-half	pulque
kvass	sake
lager beer	schenk beer
light beer	stout
malt liquor	weiss beer
mead	

.39 **wines**

abboccato	amontillado
Aglianico del Vulture	amoroso
Alba Flora	Anjou
Alban(a)	apple wine
Algarve	apricot wine
Algerian wine	Argentine wine
Alicante	Assmannshausen
Aloxe-Corton	Asti Spumante
Alsace	Aszú
altar wine	Bad Kreuznach

Badacsonyi
Banyuls
Barbaresco
Barbera
Bardolino
Barolo
Barsac
Beaujolais
Beaune
Bernkasteler
blackberry wine
blanc de blancs
blanc de noirs
Blanquette de
  Limoux
Bockstein
Bordeaux
bual
Bucelas
Burgundy
Byrrh
Cabernet
Cabernet Sauvignon
Cahors
California wine
Canary
Carignan
Castelli Romani
Catawba
Chablis
Chalonnais
Chambertin
Champagne
champagne cider
Chardonnay
Châteauneuf-du-Pape
Chenin blanc
cherry wine
Chian
Chianti
Chianti classico
Chiaretto
Chilean wine
Clairette de Die
claret
Colares
cold duck
Concord wine
Constantia
consumo
Cortaillod
Cortese
Corton
Corvo
Côte de Nuits
Côte d'Or
Côte Rotie
Côtes de Provence
Côtes du Rhone
cowslip wine
cream sherry
crémant
currant wine
damson wine
dandelion wine
Dão
Deidesheimer
Delaware
dessert wine
Dôle
Dubonnet
Échézeaux

Egri Bikavér
Eiswein
elderberry wine
Eszencia
Etna
Falerno
Fendant de Sion
Fixin
fortified wine
Frascati
Frecciarossa
frizzante
Gamay
Geisenheimer
Gewürztraminer
ginger wine
gooseberry wine
Gragano
Grands Échézeaux
Graves
Grenache
Grignolino
Grinzig
Grumello
Gumpoldskirchner
hard cider
Hattenheimer
Haut Sauternes
hawthorn wine
Hermitage
Hochheimer
hock
Hospices de Beaune
Inferno
Johannisberger
jug wine
Jura
Jurançon
Kaffia
kosher wine
Kremser
Lacrima Christi
Lambrusco
Liebfraumilch
Livermore Valley
Ljutomer
loganberry wine
Lugana
Mâcon (nais)
Madeira
Málaga
malmsey
Malvasia
Mamertino
Manzanilla
Marsala
Mavrodaphne
May wine
Médoc
Meursault
milk sherry
Monbazillac
Monchhof
Montefiascone
Montepulciano
Montmélian
Montrachet
Moroccan wine
Moselblümchen
Moselle
mulberry wine
Muscadet

Muscat
muscatel
Musigny
Nackenheimer
Napa Valley
Neckar
Neuchâtel
New York State wine
Nuits-St.-Georges
Oeil de Perdrix
oloroso
Orvieto
Pallini
Palomino
parsnip wine
Passover wine
peach wine
Peruvian wine
pink or rosé cham-
  pagne
Pinot
Pinot blanc
Pinot Chardonnay
Pinot noir
plum wine
pomace
Pomerol
Pommard
pop wine
port
Pouilly-Fuissé
Pouilly-Fumé
Priorato
Prošek
quince wine
raisin wine
raspberry wine
red wine
retsina
Reuilly
Rhenish wine
Rhine
Rhône
rhubarb wine
Ribero
Riesling
Rioja
Riquewihr
riserva
Romanée Conti
rosé
Roussillon
ruby port
Rüdesheimer
Ruppertsberger
sack
sacramental wine

.40 spirits, liquor

absinthe
alcool blanc [Fr]
Amer Picon
Angostura bitters
aquavit or akvavit
arak
Armagnac
bitters
blended whiskey
bourbon
brandy
Campari
Canadian whiskey,

sage wine
St.-Denis
St.-Émilion
St. Raphael
Sancerre
Sangiovese
Santa Clara Valley
Sassella
Saumur
sauterne
Sauternes
Sauvignon blanc
Sekt
Sémillon
sercial
Seyssel
sherry
soave
solera sherry
Somlo
Sonoma Valley
sparkling Burgundy
sparkling wine
Steinwein
stone wine
straw wine
Sylvaner
Szekszárd
Szomorodni
table wine
Tarragona
Tavel
tawny port
Tokay
Touraine
Traminer
Tulare County
Valdepeñas
Valpolicella
Valtellina
verbesserte
verdelho
Verdicchio
vermouth
Vernaccia
Vesuvio
vinho verde
vin-jaune
vin mousseux
vin ordinaire
vin rosé
Volnay
Vougeot
Vouvray
white wine
Zinfandel
zucco

Canadian
clean rum
Cognac
corn whiskey
eau de vie [Fr]
Fernet Branca
geneva
gin
Grand Champagne
Grand Fine Cham-
  pagne
grappa
grog

Holland gin, Hollands	Petite Champagne	sidecar	Tom and Jerry
Irish whiskey, Irish	plum brandy	silver fizz	Tom Collins
Jamaica gin	Punt e Mes	sling	vermouth cassis
Jamaica rum	raki	smash	vodka martini
Kirsch	rum	sour	wassail
light whiskey	rye whiskey, rye	swizzle	whiskey smash
malt whiskey	schnapps	toddy	whiskey sour
marc	Scotch whiskey,		
marc de Burgogne	Scotch		
mescal	slivovitz		
moonshine	tequila		
ouzo	vodka		
pastis [Fr]	whiskey		
Pernod			

.41 liqueurs, cordials.

anisette	Danziger Goldwasser
apple brandy	Drambuie
applejack	framboise
apricot brandy	Galliano
Benedictine	goldwater
Calvados	Grand Marnier
Chartreuse	green Chartreuse
Cointreau	Irish Mist
Cordial Médoc	Kümmel
Crema de Lima	maraschino
crème d'amande	parfait amour
crème de cacao	pear brandy
crème de cassis	poire
crème de menthe	pousse-café
crème de moka	rainbow cordial
crème de noyau	sloe gin
crème Yvette	Strega
Curaçao	Triple Sec
Danzig brandy	yellow Chartreuse

.42 mixed drinks

Americano	grasshopper
apricot sour	Green Dragon
Bacardi	Guggenheim
bishop	Harvey Wallbanger
Black Russian	highball
Bloody Mary	hot buttered rum
bourbon and branch	hot toddy
water	Irish coffee
bowle	Jersey Lily
brandy Alexander	julep
brandy and soda, BS	lamb's wool
brandy smash	Mai-Tai
Bronx cocktail	Manhattan
Bull Shot	Margarita
buttered rum	martini
champagne cocktail	mint julep
church parade	Moscow mule
cobbler	Negroni
cocktail	negus
coffee royale	old-fashioned
collins	orange blossom
cooler	pink lady
Cuba Libre	pink squirrel
Daiquiri	planter's punch
dry martini	posset
Dubonnet cocktail	purl
eggnog	rickey
fizz	rince pichon
flip	Rob Roy
gimlet	rum punch
gin and tonic	sangria
gin fizz	Sazerac
gin rickey	Scotch and soda
gin sling	Scotch and water
Glühwein	screwdriver

997. SOBRIETY

(unintoxicated state)

.1 NOUNS **sobriety, soberness;** unintoxicated-ness, uninebriatedness, undrunkenness; temperance 992.

.2 VERBS **sober up,** sober off; sleep it off; bring one down, take off a high [slang].

.3 ADJS **sober,** in one's sober senses, in one's right mind, in possession of one's faculties; **unintoxicated, uninebriated,** unine-briate, uninebrious, undrunk, undrunken, untipsy; cold sober [informal], **sober as a judge;** able to walk the chalk, able to walk the chalk mark *or* line [informal]; temperate 992.9.

.4 **unintoxicating,** nonintoxicating, uninebriating; **nonalcoholic, soft.**

998. LEGALITY

.1 NOUNS **legality, legitimacy, lawfulness, legitimateness, licitness,** rightfulness, validity, scope, applicability; **jurisdiction** 1000; actionability, justiciability, **constitutionality,** constitutional validity; legal process, legal form, **due process;** legalism, constitutionalism; **justice** 976.

.2 **legalization, legitimatization,** validation; authorization, sanction; legislation, enactment 742.13.

.3 **law,** *lex, jus* [both L], **statute,** rubric, **canon,** institution; **ordinance,** ordonnance; **act, enactment, measure,** legislation 742.13; **rule, ruling;** prescript, prescription; **regulation, règlement** [Fr]; **dictate,** dictation; form, formula, formulary, formality; standing order; bylaw, **edict, decree** 752.4; **bill** 742.17.

.4 (laws) common law, *jus commune* [Fr]; chancery law, equity; substantive law; unwritten law, *lex non scripta* [L]; written *or* statute law, *lex scripta* [L], *jus scriptum* [L], positive law; constitutional law; civil law, *jus civile* [L]; criminal law, crown law [Brit]; penal law; public law, *jus publicum* [L]; decree law; martial law; case law; international law, law of nations, *jus inter gentes* [L], *droit des gens* [Fr]; local law, law of the place, *lex loci, lex situs* [both L]; law of the land, *lex terrae* [L]; law of the domicile, *lex domicilii*

[L]; law of general application, *lex gene-ralis* [L]; law of the forum, *lex fori* [L]; mercantile law, *lex mercatorum, lex mercatoria* [both L]; commercial law, business law, corporation law, law merchant; maritime law, sea law, admiralty law; canon *or* ecclesiastical law, *jus ecclesiasticum* [L], Corpus Juris Canonici; Roman law, Corpus Juris Civilis; blue law; dry law; gag law.

.5 **code, digest,** pandect, capitulary, **body of law,** corpus juris, code of laws, digest of law; equity; codification; civil code, penal code; Napoleonic code, *Code Napoléon* [Fr].

.6 **constitution,** written constitution, unwritten constitution; constitutional amendment; Bill of Rights, constitutional guarantees.

.7 **jurisprudence, law,** legal science; nomology, nomography; forensic *or* legal medicine, medical jurisprudence, medico-legal medicine; forensic psychiatry; forensic *or* legal chemistry; criminology.

.8 VERBS **legalize, legitimize,** legitimatize, legitimate, make legal, declare lawful, validate; **authorize, sanction;** constitute, ordain, establish, put in force; prescribe, formulate; regulate, make a regulation; **decree** 752.9; **legislate, enact** 742.18.

.9 **codify,** digest.

.10 ADJS **legal, legitimate,** legit [slang], kosher [informal], competent, **licit, lawful,** rightful, according to law, within the law; actionable, justiciable, within the scope of the law; **judicial,** juridical; **authorized, sanctioned,** valid, applicable; **constitutional;** statutory, statutable; **legislative, lawmaking** 742.19; lawlike; **just** 976.8–10.

.11 jurisprudent, jurisprudential; **legalistic; forensic;** nomistic, nomothetic; criminological.

.12 ADVS **legally, legitimately, licitly, lawfully,** by law, *de jure* [L], in the eyes of the law.

999. ILLEGALITY

.1 NOUNS **illegality, unlawfulness, illicitness, lawlessness,** wrongfulness; unauthorization, impermissibility, **unconstitutionality;** legal *or* technical flaw, legal irregularity; **criminality,** criminalism; **outlawry; anarchy,** collapse *or* breakdown *or* paralysis of authority, anomie; illicit business 826.

.2 **illegitimacy, illegitimateness,** illegitimation; **bastardy,** bastardism, noth(o)–; bend *or* bar sinister, baton.

.3 **lawbreaking, violation of law,** breach of law, infringement, contravention, infraction, **transgression,** trespass, trespassing.

.4 **offense, wrong,** illegality; **violation** 769.2; **wrongdoing** 982; **crime, felony; misdemeanor;** tort; delict, delictum.

.5 VERBS **break the law, violate the law,** breach the law, infringe, contravene, infract, violate 769.4, **transgress, trespass,** disobey the law, offend against the law, fly in the face of the law, set the law at defiance, set the law at naught, circumvent the law, disregard the law, **take the law into one's own hands,** twist *or* torture the law to one's own ends *or* purposes; commit a crime; live outside the law.

.6 ADJS **illegal, unlawful, illegitimate, illicit,** nonlicit, nonlegal, lawless, wrongful, **against the law; unauthorized,** unallowed, impermissible, unwarranted, unwarrantable, unofficial; unstatutory; **unconstitutional,** nonconstitutional; flawed, irregular, contrary to law; actionable, chargeable, justiciable; triable, punishable; **criminal, felonious; outlaw, outlawed; contraband,** bootleg, black-market; under-the-table, under-the-counter; anarchic, anarchistic, anomic.

.7 **illegitimate, spurious,** false; **bastard,** misbegot, **misbegotten,** miscreated, baseborn, born out of wedlock, without benefit of clergy.

.8 ADVS **illegally, unlawfully, illegitimately, illicitly;** impermissibly; **criminally,** feloniously; contrary to law, in violation of law.

1000. JURISDICTION

(administration of justice)

.1 NOUNS **jurisdiction,** legal authority *or* power *or* right; original *or* appellate jurisdiction, exclusive *or* concurrent jurisdiction, civil *or* criminal jurisdiction, common-law *or* equitable jurisdiction, *in rem* jurisdiction, *in personam* jurisdiction; voluntary jurisdiction.

.2 **judiciary,** judicature, judicatory, legal system, the courts; **justice,** the wheels of justice, judicial process; judgment 494.

.3 **magistracy,** magistrature, magistrateship; **judgeship,** justiceship; mayoralty, mayorship.

.4 **bureau, office, department;** secretariat, ministry, commissariat; municipality, bailiwick; constabulary, constablery, sheriffry, sheriffalty, shrievalty; constablewick, sheriffwick.

.5 VERBS **administer justice,** administer, administrate; preside, preside at the board; sit in judgment 1004.17; judge 494.8.

.6 ADJS **jurisdictional,** jurisdictive; **judicatory,** judicatorial, judicative, juridic(al); **judicial, judiciary;** magisterial.

1001. TRIBUNAL

.1 NOUNS **tribunal, forum, board,** curia, Areopagus; judicature, judicatory, judiciary; council 755; inquisition, the Inquisition.

.2 **court, law court, court of law** *or* **justice,** court of arbitration, legal tribunal, judicature.

.3 (courts) circuit court, civil court, common-law court, county court, criminal court, district court, divorce court, juvenile court, police court, prize court, superior court, court of claims, court of domestic relations, family court, court of errors, court of first instance, court of record, court of requests, court of wards; appellate court, court of review, court of appeals, court of last resort; court of common pleas; assizes, court of assize; chancery, chancery court, court of chancery; conciliation court; court of inquiry, court of honor; court of conscience, equity court, court of equity; small-claims court; small-debts court; hustings, hustings court; probate court, court of probate; sessions, court of sessions, petty *or* quarter *or* special *or* general sessions; night court; traffic court; kangaroo court [informal], mock court, moot court.

.4 (US courts) Supreme Court, United States Supreme Court; United States District Court, United States Circuit Court of Appeals, Federal Court of Claims, Court of Private Land Claims.

.5 (British courts) court of admiralty, Court of Appeal, Court of Criminal Appeal, Court of Common Pleas, Court of Common Bank, Court of Common Council, Court of Divorce and Matrimonial Causes, Court of Exchequer, Court of Exchequer Chamber, Court of Queen's *or* King's Bench, Court of the Duchy of Lancaster, High Court, High Court of Appeal, High Court of Justice, High *or* Supreme Court of Judicature, Judicial Committee of the Privy Council, Lords Justices' Court, Palatine Court, Rolls Court, Stannary Court, superior courts of Westminster, Vice Chancellor's Court; court of attachments, woodmote; ward-mote, wardmote court; Green Cloth, Board of Green Cloth; Court of Session

[Scot], Teind Court [Scot]; court of pie-poudre *or* dustyfoot.

.6 (ecclesiastical courts) Papal Court, Curia, Rota, Sacra Romana Rota, Court of Arches [Brit], Court of Peculiars [Brit].

.7 **military court, court-martial,** general *or* special *or* summary court-martial, drum-head court-martial.

.8 **seat of justice, judgment seat,** mercy seat, bench; woolsack [Brit].

.9 **courthouse, court;** town hall, town house; courtroom; jury box; witness stand *or* box, dock.

.10 ADJS **tribunal, judicial,** judiciary, curial; appellate.

1002. JUDGE, JURY

.1 NOUNS **judge, magistrate, justice,** indicator, bencher, beak [Brit slang]; **justice of the peace, JP;** arbiter, arbitrator, moderator; umpire, referee; his honor, his worship, his lordship; Mr. Justice; critic 494.6, 7.

.2 (historical) tribune, praetor, ephor, archon, syndic, podesta; Areopagite; justiciar, justiciary; dempster, deemster, doomster, doomsman.

.3 [Muhammadan] mullah, ulema, hakim, mufti, cadi.

.4 (special judges) judge advocate, JA, presiding judge, probate judge, police judge *or* justice *or* magistrate, PJ; circuit judge; justice in eyre; ordinary, judge ordinary; judge *or* justice of assize; puisne judge *or* justice; military judge; lay judge; assessor, legal assessor; barmaster [Brit], chancellor, vice-chancellor, jurat, recorder, master, amicus curiae; ombudsman.

.5 Chief Justice, Associate Justice, Justice of the Supreme Court; Lord Chief Justice, Lord Justice, Lord Chancellor, Master of the Rolls, Baron of the Exchequer; Judge Advocate General.

.6 Pontius Pilate, Solomon, Minos, Rhadamanthus, Aeacus.

.7 **jury, panel,** jury of one's peers, sessions [Scot], country, twelve men in a box; inquest, jury of inquest; grand jury, petit jury, coroner's jury, special jury, trial jury, jury of the vicinage, jury of matrons *or* women, blue-ribbon jury *or* panel; police jury; jury panel, jury list, venire; hung jury.

.8 **juror, juryman,** veniremen, jurywoman; talesman; foreman of the jury, foreman, jury chancellor [Scot]; grand-juror, grand-juryman; petit-juror, petit-juryman; recognitor.

1003. LAWYER

.1 NOUNS **lawyer, attorney, attorney-at-law,** barrister, barrister-at-law, **counselor,** counselor-at-law, **counsel,** legal counselor, legal adviser, legal expert, **solicitor, advocate, pleader, mouthpiece** [slang]; member of the bar, legal practitioner, officer of the court; proctor, procurator; friend at or in court, amicus curiae; deputy, agent 781; intercessor 805.3; sea lawyer, latrine lawyer, self-styled lawyer, legalist.

.2 legist, jurist, jurisprudent, jurisconsult; law member of a court-martial.

.3 [derog terms] **shyster, ambulance chaser,** pettifogger, Philadelphia lawyer.

.4 (special lawyers) **district attorney, DA; prosecuting attorney, prosecutor;** trial judge advocate; public prosecutor; United States or US attorney; special pleader; private attorney, attorney in fact; court-appointed lawyer, public defender; **defense counsel;** criminal lawyer, mouthpiece [slang]; constitutional lawyer; corporation lawyer; law agent or writer to the signet [both Scot]; sergeant-at-law [Brit]; civilian; publicist; conveyancer; leader [Brit]; **attorney general, AG; solicitor general, SG;** Solicitor Supreme Court, SSC; King's or Queen's Counsel, KC, QC, silk, silk gown, silk-gownsman [Brit]; junior barrister or counsel, stuff gown, stuff-gownsman.

.5 **bar,** legal profession, members of the bar; representation, counsel, pleading, attorneyship.

.6 VERBS **practice law,** practice at the bar; take silk, be admitted to the bar.

.7 ADJS **lawyerly,** lawyerlike, barristerial; representing, of counsel.

1004. LEGAL ACTION

.1 NOUNS **lawsuit, suit,** suit in or at law; **litigation, prosecution, action, legal action,** proceedings, legal proceedings, legal process; legal remedy; **case,** cause, cause in court, legal case; judicial process.

.2 **summons, subpoena** 752.7; **writ, warrant** 752.6.

.3 **arraignment, indictment, impeachment;** charge 1005.1; presentment; information; bill of indictment, true bill; **bail** 772.2.

.4 **jury selection, impanelment,** venire, venire facias, venire facias de novo.

.5 **trial, jury trial,** trial by jury, trial at the bar, **hearing, inquiry, inquisition,** inquest, assize; court-martial; **examination, cross-**examination 485.11,12; mistrial; change of venue.

.6 **pleadings,** arguments at the bar; **plea,** pleading, argument; **defense,** statement of defense; demurrer, general or special demurrer; refutation 506.2; rebuttal 486.2.

.7 **declaration, statement,** allegation, allegation or statement of facts, procès-verbal; **deposition,** affidavit; claim; complaint; bill, bill of complaint; libel, narratio; nolle prosequi, nol. pros.; nonsuit.

.8 **testimony** 505.3; **evidence** 505; **argument,** presentation of the case; resting of the case; **summing up,** summation, charge to the jury, charging of the jury.

.9 **judgment, decision,** landmark decision; **verdict, sentence** 494.5; acquittal 1007; condemnation 1008, penalty 1009.

.10 **appeal,** appeal motion, application for retrial, appeal to a higher court; writ of error; certiorari, writ of certiorari.

.11 **litigant, litigator,** litigationist; **suitor, party,** party to a suit; **plaintiff** 1005.5; **defendant** 1005.6; **witness** 505.7; accessory, accessory before or after the fact; panel, parties litigant.

.12 VERBS **sue, litigate, prosecute,** go into litigation, **bring suit,** put in suit, sue or prosecute at law, **go to law,** seek in law, appeal to the law, seek justice or legal redress, implead, **bring action against,** prosecute a suit against, take or institute legal proceedings against, **take or have the law of** or **on** [informal], law [informal], take to court, bring into court, hale or haul or drag into court, bring a case before the court or bar, bring to justice, bring to trial, **put on trial,** bring to the bar, take before the judge; set down for hearing.

.13 **summons,** subpoena 752.12.

.14 **arraign, indict, impeach,** find an indictment against, present a true bill, prefer or file a claim, have or pull up [informal], bring up for investigation; **prefer charges** 1005.7.

.15 **impanel a jury,** impanel, panel.

.16 **call to witness,** bring forward, put on the stand; swear in 523.6; take oath 523.5; testify 505.10.

.17 **try,** try a case, conduct a trial, **hear,** give a hearing to; charge the jury, deliver one's charge to the jury; **judge, sit in judgment.**

.18 **plead,** implead, conduct pleadings, argue at the bar; **plead** or **argue one's case,** present one's case, make a plea, tell it to the judge [informal]; hang the jury [informal]; rest, rest one's case; sum up one's case.

.19 **bring in a verdict, pass sentence** 494.13; acquit 1007.4; convict 1008.3; penalize 1009.4.

.20 ADJS litigious, litigant, litigatory; causidical; litigable, actionable.

.21 PHRS **in litigation,** in court, in chancery, in jeopardy, **at law,** at bar, at the bar, **on trial,** up for investigation *or* hearing, before the court *or* bar *or* judge, *sub judice* [L].

1005. ACCUSATION

.1 NOUNS accusation, accusal, **charge, complaint,** plaint, count, **blame, imputation,** delation, reproach, taxing; **accusing, bringing of charges,** laying of charges, bringing to book; **denunciation,** denouncement; **impeachment, arraignment, indictment,** true bill; **allegation,** allegement; insinuation, implication, innuendo, veiled accusation, unspoken accusation; information, information against, bill of particulars; gravamen of a charge; prosecution, suit, lawsuit 1004.1.

.2 **incrimination,** crimination, **inculpation,** implication, **citation,** involvement, impugnment; attack, assault; **censure** 969.3.

.3 **recrimination,** retort, countercharge.

.4 **trumped-up charge,** false witness; **put-up job** *or* **frame-up** *or* **frame** [all slang].

.5 **accuser,** accusant, accusatrix; incriminator, delator, allegator, impugner; informer 557.6; impeacher, indictor; **plaintiff, complainant,** claimant, appellant, petitioner, libelant, suitor, **party,** party to a suit; **prosecutor,** the prosecution.

.6 **accused, defendant,** respondent, correspondent, libelee, suspect, prisoner.

.7 VERBS accuse, bring accusation; **charge, press charges, prefer** *or* **bring charges,** lay charges; complain, **lodge a complaint,** lodge a plaint; **impeach, arraign, indict,** bring in *or* hand up an indictment, return a true bill, article, **cite,** cite on several counts; book; **denounce,** denunciate; **finger** *or* point the finger at *or* put the finger on [all slang], inform on *or* against; allege, insinuate, imply; impute, fasten on *or* upon, pin on [informal], hang something on [slang], bring to book; tax, task, take to task *or* account; **reproach,** twit, taunt with; report, put on report.

.8 **blame,** blame on *or* upon [informal], hold against, **lay the blame on,** lay *or* cast blame upon, place *or* fix the blame *or* responsibility for.

.9 **accuse of, charge with,** tax *or* task with, saddle with, lay to one's charge, place to one's account, lay to one's door, bring home to, cast *or* throw in one's teeth, throw *or* thrust in the face of.

.10 **incriminate,** criminate, **inculpate,** implicate, involve; cry out against, cry out on *or* upon, cry shame upon, raise one's voice against; attack, assail, impugn; **censure** 969.13; throw a stone at, cast *or* throw the first stone.

.11 **recriminate,** countercharge, retort an accusation.

.12 **trump up a charge, bear false witness; frame,** frame up, put up a job [all slang].

.13 ADJS **accusing, accusatory,** accusative; imputative, denunciatory; recriminatory; **condemnatory** 969.23.

.14 **incriminating,** incriminatory, criminatory; delatorian; inculpative, inculpatory.

.15 **accused, charged, blamed,** tasked, taxed, reproached, **denounced, impeached, indicted, arraigned; incriminated,** inculpated, implicated, involved, in complicity; **cited,** impugned; under attack, under fire.

1006. JUSTIFICATION

.1 NOUNS **justification, vindication;** clearing, clearing of one's name, clearance, purging, purgation, destigmatizing, destigmatization, **exculpation** 1007.1; explanation, rationalization; reinstatement, restoration, rehabilitation.

.2 **defense, plea,** pleading; argument, statement of defense; answer, reply, counterstatement, response, riposte; **refutation** 506.2, **rebuttal** 486.2; demurrer, general *or* special demurrer; denial, objection, exception; **special pleading.**

.3 apology, apologia, apologetic.

.4 **excuse, cop-out** [slang], **alibi** *or* **out** [both informal]; lame excuse, poor excuse, likely story.

.5 **extenuation, mitigation, palliation,** softening; extenuative, palliative; **whitewash, whitewashing,** decontamination; gilding, gloss, varnish, color, putting the best color on; qualification, allowance; extenuating circumstances.

.6 **warrant, reason,** good reason, **cause,** call, **right, basis,** substantive *or* material basis, **ground, grounds,** foundation, substance.

.7 **justifiability, vindicability, defensibility;** explainability, explicability; **excusability,** pardonableness, forgivableness, remissibility, veniality; warrantableness, allowableness, admissibility, reasonableness, reasonability, legitimacy.

.8 **justifier, vindicator; defender,** pleader; **advocate,** successful advocate *or* defender, proponent, **champion; apologist,** apologizer, apologete; whitewasher.

.9 VERBS **justify, vindicate,** do justice to, make justice *or* right prevail; **warrant,** account for, show sufficient grounds for, give good reasons for; **rationalize,** explain; cry sour grapes, "make a virtue of necessity" [Shakespeare]; **exculpate** 1007.4; **clear,** clear one's name, purge, destigmatize, reinstate, restore, rehabilitate.

.10 **defend,** offer *or* say in defense, allege in support *or* vindication, **support, uphold, sustain, maintain,** assert; **answer,** reply, respond, riposte, counter; refute 506.5, **rebut** 486.5; **plead for,** make a plea, offer as a plea, plead one's case *or* cause; **advocate,** champion, espouse, join *or* associate oneself with, stand *or* stick up for, speak up for, contend for, speak for, argue for, urge reasons for, put in a good word for.

.11 **excuse,** alibi [informal], offer excuse for, give as an excuse, cover with excuses; plead ignorance; **apologize for,** make apology for; alibi out of [informal], crawl *or* worm *or* squirm out of, lie out of.

.12 **extenuate, mitigate, palliate,** soften, lessen, diminish, **ease,** mince; **soft-pedal;** slur over, ignore, pass by in silence, give the benefit of the doubt, not hold it against one, **gloss over,** put a gloss upon, put a good face upon, varnish, **whitewash,** color, lend a color to, put the best color on, show in the best colors; **allow for,** make allowance for; give the Devil his due.

.13 ADJS **justifying,** justificatory; **vindicative,** vindicatory, rehabilitative; **refuting** 506.6; **excusing,** excusatory; **apologetic(al); extenuating,** extenuative, **palliative.**

.14 **justifiable, vindicable, defensible; excusable, pardonable, forgivable,** expiable, remissible, exemptible, venial; **condonable,** dispensable; **warrantable,** allowable, admissible, reasonable, legitimate; unobjectionable, inoffensive.

1007. ACQUITTAL

.1 NOUNS **acquittal,** acquittance, quittance; **exculpation,** disculpation, verdict of acquittal *or* of not guilty; **exoneration, absolution, vindication,** remission, compurgation, purgation, purging, clearing, clearance, destigmatizing, destigmatization, quietus; **pardon, excuse, forgiveness; dis-**

charge, release, dismissal; quashing of the charge *or* indictment.

.2 **exemption, immunity,** impunity; **amnesty,** indemnity, nonprosecution, non prosequitur, nolle prosequi; **stay.**

.3 **reprieve,** respite, grace.

.4 VERBS **acquit, exculpate, exonerate, absolve,** give absolution, bring in *or* return a verdict of not guilty; **vindicate,** justify; **pardon, excuse, forgive;** remit, grant remission, remit the penalty of; amnesty, grant amnesty to; **discharge, release, dismiss, free, set free,** let off [informal], let go; quash the charge *or* indictment, withdraw the charge; **exempt,** grant immunity, exempt from, dispense from; clear, clear the skirts of, shrive, purge; blot out one's sins, wipe the slate clean; **whitewash,** decontaminate; destigmatize; nonpros.

.5 **reprieve,** respite, give *or* grant a reprieve.

1008. CONDEMNATION

.1 NOUNS condemnation, damnation, **doom,** guilty verdict, verdict of guilty; proscription, excommunication, anathematizing; **denunciation,** denouncement; **censure** 969.3; **conviction; sentence, judgment,** rap [slang]; death sentence, death warrant.

.2 attainder, attainture, attaintment; bill of attainder.

.3 VERBS **condemn, damn, doom; denounce,** denunciate; **censure** 969.13; **convict,** find guilty, bring home to; proscribe, excommunicate, anathematize; blacklist, put on the Index; pronounce judgment 494.13; **sentence,** pronounce sentence, pass sentence on; penalize 1009.4; attaint; sign one's death warrant.

.4 **stand condemned,** be convicted, be found guilty.

.5 ADJS **condemnatory, damnatory,** denunciatory, proscriptive; **censorious** 969.23.

1009. PENALTY

.1 NOUNS **penalty,** penalization, penance, penal retribution; **punishment** 1010; compensation, price; the devil to pay.

.2 **handicap,** disability, **disadvantage** 730.6.

.3 **fine,** mulct, amercement, sconce, damages; distress, distraint; forfeit, forfeiture; escheat, escheatment.

.4 VERBS **penalize,** put *or* impose *or* inflict a penalty on; **punish** 1010.10; **handicap,** put at a disadvantage.

.5 **fine,** mulct, amerce, sconce, estreat; distrain, levy a distress.

.6 ADVS on pain of, under or upon pain of, on or under penalty of.

1010. PUNISHMENT

.1 NOUNS **punishment**, punition, **chastisement**, **chastening**, **correction**, **discipline**, disciplinary measures or action, **castigation**, infliction, scourge, ferule, what-for [slang]; pains, pains and punishments; pay, payment; **retribution**, retributive justice, nemesis; judicial punishment; punishment that fits the crime, condign punishment, well-deserved punishment; **penalty**, penal retribution; penology; cruel and unusual punishment; judgment; deserts 960.3.

.2 (forms of punishment) penal servitude, jailing, imprisonment, incarceration, confinement; hard labor, rock pile; galleys; torture, torment, martyrdom; the gantlet, keelhauling, tar-and-feathering, railriding, picketing, the rack, impalement, dismemberment; strappado, estrapade.

.3 **slap**, smack, whack, whomp, **cuff, box**, buffet; blow 283.4; **rap on the knuckles**, box on the ear, slap in the face; slap on the wrist, token punishment.

.4 **corporal punishment**, whipping, beating, thrashing, spanking, flogging, flagellation, scourging, flailing, swingeing [dial], trouncing, basting, drubbing, buffeting, belaboring; **lashing**, **lacing**, stripes; horsewhipping; strapping, belting, rawhiding, cowhiding; **switching**; **clubbing**, cudgeling, caning, truncheoning, fustigation, bastinado; pistol-whipping; battery.

.5 [informal terms] **licking**, larruping, walloping, whaling, lathering, leathering, **hiding**, **tanning**, **dressing-down**; **paddling**.

.6 [slang terms] strap oil, hazel oil, hickory oil, birch oil; dose of strap oil, etc.

.7 **capital punishment**, execution; legal or judicial murder; **hanging**, the gallows, the rope or noose; **lynching**, necktie party or sociable [slang]; **crucifixion**; **electrocution**, the chair [informal], the hot seat [slang]; gassing, the gas chamber; **decapitation**, decollation, beheading, the guillotine, the ax, the block; **strangling**, strangulation, garrote; **shooting**, fusillade; **burning**, burning at the stake; **poisoning**, hemlock; stoning, lapidation; defenestration.

.8 **punisher**, discipliner, chastizer; **executioner**, executionist, deathsman [archaic], Jack Ketch [Brit]; **hangman**; **lyncher**; **electrocutioner**; headsman, **beheader**, de-

capitator; strangler, garroter; sadist torturer.

.9 **penologist**; jailer 761.10.

.10 VERBS **punish**, chastise, chasten, **discipline**, **correct**, **castigate**, penalize; **take to task**, bring to book, bring or call to account; deal with, settle with, settle or square accounts, **give one his deserts**, serve one right; inflict upon, visit upon; give a lesson to, make an example of; pillory; masthead.

.11 [informal terms] **attend to**, do for, take care of, serve one out, **give it to**, take or have it out of; pay, pay out, **fix**, **settle**, settle one's hash, settle the score, give one his gruel, **give one his comeuppance**; come down on or upon.

.12 [slang terms] **give what-for**, give a going-over, climb one's frame, let have it, light into, land on, mop or wipe up the floor with.

.13 **slap**, smack, whack, whomp, **cuff, box**, buffet; strike 283.13; slap the face, box the ears, give a rap on the knuckles.

.14 **whip**, give a whipping or beating or thrashing, **beat**, **thrash**, **spank**, **flog**, scourge, flagellate, flail, whale; whop or wallop or swinge [all dial], **smite**, thump, trounce, baste, **pummel**, pommel, **drub**, **buffet**, **belabor**, lay on; lash, lace, cut, stripe; horsewhip; knout; **strap**, belt, rawhide, cowhide; **switch**, birch, give the stick; **club**, **cudgel**, cane, truncheon, fustigate, bastinado; pistol-whip.

.15 [informal terms] **lick**, **larrup**, **wallop**, whale, welt, trim, flax, lather, leather, **hide**, **tan**, **tan one's hide**, dress down, give a dressing-down; **paddle**.

.16 [slang terms] **lambaste**, **clobber**, dust one s jacket, give a dose of birch oil or strap oil or hickory oil or hazel oil, take it out of one's hide or skin.

.17 **thrash soundly**, **batter**, **beat up** [slang], beat to a jelly, bruise, **beat black and blue**, beat the shit or tar out of [slang].

.18 **torture**, put to the question; rack, put on or to the rack; dismember, tear limb from limb; draw and quarter, break on the wheel, tar and feather, ride on a rail, picket, keelhaul, impale, grill.

.19 **execute**, **put to death**, inflict capital punishment; **electrocute**, burn [slang]; send to the gas chamber; **behead**, **decapitate**, decollate, guillotine, bring to the block; **crucify**; **shoot**, execute by firing squad; burn, **burn at the stake**; **strangle**, garrote, bowstring; stone, lapidate; defenestrate.

.20 **hang**, hang by the neck; **string up**, scrag

or stretch [all informal]; gibbet, noose, neck, bring to the gallows; **lynch;** hang, draw, and quarter.

.21 **be hanged,** suffer hanging, **swing,** dance upon nothing, kick the air *or* wind *or* clouds.

.22 **be punished,** suffer, suffer for, **suffer the consequences** *or* penalty, get it, **catch it** [both informal], get *or* catch it in the neck [slang]; **get one's deserts** 960.6; be doubly punished, get it coming and going [slang], sow the wind and reap the whirlwind.

.23 **take one's punishment, take the consequences, take one's medicine,** swallow the bitter pill, pay the piper, face the music [informal], make one's bed and lie on it; take the rap [slang].

.24 **deserve punishment, have it coming,** be for it *or* in for it, be heading for a fall.

.25 ADJS **punishing, chastising,** chastening, corrective, disciplinary; retributive; grueling [informal]; **penal, punitive,** punitory, inflictive; castigatory; penological.

1011. INSTRUMENTS OF PUNISHMENT

.1 NOUNS **whip, lash, scourge,** flagellum, mastig(o)–; strap, thong, rawhide, cowhide, blacksnake, kurbash, sjambok, belt, razor strap; knout; bullwhip, bullwhack; horsewhip; crop; quirt; rope's end; cat, cat-o'-nine-tails; whiplash.

.2 **rod, stick, switch; paddle,** ruler, ferule, pandybat; birch, rattan; cane; club 801.26.

.3 (devices) **pillory, stocks,** finger pillory; cucking stool, ducking stool, trebuchet; whipping post, branks, triangle *or* triangles, wooden horse, treadmill, crank.

.4 (instruments of torture) **rack,** wheel, Iron Maiden of Nuremberg; screw, thumbscrew; boot, iron heel, scarpines; Procrustean bed, bed of Procrustes.

.5 (instruments of execution) **scaffold; block, guillotine,** ax, maiden; **stake; cross; gallows,** gallows-tree, gibbet, tree, drop; **hangman's rope, noose,** rope, halter, hemp, hempen collar *or* necktie *or* bridle [slang]; **electric chair,** death chair, the chair [informal], hot seat [slang]; **gas chamber,** lethal chamber, death chamber.

1012. ATONEMENT

.1 NOUNS **atonement, reparation, amends,** making amends, **restitution, propitiation, expiation, redress, recompense,** compensation, making right *or* good, making up, squaring, redemption, reclamation, satis-

faction, quittance; indemnity, indemnification; compromise, composition; expiatory offering *or* sacrifice, piaculum, peace offering.

.2 **apology, excuse,** regrets; acknowledgment, penitence, contrition, breast-beating, mea culpa, confession 556.3; abject apology.

.3 **penance,** penitence, repentance; penitential act *or* exercise, **mortification,** maceration, flagellation, lustration; **asceticism** 991, **fasting** 995; **purgation,** purgatory, "cold purgatorial fires" [T. S. Eliot]; **sackcloth and ashes;** hair shirt; Day of Atonement, Yom Kippur.

.4 VERBS **atone, atone for, propitiate, expiate,** compensate, recompense, redress, redeem, repair, satisfy, give satisfaction, **make amends, make reparation** *or* **compensation** *or* **expiation,** make good, make right, **make up for,** make matters up, square it, square things, pay the forfeit *or* penalty, pay one's dues [informal], wipe off old scores, set one's house in order; live down.

.5 **apologize, beg pardon, ask forgiveness,** beg indulgence, express regret; take back 628.9; get *or* fall down on one's knees, get down on one's marrowbones [slang].

.6 **do penance,** flagellate oneself, mortify oneself, mortify one's flesh, shrive oneself, purge oneself, cleanse oneself of guilt, stand in a white sheet, repent in sackcloth and ashes, wear a hairshirt, wear sackcloth *or* sackcloth and ashes; receive absolution.

.7 ADJS **atoning, propitiatory, expiatory,** piacular, reparative, reparatory, restitutive, restitutory, restitutional, redressing, recompensing, compensatory, compensational, righting, squaring; redemptive, redeeming, reclamatory, satisfactional; **apologetic(al);** repentant, repenting; **penitential,** purgative, purgatorial; lustral, lustrative, lustrational, cleansing, purifying; ascetic 991.3.

1013. DEITY

.1 NOUNS **deity, divinity,** divineness; **godliness,** godlikeness; **godhood,** godhead, godship, Fatherhood.

.2 **God, the**(o)–; Lord, Jehovah, Providence, Heaven, the **Deity,** the Divinity, **the Supreme Being, God Almighty, the Almighty, Almighty God,** the All-powerful, the Omnipotent, Omnipotence, **the Infinite,** the Infinite Being, the Everlasting, the Eternal, the Eternal Being, Alpha and Omega, the Absolute, the Absolute Being, the Omniscient, Omniscience, the All-wise, the All-knowing, the All-merciful, the All-holy, the Infinite Spirit, the Supreme Soul, **King of Kings**, Lord of Lords, Lord of hosts, Demiurge, Demiourgos, I Am, the Preserver, **the Maker, the Creator,** the First Cause, Author *or* Creator of all things; the Unmoved Mover; the ground of being; ultimate concern.

.3 *Deus* [L], *Theos* [Gk], *Dieu* [Fr], *Gott* [Ger]; *Yahweh, Adonai, Elohim* [all Heb]; **Allah;** the Great Spirit, Manitou.

.4 (Hinduism) **Brahma,** the Supreme Soul, the Essence of the Universe; **Atman,** the Universal Ego *or* Self; **Vishnu,** the Preserver; **Shiva** *or* Siva, the Destroyer, the Regenerator.

.5 (Buddhism) **Buddha,** the Blessed One, the Teacher, **the Lord Buddha,** bodhisattva.

.6 (Zoroastrianism) **Ahura Mazda,** Ormazd, Mazda, the Lord of Wisdom, the Wise Lord, the Wise One, the King of Light, the Guardian of Mankind.

.7 (Christian Science) **Mind, Divine Mind,** Spirit, Soul Principle, Life, Truth, Love.

.8 **world spirit** *or* **soul,** *anima mundi* [L], universal life force, world principle, **world-self,** universal ego *or* self, infinite spirit, supreme soul *or* principle, **oversoul, nous,** archeus, Logos, World Reason.

.9 **Nature, Mother Nature,** Dame Nature, "Beldame Nature" [Milton].

.10 **Godhead, Trinity,** Holy Trinity, Triune, Triunity, Triune God, Trinity in Unity, Threefold Unity, Three in One and One in Three; **Father, Son, and Holy Ghost;** Trimurti, Hindu trinity *or* triad.

.11 **God the Father, the Father,** the All-father, the Everlasting Father, the Holy Father, Our Father, Our Father which art in Heaven, the Creator.

.12 **God the Son, Christ,** the Christ, **Jesus,** Jesu, **Jesus Christ,** Christ Jesus, Jesus of Nazareth, the Nazarene, the Galilean, the Man of Sorrows, **Messiah,** the Anointed, God-man, **Savior, Redeemer,** the Mediator, the Intercessor, the Advocate, the Judge, **Son of God, Son of Man,** Son of David, the son of Mary, the only son of Mary, the Only-Begotten, Only-Begotten Son, **Our Lord,** Lord Jesus, the Lamb, **Lamb of God, Immanuel,** Emmanuel, **the Master, King of Kings,** Lord of Lords, King of Kings and Lord of Lords, King of Heaven, King of Glory,

King of the Jews, Lord our Righteousness, the Sun of Righteousness, **Prince of Peace, the Good Shepherd,** the Risen, the Door, the Way, the Truth, the Life, the Bread of Life, the Light of the World, the Vine, the True Vine; the Christ Child, the Infant Jesus; Christo–.

.13 **the Word, Logos,** the Word Made Flesh, **the Incarnation,** the Hypostatic Union.

.14 God the Holy Ghost, **the Holy Ghost, the Holy Spirit,** the Spirit of God, the Spirit of Truth, Paraclete, the Comforter, the Consoler, the Intercessor, the Dove.

.15 (divine attributes) infinity, eternity; infinite goodness, infinite justice, infinite truth, infinite love, infinite mercy; omniscience *or* omnisciency, infinite wisdom; omnipotence *or* omnipotency, infinite power; omnipresence, ubiquity; unity, immutability; holiness, glory, light; majesty, sovereignty.

.16 (divine functions) creation, preservation, dispensation; providence, dealings *or* dispensations *or* visitations of providence.

.17 (functions of Christ) salvation, redemption; atonement, propitiation; mediation, intercession; judgment.

.18 (functions of the Holy Ghost) inspiration, unction, regeneration, sanctification, comfort, consolation, grace, witness.

.19 ADJS **divine,** heavenly, celestial, empyrean; **godly, godlike** 1028.9; **transcendent,** superhuman, supernatural; self-existent; Christly, Christlike, redemptive, salvational, propitiative, propitiatory, mediative, mediatory, intercessive, intercessional; incarnate, incarnated, made flesh.

.20 **almighty, omnipotent,** all-powerful; creating, creative, making, shaping; **omniscient,** all-wise, all-knowing, all-seeing; **infinite,** boundless, limitless, unbounded, unlimited, undefined, omnipresent, ubiquitous; eternal, everlasting, timeless, perpetual, immortal, permanent; one; immutable, unchanging, changeless, eternally the same; supreme, sovereign, highest; holy, hallowed, sacred, numinous; glorious, radiant, luminous; majestic; good, just, loving, merciful.

1014. MYTHICAL AND POLYTHEISTIC GODS AND SPIRITS

.1 NOUNS **the gods,** the immortals; the major deities, the greater gods, *di majores* [L]; the minor deities, the lesser gods, *di minores* [L]; pantheon; theogony.

.2 **god,** *deus* [L]; **deity, divinity,** immortal,

heathen god, pagan deity or divinity; **goddess,** *dea* [L]; deva, devi, the shining ones; **idol,** false god, devil-god.

.3 godling, godlet, godkin; **demigod,** half-god, hero; demigoddess, heroine.

.4 (gods and goddesses) deities of fertility 165.5; deities of the household 191.30; earth goddesses 375.10; moon goddesses 375.12; sun gods 375.14; sea gods 397.4; rain gods 394.6; wind gods 403.3; thunder gods 456.5; gods of lightning 335.17; agricultural deities 413.4; gods of commerce 827.12; war gods 797.17; love deities 931.8; gods of marriage 933.14; Muses 535.2, poetry Muses 609.12; music Muses 464.22; Fates 640.3; water gods 1014.20; forest gods 1014.21; goddesses of discord 795.1; gods of evil 1016.6; deities of the nether world 1019.5, deities of justice 976.5.

.5 (Greek and Roman deities) Olympic gods, Olympians; Zeus, Jupiter, Jove; Jupiter Fulgur or Fulminator, Jupiter Tonans, Jupiter Pluvius, Jupiter Optimus Maximus, Jupiter Fidius; Helios, Hyperion, Phaëthon; Apollo, Apollon, Phoebus, Phoebus Apollo; Mars, Ares; Mercury, Hermes; Neptune, Poseidon; Vulcan, Hephaestus; Bacchus, Dionysus; Pluto, Hades, Dis, Orcus; Saturn, Kronos or Cronus; Cupid, Amor, Eros; Hymen; Momus; Juno, Hera or Here; Demeter, Ceres; Persephone, Proserpina, Proserpine, Persephassa, Kore or Cora, Despoina; Diana, Artemis; Athena, Minerva; Nike; Venus, Aphrodite; Hestia, Vesta; Ge or Gaea or Gaia, Tellus; Ate; Mithras; Cybele, Agdistis, Great Mother, Magna Mater, Rhea, Ops.

.6 (Norse and Germanic deities) Aesir, Vanir; Balder, Bor, Bori, Bragi, Forseti, Frey or Freyr, Heimdall, Höder or Hödr, Hoenir, Loki, Nerthus or Hertha, Njorth or Njord, Odin or Woden or Wotan, Reimthursen, Thor or Donar, Tyr or Tiu, Ull or Ullr, Vali, Vitharr or Vidar, Ymir; Völund, Weland, Wayland; Wyrd; Ing; Freya or Freyja, Frigg or Frigga, Hel, Nanna, Ithunn or Idun, Sif, Sigyn.

.7 (Celtic deities) Aine, Amaethon, Angus Og, Arawn, Arianrhod, Blodenwedd, Bóann, Bodb, Brigit, Dagda, Danu, Dôn, Dylan, Epona, Goibniu, Lir, Llew Llaw Gyffes, Lug, Macha, Manannán, Morrigan, Neman.

.8 (Hindu deities) Aditi, Agni, Aryaman, Asapurna, Avalokita or Avalokitesvara, Bhaga, Bhairava, Brahma, Brihaspati, Chitragupta, Daksha, Devaki, Dharma,

Dyaus, Ganesa or Ganesha or Ganapati, Garuda, Himavat, Hanuman, Indra, Ka, Kala, Kama, Kamsa, Karttikeya, Marut, Mitra, Parjanya, Pushan, Rahu, Rhibhus, Rudra, Savitar, Shiva, Sita, Soma, Surya, Vaja, Varuna, Varuni, Vayu, Vibhu, Vishnu, Yama, Dharti Mai, Bhudevi; Devi, Bhairavi, Chandi, Durga, Gauri, Jaganmati, Kali, Parvati, Uma; Lakshmi, Sarasvati, Ushas; Asvins.

.9 (avatars of Vishnu) Buddha, Kalki, Krishna, Kurma, Matsya, Narsinh, Parshuram, Rama, Vaman, Varah; Juggernaut, Jagannath.

.10 (Egyptian deities) Anubis, Bast, Horus, Isis, Khem, Min, Neph, Nephthys, Nut, Osiris, Ptah, Ra or Amen-Ra, Set, Thoth.

.11 (Semitic deities) Adad, Adapa, Anshar, Antu, Anu, Anunaki, Ashur, Baal, Baba, Bau, Beltu, Dagon, Damkina, Dumuzi, Ea, Enki, Enkimdu, Enlil, Ereshkigal, Gibil, Girru, Gish Bar, Gishzida, Gula, Igigi, Inanna, Ishtar, Isimud, Ki, Kishar, Lahamu, Lahmu, Mama, Marduk or Bel-Merodach or Merodach, Moloch, Mylitta, Nabu or Nebo, Nammu, Namtar, Nanna, Nergal, Neti, Nina, Ningal, Ninhursag or Ninmah or Nintoo, Ninib, Ninkur, Ninlil, Ninsar, Ninshubur, Ninurta or Ningirsu, Nusku, Papsukai, Ramman, Shala, Shamash, Sin, Tammuz, Tashmit, Utnapishtim, Uttu, Utu, Zarpanit, Zubird.

.12 (animistic spirits and powers) manitou, huaca, nagual, mana, pokunt, tamanoas, wakan, zemi.

.13 (Chinese deities) Chang Fei, Chang Hsien, Chang Kuo, Ch'eng Huang, Cheng Wu, Han Chung-li, Heu Chi, Hou T'u, Hsi Wang Mu, Kuan Ti, Kuan Yin, Kuei Hsing, Lei Kung, Lung Wang, Lü Tung Pin, Ma Wang, Niu Wang, Tsai Shen, Tsao Chün, Ts'ao Kuo-ch'iu, Tung Wang Kung, T'u Ti, Wen Ch'ang, Yang Chin, Yen Lo.

.14 (Japanese deities) Amaterasu Omikami, Amatsumara, Hachiman, Hiruko, Hotei, Inari, Izanagi, Izanami, Kwannon, Ninigino-Mikoto, Susanoo.

.15 **spirit,** intelligence, supernatural being; **genius,** daemon, demon; atua; **specter** 1017; **evil spirits** 1016.

.16 **elemental,** elemental spirit; sylph, gnome, salamander, undine.

.17 **fairyfolk,** elfenfolk, shee or sidhe, **the little people** or **men,** the good folk or people, denizens of the air; **fairyland,** faerie.

.18 **fairy,** sprite, fay, fairy man or woman; **elf,**

brownie, pixie, gremlin, ouphe, hob, clu-ricaune, puca or pooka or pwca, kobold, nisse, peri; **imp, goblin** 1016.8,9; **gnome, dwarf; sylph,** sylphid; **banshee; lepre-chaun;** fairy queen; Ariel, Mab, Oberon, Titania, Béfind, Corrigan, Finnbeara.

.19 **nymph;** nymphet, nymphlin, nymph(o)– or nymphi–; **dryad,** hamadryad, wood nymph; vila or willi; tree nymph; oread, mountain nymph; limoniad, meadow or flower nymph; Napaea, glen nymph; Hyades; Pleiades, Atlantides.

.20 **water god, water spirit** or **sprite** or **nymph;** undine, nix, nixie, kelpie; naiad, limniad, fresh-water nymph; Oceanid, Nereid, sea nymph, ocean nymph, **mer-maid,** sea-maid, sea-maiden, siren; Thetis; **merman,** man fish; **Neptune,** "the old man of the sea" [Homer]; Oceanus, Po-seidon, Triton; Davy Jones, Davy.

.21 **forest god, sylvan deity,** vegetation spirit or daemon, field spirit, fertility god, corn spirit, **faun, satyr,** silenus, panisc, panis-cus, panisca; **Pan,** Faunus; Cailleac; Pria-pus; Vitharr or Vidar, the goat god.

.22 **familiar spirit,** familiar; **genius, good ge-nius,** daemon, demon, numen [L], totem; **guardian, guardian spirit, guardian angel,** angel, good angel, ministering angel, **fairy godmother, guide, control,** attendant godling or spirit, invisible helper, special providence; **tutelary** or **tutelar god** or **ge-nius** or **spirit,** tutelary; genius tutelae, ge-nius loci, genius domus, genius familiae [all L]; **household gods;** lares familiaris, lares praestites, lares compitales, lares viales, lares permarini [all L]; penates, lares and penates; ancestral spirits; manes, pitris.

.23 **Santa Claus, Santa, Saint Nicholas,** Saint Nick, Kriss Kringle, Father Christmas.

.24 **mythology,** mythicism; **legend, lore, folk-lore,** mythical lore; fairy lore, fairyism.

.25 ADJS **mythic(al), mythological,** myth-ic(o)–; **fabulous, legendary.**

.26 **divine, godlike** 1013.19,20.

.27 **fairy,** faery, **fairylike,** fairyish, fay; **sylph-ine,** sylphish, sylphy, sylphidine, sylphlike; **elfin,** elfish, elflike; gnomish, gnomelike; pixieish.

.28 **nymphic, nymphal,** nymphean, nymph-like.

1015. ANGEL, SAINT

.1 NOUNS **angel,** celestial, celestial or heav-enly being; messenger of God; **seraph,** seraphim [pl], angel of love; **cherub, cher-ubim** [pl], angel of light; principality, archangel; recording angel; **saint,** hagi-(o)–; beatified soul, canonized mortal; patron saint; martyr; redeemed or saved soul, soul in glory.

.2 **heavenly host,** host of heaven, choir invis-ible, angelic host, heavenly hierarchy, Sons of God, ministering spirits; Amesha Spentas.

.3 (celestial hierarchy of Pseudo-Dionysius) seraphim, cherubim, thrones; domina-tions or dominions, virtues, powers; prin-cipalities, archangels, angels; angelology.

.4 Azrael, angel of death, death's bright an-gel; Abdiel, Chamuel, Gabriel, Jophiel, Michael, Raphael, Uriel, Zadkiel.

.5 **Madonna, Holy Mary; Our Lady,** Notre Dame [Fr]; **Mother of God,** Dei Mater [L], Deipara, Theotokos; mater dolorosa [L], the Sorrowful Mother; Queen of Heaven, Regina Coeli [L]; Queen of An-gels, Regina Angelorum [L]; Star of the Sea, Stella Maris [L]; **the Virgin,** the Blessed Virgin, **the Virgin Mary,** the Vir-gin Mother; Sancta Virgo Virginum [L], Holy Virgin of Virgins; Virgo Sponsa Dei [L], Virgin Bride of the Lord; Virgo Clemens [L], Virgin Most Merciful; Virgo Gloriosa [L], Virgin Most Glori-ous; Virgo Potens [L], Virgin Most Pow-erful; Virgo Praedicanda [L], Virgin Most Renowned; Virgo Sapientissima [L], Virgin Most Wise; Virgo Veneranda [L], Virgin Most Venerable; hortus clu-sus [L]; Immaculate Conception; Mariol-ogy; Mariolatry.

.6 ADJS **angelic, seraphic, cherubic; heav-enly, celestial;** archangelic; **saintly, sainted,** beatified, canonized; martyred; saved, redeemed, glorified, in glory.

1016. EVIL SPIRITS

.1 NOUNS **evil spirits, demons, demonkind,** powers of darkness, spirits of the air, host of hell, hellish host, denizens of hell, in-habitants of Pandemonium, souls in hell, damned spirits, lost souls, the lost, the damned.

.2 **devil,** diable [Fr], diablo [Sp], diabolus [L], deil [Scot], Teufel [Ger], diabol(o)–.

.3 **Satan,** Satanas, **the Devil, Lucifer,** the Demon, the Fiend, the Foul Fiend, the Arch-fiend, the Wicked One, **the Evil One,** the Evil Spirit, **the Tempter,** the Adversary, the archenemy, the Common Enemy, the Old Enemy, the Devil Incar-nate, the Author or Father of Evil, the Father of Lies, the serpent, the Old Ser-pent, the Prince of the Devils, the Prince of Darkness, the Prince of this world, the Prince of the power of the air, His Satanic Majesty, the angel of the bottomless pit.

.4 [slang terms] the Deuce, the Dickens, Old Harry, Old Nick, Old Ned, Old Horny, Old Scratch, Old Gooseberry, Old Bendy, Old or Auld Clootie, Old Poker, the Old Gentleman.

.5 Beelzebub, Belial, Eblis, Azazel, Ahriman or Angra Mainyu; Mephistopheles, Mephisto; Shaitan, Sammael, Asmodeus; Abaddon, Apollyon; Lilith; Aeshma, Pisacha, Putana, Ravana.

.6 (gods of evil) Set, Typhon, Loki; Nemesis; gods of the nether world 1019.5.

.7 demon, fiend, fiend from hell, devil, satan, daeva, rakshasa, dybbuk, shedu, gyre [Scot], bad or evil spirit, unclean spirit; hellion [informal]; cacodemon, incubus, succubus; jinni, genie, genius, jinniyeh, afreet; evil genius; barghest; ghoul, lamia, Lilith, yogini, Baba Yaga, vampire, the undead.

.8 imp, pixie, sprite, elf, puck, kobold, diablotin [Fr], tokoloshe, poltergeist, gremlin, Dingbelle, Fifinella, bad fairy, bad peri; little or young devil, devilkin, deviling; erlking; Puck, Robin Goodfellow, Hob, Hobgoblin.

.9 goblin, hobgoblin, hob, ouphe.

.10 bugbear, bugaboo, bogey, bogle, boggart; booger, bugger, bug [archaic], boogerman, bogeyman, boogeyman; bête noire, fee-faw-fum, Mumbo Jumbo.

.11 Fury, avenging spirit; the Furies, the Erinyes, the Eumenides, the Dirae; Alecto, Megaera, Tisiphone.

.12 changeling, elf child.

.13 werefolk, were-animals; werewolf, lycanthrope, loup-garou [Fr]; werejaguar, jaguar-man, uturuncu; wereass, werebear, werecalf, werefox, werehyena, wereleopard, weretiger, werelion, wereboar, werecrocodile, werecat, werehare.

.14 devilishness, demonishness, fiendishness; devilship, devildom; horns, the cloven hoof, the Devil's pitchfork.

.15 Satanism, diabolism, demonism, devilry, diablerie, demonry; demonomy, demonianism; black magic; Black Mass; sorcery 1035; demonolatry, demon or devil or chthonian worship; demonomancy; demonology, diabolology or diabology, demonography, devil lore.

.16 Satanist, diabolist, demonist; demonomist, demoniast; demonologist, demonologer; demonolater, chthonian, devil worshiper, demon worshiper, Satan worshiper; sorcerer 1035.5.

.17 VERBS demonize, devilize, diabolize; possess, obsess; bewitch, bedevil 1036.10.

.18 ADJS demoniac or demoniacal, demonic(al), demonish, demonlike; devilish, devil-like; satanic, diabolic(al); hellish 1019.8; fiendish, fiendlike; ghoulish, ogreish; inhuman.

.19 impish, puckish, elfish, elvish; mischievous 738.6.

1017. SPECTER

.1 NOUNS specter, ghost, spectral ghost, spook [informal], phantom, phantasm, phantasma, wraith, shade, shadow, apparition, appearance, presence, shape, form, eidolon, idolum, revenant, larva; spirit, pneumat(o)–, psych(o)–, thymo–; sprite, shrouded spirit, disembodied spirit, departed spirit, wandering soul, soul of the dead, dybbuk; oni; Masan; astral spirit, astral; unsubstantiality, immateriality, incorporeal, incorporeity, incorporeal being or entity; walking dead man, zombie; duppy; vision, theophany; materialization; haunt or hant [both dial]; banshee; poltergeist; control, guide; manes, lemures; grateful dead.

.2 White Lady, White Lady of Avenel [Scot], White Ladies of Normandy; Brocken specter; Wild Hunt; Flying Dutchman.

.3 double, etheric double or self, co-walker, Doppelgänger [Ger], doubleganger, fetch, wraith.

.4 eeriness, ghostliness, weirdness, uncanniness, spookiness [informal].

.5 possession, obsession, spirit control.

.6 VERBS haunt, hant [dial], spook [informal]; possess, obsess.

.7 ADJS spectral, specterlike; ghostly, ghostish, ghosty, ghostlike; spiritual, psychic(al); phantomlike, phantom, phantomic(al), phantasmal, phantasmic, wraithlike, wraithy, shadowy; etheric, ectoplasmic, astral, ethereal 4.6; incorporeal 377.7; supernatural 85.15.

.8 disembodied, discarnate, decarnate, decarnated.

.9 weird, eerie, eldritch, uncanny, unearthly, macabre; spooky or spookish [both informal].

.10 haunted, hanted [dial], spooked or spooky [both informal], spirit-haunted, ghost-haunted, specter-haunted; possessed, obsessed, ghost-ridden.

1018. HEAVEN

(abode of the deity and blessed dead)

.1 NOUNS Heaven, Paradise, glory, eternity, kingdom come [informal], a better place, happy hunting ground, Land of the Leal [Scot], the happy land, the Promised Land, the world above, otherworld, better world, heaven above, high heaven, eternal home, abode of the blessed, inheritance of the saints in light, realm of light; Beulah, Beulah Land, Land of Beulah; kingdom of heaven, God's kingdom, heavenly kingdom, kingdom of God, kingdom of glory; God's presence, presence of God; Abraham's bosom.

.2 "my Father's house" [Bible], "God's residence" [Emily Dickinson], "mansions in the sky" [Isaac Watts], "the bosom of our rest" [Cardinal Newman], "the treasury of everlasting joy" [Shakespeare], "the great world of light, that lies behind all human destinies" [Longfellow].

.3 the hereafter, afterworld, afterlife 121.2.

.4 Holy City, Zion, New Jerusalem, Heavenly or Celestial City, City Celestial, Heavenly City of God, City of God, *Civitas Dei* [L], "heaven's high city" [Francis Quarles].

.5 heaven of heavens, seventh heaven, the empyrean, throne of God, God's throne, celestial throne, the great white throne.

.6 (Christian Science) bliss, harmony, spirituality, the reign of Spirit, the atmosphere of Soul.

.7 (Mormon) celestial kingdom, terrestrial kingdom, telestial kingdom.

.8 (Mohammedan) Alfardaws, Assama; Falak al aflak.

.9 (Hindu, Buddhist, and Theosophical) nirvana; Buddha-field; devaloka, land of the gods; kamavachara, kamaloka; devachan.

.10 (mythological) Olympus, Mount Olympus; Elysium, Elysian fields; fields of Aalu; Islands or Isles of the Blessed, Happy Isles, Fortunate Isles or Islands; Avalon; garden of the Gods, garden of the Hesperides, Bower of Bliss; Tir-na-n'Og, Annwfn.

.11 (Norse) Valhalla, Asgard, Fensalir, Glathsheim, Vingolf, Valaskjalf, Hlithskjalf, Thruthvang or Thruthheim, Bilskirnir, Ydalir, Sökkvabekk, Breithablik, Folkvang, Sessrymnir, Noatun, Thrymheim, Glitnir, Himinbjorg, Vithi.

.12 (removal to heaven) apotheosis, resurrection, translation, gathering, ascension, the Ascension; assumption, the Assumption; removal to Abraham's bosom.

.13 ADJS heavenly, heavenish; paradisal, paradisaic(al), paradisiac(al), paradisic(al); celestial, supernal, ethereal; unearthly, unworldly; otherworldly, extraterrestrial, extramundane, transmundane, transcendental; Elysian, Olympian; blessed, beatified, beatific(al), glorified, in glory; from on high.

.14 ADVS celestially, paradisally, supernally, ethereally; in heaven, in Abraham's bosom, *in sinu Abraham* [L], on high, among the blest, in glory.

1019. HELL

.1 NOUNS hell, Hades, Sheol, Gehenna, Tophet, Abaddon, Naraka, jahannan, avichi, perdition, Pandemonium, inferno, the pit, the bottomless pit, the abyss, "a vast, unbottom'd, boundless pit" [Robert Burns], nether world, lower world, underworld, infernal regions, abode or world of the dead, abode of the damned, place of torment, the grave, shades below; purgatory; limbo.

.2 hellfire, fire and brimstone, lake of fire and brimstone, everlasting fire or torment, "the fire that never shall be quenched" [Bible].

.3 (mythological) Hades, Orcus, Tartarus, Avernus, Acheron, pit of Acheron; Amenti, Aralu; Hel, Niflhel, Niflheim, Naströnd.

.4 (rivers of Hades) Styx, Stygian creek; Acheron, River of Woe; Cocytus, River of Wailing; Phlegethon, Pyriphlegethon, River of Fire; Lethe, River of Forgetfulness.

.5 (deities of the nether world) Pluto, Orcus, Hades or Aides or Aidoneus, Dis or Dis pater, Rhadamanthus, Erebus, Charon, Cerberus, Minos; Osiris; Persephone, Proserpine, Proserpina, Persephassa, Despoina, Kore or Cora; Hel, Loki; Satan 1016.3.

.6 VERBS damn, doom, send or consign to hell, cast into hell, doom to perdition, condemn to hell or eternal punishment.

.7 go to hell, be damned, go the other way [informal].

.8 ADJS hellish, infernal, sulfurous, chthonic, chthonian; pandemonic, pandemoniac; devilish 1016.18; Plutonic, Plutonian; Tartarean; Stygian; Lethean; Acherontic; purgatorial, hellborn.

.9 ADVS hellishly, infernally, in hell, in hellfire, below, in torment.

1020. RELIGIONS, CULTS, SECTS

.1 NOUNS **religion,** religio–; religious belief or faith, **belief, faith,** teaching, doctrine, creed, credo, theology 1023, orthodoxy 1024; system of beliefs; tradition.

.2 **cult, ism;** cultism; **mystique.**

.3 **sect** 1020.32, sectarism, religious order, **denomination, persuasion,** faction, **church,** communion, community, group, fellowship, affiliation, order, school, party, society, body, organization; branch, variety, version, segment; offshoot; **schism,** division.

.4 **sectarianism,** sectarism, **denominationalism,** partisanism, the clash of creeds; schismatism; syncretism, eclecticism.

.5 **theism; monotheism; polytheism,** multitheism, myriotheism; **ditheism,** dyotheism, dualism; **tritheism;** tetratheism; **pantheism,** cosmotheism, theopantism, acosmism; physitheism, psychotheism, animotheism; physicomorphism; hylotheism; anthropotheism, anthropomorphism; anthropolatry; allotheism; monolatry, henotheism; autotheism; zootheism, theriotheism; **deism.**

.6 **Christianity,** Christianism, Christendom; Latin *or* Roman *or* Western Christianity; Eastern *or* Orthodox Christianity; Protestant Christianity; Judeo-Christian religion *or* tradition *or* belief.

.7 **Catholicism,** Catholicity; **Roman Catholicism,** Romanism, Rome; papalism; popery, popeism, papism, papistry [all derog]; ultramontanism; Catholic Church, **Roman Catholic Church,** Church of Rome; Eastern Rites, Uniate Rites, Uniatism, Alexandrian *or* Antiochian *or* Byzantine Rite.

.8 Orthodoxy; **Eastern Orthodox Church, Holy Orthodox Catholic Apostolic Church,** Greek Orthodox Church, Russian Orthodox Church; patriarchate of Constantinople, patriarchate of Antioch, patriarchate of Alexandria, patriarchate of Jerusalem.

.9 **Protestantism,** Reform, Reformationism; Evangelicalism; Zwinglianism; dissent 522; apostasy 628.2; new theology.

.10 **Anglicanism;** High-Churchism, Low-Churchism; Anglo-Catholicism; Church of England, Established Church; High Church, Low Church; Broad Church, Free Church.

.11 **Judaism;** Hebraism, Hebrewism; Israelitism; Orthodox Judaism, Conservative Judaism, Reform Judaism, Reconstruction-ism; Hasidism; rabbinism, Talmudism; Pharisaism; Sadduceeism; Karaism *or* Karaitism.

.12 **Islam, Muhammadanism, Mohammedanism, Muslimism, Moslemism,** Islamism; Sufism, Wahabiism, Sunnism, Shiism; Black Muslimism.

.13 **Christian Science;** New Thought, Higher Thought, Practical Christianity, Mental Science, Divine Science Church.

.14 **religionist,** religioner; **believer** 1028.4; cultist, ist.

.15 **theist; monotheist; polytheist,** multitheist, myriotheist; **ditheist,** dualist; tritheist; tetratheist; **pantheist,** cosmotheist; psychotheist; physitheist; hylotheist; anthropotheist; anthropolater; allotheist; henotheist; autotheist; zootheist, theriotheist; **deist.**

.16 **Christian,** Nazarene, Nazarite.

.17 **sectarian,** sectary, **denominationalist,** factionist, schismatic.

.18 **Catholic,** Roman Catholic, RC [informal], Romanist, papist [derog]; ultramontane; Eastern-Rite Christian, Uniate.

.19 **Protestant,** non-Catholic, Reformed believer, Reformationist, Evangelical; Zwinglian; dissenter 522.3; apostate 628.5.

.20 **Jew, Hebrew,** Judaist, Israelite; Orthodox *or* Conservative *or* Reform Jew, Reconstructionist; Hasid; Rabbinist, Talmudist; Pharisee; Sadducee; Karaite.

.21 **Mormon,** Latter-day Saint, Josephite [informal].

.22 **Muslim, Muhammadan** *or* **Mohammedan** [both derog], Mussulman, Moslem, Islamite; Shiite, Shia, Sectary; Motazilite, Sunnite, Wahabi, Sufi; dervish; abdal; Black Muslim.

.23 **Christian Scientist,** Christian Science Practitioner.

.24 ADJS **religious, theistic; monotheistic; polytheistic,** ditheistic, tritheistic; **pantheistic,** cosmotheistic; physicomorphic; anthropomorphic, anthropotheistic; **deistic.**

.25 **sectarian,** sectary, **denominational,** schismatic(al).

.26 **nonsectarian, undenominational, nondenominational;** interdenominational.

.27 **Protestant,** non-Catholic, Reformed, Reformationist, Evangelical; Lutheran, Calvinist, Calvinistic, Zwinglian; dissentient 522.6; apostate 628.11.

.28 **Catholic; Roman Catholic,** RC [informal], Roman; Romish, popish, papish, papist, papistic(al) [all derog]; ultramontane.

.29 **Jewish, Hebrew,** Judaical, Israelite, Israelitic, Israelitish; Orthodox, Conservative, Reform, Reconstructionist; Hasidic.

.30 **Muslim, Islamic,** Muhammadan, Mohammedan, Moslem, Islamitic, Islamistic.

.31 (Oriental) Buddhist, Buddhistic; Brahmanic, Brahmanistic; Vedic, Vedantic; Confucian, Confucianist; Taoist, Taoistic, Shintoist, Shintoistic; Zoroastrian, Zarathustrian, Parsee.

.32 **religions and sects**

anthroposophy	Parsiism, Parsism
Babism, Babi	Reconstructionism
Bahaism	Reform Judaism
Brahmanism	reincarnationism
Brahmoism	Sabaeanism
Buddhism	Saivism
Ch'an Buddhism	Shaivite Hinduism
Chen Yen Buddhism	Shiite Muslimism
Ching-t'u Buddhism	Shin Buddhism
Christianity 1020.6,33	Shingon Buddhism
Confucianism	Shinto, Shintoism
Conservative Judaism	Sikhism
Dakshincharin Hindu-	Soka Gakkai Bud-
ism	dhism
Eleusinianism	Sufism
Ethical Culture	Taoism
Gnosticism	Tendai Buddhism
gymnosophy	Theosophy
Hinduism	Theravada or Hina-
Jainism	yana Buddhism
Jodo Buddhism	T'ien-t'ai Buddhism
Judaism 1020.11	Unitarianism
Lamaism	Vaishnavite Hinduism
Lingayat Hinduism	Vajrayana Buddhism
Magianism	Vamacharin Hindu-
Mahayana Buddhism	ism
Mandaeism	Vedanta, Vedantism
Mithraism	Wahabiism
Muhammadanism	Yoga, Yogism
1020.12	Zen, Zen Buddhism
Nichiren Buddhism	Zoroastrianism, Zo-
Orphism	roastrism
Orthodox Judaism	

.33 **Christian denominations**

Adventism, Second	Laudism, Laudianism
Adventism	Liberal Catholicism
Amish	Lutheranism
Anabaptism	Mennonitism
Anglicanism 1020.10	Methodism
Anglo-Catholicism	Moral Rearmament
antinomianism	Mormonism
Arianism	New Thought
Athanasianism	Origenism
Boehmenism	Orthodox Christianity
Calvinism	Oxford Movement
Catholicism 1020.7	Practical Christianity
Christian Science	Presbyterianism
1020.13	Puritanism
Congregationalism	Puseyism
Eastern Orthodox	Quakerism
Christianity	quietism
Episcopalianism	Roman Catholicism
Erastianism	Rosicrucianism
homoiousianism	Sabellianism
homoousianism	Salvation Army
Jansenism	Socinianism
latitudinarianism	Stundism

Swedenborgianism	Unitarianism
Tractarianism	Universalism
Trinitarianism	Wesleyanism, Wesley-
Ubiquitarianism	ism
Uniatism	

.34 **religionists**

anthroposophist	Magian, Magus
Babist	Mandaean
Brahman, Brahmanist	Muhammadan
Buddhist	1020.22
Christian 1020.16,35	Parsee
Confucianist	reincarnationist
Gentoo	Sabaean
Gheber	Shintoist
Gnostic	Sikh
gymnosophist	Taoist
Hindu	Theosophist
Jain, Jaina	Vedantist
Jew 1020.20	Yogi, Yogin, Yogist
Lamaist, Lamaite	Zoroastrian

.35 **Christian sectarians**

Adventist, Second Ad-	Huguenot
ventist	Independent
Amish, Amish Menno-	Irvingite
nite	Jacobite
Anabaptist	Jansenist
Anglican	Jehovah's Witness
Anglo-Catholic	Jovinianist
antinomian	Latitudinarian
Arian	Latter-day Saint
Athanasian	Laudist, Laudian
Baptist	Liberal Catholic
Bible Christian	Low-Churchman
Boehmenist	Lutheran
Bryanite	Mennonite
Calvinist	Methodist
Campbellite	Mormon
Catholic	Nestorian
Christadelphian	Presbyterian
Christian Scientist	Protestant 1020.19
1020.23	Protestant Episcopal
Churchman	Puritan
Congregationalist	Puseyite
Coptic Christian	Quaker
Davidist	quietist
Disciple of Christ	Restitutionist
Doukhobor	Roman Catholic
Dunker	Rosicrucian
Ebionite	Russian Orthodox
Episcopalian	Sandemanian
Erastian	Seventh-Day Adven-
Eusebian	tist
Evangelical Congrega-	Shaker
tionalist	Stundist
Familist	Swedenborgian
Friend	Tractarian
German Baptist	Trinitarian
Gideon	Ubiquitarian
Glassite	Uniate
Greek Orthodox	Unitarian
High-Churchman	Universalist
Homoiousian	Wesleyan
Homoousian	

1021. SCRIPTURE

.1 NOUNS **scripture, scriptures, sacred writings, Bible;** canonical writings or books, sacred canon.

.2 **Bible, Holy Bible,** biblic(o)–; **Scripture,**

the Scriptures, Holy Scripture, Holy Writ, the Book, the Good Book, the Book of Books, the Word, the Word of God; Vulgate, Septuagint, Douay Bible, Authorized or King James Version, Revised Version, American Revised Version; Revised Standard Version; Jerusalem Bible; Testament; canon.

.3 Old Testament, Tenach; Hexateuch, Octateuch; Pentateuch, Chumash, Five Books of Moses, Torah, the Law, the Jewish or Mosaic Law, Law of Moses; the Prophets, Nebiim, Major or Minor Prophets; the Writings, Hagiographa, Ketubim; Apocrypha, noncanonical writings.

.4 New Testament; Gospels, Evangels, the Gospel, Good News, Good or Glad Tidings; Synoptic Gospels, Epistles, Pauline Epistles, Catholic Epistles, Johannine Epistles; Acts, Acts of the Apostles; Apocalypse, Revelation.

.5 Talmud, Mishnah, Gemara; Masorah.

.6 Koran; Avesta, Zend-Avesta; Granth, Adigranth; Tripitaka, agama; Tao Tê Ching; Analects of Confucius; the Eddas; Arcana Caelestia; Book of Mormon; Science and Health with Key to the Scriptures.

.7 (Hindu) the Vedas, Veda, Rig-Veda, Yajur-Veda, Sama-Veda, Atharva-Veda; Brahmana, Upanishad, Aranyaka; Samhita; shastra, sruti, smriti, purana, tantra; Bhagavad-Gita.

.8 (Buddhist) Vinaya Pitaka, Sutta Pitaka, Abhidamma Pitaka; Dhammapada, Jataka; The Diamond-Cutter, The Lotus of the True Law, Prajna-Paramita Sutra, Pure Land Sutras.

.9 revelation, divine revelation; inspiration, afflatus, divine inspiration; theopneusty, theopneustia; theophany, theophania, epiphany; direct or immediate communication, mystical experience, mysticism, direct intuition, mystical intuition; prophecy, prophetic revelation, apocalypse.

.10 ADJS scriptural, Biblical, Old-Testament, New-Testament, Gospel, Mosaic, Yahwist, Yahwistic, Elohist, revealed, revelational, prophetic, apocalyptic(al); inspired, theopneustic; evangelic(al), evangelistic, gospel; apostolic(al); textual, textuary; canonical.

.11 Talmudic, Mishnaic, Gemaric, Masoretic; rabbinic.

.12 epiphanic, mystic(al).

.13 Koranic; Avestan; Eddic; Mormon.

.14 Vedic; tantrist.

1022. PROPHETS, RELIGIOUS FOUNDERS

.1 NOUNS prophet 543.4, vates sacer [L]; Abraham, Amos, Daniel, Ezekiel, Habakkuk, Haggai, Hosea, Isaac, Isaiah, Jacob, Jeremiah, Joel, Jonah, Joseph, Joshua, Malachi, Micah, Moses, Nahum, Obadiah, Samuel, Zechariah, Zephaniah.

.2 (Christian founders) evangelist, apostle, disciple, saint; Matthew, Mark, Luke, John; Paul; Peter; the Fathers, Apostolic Fathers, ante-Nicene Fathers, Primitive Fathers; Barnabas, Clement of Rome, Hermas, Ignatius, Papias, Polycarp; Apologetic Fathers, Justin Martyr, Theophilus, Irenaeus, Clement of Alexandria, Tertullian, Origen, Cyprian of Carthage, Dionysius of Alexandria, Gregory Thaumaturgus; post-Nicene Fathers, Eusebius of Caesarea, Athanasius, Basil, Ephrem Syrus, Cyril of Jerusalem, Gregory of Nazianzus, Gregory of Nyssa, Epiphanius of Salamis, John Chrysostom, Cyril of Alexandria, Lactantius Firmianus, Hilary of Poitiers, Ambrose of Milan, Jerome, Augustine of Hippo.

.3 Martin Luther, John Calvin, John Wycliffe, Jan Hus, John Wesley, John Knox, George Fox (Protestant reformers); Swedenborg (Church of the New Jerusalem); Mary Baker Eddy (Christian Science); Joseph Smith (Church of Jesus Christ of Latter-day Saints).

.4 Buddha, Gautama Buddha (Buddhism); Mahavira or Vardhamana or Jina (Jainism); Mirza Ali Muhammad of Shiraz or the Bab (Babism); Muhammad or Mohammed (Islam); Confucius (Confucianism); Lao-tzu (Taoism); Zoroaster or Zarathustra (Zoroastrianism); Nanak (Sikhism); Ram Mohan Roy (Brahmo-Samaj).

1023. THEOLOGY

.1 NOUNS theology, religion, divinity; theologism; doctrinism, doctrinalism, doctrinal theology; canonics; dogmatics, dogmatic theology; systematic theology, systematics; philosophical theology; dialogical theology; patristic theology, patristics; physicotheology; natural or rational theology; hierology, hagiology; hierography, hagiography; soteriology, Christology, logos theology, logos Christology; apologetics; eschatology; theological hermeneutics; secularism; rationalism; school theology, scholastic theology; Mercersburg theology; crisis theology, neoorthodox theology, neoorthodoxy; existential theology; phenomenological theology; Buddhology; Mariology, Mariolatry.

.2 **doctrine, dogma** 501.2; **creed,** credo; credenda, articles of religion or faith; Apostles' Creed, Nicene Creed, Athanasian Creed; Catechism.

.3 **theologian,** theologist, theologizer, theologer, theologician; divine; scholastic, schoolman; theological or divinity student, theological, theologue; canonist.

.4 ADJS **theological,** the(o)–, **religious,** religio–, **divine;** doctrinal, doctrinary; canonic(al); physicotheological; Buddhological; Mariological.

1024. ORTHODOXY

.1 NOUNS **orthodoxy,** orthodoxism; orthodoxness, orthodoxicalness; **soundness,** soundness of doctrine, rightness, right belief or doctrine; **authoritativeness,** authenticity, canonicalness, canonicity; traditionalism; the truth, religious truth, gospel truth.

.2 **the faith, true faith,** apostolic faith, primitive faith, "the faith once delivered unto the saints" [Bible]; old-time religion, faith of our fathers.

.3 **the Church, the true church,** Holy Church, Church of Christ, the Bride of the Lamb, body of Christ, temple of the Holy Ghost, body of Christians, members in Christ, disciples or followers of Christ; apostolic church; universal church, the church universal; church visible, church invisible; church militant, church triumphant.

.4 **true believer,** orthodox Christian; Sunni Muslim; Orthodox Jew; orthodox, orthodoxist; textualist, textuary; canonist; fundamentalist; the orthodox.

.5 **strictness,** strict interpretation, scripturalism, evangelicalism; hyperorthodoxy, puritanism, puritanicalness, purism; staunchness; straitlacedness, stiff-neckedness, hideboundness; **bigotry** 527.1; **dogmatism** 513.6; **fundamentalism,** literalism, precisianism; bibliolatry; Sabbatarianism; sabbatism.

.6 **bigot** 527.5; **dogmatist** 513.7.

.7 ADJS **orthodox,** orthodoxical; of the faith, of the true faith; **sound,** firm, faithful, true, true-blue; **Christian; evangelical; scriptural,** canonical; traditional, traditionalistic; literal, textual; standard, customary, conventional; **authoritative,** au-

thentic, accepted, received, approved; correct, right, proper.

.8 **strict,** scripturalistic, evangelical; hyperorthodox, puritanical, purist or puristic, straitlaced; staunch; hidebound, creedbound; **bigoted** 527.10; **dogmatic** 513.22; **fundamentalist,** precisianist or precisianistic, literalist or literalistic; Sabbatarian.

1025. UNORTHODOXY

.1 NOUNS **unorthodoxy, heterodoxy;** unorthodoxness, **unsoundness,** un-Scripturality; **unauthoritativeness,** unauthenticity, uncanonicalness, uncanonicity; **nonconformity** 83.

.2 **heresy, false doctrine, misbelief; fallacy, error** 518; antinomianism, Arianism, Donatism, Ebionitism, emanatism, Erastianism, Gnosticism, hylotheism, Jansenism, Jovinianism, Manichaeism or Manichaeanism, pantheism, Sabellianism, Montanism, Monophysitism or Monophysism, Pelagianism; Albigensianism, Waldensianism, Catharism; Wyclifism, Lollardy.

.3 **infidelity,** infidelism; unchristianity; gentilism; **atheism, unbelief** 1031.5.

.4 **paganism, heathenism;** paganry, heathenry; pagandom, heathendom; pagano-Christianism; allotheism; animism, animatism; idolatry 1033.

.5 **heretic, misbeliever;** heresiarch; nonconformist 83.3; antinomian, Arian, Donatist, Ebionite, emanationist, Erastian, Gnostic, hylotheist, Jansenist, Jovinian, Manichaean, pantheist, Sabellian, Montanist, Monophysite, Pelagian; Albigensian, Waldensian, Cathar; Wyclifite, Lollard.

.6 **gentile;** non-Christian; **non-Jew,** goy, goyim [pl], *shegets* [Yid masc], *shiksa* [Yid fem]; non-Muslim, non-Moslem, non-Muhammadan, non-Mohammedan, *giaour* [Turk], kaffir; zendik, zendician, zendikite; non-Mormon; infidel; unbeliever 1031.11.

.7 **pagan, heathen;** allotheist; animist; idolater 1033.4.

.8 VERBS **misbelieve, err,** stray, deviate, wander, go astray, go wrong, fall into error; be wrong, be mistaken, be in error; serve Mammon.

.9 ADJS **unorthodox,** nonorthodox, **heterodox, heretical; unsound; unscriptural,** uncanonical, apocryphal; **unauthoritative,** unauthentic, unaccepted, unreceived, unapproved; **fallacious,** erroneous 518.16; antinomian, Arian, Donatist, Ebionitist, emanationist, Erastian, Gnostic, hylotheist or hylotheistic, Jansenist or Jansenistic, Jovinianist or Jovinianistic, Manichaean, pantheist or pantheistic, Sabellian, Montanist or Montanistic, Monophysite or Monophysitic, Pelagian; Albigensian, Waldensian, Catharist; Wyclifite, Lollard.

.10 **infidel,** infidelic, misbelieving; **atheistic,** unbelieving 1031.19; **unchristian,** non-Christian; gentile, non-Jewish, goyish, uncircumcised; non-Muslim, non-Muhammadan, non-Mohammedan, non-Moslem, non-Islamic; non-Mormon.

.11 **pagan, paganish,** paganistic; **heathen, heathenish;** pagano-Christian; allotheistic; animist, animistic; idolatrous 1033.7.

1026. SANCTITY

(sacred quality)

.1 NOUNS **sanctity,** sanctitude; **sacredness, holiness,** hallowedness, numinousness; sacrosanctness, sacrosanctity; heavenliness, divineness; venerableness, **venerability, blessedness;** awesomeness, awfulness; inviolableness, **inviolability;** ineffability, unutterability, unspeakability, inexpressibility, inenarrability; godliness 1028.2; odor of sanctity.

.2 **the sacred,** the holy, the holy of holies, the numinous, the ineffable, the unutterable, the unspeakable, the inexpressible, the inenarrable.

.3 **sanctification, hallowing; purification;** beatification, beatitude, blessing; **glorification,** exaltation; **consecration,** dedication, devotion, setting apart; sainting, canonization, enshrinement; **sainthood, blessedness; grace,** state of grace; justification, justification by faith, justification by works.

.4 **redemption,** redeemedness, **salvation,** conversion, regeneration, new life, reformation, adoption; rebirth, new birth, second birth; circumcision, spiritual purification or cleansing.

.5 VERBS **sanctify, hallow; purify,** cleanse, wash one's sins away; **bless,** beatify; **glorify,** exalt; **consecrate,** dedicate, devote, set apart; saint, canonize, enshrine.

.6 **redeem,** regenerate, reform, convert, save, give salvation.

.7 ADJS **sacred,** sacr(o)–, **holy,** hier(o)–, hagi(o)–, numinous, **sacrosanct, religious, spiritual,** heavenly, divine; **venerable,** awesome, awful; inviolable, **inviolate,** untouchable; **ineffable,** unutterable, unspeakable, inexpressible, inenarrable.

.8 **sanctified, hallowed; blessed,** beatified; consecrated, devoted, dedicated, set apart; **saintly,** sainted, canonized.

.9 **redeemed, saved,** converted, regenerated, regenerate, justified, reborn, born again, renewed; circumcised, spiritually purified or cleansed.

1027. UNSANCTITY

.1 NOUNS **unsanctity,** unsanctitude; **unsacredness, unholiness,** unhallowedness, unblessedness; **profanity,** profaneness; unregenerateness, reprobation.

.2 **the profane,** the unholy; the temporal, the secular, the worldly, the fleshly, the mundane.

.3 ADJS **unsacred,** nonsacred, **unholy,** unhallowed, unsanctified, unblessed; **profane,** secular, temporal, worldly, fleshly, mundane; unregenerate, reprobate.

1028. PIETY

.1 NOUNS **piety,** piousness, pietism; **religion, faith; religiousness,** religionism, religiousmindedness; theism; **devoutness,** devotion, devotedness, worship, worshipfulness, prayerfulness, cultism; faithfulness, dutifulness, observance, churchgoing, conformity 82; **reverence,** veneration; love of God, adoration.

.2 **godliness,** godlikeness; fear of God; **sanctity,** sanctitude; odor of sanctity, beauty of holiness; **righteousness, holiness,** goodness; **spirituality,** spiritual-mindedness, holy-mindedness, heavenly-mindedness, godly-mindedness; **purity,** pureness, pureheartedness, pureness of heart; **saintliness,** saintlikeness; saintship, sainthood; **Christianity, Christliness,** Christlikeness; angelicalness, seraphicalness; heavenliness; **unworldliness,** unearthliness, otherworldliness.

.3 **zeal,** zealousness, zealotry, zealotism; **revival,** revivalism; pentecostalism, charismatic movement, charismatic renewal, baptism in the spirit; charismatic gift, gift of tongues, glossolalia; **overreligiousness,** overpiousness, overrighteousness, **overzealousness,** overdevoutness; bibliolatry; **fanaticism** 473.11; sanctimony 1029.

.4 **believer,** truster, accepter, receiver, –arian; God-fearing man, pietist, religionist, saint, theist; **devotee,** devotionalist, votary, **zealot; Christian,** good Christian; **churchgoer,** churchman, churchite; pillar of the church; communicant, daily communicant; **convert,** proselyte, neophyte, catechumen; **disciple,** follower; **fanatic** 473.17.

.5 **the believing, the faithful,** the righteous, the good; the elect, the chosen, the saved; the children of God, the children of light; Christendom.

.6 VERBS **be pious, be religious; have faith,** trust in God, love God, fear God, **believe** 501.10; keep the faith, fight the good fight, let one's light shine, praise and glorify God, walk humbly with one's God.

.7 **be converted, get religion** [informal], receive or accept Christ, stand up for Jesus, be washed in the blood of the Lamb.

.8 ADJS **pious,** pietistic; **religious,** religious-minded; theistic; **devout,** devoted, worshipful, prayerful, cultish, cultist, cultistic; **reverent,** reverential, venerative, venerational, adoring, solemn; faithful, dutiful; believing 501.21; Christian, Christianly, Christianlike.

.9 **godly, godlike; God-fearing; righteous, holy,** good; **spiritual,** spiritual-minded, holy-minded, godly-minded, heavenly-minded; **pure,** purehearted, pure in heart; **saintly,** saintlike; **Christly, Christlike; angelic(al),** seraphic(al); heavenly; **unworldly,** unearthly, otherworldly, not of the earth, not of this world.

.10 **regenerate,** regenerated, **converted, redeemed, saved,** reborn; sanctified 1026.8.

.11 **zealous,** zealotic; **overreligious,** ultrareligious, overpious, overrighteous, **overzealous,** overdevout; **fanatical** 473.32; sanctimonious 1029.5.

1029. SANCTIMONY

.1 NOUNS **sanctimony, sanctimoniousness; pietism, piety, piousness,** pietisticalness, false piety; religionism, religiosity; **self-righteousness;** goodiness or goody-goodiness [both informal]; pharisaism, pharisaicalness; Tartuffery, Tartuffism; **falseness, insincerity, hypocrisy** 616.6; affectation 903; **cant,** mummery, snivel, snuffle; unction, unctuousness, oiliness, mealy-mouthedness.

.2 **lip service, mouth honor,** lip homage, lip worship, lip devotion, lip praise, lip reverence; formalism, solemn mockery; BOMFOG, brotherhood of man and fatherhood of God.

.3 **pietist,** religionist, **hypocrite,** religious hypocrite, canting hypocrite, pious fraud, religious or spiritual humbug, whited sepulcher, **pharisee,** Holy Willie [Robert Burns], "a saint abroad and a devil at home" [Bunyan]; **canter,** ranter, snuffler,

sniveler; dissembler, dissimulator; affecter, poser 903.7,8; **lip server,** lip worshiper, formalist; Pharisee, scribes and Pharisees; Tartuffe, Pecksniff, Mawworm, Joseph Surface.

.4 VERBS be sanctimonious, be hypocritical 616.23; cant, snuffle, snivel; give mouth honor, render lip service.

.5 ADJS **sanctimonious,** sanctified, **pious, pietistic(al),** self-righteous, pharisaic(al), holier-than-thou; goody or goody-goody [both informal]; **false, insincere, hypocritical** 616.25–34; affected 903.15; Tartuffish, Tartuffian; canting, sniveling, unctuous, mealymouthed.

1030. IMPIETY

.1 NOUNS **impiety, impiousness; irreverence,** undutifulness; desertion, renegadism, apostasy, recreancy; backsliding, recidivism, lapse, fall or lapse from grace; **atheism, irreligion** 1031.1.

.2 **sacrilege, blasphemy,** impiety; **profanity,** profaneness; sacrilegiousness, blasphemousness; **desecration, profanation.**

.3 sacrilegist, **blasphemer,** Sabbath-breaker; deserter, renegade, apostate, recreant; backslider, recidivist; **atheist,** unbeliever 1031.11.

.4 VERBS **desecrate, profane,** dishonor, unhallow, commit sacrilege.

.5 **blaspheme;** vilify, abuse 972.7; curse, swear 972.6; take in vain.

.6 ADJS **impious, irreverent,** undutiful; **profane,** profanatory; **sacrilegious, blasphemous;** renegade, apostate, recreant, backsliding, recidivist or recidivistic, lapsed, fallen, lapsed or fallen from grace; atheistic, **irreligious** 1031.17.

1031. NONRELIGIOUSNESS

.1 NOUNS **nonreligiousness, unreligiousness; undevoutness;** indevoutness, indevotion, undutifulness, nonobservance; adiaphorism, indifferentism, Laodiceanism, lukewarm piety; indifference 636.

.2 **worldliness,** earthliness, earthiness, mundaneness; **unspirituality,** carnality; worldly-mindedness, earthly-mindedness, carnal-mindedness; materialism, Philistinism.

.3 **ungodliness,** godlessness, **unrighteousness, irreligion, unholiness,** unsaintliness, unangelicalness; unchristianliness, un-Christliness; impiety 1030; **wickedness, sinfulness** 981.4.

.4 **unregeneracy,** unredeemedness, **reprobacy,** gracelessness, shriftlessness.

.5 **unbelief, disbelief** 503.1; infidelity, infidelism, faithlessness; **atheism;** nullifidianism, minimifidianism; secularism.

.6 **agnosticism; skepticism, doubt, incredulity,** Pyrrhonism, Humism; scoffing 967.1.

.7 **freethinking,** free thought, **latitudinarianism; humanism,** secular humanism.

.8 **antireligion;** antichristianism, antichristianity; antiscripturism.

.9 **iconoclasm,** iconoclasticism, image breaking.

.10 **irreligionist; worldling,** earthling; **materialist** 376.6; iconoclast, idoloclast; antichristian, antichrist.

.11 **unbeliever, disbeliever,** nonbeliever; **atheist, infidel, pagan, heathen;** nullifidian, minimifidian; secularist; **gentile** 1025.6.

.12 **agnostic; skeptic, doubter,** dubitante, **doubting Thomas,** scoffer, Pyrrhonist, Humist.

.13 **freethinker, latitudinarian,** *esprit fort* [Fr]; humanist, secular humanist.

.14 VERBS **disbelieve, doubt** 503.5,6; **scoff** 967.9.

.15 ADJS **nonreligious, unreligious; undevout,** indevout, indevotional, undutiful, nonobservant; adiamorphic, indifferentist *or* indifferentistic, Laodicean, lukewarm, indifferent 636.6.

.16 **worldly, earthly,** earthy, terrestrial, **mundane,** temporal; **unspiritual, profane,** carnal, secular; worldly minded, earthly minded, carnal-minded; **materialistic,** material, Philistine.

.17 **ungodly, godless, irreligious, unrighteous, unholy,** unsaintly, unangelic(al); **unchristian,** un-Christly; **impious** 1030.6; **wicked, sinful** 981.16.

.18 **unregenerate,** unredeemed, **unconverted,** godless, reprobate, graceless, shriftless, **lost, damned.**

.19 **unbelieving, disbelieving, faithless; infidel,** infidelic; **pagan, heathen; atheistic,** atheist; nullifidian, minimifidian; unchristian.

.20 **agnostic; skeptic(al), doubtful, dubious, incredulous,** Humean, Pyrrhonic.

.21 **freethinking, latitudinarian.**

.22 **antireligious;** antichristian; antiscriptural; iconoclastic.

1032. WORSHIP

.1 NOUNS **worship,** worshiping, **adoration, devotion, homage, veneration, reverence,** "transcendent wonder" [Carlyle]; cult, cultus, cultism; latria, dulia, hyperdulia; falling down and worshiping, prostration; co-worship; idolatry 1033.

.2 **glorification,** glory, **praise,** laudation, laud, exaltation, magnification.

.3 **paean,** laud; hosanna, hallelujah, alleluia; **hymn,** hymn of praise, **doxology, psalm, anthem,** motet, canticle, chorale; **chant,** versicle; mantra, Vedic hymn *or* chant; Introit, Miserere; Gloria, Gloria in Excelsis, Gloria Patri; Te Deum, Agnus Dei, Benedicite, Magnificat, Nunc Dimittis; response, responsory, report, answer; Trisagion; antiphon, antiphony; offertory, offertory sentence *or* hymn; hymnody, hymnology, hymnography, psalmody.

.4 **prayer, supplication, invocation,** imploration, impetration, entreaty, beseechment, appeal, petition, suit, aid prayer, bid *or* bidding prayer, orison, obsecration, obtestation, rogation, **devotions;** silent prayer, meditation, contemplation, communion; intercession; **grace, thanks, thanksgiving;** litany; breviary, canonical prayers; collect, collect of the Mass, collect of the Communion; Angelus; Paternoster, the Lord's Prayer; Hail Mary, Ave, Ave Maria; Kyrie Eleison; chaplet; rosary, beads, beadroll; prayer wheel *or* machine.

.5 **benediction, blessing,** benison, invocation, benedicite; sign of the cross; laying on of hands.

.6 **propitiation,** appeasement 804.1; atonement 1012.

.7 **oblation, offering, sacrifice, immolation,** incense; libation, drink offering; burnt offering, holocaust; thank offering, votive *or* ex voto offering; heave offering, peace offering, sacramental offering, sin *or* piacular offering, whole offering; human sacrifice, mactation, infanticide, hecatomb; self-sacrifice, self-immolation; sutteeism; scapegoat, suttee; offertory, collection.

.8 **divine service, service,** public worship, **liturgy** 1040.3, office, duty, exercises, **devotions;** meeting; church service, church; **revival,** revival meeting, camp meeting, tent meeting, praise meeting; watch meeting, watch-night service, watch night; **prayer meeting,** prayers, prayer; morning devotions *or* services *or* prayers, matins, lauds; prime, prime song; tierce, undersong; sext; none, nones; novena; evening devotions *or* services *or* prayers, vesper, vespers, vigils, evensong; compline, night song *or* prayer; bedtime prayer; Mass 1040.9.

.9 **worshiper,** adorer, venerator, votary, communicant, daily communicant, celebrant, churchgoer, chapelgoer; prayer, suppliant, supplicant, supplicator, petitioner; beadsman; revivalist, evangelist; congregation; idolater 1033.4.

.10 VERBS **worship, adore, reverence, venerate, revere, honor,** do or pay homage to, pay divine honors to, do service, lift up the heart, bow down and worship, humble oneself before; **idolize** 1033.5,6.

.11 **glorify, praise, laud, exalt, extol,** magnify, bless, celebrate; praise God, praise or glorify the Lord, bless the Lord, praise God from whom all blessings flow; praise Father, Son, and Holy Ghost; sing praises, sing the praises of, sound or resound the praises of; doxologize, hymn.

.12 **pray, supplicate,** invoke, petition, make supplication; **implore, beseech** 774.11; offer a prayer, send up a prayer, commune with God; **say one's prayers;** tell one's beads, recite the rosary; **say grace, give** or **return thanks;** pray over.

.13 **bless, give one's blessing,** give benediction, confer a blessing upon, invoke benefits upon; cross, make the sign of the cross over or upon; lay hands on.

.14 **propitiate,** make propitiation; appease 804.7; **offer sacrifice,** sacrifice, make sacrifice to, immolate before, offer up an oblation.

.15 ADJS **worshipful,** worshiping; **adoring,** adorant; **devout,** devotional; **reverent,** reverential; **venerative,** venerational; solemn; at the feet of; **prayerful, supplicatory,** supplicant, suppliant, precatory, precative, imploring, on one's knees, on bended knee; prone or prostrate before, in the dust.

.16 INTERJS **hallelujah!,** alleluia!, **hosanna!, praise God!,** praise the Lord!, praise ye the Lord!, "praise ye Him ... all His hosts!" [Bible], Heaven be praised!, glory to God!, glory be to God!, glory be to God in the highest!, bless the Lord!, "bless the Lord, O my soul: and all that is within me, bless His holy name!", "hallowed be Thy Name!" [both Bible]; thanks be to God!, Deo gratias! [L]; (Hinduism) om!, om mani padme hum!

.17 O Lord!, our Father which art in heaven!; God grant!, pray God that!; God bless!, God save!, God forbid!

1033. IDOLATRY

.1 NOUNS **idolatry, idolatrousness, idolism,** idolodulia, **idol worship;** heathenism, paganism; image worship, iconolatry, iconoduly; **fetishism; demonism,** demonolatry, demon or devil worship; animal worship, snake worship, fire worship, pyrolatry, Parsiism, Zoroastrianism; sun worship, star worship, Sabaism; tree worship, plant worship, Druidism, nature worship; phallic worship, phallicism; hero worship; idolomancy; –latry.

.2 **idolization** 1033.8, fetishization; **deification,** apotheosis.

.3 **idol, idolo–** or **eidolo–; fetish,** joss; **graven image, golden calf;** devil-god, "the god of my idolatry" [Shakespeare]; Baal, Juggernaut.

.4 **idolater,** idolatress, idolizer, idolatrizer, idolist, idol worshiper; fetishist; demon or devil worshiper, demonolater, chthonian; animal worshiper, zoolater, theriolater, therolater, snake worshiper, ophiolater; fire worshiper, pyrolater, Parsi, Zoroastrian; sun worshiper, heliolater; star worshiper, Sabaist; tree worshiper, arborolater, dendrolater, plant worshiper, Druid; nature worshiper; phallic worshiper; anthropolater, archaeolater, etc.; –later.

.5 VERBS **idolatrize, idolize,** idolify, idol; fetishize, fetish; **make an idol of, deify,** apotheosize.

.6 **worship idols,** worship the golden calf, adorer le veau d'or [Fr].

.7 ADJS **idolatrous,** idolatric or idolatrical, **idol worshiping;** idolistic, fetishistic; heathen, pagan; demonolatrous, chthonian; heliolatrous; bibliolatrous; zoolatrous.

.8 **idolatries, idolization**

anthropolatry	logolatry
arborolatry	lordolatry
archaeolatry	mammonolatry
astrolatry	martyrolatry
autolatry	mobolatry
Bardolatry	monolatry
bibliolatry	neolatry
classicolatry	onolatry
cosmolatry	ophiolatry
curatolatry	Oxonolatry
demonolatry	palaeolatry
dendrolatry	papolatry
diabolatry	parsonolatry
ecclesiolatry	parthenolatry
episcopolatry	patriolatry
geniolatry	physiolatry
grammatolatry	phytolatry
gyneolatry	plutolatry
hagiolatry	pseudolatry
heliolatry	pulpitolatry
hierolatry	pyrolatry
hydrolatry	Russolatry
hygeiolatry	selenolatry
ichthyolatry	sermonolatry
iconolatry	Shakespearolatry
idiolatry	sociolatry
idolatry	statolatry
Japanolatry	staurolatry
juvenolatry	symbolatry
litholatry	taurolatry

Teutolatry
thaumatolatry
theriolatry
therolatry
titanolatry

topolatry
uranolatry
urbanolatry
verbolatry
zoolatry

1034. OCCULTISM

.1 NOUNS occultism, mysticism; esoterics, esotericism, esoterism, esotery; cabalism, cabala; yoga, yogism, yogeeism; theosophy, anthroposophy; symbolics, symbolism; anagogics; anagoge; mystery; mystification, hocus-pocus, mumbo jumbo.

.2 supernaturalism, supranaturalism, preternaturalism, transcendentalism; the supernatural, the supersensible.

.3 metaphysics, hyperphysics, transphysical science, the first philosophy or theology.

.4 psychics, psychism, psychicism; parapsychology, psychical research; metapsychics, metapsychism; psychosophy; panpsychism; psychic monism.

.5 spiritualism, spiritism; mediumism; necromancy; séance, sitting; spirit 1017.1.

.6 psychic(al) phenomena, spirit manifestation; materialization; spirit rapping, table tipping or turning; poltergeistism, poltergeist; telekinesis, psychokinesis, power of mind over matter, telesthesia, teleportation; levitation; trance speaking; psychorrhagy; automatism, psychography, automatic or trance or spirit writing; Ouija board, Ouija; planchette.

.7 ectoplasm, exteriorized protoplasm; aura, emanation, effluvium; ectoplasy.

.8 extrasensory perception, ESP; clairvoyance, lucidity, second sight, insight, sixth sense; intuition 481; foresight 542; premonition 544.1; clairsentience, clairaudience, crystal vision, psychometry, metapsychosis.

.9 telepathy, mental telepathy, mind reading, thought transference, telepathic transmission; telepathic dream, telepathic hallucination.

.10 divination 543.2,15; sorcery 1035.

.11 occultist, esoteric, mystic, mystagogue, cabalist, supernaturalist, transcendentalist; adept, mahatma; yogi, yogin, yogist; theosophist, anthroposophist.

.12 psychist, psychicist; parapsychologist; metapsychist; panpsychist; metaphysician, metaphysicist.

.13 psychic; spiritualist, spiritist, medium, ecstatic, spirit rapper, automatist, psychographist; necromancer.

.14 clairvoyant; clairaudient; psychometer, psychometrist.

.15 telepathist, mental telepathist, mind reader, thought reader.

.16 diviner 543.4; sorcerer 1035.5–9.

.17 astral body, astral, linga sharira, design body, subtle body, vital body, etheric body, bliss body, Buddhic body, spiritual body, soul body; kamarupa, desire or kamic body; causal body; mental or mind body.

.18 (seven principles of man, theosophy) spirit, atman; mind, manas; soul, buddhi; life principle, vital force, prana; astral body, linga sharira; physical or dense or gross body, sthula sharira; principle of desire, kama.

.19 spiritualization, etherealization, idealization; dematerialization, immaterialization, unsubstantialization; disembodiment, disincarnation.

.20 VERBS spiritualize, spiritize; etherealize; idealize; dematerialize, immaterialize, unsubstantialize; disembody, disincarnate.

.21 practice spiritualism, hold a séance or sitting; call up spirits 1035.11.

.22 ADJS occult, esoteric(al), mystic(al), mysterious, mystico–; anagogic(al); metaphysic(al); cabalic, cabalistic; supernatural 85.15; theosophical, theosophist.

.23 psychic(al), spiritual; spiritualistic, spiritistic; mediumistic; clairvoyant, second-sighted, clairaudient, clairsentient, telepathic; extrasensory, psychosensory; supersensible, supersensual, pretersensual; telekinetic, psychokinetic; automatist.

1035. SORCERY

.1 NOUNS sorcery, necromancy, magic, sortilege, wizardry, theurgy, gramarye [archaic], rune, glamour; witchcraft, spellcraft, spellbinding, spellcasting; witchery, witchwork, bewitchery, enchantment; voodooism, voodoo, hoodoo, wanga, juju, jujuism, obeah, obeahism; shamanism; magism, magianism; fetishism; vampirism; thaumaturgy, thaumaturgia, thaumaturgics, thaumaturgism; alchemy; white or natural magic; sympathetic magic; divination 543.2,15; spell, charm 1036.

.2 black magic, the black art; diabolism, demonism, Satanism 1016.15.

.3 (practices) magic circle; ghost dance; Sabbat, witches' meeting or Sabbath; ordeal, ordeal by battle or fire or water or lots.

.4 conjuration, conjurement, evocation, invocation; exorcism, exorcisation; exsufflation; incantation 1036.4.

.5 sorcerer, necromancer, wizard, wonderworker, warlock, theurgist; thaumaturge, thaumaturgist, miracle-worker; **conjurer; diviner** 543.4; dowser, water witch; diabolist 1016.16; Faust, Comus.

.6 **magician,** mage, magus, magian; Merlin; illusionist 619.2.

.7 **witchman,** witch master; **shaman,** shamanist; **voodoo,** voodooist, wangateur, **witch doctor,** obeah doctor, **medicine man,** mundunugu, isangoma; witchhunter, witch-finder; exorcist, exorciser; unspeller.

.8 **sorceress,** shamaness; **witch,** witchwoman [dial], witchwife [Scot], **hex, hag,** lamia; witch of Endor; coven, witches' coven, Weird Sisters [Shakespeare].

.9 **bewitcher, enchanter, charmer, spellbinder; enchantress, siren,** vampire; Circe; Medusa, Medea, Gorgon, Stheno, Euryale.

.10 VERBS sorcerize, shamanize; wave a wand, rub the ring or lamp; ride a broomstick.

.11 **conjure, conjure up,** evoke, invoke, raise, summon, call up; **call up spirits,** conjure or conjure up spirits, summon spirits, raise ghosts, evoke from the dead, "call spirits from the vasty deep" [Shakespeare].

.12 **exorcise,** lay; lay ghosts, **cast out devils;** unspell.

.13 cast a spell, bewitch 1036.7–10.

.14 ADJS sorcerous, necromantic, **magic(al),** magian, numinous, thaumaturgic(al), cantrip or weird [both Scot], wizardlike, wizardly; **shaman, shamanic, shamanist** or **shamanistic; witchlike, witchy, witch; voodoo, hoodoo** [informal], **voodooistic; incantation, incantational; talismanic.**

1036. SPELL, CHARM

.1 NOUNS **spell,** magic spell, **charm,** glamour, weird or cantrip [both Scot], wanga; hand of glory; evil eye, *malocchio* [Ital], whammy [slang]; **hex, jinx, curse;** exorcism.

.2 **bewitchment, witchery, bewitchery; enchantment, entrancement,** fascination, captivation; illusion, maya; bedevilment; **possession, obsession.**

.3 **trance,** ecstasy, ecstasis, **rapture;** yoga trance, dharana, dhyana, samadhi; hypnosis 712.7.

.4 **incantation, conjuration,** magic words or formula; hocus-pocus, abracadabra, mumbo jumbo; open sesame.

.5 **charm, amulet, talisman, fetish,** periapt, phylactery; **voodoo, hoodoo,** juju, obeah, mumbo jumbo; **good-luck charm,** good-luck piece, **lucky piece,** rabbit's-foot,

lucky bean, whammy [slang]; mascot; madstone; love charm, philter; scarab, scarabaeus, scarabee; veronica, sudarium; swastika, fylfot, gammadion.

.6 **wish-bringer,** wish-giver; **wand, magic wand,** Aaron's rod; Aladdin's lamp, magic ring, magic belt, magic spectacles, magic carpet, seven-league boots; wishing well, wishing stone; wishing cap, Fortunatus's cap; cap of darkness, Tarnkappe, Tarnhelm; fern seed; wishbone, wishing bone, merrythought [Brit].

.7 VERBS **cast a spell,** spell, **spellbind; entrance,** trance, put in a trance; **hypnotize, mesmerize.**

.8 **charm,** becharm, **enchant, fascinate,** captivate, glamour.

.9 **bewitch, witch, hex, jinx;** voodoo, hoodoo; **possess, obsess;** bedevil, diabolize, demonize; hagride; overlook, look on with the evil eye, cast the evil eye.

.10 **put a curse on,** put a hex on, put a juju on, put obeah on, give the evil eye, give the *malocchio*, give a whammy [slang].

.11 ADJS **bewitching, witching;** illusory, illusive, illusionary; **charming, enchanting, entrancing, spellbinding, fascinating,** glamorous, Circean.

.12 **enchanted, charmed,** becharmed, charmstruck, charm-bound; **spellbound,** spellstruck, spell-caught; **fascinated,** captivated; **hypnotized, mesmerized;** under a spell, in a trance.

.13 **bewitched,** witched, witch-charmed, witch-held, witch-struck; hag-ridden; **possessed, obsessed.**

1037. THE MINISTRY

.1 NOUNS **the ministry, pastorate,** pastorage, pastoral care, cure or care of souls, **the church,** the cloth, the pulpit, the desk; **priesthood,** priestship; apostleship; call, vocation, sacred calling; holy orders; rabbinate.

.2 ecclesiasticalism, ecclesiology, priestcraft.

.3 clericalism, sacerdotalism; priesthood; priestism; episcopalianism; ultramontanism.

.4 monasticism, monachism, monkery, **monkhood,** friarhood; celibacy 934.

.5 (ecclesiastical offices and dignities) cardinalate, cardinalship; primacy, primateship; prelacy, prelature, prelateship, prelatehood; archbishopric, archiepiscopate, archiepiscopacy; bishopric, bishopdom; episcopate, episcopacy; deanery, deanship; prebend, prebendaryship, prebendal stall; canonry, canonicate; curacy; rectorate, rectorship; vicariate, vicarship; pastorate, pastorship; deaconry, deaconship; archdeaconry; chaplaincy, chaplainship; abbacy; presbytery, presbyterate.

.6 papacy, papality, **pontificate,** popedom, the Vatican, Apostolic See, See of Rome.

.7 hierarchy, hierocracy; theocracy.

.8 diocese, see, archdiocese, bishopric, archbishopric; province; synod, conference; **parish.**

.9 benefice, living, **incumbency,** glebe, advowson; curacy, cure, charge, cure or care of souls; prelacy, rectory, vicarage.

.10 holy orders, orders 1038.4, major orders, apostolic orders, minor orders; calling, election, nomination, appointment, preferment, induction, institution, installation, investiture; conferment, presentation; **ordination,** ordainment, consecration, canonization, reading in [Brit].

.11 VERBS **be ordained, take holy orders,** take orders, take vows, read oneself in [Brit]; **take the veil,** wear the cloth.

.12 ordain, frock, **canonize, consecrate;** saint.

.13 ADJS **ecclesiastic(al),** churchly; **ministerial, clerical,** sacerdotal, **pastoral; priestly,** priestish; prelatic(al), prelatial; episcopal, episcopalian; archiepiscopal; canonical; capitular, capitulary; abbatical, abbatial; ultramontane; **evangelistic;** rabbinic(al); priest-ridden.

.14 monastic, monachal, **monasterial, monkish;** conventual.

.15 papal, pontifical, apostolic(al); **popish** or papist or papistic(al) [all derog], papish [dial].

.16 hierarchic(al), hierarchal; theocratic, theocratist.

.17 ordained; in orders, in holy orders, of the cloth.

1038. CLERGY

.1 NOUNS **clergy,** clerico–, **ministry,** the cloth; clerical order, clericals; **priesthood;** priestery; presbytery; prelacy; Sacred College; rabbinate.

.2 clergyman, man of the cloth, **divine, ecclesiastic, churchman, cleric, clerical;** clerk, clerk in holy orders, tonsured cleric; **minister, minister of the Gospel, parson, pastor,** abbé, curé [both Fr], **rector,** curate, man of God, servant of God, shepherd, sky pilot or Holy Joe [both slang], reverend [informal]; supply minister or preacher, supply clergy; **chaplain;** military chaplain, padre [informal]; the Reverend, the Very or Right Reverend; Doctor of Divinity, DD.

.3 preacher, sermoner, sermonizer, sermonist; pulpiter, pulpiteer; predicant, predikant; preaching friar; circuit rider.

.4 holy orders, major orders, priest or presbyter, deacon or diaconus, subdeacon or subdiaconus; minor orders, acolyte or acolytus, exorcist or exorcista, reader or lector, doorkeeper or ostiarius.

.5 priest, gallach [Heb], **father,** father in Christ, **padre,** cassock, presbyter; curé, parish priest; confessor, father confessor, spiritual father or director or leader; penitentiary.

.6 clergywoman, priestess, ministress, pastoress, parsoness, preacheress.

.7 evangelist, revivalist; **missionary,** missioner; missionary apostolic, missionary rector, colporteur.

.8 benefice-holder, beneficiary, **incumbent;** resident, residentiary.

.9 (church dignitaries) ecclesiarch, hierarch, **patriarch, high priest; pope,** pontiff, papa, Holy Father, servant of the servants of God; antipope; **cardinal,** cardinal bishop, cardinal priest, cardinal deacon, primate, exarch, metropolitan, abuna, archpriest, **archbishop, bishop,** prelate, diocesan, suffragan, coadjutor, bishop coadjutor, dean, subdean, archdeacon, prebendary, canon, rural dean, **rector, vicar, chaplain,** curate; penitentiary, Grand Penitentiary; devil's advocate, promoter of the faith.

.10 (minor and lay officers) clerk, parish clerk, Bible clerk; reader, Bible reader, lay reader, lecturer, lector, anagnost; capitular, capitulary; elder, elderman, teaching elder, lay elder, ruling elder; deacon, deaconess; churchwarden; sidesman; almoner; verger, vergeress; beadle, bedral [Scot], suisse [Fr]; sexton, shames [Yid]; sacristan, sacrist; acolyte, thurifer, choir chaplain, precentor, succentor.

.11 (Mormon) deacon, teacher, priest, elder, Seventy, high priest, bishop, patriarch, apostle; Aaronic priesthood, Melchizedek priesthood.

.12 (Jewish) **rabbi,** rabbin; chief rabbi; baal kore [Yid]; cantor; priest, kohen [Heb], high priest; Levite; scribe.

.13 (Muslim) imam, qadi, sheikh, mullah, murshid, mufti, hajji, muezzin, dervish, abdal, fakir, santon.

.14 (Hindu) Brahman, pujari, purohit, pundit, guru, bashara, vairagi or bairagi, Ramwat, Ramanandi; sannyasi; yogi, yogin; bhikshu, bhikhari.

.15 (Buddhist) bonze, bhikku, poonghie, talapoin; lama; Grand Lama, Dalai Lama, Panchen Lama.

.16 (pagan) Druid, Druidess; flamen; hierophant, hierodule, hieros, daduchus, mystes, epopt.

.17 religious, *religieux* [Fr]; monk, monastic; brother, lay brother; cenobite, conventual; caloyer, hieromonach; mendicant, friar; pilgrim, palmer; stylite, pillarist, pillar saint; beadsman; prior, claustral *or* conventual prior, grand prior, general prior; abbot; lay abbot, abbacomes; hermit 924.5; ascetic 991.2; celibate 934.2.

.18 (religious orders) Franciscan, Gray Friar, Friar Minor, Minorite, Observant, Recollect *or* Recollet, Conventual, Capuchin; Dominican, Black Friar, Friar Preacher, preaching friar *or* brother; Carmelite, White Friar; Augustinian, Augustinian Hermit, Austin Friar, begging hermit; Benedictine, Black Monk; Jesuit, Loyolite; Crutched Friar, Crossed Friar; Templar, Hospitaler; Bernardine, Bonhomme, Carthusian, Cistercian, Cluniac, Gilbertine, Lorettine, Maturine, Premonstratensian, Trappist; Brigittine; Marist; Maryknoll; Oratorian; Redemptorist.

.19 nun, sister, *religieuse* [Fr], clergywoman, conventual; abbess, prioress; mother superior, lady superior, superioress, the reverend mother; canoness, regular *or* secular canoness; novice, postulant.

1039. LAITY

.1 NOUNS laity, laymen, nonclerics, nonordained persons, seculars; brethren, people; flock, fold, sheep; congregation, parishioners, churchgoers, assembly; *minyan* [Heb]; parish, society; class.

.2 layman, laic, secular, churchman, parishioner, church member; brother, sister, lay brother, lay sister; laywoman, churchwoman; catechumen; communicant.

.3 ADJS lay, laic *or* laical; nonecclesiastical, nonclerical, nonministerial, nonpastoral, nonordained; nonreligious; secular, secularist, secularistic; temporal, popular, civil; congregational.

1040. RELIGIOUS RITES

.1 NOUNS ritualism, rituality, ceremonialism, formalism, liturgism; symbolism, symbolics; cult, cultus, cultism; sacramentalism, sacramentarianism; sabbatism, Sabbatarianism; ritualization, solemnization, solemn observance, celebration; liturgics, liturgiology.

.2 ritualist, ceremonialist, liturgist, formal-

ist, formulist, formularist; sacramentalist, sacramentarian; sabbatist, Sabbatarian; High-Churchman, High-Churchist.

.3 rite, ritual, rituality, liturgy, holy rite; order of worship; ceremony, ceremonial; observance, ritual observance; formality, solemnity; form, formula, formulary, form of worship *or* service, mode of worship; prescribed form; service, function, duty, office, practice; sacrament, sacramental, mystery; ordinance; institution.

.4 (rites) celebration, high celebration; processional; litany, greater *or* lesser litany; invocation, invocation of saints; confirmation, imposition *or* laying on of hands; confession, auricular confession, the confessional, the confessionary; sign of the cross; pax, kiss of peace; love feast, agape; reciting the rosary, telling of beads; thurification, incense; aspersion, asperges; lustration; circumcision; bar mitzvah, bas mitzvah.

.5 seven sacraments, mysteries: baptism, confirmation, the Eucharist, penance, extreme unction, holy orders, matrimony.

.6 unction, sacred unction, sacramental anointment, chrism *or* chrisom, chrismation, chrismatory; extreme unction, last rites, viaticum; ointment; chrismal.

.7 baptism, baptizement; christening; immersion, total immersion; sprinkling, aspersion, aspergation; affusion, infusion; baptism for the dead; baptismal regeneration; baptismal gown *or* dress *or* robe, chrismal; baptistery, font.

.8 Eucharist, Lord's Supper, Last Supper, Communion, Holy Communion, the Sacrament, the Holy Sacrament; intinction; consubstantiation, impanation, subpanation, transubstantiation; real presence; elements, consecrated elements, bread and wine, body and blood of Christ; Host, wafer, loaf, bread, altar bread, consecrated bread; Sacrament Sunday.

.9 Mass, *Missa* [L], Eucharistic rites; the Liturgy, the Divine Liturgy; High Mass, *Missa solemnis* [L]; Low Mass, *Missa bassa* [L]; Rosary Mass, Rosary, Rosary of the Seven Dolors of Mary; Lady Mass; Dry Mass, *Missa sicca* [L]; Liturgy of the Presanctified, *Missa praesanctificatorum* [L]; *Missa publica, Missa privata, Missa cantata, Missa media, Missa adventitia, Missa manualis, Missa capitularis, Missa legata* [all L]; requiem, Requiem Mass, dirge, Memento of the Dead.

.10 (parts of the Mass) Prayers at Foot of the Altar, Introit, Kyrie, Kyrie Eleison, Gloria, Collect, Epistle, Gradual, Alleluia, Tract, Gospel, Credo, Offertory, Lavabo, Secreta, Preface, Sanctus, Tersanctus; Canon, Memento of the Living, Consecration, Elevation of the Host, Anamnesis, Memento of the Dead; Paternoster, Fraction, Agnus Dei, Pax, Communion, Post-Communion, Dismissal, Blessing, Last Gospel.

.11 (sacred and ritualistic articles) relics, sacred relics; monstrance, ostensorium; Host; eucharistial, pyx, ciborium; tabernacle; ark; crucifix, cross, rood, holy cross or rood; osculatory, pax; Agnus Dei; icon, icon(o)– or ikon(o)– or eikon(o)–; bambino [Ital], veronica, Pietà [Ital]; sacramental; holy water; holy-water sprinkler, aspergillum, asperges, asperger; thurible, censer, incensory; cruet, urceole; rosary, beads, beadroll; chaplet; prayer wheel or machine; candle, votive candle, vigil light, paschal candle; Sanctus bell, sacring bell; Sangraal, Holy Grail; menorah, shofar, sukkah, matzo [all Heb]; tallith [Heb], prayer shawl; tefillin [Heb], phylacteries; mezuzah [Heb]; mikvah [Heb].

.12 (ritualistic manual) missal, Mass book; ritual, rituale [L], manual, formulary, church book, service book; rubric, canon, ordinal, breviary; farse; lectionary; pontifical; Virginal; prayer book; siddur, machzor, haggadah [all Heb]; Book of Common Prayer, euchologion or euchology, litany; Torah, Torah scroll, Sefer Torah [Heb].

.13 psalter, psalmbook; Psalm Book, Book of Common Order; the Psalms, Book of Psalms, the Psalter, the Psaltery.

.14 holy day, hallowday [dial], holytide; feast, fast; Sabbath; Sunday, Lord's day; saint's day; church calendar, ecclesiastical calendar.

.15 (Christian holy days) Advent; Christmas; Candlemas, Candlemas Day; Epiphany, Three Kings' Day, Twelfth-tide, Twelfthnight, Twelfth-day; Septuagesima; Shrove Tuesday, Mardi Gras, Carnival, Pancake Day; Ash Wednesday; Lent, Lententide; Quadragesima, Quadragesima Sunday; Holy Week, Passion Week; Palm Sunday, Holy Thursday or Maundy Thursday, Good Friday; Easter, Eastertide, Easter Saturday, Easter Sunday, Easter Monday; Annunciation, Annunciation Day, Lady Day; Ascension Day or Holy Thursday; Pentecost, Whitsuntide, Whitsun, Whitweek; Whitsunday, Whitmonday, Whit-Tuesday, White Sunday,

etc.; Trinity Sunday, Corpus Christi; Lammas, Lammas Day, Lammastide; Michaelmas, Michaelmas Day, Michaelmastide; Hallowmas, Allhallowmas, Allhallowtide, Halloween; Allhallows, All Saints' Day; All Souls' Day; Martinmas; Ember days.

.16 (Jewish holy days) Passover, Pesach; Pentecost, Shabuoth, Feast of Weeks; Rosh Hashanah, New Year; High Holy Days; Yom Kippur, Day of Atonement; Sukkoth, Feast of Tabernacles; Simhath Torah, Rejoicing over the Law; Hanukkah, Feast of the Dedication; Purim; Fast of Av, Ninth of Av, Tishah b'Av.

.17 (Muslim holy days) Ramadan (month), Bairam, Muharram.

.18 VERBS celebrate, observe, keep, solemnize; celebrate Mass; communicate, administer Communion; attend Communion, receive the Sacrament, partake of the Lord's Supper; attend Mass.

.19 minister, officiate, do duty, perform a rite, perform service or divine service; administer a sacrament, administer the Eucharist, etc.; anoint, chrism; confirm, impose, lay hands on; make the sign of the cross.

.20 baptize, christen; dip, immerse; sprinkle, asperge.

.21 confess, make confession, receive absolution; shrive, hear confession; absolve, administer absolution; administer extreme unction.

.22 ADJS ritualistic, ritual; ceremonial, ceremonious; formal, formular, formulary; liturgic(al), liturgistic(al); High-Church; sacramental, sacramentarian; eucharistic(al), baptismal; paschal.

1041. ECCLESIASTICAL ATTIRE

.1 NOUNS canonicals, clericals [informal], robes, cloth; vestments, vesture; liturgical garments, ceremonial attire; pontificals, pontificalia, episcopal vestments.

.2 robe, frock, mantle, gown, cloak.

.3 staff, pastoral staff, crosier, cross, crossstaff, crook, paterissa.

.4 ADJS vestmental, vestmentary.

.5 clerical garments

alb	calotte
almuce	cap
amice	capuche, capuchin
apron	cardinal's hat
bands	cassock
biretta	chasuble
bishop's ring	chimere
black gown	cincture
buskins	cingulum

clerical collar
cope
cotta
cowl
crucifix
cuculla
dalmatic
dog collar [slang]
episcopal ring
fanon
Geneva bands
Geneva cloak or gown
habit
hood
lawn sleeves
maniple
mantelletta
mantellone
miter
mozzetta
pallium
pectoral cross
rabat, rabbi
reversed collar

rochet
Roman collar
rosary
Salvation Army bonnet
sandals
scapular
scarf
shovel hat
simar
skullcap
soutane
stole
subcingulum
succinctorium
surplice
tiara
tippet
triple crown
tunic
tunicle
vakass, vagas
zucchetto

1042. RELIGIOUS BUILDINGS

.1 NOUNS church, kirk [Scot], bethel, meetinghouse, church house, house of God, place of worship, house of worship or prayer; conventicle; mission; basilica, major or patriarchal basilica, minor basilica; cathedral, cathedral church, duomo [Ital].

.2 temple, fane; tabernacle; synagogue, shul [Yid]; mosque, masjid; dewal, girja; pagoda; kiack; pantheon.

.3 chapel, chapel of ease, chapel royal, side chapel, school chapel, sacrament chapel, Lady chapel, oratory, oratorium; chantry; sacellum, sacrarium.

.4 shrine, holy place, dagoba, naos; sacrarium, delubrum; tope, stupa; reliquary, reliquaire [Fr].

.5 sanctuary, holy of holies, sanctum, sanctum sanctorum, adytum, sacrarium.

.6 cloister, monastery, house, abbey, friary; priory, priorate; lamasery; convent, nunnery.

.7 parsonage, pastorage, pastorate, manse, church house, clergy house; presbytery, rectory, vicarage, deanery; glebe.

.8 bishop's palace; Vatican; Lambeth, Lambeth Palace.

.9 (church interior) vestry, sacristy, sacrarium, diaconicon or diaconicum; baptistery; ambry, apse, blindstory, chancel, choir, cloisters, confessional, confessionary [archaic], crypt, Easter sepulcher, nave, porch, presbytery, rood loft, rood stair, rood tower or spire or steeple, transept, triforium.

.10 (church furnishings) piscina; stoup, holy-water stoup or basin; baptismal font; paten; reredos; jube, rood screen, chancel screen; altar cloth, cerecloth, chrismal; communion or sacrament cloth, corporal, fanon, oblation cloth; rood cloth; baldachin, baldacchino [Ital]; kneeling stool, prie-dieu [Fr]; prayer rug or carpet or mat.

.11 (vessels) cruet; chalice; ciborium, pyx; chrismal, chrismatory; monstrance, ostensorium; reliquary; font, holy-water font.

.12 altar, scrobis; bomos, eschara, hestia; Lord's table, holy table, Communion table, chancel table, table of the Lord, God's board; rood altar; altar desk, missal stand; credence, prothesis, table or altar of prothesis; predella; superaltar, retable, retablo, ancona, gradin; altarpiece, altar side, altar rail, altar carpet, altar stair; altar facing or front, frontal; altar slab, altar stone, mensal.

.13 pulpit, rostrum, ambo; lectern, desk, reading desk.

.14 (seats) pew; stall; mourners' bench, anxious bench or seat, penitent form; amen corner; sedilia.

.15 ADJS churchly, churchish, ecclesiastical; churchlike, templelike; cathedral-like, cathedralesque; tabernacular; synagogical, synagogal; pantheonic.

.16 claustral, cloistered; monastic, monachal, monasterial; conventual, conventical.

INDEX

HOW TO USE THIS INDEX

Numbers after index entries refer to categories and paragraphs in the front section of this book, not to page numbers. The part of the number before the decimal point refers to the category in which synonyms and related words to the word you are looking up are found. The part of the number after the decimal point refers to the paragraph or paragraphs within the category. Look at the first index entry on the next page:

aardvark 414.58, 415.8

This entry listing tells you that you can find words related to **aardvark** in paragraph 58 of category 414 and paragraph 8 of category 415.

    Words, of course, frequently have more than one meaning. Each of those meanings may have synonyms or associated related words. Look at the entry for **abhor:**

abhor dislike 867.3

hate 930.5

This tells you that you will find synonyms for **abhor** in the sense meaning "dislike" in category 867, paragraph 3. It also tells you that you will find synonyms for **abhor,** meaning "hate," in category 930, paragraph 5.

    In many cases, words are spelled the same as nouns, verbs, adjectives, etc. Look at the entry for **abandon** and notice that here you are directed to **abandon** when it is used as a noun and when it is used as a verb in a variety of meanings. Here, as in the examples above, you are referred to the category and paragraph number.

    Not all words in the main part of the book are included in the index. In order to save space, many adverbs ending with -ly have been left out of the index; but you will find the common adverbs ending in -ly here, such as lightly or easily. If you can't find the adverb ending in -ly that you are looking for, look up the word in its adjective form and go to that category. Frequently, you can use the words in the adjective paragraphs you find and convert them into the adverb you are looking for by simply adding -ly to the adjective.

    To make it easier to find phrases, we have indexed them according to their first word. You do not have to guess what the main word of the phrase is to find it in the index. Simply look up the first word in the phrase. For example, **hot air** will be found in the Hs, **fat cat** in the Fs, and **let go** in the Ls.

accompanist
accompanier 73.4
instrumentalist 464.3
accompany
go with 73.7
perform music 462.40
synchronize 118.3
accompanying
attending 73.9
coacting 177.4
happening 151.9
simultaneous 118.4
accomplice
cohort 787.3
participator 815.4
accomplish
achieve 722.4
arrive 300.6
complete 56.6
do 705.6
perform 705.8
produce 167.9
succeed with 724.10
accomplished
achieved 722.10
skilled 733.24
accomplished fact
accomplishment 722.1
act 705.3
reality 1.2
accomplishment
act 705.3
arrival 300.1
development 148.1
fulfillment 722
learning 475.4
performance 705.2
production 167.1
skill 733.8
solution 487.1
success 724.1
accord
n. agreement 26.1
compact 771.1
concord 794
conformity 82.1
consent 775.1
music 462.3
peace 803.3
relationship 9.1
unanimity 521.5
v. agree 26.6
coact 177.2
concur 521.9
conform 82.3
consent 775.2
get along 794.2
give 818.12
harmonize 462.36
make agree 26.7
permit 777.9
accordance
agreement 26.1
concord 794.1
concurrence 177.1
conformity 82.1
giving 818.1
music 462.3
observance 768.1
similarity 20.1
unanimity 521.5

uniformity 17.1
accordingly
consequently 154.9
hence 155.7
in that case 8.11
according to 82.9
according to Hoyle
according to rule 82.8
right 958.8
accordion 465.12
accost address 594.27
approach 296.3
greet 925.10
account
n. bill 845.3
bookkeeping 845
count of 87.6
credit account 839.2
description 608.3
esteem 914.3
fee 841.5
information 557.1
list 88.5
numeration 87.5
reckoning 845.2
record 570.1
statement 570.7
story 608.6
sum 86.5
worth 846.3
v. judge 494.8
accountable
attributable 155.6
interpretable 552.17
responsible 962.17
accountant
bookkeeper 845.7
calculator 87.8
financial officer 836.11
recorder 571.1
account for
attribute to 155.4
explain 552.10
justify 1006.9
accounting
n. accountancy 845.6
automation 349.7
numeration 87.1
statement 570.7
adj. bookkeeping 845.12
accouterment 659.1
accredit
attribute to 155.4
commission 780.9
place to one's credit 839.5
sanction 521.12
accredited
commissioned 780.18
well-rated 839.8
accroach
appropriate 822.19
usurp 961.8
accrue
be received 819.8
debt 840.7
increase 38.6
result from 154.6

acculturation
cultivation 691.3
culture 642.3
naturalization 189.3
accumulate
assemble 74.18
increase 38.6
join 47.5
procure 811.10
store up 660.11
accumulation
acquisition 811.2
assemblage 74.9
increase 38.1
store 660.1
accumulative
additive 40.8
cumulative 74.23
accuracy
correctness 516.3
meticulousness 533.3
particularity 8.4
accurate correct 516.15
discriminating 492.7
meticulous 533.12
accurately
correctly 516.19
meticulously 533.16
accursed 972.9
accusation 1005
accusatory 1005.13
accuse censure 969.13
charge 1005.7
accused
n. defendant 1005.6
adj. charged 1005.15
accustomed usual 84.8
wont 642.17
ace aviator 279.3
expert 733.13
friend 928.3
good thing 674.7
one 89.3
playing card 878.17
short distance 200.2
small amount 35.2
superior 36.4
acedia apathy 856.4
despair 889.2
languor 708.6
sin 982.3
unconcern 636.2
ace in the hole
advantage 36.2
reserve 660.3
aceldama
battlefield 802.2
killing site 409.12
acerbic bitter 429.6
caustic 939.21
pungent 433.6
resentful 952.24
sour 432.5
acerbity
acrimony 161.4
bitterness 952.3
causticity 939.8
pungency 433.1
sourness 432.1
unpleasant taste 429.2
acetic 432.6

ache
n. cold sensation 333.2
distress 866.5
pain 424.5
v. grieve 872.17
suffer 866.19
suffer pain 424.8
want to 634.15
wish for 634.16
achieve
accomplish 722.4
arrive 300.6
do 705.6
produce 167.9
succeed with 724.10
achievement
accomplishment 722.1
act 705.3
arrival 300.1
courageous act 893.7
heraldic insignia 569.2
performance 705.2
production 167.1
Achilles' heel 678.2
aching
cold sensation 333.2
distress 866.5
pain 424.5
yearning 634.5
achromasia 364.1
achromic 363.7
achy 424.12
acid
n. bitterness 952.3
cauterant 329.15
chemical 379.1
extinguisher 332.3
LSD 687.13
sour thing 432.2
word list 379.12
adj. acidulous 432.6
acrimonious 161.13
chemical 379.7
eloquent 600.11
ill-humored 951.17
malevolent 939.21
pungent 433.6
resentful 952.24
acidhead 642.10
acidify
react chemically 379.6
sour 432.4
acidity acrimony 161.4
bitterness 952.3
chemical 379.1
pungency 433.1
rancor 939.8
sourness 432.1
acidosis 686.20
acid rock 462.9
acid test 489.2
acidulous acid 432.6
acrimonious 161.13
rancorous 939.21
resentful 952.24
acknowledge
answer 486.4
attribute to 155.4

confess 556.7
correspond 604.12
pay 841.18
recognize 521.11
testify 505.10
thank 949.4
acknowledged
conventional 645.5
recognized 521.14
traditional 123.12
acknowledgment
answer 486.1
apology 1012.2
attribution 155.2
book 605.12
commendation 968.3
confession 556.3
due 960.2
letter 604.2
receipt 844.2
recognition 521.3
thanks 949.2
acme completion 56.5
culmination 677.3
height 207.2
ideal 25.4
summit 211.2
supremacy 36.3
acne 686.33
acolyte assistant 787.6
churchman 1038.10
holy orders 1038.4
acoustic(al)
auditory 448.14
phonic 450.17
acoustics phonics 450.5
physics 325.1
acquaint inform 557.8
introduce 927.13
acquaintance
friend 928.1
friendship 927.4
information 557.1
knowledge 475.1
acquiesce assent 521.8
be willing 622.1
consent 775.3
submit to 765.6
acquiescence
assent 521.1
belief 501.1
conformity 82.1
consent 775.1
obedience 766.1
resignation 861.2
submission 765.1
willingness 622.1
acquiescent
agreeing 521.13
conformable 82.5
consenting 775.4
obedient 766.3
resigned 861.10
submissive 765.12
willing 622.5
acquire get 811.8
incur 175.4
receive 819.6
take 822.13
acquisition gaining 811
learning 475.4
receiving 819.1

taking 822.1
acquisitive
acquiring 811.14
greedy 634.27
selfish 978.5
acquit
bring in a verdict
1004.19
exculpate 1007.4
acquittal
exculpation 1007
legal decision 1004.9
observance 768.1
payment 841.1
acquitted
forgiven 947.7
paid 841.22
acreage 179.1
acres land 385.1
much 34.3
real estate 810.7
acrid
acrimonious 161.13
bitter 429.6
caustic 939.21
hostile 929.10
pungent 433.6
sharp 258.10
acridity
acrimony 161.4
causticity 939.8
pungency 433.1
sharpness 258.1
unpleasant taste
429.2
acrimonious
acrid 161.13
caustic 939.21
resentful 952.24
acrimony acridity 161.4
animosity 929.4
bitterness 952.3
causticity 939.8
acrobat
circus artist 612.3
gymnast 878.21
acrobatics
air maneuver 278.13
sports 878.8
acronym 582.4
acropolis 799.6
across
adj. crosswise 221.9
transverse 219.19
adv. crosswise 221.13
on 216.25
transversely 219.24
prep. beyond 199.21
opposite 239.7
across the board
comprehensive 76.7
wholly 54.13
acrostic word 582.4
wordplay 881.8
acrylic 378.14
act
n. behavior 737.1
deed 705.3
doing 705.1
law 998.3
legislation 742.13
process 164.2

stage show 611.8
v. behave 737.4
do 705.4
fake 616.21
operate 164.7
perform 611.34
produce 167.9
represent 572.9
acta acts 705.3
reports 570.7
act as do duty 656.13
function as 164.8
represent 572.9
act for
be instrumental
658.5
represent 781.14
substitute for 149.5
acting
n. doing 705.1
fakery 616.3
impersonation 572.2
playing 611.9
adj. deputy 781.15
operating 164.11
performing 705.10
acting-out 690.32
actini–
actinic radiation
327.1
luminary 335.41
radiating 299.9
action activeness 707.1
automation 349.3
behavior 737.1
deed 705.3
doing 705
expedient 670.2
fight 796.4
fun 878.2
judgment 494.5
lawsuit 1004.1
mechanism 348.5
military operation
797.8
operation 164.1
story element 608.9
actionable illegal 999.6
legal 998.10
litigable 1004.20
activate atomics 326.17
energize 161.11
militarize 797.24
radioactivate 327.9
activator 161.5
active
n. voice 586.14
adj. effectual 665.20
energetic 161.12
lively 707.17
moving 267.7
observant 768.4
operating 164.11
active duty 797.13
activism action 705.1
activity 707.1
activist 707.8
activity action 705.1
activeness 707
animation 161.3
behavior 737.1
business 656.1

cause 153.10
motion 267.1
radiation 327.1
act like 22.5
act of God 639.7
act on influence 172.9
operate on 164.6
pass judgment 494.13
take action 705.5
actor affecter 903.7
deceiver 619.1
doer 718.1
player 612.2
role 611.11
act out act 611.35
represent 572.9
actress 612.2
actual certain 513.15
present 120.2
real 1.15
true 516.12
actuality
certainty 513.3
reality 1.2
truth 516.1
actually
positively 34.19
really 1.16
truly 516.17
actuarial table 511.2
actuary
accountant 845.7
calculator 87.8
insurance man 699.4
actuate impel 283.10
motivate 648.12
set in motion 267.6
actuation motion 267.1
motivation 648.2
act up 738.4
acuity alertness 533.5
intelligence 467.2
sagacity 467.4
sharpness 258.1
acumen
discrimination 492.2
sagacity 467.4
acute cunning 735.12
deep-felt 855.26
energetic 161.12
painful 424.10
pointed 258.11
sagacious 467.16
sensitive 422.15
sharp 258.10
shrill 458.14
urgent 672.21
violent 162.15
acutely 34.20
ad 559.6
AD 105.13
adage 517.1
adagio
n. music 462.25
adv. music 462.55
adamant
immovable 142.15
rigid 356.12
stone 384.10
unyielding 626.9
Adam's apple 594.19
adapt accustom 642.11

change 139.6
conform 82.3
make agree 26.7
music 462.47
orient 290.12
prepare 720.8
adaptable
changeable 141.6
conformable 82.5
handy 665.19
pliant 357.9
resilient 358.7
versatile 733.23
wieldy 732.14
adaptation
adjustment 26.4
change 139.1
conformity 82.1
development 148.3
fitting 720.2
harmonization 463.2
music 462.5
orientation 290.5
adapted
accustomed 642.17
apt 26.10
fitted 720.17
in conformity with
82.9
add adjoin 40.4
calculate 87.11
combine 52.3
addendum
adjunct 41.1
nonessential 6.2
sequel 67.1
add fuel to the flame
excite 857.11
fuel 331.8
incite 648.17
increase 38.5
stoke 329.22
addict desirer 634.12
drug user 642.10
enthusiast 635.5
addicted 642.19
addiction 642.9
addictive 642.20
adding addition 40.3
calculation 87.3
adding machine
addition 40.3
calculator 87.19
add insult to injury
aggravate 885.2
impair 692.11
offend 965.4
addition
acquisition 811.1
adjunct 41.1
affiliation 9.1
annex 41.3
augmentation 40
combination 52.1
expansion 197.1
increase 38.1
mathematics 87.4
nonessential 6.2
additional
additive 40.8
renewed 122.8
supplementary 40.10

unessential 6.4
additive
n. adjunct 41.1
adj. additional 40.8
addle confuse 532.7
make drunk 996.21
perplex 514.13
addled
intoxicated 996.30
muddled 532.13
perplexed 514.24
stupid 469.18
addlepate 471.4
addlepated
muddled 532.13
stupid 469.18
address
n. abode 191.1
behavior 737.1
greeting 925.4
mail 604.10
remark 594.4
request 774.1
skill 733.1
speech 599.2
v. court 932.19
greet 925.10
make a speech 599.9
solicit 774.14
speak to 594.27
write destination
604.14
address book 570.11
addressee
correspondent 604.9
recipient 819.3
resident 190.2
address oneself to
busy oneself with
656.11
practice 705.7
undertake 715.3
add to augment 40.5
increase 38.4
make larger 197.4
adduction 288.1
add up add 40.6
be OK 516.9
calculate 87.12
total 54.8
adenoidal 595.12
adept
n. expert 733.11
occultist 1034.11
adj. skilled in 733.25
skillful 733.20
adequate able 157.14
satisfactory 868.11
sufficient 661.6
tolerable 674.19
adhere be joined 47.11
cohere 50.6
adherence
approval 968.1
cohesion 50.1
fidelity 974.7
observance 768.1
adherent adherer 50.4
commender 968.8
follower 293.2
hanger-on 907.5
man 787.8

philosophy 500.12
adhere to fulfill 771.10
hold 813.6
observe 768.2
adhesive
n. adherent 50.4
connection 47.3
types of 50.13
adj. adherent 50.12
sticky 389.12
adhesive tape
medical dressing
687.33
tape 206.4
ad hoc 670.7
ad hominem attack
971.2
adieu
n. departure 301.4
interj. farewell! 301.23
ad infinitum
continuously 71.10
infinitely 104.4
lengthily 202.11
perpetually 112.10
throughout 56.17
¡adios! 301.23
adipose
corpulent 195.18
oily 380.9
adit channel 396.1
entrance 302.5
adjacent 200.16
adjective 586.3
adjoin add 40.4
be near 200.9
border 235.10
juxtapose 200.13
adjoining 200.16
adjourn 132.9
adjournment 132.4
adjudicate 494.8
adjunct addition 40.1
associate 787.1
attendant 73.3
component 58.2
expansion 197.1
nonessential 6.2
ornamentation 901.1
part 55.1
relationship 9.1
thing added 41
adjure entreat 774.11
place under oath
523.6
adjust accept 861.6
accustom 642.11
arrange 771.9
change 139.6
compromise 807.2
conform 82.3
equalize 30.6
make agree 26.7
mediate 805.7
organize 60.10
orient 290.12
prepare 720.8
qualify 507.3
reconcile 804.8
size 195.15
adjustable
changeable 141.6

conformable 82.5
versatile 733.23
adjusted
accustomed 642.17
fitted 720.17
adjustment
adaptation 26.4
adjustive reaction
690.34
change 139.1
compacting 771.4
compromise 807.1
condition 7.3
conformity 82.1
equalization 30.2
fitting 720.2
habituation 642.8
organization 60.2
orientation 290.5
reconciliation 804.4
adjutant 787.6
adjuvant
n. adjunct 41.1
drug 687.32
adj. helping 785.20
remedial 687.39
ad lib
n. improvisation 630.5
unpreparedness 721.1
adv. at will 621.5
extemporaneously
630.15
ad-lib
v. be unprepared
721.6
improvise 630.8
adj. extemporaneous
630.12
unprepared 721.8
adman 559.9
administer
administer justice
1000.5
apportion 816.8
execute 771.10
give 818.12
govern 741.12
impose 963.6
manage 747.11
administer to 750.13
administration
apportionment 816.2
educators 565.9
governance 739.5
government 741.1
imposition 963.2
management 747.3
performance 705.2
protectorship 699.2
administration, the
directorate 748.11
executives 748.3
the rulers 749.15
administrative
directing 747.14
governing 741.19
administrator
director 748.1
educator 565.9
admirable
lovable 931.23
praiseworthy 968.20

admiral 749.20
admiration
  approval 968.1
  love 931.1
  respect 964.1
  wonder 920.1
admire approve 968.9
  cherish 931.19
  respect 964.4
admired
  approved 968.19
  beloved 931.22
  respected 964.11
admirer devotee 635.6
  lover 931.11
  supporter 787.9
admissibility
  fitness 26.5
  inclusion 76.1
  justifiability 1006.7
  permissibility 777.8
  reasonableness 482.9
  receptivity 306.9
  satisfactoriness 868.3
  tolerableness 674.3
admissible
  acceptable 868.12
  eligible 637.24
  evidential 505.17
  justifiable 1006.14
  logical 482.20
  permissible 777.15
  receptive 306.16
  relevant 9.11
  tolerable 674.19
admission
  acknowledgment
  521.3
  admittance 306.2
  confession 556.3
  entrance 302.1
  fee 846.7
  inclusion 76.1
  naturalization 189.3
  permission 777.1
  receiving 819.1
  testimony 505.3
admissive
  disclosive 556.11
  open-minded 526.10
  permitting 777.14
  receptive 306.16
admit
  acknowledge 521.11
  allow 507.5
  confess 556.7
  enter 302.7
  include 76.3
  naturalize 189.4
  permit 777.9
  receive 819.6
  take in 306.10
  welcome 925.7
admit of
  be liable 175.3
  have a chance 156.13
admitted
  acknowledged 521.14
  approved 968.19
  conventional 645.5
  permitted 777.16
  received 819.10

  traditional 123.12
admitting 507.13
admixture
  compound 44.5
  mixture 44.1
admonish advise 754.6
  dissuade 652.3
  reprove 969.17
  warn 703.5
admonition
  advice 754.1
  dissuasion 652.1
  reproof 969.5
  warning 703.1
ado bustle 707.4
  disturbance 62.4
  excitement 857.3
  trouble 731.3
adobe
  n. building material
  378.2
  ceramic ware 576.2
  adj. earthy 385.7,13
adolescence 124.6
adolescent
  n. youngster 125.1
  adj. undeveloped
  721.11
  young 124.13
Adonis 900.9
adopt
  appropriate 822.19
  borrow 821.4
  choose 637.15
  naturalize 189.4
  usurp 961.8
adopted chosen 637.26
  naturalized 189.6
adoption
  appropriation 822.4
  borrowing 821.2
  embracement 637.4
  naturalization 189.3
  redemption 1026.4
  usurpation 961.3
adorable
  desirable 634.30
  lovable 931.23
adoration love 931.1
  piety 1028.1
  respect 964.1
  worship 1032.1
adore cherish 931.19
  enjoy 865.10
  respect 964.4
  worship 1032.10
adored beloved 931.22
  respected 964.11
adoring loving 931.25
  pious 1028.8
  reverent 964.9
  worshipful 1032.15
adorn beautify 900.14
  dignify 914.12
  make grandiloquent
  601.7
  ornament 901.8
adorned
  high-flown 601.11
  ornamented 901.11
adornment
  beautification 900.10

flowery language
  601.4
  ornamentation 901.1
adrift afloat 275.61
  astray 518.16
  bewildered 514.23
  inconstant 141.7
  irrelevant 10.6
  unfastened 49.22
adroit
  intelligent 467.14
  skillful 733.20
adsorb 306.13
adsorbent
  n. sorption 306.6
  adj. sorbent 306.17
adsorption 306.6
adulation flattery 970.1
  praise 968.5
adult
  n. grownup 127
  adj. mature 126.12
adulterate
  corrupt 692.14
  dilute 355.3
  mix with 44.13
  tamper with 616.17
  weaken 160.11
adulterated
  imperfect 678.4
  thinned 355.4
  weakened 160.19
adulterer 989.13
adulteress 989.13
adulterous 989.27
adultery
  copulation 419.8
  love affair 931.6
  unchastity 989.7
adulthood 126.2
adumbrate hint 557.10
  portend 544.10
  represent 572.8
advance
  n. approach 296.1
  course 267.2
  development 148.1
  help along 785.5
  improvement 691.1
  increase 38.1
  lending 820.1
  loan 820.2
  offer 773.1
  progression 294.1
  promotion 782.1
  v. adduce evidence
  505.13
  approach 296.3
  attack 798.17
  be expedient 670.3
  be instrumental
  658.5
  cause 153.13
  do good 674.10
  elapse 105.5
  encourage 785.17
  encroach 313.9
  evolve 148.5
  further 294.5
  get better 691.7
  increase 38.6
  lend 820.5

  make better 691.9
  make good 724.9
  move 267.5
  postulate 499.12
  progress 294.2
  promote 782.2
  propose 773.5
  prosper 728.7
  push 285.10
  interj. attack! 798.32
advanced aged 126.16
  improved 691.13
  modern 122.13
  preceding 66.4
  premature 131.8
advance guard
  guard 699.9
  the latest thing 122.2
  vanguard 240.2
advance man 611.30
advancement
  development 148.1
  furtherance 785.5
  improvement 691.1
  lending 820.1
  progression 294.1
  promotion 782.1
advance notice 703.2
advantage
  n. benefit 665.4
  expedience 670.1
  facility 785.9
  good 674.4
  leverage 287.2
  superiority 36.2
  v. be expedient 670.3
  be of use 665.17
  do good 674.10
  further 785.17
advantageous
  expedient 670.5
  gainful 811.15
  good 674.12
  useful 665.18
advantageously
  expediently 670.8
  favorably 36.19
  gainfully 811.16
  helpfully 785.24
  usefully 665.25
advent approach 296.1
  arrival 300.1
  coming 121.5
Advent 1040.15
adventitious
  chance 156.15
  circumstantial 8.7
  unessential 6.4
adventure act 705.3
  biography 608.4
  chance event 156.6
  courageous act 893.7
  event 151.2
  undertaking 715.2
adventurer
  gambler 515.17
  mercenary 800.16
  reckless person 894.4
  stock speculator
  833.11
  traveler 274.1
  upstart 919.10

adventuresome
daring 893.21
enterprising 707.23
adventuress
reckless person 894.4
unchaste woman
989.15
adventurous
daring 893.21
dynamic 707.23
enterprising 715.8
foolhardy 894.9
hazardous 697.10
adverb 586.3
adversary
n. enemy 929.6
opponent 791.1
adj. opposing 790.8
adverse contrary 15.6
opposing 790.8
untoward 729.13
adversity 729
advertent 530.15
advertise flaunt 904.17
inform 557.8
publicize 559.15
publish 559.10
advertisement 559.6
advertising 559.5
advice counsel 754
message 558.4
news 558.1
tip 557.3
advisable 670.5
advise counsel 754.5
inform 557.8
warn 703.5
advised
considered 482.21
intentional 653.9
advisement 478.2
adviser counselor 754.3
informant 557.5
advisory
admonitory 754.8
conciliar 755.5
informative 557.17
advocacy advice 754.1
patronage 785.4
promotion 559.5
recommendation
968.4
advocate
n. associate 787.9
defender 799.7
deputy 781.1
friend 928.1
justifier 1006.8
lawyer 1003.1
supporter 216.2
v. abet 785.14
advise 754.5
commend 968.11
defend 1006.10
urge 648.14
aegis armor 799.17
patronage 785.4
safeguard 699.3
aeon age 107.4
long time 110.4
aeonian 112.7
aer(o)- air 402.1

aviation 278.1
gas 401.2
aerate add gas 401.8
air 402.11
foam 405.5
aerial
n. radio 344.32
adj. aeronautic(al)
278.58
airy 402.12
high 207.19
imaginary 535.22
vaporous 401.9
aerialist
circus artist 612.3
gymnast 878.21
aerie 191.25
aeriness 401.3
aerobatics 278.13
aerodynamic(al)
aeronautic 278.58
gas 401.9
pneumatic 347.10
aerodynamics
aeronautics 278.2
dynamics 347.3
gas 401.2
pneumatics 347.5
aerography
aeronautics 278.2
meteorology 402.6
pneumatics 347.5
aerology
aeronautics 278.2
meteorology 402.6
pneumatics 347.5
aeromechanics
aeronautics 278.2
mechanics 347.1
pneumatics 347.5
aeromedicine 278.2
aeronaut aviator 279.1
balloonist 279.7
aeronautic(al) 278.58
aeronautics 278.1
aeroplane see **airplane**
aerosol
moisturizer 392.8
vaporizer 401.6
aerospace
n. aviation 278.41
adj. aeronautic 278.58
aerospace science 282.1
aerosphere
atmosphere 402.2
aviation 278.41
aerostatics
aeronautics 278.2
pneumatics 347.5
statics 347.2
aerotechnics
aeronautics 278.2
pneumatics 347.5
aery airy 402.12
ethereal 401.9
aesthete 897.6
aesthetic artistic 574.21
beautiful 900.16
tasteful 897.8
aesthetics
aesthetic taste 897.5
philosophy 500.1

aestival green 371.4
summer 128.8
warm 328.24
afar 199.15
affable agreeable 759.8
courteous 936.14
good-natured 938.14
informal 647.3
pleasant 863.6
sociable 922.18
affair business 656.1
concern 151.3
object 376.4
romance 931.6
social gathering
922.10
undertaking 715.1
affair of honor 796.7
affairs business 656.1
concerns 151.4
dealings 9.1
affect
n. emotion 855.3
mental attitude 525.1
v. affect emotionally
855.17
entail 76.4
excite pity 944.5
fake 616.21
imitate 22.5
influence 172.7
operate on 164.6
put on airs 903.12
relate to 9.5
show 555.5
stir feelings 855.16
wear 231.43
affectation
affectedness 903
behavior 737.1
fakery 616.3
grandiloquence 601.1
preciosity 589.3
style 588.2
affected elegant 589.9
falsified 616.26
grandiloquent 601.8
moved 855.25
pretentious 903.15
sanctimonious 1029.5
affecting
sympathetic 944.8
touching 855.24
unpleasant 864.20
affection
amorousness 931.3
disease 686.1
emotion 855.3
feelings 855.1
liking 634.2
love 931.1
affectionate
kind 938.13
loving 931.25
affianced
n. fiancée 931.16
adj. promised 770.8
affidavit
certificate 570.6
deposition 523.2
legal statement
1004.7

statement of belief
501.4
testimony 505.3
affiliate
n. branch 788.10
member 788.11
v. accept 637.15
ally 52.4
cooperate 786.3
join 788.14
naturalize 189.4
trace to 155.5
adj. joined 52.6
related 9.9
affiliated
associated 9.9
joined 52.6
related 11.6
affiliation
adoption 637.4
ancestry 170.4
blood relationship
11.1
combination 52.1
cooperation 786.2
naturalization 189.3
relationship 9.1
religion 1020.3
sociability 922.6
affinity accord 794.1
agreement 26.1
attraction 288.1
friendship 927.5
inclination 634.3
marriage relationship
12.1
preference 637.5
relationship 9.1
similarity 20.2
tendency 174.1
affirm
announce 559.12
assert 523.4
confirm 505.12
express belief 501.12
ratify 521.12
speak 594.24
testify 505.10
affirmation
assertion 523
confirmation 505.5
consent 775.1
deposition 523.2
premise 482.7
ratification 521.4
remark 594.4
testimony 505.3
affirmative
n. affirmative expres-
sion 521.2
consent 775.1
side of controversy
482.14
adj. agreeing 26.9
asserting 523.7
consenting 775.4
affirmed asserted 523.8
made public 559.17
ratified 521.14
affix
n. addition 41.2
morphology 582.3

v. add 40.4
  fasten 47.7
affixation
  addition 40.1
  connection 47.3
  morphology 582.3
afflatus genius 467.8
  inspiration 648.9
  poetic inspiration
    609.12
  revelation 1021.9
afflict distress 866.16
  hurt 424.7
  make grieve 872.19
  sicken 686.47
  work evil 675.6
afflicted
  distressed 866.22
  drunk 996.31
  pained 424.9
affliction
  adversity 729.1
  bane 676.1
  disease 686.1
  trouble 866.8
affluence flow 395.4
  influx 302.2
  plenty 661.2
  prosperity 728.1
  wealth 837.1
affluent flowing 395.24
  plentiful 661.7
  prosperous 728.12
  wealthy 837.13
afflux approach 296.1
  flow 395.4
  influx 302.2
afford
  able to pay 843.7
  be rich 837.10
  cost 846.15
  give 818.12
  provide 659.7
  supply 818.15
  yield 844.4
afforestation
  forestry 413.3
  woodland 411.11
affront
  n. indignity 965.2
  provocation 952.11
  v. confront 240.8
  defy 793.3
  hurt 952.20
  offend 965.4
  oppose 790.5
  stand up to 893.11
affusion
  baptism 1040.7
  wetting 392.6
afghan 228.10
aficionado
  attender 186.5
  fanatic 473.17
  specialist 81.3
  supporter 787.9
afield 199.19
afire burning 328.27
  fervent 855.23
  inspired 648.31
  zealous 635.10

afloat
  adj. adrift 275.61
  floating 275.60
  flooded 395.25
  happening 151.9
  rumored 558.15
  unfastened 49.22
  wandering 141.7
  adv. at sea 397.9
  on board 275.62
  preparation 720.23
afoot
  adj. astir 707.19
  happening 151.9
  adv. on foot 273.42
  preparation 720.23
aforementioned 64.5
aforethought
  n. intentionality 653.3
  adj. premeditated
    653.10
afoul 275.72
afraid cowardly 892.10
  irresolute 627.12
  scared 891.30
afresh anew 122.15
  once more 91.7
  repeat again 103.17
Afro 230.15
aft
  adj. rear 241.9
  adv. astern 275.69
  behind 241.14
after
  adj. rear 241.9
  subsequent 117.4
  adv. behind 241.14
  following 293.6
  subsequently 117.6
  prep. because of 155.9
  in conformity with
    82.9
  in imitation of 22.12
  in pursuit of 655.12
  subsequent to 117.8
after a fashion
  somehow 657.13
  to a degree 35.10
after all
  considering 494.17
  notwithstanding 33.8
  subsequently 117.6
afterdeath 117.5
aftereffect
  aftermath 67.3
  effect 154.4
afterglow
  aftermath 67.3
  effect 154.4
  remainder 43.1
  shine 335.2
afterimage
  aftermath 67.3
  effect 154.4
  illusion 519.5
  remainder 43.1
afterlife heaven 1018.3
  posteriority 117.1
  the future 121.2
aftermath effect 154.4
  posteriority 67.3
  sequel 117.2

yield 811.5
afternoon
  n. time of day 134
  adj. postmeridian
    134.7
afterpart rear 241.1
  sequel 67.2
aftertaste
  aftermath 67.3
  effect 154.4
  taste 427.1
afterthought
  change of mind 628.1
  delay 132.2
  mature thought
    478.5
  sequel 67.1
afterwards
  in the future 121.9
  subsequently 117.6
afterworld
  heaven 1018.3
  the future 121.2
again
  adv. additionally
    40.11
  anew 122.15
  duplication 91.7
  notwithstanding 33.8
  repetition 103.17
  then 105.11
  interj. encore! 103.18
again and again
  continuously 71.10
  frequently 135.6
  repeatedly 103.16
against
  in disagreement with
    27.10
  in preparation for
    720.24
  opposed to 790.10
  opposite to 239.7
  toward 290.28
  up against 200.25
against the grain
  backwards 295.13
  contrarily 15.9
  in opposition 790.9
  roughly 261.12
  unlikable 867.7
against the law 999.6
agape accord 794.1
  benevolence 938.4
  love 931.1
  rite 1040.4
agape astonished 920.9
  curious 528.5
  expectant 539.11
  gaping 265.19
age
  n. durability 110.1
  era 107.5
  generation 107.4
  lifetime 110.5
  long time 110.4
  oldness 123.1
  years 126
  v. become old 123.9
  grow old 126.10
aged elderly 126.16
  enduring 110.10

mature 126.13
agee 219.14
ageless old 123.10
  perpetual 112.7
agency
  commission 780.1
  instrumentality 658.2
  operation 164.1
  substitution 149.1
  trade 827.2
  workplace 719.1
agenda list 88.6
  schedule 641.2
agent assignee 780.8
  assistant 787.6
  chemical 379.1
  creator 153.4
  deputy 781.3
  doer 718.1
  instrument 658.3
  intermediary 237.4
  lawyer 1003.1
  manager 748.1
  mediator 805.3
  operator 164.4
  salesman 830.4
  substitute 149.2
  theatrical agent
    611.30
  transformer 139.4
agent provocateur
  instigator 648.11
  shill 619.5
age-old 123.10
agglomeration
  accumulation 74.9
  cohesion 50.1
  combination 52.1
  conglomeration 50.5
  joining 47.1
agglutination
  addition 40.1
  cohesion 50.1
  densification 354.3
  joining 47.1
aggrandize
  exaggerate 617.3
  expand 197.4
  glorify 914.13
  increase 38.4
  promote 782.2
aggrandized
  eminent 914.18
  exaggerated 617.4
  increased 38.7
aggravate annoy 866.13
  antagonize 929.7
  impair 692.11
  increase 38.5
  provoke 952.22
  sow dissension 795.14
  vex 864.15
  worsen 885.2
aggravated
  annoyed 866.21
  damaged 692.29
  provoked 952.25
  worsened 885.4
aggravating
  annoying 864.22
  exasperating 885.5

aggravation
  adversity 729.1
  annoyance 866.2
  excitation 857.10
  increase 38.2
  resentment 952.1
  vexatiousness 864.7
  worsening 885
aggregate
  n. accumulation 74.9
  all 54.3
  sum 86.5
  v. assemble 74.18
  total 54.8
  adj. assembled 74.21
  whole 54.9
aggregation
  accumulation 74.9
  combination 52.1
  joining 47.1
aggression attack 798.1
  enterprise 707.7
  warlikeness 797.15
aggressive
  attacking 798.30
  energetic 161.12
  enterprising 707.23
  gruff 937.7
  quarrelsome 795.17
  warlike 797.25
aggressor 798.13
aggrieve
  make grieve 872.19
  offend 952.20
  pain 866.17
  work evil 675.6
aghast astonished 920.9
  terrified 891.34
agile alert 533.14
  fast 269.19
  nimble 733.21
  quick 707.18
agility alertness 533.5
  nimbleness 733.2
  quickness 707.3
aging
  n. maturation 126.6
  adj. growing old
    126.17
agio 847.1
agitate
  discompose 63.4
  distress 866.16
  excite 857.13
  incite 648.17
  shake 324.10
  trouble 890.3
agitated active 707.20
  anxious 890.6
  distressed 866.22
  disturbed 324.16
  excited 857.21
  jittery 859.11
agitation anxiety 890.1
  bustle 707.4
  excitation 857.10
  incitement 648.4
  irregular motion 324
  nervousness 859.1
  stimulation 857.3
  trepidation 891.5
  violence 162.2

agitator
  instigator 648.11
  mixer 44.10
  rebel 767.5
  shaker 324.9
  troublemaker 943.2
agitprop
  false teacher 563.2
  instigator 648.11
aglow burning 328.27
  illuminated 335.39
  luminous 335.30
agnate kindred 9.10
  related 11.6
  similar 20.13
agnostic
  n. skeptic 1031.12
  adj. doubtful 503.9
  skeptical 1031.20
  uncertain 514.15
agnosticism
  ignorance 477.1
  skepticism 1031.6
  unbelief 503.1
Agnus Dei
  hymn 1032.3
  Mass 1040.10
  sacred article 1040.11
ago
  adj. past 119.7
  adv. since 119.15
agog astonished 920.9
  attentive 530.15
  curious 528.5
  eager 635.9
  excited 857.18
  expectant 539.11
agonistics 878.8
agonize
  be uncertain 514.9
  cause unpleasantness
    864.12
  grieve 872.17
  inflict pain 424.7
  struggle 716.11
  suffer 866.19
  suffer pain 424.8
  torture 866.18
agonized
  affected 855.25
  pained 424.9
  tortured 866.25
agonizing
  painful 424.10
  unpleasant 864.23
agonizingly
  terribly 34.21
  unpleasantly 864.28
agony despair 866.6
  dying 408.9
  pain 424.6
  sorrow 872.10
  unpleasantness 864.4
agrarian
  agricultural 413.20
  rustic 182.6
agree assent 521.8
  be willing 622.3
  coact 177.2
  coincide 14.4
  come to an agree-
    ment 521.10

  concur 521.9
  conform 26.6
  contract 771.6
  get along 794.2
  synchronize 118.3
agreeable
  acceptable 868.12
  agreeing 26.9
  beautiful 900.17
  consenting 775.4
  considerate 938.16
  courteous 936.14
  desirable 634.30
  friendly 927.14
  good-natured 938.14
  harmonious 794.3
  indulgent 759.8
  melodious 462.49
  pleasant 863.6
  submissive 765.12
  tasty 428.8
  welcome 925.12
  willing 622.5
agreed agreeing 521.13
  contracted 771.12
  so be it 521.19
agreeing
  acquiescing 521.13
  concurrent 177.4
  consenting 775.4
  in accord 794.3
  in agreement 26.9
  simultaneous 118.4
  unanimous 521.15
agreement accord 26
  assent 521.1
  combination 52.1
  compact 771.1
  concurrence 177.1
  conformity 82.1
  consent 775.1
  harmony 794.1
  identity 14.1
  promise 770.2
  similarity 20.1
  simultaneity 118.1
  unanimity 521.5
agree to assent 521.8
  consent 775.2
  contract 771.6
  promise 770.5
  strike a bargain
    827.18
agree with
  accord 521.9
  agree 521.10
  assent 521.8
  conform 82.3
  get along 794.2
  make for health
    683.4
agricultural
  agrarian 413.20
  rustic 182.6
agriculture
  deities 413.4
  farming 413
agriculturist 413.5
agronomics 413.1
agronomist 413.5
aground
  adj. fixed 142.16

  in difficulty 731.25
  adv. on the rocks
    275.73
ague
  disease symptom
    686.8
  malaria 686.12
  shaking 324.2
ah! 920.20
aha! 968.22
ahead
  adj. superior 36.12
  adv. early 131.11
  forward 294.8
  in front 240.12
  interj. command
    275.77
ahead of its time
  122.13
ahoy! attention! 530.23
  sailing 275.75
Ahura Mazda 1013.6
aid
  n. assistant 787.6
  benefactor 942.1
  help 785
  remedy 687.1
  subsidy 818.8
  support 216.1
  v. facilitate 732.6
  help 785.11
  subsidize 818.19
aid and abet
  abet 785.14
  encourage 648.21
aid and comfort 887.4
aide assistant 787.6
  commissioned officer
    749.18
ail be sick 686.43
  inflict pain 424.7
  suffer pain 424.8
  trouble 731.12
ailment 686.1
aim
  n. direction 290.1
  intention 653.1
  meaning 545.2
  objective 653.2
  v. direct 290.6
  endeavor 714.4
  head for 290.8
  intend 653.4
aim at desire 634.14
  direct 290.6
  fire upon 798.22
  intend 653.4
aimless
  discursive 593.13
  meaningless 547.6
  purposeless 156.16
  unordered 62.12
  useless 669.9
aimlessly
  chaotically 62.19
  meaninglessly 547.8
  purposelessly 156.20
  uselessly 669.15
air
  n. atmosphere 402
  aviation 278.41
  behavior 737.1

breeze 403.5
element 376.2
gas 401.2
heavens 375.2
lightness 353.2
looks 446.4
melody 462.4
milieu 233.3
spirit 4.3
v. broadcast 559.10
discuss 597.12
divulge 556.5
flaunt 904.17
make public 559.11
ventilate 402.11
airborne 278.59
air-built
imaginary 535.22
tenuous 4.6
airburst 281.9
air-condition air 402.11
refrigerate 334.10
air-conditioned 334.13
air conditioner 402.10
air conditioning
refrigeration 334.1
ventilation 402.9
air corps
air force 800.28
corps 800.20
air cover 278.11
aircraft
airplane 280.1,15
vehicle 272.1
aircraft carrier 277.8,24
aircraft engine
aviation 278.33
types of 280.17
aircrew 279.4
air current 403.1
air-cushion vehicle
aircraft 280.7
hovercraft 272.21
air express 271.3
airfield 278.22
air force
air corps 800.28
aircraft 280.9
air service 800.29
aviator 279.3
Air Force 278.7
airfreight
n. air travel 278.10
transportation 271.3
v. send 271.14
air hole
air passage 396.17
aviation 278.41
hole 265.4
airiness frailness 205.4
illusoriness 519.2
lightheartedness
870.3
lightness 353.1
rarity 355.1
unsubstantiality 4.1
windiness 403.15
airing discussion 597.7
publication 559.1
ride 273.7
ventilation 402.9
walk 273.12

air lane aviation 278.42
route 657.2
airless 268.16
airlift
n. flight 278.9
transportation 271.3
v. fly 278.45
airline 278.1
air line aviation 278.42
shortcut 203.5
straight line 250.2
air lock entrance 302.5
lock 396.11
airmail
n. mail 604.5
v. mail 604.13
send 271.14
airman 279.1
airmanship
pilotship 278.3
skill 733.1
air mass 402.5
airplane
n. aircraft 280.1,15
parts 280.16
v. fly 278.45
air pocket 278.41
air pollution
powder 361.5
unhealthfulness 684.1
airport 278.22
air raid
bombardment 798.7
flight 278.11
raid 798.4
air route 278.42
airs affectation 903.1
contempt 966.1
ostentation 904.2
air shaft 396.17
airship aircraft 280.11
parts 280.19
air show 278.1
air shuttle 278.10
airsick
aeronautic 278.58
nauseated 686.53
airspace
aviation 278.41
region 180.1
air space
headroom 179.3
space 179.4
air speed
aviation 278.40
speed 269.1
air strike 798.4
airstrip 278.23
air support 278.11
airtight
impenetrable 266.12
resistant 159.18
air-traffic controller
346.14
air travel 278.10
airway
air passage 396.17
aviation 278.42
airworthy
aeronautic 278.58
safe 698.7
airy aery 402.12

careless 534.11
high 207.19
illusory 519.9
immaterial 377.7
light 353.10
lighthearted 870.12
rare 355.4
tenuous 4.6
thin 205.16
trivial 673.16
vaporous 401.9
visionary 535.24
windy 403.25
aisle 657.4
ajar clashing 461.5
gaping 265.19
akimbo 251.6
akin in accord 794.3
related 9.10
related by blood 11.6
similar 20.13
à la 22.12
alabaster
mineral 383.19
smooth surface 260.3
white comparisons
364.2
à la carte 307.11
alacrity eagerness 635.1
hastiness 709.2
promptness 131.3
quickness 707.3
willingness 622.1
Aladdin's lamp 1036.6
à la mode
fashionably 644.17
modern 122.13
stylish 644.12
alarm
n. alarm signal 704
fear 891.1
signal 568.15
summons 568.16
warning 703.1
v. alert 704.3
frighten 891.23
alarmed aroused 704.4
frightened 891.33
alarming
dangerous 697.9
frightening 891.36
alarmist 891.8
albeit 33.8
albinism
faulty eyesight 440.1
genetic disease
686.11
whiteness 364.1
albino
n. whiteness 364.1
adj. white 364.10
album
compilation 605.4
record book 570.11
albumen
egg white 406.15
semiliquid 389.5
alchemy
conversion 145.1
sorcery 1035.1
alcohol
antifreeze 334.8

antiseptic 687.58
chemical 379.11
depressant 687.54
fuel 331.1
liquor 996.12
sedative 687.12
solvent 391.10
alcoholic
n. addict 642.10
drunkard 996.10
pathological type
690.16
adj. spirituous 996.36
alcoholism
addiction 642.9
intoxication 996.3
alcove nook 192.3
recess 257.7
summerhouse 191.13
alderman
legislator 746.3
public official 749.17
aleatory
n. music 462.5
adj. chance 156.15
circumstantial 8.7
hazardous 697.10
uncertain 514.18
Alecto Fury 1016.11
rage 952.10
alee downwind 275.68
leeward 242.9
alehouse 996.19
alert
n. alarm 704.1
v. alarm 704.3
inform 557.11
warn 703.5
adj. attentive 530.15
awake 713.8
clear-witted 467.13
prepared for 720.18
prompt 131.9
vigilant 533.14
alfresco
adj. airy 402.12
outdoor 224.7
adv. outdoors 224.10
algae plant 411.4; 412.3
types of 411.42
algebraic(al) 87.17
algesia 424.4
algid cold 333.14
feeling cold 333.15
algorithm
mathematics 87.2
number system 86.2
way 657.1
alias
n. pseudonym 583.8
adv. otherwise 16.11
alibi
n. excuse 1006.4
pretext 649.1
v. excuse 1006.11
alien
n. odd person 85.4
outsider 77.3
spaceman 282.8
stranger 78.3
adj. external 224.8
extraterrestrial 375.26

foreign 78.5
hostile 790.8
unrelated 10.5
alienate
antagonize 929.7
indoctrinate 145.15
separate 49.9
sow dissension 795.14
transfer property
817.3
alienated alone 89.8
dissenting 522.6
estranged 929.11
separated 49.21
alienation
aloneness 89.2
defense mechanism
690.30
dissent 522.1
emotional symptom
690.23
enmity 929.2
falling-out 795.4
indoctrination 145.5
insanity 473.1
property transfer
817.1
separation 49.1
alienist
insanity curing
473.18
psychologist 690.12
alight
v. descend 316.7
disembark 300.8
fly 278.52
adj. burning 328.27
illuminated 335.39
alight upon find 488.3
light on 316.10
meet 200.11
align dispose 60.9
join with 786.4
level 214.6
line 71.5
make parallel 218.5
alignment
affiliation 786.2
orientation 290.5
parallelism 218.1
alike
adj. equal 30.7
identical 14.7
indistinctive 493.6
similar 20.10
uniform 17.5
adv. identically 14.9
alimentary 309.19
alimentation
food 308.3
nutrition 309.1
alimony 818.8
aline see align
aliquot 86.8
alive alert 533.14
clear-witted 467.13
lively 707.17
living 407.11
remembered 537.23
teeming 101.9
alive and kicking
healthy 685.7

living 407.11
alive to
cognizant of 475.16
sensible 422.13
alkali 379.1
alkaline 379.7
alkalize 379.6
alkalizer 687.25
all
n. completion 56.5
everyone 79.4
the whole 54.3
universe 375.1
adj. every 79.15
whole 54.9
adv. wholly 54.13
all aboard
on board 275.62
sailing 275.75
Allah 1013.3
all-around
handy 665.19
versatile 733.23
all at once
at once 113.8
suddenly 113.9
together 73.11
allay gratify 865.6
moderate 163.6
pacify 804.7
relieve 886.5
satiate 664.4
all clear alarm 704.1
safe! 698.9
unindebted 841.23
all-comprehensive
comprehensive 76.7
infinite 104.3
universal 79.14
all-consuming 693.27
all creation 375.1
all ears
attentive 530.15
listening 448.15
vigilant 533.13
allegation
accusation 1005.1
affirmation 523.1
false claim 649.2
legal statement
1004.7
remark 594.4
testimony 505.3
allege accuse 1005.7
adduce evidence
505.13
affirm 523.4
pretext 649.3
state 594.24
testify 505.10
alleged affirmed 523.8
attributed 155.6
pretexted 649.5
supposed 499.14
allegiance duty 962.1
fidelity 974.7
obedience 766.1
allegoric(al)
fictional 608.17
implicative 546.10
meaningful 545.10

allegorize
explain 552.10
imply 546.4
narrate 608.13
allegory
comparison 491.1
fiction 608.7
implication 546.2
symbol 568.3
allegro
n. music 462.25
adv. actively 707.25
music 462.56
alleluia
n. cheer 876.2
hymn 1032.3
interj. worship
1032.16
Alleluia 1040.10
all-embracing
thorough 56.10
universal 79.14
whole 54.9
allergen allergy 686.32
antibody 687.27
allergic averse 867.8
diseased 686.57
sensitive 422.14
allergy
allergic disorder
686.32
disease 686.1
dislike 867.2
sensitivity 422.3
alleviate lighten 353.6
moderate 163.6
reduce 39.8
relieve 886.5
alleviation
decrease 39.1
lightening 353.3
moderation 163.2
relief 886.1
alleviative
n. moderator 163.3
palliative 687.10
adj. lightening 353.15
palliative 163.16
relieving 886.9
remedial 687.40
alley passageway 657.4
road 657.6
alliance
affiliation 786.2
association 788.1
blood relationship
11.1
combination 52.1
concurrence 177.1
marriage 933.1
relationship 9.1
similarity 20.1
treaty 771.2
allied akin 20.13
associated 9.9
combined 52.6
related 11.6
united 47.13
alligator 414.30,60
all in 717.8
all in all
generally 79.17

on the average 32.5
on the whole 54.14
all-inclusive
comprehensive 76.7
infinite 104.3
universal 79.14
whole 54.9
all in the mind
illusory 519.9
imaginary 535.19
alliteration
repetitiousness 103.4
rhyme 609.10
similar sound 20.6
alliterative
repetitious 103.15
rhyming 609.19
similar sounding
20.17
allocate allot 816.9
dispose 60.9
place 184.10
allocation
allotment 816.3
arrangement 60.1
placement 184.5
specification 80.6
allocution 599.2
all of a sudden
abruptly 203.13
suddenly 113.9
allopathy 688.2
allot apportion 816.9
distribute 60.9
give 818.12
allotheism
paganism 1025.4
religion 1020.5
allotment
apportionment 816.3
arrangement 60.1
portion 816.5
rations 308.6
subsidy 818.8
allotropy 19.1
all out actively 707.25
at full speed 269.24
extremely 34.22
in excess 663.23
utterly 56.16
all-out thorough 56.10
unqualified 508.2
allover 79.14
all over
completely 56.17
everywhere 179.11
in disorder 62.17
throughout 184.27
universally 79.18
all-overs anxiety 890.1
apprehension 891.4
nervousness 859.2
allow
acknowledge 521.11
concede 507.5
confess 556.7
discount 847.2
give 818.12
judge 494.8
permit 777.9

allowance
  acknowledgment 521.3
  discount 847.1
  extenuation 1006.5
  fee 841.5
  inaccuracy 518.2
  permission 777.1
  portion 816.5
  qualification 507.1
  rations 308.6
  subsidy 818.8
allowed
  acknowledged 521.14
  given 818.24
  permitted 777.16
allow for
  condone 947.4
  extenuate 1006.12
  take into account 507.5
alloy
  n. compound 44.5
  metal 383.4,22
  v. corrupt 692.14
  mix 44.11
all-pervading
  thorough 56.10
  universal 79.14
all-powerful
  godlike 1013.20
  omnipotent 157.13
all-present 186.13
all right
  acceptable 868.12
  accurate 516.15
  tolerable 674.19
  well 685.8
  yes! 521.18
all round
  all around 233.13
  everywhere 179.11
  in every direction 290.27
All Saints' Day 1040.15
all-seeing 1013.20
all set 720.16
All Souls' Day 1040.15
all the time 112.11
all the way
  as far as 199.20
  to the end 70.12
  utterly 56.16
all things considered
  generally 79.17
  judgment 494.17
  on the average 32.5
all thumbs 734.20
all together
  at once 113.8
  jointly 47.18
  simultaneously 118.6
  unanimously 521.17
allude to
  call attention to 530.10
  designate 568.18
  hint 557.10
  imply 546.4
  remark 594.25
allurement
  attraction 288.1

enticement 650
inducement 648.3
lovability 931.7
alluring
  attracting 288.5
  fascinating 650.7
  provocative 648.27
allusion 546.2
allusive figurative 551.3
  suggestive 546.6
alluvial 385.8
alluvium deposit 271.8
  land 385.1
  overflow 395.6
  sediment 43.2
ally
  n. associate 787.1
  country 181.1
  likeness 20.3
  v. cooperate 786.3
  join 52.4
  relate 9.6
alma mater 567.7
almanac 114.7
almighty
  adj. godlike 1013.20
  omnipotent 157.13
  adv. very 34.18
almond 308.38,52
almost 200.22
alms 818.6
almsgiver giver 818.11
  philanthropist 938.8
almshouse 700.4
almsman
  beneficiary 819.4
  poor person 838.4
aloft
  adv. on board 275.62
  up 207.26
  interj. sailing 275.75
aloha
  n. departure 301.4
  interj. farewell! 301.23
  greetings! 925.15
alone
  adj. secluded 924.10
  sole 89.9
  solitary 89.8
  adv. independently 762.32
  simply 45.11
  singly 89.13
along beside 242.11
  forward 294.8
  lengthwise 202.12
alongside
  adv. beside 275.70
  in parallel 218.7
  prep. beside 242.11
along with
  in addition 40.12
  together with 73.12
aloof
  adj. alone 89.8
  apathetic 856.13
  disconnected 51.4
  incurious 529.3
  reticent 613.10
  standoffish 912.12
  unsociable 923.6

adv. at a distance 199.14
  up 207.26
aloud audibly 450.18
  loudly 453.13
alp 207.7
alpen 207.23
alpha beginning 68.1
  first 68.3
alphabet basics 68.6
  representation 572.1
  writing system 581.3
alphabetarian 566.9
alphabetic(al)
  literal 581.8
  written 602.26
alphabetize
  classify 61.6
  letter 581.6
alpha particle
  atomics 326.6
  radiation 327.4
alpine 207.23
Alps 207.9
already
  previously 116.6
  until now 120.4
alright see all right
also
  adv. additionally 40.11
  conj. and 40.13
also-ran
  defeated candidate 746.9
  loser 727.5
  unsuccessful person 725.7
altar 1042.12
altarpiece
  church part 1042.12
  picture 574.12
alter be changed 139.5
  become 145.17
  castrate 42.11
  change 139.6
  qualify 507.3
alteration change 139.1
  differentiation 16.4
altercation
  contention 796.1
  quarrel 795.5
alter ego deputy 781.1
  friend 928.1
  likeness 20.3
  right-hand man 787.7
  self 80.5
alternate
  n. deputy 781.1
  substitute 149.2
  v. fluctuate 141.5
  interchange 150.4
  oscillate 323.13
  recur 137.5
  take turns 108.5
  vacillate 627.8
  adj. periodic 137.7
  reciprocal 323.19
  substitute 149.8
alternate school 567.2
alternating current 342.2

alternation
  fluctuation 141.3
  interaction 13.3
  interchange 150.1
  oscillation 323.5
  periodicity 137.2
alternative
  n. loophole 632.4
  option 637.2
  substitute 149.2
  adj. elective 637.22
  substitute 149.8
althorn 465.8
although 33.8
altimeter 207.14
altimetry
  height measurement 207.14
  mensuration 490.9
altitude
  aviation 278.44
  coordinates 490.6
  height 207.1
alto high voice 458.6
  music 462.22
  vocalist 464.13
altogether
  additionally 40.11
  completely 56.14
  generally 79.17
  wholly 54.13
altogether, the 232.3
alto-rilievo relief 256.2
  sculpture 575.3
altruism
  benevolence 938.4
  unselfishness 979.1
altruist 938.8
altruistic
  benevolent 938.15
  unselfish 979.5
alum 198.6
alumnus 566.8
alveolar
  indented 257.17
  phonetic 594.31
alveolus cavity 257.2
  indentation 257.6
  vocal organ 594.19
always constantly 135.7
  permanently 140.9
  perpetually 112.11
  regularly 17.8
  universally 79.18
AM modulation 344.14
  morning 133.1
amah maid 750.8
  nurse 699.8
amalgam alloy 383.4
  compound 44.5
amalgamate
  combine 52.3
  cooperate 786.3
  mix 44.11
amalgamation
  affiliation 786.2
  combination 52.1
  mixture 44.1
amanuensis agent 781.3
  recorder 571.1
  writer 602.13
amaranthine 112.9

amass assemble 74.18
 collect 811.10
 gather 47.5
 store up 660.11
amassed
 assembled 74.21
 stored 660.14
amateur
 n. connoisseur 897.7
 devotee 635.6
 dilettante 476.6
 nonprofessional
  718.5
 specialist 81.3
 trifler 673.9
 adj. avocational
  656.17
 half-learned 477.15
amateurish
 half-learned 477.15
 unskilled 734.16
amateur standing 656.9
Amati 465.6
amatory
 amorous 931.24
 flirtatious 932.21
amaze astonish 920.6
 perplex 514.13
amazed 920.9
amazement
 marvel 920.2
 wonder 920.1
amazing 920.12
amazon giantess 195.13
 mannish female
  420.9
ambages
 circumlocution 593.5
 convolution 254.1
 detour 321.3
ambassador 781.6
ambassadorial 781.16
amber 381.1,4
ambergris 436.2
ambi– 90.6
ambidextrous
 bilateral 91.4
 dishonest 975.21
 falsehearted 616.31
 right-left handed
  243.6
 versatile 733.23
ambience 233.1
ambient 233.8
ambiguity
 ambiguous expression
  550.2
 contrariety 15.3
 duality 90.1
 equivocacy 550
 inconsistency 27.2
 uncertainty 514.5
 unintelligibility 549.1
ambiguous
 equivocal 550.3
 mixed 44.15
 self-contradictory
  15.8
 uncertain 514.15
 unintelligible 549.13
ambit circuit 321.2
 environment 233.1

region 180.2
 sphere of influence
  172.4
ambition
 aspiration 634.10
 intention 653.1
 motive 648.1
 thing desired 634.11
ambitious
 aspiring 634.28
 enterprising 707.23
 ostentatious 904.18
ambivalence
 contrariety 15.3
 duality 90.1
 inconsistency 27.2
 irresolution 627.1
 psychological stress
  690.21
ambivalent
 irresolute 627.9
 mixed 44.15
 self-contradictory
  15.8
amble
 n. gait 273.14
 walk 273.12
 v. go slow 270.6
 ride 273.33
 walk 273.27
ambling
 n. walking 273.10
 adj. slow 270.10
ambrosia
 delicacy 308.8,49
 perfume 436.2
 salad 308.36
 sweetener 431.2
ambrosial
 fragrant 436.9
 sweet 431.4
 tasty 428.8
ambulance chaser
  1003.3
ambulatory
 n. passageway 657.4
 adj. walking 273.35
ambush
 n. concealment 615.3
 v. attack 798.15
 surprise 540.7
 waylay 615.10
ameba, amebic see
 amoeba etc.
ameliorate
 be changed 139.5
 change 139.6
 get better 691.7
 make better 691.9
amelioration
 change 139.1
 improvement 691.1
amen
 n. affirmative expres-
  sion 521.2
 interj. exactly 516.23
 so be it 521.19
 yes 521.18
amenable
 influenceable 172.15
 resigned 861.10
 responsible 962.17

willing 622.5
amend get better 691.7
 make better 691.9
 reclaim 145.12
 remedy 694.13
 revise 691.12
amendment
 improvement 691.1
 legislative clause
  742.17
 reformation 145.2
 revision 691.4
amends
 atonement 1012.1
 compensation 33.1
 payment 841.3
 reparation 694.6
 restitution 823.2
amenities
 civilities 936.7
 comfort 887.3
 etiquette 646.3
amenity courtesy 936.1
 facility 785.9
 pleasantness 863.1
 polite act 936.6
ament
 inflorescence 411.25
 simpleton 471.8
amentia 469.9
America
 New World 180.6
 United States 181.3
Americanism
 idiom 580.8
 patriotism 941.2
Americanize 189.4
American plan 307.11
amethystine 373.3
Amex 833.7
amiable friendly 927.14
 good-natured 938.14
 hospitable 925.11
 indulgent 759.8
 pleasant 863.6
 sociable 922.18
amicable
 friendly 927.14
 helpful 785.22
 in accord 794.3
 pleasant 863.6
amicus curiae
 deputy 781.1
 judge 1002.4
 lawyer 1003.1
amid among 44.18
 between 237.12
amidships
 adj. middle 69.4
 adv. midway 69.5
amigo 928.3
amino acid 309.6,24
amir see emir
amiss
 adj. disorderly 62.13
 erroneous 518.16
 adv. astray 314.7
 badly 675.13
 erroneously 518.20
amity accord 794.1
 friendship 927.1
ammo 801.8

ammonia coolant 334.7
 fertilizer 165.4
 gas 401.11
ammunition 801.8
ammunition depot
  801.2
amnesia
 failure of memory
  538.2
 trance state 690.26
amnesty
 exemption 1007.2
 pardon 947.2
amnion 229.3
amoeba germ 686.39
 microorganism
  196.18
amoebic 196.15
amok
 n. frenzy 473.7
 adj. excited 857.23
 mad 473.30
among at 184.26
 between 237.12
 mid 44.18
Amor god 1014.5
 love god 931.8
amoral
 dishonest 975.16
 unmoral 957.7
 vice-laden 981.11
amorality
 immorality 981.1
 unmorality 957.4
amorous
 passionate 931.24
 sexual 419.26
amorphous
 abnormal 85.9
 formless 247.4
 inconstant 141.7
 obscure 549.15
 unordered 62.12
 vague 514.18
amortization
 payment 841.1
 property transfer
  817.1
amortize
 pay in full 841.13
 transfer property
  817.3
amount count 28.2
 degree 29.1
 price 846.1
 quantity 28.1
 sum 86.5
 total 54.2
amount to cost 846.15
 equal 30.5
 total 54.8
amount to something
  672.11
amour 931.6
amperage 157.1
amphetamine 687.9,52
amphibian
 n. aircraft 280.8
 animal 414.32,62
 plant 411.3
 vertebrate 414.3;
  415.7

adj. froglike 414.51
amphibious
  mixed 44.15
  versatile 733.23
amphitheater
  arena 802.1
  hall 192.4
  schoolroom 567.16
  theater 611.18
ample abundant 101.8
  broad 204.6
  much 34.8
  plentiful 661.7
  satisfactory 868.11
  spacious 179.9
  sufficient 661.6
  voluminous 195.17
amplification
  aggravation 885.1
  development 148.1
  exaggeration 617.1
  expansion 197.1
  expatiation 593.6
  increase 38.1
  interpretation 552.3
  radio 344.15
amplified
  aggravated 885.4
  exaggerated 617.4
  expanded 197.10
  increased 38.7
amplifier
  audio amplifier 450.10
  electronic 343.18,20
  hearing aid 448.8
amplify
  aggravate 885.2
  develop 148.6
  electricity 342.23
  exaggerate 617.3
  expatiate 593.7
  increase 38.4
  make larger 197.4
amplitude
  aviation 278.25
  breadth 204.1
  diffuseness 593.1
  fullness 56.2
  greatness 34.1
  plenty 661.2
  quantity 28.1
  size 195.1
  sound 450.1
  spaciousness 179.5
  wave 323.4
amply
  abundantly 34.20
  satisfactorily 868.15
  sufficiently 661.8
amputate excise 42.10
  sever 49.11
amputation
  excision 42.3
  separation 49.2
  surgical operation 689.22
amputee 686.42
amuck see amok
amulet 1036.5
amuse 878.23
amused 878.28

amusement
  entertainment 878
  merriment 870.5
  pleasure 865.1
amusing
  entertaining 878.29
  humorous 880.4
ana archives 570.2
  collection 74.11
  compilation 605.4
  maxim 517.1
  selections 607.4
anabolism
  metabolism 309.10
  transformation 139.2
anachronism 115
anachronistic 115.3
anaerobe 686.39
anagram riddle 549.9
  wordplay 881.8
anal conformist 82.6
  intestinal 225.10
  tidy 59.8
analects
  compilation 605.4
  maxim 517.1
  selections 607.4
analeptic
  remedial 687.39
  restorative 694.22
  tonic 687.44
analgesia
  insensibility 423.1
  psychosomatic symptom 690.22
  relief 886.1
analgesic
  n. depressant 423.3
  sedative 687.12
  types of 687.56
  adj. deadening 423.9
  relieving 886.9
  sedative 687.45
analogous
  comparable 491.8
  parallel 218.6
  reciprocal 13.13
  similar 20.11
analogue correlate 13.4
  likeness 20.3
analogy
  comparison 491.1
  parallelism 218.1
  similarity 20.1
  substitute 149.2
analysis
  automation 349.7
  breakdown 48
  classification 61.1
  commentary 606.2
  differentiation 16.4
  discussion 597.7
  inquiry 485.1
  logic 482.3
  mathematics 87.18
  particularization 8.5
  psychoanalysis 690.8
  separation 49.5
  theorization 499.1
analyst analyzer 48.5
  psychotherapist 690.13

  tester 489.6
analytic(al)
  classificatory 48.9
  dialectic(al) 482.22
  examining 485.36
  mathematical 87.17
  reasoning 482.18
analyze
  break down 48.6
  classify 61.6
  differentiate 16.6
  discriminate 492.5
  discuss 597.12
  dissect 49.17
  grammaticize 586.16
  reason 482.15
analyzer analyst 48.5
  automatic 349.36
  separator 49.7
  tester 489.6
analyzing
  data processing 349.20
  judgment 494.3
anapest 609.9
anaphylactic 422.14
anaphylaxis 422.3
anarchic(al)
  confused 62.16
  formless 247.4
  illegal 999.6
  lawless 740.6
  revolutionary 147.6
  violent 162.17
anarchism
  lawlessness 740.2
  radicalism 745.4
  revolutionism 147.2
anarchist anarch 740.3
  radical 745.12
  revolutionist 147.3
anarchistic illegal 999.6
  lawless 740.6
  radical 745.20
anarchy confusion 62.2
  disorder 51.1
  formlessness 247.1
  illegality 999.1
  lawlessness 740.2
anathema curse 972.1
  disapproval 969.3
  hated thing 930.3
anatomic(al) 245.9
anatomize analyze 48.6
  differentiate 16.6
  dissect 49.17
  particularize 8.6
anatomy analysis 48.1
  biology 406.17
  body 376.3
  dissection 49.5
  human form 246.4
  science 245.7
  science of man 417.7
  skeleton 245.5
  structure 245.1
  zoology 415.1
ancestor
  antecedent 116.2
  parent 170.8
  precursor 66.1

ancestors
  antecedents 170.7
  producer 167.8
ancestral
  parental 170.13
  primitive 123.11
ancestry
  blood relationship 11.1
  kinsmen 11.2
  nobility 918.1
  progenitorship 170
anchor
  n. mooring 277.16
  types of 277.32
  v. fasten 47.7
  moor 275.15
  restrain 760.10
  settle 184.16
  stabilize 142.8
anchorage
  anchor 277.16
  destination 300.5
  fee 846.7
  harbor 700.6
  settlement 184.6
anchored fixed 142.14
  held 142.16
anchorite ascetic 991.2
  recluse 924.5
anchor man 344.23
anchors aweigh! 275.75
ancient
  n. man of old 123.7
  adj. aged 126.16
  enduring 110.10
  former 119.10
  old 123.10
ancient times 119.3
ancillary
  additional 40.10
  helping 785.20
and 40.13
andante
  n. music 462.25
  slowness 270.2
  tempo 463.24
  adv. music 462.55
andiron 329.12
andr(o)- 420.4
androgynous 419.33
androgyny
  effeminacy 421.2
  intersexuality 419.14
anecdotal 608.16
anecdote 608.6
anemia
  blood disease 686.18
  colorlessness 363.2
  deficiency disease 686.10
  disease symptom 686.8
  weakness 160.1
anemic colorless 363.7
  diseased 686.57
  weak 160.12
anemology
  meteorology 402.6
  wind 403.16
anemometer
  speed meter 269.7

wind instrument
403.17
anesthesia
insensibility 423.1
psychosomatic symp-
tom 690.22
relief 886.1
unfeeling 856.1
anesthetic
n. depressant 423.3
medicine 687.15,57
sleep-inducer 712.10
adj. deadening 423.9
numbing 687.47
relieving 886.9
anesthetist 688.14
anesthetize
make unfeeling 856.8
put to sleep 712.20
relieve 886.5
render insensible
423.4
anesthetized
sleepy 712.21
unfeeling 856.9
anew again 91.7
newly 122.15
repeatedly 103.17
anfractuous
spiral 254.8
winding 254.6
angel
celestial being 1015
celestial hierarchy
1015.3
endearment 932.5
financer 836.9
giver 818.11
good person 985.6
guardian angel
1014.22
innocent person
984.4
play backer 611.31
supporter 787.9
angelic innocent 984.6
lovable 931.23
pious 1028.9
seraphic 1015.6
virtuous 980.7
Angelus prayer 1032.4
signal 568.16
anger
n. heat 328.2
ill humor 951.1
sin 982.3
wrath 952.5
v. become angry
952.17
make angry 952.21
make hot 329.18
angina ache 424.5
cardiovascular disease
686.17
angle
n. aspect 446.3
aviation 278.26
corner 251.2
mental outlook 525.2
standpoint 184.2
story element 608.9
types of 251.12

viewpoint 439.7
v. bend 251.5
fish 655.10
maneuver 735.10
oblique 219.9
plot 654.10
angle for seek 485.29
solicit 774.14
angler 655.6
Anglicanism 1020.10
Anglicism idiom 580.8
patriotism 941.2
Anglicize 189.4
angling 655.3
angry annoyed 866.21
ill-humored 951.17
sore 424.11
stormy 403.26
violent 162.17
wrathful 952.26
angst anxiety 890.1
unpleasure 866.1
anguish
n. despair 866.6
pain 424.6
sorrow 872.10
unpleasure 866.1
v. make grieve 872.19
pain 866.17
suffer 866.19
suffer pain 424.8
anguished
pained 866.23
pleasureless 866.20
sorrowful 872.26
angular 251.6
angularity
angularness 251
inclination 219.2
anhydrous 393.7
anility old age 126.5
senility 469.10
anima life force 407.3
mind 466.4
psyche 690.35
animadversion 969.4
animal
n. bad person 986.7
barbarian 898.7
creature 414.2,58
prehistoric 123.26
savage 943.5
adj. animalian 414.43
carnal 987.6
cruel 939.24
lascivious 989.29
uncouth 898.12
animal diseases 686.38
animal husbandry 416
animalism
carnality 987.2
materialism 376.5
animalistic
animal 414.43
carnal 987.6
animality
animal life 414.1
carnality 987.2
cruelty 939.11
lasciviousness 989.5
uncouthness 898.3
violence 162.1

animal kingdom
animal life 414.1
class 61.4
stock 11.4
animal life 414
animal magnetism
712.8
animal noise 460
animal spirits
gaiety 870.4
life 407.1
animal worship 1033.1
animate
v. cheer 870.7
energize 161.9
impel 283.10
inspire 648.20
motivate 648.12
refresh 695.2
stimulate 857.12
vivify 407.9
adj. gender 586.10
living 407.11
organic 406.19
animated eager 635.9
energetic 161.12
gay 870.14
lively 707.17
living 407.11
motivated 648.30
refreshed 695.4
animated cartoon
cartoon 574.17
motion picture
611.16
animation
eagerness 635.1
energizing 161.7
excitation 857.10
gaiety 870.4
infusion 648.9
life 407.1
liveliness 707.2
stimulation 648.2
vivacity 161.3
vivification 407.5
animism idealism 377.3
paganism 1025.4
animist idealist 377.4
pagan 1025.7
animosity
bad feeling 855.7
bitterness 952.3
enmity 929.4
hate 930.2
animus animosity 929.4
inspiration 648.9
intention 653.1
trait of character
525.3
will 621.1
anion chemical 379.1
electrolysis 342.22
ankh 221.4
ankle joint 47.4
leg 273.16
ankle-deep deep 209.10
shallow 210.5
annalist author 602.15
chronicler 608.11
chronologist 114.10
recorder 571.2

annals chronicle 114.9
history 608.4
record 570.1
annealed
hardened 356.15
toughened 359.6
annex
n. addition 41.3
adjunct 41.1
v. acquire 811.9
add 40.4
appropriate 822.20
fasten 47.7
steal 824.13
annexation
addition 40.1
adjunct 41.1
appropriation 822.5
connection 47.3
theft 824.1
annihilate
abolish 693.13
destroy 693.14
eradicate 42.10
exterminate 2.6
kill 409.13
annihilation
death 408.1
destruction 693.6
excision 42.3
anniversary
celebration 877.1
commemoration
137.4,12
annotate
comment upon
552.11
judge 494.14
annotation
comment 552.5
record 570.4
announce affirm 523.4
forerun 116.3
presage 544.14
proclaim 559.12
report 558.11
announcement
affirmation 523.1
impartation 554.2
information 557.1
proclamation 559.2
announcer
broadcaster 344.23
harbinger 544.5
informant 557.5
precursor 66.1
proclaimer 561.3
annoy aggravate 885.2
excite 857.11
irk 866.13
provoke 952.22
vex 864.15
annoyance
adversity 729.1
aggravation 885.1
resentment 952.1
trouble 731.3
unpleasantness 864.7
vexation 866.2
annoyed
aggravated 885.4
irritated 866.21

provoked 952.25
troubled 731.19
annoying
aggravating 885.5
irritating 864.22
troublesome 731.17
worrying 890.9
annual
n. periodical 605.10
plant 411.3
record book 570.11
reports 570.7
adj. periodic 137.8
annuity
insurance 699.4
subsidy 818.8
annul abolish 693.13
divorce 935.5
neutralize 178.7
repeal 779.2
annular 253.11
annulet circlet 253.5
heraldic insignia
569.2
annulment
destruction 693.6
divorce 935.1
negation 524.2
neutralization 178.2
repeal 779.1
annum 107.2
annunciation
affirmation 523.1
proclamation 559.2
anodize 228.26
anodized 228.32
anodyne
n. pacifier 163.3
sedative 687.12
adj. palliative 163.16
relieving 886.9
sedative 687.45
anoint install 780.11
medicate 689.31
minister 1040.19
oil 380.8
anointment
accession to power
739.12
lubrication 380.6
anomalous
abnormal 85.9
eccentric 474.4
inconsistent 27.8
anomaly
abnormality 85.1
eccentricity 474.1
misfit 27.4
odd thing 85.5
unfitness 27.3
anon
in the future 121.9
soon 131.16
then 105.11
anon. 584.3
anonymity
namelessless 584
privacy 614.2
anonymous
nameless 584.3
private 614.13
anorexia 636.3

another
n. different thing 16.3
adj. additional 40.10
other 16.8
renewed 122.8
anoxia aviation 278.21
disease symptom
686.8
environmental dis-
ease 686.31
answer
n. communication
554.1
expedient 670.2
hymn 1032.3
justification 1006.2
letter 604.2
music 462.23
reaction 284.1
refutation 506.2
remark 594.4
reply 486
solution 487.1
v. agree 26.6
be expedient 670.3
be of use 665.17
communicate with
554.8
correspond 604.12
defend 1006.10
react 284.5
reciprocate 13.9
refute 506.5
relate to 9.5
reply 486.4
solve 487.2
suffice 661.4
suit 26.8
answer back
answer 486.4
be insolent 913.7
answer for
be responsible 962.9
pass for 572.7
promise 770.5
represent 781.14
ant 414.37,74
antacid
n. chemical 379.1
gastric antacid
687.25,63
neutralizer 178.3
adj. curative 687.41
neutralizing 178.9
antagonism
contrariety 15.1
counteraction 178.1
disagreement 27.1
dislike 867.2
hostility 929.3
opposition 790.2
warlikeness 797.15
antagonist actor 612.2
enemy 929.6
opponent 791.1
role 611.11
antagonistic
adverse 729.13
belligerent 797.25
contrary 15.6
counteractive 178.8
disagreeing 27.6

hostile 929.10
opposing 790.8
antagonize
contend against
790.4
counteract 178.6
provoke 929.7
ante
n. wager 515.3
v. bet 515.20
pay over 841.15
anteaters 414.58; 415.8
ante-bellum 116.5
antecede
be prior 116.3
precede 64.2
antecedent
n. ancestors 170.7
cause 153.1
precedent 116.2
precursor 66.1
adj. leading 292.3
preceding 64.4
prior 116.4
antechamber 192.20
antedate be prior 116.3
date 114.13
mistime 115.2
antediluvian
n. antiquated person
123.8
prehistoric man 123.7
adj. antiquated
123.13
prior 116.5
antelope
hoofed animal 414.5
mammal 414.58;
415.8
speed 269.6
antemeridian 133.6
antenna feeler 425.4
radar 346.22
radio 344.32
whisker 230.10
antepast
appetizer 308.9
foretaste 542.4
serving 307.10
anterior front 240.10
preceding 64.4
prior 116.4
anteroom 192.20
anthem hymn 1032.3
sacred music 462.16
song 462.13
anthill hill 207.5
pile 74.10
anthology book 605.4
collection 74.11
excerpts 607.4
poetry 609.7
anthracite 331.9
anthrax
animal disease 686.38
infectious disease
686.12
occupational disease
686.31
anthrop(o)- 417.3

anthropoid
n. prehistoric man
123.7
adj. manlike 417.11
anthropological 417.10
anthropologist
science of man 417.7
zoologist 415.2
anthropology
science of man 417.7
zoology 415.1
anthropomorphic
manlike 417.11
religious 1020.24
anthropomorphism
humanization 417.6
religion 1020.5
anthropomorphize
417.9
anti contrary 15.6
opposing 790.8
ant(i)-
counteractive 178.8
destructive 693.26
diametric 15.7
front 240.10
opposite 239.5
preventing 730.19
prior 116.4
antibiotic
n. drug 687.29,60
poison 676.3
adj. curative 687.41
antibody
antitoxin 687.27
blood 388.4
immunity 685.4
antic
n. prank 881.10
v. play 878.25
adj. frisky 870.14
queer 85.12
antichrist 1031.10
anticipate
contemplate 539.5
earliness 131.6
expect 121.6
forerun 116.3
foresee 542.5
prevent 730.14
anticipating
expectant 539.11
pregnant 169.18
anticipation
anachronism 115.1
carefulness 533.1
earliness 131.1
expectation 539.1
foresight 542.1
intuition 481.1
priority 116.1
anticipatory
early 131.7
expectant 539.11
foreseeing 542.7
prior 116.4
anticlimax 880.3
antidepressant
n. psychoactive drug
687.13
adj. psychochemical
687.46

antidote
  counteractant 178.3
  counterpoison 687.26
antiestablishment 522.6
antifreeze 334.8
antigen
  antibody 687.27
  blood 388.4
  immunity 685.4
antigravity 289.1
antihero 611.11
antihistamine 687.32
antinomian
  anarchistic 740.6
  unorthodox 1025.9
antinomy
  contrariety 15.3
  inconsistency 27.2
antipasto 308.9
antipathetic(al)
  contrary 15.6
  counteractive 178.8
  disagreeing 27.6
  hostile 929.10
  opposing 790.8
antipathy
  contrariety 15.1
  counteraction 178.1
  dislike 867.2
  hate 930.1
  hated thing 930.3
  hostility 929.3
  opposition 790.2
  unwillingness 623.1
antiphon answer 486.1
  hymn 1032.3
  music 462.23
antipodal
  diametric 15.7
  polarized 239.5
antipodes
  opposite 15.2
  poles 239.2
  remote region 199.4
Antipodes 180.6
antipole
  contraposition 239.2
  opposite 15.2
antipyretic
  n. fever reducer 687.14,64
  adj. curative 687.41
antiquarian
  n. archaist 123.5
  adj. archaeological 123.20
antiquate 123.9
antiquated
  archaic 123.13
  disused 668.10
  past 119.7
antique
  n. antiquated person 123.8
  relic 123.6
  adj. antiquated 123.13
  disused 668.10
  enduring 110.10
  old 123.10
  past 119.7

antiquity
  ancient times 119.3
  durability 110.1
  oldness 123.1
  relic 123.6
antireligion 1031.8
antireligious 1031.22
anti-Semitism
  hate 930.1
  prejudice 527.4
antiseptic
  n. disinfectant 687.21,58
  poison 676.3
  adj. disinfectant 687.43
  sanitary 681.27
antisocial 940.3
antithesis
  contraposition 239.1
  contrariety 15.1
  opposite 15.2
antithetic(al)
  contrary 15.6
  facing 239.5
  opposing 790.8
antitoxic 687.41
antitoxin
  antitoxic serum 687.27
  injection 689.18
antitype 25.1
antonym opposite 15.2
  word 582.1
anus opening 265.6
  rectum 225.4
anvil
  auditory organ 448.7
  converter 145.10
anxiety
  apprehension 891.4
  eagerness 635.1
  emotional symptom 690.23
  expectancy 539.3
  impatience 862.1
  tension 890
  trouble 731.3
  unpleasure 866.1
anxious
  concerned 890.6
  eager 635.9
  fearful 891.32
  impatient 862.6
  in suspense 539.12
  pleasureless 866.20
  troubled 731.19
anxiously
  concernedly 890.10
  eagerly 635.14
  impatiently 862.8
any
  n. anything 79.5
  some 28.3
  adj. every 79.15
  one 89.7
  quantifier 28.5
anybody 79.5
anyhow anyway 657.12
  carelessly 534.18
any old way 534.18
anyone any 79.5

whoever 79.7
anything any 79.5
  some 28.3
anytime
  whenever 105.12
  imminently 152.4
anyway 657.12
anywhere 184.21
A1
  n. superior 36.4
  adj. best 36.13
  first-rate 674.15
  seaworthy 277.18
aorta 396.14
apace fast 269.21
  hastily 709.12
  promptly 131.15
apart
  adj. alone 89.8
  distant 199.8
  secluded 924.7
  separate 49.20
  unrelated 10.5
  adv. away 199.17
  in half 92.8
  privately 614.19
  separately 49.28
  singly 89.13
apartheid
  exclusiveness 77.3
  prejudice 527.4
  seclusion 924.1
apartment 191.14
apathetic aloof 856.13
  hopeless 889.12
  incurious 529.3
  inert 268.14
  languid 708.19
  neutral 806.7
  reluctant 623.6
  unconcerned 636.7
apathy despair 889.2
  emotional symptom 690.23
  incurious 529.1
  inertia 268.4
  languor 708.6
  neutrality 806.2
  unconcern 636.2
  unfeeling 856.4
ape
  n. imitator 22.4
  mammals 415.8
  primate 414.59
  wild animal 414.28
  v. imitate 22.6
  impersonate 572.9
  resemble 20.7
  adj. enthusiastic 635.12
aperçu
  abridgment 607.1
  insight 481.1
  treatise 606.1
apéritif
  alcoholic drink 996.8
  appetizer 308.9
aperture opening 265.1
  passageway 657.4
apex height 207.2
  summit 211.2
  vertex 251.2

vocal organ 594.19
aphasia
  imperfect speech 595.6
  mental symptom 690.25
  muteness 451.2
aphorism
  conciseness 592.3
  maxim 517.1
  witticism 881.7
aphoristic(al)
  concise 592.6
  proverbial 517.6
aphrodisiac 419.7
Aphrodite
  beautiful woman 900.9
  goddess 1014.5
  love goddess 931.8
apiary 191.25
apiece 80.19
apish foolish 470.8
  imitative 22.9
  representational 572.10
aplenty
  adj. plentiful 661.7
  adv. plentifully 661.9
aplomb
  equanimity 858.3
  self-control 624.5
  stability 142.1
  verticalness 213.1
apocalypse
  disclosure 556.1
  prediction 543.1
  revelation 1021.9
Apocalypse 1021.4
apocalyptic(al)
  disclosive 556.10
  ominous 544.17
  predictive 543.11
  scriptural 1021.10
apocryphal
  spurious 616.26
  unauthoritative 514.20
  unorthodox 1025.9
apogee
  astronomy 375.16
  climax 56.5
  distance 199.2
  spacecraft 282.2
  summit 211.2
Apollo
  beautiful man 900.9
  god 1014.5
  Muse 609.12
  music patron 464.22
  spacecraft 282.14
  sun god 375.14
apologetic(al)
  atoning 1012.7
  justifying 1006.13
  penitent 873.9
apologetics
  argumentation 482.4
  theology 1023.1
apologia
  argumentation 482.4
  justification 1006.3

apologist
advocate 1006.8
arguer 482.12
defender 799.7
supporter 787.9
apologize
beg pardon 1012.5
excuse 1006.11
repent 873.7
apology
argumentation 482.4
excuse 1012.2
justification 1006.3
penitence 873.4
pretext 649.1
regret 873.1
apoplexy
cardiovascular disease
686.17
paralysis 686.25
paroxysm 162.5
seizure 686.5
stroke 324.6
apostasy change 139.1
conversion 145.3
defection 628.2
desertion 633.2
dissent 522.1
impiety 1030.1
religion 1020.9
apostate
n. defector 145.8
dissenter 522.3
impious person
1030.3
turncoat 628.5
adj. impious 1030.6
recreant 628.11
treasonable 145.20
apostatize
convert 145.13
defect 628.8
desert 633.6
apostle converter 145.9
disciple 566.2
Mormon priest
1038.11
religious founder
1022.2
apostolic(al)
papal 1037.15
scriptural 1021.10
apostrophize 594.27
apothecary
pharmacist 687.35
store 832.4
apothegm maxim 517.1
witticism 881.7
apotheosis
exaltation 317.1
glorification 914.8
ideal 25.4
idolization 1033.2
praise 968.5
removal to heaven
1018.12
respect 964.1
appall dismay 891.27
offend 864.11
terrify 891.25
appalling
disagreeable 864.19

remarkable 34.10
terrifying 891.38
appanage adjunct 41.1
endowment 818.9
property 810.2
apparatus
belongings 810.3
chemical 379.13
equipment 659.4
tool 348.1
apparel 231.1
apparent
appearing 446.11
false 616.27
illusory 519.9
manifest 555.8
probable 511.7
superficial 224.6
visible 444.6
apparently
externally 224.9
falsely 616.35
manifestly 555.14
seemingly 446.12
visibly 444.8
apparition
appearance 446.5
emergence 446.1
phantom 519.4
specter 1017.1
thing imagined 535.5
appeal
n. allurement 650.1
desirability 634.13
entreaty 774.2
legal action 1004.10
lovability 931.7
pleasantness 863.2
prayer 1032.4
v. attract 650.5
entreat 774.11
appealing
alluring 650.7
imploring 774.17
melodious 462.49
pleasant 863.7
appeal to
address 594.27
cite 505.15
demand 753.4
entreat 774.11
appear act 611.34
appear to be 446.10
attend 186.8
become visible 446.8
be revealed 556.8
be visible 444.4
manifest oneself
555.6
occur 151.6
appearance
apparition 446.5
appearing 446
arrival 300.1
exteriority 224.1
façade 446.2
fakery 616.3
form 246.3
illusoriness 519.2
manifestation 555.1
phantom 519.4
specter 1017.1

appear for 781.14
appease calm 163.7
gratify 865.6
pacify 804.7
relieve 886.5
worship 1032.14
appeasement
foreign policy 744.5
pacification 804.1
relief 886.1
worship 1032.6
appellation name 583.3
naming 583.2
append add 40.4
place after 65.3
appendage
adjunct 41.1
attendant 73.3
belongings 810.2
follower 293.2
hanger-on 907.5
nonessential 6.2
part 55.4
appendectomy 689.23
appendicitis 686.9
appendix addition 41.2
intestine 225.4
sequel 67.1
appertaining
relative 9.7
relevant 9.11
appertain to
belong to 808.7
relate to 9.5
appetite craving 634.6
eagerness 635.1
eating 307.1
sensuality 987.1
stomach 634.7
will 621.1
appetizer 308.9
appetizing
alluring 650.7
desirable 634.30
mouth-watering
428.10
applaud acclaim 968.10
assent 521.8
cheer 876.6
applause acclaim 968.2
cheer 876.2
apple of one's eye
931.15
apple-polisher 907.3
apple-polishing 907.2
appliance
equipment 659.4
facility 785.9
hard goods 831.4
instrument 658.3
machinery 348.4
use 665.1
applicable apt 26.10
legal 998.10
relevant 9.11
usable 665.22
applicant 774.7
application
attribution 155.1
engrossment 530.3
giving 963.2
industry 707.6

medical dressing
687.33
perseverance 625.1
relevance 9.4
request 774.1
study 564.3
use 665.1
appliqué
n. cover 228.4
v. sew 223.5
apply administer 963.6
attribute 155.3
cover 228.19
petition 774.10
put to use 665.11
relate 9.6
request 774.9
apply oneself
endeavor 714.4
exert oneself 716.9
apply oneself to
attend to 530.5
busy oneself with
656.11
practice 705.7
study 564.12
think about 478.11
undertake 715.3
appoint allot 816.9
assign 780.10
choose 637.20
destine 640.7
equip 659.8
prescribe 752.10
appointee 780.8
appointment
accession to power
739.12
allotment 816.3
assignment 780.2
consecration 1037.10
decree 752.4
engagement 922.8
hiring 780.4
position 656.5
selection 637.9
appointments
belongings 810.2
equipment 659.4
apportion allot 816.6
distribute 60.9
portion 49.18
quantify 28.4
share 815.6
apposite apt 26.10
relevant 9.11
apposition 200.3
appraisal analysis 48.3
judgment 494.3
measurement 490.1
valuation 846.4
appraise analyze 48.8
judge 494.9
measure 490.11
price 846.13
appraiser 490.10
appreciable
knowable 475.25
measurable 490.15
substantial 3.6
weighable 352.19

appreciably
  measurably 490.16
  to a degree 35.10
appreciate
  be grateful 949.3
  enjoy 865.10
  increase 38.6
  judge 494.9
  know 475.12
  measure 490.11
  rate highly 672.12
  respect 964.4
  savor 428.5
  understand 548.7
appreciation
  acknowledgment
    521.3
  cognizance 475.2
  commendation 968.3
  discrimination 492.1
  gratitude 949.1
  increase 38.1
  judgment 494.3
  respect 964.1
appreciative
  approbatory 968.16
  cognizant of 475.16
  discriminating 492.7
  grateful 949.5
apprehend
  arrest 761.15
  capture 822.18
  fear 891.18
  have foreboding
    544.11
  know 475.12
  sense 422.8
  understand 548.7
apprehension
  anxiety 890.1
  arrest 761.6
  doubt 503.2
  expectancy 539.3
  fearfulness 891.4
  foreboding 544.2
  idea 479.1
  intelligence 467.1
  seizure 822.2
  understanding 475.3
apprehensive
  anxious 890.6
  fearful 891.32
  in suspense 539.12
  knowing 475.15
  nervous 859.10
apprentice
  n. artisan 718.6
  novice 566.9
  producer 167.8
  trainee 68.2
  v. indenture 780.17
  train 562.14
  adj. indentured
    780.20
apprenticed 780.20
apprenticeship
  indenture 780.7
  training 562.3
apprise 557.8
apprised of 475.16
approach
  n. arrival 300.1

attempt 714.2
  coming 296
  convergence 298.1
  entrance 302.5
  imminence 152.1
  landing 278.18
  nearness 200.1
  offer 773.1
  plan 654.1
  similarity 20.1
  way 657.1
  v. accost 296.3
  address 594.27
  appear 151.6
  arrive 300.6
  attempt 714.5
  befriend 927.11
  be imminent 152.2
  be in the future
    121.6
  be near 200.8
  bribe 651.3
  communicate with
    554.8
  converge 298.2
  influence 172.9
  make advances 773.7
  near 200.7
  resemble 20.7
approachable
  accessible 296.5
  bribable 651.4
  communicative
    554.10
  possible 509.8
approaching
  arriving 300.9
  converging 298.3
  future 121.8
  imminent 152.3
  near 200.14
  nearing 296.4
approbation
  approval 968.1
  consent 775.1
  esteem 914.3
  ratification 521.4
  respect 964.1
appropriate allot 816.9
  borrow 821.4
  digest 309.16
  plagiarize 824.18
  steal 824.13
  take 822.19
  usurp 961.8
appropriate apt 26.10
  characteristic 80.13
  decorous 897.10
  due 960.8
  expedient 670.5
  relevant 9.11
  right 958.8
  timely 129.9
  useful 665.18
  well-chosen 589.7
appropriation
  allotment 816.3
  borrowing 821.2
  plagiarism 824.7
  taking over 822.4
  theft 824.1
  usurpation 961.3

approval
  approbation 968
  consent 775.1
  esteem 914.3
  ratification 521.4
  respect 964.1
approve accept 968.9
  adopt 637.15
  consent 775.2
  evidence 505.9
  ratify 521.12
approved
  accepted 968.19
  acknowledged 521.14
  authoritative 513.18
  chosen 637.26
  conventional 645.5
  orthodox 1024.7
  received 819.10
approximate
  v. approach 296.3
  be near 200.8
  resemble 20.7
  similarize 20.8
  adj. approaching
    296.4
  inaccurate 518.17
  near 200.14
  relative 9.8
  similar 20.14
approximately
  nearly 200.23
  some 28.6
  virtually 54.14
approximation
  approach 296.1
  inaccuracy 518.2
  mathematics 87.4
  measurement 490.1
  nearness 200.1
  relationship 9.1
  similarity 20.1
appurtenance
  adjunct 41.1
  component 58.2
  facility 785.9
  nonessential 6.2
  privilege 958.3
appurtenances
  belongings 810.2
  equipment 659.4
a priori back 119.12
  dialectic(al) 482.22
apron runway 278.23
  stage 611.21
  clothing 231.17
apropos
  adj. apt 26.10
  relevant 9.11
  adv. incidentally
    129.13
apse arch 252.4
  church part 1042.9
apt apposite 26.10
  inclined 525.8
  intelligent 467.14
  probable 511.6
  prompt 131.9
  skillful 733.20
  teachable 564.18
  well-chosen 589.7
aptitude fitness 26.5

intelligence 467.2
  likelihood 175.1
  probability 511.1
  talent 733.5
  teachability 564.5
  tendency 174.1
  trait of character
    525.3
aptitude test 690.11
apt to
  inclined to 174.6
  liable to 175.5
Aqua-Lung
  breathing 403.18
  diving equipment
    320.5
aquarium abode 191.24
  collection 74.11
aquatic
  water-dwelling 275.58
  watery 392.16
aquatint
  engraving process
    578.3
  print 578.6
aqueduct trench 263.2
  watercourse 396.2
aqueous 392.16
aquiculture
  botany 412.1
  oceanography 397.6
aquiline avian 414.52
  curved 252.8
Arab nomad 274.4
  waif 274.3
arabesque music 463.18
  network 221.3
  ornateness 901.2,13
Arabic numerals 86.2
arable 413.20
arbiter arbitrator 805.4
  connoisseur 897.7
  judge 1002.1
arbitrarily
  capriciously 629.7
  imperiously 739.19
arbitrary
  capricious 629.5
  discretionary 622.7
  imperious 739.16
  impulsive 630.10
arbitrate judge 494.12
  mediate 805.6
arbitration
  judgment 494.1
  mediation 805.2
arbitrator
  go-between 781.4
  judge 1002.1
  mediator 805.4
arbor axis 322.5
  summerhouse 191.13
arboreal
  branched 299.10
  treelike 411.36
arboretum
  garden 413.10
  woodland 411.11
arc curve 252.2
  electric discharge
    342.6

levitate 353.9
move 267.5
rise 315.8
ascendancy
  dominance 739.6
  influence 172.1
  superiority 36.1
  victory 726.1
ascendant
  ascending 315.14
  authoritative 739.15
  dominant 741.18
  influential 172.14
  superior 36.12
  victorious 726.8
ascending
  flowing 267.8
  high 207.19
  rising 315.14
  sloping upward
    219.17
ascension ascent 315.1
  removal to heaven
    1018.12
ascent acclivity 219.6
  course 267.2
  exaltation 317.1
  improvement 691.1
  increase 38.1
  lightness 353.1
  rise 315
ascertain decide 494.11
  learn 564.6
  make sure 513.11
  prove 505.11
ascertained
  known 475.26
  made sure 513.20
  proved 505.21
  true 516.12
ascetic
  n. abstainer 992.4
  puritan 991.2
  recluse 924.5
  religious 1038.17
  adj. abstinent 992.10
  atoning 1012.7
  austere 991.3
  in plain style 591.3
  meager 662.10
asceticism
  abstinence 992.2
  austerity 991
  penance 1012.3
ascorbic acid 309.4
ascribable
  attributable 155.6
  due 960.10
ascribe 155.3
aseptic 681.27
asexual 419.31
as far as to 199.20
  when 105.16
ash cinders 329.16
  residue 43.2
ashamed
  humiliated 906.13
  regretful 873.8
ashen burned 329.30
  colorless 363.7
  gray 366.4
  terrified 891.34

ashes cinders 329.16
  corpse 408.16
ashore 385.11
ashram
  commune 788.2
  retreat 700.5
Ash Wednesday
  1040.15
aside
  n. interjection 237.2
  soliloquy 598.1
  adv. apart 199.17
  in an undertone
    452.22
  in reserve 660.17
  on one side 242.10
  privately 614.19
  sideways 242.8
aside from
  excluding 77.9
  separately 49.28
as if 499.19
asinine foolish 470.8
  stupid 469.15
  trivial 673.16
  ungulate 414.49
as is as usual 140.10
  identically 14.9
  present 120.2
as it were
  figuratively 551.4
  so to speak 20.19
  supposedly 499.17
ask charge 846.14
  demand 753.4
  inquire 485.19
  invite 774.13
  request 774.9
  require 639.9
askance askew 219.22
  disapprovingly 969.27
  sideways 242.8
askew
  adj. asymmetric
    249.10
  disorderly 62.13
  erroneous 518.16
  oblique 219.14
  adv. awry 219.22
ask for demand 753.4
  encourage 648.21
  request 774.9
  seek 485.29
ask for it 894.5
asking price offer 773.1
  price 846.2
  stock price 834.9
asleep dead 408.30
  inattentive 531.8
  insensible 423.6
  sleeping 712.22
  unaware 477.13
  unconscious 423.8
as long as
  provided 507.15
  when 105.16
as one coactively 177.5
  cooperatively 786.6
  jointly 47.18
  simultaneously 118.6
  unanimously 521.17
aspect astrology 375.20

component 58.2
  grammatical form
    586.13
  look 446.3
  particular 8.3
  position 184.3
aspen 324.17
asperity
  bitterness 952.3
  causticity 939.8
  ill humor 951.1
  pungency 433.1
  roughness 261.1
aspersion
  baptism 1040.7
  disapproval 969.4
  indignity 965.2
  rite 1040.4
  slur 971.4
asphalt
  covering material
    228.43
  mineral 383.19
  pavement 657.7
asphyxiate die 408.24
  strangle 409.19
  suppress 760.8
asphyxiation
  disease symptom
    686.8
  suffocation 409.7
  violent death 408.6
aspic meat 308.12
  salad 308.36
aspirant desirer 634.12
  optimist 888.6
  petitioner 774.7
  political candidate
    746.9
aspirate suck 306.12
  whisper 452.10
aspiration
  ambition 634.9
  breathing 403.18
  extraction 305.3
  hope 888.1
  inhalation 306.5
  intention 653.1
  motive 648.1
  murmur 452.4
  speech sound 594.13
aspire aim at 653.4
  be ambitious 634.20
  be hopeful 888.7
  crave 634.18
  soar 315.10
aspirin analgesic 687.56
  antipyretic 687.64
aspiring
  ambitious 634.28
  high 207.19
  hopeful 888.11
ass
  beast of burden
    271.6
  buttocks 241.5
  copulation 419.8
  donkey 414.20
  fool 471.1
  obstinate person
    626.6
  sex object 419.4

assail attack 798.15
  criticize severely
    969.21
  incriminate 1005.10
assailant
  attacker 798.13
  opponent 791.1
assassin
  frightener 891.8
  killer 409.11
assassinate 409.16
assassination 409.2
assault
  n. accusation 1005.2
  attack 798.1
  berating 969.7
  violence 162.3
  v. attack 798.15
  terrorize 162.10
  thrust 283.11
assay
  n. analysis 48.1
  attempt 714.2
  test 489.2
  v. analyze 48.6
  attempt 714.5
  measure 490.11
  try out 489.8
ass-backwards
  adj. bungled 734.22
  confused 62.16
  adv. backwards 295.13
  clumsily 734.24
assemblage all 54.3
  assembling 74.14
  association 788.1
  collection 74
  composition 58.1
  hodgepodge 44.6
assemble collect 811.10
  come together 74.16
  compose 58.3
  create 167.10
  gather 74.18
  join 47.5
  sculpture 575.5
assembled
  collected 74.21
  joined 47.13
  made 167.22
assembly bunch 74.14
  collection 74.1
  composition 58.1
  council 755.1
  laity 1039.1
  legislature 742.1
  manufacture 167.3
  meeting 74.2
assembly line
  assembling 74.14
  plant 719.3
  production 167.2
assemblyman 746.3
assent
  n. acquiescence 521
  agreement 26.1
  consent 775.1
  submission 765.1
  v. acquiesce 521.8
  agree 26.6
  consent 775.2
  submit to 765.6

assenting
acquiescing 521.13
consenting 775.4
submissive 765.12
assert affirm 523.4
defend 1006.10
express belief 501.12
insist 753.7
postulate 499.12
state 594.24
assertion
affirmation 523.1
premise 482.7
remark 594.4
testimony 505.3
assertive 523.7
assert oneself 555.6
assess analyze 48.8
charge 846.14
judge 494.9
measure 490.11
price 846.13
assessed
measured 490.14
priced 846.16
assessment
analysis 48.3
fee 841.5
judgment 494.3
measurement 490.1
stock assessment
834.8
tax 846.10
valuation 846.4
assessor judge 1002.4
measurer 490.10
taxer 846.12
assets accounts 845.1
funds 835.14
property 810.8
resources 660.2
wealth 837.1
asseverate affirm 523.4
express belief 501.12
state 594.24
testify 505.10
asshole anus 265.6
fool 471.2
assiduity
attention 530.1
industry 707.6
painstakingness 533.2
perseverance 625.1
assiduous
attentive 530.15
industrious 707.22
painstaking 533.11
persevering 625.7
assign allot 816.9
appoint 780.10
assign lessons 562.18
attribute 155.3
commission 780.9
commit 818.16
locate 184.10
specify 80.11
transfer 271.9
transfer property
817.3
assignation
attribution 155.1
meeting 74.2

property transfer
817.1
rendezvous 922.9
assignee
appointee 780.8
beneficiary 819.4
assignment
accession to power
739.12
allotment 816.3
appointment 780.2
attribution 155.1
commission 780.1
commitment 818.2
lesson 562.7
placement 184.5
property transfer
817.1
specification 80.6
task 656.2
assimilate
combine 52.3
compare 491.4
conform 82.3
consume 666.2
convert 145.11
digest 309.16
include 76.3
learn 564.7
make agree 26.7
make uniform 17.4
naturalize 189.4
similarize 20.8
sorb 306.13
understand 548.7
assimilated
combined 52.5
converted 145.19
naturalized 189.6
phonetic 594.31
assimilation
adjustment 26.4
combination 52.1
consumption 666.1
conversion 145.1
digestion 309.8
inclusion 76.1
learning 564.2
metabolism 309.10
naturalization 189.3
similarity 20.1
sorption 306.6
speech sound 594.13
assist
n. helping hand 785.2
v. aid 785.11
be instrumental
658.5
subsidize 818.19
assistance aid 785.1
remedy 687.1
subsidy 818.8
assistant
academic rank 565.4
helper 785.7
partner 787.6
retainer 750.3
subordinate 764.5
assizes 1001.3
ass-kisser 907.3

associate
n. academic rank
565.4
companion 928.3
confederate 787
likeness 20.3
member 788.11
v. accompany 73.7
affiliate 788.14
be friends 927.9
be sociable 922.16
concur 177.2
cooperate 786.3
join 47.5
league 52.4
relate 9.6
associated
accompanying 73.9
communal 815.9
concurrent 177.4
corporate 788.16
joined 47.13
leagued 52.6
related 9.9
association
affiliation 786.2
combination 52.1
company 73.2
concurrence 177.1
council 755.1
participation 815.1
psychology 690.40
relationship 9.1
sociability 922.6
social grouping 922.5
society 788
thoughts 478.4
assonance
repetitiousness 103.4
rhyme 609.10
similar sound 20.6
assonant
harmonious 462.50
repetitious 103.15
rhyming 609.19
similar sounding
20.17
assort arrange 60.11
classify 61.6
assorted arranged 60.14
classified 61.8
different 16.7
diversified 19.4
assortment
grouping 60.3
hodgepodge 44.6
miscellany 74.13
assuage gratify 865.6
moderate 163.6
qualify 507.3
relieve 886.5
assuasive
palliative 163.16
qualifying 507.7
relieving 886.9
remedial 687.40
assume
appropriate 822.19
believe 501.11
borrow 821.4
don 231.42
entail 76.4

fake 616.21
imitate 22.5
imply 546.4
put on airs 903.12
receive 819.6
suppose 499.10
take command
739.14
take the liberty 961.6
undertake 715.3
usurp 961.8
assumed
falsified 616.26
implied 546.7
put-on 903.16
supposed 499.14
undertaken 715.7
assumed name 583.8
assuming that 499.19
assumption
accession to power
739.12
appropriation 822.4
belief 501.6
borrowing 821.2
conversion 145.1
entailment 76.2
exaltation 317.1
hope 888.1
implication 546.2
premise 482.7
presumption 961.2
presumptuousness
912.2
receiving 819.1
removal to heaven
1018.12
supposition 499.3
usurpation 961.3
assurance belief 501.1
certainty 513.1
comfort 887.4
confidence 513.5
encouragement 893.9
equanimity 858.3
hope 888.1
insolence 913.1
insurance 699.4
making certain 513.8
oath 523.3
promise 770.1
safety 698.1
security 772.1
assure affirm 523.5
comfort 887.6
convince 501.18
encourage 893.16
give hope 888.10
guarantee 772.9
make sure 513.11
promise 770.4
assured
believing 501.21
composed 858.13
guaranteed 772.11
hopeful 888.11
made sure 513.20
promised 770.8
sure 513.21
assuredly
adv. certainly 513.23
positively 34.19

interj. yes 521.18
Astarte
 beautiful woman
  900.9
 fertility goddess
  165.5
 love goddess 931.8
 moon goddess 375.12
astern aft 275.69
 behind 241.14
 in reverse 295.13
asteroid planet 375.9
 space hazard 282.10
as the crow flies 290.24
asthma
 allergic disorder
  686.32
 disease symptom
  686.8
 respiratory disease
  686.14
asthmatic 403.29
as though 499.19
astigmatism 440.1
astir
 adj. stirring 707.19
 adv. in motion 267.9
 preparation 720.23
astonish amaze 920.6
 surprise 540.7
astonishing
 amazing 920.12
 remarkable 34.10
 startling 540.11
astound astonish 920.6
 dismay 891.27
astounded
 astonished 920.9
 terrified 891.34
astounding
 astonishing 920.12
 terrible 891.38
astral
 n. astral body 1034.17
 specter 1017.1
 adj. celestial 375.25
 ghostly 1017.7
 immaterial 377.7
astray
 adj. bewildered
  514.23
 erroneous 518.16
 adv. afield 199.19
 amiss 314.7
 erroneously 518.20
astride 216.25
astringency
 acrimony 161.4
 constriction 198.1
 pungency 433.1
 strictness 757.1
 unkindness 939.9
 unpleasant taste
  429.2
astringent
 n. contractor 198.6
 adj. acrimonious
  161.13
 bitter 429.6
 contractive 198.11
 penetrating 857.29
 pungent 433.6

strict 757.6
 unkind 939.22
astro– aster 406.5
 star 375.8
astrogate 282.12
astrologer
 astrology 375.23
 predictor 543.4
astrology
 divining 543.2,15
 fate 640.2
 horoscopy 375.20
astronaut aviator 279.1
 spaceman 282.8
 traveler 274.1
astronautics
 aviation 278.1
 space travel 282.1
astronomic(al)
 celestial 375.25
 huge 195.20
 immeasurable 34.7
astronomy 375.19
astrophysical
 celestial 375.25
 physical 325.3
astrophysics
 astronomy 375.19
 physics 325.1
astute cunning 735.12
 discriminating 492.8
 sagacious 467.16
asunder
 adj. distant 199.8
 separate 49.20
 adv. in half 92.8
 separately 49.28
as usual as is 140.10
 normally 84.9
as well
 additionally 40.11
 equally 30.11
asylum
 hiding place 615.4
 home 700.4
 infirmary 689.27
 insane asylum 473.14
 refuge 700.1
asymmetric(al)
 distorted 249.10
 unequal 31.4
asymmetry
 distortion 249.1
 inconsistency 27.2
 inequality 31.1
asymptote 298.1
at by 184.26
 in 225.15
at all anyhow 657.12
 by any possibility
  509.10
 of any kind 61.9
at a loss
 at an impasse 731.22
 perplexed 514.24
 unprofitably 812.9
at any cost
 by any possibility
  509.10
 come what may
  624.20
 in spite of 33.9

at any rate
 anyhow 657.12
 at least 35.10
 certainly 513.23
 notwithstanding 33.8
atar see **attar**
ataraxy
 detachment 856.4
 inexcitability 858.1
 quiescence 268.1
 unconcern 636.2
at a standstill
 as is 140.10
 at an impasse 731.22
 at a stand 706.7
 immovable 142.15
 inactive 708.16
 motionless 268.13
atavism memory 537.1
 oldness 123.1
 relapse 696.1
 reversion 146.2
atavistic innate 5.7
 primitive 123.11
 reversionary 146.7
at bay cornered 731.23
 defensively 799.16
at cross-purposes
 alienated 929.12
 contrary 15.6
 disagreeing 27.6
 in opposition 790.9
 opposed to 790.10
at ease
 at one's ease 887.12
 at rest 711.11
 contented 868.7
atelier art 574.18
 studio 192.6
 workplace 719.1
at fault
 erroneous 518.16
 guilty 983.3
at hand
 convenient 200.15
 handy 665.19
 imminent 152.3
 near 200.20
 present 186.12
atheism impiety 1030.1
 nonreligiousness
  1031.5
 unbelief 503.1
 unorthodoxy 1025.3
atheist
 impious person
  1030.3
 unbeliever 1031.11
atheistic
 impious 1030.6
 unbelieving 1031.19
 unorthodox 1025.10
Athena goddess 1014.5
 war goddess 797.17
atherosclerosis
 cardiovascular disease
  686.17
 hardening 356.5
athlete 878.20
athlete's foot 686.33

athletic
 sporting 878.32
 strong 159.14
athletics exercise 716.6
 sports 878.8
at home
 n. meeting 74.2
 social gathering
  922.10
 adj. at ease 887.12
 adv. with one's family
  188.16
at home with
 acquainted 927.16
 used to 642.18
 versed in 475.19
athwart
 adj. oblique 219.19
 transverse 221.9
 adv. crosswise 221.13
 in opposition 790.9
 obliquely 219.24
 prep. opposed to
  790.10
at issue
 in opposition 790.9
 in question 485.38
 moot 514.16
 uncertain 514.17
at large
 at length 593.16
 escaped 632.11
 free 762.20
 generally 79.17
 scatteringly 75.12
 wholly 54.13
atlas map 654.4
 pillar 217.5
 reference book 605.6
Atlas giant 195.26
 rocket 281.15
 strong man 159.6
 supporter 216.3
at last discovery 488.11
 finally 70.11
at length
 at large 593.16
 finally 70.11
 fully 8.13
 lengthily 202.11
 lengthwise 202.12
at liberty free 762.20
 idle 708.17
atman life force 407.3
 psyche 466.4
 theosophy 1034.18
atmosphere
 aerosphere 402.2
 art 574.10
 gas 401.2
 milieu 233.3
 story element 608.9
atmospheric 402.12
at most 35.10
at odds
 alienated 929.12
 at variance 795.16
 different 16.7
 disagreeing 27.6
 dissenting 522.6
 in opposition 790.9
 unwilling 623.5

at the same time
additionally 40.11
at that time 105.9
notwithstanding 33.8
simultaneously 118.6
till then 109.5
when 105.16
attic garret 192.16
storage place 660.6
Attic polished 589.6
simple 902.6
tasteful 897.8
witty 881.15
attire
n. clothing 231.1
v. clothe 231.38
attitude belief 501.6
mental attitude 525
position 184.3
attitudinize 903.13
attorney deputy 781.1
lawyer 1003.1
manager 748.4
attract enamor 931.21
interest 530.12
lure 650.5
pull 288.4
attracted
approaching 296.4
interested 530.16
attraction
allurement 650.1
desirability 634.13
pull 288
pulling 286.1
attractive
alluring 650.7
attracting 288.5
beautiful 900.16
desirable 634.30
engrossing 530.20
pleasant 863.7
attributable
assignable 155.6
due 960.10
resulting from 154.8
attribute
n. characteristic 80.4
syntax 586.2
v. ascribe to 155.4
assign 155.3
attribution
designation 80.6
imputation 155
attrition abrasion 350.2
consumption 666.1
pulverization 361.4
reduction 42.2
regret 873.1
waste 39.3
weakening 160.5
attune
harmonize 462.36
make agree 26.7
prepare 720.8
put in tune 462.37
attuned
in accord 794.3
music 462.50
at variance
alienated 929.12
at odds 795.16

different 16.7
disagreeing 27.6
dissenting 522.6
in opposition 790.9
at war at odds 795.16
disagreeing 27.6
in opposition 790.9
up in arms 797.28
auburn
reddish-brown 367.4
redheaded 368.10
au courant 475.18
auction
n. sale 829.4
v. sell 829.11
auctioneer 830.8
audacious
daring 893.21
defiant 793.7
foolhardy 894.9
insolent 913.8
audacity courage 893.6
defiance 793.1
insolence 913.1
recklessness 894.3
audible
auditory 448.14
hearable 450.16
audience
attender 186.5
audition 448.2
conference 597.6
listeners 448.6
playgoer 611.32
recipient 819.3
spectator 442.2
audio 448.14
audio– hearing 448.1
sound 450.1
audio devices 344.29
audio frequency
radio frequency
344.12
tone 450.2
audio-visual 448.14
audit
n. accounting 845.6
v. check 87.14
make certain 513.12
take account of 845.9
audition
examination 485.2
hearing 448.2
sense of hearing
448.1
tryout 489.3
auditor
accountant 845.7
financial officer
836.11
listener 448.5
recipient 819.3
student 566.1
supervisor 748.2
auditorium arena 802.1
hall 192.4
schoolroom 567.16
seating 611.20
theater 611.18
auditory 448.14
auger drill 348.18
sharpness 258.3

aught any 79.5
nothing 2.2
some 28.3
augment add to 40.5
aggravate 885.2
increase 38.4
make larger 197.4
augur
n. predictor 543.4
v. hint 544.12
augur well 888.10
augury
divining 543.2,15
omen 544.3
august dignified 905.12
eminent 34.9
venerable 964.12
aunt 11.3
au pair girl 750.8
aura
illustriousness 914.6
light 335.14
milieu 233.3
occultism 1034.7
aural 448.14
aureole halo 253.2
light 335.14
auricular
auditory 448.14
confidential 614.14
aurora dawn 133.3
foredawn 133.4
light 335.14
Aurora 133.2
ausgespielt
ruined 693.28
weakened 160.18
worn-out 692.38
auspices
patronage 785.4
protectorship 699.2
supervision 747.2
auspicious
fortunate 728.14
good 674.12
of good omen 544.18
promising 888.13
timely 129.9
austere ascetic 991.3
meager 662.10
plain 902.9
plainspoken 591.3
simple 45.6
strict 757.6
unkind 939.22
austerity
asceticism 991.1
economy 851.1
meagerness 662.2
plainness 902.4
plain speech 591.1
strictness 757.1
unkindness 939.9
autarchy
absolutism 741.9
government 741.4
independence 762.5
auteur 611.28
authentic
authoritative 513.18
evidential 505.17
honest 974.14

natural 516.14
original 23.5
orthodox 1024.7
real 1.15
authenticate
confirm 505.12
ratify 521.12
authenticated
proved 505.21
ratified 521.14
true 516.12
authenticity
genuineness 516.5
originality 23.1
orthodoxy 1024.1
reality 1.2
reliability 513.4
author
n. creator 153.4
discourser 606.3
doer 718.1
producer 167.8
writer 602.15
v. originate 153.11
write 602.21
authoritarian
governmental 741.17
imperious 739.16
narrow-minded
527.10
powerful 739.15
strict 757.6
authoritative
authentic 513.18
commanding 739.15
convincing 501.26
imperious 739.16
influential 172.13
orthodox 1024.7
powerful 157.12
prescriptive 751.4
skillful 733.20
specialized 81.5
valid 516.13
versed in 475.19
authorities, the
the government
741.3
the rulers 749.15
authority
authoritativeness
739.2
certificate 570.6
commission 780.1
connoisseur 897.7
direction 747.1
expert 733.11
governance 739.5
influence 172.1
informant 557.5
power 157.1
prerogative 739
prestige 739.4
privilege 958.3
sanction 777.3
scientist 475.11
specialist 81.3
supremacy 36.3
validity 516.4
wise man 468.1

authorization
  accession to power
    739.12
  certificate 570.6
  commission 780.1
  legalization 998.2
  ratification 521.4
  sanction 777.3
  supremacy 36.3
authorize
  commission 780.9
  empower 157.10
  legalize 998.8
  prescribe 752.10
  ratify 521.12
  sanction 777.11
authorized
  authoritative 739.15
  commissioned 780.18
  empowered 777.17
  legal 998.10
authorship
  creation 167.5
  writing 602.2
autism
  defense mechanism
    690.30
  fantasy 535.7
  illusion 519.1
  selfishness 978.1
  unfeeling 856.1
  unsociability 923.1
autistic
  daydreaming 535.24
  illusory 519.9
  selfish 978.5
  unfeeling 856.9
  unsociable 923.5
auto
  automobile 272.9,24
  parts 272.25
auto–
  automatic 349.25
  automotive 272.22
  identical 14.7
  individual 80.12
autobiography 608.4
autochthonous
  beginning 68.15
  native 189.5
  primitive 123.11
autocrat 749.14
autocratic
  governmental 741.17
  imperious 739.16
  powerful 739.15
auto-da-fé
  burning 329.5
  killing 409.1
autodidactic
  educational 562.19
  learned 475.24
  studentlike 566.12
  taught 564.16
autoeroticism
  masturbation 419.9
  sexual preference
    419.12
  vanity 909.1
autograph original 23.3
  signature 583.10
  written matter 602.10

automat
  restaurant 307.15
  vending machine
    832.8
automate 349.23
automated 349.25
automatic
  n. gun 801.5,27
  robot 349.12
  adj. automated
    349.25
  habitual 642.16
  instinctive 481.6
  involuntary 639.14
  methodical 17.5
  unpremeditated
    630.11
automatically
  instinctively 481.7
  involuntarily 639.18
automatic analyzer
    349.36
automatic detector
    349.35
automatic indicator
    349.37
automatic writing
  automatism 639.5
  occultism 1034.6
  writing 602.2
automation
  electronics 343.1
  self-action 349
automatism
  automation 349.1
  habit 642.4
  involuntariness 639.5
  occultism 1034.6
automaton 349.12,29
automobile
  car 272.9,24
  parts 272.25
automotive
  self-propelled 349.26
  vehicular 272.22
autonomous
  governmental 741.17
  independent 762.21
  voluntary 622.7
autonomy
  government 741.4
  independence 762.5
  voluntariness 622.2
autopsy
  n. post-mortem
    408.18
  v. examine 485.23
autosuggestion
  hypnotism 712.8
  suggestion therapy
    690.6
autumn
  n. fall 128.4
  adj. autumnal 128.8
auxiliaries
  military reserves
    800.24
  reinforcements 785.8
auxiliary
  n. aide 787.6
  nonessential 6.2
  verb 586.4

adj. additional 40.10
  helping 785.20
  unessential 6.4
avail
  n. benefit 665.4
  good 674.4
  v. aid 785.11
  be of use 665.17
  do good 674.10
  suffice 661.4
availability
  accessibility 509.3
  presence 186.1
  utility 665.3
available
  accessible 509.8
  handy 665.19
  idle 708.17
  obtainable 811.13
  present 186.12
  vacant 187.14
avalanche
  overabundance 663.2
  plenty 661.2
  slide 316.4
  snow 333.8
avant-garde
  n. precursor 66.1
  the latest thing 122.2
  vanguard 240.2
  adj. advanced 66.4
  modern 122.13
  original 23.5
avarice greed 634.8
  sin 982.3
  stinginess 852.3
avaricious
  greedy 634.27
  stingy 852.9
avatar
  appearance 446.1
  manifestation 555.1
  transformation 139.2
  Vishnu 1014.9
Ave Maria 1032.4
avenge 956.4
avenger 956.3
avenue outlet 303.9
  passageway 657.4
  road 657.6
aver affirm 523.4
  state 594.24
  testify 505.10
average
  n. generality 79.3
  mean 32.1
  v. middle 69.3
  strike a balance 32.2
  adj. mediocre 680.8
  medium 32.3
  middle 69.4
  ordinary 79.12
  usual 84.8
average man
  common man 919.7
  generality 79.3
averse displeased 867.8
  hating 930.7
  unwilling 623.5
aversion dislike 867.2
  hate 930.1
  hated thing 930.3

  unwillingness 623.1
avert prevent 730.14
  turn aside 291.6
avian 414.52
aviary 191.23
aviate 278.45
aviation 278
aviation beacon 336.10
aviation instrument
    278.61
aviator 279
avid eager 635.9
  greedy 634.27
avidity eagerness 635.1
  greed 634.8
avidly eagerly 635.14
  greedily 634.32
avocation 656.7
avocational 656.17
avoid abstain 992.7
  pull back 284.7
  shun 631.6
  snub 966.7
avoidable 631.14
avoidance
  abstinence 992.2
  evasion 631
  retreat 284.3
avoirdupois 352.1
avoirdupois weight
    352.8
avouch affirm 523.4
  express belief 501.12
  promise 770.4
  testify 505.10
avow
  acknowledge 521.11
  affirm 523.4
  confess 556.7
  express belief 501.12
  purport 649.3
  testify 505.10
avowal
  acknowledgment
    521.3
  affirmation 523.1
  confession 556.3
  testimony 505.3
avowed
  acknowledged 521.14
  affirmed 523.8
  professed 649.5
await
  be imminent 152.2
  be in the future
    121.6
  loiter 132.12
  wait for 539.8
awake
  v. awaken 713.5
  excite 857.11
  revive 407.8
  wake up 713.4
  adj. alert 533.14
  clear-witted 467.13
  unsleeping 713.8
awaken arise 713.4
  become informed
    557.13
  disillusion 520.2
  excite 857.11
  revive 407.8

rouse 648.19
waken 713.5
awakening
disillusionment 520.1
wakening 713.2
awake to 475.16
award
n. gift 818.4
giving 818.1
judgment 494.5
reward 916.2
v. give 818.12
aware attentive 530.15
cognizant of 475.16
knowing 475.15
receptive 422.13
awareness
attention 530.1
cognizance 475.2
sensation 422.1
awash floating 275.60
flooded 395.25
soaked 392.17
away
adj. absent 187.10
distant 199.8
vanished 447.4
adv. apart 199.17
aside 242.10
at a distance 199.14
elsewhere 187.17
hence 301.21
in reverse 295.13
away from from 301.22
separately 49.28
awe
n. fear 891.1
respect 964.1
wonder 920.1
v. astonish 920.6
command respect 964.7
daunt 891.26
terrify 891.25
awe-inspiring
astonishing 920.11
grandiose 904.21
terrible 891.38
venerable 964.12
weighty 672.19
awesome
astonishing 920.11
eminent 914.18
large 34.7
sacred 1026.7
terrible 891.38
venerable 964.12
awestruck
astonished 920.9
reverent 964.9
terrified 891.34
awful
astonishing 920.11
bad 675.9
grandiose 904.21
remarkable 34.11
sacred 1026.7
terrifying 891.38
ugly 899.11
unpleasant 864.19
venerable 964.12

awfully
astonishingly 920.15
badly 675.14
distressingly 34.21
frighteningly 891.42
repugnantly 899.13
very 34.18
awkward bulky 195.19
clumsy 734.20
ignorant 477.12
inconvenient 671.7
mortifying 864.21
stilted 590.3
unwieldy 731.18
awkward age 124.7
awkwardly
clumsily 734.24
unwieldily 731.27
awning 338.1,8
AWOL
n. absence 187.4
flight 631.4
adj. absent 187.12
awry
adj. askew 219.14
disorderly 62.13
erroneous 518.16
adv. askew 219.22
ax
n. cutlery 348.2
instrument of execution 1011.5
types of 801.25
v. sever 49.11
ax, the
capital punishment 1010.7
dismissal 310.5
axial central 226.11
flowing 267.8
axiom a belief 501.2
essence 5.2
fact 1.3
maxim 517.1
premise 482.7
self-evident truth 517.2
supposition 499.3
axiomatic(al)
aphoristic 517.6
certain 513.15
manifest 555.8
axis association 788.1
aviation 278.28
axle 322.5
center 226.2
fulcrum 287.3
plant stem 411.19
straight line 250.2
aye
affirmative expression 521.2,18
consent 775.1
side of controversy 482.14
vote 637.6
azimuth
coordinates 490.6
course 290.1
direction 290.2
horizon 214.4
position 184.3

azure
n. blueness 372.1,4
heavens 375.2
heraldic insignia 569.2
adj. blue 372.3

B

Baal fertility god 165.5
idol 1033.3
Semitic deity 1014.11
Babbitt
conformist 82.2
vulgar person 898.6
babble
n. chatter 596.3
nonsense 547.2
unintelligibility 549.7
v. be incomprehensible 549.10
be insane 473.19
chatter 596.5
divulge 556.6
make a liquid sound 452.11
talk nonsense 547.5
babbling
delirious 473.31
mentally deficient 469.22
water sound 452.19
babe endearment 932.5
girl 125.6
infant 125.7
innocent person 984.4
unsophisticate 736.3
Babel dissonance 461.2
pandemonium 62.5
unintelligibility 549.7
baby
n. beginner 68.2
coward 892.5
endearment 932.5
girl 125.6
infant 125.7
little thing 196.5
weakling 160.6
youngster 125.1
adj. infantile 124.12
miniature 196.12
baby carriage 272.6
baby grand 465.13
babyish
infantile 124.12
simple-minded 469.24
Babylon 981.7
Babylonian 904.21
baby-sit 699.19
baby-sitter 699.8
baccalaureate 917.6
bacchanal
drunkard 996.10
spree 996.5
bacchic 473.30
Bacchus god 1014.5
intoxication 996.2
bachelor knight 918.5
single man 934.3
title 917.6

bachelor girl 934.4
bachelorhood 934.1
bachelor's degree 917.6
bacillus 686.39
back
n. book 605.12
dorsum 241.3
printing 603.6
rear 241.1
setting 233.2
supporter 216.2
vocal organ 594.19
v. back up 241.8
bet 515.20
commend 968.11
confirm 505.12
finance 836.15
mount 315.12
move 267.5
retreat 295.7
sail 275.34
second 785.13
sponsor 772.9
stiffen 356.9
support 216.21
support politically 744.41
adj. backward 119.12
backwoods 182.8
due 840.10
flowing 267.8
late 132.16
phonetic 594.31
rear 241.9
reversed 295.12
adv. ago 119.15
in compensation 33.7
in reserve 660.17
in reverse 295.13
interj. command 275.77
back and fill
alternate 323.13
change course 275.30
fluctuate 141.5
vacillate 627.8
back and forth
alternate 323.19
changeably 141.8
reciprocally 13.16
to and fro 323.21
backbite 971.11
backbone
courage 893.5
pluck 624.3
supporter 216.2
backbreaker 731.2
backbreaking
laborious 716.18
troublesome 731.17
back-burner 673.15
back country
hinterland 182.2
space 179.4
back-country 182.8
back door back 241.1
byway 657.5
entrance 302.6
secret passage 615.5
back-door 614.12
backdown 765.2

back down
be irresolute 627.7
recant 628.9
retreat 295.6
yield 765.7
backdrop
scenery 611.25
setting 233.2
backed
approved 968.19
hardened 356.13
backer
benefactor 942.1
financer 836.9
friend 928.1
giver 818.11
play backer 611.31
supporter 787.9
backfire
n. countermeasure
178.5
explosion 162.7
fire 328.13
recoil 284.2
v. explode 162.13
recoil 284.6
backflow 395.12
background
arena 802.1
experience 733.9
horizon 199.3
motif 901.7
setting 233.2
story element 608.9
backhanded
circuitous 321.7
insulting 965.6
oblique 219.13
backing
n. bookbinding
605.15
confirmation 505.5
course 267.2
film 577.10
financing 836.2
mounting 216.10
patronage 785.4
regression 295.3
reversion 146.1
support 216.1
supporter 216.2
adj. favoring 968.17
backlash effect 154.3
reaction 178.1
recoil 284.2
backlist 605.19
backlog firewood 331.3
reserve 660.3
store 660.1
back matter
book 605.12
part of writing 55.2
sequel 67.1
back number
antiquated person
123.8
edition 605.2
back-number
old-fashioned 123.16
trite 883.9
back of beyond
backwoods 182.8

out-of-the-way 199.9
remote region 199.4
back off 295.7
back out
abandon 633.5
be a coward 892.8
recant 628.9
retreat 295.6
backpack 273.29
backpedal retreat 295.7
slow 270.9
back scratching
exchange 150.2
obsequiousness 907.2
political influence
744.29
back-scratching 907.13
back seat back 241.1
inferiority 37.1
backseat driver
advisor 754.3
driver 274.10
meddler 238.4
backsettler 190.10
backside 241.4
backslapper
flatterer 970.4
sycophant 907.3
backslide
go wrong 981.9
regress 295.5
relapse 696.4
revert 146.4
backsliding
n. apostasy 628.2
immorality 981.1
impiety 1030.1
regression 295.1
relapse 696.2
reversion 146.1
adj. impious 1030.6
relapsing 696.5
unrighteous 981.12
backstage
n. stage 611.21
adv. theater 611.41
backstairs 614.12
back stairs byway 657.5
secret passage 615.5
stairs 315.3
backstop barrier 730.5
safety equipment
699.3
backstroke
boxing 283.5
swimming 275.11
back talk answer 486.1
insolence 913.4
back to back
behind 241.13
cooperatively 786.6
opposite 239.6
backtrack 295.7
backup
n. deputy 781.1
regression 295.3
substitute 149.2
adj. substitute 149.8
back up
confirm 505.12
go back 241.8
move 267.5

represent 781.14
retreat 295.7
second 785.13
support 216.21
support politically
744.41
backward
adj. back 119.12
conservative 140.8
dilatory 132.17
flowing 267.8
inside out 220.7
late 132.16
mentally deficient
469.22
modest 908.11
rear 241.9
reluctant 623.6
retarded 270.12
reticent 613.10
reversed 295.12
undeveloped 721.12
adv. ago 119.15
in reverse 295.13
inversely 220.8
late 132.19
rearward 241.15
backwash
aviation 278.39
eddy 395.12
effect 154.3
water travel 275.7
backwater
n. eddy 395.12
v. recant 628.9
retreat 295.7
sail 275.34
slow 270.9
back way byway 657.5
secret passage 615.5
back when 119.15
backwoods
n. hinterland 182.2
adj. country 182.8
backwoodsman 190.10
bacon 308.16
bacteria germ 686.39
microorganism
196.18
bacterial 196.15
bactericide 687.21
bacteriology 406.17
bad
n. evil 675.3
iniquity 981.3
adj. crippled 692.32
dangerous 697.9
decayed 692.41
diseased 686.56
dying 408.33
evil 675.7
excellent 674.13
inexpedient 671.5
malodorous 437.5
misbehaving 738.5
ominous 544.17
sick 686.52
unhealthful 684.5
unsavory 429.7
wicked 981.16
adv. badly 675.13

bad blood
animosity 929.4
malevolence 939.4
opposition 790.2
bad boy 738.3
bad breath 437.1
bad character 915.1
bad check 835.10
bad debt debt 840.1
nonpayment 842.1
bad deed 939.13
bad faith
falseheartedness
616.4
infidelity 975.5
violation 769.2
badge
characteristic 80.4
identification 568.11
insignia 569.1
military insignia
569.5
sign 568.2
badger annoy 866.13
wrest from 822.22
badgered 866.24
bad guy 612.2
bad habit habit 642.4
vice 981.2
bad hand 602.6
badinage 882.1
bad influence
influential person
172.6
malevolent influence
675.4
bad job bungle 734.5
slipshodness 534.3
bad language 972.3
bad lot 986.5
bad luck 729.5
badly off poor 838.7
unfortunate 729.14
bad-mouth 971.9
bad move 518.4
bad name 915.1
bad news news 558.2
trouble 866.2
undesirable person
986.1
bad notices 969.4
bad person
evildoer 943.1
undesirable 986
bad press 969.4
bad taste
literary inelegance
590.1
vulgarity 898.1
bad temper
anger 952.6
ill humor 951.1
malevolence 939.4
bad-tempered 951.18
bad time 130.2
bad turn 939.13
bad will 939.4
baffle
n. perplexity 514.3
v. be incomprehensi-
ble 549.10
disappoint 541.2

balneation
bathing 681.7
swimming 275.11
baloney
humbug 616.14
nonsense 547.3
balsa 277.11
balsam
healing ointment 687.11
medicine 687.4
ointment 380.3
perfume 436.2
remedy 687.1
balustrade fence 236.4
post 217.4
support 216.8
bamboo grass 411.5,46
material 378.4
bamboo curtain
barrier 730.5
frontier 235.5
secrecy 614.3
bamboozle
deceive 618.13
perplex 514.13
bamboozled 514.24
ban
n. curse 972.1
disapproval 969.1
exclusion 77.1
ostracism 926.3
prohibition 778.1
v. cut out 42.10
disapprove 969.10
eject 310.17
exclude 77.4
ostracize 926.6
prohibit 778.3
banal medium 32.3
trite 883.9
banality
platitude 517.3
triteness 883.3
banana 881.12
bananas 473.26
band
n. association 788.1
girdle 253.3
group 74.3
layer 227.1
line 568.6
medical dressing 687.33
orchestra 464.12
radio 344.13
strip 206.4
stripe 374.5
v. bind 47.9
cooperate 786.3
encircle 233.7
join 47.5
variegate 374.7
bandage
n. medical dressing 687.33
strip 206.4
wrapper 228.18
v. bind 47.9
blind 441.7
treat 689.30
band-aid 670.7

Band-Aid 687.33
bandeau
brassiere 231.24
heraldic insignia 569.2
supporter 216.2
banded 374.15
banderillero 800.4
bandit aircraft 280.9
thief 825.4
banditry
plundering 824.5
theft 824.3
band leader 464.17
bandog dog 414.22
watchdog 699.11
band shell 611.21
bandstand 611.21
band together
accompany 73.7
cooperate 786.3
join 52.4
bandy
v. interchange 150.4
adj. bowed 252.10
bowlegged 249.12
bandy about 559.10
bandy words
argue 482.16
converse 597.9
bane curse 676
death 408.1
evil 675.3
killing 409.1
ruin 693.2
baneful
destructive 693.26
fatal 409.23
harmful 675.12
horrid 864.19
ominous 544.17
bang
n. detonation 456.3
drug dose 687.6
explosion 162.7
explosive noise 456.1
hair 230.6
hit 283.4
narcotic injection 689.18
thrill 857.2
vim 161.2
v. blast 456.8
close 266.6
collide 283.12
hit 283.13
make explosive noise 456.6
pound 283.14
adv. suddenly 113.9
bangers 308.21
banging
crashing 456.11
huge 195.21
bangle 901.6
bang on 516.15
bangtail 414.17
bang-up 674.13
banish eject 310.17
ostracize 926.6
banishment
ejection 310.4

ostracism 926.3
banister post 217.4
support 216.8
banjo 465.4
banjo eyes 439.9
banjo-picker 464.5
bank
n. barrier 730.5
border 235.4
buttress 216.4
depository 836.12
finance 836.13
fortification 799.4
incline 219.4
lending institution 820.4
mine 383.6
pile 74.10
preserve 701.6
row 71.2
shoal 210.2
shore 385.2
side 242.1
stakes 515.5
storage place 660.6
v. align 71.5
fly 278.49
fortify 799.9
incline 219.10
pile 74.19
stoke 329.22
store 660.10
bank balance 839.2
bankbook 845.4
banker
businessman 830.1
financier 836.10
lender 820.3
banking
air maneuver 278.13
finance 836.4
bank note 835.5
bank on
be hopeful 888.7
believe in 501.16
plan on 653.6
bankroll
n. money 835.17
v. finance 836.15
bankrupt
n. insolvent 842.4
poor person 838.4
unsuccessful person 725.7
v. impoverish 838.6
ruin 842.8
adj. destitute 838.9
insolvent 842.11
ruined 693.28
wanting 662.13
bankruptcy
failure 725.1
impairment 692.1
insolvency 842.3
banned excluded 77.7
prohibited 778.7
banner
n. caption 484.2
flag 569.6
poster 559.7
rallying device 797.16
sign 568.2

adj. chief 36.14
banneret flag 569.6
knight 918.5
bannister see banister
banns betrothal 770.3
wedding 933.4
banquet
n. feast 307.9
festival 878.4
treat 865.3
v. eat 307.22
make merry 878.27
banshee fairy 1014.18
specter 1017.1
bantam
n. little thing 196.4
adj. miniature 196.12
bantamweight
n. boxing weight 352.3
pugilist 800.2
adj. lightweight 353.12
banter
n. clownishness 881.5
kidding 882
ridicule 967.1
v. kid 882.4
bantering
n. banter 882.2
adj. kidding 882.5
ridiculing 967.12
banty
n. little thing 196.4
poultry 414.34
adj. miniature 196.12
banzai
n. battle cry 797.12
interj. attack! 798.32
baptism
immersion 320.2
installation 306.2
naming 583.2
rite 1040.7
sacrament 1040.5
wetting 392.6
baptismal
introductory 306.18
ritualistic 1040.22
baptistery
baptism 1040.7
church part 1042.9
baptize clean 681.19
dilute 160.11
immerse 320.7
name 583.11
perform rites 1040.20
baptized 583.14
bar
n. barrier 730.5
blockage 266.3
currency metals 835.20
exclusion 77.1
harmonics 463.12
heraldic insignia 569.2
island 386.2
lawyers 1003.5
length 202.4
lever 287.4
line 568.6

military insignia
569.5
music 462.29
restraint 760.5
saloon 996.19
shaft 217.1
shoal 210.2
stripe 374.5
table 216.15,29
v. close 266.6
cross 221.6
eliminate 42.10
enclose 236.7
exclude 77.4
make impossible
510.6
obstruct 730.12
prevent 730.14
prohibit 778.3
stop 266.7
variegate 374.7
prep. excluding 77.9
barb arrow 801.16
barbiturate 687.12
bristle 261.3
feather part 230.17
whisker 230.10
barbarian
n. alien 78.3
boor 898.7
savage 943.5
adj. extraneous 78.5
uncouth 898.12
barbaric see **barbarous**
barbarism
literary inelegance
590.1
solecism 587.2
uncouthness 898.3
unenlightenment
477.4
word 582.6
barbarity
brutal act 939.12
cruelty 939.11
uncouthness 898.3
violence 162.1
barbarous cruel 939.24
extraneous 78.5
infelicitous 590.2
savage 162.20
uncouth 898.12
ungrammatical 587.4
unlearned 477.14
barbecue
n. meat 308.12
picnic 307.6
v. cook 330.4
barbecued 330.6
barbed 258.11
barbel bristle 261.3
feeler 425.4
whisker 230.10
barbell 716.7
barbellate 261.9
barber
n. beautician 900.12
v. cut the hair 230.22
barbershop
beauty parlor 900.13
workplace 719.1

barbican
fortification 799.4
tower 207.11
barbiturate 687.12
barbiturism 642.9
barbule
feather part 230.17
feeler 425.4
whisker 230.10
bard poet 609.13
singer 464.14
bare
v. disclose 556.4
divest 232.5
unclose 265.13
adj. in plain style
591.3
manifest 555.10
mere 35.8
naked 232.14
open 265.18
simple 45.6
unadorned 902.8
uncomplicated 45.7
vacant 187.13
worn 692.33
bareback rider 612.3
bare-boned 205.17
bared 232.12
barefaced bare 232.16
brazen 913.10
barefoot 232.15
bare-handed
bare 232.16
ill-provided 662.12
unprotected 697.14
barely nakedly 232.19
narrowly 205.22
scarcely 35.9
simply 45.11
bare minimum 661.1
bare necessities 639.2
bare of 662.13
bare possibility
improbability 512.1
possibility 509.1
small chance 156.9
barf
n. vomit 310.8
v. sicken at 867.4
vomit 310.25
barfly 996.10
barfy bad 675.8
filthy 682.23
nauseated 686.53
unsavory 429.7
bargain
n. cheap item 849.3
compact 771.1
compromise 807.1
transaction 827.5
v. confer 597.11
contract 771.6
haggle 827.17
mediate 805.6
treat with 771.7
bargain-basement 849.8
bargainer 789.3
bargain for
contract 771.6
plan on 653.6

strike a bargain
827.18
bargaining
conference 597.6
negotiation 827.3
barge haul 271.12
walk 273.27
barge in enter 302.7
intrude 238.5
baring disclosure 556.1
divestment 232.1
baritone
n. brass wind 465.8
viola 465.5
vocalist 464.13
voice 462.22
adj. deep 454.10
vocal 462.51
bark
n. animal sound 460.1
cry 459.1
detonation 456.3
hull 228.16
peel 229.2
ship 277.1,23
v. abrade 350.7
animal sound 460.2
blast 456.8
cry 459.6
injure 692.15
peel 232.8
publicize 559.15
utter 594.26
barker publicist 559.9
showman 611.28
solicitor 830.7
barley 308.4
barmaid
bartender 996.18
waiter 750.7
barmaster 1002.4
bar mitzvah 1040.4
barmy foamy 405.7
insane 473.26
leavening 353.16
barn 191.20
barnacle adherent 50.4
parasite 907.4
barnstorm act 611.34
fly 278.46
Barnumesque 857.30
barnyard 413.8
barographic 402.13
barometer
measure 490.2
testing device 489.4
weather instrument
402.8
barometric(al) 402.13
barometry 402.6
baron
businessman 830.1
nobleman 918.4
personage 672.8
superior 36.5
baroness 918.6
baronet knight 918.5
nobleman 918.4
baroque
abnormal 85.13
fanciful 535.20
ornate 901.12

barracks 191.29
barrage
n. barrier 730.5
gunfire 798.10
staccato sound 455.1
v. fire upon 798.22
barred enclosed 236.10
excluded 77.7
impossible 510.7
netlike 221.11
prohibited 778.7
striped 374.15
barrel
n. cylinder 255.4
feather part 230.17
much 34.3
v. package 236.9
put in 184.14
speed 269.8
barrel-chested 159.14
barrel of money 837.2
barrel organ 465.16
barrel roll 278.14
barrel-shaped 255.11
barren fruitless 669.12
ineffective 158.15
sterile 166.4
unimaginative 536.5
uninteresting 883.6
vacant 187.13
barrens 166.2
barricade
n. fortification 799.4
v. close 266.6
fortify 799.9
obstruct 730.12
barrier fence 236.4
fortification 799.4
obstacle 730.5
obstruction 266.3
partition 237.5
restraint 760.5
barring
n. exclusion 77.1
prep. excluding 77.9
less 42.14
barrio 183.6
barrister 1003.1
barroom 996.19
barrow hill 207.5
memorial 570.12
swine 414.9
tomb 410.16
bar sinister
bastardy 999.2
heraldic insignia
569.2
illegitimacy 171.5
stigma 915.6
bartender
drink mixer 996.18
waiter 750.7
barter
n. exchange 150.2
property transfer
817.1
trade 827.2
v. trade 827.14
transfer property
817.3
bartizan 799.4
basal basic 212.8

pack animal 271.6
beat
  n. circuit 321.2
    flutter 324.4
    meter 609.9
    music 463.26
    news 558.3
    parasite 907.4
    periodicity 137.2
    pulsation 323.3
    region 180.2
    rhythm 463.22
    round 137.3
    route 657.2
    routine 642.6
    speech accent 594.11
    sphere of work 656.4
    staccato sound 455.1
    tempo 463.24
  v. agitate 324.10
    best 36.7
    bruise 692.16
    change course 275.30
    cheat 618.17
    defeat 727.6
    fatigue 717.4
    flutter 324.12
    foam 405.5
    hunt 655.9
    make staccato sounds
      455.4
    music 462.45
    perplex 514.13
    pound 283.14
    pulsate 323.12
    pulverize 361.9
    punish 1010.14
    repeat 103.10
    sail 275.25
    triumph over 726.6
  adj. defeated 727.14
    exhausted 717.8
    nonconformist 83.6
    perplexed 514.24
    poor 838.10
beatable 697.16
beat about
  be uncertain 514.9
  change course 275.30
  grope 485.31
  have difficulty 731.10
  seek 485.29
beat around the bush
  circumlocute 593.10
  dodge 631.8
  equivocate 483.9
beat back 289.3
beat down
  bargain 827.17
  cheapen 849.6
  domineer 741.16
  make sad 872.18
  raze 693.19
  subdue 764.9
beaten bubbly 405.6
  defeated 727.14
  exhausted 717.8
  habitual 642.16
beaten path path 657.3
  routine 642.6
  tedium 884.1
beater agitator 324.9

hunter 655.5
mixer 44.10
beatification
  exaltation 317.1
  glorification 914.8
  happiness 865.2
  sanctification 1026.3
beatified
  eminent 914.18
  happy 865.13
  heavenly 1018.13
  saintly 1015.6
  sanctified 1026.8
beatify exalt 317.6
  gladden 865.7
  glorify 914.13
  sanctify 1026.5
beating
  n. defeat 727.1
    flutter 324.4
    hit 283.4
    pulsation 323.3
    pulverization 361.4
    punishment 1010.4
    staccato sound 455.1
  adj. music 463.28
    periodic 137.7
    pulsating 323.18
    staccato 455.7
beat into 562.13
beat it depart 301.9
  flee 631.11
  go away! 310.30
beatitude
  happiness 865.2
  sanctification 1026.3
beatnik 83.3
beat off 799.10
beat one's breast 875.9
beat the drum
  call to arms 797.23
  celebrate 877.2
  espouse 968.13
  music 462.45
  publicize 559.15
  signal 568.22
beat the system 724.12
beat up agitate 324.10
  make viscid 389.10
  punish 1010.17
beat-up
  dilapidated 692.35
  exhausted 717.8
  slovenly 62.15
beau dandy 903.9
  inamorato 931.12
Beau Brummel
  dandy 903.9
  fashionable 644.7
beaucoup 34.15
Beaufort scale 403.16
beaut
  beautiful person
    900.8
  good thing 674.7
beauteous 900.16
beautician 900.12
beautification
  improvement 691.2
  prettification 900.10
beautified 691.13

beautiful
  adj. artistic 574.21
    beauteous 900.16
  interj. approval
    968.22
beautiful people 644.6
beautify
  improve 691.10
  ornament 901.8
  prettify 900.14
beauty
  beautifulness 900
  beautiful person
    900.8
  literary elegance
    589.2
beauty parlor
  beauty salon 900.13
  workplace 719.1
beauty queen 900.8
beaux arts 574.1
beaver beard 230.8
  man of action 707.8
bebop 462.9
be born begin 68.13
  come forth 167.16
  come to life 407.8
becalm 268.11
becalmed 268.17
be careful
  v. be cautious 895.5
    take care 533.7
  interj. caution 895.14
because 155.10
because of 155.9
bechance 156.11
becharm delight 865.8
  enamor 931.21
  enchant 1036.8
  fascinate 650.6
becharmed
  enamored 931.26
  enchanted 1036.12
beck gesture 568.14
  running water 395.1
  summons 752.5
beck and call 752.5
beckon attract 650.5
  gesture 568.21
becloud cloud 404.6
  conceal 615.6
  confuse 532.7
  darken 337.9
  opaque 341.2
beclouded
  concealed 615.11
  muddled 532.13
become
  be converted into
    145.17
  begin 68.13
  behoove 962.4
  come to be 1.12
  convert 145.11
become of 154.5
becoming apt 26.10
  beautiful 900.17
  decent 988.5
  decorous 897.10
  due 960.8
  expedient 670.5

bed
  n. accommodations
    659.3
    bottom 212.1
    couch 216.19
    floor 212.4
    foundation 216.6
    garden 413.10
    layer 227.1
    marriage 933.1
    printing press
      603.9,26
    types of 216.33
    watercourse 396.2
  v. base 212.6
    embed 304.5
    go to bed 712.17
    house 188.10
    implant 142.9
    plant 413.18
    put to bed 712.19
    rest 711.6
    tend animals 416.7
bed and board 659.3
bedaub blemish 679.6
  coat 228.24
  color 362.13
  soil 682.16
bedazzle astonish 920.6
  blind 441.7
  confuse 532.7
  give light 335.23
bedazzled
  blinded 441.10
  dazed 532.14
bedbug 414.41,74
bedchamber 192.7
bedclothes 228.10
bedding
  bedclothes 228.10
  foundation 216.6
  underbedding 216.20
  underlayer 227.1
bedeck clothe 231.38
  ornament 901.8
bedecked
  clothed 231.44
  ornamented 901.11
bedevil annoy 866.13
  bewitch 1036.9
  demonize 1016.17
bedeviled
  insane 473.28
  tormented 866.24
bedfast 686.55
bedfellow
  associate 787.1
  companion 928.3
bedizen color 362.13
  dress up 231.41
  ornament 901.8
bedizened
  grandiloquent 601.8
  ornamented 901.11
bedlam
  insane asylum 473.14
  noise 453.3
  pandemonium 62.5
bedmate
  companion 928.3
  partner 787.2

bed of roses
comfort 887.1
prosperity 728.1
Bedouin 274.4
bedpan 311.11
bedraggle 682.19
bedraggled
slovenly 62.15
soiled 682.21
bedrape 231.38
bedridden 686.55
bedrock
n. bottom 212.1
foundation 216.6
lowest level 208.4
stability 142.6
stone 384.1
adj. bottom 212.7
deepest 209.15
vital 672.22
bedroom 192.7
bedroom eyes 439.5
bedspread 228.10
bedspring 216.20
bedstead 216.19
bedtime
eleventh hour 134.5
sleep 712.2
bedwarf 39.9
bee insect 414.38,74
party 922.13
beef
n. cattle 414.6
complaint 875.4
meat 308.13
objection 522.2
power 157.1
strength 159.2
weight 352.1
v. complain 875.13
object 522.5
beefcake 577.3
beefeater
bodyguard 699.14
household troop
800.31
beefed-up
expanded 197.10
increased 38.7
beefhead 471.4
beefheaded 469.15
beefing
n. complaint 875.4
adj. discontented
869.5
beefsteak 308.18
beef up increase 38.5
strengthen 159.11
beefy corpulent 195.18
strong 159.13
beehive apiary 191.25
workplace 719.2
bee in one's bonnet
caprice 629.1
eccentricity 474.2
beekeeper 416.4
beeline shortcut 203.5
straight line 250.2
Beelzebub 1016.5
beep
n. noise 453.4
v. honk 453.9

beer 996.15,38
beerbelly 193.3
beer garden 996.19
beery
intoxicated 996.30
sentimental 855.22
beetle
n. bug 414.36,74
pulper 390.4
v. overhang 215.7
adj. overhanging
215.11
beetle-browed
overhanging 215.11
sullen 951.24
befall happen 156.11
occur 151.5
befit
be expedient 670.3
behoove 962.4
befitting apt 26.10
expedient 670.5
timely 129.9
befog cloud 404.6
conceal 615.6
before
adv. ahead 240.12
early 131.11
formerly 119.13
in front 292.4
preceding 64.6
preferably 637.28
previously 116.6
prep. in the presence
of 186.18
prior to 116.7
beforehand
adj. ahead of time
115.3
adv. early 131.11
before long
in the future 121.9
soon 131.16
before one's eyes
in front 240.12
overtly 555.15
visible 444.6
before the house 485.38
beforetime
adj. early 131.7
adv. early 131.11
formerly 119.13
befoul defile 682.17
misuse 667.4
work evil 675.6
befouled 682.21
befriend aid 785.11
make friends with
927.10
befrilled
high-flown 601.11
ornamented 901.11
befuddle confuse 532.7
make drunk 996.21
befuddled 532.13
beg entreat 774.11
evade 631.7
scrounge 774.15
beg, borrow, or steal
658.4
beget
be productive 165.7

engender 68.14
invent 167.13
originate 153.11
procreate 169.8
beggar
n. bad person 986.2
bum 708.9
mendicant 774.8
nonworker 708.10
poor person 838.4
vagabond 274.3
v. impoverish 838.6
beggar description
baffle description
920.8
look beautiful 900.15
beggared 838.8
beggarly base 915.12
ill-provided 662.12
indigent 838.8
paltry 673.18
servile 907.13
vulgar 898.15
beggary
indigence 838.2
mendicancy 774.6
want 662.4
begging
n. beggary 774.6
adj. imploring 774.17
petitionary 774.16
begild color 362.13
yellow 370.3
begin 68.7
begin again 143.6
beginner creator 153.4
neophyte 68.2
novice 566.9
producer 167.8
beginning
n. commencement 68
creation 167.5
earliness 131.1
origin 68.4
source 153.5
adj. initial 68.15
beg leave 774.9
beg off abandon 633.5
refuse 776.3
be gone
disappear 447.2
pass 119.6
be good
behave oneself 737.5
be virtuous 980.6
beg pardon
apologize 1012.5
repent 873.7
begrime 682.15
begrudge
be parsimonious
852.5
be unwilling 623.3
envy 954.3
refuse 776.4
beg the question
dodge 631.8
equivocate 483.9
beg to differ 522.4
beguile amuse 878.23
cheat 618.17
deceive 618.13

distract 532.6
fascinate 650.6
beguiled
astonished 920.9
foolish 470.8
beguiling alluring 650.7
amusing 878.29
deceptive 618.19
wonderful 920.10
begum 918.8
behalf benefit 665.4
good 674.4
behave act 705.4
act toward 737.6
behave oneself 737.5
conduct oneself
737.4
behaved 737.7
behavior action 705.1
conditioning 690.33
conduct 737
behavioral
acting 705.10
of behavior 737.7
behaviorism
behavior 737.3
materialism 376.5
psychology 690.2
behaviorist(ic) 737.7
behead 1010.19
behemoth 195.14
behest 752.1
behind
n. buttocks 241.4
rear 241.1
adj. retarded 270.12
adv. after 293.6
in arrears 314.6
in the rear 241.13
late 132.19
prep. after 117.8
supporting 785.27
behindhand
adj. anachronous
115.3
defaulting 842.10
late 132.16
adv. in arrears 314.6
late 132.19
behind one's back
behind 241.13
furtively 614.18
behind the eight ball
731.20
behind the scenes
adj. causal 153.14
cognizant of 475.16
unseen 445.5
adv. behind 241.13
secretly 614.17
theater 611.41
behind the times
123.16
behind time
anachronous 115.3
late 132.19
behold
v. see 439.12
interj. attention!
530.22
beholden
grateful 949.5

thanks 949.2
benefaction gift 818.7
good deed 938.7
benefactor
helper 785.7
patron 942
benefice 1037.9
beneficence
auspiciousness 544.9
benevolence 938.4
beneficent
benevolent 938.15
helpful 785.22
beneficial good 674.12
healthful 683.5
helpful 785.21
useful 665.18
beneficiary
clergyman 1038.8
donee 819.4
proprietor 809.2
benefit
n. aid 785.1
estate 810.4
gift 818.7
good 674.4
good deed 938.7
theatrical perfor-
mance 611.13
use 665.4
v. aid 785.11
be expedient 670.3
be of use 665.17
do a favor 938.12
do good 674.10
benefit from 665.15
benevolence
auspiciousness 544.9
charity 938.4
forgiveness 947.1
gift 818.7
good deed 938.7
goodness 674.1
indulgence 759.2
pity 944.1
benevolent
charitable 938.15
forgiving 947.6
good 674.12
helpful 785.22
indulgent 759.8
benighted blind 441.9
ignorant 477.16
night 134.10
benign
auspicious 544.18
harmless 674.20
healthful 683.5
helpful 785.22
indulgent 759.8
kind 938.13
benignity
auspiciousness 544.9
good deed 938.7
goodness 674.1
harmlessness 674.9
indulgence 759.2
kindness 938.1
bennie 687.9
bent
n. aptitude 733.5
bias 219.3

direction 290.1
inclination 634.3
preference 637.5
prejudice 527.3
tendency 174.1
trait of character
525.3
adj. angular 251.6
curved 252.7
distorted 249.10
drunk 996.31
minded 525.8
benthonic
deep-sea 209.14
life 414.57
benthos
ocean depths 209.4
plankton 414.35
bent on
desirous of 634.22
determined upon
624.16
benumb chill 333.10
make unfeeling 856.8
relieve 886.5
render insensible
423.4
benumbed
apathetic 856.13
insensible 423.6
languid 708.19
Benzedrine 687.9,52
benzine fuel 331.1
illuminant 335.20
be off depart 301.9
go away! 310.29
start out 301.7
be on to 488.8
bequeath
transfer property
817.3
will 818.18
bequeathal
inheritance 819.2
legacy 818.10
property transfer
817.1
bequest
inheritance 819.2
legacy 818.10
be quiet! 451.14
berate 969.20
berating 969.7
bereave die 408.28
take from 822.21
widow 935.6
bereaved bereft 408.35
deprived of 812.8
indigent 838.8
bereavement
deprivation 822.6
loss 812.1
bereft bereaved 408.35
deprived of 812.8
indigent 838.8
wanting 662.13
berg 333.5
beribbon 901.9
beribboned 901.11
beriberi 686.10
berm path 657.3
shore 385.2

berry fruit 308.51
seed 411.29
berserk excited 857.23
mad 473.30
berth
n. anchorage 277.16
harbor 700.6
lodgings 191.3
position 656.5
v. house 188.10
inhabit 188.7
beseech entreat 774.11
pray 1032.12
beseechment
entreaty 774.2
prayer 1032.4
beset
v. annoy 866.13
besiege 798.19
enclose 236.5
importune 774.12
make anxious 890.4
obsess 473.24
overrun 313.6
persecute 667.6
trouble 731.12
adj. distressed 866.22
enclosed 236.10
in difficulty 731.19
infested 313.11
tormented 866.24
worried 890.7
besetting
prevalent 79.12
troublesome 731.17
beside
adv. additionally
40.11
near 200.21
prep. alongside 242.11
compared to 491.11
excluding 77.9
beside oneself
angry 952.26
distracted 532.10
excited 857.23
mad 473.30
overjoyed 865.14
beside the point
amiss 314.7
irrelevant 10.6
besiege attack 798.19
enclose 236.5
importune 774.12
besiegement 798.5
besmear blemish 679.6
coat 228.24
color 362.13
soil 682.16
besmirch blacken 365.7
blemish 679.6
soil 682.16
vilify 971.10
besmirched
blemished 679.10
dingy 365.11
soiled 682.21
unchaste 989.23
besmoke blemish 679.6
dirty 682.15
besot
make drunk 996.21

render insensible
423.4
besotted fooled 470.8
intoxicated 996.30
obsessed 473.33
bespangle
ornament 901.9
variegate 374.7
bespangled
illuminated 335.39
ornamented 901.11
spotted 374.13
bespatter
moisten 392.12
spatter 682.18
stigmatize 915.9
vilify 971.10
bespeak address 594.27
engage 780.13
evidence 505.9
indicate 568.17
mean 545.8
request 774.9
bespeckle
blemish 679.5
variegate 374.7
bespeckled 679.9
bespoke 231.47
best
v. defeat 727.6
excel 36.6
outdo 36.7
triumph over 726.6
adj. cheap 849.9
prime 674.18
superlative 36.13
best, the
good thing 674.8
superiors 36.5
best bet 156.8
bested 727.14
bestial animal 414.43
carnal 987.6
cruel 939.24
savage 162.20
uncouth 898.12
bestiality
badness 675.2
carnality 987.2
cruelty 939.11
sex act 419.9
uncouthness 898.3
be still
v. do nothing 706.2
keep quiet 268.7
interj. silence! 451.14
bestir oneself
be active 707.11
make haste 709.5
best man
assistant 787.6
wedding attendant
933.5
bestow give 818.12
impose 963.6
use 665.13
bestowal giving 818.1
imposition 963.2
bestowed 818.24
best part 54.6
bestraddle
be high 207.16

cover 228.30
mount 315.12
rest on 216.22
bestride be high 207.16
cover 228.30
dominate 741.15
mount 315.12
pass 313.8
rest on 216.22
best seller book 605.1
great success 724.3
best wishes
congratulation 948.1
greetings 925.3
regards 936.8
bet
n. wager 515.3
v. risk 156.12
wager 515.20
beta particle
electron 343.3
particle 326.6,24
radiation 327.4
beta ray 327.3
bête noire bane 676.1
evil spirit 1016.10
frightener 891.9
be that as it may 33.8
bethel 1042.1
betide happen 156.11
occur 151.5
betimes early 131.11
soon 131.16
bêtise foolishness 470.1
stupidity 469.3
betoken augur 544.12
evidence 505.9
indicate 568.17
mean 545.8
show 555.5
bet on be certain 513.9
believe in 501.16
bet 515.20
betray
be dishonest 975.14
deceive 618.13
desert 633.6
divulge 556.6
inform on 557.12
seduce 989.20
betrayal apostasy 628.2
desertion 633.2
divulgence 556.2
seduction 989.6
treason 975.8
betrayed 541.5
betrayer
criminal 986.10
informer 557.6
seducer 989.12
traitor 619.10
betroth 770.6
betrothal 770.3
betrothed
n. fiancée 931.16
adj. promised 770.8
better
v. change 139.6
excel 36.6
make better 691.9
adj. changed 139.9
improved 691.14

preferable 637.25
superior 36.12
bettered 691.13
better half
spouse 933.7
wife 933.9
betterment
change 139.1
improvement 691.1
better self
compunction 873.2
superego 80.5
betting 515.7
betting parlor 515.15
bettor 515.17
between 237.12
between the lines 546.5
between the teeth
452.22
betweentimes
meanwhile 109.5
occasionally 136.5
betwixt and between
among 237.12
mediocre 680.7
midway 69.5
bevel incline 219.4
instrument 251.4
printing 603.6
beveled 219.15
beverage
drink 308.48,49
fluid 388.2
liquor 996.12
bevue bungle 734.5
error 518.4
bevy group 74.3
large number 101.3
quail 74.6
bewail lament 875.8
regret 873.6
beware 895.7
bewhisker 230.20
bewhiskered
bearded 230.25
trite 883.9
bewilder astonish 920.6
confuse 532.7
perplex 514.12
bewildered
astonished 920.9
at an impasse 731.22
perplexed 514.23
bewildering
perplexing 514.25
wonderful 920.10
bewitch delight 865.8
demonize 1016.17
enamor 931.21
enchant 1036.9
fascinate 650.6
practice sorcery
1035.13
work evil 675.6
bewitched
astonished 920.9
enamored 931.26
enchanted 1036.13
supernatural 85.16
bewitching
alluring 650.7
enchanting 1036.11

pleasant 863.7
bey
regional governor
749.13
ruler 749.8
beyond
additionally 40.11
after 117.8
in excess of 663.26
past 199.21
unintelligible 549.26
beyond, the 121.2
**beyond a shadow of
doubt** 513.16
beyond belief
foolish 470.10
unbelievable 503.10
beyond compare
extremely 34.22
peerless 36.15
beyond control 626.12
beyond measure
extremely 34.22
superabundantly
663.24
beyond one
beyond one's power
158.20
hard to understand
549.14
impracticable 510.8
beyond question
513.16,25
beyond recall 889.15
beyond the call of duty
962.18
B-girl 989.16
biannual 137.8
bias
n. bend 219.3
deviation 291.1
diagonal 219.7
inclination 634.3
injustice 977.3
partiality 527.3
preference 637.5
tendency 174.1
trait of character
525.3
v. deflect 291.5
distort 249.6
influence 172.7
oblique 219.9
prejudice 527.9
tend 174.3
adj. diagonal 219.19
inclining 219.15
adv. diagonally 219.25
biased diagonal 219.19
distorted 249.11
inclining 219.15
prejudiced 527.12
unjust 977.11
biaxial 92.7
bib
n. apron 231.17
v. drink 307.27
tipple 996.23
bibacious 996.34
bib and tucker 231.6
bibble-babble
chatter 596.3

nonsense 547.2
bibelot
ornament 901.4
trifle 673.5
Bible
Holy Bible 1021.2
scripture 1021.1
Bible school 567.10
Biblical 1021.10
bibliographer
author 602.15
bookman 605.21
bibliographic(al) 605.25
bibliography
bibliology 605.24
book 605.12
catalog 88.3
directory 748.10
index 605.19
lore 475.9
bibliolatry
orthodoxy 1024.5
scholarship 475.5
zeal 1028.3
bibliophile
bookman 605.21
bookworm 476.4
bibliophilic 475.22
bibulous
absorbent 306.17
drinking 996.34
intemperate 993.7
bicameral
bipartite 92.7
legislative 742.19
bicentennial
anniversary 137.4
two hundred 99.8
biceps arm 287.5
muscle 159.22
bicker argue 482.16
dispute 796.22
flicker 335.25
flutter 324.12
quarrel 795.11
quibble 483.9
bickerer 800.1
bickering
n. argumentation
482.4
contention 796.1
dissension 795.3
quibbling 483.5
adj. flickering 335.36
quarrelsome 795.17
quibbling 483.14
bicolored 374.9
bicorn 252.11
bicuspid
n. tooth 258.5
adj. bisection 92.7
dental 258.16
bicycle
n. vehicle 272.8,29
v. ride 273.32
bicycling 273.6
bicyclist 274.11
bid
n. attempt 714.2
entreaty 774.2
invitation 774.4
offer 773.1

price 846.2
v. bargain 827.17
bid at auction 828.9
command 752.9
offer 773.6
bid come invite 774.13
summon 752.12
bidder 774.7
bidding
command 752.1
invitation 774.4
summons 752.5
biddy
female animal 421.9
maid 750.8
poultry 414.34
woman 421.6
bide await 539.8
be patient 861.5
continue 143.3
endure 110.6
remain 140.5
wait 132.12
bide one's time
do nothing 706.2
expect 539.8
wait 132.12
bidet horse 414.16
washing equipment
681.12
bid price price 846.2
stock price 834.9
biennial
n. anniversary 137.4
plant 411.3
adj. recurring 137.8
bier 410.13
biff
n. hit 283.4
v. hit 283.13
bifocals 443.2
bifurcation angle 251.2
bisection 92.1
duality 90.1
forking 299.3
big adult 126.12
arrogant 912.9
boastful 910.11
eminent 914.18
important 672.16
large 195.16
magnanimous 979.6
bigamist 933.12
bigamy 933.2
big bang theory 375.18
Big Board, the 833.7
Big Brother 748.2
big business 827.1
big deal triviality 673.3
what does it matter?
673.23
Big Dipper 375.28
big game
animal life 414.1
quarry 655.7
biggety
conceited 909.11
impudent 913.9
big gun 672.8
big hand 968.2
bighearted
benevolent 938.15

liberal 853.4
magnanimous 979.6
bight angle 251.2
arm of the sea 399.1
big-league 672.16
big mouth
braggart 910.5
talkativeness 596.1
big name
famous person 914.9
personage 672.8
big-name 672.16
bigot dogmatist 513.7
hater 930.4
intolerant person
527.5
obstinate person
626.6
orthodox 1024.6
bigoted
dogmatic 513.22
fanatical 473.32
narrow-minded
527.10
obstinate 626.8
orthodox 1024.8
bigotry
dogmatism 513.6
fanaticism 473.11
hate 930.1
narrow-mindedness
527.1
obstinacy 626.1
orthodoxy 1024.5
big shot 672.9
big talk boasting 910.2
exaggeration 617.1
grandiloquence 601.1
big talker 596.4
big time 878.2
big-time 672.16
big-time operator
important person
672.9
man of action 707.8
big-time spender 854.2
big top, the 611.15
big wheel
important person
672.9
influential person
172.6
bigwig personage 672.8
superior 36.5
bijou 901.6
bike
n. bicycle 272.8
v. ride 273.32
bikini 231.29
bilabial
n. speech sound
594.13
adj. phonetic 594.31
bilateral bipartite 90.6
double 91.4
sided 242.7
bile bitterness 952.3
digestion 309.8
ill humor 951.1
secretion 312.2
bilge bulge 256.3
nonsense 547.3

offal 682.9
bilingual 580.14
bilious diseased 686.57
ill-humored 951.23
bilk cheat 618.17
disappoint 541.2
bilker 619.3
bill
n. advertising 559.8
beak 256.7
debt 840.1
fee 841.5
law 998.3
legal statement
1004.7
legislative bill 742.17
list 88.5
negotiable instru-
ment 835.11
paper money 835.5
point of land 256.8
poster 559.7
schedule 641.2
statement 845.3
theatrical perfor-
mance 611.13
v. give a show 611.33
publicize 559.15
schedule 641.4
send a statement
845.11
bill and coo 932.13
billboard 559.7
bill collector
collector 74.15
creditor 839.4
billed curved 252.8
scheduled 641.6
billet
n. heraldic insignia
569.2
letter 604.2
position 656.5
wood 378.3
v. house 188.10
settle 184.16
billet-doux letter 604.3
love letter 932.12
billfold 836.14
billion
immense number
101.4
large number 86.4
number 99.12
billionaire 837.6
bill of fare list 88.5
menu 307.12
schedule 641.2
bill of health
certificate 570.6
pass 777.7
bill of lading
account 845.3
list 88.5
bill of particulars
1005.1
Bill of Rights
constitution 998.6
liberties 762.2
bill of sale 829.1
billow
n. wave 395.14

v. bulge 256.10
surge 395.22
billowy bulging 256.14
curved 252.7
wavy 254.10
billy goat goat 414.8
male animal 420.8
bin 660.6
binary 91.4
bind
n. delay 132.2
predicament 731.4
v. border 235.10
compel 756.4
indenture 780.17
obligate 962.12
promise 770.5
relate 9.6
restrain 760.10
stick together 50.9
stop 266.7
tie 47.9
binder
medical dressing
687.33
payment 841.1
wrapper 228.18
binding
n. bookbinding
605.15
connection 47.3
edging 235.7
wrapper 228.18
adj. compulsory
756.10
joining 47.16
mandatory 752.13
obligatory 962.15
prescriptive 751.4
valid 516.13
bind up bundle 74.20
tie 47.9
binge revel 878.6
spree 996.5
bingo game 878.34
game of chance 515.8
lottery 515.11
binoculars 443.3
binomial bipartite 92.7
terminological 583.17
bio– 407.1
biochemical
n. chemical 379.1
adj. chemical 379.7
biochemist 406.18
biochemistry 406.17
biodegradable
decomposable 692.48
disintegrable 53.5
biofeedback 690.5
biographer 608.11
biographical 608.18
biography 608.4
biological 406.19
biological classification
406.3
biological clock 407.3
biological urge 419.5
biologist
biology 406.18
zoologist 415.2

blather
n. chatter 596.3
nonsense 547.2
v. be unintelligent
469.12
chatter 596.5
talk nonsense 547.5
blaze
n. emotional outburst
857.8
fire 328.13
flash 328.14
glare 335.4
light 335.6
mark 568.5
notch 262.1
pointer 568.4
v. become angry
952.18
be hot 328.22
burn 329.23
give light 335.23
heat 329.24
mark 568.19
notch 262.4
proclaim 559.13
blazer 231.51
blazing
n. burning 329.5
adj. burning 328.27
flashing 335.34
blazon
n. display 904.4
heraldic insignia
569.2
v. flaunt 904.17
ornament 901.8
proclaim 559.13
bleach
n. decolorant 363.4
decoloration 363.3
types of 363.10
v. clean 681.18
decolor 363.5
lose color 363.6
whiten 364.5
bleached clean 681.25
decolored 363.8
vacant 187.13
weatherworn 692.36
bleachers 439.8
bleaching
decoloration 363.3
whitening 364.3
bleak cold 333.14
gloomy 872.24
hopeless 889.12
unpleasant 864.20
wind-blown 403.27
bleary 445.6
bleary-eyed 440.13
bleat 460.2
bleb blemish 679.1
blister 256.3
bubble 405.1
sore 686.35
blebby 405.6
bleed despoil 822.24
exploit 665.16
extract 305.12
exude 303.15
grieve 872.17

hemorrhage 311.17
let blood 689.33
overcharge 848.7
pity 944.3
suffer 866.19
take from 822.21
bleeding heart
compassionateness
944.2
despair 866.6
heartache 872.9
sentimentality 855.8
bleed white
consume 666.2
despoil 822.24
exploit 665.16
overcharge 848.7
blemish
n. disfigurement 679
fault 678.2
impairment 692.8
impurity 78.2
mark 568.5
ugly thing 899.4
v. be ugly 899.5
deform 249.7
disfigure 679.4
injure 692.15
mark 568.19
blemished
deformed 249.12
disfigured 679.8
imperfect 678.4
ugly 899.6
blench demur 623.4
flinch 891.21
pull back 284.7
suffer pain 424.8
blend
n. combination 52.1
compound 44.5
hybrid word 582.11
v. combine 52.3
harmonize 462.36
mix 44.11
blended
combined 52.5
harmonious 462.50
mixed 44.15
blend into 145.17
bless approve 968.9
congratulate 948.2
endow 818.17
give one's blessing
1032.13
gladden 865.7
praise 968.12
protect 699.18
sanctify 1026.5
thank 949.4
worship 1032.11
blessed damned 972.10
fortunate 728.14
happy 865.13
heavenly 1018.13
sanctified 1026.8
blessed event 167.7
blessed with 808.9
blessing approval 968.1
benediction 1032.5
boon 674.4
congratulation 948.1

consent 775.1
gift 818.7
godsend 811.7
good deed 938.7
prosperity 728.2
sanctification 1026.3
stroke of luck 728.3
blight
n. adversity 729.1
blast 676.2
disease 686.1
evil 675.3
v. freeze 334.11
impair 692.12
work evil 675.6
blighted
damaged 692.30
disappointed 541.5
ruined 693.28
spoiled 692.43
blighter 986.2
blimp aircraft 280.11
balloon 280.18
corpulent person
195.12
pompous person
904.9
blind
n. blinder 441.5
bridle part 659.5
concealment 615.3
pretext 649.1
shade 338.1,8
stratagem 735.3
trick 618.6
v. blind the eyes 441.7
conceal 615.6
dazzle 335.23
hoodwink 618.16
adj. closed 266.9
concealed 615.11
drunk 996.33
inattentive 531.7
involuntary 639.14
obscure 549.15
sightless 441.9
undiscerning 469.14
unpersuadable 626.13
blind, the 441.4
blind alley
impasse 731.5
obstruction 266.3
road 657.6
blinded blind 441.10
undiscerning 469.14
blinders
blindfold 441.5
bridle part 659.5
narrow-mindedness
527.1
blind faith 502.1
blindfold
n. blinder 441.5
v. blind 441.7
hoodwink 618.16
blindfolded
blinded 441.10
undiscerning 469.14
blind impulse
impulse 630.1
instinct 481.2
involuntariness 639.5

blinding
n. blindness 441.1
adj. bright 335.32
garish 362.19
obscuring 441.11
rainy 394.10
blindness
faulty eyesight 440.1
incognizance 477.3
sightlessness 441
unperceptiveness
469.2
unpersuadableness
626.5
blind spot
blindness 441.1
narrow-mindedness
527.1
radar interference
346.12
radio reception
344.21
blind to
insensible 856.10
unaware 477.13
blink
n. glance 439.4
light 335.7
reflection 335.9
v. flinch 891.21
glitter 335.24
neglect 534.8
pull back 284.7
wink 440.10
blink at be blind 441.8
be broad-minded
526.7
condone 947.4
disregard 531.2
permit 777.10
blinker 568.15
blinking
n. light 335.7
winking 440.7
adj. flickering 335.36
glittering 335.35
poor-sighted 440.11
blintz pancake 308.44
pastry 308.40
blips 346.11
bliss happiness 865.2
heaven 1018.6
pleasantness 863.1
blissful happy 865.13
pleasant 863.6
sublime 863.8
blister
n. blemish 679.1
bubble 405.1
ridge 256.3
sore 686.35
v. burn 329.24
criticize severely
969.21
blistered blistery 405.6
burned 329.30
blistering
n. burning 329.5
adj. bubbly 405.6
hot 328.25
blistery 405.6
blithe 870.11

blither 469.12
blithering 469.22
blithering idiot 471.8
blithesome 870.11
blitz
  n. attack 798.1
  bombardment 798.7
  bombing 798.8
  v. attack 798.15
  blow up 693.18
  fire upon 798.22
blitzkrieg attack 798.1
  bombardment 798.7
blizzard snow 333.8
  windstorm 403.12
bloat
  n. distension 197.2
  overextension 663.7
  v. become larger
   197.5
  increase 38.6
  make larger 197.4
bloated bulging 256.14
  corpulent 195.18
  deformed 249.12
  distended 197.13
  increased 38.7
  overfull 663.20
  pompous 904.22
  proud 905.10
blob ball 255.2
  bulge 256.3
blobby formless 247.4
  vague 514.18
bloc 788.1
block
  n. auction 829.4
  city block 183.7
  clog 266.3
  defense mechanism
   690.31
  delay 132.2
  dolt 471.3
  instrument of execu-
   tion 1011.5
  lump 195.10
  mental block 538.3
  obstacle 730.4
  plaything 878.16
  print 578.6
  set 74.12
  shares 834.3
  solid 354.6
  thought disturbance
   690.24
  tract 180.4
  v. cover 228.19
  delay 132.8
  end 144.11
  fend off 799.10
  obstruct 730.12
  prevent 730.13
  stop up 266.7
blockade
  n. closure 266.1
  enclosure 236.1
  exclusion 77.1
  hindrance 730.4
  obstruction 266.3
  siege 798.5
  v. besiege 798.19
  enclose 236.5

exclude 77.4
fortify 799.9
obstruct 730.12
stop 266.7
blockage
  defense mechanism
   690.31
  delay 132.2
  hindrance 730.1
  obstruction 266.3
  seizure 686.5
blockbuster 540.2
blocked clogged 266.11
  forgetful 538.9
  late 132.16
blockhead
  bungler 734.8
  dolt 471.4
blockheaded 469.17
blockhouse
  cottage 191.9
  stronghold 799.6
blockish 469.15
block letter 602.4
block out analyze 48.7
  form 246.7
  outline 654.12
blocky 203.10
bloke man 420.5
  person 417.3
blond
  n. hair color 362.9
  adj. fair-haired 364.9
  yellow-haired 370.5
blood ancestry 170.4
  blood relationship
   11.1
  body fluid 388.4
  class 61.2
  dandy 903.9
  diseases 686.18
  fluid 388.2
  killing 409.1
  kind 61.3
  kinsmen 11.2
  nobility 918.1
  race 11.4
  seat of life 407.3
blood and thunder
  855.9
blood-and-thunder
  857.30
blood bank
  blood 388.4
  hospital room 192.25
  transfusion 689.20
bloodbath
  carnage 409.5
  destruction 693.1
blood brother 11.3
blood clot 354.7
bloodcurdling 891.37
bloodied 866.25
bloodless
  colorless 363.7
  pacific 803.9
  uninteresting 883.6
  weak 160.12
bloodletting
  bleeding 689.26
  extraction 305.3
  killing 409.1

bloodline 170.4
bloodlust
  cruelty 939.11
  violence 162.1
bloodmobile
  blood 388.4
  transfusion 689.20
blood money fee 841.5
  recompense 841.3
blood-red 368.7
blood relationship
  consanguinity 11
  relationship 9.3
blood relative 11.2
bloodshed killing 409.1
  warfare 797.1
bloodstain
  n. blemish 679.3
  v. bloody 679.7
bloodstained 679.11
bloodstream 388.4
bloodsucker
  extortionist 822.12
  parasite 414.41
bloodthirsty
  cruel 939.24
  murderous 409.24
  warlike 797.25
blood type 388.4
blood vessel 396.14
bloody
  v. bleed 311.17
  bloodstain 679.7
  injure 692.15
  torture 866.18
  adj. bleeding 311.23
  blood red 368.7
  bloodstained 679.11
  cruel 939.24
  damned 972.9
  fluid 388.7
  murderous 409.24
  savage 162.20
  warlike 797.25
bloody-minded
  cruel 939.24
  murderous 409.24
  warlike 797.25
bloom
  n. beauty 900.1
  blossom 411.22
  flowering 411.24
  health 685.1
  heat 328.12
  reddening 368.3
  television reception
   345.5
  youth 124.1
  v. be healthy 685.5
  be hot 328.22
  evolve 148.5
  flower 411.32
  look beautiful 900.15
  mature 126.9
  reach perfection
   722.8
  thrive 728.8
blooper 518.6
blooping
  audio distortion
   450.13

television reception
  345.5
blossom
  n. bloom 411.22
  flowering 411.24
  v. evolve 148.5
  flower 411.32
  grow 197.7
  reach perfection
   722.8
  thrive 728.8
blot
  n. blemish 679.3
  obliteration 693.7
  soil 682.5
  stigma 915.6
  ugly thing 899.4
  v. be ugly 899.5
  blacken 365.7
  blemish 679.5
  dry 393.6
  obliterate 693.16
  sorb 306.13
  stigmatize 915.9
blotch
  n. blemish 679.3
  mark 568.5
  soil 682.5
  spottiness 374.3
  v. blacken 365.7
  blemish 679.5
  mark 568.19
  variegate 374.7
blotchy
  blemished 679.9
  dingy 365.11
  spotted 374.13
blot out darken 337.9
  delete 42.12
  kill 409.14
  obliterate 693.16
blotter absorbent 306.6
  record book 570.11
blotto 996.33
blouse 231.15,54
blow
  n. act 705.3
  blossom 411.22
  disappointment
   541.1
  distress 866.5
  feast 307.9
  flowering 411.24
  gust 403.6
  hit 283.4
  misfortune 729.2
  punishment 1010.3
  surprise 540.2
  windstorm 403.12
  v. be bombastic 601.6
  become exhausted
   717.5
  blare 453.9
  blunder 518.15
  boast 910.7
  breathe 403.24
  eject 310.21
  flee 631.11
  flower 411.32
  play music 462.43
  puff 310.23

reach perfection
722.8
squander 854.3
wind 403.22
blow about 559.16
blow down
knock down 318.5
raze 693.19
blower bellows 403.20
braggart 910.5
fan 403.21
ventilator 402.10
blow for blow 955.3
blowgun blower 403.20
weapon 801.5
blowhard 910.5
blow hard 910.7
blowhole
air passage 396.17
opening 265.4
outlet 303.9
blow hot and cold
be capricious 629.4
equivocate 483.9
fluctuate 141.5
vacillate 627.8
blow in 300.6
blown spoiled 692.43
tainted 692.42
wind-blown 403.27
blown up out of all
proportion 617.4
blow off boast 910.7
dissipate 75.5
blow off steam 878.26
blow one's mind
fantasy 535.17
go crazy 473.21
have hallucinations
519.8
blow one's top
become angry 952.19
get excited 857.15
go crazy 473.21
blowout banquet 307.9
ejection 310.7
explosion 162.7
festival 878.4
party 922.11
blow out eject 310.24
erupt 162.12
explode 162.13
extinguish 332.7
flow out 303.13
unclog 310.21
blow over end 70.6
knock down 318.5
stop blowing 403.22
blowpipe
blower 403.20
blowtorch 329.14
weapon 801.5
blow the whistle
be impatient 862.5
inform 557.12
put a stop to 144.11
blow to 841.19
blowtorch
aircraft 280.3
burner 329.14
blowup
explosion 162.7

increase 38.2
outburst 952.9
photoprint 577.5
blow up
become angry 952.19
come to nothing
725.12
demolish 693.18
disprove 506.4
excite 857.11
explode 162.13
get excited 857.15
increase 38.5
make larger 197.4
praise 968.12
process photos
577.15
set in 403.22
strike dead 409.18
blowy 403.25
blowzy
corpulent 195.18
red-complexioned
368.9
slovenly 62.15
blubber
n. softness 357.4
v. bubble 405.4
speak poorly 595.9
utter 594.26
weep 875.10
blubbery 380.9
bludgeon coerce 756.7
intimidate 891.28
threaten 973.2
blue
n. barbiturate 687.12
blueness 372.1
colors 372.4
trial print 603.5
v. make blue 372.2
adj. bluish 372.3
deathly 408.29
melancholy 872.23
obscene 990.9
blue, the 375.2
Bluebeard 933.12
blue blood
nobility 918.1
nobleman 918.4
blue-blooded 918.11
blue book
examination 485.2
information 557.1
official document
570.8
register 570.9
blue chip 834.2
blue-collar worker 718.2
blue devil 687.12
blue devils
delirium tremens
473.10
ill humor 951.10
sadness 872.6
bluegrass 462.10
blue in the face 857.23
bluejacket
navy man 276.4
sailor 276.1
blue language 972.3
blue movie 990.4

bluenose 903.11
blue-pencil
delete 42.12
revise 691.12
blueprint
n. diagram 654.3
outline 48.4
photograph 577.5
plan 654.1
representation 572.1
schedule 641.2
trial print 603.5
v. plot 654.11
process photos
577.15
blue ribbon
award 916.5
supremacy 36.3
blues folk music 462.10
ill humor 951.10
sadness 872.6
song 462.13
bluestocking
n. pedant 476.5
adj. book-learned
475.22
blue streak 269.6
blue velvet 687.12
bluff
n. bluster 911.1
blusterer 911.2
fakery 616.3
impostor 619.6
precipice 213.3
trick 618.6
v. bluster 911.3
deceive 618.13
fake 616.21
frighten off 891.29
adj. artless 736.5
blunt 259.3
candid 974.17
gruff 937.7
impudent 913.9
steep 219.18
blunder
n. an error 518.5
bungle 734.5
foolish act 470.4
v. bungle 734.11
err 518.14
fail 725.13
flounder 324.15
blunderhead
bungler 734.8
dolt 471.4
blunderheaded
clumsy 734.20
stupid 469.17
blunder upon
bungle 734.11
find 488.3
blunt
v. desensitize 856.7
disincline 652.4
dull 259.2
moderate 163.6
numb 423.4
weaken 160.10
adj. artless 736.5
candid 974.17
dull 259.3

free-spoken 762.22
gruff 937.7
stupid 469.16
unfeeling 856.9
blunted 259.3
blur
n. blemish 679.3
indistinctness 445.2
stigma 915.6
v. be undiscriminating
493.3
blemish 679.6
deform 247.3
lose distinctness
445.4
blurb
commendation 968.3
publicity 559.4
blurred formless 247.4
imperfectly spoken
595.12
indistinct 445.6
uncertain 514.18
blurt divulge 556.6
exclaim 459.7
remark 594.25
blurt out 630.7
blush
n. blushing 908.5
heat 328.12
reddening 368.3
warmth 362.2
v. become excited
857.17
become red 368.5
flush 908.8
look guilty 983.2
bluster
n. agitation 324.1
boasting 910.1
swagger 911
violence 162.2
v. be angry 952.15
blow 403.22
boast 910.6
intimidate 891.28
show a bold front
793.5
swagger 911.3
blustering noisy 453.12
swaggering 911.4
threatening 973.3
violent 162.17
windy 403.25
BM defecation 311.2
feces 311.4
BMOC 672.9
BO stench 437.1
sweat 311.7
boar male animal 420.8
swine 414.9
board
n. accommodations
659.3
council 755.1
directorate 748.11
edge 235.4
food 308.1
meal 307.5
rations 308.6
school board 567.17
stage 611.21

bomber
  artilleryman 800.10
  destroyer 693.8
  frightener 891.8
  violent person 162.9
bombinate 452.13
bombing attack 798.8
  flight 278.11
bombshell
  bomb 801.14
  surprise 540.2
bona fide
  authentic 516.14
  faithfully 974.25
  honest 974.14
bonanza plenty 661.2
  rich source 837.3
  source of supply
    660.4
bond
  n. compact 771.1
  connection 47.3
  contract 771.3
  debenture 834.4
  fidelity 974.7
  insurance 699.4
  joining 47.1
  pledge 772.2
  relationship 9.1
  restraint 760.4
  security 772.1
  v. join 47.5
  pledge 772.10
  secure 772.9
bondage 764.1
bondholder 833.14
bondsman
  guarantor 772.6
  slave 764.7
bone
  n. dryness 393.2
  hardness 356.6
  structure 245.6,12
  v. study 564.12
  adj. osteal 245.11
bonehead 471.4
bone of contention
  discord 795.7
  question 485.10
boner an error 518.6
  bungle 734.5
bones body 376.3
  corpse 408.16
  dice 515.9
  percussion instrument
    465.18
  refuse 669.4
  seat of affections
    855.2
  skeleton 245.5
bone to pick
  bone of contention
    795.7
  grudge 929.5
bonhomie
  cordiality 927.6
  good nature 938.2
  hospitality 925.1
bonkers 473.26
bon mot 881.7
bonny beautiful 900.17
  good 674.12

bon ton custom 642.1
  fashion 644.1
  fashionableness 644.2
bonus extra 41.4
  extra pay 841.6
  gratuity 818.5
  surplus 663.5
  windfall 811.6
bon vivant
  companion 928.4
  connoisseur 897.7
  gourmet 307.14
  sensualist 987.3
  sociable person
    922.15
bon voyage! 301.23
bony bone 245.11
  hard 356.10
  lean 205.17
boo
  n. hoot 967.3
  v. hiss 967.10
  interj. contempt
    966.10
boob dupe 620.1
  fool 471.2
  teat 256.6
boo-boo an error 518.6
  bungle 734.5
boob tube 345.11
booby fool 471.2
  loser 727.5
  teat 256.6
booby hatch 473.14
booby prize 916.2
booby trap
  concealment 615.3
  trap 618.11
boodle booty 824.11
  bribe 651.2
  money 835.2
  spoils of office
    744.35
boogie-woogie 462.9
boohoo 875.10
book
  n. book part 605.13
  part of writing 55.2
  playbook 611.26
  poetic division
    609.11
  publication 559.1
  volume 605
  wager 515.3
  v. accuse 1005.7
  engage 780.13
  keep accounts 845.8
  list 88.8
  record 570.16
  schedule 641.4
bookbinding 605.15
bookcase
  bookbinding 605.15
  bookholder 605.20
  storage place 660.6
book collector 605.21
bookdealer
  bookman 605.21
  merchant 830.3
booked
  recorded 570.18
  scheduled 641.6

book end 605.20
bookie 515.16
booking
  engagement 780.4
  playing engagement
    611.12
  recording 570.15
booking agent 611.30
bookish
  book-learned 475.22
  studentlike 566.12
  studious 564.17
bookkeeper
  accountant 845.7
  calculator 87.8
  financial officer
    836.11
  recorder 571.1
bookkeeping
  n. accounting 845.6
  adj. accounting
    845.12
book-learned 475.22
booklet 605.9
booklover
  bookman 605.21
  bookworm 476.4
bookmaker
  bookman 605.21
  gambling 515.16
bookmobile 605.17
bookrest 605.20
book review 494.2
book reviewer 606.4
books
  account book 845.4
  list 88.5
bookseller
  bookman 605.21
  merchant 830.3
bookstore
  bookshop 605.18
  store 832.4
book value 834.9
bookworm
  bibliophage 476.4
  bookman 605.21
  student 566.10
boom
  n. barrier 730.5
  business cycle 827.9
  explosion 162.7
  float 277.11
  increase 38.1
  lever 287.4
  loud noise 456.4
  prosperity 728.5
  reverberation 454.2
  v. din 453.6
  hum 452.13
  increase 38.6
  reverberate 454.7
  sail 275.48
  speed 269.8
  thrive 728.8
  thunder 456.9
  utter 594.26
boomerang
  n. recoil 284.2
  retaliation 955.1
  weapon 801.12
  v. recoil 284.6

booming
  n. boom 456.4
  hum 452.7
  reverberation 454.2
  adj. humming 452.20
  loud 453.10
  reverberating 454.11
  thriving 728.13
  thundering 456.12
boon
  n. gift 818.7
  godsend 811.7
  good 674.4
  adj. convivial 922.19
boondocks
  hinterland 182.2
  remote region 199.4
  woodland 411.11
boor
  awkward person
    734.8
  oaf 471.5
  rustic 919.9
  vulgar person 898.6
boorish churlish 898.13
  clumsy 734.20
  countrified 182.7
  discourteous 937.6
boost
  n. assist 785.2
  commendation 968.3
  improvement 691.1
  increase 38.1
  promotion 782.1
  raise 317.2
  thrust 283.2
  v. cheer 870.7
  commend 968.11
  elevate 317.5
  further 785.17
  increase 38.4
  make better 691.9
  publicize 559.15
  steal 824.13
  thrust 283.11
booster
  commender 968.8
  devotee 635.6
  dose 687.6
  injection 689.18
  publicist 559.9
  rocket 281.5
  television relay 345.9
  thief 825.1
boot
  n. an error 518.6
  footwear 231.27,60
  instrument of torture
    1011.4
  kick 283.8
  novice 566.9
  recruit 800.17
  sailor 276.4
  thrill 857.2
  v. blunder 518.15
  clothe 231.39
  dismiss 310.19
  kick 283.18
boot, the
  dismissal 310.5
  ejection 310.1
bootblack 750.5

booth
compartment 192.2
hut 191.10
store 832.3
bootleg
v. deal illicitly 826.7
make liquor 996.29
adj. illegal 999.6
bootlegger
liquor maker 996.18
racketeer 826.4
bootless
fruitless 669.12
ineffective 158.15
unsuccessful 725.17
bootlicker 907.3
booty loot 824.11
take 822.10
booze
n. liquor 996.12
v. drink 307.27
liquor 996.24
bop music 462.9
nonsense 547.3
bordello brothel 989.9
disapproved place
191.28
border
n. edge 235.4
exterior 224.2
frontier 235.5
garden 413.10
region 180.2
scenery 611.25
side 242.1
v. adjoin 200.9
edge 235.10
side 242.4
bordering
n. edging 235.7
adj. adjacent 200.16
fringing 235.11
bordering on 200.24
borderland
environment 233.1
frontier 235.5
hinterland 182.2
region 180.2
borderline 235.11
borderline case
an uncertainty 514.8
lunatic 473.15
bore
n. annoyance 866.2
boring person 884.4
puncture 265.3
thickness 204.3
wave 395.14
v. excavate 257.15
give no pleasure
866.12
leave one cold 884.6
puncture 265.16
boreal cold 333.14
northern 290.15
windy 403.25
winter 128.8
Boreas 403.3
bored incurious 529.3
languid 708.19
pleasureless 866.20
uninterested 884.11

boredom
incurious 529.1
languor 708.6
tedium 884.3
unpleasure 866.1
boring
n. puncture 265.3
adj. monotonous 17.6
wearying 884.9
born given birth 167.21
innate 5.7
thorough 56.10
borne 216.24
borne out 505.21
born for 733.27
born out of wedlock
999.7
born yesterday 736.5
borough city 183.1
district 180.5
election district
744.16
borrow
deal in money 835.27
go in debt 840.6
imitate 22.5
plagiarize 824.18
raise money 821.3
steal 824.13
borrower 840.4
borrowing debt 840.1
loan word 582.7
money market 835.16
money-raising 821
plagiarism 824.7
borrowing power 839.1
borscht circuit 611.12
borstal prison 761.8
reform school 567.14
boscage thicket 411.13
undergrowth 411.15
bosh humbug 616.14
nonsense 547.3
bos'n 276.7
bosom
n. breast 256.6
inner nature 5.4
interior 225.2
seat of affections
855.2
v. embrace 932.16
harbor 813.7
keep secret 614.7
secrete 615.7
bosomy bulging 256.14
corpulent 195.18
boss
n. knob 256.3
mark 568.7
master 749.1
political leader 746.7
relief 575.3
superior 36.4
supervisor 748.2
v. emboss 256.11
roughen 261.4
supervise 747.10
adj. excellent 674.13
governing 741.18
supervising 747.13

bossism
authoritativeness
739.3
politics 744.1
bossy
n. cow 414.6
female animal 421.9
adj. imperious 739.16
in relief 256.17
botanic(al)
herbaceous 411.33
phytological 412.8
botanist
biologist 406.18
phytologist 412.2
botany biology 406.17
phytology 412
plants 411.1
botch
n. an error 518.5
bungle 734.5
fiasco 725.6
misrepresentation
573.2
slipshodness 534.3
v. bungle 734.11
do carelessly 534.9
err 518.14
impair 692.12
misrepresent 573.4
botched
bungled 734.21
damaged 692.30
slipshod 534.12
both
n. two 90.2
adj. two 90.7
bother
n. annoyance 866.2
bustle 707.4
commotion 62.4
confusion 532.3
dither 857.5
imposition 963.1
inconvenience 671.3
perplexity 514.3
trouble 731.3
v. annoy 866.13
be unpleasant 864.15
bewilder 514.12
confuse 532.7
disquiet 890.3
distress 866.16
inconvenience 671.4
take liberties 961.7
vex 731.12
bothered
annoyed 866.21
anxious 890.6
bewildered 514.23
confused 532.12
distressed 866.22
troubled 731.19
bothersome
annoying 864.22
troublesome 731.17
worrisome 890.9
bottle
n. types of 193.12
v. enclose 236.6
package 236.9
preserve 701.9

put in 184.14
bottleneck
constriction 198.1
convergence 298.1
narrow place 205.3
obstacle 730.4
obstruction 266.3
bottle up
confine 761.12
enclose 236.6
hinder 730.10
retain 813.5
secrete 615.7
suppress 760.8
bottom
n. base 208.4
bed 212.4
bottom side 212
courage 893.5
marsh 400.1
pluck 624.3
ship 277.1
valley 257.9
adj. bottommost
212.7
cheap 849.9
bottom dollar end 70.2
funds 835.14
bottomland
lowland 208.3
marsh 400.1
plain 387.1
bottomless deep 209.11
greedy 634.27
plentiful 661.7
bottomless pit
depths 209.3
hell 1019.1
bottom line, the
crucial point 672.6
the whole story 86.5
bottom out 139.5
boudoir 192.7
bough branch 411.18
offshoot 55.4
bought 828.11
bouillabaisse
soup 308.10
stew 308.11
bouillon beef 308.13
soup 308.10
boulder 384.5
boulevard 657.6
bounce
n. elasticity 358.1
leap 319.1
lightheartedness
870.3
ostentation 904.8
radar signal 346.11
radio signal 344.10
recoil 284.2
shake 324.3
v. be elastic 358.5
bluster 911.3
dismiss 310.19
eject 310.13
jump 319.6
leap 319.5
recoil 284.6
shake 324.11

bounce back

radar 346.16
recoil 284.6
recover 694.20
reverberate 454.7

bouncing leaping 319.7
lively 707.17
recoiling 284.10
robust 685.10
strong 159.13

bound
n. leap 319.1
limit 235.3
recoil 284.2
v. border 235.10
circumscribe 234.4
enclose 236.5
leap 319.5
limit 234.5
recoil 284.6
run 269.10
separate 235.8
adj. blocked 266.11
certain 513.13
enclosed 236.10
joined 47.13
limited 234.7
obliged 962.16
promised 770.8
related 9.9
resolute 624.11
restrained 760.16

boundary
n. divider 92.3
end 70.2
fence 236.4
joint 47.4
limit 235.3
limitation 234.2
pause 144.4
adj. bordering 235.11
final 70.10

bounder
bad person 986.8
vulgar person 898.6

boundless
excessive 663.16
godlike 1013.20
infinite 104.3
large 34.7

bound over 780.20

bountiful liberal 853.4
plentiful 661.7
productive 165.9

bounty extra pay 841.6
gratuity 818.5
liberality 853.1
subsidy 818.8

bouquet bundle 74.8
compliment 968.6
flowers 411.23
fragrance 436.1

bourgeois
n. common man 919.7
conformist 82.2
townsman 190.6
vulgar person 898.6
adj. capitalist 745.23
conformist 82.6
mediocre 680.8
middle-class 919.12

vulgar 898.14

bourn boundary 235.3
destination 300.5
running water 395.1

bourse 833.7

bout boxing 796.9
contest 796.3
game 878.9
revel 878.6
spell 108.2
spree 996.5
turn 137.3

boutique 832.1

boutonniere 411.23

bovine
n. cattle 414.6
adj. complacent 868.10
inexcitable 858.10
stupid 469.15
ungulate 414.49

bow
n. bend 252.3
bulge 256.3
curve 252.2
viol 465.6
weapon 801.17
v. curve 252.6
fiddle 462.42

bow
n. crouch 318.3
front 240.3
greeting 925.4
obeisance 964.2
v. be defeated 727.12
bend 318.9
be servile 907.6
bow down 765.10
make obeisance 964.6

bowdlerize
clean 681.18
delete 42.12

bowel movement
defecation 311.2
feces 311.4

bowels depths 209.3
intestine 225.4

bower
playing card 878.17
summerhouse 191.13

bowery 411.38

bowl
n. arena 802.1
ceramic ware 576.2
pit 257.2
throw 285.4
v. be concave 257.12
make concave 257.13
push 285.10
roll 322.10
throw 285.11

bowlegged 249.12

bowl over
astonish 920.6
knock down 318.5
startle 540.8

bow out
absent oneself 187.8
dismiss 310.18
exit 303.11
leave 301.8

box
n. coffin 410.11
compartment 192.2
cottage 191.9
gift 818.4
impasse 731.5
punishment 1010.3
slap 283.7
storage place 660.6
theater part 611.20
v. contend 796.14
package 236.9
punish 1010.13
put in 184.14
restrain 760.9
slap 283.16
wrap 228.20

boxcar 272.14

boxcars 99.7

boxer 800.2

box in confine 236.6
enclose 236.5
qualify 507.3
restrain 760.9

boxing packaging 236.2
pugilism 796.9

box office
attendance 186.4
office 719.8
receipts 844.1

box springs 216.20

boy
n. child 125.5
male servant 750.4
race 418.3
interj. pleasure 865.17

boycott
n. exclusion 77.1
ostracism 926.3
protest 522.2
strike 789.7
v. object 522.5
ostracize 926.6
strike 789.9

boyfriend 931.12

boyhood
childhood 124.2
young people 125.2

boyish childish 124.11
thin 205.16

boy wonder 733.12

bra brassiere 231.24
supporter 216.2

brace
n. medical dressing 687.33
music 462.29
support 216.2,26
two 90.2
v. bind 47.9
refresh 695.2
stiffen 356.9
strengthen 159.11
support 216.21

bracelet circle 253.3
jewel 901.6

brace oneself
be determined 624.8
prepare oneself 720.13

bracer drink 996.7
refresher 695.1

supporter 216.2
tonic 687.8

braces 215.5

brace up
cheer up 870.9
encourage 893.16
recuperate 694.19
refresh 695.2
strengthen 159.11
take courage 893.14

bracing cool 333.12
energizing 161.14
healthful 683.5
refreshing 695.3
supporting 216.23
tonic 687.44

bracken 411.4,43

bracket
n. class 61.2
supporter 216.2,28
v. join 47.5
pair 90.5
parenthesize 236.8
punctuate 586.16
relate 9.6

brackish salty 433.9
unsavory 429.7

bract 411.17

brag
n. boasting 910.1
braggart 910.5
v. bluster 911.3
boast 910.6

brag about 968.12

braggart
n. blusterer 911.2
boaster 910.5
egotist 909.5
adj. boastful 910.10

bragging
n. boasting 910.1
adj. boastful 910.10

Bragi
Norse deity 1014.6
poetic inspiration 609.12

Brahma God 1013.4
Hindu deity 1014.8

Brahman
Hindu priest 1038.14
nobleman 918.4
religionist 1020.34

Brahmin
intellectual 476.1
snob 912.7

braid
n. cord 206.2
hair 230.7
weaving 222.2
v. weave 222.6

Braille 441.6

brain
n. intellect 466.1
intelligent being 467.9
seat of thought 466.6
sensory area 422.6
vitals 225.4
v. strike dead 409.18

brainchild
good idea 479.6
product 168.1

brickbat
indignity 965.2
weapon 801.12
bridal 933.19
bride 933.6
bride and groom 933.10
bridegroom 933.6
bridesmaid 933.5
bridge
n. card game 878.35
dental 258.6
music division 462.24
observation post
439.8
span 657.10
stage 611.21
viol 465.6
v. cover 228.30
join 47.5
bridgehead
outpost 240.2
stronghold 799.6
bridle
n. harness 659.5
restraint 760.4
v. affect 903.14
be arrogant 912.8
become angry 952.17
bind 47.10
drive animals 416.7
restrain 760.7
shackle 760.10
brief
n. abridgment 607.1
airmanship 278.3
record 570.7
v. abridge 607.5
advise 754.5
aviation 278.57
engage 780.13
give instructions
562.16
inform 557.8
outline 654.12
adj. abridged 607.6
concise 592.6
short 203.8
taciturn 613.9
transient 111.8
briefed
informed 475.18
prepared 720.16
briefing advice 754.1
airmanship 278.3
engagement 780.4
information 557.1
instructions 562.6
preparation 720.1
briefly concisely 592.7
shortly 203.12
transiently 111.10
brier adherent 50.4
shrubbery 411.9
thorn 258.7
brig 761.8
brigade group 74.3
military unit 800.19
brigadier 749.18
brigand 825.4
bright alert 533.14
auspicious 544.18
brilliant 335.32

cheerful 870.11
clean 681.25
colorful 362.18
gorgeous 900.19
illustrious 914.19
intelligent 467.12
optimistic 888.12
pleasant 863.10
sharp-witted 467.14
teachable 564.18
undamaged 677.8
brighten cheer 870.7
grow bright 335.27
illuminate 335.28
make pleasant 863.5
brightness
alertness 533.5
auspiciousness 544.9
beauty 900.6
brilliance 335.4
cheerfulness 870.1
colorfulness 362.4
color quality 362.6
intelligence 467.2
pleasantness 863.4
teachability 564.5
bright side
optimism 888.3
pleasantness 863.4
Brigit 1014.7
brilliance beauty 900.6
brightness 335.4
colorfulness 362.4
grandeur 904.5
illustriousness 914.6
intelligence 467.2
skill 733.1
wittiness 881.2
brilliant bright 335.32
colorful 362.18
gorgeous 900.19
illustrious 914.19
intelligent 467.14
skillful 733.20
witty 881.15
brim 235.4
brimming 56.11
brim over 395.17
brindle 374.15
brine
preservative 701.3
salt 433.4
bring be sold 829.12
bring on 153.12
cost 846.15
entail 76.4
fetch 271.15
induce 648.22
inflict 963.5
bring about
accomplish 722.5
cause 153.11
change course 275.30
do 705.6
produce 167.9
prompt 648.13
bring back fetch 271.15
remember 537.10
restore 823.4
revive 694.16
bring before
confront 240.8

propose 773.5
bring charges 1005.7
bring down
disparage 971.8
fell 318.5
humiliate 906.5
incur 175.4
raze 693.19
strike dead 409.18
bring down upon
cause trouble 731.13
incur 175.4
inflict 963.5
bring forth bear 167.14
create 167.13
elicit 305.14
indicate 555.5
originate 153.11
bring forward
adduce evidence
505.13
call to witness
1004.16
confront 240.8
indicate 555.5
make better 691.9
propose 773.5
bring home to
accuse of 1005.9
attribute to 155.4
condemn 1008.3
convince 501.18
impress upon 855.18
prove 505.11
bring in cost 846.15
harvest 413.19
introduce 306.14
yield 844.4
bring off
bring about 722.5
carry out 705.9
do 705.6
succeed with 724.10
bring on
adduce evidence
505.13
incur 175.4
induce 153.12
bring out elicit 305.14
indicate 555.5
issue 559.14
print 603.14
bring round
change course 275.30
convince 501.18
persuade 648.23
restore to health
694.15
bring to convert 145.11
revive 694.16
sail 275.24
stop 144.11
bring to light
disclose 556.4
elicit 305.14
uncover 488.4
bring to mind
imply 546.4
remember 537.10
resemble 20.7
bring to pass
bring about 722.5

cause 153.11
do 705.6
bring up begin 68.11
confront 240.8
propose 773.5
stop 144.7
train 562.14
vomit 310.25
brink 235.4
brinkmanship
foreign policy 744.5
recklessness 894.3
brio 161.3
brisk brief 111.8
cold 333.14
energetic 161.12
exciting 857.29
lively 707.17
pungent 433.7
refreshing 695.3
windy 403.25
bristle
n. barb 261.3
beard 230.8
hair 230.2
thorn 258.7
v. annoy 866.13
become angry 952.17
be sharp 258.8
provoke 952.22
rise 213.8
roughen 261.5
bristle with
be numerous 101.5
teem with 661.5
bristling crowded 74.22
rough 261.9
teeming 101.9
bristly hairy 230.24
prickly 258.12
rough 261.9
Britain 181.4
britches 231.18
brittle crisp 360.4
deteriorated 692.37
frail 160.14
transient 111.7
broach begin 68.11
extract 305.12
make public 559.11
open 265.12
propose 773.5
puncture 265.16
broad
n. girl 125.6
unchaste woman
989.14
woman 421.6
adj. broad-minded
526.8
candid 974.17
comic 880.5
compounds 204.10
extensive 79.13
general 79.11
phonetic 594.31
spacious 179.9
vague 514.18
voluminous 195.17
vulgar 990.8
wide 204.6

broadcast
 n. dispersion 75.1
  planting 413.14
  publication 559.1
  radio broadcast
   344.18
 v. communicate 554.7
  disperse 75.4
  plant 413.18
  publish 559.10
  radiobroadcast
   344.25
 adj. dispersed 75.9
  made public 559.17
broadcaster 344.23
broadcasting
  dispersion 75.1
  planting 413.14
  publication 559.1
  radio broadcasting
   344.16
broaden augment 38.4
  become larger 197.5
  generalize 79.9
  make larger 197.4
  spread 38.6
  widen 204.4
broadening 526.14
broadly
  candidly 974.23
  extensively 179.10
  far and wide 199.16
  generally 79.17
  humorously 880.6
  vaguely 514.27
broad-minded
  liberal 762.24
  tolerant 526.8
  wise 467.17
broad-shouldered
  strong 159.14
  virile 420.12
broadside
 n. advertising 559.8
  gunfire 798.10
  side 242.1
 adv. breadthwise
   204.9
  sideways 242.8
Broadway 611.1
brochure 605.9
brogue 594.9
broil
 n. commotion 62.4
  cooking 330.1
  dish 308.7
  free-for-all 796.5
  quarrel 795.5
  violence 162.2
 v. be hot 328.22
  contend 796.14
  cook 330.4
  quarrel 795.11
broiler cooker 330.10
  food 308.22
  hot day 328.8
  poultry 414.34
broke insolvent 842.11
  poor 838.10
broken
  conquered 727.16
  damaged 692.29

disconnected 51.4
discont.nuous 72.4
domesticated 191.34
in disrepair 692.39
insolvent 842.11
irregular 138.3
rough 261.6
ruined 693.28
ruptured 49.24
subdued 764.15
weak 765.15
broken-down
  dilapidated 692.35
  heartbroken 872.29
broken heart
  despair 866.6
  heartache 872.9
broken-in 642.17
broken off 72.4
broker dealer 830.9
  intermediary 237.4
  middleman 781.4
  stockbroker 833.10
brokerage fee 846.7
  stockbrokerage 833.9
  stockbroking 833.18
  trade 827.2
brolly parachute 280.13
  umbrella 228.7
bromide cliché 79.8
  platitude 517.3
bronchial tube 396.16
bronchitis
  inflammation 686.9
  respiratory disease
   686.14
bronco 414.12
broncobuster
  animal handler 416.2
  rider 274.8
Bronx cheer 967.3
bronze
 n. sculpture 575.2
 v. brown 367.2
 adj. metal 383.17
  reddish-brown 367.4
brooch 901.6
brood
 n. animal young 171.2
  family 11.5
  posterity 171.1
  race 11.4
 v. be pregnant 169.12
  consider 478.12
brooder
  birthplace 153.8
  coop 191.22
  poultry 414.34
  sad person 872.13
brood mare
  female animal 421.9
  horse 414.10
brood over
  grieve 872.17
  harbor revenge 956.5
  remember 537.13
  think over 478.13
brook
 n. running water
   395.1
 v. be broad-minded
   526.7

be patient 861.5
permit 777.10
broom 681.32
broth 308.10
brothel
  disapproved place
   191.28
  house of prostitution
   989.9
  place of vice 981.7
brother associate 787.1
  friend 928.1
  layman 1039.2
  likeness 20.3
  member 788.11
  religious 1038.17
  sibling 11.3
brotherhood
  blood relationship
   11.1
  friendship 927.2
  guild 788.3
  kindness 938.1
brotherly
  friendly 927.14
  kind 938.13
brotherly love
  accord 794.1
  benevolence 938.4
  love 931.1
brought about 167.20
brouhaha
  agitation 324.1
  commotion 62.4
  excitement 857.3
  noise 453.3
  violence 162.2
brow border 235.4
  front 240.5
  hair 230.12
  head 211.6
  looks 446.4
  summit 211.2
browbeat
  domineer 741.16
  intimidate 891.28
browbeaten 764.16
brown
 n. brownness 367.1
  colors 367.6
 v. cook 330.4
  darken 337.9
  embrown 367.2
 adj. brownish 367.3
browned-off
  angry 952.26
  annoyed 866.21
brownie cookie 308.42
  dwarf 196.6
  fairy 1014.18
  sycophant 907.3
brown-nose 907.3
brownout 337.7
brown study
  abstractedness 532.2
  dream 535.9
  thoughtfulness 478.3
browse eat 307.26
  scan 564.13
  shop 828.8
bruise
 n. contusion 692.9

discoloration 679.2
 v. mistreat 667.5
  pain 866.17
  punish 1010.17
  wound 692.16
bruiser pugilist 800.2
  roughneck 943.4
bruit about 559.10
brumal cold 333.14
  winter 128.8
brunch 307.6
brunet
 n. hair color 362.9
 adj. black-haired
   365.13
  brown 367.3
  brown-haired 367.5
brunt 283.3
brush
 n. art equipment
   574.19
  brushwood 411.14
  contact 200.5
  fight 796.4
  firewood 331.3
  hinterland 182.2
  plant beard 230.9
  tail 241.6
  tap 283.6
  touch 425.1
  wilderness 166.2
 v. dry 393.6
  graze 200.10
  speed 269.8
  sweep 681.23
  tap 283.15
  tend animals 416.7
  touch lightly 425.7
brush aside
  disregard 531.4
  reject 638.2
brush off
  disregard 531.4
  send away 289.3
  sweep 681.23
brush-off 289.2
brush up
  furbish 691.11
  groom 681.20
  refresh the memory
   537.19
  study up 564.14
brusque candid 974.17
  concise 592.6
  gruff 937.7
  taciturn 613.9
brutal animal 414.43
  bad 675.9
  carnal 987.6
  cruel 939.24
  difficult 731.16
  fatal 409.23
  savage 162.20
  uncouth 898.12
brutality badness 675.2
  barbarity 939.12
  carnality 987.2
  cruelty 939.11
  uncouthness 898.3
  violence 162.1
brutalize
  make unfeeling 856.6

wreck 162.10
brute
  n. animal 414.2
  barbarian 898.7
  savage 943.5
  violent person 162.9
  adj. animal 414.43
  carnal 987.6
  cruel 939.24
brute force force 756.2
  power 157.1
BTU 328.19
bub boy 125.5
  brother 11.3
bubble
  n. air 405
  ball 255.2
  blister 256.3
  fragility 360.2
  hope 888.5
  illusion 519.1
  lightness 353.2
  spirit 4.3
  thing imagined 535.5
  transient 111.5
  v. be enthusiastic
    635.8
  bubble up 405.4
  make a liquid sound
    452.11
bubbly bubbling 405.6
  light 353.10
  lively 707.17
buccaneer pirate 825.7
  sailor 276.1
buck
  n. boy 125.5
  goat 414.8
  hoofed animal 414.5
  jump 319.1
  male animal 420.8
  rabbit 414.29
  trestle 216.16
  US money 835.2,7
  v. contend against
    790.4
  jump 319.5
  thrust 283.11
  unseat 185.6
buckaroo
  animal handler 416.2
  rider 274.8
bucket
  n. ship 277.1
  v. ladle 271.16
  speculate in stocks
    833.23
bucket shop
  fraud 618.9
  stockbrokerage 833.9
buck fever 859.1
buckle
  n. distortion 249.1
  v. distort 249.5
  fasten 47.8
buckle down
  be determined 624.8
  exert oneself 716.9
buck-passing 735.5
buckshot 801.13
buckskin hide 229.8
  horse 414.13

buck up cheer up 870.9
  encourage 893.16
  refresh 695.2
  take courage 893.14
bucolic
  n. poem 609.6
  rustic 919.9
  adj. natural 736.6
  poetic 609.17
  rustic 182.6
bud
  n. boy 125.5
  brother 11.3
  burgeon 411.21
  source 153.7
  v. graft 304.6
  sprout 411.31
Buddha God 1013.5
  religious founder
    1022.4
  Vishnu 1014.9
  wise man 468.2
budding
  beginning 68.15
  growing 197.12
  immature 124.10
buddy boy 125.5
  brother 11.3
  co-worker 787.5
  friend 928.3
  partner 787.2
buddy-buddy 927.19
budge 267.5
budget
  n. accounts 845.1
  accumulation 660.1
  amount 28.2
  bundle 74.8
  expenses 843.3
  funds 835.14
  portion 816.5
  schedule 641.2
  v. plan expenditures
    843.5
  ration 816.10
  schedule 641.4
  adj. cheap 849.7
buff
  n. attender 186.5
  commender 968.8
  devotee 635.6
  fanatic 473.17
  follower 293.2
  specialist 81.3
  supporter 787.9
  v. polish 260.7
  rub 350.8
  adj. leather 229.7
  yellow 370.4,7
buff, the nudity 232.3
  skin 229.1
buffalo
  n. cattle 414.6
  v. perplex 514.13
buffer
  n. barrier 730.5
  neutralizer 178.3
  partition 237.5
  safety equipment
    699.3
  smoother 260.13
  tool 348.12

  v. neutralize 178.7
buffer state
  country 181.1
  partition 237.5
buffet
  counter 216.15,29
  restaurant 307.15
buffet
  n. disappointment
    541.1
  lash 283.7
  punishment 1010.3
  v. bruise 692.16
  contend against
    790.4
  mistreat 667.5
  pound 283.14
  punish 1010.13
  slap 283.16
  struggle 716.11
  whip 1010.14
buffoon comic 612.10
  fool 471.1
  mischief-maker 738.3
buffoonery
  acting 611.9
  clownishness 881.5
  foolishness 470.1
bug
  n. beetle 414.36
  computer 349.19
  enthusiast 635.5
  evil spirit 1016.10
  fanatic 473.17
  fault 678.2
  germ 686.39
  mania 473.12
  microphone 450.9
  v. annoy 866.13
  bulge 256.10
  confuse 532.7
  discompose 63.4
  importune 774.12
  listen 448.11
  nag 969.16
  spy on 485.27
bugbear bane 676.1
  evil spirit 1016.10
  false alarm 704.2
  frightener 891.9
bug-eyed
  bulging 256.15
  defective eyes 440.12
bugger
  n. bad person 986.6
  evil spirit 1016.10
  man 420.5
  mischief-maker 738.3
  sex deviant 419.17
  v. anal sex 419.24
  bungle 734.12
  disable 158.9
  spoil 692.13
buggy
  n. automobile 272.9
  adj. insane 473.26
  insectile 414.55
bughouse 473.14
bugle
  n. brass wind 465.8
  nose 256.7
  v. blare 453.9

  play music 462.43
bugle call
  call to arms 797.12
  signal 568.16
bugs
  enthusiastic 635.12
  insane 473.26
build
  n. form 246.1
  physique 246.4
  structure 245.1
  v. compose 58.3
  create 167.10
  establish 184.15
  increase 38.4
  make larger 197.4
builder
  craftsman 718.8
  producer 167.8
building
  composition 58.1
  edifice 245.2
  house 191.6
  manufacture 167.3
  structure 245.1
building block
  content 194.5
  element 376.2
  substance 3.2
build on 212.6
buildup
  commendation 968.3
  composition 58.1
  increase 38.1
  promotion 559.5
build up
  aggravate 885.2
  compose 58.3
  exaggerate 617.3
  increase 38.4
  make larger 197.4
  publicize 559.15
built beautiful 900.17
  made 167.22
bulb ball 255.2
  knob 256.3
  plant root 411.20
bulbous bulging 256.14
  globular 255.9
  herbaceous 411.33
bulge
  n. advantage 36.2
  protuberance 256.3
  v. protrude 256.10
bulging full 56.11
  rotund 255.8
  swelling 256.14
bulk
  n. greatness 34.1
  lump 195.10
  majority 100.2
  major part 54.6
  quantity 28.1
  size 195.1
  thickness 204.2
  v. assemble 74.18
  become larger 197.5
  loom 34.5
  make larger 197.4
bulkhead barrier 730.5
  entrance 302.6
  harbor 700.6

burdensome
hampering 730.18
laborious 716.18
ponderous 352.17
troublesome 731.17
unpleasant 864.24
bureau 1000.4
bureaucracy
officialism 741.11
routine 642.6
the rulers 749.15
bureaucrat 749.16
bureaucratic
governing 741.19
governmental 741.17
burg 183.1
burgeon
n. branch 411.18
bud 411.21
v. grow 197.7
vegetate 411.31
burgher
conformist 82.2
good person 985.3
townsman 190.6
burghermaster 749.17
burglar 825.3
burglarize 824.15
burglary a theft 824.10
break-in 824.4
burial
concealment 615.1
funeral 410.5
interment 410.1
submergence 320.2
tomb 410.16
buried
concealed 615.11
underground 209.12
underwater 209.13
buried in 530.17
buried treasure 811.6
burl 256.3
burlesque
n. comedy 611.6
disparagement 971.5
exaggeration 617.1
humor 881.1
imitation 22.3
misrepresentation
573.2
ridicule 967.6
theater 611.1
v. exaggerate 617.3
lampoon 971.12
misrepresent 573.3
ridicule 967.11
adj. comic 880.5
satirical 967.14
burly corpulent 195.18
strong 159.14
burn
n. burning 329.6
impairment 692.8
pain 424.3
rocketry 281.9
running water 395.1
spacecraft 282.2
v. be angry 952.15
be hot 328.22
brown 367.2
cheat 618.17

cremate 410.20
detect 488.6
dry 393.6
electrocute 1010.19
execute 1010.19
flame 329.23
give light 335.23
hurt 424.7
ignite 329.22
injure 692.15
raze 693.19
scorch 329.24
wreck 162.10
burner
blowtorch 329.14
destroyer 693.8
heater 329.10
incinerator 329.13
types of 336.12
burning
n. capital punishment
1010.7
combustion 329.5
cremation 410.2
heat 328.1
pain 424.3
adj. angry 952.27
colorful 362.18
eloquent 600.13
excited 857.20
feverish 686.54
flashing 335.34
heating 329.26
hot 328.25
in heat 419.30
luminous 335.30
near 200.14
on fire 328.27
passionate 855.23
pungent 433.7
resentful 952.24
sore 424.11
zealous 635.10
burnish polish 260.7
rub 350.8
burn out
become exhausted
717.5
burn 332.8
fatigue 717.4
burn the candle at both
ends carouse 993.6
overdo 663.10
squander 854.3
burn the midnight oil
keep late hours 132.7
study 564.12
work hard 716.13
burn up anger 952.21
annoy 866.13
burn 329.25
consume 666.2
burp 310.26
burr adherent 50.4
engraving 578.2
harsh sound 458.3
regional accent 594.9
seed vessel 411.28
thorn 258.7
burro 414.20,58
burrow
n. lair 191.26

tunnel 257.5
v. excavate 257.15
hide oneself 615.8
search 485.30
settle 184.16
bursar
financial officer
836.11
payer 841.9
burst
n. anger 952.9
break 49.4
bustle 707.4
detonation 456.3
emotional outburst
857.8
eruption 162.6
explosion 162.7
explosive noise 456.1
flash 328.14
gunfire 798.10
speed 269.3
v. blast 456.8
break 49.12
disintegrate 692.26
explode 162.13
adj. broken 49.24
damaged 692.29
burst forth
appear 446.9
begin 68.13
emerge 303.12
erupt 162.12
grow 411.31
burst in enter 302.7
intrude 238.5
open 265.15
bursting
banging 456.11
excited 857.18
explosive 162.23
full 56.11
overfull 663.20
productive 165.9
teeming 101.9
burst out erupt 162.12
exclaim 459.7
laugh 876.8
bury inter 410.19
secrete 615.7
submerge 320.7
bury the hatchet
forget 947.5
make peace 804.9
bus
n. automobile 272.9
vehicle 272.12
v. transport 271.12
travel 273.32
busboy carrier 271.5
waiter 750.7
bush brushwood 411.14
hinterland 182.2
lining 194.3
shrubbery 411.9
wilderness 166.2
woodland 411.11
bushed 717.8
bushfighter 800.15
bushfighting 797.4
bushing bearing 322.7
lining 194.3

mounting 216.10
bushman
frontiersman 190.10
prehistoric man 123.7
bush telegraph 558.10
bushwa 547.3
bushwhack
attack 798.15
surprise 540.7
bushwhacker
guerrilla 800.15
precursor 66.1
bushy hairy 230.24
shrubby 411.36
wooded 411.37
business
n. acting 611.9
activity 707.1
affair 151.3
commerce 827.1
company 788.9
duty 962.1
occupation 656
undertaking 715.1
vocation 656.6
adj. commercial
827.21
business cycle 827.9
businesslike
orderly 59.6
working 656.15
businessman 830
buss 932.17
bust
n. arrest 761.6
breast 256.6
business cycle 827.9
demotion 783.1
explosive noise 456.1
failure 725.2
figure 572.4
hard times 729.6
insolvency 842.3
memorial 570.12
revel 878.6
spree 996.5
v. arrest 761.16
bankrupt 842.8
break 49.12
demote 783.3
depose 783.4
dismiss 310.19
domesticate 764.11
explode 162.13
fail someone 725.16
go bankrupt 842.7
busted insolvent 842.11
poor 838.10
shattered 692.29
bust in enter 302.7
open 265.15
bustle
n. activity 707.4
agitation 324.1
bluster 911.1
excitement 857.3
haste 709.1
v. be active 707.12
make haste 709.5
push 709.4
bustling active 707.20
eventful 151.10

busty 195.18

busy
v. occupy 656.10
task 716.16
adj. active 707.21
meddlesome 238.9
ornate 901.12

busybody
curious person 528.2
meddler 238.4
newsmonger 558.9

busywork 656.2

but
adv. notwithstanding
33.8
conj. unless 507.16

butch
n. homosexual 419.16
mannish female
420.9
adj. bisexual 419.32

butcher
n. killer 409.11
merchant 830.3
trainman 274.13
v. bungle 734.11
destroy 162.10
murder 409.17
sever 49.11

butchered
botched 734.21
mutilated 57.5

butler
majordomo 750.10
male servant 750.4
manager 748.4

butt
n. buttocks 241.4
cigarette 434.5
end 70.2
ham 308.16
joint 47.4
laughingstock 967.7
objective 653.2
piece 55.3
push 283.2
pushing 285.1
remainder 43.1
stub 434.5
v. adjoin 200.9
fasten 47.8
push 285.10
thrust 283.11

butte 207.5

butter
n. food 308.47
pulp 390.2
semiliquid 389.5
softness 357.4
suavity 936.5
v. coat 228.24
flatter 970.6

butterfingers 734.9

butterflies 859.2

butt in intrude 238.5
talk out of turn 130.5

buttinsky advisor 754.3
intruder 238.3

buttocks 241.4

button
n. chin 240.6
fastener 47.20

insignia 569.1
knob 256.3
little thing 196.4
metal casting 383.5
trifle 673.5
v. close 266.6
fasten 47.8

buttonhole
address 594.27
bore 884.6
importune 774.12

button up
be silent 451.6
close 266.6
complete 722.6

butt out
none of your business
238.10
not interfere 762.16

buttress
n. bulwark 216.4
supporter 216.2
v. aid 785.12
confirm 505.12
strengthen 159.11
support 216.21

buxom
beautiful 900.17
corpulent 195.18
merry 870.15

buy
n. bargain 849.3
purchase 828.1
v. assent 521.8
believe 501.10
bribe 651.3
purchase 828.7

buyer 828.5

buyers' market
commerce 827.1
low prices 849.2
sale 829.1

buy in buy 828.7
invest 836.16

buy off bribe 651.3
buy 828.7

buy up purchase 828.7
stock market 833.26

buzz
n. harsh sound 458.3
monotone 71.2
rumor 558.6
sensation 426.1
sibilation 457.1
telephone call 560.13
v. bustle 707.12
fly 278.51
hum 452.13
inform 557.11
publish 559.10
sibilate 457.2
sound harshly 458.9
telephone 560.18
utter 594.26

buzzer 704.1

buzzing
n. air maneuver
278.17
hum 452.7
adj. humming 452.20

buzz off depart 301.6
go away! 310.30

insignia ...

adv. in reserve 660.17
prep. at 184.26
beside 242.11
by means of 658.7
in conformity with
82.9
through 290.29

by all means
certainly 513.23
yes 521.18

by and by
in the future 121.9
soon 131.16

by and large
generally 79.17
on the whole 54.14

by chance
haphazardly 62.18
unpredictably 156.19

by choice
preferably 637.28
voluntarily 622.10

by degrees
gradually 29.6
piece by piece 55.9

by design 653.11

by ear 630.15

by far 34.17

bygone 119.7

by heart 537.28

bylaw 998.3

by-line
attribution 155.2
avocation 656.7

by means of
by the agency of
658.7
helped by 785.25

by no means
disapproval 969.28
negation 524.9
noway 35.11
refusal 776.7

by oneself
independently 762.32
singly 89.13
solitary 924.10

bypass
n. byway 657.5
detour 321.3
road 657.6
v. detour 321.6
pass 313.8

by-product
aftermath 67.3
outgrowth 168.3
result 154.1

byre 191.20

bystander
neighbor 200.6
spectator 442.1
witness 505.7

by the book
according to rule
82.8
exactly 516.21

by the way
discursive 593.13
incidentally 129.13
occasional 129.11

by virtue of
because of 155.9
by authority of
739.20
by dint of 157.18
by means of 658.7

byway bypath 657.5
digression 593.4
road 657.6

by way of
by means of 658.7
through 290.29

byword disgrace 915.5
laughingstock 967.7
maxim 517.1
name 583.3
phrase 582.9

Byzantine devious 46.4
scheming 654.14
shrewd 467.15

C

cab 272.12

cabal clique 788.6
combination 52.1
group 74.3
intrigue 654.6

cabala
occultism 1034.1
secrets 614.5

caballero beau 931.12
knight 918.5
rider 274.8

cabaña 191.9

cabaret
amusement 878.11
saloon 996.19
theater 611.18

cabbage food 308.35,50
money 835.2

cabdriver
coachman 274.9
driver 274.10

cabin cottage 191.9
ship room 192.9

cabin boy
attendant 750.5
sailor 276.6

cabin cruiser 277.4

cabinet council 755.1
cupboard 193.19
directorate 748.11
ministry 742.8
office 719.8
radio receiver 344.3
sanctum 192.8

cable
n. communications
560.17
cord 206.2,9
electric 342.39
telegram 560.14
v. communicate
560.19

caboose kitchen 330.3
railway car 272.14

cache
n. hiding place 615.4
reserve 660.3
v. secrete 615.7
store 660.10

conjure 1035.11
elicit 305.14
enlist 780.16
evoke 648.13
excite 857.11
remember 537.10
resemble 20.7
summon 752.12
telephone 560.18
visualize 535.15
call-up assembly 74.1
call to arms 797.12
enlistment 780.6
callus callousness 856.3
tumor 686.36
calm
n. lull 268.5
moderation 163.1
uniformity 17.1
v. compose 858.6
pacify 804.7
quiet 268.8
tranquilize 163.7
adj. composed 858.12
moderate 163.13
pacific 803.9
quiescent 268.12
thoughtfree 480.4
unastonished 921.3
unnervous 860.2
calmative
n. pacifier 163.3
sedative 687.12
adj. palliative 163.16
sedative 687.45
calming
n. moderation 163.2
pacification 804.1
adj. tranquilizing
163.15
calmness
composure 858.2
moderation 163.1
peace 803.2
quiescence 268.1
unastonishment
921.1
unnervousness 860.1
calorie
thermal unit 328.19
unit of energy 161.6
calorie counter 309.11
calorie-counting 205.9
calorific 329.26
calorimetry 328.21
calumny curse 972.2
slander 971.3
calx 329.16
calypso 462.13
camaraderie 922.2
camber arch 252.4
aviation 278.25
convexity 256.1
camel
beast of burden
271.6
hoofed animal 414.5
camelback 249.3
cameo
description 608.1
relief 575.3
camera lens 443.1

photography
577.11,20
cameraman
photographer 579.5
television technician
345.13
camera tube 345.19
camouflage
n. disguise 618.10
dissemblance 21.1
v. conceal 615.6
disguise 21.3
falsify 616.16
misrepresent 573.3
camouflaged
disguised 615.13
unseen 445.5
camp
n. camping 188.4
comedy 611.6
encampment 191.29
military camp 802.3
party 788.4
political party 744.24
vulgarity 898.1
v. encamp 188.11
settle 184.16
adj. theatrical 611.40
campaign
n. cause 153.10
journey 273.5
military campaign
797.7
political campaign
744.13
v. electioneer 744.40
make war 797.21
travel 273.20
campaigner
politician 746.10
soldier 800.18
campaign for 968.13
campanile 207.11
camper
mobile home 191.18
trailer 272.18
traveler 274.1
camping 188.4
campo
city district 183.8
grassland 411.8
plain 387.1
campus arena 802.1
school 567.15
can
n. buttocks 241.5
destroyer 277.7
prison 761.9
rest room 311.10
toilet 311.11
v. be able 157.11
be allowed 777.13
dismiss 310.19
package 236.9
preserve 701.9
stow 184.14
canal
n. duct 396.13
narrow place 205.3
trench 263.2
watercourse 396.2
v. groove 263.3

canapé appetizer 308.9
sandwich 308.32
canard
fabrication 616.10
food 308.22
report 558.6
canary
n. songbird 464.23
vocalist 464.13
adj. yellow 370.4,7
cancel
n. harmonics 463.12
obliteration 693.7
repeal 779.1
v. abolish 693.13
debts 842.9
delete 42.12
end 70.7
equalize 30.6
neutralize 178.7
obliterate 693.16
repeal 779.2
stop 144.6
cancellate 221.11
cancellation
debts 842.2
deletion 42.5
network 221.3
neutralization 178.2
obliteration 693.7
postage 604.6
repeal 779.1
cancer blight 676.2
tumor 686.36
candescent
burning 328.27
luminous 335.30
candid artless 736.5
frank 974.17
free-spoken 762.22
genuine 516.14
impartial 976.10
plain-speaking 591.3
talkative 596.9
unaffected 902.7
unreserved 554.10
candidacy 744.10
candidate
aspirant 774.7
assignee 780.8
desirer 634.12
political candidate
746.9
candle
light source 336.1,8
light unit 335.21
sacred article 1040.11
taper 336.2
candlelight 134.3
candor
artlessness 736.1
fairness 976.3
frankness 554.3
honesty 974.4
plain speech 591.1
talkativeness 596.1
candy
n. drugs 687.5
sweets 308.39,54
v. solidify 356.8
sweeten 431.3

cane
n. aid for the blind
441.6
grass 411.5,46
instrument of punish-
ment 1011.2
material 378.4
plant stem 411.19
staff 217.2
supporter 216.2
v. punish 1010.14
canicular hot 328.25
summer 128.8
canine
n. animal 414.3
dog 414.22
tooth 258.5
adj. doggish 414.45
canker
n. blight 676.2
sore 686.35
v. corrupt 692.14
decay 692.25
eat away 692.24
cannibal
n. animal 414.3
killer 409.11
man-eater 307.14
savage 943.5
adj. man-eating
307.29
canniness
caution 895.1
cunning 735.1
economy 851.1
shrewdness 467.3
canning
packaging 236.2
preserving 701.2
cannon
n. artillery 801.6
impact 283.3
shot 285.5
v. backfire 284.6
collide 283.12
fire upon 798.22
cannonade
n. bombardment
798.7
boom 456.4
gunfire 798.10
v. fire upon 798.22
cannonball dive 320.1
shot 801.13
speed 269.6
cannot 158.8
canny cautious 895.8
cunning 735.12
economical 851.6
shrewd 467.15
canoe
n. boat 277.21
v. sail 275.13
canoeing 275.1
canon a belief 501.2
Bible 1021.2
clergyman 1038.9
compilation 605.4
law 998.3
measure 490.2
music 462.19
precept 751.2

ritualistic manual
1040.12
round 253.9
rule 84.4
Canon 1040.10
canoness 1038.19
canonical
doctrinal 501.27
ministerial 1037.13
orthodox 1024.7
prescriptive 751.4
scriptural 1021.10
theological 1023.4
canonicals 1041
canonicate 1037.5
canonize exalt 317.6
glorify 914.13
ordain 1037.12
sanctify 1026.5
canopy
n. cover 228.38
heavens 375.2
shade 338.8
v. cover 228.19
cant
n. angle 251.2
hypocrisy 616.6
inclination 219.2
jargon 580.9
sanctimony 1029.1
unintelligibility 549.7
v. be hypocritical
616.23
be sanctimonious
1029.4
change course 275.30
incline 219.10
sail 275.43
speak 580.16
cantabile
n. aria 462.14
adj. melodious 462.49
cantankerous
irascible 951.19
perverse 626.11
cantata
choral music 462.18
sacred music 462.16
canteen bottle 193.12
restaurant 307.15
store 832.6
canter
n. hypocrite 619.8
pietist 1029.3
speed 269.3
v. ride 273.33
run 269.10
canticle hymn 1032.3
sacred music 462.16
song 462.13
cantina 307.15
canting
hypocritic(al) 616.33
inclining 219.15
sanctimonious 1029.5
canto melody 462.4
music 462.22
poetic division
609.11
canton district 180.5
heraldic insignia
569.2

cantor
choirmaster 464.18
clergyman 1038.12
vocalist 464.13
canvas arena 802.1
art equipment 574.19
picture 574.15
sail 277.14
tent 228.8
canvass
n. assembly 74.1
political campaign
744.13
solicitation 774.5
survey 485.13
vote 637.6
v. count votes 637.18
discuss 597.12
electioneer 744.40
examine 485.23
solicit 774.14
survey 485.28
canyon 201.2
cap
n. capital 211.5
clothing 231.25,59
cover 228.5
detonator 331.7
printing 603.6
summit 211.2
top part 211.4
v. clothe 231.39
complete 722.6
cover 228.21
excel 36.6
give in kind 955.6
top 211.9
capability ability 157.2
preparedness 720.4
skill 733.1
talent 733.4
capable able 157.14
competent 733.22
fitted 720.17
capable of 175.5
capacious
spacious 179.9
voluminous 195.17
capacitance 342.15
capacitate 720.8
capacity
n. ability 157.2
electric capacitance
342.15
full measure 56.3
function 656.3
intelligence 467.1
means 658.1
role 7.5
skill 733.1
spaciousness 179.5
talent 733.4
volume 195.2
wits 466.2
adj. full 56.11
caparison harness 659.5
horsecloth 228.11
wardrobe 231.2
cape cloak 231.50
point of land 256.8
caper
n. a theft 824.10

frolic 878.5
jump 319.2
prank 881.10
v. be cheerful 870.6
jump 319.6
play 878.25
rejoice 876.5
capillary
n. blood vessel 396.14
adj. hairlike 230.23
threadlike 206.7
vascular 396.21
capital
n. center 226.7
city 183.4
funds 835.15
head 211.5,18
means 658.1
printing 603.6
resources 660.2
adj. chief 36.14
excellent 674.12
letter 581.8
monetary 835.30
most important
672.23
top 211.10
capitalism
free enterprise 745.8
noninterference
762.9
capitalist
n. financier 836.8
individualist 745.15
rich man 837.6
adj. capitalistic 745.23
capitalization
capital 835.15
financing 836.2
resources 660.2
capitalize
finance 836.15
keep accounts 845.8
letter 581.6
capitalize on
improve the occasion
129.8
profit by 811.11
take advantage of
665.15
capital punishment
1010.7
capitol 742.12
capitulate 765.8
capitulation
numeration 87.5
surrender 765.2
treaty 771.2
capping ending 70.9
superior 36.12
topping 211.11
caprice
impulsiveness 630.3
moodiness 629.2
music 462.6
whim 629
capricious erratic 138.3
impulsive 630.10
inconstant 141.7
irresolute 627.9
transient 111.7
unordered 62.12

unpredictable 514.15
unstable 18.3
whimsical 629.5
capriole
n. caper 319.2
jump 319.1
v. caper 319.6
jump 319.5
capsize overturn 220.6
tumble 316.8
upset 275.44
capstan 287.7
capstone 722.3
capsule
n. abridgment 607.1
container 193.18
hull 228.16
pill 687.7
seed vessel 411.28
spacecraft 282.2
v. abridge 607.5
package 236.9
adj. shortened 203.9
captain
n. commissioned offi-
cer 749.18
governor 749.5
naval officer 749.20
peace officer 699.15
pilot 279.1
ship's officer 276.7
v. direct 747.8
govern 741.12
Captain Kidd 825.7
captain's walk 228.6
caption
n. title 484.2
v. title 484.3
captious critical 969.24
quibbling 483.14
captivate charm 1036.8
delight 865.8
enamor 931.21
fascinate 650.6
persuade 648.23
captivated
astonished 920.9
enamored 931.26
enchanted 1036.12
captivating
alluring 650.7
pleasant 863.7
captive
n. prisoner 761.11
subject 764.7
sweetheart 931.10
adj. subjugated
764.14
captivity
imprisonment 761.3
subjection 764.1
capture
n. arrest 761.6
seizure 822.2
take 822.10
v. acquire 811.8
arrest 761.15
catch 822.18
win 726.4
car automobile 272.9
railway car 272.14

carabineer
  infantryman 800.9
  shooter 285.9
caracole
  n. jump 319.2
  v. be cheerful 870.6
  jump 319.6
  play 878.25
  rejoice 876.5
  ride 273.33
carapace 228.15
caravan
  mobile home 191.18
  procession 71.3
  trailer 272.18
  wagon 272.2
carbohydrate 309.5,22
carbon ashes 329.16
  copy 24.4
  fuel 331.1
carbonate
  add gas 401.8
  react chemically
    379.6
carbonation
  bubbling 405.3
  reaction 379.5
carbon copy copy 24.4
  the same 14.3
carbon dioxide
  coolant 334.7
  gas 401.11
carbon 14
  radioisotope 326.5
  radiotherapeutic sub-
    stance 689.9
carbon-14 dating 114.1
carbonize 329.24
carbonous 383.15
carbon tetrachloride
  332.3
carbuncle sore 686.35
  swelling 256.4
carcass body 376.3
  bomb 801.14
  corpse 408.16
  skeleton 245.5
  wreck 692.10
carcinogenic 686.57
carcinoma 686.36
card
  n. identification
    568.11
  letter 604.4
  plaything 878.17
  record 570.10
  schedule 641.2
  v. comb 681.21
cardboard 378.6,13
card-carrier 788.11
card-carrying 516.14
card game
  game of chance 515.8
  word list 878.35
cardholder
  labor unionist 789.3
  member 788.11
cardiac 225.10
cardiac arrest 686.17
cardinal
  n. clergyman 1038.9
  number 86.3

adj. chief 36.14
  most important
    672.23
  numerical 86.8
  red 368.6,12
cardiovascular disease
  686.1,17
cardsharp
  gambler 515.17
  sharper 619.4
care
  n. adversity 729.1
  affliction 866.8
  anxiety 890.1
  attention 530.1
  caution 895.1
  concern 533.1
  custody 761.5
  economy 851.1
  observance 768.1
  patronage 785.4
  protectorship 699.2
  responsibility 780.1
  sorrow 872.10
  supervision 747.2
  support 785.3
  treatment 665.2
  v. emotionally re-
    spond 855.12
  mind 533.6
careen
  n. flounder 324.8
  swing 323.6
  v. flounder 324.15
  incline 219.10
  oscillate 323.10
  overturn 220.6
  sail 275.43
  tumble 316.8
career
  n. advance 267.4
  course 267.2
  progression 294.1
  vocation 656.6
  v. flounder 324.15
  rush 269.9
  adj. accomplished
    733.24
care for doctor 689.30
  foster 785.16
  look after 699.19
  love 931.18
  serve 750.13
  treat 665.12
carefree 870.12
careful
  adj. attentive 530.15
  cautious 895.8
  conscientious 974.15
  economical 851.6
  heedful 533.10
  judicious 467.19
  interj. caution 895.14
carefully
  cautiously 895.12
  economically 851.7
  heedfully 533.15
carefulness
  caution 895.1
  economy 851.1
  heed 533
careless clumsy 734.20

inattentive 531.6
  incurious 529.3
  negligent 534.11
  reckless 894.8
  slovenly 62.15
  thoughtless 630.10
  unconcerned 636.7
  ungrammatical 587.4
  unstrict 758.4
carelessly
  haphazardly 62.18
  negligently 534.18
  on impulse 630.14
  recklessly 894.11
  unconcernedly
    636.10
carelessness
  bungling 734.4
  inattention 531.1
  incurious 529.1
  negligence 534.2
  recklessness 894.2
  slovenliness 62.6
  thoughtlessness 630.3
  unconcern 636.2
  unstrictness 758.1
care of souls
  benefice 1037.9
  the ministry 1037.1
caress
  n. contact 200.5
  endearment 932.4
  touch 425.1
  v. graze 200.10
  make love 932.14
  rub 350.6
  touch 425.8
caressing
  lovemaking 932.1
  touching 425.2
caretaker 699.6
careworn
  sorrowful 872.26
  worried 890.8
carfare 846.7
cargo burden 352.7
  charge 963.3
  freight 271.7
  impediment 730.6
  load 194.2
carhop 750.7
caricature
  n. cartoon 574.17
  exaggeration 617.1
  humor 881.1
  misrepresentation
    573.2
  ridicule 967.6
  v. exaggerate 617.3
  misrepresent 573.3
  ridicule 967.11
caricaturist
  drawer 579.3
  humorist 881.12
caries gangrene 686.37
  rotting 692.7
carillon 465.21
carmine 368.6,12
carnage
  destruction 693.1
  massacre 409.5
carnal lascivious 989.29

sensual 987.6
  sexual 419.26
  unrighteous 981.12
  worldly 1031.16
carnality
  immorality 981.1
  lasciviousness 989.5
  nonreligiousness
    1031.2
  sensuality 987.2
  sexuality 419.2
carnal knowledge 419.8
carnival festival 878.4
  show 611.15
  theater 611.1
Carnival 1040.15
carnivore animal 414.3
  flesh-eater 307.14
  mammal 415.8
carnivorous 307.29
carol
  n. Christmas song
    462.13
  song 462.13
  v. bird sound 460.5
  rejoice 876.5
  sing 462.39
carom
  n. impact 283.3
  recoil 284.2
  v. collide 283.12
  recoil 284.6
carousal
  debauchery 993.2
  revel 878.6
  spree 996.5
carouse
  n. debauchery 993.2
  revel 878.6
  spree 996.5
  v. be disorderly 62.10
  be intemperate 993.6
  go on a spree 996.27
  make merry 878.26
carousel
  amusement device
    878.15
  rotator 322.4
  tournament 878.10
carp find fault 969.15
  nag 969.16
carpe diem
  n. prodigality 854.1
  v. improve the occa-
    sion 129.8
  make no provision
    721.7
carpet
  n. floor 212.3
  floor covering
    228.9,41
  v. cover 228.22
carpetbagger 619.4
carping
  n. disapproval 969.4
  adj. critical 969.24
carriage behavior 737.1
  charge 846.8
  four-wheeler 272.4,23
  gesture 568.14
  looks 446.4
  railway car 272.14

support 216.1
transportation 271.3
vehicle 272.1
carriage trade
clientele 828.3
society 644.6
carried away
excited 857.18
frenzied 857.23
overjoyed 865.14
carrier carter 271.5
infection 686.3
mail carrier 561.6
messenger 561.1
radio wave 344.11
supporter 216.2
vector 686.41
vehicle 272.1
warship 277.8,24
carrier pigeon
carrier 271.5
message carrier 561.6
carrion corpse 408.16
filth 682.7
offal 682.9
rotting 692.7
carrottop 362.9
carry
n. range 179.2
transportation 271.3
v. adopt 637.15
be pregnant 169.12
deal in 827.15
extend 179.7
give credit 839.6
induce 648.22
keep accounts 845.8
support 216.21
transport 271.11
win 726.4
carry away
abduct 824.19
come apart 49.8
delight 865.8
enamor 931.21
fascinate 650.6
kill 409.13
remove 271.10
win 726.4
carrying
n. support 216.1
transportation 271.3
adj. armed 799.14
pregnant 169.18
supporting 216.23
carry off abduct 824.19
bring about 722.5
carry out 705.9
kill 409.13
remove 271.10
seize 822.14
succeed with 724.10
win 726.4
carry on
be angry 952.15
be disorderly 62.11
be enthusiastic 635.8
be industrious 707.15
be patient 861.4
continue 143.3
direct 747.8
endure 110.6

misbehave 738.4
operate 164.5
persevere 625.2
play 878.25
practice 705.7
rage 162.10
carry out apply 665.11
be distant 199.5
bring about 722.5
do 705.9
execute 771.10
observe 768.3
operate 164.5
carry over
keep accounts 845.8
transfer 271.9
carry through
be patient 861.4
bring about 722.5
carry out 705.9
execute 771.10
not hesitate 624.10
observe 768.3
operate 164.5
persevere 625.5
carry weight
be important 672.11
have influence 172.10
weigh 352.10
carsick 686.53
cart
n. vehicle 272.3,28
v. haul 271.12
cart away 271.10
carte blanche
full permission 777.4
latitude 762.4
right 958.4
cartel association 788.9
combination 52.1
compact 771.1
treaty 771.2
carter carrier 271.5
coachman 274.9
cartilage
structure 245.6
toughness 359.2
cartography
location 184.7
map 654.4
mensuration 490.9
carton
n. container 193.14
v. package 236.9
cartoon
caricature 574.17
diagram 654.3
motion picture
611.16
picture 574.14
cartoonist 579.3
cartridge film 577.10
shell 801.11
sound recording
450.12
sound reproduction
system 450.11
carve apportion 816.6
engrave 578.10
form 246.7
groove 263.3
produce 167.11

record 570.16
sculpture 575.5
slice 49.11
carver
printmaker 579.8
sculptor 579.6
carving 572.4
Casanova beau 931.12
deceiver 619.1
unchaste person
989.10
cascade
n. descent 316.1
eruption 162.6
waterfall 395.11
v. descend 316.5
hang 215.6
overflow 395.17
case
n. argument 482.5
bookbinding 605.15
citation 505.6
example 25.2
frame 245.4
grammatical form
586.9
hull 228.16
lawsuit 1004.1
love 931.4
odd person 85.4
particular 8.3
pillowcase 228.10
printing 603.6
sheath 228.17
sick person 686.40
state 7.1
topic 484.1
types of 193.14
v. package 236.9
reconnoiter 485.27
wrap 228.20
case, the fact 1.3
the truth 516.2
casebook
reference book 605.6
textbook 605.8
case-hardened
accustomed 642.17
callous 856.12
hardened 356.13
obstinate 626.8
wicked 981.17
case history
biography 608.4
medical history
689.11
casein 354.7
case in point
citation 505.6
example 25.2
casement frame 245.4
window 265.8
Casey Jones 274.12
cash
n. money 835.1
payment 841.1
ready money 835.18
v. cash in 835.29
pay 841.17
adv. in cash 841.25
cashbook
account book 845.4

record book 570.11
cashbox 836.12
cashier
n. banker 836.10
financial officer
836.11
payer 841.9
v. depose 783.4
dismiss 310.19
cash in on
improve the occasion
129.8
profit by 811.11
take advantage of
665.15
casino
amusement 878.11
ballroom 879.4
gambling house
515.15
resort 191.27
cask
n. cylinder 255.4
types of 193.13
v. package 236.9
casket
n. coffin 410.11
v. enclose 236.6
Cassandra
pessimist 889.7
predictor 543.4
warner 703.4
casserole 308.7
cassette 450.12
cassock 1038.5
cast
n. actors 612.11
castoff skin 229.5
characteristic 80.4
color 362.1
copy 24.6
defective vision 440.5
disposition 525.3
form 246.1
glance 439.4
group 74.3
kind 61.3
looks 446.4
medical dressing
687.33
metal casting 383.5
model 25.6
nature 5.3
role 611.11
sculpture 575.2
small amount 35.4
sum 86.5
team 788.7
tendency 174.1
throw 285.4
throw of dice 515.10
v. attack 798.28
calculate 87.11
change course 275.30
create 167.10
discard 668.7
eject 310.13
form 246.7
give birth 167.15
heat 329.24
hurl 184.12
plan 654.9

categorical
  classificational 61.7
  dialectic(al) 482.22
  unqualified 508.2
categorize analyze 48.8
  arrange 60.11
  classify 61.6
category 61.2
catenary curve 252.2
  fall 316.2
cater 659.9
catercorner
  adj. diagonal 219.19
  adv. diagonally 219.25
caterer 659.6
catering cooking 330.1
  provision 659.1
caterpillar bug 414.36
  young insect 125.10
cater to
  be servile 907.7
  help 785.18
  indulge 759.6
caterwaul
  n. cry 459.1
  shrill sound 458.4
  v. animal sound 460.2
  cry 459.6
  sound shrill 458.8
catharsis
  cleansing 681.2
  defecation 311.2
  psychocatharsis
    690.32
  release 886.2
cathartic
  n. cleaning agent
    681.17
  laxative 687.17
  adj. cleansing 681.28
  laxative 687.48
  relieving 886.9
cathedral
  n. church 1042.1
  adj. authoritative
    513.18
catheter 396.6
cathexis
  desire concentration
    690.41
  interest 530.2
cathode ray
  electronic emission
    343.5
  radiation 327.3
catholic
  broad-minded 526.8
  universal 79.14
Catholic
  n. religionist
    1020.18,35
  adj. religious 1020.28
Catholicism 1020.7,33
cathouse brothel 989.9
  disapproved place
    191.28
cation chemical 379.1
  electrolysis 342.22
catkin 411.25
cat man 825.3
cat-o'-nine-tails 1011.1
cat's-paw agent 781.3

breeze 403.5
dupe 620.1
instrument 658.3
man 787.8
sycophant 907.3
cattle animal life 414.1
  kine 414.6,69
  mammals 415.8
  rabble 919.5
cattleman
  animal raiser 416.2
  herder 416.3
cattle rustler 825.8
cattle rustling 824.3
catty
  disparaging 971.13
  feline 414.46
  ill-humored 951.21
  spiteful 939.19
cattycorner see
  catercorner
catwalk bridge 657.10
  path 657.3
Caucasian 418.3
caucus
  n. election 744.15
  meeting 74.2
  party 788.4
  political caucus 744.9
  v. politick 744.38
caudal final 70.10
  tail 241.11
caught
  engrossed 530.18
  fixed 142.16
caught short
  surprised 540.12
  unprepared 721.8
caught up in
  engrossed 530.17
  involved in 176.4
caulk 266.7
cause
  n. basis 153
  interest 153.10
  justification 1006.6
  lawsuit 1004.1
  motive 648.1
  v. compel 756.4
  effect 153.11
  produce 167.9
  prompt 648.13
caused by 154.8
causeless chance 156.15
  purposeless 156.16
causerie chat 597.4
  treatise 606.1
causeway 657.6
caustic
  n. burner 329.15
  curve 252.2
  adj. acrimonious
    939.21
  bitter 429.6
  exciting 857.29
  hostile 929.10
  ill-humored 951.17
  pungent 433.6
  resentful 952.24
  sarcastic 967.13
  sharp 161.13

cauterant
  n. burner 329.15
  adj. heating 329.26
cauterize 329.24
caution
  n. advice 754.1
  cautiousness 895
  dissuasion 652.1
  forethought 542.2
  heed 533.1
  irresolution 627.3
  pledge 772.3
  suspicion 504.1
  tip 557.3
  warning 703.1
  v. advise 754.6
  dissuade 652.3
  warn 703.5
cautious careful 533.10
  irresolute 627.11
  prudent 895.8
  slow 270.10
  suspicious 504.4
cavalcade 71.3
cavalier
  n. beau 931.12
  escort 73.5
  gallant 936.9
  knight 918.5
  rider 274.8
  adj. disdainful 912.13
  gruff 937.7
cave
  n. cavern 257.5
  destruction 693.4
  lair 191.26
  shelter 700.3
  v. collapse 198.10
  make concave 257.13
  sink 316.6
caveat advice 754.1
  dissuasion 652.1
  legal order 752.6
  warning 703.1
cave in collapse 692.27
  deflate 198.10
  make concave 257.13
  open 265.15
  sink 316.6
  weaken 160.9
  yield 765.7
cave-in
  contraction 198.4
  destruction 693.4
caveman he-man 420.6
  prehistoric man 123.7
cavern 257.5
cavernous
  abysmal 209.11
  hollow 257.16
caviar egg 406.15
  food 308.24
cavil
  n. disapproval 969.4
  quibble 483.4
  v. argue 482.16
  find fault 969.15
  quibble 483.9
cavity
  compartment 192.2
  crack 201.2
  hollow 257.2

opening 265.1
pit 209.2
cavort
  n. jump 319.2
  v. jump 319.6
  play 878.25
caw
  n. harsh sound 458.3
  v. bird sound 460.5
  sound harshly 458.9
cay 386.2
cease
  v. be destroyed 693.23
  disappear 447.2
  discontinue 144.6
  end 70.5
  give up 633.7
  quiet 268.8
  interj. stop! 144.14
cease-fire pause 144.3
  truce 804.5
ceaseless
  constant 135.5
  continuous 71.8
  perpetual 112.7
cecal closed 266.9
  intestinal 225.10
cede give up 633.7
  relinquish 814.3
  surrender 765.8
  transfer property
    817.3
ceil cover 228.21
  line 194.7
ceiling aviation 278.41
  boundary 235.3
  completion 56.5
  height 207.1
  price index 846.5
  rocketry 281.9
  roof 228.6
  visibility 444.2
celebrate
  administer rites
    1040.18
  formalize 646.5
  make merry 878.26
  observe 877.2
  praise 968.12
  proclaim 559.13
  worship 1032.11
celebrated
  famous 914.16
  notable 672.18
celebration
  ceremony 646.4
  festivity 865.3
  observance 877
  rejoicing 876.1
  revel 878.6
  rite 1040.4
  ritualism 1040.1
  spree 996.5
celebrity
  famous person 914.9
  personage 672.8
  publicity 559.4
  repute 914.1
celerity 269.1
celesta 465.18
celestial
  n. angel 1015.1

adj. angelic 1015.6
  astral 375.25
  divine 1013.19
  heavenly 1018.13
  idealized 535.23
celestial navigation
  aviation 278.6
  navigation 275.2
  position 184.3
celibacy
  abstinence 992.2
  aloneness 89.2
  chastity 988.3
  monasticism 1037.4
  singleness 934
celibate
  n. religious 1038.17
  single person 934.2
  adj. abstinent 992.10
  chaste 988.6
  childless 166.4
  sole 89.9
  unmarried 934.6
cell bioplast 406.4
  clique 788.6
  compartment 192.2
  photoelectric 343.17
  prison 761.8
  retreat 700.5
cellar basement 192.17
  storage place 660.6
cell division 406.16
cellist 464.5
cello organ stop 465.22
  viol 465.6
cellular
  cellulous 406.21
  vascular 193.4
Celsius scale 328.19
Celtic deities 1014.7
cement
  n. adhesive 50.4,13
  building material
    378.2
  ceramic ware 576.2
  hardness 356.6
  pavement 657.7
  v. cover 228.22
  fasten 47.7
  join 47.5
  plaster 228.25
  stick together 50.9
  adj. hard 356.10
cemetery 410.15
cenotaph
  memorial 570.12
  tomb 410.16
censer
  sacred article 1040.11
  scent article 436.6
censor
  n. conscience 957.5
  critic 494.7
  faultfinder 969.9
  restrictionist 760.6
  v. delete 42.12
  hush up 614.8
  suppress 760.8
censored 614.11
censorious
  blameful 969.23
  condemnatory 1008.5

disparaging 971.13
  fastidious 896.9
  prudish 903.19
censorship
  defense mechanism
    690.31
  deletion 42.5
  keeping secret 614.3
  suppression 760.2
censure
  n. accusation 1005.2
  condemnation 1008.1
  criticism 494.2
  disapproval 969.3
  stigma 915.6
  v. condemn 1008.3
  denounce 969.13
  incriminate 1005.10
  judge 494.14
  stigmatize 915.9
census
  arrangement 60.4
  assembly 74.1
  inventory 194.1
  list 88.6
  numeration 87.1
  summary 87.5
cent
  foreign money 835.9
  trifle 673.5
  US money 835.7
centenarian
  hundred 99.8
  old man 127.2
centennial
  n. anniversary 137.4
  hundred 99.8
  adj. hundred 99.29
  periodic 137.8
center
  n. athlete 878.20
  attractor 288.2
  aviation 278.27
  centrality 226.2
  essence 5.2
  interior 225.2
  mean 32.1
  middle 69.1
  middle course 806.3
  moderates 745.10
  moderatism 745.2
  v. centralize 226.9
  converge 298.2
centi– 99.29
centigrade 328.30
centigrade scale 328.19
centipede bug 414.36
  hundred 99.8
  invertebrate 415.5
central
  n. telephone 560.7
  telephone operator
    560.9
  adj. causal 153.15
  chief 36.14
  interior 225.7
  medium 32.3
  middle 69.4
  midmost 226.11
  phonetic 594.31
  vital 672.22
centrality 226

centralize center 226.9
  converge 298.2
  join 52.4
centrally
  internally 225.11
  in the center of
    226.15
  mediumly 32.4
centrifugal 299.8
centrifugal force
  force 157.6
  repulsion 289.1
centrifuge
  n. separator 49.7
  v. whirl 322.11
centripetal
  converging 298.3
  focal 226.13
centripetal force
  attraction 288.1
  force 157.6
centrist
  n. moderate 163.4
  politics 745.10
  adj. moderate 745.18
  neutral 806.7
centurion
  hundred 99.8
  noncommissioned of-
    ficer 749.19
century hundred 99.8
  long time 110.4
  period 107.2
  US money 835.7
cephalic 211.14
ceramic 576.7
ceramics arts 574.1
  ceramic ware 576.2
  pottery 576.1,8
ceramist 579.7
Cerberus
  nether world
    deity 1019.5
  watchdog 699.11
cereal
  n. food 308.34
  grass 411.5
  adj. herbaceous
    411.33
cerebellum 466.7
cerebral mental 466.8
  phonetic 594.31
cerebral cortex
  brain 466.7
  sensory area 422.6
cerebral palsy 686.23
cerebrate 478.8
cerebrum 466.7
ceremonial
  n. ceremony 646.4
  formality 646.1
  rite 1040.3
  adj. ceremonious
    646.8
  ritualistic 1040.22
ceremonious
  ceremonial 646.8
  gallant 936.15
  respectful 964.8
  ritualistic 1040.22
ceremony
  amenities 936.7

celebration 877.1
  formality 646.1
  rite 1040.3
  ritual 646.4
Ceres
  agriculture divinity
    413.4
  fertility goddess
    165.5
  goddess 1014.5
cerise 368.6
certain
  believing 501.21
  evidential 505.17
  expectant 539.11
  guaranteed 772.11
  inevitable 639.15
  particular 80.12
  plural 100.7
  quantifier 28.5
  sure 513.13
  true 516.12
  unique 89.7
certainly
  adv. inevitably 639.19
  positively 34.19
  surely 513.23
  truly 516.17
  interj. yes 521.18
certainty belief 501.1
  expectation 539.1
  inevitability 639.7
  sureness 513
certifiable 473.27
certificate
  negotiable instru-
    ment 835.11
  record 570.6
certificate of deposit
  credit instrument
    839.3
  negotiable instru-
    ment 835.11
  securities 834.1
certification
  authorization 777.3
  confirmation 505.5
  deposition 523.2
  making certain 513.8
  ratification 521.4
  record 570.6
certified
  affirmed 523.8
  guaranteed 772.11
  made sure 513.20
  proved 505.21
  ratified 521.14
  true 516.12
certify affirm 523.5
  authorize 777.11
  confirm 505.12
  make sure 513.11
  ratify 521.12
  secure 772.9
  testify 505.10
certiorari
  appeal 1004.10
  writ 752.7
cerulean
  n. heavens 375.2
  adj. blue 372.3,4

cervix
  constriction 198.1
  joint 47.4
  sex organ 419.10
  supporter 216.2
cesarean 689.24
cessation
  abandonment 633.1
  closing 70.3
  discontinuance 668.2
  discontinuity 72.2
  end 70.1
  standstill 268.3
  stopping 144
cession
  abandonment 633.3
  property transfer
    817.1
  qualification 507.1
  relinquishment 814.1
  surrender 765.2
cesspool 682.12
cetacean 414.35,64
chafe
  n. abrasion 350.2
  impairment 692.8
  irritation 866.3
  v. abrade 350.7
  be angry 952.15
  be impatient 862.4
  feel anxious 890.5
  heat 329.17
  hurt 424.7
  injure 692.15
  irritate 866.14
  provoke 952.22
chaff
  n. banter 882.1
  hull 228.16
  lightness 353.2
  rabble 919.5
  radar countermeasure
    346.13
  refuse 669.4
  residue 43.1
  trifles 673.4
  v. banter 882.4
  ridicule 967.9
chagrin
  n. mortification 866.4
  v. embarrass 866.15
chagrined
  distressed 866.22
  humiliated 906.13
chain
  n. atomics 326.7
  continuity 71.2
  curb 730.7
  fireplace 329.12
  insignia 569.1
  jewel 901.6
  mountains 207.9
  restraint 760.4
  v. bind 47.9
  connect 71.4
  join 47.5
  restrain 760.10
  stabilize 142.8
chain gang 761.11
chain of circumstances
  156.5

chain reaction
  continuity 71.2
  fission 326.8
  vicissitudes 156.5
chair
  n. instructorship
    565.11
  manager 748.5
  seat 216.17,30
  seat of authority
    739.10
  v. administer 747.11
  govern 741.12
  install 780.11
chair, the
  capital punishment
    1010.7
  electric chair 1011.5
chairman 748.5
chaise 272.4
chalet 191.9
chalice 1042.11
chalk
  n. art equipment
    574.19
  white 364.2
  writing material
    602.30
  v. mark 568.19
  picture 574.20
  record 570.16
  whiten 364.5
  whitewash 364.6
chalk talk lesson 562.7
  speech 599.2
chalk up mark 568.19
  record 570.16
chalky powdery 361.11
  white 364.7
challenge
  n. dare 793.2
  declaration of war
    797.11
  objection 522.2
  opposition 790.1
  questioning 485.11
  resistance 792.1
  v. be doubtful 503.6
  claim 753.5
  compete 796.19
  confront 240.8
  contradict 790.6
  defy 793.3
  demand 753.4
  make war on 797.19
  object 522.5
  offer resistance 792.3
  thwart 730.15
challenging
  defiant 793.7
  exciting 648.27
chamber
  bedroom 192.7
  compartment 192.2
  council 755.1
  radiation 327.13
  room 192.1
  toilet 311.11
chamberlain
  financial officer
    836.11
  majordomo 750.10

chambermaid 750.8
chamber music 462.5
chamber of commerce
  788.9
chamber pot 311.11
chambers
  apartment 191.14
  office 719.8
chameleon
  changeableness 141.4
  mind-changer 628.4
  reptile 414.60
  variegation 374.6
champ
  n. bite 307.2
  expert 733.14
  victor 726.2
  v. chew 307.25
champaign 387.1
champ at the bit
  be impatient 862.4
  wait 132.13
champion
  n. advocate 1006.8
  defender 799.7
  deputy 781.1
  expert 733.14
  protector 699.5
  superior 36.4
  supporter 787.9
  the best 674.8
  victor 726.2
  v. back 785.13
  defend 799.8
  protect 699.18
  uphold 1006.10
  adj. best 674.18
  chief 36.14
championship
  patronage 785.4
  supremacy 36.3
  victory 726.1
chance
  n. an uncertainty
    514.8
  gamble 515.1
  happenstance 156
  liability 175.1
  opportunity 129.2
  possibility 509.1
  probability 511.1
  turn 108.2
  uncertainty 514.1
  v. attempt 714.5
  gamble 515.19
  happen 156.11
  occur 151.6
  risk 697.7
  adj. uncertain 514.18
  unpredictable 156.15
Chance 156.2
chancel 1042.9
chancellery
  mastership 739.7
  office 719.8
chancellor
  diplomat 781.6
  educator 565.9
  executive 748.3
  judge 1002.4
  premier 749.6
  public official 749.17

chancery court 1001.3
  office 719.8
  registry 570.3
chance upon 488.3
chancre sore 686.35
  venereal disease
    686.16
chancy chance 156.15
  hazardous 697.10
  uncertain 514.15
  vague 514.18
chandelier 336.6,11
chandler
  merchant 830.3
  provider 659.6
  tradesman 830.2
change
  n. alteration 139
  alternate 149.2
  conversion 145.1
  differentiation 16.4
  petty cash 835.19
  substitution 149.1
  v. alter 139.6
  be changed 139.5
  convert 145.11
  differentiate 16.6
  don 231.42
  interchange 150.4
  move 267.5
  substitute 149.4
  trade 827.14
  vacillate 627.8
changeable
  changed 139.9
  fickle 629.6
  inconstant 141.7
  interchangeable
    150.5
  irregular 18.3
  irresolute 627.9
  transient 111.7
  uncertain 514.15
  variable 141.6
  weak 160.17
change course 275.30
changed altered 139.9
  converted 145.19
change hands 817.4
changeless
  godlike 1013.20
  invariable 142.17
  permanent 140.7
changeling
  evil spirit 1016.12
  substitute 149.2
change of heart
  change 139.1
  change of mind 145.2
  penitence 873.4
change of life 126.7
change of mind
  about-face 628.1
  change of heart 145.2
  irresolution 627.1
change one's mind
  repent 873.7
  reverse oneself 628.6
  vacillate 627.8
channel
  n. bed 212.4
  conduit 396

informant 557.5
information theory
  557.7
narrow place 205.3
outlet 303.9
passageway 657.4
radio 344.13
running water 395.1
seaway 275.10
trench 263.2
v. channelize 396.19
groove 263.3
pipe 271.13
chant
n. hymn 1032.3
repeat 103.5
song 462.13
v. sing 462.39
utter 594.26
chaos confusion 62.2
disorder 532.3
formlessness 247.1
lawlessness 740.2
noncohesion 51.1
outer space 375.3
violence 162.2
chaotic
confused 532.12
formless 247.4
lawless 740.6
muddled 62.16
vague 514.18
violent 162.17
chaotically
disorderly 62.19
lawlessly 740.7
nonuniformly 18.4
chap crack 201.2
man 420.5
person 417.3
chaparral 411.13
chapel church 1042.3
hall 192.4
chaperon
n. escort 73.5
guardian 699.7
maid 750.8
v. care for 699.19
escort 73.8
chapfallen
disappointed 541.5
distressed 866.22
glum 872.25
humiliated 906.13
chaplain
churchman 1038.9
clergyman 1038.2
chaps 265.5
chapter
book part 605.13
branch 788.10
church council 755.4
part of writing 55.2
topic 484.1
char
n. cleaning woman
  681.14
v. burn 329.24
work 716.12
character
n. actor 612.2
characteristic 80.4

description 608.1
eccentric 474.3
function 656.3
gene 170.6
harmonics 463.12
honesty 974.1
kind 61.3
letter 581.1
man 420.5
nature 5.3
number 86.1
odd person 85.4
person 417.3
recommendation
  968.4
repute 914.1
role 611.11
sign 568.2
status 7.5
symbol 581.2
temperament 525.3
v. describe 608.12
engrave 578.10
letter 581.6
represent 572.6
character assassination
defamation 971.2
scandal 558.8
smear campaign
  744.14
characteristic
n. habit 642.4
nature 5.3
peculiarity 80.4
sign 568.2
adj. classificational
  61.7
differentiative 16.9
peculiar 80.13
temperamental 525.7
typical 572.11
characterization
acting 611.9
description 608.1
distinction 80.8
impersonation 572.2
indication 568.1
representation 572.1
story element 608.9
characterize
describe 608.12
distinguish 80.10
indicate 568.17
represent 572.6
characterizing 16.9
characterless
formless 247.4
uninteresting 883.6
vacant 187.13
charade gesture 568.14
riddle 549.9
stage show 611.4
charcoal
art equipment 574.19
ashes 329.16
black 365.4
blacking 365.6
drawing 574.6
fuel 331.1
picture 574.14
charge
n. accusation 1005.1

arraignment 1004.3
attack 798.1
attribution 155.1
bill 840.1
burden 352.7
cathexis 690.41
commission 780.1
custody 761.5
dependent 764.6
duty 962.1
electric charge 342.5
expenses 843.3
explosive charge
  801.10
fee 846.7
full measure 56.3
heraldic insignia
  569.2
impediment 730.6
imposition 963.3
injunction 752.2
load 194.2
power 157.1
precept 751.1
price 846.1
protectorship 699.2
rocketry 281.8
supervision 747.2
task 656.2
the ministry 1037.9
thrill 857.2
v. accuse 1005.7
advise 754.6
attack 798.18
burden 352.13
command 752.9
commission 780.9
demand 846.14
electrify 342.23
fill 56.7
impose 963.4
prepare 720.9
radioactivate 327.9
receive credit 839.7
shoot 285.13
interj. attack! 798.32
charge account 839.2
charge card 839.3
charged
accused 1005.15
attributed 155.6
burdened 352.18
critical 129.10
electrified 342.31
exciting 857.28
fraught 56.12
radioactive 327.10
charge in 238.5
charge off
discount 847.2
forget 947.5
keep accounts 845.8
charger horse 414.10
war horse 800.32
charily
cautiously 895.13
economically 851.7
charisma
allurement 650.1
illustriousness 914.6
influence 172.1
power 157.1

charismatic
alluring 650.7
illustrious 914.19
influential 172.13
charismatic movement
  1028.3
charitable
benevolent 938.15
giving 818.22
gratis 850.5
pitying 944.7
tolerant 526.11
charity accord 794.1
almsgiving 818.3
benevolence 938.4
donation 818.6
love 931.1
patronage 785.4
tolerance 526.4
virtue 980.5
charity case 838.4
charivari 453.3
charlatan
n. impostor 619.6
quack doctor 688.7
adj. quack 616.28
Charley
irregular 800.15
revolutionist 147.3
watchman 699.10
charley horse 424.2
charm
n. allurement 650.1
amulet 1036.5
beauty 900.1
bird group 74.6
influence 172.1
jewel 901.6
lovability 931.7
lure 650.2
pleasantness 863.2
sorcery 1035.1
spell 1036.1
superstition 502.3
v. delight 865.8
enamor 931.21
enchant 1036.8
engross 530.13
fascinate 650.6
persuade 648.23
charmed
dreamy 535.25
enamored 931.26
enchanted 1036.12
engrossed 530.18
pleased 865.12
charmed circle 788.6
charmer
beautiful person
  900.8
bewitcher 1035.9
cunning person 735.6
deceiver 619.1
tempter 650.3
charming
alluring 650.7
bewitching 1036.11
influential 172.13
lovable 931.23
pleasant 863.7
charnel house
mortuary 410.9

tomb 410.16
Charon 1019.5
chart
　n. diagram 654.3
　list 88.2
　map 654.4
　outline 48.4
　representation 572.1
　v. organize 60.10
　plot 654.11
　represent 572.6
chart a course
　navigate 275.27
　pilot 275.14
charter
　n. exemption 762.8
　grant 777.5
　hire 780.5
　permission 777.1
　v. authorize 777.11
　commission 780.9
　hire 780.14
　rent out 780.15
chartreuse 371.4,6
chary cautious 895.9
　economical 851.6
chase
　n. groove 263.1
　horse race 796.13
　hunting 655.2
　pursuit 655.1
　woodland 411.11
　v. court 932.19
　drive out 310.14
　emboss 256.11
　follow 293.3
　hunt 655.9
　make haste 709.5
　pursue 655.8
　repulse 289.3
　sculpture 575.5
chase after 271.15
chaser act 611.8
　alcoholic drink 996.8
　pursuer 655.4
　sculptor 579.6
chasm crack 201.2
　depth 209.2
　opening 265.1
　pit 257.4
chassis bottom 212.2
　frame 245.4
　mounting 216.10
　radio receiver 344.3
chaste abstinent 992.10
　elegant 589.6
　perfect 677.6
　plain 902.6
　pure 980.8
　simple 45.6
　tasteful 897.8
　virtuous 988.4
chasten
　make plain 902.5
　moderate 163.6
　punish 1010.10
chastened
　restrained 163.11
　weak 765.15
chastise punish 1010.10
　reprove 969.17

chastity
　abstinence 992.2
　literary elegance
　　589.1
　perfection 677.1
　purity 988
　virtue 980.3
chat
　n. chatter 596.3
　conversation 597.4
　v. chatter 596.5
　converse 597.10
château 191.8
chatelaine
　governor 749.5
　jewel 901.6
　mistress 749.2
chattel property 810.1
　slave 764.7
chatter
　n. idle talk 596.3
　rattle 455.3
　speech 594.1
　v. be cold 333.9
　bird sound 460.5
　expatiate 593.8
　rattle 455.6
　shake 324.11
　speak 594.20
　talk idly 596.5
chatterbox
　chatterer 596.4
　talker 594.18
chatty
　conversational 597.13
　intimate 922.20
　talkative 596.9
chauffeur
　n. driver 274.10
　male servant 750.4
　v. ride 273.32
chauvinism
　patriotism 941.2
　prejudice 527.4
　warlikeness 797.15
chauvinist
　intolerant person
　　527.5
　militarist 800.5
　patriot 941.3
chauvinist(ic)
　militaristic 797.26
　prejudiced 527.12
　public-spirited 941.4
cheap
　disgraceful 915.11
　inexpensive 849.7
　inferior 680.9
　paltry 673.18
　stingy 852.9
　worthless 669.11
cheapen bargain 827.17
　corrupt 692.14
　depreciate 849.6
cheat
　n. deceiver 619.3
　fake 616.13
　fraud 618.8
　v. be dishonest 975.11
　deceive 618.17
check
　n. account of 87.6

bill 845.3
blemish 679.1
checkup 485.6
comparison 491.2
confinement 761.1
crack 201.2
curb 730.7
defeat 727.2
frustration 730.3
gambling 515.14
hindrance 730.1
impairment 692.8
label 568.13
making certain 513.8
mark 568.5
measure 490.2
negotiable instru-
　ment 835.11
opening 265.1
plaid 374.4
restraint 760.1
reverse 729.3
slowing 270.4
speech sound 594.13
stop 144.2
tag 835.12
　v. agree 26.6
audit 87.14
blemish 679.4
break 49.12
cleave 201.4
compare 491.5
confine 761.12
defeat 727.11
delay 132.8
examine 485.23
fend off 799.10
hinder 730.10
injure 692.15
make certain 513.12
mark 568.19
monitor 344.26
restrain 760.7
slow 270.9
stop 144.11
variegate 374.7
checkbook 835.11
checker
　be changed 139.5
　variegate 374.7
checkerboard
　check 374.4
　plaything 878.16
checkered
　changeable 141.6
　plaid 374.14
checkers 878.34
check in arrive 300.6
　die 408.20
　record 570.16
checking account
　account 839.2
　funds 835.14
checklist
　directory 748.10
　itemization 88.1
　list 88.6
checkmate
　n. defeat 727.2
　end 144.2
　frustration 730.3
　v. defeat 727.11

stop 144.11
thwart 730.15
check out audit 87.14
　be qualified 720.15
　die 408.20
　examine 485.23
　leave 301.14
　make certain 513.12
cheek buttocks 241.5
　insolence 913.3
　rashness 894.1
　side 242.1
cheeky defiant 793.7
　impudent 913.9
cheep 460.5
cheer
　n. applause 968.2
　cheerfulness 870.1
　conviviality 922.3
　cry 459.1
　food 308.1
　happiness 865.2
　hurrah 876.2
　v. applaud 968.10
　assent 521.8
　comfort 887.6
　cry 459.6
　encourage 893.16
　give hope 888.10
　gladden 870.7
　refresh 695.2
　rejoice 876.6
　urge on 648.16
cheerful
　cheering 870.16
　cheery 870.11
　happy 865.13
　homelike 191.33
　optimistic 888.12
　pleasant 863.6
cheerfully
　cheerily 870.17
　hopefully 888.14
　pleasantly 863.11
cheerfulness
　auspiciousness 544.9
　good cheer 870
　happiness 865.2
　optimism 888.3
　pleasantness 863.4
cheering
　comforting 887.13
　gladdening 870.16
　promising 888.13
　refreshing 695.3
cheerless
　hopeless 889.12
　pleasureless 866.20
　unhappy 872.21
　unpleasant 864.20
cheer up 870.9
cheery see cheerful
cheese 308.47,53
cheeseparing
　n. economizing 851.2
　parsimony 852.1
　adj. economical 851.6
　meager 102.5
　parsimonious 852.7
cheesy bad 675.8
　base 915.12
　inferior 680.9

paltry 673.18
cheetah 414.27,58
chef cook 330.2
  master 749.1
chef d'œuvre
  masterpiece 733.10
  pattern of perfection
    677.4
  product 168.1
  work of art 574.11
chemical
  n. chemistry 379.1,11
  inorganic matter
    382.3
  adj. chemistry 379.7
chemical apparatus
  379.13
chemical element
  chemical 379.1,10
  element 376.2
chemist
  drugstore 687.36
  pharmacist 687.35
  store 832.4
chemistry 379.9
cherish care for 699.19
  foster 785.16
  harbor 813.7
  hold dear 931.19
  remember 537.13
cheroot 434.4
cherry bomb 453.5
cherub angel 1015.1
  child 125.3
  endearment 932.5
che sarà sarà 640.11
chess 878.34
chest breast 256.6
  depository 836.12
  storage place 660.6
chestnut
  n. horse 414.13
  old joke 881.9
  platitude 517.3
  adj. reddish-brown
    367.4
  redheaded 368.10
chevalier gallant 936.9
  knight 918.5
  rider 274.8
chevron angle 251.2
  crookedness 219.8
  heraldic insignia
    569.2
  military insignia
    569.5
chew
  n. bite 307.2
  chewing tobacco
    434.7
  v. eat 307.25
  pulp 390.5
  reprove 969.19
  use tobacco 434.14
chewing
  n. eating 307.1
  reproof 969.6
  tobacco chewing
    434.10
  adj. masticatory
    307.30
  tobacco 434.15

chewing gum
  chicle gum 389.6
  elastic substance
    358.3
chew out 969.19
chew the fat 597.9
chewy 359.4
chi 221.4
chiaroscuro
  lighting 335.19
  picture 574.14
chic
  n. smartness 644.3
  adj. dressed up 231.45
  smart 644.13
chicanery
  dishonesty 975.2
  sophistry 483.5
  stratagem 735.3
  trick 618.6
  trickery 618.4
chichi ornate 901.12
  showy 904.19
  ultrafashionable
    644.14
chick bird 414.33
  endearment 932.5
  girl 125.6
  poultry 414.34
  woman 421.6
  young chicken 125.8
chicken
  n. coward 892.5
  effeminate male
    421.10
  food 308.22
  homosexual 419.16
  military insignia
    569.5
  poultry 414.34,67
  weakling 160.6
  v. be a coward 892.8
  adj. cowardly 892.10
  effeminate 421.14
  weak 160.12
chicken feed
  fodder 308.4
  trifles 673.4
chicle 389.6
chide 969.17
chief
  n. heraldic insignia
    569.2
  leader 749.3
  master 749.1
  potentate 749.7
  principal 672.10
  superior 36.4
  supervisor 748.2
  adj. directing 747.12
  first 68.17
  front 240.10
  governing 741.18
  leading 292.3
  main 36.14
  most important
    672.23
  preceding 64.4
  top 211.10
chiefly generally 79.17
  mainly 36.17
  normally 84.9

on the whole 54.14
  principally 68.18
chieftain 749.7
chieftaincy
  mastership 739.7
  region 181.1
chigger 414.40
chignon
  false hair 230.13
  hair 230.7
chilblain cold 333.2
  environmental dis-
    ease 686.31
  sore 686.35
child descendant 171.3
  innocent person
    984.4
  product 168.1
  unsophisticate 736.3
  youngster 125.3
childbearing 167.7
childhood origin 68.4
  youth 124.2
childish
  childlike 124.11
  senile 469.23
  simple-minded
    469.24
childishness
  childlikeness 124.4
  senility 469.10
  simple-mindedness
    469.11
  unwiseness 470.2
childless 166.4
childlike artless 736.5
  childish 124.11
  innocent 984.6
  senile 469.23
  simple-minded
    469.24
  trusting 501.22
child prodigy 733.12
children family 11.5
  posterity 171.1
  young people 125.2
child's play 673.5
chill
  n. cold 333.1
  cold sensation 333.2
  deterrent 652.2
  disease symptom
    686.8
  enmity 929.1
  indifference 636.1
  unfeeling 856.1
  unsociability 923.2
  v. be cold 333.9
  disincline 652.4
  make cold 333.10
  refrigerate 334.10
  adj. cool 333.12
  unfeeling 856.9
  unfriendly 929.9
chiller cooler 334.3
  motion picture
    611.16
chilling
  n. cold sensation
    333.2
  refrigeration 334.1

adj. frightening
    891.36
  refrigerative 334.12
chilly aloof 912.12
  cold 333.15
  cool 333.12
  reticent 613.10
  unfeeling 856.9
  unfriendly 929.9
  unsociable 923.6
chime
  n. bell 454.4
  carillon 465.21
  music 462.3
  percussion instrument
    465.18
  repetitiousness 103.4
  ringing 454.3
  v. agree 26.6
  harmonize 462.36
  ring 454.8
  say 594.23
  sound similar 20.9
chime in 238.6
chimera hope 888.5
  illusion 519.1
  mosaic 44.8
  thing imagined 535.5
chimeric(al)
  illusory 519.9
  imaginary 535.22
  tenuous 4.6
chiming
  n. music 462.3
  ringing 454.3
  adj. harmonious
    462.50
  repetitious 103.15
  ringing 454.12
  similar sounding
    20.17
chimney deposit 383.7
  fireplace 329.11
  ravine 201.2
  smoke passage 396.18
chimpanzee 414.28,59
chin
  n. front 240.6
  v. converse 597.9
  speak 594.21
china
  n. brittleness 360.2
  ceramic ware 576.2,8
  adj. ceramic 576.7
chine crest 207.6
  ridge 256.3
chink
  n. crack 201.2
  faint sound 452.3
  groove 263.1
  ringing 454.3
  vulnerable point
    697.4
  v. faint sound 452.15
  open 265.12
  ring 454.8
  stop 266.7
chinoiserie 901.2
chinook 403.7
chintzy meager 102.5
  slovenly 62.15
  tasteless 898.10

chip
n. break 49.4
flake 227.3
gambling 515.14
impairment 692.8
lightness 353.2
piece 55.3
small amount 35.3
v. break 49.12
injure 692.15
chip in give 818.14
interrupt 238.6
participate 815.5
pay 841.18
chip off the old block
copy 24.3
descendant 171.3
likeness 20.3
chip on one's shoulder
challenge 793.2
warlikeness 797.15
chipper
cheerful 870.13
healthy 685.7
lively 707.17
chippy 989.14
chips money 835.2
sailor 276.6
chiropodist 688.8
chiropractic
n. healing art 688.2
adj. medical 688.18
chiropractor 688.5
chirp
n. insect sound 458.5
v. be cheerful 870.6
bird sound 460.5
rejoice 876.5
sing 462.39
stridulate 458.7
utter 594.26
chisel
n. sculpting tool 575.4
v. cheat 618.17
engrave 578.10
form 246.7
groove 263.3
process 167.11
sculpture 575.5
chiseler 619.3
chisel in 238.5
chiseling
n. engraving 578.2
adj. deceitful 618.20
chit child 125.3
debt 840.1
letter 604.2
little thing 196.4
chitchat
conversation 597.5
gossip 558.7
chivalrous
courageous 893.17
gallant 936.15
magnanimous 979.6
noble 918.10
chivalry courage 893.1
gallantry 936.2
magnanimity 979.2
nobility 918.2
warcraft 797.10
chivy annoy 866.13

pursue 655.8
chlorinate
add gas 401.8
react chemically 379.6
sanitize 681.24
chloroform
n. anesthetic 687.57
v. kill 409.13
render insensible 423.4
chock
n. curb 730.7
v. fill 56.7
obstruct 730.12
chock-full 56.11
chocolate
n. candy 308.54
adj. brown 367.3
choice
n. free choice 762.6
judgment 494.1
loophole 632.4
selection 637
the best 674.8
will 621.1
adj. best 674.18
tasteful 897.8
choir chorus 464.16
church part 1042.9
keyboard 465.20
choirboy 464.15
choirmaster
choral director 464.18
leader 748.6
choke
n. suffocation 409.7
violent death 408.6
v. be hot 328.22
close 266.6
destroy 693.15
die 408.24
extinguish 332.7
obstruct 730.12
overload 663.15
silence 451.8
stop 266.7
strangle 409.19
chokedamp
miasma 676.4
vapor 401.1
choke on 867.4
choking
n. destruction 693.6
extinguishing 332.2
obstruction 266.3
suffocation 409.7
violent death 408.6
adj. hindering 730.17
imperfectly spoken 595.12
choler bitterness 952.3
ill humor 951.1
cholera 686.12
choleric
n. personality type 690.15
adj. ill-humored 951.23
resentful 952.24
cholesterol 309.7

chomp
n. bite 307.2
v. chew 307.25
choo-choo 272.13
choose desire 634.14
select 637.13
will 621.2
choosing
n. choice 637.1
adj. selective 637.23
choosy fastidious 896.9
selective 637.23
chop
n. cheek 242.1
grain 308.4
hit 283.4
meat 308.19
rough surface 261.2
wave 395.14
v. be changed 139.5
notch 262.4
sever 49.11
chop down fell 318.5
raze 693.19
chopfallen see chapfallen
chop logic
argue 482.16
differentiate 16.6
quibble 483.9
chopper
helicopter 280.5
motorcycle 272.8
choppy
discontinuous 72.4
irregular 138.3
jolting 324.20
nonuniform 18.3
rough 261.6
chops 265.5
choral 462.51
chorale choir 464.16
hymn 1032.3
sacred music 462.16
chord
n. harmonics 463.17
music 465.23
straight line 250.2
sympathy 855.5
v. harmonize 462.36
perform music 462.40
put in tune 462.37
chore
n. difficult thing 731.2
task 656.2
v. serve 750.13
work 716.12
chorea
nervous disorder 686.23
shaking 324.2
choreographer 611.27
choreographic 879.6
choreography
dancing 879.1
representation 572.1
chorister
choirmaster 464.18
choral singer 464.15
chorography
location 184.7

map 654.4
mensuration 490.9
chortle
n. laughter 876.4
v. laugh 876.8
chorus
n. agreement 26.1
choir 464.16
choral music 462.18
music division 462.24
poetic division 609.11
repeat 103.5
sequel 67.1
troupe 612.11
unanimity 521.5
v. imitate 22.5
say 594.23
sing 462.39
chorus girl
choral singer 464.15
dancer 879.3
entertainer 612.1
chosen
n. elect 637.12
the best 674.8
adj. selected 637.26
superior 36.12
chow 308.2
chowder soup 308.10
stew 308.11
chrismal
baptism 1040.7
church furnishing 1042.10
church vessel 1042.11
unction 1040.6
Christ
functions of 1013.17
God the Son 1013.12
christen begin 68.11
name 583.11
perform rites 1040.20
Christendom
Christianity 1020.6
the believing 1028.5
christened 583.14
christening
baptism 1040.7
naming 583.2
Christian
n. believer 1028.4
good person 985.3
religionist 1020.16,34
adj. honest 974.13
kind 938.13
orthodox 1024.7
pious 1028.8
Christian denominations 1020.33
Christianity
Christianism 1020.6,32
piety 1028.2
Christian name 583.4
Christian Science 1020.13,33
Christian Science practitioner
faith healer 688.12
religionist 1020.23

circumnavigate
 go around 321.4
 sail 275.13
circumscribe
 bound 234.4
 constrict 198.7
 limit 235.8
 qualify 507.3
 restrain 760.9
circumscription
 boundary 235.3
 bounds 235.1
 contraction 198.1
 demarcation 234
 enclosure 236.1
 exclusion 77.1
 qualification 507.1
 restriction 760.3
circumspect
 careful 533.10
 cautious 895.8
 judicious 467.19
 slow 270.10
circumstance
 component 58.2
 condition 8
 event 151.2
 fact 1.3
 pomp 904.6
 state 7.1
circumstances
 affairs 151.4
 assets 810.8
 environment 233.1
 situation 8.2
circumstantial
 conditional 8.7
 evidential 505.17
 happening 151.9
 unessential 6.4
circumstantiality
 meticulousness 533.3
 particularity 8.4
circumstantiate
 confirm 505.12
 itemize 8.6
circumvent
 deceive 618.13
 evade 631.7
 go around 321.4
 outwit 735.11
 thwart 730.15
circumvention
 avoidance 631.1
 deception 618.1
 outwitting 735.5
circus arena 802.1
 circle 253.2
 city district 183.9
 show 611.15
 theater 611.1
cirque 257.8
cirrhosis
 alcoholism 996.3
 liver disease 686.21
cirrose cloudy 404.7
 hairy 230.24
 threadlike 206.7
cirrus cloud 404.1
 curl 254.2
 filament 206.1
cist 410.16

cistern 398.1
citadel 799.6
citation
 accusation 1005.2
 attribution 155.2
 honor 916.4
 reference 505.6
 summons 752.7
cite accuse 1005.7
 call attention to
  530.10
 honor 916.8
 name 505.14
 particularize 8.6
 summon 752.12
cither 465.3
citified 183.10
citizen
 free person 762.11
 national 190.4
 noncombatant 803.5
citizenry people 417.2
 population 190.1
 the public 919.2
citizens band 344.13,29
citizenship
 nationality 189.2
 public spirit 941.1
citizenship papers 189.3
cittern 465.3
city
 n. districts of 183.6
 region 180.5
 town 183.1
 adj. urban 183.10
city dweller 190.6
city father
 legislator 746.3
 public official 749.17
city hall
 government building
  742.12
 political party 744.24
 town hall 183.5
city manager 749.17
city planner 579.10
city slicker
 sophisticate 733.16
 townsman 190.6
city-state 181.1
civic
 governmental 741.17
 political 744.43
 public 417.13
 public-spirited 941.4
 urban 183.10
civics 744.2
civil courteous 936.14
 decorous 897.10
 governmental 741.17
 lay 1039.3
 public 417.13
 sociable 922.18
civil ceremony 933.4
civil code 998.5
civilian lawyer 1003.4
 noncombatant 803.5
civility amenities 936.7
 courtesy 936.1
 cultivation 691.3
 decorousness 897.3
 etiquette 646.3

 polite act 936.6
 sociability 922.1
 social convention
  645.1
civilization
 improvement 691.3
 society 642.3
civilize humanize 417.9
 make better 691.9
 teach 562.11
civilized
 improved 691.13
 learned 475.21
 tasteful 897.9
civil rights
 liberties 762.2
 rights 958.5
civil servant 749.16
civvies 231.8
clabber
 n. curd 354.7
 semiliquid 389.5
 v. make viscid 389.10
 thicken 354.10
clack
 n. chatter 596.3
 noisemaker 453.5
 rattle 455.3
 snap 456.2
 v. bird sound 460.5
 chatter 596.5
 rattle 455.6
 snap 456.7
clacker 453.5
clad 231.44
claim
 n. demand 753.1
 estate 810.4
 extortion 305.6
 false claim 649.2
 legal statement
  1004.7
 possession 808.1
 privilege 958.3
 v. demand 753.4
 extort 305.15
 lay claim to 753.5
 possess 808.4
 pretext 649.3
 require 639.9
 take 822.13
claimant
 accuser 1005.5
 petitioner 774.7
clairvoyance
 divining 543.2
 extrasensory percep-
  tion 1034.8
 foreknowledge 542.3
 intuition 481.1
 understanding 475.3
clairvoyant
 n. occultist 1034.14
 adj. foreseeing 542.7
 intuitive 481.5
 psychic 1034.23
clam
 n. food 308.25
 invertebrate 415.5
 uncommunicative
  person 613.5
 v. fish 655.10

clambake
 electioneering 744.12
 picnic 307.6
clamber up 315.11
clammy sweaty 311.22
 viscous 389.12
clamor
 n. dissonance 461.2
 entreaty 774.2
 noise 453.3
 outcry 459.4
 v. be noisy 453.8
 complain 875.13
 vociferate 459.8
clamor for
 demand 753.4
 entreat 774.11
 require 639.9
 wish for 634.16
clamorous
 demanding 753.8
 excited 857.22
 noisy 453.12
 urgent 672.21
 vociferous 459.10
clamp
 n. contractor 198.6
 hold 813.2
 v. fasten 47.7
 squeeze 198.8
clamp down on
 domineer 741.16
 suppress 760.8
clam up be silent 451.6
 silence! 451.14
clan class 61.2
 clique 788.6
 community 788.2
 kind 61.3
 race 11.4
clandestine 614.12
clang
 n. animal sound 460.1
 harsh sound 458.3
 ringing 454.3
 v. ring 454.8
 sound harshly 458.9
clank
 n. harsh sound 458.3
 ringing 454.3
 v. ring 454.8
 sound harshly 458.9
clannish
 cliquish 788.18
 contemptuous 966.8
 exclusive 896.13
 racial 11.7
clansman 11.2
clap
 n. applause 968.2
 explosive noise 456.1
 noise 453.3
 venereal disease
  686.16
 v. applaud 968.10
 close 266.6
 hit 283.13
 make explosive noise
  456.6
 put violently 184.12

clapboard
covering material
228.43
wood 378.3
clapper bell 454.4
noisemaker 453.5
clappers 465.18
clapping 968.2
claptrap
humbug 616.14
nonsense 547.2
specious argument
483.3
claque 968.8
claqueur
applauder 968.8
playgoer 611.32
clarification
explanation 552.4
facilitation 732.4
refinement 681.4
clarify explain 552.10
make clear 548.6
refine 681.22
simplify 45.5
clarinet
organ stop 465.22
wood wind 465.9
clarion
n. brass wind 465.8
call to arms 797.12
organ stop 465.22
v. blare 453.9
play music 462.43
clarity facility 732.1
intelligibility 548.2
literary elegance
589.1
transparency 339.1
visibility 444.2
clash
n. disaccord 795.1
dissonance 461.2
explosive noise 456.1
fight 796.4
harsh sound 458.3
hostility 929.3
impact 283.3
v. be dissonant 461.3
be inharmonious
795.8
collide 283.12
conflict 362.14
contend 796.14
counteract 178.6
differ 16.5
disagree 27.5
make explosive noise
456.6
oppose 15.4
sound harshly 458.9
clashing
clashingly colored
362.20
contrary 15.6
counteractive 178.8
disaccordant 795.15
disagreeing 27.6
hostile 929.10
jarring 461.5
opposing 790.8

clasp
n. embrace 932.2
hold 813.2
v. cohere 50.6
embrace 932.16
fasten 47.8
hold 813.6
seize 822.14
stay near 200.12
class
n. biology 61.5
category 61.2
community 788.2
goodness 674.1
laity 1039.1
nomenclature 583.1
rank 29.2
school 788.5
stock 11.4
students 566.11
v. analyze 48.8
categorize 61.6
judge 494.9
classic book 605.1
classical music 462.7
literature 602.12
pattern of perfection
677.4
work of art 574.11
classic(al)
antiquated 123.13
finished 677.9
model 25.8
outright 34.12
polished 589.6
simple 902.6
tasteful 897.8
written 602.24
classicist
antiquarian 123.5
elegant writer 589.4
scholar 476.3
classification
analysis 48.3
categorization 61
nomenclature 583.1
classified
arranged 60.14
catalogued 61.8
secret 614.11
classify analyze 48.8
arrange 60.11
categorize 61.6
keep secret 614.7
classmate
companion 928.3
partner 787.2
student 566.4
classroom
n. schoolroom 567.16
adj. scholastic 567.18
classy chic 644.13
ostentatious 904.18
clatter
n. chatter 596.3
noise 453.3
rattle 455.3
v. chatter 596.5
gossip 558.12
rattle 455.6
clause
book part 605.13

condition 507.2
legislative clause
742.17
part of writing 55.2
phrase 585.1
clavichord 465.13
claw injure 692.15
seize 822.14
torture 866.18
clawed footed 212.9
grasping 813.9
tortured 866.25
claws control 741.2
governance 739.5
grasping organs 813.4
clay
n. body 376.3
ceramic material
576.3
corpse 408.16
land 385.1
mankind 417.1
mud 389.8
pipe 434.6
softness 357.4
adj. ceramic 576.7
clayey earthy 385.7
soft 357.12
clean
v. cleanse 681.18
adj. chaste 988.4
honest 974.13
innocent 984.7
skillful 733.20
thorough 56.10
trim 248.5
unsoiled 681.25
adv. absolutely 56.15
cleanly 681.29
clean-cut
clearly visible 444.7
intelligible 548.10
shapely 248.5
cleaner
cleaning agent 681.17
janitor 681.14
cleaning
n. cleansing 681.2
devices 681.32
adj. cleansing 681.28
cleanliness
chastity 988.1
cleanness 681.1
innocence 984.1
clean out clean 681.18
eject 310.21
cleanse clean 681.18
purge 886.6
sanctify 1026.5
cleanser 681.17,30
clean-shaven 232.17
cleansing
n. cleaning 681.2
release 886.2
adj. atoning 1012.7
cleaning 681.28
relieving 886.9
clean slate
innocence 984.1
revolution 147.1
void 187.3
clean sweep 147.1

clean up arrange 60.12
clean 681.18
complete 722.6
profit 811.11
clear
v. acquit 1007.4
be high 207.16
disentangle 732.8
eject 310.21
eliminate 77.5
extricate 763.7
fly 278.47
jump 319.5
manage 724.11
pay in full 841.13
profit 811.11
refine 681.22
unblock 265.13
vindicate 1006.9
adj. audible 450.16
certain 513.13
clearly visible 444.7
easy 732.12
free 762.20
innocent 984.6
intelligible 548.10
lucid 335.31
manifest 555.8
open 265.18
polished 589.6
prosperous 728.13
rid of 762.30
simple 45.7
thorough 56.10
transparent 339.4
unfastened 49.22
unhampered 762.25
unindebted 841.23
unqualified 508.2
vacant 187.13
adv. astray 199.19
clearance
acquittal 1007.1
authorization 777.3
aviation 278.44
distance 199.1
elimination 77.2
evacuation 310.6
interval 201.1
latitude 762.4
pass 777.7
payment 841.1
space 179.4
spare 179.3
vindication 1006.1
clear away
dissipate 75.5
eject 310.21
eliminate 77.5
clear-cut
clearly visible 444.7
intelligible 548.10
clearing
acquittal 1007.1
disentanglement
732.5
evacuation 310.6
extrication 763.3
field 413.9
opening 265.1
space 179.4
vindication 1006.1

clearing house 836.13
clearly audibly 450.18
  certainly 513.23
  intelligibly 548.12
  manifestly 555.14
  positively 34.19
  visibly 444.8
clear out clean 681.18
  depart 301.9
  eject 310.21
  eliminate 77.5
  flee 631.10
clear sailing 698.1
clear-sighted
  clear-eyed 439.22
  clear-witted 467.13
clear the decks
  arrange 60.12
  eject 310.21
  eliminate 77.5
  prepare 720.6
  sail 275.49
  take precautions
   895.6
clear the way
  facilitate 732.6
  prepare the way
   720.12
clear up explain 552.10
  make sure 513.11
  simplify 45.5
  solve 487.2
  tidy up 60.12
cleavage
  falling-out 795.4
  fission 326.8
  separation 49.2
cleave atomics 326.17
  bisect 92.4
  cohere 50.6
  crack 201.4
  demolish 693.17
  hold 813.6
  open 265.12
  sever 49.11
clef 463.13
cleft
  n. break 49.4
  crack 201.2
  falling-out 795.4
  notch 262.1
  opening 265.1
  adj. cut 201.7
  halved 92.6
  severed 49.23
cleft palate 249.3
clemency
  leniency 759.1
  pity 944.1
clement lenient 759.7
  pitying 944.7
clench
  n. hold 813.2
  v. hold 813.6
  seize 822.14
clerestory floor 192.23
  top 211.1
clergy 1038
clergyman 1038.2
cleric 1038.2
clerical
  ministerial 1037.13

  writing 602.28
clerical garments
  1041.5
clericalism 1037.3
clerk accountant 845.7
  agent 781.3
  churchman 1038.10
  clergyman 1038.2
  recorder 571.1
  salesman 830.4
  scholar 476.3
  secretary 602.13
clever cunning 735.12
  intelligent 467.14
  skillful 733.20
  teachable 564.18
  well-laid 733.28
  witty 881.15
cleverness
  cunning 735.1
  intelligence 467.2
  skill 733.1
  teachability 564.5
  wittiness 881.2
cliché phrase 582.9
  platitude 517.3
  triteness 883.3
  truism 79.8
click
  n. faint sound 452.3
  snap 456.2
  v. faint sound 452.15
  snap 456.7
  succeed 724.6
clicking
  n. ticking 455.2
  adj. staccato 455.7
client customer 828.4
  dependent 764.6
clientele 828.3
cliff 213.3
cliff dwelling 191.6
cliff hanger 611.4
cliff-hanging
  n. expectancy 539.3
  adj. exciting 857.28
climacteric
  n. change of life 126.7
  crisis 129.4
  adj. critical 129.10
climactic(al) 211.10
climate milieu 233.3
  pervading attitudes
   525.5
  weather 402.4
  zone 180.3
climatology
  aeronautics 278.2
  meteorology 402.6
climax
  n. completion 56.5
  culmination 677.3
  finishing touch 722.3
  important point
   672.6
  orgasm 419.8
  result 154.2
  summit 211.2
  upheaval 162.5
  v. complete 722.6
  sex 419.25
  top 211.9

climb
  n. acclivity 219.6
  ascent 315.1
  v. ascend 315.11
  fly 278.48
  incline 219.10
  move 267.5
climb down
  descend 316.7
  humble oneself 906.6
  recant 628.9
climber ascender 315.6
  traveler 274.1
  vine 411.4
climbing
  n. ambition 634.10
  ascent 315.1
  course 267.2
  adj. ascending 315.14
  sloping upward
   219.17
climb on 315.12
clime weather 402.4
  zone 180.3
clinch
  n. hold 813.2
  joint 47.4
  v. be joined 47.11
  cohere 50.6
  fasten 47.7
  hold 813.6
  make sure 513.11
  prove 505.11
  seize 822.14
clincher
  argument 506.3
  end-all 70.4
cling
  n. cohesion 50.1
  hold 813.2
  v. cohere 50.6
  hold 813.6
clinging cohesive 50.10
  retentive 813.8
cling to cohere 50.6
  harbor 813.7
  hold 813.6
  stay near 200.12
clinic hospital 689.27
  hospital room 192.25
clinical 688.18
clink
  n. faint sound 452.3
  prison 761.9
  rhyme 609.10
  ringing 454.3
  similar sound 20.6
  v. faint sound 452.15
  ring 454.8
clinker ashes 329.16
  building material
   378.2
  dissonance 461.1
  residue 43.2
Clio history 608.4
  Muse 535.2
clip
  n. hit 283.4
  piece 55.3
  rate 267.4
  v. cut off 42.10
  fasten 47.8

  harbor 813.7
  hit 283.13
  hold 813.6
  overcharge 848.7
  shorten 203.6
  speed 269.8
clipped concise 592.6
  shortened 203.9
clipping
  abbreviation 592.4
  excerpts 607.4
  piece 55.3
clique
  n. coterie 788.6
  group 74.3
  v. be sociable 922.16
cliquish
  clannish 788.18
  contemptuous 966.8
  exclusive 896.13
clitoris 419.10
cloak
  n. clothing 231.12,50
  cover 228.2
  pretext 649.1
  vestment 1041.2
  v. clothe 231.39
  conceal 615.6
  cover 228.19
  protect 699.18
cloak-and-dagger 857.30
cloak-and-dagger
  operative 781.9
cloak-and-dagger work
  485.9
cloakroom 192.15
clobber best 36.7
  hit 283.13
  overwhelm 727.8
  punish 1010.16
clock
  n. timepiece 114.6,17
  v. time 114.11
clock in 300.6
clock out 301.14
clock watcher
  idler 708.8
  shirker 631.3
clockwise
  adj. right 243.4
  adv. rightward 290.26
  round 322.16
clod body 376.3
  bungler 734.8
  dolt 471.3
  land 385.1
  lump 195.10
  meat 308.17
  oaf 471.5
  rustic 919.9
cloddish
  boorish 898.13
  countrified 182.7
  stupid 469.15
clog
  n. curb 730.7
  obstruction 266.3
  v. dance 879.5
  stop 266.7
cloister
  n. church part 1042.9
  corridor 192.18

monastery 1042.6
passageway 657.4
retreat 700.5
v. confine 761.12
enclose 236.6
cloistered
claustral 1042.16
confined 761.19
enclosed 236.10
quiescent 268.12
recluse 924.9
clone
n. copy 24.3
v. copy 24.8
clop
n. faint sound 452.3
stamp 283.9
step 273.13
v. faint sound 452.15
stamp 283.19
Clorox 363.10
close
n. cessation 144.1
completion 722.2
end 70.3
v. approach 296.3
conclude 771.9
contend 796.14
converge 298.2
end 70.5
obstruct 730.12
shut 266.6
surround 233.6
turn off 144.12
close
n. enclosure 236.3,12
road 657.6
tract 180.4
adj. airless 268.16
approximate 9.8
concealed 615.11
concise 592.6
crowded 74.22
dense 354.12
exact 516.16
fastened 47.14
friendly 927.18
imminent 152.3
meticulous 533.12
narrow 205.14
near 200.14
phonetic 594.31
secret 614.11
secretive 614.15
similar 20.14
stingy 852.9
sultry 328.28
taciturn 613.9
tight 266.12
unsociable 923.5
adv. almost 200.22
around 233.12
densely 354.15
near 200.20
close call 632.2
closed
inaccessible 510.9
inhospitable 926.7
narrow-minded
527.10
secret 614.11
shut 266.9

uninfluenceable
173.4
closed-minded 527.10
close down
close shop 266.8
stop work 144.8
closed shop 789.2
closefisted 852.9
close in approach 296.3
converge 298.2
enclose 236.5
closely densely 354.15
narrowly 205.22
nearly 200.22
closemouthed
secretive 614.15
taciturn 613.9
closeness
airlessness 268.6
density 354.1
friendship 927.5
narrowness 205.1
nearness 200.1
relationship 9.1
secrecy 614.1
similarity 20.1
stinginess 852.3
sultriness 328.6
uncommunicativeness
613.1
close out
complete 722.6
keep accounts 845.8
make impossible
510.6
sell 829.8
sell stocks 833.24
close shave 632.2
closet
n. office 719.8
privy 311.10
room 192.15
sanctum 192.8
storage place 660.6
water closet 192.26
v. enclose 236.6
adj. private 614.13
close up close 266.6
close shop 266.8
complete 722.6
converge 298.2
heal 694.21
obstruct 730.12
close-up 577.8
closing
n. cessation 144.1
closure 266.1
compacting 771.4
end 70.3
adj. ending 70.9
closure closing 266
completion 56.4
hindrance 730.1
joint 47.4
clot
n. bungler 734.8
coagulation 354.7
conglomeration 50.5
simpleton 471.8
v. cohere 50.6
come together 74.16
make viscid 389.10

thicken 354.10
cloth fabric 378.5,11
sail 277.14
scenery 611.25
vestments 1041.1
clothe cover 228.19
dress 231.38
empower 157.10
provide 659.7
clothes bedding 228.10
clothing 231.1
clothes-conscious
644.13
clotheshorse
dandy 903.9
fashionable 644.7
trestle 216.16
clothier
haberdasher 231.32
store 832.4
clothing 231
clotted
thickened 354.14
viscous 389.12
cloture
end of debate 144.5
legislative procedure
742.14
cloud
n. confusion 532.3
flock 74.6
high fog 404
large number 101.3
vapor 401.1
v. becloud 404.6
conceal 615.6
confuse 532.7
cover 228.19
darken 337.9
opaque 341.2
cloudburst 394.2
clouded cloudy 404.7
concealed 615.11
covered 228.31
dark 337.14
variegated 374.12
cloudland cloud 404.1
paradise 535.11
cloud nine
happiness 865.2
summit 211.2
cloud seeder
aviator 279.1
rainmaking 394.5
cloudy dark 337.14
muddled 532.13
nebulous 404.7
obscure 549.15
opaque 341.3
stormy 403.26
clout
n. authoritativeness
739.2
effect 154.3
force 283.1
hit 283.4
influence 172.1
power 157.1
v. hit 283.13
cloven cleft 201.7
halved 92.6
severed 49.23

clover comfort 887.1
prosperity 728.1
three 93.1
cloverleaf 221.2
clown
n. awkward person
734.8
buffoon 612.10
circus artist 612.3
fool 471.1
humorist 881.12
rustic 919.9
vulgar person 898.6
v. be foolish 470.6
cloy 664.4
cloying
oversweet 431.5
satiating 664.7
sentimental 855.22
unsavory 429.7
club
n. fellowship 788.3
instrument of punish-
ment 1011.2
plaything 878.16
resort 191.27
theater 611.18
types of 801.26
v. hit 283.17
join 52.4
punish 1010.14
clubby 922.18
clubfoot
deformity 249.3
foot 212.5
clubhouse 191.27
clubwoman
fashionable 644.7
member 788.11
sociable person
922.15
cluck 460.5
clue evidence 505.1
hint 557.4
key 568.9
tip 557.3
clump
n. bulge 256.3
bunch 74.7
faint sound 452.3
hit 283.4
lump 195.10
plants 411.2
solid 354.6
stamp 283.9
v. assemble 74.18
faint sound 452.15
hit 283.13
stamp 283.19
thicken 354.10
walk 273.27
clumsily
awkwardly 734.24
carelessly 534.18
unwieldily 731.27
clumsy
blundering 734.20
bulky 195.19
inconvenient 671.7
infelicitous 590.2
slipshod 534.12
ugly 899.9

meal 307.6
respite 711.2
coffee klatch 922.11
coffee shop 307.15
coffer
n. depository 836.12
v. store 660.10
coffin 410.11
cog inferior 37.2
pointed projection 258.4
cogency
goodness 674.1
good reasoning 482.10
power 157.1
sagacity 467.4
validity 516.4
cogent good 674.12
logical 482.20
powerful 157.12
sagacious 467.16
valid 516.13
coggle 323.10
cogitate
give the mind to 478.11
think 478.8
cognate
n. kinsmen 11.2
likeness 20.3
word 582.2
adj. kindred 9.10
related 11.6
similar 20.13
cognition 475.2
cognitive 478.21
cognizance
cognition 475.2
due 960.2
thanks 949.2
cognizant aware 475.16
grateful 949.5
knowing 475.15
sensible 422.13
cognomen name 583.3
nickname 583.7
Roman name 583.6
surname 583.5
cognoscente
connoisseur 897.7
critic 494.7
cogwheel 348.6
cohabit
copulate 419.23
inhabit 188.7
live together 933.18
cohabitation
copulation 419.8
habitation 188.1
marriage 933.1
cohere adhere 50.6
agree 26.6
be joined 47.11
coherence
agreement 26.1
cohesion 50.1
indivisibility 354.2
intelligibility 548.2
coherent agreeing 26.9
cohesive 50.10
indivisible 354.13

intelligible 548.10
cohesion
cohesiveness 50
indivisibility 354.2
cohesive
coherent 50.10
indivisible 354.13
tough 359.4
cohort
accomplice 787.3
associate 787.1
attendance 73.6
group 74.3
military unit 800.19
coif
n. hairdo 230.15
v. clothe 231.39
cover 228.21
style the hair 230.22
coiffure 230.15
coil
n. curl 254.2
hair 230.7
length 202.3
v. curl 254.5
coin
n. corner 251.2
money 835.4
v. change 139.8
create 167.13
imagine 535.14
innovate 122.5
mint 835.28
coinage coining 835.24
creation 167.5
innovation 139.3
money 835.1
neologism 582.8
product 168.1
coin a phrase 517.5
coincide
agree with 521.9
concur 177.2
conform 26.6
correspond 14.4
synchronize 118.3
coincidence
accompaniment 73.1
agreement 26.1
concurrence 177.1
identity 14.1
simultaneity 118.1
coincident
accompanying 73.9
agreeing 26.9
concurrent 177.4
identical 14.8
joint 47.12
coinciding
agreeing 26.9
identical 14.8
coin machine 832.8
coitus 419.8
coke ashes 329.16
cocaine 687.9
fuel 331.1
col ravine 201.2
ridge 207.6
colander arranger 60.5
porousness 265.9
refining equipment 681.13

cold
n. coldness 333
respiratory disease 686.14
adj. chilly 333.15
coloring 362.15
cool 333.14
dead 408.31
heartless 939.23
indifferent 636.6
insolent 913.8
reticent 613.10
unconscious 423.8
unfeeling 856.9
unfriendly 929.9
uninteresting 883.6
unsexual 419.31
unsociable 923.6
cold-blooded
cold 333.19
heartless 939.23
unfeeling 856.9
cold comfort 869.1
cold cream
cleaning agent 681.17
makeup 900.11
ointment 380.3
cold cuts 308.17
cold feet 892.4
cold frame 413.11
cold front 402.5
coldhearted
heartless 939.23
unfeeling 856.9
coldly
indifferently 636.9
inertly 268.20
unamicably 929.14
unfeelingly 856.14
coldness cold 333.1
enmity 929.1
heartlessness 939.10
indifference 636.1
reticence 613.3
sexuality 419.2
unfeeling 856.1
unsociability 923.2
cold shoulder
repulse 289.2
snub 966.2
cold-shoulder
slight 534.8
snub 966.5
cold storage
discontinuance 668.2
refrigeration 334.6
storage 660.5
cold sweat dislike 867.2
nervousness 859.2
sweat 311.7
trepidation 891.5
cold-type 603.2
cold war 797.5
cold wave
cold weather 333.3
hairdo 230.15
colic ache 424.5
disease symptom 686.8
indigestion 686.28
colicky aching 424.12
diseased 686.57

coliseum 802.1
colitis
gastrointestinal disease 686.27
inflammation 686.9
collaborate
betray 975.15
be willing 622.3
concur 177.2
cooperate 786.3
write 602.21
collaboration
concurrence 177.1
cooperation 786.1
treason 975.7
collaborator
author 602.15
cooperator 787.4
subversive 619.11
turncoat 628.5
collage 574.12
collapse
n. contraction 198.4
decrease 39.2
defeat 727.1
descent 316.1
exhaustion 717.2
failure 725.3
frailty 160.2
impairment 692.1
insolvency 842.3
ruin 693.4
sickness 686.7
v. become exhausted 717.5
become sick 686.44
break down 692.27
cave 198.10
descend 316.5
fail 725.11
fall short 314.2
fall through 314.3
go bankrupt 842.7
weaken 160.9
collapsible 198.11
collar
n. band 253.3
foam 405.2
harness 659.5
insignia 569.1
neckwear 231.64
restraint 760.4
v. arrest 761.16
capture 822.18
collate arrange 60.11
compare 491.5
make certain 513.12
collateral
n. kinsmen 11.2
nonessential 6.2
pledge 772.3
adj. accompanying 73.9
additional 40.10
connected 9.9
eventual 151.11
parallel 218.6
related 11.6
simultaneous 118.4
unessential 6.4
collation
arrangement 60.1

comparison 491.2
light meal 307.7
making certain 513.8
colleague
associate 787.1
companion 928.3
collect
n. prayer 1032.4
v. assemble 74.18
come together 74.16
conclude 494.10
procure 811.10
put together 47.5
store up 660.11
collectanea
collection 74.11
compilation 605.4
miscellany 74.13
selections 607.4
collected
assembled 74.21
joined 47.13
stored 660.14
unexcited 858.13
collection
acquisition 811.2
assembly 74.1
compilation 605.4
donation 818.6
edition 605.2
group 74.11
sacrifice 1032.7
selections 607.4
store 660.1
collection agent
collector 74.15
creditor 839.4
collective
communal 815.9
concurrent 177.4
cooperating 786.5
general 79.11
collective bargaining
labor union 789.1
negotiation 827.3
collective farm
farm 413.8
participation 815.2
collectively
cooperatively 786.6
together 73.11
wholly 54.13
collectivism
cooperation 786.1
participation 815.2
principle of government 741.8
socialism 745.6
collectivize
appropriate 822.20
communize 815.7
collector
accumulator 74.15
connoisseur 897.7
desirer 634.12
devotee 635.6
enthusiast 635.5
regional governor 749.13
transistor 343.13
colleen 125.6

college
association 788.1
school 567.7
collegiate
scholastic 567.18
studentlike 566.12
collide
be inharmonious 795.8
clash in color 362.14
contend 796.14
crash 283.12
disagree 27.5
oppose 178.6
sail 275.41
collier 383.9
collimation
orientation 290.5
parallelism 218.1
collision accident 729.2
aviation 278.20
clashing 929.3
conflict 178.1
contrariety 15.1
hostility 790.2
impact 283.3
colloid 389.7
collop piece 55.3
slice 227.2
colloquial
conversational 597.13
vernacular 580.18
colloquialism
informal language 580.5
word 582.6
colloquium
discussion 597.7
meeting 74.2
colloquy 597.1
collusion
chicanery 618.4
concurrence 177.1
cooperation 786.1
intrigue 654.6
cologne 436.3
colon
foreign money 835.9
intestine 225.4
meter 609.9
pause 144.4
colonel 749.18
Colonel Blimp 904.9
colonialism
foreign policy 744.5
government 741.4
colonist 190.9
colonization
appropriation 822.4
peopling 188.2
settlement 184.6
voting 744.18
colonize
appropriate 822.19
populate 188.9
settle 184.16
colonnade arcade 217.5
corridor 192.18
passageway 657.4
post 216.8
colony
community 788.2

flock 74.5
possession 808.1
territory 181.1
colophon book 605.12
label 568.13
mark 568.7
sequel 67.1
color
n. artistry 574.10
black 365.14
blue 372.4
brown 367.6
colorfulness 362.4
coloring matter 362.8
extenuation 1006.5
fakery 616.3
gray 366.6
green 371.6
hue 362
kind 61.3
looks 446.4
orange 369.3
ornamentation 901.1
pink 368.13
pretext 649.1
purple 373.4
red 368.12
reddish brown 367.7
redness 368.1
story element 608.9
timbre 450.3
white 364.11
yellow 370.7
v. artwork 574.20
become excited 857.17
become red 368.5
blush 908.8
distort 249.6
extenuate 1006.12
falsify 616.16
hue 362.13
influence 172.7
infuse 44.12
misrepresent 573.3
ornament 901.8
show resentment 952.14
coloration
applying color 362.11
color 362.1
implication 546.2
coloratura
n. aria 462.14
ornamentation 463.18
vocalization 462.12
voice 463.5
adj. vocal 462.51
coloratura soprano 464.13
color-blind 441.9
color blindness
defective vision 441.3
genetic disease 686.11
colored
dark-skinned 365.10
falsified 616.26
high-flown 601.11
hued 362.16
prejudiced 527.12

specious 616.27
colored person 418.3
colorfast 362.17
colorful bright 362.18
gaudy 904.20
variegated 374.9
coloring
n. applying color 362.11
blushing 908.5
color 362.1
coloring matter 362.8
fakery 616.3
falsification 616.9
meaning 545.1
misrepresentation 573.1
painting 574.5
reddening 368.3
timbre 450.3
adj. colorative 362.15
reddening 368.11
color instrument 362.24
colorless hueless 363.7
uninteresting 883.6
colors flag 569.6
flowery language 601.4
rallying device 797.16
colossal high 207.19
huge 195.20
large 34.7
tall 207.21
colosseum 802.1
colossus giant 195.13
strong man 159.6
tower 207.11
colt boy 125.5
horse 414.10
young horse 125.8
coltish childish 124.11
frisky 870.14
column base 216.8
book part 605.13
cylinder 255.4
memorial 570.12
military unit 800.19
pillar 217.5
procession 71.3
tower 207.11
columnar 255.11
columnist
author 602.15
journalist 605.22
coma stupor 712.6
unconsciousness 423.2
comatose
apathetic 856.13
asleep 712.22
sleepy 712.21
unconscious 423.8
comb billow 395.22
groom 681.21
ransack 485.32
combat
n. contention 796.1
fight 796.4
warfare 797.1
v. contend 796.14
oppose 790.4
combatant fighter 800

come to light
appear 446.8
be discovered 488.9
be revealed 556.8
come to mind
be remembered
537.16
occur to 478.18
come to nothing
be destroyed 693.23
be lost 812.6
be unproductive
166.3
fail 725.12
miscarry 314.3
neutralize 178.7
come to pass
come true 516.11
occur 151.5
come to terms
agree 521.10
make peace 804.10
strike a bargain
827.18
surrender 765.8
come true
come about 516.11
occur 151.5
come up against
contend with 796.16
find 488.3
meet 200.11
come upon
arrive at 300.7
be unexpected 540.6
find 488.3
meet 200.11
comeuppance
deserts 960.3
reprisal 955.2
come what may
necessarily 639.16
perseveringly 625.9
resolutely 624.20
without fail 513.26
comfit 308.39
comfort
n. aid 785.1
condolence 946.1
consolation 887.4
contentment 868.1
cover 228.10
ease 887
pleasure 865.1
prosperity 728.1
rest 711.1
v. abet 785.14
aid 785.11
console 946.2
reassure 887.6
comfortable
comfy 887.11
contented 868.7
homelike 191.33
pleased 865.12
prosperous 728.12
restful 711.10
wealthy 837.13
comfortably 887.14
comforter
consoler 887.5
cover 228.10

comforting
condolent 946.3
consoling 887.13
comfort station
rest room 192.26
toilet 311.10
comic
n. cartoon 574.17
comedian 612.9
humorist 881.12
adj. comical 880.5
theatrical 611.40
comical 880.5
comic book
booklet 605.9
cartoon 574.17
coming
n. advancing 296.1
advent 121.5
appearance 446.1
arrival 300.1
imminence 152.1
adj. approaching
296.4
arriving 300.9
due 960.7
emerging 303.18
eventual 151.11
future 121.8
imminent 152.3
successful 724.13
coming and going 323.5
coming out
inauguration 68.5
party 922.14
comma pause 144.4
punctuation mark
586.18
command
n. commandment 752
computer 349.19
control 741.2
direction 747.1
governance 739.5
precept 751.1
skill 733.1
supremacy 36.3
understanding 475.3
view 444.3
will 621.1
v. direct 747.8
dominate 207.16
govern 741.12
know well 475.13
order 752.9
possess 808.4
will 621.2
commandant
commissioned officer
749.18
governor 749.5
jailer 761.10
commandeer
appropriate 822.20
draft 780.16
commander
commissioned officer
749.18
governor 749.5
naval officer 749.20
ship's officer 276.7
superior 36.4

commanding
authoritative 739.15
directing 747.12
governing 741.18
imperative 752.14
commandment
command 752.1
precept 751.2
command of language
diction 588.2
eloquence 600.1
commandos 800.14
command post 226.6
comme ci comme ça
680.7
commemorate 877.2
commemoration
anniversary 137.4
celebration 877.1
memento 537.7
commemorative
celebrative 877.3
memorial 537.27
commence 68.7
commencement
beginning 68.1
ceremony 646.4
source 153.5
commend
approve 968.11
commit 818.16
commendable
good 674.12
praiseworthy 968.20
commendation
approval 968.3
commitment 818.2
commendatory 968.16
commensal
cooperating 786.5
eating 307.29
symbiotic 13.15
commensurate
agreeing 26.9
comparable 491.8
equal 30.7
satisfactory 868.11
sufficient 661.6
comment
n. commentary 606.2
communication
594.1
criticism 494.2
explanatory remark
552.5
remark 594.4
v. remark 594.25
commentary
addition 41.2
comment 552.5
treatise 606.2
commentator
broadcaster 344.23
critic 494.7
expositor 606.4
interpreter 552.7
comment upon
discuss 597.12
explain 552.11
judge 494.14
write upon 606.5

commerce
business 656.1
communication
554.1
copulation 419.8
social intercourse
922.4
trade 827
commercial
n. advertisement
559.6
announcement
344.20
radio broadcast
344.18
adj. business 827.21
vocational 656.15
commingle 44.11
commiserate
console 946.2
pity 944.3
commissar
autocrat 749.14
delegate 781.2
public official 749.17
commissary
delegate 781.2
hoard 660.1
provider 659.6
provisions 308.5
store 832.6
commission
n. commissioning 780
delegates 781.13
dividend 816.5
injunction 752.2
legislature 742.1
meeting 74.2
payment 841.7
performance 705.2
precept 751.1
receipts 844.1
task 656.2
v. authorize 780.9
command 752.9
delegate 149.7
repair 694.14
commissioner
delegate 781.2
peace officer 699.15
public official 749.17
commit
commission 780.9
consign 818.16
dedicate 816.11
do 705.6
imprison 761.17
obligate 962.12
promise 770.5
commitment
cause 153.10
commission 780.1
consignment 818.2
dedication 816.4
duty 962.1
friendship 927.7
imprisonment 761.4
promise 770.2
resolution 624.1
undertaking 715.1
unselfishness 979.1
zeal 635.2

sociability 922.6
team 788.7
workplace 719.1
comparable
analogous 20.11
approximate 9.8
comparative 491.8
relative 9.7
comparative
comparing 491.8
relative 9.7
comparatively
comparably 491.10
relatively 9.12
to a degree 35.10
compare
be comparable 491.7
liken 491.4
resemble 20.7
comparison
likening 491
similarity 20.1
substitute 149.2
compartment
chamber 192.2
ship 277.27
compartmentalize
49.18
compass
n. boundary 235.3
bounds 235.1
degree 29.1
distance 199.1
environment 233.1
gauge 490.20
guide 748.9
harmonics 463.6
range 179.2
v. accomplish 722.4
enclose 236.5
go around 321.4
succeed with 724.10
surround 233.6
compassion
kindness 938.1
leniency 759.1
pity 944.1
compassionate
kind 938.13
lenient 759.7
pitying 944.7
compatibility
accord 794.1
agreement 26.1
pleasantness 863.1
sociability 922.1
compatible
agreeing 26.9
in accord 794.3
pleasant 863.6
sociable 922.18
compatriot
associate 787.1
fellow citizen 190.5
compel
domineer 741.16
force 756.4
impel 283.10
motivate 648.12
necessitate 639.8
obsess 473.24

compelling
commanding 752.14
compulsory 756.9
motivating 648.25
obsessive 473.34
urgent 672.21
compendious
abridged 607.6
comprehensive 76.7
concise 592.6
short 203.8
compendium 607.1
compensate
atone 1012.4
equalize 30.6
interchange 150.4
make compensation
33.4
make restitution
823.5
pay 841.10
remedy 694.13
retaliate 955.5
compensating
contrary 15.6
offsetting 33.6
paying 841.21
compensation
atonement 1012.1
defense mechanism
690.30
penalty 1009.1
recompense 33
remuneration 841.3
reparation 694.6
reprisal 955.2
restitution 823.2
salary 841.4
compensatory
atoning 1012.7
offsetting 33.6
paying 841.21
restitutive 823.7
retaliatory 955.8
compete
contend against
790.4
contest 796.19
competence
ability 157.2
authority 739.1
preparedness 720.4
skill 733.1
sufficiency 661.1
competent able 157.14
authoritative 739.15
capable 733.22
fitted 720.17
legal 998.10
sufficient 661.6
competently
ably 157.16
skillfully 733.29
sufficiently 661.8
competition
opposition 790.2
rivalry 796.2
competitive
competing 796.24
opposing 790.8
competitor
athlete 878.20

combatant 800.1
opponent 791.2
compilation
book 605.4
collection 74.11
compile 74.18
complacence 868.2
complacent
contented 868.10
vain 909.8
complain
accuse 1005.7
be sick 686.43
groan 875.13
object 522.5
offer resistance 792.3
complainant
accuser 1005.5
malcontent 869.3
complainer
lamenter 875.7
malcontent 869.3
complaining
n. complaint 875.4
adj. discontented
869.5
plaintive 875.16
resistant 792.5
complaint
accusation 1005.1
disapproval 969.1
disease 686.1
grievance 875.4
legal statement
1004.7
objection 522.2
resistance 792.1
complaisant
conformable 82.5
considerate 938.16
courteous 936.14
indulgent 759.8
pleasant 863.6
soft 357.8
submissive 765.12
complement
n. adjunct 41.1
all 54.3
full measure 56.3
group 74.3
likeness 20.3
sailor 276.6
syntax 586.2
team 788.7
v. correlate 13.9
complementary
completing 56.13
reciprocal 13.13
complete
v. develop 148.6
end 70.7
execute 771.10
finish 722.6
fulfill 56.6
include 76.3
make perfect 677.5
perform 705.8
adj. accomplished
722.12
comprehensive 76.7
ended 70.8
intact 677.7

thorough 34.12
undivided 54.11
unqualified 508.2
whole 56.9
completed 722.11
completely
extremely 34.22
fully 8.13
perfectly 677.10
totally 56.14
complete works 605.4
completion
completing 722.2
execution 771.5
fulfillment 56.4
performance 705.2
result 154.2
complex
n. culture 642.3
obsession 473.13
perplex 46.2
psychological com-
plex 690.29
whole 54.1
adj. complicated 46.4
difficult 731.16
hard to understand
549.14
mixed 44.15
complexion color 362.1
looks 446.4
mode 7.4
nature 5.3
personality tendency
690.14
complexity
abstruseness 549.2
difficulty 731.1
intricacy 46
compliance
assent 521.1
conformity 82.1
consent 775.1
indulgence 759.2
obedience 766.1
observance 768.1
resignation 861.2
submission 765.1
willingness 622.1
compliant
agreeing 521.13
conformable 82.5
consenting 775.4
indulgent 759.8
obedient 766.3
observant 768.4
pliant 357.9
resigned 861.10
submissive 765.12
usable 665.22
willing 622.5
complicate add 40.4
increase 38.5
involve 46.3
make unintelligible
549.12
complicated
complex 46.4
hard to understand
549.14
complication
abstruseness 549.2

come with child
169.11
create 167.13
imagine 535.14
know 475.12
originate 153.11
phrase 588.4
suppose 499.10
think 478.8
understand 548.7
vivify 407.9
conceived
invented 167.23
known 475.26
concentrate
n. extract 305.8
v. contract 198.7
converge 298.2
densify 354.9
extract 305.16
focus 226.10
increase 38.5
pay attention 530.8
think 478.10
concentrated
attentive 530.15
central 226.14
contracted 198.12
dense 354.12
concentration
attention 530.1
centralization 226.8
contraction 198.1
convergence 298.1
densification 354.3
engrossment 530.3
extract 305.8
extraction 305.7
firmness 624.2
industry 707.6
intensification 38.2
perseverance 625.1
thoughtfulness 478.3
concentration camp
camp 191.29
killing site 409.12
prison 761.8
concentric 226.14
concept belief 501.6
idea 479.1
visualization 535.6
conception belief 501.6
creation 167.5
creative thought
535.2
idea 479.1
intellect 466.1
intelligence 467.1
plan 654.1
pregnancy 169.4
source 153.5
thought 478.1
understanding 475.3
visualization 535.6
conceptual
cognitive 478.21
ideational 479.9
imaginative 535.18
intelligent 467.12
mental 466.8
conceptualize
imagine 535.14

know 475.12
think 478.8
concern
n. affair 151.3
anxiety 890.1
business 656.1
carefulness 533.1
company 788.9
considerateness 938.3
importance 672.1
interest 530.2
relevance 9.4
study 475.10
sympathy 855.5
topic 484.1
workplace 719.1
v. involve 176.2
make attentive
530.12
relate to 9.5
trouble 731.12
upset 890.3
concerned
anxious 890.6
interested 530.16
involved 176.3
concerning 9.13
concert
n. agreement 26.1
concurrence 177.1
cooperation 786.1
music 462.3
music performance
462.34
unanimity 521.5
v. cooperate 786.3
plan 654.9
adj. music 462.52
concert artist 464.1
concerted
concurrent 177.4
cooperating 786.5
concert hall hall 192.4
theater 611.18
concertmaster 464.19
concerto 462.7
concession
acknowledgment
521.3
compromise 807.1
confession 556.3
discount 847.1
giving 818.1
grant 777.5
market 832.1
qualification 507.1
concierge 699.12
conciliar 755.5
conciliate 804.7
conciliatory
forgiving 947.6
pacificatory 804.12
unbelligerent 803.10
concise brief 592.6
short 203.8
taciturn 613.9
conclave
church council 755.4
conference 597.6
meeting 74.2
political convention
744.8

conclude arrange 771.9
complete 722.6
end 70.5
judge 494.10
resolve 624.7
suppose 499.10
conclusion
affirmation 523.1
aftermath 117.2
belief 501.6
compacting 771.4
completion 722.2
end 70.1
judgment 494.4
result 154.2
sequel 67.1
conclusive
certain 513.13
completory 722.9
convincing 501.26
evidential 505.17
final 70.10
mandatory 752.13
unqualified 508.2
concoct
construct 167.10
fabricate 616.18
imagine 535.14
invent 167.13
mix 44.11
plot 654.10
prepare 720.7
concoction
a preparation 720.3
compound 44.5
creation 167.5
fabrication 616.10
product 168.1
concomitant
n. adjunct 41.1
attendant 73.3
contemporary 118.2
adj. accompanying
73.9
concurrent 177.4
simultaneous 118.4
concord accord 794.1
agreement 26.1
cooperation 786.1
harmonics 463.17
music 462.3
order 59.1
treaty 771.2
unanimity 521.5
concordance
accord 794.1
agreement 26.1
concurrence 177.1
cooperation 786.1
music 462.3
reference book 605.6
unanimity 521.5
concordant
agreeing 26.9
concurrent 177.4
conformist 82.6
cooperating 786.5
in accord 794.3
music 462.50
pacific 803.9
unanimous 521.15

concourse
assembly 74.2
concurrence 177.1
convergence 298.1
flow 395.4
gathering 74.1
joining 47.1
concrete
n. building material
378.2
conglomeration 50.5
covering material
228.43
hardness 356.6
pavement 657.7
solid 354.6
v. cover 228.22
plaster 228.25
solidify 356.8
thicken 354.10
adj. dense 354.12
hard 356.10
particular 80.12
substantial 3.6
concubine
mistress 989.17
slave 764.7
wife 933.9
concupiscence
desire 634.1
lasciviousness 989.5
sexual desire 419.5
concur agree 521.9
collaborate 177.2
cooperate 786.3
match 26.6
synchronize 118.3
concurrence
accompaniment 73.1
assembly 74.1
assent 521.1
collaboration 177
convergence 298.1
cooperation 786.1
interaction 13.3
joining 47.1
parallelism 218.1
simultaneity 118.1
unanimity 521.5
concurrent
accompanying 73.9
collaborative 177.4
converging 298.3
cooperating 786.5
joint 47.12
parallel 218.6
simultaneous 118.4
unanimous 521.15
concurrently
concertedly 177.5
cooperatively 786.6
jointly 47.18
simultaneously 118.6
unanimously 521.17
concussion
impact 283.3
impairment 692.8
shock 162.8
condemn
censure 969.13
damn 1008.3
destroy 693.10

pass judgment 494.13
condemnation
  damnation 1008
  disapproval 969.3
  judgment 494.5
  legal decision 1004.9
condemnatory
  accusing 1005.13
  censorious 969.23
  damnatory 1008.5
condemn to death
  409.20
condensation
  abridgment 607.1
  cohesion 50.1
  contraction 198.1
  densification 354.3
  increase 38.2
  shortening 203.3
  trickle 395.7
condense abridge 607.5
  be concise 592.5
  contract 198.7
  densify 354.9
  intensify 38.5
  shorten 203.6
  solidify 356.8
  trickle 395.18
condensed
  abridged 607.6
  concise 592.6
  contracted 198.12
  dense 354.12
  shortened 203.9
condescend
  be arrogant 912.8
  consent 775.2
  deign 906.7
condescending
  arrogant 912.9
  snobbish 912.14
condescension
  arrogance 912.1
  humility 906.3
condign due 960.8
  right 958.8
condiment
  flavoring 428.3
  types of 308.55
condition
  n. circumstance 8.1
  disease 686.1
  preparedness 720.4
  provision 507.2
  rank 29.2
  role 7.5
  state 7.1
  state of affairs 151.4
  stipulation 753.2
  v. accustom 642.11
  indoctrinate 562.13
  limit 234.5
  prepare 720.8
  qualify 507.3
  repair 694.14
  stipulate 507.4
  train 562.14
conditional
  circumstantial 8.7
  dialectic(al) 482.22
  in a state 7.7
  provisional 507.8

conditioned
  accustomed 642.17
  involuntary 639.14
  limited 234.7
  qualified 507.10
  uncertain 514.17
conditioning
  n. habituation 642.8
  indoctrination 562.2
  involuntariness 639.5
  preparation 720.2
  psychological condi-
    tioning 690.33
  training 562.3
  adj. addictive 642.20
condolence
  consolation 946
  pity 944.1
  reassurance 887.4
condom 687.23
condominium
  apartment house
    191.15
  participation 815.1
condone accept 861.6
  be broad-minded
    526.7
  overlook 947.4
  permit 777.10
condoned 947.7
condoning 526.11
conduce cause 153.13
  further 785.17
  tend 174.3
conducive
  helpful 785.21
  instrumental 658.6
  tending to 174.5
conduct
  n. behavior 737.1
  management 747.1
  operation 164.1
  performance 705.2
  v. channel 396.19
  direct to 290.7
  escort 73.8
  manage 747.8
  music 462.46
  operate 164.5
  perform 705.8
  practice 705.7
  transport 271.11
conductance
  electric conduction
    342.13
  electronics 343.9
conduction
  electric conduction
    342.13
  transference 271.1
conductor
  director 748.1
  electric conduction
    342.13
  escort 73.5
  leader 748.6
  operator 164.4
  symphony 464.17
  trainman 274.13
conduit channel 396.1
  passageway 657.4

condyle 256.3
cone funnel 255.5
  inflorescence 411.25
  loudspeaker 450.8
conelrad
  civil defense 799.2
  radiotechnology
    344.2
confab
  conference 597.6
  conversation 597.3
confection
  a preparation 720.3
  compound 44.5
  sweets 308.39
confectionery
  store 832.4
  sweets 308.39
confederacy
  affiliation 786.2
  association 788.1
  combination 52.1
  intrigue 654.6
confederate
  n. accomplice 787.3
  associate 787.1
  v. accompany 73.7
  cooperate 786.3
  join 52.4
  adj. joined 52.6
confederation
  affiliation 786.2
  association 788.1
  combination 52.1
confer advise 754.5
  give 818.12
  hold conference
    597.11
  transfer property
    817.3
conference
  audition 448.2
  church council 755.4
  congress 597.6
  council 755.1
  diocese 1037.8
  discussion 597.7
confess
  acknowledge 521.11
  attend rites 1040.21
  attribute to 155.4
  express belief 501.12
  own up 556.7
confessed 521.14
confession
  acknowledgment
    521.3
  apology 1012.2
  attribution 155.2
  owning up 556.3
  profession of belief
    501.7
  rite 1040.4
  sect 788.5
confessional
  n. church part 1042.9
  adj. disclosive 556.11
  doctrinal 501.27
confessions 608.4
confessor
  penitent 873.5
  priest 1038.5

confetti 374.6
confidant advisor 754.3
  friend 928.1
  right-hand man 787.7
confide
  be hopeful 888.7
  commit 818.16
  divulge 556.5
  inform 557.11
confide in
  believe in 501.15
  trust 501.17
confidence belief 501.1
  equanimity 858.3
  expectation 539.1
  fearlessness 893.3
  hope 888.1
  secret 614.5
  sureness 513.5
confidence game 618.9
confidence man 619.4
confident
  believing 501.21
  composed 858.13
  expectant 539.11
  hopeful 888.11
  sure 513.21
  unafraid 893.19
confidential 614.14
confidentially 614.20
confiding artless 736.5
  trusting 501.22
configuration
  aspect 446.3
  characteristic 80.4
  constellation 375.5
  form 246.1
  gestalt 690.39
  outline 235.2
confine
  n. boundary 235.3
  enclosure 236.3
  v. delay 132.8
  enclose 236.6
  imprison 761.12
  limit 234.5
  narrow 205.11
  restrain 760.9
  specialize 81.4
confined
  enclosed 236.10
  imprisoned 761.19
  laid up 686.55
  limited 234.7
  local 180.9
  narrow 205.14
  restrained 760.15
  specialized 81.5
confinement
  birth 167.7
  enclosure 236.1
  imprisonment 761
  limitation 234.2
  narrowness 205.1
  punishment 1010.2
  restriction 760.3
confines bounds 235.1
  nearness 200.1
  neighborhood 180.1
confining
  enclosing 236.11
  limiting 234.9

879

restraining 760.12
confirm
accustom 642.11
collate 491.5
establish 142.9
make certain 513.12
minister 1040.19
ratify 521.12
secure 772.9
strengthen 159.11
substantiate 505.12
test 489.8
confirmation
collation 491.2
establishment 142.2
making certain 513.8
ratification 521.4
rite 1040.4
sacrament 1040.5
substantiation 505.5
confirmed
established 142.13
habituated 642.21
proved 505.21
ratified 521.14
tried 489.12
true 516.12
confiscate 822.20
conflagrate 329.22
conflagration 328.13
conflict
n. contention 796.1
contrariety 15.1
counteraction 178.1
disaccord 795.1
disagreement 27.1
fight 796.4
hostility 929.3
opposition 790.2
psychological stress
690.21
v. be dissonant 461.3
be inharmonious
795.8
clash in color 362.14
counteract 178.6
differ 16.5
disagree 27.5
oppose 15.4
conflicting
adverse 729.13
clashing 461.5
clashingly colored
362.20
contrary 15.6
counteractive 178.8
disaccordant 795.15
hostile 929.10
opposing 790.8
confluence
assembly 74.1
concurrence 177.1
convergence 298.1
flow 395.4
joining 47.1
conform agree 26.6
assent 521.9
comply 82.3
heed 768.2
obey 766.2
observe the proprie-
ties 645.4

conformation
agreement 26.1
compliance 82.1
form 246.1
shaping 246.5
structure 245.1
conformist
conformer 82.2
conventionalist 645.3
imitator 22.4
conformity
agreement 26.1
compliance 82
custom 642.1
obedience 766.1
observance 768.1
piety 1028.1
similarity 20.1
social convention
645.1
symmetry 248.1
confound
astonish 920.6
be undiscriminating
493.3
complicate 46.3
corrupt 692.14
curse 972.5
defeat 727.9
destroy 693.10
disarrange 63.3
dismay 891.27
embarrass 866.15
perplex 514.13
refute 506.5
thwart 730.15
confounded
astonished 920.9
complex 46.4
damned 972.10
defeated 727.14
disproved 506.7
perplexed 514.24
confront
approach 296.3
be imminent 152.2
compare 491.4
contrapose 239.4
defy 793.3
face 240.8
meet 200.11
offer resistance 792.3
oppose 790.5
stand up to 893.11
thwart 730.15
confrontation
comparison 491.1
conference 597.6
contraposition 239.1
contrariety 15.1
meeting 200.4
confronting
contrary 15.6
opposite 239.5
Confucius
religious founder
1022.4
wise man 468.2
confuse
be undiscriminating
493.3
complicate 46.3

deform 247.3
disorder 62.9
embarrass 866.15
fluster 532.7
make uncertain
514.14
muddle 63.3
confused
bewildered 514.23
chaotic 62.16
clashing 461.5
complex 46.4
disarranged 63.5
distressed 866.22
flustered 532.12
formless 247.4
indefinite 514.18
indistinct 445.6
shy 908.12
confusion chaos 62.2
discomfiture 727.2
fluster 532.3
formlessness 247.1
lawlessness 740.2
mortification 866.4
noncohesion 51.1
perplexity 514.3
shyness 908.4
confute
counteract 178.6
rebut 486.5
refute 506.5
con game 618.9
congeal cohere 50.6
freeze 334.11
thicken 354.10
congealed
frozen 334.14
thickened 354.14
congenial agreeing 26.9
friendly 927.14
in accord 794.3
pleasant 863.6
relative 9.7
similar 20.13
sociable 922.18
congeniality
accord 794.1
agreement 26.1
friendship 927.1
pleasantness 863.1
similarity 20.2
sociability 922.1
congenital innate 5.7
thorough 56.10
congeries
accumulation 74.9
combination 52.1
joining 47.1
congest densify 354.9
fill 56.7
overload 663.15
stop 266.7
congested
blocked 266.11
dense 354.12
full 56.11
overfull 663.20
congestion
density 354.1
fullness 56.2
obstruction 266.3

overfullness 663.3
conglomerate
n. accumulation 74.9
company 788.9
conglomeration 50.5
miscellany 74.13
rock 384.1
solid 354.6
v. assemble 74.18
cohere 50.6
mix 44.11
adj. assembled 74.21
mixed 44.15
conglomeration
accumulation 74.9
cohesion 50.1
combination 52.1
conglomerate 50.5
hodgepodge 44.6
joining 47.1
miscellany 74.13
solid 354.6
congratulate
compliment 968.14
felicitate 948.2
congratulation
compliment 948
praise 968.5
congratulations! 948.4
congregate 74.16
congregation
audience 448.6
church council 755.4
convention 74.2
gathering 74.1
laity 1039.1
worshiper 1032.9
congress assembly 74.2
communication
554.1
conference 597.6
convergence 298.1
copulation 419.8
council 755.1
legislature 742.1
social intercourse
922.4
Congress 742.2
congressional district
district 180.5
election district
744.16
congressman 746.3
congruence
agreement 26.1
sameness 14.1
congruent
agreeing 26.9
identical 14.8
congruity
agreement 26.1
conformity 82.1
symmetry 248.1
congruous
agreeing 26.9
expedient 670.5
conic(al) 255.12
conjectural
theoretical 499.13
uncertain 514.16
conjecture
n. assumption 499.3

reactionary 745.17
right-wing 243.4
unprogressive 140.8
Conservative 744.27
conservatory
arbor 191.13
nursery 413.11
school 567.9
storage place 660.6
conserve
n. sweets 308.39
v. care for 699.19
preserve 701.7
reserve 660.12
consider
allow for 507.5
be considerate 938.10
believe 501.11
care 533.6
discuss 597.12
judge 494.8
reflect 478.12
suppose 499.10
think of 478.16
considerable
authoritative 739.15
important 672.16
large 195.16
numerous 101.6
powerful 34.6
considerably 34.15
considerate
careful 533.10
courteous 936.14
judicious 467.19
thoughtful 938.16
consideration
argument 482.5
attention 530.1
belief 501.6
carefulness 533.1
contemplation 478.2
discussion 597.7
esteem 914.3
gratuity 818.5
importance 672.1
judgment 494.5
judiciousness 467.7
motive 648.1
offset 33.2
recompense 841.3
respect 964.1
thoughtfulness 938.3
considered
intentional 653.9
logical 482.21
considering 155.9
consign
commission 780.9
commit 818.16
imprison 761.17
send 271.14
transfer 271.9
transfer property
817.3
consignee agent 781.3
recipient 819.3
consignment
commission 780.1
freight 271.7
giving 818.2

property transfer
817.1
remand 761.4
consistency
agreement 26.1
conformity 82.1
continuity 50.2
density 354.1
intelligibility 548.2
symmetry 248.1
tenacity 50.3
uniformity 17.1
consistent
agreeing 26.9
consecutive 50.11
faithful 974.20
intelligible 548.10
uniform 17.5
valid 516.13
consistent with 82.9
consist of 58.3
consolation
comfort 887.4
condolence 946.1
consolation prize 916.2
console
n. automation 349.15
keyboard 465.20
radio 344.7
radio receiver 344.3
v. comfort 887.6
condole with 946.2
consolidate
combine 52.3
contract 198.7
cooperate 786.3
densify 354.9
intensify 38.5
consolidated
combined 52.5
contracted 198.12
dense 354.12
consolidation
affiliation 786.2
cohesion 50.1
combination 52.1
contraction 198.1
densification 354.3
intensification 38.2
consommé 308.10
consonance
agreement 26.1
music 462.3
rhyme 609.10
uniformity 17.1
consonant
n. speech sound
594.13
adj. agreeing 26.9
music 462.50
phonetic 594.31
uniform 17.5
consort
accompanier 73.4
agreement 26.1
associate 787.1
companion 928.3
music 462.3
spouse 933.7
consortium
association 788.9
compact 771.1

understanding 26.2
consort with
accompany 73.7
be sociable 922.16
conspectus
abridgment 203.3
synopsis 607.1
conspicuous
clearly visible 444.7
manifest 555.12
notable 672.18
prominent 914.17
striking 34.10
conspicuous
consumption 854.1
conspicuously
exceptionally 34.20
famously 914.21
importantly 672.24
manifestly 555.16
visibly 444.8
conspiracy
chicanery 618.4
combination 52.1
concurrence 177.1
intrigue 654.6
stratagem 735.3
conspirator
schemer 654.8
traitor 619.10
conspire concur 177.2
cooperate 786.3
join 52.4
plot 654.10
constable 699.15
constabulary
jurisdiction 1000.4
police 699.17
constancy
continuity 71.1
durability 110.1
fidelity 974.7
firmness 624.2
frequency 135.2
friendship 927.7
monotony 17.2
permanence 140.1
perpetuity 112.1
perseverance 625.1
regularity 137.1
stability 142.1
uniformity 17.1
constant
n. atomic 326.26
adj. dyed 362.17
enduring 110.10
exact 516.16
faithful 974.20
firm 624.12
friendly 927.7
habitual 642.16
monotonous 71.8
observant 768.4
permanent 140.7
perpetual 112.7
persevering 625.7
regular 137.6
unbroken 135.5
unchangeable 142.17
uniform 17.5
constantly always 17.8
faithfully 974.25

perpetually 112.10
regularly 137.9
steadily 135.7
unceasingly 71.10
constellation
famous persons 914.9
fate 640.2
stars 375.5,28
consternation 891.1
constipated 266.11
constipation
disease symptom
686.8
indigestion 686.28
obstruction 266.3
constituency
electorate 744.22
membership 788.12
population 190.1
sphere of influence
172.4
constituent
n. component 58.2
ingredient 194.1
material 376.2
adj. component 58.5
essential 5.8
selective 637.23
constitute
compose 58.3
create 167.12
legalize 998.8
legislate 742.18
constitution
arrangement 60.1
composition 58.1
law 998.6
legislation 742.13
nature 5.3
production 167.4
structure 245.1
temperament 525.3
constitutional
n. exercise 716.6
walk 273.12
adj. governmental
741.17
healthful 683.5
innate 5.7
legal 998.10
temperamental 525.7
constrain compel 756.4
confine 761.12
moderate 163.6
necessitate 639.8
restrain 760.7
constrained
modest 908.11
restrained 760.13
reticent 613.10
tempered 163.11
constraint
compulsion 756.1
confinement 761.1
modesty 908.3
prudence 163.1
restraint 760.1
reticence 613.3
self-control 624.5
temperance 992.1
urge 648.6
constrict close 266.6

contract 198.7
 narrow 205.11
 obstruct 730.12
constricted
 closed 266.9
 contracted 198.12
 narrow 205.14
 narrow-minded
  527.10
constriction
 contraction 198.1
 hindrance 730.1
 narrowing 205.2
construct
 n. building 245.2
 v. compose 58.3
 create 167.10
 structure 245.8
construction
 building 245.2
 composition 58.1
 interpretation 552.1
 manufacture 167.3
 meaning 545.3
 phrase 585.1
 structure 245.1
 word 582.4
constructive
 creative 167.19
 helpful 785.21
 interpretative 552.14
construe
 interpret 552.9
 render 552.12
consul 781.6
consulate house 191.6
 mastership 739.7
 office 719.8
consult 597.11
consultant
 advisor 754.3
 expert 733.11
consultation
 advice 754.1
 conference 597.6
consume burn 329.25
 deplete 812.5
 destroy 693.10
 deteriorate 692.22
 disintegrate 53.3
 eat 307.20
 shrink 198.9
 use 665.13
 use up 666.2
 waste 854.4
 wear away 39.6
consumed
 burned 329.30
 lost 812.7
 reduced 39.10
 shrunk 198.13
 used up 666.4
 wasted 854.9
consumer buyer 828.5
 eater 307.14
 user 665.9
consumerism 828.1
consuming
 destructive 693.26
 engrossing 530.20
 unpleasant 864.23

consummate
 v. accomplish 722.4
 top 211.9
 adj. complete 722.12
 outright 34.12
 perfect 677.9
 thorough 56.10
 top 211.10
consummation
 accomplishment
  722.1
 completion 56.4
 culmination 677.3
 end 70.1
 result 154.2
consumption
 destruction 693.1
 deterioration 692.4
 eating 307.1
 erosion 39.3
 loss 812.2
 shrinking 198.3
 tuberculosis 686.15
 use 665.1
 using up 666
consumptive
 n. sick person 686.40
 adj. contractive
  198.11
 destructive 693.26
 diseased 686.57
contact
 n. communication
  554.1
 go-between 781.4
 nearness 200.5
 touch 425.1
 v. be heard 448.13
 come in contact
  200.10
 communicate with
  554.8
contact lens 443.2
contagious
 communicable
  554.11
 infectious 686.58
 poisonous 684.7
 transferable 271.17
contain close 266.6
 enclose 236.5
 entail 76.4
 include 76.3
 internalize 225.6
 limit 234.5
 restrain 760.7
 total 54.8
contained in 58.4
container
 enclosure 236.3
 receptacle 193
containment
 foreign policy 744.5
 surrounding 233.5
contaminate
 adulterate 44.13
 corrupt 692.14
 defile 682.17
 infect 686.48
 radioactivate 327.9
contaminated
 diseased 686.56

 morally corrupt
  981.14
 radioactive 327.10
 unclean 682.20
 unhealthful 684.5
contemn disdain 966.3
 reject 638.2
contemplate
 consider 478.12
 expect 539.5
 foresee 542.5
 intend 653.7
 look upon 478.17
 scrutinize 439.15
 study 564.12
 think of 478.16
contemplation
 consideration 478.2
 engrossment 530.3
 expectation 539.1
 foresight 542.1
 inaction 706.1
 prayer 1032.4
 quiescence 268.1
 scrutiny 439.6
 study 564.3
contemporaneous
 present 120.2
 simultaneous 118.4
contemporary
 n. simultaneity 118.2
 adj. modern 122.13
 present 120.2
 simultaneous 118.4
contempt
 defiance 793.1
 deprecation 969.2
 disdain 966
 impudence 913.2
 indignity 965.2
 rejection 638.1
contemptible
 bad 675.9
 base 915.12
 offensive 864.18
 paltry 673.18
contemptuous
 arrogant 912.13
 condemnatory 969.23
 defiant 793.7
 disdainful 966.8
 disparaging 971.13
 impudent 913.9
 rejecting 638.4
contend affirm 523.4
 argue 482.16
 contest 796.14
 contrapose 239.4
 dispute 796.22
 insist 753.7
 oppose 790.4
 struggle 716.11
contender
 combatant 800.1
 competitor 791.2
contend for
 defend 1006.10
 strive for 796.21
 try for 714.8
contend with
 fight with 796.18
 offer resistance 792.3

 treat 665.12
content capacity 195.2
 components 194.1
content
 n. contentment 868.1
 pleasure 865.1
 v. satisfy 868.4
 adj. agreeing 521.13
 consenting 775.4
 pleased 865.12
 satisfied 868.7
 willing 622.5
contention
 argumentation 482.4
 contraposition 239.1
 disaccord 795.1
 hostility 929.3
 opposition 790.1
 quarrel 795.5
 strife 796
contentious
 aggravating 885.5
 argumentative 482.19
 quarrelsome 951.26
 warlike 797.25
contents book 605.12
 components 58.2
 list 88.2
 what is contained
  194
conterminous
 adjacent 200.16
 simultaneous 118.4
contest
 n. contention 796.1
 game 878.9
 match 796.3
 v. argue 482.16
 challenge 503.6
 contend 796.14
 contend against
  790.4
 contradict 790.6
 deny 524.4
 dispute 796.22
contestant
 combatant 800.1
 competitor 791.2
 player 878.19
context
 circumstance 8.2
 environment 233.1
contiguity
 juxtaposition 200.3
 relationship 9.1
contiguous 200.16
continence
 abstinence 992.2
 celibacy 934.1
 chastity 988.3
 limitation 234.2
 moderation 163.1
continent
 n. mainland 386
 region 180.6
 adj. abstinent 992.10
 chaste 988.6
continental
 n. mainlander 386.3
 adj. mainland 386.6
contingency
 an uncertainty 514.8

heater 329.10
kitchen 330.3
cookie 308.42
cooking cookery 330
  heating 329.1
  styles of 330.9
cookout 307.6
cook up create 167.13
  fabricate 616.18
  improvise 630.8
  plot 654.10
  prearrange 641.3
cool
  n. cold 333.1
  composure 858.2
  moderation 163.1
  stability 142.1
  unastonishment
    921.1
  v. calm 163.7
  disincline 652.4
  pacify 804.7
  refrigerate 334.10
  restrain 760.7
  adj. aloof 912.12
  calm 268.12
  cold 333.12
  coloring 362.15
  composed 858.12
  equable 163.13
  excellent 674.13
  feeling cold 333.15
  indifferent 636.6
  insolent 913.8
  reticent 613.10
  sensible 467.18
  stable 142.12
  unastonished 921.3
  unfeeling 856.9
  unfriendly 929.9
  unsociable 923.6
coolant 334.7
cooler chiller 334.3
  prison 761.9
coolie 271.5
cool it
  calm oneself 858.7
  stop 144.15
  take it easy 732.11
cool off
  calm oneself 858.7
  order 59.4
  restrain 760.7
cool one's heels
  await 539.8
  do nothing 706.2
  wait 132.14
coon's age 110.4
coop
  n. chicken house
    191.22
  enclosure 236.3
  place of confinement
    761.7
  prison 761.9
  v. confine 761.12
  enclose 236.5
co-op 832.1
cooperate agree 26.6
  be willing 622.3
  collaborate 786.3
  concur 177.2

interact 13.8
reciprocate 150.4
share 815.6
cooperation
  agreement 26.1
  collaboration 786
  concurrence 177.1
  interaction 13.3
  participation 815.2
  reciprocity 150.1
  sociability 922.6
cooperative
  n. association 788.1
  market 832.1
  adj. agreeing 26.9
  coacting 786.5
  communal 815.9
  concurrent 177.4
  helpful 785.22
  willing 622.5
co-opt 637.13
coordinate
  n. likeness 20.3
  v. equalize 30.6
  make agree 26.7
  organize 60.10
  symmetrize 248.3
  adj. concurrent 177.4
  equivalent 30.8
  symmetric 248.4
coordinated 733.20
coordinates
  bounds 235.1
  measurement 490.6
coordination
  adjustment 26.4
  automation 349.7
  equalization 30.2
  organization 60.2
  skill 733.1
  symmetrization 248.2
cop
  n. cone 255.5
  policeman 699.16
  v. steal 824.13
cop a plea
  confess 556.7
  get off 632.7
cope compete 796.19
  cover 228.19
  make shift 670.4
  survive 659.12
cope with
  behave toward 737.6
  contend with 796.18
  perform 705.8
  treat 665.12
copious
  abundant 101.8
  diffuse 593.11
  numerous 34.8
  plentiful 661.7
  productive 165.9
  voluminous 195.17
cop out
  compromise 807.2
  get off 632.7
  remain neutral 806.5
  seclude oneself 924.6
cop-out
  compromise 807.1
  excuse 1006.4

neutrality 806.1
copper
  n. currency metals
    835.20
  policeman 699.16
  US money 835.7
  adj. metal 383.17
  reddish-brown 367.4
copse bunch 74.7
  grove 411.12
  thicket 411.13
copulate
  come together 74.16
  have sex 419.23
  join 47.5
  make love 932.13
  procreate 169.8
copy
  n. diagram 654.3
  edition 605.2
  image 572.3
  imitation 22.3
  music 462.28
  news 558.3
  picture 574.12
  printer's copy 603.4
  representation 24
  reproduction 169.1
  substitute 149.2
  the same 14.3
  written matter 602.10
  v. art 574.20
  borrow 821.4
  duplicate 91.3
  imitate 22.5
  impersonate 572.9
  remake 169.7
  repeat 103.7
  replicate 14.6
  reproduce 24.8
  resemble 20.7
  write 602.19
copyboy
  attendant 750.5
  errand boy 561.4
copycat 22.4
copyhold 810.5
copying machine
  603.25
copyist artist 579.1
  imitator 22.4
  writer 602.13
copyreader
  journalist 605.22
  proofreader 603.13
copyright
  n. restriction 234.3
  right 958.4
  safeguard 699.3
  v. limit 234.5
  preserve 701.7
  protect 699.18
copywriter
  author 602.15
  publicist 559.9
coquetry
  flirtation 932.8
  trifling 673.8
coquette flirt 932.10
  sweetheart 931.10
  tempter 650.3

coquettish
  alluring 650.7
  amatory 932.21
  fickle 629.6
Cora
  agriculture divinity
    413.4
  deity of nether world
    1019.5
  goddess 1014.5
coral reef island 386.2
  point of land 256.8
  shoal 210.2
cord string 206.2,9
  wood 378.3
cordage capacity 195.2
  ropework 206.3
cordial
  n. refresher 695.1
  tonic 687.8
  types of 996.41
  adj. fervent 855.23
  genial 927.15
  good-natured 938.14
  hospitable 925.11
  informal 647.3
  pleasing 863.6
  refreshing 695.3
cordon
  n. award 916.5
  guard 699.9
  obstacle 730.4
  quarantine 761.2
  v. enclose 236.5
  quarantine 761.13
  segregate 77.6
cordon bleu
  award 916.5
  expert 733.11
corduroy
  n. fabric 378.11
  rough surface 261.2
  adj. grooved 263.4
core
  n. center 226.2
  city district 183.6
  content 194.5
  essence 5.2
  important point
    672.6
  interior 225.2
  middle 69.1
  summary 607.2
  adj. middle 69.4
cork
  n. bark 229.2
  float 277.11
  lightness 353.2
  stopper 266.4
  v. blacken 365.7
  cap 228.21
  confine 761.12
  retain 813.5
  stop 266.7
  suppress 760.8
corkscrew
  n. curl 254.2
  extractor 305.9
  opener 265.11
  v. twist 254.4
  adj. spiral 254.8

corn
n. fodder 308.4
grain 411.5,46
old joke 881.9
platitude 517.3
swelling 256.4
tumor 686.36
v. preserve 701.8
corn belt 182.1
corncob pipe 434.6
plant part 411.27
corncrib 660.7
corneous 356.10
corner
n. angle 251.2
deviation 291.1
hiding place 615.4
impasse 731.5
monopoly 808.3
nook 192.3
recess 257.7
stock manipulation
833.20
v. buy up 828.7
monopolize 808.6
place in difficulty
731.15
stock market 833.26
turn 321.5
cornered angular 251.6
at an impasse 731.23
in danger 697.13
cornerstone
foundation 216.7
important point
672.6
cornet brass wind 465.8
cone 255.5
organ stop 465.22
corn-fed 195.18
cornice 211.5,17
cornify 356.7
cornucopia
horn of plenty 661.3
source of supply
660.4
store 660.1
corny 883.9
corollary adjunct 41.1
attendant 73.3
conclusion 494.4
result 154.1
corona
chandelier 336.6
cigar 434.4
circle 253.2
flower part 411.26
light 335.14
sun 375.13
coronary
n. cardiovascular dis-
ease 686.17
adj. circular 253.11
heart 225.10
coronation
accession to power
739.12
installation 780.3
coroner
death examiner
408.18
doctor 688.6

coronet circle 253.2
heraldic insignia
569.2
jewel 901.6
royal insignia 569.3
corporal
n. church furnishing
1042.10
noncommissioned of-
ficer 749.19
adj. bodily 376.9
corporal punishment
1010.4
corporate
associated 788.16
joined 52.6
joint 47.12
corporation
company 788.9
workplace 719.1
corporeal 376.9
corps association 788.1
group 74.3
military subdivision
800.19
military unit 800.20
corpse
dead body 408.16
thin person 205.8
corpulent stout 195.18
thick 204.8
corpus all 54.3
body 376.3
collection 74.11
knowledge 475.1
money 835.15
Corpus Christi 1040.15
corpus delicti
corpse 408.16
evidence 505.2
corral acquire 811.8
assemble 74.18
drive animals 416.8
enclose 236.5
correct
v. conform 82.3
disillusion 520.2
punish 1010.10
remedy 694.13
reprove 969.17
revise 691.12
adj. accurate 516.15
conventional 645.5
grammatical 586.17
mannerly 936.16
meticulous 533.12
orthodox 1024.7
suitable 958.8
well-chosen 589.7
correction
measurement 490.1
punishment 1010.1
repair 694.6
reproof 969.5
revision 691.4
corrective
n. remedy 687.1
adj. emendatory
691.16
punishing 1010.25
remedial 687.39

correlate
n. counterpart 13.4
likeness 20.3
v. interrelate 13.6
relate 9.6
correlated
correlative 13.10
related 9.9
correlation
comparison 491.1
reciprocation 13
relationship 9.2
correlative
accompanying 73.9
comparable 491.8
correlated 13.10
relative 9.7
similar 20.13
correspond agree 26.6
coincide 14.4
communicate with
554.8
concur 177.2
conform 82.3
equal 30.5
make parallel 218.5
reciprocate 13.9
relate to 9.5
resemble 20.7
write to 604.11
correspondence
accord 794.1
agreement 26.1
communication
554.1
concurrence 177.1
conformity 82.1
correlation 13.1
equality 30.1
identity 14.1
letter writing 604
mail 604.5
record 570.1
similarity 20.1
symmetry 248.1
uniformity 17.1
correspondent
n. accused 1005.6
correlate 13.4
journalist 605.22
letter writer 604.9
likeness 20.3
adj. agreeing 26.9
analogous 20.11
equivalent 30.8
identical 14.8
reciprocal 13.13
uniform 17.5
corresponding
agreeing 26.9
analogous 20.11
conformist 82.6
equivalent 30.8
identical 14.8
in accord 794.3
reciprocal 13.13
corridor
aviation 278.42
district 180.1
entrance 302.5
hall 192.18
passageway 657.4

corrigible
improvable 691.17
manageable 765.14
remediable 694.25
corroborate 505.12
corrode decrease 39.6
disintegrate 53.3
eat away 692.24
etch 578.11
corrosion decay 692.6
decrease 39.3
disintegration 53.1
corrosive
n. caustic 329.15
adj. acrimonious
939.21
corrupting 692.45
disintegrative 53.5
harmful 675.12
ill-humored 951.17
strong 600.11
corrugated
grooved 263.4
irregular 261.6
rough 261.7
wrinkled 264.8
corrugation
groove 263.1
rough surface 261.2
wrinkle 264.3
corrupt
v. adulterate 44.13
bribe 651.3
debase 692.14
decay 692.25
defile 682.17
demoralize 981.10
indoctrinate 145.15
misteach 563.3
work evil 675.6
adj. bribable 651.4
corrupted 981.14
decayed 692.41
dishonest 975.16
erroneous 518.16
corruptible
bribable 651.4
mutable 111.7
venal 975.23
corrupting
corrosive 692.45
harmful 675.12
corruption
adulteration 44.3
bribery 651.1
colloquialism 582.6
decay 692.6
deterioration 692.2
distortion 249.2
evil 675.3
filth 682.7
improbity 975.1
indoctrination 145.5
mispronunciation
595.5
misteaching 563.1
solecism 587.2
turpitude 981.5
wordplay 881.8
corsage flowers 411.23
waist 231.15
corsair 825.7

corset supporter 216.2
  undergarment
  231.23,58
cortege
  attendance 73.6
  funeral 410.5
  procession 71.3
cortex armor 799.3
  exterior 224.2
  rind 229.2
  shell 228.15
cosm(o)– 375.1
cosmetic 900.20
cosmetics
  make-up 900.11
  sundries 831.6
cosmic(al) large 34.7
  universal 375.24
cosmology
  astronomy 375.18
  philosophy 500.1
cosmonaut 282.8
cosmopolitan
  n. citizen of the world
  190.4
  sophisticate 733.16
  adj. broad-minded
  526.8
  chic 644.13
  public 417.13
  traveled 273.39
  universal 79.14
  worldly-wise 733.26
cosmos 375.1
cossack 800.11
cosset foster 785.16
  indulge 759.6
  make love 932.14
cost
  n. expenses 843.3
  loss 812.1
  price 846.1
  v. plan expenditures
  843.5
  sell for 846.15
costly 848.11
cost of living
  economics 827.8
  expense 843.3
costume
  n. character dress
  231.9
  clothing 231.1
  suit 231.6
  theater 611.22
  v. outfit 231.40
costume designer
  designer 579.9
  theater man 611.28
costume party 922.11
cot bed 216.33
  cottage 191.9
coterie clique 788.6
  group 74.3
coterminous
  adjacent 200.16
  identical 14.8
  simultaneous 118.4
cottage
  bookbinding 605.16
  cabin 191.9
cottager 190.7

cotton fabric 378.11
  fiber 206.8
  medical dressing
  687.33
cotton belt 182.1
cottontail 414.29,58
cotton to
  be friends 927.9
  fall in love 931.20
  get along with 794.2
cottony 357.15
couch
  n. lair 191.26
  sofa 216.19,32
  v. be low 208.5
  depress 318.4
  lie down 318.11
  lurk 615.9
  phrase 588.4
  rest 711.6
couch, the 690.8
couchant low 208.7
  recumbent 214.8
cough
  n. breathing 403.18
  v. exhale 403.24
cough medicine 687.16
cough up 841.16
council
  advisory body 755
  association 788.1
  cabinet 742.8
  conference 597.6
  directorate 748.11
  meeting 74.2
  tribunal 1001.1
councilman
  legislator 746.3
  public official 749.17
counsel
  n. advice 754.1
  advisor 754.3
  bar 1003.5
  consideration 478.2
  intention 653.1
  lawyer 1003.1
  v. advise 754.5
  confer 597.11
counseling 690.5
counselor advisor 754.3
  lawyer 1003.1
count
  n. account of 87.6
  accusation 1005.1
  amount 28.2
  election returns
  744.21
  nobleman 918.4
  numeration 87.5
  particular 8.3
  sum 86.5
  v. be important
  672.11
  be judged 494.15
  have influence 172.10
  include in 76.3
  judge 494.8
  music 462.45
  number 87.10
  quantify 28.4
countenance
  n. approval 968.1

authorization 777.3
  composure 858.2
  face 240.4
  looks 446.4
  patronage 785.4
  v. abet 785.14
  accept 861.6
  approve 968.9
  encourage 648.21
  permit 777.10
counter
  n. gambling 515.14
  money 835.12
  opposite 15.2
  printing 603.6
  radiation 327.13
  radioactivity 327.6
  rear 241.7
  retaliation 955.1
  showcase 832.10
  table 216.15,29
  v. clash 15.4
  counteract 178.6
  defend 1006.10
  deny 524.4
  disagree 27.5
  fend off 799.10
  oppose 790.3
  retaliate 955.4
  thwart 730.15
  adj. adverse 729.13
  contrary 15.6
  dissimilar 21.4
  opposing 790.8
  reversed 295.12
  adv. in opposition
  790.9
  opposite 239.6
counteract clash 15.4
  contrapose 239.4
  counter 178.6
  offset 33.5
  oppose 790.3
  thwart 730.15
counteraction
  compensation 33.1
  counterworking 178
  opposition 790.1
  resistance 792.1
counterattack
  attack 798.1
  countermeasure
  178.5
counterbalance
  n. counterforce 178.4
  offset 33.2
  opposite 15.2
  weight 352.4
  v. equalize 30.6
  neutralize 178.7
  offset 33.5
  oppose 15.4
  stabilize 142.7
  weigh 352.10
counterclaim
  n. counterdemand
  33.3
  counterstatement
  486.2
  v. rebut 486.5
counterclockwise
  adj. left 244.4

adv. backwards 295.13
  leftward 290.26
  round 322.16
counter-culture 522.1
counterespionage 485.9
counterfeit
  n. copy 24.1
  counterfeit money
  835.10
  fake 616.13
  substitute 149.2
  v. affect 903.12
  coin 835.28
  fabricate 616.18
  fake 616.21
  imitate 22.5
  resemble 20.7
  adj. imitation 22.8
  similar 20.10
  substitute 149.8
  ungenuine 616.26
counterfeiter
  coiner 835.25
  deceiver 619.1
  imitator 22.4
counterfeiting
  coining 835.24
  imitation 22.1
counterforce 178.4
counterintelligence
  intelligence service
  781.12
  spying 485.9
counterirritant
  counteractant 178.3
  drug 687.32
countermand
  n. repeal 779.1
  v. repeal 779.2
  thwart 730.15
countermeasure 178.5
countermine
  n. entrenchment
  799.5
  v. plot 654.10
countermotion 295.4
countermove 670.2
counterorder 779.1
counterpane 228.10
counterpart
  correlate 13.4
  duplicate 24.3
  equal 30.4
  likeness 20.3
counterpoint
  meter 609.9
  music 462.20
  opposite 15.2
counterpose
  compare 491.4
  counteract 178.6
  oppose 15.4
counterproductive
  harmful 675.12
  hindering 730.17
  ineffective 158.15
counterrevolution
  countermeasure
  178.5
  revolution 147.1

countersign
n. identification
568.11
password 568.12
signature 583.10
v. promise 770.4
ratify 521.12
counterspy 781.9
counterstatement
justification 1006.2
rebuttal 486.2
counterstroke
countermeasure
178.5
retaliation 955.1
counter to
counteractively
178.10
in disagreement with
27.10
opposed to 790.10
countervail
be opposite 15.4
counteract 178.6
equalize 30.6
offset 33.5
oppose 790.3
countervallation 236.13
counterweight
counterforce 178.4
offset 33.2
scenery 611.25
stabilizer 142.20
counterword
ambiguous expression
550.2
portmanteau word
582.12
countess 918.6
counting
n. numeration 87.1
adj. inclusive 76.6
countinghouse 832.1
countless infinite 104.3
innumerable 101.10
much 34.8
count on
be hopeful 888.7
believe in 501.16
expect 539.6
plan on 653.6
count one's chickens
before they are
hatched
be optimistic 888.9
be rash 894.5
be wrong 518.11
mishandle 734.14
count out 77.4
countrified 182.7
country
n. jury 1002.7
nation 181
region 180.1
adj. rustic 182.6
country, the
agricultural region
182
land 385.1
country bumpkin 919.9
country club 788.3
country cousin 11.3

country gentleman
809.2
countryman
fellow citizen 190.5
peasant 919.8
country music 462.10
countryside 182.1
county country 181.1
district 180.5
county seat 183.4
coup act 705.3
expedient 670.2
instant 113.3
seizure 822.2
stratagem 735.3
coup de grâce
deathblow 409.10
end-all 70.4
ruin 693.2
coup d'état
revolt 767.4
revolution 147.1
seizure 822.2
couple
n. set 20.5
two 90.2
v. ally 52.4
come together 74.16
copulate 419.23
get married 933.16
join 47.5
join in marriage
933.15
pair 90.5
relate 9.6
coupled
accompanying 73.9
joined 47.13
leagued 52.6
married 933.22
paired 90.8
related 9.9
couplet
poetic division
609.11
two 90.2
coupling joining 47.1
joint 47.4
coupon
certificate 834.5
token 835.12
courage bravery 893
pluck 624.3
sureness 513.5
courageous
brave 893.17
plucky 624.14
courier guide 748.7
messenger 561.1
course
n. arena 802.1
aviation 278.43
career 267.2
channel 396.1
circuit 137.3
continuity 71.2
direction 290.1
dish 308.7
flow 395.4
journey 273.5
layer 227.1
manner 657.1

policy 654.5
process 164.2
progression 294.1
racecourse 878.12
route 657.2
serving 307.10
study 562.8
track 568.8
travel 273.1
trend 174.2
voyage 275.6
v. flow 395.16
hunt 655.9
travel 273.17
traverse 273.19
course of action 670.2
courser horse 414.10
hunter 655.5
speed 269.6
war horse 800.32
court
n. attendance 73.6
council 755.1
courthouse 1001.9
courtship 932.6
enclosure 236.3,12
influential persons
172.6
judiciary 1000.2
legislature 742.1
palace 191.8
playground 878.12
road 657.6
tribunal 1001.2
v. befriend 927.11
curry favor 907.8
solicit 774.14
woo 932.19
courteous polite 936.14
respectful 964.8
sociable 922.18
courtesan 989.15
courtesy
good behavior 737.2
good deed 938.7
polite act 936.6
politeness 936
respect 964.1
sociability 922.1
courthouse
court 1001.9
government building
742.12
town hall 183.5
courtier flatterer 970.4
follower 293.2
sycophant 907.3
courting
courtship 932.6
solicitation 774.5
courtliness
chivalry 936.2
etiquette 646.3
pride 905.2
courtly
dignified 905.12
flattering 970.8
gallant 936.15
court-martial
military court 1001.7
trial 1004.5
courtroom 1001.9

courtship 932.6
courtyard 236.3,12
cousin 11.3
couturier
designer 579.9
dressmaker 231.35
cove arch 252.4
arm of the sea 399.1
cave 257.5
man 420.5
nook 192.3
person 417.3
recess 257.7
coven 1035.8
covenant
n. compact 771.1
v. agree 521.10
contract 771.6
cover
n. blanket 228.10
bookbinding 605.15
concealment 615.2
covering 228.2
dish 308.7
flight 278.11
floor 212.3
hiding place 615.4
lid 228.5
pretext 649.1
protection 699.1
service 307.11
serving 307.10
shade 338.1
shelter 700.3
types of 228.38
v. be pregnant 169.12
bet 515.20
close 266.6
color 362.13
compensate 33.4
conceal 615.6
copulate 419.23
extend 179.7
include 76.3
join 47.5
overrun 313.5
protect 699.18
put on 228.19
shade 338.5
spell 505.7
stop 266.7
traverse 273.19
cover charge fee 846.7
service 307.11
cover girl 900.8
covering
n. coloring 362.12
concealment 615.1
cover 228.2
coverage 228
exterior 224.2
layer 227.2
pregnancy 169.5
adj. coating 228.34
concealing 615.15
inclusive 76.6
protecting 699.23
shading 338.6
covering material
building material
378.2
types of 228.43

cover story 649.1
covert
  n. cover 228.2
  hiding place 615.4
  lair 191.26
  plumage 230.18
  shelter 700.3
  thicket 411.13
  adj. concealed 615.11
  covered 228.31
  latent 546.5
  secret 614.12
cover up conceal 615.6
  cover 228.19
  fake 616.21
  substitute for 149.6
cover-up 649.1
covet crave 634.18
  envy 954.3
covey group 74.3
  large number 101.3
  partridges 74.6
covin chicanery 618.4
  intrigue 654.6
cow
  n. cattle 414.6
  female animal 421.9
  v. domineer 741.16
  intimidate 891.28
coward 892.5
cowardice
  cowardliness 892
  fear 891.1
  irresolution 627.4
  weakness 160.1
cowardly fearful 891.31
  irresolute 627.12
  uncourageous 892.10
  weak 160.12
cowboy herder 416.3
  rider 274.8
cowed cowardly 892.10
  terrified 891.34
cower be servile 907.6
  be weak 160.8
  crouch 318.8
  quail 892.9
cowhide 1011.1
cowl 228.2
cowlick 230.6
co-worker 787.5
cowpuncher
  herder 416.3
  rider 274.8
coxcomb comedy 611.7
  dandy 903.9
coxswain
  boatman 276.8
  pilot 748.7
coy amatory 932.21
  shy 908.12
coyote 414.25,58
cozen 618.17
cozy
  comfortable 887.11
  conversational 597.13
  homelike 191.33
  intimate 922.20
  pleased 865.12
  safe 698.7
CPA 845.7

crab
  n. animal 414.40
  lifter 317.3
  malcontent 869.3
  seafood 308.25
  windlass 287.7
  v. complain 875.13
  fly 278.49
  thwart 730.16
crabbed aged 126.18
  complex 46.4
  hard to understand
    549.14
  irascible 951.19
  sour 432.5
crabby
  discontented 869.5
  grouchy 951.22
crack
  n. attempt 714.2
  blemish 679.1
  break 49.4
  cleft 201.2
  detonation 456.3
  explosive noise 456.1
  fault 678.2
  gibe 967.2
  groove 263.1
  hit 283.4
  impairment 692.8
  instant 113.3
  opening 265.1
  remark 594.4
  short distance 200.2
  snap 456.2
  stripe 374.5
  witticism 881.7
  v. bang 456.6
  become nervous
    859.7
  be damaged 692.26
  blast 456.8
  blemish 679.4
  break 49.12
  cleave 201.4
  explain 552.10
  groove 263.3
  heat 329.24
  hit 283.13
  injure 692.15
  open 265.12
  snap 456.7
  solve 487.2
  adj. skillful 733.20
  superior 674.14
crackbrain 473.15
crack down on
  attack 798.15
  suppress 760.8
cracked
  blemished 679.8
  cleft 201.7
  damaged 692.29
  dissonant 461.4
  insane 473.25
  mentally deficient
    469.22
  raucous 458.15
  severed 49.23
cracker
  backwoodsman
    190.10

biscuit 308.30
dryness 393.2
noisemaker 453.5
crackerjack
  expert 733.13
  good person 985.2
  good thing 674.7
crackle
  n. impairment 692.8
  snap 456.2
  v. snap 456.7
crackling 456.10
crackpot
  eccentric 474.3
  lunatic 473.15
  odd person 85.4
crack shot
  expert 733.11
  shooter 285.9
crack the whip 739.13
crack up
  aviation 278.53
  become exhausted
    717.5
  become nervous
    859.7
  be separated 49.8
  collide 283.12
  disintegrate 53.3
  go mad 473.20
crack-up
  aviation 278.20
  destruction 693.4
  disruption 49.3
  exhaustion 717.2
  impact 283.3
  impairment 692.1
  mental disorder
    690.17
  misfortune 729.2
  sickness 686.7
cradle
  n. bed 216.33
  birthplace 153.8
  infancy 124.5
  native land 181.2
  origin 68.4
  refining equipment
    681.13
  v. calm 163.7
  foster 785.16
  put to bed 712.19
  support 216.21
cradlesong 462.15
craft art 574.3
  cunning 735.1
  deceit 618.3
  ship 277.1
  shrewdness 467.3
  skill 733.1
  stratagem 735.3
  technique 733.7
  vocation 656.6
craftsman artisan 718.6
  artist 579.1
  expert 733.11
  producer 167.8
  types of 718.8
craftsmanship
  manufacture 167.3
  skill 733.1
crafty cunning 735.12

dishonest 975.18
falsehearted 616.31
shrewd 467.15
underhanded 618.20
crag breccia 384.1
  pointed projection
    258.4
  precipice 213.3
craggy rough 261.7
  stony 384.11
cram densify 354.9
  eat 307.23
  fill 56.7
  gluttonize 994.4
  insert 304.7
  overload 663.15
  satiate 664.4
  study up 564.14
  thrust 283.11
  tutor 562.12
crammed
  crowded 74.22
  dense 354.12
  full 56.11
  overfill 663.20
  satiated 664.6
cramp
  n. distress 866.5
  hindrance 730.1
  pain 424.2
  restriction 760.3
  seizure 686.5
  spasm 324.6
  v. contract 198.7
  enclose 236.6
  fasten 47.7
  hamper 730.11
  restrain 760.9
  thwart 730.16
  weaken 160.10
  adj. hard to under-
    stand 549.14
  narrow 205.14
cramped
  contracted 198.12
  enclosed 236.10
  limited 234.7
  little 196.10
  narrow 205.14
  narrow-minded
    527.10
  restrained 760.15
  stilted 590.3
cramp one's style
    730.16
crane
  n. fireplace 329.12
  lifter 317.3
  v. gaze 439.16
  stretch 202.6
craniology
  anthropology 417.7
  phrenology 211.8
cranium 211.7
crank
  n. angle 251.2
  caprice 629.1
  eccentric 474.3
  eccentricity 474.2
  fanatic 473.17
  ill-humored person
    951.11

lever 287.4
malcontent 869.3
odd person 85.4
pillory 1011.3
v. angle 251.5
reel in 287.9
rotate 322.9
adj. eccentric 474.4
cranky
antagonistic 178.8
capricious 629.5
disagreeing 27.6
discontented 869.5
eccentric 474.4
irascible 951.19
cranny crack 201.2
groove 263.1
hiding place 615.4
nook 192.3
crap
n. defecation 311.2
feces 311.4
humbug 616.14
nonsense 547.3
throw of dice 515.10
v. defecate 311.13
crape 875.6
crap out 725.9
crappy bad 675.8
fecal 311.20
filthy 682.23
craps deuce 90.3
dice 515.9
game of chance 515.8
throw of dice 515.10
crash
n. addiction 642.9
aviation 278.20
decrease 39.2
defeat 727.1
descent 316.1
destruction 693.4
explosive noise 456.1
failure 725.3
impact 283.3
insolvency 842.3
misfortune 729.2
stock market 833.5
v. aviation 278.53
bang 456.6
billow 395.22
collide 283.12
descend 316.5
fail 725.11
go bankrupt 842.7
intrude 238.5
shatter 249.13
sleep 712.18
thunder 453.6
crash landing
aviation 278.20
landing 278.18
crass outright 34.12
stupid 469.15
thick 204.8
vulgar 898.11
crate
n. automobile 272.9
storage place 660.6
v. package 236.9
put in 184.14
wrap 228.20

crater basin 257.2
blemish 679.1
pit 209.2
crave desire 634.18
entreat 774.11
request 774.9
craven 892.12
craving
n. addiction 642.9
coveting 634.6
adj. coveting 634.24
craw 193.3
crawl
n. creeping 273.9
slowness 270.2
swimming 275.11
v. be low 208.5
be servile 907.6
creep 273.25
feel creepy 426.7
go slow 270.6
lie 214.5
linger 110.7
crawling
n. creeping 273.9
radio reception
344.21
adj. creeping 273.38
crowded 74.22
obsequious 907.13
permeated 186.15
recumbent 214.8
reptile 414.51
slow 270.10
teeming 101.9
crawl with
abound 661.5
be numerous 101.5
infest 313.6
pervade 186.7
crayon
art equipment 574.19
picture 574.14
craze
n. blemish 679.1
caprice 629.1
enthusiasm 635.3
excitement 857.7
fad 644.5
impairment 692.8
mania 473.12
stripe 374.5
v. blemish 679.4
injure 692.15
madden 473.23
crazy absurd 470.10
distorted 249.10
foolish 470.8
insane 473.25
mentally deficient
469.22
variegated 374.9
crazy about
enthusiastic about
635.12
fond of 931.28
crazy idea
absurd idea 479.7
caprice 629.1
creak
n. shrill sound 458.4
stridulation 458.5

v. sound shrill 458.8
stridulate 458.7
cream
n. cleaning agent
681.17
milk 308.47
ointment 380.3
semiliquid 389.5
superiors 36.5
the best 674.8
v. foam 405.5
make viscid 389.10
overwhelm 727.8
adj. whitish 364.8
yellow 370.4
cream of the crop 674.8
creamy
semiliquid 389.11
soft-colored 362.21
whitish 364.8
yellow 370.4
crease
n. fold 264.1
wrinkle 264.3
v. engrave 578.10
fold 264.5
wrinkle 264.6
create begin 68.10
cause 153.11
form 246.7
imagine 535.14
make 167.10
originate 23.4
creation
beginning 68.1
divine function
1013.16
forming 246.5
origination 167.5
product 168.1
production 167.3
structure 245.1
universe 375.1
work of art 574.11
creative
beginning 68.15
godlike 1013.20
imaginative 535.18
original 23.5
originative 167.19
productive 165.9
creativity genius 467.8
inventiveness 535.3
originality 23.1
creator artist 579.1
doer 718.1
originator 153.4
producer 167.8
creature animal 414.2
associate 787.8
entity 3.3
figurehead 749.4
inferior 37.2
instrument 658.3
organism 406.2
person 417.3
product 168.1
retainer 750.1
sycophant 907.3
creature comfort
comfort 887.3
food 308.1

pleasure 865.1
credence altar 1042.12
belief 501.1
credential
certificate 570.6
recommendation
968.4
credentials 568.11
credibility
believability 501.8
veracity 974.3
credibility gap
insincerity 975.3
unbelievability 503.3
untruthfulness 616.8
credible
believable 501.24
logical 482.20
credit
n. account entry 845.5
attribution 155.1
belief 501.1
believability 501.8
difference 42.8
due 960.2
esteem 914.3
financial credit 839
influence 172.1
receipts 844.1
thanks 949.2
token of esteem
916.1
v. attribute to 155.4
believe 501.10
keep accounts 845.8
place to one's credit
839.5
thank 949.4
creditable
honest 974.13
praiseworthy 968.20
reputable 914.15
credit card 839.3
credited
accredited 839.8
attributed 155.6
believed 501.23
creditor 839.4
credit rating
credit 839.1
financial condition
836.5
credit union
association 788.1
credit 839.1
lending institution
820.4
credo creed 1023.2
religion 1020.1
system of belief
501.3
Credo 1040.10
credulous
easy of belief 502.8
fooled 470.8
trusting 501.22
creed affirmation 523.1
doctrine 1023.2
policy 654.5
religion 1020.1
system of belief
501.3

creedbound
  narrow-minded
    527.10
  orthodox 1024.8
creek
  arm of the sea 399.1
  running water 395.1
creep
  n. creeping 273.9
  obnoxious person
    986.6
  slowness 270.2
  v. be servile 907.6
  crawl 273.25
  feel creepy 426.7
  go slow 270.6
  linger 110.7
  lurk 615.9
creeper 411.4
creep in enter 302.7
  intrude 238.5
  join 788.14
creeping
  n. crawling 273.9
  radio reception
    344.21
  slowness 270.1
  adj. crawling 273.38
  permeated 186.15
  reptile 414.51
  slow 270.10
creeps chill 333.2
  gooseflesh 426.4
  trepidation 891.5
creep up on 540.6
creep with
  abound 661.5
  be numerous 101.5
  infest 313.6
  pervade 186.7
creepy bad 675.8
  crawly 426.11
  spooky 891.39
cremate burn 329.25
  the dead 410.20
cremation
  burning 329.5
  of the dead 410.2
crenellate fortify 799.9
  notch 262.4
crêpe 308.44
crepuscule dusk 134.3
  foredawn 133.4
crescendo
  n. expansion 197.1
  increase 38.1
  loudness 453.1
  music 462.25
  v. become larger
    197.5
  din 453.6
  increase 38.6
  make larger 197.4
  adv. music 462.54
crescent
  n. city district 183.9
  curve 252.5
  heraldic insignia
    569.2
  moon 375.11
  road 657.6
  semicircle 253.8

  adj. crescent-shaped
    252.11
  growing 197.12
  waxing 38.8
crest
  n. feather 230.16
  heraldic insignia
    569.2
  notching 262.2
  peak 207.8
  summit 211.2
  top part 211.4
  wave 323.4
  v. top 211.9
crestfallen
  disappointed 541.5
  glum 872.25
  humiliated 906.13
cretin 471.8
cretinism
  gland disease 686.19
  mental deficiency
    469.9
crevasse pit 209.2
  ravine 201.2
crevice 201.2
crew aviation 279.4
  clique 788.6
  group 74.3
  staff 750.11
  team 788.7
crib
  n. abode 191.1
  bed 216.33
  brothel 989.9
  compartment 192.2
  gambling house
    515.15
  garner 660.7
  hut 191.10
  interpretation 552.3
  storage place 660.6
  v. cheat 618.17
  confine 761.12
  enclose 236.6
  imitate 22.5
  plagiarize 824.18
  steal 824.13
crick
  n. pain 424.2
  stridulation 458.5
  v. chirp 458.7
cricket
  animal 414.39,74
  fairness 976.3
  noisemaker 453.5
crier 561.3
crime illegality 999.4
  sin 982.2
  wrongdoing 982.1
criminal
  n. dishonest person
    975.10
  evildoer 943.1
  felon 986.10
  adj. dishonest 975.16
  evil 981.16
  guilty 983.3
  illegal 999.6
  improper 959.3
  sinful 982.6
criminology 998.7

crimp
  n. abductor 825.10
  fold 264.1
  hair 230.5
  sharper 619.4
  trench 263.2
  wrinkle 264.3
  v. abduct 824.19
  curl 254.5
  fold 264.5
  groove 263.3
  notch 262.4
  thwart 730.16
  wrinkle 264.6
  adj. pulverable 361.13
crimson
  v. become excited
    857.17
  become red 368.5
  blush 908.8
  make red 368.4
  adj. red 368.6
cringe be servile 907.6
  bow down before
    765.10
  cower 892.9
  flinch 891.21
  retract 297.3
  stoop 318.8
  wince 284.7
cringle hole 265.4
  sail part 277.14
crinkle
  n. convolution 254.1
  wrinkle 264.3
  v. roughen 261.5
  rustle 452.12
  twist 254.4
  wrinkle 264.6
cripple
  n. defective 686.42
  v. disable 158.9
  hamper 730.11
  impair 692.17
  weaken 160.10
crippled
  disabled 158.16
  injured 692.32
crisis
  business cycle 827.9
  critical point 129.4
  danger 697.1
  financial crisis 836.7
  important point
    672.6
  urgency 672.4
crisp
  v. curl 254.5
  fold 264.5
  adj. aphoristic 517.6
  brittle 360.4
  cold 333.14
  concise 592.6
  curly 254.9
  intelligible 548.10
  pulverable 361.13
  refreshing 695.3
crisscross
  n. cross 221.4
  v. cross 221.6
  adj. crossed 221.8
  adv. crosswise 221.13

criterion measure 490.2
  model 25.1
  rule 84.4
  test 489.2
critic author 602.15
  commentator 606.4
  connoisseur 897.7
  faultfinder 969.9
  interpreter 552.7
  judge 494.7
  specialist 81.3
critical
  commentative 606.6
  crucial 129.10
  dangerous 697.9
  difficult 731.16
  discriminating 492.7
  explanatory 552.15
  fastidious 896.9
  faultfinding 969.24
  judgmental 494.16
  meticulous 533.12
  precarious 697.12
  urgent 672.21
critical point
  crisis 129.4
  important point
    672.6
criticism
  commentary 606.2
  disapproval 969.4
  interpretation 552.8
  judgment 494.2
criticize
  disapprove 969.14
  judge 494.14
  write upon 606.5
critique
  commentary 606.2
  criticism 494.2
  iteration 103.2
critter animal 414.2
  cattle 414.6
  horse 414.10
  person 3.3
croak
  n. harsh sound 458.3
  speech defect 595.1
  v. bird sound 460.5
  complain 875.13
  die 408.20
  forebode 544.11
  kill 409.14
  sound harshly 458.9
  speak poorly 595.7
crocheting 223.6
crock
  ceramic ware 576.2
  inferior horse 414.14
crockery 576.2
crocodile tears 616.6
croft farm 413.8
  tract 180.4
croissant 308.31
crone 127.3
Cronus god 1014.5
  Time 105.2
crony associate 787.1
  companion 928.3
crook
  n. angle 251.2
  bend 219.3

sacred article 1040.11
crucifixion
  capital punishment
    1010.7
  pain 424.6
  torment 866.7
crucify execute 1010.19
  pain 424.7
  torture 866.18
  work evil 675.6
crude
  n. petroleum 380.4
  raw material 721.5
  adj. discourteous
    937.6
  garish 362.19
  infelicitous 590.2
  offensive 864.18
  ostentatious 904.20
  undeveloped 721.12
  unprepared 721.10
  vulgar 898.11
crude oil 380.4
crudity
  undevelopment 721.4
  vulgarity 898.2
cruel murderous 409.24
  painful 424.10
  pitiless 945.3
  ruthless 939.24
cruelly brutally 939.33
  distressingly 34.21
  pitilessly 945.4
cruelty
  brutal act 939.12
  pitilessness 945.1
  ruthlessness 939.11
cruet bottle 193.12
  church vessel 1042.11
  sacred article 1040.11
cruise
  n. voyage 275.6
  v. fly 278.45
  sail 275.13
  travel 273.20
cruiser boat 277.21
  motorboat 277.4
  naval vessel 277.24
  police car 272.10
  traveler 274.1
cruising aviation 278.1
  water travel 275.1
cruller 308.43
crumb
  n. minute thing 196.7
  piece 55.3
  powder 361.5
  small amount 35.3
  v. pulverize 361.9
  sprinkle 75.6
crumble
  become pulverized
    361.10
  be destroyed 693.22
  decay 692.25
  decrease 39.6
  disintegrate 53.3
  pulverize 361.9
  weaken 160.9
crumbling
  n. disintegration 53.1
  pulverization 361.4

adj. deteriorating
  692.46
  old 123.14
  weak 160.15
crumbly brittle 360.4
  frail 160.14
  pulverable 361.13
crummy bad 675.8
  base 915.12
  paltry 673.18
crumpet 308.31
crumple
  n. wrinkle 264.3
  v. distort 249.5
  roughen 261.5
  wrinkle 264.6
crumpled
  distorted 249.10
  rough 261.7
  wrinkled 264.8
crunch
  n. concussion 162.8
  critical point 129.4
  harsh sound 458.3
  impact 283.3
  predicament 731.4
  urgency 672.4
  v. collide 283.12
  shatter 49.13
  sound harshly 458.10
crunched 249.10
crupper buttocks 241.4
  harness 659.5
crusade cause 153.10
  military campaign
    797.7
crusade for 968.13
crush
  n. full measure 56.3
  liking 634.2
  love 931.4
  loved one 931.13
  pulp 390.2
  squeezing 198.2
  throng 74.4
  v. conquer 727.10
  humiliate 906.5
  make grieve 872.19
  make nervous 859.9
  pulp 390.5
  pulverize 361.9
  refute 506.5
  shatter 49.13
  squeeze 198.8
  subdue 764.9
  suppress 760.8
crushed
  conquered 727.16
  disappointed 541.5
  heartbroken 872.29
  humiliated 906.13
  powdery 361.11
  subdued 764.15
  suppressed 760.14
  unnerved 859.13
  wretched 866.26
crusher disproof 506.3
  end-all 70.4
  pulverizer 361.7
crushing
  humiliating 906.14
  laborious 716.18

mortifying 864.21
  troublesome 731.17
crust
  n. bread 308.28
  exterior 224.2
  incrustation 228.14
  insolence 913.3
  land 385.1
  v. incrust 228.27
crustacean 414.54
crusty gruff 937.7
  hardened 356.13
  impudent 913.9
  irascible 951.19
crutch fork 299.4
  staff 217.2
  supporter 216.2
crux cross 221.4
  difficulty 731.7
  dilemma 731.6
  important point
    672.6
  puzzle 549.8
cry
  n. animal sound 460.1
  call 459
  cheer 876.2
  entreaty 774.2
  lament 875.3
  phrase 582.9
  publicity 559.4
  rumor 558.6
  weeping 875.2
  v. animal sound 460.2
  call 459.6
  cheer 876.6
  cry aloud 459.9
  proclaim 559.13
  wail 875.11
  weep 875.10
crybaby 160.6
cry for demand 753.4
  entreat 774.11
  require 639.9
  wish for 634.16
cry havoc alarm 704.3
  warn 703.5
crying
  n. weeping 875.2
  adj. animal sound
    460.6
  demanding 753.8
  urgent 672.21
  vociferous 459.10
  weeping 875.17
cryo– 333.14
cryogenics cold 333.1
  physics 325.1
  refrigeration 334.1
crypt cavity 257.2
  church part 1042.9
  compartment 192.2
  tomb 410.16
cryptic
  inexplicable 549.17
  latent 546.5
  secret 614.11
crypto 619.11
cryptography
  cryptoanalysis 614.6
  interpretation 552.8
  writing 602.1

cryptologist 552.7
crystal
  n. amphetamine 687.9
  precious stone 384.6
  snow 333.8
  adj. stony 384.11
  transparent 339.4
crystal ball
  divining 543.2
  the future 121.1
crystal-clear
  clearly visible 444.7
  intelligible 548.10
  manifest 555.8
  transparent 339.4
crystal gazer 543.4
crystalline
  crystal 384.11
  intelligible 548.10
  transparent 339.4
crystallize form 59.5
  petrify 384.9
  solidify 356.8
crystallized 356.13
crystallography
  geology 384.8
  minerology 383.10
  physics 325.1
cry wolf 704.3
cub boy 125.5
  young animal 125.8
cubbyhole
  hiding place 615.4
  nook 192.3
  small place 196.3
cube dice 96.3
  triplicate 94.2
cubed 251.9
cubehead 642.10
cubes 515.9
cubic(al) angular 251.9
  spatial 179.8
cubicle bedroom 192.7
  nook 192.3
cub reporter 605.22
cuckold 989.22
cuckoldry
  adultery 989.7
  love affair 931.6
cuckoo
  n. imitator 22.4
  songbird 464.23
  v. bird sound 460.5
  adj. insane 473.26
cud bite 307.2
  chewing tobacco
    434.7
cuddle
  be loving 932.15
  snuggle 887.10
cuddly 931.23
cudgel hit 283.17
  punish 1010.14
cue clue 568.9
  hair 230.7
  hint 557.4
  mood 525.4
  playbook 611.26
  plaything 878.16
  reminder 537.6
  role 611.11
  tail 241.6

tip 557.3
cuff
n. punishment 1010.3
restraint 760.4
slap 283.7
v. punish 1010.13
slap 283.16
cuisine cooking 330.1
food 308.1
kitchen 330.3
cul-de-sac
dead end 266.3
impasse 731.5
road 657.6
culinary 330.5
culinary art 330.1
cull exclude 42.10
procure 811.10
select 637.14
separate 77.6
culling 60.3
culminate
complete 722.6
make perfect 677.5
top 211.9
culminating
completory 722.9
ending 70.9
topping 211.11
culmination
acme of perfection
677.3
completion 56.4
end 70.1
finishing 722.2
result 154.2
summit 211.2
culpability 983.1
culpable
blameworthy 969.26
guilty 983.3
culprit 986.9
cult religion 1020.2
ritualism 1040.1
system of belief
501.3
worship 1032.1
cultism piety 1028.1
religion 1020.2
ritualism 1040.1
worship 1032.1
cultist
n. religionist 1020.14
adj. pious 1028.8
cultivate
befriend 927.11
foster 785.16
improve 691.10
process 167.11
sensitize 422.9
till 413.17
train 562.14
cultivated
improved 691.13
learned 475.21
tasteful 897.9
well-bred 936.17
cultivation
agriculture 413.1
good breeding 936.4
good taste 897.1
manufacture 167.3

refinement 691.3
tilling 413.13
training 562.3
cultural 562.19
Cultural Revolution
744.6
culture
n. agriculture 413.1
cultivation 691.3
good breeding 936.4
good taste 897.1
people 418.1
scholarship 475.5
society 642.3
Stone Age 123.24
tilling 413.13
v. raise animals 416.6
till 413.17
cultured
improved 691.13
learned 475.21
tasteful 897.9
well-bred 936.17
culvert 396.2
cumbersome
bulky 195.19
clumsy 734.20
hampering 730.18
ponderous 352.17
unwieldy 731.18
cumbrous bulky 195.19
hampering 730.18
ponderous 352.17
stilted 590.3
cum laude 916.11
cumulate
assemble 74.18
store up 660.11
cumulation
acquisition 811.2
assemblage 74.9
store 660.1
cumulative
accumulative 74.23
additive 40.8
evidential 505.17
cumulus 404.1
cuneate 251.8
cuneiform
n. character 581.2
adj. wedge-shaped
251.8
cunning
n. craftiness 735
deceit 618.3
falseheartedness
616.4
shrewdness 467.3
skill 733.1
adj. crafty 735.12
deceitful 618.20
falsehearted 616.31
pretty 900.18
shrewd 467.15
skillful 733.20
well-devised 733.28
cup
n. basin 257.2
fate 640.2
memorial 570.12
trophy 916.3
types of 193.10

v. be concave 257.12
ladle 271.16
make concave 257.13
treat 689.33
cupboard
storage place 660.6
types of 193.19
cupid 931.9
Cupid god 1014.5
love god 931.8
cupidity 634.8
cupola arch 252.4
tower 207.11
cupped 257.16
cupping
bloodletting 689.26
extraction 305.3
cur bad person 986.7
mongrel 414.24
curable 694.25
curacy
church office 1037.5
the ministry 1037.9
curate
clergyman 1038.2
dignitary 1038.9
curative
remedial 687.39
restorative 694.22
curator
bookman 605.21
financial officer
836.11
guardian 699.6
manager 748.4
curb
n. border 235.6
harness 659.5
hindrance 730.7
pavement 657.7
restraint 760.1
stock exchange 833.7
v. hinder 730.10
restrain 760.7
slow 270.9
curbed 760.13
curbstone border 235.6
pavement 657.7
curd coagulation 354.7
food 308.47
semiliquid 389.5
curdle
make viscid 389.10
thicken 354.10
curdled
thickened 354.14
viscous 389.12
cure
n. commission 780.1
medical aid 689.15
protectorship 699.2
remedy 687.1
restoration 694.7
the ministry 1037.9
v. break of 643.2
dry 393.6
preserve 701.8
remedy 687.38
restore to health
694.15
tan 720.6
treat 689.30

curé clergyman 1038.2
priest 1038.5
cure-all 687.3
curfew 134.5
curing preserving 701.2
restoration 694.7
curio odd thing 85.5
trifle 673.5
curiosity desire 634.1
inquisitiveness 528
interest 530.2
marvel 920.2
odd thing 85.5
curious careful 533.10
inquiring 485.35
inquisitive 528.5
interested 530.16
odd 85.11
curiously 85.19
curl
n. coil 254.2
curve 252.2
hair 230.5
v. coil 254.5
curve 252.6
curled 254.9
curlicue 254.2
curling iron 254.3
curl up rest 711.6
snuggle 887.10
curly 254.9
currency
fashionableness 644.2
money 835.1
prevalence 79.2
publicity 559.4
usualness 84.2
current
n. course 267.2
direction 290.1
electricity 342.2
electron flow 343.6
flow 395.4
trend 174.2
wind 403.1
adj. customary 642.15
existent 1.13
fashionable 644.11
happening 151.9
made public 559.17
present 120.2
prevalent 79.12
rumored 558.15
usual 84.8
well-known 475.27
curricular 562.20
curriculum 562.8
curried cooked 330.6
pungent 433.7
curry
n. stew 308.11
v. comb 681.21
cook 330.4
tend animals 416.7
curry favor 907.8
curse
n. adversity 729.1
affliction 866.8
bad influence 675.4
bane 676.1
malediction 972
oath 972.4

spell 1036.1
v. blaspheme 1030.5
  damn 972.5
  swear 972.6
  work evil 675.6
curse, the 311.9
cursed damned 972.9
  terrible 675.10
cursing
  n. swearing 972.3
  adj. maledictory 972.8
cursive
  n. writing style 602.4
  adj. written 602.22
cursory careless 534.11
  hasty 709.9
  insignificant 35.6
  shallow 210.5
  unwilling 623.5
curt concise 592.6
  gruff 937.7
  short 203.8
  taciturn 613.9
curtail contract 198.7
  deprive 822.21
  lessen 42.9
  reduce 39.7
  restrain 760.7
  shorten 203.6
curtailed
  reduced 39.10
  shortened 203.9
curtailment
  contraction 198.1
  cutback 39.4
  deprivation 822.6
  economizing 851.2
  reduction 42.2
  restraint 760.1
  shortening 203.3
curtain
  n. act 611.8
  concealment 615.2
  cover 228.2,38
  end 70.1
  fortification 799.4
  obstacle 730.4
  scenery 611.25
  secrecy 614.3
  shade 338.1,8
  v. conceal 615.6
  cover 228.19
  shade 338.5
curtain call 611.8
curtain raiser act 611.8
  inauguration 68.5
  music 462.26
curtains death 408.1
  end 70.1
curtly concisely 592.7
  gruffly 937.9
  shortly 203.12
curtness
  conciseness 592.1
  gruffness 937.3
  shortness 203.1
  taciturnity 613.2
curtsy
  n. crouch 318.3
  greeting 925.4
  obeisance 964.2
  v. bow 318.9

bow down 765.10
  greet 925.10
  show respect 964.6
curvaceous
  beautiful 900.17
  curved 252.7
curvature 252
curve
  n. arc 252.2
  deviation 291.1
  throw 285.4
  trick 618.6
  v. deflect 291.5
  deviate 291.3
  turn 252.6
curved 252.7
curvy beautiful 900.17
  crooked 219.20
  curved 252.7
cushion
  n. alleviative 163.3
  bedding 216.20
  partition 237.5
  safety equipment 699.3
  silencer 451.4
  softness 357.4
  v. moderate 163.8
  muffle 451.9
  protect 699.18
  relieve 886.5
  soften 357.6
  support 216.21
cushioned 887.11
cushioning
  n. softening 357.5
  adj. moderating 163.14
cushy
  comfortable 887.11
  easy 732.12
cusp 258.3
cuspid 258.5
cuss
  n. curse 972.4
  v. curse 972.6
cussed irascible 951.19
  malicious 939.18
cussedness
  irascibility 951.2
  malice 939.5
  perversity 626.3
cuss out curse 972.7
  reprove 969.19
custard 308.45
custodial
  protecting 699.23
  vigilant 533.13
custodian
  cleaner 681.14
  guardian 699.6
  jailer 761.10
  manager 748.4
custody
  directorship 747.4
  imprisonment 761.5
  protectorship 699.2
  storage 660.5
  vigilance 533.4
custom
  n. behavior 737.1
  clientele 828.3

fashion 644.1
  habit 642.4
  patronage 827.6
  social convention 645.1
  tradition 123.2
  usage 642
  adj. made 167.22
customarily
  conventionally 642.22
  normally 84.9
  traditionally 645.6
customary
  conventional 645.5
  orthodox 1024.7
  traditional 123.12
  usual 84.8
  wonted 642.15
customer client 828.4
  person 417.3
custom-made
  made 167.22
  tailored 231.47
customs tax 846.11
  tax collectors 846.12
cut
  n. absence 187.4
  break 49.4
  characteristic 80.4
  cheapening 849.4
  crack 201.2
  cutback 39.4
  degree 29.1
  discount 847.1
  form 246.1
  gibe 967.2
  groove 263.1
  hit 283.4
  impairment 692.8
  indignity 965.2
  lash 283.7
  mark 568.5
  notch 262.1
  payment 841.7
  piece 55.3
  portion 816.5
  print 578.6
  reduction 42.2
  repulse 289.2
  shortcut 203.5
  slice 227.2
  snub 966.2
  sore 866.5
  thrust 798.3
  trench 263.2
  v. adulterate 44.13
  apportion 816.6
  be absent 187.9
  be sharp 258.8
  cheapen 849.6
  chill 333.10
  cleave 201.4
  cut across 219.11
  delete 42.12
  dilute 160.11
  discount 847.2
  eject 310.17
  engrave 578.10
  excise 42.10
  form 246.7
  groove 263.3

harvest 413.19
  hit 283.13
  hurt 424.7
  injure 692.15
  inscribe 570.16
  leave undone 534.7
  liquefy 391.5
  notch 262.4
  open 265.12
  pain 866.17
  punish 1010.14
  rarefy 355.3
  rebuff 776.5
  record 570.16
  reduce 39.7
  sculpture 575.5
  send away 289.3
  sever 49.11
  shorten 203.6
  slight 966.6
  till 413.17
  turn off 144.12
  adj. cheap 849.9
  cleft 201.7
  concise 592.6
  damaged 692.29
  diluted 160.19
  engraved 578.12
  grooved 263.4
  pained 866.23
  severed 49.23
  thinned 355.4
cut across
  v. cross 221.6
  cut diagonally 219.11
  take a short cut 203.7
  adj. crossed 221.8
cut-and-dried
  prearranged 641.5
  ready-made 720.19
  trite 883.9
cutaneous
  epidermal 229.6
  injection method 689.19
cutback
  economizing 851.2
  reduction 39.4
cut back reduce 39.7
  retrench 851.5
  shorten 203.6
cut corners
  neglect 534.8
  retrench 851.5
  take a short cut 203.7
cut down fell 318.5
  kill 409.13
  raze 693.19
  reduce 39.7
  retrench 851.5
  shorten 203.6
  strike dead 409.18
cute cunning 735.12
  pretty 900.18
  skillful 733.20
cuticle 229.1
cutie 125.6
cut in interrupt 238.6
  intrude 238.5
cut it 157.11
cut it out cease 144.6
  stop! 144.15

cutlery
edge tools 348.2
tableware 348.3
cutlet 308.19
cut loose
be disorderly 62.10
escape 632.6
extricate 763.7
let oneself go 762.18
make merry 878.26
run amok 162.14
sail 275.48
cutoff boundary 235.3
shortcut 203.5
stop 144.2
cut off
v. dispossess 822.23
excise 42.10
exclude 77.4
interrupt 144.10
kill 409.13
put an end to 693.12
separate 49.9
sever 49.11
take from 822.21
adj. deprived of 812.8
cut out
v. destroy 693.14
discontinue 668.4
eliminate 77.5
excise 42.10
extract 305.10
plan 654.9
run off 301.13
separate 49.9
substitute for 149.5
adj. prearranged 641.5
cut out for 733.27
cut-rate 849.9
cut short
v. put an end to
693.12
shorten 203.6
silence 451.8
stop 144.11
adj. incomplete 57.5
shortened 203.9
cutter cutlery 348.2
garmentmaker 231.33
separator 49.7
shortener 203.4
tooth 258.5
cut the mustard
be able 157.11
manage 724.11
cutthroat
n. evildoer 943.3
killer 409.11
adj. competitive
796.24
extortionate 848.12
murderous 409.24
cutting
n. abbreviation 592.4
adulteration 44.3
apportionment 816.1
excerpts 607.4
harvest 413.15
morphology 582.3
piece 55.3
plant 411.3
reduction 42.2

separation 49.2
syntax 586.2
adj. acrimonious
161.13
caustic 939.21
cold 333.14
eloquent 600.11
penetrating 857.29
pungent 433.6
sharp 258.10
solvent 391.8
violent 162.15
cutting remark 967.2
cutup humorist 881.12
mischief-maker 738.3
player 878.19
cut up
v. apportion 816.6
be disorderly 62.11
divide 49.18
find fault 969.15
make grieve 872.19
misbehave 738.4
pain 866.17
play 878.25
adj. heartbroken
872.29
wretched 866.26
cwm
mountain hollow
257.8
ravine 201.2
cyanosis blueness 372.1
disease symptom
686.8
Cybele 1014.5
cybernation
automation 349.1
control 349.3
cybernetic 349.27
cybernetics
automation 349.2
biology 406.17
cyborg 349.12
cycads 412.6
cyclamates 431.2
cycle
n. age 107.4
atomics 326.7
circle 253.2
circuit 321.2
continuity 71.2
electric current 342.2
radio frequency
344.12
round 137.3
types of 272.29
wheel 272.8
v. go around 321.4
recur 137.5
ride 273.32
cyclic(al)
atomic 326.18
circular 253.11
continuous 71.8
periodic 137.7
recurrent 103.13
cycling 273.6
cyclone
emotional outburst
857.8
storm 162.4

weather 402.5
whirlwind 403.14
cyclonic
meteorology 402.13
rotary 322.15
stormy 403.26
Cyclopean huge 195.20
strong 159.15
cyclopedia lore 475.9
reference book 605.6
cyclorama
picture 574.12
scenery 611.25
spectacle 446.7
cygnet 414.33
cylinder 255.4
cylindric(al) 255.11
cymbal
doughnut 308.43
percussion instrument
465.18
cynic disparager 971.6
misanthrope 940.2
pessimist 889.7
cynical critical 969.24
misanthropic 940.3
pessimistic 889.16
sarcastic 967.13
cynicism
misanthropy 940.1
pessimism 889.6
sarcasm 967.5
cynosure
attractor 288.2
center of attraction
226.4
famous person 914.9
guiding star 748.8
ideal 25.4
cyst swelling 256.4
tumor 686.36
cystic 193.4
cystic fibrosis 686.11
cytology 406.17
cytoplasm 406.4
czar autocrat 749.14
ruler 749.8
czarina 749.11

D

DA 1003.4
dab
n. blemish 679.3
small amount 35.2
tap 283.6
v. coat 228.24
color 362.13
smooth 260.5
tap 283.15
dabble
half-know 477.11
moisten 392.12
spatter 682.18
trifle 673.13
waste time 708.12
dabbler
dilettante 476.6
ignoramus 477.8
trifler 673.9
dacha 191.6
dactyl 609.9

dad
antiquated person
123.8
father 170.9
daddy 170.9
daddy longlegs 414.36
dado
n. base 216.8
bottom 212.2
groove 263.1
v. groove 263.3
daedal complex 46.4
skillful 733.20
variegated 374.9
daemon genius 467.8
guardian angel
1014.22
spirit 1014.15
daffiness
foolishness 470.1
insanity 473.2
daffy foolish 470.8
insane 473.26
daft foolish 470.8
insane 473.25
daftness 473.1
dagger
n. cross 221.4
cutlery 348.2,13
types of 801.22
v. stab 798.25
dago 181.7
daguerreotype
n. photograph 577.4
v. photograph 577.14
daily
n. newspaper 605.11
periodical 605.10
adj. regularly 137.8
adv. constantly 135.7
periodically 137.10
daily bread food 308.1
support 785.3
daily double 515.4
daintily prettily 900.22
weakly 160.22
daintiness
cleanness 681.1
fastidiousness 896.3
fine texture 351.3
frailty 160.2
good taste 897.1
lightness 353.1
prettiness 900.5
smallness 35.1
dainty
n. delicacy 308.8
adj. clean 681.25
delicate 35.7
edible 307.31
elegant 897.9
fastidious 896.11
frail 160.14
light 353.11
pretty 900.18
smooth 351.8
tasty 428.8
dairy larder 660.8
plant 719.3
store 832.5
dairy cows 414.6
dairy farmer 416.2

dairy-farming 416.1
dairy products 308.47
dais platform 216.13
  seat of authority
  739.10
daisy 674.7
Dalai Lama
  Buddhist priest
  1038.15
  ruler 749.8
dale 257.9
dalliance
  flirtation 932.8
  lovemaking 932.1
  slowness 270.3
  trifling 673.8
  waiting 132.3
dally dawdle 270.8
  fritter away 854.5
  make love 932.13
  trifle 673.13
  wait 132.12
  waste time 708.13
dallying
  n. idling 708.4
  slowness 270.3
  trifling 673.8
  waiting 132.3
  adj. dawdling 270.11
  dilatory 132.17
dam
  n. barrier 730.5
  body of water 398.1
  mother 170.10
  v. hinder 730.10
  stop 144.11
  stop up 266.7
damage
  n. disadvantage 671.2
  harm 675.3
  impairment 692.1
  loss 812.1
  price 846.1
  v. hurt 675.6
  impair 692.11
damaged
  impaired 692.29
  imperfect 678.4
damages
  penalty 1009.3
  recompense 841.3
damaging
  corrupting 692.45
  harmful 675.12
dame
  form of address 421.8
  girl 125.6
  instructress 565.2
  matron 421.5
  mistress 749.2
  noblewoman 918.6
  old woman 127.3
  woman 421.6
damn
  n. trifle 673.5
  v. censure 969.13
  condemn 1008.3
  curse 972.5
  destroy 693.10
  send to hell 1019.6
  vilify 972.7
  adj. cursed 972.9

interj. curse 972.11
damnable cursed 972.9
  evil 981.16
  terrible 675.10
damnation
  condemnation 1008.1
  curse 972.1
  destruction 693.1
  disapproval 969.3
damnatory
  censorious 969.23
  condemnatory 1008.5
  cursing 972.8
damned cursed 972.9
  irreligious 1031.18
damned, the 1016.1
damning 505.17
damn it! 972.11
damp
  n. deterrent 652.2
  killjoy 872.14
  moisture 392.1
  silencer 451.4
  vapor 401.1
  v. cushion 163.8
  disincline 652.4
  extinguish 332.7
  hinder 730.10
  make sad 872.18
  moderate 163.6
  moisten 392.12
  muffle 451.9
  reduce 39.7
  stabilize 17.4
  suppress 760.8
  weaken 160.10
  adj. moist 392.15
dampen cushion 163.8
  disincline 652.4
  hinder 730.10
  make sad 872.18
  moderate 163.6
  moisten 392.12
  muffle 451.9
  reduce 39.7
  weaken 160.10
damper curb 730.7
  deterrent 652.2
  fireplace 329.12
  killjoy 872.14
  silencer 451.4
dampness 392.1
damsel 125.6
dance
  n. ball 879.2
  dancing 879.1,7
  flicker 335.8
  flutter 324.4
  get-together 74.2
  music 462.9
  steps 879.8
  v. be cheerful 870.6
  dancing 879.5
  flicker 335.25
  flutter 324.12
  play 878.25
  rejoice 876.5
  adj. dancing 879.6
dance hall
  amusement 878.11
  ballroom 879.4
  hall 192.4

dancer danseur 879.3
  entertainer 612.1
dancing
  n. light 335.8
  terpsichore 879
  adj. dance 879.6
  flickering 335.36
  fluttering 324.18
  happy 865.13
dander 952.6
dandified
  foppish 903.17
  ultrafashionable
  644.14
dandruff filth 682.7
  flake 227.3
dandy
  n. fashionable 644.7
  fop 903.9
  good thing 674.7
  adj. excellent 674.13
  foppish 903.17
danger peril 697
  uncertainty 514.6
dangerous
  perilous 697.9
  unreliable 514.19
dangerous drug 687.5
dangerously 697.17
danger sign 703.3
dangle
  attach oneself to
  907.10
  flaunt 904.17
  flourish 555.5
  hang 215.6
  oscillate 323.10
dangling
  n. pendency 215.1
  adj. loose 51.5
  pendent 215.9
  swinging 323.17
Danish pastry
  bun 308.31
  pastry 308.40
dank 392.15
dankness 392.2
dapper 644.13
dapple
  n. mark 568.5
  spottiness 374.3
  v. gray 366.3
  mark 568.19
  variegate 374.7
  adj. gray 366.4
  variegated 374.12
dappled gray 366.4
  mixed 44.15
  variegated 374.12
dapple-gray
  n. horse 414.13
  adj. gray 366.4
dare
  n. challenge 793.2
  v. be insolent 913.6
  confront 240.8
  defy 793.3
  defy danger 697.7
  have courage 893.10
  presume 961.6
  try 714.7

daredevil
  n. reckless person
  894.4
  adj. foolhardy 894.9
daresay believe 501.11
  suppose 499.10
  think probable 511.5
daring
  n. courage 893.6
  defiance 793.1
  display 904.4
  recklessness 894.3
  adj. audacious 893.21
  defiant 793.7
  foolhardy 894.9
  showy 904.19
daringly
  courageously 893.22
  foolhardily 894.12
  showily 904.26
dark
  n. lightlessness 337.1
  obscurity 549.3
  unenlightenment
  477.4
  adj. black 365.8
  blind 441.9
  cloudy 404.7
  complexion 365.10
  dark-colored 365.9
  dishonest 975.16
  evil 981.16
  gloomy 872.24
  ignorant 477.16
  indistinct 445.6
  lightless 337.13
  obscure 549.15
  ominous 544.17
  opaque 341.3
  secret 614.11
  secretive 614.15
  sullen 951.24
dark age 477.4
Dark Ages 107.5
dark cloud
  heavenly body 375.7
  omen 544.6
darken
  become excited
  857.17
  blacken 365.7
  blemish 679.6
  blind 441.7
  cloud 404.6
  grow dark 337.12
  make sad 872.18
  obscure 337.9
  opaque 341.2
darkened
  blinded 441.10
  stained 679.10
darkening
  blackening 365.5
  concealment 615.1
  dimming 337.6
dark horse
  political candidate
  746.9
  small chance 156.9
  unknown quantity
  477.7
darkish blackish 365.9

deaden cushion 163.8
　desensitize 423.4
　dull 337.10
　make unfeeling 856.8
　moderate 163.6
　muffle 451.9
　relieve 886.5
　weaken 160.10
dead end
　impasse 731.5
　obstruction 266.3
dead-end 266.9
deadening
　n. moderation 163.2
　relief 886.1
　weakening 160.5
　adj. anesthetic 687.47
　moderating 163.14
　numbing 423.9
　relieving 886.9
deadeye hole 265.4
　shooter 285.9
deadfall 618.11
dead giveaway 556.2
deadhead
　freeloader 850.3
　playgoer 611.32
dead heat
　contemporary 118.2
　equality 30.3
dead language 580.2
dead letter letter 604.3
　meaninglessness
　547.1
deadline
　boundary 235.3
　crucial moment
　129.5
deadlock
　n. end 144.2
　impasse 731.5
　stalemate 30.3
　standstill 268.3
　v. prevent 730.13
　stop 144.11
deadly
　adj. deathly 408.29
　destructive 693.26
　fatal 409.23
　harmful 675.12
　poisonous 684.7
　remarkable 34.11
　adv. death 408.37
　terribly 34.21
dead march dirge 875.5
　funeral 410.5
　music 462.11
　slowness 270.2
deadness
　insensibility 423.1
　insipidness 430.1
　lusterlessness 337.5
　muffled tone 452.2
　uninterestingness
　883.1
dead of night
　darkness 337.1
　midnight 134.6
　silence 451.1
deadpan
　adj. inexpressive
　549.20

adv. unfeelingly
　856.14
dead pan
　unexpressiveness
　549.5
　unfeeling 856.1
dead reckoning
　navigation 275.2
　position 184.3
dead ringer
　image 572.3
　the same 14.3
dead set on 624.16
dead shot
　expert 733.11
　shooter 285.9
dead stop
　standstill 268.3
　stop 144.2
dead-tired 717.8
dead to
　insensible 856.10
　unaware 477.13
dead to the world
　absorbed 532.11
　asleep 712.22
　inattentive 531.7
　unconscious 423.8
deadweight
　burden 352.7
　impediment 730.6
　weight 352.1
deadwood
　branch 411.18
　refuse 669.4
deaf
　hard of hearing 449.6
　inattentive 531.7
　narrow-minded
　527.10
　unpersuadable 626.13
deaf-and-dumb
　alphabet
　gesture 568.14
　manual alphabet
　449.3
deafen din 453.6
　muffle 451.9
　stun 449.5
deafening
　intense 159.20
　loud 453.10
deaf-mute
　n. mute 451.3
　the deaf 449.2
　adj. deaf 449.6
deafness
　hardness of hearing
　449
　incognizance 477.3
　unpersuadableness
　626.5
deaf to
　insensible 856.10
　refusing 776.6
　unaware 477.13
deal
　n. amount 28.2
　bargain 827.5
　compact 771.1
　compromise 807.1
　intrigue 172.3

much 34.4
　portion 816.5
　slab 227.2
　transaction 827.4
　undertaking 715.1
　wood 378.3
　v. apportion 816.8
　distribute 60.9
　give 818.12
　hit 283.13
　trade 827.14
dealer merchant 830.2
　racketeer 826.4
　stockbroker 833.10
deal in 827.15
dealing
　commerce 827.1
　communication
　554.1
　trading 827.2
dealings acts 705.3
　affairs 151.4
　commerce 827.1
　communication
　554.1
　relationship 9.1
deal out
　apportion 816.8
　disperse 75.4
　distribute 60.9
　give 818.12
deal with
　accomplish 722.4
　behave toward 737.6
　communicate 554.6
　discourse upon 606.5
　discuss 597.12
　operate 164.5
　perform 705.8
　punish 1010.10
　relate to 9.5
　trade with 827.16
　treat 665.12
dean chief 749.3
　clergyman 1038.9
　educator 565.9
　executive 748.3
　senior 127.5
　superior 36.4
deanery
　church office 1037.5
　house 191.6
　mastership 739.7
　parsonage 1042.7
dear
　n. endearment 932.5
　loved one 931.13
　adj. beloved 931.22
　expensive 848.11
　valuable 848.10
　adv. at great cost
　848.13
dearth scarcity 662.3
　unproductiveness
　166.1
death dying 408
　end 70.1
　ruin 693.2
　symbols of 408.3
　transience 111.1
deathbed
　n. dying 408.9

adj. last-minute
　132.18
deathblow
　death stroke 409.10
　defeat 727.1
　early death 408.5
　end-all 70.4
　ruin 693.2
death-dealing 409.23
death-defying 894.9
death grip 813.2
deathless
　immortal 112.9
　indestructible 142.18
deathly
　adj. deathlike 408.29
　fatal 409.23
　adv. death 408.37
　terribly 34.21
death rate 408.13
death rattle 408.9
death sentence 1008.1
death song dirge 875.5
　swan song 408.10
death struggle
　dying 408.9
　fight 796.6
Death Valley 166.2
deathwatch
　dying 408.9
　funeral rites 410.4
death wish 872.3
deb beginner 68.2
　fashionable 644.7
debacle defeat 727.1
　descent 316.1
　disaster 693.4
　revolution 147.1
debar exclude 77.4
　obstruct 730.12
　prevent 730.14
　prohibit 778.3
debarkation 300.2
debase adulterate 44.13
　corrupt 692.14
　demote 783.3
　depress 318.4
　disgrace 915.8
　disparage 971.8
　humiliate 906.5
　lower 208.6
　misuse 667.4
debased
　depressed 318.12
　disreputed 915.12
　low 208.7
　morally corrupt
　981.14
debatable 514.16
debate
　n. contention 796.1
　discussion 597.7
　legislative procedure
　742.14
　speech 599.2
　v. be irresolute 627.7
　consider 478.12
　declaim 599.10
　discuss 597.12
debater arguer 482.12
　public speaker 599.4

morphology 582.3
refusal 776.1
declination
coordinates 490.6
descent 316.1
deterioration 692.3
deviation 291.1
obliquity 219.1
refusal 776.1
rejection 638.1
decline
n. cheapening 849.4
declivity 219.5
decrease 39.2
deterioration 692.3
end 70.3
fall 316.2
senility 469.10
shortcoming 314.1
stock prices 834.9
v. age 126.10
cheapen 849.6
decrease 39.6
degenerate 729.11
deteriorate 692.20
fail 686.45
fall short 314.2
grammaticize 586.16
incline 219.10
recede 297.2
refuse 776.3
reject 638.2
sink 316.6
weaken 160.9
declining
n. refusal 776.1
rejection 638.1
adj. aging 126.17
decreasing 39.11
descending 316.11
deteriorating 692.46
languishing 160.21
receding 297.5
sloping downward
219.16
declivitous
descending 316.11
sloping downward
219.16
declivity 219.5
decoction
a preparation 720.3
extract 305.8
extraction 305.7
heating 329.2
infusion 44.2
solution 391.3
decode 487.2
decoding
explanation 552.4
information theory
557.7
interpretation 552.3
solution 487.1
décolleté
n. nudity 232.3
adj. unclad 232.13
decoloration 363.3
decommission 804.11
decomposable
biodegradable 692.48
disintegrable 53.5

decompose
decay 692.25
disintegrate 53.3
decomposed 692.41
decomposing 53.5
decomposition
decay 692.6
disintegration 53.1
rotting 692.7
deconcentrate 75.7
decongestant 687.32
decontaminate
acquit 1007.4
sanitize 681.24
decontamination
mitigation 1006.5
radiation 327.1
sanitation 681.3
decor
ornamentation 901.1
stage scenery 611.25
decorate add 40.4
beautify 900.14
honor 916.8
make grandiloquent
601.7
ornament 901.8
decorated
high-flown 601.11
ornamented 901.11
decoration arts 574.1
award 916.5
beautification 900.10
extra 41.4
insignia 569.1
ornamentation 901.1
decorative
beautifying 900.20
ornamental 901.10
decorator 579.11
decorous
ceremonious 646.8
conventional 645.5
decent 988.5
right 958.8
solemn 871.3
tasteful 897.10
decorum decency 988.2
etiquette 646.3
good taste 897.3
propriety 958.2
social convention
645.1
decoy
n. fake buyer 828.6
lure 650.2
shill 619.5
trap 618.11
v. lure 650.4
trap 618.18
decrease
n. contraction 198.1
lessening 39
loss 812.2
reduction 42.2
v. contract 198.7
diminish 39.6
graduate 29.4
quantify 28.4
reduce 39.7
subtract 42.9
waste 812.5

decree
n. judgment 494.5
law 998.3
order 752.4
predetermination
640.1
v. command 752.9
legalize 998.8
legislate 742.18
pass judgment 494.13
will 621.2
decrement
decrease 39.1
deduction 42.7
depletion 39.3
loss 812.2
reduction 42.2
decrepit aged 126.18
dilapidated 692.35
senile 469.23
weak 160.15
decrescendo
n. decrease 39.2
faintness of sound
452.1
music 462.25
adj. decreasing 39.11
faint-sounding 452.16
adv. decreasingly
39.12
music 462.54
decretory
commanding 752.14
mandatory 752.13
decry censure 969.13
disparage 971.8
dedicate devote 816.11
sanctify 1026.5
dedicated
friendly 927.20
resolute 624.11
sanctified 1026.8
unselfish 979.5
zealous 635.10
dedication
book 605.12
devotion 816.4
duty 962.1
friendship 927.7
resolution 624.1
sanctification 1026.3
unselfishness 979.1
zeal 635.2
deduce
conclude 494.10
elicit 305.14
reason 482.15
suppose 499.10
deduct discount 847.2
reduce 39.7
subtract 42.9
deductible
n. insurance 699.4
adj. tax-free 846.18
deduction
conclusion 494.4
decrease 39.1
decrement 42.7
discount 847.1
logic 482.3
reasoning 482.1
relationship 9.1

subtraction 42.1
deductive
dialectic(al) 482.22
subtractive 42.13
deed
n. act 705.3
contract 771.3
courageous act 893.7
v. transfer property
817.3
deedholder 809.2
deem believe 501.11
judge 494.8
suppose 499.10
de-emphasize
make light of 673.11
minimize 39.9
soften 163.6
de-energize 158.9
deep
n. pit 209.2
adj. broad 204.6
colored 362.16
cunning 735.12
deep-felt 855.26
deep-toned 454.10
extensive 179.9
great 34.6
interior 225.7
learned 475.21
profound 209.10
recondite 549.16
wise 467.17
adv. beyond one's
depth 209.16
deep, the ocean 397.1
ocean depths 209.4
deep-dyed
confirmed 642.21
dyed 362.17
established 142.13
thorough 56.10
deepen aggravate 885.2
broaden 204.4
increase 38.5
lower 209.8
deepening
aggravation 885.1
increase 38.2
lowering 209.7
deep freeze 334.5
deep-freeze 334.11
deep-rooted
confirmed 642.21
deep 209.10
established 142.13
deep-sea
aquatic 275.58
deep-water 209.14
oceanic 397.8
deep-seated
confirmed 642.21
deep 209.10
established 142.13
intrinsic 5.6
deep six discard 668.3
funeral 410.5
tomb 410.16
deep-six 668.7
deep sleep 712.5
deep thought
engrossment 530.3

thoughtfulness 478.3
deer 414.5,58
de-escalation 318.1
deface blemish 679.4
  deform 249.7
  disfigure 899.5
de facto 1.15,16
defalcation
  deficiency 57.2
  misuse 667.1
  shortcoming 314.1
defamation 971.2
defamatory 971.13
defame malign 971.9
  stigmatize 915.9
default
  n. absence 187.4
  debt 840.2
  neglect 534.1
  nonobservance 769.1
  nonpayment 842.1
  shortcoming 314.1
  v. be absent 187.7
  lose 812.4
  neglect 534.6
  not pay 842.6
defeat
  n. disappointment
    541.1
  failure 725.1
  frustration 730.3
  vanquishment 727
  v. beat 36.7
  disappoint 541.2
  refute 506.5
  ruin 693.11
  thwart 730.15
  triumph over 726.6
  vanquish 727.6
defeated
  disappointed 541.5
  vanquished 727.14
defeating
  frustrating 730.20
  victorious 726.8
defeatist
  n. pessimist 889.7
  adj. pessimistic 889.16
defecate eject 310.21
  excrete 311.13
defect
  n. blemish 679.1
  deficiency 57.2
  disease 686.1
  fault 678.2
  v. apostatize 628.8
  desert 633.6
  renegade 145.13
defection
  apostasy 628.2
  change 139.1
  conversion 145.3
  desertion 633.2
  fault 678.2
  nonpayment 842.1
defective
  n. cripple 686.42
  simpleton 471.8
  adj. blemished 679.8
  faulty 518.16
  imperfect 678.4
  incomplete 57.4

insufficient 662.9
defector apostate 145.8
  turncoat 628.5
defend guard 799.8
  justify 1006.10
  protect 699.18
defendant
  accused 1005.6
  litigant 1004.11
  oppositionist 791.3
defender
  champion 799.7
  justifier 1006.8
  protector 699.5
  supporter 787.9
defense
  argumentation 482.4
  barrier 730.5
  countermeasure
    178.5
  counterstatement
    486.2
  guard 799
  justification 1006.2
  legal plea 1004.6
  protection 699.1
defense counsel 1003.4
defenseless
  forlorn 924.11
  helpless 158.18
  unprotected 697.14
defense mechanism
  avoidance 631.1
  defense 799.1
  defense reaction
    690.30
  mental block 538.3
defensible
  defendable 799.15
  just 976.8
  justifiable 1006.1
defensive
  defending 799.11
  protecting 699.23
defer 132.9
deference
  courtesy 936.1
  duty 962.1
  respect 964.1
  submission 765.1
deferential
  courteous 936.14
  dutiful 962.13
  respectful 964.8
  submissive 765.16
deferment 132.4
defer to obey 766.2
  respect 964.4
  submit to 765.9
defiance
  declaration of war
    797.11
  defying 793
  refractoriness 767.2
  resistance 792.1
  ungovernability 626.4
defiant defying 793.7
  refractory 767.10
  ungovernable 626.12
deficiency fault 678.2
  imperfection 678.1
  incompleteness 57.1

inferiority 37.3
  lack 57.2
  want 662.4
deficiency disease
  686.1,10
deficient
  imperfect 678.4
  incomplete 57.4
  inferior 37.7
  insufficient 662.9
  short of 314.5
  slipshod 534.12
deficit debt 840.2
  deficiency 57.2
  difference 42.8
  shortcoming 314.1
  want 662.4
deficit spending 843.1
defile
  n. narrow place 205.3
  passageway 657.4
  ravine 201.2
  v. corrupt 692.14
  demoralize 981.10
  dirty 682.17
  march 273.29
  misuse 667.4
  parade 71.7
  seduce 989.20
  stigmatize 915.9
  vilify 971.10
  work evil 675.6
define
  characterize 80.10
  circumscribe 234.4
  interpret 552.9
  mark 568.19
  name 583.11
  stabilize 142.9
defined
  circumscribed 234.6
  clearly visible 444.7
  intelligible 548.10
  particular 80.12
defining
  classificational 61.7
  limiting 234.9
definite audible 450.16
  certain 513.13
  circumscribed 234.6
  clearly visible 444.7
  intelligible 548.10
  particular 80.12
  resolute 624.11
  unqualified 508.2
definitely
  certainly 513.23
  exactly 516.20
  intelligibly 548.12
  particularly 80.15
  visibly 444.8
definition
  characterization 80.8
  circumscription 234.1
  intelligibility 548.2
  interpretation 552.1
  meaning 545.3
  naming 583.2
  television reception
    345.5
  visibility 444.2
definitive final 70.10

limiting 234.9
  outright 34.12
  unqualified 508.2
deflagration
  burning 329.5
  flash 328.14
deflate cheapen 849.6
  collapse 198.10
  disprove 506.4
  humiliate 906.4
  reduce 39.7
  render powerless
    158.11
deflated
  disproved 506.7
  flat 198.14
  reduced 39.10
deflation
  cheapening 849.4
  contraction 198.4
  decrease 39.1
  failure 725.3
  humiliation 906.2
deflationary 198.11
deflect curve 252.6
  dissuade 652.4
  divert 291.5
  oblique 219.9
  prevent 730.14
deflection angle 251.2
  curve 252.3
  deviation 291.2
  obliquity 219.1
  radar interference
    346.12
deflower
  corrupt 692.14
  possess sexually
    822.15
  seduce 989.20
defluxion
  descent 316.1
  flow 395.4
  outflow 303.4
defocus 445.4
defoliant 676.3
defoliate 49.14
deform blemish 679.4
  change 139.6
  distort 247.3
  misshape 249.7
deformed
  abnormal 85.13
  blemished 679.8
  malformed 249.12
  ugly 899.8
deformity
  blemish 679.1
  cripple 686.42
  disease 686.1
  malformation 249.3
  oddity 85.3
  ugliness 899.2
defraud cheat 618.17
  steal 824.13
defrauder 619.3
defray 841.18
defrayment 841.1
defrock depose 783.4
  disgrace 915.8
  dismiss 310.19
defrost 329.21

demotion
degrading 783
depression 318.1
deterioration 692.3
ejection 310.4
demulcent
n. healing ointment 687.11
ointment 380.3
adj. palliative 163.16
relieving 886.9
remedial 687.40
softening 357.16
demur
n. objection 522.2
resistance 792.1
unwillingness 623.2
v. be irresolute 627.7
be unwilling 623.4
object 522.5
demure prudish 903.19
shy 908.12
solemn 871.3
demurrer
dissenter 522.3
justification 1006.2
legal plea 1004.6
objection 522.2
demythologize 552.10
den
disapproved place 191.28
hiding place 615.4
lair 191.26
office 719.8
place of vice 981.7
retreat 700.5
sanctum 192.8
denature
adulterate 44.13
change 139.6
corrupt 692.14
deniable 514.16
denial disavowal 524.2
justification 1006.2
opposition 790.1
privation 812.1
prohibition 778.1
recantation 628.3
refusal 776.1
refutation 506.2
rejection 638.1
temperance 992.1
unbelief 503.1
denied disproved 506.7
rejected 638.3
denied to 510.9
denigrate
blacken 365.7
deprecate 969.12
vilify 971.10
denizen
n. inhabitant 190.2
v. inhabit 188.9
den of iniquity
brothel 989.9
place of vice 981.7
denomination
Christian 1020.33
indication 568.1
kind 61.3
name 583.3

naming 583.2
religion 1020.3
school 788.5
specification 80.6
denominational
partisan 788.19
religions 1020.25
denotative
indicative 568.23
meaningful 545.10
denote
designate 568.18
indicate 568.17
mean 545.8
signify 505.9
denouement end 70.1
result 154.2
solution 487.1
story element 608.9
denounce
accuse 1005.7
censure 969.13
condemn 1008.3
threaten 973.2
dense compact 354.12
crowded 74.22
growing rank 411.40
hard 356.10
stupid 469.15
substantial 3.7
thick 204.8
densify 354.9
density
compactness 354
hardness 356.1
stupidity 469.3
substantiality 3.1
dent
n. indentation 257.6
mark 568.7
tooth 258.5
v. indent 257.14
dental medical 688.18
phonetic 594.31
toothlike 258.16
dental bridge 258.6
dentate grasping 813.9
notched 262.5
dented 257.17
denti– dental 688.18
tooth 258.5
denticle 258.5
dentifrice
cleaning agent 681.17
toothpaste 687.22
dentist 688.10
dentistry 688.4,19
denture 258.6
denudant 232.18
denude despoil 822.24
divest 232.5
tear apart 49.14
denuded
deprived of 812.8
divested 232.12
denunciate
accuse 1005.7
censure 969.13
condemn 1008.3
denunciation
accusation 1005.1
condemnation 1008.1

curse 972.1
disapproval 969.3
threat 973.1
deny contradict 790.6
disbelieve 503.5
disclaim 524.4
prohibit 778.3
recant 628.9
refuse 776.4
refute 506.5
reject 638.2
deodorant
n. deodorizer 438.3
adj. deodorizing 438.6
deodorize
falsify 616.16
stop odor 438.4
depart
absent oneself 187.8
die 408.19
digress 593.9
disappear 447.2
exit 303.11
flee 631.10
leave 301.6
separate 49.9
departed absent 187.10
dead 408.30
left 301.20
past 119.7
departed, the 408.16
departed spirit 1017.1
depart from
abandon 633.5
deviate 291.3
differ 16.5
department area 180.1
jurisdiction 1000.4
region 180.2
sphere of work 656.4
department store 832.1
departure
absence 187.4
death 408.1
deviation 291.1
difference 16.1
digression 593.4
disappearance 447.1
egress 303.1
leaving 301
depend
be contingent 507.6
be uncertain 514.11
hang 215.6
dependable sure 513.17
trustworthy 974.19
unhazardous 698.5
dependence
addiction 642.9
belief 501.1
pendency 215.1
relationship 9.2
subjection 764.3
supporter 787.9
trust 888.1
dependent
n. follower 293.2
hanger-on 907.5
retainer 750.1
subject 764.6
adj. contingent 507.9
habituated 642.19

pendent 215.9
subordinate 764.13
trusting 501.22
uncertain 514.17
dependent on
contingent 507.9
habituated 642.19
liable to 175.5
resulting from 154.8
depend on
be contingent 507.6
believe in 501.16
be subject to 764.12
result from 154.6
trust 501.17
depersonalization 690.27
depict act 611.35
describe 608.12
picture 574.20
represent 572.6
depiction
description 608.1
representation 572.1
depilation 232.4
depilatory 232.4
deplane 300.8
deplete consume 666.2
eject 310.21
waste 812.5
depletion
consumption 666.1
decrease 39.3
evacuation 310.6
loss 812.2
reduction 42.2
depletion allowance 818.8
deplorable bad 675.9
disgraceful 915.11
regrettable 873.10
unpleasant 864.20
deplore lament 875.8
regret 873.6
deploy allocate 184.10
arrange evidence 505.13
diverge 299.5
order 59.4
prepare 720.6
spread 197.6
deployment
arrangement 60.1
battle array 797.6
divergence 299.1
expansion 197.1
order 59.1
placement 184.5
deplume demote 783.3
despoil 822.24
disgrace 915.8
dismiss 310.19
deponent 505.7
depopulate
eject 310.16
murder 409.17
deport eject 310.17
eliminate 77.5
emigrate 303.16
transfer 271.9
deportment 737.1
deposal dismissal 310.5

ousting 783.2
resignation 784.1
unseating 185.2
depose affirm 523.5
dislodge 185.6
dismiss 310.19
remove from office
783.4
testify 505.10
deposit
n. mineral deposit
383.7
payment 841.1
placement 184.5
pledge 772.3
precipitation 354.5
residue 43.2
sediment 271.8
v. lay eggs 169.9
pledge 772.10
precipitate 354.11
put 184.13
secrete 615.7
store 660.10
depositary
financial officer
836.11
trustee 809.5
deposition
affirmation 523.2
certificate 570.6
deposal 783.2
legal statement
1004.7
placement 184.5
residue 43.2
statement of belief
501.4
testimony 505.3
depository
storage place 660.6
treasury 836.12
depot 660.6
depravation
deterioration 692.3
turpitude 981.5
deprave corrupt 692.14
work evil 675.6
depraved base 915.12
morally corrupt
981.14
depravity
baseness 915.3
turpitude 981.5
deprecate
attach little impor-
tance to 673.11
disapprove 969.12
underestimate 498.2
deprecatory
condemnatory 969.23
disparaging 971.13
modest 908.10
depreciate
attach little impor-
tance to 673.11
cheapen 849.6
deprecate 969.12
discount 847.2
disparage 971.8
reduce 39.7
subtract 42.9

underestimate 498.2
waste 812.5
depreciation
cheapening 849.4
decrease 39.1
deprecation 969.2
deterioration 692.3
discount 847.1
disparagement 971.1
loss 812.2
reduction 42.2
underestimation
498.1
depredate
destroy 693.10
plunder 824.16
depredation
destruction 693.1
plundering 824.5
depress debase 208.6
deepen 209.8
indent 257.14
lowering 318.4
make sad 872.18
reduce 39.7
depressant 687.12,54
depressed
dejected 872.22
indented 257.17
lowered 318.12
lowness 208.7
pleasureless 866.20
unfortunate 729.14
depressed area 838.3
depressing
discouraging 872.30
unpleasant 864.20
depression
business cycle 827.9
concavity 257.1
decrease 39.1
deepening 209.7
despair 866.6
distressfulness 864.5
emotional symptom
690.23
hard times 729.6
lowering 318
lowness 208.1
notch 262.1
pit 257.2
sadness 872.3
deprivation
absence 187.1
deposal 783.2
disassembly 49.6
divestment 822.6
ejection 310.4
loss 812.1
nonexistence 2.1
poverty 838.2
refusal 776.1
want 662.4
deprive dismiss 310.19
take from 822.21
deprived
bereaved 408.35
poor 838.8
deprived of
bereft 812.8
wanting 662.13
depth deepness 209

harmonics 463.4
interiority 225.1
pit 209.2
sagacity 467.5
size 195.1
thickness 204.2
depth indicator 209.17
depthless
insignificant 35.6
shallow 210.5
depth sounding 209.5
deputation
accession to power
739.12
commission 780.1
delegates 781.13
substitution 149.1
deputize
commission 780.9
delegate 149.7
empower 157.10
get an agent 781.14
deputy agent 781
assignee 780.8
assistant 787.6
lawyer 1003.1
manager 748.1
mediator 805.3
peace officer 699.15
substitute 149.2
derange disarrange 63.2
madden 473.23
sicken 686.47
deranged
disorderly 62.13
insane 473.25
derangement
abnormality 85.1
disarrangement 63.1
disorder 62.1
insanity 473.1
derby contest 796.3
race 796.12
Derby 796.13
dereism
defense mechanism
690.30
fantasy 535.7
illusion 519.1
derelict
n. abandoned thing
633.4
bad person 986.2
bum 708.9
outcast 926.4
adj. abandoned 633.8
dilapidated 692.35
negligent 534.10
outcast 926.10
unfaithful 975.20
dereliction
desertion 633.2
infidelity 975.5
neglect 534.1
nonobservance 769.1
sin 982.2
deride
be insolent 913.6
disdain 966.3
flout 793.4
ridicule 967.8

de rigueur
conventional 645.5
obligatory 962.15
derisive
condemnatory 969.23
defiant 793.7
disparaging 971.13
disrespectful 965.5
impudent 913.9
ridiculing 967.12
derivable 482.23
derivation
ancestry 170.4
borrowing 821.2
conclusion 494.4
etymology 582.16
linguistics 580.12
morphology 582.3
receiving 819.1
result 154.1
source 153.5
word 582.2
derivative
attributed 155.6
lexical 582.20
resulting 154.7
unproductive 166.5
derive acquire 811.8
conclude 494.10
elicit 305.14
receive 819.6
derive from
borrow 821.4
receive 819.6
result from 154.6
trace to 155.5
derm(a)– 229.1
dermal 229.6
dermatitis
deficiency disease
686.10
skin disease 686.33
dermis skin 229.1
skin layer 229.4
dernier cri
the latest thing 122.2
the rage 644.4
derogation
deterioration 692.3
disparagement 971.1
reduction 42.2
derogative 971.13
derogatory
disparaging 971.13
disreputable 915.10
derrick lifter 317.3
tower 207.11
derrière 241.4
derring-do 893.6
dervish ascetic 991.2
clergyman 1038.13
Muslim 1020.22
descant
n. melody 462.4
musical part 462.22
musical piece 462.5
overture 462.26
treatise 606.1
v. discourse upon
606.5
expatiate 593.7
sing 462.39

descend
be disgraced 915.7
change hands 817.4
condescend 906.7
fly 278.52
go down 316.5
gravitate 352.15
incline 219.10
move 267.5
descendant
offspring 171.3
posterity 171.1
sequel 117.2
successor 67.4
descending
falling 316.11
flowing 267.8
sloping downward 219.16
descend upon
attack 798.15
light on 316.10
descent ancestry 170.4
continuity 71.2
course 267.2
declivity 219.5
depression 318.1
deterioration 692.3
fall 316
humiliation 906.2
posterity 171.1
reverse 729.3
rocketry 281.9
sequence 65.1
describe
characterize 80.10
interpret 552.9
portray 608.12
description
characterization 80.8
interpretation 552.1
kind 61.3
portrayal 608
descriptive
depictive 608.15
interpretative 552.14
linguistic 580.17
descry detect 488.5
see 439.12
understand 548.8
desecrate
corrupt 692.14
misuse 667.4
profane 1030.4
desecration
misuse 667.1
sacrilege 1030.2
wrong 959.2
desensitize
make unfeeling 856.7
render insensible 423.4
desert
n. plain 387.1
space 179.4
wasteland 166.2
adj. barren 166.4
dry 393.7
desert
n. goodness 674.1
reprisal 955.2
v. abandon 633.6

apostatize 628.8
be dishonest 975.12
defect 145.13
flee 631.10
deserted
abandoned 633.8
disused 668.10
forlorn 924.11
neglected 534.14
vacant 187.14
deserter apostate 145.8
desertion 633.2
impious person 1030.3
turncoat 628.5
desertion
abandonment 633.2
apostasy 628.2
defection 145.3
flight 631.4
forlornness 924.4
impiety 1030.1
deserts due 960.3
punishment 1010.1
reprisal 955.2
deserve 960.5
deserved just 976.8
warranted 960.9
deserving due 960.10
praiseworthy 968.20
desex 158.12
déshabillé 231.20
desiccate
deteriorate 692.21
dry 393.6
preserve 701.8
desideratum
intention 653.1
requirement 639.2
thing desired 634.11
design
n. arts 574.1
composition 574.10
diagram 654.3
harmonics 463.11
intention 653.1
meaning 545.2
motif 901.7
picture 574.14
plan 654.1
story element 608.9
stratagem 735.3
trick 618.6
work of art 574.11
v. create 167.13
intend 653.4
picture 574.20
plan 654.9
designate
appoint 780.10
indicate 568.18
name 583.11
nominate 637.19
specify 80.11
designation
appointment 780.2
indication 568.1
kind 61.3
name 583.3
naming 583.2
nomination 637.8
specification 80.6

designed
intentional 653.9
planned 654.13
designer planner 654.7
producer 167.8
stylist 579.9
designing
n. arts 574.1
adj. cunning 735.12
scheming 654.14
desirable
advisable 670.5
likable 634.30
pleasant 863.6
suitable 637.24
welcome 925.12
desire
n. hope 888.1
intention 653.1
love 931.1
request 774.1
sexual desire 419.5
thing desired 634.11
will 621.1
wish 634
v. be eager 635.7
be hopeful 888.7
intend 653.4
lust 419.22
request 774.9
will 621.2
wish 634.14
desirous
amorous 931.24
eager 635.9
wanting 634.21
desirous of
anxious for 634.22
envious 954.4
desist
v. cease 144.6
discontinue 668.4
give up 633.7
interj. cease! 144.14
desk
church part 1042.13
table 216.15
workplace 719.1
desolate
v. cause unpleasantness 864.12
depopulate 310.16
destroy 693.10
make grieve 872.19
adj. barren 166.4
disconsolate 872.28
forlorn 924.11
wretched 866.26
desolated
heartbroken 872.29
ruined 693.28
desolating
destructive 693.26
unpleasant 864.23
desolation agony 864.4
depopulation 310.3
despair 866.6
destruction 693.1
forlornness 924.4
sorrowfulness 872.12
wasteland 166.2

despair
n. desperation 889.2
sadness 872.3
wretchedness 866.6
v. be despondent 872.16
be hopeless 889.10
despatch, despatched
see dispatch etc.
desperado
criminal 986.10
killer 409.11
ruffian 943.3
desperate
hopeless 889.12
in trouble 731.24
mad 473.30
reckless 894.8
desperately
hopelessly 889.17
recklessly 894.11
violently 34.23
desperation 889.2
despicable bad 675.9
contemptible 915.12
offensive 864.18
paltry 673.18
despise disdain 966.3
reject 638.2
scorn 793.4
despised disliked 867.9
rejected 638.3
despite
n. contempt 966.1
defiance 793.1
disrespect 965.2
spite 939.6
prep. regardless of 33.9
despiteful
hateful 930.8
hostile 929.10
spiteful 939.19
despoil degrade 692.14
destroy 693.10
plunder 824.16
seduce 989.20
strip clean 822.24
work evil 675.6
despoliation
destruction 693.1
evil 675.3
plundering 824.5
despond
be hopeless 889.10
despair 872.16
despondency
despair 889.2
sadness 872.3
despondent
despairing 872.22
hopeless 889.12
despot 749.14
despotic
governmental 741.17
imperious 739.16
despotism
absolutism 741.9
tyranny 741.10
dessert course 307.10
delicacy 308.8

diabolize
  bewitch 1036.9
  demonize 1016.17
diacritical 16.9
diacritical mark
  586.15,19
diadem circle 253.2
  jewel 901.6
  royal insignia 569.3
diaeresis meter 609.9
  separation 49.5
diagnose
  interpret 552.9
  treat 689.30
diagnosis
  interpretation 552.1
  judgment 494.5
  medical diagnosis
  689.13
diagnostic
  differentiative 16.9
  indicative 568.23
  interpretative 552.14
diagonal
  n. line 568.6
  oblique 219.7
  straight line 250.2
  adj. transverse 219.19
diagram
  n. outline 48.4
  picture 574.14
  plan 654.3
  representation 572.1
  v. plot 654.11
  portray 574.20
  represent 572.6
diagrammatic 654.15
dial measure 490.11
  telephone 560.18
dialect
  n. diction 588.1
  idiom 580.7
  language 580.1
  adj. linguistic 580.20
dialectic
  discussion 597.7
  logic 482.2
dialectic(al)
  argumentative 482.19
  logic 482.22
dialectical materialism
  communism 745.5
  materialism 376.5
dialectics 482.2
dialogue
  conversation 597.3
  discussion 597.7
  stage show 611.4
dialysis 53.2
dialyze 53.4
diameter bisector 92.3
  middle 69.1
  size 195.1
  straight line 250.2
  thickness 204.3
diametric(al) 15.7
diamond
  gem stone 384.13
  good person 985.1
  good thing 674.5
  hardness 356.6
  playground 878.12

playing cards 878.17
diamond in the rough
  good person 985.1
  raw material 721.5
  unshaped 247.2
Diana goddess 1014.5
  moon goddess 375.12
diapason
  harmony 462.3
  interval 463.20
  organ stop 465.22
  range 179.2
  register 463.6
  tuning fork 465.25
diaper 231.19
diaphanous
  lucid 335.31
  thin 205.16
  transparent 339.4
diaphony 461.1
diaphragm
  abdomen 193.3
  contraceptive 687.23
  loudspeaker 450.8
  middle 69.1
  partition 237.5
diarist author 602.15
  chronicler 608.11
  chronologist 114.10
diarrhea
  defecation 311.2
  disease symptom
  686.8
  indigestion 686.28
diary
  autobiography 608.4
  chronicle 114.9
  periodical 605.10
  record book 570.11
diaspora 75.3
diastole
  distension 197.2
  pulse 137.3
diathermic 328.31
diathermy 689.6
diathesis heredity 170.6
  nature 5.3
  tendency 174.1
  trait of character
  525.3
diatonic scale 463.6
diatribe berating 969.7
  speech 599.2
dibble fish 655.10
  plant 413.18
dice
  n. die 515.9
  v. cube 96.3
diced 251.9
dicey chance 156.15
  hazardous 697.10
  uncertain 514.15
dichotomy
  bisection 92.1
  duality 90.1
  separation 49.2
dichromatic
  coloring 362.15
  variegated 374.9
dick detective 781.11
  policeman 699.16
dicker 827.17

dickering 827.3
dicotyledon
  plant 411.3
  seed plants 412.6
dictate
  n. axiom 517.2
  command 752.1
  law 998.3
  maxim 517.1
  precept 751.1
  v. command 752.9
  dominate 741.15
  necessitate 639.8
  oblige 756.5
  prescribe 752.10
dictator 749.14
dictatorial
  arrogant 912.11
  governmental 741.17
  imperious 739.16
dictatorship
  absolutism 741.9
  directorship 747.4
  government 741.4
  mastership 739.7
diction phrase 585.2
  speech 588
dictionary
  lexicon 605.7
  word list 88.4
dictum
  affirmation 523.1
  axiom 517.2
  decree 752.4
  judgment 494.5
  maxim 517.1
  precept 751.2
  remark 594.4
didactic advisory 754.8
  educational 562.19
  poetic 609.17
  prescriptive 751.4
didactics 562.1
diddle cheat 618.17
  copulate 419.23
  dally 708.13
  deceive 618.13
  waste time 708.12
diddle away 854.5
die
  n. base 216.8
  dice 515.9
  engraving tool 578.9
  model 25.6
  v. be destroyed 693.23
  burn out 332.8
  cease to exist 2.5
  decease 408.19
  decline 692.20
  disappear 447.2
  end 70.6
  fail 725.15
  pass 119.6
die away
  burn out 332.8
  cease to exist 2.5
  decrease 39.6
  disappear 447.2
  end 70.6
  recede 297.2
die down 268.8

diehard
  conservative 140.4
  obstinate person
  626.6
  oppositionist 791.3
  rightist 745.9
die hard
  be determined 624.8
  be obstinate 626.7
  persevere 625.6
  stand fast 792.4
die-hard
  conservative 140.8
  right-wing 745.17
die is cast, the 639.20
dielectric
  n. electric conduction
  342.13
  adj. nonconducting
  342.33
die out
  become extinct
  408.26
  burn out 332.8
  cease to exist 2.5
  disappear 447.2
dieresis see diaeresis
diesel fuel 380.4
diet
  n. council 755.1
  legislature 742.1
  meeting 74.2
  nutrition 309.11
  v. eat 307.18
  go on a diet 309.17
  slenderize 205.13
dietary 309.21
dietetic dietary 309.21
  eating 307.29
dietetics diet 309.11
  dietotherapeutics
  309.14
dieting diet 309.11
  eating 307.1
dietitian
  hospital staff 688.14
  nutritionist 309.13
differ
  be inharmonious
  795.8
  disagree 27.5
  dissent 522.4
  diversify 18.2
  not resemble 21.2
  quarrel 795.11
  vary 16.5
difference
  abnormality 85.1
  change 139.1
  disaccord 795.2
  disagreement 27.1
  dissent 522.1
  dissimilarity 21.1
  heraldic insignia
  569.2
  inequality 31.1
  nonuniformity 18.1
  product 86.5
  remainder 42.8
  unlikeness 16
different
  abnormal 85.9

differing 16.7
dissimilar 21.4
distinct 80.12
eccentric 474.4
new 122.11
nonuniform 18.3
differential
  n. characteristic 80.4
  difference 16.2
  gear 348.6
  adj. classificational
    61.7
  differentiative 16.9
  discriminating 492.7
  numerical 86.8
differentiate
  characterize 80.10
  discriminate 492.5
  distinguish 16.6
  diversify 18.2
  graduate 29.4
  signify 568.17
differentiation
  characterization 80.8
  differencing 16.4
  discrimination 492.3
  inconstancy 18.1
  indication 568.1
  mathematics 87.4
  particularity 80.1
differently
  dissimilarly 21.7
  diversely 16.10
different story 16.3
differing different 16.7
  disaccordant 795.15
  disagreeing 27.6
  dissenting 522.6
  unwilling 623.5
difficult adverse 729.13
  fastidious 896.10
  hard 731.16
  hard to understand
    549.14
  perverse 626.11
difficulties
  adversity 729.1
  poverty 838.1
difficulty
  abstruseness 549.2
  adversity 729.1
  annoyance 866.2
  disagreement 795.2
  handicap 730.6
  obstacle 730.4
  trouble 731
diffidence demur 623.2
  doubt 503.2
  fearfulness 891.3
  irresolution 627.3
  modesty 908.2
diffident
  demurring 623.7
  fearful 891.31
  irresolute 627.11
  modest 908.10
diffraction
  deflection 291.2
  dispersion 75.1
  wave phenomenon
    323.4

diffuse
  v. deflect 291.5
  disperse 75.4
  loosen 51.3
  pervade 186.7
  publish 559.10
  radiate 299.6
  shatter 49.13
  spread 271.9
  adj. copious 593.11
  deviant 291.8
  dispersed 75.9
  extensive 79.13
  plentiful 661.7
dig
  n. gibe 967.2
  hit 283.4
  pit 257.4
  push 283.2
  v. deepen 209.8
  drudge 716.14
  emotionally respond
    855.12
  excavate 257.15
  harvest 413.19
  search 485.30
  study 564.12
  thrust 283.11
  till 413.17
  understand 548.7
digest
  n. abridgment 607.1
  inventory 60.4
  law code 998.5
  v. absorb 306.13
  assimilate 309.16
  classify 61.6
  consider 478.12
  consume 666.2
  endure 861.7
  learn 564.7
  legalize 998.10
  think over 478.13
  understand 548.7
digestible 309.19
digestion
  consumption 666.1
  learning 564.2
  nutrition 309.8
  pulping 390.3
  sorption 306.6
digestive juice 312.2
diggings mine 383.6
  pit 257.4
  quarters 191.3
dig in fortify 799.9
  remain firm 624.9
dig into 485.22
digit finger 425.5
  foot 212.5
  number 86.1
digital grasping 813.9
  numerical 86.8
dignified
  eloquent 600.14
  stately 905.12
dignify formalize 646.5
  honor 914.12
dignitary 672.8
dignity
  eloquence 600.6
  formality 646.1

literary elegance
    589.1
  notability 672.2
  personage 672.8
  prestige 914.4
  pride 905.2
digress detour 321.6
  deviate 291.3
  wander 593.9
digression
  circuitousness 321.1
  departure 593.4
  detour 321.3
  deviation 291.1
  obliquity 219.1
digressive
  circuitous 321.7
  devious 291.7
  discursive 593.13
  oblique 219.13
digs 191.3
dig up assemble 74.18
  be curious 528.3
  find 488.4
  procure 811.10
  unearth 305.10
dike
  n. barrier 730.5
  body of water 398.1
  crack 201.2
  deposit 383.7
  fortification 799.4
  road 657.6
  trench 263.2
  v. excavate 257.15
  groove 263.3
dilapidated
  disintegrated 53.5
  old 123.14
  ramshackle 692.35
  slovenly 62.15
  unsteady 160.16
dilapidation
  decay 692.6
  disintegration 53.1
  impairment 692.1
dilate
  become larger 197.5
  bulge 256.10
  expatiate 593.7
  make larger 197.4
dilation
  distension 197.2
  exaggeration 617.1
  expatiation 593.6
  swelling 256.4
dilatory
  dawdling 270.11
  delaying 132.17
  indolent 708.18
  reluctant 623.6
dilemma choice 637.3
  perplexity 514.3
  predicament 731.6
  syllogism 482.6
dilettante
  connoisseur 897.7
  devotee 635.6
  half scholar 476.6
  ignoramus 477.8
  specialist 81.3
  trifler 673.9

diligence
  attention 530.1
  industry 707.6
  painstakingness 533.2
  perseverance 625.1
  studiousness 564.4
diligent
  attentive 530.15
  industrious 707.22
  painstaking 533.11
  persevering 625.7
  studious 564.17
diligently
  carefully 533.15
  industriously 707.27
  perseveringly 625.8
dilly 674.7
dillydally dally 708.13
  dawdle 270.8
  wait 132.12
diluent 391.4
dilute adulterate 44.13
  dissipate 75.5
  rarefy 355.3
  reduce 39.8
  thin 205.12
  weaken 160.11
diluted insipid 430.2
  thin 205.16
  watery 355.4
  weakened 160.19
diluvium deposit 43.2
  sediment 271.8
dim
  v. be dark 337.12
  blind 441.7
  darken 337.9
  decolor 363.5
  lose distinctness
    445.4
  adj. colorless 363.7
  darkish 337.15
  dim-sighted 440.13
  faint-sounding 452.16
  indistinct 445.6
  obscure 549.15
  stupid 469.16
dime 835.7
dime a dozen
  cheap 849.8
  paltry 673.18
  plentiful 661.7
dimension size 195.1
  space 179.1
dime store 832.1
dime-store 849.8
diminish decrease 39.6
  deteriorate 692.21
  extenuate 1006.12
  humiliate 906.5
  moderate 163.6
  narrow 205.11
  qualify 507.3
  recede 297.2
  reduce 39.7
  relieve 886.5
  subtract 42.9
diminishing
  decreasing 39.11
  moderating 163.14
  receding 297.5

dirty politics 744.14
dirty trick
  dishonesty 975.6
  trick 618.6
dirty word 972.4
dirty work
  dishonesty 975.6
  drudgery 716.4
Dis
  deity of nether world 1019.5
  god 1014.5
disability disease 686.1
  inability 158.2
  penalty 1009.2
disable cripple 692.17
  incapacitate 158.9
  sicken 686.47
disabled
  crippled 692.32
  incapacitated 158.16
  weakened 160.18
disabuse 520.2
disabused 520.5
disaccord
  n. difference 16.1
  disagreement 27.1
  dissent 522.1
  enmity 929.2
  nonconformity 83.1
  opposition 790.2
  unharmoniousness 795
  v. be inharmonious 795.8
  differ 16.5
  disagree 27.5
disaccordant
  different 16.7
  disagreeing 27.6
  opposing 790.8
  unfriendly 929.9
  unharmonious 795.15
disaccustom 643.2
disaccustomed 643.4
disadvantage
  n. impediment 730.6
  inexpedience 671.2
  penalty 1009.2
  trouble 731.3
  v. harm 675.6
  inconvenience 671.4
disadvantaged
  indigent 838.8
  inferior 37.6
disadvantaged, the
  the poor 838.3
  the underprivileged 919.6
disadvantageous
  harmful 675.12
  inexpedient 671.6
disaffected
  alienated 929.11
  averse 867.8
  unfaithful 975.20
disaffection
  dislike 867.1
  falling-out 795.4
  infidelity 975.5
disaffinity
  bad feeling 855.7

disaccord 795.1
dislike 867.1
  enmity 929.1
  repulsion 289.1
disaffirm 524.4
disaffirmation 524.2
disagree
  be inharmonious 795.8
  conflict 16.5
  differ 27.5
  dissent 522.4
  not be good for 684.4
  reject 776.3
disagreeable
  disagreeing 27.6
  irascible 951.19
  unkind 939.14
  unpleasant 864.17
  unsavory 429.5
disagreeableness
  unkindness 939.1
  unpleasantness 864.1
disagreeing
  clashing 27.6
  different 16.7
  disaccordant 795.15
  dissenting 522.6
  unwilling 623.5
disagreement
  contrariety 15.1
  difference 16.1
  disaccord 795.2
  disapproval 969.1
  discord 27
  dissent 522.1
  nonconformity 83.1
  refusal 776.1
  unwillingness 623.1
disallow deny 524.4
  disapprove 969.10
  not pay 842.6
  prohibit 778.3
  refuse 776.3
disappear
  absent oneself 187.8
  be destroyed 693.23
  be invisible 445.3
  be transient 111.6
  cease to exist 2.5
  hide oneself 615.8
  leave 301.8
  pass 119.6
  vanish 447.2
disappearance
  absence 187.4
  disappearing 447
  flight 631.4
  invisibility 445.1
disappoint
  defeat expectation 541.2
  disillusion 520.2
  dissatisfy 869.4
  make hopeless 889.11
disappointed
  disapproving 969.22
  discontented 869.5
  disillusioned 520.5
  let down 541.5

disappointing
  not up to expectation 541.6
  unsatisfactory 869.6
disappointment
  dashed hopes 541
  disapproval 969.1
  discontent 869.1
  disillusionment 520.1
  hopelessness 889.5
disapproval
  disapprobation 969
  dislike 867.1
  disparagement 971.1
  dissent 522.1
  rejection 638.1
  resentment 952.1
disapprove
  disfavor 969.10
  reject 638.2
  stigmatize 915.9
disapproved 638.3
disapprove of
  disapprove 969.10
  dislike 867.3
  disparage 971.8
  grimace 867.5
disarm
  demilitarize 804.11
  render powerless 158.11
disarmament 804.6
disarming 936.18
disarrange
  agitate 324.10
  derange 63.2
  discontinue 72.3
  dislocate 185.5
  disorder 62.9
disarranged
  confused 63.5
  dislocated 185.9
  disorderly 62.13
disarrangement
  derangement 63
  dislocation 185.1
  disorder 62.1
disarray
  n. disorder 62.1
  v. disarrange 63.2
  undress 232.7
disarticulate
  disjoint 49.16
  dislocate 185.5
  separate 49.9
disarticulated
  separated 49.21
  unordered 62.12
disassemble
  demolish 693.17
  take apart 49.15
disassembly
  demolition 693.5
  dismantlement 49.6
disassociation
  separation 49.1
  unrelatedness 10.1
disaster fatality 409.8
  misfortune 729.2
  ruin 693.4
  upheaval 162.5

disastrous
  calamitous 729.15
  convulsive 162.22
  destructive 693.26
disavow deny 524.4
  recant 628.9
disavowal denial 524.2
  recantation 628.3
disband
  demilitarize 804.11
  disperse 75.8
  part company 49.19
disbandment
  demilitarization 804.6
  dispersion 75.3
disbar depose 783.4
  dismiss 310.19
disbarment
  deposal 783.2
  ejection 310.4
disbelief
  nonreligiousness 1031.5
  unbelief 503.1
  uncertainty 514.2
disbelieve
  be incredulous 504.3
  be irreligious 1031.14
  unbelieve 503.5
disbelieving
  atheistic 1031.19
  unbelieving 503.8
disburden
  disembarrass 732.8
  lighten 353.6
  relieve 886.7
  take from 822.21
  unload 310.22
disbursal
  apportionment 816.2
  expenditure 843.1
  payment 841.1
disburse
  apportion 816.8
  spend 843.5
disc record 570.10
  sound recording 450.12
discard
  n. abandoned thing 633.4
  disuse 668.3
  elimination 77.2
  rejection 638.1
  v. abandon 633.5
  eject 310.13
  reject 638.2
  throw away 668.7
discarded
  abandoned 633.8
  disproved 506.7
  disused 668.11
  rejected 638.3
discarnate
  ghostly 1017.8
  immaterial 377.7
discern detect 488.5
  know 475.12
  see 439.12
  understand 548.8

discernible
 discoverable 488.10
 knowable 475.25
 manifest 555.8
 visible 444.6
discerning
 discriminating 492.8
 sagacious 467.16
discernment
 discrimination 492.2
 sagacity 467.4
 vision 439.1
discharge
 n. accomplishment
 722.1
 acquittal 1007.1
 detonation 456.3
 dismissal 310.5
 dispatch 705.2
 ejection 310.1
 electric discharge
 342.6
 emergence 303.2
 eruption 310.7
 excrement 311.3
 excretion 311.1
 execution 771.5
 exemption 762.8
 explosion 162.7
 outflow 303.4
 payment 841.1
 performance 768.1
 pus 388.3
 receipt 844.2
 release 763.2
 relief 886.2
 shot 285.5
 v. accomplish 722.4
 acquit 1007.4
 blast 456.8
 carry out 768.3
 disband 75.8
 dismiss 310.19
 eject 310.13
 erupt 162.12
 excrete 311.12
 execute 771.10
 exempt 762.14
 expel 310.24
 explode 162.13
 exude 303.15
 free 886.6
 pay in full 841.13
 perform 705.8
 release 763.5
 shoot 285.13
 unload 310.22
discharged
 accomplished 722.10
 paid 841.22
discharge tube
 343.11,16
disciple believer 1028.4
 convert 145.7
 follower 293.2
 man 787.8
 religious founder
 1022.2
 student 566.2
disciples 788.5
disciplinarian 749.14

disciplinary
 educational 562.19
 punishing 1010.25
 scientific 475.28
discipline
 n. government 741.1
 limitation 234.2
 orderliness 59.3
 punishment 1010.1
 science 475.10
 self-control 624.5
 sphere of work 656.4
 strictness 757.1
 study 562.8
 training 562.3
 v. be strict 757.4
 conform 82.3
 govern 741.12
 limit 234.5
 punish 1010.10
 train 562.14
disciplined
 limited 234.7
 patient 861.9
disclaim deny 524.4
 recant 628.9
 refuse 776.3
 reject 638.2
disclaimer denial 524.2
 recantation 628.3
 refusal 776.1
disclose indicate 568.17
 inform 557.8
 manifest 555.5
 reveal 556.4
 say 594.23
 testify 505.10
 unclose 265.13
 uncover 488.4
disclosed
 manifest 555.10
 open 265.18
 revealed 556.9
 visible 444.6
disclosive
 manifestative 555.9
 revealing 556.10
disclosure
 appearance 446.1
 discovery 488.1
 impartation 554.2
 indication 568.1
 manifestation 555.1
 revelation 556
 testimony 505.3
discolor blemish 679.6
 decolor 363.5
 mark 568.19
discoloration
 decoloration 363.3
 mark 568.5
 stain 679.2
discolored
 blemished 679.10
 colorless 363.7
discombobulate
 confuse 532.7
 excite 857.13
discomfit
 confuse 532.7
 defeat 727.9
 dismay 891.27

 embarrass 866.15
 thwart 730.15
discomfited
 defeated 727.14
 disorderly 62.13
 distressed 866.22
discomfiture
 confusion 532.3
 defeat 727.2
 disappointment
 541.1
 disorder 62.1
 frustration 730.3
 mortification 866.4
discomfort
 n. distressfulness
 864.5
 pain 424.1
 unpleasure 866.1
 v. cause unpleasant-
 ness 864.14
 distress 866.16
discommode
 inconvenience 671.4
 trouble 731.12
discompose
 agitate 324.10
 annoy 866.13
 bewilder 514.12
 confuse 532.7
 disarrange 63.4
 disorder 62.9
 embarrass 866.15
 excite 857.13
 give no pleasure
 866.12
discomposed
 agitated 324.16
 bewildered 514.23
 confused 532.12
 disorderly 62.13
 distressed 866.22
 excited 857.21
discomposure
 agitation 324.1
 confusion 532.3
 disarrangement 63.1
 disorder 62.1
 mortification 866.4
 perplexity 514.3
 unpleasure 866.1
disconcert
 bewilder 514.12
 confuse 532.7
 dismay 891.27
 embarrass 866.15
 excite 857.13
 mortify 864.13
 thwart 730.15
disconcerted
 bewildered 514.23
 confused 532.12
 disorderly 62.13
 distressed 866.22
disconcerting
 bewildering 514.25
 frightening 891.36
 frustrating 730.20
 mortifying 864.21
disconnect 49.9
disconnected
 discontinuous 72.4

 incoherent 51.4
 irregular 138.3
 separated 49.21
 unrelated 10.5
disconnection
 discontinuity 72.1
 psychology 690.27
 separation 49.1
 unrelatedness 10.1
disconsolate
 hopeless 889.12
 inconsolable 872.28
 wretched 866.26
disconsonant 461.4
discontent
 n. disapproval 969.1
 dissatisfaction 869
 ill humor 951.1
 resentment 952.1
 unhappiness 872.2
 unpleasure 866.1
 v. dissatisfy 869.4
 give no pleasure
 866.12
discontented
 disapproving 969.22
 dissatisfied 869.5
 ill-humored 951.17
 unhappy 872.21
discontinuance
 cessation 144.1
 disuse 668.2
 interruption 72.1
discontinue
 break the habit 643.3
 cease 144.6
 cease to use 668.4
 interrupt 72.3
 swear off 992.8
discontinued
 discontinuous 72.4
 disused 668.10
discontinuity
 change 139.1
 dislocation 185.1
 gap 57.2
 interruption 72
 interval 201.1
 irregularity 138.1
 separation 49.1
discontinuous
 disconnected 51.4
 interrupted 72.4
 irregular 138.3
 separate 49.20
 unordered 62.12
discord disaccord 795.1
 disagreement 27.1
 dissonance 461
 noise 453.3
 raucousness 458.2
discordant
 clashingly colored
 362.20
 contrary 15.6
 different 16.7
 disaccordant 795.15
 disagreeing 27.6
 dissonant 461.4
discothèque 878.11
discount
 n. price reduction 847

v. cut 847.2
  deal in money 835.27
  reject 638.2
  relax conditions
    507.5
discountenance
  n. mortification 866.4
  v. be against 790.7
    not tolerate 969.11
    thwart 730.15
discounting 42.14
discount rate 840.3
discount store 832.1
discourage
  daunt 891.26
  disincline 652.4
  make sad 872.18
  prevent 730.14
discouraging
  depressing 872.30
  dissuasive 652.5
  frightening 891.36
  preventing 730.19
discourse
  n. conversation 597.1
    lecture 599.3
    lesson 562.7
    reasoning 482.1
    speech 594.1
    treatise 606.1
  v. converse 597.9
    discourse upon 606.5
    discuss 597.12
    lecture 562.17
    make a speech 599.9
discourser
  conversationalist
    597.8
  disquisitor 606.3
  lecturer 599.5
discourteous
  disrespectful 965.5
  impolite 937.4
discourtesy
  behavior 737.2
  disrespect 965.1
  impoliteness 937
  misbehavior 738.1
discover create 167.13
  disclose 556.4
  find 488.2
  innovate 139.8
  learn 564.6
  see 439.12
discovered 167.23
discovery
  determination 488
  disclosure 556.1
  find 811.6
  innovation 139.3
discredit
  n. disrepute 915.1
    unbelief 503.1
  v. disbelieve 503.5
    disgrace 915.8
    disparage 971.8
    disprove 506.4
discredited
  disproved 506.7
  in disrepute 915.13
  not believed 503.12
discreet cautious 895.8

judicious 467.19
  reticent 613.10
  secretive 614.15
discreetly
  cautiously 895.12
  intelligently 467.20
discrepancy
  contrariety 15.1
  difference 16.1
  disagreement 27.1
  subtraction 42.8
discrepant
  contrary 15.6
  different 16.7
  disagreeing 27.6
discrete different 16.7
  disconnected 51.4
  discontinuous 72.4
  dispersed 75.9
  separate 49.20
  unrelated 10.5
discretion
  caution 895.1
  foresight 542.1
  free choice 762.6
  judiciousness 467.7
  option 637.2
  reticence 613.3
  secrecy 614.1
  will 621.1
discretionary 622.7
discriminate
  be unjust 977.8
  differentiate 16.6
  distinguish 492.5
  express prejudice
    527.8
discriminating
  differentiative 16.9
  discriminate 492.7
  fastidious 896.9
  judicious 467.19
  selective 637.23
  tasteful 897.9
discrimination
  criticalness 492
  differentiation 16.4
  fastidiousness 896.1
  good taste 897.1
  injustice 977.3
  judgment 494.1
  judiciousness 467.7
  literary elegance
    589.1
  prejudice 527.4
  selectivity 637.10
discursion
  deviation 291.1
  digression 593.4
  wandering 273.3
discursive
  circuitous 321.7
  devious 291.7
  dialectic(al) 482.22
  diffuse 593.13
  intelligent 467.12
  wandering 273.36
discus disk 253.2
  projectile 285.6
discuss confer 597.11
  debate 597.12
  discourse upon 606.5

discussion
  conference 597.6
  debate 597.7
  treatise 606.1
discussion group 755.3
disdain
  n. arrogance 912.5
    contempt 966.1
    defiance 793.1
  v. be fastidious 896.8
    deprecate 969.12
    flout 793.4
    reject 638.2
    scorn 966.3
disdainful
  arrogant 912.13
  contemptuous 966.8
  defiant 793.7
  insolent 913.8
  rejecting 638.4
disease
  n. bane 676.1
    illness 686
  v. infect 686.48
diseased morbid 686.56
  unwholesome 686.51
disembark
  anchor 275.15
  arrive 300.8
disembarkation
  arrival 300.2
  water travel 275.5
disembarrass
  disencumber 732.8
  extricate 763.7
  relieve 886.7
disembodied
  ghostly 1017.8
  immaterial 377.7
disembodiment
  dematerialization
    377.5
  occultism 1034.19
disembody
  dematerialize 377.6
  occultism 1034.20
  spiritualize 4.4
disembowel 305.13
disembowelment
  evisceration 305.4
  suicide 409.6
disembroil
  disembarrass 732.8
  extricate 763.7
  simplify 45.5
disenchant 520.2
disenchanted
  averse 867.8
  disapproving 969.22
  disillusioned 520.5
disenchantment
  disapproval 969.1
  disillusionment 520.1
  reversion 146.1
disencumber
  disembarrass 732.8
  lighten 353.6
  relieve 886.7
disencumbrance
  disembarrassment
    732.5
  relief 886.3

disendow 822.23
disenfranchise 764.8
disenfranchised 764.14
disengage detach 49.10
  disembarrass 732.8
  extricate 763.7
  retreat 295.6
  separate 49.9
disengaged
  escaped 632.11
  free 762.20
  idle 708.17
  separated 49.21
disengagement
  disembarrassment
    732.5
  extrication 763.3
  retreat 295.2
  separation 49.1
disentangle
  disembarrass 732.8
  extricate 763.7
  simplify 45.5
  solve 487.2
  straighten 250.5
  take out 305.10
disentanglement
  disembarrassment
    732.5
  extrication 763.3
  simplification 45.2
  solution 487.1
  withdrawal 305.1
disenthrall 763.4
disenthrone 783.4
disentitle 822.21
disentomb 305.11
disentwine 763.7
disesteem
  n. disapproval 969.1
    disrepute 915.1
    disrespect 965.1
  v. disrespect 965.3
disfavor
  n. disapproval 969.1
    dislike 867.1
    disrepute 915.1
    falling-out 795.4
  v. disapprove 969.10
    dislike 867.3
disfigure be ugly 899.5
  blemish 679.4
  deform 249.7
disfigured
  blemished 679.8
  deformed 249.12
  ugly 899.6
disfigurement
  blemish 679.1
  deformity 249.3
  ugliness 899.1
disgorge eject 310.24
  erupt 162.12
  relinquish 814.3
  vomit 310.25
disgorgement
  ejection 310.7
  vomiting 310.8
disgrace
  n. disparagement
    971.1
  disrepute 915.5

distracted 532.10
insane 473.25
distress
n. affliction 866.8
anxiety 890.1
appropriation 822.5
discomfort 866.5
grief 864.5
mortification 866.4
pain 424.1
penalty 1009.3
poverty 838.1
v. afflict 866.16
cause unpleasantness
864.14
hurt 424.7
trouble 731.12
work evil 675.6
worry 890.3
distressed
afflicted 866.22
pained 424.9
poor 838.7
troubled 731.19
distressing
harmful 675.12
painful 424.10
unpleasant 864.20
worrisome 890.9
distressingly
sadly 34.21
unpleasantly 864.28
distribute
apportion 816.8
deliver 818.13
disperse 75.4
dispose 60.9
publish 559.10
distributed
dispersed 75.9
made public 559.17
distribution
apportionment 816.2
arrangement 60.1
dispersion 75.1
distributive
dispersive 75.11
proportionate 816.13
distributor
intermediary 237.4
merchant 830.2
district
n. area 180.1
location 184.1
region 180.5
v. apportion 49.18
district attorney 1003.4
distrust
n. doubt 503.2
jealousy 953.2
suspicion 895.2
v. be doubtful 503.6
be jealous 953.3
distrustful
doubtful 503.9
jealous 953.4
suspicious 895.9
disturb agitate 324.10
annoy 866.13
bewilder 514.12
confuse 532.7
discompose 63.4

disorder 62.9
distress 866.16
excite 857.13
mortify 864.13
trouble 731.12
upset 890.3
disturbance
agitation 324.1
anxiety 890.1
commotion 62.4
confusion 532.3
disarrangement 63.1
disorder 62.1
excitement 857.3
mortification 866.4
perplexity 514.3
violence 162.2
disturbed
agitated 324.16
annoyed 866.21
anxious 890.6
bewildered 514.23
confused 532.12
disorderly 62.13
distressed 866.22
excited 857.21
neurotic 690.45
psychotic 473.27
disturbing
annoying 864.22
bewildering 514.25
exciting 857.28
mortifying 864.21
worrisome 890.9
disunion
disagreement 27.1
falling-out 795.4
separation 49.1
disunite separate 49.9
sow dissension 795.14
disunited
alienated 929.11
separated 49.21
disuse
n. abandonment
633.1
antiquation 123.3
disusage 668
v. discontinue 668.4
disused
abandoned 633.8
obsolete 123.15
out of use 668.10
disvalue 969.12
ditch
n. barrier 730.5
channel 396.1
crack 201.2
entrenchment 799.5
trench 263.2
v. crash land 278.52
cut 201.4
discard 668.7
evade 631.7
groove 263.3
ditchwater 682.9
ditheism 1020.5
ditheistic 1020.24
dither
n. cold sensation
333.2
disquiet 857.4

excitement 857.5
nervousness 859.2
shake 324.3
v. be cold 333.9
be unintelligent
469.12
be unsure 514.10
blabber 596.5
vacillate 627.8
ditto
n. copy 24.3
equal 30.4
repeat 103.5
the same 14.3
v. agree with 521.9
copy 24.8
duplicate 91.3
equal 30.5
imitate 22.5
repeat 103.7
reproduce 14.6
adv. again 103.17
identically 14.9
ditty 462.13
diuretic
n. cleaning agent
681.17
remedy 687.17
adj. cleansing 681.28
therapeutic 687.48
diurnal 137.8
diva lead 612.6
vocalist 464.13
divagate
be inattentive 531.3
deviate 291.3
muse 532.9
oblique 219.9
travel 273.22
wander 291.4
divan council 755.1
government 742.8
divaricate
v. deviate 291.3
differ 16.5
diverge 299.5
diversify 18.2
fork 299.7
open 265.12
adj. diverging 299.8
nonuniform 18.3
dive
n. air maneuver
278.13
brothel 989.9
cheapening 849.4
decrease 39.2
disapproved place
191.28
plunge 320.1
saloon 996.19
submergence 275.8
tumble 316.3
v. cheapen 849.6
decrease 39.6
deepen 209.8
fly 278.50
plunge 320.6
sail 275.47
swim 275.56
dive into begin 68.7
rush into 709.7

set to work 716.15
diver plunger 320.4
swimmer 275.12
diverge
be changed 139.5
deflect 291.5
deviate 291.3
differ 16.5
disperse 75.4
divaricate 299.5
diversify 18.2
fall out 795.10
oblique 219.9
part company 49.19
divergence
abnormality 85.1
change 139.1
deviation 291.1
difference 16.1
disagreement 27.1
dispersion 75.1
dissimilarity 21.1
distance 199.1
divergency 299
eccentricity 474.1
falling-out 795.4
inconstancy 18.1
obliquity 219.1
divergent
abnormal 85.9
changed 139.9
different 16.7
disagreeing 27.6
dissimilar 21.4
diverging 299.8
eccentric 474.4
nonuniform 18.3
oblique 219.9
separate 49.20
divers different 16.7
diversified 19.4
several 101.7
diverse different 16.7
dissimilar 21.4
varied 19.4
diversification
change 139.1
differentiation 16.4
multiformity 19.1
nonuniformity 18.1
diversified
different 16.7
nonuniform 18.3
varied 19.4
diversify
be changed 139.5
change 139.6
differentiate 16.6
multiformity 19.2
vary 18.2
diversion
amusement 878.1
attack 798.1
change 139.1
deviation 291.1
distraction 532.1
military tactics 797.9
misuse 667.1
diversity change 139.1
difference 16.1
disagreement 27.1
dissent 522.1

dissimilarity 21.1
multiformity 19.1
divert amuse 878.23
deflect 291.5
disincline 652.4
distract 532.6
misuse 667.4
diverted 878.28
divertissement
act 611.8
amusement 878.1
music 462.6
divest despoil 822.24
strip 232.5
take from 822.21
divested
deprived of 812.8
stripped 232.12
divestiture
disassembly 49.6
divestment 232.1
divestment
deprivation 822.6
loss 812.1
stripping 232
divide
n. mountains 207.10
v. analyze 48.6
apportion 816.6
arrange 60.11
bisect 92.4
calculate 87.11
classify 61.6
differentiate 16.6
discriminate 492.5
dissent 522.4
diverge 299.5
fall out 795.10
limit 235.8
make parts 55.6
measure 490.11
open 265.12
parcel out 49.18
partition 237.8
quantify 28.4
segregate 77.6
separate 49.9
share 815.6
sow dissension 795.14
vote 637.18
divided
alienated 929.11
halved 92.6
separated 49.21
dividend gain 811.3
payment 841.7
portion 816.5
receipts 844.1
securities 834.7
surplus 663.5
divinable 543.13
divination
forms of 543.15
occultism 1034.10
prediction 543.2
sorcery 1035.1
divinatory
foreseeing 542.7
predictive 543.11
divine
n. clergyman 1038.2
theologian 1023.3

v. augur 544.12
predict 543.9
solve 487.2
suppose 499.10
adj. godly 1013.19
gorgeous 900.19
mythological 1014.26
pleasant 863.8
sacred 1026.7
superb 674.17
theological 1023.4
diviner
occultist 1034.16
predictor 543.4
sorcerer 1035.5
divine right
authority 739.1
privilege 958.3
diving
air maneuver 278.13
plunging 320.3
swimming 275.11
diving equipment 320.5
divining rod 543.3
divinity deity 1013.1
god 1014.2
theology 1023.1
divisible
apportionable 816.12
separable 49.26
division affiliate 788.10
analysis 48.1
apportionment 816.1
bisection 92.1
class 61.2
classification 61.1
contents 194.1
differentiation 16.4
disagreement 795.2
discrimination 492.3
district 180.1
divergence 299.1
exclusiveness 77.3
faction 788.4
falling-out 795.4
group 74.3
legislative procedure
742.14
mathematics 87.4
military unit 800.19
music division 462.24
navy 800.26
part 55.1
partition 237.5
religion 1020.3
separation 49.1
vote 637.6
divisional 61.7
divisive 795.17
divisiveness 795.3
divorce
n. dissolution of mar-
riage 935
separation 49.1
v. dissolve marriage
935.5
separate 49.9
divorced
separated 49.21
unmarried 935.7
divorcée 935.2
divot 411.6

divulge indicate 555.5
make public 559.11
reveal 556.5
divulgence 556.2
divvy up
apportion 816.6
share 815.6
split up 49.18
Dixie 180.7
dizen dress up 231.41
ornament 901.8
dizziness
disease symptom
686.8
stupidity 469.5
vertigo 532.4
dizzy
v. make one's head
swim 532.8
adj. delirious 473.31
foolish 470.8
giddy 532.15
inconstant 141.7
intoxicated 996.30
scatterbrained 532.16
stupid 469.18
DJ 344.23
DNA gene 406.9
heredity 170.6
do
n. festival 878.4
v. accomplish 722.4
attend 186.8
behave 737.4
be of use 665.17
busy oneself with
656.11
cause 153.11
cook 330.4
effect 705.6
imitate 22.5
observe 768.3
perform music 462.40
practice 705.7
produce 167.9
represent 572.9
solve 487.2
suffice 661.4
suit 26.8
travel 273.18
traverse 273.19
interj. please 774.20
do a number on 971.9
do away with
exterminate 310.20
kill 409.13
put an end to 693.12
repeal 779.2
dobbin 414.10
do business
trade 827.14
work 656.12
docile
submissive 765.13
teachable 564.18
willing 622.5
dock
n. aviation 278.24
courtroom 1001.9
harbor 700.6
stage 611.21
storage place 660.6

tail 241.6
v. anchor 275.15
arrive 300.8
cut off 42.10
shorten 203.6
dockage fee 846.7
harbor 700.6
docked concise 592.6
incomplete 57.5
shortened 203.9
docket
n. document 570.5
label 568.13
list 88.6
record 570.4
record book 570.11
schedule 641.2
v. keep accounts
845.8
record 570.16
schedule 641.4
dockhand 276.9
docking arrival 300.2
spacecraft 282.2
dockyard harbor 700.6
plant 719.3
doctor
n. mender 694.10
physician 688.6
teacher 565.1
title 917.6
wise man 468.1
v. adulterate 44.13
aid 785.11
practice medicine
688.17
repair 694.14
tamper with 616.17
treat 689.30
undergo treatment
689.35
doctorate 917.6
doctored
distorted 249.11
tampered with
616.30
doctrinaire
n. dogmatist 513.7
intolerant person
527.5
theorist 499.7
adj. dogmatic 513.22
prejudiced 527.12
doctrinal
creedal 501.27
theological 1023.4
doctrine a belief 501.2
creed 1023.2
religion 1020.1
document
n. record 570.5
written matter 602.10
v. cite 505.14
confirm 505.12
particularize 8.6
documentary
n. motion picture
611.16
adj. documentational
570.19
evidential 505.17
true 516.12

documentation
confirmation 505.5
evidence 505.1
record 570.1
documented
evidential 505.17
recorded 570.18
dodder age 126.10
be weak 160.8
doddering aged 126.18
senile 469.23
unsteady 160.16
dodge
n. equivocation 483.4
evasive action 631.1
expedient 670.2
fraud 618.8
retreat 284.3
stratagem 735.3
trick 618.6
v. avoid 631.8
equivocate 483.9
live by one's wits 735.9
neglect 534.8
prevaricate 613.7
pull back 284.7
shirk 631.9
snub 966.7
dodger
corn bread 308.29
cunning person 735.6
deceiver 619.1
neglecter 534.5
safety equipment 699.3
dodging
equivocation 483.5
prevarication 613.4
shirking 631.2
dodo 123.8
doe
female animal 421.9
goat 414.8
hoofed animal 414.5
rabbit 414.29
doer
man of action 707.8
worker 718
doff detach 49.10
take off 232.6
dog
n. bad person 986.7
breeds of 414.72
canine 414.22
foot 212.5
inferior horse 414.14
male animal 420.8
ugly thing 899.4
v. annoy 866.13
follow 293.3
hunt 655.9
make anxious 890.4
obstruct 730.12
pursue 655.8
dog days
hot weather 328.7
summer 128.3
dog-eared eared 448.16
folded 264.7
worn 692.33
dog-eat-dog 945.3

dogface 800.9
dogged obstinate 626.8
persevering 625.7
tormented 866.24
worried 890.7
doggedly
obstinately 626.14
perseveringly 625.8
doggerel
n. poetry 609.5
adj. burlesque 967.14
infelicitous 590.2
dogging
annoyance 866.2
following 293.1
pursuit 655.1
doggy 414.45
doghouse
kennel 191.21
small place 196.3
dogie
abandoned thing 633.4
animal 414.6
waif 274.3
young cow 125.8
dog in the manger
hinderer 730.9
selfish person 978.3
dog-in-the-manger 869.5
dogleg angle 251.2
crookedness 219.8
deviation 291.1
dogma a belief 501.2
creed 1023.2
dogmatic
believing 501.21
certain 513.22
doctrinal 501.27
obstinate 626.8
orthodox 1024.8
prejudiced 527.12
unpersuadable 626.13
dogmatics 1023.1
dogmatism
obstinacy 626.1
orthodoxy 1024.5
sureness 513.6
unpersuadableness 626.5
dogmatist
doctrinaire 513.7
intolerant person 527.5
obstinate person 626.6
orthodox 1024.6
dogmatize 513.10
do-gooder 938.8
dog's life, a 729.1
dog tag 568.11
dog-tired 717.8
dogtrot
n. slowness 270.2
speed 269.3
v. go slow 270.6
dogwatch 108.3
dohickey 376.4
do in cheat 618.17
defeat 727.6
fatigue 717.4
kill 409.14

ruin 693.11
doing
n. act 705.3
action 705.1
affair 151.3
behavior 737.1
production 167.1
adj. happening 151.9
doings activity 707.1
acts 705.3
affairs 151.4
behavior 737.1
dojigger 376.4
do justice to
be just 976.6
do one's duty 962.10
eat 307.22
justify 1006.9
observe 768.2
dolce 462.54
doldrums calm 268.5
sadness 872.6
wind zone 403.10
dole
n. apportionment 816.2
donation 818.6
part 55.1
pittance 662.5
portion 816.5
small amount 35.2
subsidy 818.8
v. apportion 816.8
give 818.12
doleful pitiful 944.8
sorrowful 872.26
dolefully 872.36
dolittle 708.8
doll endearment 932.5
figure 572.4
girl 125.6
good person 985.2
little thing 196.5
toy 878.16
woman 421.6
dollar
British money 835.8
foreign money 835.9
US money 835.7
dollhouse
plaything 878.16
small place 196.3
doll-like 124.12
dollop 55.3
doll up beautify 900.14
dress up 231.41
ornament 901.8
dolly figure 572.4
narcotic 687.12
dolmen
memorial 570.12
tomb 410.16
dolor distress 866.5
pain 424.1
dolorous
sorrowful 872.26
unpleasant 864.20
dolphin
animal 414.35,64
mammal 415.8
dolt bungler 734.8
dunce 471.3

doltish 469.15
domain class 61.4
country 181.1
real estate 810.7
region 180.2
science 475.10
sphere of work 656.4
dome
n. arch 252.4
head 211.6
tower 207.11
v. cover 228.21
curve 252.6
domestic
n. servant 750.2
adj. home 191.32
recluse 924.9
domesticate
accustom 642.11
settle 184.16
tame 764.11
domesticated
subdued 764.15
tame 191.34
weak 765.15
domesticity 191.2
domestic science 330.1
domicile
n. abode 191.1
v. house 188.10
inhabit 188.7
dominance
ascendancy 739.6
influence 172.1
dominant
n. key 463.15
note 463.14
adj. authoritative 739.15
chief 36.14
governing 741.18
influential 172.14
most important 672.23
prevalent 79.12
victorious 726.8
dominate
be high 207.16
govern 741.15
have influence over 172.11
possess authority 739.13
prevail 79.10
subject 764.8
domination
ascendancy 739.6
control 741.2
despotism 741.10
influence 172.1
subjection 764.1
view 444.3
domineer 741.16
domineering
n. arrogance 912.1
authoritativeness 739.3
despotism 741.10
adj. arrogant 912.9
imperious 739.16
Dominican 1038.18

dominion
ascendancy 739.6
control 741.2
country 181.1
governance 739.5
ownership 808.2
precedence 64.1
region 180.2
supremacy 36.3
don
n. form of address
420.7
teacher 565.1
v. put on 231.42
Donar
Norse deity 1014.6
thunder god 456.5
donate
contribute 818.14
give 818.12
provide 659.7
donation gift 818.6
giving 818.1
done
adj. completed 722.11
cooked 330.7
ended 70.8
exhausted 717.8
produced 167.20
worn-out 692.38
phr. so be it 521.19
donee 819.4
done for dead 408.30
defeated 727.14
dying 408.33
no more 2.10
ruined 693.28
terminated 70.8
done with
disused 668.10
ended 70.8
finished 722.11
dong 454.8
Don Juan beau 931.12
deceiver 619.1
tempter 650.3
unchaste person
989.10
donkey ass 414.20,58
dolt 471.3
obstinate person
626.6
donna
form of address 421.8
woman 421.5
donnish
book-learned 475.22
pedagogical 565.12
studious 564.17
donnybrook
commotion 62.4
free-for-all 796.5
noise 453.3
quarrel 795.5
donor giver 818.11
provider 659.6
do nothing idle 708.11
not change 140.6
not stir 706.2
do-nothing
n. idler 708.8
adj. indolent 708.18

passive 706.6
Don Quixote
knight 918.5
visionary 535.13
don't 778.1
don't make waves 82.10
doodad 376.4
doodle
n. fool 471.1
picture 574.14
v. dally 708.13
picture 574.20
play music 462.43
scribble 602.20
waste time 708.12
doodlebug
dowsing 543.3
rocket bomb 281.4
doom
n. condemnation
1008.1
death 408.1
end 70.1
fate 640.2
judgment 494.5
ruin 693.2
the future 121.3
v. condemn 1008.3
destine 640.7
pass judgment 494.13
send to hell 1019.6
work evil 675.6
doomed destined 640.9
hopeless 889.13
doomful
destructive 693.26
ominous 544.17
unfortunate 729.14
doomsday 121.3
do one's duty
do what is expected
962.10
eat 307.22
do one's thing
act 705.4
specialize 81.4
door entrance 302.6
opening 265.7
outlet 303.9
doorbell 454.4
doorjamb
entrance 302.6
post 217.4
doorkeeper
gatekeeper 699.12
holy orders 1038.4
doorman 699.12
doormat mat 228.9
weakling 160.6
doorpost
entrance 302.6
post 217.4
doorstop 730.7
doorway
entrance 302.6
opening 265.7
do over convert 145.11
repeat 103.7
reproduce 169.7
dope
n. contraband 826.3
depressant 423.3

film 577.10
fuel 331.1
narcotic 687.5
stupid 471.3
v. calculate 87.11
medicate 689.31
predict 543.9
put to sleep 712.20
render insensible
423.4
solve 487.2
dope, the
information 557.1
the facts 1.4
doped sleepy 712.21
unconscious 423.8
dope fiend 642.10
dopey dazed 532.14
inert 268.14
languid 708.19
stupid 469.16
Doppelgänger
specter 1017.3
the same 14.3
do right by 938.9
dorm 191.16
dormancy
inactivity 708.1
inertness 268.4
latency 546.1
passivity 706.1
dormant asleep 712.22
do-nothing 706.6
inert 268.14
languid 708.19
latent 546.5
dormer 265.8
dormitory
abode 191.16
bedroom 192.7
dorsal back 241.10
phonetic 594.31
dorsi– 241.3
dosage 963.2
dose
n. amount 28.2
medicine 687.6
portion 55.5
venereal disease
686.16
v. impose 963.6
medicate 689.31
doss
n. bed 216.19
housing 188.3
sleep 712.2
v. snooze 712.14
dossier 570.5
dot
n. endowment 818.9
mark 568.5
music 463.12
point 196.7
small amount 35.2
spottiness 374.3
v. mark 568.19
sprinkle 75.6
variegate 374.7
dotage credulity 502.1
old age 126.5
senility 469.10
dotard old man 127.2

senile 471.9
dote be insane 473.19
be unintelligent
469.12
dote on 931.18
do the trick
accomplish 722.4
be expedient 670.3
be of use 665.17
succeed with 724.10
do time
be imprisoned 761.18
spend time 108.5
doting aging 126.17
credulous 502.8
foolish 470.8
senile 469.23
dotted spotted 374.13
sprinkled 75.10
dotty eccentric 474.4
insane 473.26
spotted 374.13
double
n. copy 24.3
fold 264.1
image 572.3
specter 1017.3
substitute 149.2
the same 14.3
turn 291.1
v. copy 24.8
duplicate 91.3
evade 631.7
fold 264.5
increase 38.5
middle 69.3
repeat 103.7
substitute for 149.5
turn back 295.8
adj. dishonest 975.21
duplicate 91.4
falsehearted 616.31
two 90.6
double agent
secret agent 781.9
traitor 619.10
double-check
make certain 513.12
verify 87.14
double cross 975.8
double-cross
betray 975.14
deceive 618.13
doubled folded 264.7
repeated 103.12
double-dealer
criminal 986.10
deceiver 619.1
traitor 619.10
double-dealing
n. dishonesty 975.6
falseheartedness
616.4
adj. dishonest 975.21
falsehearted 616.31
double-decker 272.12
double Dutch 549.7
double-edged
acrimonious 161.13
sharp 258.10
double entendre
ambiguity 550.1

equivocation 550.2
joke 881.6
double-header 878.9
double meaning 550.1
double-or-nothing 515.4
double personality
dissociation 690.27
pathological type 690.16
psychosis 473.4
double-quick
n. hastening 709.3
march 273.15
adj. fast 269.19
hurried 709.11
adv. fast 269.21
doubles 878.9
doublet two 90.2
word 582.2
double take
delay 132.2
sequel 67.1
double-talk 547.2
doublethink 90.1
double time
gratuity 818.5
hastening 709.3
march 273.15
double-time
v. make haste 709.5
adj. hurried 709.11
doubleton 90.3
double vision 440.1
doubling duality 90.1
duplication 91.1
fold 264.1
lining 194.3
repetition 103.1
doubloon 835.4
doubt
n. agnosticism 1031.6
apprehension 891.4
jealousy 953.2
skepticism 503.2
uncertainty 514.2
v. be irreligious 1031.14
be jealous 953.3
be skeptical 503.6
be uncertain 514.9
doubted 503.12
doubter
agnostic 1031.12
doubting Thomas 503.4
doubtful
agnostic 1031.20
dishonest 975.16
improbable 512.3
skeptical 503.9
unbelievable 503.10
uncertain 514.16
unsafe 697.11
doubting
skeptical 503.9
uncertain 514.15
doubting Thomas
agnostic 1031.12
doubter 503.4
doubtless
adj. believing 501.21
certain 513.16

adv. certainly 513.25
probably 511.8
doubtlessly
certainly 513.25
probably 511.8
douche
n. bath 681.8
sprinkler 392.8
washing 681.5
v. moisten 392.12
soak 392.13
wash 681.19
dough money 835.2
semiliquid 389.5
softness 357.4
doughboy 800.7
doughnut 308.43
doughy pasty 390.6
soft 357.12
viscous 389.12
dour firm 757.7
strict 757.6
sullen 951.24
unkind 939.22
unyielding 626.9
douse extinguish 332.7
immerse 320.7
take off 232.6
dousing
extinguishing 332.2
immersion 320.2
dove bird 414.33,66
innocent person 984.4
pacifist 803.6
unsophisticate 736.3
dovelike avian 414.52
innocent 984.6
weak 765.15
dovetail
n. joint 47.4
v. agree 26.6
fasten 47.8
interact 13.8
dovetailed 13.12
dovetailing 26.10
dowager mistress 749.2
old woman 127.3
widow 935.4
woman 421.5
dowdy 692.34
dower
n. endowment 818.9
talent 733.4
v. endow 818.17
do without
abstain 992.7
not use 668.5
relinquish 814.3
Dow-Jones Industrial Average 833.1
down
n. beard 230.8
descent 316.1
feather 230.19
fine texture 351.3
hill 207.5
lightness 353.2
plain 387.1
reverse 729.3
softness 357.4
v. bring down 318.5

descend 316.5
eat 307.20
endure 861.7
adj. defeated 727.14
dejected 872.22
depressing 872.30
descending 316.11
laid up 686.55
lower 208.8
recorded 570.18
sick 686.52
adv. downward 316.13
in cash 841.25
down-and-out
destitute 838.9
ruined 693.28
down at the heel
indigent 838.8
shabby 692.34
slovenly 62.15
downbeat
n. beat 137.3
music 463.26
adj. pessimistic 889.16
downcast
dejected 872.22
depressed 318.12
downturned 316.12
downdraft 403.1
downer adversity 729.1
dejection 872.3
difficulty 866.2
sedative 687.12
downfall defeat 727.1
descent 316.1
failure 725.3
rainstorm 394.2
ruin 693.3
downgrade
n. declivity 219.5
descent 316.1
v. demote 783.3
reduce 39.7
adj. sloping downward 219.16
adv. down 316.13
slantingly 219.23
downhearted 872.22
downhill
n. declivity 219.5
adj. descending 316.11
sloping downward 219.16
adv. down 316.13
slantingly 219.23
down home 188.16
down in the mouth 872.22
down pat 475.26
downpour
descent 316.1
flow 395.4
rainstorm 394.2
downright
adj. absolute 34.12
candid 974.17
thorough 56.10
unqualified 508.2
vertical 213.11
adv. down 316.13
extremely 34.22

unconditionally 508.3
Down's syndrome
genetic disease 686.11
mental deficiency 469.9
down the drain
no more 2.10
wasted 854.9
downtime
interim 109.1
respite 711.2
down-to-earth 536.6
downtown
n. city district 183.6
adj. urban 183.10
downtrodden 764.16
downturn
business cycle 827.9
decrease 39.2
descent 316.1
deterioration 692.3
down under 180.6
downward
adj. descending 316.11
flowing 267.8
adv. down 316.13
downward trend
descent 316.1
deterioration 692.3
downwind
leeward 242.9
navigation 275.68
downy feathery 230.27
fine 351.8
light 353.10
smooth 260.9
soft 357.14
dowry
endowment 818.9
talent 733.4
doxology hymn 1032.3
sacred music 462.16
doxy 989.17
doyen chief 749.3
dean 127.5
doze
n. sleep 712.2
v. sleep 712.13
dozen 99.7
doze off 712.16
DP alien 78.3
displaced person 185.4
fugitive 631.5
migrant 274.5
outcast 926.4
drab brown 367.3
lackluster 337.17
monotonous 17.6
drabness grayness 366.1
lusterlessness 337.5
Draconian 939.24
Dracula 891.9
draft
n. abridgment 607.1
demand 753.1
diagram 654.3
displacement 209.6
dose 687.6

drink 307.4
enlistment 780.6
intoxication 996.6
music 462.28
negotiable instru-
  ment 835.11
picture 574.14
pull 286.2
pulling 286.1
recruits 800.17
wind 403.1
written matter 602.10
v. enlist 780.16
  extract 305.12
  outline 654.12
  picture 574.20
  write 602.19
adj. pulling 286.6
draft animal 271.6
draftee 800.17
drafting drawing 574.6
  enlistment 780.6
  extraction 305.3
draftsman 579.3
drafty 403.25
drag
n. annoyance 866.2
  attraction 288.1
  aviation 278.36
  boring person 884.4
  burden 352.7
  friction 350.5
  gait 273.14
  hindrance 730.7
  influence 172.2
  pull 286.2
  slowing 270.4
  tobacco smoking
    434.10
v. attract 288.4
  dawdle 270.8
  delay 132.8
  follow 293.4
  go slow 270.6
  linger 110.7
  pull 286.4
  smooth 260.5
  trail 215.6
  use tobacco 434.14
  walk 273.27
dragged out
  lengthened 202.9
  protracted 110.11
draggle befoul 682.19
  pull 286.4
  trail 215.6
draggled slovenly 62.15
  soiled 682.21
drag in impose on 10.4
  interpose 237.6
dragnet search 485.14
  seizure 822.2
  snare 618.12
dragon
  ill-humored person
    951.11
  monster 85.20
  reptile 414.60
  violent person 162.9
drag on
  be tedious 884.5
  continue 143.3

linger 110.7
persist 17.3
dragoon
n. cavalryman 800.11
v. coerce 756.7
  intimidate 891.28
drag out elicit 305.14
  expatiate 593.8
  go slow 270.6
  lengthen 202.7
  postpone 132.9
  protract 110.9
drain
n. channel 396.5
  consumption 666.1
  demand 753.1
  depletion 812.2
  filth receptacle
    682.12
  outflow 303.4
v. consume 666.2
  decolor 363.5
  deplete 812.5
  despoil 822.24
  disable 158.9
  drain off 822.13
  dry 393.6
  eject 310.21
  emerge 303.13
  exploit 665.16
  extract 305.12
  subtract 42.9
  take from 822.21
drainage drying 393.3
  evacuation 310.6
  extraction 305.3
  outflow 303.4
drained barren 166.4
  bleached 363.8
  exhausted 717.8
  unhealthy 686.50
  used up 666.4
  weakened 160.18
draining
n. evacuation 310.6
  exhaustion 717.2
  extraction 305.3
adj. demanding 753.8
  deteriorating 692.46
  fatiguing 717.11
  weakening 160.20
drake
  male animal 420.8
  poultry 414.34
dram dose 55.5
  drink 307.4
  intoxication 996.6
  small amount 35.2
  unit of weight 352.23
drama
  representation 572.1
  stage show 611.4
  theater 611.1
dramatic poetic 609.17
  show business 611.38
  theatrical 904.24
  vocal 462.51
dramatics display 904.4
  theatrics 611.2
dramatist
  author 602.15
  playwright 611.27

dramatize affect 903.12
  indicate 555.5
  play up 672.15
  theatricalize 611.33
dramaturgic(al) 611.38
drape
n. cover 228.2
  hanging 215.4,13
  shade 338.1
v. clothe 231.38
  hang 215.6
draper clothier 231.32
  merchant 830.3
drapery clothing 231.1
  cover 228.2
  fabric 378.5
  ornamentation
    901.13
  pendant 215.13
  shade 338.1
drastic 162.15
draught, draughtsman,
  draughty see **draft**
  etc.
draw
n. attendance 186.4
  attraction 288.1
  equality 30.3
  pull 286.2
  ravine 201.2
  tie 118.2
v. acquire 811.8
  attract 288.4
  constrict 198.7
  describe 608.12
  equal 30.5
  extract 305.12
  influence 172.9
  lengthen 202.7
  lure 650.4
  picture 574.20
  pull 286.4
  receive 819.6
  remove 305.10
  represent 572.6
  use tobacco 434.14
draw and quarter
  tear apart 49.14
  torture 1010.18
drawback
  disadvantage 671.2
  discount 847.1
  fault 678.2
  obstacle 730.4
draw back
  flinch 891.21
  pull back 284.7
  retract 297.3
  retreat 295.6
drawbridge
  bridge 657.10
  fortification 799.4
drawer sketcher 579.3
  storage place 660.6
draw in constrict 198.7
  involve 176.2
  lure 650.4
  narrow 205.11
  reel in 287.9
  retract 297.3
  take in 306.12

drawing
n. art 574.6
  diagram 654.3
  extraction 305.1
  graphic arts 578.1
  lottery 515.11
  picture 574.14
  pulling 286.1
  representation 572.1
  suction 305.3
adj. attraction 288.5
  pulling 286.6
drawing card 650.2
drawing room
  parlor 192.5
  railway car 272.14
  society 644.6
  train room 192.10
drawl
n. regional accent
    594.9
  slowness 270.1
v. speak poorly 595.7
  utter 594.26
draw lots 515.18
drawn equal 30.7
  lengthened 202.9
  tired-looking 717.7
draw near
  approach 296.3
  be imminent 152.2
  be in the future
    121.6
  near 200.7
drawn-out
  lengthened 202.9
  protracted 110.11
draw on
  be imminent 152.2
  be in the future
    121.6
  induce 153.12
  influence 172.9
  lure 650.4
  occur 151.6
  seduce 931.21
draw out elicit 305.14
  expatiate 593.8
  extract 305.10
  lengthen 202.7
  protract 110.9
draw the line
  be unwilling 623.3
  discriminate 492.5
  express prejudice
    527.8
  limit 234.5
draw up form 59.5
  raise 317.8
  stop 144.7
  write 602.19
dray 272.2
drayage charge 846.8
  pulling 286.1
  transportation 271.3
dread
n. anxiety 890.1
  expectancy 539.3
  fear 891.1
  unpleasure 866.1
v. expect 539.5
  fear 891.18

talk nonsense 547.5
drive mad 473.23
drive on hasten 709.4
  hustle 707.13
  impel 283.10
  make one's way 294.4
  urge on 648.16
drive out 310.14
driver coachman 274.9
  male servant 750.4
  motorist 274.10
  operator 164.4
  propeller 285.7
  tyrant 749.14
driver's seat 739.10
drive up the wall
  866.13
driveway 657.6
driving
  n. operation 164.1
  riding 273.6
  adj. aggressive 707.23
  attacking 798.29
  compelling 756.9
  eloquent 600.11
  impelling 283.20
  motivating 648.25
  moving 267.7
  obsessive 473.34
  propulsive 285.15
  rainy 394.10
driving force
  impulse 283.1
  pushing 285.1
drizzle
  n. rain 394.1
  v. rain 394.9
drizzling 394.10
droit 958.3
droll humorous 880.4
  witty 881.15
drome 278.22
dromedary
  beast of burden
  271.6
  hoofed animal 414.5
drone
  n. bagpipe 465.10
  bee 414.38
  continuity 71.2
  mumbling 595.4
  music 462.22
  nonworker 708.10
  regularity 17.2
  repetitiousness 103.4
  slow person 270.5
  voice 463.5
  v. hum 452.13
  persist 17.3
  speak poorly 595.9
droning
  n. hum 452.7
  mumbling 595.4
  adj. humming 452.20
  sounding 450.15
drool
  n. nonsense 547.2
  saliva 312.3
  v. be insane 473.19
  be unintelligent
  469.12
  salivate 312.6

talk nonsense 547.5
droop
  n. fall 316.2
  gait 273.14
  hang 215.2
  v. be despondent
  872.16
  deteriorate 692.21
  fail 686.45
  get tired 717.5
  hang 215.6
  sink 316.6
  weaken 160.9
drooping
  dejected 872.22
  descending 316.11
  deteriorating 692.46
  fatigued 717.6
  hanging 215.10
  languishing 160.21
  loose 51.5
  weak 160.12
droopy dejected 872.22
  fatigued 717.6
  hanging 215.10
  languid 708.19
  weak 160.12
drop
  n. advantage 36.2
  declivity 219.5
  decrease 39.2
  descent 316.1
  deterioration 692.3
  drink 996.6
  gallows 1011.5
  leakage 303.5
  mailbox 604.7
  medicine 687.4
  minute quantity
  196.7
  pause 144.3
  plunge 320.1
  scenery 611.25
  sphere 255.3
  trickle 395.7
  v. become exhausted
  717.5
  break the habit 643.3
  decrease 39.6
  descend 316.5
  discontinue 668.4
  faint 423.5
  fell 318.5
  flow out 303.14
  give birth 167.15
  give up 633.7
  gravitate 352.15
  incline 219.10
  let fall 318.7
  lose 812.4
  plunge 320.6
  relinquish 814.3
  reproduce 169.9
  shoot 285.13
  strike dead 409.18
  take off 232.6
  trickle 395.18
  weaken 160.9
drop by 922.17
drop cloth 228.9
drop dead 408.22
drop in enter 302.7

visit 922.17
drop in on 540.7
drop in the bucket
  pittance 662.5
  small amount 35.5
  trifle 673.5
drop it cease 144.6
  no matter 673.22
  stop! 144.15
droplet drop 255.3
  minute quantity
  196.7
drop off decrease 39.6
  descend 316.5
  die 408.20
  go to sleep 712.16
dropout 83.3
drop out
  abandon 633.5
  dissent 522.4
  not conform 83.4
droppings 311.4
dropsy
  disease symptom
  686.8
  distension 197.2
drop the subject 531.4
dross ashes 329.16
  residue 43.2
drought dryness 393.1
  thirst 634.7
  want 662.4
drove
  n. flock 74.5
  v. drive animals 416.8
drover guider 748.7
  herder 416.3
drown
  come to grief 729.10
  die 408.24
  drench 392.14
  submerge 320.7
  suffocate 409.19
  suppress 760.8
drowned dead 408.32
  flooded 395.25
  soaked 392.17
  underwater 209.13
drown out 453.7
drowse
  n. sleep 712.2
  v. sleep 712.13
drowsiness
  languor 708.6
  sleepiness 712.1
drowsy sleepy 712.21
  tranquilizing 163.15
drub
  n. hit 283.4
  stamp 283.9
  v. defeat 727.6
  pound 283.14
  punish 1010.14
  stamp 283.19
drudge
  n. grub 718.3
  servant 750.2
  v. be busy 707.10
  persevere 625.3
  serve 750.13
  work hard 716.14
drudgery 716.4

drug
  n. commodity 831.2
  depressant 423.3
  medicine 687.4–32
  types of 687.52–65
  v. make unfeeling
  856.8
  medicate 689.31
  put to sleep 712.20
  render insensible
  423.4
drug addict 642.10
drug addiction 642.9
drug culture 642.9
drugged languid 708.19
  sleepy 712.21
  unconscious 423.8
  unfeeling 856.9
druggist 687.35
drug pusher 826.4
drugstore
  pharmacy 687.36
  store 832.4
drugstore cowboy 442.1
drug user addict 642.10
  pathological type
  690.16
Druid idolater 1033.4
  pagan priest 1038.16
  predictor 543.4
drum
  n. cylinder 255.4
  instrument 465.19
  staccato sound 455.1
  v. bird sound 460.5
  make staccato sounds
  455.4
  music 462.45
  pulsate 323.12
  rain 394.9
  repeat 103.10
drumbeat 455.1
drumbeating 559.5
drum major 464.17
drummer
  percussionist 464.10
  traveling salesman
  830.5
drumming
  n. hit 283.4
  pulsation 323.3
  staccato sound 455.1
  adj. rainy 394.10
  staccato 455.7
drum out depose 783.4
  dismiss 310.19
  drive out 310.14
drumstick drum 465.19
  fowl part 308.23
  leg 273.16
drunk
  n. drunkard 996.10
  spree 996.5
  adj. fervent 855.23
  intoxicated 996.30
drunkard addict 642.10
  bad person 986.2
  drinker 996.10
drunken dizzy 532.15
  drinking 996.34
  intoxicated 996.30

dummy
  n. a nobody 673.7
  deputy 781.1
  dolt 471.3
  fake 616.13
  figure 572.4
  figurehead 749.4
  imitation 22.3
  man 787.8
  model 25.5
  mute 451.3
  nonentity 4.2
  pawn 658.3
  playing cards 878.17
  substitute 149.2
  typesetting 603.2
  adj. substitute 149.8
  ungenuine 616.26
dummy up 451.6
dump
  n. armory 801.2
  disapproved place
    191.28
  filth receptacle
    682.12
  filthy place 682.11
  gibe 967.2
  hoard 660.1
  hovel 191.12
  humiliation 906.2
  indignity 965.2
  refuse heap 682.10
  storage place 660.6
  trash pile 669.6
  v. discard 668.7
  humiliate 906.5
  relinquish 814.3
  sell 829.8
  sell stocks 833.24
  unload 310.22
dumpling 308.33
dump on disdain 966.3
  humiliate 906.5
  offend 965.4
  ridicule 967.9
dumps
  ill humor 951.10
  sadness 872.6
dumpy
  corpulent 195.18
  dwarf 196.13
  stubby 203.10
dun
  n. bill 845.3
  creditor 839.4
  horse 414.13
  v. bill 845.11
  importune 774.12
  adj. brown 367.3
Dun and Bradstreet
  rating credit 839.1
  financial condition
    836.5
dunce dolt 471.3
  ignoramus 477.8
dunderhead 471.4
dune hill 207.5
  pile 74.10
dung excretion 311.4
  fertilizer 165.4
dungarees 231.56
dungeon 761.8

dunghill 682.10
dunk drench 392.14
  immerse 320.7
dunking
  immersion 320.2
  soaking 392.7
dunning
  n. importuning 774.3
  adj. importunate
    774.18
duo part music 462.17
  two 90.2
duodecimal system 86.2
duodenal
  intestinal 225.10
  twelve 99.24
duodenum 225.4
duologue
  conversation 597.3
  stage show 611.4
dupable 502.9
dupe
  n. agent 781.3
  copy 24.3
  credulous person
    502.4
  gullible person 620
  instrument 658.3
  laughingstock 967.7
  sycophant 907.3
  unsophisticate 736.3
  v. copy 24.8
  deceive 618.13
  duplicate 91.3
  gull 470.7
duplex
  n. apartment house
    191.15
  adj. double 91.4
  two 90.6
duplicate
  n. copy 24.3
  doubling 91.1
  image 572.3
  the same 14.3
  v. copy 24.8
  double 91.3
  repeat 103.7
  replicate 14.6
  reproduce 169.7
  adj. analogous 20.11
  double 91.4
  identical 14.7
duplicated
  repeated 103.12
  twin 90.6
duplication copy 24.3
  doubling 91
  duality 90.1
  imitation 22.3
  remaking 169.1
  repetition 103.1
  reproduction 24.2
  superfluity 663.4
duplicity deceit 618.3
  dishonesty 975.6
  duality 90.1
  falseheartedness
    616.4
durability
  endurance 110
  permanence 140.1

  perpetuity 112.1
  substantiality 3.1
  toughness 359.1
durable
  enduring 110.10
  permanent 140.7
  substantial 3.7
  tough 359.4
durables 831.4
duration
  durability 110.1
  permanence 140.1
  term 107.3
  time 105.1
duress coercion 756.3
  imprisonment 761.3
  necessity 639.1
  power 157.1
during 105.14
dusk
  n. darkishness 337.4
  daylight 335.10
  evening 134.3
  v. be dark 337.12
  adj. dark 365.9
  darkish 337.15
  evening 134.8
dusky dark 365.9
  darkish 337.15
  evening 134.8
dust
  n. corpse 408.16
  dirt 682.6
  dryness 393.2
  land 385.1
  lightness 353.2
  powder 361.5
  refuse 669.4
  rubbish 669.5
  v. clean 681.18
  dirty 682.15
  sprinkle 75.6
dustbin 669.7
dust bowl
  the country 182.1
  wasteland 166.2
dustheap 669.6
dust storm 403.13
dusty dirty 682.22
  dry 393.7
  gray 366.4
  old 123.14
  powdery 361.11
  tedious 884.8
  uninteresting 883.6
  wayworn 273.40
Dutch uncle 754.3
duteous dutiful 962.13
  obedient 766.3
  observant 768.4
dutiful duteous 962.13
  obedient 766.3
  observant 768.4
  pious 1028.8
  respectful 964.8
dutifully
  duteously 962.18
  obediently 766.6
duty charge 963.3
  demand 753.1
  function 665.5
  job 656.3

  military service
    797.13
  obligation 962
  respect 964.1
  rite 1040.3
  tariff 846.11
  task 656.2
  tax 846.10
  worship 1032.8
duty-bound 962.16
dwarf
  n. fairy 1014.18
  midget 196.6
  small amount 35.2
  v. minimize 39.9
  adj. little 196.13
dwarfed
  deformed 249.12
  meager 662.10
  undersized 196.13
dwell continue 110.6
  inhabit 188.7
dweller 190.2
dwell in
  be present 186.6
  exist in 1.11
dwelling
  n. abode 191.1
  habitation 188.1
  adj. resident 188.13
dwell on
  emphasize 672.13
  harbor revenge 956.5
  harp upon 884.7
  protract 110.9
  remember 537.13
  repeat 103.9
dwindle decrease 39.6
  disappear 447.2
  fail 686.45
  quiet 268.8
  recede 297.2
dwindling
  n. decrease 39.2
  adj. decreasing 39.11
  deteriorating 692.46
  quiescent 268.12
  receding 297.5
dyad 90.2
dybbuk
  evil spirit 1016.7
  specter 1017.1
dye
  n. coloring matter
    362.8
  types of 362.22
  v. color 362.13
  infuse 44.12
dyed 362.16
dyed-in-the-wool
  confirmed 642.21
  dyed 362.17
  established 142.13
  thorough 56.10
dying
  n. death 408.1
  decrease 39.1
  deterioration 692.3
  extinguishing 332.2
  terminal case 408.15
  adj. expiring 408.33
  receding 297.5

transient 111.7
dying down 268.3
dying to 634.22
dyke
　homosexual 419.16
　mannish female
　　420.9
dynamic(al)
　energetic 161.12
　enterprising 707.23
　mechanics 347.9
　powerful 157.12
dynamics forces 157.7
　mechanics 347.3
　motion 267.1
dynamism energy 161.1
　enterprise 707.7
dynamite 801.9
dynamiter 693.8
dynast 749.7
dynasty 117.2
dyne
　unit of energy 161.6
　unit of force 352.23
dys– abnormal 85.9
　bad 675.7
　difficult 731.16
dysentery
　defecation 311.2
　disease symptom
　　686.8
　indigestion 686.28
　infectious disease
　　686.12
dyspepsia
　disease symptom
　　686.8
　indigestion 686.28
dyspeptic
　n. sick person 686.40
　adj. diseased 686.57
　ill-humored 951.23
dysphasia
　mental symptom
　　690.25
　speech defect 595.1
dystopia 535.11

E

each
　adj. every 79.15
　adv. apiece 80.19
each other 13.4
eager consenting 775.4
　desirous 634.21
　expectant 539.11
　impatient 862.6
　willing 622.5
　zealous 635.9
eager beaver
　enthusiast 635.5
　man of action 707.8
eagerly willingly 622.8
　zealously 635.14
eagerness consent 775.1
　desire 634.1
　impatience 862.1
　tendency 174.1
　willingness 622.1
　zeal 635
eagle ascent 315.7

bird 414.33,66
　coin 835.4
　eye 439.11
　heraldic insignia
　　569.2
　insignia 569.1
　military insignia
　　569.5
　speed 269.6
eagle eye
　sharp eye 439.10
　vigilance 533.4
ear attention 530.1
　audition 448.2
　auditory organ 448.7
　handle 256.3
　hearing 448.1
　plant part 411.27
eardrum
　auditory organ 448.7
　membrane 229.3
eared 448.16
ear for, an
　aptitude 733.5
　good hearing 448.3
ear for music
　good hearing 448.3
　musicianship 462.32
earl 918.4
earlier
　adj. less advanced
　　208.8
　previous 131.10
　prior 116.4
　adv. formerly 119.13
　previously 116.6
earliness
　anachronism 115.1
　early hour 131
　priority 116.1
ear lobe ear 448.7
　lobe 215.4
early
　adj. anachronous
　　115.3
　backward 119.12
　beforetime 131.7
　former 119.10
　prior 116.4
　adv. beforehand
　　131.11
　long ago 119.16
　previously 116.6
early bird 131.4
earmark
　n. characteristic 80.4
　mark 568.5
　sign 568.2
　v. allot 816.9
　characterize 80.10
　label 568.20
earn acquire 811.8
　be paid 841.20
　deserve 960.5
earn a living 659.11
earnest
　n. payment 841.1
　pledge 772.2
　adj. attentive 530.15
　resolute 624.11
　serious 871.3
　weighty 672.19

zealous 635.10
earnestly
　resolutely 624.17
　solemnly 871.4
　zealously 635.15
earnestness
　attention 530.1
　resolution 624.1
　solemnity 871.1
　zeal 635.2
earnings
　acquisition 811.1
　gain 811.3
　receipts 844.1
　remuneration 841.4
ear, nose, and throat
　specialist 448.10
earphone 450.8
ear-piercing
　loud 453.10
　shrill 458.14
earring jewel 901.6
　ring 253.3
earshot earreach 448.4
　short distance 200.2
ear-splitting 453.10
earth
　n. corpse 408.16
　element 376.2
　goddesses 375.10
　ground 212.3
　horizontal 214.3
　lair 191.26
　shelter 700.3
　soil 385.1
　adj. terrestrial 385.6
Earth planet 375.9
　world 375.10
earthborn
　common 919.11
　human 417.10
earthbound
　terrestrial 385.6
　unimaginative 536.5
earthenware
　ceramics 576.8
　hard goods 831.4
earthiness
　carnality 987.2
　indecency 990.3
　nonreligiousness
　　1031.2
　practicalness 536.2
　vulgarity 898.2
earthling
　irreligionist 1031.10
　person 417.3
earthly
　materialistic 376.9
　nonreligious 1031.16
　terrestrial 385.6
earthquake 162.5
earthshaker 540.2
earthshaking
　important 672.16
　loud 453.10
earthwork barrier 730.5
　fortification 799.4
earthworm
　invertebrate 415.5
　worm 414.42,75
earthy carnal 987.6

coarse 898.11
　human 417.10
　practical 536.6
　soily 385.7
　vulgar 990.8
　worldly 1031.16
ear trumpet 448.8
ease
　n. aid 785.1
　comfort 887.1
　contentment 868.1
　eloquence 600.2
　facility 732.1
　informality 647.1
　leisure 710.1
　literary elegance
　　589.1
　pleasure 865.1
　prosperity 728.1
　relief 886.1
　rest 711.1
　v. aid 785.11
　calm 163.7
　comfort 887.6
　extenuate 1006.12
　facilitate 732.6
　lighten 353.6
　loosen 51.3
　make free 762.13
　reduce 39.8
　relax 163.9
　relieve 886.5
　soften 357.6
　unwind 711.7
ease in 304.3
easel 574.19
easement
　comfort 887.4
　estate 810.4
　lightening 353.3
　relief 886.1
ease off loosen 51.3
　relax 163.9
　slacken 711.7
　slow 270.9
　turn aside 291.6
ease out 77.4
ease up let up 711.7
　relax 163.9
　slow 270.9
ease up to 296.3
easily
　comfortably 887.14
　facilely 732.15
　slowly 270.13
　softly 357.17
easing
　n. facilitation 732.4
　lightening 353.3
　moderation 163.2
　relief 886.1
　softening 357.5
　adj. lightening 353.15
　moderating 163.14
　relieving 886.9
　softening 357.16
east
　n. direction 290.3
　adj. eastern 290.15
　adv. eastward 290.18
East Orient 180.6
　region 180.7

Easter 1040.15
easterly
  n. wind 403.9
  adj. eastern 290.15
  adv. east 290.18
Easterner 190.11
easy
  adj. at ease 887.12
  cheap 849.7
  comfortable 887.11
  contented 868.7
  eloquent 600.9
  facile 732.12
  good-natured 938.14
  gullible 502.9
  indolent 708.18
  informal 647.3
  lax 758.4
  leisurely 710.6
  lenient 759.7
  light 353.11
  loose 51.5
  nonchalant 858.15
  pleased 865.12
  polished 589.6
  prosperous 728.12
  slow 270.10
  soft 357.8
  unchaste 989.26
  adv. cautiously 895.12
  interj. caution 895.14
easy come, easy go
  854.8
easygoing
  careless 534.11
  contented 868.7
  dilatory 132.17
  free 762.20
  informal 647.3
  lax 758.4
  lenient 759.7
  nonchalant 858.15
  unconcerned 636.7
easy going 732.1
easy mark 620.1
Easy Street 728.1
eat consume 666.2
  corrode 692.24
  endure 861.7
  etch 578.11
  feed 307.18
  ingest 306.11
eat away erode 692.24
  subtract 42.9
eat crow
  humble oneself 906.6
  recant 628.9
  submit 765.11
eat, drink, and be merry
  carouse 993.6
  go on a spree 996.27
  make merry 878.27
  make no provision
    721.7
eating
  n. feeding 307
  ingestion 306.4
  adj. feeding 307.29
eat one's heart out
  872.17
eat one's words 628.9
eats 308.2

eat up
  be credulous 502.6
  consume 666.2
  eat 307.20
  enjoy 865.10
  feast 307.22
eau de Cologne 436.3
eaves 228.6
eavesdrop 448.11
eavesdropper
  curious person 528.2
  listener 448.5
eavesdropping 448.2
ebb
  n. decrease 39.2
  deterioration 692.3
  standstill 268.3
  tide 395.13
  v. decline 692.20
  decrease 39.6
  flow 395.16
  move 267.5
  quiet 268.8
  recede 297.2
ebb and flow
  n. alternation 323.5
  tide 395.13
  v. alternate 323.13
  billow 395.22
  fluctuate 141.5
ebb tide low tide 208.2
  tide 395.13
ebony
  n. black 365.4
  blackness 365.1
  tree 411.50
  wood 378.9
  adj. black 365.8
  dark 337.13
ebullient bubbly 405.6
  excited 857.18
  hot 328.25
  lively 707.17
ebullition
  agitation 324.1
  bubbling 405.3
  excitement 857.3
  heating 329.2
  violence 162.2
eccentric
  n. erratic 474.3
  odd person 85.4
  adj. abnormal 85.9
  erratic 474.4
  humorous 880.4
  inconstant 141.7
  irregular 138.3
  odd 85.11
  off-center 185.12
eccentricity
  abnormality 85.1
  foolishness 470.1
  humorousness 880.1
  idiosyncrasy 474
  inconstancy 141.2
  irregularity 138.1
  trait of character
    525.3
ecclesiastic 1038.2
ecclesiastic(al)
  churchly 1042.15
  ministerial 1037.13

ecclesiastical insignia
  569.4
echelon
  battle array 797.6
  flight formation
    278.12
  rank 29.2
echo
  n. answer 486.1
  imitator 22.4
  keyboard 465.20
  music 462.23
  radar signal 346.11
  reaction 284.1
  recurrence 103.1
  reflection 24.7
  repeat 91.2
  reverberation 454.2
  sympathy 855.5
  v. agree with 521.9
  answer 486.4
  emotionally respond
    855.12
  imitate 22.5
  radar 346.16
  recur 103.11
  repeat 103.7
  reverberate 454.7
echo chamber 454.5
echoic answering 486.6
  imitative 22.9
  lexical 582.20
  repetitious 103.14
  representational
    572.10
  reverberating 454.11
echoing
  answering 486.6
  repetitious 103.14
  reverberating 454.11
echo sounding 209.5
éclair 308.40
eclampsia seizure 686.5
  spasm 324.6
eclamptic 324.19
éclat applause 968.2
  brilliancy 904.4
  publicity 559.4
  repute 914.1
eclectic(al)
  combined 52.5
  mixed 44.15
  philosophy 500.9
  selective 637.23
eclipse
  n. covering 228.1
  disappearance 447.1
  occultation 337.8
  v. blind 441.7
  conceal 615.6
  cover 228.19
  darken 337.9
  overshadow 36.8
ecliptic
  astronomy 375.16
  circle 253.3
eco– economic 827.22
  environment 233.1
  habitat 191.5
ecological
  ecotopic 13.15
  environmental 233.9

ecology biology 406.17
  ecosystem 13.5
  environment 233.4
  zoology 415.1
economic(al)
  cheap 849.7
  economics 827.22
  thrifty 851.6
economically
  shortly 203.12
  thriftily 851.7
economics
  economic science
    827.10
  finance 836.1
economist
  economic expert
    827.11
  finance 836.8
  thrifty person 851.3
economize 851.4
economizer 851.3
economizing
  n. economization
    851.2
  adj. economical 851.6
economy
  n. economic system
    827.7
  parsimony 852.1
  thrift 851
  adj. cheap 849.7
ecosphere
  atmosphere 402.2
  biosphere 407.6
  organic matter 406.1
ecosystem ecology 13.5
  environment 233.4
ecru brown 367.3
  yellow 370.4
ecstasy
  amorousness 931.3
  excitement 857.7
  fervor 855.10
  happiness 865.2
  trance 1036.3
ecstatic excited 857.23
  overjoyed 865.14
  rapt 532.11
ectomorph 690.15
–ectomy 689.23
ectoplasm cell 406.4
  occultism 1034.7
ectoplasmic 1017.7
ecumenic(al)
  broad-minded 526.8
  cooperating 786.5
  universal 79.14
ecumenism
  broad-mindedness
    526.1
  combination 52.1
  cooperation 786.1
eczema
  allergic disorder
    686.32
  skin disease 686.33
eddy
  n. backflow 395.12
  excitement 857.3
  rotation 322.2
  v. surge 395.21

whirl 322.11
edema
  disease symptom
    686.8
  distension 197.2
  increase 38.1
  swelling 256.4
Eden 535.11
edentate 259.4
edge
  n. acrimony 161.4
  advantage 36.2
  beginning 68.1
  border 235.4
  cutting edge 258.2
  pungency 433.1
  sharpness 258.1
  straight line 250.2
  summit 211.2
  v. border 235.10
  go sideways 242.5
  sharpen 258.9
  side 242.4
edge in enter 302.7
  interpose 237.6
  intrude 238.5
edge tool cutlery 348.2
  sharp edge 258.2
  types of 348.13
edgewise 242.8
edgy excitable 857.26
  impatient 862.6
  nervous 859.10
edible
  n. food 308.1
  adj. eatable 307.31
edict
  announcement 559.2
  decree 752.4
  law 998.3
edification
  learning 475.4
  teaching 562.1
edifice dwelling 191.6
  structure 245.2
edificial
  constructional 167.18
  structural 245.9
edify
  make better 691.9
  teach 562.11
edifying 562.19
edit
  comment upon
    552.11
  delete 42.12
  revise 691.12
  rewrite 602.19
edition issue 605.2
  music 462.28
  rendition 552.2
editor bookman 605.21
  commentator 606.4
  critic 494.7
  interpreter 552.7
  journalist 605.22
editorial
  n. commentary 606.2
  adj. explanatory
    552.15
  journalistic 605.26
editorialize 602.21

educable 564.18
educate
  make better 691.9
  teach 562.11
educated
  improved 691.13
  informed 475.18
  learned 475.21
  taught 564.16
education
  cultivation 691.3
  knowledge 475.4
  learning 564.1
  teaching 562.1
educational
  informative 557.17
  instructive 562.19
educational institution
    567.1
educator 565.1
educe 305.14
edulcorate
  refine 681.22
  sweeten 431.3
eerie awesome 920.11
  creepy 891.39
  deathly 408.29
  supernatural 85.15
  weird 1017.9
eeriness
  deathliness 408.12
  frighteningness 891.2
  ghostliness 1017.4
  supernaturalism 85.7
efface 693.16
effaced 538.8
effect
  n. aspect 446.3
  end 70.1
  influence 172.1
  intention 653.1
  meaning 545.1
  power 157.1
  product 168.1
  result 154
  sequel 117.2
  v. accomplish 722.4
  cause 153.11
  create 167.12
  do 705.6
  execute 771.10
  induce 153.12
effected 722.10
effective able 157.14
  effectual 665.20
  eloquent 600.11
  influential 172.13
  operative 164.9
  powerful 157.12
  practical 670.6
effectively ably 157.16
  eloquently 600.15
  powerfully 157.15
  usefully 665.25
effectiveness
  eloquence 600.3
  power 157.1
  supremacy 36.3
  utility 665.3
effects
  merchandise 831.1
  property 810.1

effectual able 157.14
  causal 153.14
  influential 172.13
  operative 164.9
  practical 670.6
  true 516.12
  useful 665.20
effectuate
  accomplish 722.4
  cause 153.11
  create 167.12
  do 705.6
  execute 771.10
  produce 167.9
effeminate
  bisexual 419.32
  frail 160.14
  womanish 421.14
effeminize
  feminize 421.12
  unman 158.12
effervesce
  be enthusiastic 635.8
  bubble 405.4
  sibilate 457.2
effervescence
  bubbling 405.3
  excitement 857.3
  liveliness 707.2
  sibilation 457.1
effervescent
  bubbly 405.6
  excited 857.18
  lively 707.17
  sibilant 457.3
effete
  deteriorating 692.46
  ineffective 158.15
  uninteresting 883.6
  used up 666.4
  weak 160.12
  weakened 160.18
  worn-out 692.38
efficacious able 157.14
  effectual 665.20
  influential 172.13
  operative 164.9
efficiency ability 157.2
  skill 733.1
  utility 665.3
efficient able 157.14
  competent 733.22
  effectual 665.20
  operative 164.9
  practical 670.6
efficiently ably 157.16
  skillfully 733.29
  usefully 665.25
effigy 572.3
effluent
  n. excrement 311.3
  tributary 395.3
  adj. outgoing 303.19
effluvium
  miasma 676.4
  occultism 1034.7
  odor 435.1
  vapor 401.1
efflux 303.4
effort act 705.3
  attempt 714.2
  endeavor 714.1

exertion 716.1
  expedient 670.2
  undertaking 715.1
effortless 732.12
effortlessly 732.15
effrontery 913.1
effuse
  v. emerge 303.12
  excrete 311.12
  exude 303.15
  adj. plentiful 661.7
effusive diffuse 593.11
  outgoing 303.19
  talkative 596.9
  unrestrained 554.10
e.g. 505.24
egest excrete 311.12
  vomit 310.25
egg embryo 406.15
  food 308.26
  ovum 406.12
  source 153.7
eggbeater
  agitator 324.9
  helicopter 280.5
  mixer 44.10
egg cell 406.12
egghead
  intellectual 476.1
  snob 912.7
egglike 406.25
egg on 648.16
eggshell
  n. brittleness 360.2
  egg 406.15
  adj. soft-colored
    362.21
  whitish 364.8,11
egg white
  albumen 406.15
  semiliquid 389.5
ego egotism 909.3
  intellect 466.4
  psyche 690.35
  self 80.5
egocentric
  n. egotist 909.5
  adj. egotistic 909.10
egotism
  selfishness 978.1
  vanity 909.3
egotist
  selfish person 978.3
  vain person 909.5
egotistic(al)
  selfish 978.5
  vain 909.10
ego trip ego 909.1
  self-seeking 978.1
ego-trip
  self-serving 978.4
  vanity 909.6
egregious bad 675.9
  excessive 663.16
  outright 34.12
  remarkable 34.10
  thorough 56.10
egress
  n. channel 396.1
  departure 301.1
  emergence 303
  evacuation 310.6

leave 301.18
migrate 273.21
emigration egress 303.7
migration 273.4
eminence
authority 739.4
height 207.1
influence 172.1
loftiness 34.2
notability 672.2
protuberance 256.2
repute 914.5
steep 207.2
eminent
authoritative 739.15
exalted 914.18
high 207.19
important 672.18
prominent 34.9
protruding 256.13
superior 36.12
eminent domain
appropriation 822.5
ascendancy 739.6
eminently
exceptionally 34.20
illustriously 914.21
importantly 672.24
superlatively 36.16
emir
Muslim ruler 749.10
prince 918.7
title 917.3
emissary delegate 781.2
diplomat 781.6
messenger 561.1
emission ejection 310.7
emergence 303.2
excretion 311.1
emit eject 310.23
excrete 311.12
exude 303.15
issue 559.14
say 594.23
send out 401.8
emollient
n. healing ointment
687.11
ointment 380.3
adj. lubricant 380.10
relieving 886.9
remedial 687.40
softening 357.16
emote act 611.34
emotionalize 855.15
emotion
excitement 857.1
feeling 855.3
mental attitude 525.1
emotional
excitable 857.26
temperamental 525.7
visceral 855.19
emotionalism
emotionality 855.9
emotional symptom
690.23
excitability 857.9
emotionalize
act 611.34
emote 855.15

emotionally
feelingly 855.27
temperamentally
525.9
emotions 855.1
emotive
affecting 855.24
emotional 855.19
hysterical 855.20
empanel see impanel
empathetic
in accord 794.3
sensitive 422.14
empathize
emotionally respond
855.12
get along 794.2
empathy accord 794.1
sensitivity 422.3
sympathy 855.5
emperor 749.7
emphasis
importance 672.1
meter 609.9
music 463.25
speech accent 594.11
emphasize 672.13
emphatic
asserting 523.7
eloquent 600.13
emphasized 672.20
emphatically
assertively 523.9
exceptionally 34.20
emphysema 686.14
empire authority 739.5
country 181.1
government 741.1
sovereignty 739.8
empirical
experimental 489.11
philosophy 500.9
empiricism ethics 957.2
experiment 489.1
materialism 376.5
emplacement
location 184.1
placement 184.5
platform 216.13
emplane 301.16
employ
n. business 656.1
service 750.12
use 665.1
v. exert 716.8
hire 780.13
occupy 656.10
practice 705.7
spend 665.13
use 665.10
employable
instrumental 658.6
useful 665.18
employed busy 707.21
hired 780.19
used 665.23
employee
hireling 750.3
subordinate 764.5
working person 718.2
employees 750.11
employer master 749.1

user 665.9
employment
action 705.1
business 656.1
hiring 780.4
position 656.5
service 750.12
use 665.1
utilization 665.8
work 716.4
emporium
market 832.1
marketplace 832.2
empower
authorize 777.11
commission 780.9
enable 157.10
empowered
authoritative 739.15
authorized 777.17
empress 749.11
emptiness
appetite 634.7
futility 669.2
insincerity 616.5
meaninglessness
547.1
nonexistence 2.1
space 179.1
stupidity 469.6
triviality 673.3
uninterestingness
883.1
unpleasure 866.1
vacancy 187.2
empty
v. drain 305.12
eject 310.21
emerge 303.13
adj. baseless 483.13
hungry 634.25
ignorant 477.12
ineffective 158.15
inexpressive 549.20
insincere 616.32
meaningless 547.6
specious 483.10
stupid 469.19
thoughtless 480.4
trivial 673.16
uninteresting 883.6
vacant 187.13
vain 669.13
empty-handed 662.12
empty-headed
ignorant 477.12
scatterbrained 532.16
stupid 469.19
thoughtless 480.4
emptying
draining 305.3
evacuation 310.6
empty of
void of 187.18
wanting 662.13
empty pocket 838.2
emulate
be as good as 674.11
compete 796.19
follow 22.7
emulsifier
emulsion 389.7

mixer 44.10
emulsify
make viscid 389.10
mix 44.11
emulsion film 577.10
semiliquid 389.7
enable
authorize 777.11
empower 157.10
make possible 509.5
prepare 720.8
enact accomplish 722.4
act 611.35
execute 705.8
indicate 555.5
legalize 998.8
legislate 742.18
represent 572.9
enactment
display 555.2
impersonation 572.2
law 998.3
legislation 742.13
performance 705.2
enamel
n. coating 228.12
v. coat 228.24
color 362.13
adj. ceramic 576.7
enameling 362.12
enamor 931.21
enamored
charmed 931.26
fond of 931.28
en bloc 54.13
encamp 188.11
encampment
camp 191.29
camping 188.4
military camp 802.3
encapsulate 228.20
encase enclose 236.6
package 236.9
wrap 228.20
encephalic 211.14
encephalitis 686.9
enchant
bewitch 1036.8
delight 865.8
engross 530.13
fascinate 650.6
enchanted
astonished 920.9
bewitched 1036.12
dreamy 535.25
enamored 931.26
engrossed 530.18
overjoyed 865.14
supernatural 85.16
enchanter
bewitcher 1035.9
deceiver 619.1
tempter 650.3
enchanting
alluring 650.7
bewitching 1036.11
engrossing 530.20
influential 172.13
pleasant 863.7
enchantment
allurement 650.1
amorousness 931.3

bad influence 675.4
bewitchment 1036.2
happiness 865.2
influence 172.1
pleasantness 863.2
sorcery 1035.1
supernaturalism 85.8
enchantress
  beautiful person
    900.8
  bewitcher 1035.9
  tempter 650.3
enchased 578.12
encipher 614.10
encircle besiege 798.19
  enclose 236.5
  go around 321.4
  include 76.3
  surround 233.7
encircled
  circumscribed 234.6
  surrounded 233.11
encirclement
  military tactics 797.9
  siege 798.5
  surrounding 233.5
encircling
  inclusive 76.6
  surrounding 233.8
enclave
  enclosure 236.3,12
  tract 180.4
enclose
  circumscribe 234.4
  confine 761.12
  immure 236.5
  include 76.3
  internalize 225.6
  limit 235.8
  surround 233.6
enclosed
  confined 761.19
  immured 236.10
  surrounded 233.10
enclosing
  confining 236.11
  environing 233.8
  inclusive 76.6
enclosure
  confinement 236
  contents 194.6
  fortification 799.4
  pen 236.3
  prison 761.7
  surrounding 233.5
  types of 236.12
encoding 557.7
encompass
  besiege 798.19
  circle 253.10
  combine 52.3
  enclose 236.5
  extend 179.7
  go around 321.4
  include 76.3
  join 47.5
  surround 233.6
encompassed
  included 76.5
  surrounded 233.10
encore
  n. applause 968.2

repeat 91.2
repeat performance
  103.6
adv. duplication 91.7
  repetition 103.17
interj. again! 103.18
  approval 968.22
encounter
  n. contest 796.3
  impact 283.3
  meeting 200.4
  v. approach 296.3
  collide 283.12
  confront 240.8
  contend with 796.16
  experience 151.8
  find 488.3
  meet 200.11
  oppose 790.5
encounter therapy
  690.5
encourage abet 785.14
  advise 754.6
  cheer 870.7
  comfort 887.6
  further 785.17
  hearten 893.16
  motivate 648.21
encouragement
  comfort 887.4
  heartening 893.9
  incentive 648.7
  patronage 785.4
  urging 648.5
encouraging
  cheering 870.16
  comforting 887.13
  promising 888.13
  provocative 648.27
encroach intrude 238.5
  overstep 313.9
  take liberties 961.7
  usurp 961.8
encroachment
  intrusion 238.1
  overstepping 313.3
  usurpation 961.3
encrust 228.27
encumber add 40.4
  burden 352.13
  hamper 730.11
encumbered
  burdened 352.18
  indebted 840.8
encumbrance
  affliction 866.8
  burden 352.7
  dependent 764.6
  impediment 730.6
encyclical
  announcement 559.2
  letter 604.3
encyclopedia
  lore 475.9
  reference book 605.6
encyclopedic
  comprehensive 76.7
  learned 475.21
end
  n. athlete 878.20
  boundary 235.3
  completion 722.2

death 408.1
extremity 56.5
fate 640.2
objective 653.2
piece 55.3
portion 816.5
remainder 43.1
result 154.2
ruin 693.2
solution 487.1
stop 144.2
termination 70
  v. be destroyed 693.23
  cease 144.6
  complete 722.6
  destroy 693.12
  kill 409.13
  result 154.5
  terminate 70.5
end-all 70.4
endanger 697.6
endangered 697.13
endear 931.21
endearment
  lovemaking 932.4
  lure 650.2
endeavor
  n. act 705.3
  attempt 714.2
  effort 714
  exertion 716.1
  v. exert oneself 716.9
  strive 714.4
  try to 714.7
  undertake 715.3
ended
  completed 722.11
  terminated 70.8
endemic
  n. disease 686.1
  adj. contagious 686.58
  native 189.5
ending
  n. completion 722.2
  death 408.1
  halt 144.2
  termination 70.1
  adj. closing 70.9
endless
  continuous 71.8
  infinite 104.3
  innumerable 101.10
  perpetual 112.7
  wordy 593.12
endlessly
  continuously 71.10
  infinitely 104.4
  perpetually 112.10
  tediously 884.12
endocrine
  n. secretion 312.2,9
  adj. glandular 312.8
endocrinology 312.4
endomorph 690.15
endomorphic 195.18
endorse abet 785.14
  approve 968.9
  consent 775.2
  guarantee 772.9
  ratify 521.12
  support politically
  744.41

endorsement
  approval 968.1
  consent 775.1
  ratification 521.4
  signature 583.10
endorser assenter 521.7
  supporter 787.9
endow
  empower 157.10
  give to 818.17
  provide 659.7
endowed
  dowered 818.26
  possessing 808.9
  provided 659.13
  talented 733.27
endowment
  dower 818.9
  empowerment 157.8
  giving 818.1
  heredity 170.6
  provision 659.1
  support 785.3
  talent 733.4
endpaper 605.12
end result result 154.2
  solution 487.1
endue clothe 231.38
  empower 157.10
endurable 868.13
endurance
  continuance 143.1
  durability 110.1
  patience 861.1
  permanence 140.1
  perseverance 625.1
  strength 159.1
endure
  afford to pay 843.7
  be patient 861.5
  be tough 359.3
  condone 947.4
  continue 143.3
  elapse 105.5
  exist 1.9
  experience 151.8
  last 110.6
  permit 777.10
  persevere 625.2
  remain 140.5
  resist 792.2
  stay alive 407.10
enduring
  durable 110.10
  patient 861.9
  permanent 140.7
  persevering 625.7
  remembered 537.23
  substantial 3.7
endways
  adj. adjacent 200.16
  adv. lengthwise
    202.12
  vertically 213.13
enema
  cleaning agent 681.17
  clyster 687.19
  sprinkler 392.8
  washing 681.5
enemy
  n. foe 929.6
  opponent 791.1

adj. belligerent 797.25
opposing 790.8
energetic
industrious 707.22
lively 707.17
powerful 157.12
vigorous 161.12
energetically
actively 707.25
industriously 707.27
powerfully 157.15
vigorously 161.15
energetics 347.3
energize
electrify 342.23
invigorate 161.9
motivate 648.12
vivify 407.9
energized 695.4
energizer
motivator 648.10
stimulus 161.5
energizing
n. invigoration 161.7
adj. life-giving 407.12
provocative 648.27
refreshing 695.3
vitalizing 161.14
energy exertion 716.1
industry 707.6
liveliness 707.2
power 157.1
strength 159.1
vigor 161
enervate attenuate 4.4
fatigue 717.4
sicken 686.47
unman 158.12
weaken 160.10
enervated
fatigued 717.6
languid 708.19
unhealthy 686.50
unmanned 158.19
weakened 160.18
enfant terrible
bad child 125.4
mischief-maker 738.3
spoiled child 759.4
enfeeble disable 158.9
sicken 686.47
weaken 160.10
enfeebled
fatigued 717.6
weakened 160.18
enfold embrace 932.16
fold 264.5
internalize 225.6
surround 233.6
wrap 228.20
enforce apply 665.11
compel 756.4
execute 771.10
impose 963.6
enforcement
compulsion 756.1
execution 771.5
enfranchise
authorize 777.11
liberate 763.4
enfranchised
authorized 777.17

eligible 637.24
engage affiance 770.6
attempt 714.5
attract 650.5
contract 771.6
employ 780.13
engross 530.13
fight with 796.17
induce 648.22
interact 13.8
involve 176.2
occupy 656.10
promise 770.5
engaged busy 707.21
contracted 771.12
embattled 797.27
engrossed 530.17
participating 815.8
promised 770.8
engage in
busy oneself with
656.11
practice 705.7
undertake 715.3
engagement
appointment 922.8
betrothal 770.3
contest 796.3
courtship 932.7
engrossment 530.3
hiring 780.4
inducement 648.3
interaction 13.3
involvement 176.1
participation 815.1
playing engagement
611.12
position 656.5
promise 770.2
undertaking 715.1
engaging alluring 650.7
engrossing 530.20
pleasant 863.7
engender beget 68.14
be productive 165.7
cause 153.11
create 167.13
procreate 169.8
engine aircraft 280.17
converter 145.10
machinery 348.4
parts of 348.27
types of 348.26
engineer
n. military engineer
800.13
operator 164.4
producer 167.8
trainman 274.12
types of 718.9
v. accomplish 724.11
manage 747.8
maneuver 735.10
plot 654.10
produce 167.9
England 181.4
English
n. language 580.23
v. interpret 552.12
English horn
organ stop 465.22
wood wind 465.9

English-speaking 594.32
engorge destroy 693.10
eat 307.23
gluttonize 994.4
ingest 306.11
satiate 664.4
engorged 664.6
engram memory 537.1
memory trace 690.36
engrave affect 855.18
fix in the mind
537.18
groove 263.3
imprint 142.9
indent 257.14
mark 568.19
ornament 901.9
print 603.14
record 570.16
sculpture 575.5
tool 578.10
engraved grooved 263.4
indented 257.17
infixed 142.13
tooled 578.12
engraver
printmaker 579.8
recorder 571.1
engraving arts 574.1
engravement 578.2
groove 263.1
mark 568.5
picture 574.12
print 578.6
sculpture 575.1
engross absorb 530.13
buy up 828.7
fatten 197.8
monopolize 808.6
occupy the mind
478.20
sorb 306.13
stock market 833.26
write 602.19
engrossed
absorbed 530.17
absorbed in thought
478.22
abstracted 532.11
written 602.22
engrossing 530.20
engulf ingest 306.11
overflow 395.17
oversupply 663.14
overwhelm 693.21
submerge 320.7
engulfed
flooded 395.25
soaked 392.17
underwater 209.13
enhance
aggravate 885.2
increase 38.5
make better 691.9
enhanced
aggravated 885.4
improved 691.13
increased 38.7
enhancement
aggravation 885.1
exaggeration 617.1
improvement 691.1

increase 38.2
enigma dilemma 731.6
mystery 549.8
perplexity 514.3
secret 614.5
the unknown 477.7
enigmatic
ambiguous 550.3
awesome 920.10
bewildering 514.25
inexplicable 549.17
secret 614.11
unknown 477.17
enjoin advise 754.6
command 752.9
impose 963.4
prohibit 778.3
restrain 760.7
enjoy
be pleased with
865.10
possess 808.4
savor 428.5
enjoyable 863.6
enjoyment
amusement 878.1
pleasure 865.1
enlace 222.6
enlarge develop 148.6
expatiate 593.7
grow 197.5
increase 38.4
intensify 885.2
make larger 197.4
process photos
577.15
enlarged
expanded 197.10
increased 38.7
intensified 885.4
enlargement copy 24.5
development 148.1
exaggeration 617.1
expansion 197.1
expatiation 593.6
increase 38.1
intensification 885.1
photoprint 577.5
enlighten
disillusion 520.2
explain 552.10
illuminate 335.28
inform 557.8
make better 691.9
teach 562.11
enlightened
disillusioned 520.5
illuminated 335.39
informed 475.18
judicious 467.19
enlightener 557.5
enlightening
broadening 526.14
disillusioning 520.4
educational 562.19
explanatory 552.15
illuminating 335.40
informative 557.17
enlightenment
cultivation 691.3
disillusionment 520.1
explanation 552.4

individual 89.4
something 3.3
entomb enclose 236.6
inter 410.19
entombment 410.1
entomology 415.1
entourage
attendance 73.6
environment 233.1
entr'acte act 611.8
interim 109.1
entrails 225.4
entrain embark 301.16
ride 273.32
entrance access 306.3
channel 396.1
entranceway 302.5
foyer 192.19
ingress 302.1
insertion 304.1
intrusion 238.1
opening 265.7
entrance
cast a spell 1036.7
delight 865.8
fascinate 650.6
put to sleep 712.20
entranced
astonished 920.9
dreamy 535.25
overjoyed 865.14
entrancing
alluring 650.7
bewitching 1036.11
pleasant 863.7
entrant beginner 68.2
competitor 791.2
incomer 302.4
student 566.9
entrap catch 822.17
hamper 730.11
trap 618.18
entrapment
allurement 650.1
deception 618.1
entreat 774.11
entreaty appeal 774.2
prayer 1032.4
entree access 306.3
dish 308.7
entrance 302.1
serving 307.10
entrench
establish 142.9
fortify 799.9
intrude 238.5
entrenchment
establishment 142.2
fortification 799.5
intrusion 238.1
trench 263.2
entre nous
confidentially 614.20
mutually 13.17
entrepreneur
businessman 830.1
planner 654.7
entropy disorder 62.1
formlessness 247.1
information theory 557.7
noncohesion 51.1

stagnation 268.4
entrust
commission 780.9
give 818.16
give credit 839.6
entry access 306.3
account entry 845.5
entranceway 302.5
foyer 192.19
ingress 302.1
inscription 570.15
opening 265.7
race horse 414.17
record 570.4
entwine hamper 730.11
weave 222.6
enumerate
analyze 48.7
list 88.8
number 87.10
enumeration
analysis 48.2
counting 87.1
list 88.1
enumerative
analytical 48.9
numerative 87.15
enunciate affirm 523.4
proclaim 559.12
say 594.23
enunciated
affirmed 523.8
speech 594.30
enunciation
affirmation 523.1
articulation 594.6
proclamation 559.2
envelop besiege 798.19
clothe 231.38
conceal 615.6
surround 233.6
wrap 228.20
envelope exterior 224.2
illustriousness 914.6
wrapper 228.18
enveloped
covered 228.31
surrounded 233.10
envelopment
covering 228.1
enclosure 236.1
siege 798.5
surrounding 233.5
wrapper 228.18
envenom
antagonize 929.7
make ill-humored 951.16
make toxic 686.49
work evil 675.6
enviable 634.30
envious covetous 954.4
discontented 869.5
jealous 953.4
environment
circumstance 8.2
encompassment 233.5
surroundings 233
environmental
contextual 8.8
environal 233.9

environmental diseases 686.31
environs
environment 233.1
nearness 200.1
neighborhood 180.1
envisage
confront 240.8
contemplate 478.17
expect 539.5
foresee 542.5
include 76.3
intend 653.7
visualize 535.15
envision
contemplate 478.17
foresee 542.5
intend 653.7
visualize 535.15
envisioning 535.6
envoy delegate 781.2
diplomat 781.6
envy
n. covetousness 954
discontent 869.1
jealousy 953.1
sin 982.3
v. covet 954.3
enzyme digestant 309.9
types of 309.25
enzymic 353.16
eolith 123.6
eolithic 123.20
eon, eonian see aeon etc.
epact difference 42.8
time 114.5
epaulet 569.5
ephemeral
mortal 408.34
plant 411.41
transient 111.7
epic poem 609.6
story 608.6
epic(al) huge 195.20
narrative 608.16
poetic 609.17
epicure
connoisseur 897.7
gourmet 307.14
sensualist 987.3
epicurean
n. connoisseur 897.7
sensualist 987.3
adj. pleasure-loving 865.15
sensual 987.5
epicureanism
aesthetic taste 897.5
eating 307.13
gluttony 994.2
pleasure-loving 865.4
sensuality 987.1
epidemic
n. plague 686.4
adj. contagious 686.58
plentiful 661.7
prevalent 79.12
epidemiology
hygiene 683.2
infection 686.3

epidermal
cutaneous 229.6
shallow 210.5
epidermis
exterior 224.2
shallowness 210.1
skin layer 229.4
epigram
conciseness 592.3
maxim 517.1
poem 609.6
witticism 881.7
epigraph caption 484.2
lettering 581.5
motto 517.4
epilepsy
nervous disorder 686.23
seizure 686.5
spasm 324.6
epileptic
n. sick person 686.40
adj. diseased 686.57
epilogue act 611.8
addition 41.2
end 70.1
sequel 67.1
epiphany
appearance 446.1
manifestation 555.1
revelation 1021.9
visibility 444.1
Epiphany 1040.15
episcopacy
church office 1037.5
mastership 739.7
episcopal 1037.13
episode
digression 593.4
discontinuity 72.1
event 151.2
interjection 237.2
story element 608.9
episodic
discontinuous 72.4
discursive 593.13
interjectional 237.9
epistemology 500.1
epistle 604.2
epitaph 410.18
epithet
n. curse 972.4
motto 517.4
name 583.3
v. curse 972.7
epitome
abridgment 607.1
model 25.1
shortening 203.3
epitomize
set an example 25.7
shorten 203.6
epoch 107.5
epochal 137.7
equable
moderate 163.13
uniform 17.5
equal
n. equivalent 30.4
substitute 149.2
v. be as good as 674.11

match 30.5
parallel 218.4
adj. equalized 30.7
identical 14.8
interchangeable
150.5
parallel 218.6
proportionate 816.13
symmetric 248.4
uniform 17.5
equality identity 14.1
parity 30
symmetry 248.1
equalize balance 30.6
level 214.6
make agree 26.7
make uniform 17.4
smooth 260.5
symmetrize 248.3
equalizer 70.4
equalizing
n. equalization 30.2
adj. interchangeable
150.5
equally
accordingly 8.11
correspondingly
30.11
identically 14.9
justly 976.11
equal to able 157.14
competent 733.22
prepared for 720.18
satisfactory 868.11
sufficient 661.6
equanimity
composure 858.3
uniformity 17.1
equate associate 9.6
equalize 30.6
make parallel 218.5
equation equality 30.1
equalization 30.2
mathematics 86.9;
87.4
equator
astronomy 375.16
bisector 92.3
circle 253.3
hot place 328.11
latitude 180.3
middle 69.1
equatorial middle 69.4
warm 328.24
equerry
animal handler 416.2
male servant 750.4
equestrian
n. rider 274.8
adj. ungulate 414.49
equidistance
middle 69.2
parallelism 218.1
equidistant
middle 69.4
parallel 218.6
equilateral
equisized 30.10
symmetric 248.4
equilibrium
correlation 13.1
equality 30.1

equanimity 858.3
literary elegance
589.2
stability 142.1
symmetry 248.1
uniformity 17.1
equine
n. horse 414.10
adj. ungulate 414.49
equinox
astronomy 375.16
season 128.7
equip furnish 659.8
outfit 231.40
prepare 720.8
equipage
equipment 659.4
rig 272.5
equipment
electronic testing
343.23
fitting 720.2
matériel 659.4
photographic 577.19
preparation 720.1
printing 603.26
provision 659.1
ship 277.34
talent 733.4
equipoise equality 30.1
offset 33.2
equipped
prepared 720.16
provided 659.13
equispaced
equisized 30.10
parallel 218.6
equitable just 976.8
unprejudiced 526.12
equity equality 30.1
estate 810.4
justice 976.1
law 998.4
law code 998.5
stock 834.2
equivalence
agreement 26.1
comparability 491.3
correlation 13.1
equality 30.1
identity 14.1
equivalent
n. equal 30.4
likeness 20.3
offset 33.2
substitute 149.2
the same 14.3
adj. agreeing 26.9
analogous 20.11
identical 14.8
interchangeable
150.5
reciprocal 13.13
substitute 149.8
tantamount 30.8
equivocal
ambiguous 550.3
mixed 44.15
prevaricating 613.11
self-contradictory
15.8
uncertain 514.15

untruthful 616.34
equivocate
dodge 631.8
lie 616.19
prevaricate 613.7
quibble 483.9
vacillate 627.8
equivocation
ambiguous expression
550.2
avoidance 631.1
contrariety 15.3
falsification 616.9
prevarication 613.4
quibbling 483.5
sophistry 483.1
vacillation 627.2
era 107.5
eradicate annihilate 2.6
destroy 693.14
eliminate 77.5
excise 42.10
uproot 305.10
eradicative
exterminative 693.27
extractive 305.17
erase abrade 350.7
delete 42.12
kill 409.14
obliterate 693.16
erased 538.8
eraser 693.9
erasure abrasion 350.2
deletion 42.5
disappearance 447.1
obliteration 693.7
Erato Muse 535.2
music patron 464.22
poetry 609.12
ere 116.6
Erebus darkness 337.1
deity of nether world
1019.5
erect
v. create 167.10
raise 213.9
uplift 317.5
adj. honest 974.13
proud 905.8
raised 317.9
vertical 213.11
erection
elevation 317.1
erecting 213.4
house 191.6
manufacture 167.3
structure 245.2
erg 161.6
ergo 155.7
eristic(al)
argumentative 482.19
quarrelsome 795.17
ermine fur 229.8
heraldic insignia
569.2
royal insignia 569.3
erode abrade 350.7
consume 666.2
decrease 39.6
disappear 447.2
disintegrate 53.3
eat away 692.24

subtract 42.9
waste 812.5
wear 692.23
eroded
corroded 692.44
reduced 39.10
used up 666.4
wasted 812.7
weatherworn 692.36
erogenous 419.26
Eros god 1014.5
love 931.1
love god 931.8
erosion abrasion 350.2
consumption 666.1
decrease 39.3
disintegration 53.1
loss 812.2
subtraction 42.1
wear 692.5
erotic amorous 931.24
lascivious 989.29
sexual 419.26
erotica 602.12
eroticism
lasciviousness 989.5
sexual desire 419.5
err
be unorthodox
1025.8
be wrong 518.9
fail 725.13
go wrong 981.9
misjudge 496.2
sin 982.5
stray 291.4
errancy error 518.1
fallibility 514.7
errand
commission 780.1
task 656.2
errand boy
attendant 750.5
office boy 561.4
errant deviant 291.7
erroneous 518.16
uncertain 514.21
wandering 273.36
errantry
deviation 291.1
magnanimity 979.2
wandering 273.3
errata 605.12
erratic
n. eccentric 474.3
adj. abnormal 85.9
deviant 291.7
eccentric 474.4
inconstant 141.7
irregular 138.3
uncertain 514.15
uneven 18.3
unordered 62.12
erratum 518.3
erroneous false 616.25
imperfect 678.4
inaccurate 518.16
ungrammatical 587.4
unorthodox 1025.9
error bungle 734.5
computer 349.19
erroneousness 518

estranged
alienated 929.11
separated 49.21
estrogen 312.10
estrous 419.30
estruate 419.22
estrus 419.6
estuarine alluvial 385.8
aquatic 275.58
estuary 399.2
estuary
arm of the sea 399.1
outlet 303.9
et al. and others 40.14
more 100.10
etc. 40.14
et cetera
and so forth 40.14
more 100.10
etch affect 855.18
engrave 578.11
fix in the mind
537.18
imprint 142.9
etched 142.13
etching arts 574.1
engraving 578.2
engraving process
578.3
print 578.6
eternal godlike 1013.20
infinite 104.3
perpetual 112.7
eternally forever 104.4
perpetually 112.10
eternity
divine attribute
1013.15
forever 112.2
Heaven 1018.1
infinity 104.1
long time 110.4
perpetuity 112.1
timelessness 106.1
ethane 331.1
ether air 402.1
anesthetic 687.57
coolant 334.7
heavens 375.2
height 207.2
lightness 353.2
vapor 4.3
ethereal airy 402.12
ghostly 1017.7
heavenly 1018.13
high 207.19
imaginary 535.22
immaterial 377.7
light 353.10
tenuous 355.4
thin 205.16
unsubstantial 4.6
vaporous 401.9
etherealize rarefy 355.3
spiritualize 1034.20
weaken 4.4
etherize gas 401.8
render insensible
423.4
ethical dutiful 962.13
honest 974.13
moral 957.6

ethics duty 962.1
philosophy 500.1,11
principles 957
ethnic 11.7
ethnic group
party 788.4
people 418.1
ethnocentric
clannish 788.18
exclusive 77.8
ethnology 417.7
ethos belief 501.6
culture 642.3
ethics 957.1
ideology 479.8
nature 5.3
pervading attitudes
525.5
ethyl 380.4
etiology
attribution 155.1
cause 153.1
etiquette custom 642.1
good behavior 737.2
social code 646.3
social convention
645.1
étude music 462.5
treatise 606.1
etymologic(al) 582.20
etymology
derivation 582.16
linguistics 580.12
Eucharist rite 1040.8
sacrament 1040.5
eucharistic(al) 1040.22
euchre 618.17
eugenics genetics 170.6
improvement 691.1
eulogize 968.12
eulogy dirge 875.5
funeral rites 410.4
honor 916.4
praise 968.5
speech 599.2
eunuch 158.6
eupeptic
cheerful 870.11
contented 868.7
healthy 685.7
pleased 865.12
euphemism
affectation 903.5
preciosity 589.3
euphemistic 903.18
euphemize 613.7
euphonious
balanced 589.8
melodious 462.49
euphony
literary elegance
589.2
music 462.3
euphoria
contentment 868.1
emotional symptom
690.23
pleasure 865.1
euphoric
cheerful 870.11
contented 868.7
pleased 865.12

euphuism
affectation 903.5
florid style 551.1
preciosity 589.3
Eurasian 44.9
eureka! 488.11
Europe
continent 386.1
region 180.6
eurythmics
physical education
562.9
symmetry 248.1
Euterpe Muse 535.2
music patron 464.22
poetry 609.12
euthanasia death 408.7
killing 409.1
evacuate
abandon 633.5
defecate 311.13
eject 310.21
emit 310.23
leave 301.8
evacuation
abandonment 633.1
defecation 311.2
departure 301.1
voidance 310.6
evacuee fugitive 631.5
migrant 274.5
evade avoid 631.7
be dishonest 975.11
equivocate 483.9
escape 632.6
outwit 735.11
prevaricate 613.7
pull back 284.7
remain neutral 806.5
evaluate analyze 48.8
judge 494.9
measure 490.11
price 846.13
evaluation analysis 48.3
judgment 494.3
measurement 490.1
pricing 846.4
evanescent
infinitesimal 196.14
transient 111.7
vanishing 447.3
evangel
good news 558.2
herald 561.2
evangelic(al)
hyperorthodox
1024.8
orthodox 1024.7
scriptural 1021.10
evangelist
clergyman 1038.7
converter 145.9
herald 561.2
religious founder
1022.2
worshiper 1032.9
evangelistic
ministerial 1037.13
scriptural 1021.10
evaporate
be transient 111.6
cease to exist 2.5

disappear 447.2
dissipate 75.5
dry 393.6
preserve 701.8
vaporize 401.8
evaporated 393.9
evaporation
disappearance 447.1
dispersion 75.1
drying 393.3
loss 812.2
preserving 701.2
vaporization 401.5
evaporative
drying 393.10
volatile 401.10
evasion
avoidance 631.1
circumvention 735.5
equivocation 483.5
escape 632.1
neutrality 806.1
prevarication 613.4
retreat 284.3
secrecy 614.1
evasive
dishonest 975.16
elusive 631.15
equivocating 483.14
prevaricating 613.11
secretive 614.15
eve 134.2
even
v. calm 163.7
equal 30.5
equalize 30.6
level 214.6
make uniform 17.4
smooth 260.5
symmetrize 248.3
adj. equal 30.7
exact 516.16
flat 214.7
interchangeable
150.5
just 976.8
moderate 163.13
neutral 806.7
numerical 86.8
parallel 218.6
periodic 137.7
smooth 260.9
straight 250.6
symmetric 248.4
uniform 17.5
adv. exactly 516.20
indeed 36.17
interchangeably
150.6
notwithstanding 33.8
evenhanded just 976.8
unprejudiced 526.12
evening
equalization 30.2
symmetrization 248.2
evening
n. nightfall 134.2
adj. vesper 134.8
evening dress 231.11
evenly equally 30.11
horizontally 214.9
justly 976.11

repute 914.5
sanctification 1026.3
worship 1032.2
exalted cheerful 870.11
eminent 34.9
high 207.19
magnanimous 979.6
noble 918.10
overjoyed 865.14
prominent 914.18
raised 317.9
exam 485.2
examination
discussion 597.7
inspection 485.3
medical diagnosis
689.13
questioning 485.11
scrutiny 439.6
test 485.2
treatise 606.1
trial 1004.5
examine discuss 597.12
inspect 485.23
interrogate 485.20
scrutinize 439.15
study 564.12
examiner analyst 48.5
inquirer 485.15
tester 485.16
examining 485.36
example
n. citation 505.6
model 25.2
representative 572.5
taste 427.4
warning 703.1
v. cite 505.14
exasperate
annoy 866.13
provoke 952.22
trouble 864.15
exasperated
aggravated 885.4
annoyed 866.21
provoked 952.25
exasperating
aggravating 885.5
annoying 864.22
exasperation
aggravation 885.1
annoyance 866.2
excitation 857.10
incitement 648.4
resentment 952.1
unpleasantness 864.7
Excalibur 801.4
excavate deepen 209.8
dig 257.15
dig up 305.10
find 488.4
excavation
deepening 209.7
digging 257.11
discovery 488.1
extraction 305.1
hole 201.2
pit 257.4
exceed excel 36.6
loom 34.5
overdo 663.9
overrun 313.4

exceedingly
superlatively 36.16
very 34.18
excel
be expert at 733.17
surpass 36.6
excellence
goodness 674.1
good taste 897.1
nobility 914.5
superiority 36.1
excellent
adj. eminent 914.18
good 674.12
skillful 733.20
superior 36.12
tasteful 897.8
interj. approval
968.22
except
v. exclude 42.10
exempt 762.14
reject 638.2
prep. excluding 77.9
less 42.14
conj. unless 507.16
excepted
exempt 762.29
rejected 638.3
excepting
prep. excluding 77.9
less 42.14
conj. unless 507.16
exception
disapproval 969.4
exclusion 77.1
exemption 762.8
justification 1006.2
marvel 920.2
objection 522.2
odd thing 85.5
qualification 507.1
rejection 638.1
stipulation 753.2
exceptional
eccentric 474.4
exclusive 77.8
extraordinary 85.14
important 672.18
particular 80.12
remarkable 34.10
wonderful 920.10
exceptionally
extraordinarily 85.18
unusually 34.20
wonderfully 920.14
excerpt
n. extract 607.3
v. select 637.14
excess
n. exaggeration 617.1
excessiveness 663
exorbitance 848.4
intemperance 993.1
overrunning 313.1
surplus 43.4
undueness 961.1
adj. superfluous
663.17
excessive
exaggerated 617.4
inordinate 663.16

intemperate 993.7
overpriced 848.12
undue 961.10
violent 162.15
excessively
distressingly 34.21
exorbitantly 848.16
inordinately 663.22
intemperately 993.10
excessiveness
excess 663.1
exorbitance 848.4
fanaticism 473.11
intemperance 993.1
exchange
n. banter 882.1
communication
554.1
conversation 597.1
interchange 150.1
property transfer
817.1
retaliation 955.1
stock exchange 833.7
substitute 149.2
substitution 149.1
telephone number
560.12
trade 827.2
v. interchange 150.4
substitute 149.4
trade 827.14
transfer property
817.3
exchequer
depository 836.12
funds 835.14
storage place 660.6
excise
n. tax 846.11
v. cut out 42.10
extract 305.10
sever 49.11
excision
extraction 305.1
removal 42.3
separation 49.2
surgical operation
689.22
excitable
emotional 857.26
irascible 951.19
nervous 859.10
excite agitate 324.10
impassion 857.11
incite 648.17
interest 530.12
make hot 329.18
sensitize 422.9
excited agitated 324.16
fervent 855.23
impassioned 857.18
impatient 862.6
interested 530.16
excitement
agitation 324.1
emotion 857
excitation 857.10
fervor 855.10
heat 328.2
impatience 862.1
incitement 648.4

exciting alluring 650.7
desirable 634.30
eloquent 600.13
interesting 530.19
provocative 648.27
thrilling 857.28
exclaim
give an exclamation
459.7
remark 594.25
utter 594.26
exclamation
ejaculation 459.2
remark 594.4
exclamatory 459.11
exclude bar 77.4
disapprove 969.10
eject 310.13
except 42.10
expel 310.17
prevent 730.14
prohibit 778.3
reject 638.2
excluded barred 77.7
impossible 510.7
rejected 638.3
excluding
adj. exclusive 77.8
prep. barring 77.9
less 42.14
exclusion barring 77
disapproval 969.1
ejection 310.4
excision 42.3
prohibition 778.1
rejection 638.1
exclusive
n. news 558.3
adj. contemptuous
966.8
excluding 77.8
limiting 234.9
one 89.7
particular 896.13
prohibitive 778.6
unsociable 923.6
exclusively
simply 45.11
solely 89.14
exclusiveness
contempt 966.1
narrowness 77.3
particularity 896.5
partisanism 788.13
unsociability 923.3
exclusive of
excluding 77.9
less 42.14
excogitate 478.11
excommunicate
condemn 1008.3
curse 972.5
depose 783.4
eject 310.17
excoriate
criticize severely
969.21
peel 232.8
excrement
excretion 311.3
filth 682.7
excremental 311.20

past 119.7
explain
  explicate 552.10
  facilitate 732.6
  justify 1006.9
  lecture 562.17
  make clear 548.6
  solve 487.2
explanation
  example 25.2
  interpretation 552.4
  justification 1006.1
  meaning 545.3
  reason 153.2
  solution 487.1
  theorization 499.1
  theory 499.2
explanatory 552.15
expletive
  n. curse 972.4
  exclamation 459.2
  redundancy 103.3
  superfluity 663.4
  adj. superfluous
    663.17
explicable
  attributable 155.6
  interpretable 552.17
  solvable 487.3
explicate
  expatiate 593.7
  explain 552.10
  make clear 548.6
explicit candid 974.17
  intelligible 548.10
  manifest 555.8
  unqualified 508.2
explode
  become angry 952.19
  blast 456.8
  blow up 162.13
  come to nothing
    725.12
  disprove 506.4
  fuel 331.8
  get excited 857.15
exploded
  disproved 506.7
  not believed 503.12
exploit
  n. act 705.3
  courageous act 893.7
  v. overcharge 848.7
  take advantage of
    665.15
  use 665.16
exploitable
  gullible 502.9
  usable 665.22
exploitation
  overcharge 848.5
  utilization 665.8
exploration
  adventure 715.2
  reconnaissance 485.8
  search 485.14
exploratory
  examining 485.36
  preceding 66.4
explore
  investigate 485.22
  search 485.30

explorer precursor 66.1
  traveler 274.1
explosion
  detonation 456.3
  discharge 162.7
  disproof 506.1
  emotional outburst
    857.8
  increase 38.2
  outburst 952.9
explosive
  n. ammunition 801.9
  speech sound 594.13
  adj. banging 456.11
  dangerous 697.9
  excitable 857.26
  hot-tempered 951.25
  violent 162.23
exponent deputy 781.1
  example 25.2
  explainer 552.7
  representative 572.5
  supporter 787.9
exponential 86.8
export
  n. sending abroad
    303.8
  transference 271.1
  v. send 271.14
  send abroad 303.17
  transfer 271.9
expose disclose 556.4
  disillusionize 520.2
  disprove 506.4
  divest 232.5
  endanger 697.6
  stigmatize 915.9
  unclose 265.13
  uncover 488.4
exposé disclosure 556.1
  disproof 506.1
exposed airy 402.12
  disproved 506.7
  divested 232.12
  manifest 555.10
  open 265.18
  unprotected 697.15
  visible 444.6
  vulnerable 175.5
  wind-blown 403.27
exposition
  disclosure 556.1
  display 555.2
  explanation 552.4
  fair 832.2
  lesson 562.7
  music division 462.24
  spectacle 446.7
  treatise 606.1
expositive
  descriptive 608.15
  dissertational 606.6
  explanatory 552.15
expositor
  commentator 606.4
  discourser 606.3
  explainer 552.7
  lecturer 599.5
ex post facto
  back 119.12
  subsequently 117.6

expostulate
  advise 754.6
  dissuade 652.3
  object 522.5
exposure
  appearance 446.1
  disclosure 556.1
  discovery 488.1
  display 555.2
  disproof 506.1
  divestment 232.1
  film exposure 577.9
  liability 175.2
  position 184.3
  publicity 559.4
  unprotectedness
    697.3
  visibility 444.1
expound
  explain 552.10
  lecture 562.17
express
  n. carrier 271.5
  mail 604.5
  message 558.4
  messenger 561.1
  train 272.13
  v. affirm 523.4
  describe 608.12
  evidence 505.9
  extract 305.16
  indicate 568.17
  manifest 555.5
  phrase 588.4
  say 594.23
  send 271.14
  adj. exact 516.16
  fast 269.19
  intelligible 548.10
  manifest 555.8
  particular 80.12
  unqualified 508.2
  adv. posthaste 709.13
expressed 588.5
expression
  diction 588.1
  distillation 305.7
  eloquence 600.1
  extraction 305.1
  indication 568.1
  manifestation 555.1
  maxim 517.1
  music 462.31
  phrase 585.1
  remark 594.4
  word 582.1
expressionism 573.1
expressionless
  inexpressive 549.20
  reticent 613.10
expressive
  descriptive 608.15
  eloquent 600.10
  indicative 568.23
  manifestative 555.9
  meaningful 545.10
expressly exactly 516.20
  intelligibly 548.12
  manifestly 555.14
  particularly 80.15
expressway 657.6

expropriate
  appropriate 822.20
  dispossess 822.23
expulsion
  deposal 783.2
  disgorgement 310.7
  ejection 310.1
  elimination 77.2
  transference 271.1
expulsive 310.28
expunge cancel 70.7
  delete 42.12
  obliterate 693.16
expunged 70.8
expurgate clean 681.18
  delete 42.12
expurgated 681.26
exquisite
  affected 903.18
  beautiful 900.16
  chic 644.13
  fastidious 896.11
  meticulous 533.12
  pleasant 863.7
  sensitive 422.15
  superb 674.17
  tasty 428.8
exquisitely
  beautifully 900.21
  fashionably 644.18
  intensely 34.20
  meticulously 533.16
  pleasantly 863.12
  superbly 674.22
extant existent 1.13
  present 120.2
extemporaneous
  impromptu 630.12
  unprepared 721.8
extemporize
  be unprepared 721.6
  improvise 630.8
extend be distant 199.5
  be elastic 358.4
  be long 202.6
  broaden 204.4
  cover 228.30
  endure 110.6
  expatiate 593.8
  generalize 79.9
  give 818.12
  grow 197.5
  increase 38.4
  lengthen 202.7
  make larger 197.4
  offer 773.4
  postpone 132.9
  protract 110.9
  reach 179.7
  spread 197.6
  straighten 250.5
  stretch to 199.6
  sustain 143.4
extended
  expanded 197.10
  extensive 179.9
  increased 38.7
  lengthened 202.9
  meaningful 545.10
  protracted 110.11
  wordy 593.12
extension addition 41.3

factious
factional 795.17
rebellious 767.11
factor
n. agent 781.3
cause 153.1
component 58.2
gene 170.6
manager 748.4
particular 8.3
v. analyze 48.8
factory 719.3
factory town 719.2
factotum 750.9
facts evidence 505.1
information 557.1
knowledge 475.1
particulars 1.4
factual certain 513.15
evidential 505.17
real 1.15
true 516.12
faculty ability 157.2
authority 739.1
educators 565.10
intellect 466.2
privilege 958.3
talent 733.4
fad caprice 629.1
craze 644.5
momentary triumph
724.3
faddish
fashionable 644.15
fickle 629.6
faddist
enthusiast 635.5
fad 644.5
fade age 126.10
become old 123.9
bet 515.20
be transient 111.6
cease to exist 2.5
decline 692.20
decolor 363.5
deteriorate 692.21
disappear 447.2
fail 686.45
lose color 363.6
pull back 284.7
recede 297.2
weaken 160.9
fade insipid 430.2
trite 883.9
uninteresting 883.6
faded colorless 363.7
weatherworn 692.36
fade in 446.8
fade-in 344.16
fade out
cease to exist 2.5
disappear 447.2
lose color 363.6
fade-out decrease 39.1
disappearance 447.1
radio broadcasting
344.16
radio reception
344.21
fading
n. decoloration 363.3
deterioration 692.3

disappearance 447.1
radio reception
344.21
adj. aging 126.17
deteriorating 692.46
languishing 160.21
receding 297.5
transient 111.7
vanishing 447.3
faerie fairyfolk 1014.17
paradise 535.11
supernaturalism 85.7
faery 1014.27
fag
n. cigarette 434.5
drudge 718.3
drudgery 716.4
homosexual 419.16
v. drudge 716.14
fatigue 717.4
task 716.16
fag end extremity 70.2
remainder 43.1
fagged exhausted 717.8
fatigued 717.6
faggot 419.16
fagot bundle 74.8
firewood 331.3
Fahrenheit 328.30
Fahrenheit scale 328.19
fail age 126.10
be a flop 611.33
be dishonest 975.12
be inferior 37.4
be insufficient 662.8
be unsuccessful 725.8
decline 692.20
fail in health 686.45
fail someone 725.16
fall short 314.2
go bankrupt 842.7
neglect 534.6
not accomplish 723.2
weaken 160.9
failed insolvent 842.11
unsuccessful 725.17
failing
n. deterioration 692.3
fault 678.2
vice 981.2
adj. deteriorating
692.46
incomplete 57.4
insufficient 662.9
languishing 160.21
unhealthy 686.50
unsuccessful 725.17
fail-safe 698.5
failure an error 518.3
defeat 727.1
deterioration 692.3
disappointment
541.1
fault 678.2
ineffectiveness 158.3
inferiority 37.3
insolvency 842.3
insolvent 842.4
neglect 534.1
nonaccomplishment
723.1
nonobservance 769.1

nonsuccess 725
shortcoming 314.1
sin 982.2
stage show 611.4
unsuccessful person
725.7
vice 981.2
failure of memory
538.2
fain desirous 634.22
willing 622.5
faint
n. unconsciousness
423.2
v. get tired 717.5
swoon 423.5
weaken 160.9
adj. colorless 363.7
faint-sounding 452.16
fatigued 717.6
indistinct 445.6
irresolute 627.12
sick 686.52
weak 160.12
faint heart 892.4
fainthearted
cowardly 892.10
irresolute 627.12
faint praise 971.1
fair
n. festival 878.4
marketplace 832.2
adj. appropriate 960.8
auspicious 544.18
beautiful 900.17
clean 681.25
courteous 936.14
good 674.12
honest 974.13
just 976.8
legible 548.11
light 363.9
mediocre 680.7
pleasant 863.6
probable 511.6
prosperous 728.13
rainless 393.8
sunny 863.10
tolerable 674.19
unprejudiced 526.12
whitish 364.8
adv. justly 976.11
pleasantly 863.11
fair game
laughingstock 967.7
opportunity 129.2
fairly justly 976.11
legibly 548.13
mediocrely 680.11
moderately 35.10
to a degree 29.7
tolerably 674.23
fairness beauty 900.3
colorlessness 363.2
goodness 674.1
honesty 974.1
justice 976.3
unprejudicedness
526.5
whiteness 364.1
fair play 976.3
fair sex 421.3

fair shake equality 30.3
even chance 156.7
fairness 976.3
fair-spoken
flattering 970.8
suave 936.18
fair to middling
680.7,11
fair trade
commerce 827.1
price controls 846.6
fair-trade 846.13
fairway green 411.7
playground 878.12
runway 278.23
seaway 275.10
fair weather
good times 728.4
hot weather 328.7
pleasantness 863.4
weather 402.4
fair-weather friend
619.8
fairy
n. homosexual 419.16
lightness 353.2
sprite 1014.18
adj. elfin 1014.27
fairyfolk 1014.17
fairy godmother
giver 818.11
guardian angel
1014.22
fairyland
fairyfolk 1014.17
paradise 535.11
fairylike 1014.27
fairy tale fiction 608.7
lie 616.11
fait accompli
accomplishment
722.1
act 705.3
reality 1.2
faith belief 501.1
cause 153.10
fidelity 974.7
hope 888.1
obedience 766.1
orthodoxy 1024.2
piety 1028.1
promise 770.1
religion 1020.1
school 788.5
sureness 513.5
system of belief
501.3
virtue 980.5
zeal 635.2
faithful
believing 501.21
descriptive 608.15
exact 516.16
friendly 927.20
lifelike 20.16
loving 931.25
loyal 974.20
obedient 766.3
observant 768.4
orthodox 1024.7
persevering 625.7
pious 1028.8

reliable 513.17
zealous 635.10
faithfully
descriptively 608.19
exactly 516.20
loyally 974.25
obediently 766.6
perseveringly 625.8
faithful servant 907.3
faith healer 688.12
faith healing 689.3
faithless
apostate 628.11
falsehearted 616.31
nonreligious 1031.19
unbelieving 503.8
unfaithful 975.20
faithworthy
reliable 513.17
trustworthy 974.19
fake
n. affecter 903.7
copy 24.1
hoax 618.7
impostor 619.6
sham 616.13
substitute 149.2
v. affect 903.12
fabricate 616.18
imitate 22.5
improvise 630.8
sham 616.21
tamper with 616.17
adj. assumed 903.16
imitation 22.8
similar 20.10
spurious 616.26
substitute 149.8
fake out fool 618.14
overshadow 36.8
fakery falseness 616.3
imitation 22.1
fake up 534.9
fakir ascetic 991.2
clergyman 1038.13
falcate 252.11
falconry 655.2
falderal see folderol
fall
n. autumn 128.4
backsliding 696.2
declivity 219.5
decrease 39.2
defeat 727.1
descent 316.1
deterioration 692.3
failure 725.3
false hair 230.13
hang 215.2
original sin 982.4
plunge 320.1
rain 394.1
ruin 693.3
tumble 316.3
waterfall 395.11
v. be defeated 727.12
be destroyed 693.22
cheapen 849.6
decline 692.20
decrease 39.6
descend 316.5
die 408.19

fail 725.11
go wrong 981.9
hang 215.6
incline 219.10
occur 151.5
plunge 320.6
rain 394.9
relapse 696.4
tumble 316.8
fallacious
deceptive 618.19
erroneous 518.16
false 616.25
illogical 483.11
illusory 519.9
sophistical 483.10
unorthodox 1025.9
fallacy deception 618.1
error 518.1
falseness 616.1
heresy 1025.2
sophistry 483.1
specious argument
483.3
fall away
apostatize 628.8
decline 692.20
decrease 39.6
fall short 314.2
incline 219.10
fallback recoil 284.3
retreat 295.2
fall back
be behind 241.8
get worse 692.19
pull back 284.7
relapse 696.4
retreat 295.6
fall behind
be behind 241.8
follow 293.4
regress 295.5
fall by the wayside
314.3
fallen carnal 987.6
cooked 330.8
dead 408.30
defeated 727.14
depressed 318.12
impious 1030.6
prostitute 989.28
reduced 39.10
ruined 693.28
unrighteous 981.12
fallen angel 986.5
fall flat
be uninteresting
883.4
fail 725.11
fall short 314.3
tumble 316.8
fall for
be credulous 502.6
fall in love 931.20
fall from grace
backsliding 696.2
impiety 1030.1
original sin 982.4
relapse 696.4
fall guy dupe 620.1
loser 727.5
scapegoat 149.3

fallible imperfect 678.4
uncertain 514.21
fall in
break down 692.27
collapse 198.10
fail 725.11
form 59.5
line up 71.6
falling
descending 316.11
deteriorating 692.46
pendent 215.9
sloping downward
219.16
falling-out 795.4
falling sickness
epilepsy 686.5
nervous disorder
686.23
seizure 324.6
falling star 375.15
fall into
become 145.17
incur 175.4
undertake 715.3
fall into place 59.5
fall in with
acquiesce 775.3
agree with 521.9
comply 82.3
conform 82.4
converge 298.2
find 488.3
get along with 794.2
incur 175.4
fall off
apostatize 628.8
come apart 49.8
decline 692.20
decrease 39.6
descend 316.5
incline 219.10
fall on one's knees
apologize 1012.5
beg for mercy 944.6
be servile 907.6
bow 964.6
bow down before
765.10
entreat 774.11
thank 949.4
fallout atomics 326.16
powder 361.5
radiation 327.1
fall out quarrel 795.10
result 154.5
fallout shelter
atomic explosion
326.16
shelter 700.3
fallow
n. farm 413.8
v. till 413.17
adj. barren 166.4
colorless 363.7
idle 708.17
unprepared 721.14
yellow 370.4
falls 395.11
fall short
be disappointing
541.3

be imperfect 678.3
be incomplete 57.3
be inferior 37.4
be insufficient 662.8
come short 314.2
fail 725.11
fall through fail 725.11
fall short 314.3
fall to begin 68.7
eat 307.18
set to work 716.15
undertake 715.3
fall to pieces
be damaged 692.26
be destroyed 693.22
be separated 49.8
crumble 361.10
decay 692.25
disintegrate 53.3
show fragility 360.3
fall upon
arrive at 300.7
attack 798.15
be unexpected 540.6
light on 316.10
meet 200.11
false deceitful 618.20
deceptive 618.19
erroneous 518.16
falsehearted 616.31
illegitimate 999.7
illusory 519.9
sanctimonious 1029.5
unfaithful 975.20
untrue 616.25
false alarm alarm 704.2
unsuccessful person
725.7
false front
affectation 903.1
disguise 618.10
display 904.4
fakery 616.3
front 240.1
falsehearted
deceitful 618.20
dishonest 975.18
false 616.31
treacherous 975.21
falsehood
falseness 616.1
lie 616.11
untruthfulness 616.8
falsely
deceptively 618.21
erroneously 518.20
untruly 616.35
false modesty 903.6
false move 518.4
false name 583.8
falseness deceit 618.3
deception 618.1
error 518.1
falseheartedness
616.4
falsehood 616
illusoriness 519.2
infidelity 975.5
sanctimony 1029.1
false pretense 616.3
false reasoning 483.1

false show
affectation 903.1
fakery 616.3
illusoriness 519.2
false step 518.4
falsetto
n. high voice 458.6
speech defect 595.1
voice 463.5
adj. high 458.13
vocal 462.51
false witness
accusation 1005.4
liar 619.9
falsies 231.24
falsification
falsifying 616.9
misrepresentation
573.1
falsified 616.26
falsify
be dishonest 975.11
lie 616.19
misrepresent 573.3
misstate 616.16
falsity error 518.1
fakery 616.3
falseness 616.1
infidelity 975.5
lie 616.11
falter
n. demur 623.2
flounder 324.8
irresolution 627.3
shake 324.3
voice 463.19
v. be a coward 892.8
be irresolute 627.7
be unsure 514.10
dawdle 270.8
demur 623.4
despair 889.10
flounder 324.15
shake 324.11
stammer 595.8
faltering hesitant 623.7
irresolute 627.11
slow 270.10
stammering 595.13
fame eminence 34.2
notability 672.2
publicity 559.4
repute 914.1
familiar
n. friend 928.1
guardian angel
1014.22
adj. customary 642.15
friendly 927.18
informal 647.3
insolent 913.8
intimate 922.20
trite 883.9
usual 84.8
vernacular 580.18
well-known 475.27
familiarity
friendship 927.5
informality 647.1
knowledge 475.1
presumption 961.2
sociability 922.1

familiarize
accustom 642.11
inform 557.8
familiar with
used to 642.18
versed in 475.19
family
n. ancestry 170.4
biology 61.5
community 788.2
kinsmen 11.2
nomenclature 583.1
people 11.5
posterity 171.1
race 11.4
adj. lineal 170.14
racial 11.7
family planning 166.1
family tree 170.5
famine
unproductiveness
166.1
want 662.4
famished
hungry 634.25
ill-provided 662.12
famous eminent 34.9
excellent 674.12
reputable 914.16
famously
excellently 674.21
exceptionally 34.20
notably 914.21
fan
n. attender 186.5
blower 403.21
commender 968.8
cooler 334.3
devotee 635.6
fanatic 473.17
follower 293.2
fork 299.4
propeller 285.7
specialist 81.3
supporter 787.9
ventilator 402.10
v. air 402.11
excite 857.11
fail 725.9
incite 648.17
spread 197.6
fanatic believer 1028.4
enthusiast 635.5
infatuate 473.17
intolerant person
527.5
lunatic 473.15
obstinate person
626.6
odd person 85.4
fanatic(al) fiery 162.21
narrow-minded
527.10
obstinate 626.8
overeager 635.13
overzealous 473.32
zealous 1028.11
fanaticism
narrow-mindedness
527.1
obstinacy 626.1
overeagerness 635.4

overzealousness
473.11
violence 162.2
zeal 1028.3
fancied
fabricated 616.29
imaginary 535.19
fancied up 231.45
fanciful
capricious 629.5
ideational 479.9
imaginary 535.20
incredible 85.12
tenuous 4.6
unreal 2.8
fancy
n. caprice 629.1
desire 634.1
idea 479.1
illusion 519.3
imagination 535.1
impulse 630.1
inclination 634.3
love 931.1
preference 637.5
thing imagined 535.5
will 621.1
v. believe 501.11
desire 634.14
imagine 535.14
love 931.18
suppose 499.10
adj. excessive 663.16
expensive 848.11
grandiose 904.21
high-flown 601.11
ornate 901.12
ostentatious 904.18
overpriced 848.12
skillful 733.20
fancy dress 231.10
fancy man 989.18
fancy talk 910.2
fancy that! 920.22
fancywork 223.1
fanfare
bookbinding 605.16
celebration 877.1
trumpet sound 453.4
fanfaronade
bluster 911.1
boasting 910.1
celebration 877.1
display 904.4
fang
grasping organ 813.4
pointed projection
258.4
poison injector 676.5
tooth 258.5
fanged grasping 813.9
toothed 258.16
fan-jet 278.32
Fannie Mae 834.4
fanny 241.5
fan out disperse 75.4
diverge 299.5
spread 197.6
fan-shaped
diverging 299.8
spread 197.11
triangular 93.3

fantail rear 241.7
tail 241.6
fantasia 462.6
fantasize
fabricate 616.18
imagine 535.14
fantastic(al)
capricious 629.5
fabricated 616.29
fanciful 535.20
foolish 470.10
illusory 519.9
incredible 85.12
remarkable 34.10
wonderful 920.10
fantasy
n. abstractedness
532.2
caprice 629.1
defense mechanism
690.30
desire 634.1
fiction 608.7
imagination 535.1
phantom 519.4
supernaturalism 85.8
thing imagined 535.5
v. dream 535.17
muse 532.9
fan the flame
burn 329.22
excite 857.11
incite 648.17
sow dissension 795.14
far
adj. distant 199.8
adv. by far 34.17
far off 199.15
far and away
by far 34.17
superlatively 36.16
far and wide
abroad 199.16
by far 34.17
extensively 179.10
faraway
abstracted 532.11
distant 199.8
farce comedy 611.6
humor 881.1
ridicule 967.6
stuffing 308.27
trifle 673.5
farcer comedian 612.9
dramatist 611.27
farcical
burlesque 967.14
comic 880.5
theatrical 611.40
far cry difference 16.1
distance 199.2
fare
n. fee 846.7
food 308.1
traveler 274.1
v. be in a state 7.6
eat 307.18
go 273.17
result 154.5
travel 273.20
farewell
n. departure 301.4

Time 105.2
fathom
  investigate 485.22
  know 475.12
  measure 490.11
  measure depth 209.9
  solve 487.2
  understand 548.7
fathomable
  intelligible 548.9
  measurable 490.15
fathomless 209.11
fatigue
  n. disease symptom
    686.8
  languor 708.6
  tiredness 717
  weakening 160.5
  weakness 160.1
  work 716.4
  v. be tedious 884.5
  get tired 717.5
  tire 717.4
fatigued tired 717.6
  weakened 160.18
  worn-out 692.38
fatigues 231.1
fatiguing boring 884.9
  weakening 160.20
  wearying 717.11
fat of the land
  plenty 661.2
  prosperity 728.1
fatso 195.12
fatten feed 307.17
  fertilize 165.8
  increase 38.4
  make better 691.9
  make grow 197.8
  raise animals 416.6
  thicken 204.5
  thrive 728.8
fatten on eat 307.26
  sponge 907.11
fatty
  n. corpulent person
    195.12
  adj. oily 380.9
fatuity
  foolishness 470.1
  futility 669.2
  ineffectiveness 158.3
  thoughtlessness 480.1
fatuous foolish 470.8
  ineffective 158.15
  tenuous 4.6
  thoughtless 480.4
  trivial 673.16
  vain 669.13
faucet stopper 266.4
  valve 396.10
fault an error 518.3
  blemish 679.1
  crack 201.2
  defect 678.2
  fallacy 518.1
  misdeed 982.2
  vice 981.2
faultfinding
  n. complaint 875.4
  disapproval 969.4
  adj. critical 969.24

discontented 869.5
  plaintive 875.16
faultless
  accurate 516.15
  innocent 984.6
  perfect 677.6
faulty blemished 679.8
  erroneous 518.16
  guilty 983.3
  illogical 483.11
  imperfect 678.4
  ungrammatical 587.4
faun 1014.21
fauna 414.1
faux pas 518.5
favor
  n. approval 968.1
  courtesy 936.6
  esteem 914.3
  face 240.4
  gift 818.7
  good deed 938.7
  good terms 927.3
  inclination 634.3
  influence 172.2
  letter 604.2
  looks 446.4
  memento 537.7
  patronage 785.4
  pity 944.1
  preference 637.5
  prestige 172.1
  privilege 958.4
  respect 964.1
  superiority 36.1
  v. abet 785.14
  aid 785.11
  approve 968.9
  be kind 938.9
  desire 634.14
  discriminate 977.8
  do good 674.10
  further 785.17
  indulge 759.6
  make better 691.9
  oblige 785.19
  prefer 637.17
  resemble 20.7
  respect 964.4
favorable
  approving 968.17
  auspicious 544.18
  consenting 775.4
  expedient 670.5
  friendly 927.14
  good 674.12
  helpful 785.22
  promising 888.13
  timely 129.9
  willing 622.5
favorably
  advantageously 36.19
  amicably 927.21
  auspiciously 544.21
  consentingly 775.5
  helpfully 785.24
  kindly 938.18
  willingly 622.9
favored
  approved 968.19
  exempt 762.29
  fortunate 728.14

preferable 637.25
favoring
  approving 968.17
  auspicious 544.18
  instrumental 658.6
  preferential 637.25
  similar 20.10
favorite
  n. darling 931.15
  race horse 414.17
  adj. approved 968.19
  beloved 931.22
favorite son 746.9
favoritism
  injustice 977.3
  partiality 527.3
favors of office 744.36
favor with
  endow 818.17
  supply 818.15
fawn
  n. hoofed animal
    414.5
  young deer 125.8
  v. be servile 907.6
  give birth 167.15
  adj. brown 367.3
fawning
  n. flattery 970.1
  obsequiousness 907.2
  adj. flattering 970.8
  obsequious 907.13
fawn upon
  curry favor 907.8
  flatter 970.5
fay 1014.18
faze 891.26
FBI detectives 781.10
  police force 699.17
  US agency 742.11
fealty duty 962.1
  fidelity 974.7
  obedience 766.1
fear
  n. anxiety 890.1
  cowardice 892.1
  fright 891
  irresolution 627.4
  nervousness 859.1
  v. be afraid 891.18
  be irresolute 627.7
fearful afraid 891.31
  anxious 890.6
  cowardly 892.10
  frightening 891.36
  nervous 859.10
  remarkable 34.11
fear-inspiring
  frightening 891.36
  threatening 973.3
fearless 893.19
fearsome fearful 891.31
  frightening 891.36
fear-stricken 891.30
feasibility
  expedience 670.1
  possibility 509.2
  wieldiness 732.2
feasible
  expedient 670.5
  possible 509.7
  practical 670.6

wieldy 732.14
feast
  n. banquet 307.9
  festival 878.4
  food 308.1
  holiday 711.4
  holy day 1040.14
  treat 865.3
  v. eat 307.22
  gratify 865.6
  make merry 878.27
feat
  courageous act 893.7
  deed 705.3
  masterpiece 733.10
feather
  n. kind 61.3
  lightness 353.2
  plumage 230.18
  quill 230.16
  softness 357.4
  trifle 673.5
  v. fledge 230.21
  fly 278.49
  line 194.7
  ornament 901.9
  row 275.53
feather bed 357.4
featherbedding 663.4
featherbrain 471.7
featherbrained
  scatterbrained 532.16
  superficial 469.20
feathered
  ornamented 901.11
  plumaged 230.28
featheredge lip 235.4
  sharp edge 258.2
feather in one's cap
  trophy 916.3
  victory 726.1
feathers clothing 231.1
  plumage 230.18
featherweight
  n. boxing weight
    352.3
  little thing 196.4
  pugilist 800.2
  adj. lightweight
    353.12
  uninfluential 173.3
feathery light 353.10
  plumy 230.27
  soft 357.14
featly
  adj. agile 733.21
  adv. nimbly 733.29
feature
  n. aspect 446.3
  characteristic 80.4
  commodity 831.2
  component 58.2
  looks 446.4
  motion picture
    611.16
  salient point 672.7
  special 81.2
  treatise 606.1
  v. give a show 611.33
  give prominence
    672.14
  specialize 81.4

equivocate 483.9
fortify 799.9
protect 699.18
fence in confine 761.12
enclose 236.5
fence off 237.8
fence-sitter
irresolute person 627.5
neutral 806.4
fencing
equivocation 483.5
prevarication 613.4
swordplay 796.8
fend prevent 730.14
protect 699.18
ward off 799.10
fender fireplace 329.11
partition 237.5
safety equipment 699.3
fend for oneself 762.19
fend off
prevent 730.14
repulse 289.3
ward off 799.10
fenestra 265.1
fenestrated 265.20
feral cruel 939.24
excited 857.23
fatal 409.23
funereal 410.22
savage 162.20
ferment
n. agitation 324.1
alterant 139.4
anger 952.7
bubbling 405.3
bustle 707.4
excitement 857.3
leavening 353.4
reaction 379.5
types of 353.18
violence 162.2
v. agitate 324.10
bubble 405.4
incite 648.17
leaven 353.7
react chemically 379.6
seethe 162.11
sour 432.4
fermentation
agitation 324.1
bubbling 405.3
excitement 857.3
leavening 353.4
reaction 379.5
souring 432.3
fern botany 412.5
plant 411.4,43
ferocious cruel 939.24
excited 857.23
savage 162.20
warlike 797.25
ferociously
cruelly 939.33
savagely 162.26
ferocity cruelty 939.11
warlikeness 797.15
ferret sharp eye 439.11
wild animal 414.28

ferret-eyed 439.22
ferret out find 488.4
search out 485.33
ferric 383.17
ferry
n. boat 277.21
passageway 657.4
v. fly 278.45
haul 271.12
ferryman 276.5
fertile
imaginative 535.18
plentiful 661.7
productive 165.9
fertility
diffuseness 593.1
inventiveness 535.3
plenty 661.2
productiveness 165.1
fertility god
agriculture divinity 413.4
forest god 1014.21
names of 165.5
fertilization
enrichment 165.3
impregnation 169.3
fertilize enrich 165.8
impregnate 169.10
till 413.17
fertilizer 165.4
fervent
eloquent 600.13
excited 857.20
industrious 707.22
passionate 855.23
zealous 635.10
fervently
eloquently 600.15
excitedly 857.32
industriously 707.27
passionately 855.28
zealously 635.15
fervid craving 634.24
excited 857.20
fervent 855.23
zealous 635.10
fervidly
excitedly 857.32
fervently 855.28
zealously 635.15
fervor eloquence 600.5
heat 328.2
industry 707.6
love 931.1
passion 855.10
zeal 635.2
festal merry 878.30
vacational 711.10
festal board 307.9
fester
n. sore 686.35
v. decay 692.25
hurt 424.7
suppurate 311.15
festering
n. corruption 692.2
pain 424.4
pus 311.6
sore 686.35
adj. decayed 692.41
sore 424.11

suppurative 311.21
festival 878.4
festival day 711.4
festive convivial 922.19
merry 878.30
festive occasion 878.4
festivity
celebration 877.1
conviviality 922.3
festival 878.4
meeting 74.2
merrymaking 878.3
party 922.11
rejoicing 876.1
treat 865.3
festoon curve 252.2
flowers 411.23
ornamentation 901.3,13
festooned
high-flown 601.11
ornamented 901.11
fetal beginning 68.15
embryonic 406.24
fetch
n. specter 1017.3
stratagem 735.3
trick 618.6
v. accomplish 722.4
arrive 300.6
attract 650.5
bring 271.15
conclude 494.10
cost 846.15
hit 283.13
sail for 275.35
travel 273.17
fetching alluring 650.7
pleasant 863.7
fetch up arrive 300.6
sail 275.33
stop 144.7
train 562.14
fete festival 878.4
meeting 74.2
fete day 711.4
fetid bad 675.9
filthy 682.23
malodorous 437.5
offensive 864.18
unsavory 429.7
fetish charm 1036.5
idol 1033.3
fetishism
idolatry 1033.1
sexual preference 419.12
sorcery 1035.1
fetlock foot 212.5
hair 230.6
fetter
n. curb 730.7
restraint 760.4
v. bind 47.10
hamper 730.11
restrain 760.10
fettle
n. condition 7.3
v. groom 681.20
fetus 406.14
feud
n. animosity 929.4

estate 810.5
possession 808.1
quarrel 795.5
revenge 956.1
v. contend 796.14
quarrel 795.11
feudal
imperious 739.16
real 810.10
subject 764.13
feudalism
principle of government 741.8
subjection 764.1
feudal system 741.4
fever agitation 324.1
disease symptom 686.8
fever of excitement 857.6
frenzy 473.7
heat 328.1
sickness 686.6
feverish
agitated 324.16
excited 857.20
fervent 855.23
fevered 686.54
hasty 709.9
hot 328.25
overzealous 635.13
few least 37.8
not many 102.4
small 35.6
few, a
indefinite number 101.2
plurality 100.1
small number 102.2
fewer 102.6
fey eccentric 474.4
otherworldly 85.15
fiancé 931.16
fiasco
disappointment 541.1
failure 725.6
fiat
authorization 777.3
decree 752.4
fib
n. lie 616.11
v. lie 616.19
fibbing 616.8
fiber filament 206.1
flesh 406.1
nature 5.3
types of 206.8
fibrillation
disease symptom 686.8
irregularity 138.1
fibrous
threadlike 206.7
tough 359.4
fickle flighty 629.6
inconstant 141.7
irresolute 627.9
transient 111.7
uncertain 514.15
unfaithful 975.20

fiction
fabrication 616.10
lie 616.11
story 608.7
thing imagined 535.5
written matter 602.10
fictional
fabricated 616.29
fictitious 535.21
of fiction 608.17
fictionalize
imagine 535.14
narrate 608.13
fictitious
fabricated 616.29
falsified 616.26
imaginary 535.21
fictitious name 583.8
fiddle
n. viol 465.6
v. play violin 462.42
trifle 673.13
fiddle-faddle
n. nonsense 547.2
v. trifle 673.13
fiddler 464.5
fidelity accuracy 516.3
faithfulness 974.7
perseverance 625.1
zeal 635.2
Fides 976.5
fidget
be excited 857.16
be nervous 859.6
trifle 673.13
twitch 324.13
fidgets agitation 324.1
excitement 857.4
nervousness 859.1
twitching 324.5
fidgety active 707.20
agitated 324.16
jerky 324.19
jittery 859.11
restless 857.25
fiducial
fiduciary 501.25
stable 142.12
fiduciary
n. trustee 809.5
adj. believable 501.24
fiducial 501.25
in trust 772.13
fief 810.5
fiefdom 808.1
field airport 278.22
arena 802.1
battlefield 802.2
competitors 791.2
enclosure 236.3
heraldic insignia
569.2
latitude 762.4
playground 878.12
plot 180.4
region 180.2
science 475.10
setting 233.2
space 179.1
specialty 81.1
sphere of work 656.4
study 562.8

tract 413.9
field day festival 878.4
tournament 878.10
field glass 443.3
field station 489.5
fiend devil 1016.7
drug user 642.10
enthusiast 635.5
monster 943.6
violent person 162.9
fiendish cruel 939.24
devilish 1016.18
terrible 675.10
wicked 981.13
fierce
acrimonious 161.13
cruel 939.24
excited 857.23
infuriated 952.29
passionate 857.27
savage 162.20
violent 162.15
warlike 797.25
fiery eloquent 600.13
excited 857.20
fervent 855.23
feverish 686.54
hot 328.26
hot-tempered 951.25
inflammable 329.28
passionate 857.27
red 368.6
sore 424.11
violent 162.21
zealous 635.10
fiesta 878.4
fife
n. wood wind 465.9
v. play music 462.43
fifth
n. fraction 99.14
harmonics 463.20
adj. five 99.17
fifth column 619.11
fifth-column 975.22
fifth columnist
subversive 619.11
turncoat 628.5
fifty-fifty
n. even chance 156.7
half 92.2
adj. equal 30.7
mixed 44.15
neutral 806.7
proportionate 816.13
adv. in half 92.8
proportionately
816.14
fig clothing 231.1
trifle 673.5
fight
n. battle 796.4
contest 796.3
quarrel 795.5
struggle 716.3
warlikeness 797.15
v. clash in color
362.14
contend 796.14
contend against
790.4
contend for 796.21

contend with 796.18
dispute 796.22
quarrel 795.11
struggle 716.11
war 797.18
fighter
combatant 800.1
pugilist 800.2
fighting
n. boxing 796.9
contention 796.1
warfare 797.1
adj. contending
796.23
warlike 797.25
fighting man 800.6
fight shy avoid 631.6
be frightened 891.20
demur 623.4
fights, the 796.9
figment
fabrication 616.10
thing imagined 535.5
figmental
fabricated 616.29
fictitious 535.21
**figment of the
imagination**
phantom 519.4
thing imagined 535.5
fig out dress up 231.41
ornament 901.8
figural
indicative 568.23
numerical 86.8
figuration form 246.1
forming 246.5
outline 235.2
representation 572.1
figurative
high-flown 601.11
implicative 546.10
indicative 568.23
meaningful 545.10
metaphorical 551.3
numerical 86.8
representational
572.10
figuratively 551.4
figure
n. angular geometric
251.13
apparition 446.5
aspect 446.3
body 376.3
characteristic 80.4
diagram 654.3
display 904.4
famous person 914.9
figure of speech
551.1
flowery language
601.4
form 246.1
gestalt 690.39
human form 246.4
image 572.4
motif 901.7
music division 462.24
music theme 462.30
number 86.1
outline 235.2

personage 672.8
phantom 519.4
price 846.1
repute 914.1
syllogism 482.6
v. be famous 914.10
be reasonable 482.17
calculate 87.11
designate 568.18
figure of speech
551.2
form 246.7
judge 494.9
ornament 901.9
plan 654.9
represent 572.8
figured figurative 551.3
high-flown 601.11
ornamented 901.11
planned 654.13
figurehead
a nobody 673.7
deputy 781.1
front 240.3
insignia 569.1
man 787.8
nominal head 749.4
statue 572.4
figure of speech
figure 551
flowery language
601.4
types of 551.5
figure on 653.6
figure out
calculate 87.11
solve 487.2
figurer calculator 87.8
sculptor 579.6
figures
mathematics 87.2
statistics 87.7
figurine 572.4
filament
feather part 230.17
fiber 206
filamentary
hairlike 230.23
threadlike 206.7
filch 824.13
file
n. abrasive 260.14
case 193.14
catalog 88.3
document 570.5
heraldic insignia
569.2
military unit 800.19
record 570.10
registry 570.3
row 71.2
v. abrade 350.7
classify 61.6
grind 260.8
list 88.8
march 273.29
parade 71.7
record 570.16
request 774.9
sharpen 258.9
store 660.10
file away store 660.10

wear away 42.9
filed classified 61.8
 listed 88.9
 recorded 570.18
filial loving 931.25
 sonly 171.7
filiation ancestry 170.4
 blood relationship
  11.1
 collateral descendant
  171.4
 continuity 71.2
 relationship 9.1
filibuster
 n. hinderer 730.8
 legislative procedure
  742.14
 speech 599.2
 v. legislate 742.18
 outtalk 596.7
 procrastinate 132.11
filigree
 n. extra 41.4
 network 221.3
 v. ornament 901.9
filing abrasion 350.2
 classification 61.1
 legislative procedure
  742.14
 listing 88.7
filing card 570.10
filing clerk 571.1
filings powder 361.5
 refuse 43.1
 remains 669.4
filing system 88.3
fill
 n. full measure 56.3
 satiety 664.1
 v. complete 56.7
 include 76.3
 meet 768.2
 pervade 186.7
 possess 808.4
 provide 659.7
 put 184.14
 repeat 103.8
 satiate 664.4
 stop 266.7
 stuff 194.7
 superabound 663.8
filled 56.11
filler contents 194.3
 horse 414.16
 syntax 586.2
fillet band 253.3
 strip 206.4
fill in
 become shallow
  210.3
 complete 56.6
 include 76.3
 inform 557.9
 spell 108.5
 substitute for 149.5
filling
 n. contents 194.3
 extra 41.4
 redundancy 103.3
 superfluity 663.4
 weaving 222.3
 adj. completing 56.13

satiating 664.7
filling station 832.7
fillip
 n. extra 41.4
 incentive 648.7
 tap 283.6
 v. stimulate 857.12
 tap 283.15
fill out
 become larger 197.5
 complete 56.6
 execute 771.10
 expatiate 593.8
 include 76.3
 increase 38.4
 make round 255.6
 record 570.16
fill the bill
 be expedient 670.3
 be of use 665.17
 suffice 661.4
 suit 26.8
fill up
 become shallow
  210.3
 compensate 33.4
 fill 56.7
 fuel 331.8
 provision 659.9
 satiate 664.4
 stop 266.7
 supply 659.7
filly
 female animal 421.9
 girl 125.6
 horse 414.10
film
 n. coating 228.12
 fog 404.2
 layer 227.2
 motion picture
  611.16
 photography 577.10
 pornographic 990.4
 record 570.10
 v. cover 228.19
 lose distinctness
  445.4
 photograph 577.14
 adj. theatrical 611.38
film star 612.4
filmy indistinct 445.6
 membranous 227.6
 smooth 351.8
 transparent 339.4
filmy-eyed 440.13
filter
 n. light filter 338.4
 refining equipment
  681.13
 v. exude 303.15
 refine 681.22
 trickle 395.18
filter in
 infiltrate 302.10
 sorb 306.13
filtering outflow 303.6
 refinement 681.4
filth badness 675.2
 cursing 972.3
 dirt 682.7
 obscenity 990.4

filthy bad 675.9
 dirty 682.23
 obscene 990.9
filtration outflow 303.6
 refinement 681.4
fin five 99.1
 swimming 275.11
 US money 835.7
finagle cheat 618.17
 maneuver 735.10
 plot 654.10
finagler
 political intriguer
  746.6
 schemer 654.8
final
 n. examination 485.2
 adj. completory 722.9
 departing 301.19
 eventual 151.11
 evidential 505.17
 mandatory 752.13
 resulting 154.7
 terminal 70.10
 unconditional 508.2
finale act 611.8
 end 70.1
 result 154.2
final hour 408.8
finality end 70.1
 futurity 121.4
finalize complete 722.6
 end 70.7
finally
 adv. at last 70.11
 consequently 154.9
 eventually 151.12
 interj. discovery
  488.11
final stroke
 deathblow 409.10
 end-all 70.4
 finishing touch 722.3
finance
 n. money 836
 v. fund 836.15
 pay 841.18
 subsidize 818.19
 support 785.12
finance company 820.4
financer backer 836.9
 giver 818.11
finances funds 835.14
 money 836.1
financial 835.30
financial district 833.8
financier
 businessman 830.1
 moneyman 836.8
financing
 borrowing 821.1
 funding 836.2
find
 n. acquisition 811.6
 discovery 488.1
 good thing 674.5
 v. arrive 300.6
 conclude 494.10
 decide 494.11
 discover 488.2
 learn 564.6
 pass judgment 494.13

provide 659.7
finder 443.4
finding discovery 488.1
 find 811.6
 judgment 494.5
 provision 659.1
 solution 487.1
find out discover 488.2
 learn 564.6
 make sure 513.11
 solve 487.2
fine
 n. penalty 1009.3
 v. penalize 1009.5
 adj. beautiful 900.16
 discriminating 492.7
 exact 516.16
 fastidious 896.11
 good 674.12
 grandiose 904.21
 healthy 685.7
 meticulous 533.12
 ornate 901.12
 pleasant 863.6
 powdery 361.11
 rainless 393.8
 sharp 258.10
 smooth 351.8
 tasteful 897.9
 tenuous 355.4
 thin 205.16
 tiny 196.11
 adv. excellently
  674.21
 interj. approval
  968.22
 yes 521.18
fine and dandy 674.13
fine arts 574.1
fine-drawn
 smooth 351.8
 thin 205.16
fine fettle
 healthiness 685.2
 orderliness 59.3
fine-grained 351.8
fine kettle of fish 731.4
fine print 507.2
finer 36.12
finery
 good clothes 231.10
 ornamentation 901.3
fine-spoken
 flattering 970.8
 suave 936.18
finespun smooth 351.8
 thin 205.16
finesse
 n. cunning 735.1
 discrimination 492.1
 good taste 897.1
 intrigue 654.6
 skill 733.1
 v. live by one's wits
  735.9
 plot 654.10
fine writing
 calligraphy 602.5
 flowery language
  601.4
finger
 n. digit 425.5

grasping organ 813.4
v. accuse 1005.7
condemn to death
409.20
designate 568.18
touch 425.6
fingerboard
keyboard 465.20
viol 465.6
finger bowl 681.12
fingering
indication 568.1
music 462.31
touching 425.2
fingernails 813.4
finger painting
painting 574.5
picture 574.15
fingerprint 568.7
fini 70.8
finicky
attentive 530.15
detailed 8.9
fastidious 896.10
meticulous 533.12
finis 70.1
finish
n. boundary 235.3
completion 722.2
end 70.1
literary elegance
589.1
perfection 677.1
polish 260.2
skill 733.8
symmetry 248.1
texture 351.1
v. complete 722.6
consume 666.2
dispose of 693.12
end 70.7
improve 691.10
kill 409.13
polish 260.7
refute 506.5
resolve 70.5
finished
accomplished 733.24
completed 722.11
dead 408.30
elegant 589.6
ended 70.8
past 119.7
perfected 677.9
polished 260.10
ruined 693.28
symmetric 248.4
used up 666.4
finisher disproof 506.3
end-all 70.4
finishing touch 722.3
garmentmaker 231.33
finishing
n. completion 722.2
consumption 666.1
adj. completory 722.9
ending 70.9
finishing touch
end-all 70.4
final touch 722.3
finite human 417.10
limited 234.7

numerical 86.8
finitude 111.1
fink
n. informer 557.6
strikebreaker 789.6
v. break a strike
789.10
inform on 557.12
fiord see fjord
fire
n. element 376.2
eloquence 600.5
fervor 855.10
fever 686.6
fever of excitement
857.6
gunfire 798.9
heat 328.13
inspiration 648.9
light source 336.1
pain 424.3
vim 161.2
zeal 635.2
v. become angry
952.18
begin 68.7
cook 330.4
dismiss 310.19
dry 393.6
energize 161.9
excite 857.11
explode 162.13
fire upon 798.22
heat 329.17
hurl at 798.28
ignite 329.22
incite 648.17
inspire 648.20
kindle 648.18
make ceramics 576.6
rocket 281.13
shoot 285.13
throw 285.11
interj. attack! 798.32
fire and brimstone
1019.2
firearm 801.5
fireball fuel 331.1
lightning 335.17
meteor 375.15
fire bell alarm 704.1
bell 454.4
firebox 329.10
firebrand coal 328.16
instigator 648.11
lighter 331.4
violent person 162.9
firebrick
building material
378.2
ceramic ware 576.2
fire brigade 332.4
firebug 329.8
firecracker
fireworks 328.33
noisemaker 453.5
fired cooked 330.6
excited 857.18
inspired 648.31
firedamp miasma 676.4
vapor 401.1

fire-eater
fire fighter 332.4
ill-humored person
951.11
reckless person 894.4
violent person 162.9
fire escape
escape 632.3
stairs 315.3
fire extinguisher 332.3
fire fighter 332.4
fire fighting 332.2
firefly glimmer 335.7
light 336.5
fireguard
fireplace 329.11
watchman 699.10
fire hydrant
extinguisher 332.3
hydrant 396.12
fire iron 329.12
fireman
fire fighter 332.4
sailor 276.6
trainman 274.13
fireplace hearth 329.11
home 191.4
fireplug
extinguisher 332.3
hydrant 396.12
firepower gunfire 798.9
troops 157.9
fireproof
v. flameproof 332.6
strengthen 159.12
adj. flameproof
332.10
resistant 159.18
fireproofing 332.5
fireside
fireplace 329.11
home 191.4
fire tactics 797.9
firetrap 618.11
firewater 996.13
firewood
kindling 331.3
wood 378.3
fireworks fire 328.17
gunfire 798.9
types of 328.33
fire worship
idolatry 1033.1
incendiarism 329.7
firing deposal 783.2
dismissal 310.5
fuel 331.1
gunfire 798.9
ignition 329.4
incitement 648.4
inspiration 648.9
throwing 285.3
firing line 802.2
firm
n. company 788.9
workplace 719.1
v. harden 356.7
stabilize 142.7
adj. close 266.12
crowded 74.22
dense 354.12
faithful 974.20

fastened 47.14
immovable 142.15
orthodox 1024.7
permanent 140.7
reliable 513.17
resolute 624.12
rigid 356.11
sound 159.16
stable 142.12
strict 757.7
substantial 3.7
unhazardous 698.5
unyielding 626.9
firmament 375.2
firm hand 757.3
firmly densely 354.15
faithfully 974.25
resolutely 624.17
securely 47.19
strictly 757.9
strongly 159.21
unyieldingly 626.15
firm price 773.3
first
n. beginning 68.3
adj. chief 36.14
foremost 68.17
front 240.10
leading 292.3
preceding 64.4
prior 116.4
adv. in front 240.12
initially 68.18
preferably 637.28
first aid 689.15
first-born
n. oldest 127.5
adj. oldest 123.19
first-class
first-rate 674.15
superlative 36.13
first draft trial 489.2
written matter 602.10
first edition
original 23.3
rare book 605.3
firsthand
evidential 505.17
new 122.7
original 23.5
first impression 68.3
first lady 749.2
first light 133.4
first move 68.3
first name 583.4
first off 68.18
first place 36.3
first prize award 916.2
supremacy 36.3
first-rate
excellent 674.15
superlative 36.13
first refusal 828.2
first step 68.3
first string 788.7
first thing 68.18
firth 399.1
fiscal 835.30
fish
n. animal 414.35,65
dupe 620.1
food 308.24

gaseousness 401.3
grandiloquence 601.1
flatulent
  bombastic 601.9
  distended 197.13
  ejective 310.28
  pompous 904.22
flatware
  hard goods 831.4
  tableware 348.3
flaunt display 904.17
  indicate 555.5
  wave 323.11
flaunting
  n. display 904.4
  waving 323.2
  adj. garish 362.19
  gaudy 904.20
  grandiloquent 601.8
  showy 904.19
flautist 464.4
flavor
  n. characteristic 80.4
  flavoring 428.3
  odor 435.1
  taste 427.1
  v. infuse 44.12
  savor 428.7
flavored 427.9
flavorful flavored 427.9
  flavorsome 428.9
flavoring 428.3
flavorless 430.2
flavorsome
  flavorful 428.9
  pleasant 863.9
flaw
  n. blemish 679.1
  crack 201.2
  error 518.1
  fault 678.2
  gust 403.6
  vice 981.2
  v. blemish 679.4
flawed blemished 679.8
  erroneous 518.16
  illegal 999.6
  illogical 483.11
flawless
  accurate 516.15
  perfect 677.6
flay
  criticize severely
  969.21
  despoil 822.24
  peel 232.8
  tear apart 49.14
flea animal 414.40,74
  jumper 319.4
fleabag 191.16
flea-bitten 374.13
flea in one's ear
  piece of advice 754.2
  warning 703.1
flea market
  marketplace 832.2
  sale 829.3
fleck
  n. blemish 679.3
  hair 230.6
  mark 568.5
  minute thing 196.7

small amount 35.2
spottiness 374.3
v. mark 568.19
variegate 374.7
flection
  angularity 251.1
  curve 252.3
  deflection 291.2
  fold 264.1
fledge feather 230.21
  mature 126.9
fledgling
  n. animal 414.33
  beginner 68.2
  boy 125.5
  modern 122.4
  novice 566.9
  young bird 125.8
  youngster 125.1
  adj. new 122.7
  undeveloped 721.11
flee cease to exist 2.5
  disappear 447.2
  escape 632.6
  fly 631.10
  run off 301.13
fleece
  n. hair 230.2
  head of hair 230.4
  hide 229.1,8
  softness 357.4
  white 364.2
  v. cheat 618.17
  despoil 822.24
  divest 232.5
  overcharge 848.7
  plunder 824.16
fleeced 838.8
fleecy soft 357.14
  woolly 230.24
fleer
  n. gibe 967.2
  ridicule 967.4
  v. make fun of 881.13
  offend 965.4
  ridicule 967.9
fleet
  n. group 74.3
  navy 800.26
  ships 277.10
  v. be transient 111.6
  speed 269.8
  adj. agile 733.21
  fast 269.19
  transient 111.8
fleeting transient 111.7
  vanishing 447.3
flesh body 376.3
  kinsmen 11.2
  mankind 417.1
  materiality 376.1
  meat 308.12
  organic matter 406.1
  sensuality 987.2
  sexuality 419.2
  skin 229.1
flesh and blood
  kinsmen 11.2
  materiality 376.1
flesh-eater 307.14
flesh-eating 307.29
fleshly human 417.10

lascivious 989.29
materialistic 376.9
sensual 987.6
sexual 419.26
unrighteous 981.12
unsacred 1027.3
fleshpots
  disapproved place
  191.28
  place of vice 981.7
  prosperity 728.1
fleshy corpulent 195.18
  pulpy 390.6
fleur-de-lis
  heraldic insignia
  569.2
  insignia 569.1
flex
  n. bend 252.3
  v. bend 252.6
flexed 291.8
flexibility
  changeableness 141.1
  conformity 82.1
  pliancy 357.2
  resilience 358.1
  submissiveness 765.3
  unstrictness 758.2
  versatility 733.3
  wieldiness 732.2
flexible
  changeable 141.6
  conformable 82.5
  docile 765.13
  folded 264.7
  pliant 357.9
  resilient 358.7
  unstrict 758.5
  versatile 733.23
  wieldy 732.14
flexion see **flection**
flex one's muscles
  720.13
flexuous
  crooked 219.20
  pliant 357.9
  winding 254.6
flexure
  angularity 251.1
  curve 252.3
  deflection 291.2
  fold 264.1
flibbertigibbet 471.7
flick
  n. blemish 679.3
  faint sound 452.3
  jerk 286.3
  mark 568.5
  motion picture
  611.16
  tap 283.6
  touch 425.1
  v. flutter 324.12
  jerk 286.5
  tap 283.15
  touch 425.6
flicker
  n. fire 328.13
  flutter 324.4
  light 335.8
  motion picture
  611.16

v. be hot 328.22
  flutter 324.12
  glimmer 335.25
flickering
  burning 328.27
  fluttering 324.18
  glittering 335.36
  inconstant 141.7
  irregular 138.3
  transient 111.8
flier advertising 559.8
  aviator 279.1
  circus artist 612.3
  gamble 515.1
  speeder 269.5
  stock speculation
  833.19
  train 272.13
flight air force 800.28
  arrows 801.16
  aviation 278.1
  birds 74.6
  course 267.2
  defense mechanism
  690.30
  departure 301.1
  escape 632.1
  large number 101.3
  migration 273.4
  music 463.18
  rocketry 281.9
  running away 631.4
  speed 269.1
  trip 278.9
flight attendant 279.4
flight of fancy
  idealization 535.7
  imagination 535.1
flight path
  aviation 278.25
  route 657.2
flight plan 278.3
flight test 489.3
flighty fickle 629.6
  inconstant 141.7
  insane 473.25
  superficial 469.20
  volatile 532.17
flimflam
  n. caprice 629.1
  deception 618.1
  fraud 618.8
  humbug 616.14
  lie 616.11
  v. cheat 618.17
flimflam man 619.3
flimsy flaccid 357.10
  fragile 360.4
  frail 160.14
  illogical 483.12
  shaky 4.7
  tenuous 355.4
  thin 205.16
  trivial 673.16
flinch
  n. retreat 284.3
  v. be startled 540.5
  demur 623.4
  pull back 284.7
  retract 297.3
  shrink 891.21

ornament 901.9
play 878.25
walk 273.27
flounder
n. tumble 324.8
v. be uncertain 514.9
bungle 734.11
fluctuate 141.5
have difficulty 731.10
sail 275.55
trip 316.8
tumble 324.15
wallow 322.13
flour
n. powder 361.5
white 364.2
v. pulverize 361.9
sprinkle 75.6
flourish
n. display 904.4
extra 41.4
figure of speech
551.1
flowery language
601.4
improvisation 462.27
music 463.18
ornamentation 901.1
waving 323.2
v. be famous 914.10
be healthy 685.5
boast 910.6
flaunt 904.17
grow 197.7
have energy 161.10
indicate 555.5
make grandiloquent
601.7
reach perfection
722.8
thrive 728.8
vegetate 411.31
wave 323.11
flourishing
n. waving 323.2
adj. growing 197.12
luxuriant 411.40
productive 165.9
thriving 728.13
flout
n. gibe 967.2
indignity 965.2
v. defy 793.4
disobey 767.6
not observe 769.4
offend 965.4
ridicule 967.9
flow
n. aviation 278.38
course 267.2
eloquence 600.2
excretion 311.1
glide 273.8
liquidity 388.1
literary elegance
589.1
plenty 661.2
stream 395.4
tide 395.13
v. abound 661.5
elapse 105.5
enter 302.9

flow out 303.13
glide 273.34
go easily 732.9
hang 215.6
move 267.5
result from 154.6
stream 395.16
travel 273.17
flower
n. blossom 411.22,44
essence 5.2
figure of speech
551.1
parts of 411.26
the best 674.8
v. be in flower 411.32
evolve 148.5
mature 126.9
ornament 901.9
thrive 728.8
flower bed 413.10
flower child 83.3
flowered floral 411.35
ornamented 901.11
flowering
n. blossoming 411.24
development 148.1
adj. floral 411.35
growing 197.12
thriving 728.13
young 124.9
flowerlike 900.16
flower power
benevolence 938.4
power 157.1
flowers
compilation 605.4
excerpts 607.4
menstruation 311.9
flowery figurative 551.3
floral 411.35
fragrant 436.9
high-flown 601.11
ornate 901.12
flowing cursive 602.22
eloquent 600.9
fluid 388.6
harmonious 589.8
pendent 215.9
running 267.8
streaming 395.24
flown 632.11
flowoff 303.4
flow on drench 392.14
elapse 105.5
progress 294.3
flu
infectious disease
686.12
respiratory disease
686.14
flub
n. botch 734.5
v. botch 734.12
fluctuate
be capricious 629.4
intermit 138.2
oscillate 323.10
vacillate 627.8
vary 141.5
fluctuating
inconstant 141.7

irregular 138.3
oscillating 323.15
vacillating 627.10
fluctuation
irregularity 138.1
oscillation 323.1
stock prices 834.9
vacillation 627.2
variation 141.3
flue down 230.19
fireplace 329.11
lightness 353.2
smoke passage 396.18
softness 357.4
fluency
diffuseness 593.1
eloquence 600.2
flow 395.4
liquidity 388.1
literary elegance
589.1
talkativeness 596.1
fluent eloquent 600.9
flowing 267.8
harmonious 589.8
liquid 388.6
streaming 395.24
talkative 596.9
fluently
eloquently 600.15
talkatively 596.11
fluff
n. bungle 734.5
down 230.19
error in speech 518.7
fine texture 351.3
lightness 353.2
softness 357.4
v. blunder 518.15
make pliant 357.6
fluffy downy 230.27
light 353.10
smooth 351.8
soft 357.14
superficial 469.20
fluid
n. gas 401.2
liquid 388.2
vapor 401.1
adj. changeable 141.6
liquid 388.6
fluidity
changeableness 141.1
gaseousness 401.3
liquidity 388.1
fluidize liquefy 391.5
put into a gas 401.8
fluke
chance event 156.6
invertebrates 415.5
stroke of luck 728.3
fluky 156.15
flume outlet 303.9
ravine 201.2
watercourse 396.2
flummery 547.2
flummox
bewilder 514.12
confuse 532.7
fail 725.9
thwart 730.15

flump
n. faint sound 452.3
v. sink 316.6
flunk
n. fiasco 725.6
v. fail 725.8
fail someone 725.16
flunky follower 293.2
inferior 37.2
man 787.8
retainer 750.1
servant 750.6
sycophant 907.3
working person 718.2
fluoresce 335.26
fluorescence 335.13
fluorescent 335.38
fluoroscopy
radiation physics
327.7
radiotherapy 689.8
flurry
n. agitation 324.1
bluster 911.1
bustle 707.4
confusion 532.3
excitement 857.3
gust 403.6
haste 709.1
rain 394.1
snow 333.8
speed 269.1
stock prices 834.9
v. agitate 324.10
confuse 532.7
excite 857.13
flush
n. blushing 908.5
fever 686.6
health 685.1
heat 328.12
jet 395.9
playing cards 878.17
reddening 368.3
shine 335.2
thrill 857.2
warmth 362.2
washing 681.5
v. become excited
857.17
become red 368.5
be hot 328.22
blush 908.8
cheer 870.8
flow 395.16
hunt 655.9
level 214.6
make proud 905.6
show resentment
952.14
soak 392.13
thrill 857.14
wash 681.19
adj. flat 214.7
full 56.11
healthy 685.11
plentiful 661.7
red-complexioned
368.9
robust 685.10
wealthy 837.13

nominal 583.15
orderly 59.6
pompous 904.22
ritualistic 1040.22
serious 871.3
stilted 590.3
structural 245.9
stylized 646.7
formaldehyde 701.3
formalist
conformist 82.2
hypocrite 1029.3
mind-changer 628.4
pedant 476.5
ritualist 1040.2
formalistic
affected 903.18
conformist 82.6
formal 646.7
formalities
amenities 936.7
etiquette 646.3
formality
affectation 903.5
ceremony 646
law 998.3
pomp 904.6
rite 1040.3
ritual 646.4
rule 84.4
social convention
645.1
solemnity 871.1
formalize
execute 771.8
form 246.7
ritualize 646.5
standardize 84.6
format form 246.1
structure 245.1
formation
arrangement 60.1
composition 58.1
establishment 167.4
flight formation
278.12
form 246.1
forming 246.5
manufacture 167.3
order 59.1
structure 245.1
word 582.4
formational
formative 246.9
organizational 60.15
productional 167.17
formative
n. morphology 582.3
adj. beginning 68.15
causal 153.14
component 58.5
creative 167.19
formal 246.9
pliant 357.9
former older 123.19
past 119.10
preceding 64.5
prior 116.4
formidable
difficult 731.16
remarkable 34.10
terrible 891.38

weighty 672.19
formless abnormal 85.9
diffuse 593.11
shapeless 247.4
unordered 62.12
formula axiom 517.2
law 998.3
mathematics 86.9
precept 751.2
prescription 751.3
rite 1040.3
rule 84.4
formulary
n. formulas 751.3
law 998.3
rite 1040.3
rule 84.4
adj. formal 646.7
prescriptive 751.4
ritualistic 1040.22
formulate
create 167.10
legalize 998.8
phrase 588.4
say 594.23
write 602.21
formulation
arrangement 60.1
diction 588.1
manufacture 167.3
fornicate
be unchaste 989.19
copulate 419.23
fornication
adultery 989.7
copulation 419.8
for nothing 850.5,6
for real positively 34.19
real 1.15
forsake abandon 633.5
be dishonest 975.12
forsaken
abandoned 633.8
deserted 187.14
forlorn 924.11
outcast 926.10
unloved 867.10
for sale 829.16
for show 903.20
forsooth
certainly 513.23
truly 516.17
forswear
abandon 633.7
deny 524.4
recant 628.9
reject 638.2
relinquish 814.3
swear off 992.8
forsworn
deceitful 975.18
rejected 638.3
relinquished 814.5
untruthful 616.34
fort 799.6
forte
n. music 462.25
specialty 81.1
talent 733.4
adj. loud 453.10
adv. loudly 453.13
music 462.54

forth away 301.21
forward 294.8
out 303.21
forthcoming
n. appearance 446.1
approach 296.1
egress 303.1
imminence 152.1
adj. approaching
296.4
emerging 303.18
future 121.8
imminent 152.3
in preparation 720.22
for the most part
chiefly 36.17
generally 79.17
normally 84.9
on the whole 54.14
for the record 649.6
for the time being
now 120.3
temporarily 111.9
till then 109.5
forthright
adj. candid 974.17
adv. directly 290.24
forthwith
at once 113.8
promptly 131.15
fortification
confirmation 505.5
defense 799.4
strengthening 159.5
vitaminization 309.12
fortified 799.12
fortify add to 40.5
adulterate 44.13
confirm 505.12
defend 799.9
refresh 695.2
strengthen 159.11
vitaminize 309.18
fortissimo
n. music 462.25
adj. loud 453.10
adv. loudly 453.13
music 462.54
fortitude courage 893.4
patience 861.1
strength 159.1
virtue 980.5
will power 624.4
Fort Knox 836.12
fortnight fourteen 99.7
period 107.2
fortnightly
n. periodical 605.10
adj. regularly 137.8
fortress 799.6
fortuitous accessory 6.4
chance 156.15
fortuity
chance event 156.6
luck 156.1
fortunate
n. lucky person 728.6
adj. auspicious 544.18
lucky 728.14
successful 724.13
timely 129.9

fortunately
auspiciously 544.21
luckily 728.16
fortune
biography 608.4
chance 156.1
fate 640.2
gamble 515.1
prosperity 728.2
wealth 837.1
fortune hunter 978.3
fortune's child 728.6
fortune-tell 543.9
fortune-teller 543.4
forty-niner miner 383.9
traveler 274.1
forty winks 712.3
forum arena 802.1
city district 183.8
discussion 597.7
meeting 74.2
panel 755.3
tribunal 1001.1
forward
v. advance 294.5
be expedient 670.3
be instrumental
658.5
cause 153.13
deliver 818.13
encourage 785.17
hasten 709.4
impel 283.10
make better 691.9
push 285.10
send 271.14
adj. eager 635.9
foolhardy 894.9
front 240.10
immodest 990.6
insolent 913.8
meddlesome 238.9
premature 131.8
progressive 294.6
strong-willed 624.15
willing 622.5
adv. frontward 240.13
onward 294.8
forward-looking
modern 122.13
progressive 294.6
forward motion
course 267.2
progression 294.1
forward pass 285.4
fosse
entrenchment 799.5
trench 263.2
fossil
antiquated person
123.8
antiquity 123.6
remainder 43.1
fossilize
become old 123.9
harden 356.7
fossilized aged 126.18
antiquated 123.13
hardened 356.13
foster
v. advance 294.5
aid 785.16

care for 699.19
encourage 648.21
harbor 813.7
make better 691.9
motivate 648.12
nourish 307.17
train 562.14
adj. related 11.6
fosterage 785.4
foster child 171.3
foster home 700.4
foster mother 170.10
fou
n. lunatic 473.15
adj. intoxicated
996.30
foul
n. unfairness 977.2
v. catch 822.17
collide 283.12
defile 682.17
misuse 667.4
stop 266.7
adj. bad 675.9
base 915.12
blocked 266.11
cursing 972.8
decayed 692.41
evil 981.16
filthy 682.23
malodorous 437.5
obscene 990.9
offensive 864.18
stagnant 268.14
stormy 403.26
ugly 899.11
unfair 977.10
unhealthful 684.5
unsavory 429.7
fouled blocked 266.11
soiled 682.21
foul language 972.3
foul matter 682.7
foul-mouthed 990.9
foul play
chicanery 618.4
dishonesty 975.6
homicide 409.2
unfairness 977.2
foul-tasting 429.5
foul-tongued 990.9
foul up blunder 518.15
bungle 734.12
complicate 46.3
confuse 63.3
spoil 692.13
thwart 730.16
foul-up an error 518.6
bungler 734.9
confusion 62.2
foul weather 162.4
found begin 68.11
create 167.12
establish 142.9
fix 184.15
form 246.7
heat 329.24
originate 153.11
sculpture 575.5
foundation base 216.6
beginning 68.1
bottom 212.2

endowment 818.9
establishment 184.6
justification 1006.6
make-up 900.11
organization 788.8
premise 482.7
preparation 720.1
production 167.4
stability 142.6
foundation garment
corset 231.23
supporter 216.2
founded on
evidential 505.17
supported 216.24
founder
n. producer 167.8
v. capsize 275.44
break down 692.27
come to grief 729.10
fail 725.10
go lame 686.46
scuttle 320.8
sink 316.6
foundered 731.25
foundering 316.11
foundling
abandoned person
633.4
find 811.6
foundry 719.5
found wanting
imperfect 678.4
insufficient 662.9
fountain
n. ascent 315.1
jet 395.9
source 153.6
source of supply
660.4
v. shoot up 315.9
fountainhead
headwaters 395.2
source 153.6
fountain of youth 112.3
four 96
four-eyed 443.10
four-flush 616.21
four-flusher 619.6
fourfold 97.3
Four Hundred, the
nobility 918.2
society 644.6
four-letter word 972.4
fourscore 99.7
foursome four 96.1
game 878.9
foursquare four 96.4
honest 974.14
quadrangular 251.9
fourth
n. harmonics 463.20
one-fourth 98.2
adj. quarter 98.5
fourth-class 680.9
fourth dimension 179.6
fourth estate
news 558.1
the press 605.23
four-wheeler 272.4
fowl
n. bird 414.33

food 308.22
parts of 308.23
poultry 414.34
v. hunt 655.9
fox animal 414.25
cunning person 735.6
fox fire fire 328.13
phosphorescence
335.13
foxhole
entrenchment 799.5
hiding place 615.4
shelter 700.3
tunnel 257.5
fox-trot dance 879.5
run 269.10
foxy blemished 679.10
canine 414.45
cunning 735.12
reddish-brown 367.4
shrewd 467.15
foyer home 191.4
lobby 192.19
fracas commotion 62.4
free-for-all 796.5
noise 453.3
quarrel 795.5
fraction number 86.3
part 55.1
ratio 86.6
fractionate 401.8
fractious
irascible 951.19
opposing 790.8
refractory 767.10
resistant 792.5
ungovernable 626.12
unwilling 623.5
fracture
n. break 49.4
crack 201.2
impairment 692.8
v. amuse 878.23
be damaged 692.26
break 49.12
cleave 201.4
injure 692.15
fragile brittle 360.4
frail 160.14
transient 111.7
fragility
breakability 360.1
frailty 160.2
unhealthiness 686.2
fragment
n. excerpts 607.4
piece 55.3
small amount 35.2
v. demolish 693.17
pulverize 361.9
shatter 49.13
fragmentary 55.7
fragrance odor 435.1
perfume 436
fragrant aromatic 436.9
odorous 435.9
fraidy-cat 892.5
frail fragile 360.4
human 417.10
irresolute 627.12
thin 205.16
transient 111.7

unhealthy 686.50
unrighteous 981.12
weak 160.14
frailty
breakability 360.1
fault 678.2
humanness 417.5
irresolution 627.4
thinness 205.4
unhealthiness 686.2
vice 981.2
weakness 160.2
frame
n. accusation 1005.4
body 376.3
bottom 212.2
casing 245.4
film 577.10
form 246.1
human form 246.4
lip 235.4
mood 525.4
mounting 216.10
nature 5.3
skeleton 245.5
structure 245.1
v. accuse 1005.12
border 235.10
construct 167.10
create 167.13
form 246.7
phrase 588.4
plan 654.9
plot 654.10
prearrange 641.3
frame of mind 525.4
frame of reference
525.2
frame-up
accusation 1005.4
fake 616.13
intrigue 654.6
prearrangement
641.1
framework frame 245.4
frame of reference
525.2
outline 235.2
franc 835.9
franchise
n. exemption 762.8
grant 777.5
right 958.4
suffrage 744.17
voice 637.6
v. authorize 777.11
Franciscan
ascetic 991.2
religious 1038.18
frangible brittle 360.4
frail 160.14
frank
n. mail 604.5
postage 604.6
sausage 308.21
adj. artless 736.5
candid 974.17
communicative
554.10
in plain style 591.3
talkative 596.9
vulgar 990.8

Frankenstein 891.9
frankfurter 308.21
frankincense 436.4
frankly 974.23
frankness candor 974.4
  communicativeness
    554.3
  plain speech 591.1
  talkativeness 596.1
  vulgarity 990.3
frantic
  distracted 532.10
  excited 857.23
  mad 473.30
  overactive 707.24
  overzealous 635.13
  violent 162.17
frantically
  frenziedly 857.33
  turbulently 162.25
  violently 34.23
frappé 308.46
fraternal
  friendly 927.14
  kind 938.13
fraternity
  affiliation 786.2
  association 788.3
  blood relationship
    11.1
  fellowship 927.2
  sociability 922.6
fraternity house 191.16
fraternization
  affiliation 786.2
  sociability 922.6
  treason 975.7
fraternize
  be friends 927.9
  be sociable 922.16
  betray 975.15
fraternizer 619.11
fratricide 409.3
Frau
  form of address 421.8
  woman 421.5
fraud affecter 903.7
  deception 618.8
  dishonesty 975.3
  fakery 616.3
  hoax 616.13
  impostor 619.6
  theft 824.1
fraudulence
  fraud 618.8
  improbity 975.1
fraudulent
  deceitful 618.20
  dishonest 975.16
  thievish 824.20
fraught
  burdened 352.18
  loaded 56.12
Fräulein 421.8
fray
  n. fight 796.4
    impairment 692.8
  v. abrade 350.7
    injure 692.15
    wear 692.23
frayed 692.34

frazzle
  n. impairment 692.8
  v. abrade 350.7
    fatigue 717.4
    injure 692.15
    trouble 890.3
    wear 692.23
frazzled fatigued 717.6
  shabby 692.34
  worn-out 692.38
freak
  n. caprice 629.1
    desirer 634.12
    drug user 642.10
    eccentric 474.3
    enthusiast 635.5
    fanatic 473.17
    misfit 27.4
    monstrosity 85.6
    nonconformist 83.3
    specialist 81.3
  adj. abnormal 85.13
freak accident 156.6
freakish
  abnormal 85.13
  capricious 629.5
  eccentric 474.4
  inconstant 141.7
freak out delight 865.8
  enjoy 865.10
  fantasy 535.17
  go crazy 473.21
  have hallucinations
    519.8
  thrill to 857.16
freckle
  n. blemish 679.1
    mark 568.5
    spottiness 374.3
  v. blemish 679.5
    mark 568.19
    variegate 374.7
freckled
  blemished 679.9
  spotted 374.13
free
  v. acquit 1007.4
    detach 49.10
    disembarrass 732.8
    emancipate 763.4
    exempt 762.14
    extricate 763.7
    liberalize 762.13
    loosen 51.3
    release 886.6
    rescue 702.3
    unclose 265.13
  adj. at liberty 762.20
    candid 974.17
    communicative
      554.10
    escaped 632.11
    generous 853.4
    gratis 850.5
    idle 708.17
    leisure 710.5
    open 265.18
    quit 762.30
    released 763.10
    unchaste 989.25
    unfastened 49.22
    vacant 187.14

voluntary 622.7
  adv. as a gift 818.27
    gratis 850.6
    unreservedly 762.31
free and clear
  possessed 808.8
  unindebted 841.23
free and easy
  careless 534.11
  convivial 922.19
  free 762.20
  informal 647.3
  lighthearted 870.12
  nonchalant 858.15
  nonconformist 83.6
free association 690.40
freebie
  n. costless thing 850.1
  adj. gratis 850.5
freeboot pirate 824.17
  plunder 824.16
freeborn 762.20
free choice
  choice 637.1
  decision 621.1
  free will 762.6
Free Church 1020.10
freed free 762.20
  liberated 763.10
freedom candor 974.4
  facility 732.1
  leisure 710.1
  liberality 853.1
  liberty 762
  right 958.4
free enterprise
  capitalism 745.8
  noninterference
    762.9
  political policy 744.4
free-enterprise 745.23
free-for-all
  commotion 62.4
  fight 796.5
  noise 453.3
freehand
  free-acting 762.22
  pictorial 574.22
free hand
  full permission 777.4
  latitude 762.4
  liberality 853.1
freehold estate 810.6
  land 385.1
  possession 808.1
freeholder
  householder 190.7
  landowner 809.3
freeing
  disembarrassment
    732.5
  escape 632.1
  extrication 763.3
  liberation 763.1
  release 886.2
  rescue 702.1
free lance
  author 602.15
  independent 762.12
  mercenary 800.16
  working person 718.2

free-lance
  be independent
    762.19
  write 602.21
free-living 993.8
freeload 850.4
freeloader
  deadhead 850.3
  guest 925.6
  nonworker 708.10
  parasite 907.4
free love
  adultery 989.7
  love 931.1
  sex behavior 419.20
freely generously 853.5
  voluntarily 622.10
  without restraint
    762.31
freeman 762.11
freemasonry
  affiliation 786.2
  fellowship 927.2
free ride 850.1
free spirit 762.12
free-spoken
  candid 974.17
  communicative
    554.10
free-acting 762.22
  speaking 594.32
freethinker
  broad-minded person
    526.6
  independent 762.12
  latitudinarian
    1031.13
freethinking
  n. broad-mindedness
    526.2
  latitudinarianism
    1031.7
  liberalism 762.10
  adj. broad-minded
    526.9
  latitudinarian
    1031.21
  liberal 762.24
free time 710.1
freeway 657.6
freewheeling 762.21
free will choice 637.1
  freedom 762.6
  voluntariness 622.2
  will 621.1
freeze
  n. cold weather 333.3
  v. be afraid 891.19
    be cold 333.9
    be still 268.7
    chill 333.10
    ice 334.11
    make unfeeling 856.8
    perpetuate 112.5
    preserve 701.8
    render insensible
      423.4
    stabilize 142.7
    stop 144.11
    terrify 891.25
  interj. cease! 144.14
freeze-dry 701.8

973

freeze out
drive out 310.14
exclude 77.4
freezer 334.5
freeze to cohere 50.6
hold 813.6
freezing
n. preserving 701.2
refrigeration 334.1
adj. cold 333.14
refrigerative 334.12
freezing point
cold 333.1
temperature 328.3
freight
n. burden 352.7
cargo 194.2
charge 846.8
duty 963.3
impediment 730.6
shipment 271.7
train 272.13
transportation 271.3
v. burden 352.13
fill 56.7
put 184.14
send 271.14
transport 271.11
freighted
burdened 352.18
loaded 56.12
freighter carrier 271.5
ship 277.22
train 272.13
French horn 465.8
French leave
absence 187.4
flight 631.4
frenetic mad 473.30
overactive 707.24
overzealous 635.13
frenzied excited 857.23
mad 473.30
overactive 707.24
overzealous 635.13
violent 162.17
frenzy
n. confusion 532.3
excitement 857.7
insanity 473.7
overzealousness 635.4
seizure 686.5
violence 162.2
v. enrage 952.23
excite 857.11
madden 473.23
Freon 334.7
frequence
attendance 186.4
commonness 135.1
frequency
oftenness 135
oscillation 323.1
radio frequency
344.12
tone 450.2
wave 323.4
frequency band
frequency 323.1
radio 344.13
wave 323.4
frequency curve 511.2

frequent
v. attend 186.10
adj. habitual 642.16
prevalent 135.4
recurrent 103.13
frequenter
attender 186.5
guest 925.6
frequenting 186.4
frequently
commonly 135.6
habitually 642.23
repeatedly 103.16
fresco
n. coloring 362.12
picture 574.12
v. color 362.13
fresh
n. running water
395.1
violent flow 395.5
adj. additional 40.10
clean 681.25
cool 333.12
healthy 685.11
impudent 913.9
inexperienced 734.17
new 122.7
original 23.5
present 120.2
refreshing 695.3
remembered 537.23
renewed 122.8
undamaged 677.8
unused 668.12
windy 403.25
freshen air 402.11
blow 403.22
clean 681.18
refresh 695.2
refrigerate 334.10
touch up 691.11
freshman beginner 68.2
novice 566.9
student 566.6
fresh start
beginning 68.1
resumption 143.2
fret
n. ache 424.5
anger 952.7
dither 857.5
heraldic insignia
569.2
irritation 866.3
network 221.3
v. abrade 350.7
agitate 324.10
be angry 952.15
be ill-humored
951.14
be impatient 862.4
complain 875.13
feel anxious 890.5
grieve 872.17
hurt 424.7
impair 692.15
irritate 866.14
make anxious 890.4
nag 969.16
provoke 952.22
wear 692.23

fretful active 707.20
ill-humored 951.21
impatient 862.6
plaintive 875.16
fretfulness
impatience 862.1
petulance 951.5
fretted worried 890.7
woven 222.7
fretting
n. abrasion 350.2
impatience 862.1
worry 890.2
adj. abrasive 350.10
impatient 862.6
irritating 424.13
troublesome 890.9
fretwork 221.3
Frey
agriculture divinity
413.4
fertility god 165.5
Norse deity 1014.6
Freya
beautiful woman
900.9
love goddess 931.8
Norse deity 1014.6
friable brittle 360.4
pulverable 361.13
friar 1038.17
friarhood 1037.4
friary 1042.6
fribble
n. dandy 903.9
ornament 901.4
trifle 673.5
trifler 673.9
v. fritter away 854.5
trifle 673.13
waste time 708.12
adj. trivial 673.16
fricassee
n. stew 308.11
v. cook 330.4
friction
n. counteraction
178.1
disaccord 795.1
hostility 929.3
opposition 790.2
rubbing 350
touching 425.2
adj. frictional 350.9
frictionless
in accord 794.3
smooth-running
732.13
fridge 334.4
fried cooked 330.6
drunk 996.31
friend 928
friend at court
influential person
172.6
lawyer 1003.1
supporter 787.9
friendless alone 89.8
forlorn 924.11
helpless 158.18

friendly
adj. acquainted
927.16
amicable 927.14
comfortable 887.11
helpful 785.22
homelike 191.33
hospitable 925.11
sociable 922.18
adv. amicably 927.21
friendship 927
frier see **fryer**
frieze
architecture 211.17
ornamentation
901.14
Frigg
marriage goddess
933.14
Norse deity 1014.6
fright fear 891.1
ugly thing 899.4
frighten alarm 704.3
scare 891.23
startle 540.8
frightened
afraid 891.33
alarmed 704.4
nervous 859.10
frightening
n. intimidation 891.6
adj. frightful 891.36
frighten off
dissuade 652.3
scare away 891.29
frightful
frightening 891.36
remarkable 34.11
ugly 899.11
frightfully
fearfully 891.42
hideously 899.13
terribly 34.21
frigid cold 333.14
reticent 613.10
unfeeling 856.9
unsexual 419.31
unsociable 923.6
Frigid Zones
cold place 333.4
zone 180.3
frill
n. edging 235.7
extra 41.4
flowery language
601.4
fold 264.1
ornamentation 901.3
superfluity 663.4
v. fold 264.5
frilly ornate 901.12
showy 904.19
fringe
n. border 235.4
edging 235.7
exterior 224.2
hair 230.6
v. border 235.10
adj. peripheral 224.6
fringe benefit 841.6
fringed 235.12

frippery
good clothes 231.10
ornamentation 901.3
superfluity 663.4
trifle 673.5
Frisbee 878.34
frisk
n. frolic 878.5
jump 319.2
search 485.14
v. jump 319.6
play 878.25
rejoice 876.5
ride 273.33
search 485.30
frisky gay 870.14
lively 707.17
frith
arm of the sea 399.1
thicket 411.13
undergrowth 411.15
fritter 308.43
fritter away 854.5
frivolity
foolishness 470.1
merriment 870.5
triviality 673.3
wittiness 881.4
frivolous merry 870.15
scatterbrained 532.16
superficial 469.20
trivial 673.16
unordered 62.12
frizzle
n. hair 230.5
v. cook 330.4
frizzy 254.9
fro 295.13
frock dress 231.16
garment 231.3
suit 231.6
vestment 1041.2
frog
amphibian 414.32,62
Frenchman 181.7
jumper 319.4
froggy 414.51
frogman diver 320.4
sailor 276.4
swimmer 275.12
frolic
n. play 878.5
prank 881.10
v. be cheerful 870.6
play 878.25
rejoice 876.5
frolicsome
frisky 870.14
playful 878.31
from away from 301.22
less 42.14
out of 303.22
from time immemorial
119.17
from time to time
136.5
frond branch 411.18
leaf 411.17
frondeur critic 969.9
malcontent 869.3
rebel 767.5

front
n. affectation 903.1
appearances 446.2
aviation 278.41
battlefield 802.2
exterior 224.2
fakery 616.3
figurehead 749.4
fore 240
leading 292.1
mediator 805.3
political front 744.33
pretext 649.1
vanguard 240.2
weather front 402.5
v. confront 240.8
contrapose 239.4
defy 793.3
face upon 240.9
offer resistance 792.3
oppose 790.5
precede 64.2
stand up to 893.11
adj. first 68.17
frontal 240.10
phonetic 594.31
frontage front 240.1
position 184.3
frontal
n. church part
1042.12
face 240.1
adj. front 240.10
front for
represent 781.14
substitute for 149.6
frontier
n. border 235.5
boundary 235.3
front 240.1
hinterland 182.2
remote region 199.4
the unknown 477.7
adj. bordering 235.11
frontiersman
backwoodsman
190.10
precursor 66.1
fronting
adj. facing 240.11
prep. opposite 239.7
frontispiece
front 240.1
prelude 66.2
front line
battlefield 802.2
vanguard 240.2
front man
figurehead 749.4
front 240.1
mediator 805.3
front matter
book 605.12
front 240.1
part of writing 55.2
prelude 66.2
front position 64.1
front room 192.5
front-runner
precursor 66.1
vanguard 240.2
frontward 240.13

frost
n. cold weather 333.3
enmity 929.1
failure 725.2
ice 333.7
v. chill 333.10
freeze 333.11
make semitransparent
340.3
top 211.9
whiten 364.5
frostbite
n. cold sensation
333.2
environmental dis-
ease 686.31
v. chill 333.10
frostbitten 334.14
frosted
n. drink 308.48
adj. frosty 333.16
semitransparent
340.4
unfeeling 856.9
white 364.7
frosting icing 308.39
topping 211.3
whitening 364.3
frosty frostlike 333.16
reticent 613.10
semitransparent
340.4
unfeeling 856.9
unfriendly 929.9
unsociable 923.6
white 364.7
froth
n. foam 405.2
lightness 353.2
residue 43.2
saliva 312.3
sprinkle 392.5
trivia 673.4
v. foam 405.5
frothing at the mouth
excited 857.23
infuriated 952.29
mad 473.30
frothy foamy 405.7
light 353.10
showy 904.19
superficial 469.20
trivial 673.16
froufrou
ornamentation 901.3
rustle 452.6
froward
disobedient 767.8
perverse 626.11
frown
n. disapproval 969.8
resentment 952.2
scowl 951.9
v. be ill-humored
951.15
disapprove 969.10
show resentment
952.14
frowning solemn 871.3
sullen 951.24
frowsty
malodorous 437.5

spoiled 692.43
frowzy
malodorous 437.5
slovenly 62.15
spoiled 692.43
frozen cold 333.15
frozen solid 334.14
immortal 112.9
immovable 142.15
permanent 140.7
terrified 891.34
unfeeling 856.9
frozen-food locker
334.6
frozen foods 308.5
frozen in 333.18
fructify bear 167.14
be productive 165.7
enrich 165.8
fertilize 169.10
fructuous 670.5
frugal cheap 849.7
economical 851.6
meager 662.10
parsimonious 852.7
temperate 992.9
frugality
economy 851.1
parsimony 852.1
temperance 992.1
fruit
n. food 308.37,51
homosexual 419.16
posterity 171.1
product 168.1
result 154.1
seed 411.29
yield 811.5
v. bear 167.14
fruitarian
abstainer 992.4
vegetarian 307.14
fruitful 165.9
fruition
accomplishment
722.1
bearing 167.6
pleasure 865.1
fruitless barren 166.4
ineffective 158.15
unsuccessful 725.17
useless 669.12
fruitlike 411.33
fruity flavorful 428.9
fragrant 436.9
herbaceous 411.33
insane 473.26
frump
old woman 127.3
slob 62.7
frumpish 62.15
frustrate defeat 727.11
disappoint 541.2
neutralize 178.7
outwit 735.11
thwart 730.15
frustrated
disappointed 541.5
unsexual 419.31
frustrating 730.20
frustration
circumvention 735.5

defeat 727.2
disappointment
541.1
neutralization 178.2
psychological stress
690.21
thwarting 730.3
fry
n. dish 308.7
fish young 171.2
minnow 414.35
v. be hot 328.22
cook 330.4
fryer food 308.22
poultry 414.34
young chicken 125.8
fubsy 195.18
fud 123.8
fuddle
n. confusion 532.3
intoxication 996.1
v. confuse 532.7
make drunk 996.22
perplex 514.13
fuddled drunk 996.31
foolish 470.8
muddled 532.13
perplexed 514.24
fuddy-duddy
n. antiquated person
123.8
dotard 471.9
fastidious person
896.7
adj. old 123.17
fudge
n. candy 308.54
nonsense 547.2
v. cheat 618.17
do carelessly 534.8
fabricate 616.18
falsify 616.16
interpose 237.6
fuel
n. firing 331
rocketry 281.8
v. provision 659.9
stoke 331.8
fuel oil 380.11
fugacious 111.7
fugacity 111.1
fugitive
n. criminal 986.10
escapee 632.5
fleer 631.5
adj. escaped 632.11
runaway 631.16
transient 111.7
vanishing 447.3
wandering 273.36
fugleman leader 748.6
model 25.1
precursor 66.1
superior 36.4
fugue amnesia 538.2
music 462.19
trance state 690.26
führer autocrat 749.14
leader 748.6
fulcrum axis 322.5
leverage 287.3
supporter 216.2

fulfill accomplish 722.4
act on 705.9
complete 56.6
execute 771.10
observe 768.2
suffice 661.4
fulfillment
accomplishment
722.1
adjustment 690.34
completion 56.4
contentment 868.1
execution 771.5
observance 768.1
fuliginous 365.11
full
n. completeness 56.2
adj. blocked 266.11
broad 204.6
colored 362.16
complete 56.9
corpulent 195.18
crowded 74.22
detailed 8.9
great 34.6
intoxicated 996.30
loud 453.10
perfect 677.7
plentiful 661.7
replete 56.11
resonant 454.9
satiated 664.6
thick 204.8
unrestricted 762.26
adv. squarely 290.25
fullback 878.20
full blast 157.1
full-blooded
red-complexioned
368.9
strong 159.13
wellborn 918.11
full bloom
flowering 411.24
maturity 126.2
full-blown
full-size 195.22
mature 126.13
full-bodied
flavorful 428.9
thick 204.8
full circle circuit 321.2
rotation 322.1
full consent 762.6
full dress 231.11
full feather 231.10
full fig 231.1,10
full-fledged
complete 56.9
full-size 195.22
grown 197.12
mature 126.13
full-grown
complete 56.9
full-size 195.22
grown 197.12
mature 126.13
ripe 722.13
full house
full measure 56.3
playing cards 878.17
full measure fill 56.3

plenty 661.2
full nelson 813.3
fullness breadth 204.1
completeness 56.2
continuity 71.1
greatness 34.1
loudness 453.1
perfection 677.2
plenty 661.2
resonance 454.1
satiety 664.1
wholeness 54.5
full of beans
frisky 870.14
healthy 685.7
full-scale
complete 56.9
full-size 195.22
full scope 762.4
full-sized 195.22
full speed ahead
at full speed 269.24
command 275.77
full stop
standstill 268.3
stop 144.2
full swing 762.4
full tilt 707.25
full time 108.3
fully completely 56.14
in full 8.13
perfectly 677.10
plentifully 661.9
fulminate blast 456.8
explode 162.13
fuel 331.8
fulminate against
berate 969.20
censure 969.13
curse 972.5
fulsome bad 675.9
base 915.12
flattering 970.8
grandiloquent 601.8
malodorous 437.5
obscene 990.9
offensive 864.18
suave 936.18
uncritical 968.18
unsavory 429.7
fumble
n. bungle 734.5
v. bungle 734.11
confuse 63.3
grope 485.31
fumbled 734.21
fumbling
n. bungling 734.4
adj. clumsy 734.20
fume
n. agitation 324.1
anger 952.7
excitement 857.3
odor 435.1
smoke 329.16
vapor 401.1
violence 162.2
v. be angry 952.15
decolor 363.5
exhale 310.23
give off 401.8
preserve 701.8

seethe 162.11
smoke 328.23
fumigant
antiseptic 687.21
deodorant 438.3
poison 676.3
fumigate gas 401.8
sanitize 681.24
scent 436.8
stop odor 438.4
fumigation
deodorizing 438.2
sanitation 681.3
vaporization 401.5
fuming burning 328.27
infuriated 952.29
vaporous 401.9
fun
n. amusement 878.2
joke 881.6
merriment 870.5
pleasure 865.1
v. joke 881.13
adj. amusing 878.29
function
n. action 705.1
business 656.1
ceremony 646.4
intention 653.1
rite 1040.3
role 656.3
syntax 586.2
use 665.5
v. act 705.4
do duty 656.13
operate 164.7
functional
acting 705.10
grammatical 586.17
managerial 164.12
occupational 656.16
operating 164.11
operative 164.9
psychological 690.43
useful 665.18
functionalism
architecture 574.4
utilitarianism 665.6
functionary
agent 781.3
official 749.16
operator 164.4
functioning
n. action 705.1
operation 164.1
adj. acting 705.10
operating 164.11
fund
n. capital 835.15
collection 74.11
money 835.14
supply 660.2
v. finance 836.15
pay 841.18
provide 659.7
subsidize 818.19
support 785.12
fundament
bottom 212.1
foundation 216.6
fundamental
n. essence 5.2

fust become old 123.9
  stagnate 268.9
fustian
  n. bombast 601.2
  nonsense 547.2
  adj. bombastic 601.9
fustigate
  criticize severely
   969.21
  punish 1010.14
fusty malodorous 437.5
  old 123.14
  spoiled 692.43
  trite 883.9
futile foolish 470.8
  hopeless 889.13
  ineffective 158.15
  inexpedient 671.5
  trivial 673.16
  unsuccessful 725.17
  vain 669.13
futility failure 725.1
  ineffectiveness 158.3
  inexpedience 671.1
  meaninglessness
   547.1
  no hope 889.1
  triviality 673.3
  uselessness 669.2
future
  n. fate 640.2
  fiancée 931.16
  tense 586.12
  time to come 121
  adj. forthcoming
   121.8
  imminent 152.3
futures 834.11
futuristic 121.8
futurity
  eventuality 121.4
  forthcoming 152.1
  time to come 121.1
fuzee see fusee
fuzz
  n. down 230.19
  fine texture 351.3
  lightness 353.2
  policeman 699.16
  v. make uncertain
   514.14
fuzzy downy 230.27
  formless 247.4
  hairy 230.24
  indistinct 445.6
  obscure 549.15
  smooth 351.8
  vague 514.18

G

G gravity 352.5
  thousand 99.10
  US money 835.7
gab
  n. chatter 596.3
  mouth 265.5
  speech 594.1
  v. chatter 596.5
  speak 594.20
gabble
  n. chatter 596.3

imperfect speech
  595.4
nonsense 547.2
v. bird sound 460.5
  chatter 596.5
  speak poorly 595.9
  talk nonsense 547.5
gabby 596.9
Gabriel angel 1015.4
  herald 561.2
gad
  n. goad 648.8
  wanderer 274.2
  v. wander 273.22
gadabout 274.2
gad about 273.22
gadfly goad 648.8
  motivator 648.10
gadget object 376.4
  tool 348.1
Gaea
  agriculture divinity
   413.4
  Earth 375.10
  goddess 1014.5
gaff 459.4
gaffe 518.5
gaffer old man 127.2
  supervisor 748.2
gag
  n. acting 611.9
  joke 881.6
  restraint 760.4
  silencer 451.4
  v. render powerless
   158.11
  sicken at 867.4
  silence 451.8
  suppress 760.8
  vomit 310.25
gaga
  enthusiastic about
   635.12
  foolish 470.8
  insane 473.26
  scatterbrained 532.16
gage challenge 793.2
  marihuana 687.13
  pledge 772.2
gaggle
  n. geese 74.6
  v. bird sound 460.5
gag on 503.5
gaiety
  cheerfulness 870.4
  colorfulness 362.4
  conviviality 922.3
  festivity 878.3
  happiness 865.2
  ornamentation 901.3
  showiness 904.3
gain
  n. automation 349.11
  electric gain 342.16
  good 674.4
  increase 38.1
  profit 811.3
  v. acquire 811.8
  arrive 300.6
  get better 691.7
  increase 38.6
  incur 175.4

overtake 269.17
persuade 648.23
receive 819.6
win 726.4
gainer 320.1
gainful
  productive 811.15
  useful 665.21
gains profits 811.3
  receipts 844.1
  winnings 38.3
gainsay
  contradict 790.6
  deny 524.4
gain the day 726.4
gain upon
  approach 296.3
  overtake 269.17
gain weight 197.8
gait pace 273.14
  rate 267.4
gal 125.6
gala
  n. festival 878.4
  adj. festive 878.30
galactic celestial 375.25
  large 34.7
  universal 79.14
galacto– galaxy 375.6
  milk 388.3
galaxy
  famous persons 914.9
  island universe 375.6
  throng 74.4
gale breeze 403.5
  emotional outburst
   857.8
  windstorm 403.12
gall
  n. affliction 866.8
  bile 312.2
  bitterness 429.2
  ill humor 951.1
  impairment 692.8
  insolence 913.3
  irritation 866.3
  knob 256.3
  rancor 939.7
  rashness 894.1
  resentment 952.3
  v. abrade 350.7
  distress 424.7
  injure 692.15
  irritate 866.14
gallant
  n. beau 931.12
  brave person 893.8
  cavalier 936.9
  dandy 903.9
  unchaste person
   989.10
  adj. chivalrous 936.15
  courageous 893.17
  showy 904.19
  unchaste 989.25
gallantry chivalry 936.2
  courage 893.1
  courtship 932.6
  profligacy 989.3
galled annoyed 866.21
  sore 424.11
galleon 277.23

gallery art 574.18
  audience 448.6
  auditorium 192.4
  balcony 192.22
  corridor 192.18
  entrenchment 799.5
  layer 227.1
  museum 660.9
  observation post
   439.8
  passageway 657.4
  platform 216.13
  porch 192.21
  showroom 192.24
  theater part 611.20
galley kitchen 330.3
  sailboat 277.3,21
  trial print 603.5,26
  vessels 277.25
galley slave
  boatman 276.5
  drudge 718.3
  slave 764.7
galling abrasive 350.10
  annoying 864.22
  irritating 424.13
gallivant flirt 932.18
  wander 273.22
gallop
  n. gait 273.14
  speed 269.3
  v. ride 273.33
  run 269.10
galloping 269.19
gallows
  capital punishment
   1010.7
  instrument of execu-
   tion 1011.5
gallstone 686.21
galoot 471.2
galore
  adj. plentiful 661.7
  adv. greatly 34.15
galvanic
  electricity 342.27
  exciting 857.28
  provocative 648.27
galvanize
  electrify 342.23
  electrolyze 342.25
  energize 161.9
  motivate 648.12
  plate 228.26
  stimulate 857.12
galvanized 228.32
gam
  n. chat 597.4
  leg 273.16
  whales 74.5
  v. chat 597.10
gambit attempt 714.2
  beginning 68.3
  stratagem 735.3
  trick 618.6
gamble
  n. an uncertainty
   514.8
  probability 156.1
  risk 515
  v. be liable 175.3
  bet 515.20

braggart 910.5
chatterer 596.4
gas chamber
  capital punishment
    1010.7
  instrument of execu-
    tion 1011.5
  killing site 409.12
gasconade
  bluster 911.3
  boast 910.6
gaseous rarefied 355.4
  tenuous 4.6
  vaporous 401.9
gash
  n. crack 201.2
  groove 263.1
  impairment 692.8
  mark 568.5
  notch 262.1
  refuse 669.4
  v. cleave 201.4
  groove 263.3
  injure 692.15
  mark 568.10
  notch 262.4
  sever 49.11
gasify 401.8
gas jet 329.10
gasket hole 265.4
  wadding 266.5
gaslike 401.9
gaslit 335.39
gas main 396.7
gas meter 401.7
gasoline fuel 331.1
  illuminant 335.20
  petroleum 380.4
gasp
  n. breathing 403.18
  v. become exhausted
    717.5
  be hot 328.22
  breathe 403.24
  utter 594.26
gasser
  great success 724.3
  stage show 611.4
gas station 832.7
gassy boastful 910.11
  bombastic 601.9
  distended 197.13
  pompous 904.22
  talkative 596.9
  vaporous 401.9
gastric
  abdominal 193.5
  visceral 225.10
gastric juice
  digestion 309.8
  secretion 312.2
gastritis
  gastrointestinal dis-
    ease 686.27
  inflammation 686.9
gastro– 193.3
gastronome 307.14
gastronomic(al) 307.29
gastronomy
  aesthetic taste 897.5
  eating 307.13
  gluttony 994.2

gat gun 801.5
  opening 265.1
gate barrier 730.5
  conduit 396.4
  entrance 302.6
  floodgate 396.11
  metal casting 383.5
  receipts 844.1
  valve 396.10
gate, the 310.5
gâteau 308.41
gate-crasher guest 925.6
  intruder 238.3
  newcomer 78.4
gatehouse 191.10
gatekeeper 699.12
gatepost
  entrance 302.6
  post 217.4
gateway 302.6
gather
  n. fold 264.1
  v. assemble 74.18
  be imminent 152.2
  blow up 403.22
  come together 74.16
  conclude 494.10
  fold 264.5
  grow 197.7
  harvest 413.19
  join 47.5
  pick up 317.8
  procure 811.10
  suppose 499.10
gather around
  come together 74.16
  form 59.5
gathered
  assembled 74.21
  folded 264.7
  joined 47.13
  produced 167.22
  stored 660.14
gathering
  accumulation 74.9
  acquisition 811.2
  assembly 74.1
  bookbinding 605.15
  congregation 74.2
  harvest 413.15
  joining 47.1
  part of writing 55.2
  removal to heaven
    1018.12
  social gathering
    922.10
  sore 686.35
gathering clouds
  danger 697.1
  darkening 337.6
  omen 544.6
  warning sign 703.3
gator 414.30
gauche clumsy 734.20
  ignorant 477.12
gaucherie 734.5
gaucho herder 416.3
  rider 274.8
gaudiness
  appearances 446.2
  garishness 362.5
  grandiloquence 601.1

paltriness 673.2
  showiness 904.3
  vulgarity 898.2
gaudy garish 362.19
  grandiloquent 601.8
  paltry 673.18
  tawdry 904.20
  vulgar 898.11
gauge
  n. measure 490.2
  measuring device
    490.4
  size 195.1
  types of 490.20
  v. analyze 48.8
  judge 494.9
  measure 490.11
  size 195.15
gauged 490.14
gauging analysis 48.3
  judgment 494.3
  measurement 490.1
gaunt barren 166.4
  lean 205.17
gauntlet
  challenge 793.2
  gloves 231.63
  punishment 1010.2
gaup 439.16
gauss 342.9
Gautama Buddha
  1022.4
gauze fog 404.2
  medical dressing
    687.33
gauzy smooth 351.8
  thin 205.16
  transparent 339.4
gavel 739.9
gawk
  n. awkward person
    734.8
  oaf 471.5
  v. be curious 528.3
  gaze 439.16
  wonder 920.5
gawky clumsy 734.20
  lean 205.17
gay cheerful 870.14
  colorful 362.18
  convivial 922.19
  festive 878.30
  happy 865.13
  homosexual 419.32
  intoxicated 996.30
  showy 904.19
  unchaste 989.25
gay deceiver
  deceiver 619.1
  unchaste person
    989.10
gay dog 989.10
gaze
  n. stare 439.5
  v. look at 439.14
  see 439.16
  wonder 920.5
gazebo
  observation post
    439.8
  summerhouse 191.13

gazelle
  hoofed animal
    414.5,58
  jumper 319.4
  speed 269.6
gazette
  newspaper 605.11
  official document
    570.8
  periodical 605.10
gazetteer
  dictionary 605.7
  glossary 88.4
  journalist 605.22
  reference book 605.6
gazpacho 308.10
Ge see **Gaea**
gear
  n. belongings 810.3
  clothing 231.1
  cordage 206.3
  equipment 659.4
  mechanism 348.6
  rigging 277.12
  workings 348.5
  v. equip 659.8
geared 26.10
gear to conform 82.3
  make agree 26.7
gee! 920.21
geezer 127.2
Geiger counter
  photosensitive device
    343.22
  radiation counter
    327.13
geisha dancer 879.3
  entertainer 612.1
Geist 467.8
gel
  n. semiliquid 389.5
  v. thicken 354.10
gelatin
  semiliquid 389.5
  sweets 308.39
  theater lighting
    611.23
gelatinous 389.12
geld castrate 42.11
  feminize 421.12
gelded castrated 158.19
  sterile 166.4
gelding castration 42.4
  horse 414.10
  impotent 158.6
gelid cold 333.14
  frozen 334.14
gelignite 801.9
gelt 835.2
gem
  n. bun 308.31
  good person 985.1
  good thing 674.5
  jewel 901.6
  precious stone
    384.6,13
  v. ornament 901.9
Gemara 1021.5
geminate
  v. duplicate 91.3
  adj. double 91.4

talkative 596.9
glibness
  eloquence 600.1
  suavity 936.5
  talkativeness 596.1
glib tongue 735.6
glide
  n. air maneuver
    278.13
  coast 273.8
  slide 316.4
  speech sound 594.13
  v. coast 273.34
  elapse 105.5
  float 275.54
  fly 278.45
  go easily 732.9
  slide 316.9
  adj. phonetic 594.31
glider 280.12
glim 336.1
glimmer
  n. hint 557.4
  light 335.7
  v. glitter 335.24
glimmering
  n. hint 557.4
  light 335.7
  slight knowledge
    477.6
  adj. glittering 335.35
glimpse
  n. glance 439.4
  slight knowledge
    477.6
  v. glance 439.18
  see 439.12
glint
  n. light 335.6
  shine 335.2
  v. give light 335.23
  glance 439.18
glissade
  n. slide 316.4
  v. glide 273.34
  slide 316.9
glissando
  music style 462.31
  slide 316.4
glisten
  n. light 335.7
  v. glitter 335.24
glistening 335.35
glitter
  n. light 335.7
  showiness 904.3
  v. be famous 914.10
  be ostentatious
    904.13
  glimmer 335.24
glittering
  glimmering 335.35
  showy 904.19
gloaming
  darkishness 337.4
  dusk 134.3
gloat boast 910.9
  gaze 439.16
gloating
  n. boasting 910.4
  adj. boasting 910.12
gloat over boast 910.9

enjoy 865.10
global complete 56.9
  comprehensive 76.7
  spherical 255.9
  universal 79.14
  unqualified 508.2
globalize 79.9
globate 255.9
globe
  n. Earth 375.10
  lamp shade 338.3
  map 654.4
  sphere 255.2
  v. ball 255.7
globe-trot 273.20
globe-trotter 274.1
globular 255.9
globule ball 255.2
  bubble 405.1
globulin 388.4
glockenspiel 465.18
glom on to
  acquire 811.9
  seize 822.14
gloom
  n. darkness 337.2
  gloominess 872.7
  shadow 337.3
  v. be dark 337.12
  be ill-humored
    951.15
  darken 337.9
gloominess
  darkness 337.2
  gloom 872.7
  pessimism 889.6
gloomy cloudy 404.7
  dark 337.14
  dismal 872.24
  ominous 544.17
  pessimistic 889.16
glop semiliquid 389.5
  slime 682.8
gloppy 682.23
Gloria hymn 1032.3
  Mass 1040.10
glorification
  ennoblement 914.8
  praise 968.5
  sanctification 1026.3
  worship 1032.2
glorified
  eminent 914.18
  heavenly 1018.13
  saintly 1015.6
glorify ennoble 914.13
  praise 968.12
  sanctify 1026.5
  worship 1032.11
glorious eminent 34.9
  godlike 1013.20
  gorgeous 900.19
  grandiose 904.21
  illustrious 914.19
  intoxicated 996.30
  superb 674.17
glory
  n. brightness 335.4
  divine attribute
    1013.15
  eminence 34.2
  grandeur 904.5

halo 253.2
Heaven 1018.1
illustriousness 914.6
light 335.14
notability 672.2
praise 968.5
repute 914.1
token of esteem
  916.1
worship 1032.2
  v. gloat 910.9
  rejoice 876.5
glory in 905.5
gloss
  n. commentary 606.2
  dictionary 605.7
  extenuation 1006.5
  fakery 616.3
  footnote 552.5
  interpretation 552.3
  misrendering 553.1
  polish 260.2
  pretext 649.1
  shallowness 210.1
  shine 335.2
  v. coat 228.24
  color 362.13
  comment upon
    552.11
  falsify 616.16
  misinterpret 553.2
  polish 260.7
  adj. paint finish
    362.21
glossal lingual 427.10
  phonetic 594.31
glossary
  dictionary 605.7
  interpretation 552.3
  list 88.4
glossematics
  grammar 586.1
  linguistics 580.12
glossography 582.15
gloss over
  conceal 615.6
  extenuate 1006.12
  falsify 616.16
  neglect 534.6
glossy
  n. photoprint 577.5
  adj. shiny 335.33
  sleek 260.10
glottal
  n. speech sound
    594.13
  adj. phonetic 594.31
glottis 594.19
glove challenge 793.2
  handwear 231.63
glow
  n. animation 161.3
  beauty 900.1
  eloquence 600.5
  foredawn 133.4
  health 685.1
  heat 328.12
  reddening 368.3
  shine 335.2
  warmth 362.2
  v. be cheerful 870.6
  become red 368.5

be excited 857.16
be famous 914.10
be healthy 685.5
be hot 328.22
flush 857.17
give light 335.23
look beautiful 900.15
glower
  n. glare 439.5
  resentment 952.2
  scowl 951.9
  v. be ill-humored
    951.15
  glare 439.17
  show resentment
    952.14
glowering 951.24
glowing burning 328.27
  cheerful 870.11
  coloring 362.15
  eloquent 600.13
  enthusiastic 635.11
  excited 857.20
  fervent 855.23
  gorgeous 900.19
  happy 865.13
  luminous 335.30
  red 368.6
  red-complexioned
    368.9
glowworm firefly 336.5
  light 335.7
glue
  n. adherent 50.4,13
  semiliquid 389.5
  v. join 47.5
  stick together 50.9
glued 47.14
gluey adhesive 50.12
  dense 354.12
  viscous 389.12
glum morose 872.25
  sullen 951.24
glut
  n. overfullness 663.3
  satiety 664.1
  v. be tedious 884.5
  eat 307.23
  gluttonize 994.4
  overload 663.15
  satiate 664.4
gluteal 241.10
gluten 389.5
glutinous
  adhesive 50.12
  gluey 389.12
glutted overfull 663.20
  satiated 664.6
glutton eater 307.14
  gourmand 994.3
  wolverine 414.28,58
gluttonous
  eating 307.29
  excessive 663.16
  greedy 994.6
  intemperate 993.7
gluttony eating 307.1
  excess 663.1
  greed 994
  hoggishness 634.8
  intemperance 993.1
  sin 982.3

glyceride 309.7
glycerin 380.2
glyceryl ester 380.14
glyph 575.3
glyphic
  engraved 578.12
  sculptured 575.7
glyptic engraving 578.2
  sculpture 575.1
G-man
  detective 781.10
  peace officer 699.15
gnarl
  n. distortion 249.1
  knob 256.3
  v. animal sound 460.4
  distort 249.5
  roughen 261.4
  show resentment
    952.14
gnarled rough 261.8
  studded 256.16
gnash
  n. bite 307.2
  v. chew 307.25
gnash one's teeth
  lament 875.9
  show resentment
    952.14
gnat 196.7
gnaw abrade 350.7
  chew 307.25
  eat away 692.24
  hurt 424.7
gnawing
  n. ache 424.5
  pain 424.2
  adj. abrasive 350.10
  painful 424.10
gneiss 384.1,12
gnome dwarf 196.6
  fairy 1014.18
  maxim 517.1
  spirit 1014.16
gnomic
  aphoristic 517.6
  concise 592.6
gnu 414.5,58
go
  n. act 705.3
  attempt 714.2
  contest 796.3
  enterprise 707.7
  game 878.9
  spell 108.1
  success 724.1
  turn 108.2
  v. bear 290.8
  become 1.12
  be destroyed 693.23
  be distant 199.5
  cease to exist 2.5
  depart 301.6
  die 408.19
  disappear 447.2
  extend 179.7
  have place 184.8
  move 267.5
  operate 164.7
  pass 273.17
  progress 294.2
  recede 297.2

succeed 724.6
  take action 705.5
  tend 174.3
  travel 273.18
  adj. favorable 164.9
go about
  be made public
    559.16
  change course 275.30
  go around 321.4
  turn around 295.9
  undertake 715.3
  wander 273.22
go about one's business
    656.10
goad
  n. spur 648.8
  v. drive animals 416.8
  impel 283.10
  thrust 283.11
  urge 648.15
go after
  come after 117.3
  fetch 271.15
  follow 293.3
  pursue 655.8
  succeed 65.2
go against
  counteract 178.6
  oppose 790.3
go ahead begin 68.7
  get better 691.7
  hustle 707.13
  precede 64.2
  progress 294.2
go-ahead
  n. enterprise 707.7
  permission 777.1
  progression 294.1
  ratification 521.4
  adj. enterprising
    707.23
  progressive 294.6
goal destination 300.5
  end 70.1
  motive 648.1
  objective 653.2
  score 724.4
goalie 699.9
go all out
  be thorough 56.8
  do one's best 714.12
  exert oneself 716.9
  go all lengths 722.7
  go fast 269.13
  hustle 707.13
  let oneself go 762.18
  persevere 625.5
go along
  be in a state 7.6
  continue 143.3
  depart 301.6
  progress 294.2
  travel 273.17
go along with
  accompany 73.7
  acknowledge 521.11
  agree with 521.9
  be willing 622.3
  concur 177.3
  consent 775.2
  join with 786.4

submit to 765.6
goaltender 699.9
go around circle 321.4
  detour 321.6
  move 267.5
  rotate 322.9
  suffice 661.4
  surround 233.6
  turn 321.5
go around in circles
  be uncertain 514.9
  go around 321.4
go astray
  be unorthodox
    1025.8
  digress 593.9
  err 518.9
  fail 725.14
  go wrong 981.9
  miss 314.4
  stray 291.4
goat animal 414.8,58
  inferior horse 414.14
  jumper 319.4
  laughingstock 967.7
  scapegoat 149.3
  unchaste person
    989.11
go at attack 798.15
  travel 273.18
  undertake 715.3
goatee 230.8
goatherd guider 748.7
  herder 416.3
goatish
  lascivious 989.29
  lustful 419.29
  ungulate 414.49
go away
  v. depart 301.6
  disappear 447.2
  diverge 299.5
  recede 297.2
  interj. begone! 310.29
gob accumulation 74.9
  amount 28.2
  ball 255.2
  bite 307.2
  lump 195.10
  mouth 265.5
  piece 55.3
  sailor 276.4
go back back up 241.8
  be repeated 103.11
  remember 537.10
  retreat 295.6
  revert 146.5
  turn back 295.8
go back on
  abandon 633.5
  be dishonest 975.12
go back over
  re-examine 485.26
  remember 537.10
go back to
  resume 143.6
  revert to 146.6
  revisit 186.9
gobbet ball 255.2
  piece 55.3
  small amount 35.2

gobble
  bird sound 460.5
  consume 666.2
  destroy 693.10
  eat 307.21
  gluttonize 994.4
  ingest 306.11
gobbledygook
  bombast 601.2
  jargon 580.9
  nonsense 547.2
  official jargon 744.37
  unintelligibility 549.7
gobbler
  male animal 420.8
  turkey 414.34
gobbling
  gluttonous 994.6
  greedy 634.27
go before
  anticipate 131.6
  forerun 116.3
  lead 292.2
  pioneer 66.3
  precede 64.2
go-between
  instrument 658.3
  interagent 781.4
  interpreter 552.7
  liaison 237.4
  mediator 805.3
  messenger 561.1
go beyond
  exceed 663.9
  overrun 313.4
goblet 193.10
goblin evil spirit 1016.9
  fairy 1014.18
gobs 34.4
gocart 272.6,24,30
god agriculture 413.4
  commerce 827.12
  deity 1014
  discord 795.1
  earth 375.10
  evil 1016.6
  Fates 640.3
  fertility 165.5
  forest 1014.21
  good person 985.5
  household 191.30
  justice 976.5
  lightning 335.17
  love 931.8
  marriage 933.14
  moon 375.12
  Muses 535.2
  nether world 1019.5
  poetry Muses 609.12
  rain 394.6
  sea 397.4
  sun 375.14
  thunder 456.5
  war 797.17
  water 1014.20
  wind 403.3
God 1013
godawful 675.8
godchild 772.7
goddamn 972.9
goddess see god
goddess-like 900.17

godfather 772.6
God-fearing 1028.9
God forbid
  by no means 524.9
  disapproval 969.28
  worship 1032.17
godforsaken
  deserted 187.14
  forlorn 924.11
  out-of-the-way 199.9
Godhead 1013.10
godhood 1013.1
godless
  irreligious 1031.18
  ungodly 1031.17
godlike divine 1013.19
  eminent 34.9
  mythological 1014.26
  pious 1028.9
godliness deity 1013.1
  piety 1028.2
  sanctity 1026.1
  virtue 980.1
godly divine 1013.19
  pious 1028.9
  virtuous 980.7
go down
  be believed 501.20
  be defeated 727.12
  capsize 275.44
  decline 692.20
  descend 316.5
  fail 725.10
  sink 320.8
  submerge 316.6
God's country 181.2
godsend boon 811.7
  good thing 674.5
godson 772.7
Godspeed
  n. departure 301.4
  interj. farewell! 301.23
God's will 640.2
God the Father 1013.11
God the Holy Ghost
  1013.14
God the Son 1013.12
God willing 509.11
go easy caution 895.14
  take it easy 732.11
go easy on 944.4
goer outgoer 303.10
  speeder 269.5
  traveler 274.1
go far 724.9
gofer 750.5
goffer
  n. trench 263.2
  v. groove 263.3
go fly a kite 238.10
go for abet 785.14
  aim at 653.4
  attack 798.15
  be credulous 502.6
  fetch 271.15
  head for 290.10
  love 931.18
  represent 572.7
go for broke
  be determined 624.8
  be reckless 894.6
  do one's best 714.12

go all lengths 722.7
  persevere 625.5
go free get off 632.7
  go scot free 763.9
go-getter 707.8
goggle
  n. gaze 439.5
  v. bulge 256.10
  gaze 439.16
  squint 440.9
  adj. bulging 256.15
goggled bulging 256.15
  spectacled 443.10
goggle eyes
  defective eyes 440.6
  eye 439.9
goggles eyeshade 338.2
  safety equipment
    699.3
  spectacles 443.2
go-go energetic 161.12
  unreserved 762.23
  up-to-date 475.17
go in for adopt 637.15
  practice 705.7
  specialize 81.4
  study 564.15
  undertake 715.3
going
  n. death 408.1
  departure 301.1
  disappearance 447.1
  journeying 273.1
  motion 267.1
  adj. dying 408.33
  flowing 267.8
  operating 164.11
  traveling 273.35
going on
  happening 151.9
  in preparation 720.22
  in progress 294.7
  operating 164.11
goings-on activity 707.1
  affairs 151.4
  behavior 737.1
going strong
  thriving 728.13
  unweakened 159.19
go into begin 68.9
  compose 58.3
  develop 148.6
  discourse upon 606.5
  discuss 597.12
  enter 302.7
  investigate 485.22
  join 788.14
  participate 815.5
  undertake 715.3
go in with 786.4
go it alone 762.19
goiter 686.10
gold
  n. currency metals
    835.20
  metal 383.21
  money 835.1
  wealth 837.1
  yellowness 370.1
  adj. metal 383.17
  yellow 370.4

goldbrick
  n. fraud 618.9
  idler 708.8
  neglecter 534.5
  shirker 631.3
  slow person 270.5
  v. leave undone 534.7
  shirk 631.9
gold digger flirt 932.10
  miner 383.9
gold dust 383.3
golden
  auspicious 544.18
  melodious 462.49
  metal 383.17
  precious 848.10
  superb 674.17
  yellow 370.4
golden age 728.4
golden calf 1033.3
golden rule
  axiom 517.2
  ethics 957.2
  precept 751.2
golden touch, the 837.4
golden years, the 126.5
gold fever 383.8
gold-filled 383.17
gold mine mine 383.6
  rich source 837.3
  source of supply
    660.4
gold piece 835.4
gold rush 383.8
gold star 916.5
golem 471.8
Goliath giant 195.26
  strong man 159.6
Gomorrah 981.7
gonadal 312.8
gonads 419.10
go native 189.4
gondolier 276.5
gone absent 187.10
  dead 408.30
  departed 301.20
  exhausted 717.8
  hopeless 889.15
  lost 812.7
  no more 2.10
  past 119.7
  used up 666.4
  vanished 447.4
  weak 160.12
gone by ago 119.15
  obsolete 123.15
  past 119.7
gone on
  enthusiastic about
    635.12
  fond of 931.28
goner 889.8
gone to seed
  growing rank 411.40
  old 123.14
  out of practice
    734.18
gong
  n. bell 454.4
  percussion instrument
    465.18
  v. ring 454.8

Gongorism 589.3
gonif 825.1
gonorrhea 686.16
goo semiliquid 389.5
  sentimentality 855.8
goober 308.38
good
  n. welfare 674.4
  adj. auspicious 544.18
  authentic 516.14
  excellent 674.12
  expedient 670.5
  godlike 1013.20
  healthful 683.5
  honest 974.13
  just 976.8
  kind 938.13
  pious 1028.9
  pleasant 863.6
  right 958.8
  skillful 733.20
  solvent 836.17
  sufficient 661.6
  tasty 428.8
  valid 516.13
  virtuous 980.7
  adv. kindly 938.18
  interj. approval
    968.22
  yes 521.18
Good Book, the 1021.2
good-bye
  n. departure 301.4
  interj. farewell! 301.23
good chance
  gambling odds 515.6
  good opportunity
    129.3
  likelihood 156.8
  possibility 509.1
  probability 511.1
good deal 34.4
good deed 938.7
good enough
  adj. acceptable 868.12
  sufficient 661.6
  tolerable 674.19
  interj. approval
    968.22
  yes 521.18
good example 985.4
good fellow
  companion 928.4
  good person 985.1
good folk, the 1014.17
good for
  healthful 683.5
  helpful 785.21
  priced 846.16
  solvent 836.17
  useful 665.18
good form
  etiquette 646.3
  social convention
    645.1
good-for-nothing
  n. bad person 986.2
  bum 708.9
  adj. indolent 708.18
  worthless 669.11
good for you! 968.22
Good Friday 1040.15

good graces 927.3
good guy 985.2
good heavens! 920.21
good humor
    good nature 938.2
    good spirits 870.2
good-humored 938.14
good life, the 728.1
good-looking 900.17
good looks 900.4
good luck chance 156.1
    prosperity 728.2
goodly beautiful 900.17
    good 674.12
    large 195.16
    pleasant 863.6
good manners
    courtesy 936.3
    etiquette 646.3
    good behavior 737.2
good morning! 925.15
good name
    custom 827.6
    reputability 914.2
good-natured 938.14
goodness
    n. excellence 674
    healthfulness 683.1
    honesty 974.1
    kindness 938.1
    piety 1028.2
    pleasantness 863.1
    propriety 958.2
    savoriness 428.1
    virtue 980.1
    interj. wonder 920.21
good night! 301.24
good old days 119.2
good person
    benefactor 942.1
    gentleman 985
goods fabric 378.5
    freight 271.7
    merchandise 831.1
    property 810.1
goods, the ability 157.2
    genuine object 516.6
    information 557.1
    talent 733.4
good Samaritan 942.1
good shape
    good looks 900.4
    healthiness 685.2
    orderliness 59.3
good show! 948.4
good side of, the 927.3
good-size(d) 195.16
good sport 727.5
good taste
    literary elegance
    589.1
    savoriness 428.1
    taste 897.1
good terms 927.3
good time fun 878.2
    good opportunity
    129.3
good times 728.4
good turn 938.7
good vibrations 794.1
goodwill
    benevolence 938.4

custom 827.6
    good terms 927.3
    patronage 785.4
    willingness 622.1
good word
    commendation 968.3
    news 558.2
good works 938.6
goody
    n. delicacy 308.8
    wife 933.9
    adj. sanctimonious
    1029.5
    interj. pleasure 865.17
goody-goody
    n. effeminate male
    421.10
    prude 903.11
    adj. affected 903.18
    hypocritic(al) 616.33
    sanctimonious 1029.5
gooey
    sentimental 855.22
    viscous 389.12
goof
    n. an error 518.6
    bungler 734.9
    fool 471.2
    v. blunder 518.15
    bungle 734.12
    fail 725.13
goofball bungler 734.9
    sedative 687.12
go off blast 456.8
    decline 692.20
    depart 301.6
    diverge 299.5
    explode 162.13
    occur 151.5
    succeed 724.6
    turn aside 291.6
go off half-cocked
    anticipate 131.6
    be unprepared 721.6
    prejudge 495.2
    rush into 709.7
    talk out of turn 130.5
go off on a tangent
    angle 251.5
    digress 593.9
goof off dawdle 270.8
    idle 708.11
    leave undone 534.7
    shirk 631.9
goof-off idler 708.8
    neglecter 534.5
    slow person 270.5
goofy foolish 470.8
    insane 473.26
googol
    large number 86.4
    number 99.13
goo-goo eyes 932.8
gook race 418.3
    semiliquid 389.5
goon combatant 800.1
    evildoer 943.4
    man 787.8
    strike enforcer 789.5
    violent person 162.9
go on be angry 952.15
    be disorderly 62.11

behave 737.4
be in a state 7.6
chatter 596.5
continue 143.3
depart 301.6
elapse 105.5
endure 110.6
linger 110.7
manage 724.11
persevere 625.2
persist 143.5
progress 294.2
rage 162.10
go on and on
    be infinite 104.2
    last forever 112.6
    linger 110.7
go one better
    excel 36.6
    outwit 735.11
goop 389.5
goose food 308.22
    poultry 414.34,66
    silly 471.6
goose bumps
    chill 333.2
    rough surface 261.2
    sensation 426.4
    trepidation 891.5
goose egg 2.2
goose grass 258.7
goose step 273.15
goose-step 273.29
goosy avian 414.52
    fearful 891.31
    sensitive 422.14
go out be distant 199.5
    burn out 332.8
    die 408.19
    end 70.6
    exit 303.11
    extend 179.7
    obsolesce 668.9
    strike 789.9
go out for
    practice 705.7
    undertake 715.3
go over
    apostatize 628.8
    examine 485.23
    grill 485.21
    rehearse a play
    611.37
    repeat 103.8
    study 564.12
    succeed 724.6
    traverse 273.19
go over big
    please 865.5
    succeed 724.6
go overboard
    go over the side
    275.45
    overdo 663.10
go over like a lead
    balloon
    be uninteresting
    883.4
    fail 725.9
GOP 744.24
go places 724.9
go public 834.12

Gordian knot
    complex 46.2
    dilemma 731.6
gore
    n. blood 388.4
    killing 409.1
    v. attack 798.26
    pierce 265.16
gorge
    n. gullet 396.15
    obstruction 266.3
    ravine 201.2
    v. eat 307.23
    gluttonize 994.4
    overload 663.15
    satiate 664.4
gorged overfull 663.20
    satiated 664.6
gorgeous
    beautiful 900.19
    colorful 362.18
    gaudy 904.20
Gorgon 1035.9
gorilla
    combatant 800.1
    evildoer 943.4
    killer 409.11
    primate 414.59
    strong man 159.6
    violent person 162.9
gormand 994.3
gormandize 994.4
gory blood red 368.7
    bloodstained 679.11
    murderous 409.24
Goshen 535.11
gosling
    hopeless case 889.8
    poultry 414.34
    young goose 125.8
go slow idle 270.6
    make one's way 294.4
    take one's leisure
    710.4
gospel
    n. good news 558.2
    sacred music 462.16
    system of belief
    501.3
    the truth 516.2
    adj. scriptural 1021.10
Gospel
    n. Mass 1040.10
    New Testament
    1021.4
    adj. scriptural 1021.10
gossamer
    n. filament 206.1
    lightness 353.2
    weakness 160.7
    adj. smooth 351.8
    thin 205.16
    transparent 339.4
gossamery frail 160.14
    light 353.10
    smooth 351.8
    tenuous 4.6
    threadlike 206.7
    transparent 339.4
gossip
    n. chatter 596.3
    companion 928.3

size 195.15
smooth 260.5
sort 60.11
graded arranged 60.14
classified 61.8
gradient incline 219.4
rising 213.5
grading
classification 61.1
degree 29.3
gradual
gradational 29.5
slow 270.10
gradually
by degrees 29.6
slowly 270.14
graduate
n. expert 733.11
graduated student
566.8
v. get better 691.7
grade 29.4
measure 490.11
promote 782.2
size 195.15
succeed 724.6
adj. scholastic 562.20
studentlike 566.12
graduated 29.5
graduate school 567.7
graduation
ceremony 646.4
gradation 29.3
promotion 782.1
graffito 581.5
graft
n. booty 824.11
bribery 651.1
fraud 618.8
insertion 304.1
political corruption
744.34
spoils of office
744.35
theft 824.1
v. fasten 47.7
insert 304.6
grafter
corrupt politician
746.5
thief 825.1
grafting 304.1
grain
n. food 308.4
granule 361.6
grass 411.5,46
kind 61.3
minute thing 196.7
nature 5.3
seed 411.29
small amount 35.2
texture 351.1
trait of character
525.3
v. color 362.13
crumble 361.10
give texture 351.4
pulverize 361.9
graininess
coarse texture 351.2
granularity 361.2

grainy
coarse-textured 351.6
granular 361.12
rough 261.6
grammar basics 68.6
diction 588.1
linguistics 580.12
syntax 586
textbook 605.8
grammarian 580.13
grammar school
elementary school
567.5
secondary school
567.6
grammatic(al)
correct 586.17
linguistic 580.17
grammatical error 518.7
Gramophone 450.11
granary 660.7
grand
n. piano 465.13
thousand 99.10
US money 835.7
adj. dignified 905.12
eloquent 600.14
eminent 914.18
excellent 674.12
grandiose 904.21
important 672.16
large 195.16
powerful 34.6
grandchild 171.3
grande dame 903.10
grandee 918.4
grandeur
eloquence 600.6
greatness 34.1
magnificence 904.5
pride 905.2
repute 914.5
sizableness 195.6
grandfather
ancestor 170.11
old man 127.2
grandiloquence
exaggeration 617.1
long word 582.10
magniloquence 601
pompousness 904.7
style 588.2
grandiloquent
exaggerated 617.4
ostentatious 601.8
pompous 904.22
grandiose grand 904.21
grandiloquent 601.8
grandly
dignifiedly 905.14
grandiosely 904.28
importantly 672.24
grand mal 686.5
grandmother
ancestor 170.12
old woman 127.3
grandparent 170.8
Grand Prix 796.12
grand slam score 724.4
victory 726.1
grandson 171.3

grandstand
n. observation post
439.8
v. be ostentatious
904.16
grand theft 824.2
grand tour
astronautics 282.1
journey 273.5
grange farm 413.8
ranch 191.7
granite hardness 356.6
rock 384.1,12
granny
antiquated person
123.8
fastidious person
896.7
grandmother 170.12
old woman 127.3
grant
n. charter 777.5
concession 507.1
giving 818.1
right 958.4
subsidy 818.8
v. acknowledge 521.11
concede 507.5
confess 556.7
consent 775.2
give 818.12
permit 777.9
suppose 499.10
granted
acknowledged 521.14
given 818.24
supposed 499.14
granting
n. giving 818.1
conj. admitting
507.13
grantor 818.11
granular
coarse-textured 351.6
grainy 361.12
infinitesimal 196.14
granularity
coarse texture 351.2
graininess 361.2
granulate
crumble 361.10
give texture 351.4
heal 694.21
pulverize 361.9
roughen 261.4
solidify 356.8
granulated
coarse-textured 351.6
granular 361.12
hardened 356.13
rough 261.6
granule grain 361.6
small amount 35.2
grapeshot 801.13
grapevine
grapevine telegraph
558.10
informant 557.5
rumor 558.6
vine 411.4
graph
n. character 581.1

diagram 654.3
outline 48.4
picture 574.14
v. plot 654.11
graphemic letter 581.8
linguistic 580.17
graphic
descriptive 608.15
eloquent 600.10
pictorial 574.22
representational
572.10
written 602.22
graphically
descriptively 608.19
eloquently 600.15
graphic arts arts 574.1
graphics 578
printing 603.1
graphite 380.2
grapho– 602.1
graphologist 602.14
graphology 602.3
grapple
n. hold 813.2,12
v. contend 796.14
fasten 47.7
hold 813.6
seize 822.14
grapple with
contend with 796.18
fight 796.14
oppose 790.4
grasp
n. control 741.2
handle 216.11
hold 813.2
understanding 475.3
v. hold 813.6
hug 50.6
know 475.12
seize 822.14
understand 548.7
grasping
n. greed 634.8
adj. acquisitive 811.14
demanding 753.8
greedy 634.27
rapacious 822.26
retentive 813.8
selfish 978.5
grass
n. grassland 411.8
marihuana 687.13
plant 411.5,46
v. feed 307.16
grasshopper
n. animal 414.39,74
jumper 319.4
adj. improvident
721.15
grassland farm 413.8
grass 411.8
land 385.1
plain 387.1
the country 182.1
grass roots root 153.5
the country 182.1
grass widow 935.2
grassy green 371.4
verdant 411.39

groat
British money 835.8
powder 361.5
small amount 35.2
grocer 830.3
groceries
merchandise 831.7
provisions 308.5
grocery 832.5
grog 996.12,40
groggy dazed 532.14
inert 268.14
unsteady 160.16
grogshop 996.19
groin barrier 730.5
breakwater 216.4
fork 299.4
harbor 700.6
grommet circlet 253.5
hole 265.4
groom
n. animal handler
416.2
newlywed 933.6
v. arrange 60.12
preen 681.20
tend animals 416.7
train 562.14
groomed 720.16
groomer 565.7
grooming 562.3
groove
n. crack 201.2
furrow 263.1
path 657.3
printing 603.6
routine 642.6
v. cut 201.4
engrave 578.10
excavate 257.15
furrow 263.3
grooved
engraved 578.12
furrowed 263.4
groove on 865.10
groovy
adj. excellent 674.13
knowing 475.17
interj. pleasure 865.17
grope
n. feel 485.5
v. be uncertain 514.9
feel for 485.31
grope in the dark
be blind 441.8
be ignorant 477.10
feel for 485.31
groping
examining 485.36
ignorant 477.12
gross
n. gain 811.3
receipts 844.1
twelve dozen 99.8
v. profit 811.11
yield 844.4
adj. bad 675.9
base 915.12
carnal 987.6
coarse-textured 351.6
corpulent 195.18
growing rank 411.40

indecent 990.8
infelicitous 590.2
offensive 864.18
outright 34.12
stupid 469.15
thick 204.8
vulgar 898.11
whole 54.9
gross income
earnings 841.4
receipts 844.1
grossly badly 675.14
basely 915.17
exorbitantly 848.16
vulgarly 898.16
gross national product
827.7
grotesque
n. work of art 574.11
adj. abnormal 85.13
deformed 249.12
fanciful 535.20
foolish 470.10
ugly 899.8
grotesquely 85.19
grotto 257.5
grouch
n. ill-humored person
951.11
killjoy 730.9
malcontent 869.3
v. be ill-humored
951.14
complain 875.13
grouchy crabby 951.22
discontented 869.5
ground
n. arena 802.1
art equipment 574.19
bed 212.4
bottom 212.3
cause 153.1
enclosure 236.3
foundation 216.6
horizontal 214.3
justification 1006.6
land 385.1
motive 648.1
ocean depths 209.4
paint 362.8
premise 482.7
region 180.1
setting 233.2
station 184.2
v. electricity 342.26
entrench 142.9
establish 184.15
knock down 318.5
shipwreck 275.42
teach 562.11
adj. bottom 212.7
powdery 361.11
groundbreaker 66.1
ground down 764.16
grounded
aground 142.16
in difficulty 731.25
grounded on
evidential 505.17
supported 216.24
ground floor
earliness 131.1

story 192.23
groundhog
excavator 257.10
wild animal
414.28,58
groundless
baseless 483.13
unproved 506.8
unsubstantial 4.8
groundling
audience 448.6
person 417.3
playgoer 611.32
vulgar person 898.6
grounds cause 153.1
condition 507.2
evidence 505.1
foundation 216.6
green 411.7
justification 1006.6
real estate 810.7
residue 43.2
groundsel 216.9
ground swell
political movement
744.33
wave 395.14
groundwork
foundation 216.6
preparation 720.1
group
n. amount 28.2
art 574.23
association 788.1
bunch 74.7
class 61.2
clique 788.6
company 74.3
orchestra 464.12
religion 1020.3
set 20.5
v. analyze 48.8
arrange 60.11
assemble 74.18
classify 61.6
size 195.15
grouped arranged 60.14
classified 61.8
groupie 635.6
grouping analysis 48.3
arrangement 60.3
artistry 574.10
association 788.1
bunch 74.7
classification 61.1
company 74.3
division 61.2
group therapy 690.5
grouse
n. complaint 875.4
food 308.22
v. complain 875.13
grousing
n. complaint 875.4
adj. discontented
869.5
grout 228.25
grove bunch 74.7
valley 257.9
woodlet 411.12
grovel be low 208.5
be servile 907.6

be unchaste 989.19
bow down before
765.10
creep 273.25
crouch 318.8
lie 214.5
wallow 322.13
groveler 907.3
groveling
n. obsequiousness
907.2
adj. obsequious
907.13
recumbent 214.8
grow become 1.12
become higher
207.17
develop 197.7
evolve 148.5
farm 413.16
flower 411.31
increase 38.6
mature 126.9
process 167.11
raise animals 416.6
grower
agriculturist 413.5
producer 167.8
grow from 154.6
growing
n. manufacture 167.3
raising 413.12
adj. flourishing 197.12
immature 124.10
increasing 38.8
grow into 145.17
growl
n. harsh sound 458.3
reverberation 454.2
rumble 456.4
v. animal sound 460.4
complain 875.13
rumble 456.9
show resentment
952.14
sound harshly 458.9
utter 594.26
wind sound 403.23
grown adult 126.12
full-grown 197.12
manufactured 167.22
produced 167.20
grownup 127.1
grown-up adult 126.12
grown 197.12
grow old age 126.10
antiquate 123.9
growth
business cycle 827.9
conversion 145.1
development 197.3
disease symptom
686.8
increase 38.1
planting 411.2
progress 148.1
tumor 686.36
vegetation 411.30
grow together
be joined 47.11
cohere 50.6
grow up ascend 315.8

become higher
207.17
grow 197.7
mature 126.9
reach perfection
722.8
grub
n. drudge 718.3
food 308.2
young insect 125.10
v. drudge 716.14
excavate 257.15
procure 811.10
grubby dirty 682.22
infested 313.11
slovenly 62.15
grubstake
n. financing 836.2
v. finance 836.15
grub up dig up 305.10
procure 811.10
search out 485.33
grudge
n. spite 929.5
v. be parsimonious
852.5
be unwilling 623.3
envy 954.3
refuse 776.4
grudging envious 954.4
niggardly 852.8
reluctant 623.6
grudgingly 623.9
gruel cereal 308.34
semiliquid 389.5
thinness 205.7
weakness 160.7
grueling
fatiguing 717.11
laborious 716.18
punishing 1010.25
troublesome 731.17
weakening 160.20
gruesome
deathly 408.29
frightening 891.38
ugly 899.11
gruff brusque 937.7
grouchy 951.22
raucous 458.15
grum glum 872.25
sullen 951.24
grumble
n. harsh sound 458.3
reverberation 454.2
rumble 456.4
v. animal sound 460.4
complain 875.13
rumble 456.9
sound harshly 458.9
grumbler 869.3
grumbling
n. complaint 875.4
reverberation 454.2
adj. discontented
869.5
grouchy 951.22
grume blood 388.4
coagulation 354.7
grumpiness 951.6
grumpy 951.22
grungy 682.22

grunt
n. animal sound 460.1
infantryman 800.9
v. animal sound 460.3
complain 875.13
utter 594.26
G-string
clothing 231.19
supporter 216.2
G suit gravity 352.5
space suit 282.11
guarantee
n. guarantor 772.6
oath 523.3
promise 770.1
security 772.1
v. affirm 523.5
promise 770.4
protect 699.18
secure 772.9
guaranteed
assured 513.20
certified 772.11
promised 770.8
unhazardous 698.5
**guaranteed annual
income**
subsidy 818.8
welfare program
745.7
guarantor
endorser 521.7
warrantor 772.6
guaranty
n. guarantor 772.6
security 772.1
v. secure 772.9
guard
n. athlete 878.20
bodyguards 699.14
defender 799.7
defense 799.1
escort 73.5
guarder 699.9
household troops
800.31
jailer 761.10
protection 699.1
safeguard 699.3
trainman 274.13
vigilance 533.4
v. defend 799.8
escort 73.8
preserve 701.7
protect 699.18
restrain 760.7
guard against
defend 799.8
take precautions
895.6
guarded cautious 895.8
protected 699.21
restrained 760.13
reticent 613.10
suspicious 504.4
vigilant 533.13
guardedly 895.12
guardhouse 761.8
guardian
n. familiar spirit
1014.22
jailer 761.10

manager 748.4
protector 699.6
adj. protecting 699.23
guardian angel
familiar spirit
1014.22
protector 699.6
guardianship
directorship 747.4
protectorship 699.2
storage 660.5
usage 665.2
vigilance 533.4
guarding
n. custody 761.5
adj. defensive 799.11
protecting 699.23
guardrail 699.3
gubernatorial 741.17
gudgeon axis 322.5
dupe 620.1
guerrilla 800.15
guess
n. an uncertainty
514.8
unverified supposi-
tion 499.4
v. believe 501.11
conjecture 499.11
judge 494.9
predict 543.9
solve 487.2
guesser 499.8
guessing 514.23
guesswork
prediction 543.1
supposition 499.3
guest 925.6
guest house 191.16
guff chatter 596.3
nonsense 547.3
guffaw
n. laughter 876.4
v. laugh 876.8
guidance advice 754.1
direction 747.1
patronage 785.4
protectorship 699.2
teaching 562.1
guide
n. advisor 754.3
director 748.7
guardian angel
1014.22
hole 265.4
interpreter 552.7
pointer 568.4
precursor 66.1
specter 1017.1
teacher 565.1
trough 396.3
v. advise 754.5
direct 747.9
escort 73.8
go before 66.3
influence 172.8
lead 292.2
pilot 275.14
teach 562.11
guidebook
directory 748.10
handbook 605.5

information 557.1
guideline plan 654.1
precept 751.2
rule 84.4
guidepost 568.4
guiding 747.12
guiding light 648.1
guiding principle
main idea 479.4
policy 654.5
precept 751.2
guiding star
guide 748.8
motive 648.1
guild 788.3
guile cunning 735.1
deceit 618.3
guileful cunning 735.12
deceitful 618.20
shrewd 467.15
guilefully
cunningly 735.13
deceitfully 618.22
guileless artless 736.5
honest 974.18
trusting 501.22
guilelessly
artlessly 736.7
trustworthily 974.24
guillotine
n. capital punishment
1010.7
cloture 144.5
instrument of execu-
tion 1011.5
v. execute 1010.19
guilt 983
guiltily 983.5
guiltless innocent 984.6
virtuous 980.8
guiltlessly 984.9
guilty 983.3
guinea
British money 835.8
coin 835.4
guinea pig
experimentee 489.7
wild animal 414.28
guise aspect 446.3
behavior 737.1
clothing 231.1
cover 228.2
looks 446.4
mode 7.4
pretext 649.1
way 657.1
guitar 465.4
gulch ravine 201.2
watercourse 396.2
gulf
arm of the sea 399.1
concavity 257.4
gap 201.2
opening 265.1
pit 209.2
whirlpool 395.12
gull
n. dupe 620.1
v. cheat 618.17
deceive 618.13
dupe 470.7
gullet abdomen 193.3

throat 396.15
gullible
  credulous 502.9
  foolable 470.11
gully
  n. ravine 201.2
  watercourse 396.2
  v. groove 263.3
gulp
  n. breathing 403.18
  drink 307.4
  ingestion 306.4
  v. breathe 403.24
  eat 307.21
  gluttonize 994.4
  ingest 306.11
gum
  n. anatomy 258.6
  chewing gum 389.6
  elastic substance
    358.3
  resin 381.1,4
  v. chew 307.25
  stick together 50.9
  thwart 730.16
gumbo
  n. mud 389.8
  semiliquid 389.5
  soup 308.10
  adj. earthy 385.7
  gummy 389.12
gummed up
  bungled 734.22
  spoiled 692.31
gummy adhesive 50.12
  resinous 381.3
  viscous 389.12
gumption 707.7
gumshoe
  n. detective 781.11
  policeman 699.16
  v. creep 273.25
  lurk 615.9
gum up bungle 734.12
  spoil 692.13
  thwart 730.16
gun
  n. artilleryman 800.10
  end 144.2
  evildoer 943.4
  firearm 801.5,27
  killer 409.11
  makes of 801.28
  mercenary 800.16
  parts 801.29
  shooter 285.9
  shot 285.5
  v. hunt 655.9
  shoot 285.13
guncotton 801.9
gun down kill 409.14
  shoot 409.18
gunfight 798.9
gunfire attack 798.9
  shot 285.5
gun for seek 485.29
  shoot 285.13
gung ho
  n. battle cry 797.12
  adj. enthusiastic
    635.11
gunk glue 50.4

semiliquid 389.5
slime 682.8
gunman evildoer 943.3
  killer 409.11
  mercenary 800.16
  shooter 285.9
gunner
  artilleryman 800.10
  aviation 279.4
  sailor 276.6
  shooter 285.9
gunnery ballistics 801.3
  throwing 285.3
gunpowder 801.9
gunrunner 826.5
gunsel evildoer 943.4
  homosexual 419.16
  killer 409.11
  violent person 162.9
gunshot
  detonation 456.3
  short distance 200.2
  shot 285.5
gurge
  n. backflow 395.12
  rotation 322.2
  v. eddy 395.21
  whirl 322.11
gurgle bubble 405.4
  make a liquid sound
    452.11
  trickle 395.18
gurgling 452.19
guru good person 985.6
  Hindu priest 1038.14
  master 749.1
  teacher 565.1
  wise man 468.1
gush
  n. diffuseness 593.1
  eruption 162.6
  flattery 970.2
  flow 395.4
  increase 38.1
  jet 395.9
  outflow 303.4
  plenty 661.2
  talkativeness 596.1
  uprush 315.1
  v. abound 661.5
  be enthusiastic 635.8
  chatter 596.5
  emotionalize 855.15
  flow 395.16
  flow out 303.13
  jet 395.20
  upshoot 315.9
gushing
  n. diffuseness 593.1
  adj. diffuse 593.11
  flattering 970.8
  flowing 395.24
  sentimental 855.22
gussy up
  beautify 900.14
  dress up 231.41
  ornament 901.8
gust characteristic 80.4
  eagerness 635.1
  emotional outburst
    857.8
  liking 634.2

taste 427.1
wind gust 403.6
gustatory 427.8
gusto animation 161.3
  eagerness 635.1
  fervor 855.10
  gaiety 870.4
  liking 634.2
  pleasure 865.1
  savor 428.2
gusty tasty 428.8
  windy 403.25
gut
  n. abdomen 193.3
  arm of the sea 399.1
  v. destroy 693.10
  eviscerate 305.13
  plunder 824.16
  adj. basic 5.8
  emotional 855.19
  unpremeditated
    630.11
gutless
  uncourageous 892.11
  weak 160.12
gut reaction 855.3
guts contents 194.1
  courage 893.5
  eloquence 600.3
  inside parts 225.4
  intestine 225.4
  pluck 624.3
  pungency 433.2
  seat of affections
    855.2
  strength 159.1
gutsy bold 893.18
  eloquent 600.11
  plucky 624.14
  strong 159.13
gutted 329.30
gutter
  n. channel 396.5
  trench 263.2
  trough 396.3
  v. flutter 324.12
  adj. disgraceful 915.11
  vulgar 990.8
guttersnipe
  vulgar person 898.6
  waif 274.3
gutting 305.4
guttural
  n. speech sound
    594.13
  adj. imperfectly spo-
    ken 595.12
  phonetic 594.31
  raucous 458.15
guy man 420.5
  person 417.3
  supporter 216.2,26
guywire 216.2
guzzle
  n. drink 307.4
  gullet 396.15
  liquor 996.6
  spree 996.5
  v. drink 307.27
  gluttonize 994.4
  tipple 996.23
gym arena 802.1

playground 878.12
gymkhana
  contest 796.3
  tournament 878.10
gymnasium arena 802.1
  palaestra 567.11
  playground 878.12
  playroom 192.12
gymnast 878.21
gymnastic 878.32
gymnastics
  exercise 716.6
  physical education
    562.9
  sports 878.8
gyn(o)– 421.4
gynecologist 688.8
gyp
  n. dog 414.22
  female animal 421.9
  fraud 618.8
  v. cheat 618.17
gyp joint
  disapproved place
    191.28
  fraud 618.8
gypper 619.3
gypsy 274.4
gyrate move 267.5
  rotate 322.9 ∕
gyration 322.1
gyrational
  flowing 267.8
  gyratory 322.15
gyre
  n. curl 254.2
  evil spirit 1016.7
  orbiting 321.1
  rotation 322.2
  v. circuit 321.4
  rotate 322.9
gyrene marines 800.27
  sailor 276.4
gyroscope
  rotator 322.17
  stabilizer 142.20

H

habeas corpus 752.7
haberdasher
  clothier 231.32
  merchant 830.3
haberdashery 832.4
habit
  n. addiction 642.9
  clothing 231.1
  custom 642.4
  mannerism 903.2
  nature 5.3
  suit 231.6
  v. outfit 231.40
habitable 188.15
habitat
  environment 233.1
  home 191.5
habitation abode 191.1
  occupancy 188
habit-forming 642.20
habitual
  customary 642.16
  frequent 135.4

orderly 59.6
usual 84.8
habitually
    frequently 135.6
    regularly 642.23
    usually 84.9
habituate 642.11
habituated 642.19
habituating 642.20
habituation
    accustoming 642.8
    addiction 642.9
habitué attender 186.5
    guest 925.6
hachure line 568.6
    map 654.4
    network 221.3
hacienda farm 413.8
    ranch 191.7
hack
    n. breathing 403.18
    cab 272.12
    coachman 274.9
    driver 274.10
    drudge 718.3
    hack writer 602.16
    horse 414.16
    inferior horse 414.14
    mark 568.5
    notch 262.1
    petty politician 746.4
    v. exhale 403.24
    ride 273.33
    sever 49.11
hack it be able 157.11
    manage 724.11
    stand the test 489.10
    suffice 661.4
hackle
    n. feather 230.16
    plumage 230.18
    v. comb 681.21
hackneyed dull 883.9
    habitual 642.16
    trite 79.16
    well-known 475.27
Hades
    deity of nether world
        1019.5
    god 1014.5
    hell 1019.3
    nether world 1019.1
hag evildoer 943.7
    old woman 127.3
    ugly person 899.4
    witch 1035.8
haggard colorless 363.7
    deathly 408.29
    excited 857.23
    fanatical 473.32
    thin 205.20
    tired-looking 717.7
haggle
    n. negotiation 827.3
    v. bargain 827.17
haggling 827.3
hagiography
    biography 608.4
    theology 1023.1
ha-ha
    n. laughter 876.4
    trench 263.2

v. laugh 876.8
haiku 609.6
hail
    n. greeting 925.4
    ice 333.6
    large number 101.3
    v. address 594.27
    applaud 968.10
    assent 521.8
    cry 459.6
    greet 925.10
    signal 568.22
    storm 333.11
    interj. approval
        968.23
    attention! 530.23
    greetings! 925.15
hail-fellow-well-met
    922.19
Hail Mary 1032.4
hair filament 206.1
    fur 230.2
    narrowness 205.1
    short distance 200.2
    small amount 35.2
    trifle 673.5
    weakness 160.7
hairbreadth
    narrowness 205.1
    short distance 200.2
haircut boy's 230.31
    hairdo 230.15
hairdo hairstyle 230.15
    women's 230.30
hairdresser 900.12
hairiness
    difficulty 731.1
    furriness 230
hairless 232.17
hairlike
    threadlike 206.7
    trichoid 230.23
hairline difference 16.2
    line 568.6
hairpiece 230.14
hairpin
    n. crookedness 219.8
    deviation 291.1
    adj. crooked 219.20
hair-raising 891.37
hair remover 232.4
hair shirt 1012.3
hairsplitting
    n. disapproval 969.4
    overdiscrimination
        492.3
    overparticularity
        896.4
    quibbling 483.5
    adj. critical 969.24
    overparticular 896.12
    quibbling 483.14
hairstyle 230.15
hair-trigger 269.19
hairy bad 675.8
    difficult 731.16
    hirsute 230.24
    rough 261.9
    threadlike 206.7
hajj 273.5
halcyon calm 268.12
    pacific 803.9

pleasant 863.10
    prosperous 728.13
hale
    v. pull 286.4
    adj. healthy 685.10
    strong 159.13
half
    n. bisection 92.2
    middle 69.2
    portion 816.5
    adj. part 92.5
    proportionate 816.13
half-and-half
    n. half 92.2
    milk 308.47
    adj. equal 30.7
    mixed 44.15
    neutral 806.7
    proportionate 816.13
    adv. in half 92.8
    midway 69.5
    proportionately
        816.14
half-assed
    half-learned 477.15
    slipshod 534.12
    unskillful 734.15
halfback 878.20
half-baked
    half-learned 477.15
    mentally deficient
        469.22
    premature 131.8
    undeveloped 721.11
half-breed
    n. hybrid 44.9
    adj. hybrid 44.16
half-cocked
    half-learned 477.15
    premature 131.8
    undeveloped 721.11
halfhearted
    indifferent 636.6
    weak 160.17
half-life 327.1,14
half-moon
    crescent 252.5
    moon 375.11
half-pint 196.10
half time interim 109.1
    shift 108.3
halftone
    color system 362.7
    harmonics 463.20
halftone engraving
    603.1
half-truth 616.11
halfway
    adj. half 92.5
    middle 69.4
    adv. midway 69.5
halfway house
    asylum 700.4
    middle 69.2
halfway mark 92.3
half-wit 471.8
half-witted 469.22
halitosis 437.1
hall arena 802.1
    corridor 192.18
    entrance 302.5
    house 191.6

room 192.4
    school 567.15
    theater 611.18
hallelujah
    n. cheer 876.2
    hymn 1032.3
    interj. worship
        1032.16
hallmark
    n. characteristic 80.4
    label 568.13
    sign 568.2
    v. label 568.20
hall-of-famer 733.14
hallow celebrate 877.2
    sanctify 1026.5
hallowed
    godlike 1013.20
    sanctified 1026.8
    traditional 123.12
hallucinate 519.8
hallucination
    deception 618.1
    illusion 519.7
    thing imagined 535.5
    thought disturbance
        690.24
hallucinatory
    deceptive 618.19
    psychedelic 519.10
hallucinogen 687.13,53
hallucinogenic
    hallucinatory 519.10
    psychochemical
        687.46
hallway 192.18
halo circle 253.2
    illustriousness 914.6
    light 335.14
halt
    n. delay 132.2
    impasse 731.5
    prevention 730.2
    respite 711.2
    standstill 268.3
    stop 144.2
    v. arrest 144.11
    be weak 160.8
    dawdle 270.8
    discontinue 144.6
    prevent 730.13
    quiet 268.8
    stammer 595.8
    stop 144.7
    walk 273.27
    adj. crippled 692.32
    interj. cease! 144.14
halter
    n. harness 659.5
    noose 1011.5
    restraint 760.4
    v. bind 47.10
halting crippled 692.32
    irregular 138.3
    slow 270.10
    stammering 595.13
    stilted 590.3
haltingly
    irregularly 138.4
    slowly 270.13
halve bisect 92.4
    sever 49.11

hash mark 569.5
hash up bungle 734.12
  spoil 692.13
Hasidic 1020.29
hasp 47.8
hassle
  n. argumentation
    482.4
  commotion 62.4
  confusion 62.2
  quarrel 795.6
  struggle 716.3
  v. argue 482.16
  nag 969.16
  quarrel 795.12
  struggle 716.11
hassock bunch 74.7
  plants 411.2
  seat 216.30
haste hurry 709
  impatience 862.1
  impulsiveness 630.2
  prematurity 131.2
  recklessness 894.2
  speed 269.1
hasten
  accelerate 269.14
  advance 294.5
  aid 785.17
  be impatient 862.4
  facilitate 732.6
  make haste 709.5
  push 709.4
  rush 269.9
hasten off 301.11
hastily fast 269.21
  hurriedly 709.12
  impulsively 630.13
  prematurely 131.13
  recklessly 894.11
  suddenly 113.9
hastiness
  carelessness 534.2
  hurriedness 709.2
  improvidence 721.2
  impulsiveness 630.2
  prematurity 131.2
  recklessness 894.2
hasty fast 269.19
  hot-tempered 951.25
  hurried 709.9
  impatient 862.6
  impulsive 630.9
  premature 131.8
  reckless 894.8
  sudden 113.5
  unprepared 721.8
hat
  n. clothing 231.25,59
  v. clothe 231.39
  cover 228.21
hatch
  n. bird young 171.2
  entrance 302.6
  v. be born 167.16
  draw 574.20
  engrave 578.10
  fabricate 616.18
  imagine 535.14
  incubate 169.12
  mark 568.19
  originate 167.13

plot 654.10
raise animals 416.6
spawn 167.13
hatched born 167.21
  fabricated 616.29
hatchery 153.8
hatchet ax 801.25
  edge tool 348.13
hatchet-faced 205.19
hatchet job 971.5
hatchet man
  combatant 800.1
  disparager 971.6
  evildoer 943.4
  killer 409.11
  political henchman
    746.8
hatching birth 167.7
  creation 167.5
  engraving 578.2
  line 568.6
  network 221.3
hate
  n. dislike 867.2
  hated thing 930.3
  hatred 930
  hostility 929.3
  v. bear ill will 929.8
  detest 930.5
  dislike 867.3
  have deep feelings
    855.14
hateful bad 675.9
  detestable 930.8
  hostile 929.10
  malicious 939.18
  offensive 864.18
hater 930.4
hating 930.7
hat in hand
  humbly 906.15
  obsequiously 907.15
hatred dislike 867.2
  hate 930.1
  hostility 929.3
hatter 231.36
haughty arrogant 912.9
  contemptuous 966.8
  high 207.19
  proud 905.9
haul
  n. booty 824.11
  exertion 716.2
  pull 286.2
  take 822.10
  v. cart 271.12
  exert oneself 716.10
  heave 275.48
  pull 286.4
  sail 275.24
hauling
  n. pulling 286.1
  transportation 271.3
  adj. pulling 286.6
haunch 242.1
haunches 241.4
haunt
  n. resort 191.27
  specter 1017.1
  v. frequent 186.10
  make anxious 890.4
  obsess 864.16

possess 1017.6
haunted
  possessed 1017.10
  remembering 537.24
  worried 890.7
haunting
  recurrent 103.13
  unforgettable 537.26
haute couture 644.1
hauteur
  arrogance 912.1
  contempt 966.1
  height 207.1
haut monde
  nobility 918.2
  society 644.6
Havana cigar 434.4
  tobacco 434.2
have affirm 523.4
  cheat 618.17
  compel 756.4
  experience 151.8
  give birth 167.15
  harbor 813.7
  know 475.12
  permit 777.10
  possess 808.4
  receive 819.6
  recognize 537.12
  understand 548.7
have a baby 167.15
have a ball 878.24
have a mind to
  choose to 621.2
  desire 634.14
  intend 653.7
have at attack 798.15
  contend 796.15
  undertake 715.3
have coming 960.4
have in hand
  control 741.13
  have undertaken
    715.4
  possess 808.4
have in mind
  expect 539.5
  intend 653.7
  mean 545.9
  remember 537.13
  think of 478.16
have it easy 732.10
have it made 724.9
haven
  n. destination 300.5
  harbor 700.6
  refuge 700.1
  v. protect 699.18
have nothing to do with
  abstain 992.7
  avoid 631.6
  be inhospitable 926.5
  do nothing 706.4
  not concern 10.3
  refuse 776.3
have-nots, the 838.3
have one's hands full
  be busy 707.10
  have difficulty 731.10
haves, the 837.5
have to
  be compelled 756.8

must 639.10
havoc
  destruction 693.1
  evil 675.3
haw stammer 595.8
  turn aside 291.6
hawk
  n. eye 439.11
  militarist 800.5
  v. hunt 655.9
  spit 312.6
  vend 829.9
hawk-eyed
  clear-sighted 439.22
  vigilant 533.13
hawking
  n. hunting 655.2
  selling 829.2
  adj. imperfectly spo-
    ken 595.12
hawkish 797.26
hay
  n. fodder 308.4
  marihuana 687.13
  v. harvest 413.19
hay fever
  allergic disorder
    686.32
  respiratory disease
    686.14
hayloft attic 192.16
  garner 660.7
haymaker
  boxing blow 283.5
  farm hand 413.5
hayseed
  n. oaf 471.5
  rustic 919.9
  seed 411.29
  adj. countrified 182.7
haystack 74.10
haywire
  disorderly 62.13
  in disrepair 692.39
  insane 473.26
hazard
  n. chance event 156.6
  danger 697.1
  gamble 515.1
  game of chance 515.8
  obstacle 730.4
  uncertainty 514.6
  wager 515.3
  v. bet 515.20
  endanger 697.6
  gamble 515.19
  happen 156.11
  take chances 697.7
  take the liberty 961.6
hazardous
  dangerous 697.10
  gambling 515.21
  unreliable 514.19
haze
  n. confusion 532.3
  fog 404.2
  v. banter 882.4
  cloud 404.6
hazel 367.3,6
haziness
  cloudiness 404.3
  formlessness 247.1

indistinctness 445.2
vagueness 514.4
hazy dim 445.6
  foggy 404.9
  formless 247.4
  muddled 532.13
  obscure 549.15
  vague 514.18
H-blast 326.16
H-bomb 801.15,30
he male 420.4
  self 80.5
head
  n. abridgment 607.1
  book 605.12
  brain 466.6
  capital 211.5
  caption 484.2
  class 61.2
  coin 240.1
  drug user 642.10
  foam 405.2
  front 240.1
  hair 230.4
  headwaters 395.2
  inflorescence 411.25
  intellect 466.1
  intelligent being 467.9
  pate 211.6
  person 417.3
  point of land 256.8
  portrait 574.16
  pressure 283.2
  rest room 311.10
  sail part 277.14
  source 153.5
  superior 36.4
  supervisor 748.2
  topic 484.1
  top part 211.4
  water 392.3
  v. bear 290.8
  begin 68.10
  caption 484.3
  direct 747.8
  front 240.7
  govern 741.12
  gravitate 352.15
  head for 290.10
  lead 292.2
  precede 64.2
  tend 174.3
  top 211.9
  adj. directing 747.12
  first 68.17
  front 240.10
  governing 741.18
  top 211.10
headache ache 424.5
  annoyance 866.2
  boring person 884.4
  nervous disorder 686.23
  trouble 731.3
head count list 88.6
  numeration 87.5
headdress
  clothing 231.25
  hairdo 230.15
headed for 290.28
header plunge 320.1

tumble 316.3
headfirst
  precipitously 709.15
  recklessly 894.11
headgear
  clothing 231.25
  harness 659.5
head-hunter 409.11
heading
  n. aviation 278.43
  caption 484.2
  class 61.2
  direction 290.1
  front 240.1
  leading 292.1
  topic 484.1
  top part 211.4
  adj. leading 292.3
  topping 211.11
headland 256.8
headless topless 211.13
  unintelligent 469.13
headline
  n. caption 484.2
  v. caption 484.3
  give prominence 672.14
  star 611.33
headliner 612.6
headlong
  adj. fast 269.19
  impulsive 630.9
  precipitate 709.10
  reckless 894.8
  steep 219.18
  sudden 113.5
  adv. impulsively 630.13
  precipitously 709.15
  recklessly 894.11
headman
  public official 749.17
  supervisor 748.2
headmaster 565.9
headmost
  adj. chief 36.14
  front 240.10
  leading 292.3
  preceding 64.4
  top 211.10
  adv. before 292.4
  in front 240.12
head off 291.6
head of state 749.6
head over heels
  inversely 220.8
  precipitously 709.15
  recklessly 894.11
  reversed 220.7
  round 322.16
head over heels in
  engrossed 530.17
  involved in 176.4
headphone
  loudspeaker 450.8
  radiophone 560.5
headpiece
  clothing 231.25
  head 211.6
  intellect 466.1
  top part 211.4

headquarters
  center 226.6
  office 719.8
headroom 179.3
headset
  loudspeaker 450.8
  radiophone 560.5
headshrinker 690.13
headsman 1010.8
heads or tails 515.2
head start
  advantage 36.2
  earliness 131.1
headstone
  cornerstone 216.7
  memorial 570.12
headstrong
  lawless 740.5
  obstinate 626.8
head up begin 68.10
  caption 484.3
  direct 747.8
  lead 240.7
  precede 64.2
headwater
  headstream 395.2
  source 153.6
headway
  improvement 691.1
  progression 294.1
  water travel 275.9
head wind
  aviation 278.41
  counterforce 178.4
  nautical 403.11
  opposition 790.1
  wind 403.1
headwork study 564.3
  thought 478.1
heady exciting 857.28
  foamy 405.7
  intoxicating 996.35
  lawless 740.5
heal close up 694.21
  restore to health 694.15
  treat 689.30
healer
  faith healer 688.12
  therapist 688.5
healing
  n. faith healing 689.3
  restoration 694.7
  adj. remedial 687.39
health normality 84.1
  well-being 685
  types of 309.26
health food food 308.1
  types of 309.26
healthful fit 685.7
  salubrious 683.5
healthiness
  goodness 674.1
  salubrity 683.1
  soundness 685.2
health resort
  gathering place 191.27
  spa 689.29
healthy good 674.12
  healthful 685.7
  large 195.16
  salubrious 683.5

heap
  n. amount 28.2
  automobile 272.9
  much 34.4
  pile 74.10
  store 660.1
  throng 74.4
  v. be generous 853.3
  give 818.12
  pile 74.19
  put 184.14
  store up 660.11
hear
  v. be informed 557.14
  catch 448.12
  hearken to 530.7
  judge 494.12
  listen 448.11
  sense 422.8
  try 1004.17
  interj. hark! 448.17
hear a different drummer
  disagree 27.5
  not conform 83.4
hearer listener 448.5
  recipient 819.3
hearing
  n. audition 448.2
  earshot 448.4
  examination 485.2
  investigation 485.4
  sense 422.5
  sense of hearing 448
  trial 1004.5
  tryout 489.3
  adj. auditory 448.14
hearing aid 448.8
hearken
  v. listen 448.11
  interj. hark! 448.17
hearken to hark 530.7
  obey 766.2
hearsay
  n. evidence 505.2
  rumor 558.6
  adj. evidential 505.17
hearse 410.10
heart
  amphetamine 687.9
  center 226.2
  content 194.5
  courage 893.5
  diseases of 686.17
  essence 5.2
  fervor 855.10
  important point 672.6
  inner nature 5.4
  interior 225.2
  love 931.1
  meat 308.20
  middle 69.1
  mood 525.4
  psyche 466.4
  seat of affections 855.2
  seat of life 407.3
  viscera 225.4
heartache despair 866.6
  sadness 872.9

heart and soul
fervently 855.28
laboriously 716.19
resolutely 624.17
throughout 56.17
heart attack 686.17
heartbeat
palpitation 323.3
seat of life 407.3
heartbreak agony 864.4
sadness 872.9
heartbreaker 932.11
heartbreaking 864.23
heartbroken 872.29
heartburn ache 424.5
indigestion 686.28
jealousy 953.1
heart disease 686.17
hearten abet 785.14
cheer 870.7
comfort 887.6
encourage 893.16
energize 161.9
heartening
n. encouragement
893.9
adj. cheering 870.16
comforting 887.13
heart failure 686.17
heartfelt 855.26
hearth family 11.5
fireplace 329.11
home 191.4
heartily
amicably 927.21
energetically 161.15
fervently 855.28
gayly 870.18
strongly 159.21
zealously 635.15
heartland inland 225.3
region 180.1
heartless
apathetic 856.13
callous 939.23
dejected 872.22
dispassionate 856.9
pitiless 945.3
uncourageous 892.11
wicked 981.17
heartlessly
apathetically 856.15
cruelly 939.32
dejectedly 872.33
pitilessly 945.4
uncourageously
892.14
unfeelingly 856.14
heart of gold 938.1
heartrending
agonizing 864.23
pitiful 944.8
hearts-and-flowers 855.8
heart-shaped 252.15
heartsick
disconsolate 872.28
wretched 866.26
heartthrob
emotion 855.3
heartbeat 323.3
heart-to-heart 974.17

heart-warming
cheering 870.16
pleasant 863.6
hearty
n. companion 928.4
sailor 276.1
adj. convivial 922.19
cordial 927.15
energetic 161.12
fervent 855.23
gay 870.14
healthy 685.10
hospitable 925.11
strong 159.13
zealous 635.10
heat
n. anger 952.5
fervor 855.10
fever 686.6
fever of excitement
857.6
hotness 328
oestrum 419.6
race 796.12
zeal 635.2
v. cook 330.4
excite 857.11
incite 648.17
make hot 329.17
heated cooked 330.6
excited 857.20
fervent 855.23
fiery 162.21
hot 328.25
warmed 329.29
zealous 635.10
heater gun 801.5
warmer 329.10,32
heath plain 387.1
wasteland 166.2
heathen
n. pagan 1025.7
unbeliever 1031.11
adj. idolatrous 1033.7
pagan 1025.11
unbelieving 1031.19
unlearned 477.14
heathenism
idolatry 1033.1
paganism 1025.4
unenlightenment
477.4
heating
n. heat 328.1
warming 329
adj. warming 329.26
heatstroke 686.26
heat up
aggravate 885.2
antagonize 929.7
incite 648.17
increase 38.5
heat wave 328.7
heave
n. exertion 716.2
pull 286.2
raise 317.2
throw 285.4
wave 395.14
v. be excited 857.16
billow 395.22
elevate 317.5

exert oneself 716.10
hurl 798.28
lurch 275.55
pull 286.4
sail 275.48
sicken at 867.4
throw 285.11
vomit 310.25
interj. sailing 275.75
heaven
dreamland 535.11
good times 728.4
happiness 865.2
height 207.2
sky 375.2
summit 211.2
Heaven
abode of the dead
408.4
Fate 640.3
God 1013.2
Paradise 1018
the future 121.2
Heaven forbid! 969.28
heavenly
angelic 1015.6
celestial 375.25
Elysian 1018.13
godly 1013.19
gorgeous 900.19
idealized 535.23
pious 1028.9
pleasant 863.8
sacred 1026.7
superb 674.17
heavenly host 1015.2
heavily densely 354.15
dully 883.10
inertly 268.20
sadly 872.31
weightily 352.21
heavy
n. actor 612.2
corpulent person
195.12
role 611.11
adj. beautiful 900.16
burdensome 864.24
cloudy 404.7
deep 454.10
dense 354.12
excellent 674.13
growing rank 411.40
inert 268.14
laborious 716.18
languid 708.19
phonetic 594.31
powerful 34.6
pregnant 169.18
sad 872.20
serious 672.19
sleepy 712.21
stilted 590.3
stupid 469.16
substantial 3.7
theatrical 611.39
thick 204.8
troublesome 731.17
uninteresting 883.6
viscous 389.12
weighty 352.16
adv. weightily 352.21

heavy hand
despotism 741.10
strictness 757.3
heavy-handed 734.20
heavy heart
despair 866.6
sadness 872.1
heavyhearted 872.20
heavy-laden
fraught 56.12
worried 890.8
heavyset
corpulent 195.18
thick 204.8
heavyweight
n. boxing weight
352.3
corpulent person
195.12
influential person
172.6
pugilist 800.2
adj. heavy 352.16
important 672.16
hebetude apathy 856.4
languor 708.6
stupidity 469.3
Hebrew
n. Jew 1020.20
adj. Jewish 1020.29
Hecate 375.12
heckle annoy 866.13
comb 681.21
heckled 866.24
heckler 866.10
hectic
n. fever 686.6
heat 328.12
reddening 368.3
adj. excited 857.20
feverish 686.54
overactive 707.24
overzealous 635.13
red-complexioned
368.9
hector
n. blusterer 911.2
braggart 910.5
v. annoy 866.13
bluster 911.3
intimidate 891.28
hedge
n. boundary 235.3
caution 895.1
qualification 507.1
v. dodge 631.8
enclose 236.7
equivocate 483.9
limit 234.5
qualify 507.3
take precautions
895.6
hedgehop 278.51
hedging
n. caution 895.1
equivocation 483.5
qualification 507.1
adj. equivocating
483.14
hedonism ethics 957.2
pleasure-loving 865.4
sensuality 987.1

hedonist 987.3
hedonistic
philosophy 500.9
pleasure-loving 865.15
sensual 987.5
heebie-jeebies
delirium tremens 473.10
nervousness 859.2
heed
n. attention 530.1
caution 895.1
concern 533.1
observance 768.1
v. attend 530.6
care 533.6
listen 448.11
obey 766.2
observe 768.2
heedful
attentive 530.15
careful 533.10
cautious 895.8
considerate 938.16
heeding hearing 448.1
observance 768.1
heedless careless 534.11
forgetful 538.9
improvident 721.15
impulsive 630.10
inattentive 531.6
inconsiderate 939.16
incurious 529.3
unconcerned 636.7
heedlessly
carelessly 534.18
inconsiderately 939.27
on impulse 630.14
recklessly 894.11
unconcernedly 636.10
heel
n. bad person 986.6
foot 212.5
rear 241.1
stern 241.7
v. deviate 291.3
equip 659.8
follow 293.3
sail 275.43
turn around 295.9
heeler hanger-on 907.5
partisan 744.27
political henchman 746.8
heft
n. weight 352.1
v. elevate 317.5
weigh 352.10
hefty corpulent 195.18
heavy 352.16
laborious 716.18
strong 159.13
troublesome 731.17
hegira departure 301.1
flight 631.4
heifer calf 414.6
female animal 421.9
girl 125.6
height altitude 207

culmination 677.3
degree 29.1
elevation 207.2
exaltation 317.1
harmonics 463.4
size 195.1
summit 211.2
supremacy 36.3
heighten
elevate 207.18
exalt 317.5
increase 38.5
intensify 885.2
heightened
aggravated 885.4
increased 38.7
heightening
aggravation 885.1
exaggeration 617.1
increase 38.2
heinous bad 675.9
base 915.12
evil 981.16
offensive 864.18
heir descendant 117.2
heritor 819.5
posterity 171.1
successor 67.4
survivor 43.3
heir apparent
prince 918.7
successor 819.5
heiress
descendant 171.3
recipient 819.5
heirloom 819.2
heist
n. a theft 824.10
stickup 824.3
v. elevate 317.5
rob 824.14
Hekate 375.12
held engrossed 530.18
fixed 142.16
obsessed 473.33
possessed 808.8
reserved 660.15
supported 216.24
unused 668.12
held up 132.16
Helen of Troy 900.9
helical circuitous 321.7
spiral 254.8
helicopter 280.5,15
Helios god 1014.5
sun god 375.14
heliport airport 278.22
platform 216.13
helix 254.2
hell bedlam 62.5
depths 209.3
gambling house 515.15
hot place 328.11
nether world 1019
place of confinement 761.7
torment 866.7
hell-bent
determined 624.16
fast 269.21
hellcat evildoer 943.3

reckless person 894.4
violent person 162.9
witch 943.7
hellhole 981.7
hellion evildoer 943.4
evil spirit 1016.7
violent person 162.9
hellish atrocious 675.10
cruel 939.24
devilish 1016.18
infernal 1019.8
violent 162.17
wicked 981.13
hello
n. greeting 925.4
interj. attention! 530.23
greetings! 925.15
wonder 920.20
hell-raiser
evildoer 943.3
violent person 162.9
hell's kitchen 183.6
hell to pay 731.4
helm
n. control 741.2
management 747.5
seat of authority 739.10
types of 277.33
v. pilot 275.14
helmet
heraldic insignia 569.2
safety equipment 699.3
helmsman
boatman 276.8
pilot 748.7
helot slave 764.7
sycophant 907.3
help
n. aid 785.1
assistant 787.6
benefactor 942.1
remedy 687.1
servant 750.2
serving 307.10
staff 750.11
subsidy 818.8
v. aid 785.11
do a favor 938.12
do good 674.10
facilitate 732.6
prevent 730.14
serve 750.13
subsidize 818.19
helper assistant 785.7
benefactor 942.1
second 787.6
subordinate 764.5
helpful
beneficial 674.12
considerate 938.16
instrumental 658.6
serving 785.21
useful 665.18
helping
n. food 307.10
portion 816.5
adj. assisting 785.20
serving 750.14

helping hand
assist 785.2
benefactor 942.1
helpless
defenseless 158.18
drunk 996.33
forlorn 924.11
unprotected 697.14
helpmate
assistant 787.6
wife 933.9
helter-skelter
n. commotion 62.4
haste 709.1
jumble 62.3
adj. confused 62.16
adv. carelessly 534.18
hastily 709.12
in disorder 62.17
nonuniformly 18.4
recklessly 894.11
hem
n. border 235.4
edging 235.7
v. border 235.10
enclose 236.7
restrain 760.9
stammer 595.8
hem– 388.4
he-man 420.6
hem and haw
be irresolute 627.7
dodge 631.8
prevaricate 613.7
stammer 595.8
hem in confine 761.12
enclose 236.5
restrain 760.9
hemisphere half 92.2
region 180.2
hemispheric(al) 255.9
hemlock
capital punishment 1010.7
poisonous plant 676.7
hemmed in
enclosed 236.10
restrained 760.15
hemoglobin
blood 388.4
protein 309.23
hemophilia
blood disease 686.18
genetic disease 686.11
hemorrhage
n. bleeding 311.8
disease symptom 686.8
v. bleed 311.17
hemorrhaging 311.23
hemorrhoid
cardiovascular disease 686.17
sore 686.35
hemp
marihuana 687.13,53
noose 1011.5
hen
female animal 421.9
poultry 414.34

woman 421.6
hence away 301.21
  therefore 155.7
henceforth 121.10
henchman
  follower 293.2
  hanger-on 907.5
  lackey 787.8
  political henchman
    746.8
henna 367.4,7
henpeck
  domineer 741.16
  nag 969.16
henpecked
  downtrodden 764.16
  obedient 766.5
hep 475.16,17
hepatitis
  infectious disease
    686.12
  inflammation 686.9
  liver disease 686.21
Hephaestus god 1014.5
  smith 718.7
hept(a)– 99.19
her female 421.4
  self 80.5
Hera goddess 1014.5
  marriage goddess
    933.14
herald
  n. delegate 781.2
  harbinger 544.5
  heraldic official
    749.21
  messenger 561.2
  precursor 66.1
  spokesman 781.5
  v. forerun 116.3
  introduce 66.3
  presage 544.14
  proclaim 559.13
heraldry insignia 569.1
  pomp 904.6
herb medicine 687.4
  plant 411.4,47
herbaceous 411.33
herbarium 413.10
herbicide killer 409.3
  poison 676.3
herbivore animal 414.3
  vegetarian 307.14
herbivorous 307.29
Herculean
  difficult 731.16
  huge 195.20
  laborious 716.18
  strong 159.15
Hercules giant 195.26
  strong man 159.6
  supporter 216.3
herd
  n. flock 74.5
  guider 748.7
  v. direct 747.9
  drive animals 416.8
herder 416.3
herdsman guider 748.7
  herder 416.3
herd together
  be sociable 922.16

come together 74.16
confederate 73.7
here
  in this place 184.22
  now 120.3
  present 186.16
hereafter future 121.8
  in future 121.10
hereafter, the
  heaven 1018.3
  the future 121.2
here and there
  discontinuously 72.5
  in places 184.24
  scatteringly 75.12
  sparsely 102.8
hereby 658.7
hereditary
  genetic 406.20
  innate 5.7
  patrimonial 170.15
heredity gene 406.9
  heritage 170.6
heresy error 518.1
  inconsistency 27.2
  nonconformity 83.2
  unbelief 503.1
  unorthodoxy 1025.2
heretic
  misbeliever 1025.5
  nonconformist 83.3
heretical
  disagreeing 27.9
  erroneous 518.16
  nonconformist 83.6
  unbelieving 503.8
  unorthodox 1025.9
heretofore
  formerly 119.13
  previously 116.6
  until now 120.4
herewith
  by means of 658.7
  together 73.10
heritage heredity 170.6
  inheritance 819.2
hermaphrodite
  n. intersex 419.19
  adj. intersexual 419.33
Hermes god 1014.5
  god of trade 827.12
  messenger 561.1
hermetic(al)
  resistant 159.18
  sealed 266.12
  secret 614.11
hermit ascetic 991.2
  odd person 85.4
  recluse 924.5
  religious 1038.17
hermitage 700.5
hero
  brave person 893.8
  famous person 914.9
  god 1014.3
  good person 985.5
  ideal 25.4
  lead 612.6
  role 611.11
  victor 726.2
heroic
  courageous 893.17

eminent 34.9
huge 195.20
legendary 123.12
magnanimous 979.6
poetic 609.17
vocal 462.51
heroically
  courageously 893.22
  pluckily 624.18
heroics boasting 910.1
  rashness 894.1
heroin 687.12,54
heroine
  brave person 893.8
  famous person 914.9
  goddess 1014.3
  good person 985.5
  lead 612.6
  role 611.11
heroism courage 893.1
  eminence 34.2
  magnanimity 979.2
hero worship
  idolatry 1033.1
  love 931.1
  praise 968.5
  respect 964.1
hero-worship
  praise 968.12
  respect 964.4
herpes
  infectious disease
    686.12
  skin disease 686.33
herpetology 415.1
hesitant cautious 895.8
  irresolute 627.11
  uncertain 514.15
  unwilling 623.7
hesitate
  be irresolute 627.7
  be unsure 514.10
  demur 623.4
  pause 144.9
  procrastinate 132.11
  stammer 595.8
hesitating
  irresolute 627.11
  stammering 595.13
  uncertain 514.15
  unwilling 623.7
hesitation
  caution 895.1
  demur 623.2
  irresolution 627.3
  pause 144.3
  procrastination 132.5
  stammering 595.3
  uncertainty 514.1
heter(o)– different 16.7
  dissimilar 21.4
  multiform 19.3
  nonuniform 18.3
heterodox
  disagreeing 27.9
  erroneous 518.16
  nonconformist 83.6
  unorthodox 1025.9
heterogeneous
  different 16.7
  diversified 19.4
  mixed 44.15

heteronomous 741.17
heterosexual
  n. straight 419.15
  adj. sexual 419.26
heuristic
  experimental 489.11
  investigating 485.36
hew fell 318.5
  form 246.7
  sever 49.11
hex
  n. bad influence 675.4
  curse 972.1
  spell 1036.1
  witch 1035.8
  v. bewitch 1036.9
  bring bad luck 729.12
  curse 972.5
  harm 675.6
hexa– 99.18
hey! attention! 530.23
  greetings! 925.15
  wonder 920.20
heyday 728.4
H hour
  attack time 798.14
  crucial moment
    129.5
hiatus
  discontinuity 72.2
  gap 57.2
  interval 201.1
  opening 265.1
hibernal cold 333.14
  winter 128.8
hibernate
  be idle 708.15
  be latent 546.3
  sleep 712.15
  stagnate 706.2
hibernation
  inactivity 708.1
  sleep 712.2
hiccup
  n. belch 310.9
  breathing 403.18
  v. belch 310.26
  inhale spasmodically
    403.24
hick
  n. bungler 734.9
  oaf 471.5
  rustic 919.9
  unsophisticate 736.3
  adj. countrified 182.7
hickey blemish 679.1
  object 376.4
hick town 183.3
hidden
  concealed 615.11
  latent 546.5
  recondite 549.16
  secluded 924.8
  secret 614.11
  unseen 445.5
hide
  n. pelt 229.1,8
  v. conceal 615.6
  defeat 727.6
  disappear 447.2
  hide oneself 615.8
  punish 1010.15

hold water
  be proved 505.11
  be reasonable 482.17
  be true 516.7
hold with
  approve 968.9
  assent 521.8
  consent 775.2
hold your horses 132.12
hole
  n. aviation 278.41
  cave 257.5
  cavity 257.2
  cellar 192.17
  crack 201.2
  disapproved place
    191.28
  fault 678.2
  filthy place 682.11
  hiding place 615.4
  hovel 191.12
  impasse 731.5
  lair 191.26
  location 184.1
  opening 265.1
  pit 209.2
  place of vice 981.7
  room 192.2
  score 724.4
  small place 196.3
  v. puncture 265.16
hole in one 724.4
hole in the wall
  nook 192.3
  small place 196.3
hole up 615.8
holey
  perforated 265.20
  shabby 692.34
holiday
  n. absence 187.4
  celebration 877.1
  day off 711.4
  interim 109.1
  pause 144.3
  vacation 711.3
  word list 137.12
  v. vacation 711.9
  adj. vacational 711.10
holier-than-thou
  hypocritic(al) 616.33
  sanctimonious 1029.5
holiness
  divine attribute
    1013.15
  piety 1028.2
  sanctity 1026.1
holism 54.5
holistic 54.9
holler
  n. complaint 875.4
  cry 459.1
  v. complain 875.13
  cry 459.6
  object 522.5
hollow
  n. cavity 257.2
  compartment 192.2
  opening 265.1
  pit 209.2
  v. be concave 257.12
  make concave 257.13

adj. concave 257.16
  deep-pitched 454.10
  insincere 616.32
  specious 483.10
  stupid 469.19
  uninteresting 883.6
  vacant 187.13
  vain 669.13
hollow-eyed
  tired-looking 717.7
  wasted 205.20
hollow man
  affecter 903.7
  nonentity 4.2
hollow mockery 616.5
hollow ware
  hard goods 831.4
  tableware 348.3
holocaust
  carnage 409.5
  destruction 693.1
  sacrifice 1032.7
  torment 866.7
hologram 577.5
holograph
  document 570.5
  original 23.3
  written matter 602.10
holographic(al) 602.22
holus-bolus 894.11
holy godlike 1013.20
  pious 1028.9
  sacred 1026.7
Holy Bible 1021.2
Holy Communion
  1040.8
holy day holiday 711.4
  religious 1040.14
Holy Father
  God 1013.11
  pope 1038.9
Holy Ghost
  functions of 1013.18
  God the Holy Ghost
    1013.14
Holy Grail 1040.11
holy mackerel! 920.19
holy man 985.6
holy of holies
  retreat 700.5
  sanctuary 1042.5
  study 192.8
  the sacred 1026.2
holy orders
  consecration 1037.10
  major orders 1038.4
  sacrament 1040.5
  the ministry 1037.1
holy place 1042.4
Holy Sacrament, the
  1040.8
holy smoke! 920.19
Holy Spirit, the
  1013.14
holystone
  n. cleaning agent
    681.17,32
  v. wash 681.19
holy terror
  bad child 125.4
  evildoer 943.4
  frightener 891.9

  violent person 162.9
Holy Trinity 1013.10
holy war
  military campaign
    797.7
  war 797.3
homage duty 962.1
  fidelity 974.7
  obedience 766.1
  praise 968.5
  respect 964.1
  reverence 964.2
  submission 765.1
  worship 1032.1
hombre 420.4
home
  n. abode 191.4
  asylum 700.4
  grave 121.2
  habitat 191.5
  infirmary 689.27
  native land 181.2
  adj. household 191.32
homebody 924.5
home brew 996.17
homecoming 300.3
home economics
  cooking 330.1
  domestic manage-
    ment 747.6
home free 698.6
home furnishings 831.5
homeground 181.2
homegrown 189.5
home guard 800.23
home in on
  pinpoint 184.10
  use radar 346.17
homeland 181.2
homeless alone 89.8
  destitute 838.9
  displaced 185.10
  forlorn 924.11
homelike
  comfortable 887.11
  habitable 188.15
  homey 191.33
homely
  comfortable 887.11
  common 919.11
  homelike 191.33
  humble 906.9
  informal 647.3
  in plain style 591.3
  simple 902.6
  stark 45.6
  ugly 899.6
  vulgar 898.14
homemade 167.22
homemaker 749.2
homemaking
  domestic manage-
    ment 747.6
  housekeeping 191.2
homeostasis 142.1
homer
  message carrier 561.6
  score 724.4
Homeric huge 195.20
  poetic 609.17
home rule
  government 741.4

  independence 762.5
home run 724.4
homesick 634.23
homesickness 634.5
homespun
  in plain style 591.3
  made 167.22
  natural 736.6
  ordinary 902.6
  rough 261.6
  simple 45.6
  vulgar 898.14
homestead farm 413.8
  home 191.4
  house and grounds
    191.7
homesteader
  settler 190.9
  tenant 809.4
homestretch 70.3
home towner 190.5
homeward
  adj. arriving 300.9
  adv. toward 290.26
homeward bound
  arriving 300.9
  under way 275.63
homework lesson 562.7
  task 656.2
homey
  comfortable 887.11
  homelike 191.33
  informal 647.3
homicidal 409.24
homicide killer 409.11
  killing 409.3
  manslaughter 409.2
homily lecture 599.3
  lesson 562.7
  treatise 606.1
homing pigeon
  bearer 271.5
  message carrier 561.6
hominid
  mankind 417.1
  prehistoric man 123.7
hominy grits 308.34
hommage 968.5
homme 420.4
homo
  homosexual 419.16
  mankind 417.1
  person 417.3
homo– identical 14.8
  similar 20.10
  uniform 17.5
homoerotic 419.32
homogeneity
  identity 14.1
  simplicity 45.1
  uniformity 17.1
homogeneous
  similar 20.10
  simple 45.6
  uniform 17.5
homogenize
  make uniform 17.4
  mix 44.11
homogenizer 44.10
homologous
  approximate 9.8
  reciprocal 13.13

set to work 716.15
horde
  n. the people 919.3
  throng 74.4
  v. come together
  74.16
horehound 687.16
horizon distance 199.3
  sky line 214.4
  view 444.3
  vision 439.1
horizontal
  n. plane 214.3
  adj. level 214.7
  straight 250.6
hormonal 312.8
hormone drug 687.32
  kinds of 312.10
  secretion 312.2
hormonology 312.4
horn
  n. alarm 704.1
  brass wind 465.8
  loudspeaker 450.8
  noisemaker 453.5
  saddle 216.18
  wind instrument
  465.7
  v. attack 798.26
hornbook basics 68.6
  elementary instruc-
  tion 562.5
  textbook 605.8
horned
  horn-shaped 252.11
  pointed 258.11
hornet 414.38
hornet's nest
  hive 191.25
  trouble 731.3
hornify 356.7
horn in 238.5
horn of plenty 661.3
hornswaggle 618.13
horny hard 356.10
  lascivious 989.29
  lustful 419.29
  pointed 258.11
horologic(al) 114.15
horology 114.1
horoscope 375.20
horrendous
  horrid 864.19
  terrible 891.38
horrible bad 675.9
  horrid 864.19
  remarkable 34.11
  terrible 891.38
  ugly 899.11
horribly badly 675.14
  frightfully 891.42
  hideously 899.13
  terribly 34.21
  unpleasantly 864.27
horrid bad 675.9
  horrible 864.19
  terrible 891.38
  ugly 899.11
horridly badly 675.14
  frightfully 891.42
  hideously 899.13
  unpleasantly 864.27

horrified 891.34
horrify offend 864.11
  terrify 891.25
horrifying
  horrid 864.19
  terrible 891.38
horripilate
  be cold 333.9
  frighten 891.23
  roughen 261.4
horripilation
  cold sensation 333.2
  rough surface 261.2
  trepidation 891.5
horror dislike 867.2
  fear 891.1
  frightener 891.9
  torment 866.7
horror-stricken 891.34
hors de combat
  defeated 727.14
  out of action 158.17
hors d'oeuvre 308.9
horse animal 414.10
  beast of burden 271.6
  famous 414.19
  breeds of 414.68
  exercise device 716.7
  heroin 687.12
  mammal 414.58;
  415.8
  strength 159.7
  trestle 216.16,30
horse around
  be disorderly 62.11
  be foolish 470.6
  misbehave 738.4
  play 878.25
  trifle 673.13
horseback
  n. ridge 207.6
  adv. astride 216.25
  on horseback 273.43
horse blanket 228.11
horse doctor
  quack doctor 688.7
  veterinary 688.11
horsehair hair 230.2
  music 465.23
horse latitudes
  calm 268.5
  regions 180.3
  wind zone 403.10
horselaugh 876.4
horseless 349.26
horseman 274.8
horsemanship
  animal husbandry
  416.1
  riding 273.6
  skill 733.1
horse of a different
  color 16.3
horse opera
  fiction 608.7
  motion picture
  611.16
horseplay
  clownishness 881.5
  misbehavior 738.1
horsepower 157.4

horse racing
  game of chance 515.8
  racing 796.11
horse sense 467.6
horseshoe 252.5
horse trader
  cunning person 735.6
  sharper 619.4
horse trading 827.2
horsewhip
  n. whip 1011.1
  v. punish 1010.14
horsy 414.49
hortatory
  advisory 754.8
  lecturing 562.19
  persuasive 648.29
horticultural
  agriculture 413.21
  garden 411.35
horticulture
  agriculture 413.2
  flower gardening
  411.22
hosanna
  n. cheer 876.2
  hymn 1032.3
  interj. worship
  1032.16
hose
  n. hosiery 231.28
  tube 396.6
  v. moisten 392.12
hosiery hose 231.28
  types of 231.61
hospice asylum 700.4
  inn 191.16
hospitable
  comforting 887.13
  cordial 927.15
  gracious 925.11
  liberal 853.4
  receptive 306.16
  sociable 922.18
hospital 689.27
hospitality
  comfortableness
  887.2
  cordiality 927.6
  graciousness 925
  housing 188.3
  liberality 853.1
  receptivity 306.9
  sociability 922.1
hospitalization 689.15
hospitalize 686.47
hospital room 192.25
host
  n. army 800.22
  flock 74.5
  large number 101.3
  mine host 925.5
  throng 74.4
  v. entertain 925.8
Host Eucharist 1040.8
  sacred article 1040.11
hostage 772.2
hostel 191.16
hostess attendant 750.5
  aviation 279.4
  host 925.5
  waiter 750.7

hostile adverse 729.13
  antagonistic 929.10
  belligerent 797.25
  contrary 15.6
  counteractive 178.8
  disagreeing 27.6
  displeased 867.8
  opposing 790.8
hostilities 797.1
hostility
  antagonism 929.3
  bad feeling 855.7
  contention 796.1
  contraposition 239.1
  contrariety 15.1
  dislike 867.2
  opposition 790.2
  warlikeness 797.15
hostler 416.2
hot angry 952.27
  charged 342.31
  detecting 488.10
  enthusiastic about
  635.12
  excellent 674.13
  excited 857.20
  fervent 855.23
  feverish 686.54
  fiery 162.21
  fugitive 631.16
  heated 328.25
  hot-tempered 951.25
  in heat 419.30
  lascivious 989.29
  lustful 419.29
  music 463.29
  near 200.14
  pungent 433.7
  radioactive 327.10
  red 368.6
  stolen 824.22
  warmed 329.29
  zealous 635.10
hot air boasting 910.2
  bombast 601.2
  chatter 596.3
  heat 328.9
  nonsense 547.3
hotbed
  birthplace 153.8
  fertility 165.6
  nursery 413.11
hot blood
  hot temper 951.3
  sexual desire 419.5
hot-blooded
  lustful 419.29
  warm-blooded 328.29
  zealous 635.10
hotbox 322.6
hot cake 308.44
hot dog
  n. sandwich 308.32
  sausage 308.21
  show-off 904.11
  v. be ostentatious
  904.16
  interj. pleasure 865.17
hotel 191.16
hotfoot
  v. hurry 709.6
  run 269.10

sound 452.13
stammer 595.8
human
n. person 417.3
adj. kind 938.13
  mankind 417.10
  pitying 944.7
humane kind 938.13
  lenient 759.7
  pitying 944.7
human factor 80.1
human interest 855.9
humanism
  freethinking 1031.7
  mankind 417.8
  scholarship 475.5
humanist
  freethinker 1031.13
  scholar 476.3
humanitarian
n. philanthropist
  938.8
adj. benevolent
  938.15
humanitarianism 938.4
humanities 562.8
humanity
  humanness 417.5
  kindness 938.1
  leniency 759.1
  mankind 417.1
  pity 944.1
humanize 417.9
human nature
  humanness 417.5
  mankind 417.1
humanoid
n. prehistoric man
  123.7
adj. manlike 417.11
  primitive 123.11
human race 417.1
human rights
  liberties 762.2
  rights 958.5
humble
v. conquer 727.10
  demote 783.3
  humiliate 906.4
  subdue 764.9
adj. common 919.11
  inferior 37.6
  lowly 906.9
  modest 908.9
  penitent 873.9
  resigned 861.10
  unselfish 979.5
  weak 765.15
humbled
  conquered 727.16
  humiliated 906.13
  lowered 906.12
  penitent 873.9
  subdued 764.15
humbly meekly 906.15
  modestly 908.14
  penitently 873.12
humbug
n. fakery 616.3
  falsehood 616.14
  hoax 618.7
  impostor 619.6

nonsense 547.2
quackery 616.7
v. deceive 618.13
humdinger 674.7
humdrum
n. boring person 884.4
  repetitiousness 103.4
  tedium 884.1
adj. monotonous 17.6
  prosaic 610.5
  repetitious 103.15
  tedious 884.8
humid moist 392.15
  sultry 328.28
humidify 392.12
humidity
  dampness 392.2
  sultriness 328.6
humidor cigar 434.4
  humidity instrument
  392.10
humiliate
  disgrace 915.8
  humble 906.4
  mortify 864.13
  offend 965.4
  subdue 764.9
humiliated
  humbled 906.13
  subdued 764.15
humiliating
  disgraceful 915.11
  humbling 906.14
  insulting 965.6
  mortifying 864.21
humiliation
  disgrace 915.5
  humbleness 906.2
  indignity 965.2
  mortification 864.6
  snub 966.2
  subdual 764.4
humility
  humbleness 906
  inferiority 37.1
  meekness 765.5
  modesty 908.1
  resignation 861.2
  unselfishness 979.1
humming
n. hum 452.7
  vocal music 462.12
adj. droning 452.20
hummock 207.5
humor
n. blood 388.4
  body fluid 388.3
  caprice 629.1
  moisture 392.1
  mood 525.4
  nature 5.3
  personality tendency
  690.14
  wit 881.1
v. indulge 759.6
humoral
  endocrine 312.8
  fluid 388.7
humoresque 462.6
humoring 759.3
humorist author 602.15
  wit 881.12

humorless 872.21
humorous
  amusing 878.29
  funny 880.4
  witty 881.15
humorously
  amusingly 880.6
  wittily 881.18
hump
n. bulge 256.3
  mountain 207.7
v. curve 252.6
  exert oneself 716.9
  hurry 709.6
  hustle 707.14
  rush 269.9
humpbacked
  bowed 252.10
  deformed 249.13
humped bowed 252.10
  convex 256.12
  humpbacked 249.13
hun 693.8
Hun 800.7
hunch
n. bulge 256.3
  intuition 481.3
  presentiment 544.1
  unverified supposi-
  tion 499.4
v. crouch 318.8
  curve 252.6
hunchback 249.3
hunchbacked 249.13
hunched 252.10
hundred district 180.5
  number 99.8
hung 215.9
hunger
n. appetite 634.7
  craving 634.6
  eating 307.1
v. crave 634.18
  desire 634.19
  eat 307.18
hungering
  craving 634.24
  hungry 634.25
hungry craving 634.24
  ravenous 634.25
hung up
  distressed 866.22
  late 132.16
  obsessed 473.33
hunk
  accumulation 74.9
  amount 28.2
  lump 195.10
  piece 55.3
hunky-dory 674.13
hunt
n. gunning 655.2
  search 485.14
v. drive out 310.14
  go hunting 655.9
  persecute 667.6
  pursue 655.8
  search 485.30
  seek 485.29
hunt down
  discover 488.2
  hunt 655.9

trace 485.34
hunter horse 414.16
  huntsman 655.5
  pursuer 655.4
  seeker 485.17
  shooter 285.9
  sporting dog 414.23
hunting
n. automation 349.21
  gunning 655.2
  pursuit 655.1
  search 485.14
adj. pursuing 655.11
hurdle
n. jump 319.1
  obstacle 730.4
v. jump 319.5
hurdles, the 319.3
hurdy-gurdy 465.16
hurdy-gurdy man 464.9
hurl
n. throw 285.4
v. attack 798.28
  put violently 184.12
  throw 285.11
hurl a brickbat 965.4
hurly-burly
  agitation 324.1
  excitement 857.3
hurrah
n. cheer 876.2
  cry 459.1
v. cheer 876.6
interj. approval
  968.22
hurricane
  emotional outburst
  857.8
  storm 162.4
  windstorm 403.12
hurried hasty 709.9
  reckless 894.8
  rushed 709.11
hurry
n. excitement 857.3
  haste 709.1
  speed 269.1
v. accelerate 709.4
  bustle 707.12
  hasten off 301.11
  make haste 709.5
  rush 269.9
  urge on 648.16
hurry-scurry
n. excitement 857.3
  haste 709.1
v. make haste 709.5
adv. hastily 709.12
  recklessly 894.11
hurry up
v. accelerate 269.14
  hasten 709.4
  speed 709.5
interj. make haste!
  709.16
hurt
n. disadvantage 671.2
  distress 866.5
  evil 675.3
  impairment 692.1
  injury 692.8
  pain 424.1

v. ache 424.8
collide 283.12
distress 866.17
impair 692.11
injure 692.15
offend 952.20
pain 424.7
suffer 866.19
work evil 675.6
adj. damaged 692.29
distressed 866.23
pained 424.9
hurtful harmful 675.12
painful 424.10
hurting
n. impairment 692.1
pain 424.1
adj. afflicted 424.9
painful 424.10
hurtle collide 283.12
rush 269.9
throw 285.11
thrust 283.11
husband
n. married man 933.8
master 749.1
v. economize 851.4
reserve 660.12
husbandly
adj. loving 931.25
matrimonial 933.19
adv. economically
851.7
husbandry
agriculture 413.1
domestic manage-
ment 747.6
economy 851.1
management 747.1
hush
n. sibilation 457.1
silence 451.1
v. calm 163.7
fall silent 451.7
sibilate 457.2
silence 451.8
suppress 614.8
interj. silence! 451.14
hushed
quiescent 268.12
restrained 163.11
silent 451.10
hush-hush 614.11
hush money
bribe 651.2
fee 841.5
husk
n. hull 228.16
refuse 669.4
remainder 43.1
seed vessel 411.28
v. hull 232.9
husking bee 922.13
husky
n. beast of burden
271.6
adj. raucous 458.15
strong 159.13
hussar 800.11
hussy
impudent person
913.5

unchaste woman
989.14
hustle
n. dance 879.7
enterprise 707.7
haste 709.1
push 283.2
v. be active 707.13
make haste 709.5
shake 324.11
speed 709.4
thrust 283.11
work hard 716.13
hustler
man of action 707.8
prostitute 989.16
speeder 269.5
hut 191.10
hutch
n. hut 191.10
storage place 660.6
v. store 660.10
huzzah
n. cheer 876.2
v. cheer 876.6
Hyades
nymphs 1014.19
star cluster 375.8
hyaline
n. heavens 375.2
adj. glass 339.5
hybrid
n. crossbreed 44.9
hybrid word 582.11
adj. mongrel 44.16
hybridize 44.14
hydrant
extinguisher 332.3
fire hydrant 396.12
hydrate 379.6
hydrated 392.16
hydration 379.5
hydraulic
hydromechanical
347.11
water 392.16
hydraulics fluid 388.2
hydromechanics
347.4
hydro–
hydrogen 401.11
water 392.3
hydrodynamics
dynamics 347.3
hydromechanics
347.4
hydroelectric 342.27
hydrogenate
add gas 401.8
react chemically
379.6
hydrogen bomb
801.15,30
hydrologic 347.11
hydrology 347.4
hydrolysis 53.2
hydrolytic
disintegrative 53.6
electrolytic 342.29
hydrolyze 53.4
hydromechanic(al)
347.11

hydromechanics
hydraulics 347.4
mechanics 347.1
hydrometer
flowmeter 388.5
instrument 354.8
hydrometric(al) 347.11
hydrophobia
animal disease 686.38
infectious disease
686.12
phobia 891.12
rabies 473.6
hydroplane
n. aircraft 280.8
v. fly 278.45
hydroponics
agriculture 413.1
botany 412.1
hydrosphere
ocean 397.1
water 392.3
hydrostatics
aeronautics 278.2
hydromechanics
347.4
statics 347.2
hydrous 392.16
hyena
bad person 986.7
coyote 414.25,58
savage 943.5
hygiene
healthfulness 683.2
sanitation 681.3
hygienic(al)
healthful 683.5
sanitary 681.27
hygienist 683.3
hygrology 392.9
hygrometer
humidity instrument
392.10
weather instrument
402.8
hygroscopic 392.19
hymen
membrane 229.3
wedding song 933.4
Hymen god 1014.5
marriage god 933.14
hymn
n. paean 1032.3
sacred music 462.16
thanks 949.2
v. sing 462.39
worship 1032.11
hymnal
n. music 462.28
adj. vocal 462.51
hymnist 464.20
hype
n. addict 642.10
commendation 968.3
v. commend 968.11
hyped 642.19
hyper– excessive 663.16
external 224.6
fanatical 473.32
high 207.19
large 195.16
hyperactive 707.24

hyperbola 252.2
hyperbole
exaggeration 617.1
excess 663.1
misrepresentation
573.1
hyperborean
cold 333.14
northern 290.15
out-of-the-way 199.9
hypercritical
critical 969.24
overparticular 896.12
Hyperion
beautiful man 900.9
god 1014.5
sun god 375.14
hyperkinesis 707.9
hyperkinetic 707.24
hypersensitive
irascible 951.20
overparticular 896.12
sensitive 422.14
hypersensitivity
ill humor 951.4
overparticularity
896.4
sensitivity 422.3
hypertension
cardiovascular disease
686.17
disease symptom
686.8
hypertensive 686.57
hypertrophy
n. excess 663.1
oversize 195.5
v. overgrow 197.7
hyphenate
n. naturalized citizen
190.4
v. punctuate 586.16
hypnosis
hypnotic sleep 712.7
psychotherapy 690.5
suggestion therapy
690.6
trance 1036.3
hypnotic
n. sedative 687.12
sleep-inducer 712.10
adj. alluring 650.7
engrossing 530.20
mesmeric 712.24
sedative 687.45
sleep-inducing 712.23
hypnotism
hypnotherapy 690.5
mesmerism 712.8
suggestion therapy
690.6
hypnotist 712.9
hypnotize
cast a spell 1036.7
engross 530.13
fascinate 650.6
have influence over
172.11
put to sleep 712.20
hypnotized
astonished 920.9
enchanted 1036.12

engrossed 530.18
hypo 577.13
hypo–
  insufficient 662.9
  lower 208.8
hypochondria
  depression 872.4
  emotional symptom
    690.23
  neurosis 690.19
  unhealthiness 686.2
hypochondriac
  n. pathological type
    690.16
  adj. dejected 872.22
  neurotic 690.45
hypocrisy
  affectation 903.1
  deceit 618.3
  falseness 616.6
  sanctimony 1029.1
hypocrite canter 619.8
  imitator 22.4
  pietist 1029.3
hypocritical
  assumed 903.16
  canting 616.33
  pretexted 649.5
  sanctimonious 1029.5
hypodermic
  n. injection 689.18
  adj. cutaneous 229.6
hypodermis 229.4
hypoglycemia 686.19
hypostasis essence 5.2
  matter 376.2
  noun 586.5
hypostatize 3.5
hypotension 686.8
hypothesis
  premise 482.7
  supposition 499.3
hypothesize
  reason 482.15
  theorize 499.9
hypothetic(al)
  dialectic(al) 482.22
  theoretical 499.13
hypothetically 499.16
hysterectomy 689.23
hysteresis
  automation 349.11
  magnetism 342.7
hysteria
  emotional symptom
    690.23
  excitement 857.7
  neurosis 690.19
hysteric(al)
  emotionalistic 855.20
  excited 857.23
  neurotic 690.45
  overzealous 635.13
hysteron proteron
  inversion 220.3
  jumble 62.3

specious argument
  483.3

I

I one 89.3
  psyche 466.4
  self 80.5
iambic
  n. meter 609.9
  adj. metrical 609.18
ibid. 14.9
ice
  n. brittleness 360.2
  coolant 334.7
  frozen water 333.5
  ice cream 308.46
  jewelry 901.5
  smooth surface 260.3
  v. freeze 334.11
  frost 333.11
  kill 409.14
  refrigerate 334.10
  top 211.9
  adj. frozen 334.14
iceberg 333.5
icebound
  restrained 760.15
  snowbound 333.18
icebox 334.4
ice-cold frozen 334.14
  icy 333.14
ice cream 308.46
iced 334.13
icehouse 334.5
ice pack cooler 334.3
  ice 333.5
ice-skate 273.34
ice skates 272.20
ichor blood 388.4
  body fluid 388.3
  pus 311.6
ichthyologist 415.2
ichthyology 415.1
icicle 333.5
icing frosting 308.39
  topping 211.3
icky bad 675.8
  filthy 682.23
  unsavory 429.7
icon copy 24.1
  image 572.3
  picture 574.12
  sacred article 1040.11
  unit of meaning
    545.6
iconoclasm 1031.9
iconoclast
  destroyer 693.8
  irreligionist 1031.10
iconoclastic 1031.22
iconography 572.1
iconology 568.3
icterus
  disease symptom
    686.8
  liver disease 686.21
  yellow skin 370.2
ictus meter 609.9
  music 463.25
  seizure 686.5
  spasm 324.6

speech accent 594.11
icy cold 333.14
  frozen 334.14
  reticent 613.10
  unfeeling 856.9
  unfriendly 929.9
  unsociable 923.6
id instinct 481.2
  psyche 690.35
ID card 568.11
idea advice 754.1
  belief 501.6
  concept 479
  intention 653.1
  meaning 545.1
  plan 654.1
  small amount 35.4
  thought 478.1
  vague supposition
    499.5
idea, the 153.2
ideal
  n. aspiration 634.9
  good person 985.4
  idea 479.2
  idealization 535.7
  model 25.4
  motive 648.1
  pattern of perfection
    677.4
  adj. ideational 479.9
  model 25.8
  perfect 677.6
  theoretical 499.13
  utopian 535.23
idealism
  aspiration 634.9
  idea 479.2
  idealization 535.7
  immaterialism 377.3
  magnanimity 979.2
  philosophy 500.3
idealist
  n. immaterialist 377.4
  visionary 535.13
  adj. immaterialist
    377.8
idealistic(al)
  immaterialist 377.8
  magnanimous 979.6
  philosophy 500.9
  visionary 535.24
idealization
  idealism 535.7
  illusoriness 519.2
  spiritualism 1034.19
idealize
  overestimate 497.2
  spiritualize 1034.20
  utopianize 535.16
ideally perfectly 677.10
  theoretically 499.16
ideation
  intelligence 467.1
  thought 478.1
  understanding 475.3
ideational ideal 479.9
  imaginative 535.18
  intelligent 467.12
idée fixe 473.13
identical
  equivalent 30.8

same 14.7
  similar 20.10
  twin 90.6
identically alike 14.9
  equally 30.11
  similarly 20.18
identification
  analysis 48.3
  association 690.40
  identification mark
    568.11
  indication 568.1
  naming 583.2
  recognition 537.5
  sensitivity 422.3
  sympathy 855.5
  unification 14.2
identify analyze 48.8
  detect 488.5
  indicate 568.17
  make one 14.5
  name 583.11
  recognize 537.12
  relate 9.6
  use radar 346.17
identify with
  agree with 521.9
  emotionally respond
    855.12
  get along with 794.2
identity accord 794.1
  equality 30.1
  identicalness 14
  particularity 80.1
  similarity 20.1
  unity 89.1
ideogram
  character 581.2
  representation 572.1
  symbol 568.3
ideographic
  indicative 568.23
  literal 581.8
  representational
    572.10
  written 602.26
ideological 479.9
ideology
  pervading attitudes
    525.5
  system of belief
    501.3
  system of ideas 479.8
ides of March 640.2
id est 552.18
idiocy
  foolishness 470.1
  mental deficiency
    469.9
idiom dialect 580.7
  diction 588.1
  language 580.1
  phrase 585.1
idiomatic 580.20
idiosyncrasy
  eccentricity 474.1
  mannerism 903.2
  sign 568.2
  singularity 80.4
  trait of character
    525.3

idiosyncratic(al)
characteristic 80.13
differentiative 16.9
eccentric 474.4
indicative 568.23
personal 417.12
idiot lunatic 473.15
pathological type
690.16
simpleton 471.8
idiot box 345.11
idiotic foolish 470.8
mentally deficient
469.22
idle
v. do nothing 706.2
fritter away 854.5
go slow 270.6
loaf 708.11
stagnate 268.9
trifle 673.13
adj. baseless 483.13
do-nothing 706.6
inactive 708.17
leisure 710.5
motionless 268.13
slow 270.10
trivial 673.16
vain 669.13
idleness
inactivity 708.2
passivity 706.1
slowness 270.1
triviality 673.3
idler loafer 708.8
neglecter 534.5
vagrant 274.3
idle rich 708.10
idle talk chatter 596.3
gossip 558.7
idol
famous person 914.9
favorite 931.15
god 1014.2
good person 985.5
graven image 1033.3
likeness 572.3
idolater devotee 635.6
idol worshiper 1033.4
pagan 1025.7
venerator 1032.9
idolatrize 1033.5
idolatrous
idol worshiping
1033.7
pagan 1025.11
reverent 964.9
uncritical 968.18
idolatry flattery 970.3
idol worship 1033
love 931.1
paganism 1025.4
praise 968.5
respect 964.1
word list 1033.8
idolistic 1033.7
idolization
deification 1033.2
love 931.1
respect 964.1
word list 1033.8
idolize cherish 931.19

flatter 970.7
idolatrize 1033.5
praise 968.12
respect 964.4
worship 1032.10
idol worship 1033.1
idyll 609.6
idyllic pacific 803.9
poetic 609.17
i.e. 552.18
if
in the event that
151.13
provided that 507.14
supposing that
499.19
iffy chance 156.15
uncertain 514.16
if necessary 639.17
igloo arch 252.4
house 191.11
snow 333.8
igneous 328.26
ignis fatuus fire 328.13
illusion 519.1
phosphorescence
335.13
ignite
become angry 952.18
set fire to 329.22
ignited 328.27
ignition fire 328.13
kindling 329.4
rocketry 281.9
ignobility infamy 915.4
offensiveness 864.2
vulgarity 898.5
ignoble
disreputable 915.10
offensive 864.18
vulgar 898.15
ignominious
disreputable 915.10
wrong 959.3
ignominy infamy 915.4
wrong 959.2
ignoramus fool 471.1
know-nothing 477.8
novice 566.9
ignorance
inexperience 734.2
stupidity 469.1
unaccustomedness
643.1
unknowingness 477
ignorant
inexperienced 734.17
unaccustomed 643.4
unintelligent 469.13
unknowing 477.12
ignore
be broad-minded
526.7
condone 947.4
disobey 767.6
disregard 531.2
endure 861.7
exclude 77.4
extenuate 1006.12
neglect 534.6
reject 638.2
slight 966.6

ignored
neglected 534.14
rejected 638.3
unthanked 950.5
ileac 225.10
ileum 225.4
ilk kind 61.3
nature 5.3
ill
n. evil 675.3
adj. bad 675.7
ominous 544.17
sick 686.52
unkind 939.14
adv. badly 675.13
disadvantageously
671.9
unkindly 939.25
ill-advised see ill-
considered
ill at ease 866.22
ill-behaved 937.5
ill-bred
discourteous 937.6
uncouth 898.12
ill-conceived 675.11
ill-considered
botched 734.21
impulsive 630.11
inexpedient 671.5
premature 131.8
untimely 130.7
unwise 470.9
illegal prohibited 778.7
unjust 977.9
unlawful 999.6
wrong 959.3
illegality crime 999.4
injustice 977.1
unlawfulness 999
wrong 959.1
illegible 549.19
illegitimate
n. bastard 171.5
adj. illegal 999.6
spurious 999.7
ungenuine 616.26
ill-equipped
ill-provided 662.12
unfit 721.9
ill-fated 544.17
ill-favored
evil-fashioned 675.11
ugly 899.7
ill-founded 483.13
ill-gotten
dishonest 975.16
evil-fashioned 675.11
ill-gotten gains 824.11
ill health 686.2
ill humor
bad temper 951
contentiousness
482.13
discontent 869.1
ill-humored
argumentative 482.19
bad-tempered 951.18
illiberal
n. intolerant person
527.5

adj. narrow-minded
527.10
selfish 978.6
stingy 852.9
illicit illegal 999.6
prohibited 778.7
unchaste 989.27
illicit business
fraud 618.8
illegality 999.1
illegitimate business
826
illiteracy 477.5
illiterate
n. ignoramus 477.8
adj. unlearned 477.14
ill nature
ill humor 951.1
malevolence 939.4
ill-natured
ill-humored 951.18
malevolent 939.17
illness 686.1
ill off
ill-provided 662.12
poor 838.7
unfortunate 729.14
illogic 483.2
illogical
erroneous 518.16
unreasonable 483.11
ill repute 915.1
ill-suited
inappropriate 27.7
inexpedient 671.5
ill-timed
inappropriate 27.7
inexpedient 671.5
untimely 130.7
illuminant
n. light 335.20
light source 336.1
adj. luminous 335.30
illuminate color 362.13
explain 552.10
indicate 555.5
light up 335.28
ornament 901.9
illuminated
drunk 996.31
lit up 335.39
illuminating
educational 562.19
explanatory 552.15
lighting 335.40
illumination
applying color 362.11
explanation 552.4
learning 475.4
lighting 335.19
ornamentation 901.1
painting 574.5
picture 574.12
radiation 335.1
teaching 562.1
ill-use
n. mistreatment 667.2
use 665.1
v. mistreat 667.5
use badly 665.16
illusion
bewitchment 1036.2

immigrant
  incomer 302.4
  migrant 274.5
  naturalized citizen
    190.4
  newcomer 78.4
  settler 190.9
immigrate enter 302.11
  migrate 273.21
immigration
  influx 302.3
  migration 273.4
imminence
  approach 296.1
  expectation 539.1
  impendence 152
  the future 121.1
  threat 973.1
imminent
  approaching 296.4
  expected 539.13
  future 121.8
  impending 152.3
  threatening 973.3
immobile
  do-nothing 706.6
  motionless 268.13
  permanent 140.7
  stationary 142.15
immobility
  dormancy 706.1
  immovability 142.3
  inactivity 708.1
  motionlessness 268.2
  permanence 140.1
immobilize 142.7
immoderate
  excessive 663.16
  intemperate 993.7
  overpriced 848.12
  unrestrained 762.23
  violent 162.15
immodest
  conceited 909.11
  shameless 990.6
immodesty
  conceit 909.4
  shamelessness 990.2
immolate kill 409.13
  offer sacrifice
    1032.14
immolation
  killing 409.1
  oblation 1032.7
immoral
  dishonest 975.16
  vice-laden 981.11
immorality 981.1
immortal
  n. famous person
    914.9
  god 1014.2
  adj. eminent 914.18
  everlasting 112.9
  godlike 1013.20
  indestructible 142.18
  peerless 36.15
immortality
  eternal life 112.3
  indestructibility
    142.5
  life 407.1

  posthumous fame
    914.7
immortalize
  glorify 914.13
  perpetuate 112.5
immortalized 914.18
immovable firm 624.12
  rigid 356.12
  stationary 142.15
  unfeeling 856.9
  unyielding 626.9
immune
  exempt 762.29
  resistant 685.12
  safe 698.4
immunity
  exemption 1007.2
  freedom 762.8
  immunology 689.17
  pardon 947.2
  resistance 685.4
  right 958.4
  safety 698.1
immunization
  immunity 685.4
  medical treatment
    689.17
immunize 689.34
immunized 698.4
immunology 689.17
immure confine 761.12
  enclose 236.6
  imprison 761.14
immured
  enclosed 236.10
  jailed 761.21
immutable
  enduring 110.10
  godlike 1013.20
  permanent 140.7
  persevering 625.7
  rigid 356.12
  unchangeable 142.17
  uniform 17.5
  unyielding 626.9
imp bad child 125.4
  branch 55.4
  evil spirit 1016.8
  fairy 1014.18
  mischief-maker 738.3
impact
  n. collision 283.3
  concussion 162.8
  effect 154.3
  meaning 545.1
  rocketry 281.9
  v. impress 142.9
  thrust in 304.7
impair damage 692.11
  subtract 42.9
  work evil 675.6
impaired
  damaged 692.29
  imperfect 678.4
impairment
  damage 692
  disadvantage 671.2
  imperfection 678.1
  reduction 42.2
impale
  puncture 265.16
  punish 1010.18

  stab 798.25
  torture 866.18
impalpable
  immaterial 377.7
  infinitesimal 196.14
  powdery 361.11
  unsubstantial 4.5
impanel
  enroll a jury 1004.15
  list 88.8
  record 570.16
impanelment
  jury selection 1004.4
  recording 570.15
impart
  communicate 554.7
  disclose 556.4
  give 818.12
  say 594.23
  transfer 271.9
impartable
  communicable
    554.11
  giveable 818.23
  transferable 271.17
impartial just 976.10
  neutral 806.7
  unprejudiced 526.12
impartiality
  justice 976.4
  moderation 163.1
  neutrality 806.1
  unprejudicedness
    526.5
impassable 266.13
impasse corner 731.5
  dead end 266.3
impassion excite 857.11
  incite 648.17
impassioned
  amorous 931.24
  eloquent 600.13
  excited 857.18
  fervent 855.23
  zealous 635.10
impassive calm 268.12
  incurious 529.3
  inexcitable 858.10
  inexpressive 549.20
  reticent 613.10
  unfeeling 856.9
impatience
  eagerness 635.1
  impulsiveness 630.2
  restlessness 862
impatient eager 635.9
  impulsive 630.9
  restless 862.6
impatiently
  eagerly 635.14
  restlessly 862.8
impeach accuse 1005.7
  arraign 1004.14
  censure 969.13
impeachable
  blameworthy 969.26
  guilty 983.3
impeached 1005.15
impeachment
  accusation 1005.1
  arraignment 1004.3
  deposal 783.2

  disapproval 969.3
impeccable
  innocent 984.7
  perfect 677.6
impecunious 838.7
impedance 342.12
impede delay 132.8
  hamper 730.11
  hinder 730.10
  slow 270.9
impediment
  burden 730.6
  hindrance 730.1
  obstruction 266.3
impedimenta
  belongings 810.3
  equipment 659.4
  freight 271.7
  hindrances 730.6
impeding 730.18
impel compel 756.4
  motivate 648.12
  obsess 473.24
  push 285.10
  set in motion 267.6
  thrust 283.10
impelled 648.30
impelling
  driving 283.20
  motivating 648.25
  moving 267.7
  obsessive 473.34
impend
  be imminent 152.2
  expect 539.10
  overhang 215.7
impending
  imminent 152.3
  overhanging 215.11
impenetrable
  dense 354.12
  growing rank 411.40
  impervious 266.13
  impregnable 159.17
  inaccessible 510.9
  unintelligible 549.13
impenitent 874.5
imperative
  n. command 752.1
  duty 962.1
  mood 586.11
  precept 751.2
  urgent need 639.4
  adj. authoritative
    739.15
  binding 962.15
  commanding 752.14
  compelling 756.9
  eloquent 600.11
  imperious 739.16
  mandatory 752.13
  necessary 639.12
  obligatory 756.10
  urgent 672.21
imperatively
  authoritatively
    739.18
  commandingly
    752.15
  compulsively 756.12
imperceptible
  infinitesimal 196.14

take liberties 961.7
imposing
 corpulent 195.18
 dignified 905.12
 grandiose 904.21
 weighty 672.19
imposition
 demand 753.1
 fraud 618.8
 impediment 730.6
 infliction 963
 injustice 977.4
 intrusion 238.1
 presumption 961.2
 tax 846.10
 typesetting 603.2
impossibility
 inconceivability 510
 no chance 156.10
 no hope 889.1
impossible
 adj. fantastic 85.12
 hopeless 889.14
 not possible 510.7
 numerical 86.8
 unacceptable 869.7
 interj. refusal 776.7
impost demand 753.1
 tax 846.10
impostor fake 616.13
 imitator 22.4
 ringer 619.6
imposture fakery 616.3
 fraud 618.8
 imitation 22.1
 quackery 616.7
impotence
 futility 669.2
 lack of influence
  173.1
 powerlessness 158
 sexuality 419.2
 unproductiveness
  166.1
 unstrictness 758.1
 weakness 160.1
impotent
 n. weakling 158.6
 adj. powerless 158.13
 sterile 166.4
 uninfluential 173.3
 unsexual 419.31
 unstrict 758.4
 useless 669.9
 weak 160.12
impound
 appropriate 822.20
 confine 761.12
 enclose 236.5
impoverish
 bankrupt 842.8
 consume 666.2
 despoil 822.24
 pauperize 838.6
impoverished
 ill-provided 662.12
 indigent 838.8
 meager 662.10
 used up 666.4
impractical
 theoretical 499.13
 unfeasible 510.8

unwieldy 731.18
 visionary 535.24
impracticality
 idealization 535.7
 impossibility 510.2
 unwieldiness 731.8
imprecation
 curse 972.1
 entreaty 774.2
imprecatory 972.8
imprecise
 imperfect 678.4
 inaccurate 518.17
 ungrammatical 587.4
 unstrict 758.4
 vague 514.18
impregnable
 impenetrable 159.17
 indestructible 142.18
impregnate
 fertilize 165.8
 indoctrinate 562.13
 infuse 44.12
 inseminate 169.10
 soak 392.13
impregnated 169.17
impregnation
 fertilization 165.3
 imbuement 44.2
 indoctrination 562.2
 insemination 169.3
 soaking 392.7
impresario
 manager 748.1
 theater man 611.28
impress
 n. characteristic 80.4
 copy 24.5
 effect 154.3
 indentation 257.6
 mark 568.7
 print 578.6
 printing 603.3
 v. abduct 824.19
 affect emotionally
  855.17
 appropriate 822.20
 avail oneself of
  665.14
 enlist 780.16
 fix in the mind
  537.18
 grab the thoughts
  478.19
 impact 142.9
 indent 257.14
 indoctrinate 562.13
 mark 568.19
 print 603.14
impressed
 affected 855.25
 engraved 578.12
 infixed 142.13
impression
 aspect 446.3
 belief 501.6
 characteristic 80.4
 concavity 257.1
 copy 24.5
 description 608.1
 edition 605.2
 effect 154.3

emotion 855.3
 form 246.1
 hunch 481.3
 idea 479.1
 imitation 22.1
 indentation 257.6
 indoctrination 562.2
 mark 568.7
 print 578.6
 printing 603.3
 vague supposition
  499.5
impressionability
 emotional capacity
  855.4
 influenceability 172.5
 physical sensibility
  422.2
 pliancy 357.2
 teachability 564.5
impressionable
 emotionable 855.21
 influenceable 172.15
 pliant 357.9
 receptive 422.13
 teachable 564.18
impressive
 convincing 501.26
 eloquent 600.11
 exciting 857.28
 grandiose 904.21
 receptive 422.13
impressively
 eloquently 600.15
 exceptionally 34.20
 grandiosely 904.28
impressment
 abduction 824.8
 appropriation 822.5
 enlistment 780.6
imprimatur
 permit 777.6
 ratification 521.4
imprint
 n. book 605.12
 effect 154.3
 indentation 257.6
 label 568.13
 mark 568.7
 print 578.6
 printing 603.3
 v. fix in the mind
  537.18
 imbed 142.9
 indent 257.14
 mark 568.19
 print 603.14
imprinted
 engraved 578.12
 infixed 142.13
imprison enclose 236.5
 incarcerate 761.14
imprisoned
 enclosed 236.10
 jailed 761.21
imprisonment
 enclosure 236.1
 jailing 761.3
 punishment 1010.2
improbability
 inexpectation 540.1
 odd thing 85.5

small chance 156.9
 unlikelihood 512
improbable
 farfetched 10.7
 unexpected 540.10
 unlikely 512.3
improbity
 dishonesty 975
 falseheartedness
  616.4
impromptu
 n. improvisation 630.5
 music 462.27
 adj. extemporaneous
  630.12
 unprepared 721.8
 adv. extemporane-
  ously 630.15
improper bad 675.7
 evil 981.16
 inappropriate 27.7
 indecent 990.5
 inexpedient 671.5
 infelicitous 590.2
 misbehaving 738.5
 undue 961.10
 ungrammatical 587.4
 untimely 130.7
 vulgar 898.10
 wrong 959.3
improperly
 unduly 34.21
 vulgarly 898.16
 wrongly 959.4
impropriety
 indecency 990.1
 injustice 977.1
 literary inelegance
  590.1
 misbehavior 738.1
 offense 982.2
 undueness 961.1
 unfitness 27.3
 untimeliness 130.1
 vulgarity 898.1
 word 582.6
 wrong 959.1
improvable
 ameliorable 691.17
 remediable 694.25
improve
 be changed 139.5
 change 139.6
 excel 36.6
 get better 691.7
 make better 691.9
 make perfect 677.5
 recuperate 694.19
 take advantage of
  665.15
 train 562.14
improved
 bettered 691.13
 changed 139.9
improvement
 betterment 691
 change 139.1
 reformation 145.2
 restoration 694.1
 training 562.3
improvidence
 rashness 894.1

thriftlessness 721.2
improvident rash 894.7
thriftless 721.15
improvisation
creation 167.5
expedient 670.2
extemporization
630.5
music 462.27
unpreparedness 721.1
improvisational 670.7
improvisational drama
611.4
improvise
be unprepared 721.6
create 167.13
extemporize 630.8
improvised
extemporaneous
630.12
makeshift 670.7
unprepared 721.8
imprudence
foolish act 470.4
indiscrimination
493.1
rashness 894.1
unwiseness 470.2
imprudent rash 894.7
undiscriminating
493.5
unwise 470.9
impudence
defiance 793.1
disrespect 965.1
impertinence 913.2
rashness 894.1
impudent
defiant 793.7
disrespectful 965.5
impertinent 913.9
rash 894.7
impugn censure 969.13
deny 524.4
incriminate 1005.10
impugned
accused 1005.15
disproved 506.7
impulse
impulsiveness 630
instinct 481.2
involuntariness 639.5
power 157.4
prematurity 131.2
thrust 283
urge 648.6
impulsive
impelling 283.20
impetuous 630.9
inconstant 18.3
instinctive 481.6
involuntary 639.14
mercurial 141.7
motivating 648.25
precipitate 709.10
premature 131.8
sudden 113.5
transient 111.7
impulsively
impetuously 630.13
nonuniformly 18.4
precipitously 709.15

prematurely 131.13
suddenly 113.9
impulsiveness
hastiness 709.2
impetuousness 630.2
inconstancy 141.2
prematurity 131.2
impunity 1007.2
impure imperfect 678.4
infelicitous 590.2
obscene 990.9
unchaste 989.23
unclean 682.20
unrighteous 981.12
impurity
foreign body 78.2
immorality 981.1
imperfection 678.1
literary inelegance
590.1
unchastity 989.1
uncleanness 682.1
imputable
attributable 155.6
blameworthy 969.26
imputation
accusation 1005.1
attribution 155.1
disapproval 969.4
disparagement 971.4
stigma 915.6
impute accuse 1005.7
attribute 155.3
in
n. access 306.3
entrance 302.5
good terms 927.3
adj. entering 302.12
friendly 927.17
modern 122.13
adv. inside 225.12
inward 302.13
prep. into 302.14
located 184.26
within 225.15
in a bad way
in danger 697.13
sick 686.52
worn-out 692.38
inability
incapability 158.2
unskillfulness 734.1
in a bind
in a predicament
731.20
late 132.16
inaccessible
out-of-the-way 199.9
reticent 613.10
unaccessible 510.9
unsociable 923.6
inaccordant
different 16.7
disagreeing 27.6
inaccuracy
imperfection 678.1
incorrectness 518.2
misrepresentation
573.1
unmeticulousness
534.4
vagueness 514.4

inaccurate
imperfect 678.4
incorrect 518.17
unmeticulous 534.13
vague 514.18
inaction
inactiveness 708.1
motionlessness 268.2
passiveness 706
in action acting 705.10
operating 164.11
inactivate 158.9
inactive
do-nothing 706.6
idle 708.16
inert 268.14
leisurely 710.6
inactivity
inactiveness 708
leisureliness 710.2
motionlessness 268.2
passivity 706.1
rest 711.1
inadequacy fault 678.2
imperfection 678.1
inability 158.2
incompleteness 57.1
inequality 31.1
inferiority 37.3
insufficiency 662.1
shortcoming 314.1
unsatisfactoriness
869.2
unskillfulness 734.1
inadequate
imperfect 678.4
incompetent 734.19
incomplete 57.4
ineffective 158.15
inferior 37.7
insufficient 662.9
short of 314.5
unequal 31.4
unsatisfactory 869.6
inadequately
imperfectly 678.5
incompletely 57.6
insufficiently 662.14
unsatisfactorily
869.9
unskillfully 734.23
inadmissible
exclusive 77.8
inappropriate 27.7
irrelevant 10.6
unacceptable 869.7
in advance
before 292.4
early 131.11
in front 240.12
on loan 820.7
prior to 116.7
inadvertence
an error 518.4
inattention 531.1
neglect 534.1
inadvertent
impulsive 630.10
inattentive 531.6
negligent 534.10
unpremeditated
630.11

inadvertently
negligently 534.17
unpremeditatedly
630.14
inadvisable
inexpedient 671.5
unwise 470.9
inalienable
inseparable 47.15
intrinsic 5.6
unimpartable 813.10
in all conscience
candidly 974.23
in justice 976.12
positively 34.19
reasonably 482.24
rightly 958.9
in all respects
exactly 516.20
throughout 56.17
wholly 54.13
inalterable 625.7
in a manner of speaking
figuratively 551.4
so to speak 20.19
to a degree 35.10
inamorata 931.14
inamorato 931.12
inane foolish 470.8
ignorant 477.12
ineffective 158.15
insipid 430.2
meaningless 547.6
stupid 469.19
thoughtless 480.4
trivial 673.16
uninteresting 883.6
vacant 187.13
vain 669.13
inanimate
n. gender 586.10
adj. dead 408.30
inanimated 382.5
languid 708.19
inanity
foolishness 470.1
futility 669.2
ignorant 477.1
ineffectiveness 158.3
insipidness 430.1
meaninglessness
547.1
stupidity 469.6
thoughtlessness 480.1
triviality 673.3
uninterestingness
883.1
void 187.3
in a nutshell
concisely 592.8
in summary 607.7
on a small scale
196.16
in any case
anyhow 657.12
in the event that
151.13
notwithstanding 33.8
inappetence
apathy 856.4
undesirousness 636.3

inapplicable
  inappropriate 27.7
  irrelevant 10.6
  unserviceable 669.14
inapposite
  inappropriate 27.7
  irrelevant 10.6
inappreciable
  infinitesimal 196.14
  unimportant 673.15
inapprehensible 549.13
inappropriate
  inapt 27.7
  indecent 990.5
  inexpedient 671.5
  irrelevant 10.6
  undue 961.10
  untimely 130.7
  vulgar 898.10
  wrong 959.3
inappropriately 671.8
inappropriateness
  indecency 990.1
  inexpedience 671.1
  undueness 961.1
  unfitness 27.3
  untimeliness 130.1
  vulgarity 898.1
  wrong 959.1
inapt
  inappropriate 27.7
  inexpedient 671.5
  unskillful 734.15
inaptitude
  inexpedience 671.1
  unfitness 27.3
  unskillfulness 734.1
inarticulate
  imperfectly spoken
    595.12
  mute 451.12
  shy 908.12
  unintelligible 549.13
inartificial
  genuine 516.14
  natural 736.6
  plain 902.7
  undeveloped 721.13
inartistic 899.10
in a rut
  habituated 642.19
  uniformly 17.7
inasmuch as 155.10
in a spot 731.20
in a stew angry 952.28
  anxious 890.6
  bewildered 514.23
  confused 532.12
  excited 857.19
  impatient 862.6
inattention
  distraction 532.1
  heedlessness 531
  neglect 534.1
  nonobservance 769.1
  unconcern 636.2
  unwiseness 470.2
inattentive
  heedless 531.6
  negligent 534.10
  nonobservant 769.5
  unconcerned 636.7

unskillful 734.15
inaudible 451.10
inaugural
  n. ceremony 646.4
  speech 599.2
  adj. beginning 68.15
  preceding 64.4
  preliminary 66.4
inaugurate begin 68.11
  create 167.12
  innovate 122.5
  install 780.11
  instate 304.4
  originate 153.11
inauguration
  beginning 68.5
  ceremony 646.4
  initiation 306.2
  installation 184.6
  production 167.4
  taking office 780.3
inauspicious bad 675.7
  ominous 544.17
  unfortunate 729.14
  untimely 130.7
inauthentic
  illogical 483.11
  unauthoritative
    518.19
in a way
  somewhat 29.7
  so to speak 20.19
  to a degree 35.10
inbeing 5.1
inborn 5.7
inbound arriving 300.9
  entering 302.12
inbred bred 169.17
  innate 5.7
inbreed 169.8
in cahoots
  cooperatively 786.7
  joined 52.6
incalculable
  infinite 104.3
  innumerable 101.10
  uncertain 514.15
  unknown 477.17
in camera 614.19
incandesce
  be hot 328.22
  glow 335.23
incandescence
  heat 328.12
  shine 335.2
incandescent
  burning 328.27
  luminous 335.30
incantation
  conjuration 1035.4
  spell 1036.4
incapability
  inability 158.2
  unpreparedness 721.1
  unskillfulness 734.1
incapable
  n. cripple 686.42
  unskillful person
    734.7
  adj. incompetent
    734.19
  unable 158.14

unfit 721.9
incapacitate
  cripple 692.17
  disable 158.9
  sicken 686.47
incapacitated
  crippled 692.32
  disabled 158.16
  weakened 160.18
incapacity
  inability 158.2
  stupidity 469.1
  unskillfulness 734.1
  weakness 160.3
incarcerate
  enclose 236.5
  imprison 761.14
incarcerated
  enclosed 236.10
  jailed 761.21
incarceration
  enclosure 236.1
  imprisonment 761.3
  punishment 1010.2
incarnate
  v. embody 3.5
  indicate 555.5
  materialize 376.8
  represent 572.8
  adj. Christlike
    1013.19
  embodied 376.10
  innate 5.7
incarnation
  appearance 446.1
  embodiment 3.4
  impersonation 572.2
  manifestation 555.1
  materialization 376.7
in case 151.13
incautious
  inattentive 531.8
  rash 894.7
incendiarism 329.7
incendiary
  n. arsonist 329.8
  instigator 648.11
  violent person 162.9
  adj. incitive 648.28
  inflammatory 329.27
incense
  n. flattery 970.1
  fragrance 436.1
  oblation 1032.7
  rite 1040.4
  suavity 936.5
  types of 436.4
  v. excite 857.11
  incite 648.17
  provoke 952.22
  scent 436.8
incensed 952.26
incensory 436.6
incentive
  n. impulse 283.1
  inducement 648.7
  adj. incitive 648.28
inception origin 68.4
  production 167.4
  source 153.5
inceptive 68.15
incertitude 514.1

incessancy
  constancy 135.2
  continuity 71.1
  perpetuity 112.1
incessant
  constant 135.5
  continuous 71.8
  perpetual 112.7
  recurrent 103.13
incessantly
  constantly 135.7
  continuously 71.10
  perpetually 112.10
incest adultery 989.7
  sexual preference
    419.12
incestuous 989.27
inch
  n. short distance
    200.2
  v. creep 273.25
  go slow 270.6
  make one's way 294.4
in charge
  governing 741.18
  in authority 739.21
  supervising 747.13
  under arrest 761.22
inchmeal
  gradually 29.6
  piece by piece 55.9
inchoate
  beginning 68.15
  formless 247.4
  unordered 62.12
  vague 514.18
inchoative 586.13
incidence event 151.1
  frequency 135.1
incident
  circumstance 8.1
  event 151.2
  story element 608.9
incidental
  n. music 463.18
  nonessential 6.2
  particular 8.3
  adj. casual 129.11
  chance 156.15
  circumstantial 8.7
  happening 151.9
  irrelevant 10.6
  occasional 136.3
  unessential 6.4
incidentally
  by chance 156.19
  by the way 129.13
incinerate burn 329.25
  cremate 410.20
  destroy 693.10
  strike dead 409.18
incineration
  burning 329.5
  cremation 410.2
incinerator 329.13
incipiency 68.4
incipient
  beginning 68.15
  dwarf 196.13
incise cleave 201.4
  engrave 578.10
  groove 263.3

injure 692.15
notch 262.4
open 265.12
record 570.16
sever 49.11
incised
engraved 578.12
grooved 263.4
notched 262.5
incision crack 201.2
engraving 578.2
groove 263.1
impairment 692.8
notch 262.1
incisive
acrimonious 161.13
caustic 939.21
eloquent 600.11
energetic 161.12
sagacious 467.16
incisor 258.5
incite advise 754.6
excite 857.11
impel 283.10
instigate 648.17
incitement
excitation 857.10
impulse 283.1
incentive 648.7
inducement 648.4
incitive 648.28
incivility
discourtesy 937.1
uncouthness 898.3
inclemency cold 333.1
pitilessness 945.1
unkindness 939.9
violence 162.1
inclement cold 333.14
pitiless 945.3
unkind 939.22
inclination
aptitude 733.5
descent 316.1
desire 634.3
direction 290.1
injustice 977.3
obeisance 964.2
obliquity 219.2
preference 637.5
prejudice 527.3
slope 219.4
tendency 174.1
trait of character 525.3
will 621.1
incline
n. slope 219.4
stairs 315.3
v. bear 290.8
be willing 622.3
gravitate 352.15
induce 648.22
influence 172.7
lean 219.10
prefer 637.17
take an attitude 525.6
tend 174.3
inclined
desirous of 634.22
minded 525.8

motivated 648.30
oblique 219.15
prone to 174.6
tending to 174.5
willing 622.5
inclining
oblique 219.15
tending 174.4
in clover
in comfort 887.15
pleased 865.12
prosperous 728.12
include combine 52.3
comprise 76.3
enclose 236.5
internalize 225.6
join 47.5
included
comprised 76.5
involved 176.3
including
adj. composed of 58.4
containing 76.6
prep. with 40.12
inclusion
affiliation 786.2
combination 52.1
comprisal 76
enclosure 236.1
involvement 176.1
surrounding 233.5
inclusive
containing 76.6
joint 47.12
whole 54.9
inclusive of
composed of 58.4
with 40.12
incognito
n. anonymity 584.1
disguise 618.10
masquerader 619.7
privacy 614.2
adj. anonymous 584.3
disguised 615.13
private 614.13
incognizance 477.3
incognizant 477.13
incoherent
delirious 473.31
discontinuous 72.4
inconsistent 27.8
separate 49.20
uncohesive 51.4
unintelligible 549.13
vague 514.18
in cold blood
heartlessly 939.32
intentionally 653.11
unfeelingly 856.14
incombustible 332.9
income entrance 302.1
gain 811.3
receipts 844.1
remuneration 841.4
income tax 846.11
incoming
n. entrance 302.1
adj. arriving 300.9
entering 302.12
incommensurable
dissimilar 21.6

incomparable 491.9
inconsistent 27.8
unrelated 10.5
incommensurate
dissimilar 21.6
inconsistent 27.8
unsatisfactory 869.6
incommodious
inconvenient 671.7
narrow 205.14
incommunicable
indescribable 920.13
unimpartable 813.10
incommunicado 615.11
incommutable 142.17
incomparable
dissimilar 21.6
incommensurable 491.9
peerless 36.15
unrelated 10.5
incomparably
peerlessly 36.18
superlatively 36.16
incompatibility
difference 16.1
disaccord 795.1
enmity 929.1
inconsistency 27.2
unsociability 923.1
incompatible
different 16.7
disagreeing 27.6
inconsistent 27.8
unfriendly 929.9
unsociable 923.5
incompetence
inability 158.2
inferiority 37.3
insufficiency 662.1
unpreparedness 721.1
unskillfulness 734.1
incompetent
n. impotent 158.6
unskillful person 734.7
adj. incapable 734.19
inferior 37.7
insufficient 662.9
unable 158.14
unfit 721.9
incomplete
deficient 57.4
imperfect 678.4
insufficient 662.9
partial 55.7
incompletely
imperfectly 678.5
insufficiently 662.14
partially 57.6
somewhat 35.10
incompleteness
deficiency 57
discontinuity 72.1
imperfection 678.1
want 662.4
incomprehensible
fantastic 85.12
infinite 104.3
unintelligible 549.13
wonderful 920.10

incomprehension
incognizance 477.3
unperceptiveness 469.2
incompressible 354.12
inconceivable
fantastic 85.12
impossible 510.7
unbelievable 503.10
wonderful 920.10
inconclusive
illogical 483.11
unproved 506.8
unsubstantial 483.12
in condition
healthy 685.7
in order 59.7
state of being 7.8
incongruity
difference 16.1
humorousness 880.1
illogicalness 483.2
inconsistency 27.2
inexpedience 671.1
nonconformity 83.1
incongruous
clashingly colored 362.20
different 16.7
humorous 880.4
illogical 483.11
inconsistent 27.8
inexpedient 671.5
inconsequence
unimportance 673.1
unrelatedness 10.1
inconsequent
illogical 483.11
inconsistent 27.8
irrelevant 10.6
inconsequential
illogical 483.11
insignificant 35.6
unimportant 673.15
inconsiderable
insignificant 35.6
unimportant 673.15
inconsiderate
careless 534.11
discourteous 937.6
impulsive 630.10
unthoughtful 939.16
unwise 470.9
inconsistency
contrariety 15.1
difference 16.1
illogicalness 483.2
incongruity 27.2
inconstancy 141.2
noncohesion 51.1
nonconformity 83.1
nonuniformity 18.1
inconsistent
contrary 15.6
different 16.7
illogical 483.11
incoherent 51.4
incongruous 27.8
inconstant 141.7
nonuniform 18.3
inconsolable 872.28

inconsonant
different 16.7
inconsistent 27.8
inconspicuous 445.6
inconstancy
fickleness 629.3
infidelity 975.5
instability 141.2
irregularity 138.1
irresolution 627.1
nonuniformity 18.1
inconstant
changeable 141.7
fickle 629.6
irregular 138.3
nonobservant 769.5
nonuniform 18.3
transient 111.7
unfaithful 975.20
incontestable
certain 513.15
invincible 159.17
incontinence
excess 663.1
greed 634.8
intemperance 993.1
prodigality 854.1
unchastity 989.2
unrestraint 762.3
incontinent
excessive 663.16
intemperate 993.7
prodigal 854.8
unchaste 989.24
unrestrained 762.23
incontrovertible
certain 513.15
evidential 505.17
inconvenience
n. disadvantage 671.3
impediment 730.6
imposition 963.1
inexpedience 671.1
trouble 731.3
untimeliness 130.1
unwieldiness 731.8
v. discommode 671.4
take liberties 961.7
trouble 731.12
inconvenient
disadvantageous 671.7
untimely 130.7
unwieldy 731.18
inconvertible
unchangeable 142.17
unpayable 842.13
inconvincible 504.4
incorporate
combine 52.3
compose 58.3
embody 376.8
include 76.3
incorporated
associated 788.16
combined 52.5
embodied 376.10
joined 47.13
incorporation
affiliation 786.2
combination 52.1
composition 58.1

embodiment 376.7
inclusion 76.1
incorporative 52.7
incorporeal
n. immatereality 377.2
specter 1017.1
adj. ghostly 1017.7
immaterial 377.7
unsubstantial 4.5
incorporeality
immateriality 377.1
rarity 355.1
unsubstantiality 4.1
incorrect
inaccurate 518.17
infelicitous 590.2
ungrammatical 587.4
wrong 959.3
incorrectly
inaccurately 518.21
wrongly 959.4
incorrigible
confirmed 642.21
hopeless 889.15
irreclaimable 981.18
ungovernable 626.12
incorrupt
innocent 984.6
virtuous 980.9
incorruptible
immortal 112.9
indestructible 142.18
trustworthy 974.19
incrassate
v. fatten 204.5
make viscid 389.10
thicken 354.10
adj. distended 197.13
thickened 354.14
increase
n. addition 40.1
adjunct 41.1
aggravation 885.1
ascent 315.1
expansion 197.1
gain 38
multiplication 100.4
winnings 38.3
v. add to 40.5
advance 38.6
aggravate 885.2
amplify 38.4
become larger 197.5
develop 197.7
graduate 29.4
make larger 197.4
multiply 100.6
quantify 28.4
increased
aggravated 885.4
expanded 197.10
extended 38.7
multiple 100.8
increasing 38.8
increasingly 38.9
incredible
fantastic 85.12
foolish 470.10
improbable 512.3
remarkable 34.10
unbelievable 503.10

wonderful 920.10
incredibly
remarkably 34.20
unusually 85.17
wonderfully 920.14
incredulity
agnosticism 1031.6
unbelief 503.1
ungullibility 504
incredulous
skeptical 1031.20
unbelieving 503.8
ungullible 504.4
increment adjunct 41.1
increase 38.1
incremental 38.8
incriminate 1005.10
incriminating 1005.14
incrimination 1005.2
incrustation
covering 228.1
crust 228.14
incrusted 356.13
incubate 169.12
incubation 169.5
incubator 153.8
incubus burden 352.7
dream 535.9
evil spirit 1016.7
frightener 891.9
inculcate
fix in the mind 537.18
indoctrinate 562.13
inculcated 642.21
inculcation 562.2
inculpable 984.8
inculpate 1005.10
inculpated
accused 1005.15
guilty 983.3
inculpatory 1005.14
incumbency
burden 352.7
position 656.5
responsibility 962.2
the ministry 1037.9
incumbent
n. clergyman 1038.8
officeholder 746.11
resident 190.2
tenant 809.4
adj. covering 228.35
obligatory 962.14
overhanging 215.11
ponderous 352.17
incumber, incumbered, incumbrance see encumber etc.
incur 175.4
incurable
n. sick person 686.40
adj. hopeless 889.15
incuriosity
inattention 531.1
unconcern 636.2
uninquisitiveness 529
incurious
inattentive 531.6
unconcerned 636.7
uninquisitive 529.3

incursion
intrusion 238.1
overstepping 313.3
raid 798.4
incursionary 798.29
incurve
n. throw 285.4
v. be concave 257.12
curve 252.6
incurved
concave 257.16
curved 252.7
indebted in debt 840.8
insolvent 836.18
indebtedness 840.1
indebted to
grateful 949.5
obliged 962.16
indecency
eroticism 419.5
indelicacy 990
unchastity 989.1
vulgarity 898.1
indecent
indelicate 990.5
unchaste 989.23
vulgar 898.10
indecipherable 549.19
indecision
irresolution 627.1
uncertainty 514.1
indecisive
formless 247.4
inconstant 141.7
irresolute 627.9
uncertain 514.15
unproved 506.8
vague 514.18
weak 160.17
indecisiveness
formlessness 247.1
frailty 160.2
irresolution 627.1
uncertainty 514.1
vagueness 514.4
indecorous
indecent 990.5
infelicitous 590.2
vulgar 898.10
wrong 959.3
indecorum
indecency 990.1
vulgarity 898.1
wrong 959.1
indeed
adv. above all 36.17
certainly 513.23
positively 34.19
truly 516.17
interj. wonder 920.19
yes 521.18
indefatigable
continuing 143.7
industrious 707.22
persevering 625.7
indefeasible
inevitable 639.15
unchangeable 142.17
unimpartable 813.10
indefensible
unacceptable 869.7
unjust 977.12

indecency 990.1
indiscrimination
493.1
misdeed 982.2
rashness 894.1
unwiseness 470.2
indiscriminate
extensive 79.13
mixed 44.15
purposeless 156.16
undiscriminating
493.5
unordered 62.12
indiscrimination
choicelessness 639.6
indiscriminateness
493
unconcern 636.2
indispensable
n. requirement 639.2
adj. requisite 639.13
vital 672.22
indispose
disincline 652.4
sicken 686.47
indisposed sick 686.52
unwilling 623.5
indisposition
disease 686.1
unwillingness 623.1
indisputable
certain 513.15
evidential 505.17
manifest 555.8
unqualified 508.2
indistinct
faint-sounding 452.16
imperfectly spoken
595.12
obscure 549.15
uncertain 514.18
unclear 445.6
without distinction
493.6
indistinctly
unintelligibly 549.22
vaguely 514.27
indistinguishable
identical 14.7
indistinct 445.6
without distinction
493.6
indite create 167.10
write 602.21
individual
n. organism 406.2
person 417.3
something 3.3
unit 89.4
adj. indicative 568.23
one 89.7
particular 80.12
personal 417.12
individualism
capitalism 745.8
characteristic 80.4
egotism 909.3
independence 762.5
individuality 80.1
selfishness 978.1
trait of character
525.3

individualist
capitalist 745.15
egotist 909.5
independent 762.12
misfit 27.4
selfish person 978.3
individualistic
capitalist 745.23
independent 762.21
nonconformist 27.9
particular 80.12
selfish 978.5
individuality
particularity 80.1
unity 89.1
individualize
differentiate 16.6
particularize 80.9
individually
personally 80.16
singly 89.13
indivisible
inseparable 47.15
nondivisible 354.13
one 89.7
simple 45.6
indocile
insubordinate 767.9
ungovernable 626.12
unwilling 623.5
indocility
disobedience 767.1
ungovernability 626.4
unwillingness 623.1
indoctrinate
brainwash 145.15
inculcate 562.13
propagandize 563.4
indoctrinated 189.6
indoctrination
brainwashing 145.5
inculcation 562.2
misteaching 563.2
indolence
inaction 706.1
inertia 268.4
laziness 708.5
slowness 270.1
vegetation 1.6
indolent
n. lazy person 708.7
adj. lazy 708.18
slow 270.10
indomitable
invincible 159.17
persevering 625.7
ungovernable 626.12
indoor
adj. interior 225.7
adv. inside 225.14
indorse, indorsement
see **endorse** etc.
Indra
Hindu deity 1014.8
thunder god 456.5
indraft influx 302.2
wind 403.1
indubitable
certain 513.15
manifest 555.8
indubitably
certainly 513.25

positively 34.19
probably 511.8
induce advise 754.6
cause 153.12
conclude 494.10
elicit 305.14
influence 172.7
persuade 648.22
inducement
allurement 650.1
gratuity 818.5
incentive 648.7
persuasion 648.3
induct begin 68.11
enlist 780.16
insert 304.4
install 780.11
inductee novice 566.9
recruit 800.17
inductile 356.12
induction
admission 306.2
basics 68.6
conclusion 494.4
consecration 1037.10
electrostatic induc-
tion 342.14
enlistment 780.6
inauguration 68.5
installation 780.3
logic 482.3
reasoning 482.1
inductive 482.22
inductive reasoning
logic 482.3
reasoning 482.1
in due course
in time 121.11
opportunely 129.12
soon 131.16
indulge
be intemperate 993.4
enjoy 865.10
give 818.15
humor 759.6
permit 777.10
indulged
forgiven 947.7
pampered 759.9
indulgence
considerateness 938.3
forgiveness 947.1
intemperance 993.1
leniency 759.3
patience 861.1
privilege 958.4
sufferance 777.2
tolerance 526.4
indulgent
considerate 938.16
intemperate 993.7
lenient 759.8
nonrestrictive 762.24
patient 861.9
permissive 777.14
tolerant 526.11
indulge oneself
be intemperate 993.4
be lawless 740.4
be selfish 978.4
indurate
v. harden 356.7

make unfeeling 856.6
adj. hardened 356.13
indurated
callous 856.12
hardened 356.13
wicked 981.17
induration 856.3
industrial
commercial 827.21
occupational 656.16
productional 167.17
industrialist
businessman 830.1
producer 167.8
industrialization
commercialization
827.13
production 167.2
industrialize
make businesslike
827.19
produce 167.9
industrial park 719.3
industrials 834.2
industrial school
prison 761.8
reform school 567.14
vocational school
567.8
industrious
active 707.22
painstaking 533.11
persevering 625.7
industriously
actively 707.27
carefully 533.15
laboriously 716.19
perseveringly 625.8
industry
commerce 827.1
company 788.9
industriousness 707.6
painstakingness 533.2
perseverance 625.1
work 716.4
indwell
be present 186.6
inhere 5.5
indwelling
n. intrinsicality 5.1
adj. intrinsic 5.6
present 186.12
inebriant
n. liquor 996.12
adj. intoxicating
996.35
inebriate
n. drunkard 996.10
v. make drunk 996.21
adj. intoxicated
996.30
inebriation 996.1
inedible 429.8
ineducable 469.15
ineffable
extraordinary 85.14
indescribable 920.13
sacred 1026.7
ineffective
incompetent 734.19
ineffectual 158.15
unable 158.14

uninfluential 173.3
unsuccessful 725.17
useless 669.9
ineffectiveness
futility 669.2
ineffectualness 158.3
lack of influence
173.1
unskillfulness 734.1
ineffectual
incompetent 734.19
ineffective 158.15
sterile 166.4
uninfluential 173.3
unsuccessful 725.17
useless 669.9
ineffectuality
futility 669.2
ineffectiveness 158.3
lack of influence
173.1
unimportance 673.1
unskillfulness 734.1
inefficiency
inability 158.2
unskillfulness 734.1
inefficient
unable 158.14
unskillful 734.15
inefficiently 734.23
inelastic rigid 356.12
unyielding 626.9
inelegance
clumsiness 734.3
indecency 990.1
literary inelegance
590
ugliness 899.1
vulgarity 898.1
inelegant
clumsy 734.20
indecent 990.5
infelicitous 590.2
ugly 899.6
vulgar 898.10
ineluctable
certain 513.13
inevitable 639.15
inept foolish 470.8
inappropriate 27.7
inexpedient 671.5
unable 158.14
unintelligent 469.13
unskillful 734.15
ineptitude
foolishness 470.1
inability 158.2
inexpedience 671.1
stupidity 469.1
ineptly
inexpediently 671.8
unskillfully 734.23
inequality
difference 16.1
disagreement 27.1
disparity 31
injustice 977.3
nonuniformity 18.1
unevenness 261.1
inequitable 977.9
inequity
inequality 31.1

injustice 977.1
ineradicable 142.18
inerrant exact 516.16
infallible 513.19
inert do-nothing 706.6
inactive 268.14
inanimate 382.5
languid 708.19
unchangeable 142.17
inertia
immobility 142.3
inactivity 708.1
indolence 708.5
inertness 268.4
passivity 706.1
slowness 270.1
vegetation 1.6
inerudite 477.14
inescapable 639.15
inestimable 848.10
inevitability
certainty 513.1
compulsion 756.1
fate 640.2
necessity 639.7
inevitable
certain 513.13
destined 640.9
obligatory 756.10
unavoidable 639.15
inevitably
consequently 154.9
unavoidably 639.19
inexact imperfect 678.4
inaccurate 518.17
unmeticulous 534.13
vague 514.18
inexcitable
imperturbable 858.10
unastonished 921.3
unconcerned 636.7
unfeeling 856.9
uninteresting 883.6
unnervous 860.2
inexcusable 977.12
inexcusably
unduly 34.21
unjustly 977.13
inexhaustible
infinite 104.3
innumerable 101.10
plentiful 661.7
inexorable
inevitable 639.15
pitiless 945.3
strict 757.7
unyielding 626.9
inexpectation
no hope 889.1
nonexpectation 540
suddenness 113.2
inexpedience
badness 675.1
mismanagement
734.6
unfitness 671
untimeliness 130.1
unwiseness 470.2
inexpedient bad 675.7
undesirable 671.5
untimely 130.7
unwise 470.9

inexpensive 849.7
inexperience
ignorance 477.1
immaturity 124.3
unaccustomedness
643.1
unpracticedness
734.2
inexperienced
foolable 470.11
ignorant 477.12
immature 124.10
unaccustomed 643.4
unpracticed 734.17
inexpert 734.15
inexpiable 977.12
inexplicable
purposeless 156.16
unexplainable 549.18
inexpressible
indescribable 920.13
ineffable 1026.7
inexpressive 549.20
inextensible 356.12
inextinguishable 142.18
in extremis
dying 408.33
in danger 697.13
in trouble 731.24
inextricable
complex 46.5
fixed 142.16
inexplicable 549.18
in fact really 1.16
truly 516.17
infallibility
certainty 513.1
perfection 677.1
infallible exact 516.16
inerrable 513.19
perfect 677.6
infamous bad 675.9
dishonest 975.17
disreputable 915.10
evil 981.16
wrong 959.3
infamously
badly 675.14
dishonestly 975.24
disreputably 915.15
infamy disrepute 915.4
iniquity 981.3
wrong 959.2
infancy
babyhood 124.5
immaturity 124.3
legal inability 158.2
origin 68.4
infant
n. baby 125.7
beginner 68.2
innocent person
984.4
pupil 566.4
unsophisticate 736.3
youngster 125.1
adj. babyish 124.12
beginning 68.15
infantile
babyish 124.12
beginning 68.15

simple-minded
469.24
infantile paralysis
infectious disease
686.12
paralysis 686.25
infantilism
mental deficiency
469.9
simple-mindedness
469.11
infantryman
foot soldier 800.9
pedestrian 274.6
infant school 567.4
infarction 266.3
infatuate
n. enthusiast 635.5
fanatic 473.17
lover 931.11
v. enamor 931.21
fascinate 650.6
obsess 473.24
stultify 470.7
infatuated
credulous 502.8
enamored 931.26
enthusiastic 635.11
fooled 470.8
obsessed 473.33
overenthusiastic
635.13
infatuation
credulity 502.1
liking 634.2
love 931.4
making foolish 470.5
mania 473.12
overzealousness 635.4
in favor friendly 927.17
reputable 914.15
in favor of
approving 968.17
for 968.21
supporting 785.26
infect corrupt 692.14
defile 682.17
disease 686.48
harm 675.6
inspire 648.20
radioactivate 327.9
infected
diseased 686.56
radioactive 327.10
unclean 682.20
infection
corruption 692.2
defilement 682.4
disease 686.3
evil 675.3
inspiration 648.9
infectious
contagious 686.58
poisonous 684.7
infectious disease
686.1,12
infecund sterile 166.4
unimaginative 536.5
infelicitous
ill-suited 671.5
inappropriate 27.7
inelegant 590.2

ungrammatical 587.4
untimely 130.7
infelicity despair 866.6
literary inelegance
590.1
unfitness 27.3
ungrammaticalness
587.2
unhappiness 872.2
unsuitable 671.1
untimeliness 130.1
infer conclude 494.10
imply 546.4
reason 482.15
suppose 499.10
inference
conclusion 494.4
implication 546.2
logic 482.3
supposition 499.3
inferential
dialectic(al) 482.22
suggestive 546.6
inferior
n. servant 750.1
subordinate 764.5
underling 37.2
adj. bad 675.7
insignificant 673.15
lower 208.8
poor 680.9
short of 314.5
subject 764.13
subordinate 37.6
unfit 158.14
unimportant 673.14
inferiority
abnormality 85.1
badness 675.1
inability 158.2
poorness 680.3
shortcoming 314.1
subordinacy 37
subservience 764.2
unimportance 673.1
inferiority complex
690.29
infernal cruel 939.24
diabolic 981.13
hellish 1019.8
terrible 675.10
inferno hell 1019.1
hot place 328.11
inferred implied 546.7
supposed 499.14
infertile
unimaginative 536.5
unproductive 166.4
infertility
unimaginativeness
536.1
unproductiveness
166.1
infest 313.6
infestation 313.2
infested 313.11
infidel
n. gentile 1025.6
unbeliever 1031.11
adj. unbelieving
1031.19
unorthodox 1025.10

infidelity
love affair 931.6
nonreligiousness
1031.5
unbelief 503.1
unfaithfulness 975.5
unorthodoxy 1025.3
infield 878.12
infighting
bickering 795.3
boxing 796.9
infiltrate attack 798.17
filter in 302.10
infuse 44.12
intrude 238.5
soak 392.13
sorb 306.13
infiltration
attack 798.1
entrance 302.1
infusion 44.2
intrusion 238.1
military tactics 797.9
soaking 392.7
sorption 306.6
infiltrator 238.3
infinite
boundless 104.3
extensive 179.9
godlike 1013.20
huge 195.20
innumerable 101.10
large 34.7
numerical 86.8
omnipresent 186.13
perpetual 112.7
infinitely
extensively 179.10
extremely 34.22
illimitably 104.4
innumerably 101.12
perpetually 112.10
infinitesimal 196.14
infinitive 586.4
infinity distance 199.1
divine attribute
1013.15
endlessness 104
greatness 34.1
large number 86.4
length 202.1
number 86.3
omnipresence 186.2
perpetuity 112.1
infirm aged 126.18
flimsy 4.7
inconstant 141.7
irresolute 627.12
mentally deficient
469.21
unhealthy 686.50
unreliable 514.19
unrighteous 981.12
weak 160.15
infirmary 689.27
infirmity disease 686.1
fault 678.2
irresolution 627.4
mental deficiency
469.8
old age 126.5
unhealthiness 686.2

unreliability 514.6
vice 981.2
weakness 160.3
infix
n. addition 41.2
interjection 237.2
morphology 582.3
v. add 40.4
fix in the mind
537.18
implant 142.9
indoctrinate 562.13
insert 304.8
infixed
confirmed 642.21
established 142.13
intrinsic 5.6
inflame energize 161.9
excite 857.11
hurt 424.7
ignite 329.22
incite 648.17
make hot 329.18
make red 368.4
provoke 952.22
inflamed
burning 328.27
excited 857.18
feverish 686.54
fiery 162.21
red 368.6
sore 424.11
inflammable
n. fuel 331.1
adj. combustible
329.28
excitable 857.26
inflammation
disease 686.9
disease symptom
686.8
excitation 857.10
ignition 329.4
incitement 648.4
pain 424.4
inflammatory
exciting 857.28
incitive 648.28
inflaming 329.27
inflate
be bombastic 601.6
be vain 909.7
expand 197.4
increase 38.4
inflate prices 848.9
overextend 663.13
inflated
boastful 910.11
bombastic 601.9
distended 197.13
exaggerated 617.4
increased 38.7
pompous 904.22
inflation
distension 197.2
exaggeration 617.1
grandiloquence 601.1
high prices 848.3
increase 38.1
overextension 663.7
pompousness 904.7
price index 846.5

rhetoric 588.2
inflationary
expansive 197.9
overpriced 848.12
inflationary spiral
high prices 848.3
price index 846.5
inflect curve 252.6
grammaticize 586.16
modulate 594.29
inflection angle 251.2
curve 252.3
intonation 594.7
morphology 582.3
inflexibility
firmness 624.2
immobility 142.3
inevitability 639.7
rigidity 356.3
strictness 757.2
unyieldingness 626.2
inflexible firm 624.12
immovable 142.15
inevitable 639.15
rigid 356.12
strict 757.7
uninfluenceable
173.4
unyielding 626.9
inflict do 705.6
impose 963.4
wreak 963.5
infliction
affliction 866.8
bane 676.1
imposition 963.1
punishment 1010.1
in flight
aviation 278.60
fugitive 631.16
inflorescence 411.24
inflow
n. flow 395.4
influx 302.2
wind 403.1
v. enter 302.9
influence
n. authority 739.4
influentiality 172
influential person
172.6
manipulation 735.4
motivation 648.2
power 157.1
supremacy 36.3
v. affect 172.7
cause 153.13
induce 648.22
operate on 164.6
prejudice 527.9
influence peddler
corrupt politician
746.5
influence user 744.30
influential person
172.6
politician 735.8
influential
authoritative 739.15
powerful 172.13

influenza
infectious disease 686.12
respiratory disease 686.14
influx inflow 302.2
intrusion 238.1
info 557.1
in force existent 1.13
in use 665.24
operating 164.11
powerful 157.12
inform divulge 556.6
inspire 648.20
report 558.11
teach 562.11
tell 557.8
informal casual 231.46
nonconformist 83.6
slovenly 62.15
unceremonious 647.3
vernacular 580.18
informality 647
informally 647.4
informant
examinee 485.18
informer 557.5
witness 505.7
information
accusation 1005.1
arraignment 1004.3
communication 554.1
computer 349.19
data 1.4
facts 557
knowledge 475.1
news 558.1
teaching 562.1
information theory
automation 349.2
communication 554.5
communication theory 557.7
telecommunication 560.1
informative
educational 562.19
enlightening 557.17
informed
apprised 557.16
enlightened 475.18
prepared 720.16
informed of
apprised 557.16
cognizant of 475.16
informer
accuser 1005.5
betrayer 557.6
source 557.5
traitor 619.10
witness 505.7
inform on
accuse 1005.7
betray 975.14
divulge 556.6
inform against 557.12
infra 208.10
infraction
disobedience 767.1
lawbreaking 999.3

overstepping 313.3
violation 769.2
wrong 959.1
infrangible firm 159.16
indivisible 354.13
unbreakable 359.5
infrequency
fewness 102.1
rarity 136
infrequent rare 136.2
sparse 102.5
infrequently
at intervals 72.5
scarcely 102.8
seldom 136.4
infringe borrow 821.4
break the law 999.5
encroach 313.9
intrude 238.5
usurp 961.8
violate 769.4
infringement
borrowing 821.2
disobedience 767.1
impairment 692.1
intrusion 238.1
lawbreaking 999.3
overstepping 313.3
usurpation 961.3
violation 769.2
in front ahead 240.12
before 292.4
in front of 239.7
in full at length 593.16
completely 56.14
fully 8.13
in full swing
actively 707.25
astir 707.19
thriving 728.13
unweakened 159.19
in full view 444.6
in fun
for amusement 878.33
in sport 881.19
mischievously 738.7
infundibular
conical 255.12
funnel-shaped 257.16
infuriate
antagonize 929.7
enrage 952.23
excite 857.11
infuriated 952.29
infuse extract 305.16
imbue 44.12
indoctrinate 562.13
insert 304.3
inspire 648.20
liquefy 391.5
soak 392.13
infusion
admixture 44.7
baptism 1040.7
distillation 305.8
extraction 305.7
imbuement 44.2
indoctrination 562.2
insertion 304.1
inspiration 648.9
soaking 392.7

solution 391.3
in gear 13.12
in general 79.17
ingenious
cunning 735.12
imaginative 535.18
skillful 733.20
ingenue actor 612.2
role 611.11
unsophisticate 736.3
ingenuity
inventiveness 535.3
skill 733.1
ingenuous artless 736.5
candid 974.17
gullible 502.9
immature 124.10
ingest consume 666.2
eat 307.20
learn 564.7
take in 306.11
ingesta 308.1
ingestion
consumption 666.1
digestion 309.8
eating 307.1
learning 564.2
taking in 306.4
ingle fire 328.13
fireplace 329.11
home 191.4
inglorious
disreputable 915.10
humble 906.9
unrenowned 915.14
ingoing
n. entrance 302.1
adj. entering 302.12
introverted 690.46
ingot
currency metals 835.20
metal casting 383.5
ingrain color 362.13
implant 142.9
ingrained
deep-rooted 642.21
dyed 362.17
infixed 142.13
intrinsic 5.6
ingrate 950.2
ingratiate oneself
be servile 907.9
gain influence 172.12
influence 172.7
ingratiating
obsequious 907.13
suave 936.18
ingratitude 950
ingredient
component 58.2
content 194.1
ingress channel 396.1
entrance 302
inlet 302.5
ingroup clique 788.6
group 74.3
influential persons 172.6
the rulers 749.15
ingrown 142.13
inhabit exist in 1.11

occupy 188.7
populate 188.9
settle 184.16
inhabitable 188.15
inhabitant
population 190.1
resident 190.2
inhabited 188.12
inhalant 687.4
inhalation
breathing 403.18
taking in 306.5
wind 403.1
inhalator
breathing 403.18
respirator 689.37
inhale breathe 403.24
draw in 306.12
smell 435.8
use tobacco 434.14
in hand
adj. happening 151.9
operating 164.11
orderly 59.6
possessed 808.8
restrained 163.11
undertaken 715.7
unused 668.12
adv. in preparation 720.22
in production 167.25
under control 741.20
inharmonious
different 16.7
disaccordant 795.15
disagreeing 27.6
off-color 362.20
sounds 461.4
in harmony
agreeing 26.9
concurrently 177.5
in accord 794.3
in conformity with 82.9
jointly 47.18
in heat 419.30
inhere be present 186.6
exist in 1.11
indwell 5.5
inherence
intrinsicality 5.1
presence 186.1
inherent
instinctive 481.6
intrinsic 5.6
present 186.12
inherit
come into 819.7
succeed 65.2
inheritable
heritable 170.16
transferable 817.5
inheritance
bequest 818.10
heredity 170.6
heritage 819.2
inherited
hereditary 170.15
innate 5.7
inheritor
descendant 171.1
heir 819.5

interrelate 13.7
interconnection
interrelation 13.2
junction 47.2
intercosmic 375.25
intercourse
commerce 827.1
communication 554.1
conversation 597.1
copulation 419.8
interaction 13.3
joining 47.1
relationship 9.1
social intercourse 922.4
interdenominational 1020.26
interdependent 13.11
interdict
n. legal order 752.6
prohibition 778.1
restraint 760.1
v. prohibit 778.3
interdictive 778.6
interdigitation
connection 47.2
interrelation 13.2
interest
n. affair 151.3
allurement 650.1
attention 530.2
benefit 665.4
business 656.1
cause 153.10
curiosity 528.1
debt 840.3
dividend 834.7
estate 810.4
gain 811.3
good 674.4
importance 672.1
incentive 648.7
influence 172.2
partiality 977.3
party 788.4
patronage 785.4
portion 816.5
privilege 958.3
relevance 9.4
selfishness 978.1
side of controversy 482.14
v. attract 650.5
induce 648.22
involve 176.2
make attentive 530.12
relate to 9.5
interested
attentive 530.16
curious 528.5
involved 176.3
partisan 788.19
prejudiced 527.12
unjust 977.11
interesting
alluring 650.7
provocative 530.19
interests
important persons 672.8

the rulers 749.15
interface
interrelate 13.7
boundary 235.3
joint 47.4
interfere
counteract 178.6
hinder 730.10
intrude 238.5
interference
counteraction 178.1
hindrance 730.1
intrusion 238.1
radio reception 344.21
wave phenomenon 323.4
interfering 238.8
interfuse combine 52.3
interpose 237.7
interfusion
interposition 237.3
mixture 44.1
interim
n. delay 132.2
discontinuity 72.2
interval 109
pause 144.3
space 201.1
adj. temporary 109.4
interior
n. inland 225.3
inside 225.2
middle 69.1
picture 574.13
adj. inland 225.8
internal 225.7
middle 69.4
private 614.13
interior decorating 901.1
interiority depth 209.1
internalness 225
interjacent 237.10
interject insert 304.3
interpose 237.6
remark 594.25
interjection
insertion 304.1
interpolation 237.2
intrusion 238.1
part of speech 586.3
remark 594.4
interjoin
interconnect 47.6
interrelate 13.7
interlace interact 13.8
mix 44.11
weave 222.6
interlaced
webbed 221.12
woven 222.7
interlacing
n. interaction 13.3
weaving 222.1
adj. weaving 222.8
interlard
interpose 237.7
mix 44.11
interlining 194.3
interlink
interconnect 47.6
interrelate 13.7

interlinked
interrelated 13.11
related 9.9
interlock
n. safety equipment 699.3
v. agree 26.6
interconnect 47.6
interrelate 13.7
interlocked
interconnected 13.11
related 9.9
interlocking
connection 47.2
interrelation 13.2
interlocutory
conversational 597.13
mediatory 805.8
interlope 238.5
interloper 238.3
interloping 238.1
interlude act 611.8
interim 109.1
music division 462.24
pause 144.3
respite 711.2
intermarriage 933.1
intermarry 933.16
intermeddle
hinder 730.10
tamper with 238.7
intermediary
n. agent 237.4
go-between 781.4
instrument 658.3
mediator 805.3
adj. instrumental 658.6
intervening 237.10
mediatory 805.8
medium 32.3
middle 69.4
intermediate
n. gear 348.6
go-between 781.4
instrument 658.3
mediator 805.3
v. mediate 805.6
adj. intervening 237.10
mediatory 805.8
medium 32.3
middle 69.4
intermediator 805.3
interment burial 410
concealment 615.1
intermesh 13.8
intermezzo act 611.8
interim 109.1
interlude 144.3
music division 462.24
interminable
continuous 71.8
infinite 104.3
long 202.8
perpetual 112.7
protracted 110.11
interminably
continuously 71.10
for a long time 110.14
infinitely 104.4

perpetually 112.10
intermingle 44.11
intermingling 44.1
intermission act 611.8
discontinuity 72.2
interim 109.1
pause 144.3
relief 886.2
respite 711.2
intermit
fluctuate 138.2
interrupt 144.10
pause 109.3
recur 137.5
relieve 886.6
intermittence
discontinuity 72.1
interim 109.1
irregularity 138.1
pause 144.3
periodicity 137.2
intermittent
discontinuous 72.4
irregular 138.3
periodic 137.7
intermittently
discontinuously 72.5
irregularly 138.4
periodically 137.9
intermix 44.11
intern
n. doctor 688.6
interior 225.2
resident 190.2
teacher 565.5
v. imprison 761.14
practice medicine 688.17
internal
n. interior 225.2
adj. interior 225.7
intrinsic 5.6
mental 466.8
internalize 225.6
internally
intrinsically 5.9
inwardly 225.11
internal medicine
enterology 225.5
medicine 688.1,19
internal revenue agent 846.12
international
public 417.13
universal 79.14
International Date Line 114.4
internationalism
foreign policy 744.5
nationhood 181.6
universality 79.1
internationally 79.18
international relations 744.2
internecine
destructive 693.26
fatal 409.23
interned 761.21
internist 688.8
internment 761.3
internship 688.16
interplanetary 375.25

intolerable
insufferable 864.25
outright 34.12
unacceptable 869.7
unlikable 867.7
intolerably
insufferably 864.30
unduly 34.21
unsatisfactorily 869.9
intolerance
narrow-mindedness 527.2
nonendurance 862.2
obstinacy 626.1
intolerant
narrow-minded 527.11
obstinate 626.8
unforbearing 862.7
intonate inflect 594.29
sing 462.39
intonation
accent 463.25
harmonization 463.2
inflection 594.7
music 462.31
tone 450.2
vocal music 462.12
intone 462.39
intoxicate dizzy 532.8
make drunk 996.21
thrill 857.14
intoxicated
drunk 996.30
excited 857.23
fervent 855.23
intoxicating
exciting 857.28
inebriating 996.35
intoxication
excitement 857.7
happiness 865.2
inebriation 996
poisoning 686.30
intractability
disobedience 767.1
rigidity 356.3
ungovernability 626.4
intractable
insubordinate 767.9
rigid 356.12
ungovernable 626.12
intramural
internal 225.9
scholastic 567.18
intransient 110.10
intransigence 626.2
intransigent
n. obstinate person 626.6
oppositionist 791.3
adj. unyielding 626.9
intransitive
n. verb 586.4
adj. grammatical 586.17
intransmutable 142.17
intraterritorial 225.9
intravenous 689.19
intrepid 893.17
intrepidly 893.22

intricacy
abstruseness 549.2
complexity 46.1
difficulty 731.1
intricate
bewildering 514.25
complex 46.4
difficult 731.16
hard to understand 549.14
mixed 44.15
intrigue
n. dishonesty 975.3
influence 172.3
love affair 931.6
plot 654.6
stratagem 735.3
v. fascinate 650.6
maneuver 735.10
plot 654.10
intriguing
alluring 650.7
pleasant 863.7
scheming 654.14
intrinsic
characteristic 80.13
inherent 5.6
interior 225.7
intrinsically
characteristically 80.17
inherently 5.9
internally 225.11
introduce
acquaint 927.13
begin 68.11
bring in 306.14
change 139.8
go before 66.3
insert 304.3
interpose 237.6
preface 64.3
preinstruct 562.15
propose 773.5
introducer
originator 167.8
transformer 139.4
introduction
acquaintance 927.4
act 611.8
book 605.12
bringing in 306.7
elementary instruction 562.5
entrance 302.1
inauguration 68.5
innovation 139.3
insertion 304.1
interjection 237.2
legislative procedure 742.14
music 462.26
prelude 66.2
introductory
beginning 68.15
educational 562.19
initiatory 306.18
introit 462.16
Introit hymn 1032.3
Mass 1040.10
intromission
admission 306.2

insertion 304.1
intromit insert 304.3
receive 306.10
introspect 478.12
introspection 478.6
introspective
preoccupied 478.22
thoughtful 478.21
introversion
interiority 225.1
inversion 220.1
personality tendency 690.14
reticence 613.3
introvert
n. personality type 690.15
v. invert 220.5
introverted
inner-directed 690.46
reticent 613.10
reversed 220.7
intrude enter 302.7
interlope 238.5
interpose 237.6
overstep 313.9
talk out of turn 130.5
intruder
foreign body 78.2
incomer 302.4
interloper 238.3
newcomer 78.4
intrusion
entrance 302.1
extraneousness 78.1
interloping 238
interposition 237.1
overstepping 313.3
untimeliness 130.1
intrusive
entering 302.12
extraneous 78.5
interfering 238.8
overactive 707.24
untimely 130.7
intuit foreknow 542.6
sense 481.4
intuition
clairvoyance 1034.8
hunch 481.3
intuitiveness 481
intuitive
foreseeing 542.7
intuitional 481.5
premonitory 544.16
intuitively 481.7
intumescence
distension 197.2
swelling 256.4
tumor 686.36
in tune
harmonious 462.50
in accord 794.3
in turn
alternately 137.11
consecutively 71.11
in order 59.10
reciprocally 150.6
inundate
drench 392.14
engulf 395.17
make grieve 872.19

oversupply 663.14
overwhelm 693.21
raid 798.20
run over 313.7
submerge 320.7
inundated
flooded 395.25
heartbroken 872.29
soaked 392.17
underwater 209.13
inundation
overabundance 663.2
overflow 395.6
overrunning 313.1
submergence 320.2
wetting 392.6
in unison
concurrently 177.5
cooperatively 786.6
harmonious 462.50
in step 26.11
jointly 47.18
simultaneously 118.6
unanimously 521.17
inure accustom 642.11
make unfeeling 856.6
inured
accustomed 642.17
callous 856.12
wicked 981.17
invade encroach 313.9
intrude 238.5
overrun 313.6
raid 798.20
usurp 961.8
invader
assailant 798.13
intruder 238.3
invading 798.29
in vain amiss 314.7
unsuccessfully 725.18
invalid
n. impotent 158.6
recluse 924.5
sick person 686.40
v. sicken 686.47
adj. bad 675.7
illogical 483.11
ineffective 158.15
repealed 779.3
unhealthy 686.50
invalidate
abolish 693.13
disprove 506.4
disqualify 158.10
nullify 178.7
repeal 779.2
invalidated
disabled 158.16
disproved 506.7
invalidation
disproof 506.1
nullification 178.2
repeal 779.1
invaluable 848.10
invariable
tedious 884.8
unchangeable 142.17
uniform 17.5
invariably
always 112.11
permanently 140.9

regularly 17.8
universally 79.18
invasion
intrusion 238.1
overrunning 313.2
raid 798.4
usurpation 961.3
invasive
attacking 798.29
entering 302.12
intrusive 238.8
invective
n. berating 969.7
curse 972.2
sarcasm 967.5
speech 599.2
adj. condemnatory
969.23
inveigh against 969.13
inveigle lure 650.4
trap 618.18
inveiglement 650.1
invent begin 68.10
change 139.8
create 167.13
discover 488.2
fabricate 616.18
imagine 535.14
innovate 122.5
originate 23.4
invented
fabricated 616.29
originated 167.23
invention
creation 167.5
discovery 488.1
fabrication 616.10
innovation 139.3
inventiveness 535.3
music 462.5
product 168.1
thing imagined 535.5
inventive
beginning 68.15
creative 167.19
cunning 735.12
imaginative 535.18
inventiveness
cunning 735.1
invention 535.3
originality 23.1
inventor
imaginer 535.12
producer 167.8
inventory
n. account book 845.4
arrangement 60.4
assembly 74.1
contents 194.1
list 88.1
merchandise 831.1
numeration 87.5
record 570.1
store 660.1
v. check 87.14
list 88.8
summarize 87.12
take account of 845.9
inverse
n. contrary 15.2
opposite side 239.3
reverse 220.4

adj. contrary 15.6
opposite 239.5
inversely
contrarily 15.9
conversely 220.8
inversion
mathematics 87.4
reversal 220
invert
n. homosexual 419.16
v. reverse 220.5
invertebrate
n. animal 414.3
coward 892.5
weakling 160.6
adj. animal 414.54
irresolute 627.12
inverted 220.7
invest besiege 798.19
clothe 231.38
commission 780.11
empower 157.10
endow 818.17
establish 184.15
install 304.4
provide 659.7
spend 843.5
surround 233.6
venture 836.16
wrap 228.20
invested
clothed 231.44
endowed 818.26
provided 659.13
investigate
discuss 597.12
explore 485.22
investigation
discussion 597.7
research 485.4
investigative 485.36
investigator
detective 781.10
examiner 485.16
investiture
admission 306.2
clothing 231.1
consecration 1037.10
establishment 184.6
giving 818.1
installation 780.3
investment
clothing 231.1
empowerment 157.8
endowment 818.9
military tactics 797.9
provision 659.1
siege 798.5
venture 836.3
investor 836.8
inveteracy
customariness 642.7
establishment 142.2
oldness 123.1
permanence 140.1
inveterate
confirmed 642.21
enduring 110.10
established 142.13
traditional 123.12
invidious envious 954.4
jealous 953.4

malicious 939.18
in view
expected 539.13
imminent 152.3
present 186.12
visible 444.6
in view of 155.9
invigorate cheer 870.7
energize 161.9
refresh 695.2
stimulate 857.12
strengthen 159.11
invigorated 695.4
invigorating
cheering 870.16
cool 333.12
energizing 161.14
healthful 683.5
refreshing 695.3
tonic 687.44
invincibility
impregnability 159.4
indestructibility
142.5
reliability 513.4
invincible
impregnable 159.17
indestructible 142.18
peerless 36.15
persevering 625.7
reliable 513.17
inviolable
impregnable 159.17
sacred 1026.7
trustworthy 974.19
inviolate honest 974.13
permanent 140.7
sacred 1026.7
undamaged 677.8
invisibility
concealment 615.1
imperceptibility 445
infinitesimalness
196.2
invisible
imperceptible 445.5
infinitesimal 196.14
unrevealed 615.12
invisible ink 614.6
invitation
allurement 650.1
incentive 648.7
offer 773.1
request 774.4
invitational 774.19
invite
n. invitation 774.4
v. attract 650.5
bid come 774.13
encourage 648.21
incur 175.4
interest 530.12
inviting alluring 650.7
interesting 530.19
pleasant 863.7
provocative 648.27
receptive 306.16
requesting 774.19
invocation
benediction 1032.5
entreaty 774.2
exorcism 1035.4

prayer 1032.4
rite 1040.4
summons 752.5
in vogue 644.11
invoice
n. account 845.3
list 88.5
v. bill 845.11
invoke address 594.27
cite 505.15
conjure 1035.11
entreat 774.11
pray 1032.12
summon 752.12
involuntarily
instinctively 639.18
unintentionally
156.21
unpremeditatedly
630.14
unwillingly 623.8
involuntary
automatic 639.14
instinctive 481.6
obligatory 756.10
unintentional 156.17
unpremeditated
630.11
unwilling 623.5
involuted complex 46.4
winding 254.6
involution
complexity 46.1
convolution 254.1
deterioration 692.3
involvement 176.1
mathematics 87.4
involve
cause trouble for
731.14
complicate 46.3
engross 530.13
entail 76.4
entangle 176.2
evidence 505.9
hamper 730.11
imply 546.4
incriminate 1005.10
indicate 568.17
interest in 530.12
make grandiloquent
601.7
relate to 9.5
surround 233.6
involved
accused 1005.15
complex 46.4
engrossed 530.17
guilty 983.3
implicated 176.3
included 76.5
indebted 840.8
insinuated 546.7
participating 815.8
partisan 977.11
related 9.9
involvement
accusation 1005.2
complexity 46.1
engrossment 530.3
entailment 76.2
guilt 983.1

itinerary
directory 748.10
route 657.2
–itis
inflammation 686.9
tendency 174.1
itself 80.5
itsy-bitsy 196.11
IUD 687.23
ivied halls 567.7
ivories dice 515.9
keyboard 465.20
teeth 258.6
ivory
n. smooth surface
260.3
white 364.2,11
adj. whitish 364.8
ivory-carving 575.1
ivory tower 700.5
ivy
n. vine 411.4,51
adj. green 371.4
izzard 70.1

J

jab
n. gibe 967.2
hit 283.4
push 283.2
thrust 798.3
v. hit 283.13
ridicule 967.9
thrust 283.11
jabber
n. chatter 596.3
imperfect speech
595.4
nonsense 547.2
v. chatter 596.5
speak poorly 595.9
talk nonsense 547.5
jabberer 596.4
jack ass 414.20
flag 569.6
lifter 317.3
money 835.2
playing card 878.17
post 216.8
sailor 276.1
jackal coyote 414.25,58
man 787.8
sycophant 907.3
jackass ass 414.20,58
fool 471.1
jacket
n. bookbinding
605.15
clothing 231.13
hull 228.16
pelt 229.1
types of 231.51
wrapper 228.18
v. clothe 231.39
jack-in-the-box 878.16
jackknife dive 320.1
edge tool 348.13
jack-of-all-trades 733.11
jackpot award 916.2
stakes 515.5

jackrabbit
hare 414.29,58
jumper 319.4
jacks 878.16,34
jack up increase 38.4
reprove 969.19
Jacobin radical 745.12
revolutionist 147.3
jactitation
boasting 910.1
shaking 324.2
jade
n. gem stone 384.13
green color 371.6
inferior horse 414.14
unchaste woman
989.14
v. be tedious 884.5
fatigue 717.4
get tired 717.5
satiate 664.4
jaded bored 884.10
fatigued 717.6
languid 708.19
satiated 664.6
worn-out 692.38
jag
n. notch 262.1
pointed projection
258.4
spree 996.5
v. notch 262.4
Jaganmati 1014.8
jagged angular 251.6
discontinuous 72.4
nonuniform 18.3
notched 262.5
rough 261.7
jaguar
animal 414.27,58
variegation 374.6
jail
n. prison 761.8
v. enclose 236.5
imprison 761.14
jailbird criminal 986.10
prisoner 761.11
jailbreak 632.1
jailed enclosed 236.10
imprisoned 761.21
jailer guard 699.9
penology 1010.9
warder 761.10
jailing
imprisonment 761.3
punishment 1010.2
jalopy 272.9
jam
n. barrier 730.5
delay 132.2
Indian ruler 749.9
large number 101.3
obstruction 266.3
perplexity 514.3
predicament 731.4
semiliquid 389.5
state 7.1
sweets 308.39
throng 74.4
v. become fixed
142.10
be numerous 101.5

densify 354.9
drown out 453.7
fasten 47.8
fill 56.7
infix 142.9
obstruct 730.12
overload 663.15
stop 266.7
thrust 283.11
use radar 346.15
jamb leg 273.16
post 217.4
jamboree 878.4
jam in enter 302.7
thrust in 304.7
jammed
blocked 266.11
dense 354.12
fastened 47.14
fixed 142.16
late 132.16
overfull 663.20
teeming 101.9
jamming 346.13
jam-packed
crowded 74.22
dense 354.12
full 56.11
overfull 663.20
teeming 101.9
jam session 462.33
jam through 742.18
Jane 421.6
Jane Doe 583.8
jangle
n. conflict 795.1
dissonance 461.2
harsh sound 458.3
noise 453.3
ringing 454.3
v. be dissonant 461.3
clash 795.8
disagree 27.5
ring 454.8
sound harshly 458.9
jangle the nerves
make nervous 859.8
sound harshly 458.11
jangling clashing 461.5
disagreeing 27.6
sounding harsh
458.16
janitor cleaner 681.14
doorkeeper 699.12
guardian 699.6
Janus 90.1
Janus-like 91.4
Japanese deities
1014.14
japanning 362.12
jape
n. banter 882.1
gibe 967.2
joke 881.6
v. banter 882.4
joke 881.13
ridicule 967.9
jar
n. bottle 193.12
conflict 795.1
dissonance 461.2
harsh sound 458.3

shake 324.3
surprise 540.3
v. be dissonant 461.3
clash 795.8
disagree 27.5
excite 857.13
make nervous 859.8
package 236.9
preserve 701.9
shake 324.11
sound harshly 458.9
startle 540.8
jargon
n. argot 580.9
lingua franca 580.11
nonsense 547.2
unintelligibility 549.7
v. speak 580.16
jarring clashing 461.5
disagreeing 27.6
exciting 857.28
jolting 324.20
nerve-wracking
859.14
sounding harsh
458.16
surprising 540.11
jaundice
n. disease symptom
686.8
jealousy 953.1
liver disease 686.21
partiality 527.3
yellow skin 370.2
v. prejudice 527.9
yellow 370.3
jaundiced
ill-humored 951.23
jealous 953.4
prejudiced 527.12
yellow-complexioned
370.6
jaundiced eye
jealousy 953.1
partiality 527.3
jaunt
n. journey 273.5
walk 273.12
v. travel 273.20
wander 273.22
jaunty chic 644.13
lighthearted 870.12
showy 904.19
javelin 801.23
jaw
n. mouth 265.5
v. berate 969.20
chatter 596.5
speak 594.21
jawboning 648.3
jawbreaker
long word 582.10
pompous word 601.3
jawbreaking
difficult 731.16
polysyllabic 601.10
jawing 969.7
jaws
grasping organs 813.4
mouth 265.5
jaywalk 273.26
jaywalker 274.6

jazz
  n. music 462.9
  adj. music 462.52
  syncopation 463.29
Jazz Age 107.8
jazz band 464.12
jazz musician 464.2
jazz up energize 161.9
  increase 38.5
  stimulate 857.12
jazzy music 462.52
  showy 904.19
  syncopation 463.29
JD 125.4
jealous envious 954.4
  jaundiced 953.4
jealousy envy 954.1
  resentment 953
jeans 231.18,56
jeer
  n. gibe 967.2
  indignity 965.2
  v. offend 965.4
  ridicule 967.9
jeering
  n. indignity 965.2
  ridicule 967.1
  adj. ridiculing 967.12
Jehovah 1013.2
jejune barren 166.4
  insipid 430.2
  meager 662.10
  shallow 210.5
  stupid 469.19
  uninteresting 883.6
  wasted 205.20
jell
  n. semiliquid 389.5
  v. make viscid 389.10
  thicken 354.10
jellied
  thickened 354.14
  viscous 389.12
jelling 354.4
jelly
  n. semiliquid 389.5
  sweets 308.39
  v. make viscid 389.10
  thicken 354.10
jellyfish coward 892.5
  invertebrate 415.5
  irresolute person
    627.5
  weakling 160.6
jenny ass 414.20
  female animal 421.9
  spinner 206.5
jeopardize 697.6
jeopardized 697.13
jeopardy 697.1
Jeremiah
  prophet 1022.1
  warner 703.4
jerk
  n. bad person 986.6
  fool 471.2
  pull 286.3
  shake 324.3
  v. be excited 857.16
  preserve 701.8
  pull back 295.5
  throw 285.11

twitch 324.13
  yank 286.5
jerkily irregularly 138.4
  shakily 324.23
jerking
  n. preserving 701.2
  twitching 324.5
  adj. jerky 324.19
jerkwater 673.17
jerkwater town 183.3
jerky
  n. beef 308.13
  meat 308.12
  adj. discontinuous
    72.4
  irregular 138.3
  nonuniform 18.3
  paroxysmal 162.22
  twitching 324.19
jerry-built 160.14
jest
  n. banter 882.1
  gibe 967.2
  joke 881.6
  laughingstock 967.7
  trifle 673.5
  v. banter 882.4
  joke 881.13
jester buffoon 612.10
  humorist 881.12
jesting
  n. banter 882.2
  adj. witty 881.15
Jesuit religious 1038.18
  sophist 483.6
jesuitic(al)
  insincere 616.32
  sophistical 483.10
Jesus Christ 1013.12
jet
  n. aircraft 280.3,15
  ascent 315.1
  black 365.4
  ejection 310.7
  engine 348.26
  eruption 162.6
  heater 329.10
  spout 395.9
  v. ascend 315.9
  eject 310.24
  flow out 303.13
  fly 278.45
  spout 395.20
Jet Age 107.9
jeté 319.1
jet engine 281.2
jet flight 278.1
jet lag 686.31
jet-propelled
  flying 278.59
  propelled 285.17
jet propulsion
  aviation 278.33
  rocketry 281.8
  steam propulsion
    285.2
jetsam 633.4
jet set society 644.6
  traveler 274.1
jetstream
  aviation 278.41
  wind 403.1

jettison
  n. abandonment
    633.1
  discard 668.3
  ejection 310.1
  v. abandon 633.5
  discard 668.7
  eject 310.13
jetty barrier 730.5
  breakwater 216.4
  harbor 700.6
jeu d'esprit 881.7
Jew 1020.20,34
jewel
  n. bearing 322.7
  favorite 931.15
  good person 985.1
  good thing 674.5
  ornament 901.6
  v. ornament 901.9
jeweled 901.11
jeweler 830.3
jewelry 901.5
Jewish 1020.29
Jezebel
  seductress 989.15
  unchaste woman
    989.14
  witch 943.7
jib
  n. sail 277.30
  v. be frightened
    891.20
  be irresolute 627.7
  pull back 284.7
  turn aside 291.6
jibe agree 26.6
  be changed 139.5
  change course 275.30
jiffy 113.3
jig
  n. dance 879.7
  jerk 286.3
  jump 319.1
  shake 324.3
  snare 618.12
  v. fish 655.10
  jerk 286.5
  twitch 324.13
jigger
  n. animal 414.40,74
  drink 996.6
  fisher 655.6
  object 376.4
  v. jerk 286.5
  twitch 324.13
jiggle
  n. jerk 286.3
  shake 324.3
  v. jerk 286.5
  twitch 324.13
jiggler 324.9
jillion
  n. immense number
    101.4
  large number 86.4
  number 99.13
  adj. numerous 101.6
jilt
  n. deceiver 619.1
  v. abandon 633.5
  discard 668.7

jilted 867.10
jilter 619.1
Jim Crow
  exclusiveness 77.3
  prejudice 527.4
  seclusion 924.1
jim-dandy
  n. good thing 674.7
  adj. excellent 674.13
jimjams
  delirium tremens
    473.10
  nervousness 859.2
  trepidation 891.5
jimmy
  n. lever 287.4
  v. pry 287.8
jingle
  n. meter 609.9
  poem 609.6
  repetitiousness 103.4
  ringing 454.3
  similar sound 20.6
  v. poetize 609.16
  ring 454.8
jingling
  n. ringing 454.3
  adj. rhyming 609.19
  ringing 454.12
jingo
  n. chauvinist 941.3
  intolerant person
    527.5
  militarist 800.5
  adj. militaristic 797.26
jingoism
  patriotism 941.2
  warlikeness 797.15
jingoistic
  chauvinistic 941.4
  militaristic 797.26
jinni 1016.7
jinx
  n. bad influence 675.4
  spell 1036.1
  v. bewitch 1036.9
  bring bad luck 729.12
  work evil 675.6
jitney 272.12
jitters agitation 324.1
  nervousness 859.2
jittery agitated 324.16
  jumpy 859.11
jiva life force 407.3
  psyche 466.4
jive
  n. banter 882.1
  music 462.9
  v. banter 882.4
  music 462.44
job
  n. act 705.3
  affair 151.3
  a theft 824.10
  function 656.3
  position 656.5
  task 656.2
  v. deal in 827.15
  farm out 780.15
  rent 780.14
  sell 829.8
job action 789.7

jobber
  intermediary 237.4
  merchant 830.2
  stockbroker 833.10
  working person 718.2
jobbing
  Machiavellianism
    735.2
  selling 829.2
  stockbroking 833.18
  trade 827.2
jobholder 718.2
jobless 708.17
job lot 831.1
jock athlete 878.20
  common soldier
    800.7
  he-man 420.6
  supporter 216.2
jockey
  n. rider 274.8
  saddle 216.18
  speeder 269.5
  v. compete 796.19
  maneuver 735.10
jocose 881.15
jocular merry 870.15
  witty 881.15
jocularity
  merriment 870.5
  wittiness 881.2
jog
  n. gait 273.14
  jerk 286.3
  knob 256.3
  notch 262.1
  push 283.2
  shake 324.3
  slowness 270.2
  v. jerk 286.5
  shake 324.11
  thrust 283.11
  walk 273.27
joggling 324.20
jog on continue 143.3
  plod 270.7
  progress 294.3
  walk 273.26
jog the memory 537.20
jog trot routine 642.6
  slowness 270.2
  speed 269.3
jog-trot
  repetitious 103.15
  tedious 884.8
john rest room 311.10
  toilet 311.11
John Bull
  England 181.5
  the government
    741.3
John Doe alias 583.8
  people 417.2
John Hancock
  ratification 521.4
  signature 583.10
johnny man 420.5
  person 417.3
  rest room 311.10
  toilet 311.11
johnnycake 308.29
Johnny-come-lately 78.4

Johnny on the spot
  attentive 530.15
  prompt 131.9
John Q. Public
  common man 79.3
  everyone 417.2
  the people 919.2
Johnsonian 601.8
joie de vivre
  animation 161.3
  pleasure 865.1
join add 40.4
  assemble 74.18
  become a member
    788.14
  be near 200.9
  be sociable 922.16
  cohere 50.7
  combine 52.3
  compose 58.3
  concur 177.2
  connect 71.4
  cooperate 786.3
  enlist 780.16
  gather 47.5
  join in marriage
    933.15
  join together 52.4
  juxtapose 200.13
  meet 47.11
  participate 815.5
  side with 786.4
  unify 14.5
join battle
  contend against
    790.4
  fight 796.17
joined
  accompanying 73.9
  adjacent 200.16
  assembled 74.21
  coherent 50.11
  combined 52.5
  continuous 71.8
  joint 47.12
  related 9.9
  united 47.13
joiner member 788.11
  sociable person
    922.15
join forces 52.4
joining
  n. addition 40.1
  junction 47
  meeting 200.4
  union 47.4
  adj. connecting 47.16
joint
  n. brothel 989.9
  crack 201.2
  disapproved place
    191.28
  gambling house
    515.15
  juncture 47.4
  marihuana 687.13
  meat 308.12
  part 55.4
  place of vice 981.7
  v. fasten 47.8
  adj. accompanying
    73.9

assembled 74.21
combined 52.5
communal 815.9
concurrent 177.4
cooperating 786.5
joined 47.12
mutual 13.14
joint control 815.1
joint effort 786.1
jointly
  collectively 73.11
  concurrently 177.5
  cooperatively 786.6
  mutually 13.17
  together 47.18
joint operation
  cooperation 786.1
  military operation
    797.8
joint ownership 815.1
jointure
  endowment 818.9
  joining 47.1
joke
  n. banter 882.1
  jest 881.6
  laughingstock 967.7
  trifle 673.5
  v. banter 882.4
  jest 881.13
joker condition 507.2
  deceiver 619.1
  difficulty 731.7
  humorist 881.12
  legislative clause
    742.17
  man 420.5
  mischief-maker 738.3
  obstacle 730.4
  person 417.3
  playing card 878.17
  surprise 540.2
  trick 618.6
joking
  n. banter 882.2
  wittiness 881.2
  adj. witty 881.15
jollies marines 800.27
  thrill 857.2
jollity
  conviviality 922.3
  festivity 878.3
  merriment 870.5
jolly
  n. marine 276.4
  v. banter 882.4
  flatter 970.6
  make merry 878.26
  adj. convivial 922.19
  festive 878.30
  intoxicated 996.30
  merry 870.15
jollying
  n. banter 882.2
  adj. bantering 882.5
Jolly Roger 569.6
jolt
  n. drink 996.6
  push 283.2
  shake 324.3
  surprise 540.3
  v. excite 857.13

shake 324.11
startle 540.8
thrust 283.11
walk 273.27
jolting bumpy 324.20
  exciting 857.28
  surprising 540.11
Jonah
  bad influence 675.4
  prophet 1022.1
jongleur poet 609.13
  singer 464.14
joshing
  n. banter 882.2
  ridicule 967.1
  wittiness 881.2
  adj. bantering 882.5
  ridiculing 967.12
  witty 881.15
joss 1033.3
joss stick 436.4
jostle
  n. push 283.2
  shake 324.3
  v. be dissonant 461.3
  be inharmonious
    795.8
  contend 796.14
  disagree 27.5
  shake 324.11
  thrust 283.11
jot
  n. mark 568.5
  minute thing 196.7
  small amount 35.2
  v. record 570.16
jotting 570.4
jounce 324.11
journal
  account book 845.4
  autobiography 608.4
  axle 322.6
  chronicle 114.9
  periodical 605.10
  record book 570.11
journalese
  n. jargon 580.10
  adj. journalistic
    605.26
journalism news 558.1
  the press 605.23
  writing 602.2
journalist 605.22
journalistic 605.26
journey
  n. travel 273.2
  trip 273.5
  v. travel 273.20
journeyer 274.1
journeying
  n. travel 273.1
  adj. traveling 273.35
journeyman
  artisan 718.6
  expert 733.11
  producer 167.8
journey's end 300.5
joust
  n. contest 796.3
  v. contend 796.14
Jove 1014.5
jovial convivial 922.19

festive 878.30
merry 870.15
joviality
conviviality 922.3
festivity 878.3
merriment 870.5
jowl cheek 242.1
jaws 265.5
joy
n. happiness 865.2
merriment 870.5
v. be pleased 865.9
gloat 910.9
rejoice 876.5
joyful cheering 870.16
festive 878.30
happy 865.13
merry 870.15
joyfully
cheerfully 870.17
happily 865.16
joyfulness
happiness 865.2
merriment 870.5
joyless
pleasureless 866.20
unhappy 872.21
unpleasant 864.20
joylessly 872.32
joylessness
distressfulness 864.5
unhappiness 872.2
unpleasure 866.1
joyous, joyously see
joyful etc.
joyride
n. ride 273.7
v. ride 273.32
JP 1002.1
Jr. 124.15
jubilant
gloating 910.12
overjoyed 865.14
rejoicing 876.9
jubilate celebrate 877.2
gloat 910.9
rejoice 876.5
jubilation
festivity 865.3
gloating 910.4
rejoicing 876.1
jubilee
anniversary 137.4
celebration 877.1
rejoicing 876.1
Judaical 1020.29
Judaism 1020.11,32
Judas criminal 986.10
traitor 619.10
Judas-like 975.22
judge
n. adjudicator 494.6
arbitrator 805.4
connoisseur 897.7
magistrate 1002
v. administer justice
1000.5
believe 501.11
exercise judgment
494.8
mediate 805.6
try 1004.17

judgeship 1000.3
judgment
adjudication 494
belief 501.6
condemnation 1008.1
discrimination 492.2
judiciary 1000.2
legal decision 1004.9
punishment 1010.1
sagaciousness 467.7
judgmental
condemnatory 969.23
judicial 494.16
Judgment Day 121.3
judicature court 1001.2
judgment 494.1
judiciary 1000.2
tribunal 1001.1
judicial
intelligent 467.19
judiciary 494.16
jurisdictional 1000.6
legal 998.10
tribunal 1001.10
judicial process
judiciary 1000.2
lawsuit 1004.1
judiciary
n. jurisdiction 1000.2
tribunal 1001.1
adj. judicial 494.16
jurisdictional 1000.6
tribunal 1001.10
judicious
cautious 895.8
discriminating 492.8
intelligent 467.19
judicial 494.16
moderate 163.10
judiciously
cautiously 895.12
intelligently 467.20
moderately 163.17
judiciousness
caution 895.1
discrimination 492.1
moderation 163.1
sagaciousness 467.7
judo 796.10
jug bottle 193.12
ceramic ware 576.2
prison 761.9
Juggernaut idol 1033.3
Vishnu 1014.9
juggle deceive 618.13
tamper with 616.17
juggler cheat 619.3
circus artist 612.3
trickster 619.2
juggling 618.5
jughead dolt 471.4
inferior horse 414.14
jugular 396.22
juice
electric current 342.2
fluid 388.2
juiceless 393.7
juiciness
immaturity 124.3
liquidity 388.1
pleasantness 863.3
juicy fluid 388.6

immature 124.10
interesting 530.19
pleasant 863.9
tasty 428.8
jujitsu 796.10
jukebox 450.11
juke joint 878.11
jumble
n. cake 308.41
confusion 532.3
hodgepodge 44.6
scramble 62.3
unintelligibility 549.7
v. be undiscriminating
493.3
confuse 63.3
deform 247.3
disorder 62.9
make unintelligible
549.12
mix 44.11
jumbled chaotic 62.16
confused 532.12
hard to understand
549.14
mixed 44.15
jumbo
n. large animal 195.14
large thing 195.11
adj. huge 195.20
Jumbo 414.4
jump
n. advantage 36.2
ascent 315.1
flight 278.9
increase 38.1
interval 201.1
leap 319.1
step 273.13
v. attack 798.15
be eager about 635.7
be frightened 891.20
be startled 540.5
contend 796.15
escape 632.6
flee 631.10
leap 319.5
leave undone 534.7
parachute 278.56
seize on 822.16
shake 324.11
walk 273.27
jump bail 631.10
jumper athlete 878.20
clothing 231.30
diver 320.4
leaper 319.4
jump in enter 302.7
get in 315.12
jumping
n. leaping 319.3
adj. leaping 319.7
jumping-off place
end 70.2
one-horse town 183.3
remote region 199.4
jump on
reprove 969.18
suppress 760.8
jumps 859.2
jump ship 187.9

jump the gun
anticipate 131.6
be impatient 862.4
prejudge 495.2
jump to a conclusion
495.2
jump up ascend 315.9
increase 38.4
rise 213.8
jumpy active 707.20
agitated 324.16
fearful 891.31
jerky 324.19
jittery 859.11
junction addition 40.1
assembly 74.1
cohesion 50.1
combination 52.1
composition 58.1
concurrence 177.1
joining 47.1
juxtaposition 200.3
passageway 657.4
railway 657.8
relationship 9.1
juncture
circumstance 8.1
joint 47.4
pause 144.4
period 107.1
speech 594.10
jungle complex 46.2
woodland 411.11
junior
n. inferior 37.2
student 566.6
subordinate 764.5
youngster 125.1
adj. inferior 37.6
succeeding 117.4
younger 124.15
junior college 567.7
junior high school
567.6
junk
n. abandoned thing
633.4
drugs 687.5
fake 616.13
heroin 687.12
rubbish 669.5
sailing vessel 277.23
v. discard 668.8
eject 310.13
adj. worthless 669.11
junket journey 273.5
pudding 308.45
junkie 642.10
junking 668.3
junkman 830.10
junkyard 669.6
Juno goddess 1014.5
marriage goddess
933.14
Junoesque 900.17
junta clique 788.6
combination 52.1
council 755.1
group 74.3
Jupiter god 1014.5
planet 375.9
Jupiter Fidius 976.5

young goat 125.8
young person 125.2
v. banter 882.4
fool 618.14
joke 881.13
kid along 970.6
kid around joke 881.13
trifle 673.13
kidder banterer 882.3
deceiver 619.1
kidding
n. banter 882.1
deception 618.1
jesting 882.2
adj. bantering 882.5
ridiculing 967.12
kidnap abduct 824.19
seize 822.14
kidnapper 825.10
kidnapping
abduction 824.8
seizure 822.2
kidney
diseases of 686.22
kind 61.3
meat 308.20
temperament 525.3
vitals 225.4
kidney-shaped 252.16
kill
n. quarry 655.7
running water 395.1
slaughter 409.1
v. amuse 878.23
delete 42.12
end 70.7
hush up 614.8
legislate 742.18
put an end to 693.12
slay 409.13
suppress 760.8
turn off 144.12
veto 778.5
kill-crazy 162.20
killer evildoer 943.3
slayer 409.11
violent person 162.9
killer-diller 674.7
killing
n. gain 811.3
great success 724.3
slaying 409
violence 162.3
violent death 408.6
adj. fatal 409.23
fatiguing 717.11
gorgeous 900.19
laborious 716.18
killjoy hinderer 730.9
pessimist 889.7
spoilsport 872.14
kill oneself 409.22
kill time
amuse oneself 878.24
spend time 105.6
waste time 708.12
kiln
n. oven 576.5
v. dry 393.6
kilo thousand 99.10
unit of weight 352.23

kilocycle
radio frequency
344.12
thousand 99.10
kilometer
linear measure 490.17
thousand 99.10
kilowatt-hour
electric unit 342.35
unit of energy 161.6
kin class 61.2
kind 61.3
kinsmen 11.2
kind
n. nature 5.3
race 11.4
sort 61.3
adj. benevolent
938.13
forgiving 947.6
friendly 927.14
good 674.12
helpful 785.22
indulgent 759.8
kindergarten 567.4
kindergartner 566.4
kindhearted 938.13
kindle
become angry 952.18
energize 161.9
excite 857.11
ignite 329.22
incite 648.18
make hot 329.18
kindled 328.27
kindling
n. firewood 331.3
ignition 329.4
adj. inflammatory
329.27
kindly
adj. benevolent
938.13
helpful 785.22
indulgent 759.8
adv. benevolently
938.18
fervently 855.28
pleasantly 863.11
kindness
benevolence 938
forgiveness 947.1
friendship 927.1
good deed 938.7
goodness 674.1
indulgence 759.2
pity 944.1
kind of
so to speak 20.19
to a degree 29.7
kindred
n. blood relationship
11.1
kinsmen 11.2
adj. akin 11.6
related 9.10
kindred soul 20.3
kine 414.6
kinematograph
photography 577.11
projector 577.12
theater 611.19

kinescope
cinematography
577.8
picture tube 345.18
kinesic 568.24
kinesis 267.1
kinetic(al)
dynamic 347.9
energetic 161.12
kinetic energy 161.1
kinetics
aeronautics 278.2
dynamics 347.3
motion 267.1
kinfolk 11.2
king businessman 830.1
chessman 878.18
chief 672.10
playing card 878.17
potentate 749.7
prince 918.7
kingdom
biological classifica-
tion 406.3
categorization 61.5
class 61.4
country 181.1
nomenclature 583.1
kingdom come
Heaven 1018.1
paradise 535.11
kingfish 749.3
kingly dignified 905.12
noble 918.10
sovereign 739.17
kingmaker
influential person
172.6
political intriguer
746.6
kingpin 749.3
King's English, the
580.4
kingship
noble rank 918.9
sovereignty 739.8
supremacy 36.3
king-size large 34.7
oversize 195.23
king's ransom 837.2
kink
n. caprice 629.1
curl 254.2
deformity 679.1
eccentricity 474.2
imperfection 678.2
pain 424.2
v. blemish 679.4
curl 254.5
kinked
blemished 679.8
curly 254.9
kinky capricious 629.5
curly 254.9
eccentric 474.4
unconventional 83.6
kinship accord 794.1
blood ties 11.1
relationship 9.3
similarity 20.2
kinsmen 11.2
kiosk hut 191.10

store 832.3
summerhouse 191.13
kipper
n. food 308.24
salmon 414.35
v. preserve 701.8
kirk 1042.1
kishkes abdomen 193.3
viscera 225.4
kismet 640.2
kiss
n. contact 200.5
greeting 925.4
lovemaking 932.3
touch 425.1
v. graze 200.10
greet 925.10
make love 932.17
touch lightly 425.7
kissable 931.23
kiss and make up
804.10
kisser face 240.4
mouth 265.5
kiss good-bye
lose 812.4
relinquish 814.3
kit equipment 659.4
kitten 414.26
set 74.12
viol 465.6
young cat 125.8
kitchen
n. cookroom 330.3
restaurant 307.15
room 192.14
adj. cooking 330.5
kitchen cabinet
council 755.1
legislature 742.8
kitchen police 800.19
kite
n. aircraft 280.1
counterfeit 835.10
types of 280.14
v. soar 315.10
kited check 842.3
kith and kin 11.2
kitsch literature 602.12
vulgarity 898.1
work of art 574.11
kitten
n. cat 414.26
child 125.3
young animal 125.8
v. give birth 167.15
kittenish feline 414.46
feminine 421.13
infantile 124.12
kitty funds 835.14
kitten 414.26
stakes 515.5
kittycorner
adj. diagonal 219.19
adv. diagonally 219.25
Klaxon alarm 704.1
noisemaker 453.5
kleptomania 824.12
klieg light 611.23
klutz
awkward person
734.8

L
N

lap 395.8
adj. covering 228.35
water sound 452.19
lapse
n. an error 518.4
conversion 145.1
decrease 39.2
deterioration 692.3
end 70.3
fall 316.2
impiety 1030.1
misdeed 982.2
neglect 534.1
pause 144.3
regression 295.1
relapse 696.1
reversion 146.1
v. be wrong 518.9
decline 692.20
elapse 105.5
end 70.6
go wrong 981.9
neglect 534.6
pass 119.6
regress 295.5
relapse 696.4
revert 146.4
sink 316.6
lapsed carnal 987.6
impious 1030.6
past 119.7
unrighteous 981.12
lapse of memory 538.1
lapse of time 105.4
lap up
be credulous 502.6
drink 307.28
tipple 996.23
larboard 244.1
larcenous 824.20
larceny 824.2
lard
n. fat 380.13
pork 308.16
v. make better 691.9
oil 380.8
larder pantry 660.8
provisions 308.5
store 660.1
lares and penates
household gods
191.30
spirits 1014.22
large immense 34.7
liberal 853.4
sizable 195.16
largehearted
benevolent 938.15
liberal 853.4
magnanimous 979.6
largely
comprehensively
56.14
greatly 34.15
on a large scale
195.25
large-minded 526.8
largeness greatness 34.1
liberality 853.1
sizableness 195.6
size 195.1

large-scale
extensive 79.13
large 195.16
largess gratuity 818.5
liberality 853.1
largo
n. musical passage
462.25
tempo 463.24
adv. music 462.55
lariat 618.12
lark
n. ascent 315.7
revel 878.6
songbird 464.23
v. make merry 878.26
larrup pound 283.14
punish 1010.15
larva bug 414.36
embryo 406.14
specter 1017.1
young insect 125.10
larval 406.24
laryngitis
inflammation 686.9
respiratory disease
686.14
larynx 594.19
lascivious
amorous 931.24
desirous 634.21
lecherous 989.29
sexual 419.29
lash
n. blow 283.7
goad 648.8
hair 230.12
whip 1011.1
v. anchor 275.15
bind 47.9
criticize severely
969.21
drive animals 416.8
goad 648.15
punish 1010.14
restrain 760.10
lashing
connection 47.3
punishment 1010.4
lash out at 798.16
lass girl 125.6
lady love 931.14
woman 421.5
lassitude fatigue 717.1
languor 708.6
weakness 160.1
lasso
n. loop 253.2
snare 618.12
v. catch 822.17
last
n. end 70.1
model 25.6
v. elapse 105.5
endure 110.6
live 407.10
live on 1.9
persevere 625.2
remain 140.5
adj. completory 722.9
departing 301.19
eventual 151.11

final 70.10
foregoing 119.11
newest 122.14
adv. finally 70.11
lasting durable 110.10
permanent 140.7
persevering 625.7
protracted 110.11
remembered 537.23
substantial 3.7
temporal 105.7
tough 359.4
unchangeable 142.17
last minute 132.1
last-minute hasty 709.9
late 132.18
last name 583.5
last resort
last expedient 670.2
refuge 700.2
last rites
funeral rites 410.4
unction 1040.6
last straw cause 153.3
limit of patience
862.3
Last Supper 1040.8
last word
culmination 677.3
dying word 67.1
end 70.1
final proposal 773.3
last word, the
novelty 122.2
the rage 644.4
latch close 266.6
fasten 47.8
late
adj. anachronous
115.3
belated 132.16
dead 408.30
delayed 270.12
former 119.10
recent 122.12
untimely 130.7
adv. behind 132.19
late bloomer 132.6
latecomer 132.6
late lamented
n. corpse 408.16
adj. dead 408.30
lately 122.16
latency
dormancy 268.4
latent meaningfulness
546.1
lateness
anachronism 115.1
newness 122.1
posteriority 117.1
tardiness 132
untimeliness 130.1
latent
concealed 615.11
dormant 268.14
secret 614.11
underlying 546.5
unseen 445.5
later
adj. future 121.8
late 132.18

recent 122.12
subsequent 117.4
adv. in the future
121.9
subsequently 117.6
lateral
n. speech sound
594.13
throw 285.4
v. go sideways 242.5
adj. phonetic 594.31
side 242.6
sided 242.7
latest newest 122.14
present 120.2
latest thing, the
novelty 122.2
the rage 644.4
lath
n. strip 206.4
thinness 205.7
wood 378.3
v. cover 228.23
lathe converter 145.10
tool 348.12
lather
n. dither 857.5
foam 405.2
impatience 862.1
sweat 311.7
v. defeat 727.6
foam 405.5
punish 1010.15
wash 681.19
latitude breadth 204.1
broad-mindedness
526.1
coordinates 490.6
freedom 762.4
map 654.4
spare 179.3
zone 180.3
latitudinarian
n. broad-minded per-
son 526.6
freethinker 1031.13
independent 762.12
adj. broad-minded
526.9
freethinking 1031.21
nonrestrictive 762.24
latrine
rest room 311.10
toilet 311.11
latter foregoing 119.11
recent 122.12
lattice
n. atom 326.7
frame 245.4
network 221.3
reactor 326.13
window 265.8
v. net 221.7
laud
n. hymn 1032.3
praise 968.5
worship 1032.2
v. praise 968.12
worship 1032.11
laudable good 674.12
praiseworthy 968.20
laudanum 687.12,54

1050

laudatory 968.16
lauded 34.9
laugh
  n. joke 881.6
  laughter 876.4
  v. be cheerful 870.6
  be pleased 865.9
  chuckle 876.8
laughable
  foolish 470.10
  humorous 880.4
laugh at flout 793.4
  ridicule 967.8
laughing
  n. laughter 876.4
  adj. cheerful 870.11
  happy 865.13
laughingstock 967.7
laugh it up
  amuse oneself 878.24
  laugh 876.8
laugh off 531.4
laughs 878.2
laughter laughing 876.4
  merriment 870.5
launch
  n. motorboat 277.4,21
  rocketry 281.9
  v. inaugurate 68.11
  propose 773.5
  rocket 281.13
  start 285.14
  throw 285.11
launcher 801.19,27
launching 68.5
launching pad
  platform 216.13
  rocketry 281.10
launch into
  set to work 716.15
  undertake 715.3
launder 681.19
laundress 681.15
laundry
  laundering 681.6
  washery 681.11
laureate
  n. champion 733.14
  poet 609.13
  superior 36.4
  adj. honored 916.9
laurels 916.3
lava ashes 329.16
  rock 384.1,12
lavatory
  bathing place 681.10
  rest room 311.10
  room 192.26
  washing equipment
  681.12
lave soak 392.13
  wash 681.19
lavender 373.3,4
lavish
  v. give 818.12
  squander 854.3
  adj. liberal 853.4
  plentiful 661.7
  prodigal 854.8
  superabundant
  663.19
  teeming 101.9

lavishly liberally 853.5
  plentifully 661.9
  superabundantly
  663.24
lavishness
  grandeur 904.5
  overabundance 663.2
  plenty 661.2
  prodigality 854.1
lavish upon
  be generous 853.3
  give 818.15
lavish with 663.14
law
  n. axiom 517.2
  decree 752.4
  jurisprudence 998.7
  precept 751.2
  prohibition 778.1
  rule 84.4
  statute 998.3
  v. sue 1004.12
law, the 699.16
law-abiding
  honest 974.13
  obedient 766.3
law and order 803.2
lawbreaker
  criminal 986.10
  evildoer 943.1
lawbreaking
  disobedience 767.1
  illegality 999.3
  wrongdoing 982.1
law enforcement agency
  699.17
law enforcement agent
  699.15
lawful authentic 516.14
  just 976.8
  legal 998.10
  permissible 777.15
  valid 516.13
lawfully legally 998.12
  permissibly 777.19
lawfulness justice 976.1
  legality 998.1
  permissibility 777.8
lawgiver 746.3
lawless anarchic 740.5
  disobedient 767.8
  illegal 999.6
lawlessly 740.7
lawlessness anarchy 740
  disobedience 767.1
  illegality 999.1
  presumption 961.2
lawmaker 746.3
lawmaking
  n. legislation 742.13
  adj. legislative 742.19
lawn 411.7
law of averages 156.1
lawsuit
  accusation 1005.1
  legal action 1004
lawyer 1003
lax dilatory 132.17
  flaccid 357.10
  gentle 759.7
  inaccurate 518.17
  indolent 708.18

loose 51.5
  negligent 534.10
  nonrestrictive 762.24
  permissive 777.14
  phonetic 594.31
  unchaste 989.26
  unrestrained 762.23
  unstrict 758.4
  vague 514.18
laxative 687.17,62
laxity flaccidity 357.3
  inaccuracy 518.2
  looseness 51.2
  neglect 534.1
  nonobservance 769.1
  unchastity 989.4
  unstrictness 758.1
  vagueness 514.4
laxness
  dilatoriness 132.5
  flaccidity 357.3
  leniency 759.1
  looseness 51.2
  neglect 534.1
  unrestraint 762.3
  unstrictness 758
lay
  n. direction 290.1
  melody 462.4
  position 184.3
  song 462.13
  v. bet 515.20
  copulate 419.23
  exorcise 1035.12
  impose 963.4
  level 214.6
  lie 214.5
  moderate 163.6
  pacify 804.7
  place 184.11
  put 184.13
  relieve 886.5
  reproduce 169.9
  sail 275.48
  smooth 260.5
  adj. nonordained
  1039.3
lay aside
  disregard 531.4
  postpone 132.9
  put away 668.6
  remove 271.10
  segregate 77.6
lay away
  put away 668.6
  store 660.10
lay before
  confront 240.8
  propose 773.5
lay by be idle 708.15
  postpone 132.9
  prepare 720.11
  put away 668.6
  reserve 660.12
  water travel 275.17
lay down affirm 523.4
  bet 515.20
  give up 633.7
  layer 227.5
  level 214.6
  pay over 841.15
  postulate 499.12

  prescribe 752.10
  put 184.13
  sail 275.43
  store 660.10
lay down the law
  command 752.11
  direct 747.8
  dogmatize 513.10
  dominate 741.15
layer
  n. atmospheric layer
  402.3
  stratum 227
  v. laminate 227.5
layered 227.6
layette 231.30
lay figure
  art equipment 574.19
  figure 572.4
  figurehead 749.4
  model 25.5
  nonentity 4.2
lay hands on
  acquire 811.9
  attack 798.15
  bless 1032.13
  minister 1040.19
  seize 822.14
lay in sail for 275.35
  store 660.10
laying on of hands
  benediction 1032.5
  rite 1040.4
lay into attack 798.15
  contend 796.15
lay it on thick
  be bombastic 601.6
  boast 910.7
  coat 228.24
  dramatize 903.12
  exaggerate 617.3
  flatter 970.6
  overdo 663.11
lay low
  bring down 318.5
  level 214.6
  strike dead 409.18
  weaken 160.10
layman
  nonprofessional
  718.5
  secular 1039.2
layoff dismissal 310.5
  pause 144.3
  unemployment 708.3
lay off
  v. be idle 708.15
  cease 144.6
  chart 654.11
  circumscribe 234.4
  dismiss 310.19
  measure off 490.12
  stop work 144.8
  take a rest 711.8
  interj. stop! 144.15
lay of the land, the 7.2
lay on administer 963.6
  coat 228.24
  contend 796.15
  cover 228.19
  impose 963.4
  punish 1010.14

layout form 246.1
  order 59.1
  plan 654.1
  typesetting 603.2
lay out chart 654.11
  form 246.7
  kill 409.14
  knock down 318.5
  level 214.6
  measure off 490.12
  order 59.4
  prepare for burial 410.21
  render insensible 423.4
  spend 843.5
layover 188.5
lay over cover 228.19
  postpone 132.9
  sojourn 188.8
lay the foundation
  establish 184.15
  prepare the way 720.12
lay to
  attribute to 155.4
  be idle 708.15
  exert oneself 716.9
  water travel 275.17
lay to rest 410.19
lay waste
  destroy 693.10
  pillage 162.10
laze go slow 270.6
  idle 708.11
lazily 270.13
laziness
  carelessness 534.2
  indolence 708.5
  slowness 270.1
lazy
  v. idle 708.11
  adj. careless 534.11
  dilatory 132.17
  indolent 708.18
  slow 270.10
lazybones 708.7
lea 411.8
leach
  n. solution 391.3
  v. exude 303.15
  liquefy 391.5
  refine 681.22
  soak 392.13
  subtract 42.9
  trickle 395.18
leached 166.4
lead
  n. metal 383.21
  plumb 213.6
  weight 352.6
  v. weigh down 352.12
  adj. metal 383.17
lead
  n. actor 612.6
  being ahead 292.1
  clue 568.9
  direction 747.1
  harmonics 463.12
  horse 414.16
  model 25.1
  pointer 568.4

precedence 64.1
  principal 672.10
  role 611.11
  superiority 36.1
  v. bear 290.8
  begin 68.10
  be in front 240.7
  cause 153.12
  direct 747.8
  escort 73.8
  govern 741.12
  gravitate 352.15
  head 292.2
  induce 648.22
  influence 172.7
  music 462.46
  pioneer 66.3
  precede 64.2
  take precedence 36.11
  tend 174.3
lead by the nose
  dominate 741.15
  have influence over 172.11
  have subject 764.10
  influence 172.7
leaden colorless 363.7
  gray 366.4
  heavy 352.16
  inert 268.14
  languid 708.19
  metal 383.17
  stilted 590.3
  uninteresting 883.6
leader chief 749.3
  commentary 606.2
  commodity 831.2
  conductor 464.17
  director 748.6
  horse 414.16
  lawyer 1003.4
  precursor 66.1
  question 485.10
  special 81.2
  superior 36.4
leadership
  directorship 747.4
  influence 172.1
  mastership 739.7
  supremacy 36.3
leading
  n. direction 747.1
  heading 292
  adj. authoritative 739.15
  best 36.14
  directing 747.12
  dominant 741.18
  first 68.17
  front 240.10
  heading 292.3
  most important 672.23
  preceding 64.4
leading lady lead 612.6
  role 611.11
leading light
  first-rater 674.6
  principal 672.10
leading to 174.5

lead item
  commodity 831.2
  special 81.2
lead off begin 68.10
  precede 64.2
lead on direct 747.8
  influence 172.9
  lure 650.4
lead the way
  begin 68.10
  head 292.2
  set an example 25.7
lead to cause 153.13
  direct to 290.7
  entail 76.4
  extend to 199.6
lead up to 720.12
leaf
  n. advertising 559.8
  book 605.12
  frond 411.17
  layer 227.2
  paper 378.6
  tobacco 434.2
  v. vegetate 411.31
leafage 411.16
leaflet
  advertising 559.8
  booklet 605.9
  leaf 411.17
leaf metal 383.23
leaf through 485.25
leafy green 371.4
  layered 227.6
  leaved 411.38
league
  n. affiliation 786.2
  association 788.1
  combination 52.1
  treaty 771.2
  v. come together 74.16
  confederate 52.4
  cooperate 786.3
  enlist 788.14
  join 47.5
leagued
  assembled 74.21
  confederated 52.6
  joined 47.13
League of Nations
  international organi-
    zation 743.1
  supranational govern-
    ment 741.7
leak
  n. crack 201.2
  divulgence 556.2
  drip 303.5
  escape 632.1
  opening 265.1
  v. be lost 812.6
  divulge 556.6
  flow out 303.14
leakage entrance 302.1
  escape 632.1
  loss 812.2
  outflow 303.5
leak in 302.10
leak out
  be revealed 556.8
  find vent 632.10

flow out 303.14
leakproof
  resistant 159.18
  watertight 393.11
leaky 303.20
lean
  n. inclination 219.2
  v. be willing 622.3
  gravitate 352.15
  incline 219.10
  tend 174.3
  adj. in plain style 591.3
  meager 662.10
  thin 205.17
leaning
  n. aptitude 733.5
  desire 634.3
  injustice 977.3
  obliquity 219.2
  preference 637.5
  prejudice 527.3
  tendency 174.1
  trait of character 525.3
  adj. oblique 219.15
  tending 174.4
  unbalanced 31.5
lean on
  believe in 501.16
  compel 756.6
  rest on 216.22
lean-to 191.10
lean toward
  prefer 637.17
  take an attitude 525.6
leap
  n. ascent 315.1
  degree 29.1
  increase 38.1
  innovation 139.3
  interval 201.1
  jump 319
  prelude 66.2
  v. jump 319.5
  make haste 709.5
  run 269.10
leapfrog 319.5
leaping
  n. jumping 319.3
  adj. ascending 315.14
  happy 865.13
  jumping 319.7
leap year
  anniversary 137.4
  year 107.2
learn ascertain 564.6
  become informed 557.13
  be taught 564.11
  get knowledge 475.14
  understand 548.7
learn by heart 537.17
learned erudite 475.21
  studentlike 566.12
  taught 564.16
  wise 467.17
learned man 476.3
learner beginner 68.2
  student 566.1

learning
  intellectual acquire-
    ment 564
  knowledge 475.4
learn the ropes 564.9
lease
  n. estate 810.5
  hire 780.5
  possession 808.1
  v. hire out 780.15
  rent 780.14
leased 780.19
leasehold
  n. estate 810.5
  possession 808.1
  adj. real 810.11
leaseholder 809.4
lease-lend lend 820.5
  rent out 780.15
leash
  n. restraint 760.4
  trio 93.1
  v. bind 47.9
  restrain 760.10
least
  n. minority 102.3
  adj. humble 906.9
  minority 102.7
  smallest 37.8
  adv. less 37.9
leather
  n. skin 229.1,9
  toughness 359.2
  v. punish 1010.15
  adj. leathern 229.7
leatherneck
  marine 800.27
  mariner 276.4
leathery leather 229.7
  tough 359.4
leave
  n. absence 187.4
  departure 301.4
  permission 777.1
  vacation 711.3
  v. abandon 633.5
  bequeath 818.18
  depart 301.6
  die 408.28
  leave remaining 43.6
  leave undone 534.7
  permit 777.9
  plants 411.31
  resign 784.2
  separate 49.9
leave alone
  be permissive 777.12
  do nothing 706.4
  not change 140.6
  not interfere 762.16
leave behind
  abandon 633.5
  die 408.28
  leave remaining 43.6
  overtake 269.17
  surpass 36.10
leaved foliated 411.38
  green 371.4
leaven
  n. leavening 353.4,18
  transformer 139.4
  v. fill 186.7

infuse 44.12
  qualify 507.3
  raise 353.7
leavening
  n. fermentation 353.4
  adj. raising 353.16
leave no stone unturned
  be thorough 56.8
  make every effort
    714.13
  persevere 625.5
  ransack 485.32
  take precautions
    895.6
leave of absence
  absence 187.4
  vacation 711.3
leave off
  v. break the habit
    643.3
  cease 144.6
  discontinue 668.4
  give up 633.7
  interj. cease! 144.14
leave one cold
  be uninteresting
    883.4
  bore 884.6
leave out 77.4
leave-taking 301.4
leave undone 723.2
leave well enough alone
  see let well enough
    alone
leave word
  communicate 554.7
  inform 557.8
leaving
  abandonment 633.1
  absence 187.4
  departure 301.1
leaving out
  excluding 77.9
  less 42.14
leavings refuse 669.4
  remainder 43.1
lecher
  bad person 986.5
  philanderer 932.11
  unchaste person
    989.11
lecherous 989.29
lechery
  lasciviousness 989.5
  lovemaking 932.9
lectern
  church part 1042.13
  desk 216.15
lector
  churchman 1038.10
  holy orders 1038.4
  lecturer 565.8
lecture
  n. lesson 562.7
  reproof 969.5
  speech 599.3
  v. discourse 562.17
  reprove 969.17
  speak 599.11
lecturer
  academic rank 565.4
  churchman 1038.10

speaker 599.5
  teacher 565.8
lecturing
  n. public speaking
    599.1
  adj. educational
    562.19
ledge
  hidden danger 697.5
  horizontal 214.3
  layer 227.1
  lip 235.4
  shelf 216.14
ledger
  account book 845.4
  list 88.5
  record book 570.11
lee
  n. protection 699.1
  side 242.2
  adj. side 242.6
leech
  n. adherent 50.4
  bloodsucker 414.41
  doctor 688.6
  extortionist 822.12
  invertebrate 415.5
  parasite 907.4
  sail part 277.14
  v. bleed 689.33
leeching 689.26
leer
  n. look 439.3
  ridicule 967.4
  signal 568.15
  v. scrutinize 439.15
  signal 568.22
leering
  n. ridicule 967.1
  adj. ridiculing 967.12
leery cautious 895.9
  doubtful 503.9
  suspicious 504.4
lees refuse 669.4
  residue 43.2
leeward
  n. lee side 242.2
  adj. side 242.6
  adv. downwind 242.9
  sailing 275.68
  toward 290.26
leeway aviation 278.37
  distance 199.1
  interval 201.1
  latitude 762.4
  spare 179.3
  water travel 275.9
left
  n. left side 244.1
  liberalism 745.3
  liberals 745.11
  adj. abandoned 633.8
  departed 301.20
  left-hand 244.4
  remaining 43.7
  adv. to the left 244.6
left-handed
  clumsy 734.20
  insulting 965.6
  oblique 219.13
  sinistromanual 244.5

left-handed compliment
  965.2
left-hander 244.3
leftist
  n. liberal 745.11
  adj. liberal 745.19
left out 77.7
leftover
  n. remainder 43.1
  surplus 663.5
  adj. remaining 43.7
  surplus 663.18
leftward
  counterclockwise
    290.26
  to the left 244.6
left wing
  left side 244.1
  liberalism 745.3
left-wing left 244.4
  liberal 745.19
left-winger
  left side 244.1
  liberal 745.11
lefty 244.3
leg
  n. assist 785.2
  electric circuit 342.4
  fowl part 308.23
  limb 273.16
  part 55.4
  support 217.6
  voyage 275.6
  v. walk 273.26
legacy bequest 818.10
  inheritance 819.2
  result 154.1
legal just 976.8
  legitimate 998.10
  permissible 777.15
  recorded 570.18
  valid 516.13
legal age 126.2
legal counselor 1003.1
legalistic formal 646.7
  legal 998.11
legality justice 976.1
  legitimacy 998
  permissibility 777.8
legalization 998.2
legalize
  authorize 777.11
  legitimize 998.8
legally
  legitimately 998.12
  permissibly 777.19
legal system 1000.2
legal tender 835.1
legate delegate 781.2
  diplomat 781.6
legatee 819.4
legation
  commission 780.1
  diplomats 781.7
  office 719.8
legato
  n. musical passage
    462.25
  music style 462.31
  adv. music 462.54
legend biography 608.4
  caption 484.2

fiction 608.7
map 654.4
mythology 1014.24
posthumous fame
914.7
tradition 123.2
legendary
extraordinary 85.14
fabricated 616.29
famous 914.16
fictional 608.17
historical 608.18
imaginary 535.21
mythical 1014.25
traditional 123.12
legerdemain 618.5
legging 231.62
leggy 207.21
legibility 548.3
legible 548.11
legibly 548.13
legion army 800.22
large number 101.3
military unit 800.19
throng 74.4
legionary 800.6
legislate legalize 998.8
make laws 742.18
legislation law 998.3
lawmaking 742.13
legalization 998.2
legislative
congressional 742.19
legal 998.10
legislator
lawmaker 746.3
public official 749.17
legislature
council 755.1
legislation 742.13
legislative body 742
legit
n. theater 611.1
adj. legal 998.10
legitimacy
genuineness 516.5
justifiability 1006.7
legality 998.1
permissibility 777.8
right 739.1
legitimate
authentic 516.14
justifiable 1006.14
legal 998.10
logical 482.20
permissible 777.15
theatrical 611.38
valid 516.13
legitimately
genuinely 516.18
legally 998.12
permissibly 777.19
leg man 605.22
legume plant 411.4
seed vessel 411.28
legwork
investigation 485.4
walking 273.10
lei 411.23
leisure
n. ease 710
adj. idle 708.17

leisured 710.5
leisure class 708.10
leisured idle 708.17
leisure 710.5
leisurely
adj. slow 270.10
unhurried 710.6
adv. slowly 270.13
tardily 132.20
leitmotiv 462.30
lemon
n. failure 725.2
sour thing 432.2
adj. yellow 370.4
lend
deal in money 835.27
loan 820.5
lend a hand 785.11
lender 820.3
lending loaning 820
money market 835.16
lend-lease
n. lease 780.5
lending 820.1
v. lend 820.5
rent out 780.15
length distance 199.1
longness 202
size 195.1
lengthen
continue 143.4
increase 38.4
prolong 202.7
protract 110.9
lengthened
prolonged 202.9
protracted 110.11
lengthening
n. continuance 143.1
prolongation 202.5
protraction 110.2
adj. increasing 38.8
lengthwise
along 202.12
horizontally 214.9
lengthy long 202.8
tall 207.21
wordy 593.12
leniency
considerateness 938.3
indulgence 759
moderation 163.2
patience 861.1
pity 944.1
softness 357.1
tolerance 526.4
unstrictness 758.1
lenient
considerate 938.16
indulgent 759.7
patient 861.9
permissive 777.14
pitying 944.7
tolerant 526.11
unstrict 758.4
lenitive
n. alleviator 163.3
ointment 380.3
palliative 687.10
adj. lubricant 380.10
palliative 163.16
qualifying 507.7

relieving 886.9
remedial 687.40
lens eye 439.9
glass 443
lent 820.6
Lent fast 995.3
holy day 1040.15
Lenten
abstinent 992.10
fasting 995.5
meager 662.10
lento 462.55
leonine 414.46
leopard
animal 414.27,58
variegation 374.6
leper 926.4
leprechaun 1014.18
leprosy
infectious disease
686.12
skin disease 686.33
leprous 686.57
lesbian
n. homosexual 419.16
mannish female
420.9
adj. bisexual 419.32
lesbianism 419.12
lese majesty 975.7
lesion distress 866.5
impairment 692.8
sore 686.35
less
adj. fewer 102.6
inferior 37.6
reduced 39.10
adv. decreasingly
39.12
least 37.9
prep. lacking 662.17
without 42.14
lessee renter 190.8
tenant 809.4
lessen decrease 39.6
mitigate 1006.12
moderate 163.6
reduce 39.7
relieve 886.5
subtract 42.9
lessening
n. decrease 39.1
moderation 163.2
reduction 42.2
relief 886.1
adj. decreasing 39.11
moderating 163.14
lesser inferior 37.6
reduced 39.10
lesson reproof 969.5
teaching 562.7
warning 703.1
lest 175.6
let
n. hindrance 730.1
hire 780.5
v. extract 305.12
hire out 780.15
permit 777.9
rent 780.14
suppose 499.10
adj. employed 780.19

let alone
v. abstain 992.7
avoid 631.6
do nothing 706.4
leave undone 534.7
not change 140.6
not interfere 762.16
not use 668.5
prep. excluding 77.9
in addition 40.12
let be do nothing 706.4
leave undone 534.7
not change 140.6
not interfere 762.16
suppose 499.10
letdown
disappointment
541.1
humiliation 906.2
moderation 163.2
slowing 270.4
let down
v. betray 975.14
deceive 618.13
depress 318.4
desert 633.6
disappoint 541.2
get worse 692.19
humiliate 906.4
moderate 163.9
relax 711.7
slow 270.9
adj. disappointed
541.5
let drop divulge 556.6
let fall 318.7
remark 594.25
let fly shoot 285.13
throw 285.11
let fly at hurl at 798.28
lash out at 798.16
let go acquit 1007.4
discharge 75.8
discontinue 668.4
dismiss 310.19
do nothing 706.5
exempt 762.14
leave undone 534.7
let oneself go 762.18
loosen 51.3
make merry 878.26
neglect 534.6
release 763.5
relinquish 814.4
lethal fatal 409.23
harmful 675.12
lethality
deadliness 409.9
harmfulness 675.5
lethargic
apathetic 856.13
languid 708.19
sleepy 712.21
lethargy apathy 856.4
emotional symptom
690.23
languor 708.6
sleepiness 712.1
stupidity 469.3
stupor 712.6
let in receive 306.10
welcome 925.7

let in on
 disillusion 520.2
 divulge 556.5
 inform 557.11
let it all hang out
 tell the truth 556.7
 uninhibited 762.18
let it go condone 947.4
 disregard 531.4
 forget 947.5
 no matter 673.22
let loose
 let oneself go 762.18
 make merry 878.26
 release 763.5
 relinquish 814.4
let off
 v. acquit 1007.4
 exempt 762.14
 explode 162.13
 hire out 780.15
 release 763.5
 shoot 285.13
 adj. exempt 762.29
let on confess 556.7
 fake 616.21
let out disclose 556.4
 dismiss 310.19
 divulge 556.5
 extract 305.12
 give vent to 310.23
 hire out 780.15
 lengthen 202.7
 release 763.5
 say 594.23
let pass accept 861.6
 disregard 531.2
 do nothing 706.5
let ride
 do nothing 706.5
 neglect 534.6
let slide let go 706.5
 neglect 534.6
let slip disregard 531.4
 divulge 556.6
 do nothing 706.5
 lose 812.4
 neglect 534.6
letter
 n. epistle 604.2
 mail 604.5
 message 558.4
 printing 603.6
 representation 572.1
 written character 581
 written matter 602.10
 v. initial 581.6
letter carrier
 carrier 271.5
 postman 561.5
lettered learned 475.21
 literal 581.8
letterer 602.13
letterhead
 address 604.10
 label 568.13
lettering
 initialing 581.5
 writing 602.1
 writing style 602.4

letter of credit
 credit instrument
  839.3
 letter 604.3
 negotiable instru-
  ment 835.11
letter-perfect 516.15
letterpress
 imprint 603.3
 printed matter
  603.10
 printing 603.1
letters literature 602.12
 record 570.1
 scholarship 475.5
 writing system 581.3
letters of marque
 letter 604.3
 piracy 824.6
letter writer 604.9
letter writing 604.1
letting go 814.1
letup decrease 39.1
 discontinuity 72.2
 interim 109.1
 moderation 163.2
 pause 144.3
 respite 711.2
 slowing 270.4
let up
 v. decrease 39.6
 have pity 944.4
 loosen 51.3
 moderate 163.9
 pause 144.9
 relax 711.7
 slow 270.9
 interj. cease! 144.14
let well enough alone
 abstain 992.7
 avoid 631.6
 be content 868.5
 disregard 531.2
 do nothing 706.4
 not change 140.6
 not interfere 762.16
leukemia 686.18
leukocyte 388.4
Levant 180.6
levanter
 defaulter 842.5
 wind 403.9
levee barrier 730.5
 meeting 74.2
 social gathering
  922.10
level
 n. class 61.2
 degree 29.1
 floor 192.23
 horizontal 214.3
 layer 227.1
 plain 387.1
 smooth surface 260.3
 syntax 586.2
 v. be honest 974.10
 bring down 318.5
 equalize 30.6
 flatten 214.6
 make uniform 17.4
 raze 693.19
 smooth 260.5

 adj. equal 30.7
 horizontal 214.7
 just 976.8
 smooth 260.9
 straight 250.6
 uniform 17.5
 adv. horizontally
  214.9
level at 290.6
level head
 equanimity 858.3
 intelligence 467.6
levelheaded
 composed 858.13
 moderate 163.13
 sensible 467.18
lever
 n. instrument 658.3
 lifter 317.3
 pry 287.4
 v. pry 287.8
leverage
 fulcrumage 287
 influence 172.1
 mechanics 347.1
leviathan
 large animal 195.14
 ship 277.1
Leviathan 414.35
levitate ascend 315.8
 elevate 317.5
 rise 353.9
levitation ascent 315.1
 lightness 353.1
 occultism 1034.6
Levite 1038.12
levity fickleness 629.3
 inattention 531.1
 lightheartedness
  870.3
 lightness 353.1
 merriment 870.5
 ridicule 967.1
 triviality 673.3
 wittiness 881.4
levy
 n. appropriation 822.5
 call to arms 797.12
 demand 753.1
 enlistment 780.6
 recruits 800.17
 tax 846.10
 v. appropriate 822.20
 call to arms 797.23
 charge 846.14
 demand 753.4
 enlist 780.16
 impose 963.4
lewd lascivious 989.29
 obscene 990.9
lewdness
 lasciviousness 989.5
 obscenity 990.4
lex 998.3
lexeme
 unit of meaning
  545.6
 word 582.1
lexemic 545.12
–lexia 564.3
lexical meaning 545.12
 words 582.20

lexicographer
 explainer 552.7
 linguist 580.13
lexicography
 interpretation 552.8
 word study 582.15
lexicologist 580.13
lexicology
 etymology 582.15
 linguistics 580.12
 semantics 545.7
lexicon
 dictionary 605.7
 list 88.4
 vocabulary 582.14
lexigraphic(al)
 lexical 582.20
 literal 581.8
lexis 582.14
liabilities
 accounts 845.1
 expenses 843.3
liability debt 840.1
 disadvantage 671.2
 likelihood 175
 probability 511.1
 responsibility 962.2
 tendency 174.1
 unprotectedness
  697.3
liable chargeable 840.9
 probable 511.6
 responsible 962.17
 unprotected 697.15
liable to
 inclined to 174.6
 subject to 175.5
liaison
 intermediary 237.4
 joining 47.1
 love affair 931.6
 relationship 9.1
liana 411.4,51
liar 619.9
libation drink 307.4
 liquor 996.6
 oblation 1032.7
libel
 n. legal statement
  1004.7
 monstrous lie 616.12
 slander 971.3
 v. slander 971.11
libelous 971.13
liberal
 n. broad-minded per-
  son 526.6
 independent 762.12
 left winger 244.1
 progressive 745.11
 adj. broad-minded
  526.9
 extensive 79.13
 generous 853.4
 hospitable 925.11
 left-wing 244.4
 magnanimous 979.6
 nonrestrictive 762.24
 plentiful 661.7
 progressive 745.19
Liberal 744.27
liberal arts 562.8

liberalism
 broad-mindedness
  526.2
 libertarianism 762.10
 noninterference
  762.9
 progressivism 745.3
liberality
 broad-mindedness
  526.2
 generosity 853
 giving 818.1
 gratuity 818.5
 hospitality 925.1
 magnanimity 979.2
 plenty 661.2
liberalize 762.13
liberally
 generously 853.5
 magnanimously 979.8
 plentifully 661.9
liberate detach 49.10
 disembarrass 732.8
 emancipate 763.4
 release 762.13
 rescue 702.3
liberated freed 763.10
 loose 762.20
liberation escape 632.1
 freeing 763
 liberalism 762.10
 rescue 702.1
 theft 824.1
liberator 942.2
libertarian
 n. broad-minded per-
  son 526.6
 independent 762.12
 adj. broad-minded
  526.9
 liberal 762.24
libertine
 n. independent
  762.12
 philanderer 932.11
 unchaste person
  989.10
 adj. liberal 762.24
libertinism
 liberalism 762.10
 profligacy 989.3
liberty
 exemption 762.8
 freedom 762.1
 grant 777.5
 opportunity 129.2
 permission 777.1
 presumption 961.2
 right 958.4
 vacation 711.3
libidinal
 appetitive 634.21
 instinctive 481.6
 sexual 419.26
libidinous
 appetitive 634.21
 lascivious 989.29
 lustful 419.29
libido desire 634.1
 instinct 481.2
 love 931.1
 psyche 690.35

 sexuality 419.2
librarian
 bookman 605.21
 manager 748.4
 recorder 571.1
library archive 701.6
 bookroom 605.17
 collection 74.11
 edition 605.2
 room 192.6
 storage place 660.6
libration 323.1
librettist
 composer 464.20
 dramatist 611.27
 poet 609.13
libretto music 462.28
 playbook 611.26
license
 n. authority 780.1
 confusion 62.2
 exemption 762.8
 freedom 762.1
 lawlessness 740.1
 permission 777.1
 permit 777.6
 presumption 961.2
 profligacy 989.3
 right 958.4
 v. authorize 777.11
 charter 780.9
licensed
 authorized 777.17
 exempt 762.29
licentious
 intemperate 993.8
 lawless 740.5
 presumptuous 961.11
 unchaste 989.25
 unrestrained 762.23
lichen plant 411.4
 skin disease 686.33
licit legal 998.10
 permissible 777.15
lick
 n. attempt 714.2
 hit 283.4
 music 462.27
 rate 267.4
 small amount 35.4
 taste 427.2
 touch 425.1
 work 716.4
 v. best 36.7
 defeat 727.6
 drink 307.28
 lap 425.9
 perplex 514.13
 punish 1010.15
licked defeated 727.14
 perplexed 514.24
lickerish
 desirous 634.21
 lascivious 989.29
 lustful 419.29
lickety-split 269.21
licking defeat 727.1
 eating 307.1
 punishment 1010.5
lid clothing 231.25
 cover 228.5
 eyelid 439.9

 stopper 266.4
lido 385.2
lie
 n. direction 290.1
 falsehood 616.11
 position 184.3
 v. be dishonest 975.11
 be located 184.9
 be present 186.6
 extend 179.7
 falsify 616.19
 lie down 214.5
 ride at anchor 275.16
lied 462.13
lie detector 690.10
lie down couch 318.11
 lie 214.5
 rest 711.6
lief 622.9
liege
 n. master 749.1
 retainer 750.1
 subject 764.7
 adj. subject 764.13
lie in be located 184.9
 exist in 1.11
 give birth 167.15
 sail for 275.35
lie in state 410.21
lie in wait
 ambush 615.10
 await 539.8
 lurk 615.9
lie low be latent 546.3
 be low 208.5
 beware 895.7
 hide oneself 615.8
lien mortgage 772.4
 security 772.5
lie on
 be contingent 507.6
 be heavy upon
  352.11
 oppress 729.8
 rest on 216.22
lieu location 184.1
 place 184.4
lieutenant
 assistant 787.6
 commissioned officer
  749.18
 deputy 781.1
 naval officer 749.20
 peace officer 699.15
life a being 3.3
 affairs 151.4
 animation 161.3
 biography 608.4
 eagerness 635.1
 energizer 161.5
 existence 1.1
 gaiety 870.4
 lifetime 110.5
 liveliness 707.2
 living 407
 person 417.3
life after death 121.2
life-and-death 672.22
lifeblood blood 388.4
 seat of life 407.3
lifeboat escape 632.3
 life preserver 701.5

 rescue device 702.2
life cycle 407.3
life force 407.3
life-giving
 animating 407.12
 reproductive 169.15
lifeguard
 guardian 699.6
 rescuer 702.2
life jacket 701.5
lifeless dead 408.30
 inanimate 382.5
 inert 268.14
 lackluster 337.17
 languid 708.19
 uninteresting 883.6
lifelike
 authentic 516.14
 descriptive 608.15
 true to life 20.16
lifeline escape 632.3
 life preserver 701.5
 safety equipment
  699.3
lifelong 110.13
life of Riley, the 728.1
life of the party
 energizer 161.5
 humorist 881.12
 mischief-maker 738.3
 sociable person
  922.15
life-or-death 672.22
life preserver
 float 277.11
 life jacket 701.5
 safety equipment
  699.3
life principle
 life force 407.3
 theosophy 1034.18
 vital principle 466.5
lifer 761.11
lifesaver
 guardian 699.6
 preserver 701.4
 rescuer 702.2
lifesaving 702.1
life savings 835.14
life science 406.17
life-sized 195.22
life story 608.4
life-style 737.1
lifetime
 n. duration 110.5
 life 407.1
 adj. lifelong 110.13
lifework cause 153.10
 vocation 656.6
lift
 n. assist 785.2
 a theft 824.10
 atmosphere 402.2
 aviation 278.35
 elevator 317.4
 heavens 375.2
 height 207.2
 improvement 691.1
 lifter 317.3
 raise 317.2
 ride 273.7
 thrill 857.2

limit
n. boundary 235.3
capacity 195.2
completion 56.5
end 70.2
limitation 234.2
summit 211.2
v. bound 235.8
narrow 205.11
qualify 507.3
restrain 760.9
restrict 234.5
specialize 81.4
limit, the 862.3
limitation
boundary 235.3
estate 810.4
narrowness 205.1
qualification 507.1
restraint 760.3
restriction 234.2
limited
n. train 272.13
adj. little 196.10
local 180.9
meager 662.10
moderate 163.11
narrow 205.14
qualified 507.10
restrained 760.15
restricted 234.7
specialized 81.5
limiting
bordering 235.11
enclosing 236.11
final 70.10
qualifying 507.7
restraining 760.12
restricting 234.9
limitless
godlike 1013.20
greedy 634.27
infinite 104.3
unrestricted 762.26
limits 235.1
limn describe 608.12
draw 574.20
outline 235.9
represent 572.6
limner 579.2
limp
n. gait 273.14
slowness 270.2
v. be weak 160.8
go slow 270.6
walk 273.27
adj. drooping 215.10
flaccid 357.10
weak 160.12
limpet adherent 50.4
food 308.25
invertebrate 415.5
limpid
intelligible 548.10
polished 589.6
transparent 339.4
limping
crippled 692.32
slow 270.10
line
n. ancestry 170.4
artistry 574.10

battlefield 802.2
boundary 235.3
communications
560.17
conformity 82.1
cord 206.2
direction 290.1
engraving 578.2
fleet 277.10
kind 61.3
ledger line 462.29
length 202.4
letter 604.2
mark 568.6
melody 462.4
merchandise 831.1
music 462.22
poetic division
609.11
policy 654.5
political policy 744.4
posterity 117.2
procession 71.3
railway 657.8
route 657.2
row 71.2
sequence 65.1
specialty 81.1
species 11.4
story element 608.9
technique 657.1
track 568.8
trend 174.2
vanguard 240.2
vocation 656.6
v. align 71.5
arrange 60.9
border 235.10
engrave 578.10
fill 194.7
mark 568.19
outline 654.12
lineage ancestry 170.4
continuity 71.2
heirs 117.2
posterity 171.1
race 11.4
sequence 65.1
lineal consecutive 71.9
family 170.14
racial 11.7
straight 250.6
subsequent 117.4
lineaments
aspect 446.3
characteristic 80.4
exterior 224.2
face 240.4
form 246.3
looks 446.4
outline 235.2
linear consecutive 71.9
straight 250.6
linebacker 878.20
lined up 218.6
lineman athlete 878.20
electrician 342.19
telephone man
560.10
trainman 274.13
linen bedding 228.10
clothing 231.1

dry goods 831.3
underclothes 231.22
waist 231.15
liner lining 194.3
ship 277.5,22
lines artistic style 574.9
camp 191.29
harness 659.5
looks 446.4
outline 235.2
playbook 611.26
procedure 657.1
role 611.11
lineup list 88.6
order 59.1
plan 654.1
schedule 641.2
line up align 71.5
arrange 60.9
make parallel 218.5
order 59.4
queue 71.6
schedule 641.4
linger continue 143.3
dally 708.13
dawdle 270.8
follow 293.4
persist 110.7
wait 132.12
lingerer idler 708.8
slow person 270.5
lingerie 231.22
lingering
n. idling 708.4
protraction 110.2
slowness 270.3
waiting 132.3
adj. dawdling 270.11
procrastinating
132.17
protracted 110.11
reverberating 454.11
lingo jargon 580.9
language 580.1
lingua franca 580.11
lingual
linguistic 580.17
phonetic 594.31
spoken 594.30
tonguelike 427.10
linguist
linguistic scientist
580.13
polyglot 580.14
linguistic
communicational
554.9
philological 580.17
spoken 594.30
linguistics 580.12
liniment 687.11
lining
bookbinding 605.15
engraving 578.2
filling 194.3
link
n. intermediary 237.4
joint 47.4
part 55.4
relationship 9.1
torch 336.3
v. connect 71.4

couple 74.16
join 47.5
relate 9.6
linkage joining 47.1
relationship 9.1
linked continuous 71.8
joined 47.13
related 9.9
Linotype 603.2,21
lint down 230.19
medical dressing
687.33
powder 361.5
lintel 302.6
lion animal 414.27,58
brave person 893.8
heraldic insignia
569.2
idol 914.9
personage 672.8
strength 159.7
lionhearted 893.17
lionize glorify 914.13
praise 968.12
sight-see 442.6
lion's share
majority 100.2
major part 54.6
portion 816.5
lion tamer 612.3
lip
n. border 235.4
insolence 913.4
knob 256.3
wind instrument
465.7
v. be insolent 913.7
play music 462.43
say 594.23
lipid fat 309.7,23
oil 380.1,13
lipped 235.13
lip reader 449.2
lip reading 449.3
lips labia 419.10
mouth 265.5
vocal organ 594.19
lip service
hypocrisy 616.6
sanctimony 1029.2
lipstick
n. make-up 900.11
v. make red 368.4
liquefaction
liquidity 388.1
liquidization 391
liquefied 391.6
liquefy 391.5
liquefying 391.7
liqueur 996.41
liquid
n. drink 308.48
fluid 388.2
speech sound 594.13
adj. convertible
835.31
fluid 388.6
phonetic 594.31
watery 392.16
liquid assets
assets 810.8
ready money 835.18

resources 660.2
liquidate cash 835.29
  depose 783.4
  destroy 693.14
  eliminate 77.5
  kill 409.13
  murder 409.16
  pay in full 841.13
  purge 310.20
  sell stocks 833.24
liquidated paid 841.22
  purged 77.7
liquidation
  deposal 783.2
  destruction 693.6
  elimination 77.2
  homicide 409.2
  payment 841.1
  stock speculation
    833.19
liquidator
  financial officer
    836.11
  payer 841.9
liquidity 388
liquid oxygen
  coolant 334.7
  rocketry 281.8
liquor
  depressant 687.12
  drink 308.48
  fluid 388.2
  intoxicant 996.12,40
liquor-drinking 996.34
lisp
  n. sibilation 457.1
  speech defect 595.1
  v. sibilate 457.2
  speak poorly 595.7
lisping 595.12
lissome 357.9
list
  n. border 235.4
  edging 235.7
  enclosure 236.3
  enumeration 88
  inclination 219.2
  inventory 194.1
  record 570.1
  strip 206.4
  stripe 374.5
  v. border 235.10
  classify 61.6
  engage 780.16
  enumerate 88.8
  incline 219.10
  record 570.16
  sail 275.43
  till 413.17
  tumble 316.8
listen
  v. hear 448.11
  hearken to 530.7
  interj. attention!
    530.22
  hark! 448.17
listener hearer 448.5
  radio listener 344.22
  recipient 819.3
listen in
  eavesdrop 448.11
  radio 344.27

telephone 560.18
listening
  n. audition 448.2
  hearing 448.1
  adj. attentive 448.15
listen to 766.2
listing
  n. agriculture 413.13
  recording 570.15
  tabulation 88.7
  adj. inclining 219.15
  unbalanced 31.5
listless apathetic 856.13
  incurious 529.3
  languid 708.19
  unconcerned 636.7
  weak 160.12
listlessness
  apathy 856.4
  incurious 529.1
  languor 708.6
  unconcern 636.2
  weakness 160.1
list price 846.2
lit drunk 996.31
  illuminated 335.39
litany prayer 1032.4
  rite 1040.4
  ritualistic manual
    1040.12
liter 490.19
literacy 475.5
literal authentic 516.14
  lettered 581.8
  orthodox 1024.7
  unimaginative 536.5
literally 516.20
literal meaning 545.1
literal-minded 536.5
literary
  book-learned 475.22
  written 602.24
literary style 588.2
literate
  n. intellectual 476.1
  adj. learned 475.21
literati 476.2
literature
  advertising 559.8
  lore 475.9
  writing 602.12
  written matter 602.10
lithe 357.9
lithic 384.10
lithograph
  n. print 578.6
  v. engrave 578.10
lithographer 579.8
lithography
  applying color 362.11
  graphic arts 578.4
  printing 603.1
litigant
  n. litigator 1004.11
  oppositionist 791.3
  adj. litigious 1004.20
litigate 1004.12
litigation
  argumentation 482.4
  contention 796.1
  lawsuit 1004.1

litigious
  argumentative 482.19
  ill-humored 951.26
  litigant 1004.20
  quarrelsome 795.17
litter
  n. animal young 171.2
  bed 216.19
  bedding 216.20
  bier 410.13
  carrier 272.30
  jumble 62.3
  rubbish 669.5
  v. disarrange 63.2
  give birth 167.15
  tend animals 416.7
littérateur
  author 602.15
  scholar 476.3
litterbug 62.7
little
  n. short distance
    200.2
  short time 111.3
  small amount 35.2
  adj. base 915.12
  inferior 37.7
  insignificant 35.6
  narrow-minded
    527.10
  selfish 978.6
  short 203.8
  small 196.10
  unimportant 673.15
  adv. on a small scale
    196.16
  scarcely 35.9
little, a scarcely 35.9
  to a degree 29.7
little by little
  gradually 29.6
  piece by piece 55.9
  slowly 270.14
little fellow
  a nobody 673.7
  child 125.3
  common man 919.7
little known 915.14
little-minded 527.10
littleness
  baseness 915.3
  diminutiveness 196
  inferiority 37.3
  narrow-mindedness
    527.1
  selfishness 978.2
  shortness 203.1
  smallness 35.1
  unimportance 673.1
little people, the
  1014.17
littlest 37.8
littoral
  n. ocean zone 397.5
  shore 385.2
  adj. aquatic 275.58
  bordering 235.11
  seashore 385.9
liturgic(al)
  ceremonious 646.8
  ritualistic 1040.22
  vocal 462.51

liturgical music 462.16
liturgy ceremony 646.4
  rite 1040.3
  worship 1032.8
Liturgy, the 1040.9
livable 188.15
live
  v. be alive 407.7
  be famous 914.10
  endure 110.6
  exist 1.8
  inhabit 188.7
  adj. burning 328.27
  charged 342.31
  lively 707.17
  living 407.11
live and let live
  be broad-minded
    526.7
  do nothing 706.4
  not interfere 762.16
live by one's wits
  be dishonest 975.11
  cheat 618.17
  trick 735.9
lived-in 887.11
live down 1012.4
live forever 112.6
live it up 878.24
livelihood 785.3
liveliness
  activeness 707.2
  animation 161.3
  eagerness 635.1
  elasticity 358.1
  eloquence 600.4
  fervor 855.10
  gaiety 870.4
  life 407.1
  pungency 433.2
livelong 110.13
lively
  adj. active 707.17
  eager 635.9
  elastic 358.7
  eloquent 600.12
  energetic 161.12
  fast 269.19
  fervent 855.23
  gay 870.14
  interesting 530.19
  pungent 433.7
  adv. actively 707.25
liven cheer 870.7
  energize 161.9
live off of 907.11
live on eat 307.26
  endure 110.6
  persist 1.9
  postexist 121.7
live or die
  come what may
    624.20
  without fail 513.26
liver digestion 309.8
  diseases of 686.21
  meat 308.20
  vitals 225.4
liveried 231.44
livery clothing 231.7
  uniform 569.1
  wardrobe 231.2

livestock 414.1
live through
  endure 110.6
  persevere 625.4
  win through 724.12
live up to 768.2
live wire
  electric charge 342.5
  man of action 707.8
live with
  be broad-minded
   526.7
  persevere 625.4
  submit 765.6
livid angry 952.26
  black and blue
   365.12
  blue 372.3
  colorless 363.7
  deathly 408.29
  gray 366.4
  purple 373.3
living
  n. habitation 188.1
  life 407.1
  support 785.3
  the ministry 1037.9
  adj. alive 407.11
  burning 328.27
  energetic 161.12
  existent 1.13
  lifelike 20.16
  organic 406.19
  resident 188.13
living being
  animal 414.2
  organism 406.2
living quarters
  housing 188.3
  lodgings 191.3
living room 192.5
lizard 414.30,60
llano grassland 411.8
  plain 387.1
load
  n. affliction 866.8
  aviation 278.30
  burden 352.7
  contents 194.2
  explosive charge
   801.10
  freight 271.7
  full measure 56.3
  impediment 730.6
  much 34.3
  tax 963.2
  v. burden 352.13
  fill 56.7
  oppress 729.8
  prepare 720.9
  put 184.14
  shoot 285.13
  stuff 194.7
  tamper with 616.17
loaded
  burdened 352.18
  critical 129.10
  drunk 996.31
  fraught 56.12
  prepared 720.16
  wealthy 837.13
loader 276.9

loading burden 352.7
  imposition 963.1
  placement 184.5
loaf
  n. Eucharist 1040.8
  lump 195.10
  v. idle 708.11
loafer beggar 774.8
  idler 708.8
  vagabond 274.3
  vagrant 274.3
loafing 708.4
loamy earthy 385.7
  soft 357.12
loan
  n. lending 820.2
  v. lend 820.5
loaned 820.6
loaner 820.3
loaning 820.1
loan shark 820.3
loan-shark 820.5
loan-sharking
  illicit business 826.1
  lending 820.1
  overcharge 848.5
loath 623.6
loathe dislike 867.3
  hate 930.5
loathing
  n. dislike 867.2
  hate 930.1
  adj. hating 930.7
loathsome bad 675.9
  offensive 864.18
  ugly 899.11
lob elevate 317.5
  throw 285.11
lobar 215.12
lobby
  n. foyer 192.19
  influential persons
   172.6
  legislative lobby
   744.32
  v. influence 172.9
  legislate 742.18
  urge 648.14
lobbying
  inducement 648.3
  influence 172.3
  political influence
   744.29
lobbyist
  influential person
   172.6
  lobby 744.32
lobe brain 466.7
  ear 448.7
  part 55.4
  pendant 215.4
lobo 414.25
lobotomy 689.24
lobster
  invertebrates 415.5
  seafood 308.25
local
  n. branch 788.10
  labor union 789.1
  native 190.3
  railway car 272.14
  saloon 996.19

  train 272.13
  adj. dialect 580.20
  regional 180.9
local color 608.9
locale arena 802.1
  location 184.1
  setting 233.2
localism dialect 580.7
  political policy 744.4
  word 582.6
locality habitat 191.5
  location 184.1
localize locate 184.10
  restrain 760.9
localized 180.9
local yokel 190.3
locate discover 488.2
  settle 184.16
  situate 184.10
located 184.17
locating
  discovery 488.1
  placement 184.5
location
  discovery 488.1
  farm 413.8
  place 184
  placement 184.5
  position 7.1
locational
  positional 184.18
  regional 180.8
loch bay 399.1
  body of water 398.1
Loch Ness monster
  animal 414.35
  monster 85.20
lock
  n. floodgate 396.11
  hair 230.5
  restraint 760.5
  standstill 268.3
  wrestling hold 813.3
  v. agree 26.6
  close 266.6
  fasten 47.8
  obstruct 730.12
locker
  depository 836.12
  refrigerator 334.6
  storage place 660.6
locket 901.6
lock in imprison 761.14
  retain 813.5
lockjaw seizure 686.5
  tetanus 686.12
lockout exclusion 77.1
  refusing work 789.7
  stop 144.2
lock out close 266.6
  exclude 77.4
  refuse work 789.9
lock, stock, and barrel
  throughout 56.17
  wholly 54.13
lockup
  confinement 761.1
  prison 761.8
lock up close 266.6
  imprison 761.14
  secrete 615.7
loco 473.25

locomotion
  mobility 267.3
  travel 273.1
locomotive
  mechanical 347.7
  self-propelled 349.26
  vehicular 272.22
  walking 273.35
locus 184.1
locust 414.39,74
locution diction 588.1
  language 580.1
  phrase 585.1
  utterance 594.3
  word 582.1
lode deposit 383.7
  rich source 837.3
  source of supply
   660.4
lodestar
  center of attraction
   226.4
  guiding star 748.8
  magnet 288.3
  motive 648.1
  North Star 375.4
lodestone
  magnet 288.3
  thing desired 634.11
lodge
  n. association 788.10
  cottage 191.9
  house 191.6
  lair 191.26
  v. accommodate
   659.10
  become fixed 142.10
  establish 142.9
  house 188.10
  inhabit 188.7
  put 184.13
  store 660.10
lodged 188.14
lodger roomer 190.8
  tenant 809.4
lodging
  n. abode 191.1
  habitation 188.1
  housing 188.3
  quarters 191.3
  adj. resident 188.13
loess deposit 43.2
  geology 271.8
loft attic 192.16
  room 192.6
  workplace 719.1
loftily
  arrogantly 912.15
  dignifiedly 905.14
  grandiloquently
   601.12
  ostentatiously 904.25
lofty arrogant 912.9
  eloquent 600.14
  eminent 34.9
  famous 914.18
  grandiloquent 601.8
  high 207.19
  impartial 976.10
  magnanimous 979.6
  ostentatious 904.18
  proud 905.11

lubricating
　n. lubrication 380.6
　adj. lubricant 380.10
lubrication 380.6
lubricious
　lascivious 989.29
　slippery 260.11
lubritorium 380.7
lucid
　intelligible 548.10
　light 335.31
　polished 589.6
　sane 472.4
　translucent 340.5
　transparent 339.4
lucidity
　clairvoyance 1034.8
　intelligibility 548.2
　lightness 335.3
　literary elegance
　　589.1
　sanity 472.1
　translucence 340.2
　transparency 339.1
Lucifer
　morning star 375.4
　Satan 1016.3
luck chance 156.1
　gamble 515.1
　prosperity 728.2
　uncertainty 514.1
Luck 156.2
luckily
　auspiciously 544.21
　fortunately 728.16
luckless 729.14
lucky auspicious 544.18
　fortunate 728.14
　timely 129.9
lucky piece 1036.5
lucrative gainful 811.15
　paying 841.21
lucre gain 811.3
　money 835.1
　wealth 837.1
lucubration
　consideration 478.2
　study 564.3
　treatise 606.1
　written matter 602.10
ludicrous
　foolish 470.10
　humorous 880.4
lug
　n. ear 448.7
　pull 286.2
　v. pull 286.4
　transport 271.11
luggage
　belongings 810.3
　freight 271.7
　types of 193.17
lugubrious 872.26
lukewarm
　indifferent 636.6
　nonreligious 1031.15
　warm 328.24
lull
　n. calm 268.5
　discontinuity 72.2
　inactivity 708.1
　interim 109.1

pause 144.3
　respite 711.2
　silence 451.1
　v. calm 163.7
　put to sleep 712.20
　quiet 268.8
　relieve 886.5
lullaby
　cradlesong 462.15
　sleep-inducer 712.10
lulling
　n. moderation 163.2
　relief 886.1
　adj. tranquilizing
　　163.15
lulu 674.7
lumbago
　disease symptom
　　686.8
　inflammation 686.9
lumbar 241.10
lumber
　n. impediments 730.6
　rubbish 669.5
　wood 378.3
　v. flounder 734.11
　hamper 730.11
　plod 270.7
　walk 273.27
lumbering
　n. forestry 413.3
　walking 273.10
　adj. bulky 195.19
　clumsy 734.20
　slow 270.10
　stilted 590.3
lumberjack 413.7
lumberyard 660.6
lumen 335.21
luminary
　n. famous person
　　914.9
　first-rater 674.6
　light source 336.1
　principal 672.10
　adj. light 335.41
luminesce 335.26
luminescence 335.13
luminescent 335.38
luminous
　glowing 335.30
　godlike 1013.20
　illuminated 335.39
　intelligible 548.10
lummox bungler 734.9
　oaf 471.5
lump
　n. accumulation 74.9
　bulge 256.3
　bungler 734.9
　clump 195.10
　corpulent person
　　195.12
　mark 568.7
　piece 55.3
　solid 354.6
　swelling 256.4
　v. be patient 861.5
　thicken 354.10
lumpen base 915.12
　countrified 182.7
　formless 247.4

idle 708.17
　slovenly 62.15
lumpen proletariat
　common people
　　919.1
　nonworkers 708.10
lumpish boorish 898.13
　bulky 195.19
　clumsy 734.20
　countrified 182.7
　languid 708.19
　ponderous 352.17
　stupid 469.15
　thickened 354.14
lump sum 835.13
lump together
　assemble 74.18
　combine 52.3
　join 47.5
lumpy bulky 195.19
　rough 261.8
　thickened 354.14
Luna 375.12
lunacy
　foolishness 470.1
　insanity 473.1
lunar celestial 375.25
　moon-shaped 252.11
lunar module 282.2
lunatic
　n. fool 471.1
　madman 473.15
　adj. insane 473.25
lunatic fringe
　extremists 745.12
　fanatic 473.17
lunch
　n. meal 307.6
　v. eat 307.19
lunch counter 307.15
luncheon 307.6
lunchroom 307.15
lung breathing 403.19
　vitals 225.4
lunge
　n. thrust 798.3
　v. thrust at 798.16
　walk 273.27
lunkhead 471.4
lupine canine 414.45
　rapacious 822.26
lurch
　n. bend 219.3
　flounder 324.8
　gait 273.14
　swing 323.6
　v. flounder 324.15
　oscillate 323.10
　sail 275.55
　tumble 316.8
　walk 273.27
lurching irregular 138.3
　swinging 323.17
lure
　n. allurement 650.2
　attractor 288.2
　incentive 648.7
　snare 618.12
　v. attract 288.4
　entice 650.4
　induce 648.22
　trap 618.18

lurid brown 367.3
　colorless 363.7
　deathly 408.29
　garish 362.19
　gaudy 904.20
　grandiloquent 601.8
　obscene 990.9
　red 368.6
　sensational 857.30
lurk be latent 546.3
　couch 615.9
lurking
　imminent 152.3
　in hiding 615.14
　latent 546.5
luscious
　oversweet 431.5
　pleasant 863.9
　tasty 428.8
lush
　n. drunkard 996.11
　v. drink 996.24
　adj. growing rank
　　411.40
　ornate 601.11
　productive 165.9
　tasty 428.8
lust greed 634.8
　lasciviousness 989.5
　sexual desire 419.5
　sin 982.3
　will 621.1
lust after crave 634.18
　desire 634.14
　lust 419.22
luster
　n. shine 900.6
　chandelier 336.6
　illustriousness 914.6
　period 107.2
　polish 260.2
　shine 335.2
　v. give light 335.23
　polish 260.7
lusterless
　colorless 363.7
　lackluster 337.17
lustful desirous 634.21
　lascivious 989.29
　prurient 419.29
lustily
　energetically 161.15
　loudly 453.13
　strongly 159.21
lustral atoning 1012.7
　cleansing 681.28
lustrous
　illustrious 914.19
　luminous 335.30
　shiny 335.33
lusty corpulent 195.18
　energetic 161.12
　robust 685.10
　strong 159.13
lute 465.4
Lutheran 1020.27,35
lux 335.21
luxate disjoint 49.16
　dislocate 185.5
luxuriant florid 601.11
　growing rank 411.40
　ornate 901.12

plentiful 661.7
productive 165.9
luxuriate
superabound 663.8
vegetate 411.31
luxuriate in
be intemperate 993.4
enjoy 865.10
luxurious
comfortable 887.11
expensive 848.11
grandiose 904.21
ornate 901.12
pleasant 863.7
sensual 987.5
wealthy 837.13
luxury grandeur 904.5
pleasantness 863.2
pleasure 865.1
prosperity 728.1
sensuality 987.1
superfluity 663.4
lyceum hall 192.4
secondary school 567.6
lye cleanser 681.30
disinfectant 687.59
lying
n. lowness 208.1
recumbency 214.2
untruthfulness 616.8
adj. recumbent 214.8
untruthful 616.34
lying-in 167.7
lymph 388.3
lymphatic
n. duct 396.13
adj. fluid 388.7
languid 708.19
secretory 312.7
lymphocyte 388.4
lynch hang 1010.20
kill 409.13
lynching
capital punishment 1010.7
killing 409.1
lynch law 740.2
lynx animal 414.27,58
keen eye 439.11
lyre 465.3
lyric 609.6
lyric(al) choral 462.51
melodious 462.49
poetic 609.17
lyricist
composer 464.20
poet 609.13
lyric theater 462.35
lysis 693.1
Lysol 687.59

M

ma 170.10
ma'am 421.8
Mab 1014.18
macabre
deathly 408.29
terrible 891.38
weird 1017.9
macadam 657.7

macaroni dandy 903.9
food 308.33
mace club 801.26
emblem of authority 739.9
insignia 569.1
macerate pulp 390.5
soak 392.13
torture 866.18
waste away 198.9
Mach 269.2
Machiavellian
n. cunning person 735.8
deceiver 619.1
political intriguer 746.6
schemer 654.8
adj. cunning 735.12
falsehearted 616.31
scheming 654.14
machinate
maneuver 735.10
plot 654.10
machination
chicanery 618.4
intrigue 654.6
stratagem 735.4
machinator
cunning person 735.7
political intriguer 746.6
schemer 654.8
traitor 619.10
machine
n. association 788.1
automobile 272.9
converter 145.10
copying 603.25
machinery 348.4,21
political party 744.24
typesetting 603.21
writing 602.31
v. process 167.11
tool 348.10
machine-made 167.22
machinery
enginery 348.4
equipment 659.4
instrumentality 658.2
mechanism 348.5
types of 348.21
machine shop 719.3
machinist
mechanic 348.9
stage technician 611.29
machismo 420.2
macho 420.12
macrobiotic 110.10
macrocosm 375.1
maculate
blemished 679.9
spotted 374.13
unchaste 989.23
mad
n. anger 952.5
v. madden 473.23
adj. angry 952.26
excited 857.23
foolish 470.8
frenzied 473.30

insane 473.25
reckless 894.8
violent 162.17
mad about
enthusiastic about 635.12
fond of 931.28
madam
form of address 421.8
mistress 749.2
procurer 989.18
madame
form of address 421.8
title 917.4
madcap
n. humorist 881.12
reckless person 894.4
violent person 162.9
adj. fanatic 162.21
foolhardy 894.9
madden
antagonize 929.7
dement 473.23
enrage 952.23
excite 857.11
maddening 857.28
mad dog evildoer 943.3
violent person 162.9
made
man-made 167.22
produced 167.20
successful 724.13
mademoiselle
form of address 421.8
girl 125.6
made of 58.4
made-up
fabricated 616.29
invented 167.23
mad for 634.22
madhouse 473.14
madly
frenziedly 857.33
furiously 34.23
insanely 473.35
recklessly 894.11
turbulently 162.25
violently 162.24
madman 473.15
madness
excitement 857.7
foolishness 470.1
infectious disease 686.12
insanity 473.1
Madonna 1015.5
madrigal
choral music 462.18
poem 609.6
maelstrom
agitation 324.1
bustle 707.4
swirl 322.2
whirlpool 395.12
maestro musician 464.1
teacher 565.1
Mae West 701.5
maffick
be disorderly 62.11
be noisy 453.8
celebrate 877.2

Mafia
illicit business 826.1
the underworld 986.11
Mafioso
racketeer 826.4
violent person 162.9
magazine armory 801.2
periodical 605.10
storage place 660.6
magenta 373.3,4
maggot bug 414.36
caprice 629.1
eccentricity 474.2
thing imagined 535.5
white 364.2
young insect 125.10
maggoty
capricious 629.5
eccentric 474.4
fanciful 535.20
filthy 682.23
spoiled 692.43
unsavory 429.7
Magi 468.5
magic charisma 914.6
illusoriness 519.2
sorcery 1035.1
magic(al)
illustrious 914.19
sorcerous 1035.14
supernatural 85.16
magically 34.20
magic carpet 1036.6
magician
entertainer 612.1
expert 733.13
illusionist 519.2
sorcerer 1035.6
trickster 619.2
magic lantern 577.12
magic wand 1036.6
magisterial
arrogant 912.11
authoritative 513.18
chief 36.14
dignified 905.12
imperious 739.16
jurisdictional 1000.6
skillful 733.20
magistracy
district 180.5
judgeship 1000.3
mastership 739.7
magistrate
arbitrator 805.4
executive 748.3
judge 1002.1
public official 749.17
Magna Charta 762.2
magna cum laude 916.11
magnanimity
ambition 634.10
eminence 34.2
forgiveness 947.1
generosity 979.2
liberality 853.1
tolerance 526.4
magnanimous
eminent 34.9
forgiving 947.6

malaise agitation 324.1
  anxiety 890.1
  disease 686.1
  pain 424.1
  sadness 872.3
  unpleasure 866.1
malapropism
  error in speech 518.7
  figure of speech
    551.5
  solecism 587.2
  wordplay 881.8
malapropos
  inappropriate 27.7
  inexpedient 671.5
  untimely 130.7
malaria
  infectious disease
    686.12
  miasma 676.4
  vapor 401.1
malarial 686.57
malarial fever 686.12
malarkey 547.3
malcontent
  n. faultfinder 869.3
  hinderer 730.9
  lamenter 875.7
  rebel 767.5
  adj. discontented
    869.5
mal de mer 686.29
male
  n. male being 420.4
  adj. masculine 420.11
male chauvinism 527.4
male chauvinist 527.5
malediction 972.1
maledictory 972.8
malefactor
  bad person 986.9
  evildoer 943.1
maleness
  masculinity 420.1
  sex 419.1
male organs 419.10
male sex 420.3
malevolence
  badness 675.1
  enmity 929.3
  hate 930.1
  ill will 939.4
malevolent bad 675.7
  harmful 675.12
  hostile 929.10
  ill-disposed 939.17
malevolently
  harmfully 675.15
  maliciously 939.28
malfeasance
  misdeed 982.2
  mismanagement
    734.6
  misuse 667.1
  wrongdoing 982.1
malformation
  deformity 249.3
  oddity 85.3
malformed
  abnormal 85.13
  deformed 249.12
  ugly 899.8

malice enmity 929.3
  hate 930.1
  maliciousness 939.5
malicious
  hostile 929.10
  malevolent 939.18
maliciously 939.28
malign
  v. defame 971.9
  adj. fatal 409.23
  harmful 675.12
  malicious 939.18
  poisonous 684.7
  savage 162.20
malignancy
  deadliness 409.9
  harmfulness 675.5
  malice 939.5
  poisonousness 684.3
malignant
  cancerous 686.57
  fatal 409.23
  harmful 675.12
  hostile 929.10
  malicious 939.18
  poisonous 684.7
  savage 162.20
malignant growth
  686.36
malignantly
  harmfully 675.15
  malevolently 939.28
malinger
  leave undone 534.7
  shirk 631.9
malingerer
  impostor 619.6
  neglecter 534.5
  shirker 631.3
malingering
  n. shirking 631.2
  adj. evasive 631.15
mall 657.3
malleable
  changeable 141.6
  conformable 82.5
  docile 765.13
  influenceable 172.15
  pliant 357.9
  teachable 564.18
  wieldy 732.14
mallet hammer 348.19
  sculpting tool 575.4
malnutrition
  deficiency disease
    686.10
  dietary deficiency
    662.6
malocchio
  bad influence 675.4
  curse 972.1
  evil eye 1036.1
  glare 439.5
  ill will 939.4
malodorous fetid 437.5
  filthy 682.23
  odorous 435.9
  offensive 864.18
malpractice
  mismanagement
    734.6
  misuse 667.1

wrongdoing 982.1
maltreat mistreat 667.5
  work evil 675.6
maltreatment 667.2
mama 170.10
mama's boy
  effeminate male
    421.10
  spoiled child 759.4
  weakling 160.6
mammal
  animal 414.3,58
  vertebrates 415.7
mammalian
  mammary 256.18
  vertebrate 414.44
mammary 256.18
mammary gland 256.6
mammon money 835.1
  wealth 837.1
mammoth
  n. large animal 195.14
  pachyderm 414.4,58
  prehistoric animal
    123.26
  adj. huge 195.20
  large 34.7
mammy mother 170.10
  nurse 699.8
man
  n. adult 127.1
  beau 931.12
  brave person 893.8
  chessman 878.18
  follower 907.5
  henchman 787.8
  husband 933.8
  male 420.4
  male servant 750.4
  male sex 420.3
  mammals 415.8
  mankind 417.1
  person 417.3
  prehistoric 123.25
  primate 414.59
  v. equip 659.8
  fortify 799.9
  interj. pleasure 865.17
Man, the 418.3
mana
  animistic spirit
    1014.12
  power 157.1
man-about-town
  dandy 903.9
  fashionable 644.7
  sociable person
    922.15
  sophisticate 733.16
manacle
  n. restraint 760.4
  v. render powerless
    158.11
  restrain 760.10
manacled 760.16
manage
  accomplish 722.4
  come through 7.6
  contrive 724.11
  deal with 665.12
  direct 747.8
  drive animals 416.7

  economize 851.4
  govern 741.12
  handle 705.8
  make shift 670.4
  operate 164.5
  persist 143.5
  pilot 275.14
  survive 659.12
  use 665.10
manageability
  governability 765.4
  wieldiness 732.2
  workability 164.3
manageable
  cheap 849.7
  governable 765.14
  wieldy 732.14
  workable 164.10
management
  direction 747.1
  directorate 748.11
  economy 851.1
  executives 748.3
  government 741.1
  operation 164.1
  performance 705.2
  protectorship 699.2
  supremacy 36.3
  the rulers 749.15
  treatment 665.2
  utilization 665.8
manager
  businessman 830.1
  director 748.1
  governor 749.5
managerial
  directing 747.12
  operational 164.12
managership 747.4
managing
  directing 747.12
  governing 741.19
mañana
  n. the future 121.1
  adv. in the future
    121.9
man and wife 933.10
manchild 125.5
mandarin
  intellectual 476.1
  official 749.16
  snob 912.7
  wise man 468.1
mandate
  n. commission 780.1
  injunction 752.2
  legal order 752.6
  possession 808.1
  referendum 742.16
  territory 181.1
  v. command 752.9
mandated 752.13
mandatory
  binding 962.15
  commanded 752.13
  necessary 639.12
  obligatory 756.10
  prescriptive 751.4
mandibles
  grasping organs 813.4
  jaws 265.5
mandolin 465.4

fertilizer 165.4
manure pile 682.10
manuscript
n. handwriting 602.3
printer's copy 603.4
rare book 605.3
written matter 602.10
adj. written 602.22
many
n. large number 101.3
adj. different 16.7
diversified 19.4
frequent 135.4
much 34.8
numerous 101.6
plentiful 661.7
many-sided
changeable 141.6
mixed 44.15
sided 242.7
versatile 733.23
Maoism
Communism 745.5
revolutionism 147.2
Maoist
n. Communist 745.13
revolutionist 147.3
adj. Communist
745.21
revolutionary 147.6
map
n. chart 654.4
face 240.4
representation 572.1
v. plot 654.11
represent 572.6
use radar 346.17
map maker 654.4
mapped 490.14
mar be ugly 899.5
blemish 679.4
bungle 734.11
deform 249.7
impair 692.12
maraca 465.18
marathon
n. race 796.12
therapy 690.5
adj. protracted 110.11
maraud 824.16
marauder 825.6
marauding
n. plundering 824.5
adj. plunderous
824.21
marble
n. hardness 356.6
plaything 878.16
sculpture 575.2
smooth surface 260.3
variegation 374.6
v. variegate 374.7
adj. hard 356.10
white 364.7
marbled striped 374.15
variegated 374.12
marbleize 374.7
marbleized 374.15
marblelike hard 356.10
stone 384.10
marcel
n. hairdo 230.15

v. style the hair
230.22
march
n. boundary 235.3
frontier 235.5
military step 273.15
music 462.11
progression 294.1
protest 522.2
region 180.2
walk 273.12
v. border 235.10
exit 303.11
march off 301.6
march with 200.12
progress 294.3
protest 522.5
walk 273.29
march against 798.17
marcher 274.6
marching 273.10
Mardi Gras
festival 878.4
holy day 1040.15
mare
female animal 421.9
horse 414.10
plain 387.1
margarine 308.47
margin
n. border 235.4
difference 16.2
distance 199.1
interval 201.1
latitude 762.4
pledge 772.3
spare 179.3
stock margin 834.10
surplus 663.5
v. border 235.10
marginal
bordering 235.11
unimportant 673.14
marginalia
addition 41.2
record 570.4
marginally 235.15
marijuana 687.13,53
marijuana smoker
642.10
marimba 465.18
marina 700.6
marinate 701.8
marination
infusion 44.2
preserving 701.2
marine
n. navy 800.26
sailor 276.4
adj. nautical 275.57
oceanic 397.8
marine animal
414.35,63
marine biology 397.6
mariner seaman 276
traveler 274.1
marines
elite troops 800.14
sea soldiers 800.27
marionette doll 878.16
figure 572.4
marital 933.19

maritime
nautical 275.57
oceanic 397.8
mark
n. blemish 679.3
boundary 235.3
characteristic 80.4
customer 828.4
diacritical 586.19
effect 154.3
evidence 505.1
grade 29.1
harmonics 463.12
importance 672.1
indicator 568.10
kind 61.3
marking 568.5
objective 653.2
punctuation 586.18
reference 586.20
repute 914.5
sign 568.2
signature 583.10
v. blemish 679.6
celebrate 877.2
characterize 80.10
destine 640.7
differentiate 16.6
engrave 578.10
evidence 505.9
heed 530.6
indicate 568.17
judge 494.9
letter 581.6
make a mark 568.19
punctuate 586.16
specify 80.11
markdown 849.4
mark down
cheapen 849.6
record 570.16
marked
characteristic 80.13
destined 640.9
engraved 578.12
famous 914.16
notable 672.18
remarkable 34.10
superior 36.12
markedly
characteristically
80.17
conspicuously 555.16
exceptionally 34.20
importantly 672.24
visibly 444.8
marker aviation 278.19
indicator 568.10
memorial 570.12
recorder 571.1
market
n. city district 183.8
clientele 828.3
commerce 827.1
marketplace 832.2
mart 832
sale 829.1
v. deal in 827.15
sell 829.8
shop 828.8
adj. sales 829.13
market, the 833.1

marketable 829.14
market index 833.1
marketing
n. commerce 827.1
purchase 828.1
selling 829.2
adj. sales 829.13
marketplace
arena 802.1
city district 183.8
mart 832.2
market research 829.2
market value
stock price 834.9
worth 846.3
marking
characteristic 80.4
engraving 578.2
insignia 569.1
mark 568.5
mark off allot 816.9
characterize 80.10
circumscribe 234.4
differentiate 16.6
mark 568.19
measure off 490.12
plot 654.11
marksman
expert 733.11
infantryman 800.9
shooter 285.9
marksmanship 733.1
mark time await 539.8
be still 268.7
stay 132.12
time 114.11
marmalade 308.39
maroon
v. abandon 633.5
adj. red 368.6
marooned
abandoned 633.8
in difficulty 731.25
marquee poster 559.7
theater lighting
611.23
marquis 918.4
marred
blemished 679.8
damaged 692.30
deformed 249.12
ugly 899.6
marriage
combination 52.1
joining 47.1
matrimony 933
sexuality 419.2
wedding 933.4
marriageable
adult 126.12
nubile 933.21
marriage broker 933.13
marriage deities 933.14
marriage license 777.6
marriage vow 770.3
married joined 52.6
matrimonial 933.19
wedded 933.22
marrow center 226.2
content 194.5
essence 5.2
meat 308.20

marry ally 52.4
  get married 933.16
  join 47.5
  wed 933.15
Mars god 1014.5
  planet 375.9
  war god 797.17
marsh
  filthy place 682.12
  marshland 400
marshal
  n. commissioned offi-
    cer 749.18
  master of ceremonies
    878.22
  peace officer 699.15
  v. arrange evidence
    505.13
  distribute 60.9
  escort 73.8
  join 47.5
  order 59.4
  prepare 720.6
marshy moist 392.15
  swampy 400.3
marsupial
  n. animal 414.3
  adj. vascular 193.4
  vertebrate 414.44
mart city district 183.8
  market 832.1
  marketplace 832.2
martial 797.25
martial arts 796.10
martial law law 998.4
  militarization 797.14
  military government
    741.4
martinet 749.14
martyr
  n. saint 1015.1
  sufferer 866.11
  v. kill 409.13
  torment 424.7
  torture 866.18
martyrdom
  killing 409.1
  pain 424.6
  punishment 1010.2
  torment 866.7
martyred dead 408.30
  pained 424.9
  saintly 1015.6
marvel
  n. phenomenon 920.2
  wonder 920.1
  v. wonder 920.5
marvelous
  extraordinary 85.14
  remarkable 34.10
  superb 674.17
  wonderful 920.10
marvelously
  exceptionally 34.20
  extraordinarily 85.18
  superbly 674.22
  wonderfully 920.14
Marxism
  Communism 745.5
  materialism 376.5
  socialism 745.6

Marxist
  n. Communist 745.13
  materialist 376.6
  revolutionist 147.3
  socialist 745.14
  adj. Communist
    745.21
  materialist 376.11
  revolutionary 147.6
mascara 900.11
mascot 1036.5
masculine
  n. gender 586.10
  male 420.4
  adj. male 420.11
masculinity
  masculineness 420
  sex 419.1
mash
  n. fodder 308.4
  hodgepodge 44.6
  love 931.4
  meal 307.6
  pulp 390.2
  v. pulp 390.5
  pulverize 361.9
  soften 357.6
masher dandy 903.9
  philanderer 932.11
  pulper 390.4
  pulverizer 361.7
mashing 361.4
mask
  n. cover 228.2
  dance 879.2
  disguise 618.10
  party 922.11
  pretext 649.1
  safety equipment
    699.3
  sculpture 575.3
  v. conceal 615.6
  cover 228.19
  falsify 616.16
masked covered 228.31
  disguised 615.13
masochism 419.12
masochist 419.17
mason 579.6
masonry 378.2
masque dance 879.2
  masquerade 618.10
  party 922.11
  stage show 611.4
masquerade
  n. costume 231.9
  dance 879.2
  disguise 618.10
  fakery 616.3
  impersonation 572.2
  party 922.11
  v. hide oneself 615.8
  impersonate 572.9
  outfit 231.40
  pose as 616.22
masquerader 619.7
mass
  n. abundance 34.3
  accumulation 74.9
  conglomeration 50.5
  gravity 352.5
  large number 101.3

  lump 195.10
  major part 54.6
  plurality 100.2
  quantity 28.1
  sacred music 462.16
  size 195.1
  solid 354.6
  store 660.1
  substantiality 3.1
  thickness 204.2
  throng 74.4
  units 352.23
  v. assemble 74.18
  cohere 50.6
  come together 74.16
  join 47.5
  put 184.14
  adj. gravitational
    352.20
Mass parts of 1040.10
  rite 1040.9
  worship 1032.8
massacre
  n. carnage 409.5
  violence 162.3
  v. murder 409.17
massage
  n. rubbing 350.3
  v. make pliant 357.6
  rub 350.6
  touch 425.8
  treat 689.30
masses inferiors 37.2
  the people 919.3
masseur 350.4
massing cohesion 50.1
  joining 47.1
massive bulky 195.19
  dense 354.12
  heavy 352.16
  large 34.7
  ponderous 352.17
  substantial 3.7
  thick 204.8
mass murder 409.5
mass-produced 167.20
mass production 167.2
mass spectrography
  326.1
mast spar 277.13
  supporter 216.2
  tower 207.11
  types of 277.29
mastectomy 689.23
master
  n. artisan 718.6
  artist 579.1
  boy 125.5
  captain 276.7
  chief 749.3
  educator 565.9
  expert 733.13
  governor 749.5
  judge 1002.4
  lord 749
  producer 167.8
  proprietor 809.2
  superior 36.4
  teacher 565.1
  title 917.6
  victor 726.2
  wise man 468.1

  work of art 574.11
  v. conquer 727.10
  dominate 741.15
  learn 564.9
  subdue 764.9
  understand 548.7
  adj. chief 36.14
  governing 741.18
  most important
    672.23
Master
  form of address 420.7
  title 917.3
masterful
  arrogant 912.11
  finished 677.9
  imperious 739.16
  skillful 733.20
masterfully
  imperiously 739.19
  skillfully 733.29
mastermind
  n. expert 733.13
  scholar 476.3
  wise man 468.1
  v. direct 747.8
master of ceremonies
  broadcaster 344.23
  manager 748.4
  theater man 611.28
  toastmaster 878.22
masterpiece
  masterwork 733.10
  pattern of perfection
    677.4
  product 168.1
  work of art 574.11
mastership
  control 741.2
  directorship 747.4
  mastery 739.7
  skill 733.1
  supremacy 36.3
mastery conquest 727.1
  control 741.2
  influence 172.1
  mastership 739.7
  preparedness 720.4
  skill 733.1
  supremacy 36.3
  understanding 475.3
  victory 726.1
masthead 568.13
masticate chew 307.25
  pulp 390.5
mastodon
  large animal 195.14
  pachyderm 414.4
masturbate 419.24
masturbation 419.9
mat
  n. arena 802.1
  bedding 216.20
  hair 230.4
  lusterlessness 337.5
  partition 237.5
  rug 228.9
  v. dull 337.10
  weave 222.6
  adj. colorless 363.7
  lackluster 337.17

matador
bullfighter 800.4
killer 409.11
match
n. contest 796.3
equivalent 30.4
game 878.9
igniter 331.5
image 572.3
light source 336.1
marriage 933.1
two 90.2
v. agree 26.6
assemble 74.18
be comparable 491.7
coincide 14.4
compare 491.4
contrast 239.4
equal 30.5
give in kind 955.6
join in marriage
933.15
make parallel 218.5
pair 90.5
parallel 218.4
resemble 20.7
size 195.15
synchronize 118.3
matched coupled 90.8
joined 47.13
married 933.22
twin 90.6
matching
n. comparison 491.1
contest 796.3
adj. analogous 20.11
coloring 362.15
matchless best 674.18
peerless 36.15
matchmaker 933.13
mate
n. accompanier 73.4
companion 928.3
equivalent 30.4
image 572.3
likeness 20.3
partner 787.2
ship's officer 276.7
spouse 933.7
v. copulate 419.23
get married 933.16
pair 90.5
mated coupled 90.8
joined 47.13
married 933.22
material
n. content 194.5
covering 228.43
fabric 378.5,11
lore 475.9
matter 376.2
resources 378
store 660.1
substance 3.2
writing 602.30
adj. carnal 987.6
corporeal 376.9
essential 5.8
evidential 505.17
important 672.16
relevant 9.11
substantial 3.6

vital 672.22
worldly 1031.16
materialism
carnality 987.2
nonreligiousness
1031.2
philosophy 500.3
physicism 376.5
materialist
atomist 376.6
irreligionist 1031.10
materialistic
businesslike 656.15
carnal 987.6
materialist 376.11
philosophy 500.9
worldly 1031.16
materiality
existence 1.1
importance 672.1
materialness 376
matter 376.2
relevance 9.4
substantiality 3.1
materialization
appearance 446.1
corporealization
376.7
embodiment 3.4
event 151.1
manifestation 555.1
occultism 1034.6
production 167.4
specter 1017.1
materialize
appear 446.8
be discovered 488.9
be formed 246.8
corporealize 376.8
create 167.12
embody 3.5
indicate 555.5
manifest oneself
555.6
occur 151.6
matériel
equipment 659.4
materials 378.1
store 660.1
maternal loving 931.25
motherly 170.13
maternity
blood relationship
11.1
motherhood 170.3
mathematical
exact 516.16
numerical 87.17
mathematical elements
86.9
mathematician 87.9
mathematics
numeration 87.2
types of 87.18
matinee 922.10
matinee idol
actor 612.2
favorite 931.15
mating 419.8
mating call 460.1
matins morning 133.1
worship 1032.8

matri– 170.13
matriarch
antiquated person
123.8
mistress 749.2
mother 170.10
matriarchal 741.17
matriarchy 741.5
matricide 409.3
matriculate 570.16
matriculation 570.15
matrilineage 11.1
matrimonial 933.19
matrimonial bureau
933.13
matrimony
marriage 933.1
sacrament 1040.5
matrix deposit 383.7
form 246.1
model 25.6
womb 153.9
matron mistress 749.2
wife 933.9
woman 421.5
matronly
feminine 421.13
middle-aged 126.14
matte 577.5
matted complex 46.4
disorderly 62.14
hairy 230.24
matter
n. affair 151.3
body fluid 388.3
business 656.1
content 194.5
material 376.2
motive 648.1
particular 8.3
printer's copy 603.4
pus 311.6
quantity 28.1
substance 3.2
topic 484.1
trouble 731.3
written matter 602.10
v. be important
672.11
fester 311.15
matter of course 642.5
matter of fact
event 151.2
fact 1.3
prosaicness 883.2
matter-of-fact
dull 883.8
in plain style 591.3
practical 536.6
prosaic 610.5
simple 902.6
mattress 216.20
maturation aging 126.6
completion 722.2
development 148.1
growth 197.3
improvement 691.2
mature
v. complete 56.6
create 167.10
debt 840.7
develop 167.13

evolve 148.5
grow 197.7
grow up 126.9
improve 691.10
make perfect 677.5
ripen 722.8
adj. adult 126.12
complete 56.9
developed 126.13
due 840.10
experienced 733.26
finished 677.9
grown 197.12
prepared 720.16
ripe 722.13
matured complete 56.9
experienced 733.26
finished 677.9
ripe 722.13
maturing 148.8
maturity
adulthood 126.2
completion 722.2
debt 840.1
preparedness 720.4
matzo bread 308.28
ritualistic article
1040.11
maudlin foolish 470.8
intoxicated 996.30
sentimental 855.22
maul bruise 692.16
injure 692.15
mistreat 667.5
pound 283.14
terrorize 162.10
mauled 866.23
mausoleum
memorial 570.12
tomb 410.16
mauve 373.3,4
maven 897.7
maverick
n. cattle 414.6
nonconformist 83.3
obstinate person
626.6
odd person 85.4
rebel 767.5
adj. nonconformist
83.6
mavis 464.23
maw abdomen 193.3
mouth 265.5
mawkish
oversweet 431.5
sentimental 855.22
unsavory 429.7
maxi– 195.16
maxilli– 265.5
maxim a belief 501.2
aphorism 517
precept 751.2
rule 84.4
maximal
plentiful 661.7
superlative 36.13
top 211.10
maximize 38.4
maximum
n. completion 56.5
plenty 661.2

mechanical
involuntary 639.14
machinelike 348.11
mechanistic 347.7
uniform 17.5
mechanics art 733.7
physics 325.1
theoretical mechanics 347
mechanism art 733.7
control 349.34
instrument 658.3
instrumentality 658.2
machinery 348.4
materialism 376.5
works 348.5
mechanistic
materialist 376.11
mechanical 347.7
philosophy 500.9
mechanize 348.10
mechanized 348.11
medal award 916.6
insignia 569.1
relief 575.3
medalist 733.14
medallion medal 916.6
relief 575.3
meddle advise 754.5
hinder 730.10
pry 528.4
tamper with 238.7
meddler advisor 754.3
busybody 238.4
meddlesome
meddling 238.9
prying 528.6
meddling
n. intrusiveness 238.2
adj. meddlesome 238.9
media
communications 554.5
telecommunications 560.1
medial
intervening 237.10
medium 32.3
middle 69.4
median
n. mean 32.1
middle 69.1
adj. intervening 237.10
medium 32.3
middle 69.4
mediary 237.4
mediate
be instrumental 658.5
intercede 805.6
reconcile 804.8
mediating
instrumental 658.6
intercessory 805.8
mediation
instrumentality 658.2
intercession 805
pacification 804.1
mediator deputy 781.4
instrument 658.3

intermediary 237.4
intermediator 805.3
mediatory
Christlike 1013.19
intercessory 805.8
medic 688.5
Medicaid
medicine 688.1
welfare program 745.7
medical 688.18
medical examiner
death examiner 408.18
doctor 688.6
medical instrument 689.36
medical practice 688.16
Medicare
medicine 688.1
welfare program 745.7
medicate 689.31
medication
medical aid 689.15
medicine 687.4
therapy 689.1
medicinal 687.39
medicine
branches of 688.19
healing art 688
liquor 996.13
remedy 687.4
therapy 689.1
medicine man
quack doctor 688.7
sorcerer 1035.7
medico 688.6
medieval 123.13
medievalist 123.5
mediocre
imperfect 678.4
inferior 37.7
medium 32.3
middle 69.4
moderate 680.7
unskillful 734.15
mediocrity
a nobody 673.7
average 32.1
imperfection 678.1
inferiority 37.3
mediocreness 680
second-rater 680.5
unskillfulness 734.1
unskillful person 734.7
meditate
consider 478.12
intend 653.7
ponder over 478.13
meditation
consideration 478.2
engrossment 530.3
inaction 706.1
prayer 1032.4
meditative
abstracted 532.11
do-nothing 706.6
engrossed 530.17
thoughtful 478.21

medium
n. art equipment 574.19
book size 605.14
doer 718.1
environment 233.4
go-between 781.4
instrument 658.3
intermediary 237.4
matter 194.5
mean 32.1
mediator 805.3
middle course 806.3
paint 362.8
psychic 1034.13
substance 3.2
theater lighting 611.23
adj. average 32.3
cooked 330.7
intervening 237.10
mediocre 680.7
middle 69.4
medium of exchange 835.1
medley
n. hodgepodge 44.6
miscellany 74.13
music 462.6
adj. coloring 362.15
mixed 44.15
variegated 374.9
Medusa
bewitcher 1035.9
monster 85.20
meed portion 816.5
recompense 841.3
meek humble 906.10
modest 908.9
resigned 861.10
submissive 765.15
meekly humbly 906.15
modestly 908.14
resignedly 861.12
submissively 765.19
meerschaum 434.6
meet
n. assembly 74.2
contest 796.3
game 878.9
tournament 878.10
v. agree with 521.9
assemble 74.17
be joined 47.11
collide 283.12
come together 74.16
compete 796.19
conform 82.3
confront 240.8
converge 298.2
encounter 200.11
experience 151.8
observe 768.2
oppose 790.5
stand up to 893.11
suffice 661.4
adj. conventional 645.5
decorous 897.10
expedient 670.5
just 976.8
timely 129.9

meet halfway
compromise 807.2
mediate 805.6
meet head-on
contrapose 239.4
counteract 178.6
face up to 893.11
meet 200.11
offer resistance 792.3
meeting
n. assembly 74.2
conference 597.6
contest 796.3
convergence 298.1
encounter 200.4
impact 283.3
joining 47.1
rendezvous 922.9
worship 1032.8
adj. assembled 74.21
concurrent 177.4
converging 298.3
in contact 200.17
joining 47.16
meetinghouse
church 1042.1
hall 192.4
meeting of minds
agreement 26.3
unanimity 521.5
meet the eye
appear 446.8
attract attention 530.11
be visible 444.4
meg(a)– great 34.7
large 195.16
million 99.31
megacycles 344.12
megaphone 448.8
melancholia
despair 866.6
emotional symptom 690.23
mental disorder 690.17
psychosis 473.5
sadness 872.5
melancholic
n. personality type 690.15
sad person 872.13
adj. bored 884.10
sad 872.23
melancholy
n. boredom 884.3
despair 866.6
sadness 872.5
sullenness 951.8
thoughtfulness 478.3
adj. bored 884.10
sad 872.23
sullen 951.24
mélange 44.6
melanic 365.10
melanism 365.1
meld
n. combination 52.1
v. combine 52.3
melding 52.1
melee commotion 62.4
free-for-all 796.5

meliorate
  be changed 139.5
  change 139.6
  get better 691.7
  make better 691.9
mellifluous
  melodious 462.49
  pleasant 863.6
  sweet 431.4
mellow
  v. evolve 148.5
  mature 126.9
  reach perfection
    722.8
  soften 357.6
  adj. intoxicated
    996.30
  mature 126.13
  melodious 462.49
  pleasant 863.6
  resonant 454.9
  ripe 722.13
  soft 357.8
  soft-colored 362.21
mellowing
  maturation 126.6
  softening 357.5
mellowness
  pleasantness 863.1
  resonance 454.1
  softness 357.1
melodeon 465.15
melodic 462.49
melodics 463.1
melodious 462.49
melodist
  composer 464.20
  vocalist 464.13
melodrama
  emotionalism 855.9
  stage show 611.4
melodramatic
  emotionalistic 855.20
  sensational 857.30
  theatrical 611.38
melodramatics
  dramatics 611.2
  emotionalism 855.9
melody tune 462.4
  tunefulness 462.2
melt affect 855.16
  be transient 111.6
  disappear 447.2
  excite pity 944.5
  have pity 944.4
  heat 329.21
  liquefy 391.5
meltable
  liquefiable 391.9
  molten 329.31
melt away
  cease to exist 2.5
  decrease 39.6
  disappear 447.2
melt down
  extract 305.16
  liquefy 391.5
  melt 329.21
melted liquefied 391.6
  molten 329.31
  penitent 873.9

melting
  n. disappearance
    447.1
  heating 329.3
  liquefaction 391.1
  adj. liquefying 391.7
  loving 931.25
  pitying 944.7
  vanishing 447.3
melting pot
  converter 145.10
  mixer 44.10
  United States 181.3
member
  belonger 788.11
  part 55.4
membership
  inclusion 76.1
  members 788.12
  sociability 922.6
membrane layer 227.2
  skin 229.3
membranous 227.6
memento
  memorial 570.12
  remembrance 537.7
memo 570.4
memoir
  biography 608.4
  memorandum 570.4
  remembering 537.4
  treatise 606.1
memorabilia
  archives 570.2
  history 608.4
  matters of impor-
    tance 672.5
  memento 537.7
memorable
  notable 672.18
  rememberable 537.25
memorandum
  record 570.4
  reminder 537.6
memorial
  n. biography 608.4
  memento 537.7
  memorandum 570.4
  monument 570.12
  record 570.1
  adj. celebrative 877.3
  commemorative
    537.27
memorialize
  celebrate 877.2
  petition 774.10
memorize
  commit to memory
    537.17
  learn 564.8
memory
  celebration 877.1
  computer 349.17
  engram 690.36
  posthumous fame
    914.7
  remembrance 537
  retrospection 119.4
men male sex 420.3
  people 417.2
  troops 157.9
  working force 750.11

menace
  n. danger 697.1
  threat 973.1
  v. be imminent 152.2
  forebode 544.11
  threaten 973.2
  work evil 675.6
menacing
  dangerous 697.9
  imminent 152.3
  ominous 544.17
  threatening 973.3
ménage
  domestic manage-
    ment 747.6
  family 11.5
  home 191.4
menagerie
  collection 74.11
  zoo 191.19
mend
  n. improvement 691.1
  v. get better 691.7
  make better 691.9
  recover health 685.6
  repair 694.14
mendable 694.25
mendacious 616.34
mendacity lie 616.11
  untruthfulness 616.8
Mendel's law 170.6
mender 694.10
mendicancy
  beggary 774.6
  indigence 838.2
mendicant
  n. ascetic 991.2
  beggar 774.8
  nonworker 708.10
  religious 1038.17
  adj. ascetic 991.3
  begging 774.16
  indigent 838.8
mending
  n. improvement 691.1
  repair 694.6
  adj. improving 691.15
menfolk 420.3
menial
  n. servant 750.2
  working person 718.2
  adj. servile 907.12
  serving 750.14
meningitis
  infectious disease
    686.12
  inflammation 686.9
meniscus
  crescent 252.5
  lens 443.1
menopause 126.7
menorah 1040.11
mensch 985.1
menses 311.9
menstrual
  bleeding 311.24
  momentary 137.8
menstruate 311.18
menstruation 311.9
mensuration
  measurement 490.1
  metrology 490.9

menswear 231.1
mental
  cognitive 478.21
  insane 473.25
  intellectual 466.8
  temperamental 525.7
mental block
  memory obstruction
    538.3
  thought disturbance
    690.24
mental case 473.16
mental deficiency
  insanity 473.1
  mental retardation
    469.9
mental health
  health 685.1
  sanity 472.1
mental hospital
  hospital 689.27
  insane asylum 473.14
mental illness
  insanity 473.1
  mental disorder
    690.17
mentality
  intellect 466.1
  intelligence 467.1
  intelligent being
    467.9
mentally 525.9
mentally ill 473.27
mentally retarded
  469.22
mental picture 535.6
mental telepathy
  1034.9
mention
  n. honor 916.4
  information 557.1
  remark 594.4
  v. call attention to
    530.10
  inform 557.8
  remark 594.25
  specify 80.11
mentor advisor 754.3
  preparer 720.5
  teacher 565.1
  wise man 468.1
menu
  bill of fare 307.12
  list 88.5
  schedule 641.2
meow 460.2
Mephistopheles 1016.5
mercantile 827.21
mercantilism 827.12
mercantilistic 827.21
mercenary
  n. hireling 750.3
  soldier 800.16
  adj. corruptible
    975.23
  employed 780.19
  greedy 634.27
merchandise
  n. commodities 831
  provision 659.2
  v. deal in 827.15
  sell 829.8

merchandising
n. selling 829.2
trade 827.2
adj. sales 829.13
merchant
n. merchandiser 830.2
provider 659.6
adj. commercial
827.21
merchant marine
navy 800.26
ships 277.10
merci! 949.6
merciful
godlike 1013.20
lenient 759.7
pitying 944.7
mercifulness
compassionateness
944.2
leniency 759.1
merciless pitiless 945.3
savage 162.20
mercurial fast 269.19
fickle 629.6
flighty 532.17
inconstant 141.7
irresolute 627.9
lively 707.17
metal 383.17
nonuniform 18.3
mercury
changeableness 141.4
guide 748.7
speed 269.6
thermometer 328.20
Mercury god 1014.5
god of trade 827.12
messenger 561.1
planet 375.9
mercury poisoning
686.31
mercy good deed 938.7
leniency 759.1
pity 944.1
mercy killing 409.1
mere sheer 35.8
simple 45.6
merely simply 45.11
solely 89.14
to a degree 35.10
mere nothing
insignificancy 673.6
small amount 35.5
meretricious
false 616.27
gaudy 904.20
grandiloquent 601.8
paltry 673.18
prostitute 989.28
vulgar 898.11
merge assemble 58.3
become 145.17
be joined 47.11
combine 52.3
come together 74.16
cooperate 786.3
join 47.5
mix 44.11
submerge 320.7
unify 14.5
merged combined 52.5

joined 47.13
merger affiliation 786.2
combination 52.1
identification 14.2
joining 47.1
mixture 44.1
merging
n. joining 47.1
adj. combining 52.7
meridian
n. astronomy 375.16
longitude 180.3
map 654.4
noon 133.5
summit 211.2
adj. noon 133.7
top 211.10
meringue foam 405.2
icing 308.39
merit
n. dueness 960.3
goodness 674.1
importance 672.1
v. deserve 960.5
merited just 976.8
warranted 960.9
meritless 673.19
meritorious due 960.10
praiseworthy 968.20
reputable 914.15
Merlin 1035.6
mermaid
sea creature 397.4
swimmer 275.12
water god 1014.20
merrily 870.19
merriment
cheerfulness 870.5
conviviality 922.3
festivity 878.3
rejoicing 876.1
wittiness 881.4
merry festive 878.30
intoxicated 996.30
mirthful 870.15
merry chase 725.5
merry-go-round
amusement device
878.15
revel 878.7
rotator 322.4
merrymaking
n. conviviality 922.3
festivity 865.3
gaiety 878.3
adj. festive 878.30
mesa plain 387.1
plateau 207.4
mescaline 687.13,53
mesh
n. complex 46.2
interaction 13.3
network 221.3
v. catch 822.17
interact 13.8
net 221.7
trap 618.18
meshed 221.11
meshes network 221.3
snare 618.12
meshing
n. interaction 13.3

adj. fitted 26.10
mesmeric
alluring 650.7
engrossing 530.20
hypnotic 712.24
mesmerism 712.8
mesmerize
cast a spell 1036.7
engross 530.13
fascinate 650.6
have influence over
172.11
put to sleep 712.20
mesmerized
amazed 920.9
enchanted 1036.12
engrossed 530.18
mesmerizer
deceiver 619.1
hypnotist 712.9
mesmerizing 530.20
mesomorph 690.15
meson atomics 326.6
particle 196.8
radiation 327.4
mess
n. amount 28.2
bunch 74.7
bungle 734.5
complex 46.2
confusion 532.3
dining room 192.11
fiasco 725.6
filth 682.7
hodgepodge 44.6
jumble 62.3
meal 307.5
much 34.4
portion 816.5
predicament 731.4
rations 308.6
ugly thing 899.4
v. defile 682.17
disarrange 63.2
feed 307.16
message
advertisement 559.6
communication
554.1
computer 349.19
dispatch 558.4
information 557.1
letter 604.2
mess around
do carelessly 534.9
meddle 238.7
trifle 673.13
messed up
bungled 734.22
disorderly 62.14
mixed up 46.4
spoiled 692.31
messenger courier 561
delegate 781.2
harbinger 544.5
precursor 66.1
mess hall
dining room 192.11
restaurant 307.15
messiah 748.6
Messiah 1013.12
messily 534.18

messiness
formlessness 247.1
slipshodness 534.3
slovenliness 62.6
uncleanness 682.1
messmate
companion 928.3
partner 787.2
mess up bungle 734.12
complicate 46.3
defile 682.17
deform 247.3
disarrange 63.2
spoil 692.13
messy dirty 682.22
slipshod 534.12
slovenly 62.15
mestizo 44.9
metabolic
changing 139.11
plasmatic 246.10
metabolic diseases
686.20
metabolism
nutrition 309.10
transformation 139.2
metabolize
digest 309.16
transform 139.7
metal
n. element 383.21
heraldic insignia
569.2
leaf 383.23
metallics 383.3
v. cover 228.22
adj. metallic 383.16
metallic metal 383.16
raucous 458.15
metallurgical 383.18
metallurgist 383.12
metallurgy 383.11
metalworker 718.7
metalworks
foundry 719.5
works 719.4
metamorphic
changeable 141.6
changing 139.11
multiform 19.3
metamorphosis 139.2
metaphor
comparison 491.1
figure of speech
551.5
similarity 20.1
substitute 149.2
metaphorical
figurative 551.3
implicative 546.10
indicative 568.23
meaningful 545.10
metaphysical
occult 1034.22
philosophical 500.9
metaphysician
occultist 1034.12
philosopher 500.6
metaphysics
philosophy 500.1
philosophy of being
1.7

between 237.12
midterm 485.2
midtown
  n. city district 183.6
  adj. urban 183.10
mid-Victorian
  n. antiquated person
   123.8
  prude 903.11
  adj. antiquated
   123.13
  prudish 903.19
midway
  n. middle 69.2
  adj. middle 69.4
  neutral 806.7
  adv. halfway 69.5
  mediumly 32.4
midwife healer 688.5
  means 658.3
mien behavior 737.1
  exteriority 224.1
  looks 446.4
miff
  n. anger 952.7
  v. annoy 866.13
  provoke 952.22
miffed annoyed 866.21
  provoked 952.25
might
  authoritativeness
   739.2
  greatness 34.1
  power 157.1
  strength 159.1
might and main
  exertion 716.1
  power 157.1
might be 509.4
mightily
  authoritatively
   739.18
  powerfully 157.15
  strongly 159.21
  very 34.18
mighty
  adj. authoritative
   739.15
  considerable 34.6
  eminent 914.18
  huge 195.20
  powerful 157.12
  strong 159.13
  adv. very 34.18
migraine ache 424.5
  nervous disorder
   686.23
migrant bird 414.33
  migrator 274.5
  working person 718.2
migrant worker
  farm hand 413.5
  traveler 274.5
  working person 718.2
migrate 273.21
migration
  transference 271.1
  travel 273.4
migratory 273.36
mikado 749.8
mike 450.9
milady title 917.2

woman 421.5
milch 388.8
milcher 414.6
mild
  good-natured 938.14
  insipid 430.2
  lenient 759.7
  moderate 163.10
  pleasant 863.10
  soft 357.8
  warm 328.24
  weak 765.15
mildew
  n. blight 676.2
  decay 692.6
  fetidness 437.2
  v. decay 692.25
mildewed
  malodorous 437.5
  old 123.14
  spoiled 692.43
mildly meekly 765.19
  moderately 35.10
mildness
  good nature 938.2
  insipidness 430.1
  leniency 759.1
  meekness 765.5
  moderation 163.1
mileage distance 199.1
  fee 841.5
  length 202.1
milepost mark 568.10
  pointer 568.4
  post 217.4
miles per hour 269.1
milestone
  important point
   672.6
  mark 568.10
milieu arena 802.1
  atmosphere 233.3
  environment 233.1
  neighborhood 180.1
militancy activity 707.1
  warlikeness 797.15
militant
  n. combatant 800.1
  man of action 707.8
  adj. active 707.17
  warlike 797.25
militarism
  foreign policy 744.5
  military government
   741.4
  warlikeness 797.15
militarist 800.5
militaristic 797.26
militarization 797.14
militarize 797.24
military
  n. army 800.22
  adj. warlike 797.25
military court 1001.7
military insignia 569.5
military operations
  strategy 797.8
  warfare 797.1
military police 699.17
military school 567.13
military science 797.10
militate 164.7

militate against
  contend against
   790.4
  counteract 178.6
militia 800.23
milk
  n. body fluid 388.3
  fluid 388.2
  food 308.47
  white 364.2
  v. deprive 822.21
  despoil 822.24
  exploit 665.16
  extract 305.12
  overact 611.36
  tend animals 416.7
  adj. milky 388.8
milk and honey 728.1
milker 414.6
milkiness
  liquidity 388.1
  whiteness 364.1
milking 305.3
milk run 278.11
milksop coward 892.5
  effeminate male
   421.10
  fool 471.1
  weakling 160.6
milky fluid 388.8
  weak 160.17
  white 364.7
Milky Way 375.6
mill
  n. plant 719.3
  pulverizer 361.7
  types of 348.23
  US money 835.7
  v. assemble 74.16
  move around 322.12
  notch 262.4
  process 167.11
  pulverize 361.9
  tool 348.10
milled made 167.22
  powdery 361.11
millenarian
  n. optimist 888.6
  adj. optimistic 888.12
millennial
  idealized 535.23
  thousand 99.30
millennium
  good times 728.4
  paradise 535.11
  period 107.2
  thousand 99.10
millet 308.34
milli– 99.30
milliner hatter 231.36
  store 832.4
millinery
  clothing 231.25
  garment making
   231.31
milling 167.3
million
  n. immense number
   101.4
  number 99.11
  adj. numerous 101.6
millionaire 837.6

millstone burden 352.7
  pulverizer 361.7
millstone around one's
  neck
  affliction 866.8
  impediment 730.6
millstream 395.1
mill town 719.2
milord 917.2
Milquetoast
  coward 892.5
  irresolute person
   627.5
  weakling 160.6
mime
  n. actor 612.2
  comedy 611.6
  imitator 22.4
  v. act 611.34
  gesture 568.21
  imitate 22.6
  impersonate 572.9
mimeograph
  n. printing 603.1
  v. copy 24.8
  print 603.14
mimer actor 612.2
  imitator 22.4
mimetic imitative 22.9
  representational
   572.10
mimic
  n. actor 612.2
  imitator 22.4
  v. imitate 22.6
  impersonate 572.9
  resemble 20.7
  adj. imitative 22.9
mimicry acting 611.9
  imitation 22.2
  impersonation 572.2
miming acting 611.9
  impersonation 572.2
minaret 207.11
minatory 973.3
mince
  n. gait 273.14
  meat 308.12
  v. affect 903.14
  extenuate 1006.12
  grind 49.13
  speak poorly 595.7
  walk 273.27
mincing 903.18
mind
  n. belief 501.6
  desire 634.1
  intellect 466.1
  intention 653.1
  memory 537.1
  mood 525.4
  psyche 690.35
  spirit 466.4
  theosophy 1034.18
  trait of character
   525.3
  will 621.1
  v. be unwilling 623.3
  beware 895.7
  care for 699.19
  heed 530.6
  obey 766.2

minute
 n. account entry 845.5
 instant 113.3
 period 107.2
 stage 107.1
 time of day 114.2
 v. keep accounts
 845.8
 record 570.16
 adj. detailed 8.9
 meticulous 533.12
 particular 80.12
 tiny 196.11
 unimportant 673.15
minutely fully 8.13
 meticulously 533.16
 particularly 80.15
 scarcely 35.9
minutemen 800.23
minutes record 570.4
 reports 570.7
minutiae
 minute things 196.7
 particular 8.3
 small amount 35.2
 trivia 673.4
minx bad child 125.4
 impudent person
 913.5
 mischief-maker 738.3
 woman 421.6
miracle marvel 920.2
 stage show 611.4
 supernaturalism 85.8
miracle play 611.4
miracle-worker 1035.5
miraculous
 supernatural 85.16
 wonderful 920.10
miraculously 920.14
mirage
 apparition 446.5
 deception 618.1
 disappointment
 541.1
 illusion 519.6
mire
 n. filthy place 682.12
 marsh 400.1
 mud 389.8
 slime 682.8
 v. bog down 400.2
 dirty 682.15
mirror
 n. glass 443.5
 good person 985.4
 ideal 25.4
 model 25.1
 prototype 677.4
 v. imitate 22.5
 represent 572.8
 resemble 20.7
mirror image, the 15.2
mirroring image 572.3
 imitation 22.1
mirth
 amusement 878.1
 merriment 870.5
mirthful 870.15
miry dirty 682.22
 marshy 400.3
 muddy 389.14

misadventure 729.2
misalliance
 marriage 933.1
 misconnection 10.2
 unfitness 27.3
misanthrope
 hater 930.4
 man-hater 940.2
misanthropic 940.3
misanthropy
 antisociality 940
 hate 930.1
misapplication
 error 518.1
 misconnection 10.2
 misinterpretation
 553.1
 misuse 667.1
 sophistry 483.1
misapply err 518.12
 misinterpret 553.2
 misuse 667.4
 reason speciously
 483.8
misapprehend
 err 518.13
 misinterpret 553.2
misapprehension
 an error 518.3
 misinterpretation
 553.1
misappropriate 667.4
misappropriation 667.1
misbegotten
 abnormal 85.13
 bastard 999.7
 deformed 249.12
 ugly 899.8
misbehave 738.4
misbehavior 738
misbelief heresy 1025.2
 illusion 519.1
misbelieve
 be unorthodox
 1025.8
 disbelieve 503.5
misbeliever 1025.5
miscalculate err 518.9
 misjudge 496.2
miscalculation
 an error 518.3
 misjudgment 496.1
miscarriage
 an error 518.3
 failure 725.5
miscarriage of justice
 977.4
miscarry fail 725.14
 fall short 314.4
miscegenate
 get married 933.16
 hybridize 44.14
miscegenation
 crossbreeding 44.4
 marriage 933.1
miscellaneous 44.15
miscellany
 assemblage 74.13
 compilation 605.4
 hodgepodge 44.6
 selections 607.4
mischance 729.2

mischief
 disaccord 795.1
 disadvantage 671.2
 evil 675.3
 impairment 692.1
 misbehavior 738.2
 mischief-maker 738.3
mischief-maker
 instigator 648.11
 prankster 738.3
 troublemaker 943.2
mischievous
 devilish 1016.19
 harmful 675.12
 roguish 738.6
misconceive err 518.13
 misinterpret 553.2
misconception
 an error 518.3
 illusion 519.1
 misinterpretation
 553.1
misconduct
 n. misbehavior 738.1
 mismanagement
 734.6
 misuse 667.1
 wrongdoing 982.1
 v. err 518.12
 mismanage 734.13
misconstruction
 distortion 249.2
 error 518.1
 falsification 616.9
 misinterpretation
 553.1
 misjudgment 496.1
 solecism 587.2
misconstrue
 distort 249.6
 misinterpret 553.2
 misjudge 496.2
misconstrued 553.3
miscreant 986.5
miscue
 n. an error 518.4
 bungle 734.5
 v. bungle 734.11
 err 518.13
misdate
 n. anachronism 115.1
 v. mistime 115.2
misdated 115.3
misdating 115.1
misdeed 982.2
misdemeanor
 crime 999.4
 misbehavior 738.1
 misdeed 982.2
 wrongdoing 982.1
misdirect distort 249.6
 mislead 618.15
 mismanage 734.13
 misteach 563.3
misdirected
 botched 734.21
 mistaught 563.5
misdirection
 deception 618.2
 distortion 249.2
 mismanagement
 734.6

misteaching 563.1
mise-en-scène
 drama production
 611.14
 setting 233.2
 stage setting 611.24
miser collector 74.15
 niggard 852.4
miserable
 adverse 729.13
 base 915.12
 paltry 673.18
 unhappy 872.21
 wretched 866.26
miserably basely 915.17
 distressingly 34.21
Miserere 1032.3
miserly few 102.5
 greedy 634.27
 meager 662.10
 stingy 852.9
misery despair 866.6
 pain 424.1
 sorrow 872.10
 unhappiness 872.2
misfeasance error 518.1
 misdeed 982.2
 mismanagement
 734.6
 misuse 667.1
 wrongdoing 982.1
misfire
 n. failure 725.5
 v. come to nothing
 725.12
 miss 314.4
misfit intruder 78.2
 naysayer 27.4
 nonconformist 83.3
misfortune 729.2
misgiving
 n. anxiety 890.1
 apprehension 891.4
 doubt 503.2
 foreboding 544.2
 adj. anxious 890.6
 fearful 891.32
misgovern 734.13
misguidance
 deception 618.2
 mismanagement
 734.6
 misteaching 563.1
misguide
 mislead 618.15
 mismanage 734.13
 misteach 563.3
misguided
 botched 734.21
 mistaught 563.5
 unwise 470.9
mishandle
 mismanage 734.13
 mistreat 667.5
 misuse 667.4
mishandling
 mismanagement
 734.6
 misuse 667.1
mishap 729.2
mishmash
 hodgepodge 44.6

jumble 62.3
misidentify 518.13
misinform
  mislead 618.15
  misteach 563.3
misinformation
  deception 618.2
  misteaching 563.1
misinformed
  mistaught 563.5
  unlearned 477.14
misinterpret
  distort 249.6
  err 518.13
  misjudge 496.2
  misunderstand 553.2
misinterpretation
  distortion 249.2
  error 518.1
  misjudgment 496.1
  misunderstanding
    553
misjudge
  miscalculate 496.2
  misinterpret 553.2
misjudgment
  an error 518.3
  error 518.1
  misinterpretation
    553.1
  poor judgment 496
mislaid 185.11
mislay lose 812.4
  misplace 185.7
mislaying 185.3
mislead deceive 618.15
  lie 616.19
  misteach 563.3
  seduce 989.20
misleading
  n. deception 618.2
  misteaching 563.1
  adj. deceptive 618.19
  illusory 519.9
  misteaching 563.6
misled 563.5
mismanage err 518.12
  mishandle 734.13
  misuse 667.4
mismanaged 734.21
mismanagement
  mishandling 734.6
  misuse 667.1
mismatch
  n. unfitness 27.3
  v. disagree 27.5
mismatched
  inappropriate 27.7
  unequal 31.4
misname 583.12
misnomer
  n. wrong name 583.9
  v. misname 583.12
misogynist
  celibate 934.2
  hater 930.4
  woman-hater 940.2
misogyny
  celibacy 934.1
  hate 930.1
misplace lose 812.4
  mislay 185.7

misplaced
  disorderly 62.13
  inappropriate 27.7
  mislaid 185.11
  out of line 83.7
misplay
  n. an error 518.3
  v. err 518.12
misprint
  n. an error 518.3
  v. err 518.12
misprize disdain 966.3
  underestimate 498.2
misprized 867.9
mispronounce 595.11
mispronounced 595.12
mispronunciation
  error in speech 518.7
  speech defect 595.5
misquote err 518.12
  falsify 616.16
  misinterpret 553.2
  misrepresent 573.3
misquoted
  distorted 249.11
  unauthentic 518.19
misread
  v. err 518.12
  misinterpret 553.2
  adj. misinterpreted
    553.3
misreading
  misinterpretation
    553.1
  misjudgment 496.1
misremember 538.5
misrender distort 249.6
  misinterpret 553.2
misrendering 553.1
misrepresent
  belie 573.3
  distort 249.6
  falsify 616.16
misrepresentation
  distortion 249.2
  false representation
    573
  falsification 616.9
misrepresented 249.11
misrule
  n. confusion 62.2
  lawlessness 740.2
  mismanagement
    734.6
  v. mismanage 734.13
miss
  n. an error 518.3
  failure 725.4
  girl 125.6
  v. be imperfect 678.3
  be inattentive 531.2
  fail 725.13
  fall short 314.4
  leave undone 534.7
  lose 812.4
  want 662.7
Miss 421.8
missal 1040.12
Miss America 900.8
missed 534.14
misshape 249.7

misshapen
  abnormal 85.13
  deformed 249.12
  ugly 899.8
  unordered 62.12
missile
  n. names of 281.15
  projectile 285.6
  rocket 281.3,14
  weapon 801.12
  adj. projectile 285.16
missilery arms 801.1
  ballistics 801.3
  rocketry 281.1
missing absent 187.10
  incomplete 57.4
  nonexistent 2.7
  vanished 447.4
  wanting 662.13
missing link gap 57.2
  prehistoric man 123.7
mission
  n. church 1042.1
  commission 780.1
  delegates 781.13
  duty 962.1
  flight 278.11
  military operation
    797.8
  task 656.2
  undertaking 715.2
  vocation 656.6
  v. commission 780.9
missionary
  converter 145.9
  evangelist 1038.7
missive 604.2
misspeak err 518.14
  mispronounce 595.11
misspell 518.12
misspend 854.6
misspent 854.9
misstate falsify 616.16
  misrepresent 573.3
misstated 518.19
misstatement
  an error 518.3
  falsification 616.9
  misrepresentation
    573.1
misstep 518.4
miss the boat
  be late 132.7
  miscarry 314.4
  miss an opportunity
    130.6
miss the mark
  fail 725.13
  fall short 678.3
  miss 314.4
mist
  n. confusion 532.3
  fog 404.2
  obscurity 549.3
  rain 394.1
  spirit 4.3
  v. cloud 404.6
  confuse 532.7
  lose distinctness
    445.4
mistake
  n. an error 518.3

bungle 734.5
  failure 725.4
  v. err 518.13
  misinterpret 553.2
mistaken
  in error 518.18
  misinterpreted 553.3
mistaught
  misinstructed 563.5
  unlearned 477.14
misteach
  misinstruct 563.3
  misrepresent 573.3
misteaching
  n. misinstruction 563
  misrepresentation
    573.1
  adj. misinstructive
    563.6
Mister
  form of address 420.7
  title 917.3
mistime ill-time 130.4
  misdate 115.2
mistimed
  anachronous 115.3
  untimely 130.7
mistiming 115.1
mistral 403.9
mistreat ill-use 667.5
  work evil 675.6
mistreatment 667.2
mistress
  instructress 565.2
  kept woman 989.17
  lady love 931.14
  matron 749.2
  proprietor 809.2
Mistress
  form of address 421.8
  title 917.4
mistrial 1004.5
mistrust
  n. caution 895.2
  doubt 503.2
  jealousy 953.2
  v. be doubtful 503.6
  be jealous 953.3
mistrustful
  cautious 895.9
  doubtful 503.9
misty foggy 404.9
  formless 247.4
  indistinct 445.6
  insubstantial 205.16
  muddled 532.13
  obscure 549.15
  rainy 394.10
misunderstand
  err 518.13
  misinterpret 553.2
misunderstanding
  an error 518.3
  disagreement 795.2
  misinterpretation
    553.1
misunderstood
  disliked 867.9
  misinterpreted 553.3
misusage abuse 667.1
  error in speech 518.7
  solecism 587.2

misuse
  n. an error 518.3
  corruption 692.2
  distortion 249.2
  misapplication 667
  use 665.1
  v. corrupt 692.14
  distort 249.6
  err 518.12
  exploit 665.16
  misemploy 667.4
mite animal 414.40
  British money 835.8
  bug 414.36
  child 125.3
  minute quantity
    196.7
  minute thing 196.7
  pittance 662.5
  small amount 35.2
miter
  n. clerical insignia
    569.4
  joint 47.4
  v. fasten 47.8
Mithras 1014.5
mitigate
  be changed 139.5
  change 139.6
  extenuate 1006.12
  moderate 163.6
  qualify 507.3
  reduce 39.8
  relax 163.9
  relieve 886.5
  weaken 160.10
mitigating
  moderating 163.14
  qualifying 507.7
  relieving 886.9
mitigation
  change 139.1
  decrease 39.1
  extenuation 1006.5
  moderation 163.2
  pity 944.1
  relief 886.1
  weakening 160.5
mitigator 163.3
mitosis 406.16
mitzvah
  good deed 938.7
  precept 751.2
mix
  n. hodgepodge 44.6
  predicament 731.4
  v. be sociable 922.16
  be undiscriminating
    493.3
  blend 44.11
  combine 52.3
  compose 58.3
  concoct 720.7
mixable 44.17
mixed combined 52.5
  imperfect 678.4
  mingled 44.15
mixed bag 44.6
mixed-blood 44.9
mixed marriage 933.1
mixed-up complex 46.4
  confused 532.12

disordered 62.16
mixer blender 44.10
  dance 879.2
  radio 344.7
  radioman 344.24
  sociable person
    922.15
mixing blending 44.1
  radio broadcasting
    344.16
  televising 345.3
mixture
  a preparation 720.3
  blending 44
  combination 52.2
  composition 58.1
  compound 44.5
  medicine 687.4
  miscellany 74.13
  organ stop 465.22
  solution 391.3
  variety 16.1
mix up
  complicate 46.3
  confuse 532.7
  disarrange 63.3
  scramble 44.11
mix-up 62.2
mnemonic
  n. memory training
    537.9
  adj. recollective
    537.22
moan
  n. lament 875.3
  v. lament 875.8
  sigh 452.14
  wail 875.11
  wind sound 403.23
moaning
  n. lamentation 875.1
  sigh 452.8
  adj. lamenting 875.15
moat barrier 730.5
  entrenchment 799.5
  gap 201.2
  trench 263.2
mob association 788.1
  clique 788.6
  group 74.3
  large number 101.3
  throng 74.4
mob, the
  the people 919.3
  the underworld
    986.11
mobile
  n. sculpture 575.2
  work of art 574.11
  adj. changeable 141.6
  moving 267.7
mobile home
  abode 191.18
  trailer 272.18
mobile unit 345.7
mobility
  changeableness 141.1
  motivity 267.3
mobilization
  assembly 74.1
  call to arms 797.12
  enlistment 780.6

militarization 797.14
  motion 267.1
  preparation 720.1
mobilize
  assemble 74.18
  call to arms 797.23
  enlist 780.16
  join 47.5
  militarize 797.24
  prepare 720.6
  set in motion 267.6
mobilized 720.16
Möbius strip 71.2
mob rule
  government 741.4
  lawlessness 740.2
mobster bandit 825.4
  criminal 986.10
  evildoer 943.1
mock
  n. fake 616.13
  gibe 967.2
  indignity 965.2
  v. adopt 821.4
  deceive 618.13
  imitate 22.6
  joke 881.13
  offend 965.4
  ridicule 967.9
  adj. imitation 22.8
  similar 20.10
  substitute 149.8
  ungenuine 616.26
mocker 22.4
mockery
  burlesque 967.6
  imitation 22.2
  indignity 965.2
  insincerity 616.5
  laughingstock 967.7
  ridicule 967.1
  trifle 673.5
mock-heroic
  comic 880.5
  poetic 609.17
mocking
  n. imitation 821.2
  adj. ridiculing 967.12
mockingbird
  imitator 22.4
  songbird 464.23
mock-up imitation 22.3
  model 25.5
mod
  fashionable 644.11
  modern 122.13
modal 7.7
modality form 246.1
  state 7.1
mode fashion 644.1
  form 246.1
  grammar 586.11
  harmonics 463.10
  manner 7.4
  state 7.1
  style 588.2
  syllogism 482.6
  way 657.1
model
  n. beautiful person
    900.8
  duplicate 24.3

figure 572.4
  form 246.1
  good person 985.4
  harmonics 463.11
  idea 479.2
  image 572.3
  imitation 22.3
  measure 490.2
  original 23.2
  pattern 25
  v. emulate 22.7
  form 246.7
  sculpture 575.5
  adj. exemplary 25.8
  perfect 677.9
  praiseworthy 968.20
modeled 575.7
modeler 579.6
modeling
  forming 246.5
  sculpture 575.1
moderate
  n. moderation 745.10
  politics 163.4
  v. limit 234.5
  mediate 805.6
  qualify 507.3
  restrain 163.6
  slow 270.9
  adj. centrist 745.18
  cheap 849.7
  lenient 759.7
  mediocre 680.7
  medium 32.3
  mild 163.10
  neutral 806.7
  sedate 858.14
  slow 270.10
  temperate 992.9
  tolerable 674.19
moderately
  cheaply 849.10
  in moderation 163.17
  mediocrely 680.11
  slowly 270.13
  temperately 992.12
  to a degree 35.10
  tolerably 674.23
moderation
  limitation 234.2
  middle course 806.3
  restraint 163
  sedateness 858.4
  temperance 992.1
moderator
  arbitrator 805.4
  judge 1002.1
  mitigator 163.3
modern
  n. modern man 122.4
  adj. fashionable
    644.11
  new 122.13
  present 120.2
modern dance 879.1
modernist
  modern 122.4
  poet 609.13
modernization 122.3
modernize 122.6
modernized 122.13
modest cheap 849.7

decent 988.5
humble 906.9
inferior 37.6
mediocre 680.7
meek 908.9
reticent 613.10
unselfish 979.5
unwilling 623.7
modestly
humbly 906.15
mediocrely 680.11
meekly 908.14
to a degree 35.10
modesty decency 988.2
demur 623.2
humility 906.1
mediocrity 680.1
reticence 613.3
unostentatiousness
908
unselfishness 979.1
modicum piece 55.3
portion 816.5
small amount 35.2
modifiable
changeable 141.6
convertible 145.18
modification
change 139.1
diversification 16.4
qualification 507.1
speech sound 594.13
modified
changed 139.9
qualified 507.10
modifier syntax 586.2
transformer 139.4
modify change 139.6
diversify 16.6
qualify 507.3
modifying 507.7
modish
dressed up 231.45
modern 122.13
stylish 644.12
modiste 231.35
modulate
be changed 139.5
change 139.6
inflect 594.29
moderate 163.6
qualify 507.3
modulation
change 139.1
harmonization 463.2
intonation 594.7
moderation 163.2
radio 344.14
modulator 163.3
module individual 89.4
spacecraft 282.2
modus operandi 657.1
modus vivendi
truce 804.5
way of life 737.1
mogul personage 672.8
snow 333.8
moiety
community 788.2
half 92.2
middle 69.2
piece 55.3

portion 816.5
moil
n. agitation 324.1
work 716.4
v. drudge 716.14
seethe 322.12
moiré
n. variegation 374.6
adj. iridescent 374.10
moist 392.15
moisten 392.12
moistening
n. wetting 392.6
adj. wetting 392.18
moisture dampness 392
liquidity 388.1
rain 394.1
moistureproof 393.11
molar
n. tooth 258.5
adj. dental 258.16
molasses adherent 50.4
semiliquid 389.5
sweetening 431.2
mold
n. blight 676.2
characteristic 80.4
copy 24.6
decay 692.6
form 246.1
fungus 412.3
germ 686.39
kind 61.3
land 385.1
model 25.6
nature 5.3
plant 411.4,45
structure 245.1
temperament 525.3
v. conform 82.3
create 167.10
decay 692.25
form 246.7
imagine 535.14
make ceramics 576.6
sculpture 575.5
moldable docile 765.13
pliant 357.9
teachable 564.18
molded made 167.22
sculptured 575.7
molder
n. sculptor 579.6
v. become old 123.9
decay 692.25
disintegrate 53.3
quiet 268.8
moldering
dilapidated 53.5
old 123.14
quiescent 268.12
spoiled 692.43
molding copy 24.6
forming 246.5
manufacture 167.3
sculpture 575.1
structure 245.1
moldy
malodorous 437.5
old 123.14
spoiled 692.43
mole barrier 730.5

blemish 679.1
blind 441.4
breakwater 216.4
bulge 256.3
harbor 700.6
mark 568.5
tumor 686.36
molecular 196.14
molecular weight
chemistry 379.4
system of weight
352.8
molecule atomics 326.7
chemical 379.1
matter 376.2
particle 196.8
small amount 35.2
molehill hill 207.5
pile 74.10
trifle 673.5
molest annoy 866.13
harm 675.6
mistreat 667.5
persecute 667.6
mollify calm 163.7
pacify 804.7
relieve 886.5
soften 357.6
mollifying
pacificatory 804.12
softening 357.16
tranquilizing 163.15
mollycoddle
n. effeminate male
421.10
spoiled child 759.4
weakling 160.6
v. indulge 759.6
Moloch 1014.11
molt 232.10
molten liquefied 391.6
melted 329.31
mom 170.10
moment
authority 739.4
importance 672.1
impulse 283.1
influence 172.1
instant 113.3
period 107.2
short time 111.3
stage 107.1
momentarily
instantly 113.6
shortly 111.10
momentary
instantaneous 113.4
regular 137.8
transient 111.7
moment of truth
crucial moment
129.5
period 107.1
momentous
authoritative 739.15
eventful 151.10
important 672.16
influential 172.13
momentum 283.1
monad element 376.2
one 89.3
particle 196.8

person 3.3
monarch 749.7
monarchic(al)
governmental 741.17
sovereign 739.17
monarchism
political conservatism
745.1
principle of govern-
ment 741.8
monarchist 745.9
monarchy
absolutism 741.9
government 741.4
monasterial
claustral 1042.16
monastic 1037.14
monastery 1042.6
monastic
n. celibate 934.2
religious 1038.17
adj. celibate 934.6
claustral 1042.16
monkish 1037.14
monasticism
asceticism 991.1
celibacy 934.1
monkhood 1037.4
monaural system 450.11
monde 644.6
monetary 835.30
money funds 835.14
legal tender 835
wealth 837.1
moneybags
rich man 837.6
wealth 837.1
money changer
banker 836.10
broker 830.9
moneyed 837.13
money-hungry 634.27
moneylender
banker 836.10
lender 820.3
money-mad 634.27
moneymaking
n. acquisition 811.1
adj. businesslike
656.15
gainful 811.15
paying 841.21
moneyman 836.8
money market 835.16
money order 835.11
money-raising 821.1
money-saving 851.6
money's worth
bargain 849.3
worth 846.3
monger 830.2
mongolism
genetic disease
686.11
mental deficiency
469.9
mongoloid 469.22
mongoloid idiot 471.8
mongrel
n. bad person 986.7
cur 414.24
hybrid 44.9

sad person 872.13
v. be ill-humored 951.14
grieve 872.17
mopery 708.4
mopey glum 872.25
sullen 951.24
unsociable 923.5
moping glum 872.25
sullen 951.24
mop up
complete 722.6
wash 681.19
moral
n. lesson 562.7
maxim 517.1
precept 751.2
warning 703.1
adj. dutiful 962.13
ethical 957.6
honest 974.13
virtuous 980.7
moral climate
ethics 957.1
pervading attitudes 525.5
moral code 957.1
morale esprit 786.1
mood 525.4
morality 957.3
virtue 980.1
moral fiber 624.4
moralistic
advisory 754.8
ethical 957.6
morality lesson 562.7
morals 957.3
stage show 611.4
virtue 980.1
moralize judge 494.14
lecture 562.17
morals ethics 957.1
morality 957.3
moral support 216.1
moral turpitude
depravity 981.5
dishonesty 975.2
morass confusion 62.2
marsh 400.1
predicament 731.4
moratorium
debts 842.2
delay 132.2
morbid curious 528.5
diseased 686.56
gruesome 891.38
unwholesome 686.51
morbidity disease 686.1
unhealthiness 686.2
morbific 684.5
morceau
small amount 35.3
treatise 606.1
mordancy
acrimony 161.4
eloquence 600.3
pungency 433.1
unkindness 939.8
mordant
n. caustic 329.15
adj. acrimonious 161.13

eloquent 600.11
pungent 433.6
unkind 939.21
witty 881.15
more
n. plurality 100.1
adj. additional 40.10
plural 100.7
adv. additionally 40.11
increasingly 38.9
more or less
approximately 200.23
some 28.6
moreover 40.11
mores
conventions 645.2
culture 642.3
custom 642.1
etiquette 646.3
pervading attitudes 525.5
more than enough
n. overabundance 663.2
plenty 661.2
satiety 664.1
adv. superabundantly 663.24
morgue 410.9
moribund dying 408.33
languid 708.19
unhealthy 686.50
Mormon
n. polygamist 933.12
religionist 1020.21,35
adj. scriptural 1021.13
morn 133.1
morning
n. morn 133
adj. matin 133.6
moron 471.8
moronic foolish 470.8
mentally deficient 469.22
morose glum 872.25
sullen 951.24
unsociable 923.5
morpheme form 246.6
morphology 582.3
unit of meaning 545.6
Morpheus 712.11
morphine
narcotic 687.12,54
sleep-inducer 712.10
morphological
etymological 582.22
grammatical 246.11
linguistic 580.17
structural 245.9
morphologist 245.7
morphology form 246.6
grammar 586.1
linguistics 580.12
morphemics 582.3
structure 245.7
morsel bite 307.2
delicacy 308.8
piece 55.3
small amount 35.3

mortal
n. person 417.3
adj. fatal 409.23
human 417.10
perishable 408.34
transient 111.7
mortal blow 409.10
mortality
deadliness 409.9
death rate 408.13
humanness 417.5
mankind 417.1
transience 111.1
mortar
n. building material 378.2
converter 145.10
v. fire upon 798.22
plaster 228.25
mortar and pestle 361.7
mortgage
n. mortgage deed 772.4
v. pledge 772.10
mortgage company 820.4
mortgaged 840.8
mortgagee
creditor 839.4
lender 820.3
policy-holder 772.7
mortgaging 821.1
mortgagor debtor 840.4
guarantor 772.6
mortician 410.8
mortification
asceticism 991.1
chagrin 866.4
gangrene 686.37
humiliation 864.6
humility 906.2
penance 1012.3
rotting 692.7
mortified
decayed 692.41
diseased 686.56
distressed 866.22
humiliated 906.13
mortify decay 692.25
embarrass 866.15
humble 906.4
humiliate 864.13
mortifying
humbling 906.14
humiliating 864.21
mortise
n. joint 47.4
v. fasten 47.8
interact 13.8
mortuary
n. morgue 410.9
adj. deathly 408.29
funereal 410.22
mosaic
n. check 374.4
chimera 44.8
picture 574.12
adj. checked 374.14
Mosaic 1021.10
Moses 1022.1
mosey depart 301.6
go slow 270.6

Moslem
n. Muslim 1020.22
adj. Muslim 1020.30
Moslemism 1020.12
mosque 1042.2
mosquito 414.41
moss botany 412.4
marsh 400.1
plant 411.4,48
mossback
antiquated person 123.8
conservative 140.4
mossbacked 126.18
mossy 411.39
most
n. majority 100.2
major part 54.6
maximum 36.3
adj. extreme 34.13
majority 100.9
superlative 36.13
adv. extremely 34.22
most, the
n. superior 36.4
adv. superlatively 36.16
most likely 511.8
mostly chiefly 36.17
generally 79.17
normally 84.9
on the whole 54.14
mot maxim 517.1
witticism 881.7
mote impurity 78.2
lightness 353.2
minute thing 196.7
small amount 35.2
stronghold 799.6
motel 191.17
moth-eaten
aged 126.18
spoiled 692.43
stale 123.14
trite 883.9
mother
n. bad person 986.6
genetrix 170.10
originator 153.4
producer 167.8
relative 11.3
v. care for 699.19
engender 68.14
foster 785.16
reproduce 169.8
adj. maternal 170.13
mother earth 375.10
mother figure 690.38
motherhood
blood relationship 11.1
maternity 170.3
mothering 785.3
mother-in-law 12.2
motherland 181.2
motherless
bereaved 408.35
forlorn 924.11
helpless 158.18
mother lode 837.3
motherly 170.13
Mother Nature 1013.9

expedient 670.2
motion 267.1
stratagem 735.3
v. act 705.4
advise 754.6
affect 855.16
behave 737.4
budge 267.5
change residence 184.16
excite 857.11
excite pity 944.5
impel 283.10
influence 172.7
motivate 648.12
progress 294.2
propose 773.5
push 285.10
remove 271.10
sell 829.8
set in motion 267.6
travel 273.17
move away
depart 301.6
recede 297.2
move back 295.6
moved affected 855.25
excited 857.18
motivated 648.30
move in 172.12
move into 715.3
movement
activity 707.1
art 574.23
artistic style 574.9
cause 153.10
defecation 311.2
displacement 271.2
feces 311.4
gesture 568.14
group 74.3
mechanism 348.5
meter 609.9
military operation 797.8
motion 267.1
music division 462.24
political front 744.33
rhythm 463.22
story element 608.9
travel 273.1
trend 174.2
movements
action 705.1
behavior 737.1
mechanism 348.5
move out 301.6
mover doer 718.1
motivator 648.10
originator 153.4
producer 167.8
wanderer 274.2
movie
n. motion picture 611.16
adj. theatrical 611.38
moviegoer 611.32
movie house 611.19
movie star 612.4
movies, the 611.17
moving
n. displacement 271.2

motion 267.1
motivation 648.2
travel 273.1
adj. affecting 855.24
eloquent 600.14
exciting 857.28
impelling 283.20
mobile 267.7
motivating 648.25
pitiful 944.8
progressive 294.6
saddening 864.20
traveling 273.35
moving picture 611.16
moving spirit
inspiration 648.9
motivator 648.10
moving staircase 317.4
mow
n. garner 660.7
grimace 249.4
pile 74.10
scowl 951.9
v. grimace 249.8
harvest 413.19
shorten 203.6
smooth 260.5
mow down fell 318.5
raze 693.19
mowed 203.9
moxie liveliness 707.2
pluck 624.3
power 157.1
MP legislator 746.3
peace officer 699.15
police force 699.17
Mr. 420.7
Mrs. 421.8
Mrs. Grundy
conformist 82.2
conventionalist 645.3
social convention 645.1
Ms. 421.8
MS
nervous disorder 686.23
written matter 602.10
much
n. abundance 34.3
sufficiency 661.2
adj. many 34.8
plentiful 661.7
adv. greatly 34.15
much ado about nothing
overreaction 617.2
triviality 673.3
mucilage
adherent 50.4,13
lubricant 380.2
semiliquid 389.5
mucilaginous 389.12
muck
n. fertilizer 165.4
filth 682.7
mud 389.8
slime 682.8
v. dirty 682.15
muck around 673.13
mucked up
confused 62.16

mixed up 46.4
spoiled 692.31
muckrake 971.10
muckraker critic 494.7
disparager 971.6
muckraking
defamation 971.2
smear campaign 744.14
muck up
blunder 518.15
complicate 46.3
confuse 63.3
dirty 682.15
spoil 692.13
muck-up 518.6
mucky filthy 682.23
muddy 389.14
mucous 389.13
mucous membrane 229.3
mucus body fluid 388.3
filth 682.7
lubricant 380.2
secretion 312.2
semiliquid 389.5
mud dirt 682.6
marsh 400.1
slush 389.8
muddle
n. confusion 532.3
disorder 62.2
fiasco 725.6
v. be undiscriminating 493.3
bungle 734.11
complicate 46.3
disorder 62.9
fluster 532.7
make uncertain 514.14
obscure 247.3
perplex 514.13
scramble 63.3
muddled
befuddled 532.13
disordered 62.16
intoxicated 996.30
perplexed 514.24
stupid 469.18
muddlehead 471.4
muddleheaded
befuddled 532.13
stupid 469.18
muddle through
manage 724.11
move forward 294.4
muddy
v. dirty 682.15
make uncertain 514.14
adj. colorless 363.7
dingy 365.11
dirty 682.22
marshy 400.3
mucky 389.14
obscure 549.15
mud flat 400.1
mudhole
mud puddle 389.9
pit 257.3
mudlark 274.3

mudpack 900.11
mud puddle 389.9
mudslinger 971.6
mudslinging
defamation 971.2
smear campaign 744.14
muff
n. bungle 734.5
bungler 734.9
v. bungle 734.11
muffed 734.21
muffin 308.31
muffle
n. nose 256.7
silencer 451.4
v. cover 228.19
hush up 614.8
mute 451.9
silence 451.8
muffled
covered 228.31
latent 546.5
muted 452.17
muffled tone 452.2
muffler
auto part 272.25
neckwear 231.64
silencer 451.4
muffle up 231.38
mufti
clergyman 1038.13
clothing 231.8
judge 1002.3
mug
n. cup 193.10
dupe 620.1
evildoer 943.4
face 240.4
laughingstock 967.7
mouth 265.5
photograph 577.3
v. attack 798.15
grimace 249.8
overact 611.36
photograph 577.14
rob 824.14
terrorize 162.10
mugger
assailant 798.13
evildoer 943.4
robber 825.5
student 566.10
violent person 162.9
mugginess
dampness 392.2
sultriness 328.6
mugging attack 798.1
theft 824.3
muggy moist 392.15
sultry 328.28
mug shot 577.3
mugwump
apostate 628.5
independent 762.12
irresolute person 627.5
neutral 806.4
nonpartisan 744.28
procrastination 132.5
mugwumpery
irresolution 627.1

neutrality 806.1
nonpartisanism
744.26
Muhammad 1022.4
Muhammadan
n. Muslim 1020.22
adj. Muslim 1020.30
Muhammadanism
1020.12
mulatto
crossbreed 44.9
mixed race 418.4
mulch 413.17
mulct
n. penalty 1009.3
v. cheat 618.17
penalize 1009.5
mule
beast of burden
271.6
hybrid 44.9
obstinate person
626.6
spinner 206.5
sumpter mule 414.21
mulish obstinate 626.8
ungulate 414.49
mull heat 329.17
sweeten 431.3
mullion 217.4
mull over 478.13
multicolor 374.1
multicolored 374.9
multifaceted 44.15
multifarious
complex 46.4
different 16.7
multiform 19.3
numerous 101.6
multifold
multiform 19.3
multiple 100.8
numerous 101.6
multiform 19.3
multiformity 19
multilateral
angular 251.11
sided 242.7
multilingual 580.14
multimillionaire 837.6
multinational 44.15
multiparous 169.15
multipartite 49.20
multiphase 19.3
multiple
n. multiplication
100.4
adj. multiform 19.3
numerous 101.6
plural 100.8
multiple sclerosis
686.23
multiplication
increase 38.1
mathematics 87.4
multiplying 100.4
procreation 169.2
proliferation 165.2
multiplication table
100.4
multiplicity
multiformity 19.1

numerousness 101.1
multiplied
increased 38.7
plural 100.8
multiplier 100.4
multiply
be numerous 101.5
be productive 165.7
calculate 87.11
increase 38.6
procreate 169.8
proliferate 100.6
multiplying
n. multiplication
100.4
adj. increasing 38.8
multiracial 44.15
multitude
abundance 34.3
large number 101.3
populace 919.3
throng 74.4
multitudinous
much 34.8
numerous 101.6
mum mute 451.12
taciturn 613.9
mumble
n. murmur 452.4
muttering 595.4
v. chew 307.25
murmur 452.10
speak poorly 595.9
utter 594.26
mumbling
n. imperfect speech
595.4
murmur 452.4
adj. murmuring
452.18
mumbo jumbo
charm 1036.5
evil spirit 1016.10
jargon 580.9
juggling 618.5
nonsense 547.2
obscurity 549.3
occultism 1034.1
spell 1036.4
mummer actor 612.2
entertainer 612.1
masquerader 619.7
mummery acting 611.9
ceremony 646.4
disguise 618.10
hypocrisy 616.6
sanctimony 1029.1
mummification
corpse 408.16
drying 393.3
embalmment 410.3
preserving 701.2
mummified 393.9
mummify dry 393.6
prepare for burial
410.21
preserve 701.8
mummy corpse 408.16
dryness 393.2
mother 170.10
mumps
ill humor 951.10

infectious disease
686.12
sadness 872.6
munch
n. bite 307.2
v. chew 307.25
munching 307.1
mundane prosaic 610.5
unimaginative 536.5
unsacred 1027.3
worldly 1031.16
municipal 183.10
municipal building
183.5
municipality city 183.1
jurisdiction 1000.4
munificence 853.1
munificent 853.4
munition 659.8
munitions arms 801.1
equipment 659.4
store 660.1
mural
n. picture 574.12
adj. partitioned
237.11
murder
n. homicide 409.2
v. bungle 734.11
commit murder
409.16
murdered 734.21
murderer 409.11
murderous cruel 939.24
savage 162.20
slaughterous 409.24
murk
n. darkishness 337.4
obscurity 549.3
v. blacken 365.7
darken 337.9
murky darkish 337.15
dingy 365.11
discolored 679.10
obscure 549.15
murmur
n. lament 875.3
undertone 452.4
v. complain 875.13
mutter 452.10
speak imperfectly
595.9
utter 594.26
wind sound 403.23
murmured 452.16
murmurer 869.3
murmuring
n. complaint 875.4
imperfect speech
595.4
undertone 452.4
adj. discontented
869.5
whispering 452.18
muscle
n. exertion 716.1
strength 159.2
voluntary 159.22
v. exert strength
159.10
muscle-bound
rigid 757.7

strong 159.14
muscle in 238.5
muscle man
evildoer 943.4
strong man 159.6
muscular 159.14
muscular dystrophy
686.11
muscularity 159.2
musculature 159.2
muse
n. abstractedness
532.2
inspiration 535.2
v. consider 478.12
daydream 532.9
remark 594.25
Muse genius 467.8
music patrons 464.22
names of 535.2
poetic source 609.12
museum
collection 74.11
gallery 660.9
preserve 701.6
museum piece
odd thing 85.5
work of art 574.11
mush cereal 308.34
face 240.4
mouth 265.5
pulp 390.2
sentimentality 855.8
walk 273.12
mushiness
pulpiness 390.1
sentimentality 855.8
mushroom
n. botany 412.3
fungus 411.4,45
v. balloon 255.7
grow 197.7
adj. upstart 919.13
mushroom cloud
atomics 326.16
cloud 404.1
mushy pulpy 390.6
sentimental 855.22
weak 160.17
music harmonics 463.1
melody 462
patrons 464.22
score 462.28
musical
n. comedy 611.6
music drama 462.35
adj. musically inclined
462.48
tuneful 462.49
musical comedy
comedy 611.6
music drama 462.35
musicale 462.33
musical instrument 465
musicality
harmonics 463.1
melody 462.2
musical talent 462.32
music box 465.17
music director 464.17
music festival 462.33
music hall hall 192.4

national anthem
  rallying device 797.16
  song 462.13
national assembly 742.1
national debt 840.1
national emergency
  797.14
National Guard 800.23
nationalism
  foreign policy 744.5
  nationhood 181.6
  patriotism 941.2
nationalist 941.3
nationalistic 941.4
nationality
  country 181.1
  nationhood 181.6
  nativeness 189.1
  patriotism 941.2
  people 417.2
  race 418.1
nationalization
  appropriation 822.5
  communization
  815.3
  naturalization 189.3
  socialism 745.6
nationalize
  appropriate 822.20
  communize 815.7
  politicize 745.16
national park 701.6
native
  n. inhabitant 190.3
  adj. indigenous 189.5
  innate 5.7
  natural 736.6
  plain 902.7
  undeveloped 721.13
native environment
  191.5
native land 181.2
native language 580.3
nativeness 189
native tongue 580.3
nativity
  astrology 375.20
  birth 167.7
  nativeness 189.1
  origin 68.4
NATO
  international organi-
  zation 743.5
  treaty 771.2
natter
  n. chatter 596.3
  v. chatter 596.5
nattily 644.18
natty 644.13
natural
  n. hairdo 230.15
  harmonics 463.14
  odd person 85.4
  simpleton 471.8
  sure success 724.2
  talented person
  733.12
  throw of dice 515.10
  adj. artless 736.6
  authentic 516.14
  informal 647.3
  innate 5.7

  instinctive 481.6
  in the raw 721.13
  lifelike 20.16
  normal 84.7
  plain 902.7
  plainspoken 591.3
  simple 589.6
  typical 572.11
natural gas 331.1
naturalism
  authenticity 516.5
  materialism 376.5
  naturalness 736.2
  normality 84.1
naturalist
  biologist 406.18
  materialist 376.6
naturalistic
  authentic 516.14
  descriptive 608.15
  materialist 376.11
  normal 84.7
  philosophy 500.9
  typical 572.11
naturalization
  conversion 145.1
  habituation 642.8
  naturalized citizen-
  ship 189.3
naturalize
  accustom 642.11
  convert 145.11
  grant citizenship
  189.4
naturalized
  accustomed 642.17
  adopted 189.6
  converted 145.19
naturalized citizen
  190.4
natural law 84.4
naturally
  adv. artlessly 736.7
  consequently 154.9
  genuinely 516.18
  informally 647.4
  in plain words 591.4
  intrinsically 5.9
  normally 84.9
  unaffectedly 902.11
  interj. yes 521.18
naturalness
  artlessness 736.2
  authenticity 516.5
  informality 647.1
  literary elegance
  589.1
  normality 84.1
  original condition
  721.3
  plainness 902.2
  plain speech 591.1
natural right
  liberty 762.2
  privilege 958.3
natural science
  physics 325.1
  science 475.10
natural selection 148.3
natural state 721.3
natural world 376.2
nature artlessness 736.2

  character 5.3
  characteristic 80.4
  kind 61.3
  matter 376.2
  original condition
  721.3
  temperament 525.3
  universe 375.1
Nature 1013.9
naturist 232.3
naturistic naked 232.14
  normal 84.7
naught
  insignificancy 673.6
  nothing 2.2
naughty
  disobedient 767.8
  evil 981.16
  misbehaving 738.5
naughty word 972.4
nausea
  disease symptom
  686.8
  dislike 867.2
  queasiness 686.29
  unpleasure 866.1
  vomiting 310.8
nauseant
  cleaning agent 681.17
  emetic 687.18
  unsavoriness 429.3
nauseate disgust 429.4
  offend 864.11
nauseated
  disgusted 866.20
  sick 686.53
nauseating
  filthy 682.23
  offensive 864.18
  unsavory 429.7
nauseous
  nauseated 686.53
  offended 866.20
  unsavory 429.7
nautical marine 275.57
  oceanic 397.8
naval 275.57
naval academy 567.13
naval cadet 276.4
naval officer
  military officer
  749.20
  officer 276.7
naval vessel 277.6,24
navar aviation 278.6
  radar 346.2
nave axle 322.5
  center 226.2
  church part 1042.9
navel 226.2
navigable 275.59
navigate fly 278.45
  locate 184.10
  pilot 275.14
  sail 275.13
navigation
  aviation 278.6
  direction 290.1
  location 184.7
  water travel 275.1
navigational
  locational 184.18

  nautical 275.57
navigator
  aviation 279.4
  deckhand 276.6
  mariner 276.1
  pilot 748.7
  ship's officer 276.7
navvy excavator 257.10
  working person 718.2
navy
  chewing tobacco
  434.7
  fleet 277.10
  naval forces 800.26
navy man sailor 276.4
  serviceman 800.6
nay
  n. negation 524.1
  refusal 776.1
  side of controversy
  482.14
  vote 637.6
  interj. no 524.8
naysayer misfit 27.4
  oppositionist 791.3
naysaying 524.1
Nazarene 1020.16
Nazism 741.8
NB 530.22
NCO 749.19
Neanderthal
  n. barbarian 898.7
  adj. uncouth 898.12
neap
  n. low tide 208.2
  tide 395.13
  adj. low 208.7
near
  v. approach 296.3
  be imminent 152.2
  be in the future
  121.6
  come near 200.7
  resemble 20.7
  adj. approaching
  296.4
  approximate 9.8
  close 200.14
  friendly 927.18
  imminent 152.3
  left 244.4
  narrow 205.14
  similar 20.14
  stingy 852.9
  adv. nearby 200.20
  nearly 200.22
  prep. at 184.26
  close to 200.24
nearby
  adj. handy 200.15
  adv. beside 242.10
  near 200.20
Near East 180.6
nearer 200.18
nearest 200.19
nearing
  n. approach 296.1
  adj. approaching
  296.4
  close 200.14
  future 121.8
  imminent 152.3

nearly narrowly 205.22
 near 200.22
 some 28.6
 virtually 54.14
near-miss
 aviation 278.20
 failure 725.4
 meeting 200.4
 narrow escape 632.2
nearness
 approach 296.1
 closeness 200
 friendship 927.5
 narrowness 205.1
 relationship 9.1
 similarity 20.1
 stinginess 852.3
nearsighted
 narrow-minded
 527.10
 poor-sighted 440.11
 undiscerning 469.14
nearsightedness
 myopia 440.3
 narrow-mindedness
 527.1
 unperceptiveness
 469.2
neat chic 644.13
 excellent 674.13
 in plain style 591.3
 polished 589.6
 shapely 248.5
 shipshape 277.20
 simple 45.7
 skillful 733.20
 tidy 59.8
neaten 60.12
neat-fingered 733.21
neath 208.11
neatly skillfully 733.29
 smartly 644.18
neatness
 literary elegance
 589.1
 orderliness 59.3
 smartness 644.3
neb beak 256.7
 point 258.3
nebbish
 a nobody 673.7
 nonentity 4.2
 weakling 160.6
nebula
 heavenly body 375.7
 light 335.15
nebulous
 celestial 375.25
 cloudy 404.7
 general 79.11
 obscure 549.15
necessaries 639.2
necessarily
 consequently 154.9
 inevitably 639.19
 needfully 639.16
necessary
 certain 513.13
 compulsory 756.10
 inevitable 639.15
 obligatory 962.15
 requisite 639.13

 urgent 639.12
necessitate oblige 756.5
 require 639.8
necessity
 certainty 513.1
 compulsion 756.1
 indigence 838.2
 inevitability 639.7
 obligation 639
 predetermination
 640.1
 requirement 639.2
neck
 n. constriction 198.1
 fowl part 308.23
 joint 47.4
 narrow place 205.3
 supporter 216.2
 v. hang 1010.20
 make love 932.13
necking 932.1
necklace collar 253.3
 jewel 901.6
neckwear 231.64
necr(o)–
 antiquity 123.6
 atrophy 686.8
 corpse 408.16
 death 408.1
 disease 686.1
necrologic(al)
 epitaphic 410.22
 historical 608.18
 recorded 570.19
necrology
 biography 608.4
 death notice 408.14
 memorial 570.12
necromancer
 sorcerer 1035.5
 spiritualist 1034.13
necromancy
 sorcery 1035.1
 spiritualism 1034.5
necromantic
 sorcerous 1035.14
 supernatural 85.16
necrophilia 419.12
necrophiliac 419.17
necrosis
 disease symptom
 686.8
 gangrene 686.37
 rotting 692.7
nectar delicacy 308.8
 sweetener 431.2
nectarous sweet 431.4
 tasty 428.8
née 167.21
need
 n. deficiency 57.2
 desire 634.1
 indigence 838.2
 requirement 639.2
 want 662.4
 v. be poor 838.5
 must 639.10
 require 639.9
 want 662.7
needed 639.13
needful 639.13

needing
 desirous 634.21
 incomplete 57.4
 wanting 662.13
needle
 n. compass 748.9
 engraving tool 578.9
 leaf 411.17
 point 258.3
 pointer 568.4
 sound reproduction
 system 450.11
 thorn 258.7
 types of 223.8
 v. annoy 866.13
 banter 882.4
 goad 648.15
 puncture 265.16
 sew 223.4
needled 866.24
needlepoint 223.7
needless
 superfluous 663.17
 useless 669.10
needlessly
 superfluously 663.25
 uselessly 669.15
needlework 223.1,6
needleworker
 garmentmaker 231.33
 sewer 223.2
needling 648.5
need to 639.10
needy 838.8
needy, the 838.3
ne'er-do-well
 n. bad person 986.2
 bum 708.9
 adj. indolent 708.18
nefarious bad 675.9
 base 915.12
 evil 981.16
negate abolish 693.13
 contradict 790.6
 deny 524.3
 disagree 27.5
 disbelieve 503.5
 disprove 506.4
 neutralize 178.7
 refuse 776.3
negation denial 524
 destruction 693.6
 disagreement 27.1
 disproof 506.1
 nonexistence 2.1
 opposition 790.1
 refusal 776.1
negative
 n. copy 24.5
 model 25.6
 negation 524.1
 photography 577.10
 print 578.6
 prohibition 778.2
 refusal 776.1
 side of controversy
 482.14
 subtraction 42.6
 v. abolish 693.13
 deny 524.3
 disprove 506.4
 neutralize 178.7

 refuse 776.3
 veto 778.5
 adj. denying 524.5
 disagreeing 27.6
 electric 342.32
 nonexistent 2.7
 numerical 86.8
 opposing 790.8
 pessimistic 889.16
 refusing 776.6
 interj. no 524.8
negatively 524.6
negativism
 defense mechanism
 690.30
 hindrance 730.1
 negation 524.1
 pessimism 889.6
 resistance 792.1
negativist
 hinderer 730.8
 oppositionist 791.3
 pessimist 889.7
neglect
 n. mismanagement
 734.6
 negligence 534
 nonaccomplishment
 723.1
 nonobservance 769.1
 v. not accomplish
 723.2
 not observe 769.3
 overlook 534.6
 slight 966.6
neglected
 unaccomplished
 723.3
 unattended to 534.14
 unthanked 950.5
neglectful 534.10
negligee 231.20
negligence
 carelessness 534.1
 improvidence 721.2
 inaccuracy 518.2
 inattention 531.1
 mismanagement
 734.6
 nonobservance 769.1
 slovenliness 62.6
 unconcern 636.2
 unstrictness 758.1
negligent
 botched 734.21
 careless 534.10
 improvident 721.15
 inaccurate 518.17
 inattentive 531.6
 nonobservant 769.5
 slovenly 62.15
 unconcerned 636.7
 unstrict 758.4
negligible
 insignificant 35.6
 unimportant 673.15
negotiable
 convertible 835.31
 practical 509.7
 transferable 817.5
 workable 164.10

negotiable instrument
  credit instrument
    839.3
  negotiable paper
    835.11
negotiables 834.1
negotiate
  bargain 827.17
  contract 771.7
  discuss 597.11
  jump 319.5
  manage 724.11
  mediate 805.6
  transfer property
    817.3
negotiation
  commerce 827.3
  conference 597.6
  transaction 827.4
negotiator
  go-between 781.4
  labor unionist 789.3
  mediator 805.3
Negro 418.3
Negro spiritual 462.16
neigh 460.2
neighbor
  n. friend 928.1
  near 200.6
  v. adjoin 200.9
  be near 200.13
  adj. adjacent 200.16
neighborhood
  district 180.1
  environment 233.1
  nearness 200.1
neighboring
  adjacent 200.16
  surrounding 233.8
neighborliness
  friendship 927.1
  hospitality 925.1
neighborly
  friendly 927.14
  helpful 785.22
  hospitable 925.11
neither 524.7
Nembutal 687.12
nemesis bane 676.1
  justice 976.1
  punishment 1010.1
Nemesis avenger 956.3
  goddess of evil
    1016.6
  goddess of justice
    976.5
  rage 952.10
neo- abnormal 85.9
  beginning 68.15
  imitation 22.8
  new 122.7
neolith 123.6
neolithic 123.20
neologism
  innovation 139.3
  modern 122.4
  word 582.8
neonatal 124.12
neophyte beginner 68.2
  believer 1028.4
  convert 145.7
  student 566.9

neoplasm 686.36
nepenthe 538.1
nephew 11.3
nephology
  cloud study 404.4
  meteorology 402.6
nephritis
  inflammation 686.9
  kidney disease 686.22
nephrosis 686.22
ne plus ultra
  climax 56.5
  perfection 677.3
  summit 211.2
  supremacy 36.3
nepotism
  injustice 977.3
  spoils of office
    744.35
Neptune god 1014.5
  planet 375.9
  sailor 276.1
  sea god 397.4
  water god 1014.20
nerval 422.12
nerve
  n. courage 893.5
  insolence 913.3
  neuron 422.6
  self-assertion 624.6
  stability 142.1
  v. encourage 893.16
  strengthen 159.11
nerve center
  ganglion 226.5
  inner nature 5.4
nerveless
  unmanned 158.19
  unnervous 860.2
  weak 160.12
nerve-racking 859.14
nerves 859.1
nervous
  agitated 324.16
  anxious 890.6
  eloquent 600.11
  excitable 857.26
  fearful 891.31
  high-strung 859.10
  neural 422.12
  sensitive 422.14
nervous breakdown
  mental disorder
    690.17
  nervousness 859.4
  sickness 686.7
nervous disorder
  mental disorder
    690.17
  neuropathy 686.23
nervousness
  agitation 324.1
  anxiety 890.1
  eloquence 600.3
  excitability 857.9
  sensitivity 422.3
  trepidation 891.5
  uneasiness 859
nervous prostration
  exhaustion 717.2
  nervousness 859.4
  sickness 686.7

nervous system 422.6
nervous tension
  anxiety 890.1
  tension 859.3
nervous wreck
  tension 859.5
  wreck 692.10
nervy agitated 324.16
  bold 893.18
  impudent 913.9
  nervous 859.10
  strong 159.13
nescience 477.1
nest
  n. abode 191.1
  animal abode 191.25
  animal young 171.2
  birthplace 153.8
  large number 101.3
  v. inhabit 188.7
  settle 184.16
nest egg funds 835.14
  reserve 660.3
nester 190.9
nesting
  n. habitation 188.1
  adj. avian 414.52
nestle cuddle 932.15
  protect 699.18
  put to bed 712.19
  snuggle 887.10
nestling
  n. beginner 68.2
  bird 414.33
  lovemaking 932.1
  young bird 125.8
  adj. new 122.7
nestor 754.3
Nestor old man 127.2
  wise man 468.2
net
  n. difference 42.8
  gain 811.3
  network 221.3
  porousness 265.9
  price 846.2
  produce 168.2
  radio 344.8
  receipts 844.1
  snare 618.12
  weight 352.1
  v. acquire 811.8
  arrest 761.15
  catch 822.17
  fish 655.10
  hamper 730.11
  profit 811.11
  trap 618.18
  weave 222.6
  web 221.7
  yield 844.4
  adj. remaining 43.7
nether 208.8
nethermost 212.7
nether world
  deities 1019.5
  depths 209.3
  hell 1019.1
net income
  earnings 841.4
  receipts 844.1
netted 221.11

netting arrest 761.6
  network 221.3
nettle
  n. thorn 258.7
  v. annoy 866.13
  incite 648.17
  provoke 952.22
nettled
  annoyed 866.21
  provoked 952.25
network radio 344.8
  webwork 221.3
net worth assets 810.8
  worth 846.3
neur(o)- 422.6
neural 422.12
neuralgia 686.23
neuritis
  inflammation 686.9
  nervous disorder
    686.23
neurological
  medical 688.18
  neural 422.12
neurologist
  neurology 422.7
  physician 688.8
neuron 422.6
neurosis
  mental disorder
    690.17
  nervousness 859.4
  psychoneurosis
    690.19
  psychosis 473.3
neurotic
  n. pathological type
    690.16
  adj. psychoneurotic
    690.45
  psychotic 473.27
neuter
  n. gender 586.10
  neutral 806.4
  adj. do-nothing 706.6
  indifferent 636.6
  neutral 806.7
  unsexual 419.31
neutral
  n. gear 348.6
  independent 762.12
  moderate 163.4
  nonpartisan 744.28
  uncommitted person
    806.4
  adj. colorless 363.7
  do-nothing 706.6
  impartial 976.10
  indefinite 79.11
  independent 762.21
  indifferent 636.6
  nonpartisan 744.45
  uncommitted 806.7
  unprejudiced 526.12
  unsexual 419.31
  weak 160.17
neutral ground 806.3
neutrality
  avoidance 631.1
  impartiality 976.4
  inaction 706.1
  indifference 636.1

prowling 273.9
adj. noctambulant 273.37
nihilism anarchy 740.2
   pessimism 889.6
   radicalism 745.4
   thought disturbance 690.24
nihilist anarchist 740.3
   destroyer 693.8
   pessimist 889.7
   radical 745.12
   savage 943.5
nihilistic
   anarchistic 740.6
   destructive 693.26
   pessimistic 889.16
   radical 745.20
Nike 1014.5
nil 2.2
nimble agile 733.21
   alert 533.14
   fast 269.19
   intelligent 467.14
   quick 707.18
nimble-fingered 733.21
nimble-footed
   agile 733.21
   fast 269.19
nimbleness
   agility 733.2
   alertness 533.5
   intelligence 467.2
   quickness 707.3
nimble-witted
   intelligent 467.14
   witty 881.15
nimbly skillfully 733.29
   with alacrity 707.26
nimbus cloud 404.1
   illustriousness 914.6
   light 335.14
Nimrod hunter 655.5
   shooter 285.9
nincompoop 471.3
nine number 99.5
   team 788.7
nine days' wonder
   marvel 920.2
   momentary triumph 724.3
   transient 111.5
ninny 471.3
nip
   n. bite 307.2
   cold 333.1
   dose 55.5
   drink 307.4
   hold 813.2
   liquor 996.6
   pain 424.2
   pinch 198.2
   pungency 433.2
   small amount 35.3
   v. be pungent 433.5
   chill 333.10
   converge 298.2
   cut off 42.10
   freeze 334.11
   hasten off 301.11
   hold 813.6
   hurt 424.7

pinch 198.8
   put an end to 693.12
   seize 822.14
   shorten 203.6
   speed 269.8
   steal 824.13
   tipple 996.23
nip and tuck 30.7
nip in the bud
   kill 409.13
   prevent 730.13
   put an end to 693.12
nipped
   constricted 198.12
   shortened 203.9
nipper child 125.3
   grasping organ 813.4
nipple teat 256.6
   tube 396.6
nippled 256.18
nippy cold 333.14
   pungent 433.7
nirvana
   forgetfulness 538.1
   heaven 1018.9
   quiescence 268.1
   thoughtfreeness 480.1
   unconsciousness 423.2
   undesirousness 636.3
nirvanic
   desireless 636.8
   thoughtfree 480.4
   unconscious 423.8
nit animal 414.40
   disapproval 969.4
nitpick
   find fault 969.15
   quibble 483.9
nitpicker
   fastidious person 896.6
   faultfinder 969.9
   quibbler 483.7
nit-picking
   disapproval 969.4
   quibbling 483.5
nitrate
   n. fertilizer 165.4
   v. react chemically 379.6
nitration 379.5
nitrogen
   fertilizer 165.4
   gas 401.11
nitroglycerin 801.9
nitty-gritty, the fact 1.3
   fundamental 5.2
nitwit 471.3
nitwitted 469.17
nix
   n. negation 524.1
   nothing 2.2
   refusal 776.1
   water god 1014.20
   interj. no 524.10
no
   n. negation 524.1
   refusal 776.1
   side of controversy 482.14

vote 637.6
   adv. not at all 2.11
   interj. nay 524.8
   refusal 776.7
no-account
   uninfluential 173.3
   worthless 669.11
nobby chic 644.13
   excellent 674.13
nobility
   aristocracy 918.2
   eloquence 600.6
   eminence 34.2
   grandeur 904.5
   high birth 918
   honesty 974.1
   importance 914.5
   magnanimity 979.2
   mastership 739.7
   pride 905.2
   superiors 36.5
noble
   n. nobleman 918.4
   adj. aristocratic 918.10
   dignified 905.12
   eloquent 600.14
   eminent 34.9
   excellent 674.12
   grandiose 904.21
   honest 974.13
   magnanimous 979.6
   notable 672.18
   reputable 914.15
   unchangeable 142.17
nobleman 918.4
noble-minded 979.6
noblesse oblige 936.2
noblewoman 918.6
nobly
   dignifiedly 905.14
   grandiosely 904.28
   honestly 974.21
   magnanimously 979.8
   magnificently 34.20
   reputably 914.20
nobody nonentity 4.2
   no one 187.6
   unimportant person 673.7
nobody's fool
   intelligent 467.14
   ungullible 504.5
no chance
   chance 156.10
   gambling odds 515.6
   impossibility 510.1
no choice choice 637.3
   choicelessness 639.6
noct(o)- 134.4
noctambulation 273.11
nocturnal 134.9
nocturne 462.5
nod
   n. affirmative expression 521.2
   approval 968.1
   bow 318.3
   greeting 925.4
   hint 557.4
   obeisance 964.2
   ratification 521.4

signal 568.15
   stupor 712.6
   summons 752.5
   v. assent 521.8
   bow 964.6
   consent 775.2
   go to sleep 712.16
   greet 925.10
   hang 215.6
   neglect 534.6
   signal 568.22
nodding
   abstracted 532.11
   drooping 215.10
   inattentive 531.8
   sleepy 712.21
noddle brain 466.6
   head 211.6
node dilemma 731.6
   protuberance 256.5
   solid 354.6
   wave 323.4
no-deposit 666.5
no doubt
   certainly 513.25
   probably 511.8
nodular rough 261.8
   studded 256.16
nodule 256.5
nodus 731.6
noël 462.13
no end greatly 34.15
   indeed 36.17
   innumerably 101.12
   plentifully 661.9
no end to
   infinite 104.3
   innumerable 101.10
   long 202.8
noetic cognitive 478.21
   intelligent 467.12
   mental 466.8
noggin brain 466.6
   head 211.6
no go
   n. failure 725.1
   adj. hopeless 889.14
   useless 669.9
no-good
   n. bad person 986.2
   adj. worthless 669.11
nohow
   adv. anyhow 657.12
   noway 35.11
   interj. by no means 524.9
no ifs, ands, or buts
   certainly 513.23
   really 1.16
   unconditionally 508.3
noise
   n. computer 349.19
   dissonance 461.2
   information theory 557.7
   loud noise 453.3
   meaninglessness 547.1
   pandemonium 62.5
   radio reception 344.21

sound 450.1
television reception
345.5
unintelligibility 549.7
v. be noisy 453.8
sound 450.14
noise about 559.10
noiseless 451.10
noisemaker 453.5
noiseproof 159.18
noisily 453.13
noisome bad 675.9
harmful 675.12
malodorous 437.5
offensive 864.18
unhealthful 684.5
unsavory 429.7
noisy blustering 911.4
loud 453.12
vociferous 459.10
no laughing matter
672.3
nomad
n. Bedouin 274.4
adj. wandering 273.36
nomadism 273.3
no-man's-land 802.2
no matter 673.22
no matter what
by no means 524.9
whatever 79.6
nom de plume 583.8
nomen name 583.3
Roman name 583.6
nomenclature 583
nominal
n. noun 586.5
adj. cheap 849.7
grammatical 586.17
in name only 583.15
nominal charge 849.2
nominalism 80.1
nominally
cheaply 849.10
falsely 616.35
namely 80.18
nominate
appoint 780.10
choose 637.19
name 583.11
support politically
744.41
nominated 637.26
nomination
appointment 780.2
choice 637.8
consecration 1037.10
political nomination
744.11
nominative
n. case 586.9
adj. naming 583.16
nominal 583.15
nominee 780.8
no more dead 408.30
extinct 2.10
past 119.7
vanished 447.4
non(a)– 99.21
nonacceptance
refusal 776.1
rejection 638.1

nonaccomplishment
failure 725.1
nonachievement 723
nonadherent
incoherent 51.4
nonobservant 769.5
nonadmission 77.1
nonage
immaturity 124.3
nine 99.5
nonagenarian
ninety 99.7
old man 127.2
nonaggression 803.4
nonaggression pact
771.2
nonaggressive
indolent 708.18
unbelligerent 803.10
nonalcoholic 997.4
nonalcoholic beverage
308.48
nonaligned
independent 762.21
neutral 806.7
nonaligned nation
country 181.1
independent 762.12
nonalignment 806.1
nonattendance 187.4
nonattendant 187.10
nonbeliever 1031.11
nonbelieving 503.8
nonbelligerent 803.5
nonbreakable 359.5
nonce, the 120.1
nonce word 582.8
nonchalance
apathy 856.4
inexcitability 858.5
unconcern 636.2
nonchalant
apathetic 856.13
unconcerned 636.7
unexcited 858.15
nonchalantly
calmly 858.18
unconcernedly
636.10
noncoherent 51.4
noncohesion 51
noncohesive
incoherent 51.4
separate 49.20
noncom 749.19
noncombatant
n. nonbelligerent
803.5
adj. unbelligerent
803.10
noncommissioned
officer
enlisted man 800.8
sergeant 749.19
supervisor 748.2
noncommittal 895.8
noncommitted 806.7
noncommunicable
indescribable 920.13
unimpartable 813.10
noncompetitive 786.5
noncompletion 723.1

noncompliance
disobedience 767.1
nonconformity 83.1
nonobservance 769.1
refusal 776.1
noncompliant 769.5
non compos mentis
473.25
nonconducting 342.33
nonconductor 342.13
nonconforming
disobedient 767.8
dissenting 522.6
nonobservant 769.5
uncompliant 83.5
nonconformist
n. dissenter 522.3
eccentric 474.3
heretic 1025.5
misfit 27.4
odd person 85.4
original 83.3
rebel 767.5
adj. individualistic
27.9
nonuniform 18.3
opposing 178.8
nonconformity
deviation 219.1
difference 16.1
disobedience 767.1
dissent 522.1
eccentricity 474.1
extraneousness 78.1
inconsistency 27.2
individuality 80.1
noncompliance 83
nonobservance 769.1
nonuniformity 18.1
perverseness 178.1
unorthodoxy 1025.1
noncontagious 813.10
noncontiguous 49.20
nonconvergent 218.6
noncooperation
disaccord 795.1
disobedience 767.1
opposition 790.2
resistance 792.1
noncooperative
insubordinate 767.9
opposing 790.8
resistant 792.5
noncreative 166.5
nondenominational
nonsectarian 1020.26
universal 79.14
nondescript
formless 247.4
simple 902.6
nondutiable 846.18
none
n. not a one 2.3
adv. not at all 2.11
nonelastic 356.12
nonemotional 856.9
nonentity
a nobody 673.7
mediocrity 680.5
nonexistence 2.1
thing of naught 4.2
weakling 160.6

none of your business
238.10
nonessential
n. accessory 6.2
adj. accessory 6.4
circumstantial 8.7
irrelevant 10.6
needless 669.10
superfluous 663.17
unimportant 673.15
nonesuch marvel 920.2
odd thing 85.5
the best 674.8
nonetheless
anyhow 657.12
notwithstanding 33.8
nonexistence
absence 187.1
nonsubsistence 2
nonexistent
absent 187.10
imaginary 535.19
nonsubsistent 2.7
vanished 447.4
nonexpectant 540.9
nonfactual 535.21
nonfeasance
mismanagement
734.6
neglect 534.1
nonaccomplishment
723.1
nonobservance 769.1
sin 982.2
nonfertile 166.4
nonfiction 602.10
nonflammability 332.1
nonflammable 332.9
nonfulfillment
insufficiency 662.1
nonaccomplishment
723.1
nonobservance 769.1
nonfunctional 669.14
nonhuman 85.15
nonimitation 23
noninfectious 813.10
nonintellectual 477.14
noninterference
freedom 762.9
neglect 534.1
political policy 744.4
noninterruption 135.2
nonintervention
avoidance 631.1
freedom 762.9
political policy 744.4
nonintoxicating 997.4
noninvolvement
avoidance 631.1
inaction 706.1
neutrality 806.1
non-Jew 1025.6
nonliving 382.5
nonliving matter 382.1
nonmalignant 674.20
nonmandatory 622.7
nonmedical therapist
688.12
nonmedical therapy
689.3
nonmetal 383.3

dive 320.6
fly 278.50
nosegay bundle 74.8
  flowers 411.23
  fragrance 436.1
nose ring jewel 901.6
  ring 253.3
nose-tickling 433.6
nosh
  n. light meal 307.7
  v. eat 307.24
no-show 187.5
nostalgia
  sentimentality 855.8
  wistfulness 634.4
  yearning 634.5
nostalgic
  sentimental 855.22
  wistful 634.23
nostril
  air passage 396.17
  nose 256.7
  olfactory organ 435.5
no strings attached
  508.3
nostrum 687.2
no sweat 732.15
nosy
  meddlesome 238.9
  prying 528.6
  searching 485.37
not 524.8
nota bene 530.22
notability
  celebrity 914.9
  eminence 34.2
  importance 672.2
  personage 672.8
  repute 914.5
not a bit none 2.3
  not at all 35.11
notable
  n. celebrity 914.9
  personage 672.8
  adj. conspicuous
    555.12
  famous 914.16
  important 672.18
  memorable 537.25
  remarkable 34.10
notably
  conspicuously 555.16
  exceptionally 34.20
  famously 914.21
  importantly 672.24
not accept
  be incredulous 504.3
  deny 524.4
  not permit 778.4
not admit deny 524.4
  disbelieve 503.5
not allow 778.4
not all there
  insane 473.25
  mentally deficient
    469.22
notarize 521.12
notarized 521.14
notarized statement
  certificate 570.6
  deposition 523.2
notary endorser 521.7

recorder 571.1
not at all
  by no means! 524.9
  never 106.4
  none 2.11
  noway 35.11
notate 572.6
notation
  account entry 845.5
  comment 552.5
  harmonics 463.12
  mathematics 87.4
  music 462.28
  number 86.1
  record 570.4
  representation 572.1
not bad 674.19
not believe 503.5
not budge
  be obstinate 626.7
  do nothing 706.2
  stand fast 142.11
not buy
  disbelieve 503.5
  refuse 776.3
not care
  be incurious 529.2
  not mind 636.4
not care for
  dislike 867.3
  neglect 534.6
not care to 623.3
not catching 813.10
notch
  n. crack 201.2
  degree 29.1
  indentation 257.6
  mark 568.5
  nick 262
  v. indent 257.14
  mark 568.19
  nick 262.4
notched
  indented 257.17
  nicked 262.5
notching 262.2
not comparable
  dissimilar 21.6
  inferior 37.7
not compare
  be inferior 37.4
  not resemble 21.2
not concern 10.3
not count 673.10
not counting 42.14
not cricket
  not done 83.6
  unfair 977.10
not done
  unconventional 83.6
  undercooked 330.8
  wrong 959.3
note
  n. account entry 845.5
  addition 41.2
  animal sound 460.1
  certificate 570.6
  cognizance 475.2
  comment 552.5
  importance 672.1
  interval 463.20
  letter 604.2

melody 462.4
mood 525.4
musical scale 463.14
negotiable instru-
  ment 835.11
observation 439.2
paper money 835.5
record 570.4
regard 530.1
remark 594.4
repute 914.5
securities 834.1
sign 568.2
tone 463.4
treatise 606.1
undertone 233.3
v. heed 530.6
indicate 568.17
keep accounts 845.8
record 570.16
remark 594.25
not easy
  difficult 731.16
  troublesome 729.13
notebook book 605.1
  record book 570.11
noted 914.16
not enough 662.9
noteworthy
  extraordinary 85.14
  notable 672.18
  particular 80.12
  remarkable 34.10
not guilty 984.6
not have a chance
  be impossible 510.4
  not stand a chance
    156.14
not hesitate
  be willing 622.3
  remain firm 624.10
nothing
  a nobody 673.7
  insignificancy 673.6
  nil 2.2
  thing of naught 4.2
  void 187.3
nothing doing
  by no means 524.10
  disapproval 969.28
  refusal 776.7
nothing like 21.5
nothingness
  nonexistence 2.1
  space 179.1
  unconsciousness
    423.2
  void 187.3
nothing of the kind
  different thing 16.3
  dissimilar 21.5
  no! 524.8
nothing special 680.5
not hold up 518.8
notice
  n. advertisement
    559.6
  announcement 559.2
  attention 530.1
  cognizance 475.2
  commentary 606.2
  criticism 494.2

demand 753.1
information 557.1
legal order 752.6
observation 439.2
press release 559.3
warning 703.1
v. detect 488.5
heed 530.6
see 439.12
noticeable
  appreciable 490.15
  conspicuous 555.12
  manifest 555.8
  remarkable 34.10
  visible 444.6
noticeably
  appreciably 490.16
  conspicuously 555.16
  manifestly 555.14
  positively 34.19
  visibly 444.8
notification
  announcement 559.2
  impartation 554.2
  information 557.1
  legal order 752.6
  warning 703.1
notify herald 544.14
  inform 557.8
  warn 703.5
not in keeping with
  27.10
not in the habit of
  643.4
not in the mood 623.5
notion belief 501.6
  caprice 629.1
  idea 479.1
  impulse 630.1
  vague supposition
    499.5
notional
  capricious 629.5
  fanciful 535.20
  ideational 479.9
  imaginary 535.19
  imaginative 535.18
  theoretical 499.13
notions 831.6
not know 477.11
not kosher
  dishonest 975.16
  unconventional 83.6
not likely
  improbability 512.4
  refusal 776.7
not listen
  be inattentive 531.2
  disobey 767.6
not make sense 549.10
not matter
  be indifferent to
    636.5
  be unimportant
    673.10
not mind
  disobey 767.6
  not care 636.4
notoriety
  conspicuousness
    555.4
  disreputability 915.2

numeric(al)
  arithmetical 86.8
  mathematical 87.17
numerous many 101.6
  much 34.8
  plentiful 661.7
  plural 100.7
numinous
  awesome 920.11
  godlike 1013.20
  illustrious 914.19
  sacred 1026.7
  sorcerous 1035.14
  supernatural 85.15
  unintelligible 549.13
numismatic 835.30
numismatics 835.22
numskull 471.4
nun celibate 934.2
  religious 1038.19
nuncio diplomat 781.6
  messenger 561.1
nunnery 1042.6
nuptial
  matrimonial 933.19
  sexual 419.26
nuptials 933.4
nurse
  n. healer 688.13
  nursemaid 699.8
  v. care for 699.19
  cherish 813.7
  foster 785.16
  nourish 307.17
  train 562.14
  treat 689.30
nursemaid maid 750.8
  nurse 699.8
nursery bedroom 192.7
  birthplace 153.8
  hospital room 192.25
  plantation 413.11
  preschool 567.4
nurseryman 413.6
nursery rhyme 609.6
nursery school 567.4
nursing home
  asylum 700.4
  infirmary 689.27
nurture
  n. food 308.3
  support 785.3
  training 562.3
  v. care for 699.19
  cherish 813.7
  encourage 648.21
  foster 785.16
  make better 691.9
  nourish 307.17
  raise animals 416.6
  train 562.14
nut
  n. eccentric 474.3
  enthusiast 635.5
  fanatic 473.17
  food 308.38,52
  lunatic 473.15
  odd person 85.4
  plant seed 411.29
  specialist 81.3
  v. harvest 413.19
nuthouse 473.14

nutrient
  n. nutriment 309.3
  adj. nutritious 309.19
nutriment food 308.3
  nutrient 309.3
nutrition
  cooking 330.1
  eating 307.1
  nourishment 309
nutritionist 309.13
nutritious
  gastronomical 307.29
  nourishing 309.19
nutritive value 309.1
nuts 473.26
nuts about
  enthusiastic about
    635.12
  fond of 931.28
nutshell
  n. small amount 35.2
  v. abridge 607.5
nutty eccentric 474.4
  flavorful 428.9
  foolish 470.8
  insane 473.26
nuzzle cuddle 932.15
  touch 425.8
nylon fabric 378.11
  fiber 206.8
nymph bug 414.36
  fairy 1014.19
  larva 406.14
  young insect 125.10
nymphet girl 125.6
  nymph 1014.19
  unchaste woman
    989.14
nymphomania
  eroticism 419.5
  lasciviousness 989.5
nymphomaniac
  sex deviant 419.17
  unchaste woman
    989.14

O

O! 920.20
oaf
  awkward person
    734.8
  lout 471.5
  unsophisticate 736.3
oafish clumsy 734.20
  stupid 469.15
oak hardness 356.6
  strength 159.7
  tree 411.50
  wood 378.9
oak leaf 569.5
oar boatman 276.5
  paddle 277.15
oarsman 276.5
oath affirmation 523.3
  curse 972.4
  promise 770.1
oatmeal 308.34
oats fodder 308.4
  grain 411.46
obdurate
  callous 981.17

hard 356.10
  heartless 939.23
  impenitent 874.5
  insensible 423.6
  obstinate 626.10
  strict 757.7
obedience
  compliance 766
  conformity 82.1
  resignation 861.2
  submission 765.1
obedient
  compliant 766.3
  conformable 82.5
  dutiful 962.13
  resigned 861.10
  submissive 765.12
obediently
  compliantly 766.6
  conformably 82.7
  submissively 765.17
obeisance bow 318.3
  homage 964.2
  obsequiousness 907.2
  submission 765.1
obeisant
  deferential 765.16
  obsequious 907.13
  respectful 964.10
obelisk
  memorial 570.12
  tower 207.11
Oberon 1014.18
obese 195.18
obesity 195.8
obey accept 861.6
  mind 766.2
  submit 765.6
obfuscate
  confuse 247.3
  darken 337.9
  make unintelligible
    549.12
  misteach 563.3
  obscure 615.6
obituary
  n. biography 608.4
  death notice 408.14
  memorial 570.12
  adj. epitaphic 410.22
  recorded 570.19
object entity 3.3
  meaning 545.2
  objective 653.2
  syntax 586.2
  thing 376.4
object disagree 27.5
  disapprove 969.10
  offer resistance 792.3
  protest 522.5
objectify
  externalize 224.5
  visualize 535.15
objecting
  protesting 522.7
  resistant 792.5
objection
  defense 1006.2
  demur 623.2
  disapproval 969.1
  obstacle 730.4
  protest 522.2

resistance 792.1
objectionable
  offensive 864.18
  unacceptable 869.7
  unpraiseworthy
    969.25
objective
  n. intention 653.2
  lens 443.1
  will 621.1
  adj. extrinsic 6.3
  unfeeling 856.9
  unprejudiced 526.12
objectivity
  extrinsicality 6.1
  unfeeling 856.1
  unprejudicedness
    526.5
object lesson
  example 25.2
  lesson 562.7
  warning 703.1
objector
  dissenter 522.3
  oppositionist 791.3
objet d'art 574.11
oblation gift 818.4
  offering 1032.7
obligate oblige 962.12
  promise 770.5
obligated liable 840.9
  obliged 962.16
  promised 770.8
obligation
  compulsion 756.1
  condition 507.2
  debt 840.1
  duty 962.1
  good deed 938.7
  gratitude 949.1
  liability 175.1
  necessity 639.1
  promise 770.2
  undertaking 715.1
obligatory
  binding 962.15
  compulsory 756.10
  mandatory 752.13
  necessary 639.12
oblige be kind 938.9
  compel 756.5
  favor 785.19
  indulge 759.6
  necessitate 639.8
  obligate 962.12
obliged grateful 949.5
  obligated 962.16
obliging
  considerate 938.16
  courteous 936.14
  indulgent 759.8
oblique
  n. diagonal 219.7
  v. deviate 219.9
  adj. circuitous 321.7
  circumlocutory
    593.14
  slanting 219.13
  transverse 221.9
obliterate debts 842.9
  expunge 693.16
  forget 538.6

O
P

obliteration
- debts 842.2
- erasure 693.7
- forgetfulness 538.1

oblivion
- forgetfulness 538.1
- inconsiderateness 534.2
- insensibility 856.2
- thoughtfreeness 480.1
- unconsciousness 423.2

oblivious
- abstracted 532.11
- asleep 712.22
- forgetful 538.9
- inattentive 531.7
- insensible 856.10
- thoughtfree 480.4
- unconscious 423.8
- unmindful 534.11

oblong long 202.10
- quadrangular 251.9

obloquy criticism 969.4
- curse 972.2
- infamy 915.4

obnoxious bad 675.9
- base 915.12
- offensive 864.18

oboe organ stop 465.22
- wood wind 465.9

oboist 464.4

obscene cursing 972.8
- lewd 990.9
- offensive 864.18
- salacious 989.29
- vulgar 898.11

obscenity cursing 972.3
- expletive 972.4
- lasciviousness 989.5
- lewdness 990.4
- offensiveness 864.2
- vulgarity 898.2

obscure
- v. blind 441.7
- blur 247.3
- cloud 404.6
- conceal 615.6
- cover 228.19
- darken 337.9
- equivocate 483.9
- make uncertain 514.14
- make unintelligible 549.12
- misteach 563.3
- opaque 341.2
- adj. concealed 615.11
- dark 337.13
- hard to understand 549.14
- indistinct 247.4
- opaque 341.3
- shadowy 445.6
- unintelligible 549.15
- unrenowned 915.14
- vague 514.18

obscured
- blinded 441.10
- concealed 615.11
- covered 228.31

- dark 337.13
- hard to understand 549.14
- latent 546.5

obscurity
- a nobody 673.7
- darkness 337.1
- formlessness 247.1
- indistinctness 445.2
- opaqueness 341.1
- unintelligibility 549.3
- vagueness 514.4

obsequies 410.4

obsequious
- deferential 765.16
- flattering 970.8
- obeisant 964.10
- servile 907.13

observable
- manifest 555.8
- visible 444.6

observance
- attention 530.1
- celebration 877.1
- ceremony 646.4
- conformity 82.1
- custom 642.1
- execution 771.5
- keeping 768
- obedience 766.1
- observation 439.2
- piety 1028.1
- rite 1040.3
- vigilance 533.4

observant
- attentive 530.15
- dutiful 962.13
- regardful 768.4
- vigilant 533.13

observation
- attention 530.1
- idea 479.1
- keeping 768.1
- opinion 501.6
- remark 594.4
- surveillance 485.9
- viewing 439.2

observatory
- astronomy 375.17
- observation post 439.8

observe
- abide by 771.10
- administer rites 1040.18
- celebrate 877.2
- conform 82.3
- examine 485.23
- formalize 646.5
- heed 530.6
- keep 768.2
- obey 766.2
- remark 594.25
- see 439.12
- watch 439.14

observer aviator 279.3
- examiner 485.16
- spectator 442.1

obsess
- be in one's mind 537.14
- bewitch 1036.9

- cause unpleasantness 864.16
- demonize 1016.17
- engross 530.13
- haunt 1017.6
- possess 473.24

obsessed
- affected 855.25
- bewitched 1036.13
- engrossed 530.17
- haunted 1017.10
- possessed 473.33
- remembering 537.24

obsession
- bewitchment 1036.2
- emotional symptom 690.23
- engrossment 530.3
- fixation 473.13
- spirit control 1017.5

obsessive
- compelling 473.34
- engrossing 530.20
- unforgettable 537.26

obsolesce
- become old 123.9
- fall into disuse 668.9

obsolescence 668.1

obsolete disused 668.10
- out of action 158.17
- passé 123.15
- past 119.7

obstacle
- hindrance 730.4
- obstruction 266.3

obstetric(al) 688.18

obstetrician 688.8

obstinacy
- opposition 790.2
- perseverance 625.1
- refractoriness 767.2
- resistance 792.1
- resolution 624.1
- strength 159.1
- strictness 757.2
- stubbornness 626
- tenacity 50.3
- uninfluenceability 173.2
- unwillingness 623.1

obstinate
- disobedient 767.8
- opposing 790.8
- persevering 625.7
- persistent 50.12
- resolute 624.11
- strict 757.7
- strong 159.13
- stubborn 626.8
- uninfluenceable 173.4

obstreperous
- noisy 453.12
- refractory 767.10
- ungovernable 626.12
- violent 162.18
- vociferous 459.10

obstruct delay 132.8
- fend off 799.10
- hinder 730.12
- slow 270.9
- stop 266.7

obstructed
- clogged 266.11
- delayed 132.16

obstruction clog 266.3
- delay 132.2
- hindrance 730.1
- obstacle 730.4
- slowing 270.4

obstructionist
- hinderer 730.8
- oppositionist 791.3

obstructive
- hindering 730.17
- resistant 792.5

obtain acquire 811.8
- elicit 305.14
- exist 1.8
- fetch 271.15
- induce 153.12
- prevail 79.10
- receive 819.6

obtainable
- accessible 509.8
- attainable 811.13

obtrude eject 310.13
- intrude 238.5
- thrust upon 818.20

obtrusive
- conceited 909.11
- conspicuous 555.12
- gaudy 904.20
- insolent 913.8
- interfering 238.8

obtuse blunt 259.3
- insensitive 423.6
- stupid 469.16
- unfeeling 856.9

obverse
- n. counterpart 20.3
- front 240.1
- opposite 15.2
- opposite side 239.3
- adj. contrary 15.6
- opposite 239.5

obviate 730.14

obviation 730.2

obvious
- clearly visible 444.7
- manifest 555.8

obviously
- manifestly 555.14
- positively 34.19
- really 1.16
- visibly 444.8

ocarina 465.9

occasion
- n. cause 153.1
- circumstance 8.1
- event 151.2
- opportunity 129.2
- requirement 639.2
- v. cause 153.11

occasional
- causal 153.14
- circumstantial 8.7
- happening 151.9
- incidental 129.11
- infrequent 136.3

occasionally
- discontinuously 72.5
- sometimes 136.5

Occident 180.6

occidental 290.15
occipital 241.10
occlude close 266.6
  obstruct 730.12
occlusion closure 266.1
  hindrance 730.1
  stoppage 686.5
occlusive
  hindering 730.17
  phonetic 594.31
occult
  v. conceal 615.6
  cover 228.19
  darken 337.9
  adj. abtruse 549.16
  concealed 615.11
  latent 546.5
  mystical 1034.22
  otherworldly 377.7
  secret 614.11
  supernatural 85.15
occult, the
  immateriality 377.1
  mysticism 1034
  secrets 614.5
  supernaturalism 85.7
occultation
  concealment 615.1
  covering 228.1
  disappearance 447.1
  eclipse 337.8
occultism
  immateriality 377.1
  mysticism 1034
occultist 1034.11
occupancy
  habitation 188.1
  possession 808.1
occupant
  inhabitant 190.2
  tenant 809.4
occupation
  action 705.1
  business 656.1
  conquest 822.4
  habitation 188.1
  operation 164.1
  possession 808.1
  vocation 656.6
occupational 656.16
occupational disease
  686.1,31
occupational therapy
  psychotherapy 690.5
  therapy 689.2
occupied
  absorbed in thought
    478.22
  busy 707.21
  engrossed 530.17
  inhabited 188.12
occupy
  appropriate 822.19
  busy 656.10
  engross 530.13
  include 76.3
  inhabit 188.7
  pervade 186.7
  possess 808.4
  preoccupy 478.20
occur be present 186.6
  exist 1.8

happen 151.5
occur to 478.18
occurrence
  appearance 446.1
  circumstance 8.1
  event 151.2
  existence 1.1
  presence 186.1
ocean much 34.3
  sea 397
ocean depths
  ocean 397.1
  the deep 209.4
oceanic marine 397.8
  nautical 275.57
ocean liner 277.5
oceanographer
  measurer 490.10
  scientist 397.7
oceanography
  depth measurement
    209.5
  mensuration 490.9
  thalassography 397.6
Oceanus sea god 397.4
  water god 1014.20
ocelot
  animal 414.27,58
  variegation 374.6
ocherous orange 369.2
  yellow 370.4
Ockham's razor 852.1
o'clock 114.16
oct(a)– 99.20
octagonal
  angular 251.10
  eight 99.20
octane 331.1
octave eight 99.4
  harmonics 463.9
  interval 463.20
  organ stop 465.22
  poetic division
    609.11
octet eight 99.4
  electron 343.3
  group 786.1
  part music 462.17
  poetic division
    609.11
octogenarian
  eighty 99.7
  old man 127.2
octopus 414.63; 415.5
octoroon 44.9
octuple 99.20
ocular
  n. lens 443.1
  adj. visual 439.21
oculist healer 688.5
  ophthalmologist
    443.7
  physician 688.8
OD
  n. commissioned offi-
    cer 749.18
  sailor 276.1
  ship's officer 276.7
  v. be killed 409.22
  die 408.24
  take ill 686.44

odalisque
  seductress 989.15
  slave 764.7
odd dissimilar 21.4
  eccentric 474.4
  insane 473.25
  numerical 86.8
  occasional 136.3
  queer 85.11
  remaining 43.7
  sole 89.9
  unequal 31.4
oddball
  n. eccentric 474.3
  intruder 78.2
  misfit 27.4
  odd person 85.4
  adj. eccentric 474.4
  odd 85.11
oddity
  eccentricity 474.1
  odd person 85.4
  odd thing 85.5
  queerness 85.3
odd job 656.2
odds advantage 36.2
  difference 16.1
  disagreement 795.2
  even chance 156.7
  gambling odds 515.6
  inequality 31.1
  probability 511.1
odds and ends
  hodgepodge 44.6
  miscellany 74.13
  refuse 43.1
  sundries 831.6
ode 609.6
Odin
  Norse deity 1014.6
  war god 797.17
odious bad 675.9
  base 915.12
  filthy 682.23
  offensive 864.18
  unlikable 867.7
odium hate 930.1
  infamy 915.4
odor characteristic 80.4
  fragrance 436.1
  smell 435
odorize perfume 436.8
  scent 435.7
odorizer 436.6
odorless 438.5
odorous fragrant 436.9
  malodorous 437.5
  odoriferous 435.9
odyssey 273.2
Oedipus complex
  690.29
œuvre
  compilation 605.4
  product 168.1
of 9.13
of age adult 126.12
  marriageable 933.21
of consequence 672.17
of course
  certainly 513.23
  consequently 154.9
  yes! 521.18

off
  v. kill 409.14
  adj. delirious 473.31
  dissimilar 21.4
  dissonant 461.4
  erroneous 518.16
  idle 708.17
  imperfect 678.4
  inferior 680.10
  insane 473.25
  occasional 136.3
  odd 85.11
  right side 243.4
  tainted 692.42
  adv. at a distance
    199.14
  away 301.21
  oceanward 397.11
  prep. less 42.14
offal filth 682.9
  refuse 669.4
off and on
  alternately 137.11
  changeably 141.8
  irregularly 138.4
  to and fro 323.21
off-balance
  off-center 185.12
  unequal 31.5
off-base
  improper 959.3
  inappropriate 130.7
  misbehaving 738.5
offbeat
  n. music 463.26
  adj. dissimilar 21.4
  nonconformist 83.6
  unusual 85.10
off-center 185.12
off chance
  possibility 509.1
  small chance 156.9
off-color
  colored 362.20
  indecent 990.7
  sick 686.52
  wrong 959.3
off duty idle 708.17
  on one's own time
    711.12
offend affront 965.4
  anger 952.20
  be ugly 899.5
  be unpleasant 864.11
  sin 982.5
offender 986.9
offense attack 798.1
  crime 999.4
  indignity 965.2
  misdeed 982.2
  provocation 952.11
  resentment 952.2
  violation 769.2
offensive
  n. attack 798.1
  adj. attacking 798.30
  bad 675.9
  discourteous 937.6
  insulting 965.6
  malodorous 437.5
  obscene 990.9
  ugly 899.11

unpleasant 864.18
unsavory 429.7
vulgar 898.10
warlike 797.25
offer
n. attempt 714.2
giving 818.1
proposal 773
v. adduce evidence
505.13
attempt 714.5
bid 828.9
give 818.12
proffer 773.4
put to choice 637.21
offered 622.7
offering
donation 818.6
gift 818.4
oblation 1032.7
proposal 773.1
offertory
donation 818.6
hymn 1032.3
sacred music 462.16
sacrifice 1032.7
off-guard
inattentive 531.8
negligent 534.10
offhand
adj. careless 534.11
extemporaneous
630.12
informal 647.3
nonchalant 858.15
adv. carelessly 534.18
extemporaneously
630.15
informally 647.4
office aid 785.1
ceremony 646.4
commission 780.1
function 665.5
good deed 938.7
jurisdiction 1000.4
occupation 656.3
position 656.5
rite 1040.3
room 192.6
tip 557.3
workplace 719.8
worship 1032.8
office boy
attendant 750.5
errand boy 561.4
officeholder
official 749.16
politician 746.11
officer
commissioned officer
749.18
executive 748.3
official 749.16
on ships 276.7
policeman 699.15
official
n. agent 781.3
executive 748.3
officer 749.16
adj. authentic 513.18
authorized 739.15
governing 741.19

governmental 741.17
occupational 656.16
prescriptive 751.4
recorded 570.18
officialdom 749.15
officialese
jargon 580.10
official jargon 744.37
officiate
administer 747.11
do duty 656.13
judge 494.12
minister 1040.19
officious 238.9
offing distance 199.3
the future 121.1
offish aloof 912.12
reticent 613.10
unsociable 923.6
off-key 461.4
off limits limited 234.8
prohibited 778.7
offscourings offal 682.9
rabble 919.5
refuse 43.1
waste 669.4
off season 128.1
offset
n. automation 349.21
collateral descendant
171.4
counterbalance 33.2
neutralizer 178.3
offprint 603.3
opposite 15.2
printing 603.1
v. counteract 33.5
cushion 163.8
neutralize 178.7
oppose 15.4
offsetting
n. compensation 33.1
neutralization 178.2
adj. compensating
33.6
neutralizing 178.9
offshoot adjunct 41.1
affiliate 788.10
branch 55.4
by-product 168.3
collateral descendant
171.4
fork 299.4
party 788.4
plants 411.18
religion 1020.3
result 154.1
offshore 397.11
offspring child 125.3
descendant 171.3
family 11.5
posterity 171.1
product 168.1
result 154.1
sequel 117.2
off the beaten track
85.10
off the cuff 630.12,15
off the record 614.14,20
off the wall
insane 473.26
odd 85.11

off-year 130.2
often frequently 135.6
repeatedly 103.16
ogle
n. flirtation 932.8
gaze 439.5
v. be a spectator
442.5
flirt 932.18
gaze 439.16
scrutinize 439.15
ogre frightener 891.9
monster 85.20; 943.6
oh! 920.20
ohm 342.12,35
oil
n. animal 380.13
fat 380
flattery 970.1
fuel 331.1
healing ointment
687.11
illuminant 335.20
mineral 380.11
picture 574.15
vegetable 380.12
v. facilitate 732.6
flatter 970.6
fuel 331.8
grease 380.8
medicate 689.31
provision 659.9
smooth 260.5
oiling 380.6
oily flattering 970.8
greasy 380.9
hypocritic(al) 616.33
slippery 260.11
suave 936.18
ointment balm 380.3
healing ointment
687.11
money 835.2
unction 1040.6
OK
n. approval 968.1
consent 775.1
permission 777.1
ratification 521.4
v. approve 968.9
consent 775.2
permit 777.9
ratify 521.12
adj. acceptable 868.12
accurate 516.15
excellent 674.13
tolerable 674.19
interj. yes 521.18
old adult 126.12
aged 126.16
age-old 123.10
disused 668.10
experienced 733.26
former 119.10
old country, the
native land 181.2
Old World 180.6
old days 119.2
older
n. old man 127.2
senior 127.5
adj. elder 123.19

prior 116.4
oldest
n. first-born 127.5
adj. eldest 123.19
Old Faithful 328.10
old-fashioned
conservative 140.8
disused 668.10
gallant 936.15
old 123.16
old fogy
conservative 140.4
dotard 471.9
old person 123.8
old-fogy 123.17
old hand 733.15
old hat
old-fashioned 123.16
trite 883.9
old lady
girl friend 931.14
old woman 127.3
wife 933.9
old-line
conservative 140.8
established 142.13
politics 745.17
old maid
fastidious person
896.7
prude 903.11
spinster 934.4
old man
antiquated person
123.8
boy friend 931.12
elder 127.2
father 170.9
grandfather 170.11
husband 933.8
Old Man, the
commander 276.7
commissioned officer
749.18
old master artist 579.1
work of art 574.11
oldness ancientness 123
elderliness 126.5
old pro
professional 718.4
veteran 733.15
old salt sailor 276.3
veteran 733.15
old saw 517.3
old school 140.4
old story
old times 119.2
platitude 517.3
Old Testament 1021.3
old-timer
antiquated person
123.8
old man 127.2
veteran 733.15
old times 119.2
old wives' tale 502.3
old woman
antiquated person
123.8
effeminate male
421.10

fastidious person 896.7
grandmother 170.12
old lady 127.3
wife 933.9
old-world
antiquated 123.13
gallant 936.15
¡ole! 968.22
oleo 308.47
olfactories 435.5
olfactory 435.12
olio hodgepodge 44.6
stew 308.11
olive 371.4
olive branch 804.2
ology 475.10
Olympiad 878.10
Olympian aloof 912.12
detached 856.13
heavenly 1018.13
high 207.19
impartial 976.10
reticent 613.10
unsociable 923.6
Olympic gods 1014.5
Olympics contest 796.3
tournament 878.10
Olympus
heaven 1018.10
mountain 207.7
om! 1032.16
ombudsman
judge 1002.4
mediator 805.3
omega 70.1
omelet 308.26
omen
n. portent 544.3
prediction 543.1
warning sign 703.3
v. portend 544.10
ominous
harmful 675.12
inauspicious 729.14
portentous 544.17
predictive 543.12
threatening 973.3
omission an error 518.4
deficiency 57.2
deletion 42.5
exclusion 77.1
insufficiency 662.4
mismanagement 734.6
neglect 534.1
nonaccomplishment 723.1
nonobservance 769.1
sin 982.2
omit delete 42.12
exclude 77.4
leave undone 534.7
omitting 77.9
omni– multiform 19.3
universal 79.14
unqualified 508.2
omnibus
n. bus 272.12
compilation 605.4
adj. comprehensive 76.7

thorough 56.10
whole 54.9
omnifarious 19.3
omnipotence
almightiness 157.3
divine attribute 1013.15
omnipotent
almighty 157.13
godlike 1013.20
omnipresence
all-presence 186.2
completeness 56.1
divine attribute 1013.15
omnipresent
all-present 186.13
godlike 1013.20
pervasive 56.10
omniscience
divine attribute 1013.15
profound knowledge 475.6
omniscient
godlike 1013.20
knowing 475.15
omnivorous
eating 307.29
gluttonous 994.6
greedy 634.27
on
adj. happening 151.9
adv. after which 117.7
astride 216.25
forward 294.8
prep. against 200.25
at 184.26
atop 211.16
by means of 658.7
covering 228.37
in relation to 9.13
toward 290.28
on account 839.10
on account of
because of 155.9
for 785.26
on and off 141.8
on and on
constantly 135.7
continuously 71.10
increasingly 38.9
on a par 30.7
on approval
at choice 637.27
on trial 489.14
on behalf of for 785.26
instead of 149.12
on board
aboard 275.62
here 184.22
present 186.12
on call handy 665.19
in cash 841.25
on demand 753.11
once
adj. former 119.10
adv. one time 136.6
past 119.14
singly 89.13
whenever 105.12
once in a while 136.5

once upon a time 119.14
oncoming
n. approach 296.1
beginning 68.1
adj. approaching 296.4
progressive 294.6
on condition 507.12
on demand
at demand 753.11
in cash 841.25
on duty 707.21
one
n. only 89.3
person 417.3
adj. combined 52.5
godlike 1013.20
identical 14.7
married 933.22
quantifier 28.5
single 89.7
whole 54.9
one and all
n. everybody 79.4
the entirety 54.3
adj. every 79.15
adv. completely 56.14
unanimously 521.17
one and only one 89.3
sole 89.9
one-armed bandit 515.12
one by one
respectively 80.19
separately 49.28
singly 89.13
on edge
impatient 862.6
in suspense 539.12
nervous 859.10
one-horse little 196.10
petty 673.17
one-horse town 183.3
one mind 521.5
on end
continuously 71.10
vertically 213.13
oneness accord 794.1
agreement 26.1
identity 14.1
individuality 80.1
simplicity 45.1
unity 89.1
whole 54.1
one-night stand 611.12
one-piece 89.11
onerous
hampering 730.18
laborious 716.18
ponderous 352.17
troublesome 731.17
unpleasant 864.24
one's best effort 714.3
regards 936.8
oneself 80.5
one-sided
asymmetric 249.10
prejudiced 527.12
sided 242.7
unipartite 89.11
unjust 977.11

onetime 119.10
one time 136.6
one-track mind 473.13
one-two 283.5
one-upmanship
competition 796.2
cunning 735.1
superiority 36.1
one-way 290.13
ongoing
n. course 267.2
progression 294.1
adj. happening 151.9
improving 691.15
operating 164.11
progressive 294.6
on guard
cautious 895.8
defensively 799.16
vigilant 533.13
on hand handy 665.19
in store 660.16
possessed 808.8
present 186.12
on high aloft 207.26
celestially 1018.14
on ice
made sure 513.20
prearranged 641.5
on loan 820.7
onlooker
neighbor 200.6
spectator 442.1
only
adj. sole 89.9
adv. simply 45.11
solely 89.14
to a degree 35.10
onomatopoeia
echoic word 582.17
imitation 22.1
onomatopoeic
imitative 22.9
lexical 582.20
representational 572.10
on one's knees
adj. deferential 765.16
humble 906.12
obeisant 964.10
obsequious 907.13
supplicatory 774.16
worshipful 1032.15
adv. humbly 906.15
obsequiously 907.15
on one's last legs
aged 126.18
dying 408.33
exhausted 717.8
worn-out 692.38
on one's mind 478.24
on one's own
at will 621.5
independently 762.32
singlehandedly 89.13
on one's toes 533.14
on paper
theoretically 499.16
written 602.22
on purpose 653.11
on record 570.18
onrush course 267.2

password 568.12
spell 1036.4
open shop 789.2
open to
accessible 509.8
vulnerable 175.5
open to question
514.16
open up begin 68.12
confess 556.7
disclose 556.4
facilitate 732.6
let oneself go 762.18
make public 559.11
manifest oneself
555.6
open 265.12
open sesame! 265.24
propose 773.5
unfold 197.6
open warfare 797.1
opera music 462.28
music drama 462.35
product 168.1
stage show 611.4
theater 611.18
operable possible 509.7
practical 670.6
usable 665.22
workable 164.10
opera glasses 443.3
operagoer 464.21
opera house hall 192.4
theater 611.18
operant doer 718.1
operator 164.4
opera singer 464.13
operate act 705.4
function 164.7
pilot 275.14
plot 654.10
run 164.5
speculate in stocks
833.23
use 665.10
operate on
act on 164.6
treat 689.30
operatic
theatrical 611.38
vocal 462.51
operating acting 705.10
functioning 164.11
operating room 192.25
operation action 705.1
functioning 164
military operation
797.8
proceeding 705.3
production 167.1
purpose 665.5
surgical operation
689.22
transaction 827.4
undertaking 715.1
utilization 665.8
operational
acting 705.10
agential 164.12
functioning 164.11
operative 164.9

operative
n. detective 781.10
doer 718.1
operator 164.4
secret agent 781.9
adj. effectual 665.20
operational 164.9
powerful 157.12
operator doer 718.1
handler 164.4
man of action 707.8
political intriguer
746.6
schemer 654.8
stock speculator
833.11
surgeon 688.9
telephone operator
560.9
operetta 462.35
operose difficult 731.16
laborious 716.18
painstaking 533.11
ophthalm(o)– 439.9
ophthalmic
optic(al) 443.8
visual 439.21
ophthalmologist
oculist 443.7
physician 688.8
opiate depressant 423.3
narcotic 687.12
sleep-inducer 712.10
opine believe 501.11
judge 494.8
remark 594.25
suppose 499.10
opinion advice 754.1
belief 501.6
idea 479.1
judgment 494.3
mental attitude 525.1
opinionated
dogmatic 513.22
obstinate 626.8
prejudiced 527.12
opinion poll 485.13
opium
narcotic 687.12,54
sleep-inducer 712.10
opossum
mammal 414.58;
415.8
wild animal 414.28
opponent
n. adversary 791
adj. opposing 790.8
opportune apt 26.10
expedient 670.5
timely 129.9
opportunist 654.8
opportunity
chance 129.2
probability 156.1
turn 108.2
oppose
be against 790.3
compare 491.4
contrapose 239.4
counteract 178.6
deny 524.4
disapprove 969.10

dissent 522.4
go contrary to 15.4
hinder 730.10
offer resistance 792.3
opposed adverse 729.13
against 790.8
contrary 15.6
disapproving 969.22
unwilling 623.5
opposer 791.3
opposing
n. comparison 491.1
contraposition 239.1
opposition 790.1
adj. adverse 729.13
anti 790.8
contrary 15.6
counteractive 178.8
denying 524.5
disapproving 969.22
dissenting 522.6
facing 239.5
fronting 240.11
opposite
n. reverse 220.4
the contrary 15.2
adj. adverse 729.13
contrapositive 239.5
contrary 15.6
opposing 790.8
adv. poles apart 239.6
prep. against 200.25
contrary to 15.10
facing 239.7
opposite number
equal 30.4
opposite 15.2
opposites 239.2
opposition
comparison 491.1
contraposition 239.1
contrariety 15.1
counteraction 178.1
difference 16.1
disagreement 27.1
disapproval 969.1
dissent 522.1
hindrance 730.1
opponents 791.1
opposing 790
resistance 792.1
unwillingness 623.1
oppositional
contrary 15.6
counteractive 178.8
opposing 790.8
opposition party 744.24
oppress burden 352.13
domineer 741.16
go hard with 729.8
make grieve 872.19
make sad 872.18
overwork 716.16
persecute 667.6
trouble 864.16
oppressed
burdened 352.18
downtrodden 764.16
sad 872.20
subjugated 764.14
oppression
affliction 866.8

airlessness 268.6
burden 352.7
despotism 741.10
persecution 667.3
sadness 872.3
oppressive
airless 268.16
depressing 872.30
hampering 730.18
laborious 716.18
ponderous 352.17
sultry 328.28
troublesome 731.17
tyrannical 739.16
unpleasant 864.24
oppressor 749.14
opprobrium
infamy 915.4
vilification 972.2
oppugn
contradict 790.6
counteract 178.6
oppose 15.4
opt 637.13
optic 439.9
optic(al)
ophthalmic 443.8
visual 439.21
optical illusion 519.5
optical instrument
443.11
optician 443.7
optics light 335.22
optical physics 443.6
physics 325.1
optimal 674.18
optimism
cheerfulness 870.1
expectation 539.2
hope 888.3
optimist 888.6
optimistic
cheerful 870.11
expectant 539.11
hopeful 888.12
optimum
n. the best 674.8
adj. best 674.18
option
alternative 637.2
buying right 828.2
free choice 762.6
stock option 833.21
optional
discretionary 622.7
elective 637.22
optometrist
healer 688.5
oculist 443.7
optometry 443.6
opulence plenty 661.2
wealth 837.1
opulent plentiful 661.7
wealthy 837.13
opus book 605.1
music 462.5
product 168.1
written matter 602.10
or
n. heraldic insignia
569.2
yellowness 370.1

adj. yellow 370.4
conj. disjunction 637.29
OR 192.25
oracle maxim 517.1
prophet 543.7
wise man 468.1
oracular
dogmatic 513.22
predictive 543.11
oral
n. examination 485.2
adj. communicational 554.9
legendary 123.12
mouthlike 265.23
speech 594.30
orally 594.34
orange color 369
fruit 308.51
orangery 413.11
orate 599.10
oration 599.2
orator 599.6
oratorical 599.12
oratorio
choral music 462.18
sacred music 462.16
oratory chapel 1042.3
eloquence 600.1
public speaking 599.1
orb eye 439.9
region 180.2
royal insignia 569.3
sphere 255.2
sphere of work 656.4
starry host 375.4
orbit
n. astronomy 375.16
circle 253.2
circling 321.1
circuit 321.2
domain 180.2
route 657.2
spacecraft 282.2
sphere 255.2
sphere of influence 172.4
sphere of work 656.4
v. circle 253.10
go around 321.4
orbital 321.7
orbiting 321.1
orchard farm 413.8
grove 411.12
orchestra
audience 448.6
band 464.12
stage 611.21
theater part 611.20
orchestral 462.52
orchestra leader 464.17
orchestrate 462.47
orchestration
harmonization 463.2
music 462.5
orchestrator 464.20
ordain allot 816.9
appoint 780.10
command 752.9
consecrate 1037.12
destine 640.7

install 304.4
legalize 998.8
legislate 742.18
ordained
destined 640.9
ministerial 1037.17
ordeal sorcery 1035.3
test 489.2
trial 866.9
order
n. arrangement 60.1
award 916.5
biology 61.5
class 61.2
command 752.1
community 788.2
condition 7.3
demand 753.1
fellowship 788.3
harmony 59.1
instructions 562.6
judgment 494.5
literary elegance 589.2
medal 916.6
nomenclature 583.1
normality 84.1
organization 59
peace 803.2
precept 751.1
procedure 657.1
rank 29.2
relationship 11.4
religious 1037.10
school 788.5
sect 1020.3
sequence 65.1
v. arrange 60.8
classify 61.6
command 752.9
demand 753.4
direct 747.8
influence 172.8
organize 59.4
pass judgment 494.13
request 774.9
ordered arranged 60.14
harmonious 589.8
regular 137.6
systematic 59.6
uniform 17.5
ordering
arrangement 60.1
management 747.1
orderless formless 247.4
unorganized 62.12
vague 514.18
orderly
n. attendant 750.5
hospital staff 688.14
adj. arranged 60.14
coherent 50.11
harmonious 589.8
normal 84.7
pacific 803.9
precise 646.10
regular 137.6
systematic 59.6
uniform 17.5
adv. regularly 17.8
order of the day
affairs 151.4

schedule 641.2
ordinal
n. number 86.3
ritualistic manual 1040.12
adj. classificational 61.7
consecutive 71.9
numerical 86.8
ordinance decree 752.4
law 998.3
precept 751.2
rite 1040.3
ordinarily
frequently 135.6
generally 79.17
normally 84.9
plainly 902.10
ordinary
n. heraldic insignia 569.2
inn 191.16
judge 1002.4
service 307.11
adj. average 32.3
common 919.11
customary 642.15
frequent 135.4
inferior 37.6
mediocre 680.8
prevalent 79.12
prosaic 610.5
simple 902.6
usual 84.8
vulgar 898.14
ordinary, the 84.3
ordinate 490.6
ordination
appointment 780.2
consecration 1037.10
dedication 816.4
installation 306.2
organization 60.2
ordnance arms 801.1
artillery 801.6
ordure feces 311.4
filth 682.7
ore mineral 383.2
raw material 721.5
types of 383.20
or else 16.11
organ affiliate 788.10
instrument 658.3
music 465.15
part 55.4
periodical 605.10
organ(o)– life 407.1
organ 55.4
organic 406.19
organ-grinder 464.9
organic innate 5.7
structural 245.9
vital 406.19
organic matter 406
organism entity 3.3
living being 406.2
structure 245.1
organist 464.8
organization
association 788.8
composition 58.1
methodization 60.2

military unit 800.19
order 59.1
organism 406.2
plan 654.1
religion 1020.3
setting-up 167.4
structure 245.1
workplace 719.1
organizational
associational 788.17
formational 60.15
organization man 82.2
organize arrange 60.10
compose 58.3
create 167.12
join forces 52.4
order 59.4
plan 654.9
unionize 789.8
organized
arranged 60.14
drunk 996.31
organic 406.19
planned 654.13
organized crime
illicit business 826.1
the underworld 986.11
organized labor 789.1
organizer
labor unionist 789.3
originator 167.8
planner 654.7
organ player 464.8
organ stop 465.22
orgasm
excitement 857.7
paroxysm 324.6
sexual climax 419.8
orgasmic
excited 857.23
jerky 324.19
lustful 419.29
paroxysmal 162.22
violent 162.17
orgiastic carnal 987.6
excited 857.23
intemperate 993.9
unchaste 989.24
orgy debauchery 993.2
excitement 857.7
revel 878.6
spree 996.5
oriel nook 192.3
window 265.8
orient
v. accustom 642.11
take one's bearings 290.12
adj. luminous 335.30
Orient 180.6
oriental 290.15
Oriental 418.3
orientation
bearings 290.5
direction 290.1
familiarization 642.8
position 184.3
oriented 642.17
orienter 754.3
orifice 265.1
origami 264.4

origin beginning 68.1
etymology 582.16
inception 68.4
source 153.5
original
n. model 25.1
nonconformist 83.3
nonimitation 23.2
odd person 85.4
source 153.5
written matter 602.10
adj. basic 212.8
beginning 68.15
causal 153.15
fundamental 5.8
genuine 516.14
imaginative 535.18
native 189.5
new 122.7
nonconformist 83.6
preceding 66.4
uncommon 122.11
unimitated 23.5
unused 668.12
originality
inventiveness 535.3
newness 122.1
nonconformity 83.1
nonimitation 23.1
unorthodoxy 83.2
originally
initially 68.18
intrinsically 5.9
original sin 982.4
originate begin 68.13
cause 153.11
create 167.13
imagine 535.14
initiate 68.10
invent 23.4
originate from 154.6
origination
beginning 68.1
creation 167.5
inception 68.4
product 168.1
source 153.5
originative
causal 153.14
creative 167.19
imaginative 535.18
originator creator 153.4
producer 167.8
oriole 464.23
orison 1032.4
Ormazd 1013.6
ornament
n. award 916.5
decoration 901.1
extra 41.4
figure of speech
551.1
flowery language
601.4
music 463.18
music division 462.24
token of esteem
916.1
v. add 40.4
decorate 901.8
make grandiloquent
601.7

ornamental
artistic 574.21
decorative 901.10
ornamentalist 579.11
ornamentation
architectural 901.14
decoration 901
flowery language
601.4
superfluity 663.4
types of 901.13
ornamented
adorned 901.11
figurative 551.3
ornate elegant 901.12
high-flown 601.11
ornery
disobedient 767.10
irascible 951.19
malicious 939.18
perverse 626.11
ornithology 415.1
ornithopter 280.6,15
oro– mountain 207.7
mouth 265.5
orotund 601.8
orphan
n. abandoned thing
633.4
survivor 43.3
v. bereave 408.28
orphanage 700.4
orphaned 408.35
orth(o)–
metamorphic rock
384.1
right 958.8
straight 250.6
vertical 213.11
orthodontics 688.4
orthodox
n. true believer 1024.4
adj. conformist 82.6
conventional 645.5
religious 1024.7
strict 757.7
orthodoxy
conformity 82.1
religion 1020.1
right belief 1024
strictness 757.2
orthogonal
perpendicular 213.12
quadrangular 251.9
right-angled 251.7
orthography 581.4
orthopedic 688.18
orthopedist 688.8
orts refuse 43.1
waste 669.4
Oscar 916.2
oscillate
fluctuate 141.5
recur 137.5
vacillate 627.8
vibrate 323.10
oscillating
vacillating 627.10
vibrating 323.15
oscillation
fluctuation 141.3
periodicity 137.2

vacillation 627.2
vibration 323
oscillator 323.9
oscillatory
periodic 137.7
vacillating 627.10
vibrating 323.15
oscilloscope
computer 349.18
instrument 323.8
types of 346.21
osculate contact 200.10
kiss 932.17
Osiris
deity of nether world
1019.5
Egyptian deity
1014.10
–osis disease 686.1
growth 197.3
process 164.2
state 7.1
osmose 306.13
osmosis seepage 306.6
transference 271.1
ossi– 245.6
ossified bony 245.11
hardened 356.13
ossify harden 356.7
make unfeeling 856.6
ossuary tomb 410.16
urn 410.12
osteal 245.11
ostensible
apparent 446.11
conspicuous 555.12
illusory 519.9
pretexted 649.5
specious 616.27
ostensibly
allegedly 649.6
apparently 446.12
conspicuously 555.16
falsely 616.35
ostentation
conspicuousness
555.4
display 555.2
fakery 616.3
grandiloquence 601.1
ornateness 901.2
pretension 904
ostentatious
grandiloquent 601.8
ornate 901.12
pretentious 904.18
ostentatiously
grandiloquently
601.12
pretentiously 904.25
osteopath 688.5
ostracism
banishment 310.4
disapproval 969.1
exclusion 77.2
inhospitality 926.3
ostracize ban 926.6
disapprove 969.10
exclude 77.4
expel 310.17
other
n. different thing 16.3

nonessential 6.2
adj. additional 40.10
another 16.8
renewed 122.8
unrelated 10.5
other-directed
conformable 82.5
extroverted 690.47
motivated 648.30
other self friend 928.1
self 80.5
other side counter 15.2
opposite side 239.3
otherwise
adj. other 16.8
adv. contrarily 15.9
in other ways 16.11
otherworld
Heaven 1018.1
the future 121.2
otherworldly
extraterrestrial 375.26
heavenly 1018.13
immaterial 377.7
pious 1028.9
supernatural 85.15
visionary 535.24
otic 448.14
otiose fruitless 669.12
idle 708.17
trivial 673.16
unserviceable 669.14
oto– 448.7
otology 448.9
ought to 962.3
oui 521.18
Ouija 1034.6
ounce 35.2
oust depose 783.4
eject 310.13
evict 310.15
ouster
dispossession 310.2
ejector 310.11
expulsion 310.1
out
n. excuse 1006.4
outlet 303.9
v. be revealed 556.8
extinguish 332.7
adj. asleep 712.22
dislocated 185.9
dissimilar 21.4
disused 668.10
drunk 996.33
erroneous 518.16
exterior 224.6
extinguished 332.11
obsolete 123.15
odd 85.11
unconscious 423.8
adv. at a loss 812.9
audibly 450.18
away 301.21
emerging 303.21
externally 224.9
fatigued 717.12
prep. from 301.22
out of 303.22
outage 57.2
out-and-out
absolute 34.12

poor 838.7
wanting 662.13
out of practice 734.18
out of print 662.11
out of proportion
inappropriate 27.7
inconsistent 27.8
unequal 31.4
out of reach
beyond reach 199.18
inaccessible 510.9
out-of-the-way 199.9
out of season
anachronous 115.3
inappropriate 27.7
old-fashioned 123.16
scarce 662.11
seasonal 128.8
out of shape
deformed 249.12
out of practice
734.18
out of sight
adj. absent 187.10
excellent 674.13
excessive 663.16
invisible 445.5
overpriced 848.12
vanished 447.4
adv. far 199.15
out of reach 199.18
interj. pleasure 865.17
out of sorts
ill-humored 951.17
sick 686.52
unhappy 872.21
out of step 83.7
out of style 123.15
out of the blue
540.10,14
out of the ordinary
notable 672.18
unusual 85.10
out of the question
by no means! 524.9
hopeless 889.14
impossible 510.7
refusal 776.7
rejected 638.3
out of the running
disappointing 541.6
inferior 37.7
out of action 158.17
out-of-the-way
circuitous 321.7
deviant 291.7
distant 199.9
farfetched 10.7
irrelevant 10.6
nonconformist 83.6
occasional 136.3
out of reach 199.18
secluded 924.7
unexpected 540.10
unusual 85.10
out of this world
excellent 674.13
excessive 663.16
extreme 34.13
pleasant 863.8
superb 674.17
unusual 85.10

out of touch 856.9
out of whack
disagreeing 27.6
disorderly 62.13
in disrepair 692.39
out of order 7.8
unserviceable 669.14
out of work 708.17
out on a limb
in a predicament
731.20
unprotected 697.15
outpatient 686.40
outperform 36.9
outpost
environment 233.1
frontier 235.5
guard 699.9
hinterland 182.2
remote region 199.4
vanguard 240.2
outpouring
n. outflow 303.4
plenty 661.2
adj. outgoing 303.19
output
computer data
349.19
product 168.2
receipts 844.1
yield 811.5
outrage
n. crime 982.2
evil 675.3
indignity 965.2
injustice 977.4
mistreatment 667.2
v. harm 675.6
insult 965.4
mistreat 667.5
offend 952.20
outrageous bad 675.9
disgraceful 915.11
excessive 663.16
extreme 162.15
foolish 470.10
insulting 965.6
overpriced 848.12
undue 961.9
outrageously
badly 675.14
disgracefully 915.16
excessively 663.22
exorbitantly 848.16
outrank come first 64.2
take precedence
36.11
outré 470.10
outreach
deceive 618.13
outdo 36.9
outwit 735.11
stretch 202.6
outright
adj. absolute 34.12
thorough 56.10
unqualified 508.2
adv. completely 56.14
freely 762.31
outrun defeat 727.6
outdo 36.9
overtake 269.17

outset beginning 68.1
start 301.2
outshine defeat 727.6
outdo 36.9
outside
n. exterior 224.2
outdoors 224.3
adj. exterior 224.6
extraneous 78.5
extrinsic 6.3
outdoor 224.7
adv. externally 224.9
outdoors 224.10
outside chance
possibility 509.1
small chance 156.9
outside of 77.9
outsider alien 78.3
foreigner 77.3
odd person 85.4
outsize
n. oversize 195.5
adj. large 34.7
oversize 195.23
outskirts bounds 235.1
city district 183.6
environment 233.1
frontier 235.5
remote region 199.4
suburb 183.1
outsmart
deceive 618.13
outwit 735.11
outspoken artless 736.5
candid 974.17
communicative
554.10
free-spoken 762.22
speaking 594.32
outstanding
conspicuous 555.12
due 840.10
exterior 224.6
notable 672.18
prominent 914.17
protruding 256.13
remaining 43.7
remarkable 34.10
superior 36.12
outstare 893.12
outstretched 197.11
outstrip exceed 34.5
lead 292.2
outdo 36.9
overtake 269.17
outtalk outspeak 596.7
persuade 648.23
out to 714.15
outward
adj. apparent 446.11
exterior 224.6
extrinsic 6.3
formal 646.7
adv. externally 224.9
out 303.21
outwardly
apparently 446.12
externally 224.9
out 303.21
outwear 110.8
outweigh excel 36.6
overweigh 352.14

outwit deceive 618.13
outdo 36.9
outsmart 735.11
outworn
disused 668.10
obsolete 123.15
oval
n. ellipse 253.6
racecourse 878.12
adj. egg-shaped 253.12
ovarian genital 419.27
glandular 312.8
ovary 419.10
ovation applause 968.2
celebration 877.1
oven hot place 328.11
kiln 576.5
over
adj. ended 70.8
high 207.24
past 119.7
remaining 43.7
superior 36.12
surplus 663.18
adv. above 207.26
additionally 40.11
again 103.17
extremely 663.22
upside down 220.8
prep. beyond 199.21
during 105.14
in excess of 663.26
on 228.37
through 290.29
throughout 184.27
overabundance 663.2
overabundant 663.19
overact affect 903.12
overdo 663.10
overdramatize 611.36
overacted
affected 903.15
theatrical 611.38
overactive 707.24
overactivity 707.9
overage excess 43.4
surplus 663.5
overall
adj. comprehensive
76.7
cumulative 74.23
adv. generally 79.17
throughout 56.17
overambitious 635.13
over and above
additionally 40.12
in excess of 663.26
surplus 663.18
over and over 103.16
overanxious
anxious 890.6
overzealous 635.13
overassess 497.2
overawe daunt 891.26
domineer 741.16
overbearing
arrogant 912.9
imperious 739.16
overblown aged 126.15
overfull 663.20
overboard 275.74

overburden
  burden 352.13
  oppress 729.8
  overload 663.15
overburdened
  burdened 352.18
  overloaded 663.20
overcareful 895.11
overcast
  n. aviation 278.41
  cloudiness 404.3
  darkening 337.6
  v. cloud 404.6
  darken 337.9
  adj. cloudy 404.7
  dark 337.14
overcautious 895.11
overcharge
  n. exorbitance 848.5
  overfullness 663.3
  psychology 690.41
  v. exaggerate 617.3
  make grandiloquent
    601.7
  overload 663.15
  overprice 848.7
overclouded 404.7
overcoat
  clothing 231.13
  types of 231.53
overcome
  v. defeat 727.7
  excel 36.6
  triumph over 726.6
  unnerve 859.9
  adj. defeated 727.14
  drunk 996.33
  heartbroken 872.29
  overwrought 857.24
  unnerved 859.13
overcompensation
  690.30
overconfidence
  rashness 894.1
  sureness 513.5
overconfident
  rash 894.7
  sure 513.21
overconscientious
  conscientious 974.15
  overparticular 896.12
overcooked 330.7
overcount 497.2
overcritical
  critical 969.24
  overparticular 896.12
overcrossing
  bridge 657.10
  crossing 221.2
overdeveloped
  excessive 663.16
  overgrown 197.12
  oversize 195.23
overdo
  exaggerate 617.3
  go too far 663.10
  overindulge 993.5
overdone
  affected 903.15
  cooked 330.7
  exaggerated 617.4
  excessive 663.21

grandiloquent 601.8
overdose
  n. drug dose 687.6
  overabundance 663.2
  satiety 664.3
  v. oversupply 663.14
  satiate 664.4
  take sick 686.44
overdraft debt 840.2
  insolvency 842.3
overdraw
  exaggerate 617.3
  misrepresent 573.3
  overextend 663.13
  overspend 854.7
overdrawn
  exaggerated 617.4
  overdone 663.21
overdress 231.41
overdrive
  n. gear 348.6
  v. overtax 663.10
  overwork 716.16
overdue
  expected 539.13
  late 132.16
  unpunctual 115.3
overeager
  overzealous 635.13
  reckless 894.8
overeat 994.5
overelaborate
  elegant 589.9
  grandiloquent 601.8
  ornate 901.12
overemotional 855.20
overemphasis
  exaggeration 617.1
  overdoing 663.6
overemphasize
  emphasize 672.13
  overdo 663.10
overenthusiastic
  fanatical 473.32
  overzealous 635.13
  reckless 894.8
overestimate
  n. overestimation
    497.1
  v. exaggerate 617.3
  flatter 970.7
  overreckon 497.2
overestimated
  exaggerated 617.4
  overrated 497.3
overexcited 857.24
overexercise 663.10
overexert
  exert oneself 716.10
  overtax 663.10
overexpand 663.13
overexpansion 663.7
overextend
  exert oneself 716.10
  overdraw 663.13
overextension
  exertion 716.2
  overactivity 707.9
  overdrawing 663.7
overexuberant 663.19
overfed overfull 663.20
overgorged 994.7

overweight 195.23
  satiated 664.6
overfill fill 56.7
  overload 663.15
  satiate 664.4
overflow
  n. abundance 593.1
  overfullness 663.3
  plenty 661.2
  spillage 395.6
  v. abound 661.5
  flow over 395.17
  superabound 663.8
overflowing much 34.8
  overfull 663.20
  plentiful 661.7
  profuse 593.11
  teeming 101.9
overfull full 56.11
  overloaded 663.20
  satiated 664.6
overgarment
  clothing 231.12
  types of 231.50
overgrow
  grow larger 197.7
  grow rank 411.31
  overrun 313.5
  spread 197.6
  superabound 663.8
overgrown
  excessive 663.16
  growing rank 411.40
  large 34.7
  overdeveloped 197.12
  overrun 313.10
  oversize 195.23
overgrowth
  excess 663.1
  overrunning 313.1
  oversize 195.5
overhang
  n. projection 215.3
  v. be imminent 152.2
  cover 228.30
  project 215.7
overhanging
  n. projection 215.3
  adj. imminent 152.3
  projecting 215.11
overhaul
  n. examination 485.3
  repair 694.6
  v. check 87.14
  examine 485.23
  overtake 269.17
  repair 694.14
  take account of 845.9
overhead
  n. expenses 843.3
  roof 228.6
  adv. over 207.26
overhear
  be informed 557.14
  hear 448.12
overheated
  heated 329.29
  hot 328.25
overindulge
  be intemperate 993.5
  overdo 663.10
  overeat 994.5

overindulgent
  indulgent 759.8
  intemperate 993.7
  unstrict 758.4
overjoyed 865.14
overkill
  atomic attack 798.1
  exaggeration 617.1
overland 385.11
overlap
  n. agreement 26.1
  cover 228.4
  superfluity 663.4
  v. agree 26.6
  cover 228.30
overlapping
  n. cover 228.4
  adj. covering 228.35
overlarge
  exaggerated 617.4
  excessive 663.16
  oversize 195.23
overlay
  n. cover 228.4
  v. cover 228.19
  make grandiloquent
    601.7
overlie 228.30
overload
  n. burden 352.7
  overfullness 663.3
  v. burden 352.13
  make grandiloquent
    601.7
  oppress 729.8
  overfill 663.15
overloaded
  burdened 352.18
  high-flown 601.11
  overfull 663.20
overlong 110.11
overlook
  n. observation post
    439.8
  v. accept 861.6
  be broad-minded
    526.7
  be high 207.16
  bewitch 1036.9
  condone 947.4
  disregard 531.2
  examine 485.23
  front on 240.9
  neglect 534.6
  permit 777.10
  slight 966.6
  supervise 747.10
overlooked
  forgiven 947.7
  neglected 534.14
overlord master 749.1
  potentate 749.7
overly 663.22
overlying 228.35
overmaster
  domineer 741.16
  overcome 727.7
  subdue 764.9
overmatched 727.14
overmodest 903.19
overmuch
  n. excess 663.1

adj. excessive 663.16
superabundant
663.19
adv. excessively
663.22
overnice
affected 903.18
elegant 589.9
overparticular 896.12
overnight 134.11
over one's head
deep 209.16
hard to understand
549.14
overparticular 896.12
overpass
n. bridge 657.10
crossing 221.2
overrunning 313.1
passageway 657.4
v. exceed 663.9
excel 36.6
outdistance 36.10
overrun 313.4
traverse 273.19
overpay 848.8
overplay outdo 36.9
overdo 663.10
overplayed 611.38
overplus excess 43.4
surplus 663.5
overpopulation 663.2
overpower
be strong 159.8
drown out 453.7
overcome 727.7
overpowered
defeated 727.14
overexcited 857.24
overpowering
exciting 857.28
invincible 159.17
overwhelming 727.17
overprice 848.7
overpriced 848.12
overprint 603.14
overrate 497.2
overrated 497.3
overreach
deceive 618.13
exaggerate 617.3
exceed 663.9
outwit 735.11
overrun 313.4
overreact
exaggerate 617.3
overdo 663.10
overestimate 497.2
overrefined
affected 903.18
elegant 589.9
overparticular 896.12
sensitive 422.14
specious 483.10
overreligious
fanatical 473.32
zealous 1028.11
override
conquer 727.10
cover 228.30
domineer 741.16
outdo 36.9

repeal 779.2
trample 313.7
overriding 672.23
overripe aged 126.15
unsavory 429.7
overrule repeal 779.2
rule 741.14
overruling chief 36.14
imperious 739.16
most important
672.23
overrun
n. overgoing 313.1
surplus 663.5
v. conquer 822.19
exceed 663.9
grow over 411.31
infest 313.6
overflow 395.17
overgo 313.4
pervade 186.7
run over 313.7
spread 197.6
superabound 663.8
typeset 603.16
adj. growing rank
411.40
overspread 313.10
overrunning
infestation 313.2
overflow 395.6
overgoing 313
permeation 186.3
overseas
adj. absent 187.11
distant 199.11
adv. across the sea
397.10
abroad 78.6
oversee 747.10
overseer 748.2
oversell
exaggerate 617.3
oversupply 663.14
oversensitive
irascible 951.20
overparticular 896.12
sensitive 422.14
overset
n. inversion 220.2
surplus 663.5
v. capsize 275.44
overcome 727.7
overthrow 693.20
overturn 220.6
oversexed 419.26
overshadow
be high 207.16
cloud 404.6
darken 337.9
eclipse 36.8
shade 338.5
overshoot exceed 663.9
fly 278.52
overrun 313.4
oversight
an error 518.4
government 741.1
neglect 534.1
nonobservance 769.1
protectorship 699.2
supervision 747.2

oversimplification
oversimplicity 45.3
undevelopment 721.4
oversimplified 45.10
oversize
n. outsize 195.5
adj. outsize 195.23
oversleep be late 132.7
miss an opportunity
130.6
sleep 712.13
oversold 617.4
overspend
overpay 848.8
overtax 663.10
spend more than one
has 854.7
overspread
v. cover 228.19
disperse 75.4
infest 313.6
overrun 313.5
pervade 186.7
superabound 663.8
adj. overrun 313.10
overstate
exaggerate 617.3
falsify 616.16
misrepresent 573.3
overestimate 497.2
overstated 617.4
overstay 132.15
overstep exceed 663.9
overrun 313.4
take liberties 961.7
transgress 313.9
overstrain
exert oneself 716.10
fatigue 717.4
overextend 663.13
overtax 663.10
overstretch 663.13
overstuffed full 56.11
overfull 663.20
satiated 664.6
upholstered 228.33
oversubtle 483.10
oversupply
n. overabundance
663.2
surplus 663.5
v. overprovide 663.14
oversweet 431.5
overt 555.10
overt act 705.3
overtake
come after 117.3
make drunk 996.22
outstrip 269.17
overtax burden 352.13
exert oneself 716.10
overcharge 848.7
overdo 663.10
overwork 716.16
over-the-counter market
833.7
over the hill 126.15
overthrow
n. change 139.1
defeat 727.1
deposal 783.2
downthrow 318.2

inversion 220.2
refutation 506.2
revolution 147.1
ruin 693.3
upheaval 162.5
v. change 139.6
depose 783.4
destroy 693.20
overcome 727.7
overturn 220.6
refute 506.5
revolt 767.7
revolutionize 147.4
overthrown
defeated 727.14
disproved 506.7
ruined 693.28
overtime 108.3
overtire 717.4
overtired 717.9
overtly 555.15
overtone
harmonics 463.16
implication 546.2
meaning 545.1
milieu 233.3
tone 450.2
overture music 462.26
offer 773.1
prelude 66.2
overturn
n. defeat 727.1
downthrow 318.2
inversion 220.2
revolution 147.1
ruin 693.3
v. capsize 275.44
defeat 727.7
invert 220.6
overthrow 693.20
refute 506.5
revolutionize 147.4
overvalue 497.2
overview
abridgment 607.1
scrutiny 439.6
overweening
confident 513.21
excessive 663.16
insolent 913.8
presumptuous 912.10
rash 894.7
vain 909.8
overweight
n. overfullness 663.3
oversize 195.5
weight 352.1
v. burden 352.13
outweigh 352.14
overload 663.15
adj. corpulent 195.18
heavy 352.16
oversize 195.23
overwhelm
astonish 920.6
defeat 727.8
destroy 693.21
drown out 453.7
overflow 395.17
overpower 159.8
oversupply 663.14
raid 798.20

refute 506.5
sadden 872.19
subdue 764.9
submerge 320.7
overwhelmed
astonished 920.9
defeated 727.14
flooded 395.25
heartbroken 872.29
overwrought 857.24
overwhelming
astonishing 920.12
evidential 505.17
exciting 857.28
invincible 159.17
overpowering 727.17
overwork
n. overdoing 663.6
v. drive 716.16
overtax 663.10
work hard 716.13
overworked
ornate 901.12
trite 79.16
overwrought
exaggerated 617.4
grandiloquent 601.8
ornate 901.12
overdone 663.21
overexcited 857.24
overzealous
fanatical 473.32
obstinate 626.8
overeager 635.13
reckless 894.8
zealous 1028.11
ovine 414.49
oviparous 406.25
ovoid
n. oval 253.6
adj. egg-shaped 253.12
globular 255.9
ovule egg 406.15
gamete 406.12
oval 253.6
ovum egg 406.12
source 153.7
owe 840.5
owed due 960.7
unpaid 840.10
owing
attributable 155.6
due 960.7
payable 840.10
owing to
because of 155.9
resulting from 154.8
owl bird 414.33,66
omen 544.6
owlish 564.17
own
v. acknowledge 521.11
confess 556.7
possess 808.5
adj. possessed 808.8
own accord 762.7
owner 809.2
ownership 808.2
own free will 762.7
owning
n. confession 556.3
possession 808.1

adj. possessing 808.9
own up 556.7
ox
awkward person 734.8
beast of burden 271.6
bull 414.6
strength 159.7
oxcart 272.3,23
oxidation
burning 329.5
decay 692.6
reaction 379.5
oxidize corrode 692.24
heat 329.24
react chemically 379.6
oxygen 401.11
oxygenate
add gas 401.8
air 402.11
oxygen tent
breathing 403.18
respirator 689.37
oxymoron
contrariety 15.3
dilemma 731.6
impossibility 510.1
inconsistency 27.2
oyez! attention! 530.22
hark! 448.17
oyster food 308.25
fowl part 308.23
ozone 402.1

P

pa 170.9
PA 450.11
pabulum 308.3
pace
n. gait 273.14
rate 267.4
step 273.13
v. lead 292.2
measure 490.11
proceed 273.26
ride 273.33
row 275.53
walk 273.27
pacer 414.18
pacesetter 748.6
pachyderm 414.4
pacific calm 268.12
conciliatory 804.12
meek 765.15
peaceful 803.9
unbelligerent 803.10
pacification
moderation 163.2
peacemaking 804
truce 804.5
pacifier
alleviator 163.3
peacemaker 805.5
sedative 687.12
pacifism inaction 706.1
moderation 163.1
peaceableness 803.4
pacifist 803.6

pacifistic
moderate 163.10
unbelligerent 803.10
pacify calm 163.7
conciliate 804.7
quiet 268.8
regularize 59.4
pacifying
pacificatory 804.12
tranquilizing 163.15
pack
n. amount 28.2
bundle 74.8
film 577.10
flock 74.5
freight 271.7
group 74.3
impediment 730.6
large number 101.3
much 34.4
parachute 280.13
playing cards 878.17
set 74.12
v. be numerous 101.5
bundle 74.20
fill 56.7
impress 142.9
obstruct 730.12
overload 663.15
package 236.9
prearrange 641.3
put 184.14
stop 266.7
stuff 194.7
tamper with 616.17
transport 271.11
wrap 228.20
package
n. all 54.3
bundle 74.8
combination 52.1
container 236.2
v. assemble 74.20
enclose 236.9
wrap 228.20
packaged
assembled 74.21
wrapped 228.31
package deal all 54.3
combination 52.1
transaction 827.4
package tour 273.5
packaging 236.2
pack animal 271.6
pack away put 184.14
store 660.10
packed blocked 266.11
crowded 74.22
dense 354.12
full 56.11
jammed 142.16
overfull 663.20
prearranged 641.5
tampered with 616.30
teeming 101.9
packet bundle 74.8
ship 277.1,22
packet boat 561.6
pack in enter 302.7
thrust in 304.7
packing carrying 271.3

contents 194.3
packaging 236.2
placement 184.5
wadding 266.5
packing house 719.3
pack off dismiss 310.18
send away 289.3
pack of troubles 866.8
pack rat 74.15
pact 771.1
pad
n. abode 191.1
bedding 216.20
buffer 237.5
faint sound 452.3
foot 212.5
horse 414.18
mark 568.7
record book 570.11
safety equipment 699.3
v. creep 273.25
cushion 886.5
drag out 593.8
faint sound 452.15
fill 56.7
line 194.7
repeat 103.8
walk 273.26
padded 593.12
padded cell 473.14
padding contents 194.3
creeping 273.9
extra 41.4
redundancy 103.3
safety equipment 699.3
softening 357.5
superfluity 663.4
wadding 266.5
paddle
n. agitator 324.9
gait 273.14
instrument of punishment 1011.2
oar 277.15
v. churn 324.10
moisten 392.12
punish 1010.15
row 275.53
walk 273.27
paddle wheel 285.7
paddling 1010.5
paddy 413.9
paddy wagon 272.10
padlock
n. restraint 760.5
v. close 266.6
padre
clergyman 1038.2
priest 1038.5
padrone 749.1
paean hymn 1032.3
praise 968.5
rejoicing 876.2
sacred music 462.16
thanks 949.2
paella 308.11
paesano 190.5
pagan
n. heathen 1025.7
irreligious 1031.11

part of writing 55.2
phrase 585.1
treatise 606.1
v. phrase 588.4
parallel
n. entrenchment
799.5
equal 30.4
latitude 180.3
likeness 20.3
map 654.4
parallel line 218.2
v. agree 26.6
be comparable 491.7
be parallel 218.4
compare 491.4
equal 30.5
relate 9.6
resemble 20.7
adj. accompanying
73.9
analogous 20.11
comparable 491.8
equidistant 218.6
related 9.9
parallel bars 716.7
paralleling
analogous 20.11
parallel 218.6
parallelism
accompaniment 73.1
agreement 26.1
comparison 491.1
equality 30.1
equidistance 218
similarity 20.1
symmetry 248.1
parallelograph 218.3
paralogism
specious argument
483.3
syllogism 482.6
paralysis
disease symptom
686.8
inaction 706.1
paralyzation 686.25
paralytic
n. cripple 686.42
adj. diseased 686.57
do-nothing 706.6
paralyze astonish 920.6
deaden 856.8
render powerless
158.11
stupefy 423.4
terrify 891.25
paralyzed
disabled 158.16
do-nothing 706.6
drunk 996.33
terrified 891.34
paralyzing 891.37
paramedic
hospital staff 688.14
parachutist 279.8
parameter
bounds 235.1
condition 507.2
measure 490.2
paramount
n. chief 672.10

master 749.1
potentate 749.7
adj. best 674.18
chief 36.14
dominant 741.18
principal 672.23
top 211.10
paramountcy
importance 672.1
superexcellence 674.2
supremacy 36.3
paramour lover 931.11
mistress 989.17
paranoia
dissociation 690.27
mental disorder
690.17
psychosis 473.4
paranoid
n. psychotic 473.16
adj. psychotic 473.27
paranymph
assistant 787.6
deputy 781.1
supporter 787.9
wedding attendant
933.5
parapet barrier 730.5
fortification 799.4
paraphernalia
belongings 810.2
equipment 659.4
paraphilia 419.12
paraphrase
n. imitation 22.3
interpretation 552.3
v. rephrase 552.13
paraplegia 686.25
paraplegic 686.42
paraprofessional
aide 787.6
teacher 565.5
parapsychology
psychics 1034.4
psychology 690.1
parasite animal 414.40
attendant 73.6
bloodsucker 414.41
follower 293.2
nonworker 708.10
plant 411.4
sycophant 907.4
parasitic
commensal 13.15
indolent 708.18
obsequious 907.13
rapacious 822.26
symbiotic 177.4
parasitism
commensality 13.5
obsequiousness 907.2
symbiosis 177.1
parasol shade 338.1,8
umbrella 228.7
paratrooper 279.8
paratroops army 800.22
elite troops 800.14
parboiled 330.6
Parcae 640.3
parcel
n. amount 28.2
bundle 74.8

part 55.1
real estate 810.7
several 101.2
v. bundle 74.20
divide 49.18
package 236.9
quantify 28.4
share 816.6
parceled 816.12
parceling 816.1
parcel of land
field 413.9
tract 180.4
parcel out
apportion 816.8
distribute 60.9
divide 49.18
parcel post 604.5
parch be hot 328.22
burn 329.24
dry 393.6
shrink 198.9
parched burned 329.30
dried 393.9
shrunk 198.13
thirsty 634.26
parchment
brittleness 360.2
document 570.5
dryness 393.2
manuscript 602.11,29
written matter 602.10
pardner
companion 928.3
partner 787.2
pardon
n. acquittal 1007.1
excuse 947.2
pity 944.1
v. acquit 1007.4
forgive 947.3
have pity 944.4
pardonable 1006.14
pardoned 947.7
pare cheapen 849.6
cut off 42.10
peel 232.8
reduce 39.7
sever 49.11
paregoric
narcotic 687.12
sedative 687.12
parent
n. originator 153.4
progenitor 170.8
adj. ancestral 170.13
parentage 170.1
parental
ancestral 170.13
loving 931.25
protecting 699.23
parenthesis
discontinuity 72.1
interjection 237.2
inversion 220.3
parenthesize
bracket 236.8
punctuate 586.16
parenthetic(al)
discontinuous 72.4
incidental 129.11
interjectional 237.9

irrelevant 10.6
paresis paralysis 686.25
venereal disease
686.16
par excellence 36.16
parfait 308.46
parfum 436.2
parget color 362.13
plaster 228.25
pariah odd person 85.4
outcast 926.4
recluse 924.5
parietal
enclosing 236.11
partitioned 237.11
pari-mutuel
gambling 515.4
pari-mutuel machine
515.13
paring flake 227.3
piece 55.3
refuse 669.4
remnant 43.1
parish diocese 1037.8
district 180.5
laity 1039.1
parishioner 1039.2
parity equality 30.1
similarity 20.1
stock price 834.9
park
n. armory 801.2
commons 878.14
enclosure 236.3
grassland 411.8
green 411.7
preserve 701.6
woodland 411.11
v. place 184.11
settle 184.16
Parkinson's disease
686.23
parkway 657.6
parlance diction 588.1
language 580.1
parlay
n. wager 515.3
v. bet 515.20
increase 38.4
parley
n. advice 754.1
conference 597.6
peace offer 804.2
v. confer 597.11
parliament 742.1
parliamentarianism
741.8
parliamentary
governmental 741.17
legislative 742.19
parlor
living room 192.5
workplace 719.1
parlor car
railway car 272.14
train room 192.10
parlous 697.9
parochial
exclusive 77.8
local 180.9
narrow-minded
527.10

parochialism
  exclusiveness 77.3
  narrow-mindedness
    527.1
parochial school 567.10
parody
  n. humor 881.1
  imitation 22.3
  misrepresentation
    573.2
  paraphrase 22.1
  ridicule 967.6
  v. misrepresent 573.3
  ridicule 967.11
parol
  n. word of mouth
    594.3
  adj. speech 594.30
parole
  n. language 580.1
  promise 770.1
  release 763.2
  speech 594.1
  utterance 594.3
  v. release 763.5
parolee 761.11
paroxysm anger 952.8
  emotional outburst
    857.8
  fit 162.5
  frenzy 473.7
  pain 424.2
  seizure 686.5
  spasm 324.6
parquet check 374.4
  floor 212.3
  theater part 611.20
parricide 409.3
parrot
  n. conformist 82.2
  imitator 22.4
  v. imitate 22.6
  memorize 537.17
  repeat 103.7
parrotlike 103.14
parrotry 22.2
parry dodge 631.8
  equivocate 483.9
  fend off 799.10
  prevaricate 613.7
  refute 506.5
parrying
  equivocation 483.5
  prevarication 613.4
parse analyze 48.7
  grammaticize 586.16
parsimonious
  economical 851.6
  meager 662.10
  niggardly 852.7
parsimony
  economy 851.1
  meagerness 662.2
  niggardliness 852
parsing analysis 48.2
  grammar 586.1
parson 1038.2
parsonage house 191.6
  pastorage 1042.7
part
  n. allotment 816.5
  amount 28.2

book part 605.13
  component 58.2
  contents 194.1
  district 180.1
  estate 810.4
  function 656.3
  length 202.3
  music division 462.24
  music score 462.28
  portion 55
  role 611.11
  situation 7.5
  voice part 462.22
  v. apportion 816.6
  die 408.19
  disband 75.8
  divorce 935.5
  interspace 201.3
  open 265.12
  part company 49.19
  separate 49.9
  adj. half 92.5
  incomplete 57.4
  partial 55.7
  adv. partly 55.8
  to a degree 35.10
partake eat 307.18
  participate 815.5
  take 822.13
partaking
  n. participation 815.1
  sociability 922.6
  adj. participating
    815.8
part and parcel 58.2
part company
  disband 75.8
  fall out 795.10
  separate 49.19
parted 201.6
parterre
  horizontal 214.3
  theater part 611.20
parthenogenesis 169.6
Parthian shot
  gibe 967.2
  remark 594.4
  sequel 67.1
partial
  n. tone 450.2
  adj. half 92.5
  imperfect 678.4
  incomplete 57.4
  part 55.7
  partisan 788.19
  prejudiced 527.12
  unjust 977.11
partiality
  inclination 634.3
  one-sidedness 977.3
  partisanship 788.13
  preference 637.5
  prejudice 527.3
partially
  imperfectly 678.5
  incompletely 57.6
  partly 55.8
  to a degree 35.10
  unjustly 977.13
partial to
  desirous of 634.22
  fond of 931.28

partible 49.26
participant
  n. participator 815.4
  adj. participating
    815.8
participate 815.5
participating 815.8
participation
  inclusion 76.1
  partaking 815
  sociability 922.6
participator 815.4
participial 586.17
participle 586.3
particle
  minute thing 196.7
  part of speech 586.3
  piece 55.3
  small amount 35.2
  subatomic 326.24
parti-color
  n. variegation 374.1
  adj. variegated 374.9
particular
  n. citation 505.6
  event 151.2
  instance 8.3
  part 55.1
  the facts 1.4
  the specific 80.3
  adj. classificational
    61.7
  detailed 8.9
  fastidious 896.9
  meticulous 533.12
  proportionate 816.13
  selective 637.23
  special 80.12
particularity
  characteristic 80.4
  circumstantiality 8.4
  fastidiousness 896.1
  individuality 80
  meticulousness 533.3
  unity 89.1
particularization
  circumstantiation 8.5
  description 608.1
  differentiation 16.4
  logic 482.3
  specialization 80.7
particularize
  be accurate 516.10
  circumstantiate 8.6
  cite 505.14
  differentiate 16.6
  expatiate 593.7
  specialize 80.9
particularly
  chiefly 36.17
  exceptionally 34.20
  fastidiously 896.14
  fully 8.13
  singly 89.13
  specially 80.15
parting
  n. death 408.1
  departure 301.1
  disbandment 75.3
  good-by 301.4
  separation 49.1
  adj. departing 301.19

separating 49.25
parting shot gibe 967.2
  sequel 67.1
partisan
  n. follower 293.2
  friend 928.1
  guerrilla 800.15
  party member 744.27
  supporter 787.9
  adj. factional 788.19
  factious 795.17
  party 744.44
  prejudiced 527.12
  unjust 977.11
partisanism
  cliquism 788.13
  injustice 977.3
  partisanship 744.25
  politics 744.1
  religion 1020.4
partisan politics 744.1
partition
  n. apportionment
    816.1
  divider 92.3
  dividing wall 237.5
  separation 49.1
  v. apportion 816.6
  compartmentalize
    49.18
  divide 237.8
partitioned
  separate 49.20
  walled 237.11
partly
  adj. half 92.5
  adv. partially 55.8
  to a degree 35.10
part music 462.17
partner
  n. accompanier 73.4
  associate 787.2
  companion 928.3
  participator 815.4
  spouse 933.7
  v. assemble 74.18
  cooperate 786.3
  join 52.4
partner in crime 787.3
partnership
  affiliation 786.2
  association 788.1
  companionship 73.2
  company 788.9
  participation 815.1
part of speech 586.3
parts airplane 280.16
  airship 280.19
  auto 272.25
  computer 349.32
  contents 194.1
  district 180.1
  electrical 342.36
  engine 348.27
  garment 231.66
  radar 346.20
  radio receiver 344.30
  radio transmitter
    344.31
  ship 277.26
  talent 733.4

impose 963.7
outwit 735.11
transfer 271.9
pass the hat 774.15
pass through
    enter 302.8
    experience 151.8
    traverse 273.19
pass time 105.6
pass up abstain 992.7
    leave undone 534.7
    reject 638.2
    slight 966.6
password 568.12
past
    n. tense 586.12
    time 105.1
    times past 119
    adj. former 119.10
    gone 119.7
    grammar 119.9
    obsolete 123.15
    prep. after 117.8
    beyond 199.21
    in excess of 663.26
    unintelligible 549.26
pasta 308.33
past due 115.3
paste
    n. adherent 50.4,13
    compound 44.5
    fake 616.13
    food 308.33
    jewelry 901.5
    ornamentation 901.3
    pulp 390.2
    semiliquid 389.5
    v. hit 283.13
    overwhelm 727.8
    pound 283.14
    stick together 50.9
pastel
    n. art equipment
    574.19
    picture 574.14
    softness 362.3
    adj. light 363.9
    soft-colored 362.21
pasteurization 681.3
pasteurize 681.24
pasteurized 681.27
pastiche
    borrowing 821.2
    copy 24.1
    hodgepodge 44.6
    ridicule 967.6
    work of art 574.11
pastille 436.4
pastime
    amusement 878.1
    avocation 656.7
pastiness
    colorlessness 363.2
    pulpiness 390.1
    viscosity 389.2
past master
    expert 733.13
    producer 167.8
pastor 1038.2
pastoral
    n. picture 574.13
    poem 609.6

stage show 611.4
    adj. ministerial
    1037.13
    natural 736.6
    pacific 803.9
    poetic 609.17
    rustic 182.6
pastoral staff
    clerical insignia 569.4
    crosier 1041.3
    staff 217.2
pastorate
    church office 1037.5
    parsonage 1042.7
    protectorship 699.2
    the ministry 1037.1
pastrami 308.13
pastry 308.40
pasturage food 308.4
    grassland 411.8
pasture
    n. farm 413.8
    food 308.4
    grassland 411.8
    herbivorism 307.1
    v. eat 307.26
    feed 307.16
pasty
    n. pastry 308.40
    adj. colorless 363.7
    pulpy 390.6
    soft 357.12
    viscous 389.12
PA system 450.11
pat
    n. endearment 932.4
    faint sound 452.3
    lump 195.10
    tap 283.6
    v. faint sound 452.15
    make love 932.14
    tap 283.15
    adj. apt 26.10
    known 475.26
    unyielding 142.15
patch
    n. blemish 679.3
    field 413.9
    mark 568.5
    military insignia
    569.5
    ray 335.5
    small amount 35.3
    spottiness 374.3
    tract 180.4
    v. do carelessly 534.9
    repair 694.14
patch test 689.17
patchwork check 374.4
    hodgepodge 44.6
patchy
    discontinuous 72.4
    imperfect 678.4
    incomplete 57.4
    irregular 138.3
    mixed 44.15
    shabby 692.34
    spotted 374.13
pate brain 466.6
    head 211.6
pâté 308.40

patent
    n. exemption 762.8
    grant 777.5
    permission 777.1
    restriction 234.3
    right 958.4
    safeguard 699.3
    v. authorize 777.11
    limit 234.5
    preserve 701.7
    protect 699.18
    adj. clearly visible
    444.7
    manifest 555.8
patented
    authorized 777.17
    limited 234.7
    protected 699.21
patently
    manifestly 555.14
    positively 34.19
    visibly 444.8
patent medicine
    medicine 687.4
    nostrum 687.2
pater 170.9
paterfamilias
    father 170.9
    master 749.1
paternal
    fatherly 170.13
    loving 931.25
paternalism 741.9
paternity
    blood relationship
    11.1
    fatherhood 170.2
Paternoster
    Mass part 1040.10
    prayer 1032.4
path aviation 278.42
    electric circuit 342.4
    route 657.2
    track 568.8
    trail 657.3
pathetic
    affecting 855.24
    paltry 673.18
    pitiful 944.8
    unpleasant 864.20
pathfinder
    precursor 66.1
    preparer 720.5
    traveler 274.1
pathogen 686.39
pathogenic 684.5
pathological
    diseased 686.56
    unwholesome 686.51
pathologist 688.8
pathology 686.1
pathos
    distressfulness 864.5
    pity 944.1
    sadness 872.1
    sympathy 855.5
pathway 657.3
patience
    endurance 861
    forgiveness 947.1
    inexcitability 858.1
    leniency 759.1

perseverance 625.1
    tolerance 526.4
patient
    n. experimentee 489.7
    sick person 686.40
    adj. enduring 861.9
    forgiving 947.6
    inexcitable 858.10
    lenient 759.7
    persevering 625.7
    tolerant 526.11
patiently
    enduringly 861.11
    perseveringly 625.8
patina layer 227.2
    polish 260.2
    verdigris 371.2
patinate 371.3
patio 192.21
patisserie 308.40
patois dialect 580.7
    jargon 580.9
pat on the back
    n. congratulation
    948.1
    encouragement 893.9
    v. abet 648.21
    comfort 887.6
    compliment 968.14
    congratulate 948.2
    encourage 893.16
patria 181.2
patriarch
    ancestor 170.7
    antiquated person
    123.8
    clergyman 1038.9
    father 170.9
    master 749.1
    Mormon priest
    1038.11
    old man 127.2
patriarchal aged 126.16
    ancestral 170.13
    governmental 741.17
    primitive 123.11
patrician
    n. nobleman 918.4
    adj. noble 918.10
patricide 409.3
patrilineage 11.1
patrilineal 11.6
patrimonial 170.15
patrimony 819.2
patriot 941.3
patriotic 941.4
patriotism 941.2
patristics 1023.1
patrol
    n. watchman 699.10
    v. keep watch 699.20
    traverse 273.19
patrol car 272.10
patrolman
    peace officer 699.15
    watchman 699.10
patron attender 186.5
    benefactor 942.1
    commander 276.7
    customer 828.4
    financer 836.9
    giver 818.11

master 749.1
play backer 611.31
protector 699.5
provider 659.6
supporter 787.9
patronage
clientele 828.3
custom 827.6
fosterage 785.4
political patronage
744.36
protectorship 699.2
recommendation
968.4
patronize
be arrogant 912.8
finance 836.15
sponsor 785.15
trade with 827.16
patronizing
n. arrogance 912.1
adj. arrogant 912.9
snobbish 912.14
patroon 749.1
patsy
credulous person
502.4
dupe 620.1
scapegoat 149.3
patter
n. acting 611.9
faint sound 452.3
jargon 580.9
rain 394.1
sales talk 829.5
staccato sound 455.1
v. act 611.34
chatter 596.5
faint sound 452.15
gab 594.20
make staccato sounds
455.4
pound 283.14
rain 394.9
speak 580.16
pattern behavior 737.1
diagram 654.3
form 246.1
gestalt 690.39
good person 985.4
habit 642.4
harmonics 463.11
idea 479.2
measure 490.2
model 25.1
motif 901.7
original 23.2
structure 245.1
paucity fewness 102.1
scarcity 662.3
Paul 1022.2
paunch 193.3
paunchy 195.18
pauper 838.4
pauperism 838.2
pauperize 838.6
pauperized
ill-provided 662.12
indigent 838.8
pause
n. delay 132.2
demur 623.2

discontinuity 72.2
harmonics 463.12
interim 109.1
juncture 144.4
music 463.21
respite 711.2
rest 144.3
speech 594.10
v. be irresolute 627.7
demur 623.4
hesitate 144.9
recess 109.3
take a rest 711.8
pave 228.22
paved 228.31
pavement
bottom 212.3
building material
378.2
flooring 228.9,43
foundation 216.6
road 657.7
pave the way
facilitate 732.6
prepare the way
720.12
pavilion 191.10
paw
n. foot 212.5
grasping organ 813.4
v. touch 425.6
pawky cautious 895.8
cunning 735.12
fastidious 896.10
shrewd 467.15
pawn
n. chessman 878.18
inferior 37.2
instrument 658.3
pledge 772.2
v. borrow 821.3
pledge 772.10
pawnbroker
broker 830.9
lender 820.3
lending institution
820.4
pawned 772.12
pawnshop 820.4
paw print 568.7
pax peace 803.1
rite 1040.4
sacred article 1040.11
pax vobiscum!
farewell! 301.23
peace! 803.11
pay
n. punishment 1010.1
remuneration 841.4
v. be of use 665.17
be profitable 811.12
do 705.6
experience 151.8
finance 836.15
overpay 848.8
punish 1010.11
recompense 841.10
retaliate 955.5
spend 843.5
yield 844.4
payable due 960.7
owed 840.10

pay as you go
v. pay 841.17
adv. in cash 841.25
pay attention
attend to 530.5
care 533.6
court 932.19
pay heed 530.8
pay back
compensate 33.4
interchange 150.4
make restitution
823.5
repay 841.11
retaliate 955.5
pay dirt 383.7
payee 819.3
payer 841.9
paying
n. payment 841.1
adj. gainful 811.15
remunerative 841.21
paying guest
lodger 190.8
tenant 809.4
payload
aviation 278.30
freight 271.7
load 194.2
rocketry 281.3
warhead 801.10
paymaster
financial officer
836.11
payer 841.9
payment
expenditure 843.1
incentive 648.7
pay 841
punishment 1010.1
remuneration 841.4
pay no attention to
be inattentive 531.2
disobey 767.6
slight 966.6
payoff bribe 651.2
end 70.1
payment 841.1
result 154.2
pay off
be of use 665.17
be profitable 811.12
bribe 651.3
drift off course
275.29
pay in full 841.13
retaliate 955.5
sail 275.23
yield 844.4
payola 651.2
pay one's respects to
936.12
pay out
apportion 816.8
pay 841.14
punish 1010.11
settle with 841.12
spend 843.5
payroll 841.4
pay the piper
be punished 1010.23
pay 841.18

PBX 560.8
PDQ 131.15
pea 411.4
peabrain 471.4
pea-brained 469.13
peace
n. accord 794.1
agreement 26.1
comfortableness
887.2
order 59.1
peacefulness 803
quiescence 268.1
silence 451.1
truce 804.5
interj. peace be with
you! 803.11
silence! 451.14
peaceable calm 268.12
friendly 927.14
moderate 163.10
pacific 803.9
unbelligerent 803.10
weak 765.15
peace and quiet 803.2
peace be with you!
farewell! 301.23
peace! 803.11
peaceful calm 268.12
comfortable 887.11
composed 858.12
homelike 191.33
in accord 794.3
moderate 163.10
pacific 803.9
peacefully
comfortably 887.14
quietly 268.18
peacefulness
comfortableness
887.2
composure 858.2
peace 803.2
quiescence 268.1
peace lover 803.6
peace-loving 803.10
peacemaker
make-peace 805.5
pacifier 163.3
pacifist 803.6
peacemongering 804.1
peace offering
atonement 1012.1
gift 818.4
pacification 804.2
sacrifice 1032.7
peace officer 699.15
peace of mind
composure 858.2
contentment 868.1
peace of heart 803.3
peace pipe 804.2
peacetime
n. peace 803.1
adj. pacific 803.9
peach
n. beautiful person
900.8
good thing 674.7
v. divulge 556.6
inform on 557.12
adj. orange 369.2

writer 602.13
writing 602.1,30
v. confine 761.12
enclose 236.5
write 602.19
penal 1010.25
penal code 998.5
penal colony 761.8
penalize
bring in a verdict
1004.19
condemn 1008.3
handicap 1009.4
punish 1010.10
penalty discount 847.1
impediment 730.6
legal decision 1004.9
penalization 1009
punishment 1010.1
penance
atonement 1012.3
penalty 1009.1
penitence 873.4
sacrament 1040.5
pen-and-ink
picture 574.14
writing 602.1
penates
household gods
191.30
spirits 1014.22
pence 835.8
penchant
inclination 634.3
tendency 174.1
pencil
n. art equipment
574.19
artistic style 574.9
ray 335.5
v. mark 568.19
picture 574.20
write 602.19
penciled 602.22
pencil pushing 602.1
pencraft
handwriting 602.3
writing 602.2
pend
be uncertain 514.11
hang 215.6
pendant adjunct 41.1
hanger 215.4
likeness 20.3
types of 215.13
pendency 215
pendent hanging 215.9
uncertain 514.17
pending
adj. overhanging
215.11
pendent 215.9
uncertain 514.17
prep. during 105.14
pendulous
oscillating 323.15
pendent 215.9
pendulum
continuity 71.2
oscillator 323.9
penetrable
accessible 509.8

intelligible 548.9
permeable 265.22
vulnerable 697.16
penetrate affect 855.16
be remembered
537.14
be understood 548.5
chill 333.10
enter 302.8
infuse 44.12
insert 304.3
perforate 265.16
pervade 186.7
see through 488.8
understand 548.8
penetrating
acrimonious 161.13
caustic 939.21
cold 333.14
deep-felt 855.26
eloquent 600.11
exciting 857.29
intense 159.20
pungent 433.6
sagacious 467.16
shrill 458.14
strong-smelling
435.10
penetration
discrimination 492.2
entrance 302.1
infusion 44.2
insertion 304.1
perforation 265.3
permeation 186.3
sagacity 467.4
penicillin 687.60
peninsula
continent 386.1
point of land 256.8
peninsular 256.19
penis 419.10
penitence
apology 1012.2
penance 1012.3
repentance 873.4
penitent
n. confessor 873.5
adj. repentant 873.9
penitential
atoning 1012.7
compensating 33.6
repentant 873.9
penitentiary
clergyman 1038.9
priest 1038.5
prison 761.8
penmanship 602.3
pen name 583.8
pennant 569.6
pennate
feathered 230.28
fluffy 230.27
penned
enclosed 236.10
written 602.22
penniless 838.9
penny
British money 835.8
US money 835.7
penny-a-liner 602.16

penny-pinching
n. stinginess 852.3
adj. stingy 852.9
**penny-wise and pound-
foolish**
parsimonious 852.7
prodigal 854.8
pennyworth
bargain 849.3
worth 846.3
penology 1010.1
pen pal 604.9
penscript
handwriting 602.3
written matter 602.10
pension inn 191.16
subsidy 818.8
pensioned 784.3
pensioner
beneficiary 819.4
dependent 764.6
hireling 750.3
student 566.7
pension off
cause to resign 784.2
depose 783.4
discard 668.8
dismiss 310.19
subsidize 818.19
pensive
abstracted 532.11
melancholy 872.23
thoughtful 478.21
pensively sadly 872.34
thoughtfully 478.23
pensiveness
dreaminess 535.8
melancholy 872.5
thoughtfulness 478.3
penstock
floodgate 396.11
trough 396.3
pent(a)– 99.17
pentagonal 251.10
Pentagonese 580.10
pentane 331.1
Pentecost
holy day 1040.15
Jewish holiday
1040.16
penthouse
apartment 191.14
house 191.6
roof 228.6
pent-up
confined 761.19
enclosed 236.10
restrained 760.13
penumbra 337.3
penurious 852.8
penury 838.2
pen yan 687.12
peon peasant 919.8
retainer 750.1
slave 764.7
sycophant 907.3
peonage service 750.12
servility 907.1
subjection 764.1
people
n. family 11.5
folk 11.4

kinsmen 11.2
laity 1039.1
persons 417.2
population 190.1
race 418
the populace 919.2
v. populate 188.9
settle 184.16
peopled 188.12
peopling
population 188.2
settlement 184.6
pep eloquence 600.4
liveliness 707.2
vim 161.2
pepless 708.19
pepper
n. condiments 308.55
vim 161.2
v. fire upon 798.22
flavor 428.7
mark 568.19
shoot 285.13
sprinkle 75.6
variegate 374.7
pepper-and-salt 374.12
peppered holey 265.20
spotted 374.13
sprinkled 75.10
peppery
hot-tempered 951.25
pungent 433.7
pep pill 687.9
peppy eloquent 600.12
energetic 161.12
lively 707.17
pep rally 648.4
pepsin 309.9,25
pep talk
incitement 648.4
speech 599.2
peptic 309.20
peptic ulcer 686.27
peptide 309.6,23
pep up 161.9
per by means of 658.7
for each 80.20
in conformity with
82.9
perambulate
promenade 273.28
traverse 273.19
walk 273.26
perambulator 272.6
per annum 80.19
per capita each 80.19
proportionate 816.13
perceivable
manifest 555.8
visible 444.6
perceive detect 488.5
feel emotion 855.11
know 475.12
see 439.12
sense 422.8
understand 548.8
perceived 475.26
percent 86.6
percentage
benefit 665.4
discount 847.1
estate 810.4

expedience 670.1
  gain 811.3
  incentive 648.7
  part 55.1
  portion 816.5
  ratio 86.6
perceptible
  knowable 475.25
  manifest 555.8
  measurable 490.15
  visible 444.6
perceptibly
  manifestly 555.14
  measurably 490.16
  visibly 444.8
perception
  cognizance 475.2
  discrimination 492.2
  idea 479.1
  sagacity 467.4
  sensation 422.1
  vision 439.1
perceptive
  discriminating 492.8
  knowing 475.15
  sagacious 467.16
  sensible 422.13
perch
  n. birdhouse 191.23
  support 216.5
  v. descend 316.7
  inhabit 188.7
  rest on 216.22
  settle 184.16
  sit 268.10
perchance
  by chance 156.19
  possibly 509.9
percipient
  knowing 475.15
  sagacious 467.16
percolate
  be damp 392.11
  be learned 564.7
  exude 303.15
  filter in 302.10
  liquefy 391.5
  operate 164.7
  refine 681.22
  soak 392.13
  sorb 306.13
  trickle 395.18
percolation
  entrance 302.1
  liquefaction 391.1
  outflow 303.6
  refinement 681.4
  seepage 306.6
  soaking 392.7
  trickle 395.7
percolator 681.13
percussion
  concussion 162.8
  impact 283.3
  percussion instrument
    465.18
percussionist 464.10
percussive
  n. percussion instru-
    ment 465.18
  adj. crashing 283.21
per diem 80.19

perdition
  destruction 693.1
  hell 1019.1
  loss 812.1
perdurable
  enduring 110.10
  perpetual 112.7
perdure 110.6
peregrinate
  travel 273.20
  traverse 273.19
  wander 273.22
peregrine
  n. wanderer 274.2
  adj. walking 273.35
peremptory
  commanding 752.14
  dogmatic 513.22
  imperious 739.16
  mandatory 752.13
  obligatory 962.15
  unqualified 508.2
perennial
  n. plant 411.3
  adj. abiding 110.10
  constant 135.5
  continuous 71.8
  enduring 110.10
  evergreen 112.8
  plant 411.41
perennially
  constantly 135.7
  continuously 71.10
  perpetually 112.10
perfect
  n. tense 586.12
  v. complete 722.6
  develop 677.5
  end 70.7
  excel 36.6
  improve 691.10
  adj. accurate 516.15
  complete 722.12
  faultless 677.6
  outright 34.12
  thorough 56.10
  unqualified 508.2
  unrestricted 762.26
perfected ended 70.8
  finished 677.9
  improved 691.13
perfection
  accomplishment
    722.2
  accuracy 516.3
  completion 56.4
  culmination 677.3
  faultlessness 677
  good looks 900.4
  improvement 691.2
perfectionist
  n. conformist 82.2
  fastidious person
    896.6
  optimist 888.6
  adj. fastidious 896.9
  optimistic 888.12
perfectly
  absolutely 56.15
  accurately 516.19
  extremely 34.22
  faultlessly 677.10

perfect pitch 462.32
perfervid
  fanatical 473.32
  overzealous 635.13
  zealous 635.10
perfidious
  dishonest 975.21
  falsehearted 616.31
perfidy 975.6
perforate 265.16
perforated 265.20
perforation 265.3
perform
  accomplish 722.4
  act 611.34
  do duty 656.13
  execute 705.8
  indicate 555.5
  observe 768.3
  operate 164.7
  perform music 462.40
  produce 167.9
  represent 572.9
performable
  possible 509.7
  workable 164.10
performance
  accomplishment
    722.1
  acting 611.9
  action 705.2
  ceremony 646.4
  deed 705.3
  display 555.2
  impersonation 572.2
  music 462.31
  music program
    462.34
  observance 768.1
  operation 164.1
  production 167.1
  theatrical perfor-
    mance 611.13
performer
  affecter 903.7
  doer 718.1
  entertainer 612.1
  musician 464.1
performing
  n. acting 611.9
  impersonation 572.2
  operation 164.1
  adj. acting 705.10
perfume
  n. fragrance 436.1
  scent 436.2
  v. gas 401.8
  odorize 435.7
  scent 436.8
perfumed 436.9
perfumer
  fragrance 436.5
  merchant 830.3
  scent article 436.6
perfunctory
  careless 534.11
  indifferent 636.6
  reluctant 623.6
  unconcerned 636.7
  unwilling 623.5
perfuse insert 304.3
  transfer 271.9

treat 689.33
perfusion
  insertion 304.1
  transference 271.1
  transfusion 689.20
pergola corridor 192.18
  summerhouse 191.13
perhaps
  n. unverified supposi-
    tion 499.4
  adv. possibly 509.9
perigee
  astronomy 375.16
  nearness 200.3
  spacecraft 282.2
peril
  n. danger 697.1
  uncertainty 514.6
  v. endanger 697.6
perilous
  dangerous 697.9
  unreliable 514.19
perilously 697.17
perimeter
  bounds 235.1
  environment 233.1
period
  astronomy 375.16
  degree 29.1
  duration 105.1
  end 70.1
  geological 107.10
  menstruation 311.9
  meter 609.9
  music division 462.24
  pause 144.4
  phrase 585.1
  season 128.1
  time 107
  wave 323.4
periodic(al)
  continuous 71.8
  cyclic 137.7
  journalistic 605.26
  oscillating 323.15
  recurrent 103.13
periodical
  publication 559.1
  serial 605.10
periodically 137.10
periodicity
  continuity 71.2
  oscillation 323.1
  recurrence 137.2
  season 128.1
periodontic 688.18
periodontics 688.4
period style 901.7
peripatetic
  n. pedestrian 274.6
  wanderer 274.2
  adj. traveling 273.35
peripatetics 273.2
peripheral
  exterior 224.6
  outlinear 235.14
  surrounding 233.8
periphery
  bounds 235.1
  environment 233.1
  exterior 224.2
periscope 320.5

perish
become old 123.9
be destroyed 693.23
cease to exist 2.5
die 408.19
disappear 447.2
perishable
mortal 408.34
transient 111.7
perished 2.10
perish the thought!
969.28
peritoneum 229.3
peritonitis
gastrointestinal disease 686.27
inflammation 686.9
perjured
dishonest 975.18
untruthful 616.34
perjure oneself
be dishonest 975.12
swear falsely 616.20
perjurer 619.9
perjury
dishonesty 975.3
falsification 616.9
perks booty 824.11
extra pay 841.6
gain 811.3
gratuity 818.5
perk up cheer up 870.9
elevate 317.5
energize 161.9
get better 691.7
recuperate 694.19
refresh 695.2
perky conceited 909.11
lighthearted 870.12
lively 707.17
permanence
changelessness 140
durability 110.1
perpetuity 112.1
perseverance 625.1
stability 142.4
permanent
n. hairdo 230.15
adj. changeless 140.7
enduring 110.10
godlike 1013.20
perpetual 112.7
persevering 625.7
stable 142.17
permanently
perpetually 112.10
steadfastly 140.9
permeable
exudative 303.20
pervious 265.22
permeate infuse 44.12
pervade 186.7
soak 392.13
permeated
saturated 186.15
soaked 392.17
permeation
infusion 44.2
pervasion 186.3
soaking 392.7
permissible 777.15

permission
allowance 777
consent 775.1
exemption 762.8
ratification 521.4
permissive
n. mood 586.11
adj. consenting 775.4
indulgent 759.8
lax 758.4
negligent 534.10
nonrestrictive 762.24
permitting 777.14
permissiveness
indulgence 759.3
neglect 534.1
sufferance 777.2
tolerance 526.4
unrestraint 762.3
unstrictness 758.1
permit
n. license 777.6
v. allow 777.9
consent 775.2
make possible 509.5
ratify 521.12
permitted
allowed 777.16
exempt 762.29
permutable
changeable 141.6
interchangeable
150.5
permutation
interchange 150.1
transformation 139.2
pernicious fatal 409.23
harmful 675.12
pernickety 896.10
perorate
declaim 599.10
end 70.5
expatiate 593.8
peroration end 70.1
sequel 67.1
speech 599.2
peroxide
n. bleach 363.10
v. decolor 363.5
perpend 478.12
perpendicular
n. straight line 250.2
vertical 213.2
adj. orthogonal 251.7
plumb 213.12
perpetrate 705.6
perpetration 705.2
perpetual
constant 135.5
enduring 110.10
everlasting 112.7
godlike 1013.20
infinite 104.3
permanent 140.7
perpetually
constantly 135.7
everlastingly 112.10
permanently 140.9
perpetuate
preserve 112.5
sustain 143.4

perpetuation
continuance 143.1
preservation 112.4
perpetuity
constancy 135.2
durability 110.1
eternity 112
infinity 104.1
length 202.1
perplex astonish 920.6
be incomprehensible
549.10
bewilder 514.13
complicate 46.3
confuse 532.7
make doubt 503.7
thwart 730.15
trouble 731.12
perplexed
at an impasse 731.22
bewildered 514.24
complex 46.4
confused 532.12
hard to understand
549.14
perplexing
bewildering 514.25
inexplicable 549.17
perplexity
bewilderment 514.3
complexity 46.1
confusion 532.3
dilemma 731.6
obscurity 549.3
puzzle 549.8
perquisite
belonging 810.2
booty 824.11
extra pay 841.6
gain 811.3
gratuity 818.5
per se essentially 5.10
singly 89.13
persecute annoy 866.13
make anxious 890.4
oppress 667.6
work evil 675.6
persecuted
tormented 866.24
worried 890.7
persecution
annoyance 866.2
mistreatment 667.3
torment 866.7
persecutor 866.10
Persephone
agriculture divinity
413.4
deity of nether world
1019.5
goddess 1014.5
perseverance
continuance 143.1
obstinacy 626.1
patience 861.1
persistence 625
resolution 624.1
persevere
be obstinate 626.7
be patient 861.5
continue 143.5
persist 625.2

succeed 724.12
persevering
obstinate 626.8
patient 861.9
persistent 625.7
resolute 624.11
persiflage banter 882.1
witticism 881.7
persist cohere 50.6
continue 143.5
endure 110.6
insist 753.7
keep alive 407.10
live on 1.9
persevere 625.2
prevail 17.3
remain 140.5
retain 813.5
persistence
continuance 143.1
durability 110.1
insistence 753.3
permanence 140.1
perseverance 625.1
resolution 624.1
tenacity 50.3
uniformity 17.1
persistent
adhesive 50.12
continuing 143.7
demanding 753.8
habitual 642.16
long-lasting 110.10
permanent 140.7
persevering 625.7
resolute 624.11
reverberating 454.11
unforgettable 537.26
uniform 17.5
persistently
for a long time
110.14
habitually 642.23
perseveringly 625.8
resolutely 624.17
persnickety 896.10
person body 376.3
entity 3.3
grammatical form
586.7
human 417.3
individual 89.4
physique 246.4
role 611.11
persona individual 89.4
person 3.3
psyche 690.35
personable
beautiful 900.17
influential 172.13
personage chief 749.3
famous person 914.9
important person
672.8
person 417.3
role 611.11
persona grata 985.1
personal
individual 417.12
particular 80.12
private 614.13

personality
  disparagement 971.4
  entity 3.3
  individuality 80.1
  influence 172.1
  person 417.3
  personage 672.8
  psyche 690.35
personalization
  differentiation 16.4
  particularization 80.7
personalize
  differentiate 16.6
  figure of speech 551.2
  particularize 80.9
personally
  individually 80.16
  in person 186.17
persona non grata
  bad person 986.1
  outcast 926.4
  outsider 77.3
personate act 611.35
  impersonate 572.9
  represent 572.8
personation
  acting 611.9
  impersonation 572.2
personification
  embodiment 376.7
  impersonation 572.2
personify
  embody 376.8
  figure of speech 551.2
  represent 572.8
personnel
  reserves 149.2
  staff 750.11
  work force 157.9
persons 417.2
perspective
  artistry 574.10
  distance 199.1
  outlook 444.3
  station 184.2
  view 446.6
perspicacious
  discriminating 492.8
  knowing 475.15
  sagacious 467.16
perspicacity
  discrimination 492.2
  sagacity 467.4
  vision 439.1
perspicuity
  intelligibility 548.2
  literary elegance 589.1
  manifestness 555.3
  sagacity 467.4
  vision 439.1
perspicuous
  intelligible 548.10
  manifest 555.8
  polished 589.6
  sagacious 467.16
perspiration 311.7
perspire 311.16
perspiring 311.22

persuadable
  gullible 502.9
  influenceable 172.15
  open-minded 526.10
persuade advise 754.6
  convert 145.16
  convince 501.18
  induce 648.23
  influence 172.7
persuaded
  believing 501.21
  sure 513.21
persuasion
  conversion 145.6
  inducement 648.3
  influence 172.1
  kind 61.3
  religion 1020.3
  school 788.5
  strong belief 501.5
persuasive
  n. incentive 648.7
  adj. cajoling 648.29
  convincing 501.26
  influential 172.13
pert cheerful 870.13
  conceited 909.11
  defiant 793.7
  impudent 913.9
  lively 707.17
pertaining
  comparable 9.7
  relevant 9.11
pertain to
  belong to 808.7
  relate to 9.5
pertinacious
  bold 893.18
  demanding 753.8
  obstinate 626.8
  persevering 625.7
pertinacity
  courage 893.4
  insistence 753.3
  obstinacy 626.1
  perseverance 625.1
pertinence
  meaning 545.1
  relevance 9.4
pertinent
  comparable 9.7
  relevant 9.11
pertness
  animation 161.3
  conceit 909.4
  defiance 793.1
  lightheartedness 870.3
perturb agitate 324.10
  bewilder 514.12
  confuse 532.7
  discompose 63.4
  disorder 62.9
  distress 866.16
  excite 857.13
  trouble 731.12
perturbation
  agitation 324.1
  anxiety 890.1
  confusion 532.3
  discomposure 63.1
  disorder 62.1

excitation 857.10
  perplexity 514.3
  trepidation 891.5
  turmoil 857.3
perturbed
  agitated 324.16
  anxious 890.6
  bewildered 514.23
  confused 532.12
  disorderly 62.13
  distressed 866.22
  excited 857.21
  troubled 731.19
perturbing
  bewildering 514.25
  exciting 857.28
peruke 230.14
perusal
  examination 485.3
  study 564.3
peruse examine 485.23
  scrutinize 439.15
  study 564.12
pervade infuse 44.12
  permeate 186.7
pervading
  deep-felt 855.26
  pervasive 186.14
pervasion infusion 44.2
  permeation 186.3
pervasive
  pervading 186.14
  thorough 56.10
perverse contrary 15.6
  counteractive 178.8
  erroneous 518.16
  irascible 951.19
  obstinate 626.11
  opposing 790.8
  unwieldy 731.18
perversely
  ill-humoredly 951.27
  obstinately 626.16
perversion
  corruption 692.2
  distortion 249.2
  error 518.1
  falsification 616.9
  misinterpretation 553.1
  misrepresentation 573.1
  misteaching 563.1
  misuse 667.1
  sexual abnormality 419.13
  sophistry 483.1
perversity
  contrariety 15.1
  irascibility 951.2
  obstinacy 626.3
pervert
  n. bad person 986.5
  deviant 419.18
  v. corrupt 692.14
  distort 249.6
  falsify 616.16
  misinterpret 553.2
  misrepresent 573.3
  misteach 563.3
  misuse 667.4

reason speciously 483.8
perverted
  bisexual 419.32
  distorted 249.11
  erroneous 518.16
  falsified 616.26
  misinterpreted 553.3
  morally corrupt 981.14
pervious
  accessible 509.8
  exudative 303.20
  influenceable 172.15
  permeable 265.22
pes 212.5
pesky 864.22
pessimism
  cynicism 889.6
  dread 539.3
  sadness 872.3
pessimist cynic 889.7
  killjoy 872.14
pessimistic
  cynical 889.16
  dejected 872.22
pest annoyance 866.2
  bane 676.1
  blight 676.2
  boring person 884.4
  epidemic 686.4
  tormentor 866.10
pester annoy 866.13
  importune 774.12
  nag 969.16
pestered 866.24
pestering
  n. disapproval 969.4
  importuning 774.3
  adj. annoying 864.22
  importunate 774.18
pesthole
  filthy place 682.11
  plague spot 686.4
pesthouse 689.28
pesticide killer 409.11
  killing 409.3
  poison 676.3
pestiferous
  annoying 864.22
  contagious 686.58
  poisonous 684.7
  unhealthful 684.5
pestilence bane 676.1
  epidemic 686.4
pestle
  n. pulverizer 361.7
  v. pulverize 361.9
pet
  n. anger 952.7
  endearment 932.5
  favorite 931.15
  v. caress 932.14
  make love 932.13
  rub 350.6
  touch 425.8
  adj. beloved 931.22
petal
  flower part 411.26
  leaf 411.17
petcock 396.10

peter out
become exhausted
717.5
be consumed 666.3
be disappointing
541.3
be unproductive
166.3
cease to exist 2.5
fall through 314.3
weaken 160.9
petite 196.10
petit four 308.41
petition
n. prayer 1032.4
request 774.1
v. pray 1032.12
request 774.10
petitionary 774.16
petitioner
accuser 1005.5
supplicant 774.7
worshiper 1032.9
petit mal 686.5
pet name 583.7
pet peeve
complaint 875.4
grudge 929.5
hated thing 930.3
petrification
antiquity 123.6
hardening 356.5
petrifaction 384.7
petrified
antiquated 123.13
hardened 356.13
mineral 383.15
stone 384.10
terrified 891.34
petrified forest 123.6
petrify astonish 920.6
harden 356.7
lithify 384.9
mineralize 383.13
terrify 891.25
petrifying
hardening 356.14
terrifying 891.37
petrol
illuminant 335.20
petroleum 380.4
petroleum
illuminant 335.20
oil 380.4,11
petrology
geology 384.8
minerology 383.10
petticoat
n. undergarment
231.58
adj. feminine 421.13
pettifog argue 482.16
find fault 969.15
pettifogger
faultfinder 969.9
lawyer 1003.3
quibbler 483.7
sharper 619.4
pettifoggery
chicanery 618.4
sophistry 483.5

pettiness
baseness 915.3
inferiority 37.3
narrow-mindedness
527.1
selfishness 978.2
smallness 35.1
unimportance 673.1
petting
lovemaking 932.1
touching 425.2
pettish 951.21
petty base 915.12
inferior 37.7
insignificant 35.6
narrow-minded
527.10
quibbling 483.14
selfish 978.6
trivial 673.17
petty cash 835.19
petty officer 749.20
petulance
capriciousness 629.2
complaint 875.4
discontent 869.1
ill humor 951.5
petulant
capricious 629.5
discontented 869.5
ill-humored 951.21
plaintive 875.16
pew
church seat 1042.14
compartment 192.2
pewter 383.17
peyote 687.13,53
pfc. 800.8
Phaëthon deity 1014.5
sun god 375.14
phalanx group 74.3
military unit 800.19
phallic 419.27
phallic symbol 690.37
phallus 419.10
phantasm
deception 618.1
phantom 519.4
specter 1017.1
thing imagined 535.5
phantasmagoria
phantom 519.4
spectacle 446.7
phantasmagoric 519.9
phantasmal
ghostly 1017.7
illusory 519.9
imaginary 535.22
phantasy see **fantasy**
phantom
n. apparition 446.5
frightener 891.9
illusion 519.4
specter 1017.1
spirit 4.3
thing imagined 535.5
adj. ghostly 1017.7
illusory 519.9
immaterial 377.7
phantomlike
ghostly 1017.7
tenuous 4.6

pharaoh
autocrat 749.14
ruler 749.8
pharisaic(al)
hypocritic(al) 616.33
sanctimonious 1029.5
pharisee deceiver 619.8
hypocrite 1029.3
pharmaceutic(al)
687.50
pharmaceutics 687.34
pharmacist 687.35
pharmacological 687.50
pharmacologist 687.35
pharmacology
biology 406.17
pharmacy 687.34
pharmacopoeia 687.37
pharmacy
drugstore 687.36
hospital room 192.25
pharmacology 687.34
store types 832.4
pharos mark 568.10
observation post
439.8
pharyngeal
n. speech sound
594.13
adj. phonetic 594.31
pharynx gullet 396.15
vocal organ 594.19
phase 446.3
phatic 547.6
phenobarbital
687.12,54
phenomenal
eventful 151.10
extraordinary 85.14
wonderful 920.10
phenomenology 500.1
phenomenon
apparition 446.5
event 151.2
marvel 920.2
phew!
unpleasantness
864.31
wonder 920.20
Philadelphia lawyer
arguer 482.12
cunning person 735.6
lawyer 1003.3
philander
be unchaste 989.19
flirt 932.18
philanderer
beau 931.12
unchaste person
989.10
woman chaser 932.11
philandering 932.9
philanthropic
benevolent 938.15
giving 818.22
philanthropist
altruist 938.8
giver 818.11
philanthropy
benevolence 938.4
charity 818.3
philharmonic 462.48

Philharmonic 464.12
philippic
berating 969.7
speech 599.2
Philistine
n. conformist 82.2
vulgar person 898.6
adj. callous 856.12
unlearned 477.14
vulgar 898.14
worldly 1031.16
philological 580.17
philologist
linguist 580.13
scholar 476.3
philology 580.12
philosopher
names of 500.13
reasoner 482.11
scholar 476.3
thinker 500.6
types of 500.12
wise man 468.1
philosophical
composed 858.12
patient 861.9
sensible 467.18
thinking 500.8
philosophize
practice philosophy
500.7
reason 482.15
philosophy
composure 858.2
ideology 479.8
physics 325.1
reasoning 482.1
schools of 500.11
thought 500
phlebitis 686.9
phlebotomy
bloodletting 689.26
extraction 305.3
phlegm apathy 856.4
body fluid 388.3
languor 708.6
phlegmatic
n. personality type
690.15
adj. apathetic 856.13
incurious 529.3
inert 268.14
languid 708.19
phobia
fear 891.1,10–17
hated thing 930.3
neurosis 690.19
phobic 690.45
Phoebe five 99.1
moon goddess 375.12
Phoebus god 1014.5
sun god 375.14
phon 450.7
phonate 594.23
phone
n. sound 450.1
speech 594.13
telephone 560.4
types of 448.18
v. telephone 560.18
phone book
directory 748.10

pigment
n. art equipment 574.19
black 365.14
blue 372.4
brown 367.6
coloring matter 362.8
gray 366.6
green 371.6
orange 369.3
pink 368.13
purple 373.4
red 368.12
reddish brown 367.7
white 364.11
yellow 370.7
v. color 362.13

pigmentation 362.11

pigsty
filthy place 682.11
hovel 191.12

pigtail
chewing tobacco 434.7
hair 230.7,30
tail 241.6

pike peak 207.8
road 657.6

piker gambler 515.17
vagabond 274.3

pilaster pillar 217.5
post 216.8
tower 207.11

pile
n. atomics 326.13
building 245.2
cardiovascular disease 686.17
down 230.19
hair 230.2
heap 74.10
leaf 411.17
much 34.4
plant beard 230.9
post 216.8
sore 686.35
stake 217.6
store 660.1
texture 351.1
wealth 837.2
v. heap 74.19
pile in 315.12
put 184.14

pile drive 283.11
pile house 398.3
pile it on
be bombastic 601.6
exaggerate 617.3
overdo 663.11

pile out 713.6
pileup 729.2
pile up heap 74.19
shipwreck 275.42
store up 660.11

pilfer misuse 667.4
steal 824.13

pilfering misuse 667.1
theft 824.1

pilgrim
religious 1038.17
traveler 274.1

pilgrimage
n. journey 273.5
quest 715.2
v. travel 273.20

pill bad person 986.6
boring person 884.4
medicine 687.7

pill, the 687.23

pillage
n. plundering 824.5
v. plunder 824.16
seize 822.14
wreck 162.10

pillaging
n. plundering 824.5
rapacity 822.9
violence 162.3
adj. plunderous 824.21

pillar base 216.8
column 217.5
cylinder 255.4
memorial 570.12
protector 699.5
stability 142.6
tower 207.11

pillar of society
good person 985.3
personage 672.8

pillbox 799.6

pillhead 642.10

pillory
n. restraint 760.4
stocks 1011.3
v. disgrace 915.8
punish 1010.10
ridicule 967.8
stigmatize 915.9

pillow
n. bedding 216.20
softness 357.4
v. support 216.21

pillowcase 228.10

pilose 230.24

pilot
n. aviator 279.1
boatman 276.8
guide 748.7
operator 164.4
safety equipment 699.3
v. direct 747.9
fly 278.46
operate 164.5
steer 275.14
adj. experimental 489.11

pilotage aviation 278.1
direction 747.1
fee 846.7
navigation 275.2
pilotship 275.4
position 184.3

pilot balloon 489.4

pilot light 329.10

pilot model
model 25.5
original 23.2

pilot program 489.3

pilotship
airmanship 278.3
helmsmanship 275.4

pilpul 482.4

pily 351.7

pimp
n. bad person 986.5
procurer 989.18
v. be unchaste 989.21

pimping 989.8

pimple
n. blemish 679.1
mark 568.7
sore 686.35
swelling 256.4
v. roughen 261.4

pimply
blemished 679.8
rough 261.6

pin
n. axle 322.5
insignia 569.1
jewel 901.6
legs 273.16
stopper 266.4
trifle 673.5
v. fasten 47.8

pinafore 231.17,55

pinball 515.8

pinball machine 515.12

pince-nez 443.2

pincers
contractor 198.6
extractor 305.9
grasping organs 813.4

pinch
n. arrest 761.6
a theft 824.10
crisis 129.4
danger 697.1
difficulty 731.7
indigence 838.2
pain 424.2
predicament 731.4
small amount 35.2
small place 196.3
squeezing 198.2
urge 648.6
urgency 672.4
v. arrest 761.16
be parsimonious 852.5
converge 298.2
hurt 424.7
sail 275.25
squeeze 198.8
steal 824.13
adj. substitute 149.8

pinch bar 287.4

pinchbeck
n. fake 616.13
ornamentation 901.3
adj. ungenuine 616.26

pinched
constricted 198.12
in trouble 731.24
poor 838.7
thin 205.20

pinch-hit
represent 781.14
substitute for 149.5

pinch hitter
deputy 781.1
substitute 149.2

pinching
n. parsimony 852.1
theft 824.1
adj. cold 333.14
stingy 852.9

pinch pennies 852.5

pinchpenny 852.8

pindling 196.10

pin down
localize 184.10
restrain 760.10
specify 80.11
stabilize 142.7

pine deteriorate 692.21
fail 686.45
grieve 872.17
weaken 160.9
wish for 634.16

pine barrens 411.11

pine cone cone 255.5
inflorescence 411.25

pinfeather 230.16

pinhead dolt 471.4
point 196.7
top part 211.4

pinhole 265.4

pining
n. sorrow 872.10
yearning 634.5
adj. dejected 872.22
deteriorating 692.46
languishing 160.21
wistful 634.23

pinion
n. feather 230.16
wing 55.4
v. restrain 760.10

pinioned 230.28

pink
n. acme of perfection 677.3
colors 368.13
pinkness 368.2
radical 745.12
v. notch 262.4
puncture 265.16
adj. healthy 685.11
pinkish 368.8
radical 745.20

pink elephants 473.10

pink eye 686.13

pinkie 425.5

pinko 745.12

pink slip 310.5

pin money 835.19

pinnacle
completion 56.5
culmination 677.3
peak 207.8
summit 211.2
tower 207.11

pinnate 230.27

pin on accuse 1005.7
attribute to 155.4

pinpoint
n. location 184.1
point 196.7
v. attribute to 155.4
locate 184.10
use radar 346.17
adj. exact 516.16

rain 394.1
repetitiousness 103.4
staccato sound 455.1
v. flutter 324.12
make staccato sounds
455.4
rain 394.9

pity
n. leniency 759.1
sympathy 944
wrong 959.2
v. be sorry for 944.3

pitying 944.7

pivot
n. axis 322.5
center 226.2
fulcrum 287.3
important point
672.6
joint 47.4
v. rotate 322.9
turn around 295.9

pivotal causal 153.14
central 226.11
critical 129.10
urgent 672.21

pivoting 322.1

pivot on 154.6

pixie evil spirit 1016.8
fairy 1014.18
mischief-maker 738.3

pixieish 1014.27

pixilated 473.28

pizzazz liveliness 707.2
power 157.1
vim 161.2

pizzeria 307.15

pizzicato
n. music 462.25
music style 462.31
adv. music 462.54

PJ's 231.21

PKU 686.20

placable
forgiving 947.6
pacifiable 804.13

placard
n. poster 559.7
v. publicize 559.15

placate 804.7

placation 804.1

placative 804.12

place
n. abode 191.1
arena 802.1
city district 183.8
duty 962.1
function 656.3
house and grounds
191.7
location 184.1
mental outlook 525.2
opportunity 129.2
order 59.2
position 656.5
rank 29.2
region 180.1
road 657.6
serving 307.10
state 7.1
stead 184.4
turn 108.2

v. attribute 155.3
classify 61.6
dispose 60.9
impose 963.4
install 780.11
invest 836.16
locate 184.10
put 184.11
recognize 537.12

placed arranged 60.14
classified 61.8
located 184.17

placement
arrangement 60.1
attribution 155.1
classification 61.1
grouping 60.3
installation 780.3
location 184.1
positioning 184.5

placenta 67.3

placer 383.7

placid calm 268.12
composed 858.12

placidly
inexcitably 858.16
quietly 268.18

placket 265.4

plage 385.2

plagiarism
borrowing 821.2
imitation 22.1
piracy 824.7
repetition 103.1

plagiarist
deceiver 619.1
imitator 22.4
literary pirate 825.9

plagiarize borrow 821.4
imitate 22.5
pirate 824.18
repeat 103.7

plagiarized
imitation 22.8
repeated 103.12
stolen 824.22

plague
n. bane 676.1
epidemic 686.4
locusts 74.6
overrunning 313.2
v. annoy 866.13
importune 774.12
make anxious 890.4
overrun 313.6
trouble 731.12
vex 864.15

plagued
infested 313.11
remembering 537.24
tormented 866.24
troubled 731.19
worried 890.7

plaguing
n. importuning 774.3
adj. annoying 864.22
importunate 774.18
troublesome 890.9

plaid
n. check 374.4
adj. checked 374.14

plain
n. horizontal 214.3
level land 387
space 179.4
the country 182.1
adj. artless 736.5
audible 450.16
candid 974.17
champaign 387.3
clearly visible 444.7
common 919.11
dull 883.8
easy 732.12
elegant 589.6
flat 214.7
homelike 191.33
humble 906.9
informal 647.3
in plain style 591.3
intelligible 548.10
manifest 555.8
mere 35.8
ordinary 902.6
prosaic 610.5
simple 45.6
thorough 56.10
ugly 899.6
adv. absolutely 56.15

plainclothesman 781.10

plain English
intelligibility 548.2
plain speech 591.1

plain folks 919.1

plainly artlessly 736.7
audibly 450.18
candidly 974.23
informally 647.4
in plain words 591.4
intelligibly 548.12
manifestly 555.14
ordinarily 902.10
simply 45.11
visibly 444.8

plainness
artlessness 736.1
candor 974.4
communicativeness
554.3
dullness 883.2
humility 906.1
informality 647.1
intelligibility 548.2
literary elegance
589.1
manifestness 555.3
ordinariness 902
plain speech 591.1
prosaism 610.2
simplicity 45.1
ugliness 899.1
visibility 444.2

plainsman 387.2

plain speech
intelligibility 548.2
plain speaking 591

plain-spoken
candid 974.17
free-spoken 762.22
in plain style 591.3
speaking 594.32

plaint
accusation 1005.1

lament 875.3

plaintiff accuser 1005.5
litigant 1004.11
oppositionist 791.3

plaintive
mournful 875.16
sorrowful 872.26

plaintively
lamentingly 875.19
sorrowfully 872.36

plait
n. hair 230.7
layer 227.2
pleat 264.2
weaving 222.2
v. fold 264.5
weave 222.6

plaited folded 264.7
woven 222.7

plan
n. intention 653.1
meaning 545.2
outline 48.4
representation 572.1
scheme 654
story element 608.9
structure 245.1
undertaking 715.1
v. create 167.13
devise 654.9
foresee 121.6
intend 653.4
organize 60.10
prearrange 641.3
premeditate 653.8
prepare 720.6

plane
n. aircraft 280.1
degree 29.1
horizontal 214.3
smooth surface 260.3
types of 348.17
v. smooth 260.5
soar 315.10
adj. flat 214.7
smooth 260.9

planet 375.9

planetarium 375.17

planetary
celestial 375.25
universal 79.14
wandering 291.7

plangent loud 453.10
mournful 875.16
resonant 454.9
sorrowful 872.26

planimetry 490.9

plank
n. political platform
744.7
slab 227.2
strip 206.4
wood 378.3
v. cover 228.23
put violently 184.12

plank down 841.16

planking side 242.1
wood 378.3

plankton algae 411.42
animal 414.35

planless 62.12

planned devised 654.13

future 121.8
intentional 653.9
prearranged 641.5
prepared 720.16
planner designer 654.7
producer 167.8
planning
organization 60.2
prearrangement
641.1
preparation 720.1
scheme 654.1
plan on expect 539.9
figure on 653.6
plant
n. equipment 659.4
shill 619.5
vegetable 411.3
vegetation 411
workplace 719.3
v. establish 184.15
implant 413.18
infix 142.9
populate 188.9
secrete 615.7
tamper with 616.17
plantar 212.9
plantation farm 413.8
peopling 188.2
settlement 184.6
vegetation 411.2
plant-eater 307.14
planted 184.17
planter
agriculturist 413.5
farm hand 413.5
settler 190.9
planting plants 411.2
sowing 413.14
plant life 411.1
plantlike 411.33
plaque 570.12
plash
n. body of water
398.1
lap 395.8
rainstorm 394.2
sprinkle 392.5
v. lap 395.19
make a liquid sound
452.11
plashy muddy 389.14
watery 392.16
plasma 388.4
plasmic
metabolic 246.10
protoplasmic 406.20
plaster
n. adherent 50.4
building material
378.2
medical dressing
687.33
pulp 390.2
types of 228.44
v. cover 228.25
make drunk 996.22
smooth 260.5
treat 689.30
plastered 996.31
plastic
n. resin 381.1

synthetic 378.7
types of 378.14
adj. changeable 141.6
conformable 82.5
conformist 82.6
docile 765.13
formative 246.9
influenceable 172.15
mediocre 680.8
plasmatic 246.10
pliant 357.9
teachable 564.18
Plasticine 575.4
plasticity
changeableness 141.1
pliancy 357.2
submissiveness 765.3
teachability 564.5
plastic person 82.2
plastic surgery
operation 689.25
surgery 688.3
plat
n. field 413.9
pleat 264.2
real estate 810.7
tract 180.4
v. fold 264.5
plate
n. covering 228.13
engraving 578.7
false teeth 258.6
label 568.13
layer 227.2
meat 308.17
photography 577.10
printing surface 603.8
serving 307.10
shell 228.15
v. cover 228.26
plateau degree 29.1
interim 109.1
plain 387.1
tableland 207.4
plated 228.32
platen 603.9,26
platform
n. arena 802.1
horizontal 214.3
mark 568.10
policy 654.5
political platform
744.7
stage 216.13
v. make a speech
599.9
plating coating 228.13
layer 227.2
platinum blond 362.9
platinum-blond 364.9
platitude cliché 517.3
truism 79.8
platitudinous
aphoristic 517.6
banal 883.9
trite 79.16
well-known 475.27
Platonic chaste 988.6
idealist 377.8
philosophy 500.10
Platonic love
chastity 988.3

love 931.1
platoon group 74.3
military unit 800.19
team 788.7
platter 570.10
platypus 414.58; 415.8
plaudit 968.2
plausibility
believability 501.8
probability 511.3
reasonableness 482.9
superficial soundness
483.1
plausible
believable 501.24
false 616.27
logical 482.20
possible 509.6
probable 511.7
specious 483.10
play
n. action 705.1
computer 349.19
frolic 878.5
fun 878.2
gambling 515.7
game 878.9
joke 881.6
latitude 762.4
light 335.8
risk 515.1
space 179.3
stage show 611.4
wager 515.3
written matter 602.10
v. act 611.34
affect 903.12
be operative 164.7
bet 515.20
fake 616.21
flicker 335.25
gamble 515.18
jet 395.20
operate 164.5
perform action 705.4
perform music 462.40
represent 572.9
sport 878.25
trifle 673.13
use 665.10
playa plain 387.1
shore 385.2
playacting acting 611.9
fakery 616.3
playactor actor 612.2
affecter 903.7
deceiver 619.1
play around flirt 932.18
trifle 673.13
play around with
consider 478.12
try out 489.8
play ball 786.3
playbill 641.2
playbook book 605.1
script 611.26
playboy player 878.19
sociable person
922.15
playbroker 611.30
play by ear
be unprepared 721.6

improvise 630.8
perform music 462.40
play by the rules 974.9
play down
de-emphasize 673.11
minimize 39.9
moderate 163.6
play dumb
be silent 451.5
keep secret 614.7
played out
exhausted 717.8
weakened 160.18
worn-out 692.38
player actor 612.2
athlete 878.20
competitor 791.2
frolicker 878.19
gambler 515.17
musician 464.1
play favorites 977.8
playful frisky 870.14
mischievous 738.6
prankish 881.17
sportive 878.31
playfulness gaiety 870.4
mischief 738.2
wittiness 881.4
play games 735.10
play God 961.8
playgoer 611.32
playground 878.12
play havoc with
bungle 734.11
impair 692.12
work evil 675.6
play hooky 187.9
playhouse
small place 196.3
theater 611.18
playing
n. acting 611.9
gambling 515.7
impersonation 572.2
trifling 673.8
adj. flickering 335.36
playing cards 878.17
playing field 878.12
playmate
companion 928.3
mistress 989.17
partner 787.2
play-off 878.9
play on exploit 665.16
impose 963.7
play on words
n. wordplay 881.8
v. joke 881.13
play out 717.5
playroom
playground 878.12
recreation room
192.12
play safe
keep safe 698.3
take precautions
895.6
play the game
be fair 976.7
behave oneself 737.5
conform 82.4

observe the proprie-
ties 645.4
play the market 833.23
plaything dupe 620.1
instrument 658.3
toy 878.16
play up 672.15
play up to
befriend 927.11
curry favor 907.8
flatter 970.6
play with fire
be reckless 894.6
defy danger 697.7
mishandle 734.14
playwright 611.27
plaza city district 183.8
marketplace 832.2
plea argument 482.5
entreaty 774.2
justification 1006.2
legal plea 1004.6
pleach 222.6
plead
adduce evidence
505.13
argue 482.16
argue one's case
1004.18
entreat 774.11
urge 648.14
pleader deputy 781.1
justifier 1006.8
lawyer 1003.1
motivator 648.10
plead guilty
confess 556.7
repent 873.7
pleading
n. argument 482.5
justification 1006.2
lawyers 1003.1
legal plea 1004.6
adj. imploring 774.17
pleasance park 878.14
pleasantness 863.1
pleasant
cheerful 870.11
friendly 927.14
good 674.12
melodious 462.49
pleasing 863.6
rainless 393.8
pleasantly
amicably 927.21
cheerfully 870.17
pleasingly 863.11
pleasantness
cheerfulness 870.1
goodness 674.1
pleasingness 863
pleasantry banter 882.1
humor 881.1
jocularity 881.2
pleasantness 863.1
witticism 881.7
please
v. give pleasure 865.5
indulge 759.6
prefer 637.17
interj. if you please
774.20

pleased
contented 868.7
delighted 865.12
pleasing
n. indulgence 759.3
adj. beautiful 900.17
desirable 634.30
eloquent 600.9
pleasant 863.6
tasteful 897.8
tasty 428.8
welcome 925.12
pleasurable 863.6
pleasure
amusement 878.1
command 752.1
desire 634.1
enjoyment 865
option 637.2
pleasantness 863.1
will 621.1
pleasureless
joyless 866.20
unhappy 872.21
pleasure-loving
n. pleasure principle
865.4
adj. pleasure-seeking
865.15
pleasure principle
desire 634.1
pleasure-loving 865.4
psyche 690.35
sensuality 987.1
pleasure-seeker
player 878.19
sensualist 987.3
pleasure-seeking
n. sensuality 987.1
adj. pleasure-loving
865.15
sensual 987.5
pleat
n. fold 264.2
trench 263.2
v. fold 264.5
groove 263.3
pleated folded 264.7
grooved 263.4
plebe 566.6
plebeian
n. common man
919.7
adj. common 919.11
vulgar 898.14
plebiscite
referendum 742.16
vote 637.6
pledge
n. debt 840.1
drink 996.9
member 788.11
oath 523.3
promise 770.1
security 772.2
v. contribute 818.14
drink 307.27
give security 772.10
obligate 962.12
promise 770.4
toast 996.28
pledged affirmed 523.8

chargeable 840.9
obliged 962.16
promised 770.8
staked 772.12
pledget 687.33
pleiad 914.9
Pleiades
nymphs 1014.19
star cluster 375.8
plenary full 56.11
great 34.6
unrestricted 762.26
plenipotentiary
n. diplomat 781.6
adj. diplomatic 781.16
omnipotent 157.13
plenitude
continuity 71.1
fullness 56.2
greatness 34.1
intactness 677.2
plenty 661.2
quantity 34.3
store 660.1
plentiful
abundant 101.8
much 34.8
plenty 661.7
productive 165.9
superabundant
663.19
plenty
n. numerousness
101.1
overabundance 663.2
plenitude 661.2
quantity 34.3
store 660.1
adj. plentiful 661.7
sufficient 661.6
adv. greatly 34.15
plenum continuity 71.2
matter 376.2
meeting 74.2
universe 375.1
plethora fullness 56.2
overabundance 663.2
overfullness 663.3
pleura 229.3
pleurisy 686.14
plexiform 221.11
plexus ganglion 422.6
network 221.3
pliability
irresolution 627.4
pliancy 357.2
submissiveness 765.3
teachability 564.5
wieldiness 732.2
willingness 622.1
pliable docile 765.13
folded 264.7
influenceable 172.15
irresolute 627.12
pliant 357.9
teachable 564.18
usable 665.22
wieldy 732.14
pliant
conformable 82.5
docile 765.13
influenceable 172.15

pliable 357.9
unstrict 758.5
wieldy 732.14
willing 622.5
plicate
v. fold 264.5
adj. folded 264.7
pliers 305.9
plight
n. adversity 729.1
danger 697.1
perplexity 514.3
predicament 731.4
promise 770.1
state 7.1
v. affiance 770.6
promise 770.4
plighted 770.8
plinth 216.8
plod
n. slowness 270.2
v. drudge 716.14
go slowly 270.7
persevere 625.3
walk 273.27
plodder drudge 718.3
slow person 270.5
plodding
n. perseverance 625.1
adj. laboring 716.17
persevering 625.7
uninteresting 883.6
plop
v. bubble 405.4
plunge 320.6
put violently 184.12
sink 316.6
adv. squarely 290.25
suddenly 113.9
plot
n. diagram 654.3
field 413.9
intrigue 654.6
real estate 810.7
story element 608.9
stratagem 735.3
tract 180.4
v. foresee 121.6
maneuver 735.10
map 654.11
prearrange 641.3
premeditate 653.8
scheme 654.10
plotted future 121.8
measured 490.14
planned 654.13
prearranged 641.5
plotter schemer 654.8
traitor 619.10
plotting
n. intrigue 654.6
prearrangement
641.1
adj. scheming 654.14
plow
n. farm machine
348.22
v. fly 278.49
groove 263.3
till 413.17
plowland 413.8
plowman 413.5

ploy influence 172.3
  revel 878.6
  stratagem 735.3
  trick 618.6
pluck
  n. courage 893.5
  jerk 286.3
  spunk 624.3
  v. despoil 822.24
  divest 232.5
  extract 305.10
  fail someone 725.16
  harvest 413.19
  jerk 286.5
  procure 811.10
  strum 462.41
plucky bold 893.18
  resolute 624.14
plug
  n. commendation
    968.3
  hydrant 396.12
  inferior horse 414.14
  publicity 559.4
  radio 344.20
  snare 618.12
  stopper 266.4
  v. commend 968.11
  drudge 716.14
  persevere 625.3
  plod 270.7
  publicize 559.15
  shoot 285.13
  stop 266.7
plug away
  be industrious 707.15
  drudge 716.14
  persevere 625.3
plugged 266.11
plugging
  n. perseverance 625.1
  adj. laboring 716.17
  persevering 625.7
plug in 342.23
plug-ugly
  combatant 800.1
  evildoer 943.4
plum
  British money 835.8
  dividend 834.7
  good thing 674.5
  political patronage
    744.36
  purple color 373.4
  thing desired 634.11
plumage 230.18
plumb
  n. plumb line 213.6
  vertical 213.2
  weight 352.6
  v. close 266.6
  fathom 209.9
  investigate 485.22
  make vertical 213.10
  measure 490.11
  solve 487.2
  understand 548.8
  adj. perpendicular
    213.12
  thorough 56.10
  adv. absolutely 56.15
  exactly 516.20

perpendicularly
  213.14
  squarely 290.25
plumbing 659.4
plume
  n. feather 230.16
  v. groom 681.20
  ornament 901.9
plumed
  feathered 230.28
  ornamented 901.11
  topped 211.12
plummet
  n. cheapening 849.4
  plumb 213.6
  weight 352.6
  v. cheapen 849.6
  decrease 39.6
  descend 316.5
  plunge 320.6
plummeting
  n. cheapening 849.4
  descent 316.1
  adj. descending
    316.11
plump
  n. faint sound 452.3
  v. fatten 197.8
  make pliant 357.6
  plunge 320.6
  put violently 184.12
  sink 316.6
  vote 637.18
  adj. corpulent 195.18
  adv. squarely 290.25
  suddenly 113.9
plump for 785.14
plumpness 195.8
plumy 230.27
plunder
  n. booty 824.11
  pillaging 824.5
  v. pillage 824.16
plunderer 825.6
plundering
  n. pillaging 824.5
  adj. looting 824.21
plunderous 824.21
plunge
  n. cheapening 849.4
  decrease 39.2
  dive 320
  flounder 324.8
  gamble 515.1
  investment 836.3
  speed 269.3
  stock speculation
    833.19
  swimming pool
    878.13
  tumble 316.3
  v. bet 515.20
  cheapen 849.6
  decrease 39.6
  descend 316.5
  dive 320.6
  gravitate 352.15
  invest 836.16
  make haste 709.5
  move 267.5
  rush into 709.7
  sail 275.55

speculate in stocks
    833.23
  tumble 324.15
plunge into begin 68.7
  be willing 622.3
  rush into 709.7
  set to work 716.15
  stab 798.25
  study 564.12
  thrust in 304.7
  undertake 715.3
plunger diver 320.4
  gambler 515.17
  stock speculator
    833.11
plunging
  n. course 267.2
  diving 320.3
  adj. abysmal 209.11
  descending 316.11
  flowing 267.8
  perpendicular 213.12
  steep 219.18
plunk
  n. faint sound 452.3
  hit 283.4
  v. faint sound 452.15
  hit 283.13
  plunge 320.6
  put violently 184.12
  strum 462.41
  adv. squarely 290.25
  suddenly 113.9
plunk down 841.16
plural
  n. number 586.8
  plurality 100.1
  adj. more than one
    100.7
pluralism mixture 44.1
  nonuniformity 18.1
  philosophy 500.5
  plurality 100.1
  principle of govern-
    ment 741.8
pluralistic
  governmental 741.17
  mixed 44.15
  nonuniform 18.3
  plural 100.7
plurality
  large number 101.3
  majority 100.2
  major part 54.6
  pluralness 100
plus
  n. addition 40.2
  surplus 663.5
  v. add 40.4
  adj. additional 40.10
  electric 342.32
  adv. additionally
    40.11
  prep. with 40.12
plush
  n. softness 357.4
  adj. grandiose 904.21
  soft 357.15
Pluto
  deity of nether world
    1019.5
  god 1014.5

planet 375.9
plutocracy 837.5
plutocrat 837.6
pluvial 394.10
ply
  n. fold 264.1
  layer 227.2
  v. change course
    275.30
  exert 716.8
  fold 264.5
  importune 774.12
  sail 275.25
  seafare 275.13
  touch 425.6
  traverse 273.19
  urge upon 773.8
  use 665.10
ply one's trade
  trade 827.14
  work 656.12
plywood layer 227.2
  wood 378.3,10
PM afternoon 134.1
  modulation 344.14
pneuma
  life force 407.3
  psyche 466.4
pneumatic airy 402.12
  beautiful 900.17
  bulging 256.14
  gas 401.9
  mechanical 347.10
pneumatics
  aeronautics 278.2
  gas 401.2
  mechanics 347.5
  meteorology 402.6
pneumonia
  infectious disease
    686.12
  respiratory disease
    686.14
PO 604.8
poach cook 330.4
  steal 824.13
poacher 825.1
poaching
  cooking 330.1
  theft 824.1
pock
  n. blemish 679.1
  indentation 257.6
  sore 686.35
  swelling 256.4
  texture 351.1
  v. indent 257.14
pocked
  indented 257.17
  spotted 374.13
pocket
  n. aviation 278.41
  container 193.2
  funds 835.14
  pit 257.2
  purse 836.14
  v. enclose 236.5
  endure 861.7
  legislate 742.18
  put in 184.14
  take 822.13
  adj. miniature 196.12

pocketbook
  purse 836.14
  record book 570.11
pocket money 835.19
pockmark
  n. blemish 679.1
  indentation 257.6
  v. indent 257.14
pockmarked
  indented 257.17
  spotted 374.13
pocky rough 261.6
  spotted 374.13
  syphilitic 686.57
pod
  n. hull 228.16
  seals 74.5
  seed vessel 411.28
  v. husk 232.9
PO'd 952.26
podgy corpulent 195.18
  stubby 203.10
podiatrist 688.8
podium 216.13
poem
  beautiful thing 900.7
  verse 609.6
  written matter 602.10
poesy bad poetry 609.3
  poetic inspiration
    609.12
  poetic works 609.7
  verse 609.1
poet author 602.15
  imaginer 535.12
  versifier 609.13
poetaster 609.14
poetic(al) lyric 609.17
  visionary 535.24
poetic justice
  justice 976.1
  poetics 609.2
poetic license 609.2
poetics 609.2
poetize 609.15
poetry grace 600.2
  Muses 609.12
  verse 609
pogrom 409.5
poignancy
  acrimony 161.4
  distressfulness 864.5
  eloquence 600.4
  incisiveness 600.3
  pungency 433.1
poignant
  acrimonious 161.13
  deep-felt 855.26
  eloquent 600.12
  incisive 600.11
  painful 424.10
  pungent 433.6
  sensitive 422.15
  unpleasant 864.20
point
  n. acrimony 161.4
  angle 251.2
  benefit 665.4
  cutlery 348.2
  degree 29.1
  direction 290.1
  engraving tool 578.9

  extremity 70.2
  important point
    672.6
  intention 653.1
  item 89.4
  joke 881.6
  location 184.1
  mark 568.5
  meaning 545.1
  minute quantity
    196.7
  particular 8.3
  pause 144.4
  peak 207.8
  point of land 256.8
  printing 603.6
  punctuation
    586.15,18
  scout 66.1
  sculpting tool 575.4
  small amount 35.2
  summit 211.2
  time 107.1
  tip 258.3
  topic 484.1
  types of 258.18
  vanguard 240.2
  v. bear 290.8
  direct 290.6
  gravitate 352.15
  mark 568.19
  punctuate 586.16
  sharpen 258.9
  tend 174.3
point at
  call attention to
    530.10
  designate 568.18
  direct 290.6
  ridicule 967.8
point-blank
  exactly 516.20
  in plain words 591.4
  squarely 290.25
pointed angular 251.6
  aphoristic 517.6
  concise 592.6
  emphatic 672.20
  meaningful 545.10
  sharp 258.11
  witty 881.15
pointedly
  concisely 592.7
  exceptionally 34.20
  intentionally 653.11
pointer guide 748.7
  information 557.3
  sign 568.4
pointless blunt 259.3
  uninteresting 883.6
  useless 669.9
pointlessly dully 883.10
  uselessly 669.15
pointlessness
  futility 669.2
  uninterestingness
    883.1
point of departure
  301.5
point of view
  belief 501.6
  mental outlook 525.2

  viewpoint 439.7
point out
  call attention to
    530.10
  direct to 290.7
  specify 80.11
  symbolize 568.18
point to
  attribute to 155.4
  augur 544.12
  call attention to
    530.10
  designate 568.18
  direct 290.6
  evidence 505.9
  tend 174.3
point up 672.13
poise
  n. behavior 737.1
  equality 30.1
  equanimity 858.3
  gesture 568.14
  sureness 513.5
  v. equalize 30.6
  hover 315.10
poised balanced 30.9
  composed 858.13
  sure 513.21
poison
  n. bad liquor 996.14
  evil 675.3
  killer 409.11
  toxicity 684.3
  types of 676.6
  venom 676.3
  v. corrupt 692.14
  kill 409.13
  make toxic 686.49
  radioactivate 327.9
  work evil 675.6
poisoned
  diseased 686.56
  radioactive 327.10
poisoner 409.11
poisoning
  corruption 692.2
  execution 1010.7
  intoxication 686.30
  killing 409.1
poisonous
  harmful 675.12
  toxic(al) 684.7
  unsavory 429.7
poisonous plant 676.7
poison pen 971.5
poke
  n. container 193.2
  hit 283.4
  purse 836.14
  push 283.2
  signal 568.15
  v. dally 708.13
  goad 648.15
  go slow 270.6
  hit 283.13
  lash out at 798.16
  search 485.30
  signal 568.22
  thrust 283.11
  touch 425.6
poke around
  grope 485.31

  search 485.30
poker 329.12
poker face
  unexpressiveness
    549.5
  unfeeling 856.1
poker-faced 549.20
pokey 761.9
poking
  searching 485.37
  slow 270.10
poky base 915.12
  little 196.10
  petty 673.17
  slovenly 62.15
  slow 270.10
  uninteresting 883.6
pol 746.1
polar final 70.10
  magnetic 342.28
  opposite 239.5
Polaris
  guiding star 748.8
  North Star 375.4
polarity
  contraposition 239.1
  contrariety 15.1
  duality 90.1
  electric polarity 342.8
  symmetry 248.1
polarization
  contraposition 239.1
  disagreement 795.2
  electric polarity 342.8
  repulsion 289.1
polarize 239.4
polarized 239.5
polarizing 795.17
pole
  n. axis 322.5
  beam 217.3
  electric polarity 342.8
  end 70.2
  flagpole 217.1
  mast 277.13
  oar 277.15
  opposite 239.2
  post 216.8
  remote region 199.4
  shaft 217.1
  summit 211.2
  tower 207.11
  wood 378.3
  v. push 285.10
polecat
  bad person 986.7
  skunk 414.28
  stinker 437.3
polemic arguer 482.12
  argumentation 482.4
  conflict 796.1
  quarrel 795.5
polemic(al)
  argumentative 482.19
  contentious 951.26
  quarrelsome 795.17
polemicist 482.12
poles apart
  different 16.7
  opposite 239.6

dither 857.5
perplexity 514.3
v. annoy 866.13
confuse 532.7
disconcert 514.12
trouble 731.12
pothole 257.3
potholed 261.6
potion dose 687.6
drink 996.6
potluck
haphazard 156.4
matter of chance
515.2
potpourri
hodgepodge 44.6
music 462.6
scent article 436.6
potshot
n. matter of chance
515.2
shot 285.5
v. shoot 285.13
potted 996.31
potter
n. ceramist 579.7
v. fritter away 854.5
trifle 673.13
waste time 708.12
potter's field 410.15
pottery ceramics 576.1
ceramic ware 576.2
plant 719.3
potty
n. toilet 311.11
adj. insane 473.26
pouch 256.10
pouched 256.15
poultice
n. medical dressing
687.33
pulp 390.2
v. relieve 886.5
treat 689.30
poultry 414.34
pounce
n. grasping organ
813.4
leap 319.1
plunge 320.1
swoop 316.1
v. descend 316.5
jump 319.5
plunge 320.6
pounce upon
attack 798.15
be unexpected 540.6
jump 319.5
plunge 320.6
seize on 822.16
surprise 540.7
pound
n. British money
835.8
foreign money 835.9
hit 283.4
kennel 191.21
place of confinement
761.7
staccato sound 455.1
unit of weight 352.23
v. ache 424.8

attack 798.15
beat 283.14
bruise 692.16
confine 761.12
make staccato sounds
455.4
music 462.45
pulverize 361.9
repeat 103.10
sail 275.55
thrust in 304.7
poundage
capacity 195.2
charge 846.8
weight 352.1
pound away
drudge 716.14
persevere 625.3
pound-foolish 854.8
pounding
n. pulverization 361.4
staccato sound 455.1
adj. staccato 455.7
pour
n. rainstorm 394.2
violent flow 395.5
v. abound 661.5
eject 310.24
flow 395.16
give 818.12
gush 303.13
rain 394.9
transfer 271.16
pour forth
chatter 596.5
eject 310.24
say 594.23
pouring flowing 395.24
rainy 394.10
pour it on
hustle 707.14
speed 269.8
work hard 716.13
pout
n. grimace 249.4
scowl 951.9
v. be ill-humored
951.15
bulge 256.10
grimace 249.8
poverty poorness 838
scarcity 662.3
poverty-stricken 838.8
POW 761.11
powder
n. dust 361.5
explosive 801.9
make-up 900.11
medicine 687.4
v. crumble 361.10
leave 301.10
pulverize 361.9
sprinkle 75.6
powdered
powdery 361.11
sprinkled 75.10
powderiness 361
powdery 361.11
power
n. authoritativeness
739.2
control 741.2

country 181.1
eloquence 600.3
energy 161.1
governance 739.5
greatness 34.1
impulse 283.1
influence 172.1
means 658.1
personage 672.8
potency 157
prerogative 739.1
privilege 958.3
strength 159.1
supremacy 36.3
talent 733.4
will power 624.4
v. impel 283.10
powered 348.11
power elite
important persons
672.8
superiors 36.5
the rulers 749.15
powerful
authoritative 739.15
eloquent 600.11
great 34.6
influential 172.13
potent 157.12
strong 159.13
powerfully
authoritatively
739.18
eloquently 600.15
potently 157.15
strongly 159.21
very 34.18
powerhouse
man of action 707.8
power station 342.18
strong man 159.6
powerless
impotent 158.13
uninfluential 173.3
weak 160.12
power of attorney
commission 780.1
substitution 149.1
power plant
aviation 278.33
machinery 348.4
plant 719.3
powerhouse 342.18
power reactor 326.13
powers that be, the
influential persons
172.6
officeholders 746.11
the government
741.3
the rulers 749.15
power structure
hierarchy 61.4
power 157.1
rank 29.2
superiors 36.5
the rulers 749.15
powwow
n. conference 597.6
political convention
744.8
v. confer 597.11

pox 686.16
practicability
possibility 509.2
utility 665.3
workability 164.3
practicable
expedient 670.6
possible 509.7
workable 164.10
practical
businesslike 656.15
expedient 670.6
operative 164.9
possible 509.7
realistic 536.6
sensible 467.18
ungullible 504.5
usable 665.22
useful 665.18
wieldy 732.14
workable 164.10
practicality
intelligence 467.6
possibility 509.2
realism 536.2
utility 665.3
wieldiness 732.2
practical joke 881.10
practical joker
deceiver 619.1
mischief-maker 738.3
practically
approximately 200.23
expediently 670.8
usefully 665.25
practice
n. action 705.1
behavior 737.1
custom 642.1
exercise 716.6
experience 733.9
habit 642.4
mathematics 87.4
observance 768.1
operation 164.1
rite 1040.3
study 564.3
training 562.3
tryout 489.3
vocation 656.6
way 657.1
v. act 705.4
busy oneself with
656.11
exercise 705.7
experiment 489.8
observe 768.3
operate 164.5
rehearse 611.37
repeat 103.8
study 564.12
train 562.14
use 665.10
practiced
accomplished 733.24
experienced 733.26
practicing
acting 705.10
observant 768.4
practitioner 718.1
praetor 1002.2

pragmatic(al)
  expedient 670.6
  philosophy 500.9
  practical 536.6
  sensible 467.18
  useful 665.18
pragmatism
  experiment 489.1
  functionalism 665.6
  materialism 376.5
  practicalness 536.2
pragmatist 536.3
prairie grassland 411.8
  horizontal 214.3
  plain 387.1
  space 179.4
  the country 182.1
praise
  n. approval 968.5
  flattery 970.1
  honor 916.4
  thanks 949.2
  worship 1032.2
  v. flatter 970.5
  honor 916.8
  laud 968.12
  worship 1032.11
praiseworthy 968.20
pram 272.6
prana
  life principle 466.5
  soul 407.3
  theosophy 1034.18
prance
  n. gait 273.14
  jump 319.2
  v. dance 879.5
  jump 319.6
  ride 273.33
  strut 904.15
  walk 273.27
prancing
  n. leaping 319.3
  adj. leaping 319.7
prandial 307.29
prank
  n. trick 881.10
  v. dress up 231.41
  ornament 901.8
prankish
  mischievous 738.6
  waggish 881.17
prankster
  humorist 881.12
  mischief-maker 738.3
prate
  n. chatter 596.3
  nonsense 547.2
  v. chatter 596.5
  talk nonsense 547.5
pratfall an error 518.6
  failure 725.3
  tumble 316.3
prattle
  n. chatter 596.3
  nonsense 547.2
  speech 594.1
  v. blabber 596.5
  chat 597.10
  talk nonsense 547.5
prattler 596.4
prawn 308.25

praxis action 705.1
  behavior 737.1
  custom 642.1
  habit 642.4
pray
  v. entreat 774.11
  petition 774.10
  supplicate 1032.12
  interj. please 774.20
prayer entreaty 774.2
  supplication 1032.4
  worship 1032.8
prayer book
  book 605.1
  ritualistic manual
    1040.12
prayerful
  petitionary 774.16
  pious 1028.8
  worshipful 1032.15
preach advise 754.6
  discourse 562.17
  lecture 599.11
preacher
  expounder 599.5
  lecturer 565.8
  minister 1038.3
preaching
  inducement 648.3
  lecture 599.3
preachy 754.8
preamble
  n. prelude 66.2
  v. preface 64.3
prearrange plan 654.9
  precontrive 641.3
  prepare 720.6
prearranged
  precontrived 641.5
  prepared 720.16
prearrangement
  plan 654.1
  preordering 641
  preparation 720.1
precarious
  dangerous 697.12
  unreliable 514.19
precative
  imploring 774.17
  petitionary 774.16
  worshipful 1032.15
precaution
  n. forethought 895.3
  v. forewarn 703.6
precautionary
  cautious 895.10
  forewarning 703.8
precautious 895.10
precede antecede 64.2
  begin 68.10
  be prior 116.3
  go before 66.3
  lead 292.2
  outrank 36.11
precedence
  antecedence 64
  authority 739.4
  importance 672.1
  leading 292.1
  priority 116.1
  rank 29.2
  superiority 36.1

precedent
  antecedent 116.2
  judgment 494.5
  model 25.1
  precursor 66.1
preceding
  n. antecedence 64.1
  leading 292.1
  adj. antecedent 64.4
  foregoing 119.11
  leading 292.3
  preliminary 66.4
  prior 116.4
precept a belief 501.2
  directive 752.3
  legal order 752.6
  maxim 517.1
  rule 751
preceptive
  commanding 752.14
  educational 562.19
  prescriptive 751.4
precinct arena 802.1
  district 180.5
  election district
    744.16
  nearness 200.1
  region 180.2
precincts
  environment 233.1
  neighborhood 180.1
preciosity
  affectation 903.5
  formalism 646.2
  pretentiousness 589.3
precious
  n. endearment 932.5
  adj. affected 903.18
  beloved 931.22
  elegant 589.9
  outright 34.12
  punctilious 646.10
  valuable 848.10
precious stone
  gem 384.6
  jewel 901.6
precipice cliff 213.3
  peak 207.8
precipitant
  hasty 709.10
  reckless 894.8
  sudden 113.5
precipitate
  n. deposit 43.2
  result 154.1
  sedimentation 354.5
  v. deposit 354.11
  descend 316.5
  fell 318.5
  gravitate 352.15
  hasten 709.4
  rain 394.9
  adj. fast 269.19
  hasty 709.10
  impulsive 630.9
  premature 131.8
  reckless 894.8
  sudden 113.5
  unprepared 721.8
precipitation
  deposit 354.5
  downcast 318.2

hastiness 709.2
  impulsiveness 630.2
  prematurity 131.2
  rain 394.1
  recklessness 894.2
  sediment 43.2
  speed 269.1
precipitous
  hasty 709.10
  perpendicular 213.12
  reckless 894.8
  steep 219.18
  sudden 113.5
précis
  abridgment 607.1
  summary 203.3
precise
  v. be accurate 516.10
  particularize 80.9
  adj. detailed 8.9
  discriminating 492.7
  exact 516.16
  fastidious 896.9
  meticulous 533.12
  particular 80.12
  punctilious 646.10
precisely
  adv. exactly 516.20
  meticulously 533.16
  particularly 80.15
  punctually 131.14
  squarely 290.25
  thus 8.10
  interj. yes 521.18
precisian
  n. conformist 82.2
  fastidious person
    896.6
  pedant 476.5
  adj. affected 903.18
  punctilious 646.10
precision
  accuracy 516.3
  fastidiousness 896.1
  meticulousness 533.3
  specification 80.6
precisionist 476.5
preclude exclude 77.4
  prevent 730.14
  prohibit 778.3
precluding 77.9
preclusive
  exclusive 77.8
  preventing 730.19
  prohibitive 778.6
precocious 131.8
precognition
  foreknowledge 542.3
  intuition 481.1
  understanding 475.3
precognitive
  foreseeing 542.7
  intuitive 481.5
preconceive 495.2
preconceived 495.3
preconception
  partiality 527.3
  prejudgment 495.1
preconscious
  n. psyche 690.35
  adj. subconscious
    690.48

adj. at hand 186.12
existent 1.13
immediate 120.2
presentable
beautiful 900.17
giveable 818.23
tolerable 674.19
presentation
appearance 446.1
consecration 1037.10
display 555.2
gift 818.4
giving 818.1
information 557.1
introduction 927.4
offer 773.1
party 922.14
spectacle 446.7
theatrical perfor-
mance 611.13
present-day
modern 122.13
present 120.2
presentiment
emotion 855.3
foreboding 544
foreknowledge 542.3
forewarning 703.2
hunch 481.3
prediction 543.1
presently 131.16
presentment
arraignment 1004.3
display 555.2
giving 818.1
representation 572.1
theatrical perfor-
mance 611.13
preservation
conservation 701
divine function
1013.16
maintenance 140.2
perpetuation 112.4
protection 699.1
retention 813.1
storage 660.5
preservative
n. preservative me-
dium 701.3
adj. conservative
140.8
preservatory 701.10
preserve
n. refuge 700.1
reserve 701.6
sweets 308.39
v. care for 699.19
conserve 701.7
cure 701.8
perpetuate 112.5
reserve 660.12
retain 813.5
sustain 143.4
preserved kept 701.11
reserved 660.15
preserver 701.4
preshrunk 198.13
preside
administer justice
1000.5
entertain 925.8

govern 741.12
officiate 747.11
presidency
directorship 747.4
mastership 739.7
supremacy 36.3
president
educator 565.9
executive 748.3
head of state 749.6
presiding 747.14
press
n. enlistment 780.6
extractor 305.9
impulse 648.6
informant 557.5
printing 603.9,24
printing office 603.11
squeezing 198.2
throng 74.4
thrust 283.2
urgency 672.4
v. appropriate 822.20
be heavy upon
352.11
coax 648.14
compel 756.6
densify 354.9
embrace 932.16
enlist 780.16
hasten 709.4
importune 774.12
insist 753.7
smooth 260.6
squeeze 198.8
strain 716.10
thrust 283.11
urge upon 773.8
press, the news 558.1
public press 605.23
press agent agent 781.3
publicist 559.9
press charges 1005.7
pressed 709.11
pressing
n. extraction 305.7
importuning 774.3
urging 648.5
adj. compelling 756.9
demanding 753.8
motivating 648.25
urgent 672.21
press notice 559.4
press on elapse 105.5
hustle 707.13
make haste 709.5
make one's way 294.4
press release 559.3
pressure
n. adversity 729.1
authority 739.4
aviation 278.31
burden 352.7
coercion 756.3
drive 648.6
entreaty 774.3
influence 172.1
insistence 753.3
necessity 639.4
squeezing 198.2
tension 859.3
thrust 283.2

touching 425.2
urgency 672.4
urging 648.5
v. compel 756.6
importune 774.12
urge 648.14
pressure group
influential persons
172.6
interest group 744.31
party 788.4
prestidigitation
illusoriness 519.2
juggling 618.5
prestidigitator
entertainer 612.1
trickster 619.2
prestige
authority 739.4
influence 172.1
notability 672.2
repute 914.4
respect 964.1
superiority 36.1
prestigious
authoritative 739.15
influential 172.13
notable 672.18
reputable 914.15
respected 964.11
presto
n. music 462.25
tempo 463.24
adj. instantaneous
113.4
adv. music 462.56
presumable
probable 511.6
supposable 499.15
presumably
probably 511.8
supposedly 499.17
presume
be hopeful 888.7
be insolent 913.6
believe 501.11
entail 76.4
expect 539.5
imply 546.4
judge 494.8
prejudge 495.2
suppose 499.10
take the liberty 961.6
think probable 511.5
presumed
expected 539.13
implied 546.7
prejudged 495.3
supposed 499.14
presume upon
exploit 665.16
impose 963.7
take liberties 961.7
presumption
arrogance 912.2
belief 501.6
entailment 76.2
hope 888.1
implication 546.2
insolence 913.1
meddling 238.2
prejudgment 495.1

probability 511.1
recklessness 894.3
supposition 499.3
undueness 961.2
presumptive
evidential 505.17
probable 511.6
supposed 499.14
presumptuous
arrogant 912.10
foolhardy 894.9
insolent 913.8
meddlesome 238.9
undue 961.11
presuppose entail 76.4
imply 546.4
prejudge 495.2
suppose 499.10
presupposed
implied 546.7
prejudged 495.3
presupposition
implication 546.2
prejudgment 495.1
prelude 66.2
premise 482.7
supposition 499.3
pre-teens 124.2
pretend affect 903.12
fake 616.21
lay claim to 753.5
presume 961.6
pretext 649.3
try to 714.7
usurp 961.8
pretended
assumed 903.16
falsified 616.26
pretexted 649.5
pretender
affecter 903.7
impostor 619.6
usurper 961.4
pretending 616.3
pretense
affectation 903.1
fakery 616.3
ostentation 904.1
pretext 649.1
privilege 958.3
reason 153.2
pretension
affectation 903.1
fakery 616.3
grandiloquence 601.1
ostentation 904.1
pretext 649.1
privilege 958.3
pretentious
affected 903.15
boastful 910.11
elegant 589.9
grandiloquent 601.8
ostentatious 904.18
preternatural 85.15
preternaturalism
otherworldliness 85.7
supernaturalism
1034.2
pretext
n. excuse 649
fakery 616.3

affirmed 523.8
pretexted 649.5
profession
acknowledgment 521.3
affirmation 523.1
false claim 649.2
profession of belief 501.7
testimony 505.3
vocation 656.6
professional
n. expert 733.11
worker 718.4
adj. accomplished 733.24
occupational 656.16
scholastic 562.20
skillful 733.20
professionalism 656.8
professor
academic rank 565.4
expert 733.11
teacher 565.1
professorial
pedagogical 565.12
studious 564.17
professorship 565.11
proffer
n. offer 773.1
v. give 818.12
offer 773.4
proffered 622.7
proficiency
ability 157.2
preparedness 720.4
profound knowledge 475.6
skill 733.1
proficient able 157.14
expert 677.9
skillful 733.20
suited 720.17
profile
n. biography 608.4
contour 246.2
description 608.1
diagram 654.3
outline 235.2
portrait 574.16
side 242.1
v. outline 235.9
profit
n. benefit 665.4
expedience 670.1
gain 811.3
good 674.4
incentive 648.7
receipts 844.1
v. be expedient 670.3
be of use 665.17
do good 674.10
make money 811.11
profitable
expedient 670.5
gainful 811.15
good 674.12
helpful 785.21
paying 841.21
useful 665.21

profit by
improve the occasion 129.8
take advantage of 665.15
profiteer
n. predator 822.12
v. overcharge 848.7
profiteering 848.5
profitless 669.12
profit sharing 815.2
profligacy
dissoluteness 989.3
prodigality 854.1
turpitude 981.5
profligate
n. bad person 986.5
unchaste person 989.10
adj. morally corrupt 981.14
prodigal 854.8
unchaste 989.25
profound deep 209.10
deep-felt 855.26
huge 195.20
learned 475.21
outright 34.12
recondite 549.16
wise 467.17
profundity
abstruseness 549.2
depth 209.1
sagacity 467.5
sizableness 195.6
profuse diffuse 593.11
exaggerated 617.4
liberal 853.4
plentiful 661.7
prodigal 854.8
teeming 101.9
profusely
abundantly 34.20
liberally 853.5
numerously 101.12
plentifully 661.9
profusion
diffuseness 593.1
numerousness 101.1
plenty 661.2
prodigality 854.1
quantity 34.3
progenitor
ancestor 170.7
parent 170.8
progeny 171.1
prognosis
judgment 494.5
medical prognosis 689.14
prediction 543.1
prognostic
predictive 543.11
premonitory 544.16
prognosticate
predict 543.9
risk 156.12
prognosticator 543.4
program
n. announcement 559.2
list 88.6

music performance 462.34
plan 654.1
political platform 744.7
political program 744.6
schedule 641.2
undertaking 715.1
v. automate 349.23
indoctrinate 562.13
list 88.8
plan 654.9
schedule 641.4
program director 344.23
programmer
broadcaster 344.23
computer 349.22
progress
n. advance 294.1
continuance 143.1
conversion 145.1
course 267.2
development 148.1
improvement 691.1
journey 273.5
rate 267.4
travel 273.1
water travel 275.9
v. advance 294.2
evolve 148.5
get better 691.7
make good 724.9
move 267.5
prosper 728.7
travel 273.17
progressing
developing 148.8
improving 691.15
progressive 294.6
traveling 273.35
progression
advance 294
continuation 143.1
continuity 71.2
development 148.1
improvement 691.1
numbers 86.7
sequence 65.1
progressive
n. liberal 745.11
reformer 691.6
adj. consecutive 71.9
flowing 267.8
gradational 29.5
improving 691.15
liberal 745.19
modern 122.13
progressing 294.6
progressivism
liberalism 745.3
reform 691.5
prohibit exclude 77.4
forbid 778.3
make impossible 510.6
prevent 730.14
restrain 760.7
prohibited
excluded 77.7
forbidden 778.7

impossible 510.7
prohibition
exclusion 77.1
forbidding 778
obstruction 730.2
restraint 760.1
temperance 992.3
prohibitive
exclusive 77.8
overpriced 848.12
preventing 730.19
prohibiting 778.6
project
n. intention 653.1
plan 654.2
task 656.2
the future 121.1
undertaking 715.1
v. come across 555.7
extrapolate 224.5
foresee 121.6
intend 653.4
overhang 215.7
plan 654.9
protrude 256.9
represent 572.8
rocket 281.13
show 577.16
throw 285.12
projected future 121.8
intentional 653.9
planned 654.13
projectile
n. trajectile 285.6
weapon 801.12
adj. trajectile 285.16
projecting
overhanging 215.11
protruding 256.13
projection acting 611.9
defense mechanism 690.30
diagram 654.3
display 555.2
extrapolate 224.4
map 654.4
overhanging 215.3
plan 654.2
pointed projection 258.4
protuberance 256.2
representation 572.1
throwing 285.3
projector
motion-picture 577.12
planner 654.7
rocketry 281.10
weapon 801.19
proletarian
n. common man 919.7
working person 718.2
adj. middle-class 919.12
proletariat 919.1
proliferate
abound 661.5
be productive 165.7
increase 38.6
multiply 100.6
procreate 169.8

narrow-mindedness
527.1
rusticity 182.3
proving ground
rocketry 281.7
testing area 489.5
provision
n. condition 507.2
food 308.1
foresight 542.1
giving 818.1
precaution 895.3
preparation 720.1
stipulation 753.2
store 660.1
supplying 659
support 785.3
v. feed 307.16
provender 659.9
provisional
cautious 895.10
circumstantial 8.7
conditional 507.8
experimental 489.11
interim 109.4
makeshift 670.7
preparatory 720.20
substitute 149.8
unreliable 514.19
proviso condition 507.2
legislative clause
742.17
stipulation 753.2
provisory
conditional 507.8
interim 109.4
provocateur 648.11
provocation
affront 952.11
aggravation 885.1
cause 153.3
excitation 857.10
incentive 648.7
incitement 648.4
irritation 866.3
vexatiousness 864.7
provocative
aggravating 885.5
alluring 650.7
appetizing 428.10
desirable 634.30
exciting 857.28
interesting 530.19
prompting 648.27
provoke
aggravate 885.2
annoy 866.13
antagonize 929.7
be insolent 913.7
contrive 153.12
incense 952.22
incite 648.17
interest 530.12
irritate 866.14
prompt 648.13
sow dissension 795.14
stimulate 857.12
vex 864.15
provoked
aggravated 885.4
annoyed 866.21
nettled 952.25

provoking
annoying 864.22
eloquent 600.13
exciting 857.28
interesting 530.19
provocative 648.27
provost educator 565.9
executive 748.3
prow 240.3
prowess courage 893.1
skill 733.1
prowl
n. stealth 614.4
v. creep 273.25
lurk 615.9
wander 273.22
prowl car 272.10
prowler 825.1
proximate
approaching 296.4
following 65.4
near 200.14
relative 9.8
proximity
nearness 200.1
relationship 9.1
proxy
n. ballot 744.19
commission 780.1
deputy 781.1
substitute 149.2
vote 637.6
voter 744.23
adj. substitute 149.8
prude 903.11
prudence
caution 895.1
economy 851.1
expedience 670.1
foresight 542.1
judiciousness 467.7
moderation 163.1
vigilance 533.4
virtue 980.5
prudent cautious 895.8
economical 851.6
foreseeing 542.7
judicious 467.19
moderate 163.10
vigilant 533.13
prudish
fastidious 896.9
priggish 903.19
prune cut off 42.10
sever 49.11
shorten 203.6
thin out 413.17
pruned concise 592.6
shortened 203.9
prurience craving 634.6
curiosity 528.1
lasciviousness 989.5
sexual desire 419.5
prurient craving 634.24
curious 528.5
lascivious 989.29
lustful 419.29
pry
n. curious person
528.2
lever 287.4
leverage 287.1

meddler 238.4
v. be inquisitive 528.4
investigate 485.22
lever 287.8
look 439.13
meddle 238.7
search 485.30
prying
inquisitive 528.6
meddlesome 238.9
searching 485.37
pry loose from 822.22
pry open 265.15
pry out grill 485.21
search out 485.33
PS 67.1
psalm
n. hymn 1032.3
sacred music 462.16
v. sing 462.39
psalmbook book 605.1
psalter 1040.13
Psalms, the 1040.13
psalter book 605.1
psalmbook 1040.13
pseudo imitation 22.8
ungenuine 616.26
pseudo– abnormal 85.9
fictitious 535.21
illusory 519.9
similar 20.10
substitute 149.8
unsubstantial 4.5
pseudonym 583.8
psoriasis 686.33
psst! 448.17
psych discompose 63.4
solve 487.2
psych(o)– mind 466.1
psychology 690.1
spirit 1017.1
psyche intellect 466.1
psychology 690.35
spirit 466.4
psychedelic
n. hallucinogen
687.13
adj. hallucinatory
519.10
psychochemical
687.46
psyched up 720.16
psychiatric
psychological 690.43
psychotherapeutic
690.44
psychiatrist
physician 688.8
psychologist 690.12
psychotherapist
690.13
psychiatry 690.3
psychic predictor 543.4
spiritualist 1034.13
psychic(al)
ghostly 1017.7
immaterial 377.7
mental 466.8
spiritual 1034.23
supernatural 85.15
psychic(al) phenomena
1034.6

psychics
immateriality 377.1
occultism 1034.4
psycho
n. psychotic 473.16
adj. insane 473.25
psychoanalysis
psychology 690.2
psychotherapy 690.8
psychoanalyst 690.13
psychoanalytic(al)
690.44
psychoanalyze 690.42
psychodrama
catharsis 690.32
psychotherapy 690.5
stage show 611.4
psychokinesia 473.7
psychokinesis 1034.6
psychologic(al)
mental 466.8
psychiatric 690.43
psychological block
defense mechanism
690.31
thought disturbance
690.24
psychological moment
crucial moment
129.5
period 107.1
psychological test
690.11
psychological warfare
cold war 797.5
demoralization 891.6
psychology 690.1
warfare 797.4
psychologist 690.12
psychologize 690.42
psychology
mental attitude 525.1
science of man 417.7
science of mind 690
psychometrics
mensuration 490.9
psychology 690.1
psychometry 690.10
psychoneurosis 690.19
psychoneurotic
n. pathological type
690.16
adj. neurotic 690.45
psychopath
pathological type
690.16
psychotic 473.16
psychopathic
insane 473.27
psychological 690.43
psychopathy
personality disorder
690.18
psychosis 473.3
psychosis insanity 473.3
mental disorder
690.17
psychosomatic 690.43
psychotherapist 690.13
psychotherapy
psychology 690.5
therapy 689.1

psychotic
  n. lunatic 473.16
    pathological type
      690.16
  adj. insane 473.27
    psychological 690.43
psych out solve 487.2
    unnerve 859.9
ptisan 687.4
ptomaine poisoning
    686.30
pub inn 191.16
    saloon 996.19
puberty 124.6
pubescent
    adolescent 124.13
    hairy 230.24
    smooth 351.8
    soft 357.14
public
  n. clientele 828.3
    follower 293.2
    inn 191.16
    people 417.2
    populace 919.2
    population 190.1
    saloon 996.19
  adj. communal 815.9
    external 224.6
    general 417.13
    popular 898.14
    published 559.17
    well-known 475.27
public-address system
    450.11
publican
    bartender 996.18
    taxer 846.12
public assistance
    subsidy 818.8
    welfare program
      745.7
publication book 605.1
    dispersion 75.1
    impartation 554.2
    information 557.1
    manifestation 555.1
    printing 603.1
    promulgation 559
public defender 1003.4
public enemy
    criminal 986.10
    enemy 929.6
    evildoer 943.1
public health 683.2
public house
    inn 191.16
    saloon 996.19
public image
    affectation 903.1
    appearances 446.2
publicist
    commentator 606.4
    journalist 605.22
    lawyer 1003.4
    publicizer 559.9
publicity
    exposure 559.4
    information 557.1
    repute 914.1
publicize 559.15
publicizing 559.5

public knowledge 559.4
publicly
    in public 559.19
    overtly 555.15
public opinion
    belief 501.6
    political influence
      744.29
public relations 559.4
public relations man
    559.9
public school
    school 567.2
    secondary school
      567.6
public servant
    officeholder 746.11
    official 749.16
public speaker
    orator 599.6
    speechmaker 599.4
public speaking 599
public spirit 941
public-spirited 941.4
public trough
    booty 824.11
    depository 836.12
    spoils of office
      744.25
public utility 788.9
publish disperse 75.4
    divulge 556.5
    print 603.14
    promulgate 559.10
published 559.17
publisher
    bookman 605.21
    informant 557.5
publishing
    printing 603.1
    promulgation 559.1
    the press 605.23
publishing house 603.11
puce 368.6
puck bad child 125.4
    evil spirit 1016.8
    mischief-maker 738.3
Puck 1016.8
pucker
  n. anxiety 890.1
    confusion 532.3
    dither 857.5
    wrinkle 264.3
  v. constrict 198.7
    wrinkle 264.6
puckered
    constricted 198.12
    wrinkled 264.8
puckering 198.1
puckish
    devilish 1016.19
    mischievous 738.6
pudding food 308.45
    pulp 390.2
    semiliquid 389.5
    softness 357.4
puddinghead
    dolt 471.4
    ignoramus 477.8
puddle
    body of water 398.1
    mud puddle 389.9

pudency
    blushing 908.5
    decency 988.2
pudenda 419.10
pudgy
    corpulent 195.18
    stubby 203.10
puerile childish 124.11
    simple-minded
      469.24
puerility
    childishness 124.4
    simple-mindedness
      469.11
    unwiseness 470.2
puff
  n. breathing 403.18
    commendation 968.3
    distension 197.2
    foam 405.2
    make-up 900.11
    pastry 308.40
    publicity 559.4
    softness 357.4
    tobacco smoking
      434.10
    wind 403.4
  v. become exhausted
      717.5
    blow 403.22
    boast 910.6
    breathe 403.24
    exaggerate 617.3
    exhale 310.23
    make larger 197.4
    praise 968.12
    promote 968.11
    publicize 559.15
    use tobacco 434.14
puffball 411.4
puffed up
    conceited 909.11
    distended 197.13
    exaggerated 617.4
    overestimated 497.3
    proud 905.10
puffing
    breathing 403.29
    breathless 717.10
puff up
    become larger 197.5
    be vain 909.7
    make larger 197.4
    praise 968.12
puffy corpulent 195.18
    distended 197.13
    windy 403.25
pug
  n. foot 212.5
    mark 568.7
    pugilist 800.2
  adj. stubby 203.10
pugilism 796.9
pugilist athlete 878.20
    fighter 800.2
pugnacious
    quarrelsome 795.17
    warlike 797.25
pug-nosed 249.12
puissant
    authoritative 739.15
    powerful 157.12

    strong 159.13
puke
  n. vomit 310.8
  v. sicken at 867.4
    vomit 310.25
puky filthy 682.23
    nauseated 686.53
pulchritude 900.1
pule
    animal sound 460.2
    whine 875.12
puling
    animal sound 460.6
    plaintive 875.16
Pulitzer Prize 916.2
pull
  n. attraction 288.1
    draw 286.2
    drink 307.4
    exertion 716.2
    heaving 286.1
    influence 172.2
    power 157.1
    swig 996.6
    trial print 603.5
  v. attract 288.4
    deflect 291.5
    draw 286.4
    drink 307.27
    exert oneself 716.10
    extract 305.10
    lengthen 202.7
    print 603.14
    restrain 760.7
    row 275.53
    use tobacco 434.14
pull a fast one
    deceive 618.13
    outwit 735.11
pullback
    reduction 39.4
    retreat 284.3
    withdrawal 295.2
pull back demur 623.4
    dodge 631.8
    draw back 284.7
    hesitate 627.7
    regress 295.5
    retract 297.3
    retreat 295.6
    separate 49.9
pull down
    acquire 811.8
    be paid 841.20
    bring down 318.5
    depress 318.4
    raze 693.19
    receive 819.6
pullet poultry 414.34
    young chicken 125.8
pull in arrest 761.16
    arrive 300.6
    reel in 287.9
    restrain 760.7
    retract 297.3
pulling
  n. drinking 307.3
    extraction 305.1
    traction 286
  adj. attracting 288.5
    drawing 286.6

pulling power
  attraction 288.1
  pulling 286.1
Pullman car
  railway car 272.14
  train room 192.10
pull off
  bring about 722.5
  do 705.6
  succeed with 724.10
pull one's leg
  flatter 970.6
  fool 618.14
  ridicule 967.8
  trick 881.14
pull one's weight 815.6
pullout
  air maneuver 278.13
  retreat 284.3
  withdrawal 295.2
pull out abandon 633.5
  depart 301.6
  desert 633.6
  extract 305.10
  fly 278.49
  retract 297.3
  retreat 295.6
  separate 49.9
pull strings
  influence 172.9
  maneuver 735.10
pull through 694.20
pull together 786.3
pullulate
  be numerous 101.5
  be productive 165.7
  germinate 411.31
  grow 197.7
  superabound 663.8
pull up arraign 1004.14
  extract 305.10
  fly 278.49
  halt 144.11
  stop 144.7
pulmonary 403.29
pulp
  n. paste 390.2
  semiliquid 389.5
  v. mash 390.5
  soften 357.6
pulpiness
  mushiness 390
  semiliquidity 389.1
  softness 357.1
pulpit
  church part 1042.13
  platform 216.13
  the ministry 1037.1
pulpy insipid 430.2
  pulpous 390.6
  semiliquid 389.11
  soft 357.11
pulsar 375.8
pulsate
  make staccato sounds
    455.4
  pulse 323.12
  recur 137.5
pulsating
  constant 135.5
  music 463.28
  pulsing 323.18

pulsation
  frequency 135.2
  music 463.26
  periodicity 137.2
  pulse 323.3
  staccato sound 455.1
pulse
  n. beat 137.3
  legume 411.4
  music 463.26
  pulsation 323.3
  radar pulse 346.10
  v. flutter 324.12
  pulsate 323.12
  recur 137.5
  resonate 454.6
pulsing music 463.28
  periodic 137.7
  resonant 454.9
  throbbing 323.18
pulverize
  demolish 693.17
  pound 283.14
  powder 361.9
  shatter 49.13
pulverized 361.11
pulverizer 361.7
puma 414.27,58
pumice 260.8
pumice stone 681.17,32
pummel pound 283.14
  punish 1010.14
pump
  n. extractor 305.9
  heart 225.4
  types of 348.25
  v. extract 305.12
  interrogate 485.20
  make larger 197.4
  oscillate 323.14
  process 167.11
pumpkin head 471.4
pump room 689.29
pun
  n. ambiguous expres-
    sion 550.2
  similar sound 20.6
  wordplay 881.8
  v. joke 881.13
  sound similar 20.9
punch
  n. alcoholic drink
    996.8
  die 25.6
  eloquence 600.3
  engraving tool 578.9
  hit 283.4
  power 157.1
  pungency 433.2
  push 283.2
  vim 161.2
  v. hit 283.13
  indent 257.14
  mark 568.19
  puncture 265.16
  thrust 283.11
punch bowl
  basin 257.2
  liquor 996.12
punch card 349.18
punch-drunk 532.14
puncher herder 416.3

rider 274.8
punch in arrive 300.6
  indent 257.14
  record time 114.12
punching bag 716.7
punchy dazed 532.14
  vital 600.11
punctilious
  conscientious 974.15
  fastidious 896.9
  formal 646.10
  meticulous 533.12
  observant 768.4
punctual
  conscientious 974.15
  meticulous 533.12
  observant 768.4
  prompt 131.9
punctuality
  alertness 533.5
  meticulousness 533.3
  promptness 131.3
  regularity 137.1
punctuate
  emphasize 672.13
  grammaticize 586.16
  mark 568.19
punctuated 672.20
punctuation
  grammatical point
    586.15
  types of marks 586.18
  writing 602.9
puncture
  n. impairment 692.8
  mark 568.5
  perforation 265.3
  v. deflate 198.10
  disprove 506.4
  injure 692.15
  mark 568.19
  perforate 265.16
punctureproof
  impervious 266.13
  resistant 159.18
pundit
  Hindu priest 1038.14
  scholar 476.3
  specialist 81.3
  teacher 565.1
pungency
  eloquence 600.4
  odorousness 435.2
  piquancy 433
  sourness 432.1
  unpleasant taste
    429.2
  wittiness 881.2
pungent
  aphoristic 517.6
  bitter 429.6
  eloquent 600.12
  intense 159.20
  painful 424.10
  piquant 433.6
  sour 432.5
  strong-smelling
    435.10
  witty 881.15
punish chastise 1010.10
  penalize 1009.4
  retaliate 955.7

torture 866.18
punishable 999.6
punishing
  chastising 1010.25
  fatiguing 717.11
  laborious 716.18
punishment
  chastisement 1010
  penalty 1009.1
  reprisal 955.2
punitive
  punishing 1010.25
  retaliatory 955.8
  revengeful 956.6
punk
  n. a nobody 673.7
  bad child 125.4
  homosexual 419.16
  tinder 331.6
  adj. bad 675.8
  inferior 680.9
  petty 673.17
punster 881.12
punt
  n. kick 283.8
  v. bet 515.20
  kick 283.18
  row 275.53
puny frail 160.14
  little 196.10
  meager 662.10
  petty 673.17
  thin 205.20
pup
  n. boy 125.5
  dog 414.22
  impudent person
    913.5
  young dog 125.8
  v. give birth 167.15
pupa 125.10
pupil eye 439.9
  student 566.1
puppet agent 781.3
  doll 878.16
  figure 572.4
  figurehead 749.4
  instrument 658.3
  little thing 196.5
  man 787.8
  nonentity 4.2
  sycophant 907.3
puppet show 611.15
puppy boy 125.5
  dandy 903.9
  dog 414.22
  impudent person
    913.5
  young dog 125.8
puppyhood 124.2
puppyish 124.11
puppy love 931.4
purblind
  dim-sighted 440.13
  narrow-minded
    527.10
  undiscerning 469.14
purchasable
  bribable 651.4
  corruptible 975.23
purchase
  n. buying 828

intrude 238.5
put-upon 866.22
put up to 648.17
put up with
  be patient 861.5
  permit 777.10
  submit 765.6
  substitute 149.4
puzzle
  n. dilemma 731.6
  enigma 549.8
  perplexity 514.3
  the unknown 477.7
  v. perplex 514.13
  think hard 478.9
  trouble 731.12
puzzled
  astonished 920.9
  perplexed 514.24
  troubled 731.19
puzzle over
  be uncertain 514.9
  think hard 478.9
puzzler 549.8
puzzling
  bewildering 514.25
  inexplicable 549.17
  unknown 477.17
  wonderful 920.10
PX 832.6
pygmy
  n. dwarf 196.6
  race 418.3
  adj. dwarf 196.13
pylon aviation 278.19
  entrance 302.6
  tower 207.11
pyloric 225.10
pyorrhea 686.9
pyr(o)– fever 686.6
  fire 328.13
pyramid
  n. building 245.2
  hierarchy 61.4
  memorial 570.12
  pile 74.10
  tomb 410.16
  tower 207.11
  v. increase 38.4
  pile 74.19
  speculate in stocks
    833.23
pyre cremation 410.2
  fire 328.13
pyretic 686.54
pyric 328.26
pyrogenesis 329.1
pyrogenic 328.32
pyrolytic 329.30
pyromania 329.7
pyromaniac 329.8
pyrotechnics
  fireworks 328.17
  heat science 328.21
  public speaking 599.1
pyrrhic
  n. meter 609.9
  adj. metrical 609.18

Pyrrhic victory 726.1

Q

QED 505.26
quack
  n. charlatan 688.7
  impostor 619.6
  v. bird sound 460.5
  adj. quackish 616.28
quackery 616.7
quadragesimal 995.5
quadrangle
  enclosure 236.3,12
  four 96.1
  tract 180.4
quadrant
  instrument 251.4,13
  part 55.1
  semicircle 253.8
quadrat
  real estate 810.7
  typesetting 603.7
quadrate
  v. square 96.3
  adj. quadrangular
    251.9
quadratic 96.4
quadri– four 96.4
  quadrangular 251.9
  quadruplicate 97.3
quadrilateral four 96.4
  quadrangular 251.9
  sided 242.7
quadrillion
  immense number
    101.4
  number 99.13
quadriplegic 686.42
quadrisect 98.3
quadrisection 98
quadroon 44.9
quadruped
  n. animal 414.3
  adj. four 96.4
quadruple
  v. quadruplicate 97.2
  adj. quadruplicate
    97.3
quadruplicate
  n. copy 24.3
  v. copy 24.8
  quadruple 97.2
  adj. quadruple 97.3
quadruplication 97
quaff
  n. drink 307.4
  v. drink 307.27
  tipple 996.23
quagmire
  filthy place 682.12
  marsh 400.1
  predicament 731.4
quail
  n. food 308.22
  v. cower 892.9
  demur 623.4
  flinch 891.21
  pull back 284.7
quailing 892.13
quaint humorous 880.4
  odd 85.11

quake
  n. earthquake 162.5
  shake 324.3
  v. be cold 333.9
  be excited 857.16
  shake 324.11
  tremble 891.22
quaking
  n. excitement 857.4
  shaking 324.2
  trepidation 891.5
  adj. shaking 324.17
qualification
  ability 157.2
  change 139.1
  circumscription 234.2
  conditioning 720.2
  eligibility 637.11
  extenuation 1006.5
  fitness 26.5
  limitation 507
  preparedness 720.4
  restriction 760.3
  stipulation 753.2
  talent 733.4
qualified apt 26.10
  changed 139.9
  competent 733.22
  eligible 637.24
  fitted 720.17
  limited 234.7
  modified 507.10
  restrained 760.15
  warranted 960.9
qualifier 586.2
qualify be fitted 720.15
  change 139.6
  limit 234.5
  prepare 720.8
  restrain 760.9
  stipulate for 753.6
  succeed 724.6
  suffice 661.4
  suit 26.8
  temper 507.3
qualifying 507.7
quality
  characteristic 80.4
  goodness 674.1
  good taste 897.1
  milieu 233.3
  nature 5.3
  nobility 918.1
  role 7.5
quality control
  automation 349.8
  examination 485.3
qualm
  apprehension 891.4
  compunction 873.2
  conscientiousness
    974.2
  demur 623.2
  nausea 686.29
  objection 522.2
qualmish fearful 891.32
  hesitant 623.7
  nauseated 686.53
quandary
  dilemma 731.6
  perplexity 514.3

quantification
  measurement 490.1
  numeration 87.1
quantified
  measured 490.14
  quantitative 28.5
quantify
  measure 490.11
  number 87.10
  quantize 28.4
quantitative
  measuring 490.13
  quantized 28.5
quantity
  abundance 34.3
  amount 28.2
  capacity 195.2
  indefinite 28.8
  large number 101.3
  lump 195.10
  measure 490.2
  meter 609.9
  plenty 661.2
  quantum 28
  sum 86.5
  vowel quantity
    594.12
quantum
  light unit 335.21
  portion 816.5
  quantity 28.1
  unit of energy 161.6
quantum mechanics
  atomics 326.1
  mechanics 347.1
  statistics 511.2
quarantine
  n. confinement 761.2
  enclosure 236.1
  exclusiveness 77.3
  seclusion 924.1
  v. confine 761.13
  enclose 236.5
  segregate 77.6
quarantined
  confined 761.20
  enclosed 236.10
  secluded 924.7
quark 196.8
quarrel
  n. arrow 801.16
  contention 796.1
  dispute 795.5
  fight 796.4
  v. contend 796.14
  dispute 795.11
  quarrel over 796.22
quarreler
  combatant 800.1
  oppositionist 791.3
quarrelsome
  argumentative 482.19
  belligerent 797.25
  contending 796.23
  factional 795.17
  hostile 929.10
  ill humored 951.26
quarry
  n. fountainhead 153.6
  game 655.7
  mine 383.6
  objective 653.2

pit 257.4
source of supply
660.4
v. dig up 305.10
excavate 257.15
mine 383.14
quart 490.19
quarter
n. area 180.1
direction 290.1
fourth 98.2
heraldic insignia
569.2
part 55.1
period 107.2
pity 944.1
side 242.1
US money 835.7
v. divide by four 98.3
house 188.10
settle 184.16
adj. fourth 98.5
quarterback
n. athlete 878.20
v. direct 747.8
quartered
housed 188.14
quadrisected 98.4
severed 49.23
quartering
heraldic insignia
569.2
housing 188.3
quadrisection 98.1
quarterly
n. periodical 605.10
adj. momentary 137.8
quartermaster
officer 276.7
provider 659.6
quartern 98.2
quarter note 463.14
quarters 191.3
quartet
cooperation 786.1
four 96.1
orchestra 464.12
part music 462.17
quartile 96.4
quarto
book size 605.14
fourth 98.2
quasar 375.8
quash destroy 693.15
hush up 614.8
suppress 760.8
quasi
adj. imitation 22.8
nominal 583.15
similar 20.14
ungenuine 616.26
adv. imitatively 22.11
supposedly 499.17
quaternary
n. four 96.1
adj. four 96.4
quatrain 609.11
quaver
n. excitement 857.4
harmonics 463.14
music 463.19
shake 324.3

speech defect 595.1
v. be excited 857.16
shake 324.11
sing 462.39
speak poorly 595.7
tremble 891.22
quavering
n. excitement 857.4
shaking 324.2
adj. imperfectly spo-
ken 595.12
shaking 324.17
quay 700.6
queasy
fastidious 896.10
nauseated 686.53
queen bee 414.38
chessman 878.18
homosexual 419.16
playing card 878.17
princess 918.8
sovereign 749.11
termite 414.37
the best 674.8
queenly
dignified 905.12
noble 918.10
sovereign 739.17
queenship
noble rank 918.9
sovereignty 739.8
queer
n. counterfeit 835.10
homosexual 419.16
v. disable 158.9
spoil 692.13
thwart 730.16
adj. eccentric 474.4
homosexual 419.32
insane 473.25
odd 85.11
ungenuine 616.26
queer duck 85.4
queered 692.31
quell calm 163.7
conquer 727.10
destroy 693.15
subdue 764.9
suppress 760.8
quelled
conquered 727.16
restrained 163.11
subdued 764.15
suppressed 760.14
quench destroy 693.15
disincline 652.4
extinguish 332.7
gratify 865.6
suppress 760.8
querulous
discontented 869.5
ill-humored 951.21
plaintive 875.16
query
n. question 485.10
v. be curious 528.3
be doubtful 503.6
inquire 485.19
interrogate 485.20
que será será 640.11
quest
n. pursuit 655.1

search 485.14
undertaking 715.2
v. pursue 655.8
seek 485.29
question
n. an uncertainty
514.4
doubt 503.2
legislative motion
742.17
puzzle 549.8
query 485.10
remark 594.4
topic 484.1
v. be curious 528.3
be doubtful 503.6
be uncertain 514.9
communicate with
554.8
inquire 485.19
interrogate 485.20
questionable
deceptive 618.19
dishonest 975.16
doubtful 503.10
improbable 512.3
uncertain 514.16
questioner
curious person 528.2
inquirer 485.15
questioning
n. interrogation
485.11
adj. communicational
554.9
doubtful 503.9
inquiring 485.35
question mark
puzzle 549.8
question 485.10
questionnaire
n. canvass 485.13
list 88.6
v. canvass 485.28
queue
n. hair 230.7
row 71.2
sequel 67.2
tail 241.6
v. line up 71.6
quibble
n. cavil 483.4
disapproval 969.4
v. argue 482.16
cavil 483.9
find fault 969.15
quibbler caviler 483.7
faultfinder 969.9
quibbling
n. caviling 483.5
disapproval 969.4
adj. caviling 483.14
critical 969.24
quiche 308.40
quick
n. inner nature 5.4
sensitive area 422.4
adj. alert 533.14
eager 635.9
fast 269.19
hasty 709.9
hot-tempered 951.25

impulsive 630.9
intelligent 467.14
lively 707.18
living 407.11
prompt 131.9
skillful 733.20
sudden 113.5
teachable 564.18
transient 111.8
willing 622.5
adv. fast 269.21
quicken
accelerate 269.14
come to life 407.8
energize 161.9
facilitate 732.6
further 785.17
hasten 709.4
refresh 695.2
sensitize 422.9
stimulate 857.12
vivify 407.9
quickening
n. acceleration 269.4
energizing 161.7
facilitation 732.4
hastening 709.3
vivification 407.5
adj. energizing 161.14
life-giving 407.12
quickly eagerly 635.14
hastily 709.12
impulsively 630.13
promptly 131.15
shortly 111.10
swiftly 269.21
with alacrity 707.26
quickness alacrity 707.3
alertness 533.5
eagerness 635.1
hastiness 709.2
impulsiveness 630.2
intelligence 467.2
promptness 131.3
skill 733.1
speed 269.1
teachability 564.5
quicksand danger 697.1
marsh 400.1
pitfall 697.5
predicament 731.4
quicksilver
n. changeableness
141.4
speed 269.6
adj. fickle 629.6
lively 707.17
metal 383.17
quickstep 273.15
quick-tempered 951.25
quick-witted
intelligent 467.14
witty 881.15
quid bite 307.2
British money 835.8
chewing tobacco
434.7
essence 5.2
quiddity essence 5.2
quibble 483.4
quid pro quo
interaction 13.3

interchange 150.1
offset 33.2
retaliation 955.3
substitution 149.1
quiescence
immobility 140.1
inactivity 708.1
passivity 706.1
silence 451.1
stillness 268
quiescent
do-nothing 706.6
inactive 708.16
permanent 140.7
quiet 268.12
silent 451.10
quiet
n. composure 858.2
order 59.1
peace 803.2
quiescence 268.1
rest 711.1
silence 451.1
v. calm 163.7
ebb 268.8
fall silent 451.7
order 59.4
silence 451.8
adj. composed 858.12
covert 614.12
modest 908.11
pacific 803.9
quiescent 268.12
silent 451.10
soft-colored 362.21
taciturn 613.9
tasteful 897.8
vacational 711.10
weak 765.15
interj. silence! 451.14
quietening
soothing 687.45
tranquilizing 163.15
quietism
inaction 706.1
quiescence 268.1
resignation 861.2
thoughtfreeness
480.1
quietly calmly 268.18
inexcitably 858.16
meekly 765.19
modestly 908.14
silently 451.13
tastefully 897.11
quiet spell 109.1
quietude
composure 858.2
order 59.1
peace 803.2
quiescence 268.1
silence 451.1
taciturnity 613.2
quietus
acquittal 1007.1
death 408.1
defeat 727.1
end 70.1
ruin 693.2
stopper 70.4
quill
feather part 230.17

feather type 230.16
thorn 258.7,18
quilt 228.10
quilting 223.6
quilting bee 922.13
quinqu(e)– 99.17
quinsy 686.14
quintessence
content 194.5
essence 5.2
extract 305.8
pattern of perfection
677.4
the best 674.8
quintessential
best 674.18
characteristic 80.13
essential 305.18
perfect 677.9
typical 572.11
quintet
cooperation 786.1
five 99.1
orchestra 464.12
part music 462.17
quintuple
v. multiply 99.16
adj. five 99.17
quintuplet 99.1
quip
n. eccentricity 474.2
gibe 967.2
quibble 483.4
witticism 881.7
v. joke 881.13
quipster 881.12
quire 378.6
quirk caprice 629.1
characteristic 80.4
distortion 249.1
eccentricity 474.2
mannerism 903.2
quibble 483.4
quirky capricious 629.5
eccentric 474.4
quisling
n. criminal 986.10
traitor 619.10
turncoat 628.5
adj. traitorous 975.22
quit
v. abandon 633.5
cease 144.6
discontinue 668.4
leave 301.8
repay 841.11
resign 784.2
retaliate 955.5
adj. clear 762.30
quitclaim
n. relinquishment
814.2
v. relinquish 814.3
quite absolutely 56.15
exactly! 516.23
positively 34.19
to a degree 29.7
very 34.18
yes! 521.18
quits 30.7
quittance
acquittal 1007.1

atonement 1012.1
payment 841.1
receipt 844.2
recompense 841.3
reprisal 955.2
quiver
n. bundle 74.8
excitement 857.4
flutter 324.4
light 335.8
music 463.19
nervousness 859.2
shake 324.3
thrill 857.2
v. be cold 333.9
be excited 857.16
be weak 160.8
flicker 335.25
shake 324.11
tremble 891.22
quivering
n. excitement 857.4
light 335.8
shaking 324.2
part music 462.17
adj. flickering 335.36
in suspense 539.12
jittery 859.11
shaking 324.17
quixotic(al) 535.24
quiz
n. examination 485.2
questioning 485.11
v. be curious 528.3
interrogate 485.20
quizzical
bantering 882.5
curious 528.5
humorous 880.4
inquiring 485.35
ridiculing 967.12
quoin corner 251.2
cornerstone 216.7
typesetting 603.2,26
quoit circle 253.3
projectile 285.6
quondam 119.10
quorum 74.2
quota allotment 816.5
part 55.1
ratio 86.6
quotation
citation 505.6
price 846.2
repetition 103.1
stock price 834.9
quote cite 505.14
repeat 103.7
state 594.24

R

Ra
Egyptian deity
1014.10
sun god 375.14
rabbet
n. groove 263.1
joint 47.4
v. fasten 47.8
groove 263.3
rabbi
clergyman 1038.12

master 749.1
teacher 565.1
wise man 468.1
rabbinate clergy 1038.1
the ministry 1037.1
rabbinic
ministerial 1037.13
scriptural 1021.11
studious 564.17
rabbit fertility 165.6
hare 414.29,58
mammals 415.8
rabbit's-foot 1036.5
rabble
common people
919.4
throng 74.4
rabble-rouser
instigator 648.11
public speaker 599.4
rabble-rousing
n. incitement 648.4
public speaking 599.1
adj. incitive 648.28
Rabelaisian
maledictory 972.8
obscene 990.9
sarcastic 967.13
rabid excited 857.23
fanatical 473.32
infuriated 952.29
mad 473.30
rabies
animal disease 686.38
hydrophobia 473.6
infectious disease
686.12
raccoon 414.28,58
race
n. ancestry 170.4
class 61.2
contest of speed
796.12
family 11.4
flow 395.4
game 878.9
haste 709.1
kind 61.3
people 418.1
running water 395.1
speed 269.3
watercourse 396.2
v. accelerate 269.14
compete with 796.20
make haste 709.5
rush 269.9
racecourse 878.12
race horse 414.17
raceme 411.25
racer athlete 878.20
race horse 414.17
speeder 269.5
racial 11.7
racing
n. contest 796.11
adj. flowing 395.24
racism hate 930.1
prejudice 527.4
racist
n. hater 930.4
intolerant person
527.5

ragamuffin 274.3
rage
　n. excitement 857.7
　fad 644.5
　fit 952.8
　frenzy 473.7
　mania 473.12
　passion 952.10
　the latest thing 644.4
　violence 162.2
　v. be angry 952.15
　be excited 857.15
　be insane 473.19
　blow 403.22
　bluster 911.3
　storm 162.10
ragged
　nonuniform 18.3
　raucous 458.15
　rough 261.7
　severed 49.23
　shabby 692.34
　slovenly 62.15
　tormented 866.24
raggedy shabby 692.34
　slovenly 62.15
raging blustering 911.4
　excited 857.23
　infuriated 952.29
　mad 473.30
　stormy 403.26
　violent 162.17
ragman
　junk dealer 830.10
　vagrant 274.3
ragout 308.11
rag out clothe 231.38
　dress up 231.41
ragpicker 274.3
ragtag 919.4
ragtime
　n. music 462.9
　tempo 463.24
　adj. music 463.29
rah 876.2
raid
　n. attack 798.4
　plundering 824.5
　stock manipulation
　　833.20
　v. attack 798.20
　plunder 824.16
raider assailant 798.13
　plunderer 825.6
rail
　n. fence 236.4
　railway 657.8
　thinness 205.7
　v. confine 761.12
　enclose 236.7
rail at berate 969.20
　ridicule 967.9
railing
　n. fence 236.4,13
　adj. ridiculing 967.12
raillery banter 882.1
　ridicule 967.1
railroad
　n. railway 657.8
　v. hasten 709.4
　legislate 742.18
railroader 274.13

railroad man 274.13
railway 657.8
railway car 272.14
railway express 271.3
raiment
　n. clothing 231.1
　garment 231.3
　v. clothe 231.38
rain
　n. gods 394.6
　rainfall 394
　television reception
　　345.5
　water 392.3
　v. abound 661.5
　descend 316.5
　drench 392.14
　give 818.12
　precipitate 394.9
rainbow
　n. barbiturate 687.12
　iridescence 335.18
　light 335.14
　omen 544.6
　variegation 374.6
　adj. coloring 362.15
rainbowlike
　iridescent 335.37
　variegated 374.10
raindrop drop 255.3
　rain 394.1
rainfall moisture 392.1
　rain 394.1
rain forest 411.11
rain gauge 394.7
rainmaker
　aviator 279.1
　cloud seeder 394.5
rainmaking 394.5
rain or shine
　come what may
　　624.20
　perseveringly 625.9
　without fail 513.26
rainstorm
　downpour 394.2
　storm 162.4
rainy moist 392.15
　showery 394.10
　stormy 403.26
rainy day
　hard times 729.6
　wet weather 394.4
raise
　n. height 207.2
　increase 38.1
　promotion 782.1
　v. assemble 74.18
　begin 68.11
　communicate with
　　554.8
　conjure 1035.11
　create 167.10
　elevate 317.5
　emboss 256.11
　enlist 780.16
　erect 213.9
　farm 413.16
　glorify 914.13
　grow 167.11
　increase 38.4
　leaven 353.7

　make better 691.9
　make larger 197.4
　promote 782.2
　raise animals 416.6
　rouse 648.19
　say 594.23
　train 562.14
raised expanded 197.10
　grown 167.22
　increased 38.7
　in relief 256.17
　lifted 317.9
　produced 167.20
raise hell
　be angry 952.15
　be disorderly 62.11
　be noisy 453.8
　cause trouble 731.13
　confuse 532.7
　make merry 878.26
raiser
　agriculturist 413.5
　producer 167.8
raising
　n. elevation 317.1
　erection 213.4
　expansion 197.1
　growing 413.12
　manufacture 167.3
　training 562.3
　adj. leavening 353.16
raison d'être
　cause 153.10
　objective 653.2
raja 749.9
rake
　n. inclination 219.2
　pointed projection
　　258.4
　thinness 205.7
　unchaste person
　　989.10
　v. be unchaste 989.19
　comb 681.21
　fire upon 798.22
　incline 219.10
　ransack 485.32
　till 413.17
rake-off gain 811.3
　payment 841.7
　portion 816.5
rakish jaunty 904.19
　unchaste 989.25
rally
　n. call to arms 797.12
　contest 796.3
　electioneering 744.12
　meeting 74.2
　protest 522.2
　recovery 694.8
　stock prices 834.9
　tournament 878.10
　v. aid 785.11
　arrange evidence
　　505.13
　assemble 74.18
　banter 882.4
　call to arms 797.23
　come together 74.16
　dispose 60.9
　improve 691.8
　incite 648.17

　object 522.5
　recover 694.20
　recuperate 694.19
　ridicule 967.9
rallying cry
　call to arms 797.12
　cry 459.1
　signal 568.16
rally round form 59.5
　join with 786.4
ram
　n. male animal 420.8
　sheep 414.7
　v. sail 275.41
　thrust 283.11
Rama 1014.9
Ramadan fast 995.3
　holy day 1040.17
ramate 411.38
ramble
　n. amble 273.12
　wandering 273.3
　v. be insane 473.19
　chatter 596.5
　digress 593.9
　travel 273.22
　wander 291.4
rambler 274.2
rambling
　n. deviation 291.1
　discursiveness 593.3
　wandering 273.3
　adj. delirious 473.31
　discursive 593.13
　distracted 532.10
　inconstant 141.7
　irregular 138.3
　unintelligible 549.13
　traveling 273.36
　wandering 291.7
rambunctious 162.19
ram down one's throat
　compel 756.6
　thrust upon 818.20
ramification
　bisection 92.1
　branching 299.3
　complexity 46.1
　fork 299.4
　limb 411.18
　offshoot 55.4
ramify bisect 92.4
　branch 299.7
　complicate 46.3
　increase 38.5
　spread 197.6
ram in fill 56.7
　thrust in 304.7
ramjet 280.3,17
ramous
　branched 299.10
　leafy 411.38
ramp
　n. fraud 618.8
　incline 219.4
　stairs 315.3
　v. ascend 315.11
　be excited 857.15
　cheat 618.17
　jump 319.6
　rage 162.10
　rise 213.8

tenuous 4.6
thin 205.16
rarefy attenuate 355.3
dematerialize 4.4
dilute 160.11
make larger 197.4
thin 205.12
rarely
infrequently 136.4
scarcely 662.16
sparsely 102.8
unusually 85.17
raring to 635.9
rarity fewness 102.1
infrequency 136.1
marvel 920.2
odd thing 85.5
scarcity 662.3
thinness 205.4
unsubstantiality 355
unusualness 85.2
rascal
mischief-maker 738.3
scoundrel 986.3
rascally 975.17
rash
n. disease symptom
686.8
skin eruption 686.34
adj. brash 894.7
impulsive 630.9
precipitate 709.10
rasher portion 55.3
slice 227.2
rashness brashness 894
hastiness 709.2
impulsiveness 630.2
rasp
n. harsh sound 458.3
v. abrade 350.7
hurt 424.7
irritate 866.14
sound harshly 458.10
raspberry 967.3
rasping
n. abrasion 350.2
powder 361.5
refuse 669.4
adj. abrasive 350.10
irritating 424.13
sounding harsh
458.16
Rasputin 172.6
raspy 458.16
rat
n. bad person 986.6
false hair 230.13
mammal 414.58
strikebreaker 789.6
traitor 619.10
v. break a strike
789.10
desert 633.6
divulge 556.6
inform on 557.12
ratable
n. taxation 846.10
adj. chargeable 846.17
rat-a-tat
pulsation 323.3
staccato sound 455.1
ratchet 258.4

rate
n. debt 840.3
gait 267.4
price 846.1
rank 29.2
ratio 86.6
tax 846.11
worth 846.3
v. be judged 494.15
berate 969.20
classify 61.6
deserve 960.5
judge 494.9
measure 490.11
precede 64.2
price 846.13
quantify 28.4
reprove 969.17
rated classified 61.8
priced 846.16
rather
v. prefer 637.17
adv. contrarily 15.9
instead 149.11
notwithstanding 33.8
preferably 637.28
to a degree 29.7
tolerably 674.23
interj. exactly! 516.23
yes! 521.18
rathskeller 996.19
ratification
authorization 777.3
confirmation 505.5
consent 775.1
endorsement 521.4
ratified chosen 637.26
endorsed 521.14
ratify adopt 637.15
authorize 777.11
confirm 505.12
consent 775.2
endorse 521.12
rating berating 969.7
classification 61.1
credit 839.1
grade 61.2
judgment 494.3
measurement 490.1
rank 29.2
reproof 969.5
valuation 846.4
ratio
comparability 491.3
degree 29.1
intellect 466.1
proportion 86.6
ratiocination
reasoning 482.1
thought 478.1
ration
n. amount 28.2
portion 816.5
v. apportion 816.8
budget 816.10
rational
intelligent 467.12
logical 482.20
mental 466.8
numerical 86.8
practical 536.6
reasoning 482.18

sane 472.4
sensible 467.18
rationale
explanation 552.4
reason 153.2
rationalism
reasoning 482.1
theology 1023.1
rationalist 482.11
rationalistic
explanatory 552.15
philosophy 500.9
rationality
comprehension 467.1
intellect 466.1
practicalness 536.2
reasoning 482.1
sanity 472.1
sense 482.9
soundness 467.6
rationalization
defense mechanism
690.30
justification 1006.1
organization 60.2
plan 654.1
reasoning 482.1
sophistry 483.1
rationalize
deduce 482.15
explain 552.10
justify 1006.9
organize 60.10
plan 654.9
reason speciously
483.8
rationally
intelligently 467.20
reasonably 482.24
rationing
apportionment 816.1
restraint 760.1
rations food 308.6
store 660.1
rat race busyness 707.5
drudgery 716.4
futility 669.2
whirlpool 322.2
rat's nest complex 46.2
jumble 62.3
rattail hair 230.7
tail 241.6
rattan bamboo 378.4
instrument of punish-
ment 1011.2
rattle
n. chatterer 596.4
clatter 455.3
noise 453.3
noisemaker 453.5
percussion instrument
465.18
v. chatter 596.5
clatter 455.6
confuse 532.7
excite 857.13
joggle 283.11
talk nonsense 547.5
weaken 160.10
rattlebrain 471.7
rattlebrained
scatterbrained 532.16

stupid 469.19
rattletrap 692.10
rattrap 618.11
ratty infested 313.11
rodent 414.48
shabby 692.34
raucous
dissonant 461.4
harsh 458.15
raunchy 990.9
ravage
n. debauchment 989.6
destruction 693.1
overrunning 313.2
plundering 824.5
v. corrupt 692.14
destroy 693.10
overrun 313.6
plunder 824.16
seduce 989.20
ravaged
dilapidated 53.5
infested 313.11
ruined 693.28
spoiled 692.43
tired-looking 717.7
ravager
debaucher 989.12
plunderer 825.6
ravages of time
disintegration 53.1
time 105.3
wear 692.5
rave be angry 952.15
be enthusiastic 635.8
be excited 857.15
be insane 473.19
berate 969.20
bluster 911.3
rage 162.10
ravel
n. complex 46.2
v. complicate 46.3
simplify 45.5
solve 487.2
raveled 46.4
raven
n. black 365.4
omen 544.6
adj. black 365.8
raven gluttonize 994.4
hunger 634.19
plunder 824.16
ravenous
gluttonous 994.6
greedy 634.27
hungry 634.25
rapacious 822.26
ravine crack 201.2
valley 257.9
raving
n. delirium 473.8
adj. blustering 911.4
delirious 473.31
excited 857.23
gorgeous 900.19
infuriated 952.29
mad 473.30
violent 162.17
ravioli 308.33
ravish corrupt 692.14
delight 865.8

normal 84.7
philosophy 500.9
practical 536.6
typical 572.11
ungullible 504.5
reality actuality 1.2
certainty 513.3
event 151.2
truth 516.1
realizable
possible 509.7
practical 670.6
realization
accomplishment 722.1
appearance 446.1
cognizance 475.2
completion 56.4
event 151.1
inception 167.4
production 167.1
recognition 537.5
representation 572.1
realize
accomplish 722.4
be sold 829.12
cause 153.11
create 167.12
do 705.6
know 475.12
produce 167.9
profit 811.11
recognize 537.12
represent 572.8
understand 548.7
visualize 535.15
realized
accomplished 722.10
known 475.26
really
adv. actually 1.16
genuinely 516.18
positively 34.19
truly 516.17
very 34.18
interj. wonder 920.19
yes 521.18
realm class 61.4
country 181.1
region 180.2
sphere of work 656.4
real McCoy, the 516.6
Realpolitik 744.1
real property
land 385.1
real estate 810.7
real thing, the 516.6
Realtor 830.9
realty 810.7
ream
n. paper 378.6
v. anal sex 419.24
puncture 265.16
reprove 969.19
reaming-out 969.6
reap acquire 811.8
harvest 413.19
shorten 203.6
reaper 413.5
Reaper 408.3
reaping 413.15

reappear
be repeated 103.11
recur 137.5
reappearance
periodicity 137.2
repetition 103.1
reappearing
recurrent 103.13
renascent 694.24
reproductive 169.14
reappraisal
reconsideration 478.5
re-examination 485.7
reappraise
reconsider 478.15
re-examine 485.26
rear
n. back 241
buttocks 241.4
rear guard 241.2
setting 233.2
v. ascend 315.8
be high 207.15
create 167.10
elevate 317.5
erect 213.9
farm 413.16
process 167.11
raise animals 416.6
rise 213.8
sail 275.55
tower 34.5
train 562.14
adj. back 241.9
rear end back 241.1
buttocks 241.4
rearing
n. elevation 317.1
erection 213.4
growing 413.12
training 562.3
adj. ascending 315.14
vertical 213.11
rearrange 60.13
rearward
n. rear 241.1
adj. back 241.9
adv. in reverse 295.13
to the rear 241.15
reason
n. argument 482.5
cause 153.2
explanation 552.4
intellect 466.1
justification 1006.6
logical thought 482.1
motive 648.1
reasonableness 482.9
sanity 472.1
sensibleness 467.6
solution 487.1
v. conclude 494.10
confer with 597.11
discuss 597.12
logicalize 482.15
practice philosophy 500.7
think 478.8
reasonable cheap 849.7
intelligent 467.12
justifiable 1006.14
logical 482.20

moderate 163.12
practical 536.6
probable 511.7
sane 472.4
sensible 467.18
reasonably
cheaply 849.10
intelligently 467.20
logically 482.24
reasoner 482.11
reasoning
n. intellect 466.1
logical thought 482
thinking 478.1
adj. mental 466.8
rational 482.18
reasonless
illogical 483.11
impulsive 630.10
insane 473.25
unintelligent 469.13
unwise 470.9
reason to believe 505.1
reassembly 694.5
reassurance
comfort 887.4
encouragement 893.9
making certain 513.8
reassure comfort 887.6
encourage 893.16
give hope 888.10
make sure 513.11
reassuring
comforting 887.13
promising 888.13
reasty 437.5
rebarbative
offensive 864.18
unsavory 429.7
rebate
n. discount 847.1
v. discount 847.2
rebel
n. insurgent 767.5
lawless person 740.3
malcontent 869.3
revolutionist 147.3
v. revolt 767.7
adj. rebellious 767.11
rebellion
lawlessness 740.2
revolt 767.4
rebellious
discontented 869.5
mutinous 767.11
resistant 792.5
rebirth
redemption 1026.4
renewal 145.2
repetition 103.1
reproduction 169.1
revival 694.3
reborn
converted 145.19
pious 1028.10
revived 694.24
sanctified 1026.9
rebound
n. recoil 284.2
resilience 358.1
reverberation 454.2
v. recoil 284.6

reverberate 454.7
rebuff
n. defeat 727.2
recoil 284.2
refusal 776.2
rejection 638.1
repulse 289.2
resistance 792.1
snub 966.2
v. fend off 799.10
refuse 776.5
reject 638.2
repulse 289.3
resist 792.2
snub 966.5
rebuild change 139.6
remake 169.7
restore 694.18
rebuilding
reconstruction 694.5
reproduction 169.1
rebuilt 139.9
rebuke
n. reproof 969.5
v. reprove 969.17
rebus 549.9
rebut contradict 790.6
defend 1006.10
refute 506.5
rejoin 486.5
rebuttal
counterstatement 486.2
justification 1006.2
legal plea 1004.6
opposition 790.1
refutation 506.2
recalcitrance
counteraction 178.1
nonconformity 83.1
opposition 790.2
refractoriness 767.2
resistance 792.1
ungovernability 626.4
unwillingness 623.1
recalcitrant
n. reactionary 284.4
adj. counteractive 178.8
nonconforming 83.5
opposing 790.8
recoiling 284.10
refractory 767.10
resistant 792.5
ungovernable 626.12
unwilling 623.5
recall
n. referendum 742.16
remembering 537.4
repeal 779.1
v. remember 537.10
remind 537.20
repeal 779.2
summon 752.12
recant deny 524.4
reject 638.2
relinquish 814.3
repeal 779.2
retract 628.9
recantation
denial 524.2
refusal 776.1

reefer
  marihuana 687.13
  railway car 272.14
  refrigerator 334.4
reefy 210.6
reek
  n. smoke 329.16
  stench 437.1
  vapor 401.1
  v. exhale 310.23
  exude 303.15
  give off 401.8
  smell 435.6
  smoke 328.23
  stink 437.4
reeking
  n. stench 437.1
  adj. burning 328.27
  intense 159.20
  malodorous 437.5
  strong-smelling
    435.10
  vaporous 401.9
reel
  n. flounder 324.8
  rotation 322.2,17
  swing 323.6
  windlass 287.7
  v. be drunk 996.26
  eddy 395.21
  flounder 324.15
  oscillate 323.10
  pull back 284.7
  sail 275.55
  whirl 322.11
  wind in 287.9
reeling
  n. rotation 322.1
  adj. intoxicated
    996.30
  rotating 322.14
  swinging 323.17
reenact 694.11
reentry
  regression 295.1
  return 300.3
  spacecraft 282.2
reestablish
  remake 169.7
  restore 694.11
reeve
  peace officer 699.15
  public official 749.17
re-examine
  recheck 485.26
  think over 478.15
refection food 308.3
  invigoration 695.1
  refreshment 307.5
refectory 192.11
refer see **refer to**
referable
  attributable 155.6
  relative 9.7
referee
  n. arbitrator 805.4
  judge 1002.1
  umpire 494.6
  v. judge 494.12
  mediate 805.6
reference
  n. aspect 446.3

attribution 155.2
  citation 505.6
  meaning 545.1
  punctuation 586.15
  recommendation
    968.4
  relevance 9.4
  v. cite 505.15
reference book
  book 605.6
  directory 748.10
reference mark
  punctuation 586.15
  types of 586.20
referendum
  election 744.15
  political referendum
    742.16
  vote 637.6
referent 545.1
referential
  figurative 551.3
  meaningful 545.10
  suggestive 546.6
refer to
  attribute to 155.4
  avail oneself of
    665.14
  call attention to
    530.10
  cite 505.15
  confer with 597.11
  designate 568.18
  mean 545.8
  relate to 9.5
  remark 594.25
refill complete 56.6
  restore 694.11
refine extract 305.16
  finish 691.10
  make better 691.9
  melt 329.21
  process 167.11
  purify 681.22
  sensitize 422.9
  simplify 45.4
  subtract 42.9
refined
  discriminating 492.7
  exact 516.16
  fastidious 896.11
  improved 691.13
  meticulous 533.12
  perfected 677.9
  polished 589.6
  produced 167.22
  purified 681.26
  sensitive 422.14
  smooth 351.8
  tasteful 897.9
  well-bred 936.17
refinement
  accuracy 516.3
  cultivation 691.3
  difference 16.2
  discrimination 492.1
  extract 305.8
  fastidiousness 896.3
  fine texture 351.3
  good breeding 936.4
  good taste 897.1
  improvement 691.2

literary elegance
    589.1
  meticulousness 533.3
  purification 681.4
  simplification 45.2
  subtraction 42.1
refinery plant 719.3
  refining place 681.13
reflect consider 478.12
  curve 252.6
  imitate 22.5
  radar 346.16
  remark 594.25
  remember 537.10
  represent 572.8
  think over 478.13
reflection
  consideration 478.2
  curve 252.3
  disapproval 969.4
  disparagement 971.4
  idea 479.1
  image 572.3
  judiciousness 467.7
  light 335.9
  radar signal 346.11
  reaction 284.1
  reflex 24.7
  remark 594.4
  remembering 537.4
  stigma 915.6
reflective
  judicious 467.19
  thoughtful 478.21
reflector
  astronomy 375.17
  mirror 443.5
  radar 346.23
reflect upon 969.13
reflex
  n. conditioning
    690.33
  effect 154.3
  impulse 630.1
  reaction 284.1
  reflection 24.7
  v. curve 252.6
  adj. involuntary
    639.14
  reactive 284.9
  reversed 295.12
  unpremeditated
    630.11
reflex action
  involuntariness 639.5
  reaction 284.1
reflexive
  n. voice 586.14
  adj. involuntary
    639.14
  reactive 284.9
  unpremeditated
    630.11
refluent flowing 267.8
  reflex 284.9
reflux course 267.2
  eddy 395.22
  reaction 284.1
  regression 295.1
  tide 395.13
reform
  n. change 139.1

improvement 691.5
  renewal 145.2
  v. change 139.6
  change one's ways
    145.12
  make better 691.9
  purify 681.18
  repent 873.7
  restore 694.11
  sanctify 1026.6
re-form
  reconstruct 694.18
  remake 169.7
  reshape 145.12
reformation
  change 139.1
  improvement 691.5
  penitence 873.4
  redemption 1026.4
  regeneration 145.2
  restoration 694.1
reformatory
  prison 761.8
  reform school 567.14
reformed
  changed 139.9
  converted 145.19
  improved 691.13
  purified 681.26
reformer
  politician 746.1
  reformist 691.6
reform school
  prison 761.8
  school 567.14
refound 169.7
refract 291.5
refraction
  deflection 291.2
  radar interference
    346.12
refractive 291.8
refractor 375.17
refractory
  ceramic 576.7
  disobedient 767.10
  nonconforming 83.5
  opposing 790.8
  resistant 792.5
  ungovernable 626.12
  unwilling 623.5
refrain
  n. melody 462.4
  music division 462.24
  poetic division
    609.11
  repeat 103.5
  sequel 67.1
  v. abstain 992.7
  cease 144.6
  not do 706.3
  not use 668.5
refraining
  abstinence 992.2
  avoidance 631.1
refresh air 402.11
  amuse 878.23
  freshen 695.2
  refrigerate 334.10
  renovate 694.17
  revive 694.16
  strengthen 159.11

regularity
constancy 135.2
monotony 17.2
normality 84.1
order 59.1
recurrence 137
smoothness 260.1
symmetry 248.1
regularize
make uniform 17.4
normalize 84.6
order 59.4
organize 60.10
symmetrize 248.3
regularly
constantly 135.7
habitually 642.23
methodically 59.9
normally 84.9
smoothly 260.12
systematically 137.9
uniformly 17.8
regulate direct 747.8
govern 741.12
influence 172.8
legalize 998.8
make agree 26.7
make uniform 17.4
order 59.4
organize 60.10
qualify 507.3
regulation
n. adjustment 26.4
directive 752.3
government 741.1
law 998.3
management 747.1
organization 60.2
precept 751.2
rule 84.4
adj. customary 642.15
prescriptive 751.4
usual 84.8
regulator 349.14
regulatory
directing 747.12
governing 741.18
regurgitate flow 395.16
repeat 103.7
vomit 310.25
regurgitation
eddy 395.12
repetition 103.1
vomiting 310.8
rehabilitate
justify 1006.9
recondition 145.14
restore 694.11
rehabilitation
adjustment 690.34
justification 1006.1
reconditioning 145.4
restoration 694.1
reversion 146.1
rehabilitative 1006.13
rehash
n. iteration 103.2
v. paraphrase 552.13
repeat 103.8
rehearsal
drama production
611.14

iteration 103.2
narrative 608.2
numeration 87.5
training 562.3
tryout 489.3
rehearse narrate 608.13
rehearse a play
611.37
repeat 103.8
report 558.11
summarize 87.12
train 562.14
reification 3.4
reify 3.5
reign
n. authority 739.5
government 741.1
influence 172.1
prevalence 79.2
v. prevail 79.10
rule 741.14
reigning
governing 741.18
prevalent 79.12
reimburse
make restitution
823.5
repay 841.11
reimbursement
payment 841.2
restitution 823.2
rein
n. restraint 760.1
v. restrain 760.7
slow 270.9
reincarnate
embody 376.8
repeat 103.7
reincarnation
embodiment 376.7
repetition 103.1
transformation 139.2
reindeer
beast of burden
271.6
hoofed animal
414.5,58
reinforce aid 785.12
add to 40.5
confirm 505.12
increase 38.5
stiffen 356.9
strengthen 159.11
support 216.21
reinforced
hardened 356.13
increased 38.7
reinforcement
addition 40.1
adjunct 41.1
aid 785.8
conditioning 690.33
confirmation 505.5
increase 38.2
provision 659.1
strengthening 159.5
supporter 216.2
wave phenomenon
323.4
reins harness 659.5
management 747.5
restraint 760.4

reinstate justify 1006.9
restore 694.11
reinstatement
justification 1006.1
restoration 694.1
reversion 146.1
reinstitute
remake 169.7
restore 694.11
reissue
n. iteration 103.2
printing 603.3
reproduction 169.1
v. monetize 835.26
print 603.14
remake 169.7
repeat 103.8
reiterate
v. repeat 103.8
adj. repeated 103.12
reiteration
diffuseness 593.1
duplication 91.1
platitude 517.3
repetition 103.2
reiterative
diffuse 593.11
repetitious 103.14
reject
n. abandoned thing
633.4
discard 668.3
v. be incredulous
504.3
contradict 790.6
disapprove 969.10
disbelieve 503.5
discard 668.7
eject 310.13
exclude 77.4
prohibit 778.3
refuse 776.3
repudiate 638.2
vomit 310.25
rejected
discarded 668.11
disproved 506.7
outcast 926.10
repudiated 638.3
unloved 867.10
rejection
disapproval 969.1
discard 668.3
dissent 522.1
ejection 310.1
exclusion 77.1
opposition 790.1
prohibition 778.1
refusal 776.1
repudiation 638
unbelief 503.1
rejoice cheer 870.7
enjoy 865.10
jubilate 876.5
rejoicing
n. celebration 877.1
jubilation 876
adj. jubilant 876.9
merry 870.15
rejoin answer 486.4
rebut 486.5
rejoinder answer 486.1

counterstatement
486.2
rejuvenate
make young 124.8
revive 694.16
rejuvenation 694.3
rekindle burn 329.22
revive 694.16
relapse
n. falling back 696
regression 295.1
reversion 146.1
v. get worse 692.19
regress 295.5
return to 696.4
revert 146.4
relate associate 9.6
communicate with
554.8
compare 491.4
narrate 608.13
refer to 9.5
report 558.11
state 594.24
suit 26.8
summarize 87.12
related connected 9.9
germane 9.10
kindred 11.6
relation
blood relationship
11.1
comparison 491.1
connection 9
involvement 176.1
meaning 545.1
narrative 608.2
role 7.5
relations affairs 151.4
copulation 419.8
kinsmen 11.2
relationship 9.1
relationship
blood relationship
11.1
connection 9.1
relative
n. kinsman 11.2
adj. comparative
491.8
relational 9.7
relatively
comparatively 491.10
relevantly 9.12
to a degree 35.10
relativity
correlation 13.1
relationship 9.2
space 179.6
relator 608.10
relax
amuse oneself 878.24
be comfortable 887.8
be pliant 357.7
calm oneself 858.7
entertain 878.23
loosen 51.3
make pliant 357.6
moderate 163.9
relent 944.4
rest 711.7
slow 270.9

waive 507.5
relaxation
 amusement 878.1
 decrease 39.1
 looseness 51.2
 moderation 163.2
 rest 711.1
 softening 357.5
 unstrictness 758.1
 weakening 160.5
relaxed at ease 887.12
 flaccid 357.10
 informal 647.3
 leisurely 710.6
 loose 51.5
 negligent 534.10
 slow 270.10
 thoughtless 480.4
 unnervous 860.2
 unstrict 758.4
relaxing
 comfortable 887.11
 moderating 163.14
 softening 357.16
relay
 n. computer part
  349.32
 electrical part 342.36
 race 796.12
 shift 108.3
 v. transfer 271.9
relay station
 radio station 344.6
 television relay 345.9
release
 n. acquittal 1007.1
 death 408.1
 disbandment 75.3
 escape 632.1
 exemption 762.8
 information 557.1
 liberation 763.2
 message 558.4
 permission 777.1
 press release 559.3
 receipt 844.2
 relief 886.2
 relinquishment 814.1
 rescue 702.1
 v. acquit 1007.4
 detach 49.10
 disband 75.8
 dismiss 310.19
 exempt 762.14
 extricate 763.7
 free 763.5
 permit 777.9
 relieve 886.6
 relinquish 814.4
 rescue 702.3
released dead 408.30
 exempt 762.29
 free 762.20
 liberated 763.10
 relinquished 814.5
relegate commit 818.16
 eject 310.17
 exclude 77.4
relent
 be moderate 163.5
 be pliant 357.7
 have pity 944.4

submit 765.6
relentless
 industrious 707.22
 inevitable 639.15
 persevering 625.7
 pitiless 945.3
 resolute 624.11
 strict 757.7
 unyielding 626.9
relentlessness
 industry 707.6
 inevitability 639.7
 perseverance 625.1
 pitilessness 945.1
 resolution 624.1
 strictness 757.2
 unyieldingness 626.2
relevance fitness 26.5
 meaning 545.1
 pertinence 9.4
relevant apt 26.10
 pertinent 9.11
reliability
 believability 501.8
 certainty 513.4
 stability 142.1
 trustworthiness
  974.6
reliable
 believable 501.24
 evidential 505.17
 stable 142.12
 sure 513.17
 trustworthy 974.19
 unhazardous 698.5
reliance belief 501.1
 expectation 539.1
 hope 888.1
 mainstay 787.9
 support 216.1
relic
 antiquated person
  123.8
 antiquity 123.6
 memento 537.7
 record 570.1
 sacred article 1040.11
relics corpse 408.16
 remainder 43.1
relict survivor 43.3
 widow 935.4
relief aid 785.1
 consolation 887.4
 easement 886
 embossment 575.3
 interim 109.1
 lightening 353.3
 outline 235.2
 pity 944.1
 protuberance 256.2
 reinforcements 785.8
 remedy 687.1
 sculpture 575.1
 subsidy 818.8
 substitute 149.2
 turn 108.2
 welfare program
  745.7
relieve aid 785.11
 comfort 887.6
 diversify 18.2
 ease 886.5

lighten 353.6
 spell 108.5
 substitute for 149.5
 take from 822.21
religion faith 1020
 piety 1028.1
 system of belief
  501.3
 theology 1023.1
 word list 1020.32
religionist
 believer 1020.14
 pietist 1029.3
 word list 1020.34
 zealot 1028.4
religious
 n. clergyman 1038.17
 adj. conscientious
  974.15
 exact 516.16
 meticulous 533.12
 pious 1028.8
 sacred 1026.7
 theistic 1020.24
 theological 1023.4
relinquish
 abandon 144.6
 cease to use 668.4
 give up 633.7
 release 814.3
 resign 784.2
 surrender 765.8
relinquished
 disused 668.10
 released 814.5
relinquishment
 abandonment 633.3
 cessation 144.1
 discontinuance 668.2
 release 814
 resignation 784.1
 surrender 765.2
reliquary
 church vessel 1042.11
 memorial 570.12
 shrine 1042.4
 tomb 410.16
relish
 n. appetite 634.7
 fervor 855.10
 flavoring 428.3
 liking 634.2
 pleasure 865.1
 pungency 433.2
 savor 428.2
 taste 427.1
 v. eat 307.18
 enjoy 865.10
 savor 428.5
reliving 119.4
relocate
 change residence
  184.16
 move 271.10
relocation 271.2
reluct
 contend against
  790.4
 offer resistance 792.3
 revolt 767.7
reluctance
 electricity 342.12

resistance 792.1
 slowness 270.1
 unwillingness 623.1
reluctant
 grudging 623.6
 resistant 792.5
 slow 270.10
reluctantly
 grudgingly 623.9
 slowly 270.13
rely on
 be hopeful 888.7
 believe in 501.16
 rest on 216.22
 trust 501.17
remain be left 43.5
 be present 186.6
 be still 268.7
 continue 143.3
 endure 110.6
 inhabit 188.7
 persist 140.5
remainder
 difference 42.8
 estate 810.5
 part 55.1
 posteriority 117.1
 residue 43
 surplus 663.5
remaining
 continuing 143.7
 enduring 110.10
 permanent 140.7
 resident 188.13
 surplus 663.18
 surviving 43.7
remains antiquity 123.6
 corpse 408.16
 record 570.1
 residue 43.1
remake change 139.6
 reconstruct 694.18
 reproduce 169.7
remaking change 139.1
 reconstruction 694.5
 reproduction 169.1
remand
 n. commitment 761.4
 restitution 823.1
 v. commit 818.16
 imprison 761.17
 restore 823.4
remark
 n. attention 530.1
 commentary 606.2
 interjection 237.2
 statement 594.4
 v. comment 594.25
 heed 530.6
 write upon 606.5
remarkable
 extraordinary 85.14
 notable 672.18
 outstanding 34.10
 wonderful 920.10
remarkably
 exceptionally 34.20
 extraordinarily 85.18
 importantly 672.24
 wonderfully 920.14
remedial
 curative 687.39

impairment 692.8
rent money 846.9
v. charter 780.15
cleave 201.4
hire 780.14
open 265.12
adj. cleft 201.7
damaged 692.29
severed 49.23
rental hire 780.5
rent money 846.9
rent control 846.6
rented 780.19
renter lodger 190.8
tenant 809.4
renunciation
abandonment 633.3
apostasy 145.3
cessation 144.1
denial 524.2
discontinuance 668.2
recantation 628.3
relinquishment 814.1
surrender 765.2
temperance 992.1
renunciative
denying 524.5
rejecting 638.4
repudative 628.12
reoccurrence
periodicity 137.2
repetition 103.1
reorder 60.13
reorganization
rearrangement 60.7
reproduction 169.1
reorganize
rearrange 60.13
remake 169.7
repair
n. condition 7.3
reparation 694.6
v. atone 1012.4
mend 694.14
touch up 691.11
repairman 694.10
repair shop 719.6
repair to 273.24
reparable 694.25
reparation
atonement 1012.1
compensation 33.1
recompense 841.3
repair 694.6
restitution 823.2
reparative
atoning 1012.7
compensating 33.6
paying 841.21
restitutive 823.7
restorative 694.22
retaliatory 955.8
repartee answer 486.1
witticism 881.7
repast 307.5
repatriate
rehabilitate 145.14
restore 823.4
repay
be profitable 811.12
compensate 33.4

make restitution
823.5
pay 841.11
retaliate 955.5
repayment
compensation 33.1
payment 841.2
restitution 823.2
repeal
n. revocation 779
v. abolish 693.13
revoke 779.2
repeat
n. encore 91.2
repetition 103.5
replay 103.6
v. duplicate 91.3
imitate 22.5
memorize 537.17
publish 559.10
recur 137.5
redo 103.7
reproduce 169.7
resound 103.11
repeated
constant 135.5
iterated 103.12
repeatedly
frequently 135.6
often 103.16
repeater gun 801.5
returnee 146.3
voter 744.23
repel
cause dislike 867.6
disgust 429.4
disincline 652.4
fend off 799.10
offend 864.11
prevent 730.14
rebuff 776.5
reject 638.2
repulse 289.3
resist 792.2
repellent
offensive 864.18
repulsive 289.4
resistant 792.5
repelling
n. repulsion 289.1
adj. repulsive 289.4
ugly 899.11
repent 873.7
repentance
penance 1012.3
penitence 873.4
repentant
atoning 1012.7
penitent 873.9
repercussion
concussion 162.8
effect 154.3
music 462.31
reaction 178.1
recoil 284.2
repercussive
recoiling 284.10
reverberating 454.11
repertory list 88.1
numeration 87.5
storage place 660.6
store 660.1

theater 611.10
repertory company
612.11
repetition
constancy 135.2
continuance 143.1
copy 24.3
duplication 91.1
imitation 22.1
recurrence 103
regularity 137.1
reproduction 169.1
repetitious 103.14
repetitive
continuous 71.8
diffuse 593.11
habitual 642.16
monotonous 17.6
repetitious 103.14
rephrase 552.13
repine lament 875.8
regret 873.6
replace
come after 117.3
dismiss 310.19
restore 694.11
substitute for 149.5
replaceable
consumable 666.5
substitutable 149.10
replacement
exchange 149.1
restoration 694.1
substitute 149.2
successor 67.4
replacing 149.12
replay 103.6
replenish
complete 56.6
provide 659.7
restore 694.11
replete full 56.11
plentiful 661.7
satiated 664.6
repletion fullness 56.2
overfullness 663.3
plenty 661.2
satiety 664.1
replevin
n. pledge 772.2
recovery 823.3
v. appropriate 822.20
recover 823.6
replica copy 24.3
imitation 22.3
the same 14.3
replicate copy 24.8
duplicate 91.3
reproduce 14.6
replication
answer 486.1
copy 24.3
counterstatement
486.2
duplication 91.1
gene 170.6
reply
n. answer 486.1
communication
554.1
justification 1006.2
letter 604.2

reaction 284.1
retaliation 955.1
v. answer 486.4
communicate with
554.8
correspond 604.12
defend 1006.10
react 284.5
report
n. account 608.3
announcement 559.2
commentary 606.2
criticism 494.2
explosion 162.7
explosive noise 456
harmonics 463.14
hymn 1032.3
information 557.1
publicity 559.4
record 570.7
repute 914.1
rumor 558.6
v. announce 559.12
communicate 554.7
inform 557.8
narrate 608.13
pass judgment 494.13
present oneself
186.11
relate 558.11
reproach 1005.7
reportage 558.1
reported
made public 559.17
rumored 558.15
reporter
informant 557.5
journalist 605.22
newsmonger 558.9
spokesman 781.5
repose
n. leisure 710.1
moderation 163.1
recumbency 214.2
rest 711.1
sleep 712.2
stillness 268.1
v. be located 184.9
be still 268.7
exist in 1.11
lie 214.5
put 184.13
take rest 711.6
trust 501.17
reposeful
comfortable 887.11
moderate 163.13
quiescent 268.12
reposing dead 408.30
quiescent 268.12
recumbent 214.8
reposit put 184.13
store 660.10
repository friend 928.1
storage place 660.6
treasury 836.12
repossess 823.6
repossession
dispossession 822.7
recovery 823.3
repoussé
n. relief 575.3

rescript answer 486.1
  decree 752.4
  letter 604.2
  revision 691.4
rescue
  n. aid 785.1
  deliverance 702
  escape 632.1
  liberation 763.1
  v. aid 785.11
  deliver 702.3
  liberate 763.4
  redeem 694.12
rescuer lifesaver 702.2
  preserver 701.4
  savior 942.2
research
  n. investigation 485.4
  v. experiment 489.8
  search 485.30
research and
  development 489.1
research center 719.7
researcher
  experimenter 489.6
  seeker 485.17
research paper 606.1
resection
  separation 49.2
  surgical operation
    689.22
resemblance copy 24.1
  image 572.3
  similarity 20.1
resemble
  be comparable 491.7
  be like 20.7
resent 952.12
resentful
  annoyed 866.21
  discontented 869.5
  ill-humored 951.21
  resenting 952.24
resentment
  discontent 869.1
  displeasure 952
reservation
  engagement 780.4
  preserve 701.6
  qualification 507.1
  stipulation 753.2
reserve
  n. conciseness 592.1
  modesty 908.3
  preserve 701.6
  reticence 613.3
  supply 660.3
  v. allot 816.9
  engage 780.13
  not use 668.5
  postpone 132.9
  save 660.12
  adj. substitute 149.8
  unused 668.12
reserved concise 592.6
  modest 908.11
  reticent 613.10
  saved 660.15
reserves funds 835.14
  military reserves
    800.24
  reinforcements 785.8

substitute 149.2
  supply 660.3
  team 788.7
reservoir
  body of water 398.1
  reserve 660.3
  storage place 660.6
reshape change 139.6
  re-form 145.12
  remake 169.7
reside exist in 1.11
  inhabit 188.7
  settle 184.16
residence abode 191.1
  habitation 188.1
residency
  habitation 188.1
  practice of medicine
    688.16
resident
  n. clergyman 1038.8
  diplomat 781.6
  doctor 688.6
  inhabitant 190.2
  tenant 809.4
  adj. intrinsic 5.6
  residentiary 188.13
residential 191.32
residual 43.8
residue 43.1
resign deliver 818.13
  discontinue 668.4
  give up 633.7
  quit 784.2
  relinquish 814.3
  submit 765.6
resignation
  abandonment 633.3
  apathy 856.4
  contentment 868.1
  discontinuance 668.2
  patience 861.2
  relinquishment 814.1
  retirement 784
  submission 765.1
resigned
  apathetic 856.13
  contented 868.7
  disused 668.10
  patient 861.10
  submissive 765.12
resilience
  changeableness 141.1
  elasticity 358.1
  lightheartedness
    870.3
  recoil 284.2
resilient
  changeable 141.6
  elastic 358.7
  lighthearted 870.12
  recoiling 284.10
  recuperative 694.23
resin
  n. gums 381
  types of 381.4
  v. resinize 381.2
resinous 381.3
resist counteract 178.6
  hinder 730.10
  oppose 790.3
  withstand 792.2

resistance
  aviation 278.36
  defense 799.1
  defense mechanism
    690.30
  electric resistance
    342.12
  electronics 343.10
  friction 350.5
  hardness 356.1
  hindrance 730.1
  immunity 685.4
  irregular 800.15
  opposition 790.1
  reaction 178.1
  suppression 690.31
  toughness 359.1
  ungovernability 626.4
  unwillingness 623.1
  withstanding 792
resistant
  counteractive 178.8
  hard 356.10
  immune 685.12
  proof 159.18
  resisting 792.5
  tough 359.4
  ungovernable 626.12
  unwilling 623.5
resister 791.3
resolute bold 893.18
  determined 624.11
  experimental 714.14
  persevering 625.7
  zealous 635.10
resolutely
  courageously 893.22
  determinedly 624.17
  perseveringly 625.8
resolution analysis 48.2
  assay 48.1
  conversion 145.1
  courage 893.4
  decay 692.6
  determination 624
  disintegration 53.1
  end 70.1
  endeavor 714.1
  harmonization 463.2
  intention 653.1
  judgment 494.5
  legislation 742.13
  music division 462.24
  perseverance 625.1
  proposal 773.2
  reconciliation 804.4
  separation 49.5
  solution 487.1
  will 621.2
  zeal 635.2
resolvable
  convertible 145.18
  solvable 487.3
resolve
  n. intention 653.1
  resolution 624.1
  v. analyze 48.6
  decide 494.11
  determine 624.7
  end 70.5
  endeavor 714.4
  intend 653.4

outline 48.7
  reconcile 804.8
  solve 487.2
  will 621.2
resolvent
  n. solvent 391.4
  adj. disintegrative
    53.5
  solvent 391.8
resonance
  frequency 323.1
  sonorousness 454
  wave 323.4
resonant
  oscillating 323.15
  vibrant 454.9
resonate
  oscillate 323.10
  vibrate 454.6
resonator 454.5
resort
  amusement 878.11
  expedient 670.2
  haunt 191.27
  instrumentality 658.2
  means 658.1
  refuge 700.2
resort to
  avail oneself of
    665.14
  frequent 186.10
  go to 273.24
resound
  be repeated 103.11
  din 453.6
  reverberate 454.7
  sound 450.14
resounding
  n. reverberation 454.2
  adj. loud 453.10
  reverberating 454.11
resource capital 660.2
  expedient 670.2
  refuge 700.2
  reserve 660.3
  skill 733.1
  source of supply
    660.4
resourceful
  cunning 735.12
  skillful 733.20
  versatile 733.23
resources assets 810.8
  funds 835.14
  means 658.1
  supply 660.2
respect
  n. approval 968.1
  aspect 446.3
  attention 530.1
  courtesy 936.1
  duty 962.1
  esteem 914.3
  good terms 927.3
  mental outlook 525.2
  observance 768.1
  particular 8.3
  regard 964
  relevance 9.4
  viewing 439.2
  v. approve 968.9
  be considerate 938.10

observe 768.2
regard 964.4
relate to 9.5
respectable
honest 974.13
mediocre 680.7
reputable 914.15
tolerable 674.19
respectable citizen
985.3
respected
esteemed 964.11
reputable 914.15
respectful
approbatory 968.16
courteous 936.14
dutiful 962.13
regardful 964.8
respecting 9.13
respective
mutual 13.14
particular 80.12
proportionate 816.13
respectively each 80.19
mutually 13.17
proportionately
816.14
respects
compliments 936.8
regards 964.3
respiration 403.18
respirator 689.37
respire breathe 403.24
live 407.7
respite
n. delay 132.2
interim 109.1
pardon 1007.3
pause 144.3
release 886.2
rest 711.2
v. pardon 1007.5
resplendence
beauty 900.6
brightness 335.4
grandeur 904.5
illustriousness 914.6
resplendent
bright 335.32
gorgeous 900.19
illustrious 914.19
respond answer 486.4
defend 1006.10
emotionally respond
855.12
interchange 150.4
react 284.5
sense 422.8
respondent
n. accused 1005.6
answerer 486.3
adj. answering 486.6
reactive 284.9
respond to agree 26.6
behave toward 737.6
communicate with
554.8
get along with 794.2
reciprocate 13.9
response answer 486.1
communication
554.1

effect 154.3
emotion 855.3
hymn 1032.3
justification 1006.2
music 462.23
reaction 284.1
refrain 462.24
sensation 422.1
sympathy 855.5
responsibility
attribution 155.1
commission 780.1
duty 962.2
operation 164.1
supervision 747.2
trustworthiness
974.6
responsible
answerable 962.17
chargeable 840.9
liable to 175.5
trustworthy 974.19
responsive
answering 486.6
communicational
554.9
emotionable 855.21
influenceable 172.15
pliant 357.9
reactive 284.9
resilient 358.7
sensitive 422.14
willing 622.5
rest
n. death 408.1
fulcrum 287.3
leisure 710.1
music 463.21
pause 144.3
quiescence 268.1
remainder 43.1
repose 711
respite 711.2
silence 451.1
step 315.5
supporter 216.2
v. be contingent 507.6
be located 184.9
be still 268.7
calm 163.7
do nothing 706.2
exist in 1.11
pause 144.9
plead 1004.18
put 184.13
remain 43.5
ride at anchor 275.16
take it easy 711.6
rest assured
be certain 513.9
be hopeful 888.7
believe 501.14
restate
paraphrase 552.13
repeat 103.8
restaurant
dining room 192.11
eating house 307.15
rest easy
be content 868.5
persuade oneself
648.24

restful
comfortable 887.11
pacific 803.9
quiescent 268.12
tranquilizing 163.15
vacational 711.10
rest home asylum 700.4
infirmary 689.27
resting place end 70.1
supporter 216.2
tomb 410.16
restitution
atonement 1012.1
compensation 33.1
payment 841.2
recompense 841.3
restoration 694.1
return 823
reversion 146.1
restitutive
atoning 1012.7
compensatory 823.7
restorative 694.22
retaliatory 955.8
restive
discontented 869.5
impatient 862.6
obstinate 626.8
refractory 767.10
reluctant 623.6
restless 857.25
ungovernable 626.12
restless active 707.20
agitated 324.16
discontented 869.5
fidgety 857.25
impatient 862.6
inconstant 141.7
wakeful 713.7
restlessness
activeness 707.4
agitation 324.1
discontent 869.1
excitement 857.4
impatience 862.1
inconstancy 141.2
motion 267.1
wakefulness 713.1
rest on
be contingent 507.6
be heavy upon
352.11
believe in 501.16
stand on 216.22
restoration
improvement 691.1
justification 1006.1
recovery 823.3
reproduction 169.1
reestablishment 694
restitution 823.1
reversion 146.1
vitaminization 309.12
restorative
n. energizer 161.5
remedy 687.1
tonic 687.8
adj. compensatory
823.7
remedial 687.39
reparative 694.22
reproductive 169.14

tonic 687.44
restore aid 785.11
justify 1006.9
make restitution
823.4
put back 694.11
recover 823.6
reproduce 169.7
vitaminize 309.18
restrain bind 760.10
compel 756.4
confine 761.12
constrain 760.7
hinder 730.10
limit 234.5
moderate 163.6
purify 902.5
qualify 507.3
restrained
constrained 760.13
enclosed 236.10
modest 908.11
polished 589.6
reticent 613.10
subdued 163.11
tasteful 897.8
temperate 992.9
restraining
compelling 756.9
constraining 760.11
restrain oneself
be temperate 992.6
calm oneself 858.7
control 760.7
restraint
compulsion 756.1
confinement 761.1
constraint 760
defense mechanism
690.31
equanimity 858.3
good taste 897.4
hindrance 730.1
literary elegance
589.1
moderation 163.1
modesty 908.3
reticence 613.3
self-control 624.5
shackle 760.4
subjection 764.1
temperance 992.1
restraint of trade
commerce 827.1
constraint 760.1
restrict allot 816.9
confine 761.12
limit 234.5
narrow 205.11
qualify 507.3
restrain 760.9
specialize 81.4
restricted
bounded 234.7
confined 761.19
limited 234.8
narrow 205.14
qualified 507.10
restrained 760.15
secret 614.11
specialized 81.5

revert 146.4
retroflex
n. speech sound
594.13
v. curve 252.6
regress 295.5
adj. phonetic 594.31
retroflexion
inversion 220.1
regression 295.1
retrograde
v. get worse 692.19
regress 295.5
revert 146.4
adj. deteriorating
692.46
rear 241.9
regressive 295.11
reversionary 146.7
retrogress
back up 241.8
get worse 692.19
move 267.5
regress 295.5
revert 146.4
retrogression
course 267.2
deterioration 692.3
regression 295.1
reversion 146.1
retrogressive
deteriorating 692.46
flowing 267.8
regressive 295.11
reversionary 146.7
retro-rocket 282.2
retrospect
n. remembering 537.4
v. remember 537.10
retrospection
remembering 537.4
the past 119.4
retrospective
n. exhibition 555.2
adj. back 119.12
recollective 537.22
reminiscent 119.8
retroussé curved 252.9
stubby 203.10
upturned 315.15
return
n. answer 486.1
gain 811.3
homecoming 300.3
payment 841.2
periodicity 137.2
radar signal 346.11
reaction 284.1
recompense 841.3
recovery 694.8
regression 295.1
relapse 696.1
repetition 103.1
restitution 823.1
retaliation 955.1
reversion 146.1
v. answer 486.4
be repeated 103.11
give back 823.4
interchange 150.4
radar 346.16
recur 137.5

regress 295.5
restore 694.11
reverberate 454.7
revert 146.4
turn back 295.8
yield 844.4
returnable
interchangeable
150.5
reversionary 146.7
return match 103.6
returns
election returns
744.21
gain 811.3
list 88.6
receipts 844.1
reports 570.7
return to relapse 696.4
resume 143.6
revert to 146.6
revisit 186.9
reunion
reconciliation 804.3
social gathering
922.10
reunite 804.8
reupholster 228.29
reusable 665.22
rev 269.14
revaluation
monetization 835.23
reconsideration 478.5
re-examination 485.7
revalue 835.26
revamp change 139.6
renovate 694.17
revise 691.12
reveal disclose 556.4
divulge 556.5
indicate 568.17
manifest 555.5
unclose 265.13
uncover 488.4
revealed
disclosed 556.9
manifest 555.10
scriptural 1021.10
visible 444.6
revealing
n. disclosure 556.1
adj. disclosive 556.10
transparent 339.4
reveille
awakening 713.2
signal 568.16
revel
n. celebration 877.1
festivity 865.3
lark 878.6
v. enjoy 865.10
go on a spree 996.27
make merry 878.26
rejoice 876.5
revelation
appearance 446.1
disclosure 556.1
discovery 488.1
manifestation 555.1
scripture 1021.9
surprise 540.2
visibility 444.1

revelational
disclosive 556.10
manifestative 555.9
scriptural 1021.10
reveler
drunkard 996.10
player 878.19
revelry
conviviality 922.3
festivity 878.3
pleasure 865.3
revenge
n. compensation 33.1
reprisal 955.2
vengeance 956
v. avenge 956.4
revenue 844.1
revenuer
detective 781.10
taxer 846.12
reverberate
answer 486.4
be repeated 103.11
resound 454.7
reverberating 454.11
reverberation
answer 486.1
reaction 284.1
resounding 454.2
reverberator 454.5
revere cherish 931.19
respect 964.4
worship 1032.10
revered beloved 931.22
reputable 914.15
respected 964.11
reverence
n. crouch 318.3
obeisance 964.2
piety 1028.1
respect 964.1
worship 1032.1
v. respect 964.4
worship 1032.10
reverend
reputable 914.15
venerable 964.12
Reverend
n. clergyman 1038.2
title 917.5
adj. title 917.8
reverent pious 1028.8
respectful 964.9
worshipful 1032.15
reverie
abstractedness 532.2
dream 535.9
thoughtfulness 478.3
trance state 690.26
reversal
about-face 628.1
change 139.1
conversion 145.1
defeat 727.2
inversion 220.1
misfortune 729.3
regression 295.3
relapse 696.1
repeal 779.1
reversion 146.1
reverse
n. about-face 628.1

back 241.1
defeat 727.2
gear 348.6
inverse 220.4
misfortune 729.3
opposite 15.2
opposite side 239.3
regression 295.3
relapse 696.1
reversion 146.1
v. convert 145.11
counter 15.5
invert 220.5
repeal 779.2
retreat 295.7
revert 146.4
sail 275.34
adj. contrary 15.6
opposite 239.5
reversed inverted 220.7
turned around 295.12
reversible
remediable 694.25
reversionary 146.7
reversion
backward change 146
estate 810.5
inheritance 819.2
inversion 220.1
property transfer
817.2
regression 295.3
relapse 696.1
restoration 694.1
reversionary
regressive 146.7
restitutive 823.7
revert back up 241.8
be repeated 103.11
change back 146.4
regress 295.5
relapse 696.4
return to 146.6
revertible
restitutive 823.7
reversionary 146.7
review
n. abridgment 607.1
afterthought 478.5
commentary 606.2
criticism 494.2
discussion 597.7
examination 485.3
iteration 103.2
narrative 608.2
periodical 605.10
procession 71.3
re-examination 485.7
remembering 537.4
stage show 611.4
study 564.3
v. discuss 597.12
examine 485.23
judge 494.14
re-examine 485.26
refresh the memory
537.19
remember 537.10
repeat 103.8
study 564.12
think over 478.15
write upon 606.5

reviewer author 602.15
　commentator 606.4
　critic 494.7
revile berate 969.20
　curse 972.7
　ridicule 967.9
　vilify 971.10
revilement
　berating 969.7
　curse 972.2
　defamation 971.2
revise
　n. improvement 691.4
　trial print 603.5
　v. emend 691.12
　re-examine 485.26.
　remake 169.7
　rewrite 602.19
revision
　improvement 691.4
　re-examination 485.7
　reproduction 169.1
revisional
　emendatory 691.16
　reproductive 169.14
revisionism
　communism 745.5
　nonconformity 83.2
　reform 691.5
revisionist
　n. Communist 745.13
　reformer 691.6
　adj. Communist
　　745.21
　reformational 691.16
revisit 186.9
revival change 139.1
　energizing 161.7
　improvement 691.1
　piety 1028.3
　rebirth 169.1
　recovery 823.3
　reformation 145.2
　refreshment 695.1
　remembrance 119.4
　restoration 694.3
　worship 1032.8
revivalist
　evangelist 1038.7
　worshiper 1032.9
revive aid 785.11
　be changed 139.5
　change 139.6
　cheer up 870.9
　come to life 407.8
　rally 694.20
　recover 823.6
　refresh 695.2
　remake 169.7
　remember 537.10
　repeat 103.7
　restore 694.16
　stimulate 857.12
　touch up 691.11
revived changed 139.9
　refreshed 695.4
　reminiscent 119.8
　renascent 694.24
reviving 687.44
revocation denial 524.2
　recantation 628.3
　repeal 779.1

revoke abolish 693.13
　deny 524.4
　recant 628.9
　repeal 779.2
revolt
　n. counteraction
　　178.1
　rebellion 767.4
　resistance 792.1
　revolution 147.1
　strike 789.7
　v. offend 864.11
　offer resistance 792.3
　rebel 767.7
　revolutionize 147.4
　shudder at 867.5
　strike 789.9
revolted 866.20
revolting
　offensive 864.18
　ugly 899.11
revolution
　change 139.1
　circuit 321.2
　disruption 49.3
　inversion 220.2
　lawlessness 740.2
　radical change 147
　reform 691.5
　revolt 767.4
　rotation 322.1
　round 137.3
revolutionary
　n. radical 745.12
　rebel 767.5
　reformer 691.6
　revolutionist 147.3
　violent person 162.9
　adj. changed 139.9
　counteractive 178.8
　original 23.5
　radical 745.20
　rebellious 767.11
　reformational 691.16
　revolutionist 147.5
　violent 162.18
revolutionist
　n. lawless person
　　740.3
　radical 745.12
　rebel 767.5
　revolutionary 147.3
　adj. radical 745.20
　revolutionary 147.6
revolutionize
　change 139.8
　originate 23.4
　overthrow 147.4
　revolt 767.7
revolutions per minute
　322.3
revolve
　go around 321.4
　invert 220.5
　recur 137.5
　rotate 322.9
　think over 478.13
revolver 801.5,27
revolve upon 507.6
revs 322.3
revue 611.4

revulsion
　inversion 220.1
　reaction 284.1
　reversion 146.1
　revolution 147.1
revulsive reactive 284.9
　revolutionary 147.5
reward
　n. award 916.2
　death 408.1
　incentive 648.7
　recompense 841.3
　reprisal 955.2
　v. pay 841.10
　retaliate 955.5
rewarding
　gratifying 863.6
　paying 841.21
　valuable 665.21
reword
　paraphrase 552.13
　repeat 103.8
rework 691.12
rewrite
　n. revision 691.4
　v. revise 691.12
　write 602.19
rewrite man 605.22
reynard
　cunning person 735.6
　fox 414.25
RF 344.12
RF amplifier 344.10,30
RFD 604.5
Rhadamanthus
　deity of nether world
　　1019.5
　god of justice 976.5
　judge 1002.6
rhapsodic(al)
　overjoyed 865.14
　poetic 609.17
rhapsodist
　enthusiast 635.5
　poet 609.13
　singer 464.14
　visionary 535.13
rhapsodize
　be enthusiastic 635.8
　idealize 535.16
rhapsody 462.7
rhetoric diction 588.1
　eloquence 600.1
　grandiloquence 601.1
　public speaking 599.1
　style 588.2
rhetorical
　declamatory 599.12
　grandiloquent 601.8
rhetorical question
　485.10
rhetorician
　bombastic person
　　601.5
　orator 599.6
　stylist 588.3
　teacher of rhetoric
　　599.8
rheum
　body fluid 388.3
　disease symptom
　　686.8

respiratory disease
　686.14
　secretion 312.2
rheumatic
　n. sick person 686.40
　adj. diseased 686.57
rheumatic fever 686.12
rheumatism 686.9
rheumy fluid 388.7
　secretory 312.7
Rh factor
　antibody 687.27
　blood 388.4
rhinestone 901.6
rhinoceros 414.4; 415.8
rhinoplasty 689.25
rhizome 411.20
rhomboid
　n. obliquity 219.7
　adj. quadrangular
　　251.9
rhubarb
　argumentation 482.4
　food 308.35,50
　noise 453.3
　quarrel 795.6
rhyme
　n. poem 609.6
　poetry 609.1
　repetitiousness 103.4
　similar sound 20.6
　types of 609.10
　v. poetize 609.16
　sound similar 20.9
rhyming
　assonant 609.19
　repetitious 103.15
　similar sounding
　　20.17
rhythm
　literary elegance
　　589.2
　meter 609.9
　music 463.22
　periodicity 137.2
　pulsation 323.3
　speech accent 594.11
rhythm-and-blues 462.9
rhythmic(al)
　metrical 609.18
　music 463.28
　periodic 137.7
　pulsating 323.18
rhythmics 463.1
rialto city district 183.8
　marketplace 832.2
rib
　n. meat 308.17
　ridge 256.3
　wife 933.9
　v. banter 882.4
ribald
　n. vulgar person 898.6
　adj. obscene 990.9
　risqué 972.8
　vulgar 898.11
ribaldry cursing 972.3
　obscenity 990.4
　vulgarity 898.2
ribbed 263.4
ribber 882.3
ribbing 882.2

ribbon
n. award 916.5
  memorial 570.12
  ray 335.5
  strip 206.4
v. ornament 901.9
riboflavin 309.4
rice paddy 413.9
rich colorful 362.18
  expensive 848.11
  flavorful 428.9
  humorous 880.4
  interesting 530.19
  melodious 462.49
  oily 380.9
  ornate 901.12
  oversweet 431.5
  plentiful 661.7
  precious 848.10
  productive 165.9
  resonant 454.9
  wealthy 837.13
rich, the 837.5
riches 837.1
rich man
  capitalist 745.15
  wealthy man 837.6
rick
n. pile 74.10
  storage place 660.6
  store 660.1
v. pile 74.19
rickets 686.10
rickety aged 126.18
  deformed 249.12
  diseased 686.57
  loose 51.5
  unfastened 49.22
  unsteady 160.16
rickrack 262.2
ricksha 272.3
ricochet
n. recoil 284.2
v. recoil 284.6
rictus grimace 249.4
  shake 324.3
rid see **get rid of**
riddance
  elimination 77.2
  escape 632.1
  relinquishment 814.1
riddle
n. enigma 549.9
  network 221.3
  perplexity 514.3
  porousness 265.9
  refining equipment
    681.13
  sieve 60.5
  the unknown 477.7
v. be incomprehensi-
    ble 549.10
  mark 568.19
  puncture 265.16
  separate 77.6
  shoot 285.13
  sift 60.11
  solve 487.2
  strike dead 409.18
riddled 265.20
ride
n. drive 273.7

v. annoy 866.13
  banter 882.4
  drive 273.32
  float 275.54
  rest on 216.22
  ride at anchor 275.16
  ridicule 967.8
  sail 275.40
ride out
  keep safe 698.2
  sail 275.40
  stand fast 142.11
rider addition 41.2
  equestrian 274.8
  horse 414.16
  legislative clause
    742.17
ride roughshod over
  domineer 741.16
  run over 313.7
ride to hounds 655.9
ridge
n. back 241.3
  bulge 256.3
  head 211.6
  hill 207.6
  summit 211.2
  wrinkle 264.3
v. emboss 256.11
  wrinkle 264.6
ridicule
n. banter 882.1
  contempt 966.1
  deprecation 969.2
  derision 967
  disrespect 965.1
  impudence 913.2
v. be insolent 913.6
  deprecate 969.12
  deride 967.8
  disdain 966.3
  disrespect 965.3
  make fun of 881.13
ridiculing
  condemnatory 969.23
  derisive 967.12
  disparaging 971.13
  disrespectful 965.5
ridiculous
  foolish 470.10
  humorous 880.4
  impossible 510.7
  unbelievable 503.10
riding district 180.5
  driving 273.6
rife plentiful 661.7
  prevalent 79.12
  rumored 558.15
  teeming 101.9
riff music 462.27
  rapids 395.10
riffle
n. rapids 395.10
  wave 395.14
v. shuffle 63.3
riffraff offal 682.9
  rabble 919.5
  rubbish 669.5
rifle
n. gun 801.5,27
  infantryman 800.9
  soldier 800.6

v. groove 263.3
  plunder 824.16
  ransack 485.32
rifleman
  infantryman 800.9
  shooter 285.9
  soldier 800.6
rift
n. blemish 679.1
  break 49.4
  crack 201.2
  falling-out 795.4
  fault 678.2
v. open 265.12
adj. cleft 201.7
rig
n. carriage 272.5
  costume 231.9
  equipment 659.4
  ropework 277.12
  ruler 749.8
  suit 231.6
  wardrobe 231.2
v. equip 659.8
  outfit 231.40
  plot 654.10
  prearrange 641.3
  tamper with 616.17
rigamarole 547.2
rigged decked 277.17
  prearranged 641.5
  provided 659.13
  tampered with
    616.30
rigged out 231.44
rigging cordage 206.3
  equipment 659.4
  intrigue 654.6
  ropework 277.12
  stock manipulation
    833.20
  supporter 216.2
  types of 277.31
right
n. accuracy 516.3
  authority 739.1
  conservatives 745.9
  due 960.2
  estate 810.4
  justice 976.1
  justification 1006.6
  liberty 762.2
  moral rightness 958
  privilege 958.3
  right side 243.1
  stock option 833.21
v. arrange 60.8
  make agree 26.7
  remedy 694.13
adj. accurate 516.15
  apt 26.10
  conventional 645.5
  decorous 897.10
  expedient 670.5
  honest 974.13
  just 976.8
  orthodox 1024.7
  proper 958.8
  right-hand 243.4
  sane 472.4
  straight 250.6
adv. absolutely 56.15

  directly 290.24
  exactly 516.20
  excellently 674.21
  rightly 958.9
  squarely 290.25
  to the right 243.7
  very 34.18
interj. exactly 516.23
  sailing 275.76
  yes 521.18
right-about-face
n. about-face 295.3
  change of mind 628.1
v. turn around 295.10
right and left
  all round 233.13
  extensively 179.10
  sideways 242.8
right-angled
  orthogonal 251.7
  perpendicular 213.12
right away
  at once 113.8
  promptly 131.15
righteous
  honest 974.13
  pious 1028.9
  right 958.8
  virtuous 980.7
righteous, the 1028.5
righteousness
  honesty 974.1
  piety 1028.2
  propriety 958.2
  virtue 980.1
rightful
  authentic 516.14
  due 960.8
  just 976.8
  legal 998.10
  right 958.8
rightfully duly 960.11
  justly 976.11
  rightly 958.9
right hand
  right-hand man 787.7
  right side 243.1
right-hand 243.4
right-handed 243.5
right-hand man
  retainer 750.3
  right hand 787.7
  subordinate 764.5
rightist
  conservative 745.9
  diehard 140.4
rightly
  accurately 516.19
  expediently 670.8
  justly 976.11
  rightfully 958.9
right mind 472.1
right-minded
  honest 974.13
  virtuous 980.7
rightness 516.3
right-of-way road 657.6
  superiority 36.1
right on!
  congratulations 948.4
  exactly 516.23
  that's it 26.13

Right Reverend, the
  n. clergyman 1038.2
  adj. title 917.8
right side 243
right side of, the 927.3
right sort 985.1
right thing, the
  fairness 976.3
  moral rightness 958.1
  propriety 645.2
rightward
  clockwise 290.26
  to the right 243.7
right wing
  rightists 745.9
  right side 243.1
right-wing
  conservative 745.17
  diehard 140.8
  right 243.4
right-winger
  conservative 140.4
  rightist 745.9
  right side 243.1
rigid exact 516.16
  firm 159.16
  formal 646.9
  inflexible 142.15
  meticulous 533.12
  permanent 140.7
  stiff 356.11
  strict 757.7
  unyielding 626.9
rigidity accuracy 516.3
  firmness 624.2
  hardness 356.2
  immobility 142.3
  immutability 140.1
  strictness 757.2
  unyieldingness 626.2
rigidly exactly 516.20
  formally 646.12
  permanently 140.9
  strictly 757.9
  unyieldingly 626.15
rigmarole 547.2
rigor accuracy 516.3
  acrimony 161.4
  adversity 729.1
  asceticism 991.1
  cold 333.1
  difficulty 731.1
  hardness 356.2
  meticulousness 533.3
  strictness 757.2
  violence 162.1
rigorous
  acrimonious 161.13
  adverse 729.13
  cold 333.14
  difficult 731.16
  exact 516.16
  meticulous 533.12
  strict 757.7
  unyielding 626.9
  violent 162.15
rigorously
  exactly 516.20
  meticulously 533.16
  strictly 757.9
  unyieldingly 626.15
  violently 162.24

rile agitate 324.10
  annoy 866.13
  provoke 952.22
riled angry 952.26
  annoyed 866.21
rim
  n. border 235.4
  circle 253.4
  v. border 235.10
rime crack 201.2
  frost 333.7
rimed 333.16
rimose 201.7
rimple
  n. wrinkle 264.3
  v. wrinkle 264.6
rind exterior 224.2
  hull 228.16
  peel 229.2
  shallowness 210.1
  skin 229.1
ring
  n. arena 802.1
  association 788.1
  atomics 326.7
  band 253.3
  boxing 796.9
  circle 253.2
  clerical insignia 569.4
  clique 788.6
  handle 256.3
  insignia 569.1
  jewel 901.6
  light 335.14
  ringing 454.3
  telephone call 560.13
  v. din 453.6
  encircle 233.7
  telephone 560.18
  tintinnabulate 454.8
ring a bell 284.8
ringed
  circumscribed 234.6
  encircled 233.11
ringer impostor 619.6
  substitute 149.2
ring in arrive 300.6
  begin 68.11
  record time 114.12
  substitute 149.4
ringing
  n. tintinnabulation
    454.3
  adj. loud 453.10
  pealing 454.12
ringleader
  instigator 648.11
  leader 748.6
  political leader 746.7
ringlet circlet 253.5
  curl 254.2
  hair 230.5
ringmaster
  circus artist 612.3
  showman 611.28
rings 716.7
ringside 439.8
ringworm
  infectious disease
    686.12
  skin disease 686.33
rink 878.12

rinse
  n. cleaning agent
    681.17
  washing 681.5
  v. soak 392.13
  wash 681.19
rinsing refuse 669.4
  washing 681.5
  wetting 392.6
riot
  n. commotion 62.4
  free-for-all 796.5
  funny story 881.6
  great success 724.3
  plenty 661.2
  revolt 767.4
  violence 162.3
  v. be disorderly 62.10
  contend 796.14
  revolt 767.7
  vegetate 411.31
  wreck 395.14
rioter combatant 800.1
  rebel 767.5
rioting 162.3
riot of color
  colorfulness 362.4
  variegation 374.1
riotous
  growing rank 411.40
  intemperate 993.8
  plentiful 661.7
  rebellious 767.11
  superabundant
    663.19
  unrestrained 762.23
  violent 162.18
rip
  n. break 49.4
  impairment 692.8
  tide 395.13
  unchaste person
    989.10
  v. injure 692.15
  open 265.12
  speed 269.8
  tear apart 49.14
  torture 866.18
  wrest 822.22
RIP 410.24
riparian 385.9
ripe complete 56.9
  experienced 733.26
  finished 677.9
  fully developed
    722.13
  marriageable 933.21
  mature 126.13
  prepared 720.16
  timely 129.9
ripen become 145.17
  evolve 148.5
  fester 311.15
  improve 691.10
  make perfect 677.5
  mature 126.9
  reach perfection
    722.8
ripened
  experienced 733.26
  finished 677.9
rip off 824.14

rip-off fraud 618.7
  phony 616.13
  theft 824.10
riposte
  n. answer 486.1
  justification 1006.2
  witticism 881.7
  v. answer 486.4
  defend 1006.10
  react 284.5
rip out 305.10
ripping
  n. separation 49.2
  wresting 305.6
  adj. excellent 674.13
ripple
  n. rapids 395.10
  rough surface 261.2
  splash 452.5
  wave 395.14
  wrinkle 264.3
  v. agitate 324.10
  make a liquid sound
    452.11
  wrinkle 264.6
rippled 264.8
ripply 261.6
rip-roaring noisy 453.12
  violent 162.17
riptide 395.13
rise
  n. acclivity 219.6
  appearance 446.1
  ascent 315.1
  development 148.1
  height 207.2
  improvement 691.1
  increase 38.1
  promotion 782.1
  reaction 284.1
  rising 213.5
  source 153.5
  wave 395.14
  v. appear 446.8
  ascend 315.8
  begin 68.13
  be high 207.15
  billow 395.22
  din 453.6
  elevate 317.5
  get up 713.6
  incline 219.10
  increase 38.6
  levitate 353.9
  make good 724.9
  move 267.5
  result from 154.6
  revive 407.8
  revolt 767.7
  stand up 213.8
rise above accept 861.6
  be high 207.16
  exceed 34.5
  triumph over 726.6
riser 315.5
risibility laughter 876.4
  wit 881.11
risible humorous 880.4
  merry 870.15
rising
  n. acclivity 219.6
  appearance 446.1

rocking
  swinging 323.17
  tranquilizing 163.15
rocking chair 323.9
rocking horse 878.16
Rock of Gibraltar 142.6
rock the boat 83.4
rocky hard 356.10
  rough 261.7
  sick 686.52
  stony·384.11
  unsafe 697.11
  unsteady 160.16
rococo
  n. ornateness 901.2
  adj. abnormal 85.13
  fanciful 535.20
  ornate 901.12
rod atomics 326.13
  emblem of authority 739.9
  gun 801.5
  instrument of punishment 1011.2
  royal insignia 569.3
  shaft 217.1
rod and reel 655.3
rodent
  n. animal 414.3; 415.8
  adj. rodential 414.48
rodeo assembly 74.1
  show 611.15
rodlike 356.11
rodomontade
  bluster 911.1
  boasting 910.1
  bombast 601.2
  nonsense 547.2
roe egg 406.15
  female animal 421.9
  food 308.24
  hoofed animal 414.5,58
roebuck 414.5,58
roentgenograph
  diagnostic picture 689.10
  photograph 577.6
roentgenotherapy 689.7
Roentgen ray 327.3
Roger 521.18
Roget's 605.7
rogue
  inferior horse 414.14
  mischief-maker 738.3
  rascal 986.3
roguery
  dishonesty 975.2
  mischief 738.2
rogues' gallery 577.3
roguish
  dishonest 975.17
  mischievous 738.6
  prankish 881.17
roil
  n. agitation 324.1
  opaqueness 341.1
  v. agitate 324.10
  annoy 866.13
  be disorderly 62.10
  provoke 952.22
  seethe 322.12

roiled annoyed 866.21
  opaque 341.3
roily disorderly 62.13
  opaque 341.3
roister
  be disorderly 62.10
  bluster 911.3
  make merry 878.26
roisterous
  blustering 911.4
  boisterous 162.19
role capacity 7.5
  function 665.5
  occupation 656.3
  part 611.11
role-player 619.1
roll
  n. air maneuver 278.14
  boom 456.4
  bun 308.31
  bundle 74.8
  curl 254.2
  cylinder 255.4
  document 570.5
  film 577.10
  flounder 324.8
  gait 273.14
  length 202.3
  list 88.6
  money 835.17
  record 570.1
  rotation 322.1
  staccato sound 455.1
  swing 323.6
  throw of dice 515.10
  wave 395.14
  v. billow 395.22
  bird sound 460.5
  boom 456.9
  flounder 324.15
  fly 278.49
  go easily 732.9
  level 214.6
  make staccato sounds 455.4
  oscillate 323.10
  progress 294.2
  push 285.10
  reverberate 454.7
  sail 275.55
  smooth 260.6
  travel 273.17
  trundle 322.10
  walk 273.27
  wallow 322.13
roll around 137.5
rollback discount 847.1
  reduction 39.4
  regression 295.1
roll back reduce 39.7
  retrench 851.5
roll call
  legislative procedure 742.14
  list 88.6
roller cylinder 255.4
  medical dressing 687.33
  pulverizer 361.7
  rotator 322.4,17
  smoother 260.4,13

wave 395.14
roller coaster 878.15
roller-skate 273.34
roller skates 272.20
rollick
  n. frolic 878.5
  v. bluster 911.3
  play 878.25
  rejoice 876.5
rollicking
  blustering 911.4
  boisterous 162.19
  frisky 870.14
roll in arrive 300.6
  be intemperate 993.4
rolling
  n. air maneuver 278.13
  progression 294.1
  rotation 322.1
  television reception 345.5
  adj. hilly 207.23
  resonant 454.9
  rotating 322.14
  swinging 323.17
  thundering 456.12
  wavy 254.10
rolling stock 272.13
rolling stone
  changeableness 141.4
  rotator 322.4
  wanderer 274.2
roll on elapse 105.5
  progress 294.3
  travel 273.17
roll out get up 713.6
  indicate 555.5
roll up bundle 74.20
  roll 322.10
  squeeze 198.8
roly-poly
  n. corpulent person 195.12
  adj. corpulent 195.18
roman
  fictional form 608.8
  type 603.6,23
Roman candle
  fireworks 328.33
  signal 568.15
Roman Catholic
  n. Catholic 1020.18,35
  adj. Catholic 1020.28
Roman Catholicism 1020.7,33
romance
  n. fabrication 616.10
  fiction 608.7
  idealization 535.7
  love affair 931.6
  music 462.6
  thing imagined 535.5
  v. idealize 535.16
  narrate 608.13
romancer
  narrator 608.10
  visionary 535.13
Roman deities 1014.5
Roman-nosed 252.8
Roman numerals 86.2

romantic
  n. visionary 535.13
  adj. fictional 608.17
  loving 931.25
  sentimental 855.22
  visionary 535.24
romanticism
  amorousness 931.3
  idealization 535.7
  sentimentality 855.8
romanticize 535.16
romanticized
  fictional 608.17
  visionary 535.24
Romany 274.4
Rome 1020.7
Romeo 931.12
Romeo and Juliet 931.17
romp
  n. frolic 878.5
  girl 125.6
  mannish female 420.9
  v. be cheerful 870.6
  jump 319.6
  play 878.25
  rejoice 876.5
rompers 231.30,56
rondeau music 462.19
  poem 609.6
  round 253.9
rondelle 253.2
rondo music 462.19
  round 253.9
rood cross 221.4
  sacred article 1040.11
roof
  n. abode 191.1
  home 191.4
  house 191.6
  housetop 228.6
  top 211.1
  types of 228.39
  v. cover 228.21
roofed 228.31
roofing
  building material 378.2
  roof 228.6,43
rooftop roof 228.6
  top 211.1
rook
  n. chessman 878.18
  v. cheat 618.17
rookery
  birthplace 153.8
  filthy place 682.11
rookie beginner 68.2
  newcomer 78.4
  novice 566.9
  recruit 800.17
room
  n. capacity 195.2
  chamber 192
  interval 201.1
  latitude 762.4
  lodgings 191.3
  opportunity 129.2
  spare 179.3
  v. house 188.10
  inhabit 188.7

roomer lodger 190.8
  tenant 809.4
roomette
  railway car 272.14
  train room 192.10
rooming house 191.16
roommate
  companion 928.3
  partner 787.2
room-temperature
  328.24
roomy airy 402.12
  broad 204.6
  comfortable 887.11
  spacious 179.9
roorback report 558.6
  smear campaign
  744.14
roost
  n. birdhouse 191.23
  lodgings 191.3
  v. inhabit 188.7
  settle 184.16
  sit 268.10
rooster
  male animal 420.8
  poultry 414.34
root
  n. morphology 582.3
  plant root 411.20
  source 153.5
  word 582.2
  v. applaud 968.10
  base on 212.6
  become fixed 142.10
  establish 142.9
  search 485.30
  urge on 648.16
  vegetate 411.31
rooted
  confirmed 642.21
  established 142.13
  traditional 123.12
rooter
  commender 968.8
  devotee 635.6
rootlike 411.33
root out destroy 693.14
  eliminate 42.10
  eradicate 77.5
  extract 305.10
  search out 485.33
  uproot 185.6
rope
  n. capital punishment
  1010.7
  cigar 434.4
  cord 206.2,9
  latitude 762.4
  noose 1011.5
  types of 277.31
  v. bind 47.9
  catch 822.17
  lure 650.4
  restrain 760.10
rope off
  circumscribe 234.4
  quarantine 761.13
ropes 172.3
ropewalker 878.21
ropeway 657.9

ropework
  cordage 206.3
  rigging 277.12
ropy threadlike 206.7
  tough 359.4
  viscous 389.12
Rorschach test 690.11
rosary prayer 1032.4
  sacred article 1040.11
rose
  n. conduit 396.9
  emblem 569.1
  heraldic insignia
  569.2
  pinkness 368.2,13
  adj. pink 368.8
rose-colored
  optimistic 888.12
  pink 368.8
rose oil 436.2
rosette 308.40
rose water 436.3
rosé wine 996.16
Rosh Hashanah 1040.16
rosin
  n. resin 381.1
  v. resin 381.2
rosiny 381.3
roster list 88.6
  record 570.1
  schedule 641.2
rostrum beak 256.7
  church part 1042.13
  front 240.3
  platform 216.13
rosy cheerful 870.11
  healthy 685.11
  optimistic 888.12
  pink 368.8
  prosperous 728.13
  red-complexioned
  368.9
rosy-cheeked
  healthy 685.11
  red-complexioned
  368.9
rot
  n. animal disease
  686.38
  blight 676.2
  filth 682.7
  nonsense 547.3
  putrefaction 692.7
  v. decay 692.25
rota list 88.6
  record 570.1
Rota 1001.6
rotary
  n. crossing 221.2
  adj. circuitous 321.7
  flowing 267.8
  periodic 137.7
  rotational 322.15
rotary press 603.9,24
rotate fly 278.47
  invert 220.5
  move 267.5
  recur 137.5
  revolve 322.9
rotation aviation 278.8
  continuity 71.2
  revolution 322

round 137.3
  sequence 65.1
rotator rotor 322.4
  types of 322.17
rote 537.4
rotgut 996.14
Rothschild 837.7
rotogravure 603.1
rotor propeller 285.7
  rotator 322.4,17
rotor plane 280.5,15
rotten bad 675.9
  decayed 692.41
  dishonest 975.16
  filthy 682.23
  horrid 864.19
  malodorous 437.5
  morally corrupt
  981.14
  unsavory 429.7
  weak 160.15
rotten egg 437.3
rotter 986.8
rotting decayed 692.41
  putrefactive 692.40
rotund convex 256.12
  corpulent 195.18
  round 255.8
rotunda 192.1
roué 989.10
rouge
  n. makeup 900.11
  redness 368.1
  v. make red 368.4
rough
  n. combatant 800.1
  diagram 654.3
  evildoer 943.3
  rough surface 261.2
  vulgar person 898.6
  v. coarsen 261.4
  mistreat 667.5
  adj. acrimonious
  161.13
  bitter 429.6
  boisterous 162.19
  coarse-textured 351.6
  difficult 731.16
  gruff 937.7
  irregular 138.3
  jolting 324.20
  nonuniform 18.3
  pungent 433.6
  raucous 458.15
  undeveloped 721.12
  unkind 939.22
  unsmooth 261.6
  violent 162.15
  vulgar 898.11
  adv. unsmoothly
  261.11
rough-and-ready
  uncouth 898.12
  unprepared 721.8
rough-and-tumble
  n. commotion 62.4
  adj. boisterous 162.19
roughcast
  v. do carelessly 534.9
  form 246.7
  plaster 228.25

  adj. undeveloped
  721.12
  unsmooth 261.6
rough diamond
  good person 985.1
  raw material 721.5
rough draft
  picture 574.14
  trial 489.2
rough edges 723.1
roughen agitate 324.10
  coarsen 261.4
  give texture 351.4
roughhew
  do carelessly 534.9
  form 246.7
roughhewn
  undeveloped 721.12
  unsmooth 261.6
roughhouse
  n. commotion 62.4
  misbehavior 738.1
  v. be disorderly 62.11
  misbehave 738.4
rough it 188.11
roughly
  approximately 200.23
  generally 79.17
  irregularly 138.4
  unkindly 939.31
  unsmoothly 261.11
  vulgarly 898.16
roughneck
  n. evildoer 943.4
  vulgar person 898.6
  adj. boorish 898.13
roughness
  acrimony 161.4
  aviation 278.41
  coarse texture 351.2
  gruffness 937.3
  irregularity 138.1
  literary inelegance
  590.1
  pungency 433.1
  raucousness 458.2
  undevelopment 721.4
  unkindness 939.9
  unsmoothness 261
  violence 162.1
  vulgarity 898.2
rough out
  do carelessly 534.9
  form 246.7
  outline 654.12
rough sketch 489.2
rouleau bundle 74.8
  coin 835.4
  cylinder 255.4
roulette 515.8
roulette wheel 515.12
round
  n. canon 253.9
  circle 253.2
  circuit 321.2
  continuity 71.2
  degree 29.1
  drinks 996.6
  meat 308.17
  music 462.19
  playing cards 878.17
  region 180.2

revolution 137.3
rotation 322.2
route 657.2
routine 642.6
spell 108.2
sphere of work 656.4
step 315.5
v. circle 253.10
curve 252.6
go around 321.4
make round 255.6
rotate 322.9
turn 321.5
turn around 295.9
adj. candid 974.17
circuitous 321.7
circular 253.11
full 56.11
polished 589.6
rotund 255.8
unqualified 508.2
adv. around 322.16
in the vicinity 233.12
roundabout
n. amusement device
878.15
detour 321.3
rotator 322.4
adj. circuitous 321.7
devious 46.4
diffuse 593.14
peripheral 224.6
surrounding 233.8
winding 254.6
round about
adv. circuitously 321.9
in every direction
290.27
in the vicinity 233.12
round 322.16
prep. through 290.29
throughout 184.27
round and round
alternately 137.11
changeably 141.8
round 322.16
to and fro 323.21
windingly 254.11
rounded blunt 259.3
bulging 256.14
circular 253.11
phonetic 594.31
rotund 255.8
roundel circle 253.2
poem 609.6
roundelay
music 462.19
poem 609.6
rounder
intemperate person
993.3
unchaste person
989.10
vagabond 274.3
roundhouse
boxing 283.5
garage 192.27
repair shop 719.6
roundly
approximately 200.23
candidly 974.23
completely 56.14

roundness candor 974.4
circularity 253.1
sphericity 255.1
round off 722.6
round out bulge 256.10
complete 722.6
fill out 56.6
make round 255.6
round robin 604.3
round-shouldered
249.12
roundsman
peace officer 699.15
watchman 699.10
round table 755.3
round-the-clock 71.8,10
round trip circuit 321.2
journey 273.5
roundup 74.1
round up
assemble 74.18
drive animals 416.8
procure 811.10
roundworm 414.75;
415.5
rouse awake 713.4
awaken 713.5
elicit 305.14
energize 161.9
excite 857.11
incite 648.19
rousing
n. awakening 713.2
adj. energizing 161.14
provocative 648.27
refreshing 695.3
remarkable 34.11
roustabout sailor 276.6
stevedore 276.9
working person 718.2
rout
n. agitation 324.1
attendance 73.6
defeat 727.2
large number 101.3
rabble 919.4
throng 74.4
v. defeat 727.9
drive out 310.14
route 657.2
routine
n. act 611.8
continuity 71.2
habit 642.6
order 59.1
way 657.1
adj. frequent 135.4
habitual 642.16
medium 32.3
orderly 59.6
ordinary 79.12
routinely
frequently 135.6
generally 79.17
habitually 642.23
uniformly 17.7
routinize order 59.4
organize 60.10
rove
n. wandering 273.3
v. travel 273.22
wander 291.4

rover pirate 825.7
wanderer 274.2
roving
n. discursiveness 593.3
wandering 273.3
adj. discursive 593.13
inconstant 141.7
traveling 273.36
wandering 291.7
row
n. file 71.2
road 657.6
v. align 71.5
paddle 275.53
push 285.10
sail 275.13
row
n. agitation 324.1
commotion 62.4
free-for-all 796.5
noise 453.3
quarrel 795.6
violence 162.2
v. be noisy 453.8
quarrel 795.12
rowdy
n. combatant 800.1
evildoer 943.3
mischief-maker 738.3
vulgar person 898.6
adj. boisterous 162.19
boorish 898.13
misbehaving 738.5
noisy 453.12
rowing 275.1
royal
n. book size 605.14
potentate 749.7
adj. dignified 905.12
excellent 674.12
sovereign 739.17
royal insignia
insignia 569.3
royalty 739.8
royalism
political conservatism
745.1
principle of govern-
ment 741.8
royalist 745.9
royalty
aristocracy 918.1
nobility 918.2
payment 841.7
potentate 749.7
receipt 844.1
sovereignty 739.8
rpm revolutions 322.3
speed 269.1
RSVP 604.16
rub
n. bone of contention
795.7
contact 200.5
crisis 129.4
difficulty 731.7
disaccord 795.1
friction 350.1
obstacle 730.4
touch 425.1
v. abrade 350.7
affect 572.6

dry 393.6
frictionize 350.6
graze 200.10
hurt 424.7
polish 260.7
touch 425.8
treat 689.30
rubber
n. contraceptive
687.23
elastic substance
358.3
eradicator 693.9
playing cards 878.17
pliancy 357.4
types of 358.9
adj. rubbery 358.8
rubber band 358.3
rubber check 835.10
rubberize 358.6
rubberneck
n. curious person
528.2
sight-seer 442.3
traveler 274.1
v. be curious 528.3
sight-see 442.6
travel 273.20
adj. spectating 442.7
rubber stamp
n. ratification 521.4
v. ratify 521.12
rubbery
changeable 141.6
elastic 358.8
flaccid 357.10
weak 160.12
rubbing
n. copy 24.4
friction 350.1
image 572.3
reproduction 24.2
touching 425.2
adj. frictional 350.9
in contact 200.17
rubbish
abandoned thing
633.4
junk 669.5
nonsense 547.2
rabble 919.5
refuse 43.1
trifles 673.4
rubbishy
nonsensical 547.7
paltry 673.18
rubble rock 384.1
rubbish 669.5
rubdown 350.3
rub down
frictionize 350.6
tend animals 416.7
rube
n. bungler 734.9
oaf 471.5
rustic 919.9
unsophisticate 736.3
adj. countrified 182.7
rubella 686.12
rubicund red 368.6
red-complexioned
368.9

rub in 672.13
ruble 835.9
rub off abrade 350.7
  wear 692.23
rub out abrade 350.7
  delete 42.12
  kill 409.14
  obliterate 693.16
rubric
  abridgment 607.1
  caption 484.2
  class 61.2
  law 998.3
  precept 751.2
  ritualistic manual
    1040.12
  topic 484.1
rub the wrong way
  irritate 866.14
  roughen 261.5
ruby
  n. gem stone 384.13
  adj. red 368.6
ruche 264.1
ruck
  n. generality 79.3
  groove 263.1
  large number 101.3
  rabble 919.4
  throng 74.4
  wrinkle 264.3
  v. wrinkle 264.6
ruckus
  commotion 62.4
  free-for-all 796.5
  noise 453.3
  quarrel 795.6
  violence 162.2
ructation 310.9
rudder 747.5
ruddy blushing 908.13
  damned 972.10
  healthy 685.11
  red 368.6
  red-complexioned
    368.9
rude common 919.11
  discourteous 937.4
  impudent 913.9
  infelicitous 590.2
  raucous 458.15
  robust 685.10
  undeveloped 721.12
  unlearned 477.14
  vulgar 898.11
rude awakening
  arousal 713.2
  disillusionment 520.1
rudeness
  discourtesy 937.1
  impudence 913.2
  literary inelegance
    590.1
  raucousness 458.2
  undevelopment 721.4
  vulgarity 898.2
rudiment
  embryo 406.14
  foundation 216.6
  source 153.7
rudimentary
  basic 212.8

beginning 68.15
  causal 153.15
  dwarf 196.13
  undeveloped 721.12
rudiments basics 68.6
  elementary instruc-
    tion 562.5
rue 873.6
rueful regretful 873.8
  sorrowful 872.26
  unpleasant 864.20
ruff
  n. playing cards
    878.17
  staccato sound 455.1
  v. fold 264.5
ruffian
  combatant 800.1
  evildoer 943.3
  mischief-maker 738.3
  vulgar person 898.6
ruffianly
  boorish 898.13
  misbehaving 738.5
ruffle
  n. confusion 532.3
  edging 235.7
  excitement 857.3
  fold 264.1
  staccato sound 455.1
  v. agitate 324.10
  annoy 866.13
  confuse 532.7
  disarrange 63.2
  excite 857.13
  fold 264.5
  make staccato sounds
    455.4
  music 462.45
  provoke 952.22
  roughen 261.5
ruffled agitated 324.16
  annoyed 866.21
  confused 532.12
  disorderly 62.14
  excited 857.21
  folded 264.7
  rough 261.6
  winding 254.6
rug bedding 216.20
  blanket 228.10
  floor covering 228.9
  kinds of 228.41
Rugby 878.8,34
rugged difficult 731.16
  robust 685.10
  rough 261.7
  strict 757.6
  strong 159.13
  substantial 3.7
  unkind 939.22
  wrinkled 264.8
rugged individualist
  capitalist 745.15
  independent 762.12
rugous rough 261.7
  wrinkled 264.8
ruin
  n. antiquity 123.6
  defeat 727.1
  destruction 693.1
  loss 812.1

remainder 43.1
  wreck 692.10
  v. bankrupt 842.8
  defeat 727.6
  destroy 693.10
  impair 692.12
  seduce 989.20
  thwart 730.15
  wreck 162.10
ruination
  destruction 693.1
  impairment 692.1
ruined damaged 692.30
  defeated 727.14
  destroyed 693.28
  dilapidated 692.35
  hopeless 889.15
  insolvent 842.11
  old 123.14
ruinous
  destructive 693.26
  dilapidated 692.35
  disastrous 729.15
  disintegrated 53.5
  old 123.14
  ruined 693.28
  slovenly 62.15
rule
  n. average 32.1
  axiom 517.2
  custom 642.5
  decree 752.4
  directive 752.3
  government 741.1
  influence 172.1
  jurisdiction 739.5
  law 998.3
  measure 490.2,20
  model 25.1
  precept 751.2
  principle 84.4
  straightedge 250.3
  supremacy 36.3
  syllogism 482.6
  v. command 752.9
  govern 741.14
  influence 172.8
  measure off 490.12
  pass judgment 494.13
  possess authority
    739.13
  prevail 79.10
rule of thumb 489.1
rule out exclude 42.10
  make impossible
    510.6
  obliterate 693.16
  prevent 730.14
  prohibit 778.3
ruler governor 749.5
  instrument of punish-
    ment 1011.2
  potentate 749.7
  straightedge 250.3
  superior 36.4
rule the roost 741.15
ruling
  n. decree 752.4
  judgment 494.5
  law 998.3
  adj. authoritative
    739.15

chief 36.14
  governing 741.18
  influential 172.14
  powerful 157.12
  prevalent 79.12
ruling class
  mastership 739.7
  superiors 36.5
  the rulers 749.15
rum
  n. liquor 996.12,40
  adj. excellent 674.13
  odd 85.11
rumble
  n. audio distortion
    450.13
  boom 456.4
  fight 796.4
  noise 453.3
  reverberation 454.2
  rumor 558.6
  v. boom 456.9
  reverberate 454.7
  utter 594.26
rumble seat 241.1
rumbling
  n. reverberation 454.2
  adj. reverberating
    454.11
  thundering 456.12
rumen 193.3
ruminant
  n. animal 414.3
  adj. chewing 307.30
  thoughtful 478.21
  ungulate 414.49
ruminate chew 307.25
  consider 478.12
  think over 478.13
rummage
  n. search 485.14
  v. ransack 485.32
rummy 996.11
rumor
  n. report 558.6
  v. publish 559.10
  report 558.11
rumormonger 558.9
rump buttocks 241.4
  meat 308.17
  remainder 43.1
rumple
  n. wrinkle 264.3
  v. agitate 324.10
  disarrange 63.2
  roughen 261.5
  wrinkle 264.6
rumpled
  disorderly 62.14
  wrinkled 264.8
rumpus
  commotion 62.4
  free-for-all 796.5
  noise 453.3
  quarrel 795.6
  violence 162.2
rumpus room 192.12
rumrunning 826.2
run
  n. average 32.1
  continuance 143.1
  course 267.2

direction 290.1
flight 278.9
flow 395.4
freedom 762.1
generality 79.3
impairment 692.8
journey 273.5
lair 191.26
length 202.3
make 168.4
migration 273.4
music 463.18
path 657.3
playing engagement
611.12
prevalence 79.2
race 796.12
route 657.2
routine 642.6
running water 395.1
sequence 71.2
speed 269.3
trend 174.2
voyage 275.6
v. be operative 164.7
direct 747.8
elapse 105.5
endure 110.6
extend 179.7
fester 311.15
flee 631.10
float 275.54
flow 395.16
hunt 655.9
incur 175.4
injure 692.15
liquefy 391.5
make haste 709.5
melt 329.21
migrate 273.21
move 267.5
navigate 275.13
nominate 637.19
operate 164.5
pilot 275.14
print 603.14
raise animals 416.6
run for office 744.39
sail 275.22
smuggle 826.8
sprint 269.10
steer 747.9
thrust 283.11
travel 273.17
runabout 274.2
run across find 488.3
meet 200.11
run after
befriend 927.11
curry favor 907.8
fetch 271.15
pursue 655.8
run against
n. attack 798.1
v. counteract 178.6
oppose 790.3
thrust 283.11
run aground
come to grief 729.10
shipwreck 275.42
run along
go away! 310.29

run off 301.13
run amok
be disorderly 62.10
be insane 473.19
go berserk 162.14
run around 932.18
runaround, the
avoidance 631.1
circumvention 735.5
run at
n. attack 798.1
v. charge 798.18
runaway
n. fugitive 631.5
adj. escaped 632.11
fugitive 631.16
run away flee 631.10
run off 301.13
run back 295.6
rundle rotator 322.4
running water 395.1
step 315.5
rundown
airmanship 278.3
summary 607.2
run down
become exhausted
717.5
decline 692.20
discover 488.2
disparage 971.8
fail 686.45
quiet 268.8
run over 313.7
sail 275.41
trace 485.34
run-down
dilapidated 692.35
fatigued 717.6
unhealthy 686.50
weakened 160.18
worn-out 692.38
run dry 666.3
rune character 581.2
sorcery 1035.1
run for head for 290.10
sail for 275.35
run foul of
collide 283.12
contend with 796.16
meet 200.11
sail 275.41
rung degree 29.1
step 315.5
runic 609.17
run in arrest 761.16
capture 822.18
interpose 237.6
sail 275.41
thrust in 304.7
visit 922.17
run-in
n. quarrel 795.6
adj. broken-in 642.17
run into
become 145.17
collide 283.12
cost 846.15
find 488.3
meet 200.11
sail 275.41
total 54.8

runnel
running water 395.1
watercourse 396.2
runner branch 411.18
conduit 396.4
messenger 561.1
operator 164.4
part 55.4
sled part 272.19
smuggler 826.5
speeder 269.5
runner-up 726.2
running
n. candidacy 744.10
direction 747.1
heating 329.3
liquefaction 391.1
motion 267.1
operation 164.1
pus 311.6
adj. continuous 71.8
cursive 602.22
fast 269.19
flowing 267.8
operating 164.11
pouring 395.24
present 120.2
prevalent 79.12
adv. consecutively
71.11
running head
caption 484.2
label 568.13
running mate 746.9
running start
advantage 36.2
beginning 68.1
earliness 131.1
runny exudative 303.20
fluid 388.6
runoff election 744.15
game 878.9
outflow 303.4
run off flee 631.10
print 603.14
run away 301.13
run off with
abduct 824.19
steal 824.13
run of the mill 79.3
run-of-the-mill 680.8
run on chatter 596.5
connect 71.4
continue 143.3
elapse 105.5
endure 110.6
progress 294.3
run out
v. become exhausted
717.5
be consumed 666.3
be destroyed 693.23
desert 633.6
drive out 310.14
elapse 105.5
emerge 303.13
end 70.6
exit 303.11
expatiate 593.8
find vent 632.10
adj. obsolete 123.15
past 119.7

run out of steam 725.15
run over abound 661.5
browse 564.13
examine 485.23
number 87.10
overflow 395.17
repeat 103.8
think over 478.13
trample 313.7
run ragged 717.6
run rings around 36.9
run riot
be disorderly 62.10
carouse 993.6
overrun 313.5
revolt 767.7
run amok 162.14
superabound 663.8
runs 311.2
run scared 892.8
runt a nobody 673.7
dwarf 196.6
little thing 196.4
run the gauntlet 893.11
run through
browse 564.13
persist 17.3
pervade 186.7
puncture 265.16
rehearse a play
611.37
spend 843.5
squander 854.3
stab 798.25
run-through
drama production
611.14
examination 485.3
summary 607.2
run true to form 17.3
runty dwarf 196.13
low 208.7
runway airstrip 278.23
path 657.3
run wild
be disorderly 62.10
let oneself go 762.18
run amok 162.14
rupture
n. break 49.4
crack 201.2
falling-out 795.4
impairment 692.8
v. be damaged 692.26
break 49.12
cleave 201.4
injure 692.15
open 265.15
ruptured broken 49.24
damaged 692.29
rural
agricultural 413.20
natural 736.6
rustic 182.6
ruralize 182.5
ruse stratagem 735.3
trick 618.6
rush
n. attack 798.1
course 267.2
demand 753.1
eruption 162.6

sameness identity 14.1
　regularity 17.2
　similarity 20.1
　tedium 884.1
samiel
　dust storm 403.13
　hot wind 403.7
samisen 465.4
sample
　n. part 55.1
　specimen 25.3
　taste 427.4
　testing sample 489.4
　v. canvass 485.28
　taste 427.7
　try out 489.8
　adj. typical 572.11
Samson
　brave person 893.8
　strong man 159.6
samurai 918.3
sanatorium 689.27
sanctified
　eminent 914.18
　hallowed 1026.8
　pietistic 1029.5
　redeemed 1028.10
sanctify glorify 914.13
　hallow 1026.5
sanctimonious
　hypocritic(al) 616.33
　pietistic 1029.5
　prudish 903.19
　zealous 1028.11
sanctimony
　affectation 903.6
　hypocrisy 616.6
　pietism 1029
　zeal 1028.3
sanction
　n. approval 968.1
　authorization 777.3
　consent 775.1
　legalization 998.2
　ratification 521.4
　v. approve 968.9
　authorize 777.11
　consent 775.2
　legalize 998.8
　ratify 521.12
sanctioned
　authorized 777.17
　legal 998.10
sanctity piety 1028.2
　sacredness 1026
sanctuary
　hiding place 615.4
　holy of holies 1042.5
　preserve 701.6
　refuge 700.1
sanctum retreat 700.5
　room 192.8
　sanctuary 1042.5
Sanctus 1040.10
sand
　n. grain 361.6
　stone 384.2
　v. grind 260.8
　rub 350.8
sandalwood 436.4
sandbag
　n. weight 352.6

v. hit 283.17
　weigh down 352.12
sandbank
　hidden danger 697.5
　island 386.2
　shoal 210.2
sandbar
　hidden danger 697.5
　island 386.2
　sand 384.2
　shoal 210.2
sandblast abrade 350.8
　grind 260.8
sand dune hill 207.5
　sand 384.2
sander 260.13
sandhog 257.10
sanding 350.2
sandpaper
　n. rough surface 261.2
　v. grind 260.8
　rub 350.8
sandstone 384.1,12
sandstorm 403.13
sandwich
　n. food 308.32
　v. interpose 237.6
sandwich board 559.7
sandy dry 393.7
　granular 361.12
　stony 384.11
　yellow 370.4
sane intelligent 467.12
　logical 482.20
　mentally sound 472.4
　practical 536.6
　sensible 467.18
Sanforized 198.13
sangfroid
　composure 858.2
　stability 142.1
sanguinary
　bloodstained 679.11
　cruel 939.24
　murderous 409.24
　savage 162.20
　warlike 797.25
sanguine
　n. personality type
　690.15
　adj. blood red 368.7
　cheerful 870.11
　expectant 539.11
　hopeful 888.11
　red-complexioned
　368.9
sanitary clean 681.27
　healthful 683.5
sanitation
　cleansing 681.3
　hygiene 683.2
sanitize 681.24
sanity
　intelligence 467.1
　sensibleness 467.6
　saneness 472
sannyasi ascetic 991.2
　Hindu priest 1038.14
sans 662.17
sans-culotte
　radical 745.12
　revolutionist 147.3

sans serif 603.6,23
sans souci 868.7
Santa Claus
　giver 818.11
　Saint Nicholas
　1014.23
sap
　n. content 194.5
　dupe 620.1
　entrenchment 799.5
　essence 5.2
　fluid 388.2
　fool 471.2
　v. attenuate 4.4
　excavate 257.15
　impair 692.18
　undermine 693.20
　weaken 160.10
sapid flavored 427.9
　tasty 428.8
sapient
　n. wise man 468.1
　adj. wise 467.17
sapless dry 393.7
　insipid 430.2
　weak 160.12
sapling sprout 125.9
　tree 411.10
　youngster 125.1
saponaceous 380.9
saporific 427.9
sapped 160.18
sapper
　excavator 257.10
　military engineer
　800.13
sapphic bisexual 419.32
　poetic 609.17
sapphire
　n. gem stone 384.13
　adj. blue 372.3
sapphism 419.12
sappy fluid 388.6
　foolish 470.8
　immature 124.10
　sentimental 855.22
saprolite 384.1
saprophyte 411.4
saprophytic
　putrefactive 692.40
　symbiotic 177.4
sarcasm humor 881.1
　irony 967.5
sarcastic 967.13
sarcoma 686.36
sarcophagus 410.11
sardonic 967.13
sarge 749.19
sartorial 231.47
Sartrian 500.10
sash 245.4
sashay depart 301.6
　travel 273.17
　walk 273.27
sass
　n. insolence 913.4
　v. be insolent 913.7
sassy 913.9
Satan
　deity of nether world
　1019.5
　liar 619.9

the Devil 1016.3
satanic cruel 939.24
　diabolic 1016.18
　terrible 675.10
　wicked 981.13
Satanism
　diabolism 1016.15
　sorcery 1035.2
Satanist 1016.16
sate gratify 865.6
　satiate 664.4
sated languid 708.19
　satiated 664.6
satellite
　attendance 73.6
　country 181.1
　follower 293.2
　hanger-on 907.5
　list 282.14
　man 787.8
　moon 375.11
　spacecraft 282.6,14
satiate be tedious 884.5
　fill 56.7
　gratify 865.6
　overload 663.15
　sate 664.4
satiated bored 884.10
　full 56.11
　overfull 663.20
　sated 664.6
satin
　n. fine texture 351.3
　smooth surface 260.3
　softness 357.4
　adj. smooth 351.8
satiny sleek 260.10
　smooth 351.8
　soft 357.15
satire
　disparagement 971.5
　humor 881.1
　poem 609.6
　poetry 609.4
　ridicule 967.6
　sarcasm 967.5
satiric(al)
　burlesque 967.14
　sarcastic 967.13
satirist humorist 881.12
　lampooner 971.7
　poet 609.13
satirize
　lampoon 971.12
　ridicule 967.11
satisfaction
　atonement 1012.1
　compensation 33.1
　contentment 868.1
　duel 796.7
　observance 768.1
　payment 841.1
　pleasure 865.1
　recompense 841.3
　reparation 694.6
　restitution 823.2
　satiety 664.1
　sufficiency 661.1
satisfactional 1012.7
satisfactory
　convincing 501.26
　satisfying 868.11

scalded 692.29
scalding 328.25
scale
   n. break 49.4
   coating 228.12
   continuity 71.2
   crust 228.14
   degree 29.1
   flake 227.3
   harmonics 463.6
   ladder 315.4
   map 654.4
   measure 490.2,20
   range 179.2
   size 195.1
   step 315.5
   types of 352.22
   v. ascend 315.11
   break 49.12
   flake 232.11
   layer 227.5
   raid 798.20
scale down
   make small 196.9
   reduce 39.7
scaling disruption 49.3
   raid 798.4
scallop
   n. food 308.25
   notching 262.2
   shell 228.42
   v. cook 330.4
   notch 262.4
   twist 254.4
scalloped cooked 330.6
   notched 262.5
scalp peel 232.8
   speculate in stocks
     833.23
scalper salesman 830.4
   stock speculator
     833.11
scaly flaky 227.7
   powdery 361.11
scam
   n. swindle 618.8
   v. swindle 618.17
scamp
   n. mischief-maker
     738.3
   rascal 986.3
   v. be parsimonious
     852.5
   neglect 534.8
scamper
   n. haste 709.1
   speed 269.3
   v. hurry away 301.11
   make haste 709.5
   rush 269.9
scamping
   negligent 534.10
   parsimonious 852.7
scampish
   dishonest 975.17
   mischievous 738.6
scan
   n. examination 485.3
   view 444.3
   v. analyze 48.7
   browse 564.13
   examine 485.23

poetize 609.16
skim over 485.25
use radar 346.17
scandal disgrace 915.5
   gossip 558.8
   iniquity 981.3
   slander 971.3
   wrong 959.2
scandalous bad 675.9
   disgraceful 915.11
   disparaging 971.13
   evil 981.16
   wrong 959.3
scanning
   n. data processing
     349.20
   metrics 609.8
   radar operation 346.8
   televising 345.3
   adj. metrical 609.18
scansion analysis 48.2
   metrics 609.8
scant
   v. be parsimonious
     852.5
   limit 234.5
   adj. incomplete 57.4
   meager 662.10
   narrow 205.14
   sparse 102.5
   wanting 662.13
scantiness
   fewness 102.1
   insignificance 35.1
   littleness 196.1
   meagerness 662.2
   scarcity 662.3
scantling 195.1
scanty incomplete 57.4
   meager 662.10
   narrow 205.14
   scarce 662.11
   sparse 102.5
scape picture 574.13
   shaft 217.1
   view 446.6
scapegoat
   sacrifice 1032.7
   substitute 149.3
scapegrace
   bad person 986.5
   mischief-maker 738.3
scar
   n. blemish 679.1
   mark 568.5
   precipice 213.3
   v. blemish 679.4
   mark 568.19
scarab 1036.5
scarce
   insufficient 662.11
   rare 136.2
   sparse 102.5
scarcely hardly 35.9
   infrequently 136.4
   insufficiently 662.16
   sparsely 102.8
   to a degree 29.7
scarcity fewness 102.1
   rarity 136.1
   sparsity 662.3

scare
   n. fear 891.1
   v. frighten 891.23
   scare away 891.29
scarecrow figure 572.4
   frightener 891.9
   ugly thing 899.4
scared 891.30
scared stiff 891.34
scaredy-cat 892.5
scarehead 484.2
scare off 652.3
scarer 891.9
scare up 811.10
scarf
   n. joint 47.4
   neckwear 231.64
   v. fasten 47.8
scarify blemish 679.4
   criticize severely
     969.21
   mark 568.19
   notch 262.4
   torture 866.18
scariness 891.2
scarlet
   prostitute 989.28
   red 368.6
scarlet fever 686.12
scarlet woman 989.16
scarp
   fortification 799.4
   incline 219.4
   precipice 213.3
scarred 679.8
scary fearful 891.31
   frightening 891.36
scat
   n. nonsense 547.3
   vocal music 462.12
   interj. go away!
     310.29
scathe
   n. impairment 692.1
   v. criticize severely
     969.21
   work evil 675.6
scathing
   acrimonious 161.13
   caustic 939.21
scatological
   fecal 311.20
   jargonish 580.19
   obscene 972.8
scatology cursing 972.3
   jargon 580.9
scat singing 462.12
scatter
   n. deflection 291.2
   v. defeat 727.9
   deflect 291.5
   disarrange 63.2
   disband 75.8
   disperse 75.4
   loosen 51.3
   part company 49.19
   radiate 299.6
   shatter 49.13
   squander 854.3
scatterbrain 471.7
scatterbrained
   giddy 532.16

   inconstant 141.7
   stupid 469.19
scattered
   confused 62.16
   defeated 727.14
   deviant 291.8
   dispersed 75.9
   few 102.5
   separated 49.21
scattering
   n. dispersion 75.1
   disruption 49.3
   few 102.2
   noncohesion 51.1
   radiating 299.2
   adj. dispersive 75.11
scavenge 681.18
scavenger animal 414.3
   sweeper 681.16
scenario
   playbook 611.26
   project 654.2
scenario writer
   author 602.15
   dramatist 611.27
scend
   n. wave 395.14
   v. billow 395.22
   sail 275.55
scene act 611.8
   arena 802.1
   outburst 952.9
   picture 574.13
   setting 233.2
   stage scenery 611.25
   view 446.6
scenery arena 802.1
   stage scenery 611.25
   view 446.6
scenic 611.38
scent
   n. clue 568.9
   fragrance 436.1
   hint 557.4
   odor 435.1
   perfume 436.2
   sense of smell 435.4
   track 568.8
   v. detect 488.6
   odorize 435.7
   perfume 436.8
   smell 435.8
scented 436.9
scepter
   emblem of authority
     739.9
   royal insignia 569.3
schedule
   n. list 88.1
   plan 654.1
   program 641.2
   v. allot 816.9
   budget 843.5
   list 88.8
   plan 654.9
   slate 641.4
scheduled listed 88.9
   planned 654.13
   slated 641.6
schema outline 48.4
   plan 654.1
   representation 572.1

seclusion 924.1
secretness 614
secret
  n. confidence 614.5
  adj. concealed 615.11
  covert 614.11
  intrinsic 5.6
  invisible 445.5
  recondite 549.16
  secluded 924.8
  secretive 614.15
secret agent
  agent 781.9
  inquirer 485.15
secretarial 602.28
secretariat 1000.4
secretary agent 781.3
  delegate 781.2
  desk 216.15
  executive 748.3
  public official 749.17
  recorder 571.1
  writer 602.13
secrete excrete 311.12
  hide away 615.7
  keep secret 614.7
  secern 312.5
  store up 660.11
secretion
  concealment 615.1
  excretion 311.1
  secernment 312
secretive close 614.15
secretory 312.7
  uncommunicative
    613.8
secret language
  cryptography 614.6
  unintelligibility 549.7
secretly 614.17
secretory
  excretory 311.19
  secretional 312.7
secret passage 615.5
secret place
  hiding place 615.4
  interior 225.2
  retreat 700.5
  seat of affections
    855.2
secret police
  police force 699.17
  spying 485.9
secret service
  intelligence service
    781.12
  spying 485.9
Secret Service 781.10
secret society 788.3
sect party 788.4
  religion 1020.3
  school 788.5
  word list 1020.32
sectarian
  n. dissenter 522.3
  nonconformist 83.3
  religionist 1020.17,35
  adj. denominational
    1020.25
  dissenting 522.6
  partisan 788.19

sectarianism
  partisanism 788.13
  religion 1020.4
sectary
  n. dissenter 522.3
  follower 293.2
  nonconformist 83.3
  religionist 1020.17
  supporter 787.9
  adj. denominational
    1020.25
  dissenting 522.6
  partisan 788.19
Sectary 1020.22
section
  n. area 180.1
  biology 61.5
  book part 605.13
  class 61.2
  military unit 800.19
  music division 462.24
  part 55.1
  part of writing 55.2
  separation 49.2
  surgical operation
    689.22
  tract 180.4
  v. apportion 49.18
sectional partial 55.7
  partisan 788.19
  regional 180.8
sectionalism
  partisanism 788.13
  political policy 744.4
sector part 55.1
  semicircle 253.8
secular
  n. layman 1039.2
  adj. hundred 99.29
  lay 1039.3
  materialistic 376.9
  momentary 137.8
  practical 536.6
  unsacred 1027.3
  worldly 1031.16
secularism
  materialism 376.5
  nonreligiousness
    1031.5
  practicalness 536.2
  theology 1023.1
secure
  v. acquire 811.8
  close 266.6
  defend 799.8
  elicit 305.14
  fasten 47.7
  fetch 271.15
  guarantee 772.9
  protect 699.18
  receive 819.6
  restrain 760.10
  stabilize 142.8
  stop work 144.8
  adj. believing 501.21
  determinate 513.20
  fastened 47.14
  reliable 513.17
  safe 698.4
  stable 142.12
  sure 513.21
secured 772.11

securely firmly 47.19
  safely 698.8
security
  confidence 513.5
  faith 888.1
  guarantee 772
  prosperity 728.1
  reliability 513.4
  safety 698.1
  secrecy 614.3
  stability 142.1
  stocks and bonds 834
security blanket 216.1
security risk 619.11
sedate
  v. put to sleep 712.20
  adj. composed 858.14
  dignified 905.12
  solemn 871.3
sedated 712.21
sedation 712.6
sedative
  n. anesthetic 423.3
  depressant 687.12
  pacifier 163.3
  sleep-inducer 712.10
  adj. calmative 687.45
  palliative 163.16
  sleep-inducing 712.23
sedentary
  inactive 708.16
  inert 268.14
sediment
  n. deposit 271.8
  residue 43.2
  v. precipitate 354.11
sedimentary 43.8
sedimentation 354.5
sedition
  rebelliousness 767.3
  treason 975.7
seditionist 648.11
seditious 767.11
seduce debauch 989.20
  enamor 931.21
  lure 650.4
seducer beau 931.12
  debaucher 989.12
  deceiver 619.1
  philanderer 932.11
  tempter 650.3
seduction
  allurement 650.1
  debauchment 989.6
seductive
  alluring 650.7
  desirable 634.30
seductress
  tempter 650.3
  unchaste woman
    989.15
sedulous
  industrious 707.22
  painstaking 533.11
  persevering 625.7
see
  n. diocese 1037.8
  v. attend 186.8
  behold 439.12
  bet 515.20
  contemplate 478.17
  detect 488.5

heed 530.6
  know 475.12
  make sure 513.11
  sense 422.8
  understand 548.8
  visit 922.17
  visualize 535.15
  interj. attention!
    530.22
seeable manifest 555.8
  visible 444.6
see about 478.14
see after 699.19
seed
  n. ancestry 170.4
  plant seed 411.29
  posterity 171.1
  source 153.7
  sperm 406.11
  v. plant 413.18
seedbed 413.11
seeding planting 413.14
  rainmaking 394.5
seedling plant 411.3
  sprout 125.9
  tree 411.10
seedy fatigued 717.6
  inferior 680.9
  shabby 692.34
  sick 686.52
  slovenly 62.15
see fit prefer 637.17
  will 621.2
seeing that 155.10
see it through
  be thorough 56.8
  conclude 625.5
  persist 143.5
seek be curious 528.3
  endeavor 714.4
  hunt 485.29
  pursue 655.8
  solicit 774.14
seeker hunter 485.17
  petitioner 774.7
  pursuer 655.4
seem
  appear to be 446.10
  resemble 20.7
seeming
  n. aspect 446.3
  exteriority 224.1
  fakery 616.3
  illusoriness 519.2
  adj. apparent 446.11
  false 616.27
  illusory 519.9
  superficial 224.6
seemingly
  apparently 446.12
  falsely 616.35
  supposedly 499.17
seemly
  conventional 645.5
  decent 988.5
  decorous 897.10
  expedient 670.5
  right 958.8
  well-chosen 589.7
seep be damp 392.11
  exude 303.15
  trickle 395.18

elderliness 126.5
oldness 123.1
psychosis 473.3
weakness 160.3
senior
n. chief 749.3
elder 127.5
student 566.6
superior 36.4
adj. authoritative
739.15
elder 123.19
prior 116.4
senior citizen 127.2
seniority
authority 739.4
eldership 126.3
oldness 123.1
superiority 36.1
señor 420.7
señora 421.8
señorita 421.8
sensation brain 466.6
emotion 855.3
great success 724.3
marvel 920.2
sense 422.1
thrill 857.2
sensational
eloquent 600.11
emotionalistic 855.20
exciting 857.30
gaudy 904.20
grandiose 601.8
superb 674.17
wonderful 920.10
sensationalism
dramatics 611.2
emotionalism 855.9
exaggeration 617.1
grandiloquence 601.1
showiness 904.3
sense
n. discrimination
492.1
emotion 855.3
intelligence 467.1
meaning 545.1
milieu 233.3
rationality 467.6
reasonableness 482.9
sensation 422.1
v. detect 488.5
feel 855.11
intuit 481.4
perceive 422.8
understand 548.7
senseless foolish 470.8
illogical 483.11
imprudent 470.9
inanimate 382.5
insane 473.25
meaningless 547.6
unconscious 423.8
unintelligent 469.13
unordered 62.12
sense of humor 881.11
senses five senses 422.5
sanity 472.1
wits 466.2
sensibility
cognizance 475.2

discrimination 492.1
emotional capacity
855.4
pliancy 357.2
sagacity 467.4
sentience 422.2
sensible aware 475.15
cheap 849.7
cognizant of 475.16
emotionable 855.21
grateful 949.5
intelligent 467.12
logical 482.20
perceptible 422.13
practical 536.6
reasonable 467.18
sane 472.4
substantial 3.6
weighable 352.19
sensing 481.5
sensitive
discriminating 492.7
emotionable 855.21
excitable 857.26
fastidious 896.9
pliant 357.9
responsive 422.14
sensory 422.11
sore 424.11
touchy 951.20
sensitivity
discrimination 492.1
emotional capacity
855.4
excitability 857.9
fastidiousness 896.1
sensitiveness 422.3
touchiness 951.4
sensitivity to 174.1
sensitivity training
690.5
sensitize 422.9
sensory 422.11
sensual carnal 987.5
lascivious 989.29
sexual 419.26
sensualist 987.3
sensuality carnality 987
lasciviousness 989.5
sexuality 419.2
sensuous pleasant 863.7
sensory 422.11
sentence
n. condemnation
1008.1
judgment 494.5
legal decision 1004.9
maxim 517.1
part of writing 55.2
phrase 585.1
remark 594.4
v. condemn 1008.3
pass judgment 494.13
sententious
advisory 754.8
aphoristic 517.6
concise 592.6
grandiloquent 601.8
meaningful 545.10
sentience
physical sensibility
422.2

wakefulness 713.1
sentient 422.13
sentiment
attitude 525.1
belief 501.6
emotion 855.3
feeling 855.1
idea 479.1
love 931.1
sentimentality 855.8
sentimental
foolish 470.8
loving 931.25
mawkish 855.22
sentimentality
amorousness 931.3
mawkishness 855.8
sentimentalize 855.15
sentry warner 703.4
watchman 699.10
sentry box 191.10
separable 49.26
separate
v. analyze 48.6
arrange 60.11
bound 235.8
differentiate 16.6
disband 75.8
discriminate 492.5
dissent 522.4
dissolve marriage
935.5
diverge 299.5
divide 49.9
fall out 795.10
interspace 201.3
open 265.12
part company 49.19
partition 237.8
quarantine 761.13
refine 681.22
segregate 77.6
sow dissension 795.14
adj. alone 89.8
different 16.7
distinct 49.20
secluded 924.7
unrelated 10.5
separated
alienated 929.11
alone 89.8
different 16.7
disjoined 49.21
distant 199.8
interspaced 201.6
quarantined 761.20
secluded 924.7
unmarried 935.7
unrelated 10.5
separately
particularly 80.15
severally 49.28
singly 89.13
separateness
aloneness 89.2
difference 16.1
noncohesion 51.1
unrelatedness 10.1
separation analysis 48.1
differentiation 16.4
disbandment 75.3
discrimination 492.3

disjunction 49
dissolution of mar-
riage 935.1
distance 199.1
divergence 299.1
exclusiveness 77.3
falling-out 795.4
partition 237.5
quarantine 761.2
seclusion 924.1
sifting 681.4
separatism 49.1
separatist
n. apostate 628.5
dissenter 522.3
adj. repudiative 628.12
separative
differentiative 16.9
disintegrative 53.5
exclusive 77.8
separating 49.25
sepia 367.3
sepsis 686.30
sept ancestry 170.4
class 61.2
race 11.4
septal 237.11
septet
cooperation 786.1
part music 462.17
poetic division
609.11
seven 99.3
septic diseased 686.56
putrefactive 692.40
unhealthful 684.5
septicemia 686.30
septic tank 682.12
septuagenarian
old man 127.2
seventy 99.7
septum 237.5
sepulcher 410.16
sepulchral deep 454.10
funereal 410.22
sequel aftermath 117.2
continuation 67
following 293.1
result 154.1
sequence
coherence 50.2
continuity 71.2
following 293.1
order 59.2
posteriority 117.1
result 154.1
series 65
sequential
coherent 50.11
consecutive 71.9
deducible 482.23
resulting 154.7
succeeding 65.4
sequester
appropriate 822.20
separate 49.9
sequestered
concealed 615.11
private 614.13
quiescent 268.12
recluse 924.9
separated 49.21

sequitur 67.1
seraglio 933.11
seraphic angelic 1015.6
  lovable 931.23
  pious 1028.9
  virtuous 980.7
seraphim angels 1015.1
  celestial beings
  1015.3
sere
  deteriorated 692.37
  dried 393.9
  worn 692.33
serenade
  n. courtship 932.6
  song 462.13
  v. court 932.19
  sing 462.39
serendipity
  chance 156.1
  discovery 488.1
serene clear 335.31
  composed 858.12
  moderate 163.13
  pacific 803.9
serenity
  composure 858.2
  moderation 163.1
  peace 803.2
  quiescence 268.1
serf retainer 750.1
  slave 764.7
  sycophant 907.3
serfdom service 750.12
  servility 907.1
  subjection 764.1
sergeant
  noncommissioned of-
  ficer 749.19
  peace officer 699.15
serial
  n. book 605.1
  installment 605.13
  periodical 605.10
  radio broadcast
  344.18
  stage show 611.4
  adj. coherent 50.11
  consecutive 71.9
  journalistic 605.26
  periodic 137.7
series biology 61.5
  circuit 137.3
  continuity 71.2
  edition 605.2
  following 293.1
  numbers 86.7
  sequence 65.1
  set 74.12
serigraphy 578.5
serious dangerous 697.9
  eloquent 600.14
  great 34.6
  resolute 624.11
  sedate 858.14
  solemn 871.3
  thoughtful 478.21
  weighty 672.19
  zealous 635.10
seriously
  positively 34.19
  resolutely 624.17

solemnly 871.4
  zealously 635.15
seriousness
  importance 672.3
  resolution 624.1
  sedateness 858.4
  solemnity 871.1
  zeal 635.2
sermon lecture 599.3
  lesson 562.7
  reproof 969.5
sermonize
  expound 562.17
  lecture 599.11
sermonizer
  lecturer 599.5
  preacher 1038.3
serous fluid 388.7
  secretory 312.7
serpent
  bad person 986.7
  brass wind 465.8
  snake 414.31
  traitor 619.10
serpentine
  convoluted 254.7
  cunning 735.12
  curved 252.7
  flowing 395.24
  reptile 414.51
  wandering 291.7
  winding 254.6
serrate
  v. notch 262.4
  adj. angular 251.6
  notched 262.5
  rough 261.7
serration 262.2
serried continuous 71.8
  crowded 74.22
  dense 354.12
serum antitoxin 687.27
  blood 388.4
  body fluid 388.3
  transfusion 689.20
servant assistant 787.6
  hanger-on 907.5
  instrument 658.3
  retainer 750
  slave 764.7
  subordinate 764.5
  working person 718.2
serve
  n. throw 285.4
  v. act 705.4
  be expedient 670.3
  be inferior 37.4
  be instrumental
  658.5
  be of use 665.17
  copulate 419.23
  do duty 656.13
  do good 674.10
  give 818.12
  help 785.18
  soldier 797.22
  suffice 661.4
  suit 26.8
  summon 752.12
  tend 174.3
  throw 285.11
  work for 750.13

serve as 572.7
serve one right
  be just 976.6
  get one's deserts
  960.6
  punish 1010.10
  retaliate 955.5
serve time
  be imprisoned 761.18
  spend time 108.5
service
  n. agency 658.2
  aid 785.1
  benefit 665.4
  business 656.1
  ceremony 646.4
  employment 750.12
  food 307.11
  good deed 938.7
  liturgy 1040.3
  military service
  797.13
  military unit 800.21
  obedience 766.1
  portion 307.10
  position 656.5
  rigging 277.12
  subservience 764.2
  task 656.2
  throw 285.4
  worship 1032.8
  v. copulate 419.23
  repair 694.14
serviceable
  helpful 785.21
  instrumental 658.6
  useful 665.18
serviceman
  military man 800.6
  repairman 694.10
service station 832.7
servile
  deferential 765.16
  downtrodden 764.16
  inferior 37.6
  serving 750.14
  slavish 907.12
  submissive 765.12
  subservient 764.13
servility inferiority 37.1
  obedience 766.1
  obeisance 964.2
  slavishness 907
  subjection 764.1
  submissiveness 765.3
serving
  n. food 307.10
  rigging 277.12
  adj. acting 705.10
  attending 750.14
  helping 785.20
serving girl 750.8
servitude service 750.12
  subjection 764.1
servomechanism
  automation 349.13
  mechanism 348.5
  types of 349.30
sesquicentennial
  anniversary 137.4
  one-hundred-fifty
  99.8

sesquipedalian
  n. long word 582.10
  adj. high-flown 601.10
  long 202.8
  stilted 590.3
session
  church council 755.4
  conference 597.6
  meeting 74.2
  period 107.2
set
  n. all 54.3
  assemblage 74.12
  class 61.2
  clique 788.6
  cohesion 50.1
  company 74.3
  course 267.2
  direction 290.1
  edition 605.2
  flow 395.4
  form 246.1
  group 20.5
  position 184.3
  radio receiver 344.3
  setting 611.24
  sprout 125.9
  trait of character
  525.3
  trend 174.2
  v. adjust 26.7
  aim 290.8
  allot 816.9
  brood 169.12
  cohere 50.6
  designate 80.11
  direct 290.6
  establish 184.15
  fasten 47.7
  flow 395.16
  form 246.7
  heal 694.21
  impose 963.4
  incline 174.3
  place 184.11
  plant 413.18
  prepare 720.9
  prescribe 752.10
  set to music 462.47
  sharpen 258.9
  sink 316.6
  sit 268.10
  solidify 356.8
  stabilize 142.9
  thicken 354.10
  typeset 603.16
  adj. circumscribed
  234.6
  customary 642.15
  established 142.13
  fastened 47.14
  firm 624.12
  fixed 142.14
  hardened 356.13
  inveterate 642.21
  located 184.17
  made sure 513.20
  obstinate 626.8
  planned 654.13
  prepared 720.16
  sharp 258.10
  trite 883.9

Set
Egyptian deity 1014.10
god of evil 1016.6
seta bristle 261.3
hair 230.2
set about begin 68.7
set to work 716.15
undertake 715.3
set above 637.17
set against
antagonize 929.7
provoke 795.14
set an example 25.7
set apart allot 816.9
characterize 80.10
commit 816.11
differentiate 16.6
discriminate 492.5
exclude 42.10
interspace 201.3
partition 237.8
reserve 660.12
sanctify 1026.5
segregate 77.6
separate 49.9
set aside allot 816.9
disregard 531.4
exclude 42.10
postpone 132.9
put away 668.6
remove 271.10
repeal 779.2
reserve 660.12
segregate 77.6
separate 49.9
waive 507.5
setback defeat 727.2
disappointment 541.1
hindrance 730.1
regression 295.1
relapse 696.1
reverse 729.3
slowing 270.4
set back hinder 730.10
recess 257.14
restrain 760.7
slow 270.9
set before
confront 240.8
offer 637.21
prefer 637.17
propose 773.5
set down affirm 523.4
attribute 155.4
humiliate 906.5
put 184.13
record 570.16
reprove 969.17
set forth attest 505.9
describe 608.12
manifest 555.5
postulate 499.12
propose 773.5
say 594.23
start out 301.7
set in begin 68.7
gather 403.22
implant 142.9
indent 257.14
insert 304.3

set in motion
impel 283.10
motivate 648.12
move 267.6
start 285.14
setoff
counterbalance 33.2
discount 847.1
opposite 15.2
outset 301.2
printing 603.3
set off allot 816.9
beautify 900.14
border 235.10
compare 491.4
counteract 33.5
differentiate 16.6
discriminate 492.5
explode 162.13
head for 290.10
kindle 648.18
measure off 490.12
oppose 15.4
ornament 901.8
start out 301.7
set on
v. attack 798.15
base on 212.6
incite 648.17
sow dissension 795.14
adj. desirous of 634.22
determined upon 624.16
set out begin 68.7
dispose 60.9
head for 290.10
ornament 901.8
phrase 588.4
plot 654.11
start out 301.7
set right adjust 26.7
compensate 33.4
direct to 290.7
disillusion 520.2
remedy 694.13
teach 562.11
set sail begin 68.7
hoist sail 275.20
set straight
direct to 290.7
disillusion 520.2
reform 145.12
remedy 694.13
reprove 969.17
straighten 250.5
setting
n. arena 802.1
background 233.2
hardening 356.5
motif 901.7
mounting 216.10
orchestration 463.2
planting 413.14
scenery 611.24
thickening 354.4
typesetting 603.2
adj. descending 316.11
settle arrange 771.9
compromise 807.2
conform 82.3

decide 494.11
defeat 727.6
descend 316.7
fly down 278.50
gravitate 352.15
kill 409.14
light on 316.10
locate 184.16
make sure 513.11
mediate 805.7
organize 60.10
pay in full 841.13
populate 188.9
prove 505.11
punish 1010.11
reconcile 804.8
refute 506.5
resolve 624.7
ruin 693.11
sink 316.6
stabilize 142.9
transfer property 817.3
settled
contracted 771.12
defeated 727.14
ended 70.8
established 142.13
firm 624.12
fixed 142.14
inhabited 188.12
inveterate 642.21
located 184.17
made sure 513.20
paid 841.22
proved 505.21
settle down
be moderate 163.5
fly 278.52
locate 184.16
mature 126.9
sink 316.6
settle for 868.5
settle in 188.9
settlement
arrangement 771.4
community 788.2
compromise 807.1
endowment 818.9
establishment 184.6
estate 810.4
payment 841.1
peopling 188.2
proof 505.4
property transfer 817.1
reconciliation 804.4
territory 181.1
settler arrival 302.4
assigner 818.11
disproof 506.3
end-all 70.4
greenhorn 78.4
inhabitant 190.9
settle upon
attribute to 155.4
decide upon 637.16
endow 818.17
settle with
arrange 771.9
pay 841.12
punish 1010.10

retaliate 955.7
set to begin 68.7
fasten 47.7
quarrel 795.11
set to work 716.15
undertake 715.3
set-to controversy 482.4
quarrel 795.6
setup composition 58.1
easy thing 732.3
order 59.1
plan 654.1
prearrangement 641.1
structure 245.1
set up aid 785.11
begin 68.11
conceive 153.11
contrive 654.9
create 167.10
elevate 317.5
erect 213.9
establish 184.15
finance 836.15
glorify 914.13
install 167.12
order 59.4
pay for 841.19
prearrange 641.3
provoke 952.22
refresh 695.2
remedy 694.13
set upon 798.15
seven-league boots 1036.6
seventh
n. harmonics 463.20
adj. seven 99.19
seventh heaven
happiness 865.2
heaven 1018.5
summit 211.2
sever differentiate 16.6
discriminate 492.5
separate 49.11
several
n. indefinite number 101.2
plurality 100.1
adj. different 16.7
diversified 19.4
many 101.7
particular 80.12
proportionate 816.13
severally each 80.19
proportionately 816.14
separately 49.28
singly 89.13
variously 19.5
severance
differentiation 16.4
elimination 77.2
separation 49.2
severe
acrimonious 161.13
cold 333.14
difficult 731.16
exact 516.16
gruff 937.7
painful 424.10
plain 902.9

free oneself from
763.8
shaker 324.9
shakes
delirium tremens
473.10
excitement 857.4
nervousness 859.2
shaking 324.2
shake up agitate 324.10
awaken 713.5
censure 969.13
excite 857.13
fluff 357.6
rearrange 60.13
weaken 160.10
shake-up
makeshift 670.2
rearrangement 60.7
shaking
n. agitation 324.2
excitement 857.4
waving 323.2
adj. imperfectly spo-
ken 595.12
jittery 859.11
vibrating 324.17
shaky aged 126.18
cold 333.15
fearful 891.31
flimsy 4.7
imperfectly spoken
595.12
jittery 859.11
loose 51.5
shaking 324.17
unfastened 49.22
unreliable 514.19
unsafe 697.11
unsteady 160.16
shallow
n. shoal 210.2
v. become shallow
210.3
adj. half-learned
477.15
negligible 35.6
not deep 210.5
superficial 469.20
trivial 673.16
shallowness
depthlessness 210
exteriority 224.1
inattention 531.1
slight knowledge
477.6
superficiality 469.7
triviality 673.3
sham
n. affectation 903.1
display 904.4
fake 616.13
hoax 618.7
impostor 619.6
pretense 616.3
pretext 649.1
v. affect 903.12
fake 616.21
adj. assumed 903.16
imitation 22.8
ungenuine 616.26
shaman 1035.7

shamble
n. gait 273.14
slowness 270.2
v. walk 273.27
shambles
battlefield 802.2
butchery 409.4
destruction 693.1
killing site 409.12
shame
n. decency 988.2
disgrace 915.5
humiliation 906.2
iniquity 981.3
regret 873.1
wrong 959.2
v. disgrace 915.8
humiliate 906.4
shamed
humiliated 906.13
in disrepute 915.13
shamefaced
humiliated 906.13
regretful 873.8
shy 908.12
shameful bad 675.9
disgraceful 915.11
evil 981.16
regretful 873.8
wrong 959.3
shameless
brazen 913.10
dishonest 975.16
gaudy 904.20
immodest 990.6
unregretful 874.4
wicked 981.17
wrong 959.3
shampoo
n. cleaning agent
681.17
washing 681.5
v. wash 681.19
shamrock
insignia 569.1
three 93.1
shanghai abduct 824.19
coerce 756.7
seize 822.14
Shangri-la 535.11
shank leg 273.16
meat 308.17
printing 603.6
shaft 217.6
shanty 191.10
shapable 357.9
shape
n. aspect 446.3
characteristic 80.4
condition 7.3
form 246.1
human form 246.4
illusion 519.4
image 446.5
kind 61.3
mode 7.4
specter 1017.1
structure 245.1
v. be formed 246.8
conform 82.3
create 167.10
fashion 246.7

imagine 535.14
make ceramics 576.6
plan 654.9
shaped made 167.22
planned 654.13
shapeless
abnormal 85.9
formless 247.4
inconstant 141.7
obscure 549.15
ugly 899.8
unordered 62.12
vague 514.18
shapely
beautiful 900.17
well-shaped 248.5
shape up
be formed 246.8
be in a state 7.6
get better 691.7
order 59.5
shard
n. piece 55.3
refuse 669.4
v. pulverize 361.9
show fragility 360.3
share
n. allotment 816.5
amount of stock
834.3
part 55.1
v. apportion 816.6
communicate 554.7
emotionally respond
855.12
participate 815.6
sharecrop 413.16
sharecropper 413.5
sharecropping
agriculture 413.1
participation 815.2
shareholder
participator 815.4
stockholder 833.14
sharing
n. accord 794.1
apportionment 816.1
impartation 554.2
participation 815.1
sociability 922.6
sympathy 855.5
adj. participating
815.8
shark expert 733.11
fish 414.35,65
predator 822.12
savage 943.5
sharper 619.4
vertebrates 415.7
sharp
n. expert 733.11
gambler 515.17
harmonics 463.14
sharper 619.4
adj. acrimonious
161.13
alert 533.14
angular 251.6
bitter 429.6
caustic 939.21
chic 644.13
cold 333.14

cunning 735.12
deceitful 618.20
deep-felt 855.26
dissonant 461.4
gruff 937.7
intelligent 467.14
keen 258.10
painful 424.10
penetrating 857.29
pungent 433.6
quick 707.18
sensitive 422.15
shrill 458.14
steep 219.18
strong-smelling
435.10
unpleasant 864.20
violent 162.15
witty 881.15
adv. punctually
131.14
suddenly 113.9
sharp ear 448.3
sharpen
aggravate 885.2
edge 258.9
increase 38.5
sensitize 422.9
stimulate 857.12
tool 348.10
sharpener cutlery 348.2
types of 258.19
sharper deceiver 619.4
gambler 515.17
sharp eye
keen eye 439.10
vigilance 533.4
sharp-eyed
clear-sighted 439.22
vigilant 533.13
sharpness
acrimony 161.4
alertness 533.5
bitterness 864.5
causticity 939.8
chic 644.3
cold 333.1
cunning 735.1
dissonance 461.1
gruffness 937.3
intelligence 467.2
keenness 258
pungency 433.1
quickness 707.3
stridence 458.1
unpleasant taste
429.2
violence 162.1
wittiness 881.2
sharp-nosed 435.13
sharpshooter
infantryman 800.9
shooter 285.9
sharp-sighted 439.22
shatter break 360.3
demolish 693.17
madden 473.23
splinter 49.13
shattered broken 49.24
damaged 692.29
shatterproof
resistant 159.18

lateral 242.6
occasional 136.3
sideburns 230.8
side by side
cheek to cheek
242.12
cooperatively 786.6
near 200.14
parallel 218.7
together 73.10
sided 242.7
side door byway 657.5
entrance 302.6
secret passage 615.5
side effect adjunct 41.1
aftermath 67.3
side-glance
flirtation 932.8
glance 439.4
side issue adjunct 41.1
by-product 168.3
sidekick
companion 928.3
partner 787.2
sidelight
information 557.1
light 335.1
sideline
n. avocation 656.7
border 235.4
merchandise 831.1
v. put away 668.6
sidelong
adj. inclining 219.15
oblique 219.13
side 242.6
adv. beside 242.10
obliquely 219.21
sideways 242.8
sidereal 375.25
side road byway 657.5
digression 593.4
sidestep dodge 631.8
go sideways 242.5
prevaricate 613.7
pull back 284.7
quibble 483.9
step aside 291.6
side street 657.5
sidestroke 275.11
sideswipe
n. impact 283.3
v. collide 283.12
graze 200.10
sidetrack
n. digression 593.4
railway 657.8
v. turn aside 291.6
sidetracked 534.14
sidewalk 657.3
sidewalk superintendent
442.1
sideward motion 267.8
side 242.6
sideways
adj. side 242.6
adv. breadthwise
204.9
crosswise 221.13
laterally 242.8
obliquely 219.21

side with
agree with 521.9
back 785.13
join with 786.4
siding
building material
378.2
railway 657.8
side 242.1
wood 378.3
sidle
n. gait 273.14
v. approach 296.3
creep 273.25
go sideways 242.5
step aside 291.6
tilt 219.10
walk 273.27
siege
besiegement 798.5
enclosure 236.1
sierra 207.9
siesta 712.3
sieve
n. network 221.3
porousness 265.9
refining equipment
681.13
separator 49.7
sorter 60.5
v. discriminate 492.5
refine 681.22
separate 77.6
sort 60.11
sievelike 265.21
sift analyze 48.8
discriminate 492.5
discuss 597.12
explore 485.22
refine 681.22
select 637.14
separate 77.6
sort 60.11
sifter
refining equipment
681.13
sorter 60.5
sifting analysis 48.3
grouping 60.3
investigation 485.4
refinement 681.4
sigh
n. breathing 403.18
murmur 452.4
sighing 452.8
v. exhale 403.24
lament 875.8
moan 452.14
utter 594.26
whisper 452.10
wind sound 403.23
sight
n. attitude 525.2
concept 501.6
look 439.3
marvel 920.2
much 34.4
optical instrument
443.4
range of view 444.3
scene 446.6
sense 422.5

spectacle 446.7
ugly thing 899.4
vision 439.1
v. aim 290.6
see 439.12
sightless blind 441.9
unseen 445.5
sightly 900.17
sight-see
see the sights 442.6
travel 273.20
sightseer
curious person 528.2
tourist 442.3
traveler 274.1
sigmoid(al)
crescent-shaped
252.11
winding 254.6
sign
n. character 581.1
disease 686.1
evidence 505.1
harmonics 463.12
hint 557.4
indication 568.2
medical prognosis
689.14
number 86.1
omen 544.3
poster 559.7
signal 568.15
spoor 568.8
supernaturalism 85.8
symbol 149.2
unit of meaning
545.6
v. contract 771.8
inscribe 581.6
ratify 521.12
secure 772.9
signal 568.22
signal
n. computer 349.19
hint 557.4
indication 568.2
information 557.7
radar signal 346.11
sign 568.15
v. communicate 554.7
make a signal 275.52
sign 568.22
adj. notable 672.18
remarkable 34.10
telecommunicational
560.20
signaling 560.1
signalize
celebrate 877.2
evidence 505.9
honor 914.12
signal 568.22
signalizing 568.23
signal light 336.9
signalman 703.4
signature
attribution 155.2
autograph 583.10
bookbinding 605.15
book part 605.12
harmonics 463.12
identification 568.11

part of writing 55.2
radio 344.19
ratification 521.4
settlement 771.4
sign 568.2
signboard
pointer 568.4
poster 559.7
signed
contracted 771.12
ratified 521.14
signer 521.7
signet mark 568.7
ratification 521.4
royal insignia 569.3
seal 568.13
signature 583.10
significance
importance 672.1
meaningfulness 545.5
ominousness 544.7
purport 545.1
repute 914.5
significant
evidential 505.17
important 672.16
indicative 568.23
meaningful 545.10
premonitory 544.16
prominent 914.17
signification
indication 568.1
meaning 545.1
specification 80.6
signify augur 544.12
be important 672.11
evidence 505.9
indicate 568.17
mean 545.8
specify 80.11
signing 771.4
sign language
deaf-and-dumb alpha-
bet 449.3
gesture 568.14
sign off
broadcast 344.25
telegraph 560.19
sign on
broadcast 344.25
employ 780.13
enlist 780.16
install 304.4
join 788.14
telegraph 560.19
signor 420.7
signora 421.8
sign over 817.3
signpost pointer 568.4
post 217.4
sign up employ 780.13
enlist 780.16
install 304.4
join 788.14
volunteer 108.5
silage 308.4
silence
n. quiescence 268.1
silentness 451
taciturnity 613.2
v. destroy 693.15
overcome 727.7

put to silence 451.8
refute 506.5
render powerless
158.11
strike dead 409.18
suppress 760.8
interj. hush! 451.14
silencer 451.4
silent still 451.10
taciturn 613.9
unexpressed 546.9
silent film 611.16
silent majority
mediocrity 680.5
party 788.4
silhouette
n. form 246.2
outline 235.2
picture 574.14
portrait 574.16
reflection 24.7
shadow 337.3
v. outline 235.9
silicic 383.15
silicone 380.2
silicosis 686.14
silk fabric 378.5,11
fine texture 351.3
lawyer 1003.4
smooth surface 260.3
softness 357.4
silken sleek 260.10
soft 357.15
silk-screen printing
graphic art 578.5
printing 603.1
silk-stocking
n. nobleman 918.4
adj. elite 644.16
silky sleek 260.10
smooth 351.8
soft 357.15
threadlike 206.7
sill foundation 216.6
threshold 216.9
silly
n. a fool 471.6
adj. dazed 532.14
foolish 470.8
nonsensical 547.7
trivial 673.16
silo granary 660.7
rocketry 281.10
silt deposit 271.8
dregs 43.2
silvan see **sylvan**
silver
n. chemical element
379.10
currency metals
835.20
lightness 364.1
money 835.1
tableware 348.3
whiteness 364.2
v. gray 366.3
whiten 364.5
adj. eloquent 600.8
gray 366.4
metal 383.17
white 364.7
silvering 364.3

silver lining 888.3
silver plate
flatware 348.3
plating 228.13
silver-plate 228.26
silver-plated
metal 383.17
plated 228.32
silver-tongued
eloquent 600.8
melodious 462.49
silverware
hard goods 831.4
tableware 348.3
silvery gray 366.4
melodious 462.49
metal 383.17
white 364.7
silviculture
forestry 413.3
woodland 411.11
similar
approximate 9.8
comparable 491.8
like 20.10
similarity
comparability 491.3
likeness 20
relationship 9.1
similarize
approximate 20.8
make agree 26.7
similarly
additionally 40.11
correspondingly
20.18
thus 8.10
simile
comparison 491.1
figure of speech
551.5
similarity 20.1
similitude
comparison 491.1
copy 24.1
image 572.3
likeness 20.3
similarity 20.1
simmer
be angry 952.15
be hot 328.22
boil 329.20
bubble 405.4
cook 330.4
seethe 162.11
simmer down 858.7
Simon Legree 749.14
simon-pure
genuine 516.14
hypocritical 616.33
simple 45.6
simpatico 927.14
simper
n. smile 876.3
v. affect 903.14
smile 876.7
simpering 903.18
simple artless 736.5
easy 732.12
genuine 516.14
gullible 502.9
homelike 191.33

humble 906.9
ignorant 477.12
informal 647.3
intelligible 548.10
mentally deficient
469.22
mere 35.8
ordinary 902.6
plain 45.6
plain-speaking 591.3
single 89.7
soft-colored 362.21
tasteful 897.8
unaffected 589.6
simpleminded
artless 736.5
mentally deficient
469.22
simpleton 471.8
simplicity
artlessness 736.1
facility 732.1
good taste 897.4
gullibility 502.2
ignorance 477.1
informality 647.1
intelligibility 548.2
literary elegance
589.1
mental deficiency
469.9
paring down 39.1
plainness 902.1
plain speech 591.1
rusticity 182.3
unity 89.1
unmixedness 45
simplification
disentanglement 45.2
explanation 552.4
facilitation 732.4
simplified 45.9
simplify clarify 548.6
explain 552.10
facilitate 732.6
make plain 902.5
pare 39.7
streamline 45.4
simplistic
oversimplified 45.10
undeveloped 721.12
simply artlessly 736.7
easily 732.15
informally 647.4
in plain words 591.4
intelligibly 548.12
plainly 902.10
purely 45.11
solely 89.14
tastefully 897.11
to a degree 35.10
simulacrum
aspect 446.3
copy 24.1
fake 616.13
illusoriness 519.2
image 572.3
likeness 20.3
representation 616.3
simulate affect 903.12
assume 821.4
fake 616.21

imitate 22.5
resemble 20.7
simulated
assumed 903.16
falsified 616.26
similar 20.10
simulation
assumption 821.2
fakery 616.3
imitation 22.1
similarity 20.1
simultaneity
accompaniment 73.1
concurrence 177.1
instantaneousness
113.1
simultaneousness 118
simultaneous
accompanying 73.9
concurrent 118.4
simultaneously
at once 113.8
at the same time
105.9
concurrently 118.6
sin
n. error 518.1
iniquity 981.3
misconduct 982.1
wrong 982.2
v. do wrong 981.8
transgress 982.5
since
adv. ago 119.15
subsequently 117.6
until now 119.17
conj. because 155.10
sincere artless 736.5
candid 974.17
genuine 516.14
resolute 624.11
zealous 635.10
sincerity
artlessness 736.1
authenticity 516.5
candor 974.4
resolution 624.1
zeal 635.2
sinecure 732.3
sine qua non
condition 507.2
important point
672.6
sinew eloquence 600.3
muscle 159.2
power 157.1
sine wave 323.5
sinewy eloquent 600.11
strong 159.14
tough 359.4
sinful bad 675.7
evil 981.16
iniquitous 982.6
ungodly 1031.17
wrong 959.3
sing
n. music festival
462.33
v. be cheerful 870.6
be pleased 865.9
bird sound 460.5
divulge 556.6

poetize 609.15
rejoice 876.5
utter 594.26
vocalize 462.39
wind sound 403.23
singe
 n. burn 329.6
 v. blemish 679.6
 burn 329.24
singed 329.30
singer entertainer 612.1
 lead 612.6
 vocalist 464.13
singing
 n. music festival
 462.33
 vocal music 462.12
 adj. happy 865.13
 vocal 462.51
single
 n. individual 89.4
 unmarried 934.2
 adj. characteristic
 80.13
 one 89.7
 simple 45.6
 unmarried 934.7
single file 71.2
single-handed 89.8
single man 934.3
single-minded
 artless 736.5
 engrossed 530.17
 persevering 625.7
 resolute 624.11
singleness
 celibacy 934.1
 simplicity 45.1
 solitude 924.3
 unity 89.1
single out 637.14
singleton
 individual 89.4
 playing cards 878.17
single woman 934.4
sing out 459.8
singsong
 n. regularity 17.2
 repetitiousness 103.4
 adj. repetitious 103.15
 tedious 884.8
singular
 n. number 586.8
 adj. characteristic
 80.13
 eccentric 474.4
 one 89.7
 particular 80.12
 peculiar 85.11
 sole 89.9
singularity
 characteristic 80.4
 eccentricity 474.1
 oddity 85.3
 particularity 80.1
 unity 89.1
singularly
 characteristically
 80.17
 exceptionally 34.20·
 oddly 85.19
 singly 89.13

sinister adverse 729.13
 bad 675.7
 dishonest 975.16
 left 244.4
 oblique 219.13
 ominous 544.17
sinistral left 244.4
 left-handed 244.5
 oblique 219.13
sink
 n. channel 396.5
 filth receptacle
 682.12
 pit 257.2
 place of vice 981.7
 washing equipment
 681.12
 v. bankrupt 842.8
 be despondent
 872.16
 be transient 111.6
 capsize 275.44
 come to grief 729.10
 decline 692.20
 decrease 39.6
 deepen 209.8
 degenerate 729.11
 depress 318.4
 disappear 447.2
 excavate 257.15
 fade 126.10
 fail 725.10
 get tired 717.5
 go down 316.6
 gravitate 352.15
 invest 836.16
 languish 686.45
 make sad 872.18
 mess up 692.13
 plunge 267.5
 recede 297.2
 ruin 693.11
 scuttle 320.8
 submerge 320.7
 weaken 160.9
sink back 696.4
sinker biscuit 308.30
 doughnut 308.43
 throw 285.4
 weight 352.6
sinkhole 257.3
sink in
 affect emotionally
 855.17
 be remembered
 537.14
 be understood 548.5
 bog down 400.2
 impress 478.19
sinking
 n. deepening 209.7
 depression 318.1
 descent 267.2
 immersion 320.2
 adj. aging 126.17
 descending 316.11
 deteriorating 692.46
 dying 408.33
 languishing 160.21
 plunging 267.8
 receding 297.5
sinking fund 660.3

sinking stomach 891.5
sink or swim
 come what may
 624.20
 without fail 513.26
sinner
 bad person 986.9
 evildoer 943.1
sinuous curved 252.7
 winding 254.6
sinus cavity 257.2
 curve 252.2
sinusitis 686.9
sip
 n. drink 307.4
 nip 996.6
 small amount 35.4
 taste 427.2
 v. drink 307.27
 taste 427.7
 tipple 996.23
siphon
 n. extractor 305.9
 tube 396.6
 v. channel 396.19
 extract 305.12
 pipe 271.13
siphoning 305.3
sir 420.7
sire
 n. father 170.9
 originator 153.4
 producer 167.8
 senior 127.5
 title 917.3
 v. engender 68.14
 originate 153.11
 reproduce 169.8
siren
 n. alarm 704.1
 bewitcher 1035.9
 noisemaker 453.5
 sea creature 397.4
 tempter 650.3
 water god 1014.20
 witch 943.7
 adj. alluring 650.7
sirloin 308.17
sirocco
 dust storm 403.13
 hot wind 403.7
sirrah 917.3
sirup, sirupy see **syrup**
 etc.
sissified
 cowardly 892.10
 effeminate 421.14
 frail 160.14
sissy
 n. coward 892.5
 effeminate male
 421.10
 sister 11.3
 weakling 160.6
 adj. cowardly 892.10
 effeminate 421.14
sister layman 1039.2
 likeness 20.3
 member 788.11
 nun 1038.19
 nurse 688.13
 sibling 11.3

sisterhood
 association 788.3
 blood relationship
 11.1
 fellowship 927.2
 women's rights 958.6
sister-in-law 12.2
sisterly 927.14
Sisyphean task 723.1
sit be seated 268.10
 brood 169.12
 idle 708.11
 meet 74.17
Sita 1014.8
sitar 465.4
sit back 706.2
sit down
 seat oneself 318.10
 settle 184.16
 sit 268.10
 strike 789.9
sit-down strike
 stop 144.2
 strike 789.7
sit down with
 confer 597.11
 negotiate 771.7
site arena 802.1
 location 184.1
sit in object 522.5
 participate 815.5
sit-in meeting 74.2
 protest 522.2
sit in for 149.5
sit in on listen 448.11
 participate 815.5
sit on
 appropriate 822.19
 hush up 614.8
 reprove 969.19
 rest on 216.22
 suppress 760.8
sit tight
 hide oneself 615.8
 wait 132.12
sitting
 n. conference 597.6
 meeting 74.2
 pregnancy 169.5
 spiritualism 1034.5
 adv. in council 755.6
sitting duck dupe 620.1
 easy thing 732.3
sitting room 192.5
situate 184.10
situated 184.17
situation
 environment 233.1
 location 184.1
 mental outlook 525.2
 placement 184.5
 position 656.5
 state 7.1
situation comedy
 comedy 611.6
 television show 611.4
sit up rise 213.8
 straighten 250.5
 wait 132.12
six-footer 207.12

summit 211.2
sky-blue 372.3
sky dive dive 320.1
  parachute 280.13
sky-dive dive 320.6
  parachute 278.56
sky-high 207.20
skyjack 824.19
skyjacker 825.7
skyjacking 824.6
skylark 878.26
skylight roof 228.6
  shine 335.2
  window 265.8
skyline 214.4
skyrocket ascend 315.9
  get better 691.7
  rocket 281.12
skyrocketing
  ascending 315.14
  overpriced 848.12
skyscraper
  building 191.6
  structure 245.2
  tower 207.11
skyscraping 207.20
skyward aloft 207.26
  up 315.16
skyway 278.42
skywrite 559.15
skywriting 278.1
slab slice 227.2
  slime 682.8
  wood 378.3
slabber
  n. saliva 312.3
  v. salivate 312.6
slabby filthy 682.23
  muddy 389.14
  viscous 389.12
slack
  n. fuel 331.2
  refuse 669.4
  v. diminish 332.7
  ease up 163.9
  leave undone 534.7
  loosen 51.3
  relax 711.7
  shirk 631.9
  adj. apathetic 856.13
  dilatory 132.17
  indolent 708.18
  inert 268.14
  loose 51.5
  negligent 534.10
  slovenly 62.15
  slow 270.10
  unchaste 989.26
  unstrict 758.4
  weak 160.12
slacken
  become disordered
    62.8
  delay 132.8
  ease up 163.9
  get worse 692.19
  hinder 730.10
  loosen 51.3
  moderate 163.6
  reduce 39.8
  relax 711.7
  relieve 886.5

slow 270.9
slackening
  moderation 163.2
  slowing 270.4
  weakening 160.5
slacker neglecter 534.5
  shirker 631.3
slack-jawed 265.19
slack-off 270.4
slacks 231.18,56
slag ashes 329.16
  refuse 669.4
  residue 43.2
slake gratify 865.6
  relax 163.9
  relieve 886.5
  satiate 664.4
slam
  n. disapproval 969.4
  explosive noise 456.1
  gibe 967.2
  hit 283.4
  score 724.4
  v. close 266.6
  collide 283.12
  criticize 969.14
  hit 283.13
  make explosive noise
    456.6
  ridicule 967.9
slam-bang 894.11
slander
  n. defamation 971.3
  monstrous lie 616.12
  scandal 558.8
  v. libel 971.11
slanderer 971.6
slanderous 971.13
slang
  n. jargon 580.9
  substandard language
    580.6
  unintelligibility 549.7
  word 582.6
  v. bluster 911.3
  adj. jargonish 580.19
slant
  n. aspect 446.3
  deviation 291.1
  diagonal 219.7
  glance 439.4
  inclination 219.2
  mental outlook 525.2
  story element 608.9
  trait of character
    525.3
  v. cut diagonally
    219.11
  distort 249.6
  falsify 616.16
  incline 219.10
  misrepresent 573.3
  adj. diagonal 219.19
  inclining 219.15
slanted
  distorted 249.11
  inclining 219.15
slanting
  n. distortion 249.2
  misrepresentation
    573.1
  adj. inclining 219.15

slap
  n. explosive noise
    456.1
  gibe 967.2
  punishment 1010.3
  smack 283.7
  v. make explosive
    noise 456.6
  punish 1010.13
  put violently 184.12
  smack 283.16
  adv. suddenly 113.9
slapdash
  adj. hasty 709.9
  reckless 894.8
  adv. hastily 709.12
  recklessly 894.11
  sloppily 534.18
slaphappy
  dazed 532.14
  insane 473.26
slap in the face
  indignity 965.2
  provocation 952.11
  punishment 1010.3
  rebuff 776.2
slap on add 40.4
  coat 228.24
slapstick
  n. acting 611.9
  comedy 611.6
  comedy prop 611.7
  humor 881.1
  adj. comic 880.5
  theatrical 611.40
slash
  n. break 49.4
  cheapening 849.4
  diagonal 219.7
  engraving 578.2
  impairment 692.8
  line 568.6
  v. cheapen 849.6
  criticize severely
    969.21
  cut across 219.11
  gash 262.4
  injure 692.15
  sever 49.11
slashed cheap 849.9
  damaged 692.29
slashing
  n. engraving 578.2
  separation 49.2
  adj. eloquent 600.11
slat
  explosive noise 456.1
  slab 227.2
  strip 206.4
  thinness 205.7
  wood 378.3
slate
  n. ballot 744.19
  schedule 641.2
  v. cover 228.23
  schedule 641.4
slated 641.6
slather coat 228.24
  squander 854.3
slattern
  filthy person 682.13
  trollop 62.7

slatternly 62.15
slaughter
  n. butchery 409.4
  destruction 693.1
  killing 409.1
  violence 162.3
  v. destroy 162.10
  murder 409.17
  put an end to 693.12
slaughterhouse 409.12
slave
  n. drudge 718.3
  retainer 750.1
  subject 764.7
  sycophant 907.3
  tool 658.3
  v. work hard 716.13
slave driver
  supervisor 748.2
  tyrant 749.14
slaver
  n. saliva 312.3
  v. be insane 473.19
  flatter 970.5
  salivate 312.6
slavery service 750.12
  servility 907.1
  subjection 764.1
  work 716.4
slavey factotum 750.9
  servant 750.2
slavish
  downtrodden 764.16
  servile 907.12
slaw 308.36
slay amuse 878.23
  delight 865.8
  kill 409.13
slayer 409.11
slaying 409.1
sleazy 160.14
sled
  n. sleigh 272.19,31
  v. glide 273.34
  haul 271.12
sledding 273.8
sledgehammer
  v. pound 283.14
  adj. coercive 756.11
sleek
  v. polish 260.7
  adj. chic 644.13
  oily 380.9
  slick 260.10
  thriving 728.13
  tidy 59.8
sleep
  n. death 408.1
  relaxation 711.1
  rest 268.1
  slumber 712.2
  unconsciousness
    423.2
  v. neglect 534.6
  slumber 712.13
  stagnate 268.9
sleep around 989.19
sleeper
  railway car 272.14
  sedative 687.12
  slumberer 712.12

hint 44.7
hit 283.4
kiss 932.3
punishment 1010.3
slap 283.7
small amount 35.4
taste 427.1
v. collide 283.12
hit 283.13
kiss 932.17
make explosive noise 456.6
punish 1010.13
slap 283.16
taste 427.7
adv. squarely 290.25
suddenly 113.9
smacking
energetic 161.12
lively 707.17
smack of resemble 20.7
savor of 428.6
small
adj. base 915.12
humble 906.9
inferior 37.7
insignificant 35.6
little 196.10
meager 662.10
narrow-minded 527.10
selfish 978.6
thin 205.16
unimportant 673.15
adv. on a small scale 196.16
small chance
doubtfulness 512.1
gambling odds 515.6
unlikelihood 156.9
small change
petty cash 835.19
trifles 673.4
smaller fewer 102.6
reduced 39.10
smallest 37.8
small fry
little thing 196.4
nobodies 673.7
young people 125.2
small hours
foredawn 133.4
lateness 132.1
small-minded 527.10
smallness
baseness 915.3
humility 906.1
inferiority 37.3
littleness 196.1
meagerness 662.2
narrow-mindedness 527.1
selfishness 978.2
small amount 35
sparsity 102.1
unimportance 673.1
small potatoes
a nobody 673.7
mediocrity 680.5
smallpox 686.12
small print 507.2
small talk 597.5

small-time 673.17
smarm 970.2
smarmy 970.8
smart
n. pain 424.3
v. feel acutely 855.16
resent 952.12
suffer pain 424.8
adj. alert 533.14
elegant 644.13
fashionable 644.11
impudent 913.9
intelligent 467.14
quick 707.18
ridiculing 967.12
tidy 59.8
witty 881.15
smart aleck
egotist 909.5
impudent person 913.5
smart-alecky
conceited 909.11
impudent 913.9
ridiculing 967.12
smart ass
impudent person 913.5
wiseacre 468.6
smart-ass
impudent 913.9
ridiculing 967.12
smarten up 901.8
smarts intellect 466.1
intelligence 467.2
smart set 644.6
smarty 913.5
smash
n. concussion 162.8
defeat 727.1
destruction 693.4
failure 725.3
great success 724.3
hit 283.4
impact 283.3
pulp 390.2
stock market 833.5
wreck 729.2
v. collide 283.12
conquer 727.10
demolish 693.17
level 693.19
mash 357.6
pulp 390.5
pulverize 361.9
shatter 49.13
suppress 760.8
surge 395.22
smashed
conquered 727.16
damaged 692.29
drunk 996.31
suppressed 760.14
smashing
n. bookbinding 605.15
demolition 693.5
impact 283.3
pulverization 361.4
suppression 760.2
adj. concussive 283.21
excellent 674.13

smashup
destruction 693.4
impact 283.3
wreck 729.2
smattering
dabbling 673.8
slight knowledge 477.6
small amount 35.4
smear
n. blemish 679.3
defamation 971.2
soil 682.5
stigma 915.6
v. blemish 679.6
coat 228.24
color 362.13
daub 380.8
overwhelm 727.8
soil 682.16
stigmatize 915.9
vilify 971.10
smell
n. odor 435.1
sense 422.5
smelling 435.4
trace 35.4
v. be aromatic 435.6
detect 488.6
scent 435.8
sense 422.8
stink 437.4
trace 485.34
smell bad 437.4
smell good 436.7
smelly
malodorous 437.5
odorous 435.9
smelt melt 329.21
process 167.11
smelter 719.5
smelting burning 329.5
manufacture 167.3
smidgen 35.2
smile
n. greeting 925.4
grin 876.3
v. be cheerful 870.6
be pleased 865.9
grin 876.7
smile upon 785.14
smiling
n. grin 876.3
adj. cheerful 870.11
happy 865.13
smirch
n. blemish 679.3
smear 682.5
smudging 365.5
stigma 915.6
v. blemish 679.6
smudge 365.7
soil 682.16
vilify 971.10
smirched
blemished 679.10
dingy 365.11
soiled 682.21
unchaste 989.23
smirk
n. ridicule 967.4
smile 876.3

v. simper 903.14
smile 876.7
smirking happy 865.13
ridiculing 967.12
smite hit 283.13
impress 855.17
punish 1010.14
smith artisan 718.7
producer 167.8
types of 718.10
smithereen piece 55.3
small amount 35.3
smithy 719.5
smitten
enamored 931.26
fond of 931.28
smock 231.17
smog 404.2
smoke
n. black 365.4
fume 329.16
spirit 4.3
tobacco 434.3
tobacco smoking 434.10
transient 111.5
vapor 401.1
v. be angry 952.15
blacken 365.7
cloud 404.6
dirty 682.15
dry 393.6
emit 310.23
evaporate 401.8
fume 328.23
preserve 701.8
stain 679.6
use tobacco 434.14
smoke out 310.14
smoker party 922.11
railway car 272.14
smoking room 434.13
tobacco user 434.11
smoke screen
disguise 618.10
pretext 649.1
smokestack 396.18
smoking
n. preserving 701.2
tobacco smoking 434.10
vaporization 401.5
adj. burning 328.27
smoky 401.9
tobacco 434.15
smoky dingy 365.11
dirty 682.22
gray 366.4
smoking 401.9
stained 679.10
smolder
be angry 952.15
be excited 857.15
be hot 328.22
be latent 546.3
stagnate 268.9
smoldering
angry 952.27
burning 328.27
inert 268.14
smooch
n. kiss 932.3

v. laugh 876.8
snicker at 967.8
sniff
  n. breathing 403.18
  inhalation 306.5
  sibilation 457.1
  snub 966.2
  v. detect 488.6
  inhale 306.12
  sibilate 457.2
  smell 435.8
  snort 403.24
sniffle
  n. breathing 403.18
  inhalation 306.5
  sibilation 457.1
  v. inhale 306.12
  sibilate 457.2
  snort 403.24
sniffles, the 686.14
sniff out detect 488.6
  trace 485.34
sniffy breathing 403.29
  contemptuous 966.8
  snobbish 912.14
snifter 996.6
snigger
  n. laughter 876.4
  ridicule 967.4
  v. laugh 876.8
sniggle
  n. snare 618.12
  v. catch 822.17
  trap 618.18
snip
  n. minute thing 196.7
  piece 55.3
  runt 196.4
  sailor 276.6
  small amount 35.3
  v. sever 49.11
snipe criticize 969.14
  fire upon 798.22
  shoot 285.13
sniper
  infantryman 800.9
  shooter 285.9
snippet
  little thing 196.4
  minute thing 196.7
  piece 55.3
  small amount 35.3
snippy gruff 937.7
  snobbish 912.14
snitch
  n. informer 557.6
  v. inform on 557.12
  steal 824.13
snivel
  be hypocritical
   616.23
  be sanctimonious
   1029.4
  weep 875.10
sniveler 1029.3
sniveling
  n. weeping 875.2
  adj. obsequious
   907.13
  sanctimonious 1029.5
  weeping 875.17
snob 912.7

snobbery
  particularity 896.5
  priggishness 912.6
snobbish
  contemptuous 966.8
  exclusive 77.8
  particular 896.13
  priggish 912.14
snoop
  n. curious person
   528.2
  listener 448.5
  meddler 238.4
  v. meddle 238.7
  pry 528.4
snoopy
  meddlesome 238.9
  prying 528.6
snoot 256.7
snootful
  full measure 56.3
  satiety 664.1
snooty
  contemptuous 966.8
  snobbish 912.14
snooze
  n. nap 712.3
  v. get some shut-eye
   712.14
snore
  n. breathing 403.18
  harsh sound 458.3
  sibilation 457.1
  v. breathe 403.24
  sibilate 457.2
  sleep 712.13
  sound harshly 458.9
snoring
  n. breathing 403.18
  adj. breathing 403.29
  sibilant 457.3
snorkel
  diving equipment
   320.5
  extinguisher 332.3
  tube 396.6
snort
  n. drink 307.4
  intoxication 996.6
  laughter 876.4
  ridicule 967.4
  sibilation 457.1
  snub 966.2
  v. animal sound 460.3
  disdain 966.3
  inhale 403.24
  laugh 876.8
  sibilate 457.2
  utter 594.26
snot body fluid 388.3
  filth 682.7
snotty
  contemptuous 966.8
  mucous 389.13
  snobbish 912.14
snout conduit 396.9
  nose 256.7
snow
  n. cocaine 687.9
  ice 333.8
  television reception
   345.5

  white 364.2
  v. deceive 618.13
  give 818.12
  storm 333.11
snowball
  n. accumulation 74.9
  snow 333.8
  v. ball 255.7
  become larger 197.5
  increase 38.6
snowbank 333.8
snowbird 642.10
snow-blind 441.10
snowbound
  frozen 333.18
  restrained 760.15
snowcapped 333.17
snowdrift pile 74.10
  snow 333.8
snowed-in 333.18
snowfall 333.8
snowflake 333.8
snow job
  persuasion 648.3
  subterfuge 618.1
snowman figure 572.4
  snow 333.8
snowmobile 272.19
snowshoes 272.20
snowstorm snow 333.8
  storm 162.4
  television reception
   345.5
snow under
  overwhelm 727.8
  snow 333.11
snowy chaste 988.4
  snowlike 333.17
  white 364.7
snub
  n. rebuff 966.2
  repulse 289.2
  v. hinder 730.10
  ostracize 310.17
  rebuff 966.5
  refuse 776.5
  restrain 760.7
  send away 289.3
  shorten 203.6
  adj. shortened 203.9
snub-nosed
  deformed 249.12
  stubby 203.10
snuff
  n. breathing 403.18
  inhalation 306.5
  sibilation 457.1
  tobacco 434.8
  v. extinguish 332.7
  inhale 306.12
  sibilate 457.2
  smell 435.8
  snort 403.24
snuffbox 434.8
snuffle
  n. breathing 403.18
  inhalation 306.5
  sanctimony 1029.1
  sibilation 457.1
  v. be hypocritical
   616.23

  be sanctimonious
   1029.4
  inhale 306.12
  nasalize 595.10
  sibilate 457.2
  smell 435.8
  snort 403.24
snuff out
  destroy 693.15
  extinguish 332.7
snuffy
  breathing 403.29
  dirty 682.22
  tobacco 434.15
snug
  v. make comfortable
   887.9
  adj. close 266.12
  comfortable 887.11
  homelike 191.33
  safe 698.7
  seaworthy 277.18
  taciturn 613.9
  tidy 59.8
  unsociable 923.5
snuggery cottage 191.9
  nook 192.3
snuggle cuddle 932.15
  nestle 887.10
so
  adj. similar 20.12
  adv. accurately 516.19
  equally 30.11
  greatly 34.15
  in this way 657.11
  similarly 20.18
  thus 8.10
  very 34.18
  conj. intending 653.12
  provided 507.15
soak
  n. drenching 392.7
  drunkard 996.11
  v. drench 392.13
  extract 305.16
  hit 283.13
  overcharge 848.7
  overload 663.15
  tipple 996.23
soaked
  drenched 392.17
  drunk 996.31
  full 56.11
  overfull 663.20
soaker drunkard 996.10
  rainstorm 394.2
soak in
  be learned 564.7
  be understood 548.5
  filter in 302.10
  sorb 306.13
soaking
  n. drenching 392.7
  extraction 305.7
  infusion 44.2
  adj. absorbent 306.17
  soaked 392.17
  wetting 392.18
soak up drink 307.28
  dry 393.6
  learn 564.7
  sorb 306.13

adj. disintegrative
53.5
dissolvent 391.8
sound 836.17
unindebted 841.23
solving 487.1
soma 376.3
somatic(al) 376.9
somber dark 337.14
dusky 365.9
gloomy 872.24
gray 366.4
lackluster 337.17
ominous 544.17
soft-colored 362.21
solemn 871.3
some
n. quantity 28.3
adj. plural 100.7
quantifier 28.5
skillful 733.20
adv. approximately
28.6
somebody
famous person 914.9
important person
672.8
individual 417.3
somehow
by chance 156.19
in some way 657.13
someone 417.3
someplace 184.25
somersault
n. inversion 220.2
v. capsize 275.44
something being 3.3
object 376.4
personage 672.8
quantity 28.3
something else
n. different thing 16.3
marvel 920.2
adj. dissimilar 21.5
excellent 674.13
sometime
adj. former 119.10
adv. someday 121.12
sometimes 136.5
somewhat
n. quantity 28.3
adv. moderately 35.10
to a degree 29.7
somewhere 184.25
sommelier 750.7
somnambulate 273.31
somnambulism
sleep 712.2
sleepwalking 273.11
trance state 690.26
somnambulist
sleeper 712.12
sleepwalker 274.7
somnolence
languor 708.6
sleepiness 712.1
somnolent
languid 708.19
sleepy 712.21
son descendant 171.3
relative 11.3
sonance 450.1

sonant
n. speech sound
594.13
adj. phonetic 594.31
sonar
depth measurement
209.5
navigation 275.2
sonata 462.5
song melody 462.4
poem 609.6
poetry 609.1
types of 462.13
vocal music 462.12
song and dance
act 611.8
music drama 462.35
subterfuge 618.1
song and dance man
612.1
songbird
animal 414.33,66
singing bird 464.23
vocalist 464.13
songbook book 605.1
music 462.28
songster music 462.28
songbird 464.23
vocalist 464.13
song writer 464.20
sonic 450.17
sonic boom
aviation 278.40
sonics 450.6
sonics 450.6
sonic speed 269.2
son-in-law 12.2
sonnet 609.6
sonny boy 125.5
descendant 171.3
son of a bitch 986.6
Son of God 1013.12
sonority loudness 453.1
resonance 454.1
speech sound 594.13
sonorous
grandiloquent 601.8
loud 453.10
melodious 462.49
resonant 454.9
sounding 450.15
sonovox 594.17
soon
in the future 121.9
presently 131.16
soon enough 131.12
sooner
n. settler 190.9
adv. preferably 637.28
sooner or later 121.12
soot
n. ashes 329.16
black 365.4
charcoal 365.6
dirt 682.6
powder 361.5
residue 43.2
v. blacken 365.7
dirty 682.15
soothe calm 268.8
pacify 804.7
relieve 886.5

stabilize 163.7
soothing
n. moderation 163.2
pacification 804.1
relief 886.1
adj. lubricant 380.10
pacificatory 804.12
relieving 886.9
remedial 687.40
sedative 687.45
tranquilizing 163.15
soothsay 543.9
soothsayer 543.4
sooty dingy 365.11
dirty 682.22
sop
n. bribe 651.2
fool 471.1
weakling 160.6
v. soak 392.13
SOP 642.5
sophism
rationalization 483.1
specious argument
483.3
sophist casuist 483.6
philosopher 500.6,12
reasoner 482.11
sophistical
cunning 735.12
insincere 616.32
philosophical 500.8
specious 483.10
sophisticate 733.16
sophisticated
chic 644.13
disillusioned 520.5
tasteful 897.9
ungullible 504.5
worldly-wise 733.26
sophistication
experience 733.9
good taste 897.1
learning 475.4
sophistry 483.1
ungullibility 504.2
sophistry
cunning 735.1
fallacy 483.3
insincerity 616.5
misteaching 563.1
philosophy 500.1,11
reasoning 482.1
specious reasoning
483
sophomore 566.6
sophomoric(al)
half-learned 477.15
studentlike 566.12
sopor apathy 856.4
stupor 712.6
soporific
n. sedative 687.12
sleep-inducer 712.10
adj. apathetic 856.13
sedative 687.45
sleep-inducing 712.23
sleepy 712.21
sopping
n. soaking 392.7
adj. soaked 392.17
wetting 392.18

soprano
n. high voice 458.6
music 462.22
vocalist 464.13
adj. high 458.13
vocal 462.51
sorb 306.13
sorbent 306.17
sorcerer
illusoriness 519.2
occultist 1034.16
Satanist 1016.16
wizard 1035.5
sorcerous 1035.14
sorcery divining 543.2
illusoriness 519.2
occultism 1034.10
Satanism 1016.15
witchcraft 1035
sordid bad 675.9
base 915.10
greedy 634.27
niggardly 852.8
slovenly 62.15
squalid 682.25
sore
n. disease symptom
686.8
distress 866.5
impairment 692.8
lesion 686.35
pain 424.4
adj. angry 952.26
hostile 929.10
raw 424.11
resentful 952.24
unpleasant 864.20
sorehead
ill-humored person
951.11
malcontent 869.3
sorely
distressingly 34.21
unpleasantly 864.28
soreness anger 952.5
animosity 929.4
bitterness 952.3
pain 424.4
sensitivity 422.3
sore spot distress 866.5
pain 424.4
provocation 952.11
sensitive area 422.4
sorghum 431.2
sorority
affiliation 786.2
fellowship 927.2
sisterhood 788.3
sorority house 191.16
sorption 306.6
sorrel
n. horse 414.13
adj. brown 367.3
sorrow
n. affliction 866.8
grief 872.10
lamentation 875.1
regret 873.1
v. cause unpleasant-
ness 864.14
grieve 872.17
lament 875.8

shakily 324.23
spastic
 n. sick person 686.40
 adj. convulsive 162.22
  irregular 138.3
  jerky 324.19
spat
 n. fish young 171.2
  quarrel 795.5
 v. quarrel 795.11
spate eruption 162.6
  flow 395.4
  much 34.4
  overabundance 663.2
  plenty 661.2
  quantity 34.3
  rainstorm 394.2
  throng 74.4
  violent flow 395.5
spatial 179.8
spatter
 n. blemish 679.3
  sprinkle 392.5
  staccato sound 455.1
 v. blemish 679.5
  dirty 682.18
  moisten 392.12
  rain 394.9
  sprinkle 75.6
spattered
  blemished 679.9
  sprinkled 75.10
spattering
 n. sprinkling 75.1
  wetting 392.6
 adj. staccato 455.7
spatula
  art equipment 574.19
  sculpting tool 575.4
spawn
 n. egg 406.15
  fish young 171.2
 v. create 167.13
  reproduce 169.9
spay 42.11
speak address 594.27
  affirm 523.4
  communicate 554.6
  converse 597.9
  indicate 568.22
  inform 557.8
  make a speech 599.9
  remark 594.25
  signal 275.52
  sound 450.14
  talk 594.20
  use language 580.16
speakeasy 996.19
speaker
  loudspeaker 450.8
  manager 748.5
  speechmaker 599.4
  spokesman 781.5
  talker 594.18
speak for
  defend 1006.10
  represent 781.14
speak for itself
  be intelligible 548.4
  be manifest 555.7
  evidence 505.9

speaking
 n. communication
   554.1
  public speaking 599.1
  speech 594.1
  utterance 594.3
 adj. lifelike 20.16
  talking 594.32
speaking of
  incidentally 129.13
  in relation to 9.13
speak out affirm 523.4
  be honest 974.12
  manifest oneself
   555.6
  speak up 594.22
  stand up to 893.11
speak to address 594.27
  reprove 969.18
speak up affirm 523.4
  manifest oneself
   555.6
  speak out 594.22
  stand up to 893.11
speak up for 1006.10
speak well of 968.11
spear
 n. branch 411.18
  leaf 411.17
  plant stem 411.19
  types of 801.23
 v. catch 822.17
  puncture 265.16
  stab 798.25
spearhead
 n. vanguard 240.2
 v. lead 292.2
spearlike 258.14
spear side kinsmen 11.2
  male line 170.4
special
 n. commodity 831.2
  feature 81.2
  newspaper 605.11
  train 272.13
 adj. classificational
   61.7
  detailed 8.9
  notable 672.18
  other 16.8
  particular 80.12
special case
  particularity 80.2
  qualification 507.1
special delivery 604.5
Special Forces 800.14
special interests
  influential persons
   172.6
  pressure group 744.31
specialist
 n. authority 81.3
  physician 688.8
  stockbroker 833.10
 adj. specialized 81.5
speciality
  particularity 80.2
  pursuit 81.1
  talent 733.4
specialization
  differentiation 16.4
  particularization 80.7

speaking — *continued*
strong point 81.1
  vocation 656.6
specialize
  differentiate 16.6
  feature 81.4
  limit 234.5
  particularize 80.9
  specify 80.11
specialized 81.5
specialize in
  practice 705.7
  specialize 81.4
  study to be 564.15
special school 567.2
special treatment
  furtherance 785.5
  qualification 507.1
specialty
  characteristic 80.4
  component 58.2
  contract 771.3
  particularity 80.2
  pursuit 81
  science 475.10
  study 562.8
  vocation 656.6
specialty shop 832.4
specie coin 835.4
  money 835.1
species biology 61.5
  kind 61.3
  nomenclature 583.1
  race 11.4
specific
 n. characteristic 80.3
  remedy 687.1
 adj. circumscribed
   234.6
  classificational 61.7
  detailed 8.9
  particular 80.12
specifically fully 8.13
  particularly 80.15
specification
  circumscription 234.1
  condition 507.2
  description 608.1
  designation 80.6
  indication 568.1
  particularization 8.5
  qualification 507.1
specific gravity
  density 354.1
  gravity 352.5
specifics 1.4
specified 507.8
specify
  call attention to
   530.10
  circumscribe 234.4
  indicate 568.18
  itemize 8.6
  name 583.11
  stipulate 80.11
specimen
  representative 572.5
  sample 25.3
  taste 427.4
specious false 616.27
  hollow 483.10
  illusory 519.9
  pretexted 649.5

speciousness
  appearances 446.2
  fakery 616.3
  rationalization 483.1
specious reasoning
  rationality 482.1
  sophistry 483.1
speck
 n. blemish 679.3
  impurity 78.2
  mark 568.5
  minute thing 196.7
  small amount 35.2
  spottiness 374.3
 v. blemish 679.5
  mark 568.19
  sprinkle 75.6
  variegate 374.7
speckled
  blemished 679.9
  spotted 374.13
  sprinkled 75.10
specs 443.2
spectacle display 904.4
  marvel 920.2
  sight 446.7
  stage show 611.4
spectacled 443.10
spectacles 443.2
spectacular
  astonishing 920.12
  dramatic 611.38
  gaudy 904.20
  theatrical 904.24
spectator
  attender 186.5
  audience 448.6
  observer 442
  playgoer 611.32
  recipient 819.3
  witness 505.7
specter
  frightener 891.9
  ghost 1017
  illusion 519.4
  spirit 1014.15
spectral
  coloring 362.15
  ghostly 1017.7
  illusory 519.9
  variegated 374.9
spectrograph
  astronomy 375.17
  photograph 577.7
spectrometer 443.15
spectrometry
  color 362.10
  optics 443.6
spectroscope
  astronomy 375.17
  types of 443.12,15
spectroscopy
  astronomy 375.19
  color 362.10
  optics 443.6
spectrum
  color system 362.7
  continuity 71.2
  illusion 519.5
  radio frequency
   344.12
  range 179.2

v. broadcast 344.25
sportscaster 344.23
sportsman
athlete 878.20
gambler 515.17
hunter 655.5
sportsmanly 976.9
sportsmanship 976.3
sportswear
clothing 231.1
dry goods 831.3
sporty casual 231.46
showy 904.19
spot
n. advertisement
559.6
blemish 679.3
drink 996.6
location 184.1
mark 568.5
predicament 731.4
radar signal 346.11
radio 344.20
small amount 35.2
soil 682.5
state 7.1
stigma 915.6
theater lighting
611.23
variegation 374.3
v. blemish 679.5
detect 488.5
locate 184.10
mark 568.19
recognize 537.12
see 439.12
soil 682.16
spatter 682.18
sprinkle 75.6
use radar 346.17
variegate 374.7
spotless chaste 988.4
clean 681.25
honest 974.13
innocent 984.7
perfect 677.6
spotlight
n. publicity 559.4
theater lighting
611.23
v. emphasize 672.13
illuminate 335.28
indicate 555.5
spotted
blemished 679.9
dotted 374.13
located 184.17
soiled 682.21
sprinkled 75.10
spotted fever 686.12
spotter
detective 781.11
secret agent 781.9
watchman 699.10
spotty blemished 679.9
discontinuous 72.4
dotted 374.13
few 102.5
irregular 138.3
spouse 933.7
spout
n. ascent 315.1

conduit 396.8
ejection 310.7
jet 395.9
outlet 303.9
rainstorm 394.2
v. chatter 596.5
declaim 599.10
eject 310.24
erupt 162.12
flow out 303.13
jet 395.20
overact 611.36
pawn 772.10
sprain 692.15
sprawl
n. recumbency 214.2
tumble 316.3
v. lie 214.5
rest 711.6
spread 197.6
stretch 202.6
tumble 316.8
sprawling
recumbent 214.8
spread 197.11
spray
n. branch 411.18
flowers 411.23
foam 405.2
gunfire 798.10
jet 395.9
scent article 436.6
shower 392.5
sprig 55.4
sprinkler 392.8
vaporizer 401.6
volley 285.5
v. atomize 401.8
jet 395.20
moisten 392.12
spread
n. advertisement
559.6
blanket 228.10
breadth 204.1
caption 484.2
communication
271.1
dispersion 75.1
divergence 299.1
expansion 197.1
food 308.1
increase 38.1
meal 307.5
publication 559.1
size 195.1
space 179.1
stock option 833.21
v. be made public
559.16
broaden 204.4
coat 228.24
disperse 75.4
diverge 299.5
expand 197.6
extend 179.7
generalize 79.9
increase 38.6
open 265.12
publish 559.10
radiate 299.6
transfer 271.9

adj. dispersed 75.9
increased 38.7
made public 559.17
recumbent 214.8
spreading 197.11
spread eagle
heraldic insignia
569.2
military insignia
569.5
spread-eagle
knock down 318.5
sprawl 316.8
spread-out broad 204.6
sprawling 197.11
spread over
cover 228.19
overrun 313.5
spree
n. drinking bout 996.5
revel 878.6
v. go on a spree
996.27
make merry 878.26
sprig branch 411.18
spray 55.4
sprout 125.9
youngster 125.1
sprightly agile 733.21
gay 870.14
lively 707.17
witty 881.15
spring
n. ascent 315.1
bedding 216.20
elastic object 358.3
fountainhead 153.6
leap 319.1
motive 648.1
recoil 284.2
resilience 358.1
resort 191.27
season 128.2
source of supply
660.4
teal flock 74.6
types of 358.10
v. be elastic 358.5
blow up 693.18
distort 249.5
leap 319.5
open 265.12
recoil 284.6
result from 154.6
run 269.10
adj. springlike 128.8
spring apart 49.8
springboard 358.3
springbok 414.5,58
springe 618.12
spring fever 708.5
springhead 153.6
springlike green 371.4
seasonal 128.8
springtime 128.2
spring up appear 446.9
ascend 315.9
begin 68.13
grow 197.7
occur 151.6
spring upon
seize on 822.16

surprise 540.7
springy elastic 358.7
pliant 357.9
sprinkle
n. rain 394.1
spray 392.5
v. moisten 392.12
perform rites 1040.20
rain 394.9
scatter 75.6
variegate 374.7
sprinkled few 102.5
scattered 75.10
spotted 374.13
sprinkler
extinguisher 332.3
holy water 1040.11
sparger 392.8
sprinkling
admixture 44.7
baptism 1040.7
dispersion 75.1
few 102.2
small amount 35.4
wetting 392.6
sprint
n. race 796.12
speed 269.3
v. run 269.10
sprite evil spirit 1016.8
fairy 1014.18
specter 1017.1
spritz
n. jet 395.9
v. jet 395.20
sprocket 258.4
sprout
n. branch 411.18
collateral descendant
171.4
seedling 125.9
upstart 919.10
v. grow 197.7
result from 154.6
vegetate 411.31
spruce chic 644.13
cleaned 681.26
dressed up 231.45
tidy 59.8
spruce up
arrange 60.12
dress up 231.41
ornament 901.8
touch up 691.11
sprung broken 49.24
damaged 692.29
distorted 249.10
spry agile 733.21
lively 707.17
quick 707.18
spud 308.35
spume
n. foam 405.2
lightness 353.2
sprinkle 392.5
v. foam 405.5
spunk courage 893.5
enterprise 707.7
pluck 624.3
tinder 331.6
vim 161.2

spunkless
 apathetic 856.13
 uncourageous 892.11
spunk up 952.18
spunky bold 893.18
 hot-tempered 951.25
 plucky 624.14
spur
 n. branch 55.4
 goad 648.8
 peak 207.8
 pointed projection
  258.4,18
 point of land 256.8
 v. drive animals 416.8
 goad 648.15
 hasten 709.4
 sharpen 258.9
 urge on 648.16
spurious
 assumed 903.16
 false 616.26
 illegitimate 999.7
 unauthentic 518.19
spurn
 n. snub 966.2
 v. be fastidious 896.8
 be inhospitable 926.5
 disdain 966.4
 eject 310.17
 reject 638.2
 repulse 289.3
spurned rejected 638.3
 unloved 867.10
spurt
 n. ascent 315.1
 bustle 707.4
 ejection 310.7
 eruption 162.6
 jet 395.9
 short time 111.3
 speed 269.3
 v. ascend 315.9
 dash 269.16
 eject 310.24
 flow out 303.13
 jet 395.20
 make haste 709.5
spurtle
 n. jet 395.9
 trickle 395.7
 v. jet 395.20
 trickle 395.18
sputnik 282.6,14
sputter
 n. bluster 911.1
 flutter 324.4
 sibilation 457.1
 staccato sound 455.1
 v. bluster 911.3
 flutter 324.12
 make staccato sounds
  455.4
 sibilate 457.2
 speak poorly 595.9
sputtering
 fluttering 324.18
 staccato 455.7
sputum 312.3
spy
 n. informer 557.6
 secret agent 781.9

 v. detect 488.5
 pry 528.4
 reconnoiter 485.27
 search out 485.33
 see 439.12
 watch 439.14
spy glass 443.3
spying
 observation 439.2
 surveillance 485.9
squab food 308.22
 pigeon 414.33
squabble
 n. quarrel 795.5
 v. dispute 796.22
 quarrel 795.11
squad group 74.3
 military unit 800.19
 team 788.7
squad car 272.10
squadron
 air force 800.28
 military unit 800.19
 navy 800.26
squalid bad 675.9
 base 915.12
 dirty 682.25
 slovenly 62.15
squall
 n. cry 459.1
 violence 162.4
 windstorm 403.12
 v. animal sound 460.2
 blow 403.22
 cry 459.6
 utter 594.26
 wail 875.11
squally cloudy 404.7
 windy 403.25
squalor badness 675.2
 baseness 915.3
 dirtiness 682.3
 slovenliness 62.6
squander
 consume 666.2
 lavish 854.3
 spend 843.5
 waste 812.5
squandered lost 812.7
 wasted 854.9
square
 n. antiquated person
  123.8
 block 183.7
 city district 183.8
 conformist 82.2
 enclosure 236.3
 four 96.1
 straightedge 250.3
 tract 180.4
 T square 213.6
 v. agree 26.6
 atone 1012.4
 equalize 30.6
 make restitution
  823.5
 make vertical 213.10
 offset 33.5
 pay in full 841.13
 quadrate 96.3
 settle with 841.12
 adj. conformist 82.6

 corpulent 195.18
 equal 30.7
 exact 516.16
 honest 974.14
 just 976.8
 quadrangular 251.9
 trite 883.9
 adv. exactly 516.20
 perpendicularly
  213.14
 squarely 290.25
square dance
 dance 879.2,7
 four 96.1
square deal 976.3
square-dealing
 fair 976.9
 honest 974.14
squarely exactly 516.20
 right 290.25
square meal 307.8
square off
 contend 796.15
 disagree 27.5
square shooter 974.8
squaring
 adjustment 26.4
 atonement 1012.1
 four 96.1
 restitution 823.2
squash
 n. mud 389.8
 pulp 390.2
 sibilation 457.1
 v. destroy 693.15
 mash 390.5
 pulverize 361.9
 refute 506.5
 shatter 49.13
 sibilate 457.2
 silence 451.8
 soften 357.6
 stifle 614.8
 suppress 760.8
squashed flat 214.7
 suppressed 760.14
squashy muddy 389.14
 pulpy 390.6
 soft 357.13
squat
 n. crouch 318.3
 v. be low 208.5
 crouch 318.8
 inhabit 188.7
 possess 808.4
 settle 184.16
 sit down 318.10
 adj. corpulent 195.18
 dwarf 196.13
 low 208.7
 stubby 203.10
squatter
 newcomer 78.4
 settler 190.9
 tenant 809.4
squatter's right 808.1
squatting
 habitation 188.1
 possession 808.1
squaw wife 933.9
 woman 421.5

squawk
 n. complaint 875.4
 objection 522.2
 shrill sound 458.4
 v. bird sound 460.5
 complain 875.13
 cry 459.6
 object 522.5
 sound shrill 458.8
 utter 594.26
squawk box 450.11
squawky 458.15
squeak
 n. shrill sound 458.4
 v. animal sound 460.2
 sound shrill 458.8
squeak by 200.10
squeak through 632.8
squeaky 458.14
squeal
 n. audio distortion
  450.13
 cry 459.1
 loud sound 453.4
 shrill sound 458.4
 v. animal sound 460.2
 blare 453.9
 cry 459.6
 divulge 556.6
 inform on 557.12
 sound shrill 458.8
 utter 594.26
squealer 557.6
squeamish
 fastidious 896.10
 nauseated 686.53
 stickling 623.7
squeeze
 n. booty 824.11
 embrace 932.2
 hindrance 730.1
 pinch 198.2
 predicament 731.4
 v. compel 756.6
 compress 198.8
 congest 354.9
 distort 553.2
 embrace 932.16
 extract 305.16
 obstruct 730.12
 wrest from 822.22
squeeze box 465.12
squeezed
 constricted 198.12
 poor 838.7
squeeze in enter 302.7
 interpose 237.6
 intrude 238.5
 thrust in 304.7
squeezing
 compression 198.2
 extraction 305.7
 misinterpretation
  553.1
squelch
 n. rejoinder 506.2
 sibilation 457.1
 v. destroy 693.15
 refute 506.5
 sibilate 457.2
 silence 451.8
 stifle 614.8

suppress 760.8
squelcher 506.3
squelchy muddy 389.14
  pulpy 390.6
  soft 357.13
squib detonator 331.7
  disparagement 971.5
  humor 881.1
  ridicule 967.6
squint
  n. defective vision
    440.5
  obliquity 219.1
  v. look askance 439.19
  squinch 440.9
squinting askew 219.14
  poor-sighted 440.11
squire
  n. attendant 750.5
  beau 931.12
  escort 73.5
  nobleman 918.4
  proprietor 809.2
  v. court 932.19
  escort 73.8
squirm
  n. wiggle 324.7
  v. be excited 857.16
  be impatient 862.4
  wiggle 324.14
squirm out of
  excuse 1006.11
  slip away 632.9
squirmy
  impatient 862.6
  wiggly 324.21
squirrel away
  prepare 720.11
  store up 660.11
squirrel cage
  routine 642.6
  tedium 884.1
squirt
  n. a nobody 673.7
  ejection 310.7
  jet 395.9
  v. eject 310.24
  jet 395.20
squish
  n. sibilation 457.1
  v. shatter 49.13
  sibilate 457.2
squishy muddy 389.14
  pulpy 390.6
  soft 357.13
Sr.
  n. form of address
    420.7
  senior 127.5
  adj. senior 123.19
SRO full 56.11
  present 186.19
SS 800.14
SST 280.3
stab
  n. attempt 714.2
  impairment 692.8
  pain 424.2
  thrust 798.3
  unverified supposi-
    tion 499.4
  v. aggrieve 866.17

attack 798.25
  injure 692.15
  pain 424.7
  puncture 265.16
stabbing
  n. attacking 798.11
  adj. acrimonious
    161.13
  caustic 939.21
  exciting 857.29
  painful 424.10
stabile sculpture 575.2
  work of art 574.11
stability
  aviation 278.29
  continuity 71.1
  durability 110.1
  firmness 142
  moderation 163.1
  permanence 140.1
  perpetuity 112.1
  perseverance 625.1
  reliability 513.4
  strength 159.3
  substantiality 3.1
  uniformity 17.1
stabilization 142.2
stabilize calm 163.7
  immobilize 142.7
  make uniform 17.4
stabilizer
  moderator 163.3
  types of 142.20
stable
  n. barn 191.20
  filthy place 682.11
  group 74.3
  race horses 414.17
  v. enclose 236.5
  house 188.10
  adj. continuing 110.10
  faithful 974.20
  firm 159.16
  incessant 71.8
  permanent 140.7
  persevering 625.7
  reliable 513.17
  restrained 163.11
  sturdy 3.7
  substantial 142.12
  unhazardous 698.5
  uniform 17.5
stableman 416.2
staccato
  n. frequency 135.2
  harmonics 463.14
  music passage 462.25
  music style 462.31
  pulsation 323.3
  staccato sound 455
  adj. constant 135.5
  drumming 455.7
  pulsating 323.18
  adv. music 462.54
stack
  n. bookholder 605.20
  hoard 660.1
  library 192.6
  much 34.4
  pile 74.10
  smoke passage 396.18
  storage place 660.6

v. pile 74.19
  put 184.14
  tamper with 616.17
stacked
  assembled 74.21
  beautiful 900.17
  prearranged 641.5
stacked deck 641.1
stack the cards
  cheat 618.17
  prearrange 641.3
stack up
  n. landing 278.18
  v. be comparable
    491.7
  equal 30.5
  pile 74.19
  resemble 20.7
  turn out 7.6
stadium arena 802.1
  hall 192.4
staff
  n. council 755.1
  emblem of authority
    739.9
  insignia 569.1
  music 462.29
  pastoral staff 1041.3
  personnel 750.11
  post 216.8
  stick 217.2
  supporter 216.2
  v. equip 659.8
staff of life 308.28
stag
  hoofed animal 414.5
  jumper 319.4
  male animal 420.8
  party 922.11
  stock speculator
    833.11
stage
  n. arena 802.1
  layer 227.1
  period 107.1
  platform 216.13
  playing area 611.21
  rank 29.2
  setting 233.2
  stagecoach 272.12
  support 216.12
  v. dramatize 611.33
stage, the 611.1
stagecoach 272.12
stagecraft 611.3
stage fright
  fearfulness 891.3
  nervousness 859.1
  shyness 908.4
stagehand 611.29
stage manager 611.28
stage name 583.8
stage presence 611.9
stage show show 611.4
  spectacle 446.7
stagestruck 611.38
stage whisper 452.4
stag film 990.4
stagger
  n. aviation 278.25
  flounder 324.8
  gait 273.14

irregularity 138.1
  v. astonish 920.6
  be drunk 996.26
  be irresolute 627.6
  excite 857.13
  flounder 324.15
  fluctuate 141.5
  frighten 891.23
  make doubt 503.7
  startle 540.8
  tumble 316.8
  walk 273.27
  zigzag 219.12
staggered
  astonished 920.9
  crooked 219.20
  startled 540.13
staggering
  n. walking 273.10
  adj. astonishing
    920.12
  irregular 138.3
  slow 270.10
  surprising 540.11
stagnant
  do-nothing 706.6
  inert 268.14
  languid 708.19
stagnate
  do nothing 706.2
  merely exist 1.10
  vegetate 268.9
stagy affected 903.15
  ostentatious 904.24
  theatrical 611.38
staid sedate 858.14
  solemn 871.3
  unimaginative 536.5
stain
  n. blemish 679.3
  coloring matter
    362.8,23
  mark 568.5
  soil 682.5
  stigma 915.6
  v. blemish 679.6
  color 362.13
  mark 568.19
  soil 682.16
  stigmatize 915.9
stained
  blemished 679.10
  colored 362.16
  soiled 682.21
staining
  applying color 362.11
  coloring 362.12
stainless chaste 988.4
  clean 681.25
  honest 974.13
  innocent 984.7
  perfect 677.6
stair degree 29.1
  step 315.5
stairway 315.3
stake
  n. district 180.5
  estate 810.4
  financing 836.2
  horse race 796.13
  instrument of execu-
    tion 1011.5

adj. public 417.13
stated affirmed 523.8
 circumscribed 234.6
 conditional 507.8
 fixed 142.14
 made public 559.17
 made sure 513.20
statehood 181.6
statehouse 742.12
stateless person
 displaced person
  185.4
 fugitive 631.5
 migrant 274.5
stately
 ceremonious 646.8
 dignified 905.12
 eloquent 600.14
 grandiose 904.21
statement
 account 608.3
 affirmation 523.1
 announcement 559.2
 bill 845.3
 information 557.1
 legal statement
  1004.7
 list 88.5
 music division 462.24
 numeration 87.5
 premise 482.7
 record 570.7
 remark 594.4
 testimony 505.3
state of affairs
 concerns 151.4
 situation 7.2
state of mind 525.4
state of war 797.1
stateroom
 ship room 192.9
 train room 192.10
States, the 181.3
stateside 181.3
statesman
 expert 733.11
 politician 746.2
statesmanlike
 governmental 744.43
 political 746.13
 skillful 733.20
statesmanship 744.3
static
 n. audio distortion
  450.13
 pandemonium 62.5
 radio reception
  344.21
 adj. do-nothing 706.6
 electricity 342.27
 inert 268.14
 mechanical 347.8
 permanent 140.7
 quiescent 268.13
 sedentary 708.16
static electricity 342.1
statics forces 157.7
 mechanics 347.2
 physics 325.1
station
 n. class 61.2
 farm 413.8

position 656.5
 prestige 914.4
 rank 29.2
 state 7.1
 status 184.2
 v. place 184.11
stationary
 do-nothing 706.6
 immovable 142.15
 inactive 708.16
 motionless 268.13
 permanent 140.7
station break 344.19
stationery paper 378.6
 types of 602.29
station identification
  344.19
stationmaster 274.13
statistical 87.15
statistician
 calculator 87.8
 mathematician 87.9
statistics figures 87.7
 mathematical proba-
  bility 511.2
statuary
 n. figure 572.4
 sculptor 579.6
 sculpture 575.1
 adj. sculptural 575.6
statue figure 572.4
 sculpture 575.2
 work of art 574.11
statuelike
 motionless 268.13
 sculptural 575.6
statuesque
 beautiful 900.17
 dignified 905.12
 sculptural 575.6
 tall 207.21
stature authority 739.4
 height 207.1
 prestige 914.4
status class 61.2
 prestige 914.4
 rank 29.2
 role 7.5
 state 7.1
 station 184.2
status quo
 circumstance 8.2
 situation 7.2
status seeker 919.10
status-seeking 634.10
statute law 998.3
 prohibition 778.1
statutory legal 998.10
 prescriptive 751.4
staunch close 266.12
 faithful 974.20
 firm 624.12
 friendly 927.20
 orthodox 1024.8
 reliable 513.17
 solid 159.16
staunchly
 faithfully 974.25
 resolutely 624.17
 strongly 159.21
stave music 462.29

poetic division
  609.11
 staff 217.2
 step 315.5
 supporter 216.2
 wood 378.3
stave off
 fend off 799.10
 postpone 132.9
 prevent 730.14
stay
 n. corset 231.23
 curb 730.7
 delay 132.2
 exemption 1007.2
 obstruction 730.2
 pause 144.3
 respite 711.2
 sojourn 188.5
 stop 144.2
 supporter 216.2
 v. be still 268.7
 cease 144.6
 cohere 50.6
 continue 143.3
 delay 132.8
 endure 110.6
 inhabit 188.7
 obstruct 266.7
 postpone 132.9
 prevent 730.13
 remain 140.5
 settle at 184.16
 slow 270.9
 sojourn 188.8
 stop 144.11
 stay for 539.8
 support 216.21
 wait 132.12
stay-at-home
 n. recluse 924.5
 adj. recluse 924.9
 untraveled 268.15
staying power
 continuance 143.1
 perseverance 625.1
 strength 159.1
stay in line
 conform 82.4
 obey 766.2
stay put be still 268.7
 cohere 50.6
 stand fast 142.11
stay up 132.12
stay up for 539.8
stead location 184.1
 place 184.4
steadfast
 enduring 110.10
 faithful 974.20
 firm 624.12
 friendly 927.20
 permanent 140.7
 persevering 625.7
 reliable 513.17
 stable 142.12
 uniform 17.5
steadily
 constantly 135.7
 faithfully 974.25
 inexcitably 858.16
 moderately 163.17

perpetually 112.10
 regularly 137.9
 resolutely 624.17
 uniformly 17.8
steady
 n. sweetheart 931.10
 v. calm 163.7
 stabilize 142.7
 adj. continuing 143.7
 endless 71.8
 faithful 974.20
 firm 624.12
 inexcitable 858.10
 orderly 59.6
 periodic 137.7
 persevering 625.7
 regular 135.5
 reliable 513.17
 stable 142.12
 substantial 3.7
 unhazardous 698.5
 uniform 17.5
 uninterrupted 112.7
 unnervous 860.2
 interj. caution 895.14
 sailing 275.76
steady state
 automation 349.9
 continuity 71.1
 stability 142.1
steady state theory
  375.18
steak 308.18
steal
 n. a theft 824.10
 bargain 849.3
 v. borrow 821.4
 creep 273.25
 lurk 615.9
 take 822.13
 thieve 824.13
steal away 631.12
stealing
 n. booty 824.11
 creeping 273.9
 theft 824.1
 adj. lurking 615.14
steal one's thunder
  730.15
stealth cunning 735.1
 secrecy 614.4
steal the show 611.34
stealthy
 cunning 735.12
 furtive 614.12
 in hiding 615.14
steam
 n. heat 328.10
 power 157.1
 vapor 401.1
 water 392.3
 v. be hot 328.22
 cook 330.4
 exhale 310.23
 give off 401.8
 heat 329.17
 sail 275.13
steam bath 328.11
steamboat
 n. steamer 277.2
 v. sail 275.13

steamed up
enthusiastic about
635.12
excited 857.18
steamer food 308.25
steamboat 277.2,22
steaming
n. vaporization 401.5
water travel 275.1
adj. excited 857.20
fervent 855.23
vaporous 401.9
steam pipe
heater 329.10
tube 396.6
steam propulsion 285.2
steamroller
n. force 756.2
pulverizer 361.7
v. coerce 756.7
level 214.6
overwhelm 727.8
raze 693.19
adj. coercive 756.11
steam room 681.10
steamship 277.2
steam shovel 257.10
steam up excite 857.11
prepare 720.9
steamy excited 857.20
fervent 855.23
lustful 419.29
vaporous 401.9
steed 414.10
steel
n. cutlery 348.2
hardness 356.6
stock type 834.2
strength 159.7
sword 801.4
v. harden 356.7
make unfeeling 856.6
strengthen 159.11
adj. metal 383.17
steel band 464.12
steeled callous 856.12
hardened 356.13
steel mill 719.5
steel oneself
be determined 624.8
be unregretful 874.3
get up nerve 893.13
steelworks
foundry 719.5
metalworks 719.4
steely callous 856.12
firm 624.12
gray 366.4
hard 356.10
metal 383.17
strong 159.13
unyielding 626.9
steep
n. height 207.2
precipice 213.3
v. extract 305.16
infuse 44.12
soak 392.13
adj. difficult 731.16
excessive 663.16
expensive 848.11
high 207.19

perpendicular 213.12
precipitous 219.18
steeple
pointed projection
258.4
tower 207.11
steeplechase
horse race 796.13
jump 319.1
leaping 319.3
steeplechaser
race horse 414.17
rider 274.8
steer
n. bull 414.6
male animal 420.8
tip 557.3
v. bear 290.8
direct to 290.7
drive 747.9
head for 290.10
operate 164.5
pilot 275.14
steer clear of
avoid 631.6
be inhospitable 926.5
keep away 199.7
snub 966.7
turn aside 291.6
steering
automation 349.7
direction 290.1
operation 164.1
pilotage 747.1
steering committee
748.11
steersman
boatman 276.8
operator 164.4
pilot 748.7
Steinway 465.13
stela 570.12
stellar celestial 375.25
chief 36.14
theatrical 611.38
stem
n. ancestry 170.4
base 216.8
bow 240.3
fork 299.4
leg 273.16
morphology 582.3
plant stem 411.19
printing 603.6
race 11.4
root 153.5
shaft 217.1
tube 396.6
v. branch 299.7
confront 240.8
contest 790.4
progress 294.2
result from 154.6
stop 144.11
stemware 339.2
stench
n. odor 435.1
stink 437
v. stop 266.7
stencil
n. graphic art 578.5
picture 574.12

printing 603.1
v. picture 574.20
stenographer
recorder 571.1
shorthandwriter
602.17
stenography 602.8
stentorian
loud-voiced 453.11
resounding 453.10
step
n. act 705.3
attempt 714.2
dance 879.8
degree 29.1
expedient 670.2
gait 273.14
harmonics 463.20
layer 227.1
mark 568.7
process 164.2
rate 267.4
short distance 200.2
stair 315.5
tread 273.13
v. measure 490.11
run 269.10
step over 313.8
walk 273.26
step aside dodge 631.8
resign 784.2
separate 49.9
turn away 291.6
step backward 671.2
step by step
by degrees 29.6
consecutively 71.11
in order 59.10
stepchild
descendant 171.3
relative by marriage
12.3
step down
electricity 342.23
reduce 39.7
step forward
progress 294.2
volunteer 773.9
step in enter 302.7
mediate 805.6
stepladder 315.4
step lively
hustle 707.13
make haste! 709.16
run 269.10
stepmother
parent 170.10
relative by marriage
12.3
step on it
accelerate 269.14
hurry 709.6
make haste! 709.17
rush 269.9
step out
make merry 878.26
take off 232.6
steppe grassland 411.8
horizontal 214.3
plain 387.1
prairie 182.1
space 179.4

stepper horse 414.18
speeder 269.5
stepping-stone
bridge 657.10
opportunity 129.2
stair 315.3
step 315.5
steps precaution 895.3
stairs 315.3
step stool 315.5
step up
accelerate 269.14
approach 296.3
electricity 342.23
increase 38.5
step-up
acceleration 269.4
increase 38.2
stereo 450.11
stereopticon 577.12
stereoscopic
optical 443.9
spatial 179.8
stereoscopy 443.6
stereotype
n. habit 642.4
printing surface 603.8
v. fix 142.9
make plates 603.15
make uniform 17.4
stereotyped dull 883.9
habitual 642.16
indistinctive 493.6
routine 79.12
trite 79.16
stereotypy 603.1
sterile fruitless 669.12
ineffective 158.15
sanitary 681.27
uninteresting 883.6
unproductive 166.4
sterility cleanness 681.1
uninterestingness
883.1
unproductiveness
166.1
sterilization 681.3
sterilize
emasculate 158.12
sanitize 681.24
sterling
n. money 835.1
adj. genuine 516.14
honest 974.13
monetary 835.30
superb 674.17
stern
n. buttocks 241.5
rear 241.1
tail end 241.7
adj. strict 757.6
unkind 939.22
unyielding 626.9
sternway course 267.2
regression 295.1
water travel 275.9
steroid 309.7
stertor
breathing 403.18
sibilation 457.1
stertorous
breathing 403.29

raucous 458.15
stet 142.19
stethoscope 448.8
stevedore carrier 271.5
  longshoreman 276.9
stew
  n. anger 952.7
  anxiety 890.1
  brothel 989.9
  bustle 707.4
  confusion 532.3
  dither 857.5
  dive 191.28
  drunkard 996.11
  food 308.11
  hodgepodge 44.6
  impatience 862.1
  perplexity 514.3
  predicament 731.4
  prostitute 989.16
  v. be angry 952.15
  be hot 328.22
  be impatient 862.4
  boil 329.20
  cook 330.4
  feel anxious 890.5
  make drunk 996.22
  seethe 162.11
  think hard 478.9
steward
  n. agent 781.3
  attendant 750.5
  aviation 279.4
  financial officer
    836.11
  guardian 699.6
  majordomo 750.10
  manager 748.4
  provider 659.6
  sailor 276.6
  v. manage 665.12
stewardess
  attendant 750.5
  aviation 279.4
  sailor 276.6
stewardship
  directorship 747.4
  management 665.2
  protectorship 699.2
  vigilance 533.4
stewed cooked 330.6
  drunk 996.31
stick
  n. cane 217.2
  dryness 393.2
  instrument of punish-
    ment 1011.2
  marihuana 687.13
  mast 277.13
  music 465.25
  pole 217.1
  supporter 216.2
  wood 378.3
  v. become fixed
    142.10
  be patient 861.5
  be sharp 258.8
  be still 268.7
  cheat 618.17
  cohere 50.6
  fail 725.15
  fasten 47.8

hold 813.6
  injure 692.15
  insist 753.7
  overcharge 848.7
  perplex 514.13
  persevere 625.4
  place 184.11
  puncture 265.16
  remain firm 624.9
  resist 792.4
  stab 798.25
  stabilize 142.7
  stop 144.7
stick around 132.12
stick at
  be irresolute 627.7
  demur 623.4
stick by 785.13
sticker adherent 50.4
  label 568.13
  puzzle 549.8
  thorn 258.7
stick in 304.3
stick-in-the-mud
  conservative 140.4
  idler 708.8
  slow person 270.5
  untraveled 268.15
stick it out
  have courage 893.15
  not weaken 159.9
  persevere 625.4
  persist 143.5
  resist 792.4
  stand fast 142.11
stickle
  be irresolute 627.7
  be obstinate 626.7
  contend for 796.21
  demur 623.4
stickler
  fastidious person
    896.6
  obstinate person
    626.6
  tyrant 749.14
stickling
  n. demur 623.2
  adj. demurring 623.7
  irresolute 627.11
stick out
  be apparent 555.7
  be visible 444.5
  overhang 215.7
  persevere 625.4
  protrude 256.9
stickpin 901.6
sticks, the
  remote region 199.4
  the country 182.1
stick shift 348.6
stick together
  be true 516.7
  cement 50.9
  cohere 50.6
  join 47.5
stick-to-itiveness
  perseverance 625.1
  tenacity 50.3
stick to one's guns
  be obstinate 626.7
  be resolute 624.9

have courage 893.15
  persevere 625.4
  resist 792.4
  stand fast 142.11
stickum 50.4
stickup 824.3
stick up elevate 317.5
  protrude 256.9
  rise 213.8
  rob 824.14
stick up for
  back 785.13
  defend 1006.10
sticky adhesive 50.12
  moist 392.15
  sentimental 855.22
  sultry 328.28
  sweaty 311.22
  viscous 389.12
sticky-fingered 824.20
sticky wicket 731.4
stiff
  n. bad person 986.2
  bum 708.9
  corpse 408.16
  inferior horse 414.14
  vagabond 274.3
  working person 718.2
  adj. clumsy 734.20
  dead 408.31
  drunk 996.33
  excessive 663.16
  expensive 848.11
  formal 646.9
  inelegant 590.3
  out of practice
    734.18
  rigid 356.11
  seaworthy 277.18
  strict 757.7
  tough 359.4
  uninteresting 883.6
  unyielding 626.9
stiffen
  electricity 342.23
  make tough 359.3
  rigidify 356.9
  strengthen 159.11
stiffened
  hardened 356.13
  increased 38.7
stiff-necked
  obstinate 626.8
  proud 905.8
  prudish 903.19
stiffness
  expensiveness 848.1
  formality 646.1
  hardness 356.2
  strictness 757.2
  toughness 359.1
  uninterestingness
    883.1
  unyieldingness 626.2
stifle be hot 328.22
  control feelings 858.8
  destroy 693.15
  extinguish 332.7
  keep secret 614.8
  moderate 163.6
  obstruct 730.12
  silence 451.8

strangle 409.19
  suppress 760.8
stifled
  imperfectly spoken
    595.12
  muffled 452.17
  secret 614.11
  suppressed 760.14
stifling airless 268.16
  hindering 730.17
  sultry 328.28
stigma blemish 679.3
  disrepute 915.6
  flower part 411.26
  mark 568.5
  sore 686.35
stigmatize
  blemish 679.6
  brand 568.19
  defile 971.10
  designate 568.18
  slur 915.9
  variegate 374.7
stile entrance 302.6
  post 217.4
  stairs 315.3
still
  n. distillery 996.20
  photograph 577.3
  silence 451.1
  vaporizer 401.6
  v. calm 163.7
  silence 451.8
  adj. dead 408.30
  motionless 268.13
  silent 451.10
  tranquil 268.12
  adv. calmly 268.18
  notwithstanding 33.8
  until now 120.4
stillborn born 167.21
  dead 408.30
  unsuccessful 725.17
still hunt
  hunting 655.2
  search 485.14
still-hunt hunt 655.9
  seek 485.29
still life picture 574.12
  work of art 574.11
stillness
  quiescence 268.1
  silence 451.1
stilt 205.8
stilted formal 646.9
  grandiloquent 601.8
  inelegant 590.3
  pompous 904.22
  raised 317.9
stimulant drug 687.9
  energizer 161.5
  types of 687.52
stimulate elicit 305.14
  energize 161.9
  excite 857.12
  interest 530.12
  motivate 648.12
  refresh 695.2
  sensitize 422.9
stimulated
  excited 857.18
  motivated 648.30

strafe
n. bombardment
798.7
v. fire upon 798.22
straggle follow 293.4
stray 291.4
stretch 202.6
walk 273.27
wander 273.22
straggling
dispersed 75.9
stretched 202.9
unordered 62.12
wandering 273.36
straight
n. direct 250.2
heterosexual 419.15
playing cards 878.17
adj. accurate 516.15
candid 974.17
conformist 82.6
continuous 71.8
direct 290.13
honest 974.14
sexual 419.26
simple 45.7
thorough 56.10
trustworthy 974.19
undeviating 250.6
unqualified 508.2
virtuous 980.7
adv. accurately 516.19
directly 290.24
exactly 516.20
squarely 290.25
unswervingly 250.7
straight and narrow, the
980.1
straightaway
n. straight line 250.2
adj. direct 290.13
adv. at once 113.8
promptly 131.15
straightedge 250.3
straighten out
arrange 771.9
make better 691.9
mediate 805.7
rectify 250.5
reprove 969.17
straight face
solemnity 871.1
unexpressiveness
549.5
unfeeling 856.1
straight-faced 871.3
straightforward
adj. candid 974.17
direct 290.13
easy 732.12
elegant 589.6
in plain style 591.3
intelligible 548.10
simple 45.8
unaffected 902.7
adv. directly 290.24
straightjacket 760.4
straightlaced 757.7
straight man 612.2
straightness 250
straight-out
candid 974.17

unqualified 508.2
straight shooter 974.8
straight-shooting 974.14
strain
n. ancestry 170.4
anxiety 890.1
class 61.2
endeavor 714.1
enmity 929.1
exertion 716.2
fatigue 717.1
kind 61.3
lengthening 202.5
melody 462.4
music division 462.24
overdoing 663.6
overextension 663.7
people 418.1
poetic division
609.11
pull 286.2
race 11.4
stretching 358.2
style 588.2
tension 859.3
trait of character
525.3
v. be irresolute 627.7
demur 623.4
distort 249.6
endeavor 714.4
exude 303.15
falsify 616.16
injure 692.15
lengthen 202.7
overextend 663.13
refine 681.22
tax oneself 716.10
try for 714.8
strained anxious 890.6
distorted 249.11
farfetched 10.7
laborious 716.18
lengthened 202.9
tense 859.12
unfriendly 929.9
strainer
porousness 265.9
refining equipment
681.13
straining
n. distortion 249.2
exertion 716.2
falsification 616.9
filtering 303.6
overextension 663.7
purification 681.4
adj. fatiguing 717.11
irresolute 627.11
laboring 716.17
strait
n. arm of the sea
399.1
crisis 129.4
danger 697.1
narrow place 205.3
predicament 731.4
adj. limited 234.7
narrow 205.14
straiten enclose 236.6
limit 234.5
narrow 205.11

restrain 760.7
straitened
in trouble 731.24
limited 234.7
meager 662.10
poor 838.7
straitjacket
n. restraint 760.4
v. restrain 760.10
straitlaced
narrow-minded
527.10
orthodox 1024.8
prudish 903.19
strict 757.7
straits
arm of the sea 399.1
poverty 838.1
predicament 731.4
strand
n. filament 206.1
shore 385.2
v. shipwreck 275.42
stranded
aground 142.16
in difficulty 731.25
strange eccentric 474.4
extraneous 78.5
insane 473.25
new 122.11
odd 85.11
unknown 477.17
unrelated 10.5
wonderful 920.10
strangeness
atomics 326.6
eccentricity 474.1
insanity 473.1
newness 122.1
oddity 85.3
stranger alien 78.3
foreigner 77.3
strangle choke 409.19
close 266.6
constrict 198.7
destroy 693.15
die 408.24
execute 1010.19
obstruct 730.12
render powerless
158.11
suppress 760.8
strangled
constricted 198.12
hoarse 458.15
imperfectly spoken
595.12
stranglehold
hindrance 730.1
restraint 760.4
wrestling hold 813.3
strangler
executioner 1010.8
killer 409.11
strangling
n. capital punishment
1010.7
suffocation 409.7
suppression 760.2
violent death 408.6
adj. hindering 730.17

strangulated
choked 266.9
constricted 198.12
strangulation
capital punishment
1010.7
constriction 198.1
destruction 693.6
obstruction 266.3
suffocation 409.7
violent death 408.6
strap
n. stock option 833.21
strip 206.4
whip 1011.1
v. bandage 689.30
bind 47.9
punish 1010.14
restrain 760.10
sharpen 258.9
straphanger 274.1
strapless 232.13
strap oil 1010.6
strapped broke 838.10
poor 838.7
restrained 760.16
strapping
n. punishment 1010.4
adj. corpulent 195.18
strong 159.13
stratagem artifice 735.3
expedient 670.2
intrigue 654.6
pretext 649.1
trick 618.6
strategic
cunning 735.12
planned 654.13
strategist
cunning person 735.7
planner 654.7
political intriguer
746.6
strategy plan 654.1
scheme 735.3
warfare 797.9
strati– 227.1
stratification
classification 61.1
layering 227.4
stratified classified 61.8
layered 227.6
stratify 227.5
stratosphere
atmospheric layer
402.3
aviation 278.41
height 207.2
stratum
atmospheric layer
402.3
class 61.2
layer 227.1
stratus 404.1
straw
n. fodder 308.4
lightness 353.2
plant stem 411.19
refuse 43.1
trifle 673.5
tube 396.6
adj. yellow 370.4

strawberry blond 362.9
strawberry-blond 364.9
strawberry mark
  blemish 679.1
  mark 568.5
straw boss 748.2
strawhat 611.1
straw in the wind
  clue 568.9
  warning sign 703.3
straw man 903.7
straw vote
  testing device 489.4
  vote 637.6
stray
  n. waif 274.3
  v. be inattentive 531.3
  be unorthodox
    1025.8
  deviate 291.4
  digress 593.9
  err 518.9
  muse 532.9
  wander 273.22
  adj. irregular 85.9
  purposeless 156.16
  wandering 291.7
straying
  n. deviation 291.1
  wandering 273.3
  adj. erroneous 518.16
  irregular 85.9
  wandering 273.36
streak
  n. groove 263.1
  line 568.6
  nature 5.3
  ray 335.5
  stripe 374.5
  swiftness 269.6
  thinness 205.7
  trait of character
    525.3
  v. groove 263.3
  mark 568.19
  variegate 374.7
streaked netlike 221.11
  striped 374.15
streaking line 568.6
  stripe 374.5
stream
  n. aviation 278.39
  course 267.2
  current 395.4
  plenty 661.2
  procession 71.3
  ray 335.5
  running water 395
  trend 174.2
  wind 403.1
  v. abound 661.5
  come together 74.16
  course 273.17
  emerge 446.8
  flow 395.16
  move 267.5
  rain 394.9
streamer caption 484.2
  flag 569.6
  ray 335.5
streaming
  flowing 395.24

fluent 267.8
  loose 51.5
  luminous 335.30
  rainy 394.10
streamline
  n. straight line 250.2
  v. modernize 122.6
  simplify 45.4
streamlined
  modern 122.13
  simplified 45.9
  straight 250.6
streamliner 272.13
streamlining
  facilitation 732.4
  simplification 45.2
stream of consciousness
  association 690.40
  thoughts 478.4
streamy 395.23
street 657.6
street Arab 274.3
streetcar 272.15
streetcar line 657.8
street fight 796.4
streetfighter 800.1
street people 83.3
street sweeper 681.16
streetwalker 989.16
streetwalking 989.8
streetwise 475.16
strength
  authoritativeness
    739.2
  eloquence 600.3
  energy 161.1
  greatness 34.1
  might 159
  power 157.1
  pungency 433.3
  quantity 28.1
  robustness 685.3
  substantiality 3.1
  toughness 359.1
  will power 624.4
strengthen add to 40.5
  confirm 505.12
  increase 38.6
  intensify 38.5
  invigorate 159.11
  make tough 359.3
  nourish 309.15
  stiffen 356.9
strengthened
  hardened 356.13
  increased 38.7
strengthener 216.2
strengthening
  n. confirmation 505.5
  increase 38.2
  invigoration 159.5
  adj. tonic 687.44
strengthless 160.12
strenuous
  arduous 716.18
  difficult 731.16
  energetic 161.12
  industrious 707.22
strenuously
  arduously 716.19
  energetically 161.15
  industriously 707.27

with difficulty 731.26
strep throat 686.12
streptococcus 686.39
stress
  n. adversity 729.1
  aviation 278.31
  distress 866.5
  drive 648.6
  importance 672.1
  meter 609.9
  pressure 283.2
  psychological stress
    690.21
  speech accent 594.11
  strain 716.2
  tension 859.3
  urgency 672.4
  v. emphasize 672.13
  press 283.11
  strain 716.10
stressed
  emphatic 672.20
  phonetic 594.31
stressful adverse 729.13
  fatiguing 717.11
stretch
  n. distance 199.1
  elasticity 358.1
  elongation 202.5
  exercise 716.6
  extension 358.2
  length 202.1
  overextension 663.7
  period 107.1
  racecourse 878.12
  range 179.2
  spell 108.1
  strain 716.2
  term 108.4
  walk 273.12
  v. become larger
    197.5
  be elastic 358.4
  be long 202.6
  exaggerate 617.3
  hang 1010.20
  lengthen 202.7
  make larger 197.4
  overextend 663.13
  reach 179.7
  strain 716.10
  suffice 661.4
  adj. elastic 358.7
stretchable 358.7
stretched
  exaggerated 617.4
  lengthened 202.9
stretched-out
  lengthened 202.9
  protracted 110.11
  spread 197.11
stretcher 216.19
stretcher-bearer 271.5
stretching
  distension 197.2
  elasticity 358.2
  exaggeration 617.1
  lengthening 202.5
  overextension 663.7
  sleepiness 712.1
stretch of the
  imagination 535.5

stretch one's luck 894.6
stretch out
  be distant 199.5
  be long 202.6
  expatiate 593.8
  lengthen 202.7
  postpone 132.9
  protract 110.9
  reach 179.7
stretch the truth
  exaggerate 617.3
  lie 616.19
stretchy elastic 358.7
  sleepy 712.21
strew 75.4
strewn 75.9
striate groove 263.3
  mark 568.19
  variegate 374.7
striated grooved 263.4
  striped 374.15
striation groove 263.1
  line 568.6
  stripe 374.5
stricken
  affected 855.25
  heartbroken 872.29
  unnerved 859.13
  wretched 866.26
strict
  conscientious 974.15
  exact 516.16
  fastidious 896.9
  meticulous 533.12
  orthodox 1024.8
  severe 757.6
  tyrannical 739.16
strictly exactly 516.20
  meticulously 533.16
  severely 757.8
strictness
  accuracy 516.3
  conformity 82.1
  fastidiousness 896.1
  meticulousness 533.3
  orthodoxy 1024.5
  restriction 205.1
  severity 757
stricture
  constriction 198.1
  criticism 969.4
  disapproval 969.3
  hindrance 730.1
  narrowing 205.2
stride
  n. distance 199.1
  gait 273.14
  rate 267.4
  step 273.13
  v. step 273.26
  straddle 216.22
  walk 273.27
stridency
  acrimony 161.4
  shrillness 458.1
strident
  acrimonious 161.13
  dissonant 461.4
  stridulant 458.12
stridor
  dissonance 461.1
  shrillness 458.1

stridulate 458.7
stridulation
 animal sound 460.1
 cricking 458.5
strife contention 796.1
 quarrel 795.5
strigose bristly 261.9
 striped 374.15
strike
 n. attack 798.1
 discovery 488.1
 labor strike 789.7
 protest 522.2
 score 724.4
 walkout 144.2
 v. affect emotionally
  855.17
 assault 798.15
 collide 283.12
 delete 42.12
 discover 488.2
 go on strike 789.9
 hit 283.13
 impress 478.19
 march upon 798.17
 occur to 478.18
 print 603.14
 protest 522.5
 punish 1010.13
 revolt 767.7
 shoot 285.13
 stop work 144.8
strike a balance
 average 32.2
 be moderate 163.5
 be neutral 806.6
 compromise 807.2
 equalize 30.6
 keep accounts 845.8
 pay in full 841.13
 weigh 352.10
strike a bargain
 agree 521.10
 compromise 807.2
 make a deal 827.18
 transact 771.8
strike back 955.4
strikebreaker
 apostate 628.5
 scab 789.6
strike camp 301.15
strike home
 affect emotionally
  855.17
 get a reaction 284.8
strike it rich
 be fortunate 728.11
 grow rich 837.9
strike off cut off 42.10
 delete 42.12
 eliminate 77.5
 improvise 630.8
strike one
 appear to be 446.10
 occur to 478.18
strike out create 167.13
 delete 42.12
 eliminate 77.5
 fail 725.9
 head for 290.10
 lash out 798.16
 obliterate 693.16

set forth 301.7
striker 789.4
strike up 462.38
striking
 n. coining 835.24
 deletion 42.5
 adj. conspicuous
  555.12
 eloquent 600.11
 exciting 857.28
 notable 672.18
 powerful 157.12
 remarkable 34.10
 wonderful 920.10
string
 n. catch 507.2
 cord 206.2,9
 group 74.3
 horses 414.17
 line 202.4
 music 465.23
 procession 71.3
 row 71.2
 stair 315.5
 stipulation 753.2
 team 788.7
 utterance 594.3
 viol 465.6
 v. connect 71.4
 put in tune 462.37
string along
 deceive 618.13
 flatter 970.6
 follow 293.3
 join with 786.4
stringed instrument
 465.2
stringency
 acrimony 161.4
 meagerness 102.1
 strictness 757.1
 unkindness 939.9
stringent
 acrimonious 161.13
 strict 757.6
 unkind 939.22
string musician 464.5
string out align 71.5
 expatiate 593.8
 lengthen 202.7
string quartet
 music 462.5
 orchestra 464.12
strings influence 172.3
 music 465.2
 orchestra 464.12
string up 1010.20
stringy threadlike 206.7
 tough 359.4
 viscous 389.12
strip
 n. length 202.3
 line 202.4
 runway 278.23
 stock option 833.21
 strap 206.4
 stripe 568.6
 v. cut off 42.10
 despoil 822.24
 dismiss 310.19
 divest 232.5
 peel 232.8

tear apart 49.14
undress 232.7
strip down 45.4
stripe
 n. brand 61.3
 lash 283.7
 line 568.6
 military insignia
  569.5
 nature 5.3
 streak 374.5
 strip 202.4
 temperament 525.3
 v. mark 568.19
 punish 1010.14
 variegate 374.7
striped netlike 221.11
 streaked 374.15
stripling
 fledgling 122.4
 youngster 125.1
stripped
 deprived of 812.8
 divested 232.12
 indigent 838.8
stripped down 45.9
stripper
 entertainer 612.1
 nudity 232.3
 separator 49.7
striptease act 611.8
 disrobing 232.2
stripteaser
 entertainer 612.1
 nudity 232.3
strive attempt to 714.7
 contend 796.14
 endeavor 714.4
 struggle 716.11
strive against
 contend against
  790.4
 offer resistance 792.3
strive for
 contend for 796.21
 try for 714.8
striving
 n. endeavor 714.1
 intention 653.1
 adj. contending
  796.23
 laboring 716.17
stroboscopic 335.36
stroke
 n. act 705.3
 attempt 714.2
 cardiovascular disease
  686.17
 distress 866.5
 hit 283.4
 instant 113.3
 line 568.6
 maneuver 670.2
 paralysis 686.25
 paroxysm 162.5
 seizure 686.5
 spasm 324.6
 touch 425.1
 work 716.4
 v. flatter 970.6
 manipulate 665.16
 rub 350.6

touch 425.8
stroke of luck 728.3
stroll
 n. gait 273.14
 slowness 270.2
 walk 273.12
 v. go slow 270.6
 walk 273.27
 wander 273.22
stroller actor 612.2
 vehicle 272.6
 wanderer 274.2
strolling
 n. walking 273.10
 adj. slow 270.10
 traveling 273.35
 wandering 273.36
strolling player
 actor 612.2
 wanderer 274.2
strong accented 594.31
 alcoholic 996.36
 eloquent 600.11
 energetic 161.12
 forceful 159.13
 great 34.6
 influential 172.13
 malodorous 437.5
 powerful 157.12
 pungent 433.8
 rancid 692.42
 robust 685.10
 strong-smelling
  435.10
 substantial 3.7
 tough 359.4
strong arm
 coercion 756.3
 combatant 800.1
 power 157.1
strong-arm
 v. coerce 756.7
 exert strength 159.10
 adj. coercive 756.11
strongbox 836.12
strong hand 757.3
stronghold
 fortification 799.6
 refuge 700.1
strong in
 skilled in 733.25
 versed in 475.19
strong language
 cursing 972.3
 eloquence 600.3
strong man 159.6
strong-minded
 intelligent 467.12
 resolute 624.15
strong point
 good reasoning
  482.10
 specialty 81.1
 stronghold 799.6
 talent 733.4
strong room 836.12
strong-willed
 forceful 159.13
 obstinate 626.8
 resolute 624.15
strontium 90 326.5

strop
  n. strip 206.4
  v. sharpen 258.9
strophe 609.11
structural
  constructional 167.18
  formal 245.9
  linguistic 580.17
  syntactical 586.17
structural fatigue
  278.31
structure
  n. building 245.2
  composition 58.1
  construction 245
  form 246.1
  house 191.6
  intelligibility 548.2
  order 59.1
  story element 608.9
  syntax 586.2
  texture 351.1
  v. compose 58.3
  construct 245.8
  order 59.4
structuring
  arrangement 60.1
  composition 58.1
  structure 245.1
strudel 308.40
struggle
  n. contention 796.1
  endeavor 714.1
  fight 796.4
  tussle 716.3
  v. contend 796.14
  endeavor 714.4
  exert oneself 716.11
  flounder 324.15
  have difficulty 731.10
struggle against 790.4
struggle for
  contend for 796.21
  try for 714.8
struggler 800.1
struggle with 796.18
struggling
  contending 796.23
  laboring 716.17
strum 462.41
strummer 464.5
strumpet flirt 932.10
  unchaste woman
  989.14
strung out
  addicted 642.19
  insensible 423.8
  lengthened 202.9
strut
  n. gait 273.14
  ostentation 904.8
  v. swagger 904.15
  walk 273.27
strutter 904.10
strutting
  n. ostentation 904.8
  adj. swaggering 904.23
stub cigarette 434.5
  label 568.13
  stump 70.2
  tail 241.6
stubbiness 203.2

stubble beard 230.8
  bristle 261.3
  chaff 669.4
  remains 43.1
stubbled
  bearded 230.25
  rough 261.9
stubborn
  obstinate 626.8
  persevering 625.7
  rigid 356.12
  strict 757.7
  tenacious 50.12
  tough 359.4
stubbornness
  obstinacy 626.1
  perseverance 625.1
  refractoriness 767.2
  rigidity 356.3
  strictness 757.2
  tenacity 50.3
  toughness 359.1
  unwillingness 623.1
stubby 203.10
stucco 228.25
stuck
  at an impasse 731.22
  caught 142.16
  cohesive 50.10
  fastened 47.14
  in difficulty 731.25
  perplexed 514.24
stuck on 931.28
stuck-up arrogant 912.9
  conceited 909.11
stud
  n. bump 568.7
  horse 414.10
  knob 256.3
  male animal 420.8
  man 420.5
  sex object 419.4
  v. roughen 261.4
  sprinkle 75.6
  variegate 374.7
studbook
  reference book 605.6
  register 570.9
studded bristly 261.9
  illuminated 335.39
  knobbed 256.16
  knotty 261.8
  ornamented 901.11
  spotted 374.13
  sprinkled 75.10
  teeming 101.9
  textured 351.7
student pupil 566
  scholar 476.3
studied affected 589.9
  intentional 653.9
  logical 482.21
studio art 574.18
  radio station 344.6
  room 192.6
  workplace 719.1
studious
  engrossed 530.17
  learned 475.21
  scholarly 564.17
  studentlike 566.12

study
  n. branch of learning
  562.8
  concentration 478.3
  consideration 478.2
  den 719.8
  discussion 597.7
  drawing 574.14
  engrossment 530.3
  examination 485.3
  intention 653.1
  learning 564.3
  medical diagnosis
  689.13
  memorization 537.4
  music 462.5
  reverie 532.2
  room 192.6
  science 475.10
  treatise 606.1
  work of art 574.11
  v. consider 478.12
  discuss 597.12
  examine 485.23
  learn 564.12
  memorize 537.17
  pay attention 530.8
  seek 714.4
study for 564.15
study up 564.14
study with 564.11
stuff
  n. content 194.5
  drug 687.5
  essence 5.2
  fabric 378.5
  materials 378.1
  matter 376.2
  substance 3.2
  v. eat 307.23
  feed 307.17
  fill 56.7
  gluttonize 994.4
  jam 266.7
  overload 663.15
  pad 194.7
  preserve 701.8
  satiate 664.4
  thrust in 304.7
stuff and nonsense
  absurdity 470.3
  nonsense 547.2
stuffed blocked 266.11
  full 56.11
  overfull 663.20
  satiated 664.6
stuffed shirt 904.9
stuffiness
  affectation 903.6
  airlessness 268.6
  antiquation 123.3
  fetidness 437.2
  foolishness 470.2
  narrow-mindedness
  527.1
  perversity 626.3
  pompousness 904.7
  sultriness 328.6
  unimaginativeness
  536.1
  uninterestingness
  883.1

stuffing
  n. contents 194.3
  dressing 308.27
  extra 41.4
  intestines 225.4
  preserving 701.2
  wadding 266.5
  adj. gorging 994.6
stuffy airless 268.16
  conformist 82.6
  malodorous 437.5
  narrow-minded
  527.10
  old 123.17
  perverse 626.11
  pompous 904.22
  prudish 903.19
  sultry 328.28
  unimaginative 536.5
  uninteresting 883.6
stultify dupe 470.7
  frustrate 178.7
  repress 760.8
stumble
  n. an error 518.4
  bungle 734.5
  failure 725.3
  flounder 324.8
  trip 316.3
  v. be irresolute 627.6
  bungle 734.11
  err 518.9
  flounder 324.15
  stammer 595.8
  trip 316.8
stumblebum 734.9
stumble upon
  arrive at 300.7
  find 488.3
stumbling block 730.4
stump
  n. art equipment
  574.19
  end 70.2
  piece 55.3
  platform 216.13
  remainder 43.1
  v. electioneer 744.40
  make a speech 599.9
  perplex 514.13
  plod 270.7
  thwart 730.15
  walk 273.27
stumped
  at an impasse 731.22
  perplexed 514.24
stumper
  campaigner 746.10
  puzzle 549.8
stumping 744.12
stumps 273.16
stumpy
  deformed 249.12
  low 208.7
  stubby 203.10
stun astonish 920.6
  deafen 449.5
  din 453.6
  make unfeeling 856.8
  render insensible
  423.4
  startle 540.8

terrify 891.25
stung 866.23
stunned deaf 449.6
  stupefied 423.7
  terrified 891.34
stunner
  beautiful person
    900.8
  marvel 920.2
stunning
  astonishing 920.12
  deadening 423.9
  excellent 674.13
  gorgeous 900.19
  surprising 540.11
  terrifying 891.37
stunt
  n. act 705.3
  acting 611.9
  v. fly 278.49
  shorten 203.6
stunted dwarf 196.13
  meager 662.10
  undeveloped 721.12
stunt flying 278.13
stunt man 279.1
stupa memorial 570.12
  shrine 1042.4
  tomb 410.16
  tower 207.11
stupefied
  apathetic 856.13
  astonished 920.9
  stunned 423.7
  terrified 891.34
stupefy astonish 920.6
  make unfeeling 856.8
  render insensible
    423.4
  terrify 891.25
stupefying
  deadening 423.9
  extraordinary 85.14
  terrifying 891.37
stupendous
  extraordinary 85.14
  huge 195.20
  large 34.7
  wonderful 920.10
stupid
  n. dolt 471.3
  adj. foolish 470.8
  unintelligent 469.15
stupidity an error 518.5
  folly 470.1
  foolish act 470.4
  unintelligence 469.3
stupidly
  foolishly 470.12
  unintelligently
    469.25
stupor apathy 856.4
  emotional symptom
    690.23
  languor 708.6
  sleep 712.6
  trance state 690.26
  unconsciousness
    423.2
stuporific 884.9
stuporous 712.21

sturdiness
  firmness 159.3
  strength 159.1
  substantiality 3.1
sturdy firm 159.16
  robust 685.10
  strong 159.13
  substantial 3.7
stutter
  n. stammering 595.3
  v. stammer 595.8
stuttering
  n. frequency 135.2
  redundancy 103.3
  stammering 595.3
  adj. staccato 135.5
  stammering 595.13
sty blemish 679.1
  eye disease 686.13
  filthy place 682.11
  hovel 191.12
  sore 686.35
Stygian dark 337.14
  hellish 1019.8
style
  n. architectural capi-
    tals 211.18
  architecture 574.25
  art 574.24
  artistic school 574.9
  aspect 446.3
  behavior 737.1
  clothing 231.1
  engraving tool 578.9
  fashion 644.1
  flower part 411.26
  form 246.1
  kind 61.3
  manner of speaking
    588.2
  mode 7.4
  motif 901.7
  name 583.3
  preference 637.5
  protuberance 256.3
  skill 733.1
  specialty 81.1
  way 657.1
  v. name 583.11
  phrase 588.4
styled named 583.14
  phrased 588.5
styling 583.2
stylish
  dressed up 231.45
  modish 644.12
  skillful 733.20
stylist designer 579.9
  master of style 588.3
  types of 579.12
stylistics 588.2
stylize 646.5
stylized 646.7
stylus 450.11
stymie 730.13
styptic
  n. astringent 198.6
  adj. astringent 198.11
Styx
  abode of the dead
    408.4
  river of Hades 1019.4

suasive
  influential 172.13
  persuasive 648.29
suave smooth 260.9
  unctuous 936.18
sub
  n. submarine 277.9
  substitute 149.2
  v. replace 149.5
  adj. inferior 37.6
subalpine 207.23
subaltern
  n. commissioned offi-
    cer 749.18
  inferior 37.2
  adj. inferior 37.6
subatomic
  atomic 326.18
  infinitesimal 196.14
subatomic particle
  atomics 326.6
  particle 196.8
  word list 326.24
subaudible
  faint-sounding 452.16
  silent 451.10
subbasement 192.17
subclass 61.5
subcommittee
  committee 755.2
  delegates 781.13
subconscious
  n. inmost mind 466.3
  psyche 690.35
  adj. unconscious
    690.48
subcontinent 386.1
subcutaneous
  cutaneous 229.6
  injection method
    689.19
subdeb
  fashionable 644.7
  girl 125.6
subdivide analyze 48.6
  apportion 49.18
  bisect 92.4
  classify 61.6
  discriminate 492.5
subdivision
  analysis 48.1
  bisection 92.1
  category 61.2
  classification 61.1
  contents 194.1
  housing 188.3
  part 55.1
  separation 49.1
subdual conquest 726.1
  defeat 727.1
  subjugation 764.4
  suppression 760.2
subdue calm 163.7
  conquer 727.10
  moderate 163.6
  muffle 451.9
  relieve 886.5
  soften 357.6
  subjugate 764.9
  suppress 760.8
subdued
  conquered 727.16

dejected 872.22
  faint-sounding 452.16
  muffled 452.17
  restrained 163.11
  reticent 613.10
  soft-colored 362.21
  subjugated 764.15
  suppressed 760.14
  tasteful 897.8
  weak 765.15
subduer 726.2
subduing
  n. conquest 726.1
  defeat 727.1
  adj. moderating
    163.14
  relieving 886.9
  softening 357.16
subgroup class 61.2
  part 55.1
subhead
  n. caption 484.2
  v. caption 484.3
subhuman
  animal 414.43
  cruel 939.24
subjacent 208.8
subject
  n. citizen 190.4
  doer 718.1
  examinee 485.18
  experimentee 489.7
  music theme 462.30
  specialty 562.8
  story element 608.9
  study 564.3
  syntax 586.2
  topic 484.1
  vassal 764.7
  v. impose upon 963.4
  subdue 764.8
  adj. inferior 37.6
  subjugated 764.13
subjection
  inferiority 37.1
  subjugation 764
  submission 765.1
subjective intrinsic 5.6
  introverted 690.46
  mental 466.8
subjectivity 5.1
subject matter 484.1
subject to
  contingent 507.9
  liable to 175.5
  provided 507.12
subjoin add 40.4
  place after 65.3
subjoinder 594.4
subjugate
  appropriate 822.19
  conquer 727.10
  domineer 741.16
  subdue 764.8
subjugated
  conquered 727.16
  subjected 764.14
subjugation
  appropriation 822.4
  defeat 727.1
  subjection 764.1
subjunctive 586.11

vital 672.22
substitute
　n. deputy 781.1
　psychological surro-
　　gate 690.38
　replacement 149.2
　understudy 612.7
　v. exchange 149.4
　adj. alternate 149.8
substitute for
　replace 149.5
　represent 781.14
substitution
　compensation 33.1
　defense mechanism
　　690.30
　exchange 149
　replacement 149.2
substratum
　bottom 212.1
　foundation 216.6
　matter 376.2
　underlayer 227.1
substructure
　foundation 216.6
　structure 245.3
subsume 76.4
subsuming 58.4
subtend 239.4
subterfuge
　concealment 615.1
　deception 618.1
　pretext 649.1
　secrecy 614.1
　sophistry 483.5
　stratagem 735.3
　trick 618.6
subterranean 209.12
subtile cunning 735.12
　dainty 35.7
　rare 355.4
　shrewd 467.15
　tenuous 4.6
subtilize etherialize 4.4
　make distinctions
　　492.5
　rarefy 355.3
　thin 205.12
subtitle
　n. book 605.12
　caption 484.2
　v. caption 484.3
subtle cunning 735.12
　dainty 35.7
　devious 46.4
　discriminating 492.7
　exact 516.16
　meticulous 533.12
　rare 355.4
　shrewd 467.15
　soft-colored 362.21
　tasteful 897.9
　tenuous 4.6
　thin 205.16
subtlety accuracy 516.3
　complexity 46.1
　cunning 735.1
　difference 16.2
　discrimination 492.1
　good taste 897.1
　meticulousness 533.3
　shrewdness 467.3

sophistry 483.1
tenuousness 355.1
unsubstantiality 4.1
subtotal 40.2
subtract
　calculate 87.11
　deduct 42.9
　separate 49.9
subtracted 187.10
subtraction
　decrease 39.1
　deduction 42
　deprivation 187.1
　mathematics 87.4
　separation 49.1
subtractive 42.13
subtropical 328.24
subtropics
　hot place 328.11
　zone 180.3
suburb 183.1
suburban
　mediocre 680.8
　surrounding 233.8
　urban 183.10
suburbanite 190.6
suburbia
　city district 183.6
　mediocrity 680.5
　outskirts 183.1
suburbs
　city district 183.6
　environment 233.1
subvention
　maintenance 785.3
　provision 659.1
　subsidy 818.8
　support 216.1
subversion
　alienation 145.5
　destruction 693.3
　inversion 220.2
　refutation 506.2
　revolution 147.1
subversionary 693.26
subversive
　n. radical 745.12
　rebel 767.5
　revolutionist 147.3
　traitor 619.11
　adj. changed 139.9
　destructive 693.26
　radical 745.20
　rebellious 767.11
subvert alienate 145.15
　change 139.6
　overthrow 693.20
　overturn 220.6
　refute 506.5
　revolt 767.7
subway railway 657.8
　train 272.13
　tunnel 257.5
subzero 333.14
succeed
　accomplish 722.4
　be a hit 611.33
　be successful 724.6
　bring off 724.10
　change hands 817.4
　come after 117.3
　follow 65.2

inherit 819.7
manage to 724.11
prosper 728.7
substitute for 149.5
triumph 726.3
succeeding
　following 293.5
　sequential 65.4
　subsequent 117.4
　successful 724.13
success
　accomplishment
　　722.1
　prosperity 728.1
　stage show 611.4
　successfulness 724
　successful person
　　724.5
　superiority 36.1
　victory 726.1
successful
　prosperous 728.12
　succeeding 724.13
　victorious 726.8
successfully 724.14
succession
　accession to power
　　739.12
　ancestry 170.4
　continuity 71.2
　inheritance 819.2
　posteriority 117.1
　posterity 171.1
　property transfer
　　817.2
　sequence 65.1
successive
　consecutive 71.9
　following 65.4
　subsequent 117.4
successor
　follower 293.2
　heir 819.5
　replacement 67.4
　sequel 117.2
　survivor 43.3
succinct
　aphoristic 517.6
　concise 592.6
　short 203.8
succor
　n. aid 785.1
　remedy 687.1
　v. aid 785.11
succubus
　evil spirit 1016.7
　monster 891.9
succulent
　n. plant 411.4
　adj. edible 307.31
　interesting 530.19
　juicy 388.6
　pleasant 863.9
　pulpy 390.6
　tasty 428.8
succumb
　become exhausted
　　717.5
　be defeated 727.12
　be destroyed 693.23
　die 408.19
　faint 423.5

submit 765.6
yield to 765.9
such 20.3
such-and-such 584.2
such as 20.12
suchlike
　n. likeness 20.3
　adj. similar 20.12
suck
　n. guzzle 996.6
　sip 307.4
　suction 306.5
　sycophant 907.3
　v. drink 307.27
　extract 305.12
　take in 306.12
suck dry
　consume 666.2
　despoil 822.24
　exploit 665.16
sucked dry 166.4
sucked into 176.4
sucker branch 411.18
　credulous person
　　502.4
　customer 828.4
　dupe 620.1
　sprout 125.9
sucker for 635.5
suck in inhale 306.12
　involve 176.2
　lure 650.4
　suck 307.27
suckle foster 785.16
　inhale 306.12
　nurse 307.17
　suck 307.27
suckling 125.7
suck up to
　befriend 927.11
　curry favor 907.8
suction
　drawing in 306.5
　extraction 305.3
　influence 172.2
sudden abrupt 113.5
　impulsive 630.9
　precipitate 709.10
　unexpected 540.10
suddenly
　abruptly 203.13
　all at once 113.9
　impulsively 630.13
　precipitously 709.15
　unexpectedly 540.14
suddenness
　abruptness 113.2
　hastiness 709.2
　impulsiveness 630.2
sudden thought 630.1
sudorific
　n. remedy 687.30
　adj. hot 328.25
　sweaty 311.22
suds
　n. beer 996.15
　foam 405.2
　v. foam 405.5
sudsy 405.7
sue litigate 1004.12
　petition 774.10
　solicit 774.14

woo 932.19
suet 308.13
suffer be patient 861.5
be punished 1010.22
be sick 686.43
experience 151.8
feel pain 424.8
hurt 866.19
permit 777.10
sufferable 868.13
sufferance
patience 861.1
permission 777.2
sufferer
sick person 686.40
victim 866.11
suffering
n. distress 866.5
pain 424.1
adj. pained 424.9
tolerant 777.14
suffice
be of use 665.17
be satisfactory 868.6
do 661.4
sufficiency
ability 157.2
adequacy 661
satisfactoriness 868.3
tolerableness 674.3
sufficient
enough 661.6
satisfactory 868.11
tolerable 674.19
valid 516.13
suffix
n. addition 41.2
morphology 582.3
sequel 67.1
v. add 40.4
place after 65.3
suffocate be hot 328.22
destroy 693.15
die 408.24
obstruct 730.12
strangle 409.19
suppress 760.8
suffocating
n. suppression 760.2
adj. airless 268.16
strong-smelling
435.10
sultry 328.28
suffocation
destruction 693.6
smothering 409.7
violent death 408.6
suffrage
franchise 744.17
participation 815.1
vote 637.6
suffragette
suffrage 744.17
women's rightist
958.7
suffuse imbue 44.12
pervade 186.7
suffusion flush 908.5
infusion 44.2
permeation 186.3
suffusive 186.14

sugar
n. endearment 932.5
money 835.2
nutrient 309.5
sweetening 431.2
v. sweeten 431.3
sugarcoat 431.3
sugar daddy
beau 931.12
patron 818.11
sugar off 431.3
sugary 431.4
suggest advise 754.5
evidence 505.9
hint 557.10
imply 546.4
indicate 568.17
mean 545.8
promise 544.13
propose 773.5
remind 537.20
resemble 20.7
suggested 546.7
suggestible 172.15
suggestion advice 754.1
clue 568.9
disparagement 971.4
hint 557.4
implication 546.2
indication 568.1
influence 172.1
proposal 773.2
small amount 35.4
tinge 44.7
vague supposition
499.5
suggestive
allusive 546.6
eloquent 600.10
evidential 505.17
indicative 568.23
meaningful 545.10
recollective 537.22
risqué 990.7
suggestive of 20.10
suicidal
dejected 872.22
destructive 693.26
murderous 409.24
wretched 866.26
suicide killer 409.3
self-murder 409.6
sui generis
peerless 36.15
unique 16.8
unusual 85.10
suit
n. accusation 1005.1
courtship 932.6
entreaty 774.2
lawsuit 1004.1
prayer 1032.4
set 74.12
solicitation 774.5
suit of clothes 231.6
types of 231.48
v. adjust 720.8
conform 82.3
fit 26.8
outfit 231.40
suitability
eligibility 637.11

expedience 670.1
fitness 26.5
propriety 958.2
readiness 720.4
tastefulness 897.3
timeliness 129.1
suitable apt 26.10
decorous 897.10
eligible 637.24
expedient 670.5
right 958.8
sufficient 661.6
timely 129.9
suitable for 82.9
suite apartment 191.14
music 462.9
retinue 73.6
set 74.12
suited apt 26.10
competent 733.22
fitted 720.17
suit oneself 762.19
suitor accuser 1005.5
aspirant 634.12
litigant 1004.11
lover 931.11
petitioner 774.7
sukkah 1040.11
Sukkoth 1040.16
sulfa drug
types of 687.61
wonder drug 687.29
sulfonate 379.6
sulfuric 383.15
sulfurous hellish 1019.8
malodorous 437.5
mineral 383.15
sulk 951.14
sulks ill humor 951.10
sadness 872.6
unwillingness 623.1
sullen glum 872.25
obstinate 626.8
perverse 626.11
sulky 951.24
unsociable 923.5
unwilling 623.5
sullied soiled 682.21
unchaste 989.23
sully defile 682.17
demoralize 981.10
seduce 989.20
soil 682.16
stigmatize 915.9
vilify 971.10
sulphuric, sulphurous
see **sulfuric** etc.
sultan 749.10
sultanate country 181.1
sovereignty 739.8
sultry obscene 990.9
stifling 328.28
sum
n. addition 40.2
amount 28.2
extent 28.1
meaning 545.1
number 86.5
summary 607.2
sum of money 835.13
total 54.2
v. add 40.6

calculate 87.12
summa cum laude
916.11
summarily
concisely 592.7
shortly 203.12
swiftly 131.15
summarize
abridge 607.5
review 103.8
shorten 203.6
sum up 87.12
summary
n. abridgment 203.3
iteration 103.2
numeration 87.5
résumé 607.2
adj. concise 592.6
expeditious 131.9
short 203.8
summation
abridgment 203.3
addition 40.2
legal argument
1004.8
numeration 87.5
recapitulation 607.2
sum 86.5
summer
n. hot weather 328.7
season 128.3
v. spend time 105.6
adj. summery 128.8
summerhouse
arbor 191.13
nursery 413.11
summer school 567.2
summer stock 611.1
summertime 128.3
summery green 371.4
summer 128.8
warm 328.24
summing up
iteration 103.2
legal argument
1004.8
numeration 87.5
summit
completion 56.5
conference 597.6
culmination 677.3
peak 207.8
top 211.2
summon
assemble 74.17
attract 650.5
call for 752.12
conjure 1035.11
enlist 780.16
evoke 305.14
invite 774.13
summons
n. bidding 752.5
call 568.16
enlistment 780.6
invitation 774.4
legal action 1004.2
subpoena 752.7
v. litigate 1004.13
summon 752.12
summon up
elicit 305.14

excite 857.11
prompt 648.13
remember 537.10
summon 752.12
visualize 535.15
sumo 796.10
sump
  body of water 398.1
  channel 396.5
  filth receptacle
    682.12
  marsh 400.1
sumpter
  beast of burden
    271.6
  horse 414.16
  mule 414.21
sumptuary 835.30
sumptuous
  expensive 848.11
  grandiose 904.21
sum up calculate 87.12
  repeat 103.8
  shorten 203.6
sun
  n. gods 375.14
  heavenly body 375.13
  light source 336.1
  period 107.2
  year 107.2
  v. bask 329.19
  dry 393.6
sunbaked 393.9
sunbath 689.5
sunbathe 329.19
sunbeam 335.10
Sunbelt 180.7
sunburn
  n. burn 329.6
  v. brown 367.2
sunburned
  burned 329.30
  red-complexioned
    368.9
  reddish-brown 367.4
sundae 308.46
Sunday
  n. day of rest 711.5
  holy day 1040.14
  v. vacation 711.9
Sunday best 231.10
Sunday driver 274.10
Sunday painter 673.9
Sunday school 567.10
sunder
  demolish 693.17
  sever 49.11
sundered 201.7
sundown 134.2
sundowner
  alcoholic drink 996.8
  bad person 986.2
  vagabond 274.3
sundries
  miscellany 74.13
  notions 831.6
sundry diversified 19.4
  several 101.7
sunglasses
  eyeshade 338.2
  spectacles 443.2
sunk depressed 318.12

hollow 257.16
spoiled 692.31
sunken
  depressed 318.12
  hollow 257.16
  underwater 209.13
sunless 337.13
sunlight 335.10
sunlit 335.39
sunny cheerful 870.11
  luminous 335.30
  optimistic 888.12
  pleasant 863.10
  warm 328.24
sunny side 863.4
sunrise dawn 133.3
  east 290.3
sunroom 192.5
sunscreen 338.4
sunset evening 134.2
  west 290.3
sunshade shade 338.1
  umbrella 228.7
sunshine
  daylight 335.10
  good times 728.4
  happiness 865.2
sunshiny
  luminous 335.30
  warm 328.24
sunspot 375.13
sunstroke
  environmental dis-
    ease 686.31
  heatstroke 686.26
suntan 367.2
sunup 133.3
sun worship 1033.1
sun worshiper 1033.4
sup
  n. guzzle 996.6
  sip 307.4
  small amount 35.4
  taste 427.2
  v. dine 307.19
  drink 307.27
  taste 427.7
  tipple 996.23
super
  n. actor 612.7
  book size 605.14
  superintendent 748.2
  adj. superb 674.17
  superior 36.12
superable 509.7
superabound
  overabound 663.8
  overrun 313.4
superabundance
  diffuseness 593.1
  excess 663.2
  plenty 661.2
  productiveness 165.1
  quantity 34.3
superabundant
  diffuse 593.11
  excessive 663.19
  much 34.8
  plentiful 661.7
  productive 165.9
  teeming 101.9

superannuate
  become old 123.9
  depose 783.4
  discard 668.8
  dismiss 310.19
  obsolesce 668.9
  resign 784.2
superannuated
  antiquated 123.13
  disused 668.10
  retired 784.3
superb eminent 34.9
  excellent 674.17
  grandiose 904.21
superbly
  exquisitely 674.22
  grandiosely 904.28
  skillfully 733.29
supercharged
  loaded 56.12
  overfull 663.20
supercilious
  contemptuous 966.8
  disdainful 912.13
supercooled
  cold 333.14
  cooled 334.13
superego
  conscience 957.5
  psyche 690.35
  self 80.5
supereminent
  chief 36.14
  eminent 914.18
  superb 674.17
supererogatory 663.17
superficial
  apparent 446.11
  exterior 224.6
  formal 646.7
  frivolous 469.20
  half-learned 477.15
  hasty 709.9
  insignificant 35.6
  shallow 210.5
  surface 179.8
  trivial 673.16
  uninteresting 883.6
superficiality
  appearances 446.2
  exteriority 224.1
  frivolousness 469.7
  inattention 531.1
  shallowness 210.1
  slight knowledge
    477.6
  triviality 673.3
  uninterestingness
    883.1
superficially
  apparently 446.12
  externally 224.9
  hastily 709.12
  unimportantly 673.20
  vapidly 883.10
superfine
  grandiose 904.21
  superb 674.17
superfluity
  diffuseness 593.1
  excess 43.4
  extravagance 663.4

ornamentation 901.3
profusion 34.3
superfluous
  excessive 663.17
  remaining 43.7
  unessential 6.4
  useless 669.9
supergovernment 741.7
superheat
  n. heat 328.1
  v. heat 329.17
superheated 329.29
superhighway 657.6
superhuman
  divine 1013.19
  supernatural 85.15
superimpose 228.19
superimposed 228.35
superincumbent
  covering 228.35
  overhanging 215.11
  ponderous 352.17
superintend 747.10
superintendence
  directorship 747.4
  supervision 747.2
superintendent
  n. peace officer
    699.15
  supervisor 748.2
  adj. supervising
    747.13
superior
  n. chief 749.3
  head 36.4
  adj. arrogant 912.9
  authoritative 739.15
  excellent 674.14
  greater 36.12
  higher 207.24
  important 672.16
  remarkable 34.10
superiority
  abnormality 85.1
  ascendancy 739.6
  goodness 674.1
  importance 672.1
  overpassing 313.1
  power 157.1
  precedence 64.1
  preeminence 36
superlative
  n. exaggeration 617.1
  the best 674.8
  adj. consummate
    34.12
  exaggerated 617.4
  lofty 207.19
  supreme 36.13
Superman 159.6
supermarket
  market 832.1
  store 832.5
supernal
  heavenly 1018.13
  high 207.19
supernatant 353.13
supernatural
  divine 1013.19
  ghostly 1017.7
  immaterial 377.7
  occult 1034.22

unearthly 85.15
supernatural, the
occultism 1034.2
supernaturalism 85.7
supernatural being
1014.15
supernaturalism
immateriality 377.1
transcendentalism
1034.2
unearthliness 85.7
supernova 375.8
supernumerary
n. actor 612.7
adj. additional 40.10
surplus 663.18
superpatriot
chauvinist 941.3
intolerant person
527.5
superpatriotic
prejudiced 527.12
public-spirited 941.4
superphysical 85.15
superpower
country 181.1
power 157.1
supersaturate
overload 663.15
satiate 664.4
supersaturated
overfull 663.20
satiated 664.6
superscribe
address 604.14
write 602.19
superscription
address 604.10
caption 484.2
supersede 149.5
superseded 668.10
supersedure 149.1
supersensible
psychic 1034.23
supernatural 85.15
supersensitive 422.14
supersonic fast 269.20
sonic 450.17
supersonics
aeronautics 278.2
sonics 450.6
supersonic transport
280.3
superstar expert 733.13
famous person 914.9
first-rater 674.6
lead 612.6
principal 672.10
superior 36.4
superstition 502.3
superstitious 502.8
superstructure 245.2
supervene
be added 40.7
come after 117.3
supervenient 6.4
supervise govern 741.12
oversee 747.10
possess authority
739.13
supervision
government 741.1

superintendence
747.2
supervisor
public official 749.17
superintendent 748.2
supervisory
governing 741.19
overseeing 747.13
supinate invert 220.5
knock down 318.5
lie down 318.11
supine
apathetic 856.13
languid 708.19
low 208.7
recumbent 214.8
submissive 765.12
supper 307.6
supplant 149.5
supplanting 149.1
supple
changeable 141.6
cunning 735.12
mind-changing
628.10
pliant 357.9
versatile 733.23
supplement
n. adjunct 41.1
nonessential 6.2
sequel 67.1
v. add to 40.5
supplementary
additional 40.10
unessential 6.4
supplementation 40.1
suppliant
n. petitioner 774.7
worshiper 1032.9
adj. petitionary
774.16
worshipful 1032.15
supplicate
entreat 774.11
pray 1032.12
supplication
entreaty 774.2
prayer 1032.4
supplicatory
petitionary 774.16
worshipful 1032.15
supplied 659.13
supplier 659.6
supplies groceries 308.5
provision 659.2
store 660.1
supply
n. materials 378.1
means 658.1
provision 659.1
resource 660.2
v. furnish 659.7
give 818.15
supply depot 660.6
support
n. actor 612.7
aid 785.1
assent 521.1
backing 216
bearer 216.2
comfort 887.4
confirmation 505.5

financing 836.2
food 308.3
mainstay 787.9
maintenance 785.3
payment 841.8
reinforcements 785.8
subsidy 818.8
types of 216.26
upkeep 701.1
v. act opposite 611.35
afford to pay 843.7
bear 216.21
care for 699.19
commend 968.11
confirm 505.12
defend 1006.10
encourage 893.16
finance 836.15
give hope 888.10
help 785.12
maintain 701.7
pay for 841.19
provide for 659.7
ratify 521.12
strengthen 159.11
subsidize 818.19
support politically
744.41
tolerate 861.5
supportable
provable 505.20
tolerable 868.13
supporter
backer 818.11
brace 216.2
defender 799.7
financer 836.9
follower 293.2
friend 928.1
mainstay 787.9
suspender 215.5
supporting
adj. approving 968.17
bearing 216.23
confirming 505.19
prep. behind 785.27
supportive
bearing 216.23
comforting 887.13
confirming 505.19
promising 888.13
supposable
imaginable 535.26
presumable 499.15
suppose assume 499.10
believe 501.11
imagine 535.14
imply 546.4
judge 494.8
think probable 511.5
supposed
assumed 499.14
implied 546.7
supposedly 499.17
supposer 499.8
supposing
n. theory 499.3
conj. assuming that
499.19
supposition idea 479.1
implication 546.2
theory 499.3

suppositional
assumed 499.14
uncertain 514.16
supposititious
assumed 499.14
illusory 519.9
imaginary 535.19
spurious 616.26
suppress
conquer 727.10
control feelings 858.8
cushion 163.8
destroy 693.15
domineer 741.16
hinder 730.10
hush up 614.8
inhibit 813.5
moderate 163.6
prohibit 778.3
restrain 760.8
subdue 764.9
suppressed
blocked 538.9
conquered 727.16
restrained 760.14
reticent 613.10
secret 614.11
subjugated 764.14
suppression
defense mechanism
690.31
destruction 693.6
hindrance 730.1
inhibition 813.1
keeping secret 614.3
mental block 538.3
prohibition 778.1
restraint 760.2
reticence 613.3
subdual 764.4
suppressive
hindering 730.17
prohibitive 778.6
restraining 760.11
tyrannical 739.16
suppurate fester 311.15
putrefy 692.25
supra 64.6
supranational 417.13
supremacy
ascendancy 739.6
importance 672.1
influence 172.1
primacy 36.3
superexcellence 674.2
supreme
authoritative 739.15
best 674.18
dominant 741.18
godlike 1013.20
most important
672.23
omnipotent 157.13
superlative 36.13
top 211.10
Supreme Court 1001.4
surcease
cessation 144.1
release 886.2
respite 711.2
surcharge
n. burden 352.7

overcharge 848.5
overload 663.3
v. falsify accounts 845.10
overcharge 848.7
overload 663.15
surcoat 231.13
surd
n. number 86.3
speech sound 594.13
adj. deaf 449.6
numerical 86.8
phonetic 594.31
sure
adj. believing 501.21
certain 513.13
confident 513.21
evidential 505.17
guaranteed 772.11
inevitable 639.15
prepared 539.11
reliable 513.17
trustworthy 974.19
adv. certainly 513.24
interj. yes 521.18
sure-enough
authentic 516.14
certain 513.13
true 516.12
surefire reliable 513.17
successful 724.13
surefooted 733.21
surely
adv. absolutely 513.23
certainly 513.24
inevitably 639.19
interj. really! 920.19
yes 521.18
sureness belief 501.1
certainty 513.1
confidence 513.5
inevitability 639.7
trustworthiness 974.6
sure sign proof 505.4
sign 568.2
Sûreté 699.17
sure thing
n. certainty 513.2
good chance 156.8
sure success 724.2
adv. certainly 513.24
interj. yes 521.18
surety belief 501.1
certainty 513.1
guarantor 772.6
pledge 772.2
safety 698.1
security 772.1
sureness 513.5
surf foam 405.2
wave 395.14
surface
n. area 179.1
exterior 224.2
shallowness 210.1
texture 351.1
top 211.1
v. emerge 303.12
float up 315.9
sail 275.47
adj. apparent 446.11

exterior 224.6
flat 179.8
formal 646.7
shallow 210.5
surfacing
n. emergence 303.2
floor 212.3
water travel 275.8
adj. emerging 303.18
surfboard 277.11
surfeit
n. amplitude 56.2
overfullness 663.3
satiety 664.1
v. fill 56.7
overload 663.15
satiate 664.4
surfeited brimful 56.11
overfull 663.20
satiated 664.6
surfing 275.11
surge
n. ascent 315.1
crescendo 453.1
flow 395.4
increase 38.1
wave 395.14
whirl 322.2
v. ascend 315.8
billow 395.22
crescendo 453.6
flow out 303.13
gush 395.20
stream 395.16
throng 74.16
whirl 322.11
surgeon 688.9
surgery cutting 49.2
hospital room 192.25
medicine 688.3,19
surgical treatment 689.21
surgical 688.18
surgical instrument 689.36
surging 395.24
surliness
gruffness 937.3
sullenness 951.8
surly gruff 937.7
sullen 951.24
surmise
n. speculation 499.4
supposition 499.3
v. believe 501.11
suppose 499.10
surmount
ascend 315.11
be high 207.16
overcome 727.7
top 211.9
triumph over 726.6
surmountable
possible 509.7
vulnerable 697.16
surname 583.5
surpass exceed 663.9
excel 36.6
outdistance 36.10
surpassing best 674.18
consummate 34.12
superior 36.12

surplus
n. difference 42.8
excess 663.5
overrunning 313.1
superfluity 43.4
v. dismiss 310.19
adj. additional 40.10
extra 663.18
remaining 43.7
surprise
n. attack 798.2
inexpectation 540.2
wonder 920.1
v. astonish 920.6
attack 798.15
do the unexpected 540.7
surprised
astonished 920.9
startled 540.12
unprepared 721.8
surprising
astonishing 920.12
startling 540.11
sudden 113.5
surprisingly
astonishingly 920.16
startlingly 540.15
suddenly 113.9
wonderfully 34.20
surrender
n. abandonment 633.3
capitulation 765.2
compromise 807.1
giving 818.1
property transfer 817.1
relinquishment 814.1
v. compromise 807.2
deliver 818.13
relinquish 814.3
submit 765.8
transfer property 817.3
yield 633.7
surreptitious
covert 614.12
deceitful 618.20
in hiding 615.14
surrogate deputy 781.1
psychological surrogate 690.38
substitute 149.2
surround
besiege 798.19
circle 253.10
circumscribe 234.4
consume 307.20
contain 225.6
enclose 236.5
encompass 233.6
go around 321.4
limit 235.8
span 179.7
wrap 228.20
surrounded
circumscribed 234.6
encompassed 233.10
surrounding
enclosing 236.11
encompassing 233.8

environmental 8.8
surroundings 233.1
surtax 846.10
surveillance
ambush 615.3
shadowing 485.9
supervision 747.2
vigilance 533.4
survey
n. abridgment 607.1
canvass 485.13
collection 74.1
examination 485.3
measurement 490.1
scrutiny 439.6
treatise 606.1
view 444.3
v. canvass 485.28
discuss 606.5
examine 485.23
measure 490.11
scrutinize 439.15
surveying
assessment 490.1
location 184.7
mensuration 490.9
surveyor
measurer 490.10
supervisor 748.2
survival
durability 110.1
relic 123.6
remainder 43.1
survive endure 110.6
keep alive 407.10
live on 121.7
outlast 110.8
persist 143.5
recover 694.20
remain 43.5
support oneself 659.12
surviving 43.7
survivor 43.3
susceptibilities 855.1
susceptibility
ability 157.2
amorousness 931.3
emotional capacity 855.4
influenceability 172.5
liability 175.2
physical sensibility 422.2
pliancy 357.2
teachability 564.5
tendency 174.1
unprotectedness 697.3
susceptible
emotionable 855.21
influenceable 172.15
pliant 357.9
sensible 422.13
subject to 175.5
teachable 564.18
unprotected 697.15
suspect
n. accused 1005.6
v. be doubtful 503.6
be jealous 953.3
believe 501.11

supremacy 36.3
swing 323.6
v. collapse 692.27
diverge 219.9
flounder 324.15
fluctuate 141.5
incline 219.10
influence 172.7
persuade 648.23
pitch 275.55
prejudice 527.9
prompt 648.22
rule 741.14
swing 323.10
swayable 172.15
swayback 249.3
swaybacked 249.12
swayed
prejudiced 527.12
unjust 977.11
swaying
influential 172.14
swinging 323.17
swear affirm 523.5
blaspheme 1030.5
curse 972.6
express belief 501.12
promise 770.4
swear in 523.6
testify 505.10
swear by 501.16
swear in
call to witness
1004.16
place under oath
523.6
swearing cursing 972.3
deposition 523.2
swear off
break the habit 643.3
relinquish 814.3
renounce 992.8
swear to affirm 523.5
ratify 521.12
swearword 972.4
sweat
n. body fluid 388.3
bustle 707.4
confusion 532.3
impatience 862.1
nervousness 859.2
perspiration 311.7
trepidation 891.5
work 716.4
v. await 539.8
be damp 392.11
be hot 328.22
be impatient 862.4
condense 395.18
perspire 311.16
strain 714.4
work 716.16
work hard 716.13
sweat bath bath 681.8
heat therapy 689.5
sweat blood
endeavor 714.4
exert oneself 716.10
sweater 231.52
sweating
n. trickle 395.7
adj. hot 328.25

laboring 716.17
sweaty 311.22
sweat it 716.11
sweat it out
await 539.8
be impatient 862.4
not weaken 159.9
wait 132.13
sweat over 478.9
sweatshop 719.1
sweaty hot 328.25
perspiring 311.22
sweep
n. curve 252.3
deviation 291.1
glide 273.8
horse race 796.13
lottery 515.11
oar 277.15
range 179.2
sweeper 681.16
view 446.6
vision 439.1
v. clean 681.23
curve 252.6
glide 273.34
go easily 732.9
overwhelm 395.17
plunder 824.16
push 285.10
reach 179.7
speed 269.8
touch lightly 425.7
traverse 273.19
use radar 346.17
sweep away 693.14
sweeper 681.16
sweeping
n. gliding 273.8
adj. comprehensive
76.7
extensive 79.13
revolutionary 147.5
thorough 56.10
vague 514.18
sweepings refuse 669.4
remainder 43.1
sweeping statement
79.8
sweep out clean 681.18
eject 310.21
sweep 681.23
sweepstakes
award 916.2
gambling 515.4
game of chance 515.8
horse race 796.13
lottery 515.11
sweet
n. confection 308.39
endearment 932.5
sweetness 431.1
taste 427.1
adj. clean 681.25
fragrant 436.9
good-natured 938.14
harmonious 589.8
lovable 931.23
melodious 462.49
pleasant 863.6
soft-colored 362.21
sweetish 431.4

sweetbread
meat 308.20
veal 308.14
sweeten clean 681.18
dulcify 431.3
make pleasant 863.5
sweetener
gratuity 818.5
incentive 648.7
sweetening 431.2
sweetening
incentive 648.7
types of 431.2
sweetheart
endearment 932.5
good thing 674.7
lover 931.10
sweetie
endearment 932.5
sweetheart 931.10
sweetly 938.19
sweetmeat 308.39
sweetness and light
855.8
sweet nothings
endearment 932.4
flattery 970.1
sweet on 931.28
sweet potato 465.9
sweet shop 832.4
sweet sixteen 124.14
sweet-smelling 436.9
sweet talk
endearment 932.4
flattery 970.1
glibness 936.5
hypocrisy 616.6
inducement 648.3
sweet-talk
be hypocritical
616.23
make love 932.13
urge 648.14
sweet tooth 634.7
swell
n. dandy 903.9
distension 197.2
harmonics 463.12
hill 207.5
keyboard 465.20
loudness 453.1
nobleman 918.4
swelling 256.4
wave 395.14
v. be excited 857.16
be ostentatious
904.14
be vain 909.7
billow 395.22
bulge 256.10
din 453.6
expand 197.5
increase 38.6
inflate 197.4
overextend 663.13
adj. chic 644.13
excellent 674.13
grandiose 904.21
interj. approval
968.22
swelled-headed 909.11
swellhead 909.5

swelling
n. distension 197.2
increase 38.1
loudness 453.1
lump 256.4
overextension 663.7
sore 686.35
adj. bombastic 601.9
bulging 256.14
increasing 38.8
swelter
n. sultriness 328.6
sweat 311.7
v. be hot 328.22
sweat 311.16
swelterer 328.8
sweltering 328.25
swept 395.25
swept-back 241.12
swept up 530.17
swerve
n. angle 251.2
bend 219.3
deviation 291.1
v. be changed 139.5
change course 275.30
deviate 291.3
diverge 219.9
dodge 631.8
pull back 284.7
veer 251.5
swerving
n. deviation 291.1
adj. devious 291.7
swift fast 269.19
hasty 709.9
lively 707.18
prompt 131.9
sudden 113.5
transient 111.8
swiftly hastily 709.12
promptly 131.15
rapidly 269.21
transiently 111.10
with alacrity 707.26
swiftness
hastiness 709.2
promptness 131.3
quickness 707.3
speed 269.1
transience 111.2
swig
n. drink 307.4
snort 996.6
v. booze 996.24
drink 307.27
swill
n. drink 307.4
fodder 308.4
mud 389.8
offal 682.9
refuse 669.4
snort 996.6
v. booze 996.24
drink 307.27
ingest 306.11
swim
n. fashion 644.1
swimming 275.11
v. bathe 275.56
swim fins 320.5
swimmer 275.12

swimming
n. aquatics 275.11
  dizziness 532.4
  sports 878.8
adj. aquatic 275.58
  dizzy 532.15
swimmingly
  easily 732.15
  prosperously 728.15
  successfully 724.14
swimming pool 878.13
swim suit 231.29
swindle
n. fake 616.13
  fraud 618.8
  theft 824.1
v. cheat 618.17
  overcharge 848.7
  steal 824.13
swindler cheat 619.3
  criminal 986.10
  cunning person 735.6
  thief 825.1
swindle sheet 843.3
swine bad person 986.7
  breeds of 414.71
  filthy person 682.13
  pig 414.9
  sensualist 987.3
  slob 62.7
swineherd 416.3
swing
n. action 705.1
  amusement device
    878.15
  blow 283.4
  boxing 283.5
  flounder 324.8
  gait 273.14
  hang 215.2
  meter 609.9
  music 462.9
  oscillator 323.9
  rhythm 463.22
  room 179.3
  scope 762.4
  stock prices 834.9
  sway 323.6
  thrust 798.3
  trend 174.2
v. alternate 323.13
  be hanged 1010.21
  be promiscuous
    989.19
  flounder 324.15
  fluctuate 141.5
  hang 215.6
  lash out at 798.16
  manage 724.11
  music 462.44
  sail 275.55
  sway 323.10
  swivel 322.9
  tend toward 174.3
  turn around 295.9
  walk 273.27
  wave 323.11
adj. music 462.52
swing district 744.16
swinger
  libertine 989.10
  nonconformist 83.3

socialite 644.7
swinging
n. deviation 291.1
  promiscuity 989.4
  sway 323.6
  swiveling 322.1
adj. pendent 215.9
  swaying 323.17
swing shift 108.3
swing vote 744.28
swinish carnal 987.6
  filthy 682.24
  gluttonous 994.6
  greedy 634.27
  intemperate 993.7
  ungulate 414.49
swipe
n. disapproval 969.4
  gibe 967.2
  hit 283.4
v. hit 283.13
  ridicule 967.9
  steal 824.13
swirl
n. agitation 324.1
  bustle 707.4
  curl 254.2
  eddy 395.12
  excitement 857.3
  rotation 322.2
v. agitate 324.10
  eddy 395.21
  twist 254.4
  whirl 322.11
swirling
n. excitement 857.3
  rotation 322.1
adj. rotating 322.14
swish
n. sibilation 457.1
v. rustle 452.12
  sibilate 457.2
  splash 452.11
swishing 452.19
switch
n. branch 55.4
  change 139.1
  conversion 145.1
  exchange 150.2
  false hair 230.13
  rod 1011.2
  story element 608.9
  substitution 149.1
  surprise 540.2
  twig 411.18
v. apostatize 628.8
  convert 145.11
  interchange 150.4
  punish 1010.14
  substitute 149.4
  trade 827.14
  transfer 271.9
  turn aside 291.6
switchback
  crookedness 219.8
  railway 657.8
switchboard
  lightboard 611.21
  telephone 560.8
switch off
  electricity 342.23
  turn off 144.12

switch on 342.23
switch-over 145.1
swivel
n. axis 322.5
v. rotate 322.9
  turn around 295.9
swivet confusion 532.3
  dither 857.5
swollen boastful 910.11
  bombastic 601.9
  bulging 256.15
  corpulent 195.18
  distended 197.13
  full 56.11
  increased 38.7
  overfull 663.20
  pompous 904.22
  proud 905.10
swoon
n. stupor 712.6
  unconsciousness
    423.2
v. faint 423.5
swoop
n. descent 316.1
  plunge 320.1
v. descend 316.5
  plunge 320.6
swoop down upon
  attack 798.15
  seize on 822.16
sword blade 801.4
  combatant 800.1
  cutlery 348.2,13
  types of 801.24
swordlike 258.15
sword of Damocles
  precariousness 697.2
  threat 973.1
swordplay 796.8
sword side
  kinsmen 11.2
  male line 170.4
  male sex 420.3
swordsman 800.1
sword swallower 612.3
sworn affirmed 523.8
  promised 770.8
sworn off 992.10
sworn statement
  certificate 570.6
  deposition 523.3
  testimony 505.3
sworn to
  affirmed 523.8
  ratified 521.14
swot
n. drudge 718.3
v. memorize 537.17
  study 564.12
swotting 564.3
sybarite 987.3
sybaritic 987.5
sycophancy
  flattery 970.1
  obsequiousness 907.2
sycophant cajoler 970.4
  flatterer 907.3
  lackey 787.8
sycophantic
  flattering 970.8
  obsequious 907.13

syllabary
  alphabet 581.3
  representation 572.1
syllabic
n. character 581.1
adj. phonetic 594.31
syllabify 581.7
syllable
n. poetic division
    609.11
  speech sound 594.13
  word 582.1
v. spell 581.7
syllabus 607.1
syllogism logic 482.6
  reasoning 482.3
sylph fairy 1014.18
  spirit 1014.16
sylphlike fairy 1014.27
  thin 205.16
sylvan
  backwoods 182.8
  forest 411.37
sylvan deity 1014.21
symbiosis
  coaction 177.1
  cooperation 786.1
  ecology 13.5
  joining 47.1
symbiotic agreeing 26.9
  coacting 177.4
  cooperating 786.5
  ecological 13.15
symbol character 581.1
  harmonics 463.12
  insignia 569.1
  number 86.1
  psychological symbol
    690.37
  representation 572.1
  sign 568.3
  substitute 149.2
  type 25.2
  unit of meaning
    545.6
symbolic(al)
  implicative 546.10
  indicative 568.23
  meaningful 545.10
  semantic 545.12
symbolism
  designation 568.3
  implication 546.2
  occultism 1034.1
  psychological symbol
    690.37
  ritualism 1040.1
symbolize
  designate 568.18
  mean 545.8
  metaphorize 551.2
  represent 572.6
symbolizing 572.10
symmetric(al)
  balanced 248.4
  equal 30.9
  harmonious 589.8
  orderly 59.6
symmetrize
  balance 248.3
  make uniform 17.4

taboo
n. exclusion 77.1
prohibition 778.1
v. exclude 77.4
prohibit 778.3
adj. jargonish 580.19
prohibited 778.7
tabular classified 61.8
flat 214.7
tabula rasa
clean sweep 147.1
ignorant 477.1
thoughtlessness 480.1
void 187.3
tabulate classify 61.6
list 88.8
record 570.16
tabulated 88.9
tabulation
classification 61.1
listing 88.7
recording 570.15
tachometer 269.7
tachycardia
cardiovascular disease 686.17
disease symptom 686.8
tacit implicit 546.8
wordless 451.11
taciturn concise 592.6
untalkative 613.9
tack
n. cordage 206.3
deviation 291.1
direction 290.2
harness 659.5
way 657.1
v. be changed 139.5
change course 275.30
deviate 291.3
fasten 47.8
tackle
n. athlete 878.20
belongings 810.3
cordage 206.3
equipment 659.4
harness 659.5
hoist 317.3
purchase 287.6
rigging 277.12
types of 287.10
v. attempt 714.6
pursue 705.7
reel in 287.9
set to work 716.15
undertake 715.3
tack on 40.4
tacky adhesive 50.12
frail 160.14
inferior 680.9
moist 392.15
shabby 692.34
slovenly 62.15
viscous 389.12
tact
considerateness 938.3
courtesy 936.1
discrimination 492.1
sensitivity 422.3
skill 733.1

tactful
considerate 938.16
courteous 936.14
discriminating 492.7
sensitive 422.14
skillful 733.20
tactic expedient 670.2
stratagem 735.3
tactical cunning 735.12
planned 654.13
tactician
cunning person 735.7
planner 654.7
tactics behavior 737.1
machinations 735.4
plan 654.1
warfare 797.9
tactile tactual 425.10
tangible 425.11
tactless careless 534.11
discourteous 937.6
undiscriminating 493.5
tad 125.3
tadpole
amphibian 414.32
young frog 125.8
tag
n. extremity 70.2
label 568.13
name 583.3
sequel 67.1
small amount 35.3
token 835.12
trailer 67.2
v. add 40.4
allot 816.9
follow 293.3
label 568.20
name 583.11
tag along 293.3
tag line 517.4
t'ai chi chu'an 796.10
tail
n. addition 41.2
back 241.1
book part 605.12
buttocks 241.5
cauda 241.6
extremity 70.2
follower 293.2
hair 230.7
limb 55.4
rear 241.1
sequel 67.2
v. follow 293.3
trail 485.34
adj. caudal 241.11
final 70.10
rear 241.9
tailgate follow 293.3
stay near 200.12
tailing following 293.1
surveillance 485.9
tailor
n. garmentmaker 231.34
sewer 223.2
v. adapt 26.7
form 246.7
sew 223.4
tailored apt 26.10

custom-made 231.47
tailoring 231.31
tailpiece adjunct 41.1
music division 462.24
rear 241.1
sequel 67.2
tail 241.6
tails
formal clothes 231.11,51
opposite side 239.3
tailspin
air maneuver 278.15
failure 725.3
tail wind
aviation 278.41
nautical 403.11
wind 403.1
taint
n. blemish 679.3
fault 678.2
infection 686.3
peculiarity 80.4
stigma 915.6
tinge 44.7
v. blemish 679.6
corrupt 692.14
defile 682.17
infect 686.48
stigmatize 915.9
work evil 675.6
tainted
blemished 679.10
diseased 686.56
morally corrupt 981.14
soiled 682.21
spoiled 692.42
unchaste 989.23
unhealthful 684.5
take
n. booty 824.11
catch 822.10
cinematography 577.8
gain 811.3
receipts 844.1
v. acquire 811.8
become sick 686.44
believe 501.11
borrow 821.4
burn 329.23
catch 822.17
condone 947.4
eat 307.18
endure 861.7
entail 76.4
interpret 552.9
possess sexually 822.15
receive 819.6
steal 824.13
submit to 765.6
succeed 724.6
suppose 499.10
take possession 822.13
transport 271.11
understand 548.7
take aback
dismay 891.27
startle 540.8

take a crack at
attempt 714.6
lash out at 798.16
take action 705.5
take advantage of
exploit 665.16
impose 963.7
improve the occasion 129.8
use 665.15
take after emulate 22.7
resemble 20.7
take apart
demolish 693.17
disassemble 49.15
tear apart 49.14
take a powder
flee 631.11
leave 301.10
take aside
talk to 594.27
tell confidentially 614.9
take a stand 555.6
take away
remove 271.10
subtract 42.9
take from 822.21
take back
apologize 1012.5
deny 524.4
recant 628.9
recover 823.6
restore 823.4
take by storm
raid 798.20
seize 822.14
win easily 726.5
take by surprise 540.7
take care
v. be careful 533.7
beware 895.7
pay attention 530.8
interj. caution 895.14
take care of
accomplish 722.4
bribe 651.3
care for 699.19
kill 409.14
look after 533.9
operate 164.5
perform 705.8
please oneself 978.4
punish 1010.11
serve 750.13
supervise 747.10
take chances
gamble 515.19
risk 697.7
take charge
be able 157.11
take command 739.14
take-charge 161.12
take cover
hide oneself 615.8
take refuge 700.7
take down
bring down 318.5
depress 318.4
disassemble 49.15
eat 307.20

humiliate 906.5
raze 693.19
record 570.16
reprove 969.17
take effect 164.7
take exception
  disapprove 969.10
  dissent 522.4
  find fault 969.15
take five pause 109.3
  take a rest 711.8
take for believe 501.11
  suppose 499.10
take for granted
  believe 501.10
  be unastonished 921.2
  expect 539.5
  imply 546.4
  neglect 534.6
  suppose 499.10
take from reduce 39.7
  subtract 42.9
  take away from 822.21
take heart
  be comforted 887.7
  cheer up 870.9
  hope 888.8
  take courage 893.14
take-home pay
  earnings 841.4
  economics 827.8
take in accept 925.7
  attend 186.8
  be a spectator 442.5
  capture 822.18
  deceive 618.13
  eat 307.20
  encompass 47.5
  entail 76.4
  enter 302.7
  extend 179.7
  gain 819.6
  hear 448.12
  include 76.3
  learn 564.7
  receive 306.10
  see 439.12
  shorten 203.6
  sorb 306.13
  understand 548.7
take into account
  allow for 507.5
  include 76.3
  take cognizance of 530.9
take issue with
  deny 524.4
  dispute 796.22
  dissent 522.4
  oppose 790.3
take it believe 501.11
  endure 861.8
  hold 661.4
  not weaken 159.9
  submit 765.6
  suppose 499.10
take it easy
  v. be cautious 895.5
  calm oneself 858.7
  go easy 732.11

idle 708.14
rest 711.6
interj. caution 895.14
take it or leave it
  be indifferent 636.5
  have no choice 639.11
take liberties
  be insolent 913.6
  disrespect 965.3
  presume on 961.7
take notice heed 530.6
  take cognizance of 530.9
taken unawares
  surprised 540.12
  unprepared 721.8
taken with
  compared to 491.11
  fond of 931.28
  pleased 865.12
takeoff ascent 315.1
  aviation 278.8
  beginning 68.1
  departure 301.3
  imitation 22.1
  outset 301.2
  point of departure 301.5
  ridicule 967.6
take off ascend 315.10
  begin 68.7
  detach 49.10
  discount 847.2
  excise 42.10
  fly 278.47
  get better 691.7
  imitate 22.6
  impersonate 572.9
  kill 409.13
  leave 301.10
  put an end to 693.12
  remove 232.6
take off for 290.10
take off on
  imitate 22.6
  ridicule 967.11
take on adopt 821.4
  assume 819.6
  attempt 714.6
  be angry 952.15
  complain 875.13
  contend against 790.4
  employ 780.13
  engage in 705.7
  fight with 796.17
  fret 890.5
  grieve 872.17
  set to work 716.15
  undertake 715.3
take one's time
  dally 708.13
  idle 708.11
  linger 270.8
  take one's leisure 710.4
  wait 132.12
take out escort 73.8
  exclude 42.10
  extract 305.10
takeover 822.4

take over acquire 811.9
  adopt 821.4
  appropriate 822.19
  assume 819.6
  take command 739.14
  usurp 961.8
take pains
  be careful 533.7
  endeavor 714.10
take place 151.5
taker recipient 819.3
  seizer 822.11
take shape form 59.5
  shape up 246.8
take sides argue 482.16
  back 785.13
  side with 786.4
take steps
  take action 705.5
  take precautions 895.6
take stock check 87.14
  take account of 845.9
take the blame 962.9
take the bull by the horns
  attempt 714.5
  be determined 624.8
  face up to 893.11
take the opportunity 129.7
  undertake 715.3
take the cake best 36.7
  win 726.4
take the consequences 1010.23
take the edge off
  blunt 259.2
  moderate 163.6
  pacify 804.7
  weaken 160.10
take the law into one's own hands
  break the law 999.5
  defy authority 740.4
  have one's will 621.3
  not observe 769.4
take the liberty 961.6
take the rap
  be punished 1010.23
  be responsible 962.9
  substitute 149.6
take time
  spend time 105.6
  wait 132.12
take to desire 634.14
  engage in 705.7
  fall in love 931.20
  get used to 642.13
  turn to 665.14
take to task
  accuse 1005.7
  punish 1010.10
  reprove 969.17
take turns 108.5
take up acquire 811.9
  adopt 637.15
  appropriate 822.19
  begin 68.9
  collect 74.18
  deal with 606.5

discuss 597.12
engage in 656.11
engross 530.13
espouse 968.13
glean 811.10
include 76.3
patronize 785.15
pay in full 841.13
pursue 705.7
raise 317.8
sorb 306.13
undertake 715.3
take upon oneself
  be responsible 962.9
  presume 961.6
  undertake 715.3
take up with
  bear with 861.5
  befriend 927.10
  be sociable 922.16
  confer 597.11
take with a grain of salt
  allow for 507.5
  be doubtful 503.6
taking
  n. borrowing 821.2
  getting 819.1
  sexual possession 822.3
  taking possession 822
  adj. alluring 650.7
  catching 822.25
  contagious 686.58
  desirable 634.30
  pleasant 863.7
taking away loss 812.1
  subtraction 42.1
  taking 822.1
taking in
  learning 564.2
  reception 306.1
  seizure 822.2
taking over
  accession to power 739.12
  appropriation 822.4
taking place 151.9
talcum powder 900.11
tale gossip 558.7
  lie 616.11
  reckoning 86.5
  story 608.6
talebearer
  informer 557.6
  newsmonger 558.9
talebearing
  n. gossip 558.7
  adj. gossipy 558.14
talent ability 157.2
  artistry 574.8
  genius 467.8
  intelligence 467.2
  skill 733.4
  talented person 733.12
talented gifted 733.27
  intelligent 467.14
taleteller
  narrator 608.10
  newsmonger 558.9
talisman 1036.5

talk
n. address 599.2
conversation 597.3
diction 588.1
gossip 558.7
language 580.1
lesson 562.7
rumor 558.6
speech 594.1
v. chatter 596.5
communicate 554.6
discuss 597.12
divulge 556.6
gossip 558.12
make a speech 599.9
patter 594.20
speak 580.16
talkathon
legislative procedure 742.14
speech 599.2
talkative
communicative 554.10
disclosive 556.10
loquacious 596.9
speaking 594.32
wordy 593.12
talk back answer 486.4
be insolent 913.7
talk big
be bombastic 601.6
boast 910.7
exaggerate 617.3
talk dirty 972.6
talk down land 278.52
outtalk 596.7
talked-about
famous 914.16
rumored 558.15
well-known 475.27
talkee-talkee
chatter 596.3
lingua franca 580.11
ungrammaticalness 587.1
talker
conversationalist 597.8
speaker 594.18
speechmaker 599.4
talkie 611.16
talking
n. communication 554.1
speech 594.1
adj. speaking 594.32
talking point 482.5
talking-to 969.6
talk into 648.23
talk nonsense
chatter 596.5
twaddle 547.5
talk of the town
repute 914.1
rumor 558.6
talk out of 652.3
talk over confer 597.11
convince 501.18
discuss 597.12
persuade 648.23
talk show 611.4

talk to address 594.27
reprove 969.18
talk turkey 591.2
talk with 597.9
talky 596.9
tall boastful 910.11
grandiloquent 601.8
high 207.21
large 195.16
long 202.8
unbelievable 503.10
tall order 731.2
tallow 380.1
tallowy 380.9
tall ship 277.3
tall story
boasting 910.2
lie 616.11
tally
n. account 845.2
agreement 26.1
count of 87.6
label 568.13
likeness 20.3
list 88.1
reports 570.7
sum 86.5
v. add 40.6
agree 26.6
calculate 87.11
coincide 14.4
conform 82.3
list 88.8
number 87.10
tallyho
n. hunting cry 459.3
interj. hunting cry 655.13
tallying 87.1
tally sheet 88.1
Talmud
scripture 1021.5
tradition 123.2
Talmudic 1021.11
taloned footed 212.9
grasping 813.9
talons authority 739.5
control 741.2
grasping organs 813.4
tambourine 465.19
tame
v. accustom 642.11
domesticate 764.11
drive animals 416.7
moderate 163.6
adj. domesticated 191.34
dull 268.14
moderate 163.10
weak 765.15
tamed
domesticated 191.34
subdued 764.15
weak 765.15
tamer 416.2
taming
habituation 642.8
subdual 764.4
Tammany Hall
political party 744.24
politics 744.1
tamp pack in 304.7

stamp 257.14
thrust 283.11
tamper with
adulterate 44.13
bribe 651.3
falsify 616.17
meddle 238.7
tampon
medical dressing 687.33
wadding 266.5
tan
v. brown 367.2
cure 720.6
punish 1010.15
adj. brown 367.3
tandem
n. rig 272.5
adv. behind 241.13
tang characteristic 80.4
poison injector 676.5
pungency 433.2
taste 427.1
tangent borderer 200.6
convergence 298.1
straight line 250.2
tangential
converging 298.3
in contact 200.17
tangibility
manifestness 555.3
substantiality 3.1
touchableness 425.3
tangible
n. asset 810.8
substance 3.2
adj. manifest 555.8
substantial 3.6
touchable 425.11
tangle
n. complex 46.2
v. catch 822.17
complicate 46.3
contend 796.18
hamper 730.11
involve 176.2
trap 618.18
tangled 46.4
tangy 433.7
tank
n. body of water 398.1
railway car 272.14
storage place 660.6
v. package 236.9
tank car 272.14
tanked 996.31
tanker ship 277.22,24
tank corpsman 800.12
tank town 183.3
tanned 367.3
tannery 719.3
tanning 1010.5
tantalize attract 650.5
disappoint 541.2
interest 530.12
seduce 931.21
tantalizing
alluring 650.7
appetizing 428.10
desirable 634.30

disappointing 541.6
exciting 857.28
interesting 530.19
pleasant 863.7
tantamount
equivalent 30.8
reciprocal 13.13
tantrum 952.8
Taoist 1020.31
tap
n. explosive noise 456.1
faint sound 452.3
faucet 266.4
hole 265.4
outlet 303.9
plant root 411.20
rap 283.6
touch 425.1
tube 396.6
valve 396.10
v. extract 305.12
faint sound 452.15
keep time 462.45
listen 448.11
make explosive noise 456.6
open 265.12
pipe 271.13
puncture 265.16
rap 283.15
take from 822.21
touch 425.6
tap dancer 879.3
tap dancing 879.1
tape
n. medical dressing 687.33
record 570.10
sound recording 450.12
strip 206.4
v. fasten 47.5
record 570.16
tape deck 450.11
tape measure 206.4
tape memory
computer 349.17
memory 537.1
taper
n. candle 336.2
lighter 331.4
light source 336.1
narrowing 205.2
wick 336.7
v. converge 298.2
narrow 205.11
sharpen 258.9
tape recorder 450.11
tapered
cone-shaped 205.15
pointed 258.11
tapering
n. narrowing 205.2
adj. pointed 258.11
tapered 205.15
tapestry 574.12
tapeworm
appetite 634.7
invertebrate 415.5
worm 414.42,75

television
  communications
    560.3
  electronics 343.1
  informant 557.5
  news medium 558.1
  video 345
television broadcast
  345.2
television receiver parts
  345.17
television set 345.11
television show 611.4
television studio 345.6
television transmitter
  parts 345.20
telex
  n. telegram 560.14
  telegraphy 560.2
  v. communicate
    560.19
tell
  affect emotionally
    855.17
  be important 672.11
  communicate 554.7
  divulge 556.5
  evidence 505.9
  have influence 172.10
  inform 557.8
  narrate 608.13
  number 87.10
  recognize 537.12
  report 558.11
  say 594.23
tell apart 492.6
teller banker 836.10
  informant 557.5
tell fortunes 543.9
tell how 552.10
telling
  n. impartation 554.2
  narrative 608.2
  numeration 87.1
  adj. eloquent 600.11
  evidential 505.17
  exciting 857.28
  influential 172.13
  notable 672.18
  powerful 157.12
tell it like it is 974.12
tell off 969.18
tell on divulge 556.6
  inform on 557.12
telltale clue 568.9
  divulgence 556.2
  hint 557.4
  informer 557.6
  newsmonger 558.9
telltale sign
  divulgence 556.2
  sign 568.2
tell the truth
  be honest 974.11
  confess 556.7
  disillusion 520.2
tellurian
  n. person 417.3
  adj. human 417.10
  terrestrial 385.6
Tellus Earth 375.10
  goddess 1014.5

telly television 345.1
  television receiver
    345.11
Telstar 345.9
temblor 162.5
temerity 894.1
temper
  n. anger 952.6
  firmness 159.3
  hardness 356.4
  hotheadedness 951.3
  mood 525.4
  nature 5.3
  temperament 525.3
  v. harden 356.7
  infuse 44.12
  make tough 359.3
  mature 126.9
  moderate 163.6
  qualify 507.3
  strengthen 159.11
tempera paint 362.8
  picture 574.15
temperament
  disposition 525.3
  harmonics 463.6
  nature 5.3
temperamental
  capricious 629.5
  dispositional 525.7
  innate 5.7
  irascible 951.20
temperance
  control 163.1
  moderation 992
  sedateness 858.4
  sobriety 997.1
  virtue 980.5
temperate
  controlled 163.10
  cool 333.12
  moderate 992.9
  sedate 858.14
  sober 997.3
  warm 328.24
temperature 328.3
tempered
  hardened 356.15
  mature 126.13
  qualified 507.10
  restrained 163.11
  toughened 359.6
tempering
  n. admixture 44.7
  experience 733.9
  hardness 356.4
  maturation 126.6
  moderation 163.2
  preparedness 720.4
  strengthening 159.5
  toughening 356.5
  adj. moderating
    163.14
temper tantrum 952.8
tempest
  emotional outburst
    857.8
  storm 162.4
  windstorm 403.12
tempest in a teapot
  overreaction 617.2
  triviality 673.3

tempestuous
  excited 857.22
  passionate 857.27
  stormy 403.26
  violent 162.17
template 25.6
temple church 1042.2
  side 242.1
tempo music 463.24
  pulsation 323.3
temporal
  chronological 105.7
  lay 1039.3
  materialistic 376.9
  timekeeping 114.15
  transient 111.7
  unsacred 1027.3
  worldly 1031.16
temporarily 111.9
temporary
  n. working person
    718.2
  adj. interim 109.4
  makeshift 670.7
  substitute 149.8
  transient 111.7
  unreliable 514.19
temporary measure
  630.5
temporize avoid 631.13
  change one's mind
    628.7
  procrastinate 132.11
  protract 110.9
temporizing 628.10
tempt attract 650.5
  induce 648.22
  seduce 931.21
temptation
  allurement 650.1
  thing desired 634.11
tempter
  motivator 648.10
  seducer 650.3
tempting alluring 650.7
  appetizing 428.10
  desirable 634.30
  pleasant 863.7
tempt Providence
  be reckless 894.6
  take chances 697.7
temptress
  seductress 989.15
  tempter 650.3
tempus fugit 105.17
ten 99.6
tenable
  acceptable 868.12
  believable 501.24
  defensible 799.15
tenacious
  adhesive 50.12
  bold 893.18
  obstinate 626.8
  persevering 625.7
  resolute 624.11
  retentive 813.8
  tough 359.4
  viscous 389.12
tenacity cohesion 50.3
  courage 893.4
  obstinacy 626.1

  perseverance 625.1
  resolution 624.1
  retention 813.1
  toughness 359.1
  viscosity 389.2
tenancy
  habitation 188.1
  possession 808.1
tenant
  n. holder 809.4
  inhabitant 190.2
  renter 190.8
  v. inhabit 188.7
tenant farmer 413.5
ten-cent store 832.1
Ten Commandments
  ethics 957.1
  ten 99.6
tend bear 290.8
  care for 699.19
  gravitate 352.15
  have a tendency
    174.3
  heed 530.6
  look after 533.9
  serve 750.13
  tend animals 416.7
tendency
  aptitude 733.5
  direction 290.1
  inclination 174
  nature 5.3
  preference 637.5
  probability 511.1
  trait of character
    525.3
tender
  n. attendant 750.5
  railway car 272.14
  v. give 818.12
  offer 773.4
  pay 841.10
  adj. careful 533.10
  emotionable 855.21
  immature 124.10
  kind 938.13
  lenient 759.7
  light 353.11
  loving 931.25
  pitying 944.7
  seaworthy 277.18
  sensitive 422.14
  soft 357.8
  soft-colored 362.21
  sore 424.11
tender age 124.1
tenderfoot
  beginner 68.2
  ignoramus 477.8
  newcomer 78.4
  novice 566.9
  recruit 800.17
tenderhearted
  emotionable 855.21
  kind 938.13
  pitying 944.7
tenderize 357.6
tenderloin
  brothel 989.9
  city district 183.6
  meat 308.17

throwback
adversity 729.3
regression 295.1
relapse 696.1
reversion 146.2

throw down
knock down 318.5
overthrow 693.20
raze 693.19

thrower 285.8

throw in insert 304.3
interpose 237.6

throw in with
cooperate 786.4
join 52.4

throw off
break the habit 643.3
do away with 310.20
do carelessly 534.9
free oneself from 763.8
improvise 630.8
let out 310.23
say 594.23
separate 49.9
shed 232.10
take off 232.6
unseat 185.6

throw out
discard 668.7
eject 310.24
oust 310.13
reject 638.2
separate 49.9

throw over
abandon 633.5
discard 668.7
eliminate 77.5
subvert 693.20

throw stick
spear-thrower 801.18
weapon 801.12

throw together
do carelessly 534.9
improvise 630.8
mix 44.11

throw up
abandon 633.7
elevate 317.5
relinquish 814.3
vomit 310.25

thrum
n. staccato sound 455.1
v. hum 452.13
make staccato sounds 455.4
music 462.45
strum 462.41

thrumming
n. hum 452.7
staccato 455.7

thrush
songbird 464.23
infectious disease 686.12

thrust
n. acceleration 269.4
attack 798.3
aviation 278.32
drive 285.1
impulse 283.1
major part 54.6
power 157.4
push 283.2
rocketry 281.8
vim 161.2
v. attack 798.17
impel 283.10
propel 285.10
put violently 184.12
shove 283.11

thrust aside 531.4
thrust back 289.3
thruway 657.6
thrust down 318.4
thrust in drive in 304.7
enter 302.7
interpose 237.6
thrust out eject 310.13
extend 179.7
ostracize 310.17
thrust upon
force upon 818.20
urge upon 773.8

thud
n. faint sound 452.3

thug bandit 825.4
combatant 800.1
criminal 986.10
evildoer 943.3
killer 409.11
man 787.8

thumb
n. finger 425.5
v. hitchhike 273.30
touch 425.6

thumbnail sketch 607.1
thumb one's nose at
disdain 966.3
flout 793.4
thumbprint 568.7
thumbscrew 1011.4
thumbs-down
disapproval 969.1
refusal 776.1
thumbs-up 521.2
thumb through
browse 564.13
examine cursorily 485.25

thump
n. faint sound 452.3
v. hit 283.4
make staccato sounds 455.4
music 462.45
pound 283.14
punish 1010.14
thud 452.15

thumper 195.11

thumping
n. staccato sound 455.1
adj. huge 195.21
remarkable 34.11
staccato 455.7

thunder
n. gods 456.5
noise 453.3
rainstorm 394.3
reverberation 454.2
rumbling 456.5
v. boom 456.9
din 453.6
proclaim 559.13
utter 594.26

thunderbolt
lightning 335.17
speed 269.6
surprise 540.2

thundercloud
cloud 404.1
omen 544.6
warning sign 703.3

thunderous
loud 453.10
rumbling 456.12

thundering
n. reverberation 454.2
rumbling 456.5
adj. huge 195.21
intense 159.20
reverberating 454.11
rumbling 456.12

thunderstorm
rainstorm 394.3
storm 162.4
thunder 456.5

thunderstruck 920.9

thus
for instance 505.24
hence 155.7
in this way 657.11
similarly 20.18
so 8.10
thus far so far 235.16
to a degree 35.10
until now 120.4

thwack
n. explosive noise 456.1
v. hit 283.4
make explosive noise 456.6

thwart
v. defeat 727.11
disappoint 541.2
frustrate 730.15
neutralize 178.7
adj. across 221.9
deviate 219.19
adv. crosswise 221.13

thwarted 541.5

thwarting
circumvention 735.5
frustration 730.3
neutralization 178.2

thyroidal 312.8

tiara
clerical insignia 569.4
jewel 901.6
royal insignia 569.3

tic
emotional symptom 690.23
nervousness 859.1
obsession 473.13
twitch 324.3

tick
n. animal 414.41
bug 414.36
clicking 455.2
faint sound 452.3
financial credit 839.1
instant 113.3
mark 568.5
v. click 455.5
faint sound 452.15
mark 568.19
operate 164.7
pulsate 323.12

ticked off 152.26

ticker clock 114.6
heart 225.4
stock exchange 833.7
telegraphy 560.2,23

ticker tape
record 570.10
stock exchange 833.7
tape 206.4

ticket
n. ballot 744.19
certificate 570.6
dismissal 310.5
label 568.13
permission 777.1
token 835.12
v. label 568.20

ticking
n. clicking 455.2
adj. staccato 455.7

tickle
n. sensation 426.2
v. amuse 878.23
attract 650.5
delight 865.8
incite 648.17
interest 530.12
tap 283.15
thrill 857.14
titillate 426.6

tickled amused 878.28
interested 530.16
pleased 865.12

tickler 537.6

tickling
n. sensation 426.2
adj. alluring 650.7
interesting 530.19
titillative 426.9

ticklish difficult 731.16
irascible 951.20
precarious 697.12
sensitive 422.14
titillative 426.9
unreliable 514.19

ticklish spot 731.4

tick off
make angry 952.21
mark 568.19

ticktock
n. clicking 455.2
v. click 455.5
pulsate 323.12

tidal aquatic 275.58
flowing 395.24

tidal wave
election returns 744.21
oscillation 323.4

swell 395.14
upheaval 162.5
tidbit delicacy 308.8
scandalous rumor 558.8
tiddly dizzy 532.15
intoxicated 996.30
tide flow 395.4
ocean 397.1
tidal current 395.13
time 105.1
tide gate
floodgate 396.11
tideway 395.13
tidemark 490.7
tide over endure 110.6
keep safe 698.2
tidewater
n. shore 385.2
tide 395.13
adj. estuary 399.2
tidings 558.1
tidy
v. arrange 60.12
clean 681.18
adj. cleaned 681.26
large 195.16
tolerable 674.19
trim 59.8
tidy sum
large number 101.3
much 34.4
wealth 837.2
tie
n. equality 30.3
fidelity 974.7
harmonics 463.12
insignia 569.1
intermediary 237.4
joining 47.1
neckwear 231.64
relationship 9.1
security 772.1
simultaneity 118.2
v. bind 47.9
compel 756.4
equal 30.5
join 47.5
obligate 962.12
relate 9.6
restrain 760.10
secure 142.8
tied equal 30.7
fixed 142.16
joined 47.13
obliged 962.16
related 9.9
restrained 760.16
tied up busy 707.21
indebted 840.8
involved in 176.4
restrained 760.16
tie in cooperate 786.3
join 52.4
relate to 9.5
tie-in affiliation 786.2
joining 47.1
relationship 9.1
sale 829.1
tier layer 227.1
tie up anchor 275.15

arrive 300.8
bind 47.9
bundle 74.20
cooperate 786.3
monopolize 808.6
restrain 760.10
tie-up affiliation 786.2
combination 52.1
delay 132.2
splice 47.1
strike 789.7
tiff
n. anger 952.7
quarrel 795.5
v. quarrel 795.11
tiger animal 414.27,58
brave person 893.8
savage 943.5
stakes 515.5
violent person 162.9
tight
adj. close 266.12
coherent 50.11
concise 592.6
drunk 996.31
fastened 47.14
lengthened 202.9
meager 102.5
narrow 205.14
resistant 159.18
rigid 356.11
shipshape 277.20
stingy 852.9
tidy 59.8
adv. securely 47.19
tighten fasten 47.7
lengthen 202.7
reel in 287.9
restrain 760.9
squeeze 198.8
stiffen 356.9
tightening
n. deepening 38.2
squeezing 198.2
adj. increasing 38.8
tightfisted 852.9
tight-lipped 613.9
tight money 835.16
tightness
exclusiveness 77.3
meagerness 102.1
narrowness 205.1
stiffness 356.2
stinginess 852.3
tenacity 50.3
tight rein 757.3
tightrope walker
circus artist 612.3
gymnast 878.21
tights 231.9,56,61
tight spot
predicament 731.4
small place 196.3
tight squeeze
closeness 205.1
narrow escape 632.2
poverty 838.1
predicament 731.4
small place 196.3
tightwad 852.4
tigress
female animal 421.9

ill-humored woman 951.12
violent person 162.9
witch 943.7
tile
n. building material 378.2
ceramic ware 576.2
pavement 657.7
v. cover 228.23
tiling
building material 378.2
ceramic ware 576.2
flooring 228.9
till
n. booty 824.11
depository 836.12
v. cultivate 413.17
prep. until 105.15
tiller agriculturist 413.5
management 747.5
tilling 413.13
tilt
n. contest 796.3
inclination 219.2
v. charge 798.18
contend 796.14
contend with 796.18
incline 219.10
throw 285.11
tumble 316.8
tilt at windmills 669.8
tilting 219.15
timbal 465.19
timbale 308.40
timber beam 217.3
spar 277.13
tree 411.10
wood 378.3
woodland 411.11
timbered 411.37
timberland 411.11
timbre
manner of speaking 594.8
tonality 450.3
timbrel 465.19
Timbuktu 199.4
time
n. date 114.4
duration 105
generation 107.4
geological 107.10
leisure 710.1
music 463.24
opportunity 129.2
period 107.1
shift 108.3
tenure 108.4
term 107.3
time of day 114.2
turn 108.2
v. measure time 114.11
synchronize 118.3
Time 105.2
time and a half 818.5
time and motion study
efficiency engineering 747.7

time measurement 114.9
time bomb 801.14,30
timecard 114.9
time flies 105.17
time-honored
customary 642.15
traditional 123.12
venerable 964.12
time immemorial
n. antiquity 119.3
adv. for a long time 110.14
timekeeper
chronologist 114.10
chronometer 114.6
recorder 571.1
timekeeping
n. chronology 114.1
adj. chronologic(al) 114.15
time lag delay 132.2
period 107.1
timeless dateless 106.3
godlike 1013.20
old 123.10
perpetual 112.7
timelessness
datelessness 106
perpetuity 112.1
timeliness
expedience 670.1
seasonableness 129
timely expedient 670.5
opportune 129.9
time off
n. interim 109.1
vacation 711.3
v. take turns 108.5
time out
n. interim 109.1
respite 711.2
v. leave 301.14
record time 114.12
timepiece
chronometer 114.6
types of 114.17
timer
chronologist 114.10
chronometer 114.6
control mechanism 349.34
times, the affairs 151.4
the present 120.1
time-saving 851.6
timeserver
flatterer 907.3
selfish person 978.3
temporizer 628.4
traitor 619.10
time sheet 114.9
time signature 463.12
time study
efficiency engineering 747.7
time chart 114.9
timetable 114.9
timeworn aged 126.18
old 123.14
shabby 692.33
trite 883.9
time zone 114.3

timid cowardly 892.10
  fearful 891.31
  irresolute 627.11
  shy 908.12
timidity
  cowardice 892.1
  fearfulness 891.3
  shyness 908.4
timing adjustment 26.4
  chronology 114.1
  music 463.24
  skill 733.1
timorous
  cowardly 892.10
  fearful 891.31
  shy 908.12
timpani 465.19
tin
  v. package 236.9
  preserve 701.9
  adj. metal 383.17
  ungenuine 616.26
tincture
  n. admixture 44.7
  coloring matter 362.8
  heraldic insignia 569.2
  hue 362.1
  small amount 35.4
  v. color 362.13
  infuse 44.12
tinder 331.6
tin ear 448.3
tined 258.11
tinge
  n. admixture 44.7
  color 362.1
  implication 546.2
  small amount 35.4
  taste 427.3
  v. color 362.13
  influence 172.7
  infuse 44.12
  suffer pain 424.8
tinged 362.16
tingle
  n. pain 424.3
  ringing 454.3
  sensation 426
  thrill 857.2
  v. be excited 857.16
  prickle 426.5
  ring 454.8
  suffer pain 424.8
tingling
  n. pain 424.3
  ringing 454.3
  sensation 426.1
  thrill 857.2
  adj. excited 857.18
  prickly 426.8
  ringing 454.12
  sore 424.11
tinhorn
  n. gambler 515.17
  mediocrity 680.5
  adj. petty 673.17
tinker
  n. mender 694.10
  v. repair 694.14
  trifle 673.13
tinkering 673.8

tinker's damn, a 673.5
tinkle
  n. faint sound 452.3
  ringing 454.3
  v. faint sound 452.15
  ring 454.8
tinkling
  n. ringing 454.3
  adj. ringing 454.12
tinny
  adj. inferior 680.9
  sound 458.15
Tin Pan Alley 464.2
tinsel
  n. fake 616.13
  light 335.7
  adj. false 616.27
  tinselly 335.35
tint
  n. admixture 44.7
  color quality 362.6
  engraving 578.2
  shade 362.1
  v. color 362.13
  picture 574.20
tinted 362.16
tinting 362.11
tintinnabular 454.12
tintype
  n. photograph 577.4
  adj. photographic 577.17
tiny insignificant 35.6
  little 196.11
tip
  n. extra pay 841.6
  extremity 70.2
  gratuity 818.5
  inclination 219.2
  information 557.3
  piece of advice 754.2
  point 258.3
  summit 211.2
  surplus 663.5
  touch 283.6
  v. cap 228.21
  incline 219.10
  inform 557.11
  overturn 220.6
  sail 275.43
  top 211.9
  touch 283.15
tip off inform 557.11
  warn 703.5
tip-off clue 568.9
  information 557.3
  warning 703.1
tipped inclining 219.15
  topped 211.12
tipping 219.15
tipple drink 307.27
tipster n. gambler 515.17
  informant 557.5
  predictor 543.5
tipsy inclining 219.15

  intoxicated 996.30
tip the scales 352.10
tiptoe
  v. be cautious 895.5
  creep 273.25
  lurk 615.9
  adj. creeping 273.38
  adv. on tiptoe 207.26
tip-top
  n. summit 211.2
  superlative 36.13
  adj. first-rate 674.15
  uppermost 211.10
tirade berating 969.7
  lament 875.3
  outpour 593.1
  speech 599.2
tire
  n. kinds of 253.4
  v. be tedious 884.5
  cause unpleasantness 864.16
  get tired 717.5
  make tired 717.4
tired bored 884.10
  clothed 231.44
  exhausted 717.8
  fatigued 717.6
tired of bored 884.10
  satiated 664.6
  worn-out 692.38
tireless
  industrious 707.22
  persevering 625.7
tiresome
  annoying 864.22
  boring 884.9
  fatiguing 717.11
  prosaic 610.5
tiring boring 884.9
  fatiguing 717.11
tisane 687.4
tissue fabric 378.5
  flesh 406.1
  network 221.3
  structure 245.1
  weaving 222.1
tit little thing 196.4
  teat 256.6
tit for tat
  interaction 13.3
  offset 33.2
  reciprocity 150.1
  retaliation 955.3
  substitution 149.1
tithe
  n. donation 818.6
  tax 846.10
  tenth 99.14
  v. charge 846.14

titan 195.13
Titan strong man 159.6
  sun god 375.14
Titania 1014.18
titanic great 34.7
  huge 195.20

titillate amuse 878.23
  attract 650.5
  delight 865.8
  interest 530.12
  thrill 857.14
  tickle 426.6
titillating
  alluring 650.7
  amusing 878.29
  interesting 530.19
titivate dress up 231.41
  fancy 616.16
  ornament 901.8

title
  n. book part 605.12
  caption 484.2
  class 61.2
  estate 810.4
  honorific 917
  name 583.3
  possession 808.1
  privilege 958.3
  publication 605.1
  v. caption 484.3
  name 583.11
titled named 583.14
  noble 918.10
titleholder 809.2
title page book 605.12
  caption 484.4
  label 568.13
titrate 48.6
titration 48.1
titter
  n. laughter 876.4
  v. laugh 876.8
tittle mark 568.5
  minute thing 196.7
  punctuation 586.15
  small amount 35.2
tittle-tattle
  n. gossip 558.7
  jabber 596.3
  small talk 597.5
  v. chat 597.10
  gossip 558.12
  jabber 596.5
titular honorific 917.7
  nominal 583.15
tizzy confusion 532.3
  dither 857.5
TLC carefulness 533.1
  support 785.3
TM 600.5
T-man 781.10
TNT 801.9
to as far as 199.20
  intending 653.12
  into 302.14
  toward 290.28
  until 105.15
toad
  amphibian 414.32,62
  sycophant 907.3
to a degree
  relatively 9.12
  somewhat 29.7
  to a certain extent 35.10
toadstool 411.4,45
toady
  n. sycophant 907.3

toadying
v. be servile 907.6

toadying
n. obsequiousness 907.2
adj. obsequious 907.13

to a fault 663.23

to and fro
alternately 137.11
back and forth 323.21
changeably 141.8
reciprocally 13.16

to-and-fro
n. alternation 323.5
adj. alternate 323.19

toast
n. bread 308.28
celebration 877.1
drinking 996.37
fine lady 903.10
pledge 996.9
v. be hot 328.22
cook 330.4
drink 307.27
drink to 996.28
adj. brown 367.3

toastmaster 878.22

toasty 328.24

to a T exactly 516.22
to completion 722.14
to perfection 677.11

tobacco
n. smoke 434
adj. tobaccoy 434.15

tobacconist
merchant 830.3
snuffman 434.12
store 832.4

to be expected
as expected 539.14
imminently 152.4
normally 84.9

to blame
censurable 969.26
guilty 983.3
responsible 962.17

tobogganing 273.8

to come
approaching 296.4
future 121.8
imminent 152.3
scheduled 641.6

tocsin 704.1

TO'd 952.26

to date 120.4

today
n. the present 120.1
adv. now 120.3

toddle
n. gait 273.14
v. go slow 270.6
walk 273.27

toddle along
depart 301.6
go slow 270.6

toddler 125.7

toddling
n. walking 273.10
adj. slow 270.10

to-do agitation 324.1
bustle 707.4
commotion 62.4
excitement 857.3

toe bottom 212.2
foot 212.5

toehold grip 813.2
purchase 287.2
support 216.5
wrestling hold 813.3

toe the mark
conform 82.4
obey 766.2

to extremes
in excess 663.23
intemperately 993.10

toft enclosure 236.3,12
farm 413.8
home 191.4
ranch 191.7
real estate 810.7

tog 231.38

together
adj. composed 858.13
in accord 794.3
sane 472.4
adv. collectively 73.11
concurrently 177.5
continuously 71.10
cooperatively 786.6
jointly 47.18
simultaneously 118.6
unanimously 521.17

together with
among 44.18
in addition to 40.12
in agreement with 26.12
in association with 73.12

toggle
n. joint 47.4,20
v. fasten 47.8

togs clothing 231.1
garment 231.3

toil
n. snare 618.12
work 716.4
v. drudge 716.14
entrap 730.11
work 656.12

toiler
common person 919.1
working person 718.2

toilet latrine 311.10
rest room 192.26
stool 311.11

toiletries 831.6

toilette 231.1

toilet water 436.3

toiling 716.17

toilsome
difficult 731.16
fatiguing 717.11
laborious 716.18

token
n. characteristic 80.4
currency 835.12
evidence 505.1
label 568.13
memento 537.7
omen 544.3
password 568.12
record 570.1
substitute 149.2
symbol 568.3
unit of meaning 545.6
v. augur 544.12
show 555.5
adj. cheap 849.7
substitute 149.8

tokenism 616.6

token payment 772.2

tolerable
adequate 674.19
bearable 868.13
mediocre 680.7

tolerably fairly 674.23
mediocrely 680.11
satisfactorily 868.15
to a degree 35.10

tolerance
addiction 642.9
broad-mindedness 526.4
forgiveness 947.1
inaccuracy 518.2
inclusion 76.1
latitude 762.4
leniency 759.1
liberalism 762.10
patience 861.1
sufferance 777.2

tolerant
broad-minded 526.11
considerate 938.16
forgiving 947.6
lenient 759.7
liberal 762.24
patient 861.9
permissive 777.14

tolerate
be broad-minded 526.7
be lenient 759.5
be patient 861.5
permit 777.10

toll
n. fee 846.7
ringing 454.3
tax 846.10
v. ring 454.8

tollbooth hut 191.10
prison 761.8

tollgate 302.6

tolling
n. death bell 410.6
ringing 454.3
adj. ringing 454.12

tom cat 414.26
male cat 420.8
male turkey 420.8
turkey 414.34

tomato food 308.35,50
girl 125.6
woman 421.6

tomb memorial 570.12
sepulcher 410.16

tomblike 410.22

tomboy girl 125.6
mannish female 420.9

tomboyish 420.13

tombstone 570.12

tomcat cat 414.26
male animal 420.8

Tom, Dick, and Harry
common man 79.3
nobodies 673.7
the people 919.2

tome 605.1

tomfool 47.11

tomfoolery 881.5

Tommy 800.7

tomorrow
n. the future 121.1
adv. in the future 121.9

Tom Thumb 196.6

tomtit 196.4

tom-tom drum 465.19
staccato sound 455.1

tonal harmonics 463.27
phonetic 594.31
sounding 450.15

tonality
harmonics 463.4
key 463.15
lighting 335.19
melody 462.2
sound frequency 463.3
timbre 450.3

tone
n. artistry 574.10
behavior 737.1
color quality 362.6
harmonics 463.4
interval 463.20
intonation 594.7
manner of speaking 594.8
melody 462.2
milieu 233.3
mode 7.4
mood 525.4
muscle 159.2
nature 5.3
note 463.14
pitch 450.2
resilience 358.1
shade 362.1
story element 608.9
trend 174.2
way 657.1
v. color 362.13
influence 172.7

tone-deaf 449.6

tone down
decolor 363.5
dull 337.10
moderate 163.6
muffle 451.9
put in tune 462.37
soften 357.6

toneless colorless 363.7
droning 450.15

tone of voice 594.8

tone up furbish 691.11
put in tune 462.37

tongue
n. bell 454.4
language 580.1
meat 308.20
organ of taste 427.5
palate 427.1

point of land 256.8
shaft 217.1
utterance 594.3
vocal organ 594.19
v. lick 425.9
play music 462.43

tongue in cheek
n. insincerity 616.5
adj. insincere 616.32

tongue-lash 969.20
tongue-lashing 969.7
tonguelike 427.10
tongue-tied
mute 451.12
taciturn 613.9

tonic
n. drink 308.48
energizer 161.5
harmonics 463.15
medicine 687.8
refresher 695.1
adj. energizing 161.14
harmonics 463.27
healthful 683.5
phonetic 594.31
refreshing 695.3
stimulating 687.44

tonight 120.3
tonnage capacity 195.2
charge 846.8
ships 277.10
weight 352.1
tons 34.3

tonsilitis
inflammation 686.9
respiratory disease 686.14
tonsillectomy 689.23
tonsure 232.4
tontine 515.11
tonus 358.1
tony 904.18
too additionally 40.11
excessively 663.22
too bad
disgraceful 915.11
wretched 675.9

tool
n. agent 781.3
edge 348.13
gripping 813.12
instrument 348
means 658.3
sycophant 907.3
types of 348.12
v. engrave 578.10
mechanize 348.10
tooled 578.12
tooling engraving 578.2
instrumentation 348.8
too little 662.9
too much
n. excess 663.1
intemperance 993.1
adj. excessive 663.16
extreme 34.13
insufferable 864.25
intemperate 993.7
adv. excessively 663.22

too much for
beyond one 158.20
impracticable 510.8
to order 752.16
too soon
premature 131.8,13
untimely 130.7
toot
n. loud sound 453.4
revel 878.6
spree 996.5
v. blare 453.9
play music 462.43

tooth
n. anatomy 258.5
v. give texture 351.4
toothache 424.5
notch 262.4
tooth and nail
laboriously 716.19
resolutely 624.17
savagely 162.26
toothed dental 258.16
grasping 813.9
notched 262.5
toothless 259.4
pointed 258.11
toothlike 258.16
toothpaste
cleaning agent 681.17
dentifrice 687.22
toothsome
desirable 634.30
tasty 428.8
tootle
n. loud sound 453.4
v. blare 453.9
play music 462.43
too-too 663.22
tootsy 212.5

top
n. completion 56.5
cover 228.5
culmination 677.3
exterior 224.2
plaything 878.16
roof 228.6
rotator 322.4,17
summit 211.2
tent 228.8
upper side 211
v. be high 207.16
cap 211.9
cover 228.21
excel 36.6
adj. expensive 848.11
highest 211.10
superlative 36.13
top, the
important persons 672.8
the rulers 749.15
top brass
directorate 748.11
important persons 672.8
officer 749.18
the rulers 749.15

topcoat 231.13
top dog chief 749.3
paramount 672.10
superior 36.4
victor 726.2
top-drawer 674.15

top off
complete 56.6
crest 211.9
fill 56.7
fuel 331.8
perfect 722.6
provision 659.9

tope
n. grove 411.12
memorial 570.12
shrine 1042.4
tomb 410.16
tower 207.11
v. drink 996.23
topflight chief 36.14
first-rate 674.15
top-heavy
corpulent 195.18
unbalanced 31.5
topic question 485.10
story element 608.9
subject 484
topical local 180.9
present 120.2
thematic 484.4
to pieces 49.29
topknot feather 230.16
hair 230.7
top part 211.4

topless bare 232.16
headless 211.13
high 207.19
unclad 232.13
toplofty
contemptuous 966.8
high 207.19
top-notch
first-rate 674.15
superlative 36.13
topmost highest 211.10
most important 672.23
superlative 36.13
topographer 654.4
topography
location 184.7
map 654.4
mensuration 490.9
topographic(al)
locational 184.18
measuring 490.13
regional 180.8
topped 211.12
topping
n. architectural 211.17
icing 211.3
adj. crowning 211.11
first-rate 674.15
high 207.19
superior 36.12
topping-off
completion 56.4
rounding-out 722.2
topple
be destroyed 693.22
collapse 692.27
knock down 318.5
overturn 220.6
tumble 316.8
top priority 64.1
tops, the 674.8
top secret 614.11
top sergeant 749.19
top shape 685.2
topside
n. top 211.1
adv. on board 275.62
on top 211.15
topsoil land 385.1
layer 227.1

topsy-turvy
adj. confused 62.16
reversed 220.7
adv. contrarily 15.9
inversely 220.8
Torah
Old Testament 1021.3
ritualistic book 1040.12

tor mountain 207.7
peak 207.8
torch
n. blowtorch 329.14
flare 336.3,8
lighter 331.4
light source 336.1
v. fish 655.10
set fire to 329.22
torchbearer 748.6
torch singer 464.13
torch song 462.13
toreador 800.4
torment
n. agony 864.4
bane 676.1
pain 424.6
pest 866.10
punishment 1010.2
torture 866.7
worry 890.2
v. annoy 866.13
cause unpleasantness 864.12
make anxious 890.4
make grieve 872.19
pain 424.7
persecute 667.6
torture 866.18
trouble 731.12
work evil 675.6
tormented
pained 424.9
plagued 866.24
worried 890.7
tormenting
annoying 864.22
painful 424.10
troublesome 890.9
unpleasant 864.23
tormentor
scenery 611.25
torment pest 866.10
torn
affected 855.25
alienated 929.11
damaged 692.29
severed 49.23

tornado
shabby 692.34
tornado
emotional outburst 857.8
storm 162.4
whirlwind 403.14
torpedo
n. evildoer 943.4
killer 409.11
missile 281.3
types of 281.16
weapon 801.12
v. attack 798.22
ruin 693.11
shoot 285.13
torpid apathetic 856.11
changeless 140.7
inert 268.14
languid 708.19
torpor apathy 856.4
immobility 140.1
inertia 268.4
languor 708.6
vegetation 1.6
torque aviation 278.31
necklace 901.6
torrent eruption 162.6
speed 269.6
violent flow 395.5
torso 376.3
tort crime 999.4
misdeed 982.2
Torte 308.41
tortilla 308.29
tortoise
reptile 414.30,60
slow person 270.5
tortoise shell 374.6
tortoise-shell 374.10
tortuous curved 252.7
distorted 249.10
grandiloquent 601.8
winding 254.6
torture
n. agony 864.4
instruments of 1011.4
pain 424.6
punishment 1010.2
v. cause unpleasant-
ness 864.12
distort 249.6
hurt 424.7
misinterpret 553.2
punish 1010.18
torment 866.18
work evil 675.6
tortured
affected 855.25
distorted 249.11
harrowed 866.25
pained 424.9
torturing
distortion 249.2
misinterpretation 553.1
torturous
painful 424.10
unpleasant 864.23
Tory partisan 744.27
rightist 745.9
to smithereens 49.29
to spare remaining 43.7
superfluous 663.17
unused 668.12
toss
n. even chance 156.7
flounder 324.8
gamble 515.2
throw 285.4
v. be excited 857.16
billow 395.22
flounder 324.15
gamble 515.18
hurl at 798.28
oscillate 323.10
put violently 184.12
sail 275.55
search 485.32
throw 285.11
toss and turn
be excited 857.16
stay awake 713.3
tumble 324.15
toss off
do carelessly 534.9
drink 996.23
eating 307.27
improvise 630.8
toss out discard 310.13
do carelessly 534.9
improvise 630.8
toss-up
an uncertainty 514.8
even chance 156.7
gamble 515.2
tot child 125.3
drink 307.4
total
n. addition 40.2
score 86.5
sum 54.2
v. add 40.6
amount to 54.8
calculate 87.12
demolish 693.17
adj. complete 56.9
comprehensive 76.7
cumulative 74.23
great 34.6
outright 34.12
sound 677.7
thorough 56.10
universal 79.14
unqualified 508.2
whole 54.9
totalitarian
authoritative 739.15
governmental 741.17
totality
completeness 56.1
everyone 79.4
fullness 54.5
universe 375.1
whole 54.1
total loss
deprivation 812.1
destruction 693.4
failure 725.2
totally
completely 56.14
extremely 34.22
perfectly 677.10
solely 89.14
wholly 54.13
total recall 537.3
tote
n. totalizer 515.13
v. add 40.6
transport 271.11
totem
community 788.2
guardian angel 1014.22
race 11.4
symbol 568.3
tote up add 40.6
calculate 87.12
total 54.8
to the fore 240.12
to the good
gainfully 811.16
helpfully 785.24
to one's credit 839.9
to the hilt
completely 56.14
throughout 56.17
to the letter 516.20
to the point apt 26.10
concise 592.6
in plain words 591.4
relevant 9.11
to the tune of
as much as 28.7
at a price 846.19
totter
n. flounder 324.8
gait 273.14
v. age 126.10
be weak 160.8
collapse 692.27
flounder 324.15
fluctuate 141.5
go slow 270.6
tumble 316.8
vacillate 627.8
walk 273.27
tottering
n. fluctuation 141.3
oscillation 323.5
walking 273.10
adj. aged 126.18
on the decline 692.47
slow 270.10
tumbledown 316.11
unsteady 160.16
tottery aged 126.18
dilapidated 692.35
unsafe 697.11
unsteady 160.16
touch
n. admixture 44.7
communication 554.1
contact 200.5
feel 425
implication 546.2
knack 733.6
motif 901.7
music 462.31
sense 422.5
signal 568.15
small amount 35.4
tap 283.6
v. affect 855.16
beg 774.15
borrow 821.3
contact 200.10
equal 30.5
excite pity 944.5
feel 425.6
relate to 9.5
sense 422.8
signal 568.22
tap 283.15
touch and go
an uncertainty 514.8
even chance 156.7
gamble 515.2
touch-and-go
ticklish 697.12
uncertain 514.15
touch a nerve 422.10
touch bottom
be despondent 872.16
decline 692.20
fall on evil days 729.11
touchdown
landing 278.18
score 724.4
touched
affected 855.25
insane 473.25
penitent 873.9
touching
n. borrowing 821.1
contact 200.5
feeling 425.2
adj. affecting 855.24
in contact 200.17
pitiful 944.8
poignant 864.20
prep. in relation to 9.13
touch off
explode 162.13
ignite 329.22
kindle 648.18
touchstone
measure 490.2
test 489.2
touch up 691.11
touch upon
call attention to 530.10
discourse upon 606.5
examine cursorily 485.25
graze 425.7
neglect 534.8
relate to 9.5
scratch the surface 210.4
touchy
excitable 857.26

irascible 951.20
precarious 697.12
sensitive 422.14
tough
n. combatant 800.1
evildoer 943.4
strong man 159.6
violent person 162.9
549.14
adj. bold 893.18
difficult 731.16
enduring 110.10
excellent 674.13
hard 356.10
hard to understand
549.14
laborious 716.18
obdurate 626.10
persistent 50.12
resistant 359.4
strict 757.6
substantial 3.7
violent 162.15
viscous 389.12
toughen harden 356.7
make tough 359.3
strengthen 159.11
toughened
hardened 356.13
tempered 359.6
tough guy
strong man 159.6
violent person 162.9
tough it out 625.4
tough job 731.2
tough luck 729.5
tough-minded 504.5
toughness
courage 893.5
difficulty 731.1
hardness 356.1
pluck 624.3
resistance 359
strength 159.1
strictness 757.1
substantiality 3.1
tenacity 50.3
unyieldingness 626.2
viscosity 389.2
tough proposition
difficult thing 731.2
puzzle 549.8
toupee 230.14
tour
n. circuit 321.2
journey 273.5
playing engagement
611.12
route 657.2
shift 108.3
term 108.4
tower 207.11
v. travel 273.20
tour de force act 705.3
masterpiece 733.10
touring 273.35
tourism 273.1
tourist sight-seer 442.3
traveler 274.1
touristy 273.35
tournament
contest 796.3
games 878.10

tourney
n. contest 796.3
games 878.10
v. contend 796.14
tourniquet 687.33
tour of duty 108.3
tousle 63.2
tousled 62.14
tout
n. commender 968.8
gambler 515.17
informant 557.5
predictor 543.5
solicitor 830.7
v. commend 968.11
exaggerate 617.3
tout de suite 269.23
touted 617.4
tow 286.4
towage fee 846.7
pulling 286.1
toward facing 239.7
in the direction of
290.28
towel 393.6
tower
n. building 245.2
castle 191.8
landmark 568.10
observation post
439.8
protector 699.5
stability 142.6
stronghold 799.6
turret 207.11
v. ascend 315.8
be high 207.15
exceed 34.5
grow 197.7
tower above
be high 207.16
exceed 34.5
excel 36.6
towering eminent 34.9
high 207.19
huge 195.20
towhead 362.9
towheaded 364.9
to wit
by interpretation
552.18
namely 80.18
town

town
n. city 183
district 180.5
adj. urban 183.10
town crier 561.3
townee 190.6
town hall
city hall 183.5
courthouse 1001.9
town meeting
discussion 597.7
legislature 742.1
participation 815.2
township city 183.1
district 180.5
townspeople 190.6
towpath 657.3
toxemia 686.30
toxic(al)
harmful 675.12

poisonous 684.7
toxicity
harmfulness 675.5
poisonousness 684.3
toxicology 676.3
toxin bane 675.3
poison 676.3
toxoid 687.28
toy
n. caprice 629.1
dupe 620.1
instrument 658.3
laughingstock 967.7
ornament 901.4
plaything 878.16
trifle 673.5
v. make love 932.13
trifle 673.13
adj. miniature 196.12
toy with
consider 478.12
half-know 477.11
trifle 673.13
trace
n. admixture 44.7
clue 568.3
image 572.3
odor 435.1
radar signal 346.11
record 570.1
remainder 43.1
small amount 35.4
track 568.8
v. copy 24.8
discover 488.2
mark 568.19
outline 654.12
picture 574.20
represent 572.6
stalk 485.34
write 602.19
traceable 155.6
tracer atomics 326.4
bullet 801.13
radioactive substance
327.5
radiotherapeutic sub-
stance 689.9
tracery curve 252.2
network 221.3

trachea 396.16
tracheal 396.20
trachoma
blindness 441.1
eye disease 686.13
tracing image 572.3
picture 574.14
reproduction 24.2
transfer 24.4
track
n. account of 87.6
blemish 679.1
direction 290.1
effect 154.4
hint 557.4
path 657.3
racecourse 878.12
racing 796.11
railway 657.8
route 657.2
routine 642.6
school grade 566.11

spoor 568.8
sports 878.8
water travel 275.7
v. come after 117.3
hunt 655.9
trace 485.34
traverse 273.19
track down
discover 488.2
trace 485.34
tracking pursuit 655.1
radar operation 346.8
tracking station
radar station 346.6
rocketry 281.7
space station 282.5
track meet 878.10
tract booklet 605.9
field 413.9
housing 188.3
land 180.4
space 179.1
treatise 606.1
tractability
pliancy 357.2
submissiveness 765.3
willingness 622.1
tractable
conformable 82.5
docile 765.13
pliant 357.9
wieldy 732.14
willing 622.5
traction
attraction 288.1
leverage 287.2
pulling 286.1
tractor aircraft 280.2
types of 272.27
vehicle 272.17,26
tractor trailer 272.11
trade
n. bargain 827.5
business 827.2
clientele 828.3
commerce 827.1
exchange 827.6
patronage 827.6
vocation 656.6
v. deal with 827.16
do business 827.14
interchange 150.4
transfer property
817.3
adj. commercial
827.21
trade book book 605.1
edition 605.2
trade center 226.7
trade in deal in 827.15
do business 827.14
trade-in 827.5
trademark
attribution 155.2
label 568.13
mannerism 903.2
restriction 234.3
trade name 665.15
trader 830.2
trade route 657.2
trade school 567.8
tradespeople 830.11

trade union 789.1
trade unionist 789.3
trade wind 403.10
trading
n. business 827.2
exchange 150.2
property transfer 817.1
adj. commercial 827.21
trading post 832.1
tradition custom 123.2
religion 1020.1
superstition 502.3
usage 642.1
traditional
conventional 645.5
customary 642.15
historical 608.18
old 123.12
orthodox 1024.7
traditionalism
conformity 82.1
custom 123.2
orthodoxy 1024.1
traditionalist 123.8
traditionally
conformably 82.7
conventionally 645.6
traduce 971.11
traffic
n. commerce 827.1
communication 554.1
v. deal in 827.15
trade 827.14
trafficking 827.2
traffic light light 336.4
signal 568.15
traffic with
communicate 554.6
trade with 827.16
tragedian actor 612.8
dramatist 611.27
tragedy
misfortune 729.2
tragic drama 611.5
tragic disastrous 729.15
horrid 864.19
theatrical 611.39
tragicomedy 611.6
trail
n. effect 154.4
odor 435.1
path 657.3
track 568.8
wake 67.2
v. be behind 241.8
dawdle 270.8
ensue 117.3
follow 293.3
hang 215.6
hunt 655.9
linger behind 293.4
pull 286.4
trace 485.34
trail bike 272.8
trailblazer
precursor 66.1
preparer 720.5
traveler 274.1

trailer
mobile home 191.18
motion picture 611.16
sequel 67.2
vehicle 272.18
trailing
n. following 293.1
pursuit 655.1
surveillance 485.9
adj. following 293.5
train
n. attendance 73.6
military unit 800.19
procession 71.3
row 71.2
vehicle 272.13
wake 67.2
v. accustom 642.11
direct 290.6
drive animals 416.7
pull 286.4
study 564.11
teach 562.14
trainable
directable 290.14
teachable 564.18
trained
accomplished 733.24
accustomed 642.17
informed 475.18
trainee beginner 68.2
recruit 800.17
student 566.1
trainer
aircraft 280.10,15
animal handler 416.2
preparer 720.5
teacher 565.7
training
habituation 642.8
preparation 720.1
teaching 562.3
training school
prison 761.8
reform school 567.14
trainload 194.2
trainman 274.13
train of thought 478.4
traipse
n. walk 273.12
v. go slow 270.6
walk 273.26
wander 273.22
way of walking 273.27
trait characteristic 80.4
culture 642.3
looks 446.4
sign 568.2
traitor apostate 145.8
criminal 986.10
dishonest person 975.10
rebel 767.5
treasonist 619.10
turncoat 628.5
traitorous
apostate 145.20
betraying 975.22
rebellious 767.11
turncoat 628.11

trajectile 285.6
trajectory
astronomy 375.16
rocketry 281.9
route 657.2
tram railway 657.8
streetcar 272.15
trammel
n. curb 730.7
restraint 760.4
v. hamper 730.11
restrain 760.10
tramp
n. bad person 986.2
beggar 774.8
bum 708.9
odd person 85.4
vagabond 274.3
walk 273.12
v. march 273.29
plod 270.7
wander 273.22
tramping 273.10
trample run over 313.7
stamp 283.19
trampled 764.16
trampoline
elastic object 358.3
exercise device 716.7
trance
abstractedness 532.2
ecstasy 1036.3
hypnosis 712.7
stupor 712.6
types of 690.26
tranquil calm 268.12
composed 858.12
moderate 163.13
pacific 803.9
thoughtfree 480.4
tranquilize calm 163.7
order 59.4
pacify 804.7
quiet 268.8
tranquilizer
depressant 423.3
pacifier 163.3
psychoactive drug 687.13
sedative 687.12
types of 687.55
tranquilizing
calming 163.15
sedative 687.45
tranquillity
composure 858.2
moderation 163.1
order 59.1
peace 803.2
quiescence 268.1
rest 711.1
silence 451.1
thoughtlessness 480.1
transact
complete 771.10
perform 705.8
transaction act 705.3
affair 151.3
business 827.4
compact 771.1
completion 771.5
performance 705.2

transactional analysis 690.5
transanimation 139.2
transceiver 344.4,29
transcend exceed 663.9
excel 36.6
loom 34.5
transcendent
divine 1013.19
obscure 549.15
superior 36.12
transcendental
extraterrestrial 375.26
heavenly 1018.13
numerical 86.8
recondite 549.16
superior 36.12
supernatural 85.15
visionary 535.24
transcendentalism
occultism 1034.2
supernaturalism 85.7
transcendentalist
n. occultist 1034.11
adj. philosophy 500.9
transcendental meditation 690.5
transcending 36.12
transcribe copy 24.8
interpret 552.12
letter 581.6
music 462.47
write 602.19
transcribed 581.8
transcriber 602.13
transcript copy 24.4
music 462.28
written matter 602.10
transcription copy 24.4
harmonization 463.2
interpretation 552.3
lettering 581.5
music 462.28
reproduction 24.2
sound recording 450.12
written matter 602.10
transducer 145.10
transect 92.4
transept
church part 1042.9
crosspiece 221.5
transfer
n. copy 24.4
impartation 554.2
property transfer 817
transference 271.1
v. commission 780.9
communicate 554.7
deliver 818.13
transfer property 817.3
transmit 271.9
transferable
assignable 817.5
communicable 554.11
conveyable 271.17
transference
impartation 554.2
mental association 690.40

transfiguration 139.2
transfigure
make better 691.9
transform 139.7
transfix
puncture 265.16
stab 798.25
stabilize 142.7
transform change 139.7
convert 145.11
make better 691.9
transformable 145.18
transformation
change 139.2
conversion 145.1
mathematics 87.4
reform 691.5
scenery 611.25
transformed
changed 139.9
converted 145.19
improved 691.13
transformer
converter 145.10
modifier 139.4
transfuse imbue 44.12
pervade 186.7
transfer 271.9
treat 689.33
transfusion
blood transfusion
689.20
permeation 186.3
transference 271.1
transgress
break the law 999.5
disobey 767.6
not observe 769.4
overstep 313.9
sin 982.5
transgression
disobedience 767.1
lawbreaking 999.3
misdeed 982.2
overstepping 313.3
violation 769.2
transgressive 767.8
transgressor
bad person 986.9
evildoer 943.1
transience
changeableness 141.1
death rate 408.13
impermanence 111
shortness 203.1
transient
n. lodger 190.8
passerby 111.4
traveler 274.1
adj. changeable 141.6
emanent 303.18
impermanent 111.7
mortal 408.34
short 203.8
vanishing 447.3
wandering 273.36
transistor 343.13
transit
n. conversion 145.1

passage 271
property transfer
817.1
transition 139.2
travel 273.1
v. traverse 273.19
transition change 139.1
conversion 145.1
transference 271.1
transitional
convertible 145.18
moving 267.7
transitive
n. verb 586.4
adj. grammatical
586.17
transitory
changeable 141.6
impermanent 111.7
transient 111.7
translatable 552.17
translate
interpret 552.12
transfer 271.9
transform 139.7
translation
interpretation 552.3
removal to heaven
1018.12
transference 271.1
transformation 139.2
translator 552.7
transliterate
interpret 552.12
letter 581.6
transliteration
interpretation 552.3
lettering 581.5
translucence
lightness 335.3
semitransparency
340.2
translucent
intelligible 548.10
lucid 335.31
semitransparent
340.5
translucent things 339.6
transmigrate
embody 376.8
migrate 273.21
transmigration
embodiment 376.7
migration 273.4
transmission
gear 348.6,27
impartation 554.2
information 557.1
property transfer
817.1
transference 271.1
transmit
bequeath 818.18
broadcast 344.25
communicate 554.7
send 271.14
transfer 271.9

instrument 251.4
transference 271.1
travel 273.1
transition change 139.1
conversion 145.1
transference 271.1
transitional
convertible 145.18
moving 267.7
transmigratory 273.36
transmissible 552.17
transmission
gear 348.6,27
impartation 554.2
information 557.1
property transfer
817.1
transference 271.1
transmit
bequeath 818.18
broadcast 344.25
communicate 554.7
send 271.14
transfer 271.9

transfer property
817.3
use radar 346.15
transmittable
communicable
554.11
transferable 271.17
transmittal
impartation 554.2
property transfer
817.1
transference 271.1
transmute 139.7
transmuted 139.9
transom

transfer property
817.3
use radar 346.15
transmittable
communicable
554.11
transferable 271.17
transmittal
impartation 554.2
property transfer
817.1
transference 271.1
transmute 139.7
transmuted 139.9
transom

transpicuous
intelligible 548.10
transparent 339.4
transpire
be revealed 556.8
exude 303.15
occur 151.5
transplant
n. insertion 304.1
surgical operation
689.22
v. replant 413.18
transfer 271.9
transport
n. conveyance 271.3
excitement 857.7
happiness 865.2
v. convey 271.11
delight 865.8
exile 310.17
fascinate 650.6
transportable 271.17
transportation
conveyance 271.3
extradition 310.4
transported
abstracted 532.11
excited 857.23
overjoyed 865.14
transporter 271.5

transpose counter 15.5
interchange 150.4
invert 220.5
music 462.47
transfer 271.9
transposed
interchanged 150.5
reversed 220.7
transposition
interchange 150.1
inversion 220.1
transference 271.1
transformation 139.2
transsexual 419.19
transshipment 271.3
transude excrete 311.12
exude 303.15
transverse
n. crosspiece 221.5
diagonal 219.7
v. cross 221.6
adj. crosswise 221.9
diagonal 219.19
adv. crosswise 221.13
transvestite
n. sex deviant 419.17
adj. bisexual 419.32
trap
n. concealment 615.3
entrance 302.6
lure 650.2
mouth 265.5
snare 618.11
v. catch 822.17
ensnare 618.18
trap door 302.6
trapeze 716.7
trapeze artist 612.3
trapezoid(al) 251.9
trapper 655.5
trappings
belongings 810.2
harness 659.5
ornamentation 901.3
wardrobe 231.2
trapshooting 285.3
trash
abandoned thing
633.4
nonsense 547.2
rabble 919.5
rubbish 669.5
trifles 673.4
trashy
nonsensical 547.7
paltry 673.18
worthless 669.11
trattoria 307.15
trauma
impairment 692.8
psychological stress
690.21
shock 686.24
traumatic
affect emotionally
855.17
injure 692.15
traumatize
traumatize 855.17
travail
n. birth 167.7
work 716.4
v. drudge 716.14
give birth 167.15

travel
n. journeying 273
journeys 273.2
pace 267.4
progression 294.1
transference 271.1
v. journey 273.17
move 267.5
progress 294.2
traverse 273.19
traveled 273.39
traveler goer 274
traveling salesman 830.5
traveler's check 835.11
traveling
n. journeying 273.1
adj. journeying 273.35
moving 267.7
traveling salesman 830.5
travelogue 599.3
travel-worn 273.40
traverse
n. crosspiece 221.5
v. contradict 790.6
cross 221.6
oppose 790.3
sail 275.13
travel over 273.19
adj. crosswise 221.9
adv. crosswise 221.13
travesty
n. exaggeration 617.1
humor 881.1
imitation 22.3
misrepresentation 573.2
ridicule 967.6
v. exaggerate 617.3
misrepresent 573.3
ridicule 967.11
trawl
n. snare 618.12
v. fish 655.10
pull 286.4
trawling 655.3
treacherous
deceitful 618.20
dishonest 975.21
falsehearted 616.31
unreliable 514.19
unsafe 697.11
treachery
dishonesty 975.6
falseheartedness 616.4
unreliability 514.6
treacle
semiliquid 389.5
sweetening 431.2
tread
n. degree 29.1
footstep 273.13
gait 273.14
rate 267.4
stair 315.5
v. stamp 283.19
walk 273.26
treadle
n. lever 287.4
v. push 285.10

treadmill
drudgery 716.4
pillory 1011.3
regularity 17.2
routine 642.6
tedium 884.1
tread upon
domineer 741.16
trample 313.7
tread water
be still 268.7
swim 275.56
treason apostasy 145.3
betrayal 628.2
dishonesty 975.7
treasonable
apostate 145.20
rebellious 767.11
renegade 628.11
traitorous 975.22
treasure
n. collection 74.11
funds 835.14
good thing 674.5
store 660.1
wealth 837.1
v. cherish 931.19
harbor 813.7
rate highly 672.12
remember 537.13
store up 660.11
treasured
beloved 931.22
stored 660.14
treasure-house
depository 836.12
storage place 660.6
treasurer
executive 748.3
financial officer 836.11
payer 841.9
treasure trove
discovery 488.1
find 811.6
treasury
depository 836.12
hoard 660.1
ready money 835.18
storage place 660.6
treasury note
paper money 835.5
securities 834.1
treat
n. delicacy 308.8
payment 841.8
refreshment 307.5
regalement 865.3
v. behave toward 737.6
care for 689.30
deal with 665.12
discourse upon 606.5
discuss 597.12
operate on 164.6
pay for 841.19
practice medicine 688.17
prepare 720.6
remedy 687.38
treatise 606

treatment
artistry 574.10
discussion 597.7
medical aid 689.15
preparation 720.1
therapy 689.1
treatise 606.1
usage 665.2
treat with
mediate 805.6
negotiate 771.7
treaty 771.2
treble
n. high voice 458.6
melody 462.4
singing part 462.22
voice 463.5
v. triplicate 94.2
adj. high 458.13
triple 94.3
vocal 462.51
treble clef 463.13
tree
n. gallows 1011.5
genealogy 170.5
mast 277.13
timber 411.10
types of 411.50
v. corner 731.15
treed 731.23
tree farming 413.3
treelike
arboreal 411.36
branched 299.10
trefoil 93.1
trek
n. journey 273.5
migration 273.4
v. migrate 273.21
travel 273.20
trellis 221.3
tremble
n. excitement 857.4
music 463.19
nervousness 859.2
shake 324.3
v. be afraid 891.22
be cold 333.9
be excited 857.16
be nervous 859.6
be weak 160.8
shake 324.11
trembling
n. excitement 857.4
shaking 324.2
adj. fearful 891.31
jittery 859.11
shaking 324.17
tremendous
huge 195.20
large 34.7
superb 674.17
terrible 891.38
tremendously
frightfully 891.42
superbly 674.22
vastly 34.16
tremolo music 463.19
organ stop 465.22
tremor
excitement 857.4
music 463.19

shake 324.3
speech defect 595.1
thrill 857.2
tremulous
fearful 891.31
imperfectly spoken 595.12
jittery 859.11
shaking 324.17
trench
n. channel 396.1
crack 201.2
ditch 799.5
ocean depths 209.4
shelter 700.3
trough 263.2
valley 257.9
v. channel 396.19
cut 201.4
excavate 257.15
groove 263.3
intrude 238.5
trenchant
acrimonious 161.13
caustic 939.21
eloquent 600.11
energetic 161.12
pungent 433.6
sagacious 467.16
trencherman
eater 307.14
glutton 994.3
trench foot 686.31
trench mouth 686.12
trend
n. course 267.2
direction 290.1
drift 174.2
fashion 644.1
flow 395.4
v. bear 290.8
deviate 291.3
flow 395.16
tend 174.3
trend-setter 644.7
trendy 644.11
trepidation
agitation 324.1
excitement 857.4
fear 891.5
nervousness 859.1
trespass
n. intrusion 238.1
lawbreaking 999.3
misdeed 982.2
overstepping 313.3
usurpation 961.3
violation 769.2
v. break the law 999.5
intrude 238.5
not observe 769.4
overstep 313.9
sin 982.5
usurp 961.8
trespasser 238.3
trespassing
intrusion 238.1
lawbreaking 999.3
usurpation 961.3
tress 230.5
trestle horse 216.16
railway 657.8

triable 999.6
triad harmonics 463.17
  three 93.1
triage 60.3
trial
  n. adversity 729.1
  annoyance 866.2
  attempt 714.2
  contest 796.3
  examination 485.2
  experiment 489.1
  legal action 1004.5
  number 586.8
  preparation 720.1
  test 489.2
  tribulation 866.9
  adj. experimental 489.11
  tentative 714.14
  three 93.3
trial and error
  experiment 489.1
trial balloon
  question 485.10
  testing device 489.4
trial run 489.3
triangle bell 454.4
  geometry 251.13
  love affair 931.6
  percussion instrument 465.18
  pillory 1011.3
  straightedge 250.3
  three 93.1
triangular triform 93.3
  trilateral 251.8
  tripartite 95.4
triangulate
  measure 490.11
  pinpoint 184.10
triangulation
  measurement 490.1
  radar operation 346.8

tribal 11.7
tribe biology 61.5
  group 74.3
  kind 61.3
  race 11.4
tribesman 11.2
tribulation 11.2
  adversity 729.1
  trial 866.9
tribunal
  n. council 755.1
  court 1001
  platform 216.13
tribune judge 1001.10
  platform 1002.2
tributary
  n. feeder 395.3
  adj. subject 764.13
tribute
  attribution 155.2
  celebration 877.1
  demand 753.1
  fee 841.5
  gift 818.4
  honor 916.4
  praise 968.5
  tax 846.10

trice 113.3
trich(o)– 230.2
trichotomy 95.1
trick
  n. characteristic 80.4
  deception 618.6
  eccentricity 474.2
  expedient 670.2
  habit 642.4
  illusion 519.1
  intrigue 654.6
  knack 733.6
  mannerism 903.2
  number 586.8
  playing cards 878.17
  prank 881.10
  pretext 649.1
  shift 108.3
  stratagem 735.3
  style 588.2
  v. deceive 618.13
  fool 618.14
  live by one's wits 735.9
  play a practical joke 881.14

trickery
  chicanery 618.4
  juggling 618.5
  ornamentation 901.3
  stratagem 735.3
  wittiness 881.4
trickle
  n. few 102.2
  flow 395.7
  leakage 303.5
  v. dribble 395.18
  leak out 303.14
trickle away 692.22
trick out
  dress up 231.41
  falsify 616.16
  make grandiloquent 601.7
trickster
  cunning person 735.6
  deceiver 619.2
tricky cunning 735.12
  deceitful 618.20
  difficult 731.16
  dishonest 975.16
  misleading 618.19
  treacherous 975.21
  waggish 881.17
tricolor
  n. flag 569.6
  adj. variegated 374.9
tricycle 272.8,29
trident
  n. fork 299.4
  three 93.1
tried and true
  experienced 733.26
  friendly 927.20
  tested 489.12
  traditional 123.12
  trustworthy 974.19
triennial
  n. anniversary 137.4
  plant 411.3
  adj. periodic 137.8

trifle
  n. bagatelle 673.5
  pastry 308.40
  pudding 308.45
  small amount 35.5
  thing of naught 4.2
  trivia 673.4
  v. be foolish 470.6
  fritter away 854.5
  leave undone 534.7
  make love 932.13
  treat lightly 673.13
  waste time 708.12
trifle with
  disrespect 965.3
  do carelessly 534.9
  neglect 534.5
trifler dallier 673.9
  idler 708.8
trifling
  n. dallying 673.8
  adj. insignificant 35.6
  quibbling 483.14
  trivial 673.16
triform 93.3
trifurcate
  tripartite 95.4
  three 93.1

trig chic 644.13
  shipshape 277.20
  tidy 59.8
trigger kindle 648.18
  use radar 346.17
trigger-happy
  jumpy 891.31
  warlike 797.25
trigger man
  evildoer 943.4
  killer 409.11
trigonometry
  angle measurement 251.3
  mathematics 87.18
trig up 60.12
trike 272.8
trilateral sided 242.7
  triangular 251.8
  tripartite 95.4
trilingual 580.14
trill
  n. bird sound 460.5
  flow out 303.14
  make a liquid sound 452.11
  sing 462.39
trilogy 93.1
trim
  n. clothing 231.1
  condition 7.3
  ornamentation 901.1
  preparedness 720.4
  v. border 235.10
  change one's mind 628.7
  cheapen 849.6
  cut the hair 230.22
  defeat 727.6
  fasten 47.7
  ornament 901.8

  prepare 720.6
  punish 1010.15
  reel in 287.9
  remain neutral 806.5
  reprove 969.18
  sail 275.49
  shorten 203.6
  straighten up 60.12
  adj. chic 644.13
  polished 589.6
  ready 277.19
  shapely 248.5
  shipshape 277.20
  tidy 59.8
trimester period 107.2
  three 93.1
trimmed
  bordered 235.12
  defeated 727.14
  ornamented 901.11
  rigged 277.17
  shortened 203.9
trimming
  n. bookbinding 605.15
  defeat 727.1
  edging 235.7
  extra 41.4
  ornamentation 901.1
  adj. mind-changing 628.10
Trinity 1013.10
trinity
  threeness 93.2
  three 93.1
trinket ornament 901.4
  toy 878.16
  trifle 673.5
trinomial 583.17
trio cooperation 786.1
  music arrangement 462.5
  orchestra 464.12
  part music 462.17
  three 93.1
trip
  n. an error 518.4
  bungle 734.5
  flight 278.9
  flock 74.5
  illusion 519.1
  journey 273.5
  misdeed 982.2
  thing imagined 535.5
  tumble 316.3
  v. bungle 734.11
  dance 879.5
  err 518.9
  fantasy 535.17
  go wrong 981.9
  jump 319.6
  knock down 318.5
  overcome 727.7
  play 878.25
  run 269.10
  trap 618.18
  tumble 316.8
  walk 273.27
tripartite 95.4
tripe intestines 225.4
  meat 308.20
  nonsense 547.3

true
v. make agree 26.7
adj. certain 513.13
faithful 974.20
firm 624.12
friendly 927.20
observant 768.4
orthodox 1024.7
real 1.15
straight 250.6
trustworthy 974.19
unerroneous 516.12
veracious 974.16
true believer
orthodox 1024.4
truster 501.9
true blue fidelity 974.7
true-blue
faithful 974.20
orthodox 1024.7
traditional 123.12
true course
aviation 278.43
direction 290.2
true faith 1024.2
true grit 624.3
truelove
faithful love 931.1
loved one 931.13
true to form
characteristic 80.13
typical 572.11
true to life
authentic 516.14
descriptive 608.15
lifelike 20.16
true to type 572.11
truism axiom 517.2
generalization 79.8
truly
adv. certainly 513.23
in fact 516.17
in reality 1.16
positively 34.19
truthfully 974.22
interj. yes 521.18
trump
n. good person 985.2
last expedient 670.2
playing cards 878.17
v. excel 36.6
trumped-up 616.29
trumpery
nonsense 547.2
ornamentation 901.3
trifles 673.4
trumpet
n. brass wind 465.8
loud sound 453.4
organ stop 465.22
v. blare 453.9
flaunt 904.17
play music 462.43
praise 968.12
proclaim 559.13
utter 594.26
trumpeter 464.4
trump up 616.18
truncate cut off 42.10
deform 249.7
shorten 203.6

truncated
concise 592.6
deformed 249.12
incomplete 57.5
trundle push 285.10
roll 322.10
trunk base 216.8
body 376.3
communications 560.17
cylinder 255.4
nose 256.7
plant stem 411.19
railway 657.8
trunk line
communications 560.17
trunks 231.29,56
truss
n. bundle 74.8
v. bind 47.9
bundle 74.20
render powerless 158.11
trust
n. association 788.9
belief 501.1
commission 780.1
confidence 888.1
estate 810.4
financial credit 839.1
investment company 833.16
v. accept 501.10
be hopeful 888.7
believe in 501.15
confide in 501.17
delegate 818.16
give credit 839.6

trust company 836.13
trusted 501.23
trustee fiduciary 809.5
financial officer
recipient 819.3
trusteeship 780.1
truster believer 501.9
zealot 1028.4
trusting artless 736.5
credulous 502.8
trustful 501.22
trusting soul
credulous person 502.4
dupe 620.1
trustworthy
believable 501.24
dependable 974.19
reliable 513.17
unhazardous 698.5
trusty
n. honest person 974.8
prisoner 761.11
adj. believable 501.24
reliable 513.17
trusting 501.22
trustworthy 974.19
truth
axiom 517.2
certainty 513.1
reality 1.2
unfalseness 516
veracity 974.3
truthful
unerroneous 516.12
veracious 974.16
truthless false 616.25
untruthful 616.34
try
n. attempt 714.2
v. attempt 714.5
burden 729.8
judge 494.12
refine 681.22
strive for 714.8
test 489.8
try a case 1004.17
trying adverse 729.13
experimental 489.11
fatiguing 717.11
testing 485.36
troublesome 731.17
weakening 160.20
tryout audition 448.2
preparation 720.1
rehearsal 489.3
theatrical perfor-
mance 611.13

try out
experiment 489.8
give a show 611.33
prepare 720.6
tryst 922.9
tsar see czar
T square
instrument 213.6
tsunami
tidal wave 162.5
wave 395.14
tsures 866.8
tub
n. automobile 272.9
basin 193.7
bath 681.8
corpulent person
ship 277.1
washing equipment 681.12
tuba 465.8
tubby corpulent 195.18
stubby 203.10
tube
n. camera 345.19
cylinder 255.4
electron tube 343.11,16
photoelectric 343.17
picture 345.18
pipe 396.6
railway 657.8
special electronic 343.18
train 272.13
v. channel 271.13
tuber 411.20
tubercle bulge 256.3
plant root 411.20
sore 686.35

tubercular
diseased 686.57
nodular 256.16
tuberculin test 689.17
tuberculosis
disease 686.12
epidemic disease 686.4
respiratory disease 686.15
tuberosity
bulging 256.1
protuberance 256.2
tuberous
herbaceous 411.33
nodular 256.16
tub-thumper 599.4
tubular
cylindrical 255.11
pipelike 396.20
tubing 396.6
tuck
n. fold 264.1
v. fold 264.5
tucked 264.7
tucker
n. apron 231.17,64
food 308.1
v. fatigue 717.4
tuckered out 717.8
tuck in eat 307.20
insert 304.3
make comfortable 887.9
put to bed 712.19
tuft beard 230.8
clump 74.7
feather 230.16
growth 411.2
hair 230.6
tufted
feathered 230.29
verdant 411.39
tug
n. attraction 288.1
exertion 716.2
harness 659.5
pull 286.2
v. attract 288.4
exert oneself 716.10
pull 286.4
tug-of-war fight 796.4
pulling 286.1
tuition 562.1
tuitional 562.19
tumble
n. collapse 725.3
fall 316.3
flounder 324.8
jumble 62.3
v. be defeated 727.12
be destroyed 693.22
be excited 857.16
be undiscriminating 493.3
confuse 63.3
fall 316.8
find 488.3
flounder 324.15
knock down 318.5
roll about 322.13

turn on
electricity 342.23
shut off 144.12

turn on
be contingent on 507.6
begin 68.11
depend on 154.6
electricity 342.23
excite 857.11
rouse 648.19
thrill to 857.16

turn one on 550.12

turn one's back upon
abandon 633.5
avoid 631.6
be inhospitable 926.5
desert 633.6
disregard 531.4
leave 301.8
refuse 776.3
slight 534.8
snub 966.5

turn one's head
be vain 909.7
enamor 931.21
fascinate 650.6
make proud 905.6
stultify 470.7
take one's breath away 920.7

turn one's stomach
disgust 429.4
offend 864.11

turnout
attendance 186.4
meeting 74.2
railway 657.8
rig 272.5
strike 789.7
wardrobe 231.2

turn out
be in a state 7.6
come true 516.11
dismiss 310.19
eject 310.13
equip 659.8
evict 310.15
get up 713.6
happen 151.7
invert 220.5
outfit 231.40
reject 638.2
result 154.5

turnover
inversion 220.2
pastry 308.40
sale 829.1

turn over
capsize 275.44
deliver 818.13
fold 264.5
invert 220.5
overturn 220.6
sell 829.8
think over 478.13
transfer 271.9
transfer property 817.3

turn over a new leaf
change 139.6
make better 691.9
reform 145.12

turnpike road 657.6
tollgate 302.6

turn red
become excited 857.17
become red 368.5
blush 908.8

turnstile 302.6
turntable 450.11
turn tail flee 631.10
turntable 628.5
turn around 295.9

turn the corner
be changed 139.5
recuperate 694.19

turn the other cheek
condone 947.4
endure 861.7

turn the tables
change 139.6
gain influence 172.12
invert 220.5
retaliate 955.4

turn the trick
accomplish 722.4
succeed with 724.10

turn to attend to 530.5
avail oneself of 665.14
be converted into 145.17
begin 68.7
set to work 716.15
undertake 715.3

turn up appear 446.8
arrive 300.6
attend 186.8
be discovered 488.9
be unexpected 540.6
find 488.4
happen 156.11
occur 151.6
upturn 315.13

turn up one's nose at
be fastidious 896.8
disapprove 969.10
disregard 531.4
grimace 867.5
spurn 966.4

turn upside down
change 139.6
invert 220.5
overturn 220.6
ransack 485.32

turpentine 362.8

turpitude
baseness 975.2
degeneracy 981.5

turps narcotic 687.12
paint 362.8

turret 207.11
turtle 414.30,60
turtledoves 931.17
turtlelike 270.10
tush buttocks 241.5

tusk
n. tooth 258.5
v. attack 798.26

tussle
n. fight 796.4
quarrel 795.5
struggle 716.3
v. contend 796.14
struggle 716.11

tutelage
dependence 764.3
instructorship 565.11
patronage 785.4
protectorship 699.2
teaching 562.1

tutelary
n. spirit 1014.22
adj. protecting 699.23

tutor
n. academic rank 565.4
v. coach 562.12

tutorial 565.6

tutorship
instructorship 565.11
teaching 562.1

tutti-frutti 308.39,54
tutu 231.9
tuxedo 231.11

TV television 345.1
TV dinner 307.6
TV man 345.13
TV show 345.2
TV station 345.6

twaddle
n. chatter 596.3
nonsense 547.2
v. chatter 596.5
talk nonsense 547.5

twang
n. harsh sound 458.3
regional accent 594.9
speech defect 595.1
v. nasalize 595.10
sound harshly 458.9
strum 462.41
utter 594.26

twanger 464.5

twangy
imperfectly spoken 595.12
nasal 594.31

tweak
n. jerk 286.3
pain 424.2
pinch 198.2
v. hurt 424.7
jerk 286.5
pinch 198.8

tweedle
n. loud sound 453.4
v. blare 453.9
play music 462.43
sing 462.39

Tweedledum and Tweedledee
equality 30.3
twins 90.4

tweet 460.5
tweeter 450.8
tweezers 305.9
twelfth-night 1040.15
twentieth-century 122.13

twenty-four carat 516.14
twice 91.5
twice-told 103.12

twice-told tale
old joke 881.9
platitude 517.3
trite 673.13

twiddle touch 425.6

twiddle one's thumbs
do nothing 706.2
idle 708.11

twig branch 411.18
part 55.4
sprout 125.9

twiggy
n. thin person 205.8
adj. branched 411.38

twilight
n. darkishness 337.4
dusk 134.3
foredawn 133.4
adj. evening 134.8

twill fold 264.5
weave 222.6

twin
n. equivalent 30.4
image 572.3
likeness 20.3
the same 14.3
v. duplicate 91.3
adj. accompanying 73.9
analogous 20.11
double 91.4
identical 14.7
two 90.6

twine
n. cord 206.2,9
v. encircle 233.7
weave 222.6
wind 254.4

twinge
n. pain 424.2
v. suffer pain 424.8

twinkle
n. instant 113.3
light 335.7
v. glitter 335.24

twinkling
n. instant 113.3
light 335.7
adj. glittering 335.35

twins
two 90.4
twins set 20.5

twirl
n. backflow 395.12
curl 254.2
rotation 322.2
v. whirl 322.11
wind 254.4

twist
n. aspect 446.3
bend 219.3
chewing tobacco 434.7
curl 254.2
curl 206.2
deformity 679.1
deviation 291.1
distortion 249.1

eccentricity 474.2
extra 41.4
hair 230.7
partiality 527.3
story element 608.9
tendency 174.1
trait of character 525.3
v. corrupt 692.14
deflect 291.5
deform 679.4
distort 249.5
falsify 616.16
misrepresent 573.3
oblique 219.9
prejudice 527.9
rotate 322.9
torture 424.7
wander 291.4
weave 222.6
wind 254.4
twist around one's little finger
dominate 741.15
have influence over 172.11
have subject 764.10
twisted
blemished 679.8
complex 46.4
distorted 249.10
eccentric 474.4
falsified 616.26
pained 424.9
perverted 249.11
prejudiced 527.12
twister
doughnut 308.43
whirlwind 403.14
twisting
n. convolution 254.1
misinterpretation 553.1
misrepresentation 573.1
adj. wandering 291.7
weaving 222.1
winding 254.6
twist one's arm
compel 756.6
persuade 648.23
urge 648.14
twisty crooked 219.20
winding 254.6
twit
n. banter 882.1
gibe 967.2
v. banter 882.4
bird sound 460.5
reproach 1005.7
ridicule 967.9
sing 462.39
twitch
n. instant 113.3
jerk 286.3
pain 424.2
shake 324.3
v. be excited 857.16
fidget 324.13
jerk 286.5
suffer pain 424.8

twitching
n. emotional symptom 690.23
jerking 324.5
nervousness 859.1
adj. jerky 324.19
twitchy jerky 324.19
jittery 859.11
twitter
n. agitation 324.1
banterer 882.3
dither 857.5
excitement 857.4
shake 324.3
v. be excited 857.16
bird sound 460.5
shake 324.11
sing 462.39
twitting
n. banter 882.2
ridicule 967.1
adj. bantering 882.5
ridiculing 967.12
'twixt 237.12
two
n. pair 90.2
adj. double 90.6
two-bit 673.17
two bits fourth 98.2
US money 835.7
two-by-four
n. wood 378.3
adj. little 196.10
petty 673.17
two-dimensional 179.8
two-faced
deceitful 618.20
dishonest 975.21
double 91.4
falsehearted 616.31
twofer 850.2
two-fisted 420.12
twofold
adj. double 91.4
adv. doubly 91.5
two-handed 733.23
twopenny 673.18
two-ply double 91.4
layered 227.6
two shakes
instant 113.3
short time 111.3
two-sided bilateral 91.4
bipartite 90.6
sided 242.7
twosome game 878.9
pair 90.2
two-step 879.5
two-time
be false 616.24
betray 975.14
deceive 618.13
two-time loser 146.3
two-timer cheat 619.3
criminal 986.10
two-way 13.14
two-wheeler 272.3
tycoon
businessman 830.1
personage 672.8
ruler 749.8

tympanum
auditory organ 448.7
drum 465.19
eardrum 229.3
type
n. example 25.2
form 246.1
kind 61.3
measure 490.2
model 25.1
nature 5.3
odd person 85.4
omen 544.3
preference 637.5
print 603.6
representative 572.5
specialty 81.1
symbol 568.3
temperament 525.3
unit of meaning 545.6
v. classify 61.6
write 602.19
typeface 603.6,23
typescript
printer's copy 603.4
written matter 602.10
typeset 603.19
typesetter 603.12
typesetting machine 603.2
types of 603.21
type size 603.22
type style 603.23
typewriter 602.31
typewriting 602.1
typewritten 602.22
typhoid fever 686.12
Typhoid Mary 686.41
typhoon storm 162.4
whirlwind 403.14
windstorm 403.12
typhus 686.12
typical
classificational 61.7
indicative 568.23
model 25.8
normal 84.7
representational 572.11
typify augur 544.12
symbolize 568.18
typifying 572.10
typing 602.1
typist 602.18
typo 518.3
typographer 603.12
typographic(al) 603.20
typographical error 518.3
typography 603.1
typology 61.1
Tyr Norse deity 1014.6
war god 797.17
tyrannical 739.16
tyrannize
domineer 741.16
subdue 764.9
tyrannized 764.16
tyranny
absolutism 741.9
despotism 741.10

force 756.2
government 741.4
subjection 764.1
tyrant 749.14
tyro beginner 68.2
novice 566.9

U

ubiquitous
godlike 1013.20
omnipresent 186.13
pervasive 56.10
recurrent 103.13
ubiquity
completeness 56.1
divine attribute 1013.15
omnipresence 186.2
U-boat 277.9
udder 256.6
UFO 282.3
ugh! 864.13
ugly 899.5
ugliness
irascibility 951.2
raucousness 458.2
unpleasantness 864.1
unsightliness 899
ugly irascible 951.19
threatening 697.9
unpleasant 864.17
unsightly 899.6
ugly customer
evildoer 943.4
ill-humored person 951.11
violent person 162.9
UHF 344.12
ukase
announcement 559.2
decree 752.4
ukulele 465.4
ulcer
gastrointestinal disease 686.27
sore 686.35
ulcerated
decayed 692.41
diseased 686.56
ulterior
additional 40.10
extraneous 78.5
farther 199.10
secret 614.11
ultimate
n. culmination 677.3
adj. completory 722.9
eventual 151.11
farthest 199.12
final 70.10
future 121.8
irrevocable 752.13
top 211.10
ultimately
eventually 151.12
finally 70.11
in time 121.11
ultimatum
condition 507.2
demand 753.1
final proposal 773.3

ultra
warning 703.1
n. radical 745.12
adj. extreme 34.13
ultraconservative
n. conservative 140.4
adj. conservative 140.8
political principle 745.17
radical 745.20
ultramodern 122.13
ultrasonic fast 269.20
sonic 450.17
ultra-ultra
extreme 34.13
modern 122.13
ultraviolet ray 335.5
ululate
animal sound 460.2
cry 875.11
sound shrill 458.8
Ulysses 274.2
Uma 1014.8
umber 367.3
umbilical 226.11
umbilicus 226.2
umbra 337.3
umbrage foliage 411.16
resentment 952.2
shadow 337.3
umbral 337.16
umbrella
military flight 278.11
parachute 280.13
parasol 228.7
safeguard 699.3
shade 338.1,8
umpire
n. arbitrator 805.4
judge 494.6
referee 1002.1
v. judge 494.12
mediate 805.6
umpteen 101.2
umpteenth 99.25
UN 743.1
unabashed
brazen 913.10
immodest 990.6
undaunted 893.20
unabated
undiminished 34.14
unmitigated 162.16
unweakened 159.19
unable
incapable 158.14
incompetent 734.19
unabridged 54.12
unaccented 594.31
unacceptable
969.25
unsatisfactory 869.7
unwelcome 926.9
unpraiseworthy
unaccommodating
discontented 869.5
discourteous 937.4
inconsiderate 939.16
unaccompanied 89.8

unaccomplished
unachieved 723.3
unskilled 734.16
unaccountable
exempt 762.29
fantastic 85.12
inexplicable 549.18
lawless 740.5
purposeless 156.16
uncertain 514.15
unpredictable 141.7
unaccustomed
inexperienced 734.17
unfamiliar with 643.4
unacknowledged
anonymous 584.3
unthanked 950.5
unacquainted with
ignorant 477.12
inexperienced 734.17
unaccustomed 643.4
unadapted 83.5
unadapted
inappropriate 27.7
incompetent 734.19
unfit 721.9
unadorned
in plain style 591.3
mere 35.8
natural 736.6
simple 45.6
undecorated 902.8
unadulterated
genuine 516.14
perfect 677.6
simple 45.7
unadorned 902.8
unpolluted 681.25
unadventurous 895.8
unadvised
impulsive 630.11
unaware 540.9
unwise 470.9
unaesthetic
inartistic 899.10
ugly 899.6
unaffected
genuine 516.14
honest 974.18
informal 647.3
natural 736.6
plain 902.7
plain-speaking 591.3
tasteful 897.8
uninfluenced 173.5
unmoved 856.11
unyielding 626.9
unaffectionate
unfeeling 856.9
unkind 939.14
unafraid sure 513.21
unfearing 893.19
unagreeable 926.9
unaided 89.8
unalienable 5.6
unalienable rights 762.2
unalike 21.4
unallayed
unmitigated 162.16
unweakened 159.19

unallied 10.5
unallowed illegal 999.6
prohibited 778.7
unalloyed 45.7
unalluring 864.17
unalterable
rigid 356.12
unchangeable 142.17
unyielding 626.9
unaltered
permanent 140.7
unchangeable 142.17
unambiguous
certain 513.13
intelligible 548.10
unambitious
modest 908.9
undesirous 636.8
unamenable 173.4
unamiable
unfriendly 929.9
unkind 939.14
unamicable 929.9
unamusing 883.7
unanimity
agreement 26.3
likemindedness 521.5
unanimous
agreeing 26.9
of one mind 521.15
unanimously
as one 786.6
by common consent 521.17
unannounced 540.10
unanswerable
exempt 762.29
irrefutable 513.15
unanticipated
sudden 113.5
unexpected 540.10
unappealing 864.17
unappeasable
greedy 634.27
revengeful 956.6
unappetizing
unpleasant 864.17
unsavory 429.5
unappreciated 867.9
unappreciative
disapproving 969.22
ungrateful 950.4
unapprehensive 893.19
unapproachable
inaccessible 510.9
out-of-the-way 199.9
peerless 36.15
reticent 613.10
unsociable 923.6
unapproved 1025.9
unapproving 969.22
unapt
inappropriate 27.7
unskillful 734.15
unarmed unfit 721.9
unprotected 697.14
unaroused 268.14
unarranged
unordered 62.12
unprepared 721.8

unashamed
immodest 990.6
unregretful 874.4
unashamedly
flagrantly 34.21
unregretfully 874.7
unasked
neglected 534.14
unwanted 867.11
unwelcome 926.9
voluntary 622.7
unaspiring
modest 908.9
undesirous 636.8
unassailable
genuine 516.14
honest 974.18
informal 647.3
modest 908.9
natural 736.6
unassertive 765.12
unassociated
separate 49.20
unrelated 10.5
unassuming
genuine 516.14
honest 974.18
informal 647.3
modest 908.9
natural 736.6
unaffected 902.7
unassured 514.22
unastonished 921.3
unastonishment
expectation 539.1
unamazement 921
unattached free 762.20
separate 49.20
unattainable
impracticable 510.8
inaccessible 510.9
unattended alone 89.8
neglected 534.14
separate 49.20
unprotected 697.14
unattired 232.13
unattractive ugly 899.6
unpleasant 864.17
unauthentic
fallacious 483.11
spurious 616.26
unofficial 514.20
unorthodox 1025.9
unreliable 518.19
unauthenticated
unauthoritative 514.20
unauthoritative
unauthentic 514.20
unconvincing 506.8
unofficial 514.20
unauthorized
illegal 999.6
prohibited 778.7
unavailing 510.9
unavailable
inaccessible 510.9
useless 669.9
unavoidable 639.15
unaware
ignorant 477.13
insensible 856.10
unsuspecting 540.9

unhampered 762.25
unclose 265.13
unclothe 232.7
unclothed 232.13
unclouded clear 335.31
transparent 339.4
unobscured 555.11
visible 444.6
unclutter
disentangle 732.8
simplify 45.5
uncluttered 45.6
uncoached 734.16
uncoded 548.11
uncoerced free 762.23
voluntary 622.7
uncoil develop 148.7
simplify 45.5
uncollectible
nonpayment 842.1
uncolored
colorless 363.7
genuine 516.14
uncombed
disorderly 62.14
uncouth 898.12
uncomely 899.6

uncompelled
free 762.23
voluntary 622.7
uncompensated 842.12
uncomplaining
contented 868.7
resigned 861.10
submissive 765.12
uncompleted 723.3
uncompliant
insubordinate 767.9
nonconforming 83.5
nonobservant 769.5
refusing 776.6
uncomplicated
easy 732.12
simple 45.8
unadorned 902.8

uncomfortable
distressed 866.22
unpleasant 864.20
uncommendable 969.25
uncommitted
free 762.20
neutral 806.7
uncommon new 122.11
rare 136.2
remarkable 34.10
scarce 662.11
unusual 85.10
uncommonly
exceptionally 34.20
infrequently 136.4
scarcely 662.16
unusually 85.17
uncommunicative
cautious 895.8
reticent 613.8
secretive 614.15
unsociable 923.5
uncompassionate
pitiless 945.3
unkind 939.14

uncomplimentary
969.22
uncomprehending
ignorant 477.12
undiscerning 469.14
uncompromising
strict 757.7
unyielding 626.9
unconcealed
unobscured 555.11
visible 444.6
unconcern
apathy 856.4
disinterest 636.2
incuriosity 529.1
nonchalance 858.5
unconcerned
apathetic 856.13
incurious 529.3
indifferent 636.7
nonchalant 858.15
unconditional
complete 56.10
unqualified 508.2
unrestricted 762.26
unconditionally
completely 56.14
extremely 34.22

unconducive 669.14
unconfident
unbelieving 503.8
unsure 514.22
unconfined 762.26
unconfirmed
unauthoritative
514.20
unproved 506.8
unconfused 548.10
unconfuted
proved 505.22
true 516.12
uncongenial
disagreeable 27.6
reticent 613.10
unlikable 867.7
unsociable 923.5
unconnected
discontinuous 72.4
illogical 483.11
noncohesive 51.4
unintelligible 549.13
unrelated 10.5

unconquerable
invincible 159.17
undaunted 625.7
unconquered
free 762.23
victorious 726.9
unconscientious
dishonest 975.16
unmeticulous 534.13
unconscionable
dishonest 975.16
excessive 663.16
inexcusable 977.12
outrageous 162.15
outright 34.12
overpriced 848.12
unconscious
n. psyche 690.35
adj. abstracted 532.11

asleep 712.22
inanimate 382.5
inattentive 531.7
instinctive 481.6
involuntary 639.14
oblivious 856.10
senseless 423.8
subconscious 690.48
unaware 477.13
unintentional 156.17
unpremeditated
650.11
unconsenting
refusing 776.6
unwilling 623.5
unconsidered
impulsive 630.11
overlooked 534.14
unexamined 534.16
unheeded 534.15
unthought-of 480.5
unwise 470.9
unconsolable 872.28
unconsolidated 51.4
unconstitutional 999.6
unconstitutionality
999.1

unconstrained
candid 974.17
communicative
554.3
free 762.23
informal 647.23
intemperate 993.7
unconstraint
candor 974.4
communicativeness
554.3
freedom 762.3
informality 647.1
intemperance 993.1
unconsummated 677.6
uncontaminated 677.6
uncontested
believed 501.23
beyond question
513.16
unchallenged 521.15
uncontrite 874.5
uncontrived 721.8
uncontrollable
excited 857.23
inevitable 639.15
mad 473.30
ungovernable 626.12

uncontrolled
inconstant 141.7
intemperate 993.7
lawless 740.5
unrestrained 762.23
unconventional
eccentric 474.4
informal 647.3
nonconformist 83.6
unconvinced
unbelieving 503.8
uncertain 514.15
unconvincing 503.10
uncooked 721.10
uncooperative
inconsiderate 939.16
insubordinate 767.9

obstinate 626.8
opposing 790.8
refusing 776.6
resistant 792.5
uncordial
inhospitable 926.7
unfriendly 929.9
unkind 939.14
uncork 265.13
uncorroborated
unauthoritative
514.20
unproved 506.8
uncorrupted
honest 974.13
innocent 984.6
uncounted
innumerable 101.10
uncertain 514.17
uncouple 49.9
uncourageous 892.11
uncouth clumsy 734.20
countrified 182.7
inelegant 590.2
unrefined 898.12
vulgar 990.8

uncover
disclose 556.4
divest 232.5
find 488.4
greet 925.10
open 265.13
uncovered
divested 232.12
open 265.18
unprotected 697.14
uncovering
disclosure 556.1
discovery 488.1
divestment 232.1
uncreative 166.5
uncredited 950.5
uncritical
approving 968.18
credulous 502.8
undiscriminating
493.5
uncrown 783.4
uncrystallized 131.8
unction flattery 970.2
healing ointment
667.11
lubrication 380.6
ointment 380.3
rite 1040.6
sanctimony 1029.1
unctuous
flattering 970.8
hypocritic(al) 616.33
oily 380.9
sanctimonious 1029.5
suave 936.18
uncultivated
fallow 721.14
uncouth 898.12
undeveloped 721.12
unlearned 477.14
unproductive 166.4

misrepresent 573.3

understated 573.1

understatement 897.8

understatement
good taste 897.4
misrepresentation
573.1

understood
known 475.26
supposed 499.14
tacit 546.8
traditional 123.12

understructure
foundation 216.6
structure 245.3

understudy
n. actor 612.7
deputy 781.1
substitute 149.2
v. represent 781.14
substitute for 149.5

undertake agree 771.6
attempt 714.5
engage in 705.7
promise 770.5
set about 715.3
set to work 716.15

undertaken
assumed 715.7
contracted 771.12

undertaker 410.8

undertaking act 705.3
attempt 714.2
business 656.1
commitment 770.2
enterprise 715
pledge 772.2

under-the-counter
covert 614.12

under-the-table
covert 614.12
illegal 999.6

undertone
implication 546.2
meaning 545.1
milieu 233.3
murmur 452.4

undertow flow 395.4
hidden danger 697.5

undervalue 498.2

underwater 209.13

under way
at sea 275.63
happening 151.9
in motion 267.9
in preparation 720.22
undertaken 715.7

underwear 231.22

underweight
n. leanness 205.5
weight 352.1
adj. lean 205.17
lightweight 353.12

underworld
depths 209.3
hell 1019.1
organized crime
986.11

under wraps
concealed 615.11
secret 614.11

underwrite
promise 770.4
protect 699.18
ratify 521.12
secure 772.9

underwriter
endorser 521.7
guarantor 772.6
insurance man 699.4

undeserved
undue 961.9
unjust 977.9

undesignated 584.3

undesigned
unintentional 156.17
unpremeditated
650.11

undesigning
honest 974.18
natural 736.6

undesirable
n. bad person 986.1
adj. inexpedient 671.5
unacceptable 869.7
unpleasant 864.17
unwelcome 926.9

undesired 867.11

undesirous 636.8

undestroyed
permanent 140.7
undamaged 677.8

undetached
prejudiced 527.12
unjust 977.11

undetected 615.12

undetermined
chance 156.15
irresolute 627.9
uncertain 514.18
undecided 514.17
unproved 506.8

undeveloped
immature 124.10
imperfect 678.4
incomplete 57.4
inexperienced 734.17
new 122.7
unfinished 721.12

undeviating
direct 290.13
exact 516.16
straight 250.6
unchangeable 142.17
uniform 17.5

undevised 721.8

undies 231.22

undifferentiated
continuous 71.8
general 79.11
indistinctive 493.6
simple 45.6
uniform 17.5

undigested 721.11

undignified
inelegant 590.2
vulgar 898.10

undiluted 45.7

undiminished
complete 56.9
unabated 34.14
unweakened 159.19
whole 54.11

undine spirit 1014.16
water god 1014.20

undiplomatic 534.11

undirected
purposeless 156.16
unordered 62.12
wandering 291.7

undiscerning
blind 441.9

undiscernible
secret 614.11

undisciplined
disobedient 767.8
intemperate 993.7
lawless 740.5
unrestrained 141.7

undisclosable 614.11

undisclosed
secret 614.11

undiscoverable
inaccessible 510.9
unknown 477.17

undiscovered
unknown 477.17
unrevealed 615.12

undiscriminating
indiscriminate 493.5
unconcerned 636.7

undisguised
genuine 516.14
honest 974.18
unquestioned 513.16
unobscured 555.11
visible 444.6

undismayed 893.20

undisputed
believed 501.23
unquestioned 513.16

undissembling
honest 974.18
natural 736.6

undistinguished
humble 906.9
undifferentiated
493.6
unrenowned 915.14

undistorted
genuine 516.14
straight 250.6

undisturbed
calm 268.12
unexcited 858.11
untroubled 868.8

undivided joined 47.13
one 89.7
whole 54.11

undo defeat 727.6
demolish 693.17
destroy 693.13
detach 49.10
make nervous 859.9
negate 178.7
open 265.13
run 693.11
solve 487.2
take off 232.6

undoing defeat 727.1
destruction 693.1
disassembly 49.6
neutralization 178.2

undone
defeated 727.14
heartbroken 872.29
hopeless 889.15
neglected 534.14
ruined 693.28
terrified 891.34
unaccomplished
723.3

undoubted
believed 501.23
certain 513.16

undoubtedly
certainly 513.25
truly 516.17

undoubting
believing 501.21
credulous 502.8
sure 513.21

undreamed-of
unthought-of 480.5
unusual 85.10

undress
n. dishabille 231.20
plainness 902.3
v. unclothe 232.7

undressed
unadorned 902.8
unclad 232.13

undressing 232.2

undrinkable 429.8

undue excessive 663.16
overpriced 848.12
undeserved 961.9
unjust 977.9
wrong 959.3

undulant curved 252.7
periodic 137.7
rolling 254.10
waving 323.16

undulate billow 395.22
fly 278.49
recur 137.5
wave 323.11

undulating
rolling 254.10
waving 323.16

unduly
excessively 663.22
exorbitantly 848.16
improperly 34.21

unduplicated 23.6

undurable 111.7

undutiful
disobedient 767.8
impious 1030.6
nonreligious 1031.15

undying
continuing 143.7
immortal 112.9

mannish 420.13
unfetter detach 49.10
 loose 763.6
unfettered 762.27
unfilled hungry 634.25
 vacant 187.14
unfinish 721.4
unfinished
 imperfect 678.4
 unaccomplished 723.3
 undeveloped 721.12
 unskilled 734.16
unfit
 inappropriate 27.7
 incompetent 734.19
 inexpedient 671.5
 unable 158.14
 unqualified 721.9
 unserviceable 669.14
 untimely 130.7
 wrong 959.3
unfixed
 inconstant 141.7
 uncertain 514.17
 undetermined 506.8
 unfastened 49.22
unflagging
 industrious 707.22
 persevering 625.7
 unweakened 159.19
unflappable
 firm 624.12
 inexcitable 858.10
 stable 142.12
unflattering
 genuine 516.14
 honest 974.18
unflavored 430.2
unflawed 677.6
unfledged
 immature 124.10
 inexperienced 734.17
 new 122.7
 undeveloped 721.11
unflinching
 persevering 625.7
 stable 142.12
 undaunted 893.20
 unhesitating 624.13
 unnervous 860.2
unfold amplify 593.7
 develop 148.7
 disclose 556.4
 explain 552.10
 manifest 555.5
 open 265.13
 result 154.5
 spread 197.6
unfolding
 n. appearance 446.1
 development 148.2
 disclosure 556.1
 display 555.2
 expansion 593.6
 flowering 411.24
unforced
 adj. developing 148.8
 adj. free 762.23
 voluntary 622.7
 adv. at will 621.5

unforeseeable
 chance 156.15
 uncertain 514.15
 unexpected 540.10
unforeseen
 chance 156.15
 sudden 113.5
 unexpected 540.10
unforgettable
 notable 672.18
 remembered 537.26
unforgivable
 improper 981.16
 unpardonable 977.12
unforgiving 945.3
unforgotten 537.23
unformed
 immature 124.10
 undeveloped 721.12
 unshaped 247.5
unfortified simple 45.7
 unprotected 697.14
unfortunate
 n. unlucky person 729.7
 adj. inexpedient 671.5
 ominous 544.17
 unlucky 729.14
 unsuccessful 725.17
 untimely 130.7
unfortunately
 inauspiciously 544.20
 inexpediently 671.8
 inopportunely 130.8
 unluckily 729.17
unfounded
 baseless 483.13
 false 616.25
 illusory 519.9
 unauthentic 518.19
 unproved 506.8
unfree 764.14
unfreeze 329.21
unfrequented 924.7
unfriendliness
 enmity 929.1
 inhospitality 926.1
 unsociability 923.1
 warlikeness 797.15
unfriendly averse 867.8
 belligerent 797.25
 inhospitable 926.7
 inimical 929.9
 opposing 790.8
 unsociable 923.5
unfrock depose 783.4
 disgrace 915.8
 dismiss 310.19
unfrozen 328.24
unfruitful 166.4
unfulfilled
 discontented 869.5
 unaccomplished 723.3
unfurl develop 148.7
 disclose 556.4
unfurnished 721.9
unfussy plain 902.9
 unmeticulous 534.13
ungag 763.6

ungagged 762.27
ungainly clumsy 734.20
 ugly 899.9
ungallant
 discourteous 937.4
 uncourageous 892.11
ungenerous
 narrow-minded 527.10
 selfish 978.6
 stingy 852.9
ungentlemanly 937.6
ungenuine 616.26
ungettable 510.9
ungiving rigid 356.12
 unyielding 626.9
unglorified 915.14
unglue detach 49.10
 loosen 51.3
unglued 859.13
ungodliness
 immorality 981.1
 nonreligiousness 1031.3
ungodly devilish 675.10
 irreligious 1031.17
 preposterous 503.10
 unvirtuous 981.12
ungovernable
 lawless 740.5
 unrestrained 762.23
ungoverned free 762.28
ungraceful
 clumsy 734.20
 infelicitous 590.2
 ugly 899.9
ungracious
 discourteous 937.4
 inhospitable 926.7
 unkind 939.14
ungraded 62.12
ungrammatic(al) 587.4
ungrammaticalness 587
ungrateful 950.4
ungratified
 discontented 869.5
 unsatisfied 866.20
ungratifying 869.6
ungrounded
 baseless 483.13
 unsubstantial 4.8
ungrudging
 consenting 775.4
 liberal 853.4
 willing 622.6
unguarded artless 756.5
 candid 974.17
 impulsive 630.10
 inattentive 531.8
 negligent 534.10
 unintentional 156.17
 unprotected 697.14
unguent
 n. healing ointment 687.11
 ointment 380.3
 adj. oily 380.9
unguessed 540.10
ungulate
 n. animal 414.3
 adj. footed 212.9

 hoofed 414.49
unhabitable 926.8
unhallowed 1027.3
unhampered
 communicative 554.10
 unimpeded 762.25
 unrestricted 508.2
unhand release 763.5
 relinquish 814.4
unhandicapped 762.25
unhandsome 899.6
unhandy clumsy 734.20
 inconvenient 671.7
 untimely 130.7
 unwieldy 731.18
unhappiness
 disapproval 969.1
 discontent 869.1
 sadness 872.2
 unpleasure 866.1
unhappy
 disapproving 969.22
 discontented 869.5
 inexpedient 671.5
 pleasureless 866.20
 uncheerful 872.21
 unfortunate 729.14
unhappy about 873.8
unharmed safe 698.4
 undamaged 677.8
unharness 763.6
unharnessing 763.2
unhasty 710.6
unhatched 721.8
unhazardous 698.5
unhealthful 684.5
unhealthy sickly 686.50
 unhealthful 684.5
 unsafe 697.11
 unwholesome 686.51
unhearable 451.10
unheard-of new 122.11
 unknown 477.17
 unrenowned 915.14
 unusual 85.10
unhearing deaf 449.6
 unaware 477.13
unheated 333.13
unheeded 534.15
unheedful
 careless 534.11
 inattentive 531.6
unhelpful
 inconsiderate 939.16
 useless 669.14
unheralded 540.10
unheroic 892.11
unhesitating
 confident 513.21
 unfaltering 624.13
 unqualified 508.2
unhidden open 265.18
 unobscured 555.11
 visible 444.6
unhinge
 dislocate 185.5
 madden 473.23
 separate 49.16

United Kingdom
in accord 794.3
integrated 89.10
joined 47.13
United Kingdom 181.4
United Nations
international organi-
zation 743
supranational govern-
ment 741.7
United States
country 181.3
regions of 180.7
uniting
n. addition 40.1
adj. combining 52.7
concurrent 177.4
converging 298.3
unifying 89.12
unit pricing 846.4
unity accord 794.1
completeness 56.1
divine attribute
1013.15
identity 14.1
indivisibility 354.2
oneness 89
simplicity 45.1
totality 54.1
uniformity 17.1
universal
n. idea 479.2
wholeness 54.5
idealism 377.3
adj. comprehensive
76.7
cosmic 375.24
global 79.14
infinite 104.3
pervasive 56.10
total 54.9
usual 84.8
universality
completeness 56.1
generality 79.1
infinity 104.1
wholeness 54.5
universalize 79.9
universally
everywhere 179.11
generally 79.18
universe cosmos 375
frame of reference
525.2
university
n. college 567.7
adj. scholastic 567.18
univocal certain 513.13
intelligible 548.10
unipartite 89.11
unjaundiced 526.12
unjoined
discontinuous 72.4
separate 49.20
unordered 62.12
unjust 977.9
unjustifiable
unjustified 961.9
unkempt rough 261.6
slovenly 62.15
uncouth 898.12
unkind 939.14
unkindly 939.14,25

unkindness 939
unknowable
unintelligible 549.13
unknown 477.17
unknowing
ignorant 477.12
unaware 477.13
unknowingly
ignorantly 477.18
innocently 984.9
unknown
anonymous 584.3
concealed 615.11
not known 477.17
unrenowned 915.14
unknown, the
the future 121.2
the unknowable
477.7
unlabored
natural 589.6
undeveloped 721.12
unlace 49.10
unladylike 937.6
unlamented 867.9
unlatch detach 49.10
loose 763.6
open 265.13
unlawful illegal 999.6
prohibited 778.7
wrong 959.3
unlawfulness
illegality 999.1
impropriety 977.1
wrong 959.1
unlax 711.7
unlearn 538.6
unlearned
inerudite 477.14
instinctive 481.6
unleash detach 49.10
free 763.6
unless
prep. excluding 77.9
conj. excepting 507.16
unlettered 477.14
unlicensed 778.7
unlicked
immature 124.10
uncouth 898.12
undeveloped 721.12
unlikable
distasteful 867.7
hateful 930.8
unpleasant 864.17
unsavory 429.5
unlike different 16.7
dissimilar 21.4
incomparable 491.9
unlikelihood
improbability 512.1
unlikely 512.3
small chance 156.9

unlimited
godlike 1013.20
infinite 104.3
intemperate 993.7
omnipotent 157.13
unqualified 508.2
unrestricted 762.26
unlit 337.13
unliterary
unlearned 477.14
vernacular 580.18
unlivable 926.8
unload lighten 353.6
relieve 886.7
sell 829.8
sell stocks 833.24
unpack 310.22
unloading
evacuation 310.6
lightening 353.3
relief 886.3
unlock detach 49.10
explain 552.10
loose 763.6
open 265.13
solve 487.2
unlooked-for
chance 156.15
sudden 113.5
unexpected 540.10
unloosen detach 49.10
free 763.6
unloosing 763.2
unlovable 867.7
unloved 867.10
unlovely 899.6
unloving
unfeeling 856.9
unkind 939.14

unloyal
nonobservant 769.5
unfaithful 975.20
unluckily
inauspiciously 544.20
unfortunately 729.17
unlucky
ominous 544.17
unfortunate 729.14
untimely 130.7
unlucky day fate 640.2
wrong time 130.2
unmade uncreated 2.9
unprepared 721.8
unmake 693.17
unmaking 693.5
unman
domineer 741.16
frighten 891.23
make nervous 859.9
subdue 764.9
unnerve 158.12
weaken 160.10
unmanageability
clumsiness 734.3
ungovernability 626.4
unwieldiness 731.8
unmanageable
ungovernable 626.12
unwieldy 731.18
unmanly
cowardly 892.10
effeminate 421.14
unmanned
cowardly 892.10
devitalized 158.19
terrified 891.34
unnerved 859.13
untended 187.14
unmannerly 937.5

unmarked
undamaged 677.8
unheeded 534.15
unmarketable 829.15
unmarred
peerless 36.15
unmarried
n. celibate 934.2
adj. unwedded 934.7
unmask 556.4
unmasking 556.1
unmatched best 674.18
dissimilar 21.4
unmatured
immature 124.10
inexperienced 734.17
premature 131.8
unmeant 156.17
unmeasured
immeasurable 101.10
indescribable 920.13
base 915.12
unmelodious 461.4
unmelted cold 333.13
impenitent 874.5
unmentionable
base 915.12

unmentionables 231.22
unmentioned 546.9
unmerciful
heartless 939.23
pitiless 945.3
unmerited undue 961.9
unjust 977.9
unmethodical
haphazard 62.12
irregular 138.3
unmilitary 803.10
unmindful
careless 534.11
forgetful 538.9
inattentive 531.6
inconsiderate 939.16
incurious 529.3
unaware 477.13
unconcerned 636.7
ungrateful 950.4
unmingled 45.7
unmistakable
certain 513.13
clearly visible 444.7
intelligible 548.10
manifest 555.8
unqualified 508.2
unmistaken 516.12
unmitigated
changed 139.9
outright 34.12
thorough 56.10
undiminished 34.14
unqualified 508.2
unsoftened 162.16
unmixed pure 677.6
simple 45.7
unmolested 698.4
unmoor 275.18
unmoored 275.61
unmotivated 156.16
unmourned 867.9

unproficient 734.15
unprofitable
disadvantageous 671.6
fruitless 669.12
unprofitably
at a loss 812.9
disadvantageously 671.9
unprofound
shallow 210.5
superficial 469.20
unprogressive
conservative 140.8
right-wing 745.17
unprohibitive
true 516.12
unpromising
ominous 544.17
unlikely 512.3
unprompted
unintentional 156.17
voluntary 622.7
unpronounced
silent 451.10
unexpressed 546.9
unpropitious
ominous 544.17
opposing 790.8
untimely 130.7
unprosperous
poor 838.7
unfortunate 729.14
unprotected
defenseless 697.14
helpless 158.18
unprovable
uncertain 514.15
undemonstrable 506.9
unproved
erroneous 518.16
illogical 483.12
not proved 506.8
unauthoritative 514.20
unprovided
ill-provided 662.12
unfit 721.9
unprovidential
improvident 729.14
unprovincial
unprejudiced 526.8
unpublishable 614.14
unpublished 546.9
unqualified
absolute 56.10
complete 677.7
genuine 516.14
inappropriate 27.7
incompetent 734.19
insufficient 662.9
outright 34.12
unable 158.14
unconditional 508.2
unfit 721.9
unrestricted 762.26
unquelled
free 762.28
unmitigated 162.16
victorious 726.9
unquenchable
greedy 634.27
inextinguishable 142.18

unquestionable
believable 501.24
certain 513.15
unquestioned
believed 501.23
certain 513.16
unquestioning 508.2
unquiet active 707.20
agitated 324.16
impatient 862.6
pleasureless 866.20
restless 857.25
unquotable 614.14
unravel
come apart 49.8
disentangle 305.10
explain 552.10
extricate 763.7
simplify 45.5
solve 487.2
unraveling
extrication 763.3
unreachable 510.9
unread 477.14
unreadable 549.19
unready careless 534.11
inattentive 531.8
late 132.16
unexpectant 540.9
unprepared 721.8
untimely 130.7
unreal illusory 519.9
imaginary 535.19
nonexistent 2.8
tenuous 4.6
ungenuine 616.26
unreal 2.8
visionary 535.24
unrealistic
idealization 535.7
illusoriness 519.2
nonexistence 2.1
unsubstantiality 4.1
unrealizable 510.8
unrealized
unaccomplished 723.3
unseen 445.5
unreason 470.2
unreasonable
unjust 977.12
unwise 470.9
unreasonableness
excess 663.1
exorbitance 848.4
illogicalness 483.2
unwiseness 470.2
unreasoning
emotionalistic 855.20
impulsive 630.10
thoughtless 480.4
unintelligent 469.13
unrecalled 538.8

unreceptive
inhospitable 926.7
unrecognizable 445.6
unrecognized 950.5
unrecollected 538.8
unrecorded 546.9
unredeemable 981.18
unreduced
undiminished 34.14
whole 54.11
unreel 148.7
unrefined
coarse-textured 351.6
discourteous 937.6
infelicitous 590.2
rough 261.6
undeveloped 721.12
unlearned 477.14
vulgar 898.12
unreflecting
impulsive 630.10
unwise 470.9
unrefreshed 717.6
unrefutable
certain 513.15
unrefuted
proved 505.22
unregarded
neglected 534.14
unheeded 534.15
unrespected 965.7
unregenerate
irreclaimable 981.18
irreligious 1031.18
obstinate 626.8
unsacred 1027.3
unregretful 874.4
unregretted 874.4
unrelated 10.5
unrelaxed rigid 356.11
tense 859.12
unrelenting
drawn out 593.12
persevering 625.7
strict 757.7
unyielding 626.9
unreliability
fickleness 629.3
inconstancy 141.2
unbelievability 503.3
uncertainty 514.6
unsafeness 697.2
untrustworthiness 975.4
unreliable fickle 629.6
inconstant 141.7
unauthentic 518.19
uncertain 514.19
unsafe 697.11
untrustworthy 975.19
wavering 141.7

unrelieved
featureless 187.13
monotonous 17.6
outright 34.12
unremarkable 680.8
unremitting
constant 135.5
continuous 71.8
industrious 707.22
perpetual 112.7
persevering 625.7
sustained 143.7
unchangeable 142.17
uninterrupted 71.8
unremorseful
pitiless 945.3
unregretful 874.4
unremunerated 842.12
unremunerative 669.12
unrenowned 915.14
unrepeatable 990.9
unrepeated 89.9
unrepentant 874.5
unreproachful 968.18
unrequested 622.7
unrequited
needless 669.10
voluntary 622.7

unresemblance 21.1
unresembling 21.4
unresentful 947.6
unreserve candor 974.4
communicativeness 974.4
unreserved
artless 736.5
candid 974.17
communicative 554.10
unrestrained 762.23
unresolved 627.9
unrespectable 915.10
unrespected 965.7
unresponsive
heartless 939.23
unfeeling 856.9
uninfluenceable 173.4
unrest 173.4
agitation 324.1
excitement 857.4
motion 267.1
unrestful 857.25
unrestrained
candid 974.17
communicative 554.10
excessive 663.16
fervent 855.23
free 762.23
intemperate 993.7
lawless 740.5
unchaste 989.24
unconstrained 762.23
unstrict 758.4
unrestraint 762.3

unwise 470.9
weak 160.15
unsparing
industrious 707.22
liberal 853.4
strict 757.6
unkind 939.22
unspeakable evil 981.16
extraordinary 85.14
horrendous 864.19
indescribable 920.13
ineffable 1026.7
insulting 965.6
unspecified
anonymous 584.3
general 79.11
vague 514.18
unspectacular 680.8
unspent 668.12
unspiritual
carnal 987.6
materialistic 376.9
worldly 1031.16
unspoiled natural 736.6
outright 34.12
preserved 701.11
undamaged 677.8
unspoken secret 614.11
tacit 451.11
unexpressed 546.9
unsportsmanlike 977.10
unspotted chaste 988.4
clean 681.25
honest 974.13
innocent 984.7
perfect 677.6
unstable
changeable 141.7
transient 111.7
unbalanced 31.5
unreliable 514.19
unsafe 697.11
wavering 18.3
weak 160.15
unstaffed 187.14
unstained chaste 988.4
clean 681.25
honest 974.13
unsteadfast
inconstant 141.7
unfaithful 975.20
unreliable 514.19
unsteady
changeable 141.7
fluttering 324.18
inconstant 18.3
irregular 138.3
shaky 160.16
unbalanced 31.5
unreliable 514.19
unsafe 697.11
unstick detach 49.10
loosen 51.3
unstinting 853.4
unstirred
unaffected 856.11
unexcited 858.11
unstop 265.13
unstoppable 639.15
unstopped
constant 135.5
continuous 71.8
open 265.18
unstrained 860.2
unstrap detach 49.10
loose 763.6
unstressed 594.31
unstruck 856.11
unstrung
terrified 891.34
unnerved 859.13
weak 160.12
unstuck 49.22
unstudied
informal 647.3
unexamined 534.16
unpremeditated 630.11
unprepared 721.8
unsturdy 160.15
unsubject
exempt 762.29
free 762.28
unsubmissive
insubordinate 767.9
nonconforming 83.5
resistant 792.5
ungovernable 626.12
unsubstantial
frail 160.14
illogical 483.12
illusory 519.9
immaterial 377.7
intangible 4.5
tenuous 355.4
unreal 2.8
unreliable 514.19
weak 160.15
unsubstantiated 506.8
unsubtle 493.5
unsuccessful 725.17
unsuccessfulness 725.1
unsuitability
inexpedience 671.1
insufficiency 662.1
unfitness 27.3
unpreparedness 721.1
unsatisfactoriness 869.2
untimeliness 130.1
uselessness 669.1
vulgarity 898.1
wrong 959.1
unsuitable
inappropriate 27.7
inexpedient 671.5
unacceptable 869.7
unserviceable 669.14
untimely 130.7
vulgar 898.10
wrong 959.3
unsuited
inappropriate 27.7
unfit 721.9
unsullied chaste 988.4
clean 681.25
honest 974.13
innocent 984.7
natural 721.13
unsung disliked 867.9
unexpressed 546.9
unrenowned 915.14
unsupplied 662.12
unsupportable
baseless 483.13
unprovable 506.9
unsupported
alone 89.8
baseless 483.13
unproved 506.8
unsuppressed
communicative 554.10
unrestrained 762.23
unsure ignorant 477.12
uncertain 514.15
unconfident 514.22
unreliable 514.19
unsafe 697.11
unsurpassed
best 674.18
peerless 36.15
unsurprised
expectant 539.11
unastonished 921.3
unsusceptible
unchangeable 142.17
unfeeling 856.9
uninfluenceable 173.4
unsuspected
believed 501.23
unknown 477.17
unsuspecting
credulous 502.8
inexpectant 540.9
trusting 501.22
unaware 477.13
unprotected 697.14
unsuspicious
artless 736.5
credulous 502.8
trusting 501.22
unsustainable
baseless 483.13
improvable 506.9
illogical 483.12
unproved 506.8
unsustained
baseless 483.13
illogical 483.12
unproved 506.8
unswayable 173.4
unswayed
impartial 976.10
uninfluenced 173.5
unprejudiced 526.12
unsweet 432.5
unswept 682.20
unswerving
direct 290.13
firm 624.12
persevering 625.7
straight 250.6
unsymmetric(al)
distorted 249.10
nonuniform 62.12
unsympathetic
pitiless 945.3
unfeeling 856.9
unkind 939.14
unsystematic
haphazard 62.12
irregular 138.3
slovenly 62.15
untactful
inconsiderate 534.11
undiscriminating 493.5
untainted chaste 988.4
clean 681.25
innocent 984.7
perfect 677.6
unspoiled 701.11
untaken 187.14
untalented
unable 158.14
unintelligent 469.13
unskilled 734.16
untalkative 613.9
untalked-of 546.9
untamable 626.12
untamed free 762.28
savage 162.20
uncouth 898.12
untangle
extricate 763.7
simplify 45.5
solve 487.2
untangling
extrication 763.3
solution 487.1
untarnished
chaste 988.4
clean 681.25
honest 974.13
untasted 668.12
untaught
unlearned 477.14
unskilled 734.16
unteachable 469.15
untempered 162.16
untenanted 187.14
untended
neglected 534.14
unstaffed 187.14
untenable
baseless 483.13
helpless 158.18
unacceptable 869.7
untether 763.6
untested 506.8
unthankful 950.4
unthinkable
impossible 510.7
unbelievable 503.10
unthinking
careless 534.11
impulsive 630.10
inconsiderate 939.16
involuntary 639.14
thoughtless 480.4
unintelligent 469.13
unintentional 156.17
unthought-of
undreamed-of 480.5
unexpected 540.9
unthoughtful
impulsive 630.10
inconsiderate 939.16
unwise 470.9
untidy dirty 682.22
slipshod 534.12
slovenly 62.15

untie detach 49.10
  loose 763.6
untied adrift 275.61
  free 762.27
  liberated 763.10
  unfastened 49.22
until 105.15
untilled fallow 721.14
  unproductive 166.4
untimely
  inappropriate 27.7
  inexpedient 671.5
  late 132.16
  premature 131.8
  unseasonable 130.7
untimid 893.19
untired 695.5
untiring
  persevering 625.7
  tough 359.4
untold infinite 104.3
  innumerable 101.10
  secret 614.11
  uncertain 514.17
  unexpressed 546.9
untouchable
  n. outcast 926.4
  adj. out-of-the-way 199.9
  prohibited 778.7
  sacred 1026.7
  unfeeling 856.9
untouched
  impenitent 874.5
  natural 721.13
  new 122.7
  safe 698.4
  unaffected 856.11
  undamaged 677.8
  unknown 477.17
  unused 668.12
untoward
  adverse 729.13
  bad 675.7
  ominous 544.17
  untimely 130.7
untrained
  unaccustomed 643.4
  unskilled 734.16
untraveled 268.15
untreated 721.12
untried
  inexperienced 734.17
  new 122.7
  unproved 506.8
untrimmed
  honest 974.18
  unadorned 902.8
untrodden new 122.7
  unpierced 266.10
  unused 668.12
untroubled
  pacific 803.9
  still 268.12
  unbothered 868.8
  unexcited 858.11
untrue
  erroneous 518.16
  false 616.25
  nonobservant 769.5
  unfaithful 975.20
untrusting 503.9

untrustworthy
  dishonest 975.19
  unreliable 514.19
  unsafe 697.11
untruth error 518.1
  falseness 616.1
  lie 616.11
untruthful
  dishonest 616.34
  insincere 975.18
untutored
  unlearned 477.14
  unskilled 734.16
untwist simplify 45.5
  solve 487.2
unusable 669.14
unused new 122.7
  not used 668.12
  remaining 43.7
  surplus 663.18
  unaccustomed 643.4
unused to
  inexperienced 734.17
  unaccustomed 643.4
unusual new 122.11
  rare 136.2
  uncommon 85.10
unusually
  exceptionally 34.20
  uncommonly 85.17
unutterable
  indescribable 920.13
  ineffable 1026.7
unuttered
  secret 614.11
  silent 451.10
  tacit 451.11
  unexpressed 546.9
unvalued
  unappreciated 867.9
  underestimated 498.3
unvarnished
  genuine 516.14
  honest 974.18
  in plain style 591.3
  natural 736.6
  unadorned 902.8
unvarying
  constant 135.5
  permanent 140.7
  tedious 884.8
  unchangeable 142.17
  uniform 17.5
unveil disclose 556.4
  expose 232.5
  unclose 265.13
unveiling
  disclosure 556.1
  display 555.2
  inauguration 68.5
unventilated
  airless 268.16
  closed 266.9
unverified
  unauthoritative 514.20
  unproved 506.8
unversed
  ignorant 477.12
  inexperienced 734.17

unvirtuous
  unchaste 989.23
  unrighteous 981.12
unvoiced silent 451.10
  unexpressed 546.9
unwanted
  undesired 867.11
  unwelcome 926.9
unwarned 540.9
  unexpectant 540.9
  unprotected 697.14
unwarrantable
  illegal 999.6
  unjust 977.12
unwarranted
  baseless 483.13
  illegal 999.6
  overpriced 848.12
  unauthoritative 514.20
  undue 961.9
unwary artless 736.5
  inattentive 531.8
  negligent 534.10
  rash 894.7
unwashed 682.20
unwatched
  neglected 534.14
  unprotected 697.14
unwatchful
  inattentive 531.8
  negligent 534.10
unwavering
  persevering 625.7
  stable 142.12
  sure 513.21
unwearied
  unnervous 860.2
  unweakened 159.19
unweakened 159.19
  industrious 707.22
  persevering 625.7
  refreshed 695.5
unweave simplify 45.5
  solve 487.2
unwed 934.7
unweeded 411.40
unwelcome
  disliked 867.11
  unpleasant 864.17
  unwanted 926.9
unwell 686.52
unwholesome
  diseased 686.51
  unhealthful 684.5
unwieldy bulky 195.19
  clumsy 734.20
  inconvenient 671.7
  ponderous 352.17
  stilted 590.3
  unmanageable 731.18
unwilling
  disinclined 623.5
  involuntary 639.14
  refusing 776.6
unwind
  calm oneself 858.7
  develop 148.7
  relax 711.7
  simplify 45.5
unwise
  inexpedient 671.5
  injudicious 470.9

unintelligent 469.13
unwished 867.11
unwitting
  involuntary 639.14
  unaware 477.13
  unintentional 156.17
unwomanly 420.13
unwonted
  unaccustomed 643.4
  unusual 85.10
unworkable
  impracticable 510.8
  unserviceable 669.14
unworldly
  heavenly 1018.13
  immaterial 377.7
  pious 1028.9
  supernatural 85.15
unworried 868.8
unworthy
  n. bad person 986.1
  adj. evil 981.16
  undue 961.9
  unimportant 673.19
unwrap disclose 556.4
  open 265.13
  take off 232.6
unwrinkled 260.9
unwritten
  speech 594.30
  traditional 123.12
  unexpressed 546.9
unyielding firm 624.12
  immovable 142.15
  inevitable 639.15
  invincible 159.17
  obstinate 626.9
  pitiless 945.3
  resistant 792.5
  rigid 356.12
  strict 757.7
  substantial 3.7
  uninfluenceable 173.4
up
  n. increase 38.1
  v. ascend 315.8
  elevate 317.5
  increase 38.4
  make larger 197.4
  promote 782.2
  adj. awake 713.8
  adv. aloft 207.26
  upward 315.16
  vertically 213.13
  prep. toward 290.28
up-and-coming 707.23
up and down
  alternately 137.11
  perpendicularly 213.14
  to and fro 323.21
up-and-down
  alternate 323.19
  perpendicular 213.12
up-and-up 974.14
upbeat
  n. improvement 691.1
  music 463.26
  pulse 137.3
  adj. optimistic 888.12
upbraid 969.17

upbringing 562.3

upcast raised 317.9 / upturned 315.15

upchuck sicken at 867.4 / vomit 310.25

upcoming approaching 296.4 / ascending 315.14 / imminent 152.3

up-country *n.* hinterland 182.2 / inland 225.3; *adj.* country 182.8 / inland 225.8 / uncouth 182.7

update date 114.13 / modernize 122.6

updraft ascent 315.1 / wind 403.1

upend erect 213.9 / overthrow 693.20

upended 213.11

upgrade *n.* acclivity 219.6 / ascent 315.1; *v.* make better 691.9 / promote 782.2; *adj.* ascending 315.14 / sloping upward 219.17

upheaval change 139.1 / convulsion 162.5 / elevation 317.1 / emotional outburst 857.8

upheave destroy 693.10 / elevate 317.5 / erect 213.9 / get up 213.8 / surge 315.8 / ruin 693.3

upheld 216.24

uphill *n.* acclivity 219.6 / ascent 315.1; *adj.* ascending 315.14 / difficult 731.16 / laborious 716.18 / sloping upward 219.17

uphold aid 785.12 / approve 968.9 / buoy up 353.8 / confirm 505.12 / defend 1006.10 / elevate 317.5 / preserve 701.7 / support 216.21

upholder assenter 521.7 / associate 787.9 / defender 799.7 / supporter 216.2

upholster 228.28

upholstered 228.33

upholstery 228.1

UPI 605.23

up in arms *adj.* at odds 795.16 / prepared 720.16 / resistant 792.5; *adv.* at war 797.28 / in opposition 790.9

upkeep aid 785.3 / preservation 701.1 / support 216.1

upland *n.* highland 207.3 / plain 387.1 / the country 182.1; *adj.* highland 207.22 / rustic 182.6

uplift *n.* acclivity 219.6 / ascent 315.1 / elevation 317.1 / improvement 691.1; *v.* buoy up 353.8 / cheer 870.8 / elevate 317.5 / erect 213.9 / glorify 914.13 / make better 691.9 / raised 317.9

uplifted high 207.19

uplifting *n.* elevation 317.1; *adj.* elevating 317.10

upmost *n.* summit 211.2; *adj.* high 207.24 / top 211.10

upon *adv.* after which 117.7; *prep.* against 200.25 / atop 211.16 / by means of 658.7 / in relation to 9.13 / on 228.37 / toward 290.28

up on informed 475.18 / skilled in 733.25 / versed in 475.19

upper *n.* stimulant 687.9; *adj.* high 207.24 / superior 36.12

upper case 603.6

upper-case literal 581.8 / typographical 603.20

upper class nobility 918.2 / superiors 36.5

upperclassman 566.6

upper crust nobility 918.2 / society 644.6 / superiors 36.5

uppercut 283.5

upper hand advantage 36.2 / ascendancy 739.6 / influence 172.1

upper house legislature 742.1 / upper chamber 742.3

uppermost high 207.24 / most important 672.23 / superlative 36.13 / top 211.10

uppity arrogant 912.9 / insolent 913.8 / in opposition 790.9

upraise buoy up 353.8 / elevate 317.5 / erect 213.9 / raised 317.9 / vertical 213.11

upraised 317.9

uprear elevate 317.5 / erect 213.9 / raised 317.9 / vertical 213.11

upright *n.* piano 465.13 / post 217.4 / support 216.8 / vertical 213.2; *adj.* erect 213.9 / honest 974.13 / raised 317.9 / straight 250.6 / vertical 213.11 / virtuous 980.7; *adv.* vertically 213.13

uprise *v.* ascend 315.8 / become higher 207.17 / be high 207.15 / get up 213.8 / incline 219.10

uprising *n.* acclivity 219.6 / ascent 315.1 / erection 213.5 / revolt 767.4; *adj.* sloping upward 219.17

uproar commotion 62.4 / excitement 857.3 / noise 453.3 / outcry 459.4 / violence 162.2

uproarious excited 857.22 / noisy 453.12 / violent 162.17

uproot destroy 693.14 / dislodge 185.6 / extract 305.10

ups and downs alternation 323.5 / vicissitudes 156.5

upset *n.* agitation 324.1 / anxiety 890.1 / confusion 532.3 / disorder 62.1 / frustration 730.3 / inversion 220.2 / perplexity 514.3 / refutation 506.2 / revolution 147.1 / ruin 693.3 / unseating 185.2 / violence 162.2; *v.* agitate 324.10 / bewilder 514.12 / capsize 275.4 / confuse 532.7 / discompose 63.4 / disorder 62.9 / distress 866.15 / embarrass 866.16 / excite 857.13 / invert 220.6 / make nervous 859.9 / overcome 727.7 / overthrow 693.20 / refute 506.5 / revolutionize 147.4 / thwart 730.15 / trouble 890.3 / unbalance 31.3; *adj.* agitated 324.16 / bewildered 514.23 / confused 532.12 / defeated 727.14 / disorderly 62.13 / disproved 506.7 / distressed 866.22 / excited 857.21 / overwrought 857.24 / unnerved 859.13

upsetting bewildering 514.25 / exciting 857.28 / worrisome 890.9

upshot result 154.1 / solution 487.1

upside down contrarily 15.9 / inversely 220.8

upside-down confused 62.16 / reversed 220.7

upstage *v.* act 611.34 / snub 966.5; *adv.* theater 611.41

upstairs aloft 207.26 / up 315.16

upstanding honest 974.13 / vertical 213.11

upstart *n.* impudent person 913.5; *adj.* arrogant 912.9 / parvenu 919.13

upstate 315.16

upstream 315.16

upsurge *n.* ascent 315.1 / increase 38.1; *v.* ascend 315.8

upsweep *n.* ascent 315.1 / increase 38.1; *v.* ascend 315.8

upswing ascent 315.1 / improvement 691.1

increase 38.1
uptight
tense 859.12
up to able 157.14
competent 733.22
prepared for 720.18
scheming 654.14
sufficient 661.6
until 105.15
up-to-date
fashionable 644.11
informed 475.18
modern 122.13
present 120.2
up to one's ears in
busy 707.21
involved in 176.4
up-to-the-minute
fashionable 644.11
modern 122.13
present 120.2
uptown
n. city district 183.6
adj. urban 183.10
adv. up 315.16
uptrend
improvement 691.1
increase 38.1
upturn 315.2
upturn
n. business cycle 827.9
increase 38.1
inversion 220.2
uptrend 315.2
v. overturn 220.6
slope up 315.13
upturned 315.15
upward
adj. ascending 315.14
flowing 267.8
adv. aloft 207.26
up 315.16
upwards of
about 200.26
several 101.7
upwind
adj. ascend 315.8
fly 278.52
upwind
water travel 275.68
windward 242.9
uranium 327.12
uranium 235 326.5
uranology 375.19
urban 183.10
urbane
courteous 936.14
decorous 897.10
sociable 922.18
urbanite 190.6
urban renewal
housing 188.3
renovation 694.4
urchin bad child 125.4
waif 274.3
urge
n. desire 634.1
impulse 630.1
motivation 648.6
v. advise 754.6
egg on 648.16
hasten 709.4

incite 648.14
insist 753.7
pressure 774.12
urgency
dire necessity 639.4
entreaty 774.3
importance 672.4
insistence 753.3
motivation 648.6
precedence 64.1
urgent
adj. demanding 753.8
eloquent 600.13
hasty 709.9
important 672.21
motivating 648.25
necessary 639.12
pressing 774.18
interj. make hastel 709.16
urgently 753.10
urge upon 773.8
urinal rest room 311.10
toilet 311.11
urinalysis 689.13
urinary 311.20
urinate 311.14
urine body fluid 388.3
excretion 311.5
urn ceramic ware 576.2
funeral urn 410.12
ursine 414.47
urtext 25.1
USA 181.3
usable 665.22
usage
acceptation 545.4
custom 642.1
diction 588.1
employment 665.1
habit 642.4
language 580.1
phrase 585.1
treatment 665.2
word 582.1
use
n. benefit 665.4
custom 642.1
employment 665
estate 810.4
function 665.5
habit 642.4
utility 665.3
wear 692.5
v. behave toward 737.6
deal with 665.12
employ 665.10
exert 716.8
exploit 665.16
practice 705.7
used employed 665.23
lost 812.7
old 123.18
wasted 854.9
used to
accustomed 642.17
familiar with 642.18
habituated 642.19
used up
consumed 666.4
exhausted 717.8

lost 812.7
weakened 160.18
worn-out 692.38
useful
employable 665.18
expedient 670.5
good 674.12
helpful 785.21
instrumental 658.6
usefulness
expedience 670.1
goodness 674.1
helpfulness 785.10
utility 665.3
useless
disadvantageous 671.6
ineffective 158.15
pointless 669.9
unsuccessful 725.17
uselessness
failure 725.1
ineffectiveness 158.3
inexpedience 671.1
inutility 669
user addict 642.10
employer 665.9
legal right of use 665.7
use up consume 666.2
fatigue 717.4
spend 665.13
waste 854.4
usher
n. attendant 750.5
doorkeeper 699.12
escort 73.5
theater man 611.28
wedding attendant 933.5
v. escort 73.8
usher in
announce 116.3
begin 68.11
pioneer 66.3
precede 64.2
usual customary 642.15
frequent 135.4
mediocre 680.8
medium 32.3
ordinary 79.12
regular 84.8
routine 59.6
typical 572.11
usual, the 84.3
usually
customarily 642.22
frequently 135.6
generally 79.17
normally 84.9
usurer 820.3
usurious 848.12
usurp
appropriate 822.19
assume 961.8
encroach 313.9
take command 739.14
usurpation
accession to power 739.12
appropriation 822.4

overstepping 313.3
seizure 961.3
usurper arrogator 961.4
tyrant 749.14
usury
illicit business 826.1
interest 840.3
lending 820.1
overcharge 848.5
utensil container 193.1
equipment 659.4
tool 348.1
uterine genital 419.27
related 11.6
uterus sex organ 419.10
womb 153.9
utilitarian
businesslike 656.15
philosophy 500.9
useful 665.18
utility
n. company 788.9
helpfulness 785.10
machinery 348.4
usefulness 665.3
adj. substitute 149.8
utilization 665.8
utilize employ 665.10
use materials 378.8
utmost
n. completion 56.5
summit 211.2
adj. extreme 34.13
superlative 36.13
utopia
good times 728.4
hope 888.5
paradise 535.11
utopian
n. optimist 888.6
reformer 691.6
visionary 535.13
adj. idealized 535.23
optimistic 888.12
reformational 691.16
utter
v. disperse 75.4
divulge 556.5
monetize 835.26
pass counterfeit money 835.28
say 594.23
adj. outright 34.12
sound 677.7
thorough 56.10
unqualified 508.2
utterance
affirmation 523.1
articulation 594.6
phrase 585.1
remark 594.4
speaking 594.3
word 582.1
uttered 594.30
utterly
completely 56.16
extremely 34.22
U-turn
about-face 295.3

curve 252.3

V

---

vacancy
nonexistence 2.1
position 656.5
stupidity 469.6
thoughtlessness 480.1
vacuity 187.2
vacant empty 187.13
inexpressive 549.20
open 187.14
stupid 469.19
thoughtless 480.1
vacate abandon 633.5
leave 301.8
relinquish 814.3
repeal 779.2
resign 784.2
vacation
n. absence 187.4
interim 109.1
pause 144.3
repeal 779.1
rest 711.3
v. holiday 711.9
vaccinate 689.34
vaccination 689.18
vaccine
injection 689.18
medicine 687.28
vacillate
be capricious 629.4
be irresolute 627.8
be unsure 514.10
fluctuate 141.5
oscillate 323.10
vacillating fickle 629.6
inconstant 141.7
irresolute 627.10
oscillating 323.15
vacillation
fluctuation 141.3
irresolution 627.2
oscillation 323.1
uncertainty 514.1
vacuole 406.5
vacuous
ignorant 477.12
nonexistent 2.7
stupid 469.19
thoughtless 480.4
trivial 673.16
vacant 187.13
vacuum
n. nonexistence 2.1
stupidity 469.6
void 187.3
v. sweep 681.23
vacuum tube 343.11,16
vacuum tube
components 343.19
vagabond
n. bad person 986.2
vagrant 274.3
v. wander 273.22
adj. wandering 273.36
vagary caprice 629.1
obliquity 219.1
vagina duct 396.13
sex organ 419.10

vaginal covering 228.36
genital 419.27
vagrancy
indolence 708.5
wandering 273.3
vagrant
n. bad person 986.2
bum 708.9
vagabond 274.3
adj. capricious 629.5
inconstant 141.7
stray 291.7
wandering 273.36
vague formless 247.4
general 79.11
indistinct 445.6
obscure 549.15
thin 205.16
uncertain 514.18
unordered 62.12
vaguely
chaotically 62.19
indefinitely 514.27
unintelligibly 549.22
vagueness
formlessness 247.1
indefiniteness 514.4
indistinctness 445.2
obscurity 549.3
thinness 205.4
unsubstantiality 4.1
vain baseless 483.13
boastful 910.10
futile 669.13
hopeless 889.13
ineffective 158.15
proud 905.9
self-important 909.8
trivial 673.16
vainglorious
boastful 910.10
overproud 909.8
vainglory
boasting 910.3
vanity 909.1
valediction
n. departure 301.4
speech 599.2
valedictory
adj. departing 301.19
vale Earth 375.10
valley 257.9
valence 379.3
valentine 932.12
valet
n. male servant 750.4
v. serve 750.13
Valhalla 1018.11
valiant
n. brave person 893.8
adj. courageous
893.17
valid evidential 505.17
good 674.12
legal 998.10
sound 516.13

validate
authorize 777.11
confirm 505.12
legalize 998.8
make certain 513.12
ratify 521.12
test 489.8
validated
proved 505.21
ratified 521.14
true 516.12
validity goodness 674.1
legality 998.1
permissibility 777.8
power 157.1
reliability 513.4
soundness 516.4
Valkyrie 797.17
valley, glen 257.9
ravine 201.2
valor 893.1
valorous 893.17
valuable
precious 848.10
useful 665.21
valuate judge 494.9
measure 490.11

value
n. artistry 574.10
automation 349.10
benefit 665.4
color quality 362.6
goodness 674.1
importance 672.1
meaning 545.1
measure 490.2
preciousness 848.2
worth 846.3
v. judge 494.9
measure 490.11
price 846.13
rate highly 672.12
respect 964.4
valued
measured 490.14
priced 846.16
respected 964.11
valueless paltry 673.18
worthless 669.11
valve
electron tube 343.11
gate 396.10
stopper 266.4
wind instrument
465.7
valvular 396.23
vamoose
v. depart 301.9
flee 631.11
interj. go away!
310.30
vamp
n. fire fighter 332.4
flirt 932.10
improvisation 462.27
overture 462.26
seductress 989.15
sweetheart 931.10
tempter 650.3
v. fascinate 650.6
improvise 630.8
seduce 931.21
touch up 691.11

vampire
bewitcher 1035.9
extortionist 822.12
fiend 1016.7
frightener 891.9
monster 943.6
seductress 989.15
sweetheart 931.10
tempter 650.3
van front 240.2
guard 699.9
leading 292.1
railway car 272.14
wagon 272.2,26
vandal destroyer 693.8
vandalism
cruelty 939.11
destruction 693.1
misbehavior 738.1
violence 162.1
vandalize
destroy 693.10
wreck 162.10
Vandyke 230.8
vane 403.17
vanguard front 240.2
guard 699.9
precursor 66.1
the latest thing 122.2
vanish
be destroyed 693.23
be transient 111.6
cease to exist 2.5
disappear 447.2
leave 301.8
vanished absent 187.10
no more 2.10
past 119.7
vanishing
n. disappearance
447.1
adj. disappearing
447.3
vanity boasting 910.1
futility 669.2
pride 905.1
self-importance 909
triviality 673.3
vanity case 900.11
vanquish 727.10
vanquished 727.16
vanquisher 726.2
vantage
sphere of influence
172.4
superiority 36.2
viewpoint 439.7
vapid insipid 430.2
mediocre 680.7
prosaic 610.5
stupid 469.19
trivial 673.16
uninteresting 883.6
weak 160.17
vapor
n. fog 404.2
fume 401
illusion 519.1
spirit 4.3

steam 328.10
thing imagined 535.5
v. be bombastic 601.6
bluster 911.3
boast 910.6
exhale 310.23
talk nonsense 547.5
vaporization 401.5
vaporize destroy 693.10
evaporate 401.8
strike dead 409.18
vaporizer 401.6
vaporous
fanciful 535.22
gaseous 401.9
rare 355.4
tenuous 4.6
vapor trail
aviation 278.39
track 568.8
vaquero herder 416.3
rider 274.8
variability
changeability 141.2
inconstancy 18.1
irregularity 138.1
variable
changeable 141.6
inconstant 141.7
irregular 138.3
uncertain 514.15
uneven 18.3
variably
changeably 141.8
irregularly 138.4
variance
difference 16.1
disagreement 795.2
disparity 27.1
dissatisfaction 522.1
variant different 16.7
disagreeing 27.6
variation change 139.1
deviation 291.1
difference 16.1
discrimination 16.4
fluctuation 141.3
inconstancy 141.2
multiformity 19.1
music arrangement 462.5
music division 462.24
unevenness 18.1
varied different 16.7
diversified 19.4
mixed 44.15
variegate diversify 18.2
polychrome 374.7
variegated
different 16.7
many-colored 374.9
nonuniform 18.3
rainbow 362.15
variegation
comparisons 374.6
difference 16.1
multicolor 374
multiformity 19.1
nonuniformity 18.1
variety biology 61.5
change 139.1
difference 16.1

inconstancy 141.2
kind 61.3
miscellany 74.13
multiformity 19.1
nonuniformity 18.1
plurality 100.1
sect 1020.3
theater 611.1
variety store 832.1
variform 18.3
various different 16.7
diversified 19.4
nonuniform 18.3
plural 100.7
several 101.7
varmint
bad person 986.7
creature 414.2
vermin 414.3
varnish
n. art equipment 574.19
coating 228.12
extenuation 1006.5
fakery 616.3
pretext 649.1
v. color 362.13
conceal 615.6
distort 249.6
extenuate 1006.12
falsify 616.16
make grandiloquent 601.7
polish 260.7
varsity college 567.7
team 788.7
vary alternate 141.5
be changed 139.5
change 139.6
deviate 291.3
differ 16.5
differentiate 16.6
disagree 27.5
diversify 19.2
intermit 138.2
make dissimilar 21.3
vacillate 627.8
variegate 18.2
varying different 16.7
inconstant 18.3
vas 396.13
vascular tubular 396.21
vesicular 193.4
vase 576.2
vasectomy 689.23
vassal
n. feudatory 750.1
subject 764.7
adj. subject 764.13
vassalage 764.1
vast extensive 179.9
huge 195.20
large 34.7
vastly
extensively 179.10
immensely 34.16
vastness greatness 34.1
hugeness 195.7
vat 660.6
Vatican
church house 1042.8
papacy 1037.6

vaudeville
stage show 611.4
theater 611.1
vaudevillian
n. entertainer 612.1
adj. theatrical 611.38
vault
n. arch 252.4
ascent 315.1
compartment 192.2
depository 836.12
heavens 375.2
jump 319.1
storage place 660.6
tomb 410.16
v. ascend 315.9
curve 252.6
leap 319.5
vaulted 252.10
vaulter 319.4
vaulting arch 252.4
curvature 252.1
leaping 319.3
vaunt
n. boasting 910.1
display 904.4
v. boast 910.6
flaunt 904.17
Vayu
Hindu deity 1014.8
wind god 403.3
VD 686.16
veal 308.14
vector aviation 278.43
carrier 686.41
direction 290.2
infection 686.3
straight line 250.2
Vedas, the 1021.7
veer
n. angle 251.2
bend 219.3
deviation 291.1
v. angle 251.5
be changed 139.5
change course 275.30
deflect 219.9
deviate 291.3
sidle 242.5
turn around 295.9
turn aside 291.6
veering devious 291.7
irregular 138.3
vegetable
n. food 308,35,50
plant 411.3
adj. do-nothing 706.6
herbaceous 411.33
inert 708.19
vegetable kingdom
class 61.4
plants 411.1
vegetable oil oil 380.1
types of 380.12
vegetarian
n. abstainer 992.4
herbivore 307.14
adj. abstinent 992.10
eating 307.29
herbaceous 411.33
vegetarianism
abstinence 992.2

diet 309.11
herbivorism 307.1
vegetate
do nothing 706.2
grow 411.31
nature 197.7
merely exist 1.10
stagnate 268.9
vegetation
existence 1.6
growth 411.30
inaction 706.1
maturation 197.3
plants 411.1
stagnation 268.4
vehemence
acrimony 161.4
eloquence 600.5
fervor 855.10
industry 707.6
power 157.1
rage 952.10
violence 162.1
zeal 635.2
vehement
acrimonious 161.13
eloquent 600.13
industrious 707.22
passionate 857.27
violent 162.15
zealous 635.10
vehicle conveyance 272
instrument 658.3
paint 362.8
photography 577.10
stage show 611.4
vehicular 272.22
veil
n. clothing 231.26
concealment 615.2
cover 228.2,38
pretext 649.1
secrecy 614.3
shade 338.1.8
v. conceal 615.6
cover 228.19
keep secret 614.7
shade 338.5
veiled covered 228.31
latent 546.5
shaded 338.7
vague 514.18
vein
n. artery 396.14
deposit 383.7
mood 525.4
nature 5.3
source of supply 660.4
style 588.2
thinness 205.7
v. variegate 374.7
veinous 396.21
veld grassland 411.8
plain 387.1
the country 182.1
velocity gait 273.14
motion 267.1
speed 269
velvet comfort 887.1
easy thing 732.3
fine texture 351.3

print 578.6
vigor eloquence 600.3
energy 161.1
gaiety 870.4
robustness 685.3
strength 159.1
vitality 157.1
vigorous
eloquent 600.11
energetic 161.12
fervent 855.23
powerful 157.12
robust 685.10
strong 159.13
thriving 728.13
tough 359.4
viking pirate 825.7
sailor 276.1
vile bad 675.9
base 915.12
cursing 972.8
dishonest 975.17
evil 981.16
filthy 682.23
malodorous 437.5
obscene 990.9
offensive 864.18
paltry 673.18
unsavory 429.7
vulgar 898.15
vilification
berating 969.7
curse 972.2
defamation 971.2
vilify berate 969.20
blaspheme 1030.5
curse 972.7
revile 971.10
stigmatize 915.9
vilifying
condemnatory 969.23
disparaging 971.13
villa 191.8
village
n. district 180.5
hamlet 183.2
adj. urban 183.10
villager 190.6
villain actor 612.2
rascal 986.3
role 611.11
villainous bad 675.9
dishonest 975.17
evil 981.16
villainy
dishonesty 975.2
iniquity 981.3
villein 764.7
villenage
possession 808.1
subjection 764.1
villous 230.24
vim gaiety 870.4
liveliness 707.1
power 157.1
verve 161.2
vincible 697.16
vindicate acquit 1007.4
justify 1006.9
vindication
acquittal 1007.1
justification 1006.1
vindicative 1006.13
vindicator
avenger 956.3
defender 799.7
justifier 1006.8
vindictive 956.6
types of 411.51
vinegar
preservative 701.3
sour thing 432.2
vinegarish
ill-humored 951.23
sour 432.5
vineyard 413.10
viniculture 413.2
vintage 811.5
vintner
liquor dealer 996.18
merchant 830.3
viol 465.5
viola organ stop 465.22
viol 465.6
violate
break the law 999.5
corrupt 692.14
disobey 767.6
misuse 667.4
not observe 769.4
possess sexually 822.15
seduce 989.20
terrorize 162.10
work evil 675.6
violation
abomination 959.2
crime 999.4
disobedience 767.1
infraction 769.2
mistreatment 667.2
misuse 667.1
seduction 989.6
sexual possession 822.3
violence 162.3
wrong 959.1
violator 989.12
violence
acrimony 161.4
coercion 756.3
cruelty 939.11
excitability 857.9
mistreatment 667.2
rage 952.10
vehemence 162
violent
n. violent person 162.9
adj. acrimonious 161.i3
coercive 756.11
excited 857.23
mad 473.30
passionate 857.27
vehement 162.15
violently
frenziedly 857.33
furiously 34.23
vehemently 162.24
violet 373.3
violin 465.6
violinist 464.5
VIP
influential person 172.6
notable 672.8
superior 36.5
viper bad person 986.7
snake 414.31,61
virago
ill-humored woman 951.12
witch 943.7
virgin
n. girl 125.6
adj. chaste 988.6
childless 166.4
new 122.7
undamaged 677.8
unmarried 934.7
virginal chaste 988.6
immature 124.10
new 122.7
unmarried 934.7
virginity chastity 988.3
newness 122.1
original condition 721.3
unwed state 934.1
Virgin Mary, the 1015.5
virgule diagonal 219.7
line 568.6
virile 420.12
virility
masculinity 420.2
maturity 126.2
power 157.1
virtu
aesthetic taste 897.5
artistry 574.8
work of art 574.11
virtual 546.5
virtually
almost entirely 54.14
potentially 546.11
virtue chastity 988.1
courage 893.1
ethics 957.3
grace 674.1
honesty 974.1
moral goodness 980
power 157.1
virtuosity
aesthetic taste 897.5
musicianship 462.32
skill 733.1
superiority 36.1
virtuoso
n. connoisseur 897.7
expert 733.13
first-rater 674.6
musician 464.1
superior 36.4
adj. musical 462.48
skillful 733.20
virtuous chaste 988.4
good 674.12
honest 974.13
moral 980.7
virulence
animosity 929.4
bitterness 952.3
deadliness 409.9
harmfulness 675.5
poisonousness 675.10
power 157.1
violence 162.1
virulent fatal 409.23
harmful 675.12
hostile 929.10
poisonous 684.7
rancorous 939.20
resentful 952.24
rigorous 757.13
violent 162.15
virus germ 686.39
infection 686.3
organism 406.2
poison 676.3
visa certificate 570.6
pass 777.7
ratification 521.4
signature 583.10
visage face 240.4
looks 446.4
vis-à-vis
against 200.25
contrary to 239.6
opposite 15.10
versus 790.10
viscera
seat of affections 855.2
vitals 225.4
visceral
emotional 855.19
internal 225.10
viscid adhesive 50.12
dense 354.12
semiliquid 389.12
tough 359.4
viscosity solidity 354.1
tenacity 50.3
thickness 389.2
viscount 918.4
viscous
semiliquid 389.12
solid 354.12
thick 204.8
vise 198.6
viselike 813.8
Vishnu God 1013.4
Hindu deity 1014.8
incarnations of 1014.9
visibility
aviation 278.41
manifestness 555.3
visibleness 444
visible apparent 446.11
discernible 444.6
manifest 555.8
ocular 439.21
visibly by sight 439.23

adj. voluntary 622.7
voluptuous
pleasant 863.7
sensual 987.5
sexual 419.26
volute
n. curl 254.2
adj. spiral 254.8
vomit
n. emetic 687.18
vomiting 310.8
v. disgorge 310.25
erupt 162.12
flow out 303.13
jet 395.20
sicken at 867.4
vomiting
disease symptom 686.8
disgorgement 310.8
nausea 686.29
vomitory
n. outlet 303.9
adj. ejective 310.28
emetic 687.49
voodooism 1035.1
adj. sorcerous 1035.14
unsavory 429.7

voodoo
n. bad influence 675.4
charm 1036.5
sorcery 1035.1
witch doctor 1035.7
v. bewitch 1036.9
adj. sorcerous 1035.14
voracious
gluttonous 994.6
greedy 634.27
hungry 634.25
voracity gluttony 994.1
greed 634.8
vortex aviation 278.39
bustle 707.4
curl 254.2
excitement 857.3
rotation 322.2
whirlpool 395.12
vortical flowing 395.24
rotary 322.15
votary believer 1028.4
desirer 654.12
devotee 635.6
follower 293.2
man 787.8
supporter 787.9
worshiper 1032.9
vote
n. approval 968.1
choice 637.6
legislative procedure 742.14
politics 744.18
suffrage 744.17
v. cast one's vote 637.18
participate 815.5
support politically 744.41
vote in 637.20
voter elector 744.23
selector 637.7

voting choice 637.6
going to the polls 744.18
participation 815.1
voting age 126.2
votive 770.7
votive candle 1040.11
votive offering
donation 818.6
sacrifice 1032.7
vouch
n. affirmation 523.1
v. affirm 523.5
promise 770.4
testify 505.10
vouched for 523.8
voucher
certificate 570.6
negotiable instrument 835.11
receipt 844.2
recommendation 968.4
witness 505.7
vouchsafe
condescend 906.7
give 818.12
permit 777.9

vow
n. oath 523.3
promise 770.1
v. affirm 523.5
express belief 501.12
promise 770.4
vowel
n. speech sound 594.13
vox populi belief 501.6
unanimity 521.5
voyage
n. journey 273.5
water travel 275.6
v. pass over 273.19
sail 275.13
travel 273.20
voyager 274.1
voyeur
curious person 528.2
sex deviant 419.17
voyeurism
curiosity 528.1
sexual preference 419.12
VP 748.3
vs. against 790.10
opposite 239.7
V-shaped angular 251.6
forked 299.10
Vulcan god 1014.5
smith 718.7
vulcanize heat 329.24
make elastic 358.6
vulgar common 919.11
discourteous 937.6
gaudy 904.20
indecent 898.10
inelegant 590.2
inferior 37.6
uncouth 990.8
vulgarian 898.6

vulgarism
literary inelegance 590.1
tastelessness 898.1
word 582.6
vulgarity
discourtesy 937.1
indecency 898
inferiority 37.3
literary inelegance 590.1
uncouthness 990.3
vulgarize coarsen 898.9
corrupt 692.14
make clear 548.6
vulgar language
cursing 972.3
jargon 580.9
Vulgate 580.6
vulgate 1021.2
vulnerability
fragility 360.1
liability 175.2
pregnability 697.4
unpreparedness 721.1
vulnerable fragile 360.4
helpless 158.18
liable to 175.5
pregnable 697.16

vulpine canine 414.45
cunning 735.12
vulture 822.21
vulturous 822.26
vulva 419.10
vulval 419.27
V-weapon 281.4
vying
n. competition 796.2
opposition 790.2
adj. competitive 796.24

W

wacky eccentric 474.4
foolish 470.8
insane 473.26
wad
n. accumulation 74.9
lump 195.10
money 835.17
much 34.4
wealth 837.2
v. fill 56.7
line 194.7
squeeze 198.8
wadding
contents 194.3
stopping 266.5
waddle
n. gait 273.14
slowness 270.2
v. go slow 270.6
walk 273.27
wade into
attack 798.15
set to work 716.15
wade 275.56
wade through
drudge 716.14
study 564.12
wadi ravine 201.2

running water 395.1
watercourse 257.9
valley 257.9
wading 275.11
wafer cracker 308.30
Eucharist 1040.8
layer 227.2
thinness 205.7
waffle
n. pancake 308.44
v. chatter 596.5
equivocate 613.7
talk nonsense 547.5
waft
n. transportation 271.3
wind 403.4
v. be buoyed up 353.8
blow 403.22
transport 271.11
wag
n. humorist 881.12
mischief-maker 738.3
v. swing 323.6
wiggle 324.7
oscillate 323.10
wiggle 324.14

wage
n. remuneration 841.4
v. practice 705.7
wage earner 718.2
wager
n. an uncertainty 514.8
v. bet 515.3
bet 515.20
gamble 515.19
wage war battle 797.18
contend 796.14
waggery mischief 738.2
wittiness 881.4
waggish
mischievous 738.6
playful 878.31
prankish 881.17
waggle
n. swing 323.6
v. wiggle 324.7
oscillate 323.10
wiggle 324.14
wagon
n. police car 272.10
vehicle 272.2
v. haul 271.12
wagoner carrier 271.5
coachman 274.9
waif
abandoned thing 633.4
vagabond 274.3
wail
n. lament 875.3
shrill sound 458.4
v. animal sound 460.2
cry 875.11
sigh 452.14
sound shrill 458.8
utter 594.26
wind sound 403.23
wailing
n. lamentation 875.1

adj. animal sound 460.6
lamenting 875.15
shrill 458.14
wainscot
n. bottom 212.2
lining 194.3
v. line 194.7
waist middle 69.1
shirt 231.15,66
waistband
clothing 231.19
types of 231.65
waistcoat 231.14
waistline 69.1
wait
n. delay 132.2
singer 464.14
v. be patient 861.4
delay 132.12
expect 539.8
serve 750.13
waiter 750.7
waiting
n. expectancy 539.3
tarrying 132.3
adj. expectant 539.11
imminent 152.3
serving 750.14
waiting game
inaction 706.1
patience 861.1
waiting room 192.20
wait on
accompany 73.7
be servile 907.7
escort 73.8
expect 539.8
pay one's respects to 936.12
serve 750.13
waitress 750.7
wake
n. aviation 278.39
effect 154.4
funeral rites 410.4
insomnia 713.1
sequel 67.2
social gathering 922.10
track 568.8
water travel 275.7
v. awaken 713.5

excite 857.11
get up 713.4
wakeful alert 533.14
sleepless 713.7
wake up awaken 713.5
disillusion 520.2
excite 857.11
get up 713.4
rouse 648.19
wale blemish 679.1
ridge 256.3
sore 686.35
texture 351.1
walk
n. amble 273.12
arena 802.1
circuit 321.2
gait 273.14
path 657.3
race 796.12
region 180.2
route 657.2
slowness 270.2
sphere of work 656.4
vocation 656.6
v. ambulate 273.26
go slow 270.6
walkaway 726.1
walker pedestrian 274.6
vehicle 272.6
walking
n. ambulation 273.10
adj. traveling 273.35
walking papers 310.5
walking stick
staff 217.2
supporter 216.2
walk off with
steal 824.13
win easily 726.5
walk of life 656.6
walk-on actor 612.7
role 611.11
walkout
departure 301.1
desertion 633.2
stop 144.2
strike 789.7
walk out desert 633.6
exit 303.11
stop work 144.8
strike 789.9
walk over
domineer 741.16
win easily 726.5
walk-through 611.14
walk-up 191.14
walkway 657.3
wall
n. barrier 730.5
fence 236.4
partition 237.5
precipice 213.3
types of 236.13
v. enclose 236.7
fortify 799.9
partition 237.8
walled covered 228.31
enclosed 236.10
partitioned 237.11
wallet 836.14

walleye
defective eye 440.6
defective vision 440.5
eye disease 686.13
walleyed 440.12
wall in confine 761.12
cover 228.23
enclose 236.5
wallop flounder 324.15
hit 283.13
pound 283.14
punish 1010.15
thrash 1010.14
walloping
n. punishment 1010.5
adj. large 195.21
wallow
n. flounder 324.8
marsh 400.1
v. be unchaste 989.19
crouch 318.8
flounder 324.15
roll in 322.13
sail 275.55
wallow in
be intemperate 993.4
enjoy 865.10
wallpaper 228.23
Wall Street
financial district 833.8
stock exchange 833.7
stock market 833.1
Walter Mitty 532.2
waltz 879.5
wamble rotate 322.9
walk 273.27
wampum
currency 835.3
jewel 901.6
money 835.2
wan
v. lose color 363.6
adj. colorless 363.7
deathly 408.29
lackluster 337.17
languid 708.19
tired-looking 717.7
wand
divining rod 543.3
emblem of authority 739.9
insignia 569.1
wish-bringer 1036.6
wander
be inattentive 531.3
be insane 473.19
be unorthodox 1025.8
digress 593.9
err 518.9
muse 532.9
roam 273.22
stray 291.4
wanderer alien 78.3
planet 375.9
rover 274.2
wandering
n. delirium 473.8
deviation 291.1
discursiveness 593.3
roving 273.3

adj. abnormal 85.9
delirious 473.31
deviant 291.7
discursive 593.13
distracted 532.10
inconstant 141.7
insane 473.25
irregular 138.3
roving 273.36
unordered 62.12
Wandering Jew
alien 78.3
displaced person 185.4
wanderer 274.2
wanderlust 273.3
wane
n. decrease 39.2
deterioration 692.3
standstill 268.3
v. age 126.10
decrease 39.6
fail 692.20
move 267.5
quiet 268.8
recede 297.2
wangle elicit 305.14
maneuver 735.10
persuade 648.23
plot 654.10
waning aging 126.17
decreasing 39.11
deteriorating 692.46
quiescent 268.12
receding 297.5
want
n. absence 187.1
deficiency 57.2
desire 634.1
imperfection 678.1
indigence 838.2
lack 662.4
requirement 639.2
v. be inferior 37.4
be insufficient 662.8
be poor 838.5
desire 634.14
fall short 314.2
lack 662.7
require 639.9
wish to 634.15
want ad 559.6
wanted desired 634.29
requisite 639.13
wanting absent 187.10
deprived of 812.8
desirous 634.21
imperfect 678.4
incomplete 57.4
insufficient 662.9
lacking 662.13
short of 314.5
wanton
n. unchaste man 989.10
unchaste woman 989.14
v. be intemperate 993.6
be unchaste 989.19
make love 932.13
make merry 878.26

adj. capricious 629.5
inconstant 141.7
reckless 894.8
unchaste 989.26
unrestrained 762.23
unrighteous 981.12

war
n. armed conflict 797.1
contention 796.1
gods 797.17
military campaign 797.7
military science 797.10
word list 797.29
v. battle 797.18
contend 796.14

warble
n. bird sound 460.5
sing 462.39
utter 594.26
warbler bird 414.33,66
songbird 464.23
vocalist 464.13
warbling 462.12

war cry
battle cry 797.12
challenge 793.2
signal 568.16
whoop 459.1
ward custody 761.5
defense 799.1
dependent 764.6
election district 744.16
hospital room 192.25
infirmary 689.27
protectorship 699.2
stronghold 799.6
territorial division 180.5

warden
doorkeeper 699.12
executive 748.3
guardian 699.6
jailer 761.10
public official 749.17
warder guard 699.9
guardian 699.6
jailer 761.10

ward heeler
follower 293.2
hanger-on 907.5
partisan 744.27
political henchman 746.8
ward off dodge 631.8
fend off 799.10
prevent 730.14
repulse 289.3
wardrobe closet 192.15
furnishings 231.2
wardship
dependence 764.3
inability 158.2
protectorship 699.2
ware commodity 831.2
merchandise 831.1

warehouse
n. market 832.1
storage place 660.6
v. store 660.10

warfare combat 797
contention 796.1
war game 797.8
warhead
explosive charge 801.10
rocketry 281.3

war-horse
charger 800.32
horse 414.10
old woman 127.3
politician 746.1
soldier 800.18
veteran 733.15

warlike
contending 796.23
militant 797.25
warlock 1035.5
warlord 749.14

warm
v. energize 161.9
excite 857.11
heat 329.17
adj. coloring 362.15
comfortable 887.11
cordial 927.15
detecting 488.10
eloquent 600.13
excited 857.20
fervent 855.23
hospitable 925.11
hot 328.24
kind 938.13
near 200.14
red 368.6
wealthy 837.13
zealous 635.10
warm-blooded 328.29

warmed-over
heated 329.29
repeated 103.12
trite 883.9
warmer 329.10

warmhearted
cordial 927.15
emotionable 855.21
hospitable 925.11
kind 938.13
kindly 938.18

warming
n. heating 329.1
adj. heating 329.26

warmly
amicably 927.21
eloquently 600.15
excitedly 857.32
fervently 855.28
kindly 938.18
warmonger 800.5

warmongering
n. warlikeness 797.15
adj. militaristic 797.26
warm spring
hot water 328.10
spa 689.29

warmth
animation 161.3
cordiality 927.6
eloquence 600.5
fervor 855.10
glow 362.2
heat 328.1
hospitality 925.1
kindness 938.1
negotiable instrument 1004.2

warm-up begin 68.8
heat 329.17
prepare oneself 720.13

warn advise 754.6
alarm 704.3
caution 703.5
demand 753.4
dissuade 652.3
forebode 544.11
threaten 973.2

warning
n. advice 754.1
caution 703
demand 753.1
dissuasion 652.1
omen 544.4
threat 973.1
tip 557.3
adj. advisory 754.8
cautioning 703.7
premonitory 544.16

war of nerves
cold war 797.5
demoralization 891.6

warp
n. bend 219.3
blemish 679.1
deviation 291.1
distortion 249.1
tendency 174.1
trait of character 525.3
v. weaving 222.3
be changed 139.5
blemish 679.4
corrupt 692.14
defect 291.5
distort 249.5
falsify 616.16
misrepesent 573.3
prejudice 527.9
sail 275.48
tend 174.3

war paint 900.11
warp and woof
structure 245.1
weaving 222.1
warpath 797.15

warped
blemished 679.8
distorted 249.10
falsified 616.26
morally corrupt 981.14
prejudiced 527.12
unjust 977.11
warplane 280.9,15

warrant
n. authorization 777.3
certificate 570.6
commission 780.1
instrument 834.1
justification 1006.6
legal order 752.6
legal summons 1004.2
negotiable instrument 1004.2
oath 523.3
permit 777.6
ratification 521.4
receipt 844.2
right 958.4
security 772.1
v. acknowledge 521.11
affirm 523.5
authorize 777.11
commission 780.9
express belief 501.12
justify 1006.9
promise 770.4
prove 505.12
ratify 521.12
secure 772.9
testify 505.10

warrantable fair 976.8
justifiable 1006.14
permissible 777.15

warranted
acknowledged 521.14
affirmed 523.8
authorized 777.17
fair 976.8
guaranteed 772.11
justified 960.9
made sure 513.20
promised 770.8
warrantee 772.7

warrant officer
naval officer 749.20
noncommissioned officer 749.19
warrantor 772.6

warranty
authorization 777.3
certificate 570.6
promise 770.1
security 772.1

warren fertility 165.6
filthy place 682.11
tunnel 257.5

warring
n. warfare 797.1
adj. clashing 461.5
contending 796.23
warlike 797.25
warrior 800.6
warship 277.6,24
wart blemish 679.1
bulge 256.3
dwarf 196.6
little thing 196.4
tumor 686.36
wartime 797.1
wary cautious 895.9
cunning 735.12
doubtful 503.9
incredulous 504.4
vigilant 533.13

wash
n. ablution 681.5
aviation 278.39
cleaning agent 681.17
color 362.8
laundering 681.6

seaway 275.10
watercourse 396.2

water wings 701.5

water witch
diving rod 543.3
sorcerer 1035.5

waterworks plant 719.4
watercourse 396.2

watery fluid 388.6
insipid 430.2
meager 662.10
moist 392.16
secretory 312.7
thin 205.16
weak 160.17

watt 342.17,35

wattage
electric power 342.17
energy 157.1

wattle
n. network 221.3
v. weave 222.6

wave
n. billow 395.14
convolution 254.1
greeting 925.4
style the hair 230.22
undulate 323.11
ray 323.4
swing 323.6
undulation 323.2
v. billow 395.22
flaunt 904.17
flutter 324.12
indicate 555.5
oscillate 323.10
signal 568.22
style the hair 230.22
undulate 323.11

wavelength
oscillation 323.4
radio wave 344.11

waver
n. flutter 324.4
swing 323.6
v. demur 623.4
flicker 335.25
fluctuate 141.5
flutter 324.12
oscillate 323.10
vacillate 627.8

wavering
n. fluctuation 141.3
inconstancy 18.1
oscillation 323.1
vacillation 627.2
adj. changeable 141.7
flickering 335.36
fluttering 324.18
inconstant 18.3
irregular 138.3
oscillating 323.15
uncertain 514.15
vacillating 627.10

waving
n. convolution 254.1
oscillation 323.2
adj. undulating
323.16

wavy curved 252.7
inconstant 141.7
undulatory 254.10

wax
n. fit 952.8
lubricant 380.2
polish 260.14
softness 357.4
sound recording
450.12
types of 380.15
v. evolve 148.5
grow 197.7
increase 38.6
oil 380.8
polish 260.7

wax and wane
alternate 323.13
fluctuate 141.5

waxen 363.7

waxwork 572.4
way behavior 737.1
channel 396.1
continuance 143.1
custom 642.1
diction 588.2
direction 290.1
distance 199.1
entrance 302.5
habit 642.4
knack 733.6
latitude 762.4
manner 657
means 658.1
mode 7.4
nature 5.3
plan 654.1
progression 294.1
spare room 179.3
water travel 275.9
specialty 81.1
trek 273.20
wander 273.22

wayfare travel 273.17
trek 273.20

wayfarer 274.1

waylay 615.10

way off 21.5

way out
n. loophole 632.4
outlet 303.9
adj. dissimilar 21.5
extreme 34.13
modern 122.13
nonconformist 83.6

wayward
capricious 629.5
disobedient 767.8
inconstant 141.7
perverse 626.11
unchaste 989.26
unrighteous 981.12

wayworn
fatigued 717.6
travel-worn 273.40

WC toilet 311.10
washroom 192.26

weak aged 126.18
colorless 363.7
cowardly 892.10
faint-sounding 452.16
fatigued 717.6
feeble 160.12
flimsy 4.7
human 417.10
illogical 483.12
impotent 158.13
indistinct 445.6
influenceable 172.15
insipid 430.2
iresolute 627.12
mentally deficient
469.21
phonetic 594.31
thin 205.16
unhealthy 686.50
unrighteous 981.12
uninfluential 173.3
unstrict 758.4
vulnerable 697.16

weaken attenuate 4.4
blunt 259.2
disable 158.9
enfeeble 160.10
fail 686.45
fatigue 717.4
impair 692.11
languish 160.9
moderate 163.6
reduce 39.8
sicken 686.47
thin 205.12
undermine 693.20

weakened
damaged 692.29
disable 158.9
enfeebled 160.18
fatigued 717.6
reduced 39.10
unhealthy 686.50

weakening
n. decrease 39.1
enfeeblement 160.5
impairment 692.1
adj. debilitating
160.20

weaker sex 421.3
weak-eyed 440.13
weakhearted 892.10
weak-kneed
cowardly 892.10
iresolute 627.12
weakling coward 892.5
feeble person 160.6
impotent 158.6
iresolute person
627.5

weak link fault 678.2
vulnerable point
697.4

weakly
adj. feeble 160.12
unhealthy 686.50
adv. faintly 452.21
feebly 160.22
scarcely 35.9

weak-minded
iresolute 627.12
mentally deficient
469.21

weakness
colorlessness 363.2
cowardice 892.1
faintness of sound
452.1
fatigue 717.1
fault 678.2
feebleness 160
gullibility 502.2
humanness 417.5
impotence 158.1
indistinctness 445.2
influenceability 172.5
insipidness 430.1
iresolution 627.4
liability 175.1
liking 634.2
love 931.1
mental deficiency
469.8
specialty 81.1
tendency 174.1
tender feeling 855.6
thinness 205.4
unauthoritativeness
unstrictness 758.1
vice 981.2
vulnerability 697.16

weak point fault 678.2
soft spot 697.4
specious argument
483.3
vice 981.2
vulnerable point
160.4

weak sister
coward 892.5
effeminate male
421.10

impotence 158.1
indistinctness 445.2
influenceability 172.5
insipidness 430.1
iresolution 627.4
feeble person 160.6
weak-willed 627.12
weal blemish 679.1
prosperity 728.1
weald 387.1
wealth assets 810.8
gain 811.3
plenty 661.2
prosperity 661.2
riches 837
wealthy plentiful 661.7
prosperous 728.12
rich 837.13
wean convince 145.16
disaccustom 643.2
disincline from 652.4
weapon arms 801.1
sharp edge 258.2
wear
n. abrasion 350.2
clothing 231.1
deterioration 692.5
disintegration 53.1
v. abrade 350.7
affect 903.12
be tedious 884.5
change course 275.30
decrease 39.6
deteriorate 692.23
endure 110.6
fatigue 717.4
have on 231.43
waste 812.5
wear and tear
decrease 39.3
deterioration 692.5
disintegration 53.1
wear away
abrade 350.7
consume 666.2
decrease 39.6
deteriorate 692.23

wear down
disappear 447.2
disintegrate 53.3
end 70.6
subtract 42.9
waste 812.5
weaken 160.9
wear off
deteriorate 692.23
fatigue 717.4
influence 172.7
persuade 648.23
weariness
boredom 884.3
fatigue 717.1
languor 708.6
weakness 160.1
wearing apparel 231.1
wearisome
annoying 864.22
boring 884.9
fatiguing 717.11
gloomy 872.24
laborious 716.18
wear off
deteriorate 692.23
end 70.6
wear on
be tedious 884.5
fatigue 717.4
linger 110.7
wear out
cause unpleasantness 864.16
deteriorate 692.23
fatigue 717.4
wear thin
be uninteresting 883.4
weaken 160.9
wear well
be healthy 685.5
endure 110.6
weary
v. be tedious 884.5
cause unpleasantness 864.16
get tired 717.5
make tired 717.4
adj. bored 884.10
fatigued 717.6
gloomy 872.24
languid 708.19
wearying boring 884.9
fatiguing 717.11
unpleasant 864.24
weasel
n. sharp-eye 439.11
sled 272.19
wild animal 414.28,58
v. prevaricate 613.7
pull back 284.7
weasel word
ambiguous expression 550.2
prevarication 613.4
weather
n. climate 402.4
windward side 242.3
v. keep safe 698.2
ride out 275.40
sail 275.24

stand fast 142.11
wear 692.23
win through 724.12
adj. windward 242.6
weather balloon 402.8
weather-beaten 692.36
weatherboard
n. windward side 242.3
wood 378.3
v. cover 228.23
weather bureau 402.7
weathercock
changeableness 141.4
mind-changer 628.4
testing device 489.4
wind instrument 403.17
weather eye
seamanship 275.3
sharp eye 439.10
vigilance 533.4
weatherglass 692.5
weathering 692.5
weatherman 402.7
weather map
map 654.4
meteorology 402.5
weatherproof
v. proof 159.12
adj. resistant 159.18
weather report 402.7
weather the storm
keep safe 698.2
recover 694.20
sail 275.40
stand fast 142.11
win through 724.12
weather vane
changeableness 141.4
testing device 489.4
weather instrument 402.8
wind instrument 403.17
weatherworn 692.36

webbed 221.12
web-footed 221.12
Webster's 605.7
wed combine 52.4
get married 933.16
join in marriage 933.15
relate 9.6
wedded
conjugal 933.19
joined 47.13
married 933.22
paired 52.6
related 9.9
wedding
combination 52.1
marriage 933.4
wedge
n. character 581.2
v. fasten 47.8
impress 142.9
pry 287.8
wedged fastened 47.14
fixed 142.16
wedge in enter 302.7
interpose 237.6
thrust in 304.7
wedge-shaped
tapered 205.15
triangular 251.8
wedlock 933.1
wee 196.11
weed
n. intruder 78.2
marihuana 687.13
plant 411.3
refuse 669.4
types of 411.52
v. subtract 42.9
till 413.17
weed killer 676.3
weed out
eliminate 77.5
extract 305.10
till 413.17
weeds
mourning garment 875.6
widowhood 935.3
weedy
growing rank 411.40
herbaceous 411.33
week period 107.2
seven 99.3
weekend
n. vacation 711.3
v. spend time 105.6
vacation 711.9
weekly
n. newspaper 605.11
periodical 605.10
adj. regularly 137.8
weenie 308.21
weep
n. outflow 303.6
v. be damp 392.11
excrete 311.12
exude 303.15
fester 311.15
flow out 303.14
hang 215.6
lament 875.8

rain 394.9
secrete 312.5
sob 875.10
trickle 395.18
weep for console 946.2
pity 944.3
weeping
n. outflow 303.6
secretion 312.1
sobbing 875.2
adj. pendent 215.9
soaked 392.17
tearful 875.17
weepy
exudative 303.20
tearful 875.17
weevil 414.40,74
weevily insectile 414.55
spoiled 692.43
unsavory 429.7
weft fabric 378.5
network 221.3
weaving 222.3
weigh analyze 48.8
be important 672.11
compare 491.4
consider 478.12
have influence 172.10
heft 352.10
measure 490.11
weigh anchor
detach 49.10
embark 301.16
up-anchor 275.18
weigh down
hamper 730.11
oppress 729.8
weight 352.12
weighed down
burdened 352.18
sad 872.20
weigh-in 352.9
weighing 48.3
weighing instrument 352.22
weight
n. affliction 866.8
authority 739.4
charge 963.3
exercise device 716.7
formality 646.1
heaviness 352
heavy object 352.6
impediment 730.6
importance 672.1
influence 172.1
power 157.1
units 352.23
validity 516.4
v. burden 352.12
fill 56.7
heft 352.10
impose 963.6
weighted down
encumbered 352.18
sad 872.20
weightless light 353.10
unsubstantial 4.5
weightlessness
lightness 353.1
space hazard 282.10
weightlifter 878.21

weight-watch 205.13
weighty
  authoritative 739.15
  eloquent 600.14
  evidential 505.17
  heavy 352.16
  important 672.19
  influential 172.13
  large 34.7
  solemn 871.3
  unpleasant 864.24
  valid 516.13
weigh upon
  be heavy upon 352.11
  burden 352.13
  cause unpleasantness 864.16
  make sad 872.18
  oppress 729.8
weir barrier 730.5
weird
  n. fate 640.2
  spell 1036.1
  adj. awesome 920.11
  creepy 891.39
  deathly 408.29
  eerie 1017.9
  foolish 470.10
  odd 85.11
  sorcerous 1035.14
weirdo eccentric 474.3
  lunatic 473.15
Weird Sisters
  Fates 640.3
  witches 1035.8
welcome
  n. arrival 300.4
  assent 521.1
  hospitality 925.2
  liberality 853.1
  reception 306.1
  v. assent 521.8
  greet 925.9
  incur 175.4
  adj. desirable 925.12
  pleasant 863.6
  interj. greetings! 925.14
welcoming
  hospitable 925.11
  receptive 306.16
weld
  n. joint 47.4
  v. heat 329.24
  join 47.5
  sculpture 575.5
  stick together 50.9
welder
  blowtorch 329.14
  types of 348.24
welfare
  n. charity 938.5
  good 674.4
  prosperity 728.1
  subsidy 818.8
  welfare program 745.7
  adj. benevolent 938.15

welfare state
  government 741.4
  social service 938.5
  welfarism 745.7
welkin
  atmosphere 402.2
  heavens 375.2
well
  n. body of water 398.1
  overflow 395.17
  jet 395.20
  source of supply 660.4
  v. flow out 303.13
  adj. healthy 685.8
  adv. ably 157.16
  excellently 674.21
  kindly 938.18
  skillfully 733.29
  successfully 724.14
  interj. wonder 920.22
well-advised 467.19
well-balanced
  composed 858.13
  sensible 467.18
  stable 142.12
  symmetric 248.4
well-behaved 936.16
well-being
  comfort 887.1
  contentment 868.1
  good 674.4
  health 685.1
  pleasure 865.1
  prosperity 728.1
wellborn 918.11
well-bred
  genteel 936.17
  wellborn 918.11
well-built
  beautiful 900.17
  made 167.22
  strong 159.14
  substantial 3.7
well-coordinated 733.20
well-defined
  clearly visible 444.7
  intelligible 548.10
well-disposed
  approving 968.17
  friendly 927.14
  helpful 785.22
  willing 622.5
well done!
  approval 968.22
  congratulations 948.4
well-done cooked 330.7
well-dressed
  chic 644.13
  dressed up 231.45
well-earned 960.9
well-equipped 659.14
well-fed 195.18
well-fixed 837.13
well-groomed
  chic 644.13
  tidy 59.8
well-grounded
  established 142.13
  logical 482.20
  reliable 513.17
  substantial 3.7
  valid 516.13
well-informed 475.20
well-kept
  preserved 701.11
  tidy 59.8
well-known
  famous 914.16
  trite 883.9
well-laid 733.28
well-liked 931.22
well-made
  beautiful 900.17
  made 167.22
  shapely 248.5
  substantial 3.7
well-mannered
  ceremonious 646.8
  mannerly 936.16

well-meaning
  friendly 927.14
  helpful 785.22
  well-intentioned 938.17
well-off 837.13
well-oiled 732.13
well-planned 733.28
well-provided
  plentiful 661.7
  well-supplied 659.14
well-put 589.7
well-read
  versed in 475.19
well-regulated 59.6
well-set
  established 142.13
  strong 159.14
  symmetric 248.4
well-spent 665.21
well-spoken
  articulate 594.32
  eloquent 600.8
  mannerly 936.16
wellspring
  fountainhead 153.6
  source of supply 660.4
well-thought-of
  approved 968.19
  reputable 914.15
  venerated 964.11
well-timed
  expedient 670.5
  timely 129.9
well-to-do 837.13
well-understood 475.27
well-versed
  informed 475.18
  skilled in 733.25
  well-informed 475.20
well-wisher
  friend 928.1
  supporter 787.9

tidy 59.8
well-worn
  damaged 692.33
  habitual 642.16
  trite 883.9
welsh not pay 842.6
welsher defaulter 842.5
welt
  n. blemish 679.1
  edging 235.7
  ridge 256.3
  sail 275.55
  v. crouch 318.8
  flounder 324.15
welter
  n. flounder 324.8
  jumble 62.3
  v. flounder 324.15
  wallow 322.13
welterweight
  boxing weight 352.3
  pugilist 800.2
wen blemish 679.1
  swelling 256.4
  tumor 686.36
wench girl 125.6
  hussy 989.14
  maid 750.8
  woman 421.6
wenching 989.3
werewolf
  demon 1016.13
  frightener 891.9
  monster 943.6
weskit 231.14
west
  n. direction 290.3
  v. turn west 290.9
  adj. western 290.15
  adv. westward 290.15
West Occident 180.6
  region 180.7
westerly
  n. wind 403.9
  adj. western 290.15
western 290.15
Western fiction 608.7
  motion picture 611.16
West Point 567.13
westward
  n. west 290.3
  adv. west 290.19
wet
  n. drink 996.6
  moisture 392.1
  rain 394.1
  wet weather 394.4
  v. moisten 392.12
  urinate 311.14
  adj. foolish 470.8
  moist 392.15
wetback
  Mexican 181.7
  migrant 274.5
wet blanket
  boring person 884.4
  deterrent 652.2
  extinguisher 332.3
  hinderer 730.9

killjoy 872.14
wetlands 210.2
wet nurse 699.8
wet-nurse foster 785.16
wet suit
bathing suit 231.29
diving equipment 320.5

whack
n. attempt 714.2
explosive noise 456.1
hit 283.4
punishment 1010.3
turn 108.2
v. hit 283.13
make explosive noise 456.6
punish 1010.13
whack down 318.5
whacked 717.8
whacking huge 195.21
remarkable 34.11
whacky see **wacky**
whale
n. animal 414.35;
415.8
large animal 195.14
large thing 195.11
v. beat 1010.14
fish 655.10
punish 1010.15
whaler fisher 655.6
sailor 276.1
whaling
n. fishing 655.3
punishment 1010.5
adj. huge 195.21
wham
n. explosive noise 456.1
v. hit 283.13
make explosive noise 456.6
whammy
n. bad influence 675.4
charm 1036.5
curse 972.1
evil eye 1036.1
glare 439.5
malevolence 939.4
v. bring bad luck 729.12
wharf 700.6
what
n. whatever 79.6
interj. wonder 920.19
whatever
n. anything 79.6
adv. of any kind 61.9
what for 155.8
what-for
punishment 1010.1
reproof 969.6
reason 153.2
what's-his-name 584.2
what's what fact 1.3
the truth 516.2
wheal 686.35
wheat fodder 308.4
grain 411.46
wheel 865.17

wheedle cajole 774.12
flatter 970.5
urge 648.14
wheedling
n. cajolement 774.3
flattery 970.1
inducement 648.3
adj. cajoling 774.18
flattering 970.8
persuasive 648.29
wheel
n. circle 253.2
important person 672.9
instrument of torture 1011.4
management 747.5
potter's wheel 576.4
propeller 285.7
rotation 322.2
rotator 322.4
round 137.3
types of 322.18
vehicle 272.8
v. change one's mind 628.6
go around 321.4
recur 137.5
ride 273.32
rotate 322.9
turn around 295.9
whirl 322.11
wheel chair 272.7
wheeler-dealer
influential person 172.6
man of action 707.8
political intriguer 746.6
wheelhorse
horse 414.16
partisan 744.27
politician 746.1
wheeling and dealing 827.2
wheelman 276.8
wheel of fortune
Chance 156.2
changeableness 141.4
fate 640.2
gambling device 515.12
wheels
automobile 272.9
mechanism 348.5
wheels within wheels
complex 46.2
mechanism 348.5
wheelworks 348.5
wheeze
n. breathing 403.18
joke 881.6
sibilation 457.1
v. become exhausted 717.5
breathe 403.24
sibilate 457.2
wheezing
breathing 403.29
breathless 717.10
sibilant 457.3
whelk food 308.25

sore 686.35
whelm destroy 693.21
drench 392.14
overflow 395.17
oversupply 663.14
overwhelm 727.8
submerge 320.7
whelp
n. bad person 986.7
boy 125.5
dog 414.22
young dog 125.8
v. give birth 167.15
whelped 167.21
when although 33.8
at which time 105.8
while 105.16
whence away 301.21
hence 155.7
whenever
anytime 105.12
when 105.8
where 184.20
whereabouts
n. location 184.1
adv. where 184.20
whereas
n. condition 507.2
conj. because 155.10
when 105.16
wherefore
after which 117.7
hence 155.7
judgment 494.17
why 155.8
wherefore, the 153.2
where it's at
situation 7.2
the truth 516.2
wheresoever 184.21
whereupon
after which 117.7
when 105.8
wherever 184.21
wherewithal
funds 835.14
means 658.1
money 835.1
whet
n. appetizer 308.9
incentive 648.7
v. incite 648.17
increase 38.5
sensitize 422.9
sharpen 258.9
stimulate 857.12
whet the appetite
taste good 428.4
tempt 650.5
whey fluid 388.2
food 308.47
whichever 79.6
which see 505.25
whiff
n. clue 568.9
odor 435.1
wind 403.4
v. blow 403.22
smell 435.8
strike out 725.9
whiffet a nobody 673.7
wind 403.4

Whig 744.27
while
n. meantime 109.2
period 107.1
time 105.1
conj. when 105.16
while away
fritter away 854.5
use 665.13
while away the time
amuse oneself 878.24
spend time 105.6
waste time 708.12
whim caprice 629.1
eccentricity 474.2
thing imagined 535.5
whimper
n. lament 875.3
v. weep 875.10
whine 875.12
whimpering
n. weeping 875.2
adj. plaintive 875.16
weeping 875.17
whimsical
capricious 629.5
eccentric 474.4
erratic 141.7
fanciful 535.20
humorous 880.4
uncertain 514.15
witty 881.15
whimsy caprice 629.1
eccentricity 474.1
thing imagined 535.5
whim-wham
caprice 629.1
ornament 901.4
toy 878.16
trifle 673.5
whine
n. lament 875.3
shrill sound 458.4
v. animal sound 460.2
sigh 452.14
sound shrill 458.8
utter 594.26
whimper 875.12
whiner 869.3
whining
n. complaint 875.4
sigh 452.8
adj. animal sound 460.6
plaintive 875.16
shrill 458.14
whinny 460.2
whip
n. amusement ride 878.15
blow 283.7
driver 274.9
goad 648.8
lash 1011
legislator 746.3
v. agitate 324.10
defeat 727.6
drive animals 416.8
foam 405.5
goad 648.15
hasten 709.4
make viscid 389.10

pound 283.14
punish 1010.14
slap 283.16
whip hand
n. advantage 36.2
ascendancy 739.6
influence 172.1
whiplash goad 648.8
whip 1011.1
whip off 301.11
whipped bubbly 405.6
defeated 727.14
whippersnapper
a nobody 673.7
bad child 125.4
impudent person
913.5

whipping defeat 727.1
punishment 1010.4
rigging 277.12
whipping boy 149.3
whipping post 1011.3
whipsaw 833.25
whip up agitate 324.10
dash off 630.8
excite 857.11
incite 648.17
seize 822.14

whir
n. rotation 322.1
v. hum 452.13

whirl
n. backflow 395.12
bustle 707.4
curl 254.2
excitement 857.3
revel 878.7
ride 273.7
rotation 322.2
spin 322.11
turn around 295.9
twist 254.4

whirligig
amusement device
878.15
changeableness 141.4
rotator 322.4

whirling
n. rotation 322.1
adj. rotating 322.14

whirlpool
n. backflow 395.12
vortex 322.2
whirlpool bath
bath 681.8
hydrotherapy 689.4
massage 350.3

whirlwind
emotional outburst
857.8
vortex 322.2
wind 403.14
whirlybird 280.5

whirring
n. hum 452.7
adj. humming 452.20

whish
n. sibilation 457.1

v. rustle 452.12
sibilate 457.2

whisk
n. agitator 324.9
tap 283.6
v. agitate 324.10
foam 405.5
speed 269.8
sweep 681.23
tap 283.15
transport 271.11
whiskered 230.25
whiskers 230.8
whiskey 996.40
whisper
n. hint 557.4

whispering
n. imperfect speech
595.4
murmur 452.4
adj. murmuring
452.18
whispering campaign
disparagement 971.4
scandal 558.8
smear campaign
744.14

whistle
n. alarm 704.1
audio distortion
450.13
loud sound 453.4
noisemaker 453.5
shrill sound 458.4
signal 568.16
sibilation 457.1
wood wind 465.9
v. be cheerful 870.6
bird sound 460.5
blare 453.9
boo at 967.10
play music 462.43
rejoice 876.5
sibilate 457.2
sing 462.39
sound shrill 458.8
wind sound 403.23
whistle-blower 557.6
whistle for 774.9
whistle-stop
n. one-horse town
183.3
v. electioneer 744.40
whistling
n. sibilation 457.1
adj. shrill 458.14

v. inform 557.11
rumor 559.10
say 594.23
speak faintly 452.10
speak imperfectly
595.9
imperfect speech
595.4

whit 35.2
white
n. albumen 406.15
colors 364.11
race 418.3
v. whiten 364.5
whiteness 364.1
whitewash 364.6
adj. aged 126.16
blank 187.13
chaste 988.4
clean 681.25
color 364.7
colorless 363.7
comparisons 364.2
innocent 984.7
whitecaps 395.14
white-collar worker
718.2
white corpuscle 388.4
white elephant
burden 730.6
gift 818.4
white feather
coward 892.5
cowardice 892.4
white flag
peace offer 804.2
signal 568.15
white goods
dry goods 831.3
hard goods 831.4
Whitehall 741.3
white-hot fiery 162.21
hot 328.25
zealous 635.10
White House 191.6
white hunter 655.5
white lie 616.11
white lightning 996.17
white man 418.3
whiten
become excited
857.17
blanch 364.5
clean 681.18
decolor 363.5
lose color 363.6
whitening
albification 364.3
decoloration 363.3
whitewash 364.4
white paper
announcement 559.2
information 557.1
official document
570.8
white slave 989.16
white slaver 989.18
white slavery 826.1
whitewash
n. excusing 1006.5
utter defeat 727.3
whitening 364.4
v. acquit 1007.4
color 362.13
conceal 615.6
falsify 616.16
gloss over 1006.12
overwhelm 727.8
whiten 364.6

whitewashing
coloring 362.12
excusing 1006.5
utter defeat 727.3
whitening 364.3
white water 405.2
whitey 418.3
whither 184.20
Whitsuntide 1040.15
whittle
n. cutlery 348.2
v. sever 49.11
whittler 579.6
whittling 575.1
whiz
n. expert 733.13
good thing 674.7
sibilation 457.1
v. hum 452.13
sibilate 457.2
speed 269.8
who cares? 636.11
whodunit 608.7
whoever 79.7
whole
n. all 79.4
comprehensiveness
76.1
contents 194.1
quantity 28.1
sum 86.5
totality 54
adj. complete 56.9
comprehensive 76.7
healthy 685.9
one 89.7
sound 677.7
total 54.9
unqualified 508.2
wholehearted 624.11
whole hog 54.4
whole-hog 56.10
wholeness
completeness 56.1
goodness 674.1
individuality 80.1
intactness 677.2
totality 54.5
unity 89.1
whole picture 8.2
wholesale
n. sale 829.1
v. deal in 827.15
sell 829.8
adj. commercial
827.21
extensive 79.13
plentiful 661.7
sales 829.13
thorough 56.10
undiscriminating
493.5
adv. cheaply 849.10
wholesale house 832.1
wholesaler
intermediary 237.4
merchant 830.2
wholesaling
selling 829.2
trade 827.2
wholesome
healthful 683.5

healthy 685.9
reasonable 482.20
sane 472.4
whole story, the
the facts 1.4
the sum 86.5
wholism, wholistic see
holism etc.
wholly
completely 56.14
entirely 54.13
fully 8.13
perfectly 677.10
solely 89.14
whomp
n. explosive noise
456.1
impact 283.3
punishment 1010.3
v. collide 283.12
make explosive noise
456.6
overwhelm 727.8
punish 1010.13
whomp up
create 167.10
do carelessly 534.9
improvise 630.8
whoop
n. cry 459.1
v. cry 459.6
whoopee festivity 878.3
rejoicing 876.1
whooping cough
infectious disease
686.12
respiratory disease
686.14
whoop it up
be disorderly 62.11
be enthusiastic 635.8
be noisy 453.8
make merry 878.26
whoosh
n. sibilation 457.1
v. sibilate 457.2
whop
n. explosive noise
456.1
hit 283.4
v. hit 283.13
make explosive noise
456.6
overwhelm 727.8
punish 1010.14
whopper
large thing 195.11
monstrous lie 616.12
whopping
n. utter defeat 727.3
adj. huge 195.21
whore
n. bad person 986.5
flirt 932.10
prostitute 989.16
unchaste woman
989.14
v. be unchaste 989.19
whorehouse
brothel 989.9
disapproved place
191.28

whoring 989.3
whorish
prostitute 989.28
unchaste 989.26
whorl
n. curl 254.2
v. twist 254.4
whorled spiral 254.8
winding 254.6
whosoever 79.7
Who's Who 570.9
why
n. puzzle 549.8
reason 153.2
adv. wherefore 155.8
wick light 336.7
village 183.2
wicked bad 675.7
difficult 731.16
evil 981.16
malicious 939.18
sinful 982.6
ungodly 1031.17
wrong 959.3
wicked, the 986.12
wickedness
badness 675.1
evilness 981.4
malice 939.5
ungodliness 1031.3
wrong 959.1
wicket 265.8
widdershins
backwards 295.13
counterclockwise
290.26
round 322.16
wide
adj. broad 204.6
broad-minded 526.8
erroneous 518.16
extensive 79.13
general 79.11
phonetic 594.31
vast 179.9
voluminous 195.17
adv. astray 199.19
far and wide 199.16
wide-awake
alert 533.14
awake 713.8
clear-witted 467.13
wide berth 762.4
wide-eyed 920.9
widely
extensively 179.10
far and wide 199.16
widen
become larger 197.5
broaden 204.4
generalize 79.9
increase 38.6
make larger 197.4
spread 197.6
widened
expanded 197.10
increased 38.7
widening
expansion 197.1
increase 38.1
wide open 269.24
wide-open open 265.18

spread 197.11
unrestricted 762.26
wide-open spaces
plain 387.1
space 179.4
the country 182.1
widespread
customary 642.15
dispersed 75.9
extensive 79.13
spacious 179.9
spread 197.11
wide world 375.1
widget 376.4
widow
n. survivor 43.3
unmarried person
935.4
v. bereave 935.6
leave behind 408.28
widowed
bereaved 408.35
unmarried 935.7
widower survivor 43.3
unmarried person
935.4
widow's peak 230.6
widow's walk 228.6
widow's weeds
mourning garment
875.6
widowhood 935.3
width breadth 204.1
size 195.1
wield brandish 323.11
handle 425.6
use 665.10
wield authority
govern 741.12
possess authority
739.13
wieldy 732.14
wiener 308.21
wiener roast 307.6
wife 933.9
wifely loving 931.25
matrimonial 933.19
wig 230.14
wigged 230.26
wiggle
n. wriggle 324.7
v. be excited 857.16
walk 273.27
wriggle 324.14
wriggle 324.21
wiggly 324.21
wigwag
n. oscillation 323.5
signal 568.15
v. alternate 323.13
wave 323.11
wigwam 191.11
wild
n. hinterland 182.2
wilderness 166.2
adj. boisterous 162.19
country 182.8
distracted 532.10
excited 857.23
fanciful 535.20
foolhardy 894.9
foolish 470.10
infuriated 952.29

mad 473.30
overzealous 635.13
passionate 857.27
reckless 894.8
refractory 767.10
savage 162.20
turbulent 162.17
unchaste 989.25
uncouth 898.12
ungovernable 626.12
unrestrained 762.23
unruly 162.18
wild about
enthusiastic about
635.12
fond of 931.28
wild beast
animal life 414.1
violent person 162.9
wildcat
n. animal 414.27
witch 943.7
adj. hazardous 697.10
irresponsible 740.5
wilderness
complex 46.2
hinterland 182.2
space 179.4
wasteland 166.2
wildest dream
phantom 519.4
thing imagined 535.5
wild-eyed
excited 857.23
fanatical 473.32
wildflower 411.22
wild-goose chase
failure 725.5
labor in vain 669.3
wild guess 499.4
wildlife 414.1
wildly frantically 34.23
frenziedly 857.33
recklessly 894.11
violently 162.24
wild man
reckless person 894.4
savage 943.5
wild West
hinterland 182.2
region 180.7
wildwood 411.11
wile
n. cunning 735.1
falseheartedness
616.4
stratagem 735.3
trick 618.6
v. use 665.13
will
n. bequest 818.10
choice 637.1
command 752.1
desire 634.1
intention 653.1
resolution 624.1
volition 621
will power 624.4
v. bequeath 818.18
choose 621.2
resolve 624.7

willful
disobedient 767.8
intentional 653.9
lawless 740.5
obstinate 626.8
voluntary 622.7
willies 859.2
willing
consenting 775.4
game 622.5
obedient 766.3
teachable 564.18
venturesome 714.14
volitional 621.4
willingness
consent 775.1
gameness 622
obedience 766.1
teachability 564.5
tendency 174.1
will-o'-the-wisp
deception 618.1
fire 328.13
illusion 519.1
phosphorescence
335.13
willowy pliant 357.9
thin 205.16
will power
resolution 624.4
will 621.1
willy-nilly
haphazardly 72.5
in disorder 62.17
necessarily 639.16
wilt be tired 717.5
deteriorate 692.21
fail 686.45
make tired 717.4
sweat 311.16
weaken 160.9
wilted
deteriorated 692.37
sweaty 311.22
wily cunning 735.12
deceitful 618.20
shrewd 467.15
win
n. victory 726.1
v. acquire 811.8
best 36.7
be victorious 726.4
persuade 648.23
wince
n. retreat 284.3
v. demur 623.4
flinch 891.21
pull back 284.7
retract 297.3
suffer pain 424.8
winch 287.7

wind
n. air current 403
belch 310.9
breathing 403.18
fart 310.10
gods 403.3
nonsense 547.3
speed 269.6
wind instrument
465.7
v. air 402.11
blare 453.9
fatigue 717.4
play music 462.43
wind
change course 275.30
convolve 254.4
curve 252.6
prepare 720.9
rotate 322.9
trap 618.18
wander 291.4
wind around one's little
finger
have influence over
172.11
windbag braggart 910.5
chatterer 596.4
windblown 403.27
windburn 329.6
wind direction 403.16
winded 717.10
windfall find 811.6
good thing 674.5
wind gauge 269.7
wind in 287.9
winding
n. convolution 254.1
adj. convolutional
254.6
wandering 291.7
wind instrument 465.7
windjammer
braggart 910.5
chatterer 596.4
sailboat 277.3
sailor 276.1
windlass capstan 287.7
lifter 317.3
windless 268.16
window opening 265.8
radar countermeasure
346.13
window dresser 579.11
window dressing
fakery 616.3
false front 240.1
ornamentation 901.1
windowed 265.20
windowpane
glass 339.2
window 265.8
window-shop 828.8
window-shopping 828.1
wind sock
aviation 278.19
wind instrument
403.17
windstorm storm 162.4
wind 403.12
windswept 403.27
wind tunnel 396.17
windup
completion 722.2
end 70.1
wind up
complete 722.6
end 70.5
prepare 720.9

windward
n. side 242.3
adj. side 242.6
adv. side 242.9
toward 290.26
upwind 275.68
windy airy 355.4
blowy 403.25
boastful 910.11
bombastic 601.9
distended 197.13
talkative 596.9
trivial 673.16
wordy 593.12
wine
n. alcoholic beverage
996.16
types of 996.39
adj. red 368.6
wine and dine 307.16
wine cellar
cellar 192.17
storage place 660.6
wine merchant
liquor dealer 996.18
merchant 830.3
winemaking 996.20
winery plant 719.3
wing
n. affiliate 788.10
air force 800.28
annex 41.3
appendage 55.4
fowl part 308.23
group 74.3
military unit 800.19
party 788.4
protectorship 699.2
scenery 611.25
v. cripple 692.17
disable 158.9
fly 278.45
winged 269.19
winging 878.6
wing it depart 301.6
transport 271.11
improvise 630.8
wings
military insignia
569.5
stage 611.21
wink
n. glance 439.4
hint 557.4
instant 113.3
nap 712.3
signal 568.15
v. blink 440.10
signal 568.22
wink at be blind 441.8
be broad-minded
526.7
condone 947.4
consent 775.2
disregard 531.2
permit 777.10
winner
good thing 674.5
man of action 707.8

successful person
724.5
sure success 724.2
victor 726.2
winning
n. acquisition 811.1
victory 726.1
adj. alluring 650.7
desirable 634.30
lovable 931.23
persuasive 172.13
pleasant 863.7
victorious 726.8
winnings gains 38.3
profits 811.3
winning streak 726.1
win out succeed 724.12
win over
convert 145.16
convince 501.18
persuade 648.23
win 726.4
winnow
n. refining equipment
681.13
v. air 402.11
analyze 48.8
discriminate 492.5
refine 681.22
select 637.14
separate 77.6
wino 996.11
winsome alluring 650.7
cheerful 870.11
lovable 931.23
pleasant 863.7
winter
n. cold weather 333.3
season 128.6
v. spend time 105.6
adj. wintry 128.8
wintry cold 333.14
winter 128.8
wipe
n. disappearance
447.1
v. clean 681.18
dry 393.6
wipe out annihilate 2.6
clean 681.18
debts 842.9
destroy 693.14
eliminate 42.10
end 70.7
kill 409.14
obliterate 693.16
wire
n. cord 206.2
electric 342.39
telegram 560.14
v. bind 47.9
communicate 560.19
wiredrawn
smooth 351.8
thin 205.16
wireless
n. communications
560.3
radio 344.1
radiophone 560.5
radio receiver 344.3
v. broadcast 344.25

adj, radio 344.28
telecommunicational
560.20
wireman
electrician 342.19
telegraph 560.16
Wirephoto
communications
560.15
photograph 577.3
wire-puller
cunning person 735.7
influence user 744.30
influential person
172.6
political intriguer
746.6
schemer 654.8
wire-pulling
influence 172.3
intrigue 654.6
machination 735.4
political influence
744.29
wire service
news medium 558.1
telegraphy 560.2
wiretap
n. spying 485.9
v. listen 448.11
wiry strong 159.14
threadlike 206.7
tough 359.4
wisdom
expedience 670.1
maxim 517.1
sagacity 467.5
understanding 475.3
wise
n. aspect 446.3
way 657.1
adj. expedient 670.5
knowing 475.15
learned 475.21
sage 467.17
ungullible 504.5
wiseacre 468.6
wisely 467.20
wise man
intellectual 476.1
intelligent being
467.9
sage 468
wise to 475.16
wise up inform 557.8
see through 488.8
wish
n. desire 634.1
request 774.1
thing desired 634.11

will 621.1
v. desire 634.14
request 774.9
want to 635.15
will 621.2
wishbone fork 299.4
fowl part 308.23
wish-bringer 1036.6
wished-for 634.29
wish for 634.16
wish-fulfillment 535.24
wish fulfillment
defense mechanism
690.30
desire 634.1
idealization 535.7
wishful thinker 535.13
wishful thinking
credulity 502.1
deception 618.1
defense mechanism
690.30
idealization 535.7
wistfulness 634.4
wishing 634.21
wishing well 1036.6
wish well 938.11
wishy-washy
inconstant 141.7
insipid 430.2
mediocre 680.7
weak 160.17
wisp bunch 74.7
little thing 196.4
phosphorescence
335.13
wispy frail 160.14
thin 205.16
wistful
melancholy 872.23
regretful 873.8
thoughtful 478.21
wishful 634.23
wit cunning 735.1
humor 881
humorist 881.12
intelligence 467.1
skill 733.1
witch
n. hag 943.7
ill-humored woman
951.12
old woman 127.3
sorceress 1035.8
ugly thing 899.4
violent person 162.9
v. enchant 1036.9
fascinate 650.6
witchcraft 1035.1
witch doctor 1035.7
witchery
allurement 650.1
enchantment 1036.2
pleasantness 863.2
sorcery 1035.1
supernaturalism 85.7
witch-hunt
investigation 485.4
persecution 667.3
witching
n. dowsing 543.3
adj. alluring 650.7

enchanting 1036.11
pleasant 863.7
with among 44.18
by means of 658.7
in agreement with
26.12
in company with
73.12
in cooperation with
786.8
in spite of 33.9
near 184.26
plus 40.12
with a grain of salt
conditionally 507.11
doubtingly 503.13
with a vengeance
extremely 34.22
powerfully 157.15
utterly 56.16
violently 162.24
with bated breath
expectantly 539.15
fearfully 891.40
humbly 906.15
in an undertone
452.22
in suspense 539.12
secretly 614.17
with child 169.18
withdraw
back out 633.5
be secluded 89.6
dissent 522.4
extract 305.10
leave 301.8
pull back 297.3
recant 628.9
recede 297.2
repeal 779.2
resign from 784.2
retreat 295.6
separate 49.9
subtract 42.9
withdrawal
abandonment 633.1
aloneness 89.2
defense mechanism
690.30
departure 301.1
dissent 522.1
elimination 77.2
emotional symptom
690.23
extraction 305.1
incurious 529.1
recantation 628.3
recession 297.1
repeal 779.1
resignation 784.1
reticence 613.3
retreat 295.2
seclusion 924.1
separation 49.1
unfeeling 856.1
withdrawn alone 89.8
apathetic 856.13
incurious 529.3
private 614.13
reticent 613.10
secluded 924.7
unsociable 923.6

wither age 126.10
deteriorate 692.21
dry 393.6
shrink 198.9
weaken 686.45
withered aged 126.18
deteriorated 692.37
dried 393.9
shrunk 198.13
thin 205.20
withering
n. deterioration 692.4
drying 393.3
shrinking 198.3
adj. caustic 939.21
contemptuous 966.8
destructive 693.26
deteriorating 692.46
withhold abstain 992.7
be stingy 852.6
keep secret 614.7
refuse 776.4
reserve 660.12
restrain 760.7
within
adv. in 225.12
prep. in 225.15
within bounds
moderately 163.17
reasonably 482.24
temperately 992.12
within reach
accessible 509.8
near 200.20
present 186.12
with it in step 26.11
knowing 475.17
with one's eyes open
adj. disillusioned
520.5
vigilant 533.13
adv. intentionally
653.11
sleeplessly 713.9
with open arms
amicably 927.21
eagerly 635.14
hospitably 925.13
willingly 622.8
without
adv. externally 224.9
prep. excluding 77.9
lacking 662.17
minus 42.14
void of 187.18
without delay
at once 113.8
promptly 131.15
without doubt
believingly 501.28
certainly 513.25
positively 34.19
without exception
adj, comprehensive
76.7
unqualified 508.2
adv. always 112.11
regularly 17.8
universally 79.18
without fail 513.26
without foundation
flimsy 4.8

without rhyme or reason
unsupported 483.13
illogical 483.11
meaningless 547.6
capriciously 629.7
without stopping
constantly 135.7
continuously 71.10
without warning
suddenly 113.9
unexpectedly 540.14
withstand
oppose 790.3
resist 792.2
stand up to 792.3
witless
foolish 470.8
insane 473.25
scatterbrained 532.16
unaware 477.13
unintelligent 469.13
unwise 470.9
witling 881.12
wiseacre 468.6

witness
n. certificate 570.6
examinee 485.18
informant 557.5
litigant 1004.11
spectator 442.1
testifier 505.7
testimony 505.3
v. attend 186.8
see 439.12
testify 505.10
witnessing 439.2
wits 466.2
wit's end 731.5
witticism maxim 517.1
pleasantry 881.7
wittiness 881.2
wittingly
intentionally 653.11
knowingly 475.29
witty amusing 880.4
humorous 881.15
wizard
n. expert 733.13
sorcerer 1035.5
adj. excellent 674.13
wizardry skill 733.1
sorcery 1035.1
wizen age 126.10
deteriorate 692.21
dry 393.6
shrink 198.9
wizened aged 126.18
deteriorated 692.37
dried 393.9
dwarf 196.13
shrunk 198.13
thin 205.20
wobble
n. irregularity 138.1
shake 324.3
v. fluctuate 141.5
oscillate 323.10
shake 324.11
vacillate 627.8
walk 273.27
wobbly irregular 138.3
shaking 324.17
unsteady 160.16
vacillating 627.10

Woden
Norse deity 1014.6
war god 797.17
woe affliction 866.8
bane 676.1
despair 866.6
harm 675.3
sorrow 872.10
woebegone
dejected 872.22
unpleasant 864.20
wretched 866.26
woeful bad 675.9
sorrowful 872.26
unpleasant 864.20
wretched 866.26
wolf
n. animal 414.25,58
dissonance 461.1
philanderer 932.11
violent person 162.9
woman chaser 989.10
v. eat 307.21
gluttonize 994.4
wolfish canine 414.45
cruel 939.24
hungry 634.25
rapacious 822.26
Wolf-man 891.9
wolverine 414.28,58
woman adult 127.1
female 421.5
female sex 421.3
kept woman 989.17
wife 933.9
woman-hater
hater 930.4
misanthrope 940.2
womanhood
female sex 421.3
femininity 421.1
maturity 126.2
womanish
effeminate 421.14
feminine 421.13
frail 160.14

womanize
chase women 989.19
feminize 421.12
womanizer 989.10
womanly 421.13
womb
female organ 419.10
source 153.9
women's liberation
liberation 763.1
women's rights 958.6
womenswear 231.1
wonder
n. astonishment 920
first-rater 674.6
marvel 920.2
supernaturalism 85.8
v. be uncertain 514.9
marvel 920.5
not know 477.11
wonder drugs 687.29
wonderful
extraordinary 85.14
marvelous 920.10
remarkable 34.10
superb 674.17
wonderfully
amazingly 34.20
extraordinarily 85.18
marvelously 920.14
superbly 674.22
wonderfulness 920.3
wondering 920.9
wonderland 535.11
wonder-worker 1035.5
wonder-working 85.16
wondrous
marvelous 920.10
supernatural 85.16

wont
n. custom 642.1
habit 642.4
v. accustom 642.11
be used to 642.13
adj. accustomed
642.17
wonted
accustomed 642.17
customary 642.15
usual 84.8
woo court 932.19
solicit 774.14
wood firewood 331.3
lumber 378.3
types of 378.9
woodland 411.11
woodblock 578.6
wood-block 578.13
wood carving
figure 572.4
sculpture 575.1
woodcraft craft 574.3
forestry 413.3
woodcut
engraving process
578.3
print 578.6
scenery 611.25
woodcutter 413.7
wooded 411.37

wooden
inexpressive 549.20
stupid 469.16
uninteresting 883.6
woodland
n. land 385.1
the country 182.1
wood 411.11
adj. backwoods 182.8
forest 411.37
wood pulp 390.2
woods hinterland 182.2
instruments 465.9
woodland 411.11
woodsman
backwoodsman
190.10
forester 413.7
woodsy 411.37
woodwind
orchestra 464.12
wood instrument
465.9
woody 411.37

wooer 931.11
woof fabric 378.5
texture 351.1
weaving 222.3
woofer 450.8
wooing
n. allurement 650.1
courtship 932.6
solicitation 774.5
wool fabric 378.5,11
fiber 206.8
hair 230.2
softness 357.4
woolens 231.22
woolgathering
n. abstractedness
532.2
adj. abstracted 532.11
woolly hairy 230.24
soft 357.14
woozy 532.14
word
n. account 608.3
affirmation 523.1
command 752.1
information 557.1
maxim 517.1
message 558.4
news 558.1
oath 523.3
promise 770.1
remark 594.4
term 582
testimony 505.3
unit of meaning
545.6
utterance 594.3
v. phrase 588.4
say 594.23
wordage diction 588.1
vocabulary 582.14
word-coiner 582.18
worded 588.5
word-formation 582.3
word for word
authentic 516.14
exactly 516.20
word history 582.16
wordings 593.2
wordless mute 451.12
speechless 451.11
tacit 451.11
taciturn 613.9
unexpressed 546.9
word of honor 770.1
word of mouth 594.3
word-painting
description 608.1
poetry image 535.6
wordplay 881.8
words contention 796.1
conversation 597.3
quarrel 795.5
speech 594.1
vocabulary 582.14
words of wisdom 517.1
word to the wise
piece of advice 754.2
tip 557.3
warning 703.1
wordy 593.12

worthless
importance 672.1
value 846.3
adj. possessing 808.9
priced 846.16

worthless
worthless bad 675.9
disadvantageous 671.6
paltry 673.18
unimportant 673.19
useless 669.11

worthwhile
expedient 670.5
gainful 811.15
useful 665.21

worthy
n. famous person 914.9
adj. competent 733.22
dignified 905.12
eligible 637.24
honest 974.13
praiseworthy 968.20
reputable 914.15
valuable 848.10
warranted 960.9

worthy of 960.10

Wotan
Norse deity 1014.6
war god 797.17

would-be
nominal 583.15
presumptuous 912.10

wound
n. distress 866.5
impairment 692.8
sore 686.35
v. damage 675.6
grieve 866.17
hurt 424.7
injure 692.15
offend 952.20

wounded
aggrieved 866.23
pained 424.9

wound up
completed 722.11
ended 70.8
past 119.7

woven interlaced 222.7
webbed 221.12

wow
n. audio distortion 450.13
funny story 881.6
great success 724.3
v. amuse 878.23
delight 865.8
inter. pleasure 865.17
wonder 920.20

wrack
n. destruction 693.1
plant 411.4,42
wreck 693.4
v. destroy 693.10

wrack and ruin 693.1

wracked 855.25

wrack up 693.17

wraith double 1017.3
phantom 519.4
specter 1017.1

wrangle
n. quarrel 795.5
v. argue 482.16
dispute 796.22
drive animals 416.8
quarrel 795.11

wrangler arguer 482.12
combatant 800.1
herder 416.3
oppositionist 791.3
student 566.7

wrangling
n. argumentation 482.4
contention 796.1
adj. quarrelsome 795.17

wrap
n. clothing 231.20
wrapper 228.18
v. bind 47.9
clothe 231.38
cover 228.20
enclose 236.5
surround 233.6

wrapped
covered 228.31
surrounded 233.10

wrapped up
assembled 74.21
completed 722.11

wrapped up in
engrossed 530.17
fond of 931.28
involved in 176.4

wrapper binder 228.18
bookbinding 605.15
clothing 231.20

wrapping
n. covering 228.1
wrapper 228.18
adj. covering 228.34
surrounding 233.8

wraps
concealment 615.2
secrecy 614.3

wrap up bind 47.9
bundle 74.20
clothe 231.38
complete 722.6
package 228.20

wrath anger 952.5
sin 982.3

wrathful 952.26

wreak effect 705.6
inflict 963.5

wreak havoc
destroy 693.10
do harm 675.6

wreath circle 253.2
flowers 411.23
heraldic insignia 569.2
trophy 916.3
weaving 222.2

wreathe encircle 233.7
ornament 901.9
weave 222.6

wreathed
ornamented 901.11
surrounded 233.10

wreck
n. automobile 272.9
destruction 693.1
disaster 693.4
misfortune 729.2
nervous wreck 859.5
runs 692.10
v. demolish 693.17
destroy 693.10
disable 158.9
impair 692.12
rage 162.10
shipwreck 275.42

wreckage 693.5

wrecked
damaged 692.30
in difficulty 731.25
ruined 693.28

wrecker
destroyer 693.8
plunderer 825.6
savage 943.5

wrench
n. distortion 249.1
distress 866.5
impairment 692.8
jerk 286.3
types of 348.20
wresting 305.6
v. distort 249.5
exact from 305.15
injure 692.15
jerk 286.5
misinterpret 553.2
wrest 822.22

wrest
n. distortion 249.1
extraction 305.6
extort 305.15
extract 305.10
seize 822.22

wresting 305.6

wrestle
n. struggle 716.3
v. contend 796.14
struggle 716.11

wrestler athlete 878.20
fighter 800.3

wrestling 796.10

wretch
bad person 986.2
sufferer 866.11

wretched
adverse 729.13
bad 675.9
base 915.12
miserable 866.26
paltry 673.18
squalid 682.25
unhappy 872.21
unpleasant 864.20

wriggle
n. wiggle 324.7
v. be excited 857.16
wiggle 324.14

wriggler 125.10

wriggly 324.21

wright artisan 718.6

woven 222.7
producer 167.8
types of 718.11

wring
n. distortion 249.1
v. cause pain 424.7
distort 249.5
torture 866.18
twist 254.4
wrest 822.22

wringer 305.6

wringing 305.6

wrinkle
n. corrugation 264.3
extra 41.4
fad 644.5
v. age 126.10
corrugate 264.6
groove 263.3
pucker 198.7
roughen 261.5

wrinkled aged 126.16
constricted 198.12
corrugated 264.8
deteriorated 692.37
grooved 263.4
rough 261.7

wrist arm 287.5
joint 47.4

wristband
bracelet 253.3

writ document 570.5
jewel 901.6
legal action 1004.2
legal order 752.6

write author 602.21
correspond 604.11
create 167.10
describe 608.12
music 462.47
pen 602.19
record 570.16
represent 572.6

write-in 637.6

write off debts 842.9
discount 847.2
forget 947.5
repeal 779.2

write-off debts 842.2
discount 847.1
repeal 779.1

write out
draw up 602.19
record 570.16
spell 581.7

writer author 602.15
correspondent 604.9
discourser 606.3
penner 602.13

writer's cramp
nervous disorder 686.23
occupational disease 686.31

writing 602.2

write up
comment upon 606.5
publicize 559.15
record 570.16
report 558.11

write-up
commentary 606.2
publicity 559.4
writhe
be excited 857.16
distort 249.5
suffer 866.19
suffer pain 424.8
wiggle 324.14
writhing 324.21
writing
authorship 602.2
book 605.1
character 581.1
document 570.5
representation 572.1
written language 602
written matter 602.10
writing expert 602.14
writing machine 602.31
writing material 602.30
writing system
script 581.3
word list 581.9
writing 602.9
written destined 640.9
in writing 602.22
written down 570.18
wrong
n. crime 999.4
error 518.4
evil 675.3
grievance 977.4
impropriety 959
iniquity 981.3
injustice 977.1
misdeed 982.2
sinful 982.6
v. be unjust 977.7
harm 675.6
adj. bad 675.7
erroneous 518.16
evil 981.16
improper 959.3
inappropriate 671.5
mistaken 518.18
sinful 982.6
sin 982
vice 981.1
wrongful illegal 999.6
unjust 977.9
wrong 959.3
wrongdoer
bad person 986.9
evildoer 943.1
wrongdoing
crime 999.4
misbehavior 738.1
mismanagement 734.6
wrong impression
illusion 519.1
misjudgment 496.1
wrong move 518.4
wrong side 244.1

wrong time 130.2
wrong'un
bad person 986.5
trick 618.6
wroth 952.26
wrought 722.10
wrought-up
angry 952.26
excited 857.18
wrung pained 424.9
tortured 866.25
wry 219.14
wryneck
deformity 249.3
inflammation 686.9

X

x 477.7
X cross 221.4
signature 583.10
ten 99.6
Xanadu 535.10
xenophobia
exclusiveness 77.3
hate 930.1
phobia 891.10
prejudice 527.4
xerography
printing 603.1
reproduction 24.2
Xerox
n. copy 24.5
photograph 577.5
v. copy 24.8
photograph 577.14
X ray
diagnostic picture 689.10
hospital room 192.25
photograph 577.6
radiation 327.3
ray 335.5
X-ray irradiate 689.32
photograph 577.14
xylography 578.3
xylophone 465.18

Y

yacht
n. sailing vessel 277.23
v. sail 275.13
yachting 275.1
yachtsman 276.5
yak
n. cattle 414.6
chatter 596.3
v. chatter 596.5
speak 594.21
yammer
n. cry 459.1
shrill sound 458.4
v. cry 459.6
sound shrill 458.8
whine 875.12
yammering 459.10
yank
n. jerk 286.3
v. jerk 286.5
Yankee dialect 580.7

Northerner 190.11
revolutionist 147.3
yap
n. cry 459.1
mouth 265.5
v. animal sound 460.2
complain 875.13
cry 459.6
yapping
n. complaint 875.4
adj. vociferous 459.10
yard
n. enclosure 236.3,12
thousand 99.10
US money 835.7
workplace 719.3
v. enclose 236.5
yardage 202.1
yard goods 831.3
yardman 274.13
yardstick 490.2,20
yarn cord 206.2,8
joke 881.6
lie 616.11
story 608.6
yaw
n. aviation 278.28
deviation 291.1
v. change course 275.30
drift off course 275.29
fly 278.49
sail 275.55
yawn
n. gaping 265.2
opening 265.1
v. gape 265.17
yawning
n. gaping 265.2
sleepiness 712.1
adj. abysmal 209.11
gaping 265.19
sleepy 712.21
yawp
n. cry 459.1
lament 875.3
v. animal sound 460.2
cry 459.6
utter 594.26
wail 875.11
yea
n. affirmative expression 521.2
approval 968.1
vote 637.6
adv. indeed 36.17
year 107.2
yearbook
periodical 605.10
record book 570.11
reports 570.7
yearling calf 414.6
infant 125.7
yearlong 110.12
yearly 137.8
yearn for 634.16

yearning
n. love 931.1
yen 634.5
adj. wistful 634.23
years age 126.1
long time 110.4
yeast 139.4
yeasty excited 857.18
foamy 405.7
leavening 353.16
light 353.10
yecchy bad 675.8
filthy 682.23
yeuck!
contempt 966.10
unpleasantness 864.31
yegg 825.3
yell
n. cheer 876.2
cry 459.1
v. cheer 876.6
cry 459.6
utter 594.26
wail 875.11
yell at 969.20
yelling 459.10
yellow
n. barbiturate 687.12
colors 370.7
yellowness 370.1
yolk 406.15
v. turn yellow 370.3
adj. cowardly 892.10
jealous 953.4
sensational 857.30
yellowish 370.4
yellow fever 686.12
yellow-haired 370.5
yellow jacket
barbiturate 687.12
wasp 414.38,74
yellow journalism 855.9
Yellow Pages 748.10
yellow race race 418.2
yellow skin 370.2
yellow skin 370.2
yellow streak 892.4
yelp
n. cry 459.1
v. animal sound 460.2
complain 875.13
cry 459.6
utter 594.26
yelping 459.10
yen
foreign money 835.9
yearning 634.5
yen for 634.16
yenta
curious person 528.2
meddler 238.4
newsmonger 558.9
yeoman
agriculturist 413.5
attendant 750.5
bodyguard 699.14
retainer 750.1
sailor 276.6
yeoman's service 785.1

yes
n. affirmative expres-
sion 521.2
vote 637.6
v. assent 521.8
adv. consentingly
775.5
interj. yea 521.18
yeshiva 567.10
yes-man assenter 521.6
conformist 82.2
inferior 37.2
sycophant 907.3
yesterday
n. the past 119.1
adv. formerly 119.13
yesteryear 119.1
yet additionally 40.11
notwithstanding 33.8
previously 116.6
until now 120.4
yield
n. gain 811.5
produce 168.2
receipts 844.1
v. accept 861.6
acknowledge 521.11
bear 167.14
yielding
n. abandonment
633.3
be elastic 358.5
be irresolute 627.7
be lenient 759.6
be pliant 357.7
bring in 844.4
compromise 807.2
conform 82.3
give 818.12
give up 633.7
provide 659.7
relinquish 814.3
submit 765.7
weaken 160.9
adj. bearing 165.10
docile 765.13
pliant 357.9
unstrict 758.5
wieldy 732.14
yip 460.2
yippee 876.2
yippie
nonconformist 83.3
radical 745.12
yodel
n. vocal music 462.12
v. sing 462.39
yodeler 464.13
yoga exercises 716.6
occultism 1034.1
yogi ascetic 991.2
Hindu priest 1038.14
occultist 1034.11
yogurt food 308.47
health food 309.26
sour thing 432.2
yoke
n. harness 659.5

restraint 760.4
two 90.2
join 47.10
bind 47.11
join 47.5
pair 90.5
yoked coupled 90.8
joined 47.13
related 9.9
yokel
n. awkward person
734.8
oaf 471.5
rustic 919.9
unsophisticate 736.3
vulgar person 898.6
adj. countrified 182.7
yolk 406.15
Yom Kippur fast 995.3
holy day 1040.16
penance 1012.3
yonder
adj. farther 199.10
adv. in the distance
199.13
yore 119.2
you 80.5
young
n. animal young 171.2
young people 125.2
adj. juvenile 124.9
new 122.7
younger junior 124.15
subsequent 117.4
youngest 125.1
young man
beau 931.12
boy 125.5
young people 125.2
youngster
young person 125.2
youth 125.5

youth beginning 68.4
boy 125.5
youngness 124
young people 125.2
youngster 125.1
youthful
healthy 685.11
young 124.9
youngster 125.2
yourself 80.5
yowl
n. cry 459.1
lament 875.3
v. animal sound 460.2
cry 459.6
Y-shaped angular 251.6
forked 299.10
yuck 876.4
yucky 429.7
Yule 128.6
Yule log 331.3
yummy 428.8

Z

zag
n. angle 251.2
zigzag 219.8
v. angle 251.5
zigzag 219.12

zigzag
n. angle 251.2
deviation 291.1
evasive action 631.1
obliquity 219.8
v. alternate 323.13
angle 251.5
deflect 291.5
wind in and out
219.12
adj. angular 251.6
crooked 219.20
deviant 291.7

zambo 44.9
zany buffoon 612.10
fool 471.1
zap end 70.7
humorist 881.12
kill 409.14
zeal anxiety 890.1
eagerness 635.2
fervor 855.10
piety 1028.3
violence 162.2
willingness 622.1
zealot believer 1028.4
enthusiast 635.5
fanatic 473.17
odd person 85.4
zealotry
fanaticism 473.11
overzealousness 635.4
piety 1028.3
zealous anxious 890.6
eager 635.10
fanatic 162.21
fervent 855.23
industrious 707.22
pious 1028.11
willing 622.5

Zend-Avesta 1021.6
zenith height 207.2
summit 211.2
supremacy 36.3
zephyr breeze 403.5
softness 357.4
Zephyr 403.3
zeppelin 280.11
zero nothing 2.2
temperature 328.3
thing of naught 4.2
zero hour
attack time 798.14
crucial moment
129.5
zero in on
fire upon 798.22
pinpoint 184.10
zest animation 161.3
eagerness 635.1
gaiety 870.4
pleasure 865.1
pungency 433.2
savor 428.2
zestful eager 635.9
energetic 161.12
gay 870.14
pungent 433.7
refreshing 695.3
Zeus god 1014.5
rain god 394.6

zilch 2.2
zillion
n. immense number
101.4
large number 86.4
number 99.13
adj. numerous 101.6
zing
n. vim 161.2
v. go fast 269.8
zingy 707.17
Zion 1018.4
zip
n. gaiety 870.4
pungency 433.2
sibilation 457.1
vim 161.2
v. sibilate 457.2

zip code 604.10
zipper close 266.6
fasten 47.8
zippy energetic 161.12
gay 870.14
pungent 433.7
zip through 485.25
zip up close 266.6
energize 161.9
zither 463.3
zo(o)-
zodiac astrology 375.20
astronomy 375.16
zombie 1017.1
zonal 180.8
zone
n. address 604.10
astronomy 375.16
band 253.3
earth division 180.3
layer 227.1
middle 69.1
region 180.1
v. encircle 233.7
partition 49.18
zoning districting 49.1
prohibitions 778.1
zonked drunk 996.31
insensible 423.8
zoo collection 74.11
menagerie 191.19
zoological(al)
animal 414.43
zoology 415.9
zoologist
animal scientist 415.2
biologist 406.18
zoology
animal science 415
biology 406.17
zoom
n. air maneuver
278.13
v. fly 278.48
soar 315.10
speed 269.8
zounds! 920.21
zwieback 308.30
zygote 406.14

ABBREVIATIONS USED IN THIS BOOK

adj(s)	. .	adjective(s)
adv(s)	. .	adverb(s)
aero	. .	aeronautics
anat	. .	anatomy
anon	. .	anonymous
Arab	. .	Arabic
archit	. .	architecture
Ariz	. .	Arizona
astron	. .	astronomy
Austral	. .	Australian
biol	. .	biology
bot	. .	botany
Brit	. .	British
Cal	. .	California
Can	. .	Canadian
chem	. .	chemistry
Chin	. .	Chinese
conj(s)	. .	conjunction(s)
Dan	. .	Danish
derog	. .	derogatory
dial	. .	dialectal
Du	. .	Dutch
E	. .	East, Eastern
eccl	. .	ecclesiastical
Eng	. .	England, English
etc.	. .	et cetera
fem	. .	feminine
Fla	. .	Florida
Fr	. .	French
geol	. .	geology
Ger	. .	German
Gk	. .	Greek
gram	. .	grammar
Heb	. .	Hebrew
her	. .	heraldry
Hind	. .	Hindustani
Hung	. .	Hungarian
interj(s)	. .	interjection(s)
Ir	. .	Irish
Ital	. .	Italian
Jap	. .	Japanese
Ky	. .	Kentucky
L	. .	Latin
La	. .	Louisiana

masc	. .	masculine
Mass	. .	Massachusetts
math	. .	mathematics
Md	. .	Maryland
med	. .	medicine, medical
mil	. .	military
min	. .	mining
mus	. .	music
myth	. .	mythology
n	. .	noun(s)
N	. .	North, Northern
naut	. .	nautical
NC	. .	North Carolina
Norw	. .	Norwegian
Pg	. .	Portuguese
phr(s)	. .	phrase(s)
phys	. .	physics
pl	. .	plural
Pol	. .	Polish
prep(s)	. .	preposition(s)
RI	. .	Rhode Island
Rom	. .	Roman
RR	. .	railroading
Russ	. .	Russian
S	. .	South, Southern
Scot	. .	Scottish
sing	. .	singular
Skt	. .	Sanskrit
Sp	. .	Spanish
Sp Amer	. .	Spanish American
Swah	. .	Swahili
Swed	. .	Swedish
Tenn	. .	Tennessee
Turk	. .	Turkish
US	. .	United States
USSR	. .	Union of Soviet Socialist Republics
v	. .	verb(s)
Va	. .	Virginia
Vt	. .	Vermont
W	. .	West, Western
Yid	. .	Yiddish
zool	. .	zoology